Social Reform and Reaction in America

Clio Bibliography Series No. 13

Gail Schlachter, Editor
Pamela R. Byrne, Executive Editor

*Users of the Clio Bibliography Series may refer to current issues of
America: History and Life and Historical Abstracts
for continuous bibliographic coverage of the subject areas
treated by each individual volume in the series.*

1.
The American Political Process
Dwight L. Smith and Lloyd W. Garrison
1972   LC 72-77549   ISBN 0-87436-090-0

2.
Afro-American History
Dwight L. Smith
1974   LC 73-87155   ISBN 0-87436-123-0

3.
Indians of the United States and Canada
Dwight L. Smith
1974   LC 73-87156   ISBN 0-87436-124-9

4.
Era of the American Revolution
Dwight L. Smith
1975   LC 74-14194   ISBN 0-87436-178-8

5.
Women in American History
Cynthia E. Harrison
1979   LC 78-26194   ISBN 0-87436-260-1

6.
The American and Canadian West
Dwight L. Smith
1979   LC 78-24478   ISBN 0-87436-272-5

7.
European Immigration and Ethnicity
in the United States and Canada
David L. Brye
1983   LC 82-24306   ISBN 0-87436-258-X

8.
Afro-American History, Volume II
Dwight L. Smith
1981   ISBN 0-87436-314-4

9.
Indians of the United States and Canada
Volume II
Dwight L. Smith
1982   LC 73-87156   ISBN 0-87436-149-4

10.
The History of Canada
Dwight L. Smith
1983   LC 82-24307   ISBN 0-87436-047-1

11.
Urban America
Neil L. Shumsky and Timothy Crimmins
1983   LC 82-24292   ISBN 0-87436-038-2

12.
Religion and Society in North America
Robert deV. Brunkow
1983   LC 82-24304   ISBN 0-87436-042-0

13.
Social Reform and Reaction in America
1984   LC 82-24294   ISBN 0-87436-048-X

14.
American Popular Culture
Arthur Frank Wertheim
1984   LC 82-24285   ISBN 0-87436-049-8

15.
The American Presidency
1984   LC 83-12245   ISBN 0-87436-370-5

Social Reform and Reaction in America

an annotated bibliography

ABC-Clio Information Services

Santa Barbara, California
Oxford, England

Library of Congress Cataloging in Publication Data
Main entry under title:

Social reform and reaction in America.

(Clio bibliography series; no. 13)
Includes index.
1. United States—Social conditions—Bibliography.
2. Canada—Social conditions—Bibliography. 3. United
States—Economic conditions—Bibliography. 4. Canada—
Economic conditions—Bibliography. I. Series.
Z7164.S66A52 1983 [HN65] 016.306'0973 82-24294
ISBN 0-87436-048-X

©1984 by ABC-Clio, Inc.

All rights reserved. No part of this publication may be reproduced, stored in a retrieval system, or transmitted, in any form or by any means, electronic, mechanical, photo-copying, recording, or otherwise, without the prior written permission of ABC-Clio, Inc.

ABC-Clio Information Services, Inc.
2040 Alameda Padre Serra
Santa Barbara, California

Clio Press Ltd.
55 St. Thomas St.
Oxford OX1 1JG, England

Printed and bound in the United States of America.

TABLE OF CONTENTS

PREFACE vii
ABSTRACTS. 1
SUBJECT INDEX 249
AUTHOR INDEX 364
LIST OF PERIODICALS. 371
LIST OF ABSTRACTERS. 374
LIST OF ABBREVIATIONS 375

1. THE UNITED STATES AND CANADA
    General. 1
    Civil Liberties and Political Rights 10
    Economic Reform. 13
    Educational Reform 15
    Humanitarian Reform. 19
    Utopian Thought and Communalism 22
    Profiles of Reformers 23

2. THE COLONIAL EXPERIENCE
    General. 41
    Civil Liberties and Political Rights 43
    Humanitarian Reform. 45

3. CRUSADES IN THE NEW REPUBLIC, 1783-1860
    General 47
    Civil Liberties and Political Rights. 51
    The Slavery Question 52
    The First Women's Movement. 68
    Economic Reform. 70
    Educational Reform 71
    Humanitarian Reform. 73
    Religious Reform 77
    Utopian Thought and Communalism 77

4. CRISES OF MODERNIZATION, 1861-1900
    General 80
    Civil Liberties and Political Rights 92
    The Black Experience 95
    Capitalists and Labor Movements 108
    Populist Movements and Antecedents. . . 114
    Educational Reform 117
    Humanitarian Reform. 120
    Religious Reform 124
    Utopian Thought and Communalism . . . 125

5. STRUGGLES OF THE TWENTIETH CENTURY
    General 128
    Civil Liberties and Political Rights. 143
    Economic Reform. 145
    Educational Reform 153
    The Progressive Era 156
        General. 156
        Civil Liberties and Political Rights . . . 177
        Economic Reform. 180
        Educational Reform 190
    The New Era 193
    The New Deal Period. 204
    War and Reform 217
    Post World War II Reform and
        Reaction 220

6. THE CONTEMPORARY SCENE
    General 224
    Civil Liberties and Political Rights. 230
    The Black Revolution 232
    The Second Women's Movement. 241
    Economic Reform. 243
    Educational Reform 245
    Humanitarian Reform 247
    Utopian Thought and Communalism. . . 248

PREFACE

Since the 17th century, when early colonists arrived on the shores of the New World armed with little more than their hope for a new society, the creation of a different social order has been a dominant and persistent theme of North American history. Nativists and Communists, utopian schemers and Southern Redeemers, all have endeavored to direct society toward their disparate visions of right, justice, and prosperity. Individually, their successes have often been few and fleeting, but their combined impact on the development of the United States and Canada has been profound.

Modern historians, social scientists, and scholars in the humanities have been fascinated by social reform in its many guises. While traditional studies of the reformer elite continue to be written, research has also taken new directions derived from social history and ethnic studies. With insights formed by quantitative methodology, greater attention to the lives of the common folk, and sensitivity to the integrity of ethnic values, scholars have now more thoroughly investigated the efficacy of specific reforms and the reactions of groups for whose benefit reforms have been enacted.

Social Reform and Reaction in America: An Annotated Bibliography, the 13th volume in the Clio Bibliography Series, brings together the modern scholarship on social reform in the United States and Canada. It is a compendium of 2,993 abstracts of articles published during 1973-82. The abstracts are drawn from the database of ABC-Clio Information Services, the largest history database in the world, which contains abstracts of articles from over 2,000 journals in 42 languages, published in 90 countries.

Access to the scholarship summarized in this volume is enhanced by the division of the bibliography into six chapters. The chapters focus on major chronological periods, and each is subdivided by particular topics, such as educational reform, the women's movement, and the New Deal. Thus, a researcher with specific interests can turn immediately to the relevant chapter and subchapter to gain a broad insight into the scope and basic issues of the modern scholarship on the particular subject.

Chapter 1, *The United States and Canada,* encompasses general works on utopian philosophy and economic, educational, and humanitarian reform, as well as biographies of reformers. Each of the following five chapters focuses on social reform within a particular period of North American history. *The Colonial Experience,* Chapter 2, examines the roots of social reform in the period prior to the end of the American Revolution. Chapter 3, *Crusades in the New Republic, 1783-1860,* is concerned with reform prior to the Civil War, such as abolitionism and the birth of the women's movement. The fourth chapter, *Crises of Modernization, 1861-1900,* focuses on reformers' responses to the social upheavals that attended the rise of industrial capitalism. *Struggles of the Twentieth Century,* Chapter 5, includes all works on the Progressive movement, as well as purely 20th-century reform efforts, such as the New Deal. The final chapter, *The Contemporary Scene,* examines social reform since the 1960's, including the black civil rights movement and the fight for fully equal rights for women.

The articles abstracted in this volume were chosen both for the relevancy of their subjects and for their importance as contributions to modern scholarship. The editors examined every entry in the database for 1973-82 in searching for the best possible combination of article abstracts. The selection process was guided by a broad definition of social reform that encompasses efforts, both peaceful and violent, to effect changes in the structure and condition of American society. The broad selection criteria were tempered by editorial discretion in order to produce a thorough compilation of the most substantive scholarship. In-depth subject access to the abstracts in this volume is provided by ABC-SPIndex, one of the most advanced and comprehensive indexing systems in the world. ABC-SPIndex links together the key subject terms and the chronology of each abstract to form a composite index entry that furnishes a complete subject profile of the journal article. Each set of index terms is rotated so that the complete profile appears in the index under every subject term. In this way, the number of access points is increased severalfold over conventional hierarchical indexes, and works that are not relevant to a researcher's particular interests can be eliminated early in the search process. Great care has been taken during the editorial process to ensure consistency and clarity in the index terms. In addition, cross-references have been added to the subject index to facilitate rapid and accurate searching. The result is a bibliography that is both eminently usable and very thorough in its treatment of the modern periodical literature on social reform in America.

This volume represents the collaboration of a highly skilled and diverse group. Pamela R. Byrne, Executive Editor of the Clio Bibliography Series, directed the project from the initial planning stage through the complex editorial processes of the computer-assisted indexing system and machine-readable database to the final design and production of the book.

M. Joyce Baker served as a historical consultant during the early planning stages of the publication.

Historian-editor Robert deV. Brunkow selected, organized, and indexed the entries that comprise this volume and at critical points in the editorial process was expertly assisted by other ABC-Clio Information Services editors, Suzanne Robitaille Ontiveros, Lance Klass, Susan Kinnell, and Jeffrey Serena.

The Data Processing Services Department, under the supervision of Ken Baser, Director, and Deborah Looker, Production Supervisor, ably manipulated the database to fit the editorial specifications of this bibliography. Most especially, appreciation is extended to the worldwide community of scholars without whose contributions this book would not have been possible.

1. UNITED STATES AND CANADA

General

1. Bacchi, Carol. RACE REGENERATION AND SOCIAL PURITY: A STUDY OF THE SOCIAL ATTITUDES OF CANADA'S ENGLISH-SPEAKING SUFFRAGISTS. *Social Hist. [Canada] 1978 11(22): 460-474.* Most suffragists believed that woman's most valuable roles were as wife and mother. Rather than demand sexual freedom, they "upheld the Victorian idea that women stood above sex." These attitudes derived from the suffragists' origins in the Anglo-Saxon, Protestant middle class. Suffragists subscribed to the goal of a strong healthy race, but through environmental improvements rather than eugenics. Opposition to drinking and prostitution stemmed from the threat they represented to Protestant middle-class values. Primary and secondary sources; 76 notes.
D. F. Chard

2. Bendixen, Alfred. GEORGE W. CABLE AND THE GARDEN. *Louisiana Studies 1976 15(3): 310-315.* George Washington Cable (1844-1925) left New Orleans for Massachusetts in 1886 but continued his civic reforms as well as writing of fiction. One of his minor but typical interests is reflected in his book *The Amateur Garden* (1914), consisting of several previously published articles. Cable believed that maintaining a garden helped to improve its owner by giving an understanding of leisure, a sense of home and community, a respect for nature, and spiritual uplift. He recommended an annual garden contest to pursue these goals.
J. Buschen

3. Bennion, Sherilyn Cox. THE *WOMAN'S EXPONENT*: FORTY-TWO YEARS OF SPEAKING FOR WOMEN. *Utah Hist. Q. 1976 44(3): 222-239.* Utah's *Women's Exponent* (1872-1914) was one of the earliest periodicals for women in the United States. It was a forum for subjects of interest to women, including religion, fashion, politics, polygamy, and suffrage. It encouraged women writers and reported Relief Society meetings and activities. Its influence among Mormon women was largely due to the ability and dedication of its two editors. Louisa Lula Greene Richards (1849-1944) served 1872-77. Emmeline Blanche Woodward Harris Whitney Wells (b. 1828) served 1877-1914. Based on primary and secondary sources; 4 illus., 41 notes.
J. L. Hazelton

4. Bernson, Sarah L. and Eggers, Robert J. BLACK PEOPLE IN SOUTH DAKOTA HISTORY. *South Dakota Hist. 1977 7(3): 241-270.* South Dakota had few blacks, and they were prohibited from voting. After the Civil War, a few were among the advancing settlers and miners. Minor racial incidents occurred near military forts in the 1870's and 80's. There were concentrations of black people in Yankton and rural Sully County. The state had only 832 blacks in 1920. The following decade was marked by Ku Klux Klan activity and the formation of an NAACP chapter. The Great Depression was weathered through the efforts of black churches, the NAACP, and group cooperation. Following a black increase during World War II, especially at cities near military bases, discrimination in housing and services became serious issues. These problems have been legislated away. The recent national civil rights movement and black awareness have helped the black population (1,627 in 1970) establish themselves as full and equal citizens. Secondary sources; 8 photos, 95 notes.
A. J. Larson

5. Bollinger, Heil D. A NEW DIMENSION OF THE STUDENT CHRISTIAN MOVEMENT. *J. of Ecumenical Studies 1979 16(1): 169-174.* The Student Christian Movement has its roots in the 19th century. Inspired by earlier leaders such as John R. Mott, Bishop James K. Matthews, and R. H. Edwin Espy, the movement has pursued its aims of evangelism and social justice. The movement continues to crusade for ecumenism and cultural and social change through nonviolence. 6 notes.
S

6. Bolt, Christine. THE ANTI-SLAVERY ORIGINS OF CONCERN FOR THE AMERICAN INDIANS. Bolt, Christine and Drescher, Seymour, ed. *Anti-Slavery, Religion and Reform: Essays in Memory of Roger Anstey* (Folkestone, England: Dawson, 1980): 233-253. Efforts to stop the enslavement and forced resettlement of native Americans, although less well known than the movement to abolish black slavery, had the same origins as the abolitionist movement as a whole, and many of the same people were involved—William Lloyd Garrison, Wendell Phillips, Ralph Waldo Emerson, Daniel Webster, and Sarah Grimké. Even less generally known was the fact that many Indian tribes themselves kept slaves—other Indians or Negroes. 30 notes.
S

7. Buchholtz, C. W. NO TRAIL TOO STEEP: THE DREAM AND REALITY OF RECREATION IN OUR WESTERN NATIONAL PARKS. *J. of the West 1978 17(3): 95-106.* The ideals expressed by the founders of the national parks, such as John Muir, George B. Grinnell, and Frederick Law Olmsted, were that park visitors should appreciate the rugged natural beauty by active participation rather than by passive observation. The park experience, in turn, would reward the visitor with spiritual and intellectual invigoration. In fact, the general public all too frequently abused the parks by vandalizing, poaching, setting fires, and littering. Park managers responded by instituting strict regulations and providing sophisticated roads, concessions, and accommodations for the convenience of the motorized sightseer. The Wilderness Act (US, 1964) checked the advance of excessive developments and revived the aims of the preservationists. Primary and secondary sources; 8 photos, 68 notes.
B. S. Porter

8. Bullough, Vern L. CHALLENGES TO SOCIETAL ATTITUDES TOWARD HOMOSEXUALITY IN THE LATE NINETEENTH AND EARLY TWENTIETH CENTURIES. *Social Sci. Q. 1977 58(1): 29-44.*

9. Bushnell, Amy. "THAT DEMONIC GAME": THE CAMPAIGN TO STOP INDIAN PELOTA PLAYING IN SPANISH FLORIDA, 1675-1684. *Americas (Acad. of Am. Franciscan Hist.) 1978 35(1): 1-19.* Convinced that pelota, a traditional ball game played by Florida Indians, was harmful to social and political order and above all to the Indians' souls because of its violence and the sorcery, sexual license, and neglect of crops and defense it engendered, Spanish civil and religious authorities launched a campaign to eradicate it. The immediate results of the campaign are hard to assess, but the game did disappear, if only because the Indians were fast nearing extinction. Primary sources; 45 notes.
D. Bushnell

10. Clanton, O. Gene. POPULISM, PROGRESSIVISM, AND EQUALITY: THE KANSAS PARADIGM. *Agric. Hist. 1977 51(3): 559-581.* Populism and progressivism in Kansas developed from substantially different roots. Populism was a rural, radically egalitarian movement of the disadvantaged classes. Progressivism started among the small town middle class as a movement in opposition to Populist radicalism. As it developed, progressivism adopted some of the reform principles of Populism but it remained elitist, seeking more to broaden the opportunities for upward mobility than change society. Many former Populists joined the progressive movement after moderating their positions. 59 notes.
D. E. Bowers

11. Clark, Malcolm, Jr. THE BIGOT DISCLOSED: 90 YEARS OF NATIVISM. *Oregon Hist. Q. 1974 75(2): 108-190.* A history of bigotry in the Pacific Northwest, illustrated in the nativism of the period on the religious, social, and political scenes. Extreme religious sectarianism was evident at a very early date, exemplified by strong anti-Catholicism. The treatment of Chinese laborers was equally shameful, and became the subject of inflammatory journalism and oratory. Henry Francis Bowers and his American Protective Association brought bigotry into the political arena, followed in turn by the Guardians of Liberty, the I.W.W., and the revived Ku Klux Klan under the leadership of Edward Young Clark. The latter organization had phenomenal growth and influence in the 1920's, with Fred L. Gifford becoming the political boss of Oregon. Despite the Klan's demise, nativism unfortunately is not dead. 17 photos, 179 notes.
R. V. Ritter

12. Cole, Cheryl L. CHINESE EXCLUSION: THE CAPITALIST PERSPECTIVE OF THE *SACRAMENTO UNION*, 1850-1882. *California Hist.* 1978 57(1): 8-31. Traces the position of the *Sacramento Union* on the issue of Chinese exclusion. As a conservative Republican newspaper, the *Union* promoted construction of the transcontinental railroad and development of business enterprise in the state. It also defended the economic contributions of Chinese immigrants in their work on the railroad, their payment of the Foreign Miners Tax (which by 1870 accounted for half the state's total income), and their employment in occupations which did not compete with white workers, such as laundries and delta reclamation. The *Union* supported the anticipated trade with China. It condemned anti-Chinese agitation as the prejudiced view of Democratic Irish labor agitators. After a change in owners in 1875 and takeover by the Central Pacific Railroad, the *Union* came to support Chinese exclusion as a tactic of Republican political survival. The arguments centered, however, on the inability of the Chinese to assimilate culturally or socially, an argument that contributed to the congressional vote for the Chinese Exclusion Act (1882). The *Union* position 1850-80 contrasts with the more widely used San Francisco newspapers which were Democratic and opposed to Chinese immigration. Based on contemporary and secondary published works; illus., photos, 77 notes.
A. Hoffman

13. Coleman, Michael C. NOT RACE, BUT GRACE: PRESBYTERIAN MISSIONARIES AND AMERICAN INDIANS, 1837-1893. *J. of Am. Hist.* 1980 67(1): 41-60. During its first six decades of missionary activity with American Indians, the Board of Foreign Missions of the Presbyterian Church judged Indians as members of inferior, heathen cultures, but not as members of an inferior race. Presbyterian missionaries, convinced of the absolute superiority of the American republic, attempted both a secular and a spiritual transformation of their Indian charges. Missionaries blamed Indian failings upon cultural differences, not upon racial ones. Based on personal records, accounts, and correspondence of missionaries; 78 notes.
T. P. Linkfield

14. Conway, J. F. POPULISM IN THE UNITED STATES, RUSSIA, AND CANADA: EXPLAINING THE ROOTS OF CANADA'S THIRD PARTIES. *Can. J. of Pol. Sci. [Canada]* 1978 11(1): 99-124. Examines the literature on populist movements elsewhere to forge a theory to better understand the third parties of Canada's prairie west—the Social Credit in Alberta and the Co-operative Commonwealth Federation (CCF) in Saskatchewan. 102 notes.
R. V. Kubicek

15. Crouch, Archie. RACIAL-ETHNIC MINISTRY POLICIES: AN HISTORICAL OVERVIEW. *J. of Presbyterian Hist.* 1979 57(3): 272-312. The history of the Presbyterian Church in America in the field of racial and ethnic policies shows a slow movement from a mission of evangelism and civilization to advocacy and finally to an integrated Church in an integrated society. During each stage of development there were prophetic individuals who committed themselves to a vision of a different future, as they lead the church forward. The record also indicates that the church as a whole never quite managed to manifest totally the policies adopted by its assemblies. A chronological presentation is given from the colonial to the present period. Based on official reports of the church's boards and minutes of the annual General Assemblies; illus., 109 notes.
H. M. Parker, Jr.

16. Crowder, Ralph L. JOHN EDWARD BRUCE: PIONEER BLACK NATIONALIST. *Afro-Americans in New York Life and Hist.* 1978 2(2): 47-66. In many newspaper and scholarly articles, 1874-1924, black activist John Edward Bruce (1856-1924) advocated black nationalism (which entailed rejection of Americanism), economic independence, self-help, and racial solidarity.

17. Dayton, Lucille Sider and Dayton, Donald W. "YOUR DAUGHTERS SHALL PROPHESY": FEMINISM IN THE HOLINESS MOVEMENT. *Methodist Hist.* 1976 14(2): 67-92. The feminist theme permeates the literature of the Holiness Movement in America. It varied in intensity over two centuries from reserved openness, to acceptance of religious activity by women, to favoring the ordination of women. The role of women in holiness traditions was foreshadowed by Susanna Wesley's activities in the 1730's. The Holiness Movement intensified in America as early as 1827, with Phoebe Palmer later having a great impact both evangelically and as a feminist. By 1973 there was considerably less emphasis on feminism in the movement. 116 notes.
H. L. Calkin

18. Decarie, M. G. PAVED WITH GOOD INTENTIONS: THE PROHIBITIONISTS' ROAD TO RACISM IN ONTARIO. *Ontario Hist. [Canada]* 1974 66(1): 15-. Examines the prohibition movement in the late 19th century in Ontario and its effect on other aspects of reform. Traces the logic of prohibition (as distinct from temperance) from stereotyping users of alcohol to racism. 20 notes.
W. B. Whitham and S

19. Dickersin, Gail. NOTES ON NINETEENTH-CENTURY FEMINIST VERSE. *Feminist Studies* 1978 4(3): 115-126. Reprints with brief comment 10 feminist poems printed in women's periodicals, abolitionist papers, and anthologies of the 19th century. The poems offer an insight into the minds of 19th-century women, trace the growth of suffrage sentiment, and express a growing consciousness of sisterhood among American women. 14 notes.
L. M. Maloney

20. Dressner, Richard B. WILLIAM DWIGHT PORTER BLISS'S CHRISTIAN SOCIALISM. *Church Hist.* 1978 47(1): 66-82. From the Haymarket Affair until the Red Scare, the Reverend William D. P. Bliss was instrumental in organizing, researching, editing, publishing and lecturing on behalf of the coming of God's kingdom. Along with Walter Rauschenbusch and George Herron, Bliss was certainly one of the most prominent spokesmen for the left wing of the Social Gospel. Apparently, however, there was a divergence between Bliss's radical social philosophy and his political commitments to more moderate causes. Bliss was willing to accommodate his economic and social programs to political exigiencies without compromising his vision of Christian redemption. 61 notes.
M. D. Dibert

21. Dumont-Johnson, Micheline. LES COMMUNAUTÉS RELIGIEUSES ET LA CONDITION FÉMININE [Religious communities and the feminine condition]. *Recherches Sociographiques [Canada]* 1978 19(1): 79-102. As far back as the French Regime, women's religious communities played an important role in the social and cultural development of Quebec. In the second half of the 19th century one discerns the first manifestations of feminism in Quebec within the structures of these religious communities. With the present one sees their influence and importance disappear since the "Quebecoise" more and more lives within a society that offers avenues for self-development and expression unknown in the past. Based on an analysis of recent monographs; 5 tables, 4 graphs, 76 notes.
A. E. LeBlanc

22. Eaton, Clement. BREAKING A PATH FOR THE LIBERATION OF WOMEN IN THE SOUTH. *Georgia R.* 1974 28(2): 187-199. With chivalry and the Bible as its guide, the South placed enormous restraints on the rights of women. Neverless, a small group of women spoke out against the double standard applied to southern females. Leading the struggle for equal rights for women were Rebecca L. Felton, Ellen Glasgow, Gertrude T. Clanton, Belle Kearney, Kate Gordon, Laura Clay, and Kate Chopin, all of whom had a part in the liberation of women.
M. B. Lucas

23. Emery, George N. THE ORIGINS OF CANADIAN METHODIST INVOLVEMENT IN THE SOCIAL GOSPEL MOVEMENT 1890-1914. *J. of the Can. Church Hist. Soc. [Canada]* 1977 19(1-2): 104-119. The massive, rapid transformation of Canada in the early 20th century through urbanization, immigration, and industrialization brought about the growth of Methodism and other Christian denominations of the social gospel movement. There were a number of reasons. First was the decline of the evangelical tradition with the growing affluence of Methodists and the development of the higher criticism. Moreover, the strong belief in individual perfectionism evolved into concern about society as a whole. In their nationalism, pietism, optimism about the future of man, and desire to avoid theological controversy, many Methodists saw in the social gospel movement an opportunity to express their concern about the growing problems caused by the modern changes. All these factors helped bring Canadian Methodists into the forefront of the social gospel movement in Canada. Primary and secondary sources; table, 38 notes. This issue is *J. of the Can. Church Hist. Soc.* 1977 19(1-2) and *Bull. of the United Church of Can.* 1977 26.
J. A. Kicklighter

24. Erwin, Robert. REFORM FROM BELOW. *Pol. and Soc.* 1973 3(4): 463-471. Discusses the problems of reform from below in the United

States, citing historical examples ranging from the 19th-century suffrage movements, to the Massachusetts textile strike of 1912, to Cesar Chavez's Californian farmworkers' protests in the 1970's.

25. Esedebe, P. Olisanwuche. WHAT IS PAN-AFRICANISM? *J. of African Studies 1977 4(2): 167-187.* The concept of Pan-Africanism has often received inadequate definition by recent scholars. The roles of W. E. B. DuBois and George Padmore in fostering it have been emphasized to the exclusion of those of others, especially Edward Wilmot Blyden. Surveys the history of Pan-Africanism and concludes that it centers around the notion of a distinct "African personality," as discerned by Blyden. Pan-Africanism is a practical idea and movement aiming at African political and cultural unity and race solidarity. 67 notes.
L. W. Truschel

26. Ferling, John. EXCURSION IN COMPARATIVE HISTORY: THE REVOLUTIONS OF THE 1760'S-1770'S AND 1960'S-1970'S. *Social Studies 1977 68(2): 80-89.* Compares social tension amid apparent tranquility, intellectual ferment, dissatisfaction with authority, and rebellion from diverse strata of society, during the two periods.

27. Fingerhut, Eugene R. TOM WATSON, BLACKS, AND SOUTHERN REFORM. *Georgia Hist. Q. 1976 60(4): 324-343.* Traces the career of the Georgia Populist leader Thomas E. Watson from about 1880 to the early 1900's, focusing on his attitudes toward Negroes. Early in his career he supported limited rights for blacks, especially the opportunity to vote, but later on he reversed his position and became a supporter of Negro disfranchisement because that position was more useful for the reforms he was then advocating. 8 notes.
G. R. Schroeder

28. Fishbein, Leslie. HARLOT OR HEROINE: CHANGING VIEWS OF PROSTITUTION, 1870-1920. *Historian 1980 43(1): 23-35.* Reformers in the 19th century believed that through republican institutions and economic opportunity they could cure social problems in the United States, especially the persistence of prostitution. In attacking prostitution, they were torn between containing it through regulation or eradicating it entirely. The abolitionists, however, misinterpreted prostitution. Their campaign was based on the assumption that the behavior of individuals and society could be regulated and on belief in human and social perfectibility. 53 notes.
R. S. Sliwoski

29. Freedman, Estelle B. SEPARATISM AS STRATEGY: FEMALE INSTITUTION BUILDING AND AMERICAN FEMINISM, 1870-1930. *Feminist Studies 1979 5(3): 512-529.* Discusses the hypothesis that the women's community in the United States began to disintegrate during the 1920's as women began to enter the male-dominated spheres of work, politics, and social life. The history of cultural and political separatism within feminism before 1870, the transition during 1870-1929, led by Elizabeth Cady Stanton and Susan B. Anthony, and the postsuffrage period in the 1920's, all indicate that personal networks, friendships, and relationships among women enhanced feminist consciousness and feminist politics and did not detract from women's public political strategy. Only as women adopted men's attitudes and values, rejecting their own culture "in favor of men's promises of equality," did female separatism decline. 27 notes.
G. L. Smith

30. Freidel, Frank. THE OLD POPULISM AND THE NEW. *Massachusetts Hist. Soc. Pro. 1973 85: 78-90.* Discusses various aspects of agrarian protest, beginning with *Bacon's Rebellion* in 1676. Some common factors exist between the Neo-Populism of the 1970's and the Populism of the 1890's, but the new movement is urban rather than rural in its base and more akin to Progressivism.
J. B. Duff

31. Gaddy, C. Welton. SIGNIFICANT INFLUENCES OF BAPTISTS ON POLITICS IN AMERICA. *Baptist Hist. and Heritage 1976 11(2): 27-38.* Baptists fought long and successfully to obtain religious freedom in America and to get the First Amendment into the Constitution. But their emphasis on individualism in the religious experience and life has hindered most Southern Baptists from contributing any positive influence on the later American political scene. As individuals and churches they will oppose liquor and gambling, but they will not participate in fights for better housing for the poor, fair labor practices, etc. No leader has appeared among Southern Baptists, as Walter Rauschenbusch did in the North, to interpret the meaning of social Christianity and to call forth concerted efforts on major social problems. Thus the prophetic pulpit is largely absent in Southern Baptist churches. Neither a word of help or hope is extended. Some Southern Baptists have contributed much as individuals to the body politic. Urges the development of the political clout of the Southern Baptist Convention, lest that power become more a myth and less a reality. Based largely on Annual Reports of the Southern Baptist Convention and secondary sources; 23 notes.
H. M. Parker, Jr.

32. Galishoff, Stuart. TRIUMPH AND FAILURE: THE AMERICAN RESPONSE TO THE URBAN WATER SUPPLY PROBLEM, 1860-1923. Melosi, Martin V., ed. *Pollution and Reform in American Cities, 1870-1930* (Austin: U. of Texas Pr., 1980): 35-57. Discusses the development of urban water supplies in the late 19th and early 20th centuries in three American cities: Atlanta, Chicago and Newark. Atlanta was the South's leading city and the speaker of the "New South" that emerged after the Civil War. Chicago was the urban phenomenon of the period, for in just 70 years it had developed from a desolate army post into the leading commercial and industrial center of the Midwest, with a population of more than a million. Newark represents the smaller industrial cities of the Northeast. The problems these cities faced were typical. Secondary sources; fig., 63 notes.
J. Powell

33. Gear, James L. FACTORS INFLUENCING THE DEVELOPMENT OF GOVERNMENT SPONSORED PHYSICAL FITNESS PROGRAMMES IN CANADA FROM 1850 TO 1972. *Can. J. of Hist. of Sport and Physical Educ. 1973 4(2): 1-25.* A few government officials advocated physical training in the mid-1800's, but the U.S. Civil War and the threat of annexation of Canada prompted Parliament to promote military training. A trust fund of $500,000 from Lord Strathcona in 1909 stimulated physical and military training. World Wars I and II stimulated military drill in the schools. The federal government supported Provincial-Recreation Programmes in the 1930's, and a National Physical Fitness Act during World War II. In 1961 the government passed legislation to enhance amateur sport and national prestige. In the 1970's there was a strong move to encourage physical fitness to help keep down the cost of government medical services. The government has used physical fitness to accomplish various societal ends. Based on primary and secondary sources; 80 notes.
R. A. Smith

34. Gittell, Marilyn and Shtob, Teresa. CHANGING WOMEN'S ROLES IN POLITICAL VOLUNTEERISM AND REFORM OF THE CITY. *Signs 1980 5(3): supplement 67-78.* Political volunteerism in the United States began in the 1820's with a "dedicated army of urban-morality soldiers" working toward reform. Later on, national women's organizations carried on the tradition. Then, settlement houses attempted to deal with social problems; but, as was true of the Progressive Era, the reform spirit was nonpolitical. The New Activism of the 1960's, however, returned to the earlier commitment by middle-class women to work within the political sphere. Trends indicate more politicizing of volunteerism by middle- and working-class women in the future. Secondary sources; 21 notes.
S. P. Conner

35. Gold, Carol. TWO ROUTES TOWARD THE SAME PLACE. *Scandinavian Rev. 1977 65(3): 7-11.* Contrasts the history and current developments of the women's movements in Scandinavian countries with the United States. In Scandinavian countries, women acted to change laws affecting their legal status. In the United States, first efforts were aimed at women understanding themselves, with the assumption that societal changes would follow. Both groups have been successful in their goals.
J. G. Smoot

36. Gordon, Ann D. and Buhle, Mari Jo. SEX AND CLASS IN COLONIAL AND NINETEENTH-CENTURY AMERICA. Carroll, Berenice A., ed. *Liberating Women's Hist.* (Chicago: U. of Illinois Pr., 1976): pp. 278-300. Examines how changing economic conditions over three centuries altered feminist consciousness. Preindustrial colonial society concentrated a variety of essential economic activities in the family and women participated fully. In a transitional 19th-century industrial economy individual wage earners replaced families as the productive unit and sexual polarization was established. Because of their class position, wives of merchant capitalists gained control over female cultural patterns and old traditions of women's usefulness were set aside for subjugation to domesticity. This repressive femininity placed working-class women

outside the pale of respectability, where they stayed until they confronted their own class interests toward the close of the century. 46 notes.

B. Sussman

37. Gordon, Linda. THE LONG STRUGGLE FOR REPRODUCTIVE RIGHTS. *Radical Am. 1981 15(1-2): 75-88.* An adequate defense of abortion has and will be critical to free sexuality, the family, and problems of human dependancy and gender; 19th-20th centuries. 7 notes, 7 illus.

C. M. Hough

38. Grinder, Robert Dale. THE BATTLE FOR CLEAN AIR: THE SMOKE PROBLEM IN POST-CIVIL WAR AMERICA. Melosi, Martin V., ed. *Pollution and Reform in American Cities, 1870-1930* (Austin: U. of Texas Pr., 1980): 83-103. Between the 1880's and World War I in America, metropolitan centers were subject to industrial smoke pollution. The effects were at first only vaguely recognized, but soon these effects on the environment and human health became the focal concern of many. In many American cities legislation was implemented to curtail the menace. Such smoke abatement measures were either educationally or punitively oriented. Cities like Pittsburgh and St. Louis, which depended heavily on bituminous coal, would conquer the smoke problem only with the technological advances of the 1930's and 1940's. Other urban areas, such as Kansas City, saw their smoke problem disappear with the introduction of a new energy source—natural gas. Thus in most cities the smoke nuisance was conquered not so much as a result of stricter controls but because of a technological breakthrough that placed a heavier emphasis on natural gas, diesel fuel, and electricity. Secondary sources; 47 notes.

J. Powell

39. Groniowski, Krzysztof. SOCJALISTYCZNA EMIGRACJA POLSKA W STANACH ZJEDNOCZONYCH (1883-1914) [Polish socialist emigrants in the United States of America 1883-1914]. *Z Pola Walki [Poland] 1977 20(1): 3-35.* Polish Socialist activity in New York City in 1883 was contemporaneous with the first Marxist working-class party, Proletariat, in Poland. In 1886 the Association Równość [Equality] was founded in New York. In that same year the first Polish groups in the Knights of Labor were founded; their center was in Milwaukee. By 1890 the first Polish section of the American Socialist Labor Party was established; Polish centers developed in major cities and established contacts with the Socialist movement in the Prussian sector of Poland. Leadership conflicts developed within the American party over the national question. During the Revolution of 1905, a Polish Revolutionary Committee was established in the United States. It collected funds for the Polish Socialist Party. The influx of Poles after the revolution increased the splintering of the Polish Socialist movement over the issue of the home parties. The closest collaboration with the US movement took place in Milwaukee where in 1910 Socialists won the municipal elections.

J/S

40. Harper, John Paull. BE FRUITFUL AND MULTIPLY: ORIGINS OF LEGAL RESTRICTIONS ON PLANNED PARENTHOOD IN NINETEENTH-CENTURY AMERICA. Berkin, Carol Ruth and Norton, Mary Beth, ed. *Women of America: A History* (Boston: Houghton Mifflin Co., 1979): 245-269. Describes US 19th-century legal policy to suppress demands for birth control and trade in birth control devices. Some historians have claimed that this was an act to oppress women, but there is an indication that political leaders were afraid America would be underpopulated. Robert Dale Owen was a radical espouser of planned parenthood who believed birth control would improve the lot of the individual in society. Examines the place of abortion and the effect of Comstock laws. Primary sources; 10 notes.

K. Talley

41. Harrod, Frederick S. [BLACKS IN THE US NAVY].
JIM CROW IN THE NAVY (1798-1941). *US Naval Inst. Pro. 1979 105(9): 46-53.* The US Navy from its beginnings was hesitant about accepting blacks into its ranks. Blacks did serve, however, usually in the lowest ranks and doing the most menial tasks. During the War of 1812, however, blacks composed almost 20% of the Navy's enlisted force; during the Civil War, blacks made up almost eight percent of the enlisted strength of the US Navy. At all times, blacks served side by side with the white sailors in the same vessels. After the Civil War, though, and into the 20th century, the Navy restricted black enlistments, and segregation aboard ships became more evident. By 1932, there were only 441 blacks in the Navy. By this time, the few blacks that were enlisted could serve only in the messman branch. Adapted from *Manning the New Navy: The Development of a Modern Enlisted Force, 1899-1940* (Greenwood Press, 1978). 6 photos, table, 18 notes.
INTEGRATION OF THE NAVY (1941-1978). *US Naval Inst. Pro. 1979 105(10): 40-47.* During and since World War II, the role of blacks in the US Navy has changed. The Navy eventually accepted blacks for general service. In May 1949, Wesley A. Brown, became the first black midshipman to graduate from the US Naval Academy. The 1960's and 1970's saw increasing racial tension in the Navy, and the service created human relations councils and affirmative action programs to address grievances. But many black sailors today still feel they are being discriminated against and that more of the better jobs go to white sailors. Official naval figures tend to support their feelings. 10 photos, 11 notes.

A. N. Garland

42. Hayden, Dolores. CHARLOTTE PERKINS GILMAN AND THE KITCHENLESS HOUSE. *Radical Hist. Rev. 1979 (21): 225-247.* Socialist, feminist, and visionary Charlotte Perkins Gilman objected to the confining dimension of residential space, publishing plans for collective domestic life involving architectural innovations including day care centers, cooperative housekeeping, and communal kitchens; 1870-1920.

43. Hill, Ann Corinne. PROTECTION OF WOMEN WORKERS AND THE COURTS: A LEGAL CASE HISTORY. *Feminist Studies 1979 5(2): 247-273.* History of labor law pertaining to women's job protection in the United States, focusing on four periods: from 1876 (when the Massachusetts Supreme Court upheld the first piece of protective legislation for women workers) until 1923; from 1935 to 1948, when unemployment during the Depression and women working at traditionally male-held jobs during World War II raised contradictory questions in the courts about equality in the work force; from 1964 to 1971, when women challenged labor laws; and from 1974 to 1979, characterized by more Supreme Court cases on discrimination against women in the labor force than in any other period in American labor history. Examines specific court cases and legislation.

G. Smith

44. Hoig, Stan. SILAS S. SOULE: PARTIZAN OF THE FRONTIER. *Montana 1976 26(1): 70-77.* A member of the abolitionist "Jayhawkers" in Kansas, Silas S. Soule took part in raids to free imprisoned anti-slavery leaders, and led a similar attempt to rescue John Brown in 1859. Soule joined the Colorado gold rush, and was active in a volunteer force during the Civil War. Having been an unwilling participant in Chivington's attack on the Cheyennes at Sand Creek in 1864, he was assassinated soon afterward because of his testimony against the leaders of that massacre. Illus.

S. R. Davison

45. Hoxie, Frederick E. FROM PRISON TO HOMELAND: THE CHEYENNE RIVER INDIAN RESERVATION BEFORE W.W.I. *South Dakota Hist. 1979 10(1): 1-24.* The creation of the Cheyenne River Indian Reservation caused dramatic changes in the lives of the Sioux Indians who were forced to live there, especially from its founding in 1889 to World War I. Many US government programs attempted to assimilate the Indians and to destroy their Lakota culture. But rather than lead to a disintegration of tribal life, the reservation became a cultural homeland where the native Indian identity could be maintained. The Indians learned to adapt to the non-Indian institutions forced upon them and then used those institutions to defend and maintain their own traditional values and goals. Based on records of the Bureau of Indian Affairs, National Archives, Washington, D.C., and other primary sources; 6 photos, map, 48 notes.

P. L. McLaughlin

46. Huber, Joan. TOWARD A SOCIOTECHNOLOGICAL THEORY OF THE WOMEN'S MOVEMENT. *Social Problems 1976 23(4): 371-388.* Argues that the "decline in fertility and the shift of productive work from home to factory resulted in men's monopolizing the exchange of valued goods and services while, owing to their childrearing responsibility, women monopolized increasingly trivialized domestic work and second class jobs." The current women's movement is extensive in its scope and hopes to bring women into the world of work and men into the world of the home. Ref.

A. M. Osur

47. Hunt, Vilma R. A BRIEF HISTORY OF WOMEN WORKERS AND HAZARDS IN THE WORKPLACE. *Feminist Studies 1979 5(2): 274-285.* History of health hazards to women workers in industry in the United States and Europe from 1869, when Charles Dickens described conditions in a lead mill in East London, until the mid-1970's, when research on the potential health hazards of exposure to dangerous substances to workers, especially women, showed that exposure to lead, benzene, and ionizing radiation causes numerous illnesses and death. Focuses on the efforts of individuals active in improving conditions for women workers, such as Alice Hamilton, Marie Curie, and George Bernard Shaw. Instead of improving conditions for workers exposed to lead, benzene, and ionizing radiation, society excludes women workers from the workplace.
G. Smith

48. Hurwitz, Edith F. THE INTERNATIONAL SISTERHOOD. Bridenthal, Renate, ed. and Koonz, Claudia, ed. *Becoming Visible: Women in European History* (Boston: Houghton Mifflin, 1977): 325-345. Frustrated by the lack of domestic feminist reform, women established international organizations in the last third of the 19th century which aimed to override national differences and conflicting ideologies. Founded in 1888, the International Council of Women included political reformers who were interested in suffrage and social reformers who focused on issues such as temperance, educational reform, self-development, and increased career opportunities. Suffrage advocates later established their own forum in 1902 in the International Woman Suffrage Alliance. After World War I both groups were actively involved in the League of Nations. In 1925 they joined with other women's organizations to form a lobbying group, the Joint Committee of Representative Women's Organizations, and continued to strive against discrimination. Based on congress reports and secondary sources; 10 notes.
S. Tomlinson-Brown

49. Hutson, James H. WOMEN IN THE ERA OF THE AMERICAN REVOLUTION: THE HISTORIAN AS SUFFRAGIST. *Q. J. of the Lib. of Congress 1975 32(4): 290-303.* More than 50 years after the passage of the 19th amendment, the women's suffrage movement is still shaping the character of present-day writing about women during the era of the American Revolution. The first comprehensive work was *The Women of the American Revolution*, by Elizabeth F. Ellet, 1848-1850. This work was second in importance only to the *History of Woman Suffrage*, by Elizabeth Cady Stanton, Susan B. Anthony and others. The new field of women's history is largely controlled by the propagandistic work written nearly a century ago. More attention should be given to traditional information. Illus., 44 notes.
E. P. Stickney

50. Irvin, Dale T. SOCIAL WITNESS POLICIES: AN HISTORICAL OVERVIEW. *J. of Presbyterian Hist. 1979 57(3): 353-403.* In chronological fashion, embracing eight periods of ecclesiastical history, the many facets of policies regarding the "social gospel" are presented as enacted by the General Assembly of the major American Presbyterian Church. Nothing is said about the role of lesser judicatories—sessions, presbyteries, or synods—or of the numerous contributions of individuals in shaping social witness *extra ecclesiam*. Missing are the contributions of smaller Presbyterian Churches in the American tradition—Cumberland Presbyterian, "Southern" Presbyterian, and the Associate Reformed Presbyterian Church. Traces the policies for social witness from the colonial period to the present day, the latter being well represented, pointing out that General Assembly pronouncements mostly run ahead of the mood of the nation. Based on minutes and publications of the US Presbyterian Church; illus., 92 notes.
H. M. Parker, Jr.

51. Jacobs, Wilbur R. THE GREAT DESPOLIATION: ENVIRONMENTAL THEMES IN AMERICAN FRONTIER HISTORY. *Pacific Hist. Rev. 1978 47(1): 1-26.* Environmental themes should receive more attention in American history. European settlement destroyed the ecological balance wheel Indians had created, bringing soil exhaustion, timber depletion, and wildlife extermination in addition to massive Indian depopulation. By the mid-19th century, critics of the great despoliation began to be heard. Such minority voices included John Wesley Powell, George Perkins Marsh, Thorstein Veblen, and John Muir. More recent critics have included Bernard DeVoto, Carl O. Sauer, and Aldo Leopold. Historical understanding should be based on their work rather than on men such as Frederick Jackson Turner and Francis A. Walker, who have celebrated the factors responsible for the great despoliation. Based on manuscript collections, primary and secondary sources; 76 notes.
W. K. Hobson

52. Jones, Ronald W. CHRISTIAN SOCIAL ACTION AND THE EPISCOPAL CHURCH IN ST. LOUIS, MO.: 1880-1920. *Hist. Mag. of the Protestant Episcopal Church 1976 45(4): 253-274.* Analyzes movements toward social reform emanating from such American Episcopalians as Henry Codman Potter, Goerge C. Hodges, and Philo W. Sprague, and says the Episcopal Diocese of Missouri, much like the Episcopal Church across the nation, was doing little more than "nibbling at the crust of the social reform pie." Only in a few St. Louis ministries was there any activity. The church chose to minister to individuals through institutions rather than to lead actively as an agent for social change. Based on secondary materials; 78 notes, biblio.
H. M. Parker, Jr.

53. Kenneally, James J. WOMEN AND TRADE UNIONS 1870-1920: THE QUANDARY OF THE REFORMER. *Labor Hist. 1973 14(1): 42-55.* Surveys the changing role of women in the trade union movement 1870-1920, focusing primarily upon the Women's Trade Union League's struggle with the A.F.L. Trade unionists believed that women should be organized, but at the same time held that women belonged at home. Based on publications of the A.F.L. and W.T.U.L., manuscripts, and the Gompers Letterbooks; 60 notes.
L. L. Athey

54. Kessler-Harris, Alice. WOMEN, WORK, AND THE SOCIAL ORDER. Carroll, Berenice A., ed. *Liberating Women's Hist.* (Chicago: U. of Illinois Pr., 1976): pp. 330-343. Explores women's work outside the home in the context of the interaction between the fluctuations of the economy and the need for social order contingent upon the family. Traces women's participation in the labor force from colonial New England to present and contends that varying needs of the labor market determine changes in family structure and women's roles. Because the ideology of the family has always been considered crucial to the social order, the enormous number of women presently employed prompts questions about whether working women undermine family structure, and, even more importantly, whether the role of the family is to maintain the social order. 46 notes.
B. Sussman

55. Kirwan, Kent A. and Weber, Paul J. DANIEL DE LEON'S ANTI-CATHOLICISM. *Mid-Am. 1976 58(1): 20-30.* Daniel DeLeon's views concerning Catholicism were integral to his vision of the socialist state. The Church was "a political machine ambushed behind religion." Catholicism was the antithesis of socialism and a repudiation of the democratic ideal. Socialism meant individual responsibility; Catholicism, a ruling hierarchy. Education provided the key to the achievement of socialism; here the Church, the leader of capitalism's political force, was a powerful opponent. DeLeon's doctrinaire anti-Catholicism explicates his perception of capitalism. Based on DeLeon's published works and on secondary sources; 35 notes.
T. H. Wendel

56. Kline, Lawrence O. MONITORING THE NATION'S CONSCIENCE: A PERSPECTIVE ON METHODISM AND AMERICAN SOCIETY. *Methodist Hist. 1974 12(4): 44-62.* Methodism's mission to America has been reformatory from the beginning. The individual with a sense of moral liability was the basic social unit. The growing sense of Methodism's responsibility to America was paralleled with a sense of the nation's responsibility to the world. This was later complicated by the development of an American society of pluralistic values and commitments—not a unified nation measuring up to the expectations of evangelical Protestantism. 45 notes.
H. L. Calkin

57. Kraditor, Aileen S. ON THE HISTORY OF AMERICAN REFORM MOVEMENTS AND ITS LEGACY TODAY. *Continuity 1980 (1): 37-59.* Historians should not use a "good-bad" paradigm when analyzing reform movements in American history. That mode of thinking reflects too much subjective judgment. Most reformers shared common opinions of their fellow man. They perceived him as a flawed individual free to choose, but protective of the concepts of limited government and citizen responsibility. These common values stretched across three overlapping stages in US history with varying intensity: stage 1, 1780-1850; stage 2, 1828-1945; and stage 3, 1890 to the present. The underlying values should be used to research American reform movements, and because they can provide a foundation for explaining most of the inconsistencies inherent in the movements' variant branches, they may help historians minimize the possibility of incorporating their own biases into their interpretations.
W. A. Wiegand

58. Lansing, Marjorie. POLITICAL CHANGE FOR THE AMERICAN WOMAN. Iglitzin, Lynne B. and Ross, Ruth, eds. *Women in the World* (Santa Barbara, Ca.: Clio Books, 1976): pp. 175-181. The 19th-century feminist movement was begun by women abolitionists who wanted equality with men "in the state, the church and the home." After the passage of the 15th Amendment, which granted the vote to black men but not to women, the feminist movement directed its energies toward securing the vote for women. After the franchise was extended to women in 1920, the feminist movement remained largely inactive until the 1960's. Although there was no organized movement, the status of women changed dramatically during World War II when they entered the work force in large numbers. Concomitant to the rise in employment for women was a rise in the number of female voters. Moreover, the number of women voters increased as they became more educated. In recent years, women politicians have been increasingly accepted by the public. Secondary sources; 13 notes. J. Holzinger

59. Lawson, David C. and Kuehl, Warren F. JOURNALS OF THE AMERICAN PEACE SOCIETY: *ADVOCATE OF PEACE* (1837-1932). *World Affairs 1978 141(2): 183-195.* The content and perspective of the *Advocate of Peace,* the journal of the American Peace Society, changed in response to international developments and the moods of the American people.

60. Letsinger, Norman H. THE STATUS OF WOMEN IN THE SOUTHERN BAPTIST CONVENTION IN HISTORICAL PERSPECTIVE. *Baptist Hist. and Heritage 1977 12(1): 37-44.* The status of women in Southern Baptist circles has improved from a time when women were forbidden to speak in church or serve in positions of leadership to the present where a woman has been elected to a top position of leadership in the Southern Baptist Convention. Although women have not achieved a position of leadership in the Convention concomitant with their role in the local churches and in proportion to their numbers, abilities, and experiences, they have become significantly more involved as messengers (delegates) to the Convention and as members of committees, boards and commissions of the Convention. Based on annual records of the Southern Baptist Convention and records and histories of associations; 62 notes. H. M. Parker, Jr.

61. Liebman, Arthur. THE TIES THAT BIND: THE JEWISH SUPPORT FOR THE LEFT IN THE UNITED STATES. *Am. Jewish Hist. Q. 1976 65(2): 285-321.* From the 1880's through the early 1920's a massive immigrant Yiddish-speaking working class led by indigenous radicals and attuned to Marxist-socialist values emerged in the United States. Post-World War II developments have eroded this basis of the Jewish left; nevertheless, in the 1950's and beyond, the middle-class college student, comfortably American and Jewish, became the cutting edge of social action and political activism. The story of the American Communist Party and its Jewish members illustrates these changing patterns. 45 notes. F. Rosenthal

62. Luker, Ralph E. LIBERAL THEOLOGY AND SOCIAL CONSERVATISM: A SOUTHERN TRADITION 1840-1920. *Church Hist. 1981 50(2): 193-204.* James Warley Miles, an Episcopal priest and College of Charleston professor, was among the founders of a Southern intellectual tradition that found further expression in the thought of William Porcher DuBose and social reformer Edgar Gardner Murphy. This tradition sought to adopt religious ideas to modern culture, but theological assumptions were undercut because Miles, DuBose, and Murphy were viewed as spokesmen for the embattled southern social elite. 45 notes. M. D. Dibert

63. MacLeod, David. A LIVE VACCINE: THE YMCA AND MALE ADOLESCENCE IN THE UNITED STATES AND CANADA 1870-1920. *Social Hist. [Canada] 1978 11(21): 5-25.* In the 1850's and 1860's the Young Men's Christian Association (YMCA) engaged in evangelism for all ages, but as job opportunities for teenagers shrank and formal schooling increased, officials devoted more attention to middle-class adolescent boys, who needed protection from corruption, could pay fees, and would be receptive to Christianity. Around 1900, G. Stanley Hall's studies of adolescent psychology further stimulated boy's work. Workers emphasized objective, masculine religious expression, and dealt with sexuality through distraction and sublimation. During 1910-20 Taylor Statten instigated standardized programs. 87 notes. D. F. Chard

64. Magner, Lois N. WOMEN AND THE SCIENTIFIC IDIOM: TEXTUAL EPISODES FROM WOLLSTONECRAFT, FULLER, GILMAN, AND FIRESTONE. *Signs 1978 4(1): 61-80.* Leading feminists, although not trained as scientists, have used the scientific idiom to support feminist theory. Mary Wollstonecraft (1759-92), steeped in natural philosophy, asserted that a "common law of gravity" would allow the sexes to fall into their proper places once female education was provided. Transcendentalist Margaret Fuller (1810-50) presenting a model of electrical polarity, showed the androgynous nature of human beings; and social Darwinist Charlotte Perkins Gilman (1860-1935) used the methodology of physics to prove that female inferiority was cultural, not biological. Unlike earlier feminists, 20th-century radical Shulamith Firestone recommends a quantum leap, based on restructuring reproductive biology. Primary and secondary sources; 90 notes. S. P. Conner

65. Matsudaira, Martin "Mich". AN ASIAN AMERICAN PERSPECTIVE. *J. of Intergroup Relations 1976 5(4): 34-46.* Discusses subtle and overt forms of racism toward Asian Americans in employment practices, naturalization laws, and anti-Asian legislation from 1850 to the 20th century; considers problems in Asian-American ethnic identity.

66. McBeth, Harry Leon. THE ROLE OF WOMEN IN SOUTHERN BAPTIST HISTORY. *Baptist Hist. and Heritage 1977 12(1): 3-25.* Reviews the role of women in early American Baptist life, then relates Southern Baptists' reluctant acceptance of women's organized participation in denominational life. Presents especially valuable material on the gradual movement of women into influential roles in the denomination and on the contributions of women to the growth of Southern Baptists. Based largely on Southern Baptist periodicals and weeklies of the 19th century and on other secondary materials; 98 notes.
H. M. Parker, Jr.

67. McLaren, Angus. BIRTH CONTROL AND ABORTION IN CANADA, 1870-1920. *Can. Hist. Rev. [Canada] 1978 59(3): 319-340.* Based on religious, medical, legal and journalistic reports of the birth control debate. Shows why and how traditional contraceptive methods were employed by Canadian couples and, if these failed, how abortion was employed as a second line of defense against unwanted pregnancies. Reveals the importance of women's desires to control their physical functions, the view taken of women's health by the medical profession, and the differences in male and female attitudes toward sexuality. A

68. Megehee, Mark K. CREEK NATIVISM SINCE 1865. *Chronicles of Oklahoma 1978 56(3): 282-297.* Recounts the efforts by full-blood Creek Indians to wrest power from the mixed-bloods and restore a traditional culture. During 1865-1901 there were at least four rebellions, all ending in victories for the acculturation-minded mixed-bloods. Despite the impact of acculturation, some ancient traditions such as the Green Corn Dance, ball games, and "black drink" remain. Newspapers and government documents; 3 photos, 2 maps, 31 notes. M. L. Tate

69. Melosi, Martin V. REFUSE POLLUTION AND MUNICIPAL REFORM: THE WASTE PROBLEM IN AMERICA, 1880-1917. Melosi, Martin V., ed. *Pollution and Reform in American Cities, 1870-1930* (Austin: U. of Texas Pr., 1980): 105-133. Discusses efforts to resolve the refuse problem in American industrial cities. As the refuse problem grew, the first obstacle was to determine who was ultimately responsible. It was decided in most areas that it was a municipal responsibility. Often, however, this resulted in merely dumping everything in a site which was offensive to many. In the 1880's concern over the matter grew more intense, especially as the problem was linked to disease. Unless health officials were prominent in city government, however, they had problems airing their opinions and implementing effective action. The appointment of Colonel George E. Waring, Jr., as street cleaning commissioner of New York City in 1895 was the major turning point in the development of modern refuse management. By the end of his short tenure as street cleaning commissioner in 1898, Waring had generated considerable local and national attention, which led to successful solutions nationwide. Secondary sources; 3 tables, 5 fig., 64 notes. J. Powell

70. Mergen, Bernard. THE PULLMAN PORTER: FROM "GEORGE" TO BROTHERHOOD. *South Atlantic Q. 1974 73(2): 224-235.* "The organization of the Brotherhood of Sleeping Car Porters (BSCP) in the 1900's coincided with the destruction of the 'George'

stereotype in the minds of management, the American Federation of Labor (AFL), and the traveling public." A. Philip Randolph, editor of a radical Negro magazine and organizer of the BSCP, regarded the success of the BSCP and the creation of black pride and race consciousness as inextricably united. Climaxing years of struggle, Randolph succeeded in getting the AFL to grant the BSCP full equality. 42 notes.
E. P. Stickney

71. Meyer, Paul R. THE FEAR OF CULTURAL DECLINE: JOSIAH STRONG'S THOUGHT ABOUT REFORM AND EXPANSION. *Church Hist. 1973 42(3): 396-405.* Contends that Josiah Strong's support for domestic reform and overseas expansion resulted from his religious preoccupation with the idea that the Protestant Anglo-Saxon was a major contributor to civilization's progress. Only a thoroughly Anglo-Saxonized population was capable of positive influence when it inevitably became a world ruler. Strong in his early works described Anglo-Saxon cultural superiority as justification for intervention into other nations' internal affairs. As increasing industrialization created social problems, Strong's writing revealed more pessimism, undermining his earlier confidence in an ultimate Anglo-Saxon cultural victory. His early emphasis upon expansion became overshadowed in later years by his fear of Anglo-Saxon cultural decline. Based on Strong's published works; 33 notes.
S. Kerens

72. Mitchell, Norma Taylor. FROM SOCIAL TO RADICAL FEMINISM. *Methodist Hist. 1975 13(3): 21-44.* A survey of the diversity in Methodist women's organizations from the establishment of women's foreign and home missionary societies following the Civil War to the Caucus and the Commission on the Status and Role of Women in the United Methodist Church of the 1970's. Changes in the nature of feminism during this period, the accomplishments of the movement, and the problems still to be solved are discussed. 47 notes.
H. L. Calkin

73. Moens, Gabriel. DIE FORMEN DES INNERSTAATLICHEN MINDERHEITENSCHUTZES [Forms of domestic minority guarantees]. *Europa Ethnica [Austria] 1975 32(1): 2-8.* US Supreme Court decisions on minority cases from 1886 to 1972 differ in their legal interpretation, either prohibiting discrimination on individual grounds or on the basis of the rights of groups to preserve their ethnological characteristics.

74. Mohl, Raymond A. THE INTERNATIONAL INSTITUTE MOVEMENT AND ETHNIC PLURALISM. *Social Sci. 1981 56(1): 14-21.* The traditional American response to immigrants has emphasized Americanization. The doctrine of cultural pluralism made few converts until quite recently. The International Institute, a group of 55 immigrant social service agencies in American industrial cities, were among the early advocates of cultural pluralism. Unlike most agencies working with immigrants, the International Institutes accepted ethnic diversity and encouraged maintenance of immigrant languages, traditions, and folk cultures.
J

75. Mulvay, Jill C. ELIZA R. SNOW AND THE WOMAN QUESTION. *Brigham Young U. Studies 1976 16(2): 250-264.* Examines the role of Eliza Roxey Snow in originating and leading all female Latter-day Saint organizations. As wife of both Joseph Smith and Brigham Young consecutively, Mrs. Snow was in a position to help define the status of women within Mormon society. Comparisons are drawn between the woman's movement among the Mormons and the other feminist crusades stirring in America at the same time. Attention is given to Mrs. Snow's views on women's suffrage, female relief societies, business and medical efforts by Church women, and female attitudes toward polygamy.
M. S. Legan

76. Murphy, Larry George. THE CHURCH AND BLACK CALIFORNIANS: A MID-NINETEENTH-CENTURY STRUGGLE FOR CIVIL JUSTICE. *Foundations 1975 18(2): 165-183.* Discusses the role of religion in the black community in California. The black church provided opportunity for exercise of skills and expression as well as development of personal status. Black influx to California occurred with the gold rush; the first black church, St. Andrews African Methodist Episcopal, was formed in Sacramento in 1850. Expansion of A. M. E. and Baptist churches was rapid in the following decade. There was some cooperation between black churches, but union between them did not develop as some expected. The black churches considered freedom a right man received from God. Because of this, they became involved in political activity to achieve it. 74 notes.
E. E. Eminhizer

77. Noll, William T. WOMEN AS CLERGY AND LAITY IN THE 19TH CENTURY METHODIST PROTESTANT CHURCH. *Methodist Hist. 1977 15(2): 107-121.* Women, both lay and clergy, achieved significant advances in role and status in the Methodist Protestant Church before either the Methodist Episcopal Church or Methodist Episcopal Church, South. Even so their advances were never more than partial. The first constitution of the Methodist Protestant Church limited eligibility to office to white males. Women delegates to annual conferences began to appear in the 1870's, although ordination of women was a more difficult problem. 53 notes.
H. L. Calkin

78. Norton, Mary Beth. THE PARADOX OF "WOMEN'S SPHERE." Berkin, Carol Ruth and Norton, Mary Beth, ed. *Women of America: A History* (Boston: Houghton Mifflin Co., 1979): 139-149. After 1820, many aspects of women's lives changed dramatically due to technological development, providing more opportunities beyond marriage for some women. Nineteenth-century prescriptive literature can be useful as source material, but historians must be reminded to investigate social realities rather than assume that works stressing proper behavior indicate how women really lived. Although the 19th century was singularly oppressive, it also saw the foundation of the women's movement.
K. Talley

79. O'Connor, Karen and McGlen, Nancy E. THE EFFECTS OF GOVERNMENT ORGANIZATION ON WOMEN'S RIGHTS: AN ANALYSIS OF THE STATUS OF WOMEN IN CANADA, GREAT BRITAIN, AND THE UNITED STATES. *Int. J. of Women's Studies [Canada] 1978 1(6): 588-601.* Surveys the development of the legal, political, and economic status of women in the United States, Great Britain, and Canada since the mid-19th century, attributing the differences in the women's movement and acquisition of rights in the three countries to differing governmental structures.

80. Oman, Susan Staker. NURTURING LDS PRIMARIES: LOUIE FELT AND MAY ANDERSON, 1880-1940. *Utah Hist. Q. 1981 49(3): 262-275.* Louie Felt and May Anderson cooperated in the Primary Association to improve the religious education of Mormon children. Brought together by friendship between the two families, these two ladies worked closely for the remainder of their lives. From their efforts, the magazine *Children's Friend* was begun. Today, the *Friend* continues with international subscriptions. In 1921 and 1922, the Children's Convalescent Home and Day Nursery was begun as a result of their efforts to improve facilities for children. 3 photos, 47 notes.
K. E. Gilmont

81. Orr, J. Edwin. REVIVAL AND SOCIAL CHANGE. *Fides et Hist. 1974 6(2): 1-12.* Periods of religious revival have brought about social reforms. Surveys the five "awakenings" in America and Europe, discussing the various social movements emanating from them. Based on secondary sources; 31 notes.
R. Butchart

82. Penfield, Janet Harbison. WOMEN IN THE PRESBYTERIAN CHURCH: AN HISTORICAL OVERVIEW. *J. of Presbyterian Hist. 1977 55(2): 107-123.* Briefly sketches four phases of the participation of women in the life of the Presbyterian Church: 1) the rise of the "Cent" and "Praying" Societies to about 1815, 2) the development of regional and national women's boards of home and foreign missions from the Civil War to 1923, 3) the roles women played as missionaries from about 1830, and 4) the struggle of women to achieve ecclesiastical parity with men in the Presbyterian Church which ended technically in 1956. While the task of accepting women into total participation in the various areas of church life and ecclesiastical structure has not been fully accomplished, many strides have been taken. The presence today of large numbers of women in the theological seminaries is indicative that in the near future women will be more readily and widely admitted to all levels and institutional structures of the church. Based on secondary sources; picture, 57 notes.
H. M. Parker, Jr.

83. Petersen, William. CHINESE AMERICANS AND JAPANESE AMERICANS. Sowell, Thomas, ed. *Essays and Data on American Ethnic Groups* (Washington, D.C.: Urban Inst. Pr., 1978): 65-100. The

Chinese were the first immigrant group to be specifically excluded in American immigration policy and established the precedent that immigrants would be judged mainly by their place of origin. This discrimination against the Chinese and Japanese ordinarily would have resulted in ghettoization and low incomes, poor education, unstable family life, and a high crime rate, yet descendents of these immigrants have passed levels of native whites. Includes a history of preimmigration US contact with China and Japan in the 19th century, discussing movement from Hawaiian plantations and labor gangs, their social organization, internment of Japanese Americans during World War II, and their history of social mobility after 1945. Primary and secondary sources; 6 tables, 79 notes.
K. A. Talley

84. Poethig, Richard P. URBAN/METROPOLITAN MISSION POLICIES: AN HISTORICAL OVERVIEW. *J. of Presbyterian Hist. 1979 57(3): 313-352.* The mission policy of the Presbyterian Church touching the urban area did not begin until 1869. The reason was the church's preoccupation with the frontier. The United Presbyterian Church of North America did not initiate an urban mission policy until 1905. When the two churches united in 1958 the new united church was thus able to build upon existing foundations, and moved into new urban programs—inner city parishes, industrial evangelism, racial problems, ethnic groups, etc. In more recent years, largely as the result of ecclesiastical reorganization, the urban work on a national level has declined, but the responsibility has been picked up by the lesser church judicatories. Based on minutes of the General Assembly and reports of the Board of National Missions; illus., 27 notes.
H. M. Parker, Jr.

85. Powell, Thomas F. SOZIALISMUS IN AMERIKA, EINE BEWEGUNG, DIE STILLSTAND [Socialism in the USA: a movement that has never moved]. *Geschichte in Wissenschaft und Unterricht [West Germany] 1979 30(5): 284-296.* In the USA, socialism, mainly supported by Germans, has never been attractive. Its fate was sealed by the propaganda of World War I, which drove home the picture of German and un-American socialism. This failure is due to the socialists' misapprehension of what they were against. Out of their history the Americans have developed an American kind of individualism, which cannot come to terms with socialism, and they have a specific kind of private collectivism, which does not leave room for socialism. Freedom and private property are mutual preconditions in the USA against the socialist interpretation as mutually exclusive. The negative image of the state does not allow it too much power as demanded by socialism. There is no class consciousness, but a belief in social mobility depending only on the individual. 8 notes.
H. W. Wurster

86. Raeithel, Get. DER ANATOMISCHE SCHICKSALGLAUBE UND DIE AMERIKANISCHE FRAU [Belief in anatomical fate and the American woman]. *Frankfurter Hefte [West Germany] 1976 31(1): 25-34.* Discusses the current status of women in the United States (with a single reference to contemporary Canada), tracing that status through its historical development from colonial times. Emphasizes such topics as the lack of women's rights under the English common law, the slow development of female suffrage, the double standard for sexual behavior, and the Kinsey Report. Also discusses changes in sexual mores (especially those instituted by utopian religious experiments), black-white sexual relations, and the changing familial configurations of recent decades. The conclusion is that American women today are, through hard struggles, defining their new and different roles in American life. 20 notes.
J. L. Colwell

87. Reed, James. DOCTORS, BIRTH CONTROL, AND SOCIAL VALUES: 1830-1970. Vogel, Morris J. and Rosenberg, Charles E., ed. *The Therapeutic Revolution: Essays in the Social History of American Medicine* (Philadelphia: U. of Pennsylvania Pr., 1979): 109-133. From the 1830's until the early 1960's, American physicians generally discouraged methods of birth control for their patients. Historically, doctors have upheld the values and mores of society which, until the 1960's, chose to ignore the subject of birth control. Despite the descriptions of birth control methods available in medical manuals after 1865, and despite efforts by Margaret Sanger, Robert Latou Dickenson, and others in the first half of the 20th century, the medical profession remained opposed, leaving the birth control movement to lay women. Only with the marketing of the Pill in the early 1960's did doctors begin to consider birth control as a legitimate medical service. 67 notes.
G. L. Smith

88. Rosenberg, Rosalind. IN SEARCH OF WOMAN'S NATURE, 1850-1920. *Feminist Studies 1975 3(1/2): 141-154.* Antoinette Brown, America's first female minister, ordained in 1853, suffered a crisis of faith in 1854 and left the ministry to marry abolitionist Samuel Blackwell and have six children. Her crisis, similar to that of many women during the late 19th century, involved her anxiety about and search for woman's true identity. In the late 19th century Darwinism encouraged theories of different male and female natures, biologically determined, the male superior in mental capacity. Early feminists accepted female uniqueness, arguing only against the idea of female inferiority. By the late 1890's scholars such as University of Chicago psychologist Helen Thompson challenged Darwinian views, rejecting biology and emphasizing the social determinants of personality. Feminists and academics disagreed at this time, feminists insisting on an expanding role for women based on the advantages of the unique female nature. Primary and secondary sources; 28 notes.
S. R. Herstein

89. Rothman, Sheila M. OTHER PEOPLE'S CHILDREN: THE DAY CARE EXPERIENCE IN AMERICA. *Public Interest 1973 (30): 11-27.* The history of day care centers during 1854-1973 indicates that the centers may be poor institutions for promoting social reform, particularly with respect to the women's liberation movement.
S

90. Runte, Alfred. "WORTHLESS" LANDS—OUR NATIONAL PARKS: THE ENIGMATIC PAST AND UNCERTAIN FUTURE OF AMERICA'S SCENIC WONDERLANDS. *Am. West 1973 10(3): 4-11.* Establishment of most of the national parks in the United States was possible because of the abundance of worthless public land, areas that were deemed to be valueless for purposes of profitable agriculture, grazing, mining, or lumbering. This is the only explanation as to how the small minority of esthetic conservationists in a country dominated by firm commitments to the exploitation of natural resources and industrial achievement were able to achieve some success. After about 1950 when the wilderness and recreational needs of a rapidly expanding population and the deteriorating environment became apparent, the public began to push environmental issues and legislators began to heed the pressure to give more attention to the national parks. Preservation, recreational use, and exploitation are contending forces today. John Muir's 1910 dictum is important for the future of the national parks: "Nothing dollarable is safe, however guarded." 6 illus.
D. L. Smith

91. Russell, William D. A PRIESTLY ROLE FOR A PROPHETIC CHURCH: THE RLDS CHURCH AND BLACK AMERICANS. *Dialogue 1979 12(2): 37-49.* Reviews and analyzes the position of the Reorganized Church of Jesus Christ of Latter Day Saints on the ordination of women and blacks. Despite the supposed liberalism of the Reorganized Church, it has simply gone along with whatever popular feelings were present at a given moment. Very much in favor of racial equality during the Reconstruction, the church forgot the great cause in the years to follow, not reviving it until racial issues rose again during the 1960's. The RLDS, as opposed to the LDS, has preferred a priestly or pastoral mode of operation, rather than the prophetic mode chosen by the LDS. 48 notes.
V. L. Human

92. Sarkissian, Wendy. THE IDEA OF SOCIAL MIX IN TOWN PLANNING: AN HISTORICAL REVIEW. *Urban Studies [Great Britain] 1976 13(3): 231-246.* Discusses the idea of social mix in city planning, describes nine goals of the idea and evaluates the development and results of the social mix concept in England and the US since its inception, in 1845, with the proposed project for a mixed village at Ilford, England.

93. Sauer, R. ATTITUDES TO ABORTION IN AMERICA, 1800-1973. *Population Studies [Great Britain] 1974 28(1): 53-68.* "A survey of popular and professional literature indicates that there have been significant changes both in the popular and legal attitudes to abortion in America since 1800. The evolution of these attitudes may be broken into four periods: (1) the early nineteenth-century period, in which women apparently only infrequently sought abortions, even though legal norms proscribing most abortions were non-existent; (2) the mid-nineteenth-century period, in which women were seen to resort to abortion increasingly while at the same time more restrictive abortion laws were passed; (3) the late nineteenth and early twentieth-century period, in which abortion became more common even though the prevailing anti-abortion

norms still went publicly unchallenged; (4) the 1930-73 period, in which there developed, at first slowly, and then in the 1960s rapidly, an overt rejection of anti-abortion norms which was then reflected in corresponding changes of the law. Several possible factors in the liberalization of abortion attitudes are briefly presented, perhaps the most important being the development of low-fertility values evoked by the emergence of a modern industrial society." J

94. Schultz, Stanley K. and McShane, Clay. POLLUTION AND POLITICAL REFORM IN URBAN AMERICA: THE ROLE OF MUNICIPAL ENGINEERS, 1840-1920. Melosi, Martin V., ed. *Pollution and Reform in American Cities, 1870-1930* (Austin: U. of Texas Pr., 1980): 155-172. Discusses the role of sanitarians, landscape architects, and civil engineers in fighting pollution in American industrial cities. Officials in many cities granted extraordinary powers to civil engineers, for it had been demonstrated that only they were capable of solving such problems as air pollution, water pollution, and refuse, especially before the invention and widespread use of the automobile. Secondary sources; 26 notes. J. Powell

95. Seraile, William. THE POLITICAL VIEW OF TIMOTHY THOMAS FORTUNE: FATHER OF BLACK POLITICAL INDEPENDENCE. *Afro-Americans in New York Life and Hist. 1978 2(2): 15-28.* Black militant and newspaper editor Timothy Thomas Fortune (1856-1928) assumed a radical stance on black civil rights in his editorial policy, 1881-1928, on various black publications, including the New York *Globe, Freeman, Age,* and *Negro World.*

96. Shelden, Randall G. FROM SLAVE TO CASTE SOCIETY: PENAL CHANGES IN TENNESSEE, 1830-1915. *Tennessee Hist. Q. 1979 38(4): 462-478.* In 1831, Tennessee opened its first state prison with an inmate population predominantly white. With the end of slavery, prison became a kind of substitute for servitude. Blacks came to predominate as inmates, and concomitantly convicts began to be leased out as cheap labor. Similarly, urban working-class children were often placed in training schools to control them and to exploit their labor. Based on the author's unpublished PhD dissertation; 63 notes. W. D. Piersen

97. Singer, David J. AN ASSESSMENT OF PEACE RESEARCH. *Int. Security 1976 1(1): 118-137.* Discusses the thought and function of peace researchers since the late 19th century, the schism in the peace research community during the early and mid-1960's, and the three schools of thought which resulted.

98. Smylie, James H. THE BIBLE, RACE AND THE CHANGING SOUTH. *J. of Presbyterian Hist. 1981 59(2): 197-218.* Examines the principal statements of the Presbyterian Church in the United States (the Southern Presbyterian Church) to ascertain what part the Bible played in shaping the mind of this Southern denomination on racial matters. After reference to the denomination's attitudes at its beginnings in 1861, it focuses on the period after the 1930's when Southern Presbyterians felt the mounting pressure to deal with societal problems as well as race relations. Based largely on the *Minutes* of the Presbyterian Church in the United States and historical studies; illus., 47 notes.
H. M. Parker, Jr.

99. Tarr, Joel A.; McCurley, James; and Yosie, Terry F. THE DEVELOPMENT AND IMPACT OF URBAN WASTEWATER TECHNOLOGY: CHANGING CONCEPTS OF WATER QUALITY CONTROL, 1850-1930. Melosi, Martin V., ed. *Pollution and Reform in American Cities, 1870-1930* (Austin: U. of Texas Pr., 1980): 59-82. The period from 1850 to 1930 was marked both by widespread adoption of water-carriage systems by urban America and by attempts to deal with the unexpected and negative impacts of this technology. This technology was developed as such systems as public wells and pumps that utilized local groundwater supplies became inadequate, and wastewater techniques such as disposal in vaults or in nearby watercourses began to present problems. The water-carriage system had widespread political, social, and aesthetic consequences. In the area of health, it lowered substantially death rates from typhoid fever and other infectious diseases. Secondary sources; 2 tables, fig., 70 notes. J. Powell

100. Trunk, Isaiah. THE CULTURAL DIMENSION OF THE AMERICAN JEWISH LABOR MOVEMENT. *Yivo Ann. of Jewish Social Sci. 1976 (16): 342-393.* Divides the cultural history of the American Jewish labor movement into three periods. The first period, 1880's-90's, was characterized by socialism, a desire for educational achievement, and a tendency toward assimilation. The second period, 1900-20's, was caused by a new influx of immigrants coming after the Dreyfus trial and the Kishinev pogrom. As a result, they were disillusioned with socialism and tended toward cultural autonomy, radical nationalism, and Zionist socialism. A growth of the Hebrew and Yiddish press and literature characterized the Jewish labor movement during this period. The last period, extending from the 1930's to the end of World War II, saw a rise of national solidarity through such groups as the Workmen's Circle and the Jewish Labor Committee who worked against anti-Semitism. R. J. Wechman

101. Vertinsky, Patricia. THE EFFECT OF CHANGING ATTITUDES TOWARD SEXUAL MORALITY UPON THE PROMOTION OF PHYSICAL EDUCATION FOR WOMEN IN NINETEENTH CENTURY AMERICA. *Can. J. of Hist. of Sport and Physical Educ. [Canada] 1976 7(2): 26-38.* Chronicles changes in beliefs about women's health and sexuality in connection with feminism and the effects of these on promotion of women's physical education in the 19th century.

102. Walters, Ronald. MID-19TH CENTURY AMERICAN REFORM AND THE PROBLEM OF SEX. *Tr. of the Conference Group for Social and Administrative Hist. 1976 6: 57-74.* Analyzes the 19th-century entwinement of reform and sexual concerns and reformers' efforts to curb supposed prevalent sexual excess through "purity crusades" hoping to improve sexual morality.

103. Weeks, Louis B. THE SCRIPTURES AND SABBATH OBSERVANCE IN THE SOUTH. *J. of Presbyterian Hist. 1981 59(2): 267-284.* Traces a history of the use of the Bible in focusing the matter of Sabbath observance for the Presbyterian Church in the United States (the Southern Presbyterian Church). Traces the evolution in doctrine from more legalistic and proscriptive formulations in the 19th century to those that offer more freedom in the 20th. Describes the various mechanisms southern Presbyterians have employed to discern the import of biblical teaching relative to the nature of the Sabbath for church and society. Explores the ecclesiastical pronouncements to learn more generally about religious authority and the relationships of Bible, creeds, and practice. Based almost wholly on the *Minutes* of the Presbyterian Church of the United States; 45 notes. H. M. Parker, Jr.

104. Wessel, Thomas R. AGRICULTURE ON THE RESERVATIONS: THE CASE OF THE BLACKFEET, 1885-1935. *J. of the West 1979 18(4): 17-24.* In an effort to assimilate and to provide a living for the defeated Blackfoot Indians, the US government attempted to establish agricultural communities on the reservation in Montana. The government gave cattle and built extensive irrigation systems for the Indians, but the effort to make the reservation self-sufficient failed for several reasons. To the full-blood Blackfoot, status depended on ownership of horses, which they acquired by trading their cattle. Most of the Indians refused to use the irrigated land for cultivation. Finally, the vagaries of climate and market demand for beef disrupted the Blackfoot cattle industry. Based on records of the Commissioner of Indian Affairs and the Secretary of the Interior; 2 photos, 29 notes.
B. S. Porter

105. Wyatt-Brown, Bertram. JOHN BROWN, WEATHERMEN, AND THE PSYCHOLOGY OF ANTINOMIAN VIOLENCE. *Soundings 1975 58(4): 417-440.* The psychocultural theory of antinomian deviancy might be useful in explaining the behavior of individuals involved in the antislavery movement of the pre-Civil War period and the anti-Vietnam War controversy of the 1960's and 1970's. The violent antinomianism of John Brown was generated at least in part by his unhappy childhood and the unsettling conditions of the times. Similar factors might help to explain the behavior of the contemporary Weathermen. N. Lederer

106. Young, Louise M. WOMEN'S PLACE IN AMERICAN POLITICS: THE HISTORICAL PERSPECTIVE. *J. of Pol. 1976 38(3): 295-335.* Studies the social and historical changes that gave women an increasingly significant role in American political life ever since Anne

Hutchinson arrived in Boston in 1634. The social implications of the democratic principles written in the Declaration of Independence and the Constitution gradually came to be realized and implemented in the political lives of women. The whole-family involvement in the political environment was an opening wedge. Numerous aggressive and strong-willed feminist leaders carried the movement steadily forward, repeatedly demonstrating "society's urgent need for women's social energies." 73 notes.

R. V. Ritter

107. Young, Mary E. WOMEN, CIVILIZATION, AND THE INDIAN QUESTION. Deutrich, Mabel E. and Purdy, Virginia C., ed. *Clio Was a Woman: Studies in the History of American Women* (Washington, D.C.: Howard U. Pr., 1980): 98-110. Nineteenth-century US citizens labored to convert Indians to an idealized model of Christian civilization. They accomplished this by changing the Indians' relationship to property, work, and law. If Indian families could be confined to small farms and induced by private possession to work the land, they would convert millions of acres of hunting ground to land for use by white farmers. But with this sense of property, comes a sense of home, and it was felt that the female Indians, especially, should be educated according to the ideal of domestic femininity. An outstanding illustration of the US Indian Office's concern for modifying sex role definitions can be found in the work of agents and Presbyterian-Congregationalist missionaries among the Cherokee Indians: intermarriage, the rise to social prominence and political power of a mixed-blood elite of planters, merchants, millers, and ferry-keepers, and the shift to male agriculture changed the status as well as the work of the Cherokee women. A discussion summary follows. 36 notes.

J. Powell

108. —. A HISTORICAL PERSPECTIVE ABOUT THE INDIANS OF NORTH CAROLINA AND AN OVERVIEW OF THE COMMISSION OF INDIAN AFFAIRS. *North Carolina Hist. Rev. 1979 56(2): 177-187.* This survey of the early history of Indian-White relations in North Carolina reveals unrelieved repression, discrimination, and altogether reprehensible treatment of the Indians. In the late 19th and early 20th centuries, feeble attempts were made to provide education. As late as 1970, according to the census, educational barriers still existed. A major step forward was taken in 1971 when the General Assembly established the Commission of Indian Affairs to improve the quality of life for Indian people in housing, community services, and education. Some progress has been made. A paper presented by A. Bruce Jones, executive director, for the North Carolina Commission of Indian Affairs at a meeting of the North Carolina Literary and Historical Association.

R. V. Ritter

Civil Liberties and Political Rights

109. Alschuler, Albert W. PLEA BARGAINING AND ITS HISTORY. *Law and Soc. Rev. 1979 13(2): 211-245.* For most of the history of the common law, Anglo-American courts did not encourage guilty pleas but actively discouraged them. Plea bargaining emerged as a significant practice only after the American Civil War, and it generally met with strong disapproval on the part of appellate courts. This practice nevertheless became a dominant method of resolving criminal cases at the end of the 19th century and beginning of the 20th, and it attracted significant attention and criticism as a result of crime commission studies in the 1920's. In recent years, American criminal courts have become even more dependent on the guilty plea, but the good press that plea bargaining currently enjoys in legal and social science circles is a very recent development. Explores changes in guilty plea practices and in attitudes toward the guilty plea from the Middle Ages to the present. 36 notes, biblio.

J

110. Aptheker, Herbert. THE HISTORY OF ANTI-RACISM IN THE UNITED STATES. *Black Scholar 1975 6(5): 16-22.* Discusses the history of antiracist and antislavery sentiments in the United States, 1646-1974, emphasizing the works of 18th- and 19th-century abolitionists.

111. Bacchi, Carol. LIBERATION DEFERRED: THE IDEAS OF THE ENGLISH-CANADIAN SUFFRAGISTS, 1877-1918. *Social Hist. [Canada] 1977 10(20): 433-434.* The Canadian suffrage movement, initially committed to sexual equality, was infiltrated by social reformers in the 1880's. Mainly middle class traditionalists, the reformers wanted to preserve and strengthen the old order and their own positions. They regarded the family as the fundamental social unit and believed woman suffrage would give mothers a political voice and strengthen the family by doubling its representation. Feminists reactivated the movement in 1906 after an 11-year lull, but feminist concerns declined.

D. F. Chard

112. Binder, Arnold. THE JUVENILE JUSTICE SYSTEM: WHERE PRETENSE AND REALITY CLASH. *Am. Behavioral Scientist 1979 22(6): 621-652.* Discusses the rise of the juvenile court in the 19th century, the tendency to restore adult treatment and procedural protection to juvenile criminal offenders, and efforts to limit courts' jurisdiction in cases of status offense, 20th century.

113. Clifford, Deborah P. THE DRIVE FOR WOMEN'S MUNICIPAL SUFFRAGE IN VERMONT, 1883-1917. *Vermont Hist. 1979 47(3): 173-190.* Governor C. W. Gates signed the first municipal suffrage act in New England, 30 March 1917, but Governor P. W. Clement blocked efforts to make Vermont the 36th state to ratify the 19th amendment. The Vermont Women's Suffrage Association, organized in 1883, unofficially allied to the Women's Christian Temperance Union, with 276 members in 1896, collected 1500-3500 signatures for petitions for frequently defeated bills. The Vermont movement reflected the growth of favorable national opinion after 1910. 46 notes.

T. D. S. Bassett

114. Currie, James T. FROM SLAVERY TO FREEDOM IN MISSISSIPPI'S LEGAL SYSTEM. *J. of Negro Hist. 1980 65(2): 112-125.* The revolutionary impact of the Civil War and Reconstruction can be seen by comparing the legal status of Negroes in Mississippi before and after the war. Based on Mississippi state records in the Department of Archives and History; 2 tables, 55 notes.

N. G. Sapper

115. Dillard, Tom W. TO THE BACK OF THE ELEPHANT: RACIAL CONFLICT IN THE ARKANSAS REPUBLICAN PARTY. *Arkansas Hist. Q. 1974 33(1): 3-15.* Chronicles the struggle of blacks for equal participation in the state's Republican activities, 1867-1928.

S

116. DuBois, Ellen. THE RADICALISM OF THE WOMAN SUFFRAGE MOVEMENT: NOTES TOWARD THE RECONSTRUCTION OF NINETEENTH-CENTURY FEMINISM. *Feminist Studies 1975 3(1/2): 63-71.* During the 19th century the demand for the vote was considered by both feminists and antifeminists to be the most radical part of the program of the women's movement. Women were supposed to restrict their activities to the private sphere; their special contribution was to be made within the confines of the family. Men dominated the public arena, from which women were excluded. The demand for the vote, therefore, represented woman's demand for an independent voice outside her traditional family role. As voters women would participate in society as individuals, not merely as wives or mothers. The vote, therefore, would mean a change in women's concept of themselves and lead to new possibilities and a transformation of family and society. Primary and secondary sources; 26 notes.

S. R. Herstein

117. Eichler, Margrit and Nelson, Carol Ann. HISTORY AND HISTORIOGRAPHY: THE TREATMENT IN AMERICAN HISTORIES OF SIGNIFICANT EVENTS CONCERNING THE STATUS OF WOMEN. *Historian 1977 40(1): 1-15.* Examines the extent to which historians have dealt with woman suffrage in America. Two complementary approaches are taken: 1) an index search concerning suffragism as compared to other contemporaneous issues in works of general history; and 2) an examination of major reform histories and their treatment of the question. The historians examined either totally ignored woman's suffrage or dealt with it in a summary fashion. Because a lack of available information cannot be used to explain the historiographic deficiencies found, evidently sexual bias existed.

M. S. Legan

118. Elshtain, Jean Bethke. MORAL WOMAN AND IMMORAL MAN: A CONSIDERATION OF THE PUBLIC-PRIVATE SPLIT AND ITS POLITICAL RAMIFICATIONS. *Pol. and Soc. 1974 4(4): 453-473.* Outlines an Aristotelian public-political (male) versus private-nonpolitical (female) typology, filling in the paradigm with the Ma-

chiavellian divorce of morality from the public-political sphere to demonstrate that 19th- and 20th-century suffragists accepted the typologies. Suffragist arguments that the superior morality of women would purify politics show that they accepted the status quo middle- and upper-class socioeconomic conclusions of the typologies but stood antisuffragist arguments on their head. The continued acceptance of the ideologies of the paradigm will perpetuate sex and race inequalities. Based on secondary sources; 42 notes. D. G. Nielson

119. Fairweather, Gordon L. et al. CIVIL VIOLENCE AND CIVIL RIGHTS: A COMPARATIVE APPROACH TO LAW, ORDER, AND REFORM. *Am. Soc. of Int. Law Pro. 1974 68: 156-169.* Discusses the sources of violence in the US, Canada, and Mexico since the 18th century and the general problem of legally curbing violence while protecting civil rights.

120. Field, Phyllis F. REPUBLICANS AND BLACK SUFFRAGE IN NEW YORK STATE: THE GRASS ROOTS RESPONSE. *Civil War Hist. 1975 21(2): 136-147.* A statistical analysis of rank and file Whig-Republican Party voting on three New York state referenda (1846, 1860, 1869) designed to expunge clauses discriminatory against Negro suffrage from the 1821 constitution. Party leaders favored equal suffrage on each occasion, but grass roots opposition was strong in 1846, moderate in 1860, and relatively weak by 1869. The growing party solidarity on the question reflected developments during Reconstruction, but also was marked by declining political effectiveness of the party in the state.
E. C. Murdock

121. Friedman, Lawrence M. THE DEVELOPMENT OF AMERICAN CRIMINAL LAW. Hawes, Joseph M., ed. *Law and Order in American History* (Port Washington, N.Y.: Kennikat Pr., 1979): 6-24. Traces the development of American criminal law from 1776 to 1900 from the author's *A History of American Law* (New York: Simon and Schuster, 1973), and focuses on the growth and change of criminal statutes.

122. Friedman, Lawrence M. PLEA BARGAINING IN HISTORICAL PERSPECTIVE. *Law and Soc. Rev. 1979 13(2): 247-259.* This paper, using mostly data drawn from a study of the criminal work of the Superior Court of Alameda County, California, from 1880 on, explores the history of plea bargaining. Plea bargaining, it turns out, was used in Alameda County from at least 1880, though it was by no means as common in the late 19th century as it is today. There is also ample evidence of "implicit plea bargaining," that is, pleading guilty in expectation of a lighter sentence. The data from this study suggest that plea bargaining cannot be explained simply as a reaction to crowded court conditions. It is connected with structural and social changes in criminal justice, in particular, the rise of professional police and prosecutors.
J

123. Gadlin, Howard. PRIVATE LIVES AND PUBLIC ORDER: A CRITICAL VIEW OF THE HISTORY OF INTIMATE RELATIONS IN THE U.S. *Massachusetts Rev. 1976 17(2): 304-330.* Sexual liberation and the death of the family are really the transformation of a past mode of relationships. Four historical epochs mark strikingly different attitudes toward sexuality: colonial (1640-70), Jacksonian (1825-40), flapper (1920's), and contemporary (1950 on). In the first epoch, sex relationships were formal, in the second freer yet still regulated, the third, less regulated, and fourth, finally unregulated. Society must be restructured so that people do not so much look to other individuals to satisfy their needs, but give an equal amount in return. Primary and secondary sources; 21 notes. E. R. Campbell

124. Guethlein, Carol. WOMEN IN LOUISVILLE: MOVING TOWARD EQUAL RIGHTS. *Filson Club Hist. Q. 1981 55(2): 151-178.* Concentrates on the Woman Suffrage movement in Louisville and Kentucky. The author relates the role that outside speakers including Frances Wright, Lucy Stone, Elizabeth Cady Stanton, Victoria Woodhull, Susan B. Anthony, Carrie Chapman Catt, Emmaline Pankhurst, and Anna Howard Shaw played in encouraging local efforts. The Kentucky Equal Rights Association led by Laura Clay and the Louisville Woman Suffrage Association sought to improve the lot of women in the state. Their activities led to legislation in 1893 and 1894 that gave women control over their own property for the first time. The most vigorous opponent of the crusade for equal rights was Henry Watterson, editor of the Louisville *Courier-Journal.* Watterson's surprise conversion to the cause in 1918 helped to secure bipartisan support for the federal suffrage amendment in the state legislature in 1920. Based on contemporary newspapers and interviews; 122 notes. G. B. McKinney

125. Haller, Mark H. PLEA BARGAINING: THE NINETEENTH CENTURY CONTEXT. *Law and Soc. Rev. 1979 13(2): 273-279.* Plea bargaining apparently arose independently in a number of urban criminal courts in the nineteenth century. These simultaneous developments were presumably related to a number of broad structural changes that characterized American criminal justice at the time. Chief among them were the creation of urban police departments for the arrest of criminals and the development of a prison system for punishment or rehabilitation. Other developments included the reduced role of the victim, the relative independence of criminal justice from legal norms, and the corruption and political manipulation of the criminal justice system. The paper explores ways that such developments may have provided the context for the institutionalization of plea bargaining as a method of case disposition.
J

126. Harding, Vincent. OUT OF THE CAULDRON OF STRUGGLE: BLACK RELIGION AND THE SEARCH FOR A NEW AMERICA. *Soundings 1978 61(3): 339-354.* Examines the impact of black religion (mainly Christianity) on the black search for equality and freedom, from emancipation to civil rights.

127. Higginbotham, A. Leon, Jr. RACISM AND THE EARLY AMERICAN LEGAL PROCESS, 1619-1896. *Ann. of the Am. Acad. of Pol. and Social Sci. 1973 (407): 1-17.* "An understanding of the early American legal process is central to dealing with the racial disparities of today. From 1619 to 1860 the American legal process was one which expanded and protected the liberties of white Americans—while at the same time the legal process became increasingly more harsh as to the *masses* of blacks, with a steady contraction of their liberties. The United States Constitution sanctioned slavery, so that under federal law the slave 'had no rights which the white man was bound to respect.' Though the Emancipation Proclamation and the Thirteenth, Fourteenth, and Fifteenth Amendments significantly expanded the actual rights and options of blacks, nevertheless from 1865 to 1896 the legal process failed to effectuate the full potential of the rights intended and assured under the constitutional amendments."
J

128. Langbein, John H. UNDERSTANDING THE SHORT HISTORY OF PLEA BARGAINING. *Law and Soc. Rev. 1979 13(2): 261-272.* As late as the 18th century, ordinary jury trial at common law was a judge-dominated, lawyer-free procedure conducted so rapidly that plea bargaining was unnecessary. Thereafter, the rise of adversary procedure and the law of evidence injected vast complexity into jury trial and made it unworkable as a routine dispositive procedure. A variety of factors, some quite fortuitous, inclined 19th-century common law procedure to channel the mounting caseload into nontrial plea bargaining procedure rather than to refine its trial procedure as contemporary Continental legal systems were doing. 12 notes, biblio.
J

129. Larson, T. A. MONTANA WOMEN AND THE BATTLE OF THE BALLOT. *Montana 1973 23(1): 24-41.* Efforts to write woman suffrage into Montana's 1889 constitution failed. Montana women, especially "society women," did not strongly support the suffragists. Help from national leaders and from Jeannette Rankin (b. 1880), soon to be the nation's first congresswoman, led to success in 1914 when voters ratified a suffrage amendment passed by the legislature the previous year. Based on contemporary periodicals and correspondence; 46 notes.
S. R. Davison

130. Larson, T. A. THE WOMAN SUFFRAGE MOVEMENT IN WASHINGTON. *Pacific Northwest Q. 1976 67(2): 49-62.* The crusade for women's suffrage in the Pacific Northwest began in the 1850's but gained only minimal support until 1871 when Abigail Scott Duniway rekindled the movement in Washington Territory. Victory came in 1883 when the territorial legislature approved the franchise for women, but four years later the territorial supreme court overturned the act on a technicality. Mrs. Duniway's effectiveness subsequently decreased as she antagonized many potential supporters. At the same time Emma Smith

DeVoe directed a similar drive in Oregon, and despite problems created within the movement, the vote was secured in 1910. This Oregon victory prompted Washington to approve women's suffrage two years later, and both results should be credited to Mrs. DeVoe. Based on primary sources; 4 photos, 59 notes.   M. L. Tate

131. Lee, R. Alton. INDIAN CITIZENSHIP AND THE FOURTEENTH AMENDMENT. *South Dakota Hist. 1974 4(2): 198-221.* Traces the American Indian's status with regard to citizenship rights. Often considered "aliens in their own land," the 14th Constitutional Amendment (1866) and the debate which preceded its passage displayed the wide range of feelings that white Americans held toward Indians. Despite the fact that the amendment defined citizenship for all, further legal confrontations were necessary to make clear the US position in regard to earlier Indian treaties, criminal jurisdiction on reservations, authority to homestead, voting rights, and the citizenship status of reservation versus non-reservation Indians. In 1924, all Indians were granted citizenship, but Indians still do not hold first-class citizenship rights. Based on secondary sources; photo, 49 notes.   A. J. Larson

132. Mambretti, Catherine Cole. THE BATTLE AGAINST THE BALLOT: ILLINOIS WOMAN ANTISUFFRAGISTS. *Chicago Hist. 1980 9(3): 168-177.* Discusses Illinois women's antiwoman suffrage efforts in the late 19th and early 20th centuries; the Women Remonstrants of the State of Illinois (organized in 1886) became the Illinois Association Opposed to the Extension of Suffrage to Women in 1897; covers 1886-1923.

133. McKay, Robert B. RACIAL DISCRIMINATION IN THE ELECTORAL PROCESS. *Ann. of the Am. Acad. of Pol. and Social Sci. 1973 (407): 102-118.* "Nearly a century ago the Supreme Court of the United States acknowledged that the right to vote is 'a fundamental political right, because preservative of all rights.' A Court thus armed with lofty ideals might have been expected to apply the Fourteenth and Fifteenth Amendments to strike down racially discriminatory restrictions on the franchise that were adopted by many states after the Reconstruction period ended with the Hayes-Tilden Compromise of 1876. However, the Supreme Court largely confined its efforts to rhetoric and for many decades closed its eyes to the use of the white primary, literacy tests, the poll tax, and other devices to deny black citizens the vote. The white primary was at last outlawed in 1944, but Congress did not act until 1957. The Civil Rights Acts of 1957, 1960, and 1964 were well intended but not very effective. The Voting Rights Act of 1965, as amended in 1970, is now the principal vehicle for protection of the franchise against racial discrimination. It forbids literacy tests and other discriminatory tests and devices and requires federal approval of any changes in voting qualifications or procedures in states with a history of voting discrimination."   J

134. Motley, Constance B. THE CONTINUING AMERICAN REVOLUTION. *J. of Negro Hist. 1976 6(1): 7-15.* The ideological revolution begun by white colonists and Founding Fathers has been carried forward by the idealism of civil liberationists of all races throughout US history. Based on judicial opinions; 27 notes.
N. G. Sapper

135. Padilla, Fernando V. EARLY CHICANO LEGAL RECOGNITION: 1846-1897. *J. of Popular Culture 1979 13(3): 564-574.* Traces the twisted trail of legal decisions regarding citizenship and naturalization rights of Mexican Americans from the time of the Republic of Texas Constitution to the 1897 *Rodrigues* decision. The major issue in each instance was one of race versus nationality. State and federal court records; 65 notes.   D. G. Nielson

136. Penton, M. James. JEHOVAH'S WITNESSES AND THE SECULAR STATE: A HISTORICAL ANALYSIS OF DOCTRINE. *J. of Church and State 1979 21(1): 55-72.* Jehovah's Witnesses have been persecuted for refusing military service, not participating in the political system, and avoiding patriotic exercises. Their actions have been based on the concept of the secular state developed by Charles Taze Russell, who believed that Christ's return was imminent and that the secular powers would soon be destroyed. His successor as Watch Tower Society president, Joseph Franklin Rutherford, elaborated on Russell's concepts, developing the concept of higher law. The Witnesses were persecuted in the United States and Canada during World War I. Hostility to the state declined as court victories guaranteed their rights. In the 1960's, doctrine reflected this change by distinguishing between relative and absolute obedience to the state. 72 notes.   S

137. Price, Edward J., Jr. THE BLACK VOTING RIGHTS ISSUE IN PENNSYLVANIA, 1780-1900. *Pennsylvania Mag. of Hist. and Biog. 1976 100(3): 356-373.* Constitutionally disenfranchised in 1838, black Pennsylvanians did not regain the right to vote until ratification of the 15th Amendment in 1870. Although at first meeting with hostility from whites, by 1900 blacks could vote without hindrance and were exercising a small degree of political power. The franchise was useful to blacks to improve their condition but was not a panacea. Primary and secondary sources; 67 notes.   E. W. Carp

138. Rogers, T. W. JUDICIAL INTERPRETATION OF INTERNAL MIGRATION AS A CONSTITUTIONAL RIGHT IN THE UNITED STATES OF AMERICA. *Int. Migration [Netherlands] 1978 16(3-4): 131-159.* Enumerates Supreme Court cases involving the right to travel; the first arose out of efforts of a state to proscribe in-movements reflecting "an interplay between welfare, poverty and travel." Justice Story admitted specifically the power of a state to repel paupers seeking entrance. Justice Field "insisted that the rights that a state extended to its own citizens must be extended to citizens of other states within its borders." The Fifth Amendment due process includes the right to travel." In *Aptheker* [the] Court interdicted a federal statute forbidding members of the Communist party to obtain passports." The discussion of the 14th Amendment includes the position of Justice Douglas "who consistently took the position that the right to travel was a privilege and immunity of national citizenship." Since 1969, welfare residency laws have been clearly judged as interfering with a constitutional right to travel. 155 notes.   E. P. Stickney

139. Rudé, George. IDEOLOGY AND POPULAR PROTEST. *Hist. Reflections [Canada] 1976 3(2): 69-77.* The American and French Revolutions of the 18th century and the Lower Canada Rebellions of 1837-38 show that revolutions and rebellions involve a distinctive popular element. In the American Revolution the common people shared the dominant ideology which the revolutionary elites transmitted. The French Revolution also suggests the impact of the ideology of the revolutionary middle class and liberal aristocracy on the common people. The common people of France added something of their own to the notions of the French bourgeoisie. The Canadian rebellions show a popular ideology distinguishable from that of the leadership.   P. Travis

140. Shockley, Ann Allen. AMERICAN ANTI-SLAVERY LITERATURE: AN OVERVIEW—1693-1859. *Negro Hist. Bull. 1974 37(3): 232-235.* Antislavery societies, Quakers, blacks, and other individuals produced a wealth of literature instrumental in exposing the evils of slavery and bringing the peculiar institution to public attention.

141. Shofner, Jerrell H. CUSTOM, LAW, AND HISTORY: THE ENDURING INFLUENCE OF FLORIDA'S "BLACK CODE." *Florida Hist. Q. 1977 55(3): 277-298.* The black codes and Jim Crow laws of the late 19th century gave legal sanction to segregation and white supremacy attitudes which already existed in social custom. The legal justification of segregation eventually crumbled. Racial prejudice still exists but Floridians, for the most part, have rejected the violent repressive segregationist practices of the past. With time, racial equality may be not only the law, but the social custom. Based on government documents, newspapers, and secondary sources; 52 notes.
P. A. Beaber

142. Stoper, Emily and Johnson, Roberta Ann. THE WEAKER SEX AND THE BETTER HALF: THE IDEA OF WOMEN'S MORAL SUPERIORITY IN THE AMERICAN FEMINIST MOVEMENT. *Polity 1977 10(2): 192-217.* The question as to why so few women hold positions of power in American government leads the authors of this article to examine the sources and implications of one of the major arguments of American feminists: that woman's nature is morally superior to and mysteriously different from the nature of man. Although this claim has produced certain political benefits, it is argued here that the overall effect has been to limit women's role in politics as well as to perpetuate their psychological weaknesses.   J

143. Takanishi, Ruby. CHILDHOOD AS A SOCIAL ISSUE: HISTORICAL ROOTS OF CONTEMPORARY CHILD ADVOCACY MOVEMENTS. *J. of Soc. Issues 1978 34(2): 8-28.* The emergence of childhood as a social issue is barely a century old. The historical roots of current child advocacy movements can be found in an earlier period (1873-1914) characterized as the child-saving era. The emergence of this social issue during this period appears to be related to changing conceptualizations of the child, the developing "scientific" view of the child, as well as the influence of industrialization and urbanization. The child-saving era resulted in a number of problematic achievements regarding children's rights. The historical discussion points to the contributions which developmental and social psychology can make to the study of children's rights.
J

144. Tomatsu, Hidenori. BYOTOHOGO TO SHIHOSHINSA [Equal protection and judicial review: A study on judicial role in applying the equal protection clause of the US Constitution]. *Kokka Gakkai Zassi [Japan] 1977 90(7-8): 1-72; 1978 91(1-2): 1-50, (3-4): 1-31.* Part I. Studies the US Supreme Court rulings concerning the equal protection clause in the US Constitution. Part II. Discusses the criteria used in judicial reviews based on the principles of equal protection. Part III. Concludes that the judiciary is able to play a positive role in applying the equal protection clause in the Constitution because the sense of justice and the ethics against inequality are firmly established in the United States.

145. Witheridge, David E. NO FREEDOM OF RELIGION FOR AMERICAN INDIANS. *J. of Church and State 1976 18(1): 5-19.* Traces the history of Indian religious liberty from the first settlement of whites to the present time. Points out that Indians have been forced toward Christianity and deprived of their right to worship as they wish. The steps taken in recent years to restore Indian religious rights is discussed along with changing attitudes on the part of whites. 49 notes.
E. E. Eminhizer

146. Wright, James R., Jr. THE ASSIDUOUS WEDGE: WOMAN SUFFRAGE AND THE OKLAHOMA CONSTITUTIONAL CONVENTION. *Chronicles of Oklahoma 1973/74 51(4): 421-443.* Traces the Oklahoma Territory's Woman Suffrage Movement from 1870 to the Oklahoma Constitutional Convention in 1907, where it was defeated by the Southern Democrats.
S

147. Zangrando, Robert L. BLACK OUTREACH: AFRO-AMERICANS' RECRUITING EFFORTS TO ATTRACT SUPPORT ABROAD. *Phylon 1975 36(4): 368-377.* Concerns the patterns of initiative and response generated from within the black community by the repeated failure of the American political system to support and protect the civil rights of black people. Whether black leaders have chosen to work within the system, to challenge and redefine it, or to ignore and reject it, they have found it necessary to reach beyond that system itself. Black outreach has included 1) efforts designed to secure sympathy and support from abroad that might influence American public opinion, 2) efforts to invoke formal participation of external agencies such as the United Nations in the investigation and correction of racist conditions in America, and 3) actual, planned, or threatened emigration. Based on primary and secondary sources; 25 notes.
K. C. Snow

Economic Reform

148. Beauchamp, Claude. NOTES SUR L'ASSOCIATIONNISME AGRICOLE AU QUEBEC, 1760-1930 [Notes on the agricultural association movement in Quebec, 1760-1930]. *Cahiers Int. d'Hist. Écon. et Sociale [Italy] 1978 8: 87-104.* Analyzes the movement for agricultural associations in Quebec. The period from 1760 to 1900 was one of preparation for the full development of the agricultural association movement in the 20th century. The first period was marked by the formation of agricultural clubs and milk associations. In the 20th century cooperatives were formed for many products. Father Allaire founded the Confederation of Agricultural Co-operatives in 1916. Since then other important associations have been formed. Secondary sources; 22 notes, biblio.
F. X. Hartigan

149. Browne, Gary L. THE EVOLUTION OF BALTIMORE'S MARKETING CONTROLS OVER AGRICULTURE. *Maryland Hist. 1980 11(1): 1-11.* Analyzes the nexus created by Baltimore's growth as an entrepôt with the urban need for regulatory institutions over the agricultural sector in Baltimore's hinterlands. The city's increasing institutional rigidity created a "boom or bust" pattern, which endured throughout the 19th century, for the powerless agricultural sector. 21 notes.
G. O. Gagnon

150. Cassity, Michael J. SOUTHERN WORKERS AND SOCIAL CHANGE: CONCEPTS AND PROSPECTS. *Georgia Hist. Q. 1978 62(3): 200-212.* Histories of American labor have usually concentrated on the economic aspects and the labor unions. Suggests that many questions about the social implications of labor which have been asked by European labor historians should be applied to the American labor movement and particularly workers in the South. Secondary sources; 17 notes.
G. R. Schroeder

151. Goldman, Robert and Wilson, John. THE RATIONALIZATION OF LEISURE. *Pol. and Sci. 1977 7(2): 157-187.* The organization of workers' leisure time was as much a part of the rationalization of industries, of Taylorism and scientific management, as the organization of the work place. Organized recreation programs found their justification in their contribution to the general social welfare and sometimes came to resemble a moral crusade. Little attempt was made during the growth of welfare capitalism (1890-1920's), however, to conceal that the goal of these programs was to enhance production and efficiency, stabilize the class structure, and maintain the legitimacy of control. Primary and secondary sources; 97 notes.
D. G. Nielson

152. Harring, Sidney L. POLICE REPORTS AS SOURCES IN LABOR HISTORY. *Labor Hist. 1977 18(4): 585-591.* Presents eight documents from the Board of Police of Buffalo, New York, which reveal the cooperation between police and industrialists during strikes. Police reports are important sources for the social history of immigrant labor. Based on annual reports of the Buffalo, New York Board of Police; 14 notes.
L. L. Athey

153. Holford, David M. THE SUBVERSION OF THE INDIAN LAND ALLOTMENT SYSTEM, 1887-1934. *Indian Hist. 1975 8(1): 11-21.* From the passage of the General Allotment (Dawes) Act of 1887 until the Indian Reorganization Act of 1934, the policy of the US government was to detribalize, or break up the tribal Indian society and economy, and replace it with individual land holdings. In the process many millions of acres of land changed hands from tribes to the federal government to white settlers, and although the Indian was given individual land holdings, he was allowed to lease and eventually sell it, so that this, too, ended up in white hands. Although the evils of the Dawes Act were soon apparent and were pointed out by such organizations as the Indian Rights Association, it was not until 1934 that the policy was reversed. 68 notes.
E. D. Johnson

154. Holmes, Joseph J. RED BAITING AS USED AGAINST STRIKING WORKINGMEN IN THE UNITED STATES, 1871-1920. *Studies in Hist. and Soc. 1974 5(2): 1-19.* An attempt to determine the degree and extent of validity of Socialist influence charges behind labor unrest at the turn of the 20th century, and some reasons for it. The charges were widely disseminated, but are not borne out by facts. Socialists exploited unrest, but poor working conditions and economic depression were the causes. The economic overlords and their allies used the charge of Socialist influence with success because it was suited to the ideals of middle-class persons whose success in the cities had not made them happy. 91 notes.
V. L. Human

155. Holt, James. TRADE UNIONISM IN THE BRITISH AND U.S. STEEL INDUSTRIES, 1888-1912: A COMPARATIVE STUDY. *Labor Hist. 1977 18(1): 5-35.* Compares the development of labor unions in the steel industry in the United States and Great Britain. The weakness of US industrial and political labor organizations is found in the structure and policies of the steel industry's business organizations and not in a lack of class solidarity, new immigration, etc. Based on union membership rolls, government reports, and newspapers; 64 notes.
L. L. Athey

156. Isserman, Maurice. "GOD BLESS OUR AMERICAN INSTITUTIONS:" THE LABOR HISTORY OF JOHN R. COMMONS. *Labor Hist. 1976 17(3): 309-328.* John R. Commons possessed a rebellious social vision which was profoundly conservative. His central desire was to preserve the capitalist system by granting organized labor its rights as a cooperative group within the system. The central themes of Commons' works reveal historical influences leading him to develop a theory of labor history which emphasized a conservative institutionalism embracing change led by experts. His belief that workers would sacrifice long-term goals for "bread and butter" gains has not yet proved mistaken in the United States. Based on Commons' published works; 39 notes.
L. L. Athey

157. Jeffreys-Jones, Rhodri. THEORIES OF AMERICAN LABOUR VIOLENCE. *J. of Am. Studies [Great Britain] 1979 13(2): 245-264.* Historians disagree when attempting to explain those outbreaks of labor violence plaguing America during the Gilded Age and early 20th century. Some emphasized environmental forces; others stressed the impacts of race and heredity. A third group focused on clashing cultural elements, while another attributed the violence to "biological-instinctual imperatives." A fifth group claimed that ideology had insured such turmoil. 49 notes.
H. T. Lovin

158. Keller, Charles. PRISON REFORM AND INDIANS. *Indian Hist. 1976 9(1): 34-38.* Discusses similarities between imprisonment of convicted criminals and confining American Indians on reservations in the 19th century. The prison reform movement and the program to convert the Indians into farmers and craftsmen were both economic rather than humanitarian, designed to increase the labor force rather than to improve the welfare of the prisoner or Indian. 14 ref.
E. D. Johnson

159. Kessler-Harris, Alice. "WHERE ARE THE ORGANIZED WOMEN WORKERS?" *Feminist Studies 1975 3(1/2): 92-110.* Women were only a tiny percentage of the membership of trade unions as late as 1925, although the A.F.L. had been organizing for more than 40 years. Despite traditional views, the question is not why women did not organize themselves, but rather how and why they were prevented from becoming union members. Women provided a large pool of unskilled labor in the late 19th and early 20th centuries, with the added advantage of accepting low pay and poor working conditions in work situations that were often temporary. Unionists considered women a threat to their jobs and argued that they belonged at home tending to children and kitchen, not competing in the labor force. Labor committed itself to equal pay for women to protect male workers from female competition at lower wages. On the whole unions saw women as a threat to jobs and did little to promote their participation in trade unionism. Primary and secondary sources; 79 notes.
S. R. Herstein

160. Kudrle, Robert T. and Marmor, Theodore R. THE DEVELOPMENT OF WELFARE STATES IN NORTH AMERICA. Flora, Peter and Heidenheimer, Arnold J., ed. *The Development of Welfare States in Europe and America* (New Brunswick, N.J.: Transaction Books, 1981): 81-121. Seeks to identify, by comparing Canadian and US welfare state developments, "what unique characteristics distinguish the two North America countries and what common features set them apart from the countries of Western Europe" in the making of social policy, and also comments on "the future of the North American welfare state in an international context."

161. Langdon, Steven. THE EMERGENCE OF THE CANADIAN WORKING CLASS MOVEMENT, 1845-75. *J. of Can. Studies 1973 8(2): 3-13, (3): 8-26.*

162. Lawrence, Ken. THE ROOTS OF CLASS STRUGGLE IN THE SOUTH. *Radical Am. 1975 9(2): 15-36.* Discusses labor unions and organizations since 1810.
S

163. Lee, Lawrence B. ENVIRONMENTAL IMPLICATIONS OF GOVERNMENTAL RECLAMATION IN CALIFORNIA. *Agric. Hist. 1975 49(1): 223-229.* The reclamation movement in California was led by businessmen seeking to maximize their profits. Starting with the Newlands Act of 1902 the government took over the building of dams for irrigation. The 160 acre limitation has not prevented business from exploiting large quantities of land. Recently public opinion has shifted in favor of the environmentalists. 24 notes.
D. E. Bowers

164. Montgomery, David. LABOR AND THE REPUBLIC IN INDUSTRIAL AMERICA: 1860-1920. *Mouvement Social [France] 1980 (111): 201-215.* The common roots of the many sectoral struggles of workers in the deflationary phase of capitalist development, which followed the Civil War, enabled militants to inspire a sense of moral universality among *the producers,* which challenged both the ethic of acquisitive individualism and *monopoly corruption* of the republic. The changing structure of American capitalism, the recomposition of the working class, and new bourgeois strategies at the turn of the century failed to destroy working-class militancy, but they did disrupt the moral universality of the movement. In its place emerged a dominant *pure and simple* trade unionism, challenged by the Socialist Party and by direct action ideologies—minority movements which were necessarily both American and nationalist.
J

165. Montgomery, David. THE PAST AND FUTURE OF WORKERS' CONTROL. *Radical Am. 1979 13(6): 6-23.* Traces the history of the struggle for workers' control over at least part of the production process in the 19th and 20th centuries, which became increasingly difficult as mechanization and large-scale production increased labor productivity and increased the number of supervisors to overlook the workers; and briefly compares and contrasts the struggles of the 19th and 20th centuries.

166. Montgomery, David. STRIKES IN NINETEENTH-CENTURY AMERICA. *Social Sci. Hist. 1980 4(1): 81-104.* Surveys patterns of strike behavior in 19th-century America and examines what these patterns reveal of workers' changing consciousness and culture. The applicability of various generalized theories of strikes and labor protest is then tested against these specific American materials. Most of the theories are rejected as too mechanistic and positivistic. Based partly on published materials of the US Census Bureau, the Commission of Labor, and the state of Pennsylvania; 2 tables, 6 notes.
L. K. Blaser

167. Rimlinger, Gaston. LABOR AND THE GOVERNMENT: A COMPARATIVE HISTORICAL PERSPECTIVE. *J. of Econ. Hist. 1977 37(1): 210-225.* Compares the development of the workers' right to organize and bargain collectively in England, France, and the U.S. Starting with a common repressive policy, each country followed a different path toward establishing the workers' rights. The main ultimate difference lies in the extent to which the state became involved in industrial relations. In England the state remained aloof after securing very broad legal rights of collective action. The workers were left to do their own battling. In France the state came to look upon collective agreements as an aspect of public policy and became the dominant partner in labor negotiations. The American pattern lies in between: state protection extends to procedural but not to substantive issues.
J

168. Rockoff, Hugh. PRICE AND WAGE CONTROLS IN FOUR WARTIME PERIODS. *J. of Econ. Hist. 1981 41(2): 381-401.* The debate over wage and price controls has taken a highly stylized form. Advocates of controls stress the direct effect on the obvious problem, inflation, whereas critics stress the side effects. This paper measures and compares the effects of controls during the four periods when controls have been used in the United States in the 20th century. Although tentative conclusions are drawn concerning the price effects, the size of the administrative bureaucracies, and so forth, the clearest lesson, as usual, is that the issue warrants further investigation by economic historians because it is important, and because the historical record is surprisingly rich.
J

169. Schleppi, John R. "IT PAYS": JOHN H. PATTERSON AND INDUSTRIAL RECREATION AT THE NATIONAL CASH REGISTER COMPANY. *J. of Sport Hist. 1979 6(3): 20-28.* During the industrial decline of the 1890's, John H. Patterson came to realize that skilled workers were needed to build cash registers, and he initiated programs affecting the welfare of his workers. He built a factory that was lighted and that could be easily ventilated in summer; it became a model for future factories. He brought John C. Olmsted to his National Cash Register Company in Dayton, Ohio, to landscape the grounds. Physical fitness and health programs became part of the workers' lives. In 1897, an

athletic club and a bicycle club were formed. In 1905, a company baseball team was formed. Patterson's work improved working and living conditions in Dayton. Based on company publications; 24 notes.
M. Kaufman

170. Scholten, Pat Creech. THE OLD MOTHER AND HER ARMY: THE AGITATIVE STRATEGIES OF MARY HARRIS JONES. *West Virginia Hist. 1979 40(4): 365-374.* Mary Harris (Mother) Jones (1830-1930), a colorful Irish American labor organizer, used deliberate hell-raising tactics to bolster workers' morale and rouse public sympathy. She arranged "pageants of poverty" to show the exploitation of children and others, verbally abused management in public encounters, and served time in jails. Covers 1870's-1920's. Primary sources; 37 notes.
J. H. Broussard

171. Schwantes, Carlos A. LEFTWARD TILT ON THE PACIFIC SLOPE: INDIGENOUS UNIONISM AND THE STRUGGLE AGAINST AFL HEGEMONY IN THE STATE OF WASHINGTON. *Pacific Northwest Q. 1979 70(1): 24-34.* Analyzes the problems faced by the American Federation of Labor (AFL) in its attempt to organize workers in the Pacific Northwest. Its problems came not so much from conservative management as from leftist unions which had begun in the 1880's. The Western Federation of Miners and its offshoot, the American Labor Union, proved especially troublesome to the AFL. By 1920, however, the nationally organized AFL was able to displace the regional influence of the smaller indigenous unions of the Pacific Northwest. Primary and secondary sources; 6 photos, 51 notes.
M. L. Tate

172. Seretan, L. Glen. THE PERSONAL STYLE AND POLITICAL METHODS OF DANIEL DE LEON: A RECONSIDERATION. *Labor Hist. 1973 14(2): 163-201.* Reviews the literature about the "uncompromising" Daniel De Leon. De Leon was intransigent in intraparty affairs, but he was willing to compromise in working with other organizations. De Leon was no more vituperative in oral and written communications than were other contemporary labor leaders, nor was he more dictatorial. The general picture of De Leon is far too stereotyped, and a comprehensive reexamination of him is needed. Based on De Leon's writings and on secondary sources; 156 notes.
L. L. Athey

173. Shanahan, Donald G., Jr. COMPENSATION FOR THE LOSS OF THE ABORIGINAL LANDS OF THE CALIFORNIA INDIANS. *Southern California Q. 1975 57(3): 297-320.* Traces the history of Indian land claims and how the Indians of California were eventually compensated for their lands. California Indians fell victim to complex legal technicalities in the years following the American acquisition of California. Granted the use of lands rather than full title after the missions were secularized, the Indians found themselves omitted from the Treaty of Guadalupe Hidalgo and slighted by the Land Claims Commission Act of 1851. Adverse court decisions in succeeding years denied Indian contentions for compensation. Not until 1920 were federal bills introduced to devise methods of compensation for California Indians, based on equitable losses suffered because of 18 treaties unratified by the Senate in 1852. After 1928 such claims could be made, and in 1944 Indians received $5 million. Another award in 1963 provided $29 million, more than 100 years after the issue of land rights for Indians was raised. Based on published works; 65 notes.
A. Hoffman

174. Swetnam, George. LABOR-MANAGEMENT RELATIONS IN PENNSYLVANIA'S STEEL INDUSTRY, 1800-1959. *Western Pennsylvania Hist. Mag. 1979 62(4): 321-332.* Traces the labor-management relations in the ferrous metals industry from paternalism in the early 19th century to the development of strong unions in the 1950's.

175. Vecoli, Rudolph J. EMIGRATI ITALIANI E MOVIMENTO OPERAIO NEGLI USA [Italian immigrants and the workers' movement in the United States]. *Movimento Operaio e Socialista [Italy] 1976 22(1-2): 153-167.* The history of Italian Americans in the American labor movement either has been ignored totally or has represented the Italian worker as a scab or the cause of salary reductions. Attracted by hopes of saving money, Italians from Central and Southern Italy flocked to America from about 1880. Many came only for brief periods and, because they did not speak English, understand American customs, or belong to the unions, found themselves isolated and often with the worst jobs. Without formal means to protest their situation, they often staged spontaneous strikes. These had no lasting effects, but definitely prove the fallacy of the stereotypical submissive Italian worker. After 1900, Italian radicals played organizational roles in the Industrial Workers of the World and the formation of the garment workers' unions.
M. T. Wilson

176. Wells, Dave and Stodder, Jim. A SHORT HISTORY OF NEW ORLEANS DOCKWORKERS. *Radical Am. 1976 10(1): 43-69.* Despite rigid segregation and racial antipathy, white and black longshoremen united at various periods since the 1850's to work together for mutual economic gain. Racial solidarity dissolved into hostility under outside pressures and the effort of each race to achieve gains for themselves. The recent history of the New Orleans longshoremen's unions has been characterized by extreme corruption which can only be eradicated through a socialist society.
N. Lederer

177. Young, James D. DANIEL DE LEON AND ANGLO-AMERICAN SOCIALISM. *Labor Hist. 1976 17(3): 329-350.* Daniel DeLeon (1852-1914) has been misunderstood within the history of Anglo-American socialism. His fundamental ideas were at odds with Leninist ideology. DeLeon was aware of the need for a vanguard socialist party, but he did not see the workers as a herd to be led, but as a group in a stage of class consciousness development. Based on publications of Daniel DeLeon, periodicals, and secondary sources; 46 notes.
L. L. Athey

178. Zerker, Sally. THE DEVELOPMENT OF COLLECTIVE BARGAINING IN THE TORONTO PRINTING INDUSTRY IN THE NINETEENTH CENTURY. *Industrial Relations [Canada] 1975 30(1): 83-97.* Analysts of collective bargaining have tended to stress predominant functional characteristics, in general classed as marketing, governmental, and managerial theories. Less emphasis has been placed on the importance of power relationships between organizations. A careful review of the development of collective bargaining in the Toronto printing industry in the 19th century suggests that the latter is the most significant factor in the historical process.
J

Educational Reform

179. Biklen, Sari Knopp. THE PROGRESSIVE EDUCATION MOVEMENT AND THE QUESTION OF WOMEN. *Teachers Coll. Record 1978 80(2): 316-335.* The progressive education movement, whether focusing on the poor, as in its early stages, or on the well-to-do, as later, never explicitly incorporated feminist principles into its philosophy or practice. Although vocational programs involved both sexes, they stressed job-related activities for boys and domestic ones for girls. The so-called core curriculum also emphasized traditional female roles. Such women's colleges as Bennington and Sarah Lawrence sought to prepare their students for a life of creative leisure as housewives. Primary and secondary sources; 73 notes.
E. Bailey

180. Boylan, Anne M. EVANGELICAL WOMANHOOD IN THE NINETEENTH CENTURY: THE ROLE OF WOMEN IN SUNDAY SCHOOLS. *Feminist Studies 1978 4(3): 62-80.* The activities of women in the Sunday School Movement illustrate some of the ways women shaped their roles in 19th-century American society. The model of "evangelical womanhood," as one of several possible roles, was developed by these women during 1800-20. The women of the Sunday School Movement not only shaped their role but designed ways of putting it into practice and transmitting it to succeeding generations by encouraging and training other young women to follow them and by enlarging the scope of Sunday School work to include organized benevolence. A few even went from this beginning to political work for temperance, abolition, and women's rights. 34 notes.
L. M. Maloney

181. Britts, Maurice W. BLACKS ON WHITE COLLEGE CAMPUSES: 1823-PRESENT. *Negro Hist. Bull. 1974 37(4): 269-272.* Traces the growth of enrollment of blacks and treatment accorded them, from John Russwurm in 1823 to current efforts at minority recruitment.

182. Burstyn, Joan N. CATHARINE BEECHER AND THE EDUCATION OF AMERICAN WOMEN. *New England Q 1974 47(3): 386-403.* Catharine Beecher perceived that men had professionalized

their occupations, whereas women had not. Beecher did not propose to mix the sexes in all work, nor did she argue that women should be permitted employment in all occupations; each sex had a sphere reserved to it. Education was the medium of professionalization; she established schools and trained teachers for work throughout the nation. She wrote textbooks which expounded her views. Beecher was always an experimenter with new methods, but she never swerved from her view that the sexes are equal but separate. 38 notes.
V. L. Human

183. Carruthers, Iva E. CENTENNIALS OF BLACK MISEDUCATION: A STUDY OF WHITE EDUCATIONAL MANAGEMENT. *J. of Negro Educ. 1977 46(3): 291-304.* Education for Afro-Americans has always been determined by whites, and always with an eye on white rather than black interests. The priorities followed by the white educational managers have been national unity first, black uplift second. The actual shape of black education has been dependent upon compromises within the white community. The result has been the continuation of black inferiority and the assimilation of better educated blacks into the value system of white society. Secondary sources; 27 notes.
R. E. Butchart

184. Cavallo, Dom. FROM PERFECTION TO HABIT: MORAL TRAINING IN THE AMERICAN KINDERGARTEN, 1860-1920. *Hist. of Educ. Q. 1976 16(2): 147-162.* Discusses the struggle for direction in curricula and moral training in kindergarten education between those educators who subscribed to Froebelian thought and those who considered themselves progressive reformers, 1860-1920.

185. Choquette, Robert. ADÉLARD LANGEVIN ET LES QUESTIONS SCOLAIRES DU MANITOBA ET DU NORD-OUEST 1895-1915 [Adélard Langevin and questions concerning the school system in Manitoba and the North-West, 1895-1915]. *Rev. de l'Université d'Ottawa [Canada] 1976 46(3): 324-344.* In 1890, the Liberal government of Manitoba passed a law which abolished church schools; all children were to be educated in the public schools. The Catholic Church, with its own school system, opposed this. The national Conservative Party promised, if victorious in federal elections, to overturn the decision of the provincial government. Instead, the Liberal Party under Wilfrid Laurier won the 1896 elections. Laurier, though French-speaking and Catholic himself, engineered a compromise with Thomas Greenway, the Manitoba premier. All schools would be public, but there would be religious education for those who wished it between 3:30 and 4:00 PM. In addition, the French language would be used where 10 or more pupils were French-speaking (the same rights were given to other non-English-speaking groups), thus partially reversing Greenway's abolition of French as one of the official languages. Most Catholic prelates accepted the compromise, and were suported in this by the Vatican, but Louis Philippe Adélard Langevin, Archbishop of the Diocese of St. Boniface, which included the Prairie Provinces, refused to go along. He accused Laurier of being a traitor to his language and his faith, and continued to demand separate schools for Catholic students throughout his episcopate. 98 notes.
J. C. Billigmeier

186. Cole, Babalola. APPROPRIATION POLITICS AND BLACK SCHOOLS: HOWARD UNIVERSITY IN THE U.S. CONGRESS, 1879-1928. *J. of Negro Educ. 1977 46(1): 7-23.* During 1879-1928 Congress appropriated money for Howard University on a gratuity basis, with no authorizing legislation. This was questioned in the 1920's. Discusses congressional debate over authorizing legislation and analyzes the votes. Annual appropriations were authorized on 13 December 1928. 2 tables, 18 notes.
B. D. Johnson

187. Conway, Jill. PERSPECTIVES ON THE HISTORY OF WOMEN'S EDUCATION IN THE UNITED STATES. *Hist. of Educ. Q. 1974 14(1): 1-13.* Traces the history of attitudes about women's education from Puritan times to the present. Sees a historic danger in developing present-day women's studies programs, as they might tend to limit true creativity by channeling it and therefore perpetuate existing patterns of socialization. Based on primary and secondary sources; 11 notes.
L. C. Smith

188. Crouchett, Lawrence P. THE DEVELOPMENT OF THE SENTIMENT FOR ETHNIC STUDIES IN AMERICAN EDUCATION. *J. of Ethnic Studies 1975 2(4): 77-85.* "We are wrong if we assume that sentiment for ethnic studies emerged only recently," or that it is a new phenomenon peculiar to the present minorities. Bilingualism, biculturalism, and ethnic subjects were a fact of American education long before "ethnic studies" became defined in the 1960's. Cites examples as early as the 1660's showing white minority groups insisting on their own schools as a means of preserving their languages, religions, and cultures against the assimilative influences of the school systems of the dominant classes. The 19th century especially saw the Irish and Germans creating curricula in their parochial schools to combat the prevailing Protestant nativism. "Black studies" courses were offered as early as 1919 and the 100%-ism of the WWI era brought renewed stress on ethnic subjects. Surveys the efforts of W. E. B. Du Bois and Carter G. Woodson for national programs of ethnic education, and the current "revival" of white ethnic topics as a result of the civil rights movement. Based on primary and secondary sources; 23 notes.
G. J. Bobango

189. Dye, Charles M. WILLIAM GREENLEAF ELIOT AND WASHINGTON UNIVERSITY, ST. LOUIS: AN INNOVATION IN NINETEENTH CENTURY AMERICAN HIGHER EDUCATION. *Missouri Hist. Soc. Bull. 1979 35(3): 131-146.* The founder of Washington University, William Greenleaf Eliot (d. 1887), insisted that the new university avoid the classical education offered by the older universities. Washington University, consequently, focused on programs and courses designed to encourage growth and development of the West. The institution developed extensive polytechnic curricula, established preparatory programs for students lacking secondary school educations, and emphasized technical and applied science instruction. Based on Washington University archival materials; 24 notes.
H. T. Lovin

190. Elusche, Michael. ANTISLAVERY AND SPIRITUALISM: MYRTILLA MINER AND HER SCHOOL. *New-York Hist. Soc. Q. 1975 59(2): 149-172.* Founded in 1851, the Miner School for Negro Girls in Washington D.C., offered one of the few opportunities in the nation to young black girls seeking an education. Miss Miner, a sickly, intense, pious native of upstate New York, was able to establish and continue the school despite limited resources and much opposition. For a decade the school limped along until she left suddenly in 1861 for California where she became absorbed in spiritualism. Three years later she died, still hoping for the millennium. The school she founded eventually (1955) became part of the District of Columbia Teachers College, while her name is preserved on a District of Columbia elementary school. Primary and secondary sources; 4 illus., 45 notes.
C. L. Grant

191. Field, Alexander J. EDUCATION AND SOCIAL PROGRAMS. *J. of Econ. Hist. 1978 38(1): 258-261.* Presents workshop notes and discussion on the development of formal educational systems in Great Britain and the United States during 19th century-1970's. Further considers investments of "human capital" in higher education and the economic return on this investment, and how more effective means of research may be devised in testing the motivations behind those social decision processes closely related to the development of formal educational systems. Based on a workshop at the 37th annual meeting of the Economic History Association, 1977. 10 notes.
C. W. Olson

192. Findlay, James. THE SPCTEW AND WESTERN COLLEGES: RELIGION AND HIGHER EDUCATION IN MID-NINETEENTH CENTURY AMERICA. *Hist. of Educ. Q. 1977 17(1): 31-62.* An extensive study of the Society for the Promotion of Collegiate and Theological Education at the West during 1843-73. Evangelical Protestants were deeply concerned that their distinct worldview be implanted in the then-evolving system of American colleges. The Society also provided key financial support for these colleges in a time of limited state interest in higher education. The work and efforts of Theron Baldwin were particularly important to the Society. The study of the Society sheds light on the "unity, vitality, and aggressiveness" of American evangelical Protestantism itself. Based on extensive archival research and on primary and secondary sources; 84 notes.
L. C. Smith

193. Gardner, Booker T. THE EDUCATIONAL CONTRIBUTIONS OF BOOKER T. WASHINGTON. *J. of Negro Educ. 1975 44(4): 502-518.* Reviews the educational theories (1881-1915) of Booker T. Washington, who stressed practical skills for economic survival, giving rise to the charge that his principles kept blacks in menial positions.

194. Gawalt, Gerard W. MASSACHUSETTS LEGAL EDUCATION IN TRANSITION, 1766-1840. *Am. J. of Legal Hist. 1973 17(1): 27-50.* Formal legal education at such schools as Harvard College gradually replaced legal apprenticeship.

195. Gloster, Hugh M. THE BLACK COLLEGE: ITS STRUGGLE FOR SURVIVAL AND SUCCESSS. *J. of Negro Hist. 1978 63(2): 101-107.* Overview of the evolution of black colleges and universities, 1854-1978.

196. Gorelick, Sherry. CITY COLLEGE: RISE AND FALL OF THE FREE ACADEMY. *Radical Am. 1980 14(5): 21-36.* For 129 years the City University of New York (first the Free Academy in 1847 and then the City College of New York until the 50's) offered free education to New Yorkers. From 1969 until 1976 there were also open admissions. Nineteenth- and early 20th-century struggles to end this experiment in education failed. But in 1976 efforts to curtail the numbers of individuals receiving education succeeded. The end of open admission through the imposition of tuition dropped the enrollment 17% and the faculty 28% in an "orgy of official vandalism" against the college opportunities for Latinos, blacks, and other lower-class New Yorkers.
C. M. Hough

197. Graham, Patricia Albjerg. EXPANSION AND EXCLUSION: A HISTORY OF WOMEN IN AMERICAN HIGHER EDUCATION. *Signs 1978 3(4): 759-773.* Two trends—a social movement away from the norms of "true womanhood" and the expansion of higher education during 1875-1925—brought a higher proportion of women into academia than previously. As classical education expanded to include more diversity, women were accepted more readily into academia. However, when the research university of the 20th century began to develop, it became a new monolith which again generally excluded women from higher education. This trend may be reversing as lifelong learning becomes the university's primary function. Based on federal statistics and secondary sources; table, 22 notes.
S. P. Conner

198. Habibuddin, S. M. SECULARIZATION OF EDUCATION IN THE USA AND INDIA DURING THE 19TH CENTURY. *Indian J. of Pol. [India] 1976 10(1): 27-47.* The United States and India have in common a process of secularization of education that began in the 19th century. In the United States there was a gradual shift of control of schools and colleges from sectarian to secular hands. This was not accomplished without political and constitutional controversy. English education in India was controlled by missionaries in the first half of the century. The government of India early expressed a principle of neutrality and secularism, especially with the 1854 Wood Dispatch. Though this policy was challenged at times, government policy led to a remarkable growth period in Indian education. I D. K. Lambert

199. Herbst, Jurgen. NINETEENTH-CENTURY NORMAL SCHOOLS IN THE UNITED STATES: A FRESH LOOK. *Hist. of Educ. [Great Britain] 1980 9(3): 219-227.* Discusses the development of normal schools, teacher training establishments, in the United States in the 19th century. Using Merle Borrowman's argument, stresses the antagonism between supporters of liberal arts colleges and those of teachers' colleges. Points to the tendency in the East to separate normal schools from colleges and universities, and to concentrate on pedagogical professionalism. In the West there was an attempt to start a teachers' university, Illinois State Normal University. The success of normal schools depended on the desire of communities to offer publicly supported postelementary education. 29 notes.
S

200. Issel, William. THE POLITICS OF PUBLIC SCHOOL REFORM IN PENNSYLVANIA, 1880-1911. *Pennsylvania Mag. of Hist. and Biog. 1978 102(1): 59-92.* The impulse for educational reform serving conservative purposes emerged in industrial areas with a high proportion of non-English-speaking population, strikes, and class and ethnic conflict. Legitimacy-seeking interest groups desired concentration of authority over education. Their compulsory education campaign paralleled the push for child labor legislation and ultimately a comprehensive school code. Based on official records and secondary works; 61 notes.
T. H. Wendel

201. Leslie, W. Bruce. BETWEEN PIETY AND EXPERTISE: PROFESSIONALIZATION OF COLLEGE FACULTY IN THE "AGE OF THE UNIVERSITY." *Pennsylvania Hist. 1979 46(3): 245-265.* Case study of the development of faculty professionalization at Bucknell, Franklin and Marshall, Princeton, and Swathmore during 1870-1915, the "age of the university." Until 1890, little progress had been made in adopting university standards at these institutions other than an increasing insistence on specialized training for professors of science and mathematics. By 1915, these institutions conformed in many respects to the new university norms, but their faculties lacked academic freedom and security in their positions. Illus., 69 notes.
D. C. Swift

202. Melder, Keith. MASK OF OPPRESSION: THE FEMALE SEMINARY MOVEMENT IN THE UNITED STATES. *New York Hist. 1974 55(3): 261-279.* Challenges the traditional view that the female seminary movement was an instrument of women's liberation in 19th-century American society. The female seminary movement, by fostering the distinction between education for men and education for women, was actually an oppressive institution perpetuating the dependent status of women in society. Its goal of training teachers, housewives, and mothers was a male centered and sexist definition of woman's social role. Based on primary and secondary works; 4 illus., 40 notes.
G. Kurland

203. Merelman, Richard M. PUBLIC EDUCATION AND SOCIAL STRUCTURE: THREE MODES OF ADJUSTMENT. *J. of Pol. 1973 35(4): 798-829.* Examines the American educational system and its impact on class relationships in three historical phases. The upper class used education to reinforce its social position, 1787-1857. Education was an "agent for social mobility and social change," 1857-1945. Since 1945 it has become a "means of fulfilling human potential." To this incremental model is added an accretional model of organization and administration. A combination of accretion and "incomplete assimilation of overly disparate social groups" has led to a crisis in American education. Three coalitions now compete for control of educational reform under the federal government's "potential doctrine." The competitors all desire to maintain organized public education, but their quarrels may lead to the "last crisis of accretion." 2 figs., 74 notes.
A. R. Stoesen

204. Meyer, John W.; Tyack, David B.; Nagel, Joane; and Gordon, Audri. PUBLIC EDUCATION AS NATION-BUILDING IN AMERICA: ENROLLMENTS AND BUREAUCRATIZATION IN THE AMERICAN STATES, 1870-1930. *Am. J. of Sociol. 1979 85(3): 591-613.* Social movements influenced by Protestantism and Republican ideology, more than urbanization and industrialization, fostered public education in northern and western states.

205. Miller, Janet A. URBAN EDUCATION AND THE NEW CITY: CINCINNATI'S ELEMENTARY SCHOOLS, 1870 TO 1914. *Ohio Hist. 1979 88(2): 152-172.* By 1900 Cincinnati, with its 216,239 residents crowded into the basin, had evolved into a modern city. Gradually more centralized authority in the superintendent's office placed greater decisionmaking power in the hands of the professionals and facilitated efforts to reach all levels of the community with educational programs. The urban school system assumed a greater custodial role for larger numbers of children. "Perceiving different needs in the organic city, educators and city leaders sought to provide academic as well as vocational education, social and civic training, and health and welfare services through a complex educational system of elementary schools." Illus., 53 notes.
E. P. Stickney

206. Noll, Mark A. CHRISTIAN THINKING AND THE RISE OF THE AMERICAN UNIVERSITY. *Christian Scholar's Rev. 1979 9(1): 3-16.* Analyzes the change in US higher education, 1860-1930, from a broad humanistic approach with a Christian orientation to a technical, empirical orientation following the spread in belief in Social Darwinism and increase in funding from large corporations.

207. Noonan, Brian. THE CONTRIBUTION OF SEPARATE SCHOOLS TO THE DEVELOPMENT OF SASKATCHEWAN: 1870 TO THE PRESENT. *Study Sessions: Can. Catholic Hist. Assoc. [Canada] 1979 (46): 71-81.* Separate Catholic schools in Saskatchewan have provided a rallying point for minority rights, expressed religious freedom, and allowed for the democratic exercise of the religious education for Catholic youth.

208. Price, Edward J., Jr. SCHOOL SEGREGATION IN NINETEENTH-CENTURY PENNSYLVANIA. *Pennsylvania Hist. 1976 43(2): 121-137.* Pennsylvania laid the foundations of a public school system in 1834. By law, blacks had the right to attend any of these schools, but prevailing prejudice prevented them from doing so. In 1854, the legislature provided that school districts must either provide separate schools for blacks or permit them to attend regular schools. Although black teachers and some other blacks supported separate educational facilities, many others, particularly members of the Pennsylvania State Equal Rights League, demanded an end to this practice. The legislature voted to ban separate educational facilities in 1881, but segregated schools remained in Pennsylvania, particularly in the cities. This effort to end separate schools did result in the improvement of black schools. Based upon *Pennsylvania Laws*, legislative proceedings, court cases, newspapers, and other materials; illus., 55 notes. D. C. Swift

209. Ralston, Helen. RELIGION, PUBLIC POLICY, AND THE EDUCATION OF MICMAC INDIANS OF NOVA SCOTIA, 1605-1872. *Can. Rev. of Sociol. and Anthrop. [Canada] 1981 18(4): 470-498.* Examines education of the Micmac Indians of Nova Scotia in terms of the ideological perspectives that informed the decisions of public administrators and the work of the missionaries. Historical evidence indicates that both church and state policies, whether French or English, had as their goal the assimilation of the Micmac Indians to the dominant European culture that was assumed to be superior. Education was perceived as the principal means of achieving assimilation. Micmacs had no control over their own education, and virtually no say in formulating policy. J

210. Roberts, Terry. THE INFLUENCE OF THE BRITISH UPPER CLASS ON THE DEVELOPMENT OF THE VALUE CLAIM FOR SPORT IN THE PUBLIC EDUCATION SYSTEM OF UPPER CANADA FROM 1830 TO 1875. *Can. J. of Hist. of Sport and Physical Educ. 1973 4(1): 27-47.* The British upper-class elite, educated in public schools, had the means necessary to inculcate the idea that team sports build Christian character into the educational system of Upper Canada. There is little evidence of this belief 1830-75, although its existence at that time has been suggested by several writers. Similarly there is no strong evidence of the transmission of this value claim by normal schools, the Council of Public Instruction, or teachers. Sport was probably little used for educational purposes until after 1875. Based on primary and secondary sources, principally the *Journal of Education for Upper Canada;* 48 notes. R. A. Smith

211. Russell, Joseph J. SOME NOTES ON EDUCATION IN INDIANA. *Negro Hist. Bull. 1976 39(1): 511-515.* Indiana prohibited the education of Negroes at public expense until 1869, when segregated facilities were authorized. In 1877 black children were allowed to attend white schools where no separate facilities existed, or when they advanced into higher grades. But in 1927, when enough blacks advanced to secondary schools, Indianapolis opened Crispus Attucks High School for "colored" students, and other cities followed suit. Under pressure from the NAACP, the Indiana legislature outlawed segregated education in 1949, but it still exists in practice, illustrating institutional resistance to progressive legislation. Based on secondary sources; illus., 5 photos, biblio. W. R. Hively

212. Scott, Osborne. PRE- AND POST-EMANCIPATION SCHOOLS. *Urban Rev. 1976 9(4): 234-241.* The slave's education typically was limited to matters of religious salvation and perhaps reading and writing. New York City's Africa Free Schools were an exception. The day schools and black colleges which emerged after the war emphasized vocational education and black history. 6 photos. L. D. Smith

213. Simmons, Adele. EDUCATION AND IDEOLOGY IN NINETEENTH-CENTURY AMERICA: THE RESPONSE OF EDUCATIONAL INSTITUTIONS TO THE CHANGING ROLE OF WOMEN. Carroll, Berenice A., ed. *Liberating Women's Hist.* (Chicago: U. of Illinois Pr., 1976): 115-126. Establishes the connection between the prevailing ideology toward women and their opportunites for higher education. Female education was deemed important when it prepared a woman for her prescribed role. When it did not, as at the end of the 19th century when there were few jobs for college-educated women, societal reaction was not to help women use their abilities but rather to reject higher education for them. Traces this theme in women's education from the inception of the female seminary through the establishment of women's colleges, coeducational institutions, and coordinate colleges. 46 notes. B. Sussman

214. Spivey, Donald. THE AFRICAN CRUSADE FOR BLACK INDUSTRIAL SCHOOLING. *J. of Negro Hist. 1978 63(1): 1-17.* Industrial arts education was utilized in the maintenance of subordination and exploitation of black people in the US South and in Africa. It was a negative aspect of the Pan-African movement. Both white Europeans and white Southerners put industrial schooling to effective use in pursuing a world order based upon white rule. Primary materials in the Rockefeller archives and domestic and foreign secondary materials; covers 1879-1940. 82 notes. N. G. Sapper

215. Stamp, Robert M. TEACHING GIRLS THEIR "GOD GIVEN PLACE IN LIFE." *Atlantis [Canada] 1977 2(2): 18-34.* Adelaide Hoodless, an early champion of women's rights in Canada, campaigned to bring scientific information on food preparation, home management, and child care, in the form of home economics classes, to young women in public schools in the 1890's and 1900's in Canada.

216. Timberlake, C. L. THE EARLY STRUGGLE FOR EDUCATION OF THE BLACKS IN THE COMMONWEALTH OF KENTUCKY. *Register of the Kentucky Hist. Soc. 1973 71(3): 225-252.* Before the Civil War, education for black children was limited to private religious instruction. A general school law of 1837 did not even mention blacks. The first provision for financial support of black education came in 1866, and the first black high school was founded in that year. Berea College and Simmons University offered further opportunities. The Kentucky Negro Education Association, formed in 1877, led the fight for Normal Schools for blacks. State institutions for blacks were established, beginning in Frankfort in 1886. The Day Law (1904), aimed primarily at Berea, prohibited desegregated private educational institutions. Efforts to reopen opportunities for blacks succeeded most notably in the Brown decision of the Supreme Court in 1954. Based on primary and secondary sources; 39 notes. J. F. Paul

217. Tyack, David B.; Kirst, Michael W.; and Hansot, Elisabeth. EDUCATIONAL REFORM: RETROSPECT AND PROSPECT. *Teachers Coll. Record 1980 81(3): 253-269.* American education has undergone three major reform periods since 1840: the Common School movement, when education was democratized and universalized under lay control; the Progressive movement, which saw increasingly centralized control by professional educators; and the post-Sputnik era, during which the competing demands of special interests have factionalized education and loosened professional control. This factionalism, coupled with declining support for public education, is weakening the system. A more effective governance structure coupled with renewed public commitment to education is needed. Secondary sources; 36 notes. E. Bailey

218. Tyack, David B. THE SPREAD OF PUBLIC SCHOOLING IN VICTORIAN AMERICA: IN SEARCH OF A REINTERPRETATION. *Hist. of Educ. [Great Britain] 1978 7(3): 173-182.* Examines the causes of the great expansion of public schools during 1840-80 in America, paying particular attention to community involvement in organizing and maintaining the new educational system. This expansion is remarkable for its even pace and the general absence of regional variations. There are many underlying causes for this expansion, but at the same time it seems that a general popular consensus emerged in favor of developing an extensive school system which would perpetuate the standards and values associated with America's successes. 38 notes. S

219. Tyack, David B. WAYS OF SEEING: AN ESSAY ON THE HISTORY OF COMPULSORY SCHOOLING. *Harvard Educ. R. 1976 46(3): 355-389.* Discusses the role of economics, social classes, and political systems in the development of compulsory education from 1840 to the 20th century, including problems in historiography.

220. Wilke, Phyllis Kay. PHYSICAL EDUCATION FOR WOMEN AT NEBRASKA UNIVERSITY, 1879-1923. *Nebraska Hist. 1975 56(2): 193-220.* Examines the development of a program of physical education for women at the University of Nebraska, including the women and students involved. R. Lowitt

221. Zimmerman, Joan G. DAUGHTERS OF MAIN STREET: CULTURE AND THE FEMALE COMMUNITY AT GRINNELL, 1884-1917. Kelley, Mary, ed. *Woman's Being, Woman's Place: Female Identity and Vocation in American History* (Boston: G. K. Hall, 1979): 154-170. Beginning in the 1890's education in the Midwest was altered by an increasing number of women entering college. At Grinnell College in Iowa, women created a strong network comprised of various clubs and organizations, and formed a majority of the undergraduate population. Yet, their cultural impact on the college only strengthened traditional sex roles, which in turn more closely circumscribed their sphere of activity. It was clear that access to higher education alone was not enough to produce dramatic changes in the status or attitudes of women. While a college education might have served as the starting point of a professional career, instead it offered women a good set of friends and a taste for high culture. The presence of women at Grinnell between 1884 and 1917 changed college policy in order to accommodate the new student population. The college experience, however, did not significantly change women. Secondary sources; 3 tables, 25 notes.
J. Powell

Humanitarian Reform

222. Axinn, June and Levin, Herman. MONEY, POLITICS AND EDUCATION: THE CASE OF SOCIAL WORK. *Hist. of Educ. Q. 1978 18(2): 143-158.* A long-term drive has striven for recognition of social work as a profession. Early in its history, the profession moved away from an agency base for education toward university affiliation. It started with Charity Organization, the late-19th-century movement promising a "scientific method of dealing with pauperism." By 1878, the first school for training charity workers was established in New York. In the Progressive Era, President Theodore Roosevelt "rallied in the general citizenry to reform through social work." Jane Addams was a member of the Platform Committee of the Progressive Party in 1912. After World War I, social workers turned away from social reform; the emphasis shifted to personality reform. Professional organizations proliferated. By 1950, social work education grew largely at the graduate level. The social upheaval of the 1960's resulted in an enormous increase in public support. Discusses the ambivalence of the 1970's. 34 notes.
E. P. Stickney

223. Davis, Harold Eugene. ONE HUNDRED AND FIFTY YEARS OF THE AMERICAN PEACE SOCIETY. *World Affairs 1978 141(2): 93-103.* Traces the history of the American Peace Society, a nonsectarian organization dedicated to strengthening international law to preserve peace among nations, from its origins in 1816 as the Massachusetts Peace Society, to the present.

224. Duffy, John. THE AMERICAN MEDICAL PROFESSION AND PUBLIC HEALTH: FROM SUPPORT TO AMBIVALENCE. *Bull. of the Hist. of Medicine 1979 53(1): 1-22.* From the 1860's and 1870's, American physicians supported the establishment of public health agencies. The average practitioner, however, was occupied with the problems of making a living and was not able to devote attention to concerns of human welfare. The physicians' resentment of state intervention in their private practices played a major role in shaping public health policies in the 20th century. During the progressive era, the goals of organized medicine were to strengthen and broaden the powers of local and state health boards, and to create a national health department. The emergence of health centers, settlement houses, well-baby clinics and other agencies aroused the fear of private physicians. By 1917, the American Medical Association (AMA) had reversed its position, reflecting the views of the general practitioner. The AMA had become more of a guild or union devoted to improving the economic position of its members. All forms of health regulation now were suspect among organized medicine. 53 notes.
M. Kaufman

225. Eversole, Theodore W. THE CINCINNATI UNION BETHEL: THE COMING OF AGE OF THE SETTLEMENT IDEA IN CINCINNATI. *Cincinnati Hist. Soc. Bull. 1974 32(1-2): 47-59.* Outlines the history of social reform settlement houses in Cincinnati, Ohio, specifically the Jewish Cincinnati Union Bethel settlement house, 1838-1903.

226. Falk, Leslie A. A CENTURY OF SERVICE: MEHARRY MEDICAL COLLEGE. *Southern Exposure 1978 6(2): 14-18.* The founding of Meharry Medical College in Nashville, Tennessee, in 1876 was intended to produce quality physicians and leaders of the black community rather than lower level medical personnel and licensed practical nurses. Meharry was one of the few black medical colleges to remain open following the report on American medical education by Abraham Flexner in 1910. The college became deeply involved in the civil rights struggle during the 1950's-60's. The school became a leader in providing innovative health service delivery and medical education with the inauguration of Dr. Lloyd Elam as college president. Projects of the Meharry faculty and students include: the Neighborhood Health Center, an on-campus Comprehensive Health Center, the Poor People's Health Clinic, as well as supporting the Indian Health Service and the Waverly-Belmont Clinic in Nashville. Secondary sources and personal observations.
N. Lederer

227. Felton, Barbara J. and Shinn, Marybeth. IDEOLOGY AND PRACTICE OF DEINSTITUTIONALIZATION. *J. of Social Issues 1981 37(3): 158-172.* Compares the history and current status of deinstitutionalization efforts for the mentally ill, criminal offenders, and the aged in need of long-time care. Similar ideologies of deinstitutionalization have guided thinking for all three groups, but practices have diverged. Society regards all three groups negatively, but with differences that are reflected in treatment goals. Effective technologies for community treatment are available for the mentally ill, and methods for preventing institutionalization are available for the aged, but few members of even these groups receive such services. The divergence between ideology and practice for the three groups highlights both the constructive force of ideology in guiding policy and research, and its capacity to distort common perceptions of practice.
J

228. Francis, Daniel. THE DEVELOPMENT OF THE LUNATIC ASYLUM IN THE MARITIME PROVINCES. *Acadiensis [Canada] 1977 6(2): 23-38.* Considers treatment of the insane in Nova Scotia and New Brunswick in the 18th and 19th centuries. In Nova Scotia the insane were first housed in a workhouse, but the law-abiding and reasonably responsible insane were left alone. Both provinces opened asylums in the 1840's and 1850's. Moral treatment (compassion and lenience within a controlled environment) was the principal therapeutic technique. Crowding and inadequate attention, however, led to the asylums becoming filthy jails rather than hospitals. 65 notes.
D. F. Chard

229. Gibbons, Russell W. CHIROPRACTIC IN AMERICA: THE HISTORICAL CONFLICTS OF CULTISM AND SCIENCE. *J. of Popular Culture 1977 10(4): 720-731.* Discusses the difficulty which chiropractic medicine has had in gaining recognition as a valid science and medical pursuit, focusing on popular attitudes which have considered it quackery, religious fanaticism, and scientific cultism, 1850's-1970's.

230. Greene, William Robert. EARLY DEVELOPMENT OF THE ILLINOIS STATE PENITENTIARY SYSTEM. *J. of the Illinois State Hist. Soc. 1977 70(3): 185-195.* Illinois officials, responding to the national penal reform movement, established the first state penitentiary at Alton in 1831. Previously, there were only county jails and military prisons. The prison was moved to Joliet in 1860. Until 1867, the penitentiary was operated under a system whereby the building and convicts were leased. A modified contract system for prison labor prevailed until prohibited by law in 1903. 4 illus., 87 notes.
J

231. Greenstone, J. David. DOROTHEA DIX AND JANE ADDAMS: FROM TRANSCENDENTALISM TO PRAGMATISM IN AMERICAN SOCIAL REFORM. *Social Service Rev. 1979 53(4): 527-559.* Analyzes the thought and concerns of Dorothea Dix and Jane Addams, arguing that the differences between them reflect a fundamental transition in American culture from the antebellum moral certainty and self-reliance of Ralph Waldo Emerson's transcendentalism to the postbellum collective action and moral inquiry of John Dewey's pragmatism.

232. Harris, Katherine. FEMINISM AND TEMPERANCE REFORM IN THE BOULDER WCTU. *Frontiers 1979 4(2): 19-24.* Describes the social reform activities of the Boulder, Colorado, chapter of the Women's Christian Temperance Union from its organization in 1881 to 1967; objectives in addition to reform were to raise women's status and increase independence in and out of the home.

233. Heath, Frederick M. and Kinard, Harriet H. PROHIBITION IN SOUTH CAROLINA, 1880-1940: AN OVERVIEW. *Pro. of the South Carolina Hist. Assoc. 1980: 118-132.* Analyzes the background and motivation of the prohibitionists in South Carolina and the five referenda on prohibition between 1892 and 1940. After the prohibitionists won the 1892 referendum, Ben Tillman convinced the state legislature to adopt the dispensary system, whereby the state received the profits from the sale of liquor and tightly controlled it at the same time. Although the prohibition forces won subsequent referenda, the state was reluctant to close down the dispensary system because of the revenue it generated. Religious reasons as well as proximity to Charleston (the further away the country, the more likely it was to vote for prohibition), were the two major reasons for supporting prohibition in South Carolina. Based on government documents and published works; 52 notes. J. W. Thacker, Jr.

234. Henker, Fred O., III. THE EVOLUTION OF MENTAL HEALTH CARE IN ARKANSAS. *Arkansas Hist. Q. 1978 37(3): 223-239.* Describes the development of facilities and programs for the care of mental illness which began in the 1870's, focusing on the insane asylums, the medical school, and private psychiatric practice. Mentions many names and dates. Primary and secondary sources; illus., 50 notes. G. R. Schroeder

235. Hildreth, Peggy Bassett. EARLY RED CROSS: THE HOWARD ASSOCIATION OF NEW ORLEANS, 1837-1878. *Louisiana Hist. 1979 20(1): 77-92.* Founded in 1837 and incorporated in 1842, the Howard Association of New Orleans was a nonsectarian, philanthropic organization that performed medical and social work for the indigent victims of yellow fever and cholera epidemics. During its active service it cared for nearly 130,000 patients, black and white, in 11 epidemics, raised and dispensed over $750,000, and fostered 29 similar organizations in 9 states. It performed its last service in 1878, and thereafter was superseded by municipal, state, and federal health agencies. The Howard Association helped engender the national public health movement and the Public Health Service. Printed reports and secondary sources; table, 159 notes. L. N. Powell

236. Hilts, Victor L. OBEYING THE LAWS OF HEREDITARY DESCENT: PHRENOLOGICAL VIEWS ON INHERITANCE AND EUGENICS. *J. of the Hist. of the Behavioral Sci. 1982 18(1): 62-77.* Phrenologists were the first social scientists to construct a view of human nature in which the inheritability of both physical and mental qualities played a major role. Phrenologists addressed many of the same issues that were later to be addressed by Social Darwinists and eugenicists. The context within which the phrenologists addressed these issues, however, was that of early 19th-century health reform. Phrenological views of inheritance were intimately connected with the phrenological credo that humans are part of nature and therefore must live according to the laws of nature. J

237. Hunt, Marion. WOMEN AND CHILDSAVING: ST. LOUIS CHILDREN'S HOSPITAL 1879-1979. *Missouri Hist. Soc. Bull. 1980 36(2, pt. 1): 65-79.* Although 19th-century customs and cultural sanctions prescribed the sphere of women, middle-class and upper-class women found outlets in improving charitable institutions. The work of turn-of-the-century social reformers further inspired women to attack social evils. In St. Louis, women greatly advanced the St. Louis Children's Hospital. In 1919, professional clinicians took control at the hospital; they have restricted women volunteers to fund raising. Based on archival material and secondary sources; 6 photos, 41 notes. H. T. Lovin

238. Kerson, Toba Schwaber. ALMSHOUSE TO MUNICIPAL HOSPITAL: THE BALITMORE EXPERIENCE. *Bull. of the Hist. of Medicine 1981 55(2): 203-220.* The history of the Baltimore City Hospital began in 1772 with the construction of the County Almshouse. In 1794, during the yellow fever epidemic, the almshouse was used as a hospital, and when the epidemic passed, the city erected its first separate institution for the indigent sick and lunatics of Baltimore. By 1816, the city had expanded to the gates of the almshouse, and in 1820 the inmates were moved to a new site two miles outside the city limits. After the move, the Almshouse became more oriented toward illness and disease. In 1840, Dr. William Power as resident physician introduced the scientific method into health care. The institution was transformed from almshouse to asylum and then to general hospital. Based on manuscripts at the Maryland Historical Society, and upon newspapers and other sources; 121 notes. M. Kaufman

239. Kroll, Michael A. THE PRISON EXPERIMENT: A CIRCULAR HISTORY. *Southern Exposure 1978 6(4): 6-11.* The history of imprisonment in America can be divided into five distinct eras: Early American Prison (1790-1830); Penitentiary System (1830-1870); Reformatory System (1870-1900); Industrial System (1900-1935); Rehabilitative System (1935-?). Today a growing percentage of public opinion supported by many professional penologists feels that rehabilitation should be replaced by a harsher, more punitive system in which prisoners receive their "just desserts." N. Lederer

240. Lovejoy, David B., Jr. THE HOSPITAL AND SOCIETY: THE GROWTH OF HOSPITALS IN ROCHESTER, NEW YORK, IN THE NINETEENTH CENTURY. *Bull. of the Hist. of Medicine 1975 49(4): 536-555.* Details the history of hospital construction in Rochester, New York, from the 1820's to the turn of the century. Demonstrates the shift from the hospital as pesthouse to the palace of healing of modern days. During the 1850's, the availability of state funding brought a resurgence of hospital construction. As hospitals became more respectable, they began to accept private patients, rather than charity cases. Previously, hospitals were places where the poor were sent to die. Now, by the late 19th century, they were places of healing. 60 notes, charts, biblio. M. Kaufman

241. Marcus, Alan I. DISEASE PREVENTION IN AMERICA: FROM A LOCAL TO A NATIONAL OUTLOOK, 1880-1910. *Bull. of the Hist. of Medicine 1979 53(2): 184-203.* Local community-oriented disease prevention views began to disappear in the last few decades of the 19th century as American physicians and sanitarians recognized that bacteria were probable factors in the origin of disease. Community-based clean-up campaigns continued, but there were new investigations of possible extralocal disease sources, as germs could be transported in food, milk, or water, and carried long distances. Diseases carried by milk demonstrated the fallacy of a totally local disease prevention approach. Concern for pure water also helped to break down the local orientation. Establishment of local and state boards of health were some positive steps, but the Committee of One Hundred on National Health, founded in 1906, and the American Medical Association, labored for a national health department to coordinate all the local and state work in the area. In 1912, Congress established the US Public Health Service. 45 notes. M. Kaufman

242. Mennel, Robert M. "THE FAMILY SYSTEM OF COMMON FARMERS": THE ORIGINS OF OHIO'S REFORM FARM. *Ohio Hist. 1980 89(2): 125-156, (3): 279-322.* Part I. 1840-1858. The Ohio Reform Farm (now Fairfield School for Boys), established in 1858, was founded on the belief that hard agricultural work was morally edifying and that troubled boys subjected to such treatment would be quickly rehabilitated. Its predecessor was the Cincinnati House of Refuge, which was built in 1850 after a decade of efforts to arouse interest in it. Primary sources; 69 notes. Part II. 1858-1884. Discusses the values the institution's administrators sought to impart to the boys confined to the Ohio Reform Farm. The institution served as a model for other reformatories. Charles Reemelin, the first acting commissioner of the school was replaced after one year by George Edward Howe. Portrays the social and psychological characteristics of the inmates. Primary sources; 94 notes. J. Powell

243. Moyers, David M. FROM QUACKERY TO QUALIFICATION: ARKANSAS MEDICAL AND DRUG LEGISLATION, 1881-1909. *Arkansas Hist. Q. 1976 35(1): 3-26.* Arkansas, like many other states in the late 19th and early 20th centuries, moved slowly to regulate medical and pharmaceutical practice. During 1881-1909 the State Legislature, with prodding from local professional organizations, established some control over health care practitioners and drug dispensers. The goal was the elimination of outright quackery and control of the quality of physicians and pharmacists within the state. Based on medical journal and newspaper articles, legislative records, and secondary sources; 93 notes. T. L. Savitt

244. O'Gallagher, Marianna. CARE OF THE ORPHAN AND THE AGED BY THE IRISH COMMUNITY OF QUEBEC CITY, 1847

AND YEARS FOLLOWING. *Study Sessions: Can. Catholic Hist. Assoc. [Canada] 1976 43: 39-56.* Indicates the history and development of St. Bridget's Home in Quebec, and the work of Father Patrick McMahon, Irish immigrants, and the Catholic Church to provide for the needy, 1847-1972.

245. Peterson, Jon A. THE IMPACT OF SANITARY REFORM UPON AMERICAN URBAN PLANNING, 1840-1890. *J. of Social Hist. 1979 13(1): 83-103.* Reviews the influences on city planning by sanitary engineers, impelled by the "filth theory" of disease prevalent at the time. Remarks that true urban planners had not yet appeared. Covers the development of water-carried sewage, which led to the development of an integrated city concept, and sanitary surveys, which tried to locate all sources of disease in an urban complex. Notes the rise of consciousness regarding townsite location, which led to the development of parks and suburbs. Closes with the observation that the sanitary engineers were never really city planners and that their results were always less than complete. 74 notes.
V. L. Human

246. Pitsula, James M. THE EMERGENCE OF SOCIAL WORK IN TORONTO. *J. of Can. Studies [Canada] 1979 14(1): 35-42.* Nineteenth century Toronto social benevolence was largely through various private charitable societies and institutions. These did however receive municipal and provincial support. Studies one such agency as typical of the others, the House of Industry, founded in 1837, and considered by the public as the preeminent such institution. The visitors, all volunteer (28 active in 1881) were a remarkably distinguished group of men. By the 1910's and 1920's these tasks were handled by poorly paid professional social workers, mostly women. Traces the steps by which this change came as the city grew, the work being carried on first through Associated Charities, 1881-1912, and the Social Service Commission, beginning in 1912, through their paid, professional social workers. 51 notes.
R. V. Ritter

247. Plaut, Eric A. and Rubenstein, Susannah. STATE CARE FOR THE MENTALLY ILL: A BRIEF HISTORY. *State Government 1977 50(4): 192-197.* Overview of governmental involvement in medical and psychiatric care for the mentally ill, 1700-1977; touches on changing attitudes toward the nature of mental illness, evolution in treatment methods, and the introduction of psychotropic drugs in patient care.

248. Quen, Jacques M. ASYLUM PSYCHIATRY, NEUROLOGY, SOCIAL WORK, AND MENTAL HYGIENE: AN EXPLORATORY STUDY IN INTERPROFESSIONAL HISTORY. *J. of the Hist. of the Behavioral Sci. 1977 13(1): 3-11.* Explores the mental health movement and concurrent related fields, asylum psychiatry, neurology, social work, and public mental health, 1830's-1920's.

249. Radbill, Samuel X. HOSPITALS AND PEDIATRICS, 1776-1976. *Bull. of the Hist. of Medicine 1979 53(2): 286-291.* Sketches the development of foundling hospitals and identifies the leading institutions in American pediatrics. As almshouses were the antecedents of the general hospitals, so were orphanages and foundling asylums the forerunners of children's hospitals. From the early dispensaries came the first children's hospitals. The history of children's hospitals is described, focusing on New York City, Boston, and Philadelphia. 9 notes.
M. Kaufman

250. Rauch, Julia B. QUAKERS AND THE FOUNDING OF THE PHILADELPHIA SOCIETY FOR ORGANIZING CHARITY RELIEF AND REPRESSING MENDICANCY. *Pennsylvania Mag. of Hist. and Bio. 1974 98(4): 438-455.* Blaming poverty on pauperism and insisting on the necessity for character reformation, 19th-century charities failed to meet the needs of the urban poor. The activities of the Philadelphia Society for Organizing Charitable Relief and Repressing Mendicancy (SOC), founded in 1879 by Quakers, reflected the upper-class, moralistic, and repressive nature of charity relief. Since Philadelphia "Quakers did not recognize that an urban, industrialized society required social insurance and other economic security programs," they "ended up supporting a conservative, backward-looking program, one which was repressive toward the poor." Based on primary and secondary sources; 46 notes.
E. W. Carp

251. Reid, John D.; Jedlicka, Davor; Lee, Everett S.; and Shin, Yongsock. TRENDS IN BLACK HEALTH. *Phylon 1977 38(2): 105-116.* Discusses black life expectancy, the historical pattern of change in death rates, causes of death, male-female differentials and social and economic factors in black mortality. Blacks have made enormous progress since the early 19th century in improving their health and survival rates. The periods of greatest improvement have been times of national emergency and progress has been achieved through scientific advance (vaccines, inoculations, sanitation, clean water), education, and higher incomes. Presented at the W. E. B. DuBois Conference on the Health of Black Americans, Atlanta, Georgia, December 1976.
P. J. Taylorson

252. Rosenberg, Charles E. THE THERAPEUTIC REVOLUTION: MEDICINE, MEANING, AND SOCIAL CHANGE IN NINETEENTH-CENTURY AMERICA. Vogel, Morris J. and Rosenberg, Charles E., ed. *The Therapeutic Revolution: Essays in the Social History of American Medicine* (Philadelphia: U. of Pennsylvania Pr., 1979): 3-25. At the beginning of the 19th century, therapeutics were characterized by the assumptions that, 1) every part of the body was related and equilibrium of all parts was necessary for good health, and 2) normal developmental crises threatened the body's natural equilibrium. To keep the body in balance, accordingly, huge quantities of medicine were consumed. Widespread home treatments also consisted of emetics, bleeding, cathartics, and diuretics. By the end of the 19th century, such traditional therapeutic practices continued to be used, although, due to the conflict between science and therapeutics, they were reduced and drugs were prescribed in smaller doses. Doctors placed more faith in nature and the body's ability to recover without the aid of drugs or the regulation of secretions. 43 notes.
G. L. Smith

253. Rosenkrantz, Barbara Gutmann. CART BEFORE HORSE: THEORY, PRACTICE AND PROFESSIONAL IMAGE IN AMERICAN PUBLIC HEALTH, 1870-1920. *J. of the Hist. of Medicine and Allied Sci. 1974 29(1): 55-73.* The public health movement sought to retain the image of happy partnership among physicians, engineers, and others (under the banner of sanitary science), while successful measures for the control of contagious disease through biomedical intervention promoted an alternative program. The New Public Health Movement drew its reputation from its capacity to deal directly with the causes of disease. "Appropriate theories, practices, and associations for the public health professional could, in the second decade of the century, be described in terms which placed major health problems for the years to come as well as from the past, outside the purview of preventive medicine." Based on primary and secondary sources; 38 notes.
J. L. Susskind

254. Siddall, A. Clair. BLOODLETTING IN AMERICAN OBSTETRICAL PRACTICE, 1800-1945. *Bull. of the Hist. of Medicine 1980 54(1): 101-110.* Bloodletting in American obstetrical practice developed in two waves: 1800-50 and then from mid-century to 1945. The second wave saw bloodletting restricted to treatment of toxemia. William P. Dewees (1768-1841), the most influential American obstetrician, supported bloodletting for reducing the pain of the laboring patient. Thomas Denman (1733-1815) of London was the clearest spokesman for the new theories justifying the wide utilization of bloodletting in pregnancy. Toward midcentury, some physicians opposed bloodletting for treating hemorrhage. The work of Gabriel Andral (1797-1876) was crucial in destroying the old theory of a plethora of red blood cells in pregnancy. Sources include medical texts and articles in medical journals; 65 notes.
M. Kaufman

255. Smith, Becky. PROHIBITION IN ALASKA. *Alaska J. 1973 3(3): 170-179.* Discusses eras of alcoholic prohibition in Alaska 1842-1917, emphasizing the activities of the Women's Christian Temperance Union.

256. Smith, Dale C. AUSTIN FLINT AND AUSCULTATION IN AMERICA. *J. of the Hist. of Medicine and Allied Sci. 1978 33(2): 129-149.* Austin Flint (1812-86) played a significant role in the development of physical diagnosis in America. While a Harvard medical student in the early 1830's, he was influenced by Dr. James Jackson to use the stethoscope. The college already placed unusual emphasis on clinical instruction. After 1850, he auscultated and percussed his patients to eliminate thoracic disease from the possible afflictions. His explanation

257. Smith, Harold T. PROHIBITION IN NEVADA. *Nevada Hist. Soc. Q. 1976 19(4): 226-250.* Recounts struggles from the 1880's to 1918 between Nevada temperance organizations and "wets" over state-imposed prohibition in Nevada. The proponents of prohibition won the day in 1918 and were victorious again in 1919 when they persuaded the legislature to ratify the national prohibition amendment. In the 1920's, many formerly protemperance Nevadans withdrew their support because prohibition was clearly unenforceable in the state. Based on newspaper and secondary sources; 2 photos, 123 notes. H. T. Lovin

258. Sponholtz, Lloyd L. THE POLITICS OF TEMPERANCE IN OHIO, 1880-1912. *Ohio Hist. 1976 85(1): 4-27.* The Anti-Saloon League of America under the direction of Wayne B. Wheeler attempted to secure prohibition in Ohio. In conflict with the Wet forces led by the United States Brewers' Association, the ASL made its attempts through local option laws and the Constitutional Convention of 1912. The relative failure of the ASL in Ohio motivated the organization to "embark upon a campaign for a federal prohibition amendment." Based on manuscript, contemporary comments, and secondary sources; 3 illus., map, 2 tables, 56 notes. T. H. Hartig

259. Towey, Martin G. and Sullivan, Margaret LoPiccolo. THE KNIGHTS OF FATHER MATHEW: PARALLEL ETHNIC REFORM. *Missouri Hist. Rev. 1981 75(2): 168-183.* Writers have shown that immigrants contributed in some positive way to the reforms favored by the host society, but in another kind of reform, called "Parallel Reform," ethnic groups drew heavily upon their own traditions in meeting the problems they faced in America. One such example is provided by the Knights of Father Mathew, a response by Irish Americans to the problem of alcohol but one that came out of their own tradition and remained aloof from the Anglo-American prohibition crusade. Father Theobald Mathew, an Irish priest who died in 1856, toured America from 1849 to 1851; he visited St. Louis in 1850. His work led to a temperance society in St. Louis, reorganized in 1881 as the Knights of Father Mathew. Catholicity, not Irish ancestry, became the main condition of membership, although the organization kept many trappings of Irish ethnicity. It crested in 1904 and died ca. 1930. Based on articles, books, theses, dissertations, newspapers, interviews; illus., 32 notes. W. F. Zornow

260. Williams, C. Arthur, Jr. MEETING THE RISK OF UNEMPLOYMENT: CHANGING SOCIETAL RESPONSES. *Ann. of the Am. Acad. of Pol. and Social Sci. 1979 (443): 12-24.* Unemployment is enforced idleness among persons who are willing and able to work. Unemployment was not a serious problem until the Industrial Revolution produced a more complicated, interdependent, impersonal society.... Until the Great Depression society did little to help the unemployed. Friends and relatives were the major outside sources of support, other sources being private charities, public relief, and employer or trade union plans. The Great Depression produced the highest unemployment rates ever experienced and a climate favoring federal intervention. The Social Security Act of 1935 encouraged the formation of state unemployment insurance programs, now only one of several government and private efforts to control unemployment or alleviate its economic consequences. The current principal control measures are: 1) monetary and fiscal policy designed to reduce unemployment, 2) automatic stabilizers, 3) manpower development and training, 4) labor-market information, and 5) public employment. The principal alleviative measures are unemployment insurance, public assistance, and private employee benefit plans, unemployment insurance being clearly the most important. J/S

261. Zainaldin, James S. and Tyor, Peter L. ASYLUM AND SOCIETY: AN APPROACH TO INSTITUTIONAL CHANGE. *J. of Social Hist. 1979 13(1): 23-48.* Studies two 19th-century asylums in Boston, one for the poor and the other for the feeble-minded. Covers the history of the institutions, discussing the sources of institutional policy and its reformulation, institutional operation, external perception and internal fact, and the social functions which the institution provides. Closes with an examination of the conclusions of other authors and a possibly fruitful path for additional studies. 7 tables, 57 notes. V. L. Human

Utopian Thought and Communalism

262. Beauchamp, Gorman. THE IRON HEEL AND LOOKING BACKWARD: TWO PATHS TO UTOPIA. *Am. Literary Realism 1976 9(4): 307-314.* Discusses the socialistic, utopian vision of Jack London's *The Iron Heel* (1907) and Edward Bellamy's *Looking Backward 2000-1887* (1888).

263. Cary, Francine C. THE WORLD A DEPARTMENT STORE: BRADFORD PECK AND THE UTOPIAN ENDEAVOR. *Am. Q. 1977 29(4): 370-384.* Peck was one of several American businessmen of the 19th century who not only wrote a utopian novel but also sought to implement his ideas in practice. A self-made, financially successful department store owner in Lewiston, Maine, Peck was disturbed over what he viewed as the falling away of America from its founding morality and values. He was especially fearful of the leaching away of democratic and Christian ideals from the body politic. Peck labored through his writings to further cooperation which he felt would restore the harmonious, homogenous society of earlier days. He also sought to realize his goals through the founding of the Cooperative Association of America, which in turn sponsored several temporarily successful business ventures. Primary and secondary sources. N. Lederer

264. Chicoineau, Jacques C. ETIENNE CABET AND THE ICARIANS. *Western Illinois Regional Studies 1979 2(1): 5-19.* Etienne Cabet (1788-1858), born in France, was one of several founders of utopian societies in the United States as a response to the rapid rise of technology and industrialization; Cabet's Icaria, named after his book, *Voyage en Icarie (Voyage in Icaria)* (1840), first was located in Nauvoo, Illinois, later in Corning, Iowa, and finally in Sonoma County, California, where it was dissolved in 1895.

265. Jones, Russell M. VICTOR CONSIDÉRANT'S AMERICAN EXPERIENCE (1852-1869). *French-American Rev. 1976 1(1): 65-94.* Victor Prosper Considérant was a French disciple of Charles Fourier, the utopian socialist, who advocated communal organizations known as phalanxes. Considérant traveled in the United States during December 1852-July 1853. He concluded that an area in northern Texas would be ideal for establishing such a community. Returning to France, he wrote a travel book, *Au Texas,* which described the attractions of the United States to prospective emigrants and depicted the profits which could be made in investing in the western lands. Considérant would return to the United States to establish a colony in 1855. Based largely on primary sources; 118 notes. Article to be continued. R. S. Barnard

266. Kern, Louis J. IDEOLOGY AND REALITY: SEXUALITY AND WOMEN'S STATUS IN THE ONEIDA COMMUNITY. *Radical Hist. Rev. 1979 (20): 180-204.* Seemingly liberating factors in the ideology of John Humphrey Noyes's Oneida Community in New York (control over childbearing and sexuality, freedom from marriage, limited occupational flexibility, division of household labor, and laborsaving devices) actually led to the further subjugation of females within the community, because power and status still were allotted only to male members; 1848-79.

267. Pearson, Carol. WOMAN'S FANTASIES AND FEMINIST UTOPIAS. *Frontiers 1977 2(3): 50-61.* Examines similarities in utopian literature emanating from feminism, 19th-20th centuries, as well as the definition of feminist alternative consciousness.

268. Prieur, Vincent. DE NEW HARMONY À TWIN OAKS: A PROPOS DE QUELQUES RÉCURRENCES DANS L'HISTOIRE DES MOUVEMENTS COMMUNAUTAIRES AMÉRICAINS [From New Harmony to Twin Oaks: The new American communities and their roots in history]. *Mouvement Social [France] 1976 (94): 31-57.*

We all know that new American communities emerged from protest movements of the sixties. However, this movement has its roots deep in the 19th century, and has often been neglected. This is unfortunate, since such an approach would lead us to discover the sheer originality of the communitarian utopia of the United States, which can be grossly described as a slow process of Americanization. The purpose of this article is not to discover the depth and to point out the limits of this approach, but to emphasize two main examples in this process as an idea of what is done in a more thoroughgoing research.
J

269. Rodgers, James. THE RELIGIOUS ORIGINS OF AMERICAN RADICALISM AND THE IDEOLOGICAL ROOTS OF INTENTIONAL COMMUNITIES. *Rev. Française d'Etudes Américaines [France] 1976 (2): 23-29.* Explores American utopian intentional communities by examining the dissenting and religious character of American radicalism, especially as set forth in the Declaration of Independence.

270. Sargent, Lyman Tower. ENGLISH AND AMERICAN UTOPIAS: SIMILARITIES AND DIFFERENCES. *J. of General Educ. 1976 28(1): 16-22.* Compares the patterns of English and American utopias during the 19th and 20th centuries. Discusses the different attitudes and the shift in emphasis of American and English utopias toward such topics as women's rights, socialism, capitalism, religion, temperance, education, and fashion. Secondary sources; 12 notes.
N. A. Williamson

271. Thomas, Robert David. JOHN HUMPHREY NOYES AND THE ONEIDA COMMUNITY: A 19TH-CENTURY AMERICAN FATHER AND HIS FAMILY. *Psychohistory Rev. 1977-78 6(2-3): 68-87.* Describes the attempts of John Humphrey Noyes, a major utopian reformer, to create a utopian community modeled on the family and Perfectionist religious ideology at the Oneida Community in New York (1848-80). Noyes tried to create a perfect world of inner and outer harmony by regulating the sex, love, marriage, and procreative habits of his community. Order in the community was based on passivity, dependence, and familial submission to Noyes, and through him to God. Based on Noyes's writings and secondary works; 89 notes.
J. B. Street

Profiles of Reformers

272. Allen, Margaret V. THE POLITICAL AND SOCIAL CRITICISM OF MARGARET FULLER. *South Atlantic Q. 1973 72(4): 560-578.* Margaret Fuller's early life was a sheltered one. She abhorred politicians and political philosophy, with the exception of that of Thomas Jefferson, and it took time for her to develop a social conscience and an awareness of injustice. She gradually developed humanist and feminist sympathies which culminated in her book *Woman in the Nineteenth Century* in 1843. After becoming a reviewer-critic for Horace Greeley's *New York Daily Tribune*, she was exposed to poverty and exploitation, and became a political leftist. After an assignment to Italy during the Roman revolution of 1848-49 she became a political radical. 39 notes.
E. P. Stickney

273. Alsobrook, David E. MOBILE'S FORGOTTEN PROGRESSIVE: A. N. JOHNSON, EDITOR AND ENTREPRENEUR. *Alabama Rev. 1979 32(3): 188-202.* Andrew N. Johnson (1865-1922) was a reform-minded black businessman, newspaper editor, and civic leader in Mobile (Alabama) and Nashville (Tennessee). An active Republican, he opposed Alabama's lily-white faction, unsuccessfully tried to persuade President Theodore Roosevelt to remove Jim Crow proponents from patronage positions, and supported the National Negro Business League. Primary and secondary sources; 51 notes.
J. F. Vivian

274. Annunziata, Frank. DONALD R. RICHBERG AND AMERICAN LIBERALISM. *J. of the Illinois State Hist. Soc. 1974 67(5): 530-547.* Donald Randall Richberg (1881-1960), chief counsel for the National Recovery Administration (NRA), had been active in the Illinois Progressive Party before World War I. His criticism of social developments after World War II clearly reveals the limits of that original progressive vision. Richberg viewed government as an umpire to synchronize the social order. After 1940, when federal regulating power developed permanent bureaucracies, Richberg switched from battling the unregulated excesses of big business to battling the new menaces of welfare-state government and organized labor. Primary and secondary sources; 5 illus., 53 notes.
W. R. Hively

275. Annunziata, Frank. THE POLITICAL THOUGHT OF JOHN CHAMBERLAIN: CONTINUITY AND CONVERSION. *South Atlantic Q. 1975 74(1): 74-85.* John Chamberlain is the classic example of a 1920's radical becoming a 1950's conservative. His 1932 *Farewell to Reform* issued a blistering condemnation of New Deal Liberalism for attempting to rescue a foundering capitalism. Disappointment with Soviet Russia led him in *The American Stakes* (1940) to reject any state-led attempt at social salvation. Worldwide postwar repression of personal liberty pushed him to the Right as he first joined Henry Hazlitt and Susan La Follette in publishing the conservative journal *Freeman* and then supported McCarthyism. Later ties with Henry Luce made him endorse policies similar to those he denounced in 1932. Based on primary and secondary sources; 58 notes.
W. L. Olbrich

276. Apostol, Jane. HORATIO NELSON RUST, ABOLITIONIST, ARCHAEOLOGIST, INDIAN AGENT. *California History 1979-80 58(4): 304-315.* Discusses Horatio Nelson Rust (1828-1906), amateur archaeologist, collector of Native American relics, and supporter of Indian rights. Born in Massachusetts, Rust grew up a dedicated abolitionist and served in the Civil War as a medical volunteer. In 1882 he came to Pasadena, California, where he grew oranges and promoted the citrus industry. He was appointed agent for the Mission-Tule River Consolidated Agency, covering 22 California reservations, in 1889. He served four years as agent. During this time he supported practical training, education, land allotments, and assimilation for Indians. His views brought opposition from both Indians and whites. After his resignation in 1893 Rust busied himself as an archaeologist and collector of Indian artifacts. Often insensitive, Rust was nonetheless seen by many as a dedicated champion of freedmen and Indians. 7 photos, 60 notes.
A. Hoffman

277. Apostol, Jane. JEANNE CARR: ONE WOMAN AND SUNSHINE. *Am. West 1978 15(4): 28-33, 62-63.* Vermont-born Jeanne Caroline Smith Carr (1825-1903) was married to a medical scientist professor whose university assignments took them to California by way of Wisconsin. She became widely known as a feminist, author, botanist, officeholder, and educational reform activist. She met backwoods farmer John Muir while reporting on an exhibit of his inventions in Madison, Wisconsin. She became a close friend, correspondent, and mentor to Muir, whom she called "the Poet-Naturalist of our Coast." 4 illus., note, biblio.
D. L. Smith

278. Avery, Donald H. BRITISH-BORN "RADICALS" IN NORTH AMERICA, 1900-1941: THE CASE OF SAM SCARLETT. *Can. Ethnic Studies [Canada] 1978 10(2): 65-85.* Sam Scarlett, Scottish artisan immigrant to Canada in 1903, was one of many such crafts workers who were instrumental in bringing British trade union principles and socialist ideas to North America. He was associated with a variety of working-class organizations, but gained the most notoriety from his involvement with the Industrial Workers of the World and the Communist Party of Canada. A major field organizer for these organizations, and therefore a target for police and corporate harassment, he was a martyr of the imminent proletarian revolution. Partly primary sources; photo, 87 notes.
R. V. Ritter

279. Baldwin, Roger. RECOLLECTIONS OF A LIFE IN CIVIL LIBERTIES-PART I. *Civil Liberties R. 1975 2(2): 39-72.* Roger Baldwin, the founder in 1920 of the American Civil Liberties Union and its executive director until 1950, is now, at 91, the ACLU's international work adviser. He is, in addition, an energetic honorary president of The International League for the Rights of Man, of which he was a founder in 1942, and is a frequent lecturer on civil liberties at the University of Puerto Rico. This is the first of a series of Roger Baldwin's recollections to be published in *The Civil Liberties Review*. Here, he describes the events and people of his early years [1906-19] that led him to become a civil liberties activist.
J

280. Barclay, Morgan J. REFORM IN TOLEDO: THE POLITICAL CAREER OF SAMUEL M. JONES. *Northwest Ohio Q. 1978*

50(3): 79-89. Discusses Toledo, Ohio, from the 1850's and the mayoral candidacy and political career of Republican Samuel Milton Jones who served as mayor from 1897 until his death in 1904, stressing urban reform.

281. Barker-Benfield, G. J. MOTHER EMANCIPATOR: THE MEANING OF JANE ADDAMS' SICKNESS AND CURE. *J. of Family Hist. 1979 4(4): 395-420.* Describes settlement house founder and social reformer Jane Addams's life as a struggle between "the values represented by her father and those she associated with her mother." Addams overtly rejected traditional maternal and wifely roles but found close psychological substitutes in her marriage to social reform and mothering of Hull House. Covers 1880-1920. 13 notes, biblio.
T. W. Smith

282. Baxandall, Rosalynn Fraad. ELIZABETH GURLEY FLYNN: THE EARLY YEARS. *Radical Am. 1975 9(1): 97-115.* Discusses the early life of Elizabeth Gurley Flynn (1890-1964), a feminist and Communist, based on her unpublished writings and containing new evidence about her personal and political development.

283. Beatty, Bess. JOHN WILLIS MENARD: A PROGRESSIVE BLACK IN POST-CIVIL WAR FLORIDA. *Florida Hist. Q. 1980 59(2): 123-143.* John Willis Menard was typical of educated black leaders during Reconstruction. As a journalist and political and educational leader, Menard saw black improvement coming through an independent political party. His dependence on national patronage, however, kept him close to the Republicans. Menard's policies were rarely enacted, but he remained an outspoken advocate of equality. Based on Florida newspapers and state records; 51 notes.
N. A. Kuntz

284. Beck, Jeanne M. HENRY SOMERVILLE AND SOCIAL REFORM: HIS CONTRIBUTION TO CANADIAN CATHOLIC SOCIAL THOUGHT. *Study Sessions: Can. Catholic Hist. Assoc. 1975 42: 91-108.* Henry Somerville, editor of *Catholic Register* 1933-53, provided an impetus for his generation through his contributions to the development of Catholic social thought and action in Canada by combining the influences of Edwardian England and his own Canadian immigrant experiences since his arrival in 1915.

285. Beck, Leonard N. THE LIBRARY OF SUSAN B. ANTHONY. *Q. J. of the Lib. of Congress 1975 32(4): 324-336.* In 1903 Susan B. Anthony gave her personal library along with her manuscripts to the Library of Congress. Numbering less than 400 items, it has no pretensions to rarity; its interest lies in the glimpses it affords of the private person generally overshadowed by the feminist movement symbol. The review shows that she read primarily for "immediately practical information." She annotated, however, several volumes of poetry, the one which meant most to her being Elizabeth Barrett Browning's *Aurora Leigh*. Of John Stuart Mill's *The Subjugation of Women*, she wrote: "This book has been the law for me since 1869." Illus. 7 notes.
E. P. Stickney

286. Bender, George A. HENRY HURD RUSBY: SCIENTIFIC EXPLORER, SOCIETAL CRUSADER, SCHOLASTIC INNOVATOR. *Pharmacy in Hist. 1981 23(2): 71-85.* Dr. Henry Hurd Rusby (1855-1940) was professor (1888-1930) and dean (1905-30) of the College of Pharmacy of the City of New York (later the Columbia University College of Pharmacy), a botanist and pharmacognosist with Parke-Davis and a consultant to other pharmaceutical manufacturers, and an explorer of considerable repute in North and South America. Rusby's five expeditions from the 1880's to the 1920's uncovered the sources of a great variety of new vegetable drugs, many of which were accepted into the practice of pharmacy and medicine as evidenced by the US Pharmacopoeia (USP) and National Formulary entries, and other plant products with economic possibilities. During 30 years as a member of the Committee on Revision of the USP and in his research and publications, Rusby steadfastly maintained a concern for the standards of vegetable drug sources and the manufacturing and distributional quality of these drugs. He was often critical of the positions taken by government scientists and bureaucrats, pharmaceutical manufacturers, and even other physicians. Illus., 5 photos, 54 notes.
S. C. Morrison

287. Berkin, Carol Ruth. PRIVATE WOMAN, PUBLIC WOMAN: THE CONTRADICTIONS OF CHARLOTTE PERKINS GILMAN. Berkin, Carol Ruth and Norton, Mary Beth, ed. *Women of America: A History* (Boston: Houghton Mifflin Co., 1979): 150-176. Charlotte Perkins Gilman (1860-1935) wrote and lectured throughout her life in New England and California. Her *Women and Economics* (1898) was a formulation of the evolution of the social role of women. Her own personal struggle included the realization that love and social duty were not mutually exclusive. Based on Gilman's diaries and published works; 5 notes.
K. Talley

288. Bernard, Joel. AUTHORITY, AUTONOMY, AND RADICAL COMMITMENT: STEPHEN AND ABBY KELLEY FOSTER. *Pro. of the Am. Antiquarian Soc. 1980 90(2): 347-386.* Examines the various themes that affected the lives and relationships of abolitionists Stephen and Abigail Kelley Foster, particularly in the areas of personal and social authority and autonomy. Slavery dominated their consciousness, and reflected their self-perceptions and fantasies. A strong connection between their radical commitment and their personal identity is evident through the use of Freudian psychology. Based largely on the Foster Papers at the American Antiquarian Society and the Worcester Historical Museum; 87 notes.
J. A. Andrew III

289. Berrol, Selma. WHEN UPTOWN MET DOWNTOWN: JULIA RICHMAN'S WORK IN THE JEWISH COMMUNITY OF NEW YORK, 1880-1912. *Am. Jewish Hist. 1980 70(1): 35-51.* Traces the career of Julia Richman (1855-1912), first Jewish woman school principal, first Jewish district superintendent of schools, a founder of the Young Women's Hebrew Association and the National Council of Jewish Women, a director of the Hebrew Free School Association and the Educational Alliance, and a lecturer and author for the Jewish Chautauqua Society. As a Progressive reformer, Richman sought to improve secular and Jewish education to achieve a more orderly, ethical, and equitable society. She criticized East European Jewish immigrants as deficient in moral values, and was in turn criticized by them, yet she continued to work on their behalf. Her career illuminates the Progressive Era, the place of women reformers in it, and the relationship between "uptown" and "downtown" in New York City's Jewish community. Based on Richman's correspondence and writings, and other sources; 38 notes.
J. D. Sarna

290. Blackett, R. J. M. WILLIAM G. ALLEN: THE FORGOTTEN PROFESSOR. *Civil War Hist. 1980 26(1): 39-52.* Discusses William G. Allen, who was an abolitionist and defender of human rights. In ca. 1838, his education was sponsored by Gerrit Smith in Oneida (New York) Institute. As a Boston law clerk in 1847, he opposed colonization by advocating national amalgamation. First black-American professor at a white college, New York Central College at McGrawville, he married white student, Mary King, in 1853. Fleeing to Great Britain, Allen never won the usual Negro popularity; his literary-philosophical approach to lecturing and his opening the first black-led school there left him strangely destitute. The Allens remained frustrated exiles. Based on personal and society papers and secondary sources; 44 notes.
R. E. Stack

291. Blake, Cecil A. EDWARD WILMOT BLYDEN: A PRODIGY OF THE VIRGIN ISLANDS AND NEW YORK. *Afro-Americans in New York Life and Hist. 1977 1(1): 67-80.* Discusses Edward Wilmot Blyden, a black who dedicated his life to establishing an African past for American Negroes, 1850-1912; Blyden lived much of his life in Liberia and Sierra Leone.

292. Blodgett, Geoffrey. WINSTON CHURCHILL: THE NOVELIST AS REFORMER. *New England Q. 1974 47(4): 495-517.* Studies the career of novelist Winston Churchill (1871-1947) to understand the way in which he united a successful career as a novelist with his Progressive political and socioeconomic views and thereby played an important role in "catalyzing reform behavior in his adopted state of New Hampshire." Churchill's early progress toward reform and insurgency was gradual and uncharted. "Reform was what happened to him when he tried, as an affluent young outsider coming into New Hampshire at the turn of the century, to use politics as a means of fashioning his new surroundings to his taste." With some of his contemporaries he considered that the pursuit of particular personal and group goals might also advance the common welfare. 48 notes.
R. V. Ritter

293. Blumberg, Dorothy Rose. MARY ELIZABETH LEASE, POPULIST ORATOR: A PROFILE. *Kansas Hist. 1978 1(1): 1-15.* Mary Elizabeth Lease (1850-1933), long identified as a principal spokesman for Kansas Populism, emerges as a determined champion of many causes. Seldom a political theorist, Mrs. Lease was an effective political advocate. Her speeches and writings articulated the plight of farmers, urban workers, and women struggling for rights in a world run by men. Primary and secondary sources; illus., 61 notes. W. F. Zornow

294. Bogin, Ruth. SARA PARKER REMOND: BLACK ABOLITIONIST FROM SALEM. *Essex Inst. Hist. Collections 1974 110(2): 120-150.* Recounts career of this woman as an antislavery lecturer in Great Britain and the US, 1856-87. S

295. Bolin, Winifred D. Wandersee. HARRIET E. BISHOP: MORALIST AND REFORMER. Stuhler, Barbara and Kreuter, Gretchen, ed. *Women of Minnesota: Selected Biographical Essays* (St. Paul: Minnesota Historical Society Press, 1977): 7-19. In 1847, Harriet E. Bishop arrived in the frontier community of St. Paul, Minnesota. Trained by Catharine Beecher, Bishop brought with her the missionary zeal of the social reformer and a belief in the moral superiority of women. A Baptist, she established the first public school and the first Sunday School in St. Paul. Discusses her activities as a temperance advocate, largely negative attitudes toward the local Indians, efforts to help the destitute, prose and poetry, and two matrimonial opportunities. Bishop died in 1883. By then she was largely unknown in the growing metropolis, but her life "personified a whole generation of women" who tried to fulfill their destinies within the boundaries of convention and who labored to meet the responsibilities imposed by their presumed innate superiority. Primary and secondary sources; illus., 34 notes. A. E. Wiederrecht

296. Boston, Ray. MATTHEW MARK TRUMBULL: RESPECTABLE RADICAL. *J. of the Illinois State Hist. Soc. 1973 66(2): 159-176.* Matthew Mark Trumbull, Chicago lawyer and writer, was raised in England among the working class. After an unsuccessful struggle to rise out of it, he went to Montreal. Between service in the Mexican War and in the Civil War as a brevetted brigadier general from Iowa, Trumbull became a successful lawyer. As collector of internal revenue for the third congressional district of Iowa, Trumbull devoted most of his time to writing. His best-known book, *The Free Trade Struggle in England,* an economic history of the United States and England, was used as a textbook. Trumbull argued before Illinois Governor Richard James Oglesby (1824-99) for the lives of the anarchists convicted after the Haymarket Square riot (4 May 1886). Trumbull defended socialist views until his death. Based on Trumbull's autobiography, *Open Court* articles, and the *Open Court* papers in the Southern Illinois University Archives; 2 illus., 2 ports., 61 notes. A. C. Aimone

297. Bower, Robert K. JOSEPH A. DUGDALE: A FRIEND OF TRUTH. *Palimpsest 1975 56(6): 170-183.* Joseph A. Dugdale, an antislavery Hicksite Quaker minister, devoted his life to helping the oppressed. Especially active in the abolitionist movement prior to the Civil War, he turned to such crusades as women's rights, prison reform, temperance, peace, and aid to Indians in later years. He was well known for his children's conventions, which consisted of recreation, recitation, and education, and he knew many famous people of his day. Quiet and relatively anonymous during his lifetime, he has remained obscure since his death in 1896. Illus., 5 photos, note. D. W. Johnson

298. Boxerman, Burton A. ADOLPH JOACHIM SABATH IN CONGRESS: THE EARLY YEARS, 1907-1932. *J. of the Illinois State Hist. Soc. 1973 66(3): 327-340.* Sabath, a progressive reformer, represented the Fifth Congressional District of Illinois under eight presidents. A Bohemian, Sabath became an ethnic Democratic politician popular with Chicago's immigrant populations. Sabath's ardent support of the League of Nations resulted in his closest election victory (in 1920). His loyalty to presidents Franklin Delano Roosevelt and Harry S. Truman was unswerving and he became one of the most effective men in the House. Based on secondary sources and the *Congressional Record;* illus., 32 notes. Article to be continued. A. C. Aimone

299. Briceland, Alan V. DANIEL MC CALLA, 1748-1809: NEW SIDE REVOLUTIONARY AND JEFFERSONIAN. *J. of Presbyterian Hist. 1978 56(3): 252-269.* Daniel McCalla (1748-1809) was born in the midst of a Presbyterian schism. While he never figured as a major factor in his church or country, his life touched and made contributions to several important historical processes. As an academy teacher, he brought education to students with limited educational opportunities; as a chaplain, he aided the cause of the American Revolution; as a Presbyterian, he fought to establish the principle of separation of church and state; as a scholar, he published essays to enlighten and reform; as one committed to democracy, he enlisted his pen in the cause of electing Thomas Jefferson. Primary and secondary sources; 64 notes.
H. M. Parker, Jr.

300. Bromberg, Alan B. JOHN MERCER LANGSTON: BLACK CONGRESSMAN FROM THE OLD DOMINION. *Virginia Cavalcade 1980 30(2): 60-67.* Surveys the career of John Mercer Langston (1829-97), lawyer, Republican politician, educator, diplomat, orator, and crusader for civil rights—and still the only black to represent Virginia in Congress (in the House of Representatives for five months in 1890-91).

301. Brooks, Juanita, ed., and Butler, Janet G., ed. UTAH'S PEACE ADVOCATE, THE "MORMONA": ELISE FURER MUSSER. *Utah Hist. Q. 1978 46(2): 151-166.* Excerpts the writings, diaries, and letters of Elise Furer Musser (1877-1967), who was born in Switzerland, migrated to Utah in 1897, and married Burton Musser in 1911. Her social service and political career began with work in Neighborhood House. She became influential in Utah's Democratic Women's Club, serving as state senator (1933-34), and was the only woman delegate to the Buenos Aires Peace Conference in 1936. Her life puts the current women's liberation movement into perspective as a continuum rather than a new, spontaneous phenomenon. Primary sources; 5 illus., 18 notes.
J. L. Hazelton

302. Buchstein, Frederick D. JOSIAH WARREN: THE PEACEFUL REVOLUTION. *Cincinnati Hist. Soc. Bull. 1974 32(1-2): 61-71.* Discusses the philosophical anarchism and libertarianism of Cincinnatian Joseph Warren, including his participation in the utopian community of New Harmony, Indiana.

303. Bulkley, Robert D., Jr. A DEMOCRAT AND SLAVERY: ROBERT RANTOUL, JR. *Essex Inst. Hist. Collections 1974 110(3): 216-238.* Rantoul, a Massachusetts Democrat, evolved during his political career from a limited position to radical involvement in the abolition movement. S

304. Bykov, Vil'. UIL'IAM FOSTER. STRANITSY ZHIZNI I BOR'BY [William Foster: Pages from his life and struggle]. *Novaia i Noveishaia Istoriia [USSR] 1973 (4): 97-116.* Studies William Zebulon Foster of the Communist Party USA. Foster was born in 1881 in Taunton, Massachusetts, and entered the strike movement in 1895. Having worked in Texas and moved to Oregon to work in docks and on the railroads, Foster then signed on as a merchant seaman. He visited much of the world during his three years at sea. In 1904 he began homesteading in Oregon, but drought left him unable to make a living. He went into the lumber industry in Portland. Foster rose within the Socialist Party from 1904 and was strongly influenced by events in Russia and by socialist writers. As a socialist newspaper correspondent he was arrested and imprisoned in Spokane in 1908-09. He joined a left splinter group of the Socialist Party in Oregon, which obviously suffered from infantile leftism. He went to Europe and met such figures as Karl Kautsky. In Kamloops, British Columbia, he was imprisoned for preaching syndicalism. Active in the Syndicalist League, he helped to promote trade unions among loggers and others. Toward 1917 unions were developing in meat industries in many cities, due to Foster and his colleagues. In 1918-21 he was active in the Chicago (and later the national) steel industry. In 1921 he joined the American Communist Party. Based on memoirs, secondary sources, and newspaper reports; 43 notes. Article to be continued.
D. N. Collins

305. Campbell, Finley C. PROPHET OF THE STORM: RICHARD WRIGHT AND THE RADICAL TRADITION. *Phylon 1977 38(1): 9-23.* During the 1950's-60's Richard Wright, the prominent black author, was not considered an important part of the radical tradition in the United States, despite his alliance with various socialist and communist groups and causes during his career. But he should be considered the "prophet of the storm." Wright professed a personalism which enabled

him to transcend his personal consciousness into a social consciousness. He transmitted a radical ideology, which must be defined as social humanism, through his personal experiences and through his radical conception of the black experience. Primary and secondary sources; 66 notes.

B. A. Glasrud

306. Candeloro, Dominic. LOUIS POST AS A CARPETBAGGER: RECONSTRUCTION AS A FORERUNNER OF THE PROGRESSIVE MOVEMENT. *Am. J. of Econ. and Sociol. 1975 34(4): 423-432.* Louis Post was a carpetbagger in South Carolina who maintained an interest in social reform and racial equality during the Progressive era.

307. Capeci, Dominic J., Jr. FROM HARLEM TO MONTGOMERY: THE BUS BOYCOTTS AND LEADERSHIP OF ADAM CLAYTON POWELL, JR., AND MARTIN LUTHER KING, JR. *Historian 1979 41(4): 721-737.* The Harlem Bus Boycott of 1941 yields important information on Adam Clayton Powell, Jr.'s leadership before his political career. Comparing it to the Montgomery Bus Boycott of 1956 and the leadership of Martin Luther King, Jr., reveals continuity and unity in black protest and leadership. An investigation of the background and sociopsychological development of Powell and King and the boycotts provides opportunities to analyze Powell and King's leadership and black protest philosophies and tactics. Primary sources; 102 notes.

R. S. Sliwoski

308. Cavallo, Dominick. SEXUAL POLITICS AND SOCIAL REFORM: JANE ADDAMS, FROM CHILDHOOD TO HULL HOUSE. Albin, Mel, ed. *New Directions in Psychohistory: The Adelphi Papers in Honor of Erik H. Erikson* (Lexington, Mass.: Heath, 1980): 161-182. Studies social settlement worker Jane Addams's (1860-1935) childhood and adolescence, focusing on the cultural interfaces where individual life history meets social history and where biography and collective behavior interact. The problems and successes of Addams's early years were related to culturally prescribed paradigms of moral valuation and social behavior, especially the ways in which late-19th-century Americans perceived female and male social roles. The links between cultural paradigms and Addams's personal experiences, when placed in the context of late-19th-century urban and industrial changes, throw light on the relationship between her resolution of private conflicts and her decision to become a social reformer and thereby to help resolve society's public conflicts. She did this by opening Hull House, a social settlement institution, in Chicago in 1889. Secondary sources; 83 notes.

J. Powell

309. Chambers-Schiller, Lee. THE SINGLE WOMAN REFORMER: CONFLICTS BETWEEN FAMILY AND VOCATION, 1830-1860. *Frontiers 1978 3(3): 41-48.* Studies the lives and attitudes of unmarried women reformers, 1830-60, as they faced the conflicts between their work and their unmarried social status.

310. Chapman, James K. HENRY HARVEY STUART (1873-1952): NEW BRUNSWICK REFORMER. *Acadiensis [Canada] 1976 5(2): 79-104.* In his generation Henry Harvey Stuart was the most prominent and widespread voice of dissent in New Brunswick. A single theme dominated his multifarious activities: the regeneration of society through education and social reform. Stuart grew up in poverty. He began teaching in the 1890's, when his Christianity led him to socialism and the social gospel. He organized the province's first socialist party in 1902, promoted unions, edited a union newspaper, and played a role in municipal and provincial politics. 97 notes.

D. F. Chard

311. Chevigny, Bell Gale. GROWING OUT OF NEW ENGLAND: THE EMERGENCE OF MARGARET FULLER'S RADICALISM. *Women's Studies 1977 5(1): 65-100.* The radicalism of feminist writer Margaret Fuller (1810-50), which culminated with her participation in the Revolution of 1848 in Italy, was a function of her New England childhood and a reaction to the narrowness of Transcendentalism's social vision.

312. Chittenden, Elizabeth F. AS WE CLIMB: MARY CHURCH TERRELL. *Negro Hist. Bull. 1975 38(2): 351-354.* In 1892 Mary Church Terrell began the Colored Women's League of Washington, D.C., which spread to other cities and became the National Association of Colored Women. Their motto "lifting as we climb" characterized her life as an educator, suffragist and reformer. Biblio.

M. J. Wentworth

313. Christensen, Lawrence O. J. MILTON TURNER: AN APPRAISAL. *Missouri Hist. Rev. 1975 70(1): 1-19.* J. Milton Turner (1840-1915) was one of the prime figures in 19th-century blacks' struggle for equality. His career included efforts to form a Missouri Equal Rights League and to sponsor black education while serving as assistant state superintendent of schools. He was also active in raising funds to finance black migration from the South. From 1871-78 he was minister resident and consul general to Liberia. His career seemed to reach a climax during 1883-95 when he became the leader in the movement to get the Oklahoma freedmen a share of the funds that Congress had appropriated for the Cherokee Nation. Based on primary and secondary sources; illus., 84 notes.

W. F. Zornow

314. Cole, Terrence. RAYMOND ROBINS IN ALASKA: THE CONVERSION OF A PROGRESSIVE. *Pacific Northwest Q. 1981 72(2): 50-60.* In 1897 Raymond Robins set out to prospect for gold in Alaska, but in the ensuing years he gave up his dream of quick wealth and turned toward social reform. He worked to expose the corrupt political leaders of Nome and to improve the bad sanitation and overcrowded conditions of his adopted town. After leaving Alaska in 1900, Robins became active in the social settlement house movement, disarmament crusade, and the Rupublican Party. In 1917 he initiated contact with Lenin and Trotsky and worked tirelessly to gain American recognition of the Bolsheviks. Based on published family letters and newspapers; 7 photos, 46 notes.

M. L. Tate

315. Corwin, Margaret. MINNA SCHMIDT: BUSINESSWOMAN, FEMINIST, AND FAIRY GODMOTHER TO CHICAGO. *Chicago Hist. 1978-79 7(4): 226-235.* Minna Moscherosch Schmidt (1866-1961) was a German immigrant to Chicago in 1886; she owned a school of dance and later a wig and costume shop, was a devout feminist and a philanthropist to the fine arts and higher education in Chicago.

316. Cox, Steven. NATHANIEL P. ROGERS AND THE ROGERS COLLECTION. *Hist. New Hampshire 1978 33(1): 52-61.* Nathaniel Peabody Rogers (1794-1846) was New Hampshire's leading abolitionist. Diverted from a legal career by the slavery issue in the early 1830's, he helped found the Portsmouth Anti-Slavery Society in 1833, and became editor of the *Herald of Freedom* in 1838. He espoused non-resistance (pacifism) and attacked churches with southern connections. His letters are in the Quaker Collection, Haverford College Library, Haverford, Pennsylvania. Consisting of about 800 items, the collection sheds much light on Rogers' life and the abolitionist movement. Primary and secondary sources; 19 notes.

D. F. Chard

317. Craven, Martha Jacquelyn. A PORTRAIT OF EMILY TUBMAN. *Richmond County Hist. 1974 6(1): 4-10.* Presents a short biography of Emily Tubman, 1818-85, following her life as it coincided with events in Georgia and the South, and examines her efforts to aid in the establishment of Liberia. Reproduction, 27 notes.

318. Crowley, Weldon S. BENJAMIN RUSH: RELIGION AND SOCIAL ACTIVISM. *Religion in Life 1974 43(2): 227-238.* Covers 1770's-1813.

319. Culton, Donald R. LOS ANGELES' "CITIZEN FIXIT": CHARLES DWIGHT WILLARD, CITY BOOSTER AND PROGRESSIVE REFORMER. *California History 1978 57(2): 158-171.* Charles Dwight Willard (1860-1914) arrived in Los Angeles in 1888. Never particularly successful in business, Willard found his talents in newspaper work, promotion of the city's commercial potential, and moderate civic improvements. He was on the staff of several Los Angeles newspapers, secretary of the Chamber of Commerce in the 1890's, founder of the influential Sunset Club in 1895, and founder of several civic improvement groups. He started and contributed to several magazines. Because of his presence and involvement in City Council affairs, he was known as the "councilman from the 10th ward" in a nine-ward city. The *Times* uncharitably called him "Citizen Fixit." Despite declining health, Willard used his pen to urge such civic reforms as civil service, municipal ownership of services, and an end to bossism. His career delineates the "ties between promotion and reform in the progressive era." Primary and secondary sources; illus., 46 notes.

A. Hoffman

320. Curtis, Peter H. A QUAKER AND THE CIVIL WAR: THE LIFE OF JAMES PARNELL JONES. *Quaker Hist. 1978 67(1): 35-41.* Raised as a Quaker in Maine, James Parnell Jones spent two years at Haverford College, and developed a passion for antislavery and temperance reforms in reaction to the "hypocrisy" of conservative, Philadelphia Quakers. He taught school, and graduated from the University of Michigan in 1856, shifting toward the reformist tenets of Progressive or Congregational Friends in the area. When he returned to Maine in 1861 and joined its 7th Regiment, he was disowned, but felt himself still a Friend in all respects except in fighting the war for freedom and union. Based in part on letters to his family in Maine; 33 notes.
T. D. S. Bassett

321. Dahlie, Jorgen. SOCIALIST AND FARMER: OLE HJELT AND THE NORWEGIAN RADICAL VOICE IN CANADA, 1908-1928. *Can. Ethnic Studies [Canada] 1978 10(2): 55-64.* Ole Hjelt (1884-1974) settled in Instow, Saskatchewan, upon his arrival in 1908 as an immigrant from Norway. For two decades he was a spokesman for socialism among Scandinavians in Canada. He not only wrote several books calling for revolutionary change, but published voluminously in Scandinavian-language newspapers. He also traveled extensively for the Socialist Party of Canada and the Socialist Party of America. When he returned to Norway in 1928 he involved himself in Norwegian Labour Party activities. During the Nazi occupation he reversed his position, denouncing Marxism and supporting Germany. Primary sources; photo, 52 notes.
R. V. Ritter

322. Deegan, Mary Jo and Burger, John S. GEORGE HERBERT MEAD AND SOCIAL REFORM: HIS WORK AND WRITINGS. *J. of the Hist. of the Behavioral Sci. 1978 14(4): 362-372.* G. H. Mead, the eminent social psychologist, had an active civic life. His work in social reform was directly influenced by and derived from his philosophy of man and society. This facet of his life is relatively unexamined today, although most of his publications during his lifetime were concerned with the application of science for the good of the community.
J

323. DiNunzio, Mario R. IDEOLOGY AND PARTY LOYALTY: THE POLITICAL CONVERSION OF LYMAN TRUMBULL. *Lincoln Herald 1977 79(3): 95-103.* Lyman Trumbull, whose political idol was Andrew Jackson, was typical of a number of Democrats who became Republicans during the late 1850's due to the controversy over the extension of slavery into the territories. His conversion was a slow, agonizing process, but his unwillingness to support Douglas and the Kansas-Nebraska Bill finally drove Trumbull into the newly formed Illinois Republican Party in 1856. For Trumbull, the extension of slavery overshadowed all other issues. He remained an effective Republican Senator until 1872, when he left the party over the issue of increased centralization of national power at the expense of local and states rights. Photo, 53 notes.
T. P. Linkfield

324. Duke, David C. ANNA LOUISE STRONG AND THE SEARCH FOR A GOOD CAUSE. *Pacific Northwest Q. 1975 66(3): 123-137.* Committed to humanitarian causes throughout her life, Anna Louise Strong initially received inspiration from Industrial Workers of the World activities and the Seattle General Strike of 1919. But it was in the USSR of the 1920's and 1930's that she found a new sense of achievement as organizer and writer. Never a doctrinaire Marxist and never fully recognized for her achievements in the Soviet Union, Ms. Strong gradually developed an affection for the Maoist brand of communism. Her praise of the Chinese model led to deportation from the Soviet Union in 1948. Though subsequently exonerated of the charges, she chose life in China as an activist writer until her death in 1970. Based on primary and secondary sources; 2 photos, 67 notes.
M. L. Tate

325. Eberson, Frederick. CRUSADER EXTRAORDINARY: THOMAS DUCHE MITCHELL, 1791-1865. *Filson Club Hist. Q. 1978 52(3): 263-279.* Thomas Duche Mitchell was an early American doctor, medical school professor, and reformer. A graduate of the medical department of the University of Pennsylvania, Mitchell taught continuously at several schools during 1831-65. Teaching at Transylvania University medical school in Kentucky, he attempted to professionalize medicine on the frontier. At the same time Mitchell crusaded against the use of alcoholic beverages and tobacco. Based on Mitchell's published works and published biographical sketches; 31 notes.
G. B. McKinney

326. Edwards, G. Thomas. CHAMBERLAIN HOEL, ZEALOUS REFORMER. *Pacific Northwest Q. 1975 66(2): 49-60.* Chamberlain Hoel's cooperative store (a division of the New England Protective Union) was a success in 1852, but not so with his other attempts at land, educational, and medical reform until 1865 in Salem, Oregon.

327. Edwards, G. Thomas. DR. ADA M. WEED: NORTHWEST REFORMER. *Oregon Hist. Q. 1977 78(1): 5-40.* Drs. Gideon and Ada Weed, both hydropathic physicians, emigrated from New York City to Salem, Oregon, by way of California. Widely known and extremely active in many controversial causes, the Weeds lectured extensively on topics such as women's rights and prohibition, as well as medicine. Ada M. Weed carried on a lengthy debate with Asahel Bush, editor of the *Oregonian Statesman*, regarding womens' rights. Unfortunately the Weeds were unable to establish a financially successful medical practice. As a result, they returned to California. In 1870, after several years in California and Nevada, the Weeds moved to Seattle, where Ada retired from her medical career and controversial issues and became a well-known member of Seattle society. However, in 1883 Ada Weed once again became involved in womens' rights and prohibition. In 1890 the Weeds moved to Berkeley, California, where Ada Weed died in 1910. Primary sources and published secondary sources; illus., 71 notes.
D. R. McDonald

328. Endres, Kathleen. JANE GREY SWISSHELM: 19TH CENTURY JOURNALIST AND FEMINIST. *Journalism Hist. 1975-76 2(4): 128-132.* Jane Grey Swisshelm (1815-84) was a journalist and a political campaigner, particularly for the recognition of women's rights.

329. Falk, Leslie A. BLACK ABOLITIONIST DOCTORS AND HEALERS, 1810-1885. *Bull. of the Hist. of Medicine 1980 54(2): 258-272.* A number of black abolitionist doctors and healers practiced in America during 1810-85. These include James McCune Smith (1811-65), the first American black to obtain a medical degree, David Ruggles (1810-49), an early advocate of hydrotherapy, and William Wells Brown (1816-84), who lectured in England and later practiced medicine in Boston. Others were Harriet Tubman (1820-1913), a nurse and healer, and Sarah Parker Remond (b. 1826), who moved to Rome and practiced medicine there. 61 notes.
M. Kaufman

330. Finn, Barbara R. ANNA HOWARD SHAW AND WOMEN'S WORK. *Frontiers 1979 4(3): 21-25.* Describes feminist activist Anna Howard Shaw's life from 1865, when, at 18, she became a schoolteacher, until her death in 1919, focusing on the issue of equal opportunity in employment for women which she considered more important than suffrage, and her relationship with Lucy Anthony, niece of Susan B. Anthony, from their meeting in 1888, which lasted 30 years until Shaw's death; 1870's-1919.

331. Fleming, John E. SLAVERY, CIVIL WAR AND RECONSTRUCTION: A STUDY OF BLACK WOMEN IN MICROCOSM. *Negro Hist. Bull. 1975 38(6): 430-433.* Sketches the lives of three former slaves: Sojourner Truth, Susie King Taylor, and Octavia Rogers Albert. They were black women who struggled against second-class citizenship and expanded their vocation as teachers to work toward the advancement of black people. Notes.
M. J. Wentworth

332. Foner, Philip S. PETER H. CLARK: PIONEER BLACK SOCIALIST. *J. of Ethnic Studies 1977 5(3): 17-35.* After reviewing the approach of American Utopian Socialists and early German American Marxists to the questions of wage and chattel slavery before the Civil War, chronicles the career of Peter Humphries Clark (1829-1926), outstanding Cincinnati educator, editor, abolitionist, and leader of the Colored Teachers' Co-operative Association, apparently the first trade union of teachers in American history. In 1877 Clark left the Republican Party for the Workingmen's Party, where he strongly supported the railroad strikers of the great conflagration of 1877. Long excerpts of Clark's speeches as reported in William Haller's *The Emancipator,* the *Cincinnati Commercial,* and the Socialist Labor Party's *The Socialist,* are given, along with details of Clark's founding of Gaines High School for Negroes during the 1860's. Contemporary papers, secondary writings; 50 notes.
G. J. Bobango

333. Forrey, Carolyn. GERTRUDE ATHERTON AND THE NEW WOMAN. *California Hist. Q. 1976 55(3): 194-209.* Describes the career of Gertrude Atherton (1857-1948), author of 56 novels and numerous stories. Strongwilled and rebellious in her youth, Atherton found an intellectual outlet in writing fiction. Following the early death of her husband in a loveless marriage, Atherton set out to pursue a literary career. After initial unfavorable reviews she went to Europe and became a huge success there, particularly in England. A favorable reception to her novels then followed in the United States. The heroines in Atherton's novels fit the pattern of the "New Woman"—intellectually superior, athletic, independent, and sexually attractive. Such heroines greatly resembled Atherton's self-image. She had no patience with men who stereotyped women as submissive home-bound objects lacking intellectual capacity. Moreover, her heroines, in combining intellect with sexuality, represented a definition of feminism that Atherton herself attempted to fulfill throughout her long life. Based on primary and secondary sources; photos, 41 notes. A. Hoffman

334. Frederick, Peter J. A LIFE OF PRINCIPLE: ERNEST HOWARD CROSBY AND THE FRUSTRATIONS OF THE INTELLECTUAL AS REFORMER. *New York Hist. 1973 54(4): 396-423.* Ernest Howard Crosby (1856-1907) was a lawyer, poet, anti-imperialist, urban reformer, and advocate of Tolstoyan nonresistance. Son of Howard Crosby, theologian and educator, Crosby graduated from Columbia Law School in 1878, practiced law in New York City for the next 10 years, and succeeded in 1887 to Theodore Roosevelt's seat in the New York State Assembly. In 1894, Crosby read Tolstoy's *My Life*, and was so deeply affected by it that he went to Russia to meet the Count. Upon his return to America, Crosby gave up his political and legal career and moved his wife and mother to a Rhinebeck, New York, farm where he attempted to lead the simple agrarian life outlined by his mentor. Publishing many essays and poems, Crosby had a profound impact on his fellow intellectual reformers. He championed Henry George's Single-Tax movement, the Social Gospel movement, and the anti-imperialist cause. After 1898, he was prominent in the American Peace Society and served as President of the New York Anti-Imperialist League. Distrusting government, Crosby did not champion Progressive reform, and his positive impact on American reform was minimal. His career illustrates the dilemma of the intellectual reformer unable to relate to those whom he seeks to help. Based on Crosby's published work; 3 illus., 78 notes.
G. Kurland

335. Fry, Amelia R. SUFFRAGIST ALICE PAUL'S MEMOIRS: PROS AND CONS OF ORAL HISTORY. *Frontiers 1977 2(2): 82-86.* The memoirs of Alice Paul (1885-1977), suffragist and author of the proposed Equal Rights Amendment (ERA), illustrate the problems of oral history, particularly the subject's reticence on sensitive topics; part of a special issue on women's oral history.

336. Fryer, Judith. THE OTHER VICTORIA: "THE WOODHULL" AND HER TIMES. *Old Northwest 1978 4(3): 219-240.* Relates the life and times of two-time presidential candidate Victoria Claflin Woodhull (1838-1927). An advocate of free love, Woodhull, financed by Cornelius Vanderbilt (1794-1877) in New York City, published *Woodhull & Claflin's Weekly*, advocating free love, abortions, divorce, spiritualism, feminism, Communism, world government, etc. It was also a blackmail sheet. In 1871 Woodhull exposed Henry Ward Beecher's (1813-87) affair with a parishioner when he failed to stop his sisters' attacks on Woodhull. This resulted in Woodhull's arrest and trial on an obscene literature charge, for which she was acquitted. Based on Woodhull's publications and on secondary works; illus., 47 notes. J. N. Dickinson

337. Gambone, Joseph G., ed. THE FORGOTTEN FEMINIST OF KANSAS: THE PAPERS OF CLARINA I. H. NICHOLS, 1854-1885. *Kansas Hist. Q. 1973 39(3): 392-444, 39(4): 515-563, 1974 40(1): 72-135, (2): 241-292, (3): 410-459, (4): 503-562.* Continued from a previous article (see abstract 11A:3232). Part III. After returning to Kansas from the East in 1857, Mrs. Nichols became associate editor of the *Quindaro Chindowan*, a weekly Free-State journal. Her editorials are reprinted here. Giving up this position, Mrs. Nichols resumed her voluminous correspondence with prominent persons about the territorial strife in Kansas. In numerous letters to Susan B. Anthony she continued her discussion of antifeminism both in Kansas and in the nation as a whole. 142 notes. Part IV. Covers letters written during the late 1860's to the editors of the *Vermont Phoenix*, Wyandotte *Commerical Gazette*, and *Western Home Journal*, in which Mrs. Nichols discusses the status of women in Kansas and what might be done to improve their lot. She wrote at great length against the views of Rev. Eben Blachly, mustering an array of scriptural proof against his assertion that God had intended women to be inferior beings. 6 illus., 110 notes. Part V. In letters written from Wyandotte to the editors of the Topeka *Weekly Leader*, the *Kansas Daily Commonwealth*, and the *Vermont Phoenix*, Mrs. Nichols offers evidence to show that the women of Kansas did not enjoy their constitutional rights, contrary to a misconception apparently widely held in Kansas and other states at the time. She reviews scriptural evidence of the inferiority of women and again concludes that the Bible has been misinterpreted by men. She also elaborates on the ways in which homestead legislation worked to married women's disadvantage. Based on primary and secondary sources; illus., 77 notes. Part VI. Reproduces 1870-72 letters by Mrs. Nichols; from Potter Valley, California, in 1872 she described the daily life of immigrants around San Francisco. 71 notes. Part VII. Reprints more letters, 1873-80. Part VIII. Reprints letters from Mrs. Nichols' correspondence, 1881-85. W. F. Zornow and S

338. Gambone, Joseph G., ed. THE FORGOTTEN FEMINIST OF KANSAS: THE PAPERS OF CLARINA I. H. NICHOLS, 1854-1885. *Kansas Hist. Q. 1973 39(1): 12-57, (2): 220-261.* Part I. After an active career in controversy about temperance, slavery, and women's rights that began in Vermont in 1839, Mrs. Nichols moved to Kansas in 1854 "to work for a Government of equality, liberty, [and] fraternity." She spent most of her time in Kansas until poor health forced her to move to California in 1871. She helped to amend the Kansas constitution to grant women liberal property rights, equal guardianship of their children, and the right to vote. 2 illus., 140 notes. Part II. In this series of letters to prominent editors and personal friends from stopping-places between Kansas and the east coast (1855-56), Mrs. Nichols discussed her reaction to the territorial strife in Kansas and to antifeminism. Many of the letters were to Thaddeus Hyatt, a supporter of the Kansas Free-State party who in 1856 made Mrs. Nichols a relief agent in New York. 2 photos, 81 notes. Article to be continued. W. F. Zornow

339. Gardner, Bettye J. WILLIAM WATKINS: ANTEBELLUM BLACK TEACHER AND WRITER. *Negro Hist. Bull. 1976 39(6): 623-624.* William Watkins was a leader in the largest antebellum free black community in the nation in Baltimore, Maryland. He was was an active participant in the American Moral Reform Society and in the early discussions relating to the rights of the free black. Born free in 1801, he is best remembered as an educator and active worker and writer in the interests of blacks in America, but at the heart of all his ceaseless activity was his lecturing and writing. He strongly opposed black emigration as a solution to problems. Watkins died in Toronto, Canada in 1858. Photos, 18 notes. R. V. Ritter

340. Garrison, Bruce M. WILLIAM HODDING CARTER JR: A DIFFERENT PERSPECTIVE OF THE CRUSADING EDITOR. *Journalism Hist. 1976 3(3): 90-93, 96.* Newspaperman Carter's campaign against political corruption and unfair government, and his work for racial justice from the 1930's to the 1950's, led to several clashes with the authorities in Mississippi.

341. Garrison, George R. and Madden, Edward H. WILLIAM JAMES: WARTS AND ALL. *Am. Q. 1977 29(2): 207-221.* The biographers of William James have exaggerated the politically activist and social reformist aspects of his character. His opposition to American imperialism and jingoism, as well as his support of temperance, educational reform, and freedom of practice in medicine, were individualistic stands not generally associated with deep involvement in reform groups. His high sense of individualism prevented him from freely associating with others in reform actions. His understanding of social and political realities was superficial, and his assessment of the strengths and weaknesses of actors on the political scene was ambivalent. James displayed nonreformist attitudes toward civil rights for blacks, the position of the immigrant, and the women's rights movement. 42 notes. N. Lederer

342. Gersuny, Carl. A BIOGRAPHICAL NOTE ON SETH LUTHER. *Labor Hist. 1977 18(2): 239-248.* Discusses Seth Luther (1795-1863), an important labor leader in Rhode Island in the 1830's. An articulate carpenter, Luther moved from a perception of oppression to

defeat in rebellion and then to retreat from reality. A radical, Luther was involved in the labor movement, the free suffrage movement, and the Dorr Rebellion. Based on the writings of Seth Luther; 27 notes.

L. L. Athey

343. Gersuny, Carl. UPHILL BATTLE: LUCIUS F. C. GARVIN'S CRUSADE FOR POLITICAL REFORM. *Rhode Island Hist. 1980 39(2): 57-75.* Lucius F. C. Garvin (1841-1922) was a medical doctor and Rhode Island politician. A tireless but essentially unsuccessful crusader, he tried to bring his state into step with the reform currents of the time. As representative, senator, and governor he embraced such causes as black civil and political rights, public health, the abolition of child labor, and the 10-hour day. Based on unpublished materials in eight repositories, newspapers and periodicals, and published documents; 7 illus., 71 notes.

P. J. Coleman

344. Gilman, Elizabeth. CATHERYNE COOKE GILMAN: SOCIAL WORKER. Stuhler, Barbara and Kreuter, Gretchen, ed. *Women of Minnesota: Selected Biographical Essays* (St. Paul: Minnesota Historical Society Press, 1977): 190-207. Noted teacher, social worker, and feminist Catheryne Cooke Gilman was born in 1880 in the small Missouri town of Laclede. After her high school graduation in 1898, Catheryne Cooke taught social studies in Iowa and, in 1904, became a principal. Subsequently, she attended Iowa State Normal School and did graduate work at the University of Chicago where she discovered new theories, social thought, and social problems. A course by Sophonisba P. Breckinridge introduced Catheryne to feminism and to Jane Addams's Hull House. Cooke took up the new profession of social work, went to New York City's East Side House Settlement, and to the University Settlement directed by Robbins Gilman, whom she married in 1914. They settled in Minneapolis where Robbins conducted the North East Neighborhood House. Catheryne worked as a suffragist, agitated for improved maternity and infant care, and served on the Minnesota Child Welfare Commission. She became a leader of the Women's Co-operative Alliance, organized community studies, and investigated the causes of juvenile delinquency. She promoted sex education and parent-training courses in the schools. During the 1920's and 30's, she campaigned for morality laws and chaired the motion picture committee of the National Congress of Parents and Teachers. From then until her death in 1954, Catheryne Gilman remained at the North East Neighborhood House where she wrote, lectured, and worked. Primary and secondary sources; photo, 35 notes.

A. E. Wiederrecht

345. Gilman, Rhoda R. EVA MCDONALD VALESH: MINNESOTA POPULIST. Stuhler, Barbara and Kreuter, Gretchen, ed. *Women of Minnesota: Selected Biographical Essays* (St. Paul: Minnesota Historical Society Press, 1977): 55-76. During the late 1880's and early 1890's, Eva McDonald Valesh was a leading figure in Minnesota's labor and agrarian political movements. As a journalist and lecturer, Valesh worked for the Knights of Labor, the Farmers' Alliance, and the People's Party. An energetic, ambitious, impassioned lecturer and newspaper reporter, Valesh achieved political power at a time when women's suffrage was not yet seriously discussed even by third parties. She campaigned with Ignatius Donnelly, worked with editor Everett Fish, was elected State Lecturer of the Minnesota Alliance, was a national organizer for the People's Party, and worked for William Jennings Bryan's presidential campaign in 1896. That same year, she and her husband, Frank Valesh, separated. Eva moved with her son to New York City where she worked as a journalist, became involved with the Women's Trade Union League, and wed wealthy Benjamin F. Cross. After this marriage ended, Eva resumed work as a proofreader and worked for the *New York Times* until she retired, in 1951, at age 85. When she died five years later, people had long since forgotten her years of political activism in Minnesota. Primary sources; photo, 54 notes.

A. E. Wiederrecht

346. Gilpin, Patrick J. CHARLES S. JOHNSON: SCHOLAR AND EDUCATOR. *Negro Hist. Bull. 1976 39(3): 544-548.* Discusses the major achievements of Charles S. Johnson and analyzes childhood, college, and later influences on his dedication to scholarship and to improving race relations. Johnson became the first black president of Fisk University in 1947. He established an international reputation in sociology, served several Presidents, and chaired a UNESCO conference of experts on race relations in 1955. The tolls of interminable conferences, exacting scholarship, and service in race relations cut short Johnson's brilliant career in 1956, but not before the groundwork was laid for the black liberation movement that followed. Based on the Charles S. Johnson papers and other sources; illus., 23 notes.

W. R. Hively

347. Gould, Alan B. WALTER L. FISHER: PROFILE OF AN URBAN REFORMER, 1880-1910. *Mid-America 1975 57(3): 157-172.* Walter L. Fisher, son of a West Virginia minister, began his career as reformer as special assessment attorney in Chicago. He became secretary and later president of the Municipal Voters' League, president of the Fisher-organized City Club of Chicago, and a founder of the Bureau of Public Efficiency. As special traction attorney, he accomplished his most significant reforms. Based on the Fisher Papers, Library of Congress, newspapers, official records, and secondary works; 43 notes.

T. H. Wendel

348. Gounard, J.-F. LA CARRIERE MOUVEMENTÉE DE RICHARD WRIGHT: 1908-1960 [The eventful career of Richard Wright: 1908-60]. *Rev. de l'Université d'Ottawa [Canada] 1976 46(4): 520-543.* The American Richard Nathaniel Wright, a black, had an extremely traumatic youth, but rose out of it to become a great and quite prolific writer. His most famous work, *Black Boy, A Record of Childhood and Youth,* appeared in 1945. After World War II, he moved with his family to Paris, where he lived thereafter. He was the first of a new wave of black American writers who cast aside the old inferior image of blacks, refused to submit to racial restrictions, and appealed to and were read by a large number of nonblacks. 65 notes.

J. C. Billigmeier

349. Grant, Mary H. DOMESTIC EXPERIENCE AND FEMINIST THEORY: THE CASE OF JULIA WARD HOWE. Kelley, Mary, ed. *Woman's Being, Woman's Place: Female Identity and Vocation in American History* (Boston: G. K. Hall, 1979): 220-232. Presents a paradox between Julia Ward Howe's unhappy marriage and her glorification of woman's role within the home. Despite her marital experiences with a husband who refused to allow the married woman's traditional domestic prerogatives, and who withheld even affection and companionship, Howe emerged a champion of domesticity. For Howe, marriage, especially motherhood, was more significant as a vehicle than as an end in itself. Through motherhood women were responsible for the moral and mental development of their children, who would comprise the nation's future. Thus her feminism looked beyond the home as much as within. Her fame and achievement as a public figure were greatest once she was widowed. With motherhood as the key to her feminism, Howe pursued a variety of reforms for women, not the least of which was to demand that society allow women to assume their unique and critical role in spheres within and without the home. Based on the Julia Ward Howe Collection in the Library of Congress; 47 notes.

J. Powell

350. Grossman, Lawrence. IN HIS VEINS COURSED NO BOOTLICKING BLOOD: THE CAREER OF PETER H. CLARK. *Ohio Hist. 1977 86(2): 79-95.* Nineteenth-century black history in Cincinnati, Ohio, is illuminated in this biographical sketch of one of Ohio's most prominent black men. Peter H. Clark, schoolteacher and champion of antebellum Cincinnati black rights, became a figure of national importance in racial matters by the 1880's. His childhood, education, jobs, and appointment as the first black member of the Board of Trustees of The Ohio State University are discussed. Emphasizes Clark's intense involvement in politics. Based on manuscript, newspaper, contemporary, and secondary sources; illus., 55 notes.

J

351. Hancock, Harold B. MARY ANN SHADD: NEGRO EDITOR, EDUCATOR, AND LAWYER. *Delaware Hist. 1973 15(3): 187-194.* Mary Ann Shadd (d. 1893) was the daughter of Abraham D. Shadd, a Delaware Negro abolitionist prominent in the Negro convention movement. She was nursed on Quaker teachings and antislavery witness. The family moved to Ontario, Canada, in 1851, but the Shadd family maintained contacts with Wilmington (Delaware) and West Chester (Pennsylvania) friends. Mary Ann Shadd first earned her antislavery reputation by investigating the possibilities of Negro settlement in Canada to escape the baneful effects of the invigorated Fugitive Slave Act of 1850. In a pamphlet in 1852 she called attention to opportunities for Negroes in Canada, and lectured widely on the subject. Her most significant contribution was her leading role as editor, 1854-59, in the publication of the weekly *Provincial Freeman,* the first antislavery newspaper in Ontario. From its inception in 1854 the *Freeman* attacked the mismanage-

ment of experimental Negro communities, opposed segregation, and assaulted slavery in the United States. She lectured in the United States in 1855. She also taught school, initially through the American Missionary Association, participated in women's rights reform, and published articles encouraging Negroes to patronize Negro businesses. Based on newspapers and unpublished letters; 27 notes. R. M. Miller

352. Harris, Ted C. JEANNETTE RANKIN IN GEORGIA. *Georgia Hist. Q. 1974 58(1): 55-78.* Jeannette Rankin (1880-1973) of Montana, the nation's first congresswoman, chose Georgia as a retreat and second home. It became her base of operations for peace and feminism activities. 3 illus., 93 notes. D. L. Smith

353. Harris, William H. A. PHILIP RANDOLPH AS A CHARISMATIC LEADER, 1925-1941. *J. of Negro Hist. 1979 64(4): 301-315.* A. Philip Randolph emerged as a national figure in organizing the Brotherhood of Sleeping Car Porters. His later disavowal of the Communist tendencies in the National Negro Congress and his abortive March on Washington Movement made Randolph one of the best known and widely respected Afro-American leaders. Primary materials; 49 notes.
N. G. Sapper

354. Hauptman, Laurence M. ALICE JAMISON: SENECA POLITICAL ACTIVIST, 1901-1964. *Indian Hist. 1979 12(2): 15-22, 60-62.* Alice Lee Jamison, a Seneca Indian, through the work of the American Indian Federation, was a major critic of the 1930's New Deal policy developed by John Collier, and of the Bureau of Indian Affairs, 1940's-50's.

355. Hertzberg, Hazel Whitman. NATIONALITY, ANTHROPOLOGY, AND PAN-INDIANISM IN THE LIFE OF ARTHUR C. PARKER (SENECA). *Pro. of the Am. Phil. Soc. 1979 123(1): 47-72.* Arthur C. Parker (1881-1955) was one of the leading Indian intellectuals of his day, having been born on the Cattaraugus Seneca Reservation in western New York. Treats Parker's search for a vocation rather than his ultimate career as a museologist. While engaged in that search Parker made pioneering contributions to archaeology, ethnology, Pan-Indian reform, and museology. Details the many inner struggles which were interspersed with his successes and failures, until in his later years he abandoned many of his earlier principles and goals out of sheer frustration and despair, the Pan-Indian movement being one of them. Based largely on the writings of Parker, contemporary anthropologists such as Franz Boas, other Indian intellectuals, and anthropologists; 59 notes. H. M. Parker, Jr.

356. Himelhoch, Myra Samuels and Shaffer, Arthur H. ELIZABETH PACKARD: NINETEENTH-CENTURY CRUSADER FOR THE RIGHTS OF MENTAL PATIENTS. *J. of Am. Studies [Great Britain] 1979 13(3): 343-375.* Presentation of dubious evidence of insanity resulted in a three-year confinement for Elizabeth Packard (1816-97) in the Illinois State Hospital. Released in 1863, she crusaded successfully during the next 30 years for statutes which could prevent injustices within the asylums. To achieve this reform, she attacked physicians who traditionally determined mental competency, and she criticized their methods of treating asylum patients. Consequently, she was publicly maligned throughout the remainder of her lifetime. Not until the 1930's did scholars begin to acknowledge her reform achievements. Based on psychiatric and legal literature, writings of Elizabeth and Theophilus Packard, and secondary historical sources; 110 notes. H. T. Lovin

357. Hornbein, Marjorie. THE STORY OF JUDGE BEN LINDSEY. *Southern California Q. 1973 55(4): 469-482.* An account of the career of Judge Benjamin B. Lindsey (1869-1943), pioneer in the passage of child labor laws and laws for the protection of minors. Outspoken on such issues as birth control and trial marriage, Lindsey wrote a number of controversial books, including attacks on political and corporate corruption. In 1927, after 20 years as judge of the juvenile court in Denver, he was ousted from his position. He then moved to Los Angeles and was elected a superior court judge in Los Angeles County in 1934. Frustrated in his attempt to preside over the juvenile department, he settled for the Children's Court of Conciliation, a court he helped create in 1939. Lindsey advocated many ideas which shocked his contemporaries and which are still controversial today, but his reputation as a defender of the young and innocent is secure. Based on Lindsey's writings, newspapers, and published studies; photos, 116 notes. A. Hoffman

358. Hudson, Gossie Harold. NOT FOR ENTERTAINMENT ONLY. *Negro Hist. Bull. 1977 40(2): 682-683.* Josephine Baker was more than a black entertainer. Her World War II service through the Red Cross, underground intelligence, and the Free French; her postwar experiment of adopting a dozen orphans of various races and nationalities; and her work as a civil rights activist made her the personification of black contributions to the struggle for freedom for all peoples. Based on newspaper accounts and secondary sources; photo, 9 notes.
R. E. Noble

359. Hunt, Marion. WOMAN'S PLACE IN MEDICINE: THE CAREER OF DR. MARY HANCOCK MCLEAN. *Missouri Hist. Soc. Bull. 1980 36(4): 255-263.* Though her behavior defied social conventions, Mary Hancock McLean (1861-1930) was able to become a physician and surgeon in 1883. Medical education was then available to women so that, trained, they might medically attend to other women and children. Despite obstacles, she proved to the St. Louis medical fraternity that female physicians deserved a larger sphere than was traditionally granted them. Based primarily on secondary sources; 2 photos, 30 notes.
H. T. Lovin

360. Jaffe, Philip J. AGNES SMEDLEY: A REMINISCENCE. *Survey [Great Britain] 1974 20(4): 172-179.* Details Agnes Smedley's early attraction to radicalism, her life in China, dismissal by Chu Teh, whom she worshipped, and her relationship to Richard Sorge, the Soviet spy, in Tokyo which later caused her much trouble in the five years preceding the McCarthy era and finally drove her to England where she died. R. B. Valliant

361. James, Edward T. T. V. POWDERLY, A POLITICAL PROFILE. *Pennsylvania Mag. of Hist. and Biog. 1975 99(4): 443-459.* Traces the political life of Terence Vincent Powderly during 1876-1900. Originally a supporter of the Greenback-Labor party, Powderly's political impulses were largely shaped by local issues such as those he confronted while serving as mayor of Scranton. In 1879 Powderly became national head of the Knights of Labor. Its membership peaked around 1886, but shortly thereafter the Knights became more small-town and political-reform oriented rather than interested in trade unionism. Powderly flirted with both Democrats and Republicans, but in 1894 formally joined the Republicans. His political career ended as a federal officeholder in Washington when President McKinley appointed him Commissioner-General of Immigration. 65 notes. C. W. Olson

362. Jeansonne, Glen. PREACHER, POPULIST, PROPAGANDIST: THE EARLY CAREER OF GERALD L. K. SMITH. *Biography 1979 2(4): 303-327.* Gerald L. K. Smith, born and reared in Wisconsin and educated in Indiana, served as a Christian minister before becoming Huey P. Long's Share Our Wealth Society organizer in 1934. Protestant Fundamentalism and political populism and progressivism prepared Smith for political activism. His evolution from radicalism to reaction is examined and the apparent disjunction explained. J

363. Jenkins, William D. ROBERT BULKELY: PROGRESSIVE PROFILE. *Ohio Hist. 1979 88(1): 57-72.* Within the broad mainstream of progressivism stood Democratic Congressman Robert J. Bulkley. During his two terms in the House he became a recognized authority on banking and helped frame two important pieces of legislation; The Federal Reserve Act, (US, 1913) and the Federal Farm Loan Act (US, 1916). Influenced by courses studied at Harvard, Bulkley was interested in problems of the inner city. He was in sympathy with using the state as a protector of the poor, the laborer and the child. However, he was a moderate in matters of government and held a liberal stance toward social welfare, antitrust, and tariff legislation. Photo, 54 notes, ref.
H. F. Thomson

364. Johnson, James P. HERBERT HOOVER: THE ORPHAN AS CHILDREN'S FRIEND. *Prologue 1980 12(4): 193-206.* That Herbert C. Hoover was orphaned before he was 10 was a key factor in his life. As an apparent result of his unhappy childhood, Hoover developed a passion for working with and for children. This passion was evidenced throughout his life, resulting in such efforts as organizing large-scale assistance to civilian war victims as director of the Committee for Relief in Belgium, setting up a European Children's Fund to feed starving children as director of the American Relief Agency, providing food to millions of Russians

during 1921-23 under the Food and Remittance Plan, combining private volunteer groups into the American Child Health Association, and convening 2,500 delegates to a National Conference on Child Health as President. Based on Hoover public statements, Presidential personal papers, President Hoover files, newspapers, and interviews; illus., 10 photos, 84 notes.   M. A. Kascus

365. Kazymyra, Nadia O. THE DEFIANT PAVLO KRAT AND THE EARLY SOCIALIST MOVEMENT IN CANADA. *Can. Ethnic Studies [Canada] 1978 10(2): 38-54.* From 1902, Pavlo Krat (1882-1952) was involved in political uprisings in the Russian Empire, and in demonstrations against Polish authorities in Austria-Hungary before he emigrated to Canada in 1907. He revitalized Ukrainian socialists in Canada by his dynamic public speaking and articulate and voluminous writings. He combined Marxian socialism and romantic patriotism to instill social consciousness and national identity. He, however, lost leadership through unfair criticism of fellow Ukrainian immigrants for their failure to recognize his own manifest destiny in building a socialist society. His unsuccessful search for the ideal socialist state ended in his becoming a Presbyterian minister and terminating any formal association with the socialist movement. Primary sources; photo, 94 notes.
R. V. Ritter

366. Kedro, Milan James. AUTOBIOGRAPHY AS A KEY TO IDENTITY IN THE PROGRESSIVE ERA. *Hist. of Childhood Q. 1975 2(3): 391-407.* Uses the autobiographies of four reformers (Clarence S. Darrow, Richard T. Ely, Frederic C. Howe, Thomas L. Johnson), two mugwumps (Theodore Roosevelt, William Allen White), and two labor leaders (Samuel Gompers, Terence V. Powderly) to examine the psychological make-up of Progressive era leaders. While all eight individuals shared some experiences, each group generally experienced childhood and adolescence in unique ways, creating reformist, mugwump, and laborite personalities. Based on autobiographies, biographies, and other secondary sources; 82 notes.   R. E. Butchart

367. Kessler-Harris, Alice. THE AUTOBIOGRAPHY OF ANN WASHINGTON CRATON. *Signs 1976 1(4): 1019-1037.* Discusses an organizer for the socialist-dominated Amalgamated Clothing Workers of America. Ann Washington Craton, a college graduate schooled in social work, considered herself a born crusader and reformer. In the 1920's she organized factory women in the rural northeast, where mill owners had retreated with their factories to escape urban unions and take advantage of the cheap labor of coal miners' wives. Craton's autobiography reveals that the Jewish constituency in the union resented a gentile being hired as a organizer, but her background stood her in good stead when she was sent to organize the "new immigrants." Based on excerpts from Craton's autobiography; note.   J. Gammage

368. Kilde, Clarence. DARK DECADE: THE DECLINING YEARS OF WALDEMAR AGER. *Norwegian-American Studies 1979 28: 157-191.* Waldemar Theodore Ager (1868-1941) was a Norwegian immigrant steadfastly committed to three goals: total abstinence from alcohol, retention of the Norwegian language and culture by Norwegian Americans, and the creation of a genre of literature by and about Norwegian Americans in their immigrant experience. These three ideals ruled his life. For 38 years he edited *Reform*, a Norwegian-language temperance newspaper published in Eau Claire, Wisconsin. His ideals were also expressed in several novels, all written in Norwegian and all about the immigrant experience. Ager's last decade moved from twilight to darkness: depression eroded *Reform*'s subscriber list, Prohibition was repealed, and Norwegian-Americans increasingly used English. Waldemar Ager Papers, Norwegian-American Historical Association, Northfield, Minnesota; 39 notes.   D. K. Lambert

369. Knawa, Anne Marie. JANE ADDAMS AND JOSEPHINE DUDZIK: SOCIAL SERVICE PIONEERS. *Polish Am. Studies 1978 35(1-2): 13-22.* Compares the life and work of Sister Mary Theresa (Josephine Dudzik), the founder of the Franciscan Sisters of Chicago, with that of the internationally renowned Jane Addams (1860-1935). Sister Mary Theresa (1860-1918) was an indefatigable worker. Official steps are being taken for her beatification and possible canonization. Polish and English primary and secondary sources; 23 notes.   S. R. Pliska

370. Kutcher, Stan. J. W. BENGOUGH AND THE MILLENNIUM IN HOGTOWN: A STUDY OF MOTIVATION IN URBAN REFORM. *Urban Hist. Rev. [Canada] 1976 76(2): 30-49.* The career of John Wilson Bengough (1851-1923), cartoonist and author, illustrates the idealism of certain aspects of the urban reform movement. Religiously motivated, he believed in worshiping God by serving mankind. Concerned with the social conditions of Toronto, he used his weekly satirical magazine, *Grip*, to promote morality in city government. He became involved in politics by serving as an alderman for three years. Frustrated by the necessity of political compromise, he retired from office in 1909, preferring the freedom of an outside critic. Based on the Bengough Papers, secondary sources, and newspapers; 76 notes.   C. A. Watson

371. Lapitskii, M. I. BOLSHOI BILL: WILLIAM HAYWOOD (1869-1928) [Big Bill: William Haywood (1869-1928)]. *Novaia i Noveishaia Istoriia [USSR] 1974 (2): 77-97.* William Dudley Haywood held an important place in the history of the workers' and socialist movements in the late 19th and early 20th centuries in the United States. As a revolutionary he fought with reformism, took an active part in workers' movements, including the creation of trade unions, and became a prominent leader of the American proletariat. Gives an account of Haywood's ancestry and life from his birth in the far west, the development of his political ideas and activity, his emigration to the USSR in March 1921, to his death in March 1928. Primary and secondary sources; 70 notes.
L. Smith

372. Lash, Joseph P. ELEANOR ROOSEVELT'S ROLE IN WOMEN'S HISTORY. Deutrich, Mabel E. and Purdy, Virginia C., ed. *Clio Was a Woman: Studies in the History of American Women* (Washington, D.C.: Howard U. Pr., 1980): 243-253. Recounts Eleanor Roosevelt's career. Raised by a grandmother who was the epitome of Victorian female dependence and helplessness, Mrs. Roosevelt did not have a childhood upbringing which nurtured traits of independence and militancy. She was influenced in her conception of how women should participate in political life by her aunt, Mrs. Cowles, emerging as a champion of women's rights. She was also influenced to become more of a public person by the US entry into World War I and by the discovery of her husband's romance with Lucy Mercer. During the 1920's she became a leader in her own right with active participation in many organizations. The New Deal years represented a high point in women's participation in politics and government, largely because of Mrs. Roosevelt. A discussion summary follows. Based on a personal acquaintance with Mrs. Roosevelt; 26 notes.
J. Powell

373. Lawson, Alan. JOHN DEWEY AND THE HOPE FOR REFORM. *Hist. of Educ. Q. 1975 15(1): 31-66.* Chronicles John Dewey's intellectual formation, his philosophy, and social affairs, and his personal development, in order to understand his philosophy of education which balanced Instrumentalism, philosophic ideas of the 19th century, and social reform, 1909-30's.

374. LeMoignan, Michel. LA VISION AUDACIEUSE DE MGR. F.-X. ROSS, PREMIER ÉVÊQUE DE GASPÉ [The audacious vision of Monsignor F.-X. Ross, first bishop of Gaspé]. *Sessions d'Étude: Soc. Can. d'Hist. de l'Église Catholique [Canada] 1976 43: 35-47.* A biography of Bishop-founder François Xavier Ross (1869-1945), emphasizing his contributions to the educational system, medical facilities, and socioeconomic organization of Gaspé and its environs, 1923-45, and stressing the importance of his writings to the historian.

375. Lewis, Ronald L. CULTURAL PLURALISM AND BLACK RECONSTRUCTION: THE PUBLIC CAREER OF RICHARD CAIN. *Crisis 1978 85(2): 57-60, 64-65.* Richard Harvey Cain (1825-87) was a South Carolina State Senator, a US Congressman, a newspaper editor, an African Methodist Episcopal Bishop, and a college president. Born in 1825, he lived through slavery and the Civil War and worked to improve economic, political, and social conditions for blacks during Reconstruction. He died in 1887, having left a legacy of tireless effort and significant progressive change.   A. G. Belles

376. Link, Eugene P. LATTER DAY CHRISTIAN REBEL: HARRY F. WARD. *Mid-America 1974 56(4): 221-230.* Harry F. Ward, the outstanding religious social critic, played a founding role in the formation of the influential Methodist Federation for Social Service. He,

rather than Frank M. North, wrote the "Social Creed of the Churches." Ward was later a leader in the American League for Peace and Democracy in the 1930's. Ward was the most significant social Christian since Walter Rauschenbusch. Based on primary and secondary sources; 23 notes. T. D. Schoonover

377. Lojek, Helen. THE SOUTHERN LADY GETS A DIVORCE: "SANER FEMINISM" IN THE NOVELS OF AMÉLIE RIVES. *Southern Literary J. 1979 12(1): 47-69.* Discusses the changing literary characters of Amèlie Rives (1863-1945), which parallel the author's evolution from archetypal southern belle to moderate feminist.

378. Lurie, Jonathan. H. D. LLOYD: A NOTE. *Agric. Hist. 1973 47(1): 76-79.* The papers of Henry Demarest Lloyd (1847-1903) indicate his "awareness of if not actual involvement in virtually every important reform movement" of the post-Civil War era. Quotes letters to Lloyd from James B. Corruthers, a young black poet and college teacher, and reprints a fable that Lloyd read to the Sunset Club, a Chicago discussion group. Based on the Henry Demarest Lloyd Papers, in the Wisconsin State Historical Society Archives; 12 notes. D. E. Brewster

379. Lynch, Acklyn R. PAUL ROBESON: HIS DREAMS KNOW NO FRONTIERS. *J. of Negro Educ. 1976 45(3): 225-234.* Paul Robeson graduated from Rutgers University and received a law degree from Columbia University before beginning his concert career. His fights for civil liberties in the 1930's and 1940's made him very unpopular with conservative elements, and in the 1950's he was called a Communist and treated as a traitor. 15 notes. B. D. Johnson

380. Mackintosh, Barry. GEORGE WASHINGTON CARVER: THE MAKING OF A MYTH. *J. of Southern Hist. 1976 42(4): 507-528.* As in other areas of human endeavor, talented black American scientists have not obtained the recognition they deserve. George Washington Carver in reality possessed little scientific ability and a low level of achievement, but he has received great praise and recognition. Carver's work with the peanut and sweet potato transformed neither southern agrarian life nor agriculturally based industrial life, nor did he leave behind scientific-technological works permitting his alleged work to be studied, verified, or implemented. It was his personality and character—soft-spoken, deferential, submissive, and pious—which prompted whites to accept him and to build myths around him. His reputation must rest more on his social and psychological utility than on his scientific achievement. T. Schoonover

381. Maniha, John K. and Maniha, Barbara B. A COMPARISON OF PSYCHOHISTORICAL DIFFERENCES AMONG SOME FEMALE RELIGIOUS AND SECULAR LEADERS. *J. of Psychohistory 1978 5(4): 523-549.* Seeks to determine, through an examination of 26 outstanding American female leaders, why some extraordinary women choose religious rather than secular leadership roles. Female religious leaders more often came from childrearing backgrounds in which they were socialized in traditional sex roles and in which authoritarian males conveyed an image of God as an omnipotent tyrant. Female secular leaders, on the other hand, came from atypical homes in which their intellectual aspirations and abilities were supported by fathers or other males. The study examined the childhoods of Anne Hutchinson, Mary Baker Eddy, Aimee Semple McPherson, Nona Brooks, Ann Lee, Sarah Grimke, Lucy Stone, Susan B. Anthony, Jane Addams, Margaret Sanger, and others. Primary and secondary sources; tables, biblio. R. E. Butchart

382. Marable, Manning. A. PHILIP RANDOLPH & THE FOUNDATIONS OF BLACK AMERICAN SOCIALISM. *Radical Am. 1980 14(2): 6-32.* A study of the views and contributions of Asa Philip Randolph (d. 1979), black trade unionist, radical journalist, and socialist leader to black America. His career has been controversial and difficult to understand because he was often seen as compromising the very positions he had supported. Yet his accomplishments in black union organizing, militant journalism, and political protest were unequaled for many decades. Although a Marxist, he resisted Communist Party control of his cherished black causes and broke with Bolshevism. He fell into a habit of political compromise and reconciliation, and, in the end, "his ambiguous hostility toward the Negro's nationalism negated the full potential of his efforts." 7 photos, 75 notes. R. V. Ritter

383. Massey, Mary Elizabeth. THE MAKING OF A FEMINIST. *J. of Southern Hist. 1973 39(1): 3-22.* Ella Gertrude Clanton Thomas's journal of 41 years, 1848-89, is "among the most revealing records to come from the Civil War generation." It is "especially valuable for showing how and why a southern lady, reared in the tradition of the Old South, came to question its teachings and eventually to play a part in overturning many of its time-honored concepts." 81 notes. I. M. Leonard

384. Mattern, Carolyn J. MARY MACLANE: A FEMINIST OPINION. *Montana 1977 27(4): 54-63.* Mary MacLane (1881-1929) wrote three books—*The Story of Mary MacLane* (1902), *My Friend Annabel Lee* (1903), and *I, Mary MacLane* (1917)—authored numerous articles, then wrote and starred in a movie, *Men Who Have Made Love To Me* (1917). Her activities created a sensation in her hometown of Butte, Montana, and nationwide. Although atypical, she was not an eccentric woman. Her ideas arose and developed from her environment, reflected the mainstream of feminist thought, and represented ideas or feelings of educated, middle class women during that era. An unhappy, self-centered young woman, MacLane craved understanding and self-expression, believing all women should be free to live fully expressive lives. During 1902-10, MacLane found happiness in the intellectual bohemia of New York City's Greenwich Village and had several affairs with men, viewing the associations dispassionately. After her return to Butte in 1910, and a near fatal bout with scarlet fever, MacLane's writing evidenced a sense of life's fragility and her own mortality; she died lonely and forgotten in Chicago. Based on writings of Mary MacLane, contemporary newspapers and journals; 3 illus., 28 notes. R. C. Myers

385. McCarthy, Abigail. JANE GREY SWISSHELM: MARRIAGE AND SLAVERY. Stuhler, Barbara and Kreuter, Gretchen, ed. *Women of Minnesota: Selected Biographical Essays* (St. Paul: Minnesota Historical Society Pr., 1977): 34-54. Jane Grey Swisshelm was born of Scotch-Irish parents on 6 December 1815. She grew up in western Pennsylvania. Precocious, she learned to read and sew very early and became a skilled painter. In 1836, she married James Swisshelm, a prosperous farmer. They were unlike in religion, values, and temperament. The marriage proved difficult; in 1857, Jane took her daughter, left her husband, and moved to St. Cloud, Minnesota. By then, she was a noted journalist, abolitionist, and feminist. In her new home, Swisshelm resumed her newspaper career. She soon became embroiled in political controversy with Sylvanus B. Lowry, the proslavery Democratic political ruler of central Minnesota. Swisshelm's journalistic weapons of ruthless irony and vitriolic satire helped to bring about Lowry's decline. She also reported on the Sioux revolt which terrorized the state, in 1862; she advocated stern reprisals against the Indians. In 1863, Swisshelm went to Washington, D.C., and quickly became involved in Civil War nursing, an occupation which, for the first time, brought her approval and encouragement instead of criticism and controversy. Primary and secondary sources; photo, 49 notes. A. E. Wiederrecht

386. McCormick, Richard P. WILLIAM WHIPPER: MORAL REFORMER. *Pennsylvania Hist. 1976 43(1): 23-48.* By the early 1830's William Whipper (1804-76) had emerged as the leading intellectual in Philadelphia's black community. He became a wealthy lumber merchant, was active in the underground railroad, and was best known for his involvement in the national Negro conventions and the American Moral Reform Society. Whipper edited the *National Reformer*, organ of the A.M.R.S. Believing in the equality and brotherhood of all men, he opposed racially-based reform organizations, but came to accept them as necessary when his hopes for the emergence of a more just society diminished. Analysis of his career underscores the diversity of opinion that existed among Negroes in the decades prior to the Civil War. Based on the *Freedom's Journal*, the *National Reformer*, and primary and secondary sources; illus., 86 notes. D. C. Swift

387. McGinty, Garnie W. DR. MARY WILLIAMS MIMS: TEACHER, HUMANITARIAN, AND COMMUNITY ORGANIZER. *North Louisiana Hist. Assoc. J. 1976 7(4): 135-139.* Mary Williams Mims (1882-1967), the fifth of eight children born to David Samuel and Mary Eleanora (Stewart) Mims, was born and grew up on a plantation located eight miles northwest of Minden. She eventually became "an outstanding teacher and school principal, a humanitarian, and Louisiana's greatest community organizer." She retired from Louisiana State University in 1950 and spent her last 17 years in Shreveport.

She is widely regarded as "the outstanding woman in Louisiana history during the first half of the twentieth century." Primary and secondary sources; photo, 4 notes. — A. N. Garland

388. McMurry, Linda O. A BLACK INTELLECTUAL IN THE NEW SOUTH: MONROE NATHAN WORK, 1866-1945. *Phylon 1980 41(4): 333-344.* Monroe Nathan Work, a black sociologist, began his career in the early 20th century. Caught in the ideological struggle between Booker T. Washington and W. E. B. DuBois, he tried to discover where the talents of black people could best be used in the search for recognition and rights. He sought to win the support of southern whites for the black cause. Based on primary materials in the Tuskegee Institute Archives and the Library of Congress; 32 notes, biblio. — J. V. Coutinho

389. Michaels, Patricia. C. B. HOFFMAN, KANSAS SOCIALIST. *Kansas Hist. Q. 1975 41(2): 166-182.* Christian Balzac Hoffman became wealthy after 1872 by investing in milling, real estate sales, banking, farm machinery manufacturing, and publishing. He showed interest in socialistic enterprises by sponsoring a cooperative in Kansas City and a communal settlement in Mexico. When the Republican and People's Parties failed to accomplish genuine economic and social reforms, Hoffman turned to the Socialist Party after 1900 and became one of its most ardent champions. Convinced that Socialism would improve conditions of the poor and more equitably distribute wealth in the United States, Hoffman gave away most of his fortune. Based on the Hoffman papers at the University of Kansas and secondary sources; illus., 2 photos, 41 notes. — W. F. Zornow

390. Migliorino, Ellen Ginzburg and Campanaro, Giorgio G. FREDERICK DOUGLASS'S MORE INTIMATE NATURE AS REVEALED IN SOME OF HIS UNPUBLISHED LETTERS. *Southern Studies 1979 18(4): 480-487.* Some unpublished letters of black abolitionist Frederick Douglass (1817-95), recently donated to the Library of Congress, reveal aspects of his personality. One group was written by Douglass to Harriet A. Bailey, a friend residing with his family, during 1846-47; they reveal a warm, confidential relationship of close friendship and respect. They also reveal insecurity and homesickness from his residence in Great Britain. In 1894 he wrote two letters to Ruth Adams, probably the same Harriet Bailey after marriage, in which he talks of deaths in the family and remembers old times with fondness. Douglass needed to communicate with someone other than his wife, who apparently could not write. Based on the Frederick Douglass Collection in Library of Congress; 24 notes. — J. J. Buschen

391. Miller, Eugene. LEO KRZYCKI: POLISH AMERICAN LABOR LEADER. *Polish Am. Studies 1976 33(2): 52-64.* Leo Krzycki (1881-1966) contributed in no small measure to the history of political radicalism in the United States. He was vice-president of the Amalgamated Clothing Workers for 25 years. At one time he was national chairman of the executive committee of the Socialist Party. He was also active in the early organizing drives of the CIO. His fiery speeches resounded throughout Pennsylvania's Schuylkill Valley during the Depression. As a Polish American leader he dared support the Yalta agreement and the pro-Soviet regime following the end of World War II. Based on Polish and English sources; 46 notes. — S. R. Pliska

392. Miller, Rex. JOHN THOMAS CROXTON: SCHOLAR, LAWYER, SOLDIER, MILITARY GOVERNOR, NEWSPAPERMAN, DIPLOMAT AND MASON. *Register of the Kentucky Hist. Soc. 1976 74(4): 281-299.* Educated at Yale, Kentuckian John Thomas Croxton was a strong supporter of the Union with a bitter hatred of slavery. He served in the Union Army with distinction during the Civil War, and commanded the Military District of Georgia for about a year. After service, he practiced law and was active in Republican politics in Kentucky. Primary and secondary sources; 2 illus., 18 notes. — J. F. Paul

393. Mondello, Salvatore. [ISABEL CRAWFORD AND THE KIOWAS].
ISABEL CRAWFORD: THE MAKING OF A MISSIONARY. *Foundations 1978 21(4): 322-339.* Presents the early life and education of Isabel Crawford (1865-?), a missionary of the Women's American Baptist Home Missionary Society. Born in Canada, through various family moves while a child she became interested in the plight of the Indians. She received her training in Chicago, during which time she did considerable work in the slums. In June, 1893, she received word that she had been appointed to work as a missionary among the Kiowas of Elk Creek, Indian Territory. Based on the Isabel Crawford Collection, American Baptist Historical Society; 33 notes.
ISABEL CRAWFORD AND THE KIOWA INDIANS. *Foundations 1979 22(1): 28-42.* Describes the labors of Isabel Crawford among the Kiowa Indians in and near the Wichita Mountains of Oklahoma, 1893 to 1906. Her very successful work was abruptly terminated and she was forced to leave the Indians because of her questionable participation in a communion service. Based on the Isabel Crawford Collection, American Baptist Historical Society; 54 notes.
ISABEL CRAWFORD, CHAMPION OF THE AMERICAN INDIANS. *Foundations 1979 22(2): 99-115.* Discusses Isabel Crawford's life from 1907 to her death in 1961. 49 notes. — H. M. Parker, Jr./E. E. Eminhizer

394. Monteleone, Renato. SAM GOMPERS: PROFILO DI UN JINGO AMERICANO [Sam Gompers: profile of an American jingo]. *Movimento Operaio e Socialista [Italy] 1976 22(1-2): 133-152.* Defines "jingo" in its American context and says it accurately describes Samuel Gompers, founder of the American Federation of Labor. Gompers openly supported and initiated racist policies; AFL exclusion of nonqualified workers coincided with an influx of immigrant workers. Gompers fought hard to stop immigration, particularly of Orientals, because he feared for American independence and security. Along with the industrialists and financiers of his day, Gompers refused to acknowledge a connection between capitalism and imperialism and failed to recognize what was occurring in international politics. Protesting Bolshevism, he failed to comprehend the threat of a reactionary crisis of the democratic bourgeoisie and thus later suggested to American workers that fascism was a model for the reconciliation of the classes. Primary and secondary sources. — M. T. Wilson

395. Moore, N. Webster. JOHN BERRY MEACHUM (1789-1854): ST. LOUIS PIONEER, BLACK ABOLITIONIST, EDUCATOR, AND PREACHER. *Missouri Hist. Soc. Bull. 1973 29(2): 96-103.* Meachum, a Virginia slave, purchased his freedom and emigrated to St. Louis in 1815, where he joined in the efforts of a white Baptist missionary, John Mason Peck, "to reclaim the Negroes through religious instruction." In 1825, Meachum was ordained and founded the First African Baptist Church in St. Louis. He initiated educational programs for Negroes in the St. Louis area and purchased and freed about 20 slaves. Secondary sources and manuscript holdings of the Missouri Historical Society; 18 notes. — H. T. Lovin

396. Mulder, John M. THE HEAVENLY CITY AND HUMAN CITIES: WASHINGTON GLADDEN AND URBAN REFORM. *Ohio Hist. 1978 87(2): 151-174.* Examines the relationship between the social gospel and urbanization and the social gospel's influence in urban reform through the preaching and reform efforts of Washington Gladden, one of the earliest influential social gospel leaders. Gladden's activity spanned six decades and ranged from the antislavery movement of the 1850's to the New Freedom of Woodrow Wilson. His constant theme was the need for social reform. In 1882 Gladden moved to Columbus, Ohio, where he held the pulpit of the First Congregational Church for more than 30 years. The capital provided an excellent forum for Gladden's proclamations and spurred the development of ideas on urban, social, and economic reform. He became active in Columbus politics and the progressive movement until his death. Based on primary and secondary sources; 3 illus., 72 notes. — N. Summers

397. Mulvay, Jill C. THE LIBERAL SHALL BE BLESSED: SARAH M. KIMBALL. *Utah Hist. Q. 1976 44(3): 205-221.* Sarah Melissa Granger Kimball (1818-98), Utah's pioneer suffragist, president of the 15th Ward Relief Society for 40 years, is representative of her generation of Mormon women. Her life encompassed a broad spectrum of Mormon women's concerns and activities. She and others found room within the LDS system for a broad scope of activities and expression. She was shaped by, but also shaped, women's rights and responsibilities within the church and the Utah community. Based on primary and secondary sources; 3 illus., 40 notes. — J. L. Hazelton

398. Munsey, Sylvia Falconer. MARGARET KEENAN HARRAIS. *Alaska J. 1975 5(3): 144-152.* Discusses the life and charitable work of Harrais from her youth in Idaho until her marriage to an Alaskan mine owner; her social service included temperance leagues, education funds, Red Cross, and work on achieving statehood for Alaska, 1902-62.
G. A. Hewlett

399. Myhrman, Anders. SELMA JOSEFINA BORG: FINLAND: SWEDISH MUSICIAN, LECTURER, AND CHAMPION OF WOMEN'S RIGHTS. *Swedish Pioneer Hist. Q. 1979 30(1): 25-34.* Selma Josefina Borg was born in Gamlarkarleby, Finland, in 1838, the youngest of nine children in an apparently well-to-do middle-class family. She studied music in Finland, Sweden, and Switzerland. She taught music in Helsinki for some years before coming in 1864 to Philadelphia, where she established herself as a private music and language teacher. In collaboration with Marie A. Brown, she began translating current Swedish works into English. Borg joined a women's committee formed to promote the Centennial Exposition of 1876 in Philadelphia and returned to Finland in 1875 to arouse interest and possibly participation in the celebration. She had, by this time, become a champion of the rights of women and most of her lectures dealt with developments and conditions in America. Describes her lecture tour. Returning to America, she became well known as a musician and speaker on women's rights.
C. W. Ohrvall

400. Naison, Mark. CLAUDE AND JOYCE WILLIAMS: PILGRIMS OF JUSTICE. *Southern Exposure 1974 1(3/4): 38-50.* Examines the Williams' involvement in social, economic, and political reforms in the South since the 1930's, including the organizing of miners and sharecroppers in Arkansas, the integration of United Auto Workers in Detroit, and participation in voter registration and desegregation campaigns. Discusses their persecution resulting from attempts to combine the Bible with social change. Based on personal interviews; 6 illus.
G. A. Bolton

401. Nowicka, Ewa. THE JAMAICAN ROOTS OF THE GARVEY IDEOLOGY. *Acta Poloniae Hist. [Poland] 1978 37: 129-161.* Marcus Garvey (1887-1940), creator of an international Negro movement, was born and raised in Jamaica and insisted that the races should be separated, not integrated, and that the blacks, who once ruled the world, will eventually return to their own glory. Discusses the Jamaican social background of Garvey's ideas, their application to America, the British influence of his thinking, and his founding of the United Negro Improvement Association Pan-Africanism. 48 notes.
H. Heitzman-Wojcicka

402. O'Donnell, L. A. THE GREENING OF A LIMERICK MAN: PATRICK HENRY MCCARTHY. *Éire-Ireland 1976 11(2): 119-128.* Offers a biographical sketch of the Irish youth, 1860-80, of Patrick Henry McCarthy, emphasizing influences on his later development as a powerful leader in the American labor movement.

403. O'Farrell, M. Brigid and Kleiner, Lydia. ANNA SULLIVAN: TRADE UNION ORGANIZER. *Frontiers 1977 2(2): 29-36.* Anna Sullivan (b. 1904), who in 1936 began organizing the Massachusetts textile industry for the Textile Workers Union of America (TWUA), recalls her career in labor and politics; part of a special issue on women's oral history.

404. Painter, Nell and Hudson, Hosea. HOSEA HUDSON: A NEGRO COMMUNIST IN THE DEEP SOUTH. *Radical Am. 1977 11(4): 7-23.* A worker in basic industry in Birmingham, Alabama in the 1920's, Hosea Hudson remained apolitical until drawn into politics through the agitation over the Scottsboro Boys trial in the early 1930's. He became involved in clandestine Communist Party work and has remained an active member of the party until the present. As a political radical, Hudson was involved in Deep South campaigns to organize the unemployed through welfare marches and demonstrations at social welfare offices. His politically extremist activities caused him to lose a succession of factory jobs once his involvement became known. Based on extensive oral interviews with Hudson.
N. Lederer

405. Pau On Lau, Estelle. ELLEN B. SABIN: PIONEER EDUCATOR. *Pacific Hist. 1978 22(2): 145-160.* Ellen B. Sabin contributed to the development of teaching and the education of women. She simultaneously attended the University of Wisconsin and taught school during 1866-68. She moved with her family to Oregon in 1872 and continued her innovative teaching techniques in the Portland schools. In 1874 she became principal of the Old North School in Portland, where she had two problems: discipline and dirt. Visiting homes of her pupils, she imparted instruction to the family and showed mothers how to keep homes clean. Appointed head of Downer College in 1890 and Milwaukee Downer College in 1895, she guided the consolidated institutions, expanded their curriculum, and championed their commitment to educate women for their role in society. 65 notes.
R. S. Barnard

406. Penner, Norman. RECOLLECTIONS OF THE EARLY SOCIALIST MOVEMENT IN WINNIPEG, BY JACOB PENNER. *Social Hist. [Canada] 1974 7(14): 366-378.* Recollections of Jacob Penner (1880-1965), a Communist member of the Winnipeg City Council, 1933-60, except for a two-year period when jailed during World War II. Covers his youth and early manhood in Russia where he developed a Marxist consciousness, his migration to Canada in 1904, and the development of the Socialist movement in Winnipeg between 1906 and the General Strike of 1919. 10 notes.
W. K. Hobson

407. Perry, Clay. JOHN P. MITCHELL, VIRGINIA'S JOURNALIST OF REFORM. *Journalism Hist. 1977-78 4(4): 142-147, 156.* Examines the life and work of John P. Mitchell (1863-1929), editor of the *Richmond Planet*, and concentrates on his fight against racial discrimination.

408. Perry, Patsy Brewington. BEFORE *THE NORTH STAR*: FREDERICK DOUGLASS' EARLY JOURNALISTIC CAREER. *Phylon 1974 35(1): 96-107.* Before the founding of *The North Star* Frederick Douglass had contributed to two New York-based weeklies. Cites evidence that the prejudice he had met with on a western speaking tour had a great deal to do with his decision to publish a newspaper. During his months of indecision he gained valuable journalistic experience, with "an opportunity to test his ideas in print, to experience and review the various forms of racial prejudice which he would attack . . . and to explore the prospects for a newspaper such as the one he envisioned." 46 notes.
E. P. Stickney

409. Petrick, Barbara. RIGHT OR PRIVILEGE? THE ADMISSION OF MARY PHILBROOK TO THE BAR. *New Jersey Hist. 1979 97(2): 91-104.* At age 20, Mary Philbrook was interested in becoming an attorney primarily to make a living. In 1895, by an act of the legislature more than one year after she first sought admittance to the bar, she was given the right to take the qualifying examinations. Because of the attention she received as the first woman lawyer in New Jersey, Mary Philbrook soon became involved with the causes espoused by the women's movement. She acted as a legal counsel, lobbied, and gave speeches on women's rights issues, especially suffrage. One of her last acts was to fight for an equal rights provision in New Jersey's 1947 state constitution. Based on Philbrook's papers, contemporary newspaper accounts, and secondary sources; 5 illus., 30 notes.
E. R. McKinstry

410. Petryshyn, J. FROM CLERGYMAN TO COMMUNIST: THE RADICALIZATION OF ALBERT EDWARD SMITH. *J. of Can. Studies [Canada] 1978-79 13(4): 61-71.* After 32 years (1893-1924) as a Methodist pastor in western Canada, influenced by the Social Gospel, Smith passed through a Toronto People's Church to the Communist Party. By 1921, he regarded Christ as a communist thinker and teacher. His experience as a member of the Manitoba legislature (1921-23) had convinced him that a Labour Party required discipline and well-defined objectives. These he found among Communist Party members. Based on United Church Archives, Smith Papers, and secondary sources; 78 notes.
G. E. Panting

411. Phillips, J. O. C. THE EDUCATION OF JANE ADDAMS. *Hist. of Educ. Q. 1974 14(1): 49-67.* Analyzes the three determining forces in Jane Addams's life: the ideology of domestic piety, the influence of her Quaker father, and the changing mood in women's education during the 1870's. Follows these themes in her adult life, and shows how Addams' work at Hull House resulted from these early forces. Finds that Addams did not challenge "the basic assumptions of the ideology, nor the doctrines of a separate woman's sphere and a distinct female nature." Based on primary and secondary sources; 38 notes.
L. C. Smith

412. Phillips, Paul D. THE INTERRACIAL IMPACT OF MARSHALL KEEBLE, BLACK EVANGELIST, 1878-1968. *Tennessee Hist. Q. 1977 36(1): 62-74.* Marshall Keeble was an evangelist among Negroes and an ambassador between blacks and whites to improve race relations for 50 years. He followed the accommodationist, nonviolent approach of Booker T. Washington, yet he boasted of his respect for himself and his race and opposed segregation. Primary and secondary sources; 66 notes. M. B. Lucas

413. Polos, Nicholas C. SAN DIEGO'S "PORTIA OF THE PACIFIC": CALIFORNIA'S FIRST WOMAN LAWYER. *J. of San Diego Hist. 1980 2(3): 185-195.* California's first female lawyer, Clara Shortridge Foltz, moved to California at age 15 in 1872 from Indiana, was admitted to the bar in 1878 after she herself authored a bill to amend legislation not allowing women to practice law, and practised law in San Diego and elsewhere in California before running unsuccessfully for governor of California in 1930 when she was in her 70's.

414. Rader, Frank J. HARRY L. HOPKINS, THE AMBITIOUS CRUSADER: AN HISTORICAL ANALYSIS OF THE MAJOR INFLUENCES ON HIS CAREER, 1912-1940. *Ann. of Iowa 1977 44(2): 83-102.* Examines "leading conditioners" of New Dealer Harry Hopkins's (1890-1946) development from "an ambitious relief administrator into the selfless assistant president of the war years." Discusses Hopkins's family and his formal education at Grinnell College, his progressive views and social work career, the impact of his chronic poor health, his political ambitions, and "the emergency-charged ambiance of the New Deal years." Based on secondary and primary sources, including the Hopkins Papers at the Franklin D. Roosevelt Library; 3 photos, 59 notes.
P. L. Petersen

415. Rasporich, Anthony. TOMO ČAČIĆ: REBEL WITHOUT A COUNTRY. *Can. Ethnic Studies [Canada] 1978 10(2): 86-94.* Surveys the career of Tomo Čačić (1896-1969), Croatia-born radical Communist labor organizer in the western United States and western Canada. In Ontario he was a Communist Party organizer and newspaperman until his arrest and imprisonment. In 1934, he was deported to England; soon he escaped to Moscow. After three years he enlisted in the Spanish Civil War. He returned to Yugoslavia in 1941 and fought there with the Partisans throughout the war. After the war he continued his interest in the Canadian radical cause. Primary sources; 50 notes. R. V. Ritter

416. Ratcliffe, Donald J., ed. THE AUTOBIOGRAPHY OF BENJAMIN TAPPAN. *Ohio Hist. 1976 85(2): 109-157.* The first publication of Benjamin Tappan's autobiography (1840); it covers 1773-1823. Covers early life, student years, Ohio pioneering, Ohio politics from 1802, War of 1812, and other topics. The manuscript is extensively annotated. Reproduction of an original manuscript; 6 illus., 104 notes.
T. H. Hartig

417. Reverby, Susan. FROM AIDE TO ORGANIZER: THE ORAL HISTORY OF LILLIAN ROBERTS. Berkin, Carol Ruth and Norton, Mary Beth, ed. *Women of America: A History* (Boston: Houghton Mifflin Co., 1979): 289-317. An oral history of Lillian Roberts, black activist with, and a directory of, the American Federation of State, County, and Municipal Employees (AFCSME). Includes a guideline of questions for conducting the oral history. 3 notes. K. Talley

418. Reyburn, Phil. SHUBERT SEBREE, EUGENE V. DEBS, THEODORE DEBS: SOME CORRESPONDENCE. *Indiana Hist. Bull. 1975 52(5): 51-59.* Biography and correspondence of Shubert Sebree, head of the socialist movement in the early 1900's, and Indiana labor leader. S

419. Richey, Elinor. SAGEBRUSH PRINCESS WITH A CAUSE: SARAH WINNEMUCCA. *Am. West 1975 12(6): 30-33, 57-63.* Paiute Princess Sarah Winnemucca (1843?-91) attended a white school, adopted white customs, and twice married white men. When she became disillusioned with the belief, inherited from a tribal myth, that whites worked in the best interest of Indians, she began to protest. She took her protests to the highest officials, went on the lecture platform, and wrote a widely discussed book on injustices. Adapted from a forthcoming volume. 2 illus.
D. L. Smith

420. Robboy, Stanley J. and Robboy, Anita W. LEWIS HAYDEN: FROM FUGITIVE SLAVE TO STATESMAN. *New England Q. 1973 46(4): 591-613.* Describes the life and activities of Lewis Hayden (1811-89), early black slavery fighter. Born a slave, Hayden managed to escape, eventually settling in Boston. He educated himself and wholeheartedly entered the Abolition Movement, actively assisting the escape of slaves, giving speeches, and raising funds. He rose to high rank in the Masonic organization and served in the Massachusetts state senate. He fought for black rights throughout his lifetime and is now regarded as one of the greatest of black social reformers. 81 notes. V. L. Human

421. Roberts, Wayne. SIX NEW WOMEN: A GUIDE TO THE MENTAL MAP OF WOMEN REFORMERS IN TORONTO. *Atlantis [Canada] 1977 3(1): 145-164.* Provides brief portraits of activists in the Toronto women's movement before World War I; Emily Stowe, Augusta Stowe-Gullen, Flora Macdonald Denison, Helen MacMurchy, Florence Gooderham Huestis, and Mrs. Constance Hamilton; 1870's-1910's.

422. Robinson, Jo Ann. LILLIAN SMITH: REFLECTIONS ON RACE AND SEX. *Southern Exposure 1977 4(4): 43-48.* The work and writings of Lillian Smith were primarily concerned with the entwined themes of race and sex in southern life. As director of a southern girls' camp she raised female consciousness and espoused racial equality. In her books she broke taboos on race and sex. With *Killers of the Dream* Smith was systematically ostracized by southern liberal newspapers and by the New York literary establishment. In her personal life female friends were most supportive of her endeavors and most perceptive of what she was attempting to accomplish. Primary sources. N. Lederer

423. Rogers, Evelyna Keadle. FAMOUS GEORGIA WOMEN: REBECCA LATIMER FELTON. *Georgia Life 1978 5(1): 34-35.* Rebecca Latimer Felton (1835-1930), a resident of Georgia, was appointed as the first woman senator in the US Senate in 1922; discusses her career in politics and her participation in the fight for woman suffrage, 1860's-1922.

424. Rohde, Nancy Freeman. GRATIA ALTA COUNTRYMAN: LIBRARIAN AND REFORMER. Stuhler, Barbara and Kreuter, Gretchen, ed. *Women of Minnesota: Selected Biographical Essays* (St. Paul: Minnesota Historical Society Press, 1977): 173-189. Gratia Alta Countryman (1866-1953) attended the University of Minnesota where she was an active student leader and member of Phi Beta Kappa. After graduating, she became one of six assistants hired to open and operate the new Minneapolis Public Library. Gratia soon became head of the catalog department. During 1904-36 she was the head librarian, the first woman to direct a major library in the United States. Countryman especially encouraged extended library services to meet the needs of all sectors of society. She also agitated for state library laws, promoted the Minnesota Library Association, served on the State Library Commission, and was nationally renowned for her work. She served on the council, executive board, and as president of the American Library Association. A popular speaker, Countryman lectured not only on library subjects but also on woman's suffrage, social reform, and international peace. She helped organize the Minneapolis Women's Welfare League and the Business Women's Club. In 1936, she chaired the national convention of the Women's International League for Peace and Freedom. A dedicated, efficient, and decisive librarian, social reformer, and civic leader, Countryman remained active after her retirement. She died on 26 July 1953. Primary sources; photo, 54 notes. A. E. Wiederrecht

425. Roosevelt, Jinx. RANDOLPH BOURNE: THE EDUCATION OF A CRITIC: AN INTERPRETATION. *Hist. of Educ. Q. 1977 17(3): 257-274.* In his brief life, Randolph Bourne (1886-1918) attacked most established American institutions and dealt with such subjects as socialism, feminism, and progressive education. A hunchback, Bourne, feeling society's scorn for deformity, was psychologically well-suited to the role of critic, and his brilliance made him an effective one. Born into what he considered a rather cold, Calvinistic family with little discipline or attention for the children, Bourne educated himself. He was close to his younger sister, Natalie, who had defended him from the ridicule of other children when they were young. Decline in family fortunes necessitated a postponement of university education and work in factories, but during 1909-13, Bourne was a student at Columbia and thereafter wrote

for *The New Republic*. He found inspiration in the Greek and Latin classics and in the philosophy of John Dewey. Despite his not living long, Bourne's restless spirit epitomized the *Zeitgeist* of his generation. 55 notes.
J. C. Billigmeier

426. Rottier, Catherine M. ELLEN SPENCER MUSSEY AND THE WASHINGTON COLLEGE OF LAW. *Maryland Hist. Mag. 1974 69(4): 361-382.* The path to legal education for women was a slow and difficult one until 1898, "when the Washington College of Law, a school established 'primarily for women,' was founded by two pioneer female attorneys, Ellen Spencer Mussey and Emma M. Gillett." Surveys women's attempts to remove restrictive charter provisions of law schools, and gain bar recognition. The school's early years are described, and progress under various deans until 1949 when it merged with American University. Mrs. Mussey's extensive involvement in the women's rights movement and the work of the Red Cross, the Grand Army of the Republic, and temperance groups is also detailed, and the College's graduates are traced in their careers. Primary and secondary works; 11 illus., 47 notes.
G. J. Bobango

427. Rovere, Richard H. WALTER LIPPMANN. *Am. Scholar 1975 44(4): 585-603.* Walter Lippmann was an individual of wide-ranging talents and abilities. He had an incredible knowledge and passion for classical art, and was regarded as an intellectual by Europeans. He was a social activist and joined the Fabian society. As a political activist he helped in the appointment of Louis D. Brandeis to the Supreme Court. He served under General Pershing in World War I and helped to modernize psychological warfare. He supported Wilson's 14 Points. He had great physical prowess. Although he considered himself a member of the establishment, he opposed every president from Theodore Roosevelt to Richard Nixon. Lippmann represented what was best in the liberal and humanist traditions.
F. F. Harling

428. Rubinoff, Michael W. RABBI IN A PROGRESSIVE ERA: C.E.H. KAUVAR OF DENVER. *Colorado Mag. 1977 54(3): 220-239.* Russian-born (1879) and New York-educated, Rabbi Charles Eliezer Hillel Kauvar served Denver's orthodox Beth Ha Medrosh Hagodol synagogue during 1902-71. A leading progressive reformer, Kauvar founded the Jewish Consumptives' Relief Society and an orphanage, worked closely with Judge Benjamin Barr Lindsey in attacking juvenile delinquency, and was a long-time leader of Denver's Community Chest. He was a Zionist, urged ecumenism, and vigorously opposed the Ku Klux Klan in the 1920's. Primary and secondary sources; 10 illus., 51 notes.
O. H. Zabel

429. Rulon, Philip Reed and Butchart, Ronald Eugene. HENRY ELIJAH ALVORD, 1844-1904: SOLDIER, SCIENTIST AND SCHOLAR. *Chronicles of Oklahoma 1974 52(1): 61-81.* Biographical account of Henry Elijah Alvord, "soldier, farmer, teacher." Alvord was a proponent of humane treatment and educational institutions for blacks and Indians, an early environmentalist, college president, and a member of the US Department of Agriculture. He also helped to shape the land-grant university and agricultural/mechanical college systems. Primary and secondary sources; 2 photos, 40 notes.
N. J. Street

430. Russell, C. Allyn. MARK ALLISON MATTHEWS: SEATTLE FUNDAMENTALIST AND CIVIC REFORMER. *J. of Presbyterian Hist. 1979 57(4): 446-466.* Concentrates on the social concerns of Mark Allison Matthews (1867-1940), pastor of the First Presbyterian Church, Seattle, Washington. He was a strange mixture of biblical fundamentalism and social reform. Under him his congregation became the largest Presbyterian church in the United States. He was an intense critic of religious liberalism at the time of the modernist-fundamentalist controversy, yet participated actively in the civic and political life of Seattle. Describes in detail his pulpit ability, executive acumen, and fundamentalist theology. Based on the Matthews Papers (Manuscript Division of Suzzallo Library, University of Washington, Seattle); 2 photos, 66 notes.
H. M. Parker, Jr.

431. Russo, Francis X. JOHN HOWLAND: PIONEER IN THE FREE SCHOOL MOVEMENT. *Rhode Island Hist. 1978 37(4): 111-122.* John Howland was a hairdresser and self-educated. He became active in the Rhode Island free school movement in 1795, played a major role in securing legislation in 1800, and was active in Providence school affairs for the next several decades. Based on school records, recollections, and secondary accounts; 3 illus., 47 notes.
P. J. Coleman

432. San Juan, E., Jr. CARLOS BULOSAN: AN INTRODUCTION. *Asian and Pacific Q. of Cultural and Social Affairs [South Korea] 1978 10(2): 43-48.* Carlos Bulosan (1913-56) emigrated from the Philippines to the United States in 1931. His dreams of a better life under American democracy soon crumbled before the presence of repressive monopoly capitalism and the Great Depression years. Moving progressively to the left, Bulosan actively contributed to the expanding labor movement in the 1930's. His literary works embody the twin Marxist goals of criticizing bourgeois culture and creating a proletarian literary tradition. Secondary sources; 2 notes.
A. C. Migliazzo

433. Sargent, James E. CLIFTON A. WOODRUM OF VIRGINIA: A SOUTHERN PROGRESSIVE IN CONGRESS, 1923-1945. *Virginia Mag. of Hist. and Biog. 1981 89(3): 341-364.* Chronicles the political career of independent Democrat from Roanoke, Clifton A. Woodrum, who came to public attention as a lawyer, popular singer and circuit judge. In 1922 he beat a lackluster incumbent congressman by means of a superior campaign organization and platform presence, and an appeal to upwardly mobile and younger men. Woodrum neither opposed nor embraced the Byrd organization. He supported Franklin D. Roosevelt in 1932, gained seniority, and by 1940 was an acknowledged expert on steering appropriation bills, particularly that for lend-lease. The later New Deal became too liberal and urbanized for Woodrum, and his influence declined. He was frustrated by Roosevelt's refusal to make him a federal judge, and by the long tenures of Carter Glass and Harry Byrd, which blocked advancement to the Senate. Woodrum retired in 1945. Based on Woodrum papers, *Congressional Record,* and interviews; 47 notes, illus.
P. J. Woehrmann

434. Schapsmeier, Edward L. and Schapsmeier, Frederick H. RELIGION AND REFORM: A CASE STUDY OF HENRY A. WALLACE AND EZRA TAFT BENSON. *J. of Church and State 1979 21(3): 525-535.* Henry A. Wallace and Ezra Taft Benson typify moralists of both left and right who functioned fairly well when controlled by moderates, but on their own, adopted extreme moral views, consequently losing what influence they had. Considers their careers, independent of the moderating influences of presidents Roosevelt and Eisenhower. Based on the writeups and papers of Henry A. Wallace and Ezra Taft Benson; 28 notes.
E. E. Eminhizer

435. Schlup, Leonard. PHILOSOPHICAL CONSERVATIVE: PORTER JAMES MCCUMBER AND POLITICAL REFORM. *North Dakota Hist. 1978 45(3): 16-21.* A conservative Republican senator from North Dakota, Porter James McCumber was the product of the political machine of Alexander John McKenzie. Serving in the US Senate during 1898-1922, McCumber, despite his conservative beliefs and those of his Party, voted for such reforms as women's suffrage and the direct election of senators. He deeply believed in voting according to the desires of his constituents even if taking their position violated his own convictions. McCumber was a loyal party stalwart, supporting the "Old Guard" of the GOP during the factional battles with Theodore Roosevelt and the "Bull Moosers." He bitterly attacked Roosevelt for the latter's defection from Republican Party ranks. In his political philosophy McCumber favored gradual change in accordance with the Constitution.
N. Lederer

436. Scott, Ann Firor. WHAT, THEN, IS THE AMERICAN: THIS NEW WOMAN? *J. of Am. Hist. 1978 65(3): 679-703.* Analyzes the career of Emma Hart Willard (1787-1870) to demonstrate how a talented and ambitious woman could achieve a position of power and influence in the male-dominated society of pre-Civil War America. Mrs. Willard exemplified the "new women" in 19th-century America who built organizations and institutions they could control and who created networks for communication and mutual support. Mrs. Willard combined the cause of female education with her ambition for influence in the institution she created, the Troy Female Seminary in New York. Her school not only trained female teachers, it became the center for a large association of women who reflected to varying degrees Mrs. Willard's ideals. Mrs. Willard learned the secret of working within an acceptable framework of female behavior in a male-dominated society. 49 notes.
T. P. Linkfield

437. Seraile, William. BEN FLETCHER, I.W.W. ORGANIZER. *Pennsylvania Hist. 1979 46(3): 213-232.* Benjamin Harrison Fletcher (1890-1949) was an extraordinarily successful organizer of dockworkers for the Industrial Workers of the World in Philadelphia, Baltimore, and Boston. He was particularly effective in appealing to fellow blacks who were dockworkers. Sentenced to prison in 1918 with other IWW leaders for alleged violations of the Selective Service Act and Espionage Act of 1917, he was released in 1922 with a conditional commutation of his sentence. In 1933, President Franklin D. Roosevelt granted him a full pardon. Based upon Pardon Attorney files, Haywood et al. vs. U.S., and other sources; illus., 24 notes. D. C. Swift

438. Shankman, Arnold. DOROTHY TILLY, CIVIL RIGHTS, AND THE METHODIST CHURCH. *Methodist Hist. 1980 18(2): 95-108.* Dorothy Tilly (1883-1970), an outstanding woman in the Methodist Church in Georgia, was active in civil rights movements during much of her life. Through organizations of the Methodist Church and other organizations, she worked for the abolition of lynchings, the development of better education for black children, the prevention of race riots, and other civil rights movements. 56 notes. H. L. Calkin

439. Sheeler, J. Reuben. JAMES MADISON NABRIT. *Negro Hist. Bull. 1961 24(4): 75-76.* James Madison Nabrit, Jr., was an educator, civil rights advocate, and president of Howard University, 1927-60.

440. Silcox, Harry C. NINETEENTH CENTURY PHILADELPHIA BLACK MILITANT: OCTAVIUS V. CATTO (1839-1871). *Pennsylvania Hist. 1977 44(1): 53-76.* Octavius V. Catto (1839-71) was one of the most important spokesmen for Pennsylvania Negroes in the Civil War and Reconstruction years. The son of a minister, he taught at the Institute for Colored Youth, the Quaker-supported black high school in Philadelphia. Catto was the first black member of the Franklin Institute. Leading the effort to win places in the Pennsylvania National Guard for blacks, he became a major and inspector in the fifth brigade. A founder and corresponding secretary of the State Equal Rights League, Catto helped with passage of legislation ending segregation on street cars. As captain and star player for the Philadelphia Pythians baseball team, Catto developed a number of contacts with blacks in other states. He also assisted in the administration of the freedman schools in Washington. Catto was murdered during the antiblack election riots of 1871. "Catto's death brought to an end black militant behavior in 19th-century Philadelphia." Based on the Catto papers, the Pythian Baseball Club papers, and other sources; photo, 71 notes. D. C. Swift

441. Silcox, Harry C. PHILADELPHIA NEGRO EDUCATOR: JACOB C. WHITE, JR., 1837-1902. *Pennsylvania Mag. of Hist. and Biog. 1973 97(1): 75-98.* White began his career as a teacher at the Institute for Colored Youth in 1857, and was appointed principal of the Roberts Vaux Consolidated School seven years later. He held that post for the next 30 years. White was a broker between Philadelphia's white school board and the black community, and his influence and prestige grew with both groups, thus enabling him to secure acceptance of Negro teachers in black schools. White was also instrumental in easing the strain of integrating Philadelphia's schools during the 1870's and 1880's. Improvements in educational opportunity were purchased at a high price, for only by accommodating white racial prejudice and discrimination was White able to forward the cause of the Negro. Based on primary sources; 90 notes. E. W. Carp

442. Silver, George A. GEORGE ROSEN: A LIFE IN PUBLIC HEALTH. *J. of the Hist. of Medicine and Allied Sci. 1978 33(3): 266-270.* George Rosen's work on public health was his central focus of his professional life. He realized that history's purpose was to let the past teach the present, and he saw epidemics and disease as aspects of social events. As a student of Henry Sigerist, he absorbed a social concept. His work on occupational diseases, on the development of modern medical care services, and preventive medicine, were important facets of his research. He not only studied the subject as a scholar, but he immersed himself in it as a health professional. He was associated with the Health Insurance Plan of Greater New York from its inception, when health maintenance organizations were experimental. He was not only a historian of public health, but he was a public health professional whose work tried to achieve the goals he defined. 22 notes. M. Kaufman

443. Sklar, Kathryn Kish. VICTORIAN WOMEN AND DOMESTIC LIFE: MARY TODD LINCOLN, ELIZABETH CADY STANTON, AND HARRIET BEECHER STOWE. Davis, Cullom; Strozier, Charles B.; Veach, Rebecca Monroe; and Ward, Geoffrey C., ed. *The Public and the Private Lincoln: Contemporary Perspectives* (Carbondale: So. Illinois U. Pr., 1979): 20-37. Examines efforts by prominent Victorian women to limit the size of their families and their public and private activities to arrive at a qualitative rather than quantitative definition of motherhood, during 1830-80. Harriet Beecher Stowe's strategy was to abstain from sex, in part to punish her philandering husband, undertake a literary career, and foster women's education. Elizabeth Cady Stanton, like Stowe, practiced family planning and worked for feminist domestic reform, seeking the legal equality of women. Mary Todd Lincoln's approach was total commitment to her husband and children. In part she practiced family planning to aid her husband's political career, and she was indulgent of her children. She did not separate domestic from public life, participating in the political sector on Abraham's behalf, but she was unable to build an autonomous career. 40 notes. S

444. Skoglund, John E., trans. EDWIN DAHLBERG IN CONVERSATION: MEMORIES OF WALTER RAUSCHENBUSCH. *Foundations 1975 18(3): 209-218.* Transcribes an interview with Edwin Dahlberg concerning the life and work of Walter Rauschenbusch as remembered by one student. The interview centers on Rauschenbusch as teacher and social reformer. 6 notes. E. E. Eminhizer

445. Smith, Grace Ferguson. SOJOURNER TRUTH—LISTENER TO THE VOICE. *Negro Hist. Bull. 1973 36(3): 63-65.* Discusses Isabella Baumfree, who later took the name of Sojourner Truth, and her work for black civil rights, 1825-60. S

446. Smith, Kenneth and Sweet, Leonard. SHAILER MATHEWS: A CHAPTER IN THE SOCIAL GOSPEL MOVEMENT. *Foundations 1975 18(3): 219-237, (4): 296-320; 1976 19(1): 53-68, (2): 152-170.* Part I. Born in Portland, Maine, 26 May 1863, son of a Baptist businessman, Shailer Mathews was converted in a Moody revival in 1875. Strongly influenced by his grandfather, William Shailer, he attended Waterville College and Colby University. Unsure of a vocation, he attended Newton Seminary where he was introduced to lower criticism. He taught at Colby following graduation from Newton. In 1890 he studied in Germany where he was introduced to Ranke's historical method, as well as new ideas in economics and ethics. As a result he brought the new ideas to Colby and became concerned with social reform. In 1899 he joined men of similar spirit and thinking at the University of Chicago. 54 notes. Part II. Discusses Matthews' approach to dealing with the conflict that developed between religion and science in the last half of the 19th century; also his social views and theology in the context of Christian experience. The later sections are concerned with Mathews' doctrine of God. 96 notes. Part III. Discusses Mathews' view on sin and salvation, and the destiny of man as it reflects evolutionary theories. Mathews saw sin as man's "animal impulses," but man could transcend this. From this idea the article proceeds to discuss the source of sin, its consequences, and the place of Christ in changing man's condition. 88 notes. Part IV. Discusses Mathews' views on the Kingdom of God, ethics, and eschatology, as found in his *The Social Teachings of Jesus* (1897) and *Jesus on Social Institutions* (1928). E. E. Eminhizer

447. Sokolow, Jayme A. HENRY CLARKE WRIGHT: ANTEBELLUM CRUSADER. *Essex Inst. Hist. Collections 1975 111(2): 122-137.* Examines the origin of Wright's ideas on reform. Evangelical revivalism led to his interest in and advocacy of temperance, immediate abolition of slavery, women's suffrage, pacifism, and humanitarian education. Based on historical essays, newspapers, letters, journals, and Wright's work; 41 notes. R. M. Rollins

448. Spencer, Ralph W. ANNA HOWARD SHAW. *Methodist Hist. 1975 13(2): 33-51.* Anna Howard Shaw (1847-1919) was the first woman ordained in the Methodist Protestant Church, but she is best known for her work on behalf of the woman suffrage movement. Discusses her efforts to get theological and medical training, her service in the ministry, and as an exponent of the Social Gospel Movement. 41 notes. H. L. Calkin

449. Stasik, Florian. ADAM GUROWSKI'S ROAD TO ABOLITIONISM. *Acta Poloniae Hist. [Poland] 1977 35: 87-112.* Discusses Gurowski's social and political activities and their philosophical background. He fought in the November uprising, travelled in western Europe and wrote articles for radical causes. Disillusioned with the West he turned to Tsarist Russia—which also rejected his political ideas. He left for the United States in 1849 and took up Negro emancipation, writing prolifically in journals and newspapers. His radicalism intensified, antagonizing even his political partners, including President Lincoln. He died in 1866 in poor circumstances, failing to draw recognition even among the protagonists of the abolition of slavery. 90 notes.
H. Heitzman-Wojcicka

450. Stern, Sheldon M. THE EVOLUTION OF A REACTIONARY: LOUIS ARTHUR COOLIDGE, 1900-1925. *Mid-America 1975 57(2): 89-105.* A Republican progressive before World War I, Louis Arthur Coolidge, an instinctive conservative, practiced welfare capitalism as director of the United Shoe Machinery Company. His governmental wartime experiences, the Bolshevik revolution, and the growth of government led him to found the Sentinels of the Republic, through which was defeated the Child Labor Amendment, the Maternity and Infancy Act, and the Federal Education Bill. The Sentinels disbanded by 1940. Based on the Alexander Lincoln and Coolidge papers, published sources, and secondary works; 36 notes.
T. H. Wendel

451. Stevenson, Janet. LOLA MAVERICK LLOYD: "I MUST DO SOMETHING FOR PEACE!" *Chicago Hist. 1980 9(1): 47-57.* Lola Maverick Lloyd's activism in the movement for feminism and pacifism was started by a speech in 1914 by Hungarian Rosika Schwimmer of the International Suffrage Alliance, on how to stop World War I; Lloyd supported the Woman's Peace Party, the International Congress of Women, and the Women's International League for Peace and Freedom, until her death in 1944.

452. Strickland, Charles E. JULIETTE LOW, THE GIRL SCOUTS, AND THE ROLE OF AMERICAN WOMEN. Kelley, Mary, ed. *Woman's Being, Woman's Place: Female Identity and Vocation in American History* (Boston: G. K. Hall, 1979): 252-264. Employing Erik Erikson's life-cycle model, records a convergence of personal and historical crises in the life of Juliette Low (b. 1860), founder of the Girl Scouts of America. Prepared to assume the role of companion, hostess, and mother of children, Low instead faced loneliness, confronted a childless existence, and ran headlong into her husband's affair with a widow. The result was a marriage that not only brought anguish but ended in a humiliating divorce. Alone and unable to find an alternative role, Low considered her life devoid of meaning. Her opportunity to resolve her crisis of identity came only when she found in the Girl Scout movement a cause to which she could dedicate herself. Scouting might not have challenged all conventional definitions of women's role and sphere, but under Low's tutelage it did demand that women become more than delicate, helpless ornaments. 56 notes.
J. Powell

453. Stuhler, Barbara. FANNY BRIN: WOMAN OF PEACE. Stuhler, Barbara and Kreuter, Gretchen, ed. *Women of Minnesota: Selected Biographical Essays* (St. Paul: Minnesota Historical Society Press, 1977): 284-300. In 1884, three-month-old Fanny Fligelman came to Minneapolis with her Romanian Jewish parents. A serious student in high school and at the University of Minnesota, Fanny was active in the Minerva Literature Society and was elected to Phi Beta Kappa. She became a teacher, and in 1913 wed Arthur Brin, a successful businessman. Fanny raised a family, became a prominent volunteer activist, and worked for woman suffrage, world peace, democracy, and Jewish heritage. During the 1920's and 30's, she was especially active in the National Council of Jewish Women and served as director of the Minneapolis Woman's Committee for World Disarmament. Stimulated by the Nazi attack on Jews, Fanny became a strong Zionist. As the alternate delegate for the Women's Action Committee for Lasting Peace, Fanny attended the 1945 San Francisco meetings which gave birth to the United Nations. An excellent speaker, Fanny served in many organizations, promoted many causes, took civic responsibilities as serious duties, and worked to better use women and their contributions to improve world affairs. Primary and secondary sources; photo, 44 notes.
A. E. Wiederrecht

454. Swanton, Carolyn. DR. ALGERNON S. CRAPSEY: RELIGIOUS REFORMER. *Rochester Hist. 1980 42(1): 1-24.* Episcopal minister Algernon Sidney Crapsey (1847-1927) went to Rochester from New York City in 1879 to minister at St. Andrew's Church; focuses on his humanitarian work and concern for his parishioners, and his trial in an ecclesiastical court in 1906 for heresy; found guilty, he was forced to leave the church, but continued his work until his death.

455. Taylor, Richard S. BEYOND IMMEDIATE EMANCIPATION: JONATHAN BLANCHARD, ABOLITIONISM, AND THE EMERGENCE OF AMERICAN FUNDAMENTALISM. *Civil War Hist. 1981 27(3): 260-274.* Details the career of Jonathan Blanchard (1811-92), Congregationalist pastor, president of Knox College, and founder of Wheaton College. Blanchard's involvement in the temperance, antislavery and antisecret society crusades stemmed from his idea of the "moral autonomy of the individual" and demonstrated his relationship with the development of Christian evangelicalism rather than with the Social Gospel. Covers the 1830's-80's. 66 notes.
G. R. Schroeder

456. Totton, Kathryn Dunn. HANNAH KEZIAH CLAPP: THE LIFE AND CAREER OF A PIONEER NEVADA EDUCATOR, 1824-1908. *Nevada Hist. Soc. Q. 1977 20(3): 167-183.* Describes the professional and political reform activities of Hannah Keziah Clapp in Nevada. From 1881 to 1901, she was a staff member of the University of Nevada, making significant contributions to the institution by upgrading and enlarging to University's library. She also worked for kindergartens in Reno and was active in women suffrage movements, among them the Nevada Equal Suffrage Association in which she was an officer. Based on newspapers and manuscript collections at the Nevada Historical Society; 2 photos, 39 notes.
H. T. Lovin

457. Travis, Anthony R. SOPHINISBA BRECKINRIDGE, MILITANT FEMINIST. *Mid-America 1976 58(2): 111-118.* Sophinisba Breckinridge, 1866-1948, was a militant suffragette, progressive reformer, women's rights advocate, the first woman-appointee to the Kentucky bar, trade-union advocate, author of numerous works on urban-industrial problems, and professor of public welfare at the University of Chicago. Concerned for professional and working-class women as well as for prostitutes, she opposed the Equal Rights Amendment because of its possible effect on protective legislation for working women. She was influenced by Hull House and devoted her life to generous and public-spirited effort. Based on Breckinridge manuscripts, Library of Congress; 23 notes.
T. H. Wendel

458. Trefousse, Hans L. CARL SCHURZ RECONSIDERED. *Lincoln Herald 1981 83(4, i.e., 1): 563-573.* Briefly traces the public life of German-American immigrant Carl Schurz, a revolutionary leader who wanted to see a united, democratic Germany; he emigrated to the United States in 1852, settled in Wisconsin, and become involved in politics. Focuses on his private life and convictions that led him to denounce slavery, pursue reforms of the Indian Bureau, and lead a political career, 1852-1906.

459. Wallace, Les. CHARLES LENOX REMOND: THE LOST PRINCE OF ABOLITIONISM. *Negro Hist. Bull. 1977 40(3): 696-701.* Evaluates the career and thought of the Massachusetts free black, Charles Lenox Remond, who in 1838 became the first black abolitionist lecturer. His eloquence at home and abroad made him by 1841 the most noted spokesman for the black cause in America. But with the rise of Frederick Douglass, Remond was overshadowed and has never received adequate recognition. Originally a follower of Garrisonian nonviolence and abstention from politics, Remond shifted during 1848-50 to political activism and a belief that only violence would end slavery. He was also concerned with the rights of free blacks and women. He died in 1873. Based on Remond's speeches in the *Liberator* and secondary material; 4 illus., 54 notes.
R. E. Noble

460. Weales, Gerald. THE QUALITY OF MERCY, OR MRS. WARREN'S PROFESSION. *Georgia Rev. 1979 33(4): 881-894.* Mercy Otis Warren (1728-1814) was an early American writer of distinction and an advocate of equal recognition for women. The sister of James Otis and wife of James Warren, she absorbed the Revolutionary spirit of 18th-century Massachusetts, turning out popular satirical plays, of which *The*

Adulateur (1773) and *The Group* (1775) are the most notable. Warren also wrote verse tragedies and poetry in the elaborate, highly formal style of the day, and maintained a voluminous correspondence with friends such as John and Abigail Adams.　　　　　　　　　　J. N. McArthur

461. Weiss, Samuel A. THE ORDEAL OF MALCOLM X. *South Atlantic Q. 1977 76(4): 497-507.* "Physically and mentally" Malcolm X belonged to the black ghetto, and he worked to force its inhabitants out of their prison. Malcolm X blamed the white race for the terrible human misery of the ghetto, and he used racial hatred to arouse the blacks into action. He channeled his hate away from the civil rights movement, away from hypocritical Christianity, and into the puritanical self-reliance and self-improvement of Elijah Muhammad's Black Islam. After 12 years as a powerful spokesman for the Black Muslims, Malcolm X broke with this movement after a revealing trip to the Near East showed him the movement's faulty basis. He entered the American political arena with his own movement to increase black self-respect, but was murdered. His spirit still haunts the "long hot summers" of the ghettos.
　　　　　　　　　　W. L. Olbrich

462. Welch, Richard E., Jr. THE LAW, RIGHT CONDUCT, AND MOORFIELD STOREY. *Historian 1979 41(2): 225-240.* Previous biographers of Moorfield Storey (1845-1929) have failed to adequately relate his professional, legal career, with his public career. Examines Storey's ambitions as a legal reformer and his convictions regarding the legal profession, which affected his views and attitudes as a Mugwump, an anti-imperialist, and as the first president of the NAACP. Throughout his career Storey sought to demonstrate the responsibilities of lawyers to take active parts in public affairs. Primary and secondary sources; 41 notes.　　　　　　　　　　R. S. Sliwoski

463. Williams, E. Russ, Jr. JOHN RAY: FORGOTTEN SCALAWAG. *Louisiana Studies 1974 13(3): 241-262.* Studies the political career of John Ray over five decades of Louisiana politics, in which he faithfully supported his Republican Party. His scalawaggery destroyed his reputation in Louisiana and marred his record of public involvement. "Ray's accomplishment... seem inconsequential when compared to his efforts to equalize the black minority with its white counterpart. His efforts for the blacks would have made him a lasting reputation in a later century, but in his lifetime it sealed his infamy." Having supported the party least attuned to the majority, he has been almost forgotten. 92 notes.
　　　　　　　　　　R. V. Ritter

464. Wilson, J. Donald. MATTI KURIKKA AND A. B. MÄKELÄ: SOCIALIST THOUGHT AMONG FINNS IN CANADA, 1900-1932. *Can. Ethnic Studies [Canada] 1978 10(2): 9-21.* Two active Finn socialists, both newspaper editors, Matti Kurikka (1863-1915) and A. B. Mäkelä (1863-1932), emigrated to Canada before World War I. Kurikka, a utopian and theosophist, was the last of a dying breed when he reached British Columbia in 1900; there he established a utopian socialist settlement at Sointula, and edited *Aika*, the first Finnish-language newspaper in Canada. There he was joined by his Marxian socialist friend, A. B. Mäkelä. The latter, after the colony's collapse, stayed on in Canada as an editor. His socialism eventually led him into the Communist Party of Canada, but he made his major impact as a political and satirical writer rather than as an activist. Primary sources; 2 photos, 22 notes.
　　　　　　　　　　R. V. Ritter

465. Wilson, Joan Hoff. [JEANNETTE RANKIN AND AMERICAN FOREIGN POLICY].
"PEACE IS A WOMAN'S JOB": JEANNETTE RANKIN AND AMERICAN FOREIGN POLICY: THE ORIGINS OF HER PACIFISM. *Montana 1980 30(1): 28-41.* Jeannette Pickering Rankin (1880-1973), of Montana, was the first woman elected to the US House of Representatives (1916) and the only member of Congress to have opposed American entrance into both world wars. The oldest of seven children, Rankin entered the political world normally reserved for men. She experienced self-doubt and a sense of inferiority, but presented a public image of great self-confidence. Pioneer ideals of hard work, honesty, and perseverance, which she accepted as a youth, and her perceptions of women, international conflict, and the destructiveness of war, made Rankin unique in American political history, as a suffragist and pacifist. Her vote against war in 1917 influenced her political thinking for the rest of her life. Based on materials in the Swarthmore College Peace Collection, the Jeannette Rankin Papers, Schlesinger Library, Radcliff College, the Suffragist Oral History Project, Bancroft Library, University of California, Berkeley, and secondary sources; 6 illus., 55 notes.

JEANNETTE RANKIN AND AMERICAN FOREIGN POLICY: HER LIFEWORK AS A PACIFIST. *Montana 1980 30(2): 38-53.* From 1917 until her death in 1973, Rankin remained a staunch advocate of domestic reform, peace, neutrality, and disarmament. She worked privately and through such groups as the National Council for the Prevention of War and the Georgia Peace Society. Rankin admired Gandhi's work in India and opposed American involvement in Korea and Vietnam. The meaning of her life and views on foreign policy was more symbolic than practical, representing the generation of American women at the turn of the century who believed in a global society of peace. 8 illus., 59 notes.
　　　　　　　　　　R. C. Myers

466. Winestine, Belle Fligelman. MOTHER WAS SHOCKED. *Montana 1974 24(3): 70-78.* Prominent in the woman suffrage movement in Montana was Jeannette Rankin, first woman elected to Congress, whose story is recalled by her first-term secretary and campaign assistant. Political activity, especially making public speeches, was considered unladylike and distressed some families concerned. Illus.
　　　　　　　　　　S. R. Davison

467. Wolseley, Roland E. SAMUEL E. CORNISH—PIONEER BLACK JOURNALIST AND PASTOR. *Crisis 1976 83(8): 288-289.* Samuel E. Cornish (1796-1859) was born in Delaware in a nonslave home, attended Princeton University, and became a Presbyterian minister in New York City. In 1827 he was editor and copublisher, with John B. Russwurm, of the first black newspaper in the United States, *Freedom's Journal.* Cornish wrote hard-hitting editorials on any issue that he felt retarded black progress. After Russwurm left for Liberia, financial difficulties resulted in the collapse of *Freedom's Journal.* Cornish made several more attempts at journalism, but his real impact was as a strong spokesman for abolition.　　　　　　　　　　A. G. Belles

468. Wood, Randall B. AFTER THE EXODUS: JOHN LEWIS WALLER AND THE BLACK ELITE, 1878-1900. *Kansas Hist. Q. 1977 43(2): 172-192.* When writing about the Negro migration to Kansas after the Civil War, most historians have neglected the small but influential group of educated men who emerged as a black elite. John Lewis Waller (1850-1907) provides an excellent example. He practiced law, edited several black journals, held important positions in the state Republican Party, and served as US consul to Madagascar. Politics seemed the best way to serve his own interests and those of his race. Unlike many educated Negroes who turned to the Democrats and Populists when they became disillusioned with the Republicans, Waller responded instead to the imperial impulse in a futile effort to establish Negro colonies in Madagascar and Cuba. Primary and secondary sources; illus., 116 notes.
　　　　　　　　　　W. F. Zornow

469. Woywitka, Anne B. A PIONEER WOMAN IN THE LABOUR MOVEMENT. *Alberta Hist. [Canada] 1978 26(1): 10-16.* Teklia Chaban was born in the Ukraine. She moved to Alberta in 1914, the year of her marriage. Her husband worked in the Cardiff coal mines, 15 miles north of Edmonton. Follows the family for the next 10 years, with agitation for a labor organization, dealings with the United Mine Workers of America, and strikes and violence in the early 1920's. She was active in Ukrainian cultural movements that were part of the labor efforts. In the mid-1920's the family moved to Edmonton, and again was involved in agitation for labor recognition, spending some time in jail and suffering periodic unemployment for their efforts. 2 illus.　　　D. Chaput

470. Wright, W. D. THE THOUGHT AND LEADERSHIP OF KELLY MILLER. *Phylon 1978 39(2): 180-192.* Kelly Miller was one of the most important black leaders of the late 19th and early 20th centuries. He was a follower and admirer of Booker T. Washington, though he sometimes disagreed with the great Tuskegeean. He stressed progress of the Afro-American people within the existing political and economic system, while hoping and working for improvements. In the 1920's, his leadership was increasingly challenged by W. E. B. DuBois, who was a Marxist, Marcus Garvey, the Black Nationalist, and A. Philip Randolph, labor union leader and democratic socialist. 58 notes.
　　　　　　　　　　J. C. Billigmeier

471. Young, Walter D. M. J. COLDWELL, THE MAKING OF A SOCIAL DEMOCRAT. *J. of Can. Studies 1974 9(3): 50-60.* After beginning as a High Anglican and Tory in England, Major J. Coldwell went from Progressivism to Social Democracy in Western Canada. As a teacher, a school principal, and a Regina alderman, he became involved in urban and rural prairie life. This experience made it possible for him to emerge as leader of the Farmer Labor party in 1932. Based on interviews, newspapers, secondary works; 33 notes. G. E. Panting

2. THE COLONIAL EXPERIENCE

General

472. Allen, Theodore. "... THEY WOULD HAVE DESTROYED ME": SLAVERY AND THE ORIGINS OF RACISM. *Radical Am. 1975 9(3): 41-64.* Suggests that the class struggle in which poor whites and Negroes united in protest in Virginia during 1660-92, including Bacon's Rebellion (1676), led to the establishment of racial slavery as a means of social control.

473. Baker, Mary Roys. ANGLO-MASSACHUSETTS TRADE UNION ROOTS, 1130-1790. *Labor Hist. 1973 14(3): 352-396.* Labor actions and objectives from medieval through colonial times were so similar in custom, behavior, and goals that modern trade unions have distinct roots in Anglo-Massachusetts practices. Thus the basic economic goals of Anglo-American labor groups have remained practically constant for centuries. Based on court records, censuses, law compilations, and collection of documents; 90 notes.
L. L. Athey

474. Barbour, Hugh. WILLIAM PENN, MODEL OF PROTESTANT LIBERALISM. *Church Hist. 1979 48(2): 156-173.* William Penn's practical social reform combined the Quakers' radical hope for the total transforming of men, ethics, and society by God's spirit with a humanist's trust in reason and conscience already at work in all men. This was a new stance for Quakers. Best known in his own time for his practical career, Penn's ideas developed gradually in his laws and tracts. Penn's approaches to history, to toleration, and to theology and ethics cannot be claimed as unique. Yet Penn drew a unique intensity in both his universalism and his radicalism from his Quaker community, from its wrestling with "the Light within," and from his own experience of the unity of world truth and the radical depth of evil. 60 notes.
M. D. Dibert

475. Becker, Robert A. REVOLUTION AND REFORM: AN INTERPRETATION OF SOUTHERN TAXATION, 1763 TO 1783. *William and Mary Q. 1975 32(3): 417-442.* Examines the tax policies of Maryland, Virginia, North Carolina, South Carolina, and Georgia on the eve of the Revolution. Taxation heavily burdened the poor, while scandal, the growing Revolutionary movement, and back country opposition served as early stimulants for tax reform. Protest was strongest in North Carolina, which had the most regressive tax system. The need to gain public support for the Revolution and the British invasion of the South spurred tax reform. Based on legislative documents and personal correspondence; 86 notes.
H. M. Ward

476. Bradley, Michael R. THE ROLE OF THE BLACK CHURCH IN THE COLONIAL SLAVE SOCIETY. *Louisiana Studies 1975 14(4): 413-421.* The formation of the black church is the key to the beginning of Afro-American community and culture in colonial America. Because religion was an integral part of West African life, slaves used religion for the creation and recreation of community. The black church developed the concepts of group solidarity, mutual aid and assistance, and concern for everyday matters of life more highly than the white church did. The black church provided opportunities for leadership, a way of coping with slavery, a contact with a black-led group for newly arrived Africans. The church also encouraged survival, and offered a slim hope of improvement, compensation for deprivation, and ways to resist the institution of slavery. From the beginning the role of the black church in the black community has been creation, leadership, reaction to oppression, and support for the people. Based on primary and secondary sources; 28 notes.
B. A. Glasrud

477. Casino, Joseph J. ANTI-POPERY IN COLONIAL PENNSYLVANIA. *Pennsylvania Mag. of Hist. and Biog. 1981 105(3): 279-310.* Amazingly flexible, anti-Catholicism was a scapegoat for social and political crises and helped define national allegiance for both England and the colonies. Used opportunistically by different groups, anti-Catholicism was a response to change as well as a tool for maintaining political advantage. 107 notes.
T. H. Wendel

478. Christian, William A., Sr. INWARDNESS AND OUTWARD CONCERNS: A STUDY OF JOHN WOOLMAN'S THOUGHT. *Quaker Hist. 1978 67(2): 88-104.* John Woolman read devotional literature, believed his dream-visions called for personal testimony on social problems, and was unusually sensitive and self-critical. The answer to his prayers, couched in Biblical, Puritan, Quaker terms, was that God transcends the world and requires its transformation so that human beings will live as equals in one family. Mid-18th century Quaker society was comfortable and, except for a few like Woolman and Benezet, complacently dealt with internal questions of dress, speech, and discipline. "The time was ripe for Woolman to be heard" on oppression of slaves, although not for his pleas for the poor. 16 notes, 55 ref.
T. D. S. Bassett

479. Conforti, Joseph A. SAMUEL HOPKINS AND THE NEW DIVINITY: THEOLOGY, ETHICS, AND SOCIAL REFORM IN EIGHTEENTH-CENTURY NEW ENGLAND. *William and Mary Q. 1977 34(4): 572-589.* Examines the controversy among the New Divinity clerics over the nature of true virtue. The Reverend Samuel Hopkins attempted to clarify the ethical theories of Jonathan Edwards, concentrating on defects in Edwards's notions of secondary virtue. Unlike Edwards, who emphasized right affections as the essence of true virtue, Hopkins saw true virtue as right actions which would open the door to social reform. Discusses Hopkins's own position on social issues, including slavery. A unique contribution of the New Divinity was the doctrine of disinterested benevolence. Based on contemporary letters, diaries, and religious writings. 55 notes.
H. M. Ward

480. Cott, Nancy F. DIVORCE AND THE CHANGING STATUS OF WOMEN IN EIGHTEENTH-CENTURY MASSACHUSETTS. *William and Mary Q. 1976 33(4): 586-614.* Examines 229 divorce petitions for the period 1692-1786 and discusses the legal grounds for divorce. Divorces were granted by the legislature or the governor and the council. Increasingly, aggrieved spouses sought divorce through official channels rather than through the traditional means of "self divorce." More women sought divorce than men, but more men than women succeeded. Data offer perspectives on sexual, family, marriage, and property aspects. The Revolutionary era marked a decline in the double standard, and there was an improvement in the condition of wives. Stricter standards for men's marital fidelity were also evident. Based on legislative and court divorce records; 5 tables, 84 notes.
H. M. Ward

481. Ekirch, A. Roger. NORTH CAROLINA REGULATORS ON LIBERTY AND CORRUPTION, 1766-1771. *Perspectives in Am. Hist. 1977-78 11: 197-256.* The Regulator movement essentially was conservative in its values and goals. Regulators, who were organized to oppose Backcountry corrupt office-holders, were heavily influenced by the economic conditions occasioned by the French and Indian War, and by the charismatic leadership of Herman Husband. North Carolina office-holders tended to overlook the self-interest of the Backcountry office-holders, and, unable to perceive the conservative nature of the Regulator movement, thus opposed it.
W. A. Wiegand

482. Foster, Stephen. NEW ENGLAND AND THE CHALLENGE OF HERESY, 1630 TO 1660: THE PURITAN CRISIS IN TRANSATLANTIC PERSPECTIVE. *William and Mary Q. 1981 38(4): 624-660.* Religious dissension in New England did not bring about wholesale declension; rather the New England Puritans were able to accommodate a measure of reform and preserve relative unity. The Puritan ministry learned the value of social informality and keeping in touch with lay constituents. Comparisons are made between New England heresies and their counterparts in England, particularly Antinomianism and Arminianism. The essence of Puritan survival was not its stability but its maintenance of an equilibrium of contradictory impulses. 81 notes.
H. M. Ward

483. Frech, Laura P. THE REPUBLICANISM OF HENRY LAURENS. *South Carolina Hist. Mag. 1975 76(2): 69-79.* Despite wealth and social standing, Henry Laurens (1724-92) was an ardent republican and

"even something of a leveller." To assist the poor he favored abolition of slavery which he believed would reduce land prices and increase the number of small farmers. While influenced by the Enlightenment, Laurens believed that republicanism required moral regeneration, which would come with Protestant Christianity. Primary sources; 40 notes.

R. H. Tomlinson

484. Fursenko, A. A. FERMERSKIE VYSTUPLENIIA NAKANUNE VOINY ZA NEZAVISIMOST' SSHA [Farmers' action on the eve of the US War of independence]. *Novaia i Noveishaia Istoriia [USSR] 1975 (5): 77-92.* The article analyzes the causes, the course and character of the farmers' movements in the 1760's and early 1770's (Regulators of North and South Carolina and Levellers of New York State). The author comes to the conclusion that the farmers' actions were an important factor of the democratic movement in the North American colonies of England.

J

485. Herbst, Jurgen. THE AMERICAN REVOLUTION AND THE AMERICAN UNIVERSITY. *Perspectives in Am. Hist. 1976 10: 279-354.* Colonists perceived their colleges as public corporations intended to mold leaders for state and church positions. Because of this perception, mid-18th century institutions of higher education showed remarkable resiliency in weathering the American Revolution by simply transferring the object of their civic responsibilities from the old to the new governments. Radicals who saw colleges as elitist and conservative called for significant reform; but in most states, legislators were willing to protect colleges and universities by extending sufficient financial support. 83 notes.

W. A. Wiegnad

486. Herbst, Jurgen. THE CHARTER OF A PROPOSED COLLEGE IN NEWPORT, RHODE ISLAND: A CHAPTER IN THE HISTORY OF EIGHTEENTH CENTURY HIGHER EDUCATION IN AMERICA. *Newport Hist. 1976 49(2): 25-49.* An attempt by Ezra Stiles and William Ellery, Jr. to establish a college in Newport, Rhode Island, 1770, provides a record of an attempt at equal opportunity, free access, and equal treatment of minorities in the United States; reprints the original charter proposal. 3 reproductions, 34 notes.

G. A. Hewlett

487. Hornick, Nancy Slocum. ANTHONY BENEZET AND THE AFRICANS' SCHOOL: TOWARD A THEORY OF FULL EQUALITY. *Pennsylvania Mag. of Hist. and Biog. 1975 99(4): 399-421.* Traces the social thought of Anthony Benezet (1713-84) who with the Friends of Philadelphia organized the Africans' School for free Negroes in the 1770's. Benezet was ahead of his time in regarding blacks as the intellectual, moral, and spiritual equal of whites (if not social and economic). His opposition to racial prejudice was a direct result of his pioneering efforts in black education. 52 notes.

C. W. Olson

488. Humphrey, David C. THE KING'S COLLEGE MEDICAL SCHOOL AND THE PROFESSIONALIZATION OF MEDICINE IN PRE-REVOLUTIONARY NEW YORK. *Bull. of the Hist. of Medicine 1975 49(2): 206-234.* The small number of "professionals" among the numerous physicians in prerevolutionary New York City saw the rest of the physicians as unskilled and uneducated quacks. The 1760 licensing law was not enforced, and New Yorkers patronized the city's "better known empirics." There was professional scorn, social resentment, and economic rivalry between the "professionals" and the empirics. In the mid-1760's, New York's medical leaders agreed that a medical school was a feasible solution to the problem. A medical college would improve the quality of practice, give respectability to the graduates, and a competitive advantage over the unschooled empirics. The establishment of King's College Medical School was the result. The "professionals" also founded a medical society, but "beneath the surface reforms medical practice continued to look much the same to most colonists." True professionalization "awaited the scientific breakthroughs of the 19th century." 115 notes.

M. Kaufman

489. King, Anne. ANNE HUTCHINSON AND ANNE BRADSTREET: LITERATURE AND EXPERIENCE, FAITH AND WORKS IN MASSACHUSETTS BAY COLONY. *Int. J. of Women's Studies [Canada] 1978 1(5): 445-467.* Examines the lives and political, religious, and social attitudes of Anne Hutchinson (1591-1643) and Anne Bradstreet (1612-72) who, through polarizing the question of faith versus works and through questioning the position of women, introduced tensions in American life and ideology which led to eventual social change.

490. Klein, Rachel N. ORDERING THE BACKCOUNTRY: THE SOUTH CAROLINA REGULATION. *William and Mary Q. 1981 38(4): 661-680.* Continuing from where Richard Brown's *The South Carolina Regulators* (1963) left off, offers further study of social conflict and transformation of backcountry South Carolina from the eve of the rise of the Regulators to the aftermath of the movement. The backcountry settlers developed an interest in commercial agriculture. Thus the lawless element threatened the security and the profits of the settled back inhabitants. The Regulators also represented farmers against hunters. The author profiles the banditry, which the Regulators sought to end. The Regulators, in protecting their property, were not actually antiestablishment. Based on court records and newspapers; 50 notes.

H. M. Ward

491. Lang, Amy Schrager. ANTINOMIANISM AND THE "AMERICANIZATION" OF A DOCTRINE. *New England Q. 1981 54(2): 225-242.* Since its inception in the 1630's, Antinomianism has had a long history. Most recently, literary critics have employed it as an explanatory term. In so doing, they have sacrificed not only accuracy but also the doctrine's full historical relevance by ignoring its colonial context. Two 17th-century sermons, one by John Winthrop and the other by John Wheelwright, indicate that Antinomianism was preeminently a social heresy; and what in literary circles is called an Antinomian strain might better be called a Puritan strain. Puritanism in America was in itself a deviant form of Calvinism, and Antinomianism placed itself in opposition to the "Americanization" of Calvinism. 19 notes.

R. S. Sliwoski

492. Lernack, Paul. PEACE BONDS AND CRIMINAL JUSTICE IN COLONIAL PHILADELPHIA. *Pennsylvania Mag. of Hist. and Biog. 1976 100(2): 173-190.* In reaction to persecution at the hands of English authorities, the Pennsylvania Quakers established a mild criminal code. The peace bond, a legal device aimed at diverting troublemakers from the criminal justice system, was one manifestation of this lenient code. The peace bond was a form of civil or criminal bail which judges could order without criminally charging the accused. In the close-knit Quaker community, the peace bond was a flexible alternative to criminal prosecution, but by 1780, the growing anonymity of city dwellers and the inflation of the cash value of the bail nullified its flexibility and thereafter it was used infrequently. Based on primary and secondary sources; 64 notes.

E. W. Carp

493. Malmsheimer, Lonna M. DAUGHTERS OF ZION: NEW ENGLAND ROOTS OF AMERICAN FEMINISM. *New England Q. 1977 50(3): 484-504.* Traces the evolution of New England attitudes toward women from the 17th century, when they were considered morally and intellectually weaker than men, to the end of the 18th century when they were viewed as morally superior to men. Particularly important in this transformation were the sermons of Cotton Mather (1663-1728), who addressed women as individuals and reinterpreted the meaning and effect of Eve's fall. Once women were perceived to be naturally more moral and benevolent than men they were encouraged to participate in charitable activities. These activities provided women with social and political experience and a sense of self-esteem which in turn provided a basis from which they expanded their activities in the 19th century. Based on sermons and secondary sources; 40 notes.

J. C. Bradford

494. Marina, William. REVOLUTION AND SOCIAL CHANGE: THE AMERICAN REVOLUTION AS A PEOPLE'S WAR. *Literature of Liberty 1978 1(2): 5-39.* Twentieth-century scholarship approaches the independence movement from a sociological viewpoint and sees tensions among equality, inequality, and egalitarianism; discusses the basic free and prosperous society of the Revolution, the changing Revolutionary coalition, the defeat of imperial power, and post-Revolutionary society.

495. Moore, Kathryn McDaniel. THE DILEMMA OF CORPORAL PUNISHMENT AT HARVARD COLLEGE. *Hist. of Educ. Q. 1974 14(3): 335-346.* The trial and conviction in 1638 of Harvard College's first executive officer, Nathaniel Eaton, for undue and excessive use of corpo-

ral punishment was an excellent demonstration of the administration of Puritan justice and served to establish Harvard's precedent of the use of reason rather than physical punishment in student corrections.

496. Olton, Charles S. PHILADELPHIA'S FIRST ENVIRONMENTAL CRISIS. *Pennsylvania Mag. of Hist. and Biog. 1974 98(1): 90-100.* Complaints of air pollution, spoiled drinking water, and unpleasant roads led to the enactment in 1763 of Philadelphia's first comprehensive environmental law. Philadelphia's effort to clean up the environment was only temporarily successful; by 1783, the urban environment had begun to degenerate again. Based on primary and secondary sources; 48 notes.
E. W. Carp

497. Sloan, David. "A TIME OF SIFTING AND WINNOWING:" THE PAXTON RIOTS AND QUAKER NON-VIOLENCE IN PENNSYLVANIA. *Quaker Hist. 1977 66(1): 3-22.* In February 1764 armed "Paxton Boys" marched on Philadelphia demanding justice for the frontier and defense against Indians. Several hundred Quaker youths bore arms to defend the Society of Friends and the city. For three years official committees unsuccessfully tried to persuade members to recant this behavior. Instead of expelling recalcitrants they merely reaffirmed the Quaker peace testimony. 59 notes.
T. D. S. Bassett

498. Speizman, Milton D. and Kronick, Jane C., eds. A SEVENTEENTH-CENTURY QUAKER WOMEN'S DECLARATION. *Signs: J. of Women in Culture and Soc. 1975 1(1): 231-245.* Among the earliest champions of essential equality in America were the Quakers, who regarded the Britons George Fox (1624-91) and his wife Margaret Fell as cofounders of their denomination. A reflection of Fell's feminism is found in this reprinted epistle written during the 1670's in a Lancashire women's meeting and sent to the women of Philadelphia. It summarizes the Society of Friends' attitudes on sexual equality, charitable responsibility, and the organization of women's meetings. Primary and secondary sources; 11 notes.
T. Simmerman

499. Steffens, Pete. FRANKLIN'S EARLY ATTACK ON RACISM: AN ESSAY AGAINST A MASSACRE OF INDIANS. *Journalism Hist. 1978 5(1): 8-12, 31.* Benjamin Franklin's 1764 pamphlet, "A Narrative of the late Massacres in Lancaster County, or a Number of Indians, Friends of this Province, by Persons Unknown," in which he urged coexistence with the Indians, may have helped prevent repetitions of the Paxton Boys' massacre of 20 friendly Christian Indians.

500. VanHorne, John C. IMPEDIMENTS TO THE CHRISTIANIZATION AND EDUCATION OF BLACKS IN COLONIAL AMERICA: THE CASE OF THE ASSOCIATES OF DR. BRAY. *Hist. Mag. of the Protestant Episcopal Church 1981 50(3): 243-269.* The Associates of Dr. Bray (Thomas Bray, 1658-1730) had as their initial mission the task of converting and educating both slave and free Negroes. Discusses the numerous obstacles that the associates encountered in implementing their mission: attitudes held by whites toward the Christianization and education of the blacks; questions concerning the dangers inherent in educating them; doubts regarding the educability of the blacks; constraints imposed by the language barriers that separated blacks from whites; the disparity between the blacks' native religions and Christianity; the priority in the colonies of labor over education; the apathy of some whites toward the Church of England and its sacraments; the unwillingness of whites to share with the associates the financial burdens of the enterprise; and the dearth of qualified teachers willing to undertake the task. The associates did not learn from their negative experiences. Based primarily on the published American correspondence of the associates and the numerous collections of colonial statutes; 4 photos, 108 notes.
H. M. Parker, Jr.

501. Warden, G. B. LAW REFORM IN ENGLAND AND NEW ENGLAND, 1620 TO 1660. *William and Mary Q. 1978 35(4): 668-690.* The Puritan Revolution profoundly and immediately affected English law, especially laws made by Englishmen who settled in New England. Because revolutionary law reforms in England and the early New England settlements stem from similar conditions, the legal developments of the period in both places are comparable. Discusses the grievances of Puritans in England and how they were remedied in the New World. Accounts for different results in law reform in New England and England, commenting on social and intellectual differences. Based on the legal literature, codes, and contemporary accounts; 39 notes.
H. M. Ward

502. Whittenburg, James P. PLANTERS, MERCHANTS, AND LAWYERS: SOCIAL CHANGE AND THE ORIGINS OF THE NORTH CAROLINA REGULATION. *William and Mary Q. 1977 34(2): 215-238.* Examines the motivation for the Regulator movement in colonial North Carolina. Stresses the arrival of merchants and the change in the pattern of indebtedness as major factors in stirring hostility. The liaison between lawyers and merchants brought about a new elite at the expense of the planters. Domination of the colonial government by this new coalition seemed conspiratorial to the backcountry leaders. Based on local histories and records; table, 103 notes.
H. M. Ward

503. Wood, Peter H. "I DID THE BEST I COULD FOR MY DAY": THE STUDY OF EARLY BLACK HISTORY DURING THE SECOND RECONSTRUCTION, 1960 TO 1976. *William and Mary Q. 1978 35(2): 185-225.* Surveys and evaluates the quality of recent historiography concerning the study of Negroes in early American history. Areas treated are the development in individual colonies, the African slave trade, origins of colonial racism, evolution of Afro-American religion and culture, black resistance, black responses to the American Revolution, and emancipation movements. Suggests that these studies of early blacks open the need for integrating the new evidence into the larger traditional topics. Notes the numerous works on black history including articles and theses. 129 notes.
H. M. Ward

Civil Liberties and Political Rights

504. Akers, Charles W. "OUR MODERN EGYPTIANS": PHILLIS WHEATLEY AND THE WHIG CAMPAIGN AGAINST SLAVERY IN REVOLUTIONARY BOSTON. *J. of Negro Hist. 1975 60(3): 397-410.* Unnoticed by previous scholars, one of Phillis Wheatley's most eloquent letters (written in 1774) contains the three elements of her attitude toward slavery: Christian piety, Whiggish patriotism, and racial consciousness. Primary and secondary sources; 42 notes.
N. G. Sapper

505. Allain, Mathé. SLAVE POLICIES IN FRENCH LOUISIANA. *Louisiana Hist. 1980 21(2): 127-137.* The official French policy governing slaves and slavery in Louisiana was the Black Code of 1724. Neither humanitarian nor racist, it reflected the French monarchy's concerns for absolutism, order, and religious unity. This code defined bondsmen as "moveable property," yet they were definitely human beings who should not be subject to "barbarous" treatment. Essentially a product of Colbert's colonial policy and diligent French bureaucrats, the Black Code considered slaves perpetual minors, slaveholders paternalistic masters. Based on documents in the Archives Nationales, Archives des Colonies, Paris, and numerous French publications; 54 notes.
D. B. Touchstone

506. Baker, Robert A. BAPTISTS AND THE AMERICAN REVOLUTION. *Baptist Hist. and Heritage 1976 11(3): 149-159.* Political liberty would be tragically inadequate if it had not included the most important of all liberties: the right to worship according to the dictates of one's own conscience in a religiously pluralistic society. Religious liberty is the ultimate foundation of democratic institutions. All other human rights are endangered when religious liberty is questioned, hampered, or denied by any group. Emphasizes the contribution of Baptists to religious liberty in the United States. Based on secondary sources; 11 notes.
H. M. Parker, Jr.

507. Billings, Warren M. PLEADING, PROCEDURE, AND PRACTICE: THE MEANING OF DUE PROCESS OF LAW IN SEVENTEENTH-CENTURY VIRGINIA. *J. of Southern Hist. 1981 47(4): 569-584.* An analysis of the development of modern due process of law in 17th-century Virginia. The term, as well as the practice, arrived from England, where it referred merely to the processes of getting the accused through court procedures. Both term and practice lacked flexibility, but the colonists were not content to let matters stand there. Covers the development and origins of such modern ideas as the right to jury trial, defense for the accused, right of the defendant to subpoena witnesses, and the rapid clearing of court dockets. By century's end, Virginia had endorsed the processes of change in legal practice, thus opening the door for a tradition that has not yet come to an end. 39 notes.
V. L. Human

508. Brasseaux, Carl A. THE ADMINISTRATION OF SLAVE REGULATIONS IN FRENCH LOUISIANA, 1724-1766. *Louisiana Hist. 1980 21(2): 139-158.* The first slaveholders in colonial Louisiana nominally accepted the French government's Black Code, but they frequently ignored it with impunity. For example, floggings, though prohibited in the code, were accepted as part of the masters' paternal responsibilities. French officials generally used the code in the interests of slaveholders, not to protect slaves. Lessees, who were much harsher than masters in their treatment of slaves, were often brought to court by masters who seemed more concerned about the value of their leased property than about their slaves' welfare. By the 1750's the slaveholding class had gained control over making and administering regulations for blacks, and they further curtailed slaves' legal protection under the law. Based on documents in the Archives Nationales, Archives des Colonies, Paris; 91 notes. D. B. Touchstone

509. Bruns, Roger A. A QUAKER'S ANTISLAVERY CRUSADE: ANTHONY BENEZET. *Quaker Hist. 1976 65(2): 81-92.* The voices of a few antislavery Friends before 1756 were smothered by the comfortable, respectable weight of American Quakerism. Anthony Benezet believed that Friends were indifferent to the evils of slavery because they did not know them. From the 1759 publication of his first major pamphlet until his death in 1784, he was an "old white-haired busybody of good works scurrying around" to individual Friends and their meetings with letters and tracts, speaking against slave trading and holding. Discrimination continued. Although the Philadelphia Yearly Meeting (comprising Delaware, Pennsylvania, and much of New Jersey) excommmunicated slaveholding members in 1776, it did not abolish the color bar to membership until 1796. 56 notes. T. D. S. Bassett

510. Buckley, Thomas E. CHURCH AND STATE IN MASSACHUSETTS BAY: A CASE STUDY OF BAPTIST DISSENTERS, 1651. *J. of Church and State 1981 23(2): 309-322.* Discusses the Baptists' struggle for their rights, both civil and religious, in Massachusetts during 1630-55. The efforts of major leaders, John Clarke, Roger Williams, Obadiah Holms, along with some less well-known, illustrate the conflict between Baptists and the establishment. 53 notes.
E. E. Eminhizer

511. Conforti, Joseph A. SAMUEL HOPKINS AND THE REVOLUTIONARY ANTISLAVERY MOVEMENT. *Rhode Island Hist. 1979 38(2): 39-49.* A Congregational minister in Newport, Rhode Island, Samuel Hopkins, began speaking out against slavery and the slave trade in the 1770's and went on to become a leading figure in the New England antislavery movement until his death in 1803. Based on manuscripts in New Haven, Newport, New York City, Philadelphia, and Providence, newspapers, pamphlets, and Hopkins's writings; 6 illus., 37 notes.
P. J. Coleman

512. Cuddihy, William and Hardy, B. Carmon. A MAN'S HOUSE WAS NOT HIS CASTLE: ORIGINS OF THE FOURTH AMENDMENT TO THE UNITED STATES CONSTITUTION. *William and Mary Q. 1980 37(3): 371-400.* Outlines developments in English statutes and common law pertaining to search, and their application. The man's-house-as-castle ideal is derived from earlier rather than later experience. The degree of discretionary intrusion varied according to one's place in the social order—the poor had little protection against search. The 18th century witnessed a vast expansion in discretionary search. Emphasizes court cases for the mid- and third quarter of the 18th century. Relates the transplanting of English methods of search and seizure to the American colonies. General search warrants were permitted; only Massachusetts had strict confinement of search. Concludes that up to the formulating of the Bill of Rights, general search was the rule. Based on legislative and court records in England and America; 128 notes. H. M. Ward

513. Grenz, Stanley J. ISAAC BACKUS AND RELIGIOUS LIBERTY. *Foundations 1979 22(4): 352-360.* Sees a need to review New England Baptist clergyman Isaac Backus's (1724-1806) contribution to religious liberty. Recent historians have argued that his contribution was not as important as once thought. Concludes that his contributions were large, but that some of his views were not on the mark, in that truths he held were more complex than he thought. Based mostly on *Isaac Backus on Church, State, and Calvinism & Pamphlets, 1754-1789* and other sources; 35 notes. E. E. Eminhizer

514. Guggisberg, Hans R. RELIGIOUS FREEDOM AND THE HISTORY OF THE CHRISTIAN WORLD IN ROGER WILLIAMS' THOUGHT. *Early Am. Literature 1977 12(1): 36-48.* Roger Williams, the founder of Rhode Island, based his defense of religious liberty on the Holy Scriptures and the history of Christianity. His historical documentation used only those available materials which fit into his general concept of a Christian society. His aim was not universal knowledge and general understanding of the past; history simply provided the facts and examples to support his pleas for religious freedom and the separation of Church and State. Primary sources; 46 notes. J. N. Friedel

515. Higginbotham, Don and Price, William S., Jr. WAS IT MURDER FOR A WHITE MAN TO KILL A SLAVE? CHIEF JUSTICE MARTIN HOWARD CONDEMNS THE PECULIAR INSTITUTION IN NORTH CAROLINA. *William and Mary Q. 1979 36(4): 593-601.* In 1771, Martin Howard, Chief Justice of the North Carolina Superior Court, in a grand jury charge, denounced slavery. Though Howard was earlier a controversial figure in defending the Stamp Act, he was highly regarded by all factions in North Carolina. Howard did not ask for abolition, but he struck at the hypocrisy of North Carolinians in their quest for political freedom from England while denying the humanity of Negroes. He considered cruelty bad policy. Except for the fruits of his labor, a slave has all other rights of a human being. Howard's plea undoubtedly influenced the subsequent adoption of laws (1774 and 1791) in making it a crime for a white man to murder a Negro. Notes deal primarily with other legal development; 17 notes. H. M. Ward

516. Hoffer, Peter C. LAW AND LIBERTY: IN THE MATTER OF PROVOST WILLIAM SMITH OF PHILADELPHIA, 1758. *William and Mary Q. 1981 38(4): 693-701.* Reverend William Smith, provost of the College of Philadelphia, came to the aid of county court Justice William Moore, who was imprisoned for libeling the Assembly. Smith published Moore's attack (already published twice) in a German language paper, and he was charged with contempt for libeling the previous Assembly. The author discusses two briefs in defense of Smith (one by William Smith, Jr., William Livingston, and Benjamin Nicoll, and the other by William Smith, Sr., and/or William Smith, Jr.) and relates them to English libel cases and common and statute law. The chief argument of the longer brief by Smith is that provincial legislatures, which were inferior to Parliament, could not deny such rights as habeas corpus. This brief suggests that legislative authority should devolve from fixed constitutions. Reprints Smith brief. Based on various legal documents and commentaries; 50 notes. H. M. Ward

517. Jackson, Harvey H. "AMERICAN SLAVERY, AMERICAN FREEDOM" AND THE REVOLUTION OF THE LOWER SOUTH: THE CASE OF LACHLAN MCINTOSH. *Southern Studies 1980 19(1): 81-93.* In 1775 Lachlan McIntosh (b. 1728), plantation and slave owner, signed a declaration condemning slavery as unnatural and incompatible with the struggle of the American colonists against their oppressors in England. In 1787 he made another declaration, this time justifying and supporting slavery. His seeming self-contradiction, typical of many southerners, can be explained by economics. In 1775 British policies threatened McIntosh's freedom to earn a good living, and subjection of blacks who might rebel was a danger in time of revolution. In 1787 the maintenance of slavery provided the only possible means of preserving wealth for many southerners. Based on the Lachlan McIntosh Papers in University of Georgia Libraries, Henry Laurens Papers in the South Carolina Historical Society, and other primary sources; 37 notes.
J. J. Buschen

518. Jackson, Harvey H. THE DARIEN ANTISLAVERY PETITION OF 1739 AND THE GEORGIA PLAN. *William and Mary Q. 1977 34(4): 618-631.* John Mackintosh Bain and fellow Highland Scots signed an antislavery petition in 1739. Bain's 1755 petition to the Governor and Council of Georgia for permission to hold slaves accounts for his changed attitudes toward slaveholding. Discusses the economic problems of the Darien settlement, founded in 1736 on the Altamaha River. The real issue was not slavery, but rather the deficiencies of the Georgia plan. Both petitions were symptomatic of society; the latter petition shows that commercialization had taken over. Based on contemporary writings and pamphlets; 47 notes. H. M. Ward

519. Jennings, Judith. MID-EIGHTEENTH CENTURY BRITISH QUAKERISM AND THE RESPONSE TO THE PROBLEM OF SLAVERY. *Quaker Hist. 1977 66(1): 23-40.* The Seven Years' War reminded sensitive members of the Society of Friends in Britain and America of the widening contrast between their well-to-do, comfortable life-style and the sufferings of earlier members. News from American Friends of the evils of colonial slavery led British Friends in 1761 to expel members for slave-trading. The slave trade was the only part of the system directly affecting Great Britain. 90 notes. — T. D. S. Bassett

520. Koehler, Lyle. THE CASE OF THE AMERICAN JEZEBELS: ANNE HUTCHINSON AND FEMALE AGITATION DURING THE YEARS OF ANTINOMIAN TURMOIL, 1636-1640. *William and Mary Q. 1974 31(1): 55-78.* Places the Antinomian controversy into the context of female rebellion, defines the role of women in colonial Massachusetts, and describes some of Anne Hutchinson's followers. Female resistance reached its height when many women sympathized with her. The theological charges stemmed from fear of assertion of women's rights. In the aftermath of the trial, other women became assertive and were involved in cases of legal intimidation. Based on court and church records, and on Puritan writings; 70 notes. — H. M. Ward

521. Mackinley, Peter W. THE NEW ENGLAND PURITAN ATTITUDE TOWARD BLACK SLAVERY. *Old-Time New England 1973 63(3): 81-88.* Discusses the inconsistency of colonial New England Puritan attitudes toward the slave as an economic unit and as a person "subject to rights established by Hebraic precedent." As the slave population increased, Puritan legislators acted to reduce the civil and personal rights of slaves. Antislavery sentiment nevertheless prevailed and attempts to resolve the inconsistency in the Puritan attitude toward slaves proved futile, as the abolition of slavery in New England began during the American Revolution. 44 notes. — R. N. Lokken

522. Marable, Manning. DEATH OF THE QUAKER SLAVE TRADE. *Quaker Hist. 1974 63(1): 17-33.* The first admonitions to Quaker merchants by George Fox in 1656 extended his business ethic to dealing in Indian and African slaves. After Pennsylvania was settled, Friends sanctioned the trade provided all bondsmen were freed after a maximum of 14 years. Difficulties in receiving payment for West Indian slaves sold to Pennsylvania farmers, the rising prices of slaves, and fear of slave insurrection combined with a revival in sensitivity to solidify the Quaker testimony against the slave trade by 1750. 51 notes. — T. D. S. Bassett

523. Markowitz, Judith B. REFLECTIONS ON WAR IN THE REVOLUTIONARY ERA: RADICAL AND FEMINIST: MERCY OTIS WARREN AND THE HISTORIOGRAPHERS. *Peace and Change 1976 4(2): 10-21.* Examines the radical political thought of Mercy Otis Warren during the American Revolution; her historical importance lies in her radical republicanism, her belief in natural rights and equality of human beings, her recognition of the dangers threatening the establishment, and her feminism, 1760's-1805.

524. Maxwell, John Francis. THE CHARISMATIC ORIGINS OF THE CHRISTIAN ANTI-SLAVERY MOVEMENT IN NORTH AMERICA. *Quaker Hist. 1974 63(2): 108-116.* Quotes George Fox (1671), William Edmundson (1676), Philadelphia Monthly Meeting (1693), William Burling (1718), Benjamin Lay (1738), John Woolman (1762), and Anthony Benezet (1771) on slavery as a moral evil. 12 notes. — T. D. S. Bassett

525. Moore, John S. THE STRUGGLE FOR FREEDOM IN VIRGINIA. *Baptist Hist. and Heritage 1976 11(3): 160-168.* The United States became the first nation in the world to insure religious freedom for all in its organic laws. The long struggle of Baptists to achieve this required nearly two centuries, involving much sacrifice and persecution. A large amount of credit must go to the tireless and persevering Virginia Baptists. Based largely on secondary sources; 25 notes. — H. M. Parker, Jr.

526. Radbill, Kenneth A. THE ORDEAL OF ELIZABETH DRINKER. *Pennsylvania Hist. 1980 46(2): 147-172.* During the American Revolution, the Drinkers and other Philadelphia Quakers suffered at the hands of both the patriots and the British. In the summer of 1777, Pennsylvania authorities, suspecting that the Quaker pacifists were really pro-British, arrested Henry Drinker and a number of other Friends and transported them to Winchester, Virginia. This article, based on Elizabeth Drinker's *Journal,* focuses on the British occupation of the city and the eventually successful efforts of Mrs. Drinker and others to obtain the release of the Quaker prisoners in Winchester. The October 1781 assault by Philadelphia mobs on Quaker homes is also discussed. Based on the Elizabeth Drinker *Journal* and other materials; map, 113 notes. — D. C. Swift

527. Roberts, Wesley A. THE BLACK EXPERIENCE AND THE AMERICAN REVOLUTION. *Fides et Hist. 1976 8(2): 50-62.* American blacks clearly realized the potential implications of the American Revolution for their own freedom. The British sought to capitalize on that fact by giving freedom to all who would fight for the crown. Therefore, many of the colonies reluctantly accepted black enlistment. The results were limited: a few blacks achieved their freedom; northern states began abolishing slavery; and some black Baptist congregations were born. Secondary sources; 60 notes. — R. E. Butchart

528. Rosenthal, Bernard. PURITAN CONSCIENCE AND NEW ENGLAND SLAVERY. *New England Q. 1973 46(1): 62-81.* "The main efforts on behalf of slaves were likely to come from orthodox Puritans." They questioned whether Christians could be slaves—the Bible to the contrary notwithstanding. The actual conversion of Negroes was rare. John Adams in 1795 observed that theological conviction had less to do with emancipation than did the economics of the white working class. A coalition of the clergy and the white working class ended slavery in New England. 56 notes. — E. P. Stickney

529. Watson, Alan D. IMPULSE TOWARD INDEPENDENCE: RESISTANCE AND REBELLION AMONG NORTH CAROLINA SLAVES, 1750-1775. *J. of Negro Hist. 1978 63(4): 317-328.* Slaves in North Carolina continually protested their state of involuntary servitude. At the outbreak of the American Revolution many of the slaves were as eager for their freedom as white North Carolinians who prepared to seek liberation from British tyranny. Based upon public records in the North Carolina State Archives; 53 notes. — N. G. Sapper

530. Wax, Darold D. REFORM AND REVOLUTION: THE MOVEMENT AGAINST SLAVERY AND THE SLAVE TRADE IN REVOLUTIONARY PENNSYLVANIA. *Western Pennsylvania Hist. Mag. 1974 57(4): 403-429.*

Humanitarian Reform

531. Fiering, Norman S. IRRESISTIBLE COMPASSION: AN ASPECT OF EIGHTEENTH-CENTURY SYMPATHY AND HUMANITARIANISM. *J. of the Hist. of Ideas 1976 37(2): 195-218.* "Irresistible compassion" (the idea that people are moved to compassion by some inherent affective principle of their nature) was a "virtual philosophical and psychological dogma" by the mid-18th century. Though not without some ancient sources, this humanitarian dogma was only a century old when it overtook the different view of human nature associated with the Puritans and Thomas Hobbes. The Cambridge Platonists first advanced the idea and were seconded by a roll of familiar thinkers, chiefly British but including some Americans. The author refers to the religious liberalism of the 19th century, exemplified by William Ellery Channing. Published primary and secondary sources; 59 notes. — D. B. Marti

532. Gwozdz, Kathe Palmero. BENJAMIN FRANKLIN AND THE INOCULATION CONTROVERSY. *Hist. J. of Western Massachusetts 1973 2(2): 30-40.* During the controversy 1730-50 Franklin (in his private letters, *The Pennsylvania Gazette,* and his introduction to Herberden's *Pamphlet on Inoculation*) favored inoculation. Franklin used statistics effectively to prove the value of the practice. Based on Labaree's *The Papers of Benjamin Franklin;* 2 illus., 14 notes. — S. S. Sprague

533. Nash, Gary B. POVERTY AND POOR RELIEF IN PRE-REVOLUTIONARY PHILADELPHIA. *William and Mary Q. 1976 33(1): 3-30.* Discusses the growth of private and public responsibility for

the care of the increasing poor in Philadelphia in the 18th century. Emphasizes the role of the Pennsylvania Hospital for the Sick Poor. The relocation of Acadian neutrals in Philadelphia during the French and Indian War and the revival of Irish and German immigration in the 1760's added to the burden of poor relief. Quakers contributed much private philanthrophy. Also notes the new ideology regarding the poor, with some comparison to ideas in England. Based on manuscript records and secondary sources; 3 tables, 79 notes. H. M. Ward

534. Warner, Margaret Humphreys. VINDICATING THE MINISTER'S ROLE: COTTON MATHER'S CONCEPT OF THE *NISHMATH-CHAJIM* AND THE SPIRITUALIZATION OF MEDICINE. *J. of the Hist. of Medicine and Allied Sci. 1981 36(3): 278-295.* Cotton Mather used a concept of the *nishmath-chajim,* a vital spirit that formed a bridge between man's physical and spiritual components. Using this concept, he tried to make a scientific case for accepting the preacher as healer. Mather was developing this rationale for the return of the minister to the sickroom, while the well-educated physician was trying to oust him. There is no evidence that this concept received a receptive audience. 55 notes. M. Kaufman

535. Wilson, C. Edward. THE BOSTON INOCULATION CONTROVERSY: A REVISIONIST INTERPRETATION. *Journalism Hist. 1980 7(1): 16-19, 40.* Criticizes the contention that James Franklin's *New-England Courant* launched the first newspaper crusade in America over inoculation against smallpox in Boston in 1721 during a smallpox epidemic, when the paper "took an anti-inoculation stance," a position that the town government also took, and did not necessarily help free the press of government restrictions by "publishing in spite of authority" since the authority agreed with the paper.

536. —. THE TREATMENT OF THE POOR IN COLONIAL CHARLESTON. *Pro. of the South Carolina Hist. Assoc. 1980: 1-35.*
Ulmer, Barbara. BENEVOLENCE IN COLONIAL CHARLESTON, *pp. 1-12.* Examines the city's treatment of the poor from 1712 to 1775, when the vestry of St. Phillip's Parish administered poor relief, assessing parishioners according to "their land, slaves and money at interest." They tried to avoid paying the expenses of transients but did usually provide them with at least enough money to get out of the city. The motivation of the men involved seems to be more humanitarian than fear of the mob. Based on published works and the minutes of the vestry of St. Phillip's Church; 22 notes.
Fraser, Walter J., Jr. CONTROLLING THE POOR IN COLONIAL CHARLES TOWN, *pp. 13-30.* Analyzes the effects of the Charleston city government to control the poor between 1732 and 1775. Because of the rapid increase in the numbers of the poor, the merchant and professional elite believed that they were a threat to lives and property. They attempted to control them with a town watch, harsh laws, and some poor relief. Their efforts, however, were frustrated by British officials and the South Carolina assembly. Based on government documents, minutes of the vestry and published works; 47 notes.
Cart, Theodore W. and Pruden, George B., Jr. RICH AND POOR IN THE PORT CITY, *pp. 31-35.* Notes that the articles agree on the means used to deal with the poor but not the motives. A broader study of the subject would add additional insight. 3 notes.
J. W. Thacker, Jr.

3. CRUSADES IN THE NEW REPUBLIC, 1783-1860

General

537. Ashworth, John. THE JACKSONIAN AS LEVELLER. *J. of Am. Studies [Great Britain] 1980 14(3): 407-421.* Ever present in Jacksonianism was a particularistic view of equality, here described as "levelling," which Democrats refined and articulated from 1836 to 1846. Jacksonian social theory advocated equal opportunity, and, though human differences rendered the outcomes among people unequal, the societal resultant of levelling approximated true equality of conditions. Levelling, Jacksonians believed, proceeded when government allowed individual self-interest to assert itself and, in turn, members of society achieved substantial equality of wealth. These ideas particularly shaped Jacksonian era decisions on westward expansion, tariffs, immigration, and Democratic views on moral and religious questions. Primary and contemporary newspaper sources; 28 notes.
H. T. Lovin

538. Baum, Dale. KNOW-NOTHINGISM AND THE REPUBLICAN MAJORITY IN MASSACHUSETTS: THE POLITICAL REALIGNMENT OF THE 1850'S. *J. of Am. Hist. 1978 64(4): 959-986.* During the 1850's in Massachusetts, nativism and antislavery were distinct as political forces. The success of the Republican Party in Massachusetts after 1855 did not depend significantly upon attracting former Know-Nothing voters. Even though the Native American Party enjoyed a brief and phenomenal success in the state, it still represented only a temporary stop for many voters searching for a true antislavery party. The Know-Nothing Party played a minor role in the transition from a Whig to a Republican Party in Massachusetts politics. Uses ecological regression to trace voters' transitions and alignments during the 1850's. 25 tables, 53 notes.
T. P. Linkfield

539. Beeton, Beverly. TEACH THEM TO TILL THE SOIL: AN EXPERIMENT WITH INDIAN FARMS 1850-1862. *Am. Indian Q.: A J. of Anthrop., Hist., and Literature 1977-78 3(4): 299-320.* In the 1850's, the Utah Superintendency of Indian Affairs experimented with an Indian farm system. A reservation-farm system would contain and pacify Indians and employ some whites. Agent Garland Hurt brought the program to a high point in 1857, but the new Utah Superintendent of Indian Affairs, Jacob Forney, opposed the plan and mismanaged funds. In the final years, farms degenerated and cultivation virtually ceased. The program did concentrate and control Indians, possibly preventing more severe exploitation, and provided employment for settlers. Primary sources; 52 notes.
G. L. Olson

540. Bochin, Hal W. TOM CORWIN'S SPEECH AGAINST THE MEXICAN WAR: COURAGEOUS BUT MISUNDERSTOOD. *Ohio Hist. 1981 90(1): 33-53.* Discusses Thomas Corwin's eloquent and emotional appeal delivered to the US Senate on 11 February 1847. Corwin's words allied him to the growing antiwar faction in the House of Representatives. Although he was attempting to unify the Whig Party stand he was misunderstood and served to further alienate the various intraparty factions. For a while the most praised and reviled speech against the Mexican War, Corwin's address formed the core of an important issue in the 1848 presidential election. Based on the archives of the Ohio Historical Society, the Indiana State Historical Society, the Indiana State Library, and the Library of Congress, the *Congressional Globe*, and other primary sources; photo, fig., 82 notes.
L. A. Russell

541. Boles, John B. JOHN HERSEY: DISSENTING THEOLOGIAN OF ABOLITIONISM, PERFECTIONISM, AND MILLENNIALISM. *Methodist Hist. 1976 14(4): 215-234.* John Hersey (1786-1862), a devout Methodist, turned from mercantilism to preaching in his 20's. Through his preaching and his writings he was a consistent foe of slavery, urged Christians to strive for perfection in their beliefs, stressed that parenthood presented the Christian with great responsibilities, and the millennium was yet to come. Based on Hersey's books; 97 notes.
H. L. Calkin

542. Carriere, Marcus. POLITICAL LEADERSHIP OF THE LOUISIANA KNOW-NOTHING PARTY. *Louisiana Hist. 1980 21(2): 183-195.* Analysis of the age, wealth, and occupation of Louisiana's political leaders in the 1850's indicates that the American or Know-Nothing Party in this state differed significantly from its counterparts elsewhere. In Louisiana, the American Party was not exclusively the party of lawyers, businessmen, and older wealthy planters. Only in areas that lacked large concentrations of slaves did older wealth support the Americans. Moreover, Democrats and Americans in Louisiana were in many ways more similar than different. Based on 1860 US Census records; 7 tables, 44 notes.
D. B. Touchstone

543. Cirillo, Vincent J. EDWARD BLISS FOOTE: PIONEER AMERICAN ADVOCATE OF BIRTH CONTROL. *Bull. of the Hist. of Medicine 1973 47(5): 471-479.* Edward Bliss Foote, a New York physician, entered this controversy in 1858 with the first edition of his *Medical Common Sense*.
S

544. Clement, Priscilla Ferguson. THE PHILADELPHIA WELFARE CRISIS OF THE 1820's. *Pennsylvania Mag. of Hist. and Biog. 1981 105(2): 150-165.* The depression following the War of 1812 created unemployment and suffering for which Philadelphia's leaders, similar to leaders in other urban centers, blamed the "intemperate" poor and inefficient welfare officials. The harsh poor law reform of 1828 was alleviated only with the advent of better times. Based on documents in the Philadelphia City Archives, official records, printed sources, and secondary works; 27 notes.
T. H. Wendel

545. Cleveland, Len G. THE CRAWFORD-BURNSIDE AFFAIR AND THE MOVEMENT TO ABOLISH DUELING IN GEORGIA. *Res. Studies 1976 44(4): 241-247.* Offers a short history of attempts to abolish dueling in Georgia, 1809-28 and the single most important event, a duel between George W. Crawford and Thomas E. Burnside, which cinched legislation prohibiting the custom.

546. Creagh, Ronald. THE AGE OF REFORM: A REAPPRAISAL. *Rev. Française d'Etudes Américaines [France] 1978 3(5): 7-18.* Examines the role of the reformer during 1830's-50's with regard to common patterns of action: communitarian life, campaigns of propaganda, and cooperativism.

547. Danbom, David B. THE YOUNG AMERICA MOVEMENT. *J. of the Illinois State Hist. Soc. 1974 67(3): 294-306.* Young America was a loose coalition of young Democrats from the newer states in the early 1850's whose most important members were George Sanders of Kentucky and Stephen A. Douglas. Although both supported expansionism and intervention on the side of foreign republican movements, domestically they were Jeffersonian-Jacksonians. The movement's decline by 1856 was due to unsuccessful challenges to "old fogy" leaders, Douglas' failure to win the presidential nomination in 1852, an inability to deal with the slavery issue, and rising isolationism and disenchantment with reform in America. Primary and secondary sources; 2 illus., 30 notes.
L. Woolfe

548. Dublin, Thomas. WOMEN, WORK, AND PROTEST IN THE EARLY LOWELL MILLS: "THE OPPRESSING HAND OF AVARICE WOULD ENSLAVE US." *Labor Hist. 1975 16(1): 99-116.* The organization of work and the nature of housing in Lowell promoted the development of a sense of community among the women workers. The women relied upon the element of community in strikes in 1834 and 1836, and in the political action of the 1840's. The cultural traditions emergent involved preindustrial and industrial values. Based on records of the Hamilton Manufacturing Co. and on the *Lowell Offering*; 36 notes.
L. L. Athey

549. DuBois, Ellen. WOMEN'S RIGHTS AND ABOLITION: THE NATURE OF THE CONNECTION. Perry, Lewis and Fellman, Michael, ed. *Antislavery Reconsidered: New Perspectives on the Abolitionists* (Baton Rouge: Louisiana State U. Pr., 1979): 238-251. Although such

prominent feminists as Elizabeth Cady Stanton, Susan B. Anthony, Angelina Grimké, and Lucretia Mott did not receive their initial inspiration for their views on women's rights from the antislavery movement, they were ardent abolitionists and they borrowed numerous tactics and expressions of principles from the antislavery arsenal. 21 notes.   S

550. Friedman, Lawrence J. RACISM AND SEXISM IN ANTEBELLUM AMERICA: THE PRUDENCE CRANDALL EPISODE RECONSIDERED. *Societas 1974 4(3): 211-227.* In 1830 Prudence Crandall (1803-90) opened a school for black girls in Canterbury, Connecticut, which caused a storm of protest. The author reexamines the incident not only as an example of northern racism, but as an example of the problems white male abolitionists had in dealing with strong-willed women and sexuality. Discusses William Lloyd Garrison's personal and professional relationship with Crandall. 53 notes.
W. H. Mulligan, Jr.

551. Gifford, James M. SOME NEW LIGHT ON HENRY CLAY AND THE AMERICAN COLONIZATION SOCIETY. *Filson Club Hist. Q. 1976 50(4): 372-374.* Reproduces a recently discovered Henry Clay letter. Clay accepted the presidency of the American Colonization Society on 22 December 1836. In his letter Clay expressed the hope that all freed blacks would be separated from whites. The author speculates on possible political motives for Clay's acceptance. The letter is located in the Ralph R. Gurley Papers at the New York Historical Society Library. 10 notes.
G. B. McKinney

552. Gordon, Ann D. THE YOUNG LADIES ACADEMY OF PHILADELPHIA. Berkin, Carol Ruth and Norton, Mary Beth, ed. *Women of America: A History* (Boston: Houghton Mifflin Co., 1979): 68-91. Although founded by men in Philadelphia in 1787, the Young Ladies Academy offered girls an education similar to that given to boys. The founders were college-educated and felt that the education of women would raise the tenor of the entire society by cultivating reason and religion. The pupils were daughters of well-to-do families, and, although they did not go on into business or professions, the school did symbolize a recognition of the importance of women's ideas in the late 18th century. Based on published addresses of trustees and students, two of which are included; illus., 11 notes.
K. Talley

553. Green, Nancy. FEMALE EDUCATION AND SCHOOL COMPETITION: 1820-1850. *Hist. of Educ. Q. 1978 18(2): 129-142.* The fact that girls in schools prompted reconsideration of a school practice (competition for prizes) and the rejection of this practice in turn was integrated into educational theory. At first, "the argument for education of females centered on its importance for their effectiveness as mothers," but the influence of Catharine Beecher, Sarah Josepha Hale, and others broadened it to include their potential as teachers. This period saw the first public school to admit girls, followed by female seminaries which were forerunners of colleges for women. The use of prizes is discussed at length. "Emulation" (competition) slackened. By 1860, schoolmarms outnumbered schoolmasters in most states. Schooling became an avenue into a productive role for middle-class women outside the home. 54 notes.
E. P. Stickney

554. Gribbin, William. REPUBLICANISM, REFORM, AND THE SENSE OF SIN IN ANTE BELLUM AMERICA. *Cithara 1974 14(1): 25-42.* Discusses social reform movements in antebellum America and their emphasis on sin rather than injustice or inequality.   S

555. Hammett, Theodore M. TWO MOBS OF JACKSONIAN BOSTON: IDEOLOGY AND INTEREST. *J. of Am. Hist. 1976 62(4): 845-868.* Using two dissimilar mob actions occurring in Boston, discusses the interaction of ideas and interests as the main basis for ideological development. Compares the burning of an Ursuline Convent by a mob of poor, Protestant laborers on 11 August 1834 with the Massachusetts Anti-Slavery Society riot of 24 October 1835 (by "wealthier," establishment types). Contemporaries saw one as a danger to society, the latter as righteous action against society's disrupters. These two views represent society's bipartiality in developing ideological responses to events affecting it. Economics and class structure determine "rightness." 5 tables, 70 notes.
V. P. Rilee

556. Hammond, John L. REVIVALS, CONSENSUS, AND AMERICAN POLITICAL CULTURE. *J. of the Am. Acad. of Religion 1978 46(3): 293-314.* A critical analysis of 19th-century revivalism in the United States and the major interpretations which have been proposed to explain its influence on American culture politics. Past interpretations explained the revivals in terms of pietist political dispositions, as an expression of Jacksonian democracy or in terms of a common national culture. Sees weaknesses in each of these theories and concludes that revivalists primarily were attempting to moralize politics. Secondary sources; 14 notes.
E. R. Lester

557. Heriksen, Thomas H. AFRICAN INTELLECTUAL INFLUENCES ON BLACK AMERICANS: THE ROLE OF EDWARD W. BLYDEN. *Phylon 1975 36(3): 279-290.* Studies the effect of African black intellectuals in moulding black ethnic consciousness in America. This can be seen especially through a study of the career of Edward W. Blyden, who was born in the Danish West Indian Island of St. Thomas in 1832 but who moved to Liberia in 1850. He emphasized four main themes in his defense of the Negro race: "it possessed past achievements worthy of pride; its African traditions and culture must be preserved; its progress was thwarted by adherence to Christianity and enhanced by the pursuit of Islam; and it had intrinsic qualities which he termed the "African personality." Also notes others influenced by him. 69 notes.
R. V. Ritter

558. Hersh, Blanche Glassman. "AM I NOT A WOMAN AND A SISTER?" ABOLITIONIST BEGINNINGS OF NINETEENTH-CENTURY FEMINISM. Perry, Lewis and Fellman, Michael, ed. *Antislavery Reconsidered: New Perspectives on the Abolitionists* (Baton Rouge: Louisiana State U. Pr., 1979): 252-283. Surveys the many strands of philosophies, sentiments, and religious beliefs that bound feminists such as Elizabeth Cady Stanton, Lydia Maria Child, and Maria Weston Chapman to the abolition movement. Although these strong-willed women were often reviled as unsexed upstarts by opponents of abolitionism and were frequently ignored by their male colleagues, they made extremely important contributions to both the antislavery movement and feminism. 53 notes.   S

559. Holt, Michael F. THE POLITICS OF IMPATIENCE: THE ORIGINS OF KNOW NOTHINGISM. *J. of Am. Hist. 1973 60(2): 309-331.* The Know-Nothing Party was the fastest growing political force in many parts of the United States, 1853-56, probably contributing to the disintegration of the Whig Party as much as did the slavery issue. Knownothingism fed on a surge of anti-Catholic sentiment among workers and the middle class in several eastern and midwestern states. These supporters were bewildered by rapid economic and social change and opposed political manipulators and the convention system. Voters previously identified with the traditional parties were impatient at their failure to take stands, especially on the issues of temperance and public schools. When the Know-Nothing Party nominated Millard Fillmore, many of its supporters turned to the Republicans who adopted the style and some issues of Know-Nothingism. 76 notes.
K. B. West

560. Horton, James Oliver. GENERATIONS OF PROTEST: BLACK FAMILIES AND SOCIAL REFORM IN ANTE-BELLUM BOSTON. *New England Q. 1976 49(2): 242-256.* Traces the roles of the Hall, Paul, Dalton, Neit, Snowden, Bayley, and Lewis families in Boston reform movements. Early leaders established and developed entirely black educational, religious, and masonic organizations. With William Lloyd Garrison's (1805-79) establishment of the New England Anti-Slavery Society during the 1830's they changed to integrated organizations advocating abolitionism and racial integration. Following the passage of the Fugitive Slave Act of 1850 black leaders became willing to take illegal action to assist runaways. Based on the records of black organizations and on secondary sources; 29 notes.
J. C. Bradford

561. Howard, Victor B. THE DOVES OF 1847: THE RELIGIOUS RESPONSE IN OHIO TO THE MEXICAN WAR. *Old Northwest 1979 5(3): 237-267.* By the autumn of 1847, opposition to the Mexican War among Ohio Protestant clergy and churches, especially in the Western Reserve and the area around Cincinnati, where New England influence was strongest, had become almost a crusade. Antiwar propaganda in religious journals created opposition to the war by convincing religious

people that slavery was its cause and stood to profit from it; at the same time, religious journalism created opposition to slavery by convincing its readers of that institution's aggressive nature. Primary sources; 65 notes.
E. L. Keyser

562. Jable, J. Thomas. ASPECTS OF REFORM IN EARLY NINETEENTH-CENTURY PENNSYLVANIA. *Pennsylvania Mag. of Hist. and Biog. 1978 102(3): 344-363.* Intense in Pennsylvania, the Second Great Awakening's moral stewards used restrictive legislation and organization to inculcate their regenerative values during 1794-1860. They aimed at, among others, gambling, dancing, pleasure halls, horse racing, and they inculcated Sabbatarianism. Official records, printed sources, and secondary works; 72 notes.
T. H. Wendel

563. Kerber, Linda K. THE ABOLITIONIST PERCEPTION OF THE INDIAN. *J. of Am. Hist. 1975 62(2): 271-295.* Reviews the attitudes of prominent abolitionists (Lydia Child, James G. Birney, James Russell Lowell, John Greenleaf Whittier, John Quincy Adams, congressmen, Quakers, and missionaries) toward the Indian question from the 1820's to the 1880's. Many abolitionists perceived the Indian and slave questions in similar terms of race, and they advocated integration of Indians into American society rather than respect for tribal culture and identity. This oversimplification may have prevented real progress toward a practicable solution to the Indian question. Based on contemporary literature, poetry, journals, and newspapers, and on secondary works; 55 notes.
J. B. Street

564. Kremm, Thomas W. THE OLD ORDER TREMBLES: THE FORMATION OF THE REPUBLICAN PARTY IN OHIO. *Cincinnati Hist. Soc. Bull. 1978 36(3): 193-212.* The demise of the Whig Party and the growth in popularity of the Republican Party was due to anti-Catholicism, hostility toward Ohio's political system, and opposition to slavery extension, 1850's.

565. Levesque, George A. INHERENT REFORMERS—INHERITED ORTHODOXY: BLACK BAPTISTS IN BOSTON, 1800-1873. *J. of Negro Hist. 1975 60(4): 491-519.* Describes the early development of the black Baptist movement in Boston in the 1800's, including the foundation of a separate church in 1805 under the leadership of Thomas Paul and Scipio Dalton. Overt discrimination was not the principal motive for starting a new church, inasmuch as the parent churches financed and assisted the African offshoot. The black movement grew from a religious revival and an expansion of the black community, forced increasingly to live and work in one particular area. Considers how the new church was drawn into politics and the movement for social reform. 3 tables, 36 notes.
C. A. McNeill

566. Mallett, Richard P. MAINE CRUSADES AND CRUSADERS, 1830-1850. *Maine Hist. Soc. Q. 1978 17(4): 183-208.* Describes reforms of concern to citizens of Maine, during 1830-50: the peace movement, abolitionism, temperance, state and private lotteries, women's rights, problems of the insane, and capital punishment. Discusses the roles of Edward Payson and William Ladd in the peace movement, General Samuel Fessenden in the abolitionist cause, and Neal Dow in temperance reform. 34 notes.
P. C. Marshall

567. Mathews, Donald G. CHARLES COLCOCK JONES AND THE SOUTHERN EVANGELICAL CRUSADE TO FORM A BIRACIAL COMMUNITY. *J. of Southern Hist. 1975 41(3): 299-320.* Charles Colcock Jones, reformist clergyman of the antebellum period, was early disturbed by the slaveholding South in which he resided. He resolved to improve the lot of the Negro, but was sufficiently wise to recognize that any reform must enlist the support of whites. He appealed to the Christian religious conscience, hoping to remake the Negro in the white man's image. He avoided confrontation. Support was reluctantly forthcoming. Jones' personal life was exemplary, but he failed really to change anything. The future biracial Utopia he envisioned became a blueprint for postwar religious reformers. 50 notes.
V. L. Human

568. McElroy, James L. SOCIAL CONTROL AND ROMANTIC REFORM IN ANTEBELLUM AMERICA: THE CASE OF ROCHESTER, NEW YORK. *New York Hist. 1977 58(1): 17-46.* Examines reform studies of antebellum Rochester, New York, to test the paradoxical association between radical reform and conservative religious benevolence. Religious revivalism led converts first to religious benevolence and then to radical reform. The divisive anti-slavery issue, secularizaton of social control, and lessened interest in religious revivalism resulted with the decline of conservative religious benevolence. These reform movements were supported mostly by white collar groups. Younger people were attracted to radical reform. 5 illus., table, 69 notes.
R. N. Lokken

569. Moorhead, James H. SOCIAL REFORM AND THE DIVIDED CONSCIENCE OF ANTEBELLUM PROTESTANTISM. *Church Hist. 1979 48(4): 416-430.* Besides endorsing the antislavery and temperance causes, the great evangelist Charles G. Finney inspired converts to work out their salvation through useful service, including reform. Central to Finney's undertaking of reform was his belief that virtue consisted in disinterested benevolence. Benevolence was a doctrine of fermentation whose utilitarian principles potentially undermined any institutions failing to meet its rigorous test and it encouraged an open-ended search for new ways to realize its imperative. If Finney's career attested to the powerful, even volatile, potential of popular Protestantism for reform, it demonstrated equally the movement's deficiencies in providing a sustained critique of social problems and in offering policies for their improvement. 58 notes.
M. D. Dibert

570. Mott, Wesley T. EMERSON AND ANTINOMIANISM: THE LEGACY OF THE SERMONS. *Am. Literature 1978 50(3): 369-397.* Relates Ralph Waldo Emerson's spiritual tradition to his position in the broad transcendentalist impulse. Emerson's sermons reflected a spiritual position indicating the classic Puritan middle way between legalism and Antinomianism. While emphasizing faith and grace, Emerson never abandoned the idea that man must also perform works. In a similar fashion, Emerson approached the romantic social reform movements of his time as mixtures of spiritual enthusiasm and practical self-improvement. Emerson's Puritan legacy of balance shaped both his religion and his social consciousness during his intellectual evolution toward Transcendentalism. 26 notes.
T. P. Linkfield

571. Murison, Barbara C. "ENLIGHTENED GOVERNMENT": SIR GEORGE ARTHUR AND THE UPPER CANADIAN ADMINISTRATION. *J. of Imperial and Commonwealth Hist. [Great Britain] 1980 8(3): 161-180.* Discusses the role of Sir George Arthur (1784-1854) as Lieutenant Governor of Upper Canada from the Rebellion to the Union (1837-41). Coming to the post with considerable experience and a record of being a reformer, Arthur soon found that his hands were tied by the Colonial Office, but he managed to make important contributions and initiated almost every reform that was carried out by his successor. Based on the Arthur Papers and materials in the Ottawa Archives and the Colonial Office Papers at the Public Record Office, London; 87 notes.
M. D. Rosenfield

572. Park, Roberta J. THE ATTITUDES OF LEADING NEW ENGLAND TRANSCENDENTALISTS TOWARD HEALTHFUL EXERCISE, ACTIVE RECREATIONS AND PROPER CARE OF THE BODY, 1830-1860. *J. of Sport Hist. 1977 4(1): 34-50.* Examines attitudes of leading New England transcendentalists, generally finding that Ralph Waldo Emerson (1803-82), William Ellery Channing (1780-1842), Henry David Thoreau (1817-62), Amos Bronson Alcott (1799-1888), and Margaret Fuller (1810-50) agreed on the need for a healthy body. Their writings introduced a wide reading audience to ideas regarding the body as a means to attaining "higher consciousness," and to their attitudes toward health, exercise, play, and recreations. 53 notes.
M. Kaufman

573. Park, Roberta J. "EMBODIED SELVES": THE RISE AND DEVELOPMENT OF CONCERN FOR PHYSICAL EDUCATION, ACTIVE GAMES AND RECREATION FOR AMERICAN WOMEN, 1776-1865. *J. of Sport Hist. 1978 5(2): 5-41.* Starting in the 1790's, American men and women increasingly argued that women were more capable, stronger, healthier, and wiser, than was commonly believed. There was substantial interest in the health and physical education of women during 1776-1865. People advocated calisthenics, games, exercise, less confining clothes, instruction in anatomy and physiology, and healthier school and home environments. These efforts set the stage for the development of curricular physical education and extracurricular sports programs for women. 109 notes.
M. Kaufman

574. Parker, Harold M., Jr. A SCHOOL OF THE PROPHETS AT MARYVILLE. *Tennessee Hist. Q. 1975 34(1): 72-90.* In 1819 Dr. Isaac Anderson began the Southern and Western Theological Seminary in Maryville, Tennessee, with the idea of providing religious training for Presbyterian ministers in an area where there was a shortage. The seminary set a high intellectual standard, grew rapidly, and became a center of abolitionism. Failing financial support, divisions within the church, and agitation over slavery led to the demise of the seminary in the late 1850's. Secondary sources; 55 notes.   M. B. Lucas

575. Payne, John Howard. THE CHEROKEE CAUSE. *J. of Cherokee Studies 1976 1(1): 17-22.* Reprints a letter, dated 11 October 1835, in defense of the Cherokee Indians. In the late 1820's and early 1830's the Cherokees were pressured by the US federal government and the state of Georgia to cede their eastern lands and migrate west. John Howard Payne, after meeting the antiremoval leader John Ross, attacked both the United States and Georgia for forcing the Cherokees out. He defended the Cherokees as a civilized group who should be allowed to remain on their native land. The letter was read into the Congressional records of the time but otherwise has never been published before. Editorial comment; illus.
   J. M. Lee

576. Quarles, Benjamin. BLACK HISTORY'S ANTEBELLUM ORIGINS. *Pro. of the Am. Antiquarian Soc. 1979 89(1): 89-122.* Surveys efforts by blacks before the Civil War to develop their history. Black leaders denied the theory of an ignoble Afro-American past and brought forth data to refute this indictment. They accused whites of deliberately omitting black achievements and of bias in presenting a picture of black life. These efforts were primarily motivated by racial considerations, and black leaders tried to engender a sense of race pride and to develop a black self-identity. 122 notes.   J. A. Andrew

577. Reinier, Jacqueline S. REARING THE REPUBLICAN CHILD: ATTITUDES AND PRACTICES IN POST-REVOLUTIONARY PHILADELPHIA. *William and Mary Q. 1982 39(1): 150-163.* Analyzes the didactic literature pertaining to child-rearing and education of the period. British books were revised to fit the American environment. Also American lesson books extolled heroes of the American Revolution. Benjamin Rush's writings serve as an example of efforts to achieve an adaptation of republican principles to child-rearing. Protestant beliefs played a central role. Authors of children's literature combined associationist psychology with Christian doctrine. Based on educational literature and manuscripts of the period; 42 notes.   H. M. Ward

578. Reynolds, John F. PIETY AND POLITICS: EVANGELISM IN THE MICHIGAN LEGISLATURE, 1837-1861. *Michigan Hist. 1977 61(4): 322-351.* Statistical analysis of roll-call votes in the Michigan House of Representatives during 1837-60 confirms the complexity of political motive during the Jacksonian Era. Neither the class conflict theory nor the ethnocultural, or "evangelical," approach fully explains voting on such issues as slavery, temperance, adultery, and public prayer. Although non-Democrats supported evangelical legislation in greater number, the major political parties were generally similar in their stands regarding such measures. Bills and resolutions regarding slavery were the most divisive partisan issues. Although there was a degree of evangelical cleavage, neither the Democrats nor the Whigs capitalized on it. Primary sources; 30 notes, 8 illus., 2 photos, 4 tables.   D. W. Johnson

579. Rotundo, Barbara. THE RURAL CEMETERY MOVEMENT. *Essex Inst. Hist. Collections 1973 109(3): 231-240.* Discusses the rural cemetery movement in America during the early 19th century as a reform movement, and comments on cultural aesthetic significance.   S

580. Shpotov, B. M. VOSSTANIE AMERIKANSKIKH FERMEROV POD RUKOVODSTVOM D. SHEISA (1786-1787 G.G.) [The uprising of American farmers led by Daniel Shays (1786-1787)]. *Novaia i Noveishaia Istoriia [USSR] 1975 (4): 54-68.* The establishment of the USA was accompanied by the acute class struggle waged by small farmers and artisans against the ruling elite. The uprising led by Daniel Shays was the greatest popular movement in the period of the American Revolution and one of the most significant actions by farmers throughout the history of the USA. It was an attempt to deepen the bourgeois revolution in America with plebeian methods. However, it suffered fiasco as a result of which the power of the ruling bloc was strengthened and extended.   J

581. Smith, Robert E. THE CLASH OF LEADERSHIP AT THE GRAND RESERVE: THE WYANDOT SUBAGENCY AND THE METHODIST MISSION, 1820-1824. *Ohio Hist. 1980 89(2): 181-205.* In 1820 John Shaw was appointed subagent to John Johnson, Indian agent at Piqua, Ohio. The jurisdiction of the latter was over the Wyandots, Shawnees, and Seneca residing in Ohio. Shaw arrived in Upper Sandusky, Ohio, on 11 November 1820 to fill his post. A clash of wills, however, occurred between Shaw and Methodist missionary James B. Finley. Finley sought to "civilize" and Christianize the Wyandots, and then improve their standard of living. Shaw, however, sought to improve their standard of living whether they became Christians or not. Finley accused Shaw of inciting the Indians to return to their pagan ways and was successful in getting Shaw dismissed from his post in 1824. Primary sources; 57 notes.   J. Powell

582. Tyrrell, Alexander. MAKING THE MILLENNIUM: THE MID-NINETEENTH CENTURY PEACE MOVEMENT. *Hist. J. [Great Britain] 1978 21(1): 75-95.* The mid-19th century Anglo-American peace movement culminated in a series of four peace congresses convened in Brussels, Paris, Frankfurt, and London between 1848-51. The author views the peace movement as but one manifestation of a new model of Nonconformist philanthropy. In the 1830's many Nonconformists began to work for the future in explicitly millennial terms. Local groups, such as the London Peace Society, founded in 1816, grew naturally out of the Anglo-American vision of a millennial *respublica christiana*. The specific proposals of the peace movement were a mixture of practicality and idealism. Despite the best intentions of Richard Cobden (1804-65) and others, the American Civil War soon ushered in the demise of the mid-19th-century peace movement. Based on peace congress reports, committee minutes, other primary and secondary sources; 87 notes.
   L. J. Reith

583. Walters, Ronald G. THE FAMILY AND ANTE-BELLUM REFORM: AN INTERPRETATION. *Societas 1973 3(3): 221-232.* From the 1820's to after the Civil War, an unprecedented flood of nonfiction writing analyzed the family. Conservatives and reformers agreed on the redeeming value of the family and that something was wrong or about to go wrong with the family. All hoped that the family rightly ordered would lead to stability and moral progress. Concern for the family was largely the product of the turbulent economics of Jacksonian America. 16 notes.   E. P. Stickney

584. Weathersby, Robert W., II. J. H. INGRAHAM AND TENNESSEE: A RECORD OF SOCIAL AND LITERARY CONTRIBUTIONS. *Tennessee Hist. Q. 1975 34(3): 264-272.* Joseph Holt Ingraham (1809-60), though a resident of Nashville for a short duration (1847-51), made a significant and lasting contribution to Tennessee. A novelist called to the Episcopalian ministry late in life, Ingraham studied theology in Nashville where he was a schoolteacher and a vigorous advocate of penal reform and a public school system. Primary and secondary sources; 31 notes.   M. B. Lucas

585. Weinbaum, Paul O. TEMPERANCE, POLITICS, AND THE NEW YORK CITY RIOTS OF 1857. *New York Hist. Soc. Q. 1975 59(3): 246-270.* During the 1850's there was much violence in urban areas of the United States. Investigates the connection between the New York City riots of 1857, ostensibly caused by the activities of temperance forces, and local politics, particularly of the Irish and German factions. Although the temperance campaign was the chief incitement to Irish and German rioting, it was only incidental to political violence with political action that led to larger participation in city politics. Primary sources; 7 illus., 45 notes.   C. L. Grant

586. Wellman, Judith. WOMEN AND RADICAL REFORM IN ANTEBELLUM UPSTATE NEW YORK: A PROFILE OF GRASSROOTS FEMALE ABOLITIONISTS. Deutrich, Mabel E. and Purdy, Virginia C., ed. *Clio Was a Woman: Studies in the History of American Women* (Washington, D.C.: Howard U. Pr., 1980): 113-127. In 1835 women joined men petitioning in one of the largest reform campaigns of the 19th century, sending petitions to Congress for the abolition of slavery. The petitions from one small area of upstate New York, 1838-39, provide information on women within the abolition movement, almost immediately resisted. Women abolitionists faced not only hostile or ambiguous responses from many males within the movement; they also

discovered that their proslavery opponents used female political participation to demean not only women petitioners but also abolition itself. A discussion summary follows. National Archives; 3 tables, 26 notes.
J. Powell

587. Wennersten, John R. PARKE GODWIN, UTOPIAN SOCIALISM, AND THE POLITICS OF ANTISLAVERY. *New York Hist. Soc. Q. 1976 60(3/4): 107-127.* A study of the career of Parke Godwin (1816-1904) shows how the antislavery issue divided American antebellum reformers and virtually ended the movement for utopian socialism. Princetonian Godwin, a journalist and associate of William Cullen Bryant and William Leggett, became a follower of Charles Fourier and an opponent of abolitionism which, he believed, would result in interracial conflict. He became involved in Brook Farm until he broke with its members over Texas, but was forced to continue partisan political journalism to support his family. By the end of the Mexican War both Brook Farm and the socialist movement had ended; yet Godwin continued to work for economic reform and to strive for perfection. His career indicated "both the idealism and the naivete of American Fourierists." Personal writings and correspondence; 2 illus., 42 notes.
C. L. Grant

588. Whitmore, Allan R. "A GUARD OF FAITHFUL SENTINELS": THE KNOW-NOTHING APPEAL IN MAINE, 1854-1855. *Maine Hist. Soc. Q. 1981 20(3): 151-197.* Traces the rise and fall of the Know-Nothing Party in Maine from the summer of 1854 through 1855. Support for the anti-Catholic nativism grew rapidly among the working class, a result of irrational fears, the appeal of a highly secretive organization, and its leaders' demagoguery. When Know-Nothing aid helped Anson P. Morrill win the gubernatorial election of September 1854, the party reached its pinnacle. Its decline began in early 1855. Morrill generally ignored its claims, the national party's apparent proslavery position alienated Mainers, the newly formed (February 1855) Maine Republican Party had a wider appeal, and the local party was tainted with corruption and its basic fanaticism recognized. Most defectors moved into the Republican Party. Illus., 131 notes.
C. A. Watson

Civil Liberties and Political Rights

589. Barnes, Joseph W. OBEDIAH DOGBERRY, ROCHESTER FREETHINKER. *Rochester Hist. 1974 36(3): 1-24.* Obediah Dogberry fought for religious liberty and freedom of thought in Rochester, New York, through the *Liberal Advocate*, a newspaper published during 1832-34.

590. Christian, Marcus. DEMAND BY MEN OF COLOR FOR RIGHTS IN ORLEANS TREATY. *Negro Hist. Bull. 1973 36(3): 54-57.* Discusses the Treaty of Cession (1804) and the fight which Negro freedmen waged to procure civil rights.
S

591. Dennison, George M. THE DORR WAR AND POLITICAL QUESTIONS. *Supreme Court Hist. Soc. Y. 1979: 45-62.* Reviews Luther v. Borden (1849), a Supreme Court decision affecting Dorr's Rebellion, the effort of Rhode Islanders in 1842 to establish a shadow government because of restrictive voting regulations which they perceived as making legal change impossible. An influx of immigrants and an exodus of natives had changed the demographic face of the state, but the old agricultural laws remained in force. A league formed to go directly to the people voted into office its own state government, which resulted in the charter government calling out the national guard. The Suffragists, failing politically, turned to the courts. But the Supreme Court ruled against them, arguing that the constitutional right to change governments was unquestioned, but that the US Supreme Court did not have the authority to interfere in state matters. 5 illus., 77 notes.
V. L. Human

592. Edwards, Malcolm. "THE WAR OF COMPLEXIONAL DISTINCTION": BLACKS IN GOLD RUSH CALIFORNIA AND BRITISH COLUMBIA. *California Hist. Q. 1977 56(1): 34-45.* Describes how blacks in the California gold rush, disillusioned at discriminatory laws passed by the state legislature and at court decisions upholding unfair actions against them, migrated to British Columbia in the late 1850's. The state of California attempted several times to exclude free blacks from admission to California; blacks could not testify in civil and criminal actions involving whites, were excluded from jury service, and lived under other legal restrictions. Such cases as the Archy Lee case, in which the state supreme court bent the law in order to restore Lee to slave status, indicated the views of white Californians on blacks. In 1858 blacks began to migrate to British Columbia because of an indirect invitation from its Governor, James Douglas. As many as 800 blacks may have headed north. Unfortunately, although British Columbia did not codify discrimination into law, whites there displayed overt prejudice. They refused to attend integrated church services and denied blacks public accommodations. In 1864 a black militia, organized for protection of the colony against Indians, was refused permission to take part in public ceremonies. Finding their welcome little better than in California, most blacks returned to the United States after the Civil War and the enactment of new constitutional amendments. Primary and secondary sources; photos, 37 notes.
A. Hoffman

593. Erickson, Leonard. POLITICS AND THE REPEAL OF OHIO'S BLACK LAWS, 1837-1849. *Ohio Hist. 1973 82(3/4): 154-175.* Ohio's Black Laws were passed in 1804 and 1807. A movement for their repeal began in the 1830's. When the Liberty Party held the balance of power in the 1840's, the movement gained strength. In 1846 the issue attracted statewide attention. Before 1849 Western Reserve Whigs led the movement for repeal which Democrats opposed; but Whigs were insufficiently cohesive in favoring repeal to accomplish that goal. Freesoilers made inroads in 1848. In 1849 the Democrats, in control of the legislature, pushed repeal successfully in order to undercut abolition support for the Whig Party. 3 maps, 3 tables, 36 notes.
S. S. Sprague

594. Green, Jesse C., Jr. THE EARLY VIRGINIA ARGUMENT FOR SEPARATION OF CHURCH AND STATE. *Baptist Hist. and Heritage 1976 11(1): 16-26.* The struggle (ca. 1775-1810) of Virginia Baptists for the disestablishment of the state church and the privilege of freedom of religion for all men has had great implications for both the church and state in America. Three doctrines served as the foundation for the Baptist position: the nature of salvation, the nature of the church, and a belief in the necessity for the separation of civil and ecclesiastical authority. Baptists did not achieve separation of church and state alone (for the active aid of Jefferson and Madison was also a considerable factor), but did serve as a constant reminder of the necessity of securing what they believed to be the inalienable rights of men. Based largely on the writings of John Leland and other primary sources; 62 notes.
H. M. Parker, Jr.

595. Kraut, Alan M. and Field, Phyllis F. POLITICS VERSUS PRINCIPLES: THE PARTISAN RESPONSE TO "BIBLE POLITICS" IN NEW YORK STATE. *Civil War Hist. 1979 25(2): 101-118.* To examine the sources of the strength of the US two-party system, investigates the response of the Democratic and Whig parties to the third-party morality-based political challenge of the abolitionist Liberty Party in New York, 1840-47. By 1845, the Liberty Party had become strong enough to affect the outcome of elections, so the major parties forced a referendum over a proposal to remove or modify a stiff property qualification that limited Negro suffrage. Racism prevailed, the measure was soundly defeated, and the Liberty Party soon lost strength. It underwent a schism in 1847 and folded in 1848. 5 tables, 55 notes.
S

596. McBride, David. BLACK PROTEST AGAINST RACIAL POLITICS: GARDNER, HINTON, AND THEIR MEMORIAL OF 1838. *Pennsylvania Hist. 1979 46(2): 149-162.* Black abolitionists Frederick A. Hinton and Reverend Charles W. Gardner played major roles in unsuccessful efforts to resist the disfranchisement of their race proposed by the Pennsylvania Constitutional Convention of 1837-38. Their *Memorial,* reprinted here, was an eloquent attempt to persuade the convention to reject disfranchisement. Both were leaders of the Philadelphia black community, were active in local and national abolitionist circles, and should be ranked with such black leaders as Robert Purvis, James Forten, and William Whipper. Primary sources; 2 photos, 46 notes.
D. C. Swift

597. McLaughlin, Tom L. GRASS-ROOTS ATTITUDES TOWARD BLACK RIGHTS IN TWELVE NONSLAVEHOLDING STATES, 1846-1869. *Mid-America 1974 56(2): 175-181.* One test of the common wisdom that the rights of free Negroes were eroding in the North

during the age of the common man is an evaluation of the voting patterns in 22 popular referenda held in 12 northern states. The evidence suggests that the Republican Party's ideological program was not far in advance of national opinion in stressing the basic humanity of Negroes and their need for protected civil rights. Based on primary sources; table, 9 notes.
T. D. Schoonover

598. McLoughlin, William G. EXPERIMENT IN CHEROKEE CITIZENSHIP, 1817-1829. *Am. Q. 1981 33(1): 3-25.* By the terms of an 1817 treaty, 342 Cherokee heads of families in Georgia, North Carolina, Tennessee, and Alabama accepted an American offer of citizenship and 640 acres each in exchange for leaving the reservation. Frontier whites, however, forcibly ejected many of these new citizens from their land and threatened many others with violence. While the federal government can be blamed for not preparing these Cherokee for citizenship, the major reason the plan failed was opposition from within the tribe to the plan and pressure from the tribal council to stay on tribal land. The strong desire to stay in the Cherokee homeland is shown by the 1819 exchange of 3.8 million acres for a nonremoval guarantee, an exchange that was made in vain. Based on primary sources on National Archives microfilm and a register of life estates in the Georgia State Archives; 59 notes.
D. K. Lambert

599. McManus, Michael J. WISCONSIN REPUBLICANS AND NEGRO SUFFRAGE: ATTITUDES AND BEHAVIOR, 1857. *Civil War Hist 1979 25(1): 36-54.* The debated existence and extent of Republican Party involvement in Negro rights can be tested in Wisconsin. This young, heterogeneous state voted on the Negro franchise in 1857. Hard necessity forced a party dedicated philosophically to spell out the practical effects. The Democrats made sure of this. The Republican state convention exposed the split on principle. Later, party candidates avoided mentioning suffrage; party editors proclaimed it. Wisconsin blacks joined the fray. Negro suffrage was defeated, but not by Republicans, who either voted for suffrage, or simply abstained. A majority of all voters in some manner called racism into question. Based on state documents, published and unpublished, newspapers, and some secondary sources; 67 notes.
R. E. Stack

600. McQuaid, Kim. WILLIAM APES, PEQUOT: AN INDIAN REFORMER IN THE JACKSON ERA. *New England Q. 1977 50(4): 605-625.* Sketches William Apes's (b. 1798) troubled youth and shows that his religious approach to Indian-white relations and his belief in racial equality was nonconformist during the era of Indian removal. Focuses on his leadership of the Wampanoag Indians of Mashpee, Massachusetts, in their partially successful struggle for control of their own political, economic and religious affairs. Based on Apes' writings and secondary sources; 29 notes.
J. C. Bradford

601. Ruffin, Thomas F. THE COMMON MAN FIGHTS BACK. *North Louisiana Hist. Assoc. J. 1976 7(3): 91-95.* The constitution of the State of Louisiana, written in 1812, allowed an individual to vote only if he paid a state tax, or proved he had purchased Federal lands within the state from Congress, for the latter was exempt from taxation for five years. Even though land was inexpensive, those two provisions effectively disenfranchised two-thirds of those men who would otherwise have been qualified to vote. Eventually, "someone discovered" that the state constitution "required only the purchase of lands from the United States, not the continued ownership." Thus, a number of individuals banded together to buy Federal lands, in order to gain the right to vote. Another method used by the common man to gain the vote was developed by John Slidell, who used a forgotten provision of the constitution—voting in one's county, even though by the 1840's counties existed in name only. The new constitution of 1845, and another written in 1852, gave the common man a more active voice in political matters.
A. N. Garland

The Slavery Question

602. Allen, Jeffrey Brooke. DID SOUTHERN COLONIZATIONISTS OPPOSE SLAVERY? KENTUCKY 1816-1850 AS A TEST CASE. *Register of the Kentucky Hist. Soc. 1977 75(2): 92-111.* Kentucky was chosen as case study to examine conflicting testimony given on southern colonizationists' attitudes toward slavery, because the state produced Henry Clay, the president of the American Colonization Society from 1836 to 1849. Examination of the records shows that many Kentucky colonizationists did make a sincere effort to eradicate slavery in the state. Primary and secondary sources; 43 notes.
J. F. Paul

603. Allen, Jeffrey Brooke. WERE SOUTHERN WHITE CRITICS OF SLAVERY RACISTS? KENTUCKY AND THE UPPER SOUTH, 1791-1824. *J. of Southern Hist. 1978 44(2): 169-190.* This study, primarily of Kentucky clergymen, challenges the idea that the majority of white antislavery southerners were racists. Historians have neglected a large group of religious men who defended the equality of blacks. Their antislavery arguments were directed against the abolitionist and the proslavery advocate, both of whom thought in racist terms. Praises the Kentucky clergymen's challenge to racism, but concedes that their eventual conversion to African colonization came, not as a result of their conversion to racism, but because of their having to function in a racist environment.
M. S. Legan

604. Baily, Marilyn. FROM CINCINNATI, OHIO TO WILBERFORCE, CANADA: A NOTE ON ANTEBELLUM COLONIZATION. *J. of Negro Hist. 1973 58(4): 427-440.* Recounts the movement of black people out of Cincinnati after the enforcement there of legislation patterned after southern slave codes in 1829. Several families traveled to a site near London, Ontario, which they called Wilberforce. Though ultimately unsuccessful, the black colony served as a symbol of the escape from slavery and thereby contributed to the struggle against that institution. Based on secondary sources; 35 notes.
N. G. Sapper

605. Barlett, Irving H., ed. NEW LIGHT ON WENDELL PHILLIPS: THE COMMUNITY OF REFORM, 1840-1880. *Perspectives in Am. Hist. 1979 12: 1-232.* In 1977, when Crawford Blagden, a great-great nephew of Wendell Phillips, discovered a large box of family papers in his basement, he decided to send the box, which contained thousands of letters to and from Phillips, to the Houghton Library at Harvard for proper care. Based on these letters, the author reexamines Phillips's career (he wrote *Wendell Phillips: Brahmin Radical* in 1961) by reassessing 1) "The Making of an Abolitionist" and 2) "Ann and Wendell Phillips," and by quoting liberally from the letters to demonstrate new discoveries about Phillips and the abolition movement in general. Reproduces 118 letters to and from Phillips, divided into 1) "Black and White Abolitionists" with letters to demonstrate "Ambivalent Images of Blacks" and how much Phillips was "A Benefactor to the Blacks," 2) letters illustrating his "Personal Philanthropy," 3) letters demonstrating his relationship to "The Politicians, the Press and the People," with separate sections on each, plus his "Critics and Abusers" and "The Ranks of the Faithful," and 4) letters which illustrate the relationship between "Phillips and [William Lloyd] Garrison."
W. A. Wiegand

606. Barney, Robert Knight. GERMAN TURNERS IN AMERICAN DOMESTIC CRISIS. *Stadion [West Germany] 1978 4(1): 344-357.* Northern Turners (members of German gymnastic-cultural clubs) naturally supported the Turner Bund's position on the abolition of slavery because it was compatible with Jahn-inherited principles of political ideology regarding human rights, and because the social and economic environment in which they lived was conducive to such a support. On the other hand, Turners from the Lower South often compromised the identically held creed in order to meet the social and economic conditions imposed on them by their environment. In the Upper South the slavery issue was less prominent. Thus, Turners there were able to exercise their naturally held antislavery attitudes. 41 notes.
M. Geyer

607. Berfield, Karen. THREE ANTISLAVERY LEADERS OF BUREAU COUNTY. *Western Illinois Regional Studies 1980 3(1): 46-65.* Discusses the abolitionist activities of Owen Lovejoy, from 1837 to his death in 1864, John Howard Bryant, active from the 1840's to his death in 1862, and his nephew, Julian Bryant (1836-65), a commander of black soldiers in the Civil War, all of Bureau County, Illinois.

608. Billington, Louis. BRITISH HUMANITARIANS AND AMERICAN COTTON, 1840-1860. *J. of Am. Studies [Great Britain] 1977 11(3): 313-334.* The English Society of Friends helped American abolitionists to resist slavery. They organized boycotts of goods produced by slave labor. Sharing common religious and social values with American opponents of slavery, English Quakers conducted propaganda campaigns against slavery that drew heavily from the rhetoric and ideology of American abolitionism. Quaker boycotts of goods ranging from West Indian rum to American cotton had little impact, neither impressing American slaveholders nor impeding transatlantic trade. Based on archival materials and contemporary antislavery writings; 89 notes.
H. T. Lovin

609. Blackett, R. J. M. ANGLO-AMERICAN OPPOSITION TO LIBERIAN COLONIZATION, 1831-1833. *Historian 1979 41(2): 276-294.* Following the formation of the American Colonization Society (ACS) in 1816, the debate within abolitionist ranks over expatriation peaked. Monetary deficiencies prodded the ACS into commissioning Elliot Cresson, a Philadelphia colonizationist, as an emissary to Great Britain in 1831. British support would not only generate needed funds but also enhance the society's image among American abolitionists. Cresson returned in 1833 with little to show for his efforts. Defeat destroyed the possibility of British support for the ACS and the efforts in Liberia. The failure of Cresson's mission was a major success for anticolonization abolitionists at a time when contacts between British and American abolitionists were becoming increasingly important. 54 notes.
R. S. Sliwoski

610. Blackett, R. J. M. "... FREEDOM, OR THE MARTYR'S GRAVE": BLACK PITTSBURGH'S AID TO THE FUGITIVE SLAVE. *Western Pennsylvania Hist. Mag. 1978 61(2): 117-134.* Discusses Pittsburgh's Philanthropic Society, a benevolent society to aid Negroes in the community as well as a secret society of black and white abolitionists who sought to abduct slaves from southern plantations and secure their safe passage along the underground railroad, 1830's-60's.

611. Blackett, R. J. M. FUGITIVE SLAVES IN BRITAIN: THE ODYSSEY OF WILLIAM AND ELLEN CRAFT. *J. of Am. Studies [Great Britain] 1978 12(1): 41-62.* In 1848, William Craft (d. 1900) and Ellen Craft (d. 1890), slaves on a Georgia plantation, escaped to Philadelphia and later moved to Boston where they remained until Congress passed the Fugitive Slave Act of 1850. Their owners then demanded extradition of the Crafts to Georgia. Despite aid from antislavery groups, extradition appeared inevitable, forcing the Crafts to flee to Great Britain where they remained until the American Civil War ended. In England, the Crafts played prominent roles in helping British abolitionist groups oppose slavery. Based on archival, newspaper, and secondary sources; 54 notes.
H. T. Lovin

612. Blaser, Kent. NORTH CAROLINA AND JOHN BROWN'S RAID. *Civil War Hist. 1978 24(3): 197-212.* In October 1859 initial reaction to John Brown's Harpers Ferry raid in North Carolina revealed attitudes on slavery between moderation and complacency. Playing on Southern insecurity, pro-slavery extremists manufactured a Northern conspiracy; moderates retreated on issues like patrols and vigilance systems. Hysterical fear of strangers aided the main radical objective of a statewide militia system. By early 1860 even moderates were affected, and the state was armed. Relatively untouched by the Southern "Great Reaction" in the 1830's, North Carolina for the first time isolated itself from the North. Newspapers, primary family and secondary sources; 58 notes.
R. E. Stack

613. Bonacich, Edna. ABOLITION, THE EXTENSION OF SLAVERY, AND THE POSITION OF FREE BLACKS: A STUDY OF SPLIT LABOR MARKETS IN THE UNITED STATES, 1830-1863. *Am. J. of Sociol. 1975 81(3): 601-628.* Using the "split labor market" theory of ethnic and racial antagonism, this paper analyzes race relations in the pre-Civil War United States. Both slaves and free blacks are found to have been lower-priced sources of labor than whites, to whom they therefore posed a threat of displacement. Slavery was a system which gave southern capitalists total control of a cheap labor force, permitting extensive displacement. It also put the South in conflict with northern capital, because the latter depended on higher-priced (white) labor. Abolition threatened to increase competition between black and white labor, spreading the problem to all regions and segments of the economy. But manumission also made blacks more vulnerable to counterattacks by white labor in the form of either exclusion or caste. The various class interests of the three parties to split labor markets are presented for the North, South, and West on the issues of abolition, the extension of slavery, and the position of free blacks. It is argued that an understanding of the interests of the white working class and its power to implement them is of major importance for untangling race relations before the Civil War.
J

614. Brooks, George E., Jr. THE PROVIDENCE AFRICAN SOCIETY'S SIERRA LEONE EMIGRATION SCHEME, 1794-1795: PROLOGUE TO THE AFRICAN COLONIZATION MOVEMENT. *Int. J. of African Hist. Studies 1974 7(2): 183-202.* In November 1794 the African Society of Providence dispatched one of its officers, James Mackenzie, to negotiate arrangements for the settlement of American freedmen in Sierra Leone. Reverend Samuel Hopkins, a prominent Congregationalist clergyman and a well-known advocate of black emigration, was responsible for the fact that no members of the African Society subsequently emigrated, inasmuch as he refused to furnish the prospective colonists with the character references required by the governor of Sierra Leone. Primary and secondary sources; 46 notes.
M. M. McCarthy

615. Brown, Delindus R. FREE BLACKS' RHETORICAL IMPACT ON AFRICAN COLONIZATION: THE EMERGENCE OF RHETORICAL EXIGENCE. *J. of Black Studies 1979 9(3): 251-265.* The rising number of free Negroes in the 1830's caused a "peak of dialectical tension" in "rhetorical discourse" in the American Colonization Society. This tension over the society is analyzed through the "predominant motivational exigence" that blacks were subordinate to whites in American society and through the "powerful mobilizational exigence" of the threat that some whites believed that free blacks posed for the system of slavery. (252) The many "rhetorical strategies" (263) of persons for and against colonization kept the issue alive until the 1840's. Had colonization succeeded the Civil War might have been postponed until the 1910's. Primary and secondary sources; biblio.
R. G. Sherer

616. Brown, Ira V. CRADLE OF FEMINISM: THE PHILADELPHIA FEMALE ANTI-SLAVERY SOCIETY, 1833-1840. *Pennsylvania Mag. of Hist. and Biog. 1978 102(2): 143-166.* As a sequel to the founding of the American Antislavery Society, the integrated Philadelphia Female Anti-Slavery Society was organized in 1833. Lucretia Mott was its first corresponding secretary. Later members included Angelina Grimké, Mary Grew, and Sarah Pugh. The question of women's role split the national society as it did the 1840 London meeting where the excluded Mott and Elizabeth Stanton began their cooperation. Based on MSS, Philadelphia Female Anti-Slavery Society, official records, and secondary works; 99 notes.
T. H. Wendel

617. Brown, Ira V. RACISM AND SEXISM: THE CASE OF PENNSYLVANIA HALL. *Phylon 1976 37(2): 126-136.* The Garrisonian abolitionists stood wholeheartedly for racial integration and woman's liberation. The Pennsylvania State Anti-Slavery Society, formed in 1833, built a handsome new building in 1837. It was destroyed by a mob a year later when a large assembly of the Anti-Slavery Convention of American Women, organized in New York City in 1837, met in Pennsylvania Hall. The mixed company, including men and women, black and white, provoked the mob. "Not even Pennsylvania was ready for racial integration ... Southerners actually rejoiced in the burning of Pennsylvania Hall." However, the burning and other violence resulted in many previously hostile persons taking a view more sympathetic to the abolition movement. 53 notes.
E. P. Stickney

618. Burke, Ronald K. THE ANTI-SLAVERY ACTIVITIES OF SAMUEL RINGGOLD WARD IN NEW YORK STATE. *Afro-Americans in New York Life and Hist. 1978 2(1): 17-28.* Samuel Ringgold Ward, a black northern abolitionist, subscribed to the theory of Christology (becoming Christ-like in thought and action) in preaching reform in New York during 1839-51.

619. Cardinal, Eric J. ANTISLAVERY SENTIMENT AND POLITICAL TRANSFORMATION IN THE 1850'S: PORTAGE COUNTY, OHIO. *Old Northwest 1975 1(3): 223-238.* Proposes that

the slavery expansion issue became the overriding political issue in Portage County, Ohio, in the 1850's, by noting the previous failure of attempts to fuse local opposition to the national Democrats on other issues. Editor and Free Soil party leader Lyman W. Hall failed to fuse the Free Soilers and the Prohibitionists in 1853 and lost votes when he tried to fuse Republicans and Know-Nothings in 1855. Hall's striking 1856 victory in Portage County for Frémont was the result of his merger of all forces opposed to the Kansas-Nebraska Act (US, 1854). Based on Ohio newspapers, county histories, and secondary works; 38 notes.

620. Carlisle, Rodney. SELF-DETERMINATION IN COLONIAL LIBERIA AND AMERICAN BLACK NATIONALISM. *Negro Hist. Bull. 1973 36(4): 77-83.* By the mid-1840's, the American Colonization Society was willing to consider independence for Liberia, where as early as the mid-1820's there was more black participation in government than anywhere in the United States. The final draft of the constitution admitted only "persons of colour" to citizenship. The language of nationalism and the achievement of nationhood appealed to blacks in the United States; emigration to Liberia remained high in the decade after 1847. Martin Robinson Delany's interest in emigration, his major role in the conventions of the 1850's devoted to emigration, and his printed works won him lasting fame. The principle of Africa for the Africans grew in Liberia and after 1847 influenced American black nationalist thinking. Illus., 54 notes.
E. P. Stickney

621. Cousins, Leone B. WOMAN OF THE YEAR: 1842. *Nova Scotia Hist. Q. [Canada] 1976 6(4): 349-374.* Eliza Ruggles Raymond of Nova Scotia married a minister who was a missionary to escaped slaves and who eventually had a mission on Sherbro Island; she aided slaves on slaving vessels, accompanied her husband to Africa, and defended wrongly accused slaves against imprisonment, 1839-50.

622. Crow, Jeffrey J. SLAVE REBELLIOUSNESS AND SOCIAL CONFLICT IN NORTH CAROLINA, 1775 TO 1802. *Willian and Mary Q. 1980 37(1): 79-102.* Follows three lines of inquiry on race relations in North Carolina: Afro-American contribution to social upheaval; white response to the realization that independence affected the institution of slavery and slave behavior; and conflict in perception of blacks and whites that led to the slave insurrection hysteria of 1800-02. The war produced a variety of slave protest actions; many blacks ran away, some joining the British. After the war, collective resistance of blacks mounted. There was greater repression by whites. Fear of slave revolts increased. In 1802, plans for Negro insurgency were discovered in several counties, which resulted in wide-scale executions. The insurrection scare of 1802 provided the opportunity for whites to gain greater social control. Uses newspapers and colony and local archives; 66 notes.
H. M. Ward

623. Cudd, John. THE UNITY OF REFORM: JOHN GRIMES AND THE *NEW JERSEY FREEMAN*. *New Jersey Hist. 1979 97(4): 197-212.* John Grimes settled in Boonton, New Jersey in 1843 to practice medicine. He was active in the abolition movement and in 1844 began publishing the *New Jersey Freeman,* a newspaper which was a part of a network of reform journalism. In its pages Grimes discussed slavery in terms of religion, politics, economics, and patriotism. Other movements such as temperance and an equitable distribution of wealth were also considered. The Mexican War and its relation to the spread of slavery received attention, as did phrenology. Grimes's attraction to a variety of reforms was a trait that he shared with other antebellum reformers. His ideologies are placed in the context of other national movements. Based on the *New Jersey Freeman* and secondary sources; 10 illus., 38 notes.
E. R. McKinstry

624. Daniel, W. Harrison. THE METHODIST EPISCOPAL CHURCH AND THE NEGRO IN THE EARLY NATIONAL PERIOD. *Methodist Hist. 1973 11(2): 40-53.* The response of the Methodist Episcopal Church to slavery changed from severe condemnation in 1780 to acceptance in 1816. Bishop Francis Asbury (1745-1816) and Bishop Thomas Coke (1747-1814) urged that slavery be eliminated, and the church in 1784 passed resolutions against slave-holding. Later, however, the church was forced to accommodate a practice it condemned by the society of which it was a part. 76 notes.
H. L. Calkin

625. Dormon, James H. THE PERSISTENT SPECTER: SLAVE REBELLION IN TERRITORIAL LOUISIANA. *Louisiana Hist. 1977 18(4): 389-404.* Whites in the Louisiana Territory, 1801-12, feared black insurrection. There were several rumored and threatened slave revolts, but not until 1811 was there an actual rebellion, beginning at the Manuel Andry plantation, near present-day Norco. Regular and militia forces quickly suppressed it; nearly all the rebel slaves were massacred or subsequently executed. The legislature compensated owners whose slaves had been killed. In general, whites refused to believe that it was a true slave rebellion. They preferred to believe that outsiders were responsible, and rewarded blacks who had opposed the rebels. This was "the largest slave insurrection in U.S. history," but it had little chance of succeeding and represented only a small portion of the region's slaves. Yet the spectre of slave revolt persisted and "fear of revolt lay at the heart of the relationship between slaves and masters and was thus fundamental to the creation of distrust by whites, even as the whites created for their own psychic salvation the myth of the contented bondsman." Primary sources; 2 photos, map, 48 notes.
R. L. Woodward, Jr.

626. Draughon, Ralph Brown, Jr. THE MOBILE *REGISTER* INTERVIEWS JOHN BROWN. *Alabama R. 1974 27(2): 152-155.* An unidentified special correspondent for the Mobile *Register* succeeded in interviewing imprisoned John Brown. Brown denied he was insane during the interview, and admitted seeking martyrdom. The correspondent was sympathetically impressed. Based on primary and secondary sources; 6 notes.
J. F. Vivian

627. Eaklor, Vicki L. THE SONGS OF THE EMANCIPATION CAR: VARIATIONS ON AN ABOLITIONIST THEME. *Missouri Hist. Soc. Bull. 1980 36(2, pt. 1): 92-102.* In attacking slavery, pre-Civil War abolitionists produced a substantial musical literature. Although much of this material doubtless has been lost, now Vicki Eaklor has located more than 700 such antislavery songs, among them 14 song collections such as the *Emancipation Car* (Zanesville: E. C. Church, 1854; reprinted, Zanesville: Sullivan and Brown, 1874). All songs in the latter collection were ascribed to Joshua McCarter Simpson, an Oberlin-educated Negro born at Windsor, Ohio, about 1820. Many of the songs focused on American Colonization Society views that free Negroes should emigrate to Liberia. Photo, 55 notes.
H. T. Lovin

628. Eckert, Ralph Lowell. ANTISLAVERY MARTYRDOM: THE ORDEAL OF PASSMORE WILLIAMSON. *Pennsylvania Mag. of Hist. and Biog. 1976 100(4): 521-538.* Passmore Williamson was imprisoned in 1855 after liberating three slaves being transported through Philadelphia. The ensuing trials aroused national attention and highlighted the sectional conflict over federal and state statutes, the status of slaves, property rights, and the right of transit into and through states. Public opinion forced Williamson's release. Based on Passmore Williamson Scrapbook, Chester County Historical Society, other manuscripts, newspapers, and secondary sources; 57 notes.
T. H. Wendel

629. Elbert, E. Duane. THE ENGLISH BILL: AN ATTEMPT TO COMPROMISE THE LECOMPTON DILEMMA. *Kansas Hist. 1978 1(4): 219-234.* Events in Kansas in 1857-58 centered around the proslavery Lecompton constitution. Representative William H. English (1822-96) got Congress to accept a compromise involving less public land for Kansas and resubmission of the constitution to a popular vote. The plan was to satisfy advocates of popular sovereignty by the new vote and those who opposed resubmission by enabling them to say land rather than slavery was the real issue in 1858. English was trying to save his party, his political future in Indiana, and hopefully the nation by formulating a compromise. On 2 August 1858 the constitution was decisively beaten when resubmitted. Statistical studies of place of birth, age, occupation, real estate, and personal property holdings are offered to explain the decisive 12,254 to 1,915 vote against the constitution. Illus., 4 tables, 93 notes.
W. F. Zornow

630. Ely, James W., Jr. and Jordan, Daniel P. HARPER'S FERRY REVISITED: FATHER COSTELLO'S "SHORT SKETCH" OF BROWN'S RAID. *Records of the Am. Catholic Hist. Soc. of Philadelphia 1974 85(1/2): 59-67.* Presents the text of a letter by Rev. Michael A. Costello describing John Brown's 1859 Harpers Ferry raid. The letter is significant because it is descriptive rather than polemical and written from a sophisticated perspective by one whose impressions were fresh. 26 notes.
J. M. McCarthy

631. Essig, James David. CONNECTICUT MINISTERS AND SLAVERY, 1790-1795. *J. of Am. Studies [Great Britain] 1981 15(1): 27-44.* In 1790, the first Connecticut antislavery society was founded. In the next five years, it enlisted prominent Congregational clergymen such as Benjamin Trumbull and Ezra Stiles, liberal preachers such as James Dana, and many of the state's Calvinist and non-Calvinist laity. For these clerical participants, the new antislavery crusading supplied added prestige and a chance to pronounce southern society inferior to that of New England. Based on ecclesiastical writings, archival documents, and secondary sources; 61 notes.
H. T. Lovin

632. Essig, James David. THE LORD'S FREE MAN: CHARLES G. FINNEY AND HIS ABOLITIONISM. *Civil War Hist. 1978 24(1): 25-45.* Charles Grandison Finney's theology and antislavery activities reveal a surprisingly committed abolitionism joined to the conviction that indifference to slavery impeded the gospel's spread. Revivalism and abolition could hasten the millennium. His thought closely followed the march of the slavery controversy. During 1833-39, Finney attempted to persuade southerners to abolish slavery because it was sinful. Through the Civil War, detecting southern selfishness and malevolence, he turned to violent denunciation and demands for punishment. He succeeded only imperfectly, but did join evangelism to social reform. Unpublished and published papers and secondary works; 94 notes.
R. E. Stack

633. Faust, Drew Gilpin. EVANGELICALISM AND THE MEANING OF THE PROSLAVERY ARGUMENT: THE REVEREND THORNTON STRINGFELLOW OF VIRGINIA. *Virginia Mag. of Hist. and Biog. 1977 85(1): 1-17.* Southern evangelicalism in the antebellum years produced a type of reform movement significantly different from the northern counterpart. The Reverend Thornton Stringfellow had many goals similar to those of northern reformers, especially temperance, improved health, and education. But Stringfellow was also a passionate defender of the peculiar institution and viewed the defense of slavery as an intimate part of a national reform effort. Based on Stringfellow's published works, newspapers, and secondary sources; 52 notes.
R. F. Oaks

634. Fellman, Michael. REHEARSAL FOR THE CIVIL WAR: ANTISLAVERY AND PROSLAVERY AT THE FIGHTING POINT IN KANSAS, 1854-1856. Perry, Lewis and Fellman, Michael, ed. *Antislavery Reconsidered: New Perspectives on the Abolitionists* (Baton Rouge: Louisiana State U. Pr. 1979): 287-307. Surveys the attitudes and conditions that led to the friction between Kansans and Missourians over the issue of slavery in the 1850's. The residents of Kansas perceived themselves as freedom-loving, civilized, pure Anglo-Saxons opposed to the dehumanized, proslavery poor whites ("Pukes," as the Kansans called them) who roamed throughout the territory. Kansans were seen by the slave-owning elites as avaricious and lascivious profiteers who wished to deprive southerners of their rightful property—slaves—and lusted after Negro wenches. After the armed conflict between the two groups was resolved in 1856, many of the former opponents collaborated in land-grabbing schemes to enrich themselves. 47 notes.
S

635. Fellman, Michael. THEODORE PARKER AND THE ABOLITIONIST ROLE IN THE 1850'S. *J. of Am. Hist. 1974 61(3): 666-684.* In the 1850's Theodore Parker, the noted Boston preacher, entered the abolitionist ranks with a message appealing to many people. He emphasized a higher, natural law of freedom which justified the destruction, by bloodshed if necessary, of "unnatural" statutory law and institutions. Violence was seen as a means of regenerating the revolutionary spirit of Anglo-Saxon New Englanders endangered by materialism and the appearance of the degenerate Irish. Parker called for the preservation of racial purity and ideals from a southern "Spanish" type mixed with an inferior black race possessed of heightened sexuality and a slave mentality. He saw no future for blacks in a racially integrated society, but saw dangers of a future race war if slavery were not ended. 71 notes.
K. B. West

636. Finkelman, Paul. *PRIGG V. PENNSYLVANIA* AND NORTHERN STATE COURTS: ANTI-SLAVERY USE OF A PROSLAVERY DECISION. *Civil War Hist. 1979 25(1): 5-35.* This 1842 US Supreme Court decision, written by Justice Joseph Story himself, first upheld the 1793 Fugitive Slave Law and the masters' power over runaways. It struck down personal liberty laws, but the decision's *dicta* allowed state noncompliance. The slave power seemed victorious; it turned out, though, to be an antislavery tool. Chief Justice Roger Taney feared this from the start. Story's decision accelerated a legal and legislative movement against the prospect of kidnapped free blacks. It was interpreted to mean that property rights and due process could not coexist. It forced Northerners to choose free men rather than Union harmony. Based on national and state statute books and secondary sources; 100 notes.
R. E. Stack

637. Fladeland, Betty L. COMPENSATED EMANCIPATION: A REJECTED ALTERNATIVE. *J. of Southern Hist. 1976 42(2): 169-186.* One basis for labelling American abolitionists as radicals has been their unwillingness to accept compensated emancipation as compared to the "moderate" or "practical" British abolitionists who did accept it. However, the proslavery adherents were equally untractable about compensated emancipation, constantly viewing it as a radical rather than a reasonable solution for ending the institution of slavery. Only after the defeat of 1865 did some Southern congressmen propose compensated emancipation, but by then it was too late. Due to the previous widespread opposition, compensated emancipation was never a viable solution. Based on primary and secondary printed materials; 58 notes.
T. D. Schoonover

638. Foner, Eric. ABOLITIONISM AND THE LABOR MOVEMENT IN ANTEBELLUM AMERICA. Bolt, Christine and Drescher, Seymour, ed. *Anti-Slavery, Religion and Reform: Essays in Memory of Roger Anstey* (Folkestone, England: Dawson, 1980): 254-271. Although the labor movement in the North generally supported the abolition of slavery, there was a prevalent opinion that concentration on the slavery issue drew attention away from the abuses of workers in the factories of the North. Abolitionists, on the other hand, often had little sympathy for the plight of northern workers, for their labor was "voluntary" and occupied a natural place in the marketplace. While most leaders of the labor movement accepted the idea of conflict between capital and labor, most abolitionists did not. 32 notes.
S

639. Fordham, Monroe. NINETEENTH-CENTURY BLACK THOUGHT IN THE UNITED STATES: SOME INFLUENCES OF THE SANTO DOMINGO REVOLUTION. *J. of Black Studies 1975 6(2): 115-126.* The Haitian Revolution of the 1790's and an independent Haiti significantly shaped black thought and action in the United States. Reports of the revolution, especially from refugees and their slaves, encouraged many enslaved insurrectionists, who saw in Haiti a model and possible assistance. Many northern blacks depicted the revolution as a struggle against oppression and as justification for militancy in the United States. They cited Haiti's successful government as evidence of black capacity for self-rule. As emigration attracted blacks in the 1850's, Haiti seemed an asylum and the genesis of a powerful black nation that would someday redeem and represent all Africans. Primary and secondary sources; notes, biblio.
D. C. Neal

640. Franklin, Benjamin, V. THEODORE DWIGHT'S "AFRICAN DISTRESS": AN EARLY ANTI-SLAVERY POEM. *Yale U. Lib. Gazette 1979 54(1): 26-36.* The first serious antislavery poem to appear in the United States was printed anonymously in the *New-Haven Gazette,* 21 February 1788. Although brief and modest, it was the best poem ever produced by the Connecticut wit, Theodore Dwight. The most authoritative version, reprinted at the conclusion of the article, was produced by the anthologist Samuel Kettrell in *Specimens of American Poetry* (Boston, 1829). 7 notes.
D. A. Yanchisin

641. Franklin, D. Bruce. THE WHITE METHODIST IMAGE OF THE AMERICAN NEGRO EMIGRANT TO LIBERIA, WEST AFRICA, 1833-1848. *Methodist Hist. 1977 15(3): 147-166.* The first missionaries to Sierra Leone and Liberia in 1833 and supporters of colonization believed that the social, political, and economic systems of white Christian civilization were superior to the customs and habits of African black society. Negro American preachers in West Africa were expected to subordinate their activities to the Methodist Episcopal Church in America. In 1848 the whites withdrew their leadership because of inability to survive in Liberia and a desire to maintain a pious image of permitting civilized America-Liberians to carry on the evangelical work in Africa. 46 notes.
H. L. Calkin

642. Frederickson, George M. A MAN BUT NOT A BROTHER: ABRAHAM LINCOLN AND RACIAL EQUALITY. *J. of Southern Hist. 1975 41(1): 39-58.* Abraham Lincoln has been viewed as both a Negrophobe and a champion of racial equality. An examination of his racial attitudes within the intellectual context of his times and the political pressures they exerted reveals that he consistently held a racial philosophy between the two extremes throughout his public life. Beginning with his affiliation with Henry Clay's moderate position on slavery, Lincoln's speeches show a moral opposition to slavery and an acceptance of the basic humanity of blacks coupled with an underlying emotional commitment to whiteness and white supremacy. He recognized that his denial of black citizenship, though inconsistent with his basic political doctrine of natural rights, was a political necessity. Because he felt that white prejudice made social and political equality and racial harmony impossible, he advocated colonization as the only alternative. Based on speeches, letters, and secondary sources; 57 notes.
S

643. French, David. ELIZUR WRIGHT, JR., AND THE EMERGENCE OF ANTI-COLONIZATION SENTIMENTS ON THE CONNECTICUT WESTERN RESERVE. *Ohio Hist. 1976 85(1): 49-66.* Discusses colonization versus anticolonization arguments concerning a solution to slavery in the 1830's. Focuses on northeastern Ohio and discusses the American Anti-Slavery Society and early intellectual history. Based on manuscript, newspaper, and secondary sources; illus., 84 notes.
T. H. Hartig

644. Friedman, Lawrence J. ANTEBELLUM AMERICAN ABOLITIONISM AND THE PROBLEM OF VIOLENT MEANS. *Psychohistory Rev. 1980 9(1): 23-58.* Many historians have argued that abolitionist accommodation to violent means to achieve their goals resulted from a gradual retreat from pacifism toward acceptance of violent, forceful methods. Research indicates that several abolitionist proponents of moral suasion as the principal means to eradicate slavery were willing to use force in self-defense. Psychohistorical theory suggests some pacifistic abolitionists struggled with aggression. During the 1840's and 1850's accommodation to violence was a gradual process as revealed in examination of abolitionist responses to the Mexican War, the 1850 Fugitive Slave Act, "Bleeding Kansas," and John Brown's raid on the Harpers Ferry arsenal. Employs the theories of Kenneth Keniston to explain shifting abolitionist responses to violent means. Offers several explanations for changing abolitionist thought, modifying Freudian theory where appropriate. 47 notes.
J. M. Herrick

645. Friedman, Lawrence J. CONFIDENCE AND PERTINACITY IN EVANGELICAL ABOLITIONISM: LEWIS TAPPAN'S CIRCLE. *Am. Q. 1979 31(1): 81-106.* The "conservative" church-oriented abolitionists who formed Lewis Tappan's circle of reformist friends consisted of such like-minded men as William Jay, Amos Phelps, Theodore Weld, and George Cheever. Each had had positive experiences in his earlier reform activities that, coupled with his common belief in self-help and a God-ordered society, and Lewis Tappan's managerial expertise, provided a group cohesiveness that was unaffected by differences over reform specifics. Covers ca. 1830-61. Based on the journals and papers of the primary participants; 41 notes.
D. G. Nielson

646. Friedman, Lawrence J. GARRISONIAN ABOLITIONISM AND THE BOSTON CLIQUE: A PSYCHOSOCIAL INQUIRY. *Psychohistory Rev. 1978 7(2): 6-19.* Analyzes the class and social characteristics of the "Boston Clique," a small but influential congregation of persons active in the abolition movement, 1830-40. Finds there were no universal characteristics other than nonconformism among members. Diversity characterized members such as William Lloyd Garrison, Edmund Quincy, and Ellis Gray Loring. Examines the charismatic leadership of Garrison in uniting the Boston Clique, in spite of their concerns about his extremism, as well as the group solidarity promoted by Clique members' feelings of social estrangement because of their views. But group solidarity was continually threatened by internal discord resulting from Clique members' strong individualism. This resulted in tension and discord with the group. Revises modern abolitionist scholarship. 72 notes.
J. M. Herrick

647. Friedman, Lawrence J. THE GERRIT SMITH CIRCLE: ABOLITIONISM IN THE BURNED-OVER DISTRICT. *Civil War Hist. 1980 26(1): 18-38.* Gerrit Smith does not fit the Garrisonianism-Tappanite division of abolitionism. He actively pursued peace and reconciliation in the matter of the 1840 schism. Beginning in 1840-41, Smith's upstate New York abolitionist circle of like-minded professionals attempted to base themselves on the local churches, on the local solution of cultural voluntarism. They turned to national influence through the Liberty Party and failed. As all solutions failed and national affairs pressed, the group dissolved slowly by 1850. Some turned against one another in recrimination. However, they had tried to find another acceptable abolitionist solution; the widening national focus of affairs would not wait on local reforms. Based on personal papers and secondary sources; 39 notes.
R. E. Stack

648. Friedman, Lawrence J. PURIFYING THE WHITE MAN'S COUNTRY: THE AMERICAN COLONIZATION SOCIETY RECONSIDERED 1816-40. *Societas 1976 6(1): 1-24.* Reverend Robert Finley drew together a mixed following of slaveholders, Old School Federalists, Negrophobes, and antislavery philanthropists to found the American Colonization Society in 1816. The stated goal of the organization was to ease American racial difficulties by sending free blacks to Africa, but the motivations and real goals of the society were much more complex and contradictory than this stated purpose would suggest. Because the colonizationists were most ineffective in removing from the nation these allegedly impure elements, the author concludes in part, "For assurances of white purity, Negroes may have been needed as a point of contrast." Based on society's papers on the Library of Congress, and on printed primary and secondary sources; 83 notes.
J. D. Hunley

649. Fulkerson, Gerald. EXILE AS EMERGENCE: FREDERICK DOUGLASS IN GREAT BRITAIN, 1845-1847. *Q. J. of Speech 1974 60(1): 69-82.* "When Frederick Douglass fled into British exile in the summer of 1845, he was a popular but subordinate figure in the American abolition movement. When he returned to the United States in April, 1847, his Garrisonian colleagues acknowledged him as an emerging leader. This essay examines Douglass' experience in Britain in an effort to discover the factors accounting for his emergence to leadership status among American Garrisonians."
J

650. Gamble, Douglas A. GARRISONIAN ABOLITIONISTS IN THE WEST: SOME SUGGESTIONS FOR STUDY. *Civil War Hist. 1977 23(1): 52-68.* During 1842-45 a sizeable Garrisonian movement emerged in rural northeastern Ohio and southeastern Michigan. It evolved from the parent Ohio Antislavery Society. Based in Salem, Ohio, the Western Antislavery Society distained all compromise within and without abolitionism and for 16 years provided the one persistent manifestation of William Lloyd Garrison's doctrine of "No Union With Slaveholders." The Society broke with Garrison over acceptance of Republican compromise. Composed of moral suasionists, most of whom were Hicksite Quakers, the Society shows that Garrisonian abolitionism was not an Eastern monolith and may provide discriminating answers to questions about the abolitionists. Primary and secondary sources; 47 notes.
R. E. Stack

651. Gamble, Douglas A. JOSHUA GIDDINGS AND THE OHIO ABOLITIONISTS: A STUDY IN RADICAL POLITICS. *Ohio Hist. 1979 88(1): 37-56.* Congressman Joshua Reed Giddings of Ohio maintained a working relationship toward abolition with the radical Garrisonians and with the moderate antislavery politicians like Salmon F. Chase. Garrisonians, distrusting the Constitution, believed that moral suasion was more potent than political maneuvers, but were willing and eager to have the work go on through prominent politicians like Giddings. However, Giddings became disillusioned with the Free Soil Party and even with the Republican Party. By 1860 he had left Congress and joined the moral suationists. Photo, 65 notes.
H. F. Thomson

652. Genovese, Eugene D. IN THE NAME OF HUMANITY AND THE CAUSE OF FORM. *R. of Radical Pol. Econ. 1975 7(3): 84-100.* Discusses social reform of slavery in the South, 1789-1860; excerpted from the author's *Roll, Jordan Roll*.

653. George, Carol V. R. WIDENING THE CIRCLE: THE BLACK CHURCH AND THE ABOLITIONIST CRUSADE, 1830-1860. Perry, Lewis and Fellman, Michael, ed. *Antislavery Reconsidered: New Perspectives on the Abolitionists* (Baton Rouge: Louisiana

State U. Pr., 1979): 75-95. Surveys the careers of more than 40 black clergymen from 1830 to 1860 to show the multidimensional quality of their leadership. Working under extremely varied conditions—in slave states and free, as circuit preachers and permanently settled ministers, in exclusively black as well as biracial institutions, and at every level of the hierarchy—black religious leaders contributed to the abolition and civil rights movements and heightened black self-awareness among blacks. 29 notes.
S

654. Gifford, James M. BLACK HOPE AND DESPAIR IN ANTEBELLUM GEORGIA: THE WILLIAM MOSS CORRESPONDENCE. *Prologue 1976 8(3): 153-162.* During 1853-57, William Moss, a slave in Griffin, Georgia, communicated with officials of the American Colonization Society in an effort to gain financial support for promotion of the Society's activities and the raising of a group of emigrants for Liberia. His correspondence was sporadic, reflecting the disapproval of his owner and the growing exasperation of Society officials with his schemes. Moss' letters stopped in 1857 and he disappeared from view, probably dying at the age of 21 in a smallpox epidemic in Griffin. Based on correspondence in American Colonization Archives, Library of Congress.
N. Lederer

655. Gifford, James M. EMILY TUBMAN AND THE AFRICAN COLONIZATION MOVEMENT IN GEORGIA. *Georgia Hist. Q. 1975 59(1): 10-24.* Discusses the works and projects of Georgia philanthropist Emily Tubman, 1816-57, emphasizing the emancipation of her slaves and their colonization in Liberia through the African Colonization Movement.

656. Glickstein, Jonathan A. "POVERTY IS NOT SLAVERY": AMERICAN ABOLITIONISTS AND THE COMPETITIVE LABOR MARKET. Perry, Lewis and Fellman, Michael, ed. *Antislavery Reconsidered: New Perspectives on the Abolitionists* (Baton Rouge: Louisiana State U. Pr., 1979): 195-218. Although some abolitionists such as William I. Bowditch believed that the economic system of the industrialized North created a slavery almost as terrible as that of the South, most people in the antislavery movement—especially those who came from evangelical Christianity—believed that, on the positive side, marketplace competition in the United States was so fair that willing workers would not be exploited, and, on the negative side, fear of poverty and poverty itself would act as a spur to industriousness and as proof against indolence. 38 notes.
S

657. Goldstein, Leslie Friedman. RACIAL LOYALTY IN AMERICA: THE EXAMPLE OF FREDERICK DOUGLASS. *Western Pol. Q. 1975 28(3): 463-476.* This paper maintains that the concept of racial loyalty in the thought of Frederick Douglass (black American statesman, 1819-1895) provides a more viable mode of ethnic loyalty for ethnically heterogeneous nations than the more separatists concepts which are prevalent today. Douglass' argument was that members of any oppressed group must stand up for their own rights. All persons have an obligation to combat injustice, but the persons whose rights are denied have a peculiarly strong obligation to combat their own oppression. By a dignified insistence on their own rights, blacks could combat the public impression that they did not deserve those rights. Douglass' focus on justice as the basis of ethnic obligation has the advantage of tying the good-of-the-group to the good-of-the-whole-polity, and of channeling the natural sentiment of love-of-one's-own toward the more principled goal of improving the polity.
J

658. Goldstein, Leslie F. VIOLENCE AS AN INSTRUMENT FOR SOCIAL CHANGE: THE VIEWS OF FREDERICK DOUGLASS, 1817-1895. *J. of Negro Hist. 1976 6(1): 61-72.* The conventional view of Frederick Douglass' transformation from a revolutionary who opposed violence to a reformer who favored violence holds great currency, but the writings and thought of Douglass indicate an appreciation of the role of violence as an agent of social change. Douglass was a man of moral suasion, but he recognized the important power of the sword. Based on primary and secondary sources; 50 notes.
N. G. Sapper

659. Granade, Ray. SLAVE UNREST IN FLORIDA. *Florida Hist. Q. 1976 55(1): 18-36.* Slave unrest in Florida usually took the individual forms of theft, arson, running away, murder, or suicide, and only rarely the form of collective open revolt such as the Seminole Wars. Nevertheless, white Floridians, fearful of insurrection, passed strict slave codes, curtailed the actions of free blacks, and strongly resisted abolitionist activity. Based on newspaper, government document, and secondary sources; 100 notes.
P. A. Beaber

660. Greenberg, Kenneth S. REVOLUTIONARY IDEOLOGY AND THE PROSLAVERY ARGUMENT: THE ABOLITION OF SLAVERY IN ANTEBELLUM SOUTH CAROLINA. *J. of Southern Hist. 1976 42(3): 365-384.* Focuses on the tension of the revolutionary ideology of liberty and the proslavery arguments as developed and advocated in defense of South Carolina's institution of slavery. The use of avoidance measures such as the familial nature of slavery, the child-like "Sambo" description of slaves, and above all, the use of terms such as "peculiar institution," "servitude," or "African servitude," permitted South Carolinians to separate their black "slavery" from the real slavery.
T. Schoonover

661. Hackett, Derek. THE DAYS OF THIS REPUBLIC WILL BE NUMBERED: ABOLITION, SLAVERY, AND THE PRESIDENTIAL ELECTION OF 1836. *Louisiana Studies 1976 15(2): 131-160.* The presidential campaign of 1836 between Democratic candidate Martin Van Buren (1782-1862) and Whig candidate Hugh Lawson White (1773-1840) is significant because it marks the breakup of the dominant Democratic Party and inaugurates a national two-party system. In Louisiana, as an example, this situation came about for ideological reasons, especially the fear that a northerner such as Van Buren would be unable or unwilling to defend slavery. Newspapers in Louisiana during the campaign are filled with articles about fears of slave uprisings such as the "Murrell Conspiracy" of 1835 and attempts at abolition. Articles, letters to the editor, and editorials on these themes dominate in discussions of the election. Based on letters and papers in Louisiana State U. Library, Louisiana legislative records, Louisiana newspaper accounts, and secondary sources; table, 90 notes.
J. Buschen

662. Halbrooks, G. Thomas. FRANCIS WAYLAND: INFLUENTIAL MEDIATOR IN THE BAPTIST CONTROVERSY OVER SLAVERY. *Baptist Hist. and Heritage 1978 13(4): 21-35.* Francis Wayland (1796-1865) was President of Brown University, Vice-President of the Triennial Convention, and leading American Baptist spokesman for foreign missions. Describes his mediating efforts to prevent Baptists from dividing over the slavery issue. While he did view slavery as wrong, this Northerner urged that the slaveowner would be innocent if he held the slaves for their own good to prepare them for freedom. For over a decade his mediating position helped to prevent the division which finally occurred in 1845. Concludes by noting the numerous spin-offs in American Baptist history which can be attributed to him, not the least of which was Landmarkism. Based on writings of Wayland and the Manly Collection of Manuscripts at the University of Alabama; 33 notes.
H. M. Parker, Jr.

663. Hall, Kermit L. FEDERAL JUDICIAL REFORM AND PROSLAVERY CONSTITUTIONAL THEORY: A RETROSPECT ON THE BUTLER BILL. *Am. J. of Legal Hist. 1973 17(2): 166-184.* The problem of local judges and their relations with local politics was raised by the Butler Bill, which tried to adjust the federal judiciary to geographic and demographic expansion in the 1850's.

664. Hammond, John L. REVIVAL RELIGION AND ANTISLAVERY POLITICS. *Am. Sociol. R. 1974 39(2): 175-186.* Theories to explain empirical relationships between religion and political behavior (or other secular behavior) have generally asserted either that such relationships are spurious, explained by variations between religious groups in socioeconomic status, or that they are due to group identification with a religious community rather than a theology. The proposition that religious belief directly affects political attitudes and behavior is here tested with respect to revivals and antislavery voting in nineteenth-century Ohio. It has been claimed that revivals preached a new doctrine which demanded active opposition to slavery. The claim that revivalism had a direct, nonspurious effect on antislavery voting is tested in a multiple regression model which incorporates variables representing social structure, ethnicity, denominational membership, and prior political tradition. The effect of revivalism is strong despite all controls; the revivals transformed the religious orientations of those who experienced them, and this transformation affected their voting behavior.
J

665. Harris, Janet. LONGFELLOW'S POEMS ON SLAVERY. *Colby Lib. Q. 1978 14(2): 84-92.* Henry Wadsworth Longfellow's devout abolitionism resulted in the publication of *Poems on Slavery* (1842).

666. Harris, Robert L., Jr. H. FORD DOUGLAS: AFRO-AMERICAN ANTISLAVERY EMIGRATIONIST. *J. of Negro Hist. 1977 62(3): 217-234.* Afro-American emigrationists before the Civil War were found in two camps: nationalist emigrationists desiring the creation of a black nation, and antislavery emigrationists who were disillusioned by the proslavery bias of the US government. Prominent among the latter was H. Ford Douglas, a free black antislavery activist. The ultimate effort made by Douglas came with service in the Union Army during the Civil War when he became the only Afro-American captain to command combat troops. Illness contracted during the war prematurely ended his life in late 1865. Primary and secondary materials; 45 notes.
N. G. Sapper

667. Harrison, Theresa A. GEORGE THOMPSON AND THE 1851 "ANTI-ABOLITION" RIOT. *Hist. J. of Western Massachusetts 1976 5(1): 36-44.* Narrates the various popular demonstrations against the English abolitionist George Thompson during a speaking engagement in Springfield. Illus., notes.
W. H. Mulligan, Jr.

668. Harrold, Stanley C., Jr. FORGING AN ANTISLAVERY INSTRUMENT: GAMALIEL BAILEY AND THE FOUNDATION OF THE OHIO LIBERTY PARTY. *Old Northwest 1976 2(4): 371-387.* Gamaliel Bailey (ca. 1808-59) refused to form an independent abolitionist party in Ohio in the 1830's because it could not influence the policies of the major parties, could not attract votes, and would alienate public opinion on constitutional grounds. Instead he formed a Liberty Party to be the political arm of the antislavery movement and to pressure either the Whigs or the Democrats into opposing slavery. Salmon P. Chase (1808-73) became the Ohio leader of the new party, and the conceptual groundwork for the Republican Party of the 1850's was established. Based on the Library of Congress' Chase Papers, newspapers, and secondary works; 54 notes.
J

669. Harrold, Stanley C., Jr. THE PERSPECTIVE OF A CINCINNATI ABOLITIONIST: GAMALIEL BAILEY ON SOCIAL REFORM IN AMERICA. *Cincinnati Hist. Soc. Bull. 1977 35(3): 173-190.* Analyzes the political stance of Gamaliel Bailey, the influential editor of a Cincinnati abolitionist newspaper and major spokesman for the Liberty Party, as representative of a significant strain of antislavery sentiments in the 1840's.

670. Harrold, Stanley C., Jr. THE SOUTHERN STRATEGY OF THE LIBERTY PARTY. *Ohio Hist. 1978 87(1): 21-36.* Examines the Liberty Party's efforts to abolish slavery. Discusses the different—but equally radical—policies of William Lloyd Garrison and James G. Birney, two antislavery leaders in the North, but focuses on Ohio's Liberty Party leaders—Salmon P. Chase, Gamaliel Bailey, and Samuel Lewis. They used opposition to the extension of slavery to broaden the Liberty Party's appeal to both the North and South. The misconception that traditional southern governmental and moral structures could be used to abolish slavery left a legacy of historical consequence. Based on manuscript, newspaper, contemporary comments, and secondary sources; 4 illus., 71 notes.
N. Summers

671. Hewitt, John H. THE SACKING OF ST. PHILIP'S CHURCH, NEW YORK. *Hist. Mag. of the Protestant Episcopal Church 1980 49(1): 7-20.* On the night of 11 July 1834 the black Episcopal St. Philip's Church, New York City, was sacked by an antiblack, antiabolition mob. The black rector of the church was Peter Williams, Jr., who would later emerge as a leader in the abolition movement. The mob had been excited by the yellow journalism of the New York newspapers. Reveals the Jim Crow status of New York at this time, with Williams himself not being equal to the white priests in the diocese. His bishop even required him to resign offices he held in abolition societies. Nor was St. Philip's entitled to representation in the Diocesan Convention. Based largely on newspaper accounts of the incident and secondary sources; 78 notes.
H. M. Parker, Jr.

672. Hite, Roger W. VOICE OF A FUGITIVE: HENRY BIBB AND THE ANTE-BELLUM BLACK SEPARATISM. *J. of Black Studies 1974 4(3): 269-284.* Black leader Henry Bibb promoted the movement to encourage blacks to settle in Canada during the Antebellum period. 8 notes, biblio.
K. Butcher

673. Hovet, Theodore R. CHRISTIAN REVOLUTION: HARRIET BEECHER STOWE'S RESPONSE TO SLAVERY AND THE CIVIL WAR. *New England Q. 1974 47(4): 535-549.* Studies the Christian roots of Mrs. Stowe's antislavery sentiments and the charges forced upon her after the Civil War. Her views of slavery were constructed out of the tenets of Christian perfection. Her antislavery writings indicate also some of the reasons for a change from despair to optimism after the war is won, even though she must admit the ex-slaves have not actually achieved full rights; hence we may speak of the "failure of radical reform in America in the 1850's and 1860's." In her view one could never question the worth of the Civil War by finding fault with the ultimate result. 22 notes.
R. V. Ritter

674. Howard, Victor B. JAMES MADISON PENDLETON: A SOUTHERN CRUSADER AGAINST SLAVERY. *Register of the Kentucky Hist. Soc. 1976 74(3): 192-215.* Born in 1811, James Madison Pendleton rose to prominence during the 1849 campaign to abolish slavery in Kentucky. As a Baptist minister, writer, and public speaker, he did not avoid controversy. After the failure of the emancipation movement in Kentucky, Pendleton moved to Tennessee in 1856 and again became involved in controversy. Although he denied being an abolitionist, he admitted to antislavery sentiments. When the Civil War broke out, Pendleton sided with the Union and left the South. His position illustrates the divisions in the antebellum South. Primary and secondary sources; 70 notes.
J. F. Paul

675. Howard, Victor B. JOHN BROWN'S RAID AT HARPERS FERRY AND THE SECTIONAL CRISIS IN NORTH CAROLINA. *North Carolina Hist. Rev. 1978 55(4): 396-420.* John Brown's Harpers Ferry raid greatly frightened North Carolinians owing to its proximity of their state. During 1840-57 North Carolinians engaged in sporadic activities such as intercepting antislavery mail and harrassing known abolitionists. Publication of *The Impending Crisis* by fellow state resident Hinton Rowan Helper embarrassed North Carolinians and caused an intensification of these antiabolitionist efforts. John Brown's raid brought home the threat of a change of status for blacks. Reaction was especially strong in the Piedmont, though suspicion and harrassment of blacks and antislavery whites was present throughout the state. In addition, Democrats used the raid to discredit Whigs. Contemporary newspaper accounts, unpublished correspondence, published state and local records and personal papers, and secondary sources; 8 illus., map, 88 notes.
T. L. Savitt

676. Howard, Victor B. THE KENTUCKY PRESBYTERIANS IN 1849: SLAVERY AND THE KENTUCKY CONSTITUTION. *Register of the Kentucky Hist. Soc. 1975 73(3): 217-240.* Presbyterians in Kentucky were more opposed to slavery than any other denomination. Led by Robert J. and William Lewis Breckinridge, Presbyterians led the move for emancipation. Although the Emancipation Party of 1849 failed to gain its objectives, remnants of the movement formed the base for the Republican Party in Kentucky. Primary and secondary sources; 63 notes.
J. F. Paul

677. Howard, Victor B. ROBERT J. BRECKINRIDGE AND THE SLAVERY CONTROVERSY IN KENTUCKY IN 1849. *Filson Club Hist. Q. 1979 53(4): 328-343.* Robert J. Breckinridge was a consistent champion of the gradual emancipation of Kentucky's slaves. He found that his beliefs barred him from a political career in 1830, but he was a leader in the movement that persuaded the state legislature to end the importation of slaves in 1833. In 1849, he was an unsuccessful candidate for delegate to the state constitutional convention. His platform included a gradual, compensated emancipation combined with the colonization of the freed blacks in Africa. Based on the Breckinridge Family Papers at the Library of Congress and contemporary newspapers; 60 notes.
G. B. McKinney.

678. January, Alan F. THE SOUTH CAROLINA ASSOCIATION: AN AGENCY FOR RACE CONTROL IN ANTEBELLUM CHARLESTON. *South Carolina Hist. Mag. 1977 78(3): 191-201.* A small vigilance group in Charleston, 1823-50's, sought to control the actions of abolitionists, slaves, and liberal whites.

679. Jentz, John B. THE ANTISLAVERY CONSTITUENCY IN JACKSONIAN NEW YORK CITY. *Civil War Hist. 1981 27(2): 101-122.* By using the names of the male signers of 12 petitions protesting slavery in the District of Columbia that were sent to the US House of Representatives from New York City during 1829-39, it was determined that the majority of the antislavery supporters were artisans and shopkeepers, that a significant number of radicals were involved, and that the wealth and status of the signers decreased over the decade. Based on petitions, New York city directories, tax records, and other sources; 2 tables, 8 fig., 60 notes. G. R. Schroeder

680. Johnson, David W. FREESOILERS FOR GOD: KANSAS NEWSPAPER EDITORS AND THE ANTISLAVERY CRUSADE. *Kansas Hist. 1979 2(2): 74-85.* Six Kansas editors publicized the freesoil cause during territorial days. They did not entirely agree on the best means of organizing a state free from slavery, but they did agree that Providence would help this cause. Their religious allusions and imagery reassured many settlers of the inevitable outcome of territorial strife. Often, those who could not accept the idea of direct intervention by Providence found convincing these incessant reminders that God helps those who help themselves. Based on local newspapers; illus., 29 notes. W. F. Zornow

681. Johnson, Reinhard O. THE LIBERTY PARTY IN NEW HAMPSHIRE, 1840-1848: ANTISLAVERY POLITICS IN THE GRANITE STATE. *Hist. New Hampshire 1978 33(2): 123-166.* The Liberty Party, founded by abolitionists at Albany, N.Y., in 1840, became the main conduit of antislavery sentiments during the 1840's, and was a basis for many state Free Soil parties, as in New Hampshire. Although the New Hampshire party lacked strong leadership and an effective press, and drifted from election to election, it did attract unhappy Whigs and Democrats before merging with the Independent Democrats in 1846. 76 notes. D. F. Chard

682. Johnson, Reinhard O. THE LIBERTY PARTY IN MAINE, 1840-1848: THE POLITICS OF ANTISLAVERY REFORM. *Maine Hist. Soc. Q. 1980 19(3): 135-176.* Traces the origins and development of the antislavery Liberty Party in Maine politics in the 1840's. The groups involved in the state's abolition movement in the 1830's, at first reluctant to engage directly in politics, provided the strong leaders, such as Samuel Fessenden (1784-1869) and Austin Willey (1806-96), and the religious and moral convictions that characterized the party. It had a major impact on Maine politics until it merged into the Free Soil movement in the late 1840's. Based on newspapers and Willey's *History of the Antislavery Cause in State and Nation* (1886); 2 illus., 2 charts, 88 notes. C. A. Watson

683. Johnson, Reinhard O. THE LIBERTY PARTY IN VERMONT, 1840-1848: THE FORGOTTEN ABOLITIONISTS. *Vermont Hist. 1979 47(4): 258-275.* The Liberty Party won 319 votes for Birney in 1840, and soon replaced the Vermont Antislavery Society as the state abolitionist organization. Drawing first from the Whig Party and then from the Democrats, it prepared the base for the Free Soil Party of 1848-54 to "become the dominant element in Vermont state politics." Its weekly *Green Mountain Freeman,* edited by Joseph Poland, had the largest circulation of any Vermont newspaper in 1847. Based mainly on the abolitionist press; 55 notes. T. D. S. Bassett

684. Keller, Ralph A. METHODIST NEWSPAPERS AND THE FUGITIVE SLAVE LAW: A NEW PERSPECTIVE FOR THE SLAVERY CRISIS IN THE NORTH. *Church Hist. 1974 43(3): 319-339.* Because the antebellum slavery question overlapped into the churches, it is possible to learn a great deal from religious newspapers. The papers, more clearly than conference records or religious journals, show an extensive revulsion to the Fugitive Slave Law. Although the five editors cited found the law repulsive, they were in disagreement about what should be done. Their arguments were often more heated against each other than against the law. Besides being at odds over methods, religious leaders did not feel free to act or speak without concern for the consequences of the church itself. While institutional commitment often tempered the stand a churchman might take regarding a slavery problem, the crisis over slavery and the Union drew the churches into more involvement with social and political issues. Based on the five official newspapers of the Methodist Church; 89 notes. M. D. Dibert

685. Kerr, Norwood Allen. THE MISSISSIPPI COLONIZATION SOCIETY (1831-1860). *J. of Mississippi Hist. 1981 43(1): 1-30.* Describes the successes and failures of the Mississippi Colonization Society to emancipate Negroes and send them as colonists to Liberia. Organized in 1831, the state society attracted support especially from the southwestern section of Mississippi. Discusses significant state leaders who came south to promote colonization efforts. Devotes attention to campaigns to raise funds and to the local organization's financial structure. Describes the society's relations with the American Colonization Society and especially Mississippi's efforts to establish an independent colony in Africa. By 1859, 536 emancipated Negroes had been sent from Mississippi to Africa; however, the taint of abolitionism and fear of domestic emancipation worked to the disadvantage of moderate causes such as colonization. Based on reports and papers of the American Colonization Society, the *African Repository,* William Winans' Letterbooks, newspapers, and secondary sources; 81 notes. M. S. Legan

686. Kleinman, Max L. THE DENMARK VESEY CONSPIRACY: AN HISTORIOGRAPHICAL STUDY. *Negro Hist. Bull. 1974 37(2): 225-228.* Studies the slave revolt conspiracy of Denmark Vesey in Charleston, South Carolina, 1821-22, and the 1964 revisionist account of it by historian Richard Wade.

687. Kraut, Alan M. THE FORGOTTEN REFORMERS: A PROFILE OF THIRD PARTY ABOLITIONISTS IN ANTEBELLUM NEW YORK. Perry, Lewis and Fellman, Michael, ed. *Antislavery Reconsidered: New Perspectives on the Abolitionists* (Baton Rouge: Louisiana State U. Pr., 1979): 119-145. The Liberty Party, devoted exclusively to the abolition of slavery, was organized 1 April 1840 at Albany, New York, by such prominent abolitionists as Myron Holley, Gerrit Smith, Joshua Leavit, and William Goodell. Farmers, craftsmen, and professionals made up the bulk of the membership in this political party that, before its dissolution in 1848, played an important role in consolidating antislavery sentiment in early 19th-century New York. Based on poll listings from Smithfield, New York, a list of subscribers to a New York Liberal newspaper, and other primary sources; 10 tables, 43 notes. S

688. Lammen, A. BACK TO AFRICA. *Spiegel Historiael [Netherlands] 1977 12(2): 82-88.* Recounts the emigration of American blacks to Africa during the 19th century. The American Colonization Society attempted to promote this movement but with limited success. Liberia was founded by American blacks in 1821 and became a Republic in 1847. More than 20,000 blacks emigrated but many returned. The abolitionists strongly opposed these migration and colonization efforts. Illus., biblio. G. D. Homan

689. Langhorne, Elizabeth. EDWARD COLES, THOMAS JEFFERSON, AND THE RIGHTS OF MAN. *Virginia Cavalcade 1973 23(1): 30-37.* Describes Coles' manumitting and his antislavery efforts when governor of Illinois. S

690. Lee, Juliet A. BADGERS FOR A FREE KANSAS: THE WISCONSIN KANSAS EMIGRANT AID SOCIETY. *Milwaukee Hist. 1979 2(3): 65-84.* The emigrant aid movement in Wisconsin and Kansas during the 1850's was caused mostly by the Kansas-Nebraska Act (US, 1854), which repealed the Missouri Compromise of 1820 and renewed the conflict over slavery.

691. Lee, R. Alton. SLAVERY AND THE OREGON TERRITORIAL ISSUE: PRELUDE TO THE COMPROMISE OF 1850. *Pacific Northwest Q. 1973 64(3): 112-119.* Studies the treatment of the slavery question by Congress prior to 1850. John C. Calhoun in the Senate and Armistead Burt in the House based their arguments on the preservation of property rights (with the slaves understood as property), and states' rights. The southern extremists lost their gamble to trade off Oregon to free-soilers in return for the defeat of the Wilmot Proviso in the Southwest. 37 notes. R. V. Ritter

692. Lesick, Lawrence T. THE FOUNDING OF THE LANE SEMINARY. *Cincinnati Hist. Soc. Bull. 1979 37(4): 236-248.* Discusses the founding of the Lane Seminary on Walnut Hills near Cincinnati, Ohio, when Joshua L. Wilson, Ebenezer Lane, Elnathan Kemper, and Franklin Y. Vail formulated a plan for the Seminary's founding in 1829. The school is famous for the debate in 1834 between the faculty and administration,

and the students over the students' antislavery and pro-black activities, who included Theodore D. Weld, Henry B. Stanton, George Whipple, and Hiram Wilson.

693. Locke, William R. AN ABOLITIONIST AT GENERAL CONFERENCE. *Methodist Hist. 1979 17(4): 225-238.* William D. Cass was a member of the New Hampshire Conference of the Methodist Episcopal Church. He attended the 1844 General Conference of the Church at which the split over slavery occurred. As an abolitionist Cass took a position against permitting slavery within the church. His personal account of the activities is revealed in the three letters to his wife included here. 39 notes.
H. L. Calkin

694. Loomis, Sally. EVOLUTION OF PAUL CUFFE'S BLACK NATIONALISM. *Negro Hist. Bull. 1974 37(6): 298-302.* Paul Cuffe (1759-1817), a black Quaker, helped colonize black Americans in Sierra Leone in the 1810's as part of his vision for an international brotherhood that was the "African nation."

695. Loveland, Anne C. RICHARD FURMAN'S "QUESTIONS ON SLAVERY." *Baptist Hist. and Heritage 1975 10(3): 177-181.* In considering Richard Furman's views on slavery, historians have usually focused on his only published work on that subject, the *Exposition of the Views of the Baptists* (1823). But a manuscript in the Furman University Library Special Collections, "Questions on Slavery" (1807), offers insight into his earlier attitudes. His major position was that reformers should limit their efforts to improving the lot of the slave, not in abolishing slavery, as slavery gave the master the opportunity to evangelize the slave. The manuscript also provides additional evidence to support recent revisionist opinion that the evangelical proslavery argument was not a development of the 1820's, but had its roots in the post-Revolutionary period, or perhaps earlier. Based on the manuscript and *Exposition*; 8 notes.
H. M. Parker, Jr.

696. Maclear, J. F. THE EVANGELICAL ALLIANCE AND THE ANTISLAVERY CRUSADE. *Huntington Lib. Q. 1979 42(2): 141-164.* In 1846, American and British Protestants attempted to form an international organization to promote missions, reform, and benevolence. British sentiment favored excluding slaveholders, but the question was not settled prior to the organizational meeting in Liverpool, where a heated debate led to the decision to create separate national branches. While the American churchmen were personally opposed to slavery, they resented British attitudes and generally believed that religious unity was more important than abolition. Primary sources; 59 notes.
S. R. Smith

697. Maclear, J. F. THOMAS SMYTH, FREDERICK DOUGLASS, AND THE BELFAST ANTISLAVERY CAMPAIGN. *South Carolina Hist. Mag. 1979 80(4): 286-297.* Recounts the controversy in Belfast, Ireland, in 1846 between Frederick Douglass, an ex-slave and an orator of the abolition movement, and Thomas Smyth, a Charleston (South Carolina) Presbyterian minister who supported slave-holding.

698. Marszalek, John F. BATTLE FOR FREEDOM—GABRIEL'S INSURRECTION. *Negro Hist. Bull. 1976 39(3): 540-543.* Gabriel's Insurrection was the first of three great 19th century slave revolts. In 1800 Gabriel Prosser and other privileged slaves in Virginia used their freedom of movement to recruit slaves into an informal conspiracy. But the insurrection never began; rain delayed the uprising, and informers alerted Governor James Monroe, who called out the militia. Virginians responded with stricter repression and later with the American Colonization Society, dedicated to returning blacks to Africa. Based on the writings of James Monroe and other sources; 5 illus., biblio.
W. R. Hively

699. Mathews, Donald G. RELIGION AND SLAVERY: THE CASE OF THE AMERICAN SOUTH. Bolt, Christine and Drescher, Seymour, ed. *Anti-Slavery, Religion and Reform: Essays in Memory of Roger Anstey* (Folkestone, England: Dawson, 1980): 207-232. Reviews the conditions of worship and religious activities (especially of the evangelical churches—Methodist, Baptist, and Presbyterian) in the South from 1740 to 1860. Although there were some churches in which Negroes and whites worshiped together and there was considerable expression of antislavery sentiments by black and white Christians, the evangelical churches could not sustain a cohesive abolitionist movement in the South. 28 notes.
S

700. McCluskey, Audrey and McCluskey, John. FREDERICK DOUGLASS ON ETHNOLOGY: A COMMENCEMENT ADDRESS AT WESTERN RESERVE COLLEGE, 1854. *Negro Hist. Bull. 1977 40(5): 746-749.* Frederick Douglass addressed himself to genetic arguments which still remain viable.
R. Jirran

701. McFaul, John M. EXPEDIENCY VS. MORALITY: JACKSONIAN POLITICS AND SLAVERY. *J. of Am. Hist. 1975 62(1): 24-39.* Reinterprets the attitudes of the political parties toward the slavery issue during the Jackson administrations. The majority of the Jacksonian Democrats believed that government neutrality, as embodied in the Pinckney resolutions, on the slavery issue was necessary to preserve the union. Only political outsiders and some Whigs raised the slavery issue on a moral basis. In this era national parties and slavery agitation were mutually exclusive. Based on newspapers and secondary works; 45 notes.
J. B. Street

702. McKivigan, John R. THE AMERICAN BAPTIST FREE MISSION SOCIETY: ABOLITIONIST REACTION TO THE 1845 BAPTIST SCHISM. *Foundations 1978 21(4): 240-355.* Examines abolitionist relations with Northern Baptists, both before and after the 1845 schism. The American Free Baptist Mission Society was composed of those Baptists who would have no fellowship with Baptists who were in any way connected with the institution of domestic slavery—whether through slave-holding or in accepting contributions from those who held slaves. The group worked outside the normal lines of denominational missionary activity, supporting only missionaries who labored in free states. The persistence of abolitionist criticism of northern Baptists thus requires a reassessment of the denomination's pre-Civil War antislavery reputation. The number of northern Baptist associations renouncing fellowship with slaveholders steadily increased during the 1850's and helped sharpen sectional polarization, freeing northern Baptists to speak more agggressively against slavery. Based on the Annual Reports of the ABFMS and similar benevolent societies; 46 notes.
H. M. Parker, Jr.

703. McKivigan, John R. THE ANTISLAVERY "COMEOUTER" SECTS: A NEGLECTED DIMENSION OF THE ABOLITIONIST MOVEMENT. *Civil War Hist. 1980 26(2): 142-160.* Demonstrates that antislavery activity in the churches did not cease with the rise of antislavery politics in the 1840's. The various "comeouter" sects separated from the mainline denominations because they believed slaveholding was a sin and they should have no fellowship with slaveholders. The backgrounds, activities, and accomplishments of the Wesleyan Methodist Church, the Free Presbyterian Church, the American Baptist Free Missionary Society, the Franckean Evangelical Lutheran Synod, the Indiana Yearly Meeting of Anti-Slavery Friends and the Progressive Friends are discussed. Based on church publications and other sources; 56 notes.
G. R. Schroeder

704. McKivigan, John R. THE CHRISTIAN ANTI-SLAVERY CONVENTION MOVEMENT OF THE NORTHWEST. *Old Northwest 1979-80 5(4): 345-366.* The Christian Anti-Slavery Convention movement of the 1850's contradicts the prevalent notion that interdenominational abolitionist activity declined after the 1830's, giving way to antislavery politics and, under the leadership of William Lloyd Garrison, abolitionism divorced from religion. When denominational antislavery societies and the new come-outer sects replaced the American and Foreign Anti-Slavery Society as the focal point for non-Garrisonian antislavery activity, the Christian Anti-Slavery conventions in the Northwest restored some lost coordination to religious abolitionists who had become disenchanted with the diluted platform of the Free Soil campaign. The movement's most important convention took place in Chicago in 1851, but a resurgence of activity in the late 1850's culminated in the Columbus and Chicago conventions of 1859. Primary sources; 43 notes.
E. L. Keyser

705. Miller, Randall M. GEORGIA ON THEIR MINDS: FREE BLACKS AND THE AFRICAN COLONIZATION MOVEMENT IN GEORGIA. *Southern Studies 1978 17(4): 349-362.* Among free blacks, African colonization offered an escape from racial humiliation and al-

lowed for economic, social, and intellectual advancement. In 1816 the American Colonization Society, an arm of the African colonization movement, was founded. It acquired the West African settlement of Liberia. From 1816 to 1847, 206 black Georgians emigrated; from 1847 to 1860, 943 sailed. The interest in migration was fairly strong among free blacks, but the financial cost, diseases, and economic stagnation in Liberia prevented general success, despite a few individual success stories. Primary and secondary sources; 26 notes.   J. J. Buschen

706. Mitchell, Betty L. MASSACHUSETTS REACTS TO JOHN BROWN'S RAID. *Civil War Hist. 1973 19(1): 65-79.* Analyzes how Massachusetts, "the most radical antislavery state in the Union," reacted to John Brown's raid on Harpers Ferry. The response was moderate and the two major political parties spent more time reacting to each other than to Brown. After Brown's execution, the people of Massachusetts, like most northerners, soon forgot about him. Based on newspapers and secondary sources; 45 notes.   E. C. Murdock

707. Mitchell, Betty L. REALITIES NOT SHADOWS: FRANKLIN BENJAMIN SANBORN, THE EARLY YEARS. *Civil War Hist. 1974 20(2): 101-117.* An account of the involvement of Massachusetts abolitionist Franklin Benjamin Sanborn in John Brown's raid on Harpers Ferry. "More of a storybook revolutionary than a day-to-day political activist," Sanborn fled to Canada after the raid, returned, was seized by agents for a United States Senate investigating committee, but was liberated by friends. Like Brown, Sanborn thirsted for a war that would end slavery, but when war came, he "stepped back into the shadows, and did not serve." Based on the Sanborn Papers.   E. C. Murdock

708. Mitchell, Memory F. OFF TO AFRICA—WITH JUDICIAL BLESSING. *North Carolina Hist. Rev. 1976 53(3): 265-287.* Most North Carolina slaveowners who wished, in their wills, to emancipate their slaves and send them to Liberia encountered little difficulty in having these wishes acted upon. But sometimes executors encountered legal problems in which heirs contested wills and fought the bequest of freedom. It took decisions from the state supreme court to resolve these issues. The American Colonization Society was often an interested party in these court cases. Based on American Colonization Society and other manuscript collections, legal documents, and published primary and secondary materials; 6 illus., map, 120 notes.   T. L. Savitt

709. Morrison, Howard Alexander. GENTLEMEN OF PROPER UNDERSTANDING: A CLOSER LOOK AT UTICA'S ANTI-ABOLITIONIST MOB. *New York Hist. 1981 62(1): 61-82.* The antiabolitionist riot in Utica, New York on 21 October 1835 was politically motivated. Democratic politicians seeking reelection and other Democratic Party leaders led the riot in order to identify themselves and their party with the antiabolitionist majority. The Utica riot, moreover, was orchestrated by a Democratic political machine in order to strengthen the presidential candidacy of Martin Van Buren. Based on the Martin Van Buren Papers, James Watson Williams Papers, and contemporary newspapers and books; 6 illus., 52 notes.   R. N. Lokken

710. Murray, Andrew E. BRIGHT DELUSION: PRESBYTERIANS AND AFRICAN COLONIZATION. *J. of Presbyterian Hist. 1980 58(3): 224-237.* The basic flaw of the American Colonization Society (ACS) was its effort to ease the troubled consciences of white Americans while ignoring the needs and desires of black people. Points out the paradox in the life of David McDonough, an American slave whose master wanted him trained for leadership in Africa. Details the many frustrations McDonough confronted in his preparation to be a physician, due to prejudice. The ACS did not meet the needs of all blacks. For McDonough and others, colonization attempted to solve the problems of white oppressors by requiring the victims of that oppression to make major sacrifices. Covers ca. 1840-50. Based largely on McDonough's correspondence with the Board of Foreign Missions, Presbyterian Historical Society, Philadelphia, and studies on the American Colonization Society; 30 notes.   H. M. Parker, Jr.

711. Neuenschwander, John A. SENATOR THOMAS MORRIS: ANTAGONIST OF THE SOUTH, 1836-1839. *Cincinnati Hist. Soc. Bull. 1974 32(3): 121-139.* Chronicles Thomas Morris' political career in the Ohio state legislature and his lifelong agitation in favor of the antislavery movement.

712. Newton, James E. THE UNDERGROUND RAILROAD IN DELAWARE. *Negro Hist. Bull. 1977 40(3): 702-703.* Describes the structure of the Underground Railroad, the routes through Delaware, and the contributions of four Delaware participants: Harriet Tubman, Thomas Garrett, Samuel D. Burris, and John Hunn. A plaque commemorating Delaware's role was dedicated in June 1976 in Wilmington. Secondary material; 6 photos, biblio.   R. E. Noble

713. Nordin, Kenneth D. IN SEARCH OF BLACK UNITY: AN INTERPRETATION OF THE CONTENT AND FUNCTION OF "FREEDOM'S JOURNAL." *Journalism Hist. 1977-78 4(4): 123-128.* The abolitionist tag attached to the black newspaper, *Freedom's Journal,* is too narrow; it also tried to develop a fraternity and shared consciousness and culture among freed slaves, 1827-29.

714. O'Neal, David L. CHANNING'S *SLAVERY:* A BIBLIOGRAPHICAL ESSAY. *Am. Book Collector 1973 23(3): 11-14.* The father of American Unitarianism, William Ellery Channing, was at one time America's foremost man of letters; "his collected works achieved twenty-two editions by 1870." The concern here is "with the printing and publishing history of perhaps his most influential work, *Slavery,* 1835." Channing was twice repelled by close-hand encounters with slavery, but resisted the efforts of abolitionists to embroil him in their crusade until he held a critical conversation with Samuel May in 1834. By 1835 he was hard at work on *Slavery,* which was released in December 1835 by the highly respected Boston publishers, James Munroe & Co. The work went through four American editions in two years; however, the demand for it appeared spent by 1838. Forceful and judicious in argument, the book nearly destroyed Channing's reputation. Illus., 4 notes.   D. A. Yanchisin

715. Osofsky, Gilbert. ABOLITIONISTS, IRISH IMMIGRANTS, AND THE DILEMMAS OF ROMANTIC NATIONALISM. *Am. Hist. R. 1975 80(4): 889-912.* The response of Garrisonian abolitionists to substantial immigration of Roman Catholic Irish was an attempt to reach beyond traditional Protestant and anti-foreign prejudice. They secured the support of reformers in Ireland, especially the Liberator Daniel O'Connell, identified Irish and black freedom, and defended the immigrants against American nativism. But the superpatriotism of first generation immigrants, suspected of divided loyalties in both politics and religion, rejected a radical minority movement. The first major Irish American movement, supporting repeal of the legislative union of England and Ireland, was disrupted by abolitionist pressure on the contradiction of Irish support for both slavery and repeal. Moreover, individualist values limited the abolitionists' response to Irish poverty to charity and preaching the work ethic. Events were violating the romantic nationalist tradition which viewed national independence as basis for individual liberty, for neither Irish nor nativist saw any need to extend personal freedom to all. The abolitionists' efforts to harmonize a universalist and egalitarian notion of personal freedom with national self-determination trace the decline of the romantic nationalist tradition and foreshadow the Civil War.   A

716. Osofsky, Gilbert. WENDELL PHILLIPS AND THE QUEST FOR A NEW AMERICAN NATIONAL IDENTITY. *Can. Rev. of Studies in Nationalism [Canada] 1973 1(1): 15-46.* Buttressed by British and American experience, Wendell Phillips's nationalism was shaped by religion. Its ideology was derived from the European Enlightenment, as expressed by Thomas Paine, Thomas Jefferson, James Madison, and Alexander Hamilton. The Puritan ideal of a Godly Commonwealth, through a pursuit of Christian morality and justice, however, was the main influence on Phillips's nationalism. He would have fragmented the American republic to destroy slavery, and he sought to amalgamate all the American races. Thus, it was the moral end which mattered most in Phillips's nationalism. Based on newspapers, magazines, letters, and secondary sources; 85 notes.   T. Spira

717. Patterson, John S. A GARRISONIAN DISCUSSION OF PREJUDICE: "NOT ONE DARES TO RISE." *New England Q. 1975 48(4): 564-570.* Reviews an Abolitionist meeting in 1841 presided over by William Lloyd Garrison, to determine the degree of anti-Negro prejudice in New England at the time. All persons present were opposed to slavery, but a call for an antiprejudice pledge brought opposition. This was smoothed over and a unanimous vote in favor duly recorded, but such

machinations simply disguised, rather than eliminated, the fact that a large degree of racism was very much evident. 5 notes.
V. L. Human

718. Payne-Gaposchkin, Cecilia Helena. THE NASHOBA PLAN FOR REMOVING THE EVIL OF SLAVERY: LETTERS OF FRANCES AND CAMILLA WRIGHT, 1820-1829. *Harvard Lib. Bull. 1975 23(3): 221-251, (4): 429-461.* Supplies background to the establishment and abandonment of Nashoba, the west Tennessee community the Wright sisters founded to provide a self-sufficient, cooperative agricultural operation through which chosen slaves could, by amassing a surplus fund, purchase their own emancipation. Indicates the relationship of Robert Dale Owen to Nashoba and gives insight into conditions of frontier travel. Based on correspondence in the Houghton Library; 103 notes.
L. D. Smith

719. Perkal, M. Leon. AMERICAN ABOLITION SOCIETY: A VIABLE ALTERNATIVE TO THE REPUBLICAN PARTY? *J. of Negro Hist. 1980 65(1): 57-71.* The American Abolition Society molded radical abolitionism into an independent movement during 1855-58. Avoiding the disunionist sentiment of the Garrisonians, the Society exerted moral influence upon the new Republican Party. The American Abolition Society served as a link between idealism and practical politics. Based on primary materials; 57 notes.
N. G. Sapper

720. Perry, Lewis. PSYCHOLOGY AND THE ABOLITIONISTS: REFLECTIONS ON MARTIN DUBERMAN AND THE NEOABOLITIONISTS OF THE 1960'S. *Rev. in Am. Hist. 1974 2(3): 309-321.* Duberman and other neoabolitionist historians of the 1960's dismissed "the stereotype of the abolitionist as a fanatic motivated 'by an unconscious drive to gratify certain needs of his own.'" Doubting the ability of psychohistory to reveal motives for behavior, they defended the antislavery of the early 19th century as "the logical response to evil in the South." Yet their defensive forensic style of psychology ignores a wide range of motivational evidence currently used by psychohistorians such as personality, family influences, "authority, sexuality, purification, and restraint." Secondary sources; 37 notes.
T. Simmerman

721. Perry, Lewis. "WE HAVE HAD CONVERSATION IN THE WORLD": THE ABOLITIONISTS AND SPONTANEITY. *Can. R. of Am. Studies 1975 6(1): 3-26.* Examines the lives of Theodore Dwight Weld (1803-95), Amos Bronson Alcott (1799-1888), Wendell Phillips (1811-84), and other abolitionists, and the personal and professional levels on which these figures attempted to foster social spontaneity rather than social repression. Concludes that abolitionists generally preferred an orderly society but did not seek to achieve it by imposing repressive puritanical social controls. Based on writings by abolitionists and secondary sources; 64 notes.
H. T. Lovin

722. Perry, Thelma D. RACE-CONSCIOUS ASPECTS OF THE JOHN BROWN AFFAIR. *Negro Hist. Bull. 1974 37(6): 312-317.* Examines the race relations and attitudes of John Brown, the abolitionist, as exhibited in his relations with black leaders at the 1858 meeting in Canada to establish a provisional government preliminary to overthrowing the southern slave establishment, and his 1859 raid on Harpers Ferry, Virginia.

723. Pugh, Evelyn L. WOMEN AND SLAVERY: JULIA GARDINER TYLER AND THE DUCHESS OF SUTHERLAND. *Virgina Mag. of Hist. and Biog. 1980 88(2): 186-202.* Traces the controversy stemming from the reply of Julia Gardiner Tyler, wife of former President John Tyler, to the 1852 address of an English duchess which called on American women to support gradual abolition, immediate ending of the breakup of slave families, and improvement of slave education. Mrs. Tyler claimed that British social conditions were worse than those of American slaves, and attacked the British "Affectionate and Christian Address . . ." mainly as unwarranted interference in US domestic affairs. She defended southern womanhood and questioned the motivation of British appealers. 63 notes.
P. J. Woehrmann

724. Quarles, Benjamin. ANTEBELLUM FREE BLACKS AND THE "SPIRIT OF '76." *J. of Negro Hist. 1976 61(3): 229-242.* Cites examples of antebellum black spokesmen who found fault with the Declaration of Independence for inconsistency and the closely related grounds of hypocrisy and ineffectuality. Discusses negative attitudes toward Thomas Jefferson and the Fourth of July as a national holiday, and examines efforts made by blacks in the first half of the 19th century to insure that the Declaration would remain an inescapable commitment. Based mainly on periodical sources; 91 notes.
P. J. Taylorson

725. Quarles, Benjamin, ed. JOHN BROWN WRITES TO BLACKS. *Kansas Hist. Q. 1975 41(4): 454-467.* Examines a hitherto unreported aspect of John Brown's career and relates it to Frederick Douglass. In 1847 Douglass began to publish a weekly, first entitled *The North Star* and later *Frederick Douglass' Paper.* Between 25 December 1851 and 2 May 1856 Douglass published six letters to the editor from Brown, two of which contained brief postscripts by Brown's eldest, namesake son. Only one of these letters has been reproduced in a Brown reader. The letter of 17 December 1855 is particularly significant for the additional information it provides about the Wakarusa war. Based on primary and secondary sources; illus., 16 notes.
W. F. Zornow

726. Rachleff, Marshall. DOCUMENT: DAVID WALKER'S SOUTHERN AGENT. *J. of Negro Hist. 1977 62(1): 100-103.* David Walker's *Appeal* (1829), directed to blacks, had an explosive impact on the plantation aristocracy. The two letters printed here (exchanged between Wilmington, N.C., and Mobile, Ala., in November 1831) identify Walker's Wilmington agent in distributing the pamphlets as Jacob Cowan who was arrested by Wilmington authorities and sold "down the river" to Mobile, where he was allegedly implicated in a slave conspiracy. He could not be prosecuted since Alabama did not have a sedition law. Based mainly on Alabama Department of Archives and History, Montgomery, Ala.; 9 notes.
P. J. Taylorson

727. Rachleff, Marshall, ed. ECONOMIC SELF INTEREST VERSUS RACIAL CONTROL: MOBILE'S PROTEST AGAINST THE JAILING OF BLACK SEAMEN. *Civil War Hist. 1979 25(1): 84-88.* The Alabama legislature responded periodically to current white fears of slave insurrections, abolitionists, and free black sailors. In 1849, the lawmakers sought to strengthen the Mobile Harbor Act (1842) by mandating jail for visiting black crewmen. An assemblage of Mobile executives, tradesmen, and politicians joined in the chorus of protests from the North and Europe and drew up a petition. They used shipping costs as an argument to defend shipboard black crews as opposed to trouble-making whites. The legislature ignored this economic self-interest in favor of ancient fears and "public safety." Reprints the petition. Based on a primary document and secondary sources; 15 notes.
R. E. Stack

728. Reed, Harry A. FINANCING AN EARLY BACK-TO-AFRICA SCHEME. *Massachusetts Hist. Soc. Pro. 1978 90: 103-105.* For years, back-to-Africa plans were a small but important part of the philosophy of black Americans. Captain Paul Cuffe (1759-1817) organized one such controversial scheme in 1815. The author prints a document which lists the names of impoverished blacks of Boston who wished to return to Sierra Leone, along with the names of six subscribers who pledged to support their emigration financially. Based on a document in the Massachusetts Historical Society and on the general literature on return to Africa movements; 9 notes.
G. W. R. Ward

729. Reed, Harry A. THE SLAVE AS ABOLITIONIST: HENRY HIGHLAND GARNET'S *ADDRESS TO THE SLAVES OF THE UNITED STATES OF AMERICA. Centennial Rev. 1976 20(4): 385-394.* The *Address to the Slaves of the United States of America* (1843) by Henry Highland Garnet (1815-82) was not a call for insurrection but a coherent program based on the general moral and perfectionist concepts of antebellum reform. Unlike white abolitionists, ex-slave Garnet did not trust solely in concerted philosophical assaults upon the sinning slaveholder; he urged that blacks become active agents of their own emancipation rather than passive beneficiaries of white paternalism. They should demand their freedom, refuse to work if it were denied, then defend themselves against the almost inevitable violent white response. The result would be interracial warfare, but the onus would be upon masters, not slaves.
T. L. Powers

730. Reilly, Timothy F. GENTEEL REFORM VERSUS SOUTHERN ALLEGIANCE: EPISCOPALIAN DILEMMA IN OLD NEW ORLEANS. *Hist. Mag. of the Protestant Episcopal Church 1975 44(4): 437-450.* The first Episcopal church in New Orleans was founded in 1805;

the first Bishop of Louisiana, Leonidas Polk, was consecrated in 1838. His basic thrust among Negro slaves was in education. In response to the increasing sectional hostility between North and South, Polk also sought to establish a regional southern university, which was ultimately the University of the South at Sewanee, Tennessee. He was an advocate of gradual emancipation, and supported the efforts of the American Colonization Society up to the eve of the Civil War. He urged humanitarian treatment of slaves. His proselytizing efforts among them resulted in black communicants outnumbering whites in his diocese. He became a planter with slaves, and with the advent of the Civil War his program of genteel reform and educational development was considerably altered. His ministry terminated when he lost his life as a general in the Confederate Army. His religious career was governed by an emotionalism which was intermittently charged by a strong regional identification and an essential conservatism. Based on primary and secondary sources; 50 notes.
H. M. Parker, Jr.

731. Reilly, Timothy F. ROBERT L. STANTON, ABOLITIONIST OF THE OLD SOUTH. *J. of Presbyterian Hist.* 1975 53(1): 33-49. A New Englander by birth and sentiment, Robert Stanton spent nine frustrating years as a pastor in New Orleans and two years as president of Oakland College, Mississippi, prior to the Civil War. The author of a pamphlet, "New Orleans as It Is," Stanton attacked the evils of slavery as he saw it in the Crescent City. While in New Orleans he was overshadowed by B. M. Palmer of the First Presbyterian Church who supported slavery from the pulpit. Stanton held Palmer and other Presbyterian divines morally responsible for the furtherance of slavery and the secession that followed. In 1854 he left the South, settled in Ohio, and became a vociferous opponent of slavery. Based on Stanton's writings and other contemporary publications, photo, 63 notes.
H. M. Parker, Jr.

732. Reilly, Timothy F. SLAVERY AND THE SOUTHWESTERN EVANGELIST IN NEW ORLEANS (1800-1861). *J. of Mississippi Hist.* 1979 41(4): 301-317. Fundamentalism in New Orleans in the antebellum period produced mixed results. So desperate had Methodist and Baptist organizations become for converts that they were willing to proselytize among blacks and whites alike. Studies these Protestant efforts, and especially some of the clergy's liberal racial philosophies which placed them outside the mainstream in the South's defense of slavery. Key figures in New Orleans protestantism considered include: William Winans, Benjamin M. Drake, Asa C. Goldsbury, Holland McTyeire, and William Cecil Duncan. Concludes that New Orleans Catholicism and Protestantism were able to arrange a religious pluralism as the protestant clergy, with strong roots in the South's agrarian society, sought to create a religious culture which would be responsive to urban needs.
M. S. Legan

733. Reinders, Robert C. ANGLO-CANADIAN ABOLITIONISM: THE JOHN ANDERSON CASE, 1860-1861. *Renaissance and Modern Studies [Great Britain]* 1975 19: 72-97. The trial of the fugitive slave John Anderson, which led to changes in British law, illustrates the attitude of the abolition movements in Great Britain, Canada, and the United States.

734. Reinders, Robert C. THE JOHN ANDERSON CASE, 1860-1: A STUDY IN ANGLO-CANADIAN IMPERIAL RELATIONS. *Can. Hist. Rev. [Canada]* 1975 56(4): 393-415. Reexamines the John Anderson case. Reveals the close connections between British and Canadian anti-slavery societies, relations among the United States, Canada, and Great Britain, and the contentious character of Canadian politics in the early 1860's. Particularly important were the case's legal aspects and the implications of the various court decisions for Anglo-Canadian relations. 76 notes.
R. V. Ritter

735. Riach, Douglas C. DANIEL O'CONNELL AND AMERICAN ANTI-SLAVERY. *Irish Hist. Studies [Ireland]* 1976 20(77): 3-25. Although Daniel O'Connell (1775-1847) was the most important European ally of the abolitionists, expediency colored his stand and made it less than wholly consistent. Among factors which conditioned his support of antislavery were Irish American antipathy to the abolitionist movement, mutual suspicions among Irish abolitionists, hostility of the Irish American associations in the southern United States, and disillusion with his opposition to British recognition of Texas and its subsequent annexation. Based on printed and manuscript sources; 89 notes.
P. H. Hardacre

736. Riach, Douglas C. RICHARD DAVIS WEBB AND ANTI-SLAVERY IN IRELAND. Perry, Lewis and Fellman, Michael, ed. *Antislavery Reconsidered: New Perspectives on the Abolitionists* (Baton Rouge: Louisiana State U. Pr., 1979): 149-167. Richard Davis Webb (1805-72) of Dublin, Ireland, a founding member of the Hibernian Anti-Slavery Society, was one of a group of prosperous middle class men devoted to abolition. Webb campaigned against Irish American support of slavery. He appealed to the Irish love of liberty (as displayed in Ireland's struggle for independence from Great Britain) to elicit sympathy for the plight of American Negroes. 25 notes.
S

737. Richards, Leonard L. THE JACKSONIANS AND SLAVERY. Perry, Lewis and Fellman, Michael, ed. *Antislavery Reconsidered: New Perspectives on the Abolitionists* (Baton Rouge: Louisiana State U. Pr., 1979): 99-118. Examines the charge by John Quincy Adams that his defeat by Andrew Jackson in the presidential election of 1828 was a defeat rather than a victory for democracy and concludes that Adams's claim is not without merit. While northern and southern Democrats presented a generally solid front of anti-Negro and proslavery sentiment, northern Whigs were divided on these issues. Jackson's Indian policy and political maneuvers, even in engineering the election of the northerner Martin Van Buren as president, were consistently more advantageous to the South than to the North. 27 notes.
S

738. Rietveld, Ronald D. LINCOLN AND THE POLITICS OF MORALITY. *J. of the Illinois State Hist. Soc.* 1975 68(1): 27-43. Abraham Lincoln became convinced that the fight against slavery was a moral struggle by 1854. He emphasized the incompatibility of the institution existing in a free country throughout his political involvement in the 1850's, especially in his struggle for political office with the pragmatic Democrat Stephen A. Douglas. Lincoln's stand on the immorality of slavery was attuned to the intellectual climate of the time and was a great aid in making him a viable presidential candidate in 1860.
N. Lederer

739. Rosenberg, Leonard B. WILLIAM PATERSON AND ATTITUDES IN NEW JERSEY ON SLAVERY. *New Jersey Hist.* 1977 95(4): 197-206. Concludes that William Paterson reflected his fellow countrymen in his attitudes on slavery. Moderate, if not conservative, on the question, Paterson "had no clear or deep commitment or emotional feeling about the institution." A slaveowner himself, he did not see slavery as a burning moral question. Paterson, however, did what he could to limit the slave trade and in his codification of New Jersey's laws made the process of manumission easier. Primary and secondary sources; 2 illus., 19 notes.
E. R. McKinstry

740. Rozett, John M. RACISM AND REPUBLICAN EMERGENCE IN ILLINOIS, 1848-1860: A REEVALUATION OF REPUBLICAN NEGROPHOBIA. *Civil War Hist.* 1976 22(2): 101-115. Challenges the James Rawley-Eugene Berwanger thesis that Negrophobia was the predominant component in the Free Soil-Republican Party philosophy during 1848-60. While conceding that racism was a factor in the opposition to slavery extension and that the Rawley-Berwanger theory supplies an important corrective to the traditional view, the author argues that basically the antislavery parties were hostile to slavery on moral grounds and that this was not true of the Democrats. Abraham Lincoln is the best example of the free soil position although he did not believe in racial equality. Supports arguments with a quantitative analysis of Illinois elections in 1848 and 1860.
E. C. Murdock

741. Rutherford, Phillip R. THE *ARABIA* INCIDENT. *Kansas Hist.* 1978 1(1): 39-47. The New England Emigrant Aid Company was formed to bring free settlers to Kansas. Guns were brought in to fight proslavery forces. The company insisted individual members were responsible for the gunrunning, but the whole operation became so systematic and extensive it becomes impossible to separate individual and corporate responsibility. David Starr Hoyt's unsuccessful effort to bring 100 Sharps rifles to Kansas aboard the ship *Arabia* and the long legal battle to regain title to the confiscated goods clearly shows the degree to which the aid company was directly involved. Covers 1855-59. Primary and secondary sources; illus., 39 notes.
W. F. Zornow

742. Schor, Joel. THE RIVALRY BETWEEN FREDERICK DOUGLASS AND HENRY HIGHLAND GARNET. *J. of Negro*

Hist. 1979 64(1): 30-38. Ideological differences (pertaining to political action, the use of violence, and emigration) between Frederick Douglass and Henry Highland Garnet, both avid abolitionists, 1840-49, led to petty jealousies and mutual suspicions which split them politically.

743. Schwarz, Philip J. CLARK T. MOORMAN, QUAKER EMANCIPATOR. *Quaker Hist. 1980 69(1): 27-35.* An 1849 letter from his grandson, Thomas H. Tyrell of Toledo, Ohio, recalls Clark Terrell Moorman's account of how in November 1782 he manumitted his two slaves, Gloster Mingo and Peter Peters, inherited in 1766. He had a dream that a black barred him from heaven. Like other 18th-century abolitionists, Moorman emphasized the bad effects of slavery on whites rather than on blacks. Cedar Creek Monthly Meeting in Caroline County, Virginia, started its campaign to abolish slaveholding among its members in December 1777. Moorman, an average farmer, had to sell land to pay for his free labor. Ultimately, he moved to Ohio. He felt that the manumission brought spiritual blessings in spite of economic losses. County records and Quaker sources; 29 notes. T. D. S. Bassett

744. Scott, Donald M. ABOLITION AS A SACRED VOCATION. Perry, Lewis and Fellman, Michael, ed. *Antislavery Reconsidered: New Perspectives on the Abolitionists* (Baton Rouge: Louisiana State U. Pr., 1979): 51-74. Many who espoused the immediate abolition of slavery had felt sudden religious revelations that slavery was a sin and had to be extirpated. Gerrit Smith, Theodore Weld, James Birney, and H. B. Stanton were among those who, influenced by the evangelicalism of the 1820's, called from the pulpit for the swift emancipation of blacks. 32 notes.
S

745. Seaton, Douglas P. COLONIZERS AND RELUCTANT COLONISTS: THE NEW JERSEY COLONIZATION SOCIETY AND THE BLACK COMMUNITY, 1815-1848. *New Jersey Hist. 1978 96(1-2): 7-22.* Despite earlier financial and organizational problems the New Jersey Colonization Society re-established itself in 1838 as a force to be taken seriously in the effort to return blacks to Africa. Ambivalent at first, New Jersey's blacks soon defended their status in American life. While members of the New Jersey Colonization Society were certainly anti-slavery, their main motive in espousing a back to Africa movement was racial; they wanted to send blacks away as a convenience to themselves. "Colonization, therefore, rather than a reform impulse, represented a type of reactionary utopianism on their part—a unique excursion into conservative impossibilism." Based on Colonization society records and secondary sources; 4 illus., 39 notes. E. R. McKinstry

746. Sehr, Timothy J. LEONARD BACON AND THE MYTH OF THE GOOD SLAVEHOLDER. *New England Q. 1976 49(2): 194-213.* Leonard Bacon (1802-81) agreed with abolitionists that slavery was wrong, but he distinguished between sinful and innocent slaveholders, believed that southern churches mitigated slavery, and refused to condemn the entire southern people. He believed that slavery was a local institution which could only be reformed by Southerners and that abolitionists tended to alienate most Southerners thereby lessening the chances of reform. Hopes for abolition rested on making slaveholders see the sinfulness of the institution, respect their slaves' humanity, educate and free them, and repeal the state laws supporting slavery. Based on Bacon's writings; 58 notes. J. C. Bradford

747. Silverman, Jason H. "IN ISLES BEYOND THE MAIN": ABRAHAM LINCOLN'S PHILOSOPHY ON BLACK COLONIZATION. *Lincoln Herald 1978 80(3): 115-122.* From the early 1850's until his death in 1865, Abraham Lincoln advocated colonization in conjunction with emancipation as the best solution to the nation's racial problem. Both Thomas Jefferson and Henry Clay, who had enthusiastically supported colonization, provided Lincoln with inspiration. All of Lincoln's efforts to implement black colonization had failed by 1864, but he never abandoned this program as the best solution. He justified his position on political, economic, and moral grounds, claiming that both races would benefit from separation. Lincoln merely assumed that blacks would rather leave America than remain as second-class citizens. 4 photos, 28 notes.
T. P. Linkfield

748. Silverman, Jason H. KENTUCKY, CANADA, AND EXTRADITION: THE JESSE HAPPY CASE. *Filson Club Hist. Q. 1980 54(1): 50-60.* Traces the impact of several cases brought by the State of Kentucky in Canada for the return of fugitive slaves. Starting in 1793, when the first Parliament of Upper Canada passed a bill gradually abolishing slavery, Canada became a haven for escaping American slaves. After Canada passed a comprehensive extradition law in 1833, three Kentucky cases tested the limits of the new law. The most significant case was that of Jesse Happy, who was accused of stealing a horse in his escape. The Canadian government decided that it would accept only testimony given in its own courts and freed Happy. This strict testimony requirement insured that few fugitive slaves would be returned to the United States. Documentation comes from the British Colonial Office Records and the Public Archives of Canada; 29 notes. G. B. McKinney

749. Simmons, Michael K. *MAUM GUINEA:* OR A DIME NOVELIST LOOKS AT ABOLITION. *J. of Popular Culture 1976 10(1): 81-87.* Published in 1861, *Maum Guinea and her Plantation "Children;" or, Holiday Week on a Louisiana Estate, A Slave Romance,* by Mrs. Metta V. Victor, was distributed widely in England by Beadle and Adams. Although a little book in the pulp literature tradition, it was also an abolitionist tract that influenced Great Britain's decision not to recognize the Confederacy. Secondary sources; 3 notes.
D. G. Nielson

750. Sokolow, Jayme A. REVOLUTION AND REFORM: THE ANTEBELLUM JEWISH ABOLITIONISTS. *J. of Ethnic Studies 1981 9(1): 27-41.* Examines the backgrounds of pre-Civil War Jewish immigrants who became prominent speakers, writers, editors, and even guerrilla fighters in the abolition movement, finding that nearly all came from urban, cosmopolitan families in Europe and were either participants in or strongly affected by the liberal and reform ideas of the 1848 revolutions. An upwardly mobile group, active in civic life, they were the product of strong father figures as well, with a stress on duty, justice, and moral rectitude. The fact that leaders such as Sigismund Kaufman, Isaac Hartman, Theodore Weiner, Isidor Busch, and August Bondi were all Reform Jews made the slavery debate an assault on Orthodox Judaism in America as well. Table, 57 notes. G. J. Bobango

751. Stange, Douglas C. ABOLITION AS TREASON: THE UNITARIAN ELITE DEFENDS LAW, ORDER, AND THE UNION. *Harvard Lib. Bull. 1980 28(2): 152-170.* Describes pre-Civil War opposition of Unitarian conservative clergymen in Boston and St. Louis to the abolitionist movement. By championing law and order, respect for the US Constitution and state law, and separation of politics from moral influence, the ministers upheld the view of businessmen, who were mainly responsible for the fiscal well-being of the churches. The clergy, however, did accept in principle proposals to colonize slaves in foreign lands, realizing the impracticality of the idea because slaveholders would lose too much to agree. Any strong attempt at colonization would generate national disunion, a much worse evil, in the clergy's view, than slavery. Based on the James Freeman Clarke Papers, Houghton Library, Harvard University; William G. Elliot Collection, University Archives, Olin Library, Washington University, St. Louis; and files of the Missouri Historical Society, St. Louis; 81 notes. D. J. Mycue

752. Stange, Douglas C. FROM TREASON TO ANTISLAVERY PATRIOTISM: UNITARIAN CONSERVATIVES AND THE FUGITIVE SLAVE LAW. *Harvard Lib. Bull. 1977 25(4): 466-488.* Examines the dilemma faced by conservative Boston Unitarians such as Samuel A. Eliot when faced with mutually exclusive demands arising from their opposition to slavery and their commitment to the Union. Presents the actions and discussions of the group and how several individuals resolved the conflict. Notes. W. H. Mulligan, Jr.

753. Stange, Douglas C. THE MAKING OF AN ABOLITIONIST MARTYR: HARVARD PROFESSOR CHARLES THEODORE CHRISTIAN FOLLEN (1796-1840). *Harvard Lib. Bull. 1976 24(1): 17-24.* Relates the circumstances leading to Charles Theodore Christian Follen's early death which placed him in the pantheon of abolitionists. Explains how Samuel May's eulogy energized the myth of Follen's being fired from Harvard University. Based on primary and secondary sources in the Harvard U. Archives; 15 notes. L. Smith

754. Stanke, Michael J. THE BLACK ABOLITIONIST: SAVING THE PAST. *Afro-Americans in New York Life and Hist. 1979 3(1): 39-44.* Discusses works on black abolitionists active during 1830-60, a

subject which has been ignored largely and limited to studies on white abolitionists.

755. Stanley, Gerald. THE POLITICS OF THE ANTEBELLUM FAR WEST: THE IMPACT OF THE SLAVERY AND RACE ISSUES IN CALIFORNIA. *J. of the West 1977 16(4): 18-25.* Suggests that slavery and racism played a major role in California politics during 1849-60. Neither the Republicans nor the Democrats called for abolition or racial equality. Slavery extension and race, however, were issues.
R. Alvis

756. Stanley, Gerald. SLAVERY AND THE ORIGINS OF THE REPUBLICAN PARTY IN CALIFORNIA. *Southern California Q. 1978 60(1): 1-16.* The slavery issue was a major factor in the formation of California's Republican Party in 1856. Not many members of the new party came from the defunct Whig Party. Statistical evidence, while imperfect, suggests that the Republicans found their strength in recruitment of Anti-Nebraska Democrats rather than in former Whigs or the American Party. Recent studies indicate that Republican emergence in other states did not resemble the California experience, where the national slavery issue predominated over local concerns. Primary and secondary sources; table, 45 notes.
A. Hoffman

757. Stanley, Gerald. THE SLAVERY ISSUE AND ELECTION IN CALIFORNIA, 1860. *Mid-America 1980 62(1): 35-45.* In the 1860 four-party presidential election, Republicans won 32% of the total vote. The Republican Party campaigned against the extension of slavery because it encroached upon the rights of nonslave-owning whites in the West. Furthermore, they linked slavery and race to other issues such as homesteads, railroads, and daily overland mail in a deliberate appeal to race prejudice. The Democratic Party was divided, but exploitation of the slavery and race issues was the decisive factor in the Republican victory. Notes.
M. J. Wentworth

758. Stewart, James Brewer. EVANGELICALISM AND THE RADICAL STRAIN IN SOUTHERN ANTISLAVERY THOUGHT DURING THE 1820'S. *J. of Southern Hist. 1973 39(3): 379-396.* Discusses southern antislavery sentiments during the 1820's among scattered groups of devout Evangelicals, located mostly in the northernmost parts of the South. These few "radicals" believed slavery to be a cause for the decline of religious piety, a contradiction of religious creeds, a crime against humanity, an erosive force on morality and traditional values, and a cause of the diffusion of corruption and civic decay. The Evangelicals attempted to spread their gospel to purify "churchly institutions," and in the process estranged themselves from southern society. Much of the later abolitionism of the North was similar to or built upon their ideas. Based on contemporary publications and addresses, and secondary sources; 63 notes.
N. J. Street

759. Stewart, James Brewer. HEROES, VILLAINS, LIBERTY, AND LICENSE: THE ABOLITIONIST VISION OF WENDELL PHILLIPS. Perry, Lewis and Fellman, Michael, ed. *Antislavery Reconsidered: New Perspectives on the Abolitionists* (Baton Rouge: Louisiana State U. Pr., 1979): 168-191. Wendell Phillips was radicalized into eloquent and energetic abolitionism by the assassination of Elijah P. Lovejoy in 1837. He married Ann Terry Green, an iron-willed invalid bluestocking abolitionist, in 1836, and devoted his life to her and the cause of antislavery, among whose greatest enemies he numbered Daniel Webster. Phillips's philosophical ideal was manly self-control of the animal, physical self by the human, rational mind, although he admired rash activists such as Lovejoy and John Brown. 40 notes.
S

760. Stewart, James Brewer. POLITICS AND BELIEF IN ABOLITIONISM: STANLEY ELKINS' CONCEPT OF ANTIINSTITUTIONALISM AND RECENT INTERPRETATIONS OF AMERICAN ANTISLAVERY. *South Atlantic Q. 1976 75(1): 74-97.* Stanley M. Elkins located the essence of the American abolitionists in their extremely emotional rejection of all social structures which attempted to deal with slavery. This "antiinstitutionalism" destroyed any chance of a peaceful, negotiated solution to slavery. Historians in the 1960's usually rejected out of hand or ignored Elkins' theory. Current historians such as Bertram Wyatt-Brown, Lewis Perry, and the author accept it with modifications. Based on primary and secondary sources; 62 notes.
W. L. Olbrich

761. Stirn, James R. URGENT GRADUALISM: THE CASE OF THE AMERICAN UNION FOR THE RELIEF AND IMPROVEMENT OF THE COLORED RACE. *Civil War Hist. 1979 25(4): 309-328.* Briefly during 1835-37, a few Boston religious and business leaders formed, prematurely, the American Union as an alternative to Garrisonianism. Spurning quasicolonizationist views, they pushed urgent, albeit gradual, emancipation through piecemeal reforms such as education and religion, on moderates, North and South. The Union revealed Christian impatience with southern inaction. Few responded, even when the popular Reverend Leonard Bacon explained how piecemeal cessation of wicked practices would ruin slavery. Terrible disillusionment resulted. The organizers did try significant, tentative steps away from colonization toward pragmatic abolition; respectable northerners struggled, midway between old ideas, with possibilities of southern revolt and war. 84 notes.
R. E. Stack

762. Streifford, David M. THE AMERICAN COLONIZATION SOCIETY: AN APPLICATION OF REPUBLICAN IDEOLOGY TO EARLY ANTEBELLUM REFORM. *J. of Southern Hist. 1979 45(2): 201-220.* For many early 19th-century Americans, republicanism and racism united in a social theory of republicanism which demanded a homogeneous citizenry. The American Colonization Society is a good example of this. Thus, they could hold that black colonization to Africa would move the United States closer to uncontaminated republicanism, while returning blacks would impart solid republican virtues in Africa. Abolitionism challenged this early republican ideology which could not adjust to accommodate equality for blacks and whites within "one homogeneous nation of freemen." Thus, in the decades before the Civil War, northerners and southerners could both invoke republicanisms, but still be at ideological polar extremes. Printed primary and secondary sources; 54 notes.
T. D. Schoonover

763. Szasz, Ferenc M. ANTEBELLUM APPEALS TO THE "HIGHER LAW," 1830-1860. *Essex Inst. Hist. Collections 1974 110(1): 33-48.* Because slavery was written into the Constitution, Northerners and Southerners debated the nature of a "higher law" on which all law was based.
S

764. Taylor, Sally. MARX AND GREELEY ON SLAVERY AND LABOR. *Journalism Hist. 1979-80 6(4): 103-106, 122.* Discusses the thoughts on labor and slavery of Karl Marx and Horace Greeley. Both opposed slavery and expressed contempt for the British industrial system while Marx was a correspondent for Greeley's New York *Tribune* from 1851 until 1862, when Marx was dismissed due to disagreements between the two on the above issues.

765. Temperley, Howard. ANTI-SLAVERY AS A FORM OF CULTURAL IMPERIALISM. Bolt, Christine and Drescher, Seymour, ed. *Anti-Slavery, Religion and Reform: Essays in Memory of Roger Anstey* (Folkestone, England: Dawson, 1980): 335-350. The abolition movement grew out of elitist religious and philosophical ideas of 18th-century Great Britain and spread until it became a cultural attitude which was then imposed as a measuring stick on other cultures which were thereby judged for their morality—that is, their conformity to Anglo-American elitist concepts of slavery. 18 notes.
S

766. Temperley, Howard. CAPITALISM, SLAVERY AND IDEOLOGY. *Past and Present [Great Britain] 1977 (75): 94-118.* Revisionist arguments that in a capitalist economy slavery was uneconomical can be shown to be wrong. That procapitalist arguments were effectively used by abolitionists is explained by their linking of abolitionism with the ideological views (originating with Adam Smith and repeated by J. E. Cairnes) that free labor and the humanitarian treatment of labor brings greater productivity. Southern polemicists saw that capitalist ideology was inimical to slave-holding. The abolition controversy centered on a conflict of values which was not related to economic advantage at all; slavery was perfectly suited to a ruthless capitalistic interest in highest profits. Based on primary sources, Parliamentary papers, and secondary sources.
D. Levy

767. Thompson, J. Earl, Jr. ABOLITIONISM AND THEOLOGICAL EDUCATION AT ANDOVER. *New England Q. 1974 47(2): 238-261.* John Greenleaf Whittier, William Lloyd Garrison, and other abolitionists were disillusioned by Andover Seminary's rejection of orga-

nized abolitionism. Discusses in detail the development of organized antislavery reform in the seminary's curriculum until it was discontinued in 1835. 69 notes.   E. P. Stickney

768. Thompson, J. Earl, Jr. LYMAN BEECHER'S LONG ROAD TO CONSERVATIVE ABOLITIONISM. *Church Hist. 1973 42(1): 89-109.* Beecher's New School Presbyterian conservative abolitionism underwent three major developmental stages. He was first identified as a New England Colonizationist. The 1834 Lane Seminary rebellion shows Beecher in his second stage as one trying to establish cooperative links between abolitionists and colonizationists notwithstanding their fundamental differences. After the 1837 Presbyterian schism Beecher began to associate with Ohio's New School Presbyterians who by the time of the 1843-44 William Graham heresy trials accepted moderate abolitionism aimed at a gradual end to slavery among church members and, by example, throughout the nation. Based on early 19th-century association journals, newspapers, letters, Beecher's autobiography, and secondary sources; 117 notes.   S. Kerens

769. Thompson, J. Earl, Jr. SLAVERY AND PRESBYTERIANISM IN THE REVOLUTIONARY ERA. *J. of Presbyterian Hist. 1976 54(1): 121-141.* Throughout the Revolutionary epoch Presbyterians attempted to build an antislavery platform upon which the entire church could stand, to unify a young and fragile Christian community avoiding the disruption of schism which had plagued them before the Revolution, and to create a large and strong denomination. Their social goal was to maintain the tranquility, order, and racial homogeneity of white America by protecting the nation against an invasion of degraded freed blacks. They believed that they could reconcile their competing values of hostility toward slavery, fear of freedom, and loyalty to a united denomination and to a racially homogeneous America by embracing the ideology and program of gradualism. Traces the attitudes of Presbyterian leaders toward slavery—Samuel Davies, Dr. Bejamin Rush, Jacob Green, Samuel Stanhope Smith, Elias Boudinot, Samuel Miller, and David Rice. Based largely on writings of the leaders cited; 91 notes.
H. M. Parker, Jr.

770. Tillery, Tyrone. THE INEVITABILITY OF THE DOUGLASS-GARRISON CONFLICT. *Phylon 1976 37(2): 137-149.* The American Anti-Slavery Society was marred by constant disagreements. The rupture of 1851 was the product of William Lloyd Garrison's and Frederick Douglass's personalities. One of the chief causes was the purchase of Douglass's freedom by his English friends in 1846. In May 1851 at the meeting of the Society, Douglass shocked the Garrisonian abolitionists by opposing a proposition not to support any newspaper that did not assume the Constitution to be a proslavery document. Garrison moved to have Douglass's *North Star* stricken from the list. "In one instant Douglass became a heretic." His action was the result of his need for self-esteem and recognition. 87 notes.   E. P. Stickney

771. Tilly, Bette B. THE SPIRIT OF IMPROVEMENT: REFORMISM AND SLAVERY IN WEST TENNESSEE. *West Tennessee Hist. Soc. Papers 1974 (28): 25-42.* During its era of development, West Tennessee was the frontier line of the Old Southwest. Being oriented more toward the West than the South, it was more amenable to reform movements concerned with temperance, education, women's rights, and the slavery question. During the 1820's it was not certain that slavery would become a permanent social institution, but the 1830's ushered in a new period of thinking and gradually the Western District followed the rest of the South in its slavery posture. Shelby County in 1834 sent four men to the state constitutional convention, each of whom favored some plan of emancipation, but the document adopted denied even free blacks the franchise. Counties bordering the west bank of the Tennessee River retained fairly liberal attitudes towards Negroes, thus preventing antebellum West Tennessee from achieving a static society of conformism. Based on secondary sources; map, table, 35 notes.   H. M. Parker, Jr.

772. Trendel, Robert. THE EXPURGATION OF ANTISLAVERY MATERIALS BY AMERICAN PRESSES. *J. of Negro Hist. 1973 58(3): 271-290.* Considers the efforts of abolitionists to expose proslavery censorship in the publishing industry during the 1840's and 1850's. Lewis Tappan and William Jay attacked the willingness of editors, compilers, revisers, abridgers, and even authors to remove antislavery sentiments from the literature of the day. Based on primary materials in the Library of Congress and on secondary sources; 46 notes.   N. G. Sapper

773. Trendel, Robert. JOHN JAY II: ANTISLAVERY CONSCIENCE OF THE EPISCOPAL CHURCH. *Hist. Mag. of the Protestant Episcopal Church 1976 45(3): 237-252.* The Episcopal Church in New York before and during the Civil War was fearful of schism, of involvement in a divisive and sectional issue, and of offending influential members who were linked economically, socially, or through family ties to slavery interests. John Jay II forced confrontations between the church he loved and human beings he loved, regardless of the costs to his profession, his personal image, his friendships, his status in the community, or the public image of the Episcopal Church in New York. He forced his church, sometimes uncomfortably, to live in the light of truth and justice. Based largely on the John Jay II Papers, in the possession of Mrs. Arthur Iselin (Nelson, New Hampshire), and other primary sources; 49 notes.
H. M. Parker, Jr.

774. Turley, David M. "FREE AIR" AND FUGITIVE SLAVES: BRITISH ABOLITIONISTS VERSUS GOVERNMENT OVER AMERICAN FUGITIVES, 1834-61. Bolt, Christine and Drescher, Seymour, ed. *Anti-Slavery, Religion and Reform: Essays in Memory of Roger Anstey* (Folkestone, England: Dawson, 1980): 163-182. Reviews several cases in which black American slaves or Negroes brought from Africa for the United States entered British territory. Abolitionists claimed that such slaves were free by virtue of their having touched the free land and breathed the free air of Great Britain or its colonies. The legal questions and decisions involved in these cases often caused conflict between the British abolitionists and their government. 51 notes.   S

775. Tushnet, Mark. THE AMERICAN LAW OF SLAVERY, 1810-1860, A STUDY IN THE PERSISTENCE OF LEGAL AUTONOMY. *Law and Soc. R. 1975 10(1): 119-184.* Discusses American law regarding slavery and Negroes in the South from 1810-60, emphasizing state supreme courts' rulings and the role of abolitionists.

776. Tyner, Wayne C. CHARLES COLCOCK JONES: MISSION TO SLAVES. *J. of Presbyterian Hist. 1977 55(4): 363-380.* A missionary to the slaves, the Reverend Charles Colcock Jones (1804-63) was among those southern clergy who accepted slavery as a given in southern society. But while he accepted slavery, he believed that the Christian slave would be a better slave, and taught obedience to masters and contentment with the servile condition. At the same time he must not be classed with those who felt that the promise of heaven was sufficient to pacify slaves. He takes his place with those southern ministers who believed that Christianity should ameliorate the social condition of the slave. Based largely on reports and writings of Jones; illus., 63 notes.
H. M. Parker, Jr.

777. VanDeburg, William L. FREDERICK DOUGLASS: MARYLAND SLAVE TO RELIGIOUS LIBERAL. *Maryland Hist. Mag. 1974 69(1): 27-43.* Young Frederick Douglass was convinced of the omnipotence of God and His role as "Supreme Judge of the Universe." By the 1840's, however, the influence of Reason, Transcendentalism, and Unitarianism convinced him that the abolition movement must be primarily a human enterprise. Despising the passive attitude displayed by many Negro ministers, Douglass even criticized Henry Ward Beecher's reliance on God to end slavery. Increasingly enlightenment terminology crept into Douglass' writings and speeches, and his move to a humanistic theology climaxed with his address in Philadelphia's Horticultural Hall on 26 April 1870 when he lauded Wendell Phillips, Elijah Lovejoy, John Brown, and Abraham Lincoln in celebrating the recently ratified 15th Amendment. Primary and secondary sources; 8 illus., 59 notes.
G. J. Bobango

778. VanDeburg, William L. FREDERICK DOUGLASS AND THE INSTITUTIONAL CHURCH. *J. of the Am. Acad. of Religion 1977 45(2): 218.* Frederick Douglass was a black abolitionist who remained in the institutional church but was highly critical of the church over the slavery issue. The abolitionist message, for Douglass, must be a vital part of the message of the church. Only those preachers and religious groups giving such an emphasis were considered true Christians. Abstract only.   E. R. Lester

779. Walters, Ronald G. THE BOUNDARIES OF ABOLITIONISM. Perry, Lewis and Fellman, Michael, ed. *Antislavery Reconsidered: New Perspectives on the Abolitionists* (Baton Rouge: Louisiana

State U. Pr., 1979): 3-23. Traces the roots of the American antislavery movement to principles of the American Revolution and relates abolitionism to various other types of reform in the 18th and 19th centuries. Even after the Civil War, reformers continued their traditions of striving for the perfection of humanity. Abolitionists differed among themselves and they also differed from other antebellum Americans, but they were, after all, formed in the same era and society, so they thought and spoke in the terms of their contemporaries, and therefore shared similarities with their fellow Americans. 19 notes.

S

780. Walters, Ronald G. THE EROTIC SOUTH: CIVILIZATION AND SEXUALITY IN AMERICAN ABOLITIONISM. *Am. Q. 1973 25(2): 177-201.* The growth of the antislavery movement after 1830 was based on northern fears of the unrestrained power of the South. Criticism of the unbridled lasciviousness between masters and slaves was activated by northern middle-class insecurities over the expansion of the franchise to the lower-class majority. Concern for southern reform mirrored a growing reformist belief that civilization depended on controlling man's animal nature to achieve social progress. Primary and secondary sources; 47 notes.

W. D. Piersen

781. Weisberger, Bernard A. HORACE GREELEY: REFORMER AS REPUBLICAN. *Civil War Hist. 1977 23(1): 5-25.* Horace Greeley's moral guidance system sometimes pointed him simultaneously in opposed directions. This explains his curious course of thought from peaceful compromise to militancy during the secession crisis. Not wholly inconsistent, he remained faithful to humanitarianism and was offended by the slaveholders' reaction to progress and reform. He was deeply committed to the processes of law and property rights that were defied by Southern seizure of Federal installations. Finally, Greely believed in American reasonableness which he saw being thwarted by a slaveholders' conspiracy. He trod a backward path to grasp an emotional affirmation of the Union. Primary and secondary sources; 58 notes.

R. E. Stack

782. Wendler, Marilyn V. ANTI-SLAVERY SENTIMENT AND THE UNDERGROUND RAILROAD IN THE LOWER MAUMEE VALLEY. *Northwest Ohio Q. 1980 52(2): 193-208.* In the Maumee Valley in northwestern Ohio, the first antislavery society began in 1815; during the 1850's, politics and the Underground Railroad rallied local support, but the conflict between genuine humanitarianism and belief in white superiority remained for more than a century after the Civil War.

783. White, Edward. EYEWITNESS AT HARPER'S FERRY. *Am. Heritage 1975 26(2): 56-59, 94-97.* An account of John Brown's raid on Harpers Ferry written 30 years later by Edward White, an eyewitness to those events. White later joined the Confederate army in 1861. 3 illus.

J. F. Paul

784. Wiecek, William M. LATIMER: LAWYERS, ABOLITIONISTS, AND THE PROBLEM OF UNJUST LAWS. Perry, Lewis and Fellman, Michael, ed. *Antislavery Reconsidered: New Perspectives on the Abolitionists* (Baton Rouge: Louisiana State U. Pr., 1979): 219-237. In 1842 George Latimer, a fugitive slave, was detained in Boston to be returned to his master under the terms of the Fugitive Slave Act. An abolitionist lawyer, Samuel E. Sewall, attempted on various legal grounds to win Latimer's freedom from the court of the Chief Justice of Massachusetts, Lemuel Shaw, but the latter, while declaring antislavery sentiments, denied the release of Latimer, asserting that he, Shaw, was bound by oath to apply the laws as they existed regardless of his personal views. Eventually Latimer's freedom was purchased from his master, but the case exemplified the dilemma of both the private citizen and the official when confronted with the existence of morally repugnant laws. *Billy Budd, Sailor* (1891) by Herman Melville, whose father-in-law was Lemuel Shaw, reflects, in great part, a concern with precisely the same dilemma in a powerful literary parable. 39 notes.

S

785. Wiecek, William M. SLAVERY AND ABOLITION BEFORE THE UNITED STATES SUPREME COURT, 1820-1860. *J. of Am. Hist. 1978 65(1): 34-59.* The notoriety surrounding *Dred Scott* v. *Sandford* (US, 1857) has frequently hindered historians' efforts to understand the policy-making role of the antebellum Supreme Court. The *Dred Scott* case was neither exceptional nor anomalous. It was, however, the natural result of judicial doctrines and tendencies that had been developing for several years. John Marshall, though opposed to slavery in the abstract, believed that a judge's moral instincts should not influence his rulings in light of the law. Roger Taney, as Chief Justice, was determined to destroy antislavery constitutional ideas argued in cases before him. Even before the famous *Dred Scott* case, Supreme Court decisions involving *Groves* (1841), *Prigg* (1842), and *Van Zandt* (1847) consistently undermined antislavery constitutional ideas argued before the Court. The *Dred Scott* decision was no aberration. 89 notes.

T. P. Linkfield

786. Wilson, Benjamin C. KENTUCKY KIDNAPPERS, FUGITIVES, AND ABOLITIONISTS IN ANTEBELLUM CASS COUNTY MICHIGAN. *Michigan Hist. 1976 60(4): 339-358.* In the years after 1840, the black population of Cass County, located in southwestern Michigan, increased dramatically. Attracted by white defiance of discriminatory laws, by numerous Quakers, and by low-priced land, free and runaway blacks found the county an ideal haven. The situation quickly attracted the attention of southern slaveholders. In 1847 and 1849, planters from Bourbon and Boone Counties in northern Kentucky led ultimately unsuccessful raids into Cass County. On the national level, the raids helped bring about passage of the Fugitive Slave Act of 1850. Primary and secondary sources; 2 illus., 3 photos, map, 72 notes.

D. W. Johnson

787. Wiltshire, Susan Ford. JEFFERSON, CALHOUN, AND THE SLAVERY DEBATE: THE CLASSICS AND THE TWO MINDS OF THE SOUTH. *Southern Humanities Rev. 1977 11(Special Issue): 33-40.* Examines how two classical traditions in the South (the first, represented by Thomas Jefferson, closely associated with the American Enlightenment, and the second, represented by John C. Calhoun, associated with conservative reaction to economic and social change) clashed over slavery, 1830's-40's. One of the six articles in this issue on the classical tradition in the South.

788. Winston, Michael R. SELECTED DOCUMENTS ILLUSTRATIVE OF SOME ASPECTS OF THE LIFE OF BLACKS BETWEEN 1774-1841. *J. of Negro Hist. 1976 6(1): 88-97.* The first document, signed by Patrick Henry, reflects the white colonists' determination to control persons of color in 1778 during the War for Independence. A deed of emancipation recorded in Virginia in 1798 illustrates the opposite side of slavery. A marriage permit for slaves, dated 1802, reveals slaves' lack of control over their lives. A letter from Abraham Byrd to John Morgan in 1838 protests a black woman's insistence that she be treated as a human being. The resolution of the Colored Citizens of Washington, D.C., concerning Liberia insists that free black people be given a free choice to oppose or support the program of the American Colonization Society. Documents were selected from the Manuscript Division of the Moorland-Spingarn Research Center.

N. G. Sapper

789. Wyatt-Brown, Bertram. CONSCIENCE AND CAREER: YOUNG ABOLITIONISTS AND MISSIONARIES. Bolt, Christine and Drescher, Seymour, ed. *Anti-Slavery, Religion and Reform: Essays in Memory of Roger Anstey* (Folkestone, England: Dawson, 1980): 183-203. By 1800 an enlightened approach to child-rearing had been developed in many evangelical households in the United States. Although austere, this type of upbringing offered children love and fostered self-reliance and respect for authority. Children brought up in such homes often became either missionaries or abolitionists. The path chosen seemed to depend on whether, at an impressionable stage of development, the child was affected by a religious experience or a political one. Some of the notable missionaries and abolitionists considered are Henry Lyman, William Lloyd Garrison, John Greenleaf Whittier, Clara Barton, Sarah Grimké, and Elijah Lovejoy. 38 notes.

S

790. Wyatt-Brown, Bertram. PROSLAVERY AND ANTISLAVERY INTELLECTUALS: CLASS CONCEPTS AND POLEMICAL STRUGGLE. Perry, Lewis and Fellman, Michael, ed. *Antislavery Reconsidered: New Perspectives on the Abolitionists* (Baton Rouge: Louisiana State U. Pr., 1979): 308-336. Arguments on both sides of the slavery issue were written by and directed toward men of significant social standing and education in both camps. The correspondence between abolitionist Lewis Tappan and the aristocratic South Carolinian James Henry Hammond exemplifies this tendency for the elites on both sides to abjure appeals to the lower classes and blacks and to rely upon learned messages to upright, educated Christians to resolve the question of the morality of slavery. 36 notes.

S

791. Wyatt-Brown, Bertram. STANLEY ELKINS' *SLAVERY*: THE ANTISLAVERY INTERPRETATION REEXAMINED. *Am. Q. 1973 25(2): 154-176.* Reexamines Stanley M. Elkins' antislavery interpretation in *Slavery: A Problem in American Institutional and Intellectual Life* (Chicago: University of Chicago Press, 1959). Supports three of his arguments: 1) 19th-century America was iconoclastic, egocentric, and anxious; 2) abolitionists and Transcendentalists shared similar moral and intellectual priorities; and 3) a deep sense of personal guilt activated antislavery concerns. 43 notes. — W. D. Piersen

792. —. SLAVERY AND THE PROTESTANT ETHIC. *Hist. Reflections [Canada] 1979 6(1): 157-181.*
Anstey, Roger. SLAVERY AND THE PROTESTANT ETHIC, *pp. 157-172.* Analyzes the role of religious forces in the formation and expansion of antislavery movements in the United States and Great Britain and examines its influence in the abolition of the British slave trade, the West Indian emancipation, and US antislavery politics. Theological doctrines—Arminianism, redemptionism, sanctification, and postmillenialism—disposed Protestants to include the slaves among the potentially saved, to hate the institution of slavery, and to strive for earthly reform. Additionally, slavery became a denominational issue, as Anglican Evangelicals, Nonconformists, and Quakers combined to provide the political organization and strategy for abolition and emancipation. 66 notes.
DaCosta, Emilia Viotti. COMMENTARY ONE, *pp. 173-177.* Anstey's reasoning is circular and fails to distinguish causation from concomitance and real motives from the religious rhetoric in which they were dressed. 2 notes.
Davis, David Brion. COMMENTARY TWO, *pp. 177-181.* Explains Anstey's own Christian belief and the way it informed his work on the British abolitionists of the 18th and 19th centuries and their religious conception of politics. — S

The First Women's Movement

793. Bloch, Ruth H. AMERICAN FEMININE IDEALS IN TRANSITION: THE RISE OF MORAL MOTHERHOOD, 1785-1815. *Feminist Studies 1978 4(2): 100-126.* Eighteenth-century literature on women stressed their roles as helpmates or social ornaments, but said little about motherhood, except for its physical aspects (childbearing and nursing). Children's education was ascribed to parents, or particularly to fathers rather than to mothers. But beginning with the second part of Richardson's *Pamela,* the emphasis changed and a new, idealized conception of motherhood was introduced. Its impact in America began in the late 18th century in the context of an expanding literature for and about women. The concept of the "moral mother" combined older ideals with newer Enlightenment attitudes toward women. It had the ambiguous effect of confining women's role to the maternal stereotype, but also of giving women autonomy within their "sphere" and so grounding later feminist agitation. 76 notes. — L. M. Maloney

794. Dublin, Tom. WORKING WOMEN AND THE "WOMEN'S QUESTION." *Radical Hist. Rev. 1979-80 (22): 93-98.* During 1830-60, some women challenged the then-occurring articulation of women's place in American society; reprints a letter written in 1850 to feminist Caroline Dall by Harriet Farley, former textile mill worker and former coeditor of the textile companies-subsidized periodical, the *Lowell Offering.*

795. Eakin, Paul John. MARGARET FULLER, HAWTHORNE, JAMES, AND SEXUAL POLITICS. *South Atlantic Q. 1976 75(3): 323-338.* Margaret Fuller's feminist career inspired both Nathaniel Hawthorne's *The Blithedale Romance* and Henry James' *The Bostonians.* Fuller saw her own life as caught between intellectual and emotional demands. Hawthorne portrayed her as Zenobia, whose pursuit of intellectual freedom was marred by her sexual hero-worship of Hollingsworth. James made her into two heroines, Verena Tarrant and Olive Chancellor, who sought salvation through "self culture," and ended up playing sexual dominance-submission games with hero Basil Ransom. Fuller's political forays for social rights for females show how little the feminist movement has progressed. — W. L. Olbrich

796. Ginzberg, Lori D. WOMEN IN AN EVANGELICAL COMMUNITY: OBERLIN, 1835-1850. *Ohio Hist. 1980 89(1): 78-88.* Discusses the role of women at Oberlin College, the first coeducational college in the United States. Women were thought to be morally superior to men, and they were thus well suited for evangelical activities. Many of the women graduates, instilled with this sense of moral superiority, and their duty to fulfill God's mission planned on missionary work. Primary sources; 29 notes. — J. Powell

797. Hales, Jean Gould. CO-LABORERS IN THE CAUSE: WOMEN IN THE ANTE-BELLUM NATIVIST MOVEMENT. *Civil War Hist. 1979 25(2): 119-138.* Denies traditional historiographical claims that nativists refused women an active part in their movement. Argues instead that nativists sympathized with working women, urged women of all classes to join them, and, by virtue of their traditionalist belief in the moral superiority of women, regarded women as natural and valuable allies in their crusade against Catholics and foreigners. Describes the nativist careers of Pennsylvanian Harriet Probasco (1844-45) and Marylander Anna Ella Carroll (1856-61), the activities and ideology of nativists, the roles of women activists, and the resultant acceptance of the expansion of women's social and political roles. The conservative, prostability cult of true womanhood projected by nativism offered women a reassuringly safe outlet from domesticity and thus helped to engender social change. 69 notes. — S

798. Hersh, Blanche Glassman. THE "TRUE WOMAN" AND THE "NEW WOMAN" IN NINETEENTH-CENTURY AMERICA: FEMINIST-ABOLITIONISTS AND A NEW CONCEPT OF TRUE WOMANHOOD. *Maryland Hist. 1978 9(2): 27-38.* Summarizes the theoretical position of the feminist-abolitionists who sought to change society's model for women from submissive acceptance of male superiority while marrying and having children to a new ideal. The "New Woman" would be independent, equal to men and part of the world outside the home if she chose. Men, too, would change to accept this "New Woman." Based on papers of leaders of the "New Woman" movement; illus., 32 notes. — G. O. Gagnon

799. Hudson, Winthrop S. EARLY NINETEENTH-CENTURY EVANGELICAL RELIGION AND WOMEN'S LIBERATION. *Foundations 1980 23(2): 181-185.* Evangelical Christianity, which had more women than men in its membership, gave women a social and psychological "space" they had not had. The church offered women a vehicle of self-expression through societies organized to carry out its work, and thus was liberating. Covers 1800-50. 3 notes. — E. E. Eminhizer

800. Kaye, Frances W. THE LADIES' DEPARTMENT OF THE *OHIO CULTIVATOR*, 1845-1855: A FEMINIST FORUM. *Agric. Hist. 1976 50(2): 414-423.* Between 1845 and 1855 a number of profeminist articles appeared in the Ladies' Department of the *Ohio Cultivator*, a leading Midwestern agricultural journal. Under the leadership of Hannah Maria Tracy-Cutler and Frances Dana Gage, the Department printed articles on the role of women in the home, education, suffrage, and jobs for women. It was a grass-roots forum for feminism. 23 notes. — D. E. Bowers

801. Kendall, Kathleen Edgerton and Fisher, Jeanne Y. FRANCES WRIGHT ON WOMEN'S RIGHTS: ELOQUENCE VERSUS ETHOS. *Q. J. of Speech 1974 60(1): 58-68.* "Frances Wright, a Scotswoman and first woman public speaker in America, failed to persuade 1828-1830 audiences of the importance of women's rights becuase of her low extrinsic ethos. She met all the criteria for 'eloquence' defined by Longinus, and contemporary audiences granted her high intrinsic ethos; however, her radical behavior and ideas such as the invasion of the male lecture platform, association with free love practices, and attacks on organized religion violated societal norms and thereby mitigated her effectiveness." — J

802. Lebedum, Jean. HARRIET BEECHER STOWE'S INTEREST IN SOJOURNER TRUTH, BLACK FEMINIST. *Am. Literature 1973 46(3): 359-363.* Mrs. Stowe, contrary to previous opinion, was interested in feminism. This interest was sparked by feminist Soujourner Truth's work during the 1850's-60's. Stowe's attack on feminism in *My Wife and I* was directed solely at a personal enemy in the movement. In

her *The Minister's Wooing* (1859) she presents a character much like Truth, and in her magazine articles there is strong support for feminism. Based on Mrs. Stowe's works and letters.

M. Stockstill

803. Lerner, Gerda, ed. SARAH M. GRIMKÉ'S "SISTERS OF CHARITY." *Signs: J. of Women in Culture and Soc. 1975 1(1): 246-256.* At age 60 Sarah Moore Grimké (1792-1873), a pioneer in the women's rights movement and one of its earliest theoreticians, left the shelter of her family to live alone in Washington, D.C., to expose and write about sex discrimination. In this reprinted document from 1853, she "accepts the traditional argument that women, once given equal rights, will elevate society by their gentleness and nurturing qualities but repeatedly argues that women have an inherent right to self-realization . . . and calls for women's 'self-reliance.' " Based on Grimké's letters; 4 notes.

T. Simmerman

804. Matthews, Jean V. "WOMAN'S PLACE" AND THE SEARCH FOR IDENTITY IN ANTE-BELLUM AMERICA. *Can. Rev. of Am. Studies [Canada] 1979 10(3): 289-304.* Romanticist ideas, equalitarian ideologies, and redemptive Protestant notions inspired a reexamination of the relationships between men and women in antebellum American society. Alert feminist reformers then made headway by riding the crest of feminine "self-awareness and self-assertion" that the modernist social climate made fashionable. These reformers enlarged women's sphere substantially. They avoided attacks on male workplace and political redoubts, however, choosing instead to levy war on the saloon and other masculine institutions judged disruptive to home and family. Based on writings of feminist reformers and secondary sources; 30 notes.

H. T. Lovin

805. Perry, Lewis. "PROGRESS, NOT PLEASURE, IS OUR AIM": THE SEXUAL ADVICE OF AN ANTEBELLUM RADICAL. *J. of Social Hist. 1979 12(3): 354-366.* Analyzes Henry Clarke Wright's life and writings to shed light on the emerging perceptions of means to improve the relations of men and women in antebellum America. Wright was a pacifist, anarchist, abolitionist, part of the "Boston clique," was a "carrier of widely shared, if not fully articulated, ideology" about sexual self-control, enhanced intimacy, and gradual improvement of society. Wright's career as a minister and then as a traveling lecturer, and his own marriage, gave him multiple insights into the changing circumstances of women. As farm work, home manufacturing, and child labor ceased to ensure vital status for women, the focus shifted to childrearing and reform. 26 notes.

M. Hough

806. Pugh, Evelyn L. JOHN STUART MILL, HARRIET TAYLOR, AND WOMEN'S RIGHTS IN AMERICA, 1850-1873. *Can. J. of Hist. [Canada] 1978 13(3): 423-442.* Examines John Stuart Mill's writings on women, with respect to their reception in and their application to the American scene. Concentrates on the 1851 essay, "Enfranchisement of Women," and his 1869 book, *The Subjection of Women.* The former's authorship, though still disputed, is usually credited to Harriet Taylor, whom he married in 1851. It was published anonymously in the *Westminster Review,* summarizing the activities of the 1850 National Women's Rights Convention at Worcester, Massachusetts, and predicting its continuing influence. Mill became better known as a champion of women's rights during and following his election to parliament in 1866. However, his book was more theoretical than practical, and so hardly the helpful guide in the American feminist movement it otherwise might have been; nor was it as influential as the essay. 78 notes.

R. V. Ritter

807. Ruether, Rosemary Radford. THE SUBORDINATION AND LIBERATION OF WOMEN IN CHRISTIAN THEOLOGY: SAINT PAUL AND SARAH GRIMKÉ. *Soundings 1978 61(2): 168-181.* Relates beliefs about natural order, social organization, and Christian theology held by Saint Paul and compares them to the beliefs of Sarah Grimké; though working from Christian tenets, they reached radically different conclusions about women's role in society.

808. Ryan, Mary P. THE POWER OF WOMEN'S NETWORKS: A CASE STUDY OF FEMALE MORAL REFORM IN ANTEBELLUM AMERICA. *Feminist Studies 1979 5(1): 66-86.* Examines the activities and influence of the Female Moral Reform Society of Utica, New York, in the 1830's and 1840's as an example of the exercise of power by women to shape history. The social climate of Utica, a small commercial city, was ideal for the development of influence by organized women, in the transitional area between public and private organization. But the ultimate result was the development of more repressive sexual standards for women. Concludes that women's power is not always an unqualified good and draws a parallel with the New Right of the 1970's. 23 notes.

L. M. Maloney

809. Sahli, Nancy. A STICK TO BREAK OUR HEADS WITH: ELIZABETH BLACKWELL AND PHILADELPHIA MEDICINE. *Pennsylvania Hist. 1977 44(4): 335-347.* Elizabeth Blackwell, the first female medical school graduate in the United States, spent 15 important months in Philadelphia. In addition to acquiring considerable medical knowledge there, she learned something of medical organization and developed an abiding concern for social problems. Her nascent feminism was stimulated by the refusal of Philadelphia medical schools to admit her. Based on the Blackwell Papers; cover photo, 43 notes.

D. C. Swift

810. Scott, Ann Firor. THE EVER WIDENING CIRCLE: THE DIFFUSION OF FEMINIST VALUES FROM THE TROY FEMALE SEMINARY, 1822-1872. *Hist. of Educ. Q. 1979 19(1): 3-25.* Criticizes a traditional and conservative view of this early female institution. Evidence suggests that feminist and traditional values coexisted, and that Emma Willard was a powerful role model. Education was an important tool in spreading feminism. Based on the archives of the Emma Willard school in Troy, N.Y.; 3 fig., 39 notes.

L. C. Smith

811. Stern, Madeleine B. LOUISA ALCOTT'S FEMINIST LETTERS. *Studies in the Am. Renaissance 1978: 429-452.* Louisa May Alcott (1833-88) engaged in a variety of reform movements from abolitionism to temperance, but woman suffrage was her primary concern. In her correspondence, we can perceive her forceful commitment to feminism. Her activity was neither strident nor aggressive but rather "reflected the traditional values of her family. . . . Louisa Alcott's feminism of a human being impatient with indifference, apathy, and intolerance." Based on the writings and correspondence of Louisa May Alcott; 41 notes.

S. Baatz

812. Theriot, Nancy M. MARY WOLLSTONECRAFT AND MARGARET FULLER: A THEORETICAL COMPARISON. *Int. J. of Women's Studies [Canada] 1979 2(6): 560-574.* Compares the theoretical positions on sexuality of Englishwoman Mary Wollstonecraft Godwin and American feminist Margaret Fuller based on Wollstonecraft's *Vindication of the Rights of Woman* (1792) and Fuller's *Woman in the Nineteenth Century,* written from a Romantic idealist point of view.

813. Topping, Eva Catafygiotu. FRANCES WRIGHT: PETTICOAT LECTURER. *Cincinnati Hist. Soc. Bull. 1978 36(1): 43-56.* Discusses the career of Frances Wright, woman activist and social reformer in the 1820's-30's, focusing on her lectures and notoriety as the "petticoat lecturer."

814. Treckel, Paula A. JANE GREY SWISSHELM AND FEMINISM IN EARLY MINNESOTA. *Midwest Rev. 1980 2(Spr): 1-17.* Jane Grey Swisshelm (1815-84), newspaper editor, political activist, abolitionist, and feminist, spent 1857-62 in St. Cloud, Minnesota, where she edited the St. Cloud *Visitor* and spoke out against slavery and supported women's rights.

815. Vertinsky, Patricia. SEXUAL EQUALITY AND THE LEGACY OF CATHARINE BEECHER. *J. of Sport Hist. 1979 6(1): 38-49.* The ramifications of some major streams of thought on Catharine Beecher's attitude toward women and female physical education. The severity that Beecher used in defining the female role and activities may have succeeded in raising group consciousness among women and encouraged them to challenge traditional views of "women's natural sphere" and to demand greater opportunities in physical education and in sport. Popular beliefs about the poor state of health among women in the 1830's and 1840's encouraged reformers, including Beecher, to demand the development of appropriate exercise programs for women. Beecher and others were influenced by the belief that modernization and urbanization resulted in the demise of the natural order. Perfectionist thought and new

child nurture theories ruptured fatalistic beliefs that the individual lacked control over his destiny, resulting in a change in educational training. 49 notes. — M. Kaufman

816. Warner, Deborah Jean. SCIENCE EDUCATION FOR WOMEN IN ANTEBELLUM AMERICA. *Isis 1978 69(246): 58-67.* During the early 19th century, education for American women advanced remarkably. One significant aspect of this was education in science. As a result, some women (two dozen are mentioned) found careers, or partial careers, in science. 39 notes. — M. M. Vance

817. Weiner, Nella Fermi. OF FEMINISM AND BIRTH CONTROL PROPAGANDA (1790-1840). *Int. J. of Women's Studies [Canada] 1980 3(5): 411-430.* The growth of feminism in Great Britain and the United States motivated birth control propaganda during the 19th century; discusses Jeremy Bentham (1748-1842) of England, American Frances Wright (1795-1892), Francis Place (1771-1854) and Richard Carlile (1790-1843) of England, and American Robert Dale Owen (1801-77).

Economic Reform

818. Dublin, Thomas. WOMEN WORKERS AND THE STUDY OF SOCIAL MOBILITY. *J. of Interdisciplinary Hist. 1979 9(4): 647-665.* Studies the careers of women operatives in the cotton textile mills of the Hamilton Manufacturing Company in Lowell, Massachusetts, between 1836 and 1860. Simple correlations between economic opportunity and the existence of labor protest are contradicted by the evidence. For women operatives in Lowell, the existence of real opportunities for occupational mobility and wage gains did not undermine the growth of collective protest. At the end of the period the forces which kept women in the mills despite narrowing prospects made it more difficult for them to engage in collective protest. The changing circumstances also generated a different set of expectations among operatives, making mill work by the 1850's more a drab necessity than an exciting opportunity. Printed sources and the records of the Hamilton Manufacturing Company, housed in the Baker Library, Harvard Business School; 5 tables, 27 notes. — R. Howell

819. Early, Francis H. A REAPPRAISAL OF THE NEW ENGLAND LABOUR-REFORM MOVEMENT OF THE 1840'S: THE LOWELL FEMALE LABOR REFORM ASSOCIATION AND THE NEW ENGLAND WORKINGMEN'S ASSOCIATION. *Social Hist. [Canada] 1980 13(25): 33-54.* Fifteen women operatives formed the Lowell Female Labor Reform Association in 1845, after 20 years of ephemeral associations devoted to working-class causes. The Association concentrated on bread-and-butter issues, but supported other reforms, ignoring the controversy between workers and Associationists in order to advance its own objectives. In 1847 the LFLRA was absorbed by the Lowell Female Industrial Reform and Mutual Aid Society. It never had more than 500 members out of over 7,000 Lowell women mill workers, but the labor-reform mentality did not disappear. 123 notes. — D. F. Chard

820. Janiewski, Dolores. ARCHIVES: MAKING COMMON CAUSE: THE NEEDLEWOMEN OF NEW YORK, 1831-69. *Signs: J. of Women in Culture and Soc. 1976 1(3, Part 1): 777-786.* Women laborers in New York City's garment trades between 1831 and 1869 tried to deal with subsistence-level wages, exploitative homework, piecework, ruinous competition, and chronic unemployment by varying modes of organization and expression such as trade unions, producers' cooperatives dependent on public patronage, mutual aid societies, and feminist pressure groups. Some developed an analysis of class and sex oppression while others eschewed theory for publicity campaigns to attract public support. All failed to change the economic and social system, but each group in its own way tried to resist oppression. Primary sources; 5 notes. — S. E. Kennedy

821. Kulik, Gary B. PATTERNS OF RESISTANCE TO INDUSTRIAL CAPITALISM: PAWTUCKET VILLAGE AND THE STRIKE OF 1824. Cantor, Milton, ed. *American Workingclass Culture: Explorations in American Labor and Social History* (Westport, Conn.: Greenwood, 1979): 209-240. Focuses on the 1824 strike among textile workers at the Pawtucket, Rhode Island, weaving and spinning mills to demonstrate local resistance to industrialization in the textile industry and working-class opposition to the mill owners.

822. Kulik, Gary B. PAWTUCKET VILLAGE AND THE STRIKE OF 1824: THE ORIGINS OF CLASS CONFLICT IN RHODE ISLAND. *Radical Hist. Rev. 1978 (17): 5-37.* Describes the textile workers' strike of 1824 in Pawtucket, Rhode Island, in a discussion of the tradition of labor conflicts between mill owners and workers in Rhode Island.

823. Mathias, Frank F. THE RELIEF AND COURT STRUGGLE: HALF-WAY HOUSE TO POPULISM. *Register of the Kentucky Hist. Soc. 1973 71(2): 154-176.* The struggle between debtor and creditor in Kentucky during the 1820's saw an early glimmering of Populism in the relief faction, but its failure to go more than halfway resulted in its demise. In Populist terms, banks, governors, and legislatures were pawns in the struggle between the "robbers" (aristocrats, landowners) and the "robbed" (the people). In 1822, the court entered the controversy and soon the issue was primarily between the old and new court factions. Relief Governor Joseph Desha removed judges from the Court of Appeals, but the court continued in existence. In 1825-26, Kentuckians returned sufficient old court supporters to the legislature to overrule Desha, and the old court returned. Based on primary and secondary sources; 57 notes. — J. F. Paul

824. Mittlebeeler, Emmet V. THE DECLINE OF IMPRISONMENT FOR DEBT IN KENTUCKY. *Filson Club Hist. Q. 1975 49(2): 169-189.* Discusses the Kentucky legislation that outlawed *capias ad satisfaciendum* writs in 1821, thereby ending most imprisonment for debt in the state. This law was the first in the United States, but the practice had been in decline for decades. Relates the Kentucky experience to the general movement to reform debt laws. Based on published government manuscripts; 85 notes. — G. B. McKinney

825. Neufeld, Maurice F. THE PERSISTENCE OF IDEAS IN THE AMERICAN LABOR MOVEMENT: THE HERITAGE OF THE 1830S. *Industrial and Labor Relations Rev. 1982 35(2): 207-220.* In creating the first US labor movement, the craftsmen of Andrew Jackson's time advanced several ideas that challenged the emergent doctrine of extreme laissez-faire. Six of those ideas—such as the beliefs that excessive inequality of wealth and widespread monopoly existed—provided support for the idea and practice of trade unionism. These ideas have continued to be espoused by leaders and members of successive labor federations, including those of the AFL-CIO. The persistence in some form of the political, social, and economic inequities that first evoked the ideas may explain this. — J

826. Palmer, Bryan. KINGSTON MECHANICS AND THE RISE OF THE PENITENTIARY, 1833-1836. *Social Hist. [Canada] 1980 13(25): 7-32.* As early as 1830, in one of the first organized efforts of Canadian workingmen, Kingston mechanics opposed the establishment of the Kingston Penitentiary, out of fear of competition and debasement of craft skills. Aligned with the colony's reformers, the mechanics elicited a concession from a Tory paper in 1834 that convict labor should not be allowed to injure honest mechanics. When the penitentiary opened in 1835 the mechanics again petitioned against convict labor, and in 1836 formed a Mechanics' Association. By 1837 mechanics' opposition foundered, never to recover, because of economic recession, political repression and loss of leadership. 42 notes, appendix.
— D. F. Chard

827. Rich, David. THE TOLEDO MECHANICS' ASSOCIATION: THE CITY'S FIRST LABOR UNION. *Northwest Ohio Q. 1973-74 46(1): 25-31.* Austin Willey's Toledo Mechanics'. Association was a short-lived effort before the municipal elections of 1843 to unite local workingmen in an effort to protect them from exploitation and to assure a better reward for their labor. The union faded after the elections, because after the workingmen captured most of the positions they turned to regular political processes to achieve their ends. Based on newspapers; 25 notes. — W. F. Zornow

828. Vogel, Lise. ARCHIVES: THEIR OWN WORK: TWO DOCUMENTS FROM THE NINETEENTH-CENTURY LABOR MOVE-

MENT. *Signs: J. of Women in Culture and Soc. 1976 1(3, Part 1): 787-802.* Deteriorating conditions of factory work and wages in the 1840's led to efforts by labor reformers and organizers to mobilize women workers. "The Factory Bell," a poem by an unknown mill woman, contrasts the measurement of time by the relentless ringing of the factory bell with the warm rhythms of nature. *Factory Life as It is, by an Operative* sums up grievances of women textile workers and suggests solutions such as reform and organization to achieve the goals of republicanism, liberty, and equality. Based on primary and secondary works; 10 notes.
S. E. Kennedy

Educational Reform

829. Andrew, John. EDUCATING THE HEATHEN: THE FOREIGN MISSION SCHOOL CONTROVERSY AND AMERICAN IDEALS. *J. of Am. Studies [Great Britain] 1978 12(3): 331-342.* The American Board of Commissioners for Foreign Missions established a Foreign Mission School at Cornwall, Connecticut in 1816. Soon many of the students were American Indians, mostly Cherokee and Choctaws. There students received instruction in agriculture, commerce, mechanics, history, and religious studies. But disagreements plagued the institution and placed it at odds with townsmen until the school closed in 1827 amidst controversies involving some of its Indian students. The conflicts centered on the issue of whether American Indian education and missionary endeavors should focus on preserving the Indians' native culture or be directed toward producing total assimilation of the Indians into white society. Manuscript materials and secondary sources; 43 notes.
H. T. Lovin

830. Atwater, Edward C. THE PROTRACTED LABOR AND BRIEF LIFE OF A COUNTRY MEDICAL SCHOOL: THE AUBURN MEDICAL INSTITUTION, 1825. *J. of the Hist. of Medicine and Allied Sci. 1979 34(3): 334-352.* Country medical schools were established as a realistic attempt to improve the medical education of rural practitioners in the 19th century. One attempt was the short-lived Auburn Medical Institution, in New York. As early as 1810 the county medical society tried to establish a medical school at the Cayuga Academy. The legislature, however, decided to support Hamilton Oneida Academy, which became Hamilton College, and Fairfield Academy, where a medical school, the Auburn Medical Institution, was organized. In 1825, even before the legislature had been petitioned for a charter, the school was in operation. The faculty included Dr. Erastus Darwin Tuttle (1791-1829), Jedediah Smith (1796-1879), and James Douglas (1800-86). Thirty-three students enrolled at the first course of lectures. Without a charter it could not compete with Fairfield as a medical training ground, however, and its demise was hastened by the departure of Douglas. 49 notes, 3 illus.
M. Kaufman

831. Cain, Lee C. FOUNDING PUBLIC SCHOOLS IN ALABAMA: A COUNTY LED THE WAY. *Alabama Hist. Q. 1976 38(4): 243-249.* Mobile County, Alabama, established the first public schools in Alabama in 1826. 21 notes.
E. E. Eminhizer

832. Calkins, David L. BLACK EDUCATION IN NINETEENTH CENTURY CINCINNATI. *Cincinnati Hist. Soc. Bull. 1980 38(2): 115-128.* The beginnings of black education in Cincinnati during the 19th century were characterized by legal and extralegal discrimination until the struggle during the 1850's resulted in the formation of the Cincinnati Colored School system, which generated socioeconomic change in the black community but did not lead to integrated education.

833. Cauthen, Irby B., Jr. "A COMPLETE AND GENEROUS EDUCATION": MILTON AND JEFFERSON. *Virginia Q. Rev. 1979 55(2): 222-233.* Discusses John Milton's dislike of his education at St. Paul's and Cambridge and his short pamphlet, *Of Education,* in which he outlined a physical and intellectual curriculum which would provide "a complete and generous education." It called for a dramatic renovation and revolution in education. There were great similarities, and some differences, in the educational program Thomas Jefferson sponsored 200 years later. Milton's proposals were the "culmination of the English Renaissance" and Jefferson's "the epitome of the American Enlightenment." They "join in the insistence upon civic leadership and personal integrity."
O. H. Zabel

834. Darling, Arthur Burr. PRIOR TO LITTLE ROCK IN AMERICAN EDUCATION: THE *ROBERTS* CASE OF 1849-1850. *Massachusetts Hist. Soc. Pro. 1957-60 72: 126-142.* Discusses the controversy surrounding school segregation in the late 1950's by examining the case *Sarah C. Roberts* v. *The City of Boston* (1850) which dealt with the concept of "equal protection of the laws," in 1849-50.

835. Ellsworth, Edward W. LINCOLN AND THE EDUCATION CONVENTION: EDUCATION IN ILLINOIS—A JEFFERSONIAN HERITAGE. *Lincoln Herald 1978 80(2): 69-78.* Thomas Jefferson's support for universal education in a democracy provided the inspiration for Illinoisans who worked to implement that principle during 1820-55. Simultaneously, Abraham Lincoln sought a career for himself and broadened his educational horizons. In 1834 Lincoln represented Sangamon County at the Illinois General Education Convention. He developed a philosophy of education that suited not only his personal career requirements, but also those of a rapidly developing Illinois. He combined the Jeffersonian spirit of education for civic responsibility and progressive citizenship with the utilitarian needs of the frontier. 2 photos, 31 notes.
T. P. Linkfield

836. Faust, Richard H. WILLIAM MEDILL: COMMISSIONER OF INDIAN AFFAIRS, 1845-1849. *Old Northwest 1975 1(2): 129-140.* Democrat William Medill (1802-65), Commissioner of Indian Affairs during 1845-49, fought illegal liquor trade and the inequitable award system to Indians who ceded land. To "civilize" Indians he ordered hundreds of schools organized in Indian territory to stress farming and homemaking but deemphasize literature. Medill's belief in both Jeffersonian agrarianism and the Puritan ethic molded the schools, which, because of their numbers, made federal Indian educational policy irreversible. 27 notes.
J. N. Dickinson

837. Franklin, Vincent P. EDUCATION FOR COLONIZATION: ATTEMPTS TO EDUCATE FREE BLACKS IN THE UNITED STATES FOR EMIGRATION TO AFRICA, 1823-1833. *J. of Negro Educ. 1974 43(1): 91-103.* From 1816-33 there were several abortive attempts to establish schools to educate free blacks, with the idea that they would go to Africa as missionaries or settlers. These attempts failed due to lack of funds and opposition from abolitionists and blacks who opposed colonization. 47 notes.
B. D. Johnson

838. Geldbach, Erich. DIE VERPFLANZUNG DES DEUTSCHEN TURNENS NACH AMERIKA: BECK, FOLLEN, LIEBER [The transplantation of German gymnastics into America: Beck, Follen, Lieber]. *Stadion [West Germany] 1975 1(2): 331-376.* In the 1820's gymnastics became fashionable at some schools in New England, at Harvard, and among the citizens of Boston. Physical education was encouraged by medical professors, educators, reform-oriented law professors, and theologians who felt that American education had to abandon its provincialism and puritanism. It was fostered by a reorientation of academic ideals toward European, particularly German, concepts. The American reformers found enthusiastic teachers among German political emigrés, followers of the gymnastic movement of Jahn. Accordingly, gymnastics followed the German pattern of Jahn who himself declined an offer from Harvard. It is not yet clear why the interest in gymnastics waned after a few years, though the emphasis on drill may have been one of the major reasons. Based on American archives and secondary sources; 107 notes.
M. Geyer

839. Gordon, Mary MacDougall. PATRIOTS & CHRISTIANS: A REASSESSMENT OF NINETEENTH-CENTURY SCHOOL REFORMERS. *J. of Social Hist. 1978 11(4): 554-574.* The revisionist preoccupation with social control motivation in the founding of the free public educational system focuses us too much on urban concerns. The fact is that rural schools were as much the goal. Further it ignores the ties between education and nationalism. Concentrates on an educational elite throughout Massachusetts working in the American Institute for Education, founded in 1830 and instrumental before and after Horace Mann emerged through their efforts. They sought a Protestant Christian republic. 57 notes.
M. Hough

840. Griffin, Barbara J. THOMAS RITCHIE AND THE FOUNDING OF THE RICHMOND LANCASTERIAN SCHOOL. *Virginia Mag. of Hist. and Biography 1978 86(4): 447-460.* Explores the role of

Thomas Ritchie, editor of the *Richmond Enquirer,* in promoting Virginia public education. Concentrates on the Richmond Lancasterian School, which was based on the principles of Joseph Lancaster, whereby the advanced students taught the beginners. Describes Ritchie's part in promoting the free will support of public schools, which assistance was pragmatically and altruistically motivated. Suggests Ritchie as author of a favorable *Enquirer* report of Lancaster's 1819 visit to Virginia. 33 notes.

P. J. Woehrmann

841. Grossman, Lawrence. GEORGE T. DOWNING AND DESEGREGATION OF RHODE ISLAND PUBLIC SCHOOLS, 1855-1866. *Rhode Island Hist. 1977 36(4): 99-105.* George T. Downing, the black proprietor of Sea-Girt House in Newport, played a major role in desegregating public schools. Based on papers in the Boston Public Library and in private hands, newspapers, and secondary accounts; 3 illus., 16 notes.

P. J. Coleman

842. Harvey, Robert Paton. THE TEACHER'S REWARD: ALEXANDER FORRESTER AT TRURO. *Nova Scotia Hist. Q. 1975 5(1): 47-68.* A study of the career and innovative ideas of Alexander Forrester (d. 1869), the first principal of the Truro Normal School and the second Superintendent of Education in Nova Scotia. His attempts at improving teacher preparation and at selling the idea of a general property tax for the support of free education for all were strongly opposed and for a time frustrated by petty political feuding. Never during his lifetime was he properly recognized for his work and beliefs. 41 notes.

R. V. Ritter

843. Keane, Patrick. ADULT EDUCATION IN NOVA SCOTIA. *Nova Scotia Hist. Q. [Canada] 1975 5(2): 155-166.* A study of the pioneer steps by which the colonial legislature aided the education of adults. Between 1819 and 1824 the first step was taken, with an appropriation to the Central Board of Agriculture for this purpose. The Board established an agricultural library, published instructional pamphlets, and organized new societies. The movement spread to other areas: industry and commerce, and a Mechanics' Library Association. Governmental financial aid was sought and mechanics' institutes were organized. The efforts were more on the part of key individuals rather than any widespread governmental interest, yet government did make some response. 40 notes.

R. V. Ritter

844. Keane, Patrick. JOSEPH HOWE AND ADULT EDUCATION. *Acadiensis [Canada] 1973 3(1): 35-49.* Discusses the influence of publisher and educator Joseph Howe in establishing adult education in Nova Scotia, 1827-66.

845. Keane, Patrick. A STUDY IN EARLY PROBLEMS AND POLICIES IN ADULT EDUCATION: THE HALIFAX MECHANICS' INSTITUTE. *Social Hist. [Canada] 1975 8(16): 255-274.* The Halifax Mechanics' Institute, founded in 1831, reflected the hopes of its middle-class sponsors of molding the urban working class in its own image. The Institute failed to attract large numbers of mechanics, and soon became a center of occasional middle-class entertainment and recreation. It failed in its original purpose because its sponsors never came to grips with the needs and aspirations of Halifax workingmen. Based on documents in Public Archives of Nova Scotia, newspapers, and secondary sources. 98 notes.

W. K. Hobson

846. Luebbering, Ken. THE EMERGENCE OF BUREAUCRACY: THE MISSOURI SCHOOL LAW OF 1853. *Missouri Hist. Rev. 1980 74(3): 300-322.* Ellwood P. Cubberley's view that by 1860 the public schools, supported by general taxation, free and open to all, controlled American education has been challenged by Michael Katz. He found at least four organizational models. The advocates of democratic localism were beaten by the advocates of incipient bureaucracy, who wanted to upgrade education through the supervision of schools by professionals. Growing dissatisfaction of men in state government with the organization of common schools and continuing financial problems led to Missouri's school law of 1853, a victory for those favoring centralization and bureaucracy as vital elements in education. Based on books, unpublished dissertations, reports of the Superintendent of Common Schools, and Journals of the Missouri House and Senate; illus., 60 notes.

W. F. Zornow

847. Mark, Arthur. TWO LIBERTARIAN EDUCATORS: ELIZABETH BYRNE FERM AND ALEXIS CONSTANTINE FERM. *Teachers Coll. Record 1976 78(2): 264-274.* American educators Elizabeth Byrne Ferm (1857-1944) and Alexis Constantine Ferm (1869?-1971) absorbed the uniquely American philosophy of individualism developed by Jefferson and Emerson and applied it to education. Their theories offer valuable historical perspective on the current open education movement. Based on author's doctoral dissertation using primary and secondary sources; 57 notes.

E. Bailey

848. Moranian, Suzanne Elizabeth. ETHNOCIDE IN THE SCHOOLHOUSE: MISSIONARY EFFORTS TO EDUCATE INDIAN YOUTH IN PRE-RESERVATION WISCONSIN. *Wisconsin Mag. of Hist. 1981 64(4): 242-260.* Examines the attempt by Protestant and Catholic missionaries to Christianize and educate the Menominee in east Wisconsin, Chippewa and Sioux along the Mississippi River, the Winnebago around Prairie du Chien, and the Oneida, Stockbridge, and Brotherton near Green Bay. Between 1820 and 1850 the efforts were largely failures, although Catholic missionaries enjoyed more success because they made an effort to learn the Indians' language and customs, they sought to convert without imposing the white culture completely, and because they were frequently Europeans not identified with the federal government. 95 notes, 12 illus.

N. C. Burckel

849. Polos, Nicholas C. JOHN SWETT: THE RINCON PERIOD 1853-1862. *Pacific Historian 1975 19(2): 133-149.* Discusses the career of John Swett as principal of Rincon School, San Francisco. Swett was an early advocate of publicly supported education and other progressive ideas such as physical education, coeducation, better methods of teacher certification, and higher teacher salaries. He served as California's State Superintendent of Education during 1863-67. Primary sources; 32 notes.

G. L. Olson

850. Rayman, Ronald. THE WINNEBAGO INDIAN SCHOOL EXPERIMENT IN IOWA TERRITORY, 1834-1848. *Ann. of Iowa 1978 44(5): 359-387.* A movement emphasizing assimilation as the solution to the Indian "problem" began in earnest during the administration of Andrew Jackson. The history of the Winnebago school at two locations in Iowa demonstrates that assimilation was a nearly impossible task. Not only did the Winnebago Indians resist the imposition of white culture, but also the school was hampered by personal, political, economic, and Protestant-Catholic disagreements (inspired by Bureau of Indian Affairs appointment of a Presbyterian minister as first principal and refusal to allow Catholic priests to teach the Indians). The most debilitating factor was the "ambivalence and ignorance" of government officials responsible for Indian policy. Based on records of the Bureau of Indian Affairs, National Archives; 3 photos, 67 notes.

P. L. Petersen

851. Ringenberg, William C. THE OBERLIN COLLEGE INFLUENCE IN EARLY MICHIGAN. *Old Northwest 1977 3(2): 111-131.* Three Michigan schools owed their founding and character to men originally associated with Oberlin College, Ohio: Olivet, Adrian, and Hillsdale Colleges. John H. Shipherd, an Oberlin founder, established Olivet College in 1844. Asa Mahan, an early Oberlin president, took over the management of a Wesleyan school which he moved to Adrian in 1859. Freewill Baptist Elder David Marks, an Oberlin graduate, urged the hiring of another graduate, Daniel M. Graham, who became Hillsdale's president in 1844. These men carried with them Oberlin's beliefs in abolition, coeducation, Christian perfection, reform, and temperance. Based on college histories and catalogues and on secondary works; 49 notes.

J

852. Royce, Marion V. EDUCATION FOR GIRLS IN QUAKER SCHOOLS IN ONTARIO. *Atlantis [Canada] 1977 3(1): 181-192.* Provides a brief background to the Society of Friends, interest in education since 17th-century England, and discusses the interest of Quakers in Canada in organizing schools, particularly the educational opportunities for girls, in Ontario, Canada, 1790-1820.

853. Shade, William G. THE "WORKING CLASS" AND EDUCATIONAL REFORM IN EARLY AMERICA: THE CASE OF PROVIDENCE, RHODE ISLAND. *Historian 1976 39(1): 1-23.* According to this case study, educational reform after 1820 was not the product of a Jeffersonian Republican elite. Providence tradesmen and artisans, orga-

nized in the Providence Association of Mechanics and Manufacturers, were active in the school reform movement. These middle class tradesmen and artisans knew that they had obtained few educational benefits. In their memorials the Association stressed public morality, citizenship, and the state's social duty to provide schools. 3 charts, 84 notes.

M. J. Wentworth

854. Weyant, Jane G. THE DEBATE OVER HIGHER EDUCATION IN THE SOUTH, 1850-1860. *Mississippi Q. 1976 29(4): 539-558.* Discusses higher education in the South, 1850-60, emphasizing evolution in thought to include instruction in liberal arts as well as classics and the belief on the part of many elitist-minded reformers that reform in higher education would eventually diffuse to secondary and elementary levels, thus precluding the need for reform in mass public education.

855. White, Arthur O. ANTEBELLUM SCHOOL REFORM IN BOSTON: INTEGRATIONISTS AND SEPARATISTS. *Phylon 1973 34(2): 203-218.* Thomas Paul Smith led black separatists in their attempt to control the Boston "African" school mastership and undermined a movement by black and white abolitionists to integrate Boston's schools, 1848-49.

S

856. Zeigler, Earle F. CLEARING UP SOME CONFUSION ABOUT THE FIRST TEACHER TRAINING PROGRAM IN PHYSICAL EDUCATION IN THE UNITED STATES. *Can. J. of Hist. of Sport and Physical Educ. 1974 5(1): 38-46.* Attempts to clarify whether the Dio Lewis' Normal Institute for Physical Education or the Normal School of the American Gymnastic Union of the German-American Turnerbund was the first physical education training school in America. Though the Turner's first called for the establishment of a training institution in 1856, the ten-week course at Lewis' Normal Institute, opening in July 1861, was the first in operation. The American Gymnastic Union school opened in November 1866. 24 notes.

R. A. Smith

Humanitarian Reform

857. Baehre, Rainer. ORIGINS OF THE PENITENTIARY SYSTEM IN UPPER CANADA. *Ontario Hist. [Canada] 1977 69(3): 185-207.* The first penitentiary in Upper Canada opened in 1835. The penitentiary was a reform of the early justice system, conceived as a place to induce penitence (hence its name) for crimes. The motives for this reform, and the approach taken by reformers are analyzed. Notes that a legislator examined penitentiaries, which led to a legislative committee visiting the United Kingdom and the United States before defining practices to be followed in the Canadian institution. Those practices and subsequent modifications are described. An 1849 report on the institution is quoted. 101 notes.

W. B. Whitham

858. Banner, Lois W. RELIGIOUS BENEVOLENCE AS SOCIAL CONTROL: A CRITIQUE OF AN INTERPRETATION. *J. of Am. Hist. 1973 60(1): 23-41.* Religion in the post-revolutionary period has too often been viewed as a conservative force seeking "social control" not "social improvement" as the major end of benevolent schemes. This view results from a narrow preoccupation with New England Congregationalism and Lyman Beecher, and an erroneous opinion that the clergy was declining. A broader perspective shows genuine humanitarian concern among clergy of many denominations involved in education, antislavery work, and other philanthropic concerns. This benevolence was stimulated by millennarianism and a concern for a "Christian republican" nationalism. These clergymen diagnosed contemporary evils as stemming from a selfish, demagogic materialism which should be combatted through education, self-reliant religion, and voluntary associations. 53 notes.

K. B. West

859. Barron, F. L. THE AMERICAN ORIGINS OF THE TEMPERANCE MOVEMENT IN ONTARIO, 1828-1850. *Can. Rev. of Am. Studies [Canada] 1980 11(2): 131-150.* When capitalism and its new industrial order displaced the old frontier society in the province of Ontario, temperance crusades began. Temperance became a political cause at the instigation of the Ontario middle class, deriving inspiration and support from similar temperance movements in the United States. Based on writings of temperance advocates and secondary sources; 8 photos, 69 notes.

H. T. Lovin

860. Bauer, Anne. THE CHARLESTOWN STATE PRISON. *Hist. J. of Western Massachusetts 1973 2(2): 22-29.* The institution's early years were unsatisfactory; escapes, homosexuality, and overcrowding were three main problems. The Boston Prison Discipline Society, however, emphasized the ideas of penal reformers of the time and was able to transform the prison's image. The society claimed that no other prison had superior moral or religious instruction. In the 1840's prisoners had their own gardens. As the buildings grew older and reform interests were drawn elsewhere, conditions deteriorated. In the 1870's a new prison was built. Based on contemporary and secondary sources; 3 illus., 17 notes.

S. S. Sprague

861. Bernier, Jacques. FRANÇOIS BLANCHET ET LE MOUVEMENT RÉFORMISTE EN MÉDECINE AU DÉBUT DU XIXe SIÈCLE [François Blanchet and the medical reform movement of the early 19th century]. *Rev. d'Hist. de l'Amérique Française [Canada] 1980 34(2): 223-244.* In the late 18th century, the practice of medicine in Canada was monopolized by British military doctors and suffered from a lack of professional standards. François Blanchet (b. 1776), a Columbia University-trained physician, was a founder of the first professional medical society in Quebec, and one of the few doctors in the Canadian Parliament. His group worked for changes in the examination system for doctors and for the establishment of a medical school in Montreal, fought charlatans, and set up new facilities to treat contagious diseases. His efforts were a major step in the professionalization of medicine in Canada. Based on materials from archives in Quebec and the National Library of Medicine in Bethesda, Maryland; 70 notes.

R. Aldrich

862. Brewer, Paul W. VOLUNTARISM ON TRIAL: ST. LOUIS' RESPONSE TO THE CHOLERA EPIDEMIC OF 1849. *Bull. of the Hist. of Medicine 1975 49(1): 102-122.* The St. Louis cholera epidemic, which victimized at least 4,557, forced reconsideration of the voluntaristic approach to urban health and sanitation problems, and created a tentative movement toward public measures. Absence of sewers and adequate water supply made an epidemic inevitable after infected immigrants arrived, while doctors and clergy administered relief without halting the disease. When the city government failed to respond to the crisis, a citizens' Committee of Public Health assumed governmental functions and enforced sanitation regulations. Primary and secondary sources; 116 notes.

W. B. Bedford

863. Cassedy, James H. THE ROOTS OF AMERICAN SANITARY REFORM, 1843-47: SEVEN LETTERS FROM JOHN H. GRISCOM TO LEMUEL SHATTUCK. *J. of the Hist. of Medicine and Allied Sci. 1975 30(2): 136-147.* Little is known of how health reformers of the middle 19th century interacted in pursuit of their goals; however, a group of newly discovered letters from John H. Griscom of New York to Lemuel Shattuck of Boston provides details about how the activities of the two reformers helped transform "personal concerns and local reforms into a coherent national movement." 28 notes.

M. Kaufman

864. Cassedy, James H. AN EARLY AMERICAN HANGOVER: THE MEDICAL PROFESSION AND INTEMPERANCE, 1800-1860. *Bull. of the Hist. of Medicine 1976 50(3): 405-413.* Physicians played a prominent role in the temperance movement during 1800-60. Experts who could attest to the physiological effects of drinking, they were disturbed by the drinking excesses within the medical profession and sought to improve their collective image. Medical students' temperance societies were formed, along with medical temperance organizations. In the 1830's, military surgeons reported that intemperance was responsible for a large percentage of the diseases and injuries among the military, and physicians were prominent in urging military authorities to reduce consumption of alcoholic beverages. 20 notes.

M. Kaufman

865. Conklin, Forrest. PARSON BROWNLOW JOINS THE SONS OF TEMPERANCE, PART II. *Tennessee Hist. Q. 1980 39(3): 292-309.* Continued from a previous article (see entry 19A:2728). William Gannaway Brownlow's leadership in the Sons of Temperance during the 1850's gave him a base of public recognition for his east Tennessee political career. He opportunistically advocated liquor control during lulls in the political issues. For its part, the temperance movement benefited from his fine organization and oratory. Based on material in the Knoxville *Whig* and other sources; 34 notes.

W. D. Piersen

866. Conklin, Forrest. PARSON BROWNLOW JOINS THE SONS OF TEMPERANCE (PART I). *Tennessee Hist. Q. 1980 39(2): 178-194.* William Gannaway "Parson" Brownlow (1805-77) was a Methodist minister who became editor of *The Whig* (Knoxville) in 1838, and forsook his traveling ministry. At this time, efforts for greater liquor control were developing. One of the sources for temperance reform was the temperance societies. Brownlow carried on the fight for reform in the columns of his paper and in 1851 engaged in verbal debate over the issue. Largely material from the Knoxville and the Jonesboro *Whig;* 50 notes. Article to be continued. H. M. Parker, Jr.

867. Damsteegt, P. Gerard. HEALTH REFORM AND THE BIBLE IN EARLY SABBATARIAN ADVENTISM. *Adventist Heritage 1978 5(2): 13-21.* Discusses the health reform movement in early-to-mid-19th century America and the use of religious arguments in stressing the importance of healthful living.

868. Dodd, Jill Siegel. THE WORKING CLASSES AND THE TEMPERANCE MOVEMENT IN ANTE-BELLUM BOSTON. *Labor Hist. 1978 19(4): 510-531.* The working clases of ante-bellum Boston divided over temperance movements; some used "traditional" forms of collective violence to resist, others supported temperance. The evidence is analyzed in "pre-industrial" and "industrializing" terms which cut across class lines. Based on quantitative data from newspapers; 5 tables, 46 notes. L. L. Athey

869. Drachman, Virginia G. THE LOOMIS TRIAL: SOCIAL MORES AND OBSTETRICS IN THE MID-NINETEENTH CENTURY. Reverby, Susan and Rosner, David, ed. *Health Care in America: Essays in Social History* (Philadelphia: Temple U. Pr., 1979): 67-83. Dr. Horatio N. Loomis, a private practitioner in Buffalo, New York, was tried for libel in 1850. He had distributed a letter, which he may have authored, criticizing Dr. James Platt White, professor of obstetrics at Buffalo Medical College, for allowing his students to observe while he attended a woman in labor, a new practice in teaching known as demonstrative midwifery. Loomis was acquitted because his authorship could not be proved, but, more importantly, the case raised the issues of morality and the role of the male physician with women clients, the demise of midwifery, and the relationship of private practice to medical education. 49 notes. S

870. Fingard, Judith. ENGLISH HUMANITARIANISM AND THE COLONIAL MIND: WALTER BROMLEY IN NOVA SCOTIA, 1813-25. *Can. Hist. R. 1973 54(2): 123-151.* "Examines the career of Walter Bromley as a social activist in Nova Scotia and as an agent of Christian imperialism in both the Maritimes and South Australia, concentrating particularly on the response in Nova Scotia to his self-help projects for relieving the urban poor and ameliorating the condition of the Micmacs. The degree of success enjoyed by Bromley's schemes depended almost entirely on his tireless energy and dedication rather than on the support of the local population which was channelled through voluntary associations. Concludes that the colonial response to Bromley's pioneering efforts at social improvement was characterized by a parasitic reliance on the benevolence and financial assistance of the mother country." J

871. Fingard, Judith. THE RELIEF OF THE UNEMPLOYED POOR IN SAINT JOHN, HALIFAX AND ST. JOHN'S, 1815-1860. *Acadiensis [Canada] 1975 5(1): 32-53.* Overseas immigration, economic recession, and other factors forced urban poverty to the forefront of public attention in the major centers of eastern British North America after the Napoleonic Wars. Responses were influenced by "interest in economy, order, and the wider welfare of the town...." Heavy outdoor labor, such as stonebreaking, and indoor factory work were seen as solutions. Generally, however, organizations dispensed charity rather than campaigning for economic reform, and capitalists exploited patterns of unemployment. 101 notes. D. F. Chard

872. Frey, Cecile P. THE HOUSE OF REFUGE FOR COLORED CHILDREN. *J. of Negro Hist. 1981 66(1): 10-25.* The House of Refuge of Philadelphia was established in 1828 as an alternative to prison for juvenile delinquents. But no Negroes were admitted. In 1850, a House of Refuge for Colored Children was opened. It provided a program of basic education and hard work, which reflected an attitude of social control implicit in 19th-century reform movements. A. G. Belles

873. Harris, Robert L., Jr. EARLY BLACK BENEVOLENT SOCIETIES, 1780-1830. *Massachusetts Rev. 1979 20(3): 603-625.* Black benevolent societies grew simultaneously with white organizations. The first free black voluntary association, the African Union Society, was established 10 November 1780, in Newport, Rhode Island. The major features of black benevolent societies were sickness and disability benefits, pensions for deceased members' families, burial insurance, funeral direction, cemetery plots, credit unions, charity, education, moral guidance, and discussion forums. A dollar to join and a quarter per month were normal dues. Qualifications for membership included: free black male (sometimes both sexes), good moral character, 25-45 years old sometimes, and 12 months membership before obtaining benefits. They were a medium for assisting recently freed slaves to make the transition. Based on government documents, speeches, convention minutes, society minutes and bylaws, letters, and church records; 60 notes. E. R. Campbell

874. Hawes, Joseph M. PRISONS IN EARLY NINETEENTH-CENTURY AMERICA: THE PROCESS OF CONVICT REFORMATION. Hawes, Joseph M., ed. *Law and Order in American History* (Port Washington, N.Y.: Kennikat Pr., 1979): 37-52. Compares the ideas of the founders of the Auburn, New York, and Pennsylvania prison systems from 1787 to 1845; Pennsylvania prisons, with Quaker influence, "preferred a noncoercive, practically passive, approach to reform and religion," while the supporters of the Auburn believed that "religion and reform were active human pursuits."

875. Heale, M. J. THE FORMATIVE YEARS OF THE NEW YORK PRISON ASSOCIATION, 1844-1862. *New-York Hist. Soc. Q. 1975 59(4): 320-347.* Presented as a "Case Study in Antebellum Reform," indicates that the Prison Association was not easy to stereotype as an American reform movement. Formed largely as a reaction against the severity of the prison system identified with Sing Sing and Auburn after the 1820's, it began as an attempt to introduce rehabilitation of the prisoner. To do this conditions would have to be improved, discipline ameliorated, and help afforded ex-prisoners. The association recognized that society was responsible in part for the condition of law-breakers. It was one of the first groups to use statistical analysis and probably made its greatest contribution in improving prison conditions and pioneering methods of assistance to the ex-convict. Since it included members of all political parties, religious groups, and social levels (although the wealthy noticeably dominated) the association did not conform to the usual interpretation of a reform group. In addition, it was important as the predecessor of the Correctional Association of New York. Based on Prison Association minutes and reports; 5 illus., 39 notes. C. L. Grant

876. Heale, M. J. FROM CITY FATHERS TO SOCIAL CRITICS: HUMANITARIANISM AND GOVERNMENT IN NEW YORK, 1790-1860. *J. of Am. Hist. 1976 63(1): 21-41.* The humanitarian role played by the affluent of New York City altered dramatically 1790-1860. As the "well-ordered community of the early republic gave way to the sprawling and overcrowded metropolis of the mid-nineteenth century," the benevolent city fathers were forced from their political positions, based on their "natural" right to govern, and were replaced by party politics based on patronage. Philanthropic associations were formed; their activities presaging the social worker. 39 notes. V. P. Rilee

877. Heale, M. J. HARBINGERS OF PROGRESSIVISM: RESPONSES TO THE URBAN CRISIS IN NEW YORK, C. 1845-1860. *J. of Am. Studies [Great Britain] 1976 10(1): 17-36.* Analyzes the reform programs and social service work of five humanitarian organizations in New York City during the 1840's and 1850's. The groups attacked poor municipal government, crime, prostitution, gambling, and soaring death and disease rates in New York slums. In the end, the groups provided many social services which afforded relief to individuals, but their crusades failed to alter laws and make publicly controlled relief agencies more responsive. Based on publications of reform organizations and on secondary sources; 35 notes. H. T. Lovin

878. Heale, M. J. PATTERNS OF BENEVOLENCE: ASSOCIATED PHILANTHROPY IN THE CITIES OF NEW YORK, 1830-1860. *New York Hist. 1976 57(1): 53-79.* The growth of associated philanthropy in New York during 1830-60 was a response to urbanization, immigration, increasing social distance between rich and poor, and

mounting urban social problems. Describes the work of philanthropic associations in New York City, Albany, Brooklyn, Buffalo, and Rochester. 6 illus., 30 notes. — R. N. Lokken

879. Jamieson, Duncan R. CITIES AND THE AMA: THE AMERICAN MEDICAL ASSOCIATION'S FIRST REPORT ON PUBLIC HYGIENE. *Maryland Hist. 1977 8(1): 23-32.* Examines an attempt by the American Medical Association to provide impetus to the effort to relieve urban squalor by reporting on its relationship to disease. "The First Report on Public Hygiene" (1849) had little impact but became ammunition for the muckrakers of the 1880's. Based on AMA and secondary sources; 21 notes. — G. O. Gagnon

880. Jervey, Edward D. LA ROY SUNDERLAND: "PRINCE OF THE SONS OF MESMER." *J. of Popular Culture 1976 9(4): 1010-1026.* La Roy Sunderland (1804-85) became famous as a hypnotist and phrenologist in the mid-19th century in America. Sunderland's interest in mesmerism began when he worked at revival meetings in the 1820's. By the 1840's he was mesmerising patients as a treatment for illness, and he became an expert in phrenology. Sunderland felt that all illness was the result of magnetic imbalances in the body, and could be cured by nutrition and changes in mental attitudes. By the end of his life, Sunderland had come to reject any theory of supernatural agency in the cause of disease. Sunderland's early research into the treatment of psychosomatic ailments, especially his emphasis on nutrition and a positive attitude, places him above the charlatans of his age and marks him as a pioneer in medicine and psychology. Primary and secondary sources; 102 notes. — J. W. Leedom

881. Kohlstedt, Sally Gregory. PHYSIOLOGICAL LECTURES FOR WOMEN: SARAH COATES IN OHIO, 1850. *J. of the Hist. of Medicine and Allied Sci. 1978 33(1): 75-81.* In the mid-19th century, many women lectured on physiology. Their lectures included presentations on anatomy and physiology, but also discussion of diet, exercise and dress, and even comment on childbirth, menstruation, and menopause. The two letters of Sarah Coates published here give a perspective on the difficult problems of background and motivation of the itinerant female lecturers. In 1850 she became a lecturer, traveling in Ohio. She moved to Minnesota in 1851, and apparently did not lecture anymore. 19 notes. — M. Kaufman

882. Lasser, Carol S. A "PLEASINGLY OPPRESSIVE" BURDEN: THE TRANSFORMATION OF DOMESTIC SERVICE AND FEMALE CHARITY IN SALEM, 1800-1840. *Essex Inst. Hist. Collections 1980 116(3): 156-175.* The Salem Female Charitable Society, founded in 1801, directed its efforts toward providing for indigent female children: first in a semi-institutional setting, then in homes, as legally bound domestic servants. The society assisted 82 girls before the mercantile base of New England's economy eroded, necessitating dissolution of the society in 1837. Both incipient industrialization and changes in domestic service, where the structured relations of employer and employee were replacing personal bonds of benevolence and gratitude, forced the society to abandon its placement program. Extensive records provide the necessary materials for a case study of this transformation and for follow-up histories of half the girls bound out by the society. Primary sources; 45 notes. — R. S. Sliwoski

883. Lauricella, Francis, Jr. THE DEVIL IN DRINK: SWEDENBORGIANISM IN T. S. ARTHUR'S *TEN NIGHTS IN A BAR-ROOM* (1854). *Perspectives in Am. Hist. 1979 12: 353-385.* The theological doctrines articulated by Emanuel Swedenborg (1688-1772), a Swedish theologian, scientist, and mystic, influenced his followers in different ways and for different purposes. For Timothy Shay Arthur, Swedenborgianism and its tenets became a reason for joining the temperance movement. In fact, Arthur found in Swedenborgianism a foundation for taking a conservative stance that, in order to realize a stronger social bond, institutions should restrain a human's tendencies toward doing evil. — W. A. Wiegand

884. Levstik, Frank R., ed. LIFE AMONG THE LOWLY: AN EARLY VIEW OF AN OHIO POOR HOUSE. *Ohio Hist. 1979 88(1): 84-88.* Provisions for the care of the indigent were dreadfully inadequate in Ohio during the first half of the 19th century. In 1816 the legislature passed a law to authorize counties to establish poorhouses. These were increasingly necessary as immigration and economic conditions caused the rise in the numbers of helpless and destitute, but the counties were slow to build the facilities. Even in these facilities the conditions were appalling and the care negligent and often brutal. A letter written to the Governor of Ohio in 1858, by Mary Tyler Peabody Mann, quoted in full, details the conditions. Photo, fig., 7 notes, ref. — H. F. Thomson

885. Luckingham, Bradford. BENEVOLENCE IN EMERGENT SAN FRANCISCO: A NOTE ON IMMIGRANT LIFE IN THE URBAN FAR WEST. *Southern California Q. 1973 55(4): 431-443.* From almost the inception of San Francisco as a booming urban center of gold rush California, various groups banded together for mutual assistance. Organized along national, religious, or occupational lines, these benevolent associations advised newcomers, provided information about friends and relatives, gave immediate financial aid, maintained clinics, obtained jobs for the unemployed, and provided transportation to the mines or back home. Typical organizations included the French Benevolent Society, Masons, Odd Fellows, Young Men's Christian Association, and the San Francisco Ladies' Protection and Relief Society. The benevolent associations resembled the efforts of groups in older American cities, with the groups attempting to provide for the welfare of their members. Based on primary and secondary sources; 21 notes. — A. Hoffman

886. Mackey, Philip English. AN ALL-STAR DEBATE ON CAPITAL PUNISHMENT, BOSTON, 1854. *Essex Inst. Hist. Collections 1974 110(3): 181-199.* Examines the Massachusetts movement to abolish capital punishment and the open hearings which debated the topic. — S

887. Mackey, Philip English. EDWARD LIVINGSTON AND THE ORIGINS OF THE MOVEMENT TO ABOLISH CAPITAL PUNISHMENT IN AMERICA. *Louisiana Hist. 1976 16(2): 145-166.* Presents a biographical sketch of Edward Livingston (1764-1836), emphasizing his legal reform efforts in Louisiana and elsewhere, and especially his opposition to capital punishment. Traces early efforts to ban capital punishment in other states. Primary and secondary sources; photo, 33 notes. — R. L. Woodward

888. Mackey, Philip English. "THE RESULT MAY BE GLORIOUS"—ANTI-GALLOWS MOVEMENT IN RHODE ISLAND, 1838-1852. *Rhode Island Hist. 1974 33(1): 19-30.* Traces the history of the movement to abolish capital punishment and assesses the role of various factors in ending hanging in 1852. Based on records in the Rhode Island State Archives, Providence, published documents and reports, newspapers, periodicals, pamphlets, and secondary accounts. — P. J. Coleman

889. Maclear, J. F. LYMAN BEECHER IN BRITAIN. *Ohio Hist. 1976 85(4): 293-305.* Discusses Lyman Beecher's (1775-1863) trip to Great Britain in 1846 as a delegate to the World Temperance Convention and the Evangelical Alliance. Based on manuscript sources and contemporary comments; 2 illus., 22 notes. — N. Summers

890. Maestro, Marcello. A PIONEER FOR THE ABOLITION OF CAPITAL PUNISHMENT: CESARE BECCARIA. *J. of the Hist. of Ideas 1973 34(3): 463-468.* Explains the arguments in and influence of Cesare Beccaria's *Dei delitti e delle pene* (1764). Beccaria's general examination of crime and punishment included a "daring chapter" which found capital punishment without basis in natural right, less efficient than imprisonment as a deterrent to crime, and an unwholesome example of barbarism. Beccaria's book was published in London and was widely distributed in North America. Quoted by John Adams, Thomas Jefferson, and Benjamin Rush, it exerted influence on early American penal reform. Primary and secondary sources; 9 notes. — D. B. Marti

891. Marcus, Alan I. THE STRANGE CAREER OF MUNICIPAL HEALTH INITIATIVES: CINCINNATI AND CITY GOVERNMENT IN THE EARLY NINETEENTH CENTURY. *J. of Urban Hist. 1980 7(1): 3-29.* Examines the tension between the pressure for public health created by urban growth and medical advancements and traditions of private action and individualism. The initial compromise was to have limited public health during normal times with a more elaborate and powerful apparatus coming into being during times of crisis. 39 notes. — T. W. Smith

892. Mohl, Raymond A. POVERTY, PAUPERISM, AND SOCIAL ORDER IN THE PREINDUSTRIAL AMERICAN CITY, 1780-1840. Hawes, Joseph M., ed. *Law and Order in American History* (Port Washington, N.Y.: Kennikat Pr., 1979): 25-36. Focuses on the social conditions which caused social disorder in preindustrial American cities and led to our system of criminal justice.

893. Morantz, Regina Markell. MAKING WOMEN MODERN: MIDDLE CLASS WOMEN AND HEALTH REFORM IN 19TH CENTURY AMERICA. *J. of Social Hist.* 1977 10(4): 490-507. The role of middle class women in spreading health reform, particularly during the pre-Civil War era of antielitism, medical advance, and modernization, needs to be examined. Enlightenment, optimism, and Christian perfectionism mingled in motivating this effort. Concern for health reform also generated a concern for feminism. The efforts included nutrition, child-rearing, clothing styles, and sexual restraint as a means of family planning. These health reformers were the first 19th-century thinkers to prescribe restraint in sexual relations. The final irony was that this attention to modernization tended to make central the role of women, unlike the 18th-century domination by the economic demands of domestic production. 44 notes. M. Hough

894. Numbers, Ronald L. HEALTH REFORM ON THE DELAWARE. *New Jersey Hist.* 1974 92(1): 5-12. Russell Thacher Trall began his medical practice in 1844 when he established the Hygienic Institute in New York City, where he, as a Seventh-Day Adventist, emphasized nonuse of drugs; includes the diary of one of his patients, Merritt Kellogg, during his stay at another of Trall's establishments, the New York Hygeio-Therapeutic College in Florence Heights, New Jersey.

895. Phillips, Loretta and Phillips, Prentice. HE FOUGHT A HORDE OF DEMONS. *New-England Galaxy* 1977 19(1): 45-51. Describes the personal struggles of John B. Gough against Demon Rum during 1834-43. His preachings against liquor, from 1843 until his death in 1886, persuaded thousands of alcoholics to sign the pledge of total abstinence. 3 illus. P. C. Marshall

896. Rorabaugh, W. J. PROHIBITION AS PROGRESS: NEW YORK STATE'S LICENSE ELECTIONS, 1846. *J. of Social Hist.* 1981 14(3): 425-443. New York's election in 1846 serves as the best measure of broad public sentiment on prohibition. Previous studies tend to focus on middle-class leaders, chiefly ministers. Even examinations of temperance societies do not get much beyond this. In New York's election 80% of the townships voted for local non-licensing of retail liquor sales. This computer correlation of the variables of geography, politics, age, religion, class, and economic interest suggests that the larger, more urban, growing, less agricultural communities and younger voters tended to support prohibition by larger margins. Based on documents from the 1840's, including the state census of 1845; 12 tables, 43 notes. C. M. Hough

897. Rorabaugh, W. J. THE SONS OF TEMPERANCE IN ANTEBELLUM JASPER COUNTY. *Georgia Hist. Q.* 1980 64(3): 263-279. The Sons of Temperance was a secret society which flourished from 1842 to the end of the century and served as a social organization as well as encouraged abstinence from liquor. The Ocmulgee Division No. 40 in Jasper County in central Georgia was organized in 1848. Describes the characteristics of the members, comparing them with other county residents, and also the activities of the group, which was short-lived. Based on the Sons of Temperance Record Book, census data and secondary sources; 45 notes. G. R. Schroeder

898. Schlossman, Steven L. JUVENILE JUSTICE IN THE AGE OF JACKSON. *Teachers Coll. Record* 1974 76(1): 119-133. A study of the organization of the New York House of Refuge in 1825, one of the earliest reformatories, and one which brought together several theories of reform. Examines the motives and actions of the founders, and places the entire episode in the context of 19th-century literature on children and education. Notes. W. H. Mulligan, Jr.

899. Taylor, C. J. THE KINGSTON, ONTARIO PENITENTIARY AND MORAL ARCHITECTURE. *Social Hist. [Canada]* 1979 12(24): 385-408. The principle of a provincial penitentiary for Ontario was accepted in 1831, and commissioners toured the eastern United States that year to study penitentiaries. The commissioners recommended the adoption of the Auburn system, but were also influenced by the works of John Howard and the Boston Prison Discipline Society. The ideal was to design a facility embodying principles of order and harmony which would be imparted to inmates, and serve as a model to the world. 5 fig., 56 notes. D. F. Chard

900. Thavenet, Dennis. "WILD YOUNG 'UNS' IN THEIR MIDST": THE BEGINNINGS OF REFORMATORY EDUCATION IN MICHIGAN. *Michigan Hist.* 1976 60(3): 240-259. As juvenile problems mounted following statehood, Michigan's social elite initially followed the practice, popular in Jacksonian America, of segregating youthful deviants in prisons. Most citizens found this harsh approach difficult to justify; and, by 1851, prison inspectors were against placing children with hardened criminals. By 1856, Michigan's first reformatory was in operation. Characterized by order, uniformity, and obedience, the Lansing institution governed the recreational, educational, and contract labor activities of 54 enrollees by the end of its first year. Primary sources; 4 photos, 67 notes. D. W. Johnson

901. Trattner, Walter I. THE FEDERAL GOVERNMENT AND SOCIAL WELFARE IN EARLY NINETEENTH-CENTURY AMERICA. *Social Service R.* 1976 50(2): 243-255. Discusses two early charitable institutions which involved federal assistance, the Connecticut Asylum for the Deaf and Dumb (1819) and the Kentucky Deaf and Dumb Asylum (1826), showing that both private and public institutions were financed by federal funds a century before the welfare state of the New Deal.

902. Verbrugge, Martha H. THE SOCIAL MEANING OF PERSONAL HEALTH: THE LADIES' PHYSIOLOGICAL INSTITUTE OF BOSTON AND VICINITY IN THE 1850S. Reverby, Susan and Rosner, David, ed. *Health Care in America: Essays in Social History* (Philadelphia: Temple U. Pr., 1979): 45-66. The Ladies' Physiological Institute of Boston and Vicinity was founded in 1848 to instruct its members in lessons of anatomy, physiology, hygiene, and other matters of health and disease. It was part of the middle-class reform movement, representing faith in self-help. Physiological knowledge would not only prevent ill health but also promote moral and social reform. 68 notes. S

903. Whorton, James C. "CHRISTIAN PHYSIOLOGY": WILLIAM ALCOTT'S PRESCRIPTION FOR THE MILLENNIUM. *Bull. of the Hist. of Medicine* 1975 49(4): 466-481. William A. Alcott, M.D. (1798-1859) was a leading health reformer of the Jacksonian age, and a study of his ideas provides a detailed exposition of the ideology of the health reform movement. He was an advocate of "Christian Physiology" or the "directing of biological science toward the social goals of contemporary revivalism." He envisioned a Christian civilization "combining the moral and physical vigor of the Biblical days with the scientific knowledge of the modern era." 64 notes. M. Kaufman

904. Whorton, James C. 'TEMPEST IN A FLESH-POT': THE FORMULATION OF A PHYSIOLOGICAL RATIONALE FOR VEGETARIANISM. *J. of the Hist. of Medicine and Allied Sci.* 1977 32(2): 115-139. During the 1850's, America's vegetarian movement began to develop a scientific rationale in support of their practices. They maintained that God designed the human anatomy as herbivorous, that vegetable atoms were more stable and more slowly cycled through the body than meat atoms, and that vegetables were adequate for strength and were more digestible. Although "it might appear that the violence done to logic and to science by vegetarians was too clumsily masked not to be recognized," the "testimony of conversion that fills the pages of vegetarian literature rings with sincerity." 96 notes. M. Kaufman

Religious Reform

905. Carey, Patrick W. JOHN F. O. FERNANDEZ: ENLIGHTENED LAY CATHOLIC REFORMER, 1815-1820. *Rev. of Pol. 1981 43(1): 112-129.* John F. O. Fernandez was a Portuguese refugee who lived in Norfolk, Virginia, 1803-20. His views on the right of the parish laity to control the temporal affairs of the Church resulted in a clash with the bishops over the appointment of a priest to his church. Fernandez's philosophy was shaped by the teachings of the Church fathers, practices in the early Church, the Enlightenment anticlericalism of his day, and the American tradition of separation of church and state. His views were rejected by the bishops, but he was in the forefront of American Catholics who attempted to create a democratic perception of the laity. Letters and secondary sources; 43 notes. D. F. Ring

906. Gura, Philip F. THE REVEREND PARSONS COOKE AND WARE FACTORY VILLAGE: A NEW MISSIONARY FIELD. *New England Hist. & Geneal. Register 1981 135 (July): 199-212.* The early 19th century struggle of Puritanism to combat the evils of more liberal religions is characterized in the missionary work of Parsons Cooke in Ware, Massachusetts. As industrialization of such communities occurred, the social and political influence of wealthy Unitarians and Universalists became apparent. This may have obscured the important trend toward secularization during the period. 39 notes. primary and secondary sources. A. E. Huff

907. Hatch, Nathan O. THE CHRISTIAN MOVEMENT AND THE DEMAND FOR A THEOLOGY OF THE PEOPLE. *J. of Am. Hist. 1980 67(3): 545-567.* Explores the changing nature of popular religion in American society after the American Revolution by focusing on the collection of radicals known as Disciples of Christ or "Christians." Influenced by egalitarianism of the Revolutionary era, this movement attacked the traditional authority in Protestant churches by criticizing tyrannical clergy, abstract theology, and restrictive church discipline. The movement exalted public opinion and stressed the individual's right to think for himself in religion. This application of republicanism to Protestantism was part of a broader challenge to privilege and authority in American society during the Revolutionary era. Covers 1780-1820. 76 notes. T. P. Linkfield

908. Hildebrand, Reginald F. "AN IMPERIOUS SENSE OF DUTY": DOCUMENTS ILLUSTRATING AN EPISODE IN THE METHODIST REACTION TO THE NAT TURNER REVOLT. *Methodist Hist. 1981 19(3): 155-174.* Following the Nat Turner revolt, Thomas Crowder, a presiding elder of the Methodist Episcopal Church in Virginia, agreed to let the licenses of three slave preachers lapse in 1831. Seven white preachers protested this action in memorials of protest the following year: one to the Virginia Annual Conference of the Methodist Episcopal Church and one to the General Conference of the Methodist Episcopal Church. Reprints the memorials. 38 notes. H. L. Calkin

909. Hovet, Theodore R. THE CHURCH DISEASED: HARRIET BEECHER STOWE'S ATTACK ON THE PRESBYTERIAN CHURCH. *J. of Presbyterian Hist. 1974 52(2): 167-187.* Harriet Beecher Stowe conducted a prolonged debate with American churches, particularly with the Presbyterian Church. Her concern was that impersonal, intellectual, and institutional emphases were replacing personal, emotional, and individual ones. This was particularly manifest in the church response to slavery. 47 notes. D. L. Smith

910. Robertson, Darrel M. THE FEMINIZATION OF AMERICAN RELIGION: AN EXAMINATION OF RECENT INTERPRETATIONS OF WOMEN AND RELIGION IN VICTORIAN AMERICA. *Christian Scholar's Rev. 1978 8(3): 238-246.* Traces the feminization of American religion during 1820's-30's, identified as a romanticization or sentimentalization of religion by traditional historians, discussed as feminization in Barbara Welter's essay, "The Feminization of American Religion," published in 1973.

911. Ryan, Thomas R. NEWMAN'S INVITATION TO ORESTES A. BROWNSON TO BE LECTURER EXTRAORDINARY AT THE CATHOLIC UNIVERSITY OF IRELAND. *Records of the Am. Catholic Hist. Soc. of Philadelphia 1974 85(1/2): 29-47.* The project to bring Orestes A. Brownson to the Catholic University of Ireland, a project which intrigued John Henry Newman, apparently was scuttled by the furor over Brownson's 1854 article on "Native Americanism" in his *Review*. 35 notes. J. M. McCarthy

Utopian Thought and Communalism

912. Andrews, Edward Deming and Andrews, Faith. THE SHAKER CHILDREN'S ORDER. *Winterthur Portfolio 1973 (8): 201-214.* The Children's Order of the United Society of Believers (Shakers) has been neglected by scholars; yet the order is an important institution for students of American communitarianism. In their early history the Shakers accepted children under indentures. Despite legal contracts almost every Shaker community found itself confronted with angry parents, often bringing forth charges of the most hideous crimes. Life for the children was regulated, with emphasis on cleanliness, modesty, industriousness, and frugality. Education was not designed to produce scholars but to enable the student to better the community. In the early 19th century the Shaker Children's Order served a useful function. In addition to offering care, food, and shelter, the order was a testing ground for the selection of those who were ready to serve the holy cause. It was essential to the development of the Shakers. Based on primary and secondary sources; 5 illus., 34 notes. N. A. Kuntz

913. Arndt, Karl J. R. RAPP'S HARMONY SOCIETY AS AN INSTITUTION "CALCULATED TO UNDERMINE AND DESTROY THOSE FUNDAMENTAL PRINCIPLES OF FREE GOVERNMENT, WHICH HAVE CONSPICUOUSLY DISTINGUISHED US FROM ALL THE NATIONS OF THE EARTH." *Western Pennsylvania Hist. Mag. 1980 63(4): 359-366.* Reprints excerpts from George Rapp's Harmony Society's articles of association submitted to the Pennsylvania legislature to request incorporation in 1807; the request was denied.

914. Bonney, Margaret Atherton. THE SALUBRIA STORY. *Palimpsest 1975 56(2): 34-45.* Salubria, a free thought cooperative community founded in Iowa in 1839 by Abner Kneeland, failed within a few years due to land scarcity, economic adversity, a paucity of free thought advocates, competing townships, and unfavorable topography. Kneeland's controversial religious beliefs, often cited as the major cause of the colony's demise, were of secondary importance; his political activities did bring attention, however, and when combined with religious and economic factors spelled defeat for Salubria. Based on primary and secondary sources; 6 illus., 3 photos. D. W. Johnson

915. Bush, Robert D. COMMUNISM, COMMUNITY, AND CHARISMA: THE CRISIS IN ICARIA AT NAUVOO. *Old Northwest 1977 3(4): 409-428.* Describes the failure of the Icarian utopian community at Nauvoo, Illinois, under the leadership of the charismatic Etienne Cabet (1788-1865), a working-class organizer and propagandist. The community was never self-sufficient, and disputes over work sharing developed. Cabet became increasingly autocratic as criticism of his leadership mounted. He attempted to silence opponents by illegally amending the Icarian constitution. When the community divided into "Cabetists" and "Dissidents," control over the membership, and with it voting rights, became an issue. Cabet was ousted in 1856, the year of his death; and the society was dissolved. Based on memoirs, the Icarian constitution, French-language newspapers, and secondary works; table, 54 notes. J

916. Carmony, Donald F. and Elliott, Josephine M. NEW HARMONY, INDIANA: ROBERT OWEN'S SEEDBED FOR UTOPIA. *Indiana Mag. of Hist. 1980 76(3): 161-261.* Imagination and generosity motivated Robert Owen to develop the Utopian community of New Harmony, Indiana. But his skill and wealth were not sufficient to achieve all his goals of social and individual reform in the moral order. The division of labor, sluggish production, and differences over educational policy created cleavages in the community. Despite his failures to achieve all that he wished in New Harmony, Robert Owen continued to advocate

many social reforms, including women's property rights, birth control, and the cooperative movement. His fame rests as much on these as it does on New Harmony. Covers ca. 1824-58. Based on memoirs, local histories, secondary works and Robert Owen's own writings; 74 illus., 11 photos, map, chart, 90 notes. — A. Erlebacher

917. Coffey, David M. THE HOPEDALE COMMUNITY. *Hist. J. of Western Massachusetts 1975 4(1): 16-26.* Adin Ballou established Hopedale, a utopian community, (1841) so that moral and religious elements would predominate over family and material considerations. This proved unrealistic. Joint-stock industries were established and by 1846 private investors took control. Antislavery and women's rights were among the causes espoused in the community. E. D. Draper's withdrawal of investment in 1856 ended the community. Based on Heywood's and Ballou's works; 3 illus., 49 notes. — S. S. Sprague

918. Davidson, Rondel V. VICTOR CONSIDERANT AND THE FAILURE OF LA RÉUNION. *Southwestern Hist. Q. 1973 76(3): 277-296.* Disillusioned with the corrupt monarchy and laissez-faire capitalism which spawned political and social injustices in France, Victor-Prosper Considerant (1808-93) was converted to the Fourierist movement. The European Society for the Colonization of Texas, a joint stock company, established La Réunion near Dallas. This short-lived communal experiment, 1854-59, faced insurmountable problems; the colonists did not follow the plans of Considerant; the culturally elite settlers were unsuited for life in frontier Texas; isolated and desirable land was too expensive; and the scheme was not financially viable. 52 notes. — D. L. Smith

919. Douglas, Paul H. THE MATERIAL CULTURE OF THE HARMONY SOCIETY. *Pennsylvania Folklife 1975 24(3): 2-16.* Uses material culture—specifically, town planning, buildings, and artifacts—to reinterpret social customs and living patterns in Harmony Society, a 19th-century communal society in Harmony and Economy, Pennsylvania and New Harmony, Indiana. S

920. Elmen, Paul. BISHOP HILL: UTOPIA ON THE PRAIRIE. *Chicago Hist. 1976 5(1): 45-52.* Chronicles the progress of a group of Swedish immigrants known as Janssonists, who established a religious utopian colony in Bishop Hill, Illinois, 1846-60.

921. Fogarty, Robert S. ONEIDA: A UTOPIAN SEARCH FOR RELIGIOUS SECURITY. *Labor Hist. 1973 14(2): 202-227.* Examines the origins, conversion factors, and occupations of the original members of the Oneida Community. Most became leaders in the community. The main reasons for joining were related to seeking a religious security; John Humphrey Noyes' writings were an important factor. The community often had to adapt to economic realities, but an essential unity and a puritanical tenacity aided its survival. Based on the *Family Register* of Oneida and on annual inventories; 97 notes. — L. L. Athey

922. Francis, Richard. CIRCUMSTANCES AND SALVATION: THE IDEOLOGY OF THE FRUITLANDS UTOPIA. *Am. Q. 1973 25(2): 202-234.* Describes the failure in 1843 of the six-month old Fruitlands community of central Massachusetts, resulting from a misunderstanding between Amos Bronson Alcott (1799-1888) and the English transcendentalist Charles Lane (d. 1870). Lane, who believed social reform could be accelerated by gathering like-minded individuals in a "consociate family," rejected the narrowness of the biological family celebrated by Alcott—a familialism Lane had not expected when Alcott invited him to Massachusetts. 103 notes. — W. D. Piersen

923. Francis, Richard. THE IDEOLOGY OF BROOK FARM. *Studies in the Am. Renaissance 1977: 1-48.* Brook Farm was established on the philosophy and principles of Transcendentalism, but, during its brief history, it imbued the main tenets of Fourierism, both through the efforts and beliefs of leading members of the Farm community, and through association with the principal American protégés of François Fourier (1772-1837). Largely through the writings of Albert Brisbane (1809-90), the Transcendentalist ideology obtained an account of individual identity and its relationship to society. William Henry Channing (1810-84), another leading Fourierist, provided the members of Brook Farm with a moral spirit, a sense of free will, and consequently, purposiveness. Based on personal letters, memoirs and notebooks of Farm members and magazine articles; 2 plates, 145 notes. — S. Baatz

924. Friesen, Gerhard K. AN ADDITIONAL SOURCE ON THE HARMONY SOCIETY OF ECONOMY, PENNSYLVANIA. *Western Pennsylvania Hist. Mag. 1978 61(4): 301-314.* Excerpts from a German book entitled *Scenes of Life in the United States of America and Texas,* collected by Friedrich Wilhelm von Wrede, describing the Harmony Society of Economy, Pennsylvania, based on von Wrede's experiences there on a visit in 1842.

925. Grant, H. Roger, ed. THE SKANEATELES COMMUNITY: A NEW YORK UTOPIA. *Niagara Frontier 1975 22(3): 68-72.* A Utopian community in New York's Finger Lakes area was founded in 1843 by John Anderson Collins; reprints a letter by John Finch describing the surroundings and financial situation of the community in 1845.

926. Grant, H. Roger. UTOPIA AT COMMUNIA. *Palimpsest 1980 61(1): 12-17.* Founded in 1847 as a utopian community by German and Swiss Americans, Communia, in Volga Township, Iowa, had virtually disintegrated by 1854; it was dissolved by court order in 1864.

927. Grant, H. Roger. UTOPIAS THAT FAILED: THE ANTEBELLUM YEARS. *Western Illinois Regional Studies 1979 2(1): 38-51.* Describes antebellum sectarian and secular utopian communities that failed in the upper Mississippi Valley: the phalanxes, secular colonies of Charles Fourier and Albert Brisbane; the secular Garden Grove Community in Iowa; Hopewell Colony in southern Iowa; and Communia, the religious community of Jasper in Iowa.

928. Ham, F. Gerald. THE PROPHET AND THE MUMMYJUMS: ISAAC BULLARD AND THE VERMONT PILGRIMS OF 1817. *Wisconsin Mag. of Hist. 1973 56(4): 290-299.* The Vermont Pilgrims ("Mummyjums") and their prophet Isaac Bullard imbibed their religious tenets from evangelical revivalism, millennialism, and perfectionism which characterized the religious ferment in New England during the early 19th century. Bullard's faith was distinguished by extreme primitivism and the unquestioned authority of his revelations. Much of the story deals with the hardships experienced by this small band of "Mummyjums" and their leader on their journey from New England through New York, Ohio, and Missouri into the Arkansas Territory in search of the Promised Land. During these wanderings Bullard's experiment disintegrated amidst desertions and deaths. 48 notes. — N. C. Burckel

929. Hayden, Dolores. TWO UTOPIAN FEMINISTS AND THEIR CAMPAIGNS FOR KITCHENLESS HOUSES. *Signs 1978 4(2): 274-290.* Two utopian feminists, Marie Stevens Howland (b. 1836) and Alice Constance Austin, promoted kitchenless houses in order to socialize domestic work. Howland, a Lowell millworker and supporter of Fourier, worked with Albert K. Owen and architect John J. Deery to design a cooperative colony at Topolobampo, Mexico. Austin formulated plans for Llano del Rio, California, including prepared meals and innovative methods to suppress drudgery. The movement, launched between 1874 and 1917, was premature and lacked financial backing. Primary and secondary sources; 9 illus., 24 notes. — S. P. Conner

930. Kirchmann, George. UNSETTLED UTOPIAS: THE NORTH AMERICAN PHALANX AND THE RARITAN BAY UNION. *New Jersey Hist. 1979 97(1): 25-36.* The North American Phalanx, established near Red Bank, New Jersey, in 1843, was one of many communes formed in the United States during the 1840's. By 1848 this community was prosperous financially, operated a successful school, and recorded an absence of personal jealousies and bitterness. Marcus Spring had by that year become the Phalanx's largest stockholder. Through the power that went along with his holdings he tried to influence the community's religious practices. Debates over this and other matters created two factions. In 1852 Spring bought land outside Perth Amboy, New Jersey, persuaded some of the Phalanx's members to leave, and set up the Raritan Bay Union. The North American Phalanx existed until 1854, when a fire destroyed the commune. The Raritan Bay Union was finally turned into the Eagleswood Military Academy in 1859. It closed in 1867. Based on North American Phalanx records and on secondary sources; 5 illus., 29 notes. — E. R. McKinstry

931. Kolmerton, Carol A. EGALITARIAN PROMISES AND INEGALITARIAN PRACTICES: WOMEN'S ROLES IN THE AMERICAN OWENITE COMMUNITIES, 1824-1828. *J. of General*

Educ. 1981 33(1): 31-44. Owenism found fertile intellectual soil in America during the 1820's. Communities were established in Ohio, Indiana, New York, and elsewhere. In all but one of the reported communities, a constitutional provision and considerable rhetoric promoted sexual equality. It has long been assumed that the sexual equality was a reality. This research catalogs, community by community, the falsehood of the assumption. Moreover, blame for the failure of each community was placed on the shoulders of its adult females. The dream of sexual equality is far more difficult to achieve than any 19th-century Owenite ever dreamed. 29 notes.
S. A. Farmerie

932. Mathews, James W. AN EARLY BROOK FARM LETTER. *New England Q. 1980 53(2): 226-230.* In one of the few letters from the earliest era of Brook Farm in Massachusetts, George Partridge Bradford (1807-90), a teacher, in 1841 described several of his colleagues, daily life, and his adaption to the commune. Secondary sources; 18 notes.
J. C. Bradford

933. Morris, James M. COMMUNES AND COOPERATIVES: CINCINNATI'S EARLY EXPERIMENTS IN SOCIAL REFORM. *Cincinnati Hist. Soc. Bull. 1975 33(1): 57-80.* Discusses life-style experiments in utopian communes and cooperatives in the Cincinnati area 1820's-50's, including the plans of social reformer Robert Owen.

934. Myerson, Joel. TWO UNPUBLISHED REMINISCENCES OF BROOK FARM. *New England Q. 1975 48(2): 253-260.* Although George Ripley's experimental community, Brook Farm, lasted only six years, the school and educational experience of granting students perfect freedom to grow and learn as they pleased, succeeded, according to two accounts, one by Frederick Pratt, who describes the school during its first four years, the other by Mrs. Nora Schelter Blair, who recalls Brook Farm during its last days; 1841-47.

935. Nelson, Ronald E. BISHOP HILL: SWEDISH DEVELOPMENT OF THE WESTERN ILLINOIS FRONTIER. *Western Illinois Regional Studies 1978 1(2): 109-120.* Bishop Hill Colony, Illinois, a small frontier settlement of Swedish immigrants warrants study as a communalistic experiment, as an area of concentrated Swedish immigration (virtually the first of frontier America), and as a remarkable example of quick economic growth through cooperation, 1846-59.

936. Norton, John E., ed. "FOR IT FLOWS WITH MILK AND HONEY"; TWO IMMIGRANT LETTERS ABOUT BISHOP HILL. *Swedish Pioneer Hist. Q. 1973 24(3): 163-179.* Translates letters by Anders Andersson and Anders Larsson about the colony of Bishop Hill in 1847, which were published in *Aftonbladt.* Andersson, a devoted Janssonist, reported that all arrived in good health. Larsson reported that the Janssonists were laying out their new city, including communal mills, shops, and farms. Erik Jansson was accepted as the Prophet and Bishop Hill as the new spiritual Israel. Illus., notes.
K. J. Puffer

937. Pitzer, Donald E. and Elliott, Josephine M. NEW HARMONY'S FIRST UTOPIANS, 1814-1824. *Indiana Mag. of Hist. 1979 75(3): 225-300.* Discusses the communal utopian society of New Harmony, Indiana. Covers the religious mystical basis upon which the community was founded, the leadership qualities of founder George Rapp, other prominent persons, policies and procedures, art, architecture, and artifacts, eminent controversies, schisms, and eventual decline. Notes that the religion engendered at New Harmony continued for another century, and that the influence of its members extended far beyond the boundaries of the small community. 53 photos, 31 notes.
V. L. Human

938. Rollins, Richard M. ADIN BALLOU AND THE PERFECTIONIST'S DILEMMA. *J. of Church and State 1975 17(3): 459-476.* Discusses the religious attitudes of utopian socialist Adin Ballou, 1830-42, including his establishment of the Hopedale Community in Milford, Massachusetts.

939. Setterdahl, Lilly. EMIGRANT LETTERS BY BISHOP HILL COLONISTS FROM NORA PARISH. *Western Illinois Regional Studies 1978 1(2): 121-175.* Reprints a series of letters from Bishop Hill Colony, Illinois, by Swedish immigrants who settled in the commune led by Erik Jansson. The letters, dated 1847-56, are directed to relatives and friends still in Sweden and describe the sea voyage, building operations, and daily life in the community.

940. Sokolow, Jayme A. CULTURE AND UTOPIA: THE RARITAN BAY UNION. *New Jersey Hist. 1976 94(2-3): 89-100.* Discusses the origin of the Raritan Bay Union (1853-61). Theodore Weld and his wife, Angelina Grimké, Sarah Grimké, Marcus Spring, and George Arnold were early adherents. Education was the central purpose of the Union. Its well-known school was interracial and coeducational, and attempted to integrate abstract and practical learning. The school's success was counterbalanced by a lack of cohesiveness among the Union's residents. Because the community lacked a unifying ideology it failed. Based on primary and secondary sources; 4 illus., 27 notes.
E. R. McKinstry

941. Tumminelli, Roberto. ETIENNE CABET E IL MODELLO POLITICO-SOCIALE DI ICARIA [Etienne Cabet and the sociopolitical model of Icaria]. *Politico [Italy] 1979 44(1): 92-112.* Discusses Etienne Cabet's (1788-1856) communist political and social theories, his utopian experiment at Icaria in Illinois, and his newspaper career. Cabet belongs to the totalitarian democratic schools, and he represents an important conceptual connection between Gracchus Babeuf and Karl Marx.
J/S

942. Weeks, Robert P. A UTOPIAN KINGDOM IN THE AMERICAN GRAIN. *Wisconsin Mag. of Hist. 1977 61(1): 2-20.* Recounts the bizarre story of James Jesse Strang's establishment of successive utopian communities at Voree, near Burlington, Wisconsin, and then at Beaver Island in northern Lake Michigan in the 1850's. Sees this disciple of Joseph Smith, founder of the Mormon Church, in the context of four elements of the national experience: "the experimental spirit of the Founding Fathers, the utopianism of various nineteenth-century sects and socialist groups, the wild enthusiasm of American revivalism, and certain central features of...Mormonism." 7 illus., 29 notes.
N. C. Burckel

943. Wilson, Richard Guy. IDEALISM AND THE ORIGIN OF THE FIRST AMERICAN SUBURB: LLEWELLYN PARK, NEW JERSEY. *Am. Art J. 1979 11(4): 79-90.* The first planned garden suburb in the United States was Llewellyn Park, located 12 miles west of New York city in West Orange, New Jersey, on 420 acres of hills. Llewellyn S. Haskell (1815-1872) and Alexander Jackson Davis (1803-1892) designed it during 1853-57 as a commuter suburb to New York where men could commune with nature in a rustic retreat. The park's theoretical basis was utopian socialism mixed with Swedenborgianism, Fourierism, and Transcendentalism. The ideals were so much diluted, however, as to be unrecognizable. Communal activities and relationships were almost nonexistent, and what began as an ideal of relating man to man and man to nature became a source of land speculation. 10 illus., 52 notes.
J. J. Buschen

4. CRISES OF MODERNIZATION, 1861-1900

General

944. Ahern, Wilbert H. ASSIMILATIONIST RACISM: THE CASE OF THE "FRIENDS OF THE INDIAN." *J. of Ethnic Studies* 1976 4(2): 23-32. The reform movement to "save" the American Indian launched by groups such as the Indian Rights Association, the Women's National Indian Association, the Massachusetts Indian Association, and others between 1880 and 1900 enjoyed great success in implementing its plans; but those reforms were disastrous for Native Americans. Combining demands for land in severalty for Indians with educational systems which would completely assimilate them into white society, the reformers, gathering annually at Lake Mohunk, New York, "coupled ethnocentrism with egalitarianism." The Indian must disappear into white civilization and take his place in the Darwinian competitive struggle for survival on his own, based on the fallacious "sink or swim" theory also applied to educating the freemen. When Indian schools failed to produce white men, the reformers turned to beliefs in the unchanging nature of race differences, and the paradoxes in their efforts came full cycle. Primary and secondary material; 29 notes. G. J. Bobango

945. Ahern, Wilbert H. LAISSEZ FAIRE VS. EQUAL RIGHTS: LIBERAL REPUBLICANS AND LIMITS TO RECONSTRUCTION. *Phylon* 1979 40(1): 52-65. Traces the development of the Liberal Republican movement of 1872 and the reasons for the Liberal departure from the main party line. Elaborates on the role of racism, which, in contrast to other scholarship, is determined not to be the cause of the split. 42 notes. G. R. Schroeder

946. Anders, Leslie. AMERICAN PACIFISTS: THE PECULIAR BREED. *Parameters* 1980 10(3): 46-50. American pacifism, as exemplified by the pacifist movement during the Civil War, generally appears to have been more an outgrowth of war-weariness or other circumstances than a result of philosophical or religious convictions. An overwhelming pacifist sentiment swept the North at the beginning of the election year of 1864, but it quickly dissipated as the Union Army won new battles and victory seemed near. Secondary sources; 12 notes. L. R. Maxted

947. Anderson, David L. THE DIPLOMACY OF DISCRIMINATION: CHINESE EXCLUSION, 1876-1882. *California Hist.* 1978 57(1): 32-45. Traces the steps leading to the Chinese Exclusion Act (1882). The 1868 Burlingame Treaty had established the right of free immigration of Chinese to America. Pressures on Congress to prohibit Chinese immigration resulted in passage of a law limiting to 15 the number of Chinese on incoming ships; President Hayes vetoed the law. The US minister to China, George Seward, was removed because of his opposition to Chinese exclusion. In his place a diplomatic mission led by James B. Argell went to China in 1880 to revise the Burlingame Treaty. After some hard bargaining the Argell Treaty was agreed on, replacing free immigration with the right of Congress to "regulate, limit, or suspend" the immigration of Chinese laborers, while exempting students, merchants, and tourists. The treaty was approved, and was immediately followed by seven bills to exclude Chinese. President Chester A. Arthur vetoed a bill suspending immigration for 20 years but approved a substitute bill excluding Chinese for 10 years. The Chinese government, plagued by pressures from other countries and internal problems, could not retaliate. The episode reveals the use of treaties and international law to provide legitimacy for arbitrary actions against a weak country. Primary and secondary sources; illus., photos, 46 notes. A. Hoffman

948. Andrews, William D. WOMEN AND THE FAIRS OF 1876 AND 1893. *Hayes Hist. J.* 1977 1(3): 172-183. The images of the ideal American woman created at the Centennial Exposition of 1876 in Philadelphia and at the World's Columbian Exposition (Chicago, 1893) combined the values of the two apparently contradictory sides of the woman's movement—the suffragists and the domestic reformers. The displays proved the compatability of the developing image of the powerful domestic woman with her society, celebrated international sisterhood, and stressed the professional activities and educational accomplishments of American women and the significance of her domestic position. Primary and secondary sources; 10 illus., 15 notes. J. N. Friedel

949. Argersinger, Peter H. THE CONSERVATIVE AS RADICAL: A RECONSTRUCTION DILEMMA. *Tennessee Hist. Q.* 1975 34(2): 168-187. William A. Peffer provides an excellent example of the life of a common man in American history. His opposition to slavery separated him from the majority of people of his time and region. After service with the Union Army, Peffer in 1865 settled in Clarksville, Tennessee, where he opened a law office. Alienated by Governor William G. Brownlow's program, Peffer joined the conservative Unionists, but found himself opposing the Radicals for their methods more than their programs. When his conservative friends turned to violence after political losses to the Radicals, Peffer soon found himself between the extremes and eventually left Tennessee in 1869. Secondary sources; 48 notes. M. B. Lucas

950. Avillo, Philip J., Jr. BALLOTS FOR THE FAITHFUL: THE OATH AND THE EMERGENCE OF SLAVE STATE REPUBLICAN CONGRESSMEN, 1861-1867. *Civil War Hist.* 1976 22(2): 164-174. Surveys loyalty oath legislation in the Border States. The disfranchising measures gave Republicans control of the legislatures of those states and enhanced Republican control of Congress. Concludes that without this added Republican Party strength in the national legislature, important legislation such as the 13th and 14th Amendments, Civil Rights Act, Freedmen's Bureau Act, and First Reconstruction Act, would not have been passed. E. C. Murdock

951. Banning, Evelyn I. HELEN HUNT JACKSON IN SAN DIEGO. *J. of San Diego Hist.* 1978 24(4): 457-467. Describes Helen Hunt Jackson's visits to San Diego, 1882-84, and her interest in the plight of the California Indians which culminated in the novel, *Ramona* (1884).

952. Barjenbruch, Judith. THE GREENBACK POLITICAL MOVEMENT: AN ARKANSAS VIEW. *Arkansas Hist. Q.* 1977 36(2): 107-122. The Greenback movement in Arkansas was short-lived (1876-82) but significant in revealing the vicissitudes of post-Reconstruction state politics. The movement provided an alternative to the Republican and Democratic Parties. It often replaced the Republican Party by briefly allying itself with the Democrats. Major issues included national "hard money" laws, state and local politics, and race relations. The Greenback Party's greatest appeal in Arkansas was to agrarian radicals. Among its leaders were Charles E. Tobey and Rufus King Garland. Based on two contemporary Democratic Little Rock newspapers, primary and secondary sources; illus., 42 notes. T. L. Savitt

953. Benedict, Michael Les. PRESERVING THE CONSTITUTION: THE CONSERVATIVE BASIS OF RADICAL CONSTRUCTION. *J. of Am. Hist.* 1974 61(1): 65-90. In formulating means to protect the rights of ex-slaves, Republicans were conservative in their desire not to develop a permanent expansion of national power at the expense of states' rights. The 14th Amendment and the Civil Rights Act rested upon the assumption of state legislative supremacy and gave Congress no permanent power where laws were equal. More radical insistence on black suffrage was an attempt to give blacks the power to protect themselves once states were left to their own government again. The 15th Amendment limited powers of the states but did not confer powers on the national government. After 1868, though Reconstruction reeled toward disaster, Republicans would not shake off their conservative state-centeredness. 60 notes. K. B. West

954. Binning, F. Wayne. THE TENNESSEE REPUBLICANS IN DECLINE, 1869-1876. PART I. *Tennessee Hist. Q.* 1980 39(4): 471-484. Discusses political reconstruction in Tennessee, 1869-70. By controlling ballotting, DeWitt Clinton Senter earned the support of those enfranchised by his maneuvers, and was elected governor. His extension of the franchise, however, opened the way for the return of the Democrats to power. When the Democratic legislature elected in 1869 met, it undid Radical legislation. The Republican tide of 1865-69 receded. In 1870 the Democrats further extended their power with the election of John Calvin

Brown as governor. Democrats captured the legislature and Supreme Court and remodeled the state constitution to suit their needs. Primary sources; 32 notes.   J. Powell

955. Blodgett, Geoffrey. FREDERICK LAW OLMSTED: LANDSCAPE ARCHITECTURE AS CONSERVATIVE REFORM. *J. of Am. Hist. 1976 62(4): 869-889.* Frederick Law Olmsted is an example of the 19th-century cultural elite who tried to develop American society along their own static and formal philosophies without considering the "aggressive, pluralistic thrust" of the general populace. Using park landscaping to exemplify his political and social theories, Olmsted created structured, orderly, highly cultivated designs that he envisioned being used by the masses for quiet, contemplative solitude removed from the discordancies of their mundane lives. He resembled Henry Adams, Edward Atkinson, Horace White, and others in this desire to guide lesser-cultivated fellow citizens toward the higher and better things in life. His failure is mute testimonial to the determined, kaleidoscopic citizenry of his time. 68 notes.   V. P. Rilee

956. Blodgett, Geoffrey. THE MUGWUMP REPUTATION, 1870 TO THE PRESENT. *J. of Am. Hist. 1980 66(4): 867-887.* Reviews major interpretations of Republican Party (mugwump) independent reformers by historians from 1910 to 1976 and analyzes evaluations of the mugwumps by their contemporaries of the 1880's. The mugwumps enjoyed a favorable reputation among historians until 1920, when a long period of abuse began at the hands of progressive-liberal historians. Despite Richard Hofstadter's kind treatment of the mugwumps in *The Age of Reform,* their reputation declined further during the 1960's and 1970's. Only recently have American historians been more sympathetic toward the mugwumps. But the rough treatment suffered at the hands of historians has been mild in comparison to the abuse and invective the mugwumps endured from their own contemporaries. 53 notes.
T. P. Linkfield

957. Bogardus, Ralph F. and Szasz, Ferenc M. REVEREND G. D. FORSSELL AND HIS MAGIC LANTERN SHOWS: A CLUE TO AMERICA'S POPULAR IMAGINATION IN THE 1890'S. *Palimpsest 1977 58(4): 111-119.* In the early 1890's, itinerant minister G. D. Forssell toured Iowa and Minnesota delivering slide lectures on religious subjects. Forssell's presentations were simplistic in outlook and included such themes as the life of Christ, the evils of city life, and temperance. They perhaps provided a foundation for the heightened social consciousness which contributed to the rise of Progressivism. Forssell's Sears Magic Lantern and 70 slides are preserved today at Gibb Farm Museum, St. Paul, Minnesota. 11 illus., note on sources.   D. W. Johnson

958. Bordin, Ruth. "A BAPTISM OF POWER AND LIBERTY": THE WOMEN'S CRUSADE OF 1873-1874. *Ohio Hist. 1978 87(4): 393-404.* The temperance crusade sparked by Diocletian Lewis's speech in 1873 at Hillsboro, Ohio, was a watershed in the self-perception of women which represented "a real, if only partially conscious, commitment to the idea that women could legitimately function in the public realm." Linked to the national issues of abolition and revivalism in the 1830's and continued by the public debate over liquor licensing in Ohio in 1873-74, the temperance crusade, by working within the traditional bounds of home and morality, widened the accepted spheres of women's activity. Based on the Temperance and Prohibition Papers, National Headquarters file, Women's Christian Temperance Union (WCTU), and other primary sources; illus., photo, 29 notes.   L. A. Russell

959. Brodhead, Michael J. and Clanton, O. Gene. G. C. CLEMENS: THE "SOCIABLE" SOCIALIST. *Kansas Hist. Q. 1974 40(4): 475-502.* Discusses the thought and political antics of Gaspar Christopher Clemens, a radical Kansas Populist turned Socialist, 1885-90's.

960. Bromberg, Alan B. THE VIRGINIA CONGRESSIONAL ELECTIONS OF 1865: A TEST OF SOUTHERN LOYALTY. *Virginia Mag. of Hist. and Biog. 1976 84(1): 75-98.* The Congressional elections of 1865 in Virginia reveal that despite customary views of Reconstruction at least one southern state willingly accepted the inevitability of defeat. Virginia voters did not elect any former Confederate leaders, and instead chose men who could qualify taking Congress' "ironclad oath." Yet Virginians were unwilling to go so far as to show genuine repentance over secession, and it was this reluctance which provided Congressional Radicals with a rationale for Reconstruction. Based on the Pierpont Executive Papers in the Virginia State Library, newspapers, and secondary accounts; 59 notes.   R. F. Oaks

961. Burckel, Nicholas C. WILLIAM GOEBEL AND THE CAMPAIGN FOR RAILROAD REGULATION IN KENTUCKY, 1888-1900. *Filson Club Hist. Q. 1974 48(1): 43-60.* Uses the career of William Goebel to show that political ambition and reform ideas combined to form the basis of Progressivism. Goebel had built his career on a record of favoring state regulation of railroads and induced a state constitutional convention to include a railroad commission in the Kentucky constitution of 1891. In 1898, he supported a partisan election law which centralized election administration in the Democratically controlled state legislature. After Goebel received the 1899 Democratic gubernatorial nomination, the Republican candidate William S. Taylor stated that Goebel would use the election law to have himself counted into office, a charge that Goebel ignored. Taylor won the election by a small plurality, and Goebel was assassinated in the midst of his contest to overturn the results. Documentation from contemporary newspapers; 57 notes.
G. B. McKinney

962. Burstyn, Joan N. AMERICAN SOCIETY DURING THE EIGHTEEN-NINETIES: "THE WOMAN QUESTION." *Studies in Hist. and Soc. 1973 4(2): 34-40.* Deals with the great debate over the role of women during the last decade of the 19th century with emphasis on the impact of industrialization. Railroad expansion and the development of machinery helped liberate women from the drudgery of domestic life.
J. O. Baylen

963. Burton, Vernon. RACE AND RECONSTRUCTION: EDGEFIELD COUNTY, SOUTH CAROLINA. *J. of Social Hist. 1978 12(1): 31-56.* C. Vann Woodward and Eugene D. Genovese represent two historical explanations for racial adjustments during Reconstruction. Changes in race relations in Edgefield County, South Carolina, and events there during Reconstruction bring "into question the positions of both Woodward and Genovese about black acquiescence in a white dominated paternalistic system in the decade following emancipation." Instead 1867-77 was characterized by fierce competition between blacks and whites for political and economic power in Edgefield County. Explains Reconstruction violence in Edgefield County as the result of Republican-inspired land reform which was basically a class question. Land distribution more than the abolition of slavery would prevent the plantation class from retaining its hegemony. In Edgefield County's rural society Woodward's typology is reversed and Genovese's paternalism is contradicted. The success of blacks in a competitive racial system forced the whites to restore paternalism and oppressive controls when federal, state, and local political and military controls were removed. Primary and secondary sources; 42 notes.   R. S. Sliwoski

964. Campbell, Karlyn Kohrs. STANTON'S "THE SOLITUDE OF SELF": A RATIONALE FOR FEMINISM. *Q. J. of Speech 1980 66(3): 304-312.* Elizabeth Cady Stanton's "The Solitude of Self," her farewell speech to the National American Woman Suffrage Association in 1892, is analyzed as a philosophical statement of the principles underlying the 19th century struggle for woman's rights in the United States. Its rhetorical power remains undiminished because of its lyric structure and tone and its tragic, existential rationale for feminism.   J/S

965. Candeloro, Dominic. LOUIS F. POST AND THE SINGLE TAX MOVEMENT, 1872-1898. *Am. J. of Econ. and Sociol. 1976 35(4): 415-430.* The career of Louis F. Post (1849-1928), upon his return to New York following a stint as a Carpetbagger in South Carolina, became, for a time, that of publicist. Post first attempted to break into regular Republican politics, then turned to journalism on the staff of the New York *Truth*, and finally was converted to the Single Tax philosophy of Henry George in the early 1880's. Thereafter, Post became George's closest confidante and labored hard as a writer, lecturer, and political organizer to elect George and others to make the Single Tax a reality. The author's sources include Post's unpublished autobiography, the files of *The Public, The Standard* and the Cleveland *Recorder*, as well as material from the Henry George Collection in the New York Public Library.
J

966. Cangi, Ellen Corwin. PATRONS AND PROTEGES: CINCINNATI'S FIRST GENERATION OF WOMEN DOCTORS 1875-1910. *Cincinnati Hist. Soc. Bull. 1979 37(2): 89-114.* Briefly describes the relative absence of women in the medical profession in the United States, except for a few isolated cases beginning in 1835, and discusses reforms in the profession which included the admission of women to medical schools; in particular, covers the situation in Cincinnati between 1875 and 1910 (women were admitted to the Cincinnati College of Medicine and Surgery beginning in 1883).

967. Carroll, Michael P. REVITALIZATION MOVEMENTS AND SOCIAL STRUCTURE: SOME QUANTITATIVE TESTS. *Am. Sociol. R. 1975 40(3): 389-401.* After reviewing some of the methodological difficulties which have faced investigators trying to investigate the rise of revitalization movements, the methodological advantages of studying the acceptance of the Ghost Dance (circa 1889) by North American Indians are delineated. These advantages are: (1) a relatively large number of tribes (N=37) were all exposed to what was more or less the same revitalization movement; (2) information on the degree to which each tribe accepted the movement is available from a source contemporary to the event and (3) information relating to some of the social characteristics of these tribes is available from Murdock's *Ethnographic Atlas*. The sample thus provides what is probably a unique opportunity for quantitatively testing several hypotheses relating to the acceptance of revitalization movements. After ascertaining that diffusion alone could not account for acceptance of the Ghost Dance, several other hypotheses, derived from different theoretical frameworks, were tested. Thus, using a "cultural deprivation" argument, it was predicted, and found, that those tribes recently deprived (because they were living in areas in which the buffalo had only recently been exterminated) were far more likely to accept the Ghost Dance than those not recently deprived. The assertion—implicit in Worsley's analysis of Cargo Cults—that acceptance of a revitalization movement would vary inversely with degree of political centralization was *not* supported by the data. Finally, based upon a consideration of the social conditions promoting "integration" in Durkheim's sense of that word, it was predicted, and found, that acceptance varied inversely with the presence of unilineal kin groups and with the presence of a system of inheritance.
J

968. Carson, Ruth. INDIANS CALLED HER "THE MEASURING WOMAN": ALICE FLETCHER AND THE APPORTIONMENT OF RESERVATION LANDS. *Am. West 1975 12(4): 12-15.* Committing her interests, energies, and resources to the betterment of the Indians, Alice Cunningham Fletcher (1838-1923) was one of the driving forces behind the drafting and passage of the Dawes Act (1882). During the 1880's and 1890's she personally directed the survey and allotment of lands for the Omaha, Winnebago, and Nez Percé. She also gathered anthropological data and artifacts and convinced American classical archaeologists of the importance of the study of prehistory. 2 illus.
D. L. Smith

969. Carter, Dan T. FATEFUL LEGACY: WHITE SOUTHERNERS AND THE DILEMMA OF EMANCIPATION. *Pro. of the South Carolina Hist. Assoc. 1977: 49-63.* Examines the efforts of white southerners to deal with the emancipation of the slaves after the Civil War. Southerners believed that the freedmen were inherently indolent, dishonest, and unwilling to work on plantations again. "Where the Negro will work" became the crucial issue that produced the Black Codes and the election of antebellum secessionists, which in turn brought on Radical Reconstruction. Based largely on newspapers; 32 notes.
J. W. Thacker, Jr.

970. Castile, George P. EDWIN EELLS, U.S. INDIAN AGENT, 1871-1895. *Pacific Northwest Q. 1981 72(2): 61-68.* Appointed as agent to the Skokomish Indian Reservation in 1871, Edwin Eells believed strongly in breaking down Indian tribalism and replacing it with individually owned plots of land. Thirteen years before the Dawes Act (US, 1887), he introduced the policy of individual allotments among the Skokomish and worked continuously to institute the plan on a national level. Despite his efforts to preserve Indian land from the onslaught of white farmers, Eells lived long enough to see the failures of the Dawes Act, which caused the Indians of Washington State to lose most of their property. Based on Eells's annual agent reports and his memoirs; 4 photos, 35 notes.
M. L. Tate

971. Chandler, Robert. THE FAILURE OF REFORM: WHITE ATTITUDES AND INDIAN RESPONSE IN CALIFORNIA DURING THE CIVIL WAR ERA. *Pacific Hist. 1980 24(3): 284-294.* Republicans came into power in California in the 1860's and brought the belief of equality for all under the law. Reformism and the Civil War modified white attitudes toward blacks and Chinese but not Indians. Indians were thought to be both racially inferior and culturally barbaric. The Indian population rapidly declined. It was about 310,000 in 1769; by 1845 it was 150,000; by 1850 it was 100,000; and by 1900 it was only 20,000. California Indians were called "Diggers" by the Americans. Attempts were made to place some Indians on reservations. Other attempts were made to kill them or to enslave them (through apprentice programs). The whites thought that the Indians were dying out as a race and that killing them aided nature. The reformers failed because the Indian was placed so low on the scale of humanity he could not contribute to civilization and therefore did not try to. Based on local newspapers, 1850 and 1860 California Statutes; 28 notes.
G. L. Lake

972. Cimprich, John. MILITARY GOVERNOR JOHNSON AND TENNESSEE BLACKS, 1862-65. *Tennessee Hist. Q. 1980 39(4): 459-470.* The Civil War marked a turning point in Andrew Johnson's political career, increasing his national prominence and taking him into a controversial presidency. His wartime service as military governor of Tennessee turned the former proponent of slavery into a committed emancipationist. As president, however, Johnson fought against civil rights legislation. Primary sources; 32 notes.
J. Powell

973. Clark, E. Culpepper. SARAH MORGAN AND FRANCIS DAWSON: RAISING THE WOMAN QUESTION IN RECONSTRUCTION SOUTH CAROLINA. *South Carolina Hist. Mag. 1980 81(1): 8-23.* Analyzes the feminist thought and life of Sarah Ida Fowler Morgan, who published editorials in the Charleston *News and Courier*, which was edited by her future husband, Francis Warrington Dawson.

974. Cloyd, Daniel Lee. PRELUDE TO REFORM: POLITICAL, ECONOMIC, AND SOCIAL THOUGHT OF ALABAMA BAPTISTS, 1877-1890. *Alabama Rev. 1978 31(1): 48-64.* Editorial analysis of *The Alabama Baptist*, 1877-90, supports the contention that Baptists were increasingly interested in socialized religion. Although remaining theologically conservative fundamentalists, Baptists often deplored Gilded Age political corruption, encouraged education and missionary activity among the black community, and championed prohibition. Baptist concern for social issues corresponded more closely to Progressive reform than antebellum religiosity. Primary and secondary sources; 65 notes.
J. F. Vivian

975. Cook, Ramsay. HENRY GEORGE AND THE POVERTY OF CANADIAN PROGRESS. *Can. Hist. Assoc. Hist. Papers [Canada] 1977: 142-157.* Discusses the impact of the social and tax reformer, Henry George, on Canadian thinking during 1879-99, especially on the rural population and laboring classes of the industrial centers. His Canadian tours sparked great interest among all classes and resulted in heated debate of his contention that industrial "progress" and land monopoly were the causes of increasing poverty and suffering, and that a remedy could be found in the single tax and free trade. The church press had a mixed reaction, but his views proved to be increasingly compatible with liberal social gospel theology. At least he got across the notion that the economic and social status quo could not necessarily claim a divine imprimatur. 54 notes.
R. V. Ritter

976. Coray, Michael S. "DEMOCRACY" ON THE FRONTIER: A CASE STUDY OF NEVADA EDITORIAL ATTITUDES ON THE ISSUE OF NONWHITE EQUALITY. *Nevada Hist. Soc. Q. 1978 21(3): 189-204.* The State Constitution and subsequent legislation established political and cultural supremacy for whites in Nevada by 1865. However, Congress passed the Civil Rights Act of 1866, and that law, alongside other federal legislation passed in 1867 and 1868, threatened the preferential sociopolitical position of whites in Nevada. As spokesmen for white supremacy, the *Daily Territorial Enterprise* (Virginia City) and the *Humboldt Register* saw little danger from the Indians. The journals rated Chinese intrusions in Nevada a more serious threat, but believed that it was readily surmountable. On the other hand, the newspapers considered Negro intrusions calamitous to Nevada whites, for Congress had enfranchised Negroes, and Nevadans could not resist the federal will. Based on Nevada state documents and newspapers; 59 notes.
H. T. Lovin

977. Cowdrey, Albert E. PIONEERING ENVIRONMENTAL LAW: THE ARMY CORPS OF ENGINEERS AND THE REFUSE ACT. *Pacific Hist. R. 1975 44(3): 331-349.* The legislative history of the Refuse Act (1899) can be traced to a bill introduced into Congress in 1876 at the instigation of the New York Chamber of Commerce and supported by the Army Corps of Engineers. The Corps worked with sympathetic Congressmen during the 1880's in successful attempts to pass waterways regulatory measures, culminating in a comprehensive antiobstruction measure in 1890. The 1890 act proved to be poorly drafted and difficult to enforce, leading the Corps to propose a new bill, which was passed in 1899. The new bill was more sweeping than any earlier legislation, containing no express limitations on its purposes. But the Corps' enforcement policies and judicial rulings soon nullified its potential as an antipollution measure and limited its purposes to keeping the waterways open for shipping. After 1960, the act began to function as an antipollution measure when the US Supreme Court interpreted it more broadly. Based on documents in National Archives and on published government documents; 35 notes. W. K. Hobson

978. Creed, David A. RECONSTRUCTION IN MADISON PARISH. *North Louisiana Hist. Assoc. J. 1976 7(2): 39-47.* Reconstruction began in Madison Parish on 4 July 1863 with the fall of Vicksburg. One of the first results was the "lessee system," under which abandoned plantations were leased by the Federal Government for one year at a time to anyone who would support the Negroes. Soon, though, speculators and cotton thieves "roamed through the parish," and "many of the Negroes came to hate the Northerners more than they had their former masters." Jayhawker outlaw bands also created a problem, until they were overcome by a group of Confederate guerrillas commanded by Captain Joseph C. Lee. Negro schools were started in 1864, and contraband, or "Freedmen's Villages" were established to care for sick and lame Negroes. In 1865, some of the refugee planters began to return, but throughout the 1860's the Negroes and Republicans retained control in the parish. By 1874, though, the balance of power had swung to the Democrats and the whites, and the parish again went from one extreme to another. 33 notes.
A. N. Garland

979. Crider, Gregory L. WILLIAM DEAN HOWELLS AND THE ANTIURBAN TRADITION: A RECONSIDERATION. *Am. Studies 1978 19(1): 55-64.* Reviews the literature criticizing William Dean Howells as antiurban, and then analyzes Howells's vision of the city within the context of recent urban history. Although he disliked some aspects of American cities, Howells thought they could be corrected, and spent most of his adult life in Boston and New York. Howells directed his main criticism at capitalism, not urbanism, and lamented the inability of urban social institutions to keep pace with the rapid physical and economic changes. The lack of community also bothered him. Primary and secondary sources; 41 notes. J. Andrew

980. Culley, Margaret. SOB-SISTERHOOD: DOROTHY DIX AND THE FEMINIST ORIGINS OF THE ADVICE COLUMN. *Southern Studies 1977 16(2): 201-210* Dorothy Dix (Elizabeth Meriwether Gilmer, 1861-1951), who wrote the first influential and successful newspaper advice column, was an ardent feminist and suffragist. The column began in 1895 in the New Orleans *Picayune* and continued for almost 60 years. Dix later adopted the question and answer format, but in the first six years she wrote strong essays on female financial vulnerability, and the cost to women of confining social conventions and expectations. She supported women's right to work, dress reform, the franchise, improved health care, and education. When she became a nationally syndicated writer, her polemical style softened. Based on the Dix autobiography and columns from the *Picayune;* 7 notes.
J. Buschen

981. Current, Richard N. THE POLITICS OF RECONSTRUCTION IN WISCONSIN, 1865-1873. *Wisconsin Mag. of Hist. 1976-77 60(2): 82-108.* Traces the success of Wisconsin Republicans in dealing with the issues of racism, nativism, materialism, sectionalism, idealism, and antimonopolism which kept them in power during Reconstruction. The article is the concluding chapter in Current's published volume, *The History of Wisconsin, Volume II: The Civil War Era, 1848-1873.* 18 illus., 40 notes. N. C. Burckel

982. Currie, James T. THE BEGINNINGS OF CONGRESSIONAL RECONSTRUCTION IN MISSISSIPPI. *J. of Mississippi Hist. 1973 35(3): 267-286.* Describes the beginnings of Congressional Reconstruction in Mississippi between the passage of the Reconstruction Acts of 1867 and the opening of the convention in January 1868 to draw up a new state constitution. Includes the policies of Major General Edward Otho Cresap Ord, commander of the 4th Military District, who was "above all an Army officer" and was "probably more conservative than he was radical," the registration of the new electorate of 136,000, the apportionment and election of delegates to the state convention, and the composition of factions at the convention. Of the 93 delegates (of 100) whom the author classifies, 45 (including the 17 black delegates) were Radicals, 19 were "Conservative Radicals," and 29 were Conservatives. Some scholars, including James W. Garner, have argued that Ord apportioned delegates unfairly in order to guarantee a radical majority, but statistical analysis shows that these charges are "completely without basis." "Indeed, the apportionment within the 1868 Constitutional Convention was probably fairer and more equitable than that of any legislature that met in Mississippi until 1966." Based on unpublished records in the National Archives and the Mississippi Department of Archives and History.
J. W. Hillje

983. Curry, Jane. SAMANTHA "RASTLES" THE WOMAN QUESTION OR "IF GOD HAD MEANT WIMMEN SHOULD BE NOTHIN' BUT MEN'S SHADDERS, HE WOULD HAVE MADE GOSTS AND FANTOMS OF 'EM AT ONCE." *J. of Popular Culture 1974 8(4): 805-824.* Discusses the feminist and humorous writings of Marrietta Holley, 1870-1926, centering on *My Opinions and Betsy Bobbet's* (1873).

984. Curry, Richard O. THE CIVIL WAR AND RECONSTRUCTION, 1861-1877: A CRITICAL OVERVIEW OF RECENT TRENDS AND INTERPRETATIONS. *Civil War Hist. 1974 20(3): 215-238.* Analyzes recent literature on the Civil War and Reconstruction and deals with Civil War party rivalries in the North, Lincoln as war leader, and several aspects of the revisionist evaluation of Reconstruction. Holds that "Copperheads" were not traitors, that Lincoln correctly mixed his idealism with practical politics, that the traditional stereotypes of carpetbaggers and scalawags have been mercifully disposed of, and that the C. Vann Woodward thesis on the "Compromise of 1877" is basically sound. Summarizes newer writings on minor themes and current works in progress dealing with the 1861-77 years. E. C. Murdock

985. Curtis, Bruce. VICTORIANS ABED: WILLIAM GRAHAM SUMNER ON THE FAMILY, WOMEN AND SEX. *Am. Studies [Lawrence, KS] 1977 18(1): 101-122.* Did a Victorian consensus concerning sexuality exist? Sumner's life reveals many tensions and inconsistencies, although he generally supported the sexual status quo. His ideal of the middle class family, nonetheless, led him to oppose the double sexual standard and to question the idea of a stable Victorian consensus on sexuality. He supported humane divorce policies and kinder treatment for prostitutes, and recognized women as sexual beings. Primary and secondary sources; 4 notes. J. Andrew

986. Daniel, Mike. THE ARREST AND TRIAL OF RYLAND RANDOLPH: APRIL-MAY, 1868. *Alabama Hist. Q. 1978 40(3-4): 127-143.* White supremacist Ryland Randolph, editor of the Tuscaloosa *Independent Monitor* and supporter of the Ku Klux Klan, opposed Reconstruction and Radical Republican rule in Alabama. Intervening in a racially mixed fight on 28 March 1868, he stabbed a black man in self-defense. For this he was illegally tried before a military court in Selma. Civil, military, and federal authorities involved themselves in the case. For still disputed reasons, on 13 May the military acquitted Randolph. Based on contemporary newspaper articles; 67 notes.
E. E. Eminhizer

987. Daniell, Elizabeth Otto. THE ASHBURN MURDER CASE IN GEORGIA RECONSTRUCTION, 1868. *Georgia Hist. Q. 1975 59(3): 296-312.* Chronicles the political career of George W. Ashburn, and the events of the military trial of his murderers, 1868; examines his murder at the hands of anti-Radical supporters as a reflection of anti-Radical feelings in Georgia.

988. Davison, Kenneth E. PRESIDENT HAYES AND THE REFORM OF AMERICAN INDIAN POLICY. *Ohio Hist. 1973 82(3/4): 205-214.* The conclusion of the last major Indian war, the defeat of the movement to return the Indian Bureau to the Department of War, and the appointment of reform-minded Carl Schurz as Secretary of the Interior all led to a new turn in Indian policy. An investigation led to firings and reform. All Indian traders had to be bonded and licensed, and Indian education improved. Despite bad publicity from mismanagement of the removal of the Poncas and the issuance of Helen Hunt Jackson's *A Century of Dishonor*, conditions for the Indians improved under the administration of President Hayes. Based on primary and secondary sources; 3 illus., 25 notes. S. S. Sprague

989. Dawson, Joseph G., III. ARMY GENERALS AND RECONSTRUCTION: MOWER AND HANCOCK AS CASE STUDIES. *Southern Studies 1978 17(3): 255-272.* In 1867 General Joseph Anthony Mower (1827-70) was made interim commander of the 5th Military District (Texas and Louisiana) under the Military Reconstruction Act of 2 March 1867. Mower was a Radical Republican and aggressively implemented Congress' wishes. He peacefully conducted the Louisiana constitutional convention, but then removed a number of local and state officials from office. He encouraged black registration and restricted registration for whites. Winfield Scott Hancock (1824-86), a Democrat and supporter of mild reconstruction, assumed command in November, 1867. He replaced a number of radical officials with conservative Democrats, limited black registration, and allowed broad registration of whites, including many disenfranchised by Mower. Primary and secondary sources; 46 notes. J. Buschen

990. Dawson, Joseph G., III. GENERAL LOVELL H. ROUSSEAU AND LOUISIANA RECONSTRUCTION. *Louisiana Hist. 1979 20(4): 373-391.* Lovell H. Rousseau (1818-69), a Unionist Democrat from Kentucky, "was perhaps the most well-liked army officer to serve in the South during Reconstruction." Appointed commander of the Department of Louisiana in the summer of 1868 by his friend President Andrew Johnson, Rousseau quickly became popular among white Democrats because his soldiers seldom interfered with their efforts to intimidate black voters. In fact, he relaxed his supervision to the point of negligence during the November elections, facilitating a Democratic Party victory in Louisiana. The general's sudden death on 7 January 1869 kindled widespread lamenting among the conservative white citizenry. Based on contemporary newspapers, Department of Louisiana military records in the National Archives, and other archival sources; 43 notes. D. B. Touchstone

991. Dawson, Joseph G., III. GENERAL PHIL SHERIDAN AND MILITARY RECONSTRUCTION IN LOUISIANA. *Civil War Hist. 1978 24(2): 133-151.* General Philip H. Sheridan, commanding the Fifth Military District (Louisiana and Texas), interpreted the 1867 Congressional Reconstruction Acts as vesting him with all necessary powers to ensure good government and successful registration of voters for the fall 1867 constitutional conventions. Sheridan removed public officials, even governors, for obstruction or malfeasance. President Andrew Johnson, long irritated with him, replaced him in August 1867. In an unprecedented postwar situation, Sheridan was a thorough, vigorous coordinator in government and registration, strict but not harsh. He protected and encouraged the freedmen in participatory democracy. Important New Orleans newspapers gave Sheridan unexpected credit. Primary, newspaper, and other secondary sources; 54 notes. R. E. Stack

992. DuBois, Ellen, ed. ON LABOR AND FREE LOVE: TWO UNPUBLISHED SPEECHES OF ELIZABETH CADY STANTON. *Signs: J. of Women in Culture and Soc. 1975 1(1): 257-268.* Stanton (1815-1902) was the chief ideologue and theoretician of suffragism from the 1850's to the 1890's. During Reconstruction, she and other suffragists broke with their former allies, the abolitionists, and integrated the enfranchisement of women with other reforms such as labor and free love. Departing from her upper-class background in "On Labor" (1868), Stanton called poverty and wage slavery social, not natural, phenomena and advocated strikes; yet she saw "the educated classes" as the source of social change. In "On Marriage and Divorce" (1870) she criticized "external regulation of private affections" and commented favorably on the freedom in her marriage to Henry Stanton. Based on primary and secondary sources; 8 notes. T. Simmerman

993. Dunlay, Thomas W. GENERAL CROOK AND THE WHITE MAN PROBLEM. *J. of the West 1979 18(2): 3-10.* General George Crook recognized that corrupt government Indian agents, and the expansion of white settlement, did much to provoke Indian violence. Crook publicly advocated citizenship for Indians and recognition of their legal rights in courts of law. Reformers, including Crook, were overly optimistic about the Indians' ability to adapt to a settled, agricultural life. In reaction to the gross abuses of Indian agents, military men frequently suggested that Indian affairs become a function of the War Department. Crook was one of the most outspoken critics of white greed, which, as he saw it, caused most of the Indian troubles. Published sources and some government records; 4 photos, 57 notes. B. S. Porter

994. Eisenberg, John M. A HOUSE DIVIDED: SILVER DEMOCRATS AND THEIR PARTY. *West Tennessee Hist. Soc. Papers 1975 29: 86-99.* A convention of silver Democrats in Memphis called for a bimetallic meeting in Memphis during June 1895 to counteract an earlier meeting of gold Democrats which had been held in Memphis in May. More than 2,000 delegates attended. While most were Democrats, Republicans were also present, and the convention's declarations were bipartisan. The importance of the convention was that it was the first non-Congressional meeting of silver Democrats which transcended state boundaries. It also proved to be a splendid opportunity to resolve the debate between those favoring a fight within the party over the silver issue and those who wanted to leave the party. The latter group finally decided to remain in the party. The following year in Chicago William Jennings Bryan delivered his famous "Cross of Gold" speech and was subsequently nominated as the Democrats' standard-bearer, largely as the result of the Memphis convention. Based on secondary materials; 52 notes, 2 appendixes. H. M. Parker, Jr.

995. Ellis, William E. CHILDREN, YOUTH, AND THE SOCIAL GOSPEL: THE REACTION TO WASHINGTON GLADDEN. *Foundations 1980 23(3): 252-266.* Traces Congregationalist clergyman Washington Gladden's (1836-1918) attitudes toward the social responsibilities of the church, showing the influence of his own early life and religious thinking, and that of others such as Horace Bushnell, along with changing political and economic conditions. Based mostly on his sermons; 92 notes. E. E. Eminhizer

996. Fingard, Judith. MASTERS AND FRIENDS, CRIMPS AND ABSTAINERS: AGENTS OF CONTROL IN 19TH CENTURY SAILORTOWN. *Acadiensis [Canada] 1978 8(1): 22-46.* During 1850's-90's three agencies competed for control of sailors in eastern Canadian ports. Boardinghouse keepers exploited them, but enhanced their wage rates. Despised by civic elites, the keepers were tolerated as agents of control. The government shipping office, intending to reduce desertion and control wage rates, lacked the means to do either. Social reformers promoted temperance and sailors' homes, but failed because of their paternalism. By the 1880's the need for control declined as working conditions improved. 87 notes. D. F. Chard

997. Foner, Eric. CLASS, ETHNICITY, AND RADICALISM IN THE GILDED AGE: THE LAND LEAGUE AND IRISH-AMERICA. *Marxist Perspectives 1978 1(2): 6-55.* During 1880-83 the American Land League introduced Irish Americans to modern reform and labor ideologies, helped integrate them into the broader context of reform, and shaped the traditions of the Irish working class.

998. Foner, Philip S. A LABOR VOICE FOR BLACK EQUALITY: THE *BOSTON DAILY EVENING VOICE*, 1864-1867. *Sci. and Soc. 1974 38(3): 304-325.* Unique among labor publications, the *Boston Daily Evening Voice* championed unification of black and white workers and considered strong labor organization a means toward union hegemony.

999. Fox, Margery. PROTEST IN PIETY: CHRISTIAN SCIENCE REVISITED. *Int. J. of Women's Studies [Canada] 1978 1(4): 401-416.* In the 19th century, Christian Science, through its founder, Mary Baker Eddy, established a religious movement but also a women's protest movement to gain some political power.

1000. Franklin, John Hope. MIRROR FOR AMERICANS: A CENTURY OF RECONSTRUCTION HISTORY. *Am. Hist. Rev. 1980 85(1): 1-14.* For a century, historians have been writing about the Recon-

struction period. There remain, however, serious differences among them over interpretations, over the significance of major developments, and even over the very facts themselves. The principal explanation for such a state of affairs lies in the preoccupation of historians of Reconstruction with the problems of their own times. Consequently, they use Reconstruction to support their side of the argument in current disputes, such as the place of blacks in American life or the role of government in social and political reform. When Reconstruction is studied as a major historical event without attempting to use it in current disputes, the facts and the interpretations will become clearer, and then they can be very instructive. This article was delivered as the presidential address at the 94th annual meeting of the American Historical Association, held in New York, 28 December 1979. Based on Reconstruction literature, 1870-1979; 50 notes.
A

1001. Freedman, Stephen. THE BASEBALL FAD IN CHICAGO, 1865-1870: AN EXPLORATION OF THE ROLE OF SPORT IN THE NINETEENTH CENTURY CITY. *J. of Sport Hist. 1978 5(2): 42-64.* The history of baseball in Chicago during 1865-70 provides an examination of the relation between sport and the social climate of the 19th-century American city. Baseball's most vigorous supporters were businessmen, educators, journalists, and social reformers who wanted to maintain widely-held middle-class values in a time of rapid social change. Baseball was seen as a healthy way to protect the players from the evil aspects of city life. Businessmen saw it as a way to extend the same benefits to their workers. The baseball clubs that were established were supported by the middle and upper classes. When Chicago's teams began to play against teams from other cities, however, the gentlemen-players had little chance against more agile and almost professional players on other teams. Pressure began to develop for Chicago to come up with a winning team. By 1869-70, all pretense of amateurism was abandoned with the establishment of the Chicago White Stockings. Now, baseball was a symbol of the success of the city and its business community in particular. 61 notes.
M. Kaufman

1002. Fuke, Richard Paul. HUGH LENNOX BOND AND RADICAL REPUBLICAN IDEOLOGY. *J. of Southern Hist. 1979 45(4): 569-586.* The "new orthodoxy" of Radical historiography asserts that Radical ideology was conservative and unwilling to challenge northern racism. This view has slighted the progressive and genuine reform elements of Radical Republicanism. In Maryland, Hugh Lennox Bond proposed adjusting the general attitude of Marylanders to permit changes allowing "equal access to law, education and economic opportunity by both white and black citizens." While failing in the immediate post-Civil War years, Bond and others believed that progress on the race question could have induced economic progress into Maryland. Covers ca. 1861-68. Based on manuscript and printed primary and secondary sources; 97 notes.
T. D. Schoonover

1003. Gelston, Arthur Lewis. RADICAL VERSUS STRAIGHT-OUT IN POST-RECONSTRUCTION BEAUFORT COUNTY. *South Carolina Hist. Mag. 1974 75(4): 225-237.* During Reconstruction in Beaufort County, South Carolina, the radical wing of the Republican Party dominated politics with Negro and white Republicans electing congressmen and local officials. But during the 1880's, when the National Republicans adopted Reconciliation (attempting to attract conservative white southerners by dropping the Negro cause), Beaufort County Republicans divided, radicals versus reconciliationists, giving Democrats control of the county and ending Negro political power in Beaufort. Primary and secondary sources; 58 notes.
R. H. Tomlinson

1004. Gerber, Richard Allan. THE LIBERAL REPUBLICANS OF 1872 IN HISTORIOGRAPHICAL PERSPECTIVE. *J. of Am. Hist. 1975 62(1): 40-73.* Reviews major trends in the historiography on the Liberal Republicans of 1872 over the past 100 years. Earlier schools of history described the Liberal Republicans from a "Reunionist" viewpoint (James Ford Rhodes, William A. Dunning, Claude G. Bowers, Paul Buck) or from a "Reformist" viewpoint (Earl D. Ross, Matthew Josephson, Eric F. Goldman). More recent interpretations of Liberal Republicanism center around Revisionist attacks on the "Reunionists" (Robert F. Durden, James M. McPherson) and on the "Reformists" (Ari A. Hoogenboom, Matthew Downey, John G. Sproat). The recent work of Patrick Riddleberger and Michael Les Benedict shows the continued research needed to illuminate the relationship between Liberal and Radical Republicanism. Based on secondary works; 72 notes.
J. B. Street

1005. Gerteis, Louis S. SALMON P. CHASE, RADICALISM AND THE POLITICS OF EMANCIPATION, 1861-1864. *J. of Am. Hist. 1973 60(1): 42-62.* Radical Republicans may have been sincere in their desire to help southern blacks to full and meaningful freedom, but a study of the efforts of Salmon Portland Chase (1808-73) indicates that they were not successful. Chase pressed Lincoln at every turn to bring about emancipation but was content to stress military expediency as the rationale. He urged early enlistment of blacks in the Union Army, but was critical of the work of Lorenzo Thomas in utilizing landless blacks as labor in the Mississippi Valley. Chase urged the leasing of lands to blacks and supported the preemption of land by freedmen in the Sea Islands of South Carolina. He pressed the land issue in his 1864 election plans, but when his chances evaporated the land reform failed too, reflecting the weaknesses of the Radicals. The promise of the Freedmen's Bureau bill was meaningless because no land was available to implement it. 61 notes.
K. B. West

1006. Gordon, Linda. SOCIAL PURITY AND BIRTH CONTROL: THE USE OF EUGENICS IDEAS BY FEMINISTS IN THE 1890'S. *Tr. of the Conference Group for Social and Administrative Hist. 1976 6: 32-56.* Although aimed at abolishing prostitution, the social purity movement's use of eugenical arguments, race suicide, etc., contributed greatly to the acceptance of birth control.

1007. Gordon, Linda. VOLUNTARY MOTHERHOOD: THE BEGINNINGS OF FEMINIST BIRTH CONTROL IDEAS IN THE UNITED STATES. *Feminist Studies 1973 1(3/4): 5-22.* Discusses the motives and aims of the three feminist groups—the suffragists, the moral reformers, and the Free Love movement—advocating birth control during the 1870's-80's. The groups failed to challenge traditional sex roles while motherhood "remained almost exclusively a tool for women to strengthen their positions within conventional marriages and families..."
T. Simmerman

1008. Grant, H. Roger. POPULISTS AND UTOPIA: A NEGLECTED CONNECTION. *Red River Valley Hist. Rev. 1975 2(4): 481-494.* Sees a correlation between the Populist Movement during 1893-97 and the authors of Utopian novels, most of whom prove to be at least subscribers to Populism.

1009. Greene, Larry A. THE EMANCIPATION PROCLAMATION IN NEW JERSEY AND THE PARANOID STYLE. *New Jersey Hist. 1973 91(2): 108-124.* New Jersey's description as the northernmost of southern states is reinforced by its reaction to the Emancipation Proclamation. The state legislature passed "Peace Resolutions" which denied Lincoln's power to free slaves and advocated a peace settlement with the Confederacy. New Jerseyites' reverence for private property, white workers' job security, opposition to amalgamation, and a desire for limited black population were all challenged by the Emancipation Proclamation. Based on primary and secondary sources; 7 illus., 27 notes.
E. R. McKinstry

1010. Griffith, Elisabeth. ELIZABETH CADY STANTON ON MARRIAGE AND DIVORCE: FEMINIST THEORY AND DOMESTIC EXPERIENCE. Kelley, Mary, ed. *Woman's Being, Woman's Place: Female Identity and Vocation in American History* (Boston: G. K. Hall, 1979): 233-251. A woman who became the principal philosopher of the 19th-century women's movement, Elizabeth Cady Stanton's ambitions did not loom large at the outset of her marriage. Yet, even before marriage she was beginning to develop a strong sense of her own independence and looking toward total autonomy. Stanton did not enjoy an egalitarian marriage, and her feminism developed into an indictment of traditional marriage. Stanton came to believe that patriarchal marriage was the primary obstacle to female emancipation, and she pushed vigorously for reform of divorce laws. In her efforts to improve women's overall economic, legal, and social status she sought foremost to gain for women full recognition as human beings, first, and wives and mothers second. Mainly secondary sources; 64 notes.
J. Powell

1011. Hagan, William T. CIVIL SERVICE COMMISSIONER THEODORE ROOSEVELT AND THE INDIAN RIGHTS ASSOCIATION. *Pacific Hist. R. 1975 44(2): 187-200.* Theodore Roosevelt, US Civil Service Commissioner during 1889-95, contributed to the improvement of the Indian Service and acted as an ally to the Indian Rights

Association (I.R.A.). A major contributing factor was the similarity in background between Roosevelt and I.R.A. leader Herbert Welsh. Welsh requested and received Roosevelt's help in placing Indian Office personnel under Civil Service and in lobbying with Congress, the Commissioner of Indian Affairs, and the Secretary of the Interior on Indian Office personnel matters and on stopping white incursions on Indian land. Based on I.R.A. Papers, Historical Society of Pennsylvania; 61 notes.
W. K. Hobson

1012. Hall, D. J. CLIFFORD SIFTON AND CANADIAN INDIAN ADMINISTRATION, 1896-1905. *Prairie Forum [Canada] 1977 2(2): 127-151.* Preoccupied with western development, Clifford Sifton (Minister of the Interior and Superintendent General of Indian Affairs) placed unsympathetic officials in positions of authority which increased efficiency and centralized administration, but also led to animosity between the Indians and the government due to reduced spending on medical care, education, and agriculture and because of attempts at forced acculturation, 1896-1905.

1013. Harris, William C. THE CREED OF THE CARPETBAGGERS: THE CASE OF MISSISSIPPI. *J. of Southern Hist. 1974 40(2): 199-224.* The revisionist views of carpetbaggers, while "suggestive and provocative," are hypotheses based upon sparce evidence and in need of further testing. Describes in depth the ideals and objectives of the Mississippi carpetbaggers, whose ideology was rooted in the Civil War republican idealism that captured the minds of young educated Union army officers. Seeing their task as the regeneration of the South they sought to elevate loyal men to power and preserve equal rights and tolerance. Believing a public school system essential for the regeneration of Mississippi's whites and blacks, most reformers were willing to sacrifice integrated for equal schools. The reformers also struggled for economic development, a course which often won the support of Mississippi's conservatives. The reformers were dismayed by the triumph of the conservative interpretation of reconstruction. Based on manuscripts and printed primary and secondary sources; 85 notes.
T. D. Schoonover

1014. Hauptman, Laurence M. GOVERNOR THEODORE ROOSEVELT AND THE INDIANS OF NEW YORK STATE. *Pro. of the Am. Phil. Soc. 1975 119(1): 1-7.* Theodore Roosevelt's Indian-hating attitude was really an expression of sentiments held by most eastern reformers of his day. They believed that the Indian could be saved only by destroying most of his ethnic heritage. Examination of Roosevelt's attitudes towards the New York state Indians while working with the Indian Rights Association, and his instigation of the Commission of 1900, show that Roosevelt did not want to eradicate the Indian, but to assimilate him into the mainstream of white culture. Based on primary and secondary sources; 32 notes.
W. L. Olbrich

1015. Heath, William G., Jr. CYRUS BARTOL'S TRANSCENDENTAL CAPITALISM. *Studies in the Am. Renaissance 1979: 399-408.* Cyrus Bartol, minister of the Unitarian West Church in Boston, was a familiar figure in the religious, intellectual, and literary life of New England during the 19th century. He was, however, besides a religious figure, also a shrewd businessman, and had no rival "in combining the dual roles of seer and doer." Bartol became acquainted with Manchester-by-the-Sea in Massachusetts in the 1850's, and made his first important real estate purchase in 1871. Over the next quarter century Bartol bought, improved, and sold additional properties in Manchester. His business investments were to him for spiritual benefit. He used his investments as a means of putting into practice some of his strongest religious beliefs. He conceived nature as chaotic and in need of improvement by man. It is not hard to see a connection between this idea and his tremendous effect on the development of Manchester. Based on archives in the Manchester Historical Society and other primary sources; 29 notes.
J. Powell

1016. Hinckley, Ted C. "WE ARE MORE TRULY HEATHEN THAN THE NATIVES": JOHN G. BRADY AND THE ASSIMILATION OF ALASKA'S TLINGIT INDIANS. *Western Hist. Q. 1980 11(1): 37-55.* John Green Brady's Alaska career, 1878-1906, gradually shifted from missionary to secular leader. His relations with the Tlingit Indians variously included his roles as missionary-teacher, farmer-settler, businessman, judge, and governor. Brady and other like-minded allies labored to protect and civilize Alaska's natives. As a consequence of their efforts, those Indians "may well enjoy the strongest socioeconomic power base of any Amerindian group." 46 notes.
D. L. Smith

1017. Hoeveler, J. David, Jr. THE UNIVERSITY AND THE SOCIAL GOSPEL: THE INTELLECTUAL ORIGINS OF THE "WISCONSIN IDEA." *Wisconsin Mag. of Hist. 1976 59(4): 282-298.* University of Wisconsin President John Bascom was one of the most important figures in formulating the basis for the Wisconsin Idea because he 1) accepted the outlines of evolutionary science and built the "New Theology" on it, 2) took moral philosophy in new directions through a concern for the problems of government and politics, and 3) used his influence to develop a new philosophy of state which included enhanced powers for government and the state university. Gradually, through the work of Richard T. Ely, Bascom's appointment as director of the newly established School of Economics, Political Science, and History, and John R. Commons, whom Ely brought to Wisconsin, the social gospel ideas of Bascom began to take on a more secular tone. This transition became more obvious in the works of economist Commons and was completed with the ascendancy of geologist Charles R. Van Hise as President of the University and Robert M. La Follette as Governor. 8 illus., 55 notes.
N. C. Burckel

1018. Horowitz, Murray M. BEN BUTLER AND THE NEGRO: "MIRACLES ARE OCCURRING." *Louisiana Hist. 1976 17(2): 159-186.* Details the career of Democratic General Benjamin F. Butler 1861-64 and analyzes his complete reversal of positions in such a brief time. The former "pro-slavery Democrat of the worst school" had become the darling of the Radicals. The actual experiences of war in the deep South, especially his contact with Negroes, caused the reversal. Illus., 43 notes.
E. P. Stickney

1019. Horowitz, Robert F. LAND TO THE FREEDMEN: A VISION OF RECONSTRUCTION. *Ohio Hist. 1977 86(3): 187-199.* Analyzes the reconstruction plans of James M. Ashley, a Congressman from Toledo, Ohio. Appointed Chairman of the House Committee on Territories in July 1861, he became an exponent of the "territorialization" theory of reconstruction, and proposed suffrage and jury rights for blacks and confiscation and redistribution to provide freedmen with a solid economic base. When voted on in the House in 1862, the proposal was overwhelmingly defeated. Had the plan been adopted, chances for a successful reconstruction would have improved greatly and future racial problems moderated. Based on Archival and secondary sources; 3 illus., 35 notes.
N. Summers

1020. Howell, Colin D. REFORM AND THE MONOPOLISTIC IMPULSE: THE PROFESSIONALIZATION OF MEDICINE IN THE MARITIMES. *Acadiensis [Canada] 1981 11(1): 3-22.* Doctors in Canada's Maritime Provinces between 1867 and 1914 were a self-conscious elite intent upon redefining their profession to restrict competition, enhancing their professional reputations and authority, and improving the practice of medicine. They promoted the collection of vital statistics, the establishment of a provincial medical board, and improved medical training, while also attempting to deny nurses, opticians, and other professional groups the right to engage in professional improvement. By 1914 medical education had improved and approaches to the prevention of disease had become more scientific. 72 notes.
D. F. Chard

1021. Hume, Richard L. CARPETBAGGERS IN THE RECONSTRUCTION SOUTH: A GROUP PORTRAIT OF OUTSIDE WHITES IN THE "BLACK AND TAN" CONSTITUTIONAL CONVENTIONS. *J. of Am. Hist. 1977 64(2): 313-330.* Carpetbaggers were crucial in securing civil rights provisions in constitutional conventions held in former Confederate states. Carpetbaggers held a disproportionate number of committee chairmanships at these conventions, and often sponsored civil liberties provisions in Reconstruction constitutions. Originally lured to the South by economic advantages, outside whites brought Northern technical skills and liberal principles, and helped remake the South into an industrial, urban region. Primary and secondary sources; table, 74 notes.
J. W. Leedom

1022. Hume, Richard L. THE MEMBERSHIP OF THE VIRGINIA CONSTITUTIONAL CONVENTION OF 1867-1868: A STUDY OF THE BEGINNINGS OF CONGRESSIONAL RECONSTRUCTION IN THE UPPER SOUTH. *Virginia Mag. of Hist. and Biography 1978 86(4): 461-484.* Studies the 1867 Reconstruction Act-induced Convention's membership and activities. Classifies delegates as "Radicals," those voting to aid blacks, restrict ex-Confederates, or help the Republican

Party; "Conservatives," those opposing such; and non-aligned; and by hereditary class: "Outside White," "Southern White," and Negro. Concludes that Outside Whites, some Southern Whites, and Negroes made an effective coalition to pass a Radical document, notably failing only in requiring racial integration in public schools. Includes revisionist findings about delegates' education, income, and constituencies. 2 charts, 54 notes.
P. J. Woehrmann

1023. Hurt, R. Douglas. JOHN R. ROGERS: THE UNION LABOR PARTY, GEORGISM AND AGRARIAN REFORM. *J. of the West 1977 16(1): 10-15.* Reviews John R. Rogers, concentrating on his years in Kansas. As a member of the Greenback Party, and as a leader of the Union Labor Party, he attacked both major parties for unwillingness to deal with problems. While in Kansas he published the Newton *Kansas Commoner.* He left Kansas in 1890 and moved to Washington, where in 1896 he was elected governor.
R. Alvis

1024. Hurt, R. Douglas. POPULIST-ENDORSED JUDGES AND THE PROTECTION OF WESTERN LABOR. *J. of the West 1978 17(1): 19-26.* Though commonly associated with agrarianism, the Populist movement also supported urban laborers (both out of philosophy and necessity) as shown by the pro-labor rulings of populist-endorsed judges of state supreme courts in Kansas, Nebraska, Colorado, Washington, and Montana, 1893-1902.

1025. Hynson, Leon O. REFORMATION AND PERFECTION: THE SOCIAL GOSPEL OF BISHOP PECK. *Methodist Hist. 1978 16(2): 82-91.* Jesse T. Peck (1811-83), Bishop of the Methodist Episcopal Church, was a zealous spokesman for a number of social causes within Methodism. His thought became an extension and modification of the Wesleyan union of personal and social sanctification. Peck took the concept of perfection beyond the personal and individual to the social and national. Based on Peck's writings; 18 notes, biblio.
H. L. Calkin

1026. Jacobsen, Timothy C. JOSEPH BUCKNER KILLEBREW: AGRARIANISM IN THE NEW SOUTH. *Tennessee Hist. Q. 1974 33(2): 157-174.* Long before the better known leaders of the New South emerged, Joseph Buckner Killebrew, a frequent public servant in Tennessee, spoke vigorously in favor of developing the ideals of Thomas Jefferson and John Taylor in post-Civil-War southern agriculture. Killebrew advocated two themes: the yeoman farmer ideal, and the celebration of the fruitful earth itself. Primary and secondary sources; 48 notes.
M. B. Lucas

1027. James, Edward T. BEN BUTLER RUNS FOR PRESIDENT: LABOR, GREENBACKERS, AND ANTI-MONOPOLISTS IN THE ELECTION OF 1884. *Essex Inst. Hist. Collections 1977 113(2): 65-88.* Before the 1954 accession by the Library of Congress of Benjamin F. Butler's (1818-1893) papers, scholars inadequately understood his campaign as a third-party presidential candidate in 1884. Even with support from the Anti-Monopoly Convention, Greenbackers, and labor, Butler's People's Party failed to stop Grover Cleveland's nomination at the Democratic convention and subsequent election. Discusses causes for failure, chiefly the Republican subsidy. Based on the Butler Papers, primary and secondary sources; 3 illus., photo, 78 notes.
R. S. Sliwoski

1028. Jones, James P. RADICAL REINFORCEMENT: JOHN A. LOGAN RETURNS TO CONGRESS. *J. of the Illinois State Hist. Soc. 1975 68(4): 324-336.* John A. Logan, a Democratic Congressman before the Civil War, was reelected as a Radical Republican from Illinois in 1866. Allied with the anti-Johnson forces in the House, he pursued a strong line toward the former Confederate states. He was considered as a possible contender for the governorship of Illinois or even the Republican nomination for the Presidency in 1868 by some observers. Appointed as one of the managers for the House of Representatives in the impeachment of Andrew Johnson, Logan played a minor role in the deliberations. Based on primary sources.
N. Lederer

1029. Jordan, Philip D. IMMIGRANTS, METHODISTS AND A "CONSERVATIVE" SOCIAL GOSPEL, 1865-1908. *Methodist Hist. 1978 17(1): 16-43.* While accepting a social creed in the name of Christian liberality in 1908 the Methodist Episcopal Church rejected an open door policy for immigrants. After the Civil War the church saw immigration as a danger to American civilization and to the wages of the laboring classes. At the same time Methodist missionaries saw China as a vast field for evangelism, and therefore the Methodist Episcopal Church opposed American mistreatment of Asians. By 1908, however, restriction of Oriental immigration was supported. Based on Methodist publications. 39 notes.
H. L. Calkin

1030. Juhnke, James C. GENERAL CONFERENCE MENNONITE MISSIONS TO THE AMERICAN INDIANS IN THE LATE NINETEENTH CENTURY. *Mennonite Q. Rev. 1980 54(2): 117-134.* In 1880 General Conference Mennonites began missionary work among the Arapaho Indians and Cheyenne Indians in Indian Territory. Although born of prayer and self-sacrifice, the tragedy of the effort was that the best the Mennonites had to offer—education, medical aid, agricultural development, and the gospel of God's love—was inextricably bound with a massive political and cultural confrontation which turned the good news, for the most part, into bad news. Since it was their first attempt at missionary work among the Indians, the Mennonites could hardly be faulted for their numerous errors, the basic one being their insistent efforts to make whites out of red men. Based largely on Mennonite publications of the period; 55 notes.
H. M. Parker, Jr.

1031. Justin, Meryl S. THE ENTRY OF WOMEN INTO MEDICINE IN AMERICA: EDUCATION AND OBSTACLES 1847-1910. *Synthesis 1978 4(3): 31-46.* Although Elizabeth Blackwell was admitted to the Geneva Medical School in western New York in 1847, and received an M. D. degree two years later, barriers to the admission of women to medical schools, to practice, and to professional societies were lowered only slowly and grudgingly. The American Medical Association did not admit women until 1915, although in 1900 there were over 7,300 female doctors in the United States. 40 notes.
M. M. Vance

1032. Kaufman, Martin. THE ADMISSION OF WOMEN TO 19TH CENTURY AMERICAN MEDICAL SOCIETIES. *Bull. of the Hist. of Medicine 1976 50(2): 251-260.* An analysis of the debates over the admission of women to several 19th-century medical societies indicates a great deal about interrelationships within the profession. The conflict with the homeopaths played a major role in convincing Massachusetts physicians to accept women members, or possibly lose them to the irregular sects. In Pennsylvania the question of admitting women was related to the standing of the Woman's Medical College, but ultimately every case rested on the role of women in the medical profession. By 1880 there was a clear trend toward the acceptance of women as physicians and as members of the various societies, but local conditions determined when women were admitted to local societies. 35 notes.
M. Kaufman

1033. Kelly, John M. THE NEW BARBARIANS: THE CONTINUING RELEVANCE OF HENRY GEORGE. *Am. J. of Econ. and Sociol. 1981 40(3): 299-308.* By what right does anyone monopolize land? A century ago Henry George identified the land question, outlined the solution and foresaw the consequences of ignoring it. Rioting in slums, looting and other crime in cities and rural areas, rising fears, paranoia and greed bear testimony to the legacy George foresaw. Against monopoly and privilege, George raised the banner of justice and liberty, achievable only by taxing the land and untaxing labor and its products. The Intellectual Revolution fostered by the new computer technology promises to undermine myths that have enslaved the human mind.
J/S

1034. Kogan, Herman. MYRA BRADWELL: CRUSADER AT LAW. *Chicago Hist. 1974/75 3(3): 132-140.* Myra Bradwell fought for law reforms in Chicago, particularly in the areas of women's rights, taxation and penalties for crimes.
S

1035. Kohlstedt, Sally Gregory. MARIA MITCHELL: THE ADVANCEMENT OF WOMEN IN SCIENCE. *New England Q. 1978 51(1): 39-63.* Examines astronomer Mitchell's (1818-89) involvement in women's education, the Association for the Advancement of Women (AAW), and the AAW's Committee on Science. Her hope was to encourage women to become involved in science in order to provide them with "a unique intellectual challenge that could help them escape the narrowness of their lives." Focuses on 1870-89. Based on Mitchell's papers in the Maria Mitchell Science Library on Nantucket Island and on secondary sources; 74 notes.
J. C. Bradford

1036. Kolchin, Peter. SCALAWAGS, CARPETBAGGERS, AND RECONSTRUCTION: A QUANTITATIVE LOOK AT SOUTHERN CONGRESSIONAL POLITICS, 1868-1872. *J. of Southern Hist. 1979 45(1): 63-76.* Increased historical attention to Reconstruction politics has refined our image of the identity, ideology, and political behavior of the southern Republican parties without determining who—blacks, carpetbaggers, or scalawags—dominated them. Examination of the members of the U.S. House of Representatives from the 11 ex-Confederate states reveals that healthy southern Republican parties were controlled by blacks and carpetbaggers. The rise in scalawag leadership indicated an increasingly strong Democratic competition and suggested the decline of the Republican Party. Primary and secondary materials; 6 tables, 28 notes.
T. D. Schoonover

1037. Langellier, J. Phillip. CAMP GRANT AFFAIR, 1871: MILESTONE IN FEDERAL INDIAN POLICY? *Military Hist. of Texas and the Southwest 1979 15(2): 17-29.* The Camp Grant Affair in 1871 near Tucson, Arizona, over Apache raids on military posts and the violent response by the US Army, resulted in reform legislation on federal treatment of the Indians.

1038. Larmour, Jean. EDGAR DEWDNEY, INDIAN COMMISSIONER IN THE TRANSITION PERIOD OF INDIAN SETTLEMENT, 1879-1884. *Saskatchewan Hist. [Canada] 1980 33(1): 13-24.* Edgar Dewdney humanely tried to solve the difficult problems of getting the major Indian tribes in the Northwest Territories and Rupert's Land to change from buffalo hunting to agriculture. Mentions the support of public figures such as J. F. Macleod and David Laird, and problems with the American Sioux under Chief Sitting Bull until 1881, when he surrendered to US authorities. By 1884, most of the Indians were on reservations and some farming had begun. This was accomplished peacefully, due to Dewdney and the cooperation of the Indians. Primary sources; 4 photos, 54 notes.
C. H. Held/S

1039. Lavigne, Marie et al. LA FÉDÉRATION NATIONALE SAINT-JEAN-BAPTISTE ET LES REVENDICATIONS FÉMINISTES AU DÉBUT DU XXe SIÈCLE [The Saint John the Baptist National Federation and feminist demands at the start of the 20th century]. *R. d'hist. de l'Amérique française [Canada] 1975 29(3): 353-373.* Surveys the history of the Fédération Nationale Saint-Jean-Baptiste from 1907-33, and discusses the role of its founder, Marie Gérin-Lajoie (1867-1945). In order to develop in French-Canadian society, the Fédération, a feminist group, had to make alliances with the Catholic clergy and compromises with the prevailing ideology. While calling for increased political rights for women, it supported the integrity of the family and the traditional female familial role. The organization did not succeed in synthesizing these paradoxical interests, and its influence declined after 1933. Based on documents in the Archives de la Fédération Nationale Saint-Jean-Baptiste (Montréal), Archives de la Communauté des Soeurs de Notre-Dame-du-Bon Conseil (Montréal), and secondary sources; 31 notes.
L. B. Chan

1040. LeWarne, Charles P. LABOR AND COMMUNITARIANISM, 1880-1900. *Labor Hist. 1975 16(3): 393-407.* An active communitarian movement was associated with labor organizations in the late 19th century. At least 75 different communitarian experiments were founded around ideas of a just share of profits, insurance, and education. Although never a predominant philosophy, communitarianism competed with trade unionism for allegiance of laborers until the 20th century. Based on proceedings of the Knights of Labor and secondary sources; 28 notes.
L. L. Athey

1041. Lewis, Robert. FRONTIER AND CIVILIZATION IN THE THOUGHT OF FREDERICK LAW OLMSTED. *Am. Q. 1977 29(4): 385-403.* Frederick Law Olmsted, a 19th century cultural critic, felt that the United States lacked a basic serious commitment to the ideals of harmony, balance, and discipline in society. As a reformer, he felt it would be necessary for a professional, cultured elite to work through a bureaucracy in order to maintain order and discipline in America. Olmsted was frightened by the spectacle of what he termed the "frontier condition"; the unsettled, individualistic, migratory spirit that he saw imbuing rural and urban Americans alike. To counter this tendency of social behavior, he furthered the cause of "civilization." This meant efforts to practice control over and to uplift the population morally and aesthetically. Olmsted's ideas of public recreation were based on his effort to provide a genteel, uplifting environment for the masses. Primary sources.
N. Lederer

1042. Lex, Louise Moede. MARY NEWBURY ADAMS: FEMINIST FORERUNNER FROM IOWA. *Ann. of Iowa 1976 43(5): 323-341.* Through her writing, speaking, and organizational abilities, Iowan Mary Newbury Adams (1837-1901) tried to change the attitudes of 19th-century women toward themselves. Women, she believed, needed to know much more about their own history because knowledge of what women in the past had achieved would encourage succeeding generations. A forerunner in the struggle for female equality, Adams helped prepare the way for eventual improvement in the social status of women. Primary and secondary sources; 47 notes.
P. L. Petersen

1043. Luker, Ralph E. THE SOCIAL GOSPEL AND THE FAILURE OF RACIAL REFORM, 1877-1898. *Church Hist. 1977 46(1): 80-99.* Preoccupied with the ills of urban-industrial disorder, the prophets of post-Reconstruction social Christianity either ignored or betrayed the Negro and left his fate in the hands of a hostile white South. However, the concepts of the origins and nature of the social gospel make apparent the relation of the social gospel to three surviving traditions of 19th-century racial reform: 1) the home missions movement, 2) the postabolition tradition of civil equity, and 3) the colonization movement. Finally, it sheds light on the response of the social gospel prophets to the lynching problem in the 1890's. 75 notes.
M. D. Dibert

1044. Mancini, Matthew J. RACE, ECONOMICS, AND THE ABANDONMENT OF CONVICT LEASING. *J. of Negro Hist. 1978 63(4): 339-352.* Analyzes the convict lease system in Georgia as a component of that larger web of law and custom which effectively insured the South's racial hierarchy. Only when the system lost its profitability to the lessees was it finally abandoned. Covers 1868-1909. Based upon records in the Georgia Department of Archives and History; table, 2 fig., 41 notes.
N. G. Sapper

1045. Marsden, Michael T. A DEDICATION TO THE MEMORY OF HELEN HUNT JACKSON, 1830-1885. *Arizona and the West 1979 21(2): 108-112.* Helen Maria Fiske Hunt Jackson (1830-85) was a prolific and anonymous writer of children's stories, travel sketches, and magazine essays. An 1879 lecture by two Ponca Indians gave her the consuming passion of her life. She began immediately to compile material on Indian mistreatment and to write tracts, newspaper articles, and petitions at a feverish pace. Her *A Century of Dishonor* submitted massive evidence that the government was dishonest and cruel toward the Indian. Some credit the book with inspiring formation of the Indian Rights Association a year later and with leading to the Dawes Act in 1887. It continues to contribute to the romanticization of the Indian. Illus., biblio.
D. L. Smith

1046. Marsh, Margaret S. THE ANARCHIST-FEMINIST RESPONSE TO THE "WOMAN QUESTION" IN LATE NINETEENTH-CENTURY AMERICA. *Am. Q. 1978 30(4): 533-547.* Unlike mainstream feminism, the anarchist-feminists rejected any notion of significant inherent intellectual or psychological differences between the sexes. Instead, they promoted their feminist cause on the appropriateness of equality based on a shared humanity. This was integrated into a set of principles consonant with the larger anarchist movement. The career of Voltairine de Cleyre (1866-1912) furnishes an illustration of the anarchist-feminist position, both its strengths and weaknesses. They believed that the roots of inequality lay in the domestic relationship, that legal and political reform was inadequate, and that the surrender of "common humanity" as a basis for action by mainstream feminism for the sake of short-term gains worked against long-term achievement. 21 notes.
R. V. Ritter

1047. Masel-Walters, Lynne. A BURNING CLOUD BY DAY: THE HISTORY AND CONTENT OF THE "WOMEN'S JOURNAL." *Journalism Hist. 1976-77 3(4): 103-110.* Studies the success of the *Women's Journal* during 1870-1914 under the editorship of its founders, Henry B. Blackwell and Lucy Stone; discusses the political importance of this feminist magazine.

1048. Mathes, Valerie Sherer. HELEN HUNT JACKSON: OFFICIAL AGENT TO THE CALIFORNIA MISSION INDIANS. *Southern California Q. 1981 63(1): 63-82.* Describes Helen Hunt Jackson's service as an Indian agent in 1882-83. Following publication of *A Century of Dishonor* in 1881, Jackson came to California and became very concerned about the dispossession of Indians from their lands by unscrupulous whites. Commissioner of Indian Affairs Hiram Price appointed her an official agent assigned to report on the Mission Indians. Along with Abbot Kinney, Jackson visited many Indian villages in Southern California and submitted a report recommending more schools, resurveying of reservations, and purchase of land for more reservations. Finding Congress unresponsive, Jackson attracted popular attention to the Indians' plight by writing *Ramona*, a novel that combined fiction with actual events. Begun in December 1883 and completed by March 1884, *Ramona* was a popular success. Jackson died of cancer in 1885. 80 notes.
A. Hoffman

1049. McBride, Robert M. "NORTHERN, MILITARY, CORRUPT, AND TRANSITORY," AUGUSTUS E. ALDEN, NASHVILLE'S CARPETBAGGER MAYOR. *Tennessee Hist. Q. 1978 37(1): 63-67.* Augustus E. Alden (1837-86), a prototype of "carpetbaggers," was handpicked by Governor William G. Brownlow in 1867 in order to ensure his control of Nashville. A former "claims" agent who had only recently arrived in Nashville, Alden, in office 1867-69, began the Negro public schools and increased welfare programs. Nevertheless, he was hated by the citizenry and was ousted from office by a court injunction in 1869. Primary and secondary sources; 17 notes.
M. B. Lucas

1050. McCluskey, Stephen C. EVANGELISTS, EDUCATORS, ETHNOGRAPHERS AND THE ESTABLISHMENT OF THE HOPI RESERVATION. *J. of Arizona Hist. 1980 21(4): 363-390.* Describes the theoretical conflict between the dichotomous Indian policies of the 1870's and 1880's, using the personal histories of Charles A. Taylor, missionary and "civilizer," and John H. Sullivan, agent and cultural preservationist as they conflicted at the Hopi Agency. The immediate result of their conflict was the creation of a Hopi reservation and the closing of the agency. Bureau of Indian Affairs records, correspondence, and secondary sources; illus., map, 56 notes.
G. O. Gagnon

1051. McConnell, Virginia. "H. H.," COLORADO, AND THE INDIAN PROBLEM. *J. of the West 1973 12(2): 272-280.* Born and reared in New England, Helen Hunt Jackson moved to Colorado in 1873. After hearing a lecture by Chief Standing Bear on the inhumane removal of Ponca Indians, Helen launched a drive to aid the Ponca legal defense fund. She impugned Secretary of the Interior Carl Schurz on the handling of Indian titles. Schurz's successor appointed her one of the Indian commissioners sent to investigate California's Mission Indians. When her efforts did not produce political remedies, she turned to fictional writing and produced *Ramona* to carry her message to the public. 25 notes.
E. P. Stickney

1052. McKee, Delber L. "THE CHINESE MUST GO!" COMMISSIONER GENERAL POWDERLY AND CHINESE IMMIGRATION, 1897-1902. *Pennsylvania Hist. 1977 44(1): 37-51.* Terence V. Powderly, best known as leader of the Knights of Labor, served as Commissioner General of Immigration from 1897 to 1902. In that office, he worked for the reenactment and strengthening of the Chinese exclusion laws. Powderly encouraged anti-Chinese subordinates, issued new administrative regulations, and adopted legal interpretations and definitions of terms designed to reduce the number of Chinese entering the United States. Organized labor supported these efforts. Based on the Terence V. Powderly papers; photo, 43 notes.
D. C. Swift

1053. Miller, Sally M. AMERICANS AND THE SECOND INTERNATIONAL. *Pro. of the Am. Phil. Soc. 1976 120(5): 372-387.* As a rather minor segment of the movement, the American Socialist Party used the Second International for its intellectual leadership and prestige to enhance its own domestic situation. Whenever International positions ran contrary to local practices, the Americans usually either disobeyed or hedged. The Americans grudgingly agreed to the principle of the unity of all laboring peoples, but obscured their own racist exclusion practices. Most of the burning issues of the European sections failed to be of any real concern to the Americans. Based on primary and secondary sources; 49 notes.
W. L. Olbrich

1054. Moore, Robert J. GOVERNOR CHAMBERLAIN AND THE END OF RECONSTRUCTION. *Pro. of the South Carolina Hist. Assoc. 1977: 17-27.* Analyzes the end of Reconstruction in South Carolina and the factors that contributed to the decline and fall of Republican governor Daniel H. Chamberlain in 1877. Wade Hampton was supported by the men of property, the state courts, and the majority of South Carolinians while Chamberlain lost his federal support. In 1901 Chamberlain declared in the *Atlantic Monthly* that Republican Reconstruction policy was "a grievous mistake which was motivated largely by blind partisanship and less by misguided philanthropy." Based on published sources and the Chamberlain Papers; 41 notes.
J. W. Thacker, Jr.

1055. Morrison, W. R. "THEIR PROPER SPHERE": FEMINISM, THE FAMILY, AND CHILD CENTERED SOCIAL REFORM IN ONTARIO, 1875-1900. *Ontario Hist. [Canada] 1976 68(1): 45-64; (2): 65-74.* Part I. Argues that 19th-century feminists saw family instability resulting from social changes as something women should try to correct. Mentions variations of viewpoints among feminist groups and the attitudes of antifeminists. Both outlooks saw the home as central to women's lives but with varying degrees of emphasis. Also discusses the relationships between the women's movement and other social reform movements, especially the temperance movement. 88 notes. Part II. Discusses the National Council of Women, which originated as a means of coordinating the activities of several organizations. Looks at the activities of a selection of individual women (e.g., Mrs. Hoodless in education) and organizations (e.g., the Victorian Order of Nurses) which were seen as part of the women's movement specifically, and reformism in general. A final section attempts to set the movement in perspective. Photo, 35 notes.
W. B. Whitham

1056. Mugleston, William F. THE FREEDMEN'S BUREAU AND RECONSTRUCTION IN VIRGINIA: THE DIARY OF STERLING HOPKINS, A UNION OFFICER. *Virginia Mag. of Hist. and Biog. 1978 86(1): 45-102.* Hopkins, an Ohio native placed in charge of Freedmen's Bureau activities first in Prince William and then in Orange and Louisa Counties, kept a detailed diary during 1868. The diary illustrates the internal workings of the Bureau, but more importantly reveals differences between northerners and southerners, blacks and whites, and Republicans and Democrats. Edited from the original in the Alderman Library, University of Virginia; 122 notes.
R. F. Oaks

1057. Newton, Bernard. HENRY GEORGE AND HENRY M. HYNDMAN.
I: THE FORGING OF AN UNTENABLE ALLIANCE, 1882-83. *Am. J. of Econ. and Sociol. 1976 35(3): 311-324.* Henry George, an individualistic American reformer and economist, and Henry M. Hyndman, an English democratic Marxist, formed a tenuous alliance in 1882. It was based on their mutual advocacy of land nationalization and Irish land tenure reform. During the next few years, the tensions derived from differing weltanschauungen and from differing program directions gradually weakened their mutual bond, despite a continual, but grudging, mutual personal regard.
II: THE EROSION OF THE RADICAL-SOCIALIST COALITION, 1884-89. *Am. J. of Econ. and Sociol. 1977 36(3): 311-322.* While initially in support of one another, Henry George and Henry M. Hyndman eventually separated ideologically. George established the Land Restoration League, separating himself from the socialists in New York. Hyndman began a Marxian campaign within the Democratic Federation. The ultimate break came through a series of debates which highlighted their differences concerning capitalism and socialism.
J/G. A. Hewlett

1058. Oates, Stephen B. TOWARD A NEW BIRTH OF FREEDOM: ABRAHAM LINCOLN AND RECONSTRUCTION, 1854-1865. *Lincoln Herald 1980 82(1): 287-296.* Examines the phases of Abraham Lincoln's reconstruction program beginning in 1854 when the Kansas-Nebraska Act nullified the Missouri Compromise line, in terms of Lincoln's view of the Founding Fathers, and the ideals of the American Republic.

1059. Oberweiser, David. THE INDIAN EDUCATION OF LEWIS H. MORGAN. *Indian Hist. 1979 12(1): 23-28.* Chronicles the work of Lewis Henry Morgan during 1848-78, first in observing and recording the

1060. Olsen, Otto H. ABRAHAM LINCOLN AS REVOLUTIONARY. *Civil War Hist. 1978 24(3): 213-224.* Evaluates Abraham Lincoln as achieving revolutionary results, not as any radical or extremist personality. His was a strong human welfare commitment with relentless pursuit of basic social transformation within American society. Slavery expansionism threatened the national structure and ideals. Lincoln insisted he was returning to the past, but he knew better that he was engineering a basic social change. Southerners realized the revolutionary threat. Lincoln was no extremist nor did he anticipate war; his very moderate success threatened slavery dangerously. His firmness finally opposed even the national majority on peace. The war's impact was revolutionary, and Lincoln guided it. Based on secondary sources; 34 notes.
R. E. Stack

1061. Paz, D. G. MONASTICISM AND SOCIAL REFORM IN LATE NINETEENTH-CENTURY AMERICA: THE CASE OF FATHER HUNTINGTON. *Hist. Mag. of the Protestant Episcopal Church 1979 48(1): 45-66.* Traces the career of one of the most influential and radical social reformers on the national level of the Episcopal Church, the Reverend James Otis Sargent Huntington (1854-1935), founder of the Order of the Holy Cross, the first permanent monastic order for men in the American church. His career illuminates the nature of the Anglican commitment to social justice, the origins of the Order itself, and the inevitable tensions within the dual role of religious and reformer. Fr. Huntington was a great advocate of Henry George's single tax theory. Based on the Huntington Papers in the Holy Cross Archives, West Park, New York, his publications, religious studies and secular secondary sources; 92 notes.
H. M. Parker, Jr.

1062. Pennington, William D. GOVERNMENT AGRICULTURAL POLICY ON THE KIOWA RESERVATION, 1869-1901. *Indian Hist. 1978 11(1): 11-16.* Even before the passage of the Dawes Act (1887), the Kiowa Indians and their neighbors in southwestern Oklahoma were already being forced by the federal government into an individual landholding agricultural economy completely alien to their way of life. As a hunting people unaccustomed to farming, the Kiowa had little success with the new ways, despite aid and encouragement from the Bureau of Indian Affairs. The effort was a complete failure. A cattle-raising economy might have been more successful. 58 notes.
E. D. Johnson

1063. Pennington, William D. GOVERNMENT POLICY AND INDIAN FARMING: ON THE CHEYENNE AND ARAPAHO RESERVATION: 1869-1880. *Chronicles of Oklahoma 1979 57(2): 171-189.* Presents a year-by-year account of the successes and failures of farming projects on Oklahoma's Cheyenne and Arapaho Reservation during the 1870's. Though agents Brighton Darlington and John D. Miles accomplished some of their agricultural goals, the experiment faced an uphill battle against aridity, destructive weather, lack of tools, and militant factions on the reservation. Had the government offered cattle raising as an intermediate step in the acculturation of these two tribes, perhaps more success would have been attained. Based on Annual Reports of the Commissioner of Indian Affairs and archival collections; 5 photos, 91 notes.
M. L. Tate

1064. Petrella, Frank. HENRY GEORGE, THE CLASSICAL MODEL AND TECHNOLOGICAL CHANGE: THE IGNORED ALTERNATIVE TO THE SINGLE TAX IN *PROGRESS AND POVERTY*. *Am. J. of Econ. and Sociol. 1981 40(2): 191-206.* Henry George's vision of land monopolization as the source of growing rentier income was compatible with the predominant Ricardian-Millian classical distribution model, except the rent-reducing effects of technological change and Malthusian population growth as the catalyst underlying income distribution. Since George also rejected Malthusianism on ethical and philosophical grounds, his analysis focused on the autonomous nature of rent income with respect to population and technological change. George never considered the dynamic case of changing population, technology, and increasing returns, which would have contradicted his prediction of the single tax as the solution to social and economic distress.
J/S

1065. Pitsula, James M. THE TREATMENT OF TRAMPS IN LATE NINETEENTH-CENTURY TORONTO. *Hist. Papers [Canada] 1980: 116-132.* Due to the high rate of unemployment in late 19th-century Canada and the United States, tramps became a major problem in big cities. Viewed as a representation of the failure of the work ethic, middle class philanthropists sought to contain this "social evil." In Toronto, where the number of tramps was steadily increasing, groups such as the Associated Charities took measures to reduce this burden. The introduction of the labor test and the more stringent hygiene requirements did much to reduce the transient population of that city. Presented at the Annual Meeting of the Canadian Historical Association, 1980; 2 tables, 81 notes.
A. Drysdale

1066. Powell, Lawrence N. THE AMERICAN LAND COMPANY AND AGENCY: JOHN A. ANDREW AND THE NORTHERNIZATION OF THE SOUTH. *Civil War Hist. 1975 21(4): 293-308.* Examines the history of the American Land Company, founded by wartime governor John A. Andrew of Massachusetts in the fall of 1865. The company sought to develop a viable economy in the South based on free labor principles. Andrew believed northerners would move south, buy plantations for a low price, and set examples of industry and ingenuity for both whites and blacks to follow, which would lead to the revival of the South. Economic reconstruction, it was believed, would pave the way for an easy political reconstruction. But President Andrew Johnson's reconstruction program and the growing belligerence of many southerners meant the precedence of politics over economics, and the American Land Company came to grief in February 1867.
E. C. Murdock

1067. Prather, H. Leon, Sr. THE RED SHIRT MOVEMENT IN NORTH CAROLINA 1898-1900. *J. of Negro Hist. 1977 62(2): 174-184.* The disfranchisement of black voters in the South in the 1890's was marked by the linkage between poor whites and the white establishment. The example of the Red Shirt Movement in North Carolina provides an instructive lesson in the effectiveness of terrorism as an instrument of repression. North Carolina poor whites also learned the lesson of political naïvete; once poor people have served their function, it is back to business as usual. Based on period newspapers and secondary materials; 35 notes.
N. G. Sapper

1068. Rabinowitz, Howard N. FROM RECONSTRUCTION TO REDEMPTION ON THE URBAN SOUTH. *J. of Urban Hist. 1976 2(2): 169-194.* Discusses the rise, operation, and fall of Republican Party government in Southern cities during 1865-75. Primary and secondary sources; 80 notes.
T. W. Smith

1069. Reid, Robert. CHANGING INTERPRETATIONS OF THE RECONSTRUCTION PERIOD IN ALABAMA HISTORY. *Alabama R. 1974 27(4): 263-281.* The revisionist challenge to Reconstruction historiography announced by Howard K. Beale in 1940 proved slow of adoption in Alabama and was not generally accepted until the 1960's. A wealth of specific and topical studies have appeared since then, mostly supportive of revisionist conclusions. As yet no one has attempted to duplicate the synthesis achieved by Walter L. Fleming in his *Civil War and Reconstruction in Alabama* (1905). Based on published and unpublished secondary sources; 45 notes.
J. F. Vivian

1070. Riley, Stephen T. CHARLES FRANCIS ADAMS (1835-1915): CONSERVATIONIST. *Massachusetts Hist. Soc. Pro. 1978 90: 22-37.* Charles Francis Adams (1835-1915), well-known as a financier and railroad man, also had an important career as a conservationist in the late 19th century. Adams was influential in establishing parks and open spaces in his hometown of Quincy, Massachusetts, in the 1880's. Later, at the urging of Charles Eliot (1859-97) and others, he was the leader of the important committee established by the Metropolitan Park Commission Act of 1893. In the space of a few years, this commission gave Boston and its surrounding suburbs one of the most sophisticated systems of parks in the world. Based on the published autobiography of Adams, the Adams Papers at the Massachusetts Historical Society, and other primary and secondary sources; 35 notes.
G. W. R. Ward

1071. Robinson, Armstead L. BEYOND THE REALM OF SOCIAL CONSENSUS: NEW MEANINGS OF RECONSTRUCTION FOR AMERICAN HISTORY. *J. of Am. Hist. 1981 68(2): 276-297.* Republicans failed to build successful coalitions in southern states during Reconstruction because of social class tensions within both white and black communities and because of racial tensions between both groups. Georgia serves as a good example for the pattern that emerged throughout the South. Race did not overwhelm class; economic antagonisms between up-country yeomen and low-land planters proved more important at first. Racism emerged later and became the tool of one class of whites fearful of political action by another class of whites. 79 notes.

T. P. Linkfield

1072. Ross, Dorothy. SOCIALISM AND AMERICAN LIBERALISM: ACADEMIC SOCIAL THOUGHT IN THE 1880'S. *Perspectives in Am. Hist. 1977-78 11: 7-79.* American academic intellectuals briefly viewed socialism as a viable political alternative for the United States in the 1880's, but ultimately they returned to liberalism. Intellectuals such as John Bates Clark, Henry Carter Adams, and Richard T. Ely decided not to become identified with the tumultuous labor violence of the 1880's, or with the reaction against it. Instead, they opted for politically safe positions, chose their words carefully, and retained their academic posts by not alienating their university employers.

W. A. Wiegand

1073. Scott, Andrew M. HENRY GEORGE, HENRY ADAMS, AND THE DOMINANT AMERICAN IDEOLOGY. *South Atlantic Q. 1977 76(2): 234-251.* Both men critically probed the dominant American ideology for the social evils beneath its faith in material progress. Moreover, both men codified these faults into laws of social progress and decay. Henry George believed that the complex job specializations created by a developing industrial society denied equality, fostered elitism, and thereby caused social decay. Henry Brooks Adams believed that social development increased exponentially, and that social change and complexity would move too fast for human comprehension and control. Social stagnation would then set in. Neither man put much faith in piecemeal reform, but Henry George felt that his single tax would sufficiently slow the growth of elites. In their cyclical theories of history and their social criticism these two men were in advance of their times; thus, their contemporaries ignored them. 4 notes.

W. L. Olbrich

1074. Shofner, Jerrell H. A NEW JERSEY CARPETBAGGER IN RECONSTRUCTION FLORIDA. *Florida Hist. Q. 1974 52(3): 286-293.* Captain George B. Carse of New Jersey became a Freedmen's Bureau agent in Leon County after the Civil War. He was involved in Republican politics after his appointment as adjutant general in 1868, siding with Governor Harrison Reed in his political conflict with Thomas W. Osborn, leader of a competing faction of Republicans. After bribery charges were laid against him in 1870, Carse resigned, returned to New Jersey, and served three terms in that state's legislature. Manuscript, newspaper and secondary sources; 20 notes.

J. E. Findling

1075. Smith, Burton M. THE POLITICS OF ALLOTMENT: THE FLATHEAD INDIAN RESERVATION AS A TEST CASE. *Pacific Northwest Q. 1979 70(3): 131-140.* The General Allotment Act, or Dawes Act (US, 1887), carved up the various reservations and compelled Indians to establish small homesteads in the hopes that this agricultural lifestyle would acculturate them into the mainstream of American society. Though moralistic reformers promoted this legislation in behalf of Indians, western settlers also lobbied for it so that they could acquire the "surplus" reservation lands which were opened to public sales. When the law was finally applied to the Flathead Indian Reservation in 1904, it clearly demonstrated the political power of Montana businessmen and land speculators such as Joseph M. Dixon who refused to listen to Flathead complaints about the legislation. Based on archival sources; 4 photos, 32 notes.

M. L. Tate

1076. Stagg, J. C. A. THE PROBLEM OF KLAN VIOLENCE: THE SOUTH CAROLINA UP-COUNTRY, 1868-1871. *J. of Am. Studies [Great Britain] 1974 8(3): 303-318.* Analyzes several reasons for the pervasive racism which developed in up-country South Carolina after the Civil War. Political motivations, economic considerations, and common social attitudes produced solid anti-Negro alliances between professionals, the planter elite, and the poorer whites. Hence, the Klan enjoyed the support of virtually the entire "white community" for the widespread violence it perpetrated upon Negro Carolinians. Based on newspaper and secondary sources; 51 notes.

H. T. Lovin

1077. Stealey, John Edmund, III, ed. REPORTS OF FREEDMEN'S BUREAU OPERATIONS IN WEST VIRGINIA: AGENTS IN THE EASTERN PANHANDLE. *West Virginia Hist. 1980-81 42(1-2): 94-129.* Discusses the role of the Freedmen's Bureau (mostly in Jefferson and Berkeley counties), July 1865-October 1868. Several transfers of jurisdiction caused administrative instability, yet the bureau accomplished much. It helped transfer power from the old state of Virginia to the new state of West Virginia. Government reports; 2 illus., 54 notes.

J. D. Neville

1078. Trauner, Joan B. THE CHINESE AS MEDICAL SCAPEGOATS IN SAN FRANCISCO, 1870-1905. *California Hist. 1978 57(1): 70-87.* During 1870-1905, San Francisco's Chinatown was considered a breeding ground for smallpox, bubonic plague, leprosy, and other diseases. The Caucasian community considered Chinatown a threat to public health, accusing Chinese Americans of practicing low standards of hygiene, and attempted unsuccessfully during epidemic periods to have Chinatown isolated or quarantined. At the same time, public health services were denied to Chinese residents. Chinese were blamed for a bubonic plague outbreak in 1900 while politicians denied its existence, fearing that publicity would be bad for business. By 1906, when a plague epidemic followed the earthquake, the causes of diseases such as bubonic plague were better known, and accusations against the Chinese ceased. Nevertheless, the Chinese continued to be neglected by the Caucasian community in matters of public health, and had to combat discriminatory laws and racist stereotyping in order to obtain adequate medical care. Not until the 1970's did Chinatown's medical facilities become fully integrated into the general community. Based on contemporary and secondary published works; photos, charts, 83 notes.

A. Hoffman

1079. Turner, Frederick W., III. THE CENTURY AFTER A CENTURY OF DISHONOR: AMERICAN CONSCIENCE AND CONSCIOUSNESS. *Massachusetts R. 1975 16(4): 715-731.* America "needs to be saved from the conscience it has developed," partially reflected in 1881 in Helen Hunt Jackson's *A Century of Dishonor*. The book, urging justice for the Ponca, was the first pro-Indian book to have a serious impact. Bicentennial events should be used to reexamine past events so that a truly responsive culture can emerge. Based on primary and secondary sources.

M. J. Barach

1080. Walsh, Harry. THE TOLSTOYAN EPISODE IN AMERICAN SOCIAL THOUGHT. *Am. Studies 1976 17(1): 49-68.* In the late 19th century American intellectuals discovered Tolstoy, in part because his themes of morality and ethics spoke to an American conscience. William Jennings Bryan, among others, developed a lasting friendship with Tolstoy, and embraced his pacifism. The stance of American Tolstoyans resembled the major tenets of the Jeffersonian tradition, with a distrust of powerful governments, of cities, and a celebration of precapitalist economics. Primary and secondary sources; 80 notes.

J. Andrew

1081. Wetta, Frank J. "BULLDOZING THE SCALAWAGS": SOME EXAMPLES OF THE PERSECUTION OF SOUTHERN WHITE REPUBLICANS IN LOUISIANA DURING RECONSTRUCTION. *Louisiana Hist. 1980 21(1): 43-58.* Terrorism and ostracism were as important as racism in keeping Louisiana whites from Unionist or Republican sympathies during 1866-78. Coercion by groups such as the Ku Klux Klan, the Seymour Knights, and the White League drove 38 prominent southern white Republicans from public and party offices after 1868 and silenced most of their supporters. These violent tactics of "bulldozing" dealt a fatal blow (literally, in some cases) to Louisiana Republicans in the era of Reconstruction. Based on extensive archival research, census returns, contemporary newspapers, and congressional reports; 43 notes.

D. B. Touchstone

1082. Wiggins, Sarah Woolfolk. OSTRACISM OF WHITE REPUBLICANS IN ALABAMA DURING RECONSTRUCTION. *Alabama R. 1974 27(1): 52-64.* Ostracism of white Republicans was mild, perhaps nonexistent until June 1867, when the Alabama Republican Party was formed. Abuse, intimidation, and slander intensified rapidly in 1868 and remained strong throughout Reconstruction regardless of Republican political fortunes. Ostracism was not indiscriminately applied, however. It was reserved for those Northern newcomers who were politically active, as opposed to those who invested in Alabama but shunned politics;

and for scalawags more than carpetbaggers. Contemporary exaggeration notwithstanding, "ostracism was all too real for most Republicans." Based on private letters, government documents, and secondary sources; 53 notes.   J. F. Vivian

1083. Williams, Ronnie. PICTORIAL ESSAY ON THE DAWES COMMISSION. *Chronicles of Oklahoma 1975 53(2): 225-238.* Created by an act of Congress in 1893, the Dawes Commission oversaw the land allotment process for the Five Civilized Tribes of the Indian Territory. Despite much opposition from Indians and from whites who held leases on Indian land, the commission broke down tribal lands and distributed small homesteads to Indian families. Also entitled to allotments were 23,000 black freedmen, who had been slaves of the Five Civilized Tribes before the Civil War. 17 photos.   M. L. Tate

1084. Wilson, Charles Reagan. ROBERT LEWIS DABNEY: RELIGION AND THE SOUTHERN HOLOCAUST. *Virginia Mag. of Hist. and Biog. 1981 89(1): 79-89.* Analyzes the post-Civil War life of Robert Lewis Dabney, a Presbyterian theologian and philosopher at Union Seminary, Hampden-Sydney, Virginia. Dabney tried to preserve what remained of a perceived Southern ethic, and warned of moral dangers to a defeated people. Disgusted by 1881 with northern debauchery of the South, in declining health, he accepted a philosophy appointment at the new University of Texas. He taught there and helped found a seminary in Austin, but by 1890 was again disgusted by too many "Yankees" about him. In 1894 the University Regents forced him to resign because of small classes, an act likely precipitated by his enemies. He died in 1896, an example of a soul troubled by the fate of the postbellum South. 27 notes.   P. J. Woehrmann

1085. Wolfe, Nancy T. THE SINGLE TAXERS' INVASION OF DELAWARE. *Am. J. of Econ. and Sociol. 1976 35(1): 95-104.* Henry George, appalled at the misery he saw in a nation of vast wealth, sought ways for all Americans to share the benefits of the industrial boom of the late 1900's. In 1895 a contingent of Single Taxers—members of the ethical democratic social reform movement founded by George—"invaded" Delaware to achieve a successful demonstration of the efficacy of their theories by putting them into practice. Their purpose was to elect people who would implement George's Single Tax system. The campaign failed because Delaware, in the mid-90's, was an unlikely state in which to launch a third-party movement.   P. Travis

1086. —. [THE COMPROMISE OF 1877]. *J. of Am. Hist. 1973 60(1).*
Peskin, Allan. WAS THERE A COMPROMISE OF 1877?, pp. 63-75. C. Vann Woodward's *Reunion and Reaction: The Compromise of 1877 and the End of Reconstruction* (Boston: Little, Brown & Co., 1951), contains the classic and almost universally accepted interpretation of the far-reaching compromise wherein southern Democrats accepted Hayes as president in return for withdrawal of federal troops, support for internal improvements in the South, assurance of federal subsidies, appointment of a southerner as postmaster general, and the admission that the South alone could resolve its racial problems. Argues that these terms of the "compromise" were not complied with, that no compromise in fact existed, and that the southern Democrats were outwitted by Republicans.
Woodward, C. Vann. YES, THERE WAS A COMPROMISE OF 1877, pp. 215-223. The Compromise of 1877 was as real as that of 1850, the major terms were complied with, particularly home rule for the South, and if anyone was outwitted it was the Republicans. 49 notes.   K. B. West

Civil Liberties and Political Rights

1087. Adams, David Wallace. ILLINOIS SOLDIERS AND THE EMANCIPATION PROCLAMATION. *J. of the Illinois State His. Soc. 1974 67(4): 406-421.* Provides evidence that Illinois Volunteers supported the Republican Party and the Emancipation Proclamation. Their absence from the polls in 1862 was detrimental to the Republican Party's success. Based on contemporary newspaper reports, Illinois State documents, and primary and secondary sources; 2 illus., 9 photos, 51 notes.   N. J. Street

1088. Avillo, Philip J., Jr. PHANTOM RADICALS: TEXAS REPUBLICANS IN CONGRESS, 1870-1873. *Southwestern Hist. Q. 1974 77(4): 431-444.* Texas elections in 1869 gave control to the Radical Republicans in the state and its congressional delegation. The 1871 elections sent a Democratic-dominated delegation to Congress. Examines the performance of these alleged radicals. In civil rights and amnesty matters, two measures of radicalism, their records do not support the label. 53 notes.   D. L. Smith

1089. Beeton, Beverly. THE HAYES ADMINISTRATION AND THE WOMAN QUESTION. *Hayes Hist. J. 1978 2(1): 52-56.* Rutherford B. Hayes was not an advocate of women's rights; opposing the enfranchisement of women, he viewed women as an elevating influence on men. Despite the efforts of the National Woman Suffrage Association and the American Woman Suffrage Association, Hayes maintained a traditional view of women which was incompatible with political participation. The movement to outlaw the Mormon practice of polygamy, and Congress' move to take away the vote from women in Utah, resulted in Mormon women visiting President and Mrs. Hayes, and sending numerous petitions to Congress. Hayes supported Congress on the Mormon question. Secondary sources; 4 illus., 7 notes.   J. N. Friedel

1090. Beeton, Beverly. WOMAN SUFFRAGE IN TERRITORIAL UTAH. *Utah Hist. Q. 1978 46(2): 100-120.* During 1867-96, eastern suffragists promoted woman suffrage in Utah as an experiment, and as a way to eliminate polygamy. Compelling Utah motives for enfranchisement were the need to counter the image of downtrodden Mormon women and the desire to promote statehood. Advocates within Utah were William S. Godbe, Annie Thompson Godbe, Charlotte Ives Cobb Godbe, Emmeline B. Wells, Franklin D. Richards, and Emily S. Turner Richards. Utah enfranchisement moved the national suffragists closer to the Victorian Compromise and preoccupation with the franchise. Primary and secondary sources; 4 illus., 45 notes.   J. L. Hazelton

1091. Belz, Herman. THE FREEDMEN'S BUREAU ACT OF 1865 AND THE PRINCIPLE OF NO DISCRIMINATION ACCORDING TO COLOR. *Civil War Hist. 1975 21(3): 197-217.* Traces the evolution of the Freedmen's Bureau Act (1865) in Congress. Had not a provision supporting assistance to white southern refugees, sponsored by conservative rather than radical Republicans, been incorporated in the bill, it would not have passed. The original legislation dealing only with the care of freed slaves would have had insufficient backing in Congress for passage. Broadening the scope of the bill to include white refugees, an effort led by the American Union Commission and Republican Congressman Robert C. Schenck of Ohio, insured the measure's success.   E. C. Murdock

1092. Bennion, Sherilyn Cox. *THE NEW NORTHWEST* AND *WOMAN'S EXPONENT*: EARLY VOICES FOR SUFFRAGE. *Journalism Q. 1977 54(2): 286-292.* Two important newspapers, basically conservative in character but advocating woman's suffrage, were the weekly *The New Northwest,* founded in Portland, Oregon, by Abigail Scott Duniway in 1871 and edited and published by her until its demise in 1887, and the *Woman's Exponent,* issued twice a month in Utah from 1872 to 1914, first under the editorship of Louisa Greene Richards, and then under Emmeline B. Wells.

1093. Chittenden, Elizabeth F. "BY NO MEANS EXCLUDING WOMEN"; ABIGAIL SCOTT DUNIWAY, WESTERN PIONEER IN THE STRUGGLE FOR EQUAL VOTING RIGHTS. *Am. West 1975 12(2): 24-27.* A biographical sketch of suffragette Abigail Scott Duniway (b. 1834) who spearheaded the movement which culminated in

the Equal Suffrage Amendment to the constitution of Oregon in 1912. She was also active in the national movement. 2 illus., bibliographic note.
D. L. Smith

1094. Clifford, Deborah P. AN INVASION OF STRONG-MINDED WOMEN: THE NEWSPAPERS AND THE WOMAN SUFFRAGE CAMPAIGN IN VERMONT IN 1870. *Vermont Hist. 1975 43(1): 1-19.* Moderates Julia Ward Howe, Mary Livermore, Lucy Stone, and Henry Blackwell spoke to rallies in Montpelier, Rutland, Brattleboro, and Burlington in February-March 1870, in favor of the woman suffrage amendment proposed to the May 1870 constitutional convention. Editors Henry Clark (Rutland *Herald*) and the Rev. Addison Brown (Brattleboro *Phoenix*) and a few others favored it, but it was defeated 231-1. 58 notes.
T. D. S. Bassett

1095. Friedlander, Alice G. A PORTLAND GIRL ON WOMEN'S RIGHTS—1893. *Western States Jewish Hist. Q. 1978 10(2): 146-150.* In 1893 Alice G. Friedlander said there should be no question about the fundamental principal of women's equality. Any profession—such as journalism, law, medicine, education—requiring intellectual rather than manual force, is open to women. Soon they will vote and hold office, and, though lacking in parliamentary finesse, no matter how hard they try, they cannot be more ignorant and stupid than some gentleman legislators. These new skills and attainments do not conflict with women's duties in the home. Quoted from original speech at Portland (Oregon) Press Club; photo.
B. S. Porter

1096. Howard, Victor B. THE BRECKINRIDGE FAMILY AND THE NEGRO TESTIMONY CONTROVERSY IN KENTUCKY, 1866-1872. *Filson Club Hist. Q. 1975 49(1): 37-56.* Robert J. Breckinridge, Jr., and William C. P. Breckinridge, members of a distinguished Kentucky political family, were both defeated in their attempts to win public office in 1868 and 1869, because of their firm support of measures allowing blacks to testify in the state courts. William, the editor of the Lexington *Observer and Reporter*, ran for district commonwealth attorney, but his liberal stand on the testimony issue prevented him from securing the Democratic nomination. Robert won the Democratic nomination for state senator with ease, but opposition to his position on black legal rights allowed Independent Democrat Albert Gallatin Talbott to defeat him in the general election of 1869. Documentation from newspapers and the Breckinridge Family Papers at the Library of Congress; 76 notes.
G. B. McKinney

1097. Jackson, W. Sherman. REPRESENTATIVE JAMES M. ASHLEY AND THE MIDWESTERN ORIGINS OF AMENDMENT THIRTEEN. *Lincoln Herald 1978 80(2): 83-95.* Although the 13th Amendment helped revolutionize the federal Constitution concerning human rights and equality, its adoption did not signify a departure from the traditional growth of American constitutionalism. Instead it marked "a resumption of the nationalizing constitutional views of Hamilton, Marshall and the early Supreme Court." In the struggle to secure the amendment's passage in Congress in 1865, Representative James M. Ashley of Ohio played a key role. An ardent Free Soiler before turning Republican, Ashley served as House floor manager of the 13th Amendment and persuaded a number of Democrats to support it. 3 photos, 71 notes.
T. P. Linkfield

1098. Jennings, Mary Kay. LAKE COUNTY WOMAN SUFFRAGE CAMPAIGN IN 1890. *South Dakota Hist. 1975 5(4): 390-409.* In Lake County, South Dakota, the vote was denied to women in the 1890 election despite much effort to win woman's suffrage. National figures joined the state campaign and made addresses. A local newspaper in Madison was prosuffrage, a position it maintained until women were given the vote in 1918. The suffrage movement often was allied with Women's Christian Temperance Union organizations, although one of the national figures present, Susan B. Anthony, thought the two issues should be considered separately. The woman suffrage question was defeated almost two-to-one in 1890. The opposition questioned women's abilities to vote properly, and there was some fear that if women were accorded the vote, the same right would be forthcoming for Indians. Primary sources; illus., 5 photos, 56 notes.
A. J. Larson

1099. Jensen, Billie Barnes. COLORADO WOMAN SUFFRAGE CAMPAIGNS OF THE 1870'S. *J. of the West 1973 12(2): 254-271.* Colorado did not achieve woman suffrage until 1893, but the campaign of the 1870's paved the way to victory. Although the issue was widely discussed in the legislature, the newspapers provided the best forum for public opinion. The constitutional convention of 1876 denied women the right to vote in general elections but gave them the right of franchise and office-holding in school districts, provided for a referendum process, and occasioned the organization of a woman suffrage association. 91 notes.
E. P. Stickney

1100. Kersey, Harry A., Jr. THE CASE OF TOM TIGER'S HORSE: AN EARLY FORAY INTO INDIAN RIGHTS. *Florida Hist. Q. 1975 53(3): 306-318.* Describes an early attempt to promote the rights of a Seminole Indian, Captain Tom Tiger, whose horse had been stolen by a white man. A citizens group, the Friends of the Florida Seminoles, was formed in Kissimmee on 7 January 1899 to support his complaint. Although the case was lost, it dramatized the need for official attention to be given to the Seminole Indians, and also marked a turning point in the willingness of some Indians to seek legal redress for their grievances. 2 photos, 38 notes.
R. V. Ritter

1101. Kessler, Lauren. THE IDEAS OF WOMEN SUFFRAGISTS AND THE PORTLAND *OREGONIAN*. *Journalism Q. 1980 57(4): 597-605.* Issues of the Portland *Oregonian* for 1 June 1869-31 October 1905 were examined in order to study the coverage given the woman suffrage movement. Using the Oregon State Woman Suffrage Association, led by Abigail Scott Duniway, and its statements and activities as the specific points of interest, a total of 96 items were discovered. A 1905 meeting of suffragists which was attended by several prominent "Eastern leaders" apparently gave the movement the legitimacy required for the *Oregonian* to grant it access to its pages. Although the newspaper was antisuffragist in its editorials, it actually published little negative comment before the 1905 meeting, apparently in the belief that ignoring the movement was tactically sound.
J. S. Coleman

1102. Larson, T. A. WYOMING'S CONTRIBUTION TO THE REGIONAL AND NATIONAL WOMEN'S RIGHTS MOVEMENT. *Ann. of Wyoming 1980 52(1): 2-15.* In 1869, Wyoming became the first state to extend suffrage rights to women. Within a year, Wyoming had produced three female justices of the peace and several female jury members. Opposition to woman suffrage was minimal. The movement received its impetus more from men than from women. An attempt to repeal the act in 1871 was vetoed by Governor John A. Campbell. This initiated a long history of support for the suffrage issue from a majority of Wyoming governors, congressmen, and judges. During the later struggle for women's suffrage on a regional and national level, Wyoming citizens did not play as active a role as is commonly thought, although the Council of Women Voters served as an organizational focus before 1920, when the 19th Amendment assured the suffrage issue on a national level. Based on archival sources and newspapers; 9 photos, 54 notes.
M. L. Tate

1103. Lebsock, Suzanne D. RADICAL RECONSTRUCTION AND THE PROPERTY RIGHTS OF SOUTHERN WOMEN. *J. of Southern Hist 1977 43(2): 195-216.* Women's property rights in the South were not revolutionarily revised during Reconstruction. Only in Georgia, North Carolina, and South Carolina were pre-Civil War property rights of women significantly strengthened. Even in these cases, as well as the revised statutes in the other southern states, the debates of the state legislatures clearly indicate it was not from any radical or even moderate feminist position that such reforms were undertaken, but rather in order to protect the women from exploitation by "fortune hunters" or from other forms of economic hardship and disaster. Based on mss. and printed primary and secondary sources; 47 notes.
T. D. Schoonover

1104. Linford, Orma. THE MORMONS, THE LAW, AND THE TERRITORY OF UTAH. *Am. J. of Legal Hist. 1979 23(3): 213-235.* An exploratory study of the historical relationship between the Mormon Church and American law during the territorial period in Utah. Whereas Americans of the time generally were almost reverent toward law, the Mormons had a history of trouble with it. Their moves from place to place were caused by legal troubles. Utah provided a unique opportunity to establish their own system. The coming of territorial status revived the legal controversies, but the government was Mormon-dominated and therefore could get its own way on many issues. Lawyers and judges were despised. Statehood brought the territory into the national fold and Mormons gradually lost their distrust of law. 96 notes.
V. L. Human

1105. Lucie, Patricia M. L. CONFISCATION: CONSTITUTIONAL CROSSROADS. *Civil War Hist. 1977 23(4): 307-321.* Congressional debates on confiscation were more useful than the 1861-62 Acts they produced. Little property was confiscated, and the emancipation clauses were made redundant by Proclamation and Amendment. However, the debates were a seminar in Reconstruction problems. Congress developed much expertise in matching rights with remedies. The federal courts were utilized to enforce new-found constitutional rights. The courts became the "nuts and bolts" of Reconstruction legislation. Secondary sources; 35 notes.
R. E. Stack

1106. Lucie, Patricia M. L. ON BEING A FREE PERSON AND A CITIZEN BY CONSTITUTIONAL AMENDMENT. *J. of Am. Studies [Great Britain] 1978 12(3): 343-358.* During the American Civil War, feminist reformers attempted, to no avail, to fuse the issues of citizenship rights for former slaves and women's demands for political and social equality. Then the postwar constitutional amendments dealing with citizenship matters simply lifted the slaves from their earlier bondage and formally accorded them citizen privileges and immunities. In the 1870's, the US Supreme Court ruled in several cases such as *Minor* v. *Happersett* (1874) against contentions by women reformers that the new constitutional guarantees in the 14th and 15th Amendments buttressed their claims to political and civil equality with males. Based on judicial writings and secondary sources; 48 notes.
H. T. Lovin

1107. Macleod, R. C. THE SHAPING OF CANADIAN CRIMINAL LAW, 1892 TO 1902. *Hist. Papers [Canada] 1978: 64-75.* Examines the forces operating to change Canadian criminal law in the first decade after the passage of the Criminal Code in 1892. Focuses on the intention and actions of Parliament and largely ignores the development of case law. "The main object of a code is to remove the conflicts, inconsistencies and obscurities that inevitably characterize uncodified law." The changes and innovations are "numerous and of a sweeping character." It was decided that Parliament would be the principal source of change in the criminal law. A regular procedure for handling amendments was evolved by 1902. The Amendment bill of 1900 "set the pattern which prevailed until the 1950's." 72 notes.
E. P. Stickney

1108. Masel-Walters, Lynne. THEIR RIGHTS AND NOTHING MORE: A HISTORY OF *THE REVOLUTION*, 1868-70. *Journalism Q. 1976 53(2): 242-251.* The Revolution was a national weekly newspaper published by Elizabeth Cady Stanton and Susan B. Anthony. Due to coverage of topics considered radical, it served as the catalyst for the split that affected the suffrage movement for 30 years. Stanton and Anthony gave coverage to women's rights, political corruption, the condition of the poor, and the financial ideas of George Francis Train, an early benefactor. Anthony would not change the name or direction of the paper to save it, and dwindling resources forced her to sell in June, 1870. In its pages *The Revolution* carried many of the arguments for women's rights that are still being used, and it started a tradition of women's political journalism. 93 notes.
E. Gibson

1109. Mendelson, Wallace. A NOTE ON THE CAUSE AND CURE OF THE FOURTEENTH AMENDMENT. *J. of Pol. 1981 43(1): 152-158.* While the three chief congressional sponsors of the 14th Amendment agreed that they were not merely constitutionalizing the provisions of the Civil Rights Act, they disagreed on the exact meaning of the amendment. Representative John Bingham saw the amendment as protecting the privileges and immunities of all citizens and the inborn rights of all persons. Congressman Thaddeus Stevens argued that it permitted Congress to correct unjust state legislation, applying all laws equally to all persons. Senator Jacob Howard believed that it would cover all the personal rights secured by the first eight amendments. The amendment may be understood only in the context of the antiracist measures, which include all the Civil War amendments, the Civil Rights Acts of 1866, 1870, 1871, and 1875, as well as the five Reconstruction acts and Freedmen's Bureau provisions. 35 notes.
A. W. Novitsky

1110. Moses, L. G. JAMES MOONEY AND THE PEYOTE CONTROVERSY. *Chronicles of Oklahoma 1978 56(2): 127-144.* While employed by the Bureau of American Ethnology to study the Ghost Dance religion, James Mooney became an advocate of Indians' freedom to use peyote in religious services. Reformers and missionaries accused Mooney of interrupting the "civilizing process," and they debated him at every opportunity. Pressures against Mooney became so intense that he was never allowed to complete his field research among the Kiowas. He died in 1921 before the peyote issue was resolved. Based on primary sources; 4 photos, 54 notes.
M. L. Tate

1111. Noun, Louise. ANNIE SAVERY: A VOICE FOR WOMEN'S RIGHTS. *Ann. of Iowa 1977 44(1): 3-30.* Anne Savery (1831-91), wife of an Iowa hotelkeeper and land developer, struggled for woman suffrage in Iowa. During 1868-72 she and her friend Amelia Bloomer failed to secure a state referendum on the suffrage question. Savery received much blame for the negative vote in the state legislature; it was charged that her refusal to denounce free-love advocate Victoria Woodhull split the suffragist movement and thus ensured its failure. Based on newspapers and Savery-Bloomer correspondence; 5 photos, 39 notes.
P. L. Petersen

1112. Schwantes, Carlos A. FREE LOVE AND FREE SPEECH ON THE PACIFIC NORTHWEST FRONTIER. *Oregon Hist. Q. 1981 82(3): 271-293.* The *Firebrand,* published in Portland, Oregon, during 1895-97 by Henry Addis, Abraham Issak, and Abner J. Pope, advocated anarchism and radical sexual ideas. Circumstances of the newspaper's founding, publication, and demise are discussed as well as a comparison of its views with those of other Northwest radical movements, such as the International Workingmen's Association and the Puget Sound Cooperative Colony. Based on newspapers and some secondary sources; 5 illus., 39 notes.
G. R. Schroeder

1113. Spackman, S. G. F. AMERICAN FEDERALISM AND THE CIVIL RIGHTS ACT OF 1875. *J. of Am. Studies [Great Britain] 1976 10(3): 313-328.* Describes racial considerations and social and political pressures that influenced the Civil Rights Act of 1875 when Congress considered and passed it and the courts reviewed it. Authored by Charles Sumner (1811-1874) and designed to prevent discrimination against Negroes, the legislation caused major constitutional disputes about the nature and extent of federal powers to enforce the 13th and 14th Amendments. In 1883 the US Supreme Court struck down the Civil Rights Act, thus setting back the achievement of racial equality by substantially expanding federal powers to punish individuals. Based on government documents and secondary sources; 49 notes.
H. T. Lovin

1114. Spector, Robert M. WOMAN AGAINST THE LAW: MYRA BRADWELL'S STRUGGLE FOR ADMISSION TO THE ILLINOIS BAR. *J. of the Illinois State Hist. Soc. 1975 68(3): 228-242.* The unsuccessful effort of Myra Bradwell to gain admission to the Illinois bar led to her appeal to the US Supreme Court in 1873. The Court ruled that her case was not justified under the Fourteenth Amendment or the privileges and immunities clause of Section IV of the United States Constitution. Bradwell's case, however, did prepare the way for other women to be admitted to law practice in Illinois and in other states. She successfully edited the *Chicago Legal News* until her death in 1894, making this legal publication one of the most respected in the country.
N. Lederer

1115. Stephens, Lester D. EVOLUTION AND WOMAN'S RIGHTS IN THE 1890S: THE VIEWS OF JOSEPH LE CONTE. *Historian 1976 38(2): 239-252.* Analyzes the scientific arguments developed by Joseph Le Conte and his colleagues in opposition to the women's rights movement and women's suffrage in particular. He developed his argument from the thesis that "the most fundamental law of evolution is the Law of Differentiation of form and specialization and limitation of function...." Sex was not excepted from this biological law which could be projected into the social functions of the sexes in social institutions. Although he felt men must make some adjustments in their treatment of women, Le Conte believed his principles were firmly grounded in an evolutionary view of human progress. 29 notes.
R. V. Ritter

1116. Stern, Madeleine B., ed. TWO UNPUBLISHED LETTERS FROM BELVA LOCKWOOD. *Signs: J. of Women in Culture and Soc. 1975 1(1): 269-272.* These letters present a biography and the political philosophy of Belva Bennett Lockwood (1830-1917), the first woman attorney to practice law in the federal courts and before the US Supreme Court and the first woman campaigner for the presidency. Reprints her 1884 letter to the National Equal Rights Party in which she accepted the presidential nomination. In her strongly feminist and humanist platform she advocated equal political and civil rights regardless of sex or race,

equitable distribution of money and power, uniform marriage and divorce laws upholding equality of the sexes, temperance, universal peace through a court of arbitration, and citizenship for American Indians. Her vigorous campaign garnered more than 4,000 votes and helped establish the place of women in the political arena. Based on primary and secondary sources; note.
T. Simmerman

1117. Taylor, Antoinette Elizabeth. SOUTH CAROLINA AND THE ENFRANCHISEMENT OF WOMEN: THE EARLY YEARS. *South Carolina Hist. Mag. 1976 77(2): 115-126.* During 1890-1903 Virginia Durant Young of Fairfax led an unsuccessful fight for woman suffrage in South Carolina and assisted in the national movement by writing articles, testifying before the Carolina legislature, and speaking to women's groups. She argued that women would help clean up politics. Others in the movement argued that female suffrage for those who were property owners and educated would dilute the Black vote. Primary sources; 70 notes.
R. H. Tomlinson

1118. Tenney, Craig D. TO SUPPRESS OR NOT TO SUPPRESS: ABRAHAM LINCOLN AND THE CHICAGO *TIMES*. *Civil War Hist. 1981 27(3): 248-259.* Discusses the circumstances surrounding the arrest of Clement L. Vallandigham in May 1863 and the suppression of the Chicago *Times* in June 1863, both for repeated expressions of disloyal opinion, by order of General Ambrose E. Burnside. Lincoln's decision to revoke the *Times* order was apparently motivated by political considerations. Based on newspaper, other primary, and secondary sources; 63 notes.
G. R. Schroeder

1119. Thatcher, Linda, ed. "I CARE NOTHING FOR POLITICS": RUTH MAY FOX, FORGOTTEN SUFFRAGIST. *Utah Hist. Q. 1981 49(3): 239-253.* Ruth May Fox spent most of her adult life as both mother and speaker for the suffrage movement in Utah. Her interest in the suffrage movement began when she joined the Utah Women's Press Club and Reaper's Club as a writer and acquaintance of other women (Dr. Ellis R. Shipp, Dr. Ellen B. Ferguson, Emma McVicker, and Emmeline B. Wells) who proved to be major influences on her desire to improve the role of women in society. During the latter portion of the 19th century, she became active in the Utah Woman Suffrage Association, Salt Lake County Republican Committee, Second Precinct Ladies Republican Club, Deseret Agricultural & Manufacturing Society, Traveler's Aid Society, and Young Ladies' Mutual Improvement Association. Most of her later activities were with the Young Ladies' Mutual Improvement Association. A portion of her diary reveals her constant traveling and speaking to improve women's rights within the political confines of the community. She died in 1958 with little recognition for her past efforts. Photo, 69 notes.
K. E. Gilmont

1120. Wells, Merle W. LAW IN THE SERVICE OF POLITICS: ANTI-MORMONISM IN IDAHO TERRITORY. *Idaho Yesterdays 1981 25(1): 33-43.* In Idaho anti-Mormon sentiment was fueled by the average voter's attitude toward Mormon polygamy. For several years after 1884 no Idaho Mormon could vote, hold office, or serve on a jury. The anti-Mormon laws were changed only after the church authorities in Salt Lake City modified Mormon plural-marriage doctrine. Based on Idaho legal records and newspapers; 5 photos, 46 notes.
B. J. Paul

1121. Wheeler, Leslie. WOMAN SUFFRAGE'S GRAY-BEARDED CHAMPION COMES TO MONTANA, 1889. *Montana 1981 31(3): 2-13.* Henry B. Blackwell and Lucy Stone championed woman suffrage from 1850 until their respective deaths in 1909 and 1893. Their 1855 marriage provided a solid partnership in the endeavor, which included formation of the American Woman Suffrage Association and publication of *The Woman's Journal*. They campaigned for woman suffrage in Kansas, Colorado, Nebraska, North Dakota, Washington, and Montana. The author focuses on Blackwell's 1889 visit to Montana and his abortive effort to get woman suffrage included in the new state's constitution. Delegates to the constitutional convention did grant woman school suffrage and gave all tax-paying women a vote in questions concerning taxpayers. Based on the Blackwell Family Papers in the Library of congress, the Montana Constitutional Convention *Proceedings*, and contemporary newspapers; 13 illus., 36 notes.
R. C. Meyers

1122. White, G. Edward. JOHN MARSHALL HARLAN I: THE PRECURSOR. *Am. J. of Legal Hist. 1975 19(1): 1-21.* Examines Harlan's Supreme Court career, 1877-1911, focusing on his responses to the Reconstruction amendments and to the growth of large-scale industrial enterprise. Harlan evolved from an orthodox Whig to a paternalist, gradually accepting government regulation of the economy, civil rights, and liberal interpretations of the 13th, 14th, and 15th amendments. Includes a brief account of his earlier political career from the late 1850's to the mid-1870's. 104 notes.
L. A. Knafla

1123. White, Jean Bickmore. WOMAN'S PLACE IS IN THE CONSTITUTION: THE STRUGGLE FOR EQUAL RIGHTS IN UTAH IN 1895. *Utah Hist. Q. 1974 42(4): 344-369.* Reviews Utah women's struggle to acquire voting rights when the territory became a state in 1895. Initially, both political parties supported universal suffrage, but opposition soon developed. Militancy was wholly absent, and the women won because their leaders were respected members of the Mormon Church. 5 photos, 58 notes.
V. L. Human

1124. Zuber, Richard L. CONSCIENTIOUS OBJECTORS IN THE CONFEDERACY: THE QUAKERS OF NORTH CAROLINA. *Quaker Hist. 1978 67(1): 1-19.* Some 300 pacifist-abolitionist-Unionist North Carolina Quakers, ex-members, and sympathizers were exempt from conscription on payment of $500 ($100 the first year). Seven refused to pay throughout the War. Perhaps 100 labored at the coastal salt works in lieu of commutation the first year. Many "War Quakers," who joined the Society of Friends after the exemption deadline of 11 October 1862, and others who did not meet exemption requirements, were drafted; many Quakers deserted. Draft administration was as varied as Quaker reactions to the War, but generally mild. The Quakers had long made their position clear, had a positive image in the State, and had friends among Unionist Whig politicians such as William A. Graham and Jonathan Worth. 59 notes.
T. D. S. Bassett

The Black Experience

1125. Akin, Edward N. WHEN A MINORITY BECOMES THE MAJORITY: BLACKS IN JACKSONVILLE POLITICS, 1887-1907. *Florida Hist. Q. 1974 53(2): 123-145.* Develops the thesis that the dynamics of the urban setting allowed Negroes to exercise political power and rights on a broader scale than the state's rural black population, illustrated by a case study of Jacksonville politics during the late 1880's. "When given proper latitude, black leaders were just as effective in the political arena as whites." It must, however, be acknowledged that Jacksonville blacks' political success could be a unique situation. 2 illus., 2 tables, 104 notes.
R. V. Ritter

1126. Akpan, M. B. ALEXANDER CRUMMELL AND HIS AFRICAN "RACE-WORK": AN ASSESSMENT OF HIS CONTRIBUTIONS IN LIBERIA TO AFRICA'S "REDEMPTION," 1853-1873. *Hist. Mag. of the Protestant Episcopal Church 1976 45(2): 177-199.* Highlights the Liberian career of Alexander Crummell, an American Negro educator, as an example of attempts by numerous US Negroes to demonstrate practically their commitments to Africa. His failure to accomplish much stemmed from mulatto attitudes toward the native blacks. The mulattos viewed the natives as intellectually and racially inferior. The author gives insights into the philosophy behind the American Colonization Society, the hopes for the Christianization of the African Negro, and Crummell's fruitless struggle to accomplish lasting goals through his educational philosophy and labors. Based on Crummell's writings; 123 notes.
H. M. Parker, Jr.

1127. Alexander, Roberta Sue. HOSTILITY AND HOPE: BLACK EDUCATION IN NORTH CAROLINA DURING PRESIDENTIAL RECONSTRUCTION, 1865-1867. *North Carolina Hist. R. 1976 53(2): 113-132.* During Presidential Reconstruction blacks were partially successful in establishing schools on the local level with the aid of benevolent northern societies. Whites, with some violent exceptions, accepted the need for black education, mainly as a means of establishing social control over former slaves. Out of fear that northerners would force integrated schools and undesireable teachers on them, whites refused to set up a state-wide education system. Some children of both races therefore failed to receive schooling during these years. Based on Freedmen's Bureau and other manuscript papers, newspaper articles, published primary and secondary sources; 4 illus., 2 tables, 103 notes. — T. L. Savitt

1128. Aptheker, Bettina. THE SUPPRESSION OF THE *FREE SPEECH*: IDA B. WELLS AND THE MEMPHIS LYNCHING, 1892. *San José Studies 1977 3(3): 34-40.* Discusses the violent suppression of the *Free Speech,* a black newspaper in Memphis, Tennessee, whose condemnation in editorials by its publisher, Ida B. Wells, of race-related lynchings in 1892, resulted in the closure of the paper by members of the white community.

1129. Belz, Herman. LAW, POLITICS, AND RACE IN THE STRUGGLE FOR EQUAL PAY DURING THE CIVIL WAR. *Civil War Hist. 1976 22(3): 197-213.* Examines the debates leading to the passage of a law, in 1864, which for the first time authorized equal pay for both black and white Union troops. Troubled about the military ability of black troops, Congress phrased the measure ambiguously, and left the question of equal pay to be determined by Attorney General Edward Bates. Bates had a reputation for legal conservatism, but, surprisingly, he ruled that black troops should receive the same pay as white troops. He based his opinion on the Confiscation Act of 1862. This was a rather weak foundation to support such a ruling, and Bates perhaps was moved more by political than legal considerations.
— E. C. Murdock

1130. Belz, Herman. ORIGINS OF NEGRO SUFFRAGE DURING THE CIVIL WAR. *Southern Studies 1978 17(2): 115-130.* During the Civil War Negro suffrage became a major issue when Louisiana sought readmission to the Union in 1863, and the free Negro community of New Orleans, educated and property owners, demanded the right to vote. While President Lincoln's administration wished to readmit Louisiana before the final collapse of the South as a pattern for other states, radical Republicans and abolitionists opposed readmission unless Louisiana would enfranchise blacks. An administration compromise bill in 1864 which would have enfranchised black veterans in all states except Louisiana was defeated. In response, the Military Reconstruction Act of 1867 provided for universal suffrage, strongly offending white southerners. Primary and secondary sources; 54 notes. — J. Buschen

1131. Belz, Herman. PROTECTION OF PERSONAL LIBERTY IN REPUBLICAN EMANCIPATION LEGISLATION OF 1862. *J. of Southern Hist. 1976 42(3): 385-400.* Most historiographical concern over the motivation behind the Emancipation Proclamation has focused on Lincoln's motivation. Still, understanding of this crucial event can be advanced by examination of the 1862 measures of the Republican Party. These legislative items reveal little concern about Negro liberty and much about securing military advantage to the Union through depriving the South of labor. Guided by expediency, Congress no less than Lincoln's administration ignored or slighted the problem of the freed slaves' personal liberty. — T. Schoonover

1132. Bergesen, Albert. NATION-BUILDING AND CONSTITUTIONAL AMENDMENTS: THE ROLE OF THE THIRTEENTH, FOURTEENTH, AND FIFTEENTH AMENDMENTS IN THE LEGAL RECONSTITUTION OF THE AMERICAN POLITY FOLLOWING THE CIVIL WAR. *Pacific Sociol. Rev. 1981 24(1): 3-15.* The amendments (1865, 1866, 1870) solved two problems in social reconstruction: 1) establishing the ultimate political authority of the federal government over state governments and 2) legally transforming slaves into citizens.

1133. Berwanger, Eugene H. HARDIN AND LANGSTON: WESTERN BLACK SPOKESMEN OF THE RECONSTRUCTION ERA. *J. of Negro Hist. 1979 64(2): 101-115.* Chronicles the activities of William J. Hardin in northeastern Colorado and Charles H. Langston in northeastern Kansas, both black advocates for Negro suffrage, 1865-67.

1134. Berwanger, Eugene H. RECONSTRUCTION ON THE FRONTIER: THE EQUAL RIGHTS STRUGGLE IN COLORADO, 1865-1867. *Pacific Hist. R. 1975 44(3): 313-329.* Colorado blacks, led by Edward Sanderlin, Henry O. Wagoner, and William J. Hardin, successfully struggled during Reconstruction for the right to vote and to educate their children in public schools. Their petition to Congress asking that statehood be denied until equal suffrage was included in the state constitution helped the Radical Republicans in Congress in their successful attempt to forbid restricted suffrage in the territories. The victory encouraged Denver blacks to seek access to public school education. They achieved partial success in 1867 and fully integrated the schools by 1873. Based on newspapers, published government documents, and secondary sources; 67 notes. — W. K. Hobson

1135. Berwanger, Eugene H. WILLIAM J. HARDIN: COLORADO SPOKESMAN FOR RACIAL JUSTICE, 1863-1873. *Colorado Mag. 1975 52(1): 52-65.* Although now generally ignored, during 1863-73 William J. Hardin was the able and unquestioned spokesman for the black community in Denver and Colorado Territory. He aggressively supported Negro suffrage, granted in the Territories in 1867, and school integration. He also antagonized many Negroes, whom he publicly chastised for improprieties. His influence collapsed and he fled to Cheyenne in 1873 when his adultery (or bigamy) and draft evasion came to light. Based on primary sources; 3 illus., chart, 40 notes. — O. H. Zabel

1136. Binning, F. Wayne. CARPETBAGGERS' TRIUMPH: THE LOUISIANA STATE ELECTION OF 1868. *Louisiana Hist. 1973 14(1): 21-39.* Carpetbaggers and blacks were the two principal factions of the Louisiana Republican Party after the Civil War. Their struggle culminated during the election of 1868 when the Radical Republicans refused to support the party nominee, Henry Clay Warmoth, and nominated James Govan Taliaferro as an opposition candidate. The more moderate Carpetbaggers were vindicated when Warmoth strongly defeated Taliaferro. Thereafter, the "free colored class" was "effectively excluded from politics," although they kept the civil rights issue alive. Based on published documents, newspapers, and the H. C. Warmoth Papers in the Southern Collection, University of North Carolina at Chapel Hill; 3 photos, 47 notes. — R. L. Woodward

1137. Bloch, Herman D. and Banks, Carol M. THE NATIONAL LABOR UNION AND BLACK WORKERS. *J. of Ethnic Studies 1973 1(1): 13-21.* Since the rise of trade unions in the 1850's, the American labor movement has discriminated against blacks. Motivated by a belief in white supremacy and a fear of job competition, white workers attempted to keep or drive blacks from the skilled trades and bar them from union membership. The National Labor Union (1866-72), a reform-orientated federation of trades assemblies, national trade unions, and other labor and labor-reform bodies, considered the problem of the black worker and adopted the intermediate position of inviting black unions to affiliate, without openly opposing the racist practices of its constituent bodies. Blacks elected instead to form the National Colored Labor Union (1869-72). The "half-hearted reformism" of the National Labor Union and its neglect of labor solidarity contributed to its limited success and early demise. Based largely on primary sources with major secondary sources also cited; 48 notes. — T. W. Smith

1138. Borit, G. S. THE VOYAGE TO THE COLONY OF LINCONIA: THE SIXTEENTH PRESIDENT, BLACK COLONIZATION, AND THE DEFENSE MECHANISM OF AVOIDANCE. *Historian 1975 37(4): 619-632.* Abraham Lincoln was never really committed to the idea of colonization of American Negroes. He deceived himself with the colonization idea as a psychological technique by which to allay his misgivings about the place the emancipated Negro would have in American society. The idea was also politically serviceable in easing northern white fears about Negro emancipation. After emancipation in 1862 colonization became a politically valueless idea to which Lincoln gave no further public attention. 30 notes.

1139. Brier, Stephen. THE CAREER OF RICHARD L. DAVIS RECONSIDERED: UNPUBLISHED CORRESPONDENCE FROM THE *NATIONAL LABOR TRIBUNE*. *Labor Hist. 1980 21(3): 420-429.* Richard L. Davis (1864-1900), a Negro and a coal miner from Ohio, became a leader in the United Mine Workers of America in the 1890's. The letters presented here show that, while critical of the union's treatment of black miners, Davis never wavered from his belief in trade unionism as the only vehicle for black Americans to attain "final liberation." Based on Davis's letters to the *National Labor Tribune;* 10 notes.
— L. F. Velicer

1140. Brier, Stephen. INTERRACIAL ORGANIZING IN THE WEST VIRGINIA COAL INDUSTRY: THE PARTICIPATION OF BLACK MINE WORKERS IN THE KNIGHTS OF LABOR AND THE UNITED MINE WORKERS, 1880-1894. Fink, Gary M. and Reed, Merl E., eds. *Essays in Southern Labor History: Selected Papers, Southern Labor History Conference, 1976.* (Westport, Conn.; London, England: Greenwood, Pr., 1977): 18-43. A study of national unionism in the coal fields, but especially the relationship of the growth of militant, interracial local unions among southern West Virginia mine workers. Focuses on the Flat-Top Pocahontas field, 1880-94. In the latter part of the period a decline in local organization set in, largely the result of intensified economic and political repression on the part of the coal operators. For more than a decade, however, West Virginia mine workers, black and white, had flocked to the banner of trade unionism, and there was demonstrated the possibility of cooperation between black and white workers. 44 notes. R. V. Ritter

1141. Campbell, Clarice T. EXPLORING THE ROOTS OF TOUGALOO COLLEGE. *J. of Mississippi Hist.* 1973 35(1): 15-27. The American Missionary Association grew out of the abolitionist committee established to assure mutineers a fair trial in the *Amistad* case (1839-41). The events and negotiations of 1868-69 led the AMA to establish Tougaloo College, a normal-agricultural school near Jackson, Mississippi. With the financial support of the Freedmen's Bureau, the AMA established more than 500 schools in the South, chiefly for freedmen. Based on primary and secondary sources, mainly the AMA Archives at Fisk University; 51 notes. J. W. Hillje

1142. Christensen, Lawrence O. THE RACIAL VIEWS OF JOHN W. WHEELER. *Missouri Hist. R.* 1973 67(4): 535-547. Discusses the racial views of John W. Wheeler, a Republican member of the St. Louis black community and editor of the *St. Louis Palladium*. Holding a respected position within society, Wheeler was able to persuade Negroes to join the Republican Party. Like Booker T. Washington, he urged Negroes to take on the responsibility of improving themselves, maintaining high moral standards, and supporting racial solidarity. Wheeler defended blacks against racial attacks, fought segregation attempts, and opposed black emigration to Africa in 1903. Based on contemporary newspaper reports, US government documents, and secondary sources; 5 illus., photo, 54 notes. N. J. Street

1143. Christian, Garna L. THE TWENTY-FIFTH REGIMENT AT FORT MCINTOSH: PRECURSOR TO RETALIATORY RACIAL VIOLENCE. *West Texas Hist. Assoc. Y.* 1979 55: 149-161. The first resistance to racial oppression by black soldiers occurred after the rise in expectations caused by the Spanish-American War in Laredo in 1899, foreshadowing the urban riots of 1919.

1144. Cimprich, John. THE BEGINNING OF THE BLACK SUFFRAGE MOVEMENT IN TENNESSEE, 1864-65. *J. of Negro Hist.* 1980 65(3): 185-195. During the Civil War, former slaves and nonslaves in Tennessee began to hold mass meetings and conduct marches in order to achieve the right to vote. Black political leaders encouraged race pride and political consciousness to demonstrate the legitimacy of the black vote for white skeptics. Only a few whites supported black suffrage, and then only to preserve Union control, not as a right for blacks. The local efforts in Tennessee were not successful. Real progress for black voters came only after the Radical Republicans in Congress had control of national Reconstruction policies. A. G. Belles

1145. Cortada, James W. THE ABOLITION MOVEMENT AND RELATIONS BETWEEN SPAIN AND THE UNITED STATES, 1860-1868. *Lincoln Herald* 1979 81(1): 27-33. Describes the tension between the United States and Spain regarding the question of slavery, 1860-68, due to Spanish occupation of Cuba and the interest of the Confederate States in Havana.

1146. Crouch, Barry A. BLACK DREAMS AND WHITE JUSTICE. *Prologue* 1974 6(4): 255-265. "An intensive analysis of the blacks' legal response to white society and justice during the early Reconstruction years." By focusing on Negro communities in Texas and on their interaction with the Freedmen's Bureau courts one can see the need for substantial modification of conventional wisdom. Renders obsolete many popular and scholarly notions concerning the nature and scope of white dominion over slave society and of the black's capacity to function adequately in a formally free society. "That they were able to preserve an autonomous spirit throughout slavery and were ready to implement it when freedom arrived is no more clearly seen than in their use of the courts and the law in Texas." 3 photos, 32 notes. R. V. Ritter

1147. Crouch, Barry A. HIDDEN SOURCES OF BLACK HISTORY: THE TEXAS FREEDMEN'S BUREAU RECORDS AS A CASE STUDY. *Southwestern Hist. Q.* 1980 83(3): 211-226. Summarizes the 174 volumes and 44 boxes of Texas material in the records of the Bureau of Refugees, Freedmen, and Abandoned Lands, in National Archives Record Group 105. Microfilming is now underway. The records reveal much about blacks' adjustment to freedom after 1865, race relations, education, labor, family life, politics, crime, and violence. There is less material on migration, housing, medical care, social classes, and divisions within black society. 30 notes. J. H. Broussard

1148. Crouch, Barry A. SELF-DETERMINATION AND LOCAL BLACK LEADERS IN TEXAS. *Phylon* 1978 39(4): 344-355. Discusses the increasing participation of blacks in Texas politics, particularly at the local level, during and after Reconstruction from 1865 through the 1890's.

1149. Cummings, Melbourne. HISTORICAL SETTING FOR BOOKER T. WASHINGTON AND THE RHETORIC OF COMPROMISE, 1895. *J. of Black Studies* 1977 8(1): 75-82. By the mid-1890's, southern blacks were in desperate economic and political straits. Then Booker T. Washington emerged, preaching compromise and gaining the trust of whites by advocating cooperation between blacks and whites, a program of economic betterment that would benefit both races, and a utilitarian education for blacks that would not threaten whites. Washington's strategy accommodated itself to the realities of the day. This fact, along with his silence on Negro suffrage, won wide acceptance for Washington's views among most whites and blacks who now looked to the future with hope. Primary and secondary sources; biblio. D. C. Neal

1150. Dann, Martin. BLACK POPULISM: A STUDY OF THE COLORED FARMERS' ALLIANCE THROUGH 1891. *J. of Ethnic Studies* 1974 2(3): 58-71. Describes the efforts of post-Civil War blacks to break the deadlock of oppression and exploitation by organized action. The Colored Farmers' Alliance may have evolved out of secret rural societies, some of them founded by Knights of Labor organizers sent South during the 1880's. Reviews the career of Colonel R. M. Humphrey, and the spread of the Alliance from Texas into South Carolina under T. E. Pratt of Cheraw, and to Virginia under C. W. Macune. The turning point for the CFA came between the Ocala Convention and the Cincinnati Conference, when fears of whites increased in the face of cotton pickers' strikes and CFA support for a third political party. The failure of Humphrey's general strike call of September 1891 discredited the militant wing of the Alliance and brought on direct confrontation with the White Alliance which generally encouraged the brutal repression of black labor agitation, forgetting the political expediency which had originally produced limited support for black agrarianism. Based on primary news accounts, periodicals, secondary works; 43 notes. G. J. Bobango

1151. Delatte, Carolyn E. THE ST. LANDRY RIOT: A FORGOTTEN INCIDENT OF RECONSTRUCTION VIOLENCE. *Louisiana Hist.* 1976 17(1): 41-49. A riot of major proportions in St. Landry in 1868 resulted in weeks of unprecedented brutality. A majority of voters rejected the Radical constitution since the Republican Party had no roots in the parish. A small group of white radicals in St. Landry provided effective leadership for the large Negro population. "The entire white population joined ranks to insure Negro subordination." 36 notes. E. P. Stickney

1152. Drago, Edmund L. THE BLACK PRESS AND POPULISM, 1890-1896. *San Jose Studies* 1975 1(1): 97-103. Black newspapers between 1890 and 1896 were almost unanimous in their support of the Republican Party and condemnation of populism. S

1153. Elder, Arlene A. CHESNUTT ON WASHINGTON: AN ESSENTIAL AMBIVALENCE. *Phylon* 1977 38(1): 1-8. Writer Charles

W. Chesnutt's views about race relations in the United States differed from those of his black contemporary Booker T. Washington, but his public statements indicated an ambivalence about Washington and his teachings. This was because of Chesnutt's friendship with Washington and because of an original optimism about race relations. As the years progressed Chesnutt became more dissatisfied with racial conditions in the United States and with Washington's political style. Although they approached the political issues in different ways "each was essentially optimistic about an eventual solution to America's racial problems." Covers the period 1880-1915. Primary and secondary sources; 15 notes.
B. A. Glasrud

1154. Farley, Ena L. THE DENIAL OF BLACK EQUALITY UNDER THE STATES RIGHTS DICTUM: NEW YORK, 1865 TO 1873. *Afro-Americans in New York Life and Hist. 1977 1(1): 9-24.* Examines the constitutional debate over states' rights which emerged in the press, 1865-73, the nebulous focus of the states' power over blacks which led to frustration of any hope for black equality, and finally, the triumph of states' rights over federal protection. 51 notes.

1155. Fierce, Milfred C. BLACK STRUGGLE FOR LAND DURING RECONSTRUCTION. *Black Scholar 1974 5(5): 13-18.* Lack of land ownership and failure of land reform during Reconstruction has resulted in a century of economic dependence for Negroes. S

1156. Foner, Philip S. THE BATTLE TO END DISCRIMINATION AGAINST NEGROES ON PHILADELPHIA STREETCARS: BACKGROUND AND BEGINNING OF THE BATTLE. *Pennsylvania Hist. 1973 40(3): 261-292, (4): 355-379.* Part I. Discusses the first stages of the efforts to end discrimination on Philadelphia streetcars. Of the 19 street railways, 11 refused to permit blacks to enter their cars; the others permitted them to ride on the front platforms of the cars. Court challenges and petitions signed by blacks and whites led some companies to run separate cars for blacks. Two companies ended discrimination in 1864. William Still, a black merchant and abolitionist, led efforts to force other companies to do the same. Based on newspapers; 2 illus., 58 notes. Part II. In 1865 Senator Morrow B. Lowry of Erie and Crawford Counties led the fight to end segregation on Philadelphia streetcars. After two years his measure passed because the legislators knew that blacks would soon have the vote. Black organizations, particularly the State Equal Rights League, played decisive roles in winning passage of the law. Discusses the hostile attitude of most Philadelphians and the divisions within black ranks. Based largely on newspapers; illus., 51 notes.
D. C. Swift

1157. Foner, Philip S. BLACK PARTICIPATION IN THE CENTENNIAL OF 1876. *Negro Hist. Bull. 1976 39(2): 533-537.* Frederick Douglass, the nation's greatest orator, was invited to appear with dignitaries such as President Grant at the opening of the 1876 Centennial Exhibition in Philadelphia, but he barely passed the security forces at the platform. Although he was not invited to speak, his participation was greater than the general black involvement in the Centennial Celebrations. Negroes were eager to participate and to celebrate their emancipation, but their exhibition plans were discouraged. The author details their exclusion and quotes critical Centennial orations delivered by blacks throughout the country, who were still "invisible men" 100 years after American independence. Based on contemporary periodicals and other sources; 49 notes.
W. R. Hively

1158. Foner, Philip S. CAROLINE HOLLINGSWORTH PEMBERTON: PHILADELPHIA SOCIALIST CHAMPION OF BLACK EQUALITY. *Pennsylvania Hist. 1976 43(3): 227-251.* Caroline Hollingsworth Pemberton, descended from an old Quaker family and niece of Confederate General John C. Pemberton, wrote two novels and a number of letters to newspapers in favor of black equality. Her novels were *Your Little Brother James* (1896) and *Stephen the Black* (1899). She was particularly effective in defending black educational efforts and in attacking lynching, sharecropping, the hypocrisy of northern philanthropists, and derogatory assessments of the capabilities of Negroes. Late in 1901 she became a Socialist, and was assistant secretary of the Pennsylvania state committee of the Socialist Party. Pemberton attempted to combat inaccurate historical views of the black experience and segregationist attitudes that existed within Socialist ranks. After 1903 she no longer wrote for the Socialist press nor participated in party activities. Illus., 52 notes.
D. C. Swift

1159. Franklin, John Hope. THE ENFORCEMENT OF THE CIVIL RIGHTS ACT OF 1875. *Prologue 1974 6(4): 225-235.* Surveys evidence of negligence in the enforcement of the act from its inception in 1875 until the Supreme Court declared it unconstitutional in 1883. Paramount was the "lukewarm-to-indifferent attitude of the federal officials toward the Civil Rights Act." Respect for it was largely destroyed by adverse decisions by lower courts and the six-year delay by the Supreme Court in rendering a final decision. It had already "become a casualty in the war waged by white supremacists." 63 notes.
R. V. Ritter

1160. Fraser, Walter J., Jr. BLACK RECONSTRUCTIONISTS IN TENNESSEE. *Tennessee Hist. Q. 1975 34(4): 362-382.* Identifies and traces the careers of West Tennessee black activists during Reconstruction. Nine Negroes worked in a loose alliance with the Radical, white-led political machine centered in Shelby County. The frequent collapse of this alliance resulted from the blacks' belief that their white friends were more interested in them during elections than after the elections had been won. Primary and secondary sources; 59 notes.
M. B. Lucas

1161. Friedman, Lawrence J. LIFE "IN THE LION'S MOUTH": ANOTHER LOOK AT BOOKER T. WASHINGTON. *J. of Negro Hist. 1974 59(4): 337-351.* Examines the failure of the recent historians and biographers of Booker T. Washington to understand the black leader's constantly changing tactics and rhetoric, which were the result of increasing racist pressures and racial self-hate among faltering black leaders elsewhere. Based on primary sources in the Library of Congress and secondary sources; 64 notes.
N. G. Sapper

1162. Fuke, Richard Paul. A REFORM MENTALITY: FEDERAL POLICY TOWARD BLACK MARYLANDERS, 1864-1868. *Civil War Hist. 1976 22(3): 214-235.* Uses Maryland as a case study to dispute the revisionist thesis that Federal officers in the South during the Civil War and Reconstruction were opposed to bettering conditions of blacks. While admitting that government officials did not believe in racial equality, argues that they did initiate reforms that improved the former slaves' condition. By promoting black ownership of property, black civil rights, and black education, and by suppressing the apprenticeship system for black youth, the Army and Freedmen's Bureau contributed to elevating the status of the freedmen.
E. C. Murdock

1163. Gaboury, William J. GEORGE WASHINGTON MURRAY AND THE FIGHT FOR POLITICAL DEMOCRACY IN SOUTH CAROLINA. *J. of Negro Hist. 1977 62(3): 258-269.* George Washington Murray, a former slave, represented the Seventh District of South Carolina as a Republican congressman during 1893-97. Contrary to most accounts, his major political contribution was a determined struggle against the white Democrats bent upon the destruction of Negro suffrage in South Carolina. One of the first victims of the resurgent white Democrats was Congressman Murray. Primary and secondary sources; 64 notes.
N. G. Sapper

1164. Gaither, Gerald H. THE NEGRO ALLIANCE MOVEMENT IN TENNESSEE, 1888-1891. *West Tennessee Hist. Soc. Papers 1973 (27): 50-62.* Paternalism and self-interest exhibited toward black members of the national alliance movement (through the Tennessee Colored Farmers' Alliance) indicates that no racial solidarity occurred and that black participation was welcomed only peripherally as long as white economic well-being was not threatened.

1165. Gammon, Tim. BLACK FREEDMEN AND THE CHEROKEE NATION. *J. of Am. Studies [Great Britain] 1977 11(3): 357-364.* From the inception of the Cherokee Nation in 1839, the Cherokees and other Indians practiced racism against Negroes. Blacks were enslaved and, after 1866, discriminations against the Negro freedmen were practiced despite constitutional and treaty provisions to the contrary. James Milton Turner (1840-1915), a Negro lawyer from Missouri and sometime American Consul General in Liberia, challenged the restrictions successfully. In 1888, the US Congress indemnified the victims of racism. Government documents and secondary sources; 28 notes.
H. T. Lovin

1166. Gravely, William B., ed. A BLACK METHODIST ON RECONSTRUCTION IN MISSISSIPPI: THREE LETTERS BY JAMES LYNCH IN 1868-1869. *Methodist Hist. 1973 11(4): 2-18.* Reprints

three letters of 1868-69 in the Matthew Simpson Papers at the Library of Congress from James Lynch (1839-72), black minister of the Methodist Episcopal Church, to Bishop Matthew Simpson (1811-84). Lynch discussed the need to extend the work of the Methodist Episcopal Church in Mississippi during Reconstruction, the need for educational facilities for blacks, and his own political and preaching career. The editor provides biographical data on Lynch and information on the activities of the Methodist Episcopal churches in the South after the Civil War. Based on Methodist periodicals; 46 notes.
H. L. Calkin

1167. Heath, Robert L. A TIME FOR SILENCE: BOOKER T. WASHINGTON IN ATLANTA. *Q. J. of Speech 1978 64(4): 385-399.* In his Atlanta Exposition Address in 1895, Booker T. Washington (1856-1915) was conciliatory and accomomodating about race relations. His statements were appreciatively received by southern whites fearful of black resentment against post-Reconstruction segregation. Under the circumstances Washington should have refused to speak at all, because silence may be the only rhetorically effective course when conditions preclude argument. Primary and secondary sources; 74 notes.
E. Bailey

1168. Hennesey, Melinda Meek. RACE AND VIOLENCE IN RECONSTRUCTION NEW ORLEANS: THE 1868 RIOT. *Louisiana Hist. 1979 20(1): 77-92.* The New Orleans race riot, September-October 1868, grew out of efforts by white Democrats to reduce the Republican vote in New Orleans in the upcoming presidential election and to emasculate the recently created Metropolitan Police Force, one-third of whom were black. The worst phase of the violence began on the evening of 24 October 1868 in a clash between white Democratic and black Republican marching clubs, during their processions on Canal Street. During the next few nights Negroes indiscriminately attacked whites on the streets, and whites retaliated by ransacking the homes and businesses of black political leaders and relieving black citizens of their registration certificates. The crisis was defused when General Jame Steedman agreed to assume command of the Metropolitan Police Force. The result was 6-7 white deaths, at least 13 black deaths, and an overwhelming Democratic majority in the November election. Primary and secondary sources; 43 notes.
L. N. Powell

1169. Hine, William C. THE 1867 CHARLESTON STREETCAR SIT-INS, A CASE OF SUCCESSFUL BLACK PROTEST. *South Carolina Hist. Mag. 1976 77(2): 110-114.* Passage of the Military Reconstruction Act of 1867, fostered rising expectations among Negroes. In 1867, Blacks used sit-ins to protest their exclusion from the Charleston City Railway Company. While white Republicans cautioned against violence, the demonstrations and federal pressure forced the company to back down and open its cars to blacks. The policy did not change until the 20th century. Primary sources; 25 notes.
R. H. Tomlinson

1170. Holland, Antonio F. and Kremer, Gary R., eds. SOME ASPECTS OF BLACK EDUCATION IN RECONSTRUCTION MISSOURI: AN ADDRESS BY RICHARD B. FOSTER. *Missouri Hist. Rev. 1976 70(2): 184-198.* In 1933 Carter Woodson said whites no longer served a useful function in the education of blacks. Writing in 1970, Henry Bullock said the same, but both authors had also been quick to point out that there was a time after the Civil War when many sincere whites had gone south to establish schools for blacks. One of these was Richard B. Foster. Asked by the men of the 62 and 65 colored regiments to help them form a school, Foster came to Missouri in 1866 with the funds contributed by the soldiers themselves. Foster helped establish Lincoln University in Jefferson City. In this speech before the State Teachers' Association in St. Louis on 17 May 1869 Foster provided valuable insight into problems he faced in Jefferson City and the problems faced by black students in general in Missouri during this period. Based on primary and secondary sources; illus., 21 notes.
W. F. Zornow

1171. Holmes, William F. THE ARKANSAS COTTON PICKERS STRIKE OF 1891 AND THE DEMISE OF THE COLORED FARMERS' ALLIANCE. *Arkansas Hist. Q. 1973 32(2): 107-119.*

1172. Holmes, William F. THE DEMISE OF THE COLORED FARMERS' ALLIANCE. *J. of Southern Hist. 1975 41(2): 187-200.* The Colored Farmers' Alliance urged hard work, sacrifice, land ownership, and other typical farm positions to improve the lot of the Negro farmer. The Alliance spread throughout the South, during the 1880's-90's but failed because of racism, competition with other farm organizations, and divisiveness in its own leadership. A Cotton Pickers' League was formed and called a strike for higher wages. The strike failed, but whites equated it with the Alliance. Alliance members were farmers, and therefore hardly supporters of the strike. This position cost the Alliance support in Negro areas and it consequently faded away. 52 notes.
V. L. Human

1173. Holzhueter, John O. EZEKIEL GILLESPIE, LOST AND FOUND. *Wisconsin Mag. of Hist. 1977 60(3): 178-184.* Ezekiel Gillespie, a black resident of Milwaukee, unsuccessfully attempted to vote in the gubernatorial election of 1865. Ultimately he was vindicated by the state supreme court which ruled in *Gillespie* v. *Palmer* (1866) that blacks had been eligible to vote since the passage of a suffrage referendum in 1849. Photo, 19 notes.
N. C. Burckel

1174. Hornsby, Alton, Jr. THE FREEDMEN'S BUREAU SCHOOLS IN TEXAS, 1865-1870. *Southwestern Hist. Q. 1973 76(4): 397-417.* Massive Negro illiteracy, lack of a public school system in the state, prejudice against educating former slaves, and paucity of teachers were overcome by the Freedmen's Bureau in Texas, 1865-70. The bureau brought order out of chaos, reduced the illiteracy rate, and prepared for a smooth transition to state-supported schools for blacks. 63 notes.
D. L. Smith

1175. Hosmer, John H. and Fineman, Joseph. BLACK CONGRESSMEN IN RECONSTRUCTION HISTORIOGRAPHY. *Phylon 1978 39(2): 97-107.* Historians' treatment of the careers of black congressmen during Reconstruction has tended to reflect present needs rather than an objective assessment. Black writers of the 19th and early 20th centuries, if they dealt at all with these 16 senators and representatives, tended to magnify and romanticize their roles; southern white historians usually stressed their inexperience and corruption. More recently, the trend has been towards a patronizing exaggeration of the effectiveness of the black congressmen. The record suggests that black congressmen were politically impotent, accomplished little, and in general followed the leadership of white Republicans. Whether due to the legacy of slavery, white racialist attitudes, or political pressures from home constituents, this ineffectiveness remains a fact that cannot be wished away. 53 notes.
J. C. Billigmeier

1176. Howard, Victor B. THE KENTUCKY PRESS AND THE NEGRO TESTIMONY CONTROVERSY, 1866-1872. *Register of the Kentucky Hist. Soc. 1973 71(1): 29-50.* The press played a substantial role in Kentucky, after the Civil War, on deciding the right of blacks to testify in court. Despite the 13th Amendment, slave codes remained on the books in many states. The Freedmen's Bureau exerted pressure for repeal of Kentucky's slave codes and was bitterly denounced by the Democratic press. Early in 1866, all legal restrictions were removed except the provision prohibiting black testimony against whites. In April 1866, the Civil Rights Bill reversed this, but attacks from the press continued and in 1867 the Kentucky Court of Appeals declared the bill inoperative. Generally, the rural press attacked black testimony while the Louisville *Courier-Journal* was the strongest voice for it. In 1871, the issue was central to state elections, and the election of a Democratic governor led to adoption of a new law of evidence in 1872. Based on newspapers and primary sources; 91 notes.
J. F. Paul

1177. Howard, Victor B. NEGRO POLITICS AND THE SUFFRAGE QUESTION IN KENTUCKY, 1866-1872. *Register of the Kentucky Hist. Soc. 1974 72(2): 111-133.* Traces efforts to secure support for black suffrage, 1865-70, and efforts by both major parties thereafter to use or abuse black franchise. Gives Republicans the most credit for their freedom and enfranchisement. By 1872 Republican Party preference among black voters in Kentucky was ended. By 1882, the black vote was divided. Based on primary and secondary sources; 91 notes.
J. F. Paul

1178. Howard, Victor B. THE STRUGGLE FOR EQUAL EDUCATION IN KENTUCKY, 1866-1884. *J. of Negro Educ. 1977 46(3): 305-328.* Documents the efforts of blacks and whites in Kentucky to secure education for black children. State funding for black schools was eventually brought into parity with white schools, but legal precedents were established to assure segregation. Primary (including archival) and secondary sources; 94 notes. — R. E. Butchart

1179. Hudson, Gossie Harold. TWO VIGNETTES OF THE EARLY DEVELOPMENT AND HISTORY OF LINCOLN UNIVERSITY. *Crisis 1977 84(7): 367-368.* James Milton Turner, a black veteran of the Civil War, championed the cause of black education in Missouri. His collections of money resulted in a school in Jefferson City, Missouri, which became Lincoln University. The first black institution west of the Mississippi was financed by the Missouri legislature, the 62nd and 65th Colored Infantry, and private individuals. One early teacher, Lizzie A. Lindsay, wrote a blistering essay on the passage of a civil rights bill in 1875. The school was born in the tradition of black freedom in America.
— A. G. Belles

1180. Hulm, Richard L. THE FREEDMEN'S BUREAU AND THE FREEDMAN'S VOTE IN THE RECONSTRUCTION OF SOUTHERN ALABAMA: AN ACCOUNT BY AGENT SAMUEL S. GARDNER. *Alabama Hist. Q. 1975 37(3): 217-224.* Past historical treatment of the agents of the Freedmen's Bureau have not been complimentary. Reproduces a letter by an agent, Samuel S. Gardner, of 23 July 1867. This letter gives a more objective view of how the agents saw their work. 15 notes.
— E. E. Eminhizer

1181. Hurst, Marsha. INTEGRATION, FREEDOM OF CHOICE AND COMMUNITY CONTROL IN NINETEENTH CENTURY BROOKLYN. *J. of Ethnic Studies 1975 3(3): 33-55.* Educational politics in Brooklyn in the last decades of the 19th century was characterized by conflict between educational professionals "under the banner of progressivism," and those opposing centralization in favor of retaining the community-oriented, traditional, local committee system. The outcome meant either integration and phasing out of the "colored schools" which would reduce black political input to nothing on the Board of Education, or retaining the segregated schools with only token recognition on the board anyway. Little meaningful choice remained for Brooklyn's Negroes. The struggle carried into the black community as the small black bourgeoisie sided with the integrationists. School Board politics of the 1890's were closely related, and the Consolidation Bill of 1896 failed to institute borough autonomy for Brooklyn or the local committees. Progressives and reformers finally won out, which meant a significant loss of political and educational input for blacks, who were seen by the progressive centralizers as poor tenement folk deserving sympathy but not political influence, and tokenism remained the rule for black appointments. Based on Board Proceedings, newspapers, and secondary works; 58 notes.
— G. J. Bobango

1182. Jackson, W. Sherman. EMANCIPATION, NEGROPHOBIA, AND CIVIL WAR POLITICS IN OHIO, 1863-1865. *J. of Negro Hist. 1980 65(3): 250-260.* From the outset of the Civil War, Ohio Democrats conducted blatantly racist campaigns against the war, emancipation, black in-migration, and northern Republican politicians such as Abraham Lincoln. Ohioans were unwilling to grant equality to blacks. Unionist victories at the polls did not symbolize the opposite. Ohio Republicans were as strong in opposition to black progress. Negrophobia remained a rallying point in Ohio politics even after the war.
— A. G. Belles

1183. James, Felix. DECLINE AND FALL OF FREEDMEN'S VILLAGE IN ARLINGTON, VIRGINIA. *Negro Hist. Bull. 1974 37(3): 247-250.* From the termination of the Freedmen's Bureau in 1872 to 1900, whites in Arlington worked to evict blacks who had purchased land and established a community at Freedmen's Village during Reconstruction.

1184. Johnsen, Leigh Dana. EQUAL RIGHTS AND THE "HEATHEN 'CHINEE' ": BLACK ACTIVISM IN SAN FRANCISCO, 1865-1875. *Western Hist. Q. 1980 11(1): 57-68.* During Reconstruction, California's blacks, particularly those in San Francisco, pursued such American values as enfranchisement, equal education, and economic advancement. Circumstances which seemed to keep the blacks from making as much progress as they had hoped did not affect San Francisco's Chinese in the same way; and black leaders failed to form a common cause with the Chinese, whom they regarded as political, social, and economic threats and "alien corruptors of America's values." The blacks' hostility toward their Chinese neighbors was similar to that which whites often directed toward blacks and Orientals. Table, 51 notes.
— D. L. Smith

1185. Jones, Allen W. THE BLACK PRESS IN THE "NEW SOUTH": JESSE C. DUKE'S STRUGGLE FOR JUSTICE AND EQUALITY. *J. of Negro Hist. 1979 64(3): 215-228.* One of the most politically active and outspoken black editors in Alabama during the 1880's was Jesse C. Duke, founder of the Montgomery *Herald* in 1886. Duke's interest in politics was continuous and his loyalty to the Republican Party never faltered. The courageous stance of his editorials led to his departure from Alabama in fear for his life; he never returned. Based on the Booker T. Washington Papers in the Library of Congress and on the black press of Alabama; 81 notes.
— N. G. Sapper

1186. Jones, Allen W. THE ROLE OF TUSKEGEE INSTITUTE IN THE EDUCATION OF BLACK FARMERS. *J. of Negro Hist. 1975 60(2): 252-267.* Discusses the role of Booker T. Washington as a leader of the rural life activities of black people. Washington and the agriculture faculty of Tuskegee Institute educated and influenced black farmers with the Annual Negro Conferences, the Tuskegee Experiment Station, the Agricultural Short Course, the Farmers' Institutes, the Farmers' County Fairs, the Movable School, and the numerous newspapers and other publications. Based on primary materials in both the Library of Congress and the Tuskegee Institute Archives; 48 notes.
— N. G. Sapper

1187. Kann, Kenneth. THE KNIGHTS OF LABOR AND THE SOUTHERN BLACK WORKER. *Labor Hist. 1977 18(1): 49-70.* Surveys attempts 1880-87 by the Knights of Labor to organize southern blacks into unions. The racial issue was divisive, but the Knights demonstrated that southern workers of both races could be united on common interests and goals. Based on reports of the Knights of Labor and newspapers; 60 notes.
— L. L. Athey

1188. Kaushik, R. P. THE ISSUE OF POLITICAL RIGHTS OF THE BLACKS: THE FORMATIVE PERIOD, 1865-1877. *Indian J. of Am. Studies [India] 1980 10(1): 58-64.* Examines some historiographical aspects of the political rights that the 13th, 14th, and 15th Constitutional Amendments conferred on newly freed black slaves. The historian cannot reach an absolute conclusion in assessing the motives of the politicians who passed these amendments, yet the provisions of the 14th and 15th Amendments remained practically in abeyance after they had been passed. Secondary sources; 20 notes.
— L. V. Eid

1189. Kelley, Don Quinn. IDEOLOGY AND EDUCATION: UPLIFTING THE MASSES IN NINETEENTH CENTURY ALABAMA. *Phylon 1979 40(2): 147-158.* Discusses education for blacks in Alabama, 1870's-90's, detailing black frustrations, disappointments, and the success of industrial training schools run by blacks for blacks, such as Booker T. Washington's Tuskegee Institute. 41 notes.
— G. R. Schroeder

1190. Kimball, Philip Clyde. FREEDOM'S HARVEST: FREEDMEN'S SCHOOLS IN KENTUCKY AFTER THE CIVIL WAR. *Filson Club Hist. Q. 1980 54(3): 272-288.* Discusses the successful efforts of Thomas Noble and the Freedmen's Bureau to create a school system for Negroes in Kentucky. Despite the hostility of white mobs, the poor training of some teachers, and little local or state tax support, the black school system grew rapidly in 1868 and 1869. By the latter year, it had reached equality with the white school system. Although federal funding ended in 1870, black schools multiplied until full state funding was assured in 1882. Based on printed and manuscript sources in the Freedmen's Bureau collection at the National Archives; 97 notes.
— G. B. McKinney

1191. King, John L., Jr. THE FREEDMEN'S SAVINGS BANK IN ALABAMA. *Potomac Rev. 1976 7(2): 24-35.* The Freedmen's Savings Bank was established in 1865 to provide ex-slaves with the opportunity to deposit money in a reliable financial institution. An examination of the Alabama branches suggests, however, that embezzlement and mismanagement were fairly typical throughout the South. When the Bank finally terminated operations in 1874, Alabama depositors had lost more than $150,000. In spite of this, "the Freedmen's Bank apparently succeeded in instilling into many Negroes the ideal of business enterprise." 29 notes.
— M. R. Yerburgh

1192. Klingman, Peter D. JOSIAH T. WALLS AND BLACK TACTICS OF RACE IN POST CIVIL WAR FLORIDA. *Negro Hist. Bull.* *1974 37(3): 242-246.* Examines the political attitudes of the Republican Party and Josiah T. Walls, a black Florida member of the House of Representatives, during and after Reconstruction, 1867-85.

1193. Kousser, J. Morgan. A BLACK PROTEST IN THE "ERA OF ACCOMMODATION." *Arkansas Hist. Q. 1975 34(2): 149-178.* Southern Negroes, including those in Arkansas, strongly protested against proposed Jim Crow laws during the 1890's. The response of Arkansas black leadership to impending segregation laws reflects a mood different from the overtly accommodating reaction of certain national figures. Excerpts from newspaper accounts and speeches of the state's black leaders document these local attitudes. Based on primary and secondary sources; 22 notes.
T. L. Savitt

1194. Kousser, J. Morgan. SEPARATE BUT *NOT* EQUAL: THE SUPREME COURT'S FIRST DECISION ON RACIAL DISCRIMINATION IN SCHOOLS. *J. of Southern Hist. 1980 46(1): 17-44.* Despite Supreme Court Justice John Marshall Harlan's reputation for liberal opinions in Negro rights cases, in *Joseph W. Cumming, James S. Harper and John Ladeveze* v. *School Board of Richmond County, Ga.* (US, 1899), he wrote for a unanimous court that state-supported education remained under state authority. With blacks thus discouraged from seeking redress in federal courts, places such as Augusta, Georgia, offered half-day sessions for black elementary students and suspended the black high school "temporarily" for 40 years. Based on MSS. and printed primary and secondary sources; 2 tables, 63 notes.
T. D. Schoonover

1195. Kremer, Gary R. BACKGROUND TO APOSTASY: JAMES MILTON TURNER AND THE REPUBLICAN PARTY. *Missouri Hist. Rev. 1976 71(1): 59-75.* James Milton Turner, who served as minister to Liberia for seven years, looked to the Radical Republicans for financial and political support of black education and suffrage. He did not identify with those who regarded blacks as oppressed; rather, he believed that the Republicans would soon rectify whatever injustices existed. After returning from Liberia in 1877, Turner found his bid for election to the House of Representatives in 1878 blocked on racial grounds. The disillusioned Turner concluded that the party of General Grant was insincere in its dealings with blacks. Based on primary and secondary sources; illus., 34 notes.
W. F. Zornow

1196. Kremm, Thomas W. and Neal, Diane. CHALLENGES TO SUBORDINATION: ORGANIZED BLACK AGRICULTURAL PROTEST IN SOUTH CAROLINA, 1886-1895. *South Atlantic Q. 1978 77(1): 98-112.* In spite of their hopeless situation, during 1886-95 black agricultural laborers in South Carolina attempted to improve their economic position by organizing to plan boycotts and strikes. These actions were not isolated or unique to the Palmetto State, but were a part of a much larger black protest movement of the late 19th century. Although unsuccessful, these efforts were significant and afford an excellent insight into race relations in the rural South and the methods employed by blacks to improve their declining position in society. Newspaper accounts; 31 notes.
H. M. Parker, Jr.

1197. Kremm, Thomas W. and Neal, Diane. CLANDESTINE BLACK LABOR SOCIETIES AND WHITE FEAR: HIRAM F. HOOVER AND THE "COOPERATIVE WORKERS OF AMERICA" IN THE SOUTH. *Labor Hist. 1978 19(2): 226-237.* Hiram F. Hoover, a white northerner and former member of the Knights of Labor, attempted to form a clandestine society, the Cooperative Workers of America, in South Carolina and Georgia during 1886-87. Local residents responded violently; Hoover was shot and the CWA was crushed. Although a reform group, the CWA was perceived as revolutionary. Based on local newspapers; 24 notes.
L. L. Athey

1198. Kress, Sylvia H. WILL THE FREEDMEN WORK? WHITE ALABAMIANS ADJUST TO FREE BLACK LABOR. *Alabama Hist. Q. 1974 36(2): 151-163.* "Will the freedman work?" was a central question in the South following the end of the Civil War. There was concern in Alabama when many freedmen refused to go back to the plantations in the spring of 1865. Rumors of free land kept men idle until early 1866, when no division of land was made. Paying freed laborers and keeping them until after the harvest was difficult. Hard money was scarce. What developed in Alabama and much of the rest of the South was a system of share-cropping. This became the pattern of economic arrangement between former slave and former master. The new system was in full operation by 1867. 35 notes.
E. E. Eminhizer

1199. Krug, Mark M. LINCOLN, THE REPUBLICAN PARTY AND THE EMANCIPATION PROCLAMATION. *Hist. Teacher 1973 7(1): 48-61.* The Emancipation Proclamation was a turning point in the Civil War because it made slavery a central issue. Lincoln had a long record of criticizing slavery, and he wished to see it abolished. He was not forced to issue the proclamation by the Radicals; rather, he issued it to help the military situation and to right a moral wrong. The proclamation was endorsed by all factions of the Republican Party. Based on primary and secondary sources; 49 notes.
P. W. Kennedy

1200. Ledbetter, Billy D. WHITE TEXANS' ATTITUDES TOWARD THE POLITICAL EQUALITY OF NEGROES, 1865-1870. *Phylon 1979 40(3): 253-263.* White Texans resisted political equality for Negroes as long as possible because it would mean a rise in black social status as well. They finally allowed political equality in order to be readmitted to the Union, but planned to eliminate as many Negro rights as possible by state law as soon as Texas returned to the Union. 22 notes.
G. R. Schroeder

1201. Lewis, Ronald L. RACE AND THE UNITED MINE WORKERS' UNION IN TENNESSEE: SELECTED LETTERS OF WILLIAM R. RILEY, 1892-1895. *Tennessee Hist. Q. 1977 36(4): 524-536.* William R. Riley emerged during 1892-95 as a black labor leader in Tennessee. He understood the delicate position of blacks in the southern labor market and spoke pointedly in their behalf through letters to the *United Mine Workers' Journal.* Primary and secondary sources; 26 notes.
M. B. Lucas

1202. Libby, Billy W. SENATOR HIRAM REVELS OF MISSISSIPPI TAKES HIS SEAT, JANUARY-FEBRUARY, 1870. *J. of Mississippi Hist. 1975 37(4): 381-394.* Describes the reactions of the press, some US Senators, and others in 1870 to the news that the Mississippi legislature had elected a Negro, Hiram Revels, to the US Senate. After a three-day debate the Senate agreed to seat him by a vote of 48 to 8. Based on newspapers and the *Congressional Globe;* 21 notes.
J. W. Hillje

1203. Littlefield, Daniel F., Jr. and McGraw, Patricia Washington. *THE ARKANSAS FREEMAN,* 1869-1870: BIRTH OF THE BLACK PRESS IN ARKANSAS. *Phylon 1979 40(1): 75-85.* The *Arkansas Freeman* of Little Rock (1869-70) was the first black newspaper in Arkansas after the Civil War. Its editor, the Reverend Tabbs Gross, running a paper for black Republicans, supported universal suffrage and opposed the radical Republicans. Consequently, he was supported by the conservative *Daily Arkansas Gazette* and vigorously attacked by the radical *Morning Republican,* which contributed to the early cessation of the paper. Primary sources; 30 notes.
G. R. Schroeder

1204. Littlefield, Daniel F., Jr. and Underhill, Lonnie E. BLACK DREAMS AND "FREE" HOMES: THE OKLAHOMA TERRITORY, 1891-1894. *Phylon 1973 34(4): 342-357.* An account of the Negro immigration into Oklahoma Territory under the leadership of such men as Edward Preston McCabe, who hoped to make Oklahoma into a black state.
S

1205. Logue, Cal M. RACIST REPORTING DURING RECONSTRUCTION. *J. of Black Studies 1979 9(3): 335-349.* During the South Carolina Constitutional Convention, 1867-68, the white newspapers, Charleston *Daily Courier* and Charleston *Mercury,* used racist coverage of the convention to try to undermine black political power. The *Mercury,* the more blatantly racist of the two papers, ridiculed black mistakes in speech or parliamentary procedure and condemned any black who spoke unless he endorsed continued white, conservative control of the state government. Primary sources; note.
R. G. Sherer

1206. Logue, Cal M. THE RHETORICAL APPEALS OF WHITES TO BLACKS DURING RECONSTRUCTION. *Communication Monographs 1977 44(3): 241-251.* In order to maintain authority over blacks following emancipation, white spokesmen refined two forms of rhetoric: the bribe and the threat, 1865-68.

1207. Logue, Cal M. RHETORICAL RIDICULE OF RECONSTRUCTION BLACKS. *Q. J. of Speech 1976 62(4): 400-409.* After the Civil War, conservative white southerners, in an attempt to maintain their prewar status, responded to the forced enfranchisement of blacks by initiating a campaign which used the term "nigger" to play on racist attitudes. They portrayed blacks as unintelligent and immoral barbarians who were incapable of civilized self-government. Primary and secondary sources; 90 notes. E. C. Bailey

1208. Loveland, Anne C. THE "SOUTHERN WORK" OF THE REVEREND JOSEPH C. HARTZELL, PASTOR OF AMES CHURCH IN NEW ORLEANS, 1870-1873. *Louisiana Hist. 1975 16(4): 391-407.* "Like most other Northern Methodist missionaries to the South, Hartzell saw no conflict in linking religious endeavors and Republican politics." Hartzell supervised three Methodist institutions for Negroes: Union Normal School, Thomson Institute, and the Freedmen's Orphan Home which combined educational and missionary efforts. The response of Southern Whites to the educational and missionary work of the Northern Methodists among the freedmen was generally unsympathetic. Another reason for the loss of support was the Republicans ultimately abandoned the social and political goals of Reconstruction. Based largely on correspondence from the Hartzell and Baldwin Papers. Illus., 42 notes. E. P. Stickney

1209. Lovett, Bobby L. MEMPHIS RIOTS: WHITE REACTION TO BLACKS IN MEMPHIS, MAY 1865-JULY 1866. *Tennessee Hist. Q. 1979 38(1): 9-33.* The bloody racial riots in Memphis, Tennessee, on 1-2 May 1866, were the result of demographic changes caused by the influx of large numbers of black refugees, thus creating an urban black community and new race relationships. The claim that the presence of black troops caused the riots is a myth. The results of the riot were the opposite of what the white instigators desired since the riot helped convince national and state Republicans to pass protective civil rights legislation for blacks. Primary and secondary sources; 2 illus., 49 notes.
M. B. Lucas

1210. Mabee, Carleton. LONG ISLAND'S BLACK "SCHOOL WAR" AND THE DECLINE OF SEGREGATION IN NEW YORK STATE. *New York Hist. 1977 58(4): 385-411.* The attempt by blacks in Jamaica, New York, during the 1890's to force the desegregation of the Jamaica public school system led to passage of a state law limiting, but not abolishing, school segregation. Although blacks opposed the segregation of public schools in other New York cities during the 1880's-90's, Jamaica blacks were the most militant. 3 illus., 76 notes.
R. N. Lokken

1211. Magdol, Edward. LOCAL BLACK LEADERS IN THE SOUTH, 1867-75: AN ESSAY TOWARD THE RECONSTRUCTION OF RECONSTRUCTION HISTORY. *Societas 1974 4(2): 81-110.* Discusses lower-class black leadership and the community from which that leadership emerged. Suggests substantial artisan leadership in Reconstruction black communities. Based on the 1871 congressional inquiry into the Ku Klux Klan; 5 tables, 44 notes. E. P. Stickney

1212. Maidment, Richard A. *PLESSY V. FERGUSON* RE-EXAMINED. *J. of Am. Studies [Great Britain] 1973 7(2): 125-132.* Assesses the controversy over the Supreme Court's ruling on racial segregation in the case of *Plessy vs. Ferguson* (1896). The court approved segregation by race as a matter of "judicial restraint and respect for precedent" when it ruled that a Louisiana law was not in violation of the 14th Amendment. Critics contend that the court's judgment was "mere camouflage" of the judges' segregation "policy predilections." 24 notes. H. T. Lovin

1213. Marr, William L. ON THE ECONOMICS OF LINCOLN'S PROPOSAL FOR COMPENSATED EMANCIPATION. *Am. J. of Econ. and Sociol. 1976 35(1): 105-107.* Andrew Weintraub argued (see abstract 12A:2807) that the cost to the North of compensating the Southern planter for freeing his slaves would have been greater than the costs of the Civil War to the North. Such a view, according to Marr, is overstated. The value of the marginal product and land values are just as likely to rise with the emancipation of southern slaves instead of reducing land values as Weintraub suggested. The case is not as one-sided as Weintraub indicated. P. Travis

1214. Matthews, John Michael. NEGRO REPUBLICANS IN THE RECONSTRUCTION OF GEORGIA. *Georgia Hist. Q. 1976 60(2): 145-164.* The Georgia Equal Rights Association and the Union League were forerunners of the Republican Party in Georgia. Among the Republican's problems were the split between the radical and the moderate factions and the disastrous governorship of Rufus B. Bullock during 1868-71. The Party's inability to hold the allegiance of its black supporters was a significant factor in its defeat in the 1870's. The blacks were rarely rewarded with leadership or offices by the Republicans. Many blacks ended up being manipulated by the Democrats. Primary and secondary sources; 44 notes. G. R. Schroeder

1215. Matthews, Linda M. KEEPING DOWN JIM CROW: THE RAILROADS AND THE SEPARATE COACH BILLS IN SOUTH CAROLINA. *South Atlantic Q. 1974 73(1): 117-129.* Segregation existed in the South before, during, and after Reconstruction, though legally strict racial segregation began with the first Jim Crow railroad car bill in 1898 (passed after a decade of attempted legislation). There arose a dread that the younger generation of Negroes might not know their place. There also arose a feeling of insecurity among lower-class whites that Negroes were obtaining equality with them in the labor force and the factories, thus forcing them out of jobs. The long opposition to the bill had come largely from businessmen and pro-railroad men; these economic considerations were forced into the background by the fear of competition with blacks. 34 notes. E. P. Stickney

1216. McKinney, Gordon B. SOUTHERN MOUNTAIN REPUBLICANS AND THE NEGRO, 1865-1900. *J. of Southern Hist. 1975 41(4): 493-516.* The end of the Civil War witnessed Republican efforts to build a political base in the South. Reconstruction policies strengthened the Democrats everywhere but in the mountains. Republicans sought the black vote because they needed all the votes they could get. Strengthening of anti-Negro statutes forced the Republicans to disguise their position, and gradually to forsake it. There were few Negroes in the mountains; race was not an issue. Blacks were eventually excluded from all party positions, either directly or indirectly. 3 tables, 115 notes.
V. L. Human

1217. McLaurin, Melton A. THE RACIAL POLICIES OF THE KNIGHTS OF LABOR AND THE ORGANIZATION OF SOUTHERN BLACK WORKERS. *Labor Hist. 1976 17(4): 568-585.* The Knights of Labor developed a paradoxical strategy in race relations in organizing attempts in the South. The K. of L. tried both to circumvent the race issue by emphasizing economic grievances and to solve the issues by compromising its antebellum reform heritage with southern prejudices. Although the K. of L. was the first serious attempt to organize southern blacks, racial prejudice slowly forced it to become a black union —which sounded its death knell in the South. Based on the Powderly papers and newspapers; 65 notes. L. L. Athey

1218. Messner, William F. BLACK EDUCATION IN LOUISIANA, 1863-1865. *Civil War Hist. 1976 22(1): 41-59.* Explains why the Union Army played a more central role in the education of freedmen in Louisiana than elsewhere in the South. General Nathaniel Prentiss Banks, Commander of the Department of the Gulf, was concerned primarily with establishing firm control over the freedmen and sought to do this through a closely supervised free labor system. He quickly learned, however, that the blacks desired an education above all else. Banks modified his policy and, in 1863, created a school system that was carefully monitored by the army. Economic reconstruction and political reliability both were to be served. Although the project was troubled by white opposition and inadequate financing, it worked well and proved fundamental to whatever improvement in status Louisiana blacks enjoyed in the postwar years. E. C. Murdock

1219. Messner, William F. BLACK VIOLENCE AND WHITE RESPONSE: LOUISIANA, 1862. *J. of Southern Hist. 1975 41(1): 19-38.* Incidents of black unrest and black exodus from plantations during the Civil War in southern Louisiana unleashed a widespread fear of black violence. The Union Army, under the command of Major General Benjamin Franklin Butler, established a series of policies known as contraband programs to check the threat of disorder. Contrary to national law and military orders, fugitive slaves were gathered and returned to their plantations, and only slaves whose owners had committed overtly treasonable acts were confiscated. Contraband policies changed under the influence of Brigadier General John Wolcott Phelps who used blacks as a positive element in the war effort. In July 1862, all slaves who fled to the Union lines were freed and organized into military units. A wage-labor system which placed black recruits on sugar plantations under military overseers was later established. Contraband programs, including educational programs and relief measures for the unemployed, were extended throughout the Civil War, making southern Louisiana physically secure. However, the programs had negative results in that they diminished the need felt by whites for instituting new programs during Reconstruction. The stress on firm military control discouraged the development of economic and political autonomy among freedmen. Based on letters, newspaper articles, and secondary sources; 72 notes. S

1220. Messner, William F. THE VICKSBURG CAMPAIGN OF 1862: A CASE STUDY IN THE FEDERAL UTILIZATION OF BLACK LABOR. *Louisiana Hist. 1975 16(4): 371-381.* The Vicksburg campaign of 1862 has been little noted. "But despite its paucity of military gains... the Union effort is historically interesting for it was a transitional phase in the Federal utilization of black labor in the Southwest." The Vicksburg campaign was "the final instance of the Union army engaging in the practice of systematically returning slaves to their owners." Illus., 32 notes. E. P. Stickney

1221. Montesano, Philip M. SAN FRANCISCO BLACK CHURCHES IN THE EARLY 1860'S: POLITICAL PRESSURE GROUP. *California Hist. Q. 1973 52(2): 145-152.* In the late 1850's and early 1860's the three black churches in San Francisco represented the interests of the city's black community, providing spiritual leadership, economic assistance, and aid to Freedmen. They also resisted attempts to deny California blacks their civil rights. Aided by a fledgling black press, the churches successfully campaigned for the repeal of laws forbidding blacks from testifying in court cases involving whites. The Emancipation Proclamation and the increasing preoccupation of nativists with the Chinese community helped the churches' campaign. The issue of voting rights was settled by the 15th Amendment, while other issues, such as school segregation, remained to be solved. Based on primary and secondary sources; illus., photos, 31 notes. A. Hoffman

1222. Moore, James T. BLACK MILITANCY IN READJUSTER VIRGINIA, 1879-1883. *J. of Southern Hist. 1975 41(2): 167-186.* A consideration of the role of Negroes in Virginia's Readjuster Party. The party was formed to fight Virginia's massive state debt. Negro help was sought and won, but throughout the Negroes remained independent, deserting the party when such action served their interests. Continued survival of the Readjuster Party was contingent on increasing concessions to Negro causes. The party declined shortly after its greatest state victory. Negroes had become so militant that whites deserted the party, ensuring its destruction. 77 notes. V. L. Human

1223. Myers, John B. THE ALABAMA FREEDMEN AND THE ECONOMIC ADJUSTMENTS DURING PRESIDENTIAL RECONSTRUCTION, 1865-1867. *Alabama R. 1973 26(4): 252-266.* The Bureau of Refugees, Freedmen, and Abandoned Lands began operating in Alabama under the direction of General Wager Swayne in July 1865. Relief measures (food rations, shelter, and medical care) proved inadequate, due to the poverty of the state and the burden of general economic conditions. Exploitation was controlled and freedmen's response to labor was commendable, but working conditions did not widely improve, because of racial antagonism, coercive rules, and penalties adopted by the bureau. Little abandoned land was available for blacks, and the Homestead Act of 1866 proved unworkable because most public land was unsuited to agriculture. The Freedmen's Savings Bank was a limited success where it operated, but it could not overcome contemporary difficulties. The freedmen's transition from slavery to freedom required more "sincere and sustained assistance" than was available 1865-67. Based on primary and secondary sources; 46 notes.
J. F. Vivian

1224. Nelson, Larry E. BLACK LEADERS AND THE PRESIDENTIAL ELECTION OF 1864. *J. of Negro Hist. 1978 63(1): 42-58.* The presidential campaign and election of 1864 was marked by political campaigning by Afro-American leaders. Although generally denied the vote, they spoke publicly to the central issue of the campaign: the fate of black people after the Civil War. Although the Republican Party received support as the lesser of two racist evils, the political culture of Afro-Americans had its beginnings in the election of 1864. Based on periodical literature of 1864 and secondary material; 88 notes.
N. G. Sapper

1225. Nelson, Paul David. EXPERIMENT IN INTERRACIAL EDUCATION AT BEREA COLLEGE, 1858-1908. *J. of Negro Hist. 1974 59(1): 13-27.* The interracial program of Berea College upheld the total equality of Negroes while maintaining a 50-50 ratio of black and white students, 1858-92. In the later years, William G. Frost, the newly inaugurated president of Berea, placed greater emphasis upon the educational needs of white southerners. By 1908 the interracial program had been renounced for the education of white mountain youth. Based on primary materials in the Berea College Archives and on secondary sources; 60 notes. N. G. Sapper

1226. Nieman, Donald G. ANDREW JOHNSON, THE FREEDMEN'S BUREAU AND THE PROBLEM OF EQUAL RIGHTS 1865-1866. *J. of Southern Hist. 1978 44(3): 399-420.* During late 1865 one of the newly created Freedmen's Bureau's chief concerns was providing legal protection for freedmen. Given the racism of the restored southern law enforcement and judicial officials, blacks could expect summary justice. Bureau head General Oliver O. Howard was sensitive to the threat to black legal rights in the South, but he was unwilling and unable to oppose President Andrew Johnson's plan to restore southern governments to authority as soon as possible. Johnson basically opposed and resisted the efforts of the Bureau's field agents to expand the Bureau's jurisdiction over court cases involving blacks; he thus hampered efforts to provide legal protection to the ex-slaves. Manuscript and printed primary and secondary sources; 60 notes. T. D. Schoonover

1227. Nieman, Donald G. THE FREEDMEN'S BUREAU AND THE MISSISSIPPI BLACK CODE. *J. of Mississippi Hist. 1978 40(2): 91-118.* The passage of the black code by the Mississippi legislature in November 1865 created problems for the Freedmen's Bureau, which had to aid and protect the ex-slaves. Investigates the Bureau's response to the Mississippi code, particularly its efforts to shield blacks from discriminatory state laws. Summarizes struggles between the executive, legislative, and judicial branches of the federal government over Reconstruction policy. M. S. Legan

1228. Noon, Thomas R. BLACK LUTHERANS LICENSED AND ORDAINED (1865-1889). *Concordia Hist. Inst. Q. 1977 50(2): 54-63.* During the decades following the Civil War, the Lutheran Church had to adjust to the new status of the Blacks. The approaches varied slightly from one synod to another but the general movement was toward the creation of a black Lutheran clergy which would administer to the needs of the black people. The North Carolina Synod produced the most lasting results in this endeavor. Primary sources; 32 notes.
W. T. Walker

1229. Oakes, James. A FAILURE OF VISION: THE COLLAPSE OF THE FREEDMEN'S BUREAU COURTS. *Civil War Hist. 1979 25(1): 66-76.* The limited ideological framework of General Oliver Otis Howard, Bureau Commissioner, and his aides, encouraged their attempt at radical reconstruction of southern society without essential radical legislation. They thought that the elimination of all statutory inequalities, for instance, Negro court testimony, was enough to assure protection. Southern states pretended compliance on the point to end the threat of the Freedmen's Bureau courts' system. A year after the system began, the South regained control, and equal justice was a shambles. Black Codes showed the Bureau's terrible misunderstanding of reality. The freedmen tried to continue the courts' real achievements. Unfortunately, the Bureau wore blinders of classical liberalism. Based on published Congressional documents and secondary sources; 34 notes. R. E. Stack

1230. Oates, Stephen B. "THE MAN OF OUR REDEMPTION": ABRAHAM LINCOLN AND THE EMANCIPATION OF THE SLAVES. *Presidential Studies Q. 1979 9(1): 15-25.* Abraham Lincoln's political evolution from opposition to political rights for blacks (in the fear that his own political career might be affected) to steadfast belief in emancipation and equal rights led to his Emancipation Proclamation in 1863.

1231. O'Brien, John T. RECONSTRUCTION IN RICHMOND: WHITE RESTORATION AND BLACK PROTEST, APRIL-JUNE 1865. *Virginia Mag. of Hist. and Biog. 1981 89(3): 259-281.* Analyzes black political behavior in relation to fellow resident whites and the Union army of occupation. Freedmen were somewhat prepared for social and political activism by surreptitious antebellum education, by bargaining for wages in the tobacco industry, and by participation in affairs of their churches. They achieved some success in appealing to the army against the former master class, and in turning the army to their own ends, such as by securing employment. The Freedman's Bureau and Northern philanthropists assisted. The failure of the black civil rights efforts came later. Based on published documents, National Archives records, and newspapers; 97 notes.
P. J. Woehrmann

1232. Ofari, Earl. BLACK ACTIVISTS AND 19TH CENTURY RADICALISM. *Black Scholar 1974 5(5): 19-25.* Chronicles black activism, especially in labor union organizing and socialist movements.
S

1233. Oubre, Claude F. "FORTY ACRES AND A MULE:" LOUISIANA AND THE SOUTHERN HOMESTEAD ACT. *Louisiana Hist. 1976 17(2): 143-157.* One of the tragedies of reconstruction was the failure to provide the ex-slaves with economic security, especially land. The chaotic conditions prevailing in the land offices were exemplified in Louisiana. "When homesteading interfered with economic and party interests, loyal whites chose to aid railroad companies rather than press the cause of Negro land ownership." 27 notes.
E. P. Stickney

1234. Peeps, J. M. Stephen. NORTHERN PHILANTHROPY AND THE EMERGENCE OF BLACK HIGHER EDUCATION: DO-GOODERS, COMPROMISERS, OR CO-CONSPIRATORS? *J. of Negro Educ. 1981 50(3): 251-269.* The history of white philanthropy to black higher education has two distinct phases. The missionaries who founded Southern black colleges during Reconstruction had faith in black educability and insisted on traditional liberal arts education. But the wealthy industrialists, who became the primary benefactors in the 1880's and later, betrayed racist doubts about black mental abilities and funded colleges, such as Tuskegee Institute, that rejected liberal education for Negroes in favor of industrial training. Covers 1861-1920. Secondary sources; 63 notes.
R. E. Butchart

1235. Pitre, Merline. FREDERICK DOUGLASS: THE POLITICIAN VS. THE SOCIAL REFORMER. *Phylon 1979 40(3): 270-277.* Discusses the political activities of Frederick Douglass in the Republican Party during 1870-95. He held appointive offices, including member of the Santo Domingo Commission, member of the Legislative Council, Marshal of the District of Columbia, and Recorder of Deeds. While in them, Douglass seemed to make fewer comments in favor of social reform than usual. 30 notes.
G. R. Schroeder

1236. Rabinowitz, Howard N. FROM EXCLUSION TO SEGREGATION: HEALTH AND WELFARE SERVICES FOR SOUTHERN BLACKS, 1865-1890. *Social Service R. 1974 48(3): 327-354.*

1237. Rabinowitz, Howard N. FROM EXCLUSION TO SEGREGATION: SOUTHERN RACE RELATIONS, 1865-1890. *J. of Am. Hist. 1976 63(2): 325-350.* Before the resort to widespread legal segregation around 1890, de facto segregation had replaced exclusion in southern race relations. The integration stage was largely bypassed. Radical measures helped to institutionalize this shift to segregation. Both white Republicans and Redeemers came to embrace the new segregation policies, though often for different reasons. Even the attitudes of blacks helped to assure the shift. Lack of white support, black self-respect, economic pressures, tactical emphasis on securing better "separate but equal" facilities, and the development of group identity all shaped blacks' attitudes. Based on legal records, newspapers, and other sources; 141 notes.
W. R. Hively

1238. Rabinowitz, Howard N. HALF A LOAF: THE SHIFT FROM WHITE TO BLACK TEACHERS IN THE NEGRO SCHOOLS OF THE URBAN SOUTH, 1865-1890. *J. of Southern Hist. 1974 40(4): 565-594.* Examines the transformation from white to black teachers in southern schools in the post-Civil War years, using the experiences of five southern cities to provide a cross-section: Atlanta, Georgia; Raleigh, North Carolina; Nashville, Tennessee; Montgomery, Alabama; and Richmond, Virginia. Among the problems the Redeemers confronted were such matters as the removal of northern missionary ties and teachers in order to reassert southern control of the school system, the black demand for black teachers which was often accepted since it meant cheaper teachers, and the resultant black demand for equal salary for equal work, a demand usually denied. Negroes tried to obtain better quality instruction for their children, more administrative positions, and positions on the school board, but were usually unsuccessful. Ironically, since some schools became entirely black, insistence upon black instructors made it easier for the whites to discriminate. Based on manuscripts and published primary and secondary sources; 118 notes.
T. D. Schoonover

1239. Rankin, David C. THE ORIGINS OF BLACK LEADERSHIP IN NEW ORLEANS DURING RECONSTRUCTION. *J. of Southern Hist. 1974 40(3): 417-440.* While more famous black political leaders are recognized in studies of Reconstruction, the large number of secondary black politicians receive no notice. Even the major black political figures appear as people whose life begins during the Civil War. Using quantitative methodology, focuses upon the origins of 240 black leaders of New Orleans. Profiles this leadership around such characteristics as antebellum legal status, residence, birthplace, date of birth, color, occupation, wealth, and literacy. Concludes that the black politician during Reconstruction in New Orleans was already before "the Civil War a young man of unusual ancestry, uncommon wealth, and exceptional ability," and in close contact with the most sophisticated black community in mid-19th century America. Based on manuscripts and published primary and secondary sources; 9 tables, 41 notes, appendix.
T. D. Schoonover

1240. Richardson, Fredrick. AMERICAN BAPTISTS' SOUTHERN MISSION. *Foundations 1975 18(2): 136-145.* American (Northern) Baptists began missions in the South among blacks as soon as possible following the war. The first were supported by the Freedmen's Fund. Discusses the foundation of Northern Baptist educational institutions in the South for blacks. These include Shaw University, started by Henry Tupper in 1865; Wayland Seminary, 1865; Richmond Institute, started by Nathaniel Colver, 1865; Nashville Institute, started by D. W. Phillips in 1866; Augusta Institute by William Jefferson White, 1867; Leland University by Holbrook Chamberlain, 1870; Benedict Institute, 1871; Natchez Seminary, 1877; Spelman Seminary, 1881; and Bishop College, 1881. 49 notes.
E. E. Eminhizer

1241. Richardson, Joe M. THE AMERICAN MISSIONARY ASSOCIATION AND BLACK EDUCATION IN CIVIL WAR MISSOURI. *Missouri Hist. R. 1975 69(4): 433-488.* The American Missionary Association carried on antislavery work in Missouri before the Civil War, and educational programs during and after the war. In 1862 George Candee, the first educational representative, arrived in St. Louis. Real educational work did not begin until 1863 with the arrival of J. L. Richardson. After concentrating its work in St. Louis, the A.M.A. began to expand into other areas after 1864. After the war it continued modest support in Missouri but transferred most of its activities to the South. Most of the work to educate the 115,000 Negroes in Missouri fell to the blacks themselves, the state, and other benevolent societies, but they were able to build on a foundation already laid by the A.M.A. Based on primary and secondary sources; illus., 40 notes.
W. F. Zornow

1242. Richardson, Joe M. THE FAILURE OF THE AMERICAN MISSIONARY ASSOCIATION TO EXPAND CONGREGATIONALISM AMONG SOUTHERN BLACKS. *Southern Studies 1979 18(1): 51-73.* Thousands of blacks belonged to white Christian churches before the Civil War, but by 1865 almost all belonged to solely black congregations. The American Missionary Association was founded in 1846 as an evangelical, abolitionist society, which in its first years promoted education, black suffrage, and full citizenship. Association schools held nondenominational prayer meetings and taught religion. The Association ultimately failed to attract permanent black members because of its ties to Congregationalism (which was alien to emotional black religious expression), because of its insistence on white ministers, and because of its paternalistic attitudes. Based on American Missionary Association Archives at Dillard U., New Orleans, and on primary and secondary sources; 71 notes. J. J. Buschen

1243. Richardson, Joe M. FRANCIS L. CARDOZO: BLACK EDUCATOR DURING RECONSTRUCTION. *J. of Negro Educ. 1979 48(1): 73-83.* Cardozo was a freeborn South Carolina mulatto who obtained a European education before the Civil War. In 1865 he returned to Charleston, South Carolina, to direct a school under the auspices of the American Missionary Association for the newly freed blacks. His school quickly became the premier freedmen's school of South Carolina. His strong leadership abilities led him toward politics; he left his school in 1868 to serve in the state constitutional convention, and subsequently was elected to two major state offices. 37 notes. R. E. Butchart

1244. Richardson, Joe M. TO HELP A BROTHER ON: THE FIRST DECADE OF TALLADEGA COLLEGE. *Alabama Hist. Q. 1975 37(1): 19-37.* In Alabama at the end of the Civil War the outlook for black education was not promising because of a lack of teachers and money, along with strong opposition by the white community. Discusses the founding of Talladega College and the conditions under which the faculty and students lived and worked. Food was scarce, salaries were always months behind, and housing was difficult to locate. The school was sponsored by the American Missionary Association and all expenditures had to be cleared by the slow-acting New York office. The decision to make Talladega a normal school was caused by the need for teachers. The school suffered from poor leadership until 1879 when Henry S. DeForest was made president. 55 notes. E. E. Eminhizer

1245. Richardson, Joe M. "WE ARE TRULY DOING MISSIONARY WORK": LETTERS FROM AMERICAN MISSIONARY ASSOCIATION TEACHERS IN FLORIDA, 1864-1874. *Florida Hist. Q. 1975 54(2): 178-195.* The American Missionary Association led the way in aiding Florida's 62,000 freedmen by advocating full citizenship and by establishing schools throughout the state. Although few in number, American Missionary Association teachers instructed hundreds of students and with the aid of other benevolent societies and the Florida legislature, achieved an educational system for black people. Based on the Association's archives at the Amistad Reserach Center, Dillard University; 11 letters, 22 notes. P. A. Beaber

1246. Roberson, Jere W. EDWARD P. MC CABE AND THE LANGSTON EXPERIMENT. *Chronicles of Oklahoma 1973 51(3): 343-355.* Biographical sketch of Edward P. McCabe (1850-1920), promoter of Negro migration from Kansas to Langston, Oklahoma, which he founded; emphasizes the role of frontier newspapers in the migration. S

1247. Rogers, George A. and Saunders, R. Frank, Jr. THE AMERICAN MISSIONARY ASSOCIATION IN LIBERTY COUNTY, GEORGIA: AN INVASION OF LIGHT AND LOVE. *Georgia Hist. Q. 1978 62(4): 304-315.* The American Missionary Association provided aid to freedmen in Liberty County, Georgia, after the Civil War. Under the leadership of the Reverend Floyd Snelson and other dedicated teachers, the Congregational "New" Midway Church, Dorchester Academy, and several other facilities were instrumental in the education of blacks. Primary and secondary sources; 40 notes. G. R. Schroeder

1248. Roper, John Herbert. A RECONSIDERATION: THE UNIVERSITY OF SOUTH CAROLINA DURING RECONSTRUCTION. *Pro. of the South Carolina Hist. Assoc. 1974: 46-57.* Discusses the problems faced by the University of South Carolina during Reconstruction and its attempts to provide training for black leadership between 1873 and 1877. The University changed both its curriculum and its faculty, which included professional scholars and propagandists, but the attempt failed, for only 16 individuals obtained A.B. degrees during the period. Based on private papers and secondary sources; 38 ntoes.
 J. W. Thacker, Jr.

1249. Ross, Steven Joseph. FREED SOIL, FREED LABOR, FREED MEN: JOHN EATON AND THE DAVIS BEND EXPERIMENT. *J. of Southern Hist. 1978 44(2): 213-232.* Traces the history of the Davis Bend experiment in Mississippi during the Civil War. This Republican effort was designed to test an economic framework in which the needs of the freedmen, the business community, and the nation could be met and still be acceptable to the majority in Congress. Northern-born John Eaton, Jr., was given initial responsibility for developing this radical experiment in black capitalism. He envisioned transforming the South so that independent black landowners could coexist with a modified plantation system based on wage labor. Analyzes the ultimate failure of the experiment in 1866. M. S. Legan

1250. St. Hilaire, Joseph M. THE NEGRO DELEGATES IN THE ARKANSAS CONSTITUTIONAL CONVENTION OF 1868: A GROUP PROFILE. *Arkansas Hist. Q. 1974 33(1): 38-69.*

1251. Schweninger, Loren. ALABAMA BLACKS AND THE CONGRESSIONAL RECONSTRUCTION ACTS OF 1867. *Alabama Rev. 1978 31(3): 182-198.* The Reconstruction Acts prompted Alabama blacks to organize during March-October 1867 under able, moderate leadership, most of it former slaves. There was no call for retribution against whites or for forced redistribution of white lands. Republicans and Democrats alike failed to reciprocate; both parties declined to assimilate the black cause. Primary and secondary sources; 51 notes. J. F. Vivian

1252. Schweninger, Loren. BLACK CITIZENSHIP AND THE REPUBLICAN PARTY IN RECONSTRUCTION ALABAMA. *Alabama R. 1976 29(2): 83-103.* Throughout the Reconsturction era the Republican Party in Alabama was badly divided on the question of enfranchising the freedmen. A moderate wing defended the federal government and the 14th and 15th Amendments, while a conservative wing, led in part by Judge J. Haralson, an ex-slave, opposed the Constitution, the Grant Administration, and several federal patronage appointees. Tension and conflict plagued the party, and "doomed Alabama Reconstruction to failure from the outset." Based on primary and secondary sources; 88 notes. J. F. Vivian

1253. Schweninger, Loren. JAMES RAPIER AND THE NEGRO LABOR MOVEMENT, 1869-1872. *Alabama R. 1975 28(3): 185-201.* James T. Rapier, Alabama-born black politician, was vice-president of the short-lived National Negro Labor Union and leading founder of the Labor Union of Alabama. He sought creation of a federal land bureau in the interests of freedmen and reform of the public school system, but opposed westward migration as a solution to the plight of blacks. White resistance and Republican indifference precluded any favorable results. As a congressman (1872-75), he hoped for a political solution to black grievances and supported the Civil Rights Act of 1875. Based on primary and secondary sources, including the Rapier papers at Howard Univ.; 43 notes. J. F. Vivian

1254. Seraile, William. AFRO-AMERICAN EMIGRATION TO HAITI DURING THE AMERICAN CIVIL WAR. *Americas (Acad. of Am. Franciscan Hist.) 1978 35(2): 185-200.* The movement to promote black emigratrion to Haiti beginning in 1860 and during the Civil War brought about 2500 would-be settlers to Haiti but proved largely unsuccessful because of lack of resources, Haitian official inefficiency, and opposition from other black Americans; by 1864, the movement had petered out. Based on the papers of emigration promoter James Redpath in the Schomburgh Collection, New York Public Library, contemporary press, and other printed materials; 55 notes. D. Bushnell

1255. Seraile, William. THE STRUGGLE TO RAISE BLACK REGIMENTS IN NEW YORK STATE, 1861-1864. *New York Hist. Soc. Q. 1974 58(3): 215-233.* Before the end of hostilities there were three black regiments from New York, totalling over 4,000 soldiers, which saw action during the Civil War. These units had a higher casualty rate than the white regiments. Yet, initially because of opposition from Washington, and later from Governor Horatio Seymour, great difficulty was experienced in getting permission to raise the regiments. Not until February 1864 was the first, the 20th Regiment, mustered in. Only through the efforts of many influential whites in the Association for Promoting Colored Volunteers and the Union League, and through the willingness of blacks to volunteer in the face of much white opposition, did the War Department finally consent to enlist blacks, although of course with white officers. Primary sources; 8 illus., 40 notes. C. L. Grant

1256. Sewell, George A. HIRAM RHODES REVELS: ANOTHER EVALUATION. *Negro Hist. Bull. 1974/75 38(1): 336-339.* Hiram

Rhodes Revels, elected as US Senator from Mississippi, strove for conciliation with the white race. After his Senate term Revels was appointed president of Alcorn University, a new Negro college, in Alcorn, Mississippi. 21 notes. — M. J. Wentworth

1257. Sherer, Robert G. WILLIAM BURNS PATERSON: "PIONEER AS WELL AS APOSTLE OF NEGRO EDUCATION IN ALABAMA". *Alabama Hist. Q. 1974 36(2): 121-150.* William Burns Paterson (1849-1915) was a Scot who became interested in classical education for Negroes. A contemporary of Booker T. Washington, he disaqreed with Washington's stress on manual arts training. Paterson in 1878 became president of Alabama State College (Negro), a post he held until his death in 1915. He attempted to bring into this school, which was oriented primarily to teacher training, as much traditional college work as possible. Described also is his work with the Alabama State Teachers Association. 68 notes. — E. E. Eminhizer

1258. Shlomowitz, Ralph. THE ORIGINS OF SOUTHERN SHARECROPPING. *Agric. Hist. 1979 53(3): 557-575.* The author examined the records of the Bureau of Refugees, Freedmen, and Abandoned Lands, usually referred to as the Freedmen's Bureau. The Bureau approved and enforce southern labor contracts between planters and freedmen. Notable for their wide variety of terms, the contracts offered as many as seven forms of compensation: standing wages, share of the crop, sharing of time, standing rent, wages in kind, money payment per task, and explicit incentive schemes. In most of these agreements the planter contracted his labor force as a group. In this study a 5% sample of labor contracts for South Carolina was taken. Primary and secondary sources; 2 tables, 32 notes. — R. T. Fulton

1259. Shofner, Jerrell H. MILITANT NEGRO LABORERS IN RECONSTRUCTION FLORIDA. *J. of Southern Hist. 1973 39(3): 397-408.* Discusses the efforts of Negroes in Reconstruction Florida to form labor unions, often coming into conflict with white unions. Florida blacks were active in the Colored National Labor Union and the National Union of Negro Labor as well as local organizations. Agricultural labor organizations were not successful but those in the lumber and shipping industries were. The use of strikes and overt violence was common, especially in Pensacola where Canadian lumbermen were edging blacks out, and in Monroe County, where Bahamian laborers would work for lower pay. The Florida legislature often responded to union actions and passed laws to improve the workers' position. Based on contemporary newspaper reports, state and Federal government documents, primary and secondary sources; 42 notes. — N. J. Street

1260. Simon, John Y. and James, Felix. ANDREW JOHNSON AND THE FREEDMEN. *Lincoln Herald 1977 79(2): 71-75.* In 1863 Secretary of War Stanton created the American Freedmen's Inquiry Commission to study the complex problem of the increasing number of free blacks, made wards of the government because of the war. One of the persons the commission interviewed was Andrew Johnson, military governor of Tennessee. As a staunch Unionist, Johnson favored emancipation as a wartime necessity, but he scorned any measure which would give free blacks special protection or assistance from the national government. Includes Johnson's personal testimony before the commission. Photo, 13 notes. — T. P. Linkfield

1261. Smallwood, James. THE FREEDMEN'S BUREAU RECONSIDERED: LOCAL AGENTS AND THE BLACK COMMUNITY. *Texana 1973 11(4): 309-320.* Discusses the attitudes of Texans toward the Freedmen's Bureau (established by Congress in 1865) and particularly toward the efforts of bureau official William S. Kirkland during 1867 and 1868.

1263. Smallwood, James. PERPETUATION OF CASTE: BLACK AGRICULTURAL WORKERS IN RECONSTRUCTION TEXAS. *Mid-America 1979 61(1): 5-23.* At the end of the Civil War, Texas whites sought to maintain the pre-war caste status of the former slaves. In spite of work by the Freedmen's Bureau and the Army in enforcing Reconstruction laws, the former slaves were kept in a sharecropper status or as low-paid field hands. A partial reason was lack of black economic resources, but the evidence indicates that white racism was the major factor. Primary and secondary sources; 64 notes. — J. M. Lee

1264. Stealey, John Edmund, III. THE FREEDMEN'S BUREAU IN WEST VIRGINIA. *West Virginia Hist. 1978 39(2-3): 99-142.* During 1865-68 the Freedmen's Bureau was active in Berkeley and Jefferson counties, West Virginia, where freedmen were a fifth of the population. The young army officers in charge were zealous for the blacks' welfare but did not have much success in protecting their legal rights. The establishment of schools met a mixed white reception, especially where the black attendance was large; the Bureau's most significant effort was in the founding of Storer College, a Negro normal school. Based on Freedmen's Bureau records and other primary and secondary sources; 216 notes. — J. H. Broussard

1265. Stern, Mark. BLACK STRIKEBREAKERS IN THE COAL FIELDS: KING COUNTY, WASHINGTON: 1891. *J. of Ethnic Studies 1977 5(3): 60-70.* Relates the activities of the Oregon Improvement Company's recruitment and use of Negroes from Iowa and Illinois at its Newcastle and Franklin mines during the Knights of Labor-inspired strike of 1891. Contrary to the white miners' stereotypes, the blacks involved were not "collected from the slums" or "unconscious tools of the company," but were for the most part experienced coal miners who had gone through industrial conflicts before, were conscious of their role, and had some ideological justification for their actions. Local black leaders preached a philosophy of self-help and racial pride, and saw the managers of the corporation as allies against the Knights and the white workers. Events in King County contradict the dominant interpretation of the phenomenon of the black strikebreaker, and show that Booker T. Washington's creed was less a rationalization of racism than a stress on cultural pride and separateness. Primary and secondary sources; 29 notes. — G. J. Bobango

1266. Storey, John W. THE RHETORIC OF PATERNALISM: SOUTHERN BAPTISTS AND NEGRO EDUCATION IN THE LATTER NINETEENTH CENTURY. *Southern Humanities Rev. 1978 12(2): 101-108.* Southern Baptists, 1880's-90's, paternalistically supported black education, but soon even that became little more than rhetoric based on laissez-faire attitudes toward civil rights and economic betterment.

1267. Storey, John W. SOUTHERN BAPTISTS AND THE RACIAL CONTROVERSY IN THE CHURCHES AND SCHOOLS DURING RECONSTRUCTION. *Mississippi Q. 1978 31(2): 211-228.* Separation in Southern Baptist churches and opposition to equal education for blacks stemmed from the fear that equal voice in church and education would force Negroes out of "their place" in southern society and initiate a new generation of "uppity" blacks.

1268. Sweat, Edward F. THE UNION LEAGUE AND THE SOUTH CAROLINA ELECTION OF 1870. *J. of Negro Hist. 1976 61(2): 200-214.* Francis Louis Cardozo, in this document, spoke before the South Carolina Grand Council of the Union League in 1870. Dedication to equality of political rights was the basis of the Union League appeal to freedmen in South Carolina. 2 notes. — N. G. Sapper

1269. Taylor, David V. JOHN QUINCY ADAMS: ST. PAUL EDITOR AND BLACK LEADER. *Minnesota Hist. 1973 43(8): 282-296.* The *Western Appeal* (later the *Appeal*), founded after 1880, was one of the few black newspapers to achieve regional or national prominence and to survive for more than a few years. John Quincy Adams (1848-1922) was its editor for almost its entire existence. Sometime teacher, politician, and newspaper publisher, Adams published his paper simultaneously in St. Paul and Chicago. The *Appeal* conducted a "vitriolic crusade" and promoted black activism against disfranchisement, discrimination, and other injustices. 8 illus., 70 notes. — D. L. Smith

1270. Terbor-Penn, Rosalyn. NINETEENTH CENTURY BLACK WOMEN AND WOMAN SUFFRAGE. *Potomac Rev. 1977 7(3): 13-24.* Black women participated in the woman suffrage movement with far greater frequency than has generally been acknowledged. Their adherence to this cause was grounded in the belief that voting rights for women (black and white) would enhance their status in a male-oriented society. As the 20th century commenced, that rationale had grown to include the hope that suffrage for black women would uplift the lives of all American Negroes. "All this goes to say that research about black women in the suffrage movement has been merely tapped but not thoroughly investigated." 36 notes. — M. R. Yerburgh

1271. Thomas, Bettye C. PUBLIC EDUCATION AND BLACK PROTEST IN BALTIMORE, 1865-1900. *Maryland Hist. Mag. 1976 71(3): 381-391.* Reviews the efforts of the Baltimore Association for the Moral and Educational Improvement of the Colored People led by such as Isaac Myers, and Brotherhood of Liberty formed by Harvey Johnson and other Baptist ministers, to acquire public schools, have black teachers hired, secure additional school facilities, and initiate industrial education for black children. Blacks found themselves forced to support Jim Crow legislation and urge all black teachers for the colored schools because the Board of School Commissioners would not allow blacks and whites to teach in the same schools. From 1867 to 1900 black schools grew from 10 to 27 and enrollment from 901 to 9,383. The Mechanical and Industrial Association achieved success only in 1892 with the opening of the Colored Manual Training School. Black leaders were convinced by the Rev. William Alexander and his paper, the *Afro American*, that economic advancement and first-class citizenship depended on equal access to schools, and thus zealously pursued their goals in the face of a white city commission which yielded step-by-step and only very reluctantly. Primary and secondary works; 45 notes. G. J. Bobango

1272. Thompson, Ernest T. BLACK PRESBYTERIANS: EDUCATION AND EVANGELISM AFTER THE CIVIL WAR. *J. of Presbyterian Hist. 1973 51(2): 174-198.* Presbyterians' evangelization and Christian education of their former slaves after the Civil War. S

1273. Thornbery, Jerry. NORTHERNS AND THE ATLANTA FREEDMEN, 1865-69. *Prologue 1974 6(4): 236-251.* Immediately following the end of the Civil War there were several federal agencies and northern religious organizations functioning in Atlanta to aid Negroes. The first and most extensive efforts were made by the Union Army. However, the Freedmen's Bureau, the American Missionary Association, and the Methodist Episcopal Church also offered limited assistance. A rudimentary school system was established, but a study of the activities of these organizations reveals considerable limitation because of northern attitudes toward race, work, and welfare. "Northerners as well as southerners shared a responsibility for Reconstruction's failure." 4 photos, 58 notes. R. V. Ritter

1274. Toll, William. FREE MEN, FREEDMEN, AND RACE: BLACK SOCIAL THEORY IN THE GILDED AGE. *J. of Southern Hist. 1978 44(4): 571-596.* In the confused post Civil War days, the conflicts arising from judgements of freedmen as socially ill-prepared victims of slavery and from efforts by free Negroes to organize and recruit the freedmen politically were complicated by the charges that the freedmen were responsible for the inefficient southern governments. In this confused sociopolitical situation, black writers sought the characteristics or conditions which might unify black Americans. Black intellectuals like John Mercer Langston, Frederick Douglass, W. E. B. DuBois, George Washington Williams, T. Thomas Fortune, John S. Durham, and Alexander Crumwell developed varied and complex class and Pan-Africanist social theories in order to initiate understanding of the past and to project strategies for blacks in the future. Manuscript and printed primary and secondary materials; 66 notes. T. D. Schoonover

1275. Tunnell, Ted. FREE NEGROES AND THE FREEDMEN: BLACK POLITICS IN NEW ORLEANS DURING THE CIVIL WAR. *Southern Studies 1980 19(1): 5-28.* During the Civil War, free Negroes in New Orleans made a series of dramatic political shifts: from rebel militia to soldiers of the Union; from demands for suffrage for free blacks to suffrage for all blacks; from acquiescence in slavery to criticism of federal "free labor"; from support of wartime Reconstruction to approval of the Wade-Davies Bill for congressional control of Reconstruction; and from unconcern with the slave masses to interest in the freedmen. These changes reflected in part a genuine awakening of liberal conscience, but even more they resulted from a realistic perception of class interest. Based on articles in the *New Orleans Tribune*; 72 notes. J. J. Buschen

1276. Vincent, Charles. LOUISIANA'S BLACK LEGISLATORS AND THEIR EFFORTS TO PASS A BLUE LAW DURING RECONSTRUCTION. *J. of Black Studies 1976 7(1): 47-56.* Black legislators in Louisiana during Reconstruction repeatedly tried to have the state's legislature enact a "blue law," but almost yearly resolutions during 1867-75 that would have prohibited (variously) boxing, gambling, horse racing, liquor sales, amusements, and even business transactions on Sunday did not succeed in winning approval. These efforts, which were most vigorous in 1874, drew strong support among the minority of black legislators but little among their white counterparts. Based on primary and secondary sources; notes, biblio. D. C. Neal

1277. Warren, Donald R. THE U.S. DEPARTMENT OF EDUCATION: A RECONSTRUCTION PROMISE TO BLACK AMERICANS. *J. of Negro Educ. 1974 43(4): 437-451.* In 1867, the federal task of social policymaking in guaranteeing schooling to Negroes narrowed to the ineffective Department of Education.

1278. West, Earle H. THE HARRIS BROTHERS: BLACK NORTHERN TEACHERS IN THE RECONSTRUCTION SOUTH. *J. of Negro Educ. 1979 48(2): 126-138.* Discusses the teaching careers of the Harris brothers, Robert, William, and Cicero, and compares them with those of white Northern teachers who moved to the South after the Civil War to teach. The motivations of the Harris brothers were similar to those of the whites. They both wanted to teach in the South for humanitarian and religious purposes. Their activities regarding teaching were also similar. The Harris brothers spent more time with black families during their spare hours than did whites, who were more politically active. Primary sources; 65 notes. J. Powell

1279. White, Kenneth B. WAGER SWAYNE: RACIST OR REALIST? *Alabama Rev. 1978 31(2): 92-109.* Wager Swayne, controversial assistant commissioner of the Freedmen's Bureau in Alabama, was both a racist and a realist. He was racist to the extent that, like the majority of his countrymen, he insisted upon only political equality for blacks, and a realist in that he opposed few trends and generally showed a marked inclination to respect conventional standards. Moderation characterized his leadership and actions. Primary and secondary sources; 32 notes. J. F. Vivian

1280. Wilson, William J. CLASS CONFLICT AND JIM CROW SEGREGATION IN THE POSTBELLUM SOUTH. *Pacific Sociol. Rev. 1976 19(4): 431-446.* Discusses the influence of economic development and industrialization on race relations, segregation, and class conflict in the South 1865-90's.

1281. Woods, Randall B. THE BLACK AMERICAN PRESS AND THE NEW MANIFEST DESTINY: THE WALLER AFFAIR. *Phylon 1977 38(1): 24-34.* John L. Waller, a black man from Kansas who had recently been US Consul to Madagascar, challenged French imperialism in that island in 1895 and subsequently was arrested and imprisoned. The black press in the United States criticized Waller's treatment, pointed out that the US government would have done more to secure the release of a white consul, and argued that such treatment reflected the treatment of blacks in the United States. The black press believed that by taking a chauvinistic attitude toward France they could win the respect of white America. They identified Waller as an American citizen and a symbol of national sovereignty and hoped to induce the white power structure to view all black Americans as full-fledged citizens who deserved equal protection under the law. Primary and secondary sources; 58 notes. B. A. Glasrud

1282. Woods, Randall B. BLACK AMERICA'S CHALLENGE TO EUROPEAN COLONIALISM: THE WALLER AFFAIR, 1891-1895. *J. of Black Studies 1976 7(1): 57-77.* The activities of a black American, John L. Waller, first as consul and later an entrepreneur, precipitated France's annexation of Madagascar. Consul Waller, encouraged by English interests and supported by his State Department, which recognized the symbolic importance of an independent Madagascar and American economic interests there, sided with the Hova regime by challenging the French treaty right to accredit foreign consuls. The annoyed French finally intervened in 1895 when entrepreneur Waller's desire to expand American influence in Madagascar and establish a black haven from oppression, as well as Waller's desire for personal gain, led him to secure a land grant for colonization. Primary and secondary sources; notes, biblio. D. C. Neal

1283. Young, Alfred. THE EDUCATIONAL PHILOSOPHY OF BOOKER T. WASHINGTON: A PERSPECTIVE FOR BLACK LIBERATION. *Phylon 1976 37(3): 224-235.* In his first major address to the National Education Association in 1884, Booker T. Washington saw the mission of industrial education as securing the cooperation of whites and doing the best possible thing for Negroes. In his speech of 1895 Washington seemingly accepted the dominant view that blacks should remain separate in society and relegated to a second-class status. W. E. B. Du Bois considered the Atlanta speech damning to the race because of Washington's seeming acquiescence of social and political questions. However, Washington's speeches pointed out the need of Negroes for industrial education as a means to an end, the South as the best place for blacks to live. He focused on Tuskegee Institute as a prime example of industrial achievement. 43 notes. E. P. Stickney

Capitalists and Labor Movements

1284. Amsden, Jon and Brier, Stephen. COAL MINERS ON STRIKE: THE TRANSFORMATION OF STRIKE DEMANDS AND THE FORMATION OF A NATIONAL UNION. *J. of Interdisciplinary Hist. 1977 7(4): 583-616.* There is a consistent relationship between the growth and impact of trade unionism among American mine workers and the pattern of strikes in the industry in the same period. Strikes over the reordering of productive relations in mining increase as a proportion of the total, despite fluctuations in business activity. During 1881-94 miners transformed the strike into an aggressive and more broadly class-conscious tactic. Printed and manuscript sources; 3 tables, 6 figs., 53 notes. R. Howell

1285. Andersen, Arlow W. AMERICAN LABOR UNREST IN NORWAY'S PRESS: THE HAYMARKET AFFAIR AND THE PULLMAN STRIKE. *Swedish Pioneer Hist. Q. 1974 25(3/4): 208-219.* The labor movement in 19th-century America was paralleled in Norway, where it was sparked by Marcus Thrane. The Norwegian press closely followed the Haymarket affair and the Pullman strike. The reaction was generally antisocialist. The Norwegian press lacked the anti-alien prejudice and the emotionalism of the American press. Primary and secondary sources; 12 notes. K. J. Puffer

1286. Ansley, Fran and Bell, Brenda, eds. MINERS' INSURRECTIONS/CONVICT LABOR. *Southern Exposure 1974 1(3/4): 144-159.* Coal mining companies leased convicts from the state of Tennessee to replace miners and to break strikes. During 1891-93, miners waged strikes and armed resistance against the mining companies involved, especially Tennessee Coal Mining Company. Battles against the state militia, destruction of mining company equipment, and the freeing of convicts from the mines stemmed from the imposition of anti-union oaths required for employment. Eventually the state stopped leasing convicts to the highest bidder, purchasing its own mines and using convict labor. Based on oral interviews, primary and secondary sources; 11 illus., 10 notes, biblio. G. A. Bolton

1287. Baxandall, Rosalyn Fraad; Gordon, Linda; and Reverby, Susan. ARCHIVES: BOSTON WORKING WOMEN PROTEST, 1869. *Signs: J. of Women in Culture and Soc. 1976 1(3, Part 1): 803-808.* Increasing numbers of women found employment in garment manufacturing in Boston during the Civil War because of the demand for military uniforms and the absence of male workers. But, by 1869, return of men and the end of war production reduced job opportunities for women despite increasing numbers of females who were dependent on their own earnings because of war casualties. Women, therefore, expressed anger at low wages and terrible working conditions, but they also railed against the degradation of their own labor and skill through the factory system's mechanization and division of labor. Primary sources. S. E. Kennedy

1288. Blewett, Mary H. THE UNION OF SEX AND CRAFT IN THE HAVERHILL SHOE STRIKE OF 1895. *Labor Hist. 1979 20(3): 352-375.* Female stitchers, skilled workers, were among the most militant strikers against the Haverhill, Massachusetts, shoe factories in 1895. Skill, consciousness of class, and personal mobility underlaid the organizational effort which fostered a tradition of union activity among female shoeworkers in the 19th century. Based on newspapers; 49 notes. L. L. Athey

1289. Buhle, Paul. THE KNIGHTS OF LABOR IN RHODE ISLAND. *Radical Hist. Rev. 1978 (17): 39-73.* The Knights of Labor rose dramatically to power in the 1880's and practically disappeared by 1887 in Rhode Island; discusses labor and politics in Rhode Island from the Civil War to the turn of the century.

1290. Carvalho, Joseph, III. THE BAUGHMAN BOYCOTT AND ITS EFFECT ON THE RICHMOND, VIRGINIA LABOUR MOVEMENT, 1886-1888. *Social Hist. [Canada] 1979 12(24): 409-417.* The American labor movement employed strikes and boycotts as two basic tools in the 1880's. The Richmond Typographical Union was formed and included every printing office by early 1886 except for Baughman Brothers. A boycott of Baughmans severely restricted business. During this period, labor also scored numerous political victories, but a court ruling defining boycotts as a criminal conspiracy deprived labor of a powerful tool, and sounded the death-knell for the Knights of Labor in Richmond. Based on primary and secondary sources, including records of Typographical Union, No. 90, Richmond, Virginia; 54 notes. D. F. Chard

1291. Cary, Lorin Lee. ADOLPH GERMER AND THE 1890'S DEPRESSION. *J. of the Illinois State Hist. Soc. 1975 68(4): 337-343.* Coal miners in a heavily German-populated area of southern Illinois, Adolph Germer and his father were active members of the early United Mine Workers of America. Germer was a participant in the strikes of 1894 and 1897. These strikes, culminating in the killing of seven miners by company guards at Virden, Illinois, in 1898, along with the depression of the 1890's, made Germer a staunch believer in unionism and Socialism. Based on primary and secondary sources. N. Lederer

1292. Cassity, Michael J. MODERNIZATION AND SOCIAL CRISIS: THE KNIGHTS OF LABOR AND A MIDWEST COMMUNITY, 1885-1886. *J. of Am. Hist. 1979 66(1): 41-61.* Examines two railroad strikes in Sedalia, Missouri, to illustrate the impact of modernization on the Knights of Labor. Both strikes involved the Jay Gould system and demonstrated local antagonisms toward centralized authority. The first strike, in early 1885, motivated by the railroad's harsh economic policy, was spontaneous and local in origin. Because the Gould system represented a harsh, alien, and monopolistic central authority, the strikers and their union won local sympathy. The second strike, a year later, however, produced the opposite effect. The Knights shifted their goals from equality, fraternity, and community responsibility to goals which would increase workers' power in a broader, more centralized, institutional concept. This strike upheld the pattern of modernization in society and alienated the Knights from the local level. 52 notes.
T. P. Linkfield

1293. Cook, Bernard A. SECTION 15 OF THE I.W.A.: THE FIRST INTERNATIONAL IN NEW ORLEANS. *Louisiana Hist. 1973 14(3): 297-304.* Chronicles the establishment of Section 15 (the Louisiana chapter) of the International Workingmen's Association in New Orleans in 1871.

1294. Cooper, Jerry M. THE ARMY AS STRIKE BREAKER— THE RAILROAD STRIKES OF 1877 AND 1894. *Labor Hist. 1977 18(2): 179-196.* Describes the role of the Army in the strikes of 1877 and 1894. Although officers justified Army intervention as a restoration of order, the act of restoring order worked against labor. The Army's officers actually identified with middle class values on property and order. Based on Army correspondence in the National Archives and other primary sources; 28 notes. L. L. Athey

1295. Cotkin, George B. THE SPENCERIAN AND COMTIAN NEXUS IN GOMPERS' LABOR PHILOSOPHY: THE IMPACT OF NON-MARXIAN EVOLUTIONARY THOUGHT. *Labor Hist. 1979 20(4): 510-523.* Samuel Gompers's ideology was affected by the Spencerian views of Frank K. Foster and the Comtian views of Hugh McGregor, both important trade unionists. Gompers's pragmatism is more explicable from non-Marxian evolutionary thought, although some Marxian influence need not be denied. Based on the Gompers Letter Books and Files of the Tamiment Library; 25 notes. L. L. Athey

1296. Cotkin, George B. STRIKEBREAKERS, EVICTIONS AND VIOLENCE: INDUSTRIAL CONFLICT IN THE HOCKING VAL-

LEY, 1884-1885. *Ohio Hist. 1978 87(2): 140-150.* Examines the absence of violence toward strikebreakers in the Hocking Valley coal strike of 1884-85 in Ohio. Immigrant strikebreakers were brought to the coal mines by the operators and armed guards were posted on the properties, but violence against the strikebreakers was rare. When violence did appear, it was directed against the coal companies' property. Lasting over nine months, the strike ended in defeat for the miners. The strikers clearly had imposed limitations on the forms and objects of their violence. Based on manuscripts, archives, newspapers, and secondary sources; 2 illus., 43 notes. N. Summers

1297. Davies, J. Kenneth. THE SECULARIZATION OF THE UTAH LABOR MOVEMENT. *Utah Hist. Q. 1977 45(2): 108-134.* In the 1850's, the Mormon church encouraged a religiously oriented worker movement. The 1860's brought nonreligious influences: war induced inflation, large numbers of non-Mormon workers, and association with national unions. Church cooperatives, United Orders, and the Board of Trade movement reduced Mormon influence on the budding unions. Nonintercourse with Gentiles, union violence, and closed shops induced some to leave unions. Political and business secularization of the 1890's ended the church's economic program. By 1896 labor secularization was accomplished. Primary and secondary sources; 5 illus., 51 notes.
J. L. Hazelton

1298. Dawley, Alan and Faler, Paul. WORKING CLASS CULTURE AND POLITICS IN THE INDUSTRIAL REVOLUTION: SOURCES OF LOYALISM AND REVOLUTION. *J. of Social Hist. 1976 9(4): 466-480.* Discusses Lynn, Massachusetts, the center of the rapidly changing shoe industry, to study reactions to industrialization and changed behavior patterns called forth by factory work. Finds that radicalism was clear cut by the outset of the Civil War and was manifested by the rapid development of the Knights of St. Crispin after 1868. Previous students of the labor movement believe that the radicalism was muted by the particular character of the interaction between working class culture and politics. M. Hough

1299. Debouzy, Marianne. GRÈVE ET VIOLENCE DE CLASSE AUX ETATS-UNIS EN 1877 [US strikes and class violence in 1877]. *Mouvement Social [France] 1978 (102): 41-66.* By their extent, by the original forms of working-class resistance and solidarity which they produced, the 1877 strikes are a unique social phenomenon in the history of industrial conflicts in nineteenth century America. This mass movement brought to light both the deep class cleavages that divided American society at the time and the existence of circumstantial alliances between the working class and that part of the bourgeoisie which was hostile to railroad companies. These strikes raise the question of what accounts for such a high level of combativity and solidarity. The uprising involved challenge to authority, organized resistance to repression and controlled violence aimed at very precise targets. In this uprising the American working-class expressed a form of class consciousness which it would never reach again. J

1300. Dodd, Martin H. MARLBORO, MASSACHUSETTS AND THE SHOEWORKERS' STRIKE OF 1898-1899. *Labor Hist. 1979 20(3): 376-397.* The shoeworkers' strike of 1898-99 yielded a shift in Marlboro sentiment from support of labor to support for industry, thus forcing the shoeworkers to rely more on unions and less on support from other groups. The local unions were broken. Based on city directories and newspapers; 2 tables, 42 notes. L. L. Athey

1301. Doherty, William T., Jr. BERKELEY'S NON-REVOLUTION: LAW AND ORDER AND THE GREAT RAILWAY STRIKE OF 1877. *West Virginia Hist. 1974 35(4): 271-289.* During the Railway Strike of 1877, strikers seized the Baltimore and Ohio rail yard at Martinsburg, West Virginia, and halted service during July 16-19. Local militia were ineffective and federal troops were finally sent in to clear out the strikers. During and after the event, local newspapers took a moderate position, criticizing the actions of Governor Henry M. Mathews and the federal government as too pro-railroad. Local opinion sympathized with the strikers and thought the railroad was greedy, but objected to violence. Based chiefly on local newspapers; 56 notes. J. H. Broussard

1302. Eggert, Gerald G. COXEY'S MARCH ON WASHINGTON, 1894. *Am. Hist. Illus. 1977 12(6): 20-31.* Between two and three million people (20-25 percent of the nonagricultural labor force) were unemployed due to the panic of 1893. Jacob S. Coxey, greenbacker, populist, and founder of the Good Roads Association, wished the federal government to trade legal tender notes to state and local government for noninterest-bearing bonds, which would be paid off in 25 years. The money would be used to hire the unemployed to construct roads, schools, courthouses, and other public facilities. To publicize his plan, he organized a march of the unemployed on Washington, D.C. from his home in Massillon, Ohio. The marchers left Ohio in March 1894 and arrived in Washington on May Day, 1894. Between 15,000-30,000 people lined Pennsylvania Avenue as the 500 of Coxey's Army were stopped. Coxey led a second march to Washington in 1914 and spoke from the Capitol steps. He later was Mayor of Massillon, and saw his public-works-for-the-unemployed idea carried out during the New Deal. He died at age 97 in 1951. 10 illus.
D. Dodd

1303. Fink, Leon. "IRRESPECTIVE OF PARTY, COLOR OR SOCIAL STANDING": THE KNIGHTS OF LABOR AND OPPOSITION POLITICS IN RICHMOND, VIRGINIA. *Labor Hist. 1978 19(3): 325-349.* The Knights of Labor in Richmond turned to political action in 1886 by supporting a reform slate in municipal elections. A coalition with Negro Republicans threatened existing Democratic control, but racial divisions generated by the meeting of the 10th General Assembly of the Knights helped divide the coalition and ensured defeat. By 1888 the reform movement vanished, and Negroes steadily lost political influence. Based on newspapers; 50 notes. L. L. Athey

1304. Finn, J. F. A F OF L LEADERS AND THE QUESTION OF POLITICS IN THE EARLY 1890'S. *J. of Am. Studies [Great Britain] 1973 7(3): 243-265.* Unionists have debated the merits of an American "Labor Party." One faction led by Samuel Gompers (1850-1924) resisted a labor party. The other faction, heavily Socialists and "philosophical anarchists," demanded a labor party but disagreed about a "collectivist" platform for the party. Based on labor publications and manuscript sources; 117 notes. H. T. Lovin

1305. Foner, Philip S. "VATER DES MODERNEN SOZIALISMUS IN AMERIKA": FRIEDRICH ADOLPH SORGE ["Father of modern socialism in America": Friedrich Adolph Sorge]. *Beiträge Zur Geschichte Der Arbeiterbewegung [East Germany] 1978 20(1): 111-118.* Discusses the contributions of the German-born Marxist, Friedrich Adolph Sorge (1828-1906), to the early socialist movement in the United States. Sorge came to America in 1852 and was an active participant in the formation of the American section of the 1st International, the International Workingmen's Association (1869), which he served as secretary. Later Sorge helped form other Marxist organizations. After retirement from active politics Sorge served as an advisor and historian of the workers' movement. Secondary works; 27 notes. J. B. Street

1306. Fones-Wolf, Elizabeth and Fones-Wolf, Kenneth. VOLUNTARISM AND FACTIONAL DISPUTES IN THE AFL: THE PAINTERS' SPLIT IN 1894-1900. *Industrial and Labor Relations Rev. 1981 35(1): 58-69.* Some students of the American Federation of Labor (AFL) have argued that voluntarism evolved into an ideology used to justify, among other things, the stifling of rank-and-file protest within federation affiliates. Examination of the behavior of Samuel Gompers and other AFL leaders in the face of a rank-and-file movement against the leadership of the Brotherhood of Painters and Decorators during 1894 to 1900 shows that voluntaristic principles actually afforded AFL leaders a good deal of flexibility, allowing the dissident group to grow while Gompers worked to obtain a negotiated settlement between the factions. Those efforts culminated in a federation-sponsored unity conference in 1900 that set the stage for the dissident faction to assume control of the painters' union. J/S

1307. Fones-Wolf, Kenneth. BOSTON EIGHT HOUR MEN, NEW YORK MARXISTS AND THE EMERGENCE OF THE INTERNATIONAL LABOR UNION: PRELUDE TO THE AFL. *Hist. J. of Massachusetts 1981 9(2): 47-59.* Discusses the influence of Ira Steward and George McNeill, leaders in the Boston Eight Hour League, on the International Workingmen's Association (IWA) of New York during 1860-89. The IWA moved from independent political action and took up more general issues such as the eight-hour day, which was central to the emergence of the American Federation of Labor. Based on contemporary newspapers, the Ira Steward Papers (Wisconsin State Historical Society), and secondary literature. W. H. Mulligan, Jr.

1308. Frank, Miriam and Glaberman, Martin. FRIEDRICH A. SORGE ON THE AMERICAN LABOR MOVEMENT. *Labor Hist. 1977 18(4): 592-606.* Translates Friedrich A. Sorge's article on the American labor movement, 1866-76, which first appeared in *Neue Zeit*, (1891-92). 2 notes. L. L. Athey

1309. Gildemeister, Glen A. THE FOUNDING OF THE AMERICAN FEDERATION OF LABOR. *Labor Hist. 1981 22(2): 262-268.* The American Federation of Labor-Congress of Industrial Organizations (AFL-CIO) designated its founding date as 15 November 1881, the date of the founding of the AFL's predecessor, the Federation of Organized Trades and Labor Unions (FOTLU), but the latter organization had ceased to exist before the AFL came into existence. A conference of trade unionists within the Knights of Labor, joined by FOTLU members who had dissolved their organization two days earlier, created the AFL on 10 December 1886 in Columbus, Ohio. Based on contemporary newspaper accounts and other primary sources; 27 notes. L. F. Velicer

1310. Gillis, Peter. BIG BUSINESS AND THE ORIGINS OF THE CONSERVATIVE REFORM MOVEMENT IN OTTAWA, 1890-1912. *J. of Can. Studies [Canada] 1980 15(1): 93-109.* The conservative social welfare movement in Ottawa was born of the economic difficulties of the 1890's. It was a response by the city's corporate elite to events which were eroding its traditional leadership in the community. In order to reassert their leadership in mapping Ottawa's destiny as an urban and industrial society, they advocated genuinely humanitarian efforts channeled through voluntary philanthropic and religious agencies. They tried, through rationalization of these voluntary associations, to assist the "moral regeneration" of the poor in order to make them self-sufficient and useful members of the community. Recognizing that private funds were not sufficient to finance all the necessary improvements, they increasingly turned to public funding. Although their efforts were overshadowed by liberal reformers between 1900 and 1911, a severe health crisis, which was poorly handled by the liberals, allowed them to reassert their influence and to effect changes still evident today. Based on materials in the Public Archives of Canada, contemporary speeches and newspaper articles; 94 notes. R. S. Fortner

1311. Gordon, Michael A. THE LABOR BOYCOTT IN NEW YORK CITY, 1880-1886. *Labor Hist. 1975 16(2): 184-229.* The labor boycotts in New York City originated primarily in the previous agricultural experiences of Irish immigrants in their struggle for land reforms. Thus, the labor boycott was a pre-industrial mode of protection adapted to industrial conditions. The mass arrests and trials of immigrants during 1880-86 are examined. Based upon newspapers, reports of the New York Bureau of Labor Statistics and secondary sources; 79 notes. L. L. Athey

1312. Gottlieb, Amy Zahl. THE INFLUENCE OF BRITISH TRADE UNIONISTS ON THE REGULATION OF THE MINING INDUSTRY IN ILLINOIS, 1872. *Labor Hist. 1978 19(3): 397-415.* English and Scots immigrant miners settling in Illinois brought with them experience in political action and mining legislation. Their organizations supported legislation based on experience in Great Britain, and succeeded in 1872. Based on newspapers, periodicals, and legislative records; 36 notes. L. L. Athey

1313. Gutman, Herbert G. LA POLITIQUE OUVRIÈRE DE LA GRANDE ENTREPRISE AMÉRICAINE DE "L'ÂGE DU CLINQUANT": LE CAS DE LA STANDARD OIL COMPANY [The labor policy of the American corporation in the Gilded Age: The case of the Standard Oil Company]. *Mouvement Social [France] 1978 (102): 67-99.* This article calls attention to the emergence of the "large factory" in the early 1870's and examines the labor policies of one of the largest and best known of these firms, the Standard Oil Company of Ohio. It raises the question: what was the impact of the large factory on the recruitment and discipline of workers, on working conditions, methods of payment, the power of workers vis-à-vis their employers and the relations among workers? The ability of a firm like Standard Oil to adopt modern technology and machinery met with a serious obstacle: the Coopers' International Union, which was in many ways the model of a successful organization of skilled nineteenth century American craftsmen. The mechanization of the barrel industry was, on the other hand, a threat to the Coopers: it destroyed their craft and their life style. The union's strength was broken by the large oil refiners and the barrel manufacturers who sold to them. After militant struggles waged in New York, Cleveland and Pittsburgh, the coopers were crushed. Multi-plant organization, financial resources and command of the market, as well as the support Standard Oil got from the Cleveland authorities enabled Rockefeller to render the skilled and semi-skilled coopers powerless and their major weapon, the strike, ineffective. J

1314. Harvey, Fernand. UNE ENQUÊTE OUVRIÈRE AU XIXe SIÈCLE: LA COMMISSION DU TRAVAIL, 1886-1889 [A working inquiry in the 19th century: the Labour Commission, 1886-89]. *Rev. d'Hist. de l'Am. Française [Canada] 1976 30(1): 35-53.* During the latter part of December 1886, the federal government established the Royal Commission of Inquiry into the Relations between Capital and Labour. The commission investigated the poor working and living conditions of laborers in Ontario, Quebec, New Brunswick, and Nova Scotia. In February 1889, the commissioners issued reports and made recommendations. Even though federal legislation did not immediately result from the inquiry, the public nevertheless was informed about the capitalist system's abuses. Based on letters in the Public Archives of Canada (Bowell and Macdonald Papers), published government documents, newspapers, and secondary works; 2 tables, 34 notes. L. B. Chan

1315. Heap, Margaret. LE GRÈVE DES CHARRETIERS À MONTRÉAL, 1864 [The teamsters' strike in Montreal, 1864]. *Rev. d'Hist. de l'Amérique Française [Canada] 1977 31(3): 371-395.* In September 1864, the Montreal teamsters launched a spectacular, highly organized strike; the commercial life of the city was completely paralyzed. The teamsters demanded a cessation of certain monopolistic practices employed by the Grand Trunk Railway Company—practices which seriously jeopardized their livelihood. Despite the solidarity of the teamsters, the courts would not consider their demands. The rising tide of industrial capitalism continued to erode the status of the working classes. 76 notes. M. R. Yerburgh

1316. Homel, Gene Howard. "FADING BEAMS OF THE NINETEENTH CENTURY": RADICALISM AND EARLY SOCIALISM IN CANADA'S 1890S. *Labour [Canada] 1980 5(Spr): 7-32.* Describes the convictions, supporters, and organizations of Canadian radicalism during the 1890's, encompassing labor leaders, antimonopolists, single taxers, social gospellers, and the like. The radicals rejected free-market assumptions and, on the basis of their concern for ethical values and for the protection of the productive elements of the community, advocated a radically restructured society based on cooperation and brotherhood. The article explains the rise of socialist ideas against the background of traditional forms of radical protest. J/S

1317. Jebsen, Harry, Jr. THE ROLE OF BLUE ISLAND IN THE PULLMAN STRIKE OF 1894. *J. of the Illinois State Hist. Soc. 1974 67(3): 275-293.* On 29 June 1894 Eugene V. Debs delivered a strike appeal to the workers of Blue Island, a town 16 miles southwest of Chicago. The next day a striking switchman purposely derailed a Rock Island locomotive, blocking the main track out of the town and marking the first damage to railroad property in the Chicago region. Citizens, police, and town officials united behind the workers' boycott, responding to a federal injunction against the strike with jeers, violence, and the overturning of boxcars. Accounts of this incident by federal marshal John W. Arnold and a biased Chicago press convinced President Cleveland and much of the public that federal intervention was necessary in the Pullman Strike. Primary and secondary sources; 4 illus., 5 photos, 40 notes. L. Woolfe

1318. Kealey, Gregory S. ARTISANS RESPOND TO INDUSTRIALISM: SHOEMAKERS, SHOE FACTORIES AND THE KNIGHTS OF ST. CRISPIN IN TORONTO. *Can. Hist. Assoc. Hist. Papers 1973: 137-157.* Traces the part played by the Knights of St. Crispin in the organization of boat and shoe factory workers. The Crispins, beginning as a craft society, adapted to the industrialization of their trade in Toronto during the early 1870's. They were regarded as leading working class intellectuals and their spirit and tactics were carried into the Knights of Labor. Based on primary and secondary sources; 3 tables, 75 notes. G. E. Panting

1319. Kerr, K. Austin. THE MOVEMENT FOR COAL-MINE SAFETY IN NINETEENTH-CENTURY OHIO. *Ohio Hist. 1977 86(1): 3-18.* A survey of coal mine health and safety regulations from their conception. Discusses the organization of the Mining Commission in 1871, and its investigative work and early leaders, the creation of the post of State Inspector of Mines in 1874, and the attempts to have the state and federal governments assume responsibility for improving mining conditions and the political controversies involved. Based on contemporary comments and on manuscript, archival, and secondary sources; 3 illus., 44 notes.	J

1320. Kilar, Jeremy W. COMMUNITY AND AUTHORITY RESPONSE TO THE SAGINAW VALLEY LUMBER STRIKE OF 1885. *J. of Forest Hist. 1976 20(2): 67-79.* In 1885 the community of Bay City, Michigan, supported striking lumbermen politically and legally against absentee millowners. The industrial diversification of the neighboring community of Saginaw precluded such community support. Industrial relationships in the two communities seemed similar, but social, ideological, and economic structures determined the different responses to the strike. 5 illus., map, graph, 65 notes.	L. F. Johnson

1321. Lazerow, Jama. "THE WORKINGMAN'S HOUR": THE 1886 LABOR UPRISING IN BOSTON. *Labor Hist. 1980 21(2): 200-220.* In the 1886 labor uprising in Boston, Massachusetts, the Knights of Labor gained much influence and many members, and the Central Labor Union waged an unsuccessful strike for the eight-hour day. The labor movement was full of ambiguity in organization and ideology because it sought power and respectability while being conciliatory. However, a viable workers' movement was created in Boston. Based on local newspapers; 52 notes.	L. L. Athey

1322. Levstik, Frank R. THE HOCKING VALLEY MINERS' STRIKE, 1884-1885: A SEARCH FOR ORDER. *Old Northwest 1976 2(1): 55-65.* Discusses the miners' strike in the coal field of Hocking Valley, Ohio, during 1884-85, emphasizing the actions of Governor George Hoadly.

1323. Libecap, Gary D. and Johnson, Ronald N. PROPERTY RIGHTS, NINETEENTH-CENTURY FEDERAL TIMBER POLICY, AND THE CONSERVATION MOVEMENT. *J. of Econ. Hist. 1979 39(1): 129-142.* In campaigning for the establishment of the National Forests in the late 19th century, conservationists pointed to fraud and timber theft in the Pacific Northwest. In this paper we argue that the conservationists were misdirected; that it was a costly Federal land policy that encouraged fraud and theft. In the face of restrictive land laws, fraud was necessary if lumber companies were to acquire large tracts of land to take advantage of economies of scale in logging. Since fraud used real resources, it raised the actual cost of acquiring land and thus delayed the establishment of property rights. Such delays led to theft. The paper examines the public land laws, explains their selection by claimants, and calculates the added transaction costs or rent dissipation that resulted from circumventing the law.	J

1324. Lopez, David E. COWBOY STRIKES AND UNIONS. *Labor Hist. 1977 18(3): 325-340.* Although there were no enduring unions and no labor organizers of cowboys, they did strike. Most prominent among cowboy strikes were the Texas Panhandle Strike of 1883 and the Wyoming Strike of 1885. Contrary to the mythology about cowboys, their working conditions promoted a dependency upon employers; therefore unionization was not a realistic alternative. Based on newspapers and the archives of the Western History Research Center in Laramie, Wyoming; 35 notes.	L. L. Athey

1325. Luning Prak, N. PULLMAN. *Spiegel Historiael [Netherlands] 1977 12(4): 236-241.* George M. Pullman (1831-97) invented the famous sleeping car in 1858 and in 1880 established the city of Pullman near Chicago. Here his workers lived in company homes and sent their children to company schools. In 1885 and again in 1893 wages were reduced, but not rents. A strike in 1894 was supported by the American Railway Union. The strike was broken because President Cleveland called out federal troops, invoking the Sherman Anti-Trust act of 1890. Illus., biblio.	G. D. Homan

1326. Marcus, Irwin M. LABOR DISCONTENT IN TIOGA COUNTY, PENNSYLVANIA, 1865-1905: THE GUTMAN THESIS, A TEST CASE. *Labor Hist. 1973 14(3): 414-422.* Surveys labor-management relationships in Tioga County 1865-1905 and concludes that the local experience sustains the Gutman thesis that workers played an important role in the value systems of small industrial towns and had assistance from local residents in resisting dominant employers. Based on local newspapers, government reports, and secondary sources; 11 notes.	L. L. Athey

1327. McCormack, A. Ross. BRITISH WORKING-CLASS IMMIGRANTS AND CANADIAN RADICALISM: THE CASE OF ARTHUR PUTTEE. *Can. Ethnic Studies [Canada] 1978 10(2): 22-37.* Arthur Puttee was one of the many British working-class immigrants who influenced the ideological and institutional development of radical movements throughout the English-speaking world. He emigrated to Western Canada in 1888. After a brief time in the United States he returned to Canada, advocating "labourism," a persuasion consciously modelled on the policy and programs of the British Labour Party. The support his propaganda enjoyed among significant numbers of British trade unionists in prairie cities was the result of social inequalities, cultural transfer, and the sense of dislocation experienced by all immigrants. Covers ca. 1888-1913. Primary sources; photo, 60 notes.	R. V. Ritter

1328. McLaurin, Melton A. KNIGHTS OF LABOR: INTERNAL DISSENSIONS OF THE SOUTHERN ORDER. Fink, Gary M. and Reed, Merl E., eds. *Essays in Southern Labor History: Selected Papers, Southern Labor History Conference, 1976.* (Westport, Conn.; London, England: Greenwood Pr., 1977): 3-17. Weakness within the Knights of Labor contributed to its early decline, ca.1885-88, after an initial show of great strength. Most significant were the ill-defined membership requirements leading to great diversity of motives, and hence a scattering of efforts, poor leadership (often they were not actually laborers, and often they were from areas other than their areas of leadership effort), extensive internal feuding, and (equally destructive) racial polarization. 51 notes.	R. V. Ritter

1329. McQuaid, Kim. THE BUSINESSMAN AS REFORMER: NELSON O. NELSON AND THE LATE 19TH CENTURY SOCIAL MOVEMENTS IN AMERICA. *Am. J. of Econ. and Sociol. 1974 33(4): 423-435.* Nelson O. Nelson's efforts at profit-sharing and cooperatives are traced with reference to the times in which they were tried. His interest in communitarian cooperative ventures is explored. Secondary sources; 28 notes.	W. L. Marr

1330. Montgomery, David. WORKERS' CONTROL OF MACHINE PRODUCTION IN THE NINETEENTH CENTURY. *Labor Hist. 1976 17(4): 485-509.* Patterns of behavior among workers in the second or third generations of industrial experience became a form of workers' control of production, a chronic struggle which assumed three forms in the late 19th century: functional autonomy of the craftsman; the union work rule; and mutual support of diverse trades in rule enforcement and sympathetic strikes. The scientific management movement of the 20th century fundamentally disrupted the development of workers' control. Based on union minute books, labor newspapers, and secondary sources; 57 notes.	L. L. Athey

1331. Morris, James M. NO HAYMARKET FOR CINCINNATI. *Ohio Hist. 1974 83(1): 17-32.* Discusses Cincinnati's general strike of 1886 which failed because both the press and the pulpits opposed strikes and violence. About 20% of the work force struck, but the city fathers remained calm. Lack of support by major unions and a 10% pay hike for freight handlers brought the strike to a close, although a Central Labor Union was formed. Primary and secondary sources; 4 illus., 33 notes.	S. S. Sprague

1332. Morton, Desmond. THE "GLOBE" AND THE LABOR QUESTION: ONTARIO LIBERALISM IN THE "GREAT UPHEAVAL," MAY, 1886. *Ontario Hist. [Canada] 1981 73(1): 19-39.* When the *Globe* solicited comments from readers on the Labor question in 1886, it was swamped with responses. Presents the US background (Knights of Labor, Haymarket bomb, etc.) before discussing the spillover into Canada, where the movement attracted men who had been active in earlier labor movements. Indicates the political aspects of increased membership, and considers the attitude of the Toronto press (specifically the *Globe*) to this situation. Briefly analyzes the major trends in the responses published by the *Globe,* and tries to formulate consequences. 4 illus., 53 notes. W. B. Whitham

1333. Morton, Desmond. TAKING ON THE GRAND TRUNK: THE LOCOMOTIVE ENGINEERS STRIKE OF 1876-77. *Labour [Canada] 1977 2: 5-34.* Canada's first major railway strike lasted 108 hours over the New Year's weekend, 1876-77, and ended in a Brotherhood of Locomotive Engineers victory over the Grand Trunk Railway (GTR), the country's most powerful corporation. GTR General Manager Joseph Hickson sought federal intervention in vain. Prime Minister Alexander Mackenzie's refusal, a severe storm, the BLE's ability to buy off would-be strikebreakers, the tardy and inadequate mobilization of militia, municipal officials' reluctance to oppose the strikers, the "intense unpopularity" of the GTR, and the impending termination of a railroad rate-cutting war all contributed to the strike's success. Primary and secondary sources; 115 notes. W. A. Kearns

1334. Oestreicher, Richard. SOCIALISM AND THE KNIGHTS OF LABOR IN DETROIT, 1877-1886. *Labor Hist. 1981 22(1): 5-30.* Joseph Labadie and Judson Grenell, radical labor leaders in Detroit, Michigan, worked for the advancement of socialism through the Socialist Labor Party (SLP) in 1877. They and other Detroit socialists joined the Knights of Labor after 1878 to spread socialism to a wider audience. Labadie and Grenell abandoned the SLP in the early 1880's because it advocated doctrinal purity over immediate political and economic gains. Based on the Joseph Labadie Papers and other primary sources; 63 notes.
L. F. Velicer

1335. Peterson, Richard H. CONFLICT AND CONSENSUS: LABOR RELATIONS IN WESTERN MINING. *J. of the West 1973 12(1): 1-17.* An analytical account of the instability in the mining industry in eight western states during 1892-1904 and the labor priorities, policies, and attitudes of the most successful mining capitalists. Some bonanza kings preferred to cut labor costs and relied on military and judicial power to enforce and defend their policies.... However, other Western mining entrepreneurs, recognizing that a hard line policy could sometimes result in a considerable loss of life and property and build a heritage of conflict between workers and owners, adopted policies to prevent rather than to suppress the grievances of organized labor." 66 notes, appendix.
D. D. Cameron

1336. Piott, Steven L. MISSOURI AND MONOPOLY: THE 1890S AS AN EXPERIMENT IN LAW ENFORCEMENT. *Missouri Hist. Rev. 1979 74(1): 21-49.* Early antitrust movements centered at the local and state levels where an aroused public and journalistic exposure impelled policymakers toward legislative solutions. Missouri's antitrust law did not work effectively until after 1898. Public anger and newspaper revelations about excessive fire insurance rates led the attorney general to go to court to argue the unconstitutionality of a provision exempting insurance companies in St. Louis and Kansas City under the law and to claim that the Kansas City Board of Fire Underwriters regulated rates throughout the state. The test case provided a model for other state antitrust movements. 7 illus., 9 photos, 64 notes. W. F. Zornow

1337. Ray, William W. CRUSADE OR CIVIL WAR? THE PULLMAN STRIKE IN CALIFORNIA. *California History 1979 58(1): 20-37.* Describes the effect of the 1894 Pullman strike in California. Historians have overlooked events in California which highlighted public disaffection with the Central Pacific-Southern Pacific's economic and political dominance, the regional variations in the strike, and the relative effectiveness of the American Railway Union. The ARU's boycott of Pullman cars and trains which used them was most effective in Sacramento, disappointing in the Bay area, and minimal in Los Angeles. However, the strike persisted in California after the dispute ended in Pullman, Illinois, where the strike had originated. The strike brought out longstanding grievances over wage reductions but it also indicated the degree to which Californians disliked the Southern Pacific. The impact of the strike in California included the calling out of federal and state troops for the first time to maintain order, electoral successes by Populist candidates, and violence and sabotage by desperate ARU members. Railroads viewed ARU agitation as civil war; ARU supporters considered it a crusade for the rights of unskilled workers. Primary and secondary sources; 7 photos, 44 notes. A. Hoffman

1338. Roediger, David R. AMERICA'S FIRST GENERAL STRIKE: THE ST. LOUIS "COMMUNE" OF 1877. *Midwest Q. 1980 21(2): 196-206.* In July 1877 the first general strike in an American industrial city took place in St. Louis, Missouri, under the leadership of the Workingmen's Party. The strike was short-lived, however, for three reasons: an effective "citizens' militia" formed by the propertied classes, racism among white strikers, and the failure of the strike leaders to influence the mayor's selection of police deputies. Biblio.
M. E. Quinlivan

1339. Roediger, David. RACISM, RECONSTRUCTION, AND THE LABOR PRESS: THE RISE AND FALL OF THE *ST. LOUIS DAILY PRESS,* 1864-1866. *Sci. and Soc. 1978 42(2): 156-177.* The *Daily Press* originated during a period of class struggle in St. Louis, Missouri, as striking printers established the organ either as a means of winning their strike or as a beginning towards a permanent major labor voice in the city. The newspaper continued its existence after the strike as a medium for exploited white labor and was supported on an international basis. It endeavored to attract Irish workers through its espousal of the cause of Fenianism. It also tried to advocate the cause of female labor equality. It failed to become a permanent part of the St. Louis newspaper scene owing to fragmentation in labor's political ranks between the conservative Johnsonian Democrats exhibiting racism and the adherents of Radical Republicanism, many of whom were German workers. During its last days, it tried to reverse its field on racism and Radical Republicanism by championing black rights and the Republican cause, but to no avail. Its history illustrated the corroding influence of racism on labor. N. Lederer

1340. Schappes, Morris U. THE POLITICAL ORIGINS OF THE UNITED HEBREW TRADES, 1888. *J. of Ethnic Studies 1977 5(1): 13-44.* Details the origins, planning, and organizational meetings which produced the United Hebrew Trades (UHT) organization in New York City, a product of Branch 8 and Branch 17 of the Socialist Labor Party. The leaders were Yiddish-speaking workingmen such as Jacob Magidow, Lev Bandes, and Bernard Weinstein, who were products of the Jewish working class rather than the older middle-class composition of American Jewry. Demonstrates the close contacts and clearly imitative nature of the UHT and the older *Vereinigte Deutsche Gewerkschaften* (German Central Labor Union). The UHT faced opposition by Jewish middle class organs such as *The Jewish Messenger* and the *American Hebrew,* who called the Farein anarchistic. The opposition of Samuel Gompers, who objected to the socialist nature of the group's program and its religious basis, also took several years to overcome. Gompers' writings later falsely claimed him as one of the organizers of the UHT. For 25 years this union was a vital factor in organizing Jewish workers and bringing them into the American labor movement. Primary and secondary sources, 88 notes.
G. J. Bobango

1341. Scharnau, Ralph William. ELIZABETH MORGAN, CRUSADER FOR LABOR REFORM. *Labor Hist. 1973 14(3): 340-351.* Elizabeth Chambers Morgan (b. 1850), Chicago trade unionist and social reformer, rose from unskilled labor to prominence in Chicago reform and union circles. With a power base in the Ladies' Federal Labor Union and the Illinois Women's Alliance, Mrs. Morgan was partly instrumental in extending compulsory education for children, updating child labor laws, and the attack on sweatshops which resulted in the Factory and Workshop Inspection Act of 1893 in Illinois. Working with Hull House reformers and others, Mrs. Morgan helped explore detrimental health and labor conditions—for which exploration she has not received due credit. Based on the Thomas J. Morgan collection, Chicago newspapers, government reports, and secondary sources; 63 notes. L. L. Athey

1342. Scharnau, Ralph William. THOMAS J. MORGAN AND THE UNITED LABOR PARTY OF CHICAGO. *J. of the Illinois State Hist. Soc. 1973 66(1): 41-61.* In the 1880's the press depicted industrial strikers as lawless radicals and "reds." The Illinois General Assembly was particularly antilabor. Thomas J. Morgan, a socialist labor leader, favored political action to curb unfavorable political pressure. His United Labor Party worked as a labor coalition with local trade unions and Knights of Labor assemblies nationally. He helped write the 1886 national platform of the new party and made nightly speeches to workers to support the party ticket. Several state Labor Party legislature victories in Democratic districts in 1886 resulted in Democratic patronage lures to infiltrate Morgan's party. Women's suffrage, the eight-hour day for city employees, better school accommodations, and an equitable taxation system were popular party platforms. Morgan continued to spread socialist ideas through the early 1890's by his organizing genius, political interests, and speaking abilities. Based on the Morgan collection at the University of Illinois and on newspapers; 5 illus., 68 notes.   A. C. Aimone

1343. Schneirov, Richard. CHICAGO'S GREAT UPHEAVAL OF 1877. *Chicago Hist. 1980 9(1): 2-17.* During the national railroad strike of 1877, unskilled laborers (mainly Irish, German, Bohemian, and Polish) in Chicago during 23-26 July went on strike, went about in crowds to enlist other workers, and fought bloody battles with the police and the state militia; many workers won restoration of their recently cut wages.

1344. Schwantes, Carlos A. LABOR UNIONS AND SEVENTH-DAY ADVENTISTS; THE FORMATIVE YEARS, 1877-1903. *Adventist Heritage 1977 4(2): 11-19.* The opposition of the Seventh-Day Adventists to organized labor was a reaction to strikes and violence and to the presence of Catholics and Socialists in labor unions and organizations.

1345. Shotliff, Don A. THE 1894 TARIFF AND THE POTTERY STRIKE: THE REBIRTH OF THE NATIONAL BROTHERHOOD OF OPERATIVE POTTERS. *Western Pennsylvania Hist. Mag. 1975 58(3): 307-326.* Discusses the origin of the National Brotherhood of Operative Potters as a result of lowered wages because of cheap foreign labor which brought about a strike of both union and nonunion potters in 1894.

1346. Silvia, Philip T., Jr. THE POSITION OF WORKERS IN A TEXTILE COMMUNITY: FALL RIVER IN THE EARLY 1880S. *Labor Hist. 1975 16(2): 230-248.* Examines employer-dominance in the textile industry of Fall River, Massachusetts. Although a critique of labor conditions was led by Robert Howard, a muleskinner, the policies of the employers regarding grievances, wages, work conditions and company housing were maintained as a part of a laissez-faire philosophy hostile to organized labor in the 1880's. Based upon reports of the Massachusetts Bureau of Labor Statistics and Senate committees, newspapers and secondary sources; 32 notes.   L. L. Athey

1347. Skaggs, Julian C. and Ehrlich, Richard L. PROFITS, PATERNALISM, AND REBELLION: A CASE STUDY IN INDUSTRIAL STRIFE. *Business Hist. Rev. 1980 54(2): 155-174.* In the strike against the Lukens Iron Works in Coatesville, Pennsylvania, in 1886, the management's intransigence was due more to a desire to reaffirm a traditional paternalism than to the dollar cost of the workers' demands. The cause of many such confrontations of the period was a conflict over control of the firm; management saw labor's demands as threatening its own legitimate authority. Based on the Lukens Collection in the Eleutherian Mills Library; 6 graphs, 36 notes.   C. J. Pusateri

1348. Skaggs, Julian C. and Ehrlich, Richard L. PROFITS, PATERNALISM, AND REBELLION: A CASE STUDY IN INDUSTRIAL STRIFE. *Working Papers from the Regional Econ. Hist. Res. Center 1978 1(4): 1-30.* Analysis of labor unrest and an 1886 strike at the Lukens Iron Works in Coatesville, Pennsylvania, indicates that management objected not to increased wages and benefits but to the potential for worker independence and the ensuing threat to paternalism and rights of ownership.

1349. Stow, Robert N. CONFLICT IN THE AMERICAN SOCIALIST MOVEMENT, 1897-1901: A LETTER FROM THOMAS J. MORGAN TO HENRY DEMAREST LLOYD, JULY 18, 1901. *J. of the Illinois State Hist. Soc. 1978 71(2): 133-142.* Provides an annotated version of the original letter in which Morgan (1847-1912) described the status of the Socialist Labor Party and the Social Democratic Party in 1901. He was encouraged by the increasing number of converts to the socialist cause but was alarmed by developing factionalism, the cult of personality around Eugene Debs, and the failure of any faction to become a national party. 2 song sheets, 2 illus., 42 notes.   J/S

1350. Sylvain, Philippe. LES CHEVALIERS DU TRAVAIL ET LE CARDINAL ELZÉAR-ALEXANDRE TASCHEREAU [The Knights of Labor and Cardinal Elzéar-Alexandre Taschereau]. *Tr. of the Royal Soc. of Can. 1973 11: 31-42.* Records the history of Cardinal Taschereau's condemnation and later pardon of the Noble and Holy Order of the Knights of Labor for secretiveness, 1884-94, suggesting that this secret society, founded in Philadelphia in 1869, had some influence on the history of French Canadian labor unions.

1351. Sylvain, Philippe. LES CHEVALIERS DU TRAVAIL ET LE CARDINAL TASCHEREAU [The Knights of Labor and Cardinal Taschereau]. *Industrial Relations [Canada] 1973 28(3): 550-564.* The Noble and Holy Order of the Knights of Labor, formed in 1869, was one of many secret societies born of militant, discouraged workers. Elzéar Alexandre Taschereau (1820-98), Archbishop of Quebec, was among those who feared an association with Freemasonry in the rapid spread of the secret Knights of Labor. He was instrumental in having the Knights condemned by the Catholic Church in 1884. James Gibbons (1834-1918), Archbishop of Baltimore, however, as a warm supporter of the Knights journeyed to Rome and succeeded in having the ruling overturned. His efforts helped prepare the way for the encyclical *Rerum Novarum* (1891), the charter of Catholic social thought. Based on published Church documents and secondary works; 46 notes.   L. R. Atkins

1352. Turbin, Carole. AND WE ARE NOTHING BUT WOMEN: IRISH WORKING WOMEN IN TROY. Berkin, Carol Ruth and Norton, Mary Beth, ed. *Women of America: A History* (Boston: Houghton Mifflin Co., 1979): 202-222. Examines the foundation of the Collar Laundry Union of Troy, New York, in 1864 in an age when woman had little leverage to bargain with employers. During 1864-69, the lifespan of the union, the laundresses were able to raise their wages to nearly equal those of working men. They formed close alliances with the male labor movement, and their three-month strike in 1869 was highly successful. Secondary sources; 19 notes, ref.   K. Talley

1353. Ullmo, Sylvia. THE GREAT STRIKES OF 1877. *Rev. Française d'Etudes Américaines [France] 1976 (2): 49-56.* Studies the radical aspects of the massive railroad and industrial strikes of 1877 in Baltimore, Chicago, St. Louis, and Pittsburgh.

1354. Vipond, May. BLESSED ARE THE PEACEMAKERS: THE LABOUR QUESTION IN CANADIAN SOCIAL GOSPEL FICTION. *J. of Can. Studies 1975 10(3): 32-43.* Discusses the ideological evolution of social gospel Christianity in Canada in the 1890's as a reaction to increasing industrialization, including the issue of Christian responsibility toward labor.

1355. Waksmundski, John. GOVERNOR MC KINLEY AND THE WORKING MAN. *Historian 1976 38(4): 629-647.* Unlike earlier Republican Party leaders, Ohio governor William McKinley (1843-1901) sought to align himself and his party with the working class. Elected in 1891, McKinley asked the legislature to enact laws on railroad worker safety, right of employees to join labor organizations, and arbitration. McKinley was reelected in 1893 with improved Republican vote totals in counties with a substantial worker voting bloc. McKinley's careful actions dealing with striking coal miners during the 1893 depression enabled him to keep labor support. Notes.   M. J. Wentworth

1356. Walker, Samuel. TERENCE V. POWDERLY, THE KNIGHTS OF LABOR AND THE TEMPERANCE ISSUE. *Societas 1975 5(4): 279-293.* This study uses temperance as a focus but raises larger issues. It argues that for Terence V. Powderly and other leaders of the Knights of Labor, temperance was not simply a middle-class oriented, moralistic reform but was adopted as a limited policy only and was motivated in large part by pragmatic considerations having to do with the organization's stability and strength. This leads the author to support other historians (specifically David Montgomery and Warren Van Tine) in their attack on the prevailing view in 19th-century labor historiography that there existed a significant dichotomy between utopian reform unionism and pragmatic business unionism. Based on the proceedings and constitutions of the national and some local Knights of Labor organizations, Powderly's papers, and other primary and secondary sources; 56 notes.   J. D. Hunley

1357. White, W. Thomas. BOYCOTT: THE PULLMAN STRIKE IN MONTANA. *Montana 1979 29(4): 2-13.* The Pullman Strike of 1894 had a significant impact on Northern Pacific Railroad employees in

Montana. Great Northern and Union Pacific railroads experienced less disruption. American Railway Union members in Billings, Livingston, Butte, Helena, and Missoula participated. Troops from the 22d US Infantry patrolled Northern Pacific track and a major confrontation developed between the troops and citizens of Livingston. Unionized miners from western Montana communities supported A.R.U. efforts. After the strike ended, N.P. and U.P. officials blacklisted many Montana railroad employees. Six A.R.U. leaders were also convicted of violating an antistrike injunction. The Pullman Strike was a central event in the labor turbulence and political activism, which swept Montana during the 1890's, fostered by strong antirailroad populism in the state. Based on contemporary newspapers, US Army materials in the National Archives, and secondary sources; 7 illus, 41 notes. R. C. Myers

1358. —. THE WORKINGMEN'S PARTY OF CALIFORNIA, 1877-1882. *California Hist. Q. 1976 55(1): 58-73.* Presents a portfolio of 20 illustrations depicting the Workingmen's Party of California. Founded by Denis Kearney and others, the party opposed the competition of Chinese labor, called for regulation of banks and railroads, and demanded labor reforms. The Workingmen's Party participated in the framing of the 1879 State Constitution. Most of the reproductions are taken from the San Francisco *Illustrated Wasp*, which held a critical view of the movement. A. Hoffman

Populist Movement and Antecedents

1359. Abrahams, Edward H. IGNATIUS DONNELLY AND THE APOCALYPTIC STYLE. *Minnesota Hist. 1978 46(3): 102-111.* Ignatius Donnelly's view of Populism was colored by the pre-1860 concepts of an agrarian rural democracy controlled by farmers and handicraftsmen that he had imbued in his youth and early manhood. He believed in a classless society without social rank based on wealth. His political disappointments coupled with his writing of such catastrophe-tinged books as *Atlantis—The Antediluvian World* and its successor *Ragnarok: The Age of Fire and Gravel*, generated his thinking along apocalyptic lines in which he foresaw mass disaster for America if it refused to return to the innocent past. His Populist speeches and such works as *Caesar's Column* reflect this attitude. Other writings such as *Doctor Huguet, The Golden Bottle*, and *The American People's Money* deal with Populist ideas to some extent. N. Lederer

1360. Aldrich, Mark. A NOTE ON RAILROAD RATES AND THE POPULIST UPRISING. *Agric. Hist. 1980 54(3): 424-432.* Populism movement was related to changes in railroad rates on agricultural goods. Traditionally it has been believed that the Populists appeared because of long-term rising or steady railroad rates. But political science theory contends that protests occur when conditions deteriorate after a period of improvement. A look at railroad rates suggests that the political science model is correct. Railroad rates generally fell until about 1880, then began to rise into the 1890's at a time when water transportation rates were still falling. Uses railroad data and secondary sources; 3 tables, 18 notes. D. E. Bowers

1361. Bates, J. Leonard. POLITICS AND IDEOLOGY: THOMAS J. WALSH AND THE RISE OF POPULISM. *Pacific Northwest Q. 1974 65(2): 49-56.* Studies the ideology, apparent motivations, and methods of Thomas J. Walsh (1859-1933), and his move toward populism. An analysis of his early political speeches reveals a Jeffersonian Democrat of liberal ideology. Walsh often expressed populist ideas but did not join the movement, choosing rather to contribute to the liberalization of the Democratic Party while advancing his own career. 21 notes.
R. V. Ritter

1362. Bicha, Karel D. THE CONSERVATIVE POPULISTS: A HYPOTHESIS. *Agric. Hist. 1973 47(1): 9-24.* Populists were neither liberals nor reactionaries, but rather conservatives dedicated to classical laissez-faire economics. Populism offered no positive solutions to the problems of depression, unemployment, natural disasters, or welfare, believing them to be beyond the legitimate scope of government. Based mainly on newspapers, federal and State records, and correspondence; 58 notes. D. E. Brewster

1363. Bicha, Karel D. PECULIAR POPULIST: AN ASSESSMENT OF JOHN R. ROGERS. *Pacific Northwest Q. 1974 65(3): 110-117.* A study and evaluation of John R. Rogers, the Populist and Democratic governor of Washington from 1897-1901, including his significance as a publicist, ideologue, and advocate of reform. Rogers began his career as a monetary reformer and ended with a complete obsession with land use and land tenure reform. His intransigent agrarianism, as exemplified by his free homestead proposal, was socialistic in its implications, even though he was a champion of individualism. 36 notes.
R. V. Ritter

1364. Bicha, K. D. WESTERN POPULISTS: MARGINAL REFORMERS OF THE 1890'S. *Agricultural Hist. 1976 50(4): 626-635.* The People's Party of the 1890's showed little interest in reform in the legislatures of the plains and mountain states where it was strong. Except for railroad bills, Populists initiated and passed no more reform legislation than Republicans or Democrats. Populists may have encouraged other parties to sponsor reform measures but were not themselves reformers. Table, 16 notes. D. E. Bowers

1365. Bland, Gaye K. POPULISM IN THE FIRST CONGRESSIONAL DISTRICT OF KENTUCKY. *Filson Club Hist. Q. 1977 51(1): 31-43.* The combination of a relatively small black population and an economically depressed farming population made the Populist party a major factor in Kentucky's First Congressional District. The financial difficulties were caused in part by the policies of the American Tobacco Company monopoly. Populist and Republican Fusion failed to materialize, and the Democrats retained the seat in 1892. Based on contemporary newspapers; 97 notes. G. B. McKinney

1366. Bromberg, Alan B. THE WORST MUDDLE EVER SEEN IN N.C. POLITICS: THE FARMERS' ALLIANCE, THE SUBTREASURY, AND ZEB VANCE. *North Carolina Hist. Rev. 1979 56(1): 19-40.* Zebulon B. Vance's (1830-94) opposition to the Farmers' Alliance planned subtreasury in 1890 almost cost him his Senate seat and disrupted North Carolina Democratic Party politics. The Democrats were forced to discuss the substantive issue over which they were split: farmers favored the subtreasury plan, conservatives opposed it as government intervention. Before 1890 patronage and competition among state politicians had been issues dividing the party. To insure continued support and to save the party, Vance agreed to follow instructions from his legislature on the subtreasury matter, although he later broke this agreement. The Democratic Party was never the same. Journal and newspaper articles, personal letters, and secondary sources; 16 illus., 40 notes.
T. L. Savitt

1367. Brown, Thomas J. THE ROOTS OF BLUEGRASS INSURGENCY: AN ANALYSIS OF THE POPULIST MOVEMENT IN KENTUCKY. *Register of the Kentucky Hist. Soc. 1980 78(3): 219-242.* During 1870-1900, reform movements appeared in Kentucky as in the rest of the nation. Some movements (e.g., the Grange and Populism) grew large, but were only partly successful because they failed to overcome race and partisanship. Confusion of identity summarizes this era of Kentucky politics. Based on census reports and other primary materials; 2 illus., 76 notes. J. F. Paul

1368. Conway, J. F. THE PRAIRIE POPULIST RESISTANCE TO THE NATIONAL POLICY: SOME RECONSIDERATIONS. *J. of Can. Studies [Canada] 1979 14(3): 77-91.* Examines the Canadian agrarian petite bourgeoisie's resistance to the National Policy, more particularly since the 1920's, and its organization for the support of its grievances, mainly through the progressive movements or parties. 28 notes. G. P. Cleyet

1369. Crow, Jeffrey J. "POPULISM TO PROGRESSIVISM" IN NORTH CAROLINA: GOVERNOR DANIEL RUSSELL AND HIS WAR ON THE SOUTHERN RAILWAY COMPANY. *Historian 1975 37(4): 649-667.* Narrates Governor Daniel Russell's losing battle against northern control over North Carolina's railroads. Crow shows that unlike the Alabama populist experience, North Carolina's populists were reformist. With regard to political objectives they were linked to the state's progressives who during 1894-98 would not aid Russell in his railroad regulation fight but who joined the fray within 10 years. 56 notes.

1370. Erlich, Howard S. POPULIST RHETORIC REASSESSED: A PARADOX. *Q. J. of Speech 1977 63(2): 140-151.* Historians have generally denigrated Populism, finding in Populist rhetoric a simplistic nostalgia, a naive Manichaean world view, widespread belief in conspiracy, and a fear of impending apocalypse. However, the historian must balance these weaknesses with the Populist defense of the civil rights of the common man against the prevalent laissez-faire social Darwinism of big business, as well as a sincere effort to find common cause with oppressed blacks. Secondary sources; 76 notes. E. C. Bailey

1371. Gartner, Lloyd P. NAPHTALI HERZ IMBER, POPULIST. *Michael: On the Hist. of the Jews in the Diaspora [Israel] 1975 3: 88-100.* Naphtali Herz Imber (1856-1909) was a minor Hebrew poet best known for his "Hatikvah" (The Hope), which became Israel's national anthem. Much less known is his pamphlet "The Fall of Jerusalem: Reflecting upon the Present Condition of America," written shortly after his arrival in the United States in 1892 and reprinted here. It fabricates a myth of Biblical history paralleling the Populist myth of American history, exhorting Americans to heed the warning of Jewish experience and not allow their wealth to lead America to ruin. Primary and secondary sources; 5 notes. T. Sassoon

1372. Henningson, Berton E., Jr. NORTHWEST ARKANSAS AND THE BROTHERS OF FREEDOM: THE ROOTS OF A FARMER MOVEMENT. *Arkansas Hist. Q. 1975 34(4): 304-324.* To combat the declining farm prices of the post-Civil War years, the Brothers of Freedom, founded in 1882, attempted to raise northwest Arkansas farmers out of their one crop (cotton) morass through self-help. This class-oriented, anticapitalist movement of 40,000 raised farmers' hopes by instilling confidence, calling for frugality, contracting with local merchants for supplies at lower prices, and entering politics. In 1885 it merged with the Agricultural Wheel, another Arkansas farmer group. Based on primary and secondary sources; 2 illus., 40 notes. T. L. Savitt

1373. Jeffrey, Julie Roy. WOMEN IN THE SOUTHERN FARMERS' ALLIANCE: A RECONSIDERATION OF THE ROLE AND STATUS OF WOMEN IN THE LATE NINETEENTH CENTURY SOUTH. *Feminist Studies 1975 3(1/2): 72-91.* The Southern Farmers' Alliance was a major force in the 1880's and 1890's. Its goal was the revival of southern agriculture. The activities of the Alliance in North Carolina illustrate the organization's general attitude toward women. Rejecting the traditional female stereotype of pale fragile gentility, the Alliance encouraged female participation in its affairs and proposed education and economic equality for women. However, these goals for women existed within the framework of renewing southern agriculture. Women were to be coworkers on the farm, sharing agricultural tasks and prosperity rather than any equal status in the larger political world. The Alliance enlarged the traditional view of women, encouraged education and participation, but did not go further toward female equality outside farm life. Primary and secondary sources; 79 notes. S. R. Herstein

1374. Littlefield, Daniel F., Jr. and Underhill, Lonnie E. THE GRANGER MOVEMENT IN THE CHEROKEE NATION. *Red River Valley Hist. Rev. 1979 4(1): 14-25.* Discusses the granger movement in the United States during the 1870's and its effects on the Cherokee Indians in Indian Territory who shared similar interests and concerns with Anglo farmers.

1375. McCarthy, G. Michael. COLORADO'S POPULIST PARTY AND THE PROGRESSIVE MOVEMENT. *J. of the West 1976 15(1): 54-75.* Using Richard Hofstadter's hypotheses describing populism, the author examines populism in Colorado and finds some similarities and some differences. Agreeing with Hofstadter's thesis, it was found that the leaders of the Colorado populists were, by and large, professional men and professional reformers. Contrary to the thesis, few of the Colorado populists made the transition to progressivism. The stumbling block appears to have been that the doctrine of natural resource conservation ran counter to Colorado beliefs. R. Alvis

1376. McCarthy, G. Michael. THE PEOPLE'S PARTY IN COLORADO: A PROFILE OF POPULIST LEADERSHIP. *Agric. Hist. 1973 47(2): 146-155.* Colorado Populist leaders were not professional reformers. When Populism died out, they failed to make the transition to Progressivism. Most of the leaders were not farmers or silverites. Based mainly on Colorado state histories; 41 notes. D. E. Brewster

1377. McHugh, Christine. MIDWESTERN POPULIST LEADERSHIP AND EDWARD BELLAMY: "LOOKING BACKWARD" INTO THE FUTURE. *Am. Studies 1978 19(2): 57-74.* Analyzes the thrust and impact of the 1888 *Looking Backward 2000-1887,* as well as Bellamy's impact on his contemporaries. His ideas "permeated the midwestern Populist heartland." Populist editors urged readers to become familiar with Bellamy's ideas about producerism, and reprinted his articles widely. They focused on work as a divine blessing, economic grievances, and the devaluation of labor by nonproductive market forces. Primary and secondary sources; 62 notes. J. A. Andrew

1378. McLear, Patrick E. THE AGRARIAN REVOLT IN THE SOUTH: A HISTORIOGRAPHICAL ESSAY. *Louisiana Studies 1973 12(2): 443-463.* Surveys and analyzes the literature on the Agrarian Revolt in the South and notes the shortcomings of the theses. Examines economic, political, religious, and social forces to understand the Populist movement. 52 notes. G. W. McGinty

1379. McMath, Robert C., Jr. AGRARIAN PROTEST AT THE FORKS OF THE CREEK: THREE SUBORDINATE FARMERS' ALLIANCES IN NORTH CAROLINA. *North Carolina Hist. R. 1974 51(1): 41-63.* The strength of the Farmers' Alliance in the late 1880's was based on its local chapters. Farmers and rural professionals were attracted by a program of economic relief, cooperative enterprise, and fraternal organization. Statewide decline of the Alliance in 1891 was associated with increased political activity. Primary and secondary sources; illus., map, 75 notes. W. B. Bedford

1380. McMath, Robert C., Jr. PREFACE TO POPULISM: THE ORIGIN AND ECONOMIC DEVELOPMENT OF THE 'SOUTHERN' FARMERS' ALLIANCE IN KANSAS. *Kansas Hist Q. 1976 42(1): 55-65.* William F. Rightmire, a Populist whose version of the Southern Farmers' Alliance's role in Kansas usually has been accepted, based his case on two points. He claimed that he set up the Kansas Alliance after the 1888 election and that he and his friends used the Alliance to expand popular support for political insurgency. The author shows that the Southern Alliance from Texas was well organized in Kansas by 1886. He does not dismiss the political role of the Alliance but points out that it was more interested in economic reform. During 1890-92 it set up a cooperative for the sale of livestock and grain and provided cheap supplies. Farmers joined because they could save money on supplies and make more profit on their produce. Primary and secondary sources; 37 notes. W. F. Zornow

1381. Palmer, Bruce. THE ROOTS OF REFORM: SOUTHERN POPULISTS AND THEIR SOUTHERN HISTORY. *Red River Valley Hist. Rev. 1979 4(2): 33-62.* Traces Populism in the American South between the 1850's and the 1890's, and discusses the southern Populists' view of the history of the South.

1382. Palmer, Bruce. SOUTHERN POPULISTS REMEMBER: THE REFORM ALTERNATIVE TO SOUTHERN SECTIONALISM. *Southern Studies 1978 17(2): 131-149.* Southern Populists of the late 19th century looked upon the antebellum South with neither nostalgia for the Old South nor admiration for the industrialization of the New South. They were hostile to any form of aristocracy, opposed sectionalism, were antimonopoly and pro-Greenback, and were concerned with the effects of black slavery on white labor. They viewed the Civil War as necessary to destroy slavery and criticized their own period of the 1890's for enslaving blacks and whites in the new industrialization. The Civil War was an unfortunate tragedy best forgotten, not glorified. The disappearance of the Populist Party after 1896 removed the last viable political opposition to the Democratic solid South. Based on Southern newspapers and secondary sources; 72 notes. J. Buschen

1383. Perkey, Elton A. THE FIRST FARMERS' ALLIANCE IN NEBRASKA. *Nebraska Hist. 1976 57(2): 242-247.* Indicates that the birthplace of the Farmers' Alliance in Nebraska was a schoolhouse located a few miles north of Filley in Gage County. One of its organizers was Jabez Burrows, who became president of the organization in 1887 and then editor of its newspaper, the *Alliance,* until his death in 1899. R. Lowitt

1384. Piehler, Harold. HENRY VINCENT: KANSAS POPULIST AND RADICAL-REFORM JOURNALIST. *Kansas Hist. 1979 2(1): 14-25.* Much has been written about Kansas Populism, but no one has done a full study of Henry Vincent (1862-1935), the controversial editor of *The American Nonconformist and Kansas Industrial Liberator* of Winfield during 1886-91. This lack of interest is attributed to Vincent's brief stay in Kansas, his failure to seek political office, and the inaccessibility of his papers until now. Vincent now emerges as one of the most resourceful and influential men in organizing and guiding the People's Party to victory in Cowley County in 1889 and in the state of Kansas in 1890. Republican overreaction to his journalistic attacks on the GOP offers ample evidence of fear of this gadfly. Based largely on family papers in Glendora, California; illus., 77 notes. W. F. Zornow

1385. Prescott, Gerald L. FARM GENTRY VS. THE GRANGERS: CONFLICT IN RURAL CALIFORNIA. *California Hist. Q. 1977-78 56(4): 328-345.* Contrasts the California State Grange with the California State Agricultural Society in the 1870's and 1880's. The Grange campaigned against railroad rates, trusts, and middlemen, but its was not the only voice for farmers. The State Agricultural Society represented prosperous gentlemen farmers who claimed a broader understanding of such complex issues as land ownership, labor and immigration, and agricultural education. The farm elite stressed scientific farming, self-help, and hard work as the keys to success, while the Grange sought reduction of rates, cooperative effort, and an end to land monopoly. The contrast in opinions suggests that California's farm community contained a spectrum of opinion on issues affecting agriculture. Primary and secondary sources; photos, 46 notes. A. Hoffman

1386. Press, Donald E. KANSAS CONFLICT: POPULIST VERSUS RAILROADER IN THE 1890'S. *Kansas Hist. Q. 1977 43(3): 319-333.* In the 1890's, Kansas Populists alarmed railroaders by calling for maximum freight rates and state ownership of the railroads. In 1896 they won control of the governorship and both houses of the legislature, but were able to agree on railroad legislation only at a last-minute session after their defeat in 1898. At this time they created the Court of Visitation, with broad regulatory powers, which was declared unconstitutional two years later by the Republican-controlled state supreme court. Many of the measures that the Populists advocated but failed to implement in the 1890's, including a maximum freight rate, became law under the Republicans in the succeeding decade. Based on proceedings of the Kansas legislature, contemporary publications (especially *Railway Age),* and secondary sources; 2 illus., 3 tables, 42 notes. L. W. Van Wyk

1387. Pruitt, Paul, Jr. A CHANGING OF THE GUARD: JOSEPH C. MANNING AND POPULIST STRATEGY IN THE FALL OF 1894. *Alabama Hist. Q. 1978 40(1-2): 20-36.* Details the attempt of Joseph C. Manning, 1892-96, to unite populists against the Jeffersonian Democratic machine in Alabama. 80 notes. E. E. Eminhizer

1388. Reinhart, Cornel J. POPULIST IDEOLOGY: MIRROR OR PRISM OF THE GILDED AGE? *North Dakota Q. 1975 43(3): 5-15.* Discusses the ideology and rhetoric of prominent Populists during the 1870's and 80's and their appeal to northwestern farmers.

1389. Riddle, Thomas W. POPULISM IN THE PALOUSE: OLD IDEALS AND NEW REALITIES. *Pacific Northwest Q. 1974 65(3): 97-109.* A study of the rise and demise of the populist movement in Washington politics, begun among farmers and laborers of Whitman County in Eastern Washington at a meeting in Ellensburg in 1891, when they formed the Washington State People's Party. Populists were convinced that the two major parties were unwilling to regulate the arbitrary practices of commercial enterprises, felt their security on the land to be threatened, and sought legislative protection. 46 notes. R. V. Ritter

1390. Ridge, Martin. THE POPULIST AS A SOCIAL CRITIC. *Minnesota Hist. 1973 43(8): 297-302.* The depression of 1893 spawned Populist social criticism which fed upon the dissatisfaction and "monumental disillusionment" with America of midwestern and southern farmers. The Populists defined man as an economic creature, opposed monopoly, called for civil service reform, distrusted politicians, and advocated independent political action. 2 illus. D. L. Smith

1391. Schwartz, Michael H. AN ESTIMATE OF THE SIZE OF THE SOUTHERN FARMERS' ALLIANCE, 1884-1890. *Agric. Hist. 1977 51(4): 759-769.* At its height in 1890, the Southern Farmers' Alliance probably numbered about 857,000 members. This figure was reached by making estimates of state membership using average club size where actual membership was unknown and interpolating data so estimates would be for 1 January of each year. These membership figures are well below previous estimates of up to three million members, but still represent an impressive percentage of adult southern males. 2 tables, chart, 16 notes. D. E. Bowers

1392. Steelman, Lala Carr. THE ROLE OF ELIAS CARR IN THE NORTH CAROLINA FARMERS' ALLIANCE. *North Carolina Hist. Rev. 1980 57(2): 133-158.* Elias Carr (1839-1900), since 1859 master of Bracebridge Plantation, in eastern North Carolina entered state agricultural politics during the 1880's. By 1887 he was president of the newly formed North Carolina Farmers' State Association, which was absorbed the following year into the North Carolina Farmers' Alliance. Despite his upper class standing, Carr became a leader in the militant and powerful farm protest movement, first as executive committee chairman (1887-89) and then as Alliance president (1889-91). In these powerful positions, Carr, working with two other important Alliance leaders, Leonidas L. Polk (1837-92) and Sydenham B. Alexander (1840-1921), dealt with a number of tough and controversial problems, such as removing inept staff, establishing a viable business agency, boycotting the jute bagging trust, overseeing the educational programs, maintaining membership standards, and avoiding partisan politics while still supporting Senator Zebulon Vance. Though the Alliance under Carr sometimes faltered, it emerged from his presidency a stronger organization. Based primarily on Carr Papers at East Carolina University, and published proceedings of the Alliance; 14 illus., 112 notes. T. L. Savitt

1393. Thornton, Emma and Adams, Pauline. SPEAKING TO THE PEOPLE: 19TH CENTURY POPULIST RHETORIC. *J. of Popular Culture 1980 13(4): 654-658.* Examines the literary style of Populist reformer Sarah E. Van De Vort Emery (1838-95) to illustrate the power of language in shaping history. Emery, as demonstrated by her careful use of emotion-laden words in *Seven Financial Conspiracies Which Have Enslaved the American People* (1887), knew how to express the experiences of her audience in terms that would bolster her arguments. 6 notes. D. G. Nielson

1394. Trask, David Stephens. A NATURAL PARTNERSHIP: NEBRASKA'S POPULISTS AND DEMOCRATS AND THE DEVELOPMENT OF FUSION. *Nebraska Hist. 1975 56(3): 419-438.* Discusses the movement for fusion between Nebraska Democrats and Populists, consummated successfully in 1894. The party situation in the 1890's explains how the Populists in Nebraska accepted fusion with the Democrats behind Bryan before free silver became the dominant issue. R. Lowitt

1395. Trask, David Stephens. NEBRASKA POPULISM AS A RESPONSE TO ENVIRONMENTAL AND POLITICAL PROBLEMS. Blouet, Brian W. and Luebke, Frederick C., ed. *The Great Plains: Environment and Culture* (Lincoln: U. of Nebraska Pr., 1979): 61-80. Nebraska Populism developed during a period of simultaneous crises in agriculture and politics. Farmers who attempted to raise corn and hogs in dry regions of Nebraska faced economic disaster when drought occurred. When they sought relief through political means, they found the Republican Party complacent, resting on its past achievement of prosperity. The Democratic Party, meanwhile, was preoccupied with the prohibition issue. A new party seemed likeliest to provide help. 7 maps, 3 tables, 18 notes. S

1396. Turner, James. UNDERSTANDING THE POPULISTS. *J. of Am. Hist. 1980 67(2): 354-373.* Explains the development of Populism in terms of the geographic and cultural isolation of the affected areas, such as regions of East and West Texas. Populists were relatively isolated from the larger society of their state and nation. Populists felt adrift in a changing society, and they were uncertain of the new emerging order, like strangers in their own land. Their isolation bred a political movement that conflicted with the mainstream of political habits and attitudes. 2 tables, 46 notes. T. P. Linkfield

1397. Walker, Samuel. GEORGE HOWARD GIBSON, CHRISTIAN SOCIALIST AMONG THE POPULISTS. *Nebraska Hist. 1974 55(4): 553-572.* Examines the career of George Howard Gibson, a devout Christian Socialist who served as editor of the Populist official organ in Nebraska, the *Alliance-Independent* (which he renamed the *Wealth Makers*) from October 1893 to January 1896. Gibson was too extreme for most Nebraska Populists, who wished to stress free-silver and fusion. He relinquished his editorship of the paper to lead a group of Nebraskans to found the Christian Commonwealth Colony in Georgia.
R. Lowitt

1398. Wheeler, Joanne E. POPULISTS AND OTHER PEOPLE: AN ILLINOIS PORTRAIT. Plesur, Milton, ed. *An American Historian: Essays to Honor Selig Adler* (Buffalo: State U. of N.Y., 1980): 125-139. Attempts to characterize the Illinois Populist supporters of the People's Party, using electoral, economic, and biographical data of the 1880's and 1890's, and to examine their political beliefs in 1892.

1399. Wyman, Roger E. AGRARIAN OR WORKING-CLASS RADICALISM? THE ELECTORAL BASIS OF POPULISM IN WISCONSIN. *Pol. Sci. Q. 1974/75 89(4): 825-848.* "Demonstrates that Populism in Wisconsin arose out of socialist-oriented labor radicalism rather than from agricultural distress and that urban workers, not agrarians, provided the largest component of Populist supporters. His findings thus challenge the commonly held belief that Wisconsin had a long tradition of agrarian radicalism in the late nineteenth century."
J

1400. —. [AGRARIAN "POLITICAL POWER"]. *Agric. Hist. 1974 48(1): 115-129.*
Lurie, Jonathan. COMMODITY EXCHANGES, AGRARIAN "POLITICAL POWER," AND THE ANTIOPTION BATTLE, 1890-1894, pp. 115-125.
Guither, Harold D. COMMENT, pp. 126-129.
Lurie observes that agrarian thought in the late 19th century suffered from a contradiction between the idea that farmers had significant political power and the belief that they were the victims of unscrupulous businessmen. This dichotomy was manifested in the antioption struggle of the early 1890's when farmers lobbied Congress to place severe limitations on futures and option trading. Farmers confused the speculative excesses of option trading with the real benefits of futures trading. Despite the general belief that farmers had great power, antioption bills lost in Congress and the Populists failed to include the issue in their platforms. Based on primary and secondary sources; 51 notes.
D. E. Bowers

Educational Reform

1401. Adams, Paul K. JAMES P. WICKERSHAM ON EDUCATION AND CRIME IN NINETEENTH-CENTURY PENNSYLVANIA. *Pennsylvania Mag. of Hist. and Biog. 1980 104(4): 422-433.* In his work on behalf of neglected children, in his writings, and in his legislative lobbying, School Superintendent James P. Wickersham revealed his faith in intellectual and moral education in the deterrence of crime. Covers ca. 1866-81. Based on official reports and secondary sources; 107 notes.
T. H. Wendel

1402. Andrews, Andrea R. THE BALTIMORE SCHOOL BUILDING PROGRAM, 1870 TO 1900: A STUDY OF URBAN REFORM. *Maryland Hist. Mag. 1975 70(3): 260-274.* The "one-sided Progressive picture of the ward-based machine as totally corrupt and evil" needs redressing, yet the rapidly growing late-19th-century city was developing serious needs which the locally oriented city government was not equipped to meet. Analyzes the problem of providing a growing school population with buildings and equipment, describing Baltimore city and the government politically dependent school board. School commissioners were primarily ward politicians appointed by council and bound to the dictates of the machine hierarchy. Inordinate stress on budgetary economy and property tax evasion resulted in chronic deficits and lack of funds. Lack of expertise and coordination produced a shortsighted, haphazard program, with overcrowded and hazardous makeshift buildings. The reformed City Charter of 1898 created the mechanism for "centralization, independence, objectivity, and expertise" with a new Board of Estimates and a mayor-appointed board for schools, but the reform system was no guarantee that partisanship and self-interest were dead. Moreover, the popular, local control of the ward system was removed while the potential for a machine still existed. Primary and secondary works; 2 tables, 55 notes.
G. J. Bobango

1403. Barlow, William and Powell, David O. HOMEOPATHY AND SEXUAL EQUALITY: THE CONTROVERSY OVER COEDUCATION AT CINCINNATI'S PULTE MEDICAL COLLEGE, 1873-1879. *Ohio Hist. 1981 90(2): 101-113.* Of the many women physicians trained in the United States between 1860 and 1900, the majority were trained in schools sponsored by physicians who dissented from the orthodox medical therapy and who were thus branded as irregular sects by the American Medical Association. The authors discuss the controversy revolving around the admission of women into the Cincinnati homeopathic college, Pulte Medical College, from 1873 to 1879, and suggest that sexual barriers at irregular medical institutions were much more rigid than scholars have previously assumed. Reflecting the national debate over coeducation, the homeopathic wars at Pulte Medical College resulted in the adoption of a separate but equal policy for women. Based on the Pulte Medical College Papers, Cincinnati Historical Society, and other primary sources; 2 illus., 47 notes.
L. A. Russell

1404. Barney, Robert Knight. ADELE PAROT: BEACON OF THE DIOCLESIAN LEWIS SCHOOL OF GYMNASTIC EXPRESSION IN THE AMERICAN WEST. *Canadian J. of Hist. of Sport and Physical Educ. 1974 5(2): 63-73.* The impact of Dioclesius Lewis gymnastics reached the Pacific Coast through Adele Parot when she began teaching at the State Normal School in San Francisco in 1862. Suggests her influence on the first state law requiring physical education instruction in California 1866. Based on 16 primary and secondary sources.
R. A. Smith

1405. Beales, Ross W., Jr. AN INCIDENT AT THE FREEDMEN'S SCHOOL, LEXINGTON, VIRGINIA, 1867. *Prologue 1974 6(4): 252-254.* Illustrates the difficulties under which northern teachers functioned in freedmen's schools in the South. The official version of an incident at Lexington, Virginia, toned down its offensiveness, which included an armed threat, but a copy of the teacher's letter narrating the harrassment and threats in detail is a more accurate and complete statement of the facts. Photo, 7 notes.
R. V. Ritter

1406. Brabham, Robin. DEFINING THE AMERICAN UNIVERSITY: THE UNIVERSITY OF NORTH CAROLINA, 1865-1875. *North Carolina Hist. Rev. 1980 57(4): 427-455.* The University of North Carolina (UNC), along with a number of other major universities, struggled through a period of reform and redefinition as America's educational needs changed during the latter 19th century. A university now had to be more than a larger version of a country college; it had to offer more applied and advanced courses, and in areas to fit an increasingly business and technology oriented society. UNC, a successful, traditional, antebellum state school, failed to meet its constituents' curricular needs in the immediate postwar years. President David Lowry Swain began the reform process with Morrill Land Grant funds and some new ideas proposed by the trustees and faculty. Before the latter plans could be implemented, federal Reconstruction Acts caused a reorganization of the state education system, including selection of Republican-leaning trustees and president Solomom Pool. Enrollment dropped, enmity rose, and the trustees closed the school from 1871 to 1875. A new board and President Kemp P. Battle reorganized the university into six colleges leading to degrees of Bachelor of Arts, Bachelor of Science, Bachelor of Agriculture, and Master of Arts. UNC Papers and Trustee Minutes, and secondary sources; 13 illus., 73 notes.
T. L. Savitt

1407. Buchanan, Jess. HIGHER EDUCATION IN THE PALOUSE HILLS: WHY DO WASHINGTON STATE AND IDAHO RUB SHOULDERS? *Pacific Northwesterner 1980 24(2): 17-27.* Examines why Washington State University and the University of Idaho were chartered in 1890 and 1889 respectively, only nine miles apart, and opened 13 January and 3 October 1892; and traces their beginning to the Federal Land-Grant College Act, or the Morrill Act (US, 1862), one of "the most influential and far reaching piece(s) of federal educational legislation in the history of our country."

1408. Burgess, Charles. THE GODDESS, THE SCHOOL BOOK, AND COMPULSION. *Harvard Educ. R. 1976 46(2): 199-216.* Discusses compulsory education and school attendance laws in the context of social change, industrialization, and frontier expansion in the 1870's.

1409. Carper, James C. A COMMON FAITH FOR THE COMMON SCHOOL? RELIGION AND EDUCATION IN KANSAS, 1861-1900. *Mid-America 1978 60(3): 147-161.* During the latter half of the 19th century religion in education was a major issue in Kansas. Most teachers, and a majority of the population, supported the concept of religious instruction with a Protestant bias in public school systems. Bible reading, mainly from the King James Version, was a normal practice and was used as a basis for moral instruction. Catholics responded with the proposal that tax revenues be divided among the several denominations for the support of their own institutions. This proposal failed after much debate, and public schools still reflected a Protestant bias until the mid-1890's. Eventually, as Kansas society became more secular, religion was divorced from public education. Primary and secondary sources; 64 notes.
J. M. Lee

1410. Comeault, Gilbert-L. LA QUESTION DES ÉCOLES DU MANITOBA: UN NOUVEL ÉCLAIRAGE [The schools issue in Manitoba: a new light]. *Rev. d'Hist. de l'Amérique Française [Canada] 1979 33(1): 3-23.* Reexamines the schools issue in Manitoba from 1890 to 1916, refuting interpretations still given by most historians. After recalling the policy of Archbishop Msgr. A.-A. Taché, centers on the new line of action of his successor in 1894, Msgr. Adélard Langevin, who opposed the Anglo-Saxon campaign against the principle of bilingual and private schools, and mobilized the Franco-Manitoban political force to protect the other Catholic groups' faith. Based on archival documents and other primary sources; 83 notes.
G. P. Cleyet

1411. Dillingham, George A. THE UNIVERSITY OF NASHVILLE, A NORTHERN EDUCATOR, AND A NEW MISSION IN THE POST-RECONSTRUCTION SOUTH. *Tennessee Hist. Q. 1978 37(3): 329-338.* After a decade of academic inactivity by the University of Nashville following the Civil War, in 1875 Barnas Sears of the Peabody Fund fashioned an agreement whereby the University, the state of Tennessee, and the Fund would jointly conduct a normal school utilizing the University's facilities. The purpose was to make the school a model for other southern states. New York-born William Howard Payne of the University of Michigan became the school's second president (1888-1901). Under his leadership a solid foundation was laid which has characterized George Peabody College since then. Describes Payne's educational philosophy, his methodology for teacher training, the academic progress of the institution and accomplishments of some of its faculty and graduates during his tenure. More than anyone, Payne helped to vindicate the Fund's decision to devote its primary attention to teacher training. Based on the William Howard Payne file in the archives of Peabody College, College publications, and secondary sources; 39 notes.
H. M. Parker, Jr.

1412. Dye, Charles M. CALVIN WOODWARD AND MANUAL TRAINING: THE MAN, THE IDEA, AND THE SCHOOL. *Missouri Hist. Soc. Bull. 1976 32(2): 75-98.* Analyzes the educational philosophies and psychological theories of Calvin Woodward (1837-1914). Woodward implemented many of his ideas at the Manual Training School founded in St. Louis in 1879 by Washington University. Woodward's innovative curricula and pioneering pedagogical practices at the school provided models for manual arts programs in numerous secondary schools. Based on archival and secondary sources; 8 illus., 72 notes.
H. T. Lovin

1413. Foner, Philip S. A PENNSYLVANIA STATE SENATOR ON WOMEN'S RIGHTS IN 1868. *Pennsylvania Hist. 1974 41(4): 423-426.* Presents a letter written in 1868 by State Senator Morrow B. Lowry of Meadville endorsing the equal right of women to higher education. The letter was written to a resident of Smethport, Pennsylvania. Lowry, a forgotten figure in Pennsylvania history, was a philanthropist and radical abolitionist. The letter is in the Frederick Douglass papers; illus., 3 notes.
D. C. Swift

1414. Geiger, John O. THE EDGERTON BIBLE CASE: HUMPHREY DESMOND'S POLITICAL EDUCATION OF WISCONSIN CATHOLICS. *J. of Church and State 1979 20(1): 13-28.* Details the case of *State of Wisconsin ex rel. Frederick Weiss, et al.* vs. *District School Board of School District 8* (1890) concerning Bible reading in public schools, and Humphrey Desmond's (1852-1932) support of those who opposed the reading of only the King James version of the Bible by all students including Catholics. The case resulted in the elimination of Bible reading in Wisconsin schools. Covers 1888-90. 47 notes.
E. E. Eminhizer

1415. Gidney, R. D. and Lawr, D. A. EGERTON RYERSON AND THE ORIGINS OF THE ONTARIO SECONDARY SCHOOL. *Can. Hist. Rev. [Canada] 1979 60(4): 442-465.* Though the Ontario School Act (1871) is generally acknowledged as a crucial landmark in the development of Ontario's education system, it has received relatively little serious attention from historians. Examines the origins of the high school clauses of that Act and explains the changes that took place in them after 1871. During the late 1850's and 1860's, Egerton Ryerson developed a particular conception of secondary education, which he attempted to impose on the province. His efforts brought him into sustained conflict with local people who had a stake in the grammar schools. Examines the intellectual and social sources of this conflict and attempts to draw lessons from it about the nature of 19th-century governmental policymaking.
A

1416. Goedeken, Edward A. AN ACADEMIC CONTROVERSY AT IOWA STATE AGRICULTURAL COLLEGE, 1890-1891. *Ann. of Iowa 1979 45(2): 110-122.* In 1884, the Iowa Legislature called upon Iowa State Agricultural College at Ames to broaden its curriculum by including liberal arts courses. The subsequent reduction of agriculturally-related instruction produced a strong reaction from many farm groups, especially the Farmer's Alliance. Assisted by Henry Wallace, editor of the *Iowa Homestead,* the Farmer's Alliance persuaded the college faculty and Board of Trustees to reinstate a strong agriculture curriculum in 1891. The role of the Iowa Farmer's Alliance in shaping academic policy at a land-grant college is unique. Based on the records of Iowa State Agricultural College, including *General Faculty Minutes* and Board of Trustee Reports, and the *Iowa Homestead;* 3 photos, 33 notes.
P. L. Petersen

1417. Hunt, Thomas C. THE BENNETT LAW OF 1890: FOCUS OF CONFLICT BETWEEN CHURCH AND STATE. *J. of Church and State 1981 23(1): 69-93.* In 1890 a compulsory attendance law (the Bennett Law) was passed in Wisconsin that required 12 weeks of schooling and the teaching of English language. The opposition to this law by the German-speaking population found among the Lutherans and Catholics is discussed at length since it involved the schools. Those whose position favored the law are also discussed, with emphasis on the Baptists and Methodists. Mainly newspapers; 122 notes.
E. E. Eminhizer

1418. Hunt, Thomas C. METHODISM, MORAL EDUCATION AND PUBLIC SCHOOLS: A LOOK AT THE PAST. *Methodist Hist. 1981 19(2): 84-98.* The Methodist Episcopal Church in Wisconsin supported the ties between Protestant Christianity and public education for many years. It declared that the public school system was an offspring of the Bible and that Protestants should resist any assaults on the system. The author traces Methodist involvement and concern in Wisconsin from the establishment of public schools in 1846 until the Wisconsin Supreme Court in 1890 judged Bible-reading to be sectarian and therefore illegal in public schools, in a suit brought by Catholic parents against reading of the King James version of the Bible. 82 notes.
H. L. Calkin

1419. Hunt, Thomas C. THE REFORMED TRADITION, BIBLE READING AND EDUCATION IN WISCONSIN. *J. of Presbyterian Hist. 1981 59(1): 73-105.* In 1848 the Constitutional Convention of Wisconsin approved a section of the proposed constitution which forbade sectarian instruction in the public schools. In 1890 the Wisconsin Supreme Court handed down a decision which forbade Bible-reading in the schools as unconstitutional on grounds that it constituted sectarian instruction. The Bible-reading issue in Wisconsin showed that the leaders of the Congregational and Presbyterian Churches overwhelmingly supported Bible-reading in particular and Protestant-oriented public schools in general. State documents, Presbyterian records at various judicatory levels, and reactions to the 1890 decision; 105 notes.
H. M. Parker, Jr.

1420. Issel, William. AMERICANIZATION, ACCULTURATION AND SOCIAL CONTROL: SCHOOL REFORM IDEOLOGY IN INDUSTRIAL PENNSYLVANIA, 1880-1910. *J. of Social Hist. 1979 12(4): 569-590.* Analyzes school reform efforts as a consequence of dislocations caused by industrialization in Pennsylvania. It is true that elites initiated reform efforts, however, Marxists and revisionists are incorrect in asserting that economics was the motivating force. Strikes, riots, and hordes of immigrants had to be dealt with. Reformers acted to unite state, school, and community, arguing that what was good for one was good for all. The schools, therefore, stressed social control themes. Some allowance was made for the new values of immigrants as well as for those of poor native laborers. Control was designed to benefit state and society rather than industry or the individual. 54 notes. V. L. Human

1421. Johnson, Keach. ELEMENTARY AND SECONDARY EDUCATION IN IOWA, 1890-1900: A TIME OF AWAKENING. PART II. *Ann. of Iowa 1980 45(3): 171-195.* Continued from a previous article (see abstract 18A:5869). During the 1890's a consensus emerged among Iowa educators that the state's public schools needed substantial reform. Schools were called upon to identify with the democratic, scientific, and technological forces of society and to make equal educational opportunity a reality for all Iowa children. Based on *Biennial Reports of the Iowa State Superintendent of Public Instruction* and other primary sources; 3 photos, 46 notes. P. L. Petersen

1422. Johnson, Keach. ELEMENTARY AND SECONDARY EDUCATION IN IOWA, 1890-1900: A TIME OF AWAKENING. PART I. *Ann. of Iowa 1979 45(2): 87-109.* During the 1890's, several educational leaders called upon Iowans to modernize their public schools in order to meet the demands and pressures of the new industrial urban society. Although the public generally had not yet awakened to this need for modernization, Iowa educators worked throughout the decade to improve the state's elementary and secondary schools. Article to be continued. Based on *Biennial Reports of the Iowa State Superintendent of Public Instruction* and other primary sources; 6 photos, 37 notes. P. L. Petersen

1423. Johnson, Ronald M. POLITICS AND PEDAGOGY: THE 1892 CLEVELAND SCHOOL REFORM. *Ohio Hist. 1975 84(4): 196-206.* The 1892 Cleveland School reform occurred as part of the sustained political battle between the business-dominated Republican party and an increasingly immigrant-oriented Democratic organization. In 1892 the Republicans won control of a highly centralized school system. The new superintendent was Andrew S. Draper, whose primary objective was a revitalized educational process. Despite many improvements, the reform was only partially successful. Illus., 40 notes. E. P. Stickney

1424. Johnson, Ronald M. SCHOOLING THE SAVAGE: ANDREW S. DRAPER AND INDIAN EDUCATION. *Phylon 1974 35(1): 74-82.* Andrew Sloan Draper, a prominent New York schoolman, advocated Indian assimilation during 1886-1913. In the 1880's both the Indian Peace Commission and the Grant administration called for an end to tribalism as a necessary step in preparing Indians for eventual participation in American society. In this attitude Draper revealed his fear of ethnic pluralism. Nevertheless he viewed the "Indian question with grave concern." In recent years Indian assimilation and the manner in which it has been executed through schools has been increasingly and bitterly criticized by Indian spokesmen. 28 notes. E. P. Stickney

1425. Jones, Jacqueline. WOMEN WHO WERE MORE THAN MEN: SEX AND STATUS IN FREEDMEN'S TEACHING. *Hist. of Educ. Q. 1979 19(1): 47-59.* Tests stereotypes of 19th-century female teachers, particularly the idea that females were only able to offer nurturing qualities, and that they were very submissive to male authority. Discusses northern teachers who went south after the Civil War to work in freedmen schools for the American Missionary Association. Research indicates that some females questioned male authority and that their strong sense of professionalism led to some challenges in matters of curriculum. Based on extensive research in the American Missionary Association archives at Dillard University in New Orleans, LA.; 30 notes. L. C. Smith

1426. Katz, Harriet. WORKERS' EDUCATION OR EDUCATION FOR THE WORKER? *Social Service Rev. 1978 52(2): 265-274.* Jane Addams's Hull House educational programs for the working class in Chicago stressed humanities, fine arts, and folk handicrafts and reflected her educational philosophy of enrichment of social relations and human existence, 1890's.

1427. Lang, Daniel W. THE PEOPLE'S COLLEGE, THE MECHANICS' MUTUAL PROTECTION AND THE AGRICULTURAL COLLEGE ACT. *Hist. of Educ. Q. 1978 18(3): 295-321.* The People's College, chartered in 1853 in New York; the Mechanics' Mutual Protection (society), founded in 1843 in Buffalo, New York; and the Agricultural College Act (US, 1862), all were designed to insure that students could receive mechanical and/or scientific farming educations; discusses reasons for the failure of the People's College in the early 1860's.

1428. Marks, Bayly Ellen. LIBERAL EDUCATION IN THE GILDED AGE: BALTIMORE AND THE CREATION OF THE MANUAL TRAINING SCHOOL. *Maryland Hist. Mag. 1979 74(3): 238-252.* In an era when school board members, school administrators, and teachers were subject to Democratic city machine politics, the debate over manual training centered around rival educational philosophies, but was settled through political expediency. Alexander McFadden Newell, Maryland State Superintendent of Public Instruction, argued for training native youth in mechanical skills. Henry Elliot Shepherd, Baltimore City School Superintendent, insisted on intellectual and classical education as a defense against materialism. Creation of the Manual Training School in 1884, and its subsequent success preparing students for engineering colleges, reflect a shift of urban education toward science and engineering. Based on Baltimore City school records, newspapers, papers of Daniel Coit Gilman and Joshua Plaskett; 41 notes. C. B. Schulz

1429. Miller, J. R. D'ALTON MCCARTHY, EQUAL RIGHTS, AND THE ORIGINS OF THE MANITOBA SCHOOL QUESTION. *Can. Hist. R. 1973 54(4): 369-392.* Examines the historiography of the origins of provincial legislation in Manitoba to eliminate Catholic denominational education in 1890. Offers a revised view of the role of Conservative Member of Parliament D'Alton McCarthy and the Equal Rights Association in this process. There was little connection between McCarthy and the schools legislation. The 1890 Acts were the result of the social transformation of Manitoba, 1870-90. Based on newspaper, pamphlet, and manuscript sources in the Public Archives of Canada, the Public Archives of Manitoba, and the Archiepiscopal Archives of St. Boniface. A

1430. Patterson, R. S. and Rooke, Patricia. THE DELICATE DUTY OF CHILD SAVING: COLDWATER, MICHIGAN, 1871-1896. *Michigan Hist. 1977 61(3): 194-219.* The Coldwater State Public School, founded in 1874, was an example of the 19th-century humanitarian effort to save dependent children from lives of crime by teaching them Protestant, middle-class virtues. Social uplift at Coldwater focused on those from the "perishing class" of the potentially criminal. Whether the reformers were more interested in social control or social improvement remains an issue. Primary and secondary sources; 8 illus., 9 photos, 47 notes. D. W. Johnson

1431. Peitzman, Steven J. "THOROUGHLY PRACTICAL": AMERICA'S POLYCLINIC MEDICAL SCHOOLS. *Bull. of the Hist. of Medicine 1980 54(2): 166-187.* In the early 1880's polyclinic medical schools were organized in various cities. Abraham Flexner disdainfully called these schools that offered short courses on the various specialities "undergraduate repair shops." The students were taught by eminent professors, and the schools became the specialists' own colleges. These schools probably helped to cement the structure of specialization in America. Students who attended sought to catch up, by observing medical cases they had not seen in their undergraduate education. They sought practical experience, which the polyclinics provided. Sources include records of the polyclinic schools; 42 notes. M. Kaufman

1432. Raichle, Donald R. THE ABOLITION OF CORPORAL PUNISHMENT IN NEW JERSEY SCHOOLS. *Hist. of Childhood Q. 1974 2(1): 53-78.* Physical punishment was widespread in 19th-century schools. New Jersey was the first state to ban corporal punishment, abolishing it in 1867. The prohibition was opposed by educators. The loss of control and authority expected by teachers did not materialize. Primary and secondary sources; 91 notes. R. E. Butchart

1433. Rosen, F. Bruce. THE INFLUENCE OF THE PEABODY FUND ON EDUCATION IN RECONSTRUCTION FLORIDA. *Florida Hist. Q. 1977 55(3): 310-320.* The Peabody Fund encouraged public elementary education through financial support. Its most significant influence was to encourage Florida's racially segregated and unequal school system. The Fund's policy of less aid for black schools was justified on the grounds that funds for the education of black children came from the Freedmen's Bureau, charitable organizations, and the state. Primary and secondary works; 57 notes.
P. A. Beaber

1434. Sloan, Jan Butin. THE FOUNDING OF THE NAPLES TABLE ASSOCIATION FOR PROMOTING SCIENTIFIC RESEARCH BY WOMEN, 1897. *Signs 1978 4(1): 208-216.* Ida H. Hyde, American physiologist, overcame American and European sex discrimination to receive her doctorate from Heidelberg University. In 1896, she continued her work at the Naples Zoological Station, established by German scientist Anton Dohrn. The correspondence published here contains four letters from Hyde and two from Dohrn concerning the creation of an "American Women's Table" (fellowship) at the zoological station. In spite of Dohrn's support of women, he nonetheless held very traditional views of a woman's role. Based on correspondence from the Naples Zoological Station Archives, and on secondary sources; 14 notes.
S. P. Conner

1435. Stephens, Lester D. JOSEPH LE CONTE ON EVOLUTION, EDUCATION, AND THE STRUCTURE OF KNOWLEDGE. *J. of the Hist. of the Behavioral Sci. 1976 12(2): 103-119.* Joseph LeConte had an important impact on education because of the Darwinian influence upon society. LeConte maintained that society should be studied scientifically through sociology. Science should be the basis of education. LeConte developed theories of education insisting that science, art, and philosophy be included in the college curriculum. He outlined the laws of evolution in 1879 and listed seven basic differences between animals and man. Psychologists William James and G. Stanley Hall studied and commented on LeConte's theories. James stressed the active nature and adaptability of the mind. Hall stressed the importance of natural growth and urged a curriculum coinciding with the natural growth of a child. LeConte preceded John Dewey in urging reform of the school curriculum to direct students toward natural activities. Based on LeConte's articles and speeches; 46 notes.
R. I. Vexler

1436. Struna, Nancy and Remley, Mary L. PHYSICAL EDUCATION FOR WOMEN AT THE UNIVERSITY OF WISCONSIN, 1863-1913: A HALF CENTURY OF PROGRESS. *Can. J. of Hist. of Sport and Physical Educ. 1973 4(1): 8-26.* Concern for the health and physical welfare of women at the University of Wisconsin existed in 1863 when they were first admitted, but few provisions were made for them in the next 25 years. When women agitated for physical education, the university built facilities and hired instructors. By the 1890's a program had been established based on the Swedish and Delsarte systems of gymnastics, and women were pursuing many sports. By the early 1900's a women's athletic association was formed and a physical education major was initiated with 11 women enrolled. Based on primary sources including newspapers, university catalogues, and regents' reports; 66 notes.
R. A. Smith

1437. Trennert, Robert A. PEACEABLY IF THEY WILL, FORCIBLY IF THEY MUST: THE PHOENIX INDIAN SCHOOL, 1890-1901. *J. of Arizona Hist. 1979 20(3): 297-322.* A history of the founding, establishment, and first decade of the Phoenix Indian School, with Wellington Rich appointed as its first superintendent (despite no previous knowledge of Indian life or culture). The philosophy undergirding such ventures at that period of handling Indian affairs demanded the complete destruction of Indian culture and an assimilation into white society. The program of the school was geared to this goal plus providing the sort of industrial training as would give the students entrance into the white labor force. The first students were from the Maricopa and Pima tribes. In the first decade over a thousand had attended. There is little evidence of a significant mark on their lives. Primary sources; 10 photos, 35 notes.
R. V. Ritter

1438. Vaughn, William P., ed. "SOUTH CAROLINA UNIVERSITY—1876" OF FISK PARSONS BREWER. *South Carolina Hist. Mag. 1975 76(4): 225-233.* Arriving at the University of South Carolina to teach the classics in 1873, the year when Negroes first enrolled, Fisk Parsons Brewer assisted in the integration of higher education. In 1876, just prior to the collapse of reconstruction, Brewer wrote an essay extolling the virtues of the university and his preparatory program for blacks and whites. He urged the state to continue integrated education; in addition, he suggested that the college hire teaching assistants (recent college graduates) to assist experienced instructors. Primary sources; 7 notes.
R. H. Tomlinson

Humanitarian Reform

1439. Birrell, A. J. D.I.K. RINE AND THE GOSPEL TEMPERANCE MOVEMENT IN CANADA. *Can. Hist. Rev. [Canada] 1977 58(1): 23-42.* Examines the rise, message, success, and sudden downfall of D.I.K. Rine and the Gospel Temperance Movement, in Canada during 1877-82. This moral suasionist movement, begun in New England by Francis Murphy, combined religious revivalism with the temperance message in attempting to reclaim alcoholics and hard drinkers. In Canada, led by Rine, a reformed alcoholic and an ex-convict, it met with enormous success, although unlike other contemporary movements it refused to campaign for legislated prohibition. Rine's arrest for indecent assault marked the end of the movement in Canada.
A

1440. Blochowiak, Mary Ann. "WOMAN WITH A HATCHETT": CARRY NATION COMES TO OKLAHOMA TERRITORY. *Chronicles of Oklahoma 1981 59(2): 132-151.* Carry Nation entered the temperance crusade following her 1867 marriage to Charles Gloyd, a hopeless alcoholic. A second marriage led her to Richmond, Texas, where she underwent a religious awakening that fired her crusading enthusiasm. In 1899 she launched her famous "hatchet campaigns" against saloons in Kansas and Oklahoma. Nation's militancy caused various chapters of the Women's Christian Temperance Union to close their doors to her, and she responded to them with venom. Local sheriffs frequently arrested Carry Nation and her following subsided by 1906. She died alone and penniless at Leavenworth, Kansas, in 1911. Based on Oklahoma newspapers; 6 photos, 46 notes.
M. L. Tate

1441. Blocker, Jack S., Jr., ed. ANNIE WITTENMYER AND THE WOMEN'S CRUSADE. *Ohio Hist. 1979 88(4): 419-422.* Annie Turner Wittenmyer was the first president (1874-79) of the National Women's Christian Temperance Union (WCTU), the outgrowth of the Women's Temperance Crusade, a pre-Civil War spontaneous movement throughout the United States. As a recently widowed, wealthy woman, Mrs. Wittenmyer became a leader in woman's war service. After the war she returned to church-oriented work and the promotion of the Crusade. She was succeeded in the presidency of WCTU by Frances E. Willard. A brief, quoted letter explains her continued Christian social work until her death in 1900. 9 notes.
H. F. Thomson

1442. Brady, James E. FATHER GEORGE ZURCHER: PROHIBITIONIST PRIEST. *Catholic Hist. Rev. 1976 62(3): 424-433.* In 1884 the Third Plenary Council of the American Catholic Church issued a strong condemnation of the liquor trade. It encouraged Catholics to remove themselves from all aspects of this trade and also forbade the sale of alcoholic beverages at church functions. Father George Zurcher became increasingly unhappy with the widespread disregard with which this proclamation was treated. Zurcher regarded the control of alcohol as a vehicle for both assimilation and social reform. He thus turned to the state to accomplish his goal because the Church would not, he felt, follow its own teaching.
A

1443. Brenzel, Barbara M. DOMESTICATION AS REFORM: A STUDY OF THE SOCIALIZATION OF WAYWARD GIRLS, 1856-1905. *Harvard Educ. Rev. 1980 50(2): 196-213.* Fear and benevolence motivated the juvenile reform policies undertaken at the State Industrial School for Girls in Lancaster, Massachusetts.

1444. Brenzel, Barbara M. LANCASTER INDUSTRIAL SCHOOL FOR GIRLS: A SOCIAL PORTRAIT OF A NINETEENTH CENTURY REFORM SCHOOL FOR GIRLS. *Feminist Studies 1975 3(1/2): 40-53.* The mid-19th-century conviction that changes in environment could encourage rehabilitation influenced early efforts to reform

children. In 1856 the first reform school for girls was established in Lancaster, Massachusetts. It included girls who were merely poor, not actually delinquent. The majority of the girls were adolescents, between 12 and 16, with no mother at home. The school served to protect them from the possibilities of promiscuity and the life of vice which tempted the poverty stricken young woman on her own. The school provided some minimal education and attempted Protestant religious training, but was in the main a shelter for girls, rather than an educational or vocational center. Based on primary and secondary sources; 29 notes.
S. R. Herstein

1445. Campbell, Ballard C. DID DEMOCRACY WORK? PROHIBITION IN LATE NINETEENTH-CENTURY IOWA: A TEST CASE. *J. of Interdisciplinary Hist. 1977 8(1): 87-116.* An analysis of Iowa politics in the late 19th century reveals that the political parties were responsive to the prohibition issue. Lawmakers tended to represent their constituency and were not totally subservient to party pressure. Contrary to the orthodox stereotype, "democracy in the late 19th century worked better than is customarily acknowledged." Official documents, newspapers, and printed sources; 6 tables, 35 notes.
R. Howell

1446. Clark, Roger W. CINCINNATI CRUSADERS FOR TEMPERANCE: 1874. *Cincinnati Hist. Soc. Bull. 1974 32(4): 185-199.* Discusses activities and demonstrations of the Women's National Christian Temperance Union in Cincinnati, Ohio, including the role of Wesley Chapel (Methodist Church) and the Ninth Street Baptist Church.

1447. Cumbler, John T. THE POLITICS OF CHARITY: GENDER AND CLASS IN LATE 19TH CENTURY CHARITY POLICY. *J. of Social Hist. 1980 14(1): 99-112.* Male industrial elites initially controlled charities in smaller industrial cities. As women assumed positions of leadership in the organizations, they also changed policies. The Associated Charities of Lynn and Fall River, Massachusetts, during 1880-1900 reflected this trend. While men dominated, the charities stressed the work ethic and sought to prevent assistance from going to the unworthy poor. As women gained leadership positions, programs of help and social reform especially for women became more evident, and fewer of the poor were found to be unworthy of aid. 47 notes.
S

1448. Dannenbaum, Jed. THE CRUSADER: SAMUEL CARY AND CINCINNATI TEMPERANCE. *Cincinnati Hist. Soc. Bull. 1975 33(2): 136-151.* Chronicles Samuel Fenton Cary's fight against alcohol in Cincinnati, Ohio, and his active membership in temperance movements both locally and nationally, 1845-1900.

1449. Davenport, F. Gorvin. THE SANITATION REVOLUTION IN ILLINOIS, 1870-1900. *J. of the Illinois State Hist. Soc. 1973 66(3): 306-326.* Sanitation facilities in urban Illinois were begun to clear muddy water rather than to eliminate bacteria. Chicago started its water system in 1861. The reversing of the Chicago River which carried away sewage made Lake Michigan water more pure. The sanitation revolution cleaned up the milk shed and the meat market and condemned outside toilets, but it failed to produce the lasting results envisioned by sociologists such as Shailer Mathews, Jane Addams, and John Dewey. Clean food and pure water did contribute to longer life. Based on the reports of the Chicago Department of Health and annual reports of the State Board of Health of Illinois; map, 10 photos, 35 notes.
A. C. Aimone

1450. Fleckner, John A. POVERTY AND RELIEF IN NINETEENTH-CENTURY JANESVILLE. *Wisconsin Mag. of Hist. 1978 61(4): 279-299.* After surveying the existing rudimentary public welfare system and the system of privately organized charity in Janesville and Rock County, Wisconsin, discusses the founding of the Janesville Associated Charities, organized by businessmen and their wives. Much of the volunteer work was done by the well-to-do, educated women and the Associated Charities "reflected the middle-class assumption that to be poor was not a natural, if unfortunate, condition, but rather a mark of individual deviance." 9 illus., 45 notes.
N. C. Burckel

1451. Freedman, Estelle B. THEIR SISTERS' KEEPERS: AN HISTORICAL PERSPECTIVE ON FEMALE CORRECTIONAL INSTITUTIONS IN THE UNITED STATES: 1870-1900. *Feminist Studies 1974 2(1): 77-95.* The attack of 19th-century women prison reformers on the patriarchal prison system and the substitution of a matriarchal one was a "necessary intermediate route to sexual equality." In the 1820's a number of American women began efforts to reform the prisons and several states enacted reforms such as hiring female matrons and providing separate quarters for women. The post-Civil War women's prison reform movement grew out of four factors: 1) the increase in female prison population, 2) women's Civil War social service experience, 3) the charities organization movement and prison reform movement, and 4) an "embryonic feminist analysis of women's place in American society" which led to a separatist approach to female correction. Reformers argued for female superiority in correctional work and structured their reformatory programs on the traditional female virtues of domesticity and purity, which contradicted the concept of equal rights and limited their work to traditional women's roles. Today's reintegration of the correctional system should aim at equal rights, the integration of the "achievements of women's reforms into co-educational institutions" and the end to the "treatment of women as morally superior domestics." 70 notes.
J. D. Falk

1452. Fye, W. Bruce. ACTIVE EUTHANASIA: AN HISTORICAL SURVEY OF ITS CONCEPTUAL ORIGINS AND INTRODUCTION INTO MEDICAL THOUGHT. *Bull. of the Hist. of Medicine 1978 52(4): 492-502.* Late in the 19th century active euthanasia became a topic of conversation. An aspect of the conservative response to heroic medicine was the emphasis placed on palliation of disease, with attention paid to patient comfort at the time of death. Several developments set the stage for discussion of euthanasia. These included advances in diagnosis, developments in anelgesic therapy, discovery of anesthesia, and the impact of scientific discovery on theology. English essayists Samuel D. Williams, Jr., and Lionel A. Tollemache wrote on euthanasia in the 1870's. In 1879 the South Carolina Medical Association established a committee to study aspects of active euthanasia. Interest in the question continued sporadically until the end of the century. 38 notes.
M. Kaufman

1453. Gerber, David A. LYNCHING AND LAW AND ORDER: ORIGINS AND PASSAGE OF THE OHIO ANTI-LYNCHING LAW OF 1894. *Ohio Hist. 1974 83(1): 33-50.* Harry C. Smith and Albion W. Tourgée attempted to legislate lynching out of existence. Tourgée wanted to fine communities in which outrages occurred. An 1896 compromise resulted in legislation that became a model for other states. Primary and secondary sources; 3 illus., 43 notes.
S. S. Sprague

1454. Gibbons, Russell W. PHYSICIAN-CHIROPRACTORS: MEDICAL PRESENCE IN THE EVOLUTION OF CHIROPRACTIC. *Bull. of the Hist. of Medicine 1981 55(2): 233-245.* During the early years of the development of chiropractic, some medical practitioners from orthodox medical schools became associated with the new movement. They very likely recognized the inadequacy of medical education and clinical failures, and moved toward the new innovation. Of the first 15 graduates of D. D. Palmer's school of chiropractic, a third were physicians. Since the 1880's, chiropractic has followed some of the same paths as other medical sects, but instead of assimilating into orthodoxy, or disappearing, it is surviving in a period when alternative practice is gaining stature. Based on published primary sources, including registers and catalogs of chiropractic schools; 36 notes.
M. Kaufman

1455. Glassberg, David. THE DESIGN OF REFORM: THE PUBLIC BATH MOVEMENT IN AMERICA. *Am. Studies [Lawrence, KS] 1979 20(2): 5-21.* The public bath movement emerged as part of a new civic ethos in the late 19th century. The gospel of cleanliness was typically Victorian, an effort to upgrade both public health and public morality. These reforms were to transform the city and its inhabitants, and reflected an awareness of the germ theory of disease. Examines cities that led the movement. Covers ca. 1880-1910. 7 illus., 54 notes.
J. A. Andrew

1456. Harkins, Michael J. PUBLIC HEALTH NUISANCES IN OMAHA, 1870-1900. *Nebraska Hist. 1975 56(4): 471-493.* Examines the lack of sanitary control and oppressive living conditions that made for major health problems in Omaha between 1870 and 1900. Not until the 20th century did an effective board of health come into existence. Includes a discussion of patent medicines consumed by Omaha residents.
R. Lowitt

1457. Henle, Ellen Langenheim. CLARA BARTON, SOLDIER OR PACIFIST? *Civil War Hist. 1978 24(2): 152-160.* The study of Clara Barton, founder of the American Red Cross and active in three major wars, contributes new perspectives on women's future military roles. She viewed war as a fact of life and wanted women to take part in it, including military education and combat service. She believed that women's secondary citizen status was directly related to exclusion from war. A complex person, Clara Barton was attracted and repelled by war. She viewed herself as a soldier, appreciating the adventure; in a real sense, her humanitarianism provided an alternative to a military career. Yet she genuinely longed for and worked for peace, particularly through her Red Cross movement. Based on the Barton Papers and secondary sources; 31 notes.
R. E. Stack

1458. Hinckley, Ted C. ALASKA AS AN AMERICAN BOTANY BAY. *Pacific Hist. R. 1973 42(1): 1-19.* Discusses proposals for a penal colony in Alaska during the late 19th century. Public debate over the issue was encouraged by bleak economic conditions and the labor shortage in Alaska during the 1870's, along with the problem of crowded penitentiaries and concern over prison reform measures in the United States. With the Klondike rush of 1897, Alaska was obviously becoming economically profitable, and the idea no longer received serious consideration. 62 notes.
E. C. Hyslop

1459. Hollander, Russell. MENTAL HEALTH POLICY IN WASHINGTON TERRITORY, 1853-1875. *Pacific Northwest Q. 1980 71(4): 152-161.* During its territorial years, 1853-75, Washington provided care and treatment for the insane through three systems. The first was a contract system whereby the territorial legislature entrusted patient care to the lowest private bidder. By 1871 a dual management system replaced this troubled arrangement by contracting with a private agency but requiring a resident physician at each asylum. Lobbying efforts of the Medical Society of Washington Territory finally placed the entire service under the control of a medical superintendent and a board of trustees during 1875. Although many problems remained, this new arrangement assured the professionalization of patient care. Based on state government documents and newspapers; 4 photos, 41 notes.
M. L. Tate

1460. Horrall, Stan W. A POLICEMAN'S LOT IS NOT A HAPPY ONE: THE MOUNTED POLICE AND PROHIBITION IN THE NORTH-WEST TERRITORIES, 1874-91. *Tr. of the Hist. and Sci. Soc. of Manitoba [Canada] 1973-74 (30): 5-16.* Discusses the formation of the romantic and heroic myth of the Royal Canadian Mounted Police, based on their success in creating law and order on the western frontier and the reversal of their reputation after 1880 (attributed almost entirely to the enforcement of the territorial liquor laws). The stringent liquor law of 1875 primarily was intended to "protect the Indian population from the nefarious activities of the whiskey traders," but as emigration increased, white settlers were determined not to have their drinking habits dictated. The rigorous but ambiguous enforcement of the prohibition laws threatened the survival of the mounted police until about 1900, when provincial police assumed this responsibility. Based on documents in the Public Archives of Canada and secondary works; 58 notes.
S. R. Quéripel

1461. James, Janet Wilson. ISABEL HAMPTON AND THE PROFESSIONALIZATION OF NURSING IN THE 1890'S. Vogel, Morris J. and Rosenberg, Charles E., ed. *The Therapeutic Revolution: Essays in the Social History of American Medicine* (Philadelphia: U. of Pennsylvania Pr., 1979): 201-244. In 1889, Jane Addams founded Hull House in Chicago and Isabel Hampton became director of the new nursing school in Baltimore, the Johns Hopkins Hospital Training School for Nurses. These two women revolutionized social welfare and health care in the late 19th century. With the support of founder Johns Hopkins and the president of the board of trustees, Francis T. King, Hampton strove to professionalize nursing, then characterized by low pay, low status, long hours, and heavy work by working class women. Johns Hopkins, as well as other nursing institutions in the United States, based their reforms on Florence Nightingale's work at St. Thomas's Hospital's nursing school founded in London in 1860. Hampton continued working from the sidelines until her death in 1910. 113 notes.
G. L. Smith

1462. Kalberg, Stephen. THE COMMITMENT TO CAREER REFORM: THE SETTLEMENT MOVEMENT LEADERS. *Social Service R. 1975 49(4): 608-628.* Discusses the social, religious, and political attitudes of Settlement Movement reformers during the 1880's and 90's.

1463. Kaplan, Barry J. REFORMERS AND CHARITY: THE ABOLITION OF PUBLIC OUTDOOR RELIEF IN NEW YORK CITY, 1870-1898. *Social Service Rev. 1978 52(2): 202-214.* To reduce corruption in city government and the power of Tammany Hall, reformers in New York City government put public outdoor relief in the hands of private charitable organizations and subsidized it.

1464. Kerr, K. Austin. ORGANIZING FOR REFORM: THE ANTI-SALOON LEAGUE AND INNOVATION IN POLITICS. *Am. Q. 1980 32(1): 37-53.* The Anti-Saloon League, founded in 1895, was the first modern pressure group organized around one issue. Unlike earlier popular movements, it utilized bureaucratic methods learned from business to build a strong organization. The League's first leader, Howard Hyde Russell (1855-1946), believed that the best leadership was selected, not elected. He traveled to local leagues to identify and promote those he felt would be the best leaders. This organizational strategy enabled the temperance movement, in disarray before 1890, to achieve eventual success with the Prohibition amendment. Howard Hyde Russell Papers, Ohio Anti-Saloon League Papers, and other primary sources; 33 notes.
D. K. Lambert

1465. Kirkland, Edward C. "SCIENTIFIC EATING": NEW ENGLANDERS PREPARE AND PROMOTE A REFORM, 1873-1907. *Massachusetts Hist. Soc. Pro. 1974 86: 28-52.* A study of leaders in nutrition reform in the late 19th century, particularly Wilbur Olin Atwater, Edward Atkinson, and Ellen Swallow Richards. These reformers and pioneers in biochemistry were all from New England and all shared what the author terms an elitist attitude. Their work in agricultural experimentation and nutrition reform, based in large part on German theory and practice, involved them in questions of social, economic, and political reform. By 1900, these nutritionists felt that their movement was progressing well, despite several setbacks and difficulties. Based on contemporary publications and correspondence; 89 notes; indexed.
G. W. R. Ward

1466. Leavitt, Judith Walzer. THE WASTELAND: GARBAGE AND SANITARY REFORM IN THE NINETEENTH-CENTURY AMERICAN CITY. *J. of the Hist. of Medicine and Allied Sci. 1980 35(4): 431-452.* Analysis of the experience of Milwaukee, Wisconsin, with garbage demonstrates the varied processes by which America's cities assumed rsponsibility for health and sanitation in the late 19th century. Milwaukee tried all methods of garbage disposal, including food for swine, landfill, use as fertlizer, rendering, cremating, and dumping in the lake. Municipal ownership as well as the return to cremation combined to make it an engineering rather than a health problem. Medical knowledge and available technology influenced how public health reform would take place. Covers ca. 1867-1911. Based on newspapers, city records, and secondary works; 92 notes.
M. Kaufman

1467. Levenstein, Harvey. THE NEW ENGLAND KITCHEN AND THE ORIGINS OF MODERN AMERICAN EATING HABITS. *Am. Q. 1980 32(4): 369-386.* Edward Atkinson (1827-1905), manufacturer of the slow-cooking Aladdin Oven, joined with nutritionists Mary Hinman Abel and Ellen H. Richards (1842-1911) to open the New England Kitchen in Boston in 1889. This public kitchen, which stimulated similar experiments in other cities, sought to change working-class menus and demonstrate slow-cooking. These reformers believed that working-class people needed cheaper diets which incorporated alternative sources of protein and carbohydrates. Immigrants and the working class generally ignored the message and retained their traditional eating habits. Atkinson, Abel, and Richards began catering to a middle-class clientele in 1897. Based on the Edward Atkinson Papers, the Mary H. Abel Papers, the Ellen H. Richards Papers, and other primary sources; 66 notes.
D. K. Lambert

1468. MacDougall, Heather A. THE GENESIS OF PUBLIC HEALTH REFORM IN TORONTO, 1869-1890. *Urban Hist. Rev. [Canada] 1982 10(3): 1-9.* The episodic arrangements which had characterized pre-Confederation public health work in Toronto slowly gave way to a more organized approach. However, change involved continuous conflict between the supporters of privatism and growth and the advocates of intervention and amelioration. The catalyst for much of the debate was Dr. William Canniff, Toronto's first, permanent salaried medical health officer. His attempts to control disease and improve the quality of urban life were opposed by growth-oriented aldermen and their constituents but were supported by middle-class lay and medical reformers as well as the federal and provincial governments. The interplay of these forces replicated the experiences of British and American public health enthusiasts and prefigured developments in other Canadian cities.

J/S

1469. Mitchinson, Wendy. THE YWCA AND REFORM IN THE NINETEENTH CENTURY. *Social Hist. [Canada] 1979 12(24): 368-384.* The Young Women's Christian Association began operations in Canada in 1870, mainly to provide decent accommodations for young working women, but its charitable and reform objectives conflicted, and the national organization never provided strong and coordinated direction. The YWCA tended to work for women, not with them, but its concern with working women indicates an acceptance of that change in women's status. Based on primary and secondary sources, including records of the Toronto YWCA; 76 notes.

D. F. Chard

1470. Numbers, Ronald L. DR. JACKSON'S WATER CURE AND ITS INFLUENCE ON ADVENTIST HEALTH REFORM. *Adventist Heritage 1974 1(1): 11-16, 58-59.* Describes changes in Adventist health care by Ellen G. White, a leader of the sabbatarian wing of Adventists, after stays at the hydrotherapy establishment of Dr. James Caleb Jackson in Dansville, New York, in 1864 and 1865.

1471. Phaneuf, Margaret M. SANITATION AND CHOLERA: SPRINGFIELD AND THE 1866 EPIDEMIC. *Hist. J. of Western Massachusetts 1980 8(1): 26-36.* Discusses the reaction of Springfield city officials to the national cholera epidemic of 1866 with particular reference to the development of the city's sanitation system and the establishment of a city hospital. Based on newspapers, contemporary documents, and secondary sources; 42 notes.

W. H. Mulligan, Jr.

1472. Platt, Anthony. THE TRIUMPH OF BENEVOLENCE: THE ORIGINS OF THE JUVENILE JUSTICE SYSTEM IN THE UNITED STATES. Hawes, Joseph M., ed. *Law and Order in American History* (Port Washington, N.Y.: Kennikat Pr., 1979): 53-76. Traces the origins of the American juvenile justice system to the child-saving movement of the Progressive Era in the late 19th century, concluding that the juvenile justice system then, as today, failed to be humanitarian and reformist; rather it served as a means of control by the middle class with support from philanthropic industrialists.

1473. Pocock, Emil. WET OR DRY? THE PRESIDENTIAL ELECTION OF 1884 IN UPSTATE NEW YORK. *New York Hist. 1973 54(2): 174-190.* Grover Cleveland (1837-1908) won the presidential election of 1884 because he carried New York State but his plurality there was only 1,143 votes out of more than 1.1 million votes over James Gillespie Blaine (1830-93). Minimizes the usual explanations of Blaine's defeat in New York State: the Mugwump bolt, the rains that held down the turnout, and Reverend Samuel D. Burchard's "rum, Romanism and rebellion" remark that alienated the Irish in New York City. The election returns show that John P. St. John, the Prohibition Party candidate, drew 25,006 votes of which 18,665 were in normally Republican upstate New York and were enough to defeat Blaine. Primary and secondary sources; 4 illus., 7 tables, 19 notes.

G. Kurland

1474. Rauch, Julia B. WOMEN IN SOCIAL WORK: FRIENDLY VISITORS IN PHILADELPHIA, 1880. *Social Service R. 1975 49(2): 241-259.* Examines the characteristics of the women involved in the Philadelphia Society for Organizing Charitable Relief and Repressing Mendicancy during the years 1864-1909, using data obtained from schedules of the 1880 US Census.

S

1475. Romanofsky, Peter. SAVING THE LIVES OF THE CITY'S FOUNDLINGS: THE JOINT COMMITTEE AND NEW YORK CITY CHILD CARE METHODS, 1860-1907. *New York Hist. Soc. Q. 1977 61(1-2): 49-68.* At the turn of the century, the Joint Committee on the Care of Motherless Infants in New York City made considerable progress in attempting to solve the problem of the growing number of babies (orphans and the offspring of the poor) who needed care. Unfortunately its efforts, largely directed at farming out the babies to private homes, were thwarted by politics, religious differences, and by those who believed institutionalization was the proper method of care. By 1907 adherents of the "New York System" (public money given to private institutions—largely favored by Catholics) had won out and the committee ceased to function. Such progress as had been made came to an end, and public care of the children became again regressive. Primary sources; 45 notes, 3 illus.

C. L. Grant

1476. Romanofsky, Peter. "... TO RID OURSELVES OF THE BURDEN..." NEW YORK JEWISH CHARITIES AND THE ORIGINS OF THE INDUSTRIAL REMOVAL OFFICE, 1890-1901. *Am. Jewish Hist. Q. 1975 64(4): 331-343.* Various motives combined to induce the primarily German-Jewish leadership of New York Jewish charities to actively support removal of new immigrants to other parts of the country. Overcrowding, the possibility of political radicalism, and the fear of renewed antisemitism led to various programs for job training, agricultural settlements, and resettlement outside New York. Both the Industrial Removal Office of 1901 and the Galveston Plan of 1907 were created to prevent limitation of Jewish immigration to the United States. By 1914 some 70,000 men and their families had been placed outside New York City, allowing Jewish charities to expand and develop their services to the children, widows, and the sick of the Jewish community. 31 notes.

F. Rosenthal

1477. Schallhorn, Cathlyn. CHEATING THE STREETS. *Chicago Hist. 1977-78 6(4): 229-241.* Describes the life of street children in Chicago in the late 19th century and efforts by the city and private reform groups, specifically the Off-the-Street Club, founded in 1898, which was run by amateurs and operated under the philosophy that the children could best be helped by dealing with them on their own level.

1478. Skidmore, P. G. CRUSADING AND CONFORMING: THE TECHNIQUES OF TEMPERANCE. *Dalhousie Rev. [Canada] 1976 56(1): 93-102.* In discussing briefly the history of the Temperance movement and its roots in the Abolitionist movement the author investigates the techniques of local organization and action through some descriptions of temperance meetings during the 1870's in the writings of Frances Willard. The close association of the temperance movement to the Suffragist movement is also noted. 27 notes.

C. Held

1479. Stern, Norton B. THE CHARITABLE JEWISH LADIES OF SAN BERNARDINO AND THEIR WOMAN OF VALOR, HENRIETTA ANCKER. *Western States Jewish Hist. Q. 1981 13(4): 369-376.* Henrietta Ancker (1835-90) came to San Bernardino, California, with her husband Louis in 1870. She was very active in social and charitable activities, and in 1886 she helped organize the Ladies' Hebrew Benevolent Society. In tribute to her energetic leadership, the members changed the name to the Henrietta Hebrew Benevolent Society in 1891. Based on interviews and newspaper accounts; 2 photos, 34 notes.

B. S. Porter

1480. Teaham, John F. WARREN FELT EVANS AND MENTAL HEALING: ROMANTIC IDEALISM AND PRACTICAL MYSTICISM IN NINETEENTH CENTURY AMERICA. *Church Hist. 1979 48(1): 63-80.* Warren Felt Evans wrote six books that influenced the growth of New Thought, a loosely organized religious movement concerned with health and spiritual integration. His thought and therapy united idealistic philosophy and practical mysticism. As a philosophical idealist with a deeply mystical understanding of experience, Evans developed a general religious and cultural critique. The nature of Evans's mysticism influenced the practical healing techniques he employed to assist others in achieving harmonial consciousness. While influenced by romantic idealism and mysticism, Evans encountered difficulties that intense soul-searching could not alleviate. By advocating scientific and medical knowledge to supplement the cure and insisting that the patient realize that healing is not mysterious or miraculous, Evans linked his therapy with pragmatic character of later mind cure forms.

M. Dibert

1481. Vertinsky, Patricia. RHYTHMICS: A SORT OF PHYSICAL JUBILEE: A NEW LOOK AT THE CONTRIBUTIONS OF DIO LEWIS. *Can. J. of Hist. of Sport and Physical Educ. [Canada] 1978 9(1): 31-41.* Rhythmics, a sport introduced by Dio Lewis in 1860 and practiced primarily by women, consists of graceful rhythmic movements, often with the use of wands, rings, or balls; discusses the ideas of Lewis and others on health reform, exercise, sexual morality, and dress.

1482. Wetherell, Donald G. TO DISCIPLINE AND TRAIN: ADULT REHABILITATION PROGRAMMES IN ONTARIO PRISONS, 1874-1900. *Social Hist. [Canada] 1979 12(23): 145-165.* A new thrust toward rehabilitation of Ontario's prison inmates began in 1884. To ensure that the prisons themselves did not lead to further corruption of character, novices were to be separated from hardened criminals. Prisons also used work as a rehabilitative device (and as a means of defraying costs). Trades were taught and prisoners received regular religious and secular instruction. Strict discipline was imposed to build character. Table, 98 notes. D. F. Chard

1483. Whitaker, F. M. OHIO WCTU AND THE PROHIBITION AMENDMENT CAMPAIGN OF 1883. *Ohio Hist. 1974 83(2): 84-102.* Describes the founding of the Woman's Christian Temperance Union of Ohio in 1874 and its activities through the prohibition amendment campaign of 1883. In its first years the Union struggled with the liquor licensing issue and tried to avoid partisan politics. After a few years of reduced activity, the Union joined the prohibition campaign, which ended in defeat of the amendment. After the campaign of 1883 the Union became more closely associated with the Prohibition Party, and its independent influence declined. Based on minutes of the Ohio WCTU meetings, newspapers, the author's dissertation, and secondary works; 3 photos, 70 notes. J. B. Street

Religious Reform

1484. Borden, Morton. THE CHRISTIAN AMENDMENT. *Civil War Hist. 1979 25(2): 156-167.* Heeding Protestants' criticism since 1787 of the US Constitution's failure to acknowledge national dependence on God, and specifically on Christ, and accepting the common opinion that the Civil War was a punishment not only for slavery but also for that omission, Protestant fundamentalists in 1863 founded the National Reform Association to support a Christian constitutional amendment. President Abraham Lincoln proclaimed National Fast Day (30 April 1863), acknowledged the truth of the Scriptures, and urged repentance for sin, but he never supported the National Reform Association; nor did Congress. As their goal became less attainable, their supporters fell away and those who remained became fanatical. The National Reform Association persisted until 1945; its members believed that the proclamation and observance of National Fast Day had turned the tide in the Civil War and that a similar constitutional proclamation of dependence on Christ would save the nation. The public never concurred. 37 notes. S

1485. Boyd, Lois A. SHALL WOMEN SPEAK? CONFRONTATION IN THE CHURCH, 1876. *J. of Presbyterian Hist. 1978 56(4): 271-296.* The problem of women speaking in Presbyterian pulpits in the 19th century was normally solved on the scriptural injunction which denied the right. In 1876, however, the Reverend Isaac M. See permitted two women to speak from his pulpit in Newark, New Jersey. He was charged before presbytery with disobedience by a colleague. See was found guilty; subsequent appeals before the synod and general assembly sustained the action of presbytery. The "woman question" was too firmly entrenched in the political, social, and religious arenas of the 19th century for Presbyterians to have acted otherwise. Officially the cause of women suffered a setback; however, women maintained separate structures whereby mission work was supported, leadership was developed in education, and very substantial financial support was given to the Presbyterian Church. The base was laid for the 20th century when women would be ordained as officers and ministers. Based on minutes of church courts and church and secular newspapers; 47 notes. H. M. Parker, Jr.

1486. Brudnoy, David. A DECADE IN ZION: THEODORE SCHROEDER'S INITIAL ASSAULT ON THE MORMONS. *Historian 1975 37(2): 241-256.* Free-thinking Theodore Schroeder (1864-1953) began as a lawyer practicing in Salt Lake City (1889-1900) at a time when national controversies about Mormon polygamy delayed statehood for Utah Territory. Schroeder became a strident critic of Mormonism. His pamphlets and short-lived journal *Lucifer's Lantern* focused on plural marriage, and he campaigned successfully to deny polygamous Brigham Roberts the seat in Congress to which he had been elected. In the years after 1900 when he moved to New York, Schroeder became a prolific contributor to First Amendment studies and a leading advocate of free speech and press causes. The Free Speech League, which he helped form, is one of the forebears of the American Civil Liberties Union. Based on the Schroeder papers at the State Historical Society of Wisconsin, and the library of Southern Illinois University; 31 notes. N. W. Moen

1487. Davis, Rodney O. PRUDENCE CRANDALL, SPIRITUALISM, AND POPULIST-ERA REFORM IN KANSAS. *Kansas Hist. 1980 3(4): 239-254.* Prudence Crandall (1803-90) came to Elk County, Kansas, in 1877. For 13 years she was a leader in the movements for women's rights and prohibition. Her efforts in behalf of these old-fashioned issues more than offset popular resentment of her belief in spiritualist ideas that ran counter to the tenets of Christianity. She made no public appeal for support but advanced her interests in spiritualism by holding small meetings in her home. Her leading disciples waged a major effort in support of spiritualism from 1890 to 1895. Long opposed by organized clergymen, spiritualists now faced a stronger opponent. In the 1840's it was possible to have great topics discussed at any American crossroads, but by 1890 such theorizing appeared ludicrous. Knowledge was becoming the preserve of trained academics. Based on state census records and the Spiritualism File, Kansas State Historical Society, interviews, newspapers; illus., 91 notes. W. F. Zornow

1488. Golomb, Deborah Grand. THE 1893 CONGRESS OF JEWISH WOMEN: EVOLUTION OR REVOLUTION IN AMERICAN JEWISH WOMEN'S HISTORY? *Am. Jewish Hist. 1980 70(1): 52-67.* The social and philanthropic activities of 19th-century Jewish women, particularly clubwomen, coupled with a degree of anti-Semitism in the women's suffrage movement, form the background for the Congress of Jewish Women held in conjunction with the World Parliament of Religions at the World's Columbian Exposition (Chicago, 1893). Hannah G. Solomon (1858-1942) shouldered much of the responsibility for organizing the Congress. She drew inspiration from both American and Jewish sources, particularly from leading clubwoman Mrs. Charles Henrotin and from Rabbi Emil Hirsch. Though the congress did not embrace all Jewish groups—the women were predominantly Reform Jews—and though it did not resolve the tension between loyalty to Judaism or to womankind, as the address by Sadie American demonstrates, it did set the tone for a new kind of participation for Jewish women within Jewish communal life. From the gathering came the idea for a permanent organization, the National Congress of Jewish Women. 30 notes. J. D. Sarna

1489. Gorrell, Donald K. ORDINATION OF WOMEN BY THE UNITED BRETHREN IN CHRIST, 1889. *Methodist Hist. 1980 18(2): 136-143.* In 1889, the Church of the United Brethren in Christ revised its constitution. One controversial provision was the ordination of women clergy. Includes the debate regarding the provision finally adopted. Within four months, the Central Illinois Conference of the Church ordained its first woman preacher. Based on church publications, 1889; 13 notes. H. L. Calkin

1490. Headon, Christopher. WOMEN AND ORGANIZED RELIGION IN MID AND LATE NINETEENTH CENTURY CANADA. *J. of the Can. Church Hist. Soc. [Canada] 1978 20(1-2): 3-18.* Within the Christian denominations of Canada, women in the mid- and late-19th century had an alternative to their traditional role. Some served as preaching evangelists, while others joined religious orders to help the poor. The most important of all activities in which Canadian churchwomen were involved was missionary work, both foreign and domestic, in which they acted to alleviate poverty, teach the young, and eliminate as much as possible the most crude and overt forms of female subordination. Yet, there were many limitations in this advance. Women's organizations in the church were usually considered subordinate and dependent on those dominated by men; and most churchwomen conducted themselves and their activities in accordance with traditional notions of female subservience. Primary and secondary sources; 51 notes.
J. A. Kicklighter

1491. Keller, Rosemary Skinner. CREATING A SPHERE FOR WOMEN IN THE CHURCH: HOW CONSEQUENTIAL AN ACCOMMODATION? *Methodist Hist. 1980 18(2): 83-94.* The "woman issue" was the most controversial question at General Conferences of the Methodist Episcopal Church during 1869-1900. The church denied ordination for women but recognized them as helpers of men in positions of authority. In 1869, the women organized the Women's Foreign Missionary Society and began to send and support women in foreign countries. Concludes that, in developing this autonomous organization, the women began a movement which would eliminate separate spheres for men and women in the church. 26 notes.   H. L. Calkin

1492. McArthur, Benjamin. THE 1893 CHICAGO WORLD'S FAIR: AN EARLY TEST FOR ADVENTIST RELIGIOUS LIBERTY. *Adventist Heritage 1975 2(2): 11-22.* Spearheaded by Alonzo Trevier Jones, Seventh-Day Adventists protested the closing of the Chicago World's Fair on Sundays and succeeded in repealing a practice which they viewed as threatening the separation of church and state and the first step in the establishment of a national (Protestant) religion.

1493. Mitchinson, Wendy. CANADIAN WOMEN AND CHURCH MISSIONARY SOCIETIES IN THE NINETEENTH CENTURY: A STEP TOWARDS INDEPENDENCE. *Atlantis [Canada] 1977 2(2, pt. 2): 57-75.* Protestant missionary societies, the first women's groups to form on a national level, allowed women (1870's-90's) outside the sphere of their homes for the first time.

1494. Paz, D. G. A STUDY IN ADAPTABILITY: THE EPISCOPAL CHURCH IN OMAHA, 1856-1919. *Nebraska Hist. 1981 62(1): 107-130.* A study of the Episcopal Church in Omaha as an organic entity that both reflects and changes its society indicates how this well-rooted, eastern organization fared in extending its ministry. Eventually the national Episcopal Church created in the Great Plains an organization with an elected presiding bishop, a permanent central bureaucracy with control over a budget, and an annual pledge system that transformed the church's financial structure. These changes were reflected in the Diocese of Nebraska and marked "the end of the 19th century for the Episcopal Church."   R. Lowitt

1495. Semple, Neil. "THE NURTURE AND ADMONITION OF THE LORD": NINETEENTH-CENTURY CANADIAN METHODISM'S RESPONSE TO "CHILDHOOD." *Social Hist. [Canada] 1981 14(27): 157-175.* In the second half of the 19th century, the Canadian Methodist Church was becoming a far-reaching urban, social institution. In doing so, the church adopted new perceptions of childhood for the benefit of society generally and as a means of retaining children in the church. Belief in the inherent sinfulness and impurity of infants gave way to a belief that children were innocent and naturally moral creatures. Sunday schools became a key component in this approach. 87 notes.   D. F. Chard

1496. Szasz, Ferenc M. T. DEWITT TALMAGE: SPIRITUAL TYCOON OF THE GILDED AGE. *J. of Presbyterian Hist. 1981 59(1): 18-32.* Although one of the most powerful and influential pulpit masters of his day, the influence of Presbyterian Thomas DeWitt Talmage (1832-1902) hardly extended beyond his own generation. The issues and qualities which reflected his greatness do not appeal to the modern mind. His enormous success lay in his dramatic reinforcement of older views and simultaneous soothing of fears about the new. Among his major themes were labor/capital difficulties, the higher criticism of the Bible, and the theory of evolution. Even when criticizing society Talmage used Victorian rather than scriptural standards. Because he had little doctrine to support his position, he helped dilute the Protestant tradition. This weakened US Protestantism's efforts to confront the dilemmas of the 20th century. Based on the Talmage Papers of the Library of Congress, and his numerous publications; 2 photos, 54 notes.   H. M. Parker, Jr.

1497. Teaford, Jon C. TOWARD A CHRISTIAN NATION: RELIGION, LAW AND JUSTICE STRONG. *J. of Presbyterian Hist. 1976 54(4): 422-437.* William Strong (1808-95) was an Associate Justice of the US Supreme Court from 1870 until his resignation in 1880. A prosperous entrepreneur and expert in business law, he was also a Presbyterian Elder and loyal layman in a country which was beginning to deviate from traditional Christian values and the Christian way of life. He was a member of the National Reform Association which in 1864 unsuccessfully proposed an amendment to the preamble of the US Constitution which would give formal recognition to God and Jesus Christ so that there would be no doubt that the US was a Christian nation ruled by a Christian government. His efforts to promote personal piety in the midst of great social change characterized his own zeal for the moral and spiritual welfare of his country. At the same time he was woefully aware of the shortcomings of the Christian cause in the US in failing to provide religious and social provisions for the masses. He served on the boards of numerous interdenominational agencies in addition to his Presbyterian responsibilities. Based largely on Strong's writings; illus., 40 notes.
H. M. Parker, Jr.

1498. Wharton, Leslie. HERBERT N. CASSON AND THE AMERICAN LABOR CHURCH, 1893-1898. *Essex Inst. Hist. Collections 1981 117(2): 119-137.* In response to the social and economic tensions generated by the labor unrest of the late 19th century, a young Methodist seminary graduate and Socialist from Ontario, Canada, Herbert N. Casson, founded a Labor Church in Lynn, Massachusetts. Modeled after the English Labor Church, Casson's church was for the laboring poor, providing them with ideals and methods to lift themselves out of industrial slavery. Casson also tried to give his church a religious philosophy: Christian history was a struggle between the working class and the aristocrats. In the end, the church succumbed to the tensions of the labor movement, returning prosperity, and nationalist enthusiasm fostered by the Spanish-American War. Primary sources; 34 notes.
R. S. Sliwoski

Utopian Thought and Commmunalism

1499. Arndt, Karl J. R. BISMARCK'S SOCIALIST LAWS OF 1878 AND THE HARMONISTS. *Western Pennsylvania Hist. Mag. 1976 59(1): 55-70.* Following Otto von Bismarck's socialist laws of 1878, German socialist Clara Pittman applied for membership in George Rapp's Harmony Society (1879), an organization of Christian communists, headquartered in Economy, Pennsylvania.

1500. Arndt, Karl J. R. KORESHANITY, TOPOLOBAMPO, OLOMBIA, AND THE HARMONIST MILLIONS. *Western Pennsylvania Hist. Mag. 1973 56(1): 71-86.* Describes three utopian schemes which sought financial backing from the wealthy Harmony Society.
S

1501. Avrich, Paul. KROPOTKIN IN AMERICA. *Int. Rev. of Social Hist. [Netherlands] 1980 25(1): 1-34.* Among many Russian immigrants and visitors to the United States before World War I, Pëtr Kropotkin (1842-1921) left the most lasting impression. He came to North America in 1897 and 1901. On his first visit he attended several scientific conferences in Canada and the United States and lectured on social and political topics. In 1901 he lectured on Russian literature to university audiences in the East and Midwest and spoke before his usual audiences of anarchists. These visits sparked an admiration for Kropotkin in particular and anarchism in general among intellectuals and anarchists in the United States, occasionally noted to this day. Based on archival sources and newspapers; 135 notes.   G. P. Blum

1502. Blick, Boris and Grant, H. Roger. LIFE IN NEW ICARIA, IOWA: A NINETEENTH CENTURY UTOPIAN COMMUNITY. *Ann. of Iowa 1974 42(3): 198-204.* Describes the utopian community at New Icaria, Iowa, founded upon the communistic principles of Étienne Cabet (1788-1856). In the mainstream of 19th-century utopianism, the Icarians were faced with the common problems of "individualism and collectivism, the disagreement over political authority, the beckoning economic opportunities outside the pale of utopia, and ultimate failure." There were several French Icarian communities in the United States during 1848-98; the Iowa colony lasted through 1852-98. 15 notes.
C. W. Olson

1503. Egerton, John. VISIONS OF UTOPIA. *Southern Exposure 1979 7(1): 38-47.* Excerpt from John Egerton's *Visions of Utopia* (U. of Tennessee Pr., 1977) giving the biography of Julius Augustus Wayland (1854-?), and describes his founding of a utopian colony in Tennessee in 1894 which he named Ruskin after John Ruskin, Wayland's "great, loving, wise spirit"; the colony survived until 1901.

1504. Fogarty, Robert S. AMERICAN COMMUNES, 1865-1914. *J. of Am. Studies [Great Britain] 1975 9(2): 145-162.* Describes the growth and ultimate failure of American communal societies during 1865-1914. "Co-operative colonizers" founded one type of commune, "charismatic perfectionists" created another, while "political pragmatists" established their own versions of utopia. All groups shared the belief that their efforts would solve pressing social problems. They were little deterred by the unprepossessing experiences of their communatarian predecessors. Based on secondary sources; 60 notes. H. T. Lovin

1505. Fogarty, Robert S. and Grant, H. Roger. FREE LOVE IN OHIO: JACOB BEILHARDT AND THE SPIRIT FRUIT COLONY. *Ohio Hist. 1980 89(2): 206-221.* Discusses the life of Jacob Beilhardt (1846-1908), and the community he founded near Lisbon, Ohio, named the Spirit Fruit Society. Under his charismatic leadership, the utopian community attracted much publicity, mostly for its sexual philosophy. Primary sources; 49 notes. J. Powell

1506. Grant, H. Roger. HENRY OLERICH AND THE UTOPIAN IDEAL. *Nebraska Hist. 1975 56(2): 249-258.* Biographical sketch of Henry Olerich (1851-1927), and a review of his utopian novels, attempting to place them within the framework of late 19th-century Utopian literature in the United States. R. Lowitt

1507. Grant, H. Roger. THE NEW COMMUNITARIANISM: WILLIAM H. BENNETT AND THE HOME EMPLOYMENT CO-OPERATIVE COMPANY, 1894-1905. *Missouri Hist. Soc. Bull. 1976 33(1): 18-26.* Describes utopian experiments by William H. Bennett in Dallas County, Missouri. His last undertaking, the Home Employment Co-operative Company, briefly served hundreds of Ozark farm families beginning in 1895, only to be disbanded when post-Spanish American War prosperity reduced the need for cooperative utopias. Based on primary and newspaper sources; map, 2 photos, 34 notes. H. T. Lovin

1508. Grant, H. Roger. THE NEW COMMUNITARIANISM: THE CASE OF THREE INTENTIONAL COLONIES, 1890-1905. *Indiana Social Studies Q. 1977 30(1): 59-71.* Three post-Civil War communitarian settlements, the Labor Exchange, the Home Employment Cooperative Company, and the Colorado Cooperative Company, represent political pragmatism lacking in pre-Civil War communities.

1509. Grant, H. Roger. "ONE WHO DARES TO PLAN": CHARLES W. CARYL AND THE NEW ERA UNION. *Colorado Mag. 1974 51(1): 13-27.* Charles W. Caryl, businessman and reformer of the Progressive Era, centered much of his activity in Colorado. In the *New Era* (1897), he proposed an unrealistic utopia based on a meritocracy. His many reform and utopian schemes included one for "race improvement." Based on primary and secondary sources; 6 illus., 19 notes. O. H. Zabel

1510. Grant, H. Roger. PORTRAIT OF A WORKERS' UTOPIA: THE LABOR EXCHANGE AND THE FREEDOM, KANSAS, COLONY. *Kansas Hist. Q. 1977 43(1): 56-66.* G. B. De Bernardi's Labor Exchange was a popular panacea for the depression of 1893. It provided members with "labor checks" issued against their products which could be used to purchase other goods from the exchange's depositories. The Freedom Colony in Bourbon county went beyond De Bernardi's plan to show that a utopian community drawing workers out of the cities and dedicated to Labor Exchange principles was workable. The colony failed with a return of good times. Primary and secondary sources; illus., 23 notes. W. F. Zornow

1511. Grant, H. Roger. WESTERN UTOPIANS AND THE FARMER'S RAILROAD MOVEMENT, 1890-1900. *North Dakota Hist. 1979 46(1): 13-18.* Several utopian groups and individuals located in the American West during the 1880's and 1890's tried to build popular support for the construction of railroads in order to enhance the economic viability of their ventures and to break the monopolistic control over rail transportation by various companies operating in their areas. Railroad building plans were formulated by Albert Kimsey Owen in relation to his Topolobampo scheme, Colorado businessman Charles Willard Caryl, the Colorado Cooperative Company, the Freedom colony of southeastern Kansas and by North Dakota wheat farmers led by David Wellington Hines. None of the schemes ever reached actuality, although Hines's "Farmers' Railroad" venture did conduct track surveys and amass large quantities of railroad ties. N. Lederer

1512. Heath, Alden R. APOSTLE IN ZION. *J. of the Illinois State Hist. Soc. 1977 70(2): 98-113.* John Alexander Dowie (1847-1907), Scottish evangelist and founder of the Divine Healing Association, came to the United States from Australia in 1888 and established in 1899 a new communitarian settlement based on strict prohibitions against alcohol, tobacco, labor unions, and doctors. His Christian Catholic Church's experiment at Zion, Illinois, drew thousands of converts, but his own megalomania caused followers to ultimately reject his leadership of that community. 6 illus., map, 52 notes. J/S

1513. Ickstadt, Heinz. "FICTION SHOWS FACT THE FUTURE": AMERIKANISCHE UTOPIEN DES SPÄTEN 19. JAHRHUNDERTS ["Fiction shows fact the future": American Utopian novels in the late 19th century]. *Amerikastudien Am. Studies [West Germany] 1977 22(2): 295-308.* Recent criticism of utopian literature has tended to regard the utopian novel exclusively as *Langue* removed from its specific historical and social frame reference. Seen purely as a closed system and static image of perfection, it is then usually denounced as a blueprint for totalitarian society. In contrast, this essay includes the utopian novel in a pragmatic theory of fiction. In its double function as "substitute and preparation for action," fiction (whether utopian or other) cannot be separated from its communicative context. As subjective response to social change it registers the costs of that change; and by converting what is lost into images of ideal society the utopian novel makes it again available for collective action. The essay analyzes ideological structure and pragmatic dimension of utopian novels of the late 19th century in America, especially those of Bellamy, Donnelly and Howells. It then tries to link them to a process of social transformation as well as to changing concepts of fiction and reality. J

1514. Olin, Spencer C., Jr. BIBLE COMMUNISM AND THE ORIGINS OF ORANGE COUNTY. *California History 1979 58(3): 220-233.* Describes the establishment of an agricultural colony in what is now Orange County, California, by the Townerites, a dissident group of Oneida colony members, in 1881. Founded in New York in 1848 by John Humphrey Noyes, the Oneida Community achieved notoriety for its espousal of economic communism, the idea of complex marriage, and other radical social practices. The Townerites, led by James W. Towner, purchased property in the Santa Ana area and established an offshoot of the original colony. The Townerites were important in founding Orange County in 1889 and in the region's political, religious, and social life. Argues that the colony merits mention among those middle-class groups who founded Pasadena and Anaheim as expressions of the desire to create economically diversified and culturally and religiously oriented communities. Primary and secondary sources; illus., photos, 31 notes.
A. Hoffman

1515. Olin, Spencer C., Jr. THE ONEIDA COMMUNITY AND THE INSTABILITY OF CHARISMATIC AUTHORITY. *J. of Am. Hist. 1980 67(2): 285-300.* Provides a new explanation for the breakup of the Oneida Community in central New York in 1881, in terms of the social theory of Max Weber. A dispute over a successor to John Humphrey Noyes in 1875 led to a challenge of the whole concept of charismatic authority, basis for the community's political order. In Weberian terms the contest for power between Noyes and the Townerites became a struggle between charismatic authority and legal-rational authority, and led to the community's demise. Based partly on correspondence, newspaper articles, and other primary sources; 51 notes.
T. P. Linkfield

1516. Rainard, R. Lyn. CONFLICT INSIDE THE EARTH: THE KORESHAN UNITY IN LEE COUNTY. *Tampa Bay Hist. 1981 3(1): 5-16.* Describes the Koreshan Unity, a small utopian religious community in Lee County, Florida, during the late 19th and early 20th centuries, led by Cyrus Reed Teed (1839-1908), focusing on lawsuits against the group by private citizens that went unnoticed by officials in Lee County until the Koreshans tried to enter politics; with Teed's death the Koreshans disbanded.

1517. Wilson, R. Jackson. EXPERIENCE AND UTOPIA: THE MAKING OF EDWARD BELLAMY'S *LOOKING BACKWARD*. *J. of Am. Studies [Great Britain] 1977 11(1): 45-60.* Although hailed widely as an evangel of the future utopia described in *Looking Backward 2000-1887* (1888), Edward Bellamy was pessimistic about achieving utopian ends. *Looking Backward* represents Bellamy's escapism from the Gilded Age's social and economic realities. He could not come to terms with the industrial revolution and pined for America's earlier agrarian society, values, and lifestyles. Based on primary sources; 24 notes.
H. T. Lovin

1518. Wyatt, Philip R. JOHN HUMPHREY NOYES AND THE STIRPICULTURAL EXPERIMENT. *J. of the Hist. of Medicine & Allied Sci. 1976 31(1): 55-66.* The Oneida Community, established by John Humphrey Noyes (1811-86) emphasized the desire for perfection. Noyes developed four unique concepts to achieve this goal. These were male continence, complex marriage, community child care, and the stirpicultural experiment. The success of male continence freed women from unwanted pregnancies, and permitted the practice of complex marriage. To assure that children were as perfect as possible, Noyes developed the policy of stirpiculture, the culture of a new race, produced by carefully controlled selective breeding. During 1869-79, 58 live births occurred in the Oneida community as a result of the experiments in scientific breeding. There was a low infant mortality rate, indicating that the combination of selective breeding and community child care had good results. Noyes demonstrated that the nature of man could be improved by controlling the environment and man's biological inheritance. The children became exceptionally successful later in life. 26 notes.
M. Kaufman

5. STRUGGLES OF THE TWENTIETH CENTURY

General

1519. Allen, Ernest. THE CULTURAL METHODOLOGY OF HAROLD CRUSE. *J. of Ethnic Studies* 1977 5(2): 26-50. Critiques Harold Cruse's writings on integration and separation and his dialectic of material versus spiritual culture found in his contributions to *Liberator* magazine and *Studies on the Left*. Cruse's stress on the need for blacks to wrest control over ideological apparatus in order to effect structural changes in the American social system is weakened by his failure to show the steps necessary for the means to produce the end. He takes refuge instead "in essentially meaningless *pronunciamentos*." Cruse's view of integration and separation as categorical opposites does not apply in the social sense, while his use of material and spiritual culture creates "an artificial schism between thought and action which is not present in real life," and stems from his misunderstanding of Sékou Touré's writings on material and spiritual cultural production. Cruse differs from most Afro-American intellectuals in that he "studies before he thinks," and "he usually thinks incorrectly." Primary and secondary sources; 22 notes.
G. J. Bobango

1520. Annunziata, Frank. THE PROGRESSIVE AS CONSERVATIVE: GEORGE CREEL'S QUARREL WITH NEW DEAL LIBERALISM. *Wisconsin Mag. of Hist.* 1974 57(3): 220-233. George Creel (1876-1953) was a progressive Democrat long before his appointment as chairman of the Committee on Public Information during World War I, and he remained an important progressive well into the New Deal. Although an early advocate of Roosevelt and the New Deal, (in his post as chairman of the National Advisory Board, Works Progress Administration), Creel turned passionately against both during the war years 1940-45. The causes of that change in attitude included his resentment of certain advisors close to Roosevelt, his failure to win an important administrative post during the war, and the death of his first wife. Ideologically, he felt that the New Deal, by moving to create a welfare state that accommodated demands of organized interest groups, had abandoned the major tenets "of the neutral regulatory progressive state." He then called unsuccessfully for a conservative coalition of southern Democrats and Republicans to reverse the trend, and he was disappointed with the policies of both Presidents Truman and Eisenhower. 3 photos, 61 notes.
N. C. Burckel

1521. Arroyo, Luis Leobardo. CHICANO PARTICIPATION IN ORGANIZED LABOR: THE CIO IN LOS ANGELES 1938-1950. *Aztlán* 1976 6(2): 277-313. During 1938-50 Chicanos were active leaders in the Los Angeles Congress of Industrial Organizations locals and the CIO Council. They worked in close association with community organizations to help solve *Mexicano* problems, among them the Sleepy Lagoon incident and the Zoot Suit Riots. After 1943 Chicano unionists lost an effective voice in the CIO Council but continued to work on the local level. Based on newspapers, oral interviews and labor union proceedings; 101 notes.
R. Griswold del Castillo

1522. Auerbach, Jerold S. FROM RAGS TO ROBES: THE LEGAL PROFESSION, SOCIAL MOBILITY AND THE AMERICAN JEWISH EXPERIENCE. *Am. Jewish Hist. Q.* 1976 65(2): 249-284. The experiences of Jewish lawyers since 1900 illuminate the struggle for success within a profession whose elite members preferred to ostracize or exclude them. Retraces the route from "ghetto shyster and collection lawyer" to Wall Street partner, Federal and Supreme Court Justice, and government lawyer ever since the New Deal. As a result, in the 1970's Jewish lawyers have often become the spokesmen for the establishment against more recent "minorities" and the defenders of professionalism. At the same time, Jews still are overrepresented on local and national boards of civil rights organizations, to say nothing of the records of the four Jewish Supreme Court Justices. 79 notes.
F. Rosenthal

1523. Austin, Michael J. and Betten, Neil. INTELLECTUAL ORIGINS OF COMMUNITY ORGANIZING, 1920-1939. *Social Service Rev.* 1977 51(1): 155-170. The roots of contemporary community organization practice can be traced to the settlement house workers and organizers of the councils of social agencies of the early 1900's. However, the education of future organizers should include the "practice wisdom" found in the writings of the organizers and educators who wrote in the 1920's and 1930's, including Hart, Lindeman, McClenahan, Pettit, and Steiner. Students of community organizing can be guided by the insights found in the first textbooks and thereby gain a perspective similar to the well-documented history of casework practice. The early manuals on community organizing represent an important dimension of the history of social work practice.
J

1524. Avery, Donald H. and Neary, Peter. LAURIER, BORDEN AND A WHITE BRITISH COLUMBIA. *J. of Can. Studies [Canada]* 1977 12(4): 24-34. Studies Oriental immigration to British Columbia from its beginnings in the 1850's until 1914, and Dominion policy toward it under the Laurier (1896-1911; Liberal) and Borden (1911-20; Conservative) governments. The Canadian Pacific Railroad was active in recruiting, transporting, and employing unskilled Asian workers. Chinese immigration virtually ended in 1903 with the imposition of a prohibitively high entry tax, whereupon Japanese and East Indian immigration increased. Japanese immigrants were granted freedom from interference by the 1894 Anglo-Japanese treaty, but the Japanese government agreed to restrict emigration. Still, a riot in Vancouver (1907) underlined continuing hostility (based largely but not solely on economics) to *all* Asian immigration. Mentions the intervention of Theodore Roosevelt in this matter (1908). 66 notes.
L. W. Van Wyk

1525. Bammi, Vivek. NUTRITION, THE HISTORIAN, AND PUBLIC POLICY: A CASE STUDY OF U.S. NATIONAL NUTRITION POLICY IN THE 20TH CENTURY. *J. of Social Hist.* 1980 14(4): 627-648. Discusses national nutrition policy in the United States from 1906 to 1979, how government has shaped the changing trends of food production, processing, distribution, and consumption, and the consequences for the health of the population. Regulation of food quality in 1906 was a response to the commercialization of the food supply due to industrialization. During the 1930's the government became distributor as well as regulator. During World War II a national nutrition policy was manifest, but it was later discarded. The evidence of hunger in the 1960's highlighted the government's failure as a distributive agent. In this era malnutrition was recognized as a major link in the cycle of poverty. Lastly, the growing comprehension of widespread malnutrition has brought to the fore the prevalent nutritional problem of all developed societies: the need for sound nutritional guidelines. 5 notes, ref.
J. Powell

1526. Barkan, Steven E. POLITICAL TRIALS AND RESOURCE MOBILIZATION: TOWARDS AN UNDERSTANDING OF SOCIAL MOVEMENT LITIGATION. *Social Forces* 1980 58(3): 944-961. This paper integrates recent approaches to the study of social movements and of litigation by examining the use of the courts during times of social unrest. Litigation is one of several strategies available to social movements and their adversaries in the struggle for political power. After suggesting the potential and limits of social movement litigation, the paper examines political trials as one form of litigation, locating their origins in attempts to affect the distribution of resources important for the success of protest group efforts. Emphasis is placed on the jury and the press as two distinctive features of American democracy that affect decisions by social movement members to use the courts and also shape subsequent proceedings and outcomes. Finally, the paper discusses several lines of inquiry for future research. Biblio.
J

1527. Bator, Paul Adolphus. "THE STRUGGLE TO RAISE THE LOWER CLASSES": PUBLIC HEALTH REFORM AND THE PROBLEM OF POVERTY IN TORONTO, 1910 TO 1921. *J. of Can. Studies [Canada]* 1979 14(1): 43-49. Discusses the steps taken by Dr. Charles Hastings, Toronto's Medical Officer of Health from 1910 to 1929 who was determined to solve the public health crisis. To this end he led a movement to reorganize the city's splintered system of charities. He saw poverty as a major factor, and public education as his principle tool. He

was responsible for the organization of the Neighborhood Workers' Association, and through its workers and his public health nurses was able to greatly alleviate the situation although he never did get to the point of attacking the causes of poverty in addition to dealing with its results. 43 notes.
R. V. Ritter

1528. Bauman, John F. SAFE AND SANITARY WITHOUT THE COSTLY FRILLS: THE EVOLUTION OF PUBLIC HOUSING IN PHILADELPHIA, 1929-1941. *Pennsylvania Mag. of Hist. and Biog. 1977 101(1): 114-128.* Traces the development of public housing in Philadelphia. The early impetus split between practical bureaucrats and persons who envisioned revivification of the community. The latter group weakened as money poured in from Washington, D.C. The bureaucrats had their way, constructed unimaginative structures, and were concerned only with minimum standards of health and sanitation. What finally developed was new slums inhabited by persons not really in need of them. Eliminating frills also eliminated pride and character. 37 notes.
V. L. Human

1529. Berkin, Carol Ruth. NOT SEPARATE, NOT EQUAL. Berkin, Carol Ruth and Norton, Mary Beth, ed. *Women of America: A History* (Boston: Houghton Mifflin Co., 1979): 273-288. Examines the apparent disintegration of the women's liberation movement after the passage of the 19th Amendment. The media held up the flapper as an indication that women were liberated in the 1920's. Real jobs were difficult to obtain, however, and feminist leaders could not decide which issues to attack after the amendment had passed. The Depression brought with it the idea that "one unemployed woman meant one more working man." World War II brought many women back into the work force. Many resisted leaving their jobs when men returned from the war, but they were still reduced from 25% to 7.5% of the labor force. In the 1960's, a new feminist movement emerged based on the reforms of the decade.
K. Talley

1530. Bicha, Karel D. PRAIRIE RADICALS: A COMMON PIETISM. *J. of Church and State 1976 18(1): 79-94.* The "Prairie Radicals" were the activists in the plains area of the United States and Canada following the end of the populist movement. There men had no real common ideological ties. Some were leftist, some rightist, some poor, some wealthy. Argues that pietism was the common tie. There was a prominence of ministerial personnel among the radicals. Their values were pietistic. Most were Baptist, Methodist, Disciples of Christ or Pietistic Lutheran. The influence of their religious origins is analyzed in detail, showing the close similarities of each case. 59 notes.
E. E. Eminhizer

1531. Billington, Monroe. LYNDON B. JOHNSON AND BLACKS: THE EARLY YEARS. *J. of Negro Hist. 1977 62(1): 26-42.* The Johnson presidency, 1963-68, constituted a significant era in the progress of civil rights for blacks. Focuses on Lyndon B. Johnson's early relationships with and attitudes toward blacks and their rights. Questions his sincerity in pressing for civil rights legislation, issuing executive orders, and speaking out publicly. Notes the length of time he held such expressed views, the degree of consistency throughout his career, and the argument that he may have acted through political expediency in yielding to current pressures. 97 notes.
P. J. Taylorson

1532. Birch, Eugenie Ladner. RADBURN AND THE AMERICAN PLANNING MOVEMENT: THE PERSISTENCE OF AN IDEA. *J. of the Am. Planning Assoc. 1980 46(4): 424-439.* Radburn, a partially built, planned, New Jersey settlement, represents the influence of English garden city theories. Radburn's plan has become a permanent resource for planners who in every generation examine and sometimes adapt it. As a result, it has survived as testimony to the planners' vision of suburban growth. Covers 1927-present.
J/S

1533. Black, Earl. SOUTHERN GOVERNORS AND POLITICAL CHANGE: CAMPAIGN STANCES ON RACIAL SEGREGATION AND ECONOMIC DEVELOPMENT, 1950-1969. *J. of Pol. 1971 33(3): 703-734.* Examines campaign statements of successful southern gubernatorial candidates 1950-69 to determine the rate of change in attitudes toward segregation and economic development in the region. The governors are rated segregationist, moderate segregationist, and nonsegregationist, according to their racial views; and marginalist, adaptive, neopopulist marginalist, and neopopulist adaptive, according to their response to improvements in public education. The latter position is viewed as a gauge of the governor's interest in economic growth. While it is possible to find a mixture of segregationist views with a neopopulist adaptive posture on educational improvements, the major changes in both the deep and the peripheral South have come in the area of economic development. The most significant decline in segregationist campaign statements has come in the peripheral South. 4 tables, 2 figs., 34 notes.
A. R. Stoesen

1534. Blanchard, Margaret A. PRESS CRITICISM AND NATIONAL REFORM MOVEMENTS: THE PROGRESSIVE ERA AND THE NEW DEAL. *Journalism Hist. 1978 5(2): 33-37, 54-55.* Critics of the press supported the Progressive ideology of reform from within, 1890's-1920's, but during the New Deal belief that the press had subsumed journalistic ethics to economic gain led to reform moves sponsored by the federal government.

1535. Boivin, Aurélien and Landry, Kenneth. FRANÇOISE ET MADELEINE: PIONNIÈRES DU JOURNALISME FÉMININ AU QUÉBEC [Françoise and Madeleine: pioneers of feminine journalism in Quebec]. *Atlantis [Canada] 1978 4(1): 63-74.* At the beginning of the 20th century, Françoise and Madeleine, pseudonyms of Robertine Barry and Anne-Marie Gleason respectively, through their articles worked at improving the condition of women and reminded their readers of the importance of the role of women.

1536. Boydston, Jo Ann. JOHN DEWEY AND THE NEW FEMINISM. *Teachers Coll. Record 1975 76(3): 441-448.* John Dewey, long known as a leading educational reformer, was also a "forerunner" on the "woman question." His views are clearly expressed in his correspondence with Scudder Klyce. In public he restricted his comments to the issues of coeducation and suffrage, but he wrote on a broad spectrum of concerns in this correspondence.
W. H. Mulligan, Jr.

1537. Braungart, Richard G. and Braungart, Margaret M. PROTEST ATTITUDES AND BEHAVIOR AMONG COLLEGE YOUTH. *Youth and Soc. 1974 6(2): 219-248.* Examines the phenomenon of activism-prone youth among the college student population, and discusses the process of radicalization.
S

1538. Breily, Ronald. LYNN J. FRAZIER AND PROGRESSIVE REFORM: A PLODDER IN THE RANKS OF A RUGGED REGIMENT. *South Dakota Hist. 1977 7(4): 438-454.* Picked to run for governor in 1916, Lynn J. Frazier represented the Progressives, a group whose political ideals were a total faith in democracy and a contempt for corruption. As time would prove, these qualifications were not enough to bring fundamental change, although they were important factors to being elected in rural-oriented North Dakota. Frazier's views never wavered. He was elected to Congress and made chairman of a committee to evaluate the condition of American Indians. His concerns for honesty, corruption, and the abuses of big government and business were applied not only to agriculture, but also to the operation of Indian affairs. He might have evaluated the actual conditions on reservations, but instead concentrated on corruption and the rooting out of dishonesty within the institutions that saw to the Indian population. These viewpoints kept him faithful to Progressive political doctrine, but were not enough to bring about policy changes. Covers 1916-40. Primary and secondary sources; 3 photos, 53 notes.
A. J. Larson

1539. Brito, Patricia. PROTECTIVE LEGISLATION IN OHIO: THE INTER-WAR YEARS. *Ohio Hist. 1979 88(2): 173-197.* Legislative prohibition of women from certain occupations was important in the interwar years in Ohio, and more important was the provision of a minimum wage for women. A long list prohibited the employment of women in a long list of occupations. Women should go into occupations only if they were safe from physical hazards, economic exploitation, and possible moral corruption. "Ohio's minimum wage for women was never a measure of primary importance to unions.... Whatever support Ohio labor finally gave to assuring female labor a reasonable wage did not extend to assuring women an equal opportunity in the labor market." 2 illus., 82 notes.
E. P. Stickney

1540. Burgchardt, Carl R. TWO FACES OF AMERICAN COMMUNISM: PAMPHLET RHETORIC OF THE THIRD PERIOD AND THE POPULAR FRONT. *Q. J. of Speech 1980 66(4): 375-391.* Before July 1935, pamphlets of the American Communist Party demanded the overthrow of capitalism in dogmatic and distorted language. Consequently, they were not adapted well to the non-Communist public. Pamphlets published after July 1935 attempted to overcome negative impressions of communism, but they were largely unsuccessful. J

1541. Burnham, John C. THE STRUGGLE BETWEEN PHYSICIANS AND PARAMEDICAL PERSONNEL IN AMERICAN PSYCHIATRY, 1917-41. *J. of the Hist. of Medicine and Allied Sci. 1974 29(1): 93-106.* Utilizing the economists' model of supply and demand in health care, discusses the mental hygiene movement 1917-41 when the professional-nonprofessional issue was fought out between psychiatrists and nonphysicians. After 1917, demand for mental hygiene workers greatly exceeded supply; thus, social workers and psychologists became members of a mental health team. With the advent of the Depression, however, physicians were not inclined to encourage competition. Psychiatrists sought to recapture control of the profession by making the hospital once again central to practice, training, and certification. Based on primary and secondary sources; 33 notes. J. L Susskind

1542. Burson, George S., Jr. THE SECOND RECONSTRUCTION: A HISTORIOGRAPHICAL ESSAY ON RECENT WORKS. *J. of Negro Hist. 1974 59(4): 322-336.* Calls for historians to join political scientists, sociologists, journalists, and polemicists in dealing with unanswered questions surrounding the period 1954-66. Beginning with the *Brown* decision and ending with "Black Power" movement, the Second Reconstruction awaits a dispassionate and comprehensive historical interpretation. Although it is still too early to assess the long-range effects of this era, very little historical literature has dealt substantively with Negroes in the South during 1954-66. Secondary sources; 66 notes.
N. G. Sapper

1543. Butler, Johnnella and Marable, Manning. THE NEW NEGRO AND THE IDEOLOGICAL ORIGINS OF THE INTEGRATIONIST MOVEMENT. *J. of Ethnic Studies 1975 2(4): 47-55.* "The literature of the Negro Renaissance needs to be re-examined from the purview of the pervasiveness of the conflicts apparent in such ... themes as the tragic mulatto, the glorified and idealistic African past, the alienation from American culture, and an implied, and at times overt, self-hatred." Discusses the need to reevaluate the origins of the integrationist movement. W. E. B. Du Bois' contradiction, that the Negro was a new man, that he owed as much to white America as to mother Africa and should seek full integration, was extended by the Renaissance into a goal of full Americanization. But this posture placed the African American in a position as a "reactor" not an initiator of action, leading to doubts of self-worth and self-denial. Such an integrationist approach survived with few challenges into the mid-1960's, and the NAACP hierarchy and Negro intellectuals did not support Black cultural nationalism, but drew heavily "upon the ambivalences" implicit in the Renaissance. Based on primary and secondary sources; 26 notes. G. J. Bobango

1544. Butler, Matilda and Paisley, William. MAGAZINE COVERAGE OF WOMEN'S RIGHTS. *J. of Communication 1978 28(1): 183-186.* Examination of periodicals, coverage of women's rights issues, 1922-76, shows that the 1920's and the 1970's had the most coverage, but also that recent coverage (revolving primarily around the ERA) is not always in-depth or informative.

1545. Butler, Raymond V. THE BUREAU OF INDIAN AFFAIRS: ACTIVITIES SINCE 1945. *Ann. of the Am. Acad. of Pol. and Social Sci. 1978 436: 50-60.* The journey from termination, where the federal government was trying to get out of the Indian business, to Indian self-determination, where the federal government is committed to becoming a full partner to the Indian tribes, is the major theme of Indian affairs over the past several decades. The impact of Indian self-determination on the future operations of the Bureau of Indian Affairs cannot be predicted at this time. The particular nature of and direction of the change will depend upon how totally the tribes embrace its philosophy; the commitment of the Congress to the concept outlined in the Indian Self-Determination Act, as reflected in appropriations and supportive legislation; and the conversion of the Bureau from the role of policymaker to technical advisor. Present critical problems involving urban Indians, water, hunting and fishing rights, historic land claims, and the question of federal recognition of heretofore unrecognized Indian groups, will challenge every aspect of the concept of self-determination. J

1546. Buttel, Frederick H. and Flinn, William L. SOCIOPOLITICAL CONSEQUENCES OF AGRARIANISM. *Rural Sociol. 1976 41(4): 473-483.* Sees a dichotomy within the sociopolitical philosophy of agrarianism: rhetorical legitimation of the American social order but critical attitudes toward that order; agrarian criticisms have been confined to politics and the political system rather than to the private property-based stratification system, 1890's-1970's.

1547. Calderwood, William. RELIGIOUS REACTIONS TO THE KU KLUX KLAN IN SASKATCHEWAN. *Saskatchewan Hist. 1973 26(3): 103-114.* By 1926 the Ku Klux Klan was organized in most of the Canadian provinces. It fed on long-standing prejudices, but never had spectacular success. Its greatest impact was felt in Saskatchewan in 1927-30 where the prominent political issues of language, sectarianism, immigration, and control of natural resources could all be associated with a "Catholic plot." Evidence is strong that many conservative Protestants embraced and supported the principles of the KKK. 57 notes.
D. L. Smith

1548. Carlson, Oliver. RECOLLECTIONS OF AMERICAN TROTSKYIST LEADERS. *Studies in Comparative Communism 1977 10(1-2): 161-165.* Before the author left the Communist Party in 1928, he spoke with his friend, William Z. Foster. Foster agreed with objections to Moscow's dictation but wanted to reform the party from within. Before this episode, the author recalled Karl Radek insisting in Moscow in 1924 that the Politburo was always right and that this belief was essential to being a good Communist. Also mentions James P. Cannon and Max Schachtman. Covers 1920's-30's. 2 notes. D. Balmuth

1549. Carriker, Robert C. THE KALISPEL TRIBE AND THE INDIAN CLAIMS COMMISSION EXPERIENCE. *Western Hist. Q. 1978 9(1): 19-31.* The home of the precontact Kalispel Indians, affluent and independent, was a four-million-acre area in northeastern Washington, northern Idaho, and western Montana. By 1950 fewer than 100 impoverished Kalispel languished on an eight-square-mile reservation in northeastern Washington. They sought redress through the Indian Claims Commission. This brought 15 years of frustration in their dealings with government agencies and officials. The 1965 settlement of their claim removed the poverty and despair of the past but left scars. 38 notes.
D. L. Smith

1550. Carver, Joan S. WOMEN IN FLORIDA. *J. of Pol. 1979 41(3): 941-955.* Large-scale immigration since World War II has made Florida atypical of the South. On feminist issues, northern Florida remains more conservative than the southern and central regions. Only since 1960 have women made dramatic progress as power shifted from the north. During 1915-1920, 23 municipalities granted women suffrage, but feminist agitation was limited to that issue. The gains of the last two decades are attributed to an increasingly female work force; higher levels of education, especially legal training; higher voting rates and greater activism by feminist groups. Covers 1890-1978. Map, 3 tables, 22 notes.
A. W. Novitsky

1551. Chafetz, Janet Saltzman and Polk, Barbara Bovee. ROOM AT THE TOP: SOCIAL RECOGNITION OF BRITISH AND AMERICAN FEMALES OVER TIME. *Social Sci. Q. 1974 54(4): 843-853.* "The relative proportions of females to males, the bases for social recognition, educational and marital data are compared to examine the effects of changes in the formal opportunity structure and the early Women's Rights Movement ... Data from both Britain and the United States show predicted changes in education and bases of fame but that marital data suggest a lack of concomitant value changes regarding the female role."
J

1552. Colburn, David R. and Scher, Richard K. RACE RELATIONS AND FLORIDA GUBERNATORIAL POLITICS SINCE THE *BROWN* DECISION. *Florida Hist. Q. 1976 55(2): 153-169.* The quality of the governor's leadership during the racial turmoil of the mid-1950's-70's influenced the racial climate in Florida. LeRoy Collins' moderate administration during 1955-61 was followed by three administrations which made little effort to promote racial harmony. Reubin Askew's election in 1970 marked the beginning of improved racial relations in Florida. Askew has pursued equal rights policies and affirmative action in state employment. Based mainly on interviews and newspaper reports; 64 notes. — P. A. Beaber

1553. Conley, John A. BEYOND LEGISLATIVE ACTS: PENAL REFORM, PUBLIC POLICY, AND SYMBOLIC JUSTICE. *Public Hist. 1981 3(1): 26-39.* Focuses on prison reform in Oklahoma from 1910, when it constructed its penitentiary, to 1967, when it created a statewide corrections department.

1554. Cooper, Algia R. BROWN V. BOARD OF EDUCATION AND VIRGIL DARNELL HAWKINS: TWENTY-EIGHT YEARS AND SIX PETITIONS TO JUSTICE. *J. of Negro Hist. 1979 64(1): 1-20.* Chronicles the battle waged by Virgil Darnell Hawkins, 1949-76, in the Florida courts, to be admitted first to law school at the University of Florida and eventually to the Florida Bar.

1555. Coté, Joseph A. CLARENCE HAMILTON POE: THE FARMER'S VOICE, 1899-1964. *Agric. Hist. 1979 53(1): 30-41.* Coming to the staff of the *Progressive Farmer* in 1897 as "printer's devil," Clarence Hamilton Poe became editor in 1899. An aggressive spokesman for agrarian values, he viewed the farmers as the "guardians of the nation's heritage," and used the pages of his journal to propose reforms which would rejuvenate southern agriculture and end the expanding exodus from the farm. A major method which he advocated was the agricultural cooperative; however, his fertile mind and accurate analysis of problems reached out in many directions. Through his journal he championed agricultural reform measures, and brought hope and encouragement to southern farmers, including positive change. 48 notes. Comment by William Scarborough, pp. 60-61. — R. V. Ritter

1556. Courville, L. D. THE CONSERVATISM OF THE SASKATCHEWAN PROGRESSIVES. *Can. Hist. Assoc. Hist. Papers 1974: 157-181.* Discusses the underlying social and political conservatism of agrarian progressivism in Saskatchewan in the 1920's.

1557. Cox, Archibald. THE NEW DIMENSIONS OF CONSTITUTIONAL ADJUDICATION. *Massachusetts Hist. Soc. Pro. 1976 88: 60-79.* In the past 25 years, the courts have moved into new areas of activity: constitutional adjudication has been increasingly used as a means of reform, there have been many procedural changes, and the courts have imposed affirmative duties on the other branches of government. These developments lead one to ask, "What is the source of judicial power to command acceptance—for decrees which have no basis in popular consent?" The answer seems to lie in the Supreme Court's perception of the common will and its understanding of the general consensus. Based on Supreme Court cases; 30 notes, index. — G. W. R. Ward

1558. Crow, Leslie. PRESTON SCHOOL OF INDUSTRY. *Pacific Hist. 1979 23(4): 81-96.* The Preston School of Industry was founded by the state of California in 1894 in response to a growing feeling that youthful offenders should be segregated from adult criminals. As social conditions changed, Preston School programs were altered. The Junior Republic program to instill in the inmates civic responsibility was a major project. Other programs, including military training, community clubs, scouting, and religious activities were genuine efforts to rehabilitate prisoners. Based on legislative reports, reports of the Preston School of Industry, and unpublished academic studies on the institution; 8 photos, 32 notes. — H. M. Parker, Jr.

1559. Crowe-Carraco, Carol. MARY BRECKINRIDGE AND THE FRONTIER NURSING SERVICE. *Register of the Kentucky Hist. Soc. 1978 76(3): 179-191.* Personal tragedies led Mary Breckinridge to work for a family centered health care system in frontier Kentucky areas. From the mid-1920's until her death 40 years later, Breckinridge and the Frontier Nursing Service provided assistance in midwifery, general family care, and disease prevention. From small beginnings, the FNS network grew to cover an area of almost 700 square miles. Primary and secondary sources; 2 illus., 51 notes. — J. F. Paul

1560. Czuchlewski, Paul E. LIBERAL CATHOLICISM AND AMERICAN RACISM, 1924-1960. *Records of the Am. Catholic Hist. Soc. of Philadelphia 1974 85(3-4): 144-162.* During the 1920's-50's, the liberal Catholic intellectual lived in a painful tension between means and ends. An intellectual dedicated to dialogue, a religious man devoted to peace, an antitotalitarian convinced of the virtues of democratic process, and an inheritor of Jeffersonian liberalism and Thomistic organicism committed to limited government, he desired brotherhood but could not seek it through racial militancy or legislative compulsion. 30 notes. — J. M. McCarthy

1561. Dahlie, Jorgen, ed. THE ETHNIC VOICE: EYEWITNESS ACCOUNTS. *Can. Ethnic Studies [Canada] 1978 10(2): 95-106.* Six authors are excerpted "to acquaint the reader with the personality, style, and characteristic response of the individual [leftist] radical spokesmen, and to recapture something of the spirit of the times when uninhibited forms of protest were voiced against the conventional institutions of Canadian society." The excerpts are from the writings of A. B. Mäkelä (1912), Arthur Puttee (1907-10), Pavlo Krat (1914), Ole Kjelt (1920), Sam Scarlett (1926), and Tomo Čačić (1934). The excerpts are called "to a degree . . . representative." 2 photos. — R. V. Ritter

1562. Dahlie, Jorgen. THE JAPANESE CHALLENGE TO PUBLIC SCHOOLS IN SOCIETY IN BRITISH COLUMBIA. *J. of Ethnic Studies 1974 2(1): 10-23.* Reviews the history of the Japanese communities of British Columbia from 1900 until sweeping evacuation orders in 1942 shipped thousands into camps in the province's interior. Ever since the beginning of the century prejudice and discrimination were overt and thinly disguised, based on "economic, political, and social rationalizations." The constant theme was that of non-assimilability, and by the interwar years the "Oriental Menace" was a threat to a white British Columbia. The maintenance of separate Japanese-language schools and Buddhist religious centers added to the discriminatory feeling, and by the 1940's their dual nationality automatically meant fifth column activities. Paradoxically most of the Issei and Nisei coped extremely well with the restrictions and persecutions, both official and unofficial, which they experienced. The only bright spot was the work of various Christian missionary groups among the Japanese children and in the relocation camps. Since World War II conditions for minorities have improved markedly in British Columbia with the establishment of a policy of multi-culturalism. Based on contemporary sources; 58 notes. — G. J. Bobango

1563. Davidson, Charles N., Jr. GEORGE ARTHUR BUTTRICK: CHRISTOCENTRIC PREACHER AND PACIFIST. *J. of Presbyterian Hist. 1975 53(2): 143-167.* Although he has changed his mind on other matters, George Arthur Buttrick (b. 1892) has maintained his position on pacifism to the present. Traces Buttrick's pacifism from the early years of his ministry through the two world wars, concluding with a word about the dangers inherent in the idea of an "American Century," borne out by the Vietnam War. Based on an interview with Buttrick and on his writings; illus., 84 notes. — H. M. Parker, Jr.

1564. DeBenedetti, Charles. THE AMERICAN PEACE MOVEMENT AND THE NATIONAL SECURITY STATE, 1941-1971. *World Affairs 1978 141(2): 118-129.* Describes the movement in the United States, after the attack on Pearl Harbor, toward global military preparedness, and the reactions of American pacifists, both liberal and radical.

1565. Dennis, Rutledge M. DUBOIS AND THE ROLE OF THE EDUCATED ELITE. *J. of Negro Educ. 1977 46(4): 388-402.* W. E. B. DuBois's changing ideas of the role of an educated elite in gaining racial liberation are examined by dividing his intellectual migration into three periods. During the first, 1897-1904, DuBois defined his theory. During 1905-52 he sought programmatic realization of his theory through his scholarship and activism. In the last period, 1952-63, DuBois became disillusioned with the apathy of the elite, and formulated a clearer class analysis of social problems. Secondary sources; 25 notes. — R. E. Butchart

1566. Dethloff, Henry C. THE LONGS: REVOLUTION OR POPULIST RETRENCHMENT? *Louisiana Hist. 1978 19(4): 401-412.* Compares the politics of Huey P. Long (d. 1935) with Populism and

Progressivism in Louisiana. "Longism" had roots in those earlier movements, but "Longism" was more radical than Populism or Progressivism. The Long mystique was especially revolutionary. Based prinicpally on secondary sources; 36 notes.　　　　　　　　　　　R. L. Woodward

1567. Diner, Steven J. SCHOLARSHIP IN THE QUEST FOR SOCIAL WELFARE: A FIFTY-YEAR HISTORY OF THE *SOCIAL SERVICE REVIEW*. *Social Service Rev.* 1977 51(1): 1-66. This essay examines the changing purposes of social work and social welfare scholarship through the fifty years of the *Social Service Review*. The author suggests that, although the personalities and ideologies of the editors were important in determining the content of the *Review*, national and international developments and trends within the social work profession and the academic world generally have been the most important determinants.　　J

1568. Dixon, Ruth B. MEASURING EQUALITY BETWEEN THE SEXES. *J. of Social Issues* 1976 32(3): 19-32. Measures of the status of women and their potential for equality with men may be derived from women's position in five major spheres of activity—sexual relationships, reproduction, homemaking and childcare, economic production, and political decision making—and from the degree of functional independence among these spheres of activity. Some commonly used statistical indicators of the status of women in the United States from 1900 through the early 1970s are evaluated as measures of progress toward equality between the sexes, defined here as the abolition of the social division of labor based on gender, and some new measures are proposed.　　J

1569. Dobelstein, Andrew. THE EFFECTS OF THE REFORM MOVEMENT ON RELIEF ADMINISTRATION IN NORTH CAROLINA: THE CONTRIBUTIONS OF ALEXANDER WORTH MC ALISTER. *South Atlantic Q.* 1976 75(2): 245-257. Examines the role of Alexander W. McAlister in North Carolina relief programs. Discusses the reasons for success and the Unit Plan of local administration. 35 notes.　　　　　　　　　　　　　　　　　　R. W. Dubay

1570. Dunn, Joe P. PROTESTANT CHURCH SPOKESMEN, UNIVERSAL MILITARY TRAINING, AND THE ANTI-CONSCRIPTION CAMPAIGNS, 1940-1959. *Pro. of the South Carolina Hist. Assoc.* 1979: 41-58. Examines the emergence of Protestant lobbying agencies and their role in anticonscription campaigns. Traces the churches' arguments through their publications such as the *Christian Century* and *Conscription News*, a publication founded by a coalition of church groups to fight universal military training. 25 notes.
　　　　　　　　　　　　　　　　　　　　　　J. W. Thacker, Jr.

1571. Durnbaugh, Donald. ENLARGING THE CIRCLE: THE HISTORIC PEACE CHURCHES AND MILITARISM. *Mennonite Life* 1978 33(3): 16-18. The three Historic Peace Churches (Society of Friends, Mennonites, and Church of the Brethren) have worked to promote world peace in the 20th century through four main channels: education, publication, action, and witness to governments. Educational efforts have included seminars and conferences as well as support for such colleges as Haverford and Swarthmore. Propeace publications have ranged from posters to scholarly texts. Action has included devising alternate service for conscientious objectors, nonviolent resistance, and acts of civil disobedience. Peace churches have lobbied for changes in government policy. Currently the three churches are forming the New Call to Peacemaking to revitalize the peace movement. Photo.　　　B. Burnett

1572. Eyestone, Robert. CONFUSION, DIFFUSION, AND INNOVATION. *Am. Pol. Sci. Rev.* 1977 71(2): 441-447. The apparent fact that interactive effects are more common in policy innovations taking a long time to diffuse among the states, contrary to the presumed effects of interaction, suggests the existence of alternate diffusion mechanisms. Some policies diffuse directly from a federal model, while others diffuse among states via a segmented pattern of emulations. The order of state adoption of fair employment practices legislation is compared with the adoption order for three labor policies and two civil rights policies. Fair employment practice, by this test, is identified as a civil rights policy and not as a labor policy. State minimum wage legislation is discussed as a case of federal influence in the diffusion process. A first wave of diffusion was followed by a period of federally inspired court rescission. Federal legislation in 1938 began another wave of diffusion. In a third wave of innovations, states with existing laws amended those laws by emulating the new federal legislation.　　　　　　　　　　　　　　J

1573. Fairbanks, Robert B. HOUSING THE CITY: THE BETTER HOUSING LEAGUE AND CINCINNATI, 1916-1939. *Ohio Hist.* 1980 89(2): 157-180. The Cincinnati Better Housing League, established in 1916, brought better housing to the city and earned a reputation as one of the country's most effective local housing associations. At first the league was capable of assimilating newcomers from its tenement areas into used houses, which would "filter down" to the tenement dwellers. By the early 20's, the organization faced a war-induced housing shortage and the migration of thousands of blacks into the city. Houses stopped filtering down and race relations became tense in a climate of housing competition. League leader Bleeker Marquette asked for federal help, and the older sections were cleared and redeveloped. Primary sources; 59 notes.　　　　　　　　　　　　　　　　　　　　J. Powell

1574. Falcone, David J. LEGISLATIVE CHANGE AND POLICY CHANGE: A DEVIANT CASE ANALYSIS OF THE CANADIAN HOUSE OF COMMONS. *J. of Pol.* 1979 41(2): 611-632. In a Deviant Case Analysis of the Canadian House of Commons over the first 28 parliaments, it was the 16th which produced the most clearly unexpected outputs. It is possible that the remaining strength of the Progressive movement, combined with a majority government was the reason that vociferous demands for new reallocation schemes were successful. The Progressive Party's strength in the early 1920's may have crystallized attention on the need for the state to reallocate resources while the political climate inhibited such programs until bargains could be struck between the Liberal elite and the Progressives during the 16th parliament. There may have been a multiplicative effect of: a majority of seats held by the governing party, a highly competitive popular election, and the absence of a wide gap between the popular vote percentages of the two leading parties. 4 tables, 3 fig., 20 notes.　　　A. W. Novitsky

1575. Farley, Ena L. CARING AND SHARING SINCE WORLD WAR I: THE LEAGUE OF WOMEN FOR COMMUNITY SERVICES: A BLACK VOLUNTEER ORGANIZATION IN BOSTON. *Umoja* 1977 1(2): 1-12. The League of Women for Community Service, an all-black women's organization founded in Boston, Massachusetts, has a continuing record of fighting for equality, promoting civic responsibility, and sponsoring political activism, 1918-77.

1576. Ferguson, Barry and Owram, Doug. SOCIAL SCIENTISTS AND PUBLIC POLICY FROM THE 1920S THROUGH WORLD WAR II. *J. of Can. Studies [Canada]* 1980-81 15(4): 3-17. Provides a history of the social and political sciences in Canadian universities and discusses their interests in and effect on public policy formation and social reform. The depression of the 1930's led to a crisis of confidence in government, and academe was looked to for advice. Interest in these areas was encouraged by government sponsorship. Primary sources; 68 notes.
　　　　　　　　　　　　　　　　　　　　　　　J. Powell

1577. Fickle, James E. MANAGEMENT LOOKS AT THE LABOR PROBLEM: THE SOUTHERN PINE INDUSTRY DURING WORLD WAR I AND THE POSTWAR ERA. *J. of Southern Hist.* 1974 40(1): 61-76. Surveys management's view of labor conditions in the southern pine industry during 1910-20's. Troubled relations between labor and management in the pine industry before World War I continued during the war. Management would not admit the validity of labor's complaints regarding hours, wages, and working conditions, and used patriotic slogans to extract more production from the pine workers during the war. By the end of the war and afterwards, the lumber company operators sought to stem the migration of Negroes out of the South, and through the creation of an employment bureau in Chicago, actually attempted to reverse the flow of workers. Despite labor conditions, management continued to talk of the "contented workers." The views of the southern lumber operators, whether realistic or not, reflect the attitudes of influential and powerful figures toward social and economic issues during this period. Based on manuscript materials and published primary and secondary sources; 54 notes.　　　　　　　T. D. Schoonover

1578. Forbes, E. R. T. THE ORIGINS OF THE MARITIME RIGHTS MOVEMENT. *Acadiensis [Canada]* 1975 5(1): 54-66. During 1900-19 a broadly based regional protest movement developed in the

Atlantic Provinces. It climaxed in the 1920's with the Maritime Rights Movement which promoted the regionally oriented Intercolonial Railway against the national government system, and promoted the ports of Halifax and St. John as entrepots for Canada's winter trade. The clergy, labour, farm, and professional organizations espoused progressive reforms through the movement which provided an uncommon amount of regional unity. 60 notes. D. F. Chard

1579. Fowler, Robert Booth and Grossman, Joel B. LIBERALISM, LAW, AND SOCIAL CHANGE: A PREFACE. *Am. Pol. Q.* 1974 2(3): 276-312. Analyzes liberal and radical thought on liberalism, law, and social change during 1953-73. S

1580. Frederickson, Mary. THE SOUTHERN SUMMER SCHOOL FOR WOMEN WORKERS. *Southern Exposure* 1977 4(4): 70-75. From 1927 until World War II a group of middle class southern white women, led by Louise McLaren and Lois MacDonald, drew support from the Young Women's Christian Association and other agencies to run regular summer schools for southern white working women. These schools, held in Virginia and North Carolina, were designed to provide women with analytical tools necessary to understand their situation, to provide means of interrelationships between working women and to develop labor organizing skills for the southern labor movement. Participants acknowledged that their role in the school had a significant impact on their lives and thinking. Primary sources. N. Lederer

1581. French, Larry and Hornbuckle, Jim. THE HISTORICAL INFLUENCE OF THE EASTERN INDIANS ON CONTEMPORARY PAN-INDIANISM. *Indian Hist.* 1977 10(2): 23-27. As the new Indian movement gets under way, with national conferences and organizations promoting the welfare of native Americans, it is noteworthy that eastern Indians have led the struggle for Indian rights for more than 200 years. Minor tribes disappeared in the wake of white settlement, but the Cherokees, Creeks, Choctaws, and Chickasaws have survived wars, disease, removal to Oklahoma, and other major problems, to lead the American movement today. Biblio. E. D. Johnson

1582. Fretz, L. A. SOCIAL WELFARE IN THE UNITED STATES, 1932-64. *Hist. News [New Zealand]* 1977 (34): 12-15, (35): 7-11. Continued from a previous article. Part II. Discusses New Deal federal regulation, planning of public welfare, assistance to organized labor, and the initiation of social security, 1932-39. Part III. Chronicles public welfare during 1939-64, examining limitations of the New Deal, the effects of World War II, the Fair Deal, the Eisenhower era, the New Frontier, the Great Society, the Cold War, and the civil rights movement.

1583. Gavins, Raymond. HANCOCK, JACKSON, AND YOUNG: VIRGINIA'S BLACK TRIUMVIRATE, 1930-1945. *Virginia Mag. of Hist. and Biog.* 1977 85(4): 470-486. George B. Hancock, Luther P. Jackson, and Plummer B. Young have not received enough attention for their part in shaping the goals and strategies of blacks in Virginia and throughout the South. During the Depression, New Deal, and World War II, they attempted to improve the plight of blacks and to enlist white support for reform. Though essentially moderate, they were the precursors of later civil rights activists. Based on primary sources, interviews, newspapers, and secondary works; 40 notes. R. F. Oaks

1584. Genest, Jean. LA COMMISSION DES ACCIDENTS DU TRAVAIL [The Commission on Industrial Accidents]. *Action Natl. [Canada]* 1978 67(9): 710-726. In 1890, a Quebec royal commission on labor relations noted the hazards of industry. The Turgeon Commission found similar conditions in 1936-38. Quebec's Catholic bishops issued pastoral letters on the subject in 1941 and 1950. Strikes and public demonstrations in 1948, 1949, and 1972 kept the issue before the public. A Commission on Industrial Accidents was established by legislation in 1931, victims of criminal acts were indemnified in 1971, and protection was extended to victims of asbestosis and silicosis in 1975. In 1976, some 282,684 cases had been brought before the commission under the three laws. Table. A. W. Novitsky

1585. Gianakos, Perry E. THE BLACK MUSLIMS: AN AMERICAN MILLENNIALISTIC RESPONSE TO RACISM AND CULTURAL DERACINATION. *Centennial Rev.* 1979 23(4): 430-451. Traces the Black Muslims' black nationalist origins to the Marcus Garvey movement of the late 1920's and Timothy Drew's (Noble Drew Ali's) Moorish-American Science Temple, and their Islamic origins to Master Wallace Fard Muhammad in Detroit (1930-33). One faction, the Nation of Islam led by Elijah Muhammad, was called the Black Muslims, but in the 1960's "Malcolm X and other Black Muslims denied any connection with the Moorish movement and asserted Fard's uniqueness." Radical salvationists such as the Jehovah's Witnesses and the Mormons also influenced the movement. The author traces American millenarianism to antiquity and the medieval period; it is part of the Christian and Judaic tradition and as such influenced the Black Muslims. Black Muslim orthodoxy will not prevail; there will be an increasing convergence of aims and values of Muslims and black Christians. 48 notes. S

1586. Gillette, Michael L. THE RISE OF THE NAACP IN TEXAS. *Southwestern Hist. Q.* 1978 81(4): 393-416. The NAACP was revived in Texas in the late 1930's by Antonio Maceo Smith, a black Dallas insuranceman. Later, Lulu B. White of Houston and William J. Durham and Juanita Craft, both of Dallas, also joined the leadership. Helped by organizers from the national NAACP office, the Texas group challenged the exclusion of blacks from juries and Democratic primaries. By the late 1940's there were 104 branches and 30,000 members; the leaders were nearly all professionals and businessmen, with a few teachers. Primary and secondary sources; 9 illus., 48 notes. J. H. Broussard

1587. Goldstein, Jonah. PUBLIC INTEREST GROUPS AND PUBLIC POLICY: THE CASE OF THE CONSUMERS' ASSOCIATION OF CANADA. *Can. J. of Pol. Sci. [Canada]* 1979 12(1): 137-155. Examines the effectiveness of Canadian public interest groups such as the Consumers' Association of Canada from 1947 to 1977, noting that they seek to promote particular social or political policies in the name of some general good. They lack any vital economic role within the system, they are in a constant search for financial support, and they have little or no clearly defined power, unlike private interest groups and government agencies. General public interest groups and constituency groups—the latter generally being more cohesive and focused in their membership and demands—are playing an increasingly important and effective role, despite their disadvantages, in influencing public policy. 24 notes. French summary. S

1588. Gordon, Linda. THE POLITICS OF POPULATION: BIRTH CONTROL AND THE EUGENICS MOVEMENT. *Radical America* 1974 8(4): 61-98.

1589. Graebner, William. THE UNSTABLE WORLD OF BENJAMIN SPOCK: SOCIAL ENGINEERING IN A DEMOCRATIC CULTURE, 1917-1950. *J. of Am. Hist.* 1980 67(3): 612-629. Examines Benjamin Spock's *Baby and Child Care* (1946) as an analysis of American civilization between the world wars. Because the world around him during those years was unstable, Spock viewed infants as unstable—as frustrated, insecure, and "potentially destructive in... aggressive tendencies." To thwart these tendencies and to help children find a secure identity, Spock advocated natural techniques of child-rearing and discipline. He viewed the family as a democratic, decisionmaking unit in which the child would play a part. Spock was a social engineer, and his democratic methods of child-rearing were part of a broader tendency in American society between 1917 and 1940. 54 notes. T. P. Linkfield

1590. Grant, Donald L. and Grant, Mildred Bricker. SOME NOTES ON THE CAPITAL "N." *Phylon* 1975 36(4): 435-443. In the spirit of W. E. B. Du Bois' statement in 1898, "I believe that eight million Americans are entitled to a capital letter," traces the efforts of blacks to encourage publishers and editors to abandon the spelling of Negro with a belittling small "n." Because all other racial and ethnic designations were capitalized, the small "n" was simply one more form of discrimination. Then as now, however, there existed no clear agreement among blacks as to what the proper term should be. Based on the NAACP papers in the Library of Congress, the Herbert Hoover papers, and secondary sources; 51 notes. K. C. Snow

1591. Green, Dan S. W. E. B. DUBOIS' TALENTED TENTH: A STRATEGY FOR RACIAL ADVANCEMENT. *J. of Negro Educ.* 1977 46(3): 358-366. Traces W. E. B. Du Bois's idea for racial advancement through the broad liberal education of an elite cadre, the Talented Tenth, from its original statement to Du Bois's eventual disillusionment with the black elite. Secondary sources; 30 notes. R. E. Butchart

1592. Greenbaum, William. AMERICA IN SEARCH OF A NEW IDEAL: AN ESSAY ON THE RISE OF PLURALISM. *Harvard Educ. R. 1974 44(3): 411-440.* Demands by cultural and ethnic groups for equal power and political leverage in society have increased steadily between 1950 and 1970.　　　　　　　　　　　　　　　　　　　　　　S

1593. Greene, Suzanne Ellery. BLACK REPUBLICANS ON THE BALTIMORE CITY COUNCIL, 1890-1931. *Maryland Hist. Mag. 1979 74(3): 203-222.* Failure in Maryland of post-Reconstruction moves to disenfranchise blacks insured continued presence of at least one black Republican member on Baltimore's city council through 1931. Harry Sythe Cummings, John Marcus Cargill, and Hiram Watty before World War I, and William L. Fitzgerald, Warner T. McGuinn, and Walter S. Emerson afterward were regularly reelected from predominantly black wards. All fought for improved status, facilities, and faculty of segregated schools for Negroes, an improved share of patronage jobs for blacks, and against white Democratic attempts to disenfranchise blacks and institute legal residential segregation. Based on Baltimore *City Council Journals,* newspaper accounts, papers of the six councilmen, and interviews with their descendants; chart with 18 notes, 85 notes.　　　　　　C. B. Schulz

1594. Grube, John. LA LIBÉRATION ÉCONOMIQUE DU QUÉBEC [The economic liberation of Quebec]. *Action Natl. [Canada] 1980 70(4): 292-317.* François-Albert Angers saw the British ideologies of nationalism and cooperatism as the roots of Quebec's economic liberation. His economic thought derived from the practice of the Rochdale movement and the Catholic social theory of Leo XIII's *Rerum Novarum.* For Angers, cooperatism, starting with consumers and expanding to include agricultural and industrial producers, was the solution to the defects of capitalism glaringly manifested during the depression of the 1930's. He urged the creation of a network of electrical cooperatives to counter nationalization proposals introduced by Adélard Godbout in 1944 and René Lévesque in 1960. His agrarianism included demands for a rural educational system based on a simple lifestyle, a public policy supportive of family life, and government intervention in agricultural markets. 62 notes.　　　　　　　　　　　　　　　　　　A. W. Novitsky

1595. Grube, John. LES HÉROS DE LA PAIX [The heroes of peace]. *Action Natl. [Canada] 1980 69(7): 549-561.* François-Albert Angers was a heroic Quebec pacifist whose writings opposed 1) conscription during World War II, 2) European conflicts and the Cold War, and 3) war itself. His opposition to participation in World War II partially derived from the defensive neutrality of the French Canadian minority who saw conscription as a force for their assimilation into English Canada. He argued that Canada, as a small power, was in a position to preserve civilized values during a brutal era. As an ardent Catholic, he constantly recalled the traditional and contemporary teachings of the Church which stressed the ideal of Christian pacifism. 42 notes.
　　　　　　　　　　　　　　　　　　　　　　　A. W. Novitsky

1596. Hall, Dick. OINTMENT OF LOVE: OLIVER E. COMSTOCK AND TUSCON'S TENT CITY. *J. of Arizona Hist. 1978 19(2): 111-130.* Describes the efforts of the Reverend Oliver E. Comstock to care for and eventually build St. Luke's-in-the-Desert Hospital for the care of poorer citizens of Tuscon, Arizona. Early travelers lived in Tent City where medical facilities were scant. Comstock, originally an Alabama printer and preacher, started Baptist missionary work among the tubercular areas of Tuscon. Growing population, increasing concern for the health of its citizens, and support from the Daughters of the American Revolution, Red Cross, veterans of World War I, Congressman Carl Hayden, and the Veterans Administration transformed the hospital for tubercular patients, replacing Tent City. Reverend Comstock's sermon "Ointment of Love" in the Tucson *Star* (22 February 1925) was a continuing appeal for assistance for the new Comstock Hospital (known previously as Mercy Hospital). Based on author's recollections; 4 photos, 30 notes.　　　　　　　　　　　　　　　　　　　　　K. E. Gilmont

1597. Hallett, Mary E. NELLIE MCCLUNG AND THE FIGHT FOR THE ORDINATION OF WOMEN IN THE UNITED CHURCH OF CANADA. *Atlantis [Canada] 1979 4(2): 2-16.* Describes Nellie McClung's struggle with the Methodist Church beginning in 1915 and, beginning in 1925, with the United Church of Canada, made up of the Presbyterian, Methodist, and Congregational churches, for the ordination of women in Canada. McClung carried on until December 1928, and others continued until 1946 when the first married woman was ordained in the United Church.

1598. Hastie, William H. TOWARD AN EQUALITARIAN LEGAL ORDER: 1930-1950. *Ann. of the Am. Acad. of Pol. and Social Sci. 1973 (407): 18-31.* "Though the post-Civil War amendments to the Constitution promised black Americans that thereafter their rights and opportunities would not be demeaned because of race, the ensuing fifty years witnessed the comprehensive institutionalization of racial segregation and subordination by force of law. During the first quarter of this century the racist legal order was so firmly established, with the support or acquiescence of most whites, that struggle against it seemed futile. But beginning about 1930, under the leadership of the National Association for the Advancement of Colored People, a nationwide legal campaign was planned and undertaken with an equalitarian legal order as its goal. Early lawsuits served to arouse public interest and support as well as to win significant peripheral changes in the segregated legal order. Social scientists and educators were persuaded to reexamine the segregated order critically. The federal government moved from a posture of neutrality to forthright assertion that laws requiring racial segregation could not be squared with the Constitution. Responding case by case, the Supreme Court progressively eroded antecedent constitutional doctrine that sanctioned American apartheid until, by 1950, the Court appeared ready to strike down all statutes and all other governmental action that imposed racial segregation or discrimination."　　　　　　　　　　　　　　J

1599. Haymes, Howard J. POSTWAR WRITING AND THE LITERATURE OF THE WOMEN'S LIBERATION MOVEMENT. *Psychiatry 1975 38(4): 328-333.* Reviews writing about and by women in the light of Freudian analysis from 1946 to the 1970's.

1600. Haynes, John Earl. THE 'RANK AND FILE' MOVEMENT IN PRIVATE SOCIAL WORK. *Labor Hist. 1975 16(1): 78-98.* In New York City the downward pressures on wages and the increase in case loads in private social work agencies stimulated a "Rank and File" movement among social workers. Three goals emerged: unionization of social workers, reformation of social work practices, and radical political action. Although resistance by the private agencies was important, the decline of the movement began with its shifts in political action caused by the influence of Communists among rank and filers. Based on papers in the Social Welfare History Archives and on *Social Work Today*; 44 notes.
　　　　　　　　　　　　　　　　　　　　　　　L. L. Athey

1601. Hellwig, David J. AFRO-AMERICAN REACTIONS TO THE JAPANESE AND THE ANTI-JAPANESE MOVEMENT, 1906-1924. *Phylon 1977 38(1): 93-104.* The Johnson Immigration Act (1924) included a provision to effectively deny Japanese entrance into the United States. This law culminated two decades of anti-Japanese agitation. The position of most black Americans was that some immigration restrictions or quotas were probably needed, but that the Japanese ought not to be singled out for unfair treatment. Blacks readily saw similarities with their own plight and viewed the matter as a racial one. They called for "a policy applied equally to all." An exception to this general view was Howard University educator Kelly Miller, who argued that blacks would do better to identify with whites than with a group of newcomers. By the late 1920's, Miller's views seemed to dominate. Primary and secondary sources; 49 notes.　　　　　　　　　　　　　　　　　　B. A. Glasrud

1602. Henderson, Steven T. SOCIAL ACTION IN A CONSERVATIVE ENVIRONMENT: THE CHRISTIAN LIFE COMMISSION AND SOUTHERN BAPTIST CHURCHES. *Foundations 1980 23(3): 245-251.* Discusses social action in the Southern Baptist Convention through the Christian Life Commission and its antecedents, since 1907. The major issue is the contrast between Southern Baptists' individual emphasis on salvation and more collective attitude toward social action. Notes change in attitudes toward social involvement. 15 notes.
　　　　　　　　　　　　　　　　　　　　　　　E. E. Eminhizer

1603. Henson, Tom M. KU KLUX KLAN IN WESTERN CANADA. *Alberta Hist. [Canada] 1977 25(4): 1-8.* The Ku Klux Klan began in British Columbia in 1921, then moved into Alberta and Saskatchewan. Primarily anti-French at first, the Klan soon advocated immigration restriction, especially of Orientals and Eastern Europeans. The Klan also became antiunion, as most of the recent immigrants were union affiliated. The Klan was influential in several local elections, but overall lasting impact of the organization in western Canada was slight. By the early 1930's, the Klan was practically dead, due to local scandals (embezzlement) and to effective opposition from the Communist and working-class parties. 49 notes.   D. Chaput

1604. Hines, Linda O. WHITE MYTHOLOGY AND BLACK DUALITY: GEORGE W. CARVER'S RESPONSE TO RACISM AND THE RADICAL LEFT. *J. of Negro Hist. 1977 62(2): 134-146.* The myth of George Washington Carver (1864-1943) contained elements of truth along with the usual stuff of mythology. In reality, Carver felt ambivalence toward race and capitalism and his reactions to segregation in the South varied with circumstances. Although he advised white businessmen, he also formed ties with Marxian cooperatives such as Llano Cooperative Colony in Louisiana. He learned about Marxism from his close friends John Sutton and Howard Kester, yet "was a dreamer with a vision of a better world and a very dim grasp of political reality." Unfortunately, many people were willing to ignore much that Carver said and did in order to fashion a symbol, especially during the McCarthy era when a group attempted to portray him as a "commie" hater. The myth has obscured the man. Based on the George Washington Carver papers; 47 notes.   N. G. Sapper/G. Fox

1605. Hitchcock, James. THE EVOLUTION OF THE AMERICAN CATHOLIC LEFT. *Am. Scholar 1973/74 43(1): 66-84.* Compares the Catholic New Left of today with that of the 1950's when John Courtney Murray defended church and state separation. The most noted Catholic liberals of the 1960's and 1970's are the Jesuit Fathers Daniel Berrigan and Philip Berrigan. In contrast with Murray they have made a "reassertion of the central importance of religious values in political life, a denial that religion and politics can be separated in any real sense." The activist Catholic New Left has caused considerable confusion and demoralization in the American Catholic Church and has perhaps hastened the declericalization of the Church. The concern for the Gospels, sexual liberation, association with movements that are decidedly non-violent, and failure to preach to the Catholic masses has disturbed the rank-and-file and caused the Church to become more pluralistic.   C. W. Olson

1606. Hoffman, George. THE ENTRY OF THE UNITED FARMERS OF CANADA, SASKATCHEWAN SECTION INTO POLITICS: A REASSESSMENT. *Saskatchewan Hist. [Canada] 1977 30(3): 99-109.* The usual interpretation of the relationship between North American agrarian movements and politics is that during economic hard times farm organizations resort to direct political action, while in more prosperous years they act as pressure groups. There is some evidence to support this, but the movement in Saskatchewan was more complex than that. Through the activities of George Edwards, J. S. Stoneman, George Williams, and others, the conservative wing of the movement advocated direct political involvement and later became leaders in the Co-operative Commonwealth Federation (CCF). Covers the period 1930-45. 72 notes.   C. Held

1607. Hoffman, George. THE SASKATCHEWAN FARMER-LABOR PARTY, 1932-1934: HOW RADICAL WAS IT AT ITS ORIGIN? *Saskatchewan Hist. [Canada] 1975 28(2): 52-64.* While socialist and radical to some degree, in its early years the Farmer-Labor Party was moderated by the leadership of such persons as Tom Johnson, Mrs. A. Hollis of Shaunavon, Violet McNaughton, and M. J. Coldwell. There was considerable rank and file support for the social credit ideas of Major C. H. Douglas as well. "The generally held theory that the radical fathers of the party substantially moderated and compromised their ideas after 1934 needs to be seriously reassessed." 77 notes.   C. Held

1608. Hollinger, David A. THE PROBLEM OF PRAGMATISM IN AMERICAN HISTORY. *J. of Am. Hist. 1980 67(1): 88-107.* Analyzes the development and application of basic ideas in the pragmatist tradition in the first half of the 20th century. The development and spread of pragmatism as a philosophy of limited scope by Charles Sanders Peirce, William James, John Dewey, and their disciples provided American society with a coherent orientation toward science and social change. Pragmatism included several different traditions (democratic, moralistic, practical) and appealed to different types of Americans on different levels. Pragmatism helped American society face the inevitability of change. Based on the primary works of Peirce, James, and Dewey; 62 notes.   T. P. Linkfield

1609. Homel, Gene Howard. SLIDERS AND BACKSLIDERS: TORONTO'S SUNDAY TOBOGGANING CONTROVERSY OF 1912. *Urban Hist. Rev. [Canada] 1981 10(2): 25-34.* A conflict in Toronto municipal politics in 1912 centered on the question of whether the civic government should allow its toboggan slides in the parks to be used on Sunday. A well-organized and influential Sabbatarian movement forced the issue, and while labor and business leaders mobilized to protect Sunday recreation, the Sabbatarians convinced the city council to close the slides on the Lord's Day. This article examines the persistence of Sabbatarian belief as well as the increase of sentiment favorable to a more secularized view of Sunday recreation.   J

1610. Hooper, Paul F. FEMINISM IN THE PACIFIC: THE PAN-PACIFIC AND SOUTHEAST ASIA WOMEN'S ASSOCIATION. *Pacific Hist. 1976 20(4): 367-378.* The Pan-Pacific and Southeast Asia Women's Association was instrumental in establishing women's activities in the Pacific Basin. Its first meeting in 1928 established the transcultural nature of the organization. Not a militant group, PPSEAWA has worked quietly and deliberately to correct political, social, and economic problems affecting the area. Primary and secondary sources; 3 illus., 31 notes.   G. L. Olson

1611. Horn, Michiel, ed. FRANK UNDERHILL'S EARLY DRAFTS OF THE REGINA MANIFESTO 1933. *Can. Hist. R. 1973 54(4): 393-418.* Three edited documents, drafts of what in July 1933 became the manifesto and program of the Cooperative Commonwealth Federation. The final version of the Regina Manifesto is also reproduced. No drafts were believed extant until the editor found these misfiled in Professor Frank Underhill's private papers in 1972. An introduction traces the history of the drafting of the Regina Manifesto (1933). Textual comparisons show close similarities between it and the earlier drafts, and the manifesto of the League for Social Reconstruction, a social democratic group founded by intellectuals in Toronto and Montreal in 1931-32. Underhill shared the responsibility of drafting the CCF manifesto with other members of the LSR.   A

1612. Horrall, Stan W. THE ROYAL NORTH-WEST MOUNTED POLICE AND LABOUR UNREST IN WESTERN CANADA, 1919. *Can. Hist. Rev. [Canada] 1980 61(2): 169-190.* Describes the intelligence service of that force in investigating the activities of labor organizations in western Canada in the months that led up to the breaking of the Winnipeg General Strike. Information gathered by the Mounted Police did not support the view of government leaders that the strike was an attempt at revolution on the part of the One Big Union. Belief in the existence of a seditious conspiracy resulted in the establishment of the Royal Canadian Mounted Police as a nation-wide federal law enforcement and security service. Based on unpublished records of the Royal North-West Mounted Police.   A

1613. Hougland, James G., Jr.; Wood, James R.; and Mueller, Samuel A. ORGANIZATIONAL "GOAL SUBMERGENCE": THE METHODIST CHURCH AND THE FAILURE OF THE TEMPERANCE MOVEMENT. *Sociol. and Social Res. 1974 58(4): 408-416.* "Existing concepts concerning goal change do not describe organizations' adjustments to societal changes which *differentially* affect organization members, causing some to experience a given goal negatively while others continue to derive positive incentives from it. We therefore introduce the concept of 'goal submergence,' which relates goal change to executives' efforts to provide differential incentives to various organizational elements, and we illustrate this by the history of the Methodist Church in relation to the temperance movement."   J

1614. Howlett, Charles F. BROCKWOOD LABOR COLLEGE AND WORKER COMMITMENT TO SOCIAL REFORM. *Mid-America 1979 61(1): 47-66.* Brockwood Labor College was founded in 1919 by William Fincke, a pacifist minister. Its main aims were the training of labor leaders and education for social reform. It was opposed to the conservative leadership of the American Federation of Labor, calling for the unionization of all industrial workers and emphasizing reform ideology. The differences in philosophy with traditional unions led to a great decrease in funding and eventual dissolution of Brockwood in 1937. Primary and secondary sources; 44 notes.   J. M. Lee

1615. Howlett, Charles F. JOHN DEWEY AND THE CRUSADE TO OUTLAW WAR. *World Affairs 1976 138(4): 336-355.* Discusses John Dewey's pacifism, idealism, and campaign to outlaw war in US foreign policy, 1918-32.

1616. Illick, Joseph E. PERSPECTIVES ON AMERICAN STUDENT ACTIVISM. *J. of Psychohistory 1979 7(2): 175-187.* A review of student protest in American history with a discussion from a psychoanalytic perspective that is compared with more traditional interpretations that have explained such protest in terms of social conditions. Psychoanalytic tools explain conflicting and disparate themes that explain student activism. 24 notes. M. R. Strausbaugh

1617. Janick, Herbert. AN INSTRUCTIVE FAILURE: THE CONNECTICUT PEACE MOVEMENT, 1919-1939. *Peace and Change 1978 5(1): 12-22.* The peace movement in Connecticut failed, because its local hierarchy reflected upper middle class values and found it difficult to incorporate the ethnic and minority ideologies of most residents.

1618. Jones, Andrew. CLOSING PENETANGUISHENE REFORMATORY: AN ATTEMPT TO DE-INSTITUTIONALISE TREATMENT OF JUVENILE OFFENDERS IN EARLY TWENTIETH CENTURY ONTARIO. *Ontario Hist. [Canada] 1978 70(4): 227-244.* The pressure to close the reformatory came from various sources, of which the location and unsuitability of the buildings were significant. After a description of the origins and early years of the institution, analyzes these pressures and indicates the problems caused for other provincial institutions when Penetanguishene closed. Discusses a foster home project attempted as one alternative to the reformatory. Briefly remarks on the revival of the reformatory system after World War I. From archives and provincial legislative papers, mainly; 2 photos, 72 notes.
W. B. Whitham

1619. Kagan, Paul and Ziebarth, Marilyn. EASTERN THOUGHT ON A WESTERN SHORE: POINT LOMA COMMUNITY. *California Hist. Q. 1973 52(1): 4-15.* From 1897 to 1942 the Universal Brotherhood and Theosophical Society, at Point Loma, near San Diego, was a prominent utopian society. Its leader was Mrs. Katherine Augusta Westcott Tingley (1847-1929). Her brand of Theosophy combined Eastern religious and literary thought with pageantry and ceremony. The progressive school operated by the society won approval during its lifetime. Loss of financial support, dwindling membership, and the adjacent location of a U.S. naval base compelled the society to relocate. 17 photos.
A. Hoffman

1620. Kambeitz, Teresita. RELATIONS BETWEEN THE CATHOLIC CHURCH AND CCF IN SASKATCHEWAN, 1930-1950. *Study Sessions: Can. Catholic Hist. Assoc. [Canada] 1979 (46): 49-69.* Relations were spotty at best, due to Church condemnations of socialism, but economic factors and realization of the need for social reform and cooperation within the farming communities led to tolerance and even acceptance of the socialistic Co-operative Commonwealth Federation (CCF) by some Catholics.

1621. Kantowicz, Edward R. CARDINAL MUNDELEIN OF CHICAGO AND THE SHAPING OF TWENTIETH-CENTURY AMERICAN CATHOLICISM. *J. of Am. Hist. 1981 68(1): 52-68.* George Cardinal Mundelein of Chicago (d. 1939) was one of several American-born but Roman-trained bishops who, as "consolidating bishops," centralized the Church's structure and tied American Catholicism more closely to Rome. Mundelein and other 20th-century bishops brought much-needed recognition to the American Catholic Church and gave its members pride and confidence. Mundelein was famous for his administrative talents, patriotism, political influence, and princely style. 44 notes. T. P. Linkfield

1622. Kellog, Peter J. CIVIL RIGHTS CONSCIOUSNESS IN THE 1940'S. *Historian 1979 42(1): 18-41.* During the 1940's, civil rights for black people became a national issue for the first time since Reconstruction. The change, a result of specific historical circumstances, concentrated upon the issue of white prejudice rather than the place of black people in the American society. The liberal community, in which white opposition to racism developed earliest, provided the impetus and the terms of that debate. Unfortunately, the entry of civil rights into national politics in 1948 was only a temporary meeting of moral and political concerns. Primary sources; 81 notes. R. S. Sliwoski

1623. Kilson, Martin. WHITHER INTEGRATION? *Am. Scholar 1976 45(3): 360-376.* Analyzes integration since World War II, the forces that have furthered it, and the advances still needed. The most phenomenal changes have occurred during the last decade through the impetus given by the civil rights movement, the cultural shifts of the 1960's, and public policy initiatives of the Kennedy and Johnson administrations.
R. V. Ritter

1624. Kirschner, Don S. "PUBLICITY PROPERLY APPLIED": THE SELLING OF EXPERTISE IN AMERICA, 1900-1929. *Am. Studies 1978 19(1): 65-78.* Tension between democracy and expertise plagued reformers in the early 20th century. Professionals formulated intricate and technical schemes, but had to convince a public skeptical of their theories, an especially difficult task when these theories contradicted popular knowledge. Cultural barriers often frustrated professional reformers as well, and short-term elections threatened disruption. After World War I these experts turned increasingly to the electronic media, particularly films, to convey their message and reconcile tensions. Primary and secondary sources; 30 notes. J. Andrew

1625. Klehr, Harvey. LENINISM, LEWIS COREY, AND THE FAILURE OF AMERICAN SOCIALISM. *Labor Hist. 1977 18(2): 249-256.* Reviews explanations of the failure of American socialism and presents an analysis of Lewis Corey's writings on the American socialist failures. Corey argued that American radicals failed because they consistently attempted to graft European theories onto American conditions. Based on the writings of Lewis Corey; 21 notes. L. L. Athey

1626. Kleiman, Michael P. TRENDS IN RACIAL DIFFERENCES IN POLITICAL EFFICACY, 1952 TO 1972. *Phylon 1976 37(2): 159-162.* The common assumption is that the black man's life and personality are disorganized as a result of white prejudice and discrimination. "The present research ... investigates the issue of whether the relative rise in political power among blacks has indeed been matched by an increase in blacks' feelings of efficacy relative to whites." The table shows that in 1972 the percentage of blacks in the high efficacy category (53%) is much closer to the percentage of whites in that category (60.3%). In 1952 these figures had been 48.3% versus 71.2%. "Thus there is a clear increase in blacks' sense of efficacy relative to whites over the twenty year period." Table, 13 notes. E. P. Stickney

1627. Kojder, Apolonja Maria. THE SASKATOON WOMEN TEACHERS' ASSOCIATION: A DEMAND FOR RECOGNITION. *Saskatchewan Hist. [Canada] 1977 30(2): 63-74.* Women educators in Saskatchewan can point to 1918 as the date when they first demonstrated their professional responsibility and integrity with the founding of the Saskatoon Women Teachers' Association (SWTA). Because the status of elementary teachers was very low, a positive self-image was necessary. The leaders in this early movement were Victoria "Tory" Miners and Hattie Wolfe. Later important figures were Ethel Coppinger and Caroline Robins. Great strides in improving conditions and wages for all teachers were made and the influence of the SWTA was widespread. 12 notes.
C. Held

1628. Kolehmainen, John I. THE LAST DAYS OF MATTI KURIKKA'S UTOPIA: A HISTORICAL VIGNETTE. *Turun Hist. Arkisto [Finland] 1976 31: 388-396.* The collapse of the Finnish American utopian colony at Harmony Island, British Columbia, active 1901-05, was due largely to the unrealistic ideas of its founder, Matti Kurikka (1863-1913). R. G. Selleck

1629. Koppes, Clayton R. FROM NEW DEAL TO TERMINATION: LIBERALISM AND INDIAN POLICY, 1933-1953. *Pacific Hist. Rev. 1977 46(4): 543-566.* In Indian policies there was only a selective continuity of liberalism from the New Deal to the Fair Deal. Roosevelt's commissioner of Indian affairs (1933-45), John Collier, considered the loss of community the major problem of modern society. His Indian policy was in the same spirit as other early New Deal policies and programs which sought to foster cooperation and community rather than competition and individualism. By World War II liberal support for such programs had greatly eroded. The Truman administration allowed Indian

policy to return to its earlier emphasis on assimilation, in keeping with the Fair Deal's own emphasis on economic prosperity and individual competition and on individual civil rights and freedom from group identity. Based on documents in the National Archives, Yale University Library, Library of Congress, and Truman Library, and on published primary and secondary sources; 39 notes.
W. K. Hobson

1630. Lamis, Alec Peter. THE DISRUPTION OF A SOLIDLY DEMOCRATIC STATE: CIVIL RIGHTS AND SOUTH CAROLINA ELECTORAL CHANGE, 1948-1972. *J. of Pol. Sci. 1977 5(1): 55-72.* Stresses differences among counties. The realignment has left the Democrats a decided minority in South Carolina. The civil rights issue was at the heart of the electoral change. The preoccupation with race dominated South Carolina voting for president. Based on the author's M.A. thesis, Vanderbilt University, 1975; 3 tables, 2 fig., 54 notes.
T. P. Richardson

1631. Larson, Bruce L. SWEDISH AMERICANS AND FARMER-LABOR POLITICS IN MINNESOTA. Hasselmo, Nils, ed. *Perspectives on Swedish Immigration* (Chicago: Swedish Pioneer Hist. Soc. and Duluth: U. of Minnesota, 1978): 206-224. Politicians of Swedish and other Scandinavian origins were important in the history of Minnesota state politics in general and of the Farmer-Labor Party in particular. Swedish Americans Charles A. Lindbergh, Sr., Magnus Johnson, Ernest Lundeen, Elmer Benson, and Floyd Olson were key figures in the party. Swedes in Minnesota gave slightly stronger support than most other Minnesotans to the Farmer-Labor Party, especially in the peak periods of the early 1920's and the mid-1930's. The Farmer-Labor Party merged with the Democratic Party in 1944. Illus., table, fig., 37 notes, appendix.
S

1632. Layng, Anthony. VOLUNTARY ASSOCIATIONS AND BLACK ETHNIC IDENTITY. *Phylon 1978 39(2): 171-179.* Voluntary associations, groups which have formed without government sponsorship or support to work for goals in the areas of religion, welfare, culture, education, politics, or labor, have played an important role in the history of Afro-America. To a people discriminated against and devoid of government sponsorship until post-World War II, these associations were vital for spreading ethnic consciousness and pride, and for the experience and prestige given to individual personalities within the organizations. The emergence of Negroes as an important political factor in the 1960's and 1970's has been helped by the organizational skills gained in voluntary organizations. Mexican-Americans, on the other hand, who tend not to join such organizations, have been slower in electing members of their group to high political office. 53 notes.
J. C. Billigmeier

1633. Levitt, Joseph. HENRI BOURASSA AND THE PROGRESSIVE "ALLIANCE" OF 1926. *J. of Canadian Studies 1974 9(4): 17-23.*

1634. Light, Ivan. FROM VICE DISTRICT TO TOURIST ATTRACTION: THE MORAL CAREER OF AMERICAN CHINATOWNS, 1880-1940. *Pacific Hist. R. 1974 43(3): 367-394.* A study of the steps by which the Chinatowns were able to completely change their images from centers of vice, depravity, and filth to places which are clean, orderly, and attractive to tourists. There arose a mutual incompatibility between those Chinese merchants interested in developing tourism and the underworld gangs (tongs) interested in maintaining vice resorts. The merchants were finally victorious in the contest, and the tongs ultimately lent their support to commerce. 114 notes.
R. V. Ritter

1635. Lloyd, Sheila. THE OTTAWA TYPHOID EPIDEMICS OF 1911 AND 1912: A CASE STUDY OF DISEASE AS A CATALYST FOR URBAN REFORM. *Urban Hist. Rev. [Canada] 1979 8(1): 66-89.* The typhoid fever epidemics created a strong movement in Ottawa for urban health improvements. Reforms were resisted by politicians and the business element on the basis of expense and a lack of clear understanding of typhoid. Some changes were made while the crisis was fresh; once the crisis was perceived to be past, little concern was manifested. Based on municipal and federal documents; 2 illus., 74 notes.
C. A. Watson

1636. MacCarthy, Esther. CATHOLIC WOMEN AND THE WAR: THE NATIONAL COUNCIL OF CATHOLIC WOMEN, 1919-1946.

Peace and Change 1978 5(1): 23-32. Examines attitudes toward women and war in the National Catholic Welfare Conference; the National Council of Catholic Women actively participated in the peace movement, 1919-46.

1637. MacPherson, Ian. GEORGE CHIPMAN AND THE INSTITUTIONALIZATION OF A REFORM MOVEMENT. *Tr. of the Hist. and Sci. Soc. of Manitoba [Canada] 1975-76 32: 53-65.* George Chipman (1882-1935), a teacher who emigrated from the Maritimes to the prairies in 1903 and became a journalist in Winnipeg in 1905, for 26 years was editor of *The Grain Growers Guide.* He was an outspoken proponent of both the national agrarian and the cooperative movements. Into the 1920's, under his leadership, his periodical voiced western grievances and supported elements of Ontario Clear Grittism, British Fabianism, American Populism, the social gospel, prohibition, and European agrarian radicalism. Chipman supported the women's movement, educational reform, the single tax, and the initiative, recall, and referendum, and attacked tariffs, banks, farm implement manufacturers, and food trusts. An electoral defeat in 1922 increased the conservatism of both editor and journal. 36 notes.
A. W. Novitsky

1638. Manley, John. WOMEN AND THE LEFT IN THE 1930S: THE CASE OF THE TORONTO CCF WOMEN'S JOINT COMMITTEE. *Atlantis [Canada] 1980 5(2): 100-119.* Discusses the formation of the national Cooperative Commonwealth Federation (CCF) in 1932 and the Toronto CCF Women's Joint Committee (WJC) as examples of leftist political developments and the women's movement during the 1930's, in the middle of a period usually considered a time of female inactivity in Canada.

1639. Margolin, C. R. SALVATION VERSUS LIBERATION: THE MOVEMENT FOR CHILDREN'S RIGHTS IN A HISTORICAL CONTEXT. *Social Problems 1978 25(4): 441-452.* Examines the current children's rights movement in the United States. Discusses the history of child-saving, recent events concerning human rights, the conflict between salvation and liberation of children, and the various approaches to children's rights. Adults will continue to lead the children's movement, and courts and legislatures will grant more rights to younger children. Primary and secondary sources; 4 notes, ref.
A. M. Osur

1640. Margolis, Michael and Neary, Kevin. PRESSURE POLITICS REVISITED: THE ANTI-ABORTION CAMPAIGN. *Policy Studies J. 1980 8(5): 698-716.* Reviews the abortion controversy in the United States and activities of antiabortion pressure groups in Pennsylvania and compares the modern antiabortion campaign to the activities of the Anti-Saloon League.

1641. Martin, Edward A. H. L. MENCKEN AND EQUAL RIGHTS FOR WOMEN. *Georgia Rev. 1981 35(1): 65-76.* As a result of his deliberate verbal extravagances, H. L. Mencken's basically sympathetic attitudes toward women have been generally misunderstood or ignored. Mencken was sensitive to the role conflicts experienced by women because his own attraction to belles lettres was considered an unmasculine career in turn-of-the-century America. He sympathized with the humanistic concerns of feminism and the desire of women to achieve self-expression, but ridiculed the moralistic preoccupatons of the suffragettes just as he also tried to shock the conventional morality of the male middle-class "booboisie." 14 notes.
J. N. McArthur

1642. Matters, Diane L. PUBLIC WELFARE, VANCOUVER STYLE, 1919-1920. *J. of Can. Studies [Canada] 1979 14(1): 3-15.* At the beginning of the century public welfare was handled through numerous separate charitable organizations, a part of whose efforts were finally consolidated and channeled through the Associated Charities. Other associations also developed. There was some alleviation provided by World War I, but this did not solve all the problems, especially as affecting women and children. Various women's organizations rose to the challenge, supplemented by mothers' pensions. The province and federal governments were very slow to get into the act, and even after the close of the war little was forthcoming; the local authorities continued to drag their feet. Primary sources, 46 notes.
R. V. Ritter

1643. Matthews, Carl S. THE DECLINE OF THE TUSKEGEE MACHINE, 1915-1925: THE ABDICATION OF POLITICAL

POWER. *South Atlantic Q. 1976 75(4): 460-469.* The Tuskegee Institute operated as an educational center for blacks, and as a political machine. It unified blacks and gave them some sense of political influence. This machine kept Booker T. Washington in the forefront as the "One Great Leader of the Negro Race" and kept his black critics silent. Washington's secretary, Emmett Jay Scott, was the power behind the throne and expected to succeed Washington after the latter's death in 1915. The Institute's Board of Trustees, mostly whites, chose Robert Russa Moton of the Hampton Institute instead. Moton lacked Washington's charisma and failed to perpetuate the intricate webs of influence that constituted the political machine. He presided over the machine's dissolution. Primary and secondary sources; 23 notes.   W. L. Olbrich

1644. McCuaig, Katherine. "FROM SOCIAL REFORM TO SOCIAL SERVICE": THE CHANGING ROLE OF VOLUNTEERS: THE ANTI-TUBERCULOSIS CAMPAIGN, 1900-30. *Can. Hist. Rev. [Canada] 1980 61(4): 480-501.* The campaign against tuberculosis in Canada began as part of a whole urban social reform movement occurring at the turn of the century. Reformers fought the disease on two fronts: using a bacteriological approach (to eliminate the germ as the cause of the disease) and a social reform approach (attacking the underlying social causes, such as long working hours and alcoholism). This changed after the First World War. Now the bacteriological approach to the disease was pre-eminent, with federally expanded facilities, increasing provincial involvement, a growth in technology and a resulting division of labor. The federal government abdicated responsibility, leaving the provinces to act. The specialists directed the campaign, new businesslike volunteer organizations (e.g., the Rockefeller Foundation) entered the field, and lay volunteers evolved from social reformers to members of service clubs. Based on the records of the Canadian Tuberculosis Association, in the Public Archives of Canada, professional and popular periodicals (e.g., *CMAJ, Public Health Journal),* and other sources; 87 notes.   A

1645. McKillop, A. B. SOCIALIST AS CITIZEN: JOHN QUEEN AND THE MAYORALTY OF WINNIPEG, 1935. *Tr. of the Hist. and Sci. Soc. of Manitoba [Canada] 1973-74 (30): 61-80.* Discusses the political involvement of socialist John Queen from the time he arrived in Winnipeg in 1909 through his mayoralty of Winnipeg (1935-42), concentrating on the issues faced and reforms sought by his administration. After his initial campaign to readjust the tax base of the city, much of his time was spent in the provincial legislature or in Ottawa making known "the urgency of Constitutional adjustments and provincial and federal legislation necessary for the coming into being of a full measure of social justice." Primary and secondary works; 69 notes, appendix.   S. R. Quéripel

1646. Meier, August and Rudwick, Elliott. ATTORNEYS BLACK AND WHITE: A CASE STUDY OF RACE RELATIONS WITHIN THE NAACP. *J. of Am. Hist. 1976 62(4): 913-946.* In order to examine black and white interaction on an organizational basis, the authors selected the NAACP (est. 1909) as a case study. In the early days white lawyers were sought out to act for Negroes because of the vicious cycle of discrimination and inexperience affecting black lawyers. It was important that the NAACP be represented by lawyers who were competent (not only experienced but recognized as such by the courts—a recognition denied many black lawyers). Surfacing during the Dr. Ossian Sweet case of 1925-26, dissatisfaction with this system caused the retaining of three Negro lawyers (under the charge of a white lawyer) as legal representatives. During succeeding years more and more black lawyers were retained, were recognized by courts as being competent, and replaced white lawyers. The Sweet case forecasted the 1960 movement toward black separatism and black power. 117 notes.   V. P. Rilee

1647. Meier, August and Rudwick, Elliott. THE RISE OF THE BLACK SECRETARIAT IN THE NAACP, 1909-1935. *Crisis 1977 84(2): 58-69.* The NAACP began as a board-dominated organization with policy chiefly made by white progressives. By 1935 power had shifted from the board to the executive secretary. In the same period, blacks filled the post of secretary. James Weldon Johnson and Walter White had the stature, intelligence, and support to consummate the transition during 1919-35.   A. G. Belles

1648. Mesar, Joe and Dybdahl, Tom. THE UTOPIA PARK AFFAIR AND THE RISE OF NORTHERN BLACK ADVENTISTS. *Adventist Heritage 1974 1(1): 34-41, 53-54.* A separate Sabbath Day Adventist Church resulted when the First Harlem Church of James K. Humphrey, a leader in the struggle for the rights of black Adventists, was expelled from the Seventh-Day Adventists for supporting Humphrey's proposed Utopia Park settlement for blacks.

1649. Mills, Allen. THE *CANADIAN FORUM* AND SOCIALISM, 1920-1934. *J. of Can. Studies [Canada] 1978-79 13(4): 11-27.* The socialism of the *Forum,* influenced by British Fabianism, was secular, positivist, and rationalist. A voluntaristic, pluralistic, and populistic society with emphasis on market allocation of values was espoused between 1920 and 1924. After that, the emphasis was collectivist, centralist, and socialistic, accepting the state as the custodian of the public good. Despite changing editors and contributors, throughout the period there was no understanding of the place of culture in society. Based on Underhill Papers and secondary sources; 85 notes.   G. E. Panting

1650. Molander, Earl A. HISTORICAL ANTECEDENTS OF MILITARY-INDUSTRIAL CRITICISM. *Military Affairs 1976 40(2): 59-63.* Contemporary military-industrial complex criticism is part of a historical movement that has concerned itself with military-industrial integration in the arms business. Criticism, especially beginning around 1900, involved the long-standing distrust of profits, traffic in arms, and the price, quality, and delivery of military supplies sold to the government. The early attacks did not change the military-industrial domination of society but laid a solid ideological groundwork for the attacks of the 1960's. Based on primary and secondary sources; 35 notes.   A. M. Osur

1651. Mondello, Salvatore. THE INTEGRATION OF JAPANESE BAPTISTS IN AMERICAN SOCIETY. *Foundations 1977 20(3): 254-263.* American Baptists began work among the Japanese immigrants in the 1890's. They opposed discrimination against the Japanese in the National Origins Act of 1924. Deals with Baptist involvement with Japanese Americans during and after World War II. Baptists were very successful in their resettlement efforts at this time. 21 notes.   E. E. Eminhizer

1652. Moore, Jesse T., Jr. RESOLVING URBAN RACIAL PROBLEMS: THE NEW YORK URBAN LEAGUE, 1919-1959. *Afro-Americans in New York Life and Hist. 1980 4(1): 27-43.* Discusses the activities and purposes of the New York Urban League from 1919 to 1959 in its attempts to resolve the urban and racial problems of blacks in New York City.

1653. Morrison, Joseph L. W. J. CASH: THE SUMMING UP. *South Atlantic Q. 1977 76(4): 508-517.* W. J. Cash discerned an essential consensus in the South during 1830-1940 to convince white southerners to accept positive social change. He saw the southern mind self-consciously defending itself from the yankee mind, the modern mind, and the Negro's presence. Cash played the moralist and prophet in coming to understand the social changes taking place around him. Despite his eloquence and imaginative history, a new definition of the South must be made in the wake of all he foresaw.   W. L. Olbrich

1654. Moses, Wilson Jeremiah. ASSIMILATIONIST BLACK NATIONALISM, 1890-1925. *Social Studies 1977 68(6): 259-263.* Examines religious, ideological, and literary aspects of black life, as well as the role played by women, and assesses these in terms of overwhelming pressure from within the black community toward assimilation, 1890-1925.

1655. Murrah, Bill. LLANO COOPERATIVE COLONY. *Southern Exposure 1974 1(3/4): 87-104.* A group of socialists moved from California to Vernon Parish, Louisiana, to build a socialist community in 1917. Because of internal dissent over leadership and the external pressure of neighbors, the experiment ended in receivership in 1938 after several successful years. Based on interviews with participants and local residents; 13 illus., 4 notes, biblio.   G. A. Bolton

1656. O'Brien, Michael, ed. A CORRESPONDENCE: 1923-1958, EDWIN MIMS AND DONALD DAVIDSON. *Southern R. 1974*

10(4): 904-922. Discusses the agrarian movement in southern literature through the correspondence between Edwin Mims and Donald Davidson.

S

1657. Palmer, Howard. PATTERNS OF RACISM: ATTITUDES TOWARDS CHINESE AND JAPANESE IN ALBERTA 1920-1950. *Social Hist. [Canada] 1980 13(25): 137-160.* For much of the 20th century Alberta has had more Japanese and Chinese residents than any Canadian province except British Columbia. While the Chinese faced strident opposition before 1920, anti-Japanese sentiment was less intense. In the 1920's anti-Asian sentiment abated, in part because the Asian population remained small and Asians did not compete with whites. In the 1930's their urban concentration and increasing unemployment made the Chinese more obvious. World War II caused a reversal of attitudes as the war effort allowed the Chinese to prove their loyalty, and confronted Albertans with relocated Japanese. When the war ended, prodeportation sentiment declined. Although discrimination persisted, Albertans realized the value of the Japanese contribution to the economy. 77 notes.

D. F. Chard

1658. Parker, Keith A. ARTHUR EVANS: WESTERN RADICAL. *Alberta Hist. 1978 26(2): 21-29.* Arthur Evans, born in Toronto in 1889, spent years in Kansas City, Colorado, and Seattle before settling in western Canada. By the mid-1930's, he was a well-known Communist labor organizer who had spent time in prison for illegally using union funds; instead of forwarding the funds, he spent the money on food for needy families. In 1935 he was one of the organizers of the Trek from western Canada to Ottawa, where he exchanged bitter words with Prime Minister Bennett. After a riot in Regina in July, 1935, Evans was temporarily jailed on charges of being a Communist and a member of the Workers Unity League. Following his release he made a speaking tour across Canada. Evans was a shipwright and shop steward in British Columbia at the time of his death in 1944. Based on government hearings and newspaper accounts. 6 illus., 26 notes.

D. Chaput

1659. Parra, Ricardo; Rios, Victor; and Gutiérrez, Armando. CHICANO ORGANIZATIONS IN THE MIDWEST: PAST, PRESENT, AND POSSIBILITIES. *Aztlán 1976 7(2): 235-253.* Midwest Chicano institutions have developed in three successive surges. First, during 1900-40, there arose the Sociedades Mexicanas: fraternal, cultural, and mutual aid organizations. Later came groups of a frankly assimilationist character such as the League of United Latin American Citizens and the American G. I. Forum. Finally, in the 1960's and early 1970's there emerged the Chicano movement, embodied in such groups as La Raza Unida, the Brown Berets, and academically, the Centro de Estudios Chicanos at Notre Dame. Characterizes the second type of organization as "parallel", since these groups mimic similar Anglo groups, while the first and third kinds ("alternative" groups) are genuine expressions of the genius of the Chicano people. 42 notes.

L. W. Van Wyk

1660. Pavich, Paul N. JOSEPH WOOD KRUTCH: PERSISTENT CHAMPION OF MAN AND NATURE. *Western Am. Literature 1978 13(2): 151-158.* Throughout his life and his writings, Joseph Wood Krutch showed that he was very concerned about man's role in nature. He was a champion of humanity and an early defender of the ecological movement. He believed that materialism was the cause of ecological blindness—meaningful relationships to other human beings and to the land were being suppressed in a meaningless enthusiasm for things. Krutch continually emphasized man's responsibility to himself and to his environment.

M. Genung

1661. Pettigrew, Thomas F. RACIAL CHANGE AND SOCIAL POLICY. *Ann. of Am. Acad. of Pol. and Social Sci. 1979 441: 114-131.* Five major trends in contemporary American race relations are specified and discussed: 1) the discontinuities of social change, with uneven progress within and across institutions; 2) two contrasting processes, one benefitting the black middle class and the other restraining the black poor; 3) the altered nature of racial discrimination, from blatantly exclusionary practices to more subtle, procedural, ostensibly "non-racial" forms centered upon demographic trends, housing patterns, and spatial arrangements; 4) racial attitude changes, with greater rejection of racial injustice among whites combined with continued resistance to the measures needed to correct the injustice; and 5) the shifting demographic base of American race relations, from the national era of 1915-1945, through the metropolitan era of 1945-1970, to the present era of movement away from large cities, the Northeast, and the Midwest. Each of these trends are shown to intersect in important ways with the structural linchpin of modern race relations: the maldistribution of blacks and whites throughout metropolitan areas. Finally, six practical guidelines for future racial policies in urban areas are offered.

J

1662. Philp, Kenneth R. JOHN COLLIER AND THE INDIANS OF THE AMERICAS: THE DREAM AND THE REALITY. *Prologue 1979 11(1): 5-21.* As Franklin D. Roosevelt's Indian Commissioner, John Collier was interested in undertaking a hemispheric approach to bettering the lot of Indians in the Americas. His efforts, joined by like-minded individuals in other countries, especially Mexico, resulted in the creation of the Inter-American Institute in 1940. That body held three international meetings between 1940 and 1954. The IAI was to act as a coordinating body to spur projects aiding the Indians in the various American republics, and to be a publicity medium through which the plight of the Indian could be made known to policymakers. The body was always underfinanced and lacked widespread, consistent political support even in the Indian-sensitive nation of Mexico. In the United States, Collier's efforts were undercut by strong and effective opposition raised by individual members of Congress, by the lack of intrabureaucratic cooperation, and by other political priorities. The IAI was also hampered by the fact that Indians played little role in its deliberations. Based on research in National Archives.

N. Lederer

1663. Pienkos, Donald. POLITICS, RELIGION, AND CHANGE IN POLISH MILWAUKEE, 1900-1930. *Wisconsin Mag. of Hist. 1978 61(3): 178-209.* Analyzes the political behavior of Milwaukee Poles during the Progressive Era, particularly their response to progressivism and socialism. Describes the role of key leaders, including *Kuryer Polski* editor and publisher Michael Kruszka, socialist alderman Leo Krzyski, state senator Walter Polakowski, and Catholic priest and polemicist Wenceslaus Kruszka. Concludes that Poles did not always support the Democratic Party, that they often supported socialism and La Follette progressivism, that they did not always defer to the Catholic Church hierarchy, and that they were more involved with trade unionism than has previously been recognized. 23 illus., 5 tables, 74 notes.

N. C. Burckel

1664. Pitsula, James M. W. G. BROWN: "RIGHTEOUSNESS EXALTETH A NATION." *Saskatchewan Hist. [Canada] 1980 33(2): 56-70.* Discusses W. G. Brown, leader of the United Reform Movement in Saskatchewan from 1938 to 1940. Brown, Michael P. Hayes, his liberal opponent in a 1939 by-election, and W. D. Herridge receive considerable mention. Based on contemporary newspaper accounts and sermons; 121 notes.

C. H. Held

1665. Piven, Frances Fox. DEVIANT BEHAVIOR AND THE REMAKING OF THE WORLD. *Social Problems 1981 28(5): 489-508.* Describes so-called deviant behavior as a challenge to societal norms and institutions, including agitation by laborers in the early 20th century for improved working conditions, black protests in South Africa and the United States since the 1950's, and other protest movements against institutions by the aged, the disabled, and the poor since the late 1960's.

1666. Pratt, William C. WOMEN AND AMERICAN SOCIALISM: THE READING EXPERIENCE. *Pennsylvania Mag. of Hist. and Biog. 1975 99(1): 72-91.* Reviews the role of women in building the Socialist Party in Reading, Pennsylvania. The party enjoyed considerable local electoral success during 1927-36, and much of this success depended on the women's vote. Women played a larger role in Socialist Party affairs than was the case with either of the majority parties, but this role was subordinate and supportive, as the Party was neither willing nor able to break through the prevailing philosophy of male dominance. 61 notes.

V. L. Human

1667. Reid, Bill G. ARTHUR C. TOWNLEY: A STUDY IN SUCCESS AND FAILURE. *Red River Valley Hist. 1980 (Fall): 18-22.* Biography of Arthur C. Townley (1880-1959), founder and leader of the Nonpartisan League of North Dakota from 1915 to 1921 when he resigned, focusing on the League's program of state-owned industry and its support of the farmers of North Dakota, and on Townley's subsequent problems in business and politics.

1668. Richey, Susan. COMMENT ON THE POLITICAL STRATEGY OF CHRISTIAN PACIFISTS: A. J. MUSTE, NORMAN THOMAS, AND REINHOLD NIEBUHR. *Towson State J. of Int. Affairs 1977 11(2): 111-119.* Analyzes the political nature and philosophical perspectives of Christian pacifism as reflected in the writings of A. J. Muste, Norman Thomas, and Reinhold Niebuhr between World War I and World War II.

1669. Riess, Steven. PROFESSIONAL SUNDAY BASEBALL: A STUDY IN SOCIAL REFORM 1892-1934. *Maryland Historian 1973 4(2): 95-108.* Examines the pattern of social changes in Chicago, New York, and Atlanta which converted Sunday to a recreation day. As America became more urban, bureaucratized, and industrialized, religious conservatism yielded. Baseball became a working-class entertainment and an inculcator of American middle class values. Periodical and secondary sources; 55 notes. G. O. Gagnon

1670. Rivers, Larry E. THE PITTSBURGH WORKSHOP FOR THE BLIND, 1910-1939: A CASE STUDY OF THE BLINDED SYSTEM IN AMERICA. *Western Pennsylvania Hist. Mag. 1978 61(2): 135-150.* Surveys historical attitudes toward blind persons during the 19th century, the movement toward education of the blind, and a specific case, the Pittsburgh Workshop for the Blind in western Pennsylvania which sought, 1910-39, to provide employment for the blind.

1671. Rosen, George. SOCIAL SCIENCE AND HEALTH IN THE UNITED STATES IN THE TWENTIETH CENTURY. *Clio Medica [Netherlands] 1976 11(4): 245-268.* During 1860-1910 the urban population of America rose from 19 to 45 percent of the total population. The influx of European immigrants and southern blacks to industrial centers caused serious health problems. Henry W. Farnam, a Yale professor (1881-1918), urged Congress to investigate industrial diseases. In 1909 the Pittsburgh survey revealed that tuberculosis and typhoid were more likely to hit the poor living in squalid tenements. Newly established sociology departments in universities studied crime, ethnic groups, prostitution, and other urban problems. Most of these studies had chapters on public health, and in the 1930's specific works on urban health appeared. This interaction between social science and the health field has led to improvements in public health. 62 notes. A. J. Papalas

1672. Rosenof, Theodore. THE POLITICAL EDUCATION OF AN AMERICAN RADICAL: THOMAS R. AMLIE IN THE 1930'S. *Wisconsin Mag. of Hist. 1974 58(1): 19-30.* Wisconsin congressman Thomas R. Amlie served in the House of Representatives first as a La Follette Republican from 1931 to 1933 and then as a Progressive from 1935 to 1939. The author traces the intellectual evolution of Amlie's radicalism as he responded to the depression and the political philosophy of the New Deal. At first Amlie sought to alter society through the formation of a third party. He gradually abandoned that idea in hopes of transforming Franklin D. Roosevelt and the New Deal into a new radical force, but ended the decade disillusioned by 'the New Dealers' dogmatically limited solution." 5 illus., 36 notes. N. C. Burckel

1673. Rosenthal, Joel. SOUTHERN BLACK STUDENT ACTIVISM: ASSIMILATION VS. NATIONALISM. *J. of Negro Educ. 1975 44(2): 113-129.* The tension between aspiration for white middle-class status and race pride has underscored student activism in southern black colleges and universities since before 1900. The growth of southern black student activism prior to 1960 laid the groundwork for the sit-in movement, the growth of SNCC, the rise of Stokely Carmichael, and the turn to black nationalism. The violent stage of activism ended with the series of student deaths such as those at Jackson State College, 1970, and Southern University, 1972. The underlying tension has not been resolved. Primary and secondary sources; 87 notes. R. E. Butchart

1674. Roy, Patricia E. BRITISH COLUMBIA'S FEAR OF ASIANS, 1900-1950. *Social Hist. [Canada] 1980 13(25): 161-172.* British Columbia's racial intolerance was rooted in fear of Asian superiority, the province's isolation from the rest of Canada, and the newness of its society. Asian academic accomplishments, and whites' beliefs in Asian moral depravity suggested initially that children and women needed special protection. Before World War I labor organizations spearheaded anti-Asian agitation. By the 1920's and 1930's farmers and retail merchants often led the fight. By the late 1930's the Japanese faced increasing resentment as Japanese military power increased. After World War II racial hostility subsided with postwar prosperity and the dispersal of the Japanese. 74 notes. D. F. Chard

1675. Ruppert, Peter. UTOPIAN THINKING: OLD LIMITATIONS AND NEW POSSIBILITIES. *Southern Humanities Rev. 1977 11(4): 337-344.* European and American intellectual conceptions of utopias, 1930's-70's, emphasize the possibility for progressive social change and expansion of thought to include the whole of human experience.

1676. Samuels, Wilfred D. HUBERT H. HARRISON AND "THE NEW NEGRO MANHOOD MOVEMENT." *Afro-Americans in New York Life and Hist. 1981 5(1): 29-41.* "Harlem streetcorner orator and debater, political critic, and scholar" Hubert H. Harrison (b. 1883) tried to influence the direction of life for blacks; he recruited blacks into the Socialist Party of America between 1912 and 1915, formed the Liberty League of Negro Americans (LLNA) in 1917, helped form the International Colored Unity League (ICUL) in 1925, and worked on black journals; 1911-27.

1677. Sarotte, Georges-Michel. UN ÉTRANGER PARMI NOUS: L'HOMOSEXUEL DANS LA SOCIÉTÉ AMÉRICAINE [A stranger among us: the homosexual in American society]. *Rev. Française d'Études Américaines [France] 1980 5(9): 79-88.* Describes struggle for equal rights for homosexuals in American society during the 20th century.

1678. Segers, Mary C. EQUALITY AND CHRISTIAN ANARCHISM: THE POLITICAL AND SOCIAL IDEAS OF THE CATHOLIC WORKER MOVEMENT. *Rev. of Pol. 1978 40(2): 196-230.* The Catholic Worker Movement since 1933 has "consistently adopted controversial positions on contemporary social issues and has challenged Americans to think through the implications of public policy." The key to the success of the movement has been on its emphasis on "the fundamental equality and constant humanity of all men and women." The "personalism" of the Catholic Workers serves as a lesson to capitalistic society that all the "civil rights laws and all the affirmative action policies—will have relatively little impact unless there are fundamental changes in capitalist society and unless, on an attitudinal level, equality is believed and accepted as a rule of practical action." 55 notes. L. E. Ziewacz

1679. Servín, Manuel P. THE MEXICAN-AMERICAN AWAKENS: AN INTERPRETATION. *J. of the West 1975 14(4): 121-130.* Synopsis of the background of Mexican Americans and their heritage of discrimination; centers on Mexican Americans, 1930-75 and emphasizes evolving political awareness within the minority group. Biblio.

1680. Sinclair, Peter R. THE SASKATCHEWAN C.C.F. AND THE COMMUNIST PARTY IN THE 1930'S. *Saskatchewan Hist. 1973 26(1): 1-10.* The pragmatism of the Cooperative Commonwealth Federation in its programs and relations with other political organizations demonstrated that it was a political party rather than a social movement. The C.C.F. efforts in the 1930's in the Meadow Lake constituency of Saskatchewan presented a united front of opposition supporters, including the Communist Party, to the governing Liberal Party. 41 notes. D. L. Smith

1681. Sinclair, Peter R. THE SASKATCHEWAN CCF: ASCENT TO POWER AND THE DECLINE OF SOCIALISM. *Can. Hist. R. 1973 54(4): 419-433.* Examines the transformation of the Cooperative Commonwealth Federation's socialist policy, especially on land ownership, in order to appeal to a rural petit bourgeois electorate. Contributes to literature on the dilemma of parties which desire social change by electoral means. Based primarily on unpublished CCF party papers and newspapers in the Archives of Saskatchewan. A

1682. Skakkebaek, Mette. AGRARIAN RADICALISM AFTER THE POPULISTS. *Am. Studies in Scandinavia [Norway] 1979 11(1): 10-13.* Observes many similarities in agrarian radicalism among members of Populist, Socialist, Progressive, Non-Partisan League and Farmer-Labor parties, and notes shared ideological goals beyond betterment of agrarian group interests, and "latent radicalism . . . in the rural community." Further investigation of the agrarian radical population is needed to claim links among the rural protest movements. Covers ca. 1892-1930.

Based on the author's unpublished M.A. thesis, "The American Socialist Party, with Special Reference to the Elections of 1924 and 1928," University of Copenhagen, 1976; 27 notes. E. E. Krogstad

1683. Smilor, Raymond W. CACOPHONY AT 34TH AND 6TH: THE NOISE PROBLEM IN AMERICA, 1900-1930. *Am. Studies [Lawrence, KS] 1977 18(1): 23-38.* The antinoise campaign was central to Progressive efforts at environmental reform, and provides a blueprint for early consumer activism. Led by the middle class, especially women, it represented a challenge to an industrialized society and a belief in progress. Noise was primitive and inefficient, and a danger to public health. Solutions included the establishment of "quiet zones," the formation of societies, and legislative relief. Primary and secondary sources; 58 notes. J. Andrew

1684. Smilor, Raymond W. TOWARD AN ENVIRONMENTAL PERSPECTIVE: THE ANTI-NOISE CAMPAIGN, 1893-1932. Melosi, Martin V., ed. *Pollution and Reform in American Cities, 1870-1930* (Austin: U. of Texas Pr., 1980): 135-151. The antinoise campaign of 1893-1932 in American industrial cities reveals the development of an early consumer activism. Noise was a problem that affected everyone. Thus the campaign cut across social barriers and led consumers to join forces for environmental change. The middle-class reformers who directed the antinoise movement gained the support of all segments of the community because all individuals could agree on the harmful effects of noise. Noise came to represent a danger to health, a hindrance to efficiency, and an invasion of privacy. Like other progressive reformers, antinoise advocates optimistically believed that rational analysis could solve the problems of the industrial age. They put faith in law. Not until the 1920's did experts and scientists take over the campaign and begin to examine every aspect of the noise issue. Secondary sources; 57 notes.
J. Powell

1685. Spindler, George D. and Spindler, Louise S. IDENTITY, MILITANCY, AND CULTURAL CONGRUENCE: THE MENOMINEE AND KAINAI. *Ann. of the Am. Acad. of Pol. and Social Sci. 1978 436: 73-85.* Recent movements of varying degrees of militancy on the part of American Indians can be better understood if we have a grasp of the kinds of adaptations Indians have made to the long-term and continuing confrontation with white culture, white power, and white world views. Native Americans do not constitute a single group. The Menominee are taken as an example of an Indian tribe with a hitherto unaggressive record that has recently engaged in militant activity. The diversity within the Menominee population is described in terms of four major types of long-standing adaptation that were observed as dominant in the 1950s and 1960s and that emerged some time before that. Recent militancy is regarded as a fifth type of adaptive response to the continuing confrontation between Menominee and white culture. Militancy is interpreted, in part, as an assertion of identity. The responses of the Kainai, the Blood Indians of Alberta, Canada, to white culture and power are contrasted briefly at certain critical points to demonstrate the fact of diversity among American Indians in regard to current actions and to reinforce the interpretation that the degree of difference in cultures and world views between Indian cultures and white culture is a significant factor in the kinds of adaptive response to confrontation native American groups have made and will make. J

1686. Stafford, Walter W. DILEMMAS OF CIVIL RIGHTS GROUPS IN DEVELOPING URBAN STRATEGIES AND CHANGES IN AMERICAN FEDERALISM, 1933-1970. *Phylon 1976 37(1): 59-72.* Chronicles interaction of black civil rights groups in assuring urban development and in establishing viable relations with local and federal governments.

1687. Stern, Marjorie. AN INSIDER'S VIEW OF THE TEACHERS UNION AND WOMEN'S RIGHTS. *Urban Rev. 1973 6(5-6): 46-49.* The American Federation of Teachers was among the first organizations, with its foundation in 1916, to promote equal rights for women; includes a description of the structure of the union.

1688. Stinson, Robert. IDA M. TARBELL AND THE AMBIGUITIES OF FEMINISM. *Pennsylvania Mag. of Hist. and Biog. 1977 101(2): 217-239.* Ida M. Tarbell, an early convert to the suffrage movement, determined not to marry and successfully pursued a journalistic career which reached its peak when she was made managing editor of *McClure's Magazine.* After 1909, her articles and novels about women began to change. She became an advocate of home life and the family, a position she held until her death. Speculations about the reasons for her conversion fail to take into account the fact that she had not really changed but rather was reflecting another side of an ideological bipolarity that had always existed in her mind. 55 notes. V. L. Human

1689. Strong-Boag, Veronica. CANADIAN FEMINISM IN THE 1920'S: THE CASE OF NELLIE L. MC CLUNG. *J. of Can. Studies [Canada] 1977 12(4): 58-68.* Nellie L. McClung managed to be simultaneously "Canada's foremost woman warrior" and a conscientious mother. A popular novelist, she was a leading proponent of woman suffrage (achieved in 1918) and prohibition, for social reform laws, and (as an active Methodist) for the ordination of women. In 1921 she was elected to the Alberta legislature as a Liberal despite a landslide for the United Farmers of Alberta. As a legislator she was overshadowed by Irene Parlby, who was a UFA member and a cabinet minister. McClung narrowly failed to win reelection, partly because of her continued support for prohibition. The collapse in the 1920's of the moral earnestness of the war years undermined the reform movement generally, and McClung's career in particular. Based on the McClung Papers and secondary sources; 45 notes. L. W. Van Wyk

1690. Strong-Boag, Veronica. THE ROOTS OF MODERN CANADIAN FEMINISM: THE NATIONAL COUNCIL OF WOMEN, 1893-1929. *Canada 1975 3(2): 22-33.* Discusses the evolution of the National Council of Women of Canada and its role in the federation of social and political women's organizations in Canada 1893-1929.

1691. Strout, Cushing. RADICAL RELIGION AND THE AMERICAN POLITICAL NOVEL. *Clio 1976 6(1): 23-42.* Connects the biblical idea of a movement in history with modern consciousness of social change and conflicts in three American political novels of the 20th century. Ernest Poole's *The Harbor* (1915) explores the radical socialism of the Muckraking era; John Steinbeck's *In Dubious Battle* (1936), the Communist appeal of the 1930's; and E. L. Doctorow's *The Book of Daniel* (1971), the New Left of the 1960's. In each novel the hero exhibits a secular, political religion. Using millennial and apocalyptic thought, he pursues radical change or social justice in society. 35 notes.
T. P. Linkfield

1692. Stuckey, Sterling. "I WANT TO BE AFRICAN": PAUL ROBESON AND THE ENDS OF NATIONALIST THEORY AND PRACTICE, 1914-1945. *Massachusetts Rev. 1976 17(1): 81-138.* Paul Robeson (1898-1976), son of a slave, hailed as the finest bass-baritone in the world and a very fine actor, for 50 years sought to assist his fellow Negroes. Having studied African culture and languages, he included selections of folksongs in his concerts. Robeson believed that Negro culture could bring a fresh principle of human friendship. His most lasting contribution was succeeding in uniting the strands of black nationalism. He foresaw the freeing of the blacks in Africa, and was prepared to risk everything for that goal. Based on autobiographies, newspapers, interviews, and secondary works; illus., 2 plates, 120 notes.
E. R. Campbell

1693. Suderman, Elmer F. THE MENNONITE COMMUNITY AND THE PACIFIST CHARACTER IN AMERICAN LITERATURE. *Mennonite Life 1979 34(1): 8-15.* A comparison of four novels —*Erloesung* by Peter Epp, *Peace Shall Destroy Many* by Rudy Wiebe, *Mennonite Soldier* by Kenneth Reed, and *The Long Tomorrow* by Lee Brackett—and two plays—*The Blowing and the Bending* by James Juhnke and Harold Moyer, and *The Berserkers* by Warren Kliewer— shows the reactions of Mennonite pacifist communities and characters to a violent world. These worlds lack the radical pacifism that demands a commitment to love and forgiveness and do not present an admirable hero who refuses to fight nor a serious alternative to war. In most, a sense of community strength and church leadership are lacking. 2 photos, 9 notes.
B. Burnett

1694. Tanaka, June K. FRUIT OF DIASPORA: THE JAPANESE EXPERIENCE IN CANADA. *Japan Interpreter [Japan] 1978 12(1): 110-117.* Anti-Japanese prejudice and discrimination led to early anti-Japanese immigration restrictions in British Columbia, and culminated in the forced relocation of all Japanese from the Province after Pearl Harbor. Relocation proved beneficial for many Japanese Canadians. Stresses the lack of racial prejudice in eastern Canada. F. W. Iklé

1695. Taylor, John. "RELIEF FROM RELIEF": THE CITIES' ANSWER TO DEPRESSION DEPENDENCY. *J. of Can. Studies [Canada] 1979 14(1): 16-23.* Examines the procedures suggested by city mayors and the effects of attempts to avoid the dependency problems resulting from cities having largely shouldered responsibility for unemployment benefits during the worst of the Canadian Depression in the 1930's. The slogan "Relief from Relief" was more politically motivated than an actual description of the suggested procedures. "It disregarded both the complexities of 'state-willed parasitism' in an industrial society, as well as the niceties of responsibilities in a federal system." The actual result was that the cities became delivery systems and the ultimate dependents. Primary sources; 25 notes. R. V. Ritter

1696. Thomas, Richard W. THE DETROIT URBAN LEAGUE, 1916-1923. *Michigan Hist. 1976 60(4): 315-338.* The Detroit Urban League, founded in 1916 and first headed by Forrester B. Washington, sought to alleviate problems of housing, recreation, and unemployment faced by blacks arriving from the rural South. Paternalistic and possessed of urban, middle-class values, Washington urged blacks to emulate northern white culture. Under Washington's successor, John C. Dancey, the League broadened and intensified its services and, by 1939, had become an established, recognized agency in the community. Primary sources; 8 photos, 72 notes. D. W. Johnson

1697. Toll, William. THE GENIE OF "RACE": PROBLEMS IN CONCEPTUALIZING THE TREATMENT OF BLACK AMERICANS. *J. of Ethnic Studies 1976 4(3): 1-20.* Racial prejudice does not by itself account for the mistreatment of blacks. Proponents of internal colonization or caste project too static a relationship between blacks and whites. Blacks in 20th-century American cities have transformed themselves into an ethnic group organized to fight the consequences of having been perceived as a race. Charles Valentine's theme of voluntary ethnicity as a form of cultural revolution against white folk mythology is one of the more correct views of how blacks seek "the rewards of America's cosmopolitan culture" through this new social organization. Major studies of this black coalescence, such as W. E. B. Dubois' *The Philadelphia Negro,* Horace Cayton and St. Clair Drake's *Black Metropolis,* and Franklin Frazier's *Black Bourgeoisie* are surveyed. Secondary sources; 55 annotated notes. G. J. Bobango

1698. Trofimenkoff, Susan Mann. HENRI BOURASSA AND "THE WOMAN QUESTION." *J. of Can. Studies 1975 10(4): 3-11.* Discusses the opposition of writer Henri Bourassa to feminism, woman suffrage and divorce in Canada, 1913-25.

1699. Vigod, B. L. IDEOLOGY AND INSTITUTIONS IN QUEBEC: THE PUBLIC CHARITIES CONTROVERSY, 1921-1926. *Social Hist. [Canada] 1978 11(21): 167-182.* In late 1920 a brief but severe recession strained the resources of Quebec's charitable institutions. The Public Charities Act (1921) provided relief but also demanded greater accountability. The Church objected to what it saw as anticlerical state interference. The patronage-ridden regime of Premier Alexandre Taschereau, with his personal reputation for impatience and intolerance, was another cause for concern. There was also uncertainty about the most appropriate concept of social welfare. The Act provided relief, but no systematic reform occurred. 72 notes. D. F. Chard

1700. Vigod, B. L. THE QUEBEC GOVERNMENT AND SOCIAL LEGISLATION DURING THE 1930S: A STUDY IN POLITICAL SELF-DESTRUCTION. *J. of Can. Studies [Canada] 1979 14(1): 59-69.* Studies the response of the Louis Alexandre Taschereau provincial government of Quebec to the need for progressive social reform and relief policies during the Depression of the 1930's. His government's apparent indifference to human suffering probably contributed more than any other single factor to the revolt of the young Liberals. A tracing of the sequence of events in the period clearly indicates his refusal to acknowledge grim social reality; this, in turn resulting ultimately in his fall from power. 60 notes. R. V. Ritter

1701. Vodicka, John. PRISON PLANTATION: THE STORY OF ANGOLA. *Southern Exposure 1978 6(4): 32-38.* The Louisiana State Prison at Angola was founded in 1900 to replace the harsh and brutal convict lease system. It has been through the years an establishment run primarily as an agricultural business enterprise worked predominantly by black prisoners. Its history has been characterized by abysmal conditions and punitive treatment of prisoners with sporadic and short-lasting efforts at reform. Although the abuse of convict guards has been eliminated from the prison and new facilities have been constructed, Angola remains today in treatment and attitude toward convicts much as it did in 1931. N. Lederer

1702. Walker, Samuel. THE RISE AND FALL OF THE POLICEWOMEN'S MOVEMENT, 1905-1975. Hawes, Joseph M., ed. *Law and Order in American History* (Port Washington, N.Y.: Kennikat Pr., 1979): 101-111. Traces efforts to include women on police forces to 1905 when the first known woman to have full police powers was hired by the Portland, Oregon, police department, until 1975 when women were still being hired mostly as clerical workers or in juvenile divisions.

1703. Weaver, John C. ORDER AND EFFICIENCY: SAMUEL MORLEY WICKETT AND THE URBAN PROGRESSIVE MOVEMENT IN TORONTO, 1900-1915. *Ontario Hist. [Canada] 1977 69(4): 218-234.* Wickett represented the strand of urban progressivism which pressed for professionalization of urban government through the city management approach. His father had been an alderman in Toronto, on a reform ticket, in the late 19th century. Wickett's studies at University of Toronto, and postgraduate work in Vienna and then several German centers, exposed him to other influences. He returned to teach political economy at the University of Toronto for years, with time out for the family business. Details his life and services to the city government, both before and after his election as alderman in 1913. Examines his economic ideas and sets them in a broader context than local politics and interests. He died in 1915 of a heart attack, some of his work unfinished. Mainly primary sources; 92 notes. W. B. Whitham

1704. Werly, John M. PREMILLENNIALISM AND THE PARANOID STYLE. *Am. Studies [Lawrence, KS] 1977 18(1): 39-55.* Premillennialists reject reform, have no faith in social progress, and believe that all religious and secular institutions are "infested with satanic influences." The Twenties, a time of great change, produced many such groups. Among the most significant was the Ku Klux Klan. Many critics of the New Deal in the Thirties also fit this mold, such as Huey Long, Gerald L. K. Smith, and Father Charles Coughlin. After World War II Billy James Hargis and other new personalities emerged. All had a paranoid view of American society, and saw conspiracies everywhere. Primary and secondary sources; 35 notes. J. Andrew

1705. Williams, Robert J. POLITICS AND REGULATORY REFORM: SOME ASPECTS OF THE AMERICAN EXPERIENCE. *Public Administration [Great Britain] 1979 57(Spr): 55-69.* Reviews attempts to reform the US independent regulatory agencies, 1937-79, and concludes that such executive proposals often represent frustrations at the constraints on executive power, although a recent change of emphasis reflecting a widespread view that there is excessive regulation has appeared in the Ash Council report of 1971.

1706. Williams, T. Harry. HUEY, LYNDON, AND SOUTHERN RADICALISM. *J. of Am. Hist. 1973 60(2): 267-293.* The most radical mass movement and the two most radical politicians of recent history were products of an allegedly conservative, undissenting South. The black civil rights movement broke the "enveloping silence" surrounding race relations in the South and may see a greater acceptance of black equality in that region than in the North. Both Huey Long and Lyndon Johnson were products of non-affluent families in historically radical sections, both strove for economic equality for whites, and both would extend that equality to blacks. Johnson was more manipulative, working successfully within the system, while Long was authoritarian, feeling that the political system frustrated radical change. 61 notes. K. B. West

1707. Wilson, J. Donald. "NEVER BELIEVE WHAT YOU HAVE NEVER DOUBTED": MATTI KURIKKA'S DREAM FOR A NEW WORLD UTOPIA. *Turun Hist. Arkisto [Finland] 1980 34: 216-240.* A biography of the Finnish utopian socialist Matti Kurikka (1863-1915),

who founded utopian communities in Australia, 1899, and Canada, 1900-04. Kurikka was a Finnish cultural nationalist, a theosophist, and an advocate of free love. These attitudes brought him into conflict with his own followers as well as with orthodox Marxists. Based on Kurikka's letters in a private collection in Finland; 96 notes.
R. G. Selleck

1708. Winston, Michael R. CARTER GODWIN WOODSON: PROPHET OF A BLACK TRADITION. *J. of Negro Hist. 1975 60(4): 459-463.* Outlines the achievements of historian Carter Godwin Woodson (1875-1950), founder of the *Journal of Negro History.* Discusses the effectiveness of that journal as an instrument in the national movement for the study, preservation, interpretation, and dissemination of black history. Woodson's work has supported the black community in its struggle against racism and unequal opportunity, particularly his organization of programs of Negro public education. 10 notes.
C. A. McNeill

1709. Wirmark, Bo. NONVIOLENT METHODS AND THE AMERICAN CIVIL RIGHTS MOVEMENT 1955-1965. *J. of Peace Res. [Norway] 1974 11(2): 115-132.*

1710. Wolfe, Margaret Ripley. CHANGING THE FACE OF SOUTHERN APPALACHIA: URBAN PLANNING IN SOUTHWEST VIRGINIA AND EAST TENNESSEE, 1890-1929. *J. of the Am. Planning Assoc. 1981 47(3): 252-265.* Capitalistic development lifted preindustrial natives from a simple agrarian-based existence and set them down in industrial villages and towns. American and European investors exploited natural and human resources, but they also initiated urban planning and regional development which, in some instances, set the tone for subsequent growth that elevated the standard of living for the local people. Three separate planning ventures at Stonega, Virginia; Kingsport, Tennessee; and Happy Valley, Tennessee reveal striking contrasts in objectives as well as the long-term consequences.
J

1711. Ybarra-Frausto, Tomás. THE CHICANO MOVEMENT AND THE EMERGENCE OF A CHICANO POETIC CONSCIOUSNESS. *New Scholar 1977 (6): 81-110.* Chicano poetic consciousness has 19th-century origins, but the focus is on the post-1945 period. From its inception, this poetic consciousness has moved between betterment and liberation. Language, the revitalization of Chicano speech, has played a major role in this poetic development, moving toward cultural nationalism. Newspapers and presses—first Spanish-language and then Chicano—are the creative forces. Finally, this Chicano enterprise has now gone beyond cultural nationalism to a more consciously critical view of American capitalism. From a special issue, "New Directions In Chicano Scholarship." 55 notes.
D. K. Pickens

1712. Yellin, Jean Fagan. DUBOIS' *CRISIS* AND WOMEN'S SUFFRAGE. *Massachusetts R. 1973 14(2): 365-375.* William Edward Burghardt DuBois' attitudes toward women's rights were expressed in the *Crisis*, the magazine of the National Association for the Advancement of Colored People (NAACP) which he edited 1910-34. DuBois consistently sided with suffragettes, even after exposing the racism predominant in the feminist movement. He hoped to unite the women's movement with the black movement, because both groups were traditionally victims in American society. As the 19th Amendment neared ratification, DuBois urged black women to exercise their future voter's rights to the best interests of black people in general. While the amendment brought white women the franchise, it did little to uplift the status of black women. Because feminist groups continued to ignore this glaring inequity throughout the 1920's, DuBois realized that there could be no "women-Negro" alliance. 11 notes.
W. A. Wiegand

1713. Yellowitz, Irwin. MORRIS HILLQUIT: AMERICAN SOCIALISM AND JEWISH CONCERNS. *Am. Jewish Hist. 1978 68(2): 163-188.* Morris Hillquit (1869-1933), an agnostic and an American socialist leader, posed antireligious appeals and worked to neutralize this issue because it tended to drive away potential supporters. Throughout his career Hillquit, often following the advice of his friend Abraham Cahan, had to accept the reality of his ethnic political base in the New York City Jewish ghetto. Evidence from his political campaigns illustrates this thesis. Ethnic identity and concerns were a stronger influence among socialists in the Jewish community in 1930 than in 1900, and Hillquit recognized this. 42 notes.
F. Rosenthal

1714. —. AGRARIAN SOCIALISM. *Agric. Hist. 1977 51(1): 173-199.*
Burbank, Garin. AGRARIAN SOCIALISM IN SASKATCHEWAN AND OKLAHOMA: SHORT-RUN RADICALISM, LONG-RUN CONSERVATISM. *pp. 173-180.* Agrarian socialists in Oklahoma and Saskatchewan ca. 1900-45 did not want to replace capitalism with collective ownership of the land. The farmers and tenants who supported socialism wanted to better their lot rather than change the social order. 12 notes.
Calvert, Robert A. A. J. ROSE AND THE GRANGER CONCEPT OF REFORM. *pp. 181-196.* The leadership of the Texas Grange reflected southern conservatism in its stands on unions, railroad regulation, and the tariff. Like other Granges its organization was decentralized and divided. The most important Texas Granger, A. J. Rose, sought to keep the Grange out of politics. Rose emphasized educational and social activities and cooperatives along the Rochdale model which tried to avoid antagonizing merchants. When cooperatives failed, Grange membership declined and farmers turned to more radical groups such as the Alliance. 68 notes.
Hadwiger, Donald. AGRARIAN POLITICS IN THE GREAT PLAINS: A RESPONSE. *pp. 197-199.* The Saskatchewan Cooperative Commonwealth Federation and the Oklahoma Socialist Party had better success than the Texas Grangers in giving vent to frustration through political action. The Grange, on the other hand, did a better job of developing a sense of community among farmers. All three organizations may have had more influence on agrarian radicalism than Calvert or Burbank believe.
D. E. Bowers

1715. —. [WILLIAM O. DOUGLAS AND JUDICIAL ACTIVISM].
Mendelson, Wallace. MR. JUSTICE DOUGLAS AND GOVERNMENT BY THE JUDICIARY. *J. of Pol. 1976 38(4): 918-937.* Studies developments within the federal judicial process that illustrate why new liberals seem inclined to look to the judiciary for help. Their great victories have been won in court, hence it is not strange that a major element of modern activism is an effort to open more widely the gateway to the federal judiciary. Mr. Justice Douglas was a leading spokesman for this approach, and champion of the issue of access to the courts. "The old liberalism resented government by judges; neo-liberalism embraces it. Mr. Justice Douglas started out in the one camp and ended up in the other." 86 notes.
Goldman, Sheldon. IN DEFENSE OF JUSTICE: SOME THOUGHTS ON READING PROFESSOR MENDELSON'S "MR. JUSTICE DOUGLAS AND GOVERNMENT BY THE JUDICIARY." *J. of Pol. 1977 39(1): 148-158.* Questions Mendelson's characterization of Douglas as a "leading spokesman" for "neo-liberal" modern judicial activism on the Supreme Court. Douglas' decisions on certiorari, standing to sue, judicial ripeness, mootness, political questions, and substantive law consistently supported civil rights and liberties. Based on primary and secondary sources; 20 notes.
Mendelson, Wallace. A RESPONSE TO PROFESSOR GOLDMAN. *J. of Pol. 1977 (1): 159-165.* William O. Douglas emphasized his philosophy of justice over constitutional and legal standards and procedures, raising the spectre of government by an elite—the justices of the Supreme Court unaccountable to political or other judicial authority. Based on primary and secondary sources; 9 notes.
R. V. Ritter/A. W. Novitsky

Civil Liberties and Political Rights

1716. Berens, John F. THE FBI AND CIVIL LIBERTIES FROM FRANKLIN ROOSEVELT TO JIMMY CARTER: AN HISTORICAL OVERVIEW. *Michigan Academician 1980 13(2): 131-144.* The history of the Federal Bureau of Investigation since the presidency of Franklin D. Roosevelt, whose mandates in 1936 and 1939 "opened the door to massive FBI surveillance of Americans who deviated from the established and normal politics of the day," has adequately shown the dangers to individual civil liberties of the FBI's programs.

1717. Beth, Loren P. MR. JUSTICE BLACK AND THE FIRST AMENDMENT: COMMENTS ON THE DILEMMA OF CONSTI-

TUTIONAL INTERPRETATION. *J. of Pol. 1979 41(4): 1105-1124.* Justice Hugo Black attempted to confine substantive due process within the limits set by the first eight amendments, to prevent judges from substituting their policy preferences for those of the legislature or executive. His theory of the first amendment implied a place-oriented exemption covering the performance of legitimate governmental functions. While his attempts at defining the limits of the first amendment were not successful, of all recent justices, Black came closest to balancing the rule of law and the imprecise limitation it imposes on constitutional interpretation. 61 notes.
A. W. Novitsky

1718. Bodine, John J. TAOS BLUE LAKE CONTROVERSY. *J. of Ethnic Studies 1978 6(1): 42-48.* H. R. Bill 471, signed into law 15 December 1970, was the first time in the history of US-Indian relations that a claim for land, based on the practice of aboriginal religion, successfully ended in the restoration of that land to an Indian reservation. Blue Lake is not only the primary source for the water supply of the Taos Pueblo, but also the center of the annual pilgrimage for the puberty rites of the kiva society system of the tribe. The area became part of the Carson National Forest in 1906, and all attempts to regain it by the Indians failed until the 1960's when the tribal Council finally agreed to allow anthropologists and historians from outside to study the tribe closely enough to provide expert testimony. "Secrecy of religion" had been the Council's means of thwarting change and retaining power. Problems of white-Indian usage of terms such as "church" took long to clarify. To protect their religion, the Taos Pueblo were forced to reveal more of it than ever before. Primary sources; 6 notes.
G. J. Bobango

1719. Bowles, Dorothy. NEWSPAPER SUPPORT FOR FREE EXPRESSION IN TIMES OF ALARM, 1920 AND 1940. *Journalism Q. 1977 54(2): 271-279.* Editorials in large-city newspapers were generally supportive of freedom of expression during two periods of alarm in the United States; such support was not dependent on whether the threat directly affected the press, nor do the data indicate that newspaper support differed significantly across geographical areas.

1720. Furman, Necah Stewart. WOMEN'S CAMPAIGN FOR EQUALITY: A NATIONAL AND STATE PERSPECTIVE. *New Mexico Hist. Rev. 1978 53(4): 365-374.* Provides a view of the social and legal barriers to women's equality in New Mexico due to national and state legislation, and of the effects of Anglo culture on Indian and Mexican society.

1721. Geller, Gloria. THE WAR-TIME ELECTIONS ACT OF 1917 AND THE CANADIAN WOMEN'S MOVEMENT. *Atlantis [Canada] 1976 2(1): 88-106.* Describes the background of the Wartime Elections Act (Canada, 1917), which enfranchised Canadian women who were British subjects over 21 and had close relatives in the Canadian or British armed forces, and the meaning of the act for the Canadian women's movement.

1722. Hine, Darlene Clark. BLACKS AND THE DESTRUCTION OF THE DEMOCRATIC WHITE PRIMARY 1935-1944. *J. of Negro Hist. 1977 62(1): 43-59.* The adoption of the white primary by southern states in the 1890's became the most effective subterfuge to disenfranchise blacks. A 25-year legal struggle by the National Association for the Advancement of Colored People (NAACP) resulted in the victory of the Supreme Court decision in the case of *Smith* v. *Allwright* (US, 1944). 72 notes.
P. J. Taylorson

1723. Hine, Darlene Clark. THE ELUSIVE BALLOT: THE BLACK STRUGGLE AGAINST THE TEXAS DEMOCRATIC WHITE PRIMARY, 1932-1945. *Southwestern Hist. Q. 1978 81(4): 371-392.* After the Texas white primary law was ruled unconstitutional in *Nixon* v. *Herndon* (1927), the Texas Democratic Party tried every conceivable way of avoiding black voting in primaries. The state NAACP fought a losing battle against exclusion, as the Supreme Court allowed the party, but not the state, to impose a white primary: *Grovey* v. *Townshend* (1935). Nine years later the Court finally did outlaw a white primary under any pretext, in *Smith* v. *Allwright* (1944). Through this entire controversy, the state and national NAACP had led the campaign for black participation in Democratic politics. Primary and secondary sources; 49 notes.
J. H. Broussard

1724. Horn, Michiel. "FREE SPEECH WITHIN THE LAW": THE LETTER OF THE SIXTY-EIGHT TORONTO PROFESSORS, 1931. *Ontario Hist. [Canada] 1980 72(1): 27-48.* Notes that the "anti-Red" feeling in the 1920's and 30's led to confrontations with the Toronto police. Discusses the attitudes of the press, and argues that so long as only the Canadian Communist Party was subject to the consequences of confrontation, no one really cared. This changed when an interdenominational group associated with the University of Toronto was accused of running a disguised Communist meeting. This produced a public letter signed by 68 area professors, which produced much discussion. Reactions of the press to the letter and subsequent events are outlined. Similar events produced similar reactions elsewhere. Notes the long term effects. Based mainly on the contemporary press; 3 photos, 56 notes, appendix.
W. B. Whitham

1725. Lee, Carol F. THE ROAD TO ENFRANCHISEMENT: CHINESE AND JAPANESE IN BRITISH COLUMBIA. *BC Studies [Canada] 1976 (30): 44-76.* Traces the issue of Chinese and Japanese enfranchisement in British Columbia from 1935-49. Considers the events, trends, and concepts which finally eroded the long standing provincial hostility to Orientals. Enfranchisement symbolized a significant change in public attitudes and reflected a change in the prevailing conceptions of the nature of citizenship and political rights in Canada. 64 notes.
D. L. Smith

1726. Leff, Carol Skalnik and Leff, Mark H. THE POLITICS OF INEFFECTIVENESS: FEDERAL FIREARMS LEGISLATION, 1919-38. *Ann. of the Am. Acad. of Pol. and Social Sci. 1981 (455): 48-62.* Federal firearms legislation left a neutral legacy for future regulatory efforts. The 1927 statute barred handguns from the US postal system without closing off alternative shipping routes. The National Firearms Act of 1934 ultimately limited its registration provisions to "gangster" weapons, like machine guns. The more inclusive Federal Firearms Act of 1938 proved impossible to effectively enforce. The minimal impact of federal law was partially rooted in the low enforcement priorities of the Treasury Department and was in part attributable to the influence of a traditional individualist ethos hostile to the "civilizing" pretensions of federal intervention. In addition, antiregulation forces out-organized Justice Department regulators.
J/S

1727. McGovern, James R. HELEN HUNT WEST: FLORIDA'S PIONEER FOR ERA. *Florida Hist. Q. 1978 57(1): 39-53.* Helen Hunt West (1892-1964) in association with the National Women's Party, lectured and wrote on the need for an Equal Rights Amendment. Her major contribution to Florida politics was as a sponsor and supporter of a 1935 election law requiring equal participation by women at all levels of state party organization. A powerful lobbyist for the ERA in the US Congress during 1935-39, she eventually saw the endorsement of ERA by Republican and Democratic national conventions. Based mainly on the Helen Hunt West papers, Schlesinger Library; photo, 72 notes.
P. A. Beaber

1728. Nichols, John E. THE PRE-*TINKER* HISTORY OF FREEDOM OF STUDENT PRESS AND SPEECH. *Journalism Q. 1979 56(4): 727-733.* *Tinker* v. *Des Moines Community School District* (US, 1969) firmly established the right of free expression for public school and college students, but the *Blackwell* and *Burnside* cases of 1966 pointed the way toward that ruling. Both *Blackwell* and *Burnside* were decided on the basis of whether certain actions were disruptive to the educational process and could therefore be lawfully proscribed by school authorities. Previously, cases involving student expression had consistently ended with a ruling in favor of school authorities provided there was no evidence to indicate a lack of due process in the school's treatment of the student. Based on court records; 63 notes.
J. S. Coleman

1729. Prude, Jonathan. PORTRAIT OF A CIVIL LIBERTARIAN: THE FAITH AND FEAR OF ZECHARIAH CHAFEE, JR. *J. of Am. Hist. 1973 60(3): 633-656.* Chafee's dedication to freedom of speech stemmed from the xenophobia of the years after World War I. He believed he had found the rational limits of free speech in the "clear and present danger" test later propounded by Justice Holmes. A conservative, Chafee grounded his defense of free speech on its value in producing gradual social change and in alleviating otherwise festering tensions. The McCarthy hysteria of the 1950's undermined his faith in the basic rationality and tolerance of the American people and caused him temporarily to place unjustified hope in the courts to maintain civil liberties. His great contribution, in his 1941 classic *Free Speech in the United States* (New York: Atheneum Publishers, 1969), was to make people sensitive to the need for a continuous concern for free speech. 91 notes.

K. B. West

1730. Schwartz, Mildred A. CITIZENSHIP IN CANADA AND THE UNITED STATES. *Tr. of the Royal Soc. of Can. [Canada] 1976 14: 83-96.* Defines citizenship and compares attitudes in Canada and the United States concerning that status. Notes the efforts in Canada to pass a Citizenship Act and a Bill of Rights, and discusses the British tradition in Canada and the effect of the Citizenship Act on British subjects. Compares treatment of Japanese in the United States and Canada during World War II. 8 notes, biblio.

J. D. Neville

1731. Shankman, Arnold. A JURY OF HER PEERS: THE SOUTH CAROLINA WOMAN AND HER CAMPAIGN FOR JURY SERVICE. *South Carolina Hist. Mag. 1980 81(2): 102-121.* History of the struggle to allow women to serve on juries in South Carolina from 1921, when the state legislature granted women the right to vote eight months after the 19th Amendment was ratified, but excluded them from serving on juries, until 1967, when a state amendment on jury service for women was ratified.

1732. Simon, Rita James. THE AMERICAN JURY: INSTRUMENT OF JUSTICE OR OF PREJUDICE AND CONFORMITY? *Sociol. Inquiry [Canada] 1977 47(3-4): 254-293.* Examines jury decisions concerning First Amendment rights, 1940's-75, to assess whether juries truly block oppressive government and whether they reflect prejudice and ignorance.

1733. Slaughter, Sheila. THE DANGER ZONE: ACADEMIC FREEDOM AND CIVIL LIBERTIES. *Ann. of the Am. Acad. of Pol. and Social Sci. 1980 (448): 46-61.* This paper examines the way "corresponding rights and duties" surrounding academic freedom were negotiated between professional associations and organizations of university managers and trustees. The subject is approached through an analysis of the American Association of University Professors' (AAUP) major documents on academic freedom. In general terms it is argued that American academics, as intellectuals dependent on their employing institutions, have consistently sacrificed individuals and substantive principles in order to gain compliance for procedural safeguards from university officials for the profession as a whole. Restitution or reinstatement were not serious issues: the goal of the AAUP was a uniform personnel policy recognizing tenure. Even this goal was difficult to achieve. To win its acceptance, professors effectively traded civil liberties for job security.

J

1734. Trifiro, Luigi. UNE INTERVENTION À ROME DANS LA LUTTE POUR LE SUFFRAGE FÉMININ AU QUÉBEC (1922) [An appeal to Rome in the struggle for woman suffrage in Quebec (1922)]. *Rev. d'Hist. de l'Amérique Française [Canada] 1978 32(1): 1-18.* By 1922, Quebec was the only Canadian province that still denied women the right to vote. Facing strong opposition from the conservative Catholic hierarchy, a prosuffrage group launched a direct appeal to the Congress of the International Union of Catholic Women's Leagues in Rome. Despite a somewhat sympathetic hearing, the women of Quebec were refused the franchise for another 20 years. 48 notes.

M. R. Yerburgh

1735. Voisey, Paul. THE "VOTES FOR WOMEN" MOVEMENT. *Alberta Hist. 1975 23(3): 10-23.* Study of the suffrage movement in the Prairie Provinces, especially Manitoba. The movement began around the turn of the century, largely related to curtailing alcoholism, gambling, and prostitution. Leadership changed over the years, but Anglo-Saxon Protestant women dominated the movement. World War I brought many changes, as more women were employed, and the immigrant population rose considerably. Examines the power structures in the three provinces, their stakes in suffrage, and the eventual women's victory in 1916. 6 illus., 78 notes.

D. Chaput

1736. Wertheim, Larry M. NEDRICK YOUNG, ET AL. V. MPAA, ET AL.: THE FIGHT AGAINST THE HOLLYWOOD BLACKLIST. *Southern California Q. 1975 57(4): 383-418.* Traces the efforts to obtain an official judgment against the blacklisting of writers, actors, and directors by the motion picture industry. The famous Hollywood Ten actually included over 200 artists adversely affected by the Hollywood blacklist from 1948 until—for some—the 1970's. The litigation endured numerous obstacles, including lack of funds, the difficulty of proving the existence of an official blacklist, and adverse court decisions. Further hampering the effort was the view of some blacklisted writers such as Dalton Trumbo who held that everyone had suffered and that there could only be victims. Trumbo, disgusted with the legal maneuvering involved in the courts, called for individual rather than collective effort. The entire campaign was characterized by a lack of collective support, reluctance to reignite the controversy, and self-interest. The case, which began in 1960 with demands for $7.65 million in damages, was settled out of court in 1965 for $100,000. Suggests not only that Communists made no impression in Hollywood before 1947, but also that the blacklistees demonstrated a clear lack of radicalism in their efforts to reinstate themselves in the motion picture industry. Based on correspondence, documents, and other primary sources, and published records; 129 notes.

A. Hoffman

1737. —. WSPU DEPUTATION TO PRIME MINISTER BORDEN, 1912. *Atlantis [Canada] 1980 5(2): 188-195.* Brief introduction to woman suffrage activities in Canada and Great Britain during 1910-18, followed by a reprint of the account, first published in *The Champion*, a Canadian suffragist magazine, of the Women's Social and Political Union's meeting with Canadian Prime Minister Robert Laird Borden during his official visit to Britain in 1912.

Economic Reform

1738. Annunziata, Frank. THE NEW LEFT AND THE WELFARE STATE: THE REJECTION OF AMERICAN LIBERALISM. *Southern Q. 1976 15(1): 33-56.* Analyzes leftist political thinkers and philosophies during the 1930's-60's. Emphasizes New Deal legislation and the New Left demand for equality of result. 58 notes.

R. W. Dubay

1739. Arnold, Frank. HUMBERTO SILEX: CIO ORGANIZER FROM NICARAGUA. *Southwest Econ. and Soc. 1978 4(1): 3-20.* Humberto Silex (b. 1903) from 1937 to 1947 was an organizer for the International Union of Mine, Mill and Smelter Workers, CIO, out of El Paso, Texas; the federal government tried, but never was able to deport him for alleged Communist activities.

1740. Asher, Robert. JEWISH UNIONS AND THE AMERICAN FEDERATION OF LABOR POWER STRUCTURE 1903-1935. *Am. Jewish Hist. Q. 1976 65(3): 215-227.* Jewish unions, i.e., those with a substantial number of Jewish members and led by Jewish officers, until the 1930's were largely in, but not of, the mainstream of the American labor movement. Recognizing their differences with the AFL, the Jewish unions cooperated with the AFL when they could, but went their own way politically in their attempt to build a welfare state through union institutions and trade agreements with employers. By the late 1920's the Jewish unions, especially the International Ladies' Garment Workers' Union, had drifted slowly to the right and the American Federation of Labor had moved toward the left, so that the Amalgamated Clothing Workers of America could be admitted into the AFL, and the ILGWU could be allowed into the AFL power structure (executive council and resolutions committee). The accomplishments of the New Deal Democratic Party accelerated this process. 23 notes.

F. Rosenthal

1741. Babcock, Robert. SAMUEL GOMPERS AND THE FRENCH-CANADIAN WORKER, 1900-1914. *Am. Rev. of Can. Studies 1973 3(2): 47-66.* Discusses Samuel Gompers and the American Federation of Labor's policy toward trade unions and the organization of the working class in Quebec 1900-14.

1742. Baum, Gregory. THE RELEVANCE OF THE ANTIGONISH MOVEMENT TODAY. *J. of Can. Studies [Canada] 1980 15(1): 110-117.* The Antigonish Movement was a radical cooperatist response to severe economic problems in eastern Nova Scotia in the 1930's. Moses Coady exercised an extraordinary leadership in the movement through his critiques of capitalism which stressed its faulty foundations that stripped people of control of the means of production and consumption. The movement's main activity was adult education designed to assist people to devise cooperative ventures. It aimed at the transformation of consciousness and was profoundly spiritual in character. Its failure was due to its inadequate critique of capitalism which led to cooptation by the existing social order and its refusal to ally itself with socialism.

R. S. Fortner

1743. Beauchamp, Claude. LES DÉBUTS DE LA COOPÉRATION ET DU SYNDICALISME AGRICOLES, 1900-1930: QUELQUES ÉLÉMENTS DE LA PRATIQUE [The beginnings of farmer cooperatives and unions, 1900-30: a few elements of their existence]. *Recherches Sociographiques [Canada] 1979 20(3): 337-381.* The dominant ideology of the day called for the preservation of the agricultural character of Quebec by making farming more economically interesting. To do this, collective action, either through cooperatives or unions, appeared to be the only reasonable solution. A survey of the early organizations indicates, however, that their existence was precarious and that they attracted few and fluctuating numbers. This can be attributed to the nature of agriculture practiced in the province and the highly independent mentality of its farmers. Based on the records of several of these organizations, on Quebec Department of Agriculture documents, and on published works of early farmer spokesmen; 9 tables, 177 notes. A. E. LeBlanc

1744. Bellamy, Donnie D. HENRY A. HUNT AND BLACK AGRICULTURAL LEADERSHIP IN THE NEW SOUTH. *J. of Negro Hist. 1975 60(4): 464-479.* Discusses the achievements of Henry Alexander Hunt during 1890-1938 in instituting and promoting programs of social change and economic reform among the black farmers of North Carolina and Georgia, in particular his foundation of the Forth Valley High Industrial School. Apart from introducing farmers to the notion of scientific farming, Hunt was successful in persuading them to join credit unions to buy their own land, in making them aware of government loan programs, and in establishing the Flint River farms in Macon County, Georgia, a farm cooperative. 49 notes. C. A. McNeill

1745. Bercuson, David Jay. LABOUR RADICALISM AND THE WESTERN INDUSTRIAL FRONTIER: 1897-1919. *Can. Hist. Rev. [Canada] 1977 58(2): 154-175.* The frontier has been called the great leveller, but the industrial frontier in Canada was the main stimulus in the development of class consciousness and radical working-class attitudes in the Canadian west.

1746. Bercuson, David Jay. WESTERN LABOUR RADICALISM AND THE ONE BIG UNION: MYTHS AND REALITIES. *J. of Can. Studies 1974 9(2): 3-11.* Western labor radicals adopted socialist political action and industrial unionism. The One Big Union (O.B.U.) was not an industrial union and its leaders tried to discourage labor parliamentary activity. It was a tangential movement rather than a child of western labor radicalism. Based on Public Archives of Canada and of Manitoba, departmental reports, union proceedings, newspapers, secondary works; 51 notes. G. E. Panting

1747. Berney, Barbara. THE RISE AND FALL OF THE UMW FUND. *Southern Exposure 1978 6(2): 95-102.* The United Mine Workers of America Health and Retirement Fund, created in 1946, was one of the most innovative health care delivery systems in America. Beginning with a royalty of five cents per ton of coal mined, which was later raised to 40 cents per ton, the Fund collected revenues from mine operators which were used to establish a series of hospitals in the coal regions and partially to subsidize health clinics and rehabilitation services for disabled miners. The decline of the coal industry during 1950's-early 1960's caused a revenue decline resulting in the sale of the hospitals in 1962. Incompetent and even criminal mismanagement of the Fund under the leadership of Anthony Boyle created further problems of revenue flow. Under the 1977 contract the burden of health insurance was shifted to the coal operators, with miners having to pay part of the cost to subsidize health clinics. N. Lederer

1748. Betke, Carl. THE UFA: VISIONS OF A COOPERATIVE COMMONWEALTH. *Alberta Hist. [Canada] 1979 27(3): 7-14.* In the early 1930's, the agrarian leadership in Alberta supported the Cooperative Commonwealth Federation based on the nationalization of land. Leaders in this plan were United Farmers of Alberta Premier John E. Brownlee and Norman F. Priestley, head of the provincial UFA. By 1933 it became clear that the land program had no widespread support, so a compromise was reached: nationalization of some of the already publicly-owned land was recommended. Furthermore, voters, and UFA members, seemed more interested in monetary reform—the bases of UFA power was "social credit"—than in land reform. Based primarily on UFA Papers, Glenbow Alberta Institute Archives; 3 illus. D. Chaput

1749. Borisiuk, V. I. OT ZAKONA VAGNERA K ZAKONU TAFTA-KHARTLI: POVOROT K REAKTSII V TRUDOVOM ZAKONODATEL'STVE SSHA (1935-1947 GG.) [From the Wagner Act to the Taft-Hartley Act: the shift to reactionary labor legislation in the United States, 1935-47]. *Vestnik Moskovskogo U., Seriia 9: Istoriia [USSR] 1971 26(5): 15-31.* The Wagner Act (US, 1935), considered the most radical piece of labor legislation of the New Deal, generated sharp opposition from the right, manufacturers, and capital, and from their representatives in Congress. At first they sought to prove it unconstitutional; failing this they tried to amend it. They called the power of unions "un-American." During World War II there was a reactionary shift under the guise of protecting the war effort. After the war, with controls lifted, the number of strikes increased sharply. This set the stage for the victory of the right, the Taft-Hartley Act (US, 1947), which strictly regulated union activities. Based on published sources; 67 notes.

G. E. Munro

1750. Born, Kate. MEMPHIS NEGRO WORKINGMEN AND THE NAACP. *West Tennessee Hist. Soc. Papers 1974 (28): 90-107.* The Memphis chapter of the NAACP was a major influence in the attempt to raise the economic and social status of the Negro, and a consistent force in active legal protest against injustices to blacks. In 1900 almost half of Memphis' population was black. Negroes successfully operated businesses and were in all crafts and unions. The Jim Crow laws of 1905 changed this and caused the social and economic regression of the Memphis Negro until 1937. Only the NAACP stood as an advocate for the black workingman. Based on primary sources, with emphasis on the Walter F. White papers; 88 notes. H. M. Parker, Jr.

1751. Brandes, Joseph. FROM SWEATSHOP TO STABILITY: JEWISH LABOR BETWEEN TWO WORLD WARS. *Yivo Ann. of Jewish Social Sci. 1976 (16): 1-149.* Traces the growth of the Jewish labor movement from its inception, with particular emphasis on the period between World War I and World War II. Stresses the uniqueness of the Jewish labor movement and puts particular emphasis on the growth of the Jewish labor movement within the garment industry. Describes the roles of such notable labor leaders as David Dubinsky and Sidney Hillquit. Particular stress is put on the International Ladies' Garment Workers' and the United Hebrew Trades' role in the development of Jewish labor in the 1920's-30's. R. J. Wechman

1752. Brown, Lorne. PEACE AND HARMONY: BREAKING DOWN MYTHS OF CANADIAN LABOR HISTORY. *Can. Dimension 1973 9(5): 11-14.* Summarizes labor history in Canada over the last 50 years. Concentrates on violent incidents to depict inevitable violence in strikes. Includes a long interview with one of the leaders of the 1919 Winnipeg General Strike. Defends the more radical strike leaders and denigrates employers, nonstrikers, moderates, and the public. Summarizes a federal committee's report. 25 photos. W. B. Whitham

1753. Buhle, Paul. ITALIAN-AMERICAN RADICALS AND LABOR IN RHODE ISLAND, 1905-1930. *Radical Hist. Rev. 1978 (17): 121-151.*

1754. Comeau, Robert. LA CANADIAN SEAMEN'S UNION (1936-1949): UN CHAPITRE DE L'HISTOIRE DU MOUVEMENT OUVRIER CANADIEN [The Canadian Seamen's Union, 1936-49: a chapter in the history of the Canadian labor movement]. *Rev. d'Hist. de l'Amérique Française [Canada] 1976 29(4): 503-538.* During the depression period of the 1930's and the decade of the 1940's, the Canadian Seamen's Union contributed to the growth of Canadian syndicalism. Its activities illustrated the inherent polarization among militant workers who wanted to improve working conditions in the face of collusion among the shipowners, the federal government, and the corrupt directors of an international union. Discusses the important role of the militant Communists. Based on journals, newspapers, and published monographs; 73 notes. L. B. Chan

1755. Corbin, David A. "FRANK KEENEY IS OUR LEADER, AND WE SHALL NOT BE MOVED": RANK-AND-FILE LEADERSHIP IN THE WEST VIRGINIA COAL FIELDS. Fink, Gary M. and Reed, Merl E., eds. *Essays in Southern Labor History: Selected Papers, Southern Labor History Conference, 1976.* (Westport, Conn.; London, England: Greenwood Pr., 1977): 144-156. A study of the career of Frank Keeney as a labor leader in the West Virginia coal fields. His career in the United Mine Workers of America began in 1912. In 1916 he led a "rump" organization and was elected president. He forced investigation and correction of corruption among local union district leaders. He was convinced of the importance and value of indigenous leadership and acted accordingly. His independence alienated him from UMW leaders, including John L. Lewis. In 1931 his last important move, the organization of an independent union and the calling of a strike, was a failure and resulted in his ostracism by the UMW. 49 notes.
R. V. Ritter

1756. Daniel, Cletus E. RADICALS ON THE FARM IN CALIFORNIA. *Agric. Hist. 1975 49(4): 629-645.* Attempted radical union organization of California's agricultural workers in the 20th century has fallen into two distinct phases. The first such attempt, from 1909 to 1917, was by the Industrial Workers of the World (IWW). The second attempt at the organization of California's agricultural labor was by the Communist-controlled Cannery and Agricultural Workers Industrial Union during the Depression years. Members of both movements attempted to radically alter the farm workers' philosophy but failed to realize that the farm worker desires first and foremost an improvement in his lifestyle. Based on primary and secondary sources; 38 notes.
R. T. Fulton

1757. Dirks, Patricia. DR. PHILIPPE HAMEL AND THE PUBLIC POWER MOVEMENT IN QUEBEC CITY, 1929-1934: THE FAILURE OF A CRUSADE. *Urban Hist. Rev. [Canada] 1981 10(1): 17-29.* The fight over municipalization of electrical services in Quebec City waged between 1929 and 1934 grew out of the determination of a prominent dentist, Dr. Philippe Hamel, to rescue his fellow citizens from the grip of the electricity trust, the Quebec Power Company. Hamel's involvement in the French-Canadian nationalist movement and his association with L'École Sociale Populaire during the 1930's added a unique dimension to the attack he led against the electricity trust in Quebec City. The crusading nature of his drive to secure government-run competition in the electricity field proved to be an effective weapon in the hands of Quebec Power and its allies and thus contributed to the failure of the public power movement spearheaded by Hamel in Quebec City in these years.
J/S

1758. Faucher, Albert. SYNDICALISME ET COOPÉRATION DANS L'AGRICULTURE QUÉBÉCOISE [Syndicalism and cooperatives in Quebec agriculture]. *Tr. of the Royal Soc. of Can. [Canada] 1979 17: 17-30.* Compares the activities of two complementary organizations, the professional and cooperative associations, in their attempts to ameliorate social conditions in Quebec. The author notes the traditional conflict between such groups in both Canada and the United States. Based on government documents and some secondary sources; 22 notes.
J. D. Neville

1759. Feldberg, Roslyn L. "UNION FEVER": ORGANIZING AMONG CLERICAL WORKERS, 1900-1930. *Radical Am. 1980 14(3): 53-70.* As recently as 1977 only 8.2% of the clerical workers in the United States were organized. Among women, the proportion was even lower. In a period when clerical workers were not considered real workers, (because they were clerical), and not considered organizable (because they were women), difficulties were pervasive. Women moved into stenographic and typing positions during the 1890's. The job was gradually redefined. It lost its status as a career entry point for men. Collective efforts by women workers to form unions emerged many times during 1900-29. Scattered offices, close ties with employers, social views of women's role, and labor movement indifference all accounted for the difficulties in major victories. The more positive work of the Women's Trade Union League is traced. 52 notes.
C. M. Hough

1760. Fink, Gary M. THE REJECTION OF VOLUNTARISM. *Industrial and Labor Relations R. 1973 26(2): 805-819.* "'Voluntarism' is a term used to describe the philosophy said to characterize American unionism prior to the New Deal era under which the labor movement committed itself to work within the laissez-faire capitalist economy, relying on its economic power to protect and promote the interests of workers and rejecting government aid and intervention. Examination of the actual response of unions to proposed legislation to establish workmen's compensation, unemployment insurance, and so forth reveals, however, sharp divergence in behavior at the national and local levels. While national union officials rigidly opposed such government measures to assist workers, local officers and members strongly supported them. In rejecting the philosophy of voluntarism, local labor was much closer to the immediate economic and political realities of working class America."
J

1761. Fogelson, Nancy. THEY PAVED THE STREETS WITH SILK: PATERSON, NEW JERSEY SILK WORKERS, 1913-1924. *New Jersey Hist. 1979 97(3): 133-148.* In 1913, Paterson silk workers staged one of a long series of strikes that culminated in 1924 with a violent outbreak that received extensive coverage in New York newspapers. During this decade, laborers in the silk industry were unable to secure beneficial changes for themselves because so many of their number left to form their own businesses and because mill owners deserted the city in search of cheap labor available elsewhere in abundance. In addition, management did not modernize machinery or production systems, but relied on antiquated business practices that eventually led to the death of the industry in Paterson. Based on interviews, contemporary newspaper accounts, ACLU papers, and secondary sources; 3 illus., 46 notes.
E. R. McKinstry

1762. Fordham, Monroe. THE BUFFALO COOPERATIVE ECONOMIC SOCIETY, INC., 1928-1961: A BLACK SELF-HELP ORGANIZATION. *Niagara Frontier 1976 23(2): 41-49.* Discusses the Negro-owned Buffalo Cooperative Economic Society, Inc., in Buffalo, New York, 1928-61, emphasizing the role of founder Dr. Ezekiel E. Nelson.

1763. Freeman, Richard B. DECLINE OF LABOR MARKET DISCRIMINATION AND ECONOMIC ANALYSIS. *Am. Econ. R. 1973 63(2): 280-286.* Examines the changes in labor market discrimination against Negroes between 1890 and 1970.

1764. Friesen, Gerald. 'YOURS IN REVOLT': REGIONALISM, SOCIALISM AND THE WESTERN CANADIAN LABOUR MOVEMENT. *Labour [Canada] 1976 1: 139-157.* Two decades of worker militancy in western Canada culminated in 1919 with secessions from the American Federation of Labor and the Trades and Labour Congress of Canada, the establishment of One Big Union, and strikes from Winnipeg westward. Responsible for the formation of the regional labor organization, leaders of the Socialist Party of Canada saw in the strength of western consciousness the means to labor reform and possible revolution. Committed to constitutional means until the "day of revolution," they did not intend the strikes to inaugurate an overthrow of the government. Primary and secondary sources; 58 notes.
W. A. Kearns

1765. Gagnon, Gabriel. POPULISME ET PROGRÈS: LES CRÉDITISTES QUÉBÉCOIS [Populism and progress: The Quebec creditistes]. *Recherches sociographiques [Canada] 1976 17(1): 23-34.* Discusses recent interpretations of the rise of Social Credit in the Province of Quebec. Suggests that the Social Credit movement cannot be easily identified as belonging either to the right or the left. It was made up of small farmers and industrial workers affected by the expansion phase of monopolistic capitalist production, and their protests necessarily were expressed differently. 22 notes.
A. E. LeBlanc

1766. Gerber, Ellen. THE CONTROLLED DEVELOPMENT OF COLLEGIATE SPORT FOR WOMEN, 1923-1936. *J. of Sport Hist. 1975 2(1): 1-28.* Traces the development of collegiate sports for women, 1890-1936. In 1923 a national philosophy was articulated as a result of the attempt by the Amateur Athletic Union to take over women's track and field. Women physical educators asserting their own authority outlined the educational, moral, and social implications of the union and influenced the final decision. The play day form of competition was invented to implement the philosophy and by 1936 nearly all colleges engaged in intercollegiate competition. 2 illus., 89 notes.
M. Kaufman

1767. Gerstle, Gary. THE MOBILIZATION OF THE WORKING CLASS COMMUNITY: THE INDEPENDENT TEXTILE UNION IN WOONSOCKET, 1931-1946. *Radical Hist. Rev. 1978 (17): 161-172.* Gives the history and purpose of the Independent Textile Workers, an industrial trade union founded in 1931 by Belgians in Woonsocket, Rhode Island; during 1934-43 they organized Woonsocket's French-Canadian workers.

1768. Grossman, Jonathan. FAIR LABOR STANDARDS ACT: MAXIMUM STRUGGLE FOR A MINIMUM WAGE. *Monthly Labor Rev. 1978 101(6): 22-30.* The Fair Labor Standards Act (1938) guaranteed a minimum wage and a maximum number of working hours a week; chronicles amendments during 1949-77.

1769. Guth, James L. THE NATIONAL BOARD OF FARM ORGANIZATIONS: EXPERIMENT IN POLITICAL COOPERATION. *Agric. Hist. 1974 48(3): 418-440.* During its active existence from 1917-1927 the National Board of Farm Organizations coordinated the legislative work of several important farm groups and prominent rural leaders, prepared the way for the achievements of the Congressional farm bloc, and at one point, came close to attaining the status of a true "peak association." On 20 July 1917 several farm leaders created the Board, encompassing the National Farmers Union, the National Conference on Marketing and Farm Credits, the National Agricultural Organization Society, the Pennsylvania Rural Progress Association, the National Council of Farmers' Cooperative Associations, the Farmers National Congress, the dairy interests, the National Dairy Union, and the National Milk Producers Federation. The Board failed because of an unsympathetic administration and internal disagreements. Based on primary and secondary sources; 55 notes. R. T. Fulton

1770. Hield, Melissa. "UNION-MINDED": WOMEN IN THE TEXAS ILGWU, 1933-1950. *Frontiers 1979 4(2): 59-70.* Details the prounion struggles of black, Mexican American, and Anglo women in the Texas garment industry during 1933-50, based on interviews with eight women then active in the International Ladies' Garment Workers' Union.

1771. Horn, Michiel. LEONARD MARSH AND THE COMING OF A WELFARE STATE IN CANADA: A REVIEW ARTICLE. *Social Hist. [Canada] 1976 9(17): 197-204.* Reprints Leonard Marsh's *Report on Social Security for Canada* (1943) and discusses his career. He pioneered social welfare research in Canada during the 1930's, and in the 1940's he became one of the main designers of the slowly developing Canadian welfare state. Marsh was strongly influenced by Fabianism and was active in the League for Social Reconstruction which stood for a reformist and constitutionalist socialism committed to thorough-going changes in the distribution of income, wealth, and power. Secondary sources; 27 notes. W. K. Hobson

1772. Hornbein, Marjorie. JOSEPHINE ROCHE: SOCIAL WORKER AND COAL OPERATOR. *Colorado Mag. 1976 53(3): 243-260.* Sketches the life of Josephine Roche and emphasizes her labor reforms when she headed the Rocky Mountain Fuel Company. She was a classmate and friend of Francis Perkins, Denver's first policewoman, Franklin D. Roosevelt's Assistant Secretary of the Treasury and Administrator of the National Youth Administration, and a long-time United Mine Workers executive. Primary and secondary sources; 5 illus., 58 notes. O. H. Zabel

1773. Jenkins, J. Craig and Perrow, Charles. INSURGENCY OF THE POWERLESS: FARM WORKER MOVEMENTS (1946-1972). *Am. Sociol. Rev. 1977 42(2): 249-268.* Drawing on the perspective developed in recent work by Oberschall (1973), Tilly (1975) and Gamson (1975), authors analyze the political process centered around farm worker insurgencies. Comparing the experience of two challenges, they argue that the factors favored in the classical social movement literature fail to account for either the rise or outcome of insurgency. Instead, the important variables pertain to social resources—in this case, sponsorship by established organizations. Farm workers themselves are powerless; as an excluded group, their demands tend to be systematically ignored. But powerlessness may be overridden if the national political elite is neutralized and members of the polity contribute resources and attack insurgent targets. To test the argument, entries in the *New York Times Annual Index* are content coded and statistically analyzed, demonstrating how the political environment surrounding insurgent efforts alternatively contains them or makes them successful. J

1774. Kurland, Philip B. THE JUDICIAL ROAD TO SOCIAL WELFARE. *Social Service R. 1974 48(4): 481-493.* The role of the judiciary in public welfare "has been and will probably continue to be, limited to ensuring that social welfare legislation is fairly interpreted and applied." S

1775. Lapointe, Michelle. LE SYNDICAT CATHOLIQUE DES ALLUMETTIÈRES DE HULL, 1919-1924 [The Catholic matchmakers' union in Hull, 1919-24]. *Rev. d'Hist. de l'Amérique Française [Canada] 1979 32(4): 603-628.* Analysis of the matchmakers' union in Hull, Quebec, enables the researcher to develop much-needed perspective on the female Catholic workers' movement. It was a vigorous union; membership was impressive. Two strike actions were conducted in a very conservative milieu. The union played an important role in raising the consciousness of its membership and in ensuring, on a modest scale, that the needs of female workers in Canada would receive additional attention in years to come. 40 notes. M. R. Yerburgh

1776. Leman, Christopher. PATTERNS OF POLICY DEVELOPMENT: SOCIAL SECURITY IN THE UNITED STATES AND CANADA. *Public Policy 1977 25(2): 261-291.* Presents a comparative analysis of the development of social security systems in the United States and Canada. Utilizing brief histories of the evolution of social security in both nations and tracing modifications of the original systems to the present, offers explanations of how and why the two systems differ. Canada's social security systems grew out of a political process which has forced accommodation because of the nature of provincial-federal relationships. Canada has thus developed a social security system financed by contributions and out of the federal treasury. In the United States, the program has been financed entirely out of contributions. This has led to speculation about the long-range viability of the US social security system. The varying responses of both countries to political crises are studied as part of the contexts within which social security programs emerged. Primary and secondary sources; 5 notes, biblio. J. M. Herrick

1777. Leotta, Louis. ABRAHAM EPSTEIN AND THE MOVEMENT FOR OLD AGE SECURITY. *Labor Hist. 1975 16(3): 359-377.* Examines the activities of voluntary associations which promoted state old-age pension systems from 1920-35. Abraham Epstein, an important architect of old-age pension legislation, pressed for legislation through his positions with the Fraternal Order of the Eagles and then in the American Association for Old Age Security. The struggle kept the idea alive and provided part of the climate of opinion for its adoption in 1935. Based on records of the AAOAS, F.O.E. publications, and legislative records; 46 notes. L. L. Athey

1778. Lévesque, Andrée. LE QUÉBEC ET LE MONDE COMMUNISTE: COWANSVILLE 1931 [Quebec and the Communist world: Cowansville, 1931]. *Rev. d'Hist. de L'Amérique Française [Canada] 1980 34(2): 171-182.* A strike of 99 silk-workers in Cowansville in 1931 was marked by the unusual presence of several Communist organizers from Montreal and Toronto. Pressure from the Church convinced the strikers to return to work, however, and the Communist initiative left no effects. Based on Royal Commission inquiry papers, Communist Party records, and Ontario archives; 38 notes. R. Aldrich

1779. Lewis, David L. FORD AND KAHN. *Michigan Hist. 1980 64(5): 17-28.* Albert Kahn was one of the first architects to associate himself with the design of factories. Following closely the specifications of Henry Ford, Kahn innovatively designed many factories that combined aesthetic qualities with functionalism for the Ford Motor Company. 26 illus. L. E. Ziewacz

1780. MacPherson, Ian. AN AUTHORITATIVE VOICE: THE REORIENTATION OF THE CANADIAN FARMERS' MOVEMENT, 1935 TO 1945. *Hist. Papers [Canada] 1979: 164-181.* Against the background of the Depression, drought on the prairies, government ambivalence, and traditional regional, practical, philosophical, personal, and ethnic differences, the Canadian Chamber of Agriculture was founded in 1935 to promote rationalization of the marketing system for agricultural products so that farmers could receive fair and stable prices.

By 1945 Canadian agriculture was well organized and working productively within the political system; it had abandoned its traditional laissez-faire attitudes, was dealing effectively with rural social problems, and had developed a viable long-range program and marketing system. George Hoadley, P. M. Dewan, Herb Hannam, W. E. Haskins, and George Coote were among the leaders and organizers of the movement. 65 notes. French summary. S

1781. Majka, Linda C. LABOR MILITANCY AMONG FARM WORKERS AND THE STRATEGY OF PROTEST: 1900-1979. *Social Problems 1981 28(5): 533-547.* Describes the use of Japanese workers and labor militancy during 1900-15, the career of the Industrial Workers of the World during 1913-20, the depression-era militancy of Mexican, Asian and white agricultural laborers, and the successful organization of the United Farm Workers in the 1960's and 70's, primarily among Chicanos, Mexicans, and Filipinos.

1782. Makahonuk, Glen. TRADE UNIONS IN THE SASKATCHEWAN COAL INDUSTRY, 1907-1945. *Saskatchewan Hist. [Canada] 1978 31(2): 51-68.* The United Mine Workers of America, District 18, was organized in 1903. By 1907 it was active in Saskatchewan. The first strike occurred in 1908 and was considered marginally successful when only one large company recognized the union. A large, serious attempt at unionization was not mounted until the One Big Union (OBU) of 1919. This too was only temporarily successful. In 1931 the Mine Workers Union of Canada (MWUC) under J. Sloan made a more determined attempt. While not totally successful, it brought unionization much closer than ever before. Details numerous attempts to organize from 1931 to the Trade Union Act (1944), which finally made unionization possible in the mines of western Canada. 3 photos, 90 notes. C. H. Held

1783. Marden, David. FORGOTTEN BUT NOT GONE: A CASE STUDY IN THE PERSISTENCE OF REFORM. *Phylon 1974 35(1): 108-119.* Compares the Navajo-Hopi Long Range Rehabilitation Act of 1950 and the War on Poverty of the 1960's. Shows a lack of continuity between the two programs though the assumptions behind each had similarities. "Policy makers missed a chance to use the Navajo experience with the Long Range Act as what John Collier liked to call an experiment in ethnic relations." Both programs demonstrated a similar emphasis on youth. Previous proposals need to be examined as a start toward avoiding the repetition of mistakes. 45 notes. E. P. Stickney

1784. Markowitz, Gerald E. and Rosner, David. DOCTORS IN CRISIS: A STUDY OF THE USE OF MEDICAL EDUCATION REFORM TO ESTABLISH MODERN PROFESSIONAL ELITISM IN MEDICINE. *Am. Q. 1973 25(1): 83-107.* The conservatism of the modern American medical profession can be traced to the Progressive era's efforts to modernize and reform medical education. Doctors sought reorganization and reform to improve their social status, to consolidate education in university-medical school complexes, to restrict competition, and to oppose group practice and publicly financed medical care. They thereby institutionalized a two-class system which concentrated power in a small elite with little attention to public needs. 72 notes.
W. D. Piersen

1785. Mbatia, O. L. E. THE ECONOMIC EFFECTS OF FAIR EMPLOYMENT LAWS ON OCCUPATIONS: THE APPLICATION OF INFORMATION THEORY TO EVALUATE PROGRESS OF BLACK AMERICANS, 1954-1972. *J. of Black Studies 1978 8(3): 259-278.* Uses patterns of occupational distribution to measure black Americans' economic progress during 1954-72. Concepts of information theory, especially indices of racial entropy and empirical regression analysis, are more useful in understanding minority employment patterns than are numbers or percentages of persons employed. Most Negroes remain in unskilled or semiskilled occupations, but they did make economic progress, 1954-72, decreasing their representation in unskilled jobs and increasing their share in professional and managerial occupations. Fair Employment Practices "laws have a long way to go before they can effectively deal with racist employment practices." Based on published government documents and secondary sources; 4 tables, 11 notes, biblio.
R. G. Sherer

1786. McCormack, A. Ross. THE INDUSTRIAL WORKERS OF THE WORLD IN WESTERN CANADA: 1905-1914. *Can. Hist. Assoc. Hist. Papers [Canada] 1975: 167-190.* Assesses the contribution of the Industrial Workers of the World (IWW) to the radical tradition. In a continental and regional setting the IWW organized unskilled, itinerant, ethnically heterogeneous, and nonpolitical workers outside the classic labor movement. This situation led to friction with the American Federation of Labor, the Trades and Labour Congress of Canada, and the Socialist Party of Canada. Although it sought immediate improvements for workers, the IWW stood for sabotage and the general strike as weapons to defeat capitalism. Based on Frontier College Papers in the Public Archives of Canada, Public Records in the Public Archives of British Columbia, union proceedings, and secondary sources; 119 notes.
G. E. Panting

1787. McQuaid, Kim. AN AMERICAN OWENITE: EDWARD A. FILENE AND THE PARAMETERS OF INDUSTRIAL REFORM, 1890-1937. *Am. J. of Econ. and Sociol. 1976 35(1): 77-94.* Edward A. Filene introduced industrial democracy in his Boston department store in 1891. He was deposed from the presidency of the store in 1928. His experiment ceased and thereafter he was denied any effective authority. He also directed his liberal energies to local, state, and national affairs such as his ambitious plan of urban reform, "Boston 1915." Such efforts were equally unsuccessful. He was a spokesman for the New Capitalism and a supporter of the New Deal, but in both movements his integrity isolated him from his peers. His enduring contributions were the cooperative and credit union movements. P. Travis

1788. McQuaid, Kim. CORPORATE LIBERALISM IN THE AMERICAN BUSINESS COMMUNITY, 1920-1940. *Business Hist. Rev. 1978 52(3): 342-368.* Traces the activities of "corporate liberals," businessmen who favored an enlightened partnership among themselves, government, and organized labor, from World War I through the Great Depression. Disappointed with the abrupt ending of Wilson's wartime economic planning agencies, they turned to programs of welfare capitalism, efficiency, and employee representation plans. The presentation of the Swope Plan, authored by General Electric's Gerard Swope, signalled a new impetus for corporate liberalism in the early 1930's, which then promptly went into decline in the latter half of the decade. The coming of World War II, however, provided a fresh opportunity for the corporate liberals who flocked into the new war production agencies and gained renewed influence. Archival materials and government records; 47 notes.
C. J. Pusateri

1789. McQuaid, Kim. INDUSTRY AND THE CO-OPERATIVE COMMONWEALTH: WILLIAM P. HAPGOOD AND THE COLUMBIA CONSERVE COMPANY, 1917-1943. *Labor Hist. 1976 17(4): 510-529.* Assesses the efforts of William P. Hapgood (1872-1960) to establish a cooperative commonwealth between workers and management in the Columbia Conserve Company of Indianapolis. Inspired by ideas of a worker-controlled, industrial democracy, Hapgood initiated many reforms, but he was unable to successfully influence the direction of employees. The experiment ended in 1943. Based upon Hapgood publications and secondary sources; 27 notes. L. L. Athey

1790. Mergen, Bernard. "ANOTHER GREAT PRIZE": THE JEWISH LABOR MOVEMENT IN THE CONTEXT OF AMERICAN LABOR HISTORY. *Yivo Ann. of Jewish Social Sci. 1976 (16): 394-423.* Emphasizes the uniqueness of the American Jewish labor movement within the context of American labor history. Shows the various relationships between the Jewish labor movement and the American labor movement, demonstrating similarities, differences, and influences.
R. J. Wechman

1791. Mills, Allen. SINGLE TAX, SOCIALISM AND THE INDEPENDENT LABOUR PARTY OF MANITOBA: THE POLITICAL IDEAS OF F. J. DIXON AND S. J. FARMER. *Labour [Canada] 1980 5(Spr): 33-56.* The Independent Labour Party (ILP) of Manitoba was established in November 1920, mainly through the efforts of two English immigrants, Frederick John Dixon and S. J. Farmer. Dixon was the ILP's first provincial house leader and Farmer was an ILPMLA from 1922 to 1949, as well as being mayor of Winnipeg in 1923 and 1924. In their early years in Winnipeg both of them were strong supporters of Henry George's single tax doctrine and militant antisocialists. Analyzes the political ideas of Dixon and Farmer and explores the influence of their Georgeite world view on the outlook of the early ILP. J/S

1792. Nolan, Dennis R. and Jonas, Donald E. TEXTILE UNIONISM IN THE PIEDMONT, 1901-1932. Fink, Gary M. and Reed, Merl E., eds. *Essays in Southern Labor History: Selected Papers, Southern Labor History Conference, 1976.* (Westport, Conn.; London, England: Greenwood Pr., 1977): 48-79. A study designed to round out the argument previously developed which attributes to outside forces the failure of the textile unions to form stable local organizations and negotiate improvements in wages and working conditions. The workers and unions also brought on problems themselves, by "rash and poorly planned strikes, internal feuds, poor leadership, and the failure of interested groups to provide financial aid." The textile industry in the Piedmont Plateau is the locale for the study. Whatever the strength of outside forces, the workers and their organizations often were their own worst enemies. 75 notes.
R. V. Ritter

1793. Oh, John C. H. THE PRESIDENCY AND PUBLIC WELFARE POLICY. *Presidential Studies Q. 1978 8(4): 377-390.* A President's policy effectiveness depends on 1) widespread perception of a crisis, 2) public perception of the President's philosophy and commitment, 3) the public's understanding of the proposed policy, and 4) an effective relationship with Congress. These elements are reviewed in the context of presidents' welfare policy since 1933, including Roosevelt's Aid to Dependent Children (ADC), Truman's Aid to Families with Dependent Children (AFDC), the Kennedy-Johnson War on Poverty and "self-help" services strategy, and Nixon's Family Assistance Plan (FAP). Concludes that the outlook for Carter's welfare reform package is not good. 2 tables, 44 notes.
S. C. Strom

1794. Paradis, Ruth. ESDRAS MINVILLE ET LA PENSÉE COOPÉRATIVE IDÉOLOGIQUE AU QUÉBEC [Esdras Minville and ideological cooperative thought in Quebec]. *Action Natl. [Canada] 1979 69(2): 107-115.* While the Quebec cooperative movement began its greatest expansion in 1937, Esdras Minville had written of cooperatism as early as 1924, noting its success in England and Denmark. Minville was an activist as well as ideologist for the movement, having founded the first cooperative workshop in the Gaspé region. Reproaching French Canadians for their individualistic spirit, he used his positions as president of the Action Nationale, director of the École des Hautes Études, and editor of *L'Actualité Économique* to popularize the work of Lionel Groulx, Georges-Henri Lévesque, and Alphonse Desjardins. 18 notes.
A. W. Novitsky

1795. Paradis, Ruth. LA PENSÉE COOPÉRATIVE DE ESDRAS MINVILLE DE 1924 À 1943 [The cooperative thought of Esdras Minville from 1924 to 1943]. *Action Natl. [Canada] 1980 69(7): 518-526.* Esdras Minville first wrote of the cooperative movement in "Le capital étranger," *Action française* (June 1924). From then until 1943, he often wrote of the movement in foreign lands and even listed professional associations in "Agir pour vivre," *Actualité économique* (February 1930). He considered the system viable, analyzed it rigorously, participated in the creation of Quebec's first foresters' cooperative in the Gaspé, and attributed the slowness of the movement's development in Quebec to the French Canadian assimilation of American individualism. 12 notes.
A. W. Novitsky

1796. Powell, T. J. D. NORTHERN SETTLEMENT, 1929-1935. *Saskatchewan Hist. [Canada] 1977 30(3): 81-98.* "Back to the land" movements have occurred several times in Canadian history, but the one which took place from 1929 to 1935 in the pioneer region of Saskatchewan had the most governmental support and perhaps the most problems. It arose naturally from the economic hard times of the period and was supported by the hard pressed city governments in the southern part of Saskatchewan as well as the Provincial and Dominion governments. The Conservative administration of J. T. M. Anderson took most of the blame for the general failure of the movement which came about mostly because of the haste and lack of supervision which allowed unsuitable lands to be opened up. This was only partially relieved by the Liberal Gardiner administration with the Land Utilization Board and the Northern Settlers' Reestablishment Branch. Map, photo, 90 notes.
C. Held

1797. Pratt, Joseph A. GROWTH OR A CLEAN ENVIRONMENT? RESPONSES TO PETROLEUM-RELATED POLLUTION IN THE GULF COAST REFINING REGION. *Business Hist. Rev. 1978 52(1): 1-29.* Traces the environmental impact of the growth of petroleum refining along the Gulf Coast of Texas from the early 1900's-60's. Petroleum-related pollution was substantial throughout the period. Prior to World War I, no serious attempts were made to control pollution. Later the companies themselves and the American Petroleum Institute implemented unsuccessful voluntary efforts that were followed after 1940 by governmental action. Based on governmental and industry records and publications; 51 notes.
C. J. Pusateri

1798. Prendergast, James A. THE ATTEMPT AT UNIONISATION IN THE AUTOMOBILE INDUSTRY IN CANADA, 1928. *Ontario Hist. [Canada] 1978 70(4): 245-262.* Briefly describes early attempts, dating from the 1890's, to unionize (initially) the carriage making and (later) the automobile industries. Then details the 1928 strike against General Motors of Canada. Events after the strike, conflicts within the union movement, and the collapse of the various unions in 1929-30 are outlined. Mainly from contemporary newspapers; 3 photos, 58 notes.
W. B. Whitham

1799. Prickett, James R. COMMUNISTS AND THE AUTOMOBILE INDUSTRY IN DETROIT BEFORE 1935. *Michigan Hist. 1973 57(3): 185-208.* Traces the trade union activities of the Communist Party USA in Detroit automobile unionism before the formation of the United Automobile Workers in 1935. Such Communist leaders as Philip Raymond and Anthony Gerlach dominated the Automobile Workers Union in the 1920's and early 1930's. The AWU was particularly active in the wave of strikes of 1933. Communist rhetoric was tempered by pragmatism. 4 illus., 86 notes.
D. L. Smith

1800. Raynor, Bruce. UNIONISM IN THE SOUTHERN TEXTILE INDUSTRY: AN OVERVIEW. Fink, Gary M. and Reed, Merl E., eds. *Essays in Southern Labor History: Selected Papers, Southern Labor History Conference, 1976.* (Westport, Conn.; London, England: Greenwood Pr., 1977): 80-99. Textile unionization in the South has come on hard times; total disorganization and discouragement after losing ground for 25 years, is the order of the day. Studies some of the sources of past frustration in textile organizing, assesses the current state of labor relations in the industry, and projects future trends in textile unionism. The failures may be attributed to: 1) the effective (if illegal) antiunion tactics employed by mill owners, 2) a hostile political climate, and 3) the nature of the southern labor force. There have been, however, a sufficient number of significant changes in the labor situation and personnel to justify some optimism for the future. 31 notes.
R. V. Ritter

1801. Reilly, Nolan. THE GENERAL STRIKE IN AMHERST, NOVA SCOTIA, 1919. *Acadiensis [Canada] 1980 9(2): 56-77.* Between 1901 and 1906 Amherst's population doubled to 10,000 and the annual value of production rose from $1,000,000 to $4,500,000. After the 1907-08 recession, decline continued, only briefly interrupted by World War I. The purchase of Amherst industries by outside interests, particularly central Canadian, aggravated postwar dislocation. Local workers responded with the Amherst Federation of Labor, renewed interest in socialism, and the three-week general strike. The workers won some of their demands, but with Amherst's continued decline (its population dropped from 10,000 to 7,500 between 1921 and 1931), the labor movement all but disappeared by the mid-1920's. 90 notes.
D. F. Chard

1802. Rosales, Francisco A. and Simon, Daniel T. CHICANO STEEL WORKERS AND UNIONISM IN THE MIDWEST, 1919-1945. *Aztlán 1976 6(2): 267-275.* Chicano and Mexican workers comprised a large portion of the labor force in Chicago (Illinois), Gary (Indiana), and East Chicago (Indiana). Racial discrimination motivated them to actively participate in labor union organization. They played prominent roles in major strikes in the steel industry during the 1930's. Based on newspapers and secondary sources; 27 notes.
R. Griswold del Castillo

1803. Rosenthal, Star. UNION MAIDS: ORGANIZED WOMEN WORKERS IN VANCOUVER, 1900-1915. *BC Studies [Canada] 1979 (41): 36-55.* Conventional mythology held that women in the labor movement did not attempt to organize in the past, that women were "in fact unorganizable." Conventional attitudes held that women threatened male job security and that factory work was not healthy for women specifically. Women were viewed as "reactionary, materialistic and non-class-conscious." There are also obvious parallels of the history of women in the labor movement with the history of nonwhite workers. The distortions of history to the contrary and these obstacles notwithstanding, working women in Vancouver, British Columbia, did organize and carry on union activity during 1900-15. Data is scarce, but enough evidence has been discovered to warrant a reassessment of the role of women in the labor movement. 91 notes. D. L. Smith

1804. Rosenzweig, Roy. "SOCIALISM IN OUR TIME": THE SOCIALIST PARTY AND THE UNEMPLOYED, 1929-1936. *Labor Hist. 1979 20(4): 485-509.* Socialists played an important role, especially after 1932, in organizing the unemployed. Led by young socialists, practical action for relief was important in Chicago, New York, Baltimore, and other cities. The practical focus, when combined with external events such as the rise of the Nazis, led socialists toward being absorbed into New Deal liberalism. Their Depression activism should not be forgotten. Based on the Norman Thomas manuscript, Socialist Party manuscript, and files in the Tamiment Library; 39 notes. L. L. Athey

1805. Rouillard, Jacques. LE QUÉBEC ET LE CONGRÈS DE BERLIN, 1902 [Quebec and the Berlin Congress, 1902]. *Labour [Canada] 1976 1: 69-91.* At the 1902 Trades and Labour Congress of Canada in Berlin (now Kitchener), Ontario, constitutional changes caused the expulsion of all unions having concurrent jurisdiction with an international union. This victory of internationalism over the Knights of Labor, still strong in Quebec, and Canadian national unions was due in part to the "imperialist" drive of Samuel Gompers' American Federation of Labor but was also a direct result of union conflicts in Quebec, especially in Montreal, dating from 1892. Of 23 expelled organizations, 17 were from Quebec. The split in the Canadian labor movement saw the formation of a rival National Trades and Labour Congress, largely dominated by Quebec unions. Primary and secondary sources; 105 notes. W. A. Kearns

1806. St. Amant, Jean-Claude. LA PROPAGANDE DE L'ÉCOLE SOCIALE POPULAIRE EN FAVEUR DU SYNDICALISME CATHOLIQUE 1911-1949 [The propaganda of the École Sociale Populaire in favor of Catholic Syndicalism]. *Rev. d'Hist. de l'Amérique Française [Canada] 1978 32(2): 203-228.* Founded by Jesuits in Montreal, the École Sociale Populaire was an educational agency whose primary purpose was to promote improved conditions for workers. It published numerous pamphlets, tracts, and journals on a wide variety of related topics, e.g., the dangers of communism, the perils of alcohol, and the restoration of social order. The School encouraged a brand of unionism that was grounded in the Catholic faith, one that would alleviate the traditional tensions that existed between the working and proprietary classes. 76 notes. M. R. Yerburgh

1807. Sanders, Bernard, ed. VERMONT LABOR AGITATOR. *Labor Hist. 1974 15(2): 261-270.* Presents a memoir of Mose Cerasoli (1898-), a Vermont granite worker who tells the story of attempts to organize granite workers and of the brutal resistance encountered in the "pastoral state." The oral memoir covers 1913-38. L. L. Athey

1808. Sangster, Joan. THE 1907 BELL TELEPHONE STRIKE: ORGANIZING WOMEN WORKERS. *Labour [Canada] 1978 3: 109-130.* Analyzes the causes and results of the strike by Bell Canada telephone operators in Toronto, Ontario, in February 1907. There was substantial public support for the strikers' opposition to the implementation of a new policy which combined increased hours with reduced wages. A federal Royal Commission (W. L. Mackenzie King and John Winchester) conducted an investigation. Company intransigence, failure to unionize, and the attitudes of government, the middle class, and organized labor toward women workers contributed to a general lack of success. The strike led to the company's adoption of welfare capitalism in order "to kill unionization with kindness." Based on Bell Canada Historical Collection, newspapers, and other primary sources; 97 notes. W. A. Kearns

1809. Schacht, John N. TOWARD INDUSTRIAL UNIONISM: BELL TELEPHONE WORKERS AND COMPANY UNIONS, 1919-1937. *Labor Hist. 1975 16(1): 5-36.* Development of company unions in the Bell Telephone System helped prepare the way for the emergence of industrial unions after 1935. The structure of the company union helped erase distinctions between workers, and leadership and organizational skills were learned by workers. Success in converting the Bell Company union into an industrial union may help explain why other company unions failed to make the transformation. Based on oral history interviews, company publications, dissertations, and government reports; 43 notes. L. L. Athey

1810. Scott, Stanley. A PROFUSION OF ISSUES: IMMIGRANT LABOUR, THE WORLD WAR AND THE COMINCO STRIKE OF 1917. *Labour [Canada] 1977 2: 54-78.* Labor-management relations in Trail, British Columbia, were characterized by poor working conditions, poor wages, and poor living conditions. The Consolidated Mining and Smelting Company (controlled by the Canadian Pacific Railray) used various methods to maintain a nonunionized, subservient work force ideally composed of a "mixture of races which includes a number of illiterates." Nonetheless, a majority of workers joined the International Union of Mine, Mill, and Smelter Workers local in 1916 and negotiated an agreement. That pact, inflation, xenophobia, wages, hours, the Wartime Elections Act, conscription, and the paternalistic antiunion stance of management were factors behind the strike, which ended in a company victory. Primary and secondary sources, and interviews; 92 notes. W. A. Kearns

1811. Seager, Allen. THE PASS STRIKE OF 1932. *Alberta Hist. [Canada] 1977 25(1): 1-11.* The depression in the coal district by the British Columbia-Alberta border started in the early 1920's, with a decline in the price of coal. The worldwide depression led to confrontations between management and labor. In 1932, violence erupted in several mining communities, and the Mounties were called in. Management tried unsuccessfully to separate the Eastern European workers from the Canadians. An unusual aspect of the strike was the participation of women and children in parades and other demonstrations. By the mid-1930's the workers had the upper hand, and in 1936 they joined the United Mine Workers of America. 5 illus., 53 notes. D. Chaput

1812. Sinclair, Barbara Deckard. THE POLICY CONSEQUENCES OF PARTY REALIGNMENT: SOCIAL WELFARE LEGISLATION IN THE HOUSE OF REPRESENTATIVES, 1933-1954. *Am. J. of Pol. Sci. 1978 22(1): 83-105.* Burnham's theory of the policy consequences of realignments is applied to social welfare legislation during the New Deal realignment and its aftermath. As predicted, social welfare legislation does emerge as a direct response to the depression. The most clearly nonincremental programs were passed during the height of the realigning era (1935-38) and little nonincremental legislation passed during the remaining years under study. Throughout the 1930s, the increased issue distance between the parties was reflected in highly partisan voting alignments on non-labor social welfare legislation. During the 1940s, centrifugal constituency related forces reasserted themselves. By the 80th Congress, a single dominant and highly stable social welfare dimension had developed. Southern Democrats, who had been highly supportive of social welfare legislation during the 1930s, were now the least supportive regional grouping within the Democratic party. Northeastern Republicans, once the most conservative segment of the Republican party, became the most supportive while west north central Republicans followed the opposite path. J

1813. Snyder, David; Hayward, Mark D.; and Hudis, Paula M. THE LOCATION OF CHANGE IN THE SEXUAL STRUCTURE OF OCCUPATIONS, 1950-1970: INSIGHTS FROM LABOR MARKET SEGMENTATION THEORY. *Am. J. of Sociol. 1978 84(3): 706-717.* Analyzes trends in sex discrimination in the US labor market during 1950-70.

1814. Strong-Boag, Veronica. CANADA'S EARLY EXPERIENCE WITH INCOME SUPPLEMENTS: THE INTRODUCTION OF MOTHERS' ALLOWANCES. *Atlantis [Canada] 1979 4(2, part 2): 35-43.* Describes the flurry of legislation in Canada, 1916-20, which continued during the 1920's-30's, to grant mothers pensions and allowances, an important step in the history of child welfare in Canada; points out the inadequate aid for mothers in Canada during the 1960's-70's.

1815. Strong-Boag, Veronica. "WAGES FOR HOUSEWORK": MOTHERS' ALLOWANCES AND THE BEGINNINGS OF SOCIAL SECURITY IN CANADA. *J. of Can. Studies [Canada] 1979 14(1):*

24-34. The first steps in Canada's formal income support programs were directed to the needs of mother-led families with inadequate means of support in the first decades of this century. Mothers' allowance legislation was introduced in every province. There was some variation in the way the need was met, and there was a slow development in the rationale as well—often "connected to a narrow vision of human potential." Weaknesses in the present Social Security system may be one of the legacies from these early years. Primary sources; 46 notes. R. V. Ritter

1816. Struthers, James. PRELUDE TO DEPRESSION: THE FEDERAL GOVERNMENT AND UNEMPLOYMENT, 1918-29. *Can. Hist. Rev. [Canada] 1977 58(3): 277-293.* Studies Canada's economic slump in the post-World War I years and the federal government's handling of the unemployment problem. "Back-to-the-Land," and "Work or Maintenance," were the dominant emphases in Canadian social policy. The federal government considered the problem more provincial than federal, and lost its opportunity to anticipate the social and economic problems which more liberal reformers foresaw in this policy. Experience in federal leadership in labor exchanges, unemployment relief, and unemployment insurance during 1918-21 was thereby lost. 51 notes.
R. V. Ritter

1817. Tedlow, Richard S. FROM COMPETITOR TO CONSUMER: THE CHANGING FOCUS OF FEDERAL REGULATION OF ADVERTISING, 1914-1938. *Business Hist. Rev. 1981 55(1): 35-58.* The Federal Trade Commission (FTC), as envisioned at its inception in 1914, was concerned with the prevention of anticompetitive behavior in industry and not the regulation of advertising or consumer protection. However, by the 1920's federal court decisions had circumscribed FTC flexibility in antitrust areas, and advertising industry spokesmen were themselves openly calling for federal action to supplant inefficient state efforts. The passage of the Wagner-Lea amendments in 1938 gave needed support to this FTC activity by attempting a definition of false advertising and by imposing new penalties for violations of commission orders. Based principally on governmental records and contemporary periodical literature; 68 notes. C. J. Pusateri

1818. Temin, Peter. REGULATION AND THE CHOICE OF PRESCRIPTION DRUGS. *Am. Econ. Rev. 1980 70(2): 301-305.* The federal Food, Drug, and Cosmetic Act (US, 1938), has been exploited in the United States since World War II. The miracle drug explosion has been directed by drug companies, medical professionals, and public ignorance. The result is a strengthening of prescription drugs and de facto discouragement of responsible consumer participation in drug choices. Roger G. Noll's discussion, (pp. 316-317) generally agrees with Temin's findings. 8 ref. D. K. Pickens

1819. Thomas, Richard W. INDUSTRIAL CAPITALISM, INTRACLASS RACIAL CONFLICT AND THE FORMATION OF BLACK WORKING CLASS POLITICAL CULTURE. *J. of African-Afro-American Affairs 1979 3(1): 11-45.* Traces the rise of industrial capitalism during the 19th century, emphasizing the fostering of racial tension and provides a survey of the development of black labor unions during the 20th century.

1820. Thomson, Anthony. "THE LARGE AND GENEROUS VIEW": THE DEBATE ON LABOUR AFFILIATION IN THE CANADIAN CIVIL SERVICE 1918-1928. *Labour [Canada] 1977 2: 108-136.* Examines the development of and response to trade union ideology and "middle status" federal civil servants. The government was not exempt from the post-World War I militancy of labor. Postal workers were the most radical but within the civil service as a whole pro-union employees contended with those who accepted "the large and generous view" that public employees, as servants of the people, must be loyal to the government. Fought out within and between various staff associations and influenced by organized labor and government, middle-class ideology triumphed over labor ideology and the differentiation between worker ("hand") and white-collar worker ("brain") persisted. Based on civil service newspapers, primary and secondary sources; 95 notes.
W. A. Kearns

1821. Towle, W. Wilder. THE STORY OF DELMO. *Missouri Hist. Soc. Bull. 1980 36(3): 162-167.* In the 1930's, the Southern Tenant Farmers Union agitated against the plight of sharecroppers in Missouri Delta counties. One federal response to STFU demonstrations was resettlement of some sharecropper families to low-rent village complexes (called Delmo Homes) which the Farm Security Administration managed. Ownership of the complexes was transferred in 1945 to the Delmo Housing Corporation, which philanthropists founded and through which Delmo Homes tenants could eventually become owners of the homes. Based on Delmo Housing Corporation files now held by Washington University, St. Louis; 2 photos, 7 notes. H. T. Lovin

1822. Tripp, Joseph F. TOWARD AN EFFICIENT AND MORAL SOCIETY: WASHINGTON STATE MINIMUM-WAGE LAW, 1913-1925. *Pacific Northwest Q. 1976 67(3): 97-112.* Though numerous states adopted minimum wage legislation and eight-hour days for women during the Progressive Era, the state of Washington produced the most effective and lasting statutes. Reformers met only minimal resistance from Washington businessmen who recognized the small percentage of women within the labor force. Additional support for the legislation and its enforcement agency, the Industrial Welfare Commission, came from Senator George Piper and belatedly from Governor Lewis Hart who extended the commission's powers. By the mid-1920's, however, the policies were reversed by a more conservative state government. Primary sources; 4 photos, 59 notes. M. L. Tate

1823. Villemez, Wayne J. and Wiswell, Candace Hinson. THE IMPACT OF DIMINISHING DISCRIMINATION ON THE INTERNAL SIZE DISTRIBUTION OF BLACK INCOME: 1954-74. *Social Forces 1978 56(4): 1019-1034.* A number of studies have sought to ascertain the scope of black economic gains in the last two decades. The extent of these gains is still under debate, but observers agree that some gains have been made. The locus of these gains in the black sector has not been adequately demonstrated. This paper examines income data for males from 1954-74 to determine the pattern of reduction in black-white inequality and the concomitant variation of those reductions with changes in the size distribution of black income. Findings show that, in the industrial non-South, decreasing black-white inequality has been accompanied by increasing inequality among blacks, and there are indications that most black economic gains have occurred at the top of the black distribution. The data argue against the possibility of long-range improvements in the coeconomic status of blacks as a group. The theoretical and policy implications of these findings are discussed. J

1824. Walter, John C. FRANK R. CROSSWAITH AND THE NEGRO LABOR COMMITTEE IN HARLEM, 1925-1939. *Afro-Americans in New York Life and Hist. 1979 3(2): 35-49.* Frank R. Crosswaith (1892-1965), black socialist, labor organizer, and activist, founded the Negro Labor Committee in Harlem in 1935.

1825. Weed, Frank J. BUREAUCRATIZATION AS REFORM: THE CASE OF THE PUBLIC WELFARE MOVEMENT, 1900-1929. *Social Sci. J. 1979 16(3): 79-89.* During 1900-29, a struggle over the orientation of public welfare in the United States occurred between those who wanted bureaucratization, with undeviating, impersonal rules, and those who sought professionalization, whereby professionals had autonomy in determining action.

1826. Wortman, Roy T. THE RESURGENCE OF THE IWW IN CLEVELAND: A NEGLECTED ASPECT OF LABOR HISTORY. *Northwest Ohio Q. 1974/75 47(1): 20-29.* Discusses the Industrial Workers of the World in Cleveland 1918-50, especially resurgence 1934-50 due to growth in the Metal and Machinery Workers' Industrial Union (440).

1827. Woywitka, Anne B. DRUMHELLER STRIKE OF 1919. *Alberta Hist. R. 1973 21(1): 1-7.* The Alberta government, the mine companies, and the United Mine Workers of America allied to combat the threat of the One Big Union to the U.M.W.A. as the legal bargaining agent of mine workers in the Drumheller Valley. 4 illus.
D. L. Smith

1828. Woywitka, Anne B. RECOLLECTIONS OF A UNION MAN. *Alberta Hist. [Canada] 1975 23(4): 6-20.* Peter Kyforuk, a Ukrainian immigrant, came to Canada in 1912 at the age of 18. In the next decades he worked as a woodsman and railroad hand from Ontario to British Columbia. In the 1920's he became active in the Ukrainian Labour-Farmer Association in Manitoba. Later active in Farmers Unity League, he played a key role in the Hunger March on Edmonton in December 1932 and with many other leaders was arrested. By the mid-1930's Kyforuk had settled in Alberta, became a successful farmer, and remained active in the Farmer's Union of Alberta. 8 photos.   D. Chaput

1829. —. [BUSINESS AND SOCIAL WELFARE]. *J. of Econ. Hist. 1978 38(1): 120-147.*
Berkowitz, Edward D. and McQuaid, Kim. BUSINESSMAN AND BUREAUCRAT: THE EVOLUTION OF THE AMERICAN SOCIAL WELFARE SYSTEM, 1900-1940, *pp. 120-142.* Between 1900 and 1940, organized industry and the federal government, acting in conjunction with the states, created an American social welfare system. For most of the period, well developed programs of corporate bureaucracies enjoyed clear primacy. During the 1930s, an important transition occurred. Federal bureaucrats moved beyond business models and rationales. After this transformation, strong linkages between the public and private sectors remained—for example, in the early social security program. Later, however, the creation of a disability insurance plan exemplified a growing divergence between the government and private businessmen in procedure and concept. Neither side won the resulting welfare debate. By the 1940s, a mixed system of federal administrative initiative based on capitalist precedent had evolved. Businessmen and bureaucrats had arrived at an uneasy truce regarding the welfare of an industrial society.
DeCanio, Stephen J. DISCUSSION, *pp. 143-147.* Economists must take care before imputing economic motives to political actions. Often both ideas are mixed, and hasty differentiation obscures the truth. Similarly, economic policy does not always have the intended effect forecast by its authors; side-effects are not, therefore, less real or important. Berkowitz and McQuaid, for instance, sometimes fail to see beneath the propaganda of the policies which obscures the motives of the main characters in American welfare history. 5 notes.   J/J. W. Leedom

1830. —. THE HUNGRY THIRTIES: 1930-1939. *Sound Heritage [Canada] 1978 7(4): 40-59.* Examines the gains in the Canadian labor movement, particularly in British Columbia during the 1930's despite a depression, particularly the organizations established for unemployed workers, the largest of which was the National Unemployed Workers' Association, affiliated with the Workers' Unity League; also briefly mentions the participants in the labor movement and presents their versions of labor activities.

Educational Reform

1831. Aldridge, Delores P. LITIGATION AND EDUCATION OF BLACKS: A LOOK AT THE U.S. SUPREME COURT. *J. of Negro Educ. 1978 47(1): 96-112.* Chronological history of Supreme Court decisions relative to school desegregation from *Plessy* v. *Ferguson* (US, 1896) through *Brown* v. *Board of Education* (US, 1954) tp *Swann* v. *Charlotte-Mecklenburg Board of Education* (US, 1971), as well as some of the District Court responses, and the actions of the Congress, the Presidents since Eisenhower, and the Departments of Justice and HEW. Concludes that the Supreme Court has been the most activist defender of equal education. Based on court decisions, newspapers, and other primary and secondary sources; 63 notes.   R. E. Butchart

1832. Anderson, James D. NORTHERN FOUNDATIONS AND THE SHAPING OF SOUTHERN BLACK RURAL EDUCATION, 1902-1935. *Hist. of Educ. Q. 1978 18(4): 371-396.* A study of the initiation and development of northern industrialists' philanthropy in southern, black, rural education revealed programs which emphasized industrial rather than academic curricula and goals, sometimes contrary to the Negroes' interests. The philanthropists "were primarily motivated by practical interests in the relationship of black industrial education to the development of Southern agriculture and national industrial life." They sought a politically stable Southern agricultural economy without any disruption of the Southern racial hierarchy. 41 notes.
   R. V. Ritter

1833. Brown, E. Richard. HE WHO PAYS THE PIPER: FOUNDATIONS, THE MEDICAL PROFESSION, AND MEDICAL EDUCATION. Reverby, Susan and Rosner, David, ed. *Health Care in America: Essays in Social History* (Philadelphia: Temple U. Pr., 1979): 132-154. Foundations, especially the Rockefeller philanthropies, financed the most important reforms in medical education from 1910 through the 1930's. Frederick T. Gates, an agent of John D. Rockefeller, accepted the report of Abraham Flexner that American medical education was inadequate; not enough clinical research took place, and medical schools were dominated by the physicians. Consequently Gates tried to use Rockefeller money to fund full-time clinical researchers. This would not only improve the level of research but deny part-time employment for doctors in private practice. These researchers would give their loyalty completely to the medical school rather than to the organized profession as the part-timers were likely to do. Originally published in E. Richard Brown, *Rockefeller Medicine Men: Medicine and Capitalism in America* (Berkeley: U. of California Pr., 1979). 65 notes.   S

1834. Burnett, Joe R. WHATEVER HAPPENED TO JOHN DEWEY? *Teachers Coll. Record 1979 81(2): 192-210.* John Dewey's (1859-1952) impact on American education has been rather consistently overstated, primarily because of a failure to recognize two distinct strands in the development of progressive education. Romantic progressivism, which had the greater effect on educational practice, developed well before Dewey. Pragmatic progressivism, more directly Dewey's creation, was less influential partly because it was too experimental to be readily applicable. Few have noticed, moreover, that in his later, more mature writings Dewey grew pessimistic about the ability of education to foster desirable social change. Recent study of Dewey's work appears to be correcting earlier misunderstanding. Based on writings of Dewey and secondary sources; 47 notes.   E. C. Bailey

1835. Burns, Augustus M., III. GRADUATE EDUCATION FOR BLACKS IN NORTH CAROLINA, 1930-1951. *J. of Southern Hist. 1980 46(2): 195-218.* From Thomas R. Hocutt's attempt to enter the University of North Carolina's pharmacy school in 1933 until the final legal battle over the Harold Thomas Epps and Floyd B. McKissick suits in 1951, many North Carolina white leaders sought to block black efforts to enter graduate and professional training, both out of conscience and because they found it expedient to have the onus of desegregation passed on to the federal government. Based on the University of North Carolina Archives, private collections, court records, newspapers, and other sources; 73 notes.   T. D. Schoonover

1836. Carter, Doris Dorcas. CHARLES P. ADAMS AND GRAMBLING STATE UNIVERSITY: THE FORMATIVE YEARS (1901-1928). *Louisiana Hist. 1976 17(4): 401-412.* Black settlers in the vicinity of Grambling, Louisiana, organized the North Louisiana Colored Agricultural Relief Association Union in 1896 behind the leadership of Lafayette Richmond. In 1899 that organization decided to establish a coeducational industrial school at Grambling, and in 1901 they asked Booker T. Washington of Tuskegee Institute to send someone to organize the school. Washington sent Charles P. Adams, who organized the school and led it through its difficult early years. Disputes with the Agricultural Relief Organization over the nature of the school and Adams' appeals to whites for assistance led to establishment of a new school in Grambling by Adams in 1905, known as North Louisiana Agricultural and Industrial School. It began to receive Lincoln Parish funds in 1912 and became completely Parish-supported in 1918, when its name was changed to Lincoln Parish Training School. In 1928, through the efforts of Gov. Huey P. Long and State Senator Robert B. Knott, the school became a state school. Based principally on unpublished M.A. thesis by Earl Maxie, "The Development of Grambling College" (Tuskegee Institute, 1950), interviews with Maxie, and unpublished papers at Grambling University; 39 notes.   R. L. Woodward

1837. Casdorph, Paul D. CLARENCE W. MEADOWS, W. W. TRENT AND EDUCATIONAL REFORM IN WEST VIRGINIA. *West Virginia Hist. 1980 41(2): 126-141.* Governor Clarence W. Meadows and State Superintendent of Schools W. W. Trent struggled over educational reform. In his study of West Virginia schools, George D. Strayer commended its county unit system but recommended that the state superintendent be appointed rather than elected. Trent, however, successfully opposed this change, which came only after he was no longer in office. The West Virginia Education Association was also involved in the controversy. Covers 1932-58. Based on West Virginia Government documents and on newspaper accounts; 38 notes. J. D. Neville

1838. Cooper, Richard J. POLITICAL LEADERSHIP: A CATALYST FOR SPECIAL EDUCATION. *Pennsylvania Heritage 1980 6(4): 20-23.* Traces efforts for legislation for the education of handicapped children in Pennsylvania from State Senator Henry E. Lanius in 1919 until Governor George M. Leader in 1956, and discusses facilities for the education of the handicapped in Pennsylvania from 1820 to 1956.

1839. Dell, George W. ROBERT M. HUTCHINS' PHILOSOPHY OF GENERAL EDUCATION AND THE COLLEGE AT THE UNIVERSITY OF CHICAGO. *J. of General Educ. 1978 30(1): 43-58.* Discusses the development and implementation of a general education course of study consisting of the greatest books of the western world, math, the sciences, and the arts of reading, writing, thinking, and speaking. The purpose of the curriculum was to teach the student to think for himself and to lay a basis for advanced study. Primary and secondary sources; 50 notes. N. A. Williamson

1840. Desjarlais, Lionel. TOWARDS A MORE HUMANE EDUCATION. *Rev. de l'U. d'Ottawa [Canada] 1976 46(1): 24-39.* Considers the contributions of Rousseau, Pestalozzi, Froebel, Dewey, Montessori, Gandhi, Tagore, and Saiyidain to humane education. These innovators developed ideas that transcended their particular time and place, and concerned themselves more with why rather than how to educate. All of them except Dewey approached education religiously, and religion as a spirit that penetrated all life. Their basic passwords were love, understanding, and appreciation of the child as a spiritual being with inner resources to be developed. Freedom, especially of the mind, was an essential for good life, and therefore for good education. Adapted from a paper presented to the World Education Fellowship held in Bombay, India, 1 January 1975. W. R. Hively

1841. Desjarlais, Lionel. TOWARDS A MORE HUMANE EDUCATION: A COMPARATIVE ANALYSIS OF THE CONTRIBUTIONS OF SOME EASTERN AND WESTERN PHILOSOPHERS OF EDUCATION. *Rev. de l'U. d'Ottawa [Canada] 1976 46(1): 24-39.* Outlines the "creative contributions made by certain selective innovative thinkers (such as Rousseau, Pestalozzi, Froebel, Dewey, Montessori, Tagore, Ghandhi, and Saiyidain) in the East and the West to the development of a more humane education" and stresses the importance of the World Education Fellowship. Secondary sources. M. L. Frey

1842. Gonzales, Gilbert C. EDUCATIONAL REFORM AND THE MEXICAN COMMUNITY IN LOS ANGELES. *Southwest Econ. and Soc. 1978 3(3): 24-51.* Examines the curricula of the Los Angeles public schools as it served and affected the Mexican Americans in the community during the 1920's-30's.

1843. Harris, J. John, III; Figgures, Cleopatra; and Carter, David G. A HISTORICAL PERSPECTIVE OF THE EMERGENCE OF HIGHER EDUCATION IN BLACK COLLEGES. *J. of Black Studies 1975 6(1): 55-68.* Presents an overview of higher education for blacks and reviews the factors which led to the establishment of black colleges. Biblio. K. Butcher

1844. Hobson, Julius, Jr. EDUCATIONAL POLICY AND THE COURTS: THE CASE OF WASHINGTON, D.C. *Urban Rev. 1978 10(1): 5-19.* Agencies conducting Washington, D.C.'s public schools, 1804-1974, failed to provide equal education for black students despite studies which provided information on discrimination. Since 1910, D.C. residents have sought judicial relief from the "malpractice and negligence" of school officials. Although the courts have corrected many educational abuses, Washington furnishes a case study of the courts' inability to formulate and execute nondiscriminatory educational policy throughout the United States. Equal education depends upon educational agencies' fulfillment of their responsibilities. Based on published government documents and secondary studies; biblio. R. G. Sherer

1845. Homel, Michael W. THE POLITICS OF PUBLIC EDUCATION IN BLACK CHICAGO, 1910-1941. *J. of Negro Educ. 1976 45(2): 179-191.* As the black population of Chicago increased after 1910, their dissatisfaction with the public schools also increased. They worked for the next 30 years for improved facilities, integration, and representation on the Board of Education. Methods used were: white assistance, political influence, legal cases, direct action, and public verbal protest. 27 notes. B. D. Johnson

1846. Hornsby, Alton, Jr. THE "COLORED BRANCH UNIVERSITY" ISSUE IN TEXAS—PRELUDE TO SWEATT VS. PAINTER. *J. of Negro Hist. 1976 6(1): 51-60.* Texas long evaded the charge of its constitution to establish a separate but equal "university of the first class" for black Texans. After nearly three-quarters of a century (1876-1947), the state managed to establish a "branch university for colored youth" in only a few months when the black people of Texas began to seek redress in the federal courts. Despite the attempts to evade an idea whose time had come, the University of Texas was ultimately integrated as a result of the campaign. Based on primary and secondary sources; 42 notes. N. G. Sapper

1847. Howlett, Charles F. JOHN DEWEY'S OPPOSITION TO MILITARY TRAINING IN AMERICAN HIGHER EDUCATION. *Gandhi Marg [India] 1979 1(2): 87-94.* Dewey opposed college Reserve Officers' Training Corps (ROTC) programs because, he said, they encouraged a narrow nationalism and the maintenance of the status quo. This ran contrary to the primary purposes of education, to deepen sympathy and understanding among the world's peoples and to stimulate peaceful social change. Covers 1920-38. 23 notes. J. C. English

1848. Huel, Raymond. THE ANDERSON AMENDMENTS AND THE SECULARIZATION OF SASKATCHEWAN PUBLIC SCHOOLS. *Study Sessions: Can. Catholic Hist. Assoc. [Canada] 1977 44: 61-76.* Dedicated to educational reform, Premier James T. M. Anderson advanced two major amendments to Saskatchewan's School Act which prohibited religious garb and symbols in the public schools (1930) and suppressed the French language in grade one (1931). These actions occurred in a climate of anti-Catholicism and spurred nationalism among French-speaking Catholics, including those in Quebec. Covers 1929-34. G. A. Hewlett

1849. Huel, Raymond. PASTOR VS. POLITICIAN: THE REVEREND MURDOCH MACKINNON AND PREMIER WALTER SCOTT'S AMENDMENT TO THE SCHOOL ACT. *Saskatchewan Hist. [Canada] 1978 32(2): 61-73.* Originally a private exchange of letters between Presbyterian minister Murdoch MacKinnon and Premier Walter Scott, of the Liberal Party, concerning an amendment to the School Act which would force Catholics to support separate schools (thus enhancing the status of those schools) and to which MacKinnon was opposed, the controversy became a vicious public debate from 1913 to 1916. Scott wished to guarantee language and school rights to French Canadians and immigrants, while MacKinnon wished to impose Anglo-Protestant assimilation on them. Details personal vituperations on both sides. Follows MacKinnon's career up to the Church Union and his acceptance of a pastorate in Toronto in 1925. Delineates the preparation of an anti-French, anti-Catholic atmosphere which would lead to the appearance of the Ku Klux Klan in Saskatchewan in 1926. 65 notes. C. H. Held

1850. Kemper, Donald J. CATHOLIC INTEGRATION IN ST. LOUIS, 1935-1947. *Missouri Hist. Rev. 1978 73(1): 1-22.* In 1947 the Archbishop of St. Louis, Joseph E. Ritter, ordered the admission of black children to local parochial schools, an order that provoked serious resistance from parents. The success of the order came in the wake of a battle going on during the latter years of Archbishop John J. Glennon. Through the Midwest Clergy Conference on Negro Matters, some young priests had set the stage by trying to desegregate Webster College and St. Louis University. It is likely that Rome arranged the liberal Ritter's assignment to speed integration. Primary and secondary sources; illus., 58 notes. W. F. Zornow

1851. Kersey, Harry A., Jr. FEDERAL SCHOOLS AND ACCULTURATION AMONG THE FLORIDA SEMINOLES, 1927-1954. *Florida Hist. Q. 1980 59(2): 165-181.* The desire to acculturate the Seminole Indians was the motive for having their children schooled in North Carolina. Commissioner of Indian Affairs John Collier played a large role in this educational campaign. By 1950 it became apparent that the chil-

dren could not be expected to return to the reservation unchanged after experiencing the white man's education. Recent legislation recognizes the needs and values of the Seminole people. Based on the writings of John Collier, congressional hearings and other sources; 39 notes.
N. A. Kuntz

1852. Lauderdale, William B. A PROGRESSIVE ERA FOR EDUCATION IN ALABAMA, 1935-1951. *Alabama Hist. Q. 1975 37(1): 38-67.* The progressive education movement reached its peak just before World War II. Alabama became one of the most important states in the progressive movement. The first educational innovations were introduced by Dr. C. B. Smith, Director of the Division of Instruction, who developed a problem-centered approach to education. He was followed by W. Morrison McCall. Peabody College consultants aided curriculum development. The practical application of the new ideas and their effect on the community is illustrated by a case study of the schools at Cold Springs and Fairview. World War II had a negative effect, and in 1951 a conservative was elected State Superintendent. 39 notes.
E. E. Eminhizer

1853. Lindsay, Beverly and Harris, J. John, III. PROGRESSIVE EDUCATION AND THE BLACK COLLEGE. *J. of Black Studies 1977 7(3): 341-357.* When progressive education first emerged, most black institutions were preoccupied with struggles over who should control them and were dominated by the concept of industrial education. Moreover, the emphasis on educational progress for negroes as a group was antithetical to progressive education's emphasis on the individual. Black colleges in the 1920's and 30's had to provide a basic, general education and maintain (or attain) accreditation; therefore they could not experiment with a progressive education curriculum based on individualism and innovation. Primary and secondary sources; 5 notes, biblio.
D. C. Neal

1854. Lotz, Jim. THE HISTORICAL AND SOCIAL SETTING OF THE ANTIGONISH MOVEMENT. *Nova Scotia Hist. Q. [Canada] 1975 5(2): 99-116.* Studies the Antigonish Movement as a significant Canadian contribution to the theory and practice of social change. It combined educational, economic, and cooperative merchandising elements to solve serious problems developing in rural areas of eastern Nova Scotia. Traces its history from its inception in the 1920's in response to various social trends (urbanization, industrialization, and rural depopulation) as part of the social action movement of the Catholic Church, and as an alternative to the left-wing and right-wing ideologies of the period. "The Movement has acted as a model and a stimulus for grassroots organization elsewhere in Canada and throughout the world." 14 notes.
R. V. Ritter

1855. Lyons, John. THE (ALMOST) QUIET EVOLUTION: DOUKHOBOR SCHOOLING IN SASKATCHEWAN. *Can. Ethnic Studies [Canada] 1976 8(1): 23-37.* Describes efforts to bring public education to the Saskatchewan Dukhobors since 1905 and the circumstances surrounding their eventual acceptance of public schools.

1856. Melis, Caroline. J. T. M. ANDERSON, DIRECTOR OF EDUCATION AMONG NEW-CANADIANS AND THE POLICY OF THE DEPARTMENT OF EDUCATION: 1918-1923. *Saskatchewan Hist. [Canada] 1980 33(1): 1-12.* Describes J. T. M. Anderson's attempts to Canadianize the multiplicity of ethnic groups through the use of the English language and the teaching of British values in the public schools of Saskatchewan. The role of the teacher as educator, missionary, and model Canadian citizen was much emphasized in this process. Letters and contemporary newspaper accounts; illus., 52 notes.
C. H. Held

1857. Middleton, Ernest J. THE LOUISIANA EDUCATION ASSOCIATION, 1901-1970. *J. of Negro Educ. 1978 47(4): 363-378.* The Louisiana Colored Teachers Association, predecessor to the all-black Louisiana Education Association (LEA), was formed by concerned black educators such as J. B. LaFarque in 1901. It consistently fought for equality in Louisiana education, first within the framework of segregation, and then in the difficult years of white resistance to the national demand for integration. In 1969, the National Education Association disaffiliated the all-white Louisiana Teachers Association for refusal to integrate, and the LEA became the sole recognized teacher association in the state. Primary sources, including interviews, Association convention minutes, and manuscript material; 52 notes.
R. E. Butchart

1858. Orfield, Gary. IF WISHES WERE HOUSES THEN BUSING COULD STOP: DEMOGRAPHIC TRENDS AND DESEGREGATION POLICY. *Urban Rev. 1978 10(2): 108-124.* For the past decade the American "national policy on urban school desegregation" was based on three erroneous assumptions—that ghettos arose because of private choices, that housing discrimination is declining, and that "school busing on any scale will only be counterproductive." Effective school integration must include entire metropolitan areas. Such desegregation often causes stable housing desegregation, not vice versa, and can occur only through positive government action. Primary and secondary sources; 56 notes.
R. G. Sherer

1859. Ornstein, Allan C. OUR CHANGING EDUCATIONAL AIMS. *Plural Soc. [Netherlands] 1978 9(1): 37-48.* Traces the aims of education during the 20th century: 1) progressivism (1900-45), 2) focus on the academically talented (1945-50's), 3) concentration on the disadvantaged (1960's), and 4) present aims of equal opportunity (1970's).

1860. Putney, Martha S. THE BLACK COLLEGES IN THE MARYLAND STATE COLLEGE SYSTEM: QUEST FOR EQUAL OPPORTUNITY, 1908-1975. *Maryland Hist. Mag. 1980 75(4): 335-343.* Explores Maryland's record of compliance with laws and court orders on access to educational opportunities for Negroes in the state college system, a part of the state's postsecondary schools, and the efforts of blacks to improve the quality of education provided by this system, in a state which was the next to the last to provide public facilities for blacks beyond high school. Enrollments by racial composition, integration of faculties, annual expenditures per student, have all improved as a result of black agitation, Health, Education and Welfare intervention, and key court decisions which produced the 1974 *Maryland Plan for . . . Desegregation of the Public Postsecondary Education Institutions in the State.* State Board of Education Minutes, Trustee Reports, secondary studies; 33 notes.
G. J. Bobango

1861. Redford, James. ATTENDANCE AT INDIAN RESIDENTIAL SCHOOLS IN BRITISH COLUMBIA, 1890-1920. *BC Studies [Canada] 1979-80 (44): 41-56.* By 1890 education was regarded by Canadian church and government officials as the principal means of civilizing the Indians. The day schools in Indian villages of British Columbia were irregularly attended and seemed to have little effect on the cultural patterns of the students. Twenty residential schools were established in the province in the next three decades to more expeditiously assimilate the Indians. Their success or lack of it has been judged through the assumptions and conclusions of whites. This distortion can be corrected when it is balanced with the reactions and contributions of the Indians taken into consideration. 65 notes.
D. L. Smith

1862. Schudson, Michael. THE FLEXNER REPORT AND THE REED REPORT: NOTES ON THE HISTORY OF PROFESSIONAL EDUCATION IN THE UNITED STATES. *Social Sci. Q. 1974 55(2): 347-361.* ". . . concerned with these two reports written to spur reform in professional education. The Flexner report (1910) was enthusiastically received by the medical profession while the Reed report (1921) was rejected by the American bar. . . . Discusses reasons for the different receptions of the reports and examines the reports themselves, with special reference to how their views of knowledge and of democracy related to their proposals for educational reform."
J

1863. Smith, W. Elwood and Foley, Douglas E. MEXICANO RESISTANCE TO SCHOOLING IN A SOUTH TEXAS COLONY. *Educ. and Urban Soc. 1978 10(2): 145-176.* Traces the development of Mexican Americans' recognition of their power of resistance against the Anglo power structure in a city in Texas, from the 1930's to 1969, particularly Mexican American resistance in the 1950's and Chicano student activism in the late 1960's.

1864. Szasz, Margaret Connell. FEDERAL BOARDING SCHOOLS AND THE INDIAN CHILD: 1920-1960. *South Dakota Hist. 1977 7(4): 371-384.* Various theories have led to variations in the goals and operations of the federal Indian boarding schools. Originally following the ideas of assimilationists, children were taken from their families for white education to prepare them for life in urban American society. Coincidentally they provided the labor for school operation and were directed with military discipline. Crowded conditions, poor food, and hard labor led to problems, including runaway students. Improved conditions and better educational direction resulted after the Meriam Report of 1928. Ironically, some schools were closed, despite the realization that Indians' education needed to be changed to help them return to reservation life. Still, Indian educators were not used. Many Indians served in World War II both in the armed forces and in war-related industries. Training in the postwar years centered on vocational training for veterans. Especially successful was the Navajo Special Program, but it also led to resentment from other tribes. The 1969 Kennedy Report recognized the social and emotional problems of boarding school students. By the 1960's, Indians were asking for, and being given, a greater role in their own education. Primary and secondary sources; 4 photos, 31 notes. A. J. Larson

1865. Wollenberg, Charles. *MENDEZ V. WESTMINSTER*: RACE, NATIONALITY AND SEGREGATION IN CALIFORNIA SCHOOLS. *California Hist. Q. 1974 53(4): 317-332.* Studies *de jure* segregation in California as it affected Mexican American children. Though not specified by state law as was the case with other ethnic groups, Mexican American children were placed in segregated public schools in numerous districts. Justification for this practice came from beliefs that Mexican American children had poor hygiene habits, could not compete with Anglo children, and that "Mexican" schools could do better for them. In the 1930's and 1940's these views came under attack from educators who held that assimilation could best be achieved through school integration. Mexican American parents also protested the segregation of their children. In 1945 Gonzalo Mendez and four other Mexican American fathers brought suit against the Westminster School District and other districts in Orange County on charges of unconstitutional discrimination through segregation. The plaintiffs won the case and were sustained when the districts appealed. While the decision ended *de jure* segregation in California, *de facto* segregation continues to present problems yet to be solved. Based on the court decision, newspapers, and published works; 2 photos, 78 notes. A. Hoffman

1866. Yang, Kuo-shih. PROGRESSIVISM IN THE UNITED STATES GROWS OUT OF SEVERAL EUROPEAN TRADITIONS. *Bull. of Taiwan Normal U. 1974 19: 250-272.* American progressivism is deeply rooted in the intellectual traditions of the Old World. The concept of "change" and "progress" of the Ancient Greeks contributed, in a negative fashion, as much as the European Enlightenment in the formulation of this philosophy. John Dewey, the man most instrumental in bringing about progressivism in American education, was highly influenced by Charles Darwin. Together with Charles S. Peirce and William James, Dewey successfully undermined the basic principle of traditional education in America and replaced it with a philosophy based on experimentalism and pragmatism. Based on published works in English; 85 notes. R. C. Houston

The Progressive Era

General

1867. Abrahamson, James L. DAVID STARR JORDAN AND AMERICAN ANTIMILITARISM. *Pacific Northwest Q. 1976 67(2): 76-87.* Surveys the historiographical debate over American pacifist movements before World War I, and offers a new dimension to the debate by examining David Starr Jordan. Associated with peace organizations since the Spanish-American War, Jordan objected to growing militarism not on moral grounds but on the strong belief that wars were enemies of democracy. His writings reflected eugenic and euthenic theories that wars destroy the best young men of nations and create massive armies under authoritarian rule. Despite his initial opposition to World War I, Jordan supported Woodrow Wilson's policy of intervention once all diplomatic channels had been exhausted. His actions remained totally consistent with his antimilitarist philosophies that war should be avoided only until democracy is challenged by the likes of German imperialism. Photo, 50 notes. M. L. Tate

1868. Agan, Thomas. THE NEW HAMPSHIRE PROGRESSIVES: WHO AND WHAT WERE THEY? *Hist. New Hampshire 1979 34(1): 32-53.* New Hampshire's progressives emerged in the state's Republican Party in the late 19th century as a reaction to the political power of the Boston and Maine Railroad. The movement became prominent in 1906 when novelist Winston Churchill unsuccessfully sought the gubernatorial nomination but managed to create progressivism's power base. In 1910 the progressive candidate, Robert P. Bass, became governor. In many ways the progressives were similar to regular Republicans, although they were interested in some civil rights questions. Based on the Churchill and Bass collections at Dartmouth College and on secondary sources. 2 illus., 43 notes. D. F. Chard

1869. Aldrich, Mark. CAPITAL THEORY AND RACISM: FROM LAISSEZ-FAIRE TO THE EUGENICS MOVEMENT IN THE CAREER OF IRVING FISHER. *R. of Radical Pol. Econ. 1975 7(3): 33-42.* Discusses the elements of class struggle and racism in the eugenics movement and Progressivism, 1890's-1920, as embodied in the work of the economist and social reformer Irving Fisher.

1870. Aldrich, Mark. PROGRESSIVE ECONOMISTS AND SCIENTIFIC RACISM: WALTER WILLCOX AND BLACK AMERICANS, 1895-1910. *Phylon 1979 40(1): 1-14.* The scientific racism in writings on Negro economic demography by Walter F. Willcox, economics professor at Cornell University (1891-1931) and Census Bureau statistician (1899-1931), contributed to the oppression of blacks during the era of Progressivism. Primary sources; 29 notes. G. R. Schroeder

1871. Allen, Howard W. and Clubb, Jerome M. PROGRESSIVE REFORM AND THE POLITICAL SYSTEM. *Pacific Northwest Q. 1974 65(3): 130-145.* A study of Progressivism concerned with certain basic but unanswered questions: the relation between the several components of the reform movement and the isolation and identification of fundamental conflicts and differences, the sources and extent of popular support for progressive reform and the degree to which reform proposals were popularly perceived and supported, the degree to which progressive reforms were to bring about basic changes in American life, institutions, and the distribution of political and economic power within the nation. Statistical analysis of congressional response, reformer characteristics, and popular response suggest that the movement was largely one of the substantial middle class. 7 tables, 33 notes. R. V. Ritter

1872. Allen, Jodie T. THE FOOD STAMP PROGRAM: ITS HISTORY AND REFORM. *Public Welfare 1977 35(3): 33-41.* Traces the origins of the current federal food stamp program to a food voucher program begun in the 1930's, concluding that although the current program is basically sound, certain reforms are urgently needed. M. T. Wilson

1873. Appleton, Thomas H., Jr. PROHIBITION AND POLITICS IN KENTUCKY: THE GUBERNATORIAL CAMPAIGN AND ELECTION OF 1915. *Register of the Kentucky Hist. Soc. 1977 75(1): 28-54.* Prohibition was the main issue in the 1915 Democratic gubernatorial primary in Kentucky. Augustus Owsley Stanley led those who opposed statewide prohibition. Henry V. McChesney led the drys. After a heated campaign, Stanley won. In the fall election, he narrowly defeated Republican Edwin P. Morrow, in a campaign not seriously affected by the prohibition issue. Yet, by 1918, Kentucky, along with the nation, was ready for prohibition. Even Governor Stanley urged speedy approval of a state constitutional amendment. Primary and secondary sources; 100 notes. J. F. Paul

1874. Aptheker, Bettina. W. E. B. DU BOIS AND THE STRUGGLE FOR WOMEN'S RIGHTS: 1910-1920. *San Jose Studies 1975 1(2): 7-16.* Discusses the achievements of William Edward Burghardt Du Bois (1868-1963), especially in the area of human rights, and notes that a dominant theme in much of his work is the subjugation of women, especially black women, within the social, cultural, and personal milieu of contemporary America. S

1875. Ashby, LeRoy. "RECREATE THIS BOY": ALLENDALE FARM, THE CHILD, AND PROGRESSIVISM. *Mid-Am. 1976 58(1): 31-53.* The Progressive Era was deeply concerned with helping children. Princeton-educated Edward Bradley, founder of Allendale Farm, first encountered destitute city boys during his church work in

Chicago. Allendale demonstrates the influence of the social gospel. Allendale, which was governed as a junior republic, reflected Bradley's belief in environment's influence upon character—particularly rural and family values. Allendale reflected progressivism's dilemma between the social ideal and reality. Primary and secondary sources; 80 notes.

T. H. Wendel

1876. Bailey, Hugh C. HERALDS OF REFORM FROM THE NEW SOUTH. *Social Sci. 1979 54(3): 131-138.* At the turn of the century the ideals espoused by Pi Gamma Mu were exemplified in the lives of three southern reformers, Edgar Gardner Murphy, Alexander McKelway, and Walter Hines Page. Murphy wrote and spoke extensively, advocating that blacks be given an opportunity for unrepressed development, was instrumental in awakening Southerners to the child labor evil and in organizing the National Child Labor Committee, and also served as Secretary of the Southern Education Board. McKelway became an effective leader in the national crusade against child labor, which culminated in 1916 in the passage of the National Child Labor Act, and was a leading advocate of social welfare programs. Page, like Murphy, was a major figure in the Southern educational renaissance and a promoter of Woodrow Wilson's candidacy for president.

J

1877. Barnard, Kate. "STUMP" ASHBY SAVES THE DAY. *J. of the West 1973 12(2): 296-306.* Kate Barnard of Oklahoma visited the World's Fair in St. Louis in 1904 where, moved by the need for child labor laws, she began her career as a reformer. In 1908 at the annual meeting of the National Child Labor Committee she lectured to a national audience. The following year the Child Labor Law was passed in Oklahoma, and she was subsequently elected first vice-president of the newly formed Southern Conference on Woman and Child Labor. 47 notes.

E. P. Stickney

1878. Basen, Neil K. KATE RICHARDS O'HARE: THE "FIRST LADY" OF AMERICAN SOCIALISM, 1901-1917. *Labor Hist. 1980 21(2): 165-199.* Provides a biographical sketch and analysis of Carrie Katherine (Kate) Richards O'Hare. A transitional figure in American socialism, Kate O'Hare represented a paradoxical combination of primitive Christian ideals and American industrial socialism. O'Hare fell short of a Socialist-feminist synthesis, partly because US Socialists were antifeminist. Based on the Wayne State Labor History Archives and the writings of O'Hare; 65 notes.

L. L. Athey

1879. Bassett, Michael. MUNICIPAL REFORM AND THE SOCIALIST PARTY, 1910-1914. *Australian J. of Pol. and Hist. [Australia] 1973 19(2): 179-187.* Examines the mayoralty victories of Socialist Party candidates in the United States in 1910 and 1911 (e.g., Emil Seidel in Milwaukee, Lewis Duncan in Butte, George Lunn in Schenectady, Job Harriman in Los Angeles), and suggests that in each case local corruption caused voters to desert the main parties. In spite of urban reforms by the Socialist mayors, the party could not maintain the impetus, and by 1913 most of the Socialists had been defeated. Documented from newspapers.

W. D. McIntyre

1880. Bateman, Herman E. ALBERT B. CUMMINS AND THE DAVENPORT "RIOTS" OF 1907. *Arizona and the West 1976 18(2): 111-124.* Progressive Republican Governor Albert B. Cummins of Iowa challenged a veteran incumbent US Senator. Most of the state was dry, but the river counties along the Mississippi were wet. The river counties were pro-Cummins. In the summer of 1907 a series of "riots" erupted in Davenport, a river town, over local enforcement of liquor regulations. As governor, Cummins was expected to act against the lawbreaking wets. He did, and consequently lost the river counties and was defeated in the primaries of 1908. The incumbent died before the election; the governor and the progressives pushed legislation through for a special senatorial primary election; and Cummins won the senate seat he was restricted from in the regular primaries. 2 illus., 25 notes.

D. L. Smith

1881. Baum, Dale. THE NEW DAY IN NORTH DAKOTA: THE NONPARTISAN LEAGUE AND THE POLITICS OF NEGATIVE REVOLUTION. *North Dakota Hist. 1973 40(2): 4-19.* Previous historians, particularly Robert Loren Morlan in his *Political Prairie Fire: The Nonpartisan League, 1915-1922* (Minneapolis: U. of Minnesota Press, 1955), have overlooked the shortcomings of the Nonpartisan League. The league is said to have been a part of the progressive and liberal American political tradition; instead, the league tended to view the world in terms of black and white. It contributed to Upper Midwest isolationism, nativism, and anti-Semitism. 15 illus., 41 notes.

D. L. Smith

1882. Bauman, Mark K. HITTING THE SAWDUST TRAIL: BILLY SUNDAY'S ATLANTA CAMPAIGN OF 1917. *Southern Studies 1980 19(4): 385-399.* Billy Sunday's revival meetings in Atlanta, Georgia, in 1917 were his first activities in the South. Reaction to the event was generally highly enthusiastic; political, civic, business, and religious leaders united in their support of the event. A general religious revival was taking place in the South, and extensive preparation and committee work was done across denominational lines. However, segregated meetings were similar to those in other parts of the country. Based on reports in Atlanta newspapers; 31 notes.

J. J. Buschen

1883. Bean, William B. WALTER REED AND THE ORDEAL OF HUMAN EXPERIMENTS. *Bull. of the Hist. of Medicine 1977 51(1): 75-92.* Medical literature of the 1890's records outrageous abuses of medical experiments with humans. In Walter Reed's experiments on yellow fever (1900-01), however, close attention was paid to medical ethics. It was agreed that the members of the Yellow Fever Board would themselves be bitten and subjected to the risks that they would be asking others to endure. In addition, Reed developed a compact that was read and signed by the subjects, who were informed of the risks involved. 33 notes.

M. Kaufman

1884. Beardsley, Edward H. THE AMERICAN SCIENTIST AS SOCIAL ACTIVIST: FRANZ BOAS, BURT G. WILDER AND THE CAUSE OF RACIAL JUSTICE, 1900-1915. *Isis 1973 64(221): 50-66.* Documents the opposition of Columbia anthropologist Boas and Cornell anatomist Wilder to racial discrimination. The traditional view of American scientists during this period as consistent supporters of racist ideas and practices needs revision. 72 notes.

M. M. Vance

1885. Benjamin, Ludy T., Jr. THE PIONEERING WORK OF LETA HOLLINGSWORTH IN THE PSYCHOLOGY OF WOMEN. *Nebraska Hist. 1975 56(4): 493-507.* Examines the early work of Leta Hollingsworth, wife of Harry L. Hollingsworth, who in her early career as a psychologist destroyed the claims for the inferiority of women propounded by leading psychologists early in the 20th century. Her work clearly showed there were no differences in variability between males and females. When she received her Ph.D. in 1916 she had published one book and nine papers, all concerned with the psychology of women. Thereafter she shifted her research interests to the psychology of the exceptional child.

R. Lowitt

1886. Bennett, Dianne and Graebner, William. SAFETY FIRST: SLOGAN AND SYMBOL OF THE INDUSTRIAL SAFETY MOVEMENT. *J. of the Illinois State Hist. Soc. 1975 68(3): 243-256.* The industrial safety movement was a Progressive Era reform dedicated to efficiency and conservation of men and equipment, and directed and developed by businessmen. Robert J. Young of Illinois Steel is credited with having been the first to use "Safety First" as a slogan to spark a national safety campaign and to create national safety organizations. The movement placed a special emphasis on safety regulations within the mining, iron and steel, railroading, and agricultural machinery industries. By the 1930's the slogan became so overused that it had lost most of its effectiveness.

N. Lederer

1887. Bennion, Sherilyn Cox. FREMONT OLDER: ADVOCATE FOR WOMEN. *Journalism Hist. 1976-77 3(4): 124-127.* Examines the career of Fremont Older as editor of the San Francisco *Bulletin*, his deployment of female reporters on traditional male assignments, and his inclusion of women's news in the paper; covers ca. 1895-1925.

1888. Berthrong, Donald J. LEGACIES OF THE DAWES ACT: BUREAUCRATS AND LAND THIEVES AT THE CHEYENNE-ARAPAHO AGENCIES OF OKLAHOMA. *Arizona and the West 1979 21(4): 335-354.* Many Indians who received allotments under the Dawes Act (US, 1887) leased their land to farmers and ranchers for substantial sums. Work-ethic-imbued reformers reasoned that if the Indians owned less land they would be forced to earn a living as farmers. Selling the allotted land would buy farm machinery, build houses, and

help the Indians to begin farming. Congressional legislation, 1902-10, permitted sale of all allotted lands. Poor administration of these statutes created opportunities for fraud. The alienation of Cheyenne-Arapaho lands on their Oklahoma reservation in the 1910's is a vivid illustration of the national disgrace that reduced half of the Indians under the Dawes Act to a landless, rival, and economically devastated condition. 4 illus., map,. 35 notes.
　　　　　　　　　　　　　　　　　　　　　　　　　D. L. Smith

1889. Bigham, Darrel E. WAR AS OBLIGATION IN THE THOUGHT OF AMERICAN CHRISTIANS, 1898-1920. *Peace and Change 1981 7(1-2): 45-58.* From a perception of war in 1898 as a useful tool for ecclesiastical endeavors and church interests, American Christians had by 1918 shifted to a complete rejection of war, ashamed of their earlier position: disillusionment caused by the revelations of irreligion among US soldiers, the horrors of war-making and the greed of peace negotiators occasioned the shift.

1890. Breen, William J. BLACK WOMEN AND THE GREAT WAR: MOBILIZATION AND REFORM IN THE SOUTH. *J. of Southern Hist. 1978 44(3): 421-440.* Historians have slighted grassroots America during World War I. Women, especially black women, have received almost no attention. In pre-World War I years of the Wilson administration, little thought had been devoted to potential roles of women in the war effort. In late 1917, women were incorporated in more important ways. In mid-1918, Alice Dunbar Nelson was appointed to represent the Women's Committee on a tour through the South to aid in organizing black women. The role of the black women in these southern organizations could have led to social reform, but the war ended too soon for them to have much effect on southern society. Manuscripts and printed primary and secondary sources; 101 notes.
　　　　　　　　　　　　　　　　　　　　　　　　T. D. Schoonover

1891. Bryson, Thomas A. WALTER GEORGE SMITH: A CATHOLIC PROGRESSIVE. *Records of the Am. Catholic Hist. Soc. of Philadelphia 1974 85(3-4): 174-184.* Walter George Smith involved himself in municipal reform, fought for a uniform state divorce law and a uniform state commercial law, and helped raise standards of legal education in Pennsylvania. His progressivism sought no sharp change in the social structure but rather the formation of a responsible elite which was to direct the popular impulse toward change into moderate and constructive channels. 38 notes.
　　　　　　　　　　　　　　　　　　　　　　　　　J. M. McCarthy

1892. Bullough, William A. HANNIBAL VERSUS THE BLIND BOSS: THE "JUNTA," CHRIS BUCKLEY, AND DEMOCRATIC REFORM POLITICS IN SAN FRANCISCO. *Pacific Hist. Rev. 1977 46(2): 181-206.* The clash in San Francisco municipal politics during the 1890's between Democratic Blind Boss Christopher A. Buckley (1845-1922) and the Junta, an elite reform coalition, sheds light on the historiographic controversy concerning progressive reformers. Changed conditions had eroded Buckley's personal power by the 1890's, but his continued presence challenged the business and professional men who were seeking to establish their own authority and at the same time provided them with a moral issue to justify their manipulations. In reality, the reformers supplanted the Blind Boss by using more sophisticated versions of his political tactics. Based on newspapers; 71 notes.
　　　　　　　　　　　　　　　　　　　　　　　　　W. K. Hobson

1893. Burbank, Garin. THE DISRUPTION AND DECLINE OF THE OKLAHOMA SOCIALIST PARTY. *J. of Am. Studies [Great Britain] 1973 7(2): 133-152.* Traces the decline of the Socialist Party in Oklahoma 1916-18. Unlike groups in other parts of the United States, the Oklahoma group was comprised of native-born Americans of Anglo-Saxon ancestry and derived its greatest support from the less affluent agrarian elements. Despite its "grass-roots" nature, it fell victim to World War I repressions when public authorities embarked on a program of political repression in Oklahoma. Based on materials in the Western Historical Collection at the University of Oklahoma; 62 notes, appendix.
　　　　　　　　　　　　　　　　　　　　　　　　　　H. T. Lovin

1894. Burckel, Nicholas C. FROM BECKHAM TO MCCREARY: THE PROGRESSIVE RECORD OF KENTUCKY GOVERNORS. *Register of the Kentucky Hist. Soc. 1978 76(4): 285-306.* Examines the progressive attitudes and records of John C. W. Beckham (D.), Augustus E. Willson (R.), and James B. McCreary (D.), governors of Kentucky during 1899-1915. Few political reforms emerged from Beckham's administrations, while Willson's term was described as frustrating. McCreary's election in 1911, coupled with national trends toward progressivism, led to "the most progressive record of any chief executive in Kentucky up to that time." Primary and secondary sources; 56 notes.
　　　　　　　　　　　　　　　　　　　　　　　　　　J. F. Paul

1895. Burckel, Nicholas C. GOVERNOR ALBERT B. WHITE AND THE BEGINNING OF PROGRESSIVE REFORM 1901-05. *West Virginia Hist. 1978 40(1): 1-12.* The leadership of West Virginia's Republican Party in the early 20th century was in the hands of young businessmen. Albert B. White, raised in the Midwest, moved to West Virginia in 1887 and became owner-editor of the Parkersburg *State Journal*. He was elected governor in 1900 on a platform of tax reform and constitutional revision, but Republican Senator Stephen B. Elkins opposed any taxation of business. White also pushed conservation, election reform, railroad regulation, and a food and drug act, but the reluctant legislature did little on any of his recommendations. Primary and secondary sources; 28 notes.
　　　　　　　　　　　　　　　　　　　　　　　　　J. H. Broussard

1896. Burckel, Nicholas C. GOVERNOR AUSTIN LANE CROTHERS AND PROGRESSIVE REFORM IN MARYLAND 1908-1912. *Maryland Hist. Mag. 1981 76(2): 184-201.* More than any other governor of Maryland, Austin Lane Crothers succeeded in achieving progressive reforms for which individuals and groups had unsuccessfully agitated in the past, and his administration (1908-12) is even more impressive when seen "against the backdrop of volatile state politics and the racial issue which dominated the political scene" between 1896 and his election. Examines Crothers's career prior to the governorship, his legislative battles in enacting a corrupt practices act, a primary election bill, a public utilities law, and endorsement of the income tax amendment. Throughout his term, Crothers faced the opposition of powerful ex-governor John Walter Smith and leading organization Democrat Arthur P. Gorman, Jr. Crothers' death in 1912 greatly helped the decline of progressivism in Maryland. Based on the Maryland Manuals, contemporary press, and secondary works; 51 notes.
　　　　　　　　　　　　　　　　　　　　　　　　　G. J. Bobango

1897. Burckel, Nicholas C. A. O. STANLEY AND PROGRESSIVE REFORM, 1902-1919. *Register of the Kentucky Hist. Soc. 1981 79(2): 136-161.* A. O. Stanley (1867-1958) served as a US Senator from Kentucky in the post-World War I years, but made his mark as a progressive reformer earlier as a congressman and as governor of Kentucky. As a congressman during 1903-15, Stanley fought against monopolies and consolidation, and gained repute as an articulate spokesman for antitrust reform. As governor, he continued his efforts against trusts, corrupt practices, and unlimited lobbying. Other areas of concern included public service regulation, workmen's compensation, and Sunday closing of saloons. Based on primary sources including the *Congressional Record* and other records of the House and Senate.
　　　　　　　　　　　　　　　　　　　　　　　　　　J. F. Paul

1898. Burki, Mary Ann Mason. THE CALIFORNIA PROGRESSIVES: LABOR'S POINT OF VIEW. *Labor Hist. 1976 17(1): 24-37.* Reviews and reassesses the interpretations of the relationship between Progressives and organized labor in California. Although labor made gains during the Progressive Era, they were not a result of the benevolent, middle-class reformer actions, but of a powerful lobbying activity on the part of organized labor with its solid base in the San Francisco area. Based on California labor publications; 4 tables, 22 notes.　　L. L. Athey

1899. Burnham, John C. THE PROGRESSIVE ERA REVOLUTION IN AMERICAN ATTITUDES TOWARD SEX. *J. of Am. Hist. 1973 59(4): 885-908.* The "revolution" in attitudes toward sex led to an attack on the double standard of morality through antiprostitution campaigns, the abolition of red-light districts, a franker discussion of sex in literature and on the stage, and sex education in the public schools. The impetus came from feminists, "purity" reformers, and physicians such as Prince Albert Morrow (1846-1913), who were concerned about venereal disease. Morrow and others formed organizations to combat prostitution and to educate about venereal disease and sex. To some the consequence was an embarrassing flood of "Sexology" literature, but the campaign represented Progressive efforts toward moral improvement through education. 77 notes.
　　　　　　　　　　　　　　　　　　　　　　　　　　K. B. West

1900. Burns, Chester R. RICHARD CLARKE CABOT (1868-1939) AND THE REFORMATION IN AMERICAN MEDICAL ETHICS. *Bull. of the Hist. of Medicine 1977 51(3): 353-368.* In 1910 Richard C. Cabot published his findings on autopsies at Massachusetts General Hospital. He showed that many clinical diagnoses differed from his pathological findings. Cabot was criticized by physicians, and in 1916 the Massachusetts Medical Society considered expelling him for publicly advertising the faults of general practitioners. In 1906 Ida Cannon joined him to create the first significant social service department in hospitals. He developed a set of hospital ethics, which included explaining the diagnosis, prognosis, and treatment to patients and maintaining complete patient records. Patients were not to be exploited for teaching purposes. 49 notes. M. Kaufman

1901. Burran, James A. PROHIBITION IN NEW MEXICO, 1917. *New Mexico Hist. R. 1973 48(2): 133-149.* The Anti-Saloon League became active in New Mexico in 1910, two years before statehood. The prohibitionists were successful in 1917 because they argued that prohibition would save food, and because state leaders elected in 1916 favored prohibition. J. H. Krenkel

1902. Campbell, D'Ann. JUDGE BEN LINDSEY AND THE JUVENILE COURT MOVEMENT, 1901-1904. *Arizona and the West 1976 18(1): 5-20.* While serving as a law clerk and studying for the bar in Denver, Colorado, Benjamin Barr Lindsey became interested in the plight of children who were imprisoned for minor offenses. As a lawyer he secured a court appointment as guardian of orphans and other wards of the county. Later, as a judge he launched a crusade that pioneered reforms and established a juvenile court system that gained him national and international acclaim. 3 illus., 32 notes. D. L. Smith

1903. Candeloro, Dominic. L. F. POST'S DEVELOPMENT FROM THE SINGLE TAX TO BROAD PROGRESSIVISM. *Am. J. of Econ. and Sociol. 1978 37(3): 325-335.* Following a brief biographical sketch of Louis F. Post (1849-1928), this study focuses on the intellectual development of the man who became the de facto leader of the U.S. Single Tax Movement after the death of Henry George. During the period 1898-1913, Post served as editor of *The Public,* a Chicago weekly. In its analysis of Post's journalistic writings and of his books, *The Ethics of Democracy* (1905), *Social Service* (1909), and *The Ethical Principles of Marriage and Divorce* (1904), the study documents the broadening of Post's thought and suggests the influence which progressivism had on the single tax and vice versa. Single Taxers contributed greatly to the success of progressivism in America. In the process, however, many single taxers moderated their thinking to the point where the Single Tax Movement lost its separate identity. Post also participated in the 1909-1910 Reform movement in England. J

1904. Candeloro, Dominic. *THE PUBLIC* OF LOUIS F. POST AND PROGRESSIVISM. *Mid-America 1974 56(2): 109-123.* The *Public,* a progressive weekly newspaper published in Chicago during 1898-1919, was intimately involved in the life of Louis F. Post, its founder and editor from 1898-1913. Post was the de facto successor of Henry George and the single tax movement, so naturally *The Public* served the important function of being a clearing house for the world wide single tax movement. *The Public* was also significant because it reflected the reform spirit of Chicago and the nation during its two decades of existence. Based on primary and secondary sources; 52 notes. T. D. Schoonover

1905. Carney, George O. OKLAHOMA'S TERRITORIAL DELEGATES AND PROGRESSIVISM, 1901-1907. *Chronicles of Oklahoma 1974 52(1): 38-51.* Briefly outlines the goals of the Progressive movement in America and notes the role of Oklahoma territorial delegates to the House of Representatives during 1901-07. Focuses on delegates Dennis T. Flynn and Bird S. McGuire. Primary and secondary sources; 3 photos, 41 notes. N. J. Street

1906. Cary, Lorin Lee. THE BUREAU OF INVESTIGATION AND RADICALISM IN TOLEDO, OHIO: 1918-1920. *Labor Hist. 1980 21(3): 430-440.* A series of US Bureau of Investigation reports on the activities of the Industrial Workers of the World and other radical groups in Toledo, Ohio, between 1918-20, illustrates the importance of the Bureau's files for future studies of early 20th-century radicalism in Toledo and elsewhere. 14 notes. L. F. Velicer

1907. Casey, Orben J. GOVERNOR LEE CRUCE, WHITE SUPREMACY AND CAPITAL PUNISHMENT, 1911-1915. *Chronicles of Oklahoma 1974/75 52(4): 456-475.* Discusses Oklahoma Governor Lee Cruce, his attitudes on white supremacy and his actions concerning capital punishment. Cruce had been elected on a racist platform, but during his term he attempted to insure that Negroes received equal rights under state criminal laws. Cruce opposed capital punishment. Controversy and racial lynchings occurred after Cruce pardoned a convicted Negro murderer, but he continued to commute death sentences of both blacks and whites. State lawmakers questioned his use of constitutional power and public opinion was against him, but Cruce never consented to capital punishment while governor. Based on state government documents, contemporary newspaper reports, primary and secondary sources; 3 photos, chart, 99 notes. N. J. Street

1908. Casillas, Mike. MEXICAN LABOR MILITANCY IN THE U.S.: 1896-1915. *Southwest Econ. and Soc. 1978 4(1): 31-42.* Mexican Americans' militancy in the Southwestern states resulted from desire for economic parity and from perceived social, cultural, and ethnic prejudice.

1909. Cavallo, Dominick. SOCIAL REFORM AND THE MOVEMENT TO ORGANIZE CHILDREN'S PLAY DURING THE PROGRESSIVE ERA. *Hist. of Childhood Q. 1976 3(4): 509-522.* Efforts to supervise children's play and to create formal playgrounds, exemplified by the Playground Association of America and the activity of major Progressive reformers, arose from a new view of the role of play in children's lives. As a result of the work of G. Stanley Hall and his followers, play came to be conceptualized as each child's recreation of phases of man's social evolution. By directing play the positive aspects of that evolution could be more fully inculcated. Further, associated physiological theory assumed that physical conditioning was linked to moral development. Together these ideas promised Progressives a means of dealing with the social problems of urban-industrial life. Primary and secondary sources; 40 notes. R. E. Butchart

1910. Christians, Clifford G.; Schultze, Quentin J.; Sims, Norman H. COMMUNITY, EPISTEMOLOGY AND MASS MEDIA ETHICS. *Journalism Hist. 1978 5(2): 38-41, 65-66.* Questions of ethics in journalism and advertising were debated during the Progressive Era, 1890's-1920's.

1911. Clark, Nancy Tisdale. THE DEMISE OF DEMON RUM IN ARIZONA. *J. of Arizona Hist. 1977 18(1): 69-92.* After a half-century campaign Arizona adopted prohibition in December 1914. The last months of the struggle were "unmatched in . . . Arizona for sheer drama and emotional impact." 7 illus., 82 notes. D. L. Smith

1912. Clayton, John. THE SCOURGE OF SINNERS: ARTHUR BURRAGE FARWELL. *Chicago Hist. 1974 3(2): 68-77.* Social reformer and opponent of political corruption in Chicago, Arthur Burrage Farwell, was a major force within the Hyde Park Protective Association's fight for Prohibition. S

1913. Clow, Richmond L. IN SEARCH OF THE PEOPLE'S VOICE: RICHARD OLSEN RICHARDS AND PROGRESSIVE REFORM. *South Dakota Hist. 1979 10(1): 39-58.* Richard Olsen Richards (1866-1930), a leader of the progressive movement in South Dakota from 1902 to 1930, was the first South Dakota politician to use the initiative and referendum successfully as his major political strategy. Against opposition from stalwart Republicans, Richards successfully organized the voters behind his movement for primary election law reform. Remembered mostly as author of the Richards Primary Law, Richards was also a supporter of prohibition and tax reform. Although never elected to a state office because of his alienating and uncompromising attitude on progressive ideals, Richards was an important element in the liberal tradition in South Dakota. Based on the Richards Papers, Crawford Papers, and Vessey Papers at the South Dakota Historical Resource Center, Pierre, South Dakota, and other primary sources; 5 illus., photo, 56 notes. P. L. McLaughlin

1914. Clubb, Jerome M. and Allen, Howard W. COLLECTIVE BIOGRAPHY AND THE PROGRESSIVE MOVEMENT: THE "STATUS REVOLUTION" REVISITED. *Social Sci. Hist. 1977 1(4): 518-534.* Assesses the possibilities for the use of collective biography or prosopography in the quantitative assessment of history, especially as displayed by George E. Mowry in his 1963 study, *The California Progressives* and Alfred C. Chandler, Jr.'s "The Origins of Progressive Leadership" in Elting E. Morison's (ed.) *The Letters of Theodore Roosevelt* (Cambridge, 1954).

1915. Cohen, Abby. PUBLIC HEALTH AND PREVENTIVE MEDICINE IN PROVIDENCE, 1913. *Rhode Island Hist. 1977 36(2): 55-63.* Examines the Providence milk scandal of 1913 in the context of public health history, municipal corruption, and progressive reform. Published documents and secondary accounts; 22 notes.
P. J. Coleman

1916. Cotton, Carol. HELEN KELLER'S FIRST PUBLIC SPEECH. *Alabama Hist. Q. 1975 37(1): 68-72.* Helen Keller's activities are well-known. That she was a Socialist and made her first public appearance at a Socialist meeting is not. Discusses how she became a Socialist and the contents of her first speech, "The Heart and the Hand: The Right Use of Our Senses," delivered 16 February 1913 in Montclair, New Jersey. 23 notes.
E. E. Eminhizer

1917. Cox, J. Robert. "THE RHETORIC OF CHILD LABOR REFORM: AN EFFICACY-UTILITY ANALYSIS." *Q. J. of Speech 1974 60(3): 359-370.* "Two variables influenced the rhetorical choices of Progressive leaders in their fight against harsh working conditions of children: the ability of auditors to affect the aggrieved conditions (efficacy); and the valuation associated with the object of protest (utility). Success in achieving the movement's goal depended upon the adaptation of desirable objectives to groups that possessed the necessary power to induce change."
J

1918. Cripps, Thomas. THE *BIRTH OF A RACE* COMPANY: AN EARLY STRIDE TOWARD A BLACK CINEMA. *J. of Negro Hist. 1974 59(1): 28-37.* Examines the black response to David W. Griffith's *The Birth of a Nation*. Eschewing the futile gesture of demanding censorship of this offensive film, several black organizations unsuccessfully attempted to create a vehicle to counter the racism of the Griffith film. This marked the earliest efforts to provide a usable past for blacks in the film industry. Based on primary materials in the Library of Congress and on secondary sources; 25 notes.
N. G. Sapper

1919. Crofts, Daniel W. THE WARNER-FORAKER AMENDMENT TO THE HEPBURN BILL: FRIEND OR FOE OF JIM CROW? *J. of Southern Hist. 1973 39(3): 341-358.* Discusses the history of the Warner-Foraker Amendment, a provision attached to the Hepburn railroad rates bill in 1906, proposing that railroad companies must provide equal service and accommodations to all interstate passengers paying the same fare. Booker T. Washington's Committee of 12 and the Constitution League lobbied for legislation forbidding all railroad discrimination. The amendment proposed by Senator Joseph B. Foraker of Ohio was a compromise form supposed to be acceptable to both Negroes and skeptical southern legislators. The history of this amendment shows the lack of black influence on early 20th century politics and the relationship between powerlessness and factional disagreement. Based on government documents, contemporary newspaper reports, primary and secondary sources; 45 notes.
N. J. Street

1920. Crooks, James B. POLITICS AND REFORM: THE DIMENSIONS OF BALTIMORE PROGRESSIVISM. *Maryland Hist. Mag. 1976 71(3): 421-427.* Today's history is rightfully paying more attention to the local and urban side of the Progressive era reforms. Reviews the efforts of Baltimore reformers to weaken Isaac Freeman Rasin's political machine and its boss rule. From the election of Alcaeus Hooper in 1895 to the formation of the New Charter Union in 1899, progressives such as Charles J. Bonaparte and William Keyser led members of the Baltimore Reform League and the Civil Service Reform Association to pronounced victories for good government candidates. The Municipal Art Society achieved urban renewal and beautification projects, and other reformers promoted bond issues for sewage systems, civic centers, parks, paved streets, and community centers. A Board of Awards began supervising city contracts and franchises. By 1910 a city-wide congress met to coordinate physical and social planning for Baltimore. Substantial improvements came in public health, but child labor laws were delayed by businessmen, and city funds for programs were always insufficient since politicians were reluctant to upset voters by raising taxes. Reform, then, was not just ousting a corrupt boss, but "a complex movement attempting to come to grips with the realities of a rapidly urbanizing and industrializing nation." Primary and secondary sources; 17 notes.
G. J. Bobango

1921. Curtis, Bruce. SINCLAIR AND SUMNER: THE PRIVATE BACKGROUND OF A PUBLIC CONFRONTATION. *Mid-America 1978 60(3): 185-190.* Summarizes the contents of Upton Sinclair's 1904 article in *Collier's Weekly*, "The Socialist Party: Its Aims in the Present Campaign" and William Graham Sumner's rebuttal, "Reply to a Socialist," and traces the origins of the confrontation.

1922. Danbom, David B. FOR THE PERIOD OF THE WAR: THORSTEIN VEBLEN, WARTIME EXIGENCY, AND SOCIAL CHANGE. *Mid-America 1980 62(2): 91-104.* Thorstein Veblen, a radical who supported American entry into World War I, was harshly judged by his antiwar comrades and by historians generally sympathetic to him. In February 1918 Veblen accepted a post in the Statistical Division of the United States Food Administration to assess the farm labor situation in the wheat-producing Midwest states. He did this to test, firsthand, the government's willingness to sponsor social change. Veblen's perception of wartime possibilities for social change was tempered by his pessimism about the probable results of the war. 50 notes.
M. J. Wentworth

1923. Dressner, Richard B. and Altschuler, Glenn C. SENTIMENT AND STATISTICS IN THE PROGRESSIVE ERA: THE DEBATE ON CAPITAL PUNISHMENT IN NEW YORK. *New York Hist. 1975 56(2): 191-209.* Reviews the arguments for and against capital punishment during the Progressive era, emphasizing those expressed during the Constitutional Convention of New York State in 1915. 3 illus., 43 notes.
R. N. Lokken

1924. Dye, Nancy Schrom. CREATING A FEMINIST ALLIANCE: SISTERHOOD AND CLASS CONFLICT IN THE NEW YORK WOMEN'S TRADE UNION LEAGUE, 1903-1914. *Feminist Studies 1975 2(2/3): 24-38.* In 1903 a "coalition of women workers and wealthy women disenchanted with conventional philanthropic and social reform activities" formed the Women's Trade Union League of New York. There was personal, cultural, and political strife among the members, but they were not divided between trade unionists and social workers as Pauline Newman claimed in 1914. A major source of discord was the conflict between commitment to organized labor and commitment to the women's movement, although during 1903-14 the League chose to emphasize the labor movement. Based on personal papers and periodical literature, League papers, and government reports; 37 notes.
J. D. Falk

1925. Elenbaas, Jack D. THE BOSS OF THE BETTER CLASS: HENRY LELAND AND THE DETROIT CITIZENS LEAGUE, 1912-1924. *Michigan Hist. 1974 58(2): 131-150.* The thesis that the origins of Progressivism lay in the activities of the upper and upper middle classes finds support in the crusades of Henry Leland and the Detroit Citizens League. Leland thought that the upper class had a moral obligation to uplift society by freeing it from the tyranny of corrupt politicians and evil saloonkeepers. Supported by Detroit's business, professional, and Protestant religious communities, the League campaigned for a new city charter, an anti-saloon ordinance, and the open shop. Primary and secondary sources; 2 illus., 4 photos, 58 notes.
D. W. Johnson

1926. Ellis, William E. ROBERT WORTH BINGHAM AND LOUISVILLE PROGRESSIVISM, 1905-1910. *Filson Club Hist. Q. 1980 54(2): 169-195.* Robert Worth Bingham, a well-educated lawyer, was a leader in the effort to reform city government in Louisville, Kentucky. After the Kentucky Court of Appeals voided the corrupt 1905 city elections, Governor J. C. W. Beckham appointed Bingham acting mayor of Louisville in June 1907. In his four-month tenure as mayor, Bingham depoliticized the police and fire departments, exposed official corruption, and closed saloons on Sundays. While Bingham's reforms weakened the Democratic machine—the Republicans won the November 1907 election —they did not lead to permanent Progressive leadership or reforms. Based on the Bingham Papers at the Filson Club, Louisville, Kentucky, and contemporary newspapers; photo, 63 notes.
G. B. McKinney

1927. Ellis, William E. TENEMENT HOUSE REFORM: ANOTHER EPISODE IN KENTUCKY PROGRESSIVISM. *Filson Club Hist. Q. 1981 55(4): 375-382.* Describes the successful attempt by middle-class business and professional leaders to pass legislation to regulate slum housing in Louisville, Kentucky. There was no organized political opposition to this reform. Based on a city government report and the Robert Worth Bingham Papers at the Filson Club, Louisville, Kentucky; 27 notes. G. B. McKinney

1928. Engelmann, Larry. DRY RENAISSANCE: THE LOCAL OPTION YEARS, 1889-1917. *Michigan Hist. 1975 59(1-2): 69-90.* Passage of a local option law by the Michigan legislature in 1887 ushered in twenty difficult years for prohibitionists. In 1907 only one county remained under local option, but dry forces enjoyed a renaissance thereafter, and in 1916 Michigan approved statewide prohibition by a sizable majority. Ethnicity and class, rather than a rural-urban dichotomy, best explain this transformation. After 1907, counties with a relatively high percentage of native-born residents united into a single dry bloc. Prohibition was popularly accepted as a social experiment rather than a moral imperative during the local option years. Primary and secondary sources; 2 illus., 2 photos, 3 tables, graph, 26 notes. D. W. Johnson

1929. Ernst, Joy S. and Hill, Claibourne M. FEMINISM. *Foundations 1976 19(1): 24-32.* Following an introduction on the life of Claibourne M. Hill (1857-1950) is a lecture given by Hill to the Outlook Club in Berkeley, California, 19 March 1914. Hill stated that "equal freedom" was the goal of the women's movement in 1914. He described the achievements in England and America. After some comment on the movement's critics, he described support for it and lists as an example the social benefits from it—27 laws women were instrumental in getting in Colorado. 9 notes. E. E. Eminhizer

1930. Faderman, Lillian. LESBIAN MAGAZINE FICTION IN THE EARLY TWENTIETH CENTURY. *J. of Popular Culture 1978 11(4): 800-817.* In the beliefs that women were generally nonsexual (outside the procreative process) and that, given the proper man, they would marry, lesbianism and lesbian literature was commonplace and accepted in women's and popular magazines, 1900-20.

1931. Fahl, Ronald J. S. C. LANCASTER AND THE COLUMBIA RIVER HIGHWAY: ENGINEER AS CONSERVATIONIST. *Oregon Hist. Q. 1973 74(2): 101-144.* Samuel Christopher Lancaster (1864-1941) designed and built the Columbia River Highway with his engineering skills, "wedded with an artistic sense and romantic appreciation of scenic beauty," and created a great commercial artery that enabled, in his words, "tired men and women . . .[to] enjoy the wild beauty of nature's art gallery and recreate themselves." Traces his career as highway engineer and consultant and the many conflicts precipitated by bringing the Columbia River Highway and other public-oriented projects to completion. 8 photos, 132 notes. R. V. Ritter

1932. Feinstein, Karen Wolk. KINDERGARTENS, FEMINISM, AND THE PROFESSIONALIZATION OF MOTHERHOOD. *Int. J. of Women's Studies [Canada] 1980 3(1): 28-38.* Discusses the growth of the kindergarten movement in the United States between 1860 and 1920, and the effects of the movement on feminism and vice versa, due to the trends of the Progressive Era which made rapid growth and acceptance possible.

1933. Felt, Jeremy P. THE PROGRESSIVE ERA IN AMERICA: 1900-1917. *Societas 1973 3(2): 103-114.* Liberals today ought to look at "the ritual and the substance" of the earlier progressive movement to learn from their failures. Present U.S. social and governmental arrangements which rest on the concept of the Gross National Product and private enterprise cannot clear up the environment or improve the deprived, underdeveloped, or overexploited areas of the world. "It is time for Americans to try to understand, in historical perspective, what they are doing when they ask the neo-progressive question: 'How can technology be made to serve the people?' The old progressives . . . failed to understand that actions in the name of altruism may have their source in the individual's egotistic will to power." 14 notes. E. P. Stickney

1934. Felt, Jeremy P. VICE REFORM AS A POLITICAL TECHNIQUE: THE COMMITTEE OF FIFTEEN IN NEW YORK, 1900-1901. *New York Hist. 1973 54(1): 24-51.* History of the Committee of Fifteen, an upper-middle-class reform organization dedicated to the eradication of police-protected vice and gambling in New York City. To committee members, the antivice crusade was the most effective tactic in the political war against Tammany Hall. Defeat of Tammany, rather than moral reform, was their primary objective. Primary and secondary sources; 11 illus., 36 notes. G. Kurland

1935. Fernandez, Ronald. GETTING GERMANS TO FIGHT GERMANS: THE AMERICANIZERS OF WORLD WAR I. *J. of Ethnic Studies 1981 9(2): 53-68.* A study of the political and societal pressures applied to the more than eight million German Americans between 1914 and 1917 is not only intrinsically interesting, but "underlines an important point about any immigrant group, in any society, at any time," which is that even if the group is not a particular target of nativist sentiments, forces outside the group's control can easily move "patriotic" citizens to press militantly a melting pot ideology. The Iranians in the United States, or Arabs during various oil crises make this clear. "It is the wrong group, in the wrong country, at the wrong time." 55 notes. G. J. Bobango

1936. Fishbein, Leslie. FREUD AND THE RADICALS: THE SEXUAL REVOLUTION COMES TO GREENWICH VILLAGE. *Can Rev. of Am. Studies [Canada] 1981 12(2): 173-189.* After Sigmund Freud lectured at Clark University in 1909, there making his scholarly debut in America, his theories were widely popularized in the United States. Greenwich Village radicals began their own studies of his psychoanalytic ideas in 1913. But radicals such as Max Eastman, Randolph Bourne, and Walter Lippmann concluded that Freudian theories only provided tools for individual liberation instead of insights suited to Marxian sociopolitical and economic analyses. Based on the writings of Greenwich Village radicals and secondary sources; 56 notes. H. T. Lovin

1937. Folsom, Burton W. TINKERERS, TIPPLERS, AND TRAITORS: ETHNICITY AND DEMOCRATIC REFORM IN NEBRASKA DURING THE PROGRESSIVE ERA. *Pacific Hist. Rev. 1981 50(1): 53-75.* In Nebraska prohibition was of central importance in progressive politics before World War I. Many British-stock Protestants advocated prohibition as a solution to social problems, while German and other ethnic Lutherans and Catholics attacked prohibition as a menace to their social customs and personal liberty. Prohibitionists supported direct democracy to enable voters to bypass the state legislature in lawmaking. The Republican Party championed the interests of the prohibitionists, while the Democratic Party represented ethnic group interests. After 1914 the issue shifted to the Germans' opposition to Woodrow Wilson's foreign policy. Then both Republicans and Democrats joined in reducing direct democracy in order to reduce German influence in state politics. Based on contemporary newspapers, legislative journals, and other primary sources; 36 notes. R. N. Lokken

1938. Foner, Philip S. BLACK-JEWISH RELATIONS IN THE OPENING YEARS OF THE TWENTIETH CENTURY. *Phylon 1975 36(4): 359-367.* Certain well-focused events in the early 20th century forced blacks to reconsider the view they had long entertained that Jews, who also had felt the sting of prejudice, were less antiblack than other Americans. The black press reacted bitterly to Jewish involvement in efforts to disenfranchise black voters in Maryland and to the indifference of the Jewish community toward racial discrimination once they had achieved greater acceptance for their own community. Based on newspaper accounts and secondary sources; 43 notes. K. C. Snow

1939. Foner, Philip S. REVEREND GEORGE WASHINGTON WOODBEY: EARLY TWENTIETH CENTURY BLACK SOCIALIST. *J. of Negro Hist. 1976 61(2): 136-157.* The leading black socialist in the first decade of this century, George Washington Woodbey disappeared from the historical record after 1915. Previously, this exponent of Christian socialism was in the forefront of left-wing politics in the United States. Secondary sources; 60 notes. N. G. Sapper

1940. Foran, Max. BOB EDWARDS & SOCIAL REFORM. *Alberta Hist. R. 1973 21(3): 13-17.* Robert C. "Bob" Edwards, editor of

The Eye Opener, a small newspaper published intermittently from 1904 to 1922, advocated social reform. He believed that the ills of society were caused by institutions which had outlived their usefulness. He was a populist, but lacked the characteristic evangelical strident clamor. 2 illus., 39 notes.
D. L. Smith

1941. Fox, Daniel M. SOCIAL POLICY AND CITY POLITICS: TUBERCULOSIS REPORTING IN NEW YORK, 1889-1900. *Bull. of the Hist. of Medicine 1975 49(2): 169-195.* The late 19th century debate over whether tuberculosis was hereditary or contagious split the medical profession. Yet, at that time, public health advocates urged compulsory notification of tuberculosis as the first step to controlling the disease. During the 1890's, when the issue climaxed in New York, it was a time of economic stress, with the depression of 1893 adversely affecting medical incomes. New York medicine was filled with factions, and the chaotic state of the profession may have played a major role in enabling the innovations of tuberculosis control to succeed. The roles of local politics and the medical profession are examined in what is really a case study of the very early progressive period. 97 notes.
M. Kaufman

1942. Fox, Richard W. THE PARADOX OF "PROGRESSIVE" SOCIALISM: THE CASE OF MORRIS HILLQUIT, 1901-1914. *Am. Q. 1974 26(2): 127-140.* Morris Hillquit's personal career represents a microcosm of the American Socialist Party in the years prior to World War I. Next to Eugene V. Debs, he was socialism's preeminent writer and tactician. Hillquit's Marxism was revolutionary in the context of the Second International, but it was weakened in the United States "by an accommodationist political style, not only that of the office seeker in search of votes, but that of the immigrant in search of acceptance." His career epitomizes the pathos of the American Socialist Party as a whole. 25 notes.
C. W. Olson

1943. Fraser, Hugh H. J. SIDNEY PETERS: THE FIRST COMMISSIONER OF PROHIBITION IN VIRGINIA TRAVELED A ROCKY ROAD DURING FOUR YEARS OF THE GREAT EXPERIMENT. *Virginia Cavalcade 1973 22(3): 28-35.*

1944. Friedberger, Mark. THE DECISION TO INSTITUTIONALIZE: FAMILIES WITH EXCEPTIONAL CHILDREN IN 1900. *J. of Family Hist. 1981 6(4): 396-409.* Studies the growth of institutionalized care for "exceptional" children by linking institutional records and census manuscripts. Institutionalization grew because it relieved individual parents of the difficult task of rearing their handicapped children and because specialists argued that society and the child also benefit from institutional care. 3 tables, 3 notes, methodological appendix, biblio.
T. W. Smith

1945. Friesen, Steven. MENNONITE SOCIAL CONSCIOUSNESS, 1899-1905. *Mennonite Life 1975 30(2): 19-25.*

1946. Gaffield, Chad. BIG BUSINESS, THE WORKING-CLASS, AND SOCIALISM IN SCHENECTADY, 1911-1916. *Labor Hist. 1978 19(3): 350-372.* Analyzes the record of George Lunn, Socialist mayor of Schenectady, New York, and the voting patterns in the city. Socialism had its greatest strength in working-class wards, and business leaders were not unduly upset by the party victory. The demise of the Socialist Party may be more attributable to a hostile judicial system than to other factors. Based on city directories, census reports, and newspapers; 7 tables, 43 notes.
L. L. Athey

1947. Gavins, Raymond. URBANIZATION AND SEGREGATION: BLACK LEADERSHIP PATTERNS IN RICHMOND, VIRGINIA, 1900-1920. *South Atlantic Q. 1980 79(3): 257-273.* From the turn of the century through World War I and after, the Negro leaders of Richmond, Virginia, were increasingly isolated from the white community. They faced problems engendered by rapid immigration, institutional proliferation, and color oppression. Discusses the circumstances that brought the leaders to the fore and assesses their ideology and strategy. Based on manuscripts, newspapers, published primary and secondary sources.
H. M. Parker, Jr.

1948. George, Paul S. BOOTLEGGERS, PROHIBITIONISTS AND POLICE: THE TEMPERANCE MOVEMENT IN MIAMI, 1896-1920. *Tequesta 1979 39: 34-41.* Surveys attempts to enforce local and state prohibition laws in Miami, Florida, before national prohibition. Based on contemporary local newspaper articles; 34 notes.
H. S. Marks

1949. George, Paul S. A CYCLONE HITS MIAMI: CARRIE NATION'S VISIT TO "THE WICKED CITY." *Florida Hist. Q. 1979 58(2): 150-159.* Carry Nation visited Miami in 1908, attempting to establish another dry city. Her visit did not succeed. Prohibition was accomplished in 1913, but Miami flouted the law and earned a reputation as an "open city." Based on newspaper accounts and other primary sources; 57 notes.
N. A. Kuntz

1950. Gilbert, James B. COLLECTIVISM AND CHARLES STEINMETZ. *Business Hist. R. 1974 48(4): 520-540.* Charles Proteus Steinmetz "sketched a version of socialism that would combine the economic structures and organizational patterns of the modern corporation with the broader social goals of economic democracy." Traces the impact of the corporate form of organization on the utopian thought of American intellectuals prior to World War I, and shows the practical outcome as illustrated in the activities of Steinmetz, especially his relation to the National Association of Corporation Schools. 33 notes.
R. V. Ritter

1951. Gillette, Howard, Jr. THE MILITARY OCCUPATION OF CUBA, 1899-1902: WORKSHOP FOR AMERICAN PROGRESSIVISM. *Am. Q. 1973 25(4): 410-425.* The US occupation of Cuba under the military governorship of Leonard Wood (1860-1927) was a showcase for American Progressivism, and encouraged domestic reform in the United States by providing a well-publicized, successful, and cohesive program of governmental activism. However, the occupation's emphasis on urban development and governmental authority rankled the Cubans. Primary and secondary sources; 70 notes.
W. D. Piersen

1952. Glazier, Kenneth M. W. E. B. DU BOIS' IMPRESSIONS OF WOODROW WILSON. *J. of Negro Hist. 1973 58(4): 452-459.* This previously unpublished essay by W. E. B. Du Bois, written in response to a query from a researcher seeking information about Woodrow Wilson, provides insights into Du Bois' struggles for black equality. The essay is in the Hoover Institution on War, Revolution, and Peace.
N. G. Sapper

1953. Gleberzon, William I. "INTELLECTUALS" AND THE AMERICAN SOCIALIST PARTY, 1901-1917. *Can. J. of Hist. [Canada] 1976 11(1): 43-67.* Though never specifically referring to themselves as intellectuals, the faction within the American Socialist Party who were university trained became theoreticians and policymakers, causing an anti-intellectual reaction within the rank and file and resulting in the mass defection of the intellectuals from the party in 1917.

1954. Gordon, Linda. ARE THE INTERESTS OF MEN AND WOMEN IDENTICAL? *Signs 1976 1(4): 1011-1018.* During the early 20th century the Socialist Party organized women's branches in 156 party locals. At that time it was the only political party to allow women's participation and to endorse equal rights and woman suffrage. The Socialists appealed to all working-class women, not just those employed. The attempt to create a socialist feminism anchored in the working-class experience failed, in part due to the reluctance of socialist men to incorporate feminism into their program, and in part due to the legalistic middle-class women's rights movement which could not offer much to working class or radical women. The attempt to create a mass movement, however, advanced the analysis of women's situation. Based on three newspaper articles; 6 notes.
J. Gammage

1955. Gordon, Lynn. WOMEN AND THE ANTI-CHILD LABOR MOVEMENT IN ILLINOIS, 1890-1920. *Social Service Rev. 1977 51(2): 228-248.* A small group of women concerned about child labor 1890-1903 aided in the passage of three major laws against child labor and the establishment of a State Department of Factory Inspection.

1956. Gorrell, Donald K. THE METHODIST FEDERATION FOR SOCIAL SERVICE AND THE SOCIAL CREED. *Methodist Hist. 1975 13(2): 3-32.* The Methodist Federation for Social Service was organized at Washington, D.C., on 3 December 1907. The next year the Methodist Church adopted the Social Creed of Methodism. This was slightly modified and adopted by the Federal Council of Churches of Christ in America. The evolution of the Social Creed occurred because people like Frank M. North and Harry F. Ward in the Methodist Federation labored to arouse the support of Methodism and Protestantism. 88 notes.

H. L. Calkin

1957. Gould, Alan B. "TROUBLE PORTFOLIO" TO CONSTRUCTIVE CONSERVATION: SECRETARY OF THE INTERIOR WALTER L. FISHER, 1911-1913. *Forest Hist. 1973 16(4): 4-12.* In the aftermath of the Ballinger-Pinchot controversy, President William Howard Taft wisely chose Walter Lowrie Fisher (1862-1935), a progressive Republican and urban reformer, to succeed Secretary of the Interior Richard Achilles Ballinger. Fisher had opposed the administration's policies, but Taft knew he would not yield "to Pinchot and his fanatics." Fisher's conservation philosophy was one of "constructive conservation," a policy of pragmatism and enlightened compromise. By the end of Taft's administration Fisher had restored public confidence in the Interior Department and had influenced future federal resource policies. Based on personal papers, correspondence, newspapers, and secondary sources; 2 illus., 2 photos, 32 notes.

D. R. Verardo

1958. Grabowski, John J. FROM PROGRESSIVE TO PATRICIAN: GEORGE BELLAMY AND HIRAM HOUSE SOCIAL SETTLEMENT, 1896-1914. *Ohio Hist. 1978 87(1): 37-52.* Discusses the early history of Hiram House, the first social settlement in Cleveland, and how the attitudes and changing life-style of its founder and director, George Bellamy, affected its operations. Originally, dedicated to reform-oriented programs, Hiram House's success came only after it was transformed into an orderly operation by a group of businessmen which narrowed dramatically the range of programs the settlement could offer. Bellamy and the programs eventually focused on the proper development of individual character, which enabled him to avoid the progressive schemes of environmental alteration and social change. Based on archives, contemporary comments, and secondary sources; 2 illus., 47 notes.

N. Summers

1959. Graebner, William. FEDERALISM IN THE PROGRESSIVE ERA: A STRUCTURAL INTERPRETATION OF REFORM. *J. of Am. Hist. 1977 64(2): 331-357.* During the 1880's-1930's, progressives relied on uniform legislation by the states to deal with social problems. Reform was hampered because states were viewed as competing economic units and because federal legislation was seen as a threat to states' rights. Uniformity of legislation, the central methodology for progressive legislation, resulted in social protection without extending the power of the central government. Uniformity scored its greatest successes during 1908-14, when it was the only satisfactory reconciliation of interstate competition and federal ideals. Archival and secondary works; 98 notes.

J. W. Leedom

1960. Grantham, Dewey W. THE CONTOURS OF SOUTHERN PROGRESSIVISM. *Am. Hist. Rev. 1981 86(5): 1035-1059.* An interpretation of Southern Progressivism as a regional phenomenon. The essay examines the origins of the Progressive impulse in the South, the identity and motivation of the Southern Progressives, the pattern of the Progressive campaigns in the Southern states, the confluence of regional and national reforms during the presidency of Woodrow Wilson, and some of the after affects of Progressivism on Southern politics and social attitudes. The interpretation stresses 1) the instrumental role of interest-group politics in Southern Progressivism, 2) the influence of the new commercial and professional classes in the region's reform movements, 3) a classification of the Progressive campaigns in terms of organized efforts to impose social controls, to ameliorate social ills, and to promote social efficiency, and 4) the unifying function of a complex of social values and aspirations that included order, morality, humanitarianism, development, and efficiency. The author suggests that the Progressives were able to function both as agents of modernization and as guardians of Southern tradition. 80 notes.

A

1961. Grinder, Robert Dale. FROM INSURGENCY TO EFFICIENCY: THE SMOKE ABATEMENT CAMPAIGN IN PITTSBURGH BEFORE WORLD WAR I. *Western Pennsylvania Hist. Mag. 1978 61(3): 187-202.* Pittsburgh's smoke abatement movement, 1890's-1918, attracted a reform and engineering elite and gained impetus after the defeat of Corwin D. Tilbury's proposal to create the post of city smoke inspector in 1906.

1962. Grinder, Robert Dale. THE WAR AGAINST ST. LOUIS'S SMOKE 1891-1924. *Missouri Hist. R. 1975 69(2): 191-205.* After 1891 St. Louis initiated a series of "smoke abatement crusades." The movement contained professional and bureaucratic elements. The first considered smoke an engineering problem to be solved by educating businessmen; the second felt it was a problem to be solved with time and a large staff of inspectors. The movement contained a third element composed of public-minded citizens concerned about the harmful effects of smoke. They worked through such groups as the Civic League, the Business Men's Club, the women's Wednesday Club, and the Socialist Party. Based on primary and secondary sources; 65 notes.

W. F. Zornow

1963. Grosch, Anthony R. SOCIAL ISSUES IN EARLY CHICAGO NOVELS. *Chicago Hist. 1975 4(2): 68-77.* Discusses novels written during 1890-1910 by such men as Hamlin Garlin, Theodore Dreiser, Frank Norris, and Upton Sinclair.

S

1964. Grossman, Jonathan. BLACK STUDIES IN THE DEPARTMENT OF LABOR, 1897-1907. *Monthly Labor Rev. 1974 97(6): 17-27.* Between 1897 and 1903 the Labor Department, in collaboration with Atlanta University, produced a series of investigations about the condition of blacks in America; but with changed leadership and in a climate of racial strife, the effort had been abandoned by 1907.

1965. Hansen, Miriam and Christadler, Martin. DAVID WARK GRIFFITHS *INTOLERANCE* (1916): ZUM VERHÄLTNIS VON FILM UND GESCHICHTE IN DER PROGRESSIVE ERA [David Wark Griffith's *Intolerance* (1916): Concerning the relationship of motion picture and history in the Progressive Era]. *Amerikastudien/American Studies [West Germany] 1976 21(1): 7-37.* The film *Intolerance*, although a commercial failure, is presented as a typical product of the Progressive era. It reflects ambivalent contemporary attitudes towards social, political, psychological, and moral problems. Relations between the film and the contemporary social concerns with reform are discussed. Themes of love, power, violence, the city, and the quality of life and culture are examined, and finally, the notion of history, its causes, structures and directions, underlying the film's message and construction are analyzed. 88 notes.

G. Bassler

1966. Harlan, Louis R. BOOKER T. WASHINGTON AND THE "VOICE OF THE NEGRO," 1904-07. *J. of Southern Hist. 1979 45(1): 45-62.* Booker T. Washington not only was the symbol and focus for blacks in early 20th century, but also sought to dominate the thought and action of the black community. Conscious of the power of journals, he sought to control, or at least influence, the major ones reaching the black community. When the *Voice of the Negro,* a promising journal, sought to maintain a neutral ground between Washington and his enemies, Washington not only destroyed it but hounded its editor, Jesse Max Barber, long after the journal's demise. Primary and secondary materials; 83 notes.

T. D. Schoonover

1967. Hass, Paul H. THE SUPPRESSION OF JOHN F. DEITZ: AN EPISODE OF THE PROGRESSIVE ERA IN WISCONSIN. *Wisconsin Mag. of Hist. 1974 57(4): 254-309.* John F. Deitz purchased a 160 acre farm in 1900. The property included Cameron Dam on the Thornapple River which Frederick Weyerhaeuser's Chippewa Lumber and Boom Company used to float its logs to the mill. When the company refused to reimburse Deitz for his work as a company watchman, he closed the dam and demanded payment for each log passing through his property. The company refused to comply, and for the next five years Deitz and his family kept the huge company and all law enforcement officers, both local and state, at bay. During a final assault on his house in 1911, Deitz killed one of his apprehenders and received a life sentence. Because of the nationwide popularity of his cause—one small man against a giant corporation—Deitz' name remained before the public, and through the efforts of his supporters progressive Governor Francis E. McGovern commuted his sentence to 20 years. In 1921 Governor John J. Blaine pardoned Deitz. 21 illus., 77 notes.

N. C. Burckel

1968. Head, Faye E. THE THEATRICAL SYNDICATE VS. THE CHILD LABOR LAW OF LOUISIANA. *Louisiana Studies 1974 13(4): 365-374.* The Theatrical Syndicate's monopoly was opposed by the Child Labor Law (Louisiana, 1908), which had a costly though not immediate effect upon New Orleans theaters. In 1912, after a battle by Jean Gordon and a small group of women, the theatrical interests were the victors: the Child Labor Law was amended by the pressure of New York interests to permit children under 16 to act on the stages of Louisiana. Note. E. P. Stickney

1969. Hercher, Gail Pike. THE WORK CURE AT DEVEREUX MANSION. *Essex Inst. Hist. Collections 1980 116(2): 101-110.* Dr. Herbert Hall (1870-1923) believed that physical inactivity was mentally disastrous for the nervous patient. In 1912 he founded a therapeutic community at the Devereux Mansion in Marblehead, Massachusetts, where he offered the Work Cure Program—the teaching of various skills to nervously distressed people in order to restore their self-confidence and strength. A pioneer in the field of occupational therapy, Hall did succeed in creating a self-supporting industrial community where the nervously distressed could be restored to health. Primary sources; 2 photos, 17 notes. R. S. Sliwoski

1970. Hines, Linda O. and Jones, Allen W. A VOICE OF BLACK PROTEST: THE SAVANNAH MEN'S SUNDAY CLUB, 1905-1911. *Phylon 1974 35(2): 193-202.* The Savannah Men's Sunday Club was a Negro organization established in Savannah, Georgia for the dual purposes of elevating Negroes and protesting unequal treatment. The club enjoyed wide support until 1908, when a Negro boycott and subsequent white backlash caused it to gradually wither and die. Members of the club had diverse objectives; protest seemed to worsen rather than to better conditions, and a new organization had sprung up to usurp the club's more radical functions. The Sunday Club did serve to focus and crystallize discontent. 38 notes. V. L. Human

1971. Hobson, Wayne K. PROFESSIONALS, PROGRESSIVES AND BUREAUCRATIZATION: A REASSESSMENT. *Historian 1977 39(4): 639-658.* The concept of organizational synthesis was formulated primarily by Robert Wiebe and Samuel P. Hays and holds that professional leaders in the progressive era were elitist technocrats. Some questions, however, can be raised concerning the role of professionalism in Wiebe's and Hays's general interpretations of the dynamics of progressivism. The ideological position of leaders in the progressive era is directly related to their professional, bureaucratic, and business orientations. The rhetoric of professionalism, which stresses technical competence and efficiency, should be examined in light of the specific situations facing each profession. M. S. Legan

1972. Holl, Jack M. and Pederson, Roger A. THE WASHINGTON STATE REFORMATORY AT MONROE: A PROGRESSIVE ORNAMENT. *Pacific Northwest Q. 1976 67(1): 21-28.* In 1907 the state of Washington founded its first reformatory, largely through the efforts of Corwin Shank and in response to growing Progressive Era impulses. Shank found allies in Governor Albert Mead and newly elected state legislator Frank C. Jackson who negotiated the bill through the state legislature against a minimum of opposition. Despite their commitment to the idea of an intermediate correctional institution which would reform rather than merely punish youthful offenders, none of the three chief proponents had any extensive experience with penal reform. Thus, despite their good intentions, the Washington State Reformatory never attained the projected goals as it floundered on the problems of inadequate funding, political patronage, and repressive discipline. Primary sources; 4 photos, 35 notes. M. L. Tate

1973. Hoopes, James. THE CULTURE OF PROGRESSIVISM: CROLY, LIPPMANN, BROOKS, BOURNE, AND THE IDEA OF AMERICAN ARTISTIC DECADENCE. *Clio 1977 7(1): 91-111.* While Herbert Croly, Walter Lippmann, Van Wyck Brooks, and Randolph Bourne were conservative in their attacks on cultural decadence in 19th-century America, they were radical in their vision of the relationship between culture and society itself. During the early part of the 20th century they viewed social reform as an art, and envisioned a new social order in which each person possessed absolute freedom of expression. This attempt to define a new art, the art of society, led to their involvement in political issues and to their eventual frustration as critics. 36 notes. T. P. Linkfield

1974. Hougen, Harvey R. KATE BARNARD AND THE KANSAS PENITENTIARY SCANDAL, 1908-1909. *J. of the West 1978 17(1):* *9-18.* Spurred by reports of inhuman treatment in the Kansas State Penitentiary, Kate Barnard, Commissioner of Charities and Corrections for the state of Oklahoma, visited the Lansing institution to check on the welfare of Oklahoma citizens imprisoned there, found the conditions appalling, and launched a campaign which brought about much needed prison reform, 1908-09.

1975. Hoy, Suellen M. "MUNICIPAL HOUSEKEEPING": THE ROLE OF WOMEN IN IMPROVING URBAN SANITATION PRACTICES, 1880-1917. Melosi, Martin V., ed. *Pollution and Reform in American Cities, 1870-1930* (Austin: U. of Texas Pr., 1980): 173-198. Women were a significant force in the movement for sanitation reform. The movement attracted women who were satisfied with their traditional societal roles as wives, mothers, and homemakers, but were seeking ways to enlarge their sphere of action. They characteristically employed the three-pronged Progressive method of investigation, education, and persuasion to achieve their ends. Not every program they espoused was completely implemented, but women were instrumental in making the urban environment healthier and more comfortable. Secondary sources; 80 notes. J. Powell

1976. Ilkka, Richard J. RHETORICAL DRAMATIZATION IN THE DEVELOPMENT OF AMERICAN COMMUNISM. *Q. J. of Speech 1977 63(4): 413-427.* After the Bolshevik Revolution, radicals in America split away from the Socialist movement, formed a Communist Party, and developed a revolutionary rhetoric which attacked traditional socialism and, by glorifying the Russian Revolution, sought to mobilize American workers to support a proletarian revolution in the United States. Primary and secondary sources; 68 notes. E. Bailey

1977. Isaac, Paul E. MUNICIPAL REFORM IN BEAUMONT, TEXAS, 1902-1909. *Southwestern Hist. Q. 1975 78(4): 413-430.* Reviews city government reform in Beaumont, Texas. Beaumont was not a victim of the usual political ills of the time; corruption was negligible and bossism was absent. A great oil strike swelled the city's population, rendering the current governmental forms obsolete. Businessmen desired to run the city effectively and efficiently. A series of gradual reforms seemed to achieve this objective. Poll taxes wiped out the purchasable Negro vote. Greater control was gained over utilities. The Commission plan was not adopted. In sum, Beaumont followed the political attitudes of the times. Photo, 58 notes. V. L. Human

1978. Isserman, Maurice. INHERITANCE LOST: SOCIALISM IN ROCHESTER, 1917-1919. *Rochester Hist. 1977 39(4): 1-24.* Details the socialist movement among laborers in Rochester, New York, 1917-19.

1979. Jackson, Philip. BLACK CHARITY IN PROGRESSIVE ERA CHICAGO. *Social Service Rev. 1978 52(3): 400-417.* Black charities were formed in response to increasing social problems Negroes faced due, in part, to their exclusion from organized charity; covers 1890-1917.

1980. Jacoby, Robin Miller. THE WOMEN'S TRADE UNION LEAGUE AND AMERICAN FEMINISM. *Feminist Studies 1975 3(1/2): 126-140.* The Women's Trade Union League, founded in 1903 by a group of women workers and middle-class female social reformers, emphasized the power of lobbying increasingly during 1903-20. This increased reliance on the legislative process reflected the unenthusiastic support of organized labor for women workers. The WTUL supported women's suffrage and the activities of the National American Woman Suffrage Association (NAWSA) because the vote promised influence on the activities of lawmakers on state and federal levels and therefore was in itself a tool for improving working conditions for female workers. Middle-class feminists were for the most part fairly insensitive to the problems of working women, and it must be concluded that the WTUL did more for middle-class feminism than it gained from that movement. Primary and secondary sources; 49 notes. S. R. Herstein

1981. Jeffreys-Jones, Rhodri. VIOLENCE IN AMERICAN HISTORY: PLUG UGLIES IN THE PROGRESSIVE ERA. *Perspectives in Am. Hist. 1974 8: 465-583.* The Progressive Era exhibited marked bourgeois anxieties concerning potential class conflict between capital and labor, but this concern was unjustified, as the United States' size and scattered population prevented any real threat to national security. Statistics reveal the Progressive era experienced no more violence than any

other period in American history, yet Progressive reformers and politicians, including those on the US Commission on Industrial Relations, translated isolated incidents of violence into the illusion of potential revolution. In addition, conspiracy theories led to increased numbers of armed guards and labor spies, who tended to distort the threat of industrial violence. Appendix.
W. A. Wiegand

1982. Jemnitz, János. AZ AMERIKAI EGYESÜLT ÁLLAMOK MUNKÁSMOZGALMA AZ ELSŐ VILÁGHÁBORÚ ÉVEIBEN (1914-1917) [The labor movement in the United States of America during the years of the First World War (1914-1917)]. *Pártörténeti Közlemények [Hungary] 1974 20(2): 88-128.* The outbreak of the war took the American Socialist Party by surprise. They went on the wrong track by addressing the US Government to mediate for peace. The anarchists also agitated against the war. The small Socialist Labor Party (SLP) attempted to coordinate action with radicals and pacifists. The left wing of the SP, Hillquit and Lee, remained pacifist even after the sinking of the *Lusitania*, while the right wing, Upton Sinclair, Herron and A. M. Simmons, turned vehemently anti-German. Many immigrants and political exiles took active parts in these propaganda campaigns. The AFL, led by Gompers, isolated itself from the pacifists and drifted closer to the Wilson administration. When the USA entered the War in 1917 the AFL joined the National Defense Council and worked out a *modus vivendi* with Washington. The leftist union, the IWW, refused to suspend the labor struggle for the duration of the war. This union opposed the war, but allowed its members to enlist. The SP demanded that the President organize a referendum on US participation in the war. Meanwhile, the government turned on the antiwar agitators with the newly passed Espionage Law. Many SP and IWW leaders were jailed. The courts dealt severely with the anarchists who encouraged draft dodging. 146 notes.
P. I. Hidas

1983. Johnson, Abby Arthur and Johnson, Ronald M. AWAY FROM ACCOMMODATION: RADICAL EDITORS AND PROTEST JOURNALISM, 1900-1910. *J. of Negro Hist. 1977 62(4): 325-338.* The first decade of the 20th century was marked by the rivalry between the conservative view of race relations as held by Booker T. Washington and the radical view of W. E. B. DuBois and the NAACP. Contemporary Afro-American journals represented both points of view: the New York *Age* and others arguing the accommodationist position and *Voice of the Negro* and others offering protest. All of the periodicals established precedents for black journalism which persist to the present. Based on early twentieth century black periodicals; 43 notes.
N. G. Sapper

1984. Johnson, Keach. IOWA'S INDUSTRIAL ROOTS: SOME SOCIAL AND POLITICAL PROBLEMS. *Ann. of Iowa 1978 44(4): 247-277.* Although still predominantly an agricultural state, Iowa began to face the social and political problems of industrialization during 1900-10, particularly in urban-rural conflict and labor relations. Led by the State Federation of Labor and supported by organizations of professional people and women's groups, a social justice movement to secure child labor legislation marks the first major response to the changing conditions produced by industrialism. Based on publications of state agencies and secondary sources; 3 photos, map, 57 notes.
P. L. Petersen

1985. Kadzielski, Mark A. "AS A FLOWER NEEDS SUNSHINE": THE ORIGINS OF ORGANIZED CHILDREN'S RECREATION IN PHILADELPHIA, 1886-1911. *J. of Sport Hist. 1977 4(2): 169-188.* The play movement was the progressive response to urbanized society. Organized recreation for children supplied old values with new meanings at the turn of the 20th century. Boston began the play movement in 1886, and Philadelphia soon followed. Philanthropists and subsequently municipal authorities provided the impetus. 43 notes.
M. Kaufman

1986. Kann, Mark E. CHALLENGING LOCKEAN LIBERALISM IN AMERICA: THE CASE OF DEBS AND HILLQUIT. *Pol. Theory 1980 8(2): 203-222.* Revises Louis Hartz's thesis (1955) that America is a Lockean society in which socialism cannot attract mass appeal by comparing the thought of Eugene Debs and Morris Hillquit and concludes that both effectively conveyed and adapted Marxism to American Lockean political culture.

1987. Kantor, Harvey. BENJAMIN MARSH AND THE FIGHT OVER POPULATION CONGESTION. *J. of the Am. Inst. of Planners 1974 40(6): 422-429.* "Benjamin C. Marsh, a vigorous young social worker in the early years of the 20th century, attacked the extreme congestion of poor people in the nation's largest cities. In his analysis of the causes of congestion, Marsh identified the basic dynamics of large-scale crowding and offered some of the most radical solutions of taxation, land-use, and planning proposed during his day. As an early leader against the overcrowding of land, the author of the first book devoted entirely to city planning and the founder of the first National Conference on City Planning, Marsh's career points up the diversity of style and ideology that characterized the pioneers of the planning profession."
J

1988. Kennedy, David M. OVERVIEW: THE PROGRESSIVE ERA. *Historian 1975 37(3): 453-468.* Reviews the major interpretations of progressivism, noting the deficiencies therein and the problems which require further study and research. Cites the need for studying the electoral process, the nature of political participation, and the relation of the state to the economic order during the era. 31 notes.

1989. Kirschner, Don S. THE AMBIGUOUS LEGACY: SOCIAL JUSTICE AND SOCIAL CONTROL IN THE PROGRESSIVE ERA. *Hist. Reflections [Canada] 1975 2(1): 69-88.* The labels social humanitarian and amoral technocrat appear to be applicable to the reformers of the Progressive era. One impulse implied a thorough overhaul of the social structure while the other was wary of rapid substantial social change. The reformers were pulled in opposite directions. Thus as they sought to liberate the downtrodden from the shackles of society, they also sought to protect society from the threat imposed by the downtrodden. Within this ambiguity Progressives accepted social trimming in the guise of social reconstruction.
P. Travis

1990. Kirschner, Don S. THE PERILS OF PLEASURE: COMMERCIAL RECREATION, SOCIAL DISORDER AND MORAL REFORM IN THE PROGRESSIVE ERA. *Am. Studies 1980 21(2): 27-42.* Reconsiders Robert Wiebe's analysis of Progressivism and insists that the reformers did not lose their moral vision. Such reformers pointed to commercial recreation as a major factor in the collapse of family life in industrial cities. Surveys the various forms of such urban recreation, their impact on the unity of the family, and the correlation with the stages of socialization in the young. The reformers emphasized the need for self-discipline, and instituted various agencies to advance that notion. Mainly primary sources; illus., 34 notes.
J. A. Andrew

1991. Klehr, Harvey. LENIN ON AMERICAN SOCIALIST LEADERS AND ON SAMUEL GOMPERS. *Labor Hist. 1976 17(2): 265-270.* Notes Lenin's views on Eugene Debs, "Big Bill" Haywood, Samuel Gompers, and others. Lenin was hostile to Gompers and misrepresented him. Based on Lenin's writings; 34 notes.
L. L. Athey

1992. Kohler, Robert E. MEDICAL REFORM AND BIOMEDICAL SCIENCE: BIOCHEMISTRY: A CASE STUDY. Vogel, Morris J. and Rosenberg, Charles E., ed. *The Therapeutic Revolution: Essays in the Social History of American Medicine* (Philadelphia: U. of Pennsylvania Pr., 1979): 27-66. During 1890-1920, reforms in the organization of medical schools catalyzed by competition and scientific medicine, "an appropriately neutral and plausible rationale for the new economic and social order of the Progressive Age," drastically changed medical education. The once-collegiate level-medical school became a graduate course within universities, and biochemistry, one of the biomedical sciences, emerged as an area of research distinct from medical chemistry. It became a biomedical discipline because "biochemistry had a symbolic value to reformers" and "exemplified the ideals of the medical reform movement." 85 notes.
G. L. Smith

1993. Koppes, Clayton R. THE INDUSTRIAL WORKERS OF THE WORLD AND COUNTY-JAIL REFORM IN KANSAS, 1915-1920. *Kansas Hist. Q. 1975 41(1): 63-86.* A nationwide effort to jail the leaders of the Industrial Workers of the World (IWW) during World War I led to the arrest of 26 men in Kansas. They were held for two years before being brought to trial. The county jails in which they were held pending trial were antiquated pestholes. The campaign to bring about their modernization, led by the IWW, is described in detail. Based on manuscripts in the National Archives, Library of Congress, Kansas State Historical Society, and Federal Records Center, Kansas City, Missouri, and other primary and secondary sources; 4 photos, 67 notes.

W. F. Zornow

1994. Kozenko, B. D. VUDRO VIL'SON: BURZHUAZNYI REFORMATOR [Woodrow Wilson: bourgeois reformer]. *Voprosy Istorii [USSR] 1979 (4): 133-147.* During his first two years in office, President Woodrow Wilson introduced a number of reforms: the Federal Reserve System and the income tax. Despite his positivist philosophy and respect for American democracy, the progressive content of his political policies was extremely limited. He was a vain and egocentric man, and, as V. I. Lenin noted, his reformism was essentially petit bourgeois and he completely failed to understand class struggle. Covers 1913-21. Secondary sources; 99 notes.

B. Holland

1995. Kushner, Howard I. NINETEENTH-CENTURY SEXUALITY AND THE "SEXUAL REVOLUTION" OF THE PROGRESSIVE ERA. *Can. Rev. of Am. Studies [Canada] 1978 9(1): 34-49.* Victorian literature prescribed sexual conduct that suggests Americans were sexually repressed. A substantial body of evidence indicates otherwise, although historians have mostly assumed that 19th-century literature reflects prevailing mores and practices. Turn-of-the-century Progressives have been credited with promoting liberation from puritanical sex strictures, but Progressive reformers often brought repression, for they imposed their own illiberal, middle class sexual ideology on the populace. Secondary sources; 60 notes.

H. T. Lovin

1996. Kusmer, Kenneth L. THE FUNCTIONS OF ORGANIZED CHARITY IN THE PROGRESSIVE ERA: CHICAGO AS A CASE STUDY. *J. of Am. Hist. 1973 60(3): 657-678.* A study of the Charities Organization Society Movement in Chicago in the 1880's and 1890's demonstrates that in the beginning the society was concerned with transmitting the values of small-town rural America to the urban context. Values of community, country life, and the middle class were stressed by upwardly mobile charity workers from small midwestern towns whose cultural values were threatened by the many immigrant poor. The movement employed as "friendly visitors" middle-class women who applied values of the "home" to the city, and was financed by wealthy merchants, bankers, and lawyers who thought broadly of the need to avoid growing social conflict. Increasing economic dislocation and unemployment after 1890 led toward a more modern welfare system. Table, 90 notes.

K. B. West

1997. Lammen, A. CHIEF SAM EN ZIJN "BACK-TO-AFRICA"-BEWEGING [Chief Sam and his "back-to-Africa" movement]. *Spiegel Hist. [Netherlands] 1979 14(2): 100-106.* In 1913 Alfred Charles Sam (b. 1881) of the English Gold Coast colony formed an organization to transport American blacks to a new life in the Gold Coast. Sam's scheme was profoundly unrealistic but it created great enthusiasm among blacks in Oklahoma, Texas, Kansas, and Arkansas. As many as 6,000 were in some way involved and an emigration camp in Okfuskee County, Oklahoma, became the temporary home of 1,000 people. The British government made it clear from the start that they wanted no new immigrants. The American authorities must be faulted for their lack of interest in protecting black Americans. Sixty people arrived in Africa in 1915 before the scheme collapsed. Based on archival and secondary materials; 5 illus.

C. W. Wood

1998. Lamoureaux, David. *STOVER AT YALE:* AND THE GRIDIRON METAPHOR. *J. of Popular Culture 1977 11(2): 330-344.* Owen Johnson's *Stover at Yale* (1911), most often regarded as a juvenile sports story, is best read as a Progressive reform tract of the muckraking variety. The football game, as a metaphor for American society, provided the means of praising Progressive goals and reforms rooted in coordinated action and social equality, and condemning the elitism and excesses of laissez-faire capitalism. Primary and secondary sources; 53 notes.

D. G. Nielson

1999. Lane, James B. FOR GOOD GOVERNMENT: JACOB A. RIIS' URBAN REFORM ACTIVITIES IN NEW YORK CITY, 1895-1897. *Societas 1973 3(2): 143-157.* Between 1895 and 1897 Riis worked along three political paths: as general agent for the New York Council of Good-Government Clubs, as secretary to Mayor Strong's Advisory Committee on Small Parks, and as a close advisor of Theodore Roosevelt, the president of the Board of Police Commissioners. Riis was unhappy with the continuing abuses of child labor. He wanted the clubs to demand better enforcement of the law and to draw up plans for proposed reforms. He achieved some results in action against tenement-housing abuses. "His practical, humanitarian deeds established him as one of the most useful allies of the slum dweller." 40 notes.

E. P. Stickney

2000. Larson, Simeon. THE AMERICAN FEDERATION OF LABOR AND THE PREPAREDNESS CONTROVERSY. *Historian 1974 37(1): 67-81.* Although Samuel Gompers, president of the American Federation of Labor, staunchly supported Woodrow Wilson's military preparedness policies, the rank and file of American labor did not. Withstanding all pressures from the AFL organization as well as from the administration, the workers remained convinced that their stake in the American economic system was small, that wars are fought mainly for economic or imperialistic goals, and that the true struggle is that of the poor against the rich. Opposition to Wilson's defense program continued to the point of US entry into the war. Based mainly on AFL annual reports, procedures of AFL conventions, the published writings of Gompers, and trade union journals; 76 notes.

N. W. Moen

2001. Lawler, Pat. IN BOOM TOWN ANCHORAGE: RAILROAD WORKERS BATTLE "CAPITALIST WAGE SLAVERY." *Alaska J. 1980 10(3): 22-27.* Recounts the rise and fall of the socialist movement in Anchorage. When the Alaska Railroad began its activities the socialist movement was gaining strength, and in 1916 the Alaska Labor Union was founded. Many immigrants participated; the union prospered and started the *Alaska Labor News.* Lena Morrow Lewis joined its staff and through her the paper became a radical, socialist, feminist voice. The Alaska Engineering Commission began to erode the influence of the union and paper by hiring workers by contracts for specific jobs and not by an hourly wage. Then World War I nationalism made the socialist position less popular. Finally the conservative forces in the union actually came out in favor of the Allies; this helped fragment the party. By 1918 the Socialist Party was dead in Alaska. 3 photos, 9 notes.

S

2002. Lea, Arden J. COTTON TEXTILES AND THE FEDERAL CHILD LABOR ACT OF 1916. *Labor Hist. 1975 16(4): 485-494.* Cotton textile industrialists shifted their position on federal regulation of child labor during 1907-16 as a result of increased competition and a desire for uniformity and stability. The Keating-Owen Act, conservative in nature, served the interests of large industrialists who promoted use of the Federal government to stabilize the economy, although the Act was levied against business interests in a particular section of the country. Child labor and voting tables presented on pp. 492-493. Based on census reports and the *Congressional Record*; 20 notes.

L. L. Athey

2003. Leab, Daniel J. WOMEN AND THE MANN ACT. *Amerikastudien/American Studies [West Germany] 1976 21(1): 55-65.* In the Progressive Era American public opinion was anguished and excited by the concept of "women, kept in bondage for immoral purposes." In their attacks on the social evil of white slavery the Progressives looked for demons undermining what was viewed as the true America. The economic causes of prostitution were largely ignored. Middle class moral beliefs singled out the burgeoning cities and foreigners as culprits. Neither state legislation nor the Mann Act (1910) could stem the growing hysteria about white slavery. Based on primary sources; 49 notes.

G. Bassler

2004. Leavitt, Judith Walzer. BIRTHING AND ANESTHESIA: THE DEBATE OVER TWILIGHT SLEEP. *Signs 1980 6(1): 147-164.* The movement in the United States in 1914-15 to support twilight sleep (scopolamine) was an attempt by women to gain control of childbirth. Although it appeared that women were turning control over to the doctors, they were actually fighting against the prevalent use of forceps, drugs, and artificial methods. Feminists supported the cause; women organized department store rallies. Unfortunately, doctors took control by demanding safety measures; and women separated themselves from their bodies. Secondary sources; 3 illus., 76 notes.

S. P. Conner

2005. Ledbetter, Calvin R., Jr. THE CONSTITUTIONAL CONVENTION OF 1917-1918. *Arkansas Hist. Q. 1975 34(1): 3-40.* No proposed constitution-making activity has received voter approval in Arkansas since 1874. The constitutional convention of 1917-18, held during the waning period of Progressivism, produced a document with reforms such as female suffrage, prohibition, a liberalized initiative and referendum procedure, and important changes within the legislative branch. But bad weather, the influenza epidemic, preoccupation with World War I, loyalty to the 1874 constitution, opposition by organized labor, and under-representation of farmers at the convention caused defeat of the proposed constitution. Based on newspaper accounts and public documents; illus., 158 notes. T. L. Savitt

2006. Leinenweber, Charles. SOCIALISTS IN THE STREETS: THE NEW YORK CITY SOCIALIST PARTY IN WORKING CLASS NEIGHBORHOODS, 1908-1918. *Sci. and Soc. 1977 41(2): 152-171.* Socialism in New York City before World War I not only was politically oriented as part of an international radical movement but also was an integral part of the manifestation of working class culture, revealing cultural influences derived from ethnic and class traditions still vitally extant in urban neighborhoods. Socialism took to the streets through organized and spontaneous parades held to indicate neighborhood working class solidarity with striking employees, many of whom were residents of the areas of the parades. Socialist election campaigns were demonstrations of working class self-confidence and provided opportunities for neighborhood entertainment as well as being appeals for votes for radical candidates. The socialist street corner speaker provided a colorful addition to neighborhood street culture. N. Lederer

2007. Leonard, Henry B. THE IMMIGRANTS' PROTECTIVE LEAGUE OF CHICAGO, 1908-1921. *J. of the Illinois State Hist. Soc. 1973 66(3): 271-284.* The unprecedented numbers of immigrants from southern and eastern Europe were called racially inferior by people descended from northwestern Europeans. The Immigrants' Protective League, founded in Chicago in 1908 by Jane Addams and other reformers, helped the new immigrants in urban-industrial American life. The league sought broad government intervention to protect the immigrants in employment, education, and the courts. Despite some failures, the league guided immigrants in an imaginative, enlightened, and humane way that acquainted the public with their problems. Based on the league's annual reports and papers in the manuscript division of the Library of the University of Illinois, Chicago Circle; 2 photos, 34 notes.
A. C. Aimone

2008. Lewallen, Kenneth A. "CHIEF" ALFRED C. SAM: BLACK NATIONALIST ON THE GREAT PLAINS, 1913-1914. *J. of the West 1977 16(1): 49-56.* Alfred C. Sam, a member of an Akim tribe of Africa's Gold Coast, appeared on the Great Plains in August 1913 inviting Oklahoma and Kansas blacks to return to Africa. He sold stock at $25 per share. A ship was procured which ultimately landed in Liberia. Records the opposition to this movement by Oklahoma newspapers, particularly the Okemah *Independent.* R. Alvis

2009. LeWarne, Charles P. THE BOLSHEVIKS LAND IN SEATTLE: THE *SHILKA* INCIDENT OF 1917. *Arizona and the West 1978 20(2): 107-122.* A few weeks after the Bolsheviks overthrew the Kerensky revolutionary government in Russia in 1917, the *SS Shilka,* out of Vladivostok, Siberia, docked in Seattle, Washington. It was rumored that the freighter carried arms and money to support the radical movements on the Pacific Coast that had been generated by longstanding turmoil with the Industrial Workers of the World and a recent paralyzing lumber strike. At the urging of the conservative press, government officials impounded and searched the vessel. They could not find anything subversive, and the Russian crew knew little about the Bolshevik revolution. The *Shilka* incident provided insight into the growing wartime estrangement between radicals and conservatives across the nation. 5 illus., 32 notes. D. L. Smith

2010. Limón, José E. EL PRIMER CONGRESO MEXICANISTA DE 1911: A PRECURSOR TO CONTEMPORARY CHICANOISM. *Aztlán 1974 5(1/2): 85-117.* Reviews the activities of the 14-22 September 1911 El Primer Congreso Mexicanista in Laredo, Texas, as a precursor to present Mexican American political activity. S

2011. Liski, Ilkka. AMERIKAN SUOMALAINEN TYÖVÄEN YHDISTYS IMATRA I (1890-1921) [The Finnish American Workingmen's Association "Imatra I" (1890-1921)]. *Turun Hist. Arkisto [Finland] 1981 35: 7-69.* A history of the Finnish American Workingmen's Association "Imatra I" active in Brooklyn from 1890 until 1921, when the association ceased to have an ideological program. Observers have disagreed over the extent to which the association was a part of the workers' movement. Finnish American clerical and conservative groups viewed the association as virtually socialist, but after 1904 radical Finnish American socialists criticized the Brooklyn Imatra, and the nationwide federation of the same name, for their failure to accept official socialist affiliation. An examination of debates and activities within the organization suggests that the function of Imatra was to create and preserve a supportive, liberal, and nationalistic subculture for Finnish immigrants who did not wish to join either the conservative church congregations or the radical Finnish American socialist parties. Based on the archives of the Imatra Association, on Finnish American newspapers, on memoirs, and on recent monographs; 3 tables, 259 notes. English summary.
R. G. Selleck

2012. Lovin, Hugh T. THE FARMER REVOLT IN IDAHO, 1914-1922. *Idaho Yesterdays 1976 20(3): 2-15.* In the early 1900's farmers in southern Idaho were upset by the failure of irrigation projects to provide enough water to grow crops. In 1914, after fruitless efforts to gain redress from the state government, the farmers banded together and became politically active, first as Democrats and then as a third party. By the 1922 state elections, the Progressive Party had become a power in the state. Primary sources; 6 illus., 73 notes. B. J. Paul

2013. Lubove, Roy. FREDERIC C. HOWE AND THE QUEST FOR COMMUNITY. *Historian 1977 39(2): 270-291.* Frederic Clemson Howe (1867-1940) embodied liberal ideals and experience. The evolution of his thought reveals much about 20th-century American liberalism, especially the progressivism. It was inspired by the "values of agrarian equalitarianism and small-town evangelical Protestantism," but nonetheless was very complex in its origins and manifestations. Yet, through it all, there was a measure of unity: a quest for community and the restoration of social cohesion in the cities. "Howe ultimately embraced the ideal of cooperative democracy because he recognized that as the administrative and judicial prerogatives of the state expand, administrative-judicial fiat tends to supersede family and local autonomy." 66 notes.
R. V. Ritter

2014. Lucas, Stephen E. THEODORE ROOSEVELT'S "THE MAN WITH THE MUCK-RAKE": A REINTERPRETATION. *Q. J. of Speech 1973 59(4): 452-462.* "An acknowledged landmark of American public address, Theodore Roosevelt's 'The Man with the Muck-Rake' has long resisted adequate interpretation, largely because historians and rhetoricians have not resolved the apparent anomaly between Roosevelt's conservative remarks on journalism and his 'progressive' proposals for economic reform. Examining Roosevelt's rhetorical intentions resolves the anomaly, reveals the thematic unity of the address and explains its meaning as rhetorical action." J

2015. Lufkin, Jack. THE FOUNDING AND EARLY YEARS OF THE NATIONAL ASSOCIATION FOR THE ADVANCEMENT OF COLORED PEOPLE IN DES MOINES, 1915-1930. *Ann. of Iowa 1980 45(6):439-461.* Founded in 1915, the Des Moines, Iowa, branch of the National Association for the Advancement of Colored People (NAACP) grew rapidly in membership and influence. Within a year it was the ninth largest NAACP branch in the nation and was exceeded in size in the Midwest only by Chicago. With support from many white civic leaders, newspapermen, and politicans, the Des Moines NAACP challenged racial discrimination in housing, education, employment, and entertainment. Although less than total victory was achieved in these struggles, the early activities of the NAACP in Des Moines prepared the way for the modern civil rights movement. Based on Records of the NAACP, Manuscript Division, Library of Congress, and the *Iowa Bystander;* 2 photos, 39 notes. P. L. Petersen

2016. Lunardini, Christine A. STANDING FIRM: WILLIAM MONROE TROTTER'S MEETINGS WITH WOODROW WILSON, 1913-1914. *J. of Negro Hist. 1979 64(3): 244-264.* William Monroe Trotter met twice with Woodrow Wilson—in November 1913 and in November 1914. Intensification of segregation in the federal bureaucracy, despite Wilson's campaign promises to the contrary, prompted Trotter's concern. Based on the Wilson Collection at Princeton University and the Wilson Papers in the Library of Congress; 13 notes.
N. G. Sapper.

2017. Lutzker, Michael A. THE PACIFIST AS MILITARIST: A CRITIQUE OF THE AMERICAN PEACE MOVEMENT, 1898-1914. *Societas 1975 5(2): 87-104.* Focuses "on the consensus that existed between an important segment of the leaders of the peace movement and those generally perceived as having a more military orientation." In particular, "John Hays Hammond had helped found the American Society for the Judicial Settlement of International Disputes, and had been a leading participant in the National Peace Congress of 1911. But he apparently saw no conflict between his advocacy of peace and his sponsorship of the 'John Hays Hammond Cup for accuracy in bomb dropping' at the Harvard-Boston flying meet in 1910." Based on primary and secondary sources including the proceedings of peace organizations and congresses, newspapers, and MSS. collections at the Library of Congress, Columbia, Stanford, and Yale Universities, and the New York Peace Society; 46 notes.
J. D. Hunley

2018. Lynn, Kenneth S. THE REBELS OF GREENWICH VILLAGE. *Perspectives in Am. Hist. 1974 8: 335-378.* A biographical analysis of approximately 125 residents of New York's Greenwich Village during the Progressive era, challenging accepted beliefs concerning this "rebel" population. Their average age in 1912 was 31, and most were from established urban location in the East and Europe. Though all professed an aesthetic love of poverty, the majority were from middle to upper class backgrounds. 48 notes, appendix.
W. A. Wiegand

2019. MacKinnon, Jan and MacKinnon, Steve. AGNES SMEDLEY'S "CELL MATES." *Signs 1977 3(2): 531-539.* Agnes Smedley, a socialist, writer, journalist, and participant in Asian revolutionary movements, was jailed in New York City during 1918. She was charged with stirring up rebellion against British rule in India and for violating a local anti-birth control ordinance. After Margaret Sanger helped raise the $10,000 bail and Smedley was released, she wrote four short pieces entitled *Cell Mates*, depicting prison conditions and the powerful sisterhood arising out of them, her first work in the style of social realism which became her forte. Based on *Cell Mates* and secondary writings; 7 notes.
J. K. Gammage

2020. Mal'kov, V. L. TOM MUNI: UZNIK SAN-KVENTINA [Tom Mooney: prisoner of San Quentin]. *Novaia i Noveishaia Istoriia [USSR] 1975 (2): 101-115, (4): 81-94, (5): 93-103.* Part I. Gives an account of the trial of Tom Mooney following an explosion in San Francisco in 1916. Describes Mooney's life against the background of socialist activities and the labor movement in the United States. He was elected a delegate at the California Socialist Party Conference and in 1910 attended the Copenhagen Congress of the Second International. Mooney became increasingly involved in the intrigues of repression and violence which characterized industrial unrest in the 1910's. The anti-war mood made the summer of 1916 particularly tense. Secondary sources; 64 notes. Part II. Discusses hypotheses concerning the explosion in San Francisco in 1916 of which Mooney was accused and sentenced to death. After widespread protests in the United States and Russia the sentence was commuted. Describes the many unsuccessful political and legal attempts in the 1920's to free Mooney. Secondary sources; 54 notes. Part III. Stresses the heroism of Mooney in the horrific conditions of San Quentin Prison and the constant support of the International Workers' Movement until his release in 1939, interpreting his saga as the typical plight of fighters for the working class in the West. Based on letters, first-hand accounts and newspapers; 44 notes.
E. R. Sicher/V. A. Packer

2021. Marcus, Alan I. PROFESSIONAL REVOLUTION AND REFORM IN THE PROGRESSIVE ERA: CINCINNATI PHYSICIANS AND THE CITY ELECTIONS OF 1897 AND 1900. *J. of Urban Hist. 1979 5(2): 183-208.* Physicians in Cincinnati became "progressives" and took up the issue of public health in order to increase the power, prestige, and organization of their profession rather than out of interest in social justice or the common welfare. They received help from other professional groups that were engaged in comparable crusades for identical motives. 56 notes.
T. W. Smith

2022. Margulies, Herbert F. LA FOLLETTE, ROOSEVELT AND THE REPUBLICAN PRESIDENTIAL NOMINATION OF 1912. *Mid-Am. 1976 58(1): 54-76.* Despite Robert Marion La Follette's claims to the contrary, it was he and not Theodore Roosevelt who played a double game during the nomination campaign. Following the successful 1910 fall elections, La Follette created the National Progressive Republican League to work toward replacement of Taft. La Follette's strategy of a united front against Taft collapsed as Roosevelt's candidacy slowly emerged. The ill La Follette, advised by his wife, accused the Rooseveltians of treachery and continued the race. Ultimately, La Follette preferred Wilson's victory to that of his rivals; he was again the leading progressive Republican. Based on the La Follette Family Collection, Library of Congress and other MS. sources, and on published sources and secondary works; 78 notes.
T. H. Wendel

2023. Markowitz, Gerald E. PROGRESSIVISM AND IMPERIALISM: A RETURN TO FIRST PRINCIPLES. *Historian 1975 37(2): 257-275.* Almost 25 years ago, William E. Leuchtenburg advanced the thesis that instead of being opposed to-turn-of-the-century US imperialism, the majority of American progressive reformers supported it, arguing that growth, development, and reform at home were possible only in partnership with commercial expansion overseas and the regeneration of the world (particularly Asia and Latin America) along the lines of US capitalism (see Leuchtenburg's "Progressivism and Imperialism: The Progressive Movement and American Foreign Policy, 1898-1916," *Mississippi Valley Historical Review* 1952 39: 483-504). This study examines criticism of the Leuchtenburg essay, corrects two of its limitations, and finds its basic thesis to be sound. 68 notes.
N. W. Moen

2024. Martinson, Henry R. SOME MEMOIRS OF A NONPARTISAN LEAGUE ORGANIZER. *North Dakota Hist. 1975 42(2): 18-21.* Discusses activities of the Nonpartisan League and the Socialist Party in North Dakota, 1915-20's, including the formation of agricultural cooperatives.

2025. Matthews, Fred H. ROBERT PARK, CONGO REFORM AND TUSKEGEE: THE MOLDING OF A RACE RELATIONS EXPERT, 1905-1913. *Can. J. of Hist. [Canada] 1973 8(1): 37-65.* Studies the career of Robert Ezra Park, race relations expert, and his connection with the Congo Reform Association and the Tuskegee Institute.

2026. Matthews, John Michael. THE DILEMMA OF NEGRO LEADERSHIP IN THE NEW SOUTH: THE CASE OF THE NEGRO YOUNG PEOPLE'S CONGRESS OF 1902. *South Atlantic Q. 1974 73(1): 130-144.* The speakers at the congress were southern preachers who considered racial progress in terms of the individual but were not concerned about the possibilities of organization and the problems of economic bondage. "The failure of the congress of 1902 to tackle the problems that the black man confronted is thus one more indication of his debased status in Southern society." Their optimism was unjustified. 28 notes.
E. P. Stickney

2027. McArthur, Benjamin. THE CHICAGO PLAYGROUND MOVEMENT: A NEGLECTED FEATURE OF SOCIAL JUSTICE. *Social Service R. 1975 49(3): 376-395.* Discusses the movement in American cities, begun in Chicago in 1894, to develop playgrounds for urban children as "part of the Progressive's quest for social justice."
S

2028. McCarthy, G. Michael. COLORADO PROGRESSIVES AND CONSERVATION. *Mid-America 1975 57(4): 213-226.* Conservation of natural resources created a schism between eastern and western Progressives, most notably those of Colorado, since much of Colorado's lands were reserved. Conservation there seemed to inhibit rather than to enhance individualism. The easterners' "greatest good," "future generations," and "wise use" theories were seen as undermining individual rights. Eastern conservationists who did not comprehend western needs piqued Coloradans' sectional and personal pride. Based on official records, newspapers, and secondary works; 48 notes.
T. H. Wendel

2029. McClymer, John F. THE PITTSBURGH SURVEY, 1907-1914: FORGING AN IDEOLOGY IN THE STEEL DISTRICT. *Pennsylvania Hist. 1974 41(2): 169-186.* The *Pittsburgh Survey*, first published in 1909 in three issues of *Charities and the Commons*, was undertaken in 1907 by professors, social workers, charitable societies, and ethnic associations. It reflects the essentially moderate attitudes of a new class of social engineers who thought it possible to accurately measure the social effects of industrialization and to suggest viable remedies. Surveys of other industrial cities were modelled on this effort. Illus., 52 notes.
D. C. Swift

2030. McCormick, Richard L. PRELUDE TO PROGRESSIVISM: THE TRANSFORMATION OF NEW YORK STATE POLITICS, 1890-1910. *New York Hist. 1978 59(3): 253-276.* Studies the transformation from 19th-century patterns of political partisanship and public policymaking, exemplified by the political strategy of New York State Republican Party boss Thomas C. Platt, to the reforms of the progressive era. Weakening of party discipline and demands for divisive economic policies reshaped traditional New York politics. Republican Party leaders in New York State kept their party in power by compromising with the demands of independent reformers. Suggests that the progressive movement generally should be studied as the interaction between politicians in power and people who had grievances against the existing political system. 7 illus., 32 notes.
R. N. Lokken

2031. McDonnell, Janet. COMPETENCY COMMISSIONS AND INDIAN LAND POLICY, 1913-1920. *South Dakota Hist. 1980 11(1): 21-34.* The Department of the Interior, between 1913 and 1920, established several Indian competency commissions to determine which Indians were able to manage their own affairs so that they could be released from government control. The policy, although intended to promote Indian self-support and independence, actually led to their pauperization and the disintegration of the Indian estate. Approximately 20,000 Indians were persuaded or forced to accept deeds of ownership for their land allotments. The government had not relieved itself of its responsibility nor improved the condition of the Indians because most of them sold the land and became destitute. Based on the Major James McLaughlin Papers located at the Assumption Abbey Archives in Richardton, North Dakota, and other primary sources; 3 photos, 38 notes.
P. L. McLaughlin

2032. Melvin, Patricia Mooney. MAKE MILWAUKEE SAFE FOR BABIES: THE CHILD WELFARE COMMISSION AND THE DEVELOPMENT OF URBAN HEALTH CENTERS 1911-1912. *J. of the West 1978 17(2): 83-93.* Under the direction of Wilbur C. Phillips and with the backing of Milwaukee's newly elected socialist administrators, an experimental baby medical care center was established in St. Cyril's Parish. With emphasis on the neighborhood as a health unit, and after obtaining the cooperation of local doctors, the experimental center demonstrated a decline in the infant mortality rate due to nutrition and hygiene factors. The city's Child Welfare Commission advocated an expansion of the program, but the 1912 election brought in a coalition of traditional political parties that promised to end socialist programs that cost money, including the infant health care center. Primary and secondary sources; 6 photos, 2 maps, 24 notes.
B. S. Porter

2033. Miller, Larry C. WILLIAM JAMES AND TWENTIETH-CENTURY ETHNIC THOUGHT. *Am. Q. 1979 31(4): 533-555.* Before 1899, William James had only a modest interest in ethnic groups and race. His attitudes were a hodgepodge of humanitarian concerns; his response to particular groups followed no pattern. After 1899, he consistently drew attention to the treatment of ethnic minorities and made public commitments supporting brotherhood. He was especially critical of American imperialism, which, he believed, stemmed from Anglo-Saxon arrogance and bigotry. James's impact on the theory and practice of W. E. B. Du Bois, Horace M. Kallen, and Robert E. Park was significant. Based on the James Family Papers; 56 notes.
D. K. Lambert

2034. Miller, Lawrence G. PAIN, PARTURITION, AND THE PROFESSION: TWILIGHT SLEEP IN AMERICA. Reverby, Susan and Rosner, David, ed. *Health Care in America: Essays in Social History* (Philadelphia: Temple U. Pr., 1979): 19-44. Public agitation for the use of anesthesia during labor became intense by 1914. "Twilight sleep" induced by morphine and scopolamine was favored by groups such as the National Twilight Sleep Association. The twilight sleep movement failed in part from concern about the consequences of the technique and from the medical profession's hostility to lay initiative in medical practice. Debate over the use of anesthesia did have major results. Childbirth came to be perceived as a medical problem, a nine-month disease in need of correction, rather than as a natural process that should run its course. Concern for their place in society caused obstetricians to seek to professionalize their practice; midwives were regulated out of existence, and their place was taken by obstetricians rather than by general practitioners. 133 notes.
S

2035. Miller, Sally M. FROM SWEATSHOP WORKER TO LABOR LEADER: THERESA MALKIEL, A CASE STUDY. *Am. Jewish Hist. 1978 68(2): 189-205.* Theresa Serber Malkiel (1874-1949) is an example of a female Jewish leader in the labor movement and in a minor political party (Socialist Labor Party, and later the Socialist Party of America). On the Women's National Committee of the Socialist Party in the decade before 1914 she gave her greatest attention to women and the party, unionization of women workers, foreign-born women, woman suffrage, and the party commitment to sexual equality. Her most lasting accomplishment was the establishment of the Brooklyn Adult Students Association. 20 notes.
F. Rosenthal

2036. Mohler, Dorothy A. THE ADVOCATE ROLE OF THE ST. VINCENT DE PAUL SOCIETY. *Records of the Am. Catholic Soc. of Philadelphia 1975 86(1-4): 79-92.* The visitation of the poor in their homes was always the principal work of the Saint Vincent de Paul Society, and advocacy activities were special works. Work on behalf of children and Indians were two cases in which, on occasion, members of the Society exercised an advocacy role. These activities were pursued for varying lengths of time—in the case of the Indians, a relatively brief duration. Covers ca. 1900-10. 41 notes.
J. M. McCarthy

2037. Mooney-Melvin, Patricia. MOHAWK-BRIGHTON: A PIONEER IN NEIGHBORHOOD HEALTH CARE. *Cincinnati Hist. Soc. Bull. 1978 36(1): 57-72.* Wilbur C. Phillips's early venture in neighborhood health care in the Mohawk-Brighton district of Cincinnati, 1917-20, was a rallying point for neighborhood social improvement.

2038. Mugleston, William F. THE 1912 PROGRESSIVE CAMPAIGN IN GEORGIA. *Georgia Hist. Q. 1977 61(3): 233-245.* The situation of the Progressive Party in Georgia was representative of the problems Theodore Roosevelt had throughout the South during the campaign of 1912. White southerners were particularly suspicious of Progressive attitudes toward Negroes, which caused party splits in Georgia and three other states. This third party and its supporters were very weak in campaign ability and received little support in the South. Their position was even more difficult since they were opposing Woodrow Wilson who was a southern Democrat. Primary and secondary sources; 27 notes.
G. R. Schroeder

2039. Nelson, Larry E. UTAH GOES DRY. *Utah Hist. Q. 1973 41(4): 340-357.* The prohibition movement in Utah was similar to that in other states. The delay was a product of the particular political situation: although Mormons practiced total abstention themselves as an article of faith, they were reluctant to work for prohibition at the risk of revitalizing old Mormon-Gentile antagonisms. In the end, Utah's law was among the strictest state statutes and more strict than the federal Volstead Act. 7 illus., 71 notes.
D. L. Smith

2040. Neuchterlein, James A. THE DREAM OF SCIENTIFIC LIBERALISM: THE *NEW REPUBLIC* AND AMERICAN PROGRESSIVE THOUGHT, 1914-1920. *Rev. of Pol. 1980 42(2): 167-190.* The essential conflict of Progressivism "between a liberalism centered on humanitarian and moral passion and one based on an ethos of scientific analysis" was clearly reflected in the *New Republic* during 1914-20. The war caused the journal to lose "most of its naive and occasionally arrogant faith in the possibility of a scientific liberalism" but "also sacrificed analytical rigor, it and American liberalism in general were the poorer for the difference." Based mainly on articles in the *New Republic*; 78 notes.
L. E. Ziewacz

2041. Nord, David Paul. THE *APPEAL TO REASON* AND AMERICAN SOCIALISM, 1901-1920. *Kansas Hist. 1978 1(2): 75-89.* The United States had 323 socialist papers in 1912-13 with a combined circulation of 2,000,000 of which the *Appeal to Reason* of Girard, Kansas, accounted for 700,000. Employing muckraking techniques, it served up a genuine socialist creed in a manner calculated to appeal to a wide audience. Primary and secondary sources; illus., 4 tables, 103 notes, appendix.
W. F. Zornow

2042. Nord, David Paul. MINNEAPOLIS AND THE PRAGMATIC SOCIALISM OF THOMAS VAN LEAR. *Minnesota Hist. 1976 45(1): 2-10.* Thomas Van Lear's brand of socialism was flexible, reflecting his union background. He became mayor of Minneapolis in

1916 due to Mayor Nye's action against striking teamsters, franchise renewal, and the support for Wilson in the presidential contest. However, loyalty and civil rights issues during the Great War cost the local Socialist Party its standing and Van Lear his power base. Based on newspaper accounts and government documents. 4 illus., 37 notes.
S. S. Sprague

2043. Parman, Donald L. THE "BIG STICK" IN INDIAN AFFAIRS: THE BAI-A-LIL-LE INCIDENT IN 1909. *Arizona and the West 1978 20(4): 343-360.* Disagreements developed in 1907 between federal officials and a band of Navajo Indians in southeastern Utah who refused to send their children to boarding school. The Indians, whose leader was Bai-a-lil-le, a medicine man, were seized by federal troops and sent to Fort Huachuca, Arizona, where they were tried without the customary legal procedures. The Indian Rights Association took court action. Bai-a-lil-le and his followers were finally released in 1909. The incident demonstrates the nature of Indian affairs in the early years of the century, provides an insight into Indian reform organization effectiveness, and reveals much about racial attitudes. 2 illus., map, 41 notes.
D. L. Smith

2044. Pearlman, Michael. LEONARD WOOD, WILLIAM MULDOON AND THE MEDICAL PROFESSION: PUBLIC HEALTH AND UNIVERSAL MILITARY TRAINING. *New England Q. 1979 52(3): 326-344.* As a medical student, Leonard Wood (1860-1927) learned that virtue and a regulated life were the source of good health. This led him to believe that universal military training would lead to a healthier, more moral American people. His 1912 call for such training received great support from the medical community, perhaps because by doing so, doctors "could still endorse old principles that were growing professionally inappropriate." William Muldoon (1845-1933), a lay clinician who operated a health camp which stressed cold showers, simple food, strict discipline, and strenuous exercise, supported Wood's drive believing universal military training would provide the common man for free what his camp provided fee-paying aristocrats. Wood's writings and secondary sources; 38 notes.
J. C. Bradford

2045. Pendergrass, Lee F. THE FORMATION OF A MUNICIPAL REFORM MOVEMENT: THE MUNICIPAL LEAGUE OF SEATTLE. *Pacific Northwest Q. 1975 66(1): 13-25.* Throughout the tenure of its existence, 1910-20, the Municipal League of Seattle presented a genuinely progressive, nonpartisan interest in the promotion of municipal improvements, the selection of competent civic officials, the preparation of citizens for active roles in urban affairs, and the dissemination of information about Seattle.

2046. Petrov, G. D. ALEKSANDRA KOLLONTAI V SSHA [Aleksandra Kollontai in the USA]. *Novaia i Noveishaia Istoriia [USSR] 1972 (3): 128-142.* A revolutionary from early years, Kollontai (1872-1952) fled Russia in 1908. She settled, eventually, in Norway. Invited by the American Socialist Party, she departed for the USA in 1915. Throughout America she promoted Marxism-Leninism, denounced the imperialist war, and, in her meetings with Russian emigres, fostered international solidarity. At Lenin's behest she arranged the publication of Bolshevik literature. On 21 February 1916 she returned to Norway, only to leave again for the USA in August 1916 with her son. This essentially private visit she turned to political use by establishing close contact with the Socialist labor party. She tirelessly denounced the imperialist war. She left America on 27 January 1917, and news of America's joining the war reached her on the ship. She was a true internationalist, and in the USA did much useful propaganda work. Based on Lenin's work, Istoricheskii arkhiv and Inostrannaia literature; 94 notes.
A. J. Evans

2047. Piott, Steven. THE LESSON OF THE IMMIGRANT: VIEWS OF IMMIGRANTS IN MUCKRAKING MAGAZINES, 1900-1909. *Am. Studies 1978 19(1): 21-33.* Immigrants brought with them an undefiled sense of morality. Many early muckraking authors used this, and depicted innocent immigrants as victims of an industrial capitalism devoid of ethics or a sense of community. They argued for the reestablishment of a moral responsibility. A differentiated society had blinded citizens to corporate malefactors. Ordinary people could not perceive industrial patterns, and reform writers sought to implant a sense of guilt. Industrial capitalists, not the immigrants, were the true enemies. Primary and secondary sources; 36 notes.
J. Andrew

2048. Pivar, David J. CLEANSING THE NATION: THE WAR ON PROSTITUTION, 1917-21. *Prologue 1980 12(1): 29-40.* The World War I effort prompted social engineering leading to a partnership (known as the American Plan) between social hygienists in voluntary associations and their counterparts in federal government. Under section 2 of the Army Appropriation Act (US, 1916), Congress established the Council of National Defense to provide for cooperation on social hygiene between volunteer agencies and government. The Chamberlain-Kahn Act (US, 1918) created a division of venereal disease within the US Public Health Service. On 9 July 1918, an Interdepartmental Board of Social Hygiene was created by law. The new social policy was to control venereal disease and to eliminate prostitution in order to protect servicemen and keep them healthy. Based on correspondence and newspapers; 6 illus., 42 notes.
M. A. Kascus

2049. Price, David E. COMMUNITY AND CONTROL: CRITICAL DEMOCRATIC THEORY IN THE PROGRESSIVE PERIOD. *Am. Pol. Sci. Rev. 1974 68(4): 1663-1678.* Current political debate over the flaws and the fate of the American liberal tradition mirrors closely the critiques of the Progressive period. A number of those thinkers—theorists of "social control," exemplified by Ward and Ross—took aim not at the liberal-utilitarian conception of the ends of politics but rather at the notion that these goods would be produced by the politics of *laissez-faire*. A second body of critics—here termed "communitarians" and including Cooley, Royce, Croly, DuBois, and Dewey—leveled a more fundamental indictment: liberal individualism left men's needs for human sympathy, shared meanings and loyalties, and common effort unfulfilled. But the difficulties of the communitarian theorists, the range of associations on which they pinned their hopes and their fundamental ambivalence concerning politics demonstrate how little in the way of ideological or social-structural reinforcement the environment provided for one who would apply the insights of Burke or Hegel or Tönnies in America. Modern political criticism has resurrected the themes of the Progressive period, but even such bridge-builders as Dahl and McWilliams have not been sufficiently attentive to interrelationships among the persisting critiques of liberalism and to the shape ameliorative communities might assume.
J

2050. Pride, Nancy. INCIDENTS PRECEDING THE LOUISIANA CHILD LABOR LAW OF 1912. *Louisiana Hist. 1978 19(4): 437-445.* Several incidents in Louisiana illustrate the antecedents of child legislation in other states. These incidents arose from the Louisiana Child Labor Law (1908) and involved cases of children appearing on the stage in Louisiana between 1908 and 1911. These cases paved the way for the 1912 law which permitted children under 16 to act on the stage provided they received supervision. The cases made Louisiana a leader for other states.
R. L. Woodward

2051. Pumphrey, Ralph E. MICHAEL DAVIS AND THE TRANSFORMATION OF THE BOSTON DISPENSARY, 1910-1920. *Bull. of the Hist. of Medicine 1975 49(4): 451-465.* Michael M. Davis, Ph.D. (1879-1971), as director of the Boston Dispensary transformed that institution into "one of the pioneering medical institutions of the twentieth century." He improved the administration of the Dispensary, and he infused it with a progressive spirit, while being able to "relate constructively to pressures from within the medical and scientific communities.... Describes the extensive work of the Dispensary during 1910-20. 45 notes.
M. Kaufman

2052. Rakestraw, Lawrence. BEFORE MCNARY: THE NORTHWESTERN CONSERVATIONIST, 1889-1913. *Pacific Northwest Q. 1960 51(2): 49-56.* Political and social reform, utilitarianism, and ends both aesthetic and recreational, motivated the local leaders of the forest conservation movement in the Pacific Northwest even before Senator Charles McNary of Oregon promoted national legislation.
S

2053. Reese, William J. AFTER BREAD, EDUCATION: NUTRITION AND URBAN SCHOOL CHILDREN, 1890-1920. *Teachers Coll. Record 1980 81(4): 496-525.* Free lunch programs for school children developed in Great Britain and America, often at the instigation of trade unions, socialists, or women's groups. In both countries implementation was slowed by the active opposition of antisocialist proponents of private charity who believed that public programs would increase dependence on the state. Both sides agreed that undernourished children made poor students; however, opponents often advocated educating parents to better nutritional habits rather than simply providing free food. Although evaluation of the new programs was difficult, most assessments suggested that the health of students, if not necessarily their intellect, significantly improved. Based on British and American government documents, newspaper articles, and secondary sources. E. Bailey

2054. Remele, Larry. THE IMMACULATE CONCEPTION AT DEERING. *North Dakota Hist. 1980 47(1): 28-31.* Reviews various accounts of the origin of the idea for the North Dakota Nonpartisan League in 1915. Concludes that Albert E. Bowen, Jr., not Arthur Charles Townley, developed and first advocated the idea, and that the idea was outlined by Bowen at the American Society of Equity's North Dakota branch convention in Bismarck, not by Townley on the farm of F. B. Wood near Deering. The idea for the league emerged from the experience (1914-15) of frustrated radicals who sought new alternatives for farmers. Based on published accounts and contemporary publications; 2 illus., 25 notes. G. L. Olson

2055. Remele, Larry. THE NONPARTISAN LEAGUE AND THE NORTH DAKOTA PRESS: ORGANIZATION PERIOD: 1915-1916. *North Dakota Q. 1976 44(4): 30-46.* Discusses the reluctant press coverage given the Nonpartisan League by newspapers in North Dakota, 1915-16; asserts that contrary to claims of North Dakota having a "kept press" certain newspapers did give proper and fair coverage to the actions of the League.

2056. Reverby, Susan. STEALING THE GOLDEN EGGS: ERNEST AMORY CODMAN AND THE SCIENCE AND MANAGEMENT OF MEDICINE. *Bull. of the Hist. of Medicine 1981 55(2): 156-171.* Ernest Amory Codman (1869-1940) tried to make medicine more efficient by developing the end result system, following patients to determine whether the treatment has succeeded, and then to inquire, if not, why not. In 1910, Codman and Edward Martin, a clinical professor of surgery at the University of Pennsylvania, began to campaign for the implementation of the system nationwide. Codman opened a private hospital in Boston in 1911 and issued periodic studies on hospital efficiency, which he mailed to hospitals around the country. Although some hospitals did try the system, its most lasting results were achieved through the hospital standardization work of the American college of Surgeons beginning in 1916. Based on primary, including the Codman papers at the Countway Library, Boston, and secondary sources; illus., 71 notes.
M. Kaufman

2057. Ringenbach, Paul T. DISCARDING RURAL NOSTRUMS FOR CITY PROBLEMS: MOVING TOWARDS URBAN REFORM. *Rocky Mountain Social Sci. J. 1973 10(1): 33-42.* Only after social reformers attempted futile rural solutions did they try to improve urban life.
S

2058. Ritchie, Donald A. THE GARY COMMITTEE: BUSINESSMEN, PROGRESSIVES, AND UNEMPLOYMENT IN NEW YORK CITY, 1914-1915. *New-York Hist. Soc. Q. 1973 57(4): 326-347.* Disruption of trade and industry during World War I caused widespread unemployment in the United States, particularly in the Northeast and the Middle West. Most cities, some with Progressive administrations, began unemployment and relief programs. In New York City these efforts were led by Mayor John Purroy Mitchel and Elbert H. Gary, chairman of the Committee on Unemployment and Relief. The committee, composed of businessmen, promised much but never identified closely with the working class and failed to cope with basic problems. By 1917, prosperity and loss of confidence in the committee helped defeat Mitchel and bring in an urban reform movement identified with Alfred E. Smith. Primary sources; 6 illus., 45 notes. C. L. Grant

2059. Roberts, Clarence N. THE ILLINOIS INTERCOLLEGIATE PROHIBITION ASSOCIATION, 1893-1920. *J. of the Illinois State Hist. Soc. 1977 70(2): 140-148.* Member schools in this international association were usually private, church-sponsored institutions. The Association sponsored regional antialcohol debates and also encouraged establishment of academic-credit antiliquor courses on campus. After Prohibition, attempts to recruit members into other social improvement causes failed. 5 illus., 53 notes. J

2060. Romanofsky, Peter. "THE PUBLIC IS AROUSED": THE MISSOURI CHILDREN'S CODE COMMISSION, 1915-1919. *Missouri Hist. R. 1974 68(2): 204-222.* Discusses the origins and history of the Missouri Children's Code Commission, a Progressive reform movement which involved prominent educators and social workers and a coalition of citizens' groups. The first commission was appointed in 1915 to protect children from adverse conditions in labor and from delinquency, neglect, welfare and other problems, but its proposals were a failure because the more significant measures were rejected by the legislature. Appointed in 1917, the second commission revised the earlier proposals and actively engaged in an educational promotional campaign, gaining the support of various organizations such as the Women's Christian Temperance Union, The Red Cross, women's clubs, suffrage groups, and others. The Missouri Children's Code was finally passed in 1919. Based on contemporary newspaper reports, primary and secondary sources; 3 illus., 5 photos, 64 notes. N. J. Street

2061. Romanofsky, Peter. "TO SAVE... THEIR SOULS": THE CARE OF DEPENDENT CHILDREN IN NEW YORK CITY, 1900-1905. *Jewish Social Studies 1974 36(3/4): 253-261.* During 1903-05 a small number of dependent children were placed in foster homes of working class families rather than families of middle class background. The program was initiated by the United Hebrew Charities of New York City in order to cope with the increasing number of orphans and other children that needed help as Jewish immigration from Eastern Europe increased. Ideological opposition and lack of financial support terminated the program but its pioneering prepared the way for a change in the general American approach. Primary and secondary sources; 27 notes.
P. E. Schoenberg

2062. Roper, John Herbert. A CASE OF FORGOTTEN IDENTITY: ULRICH B. PHILLIPS AS A YOUNG PROGRESSIVE. *Georgia Hist. Q. 1976 60(2): 165-175.* Calls Ulrich B. Phillips, thought of as a racist, romantic, conservative historian of the antebellum South, a Progressive. While teaching at the University of Wisconsin during 1903-05, Phillips corresponded with the Atlanta *Constitution*, edited by Clark Howell. In these letters Phillips advocated the reform of the University of Georgia along the lines of the University of Wisconsin and encouraged quotas on Georgia cotton production. Despite the controversy he raised, Phillips was slightly influential. He ceased his political activism when he and Howell split because of their differing opinions of Theodore Roosevelt. Primary and secondary sources; 29 notes.
G. R. Schroeder

2063. Rosen, Ellen. SOCIALISM IN OKLAHOMA: A THEORETICAL OVERVIEW. *Pol. and Soc. 1978 8(1): 109-129.* The apparent similarities between southern populism and Oklahoma socialism masks important differences that were produced by Oklahoma's "anomalous" history. Oklahoma farmers tended to view the elites of the "electric light towns" as parasites exploiting the agricultural population. The farmers turned to socialism as a way of gaining control of the land, although they rejected immediate collectivization of it. Covers 1900's-10's. table, 63 notes. D. G. Nielson

2064. Rosen, George. THE EFFICIENCY CRITERION IN MEDICAL CARE, 1900-1920. *Bull. of the Hist. of Medicine 1976 50(1): 28-44.* During the Progressive period, an attempt was made to apply the concept of scientific management efficiency to medical care, especially regarding medical charities like the dispensary. The belief was common among physicians that patients who were able to pay for their medical care were being attended at free dispensaries. Early studies indicated that the fear was much exaggerated. Shortly after the turn of the century, studies were made of the effectiveness of the dispensary and the outpatient departments. Describes Richard C. Cabot, S. S. Goldwater, and Michael M. Davis as three leaders who attempted to improve the efficiency of medical care. These men, and especially Davis, helped "move medical care to a stage of development more appropriate to the needs of the mass of the people." 53 notes. M. Kaufman

2065. Rosenberg, Rosalind. THE ACADEMIC PRISON: THE NEW VIEW OF AMERICAN WOMEN. Berkin, Carol Ruth and Norton, Mary Beth, ed. *Women of America: A History* (Boston: Houghton Mifflin Co., 1979): 318-341. During the early 20th century, women scholars were developing critical views of assumptions about woman's nature. They sought to abolish the separate male and female worlds of the 19th century. Discusses the administrative work of Marion Talbot at the University of Chicago, and Helen Thompson's research in the social sciences, investigating the psychology of men and women. This generation produced anthropologist Margaret Mead. Based on contemporary documents; 15 notes. K. Talley

2066. Rosenberger, Homer T. THE AMERICAN PEACE SOCIETY'S REACTION TO THE COVENANT OF THE LEAGUE OF NATIONS. *World Affairs 1978 141(2): 139-152.* Describes policies of the American Peace Society after the outbreak of world war in 1914, and their mixed reactions to the 1919 Paris Peace Conference and the drafting of the League of Nations Covenant.

2067. Rowley, William D. FRANCIS G. NEWLANDS: A WESTERNER'S SEARCH FOR A PROGRESSIVE AND WHITE AMERICA. *Nevada Hist. Soc. Q. 1974 17(2): 68-79.* Discusses contributions by Senator Francis Newlands (1848-1917) to the thinking and efforts of "West Coast Progressives" in restricting immigration of Asians to the United States and in simultaneously dealing with the "Negro question." Newlands strongly supported exclusion of Asian immigrants and proposed measures to bar Negroes from American political processes. Based on the Newlands Papers and newspaper sources; 1 photo, 20 notes.
H. T. Lovin

2068. Sandos, James A. PROSTITUTION AND DRUGS: THE UNITED STATES ARMY ON THE MEXICAN-AMERICAN BORDER, 1916-1917. *Pacific Hist. Rev. 1980 49(4): 621-645.* General John J. Pershing, commander of the US Punitive Expedition into Mexico, reduced the number of venereal disease cases among his men at Columbus, New Mexico, and in Mexico by regulating prostitution to maintain troop morale and prevent infection. The venereal disease rate in his command was lower than elsewhere in the United States Army where War Department policy of abolishing prostitution in the vicinity of army camps was practiced. The ban on drugs worked better in Pershing's command than elsewhere, because Pershing isolated his men from towns and civilians, provided other diversions, and regulated prostitution. Based on the John J. Pershing Papers, reports of the Punitive Expedition in the National Archives, and other primary sources; 103 notes.
R. N. Lokken

2069. Sansoucy, Debra P. PROHIBITION AND ITS EFFECT ON WESTERN MASSACHUSETTS 1919-1920. *Hist. J. of Western Massachusetts 1975 4(1): 27-39.* Shorter factory hours and the return of servicemen were two factors for favoring prohibition in western Massachusetts. Not until 1921 did the region become relatively dry. Sixty-two deaths caused by fake wine and the successful prosecution of John Romanelli (both in 1920) led to the decline in alcohol traffic. Based on the Springfield *Union* 1919-20; 5 illus., chart, table, 41 notes.
S. S. Sprague

2070. Schiesl, Martin J. PROGRESSIVE REFORM IN LOS ANGELES UNDER MAYOR ALEXANDER, 1909-1913. *California Hist. Q. 1975 54(1): 37-56.* A study of progressive accomplishments and problems as Los Angeles moved into the status of a major metropolis. In an effort to rid the city of machine politics, reformers supported the election of George Alexander as mayor. But progressives disagreed over the goals of reform. Some supported honesty and efficiency in government, working for civil service reforms and "classless" politics. More radical reformers called for measures that promoted social welfare and economic reform. When business-oriented progressives merged their interests with the social welfare faction, the city enacted legislation creating a public utilities commission, a public power project, and other measures. However, some business-oriented progressives abandoned the reform movement, while labor leaders demanded leadership that went beyond middle-class values. Pursuing a middle course, the progressives defeated a Socialist bid for the mayoralty in 1911, and in Alexander's second term enacted additional measures benefiting the public welfare. Party regulars, however, defeated a proposed progressive city charter in 1912, and increased factionalism within progressive ranks ended progressive rule in 1913. Primary and secondary sources; illus., 65 notes. A. Hoffman

2071. Schlereth, Thomas J. BURNHAM'S *PLAN* AND MOODY'S *MANUAL:* CITY PLANNING AS PROGRESSIVE REFORM. *J. of the Am. Planning Assoc. 1981 47(1): 70-85.* Using Walter D. Moody's *Wacker's Manual of the Plan of Chicago* (1911) as an early classic in the history of American planning promotional literature, this article explores the relations of Daniel Burnham's 1909 plan for Chicago, as translated by Moody into a more democratic medium, with the intellectual concerns of progressive reformers at the turn of the 20th century. Special emphasis is given to the emerging profession of the civic promoter and his impact on urban planning. J/S

2072. Schlossman, Steven and Wallach, Stephanie. THE CRIME OF PRECOCIOUS SEXUALITY: FEMALE JUVENILE DELINQUENCY IN THE PROGRESSIVE ERA. *Harvard Educ. Rev. 1978 48(1): 65-94.* Examines sex discrimination in juvenile justice under Progressivism; some assumptions on correctional policies from that era are still present.

2073. Schlossman, Steven. END OF INNOCENCE: SCIENCE AND THE TRANSFORMATION OF PROGRESSIVE JUVENILE JUSTICE, 1899-1917. *Hist. of Educ. [Great Britain] 1978 7(3): 207-218.* Examines the educational function of juvenile corrective education as envisioned by American educationalists and jurists in this period. The juvenile court system fostered a philosophy based on the belief that a probationary officer dealing with the young offender at home was most likely to reeducate him. The belief was gradually proved wanting in many ways, and was abandoned by the 1920's. 56 notes. S

2074. Schlossman, Steven L. G. STANLEY HALL AND THE BOYS' CLUBS: CONSERVATIVE APPLICATIONS OF RECAPITULATION THEORY. *J. of the Hist. of the Behavioral Sciences 1973 9(2): 140-147.* Discusses the theories of adolescence of educational reformer G. Stanley Hall in the late 19th and early 20th centuries, emphasizing his role in the development of Boys' Clubs and the Boy Scouts of America.

2075. Schlossman, Steven L. and Cohen, Ronald D. THE MUSIC MAN IN GARY: WILLIS BROWN AND CHILD-SAVING IN THE PROGRESSIVE ERA. *Societas 1977 7(1): 1-17.* Traces the checkered career of the juvenile reformer Willis Brown, concentrating on 1910-12 in the growing industrial city of Gary, Indiana. Immigration and technological advances created concern about juvenile delinquency. Brown's controversial, and not very successful, solutions "highlighted dangers implict in Progressive child-saving ideology in general . . . " Based on collections at the Library of Congress, Indiana University, and Cornell University. Primary and secondary sources; 43 notes.
J. D. Hunley

2076. Schlup, Leonard. COE I. CRAWFORD AND THE PROGRESSIVE CAMPAIGN OF 1912. *South Dakota Hist. 1979 9(2): 116-130.* Coe Isaac Crawford (1858-1944), elected successively as a Republican Governor and Senator between 1907 and 1915, was the founder of the progressive movement in South Dakota. During the Republican Party split in 1912 Crawford supported Theodore Roosevelt while officially remaining within the Republican Party and used his influence to aid the cause of reform. When Roosevelt carried South Dakota by 10,000 votes, Crawford saw the results as a progressive victory. Although defeated by the Republican stalwarts in the 1914 senatorial primary, Crawford left behind a legacy of progressive reform in South Dakota. Primary sources; 3 illus., 5 photos, 29 notes. P. L. McLaughlin

2077. Schnell, R. L. STUDENTS AND SOCIALISM IN THE PROGRESSIVE ERA: THE INTERCOLLEGIATE SOCIALIST SOCIETY, 1905-1921. *ANZHES J. [Australia] 1979 8(1): 15-26.* Traces the history of the student movement in the United States from the Intercollegiate Socialist Society (ISS) formed in 1905 to its reorganization in 1921 as the League for Industrial Democracy (LID), a group which became the Student League for Industrial Democracy (SLID) and was the precursor of Students for a Democratic Society (SDS) formed in 1960.

2078. Schoonover, Shirley G. ALABAMA PUBLIC HEALTH CAMPAIGN, 1900-1919. *Alabama R. 1975 28(3): 218-233.* Survey of the gradual emergence of public health awareness in Alabama, which developed (1900-19) under the stimulus of national publicity, private philanthropy, and official leadership. Questions of race, rural orientations, and county options slowed progress. High incidences of tuberculo-

sis, pellagra, typhoid, hookworm, and diphtheria were commonplace until World War I, when Alabama led the nation in the number of persons rejected for military service. Progressive funding of the State Public Health Officer began in 1919. Primary and secondary sources; 50 notes.
J. F. Vivian

2079. Schullery, Paul. A PARTNERSHIP IN CONSERVATION: THEODORE ROOSEVELT AND YELLOWSTONE. *Montana 1978 28(3): 2-15.* Theodore Roosevelt became a staunch supporter and defender of wildlife conservation and Yellowstone National Park in the 1880's. With George Bird Grinnell and others, Roosevelt founded the Boone and Crockett Club and worked to preserve Yellowstone National Park as the "park for the people." He opposed railroad construction through the Park and worked to secure passage of the National Park Protective Act, 1894. As President, he visited Yellowstone from 8-24 April 1903, to relax, study wildlife, and view preservation efforts. Naturalist John Burroughs accompanied Roosevelt. As informally as possible, Roosevelt toured the Park, devoting particular attention to its wildlife. He also dedicated the stone arch entrance at Gardiner, Montana. Historians have mistakenly credited Roosevelt's 1903 visit with making the President a conservationist. In truth, he already held those beliefs. The visit merely provided lessons and inspiration. Thereafter he worked to expand all National Parks and to establish the National Park Service. Based on published letters and writings of Roosevelt and Burroughs, secondary works, and unpublished materials in the Yellowstone Park Reference Library; 13 illus., 40 notes, biblio.
R. C. Myers

2080. Severn, John K. and Rogers, William Warren. THEODORE ROOSEVELT ENTERTAINS BOOKER T. WASHINGTON: FLORIDA'S REACTION TO THE WHITE HOUSE DINNER. *Florida Hist. Q. 1976 54(3): 306-318.* Most white southerners, including Floridians, condemned Theodore Roosevelt for inviting Booker T. Washington to a White House dinner. They felt that blacks should not be denied legal rights, but were not entitled to social equality. Roosevelt never made a public apology and, indeed, continued to rely on Washington's advice. Washington did not discuss the event publicly, but the incident tended to strengthen his position among blacks. Based mainly on newspaper accounts; 46 notes.
P. A. Beaber

2081. Shahan, J. M. THE RHETORIC OF REFORM: THE 1906 GUBERNATORIAL RACE IN TENNESSEE. *Tennessee Hist. Q. 1976 35(1): 65-82.* No historian has yet adequately affirmed or denied the presence of progressivism in Tennessee. The rhetoric of the 1906 gubernatorial election cannot prove that a progressive movement existed, but can indicate the presence of popular receptivity to such a movement. Both candidates—Malcolm Rice Patterson (Dem.) and H. Clay Evans (Rep.)—advocated many political, moral, and economic reforms, and crusaded for an honest government, which indicates at least the "necessary foundation of public interest upon which to base a progressive movement." Based on the John L. Cox papers, contemporary journalism, and secondary sources; 40 notes.
W. R. Hively

2082. Shapiro, Edward S. PROGRESSIVISM AND VIOLENCE. *North Dakota Q. 1978 46(2): 47-54.* The Progressives believed that the establishment of new institutions fostering social solidarity in the 1880's-1910's would prevent the urban violence which derived from economic, class, and ethnic rivalries.

2083. Shapiro, Herbert. LINCOLN STEFFENS AND THE MCNAMARA CASE: A PROGRESSIVE RESPONSE TO CLASS CONFLICT. *Am. J. of Economics and Sociol. 1980 39(4): 397-412.* Lincoln Steffens's involvement with the McNamara case [which in 1911 exchanged a commitment to seek labor-capital understanding for prison terms for the two McNamara brothers in the *Los Angeles Times* building dynamiting] was one of the major concerns of his life. His *Autobiography* is not fully dependable regarding this incident; churches were not uniformly hostile to the settlement that ended the case and the *Los Angeles Times,* ignoring commitments to meet labor grievances, maintained its antiunion position. Steffens's experimentation with "Golden Rule" Christian love as an alternative to class conflict reflected his divergent allegiances to corporate capitalism. It also reflected his own rejection of class partisanship. Although the pledges made in the settlement were broken, Steffens remained loyal to the McNamaras and continued to argue it is futile to punish individuals for acts rooted in social conflict.
J

2084. Shumsky, Neil Larry. THE MUNICIPAL CLINIC OF SAN FRANCISCO: A STUDY IN MEDICAL STRUCTURE. *Bull. of the Hist. of Medicine 1978 52(4): 542-559.* In 1911, the Municipal Clinic of San Francisco was opened in an attempt to reduce venereal disease in the city. The San Francisco Board of Health required that every prostitute be examined twice a week, and if healthy she would be allowed to practice her profession without official harassment. If she had the disease, however, she was given free medical care and meanwhile she was forbidden to ply her trade. The St. Louis experiment of the 1870's provided precedent for this work. Analysis of the bureaucracy involved indicates that the development of the germ theory of disease, the emergence of paraprofessionals, and the coming of specialization were all factors contributing to the structuring of modern medical institutions. 38 notes.
M. Kaufman

2085. Shumsky, Neil Larry. VICE RESPONDS TO REFORM: SAN FRANCISCO, 1910-1914. *J. of Urban Hist. 1980 7(1): 31-47.* Control of prostitution was one of the prominent urban reforms of the late Progressive Era (1910-20). In the case of San Francisco, criminal elements with ties to city officials tried to subvert the reform movement to protect their own interests. They did this by bankrolling reformers who supported regimentation and by organizing petition drives through front organizations. 35 notes.
T. W. Smith

2086. Sillito, John R. WOMEN AND THE SOCIALIST PARTY IN UTAH, 1900-1920. *Utah Hist. Q. 1981 49(3): 220-238.* The Socialist movement in Utah was largely an outgrowth of suffrage activities in the early 20th century. Among the many activists were Ida Crouch-Hazlett, a newspaper reporter; Lucy Hoving, a critic of the Mormons' position on the role of women; Olivia McHugh, an active supporter of labor and peace movements; and Virginia Snow Stephen, a supporter of the Industrial Workers of the World after the Joe Hill execution. Kate S. Hilliard was particularly active in support of better labor conditions for women, better status in religious activities, and noninvolvement in military affairs. Many women worked through the Socialist Party as the only means to gain better recognition and equality. 4 photos, 44 notes.
K. E. Gilmont

2087. Silverman, Joan L. *THE BIRTH OF A NATION:* PROHIBITION PROPAGANDA. *Southern Q. 1981 19(3-4): 23-30.* The Birth of a Nation (1915) was, as much as anything else, prohibition propaganda. D. W. Griffith, the filmmaker who made the film was a prohibitionist well versed in producing temperance films. Picturing the Negro as a drunkard when liquor was available, it was necessary to pass a prohibition amendment to keep liquor from the black. Photo, 13 notes.
B. D. Ledbetter

2088. Sims, Robert C. IDAHO'S CRIMINAL SYNDICALISM ACT: ONE STATE'S RESPONSE TO RADICAL LABOR. *Labor Hist. 1974 15(4): 511-527.* Analyzes Idaho's criminal syndicalism acts which were part of the campaign against the Industrial Workers of the World (I.W.W.). The act was passed as a result of pressure from lumber and mining interests in 1917, and it was vigorously enforced from 1918 to 1920. During the 1920's there were attempts to revive the law, but opposition from organized labor helped make the law a dead issue. The I.W.W. was effectively suppressed through its use. Based upon Idaho statutes, the Moses Alexander Papers, and the *Idaho Statesman*. 50 notes.
L. L. Athey

2089. Siracusa, Joseph M. PROGRESSIVISM, IMPERIALISM, AND THE LEUCHTENBURG THESIS, 1952-1974: AN HISTORIOGRAPHICAL APPRAISAL. *Australian J. of Pol. and Hist. [Australia] 1974 20(3): 312-325.* In 1952 William E. Leuchtenburg suggested that Progressives did not oppose imperialism, but, with few exceptions, ardently supported early 20th-century American imperialist expansion. By surveying the way subsequent writers have treated this theme, the author shows that the matter was more complex. There is lack of agreement as to who were the Progressives, what constituted an imperialist issue, and how external policies were related to domestic developments. Progressivism came to be seen as a more complex movement, and US isolationism has been reemphasized. Concludes with the suggestion that the study of the factors which condition foreign policy attitudes by political sociologists and communication theorists might yield fruitful results. Documented from monographs and articles.
W. D. McIntyre

2090. Spiers, Fiona E. THE TALENTED TENTH: LEADERSHIP PROBLEMS AND THE AFRO-AMERICAN INTELLECTUALS, 1895-1919. *Bull. of the John Rylands U. Lib. of Manchester [Great Britain] 1978 61(1): 206-231.* W. E. B. Du Bois insisted that the "best" of the black race must develop in order to guide the "masses." In reality, probably only 1% of the black population identified themselves as part of the Talented Tenth, but they were influential in helping shape opinion and providing leadership. But their cohesion stemmed from their sense of elitism, not from any philosophical unanimity. Frustrated by the inadequacy of their traditional methods, by 1919 they were ready to consider more radical possibilities. Primary sources; 75 notes.

H. T. Blethen

2091. Steelman, Joseph F. ORIGINS OF THE CAMPAIGN FOR CONSTITUTIONAL REFORM IN NORTH CAROLINA, 1912-1913. *North Carolina Hist. Rev. 1979 56(4): 396-418.* Despite pressures from progressive-type legislation in much of the country and an outdated, radical republican state constitution, the North Carolina legislature resisted government reform until the 1910's. Issues such as black and poor white disfranchisement, state fiscal solvency, taxation, local and private legislation, popular elections, and judicial reform were ignored or discussed haphazardly, resulting in patchwork legislation. Through the efforts of activist historians Joseph G. de Roulhac Hamilton (1878-1961) and Enoch W. Sikes (1868-1941), as well as a number of progressive-minded people such as Josephus Daniels (1862-1948), legislators began talking of reform by 1910 and proposing constitutional amendments by 1913. Based on published and manuscript state legislative papers and documents, Joseph G. de Roulhac Hamilton and other personal papers, and newspapers; 12 illus., 82 notes.

T. L. Savitt

2092. Steinson, Barbara J. "THE MOTHER HALF OF HUMANITY": AMERICAN WOMEN IN THE PEACE AND PREPAREDNESS MOVEMENTS IN WORLD WAR I. Berkin, Carol Ruth and Lovett, Clara M., ed. *Women, War & Revolution* (New York: Holmes & Meier, 1980): 259-284. Discusses the activism and suffrage campaign during World War I which, together, increased women's awareness of their own capabilities and a feeling of sisterhood and feminism among women in organized activities. Using the ideal of the nurturant mother, focuses on this theme as applied to the Woman's Peace Party and the Woman's Section of the Navy League, two groups with different goals: the WPP formed as a feminist/pacifist organization, and the WSNL organized to promote national defense. Concludes that the idea of the nurturant mother prevented women from realizing any role other than a nurturing one; 1914-18.

G. L. Smith

2093. Stevens, Errol Wayne. THE SOCIALIST PARTY OF AMERICA IN MUNICIPAL POLITICS: CANTON, ILLINOIS, 1911-1920. *J. of the Illinois State Hist. Soc. 1979 72(4): 257-272.* Between 1911 and 1920 the depressed state of the coal industry, the abuse of city water privileges by Parlin and Orendorff, a producer of agricultural implements, and a controversy over the relocation of the Chicago, Burlington and Quincy Railroad lines all enabled the Socialist Party, despite strong opposition from nonsocialists, to elect more and more aldermen to the city council of Canton, Illinois. Finally, in 1916, when the anti-Socialist coalition split over prohibition, the Socialists succeeded in getting their candidate, Homer Whalen, elected mayor. Socialist opposition to US involvement in World War I, however, enabled the anti-Socialist coalition to regain control of Canton's municipal government. Based on local newspapers; 4 illus., photo, 61 notes.

E. L. Keyser

2094. Stevenson, James A. LETTERS TO DANIEL DE LEON: THE INTRA-PARTY CONSTITUENCY FOR HIS POLICY OF STRICT PARTY DISCIPLINE, 1896-1904. *Labor Hist. 1977 18(3): 382-396.* Daniel De Leon's position in the Socialist Labor Party of America as a strict party disciplinarian arose from within the party rather than from De Leon's personal preference. Based on the De Leon correspondence and the S.L.P.'s National Executive Committee papers; 61 notes.

L. L. Athey

2095. Stueck, William. PROGRESSIVISM AND THE NEGRO: WHITE LIBERALS AND THE EARLY NAACP. *Historian 1975 38(1): 58-78.* Describes the 43 whites who helped found the NAACP and who comprised almost 60% of the membership of its executive and general committees in 1910. Considers geographical origin, age, education, experience in elective or appointive office, political affiliation, prior involvement in the settlement house movement or in other reform activities, and commitment to and contribution to the black cause. Much of the information in the text is summarized in an appended chart. Based on a wide variety of sources; 69 notes.

N. W. Moen

2096. Suggs, Henry Lewis. P. B. YOUNG OF THE NORFOLK *JOURNAL AND GUIDE*: A BOOKER T. WASHINGTON MILITANT, 1904-1928. *J. of Negro Hist. 1979 64(4): 365-376.* Plummer B. Young became a disciple of Booker T. Washington in 1904 and upheld self-help and economic advancement throughout the 1920's. Despite the accommodating and ingratiating tone in Young's public statements, his felicitous manner of expression masked the protest quality of his thought and bridged the contradictions in his philosophy. Based on the Washington papers and the NAACP papers in the Library of Congress, and on the Norfolk *Journal and Guide*; 62 notes.

N. G. Sapper

2097. Sutherland, John F. THE ORIGINS OF PHILADELPHIA'S OCTAVIA HILL ASSOCIATION: SOCIAL REFORM IN THE "CONTENTED" CITY. *Pennsylvania Mag. of Hist. and Biog. 1975 99(1): 20-44.* An analysis of the philosophy, works, and influence of the Octavia Hill Association, a private reform group in Philadelphia dedicated to the improvement of the lot of the urban poor. The association purchased and improved homes, introduced strict sanitation measures, and meticulously avoided disrupting established neighborhoods. Its members lived in the affected neighborhoods but were socially not part of them. Their efforts were handicapped by the philosophy of the time but eventually led to governmental reform programs which enjoyed some success. 46 notes.

V. L. Human

2098. Sutherland, John F. RABBI JOSEPH KRAUSKOPF OF PHILADELPHIA: THE URBAN REFORMER RETURNS TO THE LAND. *Am. Jewish Hist. Q. 1978 67(4): 342-362.* Joseph Krauskopf (1858-1923) came to the United States as a 14-year-old. He graduated with the first class of four at Hebrew Union College in 1883 and was Philadelphia's foremost reform rabbi during 1887-1922. He introduced English into both services and the religious school, popularized the Jewish Sundry Services, and drafted the Pittsburgh Platform of 1885. His great concern with social reform led him into close cooperation with Jacob Riis. After a visit with Leo Tolstoy at Yasnaya Polyana, Krauskopf became the driving spirit of the Jewish "back-to-the land" movement and of the National Farm School, today known as the Delaware Valley College of Science and Agriculture, the only private agricultural school in the country. Thoroughly part of America's urban milieu, Krauskopf nevertheless sought to modify it with the agrarian myth, an urban-agrarian ambivalence which still influences American thought and action.

F. Rosenthal

2099. Swanson, Merwin. THE "COUNTRY LIFE MOVEMENT" AND THE AMERICAN CHURCHES. *Church Hist. 1977 46(3): 358-373.* During the Progressive Era the country life movement shared many of the urban progressives' analyses and reform plans and applied them to rural America. Progressives in the country life movement believed that even rural neighborhoods had lost their sense of community. Although the country lifers believed that the rural church should serve the rural community because such service was inherently right, they also believed that community service was essential to the survival of rural churches. Programs were instituted to transform rural churches into community centers which would serve the goals of progressive improvement and development. 30 notes.

M. D. Dibert

2100. Swart, Stanley L. EARLY EFFORTS AT STATE-LEVEL LAW ENFORCEMENT: THE FAILURE OF OHIO'S SUPERVISION OF LOCAL POLICE AUTHORITIES, 1902-1925. *Ohio Hist. 1981 90(2): 141-157.* Discusses the modern concept of "police" authorities and the gradual imposition of a statewide system by central government upon the municipal authorities. Although the initial attempt at state supervision is viewed as a failure, the concept of a strong state executive empowered to supervise local law enforcement agencies—as reflected in the ideology of the Progressive and Police Reform movements, and supported by the actions of the Ohio Supreme Court, the Ohio General Assembly, and Ohio Governors Vic Donahey and James M. Cox—survived such unpopular measures as the Prohibition statutes. Primary sources; illus., 2 tables, 43 notes.

L. A. Russell

2101. Szasz, Margaret Connell. ALBUQUERQUE CONGREGATIONALISTS AND SOUTHWESTERN SOCIAL REFORM: 1900-1917. *New Mexico Hist. Rev. 1980 55(3): 231-252.* From 1900 to 1917 the Congregationalists of the Albuquerque community participated in the rise of the social gospel and the national movement for social reform. In Albuquerque, the two primary areas of reform were prohibition and education. The Albuquerque Congregationalists, along with other state and local temperance groups, helped to pass the state constitutional amendment for prohibition in 1917. However, it was in the field of education that the Congregationalists made their most enduring contribution to New Mexico. Based on material in the Special Collections Department, University of New Mexico Library, and the First Congregational Church Archives, Albuquerque, New Mexico, and other primary sources; 3 photos, 54 notes.
P. L. McLaughlin

2102. Terrell, Karen A. EXPOSURE OF PROSTITUTION IN WESTERN MASSACHUSETTS: 1911. *Hist. J. of Massachusetts 1980 8(2): 3-11.* Focuses on the attempt by the *Chicopee News* to expose prostitution in Westfield, Massachuetts. The articles led to arrests of newspaper employees for selling obscene material. The paper quickly abandoned its crusade. Local newspapers, contemporary and secondary sources; 30 notes.
W. H. Mulligan Jr.

2103. Testi, Arnaldo. SOCIALISMO E PROGRESSISMO NEGLI STATI UNITI: ALCUNE NOTE SULLA ESPERIENZA DEL WISCONSIN (1900-1912) [Socialism and Progressivism in the United States: some notes on the experience of Wisconsin (1900-1912)]. *Storia contemporanea [Italy] 1974 5(2): 223-274.* Little attention has been paid to the role of Socialism and Socialists in the American Progressive movement. In Wisconsin, where Progressives led by Robert LaFollette dominated the state government and carried through many reforms, Socialists played a leading role. They consistently elected a Socialist Mayor of Milwaukee until 1960, and sent Victor Berger as the first Socialist to Congress. American Socialism, especially in Wisconsin, had deep roots in the German heritage of so many immigrants and their children. It also had close links with the labor unions. There is little doubt that Socialism gave Progressivism much of its driving power. 85 notes.
J. C. Billigmeier

2104. Thurner, Arthur W. THE MAYOR, THE GOVERNOR, AND THE PEOPLE'S COUNCIL: A CHAPTER IN AMERICAN WARTIME DISSENT. *J. of the Illinois State Hist. Soc. 1973 66(2): 124-143.* Pulitzer Prize-winning correspondent Louis Paul Lochner organized the People's Council of America for Democracy and Peace. The council triggered a struggle between Chicago and Springfield (city and state) political forces in 1917 as the war effort was spurred on by the press, the ruling class, patriotic groups, and the government. The First American Conference for Democracy and Terms of Peace, organized by Lochner and other pacifists in New York City in May 1917, developed into the People's Council. A national meeting was scheduled in Chicago because of opposition in other states. Chicago Mayor William Hall ("Big Bill") Thompson countermanded Illinois Governor Frank Orren Lowden's order to lock out the peace delegates. Chicago police, Illinois state militia, and Federal troops were held ready. Whether Mayor Thompson had given aid and comfort to the enemy received national press and government attention. By December 1917 the pacifist movement as a strong force had died. Based on the Louis P. Lochner papers in the State Historical Society of Wisconsin Library and contemporary newspapers; illus., 39 notes.
A. C. Aimone

2105. Tobin, Eugene M. THE PROGRESSIVE AS HUMANITARIAN: JERSEY CITY'S SEARCH FOR SOCIAL JUSTICE, 1890-1917. *New Jersey Hist. 1975 93(3-4): 77-98.* Social reformers in Jersey City are classified into three groups: private, religious, and public. The Whittier House social settlement tackled problems associated with tenement slums, crime, infant mortality, and juvenile delinquency. Protestants campaigned for broad social welfare reform, while less affluent Catholics opted for assistance on an individual basis for its immigrant communicants. A separate juvenile court was established. World War I changed the priorities of reformers. A typical Jersey City reformer was "a native-stock, middle-class Protestant who resided in the Eighth or Ninth Ward and had some college training." Based on primary and secondary sources; 7 illus., 44 notes.
E. R. McKinstry

2106. Travis, Anthony R. MAYOR GEORGE ELLIS: GRAND RAPIDS POLITICAL BOSS AND PROGRESSIVE REFORMER. *Michigan Hist. 1974 58(2): 101-130.* George E. Ellis, mayor of Grand Rapids during 1906-16, was the most dynamic, innovative, and powerful chief executive in the city's history. Forging a coalition of ethnic working class and middle class voters, Ellis strove successfully to widen the spectrum of citizen participation in politics. Ellis' career as a left-wing progressive who was both machine politician and social reformer demonstrates that the "boss" versus "reformer" typology, advanced by Samuel P. Hays, James Weinstein, and others, inadequately describes the complexity of urban politics in the progressive period. Primary and secondary sources; illus., 7 photos, map, 2 tables, 45 notes.
D. W. Johnson

2107. Travis, Anthony R. THE ORIGIN OF MOTHERS' PENSIONS IN ILLINOIS. *J. of the Illinois State Hist. Soc. 1975 68(5): 421-428.* The Illinois mothers' pensions program that began in Cook County in October 1911 served as a model for other state programs and also for the present federal program of Aid to Families with Dependent Children, which arose out of the New Deal. Despite criticism that the Illinois program violated family privacy and placed too much power in the hands of bureaucrats, investigation revealed that the program was financially superior to any other available form of charity.
N. Lederer

2108. Tucker, E. Bruce. JAMES SACKSON PUTNAM: AN AMERICAN PERSPECTIVE ON THE SOCIAL USES OF PSYCHOANALYSIS, 1895-1918. *New England Q. 1978 51(4): 527-546.* Putnam (1846-1918) played a key role in the American acceptance of Freudian psychoanalysis which led to a revival of the neurology profession in America. Putnam's philosophical orientation, like his idealism and zeal for social reform, marked him as an American progressive and separated him from European psychologists. Under Putnam, mental therapeutics became a positive process by which patients learned to extend their creative powers. Combined with his concept of health, the differences separating "well" from "unwell" are not substantive, he believed, but differences of degree, led him to emphasize the capacity of psychoanalysis to further social change. Based on Putnam's writings; 59 notes.
J. C. Bradford

2109. Tullos, Allen. THE GREAT HOOKWORM CRUSADE. *Southern Exposure 1978 6(2): 40-49.* Dr. Charles W. Stiles of the US Agriculture Department almost singlehandedly began the campaign against hookworm in the early 20th century. His contention that the inferior physical condition, low mental ability, and "laziness" of many Southern poor whites was based on infection by hookworms gained national attention through a report of one of his speeches in the *New York Sun* in December, 1902. Stiles eventually gained the attention of the Rockefeller philantropic interests through his contacts with Walter Hines Page who in turn placed Stiles in contact with Frederick Gates. The Rockefeller Sanitary Commission for the Eradication of Hookworm Disease, with Wickliffe Rose as Executive Secretary, pursued investigation and eradication of the disease during 1909-14. The Commission's educational campaign for proper sanitation gained considerable support among Southern educators and health workers.
N. Lederer

2110. Tuttle, William M., Jr. W. E. B. DU BOIS' CONFRONTATION WITH WHITE LIBERALISM DURING THE PROGRESSIVE ERA: A PHYLON DOCUMENT. *Phylon 1974 35(3): 241-258.* A previously unpublished interview conducted early in 1907 by the Progressive reformer, Ray Stannard Baker, with the black historian and economist from Atlanta University, W. E. B. DuBois, and the southern white Episcopal clergyman, Cary Breckenridge Wilmer. Despite the fact that both Baker and Wilmer were reformers, and both had indicated concern over the plight of Negroes, they appeared unwilling to support or accept DuBois' arguments for political and civil rights for blacks. Portrays the problems blacks faced in the nation when even whites who argued for reform refused to include blacks in the reformist impulse. Based on document located in Manuscript Division of the Library of Congress; 7 notes.
B. A. Glasrud

2111. Underhill, Lonnie E. HAMLIN GARLAND AND THE INDIAN. *Am. Indian Q. 1974 1(2): 103-113.* Hamlin Garland's writings on Indians, initially characterized by a mood of fatalistic determinism, came to be dominated by an optimistic attitude toward reform (1890-1923). The historical value of Garland's writing cannot be adequately assessed apart from the raw notes upon which it was based.

G. L. Olson and S

2112. Uselding, Paul. IN DISPRAISE OF THE MUCKRAKERS: UNITED STATES OCCUPATIONAL MORTALITY, 1890-1910. *Res. in Econ. Hist.* 1976 1: 334-371. Analyzes, by use of census data, the muckraker hypothesis that industrial workers suffered higher rates of mortality, and that their very occupations were the cause of the higher death rates. No reliable and comprehensive data is available on morbidity rates, but death rates for workers in manufacturing were not higher than those for the population as a whole. Mining had an even lower rate. Hence, the muckrakers are better viewed as agents for reform; their exposes hardly represent the stuff of history. 20 tables, 8 notes, ref.

V. L. Human

2113. Wagaman, David G. "RAUSCH MIT": THE I.W.W. IN NEBRASKA DURING WORLD WAR I. Conlin, Joseph R., ed. *At the Point of Production: The Local History of the I.W.W.* (Westport, Conn.: Greenwood Pr., 1981): 115-142. Details the Industrial Workers of the World's organizational campaigns in Nebraska during World War I, and examines the Justice Department's raids in September and November 1917 on the important Omaha headquarters of the union. On 15 April 1915, an IWW conference of representatives of local agricultural workers' unions in Kansas City created the Agricultural Workers Organization. After some success in Kansas, they began their campaign in Nebraska, where they were not warmly welcomed. Nebraska's agriculture-dominated economy made organization difficult for the union. The IWW was identified as a pro-German, antiwar organization engaged in sabotage. Public opinion was thus swayed against them, and made the raids of 1917 possible. By 1920 the IWW in Nebraska was practically destroyed by the ability of the federal government, along with oil, mining, and lumber interests, to sway public opinion against them. Based largely on newspaper and journal articles of the period; 79 notes.

J. Powell

2114. Walsh, James P. PETER YORKE AND PROGRESSIVISM IN CALIFORNIA, 1908. *Éire-Ireland 1975 10(2): 73-81.* Galway-born Father Peter C. Yorke championed the Catholic Church, Irish working people, and Irish nationalism in San Francisco from the 1880's until his death in 1925. Father Yorke, in his weekly newspaper *The Leader,* was a spokesman for Irish Americans who believed in political brokerage as a way to logically and democratically reconcile conflicting views. The Irish saw Progressive attempts at municipal charter revision in San Francisco in 1908 as the attempted removal of Irish political representation —by privileged, Protestant, University of California-oriented professional and business interests who thought themselves "disinterested" but did not accept cultural pluralism or political dissent. Based on *The Leader,* secondary sources, and correspondence; 28 notes.

D. J. Engler

2115. Waserman, Manfred. THE QUEST FOR A NATIONAL HEALTH DEPARTMENT IN THE PROGRESSIVE ERA. *Bull. of the Hist. of Medicine 1975 49(3): 353-380.* An intensive examination of the attempt to develop a national health department during 1906-13 indicates the significance of the role of the Committee of One Hundred, and its leader, Professor Irving Fisher of Yale. A serious problem of the supporters of a bill was that they could not agree on a well-defined, detailed plan. Thus their testimony before congressional committees seemed to be opinion rather than well-defined scientific programs. Although they failed during the Progressive period, they focused attention on national health policy and helped create future change. Illus., 119 notes.

M. Kaufman

2116. Wesser, Robert F. WOMEN SUFFRAGE, PROHIBITION, AND THE NEW YORK EXPERIENCE IN THE PROGRESSIVE ERA. Plesur, Milton, ed. *An American Historian: Essays to Honor Selig Adler* (Buffalo: State U. of N.Y., 1980): 140-148. Analyzes why women's fight for suffrage succeeded, 1911-17, when they won the vote in New York; why the campaign for prohibition was unpopular, with prohibitionist Governor Charles Whitman losing his reelection bid, in 1918, to Al Smith, during the Progressive Era, when both issues were associated with the crusade for morality in America.

2117. Wetzel, Kurt. RAILROAD MANAGEMENT'S RESPONSE TO OPERATING EMPLOYEES ACCIDENTS, 1890-1913. *Labor Hist. 1980 21(3): 351-368.* American railroads consistently opposed attempts to legislate and administer stricter safety standards in the late 19th and early 20th centuries. The industry delayed installation of safety equipment mandated by the Safety Appliances Act (US, 1893) until the courts found the companies liable for accidents caused by inoperative or missing safety equipment. Only after the Federal Employers' Liability Act (US, 1908) increased the railroads' liability for accidents did management develop a constructive program to make the operating employees' work safer. Based on articles in contemporary railroad management and union publications, and other primary sources; 41 notes.

L. F. Velicer

2118. White, Ronald C., Jr. BEYOND THE SACRED: EDGAR GARDNER MURPHY AND A MINISTRY OF SOCIAL REFORM. *Hist. Mag. of the Protestant Episcopal Church 1980 49(1): 51-70.* In November 1901 Edgar Gardner Murphy (1869-1913), Episcopal minister in Montgomery, Alabama, was invited to become executive secretary of the Southern Education Board. He had been long active in southern social reform movements. His decision to accept the invitation involved a profound religious and vocational decision. It required resigning his charge and also his vows as an Episcopal priest. But it was very clear that he was not leaving his calling to the ministry; he was merely shifting his location from the parish ministry to a ministry of social reform. The impetus for his reform efforts had been nourished by a religious motivation expressed in social consciousness. His sense of ministry continued in and through the midst of changing responsibilities. Based on the Edgar Gardner Murphy and the Southern Education Board Papers, Southern Historical Collection, University of North Carolina (Chapel Hill), Booker T. Washington Papers (Library of Congress), and on lesser primary and secondary sources; 43 notes.

H. M. Parker, Jr.

2119. Whitfield, Stephen J. MUCKRAKING LINCOLN STEFFENS. *Virginia Q. Rev. 1978 54(1): 87-103.* Steffens was the dean of American muckrakers. Analyzes his views on such items as Christianity, city bosses, Communism, democracy, liberalism, and totalitarianism. Quoting from *The Autobiography of Lincoln Steffens* and other works, the author argues that Steffens's "reputation for complexity should be seen as a mask for confusion."

O. H. Zabel

2120. Whorton, James C. "PHYSIOLOGIC OPTIMISM": HORACE FLETCHER AND HYGIENIC IDEOLOGY IN PROGRESSIVE AMERICA. *Bull. of the Hist. of Medicine 1981 55(1): 59-87.* Health reformers during the progressive era fit nicely into the intellectual components of the progressive movement, emphasizing the return to a natural existence within a civilized context, and use of scientific knowledge to improve the condition of mankind. Horace Fletcher, who was known for having "taught the world to chew," was one of the leading health reformers during that period in American history. Fletcher's works and influence helped to change America's table manners from the "gobble, gulp, and go" of the 19th century and was interested in improving nutrition. Irving Fisher's work during this period clearly benefitted from the ideas of Fletcher. Based on the works of Horace Fletcher and other primary and secondary sources; 121 notes.

M. Kaufman

2121. Williams, Marilyn Thornton. NEW YORK'S PUBLIC BATHS: A CASE STUDY IN URBAN PROGRESSIVE REFORM. *J. of Urban Hist. 1981 7(1): 49-81.* The movement to establish public baths in New York City was typical of progressive reforms in both its humanistic goals and its organizational backing. Public baths were supported by organized charities, individual reformer-philanthropists, and a welfare-minded local government. Only this combination was able to establish and maintain public baths. Covers ca. 1890-1915. Table, 4 illus., 59 notes.

T. W. Smith

2122. Williams, William J. BLOODY SUNDAY REVISITED. *Pacific Northwest Q. 1980 71(2): 50-62.* On 5 November 1916, the steamship *Verona* carried approximately 250 members of the Industrial Workers of the World (IWW) from Seattle to a rally at Everett, Washington. A large number of Everett's deputized citizens attempted to stop the landing and gunshots were fired by unidentified assailants. Seven people were killed and 47 wounded in the "Everett Massacre" before the *Verona* could escape and return to Seattle. Documents recently uncovered at the

Seattle Federal Archives and Records Center offer new eyewitness testimony about the event, but fail to answer the ultimate question of who fired the initial shots. 5 photos, map, 13 notes. — M. L. Tate

2123. Willson, Carolyn. "RATTLING THE BONES": JACK LONDON, SOCIALIST EVANGELIST. *Western Am. Literature 1976 11(2): 135-148.* Reconsiders Jack London's socialism. The years 1905-08 are the most dramatic because they represent London's most active participation as a socialist evangelist. After 1908 London redefined his conception of service to the cause of socialism and expressed his feelings only through his writings. — M. Genung

2124. Wolfe, Allis Rosenberg. WOMEN, CONSUMERISM, AND THE NATIONAL CONSUMERS' LEAGUE IN THE PROGRESSIVE ERA, 1900-1923. *Labor Hist. 1976 16(3): 378-392.* Contends that a growing consciousness about women's roles as consumers provided a base from which the National Consumers' League arose. Activities of the League were primarily in protective legislation for women and the ethical control of consumption. Never a mass organization, the League declined by 1923. Based on dissertations, records of the Massachusetts Consumers' League, and secondary sources; 29 notes. — L. L. Athey

2125. Wolfe, Margaret Ripley. THE AGRICULTURAL EXPERIMENT STATION AND FOOD AND DRUG CONTROL: ANOTHER LOOK AT KENTUCKY PROGRESSIVISM, 1898-1916. *Filson Club Hist. Q. 1975 49(4): 323-338.* Melville Amasa Scovell and Robert McDowell Allen were leaders in Kentucky's effort to control the production of unsafe foods and drugs. Both men were part of the new college-trained middle-class reform movement of the Progressive era. Using agricultural experiment stations as their base of operations, Scovell and Allen were almost uniformly successful in prosecuting businesses in Kentucky. Allen also joined in the national crusade for pure food led by Dr. Harvey W. Wiley, chief chemist of the US Department of Agriculture. Allen took part in the International Food Congress in 1904 and was a moving force behind the passage of the Heyburn Act of 1906. Based on newspapers, government reports, and the Scovell and Wiley Papers; 59 notes. — G. B. McKinney

2126. Wright, George C. THE NAACP AND RESIDENTIAL SEGREGATION IN LOUISVILLE, KENTUCKY, 1914-1917. *Register of the Kentucky Hist. Soc. 1980 78(1): 39-54.* One of the most important victories for the National Association for the Advancement of Colored People (NAACP) in its early years was the decision of the US Supreme Court on 5 November 1917 to overturn a housing ordinance legalizing segregation in Louisville. Passed by the city council in May 1914, the ordinance attempted to prevent blacks from moving into all-white neighborhoods. Before 1890, most of Louisville had been integrated, but from 1890 to 1910, segregation developed. 29 notes. — J. F. Paul

2127. Wyman, Roger E. MIDDLE-CLASS VOTERS AND PROGRESSIVE REFORM: THE CONFLICT OF CLASS AND CULTURE. *Am. Pol. Sci. Rev. 1974 68(2): 488-504.* The middle-class character of the leadership of American reform movements has been well established. While leaders of the progressive movement in early twentieth-century America also conform to this pattern, the nature of the voting base of support for progressivism has not yet been established. The purpose of this paper is twofold: first, to examine whether or not middle-class voters supported progressive candidates at the polls; and secondarily, to test the relative strength of cultural factors (i.e., ethnicity and religion) versus class considerations as determinants of voting behavior in the early twentieth century. The results demonstrate that, at least in the key progressive state of Wisconsin, middle-class voters failed to support progressive candidates in either general or primary elections; to the contrary, they provided the bulwark of support for conservative opponents of reform. Using bivariate and partial coorelational analysis, the paper also shows that ethnocultural factors remained as the most powerful determinant of voter choice among urban voters in general elections, but that class considerations often proved more influential in motivating voters in primary election contests. — J

Civil Liberties and Political Rights

2128. Bland, Sidney R. FIGHTING THE ODDS: MILITANT SUFFRAGISTS IN SOUTH CAROLINA. *South Carolina Hist. Mag. 1981 82(1): 32-43.* Details the activism of the woman suffrage movement in South Carolina which begain in the 1890's, although some organizing occurred as early as 1869, and was revitalized during the 1910's when the State Equal Suffrage League was established in 1914 as an affiliate of the National American Woman Suffrage Association (NAWSA), and when Alice Paul, using the tactics of the militant British movement led by Emmeline Pankhurst, formed the Congressional Union (later the National Woman's Party); 1890's-1919.

2129. Bosmajian, Haig A. THE ABROGATION OF THE SUFFRAGISTS' FIRST AMENDMENT RIGHTS. *Western Speech 1974 38(4): 218-232.* Covers the period 1912-19; mentions the National Women's Party. — S

2130. Bromberg, Alan B. FREE SPEECH AT MR. JEFFERSON'S UNIVERSITY: THE CASE OF PROFESSOR LEON WHIPPLE. *Virginia Mag. of Hist. and Biog. 1980 88(1): 3-20.* In November 1917, Leon Whipple, an Adjunct Professor of Journalism, was dismissed from the faculty of the University of Virginia on the charge of gross abuse of freedom of speech. Whipple, a pacifist, in an address to Sweet Briar College, had urged US withdrawal from World War I. He had sent his remarks to the press, and identified himself with the University. Branded as disloyal by Virginians in and out of his school, Whipple was removed by its Board of Visitors. Contrasts Whipple's treatment with founder Thomas Jefferson's desire that the University be based on the "illimitable freedom of the mind." 32 notes. — P. J. Woehrmann

2131. Brommel, Bernard J. KATE RICHARDS O'HARE: A MIDWESTERN PACIFIST'S FIGHT FOR FREE SPEECH. *North Dakota Q. 1976 44(1): 5-19.* Describes events leading up to the arrest, trial and conviction (1900-25) of major Socialist Party and leftist movement figure, Kate Richards O'Hare, in North Dakota for violating the Espionage Act of 1917 by speaking out against World War I.

2132. Broyles, Glen J. THE SPOKANE FREE SPEECH FIGHT, 1909-1910: A STUDY IN IWW TACTICS. *Labor Hist. 1978 19(2): 238-252.* The free speech fight in Spokane, contrary to recent historical interpretation, was a victory not for the Industrial Workers of the World but for the city and Mayor Pratt. Based on Spokane newspapers; 27 notes. — L. L. Athey

2133. Colburn, David R. GOVERNOR ALFRED E. SMITH AND THE RED SCARE, 1919-20. *Pol. Sci. Q. 1973 88(3): 423-444.* "Illuminates a little known aspect of Alfred E. Smith's public career. During the height of the Red Scare of 1919-20, the governor of New York took a strong civil-libertarian and social-reformist position, helping to dampen public fears about a Bolshevik revolution in America." — J

2134. Cumberland, William H. PLAIN HONESTY: WALLACE SHORT AND THE I.W.W. *Palimpsest 1980 61(5): 146-160.* An independent minister and the mayor of Sioux City from 1918 to 1924, Wallace Short (1866-1932) defended freedom of speech and of assembly for the Industrial Workers of the World (IWW); he defeated two recall attempts in 1918 and 1919.

2135. Daniels, Doris. BUILDING A WINNING COALITION: THE SUFFRAGE FIGHT IN NEW YORK STATE. *New York Hist. 1979 60(1): 59-80.* In the 1917 New York state referendum, the urban population provided the majority of votes for the extension of the suffrage to women. Shows how the suffragist victory in New York City resulted from a coalition of traditional suffragists, industrial workers, Eastern European immigrants, and settlement house women led by Lillian D. Wald. 6 illus., 2 tables, 53 notes. — R. N. Lokken

2136. Duram, James C. IN DEFENSE OF CONSCIENCE: NORMAN THOMAS AS AN EXPONENT OF CHRISTIAN PACIFISM DURING WORLD WAR I. *J. of Presbyterian Hist. 1974 52(1): 19-32.* Examines the early writings of Norman Thomas on civil liberties, especially his defense of conscientious objection as a tenet of Christianity and pacifism, 1915-18, in the face of universal conscription.

2137. Fowler, James H., II. CREATING AN ATMOSPHERE OF SUPPRESSION, 1914-1917. *Chronicles of Oklahoma 1981 59(2): 202-223.* Although the United States endorsed a policy of neutrality toward World War I, Americans increasingly developed an intolerance toward Germany and toward unpatriotic persons. The level of intolerance boiled over in Oklahoma as both vigilantes and respected newspapers harangued pacifists, labor union organizers, and political leftists. President Woodrow Wilson's frequent outbursts against the same groups seemingly gave legitimacy to local vigilante groups such as the Oklahoma State Council of Defense. Freedom of speech evaporated in this poisoned atmosphere. Based on Oklahoma newspapers; 3 illus., 85 notes. M. L. Tate

2138. Genini, Ronald. INDUSTRIAL WORKERS OF THE WORLD AND THEIR FRESNO FREE SPEECH FIGHT, 1910-1911. *California Hist. Q. 1974 53(2): 100-114.* After several victorious free-speech fights, the IWW clashed with authorities in Fresno, where there coexisted conservative agricultural interests and the most militant IWW local in the state. The free speech fight in Fresno consisted of confrontations from April 1910 to March 1911 between Wobblies and police over the issue of soap box speeches on street corners. Wobblies journeyed to Fresno from all parts of the country, answering the challenge of another free speech issue. More than 100 arrested Wobblies crammed the jails, demanded separate jury trials, and challenged prospective jurors. In December 1910, IWW leader Frank Little was freed after he pointed out that Fresno had no ordinance prohibiting street speaking. The city trustees instituted such a ban, but the impending influx of hundreds of additional Wobblies caused them to reconsider the move. On 2 March 1911 the ban was rescinded and all IWW prisoners were released. Most Wobblies went on to new battles elsewhere, losing the chance to build a labor organization in Fresno. Although the IWW had won its battle, the confrontations caused conservatives to view the IWW with growing concern, especially in agricultural regions. Based on contemporary articles and newspapers, interviews, and secondary sources; 61 notes. A. Hoffman

2139. Goldstein, Robert J. THE ANARCHIST SCARE OF 1908: A SIGN OF TENSIONS IN THE PROGRESSIVE ERA. *Am. Studies 1974 15(2): 55-78.* Representative of the tensions in the Progressive era, the Anarchist Scare (1908) contradicts views of this period as one of optimism and social unity. The fear of radicals and particularly anarchists, the rapid spread of radicalism before 1908, and the social instability caused by labor unrest and the depression of 1907 precipitated conservative reaction. The federal government reacted sharply, and instituted a loyalty program for aliens. Based on primary and secondary sources; 3 illus., 42 notes. J. Andrew

2140. Grandfield, Robert S. THE MASSACHUSETTS SUFFRAGE REFERENDUM OF 1915. *Hist. J. of Massachusetts 1979 7(1): 46-57.* Examines the campaign against woman suffrage in Massachusetts around the referendum of 1915 which overwhelmingly rejected extending the vote to women. Focuses especially on the anti-suffrage literature issued by women's groups. 4 illus., 50 notes. W. H. Mulligan, Jr.

2141. Grant, Marilyn. THE 1912 SUFFRAGE REFERENDUM: AN EXERCISE IN POLITICAL ACTION. *Wisconsin Mag. of Hist. 1980-81 64(2): 107-118.* Describes the work of the Wisconsin Woman Suffrage Association under Olympia Brown Willis and its more recent rival, the Political Equality League under Ada James, in support of the 1912 suffrage referendum in Wisconsin. The more assertive League organized at the grassroots level, established a speakers' bureau, distributed suffrage literature in different languages, organized a Men's League for fund-raising, led automobile junkets, and campaigned at county fairs. Even so, the referendum lost decisively. 10 illus. N. C. Burckel

2142. Hardaway, Roger D. JEANNETTE RANKIN: THE EARLY YEARS. *North Dakota Q. 1980 48(1): 62-68.* Discusses Jeannette Rankin (1880-1973), the first woman in the House of Representatives, and focuses on her fight for woman suffrage and campaign strategy on the Republican Party ticket in Montana in 1916.

2143. Hubbell, John T. A QUESTION OF ACADEMIC FREEDOM: THE WILLIAM A. SCHAPER CASE. *Midwest Q. 1976 17(2): 111-121.* The dismissal in September 1917 of William A. Schaper (1869-1955), professor of political science at the University of Minnesota, on charges of not supporting the American war effort in World War I, is a classic case of abuse of academic freedom. "Protection of academic freedom... derives from... struggle... particularly against authority which violates the law while pretending to uphold it." Secondary sources. H. S. Marks

2144. James, Louise Boyd. THE WOMAN SUFFRAGE ISSUE IN THE OKLAHOMA CONSTITUTIONAL CONVENTION. *Chronicles of Oklahoma 1978-79 56(4): 379-392.* Examines the efforts of Oklahoma leaders such as suffragette Kate H. Biggers, attorney Robert L. Owen, labor leader Peter Hanraty, and Colorado Governor Alva J. Adams to pass a woman suffrage resolution through the 1906 Oklahoma Constitutional Convention. Opponents of the resolution contended that women's domain was in the home rather than in politics. The proposal failed. Not until November 1918 did Oklahoma adopt a referendum petition which granted state-wide suffrage to women. Primary sources; 6 photos, 43 notes. M. L. Tate

2145. Jemison, Marie Stokes. LADIES BECOME VOTERS: PATTIE RUFFNER JACOBS AND WOMEN'S SUFFRAGE IN ALABAMA. *Southern Exposure 1979 7(1): 48-59.* Compares the fight for suffrage by southern women before 1920 to the civil rights and ERA struggles of the 1960's and 1970's in a brief introduction, then details the struggle for woman suffrage in the South, which was led by activist Pattie Ruffner Jacobs (1885-1938), whose biography is presented also.

2146. Juhnke, James C. MOB VIOLENCE AND KANSAS MENNONITES IN 1918. *Kansas Hist. Q. 1977 43(3): 334-350.* Discusses mob violence in central Kansas during 1918 against certain local Mennonites, some of them German-speaking, who refused on account of their pacifist convictions to buy Liberty bonds and to otherwise support the World War I effort. No legal action was ever taken against the vigilantes. Based on archival materials, interviews, contemporary newspaper accounts, and secondary sources; 5 illus., 56 notes. L. W. Van Wyk

2147. Kneeland, Marilyn. THE MODERN BOSTON TEA PARTY: THE SAN DIEGO SUFFRAGE CAMPAIGN OF 1911. *J. of San Diego Hist. 1977 23(4): 35-42.* Chronicles the California campaign for woman suffrage in 1911, and the work done in the San Diego area by Dr. Charlotte Baker and Mrs. Ella Allen to counteract the antivote feelings of Senator Leroy A. Wright.

2148. Koppes, Clayton R. THE KANSAS TRIAL OF THE I. W. W., 1917-1919. *Labor Hist. 1975 16(3): 338-358.* Although the Chicago trial of 1918 has often been cited as a major cause of the Industrial Workers of the World's decline, the Kansas trials, especially the Wichita trial of 1919, were viewed as crucial by the IWW. The trial dramatized radicals' problems in achieving justice during the Red Scare, especially when they were beset by financial woes and bereft of an effective political defense. Based on court records, newspapers, and secondary sources; 47 notes. L. L. Athey

2149. Larson, T. A. IDAHO'S ROLE IN AMERICA'S WOMEN SUFFRAGE CRUSADE. *Idaho Yesterdays 1974 18(1): 2-15.*

2150. LeWarne, Charles Pierce. THE ABERDEEN, WASHINGTON FREE SPEECH FIGHT OF 1911-1912. *Pacific Northwest Q. 1975 66(1): 1-12.* In an Industrial Workers of the World free speech fight in Aberdeen, Washington, 1911-12, IWW organizers carried on soap box harangues near hiring halls in the hope of being arrested, quickly replaced, and eventually overrunning local jails to promote their cause.

2151. LeWarne, Charles Pierce. ON THE WOBBLY TRAIN TO FRESNO. *Labor Hist. 1973 14(2): 264-289.* Presents Edward M. Clyde's account of the 1911 trek toward Fresno by the Industrial Workers of the World to support the free-speech fight. The struggle was over, and the group never reached its destination. Based on the Clyde manuscript; 9 notes. L. L. Athey

2152. Lovin, Hugh T. MOSES ALEXANDER AND THE IDAHO LUMBER STRIKE OF 1917: THE WARTIME ORDEAL OF A PROGRESSIVE. *Pacific Northwest Q. 1975 66(3): 115-122.* Representing the reformist impulse of the Progressive Era, Moses Alexander won the governorship of Idaho in 1914 and was reelected two years later. World War I disrupted his legislative programs and placed him in the arena of

conflict between "patriotic" groups and the Industrial Workers of the World. The State Council of Defense, supported by Idaho industrial interests, chided Alexander for protecting the IWW and other alleged pro-German interests, but he remained steadfast in their defense. Yet when the IWW threatened violence, he cracked down on their activities and promoted compromise at the conference table. Violence was averted and some of the barriers to labor reform were gradually overcome. Based on primary sources; photo, 34 notes.
M. L. Tate

2153. McFarland, Charles K. and Neal, Nevin E. THE RELUCTANT REFORMER: WOODROW WILSON AND WOMAN SUFFRAGE, 1913-1920. *Rocky Mountain Social Sci. J. 1974 11(2): 33-43.*

2154. Meier, August and Rudwick, Elliott. NEGRO BOYCOTTS OF SEGREGATED STREETCARS IN VIRGINIA 1904-1907. *Virginia Mag. of Hist. and Biog. 1973 81(4): 479-487.* The transit boycotts of the 1950's had precedents in the late 19th and early 20th centuries, when segregation was inaugurated on southern trolley cars. In Virginia such protests against the new Jim Crow laws occurred in several cities, though they were usually short-lived and unsuccessful. Based on newspaper accounts; 39 notes.
R. F. Oaks

2155. Morton, Michael. NO TIME TO QUIBBLE: THE JONES FAMILY CONSPIRACY TRIAL OF 1917. *Chronicles of Oklahoma 1981 59(2): 224-236.* During the summer of 1917 a group of farmers from central Oklahoma were arrested on charges of sedition. Dubbed the "Green Corn Rebellion," this insurrection resulted from the desperate economic plight of tenant farmers who had been inflamed by leftist spokesmen within the Working Class Union (WCU). The superpatriotism of World War I created an intolerant climate toward these "antiwar radicals," and resulted in a kangaroo court for the seven men arrested in Cleveland and Pottawatomie counties. Collectively known as the Jones Family, the seven were convicted on flimsy evidence. Based on Oklahoma newspapers; photo, 42 notes.
M. L. Tate

2156. Parker, James R. PATERNALISM AND RACISM: SENATOR JOHN C. SPOONER AND AMERICAN MINORITIES, 1897-1907. *Wisconsin Mag. of Hist. 1974 57(3): 195-200.* Although conservative Republican Senator John Coit Spooner of Wisconsin posed as a champion of civil rights, and his biographer has characterized him as such, the author draws a different conclusion. Spooner was first a Republican politician and then a defender of civil liberties, as his defense of President Theodore Roosevelt's action in the Brownsville incident illustrated. His attitude toward Indians and Mexican Americans was even less enlightened than toward blacks. On the issue of minority rights Spooner often had the power to affect policy, but he seldom moved beyond rhetoric to positive action. 2 illus., 40 notes.
N. C. Burckel

2157. Porter, Melba Dean. MADELINE MCDOWELL BRECKINRIDGE: HER ROLE IN THE KENTUCKY WOMAN SUFFRAGE MOVEMENT, 1908-1920. *Register of the Kentucky Hist. Soc. 1974 72(4): 342-363.* Mrs. Breckinridge was a major force in Kentucky's ratification of the 19th amendment. Working through the Federation of Women's Clubs and, after 1912, the Kentucky Equal Rights Association, she devoted her life to many reforms, but primarily to the cause of woman suffrage on both state and national levels. Replacing Laura Clay as head of the KERA in 1912, she lived to see Kentucky become the 24th state to ratify in 1920. Based on primary and secondary sources; 101 notes.
J. F. Paul

2158. Reimen, Jacqueline. RADICAL INTELLECTUALS AND REPRESSION OF RADICALISM DURING THE FIRST WORLD WAR. *Rev. Française d'Etudes Américaines [France] 1976 (2): 63-76.* Discusses radical intellectuals in America before World War I, legislative repression of them during the war, and its effects on American radicalism afterwards.

2159. Ryan, Thomas G. MALE OPPONENTS AND SUPPORTERS OF WOMAN SUFFRAGE: IOWA IN 1916. *Ann. of Iowa 1981 45(7): 537-550.* Analysis of voting behavior in woman suffrage referenda prior to the enactment of the 19th Amendment can help illuminate aspects of US political and social history. On 5 June 1916, Iowa men narrowly rejected a proposed suffrage amendment to the state constitu-

tion. An examination of voting on the county level indicates that dry counties, British-American counties, Protestant counties, and Republican counties returned the largest majorities for the amendment. Conversely, German counties, and those with large numbers of Roman Catholics and Democrats gave the least support to the measure. Community size bore almost no relationship to voting behavior. Based on Iowa Official Register and other primary sources; 3 tables, 17 notes.
P. L. Petersen

2160. Schaffer, Ronald. THE PROBLEM OF CONSCIOUSNESS IN THE WOMAN SUFFRAGE MOVEMENT: A CALIFORNIA PERSPECTIVE. *Pacific Hist. Rev. 1976 45(4): 469-494.* Studies the methods used by the leading suffragists in California who tried to make women sufficiently concerned with inequality that they would ask for the vote. Covers motivations, methods, organizational techniques, propaganda form and content, and immediate and long-range results. The most significant results related to the changes produced in the consciousness of women. It gave them their first formal education in the possibilities for change; however, it seldom got beyond a "more socially conscious maternalism," and did not move on to goals of personal equality. 46 notes.
R. V. Ritter

2161. Schwantes, Carlos A. MAKING THE WORLD UNSAFE FOR DEMOCRACY: VIGILANTES, GRANGERS AND THE WALLA WALLA "OUTRAGE" OF JUNE, 1918. *Montana 1981 31(1): 18-29.* Members of the Washington State Grange met in Walla Walla for their annual convention in 1918. Citizens of this conservative, agricultural community formed a vigilante-type group which intimidated Grangers into leaving town. They used threats of violence and denied Grangers their civil liberty of meeting peacefully. The Walla Walla press contributed to the hysteria by publicizing Granger sympathies for the Nonpartisan League (NPL) and suggested that the Grangers supported the Industrial Workers of the World (IWW). The patriotism of the NPL and IWW was suspect in the Anti-German hysteria of World War I. Central in the controversy was William Bouck, head of the Washington Grange. Based on contemporary newspapers, secondary sources, and published federal and state documents; 7 illus., 39 notes.
R. C. Myers

2162. Shanks, Rosalie. THE I.W.W. FREE SPEECH MOVEMENT: SAN DIEGO, 1912. *J. of San Diego Hist. 1973 19(1): 25-33.* During 1911 a "socialist army" dominated by the Industrial Workers of the World (I.W.W.) took over Tijuana, Mexico, for a time. Soon San Diegans feared violence and perhaps even pillage at the hands of the I.W.W. The city council prohibited free speech in a six-block area, resulting in mob action and arrests. To most people there was a tie between the red scare and the I.W.W., making restriction of civil rights respectable. Police brutality and vigilante tactics won the day and influenced laws to contain syndicalism. Based on interviews, San Diego newspapers, and secondary accounts; 3 illus., 78 notes.
S. S. Sprague

2163. Silverman, Eliane Leslau. REFORM AS A MEANS OF SOCIAL CONTROL: THEODORE ROOSEVELT AND WOMEN'S SUFFRAGE. *Atlantis [Canada] 1976 2(1): 22-36.* Discusses the idea that woman suffrage as a means of radical reform actually became a tool for middle class males to gain social and political control, citing Theodore Roosevelt's attitudes towards women's suffrage as an example of men's scorn for women's political involvement, 1899-1919.

2164. Snapp, Meredith A. DEFEAT THE DEMOCRATS: THE CONGRESSIONAL UNION FOR WOMAN SUFFRAGE IN ARIZONA, 1914 AND 1916. *J. of the West 1975 14(4): 131-139.* Discusses an attempt in 1914 and 1916 by the Congressional Union for Woman Suffrage organizers to convince women voters in Arizona (one of nine states which enfranchised women) to vote against Democratic Party candidates—the party they held responsible for inaction on the woman suffrage question. 34 notes.

2165. Sponholtz, Lloyd L. HARRY SMITH, NEGRO SUFFRAGE AND THE OHIO CONSTITUTIONAL CONVENTION: BLACK FRUSTRATION IN THE PROGRESSIVE ERA. *Phylon 1974 35(2): 165-180.* Reviews the life and career of Negro journalist and legislator Harry Smith, who single-mindedly insisted on racial integration throughout his long career. The Ohio constitutional convention of 1912 permitted Smith to once again endeavor to bring Negro suffrage to Ohio. This stand

was adopted by the convention, but the voters rejected it. Progressive movements of the times were not interested in racial or ethnic issues. Smith himself was somewhat dated; he belonged to an earlier and more militant age. Table, 41 notes.
V. L. Human

2166. Stevenson, Louise L. WOMEN ANTI-SUFFRAGISTS IN THE 1915 MASSACHUSETTS CAMPAIGN. *New England Q. 1979 52(1): 80-93.* Examines the membership and activities of the Massachusetts Association Opposed to the Further Extension of the Suffrage to Women to show that women played an important and independent role in the anti-suffrage campaign of the early 20th century. Women antisuffragists believed that a woman's identity as a woman depended on her role as a mother and homemaker. In the campaign of 1915 they charged that women suffered a loss of femininity when they entered political campaigns and that woman suffrage threatened to destroy the home. They linked woman suffrage to feminism and socialism. Based on newspapers and on society papers at the Massachusetts Historical Society; 32 notes.
J. C. Bradford

2167. Strom, Sharon Hartman. LEADERSHIP AND TACTICS IN THE AMERICAN WOMAN SUFFRAGE MOVEMENT: A NEW PERSPECTIVE FROM MASSACHUSETTS. *J. of Am. Hist. 1975 62(2): 296-315.* Describes the role of the rank and file, large and small state organizations, the reformist climate of the Progressive era, and militant English suffragist tactics in rejuvenating the Massachusetts suffrage movement after 1900. These forces played a larger part in winning passage of the 19th Amendment in 1919 in Massachusetts than betterknown leaders of the women's movement. Based on reports of suffrage organizations, newspapers, journals, and secondary works; 69 notes.
J. B. Street

2168. Sumners, Bill. SOUTHERN BAPTISTS AND WOMEN'S RIGHT TO VOTE, 1910-1920. *Baptist Hist. and Heritage 1977 12(1): 45-51.* Southern Baptists shared differing attitudes on the debate over woman suffrage. The opponents in the church believed equality at the polls would somehow mar the image of the southern lady. They further questioned the positive effects women might have on government and politics. Others quietly applauded the addition of women to the electorate, foreseeing women playing an integral role in instituting and maintaining prohibition. The Women's Christian Temperance Union and the Anti-Saloon League, both of which contained many Baptists, endorsed woman suffrage. Based largely on Baptists periodicals of the decade; 40 notes.
H. M. Parker, Jr.

2169. Taylor, Antoinette Elizabeth. SOUTH CAROLINA AND THE ENFRANCHISEMENT OF WOMEN: THE LATER YEARS. *South Carolina Hist. Mag. 1979 80(4): 298-310.* Continues account of the campaign for woman suffrage in South Carolina during 1912-20. (See abstract 15A:5700).

2170. Turcheneske, John Anthony, Jr. "IT IS RIGHT THAT THEY SHOULD SET US FREE": THE ROLE OF THE WAR AND INTERIOR DEPARTMENTS IN THE RELEASE OF THE APACHE PRISONERS OF WAR, 1909-1913. *Red River Valley Hist. Rev. 1979 4(3): 4-32.* Freedom for the Chiricahua and Ojo Caliente Apache Indians, held as prisoners of war 1886-1909, came about arduously during 1909-13 due to political battling between the Interior and War Departments over the allotment of lands formerly promised the Indians at Fort Sill, Oklahoma.

2171. White, Earl Bruce. *THE UNITED STATES V. C. W. ANDERSON ET AL.:* THE WICHITA CASE, 1917-1919. Conlin, Joseph R., ed. *At the Point of Production: The Local History of the I.W.W.* (Westport, Conn.: Greenwood Pr., 1981): 143-164. When the United States entered World War I, the Industrial Workers of the World was reorganizing itself into industrial organizations which could be controlled from Chicago headquarters. The unions were making some progress in the northern timber regions and the western copper mines, and with maritime, construction, and oil workers, when wartime legislation, patriotism, and hysteria were turned against them. They were increasingly harassed, culminating in the federal raids on IWW locals in 1917, one of which was in Wichita, Kansas. Charles W. Anderson was secretary-treasurer of the Agricultural Workers Industrial Union and the Oil Workers Industrial Union, branches of the IWW. The author details the complex events of the case of the federal government against the Wichita union. Based on court transcripts and journal articles of the period; 105 notes.
J. Powell

Economic Reform

2172. Anderson, James D. THE SOUTHERN IMPROVEMENT COMPANY: NORTHERN REFORMERS' INVESTMENT IN NEGRO COTTON TENANCY 1900-1920. *Agric. Hist. 1978 52(1): 111-131.* The Southern Improvement Company, holding land in Virginia and Alabama, was founded by northern reformers in 1900 to provide southern Negroes with the means to become independent farmers. The SIC was dissolved in 1917 because the black farmers found they couldn't operate at a profit under the company restrictions. Primary and secondary sources; 39 notes.
R. T. Fulton

2173. Asher, Robert. THE ORIGINS OF WORKMEN'S COMPENSATION IN MINNESOTA. *Minnesota Hist. 1974 44(4): 142-153.* The inefficiency and the litigation involved in employers' liability insurance, and the friction it caused, led some large companies to favor no fault workmen's compensation by 1909, the year that Governor Johnson called for an investigating commission to look into the problem. Uncertainty as to rates led to hesitancy, but by 1912 15 states approved such plans and in 1913 Minnesota passed a weak bill, a consensus reform measure. 13 illus.; 67 notes.
S. S. Sprague.

2174. Asher, Robert. PAINFUL MEMORIES: THE HISTORICAL CONSCIOUSNESS OF STEELWORKERS AND THE STEEL STRIKE OF 1919. *Pennsylvania Hist. 1978 45(1): 61-86.* Most skilled steelworkers in the Pittsburgh district remained at work during the Steel Strike of 1919. Many factors influenced their defection, but none was more important than their recollection of earlier unsuccessful confrontations with the companies. Many of the skilled steelworkers had participated in those strikes, and others had been told of the events by "old timers" in the steel towns. The skilled steelworkers who did not support the 1919 strike doubted the ability of the union leadership, respected the power and wealth of the companies, and understood the relationship between paternalism and repression. Based on interviews undertaken by David Saposs and others in 1920, US Senate hearings, recent oral history interviews, and other materials; 3 tables, 56 notes.
D. C. Swift

2175. Askol'dova, S. M. RELIGIIA I AMERIKANSKII TREDIUNIONIZM V KONTSE XIX-NACHALE XX VEKA [Religion and American trade unionism at the turn of the 20th century]. *Voprosy Istorii [USSR] 1973 (9): 89-104.* The article is devoted to the ideological rapprochement between the church seeking to "modernize" its programme and American trade unionism which renounced socialist demands and became an instrument for exerting bourgeois influence on the American proletariat. This rapprochement was aimed at achieving coordinated action in the struggle against the socialist movement in the U.S.A. The collaboration of the AFL with the Catholic Church and the various Protestant trends was adroitly used by the bourgeoisie when it resorted to the ill-famed New Deal for the sake of salvaging capitalism.
J

2176. Bailey, Kenneth R. "GRIM VISAGED MEN" AND THE WEST VIRGINIA NATIONAL GUARD IN THE 1912-13 PAINT AND CABIN CREEK STRIKE. *West Virginia Hist. 1980 41(2): 111-125.* In the 1912-13 Paint and Cabin Creek strike, because of violence between coal mine guards and members of the United Mine Workers of America, Governor William E. Glasscock declared martial law and sent in the National Guard to keep order. Based on newspaper accounts, mine workers' reports, and West Virginia government papers; 49 notes.
J. D. Neville

2177. Barkey, Fred A. SOCIALIST INFLUENCE IN THE WEST VIRGINIA STATE FEDERATION OF LABOR: THE JOHN NUGENT CASE. *West Virginia Hist. 1977 38(4): 275-290.* Challenges the common view that organized labor in the early 20th century was purely pragmatic and rejected radical class-conscious proposals to change American society. Socialists in the West Virginia State Federation of Labor showed surprising strength during 1901-14, and tried to oust state president John Nugent in 1907-08 for being insufficiently militant. By

1912 Socialists were a majority in the state labor convention. Primary and secondary sources; 64 notes. — J. H. Broussard

2178. Beeten, Neil. POLISH AMERICAN STEELWORKERS: AMERICANIZATION THROUGH INDUSTRY AND LABOR. *Polish Am. Studies 1976 33(2): 31-42.* The United States Steel Corporation in Gary, Indiana, manipulated immigrant workers under the guise of Americanization. In a final analysis, both immigrants and the employers profited from the corporation programs. Unplanned and unnoticed during the process, however, was a steady exposure of the immigrant workers to the merits of unionization, the potential benefits of organized strikes, and the necessary techniques of survival in a hard economic world. Covers ca. 1906-20. Based primarily on English newspaper accounts; 21 notes. — S. R. Pliska

2179. Bercuson, David Jay. THE ONE BIG UNION IN WASHINGTON. *Pacific Northwest Q. 1978 69(3): 127-134.* Traces the development of the One Big Union movement in the Pacific Northwest (particularly in Washington) whereby laborers in Canada and the United States would join hands in a common effort. While leftist groups such as the Industrial Workers of the World branded the movement as nonrevolutionary, leaders of the mainstream American Federation of Labor attempted to undercut its influence during 1919. The AFL's secretary Frank Morrison worked behind the scenes in the state of Washington and successfully discredited the movement which never established strong grass roots support. Primary sources; 2 photos, 26 notes. — M. L. Tate

2180. Best, Gary Dean. PRESIDENT WILSON'S SECOND INDUSTRIAL CONFERENCE, 1919-20. *Labor Hist. 1975 16(4): 505-520.* The most important proposal of the second Industrial Conference was for representation of employees through shop committees. No action was taken in the legislature, but industrialists transformed this "progressive idea" into company unions in the 1920's. Yet the idea of industrial democracy was advanced. Based on the second Industrial Conference archives, Wilson papers, and periodicals. 34 notes. — L. L. Athey

2181. Blackford, Mansel G. SCIENTIFIC MANAGEMENT AND WELFARE WORK IN EARLY TWENTIETH CENTURY AMERICAN BUSINESS: THE BUCKEYE STEEL CASTINGS COMPANY. *Ohio Hist. 1981 9(3): 238-258.* Discusses the Buckeye Steel Castings Company and the underlying progressive vision of President (1908-27) S. P. Bush. This small to medium-size corporation in Columbus had a strong impact on the surrounding social and economic environment and was able to develop an efficient, low-cost foundry operation and avoid labor unrest during the early 1900's by combining the scientific management of its steel foundry and the adoption of welfare work practices for its laborers and local community. Based on the company records, the collections of the Ohio Historical society, interviews, and other primary sources; 2 photos, 3 tables, 74 notes. — L. A. Russell

2182. Bucki, Cecelia F. DILUTION AND CRAFT TRADITION: BRIDGEPORT, CONNECTICUT, MUNITIONS WORKERS: 1915-1919. *Social Sci. Hist. 1980 4(1): 105-124.* Bridgeport, Connecticut, was a major US World War I manufacturing center. Munitions workers there responded to a series of technological innovations and managerial decisions, typical of trends in early 20th-century industrialization, which tended to "dilute" or devalue skilled workers' roles, with a variety of protest actions. Former skilled workers or artisans, rather than unskilled workers and women, dominated labor protest. Based on manuscripts in the Connecticut State Library at Bridgeport University, and other primary sources; 13 notes. — L. K. Blaser

2183. Buhle, Mari Jo. SOCIALIST WOMEN AND THE "GIRL STRIKERS," CHICAGO, 1910. *Signs 1976 1(4): 1039-1051.* The 1910 Chicago garment workers' strike showed a new determined spirit in the American labor movement. The "new immigrants," especially young women, militantly opposed the United Garment Workers' conciliations with factory owners. Contemporary newspaper articles by Nellie M. Zeh and Mary O'Reilly represented Socialist women's responses to the strike and their efforts to publicize the implications of the struggle. Their perspective was rooted in their interpretation of the historic position of women workers. They themselves had given their girlhood to commodity production and felt a sisterhood with the young strikers. They saw the actions of the "girl strikers" as a symbol of the larger tendency in the industrial working class to determine their own destiny. Based on newspaper articles; 11 notes. — J. Gammage

2184. Burke, Padraic. STRUGGLE FOR PUBLIC OWNERSHIP: THE EARLY HISTORY OF THE PORT OF SEATTLE. *Pacific Northwest Q. 1977 68(2): 60-71.* Created as a municipal corporation in 1911 the Port of Seattle represented a victory for Progressives who opposed private ownership of port facilities by monopolistic shipping companies and railroads. The first two Port commissioners, Hiram Chittenden and Robert Bridges, continued resistance against businessmen who criticized public ownership of the lucrative institution. Bridges increasingly aligned the Port's power behind liberal political causes but by 1919 more conservative commissioners outvoted him on major issues and he resigned. This signaled the Port's shift from control by liberal reformers to a domination by businessmen of the city. Primary sources; 4 photos, 51 notes. — M. L. Tate

2185. Burran, James A. LABOR CONFLICT IN URBAN APPALACHIA: THE KNOXVILLE STREETCAR STRIKE OF 1919. *Tennessee Hist. Q. 1979 38(1): 62-78.* In the period of demobilization and search for normalcy following World War I, a streetcar strike occurred in October 1919 in conservative, typically Republican, Knoxville, Tennessee. It was part of a larger movement of the American Federation of Labor which was aimed at organizing, among others, the Knoxville police. When violence broke out after strike breakers were hired, the governor called in Federal troops. The presence of troops broke the strike. Primary and secondary sources; 35 notes. — M. B. Lucas

2186. Byrkit, James W. THE IWW IN WARTIME ARIZONA. *J. of Arizona Hist. 1977 18(2): 149-170.* The Industrial Workers of the World (IWW) struck the three mining companies in Bisbee, Arizona, in summer 1917. Company-hired *agents provocateurs* infiltrated the union. Although there was no proof of overt IWW violence, the agents played upon popular fear which labeled the union as radical. Company officials prevailed upon a sheriff's posse to arrest some 2000 strikers and to send them by railway freight cars to southwestern New Mexico. The Bisbee Deportation was the most effective effort to purge Arizona of all labor influence. Other bona fide unions disintegrated and organized labor ceased to be "a substantial force in Arizona political affairs." Derived from a graduate dissertation; 5 illus., 76 notes. — D. L. Smith

2187. Candela, Joseph L., Jr. THE STRUGGLE TO LIMIT THE HOURS AND RAISE THE WAGES OF WORKING WOMEN IN ILLINOIS, 1893-1917. *Social Service Rev. 1979 53(1): 15-34.* Discusses the reform attitudes of Illinois during 1893-1917, focusing on the outcome of attempted labor legislation to protect women.

2188. Candeloro, Dominic. THE SINGLE TAX MOVEMENT AND PROGRESSIVISM, 1880-1920. *Am. J. of Econ. and Sociol. 1979 38(2): 113-127.* Henry George's Single Tax movement and the Progressive movement in the United States were inter-related. After the publication of *Progress and Poverty* a political movement developed around George. It failed, partly because George was a poor politician although he had proved a master-publicist, partly because he aroused a formidable opposition. Nevertheless the single taxers did contribute to progressive reform a specific plan for manipulating the environment in a Social Darwinistic way. George's philosophy also rejected socialism in favor of a reformed and purified capitalism—perhaps the most important theme in 20th century reform thought in America. Moreover, the Single Tax movement contributed to the democratic reform movement such leaders as Tom L. Johnson, Brand Whitlock, Louis F. Post, Frederic C. Howe, George L. Record, Newton D. Baker and Franklin K. Lane. Primary and secondary sources; 34 notes. — J

2189. Castrovinci, Joseph L. PRELUDE TO WELFARE CAPITALISM: THE ROLE OF BUSINESS IN THE ENACTMENT OF WORKMEN'S COMPENSATION LEGISLATION IN ILLINOIS, 1905-12. *Social Service R. 1976 50(1): 80-102.*

2190. Conn, Sandra. THREE TALENTS: ROBINS, NESTOR, AND ANDERSON OF THE CHICAGO WOMEN'S TRADE UNION LEAGUE. *Chicago Hist. 1980-81 9(4): 234-247.* Margaret Dreier Robins, Agnes Nestor, and Mary Anderson pooled their talents to improve working conditions for women throughout the nation from 1903 to 1920; focuses on their involvement in the National Women's Trade Union League.

2191. Conner, Valerie J. "THE MOTHERS OF THE RACE" IN WORLD WAR I: THE NATIONAL WAR LABOR BOARD AND WOMEN IN INDUSTRY. *Labor Hist. 1980 21(1): 31-54.* Analyzes the attitudes toward working women dominating the National War Labor Board during World War I. Although the NWLB advanced new government policies toward women workers and paved the way for the eventual transformation of policy in the direction of equal pay for equal work, the notion that women were born to be mothers was a powerful check on the NWLB. Based on the NWLB records, National Archives; 41 notes.
L. L. Athey

2192. Cook, Bernard A. COVINGTON HALL AND RADICAL RURAL UNIONIZATION IN LOUISIANA. *Louisiana Hist. 1977 18(2): 227-238.* Covington Hall, a socialist organizer in the Louisiana lumber industry, promoted militant labor organizations and edited radical rural labor publications in Louisiana during 1907-16. His organization of the Forest and Farm Workers Union of the Industrial Workers of the World in 1916 was a failure, and socialism in Louisiana declined thereafter. The decline resulted from national causes, the exploitation of racial issues by lumber operators, the poverty and apathy of the workers, the earlier failure of the rural labor movement in Louisiana, the organized opposition of the companies and their political adjuncts, and the prosperity of World War I. Based on Hall's unpublished manuscript, "Labor Struggles in the Deep South," in the Tulane University Library, and on published primary and secondary sources; 49 notes.
R. L. Woodward, Jr.

2193. Cook, Bernard A. and Watson, James R. THE SAILORS AND MARINE TRANSPORT WORKERS' 1913 STRIKE IN NEW ORLEANS: THE AFL AND THE IWW. *Southern Studies 1979 18(1): 111-122.* Two major types of divisions among workers in New Orleans, Louisiana, traditionally have prevented them from working together and improving their lot: racial differences and antagonism between skilled and unskilled workers. Although several attempts were made to unite the workers, and brief periods of cooperation took place, antagonism has been the general attitude. The dock strike of June-July 1913 by the Sailors' Union (American Federation of Labor) and the Marine Transport Workers (Industrial Workers of the World) against the United Fruit Company in New Orleans failed because of these antagonisms, lack of cooperation, scabbing by members, and betrayals by leadership. 47 notes.
J. J. Buschen

2194. Corbin, David A. BETRAYAL IN THE WEST VIRGINIA COAL FIELDS: EUGENE V. DEBS AND THE SOCIALIST PARTY OF AMERICA, 1912-1914. *J. of Am. Hist. 1978 64(4): 987-1009.* Even though Eugene V. Debs has enjoyed a favorable historical image in America's labor movement, his attitudes and actions concerning local affiliates and rank-and-file members actually hurt the development of the Socialist Party of America. Nowhere is this more apparent than in the West Virginia coal strike of 1912-14. Not only did the national office of the SPA ignore the strike for a year, but when Debs finally intervened with an investigating committee, he urged coal miners to accept a questionable compromise. He also exonerated Governor Hatfield of charges of having abused his power, even though a US congressional committee reached the opposite conclusion. By ignoring the wishes of the miners and by betraying local Socialist affiliates, Debs did considerable damage to Socialist solidarity in West Virginia's coal fields. 89 notes.
T. P. Linkfield

2195. Corbin, David A. *THE SOCIALIST AND LABOR STAR*: STRIKE AND SUPPRESSION IN WEST VIRGINIA, 1912-1913. *West Virginia Hist. 1973 34(2): 168-186.* The Socialist newspaper *The Socialist and Labor Star* reported the Paint Creek-Cabin Creek Strike of 1912-13 and articulated union interests in a radical fashion. Critical of labor and government establishments, it even assailed Eugene Debs for sacrificing the workers to Socialist Party solidarity. Editor Wyatt Hamilton Thompson spoke out so harshly that the military, under orders of Governor Henry D. Hatfield, destroyed the newspaper's plant and arrested Thompson. 57 notes.
C. A. Newton

2196. Corcoran, Theresa. VIDA SCUDDER AND THE LAWRENCE TEXTILE STRIKE. *Essex Inst. Hist. Collections 1979 115(3): 183-195.* During the 1912 Lawrence, Massachusetts, textile strike the Progressive Women's Club of Lawrence invited prominent speakers to address them on 4 March. No outsider stirred the conservatives more than Vida Dutton Scudder, professor at Wellesley College. A founder of the College Settlements Association and Denison House, a distinctively Boston settlement for women, a member of the Socialist Party in 1911, and author of *Socialism and Character* (1912), Scudder had moved into settlements in hopes that they might play their part in radical propaganda. In this she was discouraged, but later became convinced that Christianity offered the one solution to industrialized society, and after 1912 moved into various Christian groups for social reform. Examines Scudder's speech and the reaction to it, the Progressive Women's Club, and the textile strike. Primary and secondary sources; 30 notes.
R. S. Sliwoski

2197. Cumbler, John T. ACCOMMODATION AND CONFLICT: SHOE WORKERS IN TWENTIETH-CENTURY LYNN. *Essex Inst. Hist. Collections 1979 115(4): 232-255.* In the late 19th century, American labor was recovering from a series of defeats. To counteract further losses of membership, labor leaders sought a strategy to protect the organizations that still existed and provide a basis for future growth. They developed a policy of accommodation known as bread-and-butter unionism. The Boot and Shoe Workers Union struggle in Lynn, Massachusetts, illustrates the contradictions inherent in accommodation and the tensions between the interests of the working class and the unions. The workers' struggle demonstrates that they perceived bread-and-butter unionism as beneficial to the unions and not to the workers. Based on primary sources; 66 notes.
R. S. Sliwoski

2198. Daniel, Cletus E. IN DEFENSE OF THE WHEATLAND WOBBLIES: A CRITICAL ANALYSIS OF THE IWW IN CALIFORNIA. *Labor Hist. 1978 19(4): 485-509.* Analyzes the "hop pickers riot" in Wheatland, California, in August 1913. IWW action in Wheatland reinforced ideological and tactical deficiencies among California Wobblies and increased their powerlessness. The incident occurred in spite of IWW organizational policies and produced many more failures than successes. Based on newspapers; 50 notes.
L. L. Athey

2199. Davis, Ronald L. F. and Holmes, Harry D. INSURGENCY AND MUNICIPAL REFORM IN ST. LOUIS, 1893-1904. *Midwest Rev. 1979 1: 1-18.* Examines this example of local reform movements, particularly local taxation, the street railway system, and politics.

2200. Dearstyne, Bruce W. REGULATION IN THE PROGRESSIVE ERA: THE NEW YORK PUBLIC SERVICE COMMISSION. *New York Hist. 1977 58(3): 331-347.* The New York Public Service Commission Law (1907) benefited railroads and the public utilities. Governor Charles Evans Hughes promoted the law to defuse antirailroad and antiutility public opinion, and appointed conservative, probusiness commissioners to regulate the railroad and utility companies in the companies' interest. 4 illus., 36 notes.
R. N. Lokken

2201. Detzer, David W. BUSINESSMEN, REFORMERS, AND TARIFF REVISION: THE PAYNE-ALDRICH TARIFF OF 1909. *Historian 1973 35(2): 196-204.* In the early 20th century, reformers maintained that monopolies and protective tariffs enabled big business to raise prices and rob "the little man." Reduction of duties was considered part of progressivism, and reformers claimed credit when some rates were lowered in 1909. Actually, key businessmen,—manufacturers, shippers, publishers—not the reformers, were the most effective in bringing about this revision. Most progressive reforms, moreover, require the support of businessmen. "Without such patronage, reform laws die and are laid to rest in the congressional graveyard of unrequited dreams." Based on committee hearings, Commerce Department statistical abstracts, and the press; 28 notes.
N. W. Moen

2202. Doherty, Robert E. TEMPEST ON THE HUDSON: THE STRUGGLE FOR "EQUAL PAY FOR EQUAL WORK" IN THE NEW YORK CITY PUBLIC SCHOOLS, 1907-1911. *Hist. of Educ. Q. 1979 19(4): 413-434.* Grace Strachan, Superintendent for Districts 33 and 35, led a legislative struggle as president of the Interborough Association of Women Teachers. Although a bill to provide equal pay for New York

City public school teachers passed in both houses in 1907, the state legislature adjourned before dealing with a veto by Governor Charles Evans Hughes. Similar proposals were also introduced in 1908, 1909, and 1911 before an equal pay bill became law in 1912. Among the arguments frustrating efforts for equal pay for women were alleged exorbitant costs, the fear of feminizing school children, and the argument that men had families to support and too many alternate employment opportunities. Subsequent research suggested that students had higher achievement under women teachers. Secondary sources; 2 tables, 70 notes.

S. H. Frank

2203. Dorsey, George. THE BAYONNE REFINERY STRIKE OF 1915-1916. *Polish Am. Studies 1976 33(2): 19-30.* This strike started on 15 July 1915 at "Jersey Standard's great refinery in Bayonne" when about 100 still cleaners demanded a 15% pay increase justified by a work speedup and publicly announced anticipated company profits. When other workers joined in, the company answered by hiring armed guards from P. J. Berghoff, a New York City "industrial service." The strike, of unorganized workers, spread to other companies. In confrontations, one Pole was killed and four others were wounded. The strike ended by the end of July after promises of pay increases, a change of a foreman, and an appeal to wartime patriotism. Fifteen months later, another strike erupted to improve upon the two dollars-per-day wages. Though not apparent in 1915 and 1916, a new industrialism, one of concern for the worker, was beginning to play a recognizable role in the American economic world. Based primarily on newspaper accounts; 27 notes.

S. R. Pliska

2204. Drescher, Nuala McGann. THE WORKMEN'S COMPENSATION AND PENSION PROPOSAL IN THE BREWING INDUSTRY, 1910-1912: A CASE STUDY IN CONFLICTING SELF-INTEREST. *Industrial and Labor Relations R. 1970 24(1): 32-46.* "The United States Brewers' Association in 1910 proposed a plan for workmen's compensation and pensions for employees of the brewing industry. After negotiation over some features of the proposed plan, the leadership of the United Brewery Workers enthusiastically urged approval of the plan by union members. To the surprise of the union officials and the management of the industry, the proposal was overwhelmingly rejected by the workers. This article tells the story of the Schram plan and discusses why the industry made this proposal, unusual for its time, and the probable reasons for its rejection."

J

2205. Dye, Nancy Schrom. FEMINISM OR UNIONISM? THE NEW YORK WOMEN'S TRADE UNION LEAGUE AND THE LABOR MOVEMENT. *Feminist Studies 1975 3(1/2): 111-125.* The Women's Trade Union League of New York was founded in 1903. Made up of female social reformers and female workers, the WTUL tried, with little success, to organize women and make them part of the labor movement. The WTUL supported A.F.L. principles and patterned women's locals on that craft style model, although it was inappropriate for the majority of unskilled female workers, simply because the A.F.L. was the only successful trade union model in the United States. Separate women's unions or women's federal unions might have promoted feminist goals more successfully, but from the trade union point-of-view these models were unacceptable, because they would not have the necessary economic power base for demands to warrant serious consideration. Primary and secondary sources; 50 notes.

S. R. Herstein

2206. Eklund, Monica. MASSACRE AT LUDLOW. *Southwest Econ. and Soc. 1978 4(1): 21-30.* A strike of coal miners in 1913-14 in Ludlow, Colorado (against the Colorado Fuel and Iron Company), elicited attempted strike-breaking; mine guards, detectives, and the National Guard attacked and burned the strikers' tent city and at least 13 women and children died.

2207. Fickle, James E. RACE, CLASS, AND RADICALISM: THE WOBBLIES IN THE SOUTHERN LUMBER INDUSTRY, 1900-1916. Conlin, Joseph R., ed. *At the Point of Production: The Local History of the I.W.W.* (Westport, Conn.: Greenwood Pr., 1981): 97-113. Details the conflict between lumber workers and mill operators in eastern Texas and western Louisiana, especially from 1911 to 1912. Central to the conflict was Arthur L. Emerson, who formed his first local union at Carson in western Louisiana in 1910, leading to the founding of the Brotherhood of Timber Workers in 1911. The conflict with the mill operators reached violent proportions, as the BTW was backed by the Industrial Workers of the World and other organizations. On 7 July 1912, a gun battle erupted at an Emerson speech. Emerson and other unionists were jailed, and the operators were successful in breaking the financial and psychological strength of the union. By 1914 the BTW was practically destroyed. Mainly secondary sources; 70 notes. Portions of this chapter previously appeared in *Louisiana History* in 1975 (see entry 14A:5386).

J. Powell

2208. Foster, James C. AFL, IWW AND NOME: 1905-1908. *Alaska J. 1975 5(2): 66-77.* Describes the beginning of union organization in Nome. The first successful union was the AFL-Federal Labor Union, which had a strike for longshoremen in 1905. The Western Federation of Miners followed. Describes the conflict in the area between the American Federation of Labor and the Industrial Workers of the World. Reviews union interest and action in local politics. 11 illus., 37 notes.

E. E. Eminhizer

2209. Foster, James C. THE TREADWELL STRIKES, 1907 AND 1908. *Alaska J. 1976 6(1): 2-11.* In the early 20th century the Western Federation of Miners attempted to organize in Alaska. The mines at Douglas Island across from Juneau were a part of the effort. Failure of the WFM in Goldfield, Nevada, stimulated the interest in Alaska. Details the tactics of both sides in the strike against the Treadwell Mines. Suggests reasons for the union's failure. 10 photos., 38 notes.

E. E. Eminhizer

2210. Galvin, Miles. THE EARLY DEVELOPMENT OF THE ORGANIZED LABOR MOVEMENT IN PUERTO RICO. *Latin Am. Perspectives 1976 3(3): 17-35.* Analyzes the role of the American Federation of Labor in the early Puerto Rican labor movement. Emphasizes the importance of both Samuel Gompers and Santiago Iglesias Pantín on the changing thrust and militancy of unions and offers an explanation for the early conservatism of early unionization. The intellectual opportunism and reformist politics of both Gompers and Iglesias—as the sole paid union organizer on the island—were extremely important in diverting the thrust of the unions away from radical positions.

J. L. Dietz

2211. Glanz, Rudolph. SOME REMARKS ON JEWISH LABOR AND AMERICAN PUBLIC OPINION IN THE PRE-WORLD WAR I ERA. *Yivo Ann. of Jewish Social Sci. 1976 (16): 178-202.* Shows how the Jewish labor movement influenced American and Jewish American public opinion about the popular conception of a Jew and how it influenced the entire American labor movement.

R. J. Wechman

2212. Goldberg, Gordon J. MEYER LONDON AND THE NATIONAL SOCIAL INSURANCE MOVEMENT, 1914-1922. *Am. Jewish Hist. Q. 1975 65(1): 59-73.* Meyer London as legal counsel for the International Ladies' Garment Workers Union (ILGWU) and other unions became the principal spokesman for the labor movement and the urban immigrant. As the only Socialist representative in the 64th, 65th and 67th Congresses, London presented his party's social insurance program and waged a vigorous fight for its adoption. Although the plan was defeated, he helped educate colleagues and the public about labor reform, helping to pave the way for the New Deal.

F. Rosenthal

2213. Gowaskie, Joseph M. FROM CONFLICT TO COOPERATION: JOHN MITCHELL AND BITUMINOUS COAL OPERATORS. *Historian 1976 38(4): 669-688.* During 1898-1907 bituminous coal fields consisted of thousands of individually owned mines competing for profit and new markets. Relations between operators and unions were turbulent. After profits plunged in 1897 many operators agreed that recognition of the United Mine Workers of America, led by John Mitchell, would provide order. Employers overcame their resistance to unionization because further conflict in the soft coal industry would lead to their economic destruction. Notes.

M. J. Wentworth

2214. Graebner, William. THE ORIGINS OF RETIREMENT IN HIGHER EDUCATION: THE CARNEGIE PENSION SYSTEM. *Academe: Bull. of the AAUP 1979 65(2): 97-103.* The origins of the retirement system in higher education date to 1901 when Andrew Carnegie retired, leaving $5 million in bonds to the Carnegie Company to be spent on, among other things, pensions for loyal, long-term employees; in later years, he focused on college professors.

2215. Green, James R. THE BROTHERHOOD OF TIMBER WORKERS 1910-1913: A RADICAL RESPONSE TO INDUSTRIAL CAPITALISM IN THE SOUTHERN U.S.A. *Past and Present [Great Britain] 1973 (60): 161-200.* Analyses factors behind the struggle of the Brotherhood of Timber Workers (BTW) and Industrial Workers of the World (IWW) with the lumber companies of Louisiana and Texas, 1910-13. Both black and white workers and farmers cooperated out of hatred for the northern syndicates, which was greater than any fear of the IWW agitators' revolutionary ideas. The BTW and IWW created a radical, collective response to industrial capitalism, remarkable in an era of racial segregation. US Labor Department documents, censuses, Kirby Papers, newspapers. E. M. Sirriyeh

2216. Green, James R. TENANT FARMER DISCONTENT AND SOCIALIST PROTEST IN TEXAS, 1901-1917. *Southwestern Hist. Q. 1977 81(2): 133-154.* The growth of Socialism in Texas after 1900 was directly related to the rise of farm tenancy and the unwillingness of the established political and economic leadership to deal with this problem. Socialists moved into the vacuum with moralistic appeals against the evils of usury and excessive land rentals. They organized scores of locals in 1910-12, a renters' union and a newspaper, and Eugene Debs polled 8.5 percent of the Texas presidential vote in 1912, chiefly in the East Texas piney woods. Anger, frustration, and radicalism continued to increase among tenants, but during World War I the Socialists were crushed. By 1920 the tenant farmer was forgotten again. Primary and secondary sources; illus., 56 notes. J. H. Broussard

2217. Green, Jim. THE BROTHERHOOD. *Southern Exposure 1976 4(1-2): 21-29.* The Brotherhood of Timber Workers was founded 1911-13, in western Louisiana and eastern Texas by white and black workers who hoped to combat the repressive Southern Lumber Operators' Association.

2218. Grossman, Jonathan. THE COAL STRIKE OF 1902—TURNING POINT IN U.S. POLICY. *Monthly Labor R. 1975 98(10): 21-28.* Describes the settlement of Pennsylvania's 1902 coal strike, in which President Theodore Roosevelt, with the Commissioner of Labor, represented the federal government while acting as an arbitrator between labor and management. S

2219. Grossman, Jonathan. THE ORIGIN OF THE U.S. DEPARTMENT OF LABOR. *Monthly Labor Rev. 1973 96(3): 3-7.* Labor leaders campaigned for the creation of a federal Labor Department in the United States from 1864 until their aim was achieved in 1913.

2220. Hammett, Hugh B. LABOR AND RACE: THE GEORGIA RAILROAD STRIKE OF 1909. *Labor Hist. 1975 16(4): 470-484.* Union and management used race to further their respective position in the Georgia Railroad strike of 1909. Wage differentials based on race were used by the company to justify black employment economically. As the strike progressed, violence against black firemen was committed and the Brotherhood of Locomotive Firemen and Enginemen campaigned to remove all black firemen. Only a courageous decision by a board of arbitration led by Hilary A. Herbert which established the principle of equal pay for equal work and rejected union demands for dismissal of black firemen prevented closing of job opportunities for black firemen. Based on newspapers, union publications, and the Hoke Smith papers; 36 notes. L. L. Athey

2221. Haughton, Virginia. JOHN W. KERN: SENATE MAJORITY LEADER AND LABOR LEGISLATION, 1913-1917. *Mid-America 1975 57(3): 184-194.* Though of a rural background, John W. Kern was an early champion of labor. He ran on the defeated Bryan ticket in 1908, entered the Senate in 1911, and became Senate Majority Leader in 1913. Kern obtained Senate investigation of deplorable labor conditions in West Virginia. His most lasting achievement was the Kern-McGillicuddy Workman's Compensation Act (1916). He was instrumental in passage of the La Follette Seaman's Bill and much other prolabor legislation. Based on official records, newspapers, and secondary works; 38 notes. T. H. Wendel

2222. Helfand, Barry. LABOR AND THE COURTS: THE COMMON-LAW DOCTRINE OF CRIMINAL CONSPIRACY AND ITS APPLICATION IN THE BUCK'S STOVE CASE. *Labor Hist. 1977 18(1): 91-114.* Details the origins and development of the legal fight between the Buck's Stove and Range Co. and the American Federation of Labor during 1907-11. The decision continued the anti-labor tendency of the courts and utilized the common-law doctrine of criminal conspiracy to refute labor's defense of freedom of speech. Based upon legal records and court reports; 66 notes. L. L. Athey

2223. Hessen, Robert. THE BETHLEHEM STEEL STRIKE OF 1910. *Labor Hist. 1974 15(1): 3-18.* Details the protracted struggle between labor and management in the Bethlehem Steel strike of 1910. Triggered by the intransigence of Charles M. Schwab, the president, the strike was led by the skilled machinists. Although the company managed to maintain local support and break the strike within a three-month period, it signalled the beginning of increased federal regulation of the American steel industry. Movement of the strikers to other cities and lack of union financial resources also contributed to its failure. Based on the Bethlehem *Globe,* other newspapers and periodicals. 43 notes. L. L. Athey

2224. Hobby, Daniel T., ed. "WE HAVE GOT RESULTS": A DOCUMENT ON THE ORGANIZATION OF DOMESTICS IN THE PROGRESSIVE ERA. *Labor Hist. 1976 17(1): 103-108.* Presents a 1917 letter from Jane Street, Industrial Workers of the World organizer of domestics, as a reflection of philosophy and tactics of organizing unskilled workers. The letter, intercepted by the Post Office and sent to the Justice Department, was found in the National Archives. L. L. Athey

2225. Hurwitz, Haggai. IDEOLOGY AND INDUSTRIAL CONFLICT: PRESIDENT WILSON'S FIRST INDUSTRIAL CONFERENCE OF OCTOBER 1919. *Labor Hist. 1977 18(4): 509-524.* The First Industrial Conference of 1919 reveals the underlying ideological conflict between labor and management. Instead of pragmatic business unionism, labor delegates representing major unions argued for a broad transformation of the role of labor based on human rights. Industrialists attacked unions on the basis of property rights and managerial prerogatives designed to destroy unions. The complete ideological division represented the irreconcilable social views of labor and industry; the Conference was doomed to fail. Based on the *Proceedings* of the Conference; 41 notes. L. L. Athey

2226. Jacoby, Robin Miller. FEMINISM AND CLASS CONSCIOUSNESS IN THE BRITISH AND AMERICAN WOMEN'S TRADE UNION LEAGUE, 1890-1925. Carroll, Berenice A., ed. Liberating Women's Hist. (Chicago: U. of Illinois Pr., 1976): pp. 137-160. Discusses the influence of class consciousness on British and American trade union women when union goals for women conflicted with an ideology of class loyalty. Analyzes the different relationships of both trade union leagues to the women's suffrage movement, and the effect these differences had on the International Federation of Working Women. Despite the priority given by the British to class-based issues, and by the American to interaction between women of all classes, the British and American women were participants in the same struggle. 64 notes. B. Sussman

2227. Jaenicke, Douglas Walter. HERBERT CROLY, PROGRESSIVE IDEOLOGY, AND THE FTC ACT. *Pol. Sci. Q. 1978 93(3): 471-493.* Reexamines the origins of the Federal Trade Commission Act (US, 1914) within the context of progressive thought and argues that the act was a victory neither for equal opportunity nor for big business.

2228. Jensen, Billie Barnes. WOODROW WILSON'S INTERVENTION IN THE COAL STRIKE OF 1914. *Labor Hist. 1974 15(1): 63-77.* Assesses the factors which caused Woodrow Wilson to intervene with federal troops in the Colorado coal fields strikes of 1914. All parts of the country pressured President Wilson to intervene. His mediation attempts failed, partly as a result of mineowners obstinacy. Union and congressional outcries also increased pressure, while newspapers were generally in favor of sending federal troops. After the "Ludlow Massacre" pressure became so intense that Governor Elias Ammons finally requested federal intervention, and Wilson ordered troops in. Wilson and Ammons are characterized as men "pushed by the events." Based on the Woodrow Wilson papers in the Library of Congress. 59 notes. L. L. Athey

2229. Johnson, Keach. THE CORN BELT MEAT PRODUCERS' ASSOCIATION OF IOWA: ORIGINS OF A PROGRESSIVE PRESSURE GROUP. *Ann. of Iowa 1976 43(4): 242-260.* Denouncing what they considered to be the poor service, extortionate charges, and discriminatory practices of railroads and meatpackers, Iowa cattlemen in 1904 organized the Corn Belt Meat Producers' Association. The meat producers' support of legislation on the state and national levels (the Hepburn Act of 1906) was the result of their recognition that "they could remedy their grievances only by expanding and strengthening the regulatory powers of the state and federal governments." Consequently, the Corn Belt Meat Producers' Association became a "major force in Iowa Progressivism." Based on primary sources, newspapers, and *Wallace's Farmer* magazine; 38 notes. P. L. Petersen

2230. Kennedy, Susan Estabrook. POVERTY, RESPECTABILITY, AND ABILITY TO WORK. *Int. J. of Women's Studies [Canada] 1979 2(5): 401-418.* Discusses the reform efforts on behalf of working-class women by the Progressives, middle-class moral activists in the early 20th century, who used sociology, investigation of working conditions, and social settlement work to spur reform. They concentrated on trade unionism and self-help, and later on enacting protective legislaton until World War I when organization attempts failed.

2231. Kennedy, Susan Estabrook. "THE WANT IT SATISFIES DEMONSTRATES THE NEED OF IT": A STUDY OF *LIFE AND LABOR* OF THE WOMEN'S TRADE UNION LEAGUE. *Int. J. of Women's Studies [Canada] 1980 3(4): 391-406.* Analyzes the contents of the monthly journal published by the Women's Trade Union League from 1911 to 1921, *Life and Labor,* which focused on the union's activities, efforts to educate women workers on trade unions, and gain public support.

2232. Levi, Steven C. THE BATTLE FOR THE EIGHT-HOUR DAY IN SAN FRANCISCO. *California History 1978-79 57(4): 342-353.* From July 1916 to January 1917 the structural steel workers of San Francisco conducted a strike for the eight-hour working day. Fifty-four out of sixty-four companies agreed to the request; the ten who refused, along with other members of the business community under the blessing of the San Francisco Chamber of Commerce, organized the Law and Order Committee to maintain the nine-hour day and recreate the open shop. The Committee employed a budget of $1 million against the union and conducted an anti-union propaganda campaign. However, several of the companies found it difficult to continue with nonunion labor and capitulated to the union. The union boycotted the remaining companies. Eventually Mayor James Rolph became exasperated by Law and Order Committee tactics and sided with the union. The companies admitted defeat and accepted the eight-hour day. The Committee lasted another two years before disbanding, having alienated much of its support through endorsement of extralegal measures. Primary and secondary sources; 4 photos, 37 notes. A. Hoffman

2233. Levi, Steven. MINER CHIPMAN AND THE LAW AND ORDER COMMITTEE OF THE SAN FRANCISCO CHAMBER OF COMMERCE, 1917. *Pacific Historian 1974 18(4): 47-60.* Labor disputes in San Francisco led to the establishment of the Chamber of Commerce Law and Order Committee. Financed and supported by business interests, the Committee sought to destroy union power by instigating open-shop work policies. Miner Chipman, hired by the Committee to survey San Francisco industry, reported that both labor and management were responsible for the city's industrial problems. Chipman's report was never issued and the Committee was dissolved in 1919 after anti-union hysteria had dissipated. Table, 38 notes. S

2234. Levi, Steven C. SAN FRANCISCO'S LAW AND ORDER COMMITTEE, 1916. *J. of the West 1973 12(1): 53-70.* A detailed account of the action taken by the Law and Order Committee in San Francisco following the first major longshoremen's strike on 1 June 1916. The International Longshoremen's Association (ILA) was in conflict with the Waterfront Employers Union (WEU). "The Law and Order Committee was originally established for a single purpose: open shop. . . . Prior to July 22, 1916, the committee was a feeble power at best. Although its members represented both the Chamber of Commerce and San Francisco business and a substantial 'slush fund,' one million dollars by December, 1916, the committee did not have the support of great numbers of San Francisco businessmen. . . . By December the committee had effectively entered and ended, for better or for worse, most of the major strikes that had plagued the city six months earlier." 81 notes.
D. D. Cameron

2235. Lynch, Patrick. PITTSBURGH, THE I.W.W., AND THE STOGIE WORKERS. Conlin, Joseph R., ed. *At the Point of Production: The Local History of the I.W.W.* (Westport, Conn.: Greenwood Pr., 1981): 79-94. During the summer of 1909 a significant strike began in McKees Rocks, near Pittsburgh, Pennsylvania. The workers of the Pressed Steel Car Company demanded higher wages, the positing of wage rates, the end of a wage-pool system, and the creation of an acceptable grievance procedure. The strikers soon enlisted the help of the Industrial Workers of the World. Some historians have described the McKees Rocks strike as the incident that inspired the revival of the IWW in the East. The IWW activities in the area from 1909 through 1913 caused important developments in the Pittsburgh area, especially the stogie workers' strike of 1913. These cigar makers demanded better wages and working conditions. They won the strike, establishing the union shop and worker control of shop conditions. Based on magazine, newspaper, and journal articles of the period; 86 notes. J. Powell

2236. Maroney, James C. THE INTERNATIONAL LONGSHOREMEN'S ASSOCIATION IN THE GULF STATES DURING THE PROGRESSIVE ERA. *Southern Studies 1977 16(2): 225-232.* The International Longshoremen's Association, Gulf Coast District, maintained a conservative attitude in the early 20th century. Despite its moderation, the union movement was strongly opposed by well organized management. A powerful drive by management to promote the open shop rule almost eradicated union power by 1920. In race relations, separate and segregated locals but equal work for blacks and whites became standard. Blacks thus received more work and more opportunities for union officeholding. The black workers' gains resulted from economic rather than humanitarian factors; strikes and violence hurt white workers. Based on union records, unpublished M.A. theses, secondary sources; 19 notes.
J. Buschen

2237. Maroney, James C. THE TEXAS-LOUISIANA OIL FIELD STRIKE. Fink, Gary M. and Reed, Merl E., eds. *Essays in Southern Labor History: Selected Papers, Southern Labor History Conference, 1976.* (Westport, Conn.; London, England: Greenwood Pr., 1977): 161-172. Studies of the 1917 strike of Texas and Louisiana oil field workers as an illustration of some employers' inexorable opposition to organized labor and great resentment of all concessions made to labor by the Wilson administration. Producers gained a clear victory in opposition to the findings of the President's Mediation Commission. Union effectiveness was not to be regained before the 1930's. It all ended in employer unity, but continued division in the ranks of union members. 32 notes.
R. V. Ritter

2238. Maroney, James C. THE UNIONIZATION OF THURBER, 1903. *Red River Valley Hist. Rev. 1979 4(2): 27-32.* An account of efforts to unionize the mine workers of Thurber, Texas, in 1903, which remained a union stronghold until mining operations ended in the 1920's; also discusses the establishment of coal mining in Thurber since the 1880's.

2239. McLaughlin, Doris B. THE SECOND BATTLE OF BATTLE CREEK: THE OPEN SHOP MOVEMENT IN THE EARLY TWENTIETH CENTURY. *Labor Hist. 1973 14(3): 323-339.* Assesses the career of Charles William Post, the cereal magnate, and his activities in promoting the open shop movement in Battle Creek, Michigan. Post fought for the open shop on local and national levels, and as Battle Creek grew in population he led the effort to maintain a nonunion industrial town by paternalism and "welfare capitalism." The A.F.L. unsuccessfully tried to organize in Battle Creek in 1910-12. The experience there was the historical forerunner of the resurgence of the open shop movement in the 1920's. Based on records of Post's companies, his official publication, *The Square Deal,* and the *American Federationist;* 33 notes.
L. L. Athey

2240. McQuaid, Kim. BUSINESSMAN AS SOCIAL INNOVATOR: N. O. NELSON, PROMOTER OF GARDEN CITIES AND THE CONSUMER COOPERATIVE MOVEMENT. *Am. J. of*

Econ. and Sociol. 1975 34(4): 411-422. Describes Nelson O. Nelson's progressive business experiments around the turn of the century.

2241. Meyerhuber, Carl I., Jr. THE ALLE-KISKI COAL WARS, 1913-1919. *Western Pennsylvania Hist. Mag. 1980 63(3): 197-213.* Discusses the violent reactions to the United Mine Workers of America's unsuccessful attempts at unionization in the Allegheny-Kiskiminetas Valley.

2242. Meyerhuber, Carl I., Jr. BLACK VALLEY: PENNSYLVANIA'S ALLE-KISKI AND THE GREAT STRIKE OF 1919. *Western Pennsylvania Hist. Mag. 1979 62(3): 251-265.* Analyzes the antiunion activities and violence in the Allegheny-Kiskiminetas Valley during the Great Steel Strike of 1919.

2243. Milden, James W. WOMEN, PUBLIC LIBRARIES, AND LIBRARY UNIONS: THE FORMATIVE YEARS. *J. of Lib. Hist. 1977 12(2): 150-158.* Presents histories of several of the unions which began and ended during 1917-20, including the New York Public Library Employee's Union and the Library Workers' Union of Boston Public. Discussion of the controversies of library employees over unionization. Primary and secondary sources; 24 notes. A. C. Dewees

2244. Mohl, Raymond A. THE GREAT STEEL STRIKE OF 1919 IN GARY, INDIANA: WORKING-CLASS RADICALISM OR TRADE UNION MILITANCY? *Mid-America 1981 63(1): 36-52.* The 1919 Gary, Indiana, steel strike was notable for the absence of widespread radicalism, the lack of violence, and the moderation of the steel workers in the face of antiunion propaganda and martial law. The workers wanted better wages, shorter hours, and improved working conditions. Steel industry leaders successfully portrayed the strikers as bolshevists which alarmed the civic leaders and the local press. The US Army, led by General Leonard Wood, was called in to impose martial law on Gary. Notes. M. J. Wentworth

2245. Montgomery, David. QUELS STANDARDS? LES OUVRIERS ET LA RÉORGANISATION DE LA PRODUCTION AUX ETATS-UNIS (1900-1920) [Whose standards? Workers and the reorganization of production in the United States, 1900-20]. *Mouvement Social [France] 1978 (102): 101-127.* With the demise of customary factory management, based on the autonomy of the skilled worker and the foreman, a bitter battle developed between organized workers and management reformers over the ways in which work relations should be reshaped. The conflict reached its greatest intensity during periods of abundant employment after 1909, when scientific management spread rapidly through metal-working industries and became increasingly concerned with personnel relations. Simultaneously the level of strike activity rose rapidly, and large numbers of workers devised forms of organization which transcended traditional craft union lines and formulated their own counterplans to those of management, particularly in the realm of payment schemes. These developments intensified the employers' determination to destroy the union and contributed significantly to the ideological controversies which divided the labor movement. J

2246. Moore, John H. JACK LONDON: STRIKE METHODS: AMERICAN AND AUSTRALIAN. *Politics [Australia] 1973 8(2): 356-359.* Reprints an article by Jack London based on his personal visit to Sydney in 1908. London used the Broken Hill mining strike to demonstrate the contrasts in US and Australian disputes, with particular reference to strike-breaking, picketing, and the attitude of civil and military authorities. He also discussed the fundamental nature of labor disputes and how to achieve industrial peace. Reprinted from the *Australian Star* of 14 January 1909. C. A. McNeill

2247. Musselman, Barbara L. WORKING CLASS UNITY AND ETHNIC DIVISION: CINCINNATI TRADE UNIONISTS AND CULTURAL PLURALISM. *Cincinnati Hist. Soc. Bull. 1976 34(1): 121-143.* Chronicles attempts of working classes, 1893-1920, in Cincinnati to unify along class rather than ethnic lines; discusses the labor union movement in Cincinnati, its pre-World War I domination by German and Irish Americans, and postwar ascendancy of Russian Jews, Orientals, and blacks.

2248. Nelson, Daniel. THE MAKING OF A PROGRESSIVE ENGINEER: FREDERICK W. TAYLOR. *Pennsylvania Mag. of Hist. and Biog. 1979 103(4): 446-466.* Taylor's consulting work led him from distrust of financiers to the demand for independence from managerial interference. Influenced by Morris Cooke, Taylor in his *Principles* implied linkage between efficiency and progressive reform. Based on Taylor Papers, Stevens Institute; Cooke Papers, Franklin D. Roosevelt Library; other manuscripts; and secondary works; 78 notes. T. H. Wendel

2249. Nelson, Daniel. THE NEW FACTORY SYSTEM AND THE UNIONS: THE NATIONAL CASH REGISTER COMPANY DISPUTE OF 1901. *Labor Hist. 1974 15(2): 163-178.* Assesses the impact of the new factory system, based on "welfare work," on the workers and the unions in the National Cash Register Company. "Welfare work" did not prevent the maintenance of the old autocratic foreman methods. The latter caused the dispute of 1901 which provoked criticism of "welfare work" practices, set back the attempt to organize mass production industries, and began a new phase in the emerging "new factory system." The N.C.R. Labor Department became the first modern personnel department in American industry. Based upon the McCormick Papers, the Gompers Letterbooks, unpublished correspondence, and the Dayton Daily Journal; 55 notes. L. L. Athey

2250. Nochlin, Linda. THE PATTERSON STRIKE PAGEANT OF 1913. *Art in Am. 1974 62(3): 64-68.*

2251. Norris, John. THE VANCOUVER ISLAND COAL MINERS, 1912-1914: A STUDY OF AN ORGANIZATIONAL STRIKE. *BC Studies [Canada] 1980 (45): 56-72.* The United Mine Workers of America had difficulty organizing the Vancouver Island coal miners' strike of 1912-14. Recruiting strike breakers from among the strikers proved relatively simple; moreover, the strike's prime target, Canadian Collieries (Dunsmuir) Limited, had unusual means of resistance. Labor's attitude was changing from a resentful acceptance of circumstances to violent rebellion against the mining companies, but still lacked the strength and momentum needed for union organization. 2 tables, 34 notes. D. L. Smith

2252. O'Connell, Lucille. THE LAWRENCE TEXTILE STRIKE OF 1912: THE TESTIMONY OF TWO POLISH WOMEN. *Polish Am. Studies 1979 36(2): 44-62.* A personal account of two participants in the textile strike against the Everett Mill in Lawrence, Massachusetts, as revealed in testimony before the Committee on Rules of the House of Representatives on 2-7 March 1912. In their testimony, 14-year-old Victoria Winiarczyk and the older, more experienced Josephine Liss describe the hardships, deprivations, and dire poverty of their fellow immigrant workers. The strike radicalized many of the mill women and led them to militancy, collective action, and even membership in the Industrial Workers of the World. This strike was the first victory in the United States by unskilled, immigrant wage earners. Documented sources in English; 14 notes. S. R. Pliska

2253. Ollila, Douglas J. A TIME OF GLORY: FINNISH-AMERICAN RADICAL INDUSTRIAL UNIONISM, 1914-1917. *U. of Turku. Inst. of General Hist. Publ. [Finland] 1977 9: 31-53.* The industrial unionists in 1916 became heavily involved in the great Mesabi Iron Range strikes in Minnesota which Finnish radicals viewed as "a time of glory." But instead of ushering in the destruction of American capitalism, it was short-lived. Describes the stabilization of the Finnish-American radical industrial union movement, the evolution of its political-economic Marxist orientation to pure economic Marxism, and "an analysis of the ethnic factors related to the Mesabi strike and the ensuing challenge to the lumber industry which precipitated the eventual downfall of the IWW." Primary sources; 87 notes. E. P. Stickney

2254. Osborne, James D. PATERSON: IMMIGRANT STRIKERS AND THE WAR OF 1913. Conlin, Joseph R., ed. *At the Point of Production: The Local History of the I.W.W.* (Westport, Conn.: Greenwood Pr., 1981) 61-78. Details the history of the textile strike of 1913 in Paterson. Police, city government, and the local judiciary combined to back local manufacturers against strikers. Almost 2,000 mill hands were arrested, picket lines broken up, and workers' processions dispersed. Even strike headquarters were closed down. The Industrial Workers of the World attracted attention to the strike, bringing it before a national audience, and for a time seemed near prompting federal intervention and a favorable settlement. The central incident of the strike was the death of Valentino Modestino, an Italian metal worker who lived in Paterson's Riverside section. The strike resulted in the partial emigration of the industry, the changed ethnic composition of the workforce, and the reform of local government, particularly the police department. Based on US Bureau of Census data, journal articles; 60 notes. J. Powell

2255. Overstreet, Daphne. ON STRIKE! THE 1917 WALKOUT AT GLOBE, ARIZONA. *J. of Arizona Hist. 1977 18(2): 197-218.* Globe, Arizona, was plagued with labor-management problems which made it a center for radical labor agitation in the state. Soaring copper prices in the midst of World War I were not accompanied by improved wages and working conditions for the workers, who were locally organized by the Western Federation of Miners. Describes the walkout strike in July 1917 and its settlement. 3 illus., 57 notes. D. L. Smith

2256. Palmer, Bryan D. CLASS, CONCEPTION AND CONFLICT: THE THRUST FOR EFFICIENCY, MANAGERIAL VIEWS OF LABOR AND THE WORKING CLASS REBELLION, 1903-1922. *R. of Radical Pol. Econ. 1975 7(2): 31-49.* Considers managerial efforts to implement scientific management techniques, and to maximize efficiency at the expense of the workers, and the workers' response, such as the Illinois Central and Harriman lines Railroad Carmen's Strike (1911-15).

2257. Piott, Steven L. MODERNIZATION AND THE ANTIMONOPOLY ISSUE: THE ST. LOUIS TRANSIT STRIKE OF 1900. *Missouri Hist. Soc. Bull. 1978 35(1): 3-16.* As permitted by new state legislation passed in 1899, the United Railways Company took control of the transit lines serving St. Louis. That monopoly angered employees who organized a union, and the new corporation named the St. Louis Transit Company, signed an agreement with the union in March, 1900. The March pact only postponed a major transit employees strike for two months. The strike, accompanied by violence and killing, lasted two months and ended with reverses for the union. The strike also focused attention on the ills of monopolies. Manuscript and newspaper sources; 3 photos, 45 notes. H. T. Lovin

2258. Powell, Allan Kent. THE "FOREIGN ELEMENT" AND THE 1903-4 CARBON COUNTY COAL MINERS' STRIKE. *Utah Hist. Q. 1975 43(2): 125-154.* Finnish, Slavic, and Italian miners provided the strength behind a serious labor confrontation in Carbon County, Utah, in 1903. The Utah Fuel Company refused union recognition. The Utah National Guard was called out. Charles DeMolli, Con Kelliner, Mother Mary Jones, and Samuel H. Gilson involved themselves in the strike. The strike failed because the union lacked internal and external support and the company played on antiforeign sentiments in defending its position. Based on primary and secondary sources; 9 illus., 65 notes. J. L. Hazelton

2259. Remele, Larry. THE NORTH DAKOTA FARMERS UNION AND THE NONPARTISAN LEAGUE: BREAKDOWN OF A COALITION. *North Dakota Q. 1978 46(4): 40-50.* Though initially aligned with the Nonpartisan League because of its views toward rural development, 1916-17, the North Dakota Farmer's Union eventually (1918-19) split with the League because of disagreement over cooperatives when the League's Consumers' United Stores became private enterprises.

2260. Remele, Larry. NORTH DAKOTA'S FORGOTTEN FARMERS UNION 1913-1920. *North Dakota Hist. 1978 45(2): 4-21.* During 1913-20, the first North Dakota branch of the Farmers Educational and Cooperative Union of America played a significant role in the state's economic and political affairs. However, the organization passed so rapidly from the scene after 1920 that within a few years organizers of the second and lasting Farmers Union were almost completely unaware of the existence of their predecessor. The first Farmers Union was organized in Bismarck, largely as a result of the activity of Howard P. Knappen, editor of a local weekly. The original purposes of the Union included economic moves to end corporate control over marketing and distribution of farm goods; establishment of cooperative buying and selling agencies; discouragement of the credit and mortgage systems; and fraternal aims. Cooperatives were founded to enter into the grain elevator, flour milling, warehousing, and grocery store businesses. Some of the elevators are still in business. The Union became entangled with the political actions of the Non-Partisan League and by 1920 was defunct as a state group. N. Lederer

2261. Riell, Robert B. THE 1917 COPPER STRIKE AT GLOBE, ARIZONA. *J. of Arizona Hist. 1977 18(2): 185-196.* The Western Federation of Miners and the Industrial Workers of the World were receptive to membership that was militant socialist. On 2 July 1917, all copper mines in the country were struck, precipitating crises all over the West. Describes the strike in Globe, Arizona from the viewpoint of a company man, the paymaster. 3 illus. D. L. Smith

2262. Rocha, Guy Louis. RADICAL LABOR STRUGGLES IN THE TONOPAH-GOLDFIELD MINING DISTRICT, 1901-1922. *Nevada Hist. Soc. Q. 1977 20(1): 2-45.* Analyzes labor-management relations in one Nevada mining district during 1901-22. Stresses the expansion role of the Industrial Workers of the World (IWW) in the district. The IWW advocated better wages, hours, and working conditions, but also predicted a "revolutionary apocalypse" at Tonopah and Goldfield. Consequently, it alienated more conservative miners and helped employers to win support for governmental repression of the IWW. Economic reverses and the post-World War I Red Scare further weakened the IWW in Nevada, but IWW unions functioned in the area until 1924. Based on newspaper and secondary sources; 3 illus., 133 notes. H. T. Lovin

2263. Rodine, Floyd. LEGISLATIVE AND LEGAL STRUGGLES OF THE GRAIN COOPERATIVES IN NEBRASKA, 1900-1915. *Nebraska Hist. 1975 56(4): 457-470.* Examines the "active crusade" for grain elevators operated and owned by farmers. The monopolistic methods of private elevators had to be broken and cooperatives had to secure legal recognition and protection to operate successfully. These conditions were accomplished in Nebraska in the first 15 years of the 20th century. The Ramsay Act of 1903 compelled railroads to offer equal facilities and the passage of Nebraska's first cooperative law in 1911 combined to make possible the establishment of grain cooperatives. R. Lowitt

2264. Schmelzer, Janet. THOMAS M. CAMPBELL: PROGRESSIVE GOVERNOR OF TEXAS. *Red River Valley Hist. Rev. 1978 3(4): 52-63.* Discusses reasons for the rise of Progressivism and describes the efforts of the Democratic governor of Texas (1907-11), Thomas M. Campbell, to regulate big business.

2265. Shapiro, Herbert. THE MCNAMARA CASE: A CRISIS OF THE PROGRESSIVE ERA. *Southern California Q. 1977 59(3): 271-287.* Reasssesses the *Los Angeles Times* dynamiting case's impact on reformers and the labor movement in the Progressive Era. The American Federation of Labor rejected militancy and violence in favor of legalistic approaches to labor issues. Progressives urged capital and labor to reject extreme methods because of the possibility of class conflict. Militant unionists left the American Federation of Labor and the Socialist Party, making it possible for the labor movement to achieve moderate goals without extreme methods. The McNamara case, overlooked by labor historians, thus stands as a turning point for the labor movement and as a repudiation of violence. The case itself invites further investigation, because evidence indicates that the McNamara brothers were influenced by *agents provocateurs*. Based on primary sources and on contemporary and secondary sources; 53 notes. A. Hoffman

2266. Sharpless, John and Rury, John. THE POLITICAL ECONOMY OF WOMEN'S WORK: 1900-1920. *Social Sci. Hist. 1980 4(3): 317-346.* Examines the impact of different cultural environments in shaping women's collective responses to traditional labor issues and activities. Women lacked the formal and informal contacts outside their work situation that fostered worker mobilization among men. Women's work was mostly intermittent and a temporary life phase, furthering difficulties of organization. Finally, ethnic groups restricted women's roles outside the family. All of this limited the appeal of labor organizations and feminist groups to New York's working women in the early 20th century. Based on published federal materials on women and labor; 2 tables, 7 notes, biblio. L. K. Blaser

2267. Shofner, Jerrell H. MARY GRACE QUACKENBOS, A VISITOR FLORIDA DID NOT WANT. *Florida Hist. Q. 1980 58(3):*

273-290. Mary Grace Quackenbos was instrumental in bringing forth charges of peonage in Florida's turpentine industry. Her investigations of misleading labor recruitment in New York City forced US Attorney General Charles J. Bonaparte and the Justice Department to act. White Floridians avoided the issue by resorting to character assassination, thereby failing to realize that the state's labor practices were far out-of-step with those of the nation. Covers 1905-10. Based on papers in the National Archives, newspaper accounts and other primary sources; 39 notes. N. A. Kuntz

2268. Snyder, Robert E. WOMEN, WOBBLIES, AND WORKER'S RIGHTS: THE 1912 TEXTILE STRIKE IN LITTLE FALLS, NEW YORK. *New York Hist. 1979 60(1): 29-57.* The 1912 textile strike in Little Falls, New York, shows how immigrant women workers, Schenectady socialists, the Industrial Workers of the World, Helen Keller, and a visiting tuberculosis nurse overcame the hostility of Little Falls authorities and mill management and the indifference of native American labor to achieve reforms in wages, hours, and working conditions. 6 illus., 57 notes. R. N. Lokken

2269. Snyder, Robert E. WOMEN, WOBBLIES, AND WORKERS' RIGHTS: THE 1912 TEXTILE STRIKE IN LITTLE FALLS, NEW YORK. Conlin, Joseph R., ed. *At the Point of Production: The Local History of the I.W.W.* (Westport, Conn.: Greenwood Pr., 1981): 27-48. The Little Falls textile strike lasted from 9 October 1912 until 4 January 1913. This overview sheds light on Industrial Workers of the World strike activities, Socialist participation in working-class radicalism, and immigrant disenchantment and disillusionment. Some 70% of the strikers were women (inarticulate Poles, Slavs, Austrians, and Italians) who saw their actions only as a protest over a reduction in wages; yet the movement for protective labor legislation for women was actually the backdrop to the strike. Based on primary sources, including newspaper, magazine and journal articles of the period; 57 notes. Portions previously published in *New York History* in 1979 (see entry 17A:2402). J. Powell

2270. Sprague, Stuart Seely. UNIONIZATION STRUGGLES ON PAINT CREEK, 1912-1913. *West Virginia Hist. 1977 38(3): 185-213.* When the United Mine Workers of America tried to organize the Kanawha region coal fields in West Virginia in 1912-13, they met adamant resistance from the mine operators, who brought in guards and strike breakers. The miners responded with violence, and Governor William E. Glasscock sent in the national guard to restore order. Public opinion, which had been tolerant of the union, swung against it by early 1913 and the new Governor, Harry D. Hatfield, forced an end to the dispute. The union won recognition and a pay raise for workers. Primary and secondary sources; 163 notes. J. H. Broussard

2271. Strasser, Susan M. MISTRESS AND MAID, EMPLOYER AND EMPLOYEE: DOMESTIC SERVICE REFORM IN THE UNITED STATES, 1892-1920. *Marxist Perspectives 1978 1(4): 52-67.* Describes the rise of employment of servants during 1892-1920 in the United States and the resultant reforms.

2272. Straw, Richard A. THE COLLAPSE OF BIRACIAL UNIONISM: THE ALABAMA COAL STRIKE OF 1908. *Alabama Hist. Q. 1975 37(2): 92-114.* The United Mine Workers of America was the only large biracial union during the period 1840-1920. This policy came out of the use of Negroes as strike-breakers. The failure of the UMW in the Alabama strike of 1908 was southern racial attitudes, not the operators' actions. Details the strike, including the violence and racial conflict caused by the union's racial attitude. 64 notes. E. E. Eminhizer

2273. Suggs, George G., Jr. THE COLORADO COAL MINERS' STRIKE, 1903-1904: A PRELUDE TO LUDLOW? *J. of the West 1973 12(1): 36-52.* Describes the deplorable conditions in the coal mines of southern Colorado prior to the miners' strike of 1903-04 in Las Animas and Huerfano Counties. "The strike was a tragic mistake, not because there was insufficient justification, but because it was launched when neither the district nor national unions were powerful enough to guarantee its success.... Secondly, although state intervention undoubtedly assured the breaking of the strike, other causes more adequately explain the failure of the United Mine Workers of America in the southern fields." The failure of this strike paved the way for the struggle between the United Mine Workers and the coal companies that led to the "Ludlow massacre" in 1913-14. 59 notes. D. D. Cameron

2274. Taft, Philip. THE LIMITS OF LABOR UNITY: THE CHICAGO NEWSPAPER STRIKE OF 1912. *Labor Hist. 1978 19(1): 100-129.* Analyzes the internal division generated by the strike-lockout of Chicago newspapers in 1912. Begun by pressmen in a dispute over crew reduction on Hearst newspapers, the strike led to sympathetic walkouts by stereotypers, delivery men, and newsboys. George L. Berry of the pressman's union attempted to obtain support from Chicago newspaper unions and to broaden the strike against the Hearst chain. His efforts failed as the limits of labor unity were reached when opposition to sympathy strikes and lack of support for a National Strike, led by typographers, split labor organizations in the newspaper industry. Based on union publications, conference proceedings, and newspapers; 92 notes. L. L. Athey

2275. Tobin, Eugene M. DIRECT ACTION AND CONSCIENCE: THE 1913 PATERSON STRIKE AS AN EXAMPLE OF THE RELATIONSHIP BETWEEN LABOR RADICALS AND LIBERALS. *Labor Hist. 1979 20(1): 73-88.* The role of the judiciary, particularly in the Patrick Quinlan case, effected a closer link between IWW radicals and liberal progressives. Liberals perceived the courts as subverting justice, and an uneasy link was established between those of "hand and brain." Court records, newspapers, and the Amos Pinchot papers; 37 notes. L. L. Athey

2276. Tobin, Eugene M. IN PURSUIT OF EQUAL TAXATION. *Am. J. of Econ. and Sociol. 1975 34(2): 213-224.* Traces the attempt by Mark Fagan and George Record in Jersey City 1901-07 to use taxation to break up the railroad trust. They failed because voters were unprepared to approve the reorganization needed to overcome corporate arrogance and privilege, but the railroads accepted regulation. Based on secondary sources; 42 notes. W. L. Marr

2277. Tobin, Eugene M. THE POLITICAL ECONOMY OF GEORGE L. RECORD: A PROGRESSIVE ALTERNATIVE TO SOCIALISM. *Historian 1977 39(4): 702-716.* Traces the role of George L. Record (1859-1933) in economic reform, based on his correspondence with Theodore Roosevelt, Robert M. La Follette, Woodrow Wilson, Amos Pinchot, Lincoln Steffens, Joseph P. Tumulty, Ray Stannard Baker, and Charles E. Merriam. Believing that monopolies were the cornerstone of many of society's injustices, Record argued for, among other things, a single tax on land and government ownership of railroads. Nevertheless, his brand of reform clearly placed him between the socialists and the mainstream progressives. M. S. Legan

2278. Tobin, Eugene M. THE PROGRESSIVE AND SINGLE TAXER: MARK FAGAN AND THE JERSEY CITY EXPERIENCE, 1900-1917. *Am. J. of Econ. and Sociol. 1974 33(3): 287-297.* The Progressives' failure is dealt with through the career of Mark Fagan, mayor of Jersey City during 1901-07 and 1913-17. Explores why he and other mayors adopted the single tax late in their careers. Secondary sources; 30 notes. W. L. Marr

2279. Tobin, Eugene M. THE PROGRESSIVE AS POLITICIAN: JERSEY CITY, 1896-1907. *New Jersey Hist. 1973 91(1): 5-23.* In tracing the career of Mark Fagan, mayor of Jersey City, the author relates the failure of Progressivism in one American city. Discusses Fagan's Republican Party affiliation, his program of equal taxation, his fight with the railroads and utilities, and his demise as a leader due to a lack of patience with the customary workings of party machinery. Based on primary and secondary sources; 7 illus., 39 notes. E. R. McKinstry

2280. Tripp, Joseph F. AN INSTANCE OF LABOR AND BUSINESS COOPERATION: WORKMEN'S COMPENSATION IN WASHINGTON STATE (1911). *Labor Hist. 1976 17(4): 530-550.* Enactment of a compulsory workmen's compensation law in Washington state in 1911, was achieved through cooperation of the lumber industry and labor unions. Frequency of accidents, resultant damage suits, animosity toward casualty companies, and an inadequate legal machinery promoted the cooperation which led to a compromise between industrial and labor interests. Based on trade journals, court reports, and manuscript sources; 58 notes. L. L. Athey

2281. Usselman, Steven W. SCIENTIFIC MANAGEMENT WITHOUT TAYLOR: MANAGEMENT INNOVATIONS AT BANCROFT. *Working Papers from the Regional Econ. Hist. Res. Center 1981 4(4): 47-77.* Briefly discusses the scientific management innovations set forth by Frederick Winslow Taylor for American businesses, focusing on the scientific management techniques of management consultants Miller, Franklin, and Stevenson, an industrial engineering company from New York, which was hired in 1911 by the cotton textile finishing company, Joseph Bancroft and Sons Company of Wilmington, Delaware, after a Taylor associate was unsuccessful in streamlining the work load in several departments; reorganization was completed in 1927.

2282. Vietor, Richard H. K. BUSINESSMEN AND THE POLITICAL ECONOMY: THE RAILROAD RATE CONTROVERSY OF 1905. *J. of Am. Hist. 1977 64(1): 47-66.* Examines the controversy preceding the enactment of railroad legislation, specifically the Hepburn Act (US, 1906), which gave the Interstate Commerce Commission the power to fix rates. Identifies the business interests that opposed and supported the Hepburn Act, including the fruit, grain, lumber, livestock, and coal mining concerns. Shippers who suffered under contemporary conditions favored the act, while shippers and railroads that profited from existing rates resisted the change. 39 notes.
J. B. Reed

2283. Wagaman, David G. THE INDUSTRIAL WORKERS OF THE WORLD IN NEBRASKA, 1914-1920. *Nebraska Hist. 1975 56(3): 295-337.* Narrates the problems of the Industrial Workers of the World in Nebraska during the Wilson era. The organization was not numerically strong in Nebraska, but its presence was felt and many of its members were prosecuted.
R. Lowitt

2284. Warrick, Sherry. RADICAL LABOR IN OKLAHOMA: THE WORKING CLASS UNION. *Chronicles of Oklahoma 1974 52(2): 180-195.* Describes the Oklahoma activities of the Working Class Union, an agrarian labor organization, during 1914-17, pointing out how such radical organizations exploited workers for their own ends. By 1916 the union used violent and illegal methods to indoctrinate fellow workers and to frighten bankers and government officials. Anti-draft agitation was included in the union's program and culminated in the abortive 1917 Green Corn Rebellion. Primary and secondary sources; 3 photos, 71 notes.
N. J. Street

2285. Watson, Fred. STILL ON STRIKE: RECOLLECTIONS OF A BISBEE DEPORTEE. *J. of Arizona Hist. 1977 18(2): 171-184.* Fred Watson worked as a tool nipper at the Shattuck Mine in Bisbee, Arizona, when it was struck by the Industrial Workers of the World in 1917. He recalls the confusion of the workers over the issues, the contending forces, and his experiences as one of the several hundred who were summarily arrested and deported to New Mexico by a railway freight train. 11 illus.
D. L. Smith

2286. Weiler, N. Sue. WALKOUT: THE CHICAGO MEN'S GARMENT WORKERS' STRIKE, 1910-1911. *Chicago Hist. 1979-80 8(4): 238-249.* Examines the men's garment industry in Chicago which began growing rapidly after the Chicago Fire of 1871, particularly the division of the manufacturing process into operations performed at sweatshops for the large Chicago clothing firms such as Hart, Schaffner & Marx, The House of Kuppenheimer, the Scotch Wollen Mills, Royal Tailors, and Society Brand; focuses on the 1910-1911 men's garment workers' strikes which started when 18 year old Hannah Shapiro walked out on her sewing job.

2287. White, Earl Bruce. MIGHT IS RIGHT: UNIONISM AND GOLDFIELD, NEVADA, 1904 TO 1908. *J. of the West 1977 16(3): 75-84.* In 1904 the Western Federation of Miners (WFM) and the American Federation of Labor (AFL), rival unions, organized in Goldfield. The militant WFM had suffered a major defeat at Cripple Creek, Colorado, in 1903-04 and agreed to unite with the Industrial Workers of the World (IWW) under the leadership of Vincent St. John. The opponents of the IWW were newspaper editor Lindley C. Branson and mine owners George Wingfield, Jack Davis, and Senator George Nixon. Disputes during 1906-07 between the WFM/IWW and the mine owners, who backed the AFL, were marked by increasing hostility. Finally in December 1907 federal troops came to Goldfield at the request of Governor John Sparks and Senator Nixon. Later, a presidential commission found that the troops were not needed and that the mine owners took advantage of the military presence by reducing wages and banning the WFM. The use of the troops badly hurt the cause of industrial unionism, which was not revived until the 1930's. Based on government documents, union archival material, and other primary and secondary sources; 5 photos, 54 notes.
B. S. Porter

2288. Wold, Frances. STILL: THE "UNION CITY." *North Dakota Hist. 1978 45(3): 4-15.* Despite its size of fewer than a dozen buildings and a population never in excess of 25, Still, North Dakota, exerted a considerable social, political, and economic influence on Burleigh County and its environs. Still became the headquarters of Estherville Local 11 in 1913, a flourishing chapter of the Farmers Educational and Cooperative Union, influential in the state before and during World War I. The Local became involved in the establishment of a cooperative store, a cooperatively owned grain elevator and warehouse, as well as providing a forum for political activity and for social affairs attracting farmers from a large area around the tiny hamlet. Even following the demise of the Farmer's Union in the early 1920's. Still, dubbed "Union City," continued to influence the surrounding region through mercantile activities, the existence of a grain elevator and the presence of a meeting hall and a school. Today Still is abandoned.
N. Lederer

2289. Wollenberg, Charles. WORKING ON EL TRAQUE: THE PACIFIC ELECTRIC STRIKE OF 1903. *Pacific Hist. R. 1973 42(3): 358-369.* Discusses the pre-1910 migration of Mexican railroad workers and the Pacific Electric Railroad strike of 1903 in Los Angeles, California, which are largely ignored by scholars of Mexican American history. Mexicans were considered the most tractable workers by the railroads, primarily because they worked for lower wages than other ethnic groups, and with the aid of the railroads the Mexican-born population of Los Angeles reached nearly 20,000 in 1910. The Pacific Electric strike was "one of the first major labor disputes between Mexican workers and Anglo employers." Although the Mexican Federal Union was effective in organizing track workers to strike for higher wages, the strike was squelched when Anglo carmen affiliated with the Amalgamated Association of Street Car Employees failed to walk out, which would have shut down the entire electric railroad system owned by Henry E. Huntington. The railroad did raise wages on the Main Street line, which had highest priority, but did not rehire strikers. The tracks were completed in time for the Los Angeles fiesta, as planned, but the failure of the strike did not end conflict between Huntington and the workers on *el traque*. 47 notes.
B. L. Fenske

2290. Wortman, Roy T. THE I.W.W. AND THE AKRON RUBBER STRIKE OF 1913. Conlin, Joseph R., ed. *At the Point of Production: The Local History of the I.W.W.* (Westport, Conn.: Greenwood Pr., 1981): 49-60. The 1913 rubber industry strike in Akron was precipitated by long working hours, depersonalized working conditions, and low wages. The attempts of the workers to unionize were thwarted until 11 February 1913, when a group of 25 tire finishers walked off the job, protesting Firestone's policy of introducing new machines which produced more tires, but with a reduction in pay scale to the workers. The Industrial Workers of the World were called in to organize the strike. By 18 February the IWW claimed 12,000 members out of a total of 20,000 rubber workers. A schism developed between workers who wanted compromise with management and the more militant strike position espoused by the IWW. This led to the general failure of the strike on 25 March 1913. Based on journal articles of the period; 60 notes.
J. Powell

2291. Zamora, Emilio, Jr. CHICANO SOCIALIST LABOR ACTIVITY IN TEXAS 1900-1920. *Aztlán 1976 6(2): 221-236.* Many Chicano workers in central and south Texas organized and joined socialist labor unions influenced by Mexican and Anglo radicals. In Laredo, due to ethnic conflicts, Mexican Americans did not follow strict socialist trade union principles and engaged in numerous railway strikes. In central and south Texas Chicano organizers worked within the Renter's Union of America and the Land League. They were more concerned with bread and butter issues than the Laredo group. 55 notes.
R. Griswold del Castillo

2292. —. [THE "NEW UNIONISM"]. *J. of Social Hist. [Great Britain] 1974 7(4): 509-535.*

Montgomery, David. THE "NEW UNIONISM" AND THE TRANSFORMATION OF WORKERS' CONSCIOUSNESS IN AMERICA 1909-1922, *pp. 509-529.* By 1920 new vistas had been opened to millions of workers through the struggles of skilled workers and the wage strikes of laborers and machine tenders. It was only after a decade of continuous struggle that great masses had been enrolled in the unions and there had been infused into their consciousness a widespread aspiration to direct the operation of railroads, mines, shipyards, and factories collectively. This "new unionism" with "syndicalist tendencies" still did not have formal connections with the Industrial Workers of the World or the Socialist Party. 80 notes.

Green, James R. COMMENTS ON THE MONTGOMERY PAPER, *pp. 530-535.* Raises questions concerning Montgomery's careful dissociation of the IWW from "new unionism," and develops more fully the reasons for the limitations on the growth of the IWW, especially in employment with high immigrant worker concentrations. R. V. Ritter

2293. —. STRIKE FOR LIBERTY! SONGS, POETRY, AND COMMENTS BY WORKERS OF THE WESTERN FEDERATION OF MINERS: 1900-1907. *Southwest Econ. and Soc. 1979-80 51(1-2): 1-139.* Double issue entirely devoted to reprinting material originally published in *Miners' Magazine.*

Educational Reform

2294. Abel, Emily K. MIDDLE-CLASS CULTURE FOR THE URBAN POOR: THE EDUCATIONAL THOUGHT OF SAMUEL BARNETT. *Social Service Rev. 1978 52(4): 596-620.* Compares the ideas and activities of Samuel Augustus Barnett, founder of the first English settlement house in 1884, with American progressives, 1880's-1913.

2295. Bartow, Beverly. ISABEL BEVIER AT THE UNIVERSITY OF ILLINOIS AND THE HOME ECONOMICS MOVEMENT. *J. of the Illinois State Hist. Soc. 1979 72(1): 21-38.* Reviews the life and works of Isabel Bevier (1860-1942), especially in relation to her pioneer work in home economics at the University of Illinois during 1900-21. Covers briefly the first halting steps in the field, beginning with the acceptance of women in universities. Bevier came to the University of Illinois from a solid educational background, determined to place home management on the level of a science. Relates the steps she took to do so, the victories, and the trials and tribulations. Closes with a few notes about her later works. 10 illus., 87 notes. V. L. Human

2296. Bellamy, Donnie D. JAMES H. TORBERT: ANOTHER FORGOTTEN BENEFACTOR OF BLACK PEOPLE. *Negro Hist. Bull. 1976 39(3): 549-553.* James H. Torbert (1868-1911) joined the Fort Valley High and Industrial School staff in 1897. By the time of Torbert's accidental death in 1911, the Georgia school had grown from a shanty on four acres to seven modern buildings on 40 acres. Due largely to his efforts, it is now recognized as one of the most important industrial schools for Negroes in the South. 50 notes. W. R. Hively

2297. Berliner, Howard S. NEW LIGHT ON THE FLEXNER REPORT: NOTES ON THE AMA-CARNEGIE FOUNDATION BACKGROUND. *Bull. of the Hist. of Medicine 1977 51(4): 603-609.* Describes the close relationship between the Carnegie Foundation and the American Medical Association Council on Medical Education. The Council invited the Carnegie Foundation to survey medical education, and Henry S. Pritchett, the president of the Foundation, agreed. The Flexner Report of 1910 served to strengthen the relationship between the organizations, but later in the decade Pritchett began to disagree with the policies of the AMA regarding their ranking of medical schools. The Flexner Report has received too great attention, as the implementation of the report was more important than the report itself. The Flexner Report coupled with the money that foundations poured into medical schools between 1910-32 resulted in some reform of the existing medical education. 20 notes. M. Kaufman

2298. Bloom, Leonard. A SUCCESSFUL JEWISH BOYCOTT OF THE NEW YORK CITY PUBLIC SCHOOLS: CHRISTMAS 1906. *Am. Jewish Hist. 1980 70(2): 180-188.* When in December 1905, Principal F. F. Harding exhorted his mostly Jewish audience to be more Christlike, Jewish parents protested to the Committee on Elementary Schools of the Board of Education of the City of New York. That committee, unlike the local school board, failed to exonerate Harding and warned against sectarian teaching in the schools. The following Christmas, Jewish parents under the leadership of Albert Lucas had their children boycott closing exercises, leading the committee to a further compromise which virtually eliminated Christian doctrine from school Christmas celebrations. Primary sources; 15 notes. E. L. Keyser

2299. Candeloro, Dominic. THE CHICAGO SCHOOL BOARD CRISIS OF 1907. *J. of the Illinois State Hist. Soc. 1975 68(5): 396-406.* The election of reform Democrat Edward F. Dunne as mayor of Chicago in 1905 led to the appointment of Progressives such as Louis F. Post and Jane Addams to the School Board. The Board's reform element endeavored to implement staff and curriculum reforms in the school system and also to raise revenue through renegotiating private leases on downtown school land. Intense criticism from newspapers and business interests and the defeat for reelection of Dunne led to the removal of the reformers from the Board. Many of their reforms were implemented, however, following the appointment of Ella Flagg Young as school superintendent in 1910. N. Lederer

2300. Chapman, Paul Davis. SCHOOLS AS SORTERS: TESTING AND TRACKING IN CALIFORNIA, 1910-1925. *J. of Social Hist. 1981 14(4): 701-717.* Explores the origins of the use of intelligence tests for the purpose of classifying students into ability groups in Oakland, San Jose, and Palo Alto. In each city, tests were introduced by university psychologists and school administrators. They met with quick acceptance because testing and tracking reinforced some central values of the Progressive Era—efficiency, science, and nativism. In Oakland and San Jose especially, the publication of group intelligence scores seemed to validate widespread assumptions about the inferiority of certain ethnic groups. The most important causes of the testing movement were the increasing size and diversity of student populations. 5 tables, 37 notes. J. Powell

2301. Chipman, Donald D. YOUNG KILPATRICK AND THE PROGRESSIVE IDEA. *Hist. of Educ. Q. 1977 17(4): 407-415.* One of the most important figures in popularizing and developing the theories of progressive education espoused by John Dewey was William Heard Kilpatrick (1870?-1965). Between 1892 and 1895 at the Blakely Institute at Blakely, Georgia, Kilpatrick, then a young instructor of mathematics, became committed to progressive education. He also was inspired by the Swiss educator Johann Heinrich Pestalozzi, who held that a student was better supervised by friendship than by harsh discipline, and by Colonel Francis Parker, often called the father of progressive education. Kilpatrick used progressive methods in his own mathematics classes, and encouraged field trips to teach history, archaeology, and other sciences. Kilpatrick was no mere acolyte of Dewey, but was a creative thinker in his own right. 34 notes, biblio. J. C. Billigmeier

2302. Danbom, David B. RURAL EDUCATION REFORM AND THE COUNTRY LIFE MOVEMENT, 1900-1920. *Agric. Hist. 1979 53(2): 462-474.* The Country Life Movement wanted to improve rural life through the reform of primary education. Looking at the problem from an urban perspective, they thought that consolidating schools and broadening the curriculum to include music, art, physical education, and nature study would produce more efficient farmers and ultimately lower food costs to the cities. Rural people were slow to change and often suspicious of the motives of Country Lifers. 36 notes. D. E. Bowers

2303. De Leon, Arnoldo. BLOWOUT 1910 STYLE: A CHICANO SCHOOL BOYCOTT IN WEST TEXAS. *Texana 1974 12(2): 124-140.* In 1910 the San Angelo Board of Education prohibited the integration of Anglos and Mexicans, and the Chicanos organized in an effort to integrate the public schools. They were unsuccessful, but in 1912 the Presbyterian Church established the Mexican Presbyterian Mission School and the Chicanos pulled out of the public schools completely for several years. As time passed, they began to accept the separate school system and drifted back into public schools. Primary and secondary sources; 45 notes. B. D. Ledbetter

2304. Dixon, Blase. THE CATHOLIC UNIVERSITY OF AMERICA AND THE RACIAL QUESTION, 1914-1918. *Records of the Am. Catholic Hist. Soc. of Philadelphia 1973 84(4): 221-224.* The refusal to matriculate Charles H. Wesley in 1914 was the first known instance of racial discrimination at the Catholic University of America. Exclusion of Negroes became a policy in 1919 and the bar was not completely lifted until 1948. 10 notes.
J. M. McCarthy

2305. Dye, Charles M. CALVIN WOODWARD, MANUAL TRAINING AND THE SAINT LOUIS PUBLIC SCHOOLS. *Missouri Hist. Soc. Bull. 1975 31(2): 111-135.* Calvin Woodward (1837-1914) and a slate of reformers won control of the St. Louis Board of Education in 1897. The reformers introduced manual training into the curricula, but financial exigencies and the philosophies of the entrenched professional educationists ultimately modified Woodward's reform programs in ways of which Woodward and his reformers disapproved. Based on official Board of Education documents and on secondary sources; 97 notes.
H. T. Lovin

2306. Enck, Henry S. BLACK SELF-HELP IN THE PROGRESSIVE ERA: THE "NORTHERN CAMPAIGNS" OF SMALLER SOUTHERN BLACK INDUSTRIAL SCHOOLS, 1900-1915. *J. of Negro Hist. 1976 6(1): 73-87.* The origin of the United Negro College Fund can be found in the efforts of the administrators and agents of southern black industrial schools to obtain northern white financial support after 1900. Despite the hostile indifference of Booker T. Washington to the Association of Negro Industrial and Secondary Schools, the smaller southern black industrial schools managed to survive in the face of constant financial woes. Based on primary and secondary materials; 49 notes.
N. G. Sapper

2307. Fleming, Cynthia Griggs. A SURVEY OF THE BEGINNINGS OF TENNESSEE'S BLACK COLLEGES AND UNIVERSITIES. *Tennessee Hist. Q. 1980 39(2): 195-207.* A broad survey of the founding of schools for black Tennesseans from immediately after the Civil War to 1920. While religious denominations were eager to establish schools for the freedmen, few of the latter understood what was involved in obtaining a college education. Lack of funding hounded both students and institutions. It was not until 1912 that Tennessee established a normal school for its black residents. During 1876-1909, only 525 students had graduated from the church-related black colleges and universities. Moral development as well as intellectual was stressed in the church schools, yet most white missionaries did not feel that black graduates could hold responsible positions within the general society. Yet, with all their shortcomings, the denominational institutions provided the only local opportunities for the state's blacks to receive any college or professional training between 1865 and 1920. Secondary sources; 45 notes.
H. M. Parker, Jr.

2308. Gallagher, Edward A. ALEXIS LANGE, PROGRESSIVISM AND JUNIOR COLLEGE FUNCTIONS. *Michigan Academician 1974 7(1): 111-122.* Discusses Progressivist educator Alexis Lange, his instrumentality in the establishment of the California system of community colleges (1907), and their interrelation with the University of California.
S

2309. Gill, Mary E. and Goff, John S. JOSEPH H. KIBBEY AND SCHOOL SEGREGATION IN ARIZONA. *J. of Arizona Hist. 1980 21(4): 411-422.* Traces Joseph H. Kibbey's leadership in opposing school segregation in Arizona. As territorial governor, he vetoed the 1909 enabling legislation, and as a lawyer he represented the plaintiff in an unsuccessful challenge to segregation. Kibbey's arguments against "separate but equal" schooling anticipated those later used to overthrow segregation throughout the United States. Legislative and court records; photo, 9 notes.
G. O. Gagnon

2310. Goodman, Cary. (RE)CREATING AMERICANS AT THE EDUCATIONAL ALLIANCE. *J. of Ethnic Studies 1979 6(4): 1-28.* The largest and most heavily financed of the institutions devoted to Americanization of the New York Lower East Side Jews was the Educational Alliance. Controlled by the German Jewish capitalist "Barons," as a means of cultural imperialism and subjugation of the feared and radical immigrant masses, the Alliance especially employed sport "as a device for diverting revolutionary class consciousness." This, and the inculcation of martial virtues and the Barons' own class-bred version of nationalism and patriotism, helped subvert the traditional antagonism of the shtetl to anything military and buttress the capitalists' heavy stake in an aggressive American foreign policy. Nevertheless the Yiddish theater and press, the landsmanschaften and candy stores, and the sidewalk orators perpetuated secular East Side culture. 93 notes.
G. J. Bobango

2311. Grant, H. Roger. VIOLA OLERICH, "THE FAMOUS BABY SCHOLAR": AN EXPERIMENT IN EDUCATION. *Palimpsest 1975 56(3): 88-95.* The utopian novelist and social reformer Henry Olerich began his experiment in progressive education in 1897 when he and his wife adopted a baby girl. Olerich believed that a voluntary process which utilized educational toys and other paraphernalia was more likely to guarantee the acquisition of advanced academic skills than were orthodox pedagogical methods then in fashion. He methodically recorded his daughter's physical and mental growth, paying particular attention to verbal skills, reasoning ability, and emotional development. An early proponent of behavior modification, Olerich established a system of learning rewards. His desire for order resembled the Montessori method. Olerich had disdain for those who criticized his approach and finally ended his experiments out of discouragement. Based chiefly on an interview with Mrs. Viola Olerich Storms; 5 photos, note.
D. W. Johnson

2312. Grech, John D. DEVELOPMENT OF VOCATIONAL EDUCATION IN BUFFALO, 1907-1921. *Niagara Frontier 1978 25(4): 100-106.* History of the vocational education movement in Buffalo, New York, 1907-21, led by William B. Kamprath, when industrial growth was strong and immigration of unskilled European workers heavy.

2313. Ives, Richard. COMPULSORY EDUCATION AND THE ST. LOUIS PUBLIC SCHOOL SYSTEM: 1905-1907. *Missouri Hist. Rev. 1977 71(3): 315-329.* Missouri enacted compulsory education laws in 1905 and 1907. Discusses what groups supported or opposed the laws, whether the laws were equally enforced or were immigrants discriminated against, and whether the laws attracted new students. Newspapers, legislative voting records, and state publications reveal that the laws enjoyed wide support. Most truancy cases were settled out of court, but school administrators often were influenced by an ethnic racism. Truancy was not a serious problem. Immigrants left school at a lower percentage rate than natives because they were aware of educational values. Illus., 42 notes.
W. F. Zornow

2314. Jenkins, William D. HOUSEWIFERY AND MOTHERHOOD: THE QUESTION OF ROLE CHANGE IN THE PROGRESSIVE ERA. Kelley, Mary, ed. *Woman's Being, Woman's Place: Female Identity and Vocation in American History* (Boston: G. K. Hall, 1979): 142-153. The emergence of home economics as a formal discipline not only developed from the Progressive movement generally during 1900-20 but also was promoted by already acknowledged trends within Progressivism as varied as the child study movement, John Dewey's "New Education," the settlement house movement, and vocationalism. The introduction of home economics into secondary and collegiate curricula along with the appearance of professional associations and journals gave added recognition to the supposed science of domesticity and elevated it to the status of a discipline. It meant that traditional values concerning woman's role and place were reinforced. Progressivism supported home economics and thus indicated that woman's primary social functions were a wife and mother. Mainly secondary sources; 39 notes.
J. Powell

2315. Kostiainen, Auvo. WORK PEOPLE'S COLLEGE: AN AMERICAN IMMIGRANT INSTITUTION. *Scandinavian J. of Hist. [Sweden] 1980 5(4): 295-309.* The Finns, part of the later wave of immigrants to the United States, have proved more active in the American labor movement than most other ethnic groups. One of the key developments in the Finnish American community was the Work People's College at Smithville, Minnesota, during the 1900's; the college's links with socialism resulted in a radical and educational role, although it also facilitated the adjustment of recent immigrants to American society. Based partly on the Work People's College collection at the University of Minnesota; 48 notes.
P. J. Beck

2316. Kousser, J. Morgan. PROGRESSIVISM—FOR MIDDLE CLASS WHITES ONLY: NORTH CAROLINA EDUCATION, 1880-1910. *J. of Southern Hist. 1980 46(2): 169-194.* Quantitative analysis of tax, income, property value and education expenditure data bears out C. Vann Woodward's picture of a dramatic increase in racial discrimination around the turn of the century. Following the disfranchisement of blacks, public expenditures for black schools drastically diminished. North Carolina produced education only for middle-class whites. 12 tables, fig., 36 notes, appendix. T. D. Schoonover/S

2317. Kunitz, Stephen J. PROFESSIONALISM AND SOCIAL CONTROL IN THE PROGRESSIVE ERA: THE CASE OF THE FLEXNER REPORT. *Social Problems 1974 22(1): 16-27.* Examines the Abraham Flexner Report (1910) showing how elite members of the medical field achieved higher status for their profession. The report was a product of the Progressive era and shared concerns for professionalization and social control. Specifically, Flexner recommended a greater control of medical education and licensing procedures in medicine. Notes, biblio. A. M. Osur

2318. Ludmerer, Kenneth M. REFORM OF MEDICAL EDUCATION AT WASHINGTON UNIVERSITY. *J. of the Hist. of Medicine & Allied Sci. 1980 35(2): 149-173.* Washington University was the first school to be reformed in the aftermath of the Flexner Report (1910), and it served as an example for other institutions. Prior to the arrival of Abraham Flexner, the school had made many improvements, during which a favorable attitude toward reform was developed. The Flexner report stimulated the creation of an endowment, and the affiliation of the medical school with Barnes Hospital and St. Louis Children's Hospital. Flexner's approach stimulated the support of Robert Brookings, the university president, who became committed to important reforms in the medical school. What was needed was not a desire to reform, but a way to do so. 105 notes, including letters and documents from the Washington University archives. M. Kaufman

2319. Markowitz, Gerald E. and Rosner, David. DOCTORS IN CRISIS: MEDICAL EDUCATION AND MEDICAL REFORM DURING THE PROGRESSIVE ERA, 1895-1915. Reverby, Susan and Rosner, David, ed. *Health Care in America: Essays in Social History* (Philadelphia: Temple U. Pr., 1979): 185-205. Reform of medical education was favored by the American Medical Association. It sought the creation of a few well-funded institutions connected with university systems that would conduct ample clinical research. This reform would drive out of business the small privately operated medical schools that turned out poorly trained physicians. Reform would produce fewer and better-trained doctors and improve the status and income of physicians. 56 notes. S

2320. May, Glenn A. SOCIAL ENGINEERING IN THE PHILIPPINES: THE AIMS AND EXECUTION OF AMERICAN EDUCATIONAL POLICY, 1900-1913. *Philippine Studies [Philippines] 1976 24(2): 135-183.* Details personnel, methods, and changing goals. Policies went from a "Booker T. Washington" concept to emphasis on literary education, and then to industrial training. This back-and-forth situation was complicated by the shift from Spanish to English, which was never successful. Compared to other colonial Asian situations, the American efforts in the Philippines were successful; yet, based on Filipino needs and interests, the American system was a failure. 181 notes. D. Chaput

2321. McBride, Paul W. THE CO-OP INDUSTRIAL EDUCATION EXPERIMENT, 1900-1917. *Hist. of Educ. Q. 1974 14(2): 209-221.* Experiments with Co-op schools in Massachusetts in which students alternated classes and factory work were largely unsuccessful. Discusses the Beverly School founded in 1909 in Beverly, Massachusetts. Employers exploited a source of cheap labor and also tried to dominate the educational program to instill obedience and docility so that the future employee would not cause trouble. The experiments were resented by the community and were discontinued. Based on primary and secondary sources; 34 notes. L. C. Smith

2322. Mohl, Raymond A. SCHOOLS, POLITICS, AND RIOTS: THE GARY PLAN IN NEW YORK CITY, 1914-1917. *Paedagogica Hist. [Belgium] 1975 15(1): 39-72.* An archetypal experiment in progressive educational change occurred in New York City 1914-17 when reform mayor John Purroy Mitchel sought to introduce the much-discussed duplicate school plan first developed in Gary, Indiana. The struggle illustrates many of the tendencies revealed by the new educational historiography. 69 notes. J. M. McCarthy

2323. Muchinske, David. THE NONWHITE AS CHILD: G. STANLEY HALL ON THE EDUCATION OF NONWHITE PEOPLES. *J. of the Hist. of the Behavioral Sci. 1977 13(4): 328-336.* Although he was a significant reformer during the progressive era, a founder of various journals in psychology and pedagogy, a prolific writer, and the individual who brought Freud and Jung to the United States, G. Stanley Hall's ideas on the education of nonwhites were, for his period, quite conventional. Unlike those of some of his contemporaries, Hall's racial ideas were not overtly vicious. He argued that nonwhites were the children of the human race and that their education, like that of children of particular ages, should be based on an understanding of their indigenous culture and inherent capabilities. This argument, although reformist in tone, supported a policy of nonwhite subservience. J

2324. Mullaney, Marie Marmo. THE NEW JERSEY COLLEGE FOR WOMEN: MIDDLE CLASS RESPECTABILITY AND PROTO-FEMINISM, 1911-1918. *J. of the Rutgers U. Lib. 1980 42(1): 26-39.* The campaign for college education for New Jersey women began in 1911 and came to fruition in 1918 when the New Jersey College for Women opened. The New Jersey State Federation of Women's Clubs was the leading organization behind the movement and its chief spokesperson was Mrs. Mabel Smith Douglass (1877-1933). Proponents of the college divorced themselves from the suffrage movement and never appeared to challenge traditional views of acceptable sex roles. Their success may be attributed to a cautious, conservative approach that found favor with the male-dominated authority structure. 50 notes. R. Van Benthuysen

2325. Nelms, Willie E., Jr. CORA WILSON STEWART AND THE CRUSADE AGAINST ILLITERACY IN KENTUCKY. *Register of the Kentucky Hist. Soc. 1976 74(1): 10-29.* Cora Wilson Stewart (b. 1875) began a campaign to teach illiterates in Rowan County, Kentucky, in September, 1911. A school teacher and administrator, Stewart was most concerned with the problem of illiteracy. By 1914, she had attracted nationwide attention. One of the high points of her career came in 1914 when the legislature established the Kentucky Illiteracy Commission and she was appointed to it. She continued her work until the Commission expired in 1920. Based on primary and secondary sources; 68 notes. J. F. Paul

2326. Osterman, Paul. EDUCATION AND LABOR MARKETS AT THE TURN OF THE CENTURY. *Pol. and Soc. 1979 9(1): 103-122.* Explores the relationship of American economic and technological developments in the late 19th and early 20th centuries, and the emergence of modern compulsory education. A dramatic drop over the four decades (1890-1930) in the need for the young in the labor market, produced by the second industrial revolution and migration, removed the last resistance to progressive reformers' demands for expanded educational opportunities. This resulted in legislation providing for extended mandatory education, and a coercive bureaucracy to enforce attendance, but little corresponding change in the class structure. 60 notes. D. G. Nielson

2327. Pearlman, Michael. TO MAKE THE UNIVERSITY SAFE FOR MORALITY: HIGHER EDUCATION, FOOTBALL AND MILITARY TRAINING FROM THE 1890S THROUGH THE 1920S. *Can. Rev. of Am. Studies [Canada] 1981 12(1): 37-56.* Responding to post-Civil War industrialization, American higher education changed dramatically in the 1890's as secular universities replaced colleges designed foremost to nurture Christian morality. Disliking the changes, university officials and alumni attempted still to advance humanism, religion, and football and, failing to do so, forced military training on unenthusiastic students because martial arts substituted for the old Christian college regimen that was waning. But the new military discipline on campuses alienated students, and university administrators in the 1920's abandoned such efforts. Based on manuscripts, primarily at the Library of Congress, and secondary sources; 57 notes. H. T. Lovin

2328. Reese, William J. THE CONTROL OF URBAN SCHOOL BOARDS DURING THE PROGRESSIVE ERA: A RECONSIDERATION. *Pacific Northwest Q. 1977 68(4): 164-174.* Traces the history of educational reform in Toledo, Ohio during the Progressive Era. The Niles Bill of 1898 reduced the city's school board to five members, nominated on nonpartisan ballots and elected on a city-wide basis rather than by wards. This produced a wave of progressive victories during 1898, but the victors were just as elitist as the group they replaced. Suggests that future studies should focus on members who dominated school boards and on outside forces which influenced policy. Primary and secondary sources; 3 photos, 32 notes. M. L. Tate

2329. Reese, William J. "PARTISANS OF THE PROLETARIAT": THE SOCIALIST WORKING CLASS AND THE MILWAUKEE SCHOOLS, 1890-1920. *Hist. of Educ. Q. 1981 21(1): 3-50.* Examines the ways in which Milwaukee's exceptionally successful socialist movement, working with nonsocialist reformers, influenced public school policy during the Progressive period. Suggests that the school reforms of that period, usually understood as elitist and conservative, should also be studied in terms of working class participation. Based on published and manuscript primary and secondary sources; 150 notes. D. B. Marti

2330. Reese, William J. PROGRESSIVE SCHOOL REFORM IN TOLEDO, 1898-1921. *Northwest Ohio Q. 1975 47(2): 44-59.* Sketches the events which led to reform, despite conservative tenacity, in the Toledo school system; highlights work of local newspapers and the fights between school board member J. Kent Hamilton and Progressive Toledo school administrator William B. Gitteau. 5 photos, 64 notes.

2331. Rittenhouse, Floyd O. EDWARD A. SUTHERLAND: INDEPENDENT REFORMER. *Adventist Heritage 1977 4(2): 20-34.* Edward A. Sutherland (1865-1955), Seventh-Day Adventist educator, became president of Battle Creek College in Michigan in 1897 and helped found Madison College in 1904 in Tennessee.

2332. Seller, Maxine. THE EDUCATION OF IMMIGRANT CHILDREN IN BUFFALO, NEW YORK 1890-1916. *New York Hist. 1976 57(2): 183-199.* Examines the efforts to reform the public school education of immigrant children in Buffalo, New York during 1890-1916. School reformers, mostly of old Protestant Anglo-Saxon stock, understood little about immigrants, and thought of educational reform as part of municipal reform, and as a method of Americanizing immigrant workers and discouraging radicalism. Illus., 36 notes. R. N. Lokken

2333. Shrader, Victor L. ETHNICITY, RELIGION, AND CLASS: PROGRESSIVE SCHOOL REFORM IN SAN FRANCISCO. *Hist. of Educ. Q. 1980 20(4): 385-401.* During 1918-20, a reform movement in education was accomplished in San Francisco involving centralization of the education system. The major issue was not a simplistic contest between the so-called ruling class and the working class, but a complicated situation in which ethnicity and religion also played major roles. In 1918 the movement for reform failed; in 1920 it succeeded. The central part of this study centers around the latter effort in which anti-Catholicism played a prominent role in achieving success for the reformers. Based on the papers of Mayor John Rolph (California Historical Society, San Francisco), and the author's dissertation; 3 tables, 24 notes. H. M. Parker, Jr.

2334. Taggart, Robert J. WOODROW WILSON AND CURRICULUM REFORM. *New Jersey Hist. 1975 93(3-4): 99-114.* Woodrow Wilson, President of Princeton University, admired the tutor-student educational system of Oxford and Cambridge and believed that general education was best for Princetonians. He advocated quadrangles as the basis for student life, and criticized eating clubs as hindrances to sober reflection. Wilson felt Princeton should deemphasize its graduate program. Faculty, alumni, and trustees argued effectively against Wilson's ideas so they were never implemented. Wilson failed at educational reform because his plans did not coincide with Princeton's goals. Based on primary and secondary sources; 5 illus., 2 maps, 30 notes. E. R. McKinstry

2335. Ueda, Reed. SUBURBAN SOCIAL CHANGE AND EDUCATIONAL REFORM: THE CASE OF SOMERVILLE, MASSACHUSETTS, 1912-1924. *Social Sci. Hist. 1979 3(3-4): 167-203.* In the early 20th century, progressive reformers in Somerville, Massachusetts, spearheaded a drive for a new junior high school. This typical progressive action was led by middle class ethnic groups associated with the Democratic Party, not the elite, old stock Republicans responsible for educational reform in some other areas. Based on primary sources, especially in Somerville, Massachusetts; 10 tables, 12 notes. L. K. Blaser

2336. Urban, Wayne. ORGANIZED TEACHERS AND EDUCATIONAL REFORM DURING THE PROGRESSIVE ERA: 1890-1920. *Hist. of Educ. Q. 1976 16(1): 35-52.* Examines attitudes of teachers' organizations toward educational reform in Atlanta, Georgia, New York City, and Chicago, Illinois, during 1890-1920.

2337. Vaughn, Stephen. "TO CREATE A NATION OF NOBLE MEN": PUBLIC EDUCATION, NATIONAL UNITY, AND THE *NATIONAL SCHOOL SERVICE*, 1918-1919. *Historian 1979 41(3): 429-449.* Loyalty to one's country is not instinctive but learned and a primary vehicle for that instruction is a school. Beginning in 1918 and continuing through 1919 the government published a bulletin, the *National School Service* (NSS), to promote national unity by emphasizing the obligations of citizenship. Although the NSS has received slight attention from historians who usually view it as wartime propaganda, it made a significant effort to define the nature of citizenship in a democratic society and should be seen as an expression of reformist literature of these years. Examines the personnel that wrote and directed the NSS, the contents of the bulletin, and its impact. The NSS should not be considered solely as war propaganda but as part of the reform literature of the day. Primary and secondary sources; 76 notes. R. S. Sliwoski

The New Era

2338. Abbey, Sue Wilson. THE KU KLUX KLAN IN ARIZONA, 1921-1925. *J. of Arizona Hist. 1973 14(1): 10-30.* Established in Phoenix and Tucson in 1921, the Ku Klux Klan soon spread to smaller towns and the rural and mining areas. It campaigned for better law enforcement through prohibition and the closing of brothels and gambling halls. The Klan, alarmed at the growth of the Mexican American population and the spread of Catholicism, preached the return to "higher" moral standards and the doctrine of white supremacy. Defeated in the November 1924 elections, the Klan became a victim of its own intolerance when its violence and excesses were widely publicized. 2 illus., 86 notes. D. L. Smith

2339. Abernathy, Mollie C. SOUTHERN WOMEN, SOCIAL RECONSTRUCTION, AND THE CHURCH IN THE 1920'S. *Louisiana Studies 1974 13(4): 289-312.* Southern radical social feminists comprised a special group of southern women who combined extreme or hard-core feminism and a social reconstructionist program. Despite significant changes in the decades before World War I, the evolution of women's organizations in the South was a decade behind that of their northern sisters, though many southern women served in the Y.W.C.A. "Without the radical social feminists spurring on ordinary southern club and church-women to action little progress pertaining to women would have been accomplished during the reactionary decade of the 1920's." 60 notes. E. P. Stickney

2340. Abrams, Douglas Carl. A PROGRESSIVE-CONSERVATIVE DUEL: THE 1920 DEMOCRATIC GUBERNATORIAL PRIMARIES IN NORTH CAROLINA. *North Carolina Hist. Rev. 1978 55(4): 421-443.* The 1920 North Carolina gubernatorial Democratic primary campaign illustrates well the conservative-progressive split which existed in that state's Democratic Party politics. Three issues, "machine" politics, women's suffrage, and state press coverage of the campaign, divided the three candidates, conservative Cameron Morrison, and progressives Robert Newton Page and O. Max Gardner. While Page ran a mundane but solid campaign on the issues, Morrison and Gardner threw mud and barbs at each other and sensationalized the issues. Page was eliminated in the first primary; Gardner lost the second. Newspaper accounts, published and unpublished family papers, and secondary sources; 11 illus., 2 maps, 35 notes. T. L. Savitt

2341. Ackerman, Bruce A. *LAW AND THE MODERN MIND* BY JEROME FRANK. *Daedalus 1974 103(1): 119-127.* Reforms at Harvard Law School in the 1870's established the principle that law was a science, susceptible to study in a scientific manner. Three types of dissent arose. The third wave of criticism is best portrayed by Jerome Frank's *Law and the Modern Mind* (1930). Frank stressed the need to seek the nonrational motivations in legal decisionmaking. His work was consonant with that of other intellectuals challenging efforts to structure reality into a single determinate order. Secondary sources; 40 notes.
E. McCarthy

2342. Akpan, M. B. LIBERIA AND THE UNIVERSAL NEGRO IMPROVEMENT ASSOCIATION: THE BACKGROUND TO THE ABORTION OF GARVEY'S SCHEME FOR AFRICAN COLONIZATION. *J. of African Hist. [Great Britain] 1973 14(1): 105-127.* A number of factors were responsible for Liberia's rejection in 1924 of Marcus Garvey's colonization scheme. The Liberian economy no longer needed the Association's assistance, while its anti-colonialism crusade led to fears of British and French alienation. More importantly the ruling American-Liberian class feared that the new immigrants might challenge its entrenched and privileged position. Primary and secondary sources; 104 notes.
C. Hopkins

2343. Ashby, LeRoy. THE DISAPPEARING DRY: RAYMOND ROBBINS AND THE LAST DAYS OF PROHIBITION. *North Carolina Hist. R. 1974 51(4): 401-419.* Reviews the life and activities of Raymond Robbins. He won early wealth during the Klondike Gold Rush and then threw his energies into social reform, especially the defense of prohibition. As anti-prohibitionists gained strength, Robbins embarked on a nationwide speaking tour, after which he disappeared. He reappeared in Whittier, North Carolina, a tiny mountain town, claiming to be a victim of amnesia. Opponents argued that he was seeking sympathy for his cause. The truth remains uncertain. 8 photos, 62 notes.
V. L. Human

2344. Bauman, Mark K. PROHIBITION AND POLITICS: WARREN CANDLER AND AL SMITH'S 1928 CAMPAIGN. *Mississippi Q. 1977-78 31(1): 109-118.* Distaste for mixing religion and politics and a desire not to draw attention to anti-Prohibition elements led Methodist Episcopal Church, South, senior bishop Warren Candler to instruct the clergy in his church not to become involved in the presidential election of 1928 between Catholic, anti-Prohibition candidate Alfred E. Smith and Herbert H. Hoover.

2345. Berkowitz, Edward D. and McQuaid, Kim. BUREAUCRATS AS "SOCIAL ENGINEERS": FEDERAL WELFARE PROGRAMS IN HERBERT HOOVER'S AMERICA. *Am. J. of Economics and Sociol. 1980 39(4): 321-335.* Historians interested in 20th century American reform often seek to analyze the ideologies of political leaders separately from the institutions that these same leaders created. Such emphases on ideas, as opposed to actions, has, for example, led "revisionist" American historians to argue that the presidencies of Herbert Hoover and Franklin D. Roosevelt were "conceptually continuous." Our examination of the major social welfare programs undertaken by the federal government in the 1920's disputes this claim. Examination of the operations of the federal bureaucracy instead of the rhetoric of politicians demonstrates the existence of decided policy difference between the Hoover and Roosevelt eras. "Efficiency" analogues dominant during the Hoover era were replaced with "direct service-provider" approaches which created a clear distinction between private and public welfare programs. Elements of "continuity" between the two eras have been overdrawn. Background is provided for increased understanding of some of the policy implications of America's contemporary welfare debate—particularly about "rehabilitation" strategies and/or rationales for action in the social welfare field.
J

2346. Brackenridge, R. Douglas. EQUALITY FOR WOMEN? A CASE STUDY IN PRESBYTERIAN POLITY, 1926-1930. *J. of Presbyterian Hist. 1980 58(2): 142-165.* In 1930 women for the first time were eligible for ordination as Ruling Elders in the Presbyterian Church in the United States. Before then, they had raised and contributed substantial amounts of money for the church's benevolent programs, and had served in many unordained capacities. Discusses the appointment of the Committee of Four in 1926 by the General Assembly to look into the matter of ordaining women as Elders. The committee consisted of Robert E. Speer, Lewis S. Mudge, Katherine Bennett, and Margaret Hodge. All were conservative, evangelical, and ecumenical. Details the work of the committee and the General Assemblies of 1926-29 that finally approved the ordination of women as Elders. Emphasizes the difficult context in which the Committee of Four functioned. Based on the Minutes of the General Assembly, numerous personal collections, such as the Mudge Papers, Presbyterian Historical Society, Philadelphia, and the Speer Papers, Princeton Theological Seminary, and contemporary church newspapers; 77 notes.
H. M. Parker, Jr.

2347. Brown, Lawrence L. TEXAS BISHOP VETOES WOMEN COUNCIL DELEGATES IN 1921. *Hist. Mag. of the Protestant Episcopal Church 1979 48(1): 93-102.* At the Annual Council of the Episcopal Diocese of Texas in 1921 an amendment to the constitution which would have allowed women as delegates to the Council was adopted by lay and clerical votes, but was vetoed by Bishop George Herbert Kinsolving. Traces the drive for women's rights in the diocese, the origin of the power of the bishop to veto, and why the bishop vetoed the measure: he felt that the church was moving with secular trends, and not in harmony with apostolic precept. It was not until 1969 that the council authorized women as delegates, and the provision was made operative the next year. Based on the Journal of the Annual Council of the Diocese of Texas; 41 notes.
H. M. Parker, Jr.

2348. Brown, Thomas Elton. PATRIOTISM OR RELIGION. *Michigan Hist. 1980 64(4): 36-42.* In 1920 an attempt was made to force compulsory education upon Michigan children. The proposed state amendment in fact attempted to stem the power of the Catholic Church. Although Lutherans, Seventh Day Adventists, and other congregations rallied against the proposal, the Catholic Church spearheaded the opposition. Defeated in 1920, the issue resurfaced in 1924. This time Catholics abandoned the interdenominational approach and concentrated on their own vote. They succeeded in defeating the amendment. On 1 June 1925 the US Supreme Court declared a similar statute in Oregon unconstitutional, thus ending further agitation in Michigan on this issue. The politicization of Michigan Catholics presaged "the growing political maturity of American Catholics." It subsequently benefited the Democratic Party in Michigan. 7 photos, 62 notes.
L. E. Ziewacz

2349. Buhle, Paul and Celenza, James, eds. "BORN OUT OF STRIKES": AN INTERVIEW WITH LUIGI NARDELLA. *Radical Hist. Rev. 1978 (17): 153-160.* Luigi Nardella recounts his experiences in the textile strike of 1922 in Rhode Island.

2350. Bukowski, Douglas. WILLIAM DEVER AND PROHIBITION: THE MAYORAL ELECTIONS OF 1923 AND 1927. *Chicago Hist. 1978 7(2): 109-118.* Efforts of Chicago mayor William Dever to impose a reform-minded and prohibitionist city government following his election in 1923 led to discontent within the electorate, erosion of support from ethnic groups and blacks, and his defeat in 1927.

2351. Burkett, Randall K. RELIGIOUS DIMENSIONS OF THE UNIVERSAL NEGRO IMPROVEMENT ASSOCIATION AND AFRICAN COMMUNITIES LEAGUE. *Afro-Am. in New York Life and Hist. 1977 1(2): 167-182.* Examines the religious dimension of the Universal Negro Improvement Association, under the leadership of Marcus Garvey, through exploration of meeting structure, format, vocabulary of UNIA members when addressing issues, the role of chaplains, and the religiopolitical symbols of nationhood in the organization, 1920's.

2352. Candeloro, Dominic. LOUIS F. POST AND THE RED SCARE OF 1920. *Prologue 1979 11(1): 41-55.* In 1920 as Assistant Secretary of Labor, 71-year-old Louis F. Post successfully thwarted the arbitrary and capricious enforcement of the Alien Anarchist Act (US, 1918), by which scores of foreign-born radicals were deported under the aegis of Attorney General Mitchell Palmer and his assistant J. Edgar Hoover. Post, a long-time sympathizer with left-wing causes and a public admirer of the Russian Revolution, came under intensive Congressional scrutiny for his stand and an effort was made to remove him from office through impeachment proceedings. The effort failed, owing in large part to Post's own inspired defense of his position before Congressional committees. Post's insistence that due process and a rigid adherence to law mark governmental operations against foreign-born radicals did a great deal to stem the tide of wanton and arbitrary deportation of dissenters resident in the United States. Based mainly on research in the National Archives. N. Lederer

2353. Carpenter, Gerald. PUBLIC OPINION IN THE NEW ORLEANS STREET RAILWAY STRIKE OF 1929-1930. Fink, Gary M. and Reed, Merl E., eds. *Essays in Southern Labor History: Selected Papers, Southern Labor History Conference, 1976.* (Westport, Conn.; London, England, Greenwood Pr., 1977): 191-207. Studies the New Orleans Street Railway Strike of 1929-30 as an illustration of the incorrectness of the usual stereotype of southern public opinion as united against trade unionism. This is seen both in company (New Orleans Public Service, Inc.) appeals which reflected the public's acceptance of unionism and in union (Street and Electric Railway Employees of America) appeals for support resting on "positive concern for the principles of organized labor and negative objections to outside control." The usual generalizations therefore must be examined more critically. 65 notes.
R. V. Ritter

2354. Carper, N. Gordon. MARTIN TABERT, MARTYR OF AN ERA. *Florida Hist. Q. 1973 52(2): 115-131.* Martin Tabert, arrested in 1921 for riding a train without a ticket, became subject to the Leon County convict-leasing system in Florida. Under this practice, convicts were distributed to local industries and often treated very harshly. In Tabert's case, harsh treatment resulted in death. Subsequent investigations by the Florida legislature revealed widespread brutality in convict-leasing, and in 1923 the lease system and corporal punishment for county convicts were abolished. Primary sources, newspapers, legislative and court records; 82 notes.
J. E. Findling

2355. Carter, L. Edward. RISE AND FALL OF THE INVISIBLE EMPIRE: KNIGHTS OF THE KU KLUX KLAN. *Great Plains J. 1977 16(2): 82-106.* Discusses the revived Ku Klux Klan of the early 1920's, especially in Lawton, Comanche County, Oklahoma. The Klan appeared in Lawton in 1921. Its parades, meetings, support of morality, religious overtones, and philanthropy "helped it gain widespread acceptance." In the later 1920's it fell apart, and by 1929 had lost virtually all influence. 4 illus., 62 notes.
O. H. Zabel

2356. Carter, Paul A. PROHIBITION AND DEMOCRACY: THE NOBLE EXPERIMENT REASSESSED. *Wisconsin Mag. of Hist. 1973 56(3): 189-201.* Challenges the traditional view of prohibition as a battle of liberal wets fighting for democratic principles against a conservative and well organized fanatic minority that imposed the 18th Amendment on an unsuspecting public. Examines prohibitionists' literature, leaders, and opponents, and argues that the prohibition movement used many of the arguments of future New Dealers and radicals. Explores the role of women's organizations in the prohibition controversy. 8 illus., 45 notes.
N. C. Burckel

2357. Cary, Lorin Lee. THE REORGANIZED UNITED MINE WORKERS OF AMERICA, 1930-1931. *J. of the Illinois State Hist. Soc. 1973 66(3): 244-270.* The Reorganized United Mine Workers of America was founded in 1930 by a coalition of traditionalists and radicals dissatisfied with the leadership of United Mine Workers of America president John L. Lewis. The reorganized union lasted for only one year, in which it illustrated the unusual problems of labor unions during the Depression. Inadequate funds, personality clashes, and membership distrust particularly hindered the establishment of a strong anti-Lewis union. 5 illus., 72 notes.
A. C. Aimone

2358. Clarke, John Henrik. MARCUS GARVEY: THE HARLEM YEARS. *Black Scholar 1973/74 5(4): 17-24.* Marcus Garvey's Universal Negro Improvement Association centered in Harlem 1919-26. S

2359. Cofer, Richard. BOOTLEGGERS IN THE BACKWOODS: PROHIBITION AND THE DEPRESSION IN HERNANDO COUNTY. *Tampa Bay Hist. 1979 1(1): 17-23.* Illegal manufacture of alcohol (moonshining) and rum-running were common in Hernando County, Florida, with the sanction of (or at least unchallenged by) local law enforcement because of the lucrative nature of the business; 1929-33.

2360. Colburn, David R. GOVERNOR ALFRED E. SMITH AND PENAL REFORM. *Pol. Sci. Q. 1976 91(2): 315-327.* Discusses Governor Alfred E. Smith of New York as a prison reformer far ahead of his time, especially in his advocacy of a penal program to rehabilitate prisoners and return them as meaningful contributors to society.
J

2361. Cook, Sylvia. GASTONIA: THE LITERARY REVERBERATIONS OF THE STRIKE. *Southern Literary J. 1974 7(1): 49-66.* Poor whites and communism are combined in six novels about the 1929 strike of textile workers in Gastonia, North Carolina.
S

2362. Critchlow, Donald T. LEWIS MERIAM, EXPERTISE, AND INDIAN REFORM. *Historian 1981 43(3): 325-344.* After years of vehement criticism of the US Indian Service, Secretary of the Interior Hubert Work asked Lewis Meriam of the Institute for Government Research to undertake a major investigation of the social conditions of Indians. Meriam's report, *The Problem of Indian Administration* (1928), recommended improving conditions through better administration and personnel within the Indian Service. Two significant issues dominated the report: Progressivism's concern for efficiency and economy and the subtle relationship between administrative reform advocated by scientific experts and the popular reform movement. Includes a short biographical sketch of Meriam from college at Harvard to the Institute for Government Research. Primary sources; 66 notes.
R. S. Sliwoski

2363. Cuddy, Edward. THE IRISH QUESTION AND THE REVIVAL OF ANTI-CATHOLICISM IN THE 1920's. *Catholic Hist. Rev. 1981 67(2): 236-255.* Details the causal connection between the Irish Question and the resurgent anti-Catholicism of the 1920's. The agitation of Irish-Americans for a free Ireland, and the Protestant-Catholic conflict in Ireland, herself, and the unprecedented support of American Catholic leaders for the Irish cause, revived sectarian discord in the United States. These factors were related to the increasing anxieties of American nativists under the impact of urbanization. The tidy world of rural, Protestant America was giving way to the city. And, it was in the city, that the power of Roman Catholicism and of the Irish political machines was most painfully visible. These fears, crystallized by the tug of war over Ireland, were a significant force in reviving the anti-Catholicism of postwar America.
A

2364. Dillard, Tom W. FIGHTING THE LILY WHITES: RACIAL CONFRONTATION IN THE ARKANSAS REPUBLICAN PARTY, 1920-1924 DOCUMENTS. *Red River Valley Hist. Rev. 1979 4(2): 63-71.* Traces efforts by white Republicans to eliminate black participation in the party between the 1890's and 1920, and the resulting counteroffensive by blacks between 1920 and 1924, based on documents now in the Pratt C. Remmel Collection at the University of Arkansas Library Special Collections, which show how hard the blacks fought.

2365. Drake, Douglas C. HERBERT HOOVER, ECOLOGIST: THE POLITICS OF OIL POLLUTION CONTROL, 1921-1926. *Mid-Am. 1973 55(3): 207-228.* Commerce Secretary Herbert Hoover, representing conflicting shipping and fishing interests, initiated an antipollution bill 7 June 1924. Although it died on the books, it nevertheless represented the birth of the modern ecology movement. An earlier conference covened by Hoover led to complex congressional hearings and politicking in which the American Petroleum Institute played a significant role. Major legislative issues included inclusion of shore plants, separators, and enforcement. Delay and compromises were the politics of oil pollution control. Based on the Herbert Hoover Papers, Herbert Hoover Presidential Library, and printed sources. 44 notes.
T. H. Wendel

2366. Ebner, Michael H. STRIKES AND SOCIETY: CIVIL BEHAVIOR IN PASSAIC, 1875-1926. *New Jersey Hist. 1979 97(1): 7-24.* Puts into historical perspective the 1926 textile strike in Passaic. Soon after the mills began operating in that city, questions arose about working conditions. Low wages, seasonal employment fluctuations, and unhealthy plant surroundings were concerns. Labor attempted to organize the industry, and strikes occurred. Local officials succeeded in quelling these disturbances, though the Red Scare, a post-World War I phenomenon, and suspicions of left-wing influences made them put constraints on labor's activities. The textile industry was at first thought of as a constructive and integral part of Passaic's life, but by 1926 these suppositions were

being questioned. Based on government records, contemporary newspaper accounts, manuscript collections, and secondary sources; 9 illus., 33 notes.
E. R. McKinstry

2367. Edgar, Irving I. BEGINNINGS OF DETROIT JEWISH WELFARE FEDERATION. *Michigan Jewish Hist. 1975 15(2): 6-8.* Minutes of the 5 May 1926 organization meeting of the Jewish Welfare Federation of Detroit.
S

2368. Everett, Dianna. THE WETTEST DROUGHT IN THE HISTORY OF TEXAS: A SURVEY OF THE ENFORCEMENT OF THE EIGHTEENTH AMENDMENT AND THE DEAN ACT, 1920-1933. *Panhandle-Plains Hist. Rev. 1979 52: 39-61.* Efforts to end liquor production and consumption in Texas paralleled the development of a national prohibition movement during the early 20th century. Texas joined a growing list of states when in 1918 it enacted a prohibition law, but problems of constitutionality and enforcement undercut its effectiveness. In 1919, Texas legislators passed the Dean Act to supplement the national Volstead Act and insure greater enforcement of prohibition. Too few agents, too many bootleggers, and too much public demand for alcohol forced a repeal of the 18th Amendment in 1933. Based on newspapers and government reports; 101 notes.
M. L. Tate

2369. Feinman, Ronald L. THE PROGRESSIVE REPUBLICAN SENATE BLOC AND THE PRESIDENTIAL ELECTION OF 1932. *Mid-America 1977 59(2): 73-91.* During the early 1930's the progressive Republican Senate bloc consisted of 12 senators from Midwestern and Western states. Most of them opposed Herbert Hoover's policies and sought options which would further progressivism. A third party alternative was rejected. Several considered opposing Hoover in the 1932 primaries, but this failed to materialize. Only two of the 12, Charles McNary of Oregon and Arthur Capper of Kansas, actively supported Hoover during the Presidential campaign. The others remained neutral or supported Roosevelt as the most progressive candidate. Based on archival material; 43 notes.
J. M. Lee

2370. Fetner, Gerald. PUBLIC POWER AND PROFESSIONAL RESPONSIBILITY: JULIUS HENRY COHEN AND THE ORIGINS OF THE PUBLIC AUTHORITY. *Am. J. of Legal Hist. 1977 21(1): 15-39.* Judge Leonard Crouch's decision in *Muller* v. *New York Housing Authority* (1936) was the first judicial statement to establish housing as a public use subject to the power of eminent domain. Marking a departure from previous policy, allowing local communities to establish housing authorities for low-cost public projects offered a more constitutionally acceptable method for using the state's power of eminent domain and a more rational approach to resolving slum conditions. The initial legislation was drafted by Julius Henry Cohen in the early 1920's. Focuses on Cohen's philosophy, work, and development of the state housing agency. Concludes that the state authority developed by Cohen "represented an important period piece between Progressive era regulation designed to democraticize business and maintain the American ideal of competition, and New Deal era legislation focused more on managing an economy disrupted by depression." Based on original sources; 75 notes.
L. A. Knafla

2371. Filesi, Teobaldo. IL MOVIMENTO PAN-NEGRO E LA POLITICA COLONIALE ITALIANA NEL 1920-1923 [The Pan-Negro movement and the Italian colonial policy, 1920-23]. *Africa [Italy] 1975 30(2): 159-197.* After World War I the problem of the Negro race in general and of Africa and the Africans in particular had gained ground especially in the United States where two organizations had become active: The National Association for the Advancement of Colored People, led by W. E. B. Du Bois and the Universal Negro Improvement Association led by Marcus Garvey. The latter soon became very popular thanks to its strong claims and the revolutionary charm of its leader, who between 1920 and 1922 organized three very effective conferences in New York City. Marcus Garvey wanted the colonial powers to be present at the third congress and had asked the governments of Great Britain, France, Belgium, Portugal, and Italy to send an official representative to the Pan Negro Conference. The invitation was not accepted by these powers which looked with suspicion on Garvey's movement. After a presentation of the Pan Negro leader and of the main features of the Universal Negro Improvement Association, the author gives an account of the reactions of the government and public opinion in Italy to the invitation and the activities of Garvey, analyzing the contents and results of the third Pan Negro Congress, and the subsequent decay of the association. Based mainly on the papers of the former Italian Ministry for the Colonies.
J

2372. Filippelli, Ronald L. DIARY OF A STRIKE: GEORGE MEDRICK AND THE COAL STRIKE OF 1927 IN WESTERN PENNSYLVANIA. *Pennsylvania Hist. 1976 43(3): 253-266.* The bituminous coal strike that began in 1925 involved most of the nation's fields, but its greatest impact was felt in Pennsylvania. The United Mine Workers were severely damaged as operators were often successful in forcing the union from their mines. By 1929 most of the Pennsylvania bituminous coal industry was nonunion. U.M.W.A. membership in the nation stood at about one-fourth of what it had been in 1920. The 1927 diary entries presented here are those of George Medrick, then a U.M.W.A. agent active in the Pittsburgh area. Based on the George Medrick Papers; illus., 18 notes.
D. C. Swift

2373. Flanders, Jane. KATHERINE ANNE PORTER'S FEMINIST CRITICISM: BOOK REVIEWS FROM THE 1920'S. *Frontiers 1979 4(2): 44-48.* Discusses author Katherine Anne Porter's career as a feminist-oriented literary critic during the 1920's, using her reviews of Emily Post's *Parade* (1925), W. L. George's *The Story of Woman,* and others to reveal her views on women's rights, sex roles, and her social milieu.

2374. Freedman, Estelle B. THE NEW WOMAN: CHANGING VIEWS OF WOMEN IN THE 1920'S. *J. of Am. Hist. 1974 61(2): 372-393.* Historians have not been consistent in their evaluation of the women's movement in the 1920's. They have differed in their evaluation of the uses to which women put the newly acquired economic parity with men, and in their attitudes toward the reality of the sexual revolution of the 20's. Most recent works by William O'Neill and William Chafe see women as having made little progress in either the political or nonpolitical realms in the period, though they differ in whether this failure should be attributed to splits within the feminist movement or to social barriers to full emancipation. Common to nearly all studies is a tendency toward broad and unsubstantiated generalizations about women without fully recognizing class, race, region, and ethnicity. 63 notes.
K. B. West

2375. Garson, Robert A. POLITICAL FUNDAMENTALISM AND POPULAR DEMOCRACY IN THE 1920'S. *South Atlantic Q. 1977 76(2): 219-233.* The 1920's fundamentalist backlash against cosmopolitan modernity was an expression of popular democracy in the Jacksonian tradition. Alienated and frustrated by the crumbling of Victorian mores, the fundamentalists, including pietistic Christian evangelists and the Ku Klux Klan, attempted to preserve traditional ways at the local level. Their vigilantism was intended to keep unpopular new ideas out of local communities and to silence any local adherents. Not sophisticated enough to focus their attack on the mass media, they spent most of their efforts in minimizing the effects of the professional elites in public education on local youth and in carrying punishment to the moral lawbreakers left untouched by civil authorities. In this the fundamentalists evoked the issue of accountability in local education and politics. 24 notes.
W. L. Olbrich

2376. Geidel, Peter. THE NATIONAL WOMAN'S PARTY AND THE ORIGINS OF THE EQUAL RIGHTS AMENDMENT, 1920-1923. *Historian 1980 42(4): 557-582.* With the attainment of woman suffrage in 1920, the tenable alliance between the Social Feminists and the Feminists collapsed. The Feminists, represented by the National Woman's Party, now sought equality for women in all fields, while the Social Feminists considered feminism as only a part of their reform program. Instrumental in the passage of Wisconsin's Equal Rights Bill in 1921, the National Woman's Party sought blanket bills in other states and supported a federal equal rights amendment. The Social Feminists refused to cooperate and believed that an equal rights amendment was an infringement upon states' rights. Failure to secure an equal rights amendment along with the absence of an official magazine contributed to the eventual demise of the National Woman's Party. Primary sources; 88 notes.
R. S. Sliwoski

2377. Gerz, Richard J., Jr. URBAN REFORM AND THE MUSSER COALITION IN THE CITY OF LANCASTER, 1921-1930. *J. of the Lancaster County Hist. Soc. 1974 78(2): 49-110.* Analyzes the nature of the urban reform movement in Lancaster, Pennsylvania, 1921-30, drawing parallels to the national movement, 1900-16; chronicles and compares the concurrent Coalition Movement in which members of the Republican Party grew dissatisfied with the party machine and switched to the Democratic Party, forming a Coalition Party in order to bring about modernization and progressivism to Lancaster. 4 photos, 274 notes, 10 appendixes, biblio.
G. A. Hewlett

2378. Glaser, Martha. PATERSON, 1924: THE A.C.L.U. AND LABOR. *New Jersey Hist. 1976 94(4): 155-172.* Loom assignments and low wages caused the Paterson silk strike of 1924. The American Civil Liberties Union (ACLU) involved itself on behalf of labor after the strike committee of the Associated Silk Workers Union asked for assistance. By taking legal action, by publicizing events in Paterson throughout the country, and by confronting the owners of the factories and local authorities who made it difficult to assemble for strike meetings, the ACLU demonstrated its tactics in handling the problems of free speech and assembly that arose from labor-management clashes. Although the owners were victorious in this instance, the ACLU won the right to assemble and to listen to any speaker desired for the union. Primary and secondary sources; 3 illus., 47 notes.
E. R. McKinstry

2379. Goodenow, Ronald K. THE PROGRESSIVE EDUCATOR AS RADICAL OR CONSERVATIVE: GEORGE S. COUNTS AND RACE. *Hist. of Educ. [Great Britain] 1978 7(1): 45-57.* Outlines the ideas of George S. Counts, a social reconstructionist and educational reformer, who conducted empirical research into the economic and political roots of social conflict, and the divisions of US society. Examines the complex nature of his liberalism, with particular reference to his theories on race. Discusses the ways in which he believed that education and democracy could shape a new set of social attitudes and considers the relationship of his ideas to those of the progressive movement. 53 notes.
C. A. McNeill

2380. Griffin, William. THE MERCY HOSPITAL CONTROVERSY AMONG CLEVELAND'S AFRO-AMERICAN CIVIC LEADERS, 1927. *J. of Negro Hist. 1976 61(4): 327-350.* In Cleveland, the campaign to eliminate racial discrimination in health care institutions focused attention upon the municipal hospital which excluded Negroes from its staff and training programs. Black leaders in Cleveland were divided in their support of the proposed Negro institution, Mercy Hospital. The controversy focused attention on discrimination in hospitals, and by 1930, under pressure from black civic leaders, the Cleveland City Hospital was ordered to change its racial policies. Based upon primary materials in the Western Reserve Historical Society Library and the Library of Congress Manuscript Collection; 105 notes.
N. G. Sapper

2381. Hansen, James E., II. MOONSHINE AND MURDER: PROHIBITION IN DENVER. *Colorado Mag. 1973 50(1): 1-23.* Studies the prohibition experience of Denver, Colorado, in relation to the report of the Wickersham Committee of 1931. The Denver situation exemplified the committee's conclusions that prohibition was not living up to expectations. There was general resistance in the city; "undermanned, poorly organized and sometimes corrupt law enforcement; congested courts; conflicts between temperance and civil liberties; and failure to educate the public to the reform's merits." 7 illus., 85 notes.
O. H. Zabel

2382. Hellwig, David J. BLACK LEADERS AND UNITED STATES IMMIGRATION POLICY, 1917-1929. *J. of Negro Hist. 1981 66(2): 110-127.* Many black Americans felt that World War I would result in more democracy, economic improvement, and recognition for wartime contributions. However, some of the expected gains would be lost if immigration levels were increased. Therefore, many black leaders supported legislation restricting immigration even though the policies were often racist and contrary to the American tradition.
A. G. Belles

2383. Hendrick, Irving G. EARLY SCHOOLING FOR CHILDREN OF MIGRANT FARMWORKERS IN CALIFORNIA: THE 1920'S. *Aztlán 1977 8: 11-26.* As State Superintendent of Schools, Georgiana Carden worked diligently to enforce legislation funding mandatory elementary education for the children of Mexican American farmworkers in order to encourage assimilation and guarantee equality of education in California.

2384. Hill, Charles. FIGHTING THE TWELVE-HOUR DAY IN THE AMERICAN STEEL INDUSTRY. *Labor Hist. 1974 15(1): 19-35.* Reviews the movement against the twelve-hour day in the steel industry and details the intricate maneuvering of a diverse group of opponents and supporters ranging from John A. Fitch, President Harding, Secretary of Commerce Herbert Hoover, Paul Kellogg, and others during 1923. The reform was achieved, and the steel companies had little difficulty in making the changeover to the eight-hour day. Based on the files of the War Labor Policies Board, the Samuel McCune Lindsay papers, the Herbert Hoover papers, and *The Survey.* 96 notes.
L. L. Athey

2385. Hine, Darlene Clark. THE N.A.A.C.P. AND THE SUPREME COURT: WATLER F. WHITE AND THE DEFEAT OF JUDGE JOHN J. PARKER, 1930. *Negro Hist. Bull. 1977 40(5): 753-757.* The NAACP and Walter F. White established themselves on the national scene as well as in North Carolina when they defeated the appointment of Judge John J. Parker to the Supreme Court.
R. Jirran

2386. Jackson, Joy J. PROHIBITION IN NEW ORLEANS: THE UNLIKELIEST CRUSADE. *Louisiana Hist. 1978 19(3): 261-284.* Presidential address, 20th Annual Meeting of the Louisiana Historical Association, Alexandria, Louisiana, 10 March 1978. The Louisiana legislature ratified the 18th Amendment in August 1918 by a narrow margin, as north and central Louisiana "dry" interests defeated the "wet" votes of southern Louisiana and New Orleans. New Orleans opposed prohibition and was a center for bootlegging to dry regions throughout the Gulf South. Many establishments in the city secretly and openly defied the ban on alcoholic beverages. Despite heavy enforcement efforts, wine, beer, and liquor remained widely available throughout the period, and prohibition violation contributed to the rise of organized crime, gangsterism and bribery of public officials in New Orleans as in other large cities. Details enforcement efforts as well as popular opposition and flaunting of prohibition. Primary sources; 86 notes.
R. L. Woodward, Jr.

2387. Jones, Bartlett C. NULLIFICATION AND PROHIBITION, 1920-1933. *Southwestern Social Sci. Q. 1964 44(4): 389-398.* They never explicitly prescribed nullification of federal law (in this case, the 18th amendment), but pronullification forces advocated cooperative action between Congress and the states, passive resistance of states, and aggressive resistance by individuals, to secure the repeal of Prohibition, 1920-33.

2388. Jones, Walter R. CASPER'S PROHIBITION YEARS. *Ann. of Wyoming 1976 48(2): 264-273.* Attempts to enforce national Prohibition in Casper, Wyoming produced 14 troubled years, 1919-33, as many citizens refused to abide by the law. Bootlegging led to arrests and the death of a deputy sheriff, but high profits kept the illicit trade alive. Charges of corruption reached a peak by early 1933 when the sheriff and mayor were indicted along with 34 other persons. Though the trials produced no convictions, disrespect for these public officials continued even after the repeal of Prohibition at the end of 1933. Based on primary sources; 3 photos, 21 notes.
M. L. Tate

2389. Jordan, Daniel P. THE MINGO WAR: LABOR VIOLENCE IN THE SOUTHERN WEST VIRGINIA COAL FIELDS, 1919-1922. Fink, Gary M. and Reed, Merl E., eds. *Essays in Southern Labor History: Selected Papers, Southern Labor History Conference, 1976.* (Westport, Conn.; London, England: Greenwood Pr., 1977): 102-143. Chronicles the Mingo War, discusses the major adversaries' views of issues, their strategy, tactics, and weapons, and analyzes the war's effects and significance. The fundamental issue was unionization or "the right to belong to a labor union," but also included many related issues. The United Mine Workers of America operated under serious handicaps. Though largely typical, the conflict had several distinctive elements: its single issue, the exceptionally great amount of violence, the lack of radical issues despite a fairly large number of blacks in both camps, and the lack of outside radical participants. 129 notes.
R. V. Ritter

2390. Kanarek, Harold K. DISASTER FOR HARD COAL: THE ANTHRACITE STRIKE OF 1925-1926. *Labor Hist. 1974 15(1): 46-*

62. Details the struggle between the mine owners, the U.M.W.A., and the federal government during the anthracite strike of 1925-26. The owners and the unions lacked foresight and precipitated a strike which disastrously affected the whole industry. Only Gifford Pinchot, among public officials, consistently tried to protect the interests of the public and the worker. The federal government did not support this view. Based on the Gifford Pinchot, Coolidge, and W. Jett Lauck papers, and on the *Congressional Record.* 83 notes.
L. L. Athey

2391. Kanarek, Harold K. THE PENNSYLVANIA ANTHRACITE STRIKE OF 1922. *Pennsylvania Mag. of Hist. and Biog.* 1975 99(2): 207-225. Studies the way mining operators met the miners' demands and their failure to understand their own best interests, which opened the way for competitors (gas, oil, and electricity) to capture the market. Various factors were involved: the dangers of an unregulated monopoly, the operators concentration on weakening the union, preoccupation with wages on the part of the United Mine Workers, and total disinterest on the part of both Congress and the White House. 73 notes.
R. V. Ritter

2392. Kane, Richard D. THE FEDERAL SEGREGATION OF THE BLACKS DURING THE PRESIDENTIAL ADMINISTRATIONS OF WARREN G. HARDING AND CALVIN COOLIDGE. *Pan-African J.* [Kenya] 1974 7(2): 153-171. Condemns the federal government for its discrimination against black Americans during 1897-1927, particularly those blacks employed by the federal government. Cases of abuse are cited in all administrations during that era. 102 notes.
H. G. Soff

2393. Kearnes, John. UTAH, SEXTON OF PROHIBITION. *Utah Hist. Q.* 1979 47(1): 5-21. Utah, whose Mormon majority espoused abstinence, was the 36th state to ratify the 21st amendment, which repealed the 18th (Prohibition) amendment. Urban majorities prevailed over rural prohibitionists in spite of concerted efforts of secular and religious leaders. Wets pointed to disrespect for law created by Prohibition. They argued that additional revenue repeal would provide toward recovery from the depression, and made Prohibition a poltical, not a religious, issue. Drys rejected the economic appeal, pointed out evils rampant before Prohibition, and made prohibition a moral and religious obligation. Covers 1932-33. 8 illus., 59 notes.
J. L. Hazelton

2394. Keeran, Roger R. COMMUNIST INFLUENCE IN THE AUTOMOBILE INDUSTRY, 1920-1933: PAVING THE WAY FOR AN INDUSTRIAL UNION. *Labor Hist.* 1979 20(2): 189-225. Although small in number, the Communists formed a nucleus in the auto industry in the 1920's which challenged "welfare capitalism." Through shop activity, newspapers, strike support, and fraternal society meetings, the Communists spread the idea of industrial unionism and established the base for success of unionism in the 1930's. Based on the records of the Auto Workers Union, newspapers, and oral history; 58 notes.
L. L. Athey

2395. Kohn, Lawrence A. GOITER, IODINE AND GEORGE W. GOLER: THE ROCHESTER EXPERIMENT. *Bull. of the Hist. of Medicine* 1975 49(3): 389-399. On 24 April 1923 sodium iodide was added to the water supply of Rochester, New York, "the first recorded community act against human disease other than the infections." George W. Goler, Rochester's health officer from 1896 to 1932, was primarily responsible for this attempt to reduce the incidence of goiter in the community. With the endorsement of George H. Whipple, dean of the University's medical school, and the assistance of Beekman C. Little, superintendent of the water department from 1901 to 1926, Goler proposed the plan, and put it into action. The opposition is described, including the American Medical Liberty League, the Christian Scientists, and the home-brewing industry, who complained that iodized water prevented the development of a decent "head" on their beer. When the goiter count fell, opposition disappeared. In 1933, the program was dropped. 52 notes.
M. Kaufman

2396. Kyvig, David E. WOMEN AGAINST PROHIBITION. *Am. Q.* 1976 28(4): 465-482. Women were influential in the fight to repeal national prohibition, especially through the Women's Organization for National Prohibition Reform (WONPR). Led by Mrs. Pauline Sabin, the group consisted primarily of middle and upper class women who viewed prohibition as a failure in terms of diminishing the consumption of alcoholic beverages, feared the influence of the speakeasy on the morals of the young, and believed taxes on alcoholic beverages were a needed source of government revenue. The WONPR combated the propaganda of the Women's Christian Temperance Union, supported anti-prohibition candidates for political office, and generally operated in an independent fashion. The group's activities during the late 1920's and early 1930's suggest a revision of the view that the women's movement declined in strength and influence following the adoption of the woman suffrage amendment. Primary and secondary sources; 77 notes.
N. Lederer

2397. Lamon, Lester C. THE BLACK COMMUNITY IN NASHVILLE AND THE FISK UNIVERSITY STUDENT STRIKE OF 1924-1925. *J. of Southern Hist.* 1974 40(2): 225-244. Discusses Fisk University students' struggle to obtain freedom from paternalistic control of their clubs, publications, and dress codes and to secure student participation in school administration through a student council, student publications, and an athletic association. With the white administration unwilling to make any appreciable concessions, the resultant friction and confrontation moved the struggle into the community. The administration sought support from the whites in Nashville, while the students sought support from the black community in Nashville. With solid local and national black support, Fisk President Fayette Avery McKenzie was forced to resign in 1925. Although not replaced with a black, the new president granted most of the students' previous demands. Based on manuscripts and printed primary and secondary sources; 46 notes.
T. D. Schoonover

2398. Landes, Elisabeth M. THE EFFECT OF STATE MAXIMUM-HOURS LAWS ON THE EMPLOYMENT OF WOMEN IN 1920. *J. of Pol. Econ.* 1980 88(3): 476-494. Strict enforcement of state maximum hours laws in 1920 led to reduced work hours and employment among women and was most dramatically felt among foreign-born females, indicating a hostility toward immigration and immigrants within the American labor movement.

2399. Laska, Lewis L. MR. JUSTICE SANFORD AND THE FOURTEENTH AMENDMENT. *Tennessee Hist. Q.* 1974 33(2): 210-227. Edward Terry Sanford (1865-1930) was one of Tennessee's most distinguished jurists. Born in Knoxville of Unionist parents, he graduated from the University of Tennessee and later Harvard Law School, was a strong supporter of higher education, and an outstanding public speaker. After a successful law practice, Sanford was appointed to the US Supreme Court where his most famous decision was his defense of civil liberties in *Gitlow* v. *New York* (US, 1925). Primary and secondary sources; 52 notes.
M. B. Lucas

2400. Lawson, Steven F. PROGRESSIVES AND THE SUPREME COURT: A CASE FOR JUDICIAL REFORM IN THE 1920S. *Historian* 1980 42(3): 419-436. After World War I, the Supreme Court, faced with legal issues brought forth by the extraordinary centralization of state authority during the war, followed a double standard of striking down government restrictions on the disposal of private property while curbing freedom of speech, emasculating progressive economic legislation, and limiting efforts at unionization. The Progressives, led by Senator Robert M. La Follette, Sr., attempted to limit Supreme Court judicial hegemony through congressional supremacy. A leaderless coalition by 1925 and splintered by differing conceptions of judicial functions, the Progressives were badly outmaneuvered by Chief Justice William H. Taft and soundly defeated. Primary sources; 87 notes.
R. S. Sliwoski

2401. Lemons, J. Stanley. SOCIAL FEMINISM IN THE 1920S: PROGRESSIVE WOMEN AND INDUSTRIAL LEGISLATION. *Labor Hist.* 1973 14(1): 83-91. Surveys the continuing struggle for industrial legislation in the 1920's. A group of women's organizations pressed for many reforms including the elimination of child labor, maternity and infant care, nightwork laws, and labor legislation. Although attacked bitterly, the groups kept alive the hope for industrial legislation which was finally realized under the impetus of the Depression. Based on periodicals, proceedings of organizations, and a doctoral dissertation; 21 notes.
L. L. Athey

2402. Lewis, Vashti. MARCUS GARVEY'S IMPOSSIBLE DREAM. *Negro Hist. Bull. 1977 40(6): 770-773.* In 1926, Liberia leased the tracts of land previously allocated to the Universal Negro Improvement Association to Harvey S. Firestone.
R. J. Jirran

2403. Livingston, John C. GOVERNOR WILLIAM SWEET: PERSISTENT PROGRESSIVISM VS. PRAGMATIC POLITICS. *Colorado Mag. 1977 54(1): 1-25.* William Sweet, a progressive Democrat, was elected Colorado governor (1922) with the support of farmers, labor, and middle-class Progressives. Senator Samuel D. Nicholson's death (1923) caused Governor Sweet to balance progressive commitment with practical politics by appointing Pueblo resident and semiconservative Alva B. Adams to the Senate. Sweet was defeated in his 1924 reelection bid. Primary sources; 6 photos, 47 notes.
O. H. Zabel

2404. Lovin, Hugh T. THE BANISHMENT OF KATE RICHARDS O'HARE. *Idaho Yesterdays 1978 22(1): 20-25.* Kate Richards O'Hare, Socialist orator, planned to visit Twin Falls, Idaho, on a speaking tour in the summer of 1921. She was speaking on her recent prison experiences. After legal attempts to block her speech failed, some Twin Falls citizens kidnapped O'Hare and transported her into Utah, where she was released. Her demands for justice were ignored and the incident was eventually forgotten. Primary and secondary sources; 3 illus., 33 notes.
B. J. Paul

2405. Lovin, Hugh T. IDAHO AND THE "REDS," 1919-1926. *Pacific Northwest Q. 1978 69(3): 107-115.* The collapse of the 1919 Seattle general strike alarmed Idaho citizens who feared that the Industrial Workers of the World and other leftist groups would soon flood their state. Idaho Governor David W. Davis mobilized public opinion and organized a roundup of Wobblies. Idaho's Socialist Party and Nonpartisan League also received pressure, but the "red-baiting" gradually declined during the early 1920's. Primary sources; 4 photos, 37 notes.
M. L. Tate

2406. Lovin, Hugh T. RAY MCKAIG: NONPARTISAN LEAGUE INTELLECTUAL AND RACONTEUR. *North Dakota Hist. 1980 47(3): 12-20.* A former minister, Robert Raymond McKaig was a successful rancher who became a leading spokesman for the Nonpartisan League in North Dakota and Idaho. He spent more than 20 years, between the early 1920's and 1945, writing and attempting to publish a novel based on farmers' problems and Nonpartisan solutions. Based on the McKaig Papers in Idaho State Historical Society; 6 illus., 48 notes.
G. L. Olson

2407. Luodesmeri, Varpu. AMERIKANSUOMALAISTEN TYÖVÄENJÄRJESTÖJEN SUHTAUTUMINEN SUOMESTA VUODEN 1918 SODAN JÄLKEEN TULLEISIIN SIIRTOLAISIIN: "HILJAN SUOMESTA TULLEITTEN TUTKIJAKOMITEAT" [The attitudes of the Finnish American workers' movement toward immigrants coming from Finland after the 1918 war: the "Committees of examination of recent arrivals from Finland"]. *Turun Hist. Arkisto [Finland] 1974 29: 63-113.* Describes radical labor organizations of Finnish immigrants in the United States and Canada. Recent immigrants were screened to determine their roles in the 1918 Finnish civil war before that person was allowed to join the local organization. At least 68 local committees were established, ceasing in the United States after 1924, but continuing longer in Canada. Based on newspapers, manuscripts and interviews collected at Turku University, Finland; map, 195 notes, English summary.
R. G. Selleck

2408. Margulies, Herbert F. THE ARTICLES OF WAR, 1920: THE HISTORY OF A FORGOTTEN REFORM. *Military Affairs 1979 43(2): 85-89.* Discusses the legislative history of the 1920 Articles of War and places them in the context of Progressivism. The 1920 Articles liberalized the code of military law and courts-martial procedure in the Army. Adoption was due to the efforts of Samuel T. Ansell, Judge Advocate General Enoch H. Crowder, Senator George Chamberlain of Oregon, and Senator Irvine L. Lenroot of Wisconsin. The limitations in the Articles were serious, reflecting the effects of compromise and some short-sightedness, yet they represented measurable progress. Primary and secondary sources; 33 notes.
A. M. Osur

2409. Mathews, Allan. AGRARIAN RADICALS: THE UNITED FARMERS LEAGUE OF SOUTH DAKOTA. *South Dakota Hist. 1973 3(4): 408-421.* Discusses farm protest against foreclosure and other economic and social ills during the Great Depression. The United Farmers League [before 1930 the United Farmers Educational League] gained the ascendency in northeastern South Dakota, attracting many farmer members with its relief programs as well as rhetoric, despite its Communist affiliation. Political organization, a protest march to the state capitol, physical violence, and an emotional trial all took place before the UFL's power and attractiveness faded. The league ran candidates in 1934, but its Communist affiliation plus the New Deal's farm programs combined to dissolve its support. Primary and secondary sources; 3 illus., 28 notes.
A. J. Larson

2410. McDonald, Rita and Dunbar, Robert G. THE INITIATION OF THE MCNARY-HAUGEN MOVEMENT IN MONTANA AND THE PACIFIC NORTHWEST. *Pacific Northwest Q. 1980 71(2): 63-71.* Declining crop prices and rising costs of production during the early 1920's hit Pacific Northwest wheat farmers especially hard and they began organizing to discuss marketing remedies. A plan suggested by George N. Peek and Hugh S. Johnson of the Moline Plow Company called for new tariffs to protect farmers from foreign producers and a federal program for price supports. Secretary of Agriculture Henry C. Wallace and Henry C. Taylor, head of the Bureau of Agricultural Economics, rallied behind the plan which formed the basis for the McNary-Haugen bill. Although the McNary-Haugen bill failed passage during the Republican administrations of the 1920's, it became the basis for subsequent New Deal legislation. Based on newspapers and archival sources; 5 photos, 37 notes.
M. L. Tate

2411. McMahan, Ronald L. "RANG-U-TANG": THE I.W.W. AND THE 1927 COLORADO COAL STRIKE. Conlin, Joseph R., ed. *At the Point of Production: The Local History of the I.W.W.* (Westport, Conn.: Greenwood Pr., 1981): 191-212. Employs the historical record, ethnographic accounts, and scholarly works in an attempt to get at the heart of the issues raised by the 1927 Colorado coal strike. Examines the conditions that created the environment enabling the Industrial Workers of the World to organize a massive strike, the goals of the IWW, the success of their activities in achieving those goals, and the decline and virtual disappearance of Socialist influence within the American labor movement. The IWW failed to establish and maintain a viable organization in Colorado because of the anarcho-syndicalist ideology and strategy they employed. Based on ethnographic accounts, newspaper and journal articles; 49 notes.
J. Powell

2412. McQuaid, Kim. YOUNG, SWOPE AND GENERAL ELECTRIC'S 'NEW CAPITALISM': A STUDY IN CORPORATE LIBERALISM, 1920-33. *Am. J. of Econ. and Sociol. 1977 36(3): 323-334.* The General Electric Co. espoused "New Capitalism," 1920-33, which attempted employee "welfare work" programs, company unionism, and industrial "self-regulation" under the direction, but not regulation, of the federal government; discusses the patterns of power and perception formulated before the Depression, which forced corporate definitions of capitalist normalcy.

2413. Melcher, Daniel P. THE CHALLENGE TO NORMALCY: THE 1924 ELECTION IN CALIFORNIA. *Southern California Q. 1978 60(2): 155-182.* Analyzes the influence of the La Follette Progressive Party ticket on California in the 1924 presidential election. The third party movement was supported by Republicans who failed to share in Coolidge prosperity, including workers in the depressed gold, timber, and agricultural industries, plus urban working class voters. Their vote was a protext against the upper and middle class orientation of the Republican party; disaffected Democrats also turned to the Progressives in the belief that the Democratic party failed to represent their needs. The La Follette ticket provided the means for a major realignment in the electorate as Republicans went through the Progressive Party in 1924 and into the Democratic party in 1928. "More than any other factor, the election of 1924 turned on the economic well-being of the electorate." Thus the Progressives were not a reminder of prewar reform as much as the beginnings of what by 1932 became a Democratic coalition. Census and voting records, contemporary and secondary published works; 6 tables, 59 notes.
A. Hoffman

2414. Millett, Stephen M. THE MIDWEST ORIGINS OF THE AMERICAN COMMUNIST PARTY: THE LEADERSHIP OF CHARLES E. RUTHENBERG, 1919-1927. *Old Northwest 1975 1(3): 253-290.* Relates the activities of Charles Emil Ruthenberg (1882-1927), Cleveland, Ohio, as first executive secretary of the American Communist Party, 1919-27. Ruthenberg strove for a united party, above ground, emphasizing propaganda, and always subservient to the Kremlin. Although neither an intellectual nor a theorist, and without strong labor support, he dominated the American Communist movement by 1923. He defeated the attempt of William Z. Foster (1881-1961) to oust him when the Kremlin intervened in his behalf. Based on the Ohio Historical Society's Ruthenberg Papers, Congressional hearings, newspapers, and secondary works; 109 notes. J. N. Dickinson

2415. Mitchell, Gary. WOMEN STANDING FOR WOMEN: THE EARLY POLITICAL CAREER OF MARY T. NORTON. *New Jersey Hist. 1978 96(1-2): 27-42.* Before her election to Congress in 1924 as a representative from Frank Hague's Hudson County, Mary T. Norton worked with working class women in Jersey City, New Jersey, organized women for the Democratic Party, served on New Jersey's Democratic State Committee, and became a county freeholder. During her early congressional career she introduced legislation designed to help women achieve equality on the District of Columbia's police force and on its juries. She spoke out on immigration equalization for women and introduced legislation to increase pensions for Civil War veteran's widows. Norton fought throughout her career to be judged by her record, not her sex. She urged women everywhere to become involved in politics. Based on the Mary Norton papers and secondary sources; 5 illus., 39 notes. E. R. McKinstry

2416. Mugleston, William F. THE PRESS AND STUDENT ACTIVISM AT THE UNIVERSITY OF GEORGIA IN THE 1920S. *Georgia Hist. Q. 1980 64(3): 241-252.* An alliance between Julian LaRose Harris of the Columbus *Enquirer-Sun* and certain students at the University of Georgia called attention to various problems and abuses on the campus, which were gradually corrected. Based on correspondence, newspapers and secondary sources; 30 notes. G. R. Schroeder

2417. Mullins, William H. SELF-HELP IN SEATTLE, 1931-1932: HERBERT HOOVER'S CONCEPT OF COOPERATIVE INDIVIDUALISM AND THE UNEMPLOYED CITIZENS' LEAGUE. *Pacific Northwest Q. 1981 72(1): 11-19.* The Unemployed Citizens' League (UCL) of Seattle, Washington, created in 1931, closely paralleled President Herbert C. Hoover's call for voluntary, self-help programs to solve the problems of the Depression. Mayor Robert Harlin agreed with the program and appointed I. F. Dix to coordinate public and private relief efforts. Initial UCL success in creating jobs was shortlived, however, as internal strife, local politics, loss of funding sources, and the leftward turn of UCL leaders undermined its efforts. By the end of 1932 the organization had lost its popular following and its power. Primary sources; 3 photos, 39 notes. M. L. Tate

2418. Nitoburg, E. L. GARVIZM [The Garvey movement]. *Voprosy Istorii [USSR] 1977 (7): 137-151.* Deals with the controversial philosophy of Marcus Garvey (1887-1940) based on his doctrine of black racial purity and separatism. Garvey's utopian plans of American Negroes returning to Africa, his disinterest in improving the social conditions in the United States or the fight for civil rights, brought him close to the most virulent antiblack elements, including the Ku Klux Klan. While appealing primarily to ghetto Negroes, his claims that white workers were the principal enemies of blacks alienated the working class and led him, eventually, to endorse bourgeois capitalist positions. However, his attempts to create racial barriers between pure blacks and mulattoes as well as blacks and whites antagonized the black middle-class, and his back-to-Africa movement found no support among American Negroes who felt no ties to Africa. Garvey's initial success in the early 1920's proved ephemeral and his Universal Negro Improvement Association, founded in 1914, did not survive him. 79 notes. N. Frenkley

2419. Novitsky, Anthony. PETER MAURIN AND THE GREEN REVOLUTION. *R. of Pol. 1975 27(1): 83-103.* The ideology of the Catholic Worker Movement is a product of the European Right and not the American Left. The "Easy Essays" of Peter Maurin reflect the ideology of reactionary French Social Catholicism and a repudiation of Enlightenment ideas which underlie American political and social thought. For Maurin, social reconstruction is based on Christian concepts and a rejection of capitalism, a position that is "so old that it looks new." L. E. Ziewacz

2420. Nyden, Linda. BLACK MINERS IN WESTERN PENNSYLVANIA, 1925-1931: THE NATIONAL MINERS UNION AND THE UNITED MINE WORKERS OF AMERICA. *Sci. and Soc. 1977 41(1): 69-101.* The National Miners Union kept the spirit of unionism in the coal fields alive during the late 1920's and early 1930's when open shop efforts by operators, coupled with poor and dispirited leadership of the United Mine Workers of America, threatened to drive collective bargaining from the region. The NMU was a class struggle trade union which organized the unorganized, fought wage cuts, and led mass picket lines. It successfully organized and elevated blacks to leadership positions in the union at a time when the UMW segregated them from a meaningful role in its ranks and operators employed huge numbers of blacks as strikebreakers. Without the efforts of the NMU, conditions for the miners would have been far worse and the situation would not have been readied for the later resurgence of the UMW. N. Lederer

2421. O'Brien, Patrick G. SENATOR JOHN J. BLAINE: AN INDEPENDENT PROGRESSIVE DURING "NORMALCY." *Wisconsin Mag. of Hist. 1976 60(1): 25-41.* Analyzes John J. Blaine's record as Senator 1927-33 and concludes that he was an insurgent Republican whose progressivism, as reflected in key Congressional votes, was exceeded only by a few Republicans during his single term in office. Some of the major issues which reflected Blaine's stand included his repudiation of Hoover for President, his opposition to the Republican party's choice for president pro tempore of the Senate and for committee assignments, his defense of civil liberties and opposition to the Ku Klux Klan, his support for an excess-profits tax to end privilege and redistribute income, and his opposition to "dollar diplomacy" which he saw as the policy of imperialism and colonialism. 10 illus., 78 notes. N. C. Burckel

2422. Offiong, Daniel A. GARVEYISM AND NKRUMAHISM: THE QUEST FOR BLACK IRREDENTISM. *Pan-African J. [Kenya] 1975 8(1): 89-102.* Marcus Garvey's philosophy of racial pride and African nationalism is fundamentally related to black irredentism in Africa. Kwame Nkrumah of Ghana, was a disciple of Garvey's ideas, and there are many similarities between Garveyism and Nkrumahism. Considers in particular two similarities: 1) their concern with the degradation of the black race by the distortion of its history, and 2) their wish for a United States of Africa as an instrument of restoring black pride. Such ideas have had a significant effect on the present generation of black Africans and Americans. Covers 1920's-75. 60 notes. S

2423. Olssen, Erik. THE PROGRESSIVE GROUP IN CONGRESS, 1922-1929. *Historian 1980 42(2): 244-263.* While historians have argued over the effectiveness of Congressional "progressives" during the 1920's, most agree that they held the balance of power during this time. Yet little is known about the composition and character of this group. A systematic analysis of the voting behavior of all senators during the first sessions of the 68th, 69th and 70th Congresses revealed "a sizable and cohesive proreform group with a relatively stable membership, although the group did not include all those whom historians have described as 'progressive.' " Shows why the group was formed, how it came to enjoy the services of a research bureau, the People's Legislative Service, and the way in which it functioned during the 1920's. Primary sources; 3 tables, 85 notes. R. S. Sliwoski

2424. Pacyga, Dominic A. CRISIS AND COMMUNITY: THE BACK OF THE YARDS, 1921. *Chicago Hist. 1977 6(3): 167-176.* Polish Americans living in the Back of the Yards district of Chicago, Illinois, though Catholic and conservative working class, were instrumental in labor organization and especially in organizing and carrying out a strike of the meat packing workers in 1921.

2425. Palmer, Bryan D. "BIG BILL" HAYWOOD'S DEFECTION TO RUSSIA AND THE IWW: TWO LETTERS. *Labor Hist. 1976 17(2): 271-278.* Presents two letters from John Grady, Secretary-Treasurer of the IWW, to Mont Schuyler, Haywood's US agent, which reveal the financial and social disruption of the IWW caused by Haywood's defection. Letters are from the Archives of Labor History and Urban Affairs at Wayne State University. 11 notes. L. L. Athey

2426. Pearson, Ralph L. COMBATTING RACISM WITH ART: CHARLES S. JOHNSON AND THE HARLEM RENAISSANCE. *Am. Studies [Lawrence, KS] 1977 18(1): 123-134.* Johnson, editor of *Opportunity,* expected "the revelation of black artistic talent to be a liaison between the races." It would also improve the self-image of blacks as an ethnic group. He sought mutual understanding, and thought that black racial pride could help achieve equality in the 1920's. White racism, however, refused to be affected, and thwarted Johnson's efforts. Primary and secondary sources; 50 notes.
J. Andrew

2427. Philp, Kenneth R. JOHN COLLIER AND THE CRUSADE TO PROTECT INDIAN RELIGIOUS FREEDOM, 1920-1926. *J. of Ethnic Studies 1973 1(1): 22-38.* As part of the general program of Americanizing the Indian population, the Indian Bureau in the 1920's attempted to suppress various aspects of Indian culture, including the ceremonial dances of the Pueblos. These actions were supported by several missionary-oriented groups such as the Indian Rights Association and the YWCA Indian Department, which considered the dances as immoral and pagan. Defending the native practices of the Indians was John Collier, whose interest in subculture norms had originated from his experience as a social worker among immigrants in New York City. He formed the American Indian Defense Association in 1923 to provide legal aid and to lobby for Indian rights. Although unable to secure positive legislation to guarantee Indian religious freedom, Collier and the association forced the Indian Bureau to curb its program of cultural assimilation and to end its religious persecutions. Based on extensive primary sources, including unpublished papers of John Collier; 76 notes.
T. W. Smith

2428. Pitcher, Brian L. THE HAWTHORNE EXPERIMENTS: STATISTICAL EVIDENCE FOR A LEARNING HYPOTHESIS. *Social Forces 1981 60(1): 133-149.* The historical productivity data from the Hawthorne First Relay Assembly Test Room experiments permit the statistical evaluation of the hypotheses of the original experimenters and others by conducting appropriate time-series analyses. The introduction of rest pauses in the test room led to the more productive use of work time. Overall, the conditions motivating increased learning (increased status and new economic incentives and regular performance feedback) were the primary causes of increased output.
J/S

2429. Powell, Allan Kent. UTAH AND THE NATIONWIDE COAL MINERS' STRIKE OF 1922. *Utah Hist. Q. 1977 45(2): 135-157.* Union organizers felt union strength in Carbon County, Utah, was too weak to be included in the nationwide strike of the United Mine Workers of America in 1922. Utah miners protesting a 30 percent wage reduction struck anyway. Shooting incidents forced Governor Charles R. Mabey to call in the National Guard. Although the strikers gained a temporary restoration of the pay scale, the strike failed to achieve union recognition. Primary and secondary sources; 3 illus., 67 notes.
J. L. Hazelton

2430. Rainbolt, Rosemary. WOMEN AND WAR IN THE UNITED STATES: THE CASE OF DOROTHY DETZER, NATIONAL SECRETARY WOMEN'S INTERNATIONAL LEAGUE FOR PEACE AND FREEDOM. *Peace and Change 1977 4(3): 18-22.* Examines Dorothy Detzer's political clout, 1920-34, in the Women's International League for Peace and Freedom, on Capitol Hill as a major lobbyist and political analyst, and in the Nye Munitions Investigation of 1934.

2431. Reilly, John M. IMAGES OF GASTONIA: A REVOLUTIONARY CHAPTER IN AMERICAN SOCIAL FICTION. *Georgia R. 1974 28(3): 498-517.* Six radical novelists wrote about the 1929 Gastonia textile strike with the intent of conveying Marxian revolutionary concepts. The strike had been called by a Communist organized union. To make the story fit the theme, however, inevitably led to a certain amount of predictability.
M. B. Lucas

2432. Rice, Hazel F. A MEMO FROM MEMORY: WORKING WITH THE NORTH DAKOTA WORKMEN'S COMPENSATION BUREAU, 1919-1922. *North Dakota Hist. 1979 46(2): 22-29.* The author became the first Secretary of the North Dakota Minimum Wage Department in 1919. Her bureau was created by the state government brought into power through the successful electoral efforts of the Non-Partisan League. The author had sporadic contacts with officials of the Bureau, especially Board Member Laureas J. Wehe, but she basically worked alone in journeying throughout the state to investigate working conditions. Her letters to her family in New England during her tenure of service describe the arduous efforts necessary to travel from place to place in a state served by three railroads but ill-served by any other rapid transportation. The author's work was greatly inconvenienced by abysmal weather conditions and by the lack of adequate lodging for women in towns and villages.
N. Lederer

2433. Rocha, Guy Louis. THE IWW AND THE BOULDER CANYON PROJECT: THE FINAL DEATH THROES OF AMERICAN SYNDICALISM. *Nevada Hist. Soc. Q. 1978 21(1): 2-24.* Construction began in 1931 on the Boulder Canyon project (later, Hoover Dam) on the Colorado River, a project that Bureau of Reclamation officials speeded to create employment. Genuine grievances about living and working conditions developed among the workers. Industrial Workers of the World (IWW) organizers fanned the discontent and provoked repressive measures by Las Vegas townsmen and civil authorities. The workers went on strike 8-14 August 1931 and obtained redress of part of their grievances. Despite IWW aid and leadership of the strike, most workers never joined the IWW and (in 1933) ignored a second IWW strike call on the Boulder Canyon project. Newspaper and secondary sources; 4 photos, 59 notes.
H. T. Lovin

2434. Rocha, Guy Louis. THE I.W.W. AND THE BOULDER CANYON PROJECT: THE DEATH THROES OF AMERICAN SYNDICALISM. Conlin, Joseph R., ed. *At the Point of Production: The Local History of the I.W.W.* (Westport, Conn.: Greenwood Pr., 1981): 213-234. Nevada was the site of the birth and death of the Industrial Workers of the World. The first major organizational campaigns took place within the state, in 1905. On 16 August 1931, the final significant organizational activity of the IWW in the state terminated with an unsuccessful strike at the Boulder Canyon Project, one of the last important IWW activities in America. The working conditions at the Boulder Canyon Project, constructing Hoover Dam, were extremely hazardous. In 1930 President Herbert C. Hoover felt it necessary to 1) employ some of the vast number of jobless Americans on the project and 2) rush the project. The Six Companies, Inc., of San Francisco, exploited the workers, leading to the IWW-backed strike, 7-16 August. Based on newspaper and journal articles; 59 notes.
J. Powell

2435. Saito, Makoto. PRINCETON KOTOKENKYUSHO NO SETSURYTSU: AMERICASHI NO NAKANO "MUYONOGAKU NO YOU" [The establishment of Princeton's Institute for Advanced Study: "The usefulness of useless pursuits"]. *Kokka Gakkai Zassi [Japan] 1979 92(7-8): 76-89.* The establishment of the Institute for Advanced Study in Princeton, New Jersey, in the context of American history, was an epoch-making event. The establishment in 1930 of a research institute devoted to intellectual pursuits regarded as "useless"—studies of no immediate use—contravened the American traditional concept of education and research. The establishment of the Institute may be regarded as a turning point in intellectual endeavors in the United States.
T. Kobayashi

2436. Scott, William R. RABBI ARNOLD FORD'S BACK-TO-ETHIOPIA MOVEMENT: A STUDY OF BLACK EMIGRATION, 1930-1935. *Pan-African J. [Kenya] 1975 8(2): 191-202.* An account of the career of Rabbi Arnold Ford (1876-1935), early black Nationalist and leader of the back-to-Ethiopia movement. Accompanied by three other members of his congregation, Rabbi Ford arrived in Addis Ababa in 1930 in an attempt to obtain concessions for the rest of his group, who, it was hoped, would follow soon after. Records the difficulties encountered by those 60 members who made the journey to Addis Ababa during 1930-34. Twenty-five members returned shortly after their arrival and none remained after Ford's death in 1935 and the outbreak of the Italo-Ethiopian War. Primary and secondary sources; 52 notes.
M. Feingold

2437. Searle, R. Newell. AUTOS OR CANOES? WILDERNESS CONTROVERSY IN THE SUPERIOR NATIONAL FOREST. *J. of Forest Hist. 1978 22(2): 68-77.* The forested lakelands of Superior National Forest in northeastern Minnesota provided the focal point of a wilderness controversy during 1923-26. Although landscape architect Arthur H. Carhart recommended in 1921 that the Forest Service should manage the forest primarily for canoeists and nonmotorized recreation,

surrounding communities favored the development of roads, resorts, and such traditional economic activities as logging and mining. Local Forest Service officials were inclined to favor multiple use, but a persuasive campaign by downstate conservationists, led by the Izaak Walton League and by Paul B. Riis, pressured a wavering Forest Service into designating a roadless area in 1926. Aldo Leopold, who had ties with both groups, helped effect the compromise solution. The road controversy helped to shape Forest Service wilderness policy in the 1920's. Forest Service records and other primary and secondary sources; 5 illus., 2 maps, 39 notes.
R. J. Fahl

2438. Sexton, Robert F. THE CRUSADE AGAINST PARI-MUTUEL GAMBLING IN KENTUCKY: A STUDY OF SOUTHERN PROGRESSIVISM IN THE 1920'S. *Filson Club Hist. Q. 1976 50(1): 47-57.* Documents a continued Progressive movement in Kentucky in the 1920's. The anti-gambling crusade sprang from the religious attack on machine politics led by Helm Bruce and the Louisville Churchmen's Federation. The reformers had their greatest support in rural Kentucky, with support from the Ku Klux Klan and fundamentalist clergymen. Alben Barkley became the political spokesman of the anti-gambling group and nearly secured the Democratic gubernatorial nomination in 1923; four years later, former governor J. C. W. Beckham won the party's nomination as the anti-gambling candidate. Urban Democrats deserted Beckham, however, and Republican Slem Sampson was elected. Beckham's defeat marked the end of the Progressive movement in Kentucky. Documented from newspapers and the Barkley Papers at the University of Kentucky; 34 notes.
G. B. McKinney

2439. Shankman, Arnold. JULIAN HARRIS AND THE NEGRO. *Phylon 1974 35(4): 442-456.* Julian Harris, the son of Joel Chandler Harris, became editor and owner of the Columbus (Georgia) *Enquirer-Sun* in 1920, and controlled that newspaper until 1929 when he was forced to sell because of bankruptcy. During those years he fought the Ku Klux Klan, demanded that lynchings be outlawed, argued that blacks should be paid living wages, and supported equal housing and educational facilities. As a result, this courageous crusading editor, who demanded justice for blacks in the South when it was neither popular nor safe to do so, received in 1925 the Pulitzer Prize. However, his fights led to loss of subscriptions and advertising, and in 1929 he sold his interest in the paper. During the last years of his life Harris became unhappy, bitter, and increasingly conservative. Based on primary and secondary sources; 40 notes.
B. A. Glasrud

2440. Smith, John S. H. CIGARETTE PROHIBITION IN UTAH, 1921-23. *Utah Hist. Q. 1973 41(4): 358-372.* The tobacco prohibition movement was a lesser known attempt to legislate morality. Utah was one of more than a dozen states to enact such legislation. Traces the movement in the state from 1896 to 1923. In addition to the usual reasons for opposing the use of tobacco, it was a basic tenet of the Mormon Church. It was impossible to keep Mormon-Gentile antagonisms out of the issue. 4 illus., 53 notes.
D. L. Smith

2441. Smith, Norman W. THE KU KLUX KLAN IN RHODE ISLAND. *Rhode Island Hist. 1978 37(2): 35-45.* The Ku Klux Klan flowered briefly in Rhode Island during the 1920's and may have continued in the early 1930's. It attracted more rural than urban supporters, received encouragement from the Protestant clergy, had some links to the Republican Party, and was overwhelmingly anti-Catholic rather than anti-Jew or Negro. Based on interviews, manuscripts in the Rhode Island Historical Society (Providence), newspapers, and secondary accounts; 3 illus., 80 notes.
P. J. Coleman

2442. Springer, W. F. THE OMAHA INDIANS: WHAT THEY ASK OF THE UNITED STATES GOVERNMENT. *Indian Hist. 1976 9(1): 30-33.* An address by an Omaha Indian leader to the Nebraska Historical Society in 1928. Summarizes the history of the Omaha Indians and their decline from a populous tribe occupying most of the state to a few scattered individuals by the 1920's. Notes that a new organization, the Returned Students of Omaha, would attempt to get the federal government to reconstitute the Omaha Tribe and give it full civil rights.
E. D. Johnson

2443. Stark, Rodney; Bainbridge, William Sims; and Kent, Lori. CULT MEMBERSHIP IN THE ROARING TWENTIES: ASSESSING LOCAL RECEPTIVITY. *Sociol. Analysis 1981 42(2): 137-162.* A series of strangely neglected nationwide census studies of religion conducted by the Census Bureau during the first four decades of this century permits examination of the specific historical development of a number of important American cult movements. It also permits for the first time an analysis of cult membership rather than use of more inferential measures of cult activity and strength. The amazing stability in cult activity between the 1920's and the 1970's suggests the need for more basic theories of cult formation than those suggested by scholars who regard the rise of new religions as a new phenomenon.
J/S

2444. Stefon, Frederick J. SIGNIFICANCE OF THE MERIAM REPORT OF 1928. *Indian Historian 1975 8(3): 2-7, 46.* The Meriam Report (1928), compiled under the direction of Dr. Lewis Meriam for the Department of the Interior, studied the US Bureau of Indian Affairs and the conditions of the American Indians under its direction. The report revealed terrible conditions and resulted in the passage of the Indian Reorganization Act (1934), which reversed the government's policy of detribalization and brought about a new era in Indian-government relations. 37 notes, biblio.
E. D. Johnson

2445. Stegh, Leslie J. A PARADOX OF PROHIBITION: ELECTION OF ROBERT J. BULKLEY AS SENATOR FROM OHIO, 1930. *Ohio Hist. 1974 83(3): 170-182.* Analyzes the impact of the repeal issue on the election of the "wet" Democrat Robert J. Bulkley to the US Senate from Ohio in 1930. Though repeal gained nationwide attention in the campaign, many other factors played a role in Bulkley's victory: the economy, the Hawley-Smoot tariff, agricultural relief, personalities, and other issues. Based on the Bulkley papers, newspapers, and journals; table, photo, 32 notes.
J. B. Street

2446. Stein, Gary C. THE INDIAN CITIZENSHIP ACT OF 1924. *New Mexico Hist. R. 1972 47(3): 257-274.* President Calvin Coolidge on 2 June 1924 signed an act stating "that all noncitizen Indians born within the territorial limits of the United States" were to be US citizens "provided that the granting of such citizenship shall not in any manner impair or otherwise affect the right of any Indian to tribal or other property." The citizenship act did little to improve the condition of the Indian. The act seems to have been intended as a reform measure and not as reward for the Indians for their service in World War I or as a means to get their votes as some writers have claimed.
J. H. Krenkel

2447. Straw, Richard A. AN ACT OF FAITH: SOUTHEASTERN OHIO MINERS IN THE COAL STRIKE OF 1927. *Labor Hist. 1980 21(2): 221-238.* Studies the living conditions of miners in the Hocking Valley during the strike of 1927. Although miners were feverishly loyal to the United Mine Workers of America (UMW), the union lost the strike, a severe blow to the local and the national UMW, led by John L. Lewis. Based on government documents and local newspapers; 56 notes.
L. L. Athey

2448. Straw, Richard A. THE UNITED MINE WORKERS OF AMERICA AND THE 1920 COAL STRIKE IN ALABAMA. *Alabama R. 1975 28(2): 104-128.* The United Mine Workers ordered a general strike in Alabama in September, 1920 for higher wages and collective bargaining rights. Coal operators refused to negotiate, persuaded Governor Thomas E. Kilby to call out troops, and won a court injunction against the union. Strike forces weakened by February, 1921, with public opinion and state officials taking an anti-union stand, although the Birmingham press was more moderate and tried to promote a compromise. As in 1904 and 1908, the union failed in its objectives; only one United Mine Workers local functioned in Alabama by 1929, allowing mine operators to maintain open shop. Based on primary and secondary sources; 59 notes.
J. F. Vivian

2449. Swallow, Craig A. THE KU KLUX KLAN IN NEVADA DURING THE 1920S. *Nevada Hist. Soc. Q. 1981 24(3): 202-220.* During the 1920's, the Ku Klux Klan, using rhetoric against Orientals, attracted sympathizers in northern Nevada. It had limited influence, however, and functioned primarily as a social and fraternal organization. Conversely, the Klan prospered in southern Nevada. Its larger membership remained stable, participating in municipal politics and vigilantism. Based on newspaper sources and interviews; photo, 58 notes.
H. T. Lovin

2450. Swenson, Mary E. TO UPLIFT A STATE AND NATION: THE FORMATIVE YEARS OF THE ALABAMA LEAGUE OF WOMEN VOTERS, 1920-1921. *Alabama Hist. Q. 1975 37(2): 115-135.* The most difficult section the woman suffrage movement had to deal with was the South. When it appeared that the national government was going to enfranchise women, the National American Woman Suffrage Association began to plan for it. The League of Women Voters was organized at the NAWSA meeting in 1919. Its basic ideas included compulsory education to age 16, adult education, and citizenship. Following a period of internal dissension and opposition from the political parties, the League began to move forward. 83 notes.
E. E. Eminhizer

2451. Taggart, Robert J. PHILANTHROPY AND BLACK PUBLIC EDUCATION IN DELAWARE, 1918-1930. *Pennsylvania Mag. of Hist. and Biog. 1979 103(4): 467-483.* Gifts of Pierre du Pont improved black education, particularly in the building of schools. A side-effect was more viable segregation, yet du Pont's philanthropy ensured the rights of blacks to a decent schooling. Based on Longwood MS. and others, Eleutherian Mills Historical Library, official records, newspapers, and secondary works; 51 notes.
T. H. Wendel

2452. Taggart, Robert J. PIERRE S. DU PONT AND THE GREAT SCHOOL FIGHT OF 1919-1921. *Delaware Hist. 1977 17(3): 155-178.* Reviews Delaware's educational practices in the late 19th and early 20th centuries. The efforts of Pierre S. duPont and other reformers led to a modern state system of education through legislation enacted during 1919-21. The school laws transferred the funding and control from "a democratic and locally controlled system to a centralized and professionalized state system." Based largely on duPont correspondence and state records; 105 notes.
R. M. Miller

2453. Tanaka, Stefan. THE TOLEDO INCIDENT: THE DEPORTATION OF THE NIKKEI FROM AN OREGON MILL TOWN. *Pacific Northwest Q. 1978 69(3): 116-126.* During the mid-1920's the Pacific Spruce Corporation of Toledo, Oregon, began to import Japanese Americans for lumber mill work. Local white citizens established a nativist organization to stop the Oriental influx and this led to a riot during July, 1925. Though the Japanese were driven from Toledo, they received financial compensation for damages a year later. Based on newspapers and interviews; map, 4 photos, 43 notes.
M. L. Tate

2454. Thomison, Dennis. THE PRIVATE WARS OF CHICAGO'S BIG BILL THOMPSON. *J. of Lib. Hist. 1980 15(3): 261-280.* Describes a censorship campaign against Chicago school and library books conducted during and after the reelection of William Hale Thompson as mayor in 1927. Accusations focused on works leaning toward British interpretations of historical events, thus becoming a political issue in a city lacking a large anglophile constituency. Aided by William Randolph Hearst's newspaper and by patriotic organizations, the campaign met favor with the Chicago Public Library director and the head of the Municipal Reference Library. Soon, however, activities turned bizarre: attempts to replace teachers with civil servants; suspension of the superintendent of schools; a weird inquest into the matter by the school board; vituperative attacks on publications of the Chicago-based American Library Association, whose president then was a Canadian; an investigation of the Public Library collection by the library board; and the burning of a copy of Arthur M. Schlesinger, Sr.'s *New Viewpoints in American History* by one of its members. Upon the release of a pamphlet by opposing library board members revealing that Queen Victoria and prominent Britons had helped rebuild the Chicago Public Library following the 1871 fire, Chicagoans began viewing the campaign as ridiculous. It, consequently, died out as library circulation rose to unprecedented numbers. 85 notes.
D. J. Mycue

2455. Tolbert, Emory. OUTPOST GARVEYISM AND THE UNIA RANK AND FILE. *J. of Black Studies 1975 5(3): 233-253.* Studies the appeal to blacks in Los Angeles of Marcus Garvey's Universal Negro Improvement Association. He finds that the movement appealed mainly to upwardly-mobile Negroes and that it was more conservative than some of the chapters in the East. In Los Angeles the UNIA appealed to religious family men and acted in many ways as a black fraternity. Notes, biblio.
K. Butcher

2456. Toll, William. PROGRESS AND PIETY: THE KU KLUX KLAN AND SOCIAL CHANGE IN TILLAMOOK, OREGON. *Pacific Northwest Q. 1978 69(2): 75-85.* During the early 1920's the small Oregon town of Tillamook produced a sizable Ku Klux Klan membership. Its targets were not new racial or ethnic groups, which were virtually nonexistent in the community. Rather the local Klan attempted to preserve deep-rooted traditions against the influx of new "threats" such as the automobile, liquor, and transient-types employed in lumbering. The local Klan declined rapidly after 1925 as the citizens became less fearful of the outside threats. Primary and secondary sources; 2 photos, 3 tables, 31 notes.
M. L. Tate

2457. Toth, Charles W. SAMUEL GOMPERS, EL COMUNISMO Y LA FEDERACIÓN PANAMERICANA DEL TRABAJO [Samuel Gompers, Communism, and the Pan American Federation of Labor]. *Rev. de Ciencias Sociales [Puerto Rico] 1973 17(1): 95-101.* The threat of radical socialism was less dangerous than people thought in the 1920's, but it had some potential; Samuel Gompers saw the Pan American Federation of Labor as a bulwark against leftist dictatorships.

2458. Watkins, Ralph. THE MARCUS GARVEY MOVEMENT IN BUFFALO, NEW YORK. *Afro-Americans in New York Life and Hist. 1977 1(1): 37-48.* A rift occurred within the black community in Buffalo between established community members and many who migrated north during the 1920's: some of the migrants decided to organize an affiliate of Marcus Garvey's United Negro Improvement Association and African Communities League, to the displeasure of local black clergy who saw their power over community affairs in danger.

2459. Weisbord, Vera Buch. GASTONIA 1929: STRIKE AT THE LORAY MILL. *Southern Exposure 1974 1(3/4): 185-203.* The author, a labor organizer, views the textile workers' strike in which she was harassed, jailed, and tried on charges stemming from her participation in the strike. The National Textile Workers Union organized the strike which also was supported by International Labor Defense and the Young Communist League. Tension between white and black workers was exploited, while the National Guard were used as strikebreakers. The mills had not been unionized by 1974. Based on unpublished autobiography and oral interviews; 8 illus.
G. A. Bolton

2460. Whisenhunt, Donald W. THE TEXAN AS A RADICAL, 1929-1933. *Social Sci. J. 1977 14(3): 61-72.* Discusses the political reaction of Texans in the initial stages of the Depression, 1929-33, concentrating on radical reactions, demands for government action and general feelings of malaise for the capitalistic system and American traditions.

2461. Williams, David. THE BUREAU OF INVESTIGATION AND ITS CRITICS, 1919-1921: THE ORIGINS OF FEDERAL POLITICAL SURVEILLANCE. *J. of Am. Hist. 1981 68(3): 560-579.* Federal Bureau of Investigation surveillance of political dissent originated with American involvement in World War I, not with the Cold War. Investigations by J. Edgar Hoover, chief of the General Intelligence Division during the Red Scare, were systematic and pervasive and revealed the extreme antiradicalism in the bureau. Hoover learned that Congress and the president would tolerate the bureau's antiradical activities as long as they remained secret. Based in part on FBI files secured through the Freedom of Information Act; 49 notes.
T. P. Linkfield

2462. Williams, Lillian S., ed. ATTICA PRISONERS SEEK AID FROM NAACP (1932). *Afro-Am. in New York Life and Hist. 1977 1(2): 211-212.* Reprints a letter by black inmates of New York's Attica State Prison in 1932 asking the NAACP to investigate prison conditions of blacks.

2463. Woodruff, Nan E. THE FAILURE OF RELIEF DURING THE ARKANSAS DROUGHT OF 1930-1931. *Arkansas Hist. Q. 1980 39(4): 301-313.* Coming before real recovery from the disastrous Mississippi River flood of 1927, the drought of 1930 almost wiped out the plantation economy in the Arkansas Delta. Red Cross relief programs relied on the local planters' opinions and they minimized the sufferings of the starving black sharecroppers, delaying relief until after the harvest season so that the planters could get as much work out of the blacks as possible. Red Cross papers and secondary sources; 38 notes.
G. R. Schroeder

2464. Zanger, Martin. UPTON SINCLAIR AS CALIFORNIA'S SOCIALIST CANDIDATE FOR CONGRESS, 1920. *Southern California Q. 1974 56(4): 359-373.* Contrary to the view that prior to the 1934 gubernatorial campaign Upton Sinclair made only a token effort in several elections, Sinclair's ideas and plans of 1934 have clear antecedents in 1920, and the issues of the earlier race invite investigation. In 1920 Sinclair, despite the certainty that he would not win, consented to having his name placed on the ballot as the Socialist Party's candidate for Congress. He made several speeches attacking the Los Angeles *Times*, inflation, and poverty, advocating taxing excessive land ownership and banks run for private profit. Despite defeat, Sinclair's campaign made some achievements. He received more than twice as many Socialist votes as the previous Socialist candidate and ran ahead of presidential candidate Eugene V. Debs. Based on primary and secondary sources; illus., 34 notes.
A. Hoffman

2465. Zieger, Robert H. HERBERT HOOVER, THE WAGE-EARNER, AND THE "NEW ECONOMIC SYSTEM," 1919-1929. *Business Hist. Rev. 1977 51(2): 161-189.* Herbert Hoover regarded the labor issue as the greatest challenge facing American capitalism, feared union militancy as "wasteful and authoritarian," and favored employee representation systems in industry. During the 1920's, however, he was "curiously silent" on the subject, apparently unwilling to seriously examine the real nature of representation plans. Attributes this inaction in large part to Hoover's natural affinity for the new corporate managers who were the sponsors of welfare capitalism and company-sponsored unions. Based on Hoover papers and writings as well as other contemporary sources; 62 notes.
C. J. Pusateri

The New Deal Period

2466. Accinelli, Robert D. MILITANT INTERNATIONALISTS: THE LEAGUE OF NATIONS ASSOCIATION, THE PEACE MOVEMENT, AND U.S. FOREIGN POLICY, 1934-38. *Diplomatic Hist. 1980 4(1): 19-38.* During the 1930's, as pacifists and isolationists worked to prevent political involvement abroad, a less publicized wing of the American peace movement was advocating international cooperation. The most dynamic group in this coalition, the League of Nations Association, played a significant, if ultimately ineffectual, role, by keeping the internationalist viewpoint before Congress, president, and public in a time of rising isolationism. 67 notes.
T. L. Power

2467. Allen, John E. EUGENE TALMADGE AND THE GREAT TEXTILE STRIKE IN GEORGIA, SEPTEMBER 1934. Fink, Gary M. and Reed, Merl E., eds. *Essays in Southern Labor History: Selected Papers, Southern Labor History Conference, 1976.* (Westport, Conn.; London, England: Greenwood Pr., 1977): 224-243. Studies the history of the southern textile industry before and during the early years of the National Recovery Administration (NRA) as the setting for the strike of 1934, the course of the strike, and Governor Eugene Talmadge's role in getting the strike settled. That role was based philosophically in his staunchly conservative opposition to the whole NRA concept. The strike was an unmitigated disaster for Georgia's textile workers; no union men were rehired. Talmadge's duplicity regarding his intentions and "the brutality and flamboyance with which he suppressed the strike" was unprecedented. The workers were not fooled as to where his real loyalties lay, but the damage had been done. 74 notes.
R. V. Ritter

2468. Allen, William R. IRVING FISHER, F.D.R., AND THE GREAT DEPRESSION. *Hist. of Pol. Econ. 1977 9(4): 560-587.* Presents Professor Fisher's (1867-1947) analysis of and prescriptions for the Great Depression. Perhaps "the country's greatest scientific economist," he favored monetary remedies for the depression: reflation and stabilization of the dollar. He proposed 100% reserves against demand deposits in commercial banks, thus enabling monetary authorities to control the volume of money. His efforts were seconded by other leading economists, but the imminence of World War II blocked possible completion. 114 notes.
J. Tull

2469. August, Jack. THE ANTI-JAPANESE CRUSADE IN ARIZONA'S SALT RIVER VALLEY, 1934-35. *Arizona and the West 1979 21(2): 113-136.* The Japanese were highly successful and competitive farmers in Arizona's Salt River Valley. They circumvented state alien land laws through lease contracts and through their American-born children. The combination of their agricultural excellence and the depressed economic conditions of the 1930's evoked white militant reaction in 1934-35. Local white farmers organized to oust the Japanese farmers from the valley. Threats, terrorism, court and legal maneuvers, national press coverage, and political opportunism created a hostile anti-foreigner situation. The federal government applied pressure to quell the disturbance. The Salt River Valley anti-Japanese episode was not unique in western states. 4 illus., 52 notes.
D. L. Smith

2470. Avery, Inda. SOME SOUTH DAKOTANS' OPINIONS ABOUT THE NEW DEAL. *South Dakota Hist. 1977 7(3): 309-324.* Traces South Dakota's economy during the Great Depression, and discusses responses to a 14-point questionnaire about the hardships and attitudes about New Deal relief policies. South Dakotans share in a "western split personality:" they boast of individualistic self-sufficiency and vote conservatively in local elections, yet they send liberals to Congress and readily accept welfare from the national level. Notes reluctance to admit accepting relief along with the admission that their friends do. 164 persons in 55 counties responded to 500 questionnaires. 3 photos, 8 notes, appendix.
A. J. Larson

2471. Babu, B. Ramesh. UNEMPLOYMENT INSURANCE IN THE UNITED STATES: AN ANALYSIS OF THE BEGINNING. *J. of the U. of Bombay [India] 1975-76 44-45(80-81): 139-172.* The Social Security Act (US, 1935), which provided for unemployment insurance, was part of Franklin D. Roosevelts second New Deal. Although intended to counter criticism from the left, the Act was in fact a middle-of-the-road policy. It was preceded in 1934 by two attempts at unemployment insurance which failed to secure Congressional approval: the Wagner-Lewis Bill, intended to encourage the states to provide benefits, and the Lundeen Bill, which proposed coverage for persons who had been unable to secure employment for a minimum period. The Committee on Economic Security, appointed in 1934 to advise Roosevelt on social security, placed more emphasis on job creation than on unemployment insurance. They recommended a federal-state system based on tax credits. The Social Security Act, based on their recommendations but modified somewhat by the House of Representatives and the Senate, became law on 14 August 1935. Although the unemployment insurance provisions, criticized by the left and the right, were less impressive than some of its others, the Act as a whole was a major development in the evolution of the United States as a welfare state. Published government documents, contemporary newspapers and journals and secondary works; 87 notes.
J. F. Hilliker

2472. Barber, Henry E. THE ASSOCIATION OF SOUTHERN WOMEN FOR THE PREVENTION OF LYNCHING, 1930-1942. *Phylon 1973 34(4): 378-389.* Studies the effects of the Association of Southern Women for the Prevention of Lynching, 1930-42.
S

2473. Baskerville, Stephen W. FRANKFURTER, KEYNES AND THE FIGHT FOR PUBLIC WORKS, 1932-1935. *Maryland Hist. 1978 9(1): 1-16.* Summarizes the campaign led by Felix Frankfurter and assisted by John Maynard Keynes to influence New Deal decisions on public works and other policies. The ideas of Keynes were injected into policy because of the constant efforts of Frankfurter and Keynes's willingness to market them in the press and other public forums. Based on correspondence and secondary sources; photo, 58 notes.
G. O. Gagnon

2474. Baughman, James L. CLASSES AND COMPANY TOWNS: LEGENDS OF THE 1937 LITTLE STEEL STRIKE. *Ohio Hist. 1978 87(2): 175-192.* Examines events in Canton, Youngstown, and Warren (Ohio) during the 1937 "Little Steel" strike, the first major strike since 1919. Discusses the relationship of the communities to the month-long labor-management conflict. After the strike of the Youngstown Sheet and Tube, Inland Steel, and Republic Steel, not solidarity but demoralization and internal division characterized the employees. The union never came close to victory—after four weeks the laborers began filing back into the mills and the managers had halted the impressive advance for CIO organization in the nation's basic industries. Through examination of the communities involved, discusses why the union lost. Based on primary and secondary sources; 3 illus., 48 notes.
N. Summers

2475. Bauman, John F. BLACK SLUMS/BLACK PROJECTS: THE NEW DEAL AND NEGRO HOUSING IN PHILADELPHIA. *Pennsylvania Hist. 1974 41(3): 311-338.* The first two New Deal housing projects in Philadelphia were restricted to whites despite the fact that black housing conditions in the city were deplorable. The Philadelphia chapter of the National Negro Congress and the Tenants League led efforts to assure that future federal housing would be used to help Philadelphia Negroes. The fact that black votes had contributed to Democratic victories in Philadelphia was not lost upon New Deal policymakers, and federal funds made available through the Wagner-Steagall Act of 1938, built two housing projects for blacks. Notes that the projects were developed in such a way as to limit the expansion of black neighborhoods and reinforce segregation patterns. Based on Housing Division Records, Housing Association Papers, government reports and other materials; 2 illus., 31 notes.   D. C. Swift

2476. Beddow, James B. DEPRESSION AND NEW DEAL: LETTERS FROM THE PLAINS. *Kansas Hist. Q. 1977 43(2): 140-153.* Statistics show the impact of the depression and New Deal on farmers of the Great Plains, but they do not capture the emotional trauma and attitudinal change effected by hard times. Few farmers bothered to write national and state legislators during the booming 1920's, but during the 1930's files bulge with letters from rural constituents explaining the causes of the depression, expounding on the discrimination that broke small farmers and enriched speculators and corporate farmers, and aiming shafts at the New Deal's reliance on nonagricultural theorists and the regimentation of the AAA. Archival material in Washington, D.C., Minnesota, South Dakota, North Dakota, and Kansas; 52 notes.
W. F. Zornow

2477. Beezer, Bruce G. ARTHURDALE: AN EXPERIMENT IN COMMUNITY EDUCATION. *West Virginia Hist. 1974 36(1): 17-36.* The Arthurdale community was a New Deal experiment in rural homesteading which resettled 200 poor West Virginia coal mining families. Run by a succession of government agencies in the 1930's and with the heavy unofficial involvement of Eleanor Roosevelt, Arthurdale cost far more than expected and failed chiefly because there was no industry located there to provide permanent jobs. The Arthurdale school, run by Elsie Ripley Clapp, tried with some limited success to apply John Dewey's educational ideas about community-oriented schooling. Based on Clapp's own account and contemporary articles; 76 notes.
J. H. Broussard

2478. Biebel, Charles D. PRIVATE FOUNDATIONS AND PUBLIC POLICY: THE CASE OF SECONDARY EDUCATION DURING THE GREAT DEPRESSION. *Hist. of Educ. Q. 1976 16(1): 3-34.* To bring about social change within secondary education during the 1930's, John D. Rockefeller's General Education Board used manipulation and control of established institutions and educational associations.

2479. Birch, Eugenie Ladner. WOMAN-MADE AMERICA: THE CASE OF EARLY PUBLIC HOUSING POLICY. *J. of the Am. Inst. of Planners 1978 44(2): 130-144.* The 1937 Wagner-Steagall Act provided for the first permanent public housing program subsidized by the federal government. Although immediate economic conditions caused by the Depression provided the direct impetus for its passage, a painstakingly constructed intellectual background and grass-roots political support created the climate for its acceptance. This atmosphere was the product of the work of many housing reformers. However, two women, Edith Elmer Wood and Catherine Bauer, stand out as leaders having the most significant impact on the formulation of the new policy. As women, they contributed two major facets to it: the recognition of the need for government construction of dwellings when the private sector did not build; the demand that publicly constructed homes be positively supportive of family life.   J

2480. Blayney, Michael S. "LIBRARIES FOR THE MILLIONS": ADULT PUBLIC LIBRARY SERVICES AND THE NEW DEAL. *J. of Lib. Hist. 1977 12(3): 235-249.* New Deal library programs created jobs for many white-collar workers and helped put culture back into the everyday life of the working people. New Deal library projects were initiated through expanded public library services in adult education and rural extension. These changes had a lasting impact on the library profession. Based on primary and secondary sources; 37 notes.
A. C. Dewees

2481. Bonthius, Andrew. ORIGINS OF THE INTERNATIONAL LONGSHOREMEN'S AND WAREHOUSEMEN'S UNION. *Southern California Q. 1977 59(4): 379-426.* Traces the organization of longshoremen and warehousemen on the Pacific Coast from the founding of the International Longshoremen's Union in 1934 to the merger of their union and warehousemen's union into the International Longshoremen's and Warehousemen's Union in 1937. Longshoremen had been neglected by American Federation of Labor leadership for decades; they endured company unions, low wages, and wretched working conditions. Under radical and Communist leadership, the ILA made dramatic gains in the mid-1930's, eventually achieving affiliation with the Congress of Industrial Organizations. Finding duplication in their work, the ILA and the warehousemen's union worked for common goals and eventual merger. Opposition came from the AFL hierarchy and the International Brotherhood of Teamsters. In an era filled with strikes, violence, and internecine labor struggles, the ILWU emerged as a powerful, militant union which successfully achieved a working relationship with the forces of capital. Primary and secondary sources; 131 notes.   A. Hoffman

2482. Boryczka, Ray. MILITANCY AND FACTIONALISM IN THE UNITED AUTO WORKERS UNION, 1937-1941. *Maryland Hist. 1977 8(2): 13-25.* Traces the impact of factionalism on United Automobile Workers of America efforts to generate consistent rank and file militancy. Concludes that pragmatic, self-serving factionalism prevented organized militancy. Based on oral and printed primary sources and secondary sources; illus., 33 notes.   G. O. Gagnon

2483. Brax, Ralph S. WHEN STUDENTS FIRST ORGANIZED AGAINST WAR. *New-York Hist. Soc. Q. 1979 63(3): 228-255.* College student unrest was not new in the 20th century. However, before the 1930's it usually was directed against campus problems. During the Great Depression unrest increased, not, as one might have expected, against the economic system, but concentrating by the mid-1930's on an opposition to war. Sparked at first by socialist and communist groups, three nationwide student strikes were held, the last in 1936 supposedly including half a million students, but probably no more than 350,000. The majority of the million college students took little or no active part. Yet, some success was attained even though the movement collapsed when the nation found itself in World War II. Primary sources; 4 illus., 56 notes.
C. L. Grant

2484. Bremer, William W. ALONG THE "AMERICAN WAY": THE NEW DEAL'S WORK RELIEF PROGRAMS FOR THE UNEMPLOYED. *J. of Am. Hist. 1975 62(3): 636-652.* Describes the ideal of a constructive and psychologically supportive work relief program formulated by New Deal administrators and social workers, including Harry Hopkins, William Matthews, and Homer Folks, and its partial and temporary implementation in the Civil Works Administration of 1933-34. Political and budgetary pressures soon ended the CWA experiment. Instead, more traditional relief practices were adopted which kept work relief less attractive than private employment and retained the animus of charity. New Dealers did not view work relief as a permanent policy which guaranteed a "right to work." Based on collected papers, journals, and secondary works; 70 notes.   J. B. Street

2485. Brinkley, Alan. HUEY LONG, THE SHARE OUR WEALTH MOVEMENT, AND THE LIMITS OF DEPRESSION DISSIDENCE. *Lousiana Hist. 1981 22(2): 117-134.* From his entrance into the US Senate in 1932 until his death in 1935, Huey P. Long of Louisiana was the head of a powerful national movement. At the center of this movement were the Share Our Wealth clubs. The Share Our Wealth plan called for high income taxes, estate taxes, and capital levies to limit fortunes. This money would be redistributed to the poor. The movement, however, was ideologically diverse and organizationally loose. Thus, though it enjoyed support, that support was not as focused as in many mass movements. Primary sources; 44 notes.   J. Powell

2486. Bromert, Roger. THE SIOUX AND THE INDIAN-CCC. *South Dakota Hist. 1978 8(4): 340-356.* Studies measures taken to improve the condition of Indians, economically, educationally, and in health. The special Civilian Conservation Corps (Indian Division) programs were very popular with the Sioux Indians, 1933-42. The projects significantly helped the reservations by way of road building, dams, reclamation projects, etc., in addition to the value to the Indians personally.

The educational values incidental to carrying out the other projects were of major consequence. 7 photos, 38 notes.
R. V. Ritter

2487. Bulkley, Peter B. AGRARIAN CRISIS IN WESTERN NEW YORK: NEW DEAL REINFORCEMENT OF THE FARM DEPRESSION. *New York Hist. 1978 59(4): 391-407.* Examines the effect of New Deal farm policy on Allegany, Cattaraugus, and Chautauqua counties during 1934, and concludes that the policies of the Agricultural Adjustment Administration prolonged the agricultural depression in those counties. The problem in western New York was not a farm surplus but oligopoly in the field of distribution. The AAA's response to the problem was to stress urban consumption rather than restoration of the farmers' purchasing power. The AAA benefited the large commodity farms in the south and west rather than the small, diversified farms that prevailed in western New York. 5 tables, 7 illus., 54 notes.
R. N. Lokken

2488. Carlisle, Rodney P. WILLIAM RANDOLPH HEARST: A FASCIST REPUTATION RECONSIDERED. *Journalism Q. 1973 50(1): 125-133.* There was little change in the Progressivism of William Randolph Hearst during the New Deal—his break with Roosevelt was a consequence of the 1935 Wealth Tax.
S

2489. Carr, Joe Daniel. LABOR CONFLICT IN THE EASTERN KENTUCKY COAL FIELDS. *Filson Club Hist. Q. 1973 47(2): 179-192.* Analyzes the industrial conflict in Harlan and Bell counties in eastern Kentucky during the 1930's, providing graphic examples of the exploitation of miners by the mining corporations. Violent confrontations at Evarts in 1931 and at Stanfill in 1939 are investigated in depth, and the roles of the United Mine Workers, the National Recovery Administration, and the National Labor Relations Board are also explored. Exposes the failure of the judicial system and the corruption of Harlan County sheriff Theodore Middleton. Based on the Louisville *Courier-Journal* and the New York *Times*; 58 notes.
G. B. McKinney

2490. Cassity, Michael J. HUEY LONG: BAROMETER OF REFORM IN THE NEW DEAL. *South Atlantic Q. 1973 72(2): 255-269.* "In his criticism of the New Deal, Long focused on what appeared to be a centralization of wealth and power." He assailed the establishment of regulatory commissions under the NRA as a reversal of the intent of the antitrust legislation. He contended that this sort of legislation removed public control, thus threatening democracy. In agriculture the New Deal did not respond to the needs of small farmers. Instead of the Civilian Conservation Corps he proposed giving young men an education. "Instead of widening the chasm between the very rich and the very poor he proposed to limit the depths to which a person could fall and to put a maximum on the profits he could accumulate." He was an eloquent spokesman for the progressive tradition of reform. 54 notes.
E. P. Stickney

2491. Christie, Jean. NEW DEAL RESOURCES PLANNING: THE PROPOSALS OF MORRIS L. COOKE. *Agric. Hist. 1979 53(3): 597-606.* Morris L. Cooke, independently wealthy former advisor to Pennsylvania Governor Gifford Pinchot, served as head of a number of New Deal agencies dealing with land and water conservation. Cooke's approach to conservation was a regional one. He believed in the watershed and river valley as the smallest division of a conservation unit. Cooke served with the Rural Electrification Administration and other government agencies until the era of conservation reform ended under President Harry S. Truman, who was preoccupied with the Korean War. Primary and secondary sources; 23 notes.
R. T. Fulton

2492. Coode, Thomas H. and Fabbri, Dennis E. THE NEW DEAL'S ARTHURDALE PROJECT IN WEST VIRGINIA. *West Virginia Hist. 1975 36(4): 291-308.* Arthurdale was the first self-help project funded under the National Industrial Recovery Act's Subsistence Homesteads Program to resettle unemployed miners on subsistence farms. Families were selected only after thorough investigation, and only native whites were allowed. From the beginning, Arthurdale suffered from mismanagement, delays, and cost overruns. Mrs. Eleanor Roosevelt and Louis Howe, though having no official connection with the project, intervened continually. Plans to attract industry never worked out, and cooperative farming failed also. Arthurdale was the most publicized project in the country and was extremely controversial. Finally, the government sold off the houses during World War II at a great loss. Based on Bushrod Grimes MSS and other primary sources; 49 notes.
J. H. Broussard

2493. Cooney, Terry A. COSMOPOLITAN VALUES AND THE IDENTIFICATION OF REACTION: *PARTISAN REVIEW* IN THE 1930S. *J. of Am. Hist. 1981 68(3): 580-598.* Examines the shift in editorial emphasis in the *Partisan Review* from Communism to anti-Stalinism during the 1930's. The commitment by editors like William Phillips and Philip Rahv to cosmopolitan cultural values provided a basic continuity to the shift. First Communism and then anti-Stalinist socialism stood for cosmopolitan cultural values. 40 notes.
T. P. Linkfield

2494. Damiani, Alessandro. I COMMUNISTI E IL MOVIMENTO OPERAIO DENTRO LA CRISI: LA LIQUIDAZIONE DEI SINDICATI ROSSI, 1933-1935 [The communists and the workers' movement during the crisis: the liquidation of the red unions, 1933-1935]. *Movimento Operaio e Socialista [Italy] 1976 22(1-2): 87-110.* The year 1933 signaled the growth of worker agitation in the United States. The communist Trade Union Unity League (TUUL), which grew rapidly and proportionately more than the American Federation of Labor, was unable to keep in step with the increased radicalism of its members and the leadership necessary for a true revolutionary party of the masses. By late 1933 the Communist Party was vigorously supporting its old policy of "bore from within." The National Executive Committee of the TUUL proposed in October of 1934 to unify all unions, ultimately leading to the dissolution of the TUUL and many other independent unions. The entrance of large numbers of Communists into the AFL was undoubtedly an important cause of the breakup of the union movement and the eventual formation of the Committee for Industrial Organization, thus representing the first determining role ever played by the Communist Party in the workers' movement. Primary and secondary sources; 44 notes.
M. T. Wilson

2495. Daniel, Cletus E. AGRICULTURAL UNIONISM AND THE EARLY NEW DEAL: THE CALIFORNIA EXPERIENCE. *Southern California Q. 1977 59(2): 185-215.* Argues that the Franklin D. Roosevelt administraton, in the first phase of its New Deal policies, undercut the development of agricultural unionism in California. New Deal economic planners at first envisioned a harmonious relationship between employers and workers brought about through active federal mediation under the National Industrial Recovery Act (NIRA). Although New Deal labor policy dramatically changed after the end of the NIRA and the passage of the Wagner Act, California's agricultural labor movement suffered irreparably from the involvement of George Creel, self-styled NIRA mediator, in the San Joaquin cotton strike of October 1933. Creel effected a compromise which the Communist-led union accepted, and the chance to create an effective agricultural workers' union was lost. The Department of Labor sent Pelham Glassford to mediate labor disputes in the Imperial Valley. In 1934 he undercut the union by endorsing a company union, only to find that employers rejected both federal involvement and the company union. Thus the New Deal, remembered for its liberalism and reform, promoted the destruction of a vigorous effort to organize California agriculture. Primary and secondary sources; 68 notes.
A. Hoffman

2496. Daniel, Cletus E. WOBBLIES ON THE FARM: THE IWW IN THE YAKIMA VALLEY. *Pacific Northwest Q. 1974 65(4): 166-175.* A study of the 1933 efforts of the reactivated Industrial Workers of the World ("Wobblies") to organize the fruit workers of the Yakima Valley. When picket lines were formed to enforce a strike the farmers organized into vigilante groups. The most notable and violent confrontation was at Congdon's Orchard, in the course of which a large number of strikers were turned over to county authorities for arrest and trial. The farmers gained the sympathies of the area on "patriotic" grounds as a mask for their antiunionism, and the "Wobblies" were never again able to successfully revive their efforts. 51 notes.
R. V. Ritter

2497. Davin, Eric Leif and Lynd, Staughton. PICKET LINE AND BALLOT BOX: THE FORGOTTEN LEGACY OF THE LOCAL LABOR PARTY MOVEMENT, 1932-1936. *Radical Hist. Rev. 1979-80 (22): 43-63.* Using Berlin, New Hampshire, as a case study, discusses the widespread working-class participation in state and local politics through the formation of independent labor and farmer-labor parties during 1932-36, and the destruction of the movement in 1936 by the Congress of Industrial Organizations through the Non-Partisan League.

2498. De Marco, Joseph P. THE RATIONALE AND FOUNDATION OF DU BOIS'S THEORY OF ECONOMIC CO-OPERATION. *Phylon 1974 35(1): 5-15.* In 1940 W. E. B. DuBois evolved a careful, rational, and realistic plan for the economic betterment of a minority group during a severe depression. His plan called for a segregated racial economic cooperative. He rejected a communist solution. Cooperation was a primary aspect of African tribal life which carried over into slavery. He believed segregation could be overcome only if it was used to advantage through cooperation. "Partly through his examination of the effectiveness of boycotts he considered that the economic cycle began not with production, as most Americans assumed, but with consumption." A racial consumers' cooperative would be sound because it based production on consumer needs. He failed to foresee the adoption of new economic policies by the government. 46 notes. E. P. Stickney

2499. DeWitt, Howard A. THE FILIPINO LABOR UNION: THE SALINAS LETTUCE STRIKE OF 1934. *Amerasia J. 1978 5(2): 1-21.* The Salinas, California, lettuce strike of 1934, though easily broken, was "a seminal turning point" in the evolution of organized Filipino labor. For the first time, a Filipino organization, the Filipino Labor Union, retained its structure and cohesion throughout the conflict. Despite the Salinas defeat, Filipino labor became more militant afterward, and destroyed the stereotype of the happy immigrant content to labor long hours at menial tasks for low wages. 68 notes. T. L. Powers

2500. Dinwoodie, D. H. DEPORTATION: THE IMMIGRATION SERVICE AND THE CHICANO LABOR MOVEMENT IN THE 1930S. *New Mexico Hist. Rev. 1977 52(3): 193-206.* During the 1930's, Chicanos were the object of much investigation as to whether they had entered the United States illegally. The investigations generally took place when the immigrants organized labor unions. In 1935, Julio Herrera was deported on charges that he had entered the United States illegally. The following year Jesus Pallares was deported, after subversion charges were brought against him. Actually he was deported as a result of his activities in organizing the *Liga Obrera de Habla Español.* Chicanos were encouraged to organize labor unions by the policies of the New Deal, although local authorities were opposed to these policies. 39 notes.
J. H. Krenkel

2501. Doenecke, Justus D. NON-INTERVENTION OF THE LEFT: THE KEEP AMERICA OUT OF THE WAR CONGRESS, 1938-41. *J. of Contemporary Hist. [Great Britain] 1977 12(2): 221-236.* After Norman Thomas visited Europe in 1937, he was ordered by the Socialist Party to form an antiwar coalition. Accordingly, the Keep America Out of War Congress was officially founded in New York on 6 March 1938, under the veteran pacifist reformer, Oswald Garrison Villard. The KAOWC was a makeshift coalition of left-wing pacifist groups. Its ideological tenets were also a potpourri: jobs at home rather than abroad, anti-Asian involvement, neutrality, food not guns, etc. With the proximity of war, the movement dwindled. It died after Pearl Harbor. Based on materials in the Papers of the Socialist Party, Duke University; 51 notes.
M. P. Trauth

2502. Duram, James C. CONSTITUTIONAL CONSERVATISM: THE KANSAS PRESS AND THE NEW DEAL ERA AS A CASE STUDY. *Kansas Hist. Q. 1977 43(4): 432-447.* Analyzes the editorial treatment of constitutional law issues of the New Deal in 46 Kansas newspapers in 1934-35. The editorial response of the Kansas press to the New Deal was the product of the Republican backgrounds and probusiness attitudes of the editors. Many editorials excoriated the New Deal for excessive regulation of business, wild spending, socialistic concepts, dangerous experimentation, and hastily drawn legislation. Most of the Kansas papers welcomed the Supreme Court's decisions on legislation, and criticized some decisions for not being more conservative than they were. Primary sources; 2 tables, 46 notes. A. W. Howell

2503. Duram, James C. THE LABOR UNION JOURNALS AND THE CONSTITUTIONAL ISSUES OF THE NEW DEAL: THE CASE FOR COURT RESTRICTION. *Labor Hist. 1974 15(2): 216-238.* Assesses the editorial position of labor union periodicals on the constitutional issues posed by the New Deal between 1935 and 1937. A liberal interpretation of the constitution was demanded which would allow comprehensive economic and social legislation. The journals reacted to specific court decisions and carried general articles on judicial reform. During the court fight of 1937, labor union journals favored reorganization of the judiciary. The editorials reflect a relationship between the group's economic and constitutional positions and the fact that labor gave up its traditional independent approach to politics in the 1930's. 70 notes, appendix. L. L. Athey

2504. Echols, James P. JACKSON RALSTON AND THE LAST SINGLE TAX CAMPAIGN. *California History 1979 58(3): 256-263.* Describes the effort of Jackson Ralston (1857-1946) to base California's tax structure on land values. A successful lawyer favorable to labor, civil rights, and international legal issues, Ralston retired to California in 1924. With the Great Depression, Ralston came to oppose California's Riley-Stewart Amendment which collected a state sales tax. Ralston commenced a struggle to remove the regressive tax and instead base the revenue tax on land values, reviving Henry George's famous idea. In using the initiative process Ralston and his supporters faced an uphill struggle in obtaining signatures, fighting legal technicalities, and meeting an active coalition of opponents. After long delays Ralston succeeded in placing his amendment on the 1938 election ballot, only to see it defeated by a 5 to 1 margin as Californians who may have appreciated the plan failed to vote for it. Ralston's effort illustrated the difficulty of enacting grass-roots reform measures through initiatives. Primary and secondary sources; illus., photos, 22 notes. A. Hoffman

2505. Filippelli, Ronald L. UE: THE FORMATIVE YEARS, 1933-1937. *Labor Hist. 1976 17(3): 351-371.* Study of the formation of the United Electrical and Radio Workers of America reveals its origins in the Philadelphia Philco strike of 1933, the early struggles over industrial vs. craft unionism, and three major groups for union activities among the U.E. All the elements for later internecine warfare were prevalent in the U.E. before 1937. Based on files of the U.E., oral interviews, and the Pennsylvania State University Labor Collection; 60 notes.
L. L. Athey

2506. Finkle, Lee. QUOTAS OR INTEGRATION: THE NAACP VERSUS THE PITTSBURGH "COURIER" AND THE COMMITTEE ON PARTICIPATION OF NEGROES. *Journalism Q. 1975 52(1): 76-84.* In 1938, the Pittsburgh *Courier* began a movement to open all branches of the Army to blacks on a percentage basis. It supported the Committee on Participation of Negroes in the National Defense Program. The National Association for the Advancement of Colored People had no positive program, but it participated in a move to insert a non-discrimination clause in the conscription bill. Blacks considered the White House announcement sanctioning Army segregation an insult, and the *Courier* altered its position to advocate integration. Primary and secondary sources; 55 notes. K. J. Puffer

2507. Fram, Leon. DETROIT JEWRY'S FINEST HOUR. *Michigan Jewish Hist. 1978 18(2): 14-19.* The author reminisces about his leadership role in Detroit's League for Human Rights during 1930's-40's, boycotting Nazi goods and services, and organizing a campaign of resistance to Nazism.

2508. Fry, Joseph A. RAYON, RIOT, AND REPRESSION: THE COVINGTON SIT-DOWN STRIKE OF 1937. *Virginia Mag. of Hist. and Biog. 1976 84(1): 3-18.* The attempt by the Textile Workers Organizing Committee to organize the Industrial Rayon Corporation's plant in Covington, Virginia, illustrates the problems which faced union leaders in the South. Though the movement did result in Virginia's first significant sit-down strike, the support of state officials and police for the management produced violence and ultimate failure. Based on the George C. Peery Papers, Virginia State Library, interviews with participants, newspapers, and additional primary sources; 55 notes.
R. F. Oakes

2509. Furlow, John W., Jr. CORNELIA BRYCE PINCHOT: FEMINISM IN THE POST-SUFFRAGE ERA. *Pennsylvania Hist. 1976 43(4): 329-346.* In the 1920's, Cornelia Pinchot was drawn into politics through her husband, Gifford Pinchot, and she became an effective public speaker. The first woman to serve on the Republican state committee, she also helped found the Pennsylvania Council of Republican Women. In the 1930's, Mrs. Pinchot increasingly pursued an independent course by advocating a variety of social reforms. She is considered a social feminist because she considered social justice programs more important than measures that provided women with legal and employment equality with men. Based on the Cornelia Bryce Pinchot Papers and other materials; illus., 70 notes.

D. C. Swift

2510. Garvey, Timothy J. THE DULUTH HOMESTEADS: A SUCCESSFUL EXPERIMENT IN COMMUNITY HOUSING. *Minnesota Hist. 1978 46(1): 2-16.* Duluth's suburban federal subsistence homestead program started in 1936 and remained under various forms of government control until the homesteads were turned over to private interests in 1947. In mid-March 1938 84 homesteads were occupied by persons contracting to buy their government-built homes and adjacent land on an installment basis and to live in accordance with the rules of a community-based association of home owners. The residents appear to have been carefully selected for the venture and represented a group of "achievers" who maintained and improved their property. Most of the residents worked as part-time farmers and held other jobs whenever they could to pay off the considerable amounts charged by the government for the properties involved. The Duluth homestead project was among the most successful ventures of its type inaugurated by the New Deal, initially under the Interior Department and later by the Resettlement Administration. Primary research and oral interviews.

N. Lederer

2511. Gilbert, Jess and Brown, Steve. ALTERNATIVE LAND REFORM PROPOSALS IN THE 1930S: THE NASHVILLE AGRARIANS AND THE SOUTHERN TENANT FARMERS' UNION. *Agric. Hist. 1981 55(4): 351-369.* The Nashville Agrarians and Southern Tenant Farmers' Union presented alternatives to the New Deal's farm programs that attacked corporate capitalism and urged land reform. The Nashville Agrarians, a group of southern writers and social scientists who wrote *I'll Take My Stand,* opposed industrialism and sought a return to the small, diversified, self-sufficient farms of the early republic. The Southern Tenant Farmers' Union, an Arkansas-based group with socialist roots, wanted the government to buy farmland and lease it to small farmers, tenants, and cooperatives. Neither organization was able to get a strong farm tenant law through Congress, and by the late 1930's the movement had subsided. 50 notes.

D. E. Bowers

2512. Goodenow, Ronald K. PARADOX IN PROGRESSIVE EDUCATIONAL REFORM: THE SOUTH AND THE EDUCATION OF BLACKS IN THE DEPRESSION YEARS. *Phylon 1978 39(1): 49-65.* Progressive educational reforms in the South seemingly functioned to serve modernization, but paradoxically maintained racist patterns which were contradictory to progressive ideology. White educators emphasized occupational training for blacks at the expense of academic preparation and also advocated a biracial, segregated South. Black criticism of progressive education has called for testing the democratic ideology against the real conditions of oppression. Primary and secondary sources; 74 notes.

J. Moore

2513. Goodenow, Ronald K. THE PROGRESSIVE EDUCATOR, RACE AND ETHNICITY IN THE DEPRESSION YEARS: AN OVERVIEW. *Hist. of Educ. Q. 1975 15(4): 365-394.* Focuses on the positions of progressive educators regarding race and ethnicity in the United States during the Depression and their subsequent influence on education and society.

2514. Gower, Calvin W. THE STRUGGLE OF BLACKS FOR LEADERSHIP POSITIONS IN THE CIVILIAN CONSERVATION CORPS: 1933-1942. *J. of Negro Hist. 1976 61(2): 123-135.* The efforts of Negroes to gain equal opportunities through leadership positions in the Civilian Conservation Corps were not successful. This experience reflects the general failure of Afro-Americans to obtain significant improvement for themselves during the New Deal. Based on the records of the Civilian Conservation Corps; 24 notes.

N. G. Sapper

2515. Green, Joe L. THE EDUCATIONAL SIGNIFICANCE OF HUEY P. LONG. *Louisiana Studies 1974 13(3): 263-277.* Studies the influence of Huey P. Long on education. What was "the meaning of his leadership as a phenomenon of culture in his native Louisiana, the residual effects of which have extended into the present?" Based on a schematic model of "the hero in history," concludes that "his appeal to the people was through actions which sought to rectify the deplorable educational situation" in which the economic elite exploited the ignorance of the masses. "His aim . . . was to liberate the oppressed masses through better and more accessible education." Diagram, 41 notes.

R. V. Ritter

2516. Hall, Jacquelyn Dowd. A TRULY SUBVERSIVE AFFAIR: WOMEN AGAINST LYNCHING IN THE TWENTIETH-CENTURY SOUTH. Berkin, Carol Ruth and Norton, Mary Beth, ed. *Women of America: A History* (Boston: Houghton Mifflin Co., 1979): 360-388. Texas suffragist Jessie Daniel Ames founded the Association of Southern Women for the Prevention of Lynching (ASWPL) in 1930 in reaction to the southern tradition of extralegal racial violence. Earlier organizations had existed, connected with the Methodist Woman's Missionary Council and black YWCA. Jessie Ames also wished to kill the chivalric assumptions inherent in lynchings, which were a potent symbol of white male supremacy and an expression of a "Southern rape complex." Based on ASWPL papers; 2 tables, 15 notes.

K. Talley

2517. Heinemann, Ronald L. BLUE EAGLE OR BLACK BUZZARD? THE NATIONAL RECOVERY ADMINISTRATION IN VIRGINIA. *Virginia Mag. of Hist. and Biog. 1981 89(1): 90-100.* Interprets the rise and fall of the National Recovery Administration (NRA). Initial enthusiasm for this New Deal program in mid-1933 faded when resistance to enforcement of many of its codes developed, mostly over wage and hour violations. The NRA simultaneously fought the customary southern versus northern wage differential, cut hours and discharges instead of wage rates, a mixed reaction from business, and a generally hostile press. In May 1935 the US Supreme Court declared the NRA unconstitutional. 29 notes.

P. J. Woehrmann

2518. Hendrick, Irving G. CALIFORNIA'S RESPONSE TO THE "NEW EDUCATION" IN THE 1930's. *California Hist. Q. 1974 53(1): 25-40.* During the 1930's California educators responded favorably to the idea of "progressive education." California became a leader in implementation of progressive education programs, encouraged by State Superintendent of Public Instruction Vierling Kersey and Helen Heffernan, chief of the State Bureau of Elementary Education. Efforts were made to relieve school curricula from excessive rigidity in course content and methods of grading. The public accepted the movement, though educators themselves were cautious of favoring fads and frills over basic subjects. The overall effect of the "new" education was less impressive than the rhetoric about it, due to bureaucratic inertia and the control of a wide range of sanctioning bodies with various policy positions. Many current ideas regarding educational reform are similar to those of the 1930's, the chief difference being that in the 1930's educators were accepted as the makers of their own reforms. Based on government reports and published studies; illus., photo, 52 notes.

A. Hoffman

2519. Hendrickson, Kenneth E., Jr. THE CIVILIAN CONSERVATION CORPS IN SOUTH DAKOTA. *South Dakota Hist. 1980 11(1): 1-20.* Discusses the administration, organization, and achievements of the Civilian Conservation Corps (CCC) in South Dakota between 1933 and 1942. The CCC was one of the most effective federal relief programs in South Dakota. The program provided employment for more than 26,000 men and distributed over six million dollars to their families. The program also improved the South Dakota environment, particularly through soil conservation, timber stand improvement, and control of forest fires. Based on the records of the Civilian Conservation Corps-South Dakota in the National Archives, Washington, D.C., and other primary sources; 12 photos, 37 notes.

P. L. McLaughlin

2520. Herman, Alan. DUST, DEPRESSION AND DEMAGOGUES: POLITICAL RADICALS OF THE GREAT PLAINS, 1930-1936. *J. of the West 1977 16(1): 57-62.* Biographical sketches of several Great Plains radical politicians of the 1930's. Included are John Romulus Brinkley and "Alfalfa Bill" Murray of Oklahoma, William Langer and William Lemke of North Dakota, and Jim Ferguson and Miriam A. Ferguson of Texas.

R. Alvis

2521. Hodges, James A. GEORGE FORT MILTON AND THE NEW DEAL. *Tennessee Hist. Q. 1977 36(3): 383-409.* Though he had been skeptical of Roosevelt during the 1932 campaign, George Fort Milton became an active New Dealer as a result of the Hundred Days. He used his editorial page to vigorously support New Deal measures across the board, including racial liberalism, though moderately. He lived and wrote, however, in Tennessee, an area that was unfriendly to most of his liberalism. Primary and secondary sources; 118 notes.

M. B. Lucas

2522. Hoffman, Abraham. THE EL MONTE BERRY PICKERS' STRIKE, 1933: INTERNATIONAL INVOLVEMENT IN A LOCAL LABOR DISPUTE. *J. of the West 1973 12(1): 71-84.* A detailed account of the 1933 berry pickers' strike in El Monte, California, which involved "Mexican laborers, Communist agitators, Japanese employers, Los Angeles Chamber of Commerce and business representatives, and state and federal mediators . . . over issues of wages, hours, and working conditions. . . . The El Monte strike, however, claimed the distinction of direct involvement by the government of Mexico, in the form of diplomatic pressure, monetary assistance, and consular intervention. . . . In contrast to the active assistance of the Mexican consuls, the Japanese consul maintained a low profile, probably because of his awareness that excessive publicity would raise questions about Japanese leasing of property in a state that had already endorsed two alien land laws." 44 notes.

D. D. Cameron

2523. Homel, Michael W. THE LILYDALE SCHOOL CAMPAIGN OF 1936: DIRECT ACTION IN THE VERBAL PROTEST ERA. *J. of Negro Hist. 1974 59(3): 228-241.* During the 1960's black people marched, boycotted, sat-in, and took other forms of direct action to implement public school integration and to assure improved education for their children. Among earlier precedents for such direct action was an effort by black Chicagoans in 1936, at a time when most civil rights activity was verbal. Based on secondary sources; 33 notes.

N. G. Sapper

2524. Hurd, Richard W. NEW DEAL LABOR POLICY AND THE CONTAINMENT OF RADICAL UNION ACTIVITY. *Rev. of Radical Pol. Econ. 1976 8(3): 32-43.* New Deal labor policies were designed to impart support for working class movements to discourage activism and militance on the part of labor radicals, 1930's.

2525. Jacklin, Thomas M. MISSION TO THE SHARECROPPERS: NEO-ORTHODOX RADICALISM AND THE DELTA FARM VENTURE, 1936-1940. *South Atlantic Q. 1979 78(3): 302-316.* The episode whereby northern neoorthodox theologians attempted to aid the southern sharecropper in the late 1930's provides a revealing commentary on the way in which the proponents of the new theology sought in a concrete manner to connect the Word with the world around them. In spite of purchasing two large farms in the Mississippi State delta area which were settled by both white and black tenant farmers, and in spite of the constant infusion of northern money into the operation to keep it solvent, the attempt of the theologians—who acted like absentee landlords—to provide a model whereby the plight of the sharecropper might be lifted up failed. They forgot that the way of righteousness can be as thorny as the way of sin, a truth which the neoorthodox critics labored long to impress on their liberal colleagues. Based largely on the Reinhold Niebuhr Papers (Manuscript Division), Library of Congress, and contemporary articles in the *Christian Century;* 40 notes.

H. M. Parker, Jr.

2526. Jeansonne, Glen. CHALLENGE TO THE NEW DEAL: HUEY P. LONG AND THE REDISTRIBUTION OF NATIONAL WEALTH. *Louisiana Hist. 1980 21(4): 331-339.* While earlier studies of Huey P. Long have emphasized positive results of his political career, the "long-range results of Longism" produced more corruption and insincerity in Louisiana politics than improvement or reform. The real goal of Longism was power for Long in the national government to equal his control over Louisiana. Had Long lived, he would have divided the nation and created animosity without accomplishing anything. Rather than aiding the needy, Long's Share-Our-Wealth movement would have reduced the availability of capital needed for investment. Additionally, his program required a huge federal government resembling a police state. Based on Huey P. Long's *Every Man a King* and *My First Days in the White House;* 14 notes.

R. H. Tomlinson

2527. Jeansonne, Glen. GERALD L. K. SMITH AND THE SHARE OUR WEALTH MOVEMENT. *Red River Valley Hist. Rev. 1978 3(3): 52-65.* Discusses the ecclesiastical-turned-political evangelist Gerald L. K. Smith of Louisiana and the Share-Our-Wealth movement which he inherited after the assassination of Huey P. Long in 1935.

2528. Johnson, Charles. THE ARMY, THE NEGRO, AND THE CIVILIAN CONSERVATION CORPS: 1933-1942. *Military Affairs 1972 36(3): 82-88.* The problem of implementation of the nondiscrimination provisions of its organic act lasted throughout the life of the CCC. The Army, which operated the camps, followed no consistent policy on integration or segregation of individual companies. Because of local pressures, the recruiting of Negroes was limited after 1935 and the Army found it difficult to get local communities to accept the stationing of Negro companies in their midst. The Army believed that Negro troops performed best under white officers. In 1935 a limited number of Negro reserve medical officers and chaplains was authorized; but few would serve. In 1936 President Franklin Delano Roosevelt ordered the establishment of wholly Negro-operated camps, but only two were formed. Based on War Department records, memoirs, and monographs; 30 notes.

K. J. Bauer

2529. Kahn, Lawrence M. UNIONS AND INTERNAL LABOR MARKETS: THE CASE OF THE SAN FRANCISCO LONGSHOREMEN. *Labor Hist. 1980 21(3): 369-391.* West Coast longshoremen's unions transformed longshoring in San Francisco, California, in the 1930's from a secondary job characterized by low earnings and poor working conditions, to a primary job offering high relative earnings, job stability, and improved working conditions. The key to this transformation was the 1934 West Coast longshoremen's strike. Based on Bureau of Labor Statistics data, Works Progress Administration surveys, and other primary sources; 6 tables, 48 notes.

L. F. Velicer

2530. Kelly, Lawrence C. THE INDIAN REORGANIZATION ACT: THE DREAM AND THE REALITY. *Pacific Hist. R. 1975 44(3): 291-312.* The Indian Reorganization Act (1934) fell short of the revolutionary changes in federal Indian policy attributed to it by John Collier, Commissioner of Indian Affairs 1933-45, and by historians who have accepted his interpretation. Collier aimed to completely reverse the previous assimilationist policy. Assimilated Indians successfully opposed extension of the Act to themselves. In referenda on the Act, less than half of the eligible Indians voted to establish tribal constitutions and even fewer voted to place themselves under the economic provisions of the Act. When Collier attempted to get around the limitations of the Act by administrative action, Congress refused to appropriate the necessary funds. Based on documents in the National Archives, on Congressional hearings and other published government documents, and on secondary sources; table, 32 notes.

W. K. Hobson

2531. Keubler, Edward J. THE DESEGREGATION OF THE UNIVERSITY OF MARYLAND. *Maryland Hist. Mag. 1976 71(1): 37-49.* A study of the case of Donald G. Murray, the first black since the passage of the "separate but equal" doctrine to enter a southern university. After the exchange of a typical pattern of form letters with the admissions officials of the University of Maryland, Murray was denied entrance to the School of Law and referred to the all-Negro Morgan College and a virtually nonexistent black scholarship fund. The NAACP, with Thurgood Marshall coordinating the case, challenged the university in the Maryland courts in June 1935, and a writ of mandamus ordered Murray's admission. In the following year this writ was upheld in the Court of Appeals. Murray himself was watched carefully by the NAACP, tutored in his studies, and guided in legal procedures by Marshall and Charles H. Houston of Howard University. Winning acceptance by his classmates and graduating in 1938, Murray passed his bar exam and devoted himself to a simple life of public service in Baltimore, not seeking notoriety. His case, however, set the precedent for the NAACP to continue its fight against unequal education for blacks, even though full desegregation was a long time away. Primary sources; 82 notes.

G. J. Bobango

2532. Kirby, John B. RALPH J. BUNCHE AND BLACK RADICAL THOUGHT IN THE 1930'S. *Phylon 1974 35(2): 129-141.* Reviews the political thought of Negro leader Ralph Bunche during the New Deal era. Bunche was decidedly further Left at the time. He considered the Negro's problems to be economic and social rather than racial; Bunche took a class position. He saw little hope in the labor unions or early New Deal policies. He created the National Negro Congress, but became

disillusioned with its racial stress. Bunche's philosophy won few followers. As the decade drew to an end, he came more and more to support the New Deal program. 49 notes.
V. L. Human

2533. Koeniger, A. Cash. CARTER GLASS AND THE NATIONAL RECOVERY ADMINISTRATION. *South Atlantic Q. 1975 74(3): 349-364.* The usual view of New Deal liberals calmly carrying out the programs of earlier Progressives is not borne out in the example of Senator Carter Glass' struggle with the National Industrial Recovery Act and its administrative organization, the National Recovery Administration. Glass despised the program and fought it until the Supreme Court ruled it unconstitutional. Glass, like many Progressives, viewed the New Deal not as a reform program building evolutionarily on the past, but rather as a complete break with the past and the beginning of Fascist collectivism. This argument was at the heart of his objections. 38 notes.
V. L. Human

2534. Kreider, Robert. THE HISTORIC PEACE CHURCHES' MEETING IN 1935. *Mennonite Life 1976 31(2): 21-24.* In the fall of 1935 representatives of the Mennonites, Dunkards (Church of the Brethren), and Quakers met in Newton, Kansas, to discuss the possibilities for peace in a world threatened by war. Mennonite leader H. P. Krehbiel convened the meeting and was instrumental in changing the name of the group from Conference of Pacifist Churches to Historic Peace Churches in response to fundamentalist criticism of "pacifism" as a "secular" word. The conference drafted a message to the Methodist General Conference of 1936 (reprinted) and planned future meetings. 2 photos.
R. Burnett

2535. Kruman, Marie W. QUOTAS FOR BLACKS: THE PUBLIC WORKS ADMINISTRATION AND THE BLACK CONSTRUCTION WORKER. *Labor Hist. 1975 16(1): 37-51.* Harold Ickes instituted quotas for hiring skilled and unskilled blacks in construction financed through the Public Works Administration (PWA). Resistance from employers and unions was partially overcome by negotiations and implied sanctions. Although results were ambiguous, the plan helped provide blacks with employment, especially among unskilled workers. Based on files of the PWA in the National Archives; tables of compliance, 30 notes.
L. L. Athey

2536. Kyvig, David E. RASKOB, ROOSEVELT, AND REPEAL. *Historian 1975 37(3): 469-487.* A prohibition repeal advocate, John J. Raskob exploited his chairmanship (1928-32) of the Democratic National Committee to secure repeal of the 18th Amendment. In so doing he collided with the presidential course of Franklin D. Roosevelt who mistakenly questioned the political wisdom of making any party commitment to repeal. However, Raskob was successful, first at the Democratic National Convention of 1932 with passage of a strong anti-prohibition plank to which Roosevelt gave opportunistic endorsement, and finally with the actual repeal on 5 December 1933. 83 notes.

2537. Lambert, Roger C. THE ILLUSION OF PARTICIPATORY DEMOCRACY: THE AAA ORGANIZES THE CORN-HOG PRODUCERS. *Ann. of Iowa 1974 42(6): 468-477.* Discusses the New Deal efforts under Secretary of Agriculture Henry A. Wallace to create farmer support and involvement in a program to control commodity production. The economic situation was particularly acute in the interrelated hog and corn-growing sector. Iowa farmers created a pressure group under the leadership of Roswell Garst and Donald Murphy, the editor of *Wallaces' Farmer.* They supported production control in return for federal cash assistance, as in the Agricultural Adjustment Act (1933). 31 notes.
C. W. Olson

2538. Lauderbaugh, Richard A. BUSINESS, LABOR, AND FOREIGN POLICY: U.S. STEEL, THE INTERNATIONAL STEEL CARTEL, AND RECOGNITION OF THE STEEL WORKERS ORGANIZING COMMITTEE. *Pol. and Soc. 1976 6(4): 433-457.* "Private" foreign diplomacy led to the US Steel Corp.'s collective bargaining agreement with the Steel Workers Organizing Committee (SWOC) in early 1937. The agreement with the SWOC depended upon a verbal commitment to join the Entente Internationale de L'Acier (International Steel Cartel). In contravention of New Deal policies and US antitrust laws, the agreement included import restrictions, thereby controlling competition in the international steel market, and in turn protecting the US market. The agreement with SWOC served to camouflage the international aspects of the "invisible tariff" protecting the US steel market from the eyes of Roosevelt's New Dealers. 48 notes.
D. G. Nielson

2539. Lepawsky, Albert. THE PLANNING APPARATUS: A VIGNETTE OF THE NEW DEAL. *J. of the Am. Inst. of Planners 1976 42(1): 16-32.* Despite a lack of sophistication in the field of economic planning, the New Deal remains the high watermark of American planning thought and planning practice. This was most apparent in the realm of social and socioeconomic planning, including social security; in the planned use and development of natural resources and the related field of ecologic-environmental planning; in the correlation of national plans with local, state, regional, and international, including strategic, planning; and in the realm of political planning, that is, in the realization of progressive societal values through innovative public policy and adaptive planning technique. In search of a causative explanation for this unique American experience in the use of political intelligence and administrative expertise, the author offers this vignette of the New Deal and its planning apparatus.
J

2540. Levenstein, Harvey. LENINISTS UNDONE BY LENINISM: COMMUNISM AND UNIONISM IN THE UNITED STATES AND MEXICO, 1935-1939. *Labor Hist. 1981 22(2): 237-261.* The Communist Party in the United States and Mexico during the Popular Front period (1935-39) encouraged its members to cooperate with other leftists and moderates in the organizing of workers in the two countries. The Communist Party's leadership, however, actively discouraged Communists from gaining and maintaining powerful positions in such US unions as the United Steelworkers and United Automobile Workers and in the *Confederación de Trabajadores Mexicanos* in Mexico. The restraint preached by its leadership weakened the Communist Party's position in union activities enough to facilitate a purge of all Communists from these unions in the 1940's. Based on the Earl Browder Papers and other primary sources; 44 notes.
L. F. Velicer

2541. Lovin, Hugh T. AGRARIAN RADICALISM AT EBB TIDE: THE MICHIGAN FARMER-LABOR PARTY, 1933-1937. *Old Northwest 1979 5(2): 149-166.* During Franklin Delano Roosevelt's first term as president (1933-37), agrarian rebel groups in Michigan, such as the Farmers' Educational and Cooperative Union, the Farmers' Holiday Association, and the Farmer-Laborites of Wisconsin Congressman Thomas Amlie, cooperated to form a Farmer-Labor Party to oppose New Deal programs. Party secretary D. D. Alderdyce, however, tried to sever ties with Amlie's national movement, and although his demotion and the support of the United Automobile Workers helped, Committee for Industrial Organization President John L. Lewis's support for Roosevelt hurt. The presidential candidacy of Union Party member William Lenke made party unity impossible. Based on the Thomas R. Amlie Papers, State Historical Society of Wisconsin, Madison, the Howard Y. Williams Papers, Minnesota Historical Society, St. Paul, and other primary sources; 41 notes.
E. L. Keyser

2542. Lovin, Hugh T. THE AUTOMOBILE WORKERS UNIONS AND THE FIGHT FOR LABOR PARTIES IN THE 1930S. *Indiana Mag. of Hist. 1981 77(2): 123-149.* When the automobile workers began to organize unions in the mid-1930's there were strong disputes about whether these industrial unions should join one of the new labor-liberal parties or continue to reflect the nonpolitical bread and butter issues of the American Federation of Labor. After many experiments and some indecision the United Automobile Workers of America in Indiana and Ohio went along with the Democratic New Deal, but without much enthusiasm. Based on official proceedings, monographs, manuscripts, and newspapers; 2 illus., 57 notes.
A. Erlebacher

2543. Lovin, Hugh T. THE OHIO "FARMER-LABOR" MOVEMENT IN THE 1930'S. *Ohio Hist. 1978 87(4): 419-437.* Discusses Thomas Amlie and Herbert Hard's attempts to build a viable farmer-labor coalition as a third party to the left of the New Deal. Ohio Farmer-Labor Progressive Federation (1933-36) leaders viewed Ohio as a crucial state in their movement and hoped to draw on the well-organized movement of the unemployed and the rebellious union consciousness of the industrial worker to combat the conservative and intractable records of Governors White and Davey. The subsequent failure of the movement

resulted not only from the personal popularity of FDR, the power of the CIO, the New Deal support of the AFL, Grange, and Farm Bureau, and the party schism created by the Communist-sponsored 1935 Popular Front, but from the leadership's inability to work with or appeal to the ethnic and urban laborites who dominated Ohio's work force. Based on the archives of Wayne State University, the Minnesota Historical Society, the State Historical Society of Wisconsin, and other primary sources; 44 notes.
L. A. Russell

2544. Lovin, Hugh T. THOMAS R. AMLIE'S CRUSADE AND THE DISSONANT FARMERS: A NEW DEAL WINDFALL. *North Dakota Q. 1981 49(1): 91-105.* Discusses Wisconsin Congressman Thomas Ryum Amlie's crusade to attract disgruntled farmers to the Farmer Labor Party, in the 1930's, which was a failure and resulted in a windfall for the New Deal administration which attracted Amlie's Farmer Laborites, farm conservatives, and North Dakota Congressman Wiliam Lemke's old Unionists.

2545. Lovin, Hugh T. TOWARD A FARMER-LABOR PARTY IN OREGON, 1933-38. *Oregon Hist. Q. 1975 76(2): 135-151.* Analyzes the failure of attempts to establish a branch of the Farmer-Labor Party in Oregon. This party was composed of agrarians and labor unionists discontented with the New Deal's failure to combat the depression. It proposed as a cure an "economy of abundance" achieved by government encouragement of cooperatives and legislation ensuring the production of goods "for use" rather than "for profit." In 1937 opponents of the New Deal formed the Oregon Commonwealth Federation but the new party failed because of its radical reputation, weak backing from agrarians and the American Federation of Labor, and a disinclination toward third parties. Many of the reform-oriented goals were ultimately achieved through political activities within the Oregon Democratic Party. Based on manuscript collections, newspapers, unpublished theses, and secondary sources; 57 notes.
J. D. Smith

2546. Lynd, Staughton. THE UNITED FRONT IN AMERICA: A NOTE. *Radical America 1974 8(4): 29-37.* Radicalism, labor organizing, and the New Deal in the 1930's.
S

2547. Mal'kov, V. L. KOMMUNISTY, SOTSIALISTY I "NOVYI KURS" RUZVEL'TA: IZ ISTORII BOR'BY ZA EDINSTVO ANTIMONOPOLISTICHESKIKH SIL V SSHA [Communists, socialists and Roosevelt's "New Deal": From the history of the struggle for the unity of antimonopolist forces in the United States]. *Novaia i Noveishaia Istoriia [USSR] 1974 (5): 39-54.* The 7th Congress of Comintern in 1935 decreed that a united front of workers' and antifascist organizations was to be created. Aims to demonstrate the effect of this decree on the American Workers' movement in the 1930's. They attempted to establish a progressive antimonopolistic bloc in the decade before World War II. In November 1935 the Communist and Socialist parties in the United States cemented an alliance at a 20,000-strong meeting in New York. The two parties had hitherto been antagonistic: the Communists determined on revolution, the Socialists, permeated with evangelistic Christianity, were dedicated to a gradualist approach. The New Deal revealed their different approaches. The Communist Party stressed its negative features, the Socialist Party approved of its socialistic content. The Socialists, realizing the class character of the reforms, began to move toward the Communist position, especially in view of extreme right wing threats, they wavered. Discussions were held with the Communists about the creation of a united workers' and farmers' party. The Socialist Party's leadership eventually decided not to support the Communists, and the party membership fell drastically. Based on the papers of N. Thomas, Chairman of the Socialist Party (New York Public Library) and on published sources; 60 notes.
D. N. Collins

2548. Martin, Charles H. COMMUNISTS AND BLACKS: THE ILD AND THE ANGELO HERNDON CASE. *J. of Negro Hist. 1979 64(2): 131-141.* The International Labor Defense, a Communist-supported legal defense organization, secured the freedom of Angelo Herndon, an Atlanta, Georgia, black arrested on that state's outmoded anti-insurrection laws, but failed to gain the continued support of Atlanta blacks due to contradictory actions in other similar cases, 1932-37.

2549. Martin, Charles H. SOUTHERN LABOR RELATIONS IN TRANSITION: GADSDEN, ALABAMA, 1930-1943. *J. of Southern Hist. 1981 47(4): 545-568.* A review of labor organizing and the rise of unionism in Gadsden, Alabama. The town was dominated by three industries, which acted in concert to oppose all unionization efforts. Covers the early failures of organizers, the accompanying violence, and the influence of big wartime contracts in enabling the federal government to force the industries to comply. The Southern story was not very different from the Northern variety, except that Southern workers were mildly less enthusiastic about unionization, and the local "establishment" worked the "outsider" and "Northern carpetbagger" themes intensively, and to considerable effect. 47 notes.
V. L. Human

2550. McQuaid, Kim. COMPETITION, CARTELLIZATION AND THE CORPORATE ETHIC: GENERAL ELECTRIC'S LEADERSHIP DURING THE NEW DEAL ERA, 1933-1940. *Am. J. of Econ. and Sociol. 1977 36(4): 417-428.* Relations between General Electric Co. leaders and New Deal economic advisors and agencies resulted in sincere attempts at humanizing the managerial-capitalist order, an ideal which did not last long within the corporate structure.

2551. Miller, John E. GOVERNOR PHILIP F. LA FOLLETTE'S SHIFTING PRIORITIES FROM REDISTRIBUTION TO EXPANSION. *Mid-Am. 1976 58(2): 119-126.* Utilizing Frederick Jackson Turner's frontier thesis, Wisconsin Governor Philip F. LaFollette early subscribed to the mature-economy thesis propounded in Franklin D. Roosevelt's 1932 *Commonwealth Club Address.* LaFollette prescribed redistribution of purchasing power. By 1938, as the standard-bearer of the National Progressives of America, he had shifted to expansion because he opposed federal crop reduction policies, New Deal relief programs, and Huey P. Long's and Francis E. Townsend's redistribution plans, and because redistribution rhetoric hurt his national political ambitions. Based on LaFollette manuscripts, State Historical Society of Wisconsin, newspapers, and secondary sources; 21 notes.
T. H. Wendel

2552. Miller, John E. PROGRESSIVISM AND THE NEW DEAL: THE WISCONSIN WORKS BILL OF 1935. *Wisconsin Mag. of Hist. 1978 62(1): 25-40.* Uses the controversy surrounding the unsuccessful Wisconsin Works Bill as a means of studying the leadership of Governor Philip F. LaFollette; "the anomalous relationship between the Wisconsin progressives and the New Deal; the effectiveness of President Franklin Delano Roosevelt's strategy in co-opting potential left-wing opposition; and the declining influence of the states within the federal system." 10 illus., 43 notes.
N. C. Burckel

2553. Miller, Kathleen Atkinson. THE LADIES AND THE LYNCHERS: A LOOK AT THE ASSOCIATION OF SOUTHERN WOMEN FOR THE PREVENTION OF LYNCHING. *Southern Studies 1978 17(3): 221-240.* In 1930 Jessie Daniel Ames (b. 1893), Director of Woman's Work for the Commission on Interracial Cooperation (CIC), helped found the Association of Southern Women for the Prevention of Lynching (ASWPL). Until 1942 this association of Southern white women, working through church and civic groups, attempted to curb lynchings by educating the public and officials and by eliciting and publicizing commitments against lynching by prominent citizens, public officials, and newspapers. The basic reasons for the increased lynchings during the Depression were economic rivalry and racial antipathy. Based on papers of ASWPL at Atlanta U., primary and secondary sources; 72 notes.
J. Buschen

2554. Moehring, Eugene P. PUBLIC WORKS AND THE NEW DEAL IN LAS VEGAS, 1933-1940. *Nevada Hist. Soc. Q. 1981 24(2): 107-129.* From 1933 to 1940, New Deal expenditures for public works programs in Nevada exceeded the federal government's per-capita spending in the rest of the states. Because Las Vegas city officials and the local Chamber of Commerce lobbied and waged particularly effective publicity campaigns, they secured ambitious public works projects that vastly improved the city and suburban enclaves, enhanced the city's acceptability to tourists, and stimulated the local economy sufficiently so that Las Vegas lost little momentum in its drive to achieve metropolitan standing. Based on newspapers and archival materials at the University of Nevada, Las Vegas; 2 photos, 2 maps, 64 notes.
H. T. Lovin

2555. Moore, James R. SOURCES OF NEW DEAL ECONOMIC POLICY: THE INTERNATIONAL DIMENSION. *J. of Am. Hist. 1974 61(3): 728-744.* In the earliest months of the New Deal, Franklin

D. Roosevelt developed his pragmatic economic policies within an international dimension. He and his economic advisors advocated schemes for global public works programs backed by continued American loans, stabilization of currency exchange rates at devalued levels, a tariff "truce," and settlement of the thorny war debts issue. Pressed by a Congress that advocated inflationary action and faced with an attitude of non-cooperation from France and Britain, Roosevelt turned to a frankly nationalistic economic policy. 50 notes. K. B. West

2556. Morgan, Thomas S., Jr. A "FOLLY... MANIFEST TO EVERYONE": THE MOVEMENT TO ENACT UNEMPLOYMENT INSURANCE LEGISLATION IN NORTH CAROLINA, 1935-1936. *North Carolina Hist. R. 1975 52(3): 283-302.* As part of Franklin D. Roosevelt's New Deal program, the Social Security Act (1935) provided unemployment insurance compensation to workers based on state compliance with certain stipulations by 1 January 1936. North Carolina was near the close of its biennial legislative session when Congress passed the law. For political and financial reasons, Governor J. C. B. Ehringhaus opposed calling a special session, but he was forced to in December 1937, only weeks before the regular session. Based on manuscript and printed public papers, newspaper accounts, and secondary sources; 5 illus., 70 notes. T. L. Savitt

2557. Mulder, Ronald A. THE PROGRESSIVE INSURGENTS IN THE UNITED STATES SENATE, 1935-1936: WAS THERE A SECOND NEW DEAL? *Mid-America 1975 57(2): 106-125.* Though the bills fell short of their hopes, the insurgents voted 96.8% for the 1935 Public Utility Holding, Banking, and Wealth Tax Acts and the 1936 Revenue Act among others. Franklin D. Roosevelt, they believed, had discovered that big business and high finance were the enemy, yet they were uneasy with New Deal centralizing and they could not embrace the welfare state. Based on the Hiram Johnson, Roosevelt and Bronson Cutting papers, newspapers, published sources and secondary works; 47 notes. T. H. Wendel

2558. Mulder, Ronald A. RELUCTANT NEW DEALERS: THE PROGRESSIVE INSURGENTS IN THE UNITED STATES SENATE, 1933-1934. *Capitol Studies 1974 2(2): 5-22.* Details efforts of progressives in the Senate to revise presidential proposals and to retain traditional congressional prerogatives during the first years of the New Deal. S

2559. Myers, Constance Ashton. AMERICAN TROTSKYISTS: THE FIRST YEARS. *Studies in Comparative Communism 1977 10(1-2): 133-151.* Trotskyists were involved in the organization of the Workers' Party, a result of fusion with A. J. Muste's Conference for Progressive Labor Action. In 1935 the Trotskyists expelled those who opposed the "French turn" (coalition with the socialists). They moved to take over the Socialist Party but were expelled in 1937. Thereafter the Trotskyists split in 1940 on the issue of Soviet Russia and on organizational issues. The two groups were the unorthodox Schachtman wing and the Cannon unorthodox wing. Trotskyism influenced many writers in the 1930's. Cannon's Socialist Workers' Party played a role in opposing the Vietnam War. 44 notes. D. Balmuth

2560. Myhra, David. REXFORD GUY TUGWELL: INITIATOR OF AMERICA'S GREENBELT NEW TOWNS, 1935 TO 1936. *J. of the Am. Inst. of Planners 1974 40(3): 176-188.* "Between 1935 and 1936, the United States Department of Agriculture (USDA) initiated a public housing program that resulted in the construction of planned new communities called Greenbelt Towns. The prime mover behind this effort was Rexford Tugwell. The significance of this idea was his advanced concept of resettling the rural poor in planned towns at the edge of urban areas. Tugwell recognized, earlier perhaps than many of his colleagues, the 'push-pull' tendencies emerging in American society in the 1930s. Arguing that urban growth was inevitable, Tugwell's Greenbelt concept was to demonstrate how housing could be surrounded with a more pleasing environment in order to accommodate the expanding rural to urban migration. In less than two years Tugwell's Resettlement Administration planned and constructed three new communities and litigated a fourth. By all standards, these accomplishments demonstrate an unprecedented speed record for action by a bureaucracy." J

2561. Naison, Mark. COMMUNISM AND BLACK NATIONALISM IN THE DEPRESSION: THE CASE OF HARLEM. *J. of Ethnic Studies 1974 2(2): 24-36.* "The political struggle between nationalists and communists in Harlem had its roots in the Twenties. Communists in the African Blood Brotherhood... waged a bitter ideological struggle with Marcus Garvey... over questions of race loyalty vs. class loyalty." The Garvey movement and its spinoffs were business-oriented, seeking to develop a Negro entrepreneur class. Its answer to massive black unemployment was the "Don't Buy Where You Can't Work" campaign pushed by the Harlem Business Men's Club and the *Negro World*. By 1933 a picket campaign against stores was going on. The Party insisted on black-white working class solidarity, and along with the Young Liberators and the League of Struggle for Negro Rights maintained separate picketing operations. Meanwhile a Citizen's League under Harlem ministers and the *New York Age* sought to unite diverse organizations. The March 1935 riots brought the Party new acceptance as they helped in exposing social conditions in the community during the postriot investigations. From then to 1939 the Party played a role in every major coalition of protest, but its political "victory" over Negro nationalism "was never really secure." Contemporary and secondary sources; 46 notes. G. J. Bobango

2562. Naison, Mark. COMMUNISM AND HARLEM INTELLECTUALS IN THE POPULAR FRONT: ANTI-FASCISM AND THE POLITICS OF BLACK CULTURE. *J. of Ethnic Studies 1981 9(1): 1-25.* Explores the Communist Party approach to the Harlem intelligentsia and middle class in the late depression years, through incorporating the black community into anti-Fascist alliances with white liberals and radicals. The most successful efforts resulted from abandoning the party line of class struggle and striving for a "Negro People's Front," through organizations such as the United Aid for Ethiopia and the new National Negro Congress, but the Party's greatest source of prestige came from its attempts to gain institutional support for the black arts, centered primarily on the WPA Artists and Writers' Project. Based on contemporary newspapers, secondary sources; 59 notes. G. J. Bobango

2563. Naison, Mark. HARLEM COMMUNISTS AND THE POLITICS OF BLACK PROTEST. *Marxist Perspectives 1978 1(3): 20-51.* Because of the active protest against economic conditions and in favor of civil rights by the Communist Party, many black political leaders in Harlem supported and were active in Communist affairs in the 1930's.

2564. Naison, Mark. LEFTIES AND RIGHTIES: THE COMMUNIST PARTY AND SPORTS DURING THE GREAT DEPRESSION. *Radical Am. 1979 13(4): 47-59.* Under the aegis of the Communist Party, youth, fraternal, and trade union organizations during the period of the 1920's to the 1940's supported independent sports leagues in various cities, took part in the boycott of two Olympics, supported many track meets and benefit games for political prisoners, and took part in a vigorous campaign to open the ranks of major league baseball teams to blacks. The sports leagues, manned mainly by immigrants, were but a small shadow of their counterparts in Europe. In the 1930's Communist publications such as *Young Worker* and *Daily Worker* moved in their sports coverage to "Americanize" their approach, eschewing dogma in favor of relatively impartial coverage of sports. The Communists played an important role in bringing about the integration of major league baseball in the 1940's. Based mainly on printed primary sources. N. Lederer

2565. Nelson, Daniel, ed. THE BEGINNINGS OF A SITDOWN ERA: THE REMINISCENCES OF REX MURRAY. *Labor Hist. 1974 15(1): 89-97.* Reviews the use of the "sit-down" as a strike tactic and presents Rex Murray's reminiscences of the 1934 General Tire strike. The initial "sit down" occurred in 1934 rather than 1935, and the strike was not a spontaneous protest as previously believed. Based on Rex Murray's oral history memoirs at the University of Akron; 23 notes. L. L. Athey

2566. Nelson, H. Viscount. THE PHILADELPHIA NAACP: RACE VERSUS CLASS CONSCIOUSNESS DURING THE THIRTIES. *J. of Black Studies 1975 5(3): 255-276.* Correspondence of the Philadelphia chapter of the NAACP from the 1930's shows that its membership was made up of middle- and upper-class blacks who were almost totally unconcerned with the plight of poorer blacks. Their main concern was fund-raising and keeping on good terms with members of the white community. Though they took stands on blatantly racist issues they generally avoided taking positions which would jeopardize their social standing in the community. Notes, biblio.   K. Butcher

2567. Nelson, Lawrence J. NEW DEAL AND FREE MARKET: THE MEMPHIS MEETING OF THE SOUTHERN COMMISSIONERS OF AGRICULTURE, 1937. *Tennessee Hist. Q. 1981 40(3): 225-238.* Following apparent recovery in 1936, cotton farmers in the South forgot about acreage reduction and expanded production in the following year. The result was predictable—prices fell. Southerners then looked to the Roosevelt administration for financial relief. In September, the Association of Southern Commissioners of Agriculture meeting in Memphis amidst considerable agitation found one of the leading cotton planters, Oscar G. Johnston of Mississippi, to be a persuasive advocate of federal policy based upon a combination of allotments and subsidies. The resulting controversy indicated that Southern opposition to New Deal farm policies was based more on a pragmatic approach to the economic programs than on opposition to the philosophy behind the New Deal. In a short time Southerners had begun to expect federal assistance. Mainly letters and newspapers; 54 notes.   C. L. Grant

2568. Newbill, James G. FARMERS AND WOBBLIES IN THE YAKIMA VALLEY, 1933. *Pacific Northwest Q. 1977 68(2): 80-87.* During August 1933 farm workers struck the Congdon Orchards in the Yakima Valley of Washington. Led by the Industrial Workers of the World (IWW), the workers sought higher wages, amounting to between 35 and 50 cents per hour. Farm owners, receiving close cooperation from the sheriff's department, resisted and a bloody fight broke out. State police and National Guardsmen restored order, but not before the power of the IWW had been totally destroyed in Yakima Valley. Owners ultimately raised wages slightly, but economic difficulties made it impossible for them to fully meet the strikers' demands. Based on interviews and newspapers; 3 photos, 33 notes.   M. L. Tate

2569. Newbill, James G. YAKIMA AND THE WOBBLIES, 1910-1936. Conlin, Joseph R., ed. *At the Point of Production: The Local History of the I.W.W.* (Westport Conn.: Greenwood Pr., 1981): 167-190. Describes confrontations between the Industrial Workers of the World and ranchers and farmers in Yakima before 1933, the combination of depression economics and racism which led to mass meetings and eventual violence, fruit rancher-laborer difficulties in July and August 1933, and the "Congdon orchards battle" of 24 August 1933, and its aftermath. The major confrontation at Congdon resulted from a distorted image the IWW held of their own strength, and the fear of the farming community of the union. The confrontation and legal actions against the union in 1933 resulted in the collapse of the union's power in the Yakima Valley. Based on newspaper, journal, and personal accounts; 53 notes.
J. Powell

2570. Ostrower, Gary B. THE AMERICAN DECISION TO JOIN THE INTERNATIONAL LABOR ORGANIZATION. *Labor Hist. 1975 16(4): 495-504.* Support for American membership in the International Labor Organization arose from the Department of Labor under Frances Perkins. With the support of the Department of State and Franklin D. Roosevelt, opposition from isolationist sentiment and financial conservatives was overcome by 1934. Suggests that the New Deal may have been less isolationist than generally characterized. Based on archives of Departments of Labor and State; 23 notes.   L. L. Athey

2571. Papanikolas, Helen Z. UNIONISM, COMMUNISM, AND THE GREAT DEPRESSION: THE CARBON COUNTY COAL STRIKE OF 1933. *Utah Hist. Q. 1973 41(3): 254-300.* In 1933 the United Mine Workers of America and the National Miners Union attempted to unionize the bituminous coal fields of Carbon County. Immigrant laborers were attracted to the NMU. A strike set for Labor Day spread unrest, protests, and violence throughout the county. Mine operators called for the National Guard, maintaining that strikers were anarchists and communists. Many strikers were arrested and placed in bullpens at a ball park. While the NMU was involved with the strike the UMWA negotiated with operators on a coal code, which was adopted in October. The NMU declined in importance thereafter. Significant gains for labor did occur in Carbon County in 1933. Map, illus., 147 notes.
H. S. Marks

2572. Parrish, E. THE HUGHES COURT, THE GREAT DEPRESSION, AND THE HISTORIANS. *Historian 1978 40(2): 286-308.* Analyzes several groups of historians who have concerned themselves with the Supreme Court under Chief Justice Charles Evans Hughes in the 1930's. One group, typified by Merlo Pusey and Samuel Hendel, was inclined to be generous with the Court, especially Hughes and Owen Roberts. They blamed the New Dealers for the constitutional difficulties. Another contingent, which included Edward Corwin, Robert Stern, Thomas Reed Powell, and others, were New Dealers who defended Roosevelt at the Court's expense. A later group, the revisionist historians of the 1960's, often failed to confront judicial issues, and consequently have ignored the significant civil rights and civil liberties stands of the 1930's Court. Evaluating the quantity and quality of the works on the Hughes Court, concludes that the body of literature is small and the works are of varying significance.   M. S. Legan

2573. Patenaude, Lionel. THE NEW DEAL: ITS EFFECT ON THE SOCIAL FABRIC OF TEXAS SOCIETY, 1933-1939. *Social Sci. J. 1977 14(3): 51-60.* Discusses the condition of labor, the economy, and social issues in Texas during the New Deal; concludes that though Texans suffered during the Depression, relatively it was less drastic than for the remainder of the country.

2574. Philp, Kenneth R. THE NEW DEAL AND ALASKAN NATIVES, 1936-1945. *Pacific Hist. Rev. 1981 50(3): 309-327.* The Indian Reorganization Act of 1934 delayed social justice for Alaskan Indians, Aleuts, and Eskimos. New Deal policy was to create new reservations, but most Alaskan aborigines were small family groups resident on town lots in villages, lacked tribal cohesiveness, and were Americanized and of mixed blood. The attempt to create reservations failed because of native opposition. Natives received benefits from the Alaska Reorganization Act (US, 1936), but Interior Department inefficiency created problems. The Interior Department's intention to protect the natives' fishing and hunting rights probably erred in failing to obtain the full cooperation of the Congress and the Justice Department. Based on records of the Solicitor's Office, Alaska Native rights, other sources in the National Archives, and other primary sources; 87 notes.   R. N. Lokken

2575. Quinn, Larry. THE END OF PROHIBITION IN IDAHO. *Idaho Yesterdays 1974 17(4): 6-13.*

2576. Raper, Arthur F. THE SOUTHERN NEGRO AND THE NRA. *Georgia Hist. Q. 1980 64(2): 128-145.* Discusses the effect of the National Recovery Administration's wage regulations on Negro labor in the South in 1933-34, including wage differentials between North and South, benefits and disadvantages to Negroes, Negroes' fears, employers' evasion of the rules, and why employees went along with lower wages. This article was written in 1934. Based on fieldwork.
G. R. Schroeder

2577. Rosenzweig, Roy. RADICALS AND THE JOBLESS: THE MUSTEITES AND THE UNEMPLOYED LEAGUES, 1932-1936. *Labor Hist. 1975 16(1): 52-77.* The Unemployed Leagues (UL), formed under the direction of Abraham J. Muste, illustrate the dilemmas faced by radicals in efforts to build mass organizations of the jobless. Initial growth of the UL was fostered by the emphasis upon meeting local needs for jobs, relief, etc. When the radical leaders shifted to revolutionary tactics, the leagues split along ideological lines because the rank and file were not prepared for revolution. Besides organizational problems, the leagues demonstrate some limited successes of the radical movement in the 1930's. Based on papers and publications of the UL and Musteites, and on interviews; 45 notes.   L. L. Athey

2578. Ross, B. Joyce. MARY MC LEOD BETHUNE AND THE NATIONAL YOUTH ADMINISTRATION: A CASE STUDY OF POWER RELATIONSHIPS IN THE BLACK CABINET OF FRANKLIN D. ROOSEVELT. *J. of Negro Hist. 1975 60(1): 1-28.* Argues that the 1930's rather than the 1960's should be termed the beginning of the "Second Reconstruction" because of the revival of federal support for racial equality. The existence of a so-called New Deal "Black Cabinet" was illustrated by the career of Mary McLeod Bethune with the National Youth Administration (NYA). As Director of the NYA's Division of Negro Affairs, Bethune was a symbol of black aspiration in the earliest years of the "Second Reconstruction." Based on primary sources in the records of the NYA in the National Archives; 39 notes. N. G. Sapper

2579. Ryan, James Gilbert. THE MAKING OF A NATIVE MARXIST: THE EARLY CAREER OF EARL BROWDER. *Rev. of Pol. 1977 39(3): 332-362.* Earl Browder, an advocate of "Stalinist Orthodoxy," emerged as a darkhorse candidate for the general secretary of the American Communist Party in 1934. Ironically, he would be removed 11 years later because of his "evolution toward an independent, unorthodox, Marxism" and because he replaced "revolutionary rhetoric and programs with those of domestic reform." 67 notes.
L. E. Ziewacz

2580. Ryon, Roderick M. AN AMBIGUOUS LEGACY: BALTIMORE BLACKS AND THE CIO, 1936-1941. *J. of Negro Hist. 1980 65(1): 18-33.* Black people in Baltimore largely were left untouched by the Congress of Industrial Organizations (CIO) membership campaigns. Despite its shortcomings, the CIO was perceived as a friend of black workers by white workers who feared integrated unions. As World War II approached, the character of the CIO changed with beginning of the war boom. Large numbers of black migrants swelled the ranks of the CIO and were vital ingredients to its success. 49 notes. N. G. Sapper

2581. Saloutos, Theodore. NEW DEAL AGRICULTURAL POLICY: AN EVALUATION. *J. of Am. Hist. 1974 61(2): 394-416.* An analysis of the manifold aspects of New Deal farm policy demonstrates that efforts of the first Agricultural Adjustment Administration to raise prices to parity were not very successful, that acreage reduction was countered by expansion of yield per acre, that relatively few acres of crop land subject to erosion were in fact covered by plans of the Soil Conservation Service, and that the concept of the second AAA's "ever normal granary" did develop reserves and seemed to operate successfully. In spite of the "agricultural establishment," more was done for tenant farmers, sharecroppers, and farm laborers than is commonly supposed. On the whole, the New Deal constituted "the greatest innovative epoch in the history of American agriculture." 72 notes. K. B. West

2582. Sato, Susie. BEFORE PEARL HARBOR: EARLY JAPANESE SETTLERS IN ARIZONA. *J. of Arizona Hist. 1973 14(4): 317-334.* Issei (natives of Japan) began to come into the Salt River Valley of Arizona at the turn of the century. Like their white counterparts, the Issei cleared land and settled as farmers. Arizona's alien land law of 1921 was designed to discourage their residence and to prohibit their owning or leasing agricultural lands. It was used by militant farmers in 1934-35 to drive out the Japanese farmers. There was resentment among whites that the Japanese farmers were also enjoying profits of the agricultural prosperity of those years. When the state supreme court reversed all previous decisions against the Japanese in lower courts, stiff legislation was introduced to further restrict the Japanese. Its eventual defeat only deepened racial animosities among white farmers. 63 notes.
D. L. Smith

2583. Schneider, Albert J. "THAT TROUBLESOME OLD COCKLEBUR": JOHN R. BRINKLEY AND THE MEDICAL PROFESSION OF ARKANSAS, 1937-1942. *Arkansas Hist. Q. 1976 35(1): 27-46.* Dr. John R. Brinkley (1885-1942) and his staff of quasi-doctors and nurses treated patients in the South from the 1920's to the early 1940's. He became rich on "goat gland" operations and Formula No. 1020. Eventually the Arkansas authorities, his patients, and the American Medical Association caught up with him. Interestingly, the Arkansas Medical Society avoided legal confrontation with quacks during this period, and played only a minor role in discouraging quackery in Arkansas. Based on medical journal and newspaper articles, public legal records, and secondary sources; 3 illus., 48 notes. T. L. Savitt

2584. Schwartz, Bonnie Fox. NEW DEAL WORK RELIEF AND ORGANIZED LABOR: THE CWA AND THE AFL BUILDING TRADES. *Labor Hist. 1976 17(1): 38-57.* The Civil Works Administration, a first attempt at work relief, faced immediate problems of hiring and wage practices in their relationship to the American Federation of Labor's building trades. Under the leadership of John Carmody federal regulations attempted to protect labor's right to organize and uphold the prevailing wage rates, while mollifying the opposition of local employers. The CWA provided a "first forum" to alleviate organized labor's suspicions of work relief. Based on the CWA papers and the oral memoir of John Carmody; 41 notes. L. L. Athey

2585. Schwieder, Dorothy. THE GRANGER HOMESTEAD PROJECT. *Palimpsest 1977 58(5): 149-161.* In March 1934, Granger, Iowa, was chosen as the site of a Federal Subsistence Homesteads Corporation project. Granger, located in the heart of Iowa's depressed coal-mining region, was ideally suited for the experiment because severe unemployment, substandard housing, and inadequate social and educational opportunities were chronic problems. Conceived initially by Father Luigi Ligutti as a self-help project designed to promote cooperative rural living, the endeavor soon became a New Deal showplace. It did not fulfill Father Ligutti's high expectations, but was very significant as a successful social experiment. 3 photos, note on sources. D. W. Johnson

2586. Sears, James M. BLACK AMERICANS AND THE NEW DEAL. *Hist. Teacher 1976 10(1): 89-105.* A discussion of black support for Franklin D. Roosevelt and the New Deal. Blacks, disenchanted with the Hoover administration, anticipated inclusion in New Deal efforts to create jobs for the unemployed. Blacks benefitted from the New Deal in perhaps greater measure than they had anticipated. Without specifically committing himself, Roosevelt gave black Americans a stake in the governmental process. Black political and religious leaders, the black press and organizations, and Roosevelt's charisma helped place Negroes firmly in the Democratic party. Based on primary and secondary sources; 63 notes, biblio. P. W. Kennedy

2587. Selvin, David F. CAREY MCWILLIAMS: REFORMER AS HISTORIAN. *California Hist. Q. 1974 53(2): 173-180.* Reviews McWilliams' *Factories in the Field* (Salt Lake City: Peregrine Smith, Inc., 1971, reprint of 1939 edition) and appraises his contributions to labor and ethnic history. As a young lawyer McWilliams defended striking Mexican citrus workers; his interest expanded as he explored deeper into the problems of California farm labor. The coincidence of timing which saw *Factories in the Field* published in the same year as *Grapes of Wrath* brought additional controversy and accusations of conspiracy from growers. World War II sidetracked the issue of farm workers' rights and other questions raised by McWilliams and Steinbeck, but the problems are still alive in the 1970's as Cesar Chavez, the Teamsters, and the agribusinessmen continue the complex struggle. Includes McWilliams' foreword to the 1971 reprint edition of *Factories in the Field* and a partial listing of his writings. Photos. A. Hoffman

2588. Shankman, Arnold. BLACK PRIDE AND PREJUDICE: THE AMOS 'N' ANDY CRUSADE. *J. of Popular Culture 1978 12(2): 236-252.* Protest directed at the popular radio program, *Amos 'n' Andy*, by black groups made the public aware of the stereotypes used to portray blacks, taught blacks valuable lessons about economic boycotts of radio advertiser's products, and caused blacks to question demeaning stereotypes used in popular comic strips, 1930's.

2589. Shankman, Arnold. THE FIVE-DAY PLAN AND THE DEPRESSION. *Historian 1981 43(3): 393-409.* One panacea proposed to alleviate the Depression was the Five-Day Plan. Developed by Mary (1874-1966) and Mildred (1888-1960) Hicks, two Socialists living in Bainbridge, Georgia, the plan attracted only modest attention during the 1930's. Inspired by Charles and Mary Beard's *Rise of American Civilization*, which argued that shifting taxes could transfer wealth from one class to another, the Hicks Five-Day Plan of 1931 proposed a 100% tax on all income above $50,000 and a 100% tax on all bequests above $100,000. Dissatisfaction with the trends of Roosevelt's New Deal turned the Hickses toward Huey Long and his Share-Our-Wealth society. His death effectively signaled the end of the Hicks Plan. Primary sources; 63 notes. R. S. Sliwoski

2590. Shapiro, Edward S. CATHOLIC AGRARIAN THOUGHT AND THE NEW DEAL. *Catholic Hist. Rev. 1979 65(4): 583-599.* The American Catholic rural movement welcomed the election of Franklin D. Roosevelt in 1932. It believed the New Deal would embark upon an extensive program of rural rehabilitation, the restoration of the widespread ownership of productive property, and demographic decentralization. While initially favorably disposed toward the Agricultural Adjustment Act, the National Industrial Recovery Act, and other New Deal measures, Catholic ruralists had by the end of the 1930's concluded that the New Deal was a pragmatic response directed at propping up American capitalism rather than embarking upon a fundamental reconstruction of the economy along Catholic and Jeffersonian lines. A

2591. Shapiro, Edward S. THE CATHOLIC RURAL LIFE MOVEMENT AND THE NEW DEAL FARM PROGRAM. *Am. Benedictine Rev. 1977 28(3): 307-332.* Analyzes the Catholic agrarian movement of the 1930's and compares its goals with New Deal farm programs. The New Deal did not alleviate the problems noted by the Catholic agrarian movement. Based on original and secondary sources; 35 notes.
J. H. Pragman

2592. Singer, Donald L. UPTON SINCLAIR AND THE CALIFORNIA GUBERNATORIAL CAMPAIGN OF 1934. *Southern California Q. 1974 56(4): 375-406.* An account of the 1934 California gubernatorial campaign. Persuaded to change his affiliation from Socialist to Democrat, Upton Sinclair captured the party's nomination in a major primary victory. His End Poverty In California (EPIC) program, however, alarmed conservatives, although the Democrats modified and compromised it. Sinclair was smeared viciously; his only editorial support came from his own *EPIC News*, and almost all the state's newspapers denied him coverage. Not only Republicans but Communists feared his candidacy. He failed to receive endorsement from President Franklin Roosevelt, and his opponent, Governor Frank Merriam, let underlings carry on smear tactics. Having lost by some 250,000 votes, Sinclair attributed his defeat to defections by prominent Democrats, the smear campaign, and lack of newspaper coverage. Despite its defeat, the EPIC campaign indirectly helped turn the New Deal towards social welfare legislation, increased California's registration of Democrats, and gave budding Democratic leaders a boost in politics. Based on primary and secondary sources; 155 notes.
A. Hoffman

2593. Sivachev, N. V. RABOCHAIA POLITIKA PRAVITEL'STVA SSHA V NACHALE VTOROI MIROVOI VOINY (SENTIABR' 1939 G.-DEKABR' 1941 G.) [The labor policy of the US government at the beginning of World War II, September 1939-December 1941]. *Vestnik Moskovskogo U., Seriia 9: Istoriia [USSR] 1971 26(6): 18-37.* During this 27-month period the liberal-progressive labor policy of the 1930's (Wagner Act, etc.) began a reactionary shift led by Congressman Smith of Virginia. The large corporations sought strict limitations on the rights of labor unions, all in the interest of national defense. The National Labor Relations Board was instituted to handle disputes. When strikes continued to occur, President Franklin D. Roosevelt called out military forces on two occasions to work in defense-related industries in the absence of striking workers. In 1940 the National Defense Advisory Commission (NDAC) and in 1941 the Office of Production Management (a branch of the NDAC) were created. By 7 December 1941, the reactionary forces had won. 106 notes.
G. E. Munro

2594. Smith, Elaine M. MARY MCLEOD BETHUNE AND THE NATIONAL YOUTH ADMINISTRATION. Deutrich, Mabel E. and Purdy, Virginia C., ed. *Clio Was a Woman: Studies in the History of American Women* (Washington, D.C.: Howard U. Pr., 1980): 149-177. The National Youth Administration existed during 1935-44 primarily to assist youth aged 16 to 24 in getting work. Mary McLeod Bethune persuaded the agency to recognize Negro leadership both by expanding the Office of Negro Affairs and by employing black administrative assistants in more than 25 states. Under her aegis, too, it addressed blacks' needs notably through the Special Graduate and Negro College Fund. She also promoted a policy which assured blacks the same defense training and placement opportunities as whites. A discussion summary follows. 107 notes.
J. Powell

2595. Snyder, Robert E. HUEY LONG AND THE PRESIDENTIAL ELECTION OF 1936. *Louisiana Hist. 1975 16(2): 117-143.* The rise in popularity of Huey Long's Share Our Wealth movement caused Franklin D. Roosevelt and his supporters well-founded concern as the election of 1936 approached, not because Long (1893-1935) had any chance of winning the presidency, but because his candidacy could have given a strong Republican a better chance. Moreover, Long's movement would have kept other pro-Roosevelt politicians from winning office. Based on primary and secondary sources; 73 notes.
R. L. Woodward

2596. Stetson, Frederick W. THE CIVILIAN CONSERVATION CORPS IN VERMONT. *Vermont Hist. 1978 46(1): 24-42.* Most Vermont politicians opposed New Deal programs, but "Vermonters found the C. C. C. both justifiable and popular." It provided steady jobs for disproportionately large numbers in Vermont, poured millions into the depressed Vermont economy, developed skills useful in World War II, and helped lay the foundations of Vermont's postwar recreation industry. 9 illus., table, 73 notes.
T. D. S. Bassett

2597. Swain, Martha H. THE HARRISON EDUCATION BILLS, 1936-1941. *Mississippi Q. 1977-78 31(1): 119-132.* Though commonly held to be a staunch conservative, Mississippi senator Byron Patton Harrison was responsible for several federal aid to education bills during 1936-41.

2598. Swain, Martha H. PAT HARRISON AND THE SOCIAL SECURITY ACT OF 1935. *Southern Q. 1976 15(1): 1-14.* Examines Mississippi Senator Pat Harrison's efforts to secure the passage of the 1935 Social Security Act. His managerial abilities and role as chairman of the Senate Committee on Finance receive focus. Conflicting views concerning the measure are considered. Frances Perkins, Francis E. Townsend, and William Green are among the more notable personalities mentioned. 29 notes.
R. W. Dubay

2599. Taylor, Graham D. ANTHROPOLOGISTS, REFORMERS, AND THE INDIAN NEW DEAL. *Prologue 1975 7(3): 151-162.* Bureau of Indian Affairs Commissioner John Collier has been considered as one of the New Deal administrators who applied social sciences principles to the federal government for the first time. However, his analysis of Indian culture was prescriptive rather than descriptive. Collier was not completely successful in his reversal of previous policies aimed at assimilating Indians into white society. Anthropologists who shared his reformist commitment to preserve traditional cultures functioned effectively in the bureaucracy; those committed to professional academic standards and current methodology encountered hostility. The hypothesis of conflict between old-line administrators and young reformers is simplistic and inaccurate. Based on primary and secondary sources; 2 photos, 51 notes.
W. R. Hively

2600. Taylor, Graham D. THE TRIBAL ALTERNATIVE TO BUREAUCRACY: THE INDIAN'S NEW DEAL, 1933-1945. *J. of the West 1974 13(1): 128-156.* A critical analysis of the steps taken under the new Commissioner of Indian Affairs, John Collier, to change what had become "a frightening example of an arrogant, corrupt, and undirected bureaucracy" that left the Indians "mired in poverty and despair." Proponents of the New Deal saw the Indian tribes as a convenient "laboratory" for experimenting with planned political and economic development. Although Collier attempted "a genuine and farsighted effort to bridge a cultural chasm and allow the Indians to build a new society on the foundations of traditional institutions," the reorganization foundered on the lack of understanding of Indian tribal and political patterns and the great variety represented. The result was "a revival of bureaucratic control and Congressional exploitation." 54 notes.
R. V. Ritter

2601. Taylor, Paul F. LONDON: FOCAL POINT OF KENTUCKY TURBULENCE. *Filson Club Hist. Q. 1975 49(3): 256-265.* London was the site of the federal court for southeastern Kentucky, and the author concentrates on two important cases tried there in the 1930's. The first occurred in 1932 when the American Civil Liberties Union enjoined Bell County officials to let them enter the county. The ACLU lost the case. In 1938 mine owners and law enforcement officals were placed on trial for violating the civil rights of coal miners. The sensational trial made London the center of national attention and resulted in hung juries and the freeing of the defendants. Documentation from newspapers; 55 notes.
G. B. McKinney

2602. Thrasher, Sue and Wise, Leah. THE SOUTHERN TENANT FARMERS' UNION. *Southern Exposure 1974 1(3/4): 5-32.* During the Depression, black and white sharecroppers organized the Southern Tenant Farmers' Union which became a mass movement. Explores the plight of the tenants and the union's relationships with the Communist Party, American Federation of Labor, Congress of Industrial Organizations, and black and white sharecroppers. The Agricultural Adjustment Administration caused the eviction of thousands of sharecroppers who then sought work in industrial plants outside the South during World War II. Based on papers in Southern Historical Collection, University of North Carolina, and oral interviews; 12 illus., 3 notes, biblio.

G. A. Bolton

2603. Tomlins, Christopher L. AFL UNIONS IN THE 1930S: THEIR PERFORMANCE IN HISTORICAL PERSPECTIVE. *J. of Am. Hist. 1979 65(4): 1021-1042.* Challenges traditional interpretations and suggests a new analytic framework to explain American Federation of Labor (AFL) successes. Historically, AFL unions had adapted to the changing industrial environment; this tendency continued in the 1930's when the AFL faced Congress of Industrial Organizations (CIO) competition. AFL unions made major contributions to the growth of the organized labor movement in the 1930's, especially in transport, communications, service trades, and retail trades. 4 tables, 50 notes.

T. P Linkfield

2604. Toy, Eckard, V., Jr. THE OXFORD GROUP AND THE STRIKE OF THE SEATTLE LONGSHOREMEN IN 1934. *Pacific Northwest Q. 1978 69(4): 174-184.* Traces the development of the Oxford Group from its founding in 1921 as a Christian mediation group devoted to settling labor and international problems. During the 1934 longshoremen's strike in Seattle, Oxford Group leaders George Light, James Clise, and Walter Horne worked themselves into a mediating role which helped end the deadlock by June. Throughout the negotiations, they unabashedly supported management over labor which was consistent with the entire Oxford Group movement. Primary and secondary sources; 2 photos, 41 notes.

M. L. Tate

2605. Valerina, A. F. ROL' BESPARTIINOI RABOCHEI LIGI VO VNUTRENNEI POLITICHESKOI BOR'BE S. SH. A. (1936-1938 GG.) [The role of the Labor Non-Partisan League in the internal political struggle in the US, 1936-38]. *Vestnik Moskovskogo U., Seriia 9: Istoriia [USSR] 1975 30(6): 38-57.* Outlines the activities of the League, the most progressive labor organization in the United States during the 1930's. It represented the true feelings of the workers, tried to provide them with independent political representation, and stimulated important legislation which improved working conditions in the country. 129 notes.

N. Dejevsky

2606. Wallis, John Joseph and Benjamin, Daniel K. PUBLIC RELIEF AND PRIVATE EMPLOYMENT IN THE GREAT DEPRESSION. *J. of Econ. Hist. 1981 41(1): 97-102.* The unemployment relief programs introduced by the federal government in the 1930's were the largest single factor in the growth of the federal budget over the decade. Cross-sectional data bearing on the operation of the Federal Emergency Relief Administration rejects the hypothesis that the federal relief programs reduced private employment. Individuals did respond to the incentives of relief benefits, but only by moving between relief and non-relief unemployment.

J

2607. Weeks, Charles J. THE EASTERN CHEROKEE AND THE NEW DEAL. *North Carolina Hist. Rev. 1976 53(3): 303-319.* Though the Indian New Deal offered a program designed to reverse misguided policies of the previous 50 years, it failed to have a significant impact on the social and economic condition of the Cherokees of western North Carolina. The influx of public money discouraged farming and handicraft work, thereby weakening the tribe's economic base. For personal, political, and economic reasons "white" Cherokees (mixed bloods who had adopted local white culture) resisted reforms offered by the New Deal. Based on manuscript archival records, published government documents, and secondary sources; 12 illus., 60 notes.

T. L. Savitt

2608. Weiss, Stuart L. KENT KELLER, THE LIBERAL BLOC, AND THE NEW DEAL. *J. of the Illinois State Hist. Soc. 1975 68(2): 143-158.* Keller was a stalwart member of the unofficial "liberal bloc" of Democrats, progressive Republicans and independents in Congress during 1930-40. Representing "Egypt," the 25th District in southern Illinois, he supported almost every item of New Deal legislation that would benefit his coal-miner and small-farmer constituents. Believing that public works projects would alleviate the mass unemployment in his area, he supported a scheme to provide cheap electric power for his district through the construction by the federal government of a "little TVA" on Crab Orchard Creek. By 1938 the liberal bloc had largely been dismantled in Congress and the defeat of Keller and other Congressmen in 1940 and 1942 marked the ascendancy of a conservative Congress hostile to the New Deal.

N. Lederer

2609. Weiss, Stuart L. THOMAS AMLIE AND THE NEW DEAL. *Mid-Am. 1977 59(1): 19-38.* Sketches the political career of Thomas Amlie, US Representative from Wisconsin's First District. In 1931, Amlie began as a Republican; but he soon founded the Wisconsin Progressive Party and ended his career as a Democrat. During the 1930's he was an ardent New Dealer and proposed radical economic programs based on "production for use" and preserving "democratic values." His nomination to the Interstate Commerce Commission in 1939 was withdrawn at his own request because of conservative criticism from his home state. Amlie was a realistic liberal. Primary and secondary sources; 125 notes.

J. M. Lee

2610. Wennersten, John R. THE BLACK SCHOOL TEACHER IN MARYLAND—1930'S. *Negro Hist. Bull. 1975 38(3): 370-373.* During the 1930's black teachers in Maryland grappled with limited intellectual preparation, job opportunities, and salary. In 1938 the black teachers association joined with the National Association for the Advancement of Colored People to bring salary equalization before the state court. These court cases, leading to salary equalization, were an essential part of the black teacher's experience.

M. J. Wentworth

2611. Whisenhunt, Donald W. THE CONTINENTAL CONGRESS OF WORKERS AND FARMERS, 1933. *Studies in Hist. and Soc. 1974-75 6(1): 1-14.* The 1933 congress, modelled after the 1776 Second Continental Congress, was organized by Clarence Senior, with support from leading Socialists including Norman Thomas. Planned in the aftermath of the 1932 presidential election, when Franklin D. Roosevelt appeared only slightly less conservative than Herbert Hoover, the Congress convened two months after Roosevelt took office—the period during which the New Deal was most active and least opposed. Unclear goals, exclusion of Communists, uncertainty over the best means of promoting Socialist politics, and poor timing with regard to the New Deal prevented permanent gains for the Socialist Party of America and allied groups. Based on primary sources; 98 notes.

G. H. Libbey

2612. White, Larry. THE RETURN OF THE THIEF: THE REPEAL OF PROHIBITION AND THE ADVENTIST RESPONSE. *Adventist Heritage 1978 5(2): 34-47.* Discusses the response (1932-34) of Seventh-Day Adventists to the campaign for repeal of Prohibition and its aftermath.

2613. Wyche, Billy H. SOUTHERN INDUSTRIALISTS VIEW ORGANIZED LABOR IN THE NEW DEAL YEARS, 1933-1941. *Southern Studies 1980 19(20): 151-171.* Although the NIRA, or National Industrial Recovery Act (US, 1933), was at first greeted with enthusiasm by southern industrialists, they soon came to attack Section 7(a), which provided for collective bargaining. The general textile strike of 1934 and the emergence of the CIO (Congress of Industrial Organizations) aroused great fear and anger among the industrialists, who opposed the NLRA, or National Labor Relations Act (US, 1935), from the beginning. Economic rather than ideological factors played the leading role in shaping these views. Textiles, the leading industry of the South, had overexpanded and overproduced for many years, and costs had to be reduced. Union and management journals and other primary sources; 88 notes.

J. J. Buschen

2614. Wyche, Billy H. SOUTHERN NEWSPAPERS VIEW ORGANIZED LABOR IN THE NEW DEAL YEARS. *South Atlantic Q. 1975 74(2): 178-196.* Southern newspapers presented a full spectrum of opinion on labor problems during the 1930's. Most of them broadly supported the New Deal in principle, but were sometimes less enthusiastic when its programs were put into practice. Strikes were almost unanimously abhorred, especially when violent, but violence against strikers was seldom condemned. The Congress of Industrial Organizations was generally disliked. The fulcrum of newspaper opinion moved more and more to an antilabor position as the decade advanced. 90 notes.

V. L. Human

2615. Zieger, Robert H. THE LIMITS OF MILITANCY: ORGANIZING PAPER WORKERS, 1933-1935. *J. of Am. Hist. 1976 63(3):*

638-657. Analyzes efforts to organize workers in the converted paper industry in the early years of the New Deal. The mid-1930's form a discrete segment of transitional trial-and-error organizational techniques in which grass roots militancy played a major role. This early militancy lacked staying power and represented a false start. The claims of militancy conflicted with those of permanent organization and erratic, ineffective local unions quarreled with the international organization, the International Brotherhood of Pulp, Sulphite, and Paper Mill Workers, AFL. Primary and secondary sources; 44 notes. W. R. Hively

War and Reform

2616. Abbott, Carl. PORTLAND IN THE PACIFIC WAR: PLANNING FROM 1940 TO 1945. *Urbanism Past & Present 1980-81 6(1): 12-24.* Portland grew extraordinarily during World War II as a result of the shipbuilding industry. Rapid growth combined with national shortages of men and materials to create a crisis for the local government. Portland defined its goals for the home front in terms of short-range solutions. In 1941 and 1942, the city's goal was more housing, not more and better housing. In 1943 and 1944, the city limited itself to schemes to ease the unemployment of returning veterans rather than devising strategies to restructure the metropolitan economy. Wartime pressures caused planners to seek engineering solutions to the problems of metropolitan growth. Portland Census tracts, Portland Planning Commission Annual Reports, Portland Planning Commission Minutes, Portland City Council Proceedings; 2 maps, 52 notes. B. P. Anderson

2617. Bailey, Robert J. THEODORE G. BILBO AND THE FAIR EMPLOYMENT PRACTICES CONTROVERSY: A SOUTHERN SENATOR'S REACTIONS TO A CHANGING WORLD. *J. of Mississippi Hist. 1980 42(1): 27-42.* During World War II, President Franklin Roosevelt, in an effort to integrate minority groups into the war effort, created the Fair Employment Practices Committee by executive order in 1941, and enlarged its responsibilities in 1943. However, only congressional action could extend its life beyond the war years. Senator Dennis Chavez of New Mexico introduced a bill to establish a permanent FEPC in 1945 which set off a national controversy over how much control the federal government should have in employment practices. Some members of Congress, especially southern Democrats, viewed the bill as a step toward social equality of the races. Leading the opposition was Senator Theodore G. Bilbo of Mississippi who vowed he would beat the "damnable, unAmerican and unconstitutional" FEPC to death. Describes Bilbo's arguments and efforts to defeat the bill as well as the bill's supporters' criticisms of the Mississippian's race-baiting. Although the bill was withdrawn from consideration after a 24-day filibuster, concludes that Bilbo had become an anachronism, for by 1946 racism was becoming more subtle in American politics. M. S. Legan

2618. Barnes, William R. A NATIONAL CONTROVERSY IN MINIATURE: THE DISTRICT OF COLUMBIA STRUGGLE OVER PUBLIC HOUSING AND REDEVELOPMENT, 1943-46. *Prologue 1977 9(2): 91-104.* The conflict over public housing in the District of Columbia, although generated by local needs resulting from a wartime boom and consequent housing shortage, had a much broader significance than that of reconciling black and white interests and of inaugurating planning in the nation's capital. National pro- and antipublic housing advocates used the issue as a forum on which to discuss and bitterly fight over the postwar nature of the role of public housing in meeting national needs. Knowing that this issue would be an important one after the war, social reformers and representatives of private real estate interests were keenly concerned over the fate of public housing in the capital and fully participated in debates regarding the issue. The resultant clash of ideologies was revealing of the role which private interests play in the development of a city and of their employment of the device of redevelopment as a reform measure to avoid more public oriented legislation. N. Lederer

2619. Capeci, Dominic J. FROM DIFFERENT LIBERAL PERSPECTIVES: FIORELLO H. LAGUARDIA, ADAM CLAYTON POWELL, JR., AND CIVIL RIGHTS IN NEW YORK CITY, 1941-1943. *J. of Negro Hist. 1977 62(2): 160-173.* Mayor Fiorello LaGuardia and Councilman Adam Clayton Powell, Jr., were embroiled in political warfare during Powell's term as a councilman in New York City during 1941-43. Ironically, although both were liberals, their personalities, philosophies, and styles were so alike as to prove the physical law of magnetism that likes repel. Based on documents in the Fiorello H. LaGuardia Papers and secondary sources; 92 notes. N. G. Sapper

2620. Cook, James F. THE EUGENE TALMADGE-WALTER COCKING CONTROVERSY. *Phylon 1974 35(2): 181-192.* Reviews the disagreement between Governor Eugene Talmadge of Georgia and Walter Cocking of the University of Georgia. By request of his supervisors, Cocking drafted a report on the higher education of Negroes in Georgia, in which he found the current system lacking and advocated improvements. Talmadge was incensed; he accused Cocking of advocating the integration of schools. The Governor determined to get rid of Cocking, and finally did so by means of a packed Board of Regents. There followed a general academic purge which seriously damaged the state's intellectual reputation. Covers the period 1937-43. 69 notes.
V. L. Human

2621. Cripps, Thomas and Culbert, David. *THE NEGRO SOLDIER* (1944): FILM PROPAGANDA IN BLACK AND WHITE. *Am. Q. 1979 31(5): 616-640.* Discusses the symbiotic relationship among the army, blacks, social scientists, and the Hollywood film community that made the World War II army orientation film *The Negro Soldier* in 1944. Frank Capra chose Stuart Heisler to direct it. The result was a 43-minute documentary of high technical quality that portrayed blacks with middle class values and stressed black history. Both black and white troops were enthusiastic, as were most civilian audiences. The impact of *The Negro Soldier* with its well-executed theme of racial integration extended into three areas: promotion, in that black pressure groups learned that film could be a tool for social change; production of "message films"; and the demise of "race movies." 6 photos, 74 notes. S

2622. Critchlow, Donald T. COMMUNIST UNIONS AND RACISM. *Labor Hist. 1976 17(2): 230-244.* Studies the responses of the United Electrical Radio and Machine Workers and the National Maritime Union to the "Black Question" during World War II. The U.E. ignored Negroes while the N.M.U. prided itself on its black members. This ambiguity of policy casts doubt on the assumption that "Communist-dominated" unions were essentially identical in interests. Based on proceedings of the U.E. and the N.M.U.; 38 notes. L. L. Athey

2623. Cuneo, Carl J. STATE, CLASS, AND RESERVE LABOUR: THE CASE OF THE 1941 CANADIAN UNEMPLOYMENT INSURANCE ACT. *Can. Rev. of Sociol. and Anthrop. [Canada] 1979 16(2): 147-170.* Uses the Canadian Unemployment Insurance Act (1941) as a case study comparing the validity of the Marxist instrumental and structural theories of the capitalist state. Examines the interests of capital accumulation, social control of labor, and labor's wage subsistence on this legislation. Shows that the federal state introduced unemployment insurance to control unrest among the unemployed and to assist its own accumulation of capital in the context of World War II. The capitalist class consistently opposed state unemployment insurance during 1920-41, although its opposition weakened somewhat during the Depression of the 1930's. Labor organizations have consistently supported unemployment insurance since 1919. The radicalism of some of their proposals reached a high point during the Depression. Concludes that because the federal state introduced unemployment insurance largely over the objections of Canadian business, Marxist structural theory, in which the state displays a relative autonomy from business and thereby accommodates some working-class demands, is the most valid theory for this case. J/S

2624. Droker, Howard A. SEATTLE RACE RELATIONS DURING THE SECOND WORLD WAR. *Pacific Northwest Q. 1976 67(4): 163-174.* Seattle's relatively small black population doubled during World War II as thousands of people came for jobs in defense industries. Jim Crowism became more prevalent and racial tension increased. To combat the possibility of race riots, Mayor William Devin created the Civic Unity Committee in February 1944. This multiracial group, dominated by conservatives, avoided conflict as it worked to defuse potential problems. Its quiet, behind-the-scenes efforts achieved limited success for black employment opportunities, but it never solved the discriminatory housing practices. The committee's efforts in behalf of displaced Japanese Americans in 1945 insured its credibility as a broad-based race relations organization which could effectively accomplish its goals. Primary and secondary sources; 6 photos, 51 notes. M. L. Tate

2625. Finkle, Lee. THE CONSERVATIVE AIMS OF MILITANT RHETORIC: BLACK PROTEST DURING WORLD WAR II. *J. of Am. Hist. 1973 60(3): 692-713.* Black newspapers were often accused of advocating radical action in pressing for an immediate end to segregation and an "overnight revolution" in race relations. In fact, because of the betrayal of promises after World War I, unemployment, and the continued riots and segregation in the armed forces, many black Americans were disillusioned with democracy at home and were half-hearted about fighting to promote it abroad. As a result, black editors adopted a militant rhetoric and promoted a "double V" program of urging young black soldiers to fight while their fellows at home worked to secure liberties. Black newspapers were patriotic and generally denounced the more militant all-black approach of Asa Philip Randolph. 90 notes.
K. B. West

2626. Hachey, Thomas. WALTER WHITE AND THE AMERICAN NEGRO SOLDIER IN WORLD WAR II: A DIPLOMATIC DILEMMA FOR BRITAIN. *Phylon 1978 39(3): 241-249.* World War II was in part a crusade against Nazi-Fascist racism, and it had as a by-product the end of colonial domination of colored peoples by European empires. Yet American black soldiers were still the victims of much racial discrimination. In 1944, Walter F. White, executive secretary of the National Association for the Advancement of Colored People, traveled to Great Britain to investigate race discrimination in the US Army. White's journey deeply concerned the British Foreign Office who kept close watch on his movements. After interviewing black GI's, he wanted to go to India but was dissuaded, being told he would not be able to see interned nationalist leaders, including Gandhi. He did, however, travel widely in Africa. The Foreign Office, though worried by his presence there, told its people in the capitals of Africa to "show him every courtesy." Walter White's sojourn in England was an important contribution to the process which led to President Truman's order to desegregate the Armed Forces in 1948. 23 notes. J. C. Billigmeier

2627. Harris, William H. FEDERAL INTERVENTION IN UNION DISCRIMINATION: FEPC AND WEST COAST SHIPYARDS DURING WORLD WAR II. *Labor Hist. 1981 22(3): 325-347.* Describes the effects of the Fair Employment Practices Committee (FEPC) to eliminate racial discrimination by unions and shipbuilding companies against blacks who came west during World War II. An auxiliary union membership system kept blacks separated from white union members, and the West Coast Master Agreement gave AFL (American Federation of Labor) unions a nearly closed shop in the shipyards. Blacks' complaints to the FEPC eventually spurred investigations, a reorganization of the FEPC, hearings before the FEPC, and lawsuits in state courts. The California Supreme Court's right to work decision reinforced the FEPC findings of racial discrimination and led to an end of that practice by unions. Covers 1939-46. Based on FEPC West Coast Hearings and other primary sources; table, 48 notes. L. F. Velicer

2628. Hartmann, Susan M. WOMEN IN THE MILITARY SERVICE. Deutrich, Mabel E. and Purdy, Virginia C., ed. *Clio Was a Woman: Studies in the History of American Women* (Washington, D.C.: Howard U. Pr., 1980): 195-205. The admission of women into the US military constituted one of World War II's most noted expansions in sex roles. The legislative history of the women's corps, including policies and procedures regarding female personnel, and the roles assigned to women in the armed services, are used to assess the relative significance of military expediency, public attitudes, and women's own ambitions in promoting attitudinal and material alterations in women's status. A discussion summary follows. Secondary sources; 20 notes. J. Powell

2629. Hartmann, Susan M. WOMEN'S ORGANIZATIONS DURING WORLD WAR II: THE INTERACTION OF CLASS, RACE, AND FEMINISM. Kelley, Mary, ed. *Woman's Being, Woman's Place: Female Identity and Vocation in American History* (Boston: G. K. Hall, 1979): 313-328. Examines the ideologies of feminist organizations during World War II. Active a century after the beginning of women's involvement in reform movements of the 19th century, these organizations pointed to changes as well as continuities in women's experiences. They also provide a means by which two interrelated questions can be addressed. How did the war affect the experiences of women? Perhaps most obvious was the impact of the entrance of millions of women into the labor force. Another major question is: what was the response of women's organizations to these altered circumstances? A broad spectrum of organizations engaged in efforts to broaden women's opportunities for employment and to increase their representation in administrative and policymaking positions. The significant role played by social classes and race as obstacles to female solidarity are pointed out. 18 notes.
J. Powell

2630. Henderson, Alexa B. FEPC AND THE SOUTHERN RAILWAY CASE: AN INVESTIGATION INTO DISCRIMINATORY PRACTICES DURING WORLD WAR II. *J. of Negro Hist. 1976 61(2): 173-187.* For the first time, hearings into discrimination by railroad employers, all members of the Southeastern Carriers Conference, were held by the Fair Employment Practice Committee during World War II. Hundreds of black rail workers cooperated with the field investigators in building the FEPC's case against the railroads and all-white unions. However, the resolve of the FEPC was undermined by presidential vacillation. Based on the records of the FEPC; 45 notes.
N. G. Sapper

2631. Johnson, Clyde. CIO OIL WORKERS' ORGANIZING CAMPAIGN IN TEXAS, 1942-1943. Fink, Gary M. and Reed, Merl E., eds. *Essays in Southern Labor History: Selected Papers, Southern Labor History Conference, 1976.* (Westport, Conn.; London, England: Greenwood Pr., 1977): 173-188. A narrative (by an ex-organizer) of strategies and results in the efforts of the Congress of Industrial Organizations to organize oil workers in Texas in the early years of World War II. Covers the campaigns in Port Arthur, the Pan American campaign in Texas City, the Southport campaign, the Ingleside Humble campaign, the Baytown Humble Oil campaign, and the Gulf oil campaign. Notable were the company's exploitation of race issues and its appeals to "patriotism."
R. V. Ritter

2632. Keim, Albert N. SERVICE OR RESISTANCE? THE MENNONITE RESPONSE TO CONSCRIPTION IN WORLD WAR II. *Mennonite Q. Rev. 1978 52(2): 141-155.* Mennonites' experiences during World War I caused them to seek an alternative military conscription in the event of another war, an impulse which quickened as World War II approached during the 1930's. Representatives of the Peace Churches approached the federal government with a plan for alternative service in the United States. Neither Congress nor President Roosevelt was enthusiastic about it, but eventually it was adopted. The Mennonites were satisfied with this solution, because they opposed not conscription but war. Some Quakers were more reserved. Ironically, the civilian service units operated under military control, although the individual churches acted as "camp managers." 52 notes. V. L. Human

2633. Lebowitz, Neil H. "ABOVE PARTY, CLASS, OR CREED": RENT CONTROL IN THE UNITED STATES, 1940-1947. *J. of Urban Hist. 1981 7(4): 439-470.* Analyzes the rent controls imposed by the federal government during World War II. It was "the most effective of all the wartime stabilization programs." Rent control helped to equalize the economic burdens of the war and helped to maintain domestic morale. 75 notes. T. W. Smith

2634. MacDowell, Laurel Sefton. THE FORMATION OF THE CANADIAN INDUSTRIAL RELATIONS SYSTEM DURING WORLD WAR TWO. *Labour [Canada] 1978 3: 175-196.* Union membership more than doubled during World War II, a period marked by labor unrest and antagonistic government-labor relations. Union opposition to wage controls and government's failure to enact collective bargaining legislation or to provide for labor representation on policymaking boards united the Trades and Labour Congress and the Canadian Labour Congress in a common front. The latter organization entered politics through an alliance with the Cooperative Commonwealth Federation. Strikes, political action, and Ontario legislation convinced the government to change its position; in 1944, it enacted an order-in-council to provide protection and legal status for union organizing and collective bargaining. The new policy became a model for postwar legislation. Primary sources; 74 notes.
W. A. Kearns

2635. Martin, Tony. MARCH ON WASHINGTON MOVEMENT. *J. of African-Afro-American Affairs 1979 3(1): 63-69.* Originally organized in 1941 by A. Philip Randolph and Milton Webster, the March on Washington Movement (which threatened a massive march on Washington, DC, of 10,000 blacks) succeeded in obtaining Executive Order 8802 which proscribed discrimination in defense-related industries and indirectly influenced the establishment of the Fair Employment Practices Committee and then began efforts to end segregation in the armed forces before it lost momentum in 1944.

2636. McGuire, Phillip. JUDGE HASTIE, WORLD WAR II, AND ARMY RACISM. *J. of Negro Hist. 1977 62(4): 351-362.* William Hastie, the first Afro-American appointed to the federal bench as US District Court Judge for the Virgin Islands (1937-39), left the deanship of the Howard University Law School to serve as a civilian aide to the Secretary of War (1940-43). Although Secretary Henry L. Stimson asked Hastie to be responsible for all black military personnel, most of Hastie's activities related to the US Army. The aide resigned in 1943 in protest against the racism of the military establishment. The integration of the armed forces by executive order in 1948 was the legacy of Hastie's efforts. Based on primary materials in the Library of Congress, National Archives, the Yale University Library, and secondary sources; 34 notes.
N. G. Sapper

2637. McGuire, Phillip. JUDGE WILLIAM H. HASTIE CIVILIAN AIDE TO THE SECRETARY OF WAR, 1940-1943. *Negro Hist. Bull. 1977 40(3): 712-713.* Evaluates William H. Hastie's fight against racism in the armed forces during World War II. Although unable to convince the War Department to integrate the Army, he helped bring about military reform: the admission of Blacks to officer candidate schools, acceptance of Blacks as blood donors, integration of some recreational facilities, the commissioning of black doctors in the Army Medical Reserve, the training of black pilots as heavy bombardment fliers, the participation of black schools in the Air Force enlistment program, and the beginning of experiments with integrated units. Based on the author's unpublished dissertation; photo, note, biblio.
R. E. Noble

2638. McGuire, Phillip. JUDGE WILLIAM H. HASTIE AND ARMY RECRUITMENT, 1940-1942. *Military Affairs 1978 42(2): 75-79.* Discusses the work of Judge William H. Hastie, Civilian Aide to the Secretary of War, to persuade the War Department to include the black press in its military recruitment program during 1940-42. Hastie was charged with helping form and implement policies to effectively utilize blacks in the Army. Hastie considered the black press the best medium to aid him in his recruitment campaign. He did increase the number of blacks in the Army, although with great difficulty. Based on the papers of the Civilian Aide and NAACP; 27 notes.
A. M. Osur

2639. Mihelich, Dennis N. WORLD WAR II AND THE TRANSFORMATION OF THE OMAHA URBAN LEAGUE. *Nebraska Hist. 1979 60(3): 401-423.* Examines the activities of the Omaha Urban League which was started in 1928. Indicates that while the league entered the war period as a dispenser of social services, it emerged from it as a mediator for social justice. In the former capacity it enhanced the quality of life for a significant number in the black community; in the latter capacity it helped to initiate the struggle to include blacks in the mainstream of American life. 4 photos, map, 54 notes.
R. Lowitt

2640. Nuechterlein, James A. THE POLITICS OF CIVIL RIGHTS: THE FEPC, 1941-46. *Prologue 1978 10(3): 171-191.* Despite his lack of a strong political commitment to civil rights, Roosevelt bent to black pressures in 1941 to establish the Fair Employment Practices Committee through Executive Order 8802. The FEPC had no direct enforcement powers to curb job discrimination in war industries and was therefore forced to rely on other governmental agencies to cancel the war contracts of offenders. The principal weapon of the committee was publicity generated through media exposure of their hearings. Placing the FEPC under the supervision and control of hostile Paul V. McNutt, director of the War Production Board, in 1942 brought tensions between the committee and other government agencies to a head. An explosion resulted from McNutt's cancellation of committee hearings into railroad employment discrimination. Roosevelt was forced to step in, reconstituting the FEPC with a larger budget but still without enforcement powers. Between 1943 and the committee's demise in 1946, the body was under continual Congressional attack from conservative Southern Democrats who ended the FEPC in 1946. Based on research in the National Archives.
N. Lederer

2641. Okihiro, Gary Y. TULE LAKE UNDER MARTIAL LAW: A STUDY IN JAPANESE RESISTANCE. *J. of Ethnic Studies 1977 5(3): 71-85.* Examines the "orthodox interpretation" of the wartime internment of American Japanese, and the simplistic categorizations of Issei, Kibei, and Nisei found at the base of most treatments of the topic. Also attacks the "myth of the model minority" relative to Japanese Americans, especially as seen in *The Spoilage* by Thomas and Nishimoto. Analyzes the period of military rule by the Army at the Tule Lake Camp for "segregees" or "disloyals" during November 1943-January 1944, with the arrest and detention of the democratically elected representative body for the internees, the *Daihyo Sha Kai,* and the substitution of Army-named "block managers" for maintaining order. The authorities manipulated the famous "Status Quo" ballot of 11 January 1944, but the basic unity of purpose among factions of the internees did not waver; various groupings among the prisoners simply held different approaches to the same goal, that of gaining respect for their basic human rights and bringing reforms into camp administration. Primary sources; 44 notes.
G. J. Bobango

2642. Prickett, James R. COMMUNIST CONSPIRACY OR WAGE DISPUTE?: THE 1941 STRIKE AT NORTH AMERICAN AVIATION. *Pacific Hist. Rev. 1981 50(2): 215-233.* The strike at the North American Aviation plant in Inglewood, California, in the summer of 1941 resulted from an attempt to bring aircraft workers into the United Automobile Workers of America (UAW) and to increase wages. The union's negotiating committee twice postponed the strike while trying to work out a settlement with the National Defense Mediation Board, but the union voted to strike when the board proved to be dilatory. US Army forces broke the strike, and the UAW organizer of aircraft workers, a Communist, advised the strikers to return to work. There is no evidence that the strike was Communist-inspired. Communist leaders in the UAW in southern California had tried to prevent the strike. Based on oral history interviews, labor union records and publications, and other primary sources; 76 notes.
R. N. Lokken

2643. Ramsey, B. Carlyle. THE UNIVERSITY SYSTEM CONTROVERSY REEXAMINED: THE TALMADGE-HOLLEY CONNECTION. *Georgia Hist. Q. 1980 64(2): 190-203.* Georgia Governor Eugene Talmadge began his third term in 1941 with an effort to rid the Georgia University system of individuals promoting racial equality. His particular focus was Dr. Walter D. Cocking, Dean of the College of Education at the University of Georgia, who was dismissed in July 1941. In these endeavors, Talmadge was supported by Joseph Winthrop Holley, the black president of Georgia Normal College in Albany, to the disgust of other blacks. Based on interviews, newspapers and other sources; 62 notes.
G. R. Schroeder

2644. Reed, Merl E. FEPC AND THE FEDERAL AGENCIES IN THE SOUTH. *J. of Negro Hist. 1980 65(1): 43-56.* Despite the emergency of World War II, employment discrimination on the basis of race was a way of life in the South. The efforts of the Fair Employment Practices Committee (FEPC) in behalf of nondiscrimination were revolutionary, but a quarter of a century would pass before those efforts were enforced by later agencies. Based on primary materials in the Archives of the U.S. and the Atlanta Federal Records Center; 37 notes.
N. G. Sapper

2645. Rockoff, Hugh. THE RESPONSE OF THE GIANT CORPORATIONS TO WAGE AND PRICE CONTROLS IN WORLD WAR II. *J. of Econ. Hist. 1981 41(1): 123-128.* Reexamines the extent to which the giant corporations cooperated with wage and price controls during World War II, an issue to which John Kenneth Galbraith first drew attention. The compliance record could be characterized as a good one, but this achievement depended on the constraints on allocation and collective bargaining that existed during the war. Based on a sample of court cases involving the Office of Price Administration and large corporations, and monographs in which former administrators reflected on their wartime experiences.
J/S

2646. Rothwell, David R. UNITED CHURCH PACIFISM OCTOBER 1939. *Bull. of the United Church of Can. 1973 (22): 36-55.* Examines the reasons for the issuance of "A Witness Against War," a manifesto signed by 68 United Church of Canada ministers in October 1939 proclaiming opposition to Canadian participation in World War II. The central figure was Reverend R. Edis Fairbairn, who hoped to force the church to recognize the moral dilemma posed by the war and to advertise his conscientious commitment. The manifesto called for no action but sought merely "to bring into fellowship . . . all the Christian pacifists in the United Church." The church moderator suggested that "it is a very serious thing for a minister to split his congregation through controversy," but counselled "tolerance and acceptance of the conscientious rights of others." Concludes that "the pure form of idealism that underlay both the effort to Christianize the social order and to reform international affairs by pacific means was largely a victim of the Second World War." Based on newspapers, interviews and secondary sources; 90 notes.
B. D. Tennyson

2647. Roy, Patricia E. THE SOLDIERS CANADA DIDN'T WANT: HER CHINESE AND JAPANESE CITIZENS. *Can. Hist. Rev. [Canada] 1978 59(3): 341-358.* Draws on the records of many federal government departments and politicians as well as British Columbia sources. Argues that the Mackenzie King government was reluctant to enlist Chinese and Japanese Canadians in the armed forces during World War II partly for considerations of military morale but especially because of its sympathies with British Columbia's fears that military service would give Asian Canadians a strong claim to the franchise. Only late in the war, and under special circumstances, were Chinese and Japanese recruited.
A

2648. Sivachev, N. V. NEGRITIANSKII VOPROS V SSHA V GODY VTOROI MIROVOI VOINY [The negro question in the United States during the Second World War]. *Novaia i Noveishaia Istoriia [USSR] 1976 (6): 50-65.* Recent US historiography on the position of Negroes in the New Deal era, unlike the earlier adulation of Roosevelt, attacks the Democrats' racial policies of 1933-45. Soviet works have not discussed the negroes' position in detail. Investigates the negroes' attitudes toward World War II, their position in the armed forces and at home, and the struggle against discrimination and segregation. Drawing on many sources the analysis gives statistics on blacks in the forces, and their unequal treatment, especially regarding promotion. Instances of racial fights in war zones are stressed, as is the fact that no negroes received high decorations for valour. Figures also show discrimination in civilian occupations. However, the participation of the USSR in the war, the rise of national-liberation movements among colored peoples, prepared the ground for a future struggle to end segregation and racial discrimination in America. Based on many American newspapers, papers of H. S. Truman (Truman Library), US National Archives RG-228, and published studies; 89 notes.
D. N. Collins

2649. Skinner, James M. THE TUSSLE WITH RUSSELL: *THE OUTLAW* AS A LANDMARK IN AMERICAN FILM CENSORSHIP. *North Dakota Q. 1981 49(1): 4-12.* Provides a brief background of movie censorship during the 1940's, focusing on the controversy surrounding Howard Hughes's film, *The Outlaw*, starring the then-unknown Jane Russell, and Hughes's battle with the Hays Office, officially the Motion Picture Producers and Distributors of America (the MPPDA), and the Legion of Decency.

2650. Straub, Eleanor F. WOMEN IN THE CIVILIAN LABOR FORCE. Deutrich, Mabel E. and Purdy, Virginia C., ed. *Clio Was a Woman: Studies in the History of American Women* (Washington, D.C.: Howard U. Pr., 1980): 206-226. The establishment of the War Manpower Commission (WMC) in April 1942 allowed the development of a unified approach to the problems of civilian labor supply. The mobilization of women workers became a pressing chore. The United States, however, never adopted compulsory measures or sanctions to force women to work during World War II. The mobilization of women depended on effective publicity, special promotions, and public relations techniques. A discussion summary follows. 105 notes.
J. Powell

2651. Walker, Samuel. COMMUNISTS AND ISOLATIONISM: THE AMERICAN PEACE MOBILIZATION, 1940-1941. *Maryland Historian 1973 4(1): 1-12.* The short-lived American Peace Mobilization (APM) was dominated by the Communist Party USA. The history of the APM exemplifies the decline of noninterventionism in America and illustrates the problems of the American Communist movement after the signing of the Russo-German nonaggression pact. Based on secondary sources; 50 notes.
G. O. Gagnon

2652. Wollenberg, Charles. BLACKS VS. NAVY BLUE: THE MARE ISLAND MUTINY COURT MARTIAL. *California Hist. 1979 58(1): 62-75.* Describes the court martial in 1944 of 50 black sailors who refused to load ammunition ships at Port Chicago Naval Magazine on San Francisco Bay, 15 miles east of Mare Island, after two ships exploded with the loss of more than 300 men. Their trial embodied such issues as exclusive use of black sailors in loading ammunition ships, the Navy's segregation policies, and whether the men actually had mutinied. The trial proceedings were marred by admission of hearsay evidence and expressions of prejudice by the prosecution. All 50 men were found guilty. Subsequent appeals reduced the initially harsh sentences, while protests from the black community and the NAACP brought the affair to national attention. Eventually Secretary of the Navy James Forrestal, sensitive to race relations in the Navy, provided amnesties for almost all the men. Forrestal's efforts helped moved the Navy from its segregation policies to one of technical integration before President Truman's 1948 order to integrate the armed forces. Primary and secondary sources; 4 photos, 37 notes.
A. Hoffman

2653. Wollenberg, Charles. JAMES VS. MARINSHIP: TROUBLE ON THE NEW BLACK FRONTIER. *California History 1981 60(3): 262-279.* Describes the efforts of black shipyard workers to become full members in the International Brotherhood of Boilermakers, Iron Shipbuilders and Helpers of America. During World War II, thousands of blacks came to the San Francisco Bay area to work at skilled jobs for good wages. At the Marinship shipyard in Sausalito the boilermakers granted union clearances to black workers for employment but limited their union affiliation to auxiliary status. Led by Joseph James, a shipyard welder and NAACP leader, blacks argued for their right to full union membership. The issue went to court and in *James* v. *Marinship* (California, 1945), Negroes' right to full union membership was upheld. Ironically, the end of the war marked a decline in shipyard work, with the growing black population finding only unskilled employment at low wages in the postwar years. 10 photos, 54 notes.
A. Hoffman

2654. Young, Michael. FACING A TEST OF FAITH: JEWISH PACIFISTS DURING THE SECOND WORLD WAR. *Peace and Change 1975 3(2/3): 34-40.* Pacifist convictions and the necessity to fight the Nazis created a dilemma for the Jews of the Jewish Peace Fellowship in 1943.

2655. Zeitzer, Glen. THE FELLOWSHIP OF RECONCILIATION ON THE EVE OF THE SECOND WORLD WAR: A PEACE ORGANIZATION PREPARES. *Peace and Change 1975 3(2/3): 46-51.* The Fellowship of Reconciliation prepared a program of non-violent resistance during 1940-41 and tried to find solutions to end World War II.

Post World War II Reform and Reaction

2656. Baldasty, Gerald J. and Winfield, Betty Houchin. INSTITUTIONAL PARALYSIS IN THE PRESS: THE COLD WAR IN WASHINGTON STATE. *Journalism Q. 1981 58(2): 273-278, 285.* Examines press coverage of the Washington State Committee on Un-American Activities and its investigation of Communist influence at the University of Washington during the 1940's. The newspapers under study exhibited some degree of hostility toward the implicated faculty members. These negative feelings were reflected in the contents of the stories themselves, the placement of the stories, and the sources consulted. 4 tables, 27 notes.
J. S. Coleman

2657. Beeler, Dorothy. RACE RIOT IN COLUMBIA, TENNESSEE: FEBRUARY 25-27, 1946. *Tennessee Hist. Q. 1980 39(1): 49-61.* The February 1946 race riot in Columbia, Tennessee, mobilized many

civil rights organizations to use increasing black political power to force President Harry S. Truman into a stronger civil rights stance. The incident and reaction to it, major events of the period, helped create a base from which black orgnizations gained strength for the civil rights push of the 1950's and 1960's. Civil rights had become a national issue. Based on *Journal, Headquarters, Second Infantry Brigade, Nashville, Tennessee* and *Second Brigade Task Force, Columbia, Tennessee*, contemporary newspaper accounts, and secondary sources; 39 notes.
                   H. M. Parker, Jr.

2658. Berkowitz, Edward. GROWTH OF THE U. S. SOCIAL WELFARE SYSTEM IN THE POST-WORLD WAR II ERA: THE UMW REHABILITATION, AND THE FEDERAL GOVERNMENT. *Res. in Econ. Hist. 1980 5: 233-247.* The fact that government social welfare expenditures tripled between 1945 and 1956 contradicts the implicit assertion of political historians that those years were marked by conservatism and inactivity. The relationship between the federal government and the UMW's [United Mine Workers of America] Welfare and Retirement Fund was one source of the growth of federal expenditures which is often overlooked. Federal officials helped create the fund in 1946, and many federal officials worked for the fund after 1946. One focus of the fund's efforts was rehabilitation. A special relationship between the fund and the vocational rehabilitation program resulted in favored treatment of coal miners by the program and increased appropriations for the program. This relationship influenced the passage of three major pieces of federal social welfare legislation in the 1950's, including disability insurance.   J

2659. Berkowitz, Edward D. and McQuaid, Kim. WELFARE REFORM IN THE 1950'S. *Social Service Rev. 1980 54(1): 45-58.* Discusses the Eisenhower administration's policy to use federal money to reform welfare legislation, particularly programs dealing with disability, and notes that this policy was based on those established during the New Deal.

2660. Boender, Debra R. TERMINATION AND THE ADMINISTRATION OF GLENN L. EMMONS AS COMMISSIONER OF INDIAN AFFAIRS, 1953-1961. *New Mexico Hist. Rev. 1979 54(4): 287-304.* During an era when Congress favored the policy of "termination" for Indian tribes, Glenn L. Emmons (b. 1895) as Commissioner of Indian Affairs implemented his program of "readjustment with security." The three-point "Emmons plan," designed to improve the health, education, and economy of federally recognized Indian tribes, was successfully implemented during his term in office from 1953 to 1961. Although no permanent solution to federal Indian policy emerged from Emmons's administration, the success of his program brought about the end of termination as an official policy. Primary sources; photo, 3 tables, 45 notes.   P. L. McLaughlin

2661. Burt, Larry W. FACTORIES ON RESERVATIONS: THE INDUSTRIAL DEVELOPMENT PROGRAMS OF COMMISSIONER GLENN EMMONS, 1953-1960. *Arizona and the West 1977 19(4): 317-332.* Under Glenn L. Emmons, Commissioner of Indian Affairs, 1953-60, the Bureau of Indian Affairs initiated programs to prepare Indians for greater self-determination and federal withdrawal. By encouraging private industry to establish plants near the reservations, Emmons hoped to raise living standards of the Indians. This strategy faltered and government aid was necessary to bolster the program. Government involvement in tribal affairs expanded. The commissioner's efforts did, however, establish a precedent and pattern which later attracted factories and industries to Indian areas. 4 illus., 38 notes.   D. L. Smith

2662. Cleveland, Len G. GEORGIA BAPTISTS AND THE 1954 SUPREME COURT DESEGREGATION DECISION. *Georgia Hist. Q. 1975 59(Supplement): 107-117.* Discusses the reaction of Georgia's Baptist Church to the Supreme Court's *Brown* v. *Board of Education* decision during 1954-61.

2663. Cleveland, Mary L. A BAPTIST PASTOR AND SOCIAL JUSTICE IN CLINTON, TENNESSEE. *Baptist Hist. and Heritage 1979 14(2): 15-19.* Describes the efforts of Baptist pastor Paul Turner in dealing with the violence resulting from forced desegregation in the community of Clinton, Tennessee, in 1956.

2664. Coleburn, David R. and Scher, Richard K. AFTERMATH OF THE BROWN DECISION: THE POLITICS OF INTERPOSITION IN FLORIDA. *Tequesta 1977 (37): 62-81.* In 1957 the Florida state legislature passed an interposition resolution against the US Supreme Court decision in *Brown* v. *Board of Education* (US, 1954). Governor LeRoy Collins opposed the resolution, stating that it was meaningless and would fail. Time proved him correct.   H. S. Marks

2665. Dudley, J. Wayne. "HATE" ORGANIZATIONS OF THE 1940S: THE COLUMBIANS, INC. *Phylon 1981 42(3): 262-274.* A wave of racial violence followed World War II. A number of racist organizations emerged to promote patriotism, faith, and the white community. In 1946, several white men chartered the Columbians in Atlanta, Georgia. To join, one had to hate Negroes and Jews and have three dollars. While the Columbians stirred up Atlanta for several months, the city and state governments, local politicians, and the city's newspapers attacked the group until it was legally disbanded, June 1947.
                     A. G. Belles

2666. Faust, Clarence and Ward, F. Champion. ASPEN COLLEGE. *J. of General Educ. 1978 30(2): 67-72.* Explains the origin and content of a plan to establish a college in Aspen, Colorado, conceived and promoted during the late 1940's and early 50's by the American industrialist, Walter Paepcke. While the plan never materialized, it continues to raise important questions about the value and direction of undergraduate education in the United States. Specifically, Paepcke envisioned reforms in students' living conditions, the college library, laboratory facilities, the curriculum, and, most importantly, teaching to assure that students' liberal education is a truly liberalizing and civilizing experience. Unfortunately, financial and organizational obstacles prevented Paepcke from bringing his plan to fruition.   A. Howell

2667. Freeman, Ruges R. EDUCATIONAL DESEGREGATION IN ST. LOUIS. *Negro Hist. Bull. 1975 38(3): 364-369.* Summarizes the author's doctoral dissertation on the 1954-55 St. Louis desegregation plan. School desegregation in St. Louis was significant because planning for orderly integration was underway before the May 1954 Supreme Court decision.   M. J. Wentworth

2668. Grafton, Carl. JAMES E. FOLSOM AND CIVIL LIBERTIES IN ALABAMA. *Alabama Rev. 1979 32(1): 3-27.* James E. Folsom, two-term governor of Alabama, 1947-50 and 1955-58, consistently advocated a gradual extension of civil liberties to blacks and women. Folsom was not a moderate on these subjects, and contrary to some writers and interpreters he was neither populist nor opportunist. He sincerely opposed racial discrimination and less outspokenly, sexual inequality. Primary and secondary sources and personal interviews, including Governer Folsom; 68 notes.   J. F. Vivian

2669. Grant, Philip A., Jr. CATHOLIC CONGRESSMEN, CARDINAL SPELLMAN, ELEANOR ROOSEVELT, AND THE 1949-1950 FEDERAL AID TO EDUCATION CONTROVERSY. *Records of the Am. Catholic Hist. Soc. of Philadelphia 1979 90(1-4): 3-14.* Passage of a comprehensive federal aid to education bill by Congress failed in 1950 because the divisive issue of aid to parochial schools was raised. Francis Cardinal Spellman and Eleanor Roosevelt engaged in ugly polemics rather than true leadership behavior, and Catholic members of Congress avoided expressing opinions on an issue that had become virtually insoluble. The ineptness of congressional leaders greatly contributed to failure of the bill. Based on public documents and newspapers; 47 notes.
                  J. M. McCarthy

2670. Hunsaker, David M. THE RHETORIC OF BROWN VS. BOARD OF EDUCATION: PARADIGM FOR CONTEMPORARY SOCIAL PROTEST. *Southern Speech Communications J. 1978 43(2): 91-109.* Analyzes desegregation arguments in *Brown* v. *Board of Education* (US, 1954); the paradigm set up in this court case is representative of the rhetoric of all social protest, 1954-78.

2671. Johnson, Whittington B. THE VINSON COURT AND RACIAL SEGREGATION, 1946-1953. *J. of Negro Hist. 1979 63(3): 220-230.* Decisions of the Supreme Court under the leadership of Frederick M. Vinson made the state action concept the bulwark of protection of civil rights for blacks and rendered the separate-but-equal doctrine invalid, 1946-53.

2672. Katz, Jonathan. THE FOUNDING OF THE MATTACHINE SOCIETY: AN INTERVIEW WITH HENRY HAY. *Radical Am. 1977 11(4): 27-40.* Henry Hay was a prominent figure in the founding of the Mattachine Society in 1950, an organization that remained the principal homosexual rights group until the late 1960's. His recruiting efforts for the society were spurred on by his own deep involvement in Communist Party activities and his belief that homosexuals would become a major target of McCarthyite attacks. The involvement of Hay and other early organizers of the society in politically extremist activities generated additional public hostility toward the society as well as criticism from otherwise responsive homosexuals. The original purpose of the society and of the Foundation which spearheaded the group's activities was to identify homosexuals as a self-conscious group, confident of their place in history and working collectively as a positive force in relationship to the heterosexual majority. Hay left the society and dissolved the Foundation in 1953 when he became convinced that internal dissension was masking the original intent of the society. N. Lederer

2673. Kellog, Peter J. THE AMERICANS FOR DEMOCRATIC ACTION AND CIVIL RIGHTS IN 1948: CONSCIENCE IN POLITICS OR POLITICS IN CONSCIENCE? *Midwest Q. 1978 20(1): 49-63.* The issue of civil rights was prominent in US politics in 1948; examines the motives of members of Americans for Democratic Action in the 1940's and the impact of this group on awareness of racism.

2674. Kurtz, Michael L. GOVERNMENT BY THE CIVICS BOOK: THE ADMINISTRATION OF ROBERT F. KENNON, 1952-1956. *North Louisiana Hist. Assoc. J. 1981 12(2-3): 52-61.* Democrat Robert F. Kennon promised clean government when he ran for governor of Louisiana against the Long machine candidate in 1952. His efforts in civil service and penal reform, and his antigambling crusade made clear his commitment to good government, but an early appraisal indicates that his reforms were not enduring. His opposition to civil rights led to his support for Eisenhower in 1952 and his vocal opposition to the *Brown* decision in 1954. Based on interviews, voting records, and secondary sources; illus., 50 notes. J. F. Paul

2675. McAuliffe, Mary S. LIBERALS AND THE COMMUNIST CONTROL ACT OF 1954. *J. of Am. Hist. 1976 63(2): 351-367.* The Communist Control Act (1954), drafted and supported by liberals, illustrates how deeply McCarthyism penetrated American society. When Senator Hubert H. Humphrey and others defended the Act as a civil libertarian measure, they failed to comprehend the basic dangers of the Red Scare. Joseph R. McCarthy's technique of guilt by association had caught liberals as well as radicals. Liberals wanted to silence their enemies on the right while limiting the catch to Communist Party members. The Act thus confirms liberals' acquiescence to and participation in the postWorld War II Red Scare. Based on the *Congressional Record,* interviews, newspapers, and other sources; 57 notes. W. R. Hively

2676. McFadyen, Richard E. THE FDA'S REGULATION AND CONTROL OF ANTIBIOTICS IN THE 1950S: THE HENRY WELCH SCANDAL, FÉLIX MARTÍ-IBÁÑEZ, AND CHARLES PFIZER & CO. *Bull. of the Hist. of Medicine 1979 53(2): 159-169.* In late 1959, Dr. Henry Welch, a high official of the Food and Drug Administration, was charged with conflict of interest involving the federal regulation of antibiotics. The scandal indicated that it was dangerous for the agency to be closely intertwined with the industry it was supposed to regulate. Welch, who was chief regulator of the antibiotics industry, was chief editor of scientific papers sponsored by drug companies and which appeared in periodicals supported by the drug companies' own advertising and purchases of reprints. This went on from 1953 to 1960. The Kefauver investigation revealed the degree to which Welch was indebted to the drug industry, and Welch resigned and received a federal disability pension. In 1962, amendments to the Food and Drug law revised the status of the agency and revitalized its regulation of drugs. 44 notes. M. Kaufman

2677. Melton, Thomas R. WALTER SILLERS AND NATIONAL POLITICS (1948-1964). *J. of Mississippi Hist. 1977 39(3): 213-225.* Describes the actions of Walter Sillers, the powerful Speaker of the Mississippi House of Representatives, 1944-66, to oppose civil rights and to defend conservatism and states' rights during the presidential elections from 1948 through 1964. A leader of the 1948 Dixiecrat revolt, Sillers staunchly opposed integration and by 1956 was disillusioned with both national political parties. Based largely on the Walter Sillers Papers at Delta State University; 59 notes. J. W. Hillje

2678. Morantz, Regina Markell. THE SCIENTIST AS SEX CRUSADER: ALFRED C. KINSEY AND AMERICAN CULTURE. *Am. Q. 1977 29(5): 563-596.* Summarizes the origins of sex research in the United States and analyzes its acceptance in US culture and Alfred C. Kinsey's contribution to that acceptance. To understand the whole picture it is necessary to understand the man, his methods, and the content of his reports, together with the critical response they evoked. His publication of his findings brought strong reactions not simply on the ground of its violation of Victorian sex mores, but also from biologists, physicians, psychiatrists, theologians, and humanists. His occasional departure from reporting findings to expressions of his own liberal biases often made him vulnerable to such criticism. The full implications of his findings in related sociological analyses remain to be explored. 68 notes. R. V. Ritter

2679. Muller, Mary Lee. NEW ORLEANS PUBLIC SCHOOL DESEGREGATION. *Louisiana Hist. 1976 17(1): 69-88.* The *Brown* decision of 1954 prohibiting school segregation was a much resented intrusion of federal authority in local New Orleans affairs. The integration issue divided the white community into two opposing camps. The city's leadership sanctioned the fight against court-ordered desegregation by shunning acceptance of the order. When finally compelled to implement desegregation, the school board chose to limit racial mixing through pupil placement in the ninth ward, seemingly the course of least liability—politically, economically, and socially. 88 notes. E. P. Stickney

2680. Musselman, Thomas H. A CRUSADE FOR LOCAL OPTION: SHREVEPORT, 1951-1952. *North Louisiana Hist. Assoc. J. 1975 6(2): 59-73.* During the early 1950's, an active political campaign was waged "for the purpose of 'drying up' Shreveport" by members and supporters of the Shreveport Ministerial Association. "Both supporters and opponents of prohibition resorted to unsavory campaign tactics," and the "local option campaign of 1951 and 1952 was bitterly fought and roughly contested." At the end, on election day, 16 July 1952, "voters turned out in near record numbers to defeat prohibition in Shreveport with a total of 28,806 going to the polls." 77 notes.
A. N. Garland

2681. Pace, David. LENOIR CHAMBERS OPPOSES MASSIVE RESISTANCE: AN EDITOR AGAINST VIRGINIA'S DEMOCRATIC ORGANIZATION, 1955-1959. *Virginia Mag. of Hist. and Biog. 1974 82(4): 415-429.* The Supreme Court's 1954 decision outlawing racial segregation in public schools led to a campaign in Virginia to prevent implementation of the decision. Lenoir Chambers, editor of the *Norfolk Virginian-Pilot*, waged an editorial struggle against the plan backed by Senator Harry F. Byrd to close schools before accepting integration. Chambers' position resulted not from racial liberalism but from a traditional respect for law and order. Based on primary sources; photo, 34 notes. R. F. Oaks

2682. Rand, Ivan C. DÉCISION TOUCHANT LA SÉCURITÉ SYNDICALE DANS LE CONFLIT FORD 1946 [Decision concerning union security in the Ford conflict, 1946]. *Industrial Relations [Canada] 1975 30(4): 761-771.* Presents the text of the famous Judge Rand decision, 29 January 1946, in the arbitration between the Ford Motor Company of Canada Limited and the International United Automobile Workers (Canadian Region). Develops a general philosophy of labor relations in a democratic industrial society, and considers individual rights and social duty. Lays out principles for management and labor, asserting that labor unions are natural and necessary organizations, and that collective negotiation is an accepted and desirable social institution. Some points include: mandatory payment of union dues through employer salary deduction, worker freedom to participate in activities, equal vote of all members in strike decision, and simple majority in strike decision. This decision sets new principles where none were yet established, and reinforces the security of unionism. S. Sevilla

2683. Scott, William B. JUDGE J. WATIES WARING: ADVOCATE OF "ANOTHER" SOUTH. *South Atlantic Q. 1978 77(3): 320-334.* Federal Judge J. Waties Waring (1880-1968) was responsible for declaring the white Democratic Party primary system in his native South Carolina unconstitutional in 1947 and he later struck down segregation in the state's public schools. Far from being a well-intentioned old man, he found the racial conditions of South Carolina standing in stark contrast to his fundamental beliefs, which had been arrived at both by political heritage and religious (Episcopal) conviction. He was also supported by his second wife, who was much more outspoken in her denunciation of the racial situation. Waring thus ceased trying to find any accommodation and rejected segregation as entirely unjust. In so doing he merely anticipated the responses of large numbers of southern whites following World War II. Based on the Marion A. Wright Papers (Linville, N. C.), Waring's "Reminiscences" in the Oral History Institute, Columbia University, state and federal documents and newspapers; 29 notes.

H. M. Parker, Jr.

2684. Smith, Ronald A. THE PAUL ROBESON-JACKIE ROBINSON SAGA AND A POLITICAL COLLISION. *J. of Sport Hist. 1979 6(2): 5-27.* In 1949, the House Committee on Un-American Activities asked Jackie Robinson (1919-72) to help eliminate Paul Robeson's (1898-1976) leadership role among Negroes by criticizing Robeson's statements that Negroes would refuse to fight against the USSR. Robeson helped to desegregate baseball, and it was ironic that later Robinson, the first black to play in the Major Leagues in the 20th century, agreed to counter Robeson's pro-Soviet viewpoints. Robinson desegregated baseball under white terms, while Robeson fought for human rights under free political terms. The attacks on Robeson were part of the Cold War hysteria. Both men fought in their own ways for equal rights for blacks. 2 illus., 100 notes.

M. Kaufman

2685. Theoharis, Athan. THE TRUMAN ADMINISTRATION AND THE DECLINE OF CIVIL LIBERTIES: THE FBI'S SUCCESS IN SECURING AUTHORIZATION FOR A PREVENTIVE DETENTION PROGRAM. *J. of Am. Hist. 1978 64(4): 1010-1030.* Uses the history of the Federal Bureau of Investigation's preventive detention program to demonstrate the possible lack of effective executive control over internal security policy during the Cold War. Top level bureaucrats in the FBI and the Justice Department may have made policy decisions regarding the compilation and use of lists of suspected subversives without informing the President. The FBI's desire for written authorization from the Justice Department to ignore the restrictions of the Internal Security Act of 1950 may have been pursued without President Truman's knowledge. Bureaucrats, operating in a vacuum, may have made national security decisions without regard to their constitutionality or to the need for high-level authorization. 31 notes.

T. P. Linkfield

2686. Tomberlin, Joseph A. FLORIDA AND THE SCHOOL DESEGREGATION ISSUE, 1954-1959: A SUMMARY VIEW. *J. of Negro Educ. 1974 43(4): 457-467.* By 1959 Florida had not fully adhered to the 1954 Supreme Court ruling on desegregation in schools, and it was not until the Civil Rights Act of 1964 that desegregation was stepped-up appreciably.

2687. Vaughan, Philip H. THE TRUMAN ADMINISTRATION'S FAIR DEAL FOR BLACK AMERICA. *Missouri Hist. Rev. 1976 70(3): 291-305.* When he sponsored a Fair Deal in 1949 President Harry S. Truman insisted that a meaningful civil rights program had to be an integral part of it. Such a program was before Congress during 1949 and the first half of 1950. Except for certain provisions of the Housing Act of 1949, Truman had to be content with civil rights' victories achieved by executive order or through the courts. Nevertheless, by continuing appeals to Congress for civil rights legislation, Truman helped reverse the long acceptance of segregation and discrimination by establishing integration as a moral principle. Primary and secondary sources; illus., 47 notes.

W. F. Zornow

2688. Wagy, Thomas R. GOVERNOR LEROY COLLINS OF FLORIDA AND THE LITTLE ROCK CRISIS OF 1957. *Arkansas Hist. Q. 1979 38(2): 99-115.* LeRoy Collins was governor of Florida from 1954 to 1961. During the school integration crisis in Little Rock, Arkansas, in the fall of 1957, Collins championed a moderate position. He opposed southerners who resisted court integration orders. Describes several of his speeches. The South chose defiance rather than moderation, and Collins never held elective office again. Primary and secondary sources; 56 notes.

G. R. Schroeder

2689. Walker, Samuel. THE ORIGINS OF THE AMERICAN POLICE-COMMUNITY RELATIONS MOVEMENT: THE 1940S. *Criminal Justice Hist. 1980 1: 225-246.* The basis for the development of early police-community relations emanated from the perceived necessity to placate animosities of racial minorities. The initial theory concerned the need for police to separate opposing racial groups once an outbreak of violence occurred. The year 1940 witnessed an upsurge of racial conflict requiring novel approaches. Police administrators possessing enlightened attitudes began structuring police training and retraining programs designed to alter traditional police attitudes toward racial conflict. Most police administrators of this era targeted upper echelon command officers for receipt of community relations training when this reeducation should have been directed toward a larger percentage of police officers. Table, 49 notes.

J. L. Ingram

2690. Weaver, Bill L. THE BLACK PRESS AND THE ASSAULT ON PROFESSIONAL BASEBALL'S "COLOR LINE," OCTOBER, 1945-APRIL, 1947. *Phylon 1979 40(4): 303-317.* Focuses on the responses of the black press to the first black in 20th-century professional baseball, Jack Roosevelt "Jackie" Robinson, who was signed by Branch Rickey for the minor league Montreal Royals in 1945 and moved to the major league Brooklyn Dodgers in 1947. Based mainly on newspapers; 69 notes.

G. R. Schroeder

2691. Wolman, Philip J. THE OAKLAND GENERAL STRIKE OF 1946. *Southern California Q. 1975 57(2): 147-178.* Examines the causes and events concerning the general strike in Oakland, California, 3-5 December 1946. Part of a nationwide series of strikes in 1946, the Oakland incident involved most city workers whole-heartedly endorsing a strike which for 54 hours shut down most economic activity in the city. Essential facilities were maintained at minimum levels while city leaders and national union officials worked to end the strike, but its official termination neither resolved smoldering issues nor penetrated worker discontent. In the 1947 municipal election a labor slate of candidates defeated the incumbents. Suggests that the general strike was occasioned by an emotional outburst against business' failure to effect long-postponed social changes. Primary sources, including personal interviews, and secondary studies; 99 notes.

A. Hoffman

6. THE CONTEMPORARY SCENE

General

2692. Aron, William S. STUDENT ACTIVISM OF THE 1960'S REVISITED: A MULTIVARIATE ANALYSIS RESEARCH NOTE. *Social Forces 1974 52(3): 408-414.* The present study finds that there is very little direct effect on activism by social background, indicating that past studies of student political activism have overemphasized the influence of social background factors. Social background explains more of the variation in political attitudes and beliefs than it explains variation in political activism. This is not to say the social background is not important or influential in the development of an activist political commitment —merely that no univalent rules exist which link social background characteristics with an individual's involvement in politics. There are too many intervening factors, such as political attitudes and beliefs (and others not accounted for here) which influence individuals in numberless ways. J

2693. Aubéry, Pierre. NATIONALISME ET LUTTE DES CLASSES AU QUEBEC [Nationalism and class struggle in Quebec]. *Am. Rev. of Can. Studies 1975 5(2): 130-145.* Intellectuals in Quebec are trying to help the proletariat French-speaking community bring about social, political, and economic equality for all Quebecois, 1960's-70's.

2694. Auger, Deborah A. THE POLITICS OF REVITALIZATION IN GENTRIFYING NEIGHBORHOODS: THE CASE OF BOSTON'S SOUTH END. *J. of the Am. Planning Assoc. 1979 45(4): 515-522.* Federal and local officials have in recent years enacted programs to escalate the middle-class resettlement of city neighborhoods. Enamoured with the physical and economic benefits promised by the back-to-the-city movement, they have underestimated the shortcomings of this neighborhood revitalization strategy. The experience of Boston's South End with publicly supported middle-class resettlement illustrates the severe social and political strains that can develop between incumbents and more affluent "pioneers"—strains which can ultimately inflict damage on the neighborhood's poor. Officials must direct current resources to aid the cities' poorer residents and avoid stimulating gentrification until its adverse side effects can be controlled. J

2695. Balswick, Jack. THE JESUS PEOPLE MOVEMENT: A GENERATIONAL INTERPRETATION. *J. of Social Issues 1974 30(3): 23-42.* The Jesus People, as members of a distinctive age stratum, exhibit many attributes common to the counterculture: subjectivism, informality, spontaneity, new forms and media of communication. As members of a distinctive religious orientation, they exhibit attributes common to a fundamentalist and Pentecostal Christianity: the inerrancy of scripture, emphasis on the Holy Spirit, and a commitment to "one way" to God. This phenomenological study of the Jesus People suggests that the movement can best be seen as the result of a youthful cohort's "fresh contact" (using Mannheim's concept) with the fundamentalist tradition in Christianity, set within the context to structural conditions in American society in the 1960s and in organized American religion, plus the distinctive life style and orientations of the broader youth counterculture movement. It is suggested that this unique generational movement represents a potential for change in American religious institutions. J

2696. Baral, J. K. ANTI-VIETNAM WAR STUDENT MOVEMENT IN AMERICA 1965-1971. *Indian Pol. Sci. Rev. [India] 1978 12(1): 43-58.* The student anti-Vietnam War movement was one part of the New Left. Demonstrations in October and November 1969 marked the height of its success. The movement did voice other concerns of the New Left, such as antiracism and student freedom, but it was motivated considerably by opposition to the draft. As draft calls declined, so did the movement. Throughout its history it was divided as to goals and means and it failed to gain the support of workers and most blacks.
J. C. English

2697. Barron, Milton L. RECENT DEVELOPMENTS IN MINORITY AND RACE RELATIONS. *Ann. of the Am. Acad. of Pol. and Social Sci. 1975 (420): 125-176.* A review of minority and race developments during the years 1968-73. Accords especial emphasis to the Negroes' retreat from radicalism and violence in favor of a separate subculture within the larger community. Real progress remains questionable. Lesser attention is given the struggles of American Indians, Mexican Americans, Asian Americans, Puerto Rican immigrants, white minorities, and religious groups. A general pattern of confusion and uncertainty emerges. 5 tables, 117 notes.
V. L. Human

2698. Bell, Carolyn. IMPLEMENTING SAFETY AND HEALTH REGULATIONS FOR WOMEN IN THE WORKPLACE. *Feminist Studies 1979 5(2): 286-301.* Discusses whether the Occupational Safety and Health Act (US, 1970), designed to assure workers of uniform health and safety protection, has protected or restricted workers, particularly women, in the labor force, the topic of a conference among students and faculty at Smith College in 1976. Briefly discusses the regulatory policies of the Environmental Protection Agency (EPA) and the Equal Employment Opportunity Commission (EEOC) as well as OSHA, focusing on OSHA's standards for certain dangerous chemicals and the problems of implementing policy standards of the nearly 70,000 chemicals, with 2,000 added each year, used in the workplace.
G. Smith

2699. Briscoe, Jerry B. THE POLITICS OF PLANNING: IN CALIFORNIA COMMUNITY CONSERVATIONISM IS STIRRING. *Pacific Hist. 1977 21(1 supplement): 19-26.* California's history is replete with stories of attacks on the environment, but the era of unquestioned growth is coming to an end. Describes the current community conservation movement and suggests examples of strength in California such as historic preservation districts and limited growth. Secondary sources; 23 notes.
G. L. Olson

2700. Brym, Robert J. REGIONAL SOCIAL STRUCTURE AND AGRARIAN RADICALISM IN CANADA: ALBERTA, SASKATCHEWAN, AND NEW BRUNSWICK. *Can. Rev. of Sociol. and Anthrop. [Canada] 1978 15(3): 339-351.* In this paper it is suggested that regional variations in Canadian populist ideologies are largely a function of variations in the social organization of farmers. Of particular importance in this connection are (a) the degree of social *connectivity* among farmers; (b) the degree to which farmers are able to retain their position as *independent* commodity producers; and (c) the density of *inter-class* ties between farmers and others. It is tentatively concluded through an examination of agrarian organization and unrest in Alberta, Saskatchewan, and New Brunswick that (a) the greater the degree of social connectivity, the greater the degree of radicalism (left or right); (b) the greater the degree of independence, the more likely it is that radicalism will take on a right-wing colouring; (c) the greater the density of ties between farmers and urban workers, the more likely it is that left-wing populism will emerge; and (d) the greater the density of ties between farmers and non-working-class urban groups, the more likely it is that right-wing populism will emerge. J

2701. Cavaioli, Frank J. CHICAGO'S ITALIAN AMERICANS RALLY FOR IMMIGRATION REFORM. *Italian Americana 1980 6(2): 142-156.* Brief history of the American Committee on Italian Migration (ACIM), focusing on the Chicago chapter formed in 1952, particularly the group's Immigration Legislation Rally in 1963 to protest against the national origins-quota system established in the United States in the 1920's, which limited the number of immigrants from southern and eastern European countries much more than the number from Anglo-Saxon nations; 1952-67.

2702. Clark, S. D. THE ATTACK ON THE AUTHORITY STRUCTURE OF THE CANADIAN SOCIETY. *Tr. of the Royal Soc. of Can. [Canada] 1976 14: 3-15.* Discusses the effect of the protest movements of the 1960's on Canadian society. In Canada the middle class was more narrowly based than in the United States; hence, there was less opportunity for individual advancement. Dissatisfied Canadians, both working class and middle class, sought opportunities to the south. After World War II there were more economic opportunities in Canada with the

resulting population shift from rural to urban; but, in the 1960's, more young people entered the work force than there were positions. At the same time, dissatisfied Americans emigrated to Canada where they became leaders in opposition to the old order. Although in the United States the protest movement was more violent, in Canada it had a more lasting effect because many Canadian officials had little experience in running newly created educational and governmental agencies and more readily yielded to pressure. 2 notes.
J. D. Neville

2703. Debo, Angie. "TO ESTABLISH JUSTICE." *Western Hist. Q. 1976 7(4): 405-412.* The author recounts her personal efforts to enlist concerned citizens in support for Indians, specifically: the Alaska Eskimos, Indians, and Aleuts; the Havasupai of Arizona; and the Pima of southern Arizona. What is needed is "a unified and proficient Indian leadership supported by public sensitivity to Indian aspirations... [to] bring about a change in governmental structure and policy." Only then can general reform be achieved.
D. L. Smith

2704. DelCastillo, Adelaida R. STERILIZATION: AN OVERVIEW. Mora, Magdalena and DelCastillo, Adelaida R., ed. *Mexican Women in the United States: Struggles Past and Present* (Los Angeles: U. of California Chicano Studies Res. Center, 1980): 65-70. Discusses the predominantly punitive rationale underlying the advocacy of sterilization in the United States, especially involving Mexican women. The first sterilization bill was passed in the United States in 1907. More recently, legislators, judges, and doctors have advocated and mandated forced sterilization for other than eugenic purposes. The poor and ethnic minorities, by extension, have come to be seen as social misfits and an economic drain on the state. Their sterilization has been advocated even though it violates a number of juridical precedents, laws, and constitutional rights that protect the fundamentals of privacy and procreation. 40 notes.
J. Powell

2705. Deleon, David. THE AMERICAN AS ANARCHIST: SOCIAL CRITICISM IN THE 1960'S. *Am. Q. 1973 25(5): 516-537.* Anarchistic responses of right, left, and youth groups during the 1960's were extreme exaggerations of the philosophical method of American liberalism as is evidenced in the group's middle-class constituency and audience, methods of analysis, and the educational and pacifistic content of their programs. Under such prodding the American bourgeoise traditionally act constructively and minimally to reduce discomforting disparity between the real and ideal. Primary and secondary sources; 32 notes.
W. D. Piersen

2706. Deloria, Vine, Jr. LEGISLATION AND LITIGATION CONCERNING AMERICAN INDIANS. *Ann. of the Am. Acad. of Pol. and Social Sci. 1978 436: 86-96.* The period 1957-77 witnessed an increasing tendency to include Indians in programs and legislation that affected all Americans, particularly in the field of social welfare and development. Indians, as a whole, made good use of their eligibility for these new opportunities, and entered the mainstream of public social concern. Legislation dealing specifically with Indian rights and legal status was generally trivial because no administration made more than a perfunctory effort to define the larger philosophical issues that might have clarified and modernized the Indian legal status. In litigation Indians were unusually successful in some of their efforts, although, again, truly definitive cases that might have proved a fertile ground for long-term gains in the development of contemporary understanding were sparse. Generally, those cases which might have produced landmark theories or doctrines, the Supreme Court refused to take and the decisions, remaining on the federal circuit level, are not sufficiently strong or clear to provide a basis for further development. The era ended with a state of benign confusion, in which Indians seemed more concerned with funding programs than sketching out in broader and more comprehensive terms the ideologies and theories that are necessary for sustained growth. It was, basically, an undistinguished era, but one of maturing and awareness.
J

2707. DiClerico, Robert. THE NEW LEFT: AN ALTERNATIVE VISION. *South Atlantic Q. 1976 75(3): 339-350.* The American New Left proposed to replace representative democracy with participatory democracy, "whereby people propose, discuss, decide, plan, and implement those decisions that affect their lives." However, the New Left never probed the problems inherent in participatory democracy concerning the relationships of equity of participation, equity of interest, equity of need, or equity of competence. Their failure to resolve these problems prevented American society from undergoing the traumatic experience of the radical alteration of its institutions. Primary sources; 27 notes.
W. L. Olbrich

2708. Dolgoff, Sam. LE NÉO-ANARCHISME AMÉRICAIN: NOUVELLE GAUCHE ET GAUCHE TRADITIONNELLE [American neo-anarchism: The new left and the traditional left]. *Mouvement Social [France] 1973 (83): 181-199.* Neoanarchism was born out of the youth battle against war, racism, false values, crime, and other negative aspects of the Establishment. The movement developed without differing greatly from the leftist movement. The libertarian rightist anarchists arose out of the 28-29 August 1969 Young Americans for Freedom Conference held in St. Louis, where a political split revealed the anarcho-libertarian stream led by economist Murray N. Rothbard, journalist Karl Hess, writer Jerome Tuccille, and others. They later formed the Society for Individual Liberty. Also distinguishes the old school anarchists, a group of diffuse individuals linked by underground newspapers, and the pacifist-anarchists, who defend the Third World. Contrasts this movement with the goals and philosophy of collectives and communes. Based on underground newspapers and on secondary sources; 10 notes.
S. Sevilla

2709. Dollar, Clyde D. THE SECOND TRAGEDY AT WOUNDED KNEE: A 1970S CONFRONTATION AND ITS HISTORICAL ROOTS. *Am. West 1973 10(5): 4-11, 58-61.* For 70 days from 27 February 1973 the militant American Indian Movement occupied Wounded Knee, a remote hamlet on the Pine Ridge Sioux Reservation in South Dakota, in opposition to the Oglala Sioux elected tribal council and the federal government. The attempt to focus world attention on Indian mistreatment became "Indian mistreatment of Indians and a cul-de-sac for Indian hope." The blustering threats and demands of the AIM spokesmen turned into "silly rantings of petty demagogues." Reversion to prereservation warrior society behavior patterns likely will not produce long-range benefits, but will threaten the culture of the Sioux with extinction. AIM succeeded in catapulting itself into a pre-eminent political position of leadership with the Indians, but has little chance of effective negotiation with the federal government; revival of tribal warrior culture patterns threatens the mechanism which offers the most hope for the Indians today, the democratic process. The cost of the tragic affair exceeds seven million dollars. 8 illus., note.
D. L. Smith

2710. Donahue, Francis. ANATOMY OF CHICANO THEATER. *San José Studies 1977 3(1): 37-48.* Discusses guerrilla theater used by Mexican Americans to bring about social consciousness and social change; examines the types of dramatic presentations used, and characterizations, 1965-76.

2711. Donahue, Francis. THE CHICANO STORY. *Colorado Q. 1973 21(3): 307-316.* Chicanos are the second largest minority group in the United States and total 3% of the population. Most Chicanos live in the Southwest where they receive fewer benefits from the American lifestyle. Discusses the career of Cesar Chavez (b. 1927) and the establishment of La Raza Unida Party in 1968. The four goals of the Chicano movement are 1) self-identity, 2) pluralistic philosophy of subculture, 3) social protest, and 4) unity within the movement.
B. A. Storey

2712. Feaver, George. [THE AMERICAN INDIANS AND THE NEW TRIBALISM].
WOUNDED KNEE AND THE NEW TRIBALISM: THE AMERICAN INDIANS (I), *Encounter [Great Britain] 1975 44(2): 28-35.*
WOUNDED KNEE AND THE NEW TRIBALISM: THE AMERICAN INDIANS (II), *Encounter [Great Britain] 1975 44(3): 16-24.*
VINE DELORIA: THE AMERICAN INDIANS (III), *Encounter [Great Britain] 1975 44(4): 33-46.*
AN INDIAN MELODRAMA: THE AMERICAN INDIAN (IV), *Encounter [Great Britain] 1975 44(5): 23-34.*
THE TRUE ADVENTURE: EPILOGUE TO "THE AMERICAN INDIAN," *Encounter [Great Britain] 1975 45(4): 25-32.*
Against the background of Indian history since 1877, explores the ideology of the American Indian Movement (AIM) and of Sioux spokesman Vine Deloria, Jr., focusing on the rise of Red Power since 1969 and the occupation of Wounded Knee on the Pine Ridge Indian Reservation

in South Dakota. Analyzes the American fascination with adventurism which has led to the formation of a 20th-century "noble savage" image for American Indians, elevating AIM and Red Power to one of the leading civil rights causes of the 1970's.

2713. Fendrich, James M. BLACK AND WHITE ACTIVISTS TEN YEARS LATER: POLITICAL SOCIALIZATION AND ADULT LEFT-WING POLITICS. *Youth & Soc. 1976 8(1): 81-104.* Although student activism is a good predictor of the degree of black political participation, it is not related to black radicalism. The civil rights movement was the key determinant in later white radicalism. This difference appears primarily due to adult black politics' emphasizing the single issue of advancement of the race, and to the fact that blacks are a more homogeneous group. Based on a 1971-72 survey of former students in one of the major centers of the civil rights movement, and on primary and secondary works; 2 tables, fig., 14 notes, biblio.   J. H. Sweetland

2714. Fendrich, James M. KEEPING THE FAITH OR PURSUING THE GOOD LIFE: A STUDY OF THE CONSEQUENCES OF PARTICIPATION IN THE CIVIL RIGHTS MOVEMENT. *Am. Sociol. Rev. 1977 42(1): 144-157.* Examines the long-range political consequences of the earliest phase of the student movement—the civil rights movement before 1965. The research focused on a relatively homogeneous group of black and white activists who participated in demonstrations in one of the leading centers of the civil rights movement. A theoretical causal model was developed and tested using nine exogenous and intervening variables to explain adult radical political attitudes and leftist behavior. The model accounts for 45.6 percent of the variance in radical attitudes and 22.2 percent of the variance in leftist behavior. Racial differences in adult politics are explained. Tentative conclusions concerning the consequences of participation in left-wing student politics are presented.   J

2715. Fendrich, James M. and Tarleau, Alison T. MARCHING TO A DIFFERENT DRUMMER: OCCUPATIONAL AND POLITICAL CORRELATES OF FORMER STUDENT ACTIVISTS. *Social Forces 1973 52(2): 245-253.* This study reports on long-range consequences of student political activism. Three groups were selected: (1) former civil rights activists, (2) student government members, and (3) apolitical undergraduates. It was hypothesized that variation in political activism would be linked with differing occupations and political orientations. Former civil rights activists are heavily concentrated in the knowledge and human service occupations and are politically radical to liberal in their attitudes and behavior.   J

2716. Floyd, Charles F. BILLBOARD CONTROL UNDER THE HIGHWAY BEAUTIFICATION ACT—A FAILURE OF LAND USE CONTROLS. *J. of the Am. Planning Assoc. 1979 45(2): 115-126.* Billboard control and removal under the Highway Beautification Act has largely been a failure, achieving little toward the accomplishment of stated Congressional goals. Crippling amendments, "loopholes" in the designation of commercial and industrial zones, the exemption of on-premise signs, a lack of national standards, reliance upon the use of eminent domain rather than the police power to remove noncomforming signs, inadequate appropriations for the program, and general indifference among former supporters have been the main causes of the Act's ineffectiveness. Extensive amendment and vigorous administration are essential if the Act is ever to be effective.   J

2717. Fox, Daniel M. and Stone, Judith F. BLACK LUNG: MINER'S MILITANCY AND MEDICAL UNCERTAINTY, 1968-1972. *Bull. of the Hist. of Medicine 1980 54(1): 43-63.* The passage of the Coal Mine Health and Safety Act (US, 1969; amended, 1972) resulted from strikes and demonstrations by miners who persuaded public officials to accept theirs, rather than medical men's, definition of disease. The curtailment of the United Mine Workers of America health care and pension system was a threat to miners, as were the decline of the coal industry and periodic mine disasters. After three weeks of wildcat strikes in February 1969, the West Virginia legislature accepted the miners' demands for recognition of black lung disease as a compensable occupational disease. The federal law of 1969 resulted from the miners' strength as well as the shrewd political stance of the mine operators. In this case, decisions were not medical but political. Sources include government documents and interviews; 54 notes.   M. Kaufman

2718. Frieden, Bernard J. THE CONSUMER'S STAKE IN ENVIRONMENTAL REGULATION. *Ann. of the Am. Acad. of Pol. and Social Sci. 1980 451(Sept): 36-44.* Local governments across the country have been enacting new growth control regulations, usually in the name of environmental protection. The effects of these new controls can be seen most clearly in northern California, where a large number of San Francisco suburbs have all tightened their restrictions on home building. The new control systems have made it easy for groups that oppose growth to block or curtail new housing developments. Growth control tactics and the environmental politics that surround them have succeeded in reducing the amount of housing built in many new developments, restricting competition among home builders, raising costs to consumers, and restricting the locational choices available to families with average incomes. At the same time, they have contributed little to the improvement of the public environment, but have protected many established suburban communities against the inconveniences of growth and the loss of open land. By blocking growth in locations close to job centers, opponents have shifted home building to the suburban fringe, where the environmental costs are usually greater.   J

2719. Game, Kingsley W. CONTROLLING AIR POLLUTION: WHY SOME STATES TRY HARDER. *Policy Studies J. 1979 7(4): 728-738.* Study of rates of compliance with Clean Air Amendments was measured, concluding that organization, bureaucracy, demography, and energy scarcity rather than actual pollution or party politics were more important in determining spending levels for compliance, 1970-79.

2720. Gordon, Fred. A CLASS ANALYSIS OF THE RADICAL STUDENT MOVEMENT. *New Scholar 1973 4(1): 5-27.* Outlines three basic theories of student behavior: humanist, irrationalistic, and class. Using a synthesis of these theories, the author describes the progressive and reactionary natures of the student rebellions in the 1960's and the history of the Students for a Democratic Society via its political alliances. Bibliographically the students' revolt began in the 1950's with their reading of the works of David Riesman, C. Wright Mills, and Kenneth Keniston which led to a crisis in the students' petit bourgeois outlook.   D. K. Pickens

2721. Grabowski, Harry G. and Vernon, John M. CONSUMER PRODUCT SAFETY REGULATION. *Am. Econ. Rev. 1978 68(2): 284-289.* While the early evidence is inconclusive, the current emphasis on direct controls (product standards and bans) contributes to a serious misallocation of resources. In addition to ignoring the costs of such controls the Consumer Product Safety Commission does not deal effectively with products (such as microwave ovens) whose hazards to the consumer are more subtle and poorly defined. Information on the safety of such products is rare and difficult to locate. Ref.
   D. K. Pickens

2722. Granberg, Donald and Granberg, Beth Wellman. PRO-LIFE VERSUS PRO-CHOICE: ANOTHER LOOK AT THE ABORTION CONTROVERSY IN THE U.S. *Sociol. and Social Res. 1981 65(4): 424-434.* The prolife assertion that disapproval of abortion reflects a general prolife ideology received support if one considers this ideology as including favoring large families and disapproving of suicide and euthanasia. It does not include opposition to capital punishment or the military, and it does not include favoring gun control or increased spending on health. The prochoice assertion that approval of legalized abortion reflects general support for civil liberties received consistent support.
   J/S

2723. Greer, Edward. AIR POLLUTION AND CORPORATE POWER: MUNICIPAL REFORM LIMITS IN A BLACK CITY. *Pol. and Soc. 1974 4(4): 483-510.* Presents a case study of Gary, Indiana, considered a prototypical industrial city. Outlines the city's political impotency before and since the election of black reform mayor Richard Hatcher in face of US Steel's resistance to implementing air pollution controls at its Gary Works. The corporation's strategy did not change until the federal government provided the means of passing the costs for pollution abatement along to the consumer. Based on primary and secondary sources; 136 notes.   D. G. Nielson

2724. Gross, Harriet. JANE KENNEDY: MAKING HISTORY THROUGH MORAL PROTEST. *Frontiers 1977 2(2): 73-81.* Jane

Kennedy describes her career as a political activist since 1964, including her involvement in the civil rights movement, the anti-Vietnam War movement, and her two prison terms; part of a special issue on women's oral history.

2725. Hagan, John and Bernstein, Ilene N. CONFLICT IN CONTEXT: THE SANCTIONING OF DRAFT RESISTERS, 1963-76. *Social Problems 1979 27(1): 109-122.* Describes the period from 1963 through 1968 as one of coercive control, as shown by the imprisonment of US draft resisters; while from 1969 to 1976, a period of decline in demonstrations and increase in reform-oriented articles in the press, use of probation increased.

2726. Harakas, Stanley S. SOCIAL CONCERN AND THE GREEK ORTHODOX ARCHDIOCESE. *Greek Orthodox Theological Rev. 1980 25(4): 377-408.* Surveys Archbishop Iakovos's keynote addresses at the 10 clergy-laity congresses held during 1960-80, with stress on social and moral issues, including world peace and the state of the American family.

2727. Hayes, James R. THE DIALECTICS OF RESISTANCE: AN ANALYSIS OF THE GI MOVEMENT. *J. of Social Issues 1975 31(4): 125-139.* Little attention has been given by social scientists to the attempt by a minority of military personnel to create an antiwar, antimilitary protest movement in the Vietnam-era military. The purpose of this article is to briefly describe and analyze the GI movement. Particular attention is focused on: (a) some of the factors that were instrumental in the genesis and development of the GI movement, and (b) the military's response to internal resistance. The article concludes with an assessment of the movement and a discussion of some of the reasons why the GI movement was less than successful in mobilizing resistance on a large scale. J

2728. Hertz, Edwin. IDEOLOGICAL LIBERALS IN REFORM POLITICS: A NOTE ON THE BACKGROUND AND MOVEMENT OF POLITICAL OUTSIDERS INTO MAJOR PARTY POLITICS. *Int. J. of Contemporary Sociol. 1974 11(1): 1-11.* Discusses the political participation of working class Jews, Negroes, and Puerto Rican Americans as pressure groups in social reform and civil rights issues in New York City, 1963-70's.

2729. Koller, Norman B. and Retzer, Joseph D. THE SOUNDS OF SILENCE REVISITED. *Sociol. Analysis 1980 41(2): 155-161.* Research conducted in California near the peak of social activism in the late 1960's concluded that sermons tended not to address controversial social and political issues. This study, conducted a decade later in North Carolina, found much higher levels of sermonizing on a broad range of social issues. Furthermore, "conservative" clergy are as likely as are "liberal" clergy to address social issues from the pulpit, although some clearly discernible foci of interest are apparent. J/S

2730. Kopkind, Andrew. ACORN CALLING: DOOR-TO-DOOR ORGANIZING IN ARKANSAS. *Working Papers for a New Soc. 1975 3(2): 13-20.* Describes the work of the Arkansas Community Organizations for Reform Now (ACORN) during the 1960's and the social and political reforms they have fought for, from improved street drainage to revised property taxes. S

2731. Ladd, Everett Carll, Jr. LIBERALISM UPSIDE DOWN: THE INVERSION OF THE NEW DEAL ORDER. *Pol. Sci. Q. 1976-77 91(4): 577-600.* Contends that in the last decade, support for liberal causes and candidates has been most forthcoming from voters at the highest socio-economic levels. This pattern is in contrast to the New Deal era, when such causes and candidates drew their strongest support from lower-status voters. J

2732. Levi, Margaret. POOR PEOPLE AGAINST THE STATE. *R. of Radical Pol. Econ. 1974 6(1): 76-98.* In the 1960's political organizations of the urban poor proliferated. The history of groups such as JOIN Community Union in Chicago, the South End Tenants Council in Boston, the National Welfare Rights Organization, and prisoners' associations, challenged bourgeois notions that the poor are incapable of sustained collective action. The state response to such pressure, ranging from minor concession to violent repression, teaches the poor the value of organization and reveals to them the social control practiced by state agencies. 22 notes. P. R. Shergold

2733. Lewis, Diane K. A RESPONSE TO INEQUALITY: BLACK WOMEN, RACISM, AND SEXISM. *Signs 1977 3(2): 339-361.* Recent developments indicate that after initial rejection of the women's movement, black women are now reacting more favorably to it. As blacks began to participate more fully in public activities previously reserved to whites, black women, particularly those in the middle class, began to perceive that sexism was an obstacle to their progress. The shared experience of racism has tended to blur class lines among blacks, so that both poor and middle-class black women tend to agree regarding women's rights, whereas working class white women manifest low interest in women's rights, 1960-75. Based on census records, recently published and unpublished papers; 70 notes, 10 tables. J. K. Gammage

2734. Lilley, William, III, and Miller, James C., III. THE NEW "SOCIAL REGULATION." *Public Interest 1977 (47): 49-61.* During 1970-75 the growth of federal regulation has been dramatic. The new-style regulation is social rather than economic, extends to far more industries than before, and involves the government in the detailed facets of the production process. The benefit from this escalating activity is lower than it should be. The new regulation is a threat to the democratic process because it concentrates enormous power in the president and overstrengthens government in a way that may cause a backlash against all government. Regulatory decisionmaking is inefficient and leads to higher costs because decisions are made on grossly inadequate information and do not necessarily reflect rational judgments concerning costs and benefits. Also, because the type of people who become regulators through the civil service system are risk-averse and security-conscious, there is resistance to the consideration of alternatives and innovative approaches. 16 notes. S. Harrow

2735. Marin, Christine. RODOLFO "CORKY" GONZALES: THE MEXICAN AMERICAN MOVEMENT SPOKESMAN, 1966-1972. *J. of the West 1975 14(4): 107-120.* Discusses the founding of the Crusade for Justice in Denver, Colorado, by Rodolfo "Corky" Gonzales and the political and social work which was done for Mexican Americans by the organization throughout the west and southwest. 52 notes.

2736. McGregor-Alegado, Davianna. HAWAIIANS: ORGANIZING THE 1970S. *Amerasia J. 1980 7(2): 29-55.* Chronicles the political organization of native Hawaiians from 1900 to 1980. Native political power declined in the first half of this century due to Hawaiian royalty activity and to Americanization of the political and educational institutions. In more recent decades, native Hawaiians have organized to advocate native concerns, and have been successful in achieving passage of the Hawaiian Affairs amendment to the state constitution. 2 tables, 61 notes, appendix (chronology of Hawaiian Community Struggles). E. S. Johnson

2737. McInerny, Dennis Q. THOMAS MERTON AND THE AWAKENING OF SOCIAL CONSCIOUSNESS. *Am. Studies (Lawrence, KS) 1974 15(2): 37-53.* Thomas Merton, a notable American churchman, experienced an awakening of social consciousness in the 1960's and subsequently tried to bring other people to a similar awakening. Merton was concerned with social conditions in the United States, particularly in the cities, and strongly opposed the Vietnam War. He remained an avid social critic to his death in 1968, and he also dedicated himself to nonviolence. Based on primary and secondary sources; 35 notes. J. Andrew

2738. Medicine, Bea. NATIVE AMERICAN RESISTANCE TO INTEGRATION: CONTEMPORARY CONFRONTATIONS AND RELIGIOUS REVITALIZATION. *Plains Anthropologist 1981 26(94 part I): 277-286.* Most studies dealing with North American Indian integration often focus upon efforts directed at tribal groups by a dominant society in forced acculturation. This paper seeks to examine current trends initiated by tribal groups and members to resist integration. Aspects for consideration include confrontative efforts, including Alcatraz, Wounded Knee II, and the "Longest Walk." The recent efforts of religious revitalization, including the Sioux Sun Dance, which form a part of enhanced efforts toward developing a new "native ethic" in combatting integration and assimilation, increasingly form an ethnic marker to many Native Americans. Covers 1964-78. J/S

2739. Miller, Michael V. CHICANO COMMUNITY CONTROL IN SOUTH TEXAS: PROBLEMS AND PROSPECTS. *J. of Ethnic Studies 1975 3(3): 70-89.* Attempts to assess the political prospects for Chicanismo in South Texas. Poverty, illiteracy, substandard housing, and general economic exploitation have prevented interest-oriented political activity until recent years. Anglo techniques of electoral manipulation and illicit use of poll taxes severely hampered attempts at ethnic power-bloc formation. Other debilitating factors have been strong psychosocial attachments to Mexico by Chicanos, and the cultural trait of *envidia* which weakened any emerging ethnic leadership. Analyzes Crystal City as a "case history of organizational success," with its "revolutions" in 1963 and 1970. The Anglo establishment was ousted by an all Mexican American slate, which took control of city government and the school system. Reasons for this success centered on catching the Anglo city manager off guard through organized poll tax payments by Chicanos' groups, and the fact that, unlike other South Texas cities, Crystal City had a union organization independent of local economic constraints. Finally *La Raza Unida* under José Gutierrez provided solid leadership. Whether other towns will be as successful, however, is dubious at this time. Primary and secondary sources; 20 notes.
G. J. Bobango

2740. Mount, Eric, Jr., and Bos, Johanna W. H. SCRIPTURE ON SEXUALITY: SHIFTING AUTHORITY. *J. of Presbyterian Hist. 1981 59(2): 219-244.* Focuses on General Assembly statements of the two largest Presbyterian bodies in America—United Presbyterian Church in the United States of America and the Presbyterian Church in the United States—which suggest where these two churches have stood in recent years in their formal treatments of human sexuality. Through the legislation which they have passed, a subtle shift in the positions of Presbyterian leadership on biblical authority may be occurring. Most of the discussion is limited to the handling of the homosexual issue by the two denominations, since this perhaps provides the best indication of where they stand on biblical authority in relation to views on human sexuality and sex ethics. Based largely on study papers and minutes of the United Presbyterian Church and the Presbyterian Church, United States; 5 illus., 33 notes.
H. M. Parker, Jr.

2741. Neitz, Mary Jo. FAMILY, STATE, AND GOD: IDEOLOGIES OF THE RIGHT-TO-LIFE MOVEMENT. *Sociol. Analysis 1981 42(3): 265-276.* Examines the differences between ideologies of elite and mass publics in the case of the abortion issue. Within the Right-to-Life movement exist two conceptual frameworks: a "prolife" framework advocated by the elite, and a "profamily" framework advocated by the mass. Ethnographic data from a Catholic Charismatic prayer group shows that the profamily framework demonstrates both range and centrality, but in regard to concerns quite different from those of the elite.
J/S

2742. O'Riordan, Timothy. PUBLIC ENVIRONMENTAL INTEREST GROUPS IN THE UNITED STATES AND BRITAIN. *J. of Am. Studies [Great Britain] 1979 13(3): 409-438.* During the 1970's, British and American environmental groups shared a common outlook and succeeded in effecting major shifts in public policy away from encouraging growth and consumption of resources. However, the American and British groups achieved such results in different ways, primarily because divergent policymaking style prevails in the two nations. Environmental lobbyists were less able to exert political pressure in Britain than in America. At the end of the 1970's, America environmentalists appeared more entrenched than their British counterparts, but American environmental precepts had increasingly aroused public opposition. Based on contemporary environmentalists' writings and on secondary sources; 2 tables, 54 notes.
H. T. Lovin

2743. Parman, Donald L. AMERICAN INDIANS AND THE BICENTENNIAL. *New Mexico Hist. Rev. 1976 51(3): 233-249.* During the past 15 years complex social changes have taken place in government policies concerning Indians. In general there has been a shift from the reservations to urban areas. The Indians have forged a new image for themselves. Indians are no longer patient, humble, or silent. They still desire to be Indians, but hope to somehow remind the government that it has not fulfilled its obligations to the original Americans.
J. H. Krenkel

2744. Payne, William C. IMPLEMENTING FEDERAL NONDISCRIMINATION POLICIES IN THE DEPARTMENT OF AGRICULTURE, 1964-1976. *Policy Studies J. 1978 6(4): 507-509.* Assesses attempts at integration and nondiscriminatory federal policy followed by the Agriculture Department's personnel policy, 1964-76. One of 16 articles in this issue on agricultural policy.

2745. Perret, Karen. THE ALASKA NATIVE CLAIMS SETTLEMENT ACT. *Indian Hist. 1978 11(1): 3-10.* The Alaska Native Claims Settlement Act (1971) was designed to assure the Alaska Natives permanent possession of 40 million acres of Alaskan land, and millions in cash in payment for the remainder of their claims. Unfortunately, the Act also forced the Eskimos, Aleuts, and Alaskan Indians into a new capitalistic economy, and moved them into a social system alien to their heritage. Additional legislation is needed to protect the Natives, but a thorough study of their present and future needs should be made before passing such legislation. Biblio.
E. D. Johnson

2746. Pickvance, C. G. ON THE STUDY OF URBAN SOCIAL MOVEMENTS. *Social Rev. [Great Britain] 1975 23(1): 29-49.* Discusses the growth of community organizations in dealing with local social problems in Great Britain and the United States in the 1960's-70's.

2747. Powell, Elwin H. PROMOTING THE DECLINE OF THE RISING STATE: DOCUMENTS OF RESISTANCE AND RENEWAL FROM THE ALTERNATIVE COMMUNITY: BUFFALO, 1965-76. *Catalyst [Canada] 1977 (9): 59-98.* Chronicles political protest movements in Buffalo, New York, 1965-76, primarily antiwar and antinuclear weaponry, as representations of rising social consciousness and resistance to social and political control by the federal government.

2748. Quinley, Harold E. THE DILEMMA OF AN ACTIVIST CHURCH: PROTESTANT RELIGION IN THE SIXTIES AND SEVENTIES. *J. for the Sci. Study of Religion 1974 13(1): 1-21.* Discusses sources of political and social activism in the church during the 1960's and 70's; based on a 1968 survey of Protestant clergymen.

2749. Roos, Philip D.; Smith, Dowell H.; Langley, Stephen; and McDonald, James. THE IMPACT OF THE AMERICAN INDIAN MOVEMENT ON THE PINE RIDGE INDIAN RESERVATION. *Phylon 1980 41(1): 89-99.* Considering its political and economic goals, the occupation of Wounded Knee in 1975 was counterproductive. By reviving a sense of community, however, the American Indian Movement made inhabitants of the Pine Ridge Indian Reservation newly sensitive to native culture. Socially, then, it benefitted the local Indians. Covers 1972-75. 34 notes.
N. G. Sapper

2750. Rothman, Stanley. INTELLECTUALS AND THE STUDENT MOVEMENT: A POST MORTEM. *J. of Psychohistory 1978 5(4): 551-566.* Most social science investigations of the student movement of the 1960's concluded that the young radicals were liberal, tolerant, humane, intellectually democratic, autonomous, warm, etc. The studies were seriously flawed, however, and missed the shifting character of the movement as it spread from the elite universities to the broader student population. Neither the descriptions of the movement nor its presumed psychodynamic base bear close scrutiny. Secondary sources and original research; 39 notes.
R. E. Butchart

2751. Rowland, Andrew. TANNING LEATHER, TANNING HIDES: HEALTH AND SAFETY STRUGGLE IN A LEATHER FACTORY. *Radical Am. 1980 14(6): 23-37.* Notes the circumstances in a California tannery and the 20th-century history of the industrial safety and insurance industry theory designed to place responsibility for accidents almost exclusively on the "careless" worker, and the lack of accountability for poor industrial design. The division of safety into short-run physical safety and long-run health considerations becomes even more questionable with the growing introduction of exotic chemicals into virtually every industrial process. Based on six months on site as a safety researcher; 4 illus., 22 notes.
C. M. Hough

2752. Schreiber, E. M. ANTI-WAR DEMONSTRATIONS AND AMERICAN PUBLIC OPINION ON THE WAR IN VIETNAM. *British J. of Sociol. [Great Britain] 1976 27(2): 225-236.* Questions whether anti-Vietnam War demonstrations altered American public opinion on the Vietnam War.

2753. Shaffer, Stephen D. THE POLICY BIASES OF POLITICAL ACTIVISTS. *Am. Pol. Q. 1980 8(1): 15-33.* The nature of policy differences between political strata are examined with survey data from 1952 to 1976. In identifying policy biases, one must consider the interaction between issue area, time period, and partisan grouping. Prior to 1966, a conservative bias on domestic economic issues existed among the more active, due to the conservative bias of the higher SES and hyperactivity among conservative Republicans. After 1966, no consistent bias on domestic economic issues existed among the more active, due to hyperactivity among liberal Democrats as well as conservative Republicans. After 1966 a definite liberal bias existed among activists on black rights and social-cultural issues, because of the greater liberalism of the more educated, and hyperactivity among Democratic liberals. Foreign affairs patterns are more complex, though there is usually an internationalist bias among activists, due to the greater internationalism of the more educated. 5 tables, fig., 3 notes. J

2754. Skidmore, Max J. THE TUMULTUOUS DECADE: THE AMERICAN OF THE 1960S. *Indian J. of Am. Studies [India] 1979 9(2): 38-50.* Describes America from the nomination of John F. Kennedy in 1960 to the inauguration of Richard M. Nixon in 1969. In this period of ferment, old ideas mixed with new ideas derived from them. The New Left itself had many antecedents. Consumerism, the civil rights movement, participatory democracy, the peace movement, and the women's movement all had long histories in the intellectual and cultural life of the nation. Nixon's presidency introduced great changes in tone and feeling as much as substance, but the America of the Eisenhower years was irreversibly gone; technology, popular culture, political administrations, and social movements had brought about social change. 6 notes.
L. V. Eid

2755. Smith, Robert T. THE BIG SKY DEVELOPMENT: A LESSON FOR THE FUTURE. *Am. West 1975 12(5): 46-47, 62-63.* Chet Huntley, well-known television news broadcaster, was the prime mover in the Big Sky development in Montana. Big Sky was a "dream" resort enterprise designed to balance recreation and conservation. The 1970-73 launching of the enterprise taught some important lessons. Conservationists learned that they could not defend the position that "the only good environment was one untouched by human hands"; that they should be wary of those who tried to use conservation as a soapbox; and that if they chose their targets wisely their efforts could be effective. The promoters learned that the watchful conservationists forced them to exercise a higher level of public concern; and if they behaved responsibly toward the environment, public support was assured. The federal government learned that altruistic legislation was one thing, but that putting it into operation was another. Illus.
D. L. Smith

2756. Stein, Peter R. GREENING OF THE CITY. *Hist. Preservation 1980 32(1): 24-29.* Since 1975, the Trust for Public Land has provided technical and legal assistance to neighborhood groups committed to creating or reclaiming green spaces for communal use. Modeled after "town commons," land trusts have for the past century helped preserve land in rural and suburban communities; now they are contributing to urban revitalization. Collective action inspires a cooperative spirit, as well as pride in, and hope for, communities and so for cities themselves. 6 photos. S

2757. Talbot, Steve. FREE ALCATRAZ: THE CULTURE OF NATIVE AMERICAN LIBERATION. *J. of Ethnic Studies 1978 6(3): 83-96.* Analyzes the occupation of Alcatraz Island by Indians and Eskimos during November, 1969, and its implications for the culture of Native American liberation, especially in its ideological dimension. The Indian view of liberation includes self-determination, educating the American public, peaceful coexistence, all-Indian unity, educational opportunity, and cultural revitalization. Moreover, clearly the common enemy is the monolithic Bureau of Indian Affairs, which should either be abolished or drastically reformed to the extent that Indian people take over its functions. The impact of the Alcatraz landing on the general public and on its participants 10 years later remains significant, given its important role in furthering the ethos of the liberation movement. Based on personal contacts with the Alcatraz occupiers, secondary works; 6 notes.
G. J. Bobango

2758. Tanaka, Ron. CULTURE, COMMUNICATIONS AND THE ASIAN MOVEMENT IN PERSPECTIVE. *J. of Ethnic Studies 1976 4(1): 37-52.* Defines assimilation as "the integration of a dominated communications system into a dominating one through the process of reconceptualization," with stress on the great difference between knowing the words and phrases of a language and sharing its conceptual understandings. The Asian Movement which climaxed during 1968-72 created a conceptual problem of communication through its politics and phraseology borrowed from White, Black, Vietnamese and Red Chinese models, and the Sansei youth who formed its core found themselves isolated from their own Japanese culture while unable to be more than marginal participants in the new set of concepts shared by the anti-Establishment community. At the same time the Sansei goal of system survival for Japanese Americans did not succeed, as evidenced especially by the sizeable increase of intermarriage with Caucasians during the very years that the Movement peaked. Meanwhile its other goal, of combatting racism against Asians, has meant more control than ever before by the majority, as Sansei and Yonsei will continue to abandon Japanese culture. Secondary sources; 8 notes.
G. J. Bobango

2759. Tatalovich, Raymond. AFTER MEDICARE: THE POLITICS OF BUREAUCRATIC ADAPTATION IN THE AMERICAN MEDICAL ASSOCIATION. *Int. Rev. of Hist. and Pol. Sci. [India] 1974 11(1): 1-18.* Policymaking in the American Medical Association may be described as goal displacement. Responding to outside pressures, the American Medical Association has, in the course of the years, changed its goals only after a series of deliberate but gradual adjustments. In no case was reform complete. Future changes will result only from intense societal pressures and will always be tempered by conservative decision-making. Primary and secondary sources; 31 notes.
E. McCarthy

2760. Tokarczyk, Roman. NARODZINY I UPADEK "NOWEJ LEWICY" AMERYKANSKIEJ [The growth and downfall of the American New Left]. *Studia Nauk Politycznych [Poland] 1978 (5): 85-113.* Covers the New Left and its antecedents, including the Intercollegiate Socialist Society (1905), the National Student League, the Student League for Industrial Democracy (with which it was united in 1935 into the American Student Union), and the radical leftist Students for a Democratic Society. Movements of American youth of the sixties passed through reorganization (1960-62), attempts to reform (1962-64), resistance (1964-68), and revolt (1968-70). The ideology of the New Left was the amalgam of theoretical ideas and practical experience of the representatives of the intellectual left and the participants in these movements.
J/S

2761. Vasquez, John A. A LEARNING THEORY OF THE AMERICAN ANTI-VIETNAM WAR MOVEMENT. *J. of Peace Res. [Norway] 1976 13(4): 299-314.* This paper is concerned with how individuals and groups become radicalized. While there has been considerable research on why individuals join radical groups and why different groups and individuals engage in violence there has been little attention devoted to why groups adopt non-violent strategies and the relationship between these non-violent strategies and violence. This paper employs insights derived from learning theory to explain and predict what strategies will be adopted by radical groups and in what sequence they will be adopted given various environmental conditions. A formal model of radical social movements is presented and applied in detail to the American Anti-Vietnam War Movement. The case study lends considerable credence to numerous propositions in the model. J

2762. Vietor, Richard H. K. ENVIRONMENTAL POLITICS IN PENNSYLVANIA: THE REGULATION OF SURFACE MINING, 1961-1973. *Pennsylvania Hist. 1978 45(1): 19-46.* Discusses the passage of Pennsylvania's basic surface mining legislation in 1961 and 1963-73. Analyzes legislative votes and discusses the campaign for strip mining legislation. The Bureau of Surface Mine Reclamation developed a body of regulatory policy through a process of bargaining with the industry, and "a smoothly functioning 'cliental' relationship" emerged between the BSMR and the industry. Analyzes the agency's enforcement record with quantitative methods. Based on legislative records, interviews, surveys, and BSMR records; 2 photos, 5 tables, 49 notes.
D. C. Swift

2763. Vietor, Richard H. K. THE EVOLUTION OF PUBLIC ENVIRONMENTAL POLICY: THE CASE OF "NO SIGNIFICANT

DETERIORATION." *Environmental Rev. 1979 3(2): 2-19.* The "no significant deterioration" concept (which regulates the air quality standards pertaining to allowable air pollution levels) is traced through national environmental policy dictated by the Air Quality Act (US, 1967) and the Clean Air Act (US, 1970); although it was originally a minor aspect of overall policy, it became the primary determining standard in recent legislation and policymaking; 1967-78.

2764. Zarefsky, David. THE GREAT SOCIETY AS A RHETORICAL PROPOSITION. *Q. J. of Speech 1979 65(4): 364-378.* The Great Society programs of President Lyndon Johnson reflected commitment to the quality of life, the idea of affirmative action, and government's role as stimulus and guarantor of social change. Obstacles to adopting the programs were overcome by employing conservative themes, claiming a moral imperative to act, and distinguishing the Great Society from older programs.   J

Civil Liberties and Political Rights

2765. Bosmajian, Haig A. RESTRICTING *STANLEY* AND FREEDOM OF SPEECH. *Midwest Q. 1979 20(3): 228-240.* Provides the background of the US Supreme Court's *Stanley* v. *Georgia* (US, 1969), in which Robert Stanley's 1968 obscenity conviction for private possession of three films was reversed; discusses the significance of the Stanley case in 1979.

2766. Bouthillier, Guy. L'AN 1 DE LA LOI 101 [The first year of Law 101]. *Action Natl. [Canada] 1979 68(5): 416-423.* Anglo-Canadians are not enthusiastic about Law 101, the Charter of the French Language (1977), which emphasizes French as the official language of Quebec; however, they have obeyed the law. Neither the federal nor the other nine provincial governments have contested the law; there have been no official protests; the parliamentary opposition has not challenged the enforcement of the law; and the Protestant School Board of Montreal has not questioned the constitutionality of such legislation. Leaders of the Liberal Party have supported it. In the 5 July by-elections, only 24% of the voters supported a candidate who opposed the law. 11 notes.

A. W. Novitsky

2767. Earle, Valerie A. and Earle, Chester B. THE SUPREME COURT AND THE ELECTORAL PROCESS. *World Affairs 1977 140(1): 25-40.* The Supreme Court has extended the power of Congress to enforce the 14th and 15th Amendments in a series of court cases stemming from the Voting Rights Act (1965) and the Federal Election Campaign Acts (1971, 1974).

2768. Erskine, Hazel and Siegel, Richard L. CIVIL LIBERTIES AND THE AMERICAN PUBLIC. *J. of Social Issues 1975 31(2): 13-29.* Important new survey findings show the American public's restrictive approach to the First Amendment rights of people who express deviant views to be moderating over the last two decades. This mellowing is backed up by parallel findings of major liberalizing of the consensus in other areas, notably equality and sexual freedom. Liberalization has been limited in such areas as criminal justice and separation of church and state. Post-McCarthy and post-Watergate developments are credited, along with educational progress, with much of the advance. Reduced value consensus and a growing sense of self-interest in civil liberties seem to have contributed to the trends in support of civil liberties.

2769. Flowers, Ronald B. FREEDOM OF RELIGION VERSUS CIVIL AUTHORITY IN MATTERS OF HEALTH. *Ann. of the Am. Acad. of Pol. and Social Sci. 1979 (446): 149-161.* Decisions of the United States Supreme Court in 1963 and 1972 expanded the scope of the free exercise clause of the First Amendment beyond any previous interpretation of that clause in American judicial history. Although it is still understood that government may prohibit religiously motivated behavior which represents harm to individuals or to the public welfare, civil authorities now may intervene only when the religious activity threatens a compelling state interest. The possibilities of religious activity are abundant, and government intervention is limited to only the gravest offenses of the public order. This article examines some of the areas of health, broadly defined, in which religious attitudes have conflicted with state interests: the handling of poisonous snakes and drinking of poison in religious worship, the use of prohibited drugs in worship, compulsory blood transfusions for those who have theological objections to them, and the application of public health laws to those whose theology rejects medicine altogether. In the light of these cases, as much as the American constitutional system exalts religious liberty, it can never be unfettered. But, even in this area, it is imperative that our governmental units make religious liberty the rule and its curtailment the exception.   J

2770. Galliher, John F. and Basilick, Linda. UTAH'S LIBERAL DRUG LAWS: STRUCTURAL FOUNDATIONS AND TRIGGERING EVENTS. *Social Problems 1979 26(3): 284-297.* Describes the passage in 1969 and 1971 of Utah bills reducing possession of marijuana to a misdemeanor and dropping the mandatory minimum penalties for all drug offenses, and notes how such innovative legislation was especially unexpected in a state whose Mormon faithful cherish the family and oppose all drugs.

2771. Gietschier, Steven P. THE 1951 SPEAKER'S RULE AT OHIO STATE. *Ohio Hist. 1978 87(3): 294-309.* Discusses the appearance of Harold Ordway Rugg at the sixth Boyd H. Bode Conference on Education (July 1951), the "Rugg Controversy," and the "Speaker's Rule" that resulted. The rule—which required that the Ohio State University president approve any speaker to appear at the university—was in line with OSU's traditional emphasis on the practical arts rather than the humanities and was a result of the Cold War mentality of the OSU Board of Trustees who preferred to restrict academic freedom while favoring the protection of national security and the insulation of the university from indoctrination and propaganda. Based on the archives of Ohio State University, author questionnaires, and other primary sources; photo, 45 notes.

L. A. Russell

2772. Graham, Hugh Davis. LIBERTY, EQUALITY, AND THE NEW CIVIL RIGHTS. *South Atlantic Q. 1980 79(1): 82-92.* The rights revolution of the 1960's spawned such congeries of competing rights— new against old, group against individual, children against parents, fetuses against mothers, animals against humans—that, increasingly, contradictions were embraced and important distinctions were blurred, especially between civil rights and civil liberties and their relationship to freedom's historic goals of liberty and equality. For years, elitist judicial activism subordinated substantive equality to procedural liberty. It is ironical that an egalitarian judicial system should increasingly subordinate individual to collective rights, seeking to redress the imbalance in a well-intentioned excess of zeal which, in the name of equality, may enmesh Americans firmly in more intricate bonds.

H. M. Parker, Jr.

2773. Haas, Kenneth C. THE "NEW FEDERALISM" AND PRISONERS' RIGHTS: STATE SUPREME COURTS IN COMPARATIVE PERSPECTIVE. *Western Pol. Q. 1981 34(4): 552-571.* Utilizes a comparative perspective to evaluate the strength and breadth of the "new federalism"—the willingness of some state supreme courts to take a more expansive approach than that adopted by the federal courts in the protection of individual liberties. A textual analysis of state supreme court decisions in the area of corrections law from 1969 to 1980 reveals that these courts have proved to be unsympathetic toward prisoners' efforts to seek judicial redress of their grievances. It thus appears that the spirit of state court activism which has been evident in many other areas of law has bypassed an entire class of litigants. The article concludes with some predictions concerning the future of the new federalism and the prisoners' rights movement.   J

2774. Hayden, J. Carleton. NEW MEN, STRANGE FACES, OTHER MINDS: THE HUMAN RIGHTS REVOLUTION, 1954-1978. *Hist. Mag. of the Protestant Episcopal Church 1980 49(1): 71-81.* After World War II people of color emerged worldwide in aggressive demands for justice and self-determination which led to the collapse of colonialism. In the United States this emergence was expressed by the civil rights movement in 1954 which drew upon a powerful black protest tradition intimately connected with traditional Afro-American religion. This movement provided a paradigm for other oppressed people, and all human rights groups later drew upon the black model, for they likened themselves to blacks in their effort to interpret their plight to others as well as to convince other members of the groups to solidify around a common heritage and condition. Demonstrates this impact on such movements as the women's, student protest, the handicapped, Asian Americans, and the Chicano Power movement. Secondary sources; 42 notes.

H. M. Parker, Jr.

2775. Heck, Edward V. CIVIL LIBERTIES VOTING PATTERNS IN THE BURGER COURT, 1975-78. *Western Pol. Q. 1981 34(2): 193-202.* Evaluations of the civil liberties record of the Warren E. Burger Supreme Court have often been based on analysis of the outcome of selected cases rather than on an entire set of civil liberties cases. This paper focuses on the voting record of individual justices and the Court as whole between the appointment of Justice Stevens and the end of the 1977-78 term. Despite a few libertarian advances, this Court was markedly hostile to libertarian claims and the prospects for change via the appointment process are far from realization.

J/S

2776. Hinckley, Ted C. THE UNITED STATES AND THE PACIFIC TRUST TERRITORY. *J. of the West 1981 20(1): 41-51.* In 1947 the vast Micronesian island region became the US Trust Territory of the Pacific Islands in a UN decision. Both the United States and the UN hoped for the eventual self-determination of the natives, but divisions of language, culture, and distance precluded a united Micronesia. Infusion of American dollars and consumer goods irrevocably changed the traditional cultures and caused some islanders to seek political union with the United States. The political destiny of the islands is yet unknown, but the United States insists that it will be self-determined. Published sources; map, 9 photos, 33 notes.

B. S. Porter

2777. Isaac, Amos. THE ISSUE IS NOT BUSING BUT THE FOURTEENTH AMENDMENT: STRATEGIES FOR EVASION. *Educ. and Urban Soc. 1977 9(3): 259-276.* Reviews efforts to escape federally mandated forced busing since *Brown* v. *Board of Education* (US, 1954). Outlines the Southern response and the Northern response, using Chicago as an example. Concludes that: resistance comes primarily from the majority community whose special resources are threatened; low income whites tend to be the "victims" of such efforts; the rewards for merely being white remain significant enough to prevent meaningful cooperation between poor whites and blacks; and when traditional sources of power and leadership in a community support desegregation it is successful. The general benefits of American society are not available to the impoverished and the media tends to emphasize opposition to desegregation rather than successful school integration. 8 tables, note, 15 ref.

C. D'Aniello

2778. Jones, Edward D., III. THE DISTRICT OF COLUMBIA'S "FIREARMS CONTROL REGULATIONS ACT OF 1975": THE TOUGHEST HANDGUN CONTROL LAW IN THE UNITED STATES—OR IS IT? *Ann. of the Am. Acad. of Pol. and Social Sci. 1981 (455): 138-149.* The District of Columbia's Firearms Control Regulations Act (1975) had two legislative objectives: to reduce the potential of firearms-related crimes and to monitor more effectively firearms' trafficking. In July 1980, the US Conference of Mayors reported that the act significantly reduced firearm and handgun crime. This report met largely with opposition. The author relates the provisions and legislative history of the Firearms Control Regulations Act, analyzes the deficiencies in the Conference of Mayors' research methods and assumptions, and discusses any beneficial effects and weaknesses of the act.

J/S

2779. Lamb, Charles M. LEGAL FOUNDATIONS OF CIVIL RIGHTS AND PLURALISM IN AMERICA. *Ann. of the Am. Acad. of Pol. and Social Sci. 1981 (454): 13-25.* Addresses the question of legal protections for minorities in the context of the transformation of the concept of equal protection since *Plessy* v. *Ferguson* (1896). Certainly the legal metamorphosis from the "separate but equal" doctrine to the current status of minority rights is profound. Particularly important in recent years is the issue of affirmative action. Traces the progression of the equal protection principle with emphasis on the three most recent affirmative action decisions announced by the Court: *University of California Regents* v. *Bakke* (1978), *United Steelworkers of America* v. *Weber* (1979), and *Fullilove* v. *Klutznick* (1980).

J/S

2780. Levy, Joanne. IN SEARCH OF ISOLATION: THE HOLDEMAN MENNONITES OF LINDEN, ALBERTA AND THEIR SCHOOL. *Can. Ethnic Studies [Canada] 1979 11(1): 115-130.* Just as Canadian history and political events are sometimes viewed as dull and ordinary, so are the courts criticized as less than innovative. But in February 1977, the Assistant Chief Provincial Court Judge of Alberta made a decision on a disputed point in Mennonite history in Canada, giving new recognition to the civil rights of a minority group and made Canadian legal history. For the first time a provincial Bill of Rights was used to override part of another provincial statute. Freedom of religion triumphed over compulsory attendance regulations contained in the School Act. As a result the Holdeman Mennonites of Linden, Alberta, were allowed to retain a school unauthorized by provincial legislation.

J/S

2781. Lewis, Anthony. THE PRESS AND SOCIETY: THE FARBER CASE. *Massachusetts Hist. Soc. Pro. 1978 90: 89-99.* The jailing in 1975 of Myron Farber of *The New York Times* for refusing to reveal the identity of his sources as a journalist raises many questions concerning the meaning of freedom of the press. The many aspects of this case are discussed in light of current judicial opinion and the author's own values. Based on an analysis of several court cases concerning related issues, and written and spoken opinions of judges and others.

G. W. R. Ward

2782. Maidment, R. A. THE US SUPREME COURT AND AFFIRMATIVE ACTION: THE CASES OF BAKKE, WEBER AND FULLILOVE. *J. of Am. Studies [Great Britain] 1981 15(3): 341-356.* Challenges to affirmative action laws and discriminatory procedures which favored minorities reached the Supreme Court during the 1970's. Important cases before the court included: *Regents of the University of California* v. *Bakke; United Steelworkers of America* v. *Weber;* and *Fullilove* v. *Klutznick.* In these cases, jurists were forced to confront problems raised by their desire to uphold affirmative action procedures and sanction discrimination on behalf of minorities, although the court's own 1954 dicta in *Brown* v. *Board of Education* required nondiscrimination. 35 notes.

H. T. Lovin

2783. Moore, Kenny. THE CAMPAIGN FOR ATHLETES' RIGHTS. *Ann. of the Am. Acad. of Pol. and Social Sci. 1979 (445): 59-65.* Amateur athletes who pursue their sport primarily for its own sake feel they have, or ought to have, the right to compete wherever they are physically qualified. Yet, as reported by athletes' groups and confirmed by the President's Commission on Olympic Sports (1975-1977), this freedom has been abridged by practically all major amateur sports organizations such as the NCAA (The National Collegiate Athletic Association) and AAU (Amateur Athletic Union). The President's Commission recommended statutory guarantees of the right to compete in international competition, but the campaign for such a law ran into the lobbying power of the NCAA. A compromise was effected, permitting the Amateur Sports Act of 1978 to pass, thus reorganizing much of American amateur sport. But athletes' rights do not yet enjoy the protection in law desired by most athletes.

J

2784. Pierce, Glenn L. and Bowers, William J. THE BARTLEY-FOX GUN LAW'S SHORT-TERM IMPACT ON CRIME IN BOSTON. *Ann. of the Am. Acad. of Pol. and Social Sci. 1981 (455): 120-137.* Examines the effects of the Bartley-Fox Amendment of 1975, which made the illicit carrying of a firearm punishable with a one-year mandatory prison term. The law substantially reduced the incidence of gun assaults, but produced a more than offsetting increase in nongun armed assaults. It resulted in a reduction in gun robberies, accompanied by a less than corresponding increase in nongun armed robberies. It reduced gun homicides with no increase in nongun homicides. Publicity about the law's intent rather than the punishments was responsible for the reductions in gun-related crimes; 1974-76.

J/S

2785. Pilling, Arnold R. NATIVE AMERICAN RELIGIOUS RIGHTS: CONSTITUTIONAL CONSIDERATIONS. *Indian Hist. 1979 12(1): 13-19.* General overview of Supreme Court rulings on religious liberty (under the 1st amendment) is applied to the case of the Eight Mile-Blue Creek land of California containing Indians' sacred areas, where the US Forest Service proposed road construction and logging, 1975.

2786. Rickabaugh, Carey G. THE FURTHER EXAMINATION OF REVERSE DISCRIMINATION: AFTER *WEBER* AND *FUL-*

LILOVE: WHAT SCENARIO NOW? *South Atlantic Q. 1981 80(3): 243-256.* Reappraises the previously reappraised axioms of *Plessy* v. *Ferguson* (US, 1896). The affirmative action/reverse discrimination issue is a late 20th-century variation of the historic clash of "vested interests" and the "public interest." Presents some of the arguments for and against affirmative action and explores the evolving legal doctrine of "substantive equal protection" in the context of reverse discrimination. After examining both *Kaiser-USWA* v. *Weber* (US, 1979) and *Fullilove* v. *Weber* (US, 1980) in terms of what they did and did not involve, concludes by evaluating the bottom line residuals of reverse discrimination, the dangers that lie ahead, and the limited role possible for the judiciary in the ongoing American racial dilemma. Based on opinions and decisions in cases involving reverse discrimination as well as articles in law reviews; 25 notes.
H. M. Parker, Jr.

2787. Robbins, Thomas. CHURCH, STATE AND CULT. *Sociol. Analysis 1981 42(3): 209-225.* The problems posed by cults must be understood in terms of the social conditions which facilitate the growth of these movements, and in particular, the decline of traditional "mediating structures" in US society. Cults meet genuine needs, but in doing so they may perpetrate abuses, perhaps eliciting from devotees a diffuse obligation and a strong dependency, which may encourage exploitation. Communal sects come into conflict with a number of groups and institutions including families, churches, and licensed psychotherapists and highlight tensions between church and state. As the state increasingly regulates "secular" organizations, the exemptions of "churches" take on heightened controversiality. J/S

2788. Rodgers, Harrell R., Jr. PRELUDE TO CONFLICT: THE EVOLUTION OF CENSORSHIP CAMPAIGNS. *Pacific Sociol. Rev. 1975 18(2): 194-205.* Investigates the causes and effects of censorship movements in the United States which have many characteristics of social movements; based on studies in 18 American cities and previous 1960's studies.

2789. Rogers, Raymond S. and Lujan, Phillip. NATURAL LAW, SANTA CLARA, AND THE SUPREME COURT. *J. of Ethnic Studies 1981 9(3): 71-77.* The case of *Santa Clara Pueblo* v. *Martinez* (US, 1977), focusing on a 1939 Pueblo tribal ordinance barring tribal membership to children of female members who married nonmembers brought into conflict two fundamental theories of self-evident natural law: that of a sovereign tribe to determine its own membership, and the 14th-Amendment guarantee of equal protection of the law embodied in the Indian Civil Rights Act (US, 1968). Consideration of Hans Kelsen's distinction between two normative systems, the static and the dynamic, shows that Native Americans, despite the trappings of a positive legal order, see their own normative system as static. The Supreme Court's upholding of the Pueblo ordinance gives rise to meaningful implications for the future of the Bill of Rights. Based on court briefs of the litigants and amici curiae; 21 notes.
G. J. Bobango

2790. Steamer, Robert J. CONTEMPORARY SUPREME COURT DIRECTIONS IN CIVIL LIBERTIES. *Pol. Sci. Q. 1977 92(3): 425-442.* Current literature is concerned with measuring erosion to civil liberties since the Warren years, but the Burger Court is in fact more like than unlike the Warren Court. The Burger Court is skewed toward a "conservative-restraint" position, but it has not yet broken out of old Warren pathways. Where the two courts differ, the Burger Court has often taken a sensible position. There are indications that the Court is moving away from expanded judicial review in some areas, recognizing that judges cannot become administrators or budgetmakers without eroding their political immunity. Based on Burger Court decisions and on secondary sources; 100 notes.
W. R. Hively

2791. Switzer, Walter E. CAPITAL PUNISHMENT. *Pacific Hist. 1979 23(4): 45-80.* On 18 February 1972 the California Supreme Court seemingly brought to an end a judicial and political struggle to prohibit capital punishment in California, a situation that had been building in intensity since the execution of Caryl Chessman in 1960. It declared that the California Constitution prohibited capital punishment. Nine months later California voters negated the decision by approving a constitutional amendment that expressly allowed the death penalty. Examines the events and judicial actions leading up to these two occurrences. Based on federal and state cases and secondary sources; 212 notes, biblio.
H. M. Parker, Jr.

2792. Unsigned. THE TROBRINER DECISION. *Indian Historian 1973 6(4): 26-31.* Transcript: California Supreme Court Judge Trobriner reversed conviction of Navajo Indians arrested for religious ceremonial use of peyote. S

The Black Revolution

2793. Abeles, Ronald P. RELATIVE DEPRIVATION, RISING EXPECTATIONS, AND BLACK MILITANCY. *J. of Social Issues 1976 32(2): 119-137.* The anomalous relationship between improvements in the socioeconomic condition of blacks and the rise of the civil rights movement and urban riots of the 1960s is frequently explained by social scientists in terms of theories of relative deprivation (RD) and rising expectations (RE). The present paper investigates the role of RD and RE as mediating variables between social structure and black militancy through secondary analyses of survey data of blacks living in Cleveland and Miami in the late 1960s. While the results are generally supportive, the mediating roles of RD and RE are not as important as originally anticipated. Alternative explanations and implications derived from the present data and the theories for the future of black militancy are discussed. J

2794. Allen, Bernadene V. BAKKE VS. MINORITY STUDENTS: DID THE SUCCESS OF MINORITY RECRUITMENT PROGRAMS CREATE THE BAKKE CASE? *San José Studies 1978 4(3): 97-107.* Maintains that the Bakke social case was a reaction to the visible signs of the success of mandated social change but that invisible racist attitudes still keep minority groups in low-paying jobs, out of professional positions, and minimally represented on college and university campuses.

2795. Alvis, Joel L., Jr. RACIAL TURMOIL AND RELIGIOUS REACTION: THE RT. REV. JOHN M. ALLIN. *Hist. Mag. of the Protestant Episcopal Church 1981 50(1): 83-96.* The involvement of John M. Allin, Bishop Coadjutor of the Episcopal Diocese of Mississippi (1961-66) and Bishop of the Diocese (1966-74) poses a problem in interpreting the role of the Southern moderate in the civil rights crisis. As a participant in an indigenous attempt to respond to racial violence he was perceived by many fellow Mississippians, especially those outside the Episcopal Church, as a liberal. As an official of a denomination in the National Council of Churches which questioned the procedures and attitudes of Council activity in his own diocese, however, he appeared as a defender of the status quo. Based largely on the archives of the Diocese of Mississippi, particularly the Committee of Concern File, St. Andrew's Cathedral, Jackson, Mississippi; 80 notes.
H. M. Parker, Jr.

2796. Ammerman, Nancy T. THE CIVIL RIGHTS MOVEMENT AND THE CLERGY IN A SOUTHERN COMMUNITY. *Sociol. Analysis 1980 41(4): 339-350.* Seventy-two of Tuscaloosa, Alabama's white clergymen were interviewed regarding the civil rights movement and integration in their community. Civil rights activism was shown to be the strongest predictor of decreased localism, mediating the effects of education and urban backgrounds. For the minority of these clergymen who were active in the movement, a supportive reference group of clergy colleagues and mainline denominations was important. This countered their isolation from the rest of the religious community and lack of agreement with their laity. This minority represents an important alternative definition of the Southern religious world. J/S

2797. Anderson, William A. and Dynes, Russell R. CIVIL DISTURBANCES AND SOCIAL CHANGE: A COMPARATIVE ANALYSIS OF THE UNITED STATES AND CURAÇAO. *Urban Affairs Q. 1976 12(1): 37-56.* Argues that civil disturbances in Curaçao, May 1969, and the United States, mid-1960's, were general attacks by the disadvantaged on traditional societal arrangements and were also part of broader political and social movements. They developed specific political demands and ushered in periods of nonwhite innovation which engendered reform and counterprotest activity. The Curaçaon disturbance had the greater immediate impact because of its rapid politization, undeveloped indigenous social control mechanisms, and the larger percentage of total population involved. Concludes that networks of organization are crucial to the crystallization of new movements. Based on semistructured interviews and on published primary and secondary sources; 4 notes, biblio.
L. N. Beecher

2798. Anderson, William A. THE REORGANIZATION OF PROTEST: CIVIL DISTURBANCES AND SOCIAL CHANGE IN THE BLACK COMMUNITY. *Am. Behavioral Scientist 1973 16(3): 426-440.* Discusses the new political consciousness of the black community arising from the civil disturbances of the 1960's. S

2799. Arnez, Nancy L. IMPLEMENTATION OF DESEGREGATION AS A DISCRIMINATORY PROCESS. *J. of Negro Educ. 1978 47(1): 28-45.* Although ostensibly impelmented to end educational discrimination, desegregation has in practice been highly discriminatory, resulting in high incidence of discipline against black students, demotions and dismissals for black educators, and ability grouping inimical to blacks. The desegregation efforts in Louisville, Kentucky, are analyzed as a case study. Newspapers, NEA and HEW documents, and other primary and secondary sources; 38 notes. R. E. Butchart

2800. Bellamy, Donnie D. WHITES SUE FOR DESEGREGATION IN GEORGIA: THE FORT VALLEY STATE COLLEGE CASE. *J. of Negro Hist. 1979 64(4): 316-341.* Hunnicutt et al. v. Burge et al, the legal action initiated in 1972 and aimed at Fort Valley State College in Peach County, Georgia, was grounded in white resentment of the political power held by students at that historically black college. Seeking the dissolution of Fort Valley State College as a segregated institution which discriminated against whites, the lawsuit was an expression of white backlash against the idea of sharing political power with blacks. Based on court records and primary materials; 91 notes. N. G. Sapper

2801. Binion, Gayle. THE IMPLEMENTATION OF SECTION 5 OF THE 1965 VOTING RIGHTS ACT: A RETROSPECTIVE ON THE ROLE OF COURTS. *Western Pol. Q. 1979 32(2): 154-173.* The 1965 Voting Rights Act (amended 1970, 1975) has proven to be the most important federal legislation protecting the right to vote. The specific focus here is on the roles played by the courts in the implementation of Section 5 of the Act, which was virtually ignored during the first five years after its passage. It was not until the U.S. Supreme Court rendered decisions interpreting broadly the reach of Section 5 that compliance began. Three specific functions of the courts are analyzed: first, they were crucial actors in securing compliance when covered jurisdictions refused to submit their electoral changes for preclearance. Second, they have been important in immunizing court-ordered electoral changes (i.e., reapportionment) from the preclearance requirements of Section 5. Third, the decisions of the U.S. Supreme Court in 1975 and 1976 have placed limitations on the power of the Attorney General to object to electoral changes which he has reviewed. The paper involves both an analysis of all of the reported decisions of courts on Section 5 and a critique of their strengths and weaknesses. J

2802. Black, Merle. RACIAL COMPOSITION OF CONGRESSIONAL DISTRICTS AND SUPPORT FOR FEDERAL VOTING RIGHTS LEGISLATION IN THE AMERICAN SOUTH. *Social Sci. Q. 1978 59(3): 435-450.* Such support is related to racial composition in three time periods: (1) prior to the emergence of massive participation by blacks (1957 and 1960), (2) during the rapid expansion of the black electorate (1965 and 1969-1970) and (3) a decade after passage of the original act (1975). The research shows how the relationship between approval of the principle of federal intervention and district racial composition has been altered over time. J

2803. Black, Merle. REGIONAL AND PARTISAN BASES OF CONGRESSIONAL SUPPORT FOR THE CHANGING AGENDA OF CIVIL RIGHTS LEGISLATION. *J. of Pol. 1979 41(2): 665-679.* In each Congress from the 88th through the 92nd (1963-72), regional (North-South) cleavages were stronger on civil rights legislation than were partisan (Democratic-Republican) differences. Since the 89th congress, Democrats have consistently provided more support for all civil rights legislation. Extreme regional polarization last occurred in the 88th congress, remained stable from the 89th through the 91st congress, and substantially declined in the 92nd, as national school desegregation and busing monopolized the agenda. 2 illus., 2 tables, 24 notes. A. W. Novitsky

2804. Blackwelder, Julia Kirk. SOUTHERN WHITE FUNDAMENTALISTS AND THE CIVIL RIGHTS MOVEMENT. *Phylon 1979 40(4): 334-341.* Analyzes the response to the civil rights movement of the 1950's and 1960's by the Southern Presbyterian Church, the Church of God, and the Assemblies of God, as seen through articles in their respective denominational publications, *Southern Presbyterian Journal, Church of God Evangel,* and *Pentecostal Evangel.* 21 notes. G. R. Schroeder

2805. Blume, Norman. UNION WORKER ATTITUDES TOWARD OPEN HOUSING: THE CASE OF THE UAW IN THE TOLEDO METROPOLITAN AREA. *Phylon 1973 34(1): 63-72.* United Auto Workers approve of open housing for Negroes in theory but balk at it in practice (1967-73). S

2806. Boffard, Jean-Claude; Bowen, Norman; and Armand, Laura. ELEVEN YEARS AFTER MEMPHIS, WHERE IS BLACK AMERICA? *Rev. Française d'Études Américaines [France] 1980 5(9): 35-46.* Examines the Civil Rights Movement during the 11 years since the assassination of Martin Luther King, Jr.; finding that little has changed, documents reasons for political and social pessimism concerning the demoralized black minority.

2807. Bosmajian, Haig A. THE RHETORIC OF MARTIN LUTHER KING'S "LETTER FROM A BIRMINGHAM JAIL." *Midwest Q. 1979 21(1): 46-62.* Martin Luther King, Jr.'s "Letter from Birmingham Jail" (1963) ranks among the classics of the public letter tradition. Rhetorical analysis demonstrates King's mastery of the form: his appreciation of both the ideals and the literary techniques of Greek, Christian, and American philosophers to whom he alluded, and his recognition of the occasion, demanding a balance of logic, fact, and passion, had the intended effect on his audience, appealing to Americans in the cause of civil rights, which is to say, humanity. First published in *Midwest Quarterly,* 1967 (see abstract 4:1581). S

2808. Boulton, Scot W. DESEGREGATION OF THE OKLAHOMA CITY SCHOOL SYSTEM. *Chronicles of Oklahoma 1980 58(2): 192-220.* Oklahoma City formally desegregated its public schools in 1955, but the actual integration process soon slowed down. Black frustration led Dr. A. L. Dowell to file suit in behalf of his son in 1961. The National Association for the Advancement of Colored People joined the crusade which reached the court of Federal District Judge Luther Bohanon. Judge Bohanon not only ruled in Dowell's favor and called for an end to segregationist barriers that placed black students in certain schools, he also ordered an affirmative action program for the assignment of black teachers, principals and other school employees. Though white opposition to the court ruling made the first year difficult, subsequent court rulings reinforced Bohanon's decision and helped undercut further opposition. Based on newspapers and court documents; photo, 125 notes. M. L. Tate

2809. Braden, Anne. BIRMINGHAM, 1956-1979: THE HISTORY THAT WE MADE. *Southern Exposure 1979 7(2): 48-54.* The Reverend Fred L. Shuttlesworth, a black minister active in the southern civil rights movement, participated in integration attempts and sit-ins on buses and joined Martin Luther King, Jr., and Ralph Abernathy in organizing protests in Birmingham, Alabama.

2810. Bullock, Charles S., III and Rodgers, Harrell R., Jr. INSTITUTIONAL RACISM: PREREQUISITE, FREEZING, AND MAPPING. *Phylon 1976 37(3): 212-223.* Overt discrimination has been attacked successfully by civil rights protesters but a second form of racism ("institutional racism") increasingly is apparent. "Freezing" occurs when standards are rigorously applied to all applicants, "but only after most whites qualified during a period of less stringent requirements." "Mapping" is "drawing geographical lines so as to concentrate blacks in an area while excluding them from others." In housing, severe crowding exists for three times as many black families as white, "because of low and moderate incomes. The federal government has acted to counter freezing by elimination of literacy tests for voting, and in the area of employment." As to "mapping," minorities have sought a fairer distribution of school revenue and fairer zoning ordinances. 30 notes. E. P. Stickney

2811. Bullock, Charles S., III, and Stewart, Joseph, Jr. THE JUSTICE DEPARTMENT AND SCHOOL DESEGREGATION: THE IMPORTANCE OF DEVELOPING TRUST. *J. of Pol. 1977 39(4): 1036-1043.* School desegregation lawsuits by the federal Justice Department during 1964-68 strongly paralleled the geographic location of suits concerning voting rights in 1957-64 throughout the South. Involvement in voting cases was contingent upon black complaints, and enabled Justice to develop a record of trustworthiness. The pattern of suits enforcing the 1964 school desegregation provisions, gradually widening circles from the counties where voting suits had been filed, indicates that without the sanction of Health, Education and Welfare Department regulations, progress in the Deep South would have been slower and less uniform. Primary and secondary sources; map, table, 10 notes.

A. W. Novitsky

2812. Burman, Stephen. THE ILLUSION OF PROGRESS: RACE AND POLITICS IN ATLANTA, GEORGIA. *Ethnic and Racial Studies [Great Britain] 1979 2(4): 441-454.* Using the example of Atlanta from the 1960's to 1973, argues that contrary to the thesis of Talcott Parsons, political change has led not to black incorporation but to an illusionary racial and economic progress.

2813. Burstein, Paul. PUBLIC OPINION, DEMONSTRATIONS, AND THE PASSAGE OF ANTIDISCRIMINATION LEGISLATION. *Public Opinion Q. 1979 43(2): 157-172.* This paper considers the relationship of public opinion and demonstrations to the passage of federal civil rights legislation since World War II. Congress passed such legislation when substantial majorities of the population favored equal rights *and* the proportion favoring equal rights was clearly increasing. The evidence is consistent with the notion that civil rights demonstrations played a significant role in the passage of the legislation. Both demonstrations and changes in public opinion appear to have been necessary components of the drive to provoke congressional action... The data utilized in this paper were made available in part by the Roper Public Opinion Research Center, the National Opinion Research Center, and Inter-University Consortium for Political Research. J

2814. Button, James and Scher, Richard K. IMPACT OF THE CIVIL RIGHTS MOVEMENT: PERCEPTIONS OF BLACK MUNICIPAL SERVICE CHANGES. *Social Sci. Q. 1979 60(3): 497-510.* Analyzes the effect of the civil rights movement on black municipal services (police protection, streets, parks, fire protection, water and sewage, and employment) in six Florida cities, utilizing the perceptions of community knowledgables. The civil rights movement did not affect the level of municipal services to blacks as much as proponents have claimed. Based on 110 interviews; 3 tables, 4 notes, biblio. L. F. Velicer

2815. Carter, George E. MARTIN LUTHER KING: INCIPIENT TRANSCENDENTALIST. *Phylon 1979 40(4): 318-324.* Overemphasis on the influence of Henry David Thoreau's *Civil Disobedience* on Martin Luther King, Jr., has obscured King's resemblance to other Transcendentalists in the areas of: the church leading social change, the concept of God and inner light, and the principle of higher law. Based on King's works and on secondary sources; 44 notes.

G. R. Schroeder

2816. Chafe, William. THE GREENSBORO SIT-INS. *Southern Exposure 1978 6(3): 78-87.* The sit-ins were based on a long tradition in the Greensboro, North Carolina, black community of overt and covert opposition to segregation and discrimination. Black leaders either openly opposed violations of civil rights before 1960 or worked within the system to change conditions. The issue of school desegregation in the late 1950's and resultant white procrastination and hypocrisy on this issue prepared the way for the sit-ins which rapidly united and at times divided the black community. The sit-ins also resulted in white concessions in the area of segregation, but black community actions were of far greater significance than were white reactions. N. Lederer

2817. Cohen, David K. SEGREGATION, DESEGREGATION AND 'BROWN': A TWENTY YEAR RETROSPECTIVE. *Society 1974 12(1): 34-40.* Discusses the role of the Supreme Court case *Brown v. Board of Education* (US, 1954) in altering discrimination against Negroes, and its unsettling impact on concepts of equality. S

2818. Condran, John G. CHANGES IN WHITE ATTITUDES TOWARD BLACKS: 1963-1977. *Public Opinion Q. 1979 43(4): 463-476.* This paper investigates white attitudes toward blacks from national survey data collected in 1963, 1972, and 1977. Five attitude items are examined with respect to a full multivariate framework including age, educational attainment, region of residence, and time as independent variables. The results generally show large effects for each independent variable on each attitude item, net of the others. Variations from this pattern are also explored. There is evidence that racial liberalism among whites is slowing its growth in the 1970's and even reversing in some cases. The results are discussed and tentative conclusions suggested.

J

2819. Coombs, David W.; Alsikafi, M. H.; Bryan, C. Hobson; and Webber, Irving L. BLACK POLITICAL CONTROL IN GREENE COUNTY, ALABAMA. *Rural Sociol. 1977 42(3): 398-406.* Examines the 1971-72 change in political decisionmaking power from white majority to black majority in Greene County, Alabama, and compares the findings to two other Alabama counties, Bullock and Wilcox.

2820. Corner, George W. THE BLACK COALITION: AN EXPERIMENT IN RACIAL COOPERATION, PHILADELPHIA, 1968. *Pro. of the Am. Phil. Soc. 1976 120(3): 178-186.* During April 1968-March 1969 32 black and white community leaders in Philadelphia attempted to prevent race riots. The white businessmen produced over one million dollars for the blacks—who called themselves the "Black Coalition"—to run 25 prototype business and social programs. The majority of the programs which were well run, received adequate funds, and produced admirable results. Some of the programs failed for the lack of funds, and three—which received over half the available funds—failed because of total mismanagement. Developing interracial trust and identifying black community leaders proved the most durable result.

W. L. Olbrich

2821. Couto, Richard. FAYETTE COUNTY, TENNESSEE: SICK FOR JUSTICE. *Southern Exposure 1978 6(2): 73-76.* The Rossville Health Center in Fayette County, Tennessee is in many ways an outgrowth of the civil rights movement. The center was established by a group of blacks organized as the Poor People's Health Council which still runs the enterprise. The desperate need for community based medical care in the county was met through the efforts of Square Mormon and other community leaders. The integrated clinic has improved race relations in the county. Interview of Square Mormon. N. Lederer

2822. Dikshit, Om. THE IMPACT OF MAHATMA GANDHI ON MARTIN LUTHER KING, JR. *Negro Hist. Bull. 1975 38(2): 342-344.* Martin Luther King's leadership of the civil rights movement was profoundly affected by his study and practice of Mahatma Gandhi's philosophy of nonviolent social change. After a 1959 trip to India, King returned to the United States convinced that nonviolent resistance to oppression was the most potent weapon available in the struggle for justice. 23 notes. M. J. Wentworth

2823. Dinnerstein, Leonard. SOUTHERN JEWRY AND THE DESEGREGATION CRISIS, 1954-1970. *Am. Jewish Hist. Q. 1973 62(3): 231-241.* Despite the participation of many Jews in the civil rights movement, the level of commitment varied widely. Southern Jews, many of them merchants dependent upon the goodwill of their neighbors, were circumspect in their allegiance to equal rights, except in a few areas like Atlanta and among some college groups. In the early 1960's, perhaps six to 10 rabbis in the South worked for the cause, including Jacob Rothschild, Emmet Frank, Perry Nussbaum, and Charles Mantninband. Based on correspondence of southern rabbis at the American Jewish Archives; 32 notes. F. Rosenthal

2824. Edelman, Marian Wright. SOUTHERN SCHOOLS DESEGREGATION, 1954-1973: A JUDICIAL-POLITICAL OVERVIEW. *Ann. of the Am. Acad. of Pol. and Social Sci. 1973 (407): 32-42.* "Following the *Brown* decisions of 1954 and 1955, the Supreme Court refrained from ordering immediate dismantlement of the dual school system, leaving formulation of specific orders with regard to school desegregation in the hands of district courts. Obstruction and delay resulted, with massive southern resistance and a weak federal response. It was not until passage of the Civil Rights Act of 1964, when federal desegregation standards were adopted, that substantial desegregation could begin. Soon both the Department of Health, Education, and Welfare and the federal courts took a unified stand behind the law, attacking 'free choice' and southern delay. Progress finally seemed at hand. However, under the Nixon administration, federal enforcement efforts have been undercut. Major responsibility for enforcing school desegregation has been shifted from HEW to the slower judicial efforts of the Justice Department. Negative executive leadership has set a tone of national retreat. The current issue of busing and neighborhood schools threatens to erase desegregation progress already made in the South as well as to defeat efforts at making *Brown* a nationally applied policy. However, strong national and local leadership could maintain desegregation progress." J

2825. Edelstein, Frederick S. FEDERAL AND STATE ROLES IN SCHOOL DESEGREGATION. *Educ. and Urban Soc. 1977 9(3): 303-326.* The roles of the states and the federal government in initiating and enforcing school integration are discussed historically and in contemporary context. Concludes that the federal government has by far played the more significant role, although state involvement is increasing. Nonetheless, the federal government must remain the conscience and primary financial support for such efforts. Policy suggestions are offered for enhancing the role of each as well as their cooperation. 2 notes, 23 ref.
C. D'Aniello

2826. Edmund, T. MARTIN LUTHER KING AND THE BLACK PROTEST MOVEMENT. *Gandhi Marg [India] 1976 20(4): 235-249.* King believed that the Christian doctrine of love operating through Gandhian nonviolence was one of the most potent weapons available to black Americans in their struggle for freedom. Although he mobilized support among Negroes belonging to the middle and upper classes and in the South, he did not attract the support of blacks living in the ghettoes of the northern states, who were interested primarily in economic issues, not civil rights.
J. C. English

2827. Efthim, Helen. PONTIAC DESEGREGATION: MYTH AND REALITY. *Urban R. 1975 8(2): 155-159.* Since Pontiac, Michigan's public schools were desegregated by busing in 1971, there has been an improvement in race relations and attitudes.

2828. Fairclough, Adam. THE SOUTHERN CHRISTIAN LEADERSHIP CONFERENCE AND THE SECOND RECONSTRUCTION, 1957-1973. *South Atlantic Q. 1981 80(2): 177-194.* Discusses the peculiarities of the Southern Christian Leadership Conference, (SCLC), particularly comparing it to other such contemporary organizations as NAACP, SNCC, and CORE. The basic characteristic and weakness was its lack of organization. The leadership of Dr. Martin Luther King, Jr., was more charismatic than professional. So long as SCLC worked in the South, where its limited funds were adequate to support its program, it was fairly successful, particularly in spreading its doctrine of nonviolence. But upon entering the North, particularly Chicago, lack of funds as well as encounter with a black mentality quite at variance with that of the Southern black prevented success. King's death fractured the fragile structure, and its effectiveness experienced a gradual demise. Based on the King Papers (Boston University), contemporary newspaper accounts, and secondary sources; 46 notes.
H. M. Parker, Jr.

2829. Farley, Reynolds. TRENDS IN RACIAL INEQUALITIES: HAVE THE GAINS OF THE 1960'S DISAPPEARED IN THE 1970'S? *Am. Sociol. Rev. 1977 42(2): 189-208.* Since the end of the Depression the black population has become urbanized, and black leaders increasingly have stressed civil rights grievances. Federal courts have overturned many segregationist practices, and Congress has enacted encompassing civil rights legislation. The nations's economy expanded rapidly in the 1960's, and economic growth may account for the improvements in the status of blacks registered in that decade. We would anticipate that the improvements of the 1960's would be negated in the recession of the 1970's. Investigation of recent trends in education, employment, occupations, family income and personal earnings shows that gains made in the 1960's did not disappear. Indeed, racial differences attenuated in the lean 1970's just as they did in the prosperous 1960's. The changes of the post-Depression period apparently mean that even during a pervasive recession blacks did not lose the gains they previously experienced. Despite these improvements, racial differences remain large and will not disappear soon. J

2830. Fitzgerald, Michael R. and Morgan, David R. CHANGING PATTERNS OF URBAN SCHOOL DESEGREGATION. *Am. Pol. Q. 1977 5(4): 437-464.* That desegregation has worked better in certain places indicates the operation of forces other than federal pressure. Analyzes forces in many northern and southern cities. In the North, cities with segregated housing, large school districts, and more black students proved most resistant. In the South, factors are more complex. School district size proved to be negative, but "southern desegregation engulfed the whole community." 3 tables, 11 notes, ref.
R. V. Ritter

2831. Freeman, Richard B. POLITICAL POWER, DESEGREGATION, AND EMPLOYMENT OF BLACK SCHOOL TEACHERS. *J. of Pol. Econ. 1977 85(2): 299-322.* Examines the impact of de jure desegregation on education in the South and of increased black voting power on the demand for black schoolteachers in the United States. Because changes in the black share of voters in the post-World War II South are due largely to "exogenous" national laws (the Voting Rights Act of 1965, in particular), the paper provides a unique test of the impact of changes in political power on public decisionmaking. The main finding is that increased black voting power appears to have raised demand for black schoolteachers in the 1960's. There is additional suggestive evidence that black voting power operated in part through election of black officials. The increase in demand due to the changes in voting offset most of the reduction in demand due to desegregation of schooling in the South, averting the potential dire effects of desegregated education on employment of black teachers. Instead of declining, relative employment of blacks in teaching was maintained, and relative incomes rose in the 1950's and 1960's. These results are consistent with the broad "governmental discrimination" hypothesis that much of the economic progress or retrogression of blacks in the United States is explicable in terms of black political power and resultant governmental activity. J

2832. Geschwender, James A. THE LEAGUE OF REVOLUTIONARY BLACK WORKERS: PROBLEMS OF CONFRONTING BLACK MARXIST-LENINIST ORGANIZATIONS. *J. of Ethnic Studies 1974 2(3): 1-23.* Analyzes the five-year career of the Detroit-based League of Revolutionary Black Workers, formed by the integration of the Dodge Revolutionary Union Movement at the Hamtramck Assembly Plant with the component Ford and Eldon Avenue Movements in 1968; it was designed to fight racism and the oppression of Negroes in the automobile industry. Led by John Watson, General G. Baker, Jr., Luke S. Tripp, Jr., and using their periodical, *The Inner City Voice*, they called wildcat strikes, sought to raise black worker consciousness of their economic power, and organized the Detroit Branch of the Black Panther Party. Control of the Wayne State University student paper, and cooperation with the National Black Economic Development Conference followed. Ideological disagreements between adherents of a capitalist exploitation model, with socialist revolution as its goal, and the colonial model favoring a black separatist state led to the League's demise, but the stimulus it provided has not been lost. Based largely on first-hand newspaper accounts, interviews with participants; 70 notes.
G. J. Bobango

2833. Giles, Michael W. and Walker, Thomas G. JUDICIAL POLICY-MAKING AND SOUTHERN SCHOOL SEGREGATION. *J. of Pol. 1975 37(4): 917-936.* The authors test four hypotheses to discover possible correlates of decisions in desegregation cases. These are the social background of the judges, variables from their environments, community linkages, and school district variables. Social background refers to elements in the judges' associations with the traditional southern culture. Except for education in the South, none of these factors appears to be related to levels of school desegregation in the recent period under study. Environmental factors, such as the proportion of Blacks in the school district population or the 1968 vote for George Wallace, do not suggest a significant relationship. Community linkages appear to yield some results: Judges often allow substantially more segregation in their own communities than in neighboring districts. The largest amount of variance, however, is explained by the Black concentration within the schools and the size of the school district. J

2834. Giles, Michael W. RACIAL STABILITY AND URBAN SCHOOL DESEGREGATION. *Urban Affairs Q. 1976 12(4): 499-510.* Studies Florida's Jacksonville area to test the assumption that school desegregation produces white withdrawal and resegregation. Desegregation was ordered in 1963 and began in 1972, when a court ordered plan was implemented. Initial white withdrawal was evident in previously all black public schools, but was not apparent when blacks were integrated into previously all white schools. An increased but stable percentage of students are sent to private schools. Expansion of the ghetto explains why some schools have shown a five percent or more increase in black students since 1972. Desegregation can be attained without substantial resegregation. Primary and secondary sources; 2 tables, 7 notes, biblio.

L. N. Beecher

2835. Graves, Carl R. THE RIGHT TO BE SERVED: OKLAHOMA CITY'S LUNCH COUNTER SIT-INS, 1958-1964. *Chronicles of Oklahoma 1981 59(2): 152-166.* Six years of struggle to integrate the lunch counters of downtown Oklahoma City began in August 1958 when Clara Luper and 13 black children sat down at Katz Drugstore and requested food service. Continued sit-ins compelled other restaurants to end their segregationalist practices, and those that refused were met by a fairly unified black boycott. Although confrontationist in nature, the NAACP-directed sit-ins achieved beneficial results without violence. The discipline and youth of the demonstrators helped win respect from many whites and minimized the possibility of bloodshed. Based on Oklahoma City newspapers; 4 photos, 48 notes.

M. L. Tate

2836. Gray, Noel. BLACK AND WHITE: A LATE TWENTIETH CENTURY REVOLUTION. *Louisiana Hist. 1977 18(3): 277-285.* Among the many humanistic changes that have "swept across the spectrum of American life in this century," the black-white revolution in the area of civil rights "can be registered as a plus for America." Questions, however, the wisdom of forced busing, which "remains a contradiction to the American spirit." The Women's liberation movement resulted from the black-white revolution, affecting women of both races, but to date results have been mixed. Blacks' recognition of their own heritage has produced a mixture of pride and militancy, along with a white reaction, but the American tradition of accepting change is working to "compromise a kind of silent revolution." 2 notes.

R. L. Woodward, Jr.

2837. Hamilton, Charles V. BLACKS AND THE CRISIS OF POLITICAL PARTICIPATION. *Public Interest 1974 (34): 188-210.* Traces the efforts of increasingly politicized Negroes in the 1960's working for voter participation in the South, access to the delegation selection process in the Democratic Party, and participation in the administration of local poverty programs.

2838. Haney, James E. THE EFFECTS OF THE BROWN DECISION ON BLACK EDUCATORS. *J. of Negro Educ. 1978 47(1): 88-95.* Desegregation resulting from *Brown* v. *Board of Education* (US, 1954) has had a negative impact on black educators. As black students entered formerly white facilities, their black teachers were demoted or dismissed in large numbers. Black principals were hit particularly hard. Secondary sources; 19 notes.

R. E. Butchart

2839. Hardy, Richard J. and McCrone, Donald J. THE IMPACT OF THE CIVIL RIGHTS ACT OF 1964 ON WOMEN. *Policy Studies J. 1978 7(2): 240-243.* Attempts to determine if the relative income of black women has improved systematically since the implementation of Title 7 of the Civil Rights Act of 1964.

2840. Hart, John. KENNEDY, CONGRESS AND CIVIL RIGHTS. *J. of Am. Studies [Great Britain] 1979 13(2): 165-178.* President John F. Kennedy took into account the roadblocks to implementing the broad civil rights plank in the Democratic Party platform of 1960. He campaigned in 1960 not for sweeping civil rights legislation but expanded employment and educational opportunities for minorities. After the election, Kennedy cajoled and bargained with an unreceptive Congress until his "moderate and pragmatic" civil rights proposals were headed for Congressional approval when Kennedy was assassinated in 1963. Archival materials and secondary sources; 39 notes.

H. T. Lovin

2841. Herbst, Robert L. THE LEGAL STRUGGLE TO INTEGRATE SCHOOLS IN THE NORTH. *Ann. of the Am. Acad. of Pol. and Social Sci. 1973 (407): 43-62.* "The struggle to integrate public schools in the North has been conducted largely in the federal courts. While the landmark case of *Brown* v. *Board of Education* and its progeny have clearly outlawed 'de jure' or state-imposed school segregation, the Supreme Court has not yet clarified whether its constitutional proscription extends to racial imbalance which results from the application of neighborhood school principles to racially imbalanced residential areas—so-called 'de facto' segregation. In the early phase of northern litigation, the NAACP (National Association for the Advancement of Colored People) lawyers who led the legal struggle sought, largely unsuccessfully, to vindicate their theory that racial imbalance in the public schools, whether caused directly by state officials or not, unconstitutionally deprived black children of equal educational opportunity. Recently, the NAACP has changed its strategy and has attempted to prove in every case that school officials have taken at least some intentionally discriminatory actions which have helped isolate black children in black schools, and its lawyers have managed to convince a more sympathetic judiciary to grant comprehensive integration relief."

J

2842. Hornsby, Alton, Jr. THE DRUM MAJOR ON THE MOUNTAINTOP: A TRIBUTE TO DR. MARTIN LUTHER KING, JR. *J. of Negro Hist. 1977 62(3): 213-216.* Martin Luther King, Jr., delivered a sermon at his Ebenezer Baptist Church in Atlanta on 4 February 1968. He indicated that he wished his funeral, when it was held, to be short and simple. He asked to be remembered as a drum major for justice, peace, and righteousness. In early April 1968, King's funeral was held. Based on the last sermons of Martin Luther King, Jr. and secondary materials; 9 notes.

N. G. Sapper

2843. Hornsby, Alton, Jr. THE DRUM MAJOR ON THE MOUNTAINTOP: A TRIBUTE TO DR. MARTIN LUTHER KING, JR. *J. of Negro Hist. 1978 63(2): 108-117.* Discusses the actions of Martin Luther King, Jr., following a march led in 1962 in Birmingham, Alabama, in protest of Jim Crow laws; reprints King's "Letter from Birmingham Jail" which addressed members of the Southern Christian Leadership Conference, explained and defended his actions, and expounded on his philosophy of nonviolent "massive direct action."

2844. Hunt, Larry L. and Hunt, Janet G. BLACK RELIGION AS BOTH OPIATE AND INSPIRATION OF CIVIL RIGHTS MILITANCY: PUTTING MARX'S DATA TO THE TEST. *Social Forces 1977 56(1): 1-14.* This research evaluates the claim of a general tension between religiosity and civil rights militance among black Americans through a secondary analysis of the 1964 Gary Marx data. It shows that when important secular factors are controlled, Marx's findings of (a) greater militance in largely white denominations (Episcopalian, Presbyterian, Congregationalist, and Roman Catholic), and (b) an inverse correlation between militance and both church attendance and orthodoxy of belief essentially disappear. Additional lines of analysis support the proposal of Nelsen et al. (b) that only a sectlike orientation corrodes militance, while a churchlike orientation actually makes for greater militance.

J

2845. Jones, Faustine C. IRONIES OF SCHOOL DESEGREGATION. *J. of Negro Educ. 1978 47(1): 2-27.* An overview of black education in the United States, particularly in relation to desegregation and affirmative action, and an analysis of the current situation and necessary actions in the future to protect the gains of the last two decades. Notes the federal retreat from desegregation, trends in recent court decisions, and the historical ironies related to the question of educational equality. Secondary sources; 49 notes.

R. E. Butchart

2846. Jones, Leon. BROWN REVISITED: FROM TOPEKA, KANSAS, TO BOSTON, MASSACHUSETTS. *Phylon 1976 37(4): 343-358.* The *Brown* decision of 1954 embodied the concept of the 14th Amendment adopted in 1868. Ten years after *Brown* the number of black students in formerly all-white schools totaled less than 2% of the students, but after the Civil Rights Act of 1964, 26.3% of the students in schools in the Deep South were black. The Coleman Report of 1966, showing that racial integration is an important factor in improving the educational achievement of black students, must be credited with precipitating the white flight to the suburbs and the current busing crisis. Concludes that "the desegregation of the American public school is a long way from completion." 34 notes.

E. P. Stickney

2847. Jones, Mack H. BLACK POLITICAL EMPOWERMENT IN ATLANTA: MYTH AND REALITY. *Ann. of the Am. Acad. of Pol. and Social Sci. 1978 (439): 90-117.* Much of the scholarly literature on black political life in the United States may be appropriately classified as atheoretical. This paper develops a theoretical framework for understanding black politics and assessing black power in America. The distinguishing characteristic of black political life in the subordination of blacks by whites and the concomitant institutionalized belief that white domination is a function of the inherent superiority of whites. Given this as a frame of reference, the evolution of black political power in Atlanta is traced. The discussion is divided into two periods, the first beginning in 1965 and extending to 1973, when Atlanta elected its first black mayor, Maynard Jackson, and the second covering the first four years of the latter's incumbency. J

2848. Joubert, Paul E. and Crouch, Ben M. MISSISSIPPI BLACKS AND THE VOTING RIGHTS ACT OF 1965. *J. of Negro Educ. 1977 46(2): 157-167.* Blacks registered to vote in great numbers in Mississippi after the Voting Rights Act (1965), especially in those counties which were assigned federal examiners. By 1970, 71 percent of eligible Mississippi blacks were registered. Whites' control of the economy, however, still affects black political power. 21 notes, 4 tables.
B. D. Johnson

2849. Kater, John L., Jr. DWELLING TOGETHER IN UNITY: CHURCH, THEOLOGY, AND RACE 1950-1965. *Anglican Theological Rev. 1976 58(4): 444-457.* Examines the response of the Episcopal Church to the Freedom Movement during 1950-65 and links this response to the Church's heritage reaching back to the 1800's.

2850. Kater, John L., Jr. EXPERIMENT IN FREEDOM: THE EPISCOPAL CHURCH AND THE BLACK POWER MOVEMENT. *Hist. Mag. of the Protestant Episcopal Church 1979 48(1): 67-81.* Explores the Episcopal Church's response to the later phase of the movement for black freedom, and describes the course of its history in light of the Church's social theology. The endorsement of the General Convention Special Program of the principle of black self-determination and the commitment of financial support meant that the many older programs at home and abroad had to be curtailed. There is little internal impetus toward a substantive role for the Episcopal Church in the social crises of the present; and it is uncertain whether another period of rapid change would call forth a reassertion of the theological categories of the past for interpreting the Church's place in society. For the present, the challenge lives on in a world where justice and unity and freedom remain unfulfilled dreams for many. Based on Episcopal documents and literature; 41 notes.
H. M. Parker, Jr.

2851. Kelly, William R. and Snyder, David. RACIAL VIOLENCE AND SOCIOECONOMIC CHANGES AMONG BLACKS IN THE UNITED STATES. *Social Forces 1980 58(3): 739-760.* This paper reports an inquiry into the relationship between racial violence and the socioeconomic gains among blacks that occurred in the United States during the 1960's. The few previous studies of the effects of racial disorders are limited in scope and are marred by methodological problems. We take the resource management framework, which conceptualizes violence as a potential political resource for its users, as a substantive warrant to examine this relationship. We also locate the analysis in the general (though largely neglected) arena of violence and social change. We argue that the effects of violence are likely conditional on other factors, and develop hypotheses concerning the differential influence of racial disorders according to the political structure of American cities and the public versus private sector location of socioeconomic changes. We analyze the effects of racial violence frequency and severity on changes between 1960 and 1970 in three socioeconomic variables: nonwhite income, unemployment rates, and the racial composition of selected occupations. These analyses are estimated separately for cities in the South and those in other regions. Our results consistently indicate no relationship between racial violence and black socioeconomic gains *at the local level*. These findings suggest that earlier evidence of reform responses to disorder in some cities may have reflected attempts to cool out black protest but did not result in substantive changes. Our conclusions on the effects of racial violence therefore parallel those on its causes: *if* there were socioeconomic consequences, they must have operated at the national level and affected blacks uniformly across local communities. 3 tables, 23 notes, biblio. J

2852. Kirp, David L. LAW, POLITICS, AND EQUAL OPPORTUNITY: THE LIMITS OF JUDICIAL INVOLVEMENT. *Harvard Educ. Rev. 1977 47(2): 117-137.* Analyzes the relationship of judicial interpretation, legislation, educational policy, and equal opportunity since 1954.

2853. Kopkind, Andrew. A LONG TIME COMING. *Working Papers for a New Soc. 1975 2(4): 13-20.* History of the black power movement in Alabama's Lowndes County, 1965-75, its problems, achievements, and failings. S

2854. Koroleva, A. P. MARTIN LIUTER KING I REBUSY AMERIKANSKOI DEMOKRATII [Martin Luther King and abuses of American democracy]. *Voprosy Istorii [USSR] 1978 (10): 122-140.* The Reverend Martin Luther King, Jr. (1929-68), was noted for his criticism of the US social and legal system and for advocating civil rights. His utopian ideas drew hatred from white racists and from black nationalists. During 1955-68, King's marches and sit-in strikes provoked clashes with racists. Shadowed by the FBI, and the target of smear campaigns, King was finally murdered in mysterious circumstances. 74 notes.
A. P. Oxley

2855. Lawson, Steven F. and Gelfand, Mark I. CONSENSUS AND CIVIL RIGHTS: LYNDON B. JOHNSON AND THE BLACK FRANCHISE. *Prologue 1976 8(2): 65-76.* President Lyndon B. Johnson was personally committed to working for civil rights for Negroes, but was determined to work within the existing political structure to achieve reform in a gradual, orderly manner. He used the authority of his office to clear away many of the legal barriers to black voting, but his political instincts and his sense of the federal system prevented him from using the Voting Rights Act of 1965 as a catalyst for southern political change. Based on primary and secondary sources.
N. Lederer

2856. Lazin, Frederick A. FEDERAL LAW—INCOME HOUSING ASSISTANCE PROGRAMS AND RACIAL SEGREGATION: LEASED PUBLIC HOUSING. *Public Policy 1976 24(3): 337-360.* Study of the implementation of Section 23 of the Housing and Urban Development Act of 1965 which authorized the Federal Public Housing Authority to make funds available to local housing authorities, to lease privately owned dwelling units for public housing. Using the Chicago Housing Authority operation of Section 23 during 1965-73, finds racial "segregation was furthered." Negroes were unable to obtain housing in white communities in Chicago. Analysis of the ability of local constituencies to coopt federal agencies in the implementation of federal programs reveals the strength of federalism. Administrative regulations governing Section 23's operation which encouraged continued patterns of segregation in leased housing are criticized and solutions are offered. Black community response to the program is detailed. Based on original research, interviews, primary and secondary material; table, 86 notes.
J. M. Herrick

2857. Lipsky, Michael and Olson, David J. THE PROCESSING OF RACIAL CRISIS IN AMERICA. *Pol. and Soc. 1976 6(1): 79-103.* Views the political responses of officials to the riots of the 1960's as an elitist process designed to make their political impact negligible while giving the appearance of liberal sympathy for black political demands. This process, best seen in the structure and work of riot commissions and analyzed from a conflict perspective, better explains declining political concern over race relations in the 1970's than assertions to the effect that the status of Negroes has improved, or that the crises of the 1960's were part of a cyclical "issue-attention" process. Primary and secondary sources; 38 notes.
D. G. Nielson

2858. Lord, Donald C. JFK AND CIVIL RIGHTS. *Presidential Studies Q. 1978 8(2): 151-163.* Examines the executive tools employed by the John F. Kennedy administration to further minority voting rights, employment, and desegregation of public accommodations. While building goodwill among blacks, the limited success of this method in 1961 and 1962 convinced Kennedy of the need for stronger civil rights legislation. Public climate made it impossible to strengthen federal civil rights laws before the racial confrontations of 1963. However, the legislative strategy which secured passage of the Civil Rights Act of 1964 was devised by Kennedy in early 1963. Using the authority of his office and appealing to public opinion, Kennedy persuaded doubtful Senators to support a cloture motion resulting in a defeat for the southern filibuster in 1964. 76 notes.
S. C. Strom

2859. MacDonald, A. P., Jr. BLACK POWER. *J. of Negro Educ. 1975 44(4): 547-554.* Studies the sociology of black protest and self-improvement in the 1960's and 70's—from shiftless "Negroes" to blacks on the way to upgrading their lives.

2860. McCormack, Donald J. STOKELY CARMICHAEL AND PAN-AFRICANISM: BACK TO BLACK POWER. *J. of Pol.* 1973 35(2): 386-409. Examines the failure of black power advocate Stokely Carmichael to produce an effective political ideology. The essence of his failure lay in his entrapment in "group theory." Instead of offering a challenge to the American system, Carmichael merely called for "more of the same." He became an advocate of ultra-American "equality and freedom through interest-group liberalism," which, in effect, made him a backer of the status quo. This created a "gap between thought and action" which Carmichael could not close. Carmichael has since sought to escape his "theoretical *cul-de-sac*" by moving toward the advocacy of Pan-Africanism. 38 notes. A. R. Stoesen

2861. McCrone, Donald J. and Hardy, Richard J. CIVIL RIGHTS POLICIES AND THE ACHIEVEMENT OF RACIAL ECONOMIC EQUALITY, 1948-1975. *Am. J. of Pol. Sci.* 1978 22(1): 1-17. The purpose of this article is to determine whether civil rights policies since 1964 have succeeded in systematically decreasing the gap between black and white male incomes, both nationally and regionally. We employ time-series regression analysis to separate the effects of cyclical economic conditions (unemployment and growth in the Gross National Product) from policy induced changes in the ratio of black to white income. We conclude that civil rights policies since 1964 have decreased the gap between black and white incomes, but that this effect is confined to the South. J

2862. McGinnis, Ronald L. CLASS ACTION LITIGATION ON DESEGREGATION. *Negro Hist. Bull.* 1976 39(7): 639-641. Reviews class action suits and some problems attending them. By the mid-1960's class action was popular. Recent court cases have dampened this early ardor and have brought up the question of precisely what constitutes a class. Race seems an inadequate criterion. The recent state of reverse discrimination charges and court challenges relating to affirmative action programs gives the question a new urgency. 2 photos, 35 notes.
V. L. Human

2863. McMillen, Neil R. BLACK ENFRANCHISEMENT IN MISSISSIPPI: FEDERAL ENFORCEMENT AND BLACK PROTEST IN THE 1960'S. *J. of Southern Hist.* 1977 43(3): 351-372. Mississippi has been more recalcitrant than other southern states with regard to voter registration and compliance with the Voting Rights Act (1965). Despite little support from the Justice Department or the Kennedy administration, an uneasy coalition of black groups with some support from white college students found various means of attracting public attention to the black situation in Mississippi's political process. Despite warnings to the contrary, the Voting Rights Act of 1965 was ultimately, if slowly, implemented without much violent resistance from Mississippi whites. Still the history of the struggle of Mississippi blacks to obtain the vote emphasizes the durability of Jim Crow. Based upon manuscripts, printed primary and secondary sources; 68 notes. T. D. Schoonover

2864. Meyers, Michael. BLACK EDUCATION AT ANTIOCH COLLEGE. *Youth & Soc.* 1974 5(4): 379-396. A former Negro student at Antioch College in Yellow Springs, Ohio, describes his 1966-69 campaign against racial segregation advocated by both Negroes and whites at the college. S

2865. Mims, Jasper, Jr. and Jennings, Clara Murphy. SCHOOL DESEGREGATION: BUSING. *Negro Hist. Bull.* 1976 39(7): 634-637. Reviews the school busing controversy and progress in school integration. Little progress has been made; the nation seems to be embarking on an apartheid course. Recent Supreme Court decisions have been unfavorable, researchers are publishing grim reports about integrated schools, and whites continue to flee schools having large black populations. Many Negroes are turning to the concept of all-black schools with black teachers. Two decades of integration efforts have produced few tangible results. 3 photos, 21 notes. V. L. Human

2866. Miroff, Bruce. PRESIDENTIAL LEVERAGE OVER SOCIAL MOVEMENTS: THE JOHNSON WHITE HOUSE AND CIVIL RIGHTS. *J. of Pol.* 1981 43(1): 2-23. While no other administration achieved as much in the field of civil rights as did that of Lyndon Baines Johnson, when activists defined black emancipation in terms alien to the administration's, the confident exercise of presidential leadership was frustrated. Fearing mass activism and defining the racial issue in terms of consensus politics, the Johnson White House sought a shift in black activity from civil rights to party politics. A black Democratic network was to serve as a means of both riot prevention and electoral gains. The administration lost control over the issue by mid-1966 as the movement turned militant and both the Vietnam War and resistance to it preoccupied Washington. 35 notes. A. W. Novitsky

2867. Mithun, Jacqueline S. BLACK POWER AND COMMUNITY CHANGE: AN ASSESSMENT. *J. of Black Studies* 1977 7(3): 263-280. The Black Power movement of the 1960's helped increase black self-worth, accelerate change in the black community, and encourage indigenous leadership. The movement also had tangible results in education, economic self-development, and politics. As a consequence of Black Power social change may involve a more positive self-image for Negroes, urban development, and political action. By their response to the Black Power movement, whites may determine whether or not these constructive ends are attained. Primary and secondary sources; biblio.
D. C. Neal

2868. Morris, Aldon. BLACK SOUTHERN STUDENT SIT-IN MOVEMENT: AN ANALYSIS OF INTERNAL ORGANIZATION. *Am. Sociol. Rev.* 1981 46(6): 744-767. Though it appears to have developed in the spontaneous manner described by classic collective behavior theory, the Southern sit-in movement of 1960 actually grew out of pre-existing institutions and organizational forms. Factors internal to the black community—churches, colleges, protest organizations, and leaders —were responsible for nurturing and developing the movement. Based on primary data collected from archives and interviews with civil rights leaders. J

2869. Mott, Wesley T. THE RHETORIC OF MARTIN LUTHER KING, JR.: *LETTER FROM BIRMINGHAM JAIL*. *Phylon* 1975 36(4): 411-421. Examines closely the oral traditions behind *Letter from Birmingham Jail* and analyzes King's thorough grasp of the emotional intensity his speeches and sermons generated. King's careful wielding of this emotional intensity allowed him to make his powerful denunciations of racism and injustice in America and yet win his audience over to his side and exhort them to action. At a time when prominent black activists have proclaimed King's nonviolence as irrelevant to the black movement, King's style of sustained eloquence has set the stage for general acceptance and recognition of Malcolm X's *Autobiography* and Eldridge Cleaver's *Soul On Ice* as modern masterpieces. Based on secondary sources; 22 notes. K. C. Snow

2870. Muir, Donal. THROUGH THE SCHOOL-HOUSE DOOR: TRENDS IN INTEGRATION, ATTITUDES ON A DEEP-SOUTH CAMPUS DURING THE FIRST DECADE OF DESEGREGATION. *Sociol. and Social Res.* 1974 58(2): 113-121. "Four surveys of the attitudes of the white students on the main campus of the University of Alabama, begun in 1963 and taken at three-year intervals, consistently indicate increasing acceptance of blacks. Most of these students now approve of desegregation in all major areas, have rejected the classic Southern stereotype of blacks, and uphold ideals of political and economic equality. Blacks are strongly accepted on campuses as students, but still tend to be rejected as roommates, social intimates, or dates. The data indicate, however, that social distance is rapidly decreasing. It would appear that the desegregation of any social system, including educational systems, tends to result in rapid rejection of 'racial' roles for interaction, assuming that the setting has been politically neutralized." J

2871. Murray, Hugh T., Jr. THE STRUGGLE FOR CIVIL RIGHTS IN NEW ORLEANS IN 1960: REFLECTIONS AND RECOLLECTIONS. *J. of Ethnic Studies* 1978 6(1): 25-41. Narrative of author's student days at Tulane University and involvement with the Tulane Interfaith Council, the Inter-Collegiate Council for Inter-Racial Cooperation, and the NAACP Youth Chapter. His work with voter registration taught him the many devices used to keep blacks away from the polls and his friendship with a black girl exposed him to direct discrimination in public transportation, parks, and restaurants. In the summer of 1960, he attended a CORE workshop in Miami to learn the techniques of nonviolent protest which were then tested in the Shell's City sit-in and white churches. Throughout these events the New Orleans student groups were peripherally in contact with national figures in the civil rights movement. G. J. Bobango

2872. Nam, Tae Y. A MANIFESTO OF THE BLACK STUDENT ACTIVISTS IN A SOUTHERN BLACK COLLEGE UNDER THE INTEGRATION ORDER. *J. of Negro Educ. 1977 46(2): 168-185.* In 1972 students at predominantly black University of Arkansas at Pine Bluff rebelled against merger of the former Arkansas Agricultural, Mechanical, and Normal College into the University. Details their drive for black separatism and attacks on U.A.P.B. administrators. The student activists compromised with the administration, and separatism lost. 50 notes.
B. D. Johnson

2873. Norrell, R. Jefferson. REPORTERS AND REFORMERS: THE STORY OF THE *SOUTHERN COURIER*. *South Atlantic Q. 1980 79(1): 93-104.* The *Southern Courier* was a weekly newspaper published by young white northern liberals working in Alabama, July 1965-December 1968. Its first editorial stated that the paper "cannot ignore that most of Alabama's Negroes are denied . . . basic equalities. Therefore we will publish information to help erase the injustice of segregation and prejudice." Articles were critical; together they suggest that Alabama and the civil rights movement were characterized by success and failure, good and evil, but also a realistic measure of ambiguity. At first the staff was completely white; but near the end of the paper's existence all staff members but one were black. Despite its short life, the *Courier* made significant contributions as a journalistic institution, informing blacks and enlightening whites in a very critical period of domestic American history. Articles from the *Courier* and the *Courier* files at the Tuskegee Institute; 25 notes.
H. M. Parker, Jr.

2874. O'Kelly, Charlotte G. BLACK NEWSPAPERS AND THE BLACK PROTEST MOVEMENT, 1946-1972. *Phylon 1980 41(4): 313-324.* Little systematic study has been made of the relationship between the black press and the black protest movement. An analysis of 1,623 editorial pages of four large regional newspapers shows that the black press devoted much of its content to publicizing movement activities and problems. Greatest attention was given to the National Association for the Advancement of Colored People and the Urban League. The black press has been overwhelmingly integrationist and nonviolent. 6 tables, 4 notes.
J. V. Coutinho

2875. O'Kelly, Charlotte G. THE BLACK PRESS: CONSERVATIVE OR RADICAL, REFORMIST OR REVOLUTIONARY? *Journalism Hist. 1977-78 4(4): 114-116.* Discusses the black press as a stimulating or inhibiting factor on the black protest movement since the 1950's, and adaptability to the changes in goals and methods of that movement.

2876. Peterson, Paul E. ORGANIZATIONAL IMPERATIVES AND IDEOLOGICAL CHANGE: THE CASE OF BLACK POWER. *Urban Affairs Q. 1979 14(4): 465-484.* The principal explanations for ideological change in the black community assume either mass despair or a lower class uprising against traditional and wealthier black leaders. Argues instead that black power was the result of the political activism in the community generated by the civil rights movement. By stressing racial unity rather than horizontal differences, the black power ideology provided a vehicle for harnessing mass enthusiasm to the task of elevating black elites to positions of power and influence. Compares this process to the emergence of an independent British Labor Party in 1918 so that trade unionists could obtain official acceptance. Similarly, the black power ideology might contribute to the cooptive capabilities of the American regime. 2 notes, biblio.
L. N. Beecher

2877. Polsby, Daniel D. THE DESEGREGATION OF SCHOOL SYSTEMS: WHERE THE COURTS ARE HEADED. *Urban Rev. 1978 10(2): 136-148.* A survey of Supreme Court decisions affecting urban school desegregation shows that no one, "not even, probably, the Supreme Court" knows definitely where the courts are going. Recent decisions have generally narrowed the *Brown v. Board of Education* ruling that "the very idea of unequality is contained in the fact of separation." Partly because of the ambiguity in court decisions, the next major move will probably come from Congress, not the courts. Primary sources; 21 notes.
R. G. Sherer

2878. Rao, K. L. Seshagiri. NONVIOLENT RESISTANCE IN NORTH AMERICA. *Gandhi Marg [India] 1979 1(9): 601-606.* Martin Luther King, Jr. (d. 1968), adapted Gandhian methods of nonviolence to the North American situation with spectacular success in the 1950's and 1960's.

2879. Ravitch, Diane. THE EVOLUTION OF SCHOOL DESEGREGATION POLICY: 1964-1978. *Hist. of Educ. [Great Britain] 1978 7(3): 229-236.* Examines the changing nature of school desegregation in America since the early 1960's, noting the remarkable advances made, but also pointing out emerging complications. Black consciousness and resulting social transformations have strengthened other kinds of ethnic consciousness, thereby creating a new impediment to the realization of a culturally and ethnically integrated America. 10 notes.
S

2880. Reagon, Bernice Johnson and Cluster, Dick. THE BORNING STRUGGLE: THE CIVIL RIGHTS MOVEMENT: AN INTERVIEW WITH BERNICE JOHNSON REAGON. *Radical Am. 1978 12(6): 8-25.* Story of Bernice Johnson Reagon's involvement in the civil rights movement, beginning in 1960 when a junior chapter of the National Association for the Advancement of Colored People (NAACP) was formed in the Harlem district of Albany, Georgia; mentions the formation of the Albany Movement, and her membership in the Freedom Singers.

2881. Romero, Patricia W. W. E. B. DU BOIS, PAN-AFRICANISTS, AND AFRICA 1963-1973. *J. of Black Studies 1976 6(4): 321-336.* Modern scholarship lacks a definitive account of Pan-Africanism prior to 1956, especially the part played by T. Ras Makonnen. A new interpretation of Africa's conception of early Pan-Africanists, particularly W. E. B. DuBois, is also called for. Based on primary and secondary sources; notes, biblio.
D. C. Neal

2882. Rothschild, Mary Aickin. WHITE WOMEN VOLUNTEERS IN THE FREEDOM SUMMERS: THEIR LIFE AND WORK IN A MOVEMENT FOR SOCIAL CHANGE. *Feminist Studies 1979 5(3): 466-495.* Briefly discusses the 1960 origins of the Freedom Summers of 1964 and 1965, when students, sponsored by the Congress of Racial Equality, the Southern Christian Leadership Conference, and the Student Non-Violent Coordinating Committee, became active in the civil rights movement. Details the participation of 650 northern working women in the Freedom Summers. In the civil rights movement that saw inequality in terms of race and color rather than sex, these women faced institutional sexism. White, mostly well-educated students and teachers, with secure incomes, they considered themselves liberal. They performed menial office work without participating in policy decisions, received sexual advances from black men in the movement, and experienced all the hostility blacks in the movement felt for whites. 75 notes.
G. L. Smith

2883. Runcie, John. THE BLACK CULTURE MOVEMENT AND THE BLACK COMMUNITY. *J. of Am. Studies [Great Britain] 1976 10(2): 185-214.* Traces the efforts of militant contemporary Afro-American organizations—Black Muslims and Black Panthers—and of moderate groups (such as the Urban League, NAACP, and Congress of Racial Equality) to encourage black culture in the United States. A black cultural renaissance developed in the 1960's, only to subside in the 1970's; but the renaissance enhanced "ethnic consciousness" of blacks, leaving them better prepared to strengthen the movement which was built in the 1960's. Based on newspaper, magazine, and secondary sources; 115 notes.
H. T. Lovin

2884. Salamon, Lester M. LEADERSHIP AND MODERNIZATION: THE EMERGING BLACK POLITICAL ELITE IN THE AMERICAN SOUTH. *J. of Pol. 1973 35(3): 615-646.* Data from black political candidates in Mississippi 1965-70 suggests parallels between that state and developing nations. The pattern involves initial action by a "radical, cosmopolitan elite" which is replaced by a conservative, traditional elite when basic goals are achieved. In Mississippi the civil rights movement was led by outsiders whom traditional black leaders opposed. After reenfranchisement the latter gained control of most black leadership positions and limited the pace of change. Nevertheless the old elite's monopoly was challenged and partially diminished, forcing them to take a more progressive stance. The demand for change placed in an electoral context results in continued stability, protection of the traditional system, and a "blunting of the reform impetus." Mississippi illustrates how a new social force can be accommodated into an "orderly progression" of events. 7 tables, 47 notes.
A. R. Stoesen

2885. Sawyer, Jack and Senn, David J. INSTITUTIONAL RACISM AND THE AMERICAN PSYCHOLOGICAL ASSOCIATION. *J. of Social Issues 1973 29(1): 67-80.* "Institutional racism—institutional practice that perpetuates racial inequality—does not require individual prejudice or institutional intent, but is a by-product of business as usual. Psychologists for Social Action showed how APA practices institutional racism by condoning employment practices of Lancaster Press, APA's major printer. In May 1969, the Press employed one black person ('wash-up man') out of 300 employees, though Lancaster's 63,000 population included over 15 percent blacks and Puerto Ricans. Both the Press and the APA Central Office attributed this to low educational level. The authors met with representatives of Lancaster minority communities and together with them influenced the Press to hire 9 black persons out of 18 new employees between October 1, 1969 and September 30, 1970. A May 1973 postscript documents APA's continued hesitancy to influence its suppliers toward equal employment practices. [One of seven articles in this issue on 'The White Researcher in Black Society.']." J

2886. Smith, Charles U. PUBLIC SCHOOL DESEGREGATION AND THE LAW. *Social Forces 1975 54(2): 317-327.* Contrary to the still persisting views of William Graham Sumner, stateways can make folkways. Despite evasive reactions (recapitulating the tactics of a century past), a surprising amount of court-ordered desegregation has occurred in southern and border states. Public colleges and universities, however, have lagged behind. But with continued pressure and firmer executive action, law can be an instrument for forging a new morality in support of equal educational opportunity. J

2887. Smith, Douglas C. IN QUEST OF EQUALITY: THE WEST VIRGINIA EXPERIENCE. *West Virginia Hist. 1976 37(3): 211-220.* The West Virginia Human Rights Commission was created in 1961 to deal with problems in race relations. Its appointees, required by law to be of both political parties and races, and of all major denominations, were overwhelmingly well-educated, of above-average income, and politically moderate. The Commission attacked discrimination in every form by setting up local human relations commissions and waging a statewide educational campaign. J. H. Broussard

2888. Spiegel, S. Arthur. AFFIRMATIVE ACTION IN CINCINNATI. *Cincinnati Hist. Soc. Bull. 1979 37(2): 78-88.* Describes action by Cincinnati's city council and mayor's office to end employment discrimination against Negroes, starting in 1963, which culminated in the concept of affirmative action in 1965, then known as fair employment practices, and follows Cincinnati's affirmative action programs 1967.

2889. Stoper, Emily. THE STUDENT NONVIOLENT COORDINATING COMMITTEE: RISE AND FALL OF A REDEMPTIVE ORGANIZATION. *J. of Black Studies 1977 8(1): 13-34.* After a peak of success in 1964, the Student Nonviolent Coordinating Committee (SNCC) went rapidly into decline because of insoluble tension between its sect-like characteristics and its pursuit of political objectives. SNCC members totally committed themselves to the organization's values, and SNCC members came to view those values in highly moral terms that allowed no compromise. Five crises fatally exposed this tension. They were the Mississippi delegation fight at the 1964 Democratic National Convention, a sudden influx of hundreds of whites into SNCC, frictions with other civil rights groups, an abortive attempt to begin activism in northern cities, and erosion of the organization's financial base. Primary and secondary sources; biblio. D. C. Neal

2890. Storey, John W. TEXAS BAPTIST LEADERSHIP, THE SOCIAL GOSPEL, AND RACE, 1954-1968. *Southwestern Hist. Q. 1979 83(1): 29-46.* The Southern Baptist Convention's "crisis statement" of June, 1968, stressing the church's social involvement, came after 14 years of maneuvering and debate. Since 1954 several Texas Baptist leaders—Ewing S. James, Thomas B. Maston, Acker C. Miller, and Foy Valentine—had pushed the church toward more concern for racial equality. Their course illustrates Walter Rauschenbusch's idea that social action is compatible with conservative theology. Based on interviews and other primary sources; 35 notes. J. H. Broussard

2891. Sveino, Per. MARTIN LUTHER KING: A CREATIVE EXTREMIST. *Norwegian Contributions to Am. Studies 1973 4: 361-377.* Martin Luther King's violent death in Memphis, Tennessee, 4 April 1968, meant that "the principle of nonviolence in race relations had suffered a blow, ... in the whole world. Though ... his attempts at carrying out his ideas, should by no means be underrated, it is the validity of the ideological basis of his action that must decide whether King's mission will have lasting value." Despite world-wide recognition of King's work (including the 1964 Nobel Peace Prize), his last years were "progress through pain." His principle and tactics of nonviolence were increasingly disputed by blacks and whites. King defined nonviolent resistance as a reconciliation of opposites—acquiescence and violence—while avoiding the extremes and immoralities of both. King "was one of those ... 'creative extremists' who in the best American tradition had a dream of 'the beloved community' to be realized by 'white and black' together ...." 70 notes.
D. D. Cameron

2892. Terchek, Ronald J. POLITICAL PARTICIPATION AND POLITICAL STRUCTURES: THE VOTING RIGHTS ACT OF 1965. *Phylon 1980 41(1): 25-35.* The 24th Amendment (1964) abolished the poll tax as a prerequisite for voting, but hardly affected voter registration. The Voting Rights Act (US, 1965) did precipitate the anticipated increase. 4 tables, 29 notes. N. G. Sapper

2893. Tulsky, Fredric. STANDING UP TO FEAR IN MISSISSIPPI. *Southern Exposure 1978 6(3): 68-72.* Founded in 1966 by Alfred Robinson, the black United League has been seeking to consolidate the black community in northern Mississippi in order to effect political, economic, and civil rights goals. A major concern has been alleged police brutality and murder practiced against Negroes. The United League has recently been deeply involved in an economic boycott by blacks of white merchants in Tupelo, Mississippi, an action designed to bring about police reform. This campaign has engendered a white backlash in the form of a revived Ku Klux Klan. Various clashes have occurred between these two contending groups. N. Lederer

2894. Useem, Bert. MODELS OF THE BOSTON ANTI-BUSING MOVEMENT: POLITY/MOBILIZATION AND RELATIVE DEPRIVATION. *Sociol. Q. 1981 22(2): 263-274.* Provides data on the Boston antibusing movement collected during interviews with white Boston residents between the ages of 25 and 53 during 1977-78, which supports polity/mobilization theory and relative deprivation theory, and presents a new model that incorporates elements of both theories for analyzing participation in social movements.

2895. Useem, Bert. SOLIDARITY MODEL, BREAKDOWN MODEL, AND THE BOSTON ANTI-BUSING MOVEMENT. *Am. Sociol. Rev. 1980 45(3): 357-369.* "Breakdown theorists" assert that actors who are weakly integrated into their community and experience discontent are likely to join a protest movement. These analysts also maintain that disorganization increases discontent. "Solidarity theorists," on the other hand, argue that isolated individuals are less likely to protest than others and that discontent is unrelated to protest. Data from a survey of Boston residents provide support for the solidarity theorists' argument that social cohesion increases protest. The Boston data, however, support the breakdown theorists' hypothesis that discontented individuals are more likely to protest than others. Finally, the data undercut the breakdown theorists' hypothesis that disorganization increases discontent. J

2896. VanValey, Thomas L.; Roof, Wade Clark; and Wilcox, Jerome E. TRENDS IN RESIDENTIAL SEGREGATION: 1960-70. *Am. J. of Sociol. 1977 82(4): 826-844.* The literature on racial residential segregation in American metropolitan areas reports contradictory findings on the decade of the sixties. Some researchers have concluded that average scores declined between 1960 and 1970, while others point to evidence of increases. This paper presents tract-based indexes for all 237 SMSAs (and their central cities) in 1970 and a comparable set of indexes for 1960. These are also cross-tabulated against region, population size, and minority proportion. Several conclusions are drawn: (1) overall, the data indicate a general decline in the average level of segregation between 1960 and 1970; (2) much of that decline is due to the relatively low scores among SMSAs added during the decade; (3) contradictory findings reported in the literature are likely to be due to sampling or other methodological inconsistencies; and (4) clear variations in levels of segregation persist with regard to region, population size, and minority proportion. The importance of these findings for future research is discussed. J

2897. Wagy, Thomas R. GOVERNOR LEROY COLLINS OF FLORIDA AND THE SELMA CRISIS OF 1965. *Florida Hist. Q. 1979 57(4): 403-420.* LeRoy Collins (b. 1909), as head of the Community Relations Service (CRS) was instrumental in designing a compromise plan for the proposed Selma-to-Montgomery, Alabama, march of 9 March 1965. His compromise stopped bloodshed and allowed both sides to claim victory by drawing moderate Southerners to the side of integration. Collins's role was harmful to his campaign for the US Senate in 1968. Primary and secondary sources; 81 notes.   N. A. Kuntz

2898. Warheit, George J.; Swanson, Edith; and Schwab, John J. A STUDY OF RACIAL ATTITUDES IN A SOUTHEASTERN COUNTY: A CONFIRMATION OF NATIONAL TRENDS. *Phylon 1975 36(4): 395-406.* Reviews earlier research on social distance and racial attitudes in the United States and corroborates with recent findings changes toward a growing inclusiveness of racial attitudes among whites over the last 50 years. However, the study recognizes that a change in attitudes does not necessarily mean behavior will change. Attitudinal changes occurred following the historic 1954 Supreme Court decision and a decade of Civil Rights legislation. The political climate today is different inasmuch as "forced busing" has become an explosive political issue and may signal a reemergence of more exclusive racial attitudes on the part of white Americans. Based on primary research and secondary sources; 7 tables, 16 notes.   K. C. Snow

2899. Wasserman, Ira M. A REANALYSIS OF THE WALLACE MOVEMENT. *J. of Pol. and Military Sociol. 1979 7(2): 243-256.* The standard interpretation of the Wallace movement of the 1960s and the 1970s was that it represented a movement of racists and bigots opposed to blacks and other minority groups. An alternative explanation has been that it was a neo-Populist movement that mobilized the masses against the established order within the federal government and the political parties. This paper challenges both of these positions. Employing Baran and Sweezey's classic Marxian analysis of race relations in Monopoly Capital as a theoretical framework, the paper argues that the movement was a potential counterrevolutionary movement which mobilized mass white support against government civil rights policies which directly threatened their vested interests. Calling forth the 'fury of private interests,' the movement attempted to mobilize these groups against government intervention in social areas. The ultimate failure of the movement was brought about by the end of the racial turmoil in the late 1960s.   J

2900. Welsh, Matthew E. CIVIL RIGHTS AND THE PRIMARY ELECTION OF 1964 IN INDIANA: THE WALLACE CHALLENGE. *Indiana Mag. of Hist. 1979 75(1): 1-27.* Matthew E. Welsh, former governor of Indiana, discusses his favorite-son candidacy in the Indiana Democratic primary of 1964. Welsh decided to resist the candidacy of Alabama Governor George C. Wallace, fearing that Wallace's candidacy would resurrect racial hatreds in Indiana and reverse recent improvements in race relations. Welsh's successful campaign stanched sentiment against the Civil Rights Act (US, 1964) and set the stage for Lyndon Johnson's nomination as the Democratic presidential nominee. 28 notes.   J. Moore

2901. Willhelm, Sidney M. MARTIN LUTHER KING, JR. AND THE BLACK EXPERIENCE IN AMERICA. *J. of Black Studies 1979 10(1): 3-19.* Martin Luther King, Jr.'s *Where Do We Go From Here?* (1968) was a better assessment of US race relations than scholars' studies because King correctly noted that relations were getting worse, he stressed justice over equality, and he showed how capitalists used automation to exploit blacks. But King underestimated the extent of racism, especially the US willingness to use "conditional genocide" against blacks who resist white attempts to put blacks onto "reservations" of ghettos or college campuses. biblio.   R. G. Sherer

2902. —. CIVIL RIGHTS PROTESTS IN TAMPA: ORAL MEMOIRS OF CONFLICT AND ACCOMMODATION. *Tampa Bay Hist. 1979 1(1): 37-54.* Presents two interviews, one with Clarence Fort, a civil rights activist, the other with Julian Lane, a former mayor of Tampa, Florida, in which both discuss civil rights in general and protests in Tampa which resulted (because of peaceful demonstrations led by Fort and the work of Tampa's Biracial Committee, led by Lane) in desegregation of lunch counters, municipal facilities, and theaters, 1960.

The Second Women's Movement

2903. Agre, Gene P. and Finkelstein, Barbara. FEMINISM AND SCHOOL REFORM: THE LAST FIFTEEN YEARS. *Teachers Coll. Record 1978 80(2): 307-315.* Two distinct lines of argument appear in the statements of feminists on education: "domestic feminism" asserts the importance of better training women for traditional nurturing and service roles; "economic feminism" stresses the necessity of making women economically independent. Recent heavy emphasis on the latter concern has caused most feminists to ignore or denigrate women in domestic roles. This imbalance should be corrected. Secondary sources; 20 notes.   E. Bailey

2904. Arendale, Marirose. TENNESSEE AND WOMEN'S RIGHTS. *Tennessee Hist. Q. 1980 39(1): 62-78.* While the Tennessee legislature dragged its feet in adopting the proposed 19th Amendment to the Constitution, it was the 10th legislature to pass on the Equal Rights Amendment. But reaction set in, and two years later, in 1974, the legislature rescinded its action. The arguments in both campaigns suggest that Tennessee, a border state with ties to the deep South, retains the regional conviction that a woman is the fulcrum around which family life revolves. Buttressed by Biblical references, this concept has stubbornly resisted contemporary pressures for change. Based largely on contemporary newspaper accounts; 2 illus., 44 notes.   H. M. Parker, Jr.

2905. Evans, Sara M. THE ORIGINS OF THE WOMEN'S LIBERATION MOVEMENT. *Radical Am. 1975 9(2): 1-14.* Considers changes in sex roles since the 1950's as women entered the service sector of the economy and participated in the Civil Rights Movement.   S

2906. Evans, Sara M. TOMORROW'S YESTERDAY: FEMINIST CONSCIOUSNESS AND THE FUTURE OF WOMEN. Berkin, Carol Ruth and Norton, Mary Beth, ed. *Women of America: A History* (Boston: Houghton Mifflin Co., 1979): 390-417. Examines the role of feminist movements of the 1960's, primarily the National Organization for Women. Some organizations grew out of the student activist groups such as the SDS Economic Research and Action Project (ERAP) and involvement with the Student Nonviolent Coordinating Committee. Others, such as the Boston organization 9 to 5, evolved from women's desires for equality in their work. Primary sources, including SNCC documents; 14 notes.   K. Talley

2907. Evans, Sara M. WOMEN'S CONSCIOUSNESS AND THE SOUTHERN BLACK MOVEMENT. *Southern Exposure 1977 4(4): 10-18.* A women's social movement arose out of both the abolition crusade and the civil rights movement of the 1960's. In both instances female participation in the struggle for racial equality allowed women to develop political skills and a belief in human rights that could be employed to justify female claims for equality. The extent to which northern and southern white women participated in the southern civil rights movement eventually spurred the opposition of black female participants because of the relationships formed between black males and white females in the organizations. Pressures exerted by black women coupled with the rise of black nationalism generated the departure of white women from the movement. Mainly based on oral interviews.   N. Lederer

2908. Featherman, David L. and Hauser, Robert M. SEXUAL INEQUALITIES AND SOCIOECONOMIC ACHIEVEMENT IN THE U.S., 1962-1973. *Am. Sociol. Rev. 1976 41(3): 462-483.* Intercohort shifts in mean education, occupational status and earnings for married persons in the experienced civilian labor forces of 1962 and 1973 represent socioeconomic improvements for both men and women. While the occupational and educational achievements of women have kept pace with men's and indeed exceed the male means, the ratio of female to male earnings has declined from 0.39 to 0.38 for persons in the ECLF. Causal models of the processes of socioeconomic achievement show men and women to be allocated to levels of education and occupational status in much the same manner. Women's achievements are somewhat less related to their family origins, especially farm origins, than are men's, and the net effect of educational attainment on occupational status is larger for women. Intercohort changes in the process of occupational achievement have affected both sexes and include an increase in the net occupational status benefit of an additional year of schooling and a decline in the occupational handicap of farm origins. Equality of economic opportunity for women has not followed from women's opportunities for schooling and occupational status. While the net returns to education have improved more noticeably for women than men, the inter-temporal increases in returns to occupational status have benefited only men. Sexual "discrimination" accounts for 85% of the earnings gap in 1962 and 84% in 1973. J

2909. Gammage, Judie K. PRESSURE GROUP TECHNIQUES: THE TEXAS EQUAL LEGAL RIGHTS AMENDMENT. *Great Plains J. 1976 16(1): 45-65.* Describes the long battle during 1957-72 in which the Texas Federation of Business and Professional Women's Clubs, led by Attorney Hermine Tobolowsky, pressed for passage and ratification of the Equal Legal Rights Amendment in Texas. Excellent political organization and growing national support for womens' rights led to victory in 1972. Primary materials; 64 notes. O. H. Zabel

2910. Gates, Margaret J. OCCUPATIONAL SEGREGATION AND THE LAW. *Signs: J. of Women in Culture and Soc. 1976 1(3, Part 2): 61-74.* Past and present laws and judicial attitudes directly or indirectly contribute to occupational segregation. Twenty-six states require limiting certain job categories to one sex; discriminatory laws touch policing, veterans' preferences, military service, and serving liquor. Protective legislation and domestic relations laws contribute to sex segregation in employment. Laws and decisions since 1964 offer remedies for gender-related barriers in the work force, but it is still early to judge the results of these, except in police patrol where women have increased markedly. Based on court decisions; 36 notes. S. E. Kennedy

2911. Gelb, Joyce and Palley, Marian Lief. WOMEN AND INTEREST GROUP POLITICS: A COMPARATIVE ANALYSIS OF FEDERAL DECISION-MAKING. *J. of Pol. 1979 41(2): 362-392.* The role of women activists has changed and increased in the 1970's. Analysis of campaigns for the Equal Credit Opportunity Act of 1974, antisex discrimination provisions of Title IX of the Education Amendment of 1972, antiabortion Hyde Amendments of 1976 and 1977, and the Amendment to Title VII of the Civil Rights Act of 1964 banning pregnancy-related discrimination in employment, indicates greatest success when there is no fundamental value split in society, and no strong organizational support for the status quo. Success was also enhanced when issues were perceived as dealing with role equity rather than role change for women. 45 notes. A. W. Novitsky

2912. Harding, Susan. FAMILY REFORM MOVEMENTS: RECENT FEMINISM AND ITS OPPOSITION. *Feminist Studies 1981 7(1): 57-75.* Feminists and their opponents employ two distinct perspectives and strategies in attempting to reform family organization. Feminist strategy (set of plans) reduces the family's role in defining woman's life and identity. Feminist ("egalitarian") perspective emphasizes individuality and equality. Their opponents emphasize deference to authority and inevitability of marriage and children. This "hierarchal" perspective centralizes the family's role in woman's identity. In general, women combine "egalitarian" and "hierarchal" ideas. An uneasy truce is likely between competing strategies. Another consciousness is emerging: kinship reaching beyond the family for identity, intimacy, sexuality, and reproduction. Covers ca. 1960-80. Secondary sources; 23 notes. P. D. Hinnebusch

2913. Ingram, Anne G. AN ORAL HISTORY STUDY OF THE WOMEN'S EQUITY MOVEMENT, UNIVERSITY OF MARYLAND, COLLEGE PARK (1968-1978). *Maryland Hist. 1978 9(2): 1-25.* Analyzes a decade of feminism at the University of Maryland through edited conversations with eight women who led the movement. Provides a prologue and epilogue placing the interviews in context. Concludes that the situation has improved but that discrimination against women continues at all levels. Interviews and primary sources; 12 notes. G. O. Gagnon

2914. Jamieson, Kathleen. MULTIPLE JEOPARDY: THE EVOLUTION OF A NATIVE WOMEN'S MOVEMENT. *Atlantis [Canada] 1979 4(2, part 2): 157-178.* Discusses Indian women's lack of political participation in Canada due to the Indian Act, 1869-1951, until Indians received the franchise in 1960, and the increase in native political participation, 1970's. The native women's movement gained momentum in 1970 when Jeannette Lavell, an Ojibwa Indian, contested a section of the Indian Act in the courts; traces the development of the native women's movement as a separate women's movement.

2915. Lavine, T. Z. IDEAS OF REVOLUTION IN THE WOMEN'S MOVEMENT. *Am. Behavioral Scientist 1977 20(4): 535-566.* Explores the growth of the women's liberation movement out of the youth and civil rights movements of the 1960's; this third wave of feminism hopes to establish revolutionary concepts for liberation.

2916. Lockett, Darby Richardson. FEMINIST FOOTHOLDS IN RELIGION. *Foundations 1976 19(1): 33-39.* Reviews the feminist movement in American Judaism, Catholicism, and Protestantism. Mentions their gains but stresses the general antifeminist attitude found in most religious organizations. Makes suggestions for changing attitudes. Biblio. E. E. Eminhizer

2917. Lynch, John E. THE ORDINATION OF WOMEN: PROTESTANT EXPERIENCE IN ECUMENICAL PERSPECTIVE. *J. of Ecumenical Studies 1975 12(2): 173-197.* Presents the issue of the ordination of women to the professional office of ministry in world Protestantism and the World Council of Churches within the past 10 years. Many churches accept women ministers, but some still hesitate. Scandinavia appears to be more progressive in this regard than either the US or England. Theological and sociological arguments favor the ordination of women, and encourage churches to keep up with social change.
 J. A. Overbeck

2918. Marecek, Jeanne and Kravetz, Diane. WOMEN AND MENTAL HEALTH: A REVIEW OF FEMINIST CHANGE EFFORTS. *Psychiatry 1977 40(4): 323-329.* Reviews the negative effects of social conditions on women's psychological well-being and discusses areas in which feminists are striving to change the mental health system.

2919. Mason, Karen Oppenheim; Czajka, John L.; and Arber, Sara. CHANGE IN U.S. WOMEN'S SEX-ROLE ATTITUDES, 1964-1974. *Am. Sociol. Rev. 1976 41(4): 573-596.* This paper uses data from five sample surveys taken between 1964 and 1974 to investigate recent change in U.S. women's sex-role attitudes. It employs several statistical techniques to insure comparability among samples before making inferences about attitude change. The results of the analysis suggest there has been considerable movement toward more egalitarian role definitions in the past decade, with such change occurring equally among higher and lower status women. The analysis also finds evidence that women's attitudes about their rights in the labor market are becoming more strongly related to their attitudes about their roles in the home and shows that educational attainment and employment are among the most important individual-level predictors of attitudes at a given point in time. Little evidence is found for the unique influence of the women's movement on change in women's sex-role attitudes, but the sizable changes in these attitudes since 1964 may help explain the rise of the movement. J

2920. Robinson, Donald Allen. TWO MOVEMENTS IN PURSUIT OF EQUAL EMPLOYMENT OPPORTUNITY. *Signs 1979 4(3): 413-433.* After passage in 1964, Title VII of the Civil Rights Act made only "statutory promises" to women. Because of the strange coalition formed by woman's rights advocate Martha Griffiths and southern obstructionist Howard "Judge" Smith, the word "sex" had been added successfully to the bill. Little was done for women until the volume of complaints to the Equal Employment Opportunity Commission reached over 25% and feminist action groups exerted pressure. Between 1968 and 1971, the EEOC began to make important policy decisions, creating a "magna carta" of the working woman. By 1974, however, limited resources divided between blacks and women and ineffective leadership plagued the Commission. Based on US government sources and on personal correspondence with participants; 69 notes. S. P. Conner

2921. Schroeder, Fred E. H. FEMININE HYGIENE, FASHION, AND THE EMANCIPATION OF AMERICAN WOMEN. *Am. Studies 1976 17(2): 101-110.* Examines the public depiction of behavior patterns surrounding menstruation in television commercials and in contemporary advertising. All devolve from the theme of women's liberation and the New Freedom. Fashions have generally followed suit. Primary and secondary sources; 30 notes. J. Andrew

2922. Zangrando, Joanna Schneider. WOMEN IN ARCHIVES: AN HISTORIAN'S VIEW ON THE LIBERATION OF CLIO. *Am. Archivist 1973 36(2): 203-214.* Asks why women have not been given more consideration in the historical treatment of men and women. Explains the role of the Coordinating Committee of Women in the History Profession, part of the American Historical Association (AHA), and describes the impact of the women's rights movement on the AHA. More research on women is necessary to increase information and to help women understand their roles. Discusses methods of research in women's history and suggests that archivists can promulgate information about sources. Table, 17 notes. D. E. Horn

Economic Reform

2923. Cherry, Robert. CLASS STRUGGLE AND THE NATURE OF THE WORKING CLASS. *R. of Radical Pol. Econ. 1973 5(2): 47-86.* Defines a leftist political program based on analysis of the working class's standard of living and their demands for reform from the late 1950's to 1973.

2924. Ferrari, Art. SOCIAL PROBLEMS, COLLECTIVE BEHAVIOR AND SOCIAL POLICY: PROPOSITIONS FROM THE WAR ON POVERTY. *Sociol. and Social Res. 1975 59(2): 150-162.* "Propositions are presented on the rise of the social problem of poverty and antipoverty policy during the 1960s, derived from four of five issues raised by Herbert Blumer in viewing social problems as collective behavior: emergence, legitimation, mobilization of action, and formation of an official plan. The propositions suggest the crucial role of political authorities, especially when there is little public interest in the problem, how misinterpretation of protester grievances can lead to policies that escalate conflict, the role of mass media after legitimation of a problem, the political integration aspects of social policy, the mobilization of action before a problem emerges, the mobilization of support after a problem emerges, and the power of political elites to have their definition and policy accepted." J

2925. Friedland, Roger. CLASS POWER AND SOCIAL CONTROL: THE WAR ON POVERTY. *Pol. and Soc. 1976 6(4): 459-489.* Views the War on Poverty as a co-optive program of social control to defuse the political threat of the urban poor and nonwhites to the accommodations between monopoly capital and organized labor in the 1960's. Analyzes the conditions under which poor and nonwhite groups could influence political outcomes. Through statistical analysis of funding levels provided under War on Poverty programs, argues that the presence of powerful labor and corporate forces attended large allocations of funds to poverty agencies. These new bureaucracies allowed for some influence by poor and nonwhites on their operation, thereby deflecting any real influence upon the traditional class power structure. Based on secondary sources; tables, diagram, 46 notes. D. G. Nielson

2926. Fugita, Stephen S. A PERCEIVED ETHNIC FACTOR IN CALIFORNIA'S FARM LABOR CONFLICT: THE NISEI FARMER. *Explorations in Ethnic Studies 1978 1(1): 50-72.* Examines the conflict between the Nisei Farmers League and the United Farm Workers Union in California's San Joaquin Valley over agricultural labor, 1971-77.

2927. Gehley, Dennis M. REFLECTIONS ON THE GROWTH MYTH: ECONOMIC AND SOCIAL DEVELOPMENT IN APPALACHIA. *Potomac Rev. 1979 8(2): 1-11.* Studies the implementation of the Appalachian Regional Development Act (US, 1965) through 1975. A major weakness of the act is the requirement that public investment be concentrated in areas where there is "significant potential for future growth, and where the expected return on public dollars will be greatest." Thus a disproportionate amount of money has gone to areas with high per-capita income—sometimes close to the national average—while neglecting poorer, rural areas. Suggests a reevaluation of our thinking about the values to be served in framing and modifying this and similar legislation. Based on US government documents and secondary sources; 19 notes. L. Van Wyk

2928. Gilbert, Neil. THE TRANSFORMATION OF SOCIAL SERVICES. *Social Service Rev. 1977 51(4): 624-641.* Since the Public Welfare Amendments (1962), profound change has occurred in the basic aspects of social services: increased clientele, diversification of services, increased purchase of services from private agencies, increased funding proportionate to population, and increased state participation in planning.

2929. Goodwin, Leonard and Moen, Phyllis. THE EVOLUTION AND IMPLEMENTATION OF FAMILY WELFARE POLICY. *Policy Studies J. 1980 8(4, Special no. 2): 633-651.* Examines federal public welfare programs enacted since 1962, their implementation, and the attitudes of welfare recipients.

2930. Grant, Jim. THE ORGANIZED UNORGANIZED. *Southern Exposure 1976 4(1-2): 132-135.* Examines unionization movements in the South since the 1920's; mentions northern industries which moved south to avoid organization and members' and organizers' stepped-up efforts to maintain union organization, 1968-74.

2931. Grube, John. UNE SÉCURITÉ SOCIALE BIEN DE CHEZ NOUS [A good social security program for us]. *Action Natl. [Canada] 1980 69(9): 690-706.* François-Albert Angers argued that Catholicism should inspire not only the outward religious practice of Quebec, but also the public welfare policies of the province. In accord with Catholic social justice teachings, he: espoused the principle of a just family wage, supported private, voluntary charity while considering state welfare programs as a drug inhibiting individual freedom and responsibility, asserted that modern poverty resulted from the destruction of medieval institutions and relationships, and suggested that compensation programs differentiate among seasonal, structural, cyclical, and technological unemployment. He believed that each of these principles militated against the centralizing tendencies of federal welfare programs. 48 notes.
A. W. Novitsky

2932. Heins, Marjorie. THE FOURTEEN-YEAR FUROR OVER EQUAL EMPLOYMENT. *Working Papers for a New Soc. 1978 6(4): 61-71.* Discusses progress to end employment discrimination against women and minorities since the Civil Rights Act (1964, Title VII); cites court cases.

2933. Hertz, Susan H. THE POLITICS OF THE WELFARE MOTHERS MOVEMENT: A CASE STUDY. *Signs: J. of Women in Culture and Soc. 1977 2(3): 600-611.* Prior to the 1960's welfare clients had not organized to lobby in their own interest and had minimal influence on either local or national policy. The Welfare Mothers Movement in Minnesota represents one organizational response to the problem. Welfare recipients were organized in an attempt to change both their public and self-images. Strategies were developed leading to political action by recipients, influencing policy decisions, and contributing to the reform of the system. The movement involved the client in changing a system which previously had never responded directly to client demand. Primary and secondary sources; 12 notes. S. R. Herstein

2934. Hurd, Richard W. ORGANIZING THE WORKING POOR —THE CALIFORNIA GRAPE STRIKE EXPERIENCE. *R. of Radical Po. Econ. 1974 6(1): 50-75.* Examines the development of the United Farm Workers Union from the early 1960's, particularly during the California grape strikes (1966-70). The manner in which community and union organizing were combined to achieve grass roots participation, the emphasis upon non-violence, and the successful use of boycott tactics suggest important lessons for future organizers. Secondary and primary materials, especially newspapers; 109 notes. P. R. Shergold

2935. Kerstein, Robert J. and Judd, Dennis R. ACHIEVING LESS INFLUENCE WITH MORE DEMOCRACY: THE PERMANENT LEGACY OF THE WAR ON POVERTY. *Social Sci. Q. 1980 61(2): 208-220.* Assesses the War on Poverty program in St. Louis, Missouri. The Human Development Corporation benefited city officials and other black elites, but not the poor for whom the program was initially intended. In contrast to the optimism of the Economic Opportunity Act, the War on Poverty program failed to provide both short- and long-term solutions to the employment problems of the urban poor. Covers 1964-75. Based on committee records of the Human Development Corporation,

job placement data and funds distribution by area and activity; 36 notes.
M. Mtewa

2936. Levitan, Sar A. and Taggart, Robert. THE GREAT SOCIETY DID SUCCEED. *Pol. Sci. Q. 1976-77 91(4): 601-618.* Report on their extensive reevaluation of the Johnson administration's Great Society programs. Their conclusion is that the Great Society programs did not fail —as has been widely charged in recent years—but that despite some deficiencies, the programs led to substantial improvements in the living conditions of the poor, the sick, the elderly, and the members of minority groups.
J

2937. MacDonald, Maurice. FOOD STAMPS: AN ANALYTICAL HISTORY. *Social Service Rev. 1977 51(4): 642-658.* Reviews the history of the food stamp program, begun in 1939 to absorb food surpluses; discusses the origins and motives behind the 1964 Food Stamp Act (and its subsequent modification), and quantifies its massive growth during 1967-75.

2938. McConville, Ed. OLIVER HARVEY: "GOT TO TAKE SOME RISKS." *Southern Exposure 1978 6(2): 24-28.* Harvey was involved for many years in the effort to organize a union of health service workers at the Duke University Medical Center in Durham, North Carolina. Despite poor working conditions at Duke, unionization was an uphill battle given to the hostile attitude of the power establishment in Durham and the intransigent anti-union attitude of the Duke Hospital administration. Harvey also became involved in local civil rights agitation during the 1960's. The fight for union recognition at Duke, including the demand for a minimum wage of $1.60 per hour, culminated in a strike supported by students and faculty in 1968. The union finally came to Duke as a result of a NLRB election in 1972. Oliver Harvey, now retired, continues to work for the betterment of health service workers on an unofficial basis. Based on oral interviews.
N. Lederer

2939. McFadyen, Richard E. ESTES KEFAUVER AND THE TRADITION OF SOUTHERN PROGRESSIVISM. *Tennessee Hist. Q. 1978 37(4): 430-443.* Tennessee Senator Estes Kefauver's (1903-63) work on the Senate Subcommittee on Antitrust and Monopoly gives insight into his posture as a southern Progressive. As a true Progressive, Kefauver opposed monopolies and businesses which were overly-protected by government regulations at the expense of the taxpayer. His investigation of the pharmaceutical industry brought him to the forefront of the modern consumer movement. Details the intricacies of the struggle which ultimately led in 1962 to the Kefauver-Harris amendments to the Food, Drug and Cosmetic Act, largely over the opposition of President John F. Kennedy who was allied with the pharmaceutical giants. Based on Federal documents, particularly the *Congressional Record,* the Kefauver Collection at the University of Tennessee Library and secondary sources; 48 notes.
H. M. Parker, Jr.

2940. Perrotta, John A. MACHINE INFLUENCE ON A COMMUNITY ACTION PROGRAM: THE CASE OF PROVIDENCE, RHODE ISLAND. *Polity 1977 9(4): 481-502.* The alleged absence of participation by low-income groups and minorities in the decision-making process has been a major argument against community power studies of the pluralist variety. Perrotta examines the theses of the pluralists and their critics through his case study of the Community Action Program in Providence from 1965 to 1969. He finds that members of minority groups, particularly blacks, were able to broaden their power base through the federally sponsored CAP against the centralized political structure of the city. His study provides no evidence that deprived groups are excluded from the decision-making process in Providence.
J

2941. Piven, Frances Fox and Cloward, Richard. DILEMMAS OF ORGANIZATION BUILDING: THE CASE OF WELFARE RIGHTS. *Radical Am. 1977 11(5): 39-61.* The organization of working class and poor people for political action embodies a fatal flaw in that the drive is invariably to create a formal organization as a vehicle of power. This trend is exemplified in the history of the National Welfare Rights Organization, 1967-74. The establishment of a formal organizational structure for the NWRO resulted in the creation of a protest bureaucracy and the moderation of the originally vital protest energies of the militant members. The movement was suborned by the power structure which always seeks to temper oppositional politics. In the last analysis the work of the NWRO was of little lasting benefit to its intended constituencies.
N. Lederer

2942. Resnick, Philip. SOCIAL DEMOCRACY IN POWER: THE CASE OF BRITISH COLUMBIA. *BC Studies [Canada] 1977 (34): 3-20.* The New Democratic Party (NDP), Canada's principal left party, has been largely regional in its success. During 1972-75, the NDP government in British Columbia furnished a test case for the study of social democracy in practice in Canada. The NDP stood for a mixed economy, with increased government involvement in some sectors and tighter regulation and taxation in the area of natural resources. After instituting reforms in labor's favor, the NDP passed back-to-work and cooling-off-before-strikes legislation for "essential services." Programs in social policy ranged from achieving essential reform in some areas to "fundamental bankruptcy" and bungling in others. In performance, the NDP left "a trail of disappointment. Social democracy is not the easy road to socialism." 4 tables, 2 graphs, 29 notes.
D. L. Smith

2943. Ritti, R. Richard and Hyman, Drew W. THE ADMINISTRATION OF POVERTY: LESSONS FROM THE WELFARE EXPLOSION, 1967-1973. *Social Problems 1977 25(2): 157-175.* Using the Pennsylvania Public Welfare Department as an example, argues the public welfare explosion, 1967-73, resulted from the redefinition of welfare and the socially sensitive political environment at the time, not from welfare cheating.

2944. Robbins, Lynn A. NAVAJO LABOR AND THE ESTABLISHMENT OF A VOLUNTARY WORKERS ASSOCIATION. *J. of Ethnic Studies 1978 6(3): 97-112.* As a result of a series of actions initiated by Navajo workers in 1971 at the Navajo Project near Page, Arizona, rectifications of employment discrimination and irregularities in hiring and firing practices were effected. Associations between the Navajo Nation, international unions, and major contracting companies were altered, a factor which has become a landmark in Navajo labor relations and has had a profound effect on other tribes involved in major energy projects. Events of the past decade have seen Navajo worker independence institutionalized in the Office of Navajo Labor Relations, and the one labor movement which had genuine grass-roots vitality has produced the Navajo Construction Workers Associations. From interviews of workers and union officials, Navajo Nation reports, and *The Navajo Times;* 5 notes, biblio.
G. J. Bobango

2945. Robbins, Lynn Arnold. NAVAJO WORKERS AND LABOR UNIONS. *Southwest Econ. and Soc. 1978 3(3): 4-23.* Traces the formation of voluntary labor organizations among the Navajo Indians in the Southwest and their relationship with national labor unions, 1958-78.

2946. Schiller, Bradley R. WELFARE: REFORMING OUR EXPECTATIONS. *Public Interest 1981 (62): 55-65.* Public welfare programs have promised much yet delivered little since the 1930's. Despite such innovations as the Work Incentive Program, welfare rolls have not declined. Contemporary welfare reform proposals aim to provide employment for all able-bodied recipients based on the erroneous assumption that those receiving welfare are lazy "chiselers." Recent programs aim to provide job and work-experience opportunities for recipients without many of the counseling, training, and educational services offered in the early days of WIN. Early results indicate provision of jobs alone will not satisfy the goal of decreasing the welfare rolls. While the welfare system has helped millions of people, it has not substantially decreased welfare rolls. We must abandon our unrealistic expectations for welfare reform. Secondary sources; 2 notes.
J. M. Herrick

2947. Sclar, Elliott; Behr, Ted; Torto, Raymond; and Edid, Maralyn. TAXES, TAXPAYERS, AND SOCIAL CHANGE: THE POLITICAL ECONOMY OF THE STATE SECTOR. *R. of Radical Pol. Econ. 1974 6(1): 134-153.* Since the late 1960's various efforts have been made to effect tax reform at the state and local level. Groups such as the Seattle Liberation Front, the Coalition for Tax Reform (Massachusetts), and the Citizens Action Program (Chicago), organized opposition to a system in which local governments had to provide key public services from the most regressive taxes. The movements' failure indicates that it is insufficient to articulate the objective conditions, but that it is also necessary to understand the voters' subjective perception of those conditions. 12 notes.
P. R. Shergold

2948. Skogstad, Grace. AGRARIAN PROTEST IN ALBERTA. *Can. Rev. of Sociol. and Anthrop. [Canada] 1980 17(1): 55-73.* Demonstrates the direct links between the protest activity of individual Alberta farmers and economic discontent, populist beliefs, and political alienation. The current relevance of the three themes preeminent in accounts of agrarian movements on the Canadian prairies prior to 1950 derives from the contemporary structure of farming. More specifically, it is claimed that the structure of farming today equally facilitates protest action. Statistical analyses of data gathered on 133 Alberta farmers in 1974 yield two important findings. First, the three themes are linked to protest activity. Second, the paths to protest activity differ for older (45 years and over) and younger (under 45 years) farmers. For older farmers, membership in a protest union is a function of anticipated future deprivation, of ideological congruence, and of estrangement from the provincial government. For younger farmers, relative deprivation with respect to aspirations as well as political estrangement are potent factors inducing membership. J/S

2949. Smith, Arthur B., Jr. THE LAW AND EQUAL EMPLOYMENT OPPORTUNITY: WHAT'S PAST SHOULD NOT BE PROLOGUE. *Industrial and Labor Relations Rev. 1980 33(4): 493-505.* This article explores the debate over the role of law in insuring equal employment opportunity. The author describes the constant change in judicial and administrative regulation on this subject that has resulted, he believes, from the absence of consensus on whether the goal of public policy should be to promote equal treatment or equal achievement in the workplace. He argues that the overlapping and conflicting regulations, inconsistent results, and general confusion produced by the past encounters between the law and discriminatory employment practices should not be the model for future development of policy. J

2950. Smith, Lawrence B. CANADIAN HOUSING POLICY IN THE SEVENTIES. *Land Econ. 1981 57(3): 338-352.* Reviews a number of federal housing programs initiated in Canada. The programs were designed to promote home ownership, restrict private ownership of rental property, and redistribute income toward lower-income households. Some of these goals were achieved, but the programs also reduced private investment in housing and left the government with a growing financial deficit and impaired the home mortgage loan insurance program. 4 tables, 30 notes, biblio. E. S. Johnson

2951. Thurow, Lester C. THE POLITICAL ECONOMY OF INCOME REDISTRIBUTION POLICIES. *Ann. of the Am. Acad. of Pol. and Social Sci. 1973 (409): 146-155.* "During the decade of the 1960's, a variety of public policies were adopted to alter the American distribution of income. A history of these policies begins with the manpower programs of the early Kennedy administration and ends with President Nixon's 1974 budget. An examination of the economic and political history of these programs reveals a variety of reasons for their publicly proclaimed failure. Means and ends were never sufficiently distinguished; no consistent decision was ever made about the aspects of the income distribution to be altered; the political process wanted to pretend that income could be redistributed without reducing anyone's economic position; funds could never be concentrated enough to have a visible impact; and the public was simply unwilling to make investments of the size that would have been necessary to solve the problem. The elimination of poverty may be a good investment socially; financially, it is a bad investment. Increases in productivity do not cover the costs of the necessary programs. The Family Assistance Plan was a radical departure from previous attempts to alter the distribution of income, but it was fatally flawed by internal contradictions. Eventually, it proved to be a political liability for politicians of all parties." J

2952. Uslaner, Eric M. and Weber, Ronald E. THE "POLITICS" OF REDISTRIBUTION: TOWARD A MODEL OF THE POLICY-MAKING PROCESS IN THE AMERICAN STATES. *Am. Pol. Q. 1975 3(2): 130-170.* Discusses the roles of partisanship, legislative professionalism, and liberalism in the formulation of policy on public welfare redistribution issues in state governments in the 1960's and 70's.

2953. Vogel, David. THE PUBLIC-INTEREST MOVEMENT AND THE AMERICAN REFORM TRADITION. *Pol. Sci. Q. 1980-81 95(4): 607-627.* Examines the political perspectives of the contemporary public-interest movement's effort to challenge business's influence over the regulatory process. The strategies the movement has developed reflect both the strengths and limitations of the American reform tradition. J

2954. Zarefsky, David. PRESIDENT JOHNSON'S WAR ON POVERTY: THE RHETORIC OF THREE "ESTABLISHMENT" MOVEMENTS. *Communication Monographs 1977 44(4): 352-373.* Most rhetorical critics feel that social movements arise from disaffected minority groups, but social reform also can be generated from within the establishment, as shown by President Lyndon B. Johnson's War on Poverty; the rhetorical and activist measures of the War on Poverty were identical, which indicates a need to study further the rhetoric and origins of social movements.

2955. —. COOPÉRATION ET DÉVELOPPEMENT AU QUÉBEC [Cooperation and development in Quebec]. *Action Natl. [Canada] 1979 69(4): 304-314.* With a provincial population of 6.25 million, there are nearly .25 million members of cooperatives in Quebec. The cooperative movement, based on Christian social teachings, is a manifestation of a distinctly Quebec culture. The social, economic, cultural, and political transformations of the past few decades have called for new institutions neither capitalist nor Marxist. Cooperatives uniquely recognize people in all dimensions: physical and spiritual; individual and collective, as responsible and participating members of society. Pastoral declaration on the occasion of the Congress of the Fédération de Québec des caisses populaires Desjardins, Quebec 22-24 May 1978. A. W. Novitsky

2956. —. [EVALUATING CONSUMER PROTECTION LEGISLATION: THE 1962 DRUG AMENDMENTS]. *J. of Pol. Econ. 1975 83(3): 655-667.*
McGuire, Thomas; Nelson, Richard; and Spavins, Thomas. "AN EVALUATION OF CONSUMER PROTECTION LEGISLATION: THE 1962 DRUG AMENDMENTS": A COMMENT, pp. 655-662.
Peltzman, Sam. "AN EVALUATION OF CONSUMER PROTECTION LEGISLATION: THE 1962 DRUG AMENDMENTS": A REPLY, pp. 663-667.
Evaluates the methodology and findings of Sam Peltzman's article, "An Evaluation of Consumer Protection Legislation: The 1962 Drug Amendments" (see abstract 12A:3494), on the cost to consumers of the 1962 changes in the federal regulations on drugs.

Educational Reform

2957. Almaraz, Felix D., Jr. BILINGUAL EDUCATION IN NEW MEXICO: HISTORICAL PERSPECTIVE AND CURRENT DEBATE. *New Mexico Hist. Rev. 1978 53(4): 347-360.* Discusses the background to bilingual education in New Mexico, and projects beginning with the Bilingual Education Act (US, 1968).

2958. Burger, Robert H. THE KANAWHA COUNTY TEXTBOOK CONTROVERSY: A STUDY OF COMMUNICATION AND POWER. *Lib. Q. 1978 48(2): 143-162.* The Kanawha County, West Virginia, textbook controversy (1974) is examined from the point of view of communication theory in order to determine why communication broke down between school officials and the local community. Major messages and events are identified and analyzed within the framework of the Lasswell communication model. The article contends that communication broke down for two reasons: (1) each side developed a distinctive style of communication or means by which its leaders attempted to persuade both their own constituents and their opponents; and (2) there was a whole set of contrasting assumptions on both sides relating to authority of school officials, effects of reading on behavior, and effects of particular means of communication, all of which time and again set each side against the other. Suggestions for avoiding future conflicts are offered. J

2959. Chalmers, John W. FEDERAL, PROVINCIAL AND TERRITORIAL STRATEGIES FOR CANADIAN NATIVE EDUCATION, 1960-1970. *J. of Can. Studies [Canada] 1976 11(3): 37-49.* A marked increase in Indian and Métis populations during the 1940's forced the federal government to take control of native school children away from local authorities. In the 1960's, native education became compulsory, universal, and racially integrated; and day schools replaced residential ones. However, the white man's curriculum did not provide for the social integration of native children, and their parents were dissatisfied with their own exclusion from educational decisions. Based on government reports and author's data; 3 tables, 3 notes. G. E. Panting

2960. Cohen, David K. and Farrar, Eleanor. POWER TO THE PARENTS? THE STORY OF EDUCATION VOUCHERS. *Public Interest 1977 (48): 72-97.* Education vouchers are direct aids to families so that they can enroll their children in schools of their own choice. The vouchers provide an alternative to the requirement of either mandatory public school attendance or additional outlays for private schools. Vouchers were to promote competition, thereby encouraging schools to improve curricula and increase responsiveness, and help shift the balance of power from professional educators to parents. The idea gained the attention of reformers in the 1960's and a federal effort was begun in 1969. An outstanding experience with vouchers took place in Alum Rock, California, in 1972. Because the voucher idea overestimated popular discontent and the demand for educational change, it was the professional educators in Alum Rock who emerged from the experience with increased power. The parents did have more alternatives and freedom of choice, but within an authoritative framework provided by professionals. 8 notes.
S. Harrow

2961. Datta, Lois-Ellin. CHANGING TIMES: THE STUDY OF FEDERAL PROGRAMS SUPPORTING EDUCATIONAL CHANGE AND THE CASE FOR LOCAL PROBLEM SOLVING. *Teachers Coll. Record 1980 82(1): 101-116.* A 1973 RAND Corporation study, *Federal Programs Supporting Educational Change,* found that most federally supported innovative programs did not persist after federal funding ceased. The study blamed this impermanence on lack of local control over the projects, prompting the federal government to reverse its earlier emphasis on centralized development and dissemination of educational innovations. A careful analysis of the study, however, indicates substantial local control over most of the projects examined and little use of federally developed programs or outside experts. Based on the RAND study and on secondary sources; 28 notes. E. C. Bailey, Jr.

2962. Eger, Martin. THE CONFLICT IN MORAL EDUCATION: AN INFORMAL CASE STUDY. *Public Interest 1981 (63): 62-80.* Uses an upstate New York community debate over the implementation of a values clarification course in the public schools to assess contemporary dilemmas concerning the teaching of moral education. Opponents of the value clarification approach feel it favors moral relativism. Proponents feel the process of values clarification is based on principles of scientific reasoning and needs no justification. 13 notes.
J. M. Herrick

2963. Havighurst, Robert J. INDIAN EDUCATION SINCE 1960. *Ann. of the Am. Acad. of Pol. and Social Sci. 1978 436: 13-26.* Since 1960 there has been a growing policy of Indian self-determination in the field of education of Indian youth. Two major federal government laws have put money behind this policy—The Indian Education Act (1972) and the Indian Self-Determination and Educational Assistance Act (1975). This leads to a policy of local self-determination for Indian tribes and Indian communities, and to greater responsibility of Indians as teachers and administrators. During this same period there has been a rapid expansion of the number of Indian students in college, most of them aided by government scholarship funds. There has also been a growth of schools on reservations, which are operated by local native school boards, with government funds. There remains the question of the basic goal of the education of Indian youth—assimilation into the Anglo society or separate economic and social activity, based on tribal culture and tradition. Some form of cultural pluralism will be worked out, located between these two poles. The American Indian Policy Review Commission, established by Congress for the 1975-77 period, has recommended a maximum of self-determination for Indians in their economic, social, and educational life. For the next 20 years, it appears that the Indian tribes and communities will be finding their places in a permissive American society. However, the fact that more and more Indians are moving to large cities and trying to find a place in urban society, will tend to favor a degree of assimilation in the mainstream of economic and social life. An especially important and significant situation is provided by the Alaska Native Land Claims Settlement, which gives Alaskan Eskimos, Aleuts, and Indians a relatively large amount of money and land in return for the oil and minerals and land which has been and will be taken by the Anglo economy. Here, in contrast to nineteenth century dealings between the United States government and Indian tribes, the native Americans are receiving a fairly large amount of money and property, which goes to them as members of native corporations, or regional resident groups. What forms of personal and village or communal life will emerge from this situation?
J

2964. Holzner, Burkart and Salmon-Cox, Leslie. CONCEPTIONS OF RESEARCH AND DEVELOPMENT FOR EDUCATION IN THE UNITED STATES. *Ann. of the Am. Acad. of Pol. and Social Sci. 1977 434: 88-100.* In the early 1960s, spurred by federal initiatives and funding, a movement got underway to place educational practice on a foundation of scientifically based knowledge. The Research and Development Centers program was the first of several institutional approaches to what came later to be known as the knowledge production and use (KPU) system in education. Based on their thirteen years of case study experience of one such center, and their application of a sociology of knowledge framework to some of the larger policy issues, the authors trace some of the positive and negative effects of this attempt to place education in the domain of "big science." They discuss the evolution of models for educational R&D, which are presciptive, rather than descriptive, of intellectual activity. The development of epistemic communities and ensuing standards of judgment in the one institution are also seen to have been crucial to its development. While a final judgment of the efficacy of the Research and Development Centers program and other related efforts is not possible, some of the products and outcomes of these programs are now visibly available. J

2965. Krasner, Michael A. TWO DISTRICTS: ANOTHER LOOK AT SCHOOL DECENTRALIZATION. *New York Affairs 1980 6(1): 58-68.* Discusses how School District One on Manhattan's Lower East Side, a largely Puerto Rican area with some blacks, was able to gain some control over the school board on decisions affecting curriculum, budget, and personnel decisions, and compares District One's victory to the lack of control of the community in Brooklyn's District 14. These situations reflect the predicament of minorities whose community school boards are controlled by white majorities since the Decentralization Act (1969) passed by the New York State Legislature.

2966. Lau, Estelle Pau-on. CALIFORNIA'S CONTRIBUTION TO BILINGUAL EDUCATION: LAU VS. NICHOLS. *Pacific Hist. 1980 24(1): 45-54.* Using the 1974 Supreme Court decision *Lau v. Nichols* (US, 1974), as a base, discusses recent developments in bilingual bicultural education. This decision stated that students who do not understand English are denied a meaningful opportunity to obtain an education. The Court ruled that to deny instruction to students in their own language violated the Civil Rights Act (US, 1964). California enacted the Chacone-Moscone Bilingual Bicultural Education Act (1976), which requires bilingual learning opportunities for all students with limited facility in English. US and California Codes, Statutes, and court decisions; 41 notes.
G. L. Lake

2967. Lillard, Richard G. CONFRONTATION AND INNOVATION ON THE CAMPUS: AN EVENTFUL DECADE FOR WESTERN UNIVERSITIES. *Am. West 1974 11(1): 10-17, 62-64.* In the decade 1964-74, higher education became big news. Motivated by the assassination of John F. Kennedy, students became actively concerned with matters of power, war, justice, affluence, and the nature and meaning of education. They engaged in confrontation and direct social action. Using western universities, including those of Hawaii and Alaska, as examples, examines resulting changes, failures to change, and losses. 3 illus. D. L. Smith

2968. McLaughlin, Milbrey Wallin. IMPLEMENTATION OF ESEA TITLE I: A PROBLEM OF COMPLIANCE. *Teachers Coll. Record 1976 77(3): 398-415.* Title I of the Elementary and Secondary Education Act (1965) has failed to produce significant educational improvement because it never has been implemented properly. This lack of implementation resulted from lack of common goals, inadequate knowledge, weak enforcement of regulations, and improper local use of funds. Primary and secondary sources; 25 notes. E. Bailey

2969. Noblit, George W. and Collins, Thomas W. SCHOOL FLIGHT AND SCHOOL POLICY: DESEGREGATION AND RESEGREGATION IN THE MEMPHIS CITY SCHOOLS. *Urban Rev. 1978 10(3): 203-212.* Current debate on "white flight" after desegregation of public schools is based on quantitative studies of city school systems, such as O. Z. Stephens's 1976 report on Memphis schools. Ethnographic case studies of specific schools are also needed to understand the impact of desegregation. For white parents who removed their children from one Memphis public school the main "pull" factor was the establishment of white, private academies, usually in congregational Protestant churches. The main "push" factors were the parents' desires for "quality" education, i.e. discipline and a flexible curriculum offering advanced or honors courses, and for control of the schools' student organizations. Primary and secondary sources; 3 notes, biblio.
R. G. Sherer

2970. Ravitch, Diane. FORGETTING THE QUESTIONS: THE PROBLEM OF EDUCATIONAL REFORM. *Am. Scholar 1981 50(3): 329-340.* The current public perception of American public education as a "failure" is the result of the schools trying to be all things to all people. The unwarranted optimism about what schools might do has been a failure. Schools are limited institutions and do not have total power.
F. F. Harling

2971. Sakolsky, R. THE MYTH OF GOVERNMENT-SPONSORED REVOLUTION: A CASE STUDY OF INSTITUTIONAL SAFETY VALVES. *Educ. and Urban Soc. 1973 5(3): 321-344.* Presents a case study on the Ocean Hill-Brownsville school decentralization controversy in New York City.
S

2972. Tremblay, Marc-Adélard. L'EDUCATION DES INDIENS: UN MODÈLE D'ANALYSE DE L'ÉCHEC DES AGENCES BLANCHES [Indian education: a model analyzing the failure of the white agencies]. *Tr. of the Royal Soc. of Can. [Canada] 1978 16: 171-193.* Notes the failure of the educational system of whites in the education of Indians, mentioning problems caused by conflicts of interest, failures to adapt to their needs, and stereotyping. After many years' experience, education has had a negative effect. 8 notes, biblio.
J. D. Neville

2973. Waldrip, Donald R. THE CINCINNATI ALTERNATIVE SCHOOLS. *Cincinnati Hist. Soc. Bull. 1980 38(2): 129-135.* Discusses the interest expressed by the Cincinnati School Board in establishing alternative or magnet schools beginning in 1972 based on programs in other cities in the United States, and gives numerous reasons supporting the positive aspects of alternative schools.

2974. Ward, Paul L. EDUCATION'S ROLE IN RECENT SOCIAL CHANGE. *Hist. Mag. of the Protestant Episcopal Church 1978 47(4): 403-414.* Traces and evaluates the role of higher education during the rise of relativism, the flight from the humanities, fading anti-intellectualism, the thirst for social justice, and the evangelical and charismatic revival which characterized the 1960's-70's. Notes certain positive forces in society such as the search for social justice and the yearning for authentic religion. Concludes that prospects are not necessarily dim for education's role in the next decade. Secondary materials; 28 notes.
H. M. Parker, Jr.

Humanitarian Reform

2975. Aday, Lu Ann and Andersen, Ronald. FOSTERING ACCESS TO MEDICAL CARE. *Pro. of the Acad. of Pol. Sci. 1977 32(3): 29-41.* Analyzes the results of three national health surveys of health care utilization and expenditures three years before, four years after, and 10 years after the enactment of Medicaid and Medicare legislation. The purpose was to determine how access to care may have changed for the elderly and the medically indigent in response to these programs and to identify groups for which inequities continue to exist. The situation of the low-income population has improved considerably. In 1976, however, the poor were still less apt to have a particular provider, and to have long office waits. The proportion of the poor whose most recent contact was preventive, was less than that of the more affluent. During the 1960's there were movements toward equity; in the 1970's "more attention should be directed to the organization of care and the noneconomic barriers to access that certain groups continue to experience." 5 tables.
R. V. Ritter

2976. Berkowitz, Edward D. THE POLITICS OF MENTAL RETARDATION DURING THE KENNEDY ADMINISTRATION. *Social Sci. Q. 1980 61(1): 128-143.* President John F. Kennedy's (1917-63) special attention to mental retardation legislation culminated in the passage of the Mental Retardation Amendments of 1963. Motivated by the Kennedy family's interest in mental retardation, the President altered domestic policymaking routines by using the power of his office to push mental retardation to the forefront of health politics. Based on the Myer Feldman Papers, the John F. Kennedy Library Oral History Collection, and secondary works; 28 notes, biblio.
L. F. Velicer

2977. Blumenthal, Dan. LEE COUNTY, ARK.: BUILDING A BASE FOR REFORM. *Southern Exposure 1978 6(2): 83-89.* The establishment of the Lee County, Arkansas, Cooperative Clinic in 1969 to serve the medical care needs of poor Negroes was bitterly opposed by many local white interests. Formed under the impetus of a VISTA team, the clinic was intended as a first step in creating a sense of self-help among the black community which could eventually have political manifestations. Olly Neal, Jr., the first clinic administrator, provided the skillful leadership as a native black necessary to enable the clinic to survive and to have an impact on the region. Following considerable trouble, including violence, the clinic's place was accepted by most of the whites resident in the area. Based on recollections by the first doctor at the clinic.
N. Lederer

2978. Covell, Ruth M. THE IMPACT OF REGULATION ON HEALTH CARE QUALITY. *Pro. of the Acad. of Pol. Sci. 1980 33(4): 111-125.* Surveys federal regulation of health care quality in cost control, utilization control, access control, and funding control. In each area, regulation has had unintended and often negative effects. Emphasizes the Professional Standards Review Organization Program (PSRO), a plan established by the 1972 Amendments to the Social Security Act to review medical care. Composed of physicians, the PSRO's evaluate all levels of care in hospitals and nursing homes. PSRO's can improve the quality of health care, but a number of factors have hindered their effectiveness. The author details how PSRO's can be better utilized and how other federal regulatory programs can be improved. Based on HEW Reports.
D. F. Ring

2979. Decker, Barry. FEDERAL STRATEGIES AND THE QUALITY OF LOCAL HEALTH CARE. *Pro. of the Acad. of Pol. Sci. 1977 32(3): 200-214.* Studies the quality of personal health services as affected by federal programs, seeking to identify the trends and consequences of health legislation in recent years. Evaluates the quality impacts of the following federal efforts: biomedical research, resource expansion, financing of health services, and rationalization of the health delivery system. When legislation focuses on any one of these it is likely "to have inadvertent consequences which will diminish some important aspects of the quality of the health delivery system." Current emphases bypass these problems but their preservation and improvement will "require a system that provides individual access to competent and appropriate continuing care at an acceptable cost."
R. V. Ritter

2980. Kimble, Cary. IN PURSUIT OF WELL-BEING. *Wilson Q. 1980 4(2): 61-74.* Traces the concept of health from the 17th-century idea of sickness as the result of sin to the 20th-century dream of the total eradication of disease and suffering and discusses government activity in the health services, the World Health Organization, the ethical issues of euthanasia and environmental pollution, and the naiveté of the modern view of disease.

2981. Moore, Carol and Winer, Jane L. DR. PRESTON E. HARRISON: PIONEER TRAILBLAZER FOR MENTAL HEALTH IN WEST TEXAS. *West Texas Hist. Assoc. Year Book 1979 55: 49-58.* Discusses the work and humanistic philosophy of Dr. Preston E. Harrison, superintendent of Big Spring State Hospital, where he directed the medical care of the mentally ill from 1953 to 1975.

2982. Myers, Beverlee A. HEALTH CARE FOR THE POOR. *Pro. of the Acad. of Pol. Sci. 1977 32(3): 68-78.* A study of the development of programs designed to provide a measure of medical care for the poor. The most significant programs were developed during the 1960's as a part of the "War on Poverty" and the "Great Society" programs. Medicare and Medicaid were most important in the latter. Analysis of Medicaid reveals serious impairments of performance and many problems. Concludes that "Medicaid is a poor program for poor people." Its main flaw is its "basic welfare image." There is needed "some form of national health program that treats everyone equally."
R. V. Ritter

2983. Scull, Andrew T. THE DECARCERATION OF THE MENTALLY ILL: A CRITICAL VIEW. *Pol. and Soc. 1976 6(2): 173-212.* Explores the reasons behind the move in the last quarter-century toward community-based treatment of mental illness. Dismisses the usual explanation that the deinstitutionalization trend stems from the realization that asylums are basically antitherapeutic and from the introduction in the 1950's of antipsychotic medications, and finds the basic causes in the need to cut the rising cost of incarceration. Provides comparative information and data among several states and between the United States and Britain. Based on primary and secondary sources; tables, 131 notes.
D. G. Nielson

2984. Scull, Andrew T. DEINSTITUTIONALIZATION AND THE RIGHTS OF THE DEVIANT. *J. of Social Issues 1981 37(3): 6-20.* The deinstitutionalization movement has been widely hailed as a beneficent reform which reflected advances in understanding produced by social scientific research. Yet close attention to the achievements rather than the rhetoric of the movement suggests a much bleaker picture. For neither the mentally ill nor the criminal has the outcome matched proponents' expectations and intentions.
J

2985. Starr, Paul. THE UNDELIVERED HEALTH SYSTEM. *Public Interest 1976 (42): 66-85.* In 1971 President Nixon endorsed a federal health policy based on the encouragement of "health maintenance organizations" (HMO's), which are "programs which provide a wide range of hospital and medical services to a defined group of subscribers in return for an annual premium." Such prepaid plans, long identified with the political left, were endorsed by cost-minded free market advocates because they brought health care expenses under control through innovative management and competition. This health program never developed. The HMO Act (1971) attempted to open new markets to the HMO's by requiring that employers of over 25 who offered their employees health benefits also include a local qualifying HMO as an alternative. However, the Act set such unrealistically demanding qualifications on the services offered by the HMO's that their growth was discouraged. Since government regulation has been the main cause of the failure of the HMO's, the policymaking role of each HMO should be assumed by its membership. Success for the HMO's is not likely, and they may fall before pressure for a national health service.
S. Harrow

Utopian Thought and Communalism

2986. Berger, Alan L. HASIDISM AND MOONISM: CHARISMA IN THE COUNTERCULTURE. *Sociol. Analysis 1980 41(4): 375-390.* Examines the mechanism of charismatic authority and the nature of religious life as advocated by two genres of charismatic religion: Hasidism and the Holy Spirit Association for the Unification of World Christianity. Both the Jewish and Neo-Christian examples achieved prominence in the counterculture during the 1970's.
J/S

2987. Berger, Bennett M. AMERICAN PASTORALISM, SUBURBIA, AND THE COMMUNE MOVEMENT. *Society 1979 16(5): 64-69.* Connects the commune movement of the 1960's and 1970's, the suburban trend of the 1950's, and the concept of American pastoralism, and examines these trends in terms of the sociology of ideas.

2988. Bodemann, Y. Michal. MYSTICAL, SATANIC, AND CHILIASTIC FORCES IN COUNTERCULTURAL MOVEMENTS: CHANGING THE WORLD—OR RECONCILING IT. *Youth & Soc. 1974 5(4): 433-447.* Discusses the impact on social reform of the mystical, satanic and chiliastic trends developing in American counterculture.
S

2989. Séguy, Jean. À PROPOS DES COMMUNAUTÉS AMÉRICAINES [On American communes]. *Communautés: Arch. Int. de Sociol. de la Coopération et du Développement [France] 1973 (33): 163-201.* Comments on a comprehensive bibliography (listed) on the history and development of the American commune movement, 1963-73, as a counterculture movement, a means of radical protest, and a tool for social change.

2990. Spates, James L. COUNTERCULTURE AND DOMINANT CULTURE VALUES: A CROSS-NATIONAL ANALYSIS OF THE UNDERGROUND PRESS AND DOMINANT CULTURE MAGAZINES. *Am. Sociol. Rev. 1976 41(5): 868-883.* A content analysis of values in dominant culture magazines in the United States, Canada and Great Britain during 1957-59, 1967-69 and 1970-72 indicated a priority on instrumentalism and little shifting in overall value preference over time. This appears to be contrary to predictions made by counterculture observers that Western society was changing rapidly toward a countercultural ideology. A similar analysis of the underground press in the same countries during 1967-69 and 1970-72 revealed a marked shift from expressive priorities during the earlier period to political priorities during the later period. These findings and their implications are discussed.
J

2991. Xenakis, Jason. HIPPIES AND CYNICS. *Inquiry [Norway] 1973 16(1): 1-15.* Hippiedom is the latest Cynic apparition. Both make fun of the rat race, money-making, accumulation, consumerism, uptightness, egodependence, puritanism, racism, nationalism, sexism. Their rebellions transcend particular times and places and share a common target. Even the expressions of rebellion are largely the same, from long hair to panhandling to sexualizing in public. Of course there are differences. Thus the Cynics were not social dropouts, although remember hippie offshoots like the yippies. Nor did they go for artificially-induced highs and self-confidence, though to them guts and freedom (as liberation, not primarily as option or responsibility) were the wildest things, man.
J

2992. Zashin, Elliot M. POLITICAL THEORIST AND DEMIURGE: THE RISE AND FALL OF KEN KESEY. *Centennial R. 1973 17(2): 199-213.* In Thomas Kennerly Wolfe, Jr.'s *The Electric Kool-Aid Acid Test* (New York: Farrar, Straus and Giroux, 1968) the hero, Ken Kesey, sought to create a "new social reality." Through the use of LSD he and his followers envisioned a "counter-community" based on a "group-mind" possessing "continual intuitive intersubjectivity." Kesey failed because of his reliance on LSD as a medium, because he sought not only to found a new society but also to make it work, and because he "could not simultaneously be a politico and an embodiment of the new consciousness." Kesey was in line with earlier thinkers in his desire to see the world transformed, particularly with Plato and Rousseau who believed that a group reaction or "being" was needed to bring about social change. 15 notes.
A. R. Stoesen

2993. —. [ANARCHISM, UTOPIANISM AND THE COUNTER CULTURE IN IRELAND AND THE UNITED STATES]. *Studies [Ireland] 1974 63(252): 323-341.*
Bennett, Donald C. ANARCHY AS UTOPIA, *pp. 323-335.*
Walsh, Brian. COMMENT, *pp. 336-338.*
Torode, Brian. THE POVERTY OF UTOPIANISM, *pp. 339-341.*
  Evaluates the advocacy by counterculture spokesmen of anarchism, utopianism, and mysticism as a response to an overemphasis on industrialization, rationalism, and government centralization in the United States and elsewhere in the 1970's.

SUBJECT INDEX

Subject Profile Index (ABC-SPIndex) carries both generic and specific index terms. Begin a search at the general term but also look under more specific or related terms. Cross-references are included.

Each string of index descriptors is intended to present a profile of a given article; however, no particular relationship between any two terms in the profile is implied. Terms within the profile are listed alphabetically after the leading term. The variety of punctuation and capitalization reflects production methods and has no intrinsic meaning; e.g., there is no difference in meaning between "History, study of" and "History (study of)."

Cities, towns, and counties are listed following their respective states or provinces; e.g., "Ohio (Columbus)." Terms beginning with an arabic numeral are listed after the letter Z. The chronology of the bibliographic entry follows the subject index descriptors. In the chronology, "c" stands for "century"; e.g., "19c" means "19th century."

Note that "United States" is not used as a leading index term; if no country is mentioned, the index entry refers to the United States alone. When an entry refers to both Canada and the United States, both "Canada" and "USA" appear in the string of index descriptors, but "USA" is not a leading term. When an entry refers to any other country and the United States, only the other country is indexed.

The last number in the index string, in italics, refers to the bibliographic entry number.

A

Abel, Mary Hinman. Aladdin Ovens. Atkinson, Edward. Food Consumption. Massachusetts (Boston). New England Kitchen. Richards, Ellen H. Working Class. 1889-97. *1467*
Abernathy, Ralph. Alabama (Birmingham). Civil rights. Demonstrations. King, Martin Luther, Jr. Shuttlesworth, Fred L. 1956-79. *2809*
Abolition Movement *See also* Antislavery Sentiments; Emancipation.
—. Africa. American Colonization Society. Colonization. Racism. Republicanism. ca 1815-35. *762*
—. American Abolition Society. Republican Party. 1855-58. *719*
—. American Anti-Slavery Society. Douglass, Frederick. Garrison, William Lloyd. 1833-51. *770*
—. American Colonization Society. Colonization. Cresson, Elliot. Great Britain. Liberia. 1831-33. *609*
—. American Free Baptist Mission Society. Baptists. Missions and Missionaries. Schisms. 1830-69. *702*
—. American Revolution. Friends, Society of. Pennsylvania. Woolman, John. 1758-88. *530*
—. American Revolution. Reform. ca 1770-1899. *779*
—. American Union for the Relief and Improvement of the Colored Race. Massachusetts (Boston). 1835-37. *761*
—. Anderson, Isaac. Presbyterian Church. Southern and Western Theological Seminary. Tennessee (Maryville). 1819-50's. *574*
—. Anderson, John. Canada. Foreign Relations. Great Britain. Politics. USA. 1860-61. *734*
—. Anderson, John. Canada. Fugitive Slaves. Great Britain. Trials. USA. 1860-61. *733*
—. Andover Seminary. Massachusetts. Theology. 1825-35. *767*
—. Anthony, Susan B. Grimké, Angelina. Mott, Lucretia. Stanton, Elizabeth Cady. Woman Suffrage. ca 1820-60. *549*
—. Anti-Catholicism. Ideology. Massachusetts (Boston). Riots. Social Classes. 1834-35. *555*
—. Antiwar sentiment. Mexican War. Ohio. Propaganda. Protestant Churches. 1847. *561*
—. Artifacts. California. Citrus industry. Indians (agencies). Rust, Horatio Nelson. 1850's-1906. *276*
—. Assassination. Green, Ann Terry. Lovejoy, Elijah P. Marriage. Phillips, Wendell. 1830-67. *759*
—. Attitudes. Competition. Economic Structure. Poverty. ca 1830-60. *656*
—. Attitudes. Labor movement. North. 1820-65. *638*
—. Bacon, Leonard. Slaveholders. 1830-61. *746*
—. Beecher, Lyman. Colonization. Presbyterian Church. 1820-50. *768*
—. Birney, James. Clergy. Evangelicalism. Smith, Gerrit. Stanton, H. B. Weld, Theodore Dwight. 1820-50. *744*
—. Blanchard, Jonathan. Evangelicalism. 1830's-80's. *455*

—. "Boston Clique". Garrison, William Lloyd. Individualism. Interpersonal Relations. 1830-40. *646*
—. Breckinridge, Robert J. Breckinridge, William Lewis. Constitutions, State. Emancipation Party. Kentucky. Presbyterians. 1849. *676*
—. Brown, John. Civil War (antecedents). Harpers Ferry raid. Sanborn, Franklin Benjamin. 1854-60. *707*
—. Brown, John. Harpers Ferry raid. North Carolina. Sectional Conflict. State Politics. 1840-60. *675*
—. Bryant, John Howard. Bryant, Julian. Civil War. Illinois (Bureau County). Lovejoy, Owen. Military Service. Negroes. 1831-65. *607*
—. Cass, William D. Letters. Methodist Episcopal Church (General Conference). 1844. *693*
—. Channing, William Ellery *(Slavery)*. 1830-38. *714*
—. Chapman, Maria Weston. Child, Lydia Maria. Feminism. Stanton, Elizabeth Cady. ca 1830-40. *558*
—. Christian Anti-Slavery Convention. Old Northwest. 1830-60. *704*
—. Christianity. Douglass, Frederick. 1830's-60's. *778*
—. Christianity. Enlightenment. Morality. Nationalism. Phillips, Wendell. 1830-84. *716*
—. Christology. Negroes. New York. Ward, Samuel Ringgold. 1839-51. *618*
—. Civil War (antecedents). Garrison, William Lloyd. Ohio. Western Antislavery Society. 1835-61. *650*
—. Civil War (antecedents). New England. Parker, Theodore. Violence. 1850-60. *635*
—. Civil War (antecedents). Presbyterian Church. South. Stanton, Robert. 1840-55. *731*
—. Clergy. Negroes. 1830-60. *653*
—. Confederate States of America. Cuba. Foreign Relations. Spain. 1860-68. *1145*
—. Congregationalism. Evangelism. Finney, Charles Grandison. South. 1833-69. *632*
—. Connecticut (Canterbury). Crandall, Prudence. Garrison, William Lloyd. Racism. Sexism. 1830-40. *550*
—. Constitutional Amendments (15th). Douglass, Frederick. Negroes. Theology. 1825-86. *777*
—. Constitutional conventions, state. Disfranchisement. Gardner, Charles W. Hinton, Frederick A. Negroes. Pennsylvania. 1838. *596*
—. Cornish, Samuel E. *Freedom's Journal* (newspaper). Journalism. Negroes. Presbyterian Church. 1820's-59. *467*
—. Craft, Ellen. Craft, William. Fugitive slaves. Great Britain. 1848-65. *611*
—. Democratic Party. New York (Utica). Proslavery Sentiments. Riots. 1835. *709*
—. Douglass, Frederick. Garnet, Henry Highland. Negroes. Political Factions. 1840-49. *742*
—. Douglass, Frederick. Great Britain. 1845-47. *649*
—. Douglass, Frederick. Ireland (Belfast). Presbyterian Church. Smyth, Thomas. 1846. *697*
—. Dugdale, Joseph A. Friends, Society of. Reform. 1810-96. *297*
—. Elkins, Stanley M. Historiography. 1829-60. 1954-76. *760*

—. Emancipation. Proslavery Sentiments. Radicals and Radicalism. 1790-1865. *637*
—. Evangelism. Friendship. Tappan, Lewis. 1830-61. *645*
—. Feminism. Journalism. Lowry, Sylvanus B. Minnesota. Swisshelm, Jane Grey. 1815-84. *385*
—. Feminism. Minnesota. St. Cloud *Visitor* (newspaper). Swisshelm, Jane Grey. 1857-62. *814*
—. Feminism. Pennsylvania. Philadelphia Female Anti-Slavery Society. 1833-40. *616*
—. Feminism. Sex roles. Social Change. 1820's-80. *798*
—. Fessenden, Samuel. Free Soil movement. Liberty Party. Maine. State Politics. Willey, Austin. 1830's-48. *682*
—. Follen, Charles Theodore Christian. Harvard University. May, Samuel. 1824-42. *753*
—. Foster, Abigail Kelley. Foster, Stephen Symonds. Psychohistory. Radicals and Radicalism. 1820-77. *288*
—. Freedmen. Labor. Race relations. Slavery. 1830-63. *613*
—. Garnet, Henry Highland. Reform. Speeches, Addresses, etc. 1843. *729*
—. Garrison, William Lloyd. New England. Racism. 1841. *717*
—. German Americans. Gymnastics. Turnverein (club). 1850-70. *606*
—. Giddings, Joshua Reed. Ohio. Radicals and Radicalism. State Politics. 1840-60. *651*
—. Great Britain. Historiography. Protestantism. 18c-19c. *792*
—. Great Britain. Novels. Victor, Metta V. 1861. *749*
—. *Green Mountain Freeman* (newspaper). Liberty Party. Poland, Joseph. State politics. Vermont. 1840-48. *683*
—. Grimes, John. *New Jersey Freeman* (newspaper). Reform. 1844-50. *623*
—. Gurowski, Adam. Poland. Radicals and Radicalism. 1849-66. *449*
—. Harvard University, Houghton Library, Blagden Papers. Letters. Phillips, Wendell. 1840-80. 1977-79. *605*
—. Haverford College Library (Quaker Collection). New Hampshire. Portsmouth Anti-Slavery Society. Rogers, Nathaniel Peabody. 1830-46. *316*
—. Hayden, Lewis. Massachusetts (Boston). 1811-89. *420*
—. Hersey, John. Methodist Church. Millenarianism. Perfectionism. 1786-1862. *541*
—. Historiography. Negroes. 1830-60. *754*
—. Ideology. Proslavery Sentiments. South Carolina. 1776-1861. *660*
—. Jews. Reform. 1850-63. *750*
—. Keniston, Kenneth. Pacifism. Violence. 1830-65. *644*
—. Liberty Party. New York. 1840-48. *687*
—. Liberty Party. Ohio. South. 1838-50. *670*
—. Massachusetts. Negroes (free). Remond, Charles Lenox. 1838-63. *459*
—. Massachusetts (Springfield). Riots. Thompson, George. 1851. *667*
—. Negroes. Truth, Sojourner. 1825-60. *445*
—. New York, upstate. Petitions. Political participation. Women. 1838-39. *586*

Abolition Movement

—. New York (upstate). Smith, Gerrit. 1840-50. *647*
—. Ohio, northeastern. Wright, Elizur, Jr. 1829-32. *643*
—. Pennsylvania Hall. Pennsylvania (Philadelphia). Riots. Women. 1833-37. *617*
—. Political Participation. Rantoul, Robert, Jr. 1820's-56. *303*
—. Reform. Sexuality. 1830-65. *780*
—. Schisms. Sects, Religious. ca 1840-60. *703*
Abolitionists. Alcott, Amos Bronson. Civil War (antecedents). Phillips, Wendell. Weld, Theodore Dwight. 1830-60. *721*
—. Antislavery materials. Censorship. Publishers and Publishing. 1852-55. *772*
—. Antislavery sentiments. Racism. 1646-1974. *110*
—. Assimilation. Indians. 1820-80. *563*
—. Brown, William Wells. Medicine. Negroes. Remond, Sarah Parker. Ruggles, David. Smith, James McCune. Tubman, Harriet. 1810-85. *329*
—. Childhood. Missions and Missionaries. 1800-60. *789*
—. Elkins, Stanley M. (review article). Slavery. Transcendentalism. 1830-63. 1959-73. *791*
—. Fugitive slaves. Government. Great Britain. Law. Slave Trade. 1834-61. *774*
—. Fugitive Slaves. Negroes. Pennsylvania (Pittsburgh). Philanthropic Society. 1830's-60. *610*
—. Historians. Psychohistory. 1800-60. 1930's-60's. *720*
—. Immigrants. Irish Americans. Nationalism. ca 1830's-50's. *715*
—. Law. Slavery. South. Supreme courts, state. 1810-60. *775*
Abortion. Antiabortion movement. Anti-Saloon League. Pennsylvania. Politics. Pressure groups. Prohibition. 1890-1978. *1640*
—. Birth control. Canada. 1870-1920. *67*
—. Family. Sex roles. 19c-20c. *37*
—. Ideology. 1965-80. *2722*
—. Ideology. Social Classes. 1970's. *2741*
—. Public Opinion. 1800-1973. *93*
Abyssinia. *See* Ethiopia.
Academic freedom. American Association of University Professors. Civil Rights. Tenure. 1915-70. *1733*
—. Minnesota, University of. Schaper, William A. World War I. 1917. *2143*
—. National security. Ohio State University. Rugg, Harold Ordway. Speeches, Addresses, etc. 1951. *2771*
Accidents *See also* specific kinds of accidents.
—. California. Industrial safety. Tanneries. Working Conditions. 1901-80. *2751*
—. Courts. Federal Employers' Liability Act (US, 1908). Management. Railroads. Safety Appliances Act (US, 1893). Working Conditions. 1890-1913. *2117*
Acculturation *See also* Assimilation.
—. American Indian Defense Association. Collier, John. Indians. Religious liberty. 1920-26. *2427*
—. Canada. Federal Policy. Indians. Sifton, Clifford. 1896-1905. *1012*
—. Collier, John. Florida. Indians. North Carolina. Schools. Seminole Indians. 1927-54. *1851*
—. Creek Indians. Indians (tribal warfare). 1865-1978. *68*
—. Educational Reform. Ideology. Industrialization. Pennsylvania. Social control. 1880-1910. *1420*
Actualité Économique (periodical). Cooperative movement. Individualism. Minville, Esdras. Nationalism. Quebec (Gaspé Peninsula). 1924-40. *1794*
—. Cooperative movement. Individualism. Minville, Esdras. Quebec (Gaspé Peninsula). 1924-43. *1795*
Adams, Alva B. Colorado. Progressivism. State Politics. Sweet, William. 1922-24. *2403*
Adams, Charles Francis. Conservation. Massachusetts (Boston; Quincy). Parks. 1880's-90's. *1070*
Adams, Charles P. Colleges and Universities. Grambling State University. Louisiana. Negroes. 1896-1928. *1836*
Adams, Henry Brooks. George, Henry. Ideology. Industrialization. Philosophy of History. Social criticism. 1870's-1910's. *1073*
Adams, John Quincy. Democratic Party. Elections (presidential). Jackson, Andrew. Slavery. Whig Party. 1828-44. *737*

Adams, John Quincy (1848-1922). Minnesota (St. Paul). Negroes. *Western Appeal* (newspaper). 1888-1922. *1269*
Addams, Mary Newbury. Iowa. Self-image. Social status. Women. 1850-1900. *1042*
Addams, Jane. Dewey, John. Dix, Dorothea. Emerson, Ralph Waldo. Pragmatism. Transcendentalism. 1830's-1960's. *231*
—. Dudzik, Mary Theresa. Franciscan Sisters of Chicago. Illinois. Polish Americans. Social Work. 1860-1918. *369*
—. Education. Hull House. Ideology. Illinois (Chicago). Women. 1875-1930. *411*
—. Education. Hull House. Illinois (Chicago). Working class. 1890's. *1426*
—. Hampton, Isabel. Illinois (Chicago). Johns Hopkins Hospital Training School for Nurses. Maryland (Baltimore). Nurses and Nursing. Professionalization. Social Work. 1889-1910. *1461*
—. Sex roles. Values. 1880-1920. *281*
—. Sex roles. Women. Youth. 1860-89. *308*
Adolescence *See also* Youth.
—. Boy Scouts of America. Boys' Clubs. Educational reform. Hall, G. Stanley. ca 1890-1910. *2074*
—. Boys. Canada. Protestantism. USA. Young Men's Christian Association. 1870-1920. *63*
Adoption. Baker, Josephine. Civil rights. Entertainers. Negroes. World War II. 1940-75. *358*
Adrian College. Hillsdale College. Michigan. Oberlin College. Ohio. Olivet College. 1833-70. *851*
Adult education. Antigonish Movement. Capitalism. Coady, Moses. Cooperatives. Nova Scotia, eastern. 1930-40. *1742*
—. Colonial Government. Nova Scotia. ca 1820-35. *843*
—. Educators. Howe, Joseph. Nova Scotia. 1827-66. *844*
—. Halifax Mechanics' Institute. Middle Classes. Nova Scotia. Working class. 1830's-40's. *845*
Adventists. Battle Creek College. Madison College. Michigan. Sutherland, Edward A. Tennessee. 1897-1904. *2331*
—. Bible. Medical reform. 1800's-63. *867*
—. Constitutional Amendments (21st). Prohibition. 1932-34. *2612*
—. Humphrey, James K. New York City (Harlem). Race Relations. Sabbath Day Adventist Church. Utopia Park. 1920's-30's. *1648*
—. Hydrotherapy. Jackson, James Caleb. Medical reform. New York (Dansville). White, Ellen G. 1864-65. *1470*
—. Illinois. Jones, Alonzo Trevier. Religious liberty. Sunday. World's Columbian Exposition (Chicago, 1893). 1893. *1492*
—. Kellogg, Merritt (diary). Medicine (practice of). Trall, Russell Thacher. 1844-77. *894*
—. Labor unions and organizations. 1877-1903. *1344*
Advertising *See also* Commercials; Marketing; Propaganda; Publicity.
—. Ethics. Journalism. Progressivism. 1890's-1920's. *1910*
—. Federal Trade Commission. 1914-38. *1817*
Advice columns. Dix, Dorothy. Feminism. Louisiana. New Orleans *Picayune* (newspaper). 1895-1900. *980*
Advocate of Peace (periodical). American Peace Society. Foreign Relations. Pacifism. Public Opinion. 1837-1932. *59*
Affirmative action. City Government. Discrimination, employment. Negroes. Ohio (Cincinnati). 1963-67. *2888*
—. Civil rights. Pluralism. Supreme Court. 1970-80. *2779*
—. Discrimination. *Fullilove* v. *Klutznick* (US, 1980). Minorities. *Regents of the University of California* v. *Allan Bakke* (US, 1978). Supreme Court. *United Steelworkers of America* v. *Weber* (US, 1979). 1970's. *2782*
—. Education. Negroes. School Integration. 17c-20c. *2845*
—. *Fullilove* v. *Klutznick* (US, 1980). *United Steelworkers of America* v. *Weber* (US, 1979). 1979-81. *2786*
Africa *See also* Pan-Africanism.
—. Abolition Movement. American Colonization Society. Colonization. Racism. Republicanism. ca 1815-35. *762*
—. American Colonization Society. Colonization. McDonough, David. Medical Education. Presbyterian Church. Slavery. 1840-50. *710*

—. Blyden, Edward Wilmot. Ethnic consciousness. Intellectuals. Negroes. ca 1832-65. *557*
—. Colonization. Cuffe, Paul. Massachusetts (Boston). Negroes. 1810-15. *728*
—. Colonization. Negroes. New Jersey Colonization Society. 1815-48. *745*
—. Colonization. Negroes (free). Schools. 1816-33. *837*
—. DuBois, W. E. B. Makonnen, T. Ras. Pan-Africanism. USA. 1919-73. *2881*
—. Garvey, Marcus. Negroes. Nkrumah, Kwame. 1920's-75. *2422*
—. Industrial arts education. Pan-Africanism. Racism. South. 1879-1940. *214*
Africa, West. Black Nationalism. Colonization. Newspapers. Oklahoma. Sam, Alfred Charles. 1913-14. *2008*
—. Blyden, Edward Wilmot. Negroes. New York. 1850-1912. *291*
African Baptist Church. Education. Emancipation. Meachum, John Berry. Missouri (St. Louis). Negroes. 1815-54. *395*
African Colonization Movement. Emancipation. Georgia. Liberia. Tubman, Emily. 1816-57. *655*
African Society. Colonization. Freedmen. Hopkins, Samuel. Rhode Island (Providence). Sierra Leone. 1789-95. *614*
Africans' School. Benezet, Anthony. Education. Friends, Society of. Negroes. Pennsylvania (Philadelphia). 1770's-80's. *487*
Afro-American history. Identity. 1800-60. *576*
Afro-American Studies. Education. Negroes. 1674-1917. *212*
Afro-Americans. *See* Negroes.
Aged *See also* Pensions; Public Welfare.
—. Crime and Criminals. Deinstitutionalization. Mental Illness. 19c-20c. *227*
Ager, Waldemar Theodore. Editors and Editing. Norwegian Americans. Novels. *Reform* (newspaper). Temperance Movements. 1893-1941. *368*
Agrarianism. Angers, François-Albert. Cooperatives. Economic Theory. Quebec. 1930-80. *1594*
—. Attitudes. Politics. Social Organization. 1890's-1970's. *1546*
—. Bellamy, Edward (*Looking Backward 2000-1887*). Industrial revolution. Utopias. ca 1865-1900. *1517*
—. Davidson, Donald. Literature. Mims, Edwin. South. 1923-58. *1656*
—. Killebrew, Joseph Buckner. New South movement. South. ca 1870-1910. *1026*
—. Land reform. Southern Tenant Farmers' Union. 1933-40. *2511*
—. Neo-Populism. Political Change. Populism. Progressivism. 1676-1972. *30*
—. Populism. Radicals and Radicalism. Wisconsin. Working class. 19c. *1399*
—. Populism. South. 1865-1900. *1378*
Agricultural Adjustment Act (1933). Federal Programs. Iowa. New Deal. Wallace, Henry Agard. 1933-34. *2537*
Agricultural Adjustment Administration. Depressions. Farmers. Federal Policy. New Deal. New York, western. 1934. *2487*
—. Depressions. Labor Unions and Organizations. Sharecroppers. Southern Tenant Farmers' Union. ca 1930's. *2602*
—. New Deal. Soil Conservation Service. 1933-41. *2581*
Agricultural College Act (US, 1862). Agriculture. Labor. Mechanics' Mutual Protection (society). New York. People's College. 1843-60's. *1427*
Agricultural Cooperatives. Consumers' United Stores. Farmers Educational and Cooperative Union of America. Nonpartisan League. North Dakota. 1916-19. *2259*
—. Farmers Educational and Cooperative Union of America. Labor Unions and Organizations. North Dakota (Burleigh County; Still). 1913-78. *2288*
—. Grain elevators. Nebraska. 1900-15. *2263*
—. Labor Unions and Organizations. Quebec. 1900-30. *1743*
—. Nonpartisan League. North Dakota. Socialist Party. 1915-20's. *2024*
—. Quebec. Syndicalism. 1922-79. *1758*
Agricultural Labor *See also* Migrant Labor.
—. Boycotts. Labor Unions and Organizations. Race relations. South Carolina. 1886-95. *1196*
—. California. Cannery and Agricultural Workers Industrial Union. Industrial Workers of the World. Radicals and Radicalism. 1909-39. *1756*

Agricultural Labor

—. California. Historians. McWilliams, Carey. 1939. *2587*
—. California. Labor Unions and Organizations. National Industrial Recovery Act (US, 1933). 1933-34. *2495*
—. California (Salinas). Filipino Labor Union. Lettuce. Strikes. 1934. *2499*
—. California (San Joaquin Valley). Japanese Americans. Mexican Americans. Nisei Farmers League. United Farm Workers Union. 1971-77. *2926*
—. Economic Structure. Freedmen. Racism. Reconstruction. Texas. 1865-74. *1263*
—. Elites. Political Culture. 1946-72. *1773*
—. Farmers. Industrial Workers of the World. Labor Disputes. Ranchers. Washington (Yakima Valley). 1910-36. *2569*
—. Labor Unions and Organizations. 1900-79. *1781*

Agricultural Organizations *See also* names of agricultural organizations, e.g. 4-H Clubs, Grange, etc.
—. Farmers' Alliance. Historiography. North Carolina. ca 1888-91. *1379*
—. Lobbying. National Board of Farm Organizations. 1917-27. *1769*
—. North Carolina. Southern Farmers' Alliance. Women. ca 1880-1900. *1373*
—. Quebec. 1760-1930. 1900H. *148*

Agricultural Policy. Association of Southern Commissioners of Agriculture. Cotton. New Deal. South. Tennessee (Memphis). 1936-37. *2567*
—. Dawes Act (US, 1887). Federal government. Indians (reservations). Kiowa Indians. Oklahoma. 1869-1901. *1062*

Agricultural Production. Cities. Country Life Movement. Educational Reform. Rural Schools. 1900-20. *2302*

Agricultural Reform *See also* Land Reform.
—. Arkansas. Colored Farmers' Alliance. Cotton. Humphrey, R. M. Strikes. 1891. *1171*
—. Catholic Church. New Deal. Roosevelt, Franklin D. (administration). Social Theory. 1933-39. *2590*
—. Editors and Editing. Farmers. Poe, Clarence Hamilton. *Progressive Farmer* (periodical). South. 1899-1964. *1555*
—. Georgia. Hunt, Henry Alexander. Negroes. North Carolina. 1890-1938. *1744*

Agricultural Technology and Research. Alvord, Henry Elijah. Colleges and Universities (land grant). 1860's-1904. *429*

Agriculture *See also* Agricultural Labor; Agricultural Organizations; Conservation of Natural Resources; Farms; Forests and Forestry; Land; Land Tenure; Plantations; Rural Development.
—. Agricultural College Act (US, 1862). Labor. Mechanics' Mutual Protection (society). New York. People's College. 1843-60's. *1427*
—. Arizona (Salt River Valley). Discrimination. Japanese (Issei). Race Relations. 1934-35. *2582*
—. Blackfoot Indians. Cattle Raising. Indians (reservations). Montana. 1885-1935. *104*
—. Boys. Fairfield School for Boys. Juvenile Delinquency. Ohio. Reformatories. Values. 1840-84. *242*
—. Cheyenne and Arapaho Reservation. Federal Policy. Indians. Oklahoma. 1869-80. *1063*
—. Convict Labor. Louisiana State Prison (Angola). Prisons. Working Conditions. 1900-78. *1701*
—. Dewdney, Edgar. Hunting. Indians (reservations). Northwest Territories. Saskatchewan. 1879-84. *1038*
—. Droughts. Nebraska. Politics. Populism. 1880's-90's. *1395*
—. Freight and Freightage. Populism. Prices. Railroads. 1870-97. *1360*
—. Government Regulation. Maryland (Baltimore). 1750-1820. *149*
—. Industrial Arts Education. Negroes. North. Philanthropy. South. 1902-35. *1832*
—. Judaism. Krauskopf, Joseph. Reform. 1880's-1923. *2098*
—. New England. Nutrition. Reformers. 1873-1907. *1465*

Agriculture and Government. Antioption struggle. Commodity exchanges. Trade Regulations. 1890-94. *1400*
—. Canadian Chamber of Agriculture. Marketing. 1935-45. *1780*

Agriculture Department. Employment. Equal opportunity. Federal policy. 1964-76. *2744*
—. Greenbelt new towns. Poor. Tugwell, Rexford Guy. 1935-36. *2560*

Aid to Families with Dependent Children. Illinois (Cook County). Mothers' pensions. Public Welfare. 1911-75. *2107*

Air pollution. Cities. Energy. Industry. Legislation. 1880-1920. *38*
—. City Government. Indiana (Gary). Reform. US Steel Corporation. 1956-73. *2723*
—. Clean Air Act (US, 1970). Demography. Energy. Fiscal Policy. State Government. 1970-79. *2719*
—. Elites. Pennsylvania (Pittsburgh). Reform. Smoke. Tilbury, Corwin D. 1890's-1918. *1961*
—. Environment. Legislation. Public Policy. 1967-78. *2763*
—. Missouri (St. Louis). Smoke. 1891-1924. *1962*

Alabama *See also* South; South Central and Gulf States.
—. American Missionary Association. Education. Negroes. Talladega College. 1865-79. *1244*
—. Banking. Freedmen's Savings Bank. Negroes. 1865-74. *1191*
—. Baptists, Southern. Reform. Social Conditions. 1877-90. *974*
—. Brown, John. Mobile *Register* (newspaper). 1859. *626*
—. Bureau of Refugees, Freedmen, and Abandoned Lands. Freedmen. Reconstruction. 1865-67. *1223*
—. Civil Rights. Democratic Party. Folsom, James E. Negroes. State Government. Women. 1947-58. *2668*
—. Civil rights movement. Reporters and Reporting. *Southern Courier* (newspaper). 1965-68. *2873*
—. Coal. Kilby, Thomas E. Strikes. United Mine Workers of America. 1890-1929. *2448*
—. Democratic Party. Manning, Joseph C. Populism. State Politics. 1892-96. *1387*
—. Diseases. Public health. 1839-1930. *2078*
—. Duke, Jesse C. Editors and Editing. Montgomery *Herald* (newspaper). Negroes. Political Commentary. Republican Party. 1886-1916. *1185*
—. Education. 1930-51. *1852*
—. Farmers. Negroes. Southern Improvement Company. Virginia. 1900-20. *2172*
—. Freedmen. Labor. Plantations. Sharecropping. 1865-67. *1198*
—. Freedmen's Bureau. Gardner, Samuel S. (letter). Negro Suffrage. Reconstruction. 1867. *1180*
—. Freedmen's Bureau. Racism. Reconstruction. Swayne, Wager. 1865-68. *1279*
—. Haralson, J. Negro Suffrage. Reconstruction. Republican Party. 1867-82. *1252*
—. Historiography. Reconstruction. Revisionism. 1884-1971. *1069*
—. Industrial Arts Education. Negroes. Tuskegee Institute. Washington, Booker T. 1870's-90's. *1189*
—. Jacobs, Pattie Ruffner. Woman suffrage. 1900's-20. *2145*
—. Labor Union of Alabama. National Negro Labor Union. Negroes. Politics. Rapier, James T. Reconstruction. 1837-75. *1253*
—. League of Women Voters. National American Woman Suffrage Association. Woman Suffrage. 1919-21. *2450*
—. Legislation. Political Parties. Reconstruction. 1867. *1251*
—. Military. Racism. Randolph, Ryland. Reconstruction. Trials. Tuscaloosa *Independent Monitor*. 1868. *986*
—. Mobile Harbor Act (Alabama, 1842). Negroes. Petitions. Prisons. Seamen. State Legislatures. 1849. *727*
—. Ostracism. Politics. Reconstruction. Republican Party. 1865-80. *1082*

Alabama (Birmingham). Abernathy, Ralph. Civil rights. Demonstrations. King, Martin Luther, Jr. Shuttlesworth, Fred L. 1956-79. *2809*
—. Civil Rights. King, Martin Luther, Jr. Negroes. Nonviolence. Political Protest. 1962. *2843*
—. Communist Party. Hudson, Hosea. Negroes. South. 1920's-70's. *404*

Alabama (Bullock, Greene, Wilcox counties). Decisionmaking. Local Politics. Negroes. 1971-72. *2819*

Alabama (Gadsden). Labor Unions and Organizations. 1930-43. *2549*

Alabama (Lowndes County). Black Power. Civil Rights. Political Protest. 1965-75. *2853*

Alabama (Mobile). Black Capitalism. Editors and Editing. Johnson, Andrew N. Republican Party. Tennessee (Nashville). 1890-1920. *273*
—. Cowan, Jacob. North Carolina (Wilmington). Slave Revolts. Walker, David *(Appeal)*. 1829-31. *726*

Alabama (Mobile County). Public schools. 1826. *831*

Alabama (Montgomery). Boycotts. King, Martin Luther, Jr. Leadership. Negroes. New York City (Harlem). Powell, Adam Clayton, Jr. 1941-56. *307*

Alabama (Selma). Civil Rights. Collins, LeRoy. Community Relations Service. Demonstrations. Florida. 1965-68. *2897*

Alabama State College. Education. Negroes. Paterson, William Burns. 1878-1915. *1257*

Alabama (Tuscaloosa). Civil rights movement. Clergy. Integration. 1976-77. *2796*

Alabama, University of. Attitudes. Desegregation. Students. 1963-74. *2870*

Aladdin Ovens. Abel, Mary Hinman. Atkinson, Edward. Food Consumption. Massachusetts (Boston). New England Kitchen. Richards, Ellen H. Working Class. 1889-97. *1467*

Alaska *See also* Far Western States.
—. 1870's-1897. *1458*
—. Assimilation. Brady, John Green. Economic Conditions. Indian-White Relations. Tlingit Indians. 1878-1906. *1016*
—. Prohibition. Women's Christian Temperance Union. 1842-1917. *255*

Alaska (Anchorage). Labor Unions and Organizations. Lewis, Lena Morrow. Railroads. Socialist Party. World War I. 1916-18. *2001*

Alaska (Douglas Island). Gold Mines and Mining. Labor Unions and Organizations. Strikes. Treadwell Mines. Western Federation of Miners. 1905-10. *2209*

Alaska Native Claims Settlement Act (US, 1971). Aleuts. Eskimos. Indians. 1971-78. *2745*

Alaska (Nome). American Federation of Labor. Industrial Workers of the World. Labor Unions and Organizations. 1905-20. *2208*
—. Progressivism. Robins, Raymond. 1897-1925. *314*

Alaska Reorganization Act (US, 1936). Aleuts. Eskimos. Federal Policy. Indians. 1936-45. *2574*

Alaska (Valdez). Harrais, Margaret Keenan. 1902-62. *398*

Alberta *See also* Prairie Provinces.
—. Alienation. Economic Conditions. Farmers. Political Protest. 1921-79. *2948*
—. Blackfoot Indians (Blood). Identity. Indians. Menominee Indians. Militancy. Wisconsin. 1950's-60's. *1685*
—. British Columbia. Coal Mines and Mining. Depressions. Pass Strike of 1932. 1920's-30's. *1811*
—. Chinese Canadians. Japanese Canadians. Racism. 1920-50. *1657*
—. Cooperative Commonwealth Federation. Land reform. Leadership. Social credit. United Farmers of Alberta. 1930's. *1748*
—. Cooperative Commonwealth Federation. Populism. Russia. Saskatchewan. Social Credit Party. USA. 1870's-1940's. *14*
—. Edwards, Robert C. "Bob". *Eye Opener* (newspaper). Populist. 1904-22. *1940*
—. New Brunswick. Populism. Radicals and Radicalism. Saskatchewan. Social organization. 1950's-70's. *2700*

Alberta (Cardiff, Edmonton). Chaban, Teklia. Coal Mines and Mining. Labor Unions and Organizations. Ukrainian Canadians. 1914-20's. *469*

Alberta (Drumheller Valley). Labor disputes. One Big Union. United Mine Workers of America. 1919. *1827*

Alberta (Edmonton). Farmer's Union of Alberta. Kyforuk, Peter. Manitoba. Ukrainian Labour-Farmer Association. 1912-30's. *1828*

Alberta (Linden). Church Schools. Courts. Mennonites. Religious Liberty. 1977-78. *2780*

Alcohol. Massachusetts, western. Prohibition. Romanelli, John. 1919-20. *2069*

Alcorn University. Mississippi. Negroes. Race Relations. Revels, Hiram Rhodes. Senate. ca 1870's. *1256*

Alcott, Amos Bronson. Abolitionists. Civil War (antecedents). Phillips, Wendell. Weld, Theodore Dwight. 1830-60. *721*
—. Fruitlands (community). Lane, Charles. Massachusetts. Transcendentalism. Utopias. 1840-50. *922*

Alcott, Louisa May. Feminism. Letters. Woman suffrage. 1853-85. *811*
Alcott, William A. "Christian Physiology". Health reform. ca 1829-60. *903*
Alden, Augustus E. Brownlow, William G. Carpetbaggers. City Government. Education. Public welfare. Reconstruction. Republican Party. Tennessee (Nashville). 1865-69. *1049*
Aleuts. Alaska Native Claims Settlement Act (US, 1971). Eskimos. Indians. 1971-78. *2745*
—. Alaska Reorganization Act (US, 1936). Eskimos. Federal Policy. Indians. 1936-45. *2574*
Alexander, George. California (Los Angeles). City Government. Progressivism. Reform. ca 1909-13. *2070*
Alexander, Moses. Idaho. Industrial Workers of the World. Labor reform. 1914-17. *2152*
Alexander, Sydenham B. Carr, Elias. Farmers' Alliance. Leadership. North Carolina. Polk, Leonidas L. Upper Classes. 1887-95. *1392*
Alien Anarchist Act (US, 1918). Anti-Communist Movements. Congress. Law Enforcement. Leftism. Post, Louis F. 1919-20. *2352*
Alienation. Alberta. Economic Conditions. Farmers. Political Protest. 1921-79. *2948*
Allen, Ella. Baker, Charlotte. California (San Diego). Political Campaigns. Woman suffrage. 1911. *2147*
Allen, Robert McDowell. Food Adulteration and Inspection. Kentucky. Progressivism. Scovell, Melville Amasa. 1898-1916. *2125*
Allen, William G. Attitudes. Colonization. Exiles. Great Britain. Negroes. New York Central College at McGrawville. 1820-78. *290*
Allendale Farm. Boys. Bradley, Edward. Progressivism. 1894-1937. *1875*
Alliance-Independent (newspaper). Burrows, Jabez. Farmers' Alliance. Nebraska (Gage County). 1887-99. *1383*
—. Christian Socialism. Gibson, George Howard. Nebraska. Populism. *Wealth Makers* (newspaper). 1893-96. *1397*
Allin, John M. Civil rights. Clergy. Episcopal Church, Protestant. Mississippi. Political Attitudes. 1964-73. *2795*
Alta California. *See* California.
Alternative schools. Cincinnati School Board. Ohio. 1972-79. *2973*
Altruism. Progressive movement. Public policy. Technology. 1900-17. 1973. *1933*
Alvord, Henry Elijah. Agricultural Technology and Research. Colleges and Universities (land grant). 1860's-1904. *429*
Amalgamated Clothing Workers of America. Craton, Ann Washington. Northeastern or North Atlantic States. Women. 1915-44. *367*
Amateur Athletic Union. Colleges and Universities. Sports. Women. 1890's-1936. *1766*
Amateur Sports Act (US, 1978). Competition. President's Commission on Olympic Sports. Sports. 1960's-70's. *2783*
American Abolition Society. Abolition Movement. Republican Party. 1855-58. *719*
American Anti-Slavery Society. Abolition Movement. Douglass, Frederick. Garrison, William Lloyd. 1833-51. *770*
American Association of University Professors. Academic freedom. Civil Rights. Tenure. 1915-70. *1733*
American Board of Commissioners for Foreign Missions. Assimilation. Connecticut (Cornwall). Foreign Mission School. Indian-White Relations. Students. 1816-27. *829*
American Civil Liberties Union. Associated Silk Workers Union. Freedom of Assembly. Freedom of Speech. New Jersey (Paterson). Strikes. 1924. *2378*
—. Baldwin, Roger (recollections). Civil Rights. 1906-19. *279*
—. Civil rights. Kentucky (Bell County, London). Miners. Trials. 1932-38. *2601*
American Colonization Society. Abolition Movement. Africa. Colonization. Racism. Republicanism. ca 1815-35. *762*
—. Abolition Movement. Colonization. Cresson, Elliot. Great Britain. Liberia. 1831-33. *609*
—. Africa. Colonization. McDonough, David. Medical Education. Presbyterian Church. Slavery. 1840-50. *710*
—. Black nationalism. Delany, Martin Robinson. Liberia. 1820-58. *620*
—. Clay, Henry (letter). 1836. *551*
—. Colonization. Georgia. Liberia. Negroes. 1816-60. *705*
—. Crummell, Alexander. Education. Liberia. Negroes. 1853-73. *1126*

—. Emancipation. Liberia. North Carolina. Slaveholders. 1800-60. *708*
—. Emigration. Liberia. Negroes. 19c. *688*
—. Finley, Robert. Racism. 1816-40. *648*
—. Gabriel's Insurrection. Monroe, James. Prosser, Gabriel. Slave revolts. Virginia. 1800. *698*
—. Georgia (Griffin). Liberia. Moss, William (letters). Slavery. 1853-57. *654*
—. Negroes, free. Rhetoric. Slavery. Social Status. Whites. 1831-34. *615*
American Committee on Italian Migration. Illinois (Chicago). Immigration. Italian Americans. Reform. 1952-67. *2701*
American Federation of Labor. 1930's. *2603*
—. Alaska (Nome). Industrial Workers of the World. Labor Unions and Organizations. 1905-20. *2208*
—. American Labor Union. Leftism. Washington. Western Federation of Miners. 1880's-1920. *171*
—. Armies. Industrial Workers of the World. Labor Disputes. Nevada (Goldfield). Western Federation of Miners. 1904-08. *2287*
—. Armies. Police. Streetcars. Strikes. Tennessee (Knoxville). 1919-20. *2185*
—. Bombing. California (Los Angeles). Labor movement. *Los Angeles Times*. McNamara case. Progressives. 1910-14. *2265*
—. Brotherhood of Painters and Decorators. Gompers, Samuel. Labor Disputes. Voluntarism. 1894-1900. *1306*
—. Brotherhood of Sleeping Car Porters. Negroes. Randolph, A. Philip. 1867-1935. *70*
—. Buck's Stove and Range Company. Courts. Labor Law. 1907-11. *2222*
—. Carmody, John. Civil Works Administration. Labor. New Deal. 1933-34. *2584*
—. Communist Party. Labor Unions and Organizations. Radicals and Radicalism. Trade Union Unity League. 1933-35. *2494*
—. Discrimination, Employment. Fair Employment Practices Committee. Federal Government. Labor Unions and Organizations. Shipbuilding. West Coast Master Agreement. World War II. 1939-46. *2627*
—. Fascism. Gompers, Samuel. Immigration. Jingoism. Racism. 1850-1924. *394*
—. Federation of Organized Trades and Labor Unions. Knights of Labor. Labor Unions and Organizations. Ohio (Columbus). 1881-86. *1309*
—. French Canadians. Gompers, Samuel. Quebec. 1900-14. *1741*
—. Gompers, Samuel. Iglesias Pantín, Santiago. Labor Unions and Organizations. Puerto Rico. 1897-1920's. *2210*
—. Gompers, Samuel. Labor. Socialism. 1893-95. *1304*
—. Gompers, Samuel. Labor Unions and Organizations. Military. Preparedness. Wilson, Woodrow. 1914-17. *2000*
—. Industrial Workers of the World. Louisiana. Marine Transport Workers. Sailors' Union. Strikes. United Fruit Company. 1913. *2193*
—. Industrial Workers of the World. One Big Union. Washington. 1919. *2179*
—. International Brotherhood of Pulp, Sulphite, and Paper Mill Workers. Labor Unions and Organizations. Militancy. Paper industry. 1933-35. *2615*
—. International Ladies' Garment Workers' Union. Jews. Labor Unions and Organizations. 1930's. *1740*
American Federation of State, County, and Municipal Employees. Negroes. Oral history. Roberts, Lillian. 1920's-70's. *417*
American Federation of Teachers. Teachers. Women's Liberation Movement. 1916-73. *1687*
American Free Baptist Mission Society. Abolition Movement. Baptists. Missions and Missionaries. Schisms. 1830-69. *702*
American Freedmen's Inquiry Commission. Civil War. Freedmen. Johnson, Andrew. 1863. *1260*
American Historical Association (Coordinating Committee of Women in the History Profession). Women. 1966-72. *2922*
American Indian Defense Association. Acculturation. Collier, John. Indians. Religious liberty. 1920-26. *2427*
American Indian Federation. Bureau of Indian Affairs. Collier, John. Indians. Jamison, Alice Lee. New Deal. Political activism. 1930's-50's. *354*

American Indian Movement. Deloria, Vine, Jr. Federal Government. Indians. Political Protest. South Dakota. Wounded Knee (occupation). 1877-1970's. *2712*
—. Indians. Pine Ridge Indian Reservation. South Dakota. Wounded Knee (occupation). 1972-75. *2749*
—. Indians. Sioux Indians (Oglala). South Dakota (Wounded Knee). 1973. *2709*
American Institute for Education. Educational Reform. Elites. Massachusetts. Nationalism. Rural schools. 1830-37. *839*
American Labor Union. American Federation of Labor. Leftism. Washington. Western Federation of Miners. 1880's-1920. *171*
American Land Company. Andrew, John A. Politics. Reconstruction. South. 1865-67. *1066*
American League for Peace and Democracy. Methodist Federation for Social Service. Social criticism. Ward, Harry F. 1900-40. *376*
American Medical Association. Arkansas Medical Society. Brinkley, John R. Medicine (practice of). Quackery. 1920-42. *2583*
—. Bureaucracies. Decisionmaking. Reform. 1960's. *2759*
—. Carnegie Foundation. Flexner Report. Medical education. Reform. 1910-32. *2297*
—. Cities. Hygiene. Public Health. 1820-80. *879*
—. Medical education. Medical reform. 1895-1915. *2319*
—. Medicine. Sex Discrimination. 1847-1910. *1031*
—. Medicine and State. Public health. 1860's-1917. *224*
American Missionary Association. Alabama. Education. Negroes. Talladega College. 1865-79. *1244*
—. Cardozo, Francis Louis. Education. Freedmen. Reconstruction. South Carolina (Charleston). State Politics. 1865-70. *1243*
—. Civil Rights. Education. Florida. Freedmen. 1864-74. *1245*
—. Civil War. Education. Missouri. Negroes. 1862-65. *1241*
—. Colleges and Universities. Freedmen's Bureau. Mississippi. Negroes. Tougaloo College. 1865-69. *1141*
—. Congregationalism. Freedmen. Georgia (Liberty County). 1870-80's. *1247*
—. Congregationalism. Negroes. South. 1846-80. *1242*
American Moral Reform Society. Civil Rights. Maryland (Baltimore). Negroes (free). Watkins, William. 1801-58. *339*
—. Negroes. Pennsylvania (Philadelphia). Reform. Whipper, William. 1830-76. *386*
American Peace Mobilization. Communist Party USA. Isolationism. World War II (antecedents). 1939-41. *2651*
American Peace Society. *Advocate of Peace* (periodical). Foreign Relations. Pacifism. Public Opinion. 1837-1932. *59*
—. International law. 1816-1978. *223*
—. League of Nations Covenant. Pacifism. Paris Peace Conference. 1914-19. *2066*
American Petroleum Institute. Ecology. Hoover, Herbert C. Oil Industry and Trade. Politics. Pollution. 1921-26. *2365*
—. Oil Industry and Trade. Pollution. Texas (Gulf Coast). 1900-70. *1797*
American Plan. Council of National Defense. Federal government. Prostitution. Social policy. Venereal disease. Voluntary associations. World War I. 1917-21. *2048*
American Psychological Association. Equal opportunity. Lancaster Press. Psychologists for Social Action. Racism. 1969-73. *2885*
American Railway Union. California. Illinois (Pullman). Strikes. 1893-94. *1337*
—. Montana. Railroads. Strikes. 1894. *1357*
American Revolution *See also* Treaty of Paris (1783); Declaration of Independence; Fourth of July.
—. Abolition Movement. Friends, Society of. Pennsylvania. Woolman, John. 1758-88. *530*
—. Abolition Movement. Reform. ca 1770-1899. *779*
—. Antislavery Sentiments. Congregationalism. Hopkins, Samuel. Rhode Island (Newport). ca 1770-1803. *511*
—. Antislavery sentiments. Presbyterian Church. Racism. 1750-1818. *769*
—. Attitudes. McIntosh, Lachlan. Slavery. South. Wealth. 1775-87. *517*
—. Baptists. Religious liberty. 1775-1800. *506*

American Revolution

—. Canada. French Revolution. Ideology. 1775-1838. *139*
—. Civil Rights. Constitutional Law. Ideology. 1776-1976. *134*
—. Colleges and universities. Public Opinion. State Legislatures. 1775-83. *485*
—. Diaries. Drinker family. Friends, Society of. Pennsylvania (Philadelphia). Prisoners. Virginia (Winchester). 1777-81. *526*
—. Egalitarianism. Historiography. Social change. 1775-83. 20c. *494*
—. Feminism. Political theory. Republicans (Radical). Warren, Mercy Otis. 1760's-1805. *523*
—. Historiography. Women. 1770's-1970's. *49*
—. Letters. Literature. Massachusetts. Warren, Mercy Otis. 1740-1814. *460*
—. Massachusetts (Boston). Slavery. Wheatley, Phillis (letter). Whigs. 1767-80. *504*
—. Military Recruitment. Negroes. 1770-1802. *527*
—. North Carolina. Race relations. Slave revolts. 1775-1802. *622*
—. North Carolina. Slave revolts. 1750-1775. *529*
—. Revolution. 1760's-70's. 1960's-70's. *26*

American Revolution (antecedents). Conservatism. Liberty. North Carolina. Political Corruption. Regulators. 1766-71. *481*
—. Farmers. New York. North Carolina. South Carolina. 1760's-70's. *484*
—. South. Taxation. 1755-85. *475*

American, Sadie. Congress of Jewish Women. Jews. Solomon, Hannah G. Women. World Parliament of Religions. World's Columbian Exposition (Chicago, 1893). 1893. *1488*

American Socialist Party. Hillquit, Morris. Marxism. Political Reform. Socialism. 1901-14. *1942*

American Tobacco Company. Elections (congressional). Kentucky. Populism. 1886-92. *1365*

American Union for the Relief and Improvement of the Colored Race. Abolition Movement. Massachusetts (Boston). 1835-37. *761*

Americanization. Educational Alliance. Jews. New York City (Lower East Side). 1890-1914. *2310*
—. German Americans. World War I. 1914-17. *1935*
—. Indiana (Gary). Labor Unions and Organizations. Polish Americans. United States Steel Corporation. 1906-20. *2178*

Americans for Democratic Action. Civil rights. Politics. 1948. *2673*

Americas (North and South). Bureau of Indian Affairs. Collier, John. Indians. Inter-American Institute. 1930's-50's. *1662*
—. Columbia University College of Pharmacy. Medicine. Pharmacy. Rusby, Henry Hurd. Scientific Expeditions. ca 1880-1930. *286*

Ames, Jessie Daniel. Association of Southern Women for the Prevention of Lynching. Lynching. Racism. South. Women. 1930's. *2516*
—. Association of Southern Women for the Prevention of Lynching. Lynching. South. Women. 1928-42. *2553*

Amherst Federation of Labor. Economic Conditions. Labor Unions and Organizations. Nova Scotia (Amherst). Strikes. 1901-31. *1801*

Amlie, Thomas. Economic programs. Liberals. New Deal. Politics. Wisconsin. 1931-39. *2609*
—. Farmer-labor Party. Hard, Herbert. New Deal. Ohio Farmer-Labor Progressive Federation. Third Parties. 1930-40. *2543*
—. Farmer-Labor Party. New Deal. Wisconsin. 1930-38. *2544*
—. New Deal. Radicals and Radicalism. Roosevelt, Franklin D. Wisconsin. 1930-39. *1672*

Ammons, Elias. Coal. Colorado. Federal Government. Strikes. Wilson, Woodrow. 1914. *2228*

Amos 'n' Andy (program). Boycotts. Comic strips. Negroes. Radio. Stereotypes. 1930's. *2588*

Anarchism and Anarchists *See also* Communism.
—. deCleyre, Voltairine. Feminism. Human Rights. 1800's-90's. *1046*
—. Indiana (New Harmony). Libertarianism. Ohio (Cincinnati). Utopias. Warren, Joseph. 1818-74. *302*
—. Intellectuals. Kropotkin, Pëtr. Lectures. Russia. 1897-1901. *1501*
—. Liberalism. Political Protest. Social criticism. 1960-68. *2705*
—. New Left. Rightists. Youth Movements. 1968-73. *2708*
—. Newspapers. Oregon. Portland *Firebrand* (newspaper). Radicals and Radicalism. 1895-98. *1112*

Anarchist Scare (1908). Progressivism. Radicals and Radicalism. Social movements. 1900-10. *2139*

Ancker, Henrietta. California (San Bernardino). Charities. Henrietta Hebrew Benevolent Society. Jews. 1870-91. *1479*

Anderson, Isaac. Abolition Movement. Presbyterian Church. Southern and Western Theological Seminary. Tennessee (Maryville). 1819-50's. *574*

Anderson, James T. M. Anglicization. English language. Ethnic groups. Immigrants. Public schools. Saskatchewan. 1918-23. *1856*
—. Anti-Catholicism. Public schools. Saskatchewan. School Act (amended). Secularization. 1929-34. *1848*

Anderson, John. Abolition Movement. Canada. Foreign Relations. Great Britain. Politics. USA. 1860-61. *734*
—. Abolition movement. Canada. Fugitive Slaves. Great Britain. Trials. USA. 1860-61. *733*

Anderson, Mary. Illinois (Chicago). Labor Unions and Organizations. Nestor, Agnes. Robins, Margaret Dreier. Women. Women's Trade Union League. Working conditions. 1903-20. *2190*

Anderson, May. *Children's Friend* (periodical). Felt, Louie. Periodicals. Primary Association. Religious education. Utah. 1880-1940. *80*

Andover Seminary. Abolition Movement. Massachusetts. Theology. 1825-36. *767*

Andral, Gabriel. Bloodletting. Denman, Thomas. Dewees, William P. Medicine (practice of). Obstetrics. 1800-1945. *254*

Andrew, John A. American Land Company. Politics. Reconstruction. South. 1865-67. *1066*

Andry plantation. Louisiana. Slave revolts. 1801-12. *625*

Anesthesia. Childbirth. Medicine (practice of). Twilight sleep movement. Women. 1902-23. *2034*

Angers, François-Albert. Agrarianism. Cooperatives. Economic Theory. Quebec. 1930-80. *1594*
—. Canada. Catholic Church. French Canadians. Pacifism. Values. 1940-79. *1595*
—. Catholic Church. Public welfare. Quebec. Social justice. 1950-80. *2931*

Anglicization. Anderson, James T. M. English language. Ethnic groups. Immigrants. Public schools. Saskatchewan. 1918-23. *1856*

Anglophobia. Censorship. City Politics. Illinois (Chicago). Libraries. Public Schools. Thompson, William Hale. 1927. *2454*

Anglo-Saxonism. Interventionism. Reform. Strong, Josiah. 1885-1915. *71*

Ansell, Samuel T. Chamberlain, George. Congress. Crowder, Enoch H. Lenroot, Irvine L. Military law. Progressivism. 1916-20. *2408*

Anthony, Lucy. Employment. Equal opportunity. Feminism. Shaw, Anna Howard. 1865-1919. *330*

Anthony, Susan B. Abolition Movement. Grimké, Angelina. Mott, Lucretia. Stanton, Elizabeth Cady. Woman Suffrage. ca 1820-60. *549*
—. Book Collecting. Feminism. 1869-1903. *285*
—. Journalism. *Revolution* (newspaper). Stanton, Elizabeth Cady. Woman Suffrage. 1868-70. *1108*

Anthropology *See also* Acculturation; Ethnology; Race Relations; Social Change.
—. Indians. Pan-Indianism. Parker, Arthur C. Seneca Indians. 1881-1925. *355*

Antiabolition sentiments. Clergy. Conservatism. Constitutions. Massachusetts (Boston). Missouri (St. Louis). Unitarianism. 1828-57. *751*

Antiabortion movement. Abortion. Anti-Saloon League. Pennsylvania. Politics. Pressure groups. Prohibition. 1890-1978. *1640*

Antibiotics. Conflict of interest. Federal regulation. Food and Drug Administration. Periodicals. Pharmacy. Welch, Henry. 1953-62. *2676*

Antibusing movement. Massachusetts (Boston). Models. Political Protest. Social Organizations. 1970's. *2895*

Anti-Catholicism. Abolition Movement. Ideology. Massachusetts (Boston). Riots. Social Classes. 1834-35. *555*
—. Anderson, James T. M. Public schools. Saskatchewan. School Act (amended). Secularization. 1929-34. *1848*
—. Capitalism. DeLeon, Daniel. Socialism. 1891-1914. *55*
—. Chinese Americans. Nativism. Pacific Northwest. Racism. ca 1840-1945. *11*
—. Clergy. Ku Klux Klan. Protestantism. Republican Party. Rhode Island. 1915-32. *2441*
—. Education, Finance. MacKinnon, Murdoch. Saskatchewan. School Act (amended). Scott, Walter. 1913-26. *1849*
—. Ireland. Urbanization. 1920-29. *2363*
—. Know-Nothing Party. Maine. Morrill, Anson P. Nativism. Working class. 1854-55. *588*
—. Ku Klux Klan. Protestantism. Saskatchewan. 1927-30. *1547*
—. Ohio. Political Systems. Republican Party. Slavery. Whig Party. 1850's. *564*
—. Pennsylvania. Politics. Social Change. 1682-1774. *477*

Anti-Communist Movements. Alien Anarchist Act (US, 1918). Congress. Law Enforcement. Leftism. Post, Louis F. 1919-20. *2352*
—. Freedom of Speech. Letters. Ontario (Toronto). Police. Political Repression. 1931. *1724*
—. House Committee on Un-American Activities. Negroes. Robeson, Paul. Robinson, Jackie. USSR. 1949. *2684*
—. Newspapers. Washington State Committee on Un-American Activities. 1948-49. *2656*

Antiforeign sentiments. Strikes. Utah (Carbon County). Utah Fuel Company. 1902-04. *2258*

Anti-German sentiment. Bouck, William. Freedom of Assembly. Grange. Public Opinion. Vigilantes. Washington (Walla Walla). World War I. 1918. *2161*

Antigonish Movement. Adult education. Capitalism. Coady, Moses. Cooperatives. Nova Scotia, eastern. 1930-40. *1742*
—. Catholic Church. Nova Scotia. Rural Development. Social change. ca 1928-73. *1854*

Anti-Imperialism *See also* Imperialism; Nationalism.
—. Attitudes. Law Reform. Mugwumps. NAACP. Storey, Moorfield. 1870's-1929. *462*

Antilabor sentiments. Canada, western. Elections. Immigration. Ku Klux Klan. 1921-30's. *1603*

Anti-lynching law of 1894. Law Reform. Ohio. Smith, Harry C. Tourgée, Albion W. 1890-96. *1453*

Antimilitarism. Democracy. Jordan, David Starr. World War I. 1898-1917. *1867*

Anti-Nazi Movements. Boycotts. Fram, Leon (reminiscences). Jews. League for Human Rights. Michigan (Detroit). 1930's-40's. *2507*

Antinomian controversy. Hutchinson, Anne. Massachusetts Bay Colony. Women. 1630-43. *520*

Antinomianism. Arminianism. New England. Puritans. 1630-60. *482*
—. Emerson, Ralph Waldo. Puritans. Sermons. 1820's-30's. *570*
—. Puritans. 1630's. *491*

Antioch College. Colleges and Universities. Negroes. Ohio (Yellow Springs). Segregation. 1966-69. *2864*

Antioption struggle. Agriculture and Government. Commodity exchanges. Trade Regulations. 1890-94. *1400*

Anti-Radicals. Ashburn, George W. (murder). Georgia. Reconstruction. Trials. 1868. *987*

Anti-Saloon League. Abortion. Antiabortion movement. Pennsylvania. Politics. Pressure groups. Prohibition. 1890-1978. *1640*
—. New Mexico. Prohibition. 1910-17. *1901*
—. Organizations. Russell, Howard Hyde. Temperance movements. 1895-1900. *1464*
—. Peters, J. Sidney. Prohibition. Virginia. 1916-20. *1943*

Anti-Saloon League of America. Ohio. Prohibition. 1880-1912. *258*

Antislavery movement. Abolitionists. Censorship. Publishers and Publishing. 1852-55. *772*
—. Brown, John. Harpers Ferry Raid. Vietnam War. Violence. Weathermen. 1800-61. 1960-75. *105*
—. Morris, Thomas. Ohio. State Legislatures. 1836-39. *711*

Antislavery Sentiments *See also* Abolition Movement; Proslavery Sentiments.
—. Abolitionists. Racism. 1646-1974. *110*

Antislavery Sentiments

—. American Revolution. Congregationalism. Hopkins, Samuel. Rhode Island (Newport). ca 1770-1803. *511*
—. American Revolution. Presbyterian Church. Racism. 1750-1818. *769*
—. *Arabia* (vessel). Arms Trade. Hoyt, David Starr. Kansas. New England Emigrant Aid Company. 1855-59. *741*
—. Bailey, Gamaliel. Chase, Salmon Portland. Liberty Party. Ohio. Republican Party. 1836-60. *668*
—. Bailey, Gamaliel. Ohio (Cincinnati). 1840's. *669*
—. Bain, John Mackintosh. Economic Conditions. Georgia (Darien). Petitions. 1736-55. *518*
—. Baptists. Methodist Church. Presbyterian Church. South. 1740-1860. *699*
—. Benezet, Anthony. Friends, Society of. 1759-84. *509*
—. Boycotts. Cotton. Friends, Society of. Great Britain. 1840-60. *608*
—. British North America. Friends, Society of. Social problems. Woolman, John. 1720-72. *478*
—. Brook Farm. Godwin, Parke. Utopias. 1837-47. *587*
—. Brown, John. Douglass, Frederick. Letters. 1851-56. *725*
—. Brown, John. Harpers Ferry raid. Massachusetts. 1859. *706*
—. Christianity. Civil War. Stowe, Harriet Beecher. ca 1850-80. *673*
—. Civil War. Douglas, H. Ford. Emigration. Military Service. Negroes. 1854-65. *666*
—. Civil War. Episcopal Church, Protestant. Jay, John, II. 1840-65. *773*
—. Civil War. Friends, Society of. Jones, James Parnell. Maine. Military Service. 1850's-64. *320*
—. Clergy. Congregationalism. Connecticut. South. 1790-95. *631*
—. Clergy. Kentucky. Racism. 1791-1824. *603*
—. Coles, Edward. Illinois. Jefferson, Thomas. 1809-68. *689*
—. Connecticut. Dwight, Theodore. Poetry. 1788-1829. *640*
—. Cultural imperialism. Elites. Great Britain. 18c-19c. *765*
—. Debates. Lane Seminary. Ohio (Cincinnati; Walnut Hills). 1829-34. *692*
—. Editors and Editing. Kansas. Newspapers. Religion. Rhetoric. 1855-58. *680*
—. Eliot, Samuel A. Fugitive Slave Act (US, 1850). Massachusetts (Boston). Patriotism. Unitarianism. 1850-60. *752*
—. *Emancipation Car* (collection). Music. Simpson, Joshua McCarter. 1854. *627*
—. Evangelicalism. Religion. South. 1820-30. *758*
—. Free Soil Party. Illinois. Racism. Republican Party. 1848-60. *740*
—. Friends, Society of. North America. 1671-1771. *524*
—. Great Britain. Greeley, Horace. Labor. Marx, Karl. New York *Tribune*. 1851-62. *764*
—. Great Britain. Massachusetts (Salem). Negroes. Remond, Sarah Parker. Women. 1856-87. *294*
—. Great Britain. Protestantism. 1846. *696*
—. Great Britain. Sutherland, Duchess of (Harriet Howard). Tyler, Julia Gardiner. Women. 1842-89. *723*
—. Hall, Lyman W. Kansas-Nebraska Act (US, 1854). Ohio (Portage County). Political Parties. 1852-56. *619*
—. Hibernian Anti-Slavery Society. Ireland. Webb, Richard Davis. 1837-61. *736*
—. Indians. 1830-94. *6*
—. Ireland. Irish Americans. O'Connell, Daniel. 1824-44. *735*
—. Kentucky. Pendleton, James Madison. Tennessee. 1849-60. *674*
—. Know-Nothing Party. Massachusetts. Nativism. Republican Party. Voting and Voting Behavior. 1850's. *538*
—. Liberty Party. New Hampshire. State Politics. 1840-48. *681*
—. Longfellow, Henry Wadsworth *(Poems on Slavery).* Massachusetts (Cambridge). 1842. *665*
—. Negroes. Newspapers. Ontario. *Provincial Freeman* (newspaper). Shadd, Mary Ann. 1852-93. *351*
—. New York City. Petitions. 1829-39. *679*
—. Ohio. Political attitudes. Revivals. Voting and Voting Behavior. 1825-70. *664*

—. Ohio (Lower Maumee Valley). Underground Railroad. 1815-67. *782*
—. Pennsylvania (Philadelphia). Slavery. Trials. Williamson, Passmore. 1855. *628*
—. Propaganda. 1693-1859. *140*

Antitrust

Antitrust. Courts. Fire insurance. Kansas City Board of Fire Underwriters. Law enforcement. Missouri. 1889-99. *1336*
—. French Canadians. Hamel, Philippe. Nationalism. Public Utilities. Quebec (Quebec). 1929-34. *1757*
—. Local Government. New Jersey (Jersey City). Railroads. Taxation. 1901-07. *2276*

Antiwar Sentiment *See also* Peace Movements.

—. Abolition Movement. Mexican War. Ohio. Propaganda. Protestant Churches. 1847. *561*
—. Christianity. Public Opinion. World War I. 1898-1918. *1889*
—. Civil rights. Kennedy, Jane. Oral history. Political Protest. Vietnam War. Women. 1964-77. *2724*
—. Colleges and Universities. Leftism. Political Protest. 1920-36. *2483*
—. Conscription, Military. New Left. Students. Vietnam War. 1965-71. *2696*
—. Fellowship of Reconciliation. World War II. 1940-41. *2655*
—. Keep America Out of War Congress. Socialist Party. Thomas, Norman. Villard, Oswald Garrison. World War II (antecedents). 1938-41. *2501*
—. Labor Unions and Organizations. Socialism. World War I. 1914-17. *1982*
—. Radicals and Radicalism. Vietnam War. Violence. 1960's-70's. *2761*

Apache Indians (Chiricahua, Ojo Caliente). Fort Sill. Interior Department. Land allotment. Oklahoma. Prisoners of war. War Department. 1909-13. *2170*
Apes, William. Indian-white relations. Massachusetts (Mashpee). Reform. Wampanoag Indians. 1830-40. *600*
Appalachia. City Planning. Regional development. Tennessee, eastern. Virginia, southwestern. 1890-1929. *1710*
—. Negroes. Reconstruction. Republican Party. State Politics. 1865-1900. *1216*
Appalachian Regional Development Act (US, 1965). Economic Development. Regional development. Social Conditions. 1965-75. *2927*
Appeal to Reason (newspaper). Journalism. Kansas (Girard). Muckraking. Socialism. 1901-20. *2041*
Apportionment. Attorneys General. Courts. Election Laws. Intergovernmental Relations. Voting Rights Act (US, 1965; Section 5). 1965-77. *2801*
Arabia (vessel). Antislavery Sentiments. Arms Trade. Hoyt, David Starr. Kansas. New England Emigrant Aid Company. 1855-59. *741*
Arapaho Indians. Cheyenne Indians. Dawes Act (US, 1887). Fraud. Indians (agencies). Land allotment. Oklahoma. 1910's. *1888*
—. Cheyenne Indians. Indians. Mennonites. Missions and Missionaries. 1880-1900. *1030*
Architecture *See also* Construction.
—. Attitudes. Boston Prison Discipline Society. Crime and Criminals. Howard, John. Kingston Penitentiary. Ontario. ca 1830-50. *899*
—. Automobile Industry and Trade. Factories. Ford, Henry. Kahn, Albert. 1869-1942. 1900H. *1779*
—. Communalism. Feminism. Gilman, Charlotte Perkins. Housing. 1870-1920. *42*
Archives, National. Freedmen's Bureau. Public Records. Reconstruction. Texas. 1865-76. *1147*
Argell, James B. Chinese Exclusion Act (US, 1882). Congress. Diplomacy. Immigration. 1876-82. *947*
Arizona *See also* Far Western States.
—. Assimilation. Education. Indians. Industrial Arts Education. Phoenix Indian School. 1890-1901. *1437*
—. Bai-a-lil-le (medicine man). Civil Rights. Courts. Education. Fort Huachuca. Indian Rights Association. Navajo Indians. Utah, southeastern. 1906-09. *2043*
—. Congressional Union for Woman Suffrage. Democratic Party. Political Campaigns. Women. 1914. 1916. *2164*
—. Kibbey, Joseph H. Schools. Segregation. 1908-12. *2309*
—. Ku Klux Klan. 1921-25. *2338*
—. Prohibition. 1914. *1911*

Arizona (Bisbee). Industrial Workers of the World. Labor Unions and Organizations. Mining. Strikes. 1917. *2186*
—. Industrial Workers of the World. Shattuck Mine. Strikes. 1917. *2285*
Arizona (Globe). Copper Mines and Mining. Strikes. Western Federation of Miners. 1917. *2261*
—. Copper Mines and Mining. Strikes. Western Federation of Miners. World War I. 1917. *2255*
Arizona (Page). Discrimination, employment. Indians. Industrial Relations. Navajo Construction Workers Associations. Office of Navajo Labor Relations. 1971-77. *2944*
Arizona (Salt River Valley). Agriculture. Discrimination. Japanese (Issei). Race Relations. 1934-35. *2582*
—. Depressions. Farmers. Japanese Americans. Race Relations. 1934-35. *2469*
Arizona (Tucson). Camp Grant Affair. Federal Policy. Indian Wars. 1871. *1037*
Arizona (Tucson; Tent City). Baptists. Comstock, Oliver E. Medical care. St. Luke's-in-the-Desert Hospital. 1907-37. *1596*
Arkansas *See also* South; South Central and Gulf States.
—. Agricultural Reform. Colored Farmers' Alliance. Cotton. Humphrey, R. M. Strikes. 1891. *1171*
—. Constitutions, State (conventions). Negroes. Reconstruction. 1868. *1250*
—. Constitutions, State (proposed). Political Reform. Progressivism. 1917-18. *2005*
—. Disasters. Droughts. Negroes. Plantations. Red Cross. Sharecroppers. 1930-31. *2463*
—. Garland, Rufus King. Greenback Party. State politics. Tobey, Charles E. 1876-82. *952*
—. Jim Crow laws. Negroes. Political Leadership. Segregation. 1890's. *1193*
—. Medical care. Mental illness. 1870's-1970's. *234*
—. Medical Reform. Pharmacy. Physicians. 1880-1910. *243*
—. Negroes. Race Relations. Republican Party. 1867-1928. *115*
—. Race Relations. Republican Party. 1890's-1924. *2364*
Arkansas Agricultural, Mechanical, and Normal College. Arkansas, University of, Pine Bluff. Black Nationalism. Colleges and Universities. Student activism. 1972-73. *2872*
Arkansas Community Organizations for Reform Now. Community Participation in Politics. Political reform. 1960's-70. *2730*
Arkansas Freeman (newspaper). Gross, Tabbs. Negroes. Political Commentary. Reconstruction. Republican Party. 1869-70. *1203*
Arkansas (Lee County). Clinics. Cooperatives. Medical care. Negroes. 1960's-70's. *2977*
Arkansas (Little Rock). Collins, LeRoy. Courts. Federal Government. Florida. Political Speeches. School integration. 1957. *2688*
Arkansas Medical Society. American Medical Association. Brinkley, John R. Medicine (practice of). Quackery. 1920-42. *2583*
Arkansas (northwestern). Brothers of Freedom. Farmers. 1880's. *1372*
Arkansas, University of, Pine Bluff. Arkansas Agricultural, Mechanical, and Normal College. Black Nationalism. Colleges and Universities. Student activism. 1972-73. *2872*
Armaments Industry. Connecticut (Bridgeport). Industrial Relations. Technology. World War I. 1915-19. *2182*
—. Military-industrial complex. 1900-60's. *1650*
Armed Forces. *See* Military.
Armies *See also* National Guard.
—. American Federation of Labor. Industrial Workers of the World. Labor Disputes. Nevada (Goldfield). Western Federation of Miners. 1904-08. *2287*
—. American Federation of Labor. Police. Streetcars. Strikes. Tennessee (Knoxville). 1919-20. *2185*
—. Banks, Nathaniel Prentiss. Civil War. Education. Louisiana. 1863-65. *1218*
—. Bates, Edward. Civil War. Negroes. Politics. Wages. 1861-64. *1129*
—. Civil War. Freedmen's Bureau. Maryland. Reconstruction. Reform. 1864-68. *1162*
—. Discrimination. Great Britain. White, Walter F. World War II. 1943-44. *2626*
—. Drugs. Mexico. New Mexico (Columbus). Pershing, John J. Prostitution. Venereal disease. 1916-17. *2068*

Armies

—. Films (documentaries). Heisler, Stuart. *Negro Soldier* (film). Propaganda. Race Relations. World War II. 1944. *2621*
—. Hastie, William H. Military recruitment. Negroes. Press. World War II. 1940-42. *2638*
—. Railroads. Strikes. Values. 1877. 1894. *1294*
Arminianism. Antinomianism. New England. Puritans. 1630-60. *482*
Arms Trade *See also* Armaments Industry.
—. Antislavery Sentiments. *Arabia* (vessel). Hoyt, David Starr. Kansas. New England Emigrant Aid Company. 1855-59. *741*
Army. Civilian Conservation Corps. Military Organization. Negroes. 1933-42. *2528*
—. Committee on Participation of Negroes in the National Defense Program. NAACP. Negroes. Pittsburgh *Courier* (newspaper). Segregation. 1937-40. *2506*
Army Corps of Engineers. Environmental law. Refuse Act (US, 1899). Waterways. 1876-1971. *977*
Art *See also* Architecture.
—. Harlem Renaissance. Johnson, Charles S. Racism. 1920's. *2426*
Art criticism. Culture. Progressivism. 1900's. *1973*
Arthur, George. Colonial Government. Great Britain. Ontario (Upper Canada). Reform. 1837-41. *571*
Arthur, Timothy Shay *(Ten Nights in a Bar-Room).* Swedenborg, Emanuel. Temperance Movements. 18c. 1854. *883*
Artifacts. Abolition Movement. California. Citrus industry. Indians (agencies). Rust, Horatio Nelson. 1850's-1906. *276*
—. Dawes Act (US, 1887). Fletcher, Alice Cunningham. Indians (reservations). 1880's-90's. *968*
Artisans. Convict labor. Kingston Penitentiary. Machinists. Ontario. Petitions. 1833-36. *826*
Asbury, Francis. Coke, Thomas. Methodist Episcopal Church. Slavery. 1780-1816. *624*
Ashburn, George W. (murder). Anti-Radicals. Georgia. Reconstruction. Trials. 1868. *987*
Ashley, James M. Civil War. House of Representatives. Negro Suffrage. Ohio (Toledo). Reconstruction. 1861-62. *1019*
—. Constitutional Amendments (13th). House of Representatives. Nationalism. Ohio. Political Parties. 1848-65. *1097*
Asian Americans. Employment. Ethnicity. Legislation. Naturalization. Racism. 1850-20c. *65*
Asian Canadians. British Columbia. Immigration. Politics. Racism. 1850-1914. *1524*
—. British Columbia. Racism. 1900-50. *1674*
Asians. Conservatism. Immigration. Methodist Episcopal Church. Social Gospel. 1865-1908. *1029*
—. Immigration. Negroes. Newlands, Francis. Progressives. West Coast. 1904-17. *2067*
Assassination *See also* Murder.
—. Abolition Movement. Green, Ann Terry. Lovejoy, Elijah P. Marriage. Phillips, Wendell. 1830-67. *759*
Assemblies of God. Church of God. Civil rights movement. Periodicals. Presbyterian Church, Southern. South. 1950's-60's. *2804*
Assimilation *See also* Acculturation; Integration.
—. Abolitionists. Indians. 1820-80. *563*
—. Alaska. Brady, John Green. Economic Conditions. Indian-White Relations. Tlingit Indians. 1878-1906. *1016*
—. American Board of Commissioners for Foreign Missions. Connecticut (Cornwall). Foreign Mission School. Indian-White Relations. Students. 1816-27. *829*
—. Arizona. Education. Indians. Industrial Arts Education. Phoenix Indian School. 1890-1901. *1437*
—. Black nationalism. Ideology. Literature. Religion. Women. 1890-1925. *1654*
—. British Columbia. Indians. Schools. 1890-1920. *1861*
—. Cheyenne River Indian Reservation. Federal Programs. Identity. Indians. Sioux Indians. 1889-1917. *45*
—. Collier, John. Federal Policy. Indian Reorganization Act (US, 1934). 1933-45. *2530*
—. Draper, Andrew Sloan. Education. Indians. 1880's-1913. *1424*
—. Education. Indians. Micmac Indians. Nova Scotia. Public policy. Religion. 1605-1872. *209*

—. Education. Indians. Self-determination. 1960's-70's. *2963*
—. Education. Jews. Labor movement. Socialism. 1880's-1945. *100*
—. Finley, James B. Indians (agencies). Methodist Church. Missions and Missionaries. Ohio. Shaw, John. 1820-24. *581*
—. Indian Rights Association. New York. Roosevelt, Theodore. 1890-1910. *1014*
—. Indians. Racism. Reform. 1880-1900. *944*
—. Japanese Americans (Sansei). Social Customs. 1968-76. *2758*
Associated Charities. Charities. Leadership. Massachusetts (Fall River, Lynn). Men. Social Policy. Women. 1880-1900. *1447*
Associated Silk Workers Union. American Civil Liberties Union. Freedom of Assembly. Freedom of Speech. New Jersey (Paterson). Strikes. 1924. *2378*
Associates of Dr. Bray. Bray, Thomas. Church of England. Education. Missions and Missionaries. Negroes. 1717-77. *500*
Association for Promoting Colored Volunteers. Civil War. Military Recruitment. Negroes. New York. Race Relations. Union League. 1861-65. *1255*
Association for the Advancement of Women. Education. Mitchell, Maria. Science. Women. 1870-89. *1035*
Association of Southern Commissioners of Agriculture. Agricultural Policy. Cotton. New Deal. South. Tennessee (Memphis). 1936-37. *2567*
Association of Southern Women for the Prevention of Lynching. Ames, Jessie Daniel. Lynching. Racism. South. Women. 1930's. *2516*
—. Ames, Jessie Daniel. Lynching. South. Women. 1928-42. *2553*
—. Lynching. Negroes. South. Women. 1930-42. *2472*
Asylums. Decarceration. Mental illness. 1950's-75. *2983*
—. Massachusetts (Boston). Mental Illness. Poor. 1847-1920. *261*
—. Mental Illness. New Brunswick. Nova Scotia. 1749-1900. *228*
Atheism. *Lucifer's Lantern* (periodical). Mormons. Schroeder, Theodore. Utah. 1889-1900. *1486*
Atherton, Gertrude. Authors. Feminism. Novels. 1890's-1910's. *333*
Athletics. *See* Physical Education and Training; Sports.
Atkinson, Edward. Abel, Mary Hinman. Aladdin Ovens. Food Consumption. Massachusetts (Boston). New England Kitchen. Richards, Ellen H. Working Class. 1889-97. *1467*
Atlanta University. Labor Department. Negroes. Social Conditions. 1897-1907. *1964*
Atlantic Provinces *See also* Maritime Provinces; New Brunswick; Newfoundland; Nova Scotia.
—. Boardinghouses. Government. Labor. Merchant Marine. ca 1850's-90's. *996*
—. Maritime Rights Movement. Reform. Regionalism. 1900-25. *1578*
Attica State Prison. NAACP. Negroes. New York. Prisons. 1932. *2462*
Attitudes *See also* Political Attitudes; Public Opinion; Values.
—. Abolition Movement. Competition. Economic Structure. Poverty. ca 1830-60. *656*
—. Abolition Movement. Labor movement. North. 1820-65. *638*
—. Agrarianism. Politics. Social Organization. 1890's-1970's. *1546*
—. Alabama, University of. Desegregation. Students. 1963-74. *2870*
—. Allen, William G. Colonization. Exiles. Great Britain. Negroes. New York Central College at McGrawville. 1820-70. *290*
—. American Revolution. McIntosh, Lachlan. Slavery. South. Wealth. 1775-87. *517*
—. Anti-Imperialism. Law Reform. Mugwumps. NAACP. Storey, Moorfield. 1870's-1929. *462*
—. Architecture. Boston Prison Discipline Society. Crime and Criminals. Howard, John. Kingston Penitentiary. Ontario. ca 1830-50. *899*
—. Baptists. Church and Social Problems. Furman, Richard. Slavery. 1807-23. *695*
—. Blind. Education. Employment. Pennsylvania. Pittsburgh Workshop for the Blind. 19c-1939. *1670*
—. Boundaries. Civil War (antecedents). Kansas. Missouri. Slavery. 1854-56. *634*
—. Canada. Citizenship. Japanese. USA. World War II. 1941-58. *1730*
—. Canada. English Canadians. Race. Sex. Woman Suffrage. ca 1877-1918. *1*

—. Canada, western. Industrialization. Labor Unions and Organizations. Radicals and Radicalism. Working class. 1897-1919. *1745*
—. Capitalism. Cities. Howells, William Dean. 1860-1900. *979*
—. Chiropractic. Cults. Medicine (practice of). Science. 1850's-1970's. *229*
—. Civil Rights. Declaration of Independence. Fourth of July. Jefferson, Thomas. Negroes. 1776. 1800-50. *724*
—. Civil rights. Johnson, Lyndon B. Negroes. 1930's-68. *1531*
—. Colonization. Kentucky. Slavery. South. 1816-50. *602*
—. Democracy. Federal Reserve System. Income tax. Reform. Wilson, Woodrow. 1913-21. *1994*
—. Dewey, John. Higher education. Reserve Officers' Training Corps. 1920-38. *1847*
—. Domesticity. Lincoln, Mary Todd. Stanton, Elizabeth Cady. Stowe, Harriet Beecher. 1830-80. *443*
—. Economic Growth. Governors. Segregation. South. 1950-69. *1533*
—. Education. Socialization. Women's studies. 1600-1974. *187*
—. Equality. Lincoln, Abraham. 1830's-65. *642*
—. Exercise. Health. New England. Recreation. Transcendentalism. 1830-60. *572*
—. Family. Federal Government. Public welfare. 1962-80. *2929*
—. Films. *Intolerance* (film). Progressivism. 1916. *1965*
—. Florida. Roosevelt, Theodore. South. Washington, Booker T. 1901. *2080*
—. Friends, Society of. New York (Auburn). Pennsylvania. Prisons. Reform. Religion. 1787-1845. *874*
—. Homosexuality. 1870's-1900's. *8*
—. Housing. Negroes. Ohio (Toledo). Racism. United Automobile Workers of America. 1967-73. *2805*
—. Howard, Martin. Law. Murder. North Carolina. Slavery. 1765-91. *515*
—. Indians. Missions and Missionaries. Presbyterian Church. 1837-93. *13*
—. Industrialization. Rhode Island (Pawtucket). Strikes. Textile industry. Working Class. 1824. *821*
—. Industry. National War Labor Board. Public Policy. Sex roles. Wages. Women. World War I. 1918-19. *2191*
—. Intellectuals. Letters. Slavery. Social Classes. 1830-60. *790*
—. Janesville Associated Charities. Middle Classes. Poor. Wisconsin. 1870-1900. *1450*
—. Judges. School Integration. South. 1954-70. *2833*
—. Kinsey, Alfred C. Scientific Experiments and Research. Sex. ca 1940-77. *2678*
—. Mather, Cotton. New England. Sermons. Women. 1650-1800. *493*
—. Morrow, Prince Albert. Sex. 1890-1915. *1899*
—. Negroes. Political Power. 1952-72. *1626*
—. Negroes. Whites. 1963-77. *2818*
—. New England. Puritans. Slavery. 1641-1776. *521*
—. New Jersey. Paterson, William. Slavery. 1785-1804. *739*
—. Reform. Slavery. Tennessee, western. 1820-40. *771*
—. Sexuality. 1650-1976. *123*
—. Sin. 1830's-60's. *554*
Attorneys General. Apportionment. Courts. Election Laws. Intergovernmental Relations. Voting Rights Act (US, 1965; Section 5). 1965-77. *2801*
Auburn Medical Institution. Medical Education. New York. 1825. *830*
Austin, Alice Constance. California (Llano del Rio). Feminism. Housework. Howland, Marie Stevens. Mexico (Topolobampo). Utopias. 1874-1917. *929*
Australia. Canada. Finland. Kurikka, Matti. Utopias. 1883-1915. *1707*
—. London, Jack. Strikes. 1908-09. *2246*
Authority. Charisma. Counter Culture. Hasidism. Unification Church. 1960-80. *2986*
—. Charisma. Noyes, John Humphrey. Oneida Community. 1875-81. *1515*
—. Citizenship. Constitutional Amendments (13th, 14th, 15th). Federal government. Freedmen. Reconstruction. 1865-70. *1132*
—. Communications Behavior. Parents. Public Schools. Textbooks. West Virginia (Kanawha County). 1974. *2958*

—. Constitutional Amendments (1st). Health. Religious liberty. Supreme Court. 1963-79. *2769*
—. Disciples of Christ. Egalitarianism. Republicanism. 1780-1820. *907*
—. Freedmen. South. Teaching. Women. 1865-70. *1425*
—. Lukens Iron Works. Paternalism. Pennsylvania (Coatesville). Profits. Strikes. 1886. *1347*
—. Race Relations. Reconstruction. Rhetoric. 1865-68. *1206*
Authors *See also* names of individual authors.
—. Atherton, Gertrude. Feminism. Novels. 1890's-1910's. *333*
—. Churchill, Winston (1871-1947). New Hampshire. Progressivism. ca 1900-47. *292*
Autobiography *See also* Personal Narratives.
—. Identity. Progressivism. Psychohistory. Reformers. ca 1860-1920. *366*
—. Ohio. Tappan, Benjamin. 1773-1823. *416*
Automobile Industry and Trade. Architecture. Factories. Ford, Henry. Kahn, Albert. 1869-1942. *1900H. 1779*
—. Canada. General Motors. Labor Disputes. 1927-30. *1798*
—. Communist Party. Labor Unions and Organizations. 1920-33. *2394*
—. Communist Party USA. Labor Unions and Organizations. Michigan (Detroit). 1920's-1935. *1799*
—. Indiana. Labor. New Deal. Ohio. United Automobile Workers of America. 1935-40. *2542*
—. Labor Unions and Organizations. League of Revolutionary Black Workers. Michigan (Detroit). Negroes. 1968-73. *2832*

B

Backus, Isaac. Baptists. New England. Religious liberty. 1754-89. *513*
Bacon, Leonard. Abolition Movement. Slaveholders. 1830-61. *746*
Bacon's Rebellion. Class struggle. Racism. Slavery. Social control. Virginia. 1660-92. *472*
Bacteriology. Canada. Cities. Public Health. 1900-30. *1644*
Bai-a-lil-le (medicine man). Arizona. Civil Rights. Courts. Education. Fort Huachuca. Indian Rights Association. Navajo Indians. Utah, southeastern. 1906-09. *2043*
Bailey, Gamaliel. Antislavery Sentiments. Chase, Salmon Portland. Liberty Party. Ohio. Republican Party. 1836-60. *668*
—. Antislavery sentiments. Ohio (Cincinnati). 1840's. *669*
Bain, John Mackintosh. Antislavery Sentiments. Economic Conditions. Georgia (Darien). Petitions. 1736-55. *518*
Baker, Charlotte. Allen, Ella. California (San Diego). Political Campaigns. Woman suffrage. 1911. *2147*
Baker, Josephine. Adoption. Civil rights. Entertainers. Negroes. World War II. 1940-75. *358*
Baker, Ray Stannard. Civil rights. DuBois, W. E. B. Liberalism. Negroes. Wilmer, Cary Breckenridge (interview). 1900-10. *2110*
Bakke, Allan. Racism. *Regents of the University of California v. Allan Bakke* (US, 1978). Social change. 1960's-78. *2794*
Baldwin, Roger (recollections). American Civil Liberties Union. Civil rights. 1906-19. *279*
Baldwin, Theron. Higher education. Protestantism. Society for the Promotion of Collegiate and Theological Education at the West. 1843-73. *192*
Ballinger-Pinchot Controversy. Conservation. Fisher, Walter Lowrie. Interior Department. 1911-13. *1957*
Ballou, Adin Augustus. Draper, E. D. Hopedale Community. Massachusetts (Milford). Utopias. 1824-56. *917*
—. Hopedale Community. Massachusetts (Milford). Religion. Utopias. 1830-42. *938*
Baltimore and Ohio Railroad. Mathews, Henry M. Railroads. Strikes. West Virginia (Martinsburg, Berkeley County). 1877. *1301*
Baltimore City Hospital. Hospitals. Maryland. 1772-1964. *238*
Bancroft, Joseph and Sons Company. Delaware (Wilmington). Miller, Franklin, and Stevenson (firm). Scientific management. Textile Industry. 1911-27. *2281*
Banking *See also* Federal Reserve System; Investments.

—. Alabama. Freedmen's Savings Bank. Negroes. 1865-74. *1191*
—. Bulkley, Robert J. Federal Farm Loan Act (US, 1916). Federal Reserve Act (US, 1913). Progressivism. 1906-30. *363*
Banks, Nathaniel Prentiss. Armies. Civil War. Education. Louisiana. 1863-65. *1218*
Baptists. Abolition Movement. American Free Baptist Mission Society. Missions and Missionaries. Schisms. 1830-69. *702*
—. American Revolution. Religious liberty. 1775-1800. *506*
—. Antislavery sentiments. Methodist Church. Presbyterian Church. South. 1740-1860. *699*
—. Arizona (Tucson; Tent City). Comstock, Oliver E. Medical care. St. Luke's-in-the-Desert Hospital. 1907-37. *1596*
—. Attitudes. Church and Social Problems. Furman, Richard. Slavery. 1807-23. *695*
—. Backus, Isaac. New England. Religious liberty. 1754-89. *513*
—. Bishop, Harriet E. Minnesota (St. Paul). Women. 1847-83. *295*
—. *Brown v. Board of Education* (US, 1954). Desegregation. Georgia. Supreme Court. 1954-61. *2662*
—. Church and state. Massachusetts. 1630-60. *510*
—. Church and state. Virginia. 1775-1810. *594*
—. Crawford, Isabel. Indians. Kiowa Indians. Missions and Missionaries. Oklahoma (Wichita Mountains). Women's American Baptist Home Missionary Society. 1893-1961. *393*
—. Dahlberg, Edwin (interview). Rauschenbusch, Walter. 1914-18. *444*
—. Desegregation. Tennessee (Clinton). Turner, Paul. Violence. 1956. *2663*
—. Discrimination. Japanese Americans. Resettlement. World War II. 1890-1970. *1651*
—. Education. Missions and Missionaries. Negroes. South. 1862-81. *1240*
—. Massachusetts (Boston). Negroes. 1800-73. *565*
—. Religious Liberty. Virginia. 1600-1800. *525*
—. Slavery. Wayland, Francis. 1830-45. *662*
Baptists, Southern. Alabama. Reform. Social Conditions. 1877-90. *974*
—. Christian Life Commission. 1907-79. *1602*
—. Churches. Education. Racism. Reconstruction. 1865-76. *1267*
—. Education. Negroes. Paternalism. 1880's-90's. *1266*
—. Individualism. Politics. Social problems. 18c-1976. *31*
—. Leadership. Race Relations. Texas. 1954-68. *2890*
—. Woman suffrage. 1910-20. *2168*
—. Women. 1700-1974. *66*
Barber, Jesse Max. Negroes. *Voice of the Negro* (periodical). Washington, Booker T. 1904-07. *1966*
Barkley, Alben. Gambling. Kentucky. Louisville Churchmen's Federation. Progressivism. 1917-27. *2438*
Barnard, Kate. Child labor. Law Reform. Oklahoma. 1904-24. *1877*
—. Kansas State Penitentiary. Oklahoma. Prisons. Reform. 1908-09. *1974*
Barnett, Samuel Augustus. Cities. Education. Great Britain. Poor. Progressivism. 1880's-1913. *2294*
Barry, Robertine (pseud. Françoise). Feminism. Gleason, Anne-Marie (pseud. Madeleine). Journalism. Quebec. Social Conditions. 1900-19. *1535*
Bartol, Cyrus. Investments. Massachusetts (Boston, Manchester). Real estate. Transcendentalism. 1850-96. *1015*
Barton, Clara. Red Cross. War. Women. 1860's-90's. *1457*
Bascom, John. Commons, John R. Ely, Richard T. Social gospel. Wisconsin, University of. 1870-1910. *1017*
Baseball. Brooklyn Dodgers (team). Integration. Montreal Royals (team). Negroes. Press. Rickey, Branch. Robinson, Jackie. 1945-47. *2690*
—. Business. City life. Illinois (Chicago). Social change. Values. 1865-70. *1001*
—. Religion. Social change. Values. 1892-1934. *1669*
Bass, Robert P. Boston and Maine Railroad. Churchill, Winston (1871-1947). New Hampshire. Progressivism. Republican Party. 1890-1912. *1868*

Bates, Edward. Armies. Civil War. Negroes. Politics. Wages. 1861-64. *1129*
Battle Creek College. Adventists. Madison College. Michigan. Sutherland, Edward A. Tennessee. 1897-1904. *2331*
Bauer, Catherine. Federal Policy. Public housing. Reform. Wagner-Steagall Act (US, 1937). Wood, Edith Elmer. 1890's-1940's. *2479*
Baughman Brothers (company). Boycotts. Knights of Labor. Richmond Typographical Union. Virginia. 1886-88. *1290*
Becarria, Cesare. Capital punishment. Italy. Penal reform. 1764-97. *890*
Beckham, John C. W. Kentucky. McCreary, James B. Progressivism. State Government. Willson, Augustus E. 1899-1915. *1894*
Beecher, Catharine. Education. Employment. Professionalization. Women. 1823-75. *182*
—. Physical Education and Training. Sex roles. Women. 1830's-40's. *815*
Beecher, Henry Ward. Feminism. New York City. Radicals and Radicalism. Sex. Vanderbilt, Cornelius. Woodhull, Victoria Claflin. 1868-90's. *336*
Beecher, Lyman. Abolition Movement. Colonization. Presbyterian Church. 1820-50. *768*
—. Evangelical Alliance. Great Britain. Temperance Movements. World Temperance Convention. 1846. *889*
Behavior. Censorship. Cities. Social Psychology. 1960's-70's. *2788*
—. Child development. Education, Experimental Methods. Olerich, Henry. 1897-1902. *2311*
—. Counter Culture. Occult Sciences. 1960's-70's. *2988*
—. Labor. Management, scientific. 1870-1920. *1330*
—. Progressivism. Reform. Sex. 1890-1920. *1995*
Beilhardt, Jacob. Ohio (Lisbon). Sex. Spirit Fruit Society. Utopias. 1865-1908. *1505*
Belgian Americans. French Canadian Americans. Independent Textile Workers. Rhode Island (Woonsocket). Working Class. 1931-50's. *1767*
Bell Canada. Ontario (Toronto). Strikes. Telephone operators. Women. 1907. *1808*
Bell Telephone System. Labor Unions and Organizations. Labor Unions and Organizations. 1919-37. *1809*
Bellamy, Edward. London, Jack. Socialism. Utopias. 1888-1920. *262*
—. Bellamy, Edward (*Looking Backward 2000-1887*). Agrarianism. Industrial revolution. Utopias. ca 1865-1900. *1517*
—. North Central States. Populism. 1880's-90's. *1377*
Bellamy, George. Hiram House. Ohio (Cleveland). Settlement houses. 1896-1914. *1958*
Benezet, Anthony. Africans' School. Education. Friends, Society of. Negroes. Pennsylvania (Philadelphia). 1770's-80's. *487*
—. Antislavery Sentiments. Friends, Society of. 1759-84. *509*
Bengough, John Wilson. City government. *Grip* (periodical). Ontario (Toronto). Political Reform. Protestantism. 1873-1910. *370*
Bennett Law (Wisconsin, 1890). Church and state. Compulsory Education. Wisconsin. 1890. *1417*
Bennett, William H. Communitarianism. Home Employment Cooperative Company. Missouri (Dallas County). Utopias. 1894-1905. *1507*
Benson, Ezra Taft. Morality. Mormons. Political Leadership. Presbyterian Church. Wallace, Henry A. 1933-60. *434*
Bentham, Jeremy. Birth control. Carlile, Richard. Feminism. Great Britain. Owen, Robert Dale. Place, Francis. Propaganda. Wright, Frances. 1790-1840. *817*
Berea College. Education. Kentucky. Negroes. 1858-1908. *1225*
Berrigan, Daniel. Berrigan, Philip. Catholic Church. Church and state. Leftism. Murray, John Courtney. 1950's-70's. *1605*
Berrigan, Philip. Berrigan, Daniel. Catholic Church. Church and state. Leftism. Murray, John Courtney. 1950's-70's. *1605*
Berry, George L. Illinois (Chicago). Newspapers. Strikes. 1912-14. *2274*
Berry pickers. California (El Monte). Foreign Relations. Japan. Mexico. Strikes. 1933. *2522*
Beth Ha Medrosh Hagodol synagogue. Colorado (Denver). Judaism. Kauvar, Charles E. H. Progressivism. 1902-71. *428*

Bethune, Mary McLeod. Equal opportunity. National Youth Administration. Negroes. Public Policy. Youth. 1935-44. *2594*
—. National Youth Administration. Negroes. New Deal. 1930-40. *2578*
Beverly School. Education, Experimental Methods. Industry. Massachusetts. 1900-17. *2321*
Bevier, Isabel. Home economics. Illinois, University of. Women. 1900-21. *2295*
Bias. Political activism. Public Policy. 1952-76. *2753*
Bibb, Henry. Canada. Emigration. Negroes. Separatism. USA. 1830-60. *672*
Bible. Adventists. Medical reform. 1800's-63. *867*
—. Catholic Church. Desmond, Humphrey. Protestantism. Religion in the Public Schools. Wisconsin. *Wisconsin ex rel. Frederick Weiss et al.* vs *District School Board of School District 8* (1890). 1888-90. *1414*
—. Constitutional Amendments (19th). Equal Rights Amendment. State Legislatures. Tennessee. Women. 1876-1974. *2904*
—. Constitutions, State. Presbyterian Church. Religious Education. Supreme courts (state). Wisconsin. 1848-90. *1419*
—. Imber, Naphtali Herz *(The Fall of Jerusalem)*. Myths and Symbols. Populism. 1856-1909. *1371*
—. Methodist Church. Religion in the Public Schools. Wisconsin. 1846-90. *1418*
—. Presbyterian Church. Sexuality. 1975-80. *2740*
—. Presbyterian Church, Southern. Race relations. South. 1861-1980. *98*
—. Presbyterian Church, Southern. Sabbath. South. 1861-1959. *103*
Bibliographies. Communes. Counter culture. Political Protest. Social change. 1963-73. *2989*
Big Sky development. Conservation. Huntley, Chet. Montana. Resorts. 1970-73. *2755*
Big Spring State Hospital. Harrison, Preston E. Medical care. Mental Illness. Texas (western). 1946-77. *2981*
Bilbo, Theodore G. Employment. Fair Employment Practices Committee. Filibusters. Mississippi. Racism. Senate. 1941-46. *2617*
Bilingual education. California. Chacone-Moscone Bilingual Bicultural Education Act (1976). Civil Rights Act (US, 1964). *Lau v. Nichols* (US, 1974). Supreme Court. 1965-76. *2966*
—. New Mexico. Spanish language. 1968-78. *2957*
Billboards. Congress. Federal Regulation. Highway Beautification Act (US, 1965). Land use. 1965-79. *2716*
Bimetallism. Democrats, silver. Tennessee (Memphis). 1895-96. *994*
Bingham, Robert Worth. City government. Kentucky (Louisville). Progressivism. Reform. 1905-10. *1926*
Biochemistry. Medical Education. Medical Reform. 1890-1920. *1992*
Birney, James. Abolition Movement. Clergy. Evangelicalism. Smith, Gerrit. Stanton, H. B. Weld, Theodore Dwight. 1820-50. *744*
Birth Control. Abortion. Canada. 1870-1920. *67*
—. Bentham, Jeremy. Carlile, Richard. Feminism. Great Britain. Owen, Robert Dale. Place, Francis. Propaganda. Wright, Frances. 1790-1840. *817*
—. Dickenson, Robert Latou. Physicians. Sanger, Margaret. Values. Women. 1830-1970. *87*
—. Eugenics. Feminism. Prostitution. 1890's. *1006*
—. Eugenics movement. Feminism. Politics. 1915-74. *1588*
—. Feminism. Sex roles. 1870's-80's. *1007*
—. Foote, Edward Bliss. Medicine. New York. 1858-1906. *543*
—. Law. Medicine and State. Public Policy. 19c. *40*
Birth of a Nation (film). Films. Griffith, David W. Negroes. Temperance Movements. 1900-20. *2087*
Bishop, Harriet E. Baptists. Minnesota (St. Paul). Women. 1847-83. *295*
Bishop Hill Colony. Communalism. Economic growth. Illinois. Swedish Americans. Westward Movement. 1846-59. *935*
—. Daily life. Illinois. Jansson, Erik. Letters. Swedish Americans. Utopias. 1847-56. *939*
—. Illinois. Immigrants. Janssonists. Swedish Americans. Utopias. 1846-60. *920*
—. Illinois. Janssonists. Letters. Swedes. 1847. *936*

Bishops. Methodist Episcopal Church. Peck, Jesse T. Social gospel. 1850-83. *1025*
Black Capitalism. Alabama (Mobile). Editors and Editing. Johnson, Andrew N. Republican Party. Tennessee (Nashville). 1890-1920. *273*
—. Civil War. Davis Bend colony. Eaton, John, Jr. Freedmen. Mississippi. 1862-66. *1249*
Black, Hugo. Constitutional Amendments (1st). Due process. Judicial Administration. 1936-79. *1717*
Black Laws (Ohio, 1804, 1807). Ohio. State Politics. 1837-49. *593*
Black lung disease. Coal Mine Health and Safety Act (US, 1969; amended, 1972). Coal Mines and Mining. Medicine. Strikes, wildcat. United Mine Workers of America. Workmen's Compensation. 1968-72. *2717*
Black Muslims. Christianity. Millenarianism. 1920-79. *1585*
—. Ghettos. Malcolm X. Political Leadership. Race Relations. 1940-65. *461*
Black Nationalism *See also* Black Muslims.
—. Africa, West. Colonization. Newspapers. Oklahoma. Sam, Alfred Charles. 1913-14. *2008*
—. American Colonization Society. Delany, Martin Robinson. Liberia. 1820-58. *620*
—. Arkansas Agricultural, Mechanical, and Normal College. Arkansas, University of, Pine Bluff. Colleges and Universities. Student activism. 1972-73. *2872*
—. Assimilation. Ideology. Literature. Religion. Women. 1890-1925. *1654*
—. Bruce, John Edward. Economic independence. Self-help. 1874-1924. *16*
—. Colleges and universities. South. Student activism. 1890-1972. *1673*
—. Colonization. Cuffe, Paul. Friends, Society of. Sierra Leone. 1810's. *694*
—. Communism. Depressions. Garvey, Marcus. New York City (Harlem). 1931-39. *2561*
—. Culture. Ethnic consciousness. 1960-75. *2883*
—. Garvey, Marcus. 1914-30's. *2418*
—. Garvey, Marcus. New York City (Harlem). Universal Negro Improvement Association. 1919-26. *2358*
—. Musicians. Negroes. Robeson, Paul. 1914-45. *1692*
Black Power. Alabama (Lowndes County). Civil Rights. Political Protest. 1965-75. *2853*
—. Carmichael, Stokely. Pan-Africanism. Political Theory. 1965-73. *2860*
—. Church and Social Problems. Economic Aid. Episcopal Church, Protestant. General Convention Special Program. Self-determination. 1963-75. *2850*
—. Civil Rights. Historiography. South. 1954-72. *1542*
—. Ideology. Political Leadership. 1960's-79. *2876*
—. Political Protest. Self-improvement. Sociology. 1960's-70's. *2859*
—. Social change. 1963-68. *2867*
Blackfoot Indians. Agriculture. Cattle Raising. Indians (reservations). Montana. 1885-1935. *104*
Blackfoot Indians (Blood). Alberta. Identity. Indians. Menominee Indians. Militancy. Wisconsin. 1950's-60's. *1685*
Blacklisting. Communists. Courts. Film industry. Hollywood Ten. *Young v. MPAA* (US, 1965). 1947-73. *1736*
Blacks. *See* Negroes.
Blackwell, Elizabeth. Feminism. Medical Education. Pennsylvania (Philadelphia). 1821-1910. *809*
Blackwell, Henry B. Constitutional conventions, state. Montana. Woman suffrage. 1889. *1121*
—. Editors and Editing. Feminism. Politics. Stone, Lucy. *Women's Journal* (periodical). 1870-1914. *1047*
Blackwell v. Issaquena County Board of Education (US, 1966). *Burnside* v. *Byars* (US, 1966). Courts. Freedom of Speech. Students. *Tinker v. Des Moines Community School District* (US, 1969). 1870-1969. *1728*
Blaine, John J. Progressivism. Republican Party. Senate. Wisconsin. 1927-33. *2421*
Blair, Nora Schelter. Brook Farm. Education, Experimental Methods. Massachusetts. Personal narratives. Pratt, Frederick. Ripley, George. Utopias. 1841-47. *934*
Blakely Institute. Dewey, John. Georgia. Kilpatrick, William Heard. Progressive education. 19c-20c. *2301*

Blanchard, Jonathan. Abolition Movement. Evangelicalism. 1830's-80's. *455*
Blanchet, François. Medical reform. Quebec. 1776-1824. *861*
Blind. Attitudes. Education. Employment. Pennsylvania. Pittsburgh Workshop for the Blind. 19c-1939. *1670*
Bliss, William D. P. Christianity. Leftism. Social Gospel. 1876-1926. *20*
Bloodletting. Andral, Gabriel. Denman, Thomas. Dewees, William P. Medicine (practice of). Obstetrics. 1800-1945. *254*
Bloomer, Amelia. Iowa. Savery, Anne. State Politics. Woman suffrage. Woodhull, Victoria Claflin. 1868-72. *1111*
Blue law. Legislators. Louisiana. Negroes. Reconstruction. State Legislatures. 1867-75. *1276*
Blumer, Herbert. Poverty. Public Policy. Social problems. 1960's-73. *2924*
Blyden, Edward Wilmot. Africa. Ethnic consciousness. Intellectuals. Negroes. ca 1832-65. *557*
—. Africa, West. Negroes. New York. 1850-1912. *291*
—. DuBois, W. E. B. Padmore, George. Pan-Africanism. 1776-1963. *25*
Boarding schools. Children. Federal Government. Indians. 1920-60's. *1864*
Boardinghouses. Atlantic Provinces. Government. Labor. Merchant Marine. ca 1850's-90's. *996*
Boas, Franz. Discrimination. Scientists. Wilder, Burt G. 1900-15. *1884*
Bohanon, Luther. Courts. Oklahoma (Oklahoma City). School Integration. 1955-79. *2808*
Bombing. American Federation of Labor. California (Los Angeles). Labor movement. *Los Angeles Times*. McNamara case. Progressives. 1910-14. *2265*
—. California (San Francisco). Mooney, Tom. San Quentin Prison. Socialist Party. Trials. 1916-42. *2020*
Bond, Hugh Lennox. Ideology. Maryland. Racism. Republicans (Radical). ca 1861-68. *1002*
Book Collecting. Anthony, Susan B. Feminism. 1869-1903. *285*
Book reviews. Feminism. Literary Criticism. Porter, Katherine Anne. 1922-29. *2373*
Books *See also* Authors; Libraries; Literature; Manuscripts; Press; Printing; Publishers and Publishing; Textbooks.
—. Child-rearing. Education. Pennsylvania (Philadelphia). Protestantism. Republicanism. 1780-1835. *577*
Boosterism. California (Los Angeles). City Government. Journalism. Progressivism. Willard, Charles Dwight. 1888-1914. *319*
Bootlegging. Depressions. Florida (Hernando County). Law enforcement. Liquor. Prohibition. 1929-33. *2359*
Borden, Robert Laird. Canada. *Champion* (periodical). Great Britain. Woman suffrage. Women's Social and Political Union. 1910-18. *1737*
Border States. Congress. Legislation. Loyalty oath. Republican Party. South. 1861-67. *950*
Borg, Selma Josefina. Centennial Exposition of 1876. Finnish Americans. Lectures. Music. Pennsylvania (Philadelphia). Women's rights. 1858-90. *399*
Boston and Maine Railroad. Bass, Robert P. Churchill, Winston (1871-1947). New Hampshire. Progressivism. Republican Party. 1890-1912. *1868*
"Boston Clique". Abolition movement. Garrison, William Lloyd. Individualism. Interpersonal Relations. 1830-40. *646*
Boston Daily Evening Voice (newspaper). Equality. Labor Unions and Organizations. Massachusetts. Race Relations. Working Class. 1864-67. *998*
Boston Dispensary. Clinics. Davis, Michael M. Massachusetts. 1910-20. *2051*
Boston Eight Hour League. International Workingmen's Association. Labor Unions and Organizations. Marxism. McNeill, George. New York. Steward, Ira. 1860-89. *1307*
Boston Prison Discipline Society. Architecture. Attitudes. Crime and Criminals. Howard, John. Kingston Penitentiary. Ontario. ca 1830-50. *899*
—. Charlestown State Prison. Massachusetts. Penal reform. 1804-78. *860*
Bouck, William. Anti-German sentiment. Freedom of Assembly. Grange. Public Opinion. Vigilantes. Washington (Walla Walla). World War I. 1918. *2161*

Boulder Canyon Project. Colorado River. Hoover Dam. Industrial Workers of the World. Nevada. Strikes. 1931. *2433*
—. Hoover Dam. Industrial Workers of the World. Nevada. Six Companies, Inc. Strikes. 1931. *2434*
Boundaries. Attitudes. Civil War (antecedents). Kansas. Missouri. Slavery. 1854-56. *634*
Bourassa, Henri. Canada. Divorce. Feminism. Woman suffrage. 1913-25. *1698*
—. Canada. Parliaments. Progressives. 1926. *1633*
Bourgeoisie. See Middle Classes.
Bourne, Randolph. Feminism. Political Commentary. Progressive education. Socialism. 1886-1918. *425*
Bowen, Albert E., Jr. Farmers. Nonpartisan League. North Dakota. Townley, Arthur C. 1914-15. *2054*
Boy Scouts of America. Adolescence. Boys' Clubs. Educational reform. Hall, G. Stanley. ca 1890-1910. *2074*
Boycotts. Agricultural labor. Labor Unions and Organizations. Race relations. South Carolina. 1886-95. *1196*
—. Alabama (Montgomery). King, Martin Luther, Jr. Leadership. Negroes. New York City (Harlem). Powell, Adam Clayton, Jr. 1941-56. *307*
—. *Amos 'n' Andy* (program). Comic strips. Negroes. Radio. Stereotypes. 1930's. *2588*
—. Anti-Nazi Movements. Fram, Leon (reminiscences). Jews. League for Human Rights. Michigan (Detroit). 1930's-40's. *2507*
—. Antislavery Sentiments. Cotton. Friends, Society of. Great Britain. 1840-60. *608*
—. Baughman Brothers (company). Knights of Labor. Richmond Typographical Union. Virginia. 1886-88. *1290*
—. Christianity. Elementary Education. Jews. New York City. Religion in the Public Schools. 1905-06. *2298*
—. Immigrants. Irish Americans. Labor. New York City. Working conditions. 1880-86. *1311*
—. Mass Transit. Negroes. Segregation. Virginia. 1904-07. *2154*
—. Mexican Americans. Presbyterian Church. Public schools. Segregation. Texas (San Angelo). 1910-15. *2303*
—. Mississippi. Negroes. Police brutality (alleged). Robinson, Alfred. United League. 1966-78. *2893*
Boys. Adolescence. Canada. Protestantism. USA. Young Men's Christian Association. 1870-1920. *63*
—. Agriculture. Fairfield School for Boys. Juvenile Delinquency. Ohio. Reformatories. Values. 1840-84. *242*
—. Allendale Farm. Bradley, Edward. Progressivism. 1894-1937. *1875*
Boys' Clubs. Adolescence. Boy Scouts of America. Educational reform. Hall, G. Stanley. ca 1890-1910. *2074*
Bradford, George Partridge. Brook Farm. Daily life. Letters. Massachusetts. Utopias. 1841. *932*
Bradley, Edward. Allendale Farm. Boys. Progressivism. 1894-1937. *1875*
Bradstreet, Anne. Hutchinson, Anne. Literature. Massachusetts Bay Colony. Religion. Social change. Women. 1630's-70's. *489*
Bradwell, Myra. Illinois. Lawyers. Sex Discrimination. Supreme Court (decision). 1873-1894. *1114*
—. Illinois (Chicago). Law reform. Women's rights. 1855-92. *1034*
Brady, John Green. Alaska. Assimilation. Economic Conditions. Indian-White Relations. Tlingit Indians. 1878-1906. *1016*
Bray, Thomas. Associates of Dr. Bray. Church of England. Education. Missions and Missionaries. Negroes. 1717-77. *500*
Breckinridge, Madeline McDowell. Federation of Business and Professional Women's Clubs. Kentucky Equal Rights Association. Woman suffrage. 1908-20. *2157*
Breckinridge, Mary. Frontier Nursing Service. Kentucky. Nurses and Nursing. 1925-65. *1559*
Breckinridge, Robert J. Abolition Movement. Breckinridge, William Lewis. Constitutions, State. Emancipation Party. Kentucky. Presbyterians. 1849. *676*
—. Emancipation. Kentucky. State Politics. 1830-49. *677*

Breckinridge, Robert J., Jr. Breckinridge, William C. P. Courts. Elections. Kentucky. Negroes. Testimony. 1866-69. *1096*
Breckinridge, Sophinisba. Feminism. 1880's-1948. *457*
Breckinridge, William C. P. Breckinridge, Robert J., Jr. Courts. Elections. Kentucky. Negroes. Testimony. 1866-69. *1096*
Breckinridge, William Lewis. Abolition Movement. Breckinridge, Robert J. Constitutions, State. Emancipation Party. Kentucky. Presbyterians. 1849. *676*
Brewer, Fisk Parsons. Higher education. Integration. South Carolina, University of. 1873-76. *1438*
Brewing industry. Labor Unions and Organizations. Workmen's compensation. 1910-12. *2204*
Brin, Fanny Fligelman. Jews. Minnesota (Minneapolis). Peace. Women. 1913-60's. *453*
Brinkley, John R. American Medical Association. Arkansas Medical Society. Medicine (practice of). Quackery. 1920-42. *2583*
Brisbane, Albert. Brook Farm. Channing, William Henry. Transcendentalism. 1840-46. *923*
British Columbia. Alberta. Coal Mines and Mining. Depressions. Pass Strike of 1932. 1920's-30's. *1811*
—. Asian Canadians. Immigration. Politics. Racism. 1850-1914. *1524*
—. Asian Canadians. Racism. 1900-50. *1674*
—. Assimilation. Indians. Schools. 1890-1920. *1861*
—. California. Discrimination. Gold Rushes. Negroes. Race Relations. 1849-66. *592*
—. Canada. Chinese Canadians. Japanese Canadians. Military Service. World War II. 1939-45. *2647*
—. Chinese. Immigration. Japanese. Suffrage. 1935-49. *1725*
—. Depressions. Industrial Relations. National Unemployed Workers' Association. Unemployment. Workers' Unity League. 1930-39. *1830*
—. Japanese Canadians. Minorities. Public schools. 1900-72. *1562*
—. Labor. Legislation. Natural resources. New Democratic Party. Public Policy. Social Democracy. Taxation. 1972-75. *2942*
British Columbia (Harmony Island). Finnish Americans. Kurikka, Matti. Utopias. 1901-05. *1628*
British Columbia (Trail). Consolidated Mining and Smelting Company. Immigration. Mine, Mill and Smelter Workers, International Union of. Strikes. World War I. 1916-17. *1810*
British Columbia (Vancouver). Labor Unions and Organizations. Women. 1900-15. *1803*
—. Public welfare. 1919-20. *1642*
British Columbia (Vancouver Island). Canadian Collieries (Dunsmuir) Limited. Coal Mines and Mining. Labor Unions and Organizations. Strikes. United Mine Workers of America. 1912-14. *2251*
British North America See also Canada; North America.
—. Antislavery Sentiments. Friends, Society of. Social problems. Woolman, John. 1720-72. *478*
—. Friends, Society of. Great Britain. Slavery. 1757-61. *519*
Brockwood Labor College. Education. Fincke, William. Labor. 1919-37. *1614*
Bromley, Walter. Charities. Micmac Indians. Nova Scotia. Poverty. Self-help. 1813-25. *870*
Brook Farm. Antislavery Sentiments. Godwin, Parke. Utopias. 1837-47. *587*
—. Blair, Nora Schelter. Education, Experimental Methods. Massachusetts. Personal narratives. Pratt, Frederick. Ripley, George. Utopias. 1841-47. *934*
—. Bradford, George Partridge. Daily life. Letters. Massachusetts. Utopias. 1841. *932*
—. Brisbane, Albert. Channing, William Henry. Transcendentalism. 1840-46. *923*
Brookings, Robert. Flexner Report. Medical education. Missouri (St. Louis). Reform. Washington University. 1910-16. *2318*
Brooklyn Dodgers (team). Baseball. Integration. Montreal Royals (team). Negroes. Press. Rickey, Branch. Robinson, Jackie. 1945-47. *2690*
Brotherhood of Locomotive Engineers. Canada. Grand Trunk Railway. Strikes. 1876-77. *1333*

Brotherhood of Painters and Decorators. American Federation of Labor. Gompers, Samuel. Labor Disputes. Voluntarism. 1894-1900. *1306*
Brotherhood of Sleeping Car Porters. American Federation of Labor. Negroes. Randolph, A. Philip. 1867-1935. *70*
—. March on Washington Movement. National Negro Congress. Negroes. Randolph, A. Philip. 1925-41. *353*
Brotherhood of Timber Workers. Emerson, Arthur L. Industrial Workers of the World. Labor Disputes. Louisiana, western. Lumber and Lumbering. Texas, eastern. 1900-16. *2207*
—. Industrial Workers of the World. Louisiana. Lumber and Lumbering. Race Relations. Texas. 1910-13. *2215*
—. Louisiana, western. Lumber and Lumbering. Race Relations. Southern Lumber Operators' Association. Texas, eastern. 1911-13. *2217*
Brothers of Freedom. Arkansas (northwestern). Farmers. 1880's. *1372*
Browder, Earl. Communist Party. 1934-45. *2579*
Brown, John. Abolition Movement. Civil War (antecedents). Harpers Ferry raid. Sanborn, Franklin Benjamin. 1854-60. *707*
—. Abolition Movement. Harpers Ferry raid. North Carolina. Sectional Conflict. State Politics. 1840-60. *675*
—. Alabama. Mobile *Register* (newspaper). 1859. *626*
—. Antislavery movement. Harpers Ferry Raid. Vietnam War. Violence. Weathermen. 1800-61. 1960-75. *105*
—. Antislavery Sentiments. Douglass, Frederick. Letters. 1851-56. *725*
—. Antislavery Sentiments. Harpers Ferry raid. Massachusetts. 1859. *706*
—. Civil War (antecedents). Harpers Ferry raid. North Carolina. Slavery. Social Psychology. 1859-60. *612*
—. Civil War (antecedents). Harpers Ferry raid. West Virginia. White, Edward. 1859. *783*
—. Costello, Michael A. (letter). Harpers Ferry raid. 1859-60. *630*
—. Harpers Ferry raid. Race relations. 1858-59. *722*
Brown v. *Board of Education* (US, 1954). Baptists. Desegregation. Georgia. Supreme Court. 1954-61. *2662*
—. Collins, LeRoy. Florida. State Legislatures. Supreme Court. 1954-61. *2664*
—. Constitutional Amendments (14th). Illinois (Chicago). School integration. South. 1954-77. *2777*
—. Desegregation. Equality. Negroes. Public Schools. 1950's-74. *2817*
—. Educators. Negroes. School Integration. 1954-75. *2838*
—. Rhetoric. School Integration. 1954-78. *2670*
Brown, W. G. Hayes, Michael P. Herridge, W. D. Saskatchewan. United Reform Movement. 1938-40. *1664*
Brown, William Wells. Abolitionists. Medicine. Negroes. Remond, Sarah Parker. Ruggles, David. Smith, James McCune. Tubman, Harriet. 1810-85. *329*
Brown, Willis. Indiana (Gary). Juvenile delinquency. 1910-12. *2075*
Brownlow, William G. Alden, Augustus E. Carpetbaggers. City Government. Education. Public welfare. Reconstruction. Republican Party. Tennessee (Nashville). 1865-69. *1049*
Brownlow, William Gannaway. Editors and Editing. Temperance Movements. Tennessee. *Whig* (newspaper). 1838-51. *866*
—. Sons of Temperance. Temperance Movements. Tennessee. 1851-67. *865*
Brownson, Orestes A. Catholic University of Ireland. Great Britain. Ireland. Newman, John Henry. 1853-54. *911*
Bruce, John Edward. Black nationalism. Economic independence. Self-help. 1874-1924. *16*
Bryant, John Howard. Abolition Movement. Bryant, Julian. Civil War. Illinois (Bureau County). Lovejoy, Owen. Military Service. Negroes. 1831-65. *607*
Bryant, Julian. Abolition Movement. Bryant, John Howard. Civil War. Illinois (Bureau County). Lovejoy, Owen. Military Service. Negroes. 1831-65. *607*
Buckeye Steel Castings Company. Bush, S. P. Management, scientific. Ohio (Columbus). Social Work. Steel Industry. 1890-1920. *2181*
Buckley, Christopher A. California (San Francisco). City Politics. Political Reform. Progressivism. 1890's. *1892*

Buck's Stove and Range Company. American Federation of Labor. Courts. Labor Law. 1907-11. *2222*
Buffalo Cooperative Economic Society, Inc. Negroes. Nelson, Ezekiel E. New York (Buffalo). 1928-61. *1762*
Buffalo Medical College. Libel. Loomis, Horatio N. Medical Education. Midwifery. New York. Obstetrics. White, James Platt. 1850. *869*
Bulkley, Robert J. Banking. Federal Farm Loan Act (US, 1916). Federal Reserve Act (US, 1913). Progressivism. 1906-30. *363*
—. Elections. Ohio. Prohibition. Senate. 1918-30. *2445*
Bullard, Isaac. Christianity. Vermont Pilgrims ("Mummyjums"). 1817-24. *928*
Bulosan, Carlos. Labor. Literature. Marxism. 1931-56. *432*
Bunche, Ralph. National Negro Congress. Negroes. New Deal. Political Attitudes. 1930-39. *2532*
Bureau of American Ethnology. Ghost Dance. Indians. Mooney, James. Peyote. Research. 1891-1921. *1110*
Bureau of Indian Affairs. American Indian Federation. Collier, John. Indians. Jamison, Alice Lee. New Deal. Political activism. 1930's-50's. *354*
—. Americas (North and South). Collier, John. Indians. Inter-American Institute. 1930's-50's. *1662*
—. California (Alcatraz Island). Eskimos. Ideology. Indians. Political Protest. 1969-78. *2757*
—. Christianity. Indian-White Relations. Iowa. Schools. Winnebago Indians. 1834-48. *850*
—. Collier, John. Indians. New Deal. 1933-45. *2600*
—. Collier, John. New Deal. Public Administration. Social sciences. 1933-45. *2599*
—. Educational policy. Indians. Medill, William. 1845-49. *836*
—. Emmons, Glenn L. Indians. Social Policy. Tribes. 1953-61. *2660*
—. Emmons, Glenn L. Indians (reservations). Industrialization. 1953-60. *2661*
—. Indian Reorganization Act (US, 1934). Meriam Report (1928). 1928-34. *2444*
—. Indians. Self-determination. 1945-75. *1545*
Bureau of Refugees, Freedmen, and Abandoned Lands. Alabama. Freedmen. Reconstruction. 1865-67. *1223*
Bureau of Surface Mine Reclamation. Legislation. Mining. Pennsylvania. 1961-73. *2762*
Bureaucracies. American Medical Association. Decisionmaking. Reform. 1960's. *2759*
—. Business. Disability insurance. Federal government. Social Security. 1900-40. *1829*
—. California (San Francisco). Medicine (practice of). Municipal Clinic. Venereal disease. 1911. *2084*
—. Centralization. Legislation. Missouri. Public schools. State government. 1853. *846*
—. Corporations. Labor. Poor. Social Classes. War on Poverty. 1960's. *2925*
—. Professionalization. Public welfare. 1900-29. *1825*
Bureaucrats. Pennsylvania (Philadelphia). Public housing. 1929-41. *1528*
Burger, Warren E. Civil Rights. Supreme Court. 1975-78. *2775*
—. Civil Rights. Supreme Court. ca 1970-75. *2790*
Burnham, Daniel Hudson. City planning. Illinois (Chicago). Moody, Walter D. *(Wacker's Manual of the Plan of Chicago)*. Progressivism. Publicity. Reform. 1909-11. *2071*
Burnside, Thomas E. Crawford, George W. Dueling. Georgia. Law. 1809-28. *545*
Burnside v. *Byars* (US, 1966). *Blackwell* v. *Issaquena County Board of Education* (US, 1966). Courts. Freedom of Speech. Students. *Tinker* v. *Des Moines Community School District* (US, 1969). 1870-1969. *1728*
Burris, Samuel D. Delaware. Garrett, Thomas. Hunn, John. Tubman, Harriet. Underground Railroad. 1820-60. *712*
Burrows, Jabez. *Alliance-Independent* (newspaper). Farmers' Alliance. Nebraska (Gage County). 1887-99. *1383*
Burt, Armistead. Calhoun, John C. Compromise of 1850. Congress. Oregon. Slavery. Wilmot Proviso. ca 1846-60. *691*
Bush, S. P. Buckeye Steel Castings Company. Management, scientific. Ohio (Columbus). Social Work. Steel Industry. 1890-1920. *2181*

Bushnell, Horace. Christianity. Economic conditions. Gladden, Washington. Politics. Social gospel. Youth. 1836-1918. *995*
Business *See also* Advertising; Banking; Consumers; Corporations; Management; Marketing.
—. Baseball. City life. Illinois (Chicago). Social change. Values. 1865-70. *1001*
—. Bureaucracies. Disability insurance. Federal government. Social Security. 1900-40. *1829*
—. California (San Francisco). Construction. Eight-hour day. Law and Order Committee. Strikes. 1916-17. *2232*
—. Campbell, Thomas M. Democratic Party. Progressivism. State Government. Texas. 1907-11. *2264*
—. Canada. Federal Government. Labor Unions and Organizations. Social control. Unemployment Insurance Act (Canada, 1941). Wages. 1910-41. *2623*
—. Capitalism. Illinois. Legislation. Workmen's compensation. 1905-12. *2189*
—. Civil rights. Populism. Rhetoric. 1870-1900. *1370*
—. Construction. Farmers. Railroads. Utopias. Western States. 1880's-90's. *1511*
—. Consumer cooperative movements. Garden City Movement. Nelson, Nelson O. Progressivism. 1890's-1918. *2240*
—. Cooperative Association of America. Democracy. Morality. Peck, Bradford *(World a Department Store)*. Utopias. 1880-1925. *263*
—. Croly, Herbert. Equal opportunity. Federal Trade Commission Act (US, 1914). Progressivism. 1900's-10's. *2227*
—. Economic planning. Government. Labor Unions and Organizations. Liberalism. 1920-40. *1788*
—. Farmers. Nonpartisan League. North Dakota. Politics. Townley, Arthur C. 1880-1959. *1667*
—. Federal Regulation. Freight and Freightage. Hepburn Act (US, 1906). Interstate Commerce Commission. 1905-06. *2282*
—. Feminism. Illinois (Chicago). Philanthropy. Schmidt, Minna Moscherosch. 1886-1961. *315*
—. Government regulation. Pressure Groups. Public interest. 1975-79. *2953*
—. Labor Unions and Organizations. New Deal. Taft-Hartley Act (US, 1947). Wagner Act (US, 1935). World War II. 1935-47. *1749*
Businessmen. Cooperatives. Nelson, Nelson O. Profit-sharing. 1886-1904. *1329*
—. Payne-Aldrich Tariff (1909). Reformers. Tariff. 1905-09. *2201*
—. Ports. Progressives. Washington (Seattle). 1911-20. *2184*
Busing. Community Participation. Massachusetts (Boston). Political Protest. 1977-78. *2894*
Butler, Benjamin F. Civil War. Proslavery Sentiments. 1861-64. *1018*
Butler, Benjamin F. (papers). Elections (presidential). People's Party. Third Parties. 1884. *1027*
Butler Bill. Judiciary. Local politics. Proslavery Sentiments. 1850's. *663*
Buttrick, George Arthur. Pacifism. Presbyterian Church. 1915-74. *1563*
Byrd, Harry F. Chambers, Lenoir. Editors and Editing. School Integration. Virginia. 1955-59. *2681*

C

Cabet, Etienne. France. Icarians. Iowa (New Icaria, Corning). Utopias. 1852-98. *1502*
—. Icaria (colony). Illinois. Newspapers. Political Theory. Social Theory. Utopias. 1820's-56. *941*
—. Icaria (colony). Illinois (Nauvoo). Utopias. 1848-56. *915*
—. Icaria (colony). Utopias. 1840-95. *264*
Cable, George Washington. Fiction. Gardens. 1886-1925. *2*
Cabot, Richard C. Medical ethics. 1906-16. *1900*
Čačić, Tomo. Canada. Communist Party. Croatians. Yugoslavia. ca 1913-69. *415*
—. Ethnic Groups. Kjelt, Ole. Krat, Pavlo. Leftism. Mäkelä, A. B. Political Protest. Puttee, Arthur. Scarlett, Sam. 1907-34. *1561*
Cain, Richard Harvey. Negroes. Politics. Reconstruction. Social conditions. South Carolina. 1850's-87. *375*
Calhoun, John C. Burt, Armistead. Compromise of 1850. Congress. Oregon. Slavery. Wilmot Proviso. ca 1846-60. *691*

—. Jefferson, Thomas. Slavery. South. 1830's-40's. *787*
California *See also* Far Western States.
—. Abolition Movement. Artifacts. Citrus industry. Indians (agencies). Rust, Horatio Nelson. 1850's-1906. *276*
—. Accidents. Industrial safety. Tanneries. Working Conditions. 1901-80. *2751*
—. Agricultural labor. Cannery and Agricultural Workers Industrial Union. Industrial Workers of the World. Radicals and Radicalism. 1909-39. *1756*
—. Agricultural labor. Historians. McWilliams, Carey. 1939. *2587*
—. Agricultural Labor. Labor Unions and Organizations. National Industrial Recovery Act (US, 1933). 1933-34. *2495*
—. American Railway Union. Illinois (Pullman). Strikes. 1893-94. *1337*
—. Bilingual education. Chacone-Moscone Bilingual Bicultural Education Act (1976). Civil Rights Act (US, 1964). *Lau* v. *Nichols* (US, 1974). Supreme Court. 1965-76. *2966*
—. British Columbia. Discrimination. Gold Rushes. Negroes. Race Relations. 1849-66. *592*
—. Capital punishment. Courts. Elections. 1954-72. *2791*
—. Carr, Jeanne Caroline Smith. Muir, John. Wilderness. Wisconsin. 1850's-1903. *277*
—. Chinese. Constitutions, State. Federal Regulation. Labor reform. Workingmen's Party of California. 1877-82. *1358*
—. Chinese Americans. Immigration. Nativism. *Sacramento Union* (newspaper). 1850-82. *12*
—. Civil War. Indian-White Relations. Reform. Republican Party. 1860-70. *971*
—. Community Participation in Politics. Conservation movement. Preservation. 1970's. *2699*
—. Compensation. Indians. Land claims. 1821-1963. *173*
—. Courts. Navajo Indians. Peyote. Religious Liberty. 1964. *2792*
—. Democratic Party. End Poverty In California (program). Political Campaigns (gubernatorial). Sinclair, Upton. ca 1933-34. *2592*
—. Ecology. Reclamation Movement. 1874-1974. *163*
—. Editors and Editing. Older, Fremont. Reporters and Reporting. San Francisco *Bulletin.* Women. 1895-1925. *1887*
—. Education. Preston School of Industry. Prisons. Rehabilitation. Youth. 1894-1955. *1558*
—. Educational Tests and Measurements. Ethnic groups. IQ tests. Progressivism. Students. 1917-21. *2300*
—. Elections. Ralston, Jackson. Reform. Single tax. 1932-38. *2504*
—. Elections (presidential). Progressive Party. 1924. *2413*
—. Elections (presidential). Racism. Republican Party. Slavery. 1860. *757*
—. Equality. Woman suffrage. 1895-1911. *2160*
—. Feminism. Gilman, Charlotte Perkins. New England. 1880's-1935. *287*
—. Grape industry. Labor Unions and Organizations. Strikes. United Farm Workers Union. 1966-70. *2934*
—. Indians. Jackson, Helen Hunt *(Ramona)*. Mission Indians. Ponca Indians. Removals, forced. Schurz, Carl. 1873-84. *1051*
—. Indian-White Relations. Paiute Indians. Winnemucca, Sarah (Paiute). 1840's-91. *419*
—. Junior Colleges. Lange, Alexis. Progressivism. 1890-1920. *2308*
—. Labor Unions and Organizations. Lobbying. Progressives. 1900-19. *1898*
—. Negroes. Political activism. Religion. 1850-73. *76*
—. North Carolina. Sermons. Sermons. Social Conditions. 1969-78. *2729*
—. Political Campaigns (congressional). Sinclair, Upton. Socialist Party. ca 1920. *2464*
—. Progressive education. ca 1930-40. *2518*
—. Racism. Slavery. State Politics. 1849-60. *755*
—. Republican Party. Slavery. 1852-56. *756*
California (Alameda County). Courts. Plea bargaining. Sentencing. 1880-1970's. *122*
California (Alcatraz Island). Bureau of Indian Affairs. Eskimos. Ideology. Indians. Political Protest. 1969-78. *2757*
California (Alum Rock). Education. Parents. Public Schools. Vouchers. 1960's-70's. *2960*

California (Eight Mile, Blue Creek). Forest Service. Indians. Religious liberty. Supreme Court. 1975. *2785*
California (El Monte). Berry pickers. Foreign Relations. Japan. Mexico. Strikes. 1933. *2522*
California (Fresno). Clyde, Edward M. Freedom of speech. Industrial Workers of the World. 1911. *2151*
—. Freedom of speech. Industrial Workers of the World. 1910-11. *2138*
California (Inglewood). Communist Party. North American Aviation. Strikes. United Automobile Workers of America. 1941. *2642*
California (Llano del Rio). Austin, Alice Constance. Feminism. Housework. Howland, Marie Stevens. Mexico (Topolobampo). Utopias. 1874-1917. *929*
California (Los Angeles). Alexander, George. City Government. Progressivism. Reform. ca 1909-13. *2070*
—. American Federation of Labor. Bombing. Labor movement. *Los Angeles Times*. McNamara case. Progressives. 1910-14. *2265*
—. Boosterism. City Government. Journalism. Progressivism. Willard, Charles Dwight. 1888-1914. *319*
—. Children's Court of Conciliation. Judges. Lindsey, Benjamin Barr. 1894-1943. *357*
—. Congress of Industrial Organizations. Labor Unions and Organizations. Mexican Americans. 1938-50. *1521*
—. Curricula. Educational reform. Mexican Americans. Public schools. 1920's-30's. *1842*
—. Garvey, Marcus. Negroes. Universal Negro Improvement Association. 1920's. *2455*
—. Mexican Americans. Pacific Electric Railroad. Strikes. 1900-03. *2289*
California (Oakland). Social change. Strikes. 1946-47. *2691*
California (Orange County). *Mendez* v. *Westminster* (California, 1946). Mexican Americans. Public schools. Segregation *(de jure, de facto)*. 1850-1970's. *1865*
—. Middle Classes. Oneida Community. Religion. Social Organization. Townerites. 1848-1900's. *1514*
California (Point Loma). Communes. Theosophy. Tingley, Katherine Augusta Westcott. Universal Brotherhood and Theosophical Society. 1897-1942. *1619*
California (Salinas). Agricultural Labor. Filipino Labor Union. Lettuce. Strikes. 1934. *2499*
California (San Bernardino). Ancker, Henrietta. Charities. Henrietta Hebrew Benevolent Society. Jews. 1870-91. *1479*
California (San Diego). Allen, Ella. Baker, Charlotte. Political Campaigns. Woman suffrage. 1911. *2147*
—. Foltz, Clara Shortridge. Lawyers. Women. 1872-1930. *413*
—. Freedom of speech. Industrial Workers of the World. Mexico (Tijuana). 1911-12. *2162*
—. Indians. Jackson, Helen Hunt *(Ramona)*. 1882-84. *951*
California (San Francisco). Bombing. Mooney, Tom. San Quentin Prison. Socialist Party. Trials. 1916-42. *2020*
—. Buckley, Christopher A. City Politics. Political Reform. Progressivism. 1890's. *1892*
—. Bureaucracies. Medicine (practice of). Municipal Clinic. Venereal disease. 1911. *2084*
—. Business. Construction. Eight-hour day. Law and Order Committee. Strikes. 1916-17. *2232*
—. Catholic Church. City Politics. Irish Americans. Progressivism. Yorke, Peter C. 1900's. *2114*
—. Chamber of Commerce Law and Order Committee. Chipman, Miner. Labor disputes. 1915-19. *2233*
—. Charities. Immigration. Voluntary Associations. ca 1850-60. *885*
—. Chinatowns. Chinese Americans. Public health. Racism. 1870-1970. *1078*
—. Chinese Americans. Law. Negroes. Political Leadership. Racism. 1865-75. *1184*
—. Churches. Civil rights. Negroes. Pressure groups. 1860's. *1221*
—. City Government. Crime and Criminals. Progressivism. Prostitution. 1910-14. *2085*
—. Educational Reform. Ethnicity. Religion. 1918-20. *2333*
—. Educational Reform. Rincon School. Swett, John. 1853-62. *849*
—. Gymnastics. Lewis, Diocleius. Parot, Adele. 1860's-70's. *1404*

—. Labor Disputes. Law and Order Committee. Longshoremen. Strikes. 1916. *2234*
—. Longshoremen. Strikes. 1934-39. *2529*
California (San Francisco Bay). Courts Martial and Courts of Inquiry. Mare Island Mutiny. Navies. Negroes. Port Chicago Naval Magazine. Race relations. 1944-48. *2652*
California (San Francisco Bay area). Consumers. Environmental protection. Government regulation. Housing. Local government. Suburbs. 1940-80. *2718*
California (San Joaquin Valley). Agricultural labor. Japanese Americans. Mexican Americans. Nisei Farmers League. United Farm Workers Union. 1971-77. *2926*
California (Sausalito). Discrimination. International Brotherhood of Boilermakers, Iron Shipbuilders and Helpers of America. *James* v. *Marinship* (California, 1945). Labor. Negroes. Shipbuilding. 1940-48. *2653*
California, southern. Indians (agencies). Jackson, Helen Hunt *(Century of Dishonor; Ramona)*. 1881-84. *1048*
California State Agricultural Society. Elites. Farmers. Grange. 1870's-80's. *1385*
California (Wheatland). Industrial Workers of the World. Migrant Labor. State Government. Strikes. Trials. 1913-17. *2198*
Camp Grant Affair. Arizona (Tucson). Federal Policy. Indian Wars. 1871. *1037*
Campaigns, Political. *See* Political Campaigns.
Campbell, Thomas M. Business. Democratic Party. Progressivism. State Government. Texas. 1907-11. *2264*
Canada *See also* individual provinces; Atlantic Provinces; British North America; North America; Northwest Territories; Prairie Provinces.
—. Abolition Movement. Anderson, John. Foreign Relations. Great Britain. Politics. USA. 1860-61. *734*
—. Abolition movement. Anderson, John. Fugitive Slaves. Great Britain. Trials. USA. 1860-61. *733*
—. Abortion. Birth control. 1870-1920. *67*
—. Acculturation. Federal Policy. Indians. Sifton, Clifford. 1896-1905. *1012*
—. Adolescence. Boys. Protestantism. USA. Young Men's Christian Association. 1870-1920. *63*
—. American Revolution. French Revolution. Ideology. 1775-1838. *139*
—. Angers, François-Albert. Catholic Church. French Canadians. Pacifism. Values. 1940-79. *1595*
—. Attitudes. Citizenship. Japanese. USA. World War II. 1941-58. *1730*
—. Attitudes. English Canadians. Race. Sex. Woman Suffrage. ca 1877-1918. *1*
—. Australia. Finland. Kurikka, Matti. Utopias. 1883-1915. *1707*
—. Automobile Industry and Trade. General Motors. Labor Disputes. 1927-30. *1798*
—. Bacteriology. Cities. Public Health. 1900-30. *1644*
—. Bibb, Henry. Emigration. Negroes. Separatism. USA. 1830-60. *672*
—. Borden, Robert Laird. *Champion* (periodical). Great Britain. Woman suffrage. Women's Social and Political Union. 1910-18. *1737*
—. Bourassa, Henri. Divorce. Feminism. Woman suffrage. 1913-25. *1698*
—. Bourassa, Henri. Parliaments. Progressives. 1926. *1633*
—. British Columbia. Chinese Canadians. Japanese Canadians. Military Service. World War II. 1939-45. *2647*
—. Brotherhood of Locomotive Engineers. Grand Trunk Railway. Strikes. 1876-77. *1333*
—. Business. Federal Government. Labor Unions and Organizations. Social control. Unemployment Insurance Act (Canada, 1941). Wages. 1910-41. *2623*
—. Čačić, Tomo. Communist Party. Croatians. Yugoslavia. ca 1913-69. *415*
—. Catholic Church. Journalism. Social Theory. Somerville, Henry. 1915-53. *284*
—. Catholic Church. Knights of Labor. Labor Unions and Organizations. Taschereau, Elzéar-Alexandre. 1884-94. *1350*
—. Child welfare. Income. Legislation. Mothers. 1916-70's. *1814*
—. Children. Methodism. 1850-1900. *1495*
—. Christianity. Fiction. Labor. Social gospel. 1890's. *1354*
—. Christianity. Missions and Missionaries. Sex roles. Women. 1815-99. *1490*

—. Citizen Lobbies. Consumers' Association of Canada. Public policy. 1947-77. *1587*
—. City Government. Depressions. Public Welfare. ca 1930-40. *1695*
—. Civil Rights. Feminism. Government. Great Britain. USA. 1850-20c. *79*
—. Civil rights. Law. Mexico. USA. Violence. 18c-1974. *119*
—. Civil service. Ideology. Labor Unions and Organizations. Middle Classes. 1918-28. *1820*
—. Coldwell, Major J. Farmer Labor party. Political Leadership. Progressivism. Social Democracy. 1907-32. *471*
—. Colleges and Universities. Public policy. Social Sciences. 1920-49. *1576*
—. Communist Party. Industrial Workers of the World. Labor Unions and Organizations. Scarlett, Sam. 1900-41. *278*
—. Communist Party. Labour Party. Methodism. Smith, Albert Edward. Social Gospel. 1893-1924. *410*
—. Counter Culture. Great Britain. Press, underground. USA. 1957-72. *2990*
—. Courts. Extradition. Fugitive slaves. Happy, Jesse. Kentucky. Testimony. 1793-1838. *748*
—. Courts. Indians. Lavell, Jeannette. Political participation. Women's Liberation Movement. 1869-1979. *2914*
—. Criminal law. Parliaments. 1892-1902. *1107*
—. Economic opportunity. Political Protest. Social Classes. USA. 1960-74. *2702*
—. Economic Reform. George, Henry. Industry. Poverty. Progress (concept). Social gospel. ca 1879-99. *975*
—. Editors and Editing. Finnish Canadians. Kurikka, Matti. Mäkelä, A. B. Newspapers. Socialism. 1900-32. *464*
—. Education. Federal government. Indians. Métis. 1940-70. *2959*
—. Education. Indian-White Relations. 1978. *2972*
—. English Canadians. Family. Woman suffrage. 1877-1918. *111*
—. English Canadians. Immigrants. Propaganda. Puttee, Arthur. Radicals and Radicalism. Water Conservation. ca 1888-1913. *1327*
—. Europe, Western. Social policy. USA. Welfare state. 1890-1970. *160*
—. Fairbairn, R. Edis. Pacifism. United Church of Canada. World War II. 1939. *2646*
—. Federal government. Physical Education and Training. 1850-1972. *33*
—. Federal government. Social policy. Unemployment. 1918-21. *1816*
—. Federal Policy. Housing. 1970-79. *2950*
—. Feminism. Literature. McClung, Nellie L. Politics. Reform. 1873-1930's. *1689*
—. Feminism. National Council of Women of Canada. 1893-1929. *1690*
—. Finns. Immigrants. Labor Unions and Organizations. Radicals and Radicalism. 1918-26. *2407*
—. Germany. Hjelt, Ole. Labour Party. Nazism. Norway. Socialism. 1908-28. *321*
—. Girls. Home economics. Hoodless, Adelaide. Public schools. 1890's-1900's. *215*
—. Gospel Temperance Movement. Revivalism. Rine, D.I.K. 1877-82. *1439*
—. Great Britain. Wartime Elections Act (Canada, 1917). Woman Suffrage. 1917. *1721*
—. Great Plains. Pietism. Prairie Radicals. 1890-1975. *1530*
—. House of Commons. Legislation. Liberal Party. Political Change. Progressive Party. 1920's. *1574*
—. Income. Legislation. Mothers. Public Welfare. ca 1900-39. *1815*
—. Japanese Canadians. Race Relations. Removals, forced. World War II. 1890's-1940's. *1694*
—. Krat, Pavlo. Socialism. Ukrainian Canadians. ca 1902-52. *365*
—. Labor Reform. Royal Commission of Inquiry into the Relations between Capital and Labour. 1886-89. *1314*
—. Labor Unions and Organizations. Working class. 1845-75. *161*
—. Marsh, Leonard *(Report)*. Social Security. Socialism. Welfare state. 1930-44. *1771*
—. McClung, Nellie L. Methodist Church. Ordination. United Church of Canada. Women. 1915-46. *1597*
—. Methodism. Social gospel. 1890-1914. *23*
—. Public Policy. Social security. USA. 1935-75. *1776*

Canada

—. Radicals and Radicalism. Socialism. 1890-99. *1316*
—. Strikes. Winnipeg General Strike (1919). 1920-70. *1752*
—. Women. Young Women's Christian Association. 1870-1900. *1469*
Canada, western. Antilabor sentiments. Elections. Immigration. Ku Klux Klan. 1921-30's. *1603*
—. Attitudes. Industrialization. Labor Unions and Organizations. Radicals and Radicalism. Working class. 1897-1919. *1745*
—. Communist Party. Evans, Arthur. Labor. 1930's. *1658*
—. Conspiracy. Intelligence service. Labor Disputes. One Big Union. Royal Canadian Mounted Police. 1919. *1612*
—. Industrial Workers of the World. Labor Unions and Organizations. Radicals and Radicalism. 1905-14. *1786*
—. Labor reform. Regionalism. Socialism. 1918-19. *1764*
—. Labor Unions and Organizations. One Big Union. Radicals and Radicalism. Socialism. 1917-19. *1746*
Canadian Chamber of Agriculture. Agriculture and Government. Marketing. 1935-45. *1780*
Canadian Collieries (Dunsmuir) Limited. British Columbia (Vancouver Island). Coal Mines and Mining. Labor Unions and Organizations. Strikes. United Mine Workers of America. 1912-14. *2251*
Canadian Forum. Culture. Socialism. 1920-34. *1649*
Canadian Labour Congress. Cooperative Commonwealth Federation. Federal Government. Industrial relations. Trades and Labour Congress of Canada. World War II. 1939-46. *2634*
Canadian Seamen's Union. Communists. Syndicalism. 1936-49. *1754*
Candler, Warren A. Methodist Episcopal Church, South. Political Campaigns (presidential). Prohibition. Religion. Smith, Alfred E. 1928. *2344*
Cannery and Agricultural Workers Industrial Union. Agricultural labor. California. Industrial Workers of the World. Radicals and Radicalism. 1909-39. *1756*
Canniff, William. Medical Reform. Ontario (Toronto). Public health. 1869-90. *1468*
Capital punishment. Beccaria, Cesare. Italy. Penal reform. 1764-97. *890*
—. California. Courts. Elections. 1954-72. *2791*
—. Constitutional Conventions, state. New York. Progressivism. 1915. *1923*
—. Cruce, Lee. Governors. Negroes. Oklahoma. White supremacy. 1911-15. *1907*
—. Law Reform. Public Opinion. Rhode Island. 1838-52. *888*
—. Livingston, Edward. Public Opinion. ca 1800-30. *887*
—. Massachusetts (Boston). Public Opinion. 1836-54. *886*
Capitalism *See also* Socialism.
—. Adult education. Antigonish Movement. Coady, Moses. Cooperatives. Nova Scotia, eastern. 1930-40. *1742*
—. Anti-Catholicism. DeLeon, Daniel. Socialism. 1891-1914. *55*
—. Attitudes. Cities. Howells, William Dean. 1860-1900. *979*
—. Business. Illinois. Legislation. Workmen's compensation. 1905-12. *2189*
—. Carver, George Washington. Marxism. Myths and Symbols. Race Relations. South. 1896-1950's. *1604*
—. Conservatism. Coolidge, Louis Arthur. Sentinels of the Republic. 1900-25. *450*
—. Corporations. Federal government. General Electric Company. Labor Unions and Organizations. Liberalism. 1920-33. *2412*
—. Depressions. Political Attitudes. Radicals and Radicalism. Texas. 1929-33. *2460*
—. George, Henry. Politics. Progressivism. Single tax. 1880-1920. *2188*
—. Ideology. Slavery. South. 19c. *766*
—. Labor. Leisure. Social Organization. 1890-1920's. *151*
—. Labor movement. 1860-1920. *164*
Carbon County Coal Strike (1933). National Miners Union. Strikes. United Mine Workers of America. Utah. 1900-39. *2571*
Carden, Georgiana. Compulsory Education. Elementary education. Mexican Americans. Migrant Labor. 1920's. *2383*

Cardozo, Francis Louis. American Missionary Association. Education. Freedmen. Reconstruction. South Carolina (Charleston). State Politics. 1865-70. *1243*
—. Freedmen. Political rights. Reconstruction. South Carolina. Union League. 1870. *1268*
Carlile, Richard. Bentham, Jeremy. Birth control. Feminism. Great Britain. Owen, Robert Dale. Place, Francis. Propaganda. Wright, Frances. 1790-1840. *817*
Carlson, Oliver (reminiscences). Communist Party. Foster, William Z. Politburo. Radek, Karl. Trotskyism. USSR. 1924-35. *1548*
Carmichael, Stokely. Black Power. Pan-Africanism. Political Theory. 1965-73. *2860*
Carmody, John. American Federation of Labor. Civil Works Administration. Labor. New Deal. 1933-34. *2584*
Carnegie, Andrew. Higher education. Pensions. Retirement. 1901-18. *2214*
Carnegie Foundation. American Medical Association. Flexner Report. Medical education. Reform. 1910-32. *2297*
Carpetbaggers. Alden, Augustus E. Brownlow, William G. City Government. Education. Public welfare. Reconstruction. Republican Party. Tennessee (Nashville). 1865-69. *1049*
—. Civil rights. Constitutional conventions, state. Industrialization. Reconstruction. South. 1867-69. *1021*
—. Equality. Post, Louis F. Progressive era. Reconstruction. 1868-1925. *306*
—. Historiography. Ideology. Mississippi. Reconstruction. Reformers. 1865-76. *1013*
—. House of Representatives. Negroes. Reconstruction. Republican Party. Scalawags. South. 1868-72. *1036*
—. Louisiana. Negroes. Republican Party. State Politics. 1868. *1136*
Carr, Elias. Alexander, Sydenham B. Farmers' Alliance. Leadership. North Carolina. Polk, Leonidas L. Upper Classes. 1887-95. *1392*
Carr, Jeanne Caroline Smith. California. Muir, John. Wilderness. Wisconsin. 1850's-1903. *277*
Carroll, Anna Ella. Nativism. Probasco, Harriet. Women. 1840's-61. *797*
Carse, George B. Florida (Leon County). Freedmen's Bureau. Reconstruction. Republican Party. 1867-70. *1074*
Carter, William Hodding, Jr. Editors and Editing. Mississippi. Political Reform. Race Relations. ca 1930-60. *340*
Carver, George Washington. Capitalism. Marxism. Myths and Symbols. Race Relations. South. 1896-1950's. *1604*
—. Negroes. Scientists. 1900-75. *380*
Cary, Samuel Fenton. Ohio (Cincinnati). Temperance movements. 1845-1900. *1448*
Caryl, Charles W. Colorado. New Era Union. Progressive Era. Racial thought. Utopias. 1858-1926. *1509*
Cash, W. J. Historiography. Social change. South. 1830-1940. *1653*
Cass, William D. Abolition Movement. Letters. Methodist Episcopal Church (General Conference). 1844. *693*
Casson, Herbert N. Labor Church. Massachusetts (Lynn). Socialism. Working class. 1893-98. *1498*
Catholic Church *See also* religious orders by name, e.g. Franciscans, Jesuits, etc.
—. Agricultural Reform. New Deal. Roosevelt, Franklin D. (administration). Social Theory. 1933-39. *2590*
—. Angers, François-Albert. Canada. French Canadians. Pacifism. Values. 1940-79. *1595*
—. Angers, François-Albert. Public welfare. Quebec. Social justice. 1950-80. *2931*
—. Antigonish Movement. Nova Scotia. Rural Development. Social change. ca 1928-73. *1854*
—. Berrigan, Daniel. Berrigan, Philip. Church and state. Leftism. Murray, John Courtney. 1950's-70's. *1605*
—. Bible. Desmond, Humphrey. Protestantism. Religion in the Public Schools. Wisconsin. *Wisconsin ex rel. Frederick Weiss et al. vs. District School Board of School District 8* (1890). 1888-90. *1414*
—. California (San Francisco). City Politics. Irish Americans. Progressivism. Yorke, Peter C. 1900's. *2114*
—. Canada. Journalism. Social Theory. Somerville, Henry. 1915-53. *284*
—. Canada. Knights of Labor. Labor Unions and Organizations. Taschereau, Elzéar-Alexandre. 1884-94. *1350*

—. Church and State. Compulsory education. Michigan. Politics. 1920-25. *2348*
—. Church and State. French language. Langevin, Adélard. Manitoba. Politics. Private schools. 1890-1916. *1410*
—. Church and State. Provincial Government. Public Charities Act (Canada, 1921). Quebec. Recessions. 1921-26. *1699*
—. Church Schools. Congress. Federal aid to education. Roosevelt, Eleanor. Spellman, Francis J. 1949-50. *2669*
—. Church schools. French language. Langevin, Louis Philippe Adélard. Laurier, Wilfrid. Liberal Party. Prairie Provinces. Religion in the Public Schools. 1890-1915. *185*
—. Church Schools. Glennon, John J. Missouri (St. Louis). Ritter, Joseph E. School Integration. 1935-47. *1850*
—. Church Schools. Manitoba. McCarthy, D'Alton. Provincial legislatures. 1870-90. *1429*
—. Cooperative Commonwealth Federation. Saskatchewan. Socialism. 1930-50. *1620*
—. Democracy. Intellectuals. Liberalism. Racism. 1924-59. *1560*
—. École Sociale Populaire. Propaganda. Quebec (Montreal). Syndicalism. Working Class. 1911-49. *1806*
—. Farms. New Deal. 1930's. *2591*
—. Fédération Nationale Saint-Jean-Baptiste. Feminism. Gérin-Lajoie, Marie. Quebec. 1907-33. *1039*
—. Feminism. Quebec. Religious Orders. Women. 1640-1975. *21*
—. Fernandez, John F. O. Laity. Parishes. Virginia (Norfolk). 1815-20. *905*
—. Gibbons, James. Knights of Labor. Social Theory. Taschereau, Elzéar Alexandre. 1880's. *1351*
—. Illinois (Chicago). Mundelein, George. 20c. *1621*
—. Immigrants. Irish Americans. McMahon, Patrick. Poor. Quebec (Quebec). St. Bridget's Home. 1847-1972. *244*
—. International Union of Catholic Women's Leagues (congress). Italy (Rome). Quebec. Woman suffrage. 1922. *1734*
—. Kansas. Protestantism. Religion in the Public Schools. 1861-1900. *1409*
—. Labor Unions and Organizations. Polish Americans. Political Leadership. Progressivism. Socialism. Wisconsin (Milwaukee). 1900-30. *1663*
—. Lawyers. Pennsylvania. Progressivism. Smith, Walter George. 1900-22. *1891*
—. National Catholic Welfare Conference. National Council of Catholic Women. Peace Movements. Women. 1919-46. *1636*
—. Prohibition. Zurcher, George. 1884-1920's. *1442*
—. Quebec (Gaspé Peninsula). Ross, François Xavier. Social Conditions. 1923-45. *374*
—. Religious Education. Saskatchewan. Youth. 1870-1978. *207*
Catholic University of America. Colleges and Universities. Discrimination. District of Columbia. Negroes. Wesley, Charles H. 1914-48. *2304*
Catholic University of Ireland. Brownson, Orestes A. Great Britain. Ireland. Newman, John Henry. 1853-54. *911*
Catholic Worker Movement. Equality. Human Rights. Public policy. 1933-78. *1678*
—. Maurin, Peter ("Easy Essays"). Political Theory. 1920's-33. *2419*
Cattle Raising. Agriculture. Blackfoot Indians. Indians (reservations). Montana. 1885-1935. *104*
Cattlemen. Corn Belt Meat Producers' Association. Hepburn Act (US, 1906). Iowa. 1900-10. *2229*
Catto, Octavius V. Civil Rights. Militancy. Pennsylvania (Philadelphia). 1861-71. *440*
Cedar Creek Monthly Meeting. Emancipation. Farms. Friends, Society of. Moorman, Clark Terrell. Ohio. Virginia (Caroline County). 1766-1814. *743*
Cemeteries. Rural Cemetery Movement. 1804-35. *579*
Censorship *See also* Freedom of Speech; Freedom of the Press.
—. Abolitionists. Antislavery materials. Publishers and Publishing. 1852-55. *772*
—. Anglophobia. City Politics. Illinois (Chicago). Libraries. Public Schools. Thompson, William Hale. 1927. *2454*
—. Behavior. Cities. Social Psychology. 1960's-70's. *2788*

—. Chicago *Times*. Civil War. Lincoln, Abraham. Newspapers. 1863-64. *1118*
—. Hughes, Howard. Legion of Decency. Motion Picture Producers and Distributors of America. *Outlaw* (film). Russell, Jane. 1940-49. *2649*
Census. Cults. 1920-79. *2443*
Census Bureau. Cornell University. Economics. Negroes. Progressivism. Racism. Willcox, Walter F. 1895-1910. *1870*
Centennial Celebrations. Douglass, Frederick. Negroes. Pennsylvania (Philadelphia). 1876. *1157*
—. Indian-White Relations. Jackson, Helen Hunt. National Self-image. 1881. 1975. *1079*
Centennial Exposition of 1876. Borg, Selma Josefina. Finnish Americans. Lectures. Music. Pennsylvania (Philadelphia). Women's rights. 1858-90. *399*
—. Sex roles. Values. Women. World's Columbian Exposition (Chicago, 1893). 1876-93. *948*
Central Labor Union. Eight-hour day. Knights of Labor. Labor Unions and Organizations. Massachusetts (Boston). Strikes. 1886. *1321*
—. Ohio (Cincinnati). Strikes. 1886. *1331*
Centralization. Bureaucracies. Legislation. Missouri. Public schools. State government. 1853. *846*
Cerasoli, Mose (memoir). Granite Industry. Labor. Labor Disputes. Vermont. 1913-38. *1807*
Chaban, Teklia. Alberta (Cardiff, Edmonton). Coal Mines and Mining. Labor Unions and Organizations. Ukrainian Canadians. 1914-20's. *469*
Chacone-Moscone Bilingual Bicultural Education Act (1976). Bilingual education. California. Civil Rights Act (US, 1964). Lau v. Nichols (US, 1974). Supreme Court. 1965-76. *2966*
Chafe, William. Feminism. Historiography. O'Neill, William. Sexual revolution. ca 1920-70. *2374*
Chafee, Zechariah, Jr. Civil Rights. Freedom of speech. 1919-57. *1729*
Chamber of Commerce Law and Order Committee. California (San Francisco). Chipman, Miner. Labor disputes. 1915-19. *2233*
Chamberlain, Daniel H. Hampton, Wade. Reconstruction. South Carolina. State Politics. 1877. *1054*
Chamberlain, George. Ansell, Samuel T. Congress. Crowder, Enoch H. Lenroot, Irvine L. Military law. Progressivism. 1916-20. *2408*
Chamberlain, John. Conservatism. Political Theory. Radicals and Radicalism. 1920's-65. *275*
Chambers, Lenoir. Byrd, Harry F. Editors and Editing. School Integration. Virginia. 1955-59. *2681*
Champion (periodical). Borden, Robert Laird. Canada. Great Britain. Woman suffrage. Women's Social and Political Union. 1910-18. *1737*
Channing, William Ellery *(Slavery)*. Abolition Movement. 1830-38. *714*
Channing, William Henry. Brisbane, Albert. Brook Farm. Transcendentalism. 1840-46. *923*
Chapman, Maria Weston. Abolition movement. Child, Lydia Maria. Feminism. Stanton, Elizabeth Cady. ca 1830-40. *558*
Charisma. Authority. Counter Culture. Hasidism. Unification Church. 1960-80. *2986*
—. Authority. Noyes, John Humphrey. Oneida Community. 1875-81. *1515*
Charities *See also* Philanthropy; Public Welfare; Red Cross.
—. Ancker, Henrietta. California (San Bernardino). Henrietta Hebrew Benevolent Society. Jews. 1870-91. *1479*
—. Associated Charities. Leadership. Massachusetts (Fall River, Lynn). Men. Social Policy. Women. 1880-1900. *1447*
—. Bromley, Walter. Micmac Indians. Nova Scotia. Poverty. Self-help. 1813-25. *870*
—. California (San Francisco). Immigration. Voluntary Associations. ca 1850-60. *885*
—. Church of England. City government. Poor. South Carolina (Charleston; St. Phillip's Parish). 1712-75. *536*
—. City government. New York City. Reform. Subsidies. 1870-98. *1463*
—. Friends, Society of. Pennsylvania. Pennsylvania (Philadelphia). Society for Organizing Charitable Relief and Repressing Mendicancy. 1800-1900. *250*
—. Galveston Plan of 1907. Immigration. Industrial Removal Office. Jews. Migration, Internal. New York City. 1890-1914. *1476*
—. Illinois (Chicago). Negroes. Social problems. 1890-1917. *1979*

—. Institutions. Ontario (Toronto). Social work. ca 1875-1920. *246*
—. Jewish Welfare Federation of Detroit. Michigan. Social Organizations. 1926. *2367*
—. Medical care. Progressivism. Scientific management. 1900-20. *2064*
—. New Brunswick (Saint John). Newfoundland (Saint John's). Nova Scotia (Halifax). Poverty. Unemployment. 1815-60. *871*
—. Ontario (Toronto). Social Control. Tramps. 1870-90. *1065*
—. Pennsylvania (Philadelphia). Social work. Society for Organizing Charitable Relief and Repressing Mendicancy. Women. 1864-1909. *1474*
Charities and the Commons (periodical). Industrialization. Pennsylvania. *Pittsburgh Survey* (1909). Social Surveys. 1907-14. *2029*
Charities Organization Society Movement. Illinois (Chicago). Public Welfare. 1880-1930. *1996*
Charleston City Railway Company. Desegregation. Negroes. Reconstruction. South Carolina. Streetcars. 1867. *1169*
Charleston *Daily Courier* (newspaper). Charleston *Mercury* (newspaper). Constitutional conventions, state. Racism. Reconstruction. South Carolina. 1867-68. *1205*
Charleston *Mercury* (newspaper). Charleston *Daily Courier* (newspaper). Constitutional conventions, state. Racism. Reconstruction. South Carolina. 1867-68. *1205*
Charleston *News and Courier* (newspaper). Dawson, Francis Warrington. Dawson, Sarah Morgan. Feminism. Reconstruction. South Carolina. 1870's. *973*
Charlestown State Prison. Boston Prison Discipline Society. Massachusetts. Penal reform. 1804-78. *860*
Charter of the French Language (1977). French language. Politics. Provincial government. Quebec. 1977-78. *2766*
Chase, Salmon Portland. Antislavery Sentiments. Bailey, Gamaliel. Liberty Party. Ohio. Republican Party. 1836-60. *668*
—. Emancipation. Republicans, Radical. 1861-64. *1005*
Chavez, Cesar. La Raza Unida Party. Mexican Americans. 1968-73. *2711*
Cherokee Indians. Christianity. Indian-White Relations. Missions and Missionaries. Property. Social Change. Women. 19c. *107*
—. Citizenship. Indians. South. 1817-29. *598*
—. Farmers. Grange. Indian Territory. 1870's. *1374*
—. Federal government. Georgia. Land (cessions). Payne, John Howard (letter). Ross, John (chief). 1820's-30's. *575*
—. Federal Policy. Indians. New Deal. North Carolina, western. 1930's. *2607*
—. Freedmen. Indian Territory. Racism. 1839-88. *1165*
Chesnutt, Charles W. Politics. Race relations. Washington, Booker T. 1880-1915. *1153*
Cheyenne and Arapaho Reservation. Agriculture. Federal Policy. Indians. Oklahoma. 1869-80. *1063*
Cheyenne Indians. Arapaho Indians. Dawes Act (US, 1887). Fraud. Indians (agencies). Land allotment. Oklahoma. 1910's. *1888*
—. Arapaho Indians. Indians. Mennonites. Missions and Missionaries. 1880-1900. *1030*
Cheyenne River Indian Reservation. Assimilation. Federal Programs. Identity. Indians. Sioux Indians. 1889-1917. *45*
Chicago *Times*. Censorship. Civil War. Lincoln, Abraham. Newspapers. 1863-64. *1118*
Chicago, University of. Curricula. Education. Hutchins, Robert M. 1930-77. *1839*
Chicanos. *See* Mexican Americans.
Chicopee News. Massachusetts, western. Massachusetts (Westfield). Newspapers. Prostitution. 1911. *2102*
Chief Justices. *See* Judges; Supreme Court.
Child Care Centers. Women's Liberation Movement. 1854-1973. *89*
Child development. Behavior. Education, Experimental Methods. Olerich, Henry. 1897-1902. *2311*
Child labor. Barnard, Kate. Law Reform. Oklahoma. 1904-24. *1877*
—. Illinois. Law. Women. 1890-1920. *1955*
—. Industrialization. Iowa. Labor Unions and Organizations. Women. 1900's. *1984*
—. Louisiana Child Labor Laws (1908-1912). Theater. 1908-12. *2050*
Child Labor Act (US, 1916). Cotton. Federal regulation. Textile Industry. 1907-16. *2002*

Child Labor Law (Louisiana, 1908). Gordon, Jean. Louisiana (New Orleans). New York. Theatrical Syndicate. 1908-12. *1968*
Child, Lydia Maria. Abolition movement. Chapman, Maria Weston. Feminism. Stanton, Elizabeth Cady. ca 1830-40. *558*
Child Welfare *See also* Child Care Centers; Child Labor; Children; Juvenile Deliquency.
—. Canada. Income. Legislation. Mothers. 1916-70's. *1814*
—. Children's Code Commission. Missouri. 1915-19. *2060*
—. Family. Foster homes. Immigration. Jews. New York City. Working class. 1900-05. *2061*
—. Hoover, Herbert C. Voluntary associations. War relief. 1914-31. *364*
—. Human Rights. Law. Pressure Groups. 1978. *1639*
—. Human Rights. Psychology. 1873-1914. 1970's. *143*
—. Illinois (Chicago). Off-the-Street Club. 1890's. *1477*
—. Joint Committee on the Care of Motherless Infants. New York City. 1860-1907. *1475*
Child Welfare Commission. Medical care. Socialism. Wisconsin (Milwaukee). 1911-12. *2032*
Childbirth. Anesthesia. Medicine (practice of). Twilight sleep movement. Women. 1902-23. *2034*
—. Medical Reform. Twilight sleep. Women. 1914-15. *2004*
Childhood. Abolitionists. Missions and Missionaries. 1800-60. *789*
—. Leadership. Religion. Secularism. Sex roles. Women. 1636-1930. *381*
Child-rearing. Books. Education. Pennsylvania (Philadelphia). Protestantism. Republicanism. 1780-1835. *577*
—. Democracy. Family. Infants. Spock, Benjamin (*Baby and Child Care*). 1917-50. *1589*
Children *See also* Education; Handicapped Children; Kindergarten; Television; Youth.
—. Boarding schools. Federal Government. Indians. 1920-60's. *1864*
—. Canada. Methodism. 1850-1900. *1495*
—. Coldwater State Public School. Crime and Criminals. Michigan. Protestantism. 1874-96. *1430*
—. Education. Great Britain. Nutrition. 1890-1920. *2053*
—. Education. New York House of Refuge. Reformatories. 1800-30. *898*
—. Education. Shakers. 1780-1900. *912*
—. Hall, G. Stanley. Playgrounds. Progressivism. 1880-1920. *1909*
—. Hospitals. Massachusetts (Boston). New York City. Pediatrics. Pennsylvania (Philadelphia). 1776-1976. *249*
—. Indians. Poor. Saint Vincent de Paul Society. 1900-10. *2036*
—. Labor reform. Progressivism. Rhetoric. 1904-16. *1917*
—. Massachusetts (Boston). Pennsylvania (Philadelphia). Progressivism. Recreation. 1886-1911. *1985*
—. Michigan. Prisons. Reformatories. 1851-58. *900*
—. Missouri. St. Louis Children's Hospital. Women. 1879-1979. *237*
Children's Code Commission. Child Welfare. Missouri. 1915-19. *2060*
Children's Court of Conciliation. California (Los Angeles). Judges. Lindsey, Benjamin Barr. 1894-1943. *357*
Children's Friend (periodical). Anderson, May. Felt, Louie. Periodicals. Primary Association. Religious education. Utah. 1880-1940. *80*
China. Chu Teh. Communism. Smedley, Agnes. Sorge, Richard. 1893-1950. *360*
—. Maoism. Strong, Anna Louise. USSR. 1919-70. *324*
Chinatowns. California (San Francisco). Chinese Americans. Public health. Racism. 1870-1970. *1078*
—. Tourism. ca 1880-1940. *1634*
Chinese. British Columbia. Immigration. Japanese. Suffrage. 1935-49. *1725*
—. California. Constitutions, State. Federal Regulation. Labor reform. Workingmen's Party of California. 1877-82. *1358*
—. Immigration. Labor Unions and Organizations. Powderly, Terence V. 1897-1902. *1052*
Chinese Americans. Anti-Catholicism. Nativism. Pacific Northwest. Racism. ca 1840-1945. *11*

Chinese Americans

—. California. Immigration. Nativism. *Sacramento Union* (newspaper). 1850-82. *12*
—. California (San Francisco). Chinatowns. Public health. Racism. 1870-1970. *1078*
—. California (San Francisco). Law. Negroes. Political Leadership. Racism. 1865-75. *1184*
—. Discrimination. Economic Conditions. Japanese Americans. Nativism. Social Status. 1840's-1978. *83*
Chinese Canadians. Alberta. Japanese Canadians. Racism. 1920-50. *1657*
—. British Columbia. Canada. Japanese Canadians. Military Service. World War II. 1939-45. *2647*
Chinese Exclusion Act (US, 1882). Argell, James B. Congress. Diplomacy. Immigration. 1876-82. *947*
Chipman, George. Editors and Editing. *Grain Growers Guide* (periodical). Manitoba (Winnipeg). Reform. Social movements. 1905-30. *1637*
Chipman, Miner. California (San Francisco). Chamber of Commerce Law and Order Committee. Labor disputes. 1915-19. *2233*
Chippewa Lumber and Boom Company. Deitz, John F. Individualism. Weyerhaeuser, Frederick. Wisconsin (Cameron Dam). 1900-24. *1967*
Chiropractic. Attitudes. Cults. Medicine (practice of). Science. 1850's-1970's. *229*
—. Physicians. 1885-1980. *1454*
Cholera. City Government. Hospitals. Massachusetts (Springfield). Sanitation. 1865-70. *1471*
—. Epidemics. Missouri (St. Louis). Public Health. 1849-67. *862*
—. Howard Association. Louisiana (New Orleans). Philanthropy. Public health. Yellow fever. 1837-78. *235*
Christian Anti-Slavery Convention. Abolition Movement. Old Northwest. 1830-60. *704*
Christian Catholic Church. Dowie, John Alexander. Evangelism. Illinois (Zion). 1888-1907. *1512*
Christian Life Commission. Baptists, Southern. 1907-79. *1602*
"Christian Physiology". Alcott, William A. Health reform. ca 1829-60. *903*
Christian Science. Eddy, Mary Baker. Political power. Women. 1879-99. *999*
Christian Socialism. *Alliance-Independent* (newspaper). Gibson, George Howard. Nebraska. Populism. *Wealth Makers* (newspaper). 1893-96. *1397*
Christianity *See also* Catholic Church; Councils and Synods; Missions and Missionaries; Protestantism; Theology.
—. Abolition Movement. Douglass, Frederick. 1830's-60's. *778*
—. Abolition Movement. Enlightenment. Morality. Nationalism. Phillips, Wendell. 1830-84. *716*
—. Antislavery sentiments. Civil War. Stowe, Harriet Beecher. ca 1850-80. *673*
—. Antiwar Sentiment. Public Opinion. World War I. 1898-1918. *1889*
—. Black Muslims. Millenarianism. 1920-79. *1585*
—. Bliss, William D. P. Leftism. Social Gospel. 1876-1926. *20*
—. Boycotts. Elementary Education. Jews. New York City. Religion in the Public Schools. 1905-06. *2298*
—. Bullard, Isaac. Vermont Pilgrims ("Mummyjums"). 1817-24. *928*
—. Bureau of Indian Affairs. Indian-White Relations. Iowa. Schools. Winnebago Indians. 1834-48. *850*
—. Bushnell, Horace. Economic conditions. Gladden, Washington. Politics. Social gospel. Youth. 1836-1918. *995*
—. Canada. Fiction. Labor. Social gospel. 1890's. *1354*
—. Canada. Missions and Missionaries. Sex roles. Women. 1815-99. *1490*
—. Cherokee Indians. Indian-White Relations. Missions and Missionaries. Property. Social Change. Women. 19c. *107*
—. Church and Social Problems. Labor Unions and Organizations. Socialism. 1880-1913. *2175*
—. Civil rights. Equality. Negroes. 19c-20c. *126*
—. Civil Rights. King, Martin Luther, Jr. Transcendentalism. 1840's-50's. 1950's-60's. *2815*

—. Class Struggle. *Los Angeles Times*. McNamara case. Progressivism. Radicals and Radicalism. Steffens, Lincoln. 1908-12. *2083*
—. Communes. Harmony Society. Pennsylvania (Economy). Pittman, Clara. Socialist Laws (Germany, 1878). 1878-79. *1499*
—. Conscientious objectors. Pacifism. Thomas, Norman. World War I. 1915-18. *2136*
—. Corporations. Education, Finance. Higher education. Social Darwinism. 1860-1930. *206*
—. Education. Freedmen. Presbyterians. 1872-1900. *1272*
—. Grimké, Sarah Moore. Nature. Paul, Saint. Social organization. Women. 1c. 1830's. *807*
—. History. Religious liberty. Rhode Island. Williams, Roger. 17c. *514*
—. Industrial Relations. Massachusetts (Lawrence). Scudder, Vida Dutton. Women. 1912. *2196*
—. Jesus People. Youth Movements. 1960's. *2695*
—. Longshoremen. Oxford Group movement. Strikes. Washington (Seattle). 1921-34. *2604*
—. Muste, Abraham J. Niebuhr, Reinhold. Pacifism. Political Theory. Thomas, Norman. 1914-38. *1668*
—. Presbyterian Church. Strong, William. Supreme Court. 1864-80. *1497*
—. Slavery. Social Organization. 1740-76. *476*
Christology. Abolition Movement. Negroes. New York. Ward, Samuel Ringgold. 1839-51. *618*
Chu Teh. China. Communism. Smedley, Agnes. Sorge, Richard. 1893-1950. *360*
Church and Social Problems. Attitudes. Baptists. Furman, Richard. Slavery. 1807-23. *695*
—. Black power. Economic Aid. Episcopal Church, Protestant. General Convention Special Program. Self-determination. 1963-75. *2850*
—. Christianity. Labor Unions and Organizations. Socialism. 1880-1913. *2175*
—. Clergy. Protestant Churches. Reform. 1960's-70's. *2748*
Church and State *See also* Religion in the Public Schools; Religious Liberty.
—. Baptists. Massachusetts. 1630-60. *510*
—. Baptists. Virginia. 1775-1810. *594*
—. Bennett Law (Wisconsin, 1890). Compulsory Education. Wisconsin. 1890. *1417*
—. Berrigan, Daniel. Berrigan, Philip. Catholic Church. Leftism. Murray, John Courtney. 1950's-70's. *1605*
—. Catholic Church. Compulsory education. Michigan. Politics. 1920-25. *2348*
—. Catholic Church. French language. Langevin, Adélard. Manitoba. Politics. Private schools. 1890-1916. *1410*
—. Catholic Church. Provincial Government. Public Charities Act (Canada, 1921). Quebec. Recessions. 1921-26. *1699*
—. Cults, religious. 1970's. *2787*
—. Education. Great Britain. India. Secularization. 19c. *198*
—. Government, Resistance to. Jehovah's Witnesses. Persecution. Theology. 1870's-1960's. *136*
Church Councils. *See* Councils and Synods.
Church of England *See also* Puritans.
—. Associates of Dr. Bray. Bray, Thomas. Education. Missions and Missionaries. Negroes. 1717-77. *500*
—. Charities. City government. Poor. South Carolina (Charleston; St. Phillip's Parish). 1712-75. *536*
Church of God. Assemblies of God. Civil rights movement. Periodicals. Presbyterian Church, Southern. South. 1950's-60's. *2804*
Church Schools *See also* Religious Education.
—. Alberta (Linden). Courts. Mennonites. Religious Liberty. 1977-78. *2780*
—. Catholic Church. Congress. Federal aid to education. Roosevelt, Eleanor. Spellman, Francis J. 1949-50. *2669*
—. Catholic Church. French language. Langevin, Louis Philippe Adélard. Laurier, Wilfrid. Liberal Party. Prairie Provinces. Religion in the Public Schools. 1890-1915. *185*
—. Catholic Church. Glennon, John J. Missouri (St. Louis). Ritter, Joseph E. School Integration. 1935-47. *1850*
—. Catholic Church. Manitoba. McCarthy, D'Alton. Provincial legislatures. 1870-90. *1429*
—. Colleges and universities, black. Negroes. Tennessee. 1865-1920. *2307*
Churches. Baptists, Southern. Education. Racism. Reconstruction. 1865-76. *1267*

—. California (San Francisco). Civil rights. Negroes. Pressure groups. 1860's. *1221*
Churchill, Winston (1871-1947). Authors. New Hampshire. Progressivism. ca 1900-47. *292*
—. Bass, Robert P. Boston and Maine Railroad. New Hampshire. Progressivism. Republican Party. 1890-1912. *1868*
Cigar industry. Industrial Workers of the World. Pennsylvania (McKees Rocks, Pittsburgh). Pressed Steel Car Company. Steel Industry. Strikes. 1909-13. *2235*
Cincinnati Better Housing League. Housing. Ohio. Race relations. 1916-39. *1573*
Cincinnati College of Medicine and Surgery. Medical Education. Ohio. Women. 1875-1910. *966*
Cincinnati Colored School system. Discrimination, Educational. Economic Conditions. Negroes. Ohio. Social Change. 19c. *832*
Cincinnati School Board. Alternative schools. Ohio. 1972-79. *2973*
Cincinnati Union Bethel. Jews. Ohio. Settlement houses. 1838-1903. *225*
Cities *See also* terms beginning with the word city and the word urban; names of cities and towns by state; Chinatowns; Ghettos; Housing; Metropolitan Areas; Neighborhoods; Sociology; Suburbs.
—. Agricultural Production. Country Life Movement. Educational Reform. Rural Schools. 1900-20. *2302*
—. Air pollution. Energy. Industry. Legislation. 1880-1920. *38*
—. American Medical Association. Hygiene. Public Health. 1820-80. *879*
—. Attitudes. Capitalism. Howells, William Dean. 1860-1900. *979*
—. Bacteriology. Canada. Public Health. 1900-30. *1644*
—. Barnett, Samuel Augustus. Education. Great Britain. Poor. Progressivism. 1880's-1913. *2294*
—. Behavior. Censorship. Social Psychology. 1960's-70's. *2788*
—. Citizen Lobbies. Consumers. Environment. Noise pollution. Reform. 1893-1932. *1684*
—. Civil disturbances. Negroes. Political Participation. Social change. 1960's-70's. *2798*
—. Civil Engineering. Political reform. Pollution. 1840-1920. *94*
—. Civil rights movement. Federal government. Local Government. Negroes. 1933-70. *1686*
—. Community organizations. Great Britain. Social problems. 1960's-70's. *2746*
—. Congregationalism. Gladden, Washington. Ohio (Columbus). Reform. Social gospel. 1850's-1914. *396*
—. Criminal Law. Poverty. 1780-1840. *892*
—. Democracy. Howe, Frederic C. Liberalism. Progressivism. ca 1890-1940. *2013*
—. Educational Reform. Negroes. Public Schools. South. Teachers. 1865-90. *1238*
—. Ethnicity. Negroes. Race Relations. Social organization. Valentine, Charles. 1865-1975. *1697*
—. Family. Morality. Progressivism. Recreation. Reform. Socialization. 1890-1920. *1990*
—. Georgia (Atlanta). Illinois (Chicago). New Jersey (Newark). Water supply. 1860-1923. *32*
—. Illinois (Chicago). Playgrounds. Progressivism. 1894-1917. *2027*
—. Merton, Thomas. Nonviolence. Reform. Social criticism. 1960's. *2737*
—. Morality. Public baths. Public health. 1880-1910. *1455*
—. Neighborhoods. Public Lands. Trust for Public Land. 1975-80. *2756*
—. New York. Philanthropy. Social problems. 1830-60. *878*
—. New York City. Pollution. Public Health. Reform. Refuse disposal. Waring, George E., Jr. 1880-1917. *69*
—. Noise pollution. Progressivism. Reform. 1900-30. *1683*
—. North. School Integration. South. 1954-77. *2830*
—. Politics. Volunteerism. Women. 1820-1978. *34*
—. Public Health. Technology. Wastewater. Water Supply. 1850-1930. 1900H. *99*
—. Reform. Sanitation. Women. 1880-1917. *1975*
Citizen Lobbies *See also* Community Participation in Politics.
—. Canada. Consumers' Association of Canada. Public policy. 1947-77. *1587*

Citizen Lobbies / SUBJECT INDEX / Civil Rights

—. Cities. Consumers. Environment. Noise pollution. Reform. 1893-1932. *1684*
—. Conscription, Military. Periodicals. Political Protest. Protestant Churches. 1940-59. *1570*
Citizenship *See also* Naturalization; Patriotism; Suffrage.
—. Attitudes. Canada. Japanese. USA. World War II. 1941-58. *1730*
—. Authority. Constitutional Amendments (13th, 14th, 15th). Federal government. Freedmen. Reconstruction. 1865-70. *1132*
—. Cherokee Indians. Indians. South. 1817-29. *598*
—. Civil Rights. Crook, George. Indians (agencies). Political Corruption. Whites. 1870's-80's. *993*
—. Constitutional Amendments (14th). Indians. Law. ca 1776-1934. *131*
—. Coolidge, Calvin. Indian Citizenship Act (US, 1924). Political Reform. 1924. *2446*
—. Courts. Mexican Americans. Nationality. Race. 1846-97. *135*
Citrus industry. Abolition Movement. Artifacts. California. Indians (agencies). Rust, Horatio Nelson. 1850's-1906. *276*
City Government *See also* Cities; City Politics; Public Administration.
—. Affirmative action. Discrimination, employment. Negroes. Ohio (Cincinnati). 1963-67. *2888*
—. Air pollution. Indiana (Gary). Reform. US Steel Corporation. 1956-73. *2723*
—. Alden, Augustus E. Brownlow, William G. Carpetbaggers. Education. Public welfare. Reconstruction. Republican Party. Tennessee (Nashville). 1865-69. *1049*
—. Alexander, George. California (Los Angeles). Progressivism. Reform. ca 1909-13. *2070*
—. Bengough, John Wilson. *Grip* (periodical). Ontario (Toronto). Political Reform. Protestantism. 1873-1910. *370*
—. Bingham, Robert Worth. Kentucky (Louisville). Progressivism. Reform. 1905-10. *1926*
—. Boosterism. California (Los Angeles). Journalism. Progressivism. Willard, Charles Dwight. 1888-1914. *319*
—. California (San Francisco). Crime and Criminals. Progressivism. Prostitution. 1910-14. *2085*
—. Canada. Depressions. Public Welfare. ca 1930-40. *1695*
—. Charities. Church of England. Poor. South Carolina (Charleston; St. Phillip's Parish). 1712-75. *536*
—. Charities. New York City. Reform. Subsidies. 1870-98. *1463*
—. Cholera. Hospitals. Massachusetts (Springfield). Sanitation. 1865-70. *1471*
—. Civil rights movement. Florida. Negroes. Public services. 1960-76. *2814*
—. Construction. Maryland (Baltimore). Schools. Urban reform. 1870-1900. *1402*
—. Editorials. Franklin, James. Freedom of the Press. Inoculation. Massachusetts (Boston). *New England Courant* (newspaper). Smallpox. 1721. *535*
—. Elites. Human Development Corporation. Missouri (St. Louis). Negroes. Poor. War on Poverty. 1964-75. *2935*
—. Ellis, George E. Michigan (Grand Rapids). Progressivism. 1894-1921. *2106*
—. Fisher, Walter L. Illinois (Chicago). Reform. 1880-1910. *347*
—. Health. New York City. Progressivism. Public baths. 1890-1915. *2121*
—. Humanitarianism. New York City. 1790-1860. *876*
—. Jones, Samuel Milton. Ohio (Toledo). Reform. 1850's-1904. *280*
—. Louisiana (New Orleans). School Integration. 1952-61. *2679*
—. Maryland (Baltimore). Negroes. Political protest. Public schools. 1865-1900. *1271*
—. Maryland (Baltimore). Negroes. Republican Party. 1890-1931. *1593*
—. Medicine. Reform. Refuse disposal. Sanitation. Technology. Wisconsin (Milwaukee). 1867-1911. *1466*
—. Missouri (St. Louis). Political Reform. Progressivism. 1893-1904. *2199*
—. Municipal League of Seattle. Progressivism. Reform. Washington (Seattle). 1910-20. *2045*
—. Ohio (Cincinnati). Public health. ca 1800-50. *891*
—. Ontario (Toronto). Progressivism. Wickett, Samuel Morley. 1900-15. *1703*

—. Political attitudes. Reform. Texas (Beaumont). 1902-09. *1977*
—. Reconstruction. Republican Party. South. 1865-75. *1068*
City life. Baseball. Business. Illinois (Chicago). Social change. Values. 1865-70. *1001*
—. Environmentalism. Law. Pennsylvania (Philadelphia). 1750-84. *496*
City Planning *See also* Housing; Social Surveys.
—. Appalachia. Regional development. Tennessee, eastern. Virginia, southwestern. 1890-1929. *1710*
—. Burnham, Daniel Hudson. Illinois (Chicago). Moody, Walter D. (*Wacker's Manual of the Plan of Chicago*). Progressivism. Publicity. Reform. 1909-11. *2071*
—. Communes. Harmony Society. Indiana (New Harmony). Pennsylvania (Economy, Harmony). Social customs. 1820's-1905. *919*
—. Diseases. Sanitation. 1840-90. *245*
—. Garden cities. New Jersey. Radburn (settlement). Suburbs. 1927-79. *1532*
—. Great Britain. 1845-1974. *92*
—. Marsh, Benjamin C. National Conference on City Planning. Poor. Population. 1900-17. *1987*
—. Oregon (Portland). World War II. 1940-45. *2616*
City Politics *See also* City Government; Community Participation in Politics; Minorities in Politics.
—. Anglophobia. Censorship. Illinois (Chicago). Libraries. Public Schools. Thompson, William Hale. 1927. *2454*
—. Buckley, Christopher A. California (San Francisco). Political Reform. Progressivism. 1890's. *1892*
—. California (San Francisco). Catholic Church. Irish Americans. Progressivism. Yorke, Peter C. 1900's. *2114*
—. Civil rights. LaGuardia, Fiorello. Liberalism. New York City. Powell, Adam Clayton, Jr. 1941-43. *2619*
—. Community Action Programs. Decisionmaking. Minorities. Rhode Island (Providence). 1965-69. *2940*
—. Draper, Andrew Sloan. Educational Reform. Ohio (Cleveland). 1892-94. *1423*
—. Elections, municipal. Knights of Labor. Negroes. Political Reform. Virginia (Richmond). 1886-88. *1303*
—. Fagan, Mark. New Jersey (Jersey City). Progressivism. 1896-1907. *2279*
—. Freedom of speech. Industrial Workers of the World. Iowa (Sioux City). Short, Wallace. 1918-24. *2134*
—. Georgia (Atlanta). Jackson, Maynard. Negroes. Political Leadership. 1965-77. *2847*
—. Illinois (Canton). Prohibition. Socialist Party. Whalen, Homer. 1911-20. *2093*
—. Maryland (Baltimore). Progressivism. 1895-1911. *1920*
—. New York City. Public Health. Social policy. Tuberculosis. 1889-1900. *1941*
—. Ontario (Ottawa). Public Health. Reform. Typhoid fever. 1911-12. *1635*
—. Pennsylvania (Lancaster). Urban reform. 1921-80. *2377*
Civic Unity Committee. Defense industries. Japanese Americans. Negroes. Race relations. Washington (Seattle). World War II. 1940-45. *2624*
Civil Disobedience. King, Martin Luther, Jr. Nonviolence. Race relations. 1954-68. *2891*
Civil Disturbances *See also* Revolution; Riots.
—. Cities. Negroes. Political Participation. Social change. 1960's-70's. *2798*
—. Conscription, Military. Law Enforcement. 1963-76. *2725*
—. Farmers. Regulators. South Carolina. 1730-80. *490*
Civil Engineering *See also* Highway Engineering; Irrigation; Water Supply.
—. Cities. Political reform. Pollution. 1840-1920. *94*
Civil Liberty. *See* Civil Rights.
Civil Rights *See also* Academic Freedom; Equal Rights Amendment; Freedom of Assembly; Freedom of Speech; Freedom of the Press; Human Rights; Religious Liberty.
—. Abernathy, Ralph. Alabama (Birmingham). Demonstrations. King, Martin Luther, Jr. Shuttlesworth, Fred L. 1956-79. *2809*
—. Academic freedom. American Association of University Professors. Tenure. 1915-79. *1733*
—. Adoption. Baker, Josephine. Entertainers. Negroes. World War II. 1940-75. *358*
—. Affirmative action. Pluralism. Supreme Court. 1970-80. *2779*

—. Alabama. Democratic Party. Folsom, James E. Negroes. State Government. Women. 1947-58. *2668*
—. Alabama (Birmingham). King, Martin Luther, Jr. Negroes. Nonviolence. Political Protest. 1962. *2843*
—. Alabama (Lowndes County). Black Power. Political Protest. 1965-75. *2853*
—. Alabama (Selma). Collins, LeRoy. Community Relations Service. Demonstrations. Florida. 1965-68. *2897*
—. Allin, John M. Clergy. Episcopal Church, Protestant. Mississippi. Political Attitudes. 1964-73. *2795*
—. American Civil Liberties Union. Baldwin, Roger (recollections). 1906-19. *279*
—. American Civil Liberties Union. Kentucky (Bell County, London). Miners. Trials. 1932-38. *2601*
—. American Missionary Association. Education. Florida. Freedmen. 1864-74. *1245*
—. American Moral Reform Society. Maryland (Baltimore). Negroes (free). Watkins, William. 1801-58. *339*
—. American Revolution. Constitutional Law. Ideology. 1776-1976. *134*
—. Americans for Democratic Action. Politics. 1948. *2673*
—. Antiwar Sentiment. Kennedy, Jane. Oral history. Political Protest. Vietnam War. Women. 1964-77. *2724*
—. Arizona. Bai-a-lil-le (medicine man). Courts. Education. Fort Huachuca. Indian Rights Association. Navajo Indians. Utah, southeastern. 1906-09. *2043*
—. Attitudes. Declaration of Independence. Fourth of July. Jefferson, Thomas. Negroes. 1776. 1800-50. *724*
—. Attitudes. Johnson, Lyndon B. Negroes. 1930's-68. *1531*
—. Baker, Ray Stannard. DuBois, W. E. B. Liberalism. Negroes. Wilmer, Cary Breckenridge (interview). 1900-10. *2110*
—. Black Power. Historiography. South. 1954-72. *1542*
—. Burger, Warren E. Supreme Court. 1975-78. *2775*
—. Burger, Warren E. Supreme Court. ca 1970-75. *2790*
—. Business. Populism. Rhetoric. 1870-1900. *1370*
—. California (San Francisco). Churches. Negroes. Pressure groups. 1860's. *1221*
—. Canada. Feminism. Government. Great Britain. USA. 1850-20c. *79*
—. Canada. Law. Mexico. USA. Violence. 18c-1974. *119*
—. Carpetbaggers. Constitutional conventions, state. Industrialization. Reconstruction. South. 1867-69. *1021*
—. Catto, Octavius V. Militancy. Pennsylvania (Philadelphia). 1861-71. *440*
—. Chafee, Zechariah, Jr. Freedom of speech. 1919-57. *1729*
—. Christianity. Equality. Negroes. 19c-20c. *126*
—. Christianity. King, Martin Luther, Jr. Transcendentalism. 1840's-50's. 1950's-60's. *2815*
—. Citizenship. Crook, George. Indians (agencies). Political Corruption. Whites. 1870's-80's. *993*
—. City Politics. LaGuardia, Fiorello. Liberalism. New York City. Powell, Adam Clayton, Jr. 1941-43. *2619*
—. Civil War. Constitutional Amendments (14th, 15th). Slavery. Supreme Court. Woman Suffrage. 1863-75. *1106*
—. Civil War. Emancipation Proclamation. Lincoln, Abraham. 1854-63. *1230*
—. Clark, Peter Humphries. Negroes. Ohio (Cincinnati). Politics. 1880's-1925. *350*
—. Cold War. Detention. Federal Bureau of Investigation. National security. Truman, Harry S. (administration). 1945-52. *2685*
—. Columbus *Enquirer-Sun* (newspaper). Georgia. Harris, Julian LaRose. Journalism. 1920's. *2439*
—. Communist Party. Economic conditions. Negroes. New York City (Harlem). Political Protest. 1930's. *2563*
—. Congress. Democratic Party. Kennedy, John F. 1960-63. *2840*
—. Congress. Democratic Party. Legislation. Partisanship. Regionalism. Republican Party. 1963-72. *2803*
—. Congress. Demonstrations. Legislation. Public opinion. 1957-77. *2813*

Civil Rights

—. Congress. Discrimination, employment. Fair Employment Practices Committee. Roosevelt, Franklin D. (administration). World War II. 1941-46. *2640*
—. Congress. Negroes. Truman, Harry S. 1949-50. *2687*
—. Constitutional Amendments (1st). Liberalism. Political Attitudes. 1954-74. *2768*
—. Constitutional Amendments (13th, 14th, 15th). Freedmen. Politics. Reconstruction. 1865-77. *1188*
—. Constitutional Amendments (14th). *Gitlow* v. *New York* (US, 1925). Sanford, Edward Terry. Supreme Court. ca 1890-1930. *2399*
—. Constitutional Amendments (14th). Judicial review. Supreme Court. 19c-20c. *144*
—. Constitutional Amendments (14th). Reconstruction. 1865-68. *1109*
—. Constitutional Law. Douglas, William O. Judicial process. Liberalism. Supreme Court. 1928-77. *1715*
—. Constitutions. 1930-50. *1598*
—. Constitutions. Migration, internal. Supreme Court. 1780's-1977. *138*
—. Democratic Party. Elections (presidential). South Carolina. 1948-72. *1630*
—. Demonstrations. Desegregation. Florida (Tampa). Fort, Clarence. Lane, Julian. Negroes. 1960. *2902*
—. Demonstrations. Negroes. Oklahoma (Oklahoma City). Restaurants. 1958-64. *2835*
—. Discrimination. Equality. Negroes. Political Attitudes. Reconstruction. Texas. 1865-70. *1200*
—. Duke University Medical Center. Harvey, Oliver. Labor Unions and Organizations. North Carolina (Durham). 1930's-70's. *2938*
—. Ebenezer Baptist Church. Georgia (Atlanta). King, Martin Luther, Jr. (tribute). 1968. 1977. *2842*
—. Economic conditions. Income. Public Policy. 1948-75. *2861*
—. Economic Conditions. Negroes. 1960's-70's. *2829*
—. Economic Research and Action Project. Feminism. National Organization for Women. Student Nonviolent Coordinating Committee. 1960's. *2906*
—. Editors and Editing. Fortune, Timothy Thomas. Negroes. 1881-1928. *95*
—. Employment. Federal Government. Public Policy. State Government. 20c. *1572*
—. Equality. Judicial Process. Liberty. 1960-79. *2772*
—. Executive Power. Kennedy, John F. Legislation. 1961-64. *2858*
—. Federal Bureau of Investigation. Roosevelt, Franklin D. 1936-80. *1716*
—. Federal Policy. Interest Groups. Populism. Private sector. Racism. Wallace, George C. 1960's. *2899*
—. Five Civilized Tribes. Indian-White Relations. 18c-20c. *1581*
—. Florida (Kissimmee). Friends of the Florida Seminoles. Indians. Seminole Indians. Tiger, Tom. 1898-99. *1100*
—. Freedmen. Louisiana Purchase. Treaty of Cession (1804). 1797-1804. *590*
—. Georgia. Methodist Church. Tilly, Dorothy. 1900's-70. *438*
—. Governors. Johnson, Andrew. Negroes. Tennessee. 1862-65. *972*
—. Hancock, George B. Jackson, Luther P. Negroes. Virginia. Young, Plummer B. 1930-45. *1583*
—. Harlan, John Marshall. Supreme Court. 1877-1911. *1122*
—. Howard University. Nabrit, James Madison, Jr. Negroes. 1927-60. *439*
—. Human rights. Negroes. Political Protest. 1954-78. *2774*
—. Indian Civil Rights Act (US, 1968). Natural law. Pueblo Indians. *Santa Clara Pueblo* v. *Martinez* (US, 1977). Tribal government. 1939-77. *2789*
—. Institutions. Negroes. Organizations. Sit-ins. South. 1960. *2868*
—. Johnson, Lyndon B. Negro Suffrage. Political Reform. 1960's. *2855*
—. Johnson, Lyndon B. (administration). Negroes. 1963-69. *2866*
—. Kentucky. Negroes. Newspapers. Reconstruction. 1866-72. *1176*
—. King, Martin Luther, Jr. Negroes. Nonviolence. 1950's-68. *2826*
—. King, Martin Luther, Jr. Political Protest. 1955-68. *2854*
—. King, Martin Luther, Jr. ("Letter from Birmingham Jail"). Literature. Rhetoric. 1963. *2807*
—. Labor Unions and Organizations. Mexican Americans. North Central States. Social Organizations. 1900-76. *1659*
—. Leftism. Negroes. Robeson, Paul. Singers. 1898-1976. *379*
—. Legislation. Population. Race Relations. Riots. Tennessee (Memphis). 1865-66. *1209*
—. Liberals. Minorities in Politics. New York City. 1963-70's. *2728*
—. Massachusetts (Boston). Roberts, Sarah C. *Sarah C. Roberts* v. *City of Boston* (Massachusetts, 1850). School Integration. 1849-50. 1950's. *834*
—. Militancy. Negroes. Religion. 1960's-70's. *2844*
—. Minorities. Supreme Court. 1886-1972. *73*
—. Nebraska (Omaha). Negroes. Quality of life. Social services. Urban League. World War II. 1928-50. *2639*
—. Negroes. Newspapers. 1946-82. *2874*
—. Negroes. Pemberton, Caroline Hollingsworth. Pennsylvania (Philadelphia). Socialist Party. 1896-1903. *1158*
—. Negroes. Political Protest. Press. 1950-76. *2875*
—. Negroes. Politics. Racism. 1940's. *1622*
—. Negroes. Republican Party. Voting and Voting Behavior. 1846-69. *597*
—. Negroes. Sociology. South. Work, Monroe Nathan. 1900-45. *388*
—. Negroes. Turner, James Milton. 1865-1915. *313*
—. New federalism. Prisoners. Supreme courts, state. 1969-80. *2773*
—. Public Opinion. Racism. 1820-1975. *147*
—. Race Relations. 1960-70's. *2836*
—. Racism. Spooner, John Coit. 1897-1907. *2156*
—. Red scare. Smith, Alfred E. 1919-20. *2133*
—. Segregation. Supreme Court. Vinson, Frederick M. 1946-53. *2671*
Civil Rights Act (US, 1866). Constitutional Amendments (14th, 15th). Negroes. Reconstruction. Republican Party. States' rights. ca 1865-77. *953*
Civil Rights Act (US, 1875). Constitutional Amendments (13th, 14th). Federal Government. Negroes. 1875-83. *1113*
—. Law Enforcement. Supreme Court. 1875-83. *1159*
Civil Rights Act (US, 1964). Bilingual education. California. Chacone-Moscone Bilingual Bicultural Education Act (1976). *Lau* v. *Nichols* (US, 1974). Supreme Court. 1965-76. *2966*
—. Democratic Party. Indiana. Primaries (presidential). Wallace, George C. Welsh, Matthew E. 1964. *2900*
—. Florida. School Integration. Supreme Court decisions. 1954-64. *2686*
Civil Rights Act (US, 1964; Title VII). Courts. Discrimination, employment. Equal opportunity. 1964-78. *2932*
Civil Rights Act (US, 1964; Title VIII). Discrimination, Employment. Income. Negroes. Women. 1964-70's. *2839*
Civil rights movement. Alabama. Reporters and Reporting. *Southern Courier* (newspaper). 1965-68. *2873*
—. Alabama (Tuscaloosa). Clergy. Integration. 1976-77. *2796*
—. Assemblies of God. Church of God. Periodicals. Presbyterian Church, Southern. South. 1950's-60's. *2804*
—. Cities. Federal government. Local Government. Negroes. 1933-70. *1686*
—. City Government. Florida. Negroes. Public services. 1960-76. *2814*
—. Employment. Sex roles. Women's Liberation Movement. 1950's-75. *2905*
—. Episcopal Church, Protestant. Race Relations. Theology. 1800-1965. *2849*
—. Freedom Singers. Georgia (Albany; Harlem district). NAACP. Reagon, Bernice Johnson (interview). 1960-77. *2880*
—. Freedom Summers. Sex Discrimination. Women. 1960-65. *2882*
—. Gandhi, Mahatma. King, Martin Luther, Jr. Nonviolence. Political Protest. 1950's-60's. *2878*
—. Gandhi, Mahatma. King, Martin Luther, Jr. Social change. 1959-68. *2822*
—. Illinois (Chicago). Negroes. School integration. 1936. *2523*
—. Integration. Public policy. 1945-76. *1623*
—. Jews. South. 1954-70. *2823*
—. Johnson, Lyndon B. Long, Huey P. Radicals and Radicalism. South. 1920-70. *1706*
—. King, Martin Luther, Jr. Negroes. Social Conditions. 1968-79. *2806*
—. Leftism. Models. Political attitudes. Students. 1960's-70's. *2714*
—. NAACP. Negroes. South Dakota. 1804-1970. *4*
—. Negroes. Nonviolence. Political Protest. 1955-65. *1709*
—. Negroes. Politics. Riots. Tennessee (Columbia). Truman, Harry S. 1946. *2657*
—. Political socialization. Radicals and Radicalism. Student activism. ca 1955-75. *2713*
—. Race Relations. South. Women. 1960's. *2907*
Civil Rights Organizations. Discrimination. Florida (Miami). Louisiana (New Orleans). Murray, Hugh T., Jr. (reminiscences). 1959-60. *2871*
—. King, Martin Luther, Jr. Leadership. Negroes. Southern Christian Leadership Conference. 1957-73. *2828*
Civil Service *See also* Federal Government; Public Administration.
—. Canada. Ideology. Labor Unions and Organizations. Middle Classes. 1918-28. *1820*
—. Conscription, military. Mennonites. World War II. 1930's-45. *2632*
Civil Service Commissioner. Indian Rights Association. Indian-White Relations. Roosevelt, Theodore. Welsh, Herbert. 1889-95. *1011*
Civil War *See also* battles and campaigns by name; Confederate States of America; Reconstruction; Secession; Slavery.
—. Abolition Movement. Bryant, John Howard. Bryant, Julian. Illinois (Bureau County). Lovejoy, Owen. Military Service. Negroes. 1831-65. *607*
—. American Freedmen's Inquiry Commission. Freedmen. Johnson, Andrew. 1863. *1260*
—. American Missionary Association. Education. Missouri. Negroes. 1862-65. *1241*
—. Antislavery sentiments. Christianity. Stowe, Harriet Beecher. ca 1850-80. *673*
—. Antislavery Sentiments. Douglas, H. Ford. Emigration. Military Service. Negroes. 1854-65. *666*
—. Antislavery Sentiments. Episcopal Church, Protestant. Jay, John, II. 1840-65. *773*
—. Antislavery Sentiments. Friends, Society of. Jones, James Parnell. Maine. Military Service. 1850's-64. *320*
—. Armies. Banks, Nathaniel Prentiss. Education. Louisiana. 1863-65. *1218*
—. Armies. Bates, Edward. Negroes. Politics. Wages. 1861-64. *1129*
—. Armies. Freedmen's Bureau. Maryland. Reconstruction. Reform. 1864-68. *1162*
—. Ashley, James M. House of Representatives. Negro Suffrage. Ohio (Toledo). Reconstruction. 1861-62. *1019*
—. Association for Promoting Colored Volunteers. Military Recruitment. Negroes. New York. Race Relations. Union League. 1861-65. *1255*
—. Black capitalism. Davis Bend colony. Eaton, John, Jr. Freedmen. Mississippi. 1862-66. *1249*
—. Butler, Benjamin F. Proslavery Sentiments. 1861-64. *1018*
—. California. Indian-White Relations. Reform. Republican Party. 1860-70. *971*
—. Censorship. Chicago *Times*. Lincoln, Abraham. Newspapers. 1863-64. *1118*
—. Civil Rights. Constitutional Amendments (14th, 15th). Slavery. Supreme Court. Woman Suffrage. 1863-75. *1106*
—. Civil Rights. Emancipation Proclamation. Lincoln, Abraham. 1854-63. *1230*
—. Confiscations. Congress. Constitutional Law. Debates. Reconstruction. 1861-65. *1105*
—. Constitutional Amendments. Fundamentalism. Lincoln, Abraham. National Fast Day. National Reform Association. 1787-1945. *1484*
—. Contraband programs. Fugitive slaves. Louisiana, southern. Military Occupation. 1862-65. *1219*
—. Croxton, John Thomas. Kentucky. Law. Military Service. Republican Party. 1855-74. *392*
—. Elections (presidential). Negroes. Political Participation. Republican Party. 1864. *1224*
—. Emancipation. Ohio. Racism. State Politics. 1863-65. *1182*

Civil War

—. Emancipation Proclamation. Illinois Volunteers. Republican Party. 1862-63. *1087*
—. Emigration. Haiti. Negroes. 1860-64. *1254*
—. Freedmen. Louisiana (New Orleans). Negroes, free. Political Attitudes. Politics. Social Classes. 1860-65. *1275*
—. Historiography. Reconstruction. 1861-77. ca 1950-74. *984*
—. Labor. Mississippi. Negroes. Vicksburg (battle). 1862. *1220*
—. Law. Mississippi. Negroes. Reconstruction. 1857-70. *114*
—. Lincoln, Abraham. Louisiana (New Orleans). Negroes. Reconstruction. Suffrage. 1860-67. *1130*
—. Lincoln, Abraham. Political Theory. Revolution. Slavery. Social change. 1850-65. *1060*
—. Negroes. Political Protest. State Politics. Suffrage. Tennessee. 1864-65. *1144*
—. Negroes. Reconstruction. Slavery. Women. 19c. *331*
—. North. Pacifism. 1864. *946*
Civil War (antecedents). Abolition Movement. Brown, John. Harpers Ferry raid. Sanborn, Franklin Benjamin. 1854-60. *707*
—. Abolition Movement. Garrison, William Lloyd. Ohio. Western Antislavery Society. 1835-61. *650*
—. Abolition Movement. New England. Parker, Theodore. Violence. 1850-60. *635*
—. Abolition Movement. Presbyterian Church. South. Stanton, Robert. 1840-55. *731*
—. Abolitionists. Alcott, Amos Bronson. Phillips, Wendell. Weld, Theodore Dwight. 1830-60. *721*
—. Attitudes. Boundaries. Kansas. Missouri. Slavery. 1854-56. *634*
—. Brown, John. Harpers Ferry raid. North Carolina. Slavery. Social Psychology. 1859-60. *612*
—. Brown, John. Harpers Ferry raid. West Virginia. White, Edward. 1859. *783*
—. Constitutions. Law. Slavery. 1830-60. *763*
—. Greeley, Horace. Reform. Secession. Slavery. 1860-61. *781*
Civil Works Administration. American Federation of Labor. Carmody, John. Labor. New Deal. 1933-34. *2584*
—. Labor. New Deal. 1933-39. *2484*
Civilian Conservation Corps. Army. Military Organization. Negroes. 1933-42. *2528*
—. Economic Conditions. New Deal. Vermont. 1933-42. *2596*
—. Employment. Environment. South Dakota. 1933-42. *2519*
—. Equal opportunity. Negroes. New Deal. 1933-42. *2514*
Civilian Conservation Corps (Indian Divison). Depressions. Indians (reservations). Sioux Indians. South Dakota. 1933-42. *2486*
Civil-Military Relations. Labor. Publicity. War Manpower Commission. Women. World War II. 1942-45. *2650*
Clapp, Elsie Ripley. Education. Homesteading and Homesteaders. New Deal. Roosevelt, Eleanor. West Virginia (Arthurdale). 1933-44. *2477*
Clapp, Hannah Keziah. Educators. Nevada, University of. Woman Suffrage. 1824-1908. *456*
Clark, Peter Humphries. Civil Rights. Negroes. Ohio (Cincinnati). Politics. 1880's-1925. *350*
—. Education. Negroes. Ohio (Cincinnati). Socialism. 1849-81. *332*
Class action suits. Courts. Desegregation. Discrimination, reverse. 1965-76. *2862*
Class conflict. Commission on Industrial Relations. Plug-uglies. Progressive era. Violence. 1890-1920. *1981*
—. Race relations. Segregation. South. 1865-90's. *1280*
—. Rhode Island (Pawtucket). Strikes. Textile Industry. 1790-1824. *822*
Class consciousness. Feminism. Great Britain. Labor Unions and Organizations. USA. Women's Trade Union League. 1890-1925. *2226*
—. NAACP. Negroes. Pennsylvania (Philadelphia). Race. 1930's. *2566*
Class struggle. Bacon's Rebellion. Racism. Slavery. Social control. Virginia. 1660-92. *472*
—. Christianity. *Los Angeles Times*. McNamara case. Progressivism. Radicals and Radicalism. Steffens, Lincoln. 1908-12. *2083*
—. Equality. French language. Intellectuals. Nationalism. Quebec. 1960's-70's. *2693*

SUBJECT INDEX

—. Eugenics. Fisher, Irving. Progressivism. Racism. 1890's-1920. *1869*
—. Labor unions and organizations. South. 1810-1975. *162*
—. Reform. Standard of living. Working class. 1950's-73. *2923*
Clay, Henry (letter). American Colonization Society. 1836. *551*
Clean Air Act (US, 1970). Air pollution. Demography. Energy. Fiscal Policy. State Government. 1970-79. *2719*
Clemens, Gaspar Christopher. Kansas. Socialism. 1885-90's. *959*
Clergy *See also* specific denominations by name.
—. Abolition Movement. Birney, James. Evangelicalism. Smith, Gerrit. Stanton, H. B. Weld, Theodore Dwight. 1820-50. *744*
—. Abolition Movement. Negroes. 1830-60. *653*
—. Alabama (Tuscaloosa). Civil rights movement. Integration. 1976-77. *2796*
—. Allin, John M. Civil rights. Episcopal Church, Protestant. Mississippi. Political Attitudes. 1964-73. *2795*
—. Antiabolition sentiments. Conservatism. Constitutions. Massachusetts (Boston). Missouri (St. Louis). Unitarianism. 1828-57. *751*
—. Anti-Catholicism. Ku Klux Klan. Protestantism. Republican Party. Rhode Island. 1915-32. *2441*
—. Antislavery Sentiments. Congregationalism. Connecticut. South. 1790-95. *631*
—. Antislavery Sentiments. Kentucky. Racism. 1791-1824. *603*
—. Church and Social Problems. Protestant Churches. Reform. 1960's-70's. *2748*
—. Community affairs. Garvey, Marcus. Negroes. New York (Buffalo). Universal Negro Improvement Association. 1830's-1920's. *2458*
—. Episcopal Church, Protestant. Ingraham, Joseph Holt. Novels. Penal reform. Public Schools. Tennessee (Nashville). 1847-51. *584*
—. Equality. Mormons. Negroes. Women. 1860-1979. *91*
—. Lutheran Church (North Carolina Synod). Negroes. 1865-89. *1228*
—. Mather, Cotton. Medicine. *Nishmath-chajim* (concept). 1700-22. *534*
—. Ordination. United Brethren in Christ. Women. 1889. *1489*
Clerical workers. Labor Unions and Organizations. Women's Trade Union League. 1900-30. *1759*
Clinics. Arkansas (Lee County). Cooperatives. Medical care. Negroes. 1960's-70's. *2977*
—. Boston Dispensary. Davis, Michael M. Massachusetts. 1910-20. *2051*
Clyde, Edward M. California (Fresno). Freedom of speech. Industrial Workers of the World. 1911. *2151*
Coady, Moses. Adult education. Antigonish Movement. Capitalism. Cooperatives. Nova Scotia, eastern. 1930-40. *1742*
Coal. Alabama. Kilby, Thomas E. Strikes. United Mine Workers of America. 1890-1929. *2448*
—. Ammons, Elias. Colorado. Federal Government. Strikes. Wilson, Woodrow. 1914. *2228*
Coal, anthracite. Mining. Pennsylvania. Strikes. United Mine Workers of America. 1922-23. *2391*
—. Pinchot, Gifford. Strikes. United Mine Workers of America. 1925-26. *2390*
Coal Mine Health and Safety Act (US, 1969; amended, 1972). Black lung disease. Coal Mines and Mining. Medicine. Strikes, wildcat. United Mine Workers of America. Workmen's Compensation. 1968-72. *2717*
Coal miners. Germer, Adolph. Illinois (Virden). Socialism. Strikes. United Mine Workers of America. 1893-1900. *1291*
—. Labor Unions and Organizations. Strikes. 1881-94. *1284*
Coal Mines and Mining. Alberta. British Columbia. Depressions. Pass Strike of 1932. 1920's-30's. *1811*
—. Alberta (Cardiff, Edmonton). Chaban, Teklia. Labor Unions and Organizations. Ukrainian Canadians. 1914-20's. *469*
—. Black lung disease. Coal Mine Health and Safety Act (US, 1969; amended, 1972). Medicine. Strikes, wildcat. United Mine Workers of America. Workmen's Compensation. 1968-72. *2717*

Cold War

—. British Columbia (Vancouver Island). Canadian Collieries (Dunsmuir) Limited. Labor Unions and Organizations. Strikes. United Mine Workers of America. 1912-14. *2251*
—. Colorado. Industrial Workers of the World. Strikes. 1927. *2411*
—. Colorado. Labor reform. Roche, Josephine. Roosevelt, Franklin D. (administration). Social work. 1886-1976. *1772*
—. Colorado Fuel and Iron Company. Ludlow Massacre. National Guard. Strikes. 1913-14. *2206*
—. Colorado (Las Animas, Huerfano counties). Strikes. United Mine Workers of America. 1904-14. *2273*
—. Convict labor. State Government. Strikes. Tennessee. 1891-93. *1286*
—. Davis, Richard L. Labor Unions and Organizations. Letters-to-the-editor. *National Labor Tribune*. Negroes. United Mine Workers of America. ca 1890-1900. *1139*
—. Debs, Eugene V. Socialist Party. Strikes. West Virginia. 1912-14. *2194*
—. Diaries. Medrick, George. Pennsylvania, western. Strikes. United Mine Workers of America. 1927. *2372*
—. Employment. Mitchell, John. United Mine Workers of America. 1897-1907. *2213*
—. Federal government. Pennsylvania. Roosevelt, Theodore. Strikes. 1902. *2218*
—. Glasscock, William E. Martial law. National Guard. United Mine Workers of America. Violence. West Virginia (Cabin Creek, Paint Creek). 1912-13. *2176*
—. Government. Health and safety regulations. Ohio. 1869-81. *1319*
—. Great Britain. Illinois. Labor Unions and Organizations. Legislation. Lobbying. 1861-72. *1312*
—. Hoadly, George. Ohio (Hocking Valley). Strikes. 1884-85. *1322*
—. Hocking Valley. Lewis, John Llewellyn. Ohio, southeastern. Strikes. United Mine Workers of America. 1927. *2447*
—. Keeney, Frank. United Mine Workers of America. West Virginia. 1916-31. *1755*
—. Kentucky (Bell, Harlan counties). Labor Disputes. Political Corruption. 1920-39. *2489*
—. Knights of Labor. Race Relations. United Mine Workers of America. West Virginia, southern. 1880-94. *1140*
—. Labor Disputes. Mingo War. United Mine Workers of America. Violence. West Virginia (southern). 1919-22. *2389*
—. Labor Unions and Organizations. One Big Union. Saskatchewan. 1907-45. *1782*
—. Labor Unions and Organizations. Racism. Strikes. United Mine Workers of America. 1894-1920. *2272*
—. Labor Unions and Organizations. Texas (Thurber). 1880's-1920's. *2238*
—. Medical care. United Mine Workers of America (Welfare and Retirement Fund). 1946-78. *1747*
—. Negroes. Oregon Improvement Company. Strikebreakers. Washington (King County). 1891. *1265*
—. Ohio (Hocking Valley). Strikebreakers. Violence. 1884-85. *1296*
—. State Government. Strikes. United Mine Workers of America. West Virginia (Paint Creek). 1912-13. *2270*
Coates, Sarah (letters). Lectures. Ohio. Physiology. Women. 1850. *881*
Cobden, Richard. Great Britain. Millenarianism. Nonconformists. Peace movements. 1840-60. *582*
Cocking, Walter D. Georgia. Higher education. Negroes. Talmadge, Eugene. 1937-43. *2620*
—. Georgia, University of. Holley, Joseph Winthrop. Racism. Talmadge, Eugene. 1941. *2643*
Codman, Ernest Amory. Hospitals. Medicine (practice of). 1910-23. *2056*
Coeducation *See also* Education; Women.
—. Homeopathy. Medical Education. Ohio (Cincinnati). Pulte Medical College. 1873-79. *1403*
Cohen, Julius Henry. Eminent domain. Housing. New York. 1920's-30's. *2370*
Coke, Thomas. Asbury, Francis. Methodist Episcopal Church. Slavery. 1780-1816. *624*
Cold War. Civil Rights. Detention. Federal Bureau of Investigation. National security. Truman, Harry S. (administration). 1945-52. *2685*

Coldwater State Public School. Children. Crime and Criminals. Michigan. Protestantism. 1874-96. *1430*

Coldwell, Major J. Canada. Farmer Labor party. Political Leadership. Progressivism. Social Democracy. 1907-32. *471*

Coles, Edward. Antislavery Sentiments. Illinois. Jefferson, Thomas. 1809-68. *689*

Collar Laundry Union. Industrial Relations. Irish Americans. New York (Troy). Women. 1864-69. *1352*

Collective Bargaining *See also* Labor Unions and Organizations; Strikes.
—. France. Great Britain. Labor. 18c-20c. *167*
—. Ontario (Toronto). Organizational Theory. Printing. 19c. *178*

Collectivism. Glass, Carter. Liberals. National Recovery Administration. New Deal. 1933-35. *2533*
—. Intellectuals. National Association of Corporation Schools. Steinmetz, Charles Proteus. Utopias. 1910-17. *1950*

Colleges and Universities *See also* names of individual institutions; Coeducation; Higher Education; Junior Colleges; Students.
—. Adams, Charles P. Grambling State University. Louisiana. Negroes. 1896-1928. *1836*
—. Amateur Athletic Union. Sports. Women. 1890's-1936. *1766*
—. American Missionary Association. Freedmen's Bureau. Mississippi. Negroes. Tougaloo College. 1865-69. *1141*
—. American Revolution. Public Opinion. State Legislatures. 1775-83. *485*
—. Antioch College. Negroes. Ohio (Yellow Springs). Segregation. 1966-69. *2864*
—. Antiwar sentiment. Leftism. Political Protest. 1920-36. *2483*
—. Arkansas Agricultural, Mechanical, and Normal College. Arkansas, University of, Pine Bluff. Black Nationalism. Student activism. 1972-73. *2872*
—. Black Nationalism. South. Student activism. 1890-1972. *1673*
—. Canada. Public policy. Social Sciences. 1920-49. *1576*
—. Catholic University of America. Discrimination. District of Columbia. Negroes. Wesley, Charles H. 1914-48. *2304*
—. Curricula. Education. Individualism. Negroes. 1890-1970's. *1853*
—. Douglass, Mabel Smith. Lobbying. Middle Classes. New Jersey College for Women. Women. 1911-18. *2324*
—. Education. Ideology. Sex roles. Women. 19c-20c. *213*
—. Education, Experimental Methods. Minorities. New York, City University of. 1847-1980. *196*
—. Educational Reform. Industrialization. North Carolina, University of. Social Change. 1850-75. *1406*
—. Educational Reform. Political Protest. West. 1964-74. *2967*
—. Educators. New Jersey. Pennsylvania. Professionalization. 1870-1915. *201*
—. Ellery, William, Jr. Rhode Island (Newport). Stiles, Ezra. 1770. *486*
—. Equal opportunity. Maryland. Negroes. 1908-75. *1860*
—. Evangelicalism. Oberlin College. Ohio. Women. 1835-50. *796*
—. Grinnell College. Iowa. Sex roles. Women. 1884-1917. *221*
—. Illinois Intercollegiate Prohibition Association. Prohibition. Protestantism. 1893-1920. *2059*
—. Intellectuals. Liberalism. Political Attitudes. Socialism. 1880-95. *1072*
—. Intellectuals. Political Protest. Radicals and Radicalism. Students. 1963-77. *2750*
—. Law. School Integration. 19c-20c. *2886*
—. Nebraska, University of. Physical Education and Training. Women. 1879-1923. *220*
—. Negroes. Russwurm, John. 1823-1973. *181*
—. Political Attitudes. Radicals and Radicalism. Students. 1943-70. *1537*

Colleges and universities, black. Church Schools. Negroes. Tennessee. 1865-1920. *2307*
—. Fort Valley State College. Georgia (Peach County). *Hunnicutt et al. v. Burge et al.* (Georgia, 1972). Racism. School Integration. 1972-78. *2800*
—. Negroes. 1854-1978. *195*
—. Negroes. 1890-1974. *1843*
—. Segregation. State Government. Texas. 1876-1947. *1846*

Colleges and Universities (land grant). Agricultural Technology and Research. Alvord, Henry Elijah. 1860's-1904. *429*

Collier, John. Acculturation. American Indian Defense Association. Indians. Religious liberty. 1920-26. *2427*
—. Acculturation. Florida. Indians. North Carolina. Schools. Seminole Indians. 1927-54. *1851*
—. American Indian Federation. Bureau of Indian Affairs. Indians. Jamison, Alice Lee. New Deal. Political activism. 1930's-50's. *354*
—. Americas (North and South). Bureau of Indian Affairs. Indians. Inter-American Institute. 1930's-50's. *1662*
—. Assimilation. Federal Policy. Indian Reorganization Act (US, 1934). 1933-45. *2530*
—. Bureau of Indian Affairs. Indians. New Deal. 1933-45. *2600*
—. Bureau of Indian Affairs. New Deal. Public Administration. Social sciences. 1933-45. *2599*
—. Federal Government. Indians. Liberalism. Roosevelt, Franklin D. (administration). Truman, Harry S. (administration). 1933-53. *1629*

Collier's Weekly. Sinclair, Upton. Socialism. Sumner, William Graham. 1900-04. *1921*

Collins, LeRoy. Alabama (Selma). Civil Rights. Community Relations Service. Demonstrations. Florida. 1965-68. *2897*
—. Arkansas (Little Rock). Courts. Federal Government. Florida. Political Speeches. School integration. 1957. *2688*
—. *Brown* v. *Board of Education* (US, 1954). Florida. State Legislatures. Supreme Court. 1954-61. *2664*

Colonial Government *See also* Imperialism.
—. Adult education. Nova Scotia. ca 1820-35. *843*
—. Arthur, George. Great Britain. Ontario (Upper Canada). Reform. 1837-41. *571*
—. Elites. North Carolina. Regulator movement. Social change. 1760-75. *502*

Colonial policy. Garvey, Marcus. Italy. Pan-Africanism. Universal Negro Improvement Association. USA. 1920-23. *2371*

Colonialism *See also* Imperialism.
—. France. Madagascar. Waller, John L. 1891-95. *1282*

Colonization *See also* Settlement.
—. Abolition Movement. Africa. American Colonization Society. Racism. Republicanism. ca 1815-35. *762*
—. Abolition Movement. American Colonization Society. Cresson, Elliot. Great Britain. Liberia. 1831-33. *609*
—. Abolition Movement. Beecher, Lyman. Presbyterian Church. 1820-50. *768*
—. Africa. American Colonization Society. McDonough, David. Medical Education. Presbyterian Church. Slavery. 1840-50. *710*
—. Africa. Cuffe, Paul. Massachusetts (Boston). Negroes. 1810-15. *728*
—. Africa. Negroes. New Jersey Colonization Society. 1815-48. *745*
—. Africa. Negroes (free). Schools. 1816-33. *837*
—. Africa, West. Black Nationalism. Newspapers. Oklahoma. Sam, Alfred Charles. 1913-14. *2008*
—. African Society. Freedmen. Hopkins, Samuel. Rhode Island (Providence). Sierra Leone. 1789-95. *614*
—. Allen, William G. Attitudes. Exiles. Great Britain. Negroes. New York Central College at McGrawville. 1820-78. *290*
—. American Colonization Society. Georgia. Liberia. Negroes. 1816-60. *705*
—. Attitudes. Kentucky. Slavery. South. 1816-50. *602*
—. Black nationalism. Cuffe, Paul. Friends, Society of. Sierra Leone. 1810's. *694*
—. Emancipation. Lincoln, Abraham. Negroes. 1852-65. *747*
—. Emancipation. Lincoln, Abraham. Negroes. 1861-65. *1138*
—. Emancipation. Mississippi Colonization Society. 1831-60. *685*
—. Garvey, Marcus. Liberia. Negroes. Universal Negro Improvement Association. 1914-24. *2342*
—. Gold Coast. Negroes. Sam, Alfred Charles. 1913-16. *2011*
—. Liberia. Methodist Episcopal Church. Missions and Missionaries. Negroes. Sierra Leone. 1833-48. *641*

—. Negroes. Ohio (Cincinnati). Ontario (Wilberforce). 1829-56. *604*

Colorado *See also* Western States.
—. Adams, Alva B. Progressivism. State Politics. Sweet, William. 1922-24. *2403*
—. Ammons, Elias. Coal. Federal Government. Strikes. Wilson, Woodrow. 1914. *2228*
—. Caryl, Charles W. New Era Union. Progressive Era. Racial thought. Utopias. 1858-1926. *1509*
—. Coal Mines and Mining. Industrial Workers of the World. Strikes. 1927. *2411*
—. Coal Mines and Mining. Labor reform. Roche, Josephine. Roosevelt, Franklin D. (administration). Social work. 1886-1976. *1772*
—. Conservation of natural resources. Individualism. Progressives. 1896-1910. *2028*
—. Equal rights. Negroes. Reconstruction. 1865-67. *1134*
—. Hofstadter, Richard. Populism. Progressive movement. 1890-1910. 1950's. *1375*
—. Indian Wars. Sand Creek Massacre. Soule, Silas S. 1859-65. *44*
—. Newspapers. Public opinion. Woman suffrage. 1870's. *1099*
—. Populism. Progressivism. 1900. *1376*

Colorado (Aspen). Educational Reform. Higher Education. Paepcke, Walter. 1949-51. *2666*

Colorado (Boulder). Feminism. Women's Christian Temperance Union. 1881-1967. *232*

Colorado Cooperative Company. Communitarianism. Home Employment Cooperative Company. Labor Exchange. Politics. Pragmatism. 1890-1905. *1508*

Colorado (Denver). Beth Ha Medrosh Hagodol synagogue. Judaism. Kauvar, Charles E. H. Progressivism. 1902-71. *428*
—. Hardin, William J. Negroes. 1863-73. *1135*
—. Juvenile Courts. Lindsey, Benjamin Barr. 1901-20's. *1902*
—. Prohibition. Wickersham Committee (1931). 1907-33. *2381*

Colorado Fuel and Iron Company. Coal Mines and Mining. Ludlow Massacre. National Guard. Strikes. 1913-14. *2206*

Colorado (Las Animas, Huerfano counties). Coal Mines and Mining. Strikes. United Mine Workers of America. 1904-14. *2273*

Colorado, northeastern. Hardin, William J. Kansas, northeastern. Langston, Charles H. Negro suffrage. 1865-67. *1133*

Colorado River. Boulder Canyon Project. Hoover Dam. Industrial Workers of the World. Nevada. Strikes. 1931. *2433*

Colored Farmers' Alliance. Agricultural Reform. Arkansas. Cotton. Humphrey, R. M. Strikes. 1891. *1171*
—. Farmers. Negroes. South. ca 1886-95. *1172*
—. Humphrey, R. M. Labor Unions and Organizations. Negroes. South. Strikes. 1876-91. *1150*
—. Race Relations. Tennessee. 1888-91. *1164*

Colored National Labor Union. Florida. Labor Unions and Organizations. National Union of Negro Labor. Negroes. Race Relations. Reconstruction. 1865-75. *1259*

Columbia Conserve Company. Hapgood, William P. Indiana (Indianapolis). Industrial Relations. 1917-43. *1789*

Columbia University College of Pharmacy. Americas (North and South). Medicine. Pharmacy. Rusby, Henry Hurd. Scientific Expeditions. ca 1880-1930. *286*

Columbia University (Medical School). Medical education. New York City. Professionalization. 1760's. *488*

Columbians, Inc. Georgia (Atlanta). Patriotism. Racism. 1946-47. *2665*

Columbus *Enquirer-Sun* (newspaper). Civil Rights. Georgia. Harris, Julian LaRose. Journalism. 1920's. *2439*
—. Georgia, University of. Harris, Julian LaRose. Student activism. 1920-29. *2416*

Comic strips. *Amos 'n' Andy* (program). Boycotts. Negroes. Radio. Stereotypes. 1930's. *2588*

Comintern (7th Congress). Communist Party. New Deal. Socialist Party. 1935-39. *2547*

Commercials *See also* Advertising.
—. Fashion. Hygiene. Television. Women. Women's Liberation Movement. 1970's. *2921*

Commission on Industrial Accidents. Industry. Provincial Government. Quebec. Workmen's Compensation. 1890-1978. *1584*

Commission on Industrial Relations. Class conflict. Plug-uglies. Progressive era. Violence. 1890-1920. *1981*

Commission on the Status and Role of Women in the United Methodist Church. Feminism. Methodism. Social Organizations. 1869-1974. *72*

Committee of Fifteen. Local Politics. New York City. Tammany Hall. 1900-01. *1934*

Committee on Participation of Negroes in the National Defense Program. Army. NAACP. Negroes. Pittsburgh *Courier* (newspaper). Segregation. 1937-40. *2506*

Commodity exchanges. Agriculture and Government. Antioption struggle. Trade Regulations. 1890-94. *1400*

Common law. Constitutional Amendments (4th). Great Britain. Searches. 15c-18c. *512*

Commons, John R. Bascom, John. Ely, Richard T. Social gospel. Wisconsin, University of. 1870-1910. *1017*

—. Conservatism. Institutions. Labor history. 1884-1935. *156*

Communalism See also Communes.
—. Architecture. Feminism. Gilman, Charlotte Perkins. Housing. 1870-1920. *42*
—. Bishop Hill Colony. Economic growth. Illinois. Swedish Americans. Westward Movement. 1846-59. *935*
—. Cooperatives. Propaganda. 1830's-50's. *546*

Communes See also names of individual communes; Counter Culture; Utopias.
—. Bibliographies. Counter culture. Political Protest. Social change. 1963-73. *2989*
—. California (Point Loma). Theosophy. Tingley, Katherine Augusta Westcott. Universal Brotherhood and Theosophical Society. 1897-1942. *1619*
—. Christianity. Harmony Society. Pennsylvania (Economy). Pittman, Clara. Socialist Laws (Germany, 1878). 1878-79. *1499*
—. City Planning. Harmony Society. Indiana (New Harmony). Pennsylvania (Economy, Harmony). Social customs. 1820's-1905. *919*
—. Considerant, Victor Prosper. France. Land. Texas, northern. Travel. 1852-69. *265*
—. Considerant, Victor Prosper. Reunion (community). Texas. 1854-59. *918*
—. Llano del Rio Co-operative Colony. Louisiana (Vernon Parish). Socialism. 1917-38. *1655*
—. New Jersey (Perth Amboy, Red Bank). North American Phalanx. Raritan Bay Union. Spring, Marcus. 1843-59. *930*
—. Ohio (Cincinnati). Owen, Robert Dale. Utopias. 1820's-50's. *933*
—. Owen, Robert Dale. Sex roles. Women. 1824-28. *931*
—. Pastoralism. Suburbs. 1950's-1970's. *2987*
—. Social Organization. 19c-1976. *268*
—. Social problems. Utopias. 1865-1914. *1504*

Communia (settlement). German Americans. Iowa (Volga Township). Swiss Americans. Utopias. 1847-64. *926*

Communications Behavior. Authority. Parents. Public Schools. Textbooks. West Virginia (Kanawha County). 1974. *2958*

Communism See also Anarchism and Anarchists; Anti-Communist Movements; Comintern; Leftism; Maoism; Marxism; Socialism; Stalinism; Trotskyism.
—. Black nationalism. Depressions. Army. Garvey, Marcus. New York City (Harlem). 1931-39. *2561*
—. China. Chu Teh. Smedley, Agnes. Sorge, Richard. 1893-1950. *360*
—. Farmers. Political Protest. South Dakota. United Farmers League. 1923-34. *2409*
—. Feminism. Flynn, Elizabeth Gurley. ca 1890-1920. *282*
—. Gompers, Samuel. Pan American Federation of Labor. Political Attitudes. 1920's. *2457*
—. Kollontai, Aleksandra. Norway. Propaganda. Russia. World War I. 1915-16. *2046*
—. North Carolina (Gastonia). Novels. Poor. Strikes. Textile Industry. Whites. 1929-34. *2361*

Communist Control Act (US,1954). Humphrey, Hubert H. Liberalism. McCarthy, Joseph R. 1954. *2675*

Communist International. See Comintern.

Communist Party. Alabama (Birmingham). Hudson, Hosea. Negroes. South. 1920's-70's. *404*
—. American Federation of Labor. Labor Unions and Organizations. Radicals and Radicalism. Trade Union Unity League. 1933-35. *2494*
—. Automobile Industry and Trade. Labor Unions and Organizations. 1920-33. *2394*
—. Browder, Earl. 1934-45. *2579*

—. Čačić, Tomo. Canada. Croatians. Yugoslavia. ca 1913-69. *415*
—. California (Inglewood). North American Aviation. Strikes. United Automobile Workers of America. 1941. *2642*
—. Canada. Industrial Workers of the World. Labor Unions and Organizations. Scarlett, Sam. 1900-41. *278*
—. Canada. Labour Party. Methodism. Smith, Albert Edward. Social Gospel. 1893-1924. *410*
—. Canada, western. Evans, Arthur. Labor. 1930's. *1658*
—. Carlson, Oliver (reminiscences). Foster, William Z. Politburo. Radek, Karl. Trotskyism. USSR. 1924-35. *1548*
—. Civil rights. Economic conditions. Negroes. New York City (Harlem). Political Protest. 1930's. *2563*
—. Comintern (7th Congress). New Deal. Socialist Party. 1935-39. *2547*
—. Cooperative Commonwealth Federation. Elections (provincial). Saskatchewan. 1930's. *1680*
—. Culture. Intellectuals. Negroes. New York City (Harlem). Popular Front. 1935-39. *2562*
—. Depressions. Sports. 1920's-40's. *2564*
—. Foster, William Z. Socialist Party. 1881-1921. *304*
—. Georgia (Atlanta). Herndon, Angelo. International Labor Defense. Negroes. 1932-37. *2548*
—. Hay, Henry (interview). Homosexuality. Mattachine Society. 1950-53. *2672*
—. Labor Unions and Organizations. Mexico. 1935-39. *2540*
—. National Maritime Union. Negroes. Racism. United Electrical, Radio and Machine Workers of America. World War II. 1941-45. *2622*
—. North Central States. Political Leadership. Ruthenberg, Charles Emil. USSR. 1919-27. *2414*
—. Ontario. Quebec (Cowansville). Silk industry. Strikes. 1931. *1778*
—. Pamphlets. Rhetoric. 1929-39. *1540*
—. Revolution. Rhetoric. Russian Revolution. 1917-20. *1976*

Communist Party USA. American Peace Mobilization. Isolationism. World War II (antecedents). 1939-41. *2549*
—. Automobile Industry and Trade. Labor Unions and Organizations. Michigan (Detroit). 1920's-1935. *1799*
—. Communists. Blacklisting. Courts. Film industry. Hollywood Ten. *Young* v. *MPAA* (US, 1965). 1947-73. *1736*
—. Canadian Seamen's Union. Syndicalism. 1936-49. *1754*
—. New York City. Radicals and Radicalism. "Rank and File" movement. Social work. 1931-51. *1600*

Communitarianism. Bennett, William H. Home Employment Cooperative Company. Missouri (Dallas County). Utopias. 1894-1905. *1507*
—. Colorado Cooperative Company. Home Employment Cooperative Company. Labor Exchange. Politics. Pragmatism. 1890-1905. *1508*
—. Democracy. Liberalism. Progressive Era. 1890-1920's. *2049*
—. Labor Unions and Organizations. 1880-1900. *1040*

Community Action Programs. City Politics. Decisionmaking. Minorities. Rhode Island (Providence). 1965-69. *2940*

Community affairs. Clergy. Garvey, Marcus. Negroes. New York (Buffalo). Universal Negro Improvement Association. 1830's-1920's. *2458*

Community centers. Country life movement. Progressives. Religion. Rural Settlements. 1900's-20's. *2099*

Community control. Education. Integration. Negroes. New York City (Brooklyn). Politics. 1882-1902. *1181*
—. Elections. Mexican Americans. Texas (Crystal City). 1910-75. *2739*

Community organizations. Cities. Great Britain. Social problems. 1960's-70's. *2746*

Community organizing. Education. Social work. 1920-39. *1523*

Community Participation. Busing. Massachusetts (Boston). Political Protest. 1977-78. *2894*

Community Participation in Politics. Arkansas Community Organizations for Reform Now. Political reform. 1960's-70. *2730*
—. California. Conservation movement. Preservation. 1970's. *2699*

—. Lumber and Lumbering. Michigan (Bay City, Saginaw). Strikes. 1880's. *1320*

Community relations. Police. Race Relations. Riots. 1940-49. *2689*

Community Relations Service. Alabama (Selma). Civil Rights. Collins, LeRoy. Demonstrations. Florida. 1965-68. *2897*

Community services. Education. Housing. Indian-White relations. North Carolina Commission of Indian Affairs. ca 1700-1978. *108*

Company towns. Ohio. Social Classes. Steel Industry. Strikes. 1937. *2474*

Compensation. California. Indians. Land claims. 1821-1963. *173*

Competency commissions. Federal Policy. Indians. Land allotment. 1913-20. *2031*

Competition. Abolition Movement. Attitudes. Economic Structure. Poverty. ca 1830-60. *656*
—. Amateur Sports Act (US, 1978). President's Commission on Olympic Sports. Sports. 1960's-70's. *2783*

Compromise of 1850. Burt, Armistead. Calhoun, John C. Congress. Oregon. Slavery. Wilmot Proviso. ca 1846-60. *691*

Compromise of 1877. Democratic Party. Elections (presidential). Reconstruction. Republican Party. Woodward, C. Vann. 1876-77. *1086*

Compulsory Education See also Child Labor; Schools.
—. Bennett Law (Wisconsin, 1890). Church and state. Wisconsin. 1890. *1417*
—. Carden, Georgiana. Elementary education. Mexican Americans. Migrant Labor. 1920's. *2383*
—. Catholic Church. Church and State. Michigan. Politics. 1920-25. *2348*
—. Educational reform. Interest groups. Pennsylvania. Social Problems. 1880-1911. *200*
—. Frontier and Pioneer Life. Industrialization. Social change. 1870's. *1408*
—. Immigrants. Missouri (St. Louis). Public Schools. Truancy. 1905-07. *2313*
—. Industrialization. Labor. 1890-1930. *2326*

Comstock, Oliver E. Arizona (Tucson; Tent City). Baptists. Medical care. St. Luke's-in-the-Desert Hospital. 1907-37. *1596*

Comte, Auguste. Foster, Frank K. Gompers, Samuel. Ideology. Labor Unions and Organizations. McGregor, Hugh. Spencer, Herbert. 1876-1900. *1295*

Confederate States of America See also names of individual states; Reconstruction.
—. Abolition movement. Cuba. Foreign Relations. Spain. 1860-68. *1145*
—. Conscientious objectors. Friends, Society of. North Carolina. 1861-65. *1124*

Confiscations. Civil War. Congress. Constitutional Law. Debates. Reconstruction. 1861-65. *1105*

Conflict and Conflict Resolution. Ontario School Act (1871). Ryerson, Egerton. Secondary education. 1850's-80's. *1415*

Conflict of interest. Antibiotics. Federal regulation. Food and Drug Administration. Periodicals. Pharmacy. Welch, Henry. 1953-62. *2676*

Congo Reform Association. Park, Robert Ezra. Race relations. Tuskegee Institute. 1905-13. *2025*

Congregationalism See also Friends, Society of; Puritans; Unitarianism.
—. Abolition Movement. Evangelism. Finney, Charles Grandison. South. 1833-69. *632*
—. American Missionary Association. Freedmen. Georgia (Liberty County). 1870-80's. *1247*
—. American Missionary Association. Negroes. South. 1846-80. *1242*
—. American Revolution. Antislavery Sentiments. Hopkins, Samuel. Rhode Island (Newport). ca 1770-1803. *511*
—. Antislavery Sentiments. Clergy. Connecticut. South. 1790-95. *631*
—. Cities. Gladden, Washington. Ohio (Columbus). Reform. Social gospel. 1850's-1914. *396*
—. Education. New Mexico (Albuquerque). Prohibition. Social gospel. 1900-17. *2101*

Congress See also House of Representatives; Legislation; Senate.
—. Alien Anarchist Act (US, 1918). Anti-Communist Movements. Law Enforcement. Leftism. Post, Louis F. 1919-20. *2352*
—. Ansell, Samuel T. Chamberlain, George. Crowder, Enoch H. Lenroot, Irvine L. Military law. Progressivism. 1916-20. *2408*

—. Argell, James B. Chinese Exclusion Act (US, 1882). Diplomacy. Immigration. 1876-82. *947*
—. Billboards. Federal Regulation. Highway Beautification Act (US, 1965). Land use. 1965-79. *2716*
—. Border States. Legislation. Loyalty oath. Republican Party. South. 1861-67. *950*
—. Burt, Armistead. Calhoun, John C. Compromise of 1850. Oregon. Slavery. Wilmot Proviso. ca 1846-60. *691*
—. Catholic Church. Church Schools. Federal aid to education. Roosevelt, Eleanor. Spellman, Francis J. 1949-50. *2669*
—. Civil rights. Democratic Party. Kennedy, John F. 1960-63. *2840*
—. Civil rights. Democratic Party. Legislation. Partisanship. Regionalism. Republican Party. 1963-72. *2803*
—. Civil rights. Demonstrations. Legislation. Public opinion. 1957-77. *2813*
—. Civil rights. Discrimination, employment. Fair Employment Practices Committee. Roosevelt, Franklin D. (administration). World War II. 1941-46. *2640*
—. Civil rights. Negroes. Truman, Harry S. 1949-50. *2687*
—. Civil War. Confiscations. Constitutional Law. Debates. Reconstruction. 1861-65. *1105*
—. Constitutional Amendments (14th, 15th). Elections. Federal Election Campaign Act (US, 1971, 1974). Supreme Court. Voting Rights Act (US, 1965). 1965-75. *2767*
—. Constitutions, State. English, William H. Kansas. Proslavery Sentiments. 1857-58. *629*
—. Courts. School Integration. 1950's-70's. *2877*
—. District of Columbia. Education, Finance. Howard University. Politics. 1879-1928. *186*
—. Equal Employment Opportunity Commission. Feminism. Sex Discrimination. 1964-74. *2920*
—. Fisher, Irving. Progressive era. Public health. 1906-13. *2115*
—. Freedmen's Bureau Act (US, 1865). Refugees. 1864-65. *1091*
—. Hayes, Rutherford B. Mormons. Polygamy. Woman Suffrage. 1877-81. *1089*
—. Historiography. Negroes. Reconstruction. South. 1860's-1978. *1175*
—. Illinois. Keller, Kent. Liberalism. New Deal. 1930-42. *2608*
—. International Ladies' Garment Workers' Union. London, Meyer. Socialism. 1914-22. *2212*
—. Judicial reform. Progressivism. Supreme Court. Taft, William H. 1920-25. *2400*
—. Montana. Rankin, Jeannette. Woman suffrage. 1913-18. *466*
—. New Deal. Roosevelt, Franklin D. Social Security Act (US, 1935). Unemployment insurance. 1934-35. *2471*
—. People's Legislative Service. Progressivism. Roll-call voting. 1922-29. *2423*
Congress of Industrial Organizations. California (Los Angeles). Labor Unions and Organizations. Mexican Americans. 1938-50. *1521*
—. Labor. New Hampshire (Berlin). Nonpartisan League. Political Parties. 1932-36. *2497*
—. Labor Disputes. New Deal. Newspapers. South. 1930-39. *2614*
—. Labor Unions and Organizations. Management. National Industrial Recovery Act (US, 1933). National Labor Relations Act (US, 1935). South. Textile Industry. 1933-41. *2613*
—. Maryland (Baltimore). Negroes. 1930-41. *2580*
—. Oil Industry and Trade. Texas. World War II. 1942-43. *2631*
Congress of Jewish Women. American, Sadie. Jews. Solomon, Hannah G. Women. World Parliament of Religions. World's Columbian Exposition (Chicago, 1893). 1893. *1488*
Congressional Union for Woman Suffrage. Arizona. Democratic Party. Political Campaigns. Women. 1914. 1916. *2164*
Congressmen. New Deal. Politics. Roosevelt, Franklin D. Virginia. Woodrum, Clifton A. 1922-45. *433*
Connecticut *See also* New England; Northeastern or North Atlantic States.
—. Antislavery Sentiments. Clergy. Congregationalism. South. 1790-95. *631*
—. Antislavery Sentiments. Dwight, Theodore. Poetry. 1788-1829. *640*
—. Elections. Peace Movements. 1919-39. *1617*

Connecticut Asylum for the Deaf and Dumb. Federal government. Kentucky Deaf and Dumb Asylum. Public Welfare. 1819-26. *901*
Connecticut (Bridgeport). Armaments Industry. Industrial Relations. Technology. World War I. 1915-19. *2182*
Connecticut (Canterbury). Abolition Movement. Crandall, Prudence. Garrison, William Lloyd. Racism. Sexism. 1830-40. *550*
Connecticut (Cornwall). American Board of Commissioners for Foreign Missions. Assimilation. Foreign Mission School. Indian-White Relations. Students. 1816-27. *829*
Conscientious Objectors *See also* Conscription, Military.
—. Christianity. Pacifism. Thomas, Norman. World War I. 1915-18. *2136*
—. Confederate States of America. Friends, Society of. North Carolina. 1861-65. *1124*
—. Espionage Act of 1917. North Dakota. O'Hare, Kate Richards. Pacifism. World War I. 1900-25. *2131*
Conscription, Military *See also* Conscientious Objectors; Military Recruitment.
—. Antiwar Sentiment. New Left. Students. Vietnam War. 1965-71. *2696*
—. Citizen Lobbies. Periodicals. Political Protest. Protestant Churches. 1940-59. *1570*
—. Civil Disturbances. Law Enforcement. 1963-76. *2725*
—. Civil service. Mennonites. World War II. 1930's-45. *2632*
Conservation. Adams, Charles Francis. Massachusetts (Boston, Quincy). Parks. 1880's-90's. *1070*
—. Ballinger-Pinchot Controversy. Fisher, Walter Lowrie. Interior Department. 1911-13. *1957*
—. Big Sky development. Huntley, Chet. Montana. Resorts. 1970-73. *2755*
Conservation movement. California. Community Participation in Politics. Preservation. 1970's. *2699*
—. Federal Policy. Lumber and Lumbering. Pacific Northwest. Property rights. Public Lands. 1870's-90's. *1323*
Conservation of Natural Resources *See also* types of resource conservation, e.g. Soil Conservation, Water Conservation, Wildlife Conservation, etc.; Ecology; Environment; Forests and Forestry.
—. Colorado. Individualism. Progressives. 1896-1910. *2028*
—. Cooke, Morris L. New Deal. Rural Electrification Administration. 1933-51. *2491*
—. Economic Growth. National Parks and Reserves. 1870's - 1973. *90*
—. Forests and Forestry. Pacific Northwest. 1889-1913. *2052*
Conservatism. American Revolution (antecedents). Liberty. North Carolina. Political Corruption. Regulators. 1766-71. *481*
—. Antiabolition sentiments. Clergy. Constitutions. Massachusetts (Boston). Missouri (St. Louis). Unitarianism. 1828-57. *751*
—. Asians. Immigration. Methodist Episcopal Church. Social Gospel. 1865-1908. *1029*
—. Capitalism. Coolidge, Louis Arthur. Sentinels of the Republic. 1900-25. *450*
—. Chamberlain, John. Political Theory. Radicals and Radicalism. 1920's-65. *275*
—. Commons, John R. Institutions. Labor history. 1884-1935. *156*
—. Constitutional law. Kansas. New Deal. Newspapers. Supreme Court. 1934-35. *2502*
—. Creel, George. New Deal. Progressivism. Works Progress Administration. 1900-53. *1520*
—. Democratic Party. North Carolina. Primaries, gubernatorial. Progressivism. 1890-1920. *2340*
—. DuBois, W. E. B. Negroes. Periodicals. Race relations. Radicals and Radicalism. Washington, Booker T. 1900-10. *1983*
—. DuBose, William Porcher. Episcopal Church, Protestant. Miles, James Warley. Murphy, Edgar Gardner. South. Theology. 1840-1920. *62*
—. Elections, presidential. Mississippi. Segregation. Sillers, Walter. State Legislatures. 1948-64. *2677*
—. Elites. Ontario (Ottawa). Political Leadership. Public Welfare. 1880-1912. *1310*
—. Individualism. Olmsted, Frederick Law. 19c. *1041*

—. McCumber, Porter James. McKenzie, Alexander John. North Dakota. Political reform. Republican Party. Suffrage. Women. 1898-1933. *435*
—. Progressivism. Saskatchewan. 1920's. *1556*
Considerant, Victor Prosper. Communes. France. Land. Texas, northern. Travel. 1852-69. *265*
—. Communes. Reunion (community). Texas. 1854-59. *918*
Consolidated Mining and Smelting Company. British Columbia (Trail). Immigration. Mine, Mill and Smelter Workers, International Union of. Strikes. World War I. 1916-17. *1810*
Conspiracy. Canada, western. Intelligence service. Labor Disputes. One Big Union. Royal Canadian Mounted Police. 1919. *1612*
Constitution League. Discrimination. Foraker, Joseph B. Hepburn Bill, Warner-Foraker Amendment (1906). Jim Crow laws. Negroes. Railroads. Washington, Booker T. (and Committee of 12). 1906. *1919*
Constitutional Amendments *See also* specific amendments, e.g. Constitutional Amendment (14th).
—. Civil War. Fundamentalism. Lincoln, Abraham. National Fast Day. National Reform Association. 1787-1945. *1484*
Constitutional Amendments (1st). Authority. Health. Religious liberty. Supreme Court. 1963-79. *2769*
—. Black, Hugo. Due process. Judicial Administration. 1936-79. *1717*
—. Civil Rights. Liberalism. Political Attitudes. 1954-74. *2768*
—. Decisionmaking. Jury. 1940's-75. *1732*
Constitutional Amendments (4th). Common law. Great Britain. Searches. 15c-18c. *512*
Constitutional Amendments (13th). Ashley, James M. House of Representatives. Nationalism. Ohio. Political Parties. 1848-65. *1097*
Constitutional Amendments (13th, 14th). Civil Rights Act (US, 1875). Federal Government. Negroes. 1875-83. *1113*
Constitutional Amendments (13th, 14th, 15th). Authority. Citizenship. Federal government. Freedmen. Reconstruction. 1865-70. *1132*
—. Civil Rights. Freedmen. Politics. Reconstruction. 1865-77. *1188*
Constitutional Amendments (14th). *Brown* v. *Board of Education* (US, 1954). Illinois (Chicago). School integration. South. 1954-77. *2777*
—. Citizenship. Indians. Law. ca 1776-1934. *131*
—. Civil rights. *Gitlow* v. *New York* (US, 1925). Sanford, Edward Terry. Supreme Court. ca 1890-1930. *2399*
—. Civil Rights. Judicial review. Supreme Court. 19c-20c. *144*
—. Civil Rights. Reconstruction. 1865-68. *1109*
Constitutional Amendments (14th, 15th). Civil Rights. Civil War. Slavery. Supreme Court. Woman Suffrage. 1863-75. *1106*
—. Civil Rights Act (US, 1866). Negroes. Reconstruction. Republican Party. States' rights. ca 1865-77. *953*
—. Congress. Elections. Federal Election Campaign Act (US, 1971, 1974). Supreme Court. Voting Rights Act (US, 1965). 1965-75. *2767*
Constitutional Amendments (15th). Abolition movement. Douglass, Frederick. Negroes. Theology. 1825-86. *777*
Constitutional Amendments (18th). Dean Act (1919). Prohibition. State Legislatures. Texas. 1917-33. *2368*
—. Prohibition. 1920-33. *2387*
Constitutional Amendments (18th, 21st). Democratic Party. Prohibition. Raskob, John J. Roosevelt, Franklin D. 1928-33. *2536*
Constitutional Amendments (19th). Bible. Equal Rights Amendment. State Legislatures. Tennessee. Women. 1876-1974. *2904*
—. *Crisis* (periodical). DuBois, W. E. B. Negroes. Woman Suffrage. 1910-34. *1712*
Constitutional Amendments (19th; ratification). Massachusetts. Woman suffrage. 1900-19. *2167*
Constitutional Amendments (21st). Adventists. Prohibition. 1932-34. *2612*
—. Mormons. Prohibition. Utah. 1932-33. *2393*
Constitutional Amendments (24th). Negroes. Political participation. Voter registration. Voting Rights Act (US, 1965). 1964-67. *2892*
Constitutional conventions. Negroes. Ohio. Progressive era. Smith, Harry. Suffrage. 1863-1912. *2165*

Constitutional conventions, state. Abolition Movement. Disfranchisement. Gardner, Charles W. Hinton, Frederick A. Negroes. Pennsylvania. 1838. *596*
—. Blackwell, Henry B. Montana. Woman suffrage. 1889. *1121*
—. Capital punishment. New York. Progressivism. 1915. *1923*
—. Carpetbaggers. Civil rights. Industrialization. Reconstruction. South. 1867-69. *1021*
—. Charleston *Daily Courier* (newspaper). Charleston *Mercury* (newspaper). Racism. Reconstruction. South Carolina. 1867-68. *1205*
—. Delegates. Reconstruction. Virginia. 1867-68. *1022*
—. Democrats. Oklahoma. Woman Suffrage. 1870-1907. *146*
—. Oklahoma. Politics. Woman suffrage. 1906. *2144*
Constitutional Law *See also* Citizenship; Civil Rights; Democracy; Eminent Domain; Federal Government; Legislation; Referendum; Suffrage.
—. American Revolution. Civil Rights. Ideology. 1776-1976. *134*
—. Civil rights. Douglas, William O. Judicial process. Liberalism. Supreme Court. 1928-77. *1715*
—. Civil War. Confiscations. Congress. Debates. Reconstruction. 1861-65. *1105*
—. Conservatism. Kansas. New Deal. Newspapers. Supreme Court. 1934-35. *2502*
—. Government. Supreme Court. 1950-75. *1557*
Constitutions. Antiabolition sentiments. Clergy. Conservatism. Massachusetts (Boston). Missouri (St. Louis). Unitarianism. 1828-57. *751*
—. Civil Rights. 1930-50. *1598*
—. Civil Rights. Migration, internal. Supreme Court. 1780's-1977. *138*
—. Civil War (antecedents). Law. Slavery. 1830-60. *763*
—. Editorials. Labor Unions and Organizations. New Deal. Periodicals. Supreme Court. 1935-37. *2503*
Constitutions, State. Abolition Movement. Breckinridge, Robert J. Breckinridge, William Lewis. Emancipation Party. Kentucky. Presbyterians. 1849. *676*
—. Bible. Presbyterian Church. Religious Education. Supreme courts (state). Wisconsin. 1848-90. *1419*
—. California. Chinese. Federal Regulation. Labor reform. Workingmen's Party of California. 1877-82. *1358*
—. Congress. English, William H. Kansas. Proslavery Sentiments. 1857-58. *629*
—. Duniway, Abigail Scott. Oregon. Voting rights. Woman Suffrage. 1860's-1912. *1093*
—. Jury. Lobbying. South Carolina. Women. 1921-67. *1731*
—. Louisiana. Slidell, John. Suffrage. 1812-52. *601*
—. Montana. Rankin, Jeannette. Woman suffrage. 1889-1914. *129*
—. Vermont. Woman suffrage. 1870. *1094*
Constitutions, State (conventions). Arkansas. Negroes. Reconstruction. 1868. *1250*
Constitutions, State (proposed). Arkansas. Political Reform. Progressivism. 1917-18. *2005*
Constitutions, State (reform). Hamilton, Joseph G. de Roulhac. North Carolina. Progressivism. Sikes, Enoch W. State Legislatures. 1898-1913. *2091*
Construction *See also* Architecture.
—. Business. California (San Francisco). Eight-hour day. Law and Order Committee. Strikes. 1916-17. *2232*
—. Business. Farmers. Railroads. Utopias. Western States. 1880's-90's. *1511*
—. City government. Maryland (Baltimore). Schools. Urban reform. 1870-1900. *1402*
—. Employment. Ickes, Harold. Negroes. Public Works Administration. Quotas. 1933-40. *2535*
Consumer cooperative movements. Business. Garden City Movement. Nelson, Nelson O. Progressivism. 1890's-1918. *2240*
Consumer Product Safety Commission. Federal Regulation. Safety. 1972-77. *2721*
Consumer protection. Drugs. Federal regulation. Legislation. Methodology. 1962-73. *2956*
Consumers *See also* Citizen Lobbies.
—. California (San Francisco Bay area). Environmental protection. Housing. Local government regulation. Housing. Local government. Suburbs. 1940-80. *2718*

—. Cities. Citizen Lobbies. Environment. Noise pollution. Reform. 1893-1932. *1684*
—. Drugs. Food, Drug, and Cosmetic Act (US, 1938). Regulation. 1938-78. *1818*
—. National Consumers' League. Progressive era. Women. 1900-23. *2124*
Consumers' Association of Canada. Canada. Citizen Lobbies. Public policy. 1947-77. *1587*
Consumers' United Stores. Agricultural Cooperatives. Farmers Educational and Cooperative Union of America. Nonpartisan League. North Dakota. 1916-19. *2259*
Continental Congress of Workers and Farmers. Senior, Clarence. Socialist Party. 1933. *2611*
Contraband programs. Civil War. Fugitive slaves. Louisiana, southern. Military Occupation. 1862-65. *1219*
Contracts. Freedmen's Bureau. Planters. Sharecropping. South. 1865-68. *1258*
Converts. Evangelism. Louisiana (New Orleans). Protestant Churches. Slavery. 1800-61. *732*
Convict Labor. Agriculture. Louisiana State Prison (Angola). Prisons. Working Conditions. 1900-78. *1701*
—. Artisans. Kingston Penitentiary. Machinists. Ontario. Petitions. 1833-36. *826*
—. Coal Mines and Mining. State Government. Strikes. Tennessee. 1891-93. *1286*
Convict lease system. Corporal punishment. Florida (Leon County). Law Reform. Tabert, Martin. 1921-23. *2354*
—. Economic Conditions. Georgia. Prisons. Racism. 1868-1909. *1044*
Cooke, Morris L. Conservation of Natural Resources. New Deal. Rural Electrification Administration. 1933-51. *2491*
Cooke, Parsons. Industrialization. Massachusetts (Ware). Missions and Missionaries. Puritans. 19c. *906*
Coolidge, Calvin. Citizenship. Indian Citizenship Act (US, 1924). Political Reform. 1924. *2446*
Coolidge, Louis Arthur. Capitalism. Conservatism. Sentinels of the Republic. 1900-25. *450*
Cooperative Association of America. Business. Democracy. Morality. Peck, Bradford (*World a Department Store*). Utopias. 1880-1925. *263*
Cooperative Commonwealth Federation. Alberta. Land reform. Leadership. Social credit. United Farmers of Alberta. 1930's. *1748*
—. Alberta. Populism. Russia. Saskatchewan. Social Credit Party. USA. 1870's-1940's. *14*
—. Canadian Labour Congress. Federal Government. Industrial relations. Trades and Labour Congress of Canada. World War II. 1939-46. *2634*
—. Catholic Church. Saskatchewan. Socialism. 1930-50. *1620*
—. Communist Party. Elections (provincial). Saskatchewan. 1930's. *1680*
—. Feminism. Leftism. Ontario (Toronto). Women's Joint Committee. 1930's. *1638*
—. League for National Reconstruction. Regina Manifesto. Saskatchewan. Underhill, Frank. 1933. *1611*
—. Political Participation. Saskatchewan. United Farmers of Canada. 1930-45. *1606*
—. Political Parties. Saskatchewan. Socialism. 1928-44. *1681*
Cooperative movement. *Actualité Économique* (periodical). Individualism. Minville, Esdras. Nationalism. Quebec (Gaspé Peninsula). 1924-40. *1794*
—. *Actualité Économique* (periodical). Individualism. Minville, Esdras. Quebec (Gaspé Peninsula). 1924-43. *1795*
Cooperative Workers of America. Georgia. Hoover, Hiram F. Negroes. Secret Societies. South Carolina. 1886-87. *1197*
Cooperatives *See also* Agricultural Cooperatives.
—. Adult education. Antigonish Movement. Capitalism. Coady, Moses. Nova Scotia, eastern. 1930-40. *1742*
—. Agrarianism. Angers, François-Albert. Economic Theory. Quebec. 1930-80. *1594*
—. Arkansas (Lee County). Clinics. Medical care. Negroes. 1960's-70's. *2977*
—. Businessmen. Nelson, Nelson O. Profit-sharing. 1886-1904. *1329*
—. Communalism. Propaganda. 1830's-50's. *546*
—. DuBois, W. E. B. Economic Theory. Negroes. 1940. *2498*
—. Hoel, Chamberlain. Oregon (Salem). Reform. 1852-65. *326*

—. Quebec. 1940-78. *2955*
Coopers' International Union. Industrial Relations. Mechanization. Standard Oil Company of Ohio. 1870's. *1313*
Copper Mines and Mining. Arizona (Globe). Strikes. Western Federation of Miners. 1917. *2261*
—. Arizona (Globe). Strikes. Western Federation of Miners. World War I. 1917. *2255*
Corey, Lewis. Socialism. 1940-53. *1625*
Corn Belt Meat Producers' Association. Cattlemen. Hepburn Act (US, 1906). Iowa. 1900-10. *2229*
Cornell University. Census Bureau. Economics. Negroes. Progressivism. Racism. Willcox, Walter F. 1895-1910. *1870*
Cornish, Samuel E. Abolition Movement. *Freedom's Journal* (newspaper). Journalism. Negroes. Presbyterian Church. 1820's-59. *467*
Corporal punishment. Convict lease system. Florida (Leon County). Law Reform. Tabert, Martin. 1921-23. *2354*
—. Eaton, Nathaniel. Harvard University. Massachusetts (Cambridge). Puritans. Trials. 1638. *495*
—. Educational Reform. New Jersey. Schools. 1800-1972. *1432*
Corporations *See also* Public Utilities.
—. Bureaucracies. Labor. Poor. Social Classes. War on Poverty. 1960's. *2925*
—. Capitalism. Federal government. General Electric Company. Labor Unions and Organizations. Liberalism. 1920-33. *2412*
—. Christianity. Education, Finance. Higher education. Social Darwinism. 1860-1930. *206*
—. Employment. Hoover, Herbert C. Labor Unions and Organizations. 1919-29. *2465*
—. General Electric Company. New Deal. 1933-40. *2550*
—. Wage-price controls. World War II. 1941-45. *2645*
Corruthers, James B. (letters). Lloyd, Henry Demarest. 1870-1903. *378*
Corwin, Thomas. Mexican War. Political Speeches. Whig Party. 1847. *540*
Costello, Michael A. (letter). Brown, John. Harpers Ferry raid. 1859-60. *630*
Cotton. Agricultural Policy. Association of Southern Commissioners of Agriculture. New Deal. South. Tennessee (Memphis). 1936-37. *2567*
—. Agricultural Reform. Arkansas. Colored Farmers' Alliance. Humphrey, R. M. Strikes. 1891. *1171*
—. Antislavery Sentiments. Boycotts. Friends, Society of. Great Britain. 1840-60. *608*
—. Child Labor Act (US, 1916). Federal regulation. Textile Industry. 1907-16. *2002*
—. Educational Reform. Howell, Clark. Phillips, Ulrich B. Progressivism. 1903-05. *2062*
—. Hamilton Manufacturing Company. Labor Disputes. Massachusetts (Lowell). Social mobility. Textile Industry. Women. 1836-60. *818*
Council of National Defense. American Plan. Federal government. Prostitution. Social policy. Venereal disease. Voluntary associations. World War I. 1917-21. *2048*
Councils and Synods. Delegates. Episcopal Church, Protestant. Kinsolving, George Herbert. Texas. Veto. Women. 1921-70. *2347*
Counter Culture *See also* Communes.
—. Authority. Charisma. Hasidism. Unification Church. 1960-80. *2986*
—. Behavior. Occult Sciences. 1960's-70's. *2988*
—. Bibliographies. Communes. Political Protest. Social change. 1963-73. *2989*
—. Canada. Great Britain. Press, underground. USA. 1957-72. *2990*
—. Cynics. Hippies. 1960's-73. *2991*
—. Ireland. ca 1970's. *2993*
—. Kesey, Ken. LSD. Political Theory. Wolfe, Thomas Kennerly, Jr. 1964-68. *2992*
Country Life Movement. Agricultural Production. Cities. Educational Reform. Rural Schools. 1900-20. *2302*
—. Community centers. Progressives. Religion. Rural Settlements. 1900's-20's. *2099*
Countryman, Gratia Alta. Libraries (public). Minnesota (Minneapolis). Reform. Women. 1890's-1953. *424*
Counts, George S. Educational reform. Liberalism. Race. 1929-34. *2379*
Court of Visitation. Kansas. Populism. Railroads. Republican Party. State Legislatures. 1890-1900. *1386*

Courts *See also* Courts Martial and Courts of Inquiry; Judges; Judicial Administration; Judicial Process; Jury; Juvenile Courts; Supreme Court.
—. Accidents. Federal Employers' Liability Act (US, 1908). Management. Railroads. Safety Appliances Act (US, 1893). Working Conditions. 1890-1913. *2117*
—. Alberta (Linden). Church Schools. Mennonites. Religious Liberty. 1977-78. *2780*
—. American Federation of Labor. Buck's Stove and Range Company. Labor Law. 1907-11. *2222*
—. Antitrust. Fire insurance. Kansas City Board of Fire Underwriters. Law enforcement. Missouri. 1889-99. *1336*
—. Apportionment. Attorneys General. Election Laws. Intergovernmental Relations. Voting Rights Act (US, 1965; Section 5). 1965-77. *2801*
—. Arizona. Bai-a-lil-le (medicine man). Civil Rights. Education. Fort Huachuca. Indian Rights Association. Navajo Indians. Utah, southeastern. 1906-09. *2043*
—. Arkansas (Little Rock). Collins, LeRoy. Federal Government. Florida. Political Speeches. School integration. 1957. *2688*
—. Blacklisting. Communists. Film industry. Hollywood Ten. *Young* v. *MPAA* (US, 1965). 1947-73. *1736*
—. *Blackwell* v. *Issaquena County Board of Education* (US, 1966). *Burnside* v. *Byars* (US, 1966). Freedom of Speech. Students. *Tinker* v. *Des Moines Community School District* (US, 1969). 1870-1969. *1728*
—. Bohanon, Luther. Oklahoma (Oklahoma City). School Integration. 1955-79. *2808*
—. Breckinridge, Robert J., Jr. Breckinridge, William C. P. Elections. Kentucky. Negroes. Testimony. 1866-69. *1096*
—. California. Capital punishment. Elections. 1954-72. *2791*
—. California. Navajo Indians. Peyote. Religious Liberty. 1964. *2792*
—. California (Alameda County). Plea bargaining. Sentencing. 1880-1970's. *122*
—. Canada. Extradition. Fugitive slaves. Happy, Jesse. Kentucky. Testimony. 1793-1838. *748*
—. Canada. Indians. Lavell, Jeannette. Political participation. Women's Liberation Movement. 1869-1979. *2914*
—. Citizenship. Mexican Americans. Nationality. Race. 1846-97. *135*
—. Civil Rights Act (US, 1964; Title VII). Discrimination, employment. Equal opportunity. 1964-78. *2932*
—. Class action suits. Desegregation. Discrimination, reverse. 1965-76. *2862*
—. Congress. School Integration. 1950's-70's. *2877*
—. Debts. Desha, Joseph. Kentucky. 1819-26. *823*
—. Democratic Party. Primaries. Segregation. South Carolina. Waring, J. Waties. 1947-52. *2683*
—. Discrimination, Educational. District of Columbia. Negroes. Public schools. 1804-1974. *1844*
—. Discrimination, educational. Florida, University of. Hawkins, Virgil Darnell. Lawyers. Legal education. 1949-76. *1554*
—. Discrimination, Employment. Labor law. Women. 1876-1979. *43*
—. Farber, Myron. Freedom of the press. *New York Times* (newspaper). Reporters and Reporting. 1975-79. *2781*
—. Freedmen's Bureau. Howard, Oliver Otis. Reconstruction. South. 1865-68. *1229*
—. Freedmen's Bureau. Justice. Negroes. Reconstruction. Texas. 1865-68. *1146*
—. Industrial Workers of the World. Labor. New Jersey (Paterson). Progressivism. Quinlan, Patrick. 1913-17. *2275*
—. Industrialists. Juvenile Delinquency. Middle Classes. Philanthropy. Reform. 1890-99. *1472*
—. North. *Prigg* v. *Pennsylvania* (US, 1842). Slavery. Supreme Court. 1842-57. *636*
—. Plea bargaining. Sentencing. 19c. *125*
—. Public welfare. 1925-75. *1774*
Courts Martial and Courts of Inquiry *See also* Military Law.
—. California (San Francisco Bay). Mare Island Mutiny. Navies. Negroes. Port Chicago Naval Magazine. Race relations. 1944-48. *2652*

Cowan, Jacob. Alabama (Mobile). North Carolina (Wilmington). Slave Revolts. Walker, David *(Appeal)*. 1829-31. *726*
Cowboys. Strikes. Western States. Working conditions. 1870-90. *1324*
Coxey, Jacob S. District of Columbia. Political Protest. Unemployment. 1894. *1302*
Craft, Ellen. Abolition Movement. Craft, William. Fugitive slaves. Great Britain. 1848-65. *611*
Craft, Juanita. Durham, William J. NAACP. Smith, Antonio Maceo. Texas. White, Lulu B. 1933-50. *1586*
Craft, William. Abolition Movement. Craft, Ellen. Fugitive slaves. Great Britain. 1848-65. *611*
Crafts. *See* Home Economics.
Crandall, Prudence. Abolition Movement. Connecticut (Canterbury). Garrison, William Lloyd. Racism. Sexism. 1830-40. *550*
—. Kansas (Elk County). Spiritualism. Temperance Movements. Women's rights. 1877-95. *1487*
Crapsey, Algernon Sidney. Episcopal Church, Protestant. Heresy. New York (Rochester). Reform. St. Andrew's Church. Trials. 1879-1927. *454*
Craton, Ann Washington. Amalgamated Clothing Workers of America. Northeastern or North Atlantic States. Women. 1915-44. *367*
Crawford, Coe Isaac. Progressivism. Republican Party. Roosevelt, Theodore. South Dakota. State Politics. 1912-14. *2076*
Crawford, George W. Burnside, Thomas E. Dueling. Georgia. Law. 1809-28. *545*
Crawford, Isabel. Baptists. Indians. Kiowa Indians. Missions and Missionaries. Oklahoma (Wichita Mountains). Women's American Baptist Home Missionary Society. 1893-1961. *393*
Creek Indians. Acculturation. Indians (tribal warfare). 1865-1978. *68*
Creel, George. Conservatism. New Deal. Progressivism. Works Progress Administration. 1900-53. *1520*
Cresson, Elliot. Abolition Movement. American Colonization Society. Colonization. Great Britain. Liberia. 1831-33. *609*
Crime and Criminals *See also* names of crimes, e.g. Murder, etc.; Capital Punishment; Criminal Law; Juvenile Delinquency; Police; Prisons; Riots; Terrorism; Trials.
—. Aged. Deinstitutionalization. Mental Illness. 19c-20c. *227*
—. Architecture. Attitudes. Boston Prison Discipline Society. Howard, John. Kingston Penitentiary. Ontario. ca 1830-50. *899*
—. California (San Francisco). City Government. Progressivism. Prostitution. 1910-14. *2085*
—. Children. Coldwater State Public School. Michigan. Protestantism. 1874-96. *1430*
—. Deinstitutionalization. Mental Illness. 1960's-70's. *2984*
—. Education. Morality. Pennsylvania. Wickersham, James P. 1866-81. *1401*
—. Fletcher, Benjamin Harrison. Industrial Workers of the World. Labor. Longshoremen. Negroes. 1910-33. *437*
—. Florida. Rebellions. Slavery. ca 1820-65. *659*
—. Friends, Society of. Peace bonds. Pennsylvania (Philadelphia). 1680-1829. *492*
—. George, Henry. Land. Monopolies. Property. Technology. 19c-20c. *1033*
—. Great Britain. Plea bargaining. 17c-20c. *109*
—. Gun Control. Massachusetts (Boston). 1974-76. *2784*
—. Idaho. Industrial Workers of the World. Labor Law. State Government. 1917-33. *2088*
—. Louisiana (New Orleans). Prohibition. 1918-33. *2386*
—. Ontario (Upper Canada). Prisons. Reform. 1835-50. *857*
Criminal Law *See also* Capital Punishment; Jury; Trials.
—. 1776-1900. *121*
—. Canada. Parliaments. 1892-1902. *1107*
—. Cities. Poverty. 1780-1840. *892*
Crisis (periodical). Constitutional Amendments (19th). DuBois, W. E. B. Negroes. Woman Suffrage. 1910-34. *1712*
Croatians. Čačić, Tomo. Canada. Communist Party. Yugoslavia. ca 1913-69. *415*
Croly, Herbert. Business. Equal opportunity. Federal Trade Commission Act (US, 1914). Progressivism. 1900's-10's. *2227*

Crook, George. Citizenship. Civil Rights. Indians (agencies). Political Corruption. Whites. 1870's-80's. *993*
Crosby, Ernest Howard. Intellectuals. Reformers. Tolstoy, Lev Nikolaevich, Count. 1878-1907. *334*
Crosswaith, Frank R. Negro Labor Committee. New York City (Harlem). 1925-39. *1824*
Crothers, Austin Lane. Governors. Maryland. Progressivism. 1904-12. *1896*
Crowder, Enoch H. Ansell, Samuel T. Chamberlain, George. Congress. Lenroot, Irvine L. Military law. Progressivism. 1916-20. *2408*
Croxton, John Thomas. Civil War. Kentucky. Law. Military Service. Republican Party. 1855-74. *392*
Cruce, Lee. Capital punishment. Governors. Negroes. Oklahoma. White supremacy. 1911-15. *1907*
Crummell, Alexander. American Colonization Society. Education. Liberia. Negroes. 1853-73. *1126*
Crusade for Justice. Gonzales, Rodolfo "Corky". Mexican Americans. Southwest. 1966-72. *2735*
Cruse, Harold. Culture. Intellectuals. Methodology. Negroes. 1910-75. *1519*
Cuba. Abolition movement. Confederate States of America. Foreign Relations. Spain. 1860-68. *1145*
—. Medical ethics. Medical research. Reed, Walter. Yellow fever. 1900-01. *1883*
—. Military occupation. Progressivism. Wood, Leonard. 1899-1902. *1951*
Cuffe, Paul. Africa. Colonization. Massachusetts (Boston). Negroes. 1810-15. *728*
—. Black nationalism. Colonization. Friends, Society of. Sierra Leone. 1810's. *694*
Cults. Attitudes. Chiropractic. Medicine (practice of). Science. 1850's-1970's. *229*
—. Census. 1920-79. *2443*
Cults, religious. Church and state. 1970's. *2787*
Cultural imperialism. Antislavery Sentiments. Elites. Great Britain. 18c-19c. *765*
Culture *See also* Education; Popular Culture; Scholarship.
—. Art criticism. Progressivism. 1900's. *1973*
—. Black Nationalism. Ethnic consciousness. 1960-75. *2883*
—. *Canadian Forum*. Socialism. 1920-34. *1649*
—. Communist Party. Intellectuals. Negroes. New York City (Harlem). Popular Front. 1935-39. *2562*
—. Cruse, Harold. Intellectuals. Methodology. Negroes. 1910-75. *1519*
Cummins, Albert B. Government regulation. Iowa (Davenport). Law Enforcement. Liquor. Riots. State Politics. 1907-08. *1880*
Curaçao. Negroes. Political Protest. Social change. 1960's-70's. *2797*
Curricula. California (Los Angeles). Educational reform. Mexican Americans. Public schools. 1920's-30's. *1842*
—. Chicago, University of. Education. Hutchins, Robert M. 1930-77. *1839*
—. Colleges and Universities. Education. Individualism. Negroes. 1890-1970's. *1853*
—. Domesticity. Home economics. Progressivism. Sex education. 1900-20. *2314*
—. Eliot, William Greenleaf. Higher education. Missouri (St. Louis). Trans-Mississippi West. Washington University. 1853-87. *189*
—. Farmers' Alliance. Iowa State Agricultural College. State Legislatures. Wallace, Henry. 1884-91. *1416*
—. Kindergarten. Morality. Progressive education. 1860-1920. *184*
Cynics. Counter Culture. Hippies. 1960's-73. *2991*

D

Dabney, Robert Lewis. Morality. Presbyterian Church. South. Texas, University of (Austin). Union Seminary. 1865-96. *1084*
Dahlberg, Edwin (interview). Baptists. Rauschenbusch, Walter. 1914-18. *444*
Daily Life *See also* Popular Culture.
—. Bishop Hill Colony. Illinois. Jansson, Erik. Letters. Swedish Americans. Utopias. 1847-56. *939*
—. Bradford, George Partridge. Brook Farm. Letters. Massachusetts. Utopias. 1841. *932*
Dakota Indians. *See* Sioux Indians.
Dall, Caroline. Farley, Harriet. Feminism. Letters. Working Class. 1850. *794*

Dancey, John C. Discrimination. Michigan (Detroit). Urban League. Washington, Forrester B. 1916-39. *1696*

Darwinism. Feminism. Women. 1850-1920. *88*

Davidson, Donald. Agrarianism. Literature. Mims, Edwin. South. 1923-58. *1656*

Davis, Alexander Jackson. Garden cities. Haskell, Llewellyn S. Idealism. New Jersey (West Orange; Llewellyn Park). Suburbs. 1853-57. *943*

Davis Bend colony. Black capitalism. Civil War. Eaton, John, Jr. Freedmen. Mississippi. 1862-66. *1249*

Davis, David W. Idaho. Industrial Workers of the World. Nonpartisan League. Public opinion. Socialist Party. 1919-26. *2405*

Davis, Michael M. Boston Dispensary. Clinics. Massachusetts. 1910-20. *2051*

Davis, Richard L. Coal Mines and Mining. Labor Unions and Organizations. Letters-to-the-editor. *National Labor Tribune*. Negroes. United Mine Workers of America. ca 1890-1900. *1139*

Dawes Act (US, 1887). Agricultural policy. Federal government. Indians (reservations). Kiowa Indians. Oklahoma. 1869-1901. *1062*

—. Arapaho Indians. Cheyenne Indians. Fraud. Indians (agencies). Land allotment. Oklahoma. 1910's. *1888*

—. Artifacts. Fletcher, Alice Cunningham. Indians (reservations). 1880's-90's. *968*

—. Eells, Edwin. Indians (agencies). Land Tenure. Skokomish Indian Reservation. Washington. 1871-95. *970*

—. Flathead Indian Reservation. Indians. Land Tenure. Montana. Salish (Flathead) Indians. 1887-1904. *1075*

—. Indian Reorganization Act (US, 1934). Indian Rights Association. Indians. Land allotment. 1887-1934. *153*

Dawes Commission. Five Civilized Tribes. Freedmen. Homesteading and Homesteaders. Indian Territory. 1893-1905. *1083*

Dawson, Francis Warrington. Charleston *News and Courier* (newspaper). Dawson, Sarah Morgan. Feminism. Reconstruction. South Carolina. 1870's. *973*

Dawson, Sarah Morgan. Charleston *News and Courier* (newspaper). Dawson, Francis Warrington. Feminism. Reconstruction. South Carolina. 1870's. *973*

Dean Act (1919). Constitutional Amendments (18th). Prohibition. State Legislatures. Texas. 1917-33. *2368*

Death Penalty. *See* Capital Punishment.

Debates. Antislavery Sentiments. Lane Seminary. Ohio (Cincinnati; Walnut Hills). 1829-34. *692*

—. Civil War. Confiscations. Congress. Constitutional Law. Reconstruction. 1861-65. *1105*

DeBernardi, G. B. Depressions. Freedom Colony. Kansas. Labor Exchange. Utopias. 1894-1905. *1510*

Debo, Angie (personal account). Federal Government. Indians. Public Opinion. Reform. 1969-76. *2703*

Debs, Eugene V. Coal Mines and Mining. Socialist Party. Strikes. West Virginia. 1912-14. *2194*

—. Debs, Theodore. Labor Unions and Organizations. Sebree, Shubert (letters). 1890-1930's. *418*

—. Federal Government. Illinois (Blue Island). Pullman Strike. Strikes. 1894. *1317*

—. Hartz, Louis. Hillquit, Morris. Liberalism. Locke, John. Marxism. Political culture. 20c. *1986*

Debs, Theodore. Debs, Eugene V. Indiana. Labor Unions and Organizations. Sebree, Shubert (letters). 1890-1930's. *418*

Debts. Courts. Desha, Joseph. Kentucky. 1819-26. *823*

—. Kentucky. Law Reform. Legislation. 1790-1839. *824*

Decarceration. Asylums. Mental illness. 1950's-75. *2983*

Decentralization. Educational Policy. New York City (Brownsville, Ocean Hill). Public Opinion. 1962-71. *2971*

Decentralization Act (1969). Minorities. New York City (Brooklyn, Lower East Side). Public Schools. School boards. 1969-73. *2965*

Decisionmaking *See also* Elites; Foreign Policy.

—. Alabama (Bullock, Greene, Wilcox counties). Local Politics. Negroes. 1971-72. *2819*

—. American Medical Association. Bureaucracies. Reform. 1960's. *2759*

—. City Politics. Community Action Programs. Minorities. Rhode Island (Providence). 1965-69. *2940*

—. Constitutional Amendments (1st). Jury. 1940's-75. *1732*

—. Democracy. Federal regulation. Social policy. 1970-75. *2734*

—. Desegregation. Negroes. Political power. South. Teachers. Voting and Voting Behavior. 1950's-60's. *2831*

—. Federal Government. Interest Groups. Legislation. Politics. Women. 1970's. *2911*

Declaration of Independence. Attitudes. Civil Rights. Fourth of July. Jefferson, Thomas. Negroes. 1776. 1800-50. *724*

—. Ideology. Radicals and Radicalism. Religion. Utopias. 1730's-1890's. *269*

deCleyre, Voltairine. Anarchism and Anarchists. Feminism. Human Rights. 1800's-90's. *1046*

Defense industries. Civic Unity Committee. Japanese Americans. Negroes. Race relations. Washington (Seattle). World War II. 1940-45. *2624*

—. Discrimination. Executive Order 8802. March on Washington Movement. Military. Randolph, A. Philip. Webster, Milton. 1941-44. *2635*

Defense Policy *See also* National Security.

—. Federal Policy. Industry. Labor Unions and Organizations. World War II. 1939-41. *2593*

Deinstitutionalization. Aged. Crime and Criminals. Mental Illness. 19c-20c. *2712*

—. Crime and Criminals. Mental Illness. 1960's-70's. *2984*

Deitz, John F. Chippewa Lumber and Boom Company. Individualism. Weyerhaeuser, Frederick. Wisconsin (Cameron Dam). 1900-24. *1967*

Delany, Martin Robinson. American Colonization Society. Black nationalism. Liberia. 1820-58. *620*

Delaware. Burris, Samuel D. Garrett, Thomas. Hunn, John. Tubman, Harriet. Underground Railroad. 1820-60. *712*

—. DuPont, Pierre S. Educational Reform. Legislation. 1890's-1921. *2452*

—. DuPont, Pierre S. Negroes. Philanthropy. Public Schools. 1918-30. *2451*

—. George, Henry. Political Parties. Reform. Single Tax movement. 1890's. *1085*

Delaware (Wilmington). Bancroft, Joseph and Sons Company. Miller, Franklin, and Stevenson (firm). Scientific management. Textile Industry. 1911-27. *2281*

Delegates. Constitutional conventions, state. Reconstruction. Virginia. 1867-68. *1022*

—. Councils and Synods. Episcopal Church, Protestant. Kinsolving, George Herbert. Texas. Veto. Women. 1921-70. *2347*

DeLeon, Daniel. Anti-Catholicism. Capitalism. Socialism. 1891-1914. *55*

—. Great Britain. Socialism. 1880-1917. *177*

—. Labor Unions and Organizations. 1893-1908. *172*

—. Letters. Socialist Labor Party. 1896-1904. *2094*

Delinquency. *See* Juvenile Delinquency.

Delmo Housing Corporation. Farm Security Administration. Missouri. Southern Tenant Farmers' Union. Tenancy. 1939-80. *1821*

Deloria, Vine, Jr. American Indian Movement. Federal Government. Indians. Political Protest. South Dakota. Wounded Knee (occupation). 1877-1970's. *2712*

Democracy *See also* Federal Government; Middle Classes; Referendum; Socialism; Suffrage.

—. Antimilitarism. Jordan, David Starr. World War I. 1898-1917. *1867*

—. Attitudes. Federal Reserve System. Income tax. Reform. Wilson, Woodrow. 1913-21. *1994*

—. Business. Cooperative Association of America. Morality. Peck, Bradford *(World a Department Store)*. Utopias. 1880-1925. *263*

—. Catholic Church. Intellectuals. Liberalism. Racism. 1924-59. *1560*

—. Child-rearing. Family. Infants. Spock, Benjamin *(Baby and Child Care)*. 1917-50. *1589*

—. Cities. Howe, Frederic C. Liberalism. Progressivism. ca 1890-1940. *2013*

—. Communitarianism. Liberalism. Progressive Era. 1890-1920's. *2049*

—. Decisionmaking. Federal regulation. Social policy. 1970-75. *2734*

—. Democratic Party. Ethnicity. Nebraska. Prohibition. Republican Party. 1907-20. *1937*

—. Education. Fundamentalism. Local Politics. Social Change. Vigilantism. 1920's. *2375*

—. Institutions. New Left. 1965-72. *2707*

—. Mass Media. Publicity. Reform. 1900-29. *1624*

—. Political Speeches. Prohibition. Women. 1920-34. *2356*

—. Politics. Social Change. Women. 1634-1935. *106*

Democratic Party. Abolition Movement. New York (Utica). Proslavery Sentiments. Riots. 1835. *709*

—. Adams, John Quincy. Elections (presidential). Jackson, Andrew. Slavery. Whig Party. 1828-44. *737*

—. Alabama. Civil Rights. Folsom, James E. Negroes. State Government. Women. 1947-58. *2668*

—. Alabama. Manning, Joseph C. Populism. State Politics. 1892-96. *1387*

—. Arizona. Congressional Union for Woman Suffrage. Political Campaigns. Women. 1914. 1916. *2164*

—. Business. Campbell, Thomas M. Progressivism. State Government. Texas. 1907-11. *2264*

—. California. End Poverty In California (program). Political Campaigns (gubernatorial). Sinclair, Upton. ca 1933-34. *2592*

—. Civil rights. Congress. Kennedy, John F. 1960-63. *2840*

—. Civil rights. Congress. Legislation. Partisanship. Regionalism. Republican Party. 1963-72. *2803*

—. Civil rights. Elections (presidential). South Carolina. 1948-72. *1630*

—. Civil Rights Act (US, 1964). Indiana. Primaries (presidential). Wallace, George C. Welsh, Matthew E. 1964. *2900*

—. Compromise of 1877. Elections (presidential). Reconstruction. Republican Party. Woodward, C. Vann. 1876-77. *1086*

—. Conservatism. North Carolina. Primaries, gubernatorial. Progressivism. 1890-1920. *2340*

—. Constitutional Amendments (18th and 21st). Prohibition. Raskob, John J. Roosevelt, Franklin D. 1928-33. *2536*

—. Courts. Primaries. Segregation. South Carolina. Waring, J. Waties. 1947-52. *2683*

—. Democracy. Ethnicity. Nebraska. Prohibition. Republican Party. 1907-20. *1937*

—. Douglas, Stephen A. Political Factions. Sanders, George. Young America movement. 1850's. *547*

—. Educational reform. Ethnic groups. Junior High Schools. Massachusetts (Somerville). Middle Classes. Progressivism. 1912-24. *2335*

—. Elections. Louisiana. Military Occupation. Reconstruction. Rousseau, Lovell H. 1868-69. *990*

—. Equal opportunity. Jacksonianism. Social theory. Wealth. 1836-46. *537*

—. Farmers' Alliance. North Carolina. State Politics. Vance, Zebulon B. 1880-90. *1366*

—. House of Representatives. Human Rights. New Jersey. Norton, Mary T. Women. 1920-30. *2415*

—. Illinois. Republican Party. Slavery. Trumbull, Lyman. 1855-72. *323*

—. Liberty Party. Negro suffrage. New York. Referendum. Whig Party. 1840-47. *595*

—. NAACP. Negro Suffrage. Primaries. *Smith* v. *Allwright* (US, 1944). South. Supreme Court. 1890's-1944. *1722*

—. NAACP. Negro Suffrage. Primaries. Supreme Court. Texas. 1927-45. *1723*

—. Nebraska. Political Parties. Populism. 1890's. *1394*

—. Negroes. Political participation. Poverty. South. 1960's. *2837*

Democrats. Constitutional Conventions, state. Oklahoma. Woman Suffrage. 1870-1907. *146*

Democrats, silver. Bimetallism. Tennessee (Memphis). 1895-96. *994*

Demography *See also* Birth Control; Mortality; Population.

—. Air pollution. Clean Air Act (US, 1970). Energy. Fiscal Policy. State Government. 1970-79. *2719*

Demonstrations *See also* Riots; Youth Movements.

—. Abernathy, Ralph. Alabama (Birmingham). Civil rights. King, Martin Luther, Jr. Shuttlesworth, Fred L. 1956-79. *2809*

Demonstrations

—. Alabama (Selma). Civil Rights. Collins, LeRoy. Community Relations Service. Florida. 1965-68. *2897*
—. Civil rights. Congress. Legislation. Public opinion. 1957-77. *2813*
—. Civil rights. Desegregation. Florida (Tampa). Fort, Clarence. Lane, Julian. Negroes. 1960. *2902*
—. Civil Rights. Negroes. Oklahoma (Oklahoma City). Restaurants. 1958-64. *2835*
—. Ohio (Cincinnati). Protestant Churches. Temperance Movements. Women's Christian Temperance Union. 1874. *1446*
—. Peace movements. Public opinion. Vietnam War. ca 1965-73. *2752*
Denman, Thomas. Andral, Gabriel. Bloodletting. Dewees, William P. Medicine (practice of). Obstetrics. 1800-1945. *254*
Deportation. Immigrants. Labor Unions and Organizations. Mexican Americans. New Deal. 1930's. *2500*
Depressions *See also* Recessions.
—. Agricultural Adjustment Administration. Farmers. Federal Policy. New Deal. New York, western. 1934. *2487*
—. Agricultural Adjustment Administration. Labor Unions and Organizations. Sharecroppers. Southern Tenant Farmers' Union. ca 1930's. *2602*
—. Alberta. British Columbia. Coal Mines and Mining. Pass Strike of 1932. 1920's-30's. *1811*
—. Arizona (Salt River Valley). Farmers. Japanese Americans. Race Relations. 1934-35. *2469*
—. Black nationalism. Communism. Garvey, Marcus. New York City (Harlem). 1931-39. *2561*
—. Bootlegging. Florida (Hernando County). Law enforcement. Liquor. Prohibition. 1929-33. *2359*
—. British Columbia. Industrial Relations. National Unemployed Workers' Association. Unemployment. Workers' Unity League. 1930-39. *1830*
—. Canada. City Government. Public Welfare. ca 1930-40. *1695*
—. Capitalism. Political Attitudes. Radicals and Radicalism. Texas. 1929-33. *2460*
—. Civilian Conservation Corps (Indian Divison). Indians (reservations). Sioux Indians. South Dakota. 1933-42. *2486*
—. Communist Party. Sports. 1920's-40's. *2564*
—. DeBernardi, G. B. Freedom Colony. Kansas. Labor Exchange. Utopias. 1894-1905. *1510*
—. Economic Reform. Fisher, Irving. Roosevelt, Franklin D. 1930's. *2468*
—. Employment. Federal Emergency Relief Administration. 1933-40. *2606*
—. Ethnicity. Progressive education. Race. 1929-45. *2513*
—. Farmer-Labor Party. New Deal. Oregon Commonwealth Federation. Political Factions. 1933-38. *2545*
—. Farmers. Government. Great Plains. Letters. New Deal. 1930-40. *2476*
—. Frankfurter, Felix. Keynes, John Maynard. New Deal. Public works. 1932-35. *2473*
—. General Education Board. Public policy. Rockefeller, John D. Secondary education. Social change. 1930's. *2478*
—. Great Plains. Radicals and Radicalism. State Politics. 1930-36. *2520*
—. Historiography. Hughes, Charles Evans. New Deal. Supreme Court. 1930's. 1950's-60's. *2572*
—. LaFollette, Philip F. New Deal. Progressivism. Roosevelt, Franklin D. Wisconsin Works Bill (1935). 1935. *2552*
—. Legislation. Provincial government. Public Welfare. Quebec. Taschereau, Louis Alexandre. ca 1934-36. *1700*
—. Liberalism. New Deal. Political activism. Socialist Party. Unemployment. 1929-36. *1804*
—. Long, Huey P. Louisiana. Politics. Share-Our-Wealth movement. Smith, Gerald L. K. 1930's. *2527*
—. Negroes. Progressive education. South. 1930-45. *2512*
—. Pennsylvania (Philadelphia). Public Welfare. 1820-28. *544*
Desegregation *See also* Segregation.
—. Alabama, University of. Attitudes. Students. 1963-74. *2870*
—. Baptists. *Brown* v. *Board of Education* (US, 1954). Georgia. Supreme Court. 1954-61. *2662*

SUBJECT INDEX

—. Baptists. Tennessee (Clinton). Turner, Paul. Violence. 1956. *2663*
—. *Brown* v. *Board of Education* (US, 1954). Equality. Negroes. Public Schools. 1950's-74. *2817*
—. Charleston City Railway Company. Negroes. Reconstruction. South Carolina. Streetcars. 1867. *1169*
—. Civil rights. Demonstrations. Florida (Tampa). Fort, Clarence. Lane, Julian. Negroes. 1960. *2902*
—. Class action suits. Courts. Discrimination, reverse. 1965-76. *2862*
—. Decisionmaking. Negroes. Political power. South. Teachers. Voting and Voting Behavior. 1950's-60's. *2831*
—. Discrimination, Educational. Graduate schools. Lawsuits. Negroes. North Carolina. Professional training. 1930-51. *1835*
—. Federal Government. Law enforcement. Public Schools. South. 1954-73. *2824*
—. Florida (Jacksonville). Public schools. Students. 1960's-70's. *2834*
—. North Carolina (Greensboro). Political Protest. Sit-ins. 1950's-60's. *2816*
Desha, Joseph. Courts. Debts. Kentucky. 1819-26. *823*
Desmond, Humphrey. Bible. Catholic Church. Protestantism. Religion in the Public Schools. Wisconsin. *Wisconsin ex rel. Frederick Weiss et al.* vs. *District School Board of School District 8* (1890). 1888-90. *1414*
Detention. Civil Rights. Cold War. Federal Bureau of Investigation. National security. Truman, Harry S. (administration). 1945-52. *2685*
Determinism. Garland, Hamlin. Indians. Reform. 1890-1923. *2111*
Detroit Citizens League. Leland, Henry. Michigan. Progressivism. Social Classes. 1912-24. *1925*
Detzer, Dorothy. Nye Committee. Peace Movements. Politics. Women's International League for Peace and Freedom. 1920-34. *2430*
Dever, William. Elections (mayoral). Ethnic groups. Illinois (Chicago). Negroes. Prohibition. 1923-27. *2350*
Devereux Mansion. Hall, Herbert. Massachusetts (Marblehead). Mental Illness. Occupational therapy. Work Cure Program. 1912-23. *1969*
DeVoe, Emma Smith. Duniway, Abigail Scott. Pacific Northwest. Woman suffrage. 1854-1912. *130*
Dewdney, Edgar. Agriculture. Hunting. Indians (reservations). Northwest Territories. Saskatchewan. 1879-84. *1038*
Dewees, William P. Andral, Gabriel. Bloodletting. Denman, Thomas. Medicine (practice of). Obstetrics. 1800-1945. *254*
Dewey, John. Addams, Jane. Dix, Dorothea. Emerson, Ralph Waldo. Pragmatism. Transcendentalism. 1830's-1960's. *231*
—. Attitudes. Higher education. Reserve Officers' Training Corps. 1920-38. *1847*
—. Blakely Institute. Georgia. Kilpatrick, William Heard. Progressive education. 19c-20c. *2301*
—. Education. Philosophy. 1909-30's. *373*
—. Education. Progressivism. Social change. 1890-1979. *1834*
—. Educational Reform. Europe. Progressivism. 1800-1960. *1866*
—. Foreign policy. Pacifism. War. 1918-32. *1615*
Dewey, John (letters). Feminism. Klyce, Scudder. 1915-31. *1536*
Diaries *See also* Personal Narratives.
—. American Revolution. Drinker family. Friends, Society of. Pennsylvania (Philadelphia). Prisoners. Virginia (Winchester). 1777-81. *526*
—. Coal Mines and Mining. Medrick, George. Pennsylvania, western. Strikes. United Mine Workers of America. 1927. *2372*
—. Fox, Ruth May. Suffrage. Utah. Women. 1865-95. *1119*
—. Freedmen's Bureau. Hopkins, Sterling. Reconstruction. Virginia. 1868. *1056*
—. Mormons. Musser, Elise Furer. Political Leadership. Utah. 1897-1967. *301*
Dickenson, Robert Latou. Birth control. Physicians. Sanger, Margaret. Values. Women. 1830-1970. *87*
Diet. *See* Food Consumption.
Diplomacy. Argell, James B. Chinese Exclusion Act (US, 1882). Congress. Immigration. 1876-82. *947*

Discrimination

Disability insurance. Bureaucracies. Business. Federal government. Social Security. 1900-40. *1829*
Disasters *See also* names of particular disasters, e.g. San Francisco Earthquake and Fire (1906).
—. Arkansas. Droughts. Negroes. Plantations. Red Cross. Sharecroppers. 1930-31. *2463*
Disciples of Christ. Authority. Egalitarianism. Republicanism. 1780-1820. *907*
Discrimination *See also* Civil Rights; Minorities; Racism; Segregation; Sex Discrimination.
—. Affirmative action. *Fullilove* v. *Klutznick* (US, 1980). Minorities. *Regents of the University of California* v. *Allan Bakke* (US, 1978). Supreme Court. *United Steelworkers of America* v. *Weber* (US, 1979). 1970's. *2782*
—. Agriculture. Arizona (Salt River Valley). Japanese (Issei). Race Relations. 1934-35. *2582*
—. Armies. Great Britain. White, Walter F. World War II. 1943-44. *2626*
—. Baptists. Japanese Americans. Resettlement. World War II. 1890-1970. *1651*
—. Boas, Franz. Scientists. Wilder, Burt G. 1900-15. *1884*
—. British Columbia. California. Gold Rushes. Negroes. Race Relations. 1849-66. *592*
—. California (Sausalito). International Brotherhood of Boilermakers, Iron Shipbuilders and Helpers of America. *James* v. *Marinship* (California, 1945). Labor. Negroes. Shipbuilding. 1940-48. *2653*
—. Catholic University of America. Colleges and Universities. District of Columbia. Negroes. Wesley, Charles H. 1914-48. *2304*
—. Chinese Americans. Economic Conditions. Japanese Americans. Nativism. Social Status. 1840's-1978. *83*
—. Civil Rights. Equality. Negroes. Political Attitudes. Reconstruction. Texas. 1865-70. *1200*
—. Civil Rights Organizations. Florida (Miami). Louisiana (New Orleans). Murray, Hugh T., Jr. (reminiscences). 1959-60. *2871*
—. Constitution League. Foraker, Joseph B. Hepburn Bill, Warner-Foraker Amendment (1906). Jim Crow laws. Negroes. Railroads. Washington, Booker T. (and Committee of 12). 1906. *1919*
—. Dancey, John C. Michigan (Detroit). Urban League. Washington, Forrester B. 1916-39. *1696*
—. Defense industries. Executive Order 8802. March on Washington Movement. Military. Randolph, A. Philip. Webster, Milton. 1941-44. *2635*
—. Editors and Editing. Negro (term). Publishers and Publishing. 1898-1975. *1590*
—. Equal rights. Homosexuals. 20c. *1677*
—. Fair Employment Practices Committee. Negroes. Railroads. Southeastern Carriers Conference. World War II. 1941-45. *2630*
—. Federal Policy. Freedmen's Bureau. Mississippi. Reconstruction. State Government. 1865. *1227*
—. Freedmen's Bureau. Johnson, Andrew. Law. Reconstruction. 1865-66. *1226*
—. Hospitals. Mercy Hospital (proposed). Negroes. Ohio (Cleveland). 1927-30. *2380*
—. Idaho. Mormons. Politics. 1880-95. *1120*
—. Jews. Negroes. Racism. 1890-1915. *1938*
—. Labor Unions and Organizations. Mexican Americans. North Central States. Steel Industry. 1919-45. *1802*
—. Labor Unions and Organizations. National Colored Labor Union. National Labor Union. Negroes. 1866-72. *1137*
—. Mexican Americans. Political Participation. 1930-75. *1679*
—. Negroes. Public Welfare. South. 1865-90. *1236*
—. Voting and Voting Behavior. -1973. *133*
Discrimination, Educational. Cincinnati Colored School system. Economic Conditions. Negroes. Ohio. Social Change. 19c. *832*
—. Courts. District of Columbia. Negroes. Public schools. 1804-1974. *1844*
—. Courts. Florida, University of. Hawkins, Virgil Darnell. Lawyers. Legal education. 1949-76. *1554*
—. Desegregation. Graduate schools. Lawsuits. Negroes. North Carolina. Professional training. 1930-51. *1835*
—. Disfranchisement. Middle Classes. Negro Suffrage. North Carolina. Progressivism. Public Finance. Whites. 1880-1910. *2316*
—. Female seminary movement. Women. 1818-91. *202*

Discrimination

—. Harlan, John Marshall. *Joseph W. Cumming, James S. Harper and John Ladeveze* v. *School Board of Richmond County, Ga.* (US, 1899). Public Schools. Supreme Court. ca 1896-1907. *1194*
—. Indiana. NAACP. Negroes. ca 1869-1975. *211*
Discrimination, employment. Affirmative action. City Government. Negroes. Ohio (Cincinnati). 1963-67. *2888*
—. American Federation of Labor. Fair Employment Practices Committee. Federal Government. Labor Unions and Organizations. Shipbuilding. West Coast Master Agreement. World War II. 1939-46. *2627*
—. Arizona (Page). Indians. Industrial Relations. Navajo Construction Workers Associations. Office of Navajo Labor Relations. 1971-77. *2944*
—. Civil rights. Congress. Fair Employment Practices Committee. Roosevelt, Franklin D. (administration). World War II. 1941-46. *2640*
—. Civil Rights Act (US, 1964; Title VII). Courts. Equal opportunity. 1964-78. *2932*
—. Civil Rights Act (US, 1964; Title VIII). Income. Negroes. Women. 1964-70's. *2839*
—. Courts. Labor law. Women. 1876-1979. *43*
—. Equal opportunity. Law. Public policy. 1964-72. *2949*
—. Fair Employment Practices Committee. Minorities. South. World War II. 1941-45. *2644*
—. Georgia Railroad. Negroes. Strikes. 1909. *2220*
—. Jim Crow laws. NAACP. Negroes. Tennessee (Memphis). 1900-37. *1750*
—. Military Service (enlistees). Navies. Negroes. Race Relations. Segregation. 1798-1970's. 1970D 1900H. *41*
—. Negroes. 1890-1970. *1763*
Discrimination, housing. Metropolitan areas. School integration. 1945-77. *1858*
Discrimination, reverse. Class action suits. Courts. Desegregation. 1965-76. *2862*
Diseases *See also* names of diseases, e.g. diphtheria, etc.; Epidemics; Medicine (practice of).
—. Alabama. Public health. 1839-1930. *2078*
—. City planning. Sanitation. 1840-90. *245*
—. Public health. 1870-1920. *253*
Disfranchisement. Abolition Movement. Constitutional conventions, state. Gardner, Charles W. Hinton, Frederick A. Negroes. Pennsylvania. 1838. *596*
—. Discrimination, Educational. Middle Classes. Negro Suffrage. North Carolina. Progressivism. Public Finance. Whites. 1880-1910. *2316*
District of Columbia. Catholic University of America. Colleges and Universities. Discrimination. Negroes. Wesley, Charles H. 1914-48. *2304*
—. Congress. Education, Finance. Howard University. Politics. 1879-1928. *186*
—. Courts. Discrimination, Educational. Negroes. Public schools. 1804-1974. *1844*
—. Coxey, Jacob S. Political Protest. Unemployment. 1894. *1302*
—. Education. Miner, Myrtilla. Negroes. Spiritualism. 1851-1955. *190*
—. Firearms Control Regulations Act (US, 1975). Gun control. Methodology. US Conference of Mayors (report). 1975-80. *2778*
—. Gillett, Emma M. Legal education. Mussey, Ellen Spencer. Washington College of Law. Women. 1869-1949. *426*
—. Public housing. Redevelopment. 1943-46. *2618*
Divorce *See also* Family; Marriage.
—. Bourassa, Henri. Canada. Feminism. Woman suffrage. 1913-25. *1698*
—. Feminism. Marriage. Reform. Stanton, Elizabeth Cady. 1840-90. *1010*
—. Law. Massachusetts. Women. 1692-1786. *480*
Dix, Dorothea. Addams, Jane. Dewey, John. Emerson, Ralph Waldo. Pragmatism. Transcendentalism. 1830's-1960's. *231*
Dix, Dorothy. Advice columns. Feminism. Louisiana. New Orleans *Picayune* (newspaper). 1895-1900. *980*
Dix, I. F. Hoover, Herbert C. Local politics. Self-help. Unemployed Citizens' League. Washington (Seattle). 1931-32. *2417*
Dixon, Frederick John. Farmer, S. J. Independent Labour Party. Manitoba. Single tax. 1920-49. *1791*
Documents *See also* Manuscripts.

SUBJECT INDEX

—. Methodist Episcopal Church. Slave Revolts. Turner, Nat. Virginia. 1831-32. *908*
—. Negroes. Slavery. Social Conditions. 1774-1841. *788*
Dogberry, Obediah. *Liberal Advocate* (newspaper). New York (Rochester). Religious liberty. 1832-34. *589*
Dohrn, Anton. Hyde, Ida H. Italy. Naples Zoological Station. Scientific Experiments and Research. Women. 1896-97. *1434*
Domestic Policy *See also* Federal Policy.
—. Kennedy, John F. Mental Retardation Facilities and Community Mental Health Centers Construction Act (US, 1963). Politics. Social Security Act (US, 1935; amended, 1963). 1961-63. *2976*
Domesticity. Attitudes. Lincoln, Mary Todd. Stanton, Elizabeth Cady. Stowe, Harriet Beecher. 1830-80. *443*
—. Curricula. Home economics. Progressivism. Sex roles. 1900-20. *2314*
—. Economic independence. Education. Feminism. 1960's-70's. *2903*
—. Feminism. Howe, Julia Ward. Motherhood. Reform. 1844-85. *349*
Domestics. Female Charitable Society. Girls. Industrialization. Massachusetts (Salem). 1800-40. *882*
—. Industrial Workers of the World. Labor Unions and Organizations. Progressive era. Street, Jane (letter). 1917. *2224*
Donnelly, Ignatius. Literature. Populism. 1831-90's. *1359*
Dorr's Rebellion. Election Laws. *Luther* v. *Borden* (US, 1849). Rhode Island. State government. Supreme Court. 1842-49. *591*
Douglas, H. Ford. Antislavery Sentiments. Civil War. Emigration. Military Service. Negroes. 1854-65. *666*
Douglas, Stephen A. Democratic Party. Political Factions. Sanders, George. Young America movement. 1850's. *547*
—. Lincoln, Abraham. Morality. Political Attitudes. Slavery. 1850's. *738*
Douglas, William O. Civil rights. Constitutional Law. Judicial process. Liberalism. Supreme Court. 1928-77. *1715*
Douglass, Frederick. Abolition Movement. American Anti-Slavery Society. Garrison, William Lloyd. 1833-51. *770*
—. Abolition Movement. Christianity. 1830's-60's. *778*
—. Abolition movement. Constitutional Amendments (15th). Negroes. Theology. 1825-86. *777*
—. Abolition Movement. Garnet, Henry Highland. Negroes. Political Factions. 1840-49. *742*
—. Abolition movement. Great Britain. 1845-47. *649*
—. Abolition movement. Ireland (Belfast). Presbyterian Church. Smyth, Thomas. 1846. *697*
—. Antislavery Sentiments. Brown, John. Letters. 1851-56. *725*
—. Centennial Celebrations. Negroes. Pennsylvania (Philadelphia). 1876. *1157*
—. Ethnicity. Justice. 19c. 1975. *657*
—. Ethnology. Speeches, Addresses, etc. 1854. *700*
—. Human Relations. Letters. 1846-94. *390*
—. Journalism. New York City. Racism. 1841-47. *408*
—. Patronage. Politics. Republican Party. 1870-95. *1235*
—. Social change. Violence. ca 1840-95. *658*
Douglass, Mabel Smith. Colleges and Universities. Lobbying. Middle Classes. New Jersey College for Women. Women. 1911-18. *2324*
Dowie, John Alexander. Christian Catholic Church. Evangelism. Illinois (Zion). 1888-1907. *1512*
Downing, George T. Negroes. Public schools. Rhode Island (Newport). School Integration. 1855-66. *841*
Draper, Andrew Sloan. Assimilation. Education. Indians. 1880's-1913. *1424*
—. City Politics. Educational Reform. Ohio (Cleveland). 1892-94. *1423*
Draper, E. D. Ballou, Adin Augustus. Hopedale Community. Massachusetts (Milford). Utopias. 1824-56. *917*
Dred Scott v. *Sandford* (US, 1857). Marshall, John. Slavery. Supreme Court. Taney, Roger Brooke. 1820-60. *785*
Drinker family. American Revolution. Diaries. Friends, Society of. Pennsylvania (Philadelphia). Prisoners. Virginia (Winchester). 1777-81. *526*

Eaton

Droughts. Agriculture. Nebraska. Politics. Populism. 1880's-90's. *1395*
—. Arkansas. Disasters. Negroes. Plantations. Red Cross. Sharecroppers. 1930-31. *2463*
Drugs. Armies. Mexico. New Mexico (Columbus). Pershing, John J. Prostitution. Venereal disease. 1916-17. *2068*
—. Consumer protection. Federal regulation. Legislation. Methodology. 1962-73. *2956*
—. Consumers. Food, Drug, and Cosmetic Act (US, 1938). Regulation. 1938-78. *1818*
—. Federal regulation. Kefauver, Estes. Senate Subcommittee on Antitrust and Monopoly. South. 1950's-60's. *2939*
—. Law Enforcement. Utah. 1967-71. *2770*
DuBois, W. E. B. Africa. Makonnen, T. Ras. Pan-Africanism. USA. 1919-73. *2881*
—. Baker, Ray Stannard. Civil rights. Liberalism. Negroes. Wilmer, Cary Breckenridge (interview). 1900-10. *2110*
—. Blyden, Edward Wilmot. Padmore, George. Pan-Africanism. 1776-1963. *25*
—. Conservatism. Negroes. Periodicals. Race relations. Radicals and Radicalism. Washington, Booker T. 1900-10. *1983*
—. Constitutional Amendments (19th). *Crisis* (periodical). Negroes. Woman Suffrage. 1910-34. *1712*
—. Cooperatives. Economic Theory. Negroes. 1940. *2498*
—. Education. Negroes. Social problems. 1897-1963. *1565*
—. Education. Ethnic studies. German Americans. Irish Americans. Woodson, Carter G. 1649-1972. *188*
—. Elites. Intellectuals. Negroes. Talented Tenth strategy. 1895-1919. *2090*
—. Elites. Liberal education. Negroes. Talented Tenth strategy. 1890's-1963. *1591*
—. Equality. Wilson, Woodrow. 1911-18. *1952*
—. Human rights. Negroes. Women. 1910-20. *1874*
—. Ideology. Integration. Negro Renaissance. 1903-74. *1543*
DuBose, William Porcher. Conservatism. Episcopal Church, Protestant. Miles, James Warley. Murphy, Edgar Gardner. South. Theology. 1840-1920. *62*
Dudzik, Mary Theresa. Addams, Jane. Franciscan Sisters of Chicago. Illinois. Polish Americans. Social Work. 1860-1918. *369*
Due process. Black, Hugo. Constitutional Amendments (1st). Judicial Administration. 1936-79. *1717*
—. Law. Virginia. 1634-1700. *507*
Dueling. Burnside, Thomas E. Crawford, George W. Georgia. Law. 1809-28. *545*
Dugdale, Joseph A. Abolition movement. Friends, Society of. Reform. 1810-96. *297*
Duke, Jesse C. Alabama. Editors and Editing. Montgomery *Herald* (newspaper). Negroes. Political Commentary. Republican Party. 1886-1916. *1185*
Duke University Medical Center. Civil rights. Harvey, Oliver. Labor Unions and Organizations. North Carolina (Durham). 1930's-70's. *2938*
Dukhobors. Public schools. Saskatchewan. 1905-50. *1855*
Duniway, Abigail Scott. Constitutions, State. Oregon. Voting rights. Woman Suffrage. 1860's-1912. *1093*
—. DeVoe, Emma Smith. Pacific Northwest. Woman suffrage. 1854-1912. *130*
—. Newspapers. Oregon (Portland). Utah. Wells, Emmeline B. Woman suffrage. 19c. *1092*
Dunkards. Friends, Society of. Mennonites. Militarism. Pacifism. 1900-78. *1571*
Dunne, Edward F. Educational Reform. Illinois (Chicago). Progressives. 1905-10. *2299*
DuPont, Pierre S. Delaware. Educational Reform. Legislation. 1890's-1921. *2452*
—. Delaware. Negroes. Philanthropy. Public Schools. 1918-30. *2451*
Durham, William J. Craft, Juanita. NAACP. Smith, Antonio Maceo. Texas. White, Lulu B. 1933-50. *1586*
Dwight, Theodore. Antislavery Sentiments. Connecticut. Poetry. 1788-1829. *640*

E

Eaton, John, Jr. Black capitalism. Civil War. Davis Bend colony. Freedmen. Mississippi. 1862-66. *1249*

Eaton, Nathaniel. Corporal punishment. Harvard University. Massachusetts (Cambridge). Puritans. Trials. 1638. *495*

Ebenezer Baptist Church. Civil Rights. Georgia (Atlanta). King, Martin Luther, Jr. (tribute). 1968. 1977. *2842*

École Sociale Populaire. Catholic Church. Propaganda. Quebec (Montreal). Syndicalism. Working Class. 1911-49. *1806*

Ecology *See also* Conservation of Natural Resources; Environment; Pollution; Wilderness.
—. American Petroleum Institute. Hoover, Herbert C. Oil Industry and Trade. Politics. Pollution. 1921-26. *2365*
—. California. Reclamation Movement. 1874-1974. *163*
—. Krutch, Joseph Wood. Materialism. Values. 1920's-70. *1660*

Economic Aid. Black power. Church and Social Problems. Episcopal Church, Protestant. General Convention Special Program. Self-determination. 1963-75. *2850*

Economic Conditions *See also* terms beginning with Economic; Natural Resources.
—. Alaska. Assimilation. Brady, John Green. Indian-White Relations. Tlingit Indians. 1878-1906. *1016*
—. Alberta. Alienation. Farmers. Political Protest. 1921-79. *2948*
—. Amherst Federation of Labor. Labor Unions and Organizations. Nova Scotia (Amherst). Strikes. 1901-31. *1801*
—. Antislavery Sentiments. Bain, John Mackintosh. Georgia (Darien). Petitions. 1736-55. *518*
—. Bushnell, Horace. Christianity. Gladden, Washington. Politics. Social gospel. Youth. 1836-1918. *995*
—. Chinese Americans. Discrimination. Japanese Americans. Nativism. Social Status. 1840's-1978. *83*
—. Cincinnati Colored School system. Discrimination, Educational. Negroes. Ohio. Social Change. 19c. *832*
—. Civil rights. Communist Party. Negroes. New York City (Harlem). Political Protest. 1930's. *2563*
—. Civil rights. Income. Public Policy. 1948-75. *2861*
—. Civil rights. Negroes. 1960's-70's. *2829*
—. Civilian Conservation Corps. New Deal. Vermont. 1933-42. *2596*
—. Convict lease system. Georgia. Prisons. Racism. 1868-1909. *1044*
—. Employment. Equal opportunity. Law. Negroes. Occupations. 1954-72. *1785*
—. Feminism. Sex. Social Classes. 1600-1900. *36*
—. Georgia (Atlanta). Political change. Race Relations. 1960's-73. *2812*
—. Labor. New Deal. Texas. 1929-39. *2573*
—. Letters. Mann, Mary Tyler Peabody. Ohio. Poorhouses. 1795-1858. *884*
—. National Recovery Administration. New Deal. Supreme Court. Virginia. 1933-35. *2517*
—. Negro suffrage. Race Relations. Washington, Booker T. 1895. *1149*
—. Negroes. Race Relations. Social change. Violence. 1960's. *2851*
—. Racism. Reconstruction. Social Classes. South. 1865-76. *1071*

Economic dependence. Land reform. Negroes. Reconstruction. 1861-1900. *1155*

Economic Development. Appalachian Regional Development Act (US, 1965). Regional development. Social Conditions. 1965-75. *2927*
—. Forest Service. Minnesota, northeastern. Public Policy. Superior National Forest. Wilderness. 1923-26. *2437*

Economic Growth *See also* Economic Policy; Industrialization; Modernization.
—. Attitudes. Governors. Segregation. South. 1950-69. *1533*
—. Bishop Hill Colony. Communalism. Illinois. Swedish Americans. Westward Movement. 1846-59. *935*
—. Conservation of Natural Resources. National Parks and Reserves. 1870's - 1973. *90*

Economic History Association (annual meeting). Great Britain. Higher Education. Research. 19c-20c. 1977. *191*

Economic independence. Black nationalism. Bruce, John Edward. Self-help. 1874-1924. *16*
—. Domesticity. Education. Feminism. 1960's-70's. *2903*

Economic opportunity. Canada. Political Protest. Social Classes. USA. 1960-74. *2702*

—. Educational achievements. Men. Sex Discrimination. Women. 1962. 1973. *2908*

Economic Planning *See also* City Planning.
—. Business. Government. Labor Unions and Organizations. Liberalism. 1920-40. *1788*
—. New Deal. Public policy. 1932-41. *2539*

Economic Policy *See also* Agricultural Policy; Industrialization; Modernization; Tariff.
—. Foreign Policy. New Deal. Public works. Roosevelt, Franklin D. 1933. *2555*
—. Indians (reservations). Prisons. Reform. 19c. *158*
—. Populism. Prairie Provinces. Tariff. 1879. 1920-79. *1368*

Economic programs. Amlie, Thomas. Liberals. New Deal. Politics. Wisconsin. 1931-39. *2609*

Economic Reform. Canada. George, Henry. Industry. Poverty. Progress (concept). Social gospel. ca 1879-99. *975*
—. Depressions. Fisher, Irving. Roosevelt, Franklin D. 1930's. *2468*
—. Five-Day Plan. Hicks, Mary. Hicks, Mildred. 1931-40. *2589*
—. Hoffman, Christian Balzac. Kansas. Socialism. 1872-1915. *389*
—. Kansas. Politics. Rightmire, William F. Southern Farmers' Alliance. 1886-92. *1380*
—. Long, Huey P. Share-Our-Wealth movement. 1932-35. *2485*
—. Progressives. Record, George L. 1859-1933. *2277*

Economic Regulations *See also* Federal Regulation; Trade Regulations.
—. Labor. National Recovery Administration. Negroes. South. Wages. 1933-34. *2576*

Economic Research and Action Project. Civil Rights. Feminism. National Organization for Women. Student Nonviolent Coordinating Committee. 1960's. *2906*

Economic Structure. Abolition Movement. Attitudes. Competition. Poverty. ca 1830-60. *656*
—. Agricultural Labor. Freedmen. Racism. Reconstruction. Texas. 1865-74. *1263*

Economic Theory. Agrarianism. Angers, François-Albert. Cooperatives. Quebec. 1930-80. *1594*
—. Bellamy, Edward *(Looking Backward 2000-1887)*. North Central States. Populism. 1880's-90's. *1377*
—. Cooperatives. DuBois, W. E. B. Negroes. 1940. *2498*
—. George, Henry. Income. Landlords and Tenants. Population. Taxation. Technology. 1871-83. *1064*

Economics *See also* Business; Commerce; Depressions; Income; Industry; Labor; Land; Monopolies; Population; Prices; Property; Socialism.
—. Census Bureau. Cornell University. Negroes. Progressivism. Racism. Willcox, Walter F. 1895-1910. *1870*
—. Education. Historiography. Political systems. Social classes. 1840-20c. *219*
—. Emancipation. South. 1860's. *1213*
—. Populism. 1880-1900. *1362*

Ecumenism. Evangelism. Protestantism. Social change. Social justice. Student Christian Movement. 19c-20c. *5*

Eddy, Mary Baker. Christian Science. Political power. Women. 1879-99. *999*

Editorials. City Government. Franklin, James. Freedom of the Press. Inoculation. Massachusetts (Boston). *New England Courant* (newspaper). Smallpox. 1721. *535*
—. Constitutions. Labor Unions and Organizations. New Deal. Periodicals. Supreme Court. 1935-37. *2503*
—. Freedom of the Press. Newspapers. 1920. 1940. *1719*
—. Labor. *Miners' Magazine.* Poetry. Songs. Western Federation of Miners. 1900-07. *2293*

Editors and Editing *See also* Press; Reporters and Reporting.
—. Ager, Waldemar Theodore. Norwegian Americans. Novels. *Reform* (newspaper). Temperance Movements. 1893-1941. *368*
—. Agricultural reform. Farmers. Poe, Clarence Hamilton. *Progressive Farmer* (periodical). South. 1899-1964. *1555*
—. Alabama. Duke, Jesse C. Montgomery *Herald* (newspaper). Negroes. Political Commentary. Republican Party. 1886-1916. *1185*
—. Alabama (Mobile). Black Capitalism. Johnson, Andrew N. Republican Party. Tennessee (Nashville). 1890-1920. *273*

—. Antislavery Sentiments. Kansas. Newspapers. Religion. Rhetoric. 1855-58. *680*
—. Blackwell, Henry B. Feminism. Politics. Stone, Lucy. *Women's Journal* (periodical). 1870-1914. *1047*
—. Brownlow, William Gannaway. Temperance Movements. Tennessee. *Whig* (newspaper). 1838-51. *866*
—. Byrd, Harry F. Chambers, Lenoir. School Integration. Virginia. 1955-59. *2681*
—. California. Older, Fremont. Reporters and Reporting. San Francisco *Bulletin.* Women. 1895-1925. *1887*
—. Canada. Finnish Canadians. Kurikka, Matti. Mäkelä, A. B. Newspapers. Socialism. 1900-32. *464*
—. Carter, William Hodding, Jr. Mississippi. Political Reform. Race Relations. ca 1930-60. *340*
—. Chipman, George. *Grain Growers Guide* (periodical). Manitoba (Winnipeg). Reform. Social movements. 1905-30. *1637*
—. Civil rights. Fortune, Timothy Thomas. Negroes. 1881-1928. *95*
—. Discrimination. Negro (term). Publishers and Publishing. 1898-1975. *1590*
—. Liberalism. Milton, George Fort. New Deal. Tennessee. 1930's. *2521*
—. Mitchell, John P. Race Relations. *Richmond Planet* (newspaper). Virginia. ca 1883-1929. *407*
—. Mormons. Utah. *Woman's Exponent* (periodical). Women. 1872-1914. *3*
—. *Partisan Review* (periodical). Socialism. Stalinism. 1930's. *2493*

Education *See also* headings beginning with education and educational; Adult Education; Bilingual Education; Coeducation; Colleges and Universities; Curricula; Discrimination, Educational; Elementary Education; Federal Aid to Education; Higher Education; Illiteracy; Industrial Arts Education; Physical Education and Training; Progressive Education; Religious Education; Scholarship; Schools; Secondary Education; Special Education; Teaching; Textbooks; Vocational Education.
—. 20c. *1859*
—. Addams, Jane. Hull House. Ideology. Illinois (Chicago). Women. 1875-1930. *411*
—. Addams, Jane. Hull House. Illinois (Chicago). Working class. 1890's. *1426*
—. Affirmative action. Negroes. School Integration. 17c-20c. *2845*
—. African Baptist Church. Emancipation. Meachum, John Berry. Missouri (St. Louis). Negroes. 1815-54. *395*
—. Africans' School. Benezet, Anthony. Friends, Society of. Negroes. Pennsylvania (Philadelphia). 1770's-80's. *487*
—. Afro-American Studies. Negroes. 1674-1917. *212*
—. Alabama. 1930-51. *1852*
—. Alabama. American Missionary Association. Negroes. Talladega College. 1865-79. *1244*
—. Alabama State College. Negroes. Paterson, William Burns. 1878-1915. *1257*
—. Alden, Augustus E. Brownlow, William G. Carpetbaggers. City Government. Public welfare. Reconstruction. Republican Party. Tennessee (Nashville). 1865-69. *1049*
—. American Colonization Society. Crummell, Alexander. Liberia. Negroes. 1853-73. *1126*
—. American Missionary Association. Cardozo, Francis Louis. Freedmen. Reconstruction. South Carolina (Charleston). State Politics. 1865-70. *1243*
—. American Missionary Association. Civil Rights. Florida. Freedmen. 1864-74. *1245*
—. American Missionary Association. Civil War. Missouri. Negroes. 1862-65. *1241*
—. Arizona. Assimilation. Indians. Industrial Arts Education. Phoenix Indian School. 1890-1901. *1437*
—. Arizona. Bai-a-lil-le (medicine man). Civil Rights. Courts. Fort Huachuca. Indian Rights Association. Navajo Indians. Utah, southeastern. 1906-09. *2043*
—. Armies. Banks, Nathaniel Prentiss. Civil War. Louisiana. 1863-65. *1218*
—. Assimilation. Draper, Andrew Sloan. Indians. 1880's-1913. *1424*
—. Assimilation. Indians. Micmac Indians. Nova Scotia. Public policy. Religion. 1605-1872. *209*
—. Assimilation. Indians. Self-determination. 1960's-70's. *2963*
—. Assimilation. Jews. Labor movement. Socialism. 1880's-1945. *100*

Education

—. Associates of Dr. Bray. Bray, Thomas. Church of England. Missions and Missionaries. Negroes. 1717-77. *500*
—. Association for the Advancement of Women. Mitchell, Maria. Science. Women. 1870-89. *1035*
—. Attitudes. Blind. Employment. Pennsylvania (Pittsburgh). Pittsburgh Workshop for the Blind. 19c-1939. *1670*
—. Attitudes. Socialization. Women's studies. 1600-1974. *187*
—. Baptists. Missions and Missionaries. Negroes. South. 1862-81. *1240*
—. Baptists, Southern. Churches. Racism. Reconstruction. 1865-76. *1267*
—. Baptists, Southern. Negroes. Paternalism. 1880's-90's. *1266*
—. Barnett, Samuel Augustus. Cities. Great Britain. Poor. Progressivism. 1880's-1913. *2294*
—. Beecher, Catharine. Employment. Professionalization. Women. 1823-75. *182*
—. Berea College. Kentucky. Negroes. 1858-1908. *1225*
—. Books. Child-rearing. Pennsylvania (Philadelphia). Protestantism. Republicanism. 1780-1835. *577*
—. Brockwood Labor College. Fincke, William. Labor. 1919-37. *1614*
—. California. Preston School of Industry. Prisons. Rehabilitation. Youth. 1894-1955. *1558*
—. California (Alum Rock). Parents. Public Schools. Vouchers. 1960's-70's. *2960*
—. Canada. Federal government. Indians. Métis. 1940-70. *2959*
—. Canada. Indian-White Relations. 1978. *2972*
—. Chicago, University of. Curricula. Hutchins, Robert M. 1930-77. *1839*
—. Children. Great Britain. Nutrition. 1890-1920. *2053*
—. Children. New York House of Refuge. Reformatories. 1800-30. *898*
—. Children. Shakers. 1780-1900. *912*
—. Christianity. Freedmen. Presbyterians. 1872-1900. *1272*
—. Church and State. Great Britain. India. Secularization. 19c. *198*
—. Clapp, Elsie Ripley. Homesteading and Homesteaders. New Deal. Roosevelt, Eleanor. West Virginia (Arthurdale). 1933-44. *2477*
—. Clark, Peter Humphries. Negroes. Ohio (Cincinnati). Socialism. 1849-81. *332*
—. Colleges and Universities. Curricula. Individualism. Negroes. 1890-1970's. *1853*
—. Colleges and Universities. Ideology. Sex roles. Women. 19c-20c. *213*
—. Community control. Integration. Negroes. New York City (Brooklyn). Politics. 1882-1902. *1181*
—. Community organizing. Social work. 1920-39. *1523*
—. Community services. Housing. Indian-White relations. North Carolina Commission of Indian Affairs. ca 1700-1978. *108*
—. Congregationalism. New Mexico (Albuquerque). Prohibition. Social gospel. 1900-17. *2101*
—. Crime and Criminals. Morality. Pennsylvania. Wickersham, James P. 1866-81. *1401*
—. Democracy. Fundamentalism. Local Politics. Social Change. Vigilantism. 1920's. *2375*
—. Dewey, John. Philosophy. 1909-30's. *373*
—. Dewey, John. Progressivism. Social change. 1890-1979. *1834*
—. District of Columbia. Miner, Myrtilla. Negroes. Spiritualism. 1851-1955. *190*
—. Domesticity. Economic independence. Feminism. 1960's-70's. *2903*
—. DuBois, W. E. B. Negroes. Social problems. 1897-1963. *1565*
—. DuBois, W. E. B. Ethnic studies. German Americans. Irish Americans. Woodson, Carter G. 1649-1972. *188*
—. Economics. Historiography. Political systems. Social classes. 1840-20c. *219*
—. Education Department. Negroes. Reconstruction. 1867. *1277*
—. Elementary and Secondary Education Act (Title I; US, 1965). 1965-76. *2968*
—. Employment. Sex roles. Social Classes. Women. 1964-74. *2919*
—. Episcopal Church, Protestant. Louisiana (New Orleans). Polk, Leonidas L. Slavery. 1805-65. *730*
—. Evolution. LeConte, Joseph. 1875-1900. *1435*

SUBJECT INDEX

—. Farmers. Negroes. Tuskegee Institute. Washington, Booker T. 1881-1915. *1186*
—. Feminism. Troy Female Seminary. Values. Willard, Emma Hart. 1822-72. *810*
—. Ferm, Alexis Constantine. Ferm, Elizabeth Byrne. Individualism. 1880's-1970's. *847*
—. Fort Valley High and Industrial School. Georgia. Negroes. Torbert, James H. 1897-1911. *2296*
—. Freedmen's Bureau. Negroes. Texas. 1865-70. *1174*
—. Friends, Society of. Girls. Ontario. 1790-1820. *852*
—. Great Britain. Jefferson, Thomas. Milton, John. 17c-19c. *833*
—. Hall, G. Stanley. Minorities. Social Status. 1870's-1920. *2323*
—. Illinois. Jefferson, Thomas. Lincoln, Abraham. 1820-62. *835*
—. Illiteracy. Kentucky Illiteracy Commission. Kentucky (Rowan County). Stewart, Cora Wilson. 1910-20. *2325*
—. Indians. Manuscripts. Wisconsin. 1820-50. *848*
—. Juvenile Courts. Probation. 1899-1917. *2073*
—. Kentucky. Negroes. 1800-1954. *216*
—. Lincoln University. Lindsay, Lizzie A. Missouri (Jefferson City). Negroes. Turner, James Milton. 1865-75. *1179*
—. Long, Huey P. Louisiana. Working Class. 1928-35. *2515*
—. Management. Negroes. Whites. 1652-1972. *183*
—. Manual Training School. Maryland (Baltimore). Newell, Alexander McFadden. Politics. Shepherd, Henry Elliot. 1876-94. *1428*
—. Models. Research and Development Centers program. 1960's-70's. *2964*
—. Negroes. North Carolina. Reconstruction. School Integration. 1865-67. *1127*
—. New Brunswick. Socialism. Stuart, Henry Harvey. 1873-1952. *310*
—. New Jersey. Raritan Bay Union. Utopias. 1853-61. *940*
—. New York. Troy Female Seminary. Willard, Emma Hart. Women. 1809-70. *436*
—. Pennsylvania (Philadelphia). Women. Young Ladies Academy. 1780's-90's. *552*
—. Philosophy. 18c-20c. *1841*
—. Reform. 1870's-1970's. *222*
—. Science. Women. ca 1800-60. *816*
Education Department. Education. Negroes. Reconstruction. 1867. *1277*
Education, Experimental Methods *See also* Free Schools.
—. Behavior. Child development. Olerich, Henry. 1897-1902. *2311*
—. Beverly School. Industry. Massachusetts. 1900-17. *2321*
—. Blair, Nora Schelter. Brook Farm. Massachusetts. Personal narratives. Pratt, Frederick. Ripley, George. Utopias. 1841-47. *934*
—. Colleges and Universities. Minorities. New York, City University of. 1847-1980. *196*
—. Federal programs. Local Government. RAND Corporation. 1965-80. *2961*
Education, Finance *See also* Federal Aid to Education.
—. Anti-Catholicism. MacKinnon, Murdoch. Saskatchewan. School Act (amended). Scott, Walter. 1913-26. *1849*
—. Christianity. Corporations. Higher education. Social Darwinism. 1860-1930. *206*
—. Congress. District of Columbia. Howard University. Politics. 1879-1928. *186*
—. Kentucky. Negroes. Segregation. State Government. 1865-1954. *1178*
Educational achievements. Economic opportunity. Men. Sex Discrimination. Women. 1962. 1973. *2908*
Educational Administration. George Peabody College. Nashville, University of. Payne, William Howard. Teacher training. Tennessee. 1875-1901. *1411*
Educational Alliance. Americanization. Jews. New York City (Lower East Side). 1890-1914. *2310*
Educational policy. Bureau of Indian Affairs. Indians. Medill, William. 1845-49. *836*
—. Decentralization. New York City (Brownsville, Ocean Hill). Public Opinion. 1962-71. *2971*
—. Equal opportunity. Law. 1954-74. *2852*
—. Industrial Arts Education. Negroes. Speeches, Addresses, etc. Washington, Booker T. 1884-1904. *1283*

Educators

—. Lancaster, Joseph. Public schools. *Richmond Enquirer* (newspaper). Ritchie, Thomas. Virginia. 1803-50. *840*
—. Philippines. USA. 1900-13. *2320*
—. Public schools. 1840's-80's. *218*
Educational Reform *See also* Compulsory Education; Education; Educators; Free Schools; School Integration.
—. 1840-1980. *217*
—. Acculturation. Ideology. Industrialization. Pennsylvania. Social control. 1880-1910. *1420*
—. Adolescence. Boy Scouts of America. Boys' Clubs. Hall, G. Stanley. ca 1890-1910. *2074*
—. Agricultural Production. Cities. Country Life Movement. Rural Schools. 1900-20. *2302*
—. American Institute for Education. Elites. Massachusetts. Nationalism. Rural schools. 1830-37. *839*
—. California (Los Angeles). Curricula. Mexican Americans. Public schools. 1920's-30's. *1842*
—. California (San Francisco). Ethnicity. Religion. 1918-20. *2333*
—. California (San Francisco). Rincon School. Swett, John. 1853-62. *849*
—. Cities. Negroes. Public Schools. South. Teachers. 1865-90. *1238*
—. City Politics. Draper, Andrew Sloan. Ohio (Cleveland). 1892-94. *1423*
—. Colleges and Universities. Industrialization. North Carolina, University of. Social Change. 1850-75. *1406*
—. Colleges and Universities. Political Protest. West. 1964-74. *2967*
—. Colorado (Aspen). Higher Education. Paepcke, Walter. 1949-51. *2666*
—. Compulsory Education. Interest groups. Pennsylvania. Social Problems. 1880-1911. *200*
—. Corporal punishment. New Jersey. Schools. 1800-1972. *1432*
—. Cotton. Howell, Clark. Phillips, Ulrich B. Progressivism. 1903-05. *2062*
—. Counts, George S. Liberalism. Race. 1929-34. *2379*
—. Delaware. DuPont, Pierre S. Legislation. 1890's-1921. *2452*
—. Democratic Party. Ethnic groups. Junior High Schools. Massachusetts (Somerville). Middle Classes. Progressivism. 1912-24. *2335*
—. Dewey, John. Europe. Progressivism. 1800-1960. *1866*
—. Dunne, Edward F. Illinois (Chicago). Progressives. 1905-10. *2299*
—. Elites. Niles Bill (Ohio, 1898). Ohio (Toledo). Progressive Era. School boards. 1890's. *2328*
—. Free Schools. Howland, John. Legislation. Rhode Island. 1757-1838. *431*
—. Georgia (Atlanta). Illinois (Chicago). New York City. Progressivism. Teachers. 1890-1920. *2336*
—. Immigrants. New York (Buffalo). Public Schools. 1890-1916. *2332*
—. Iowa. Public schools. 1890-1900. *1421*
—. Jews. New York City. Richman, Julia. Women. 1880-1912. *289*
—. Manual training. Missouri (St. Louis). Woodward, Calvin. 1897-1914. *2305*
—. Massachusetts (Boston). Negroes. Separatist Movements. Smith, Thomas Paul. 1848-49. *855*
—. Meadows, Clarence W. Public Schools. Strayer, George D. Trent, W. W. West Virginia Education Association. 1932-58. *1837*
—. Mitchel, John Purroy. New York City. 1914-17. *2322*
—. Negroes. Pennsylvania (Philadelphia). White, Jacob C., Jr. 1857-1902. *441*
—. New Jersey. Princeton University. Wilson, Woodrow. 1902-10. *2334*
—. Providence Association of Mechanics and Manufacturers. Rhode Island. Working Class. 1790's-1850. *853*
—. Public Opinion. 1960-80. *2970*
—. Public Schools. Social Classes. 1787-1973. *203*
Educational Tests and Measurements. California. Ethnic groups. IQ tests. Progressivism. Students. 1917-21. *2300*
Educational Theory. Missouri (St. Louis). Vocational Education. Washington University (Manual Training School). Woodward, Calvin. 1879-1910. *1412*
—. Negroes. Washington, Booker T. 1881-1915. *193*
Educators *See also* Teachers.
—. 18c-20c. *1840*

Educators

—. Adult education. Howe, Joseph. Nova Scotia. 1827-66. *844*
—. *Brown* v. *Board of Education* (US, 1954). Negroes. School Integration. 1954-75. *2838*
—. Clapp, Hannah Keziah. Nevada, University of. Woman Suffrage. 1824-1908. *456*
—. Colleges and Universities. New Jersey. Pennsylvania. Professionalization. 1870-1915. *201*
—. Ethnographers. Evangelism. Indians (reservations). Pueblo Indians (Hopi). Sullivan, John H. Taylor, Charles A. 1870-89. *1050*
—. Forrester, Alexander. Nova Scotia (Truro). ca 1848-69. *842*
—. Iowa. Modernization. Public schools. 1890-1900. *1422*
Edwards, Jonathan. Hopkins, Samuel. New Divinity (doctrines). New England. Theology. 1730-1803. *479*
Edwards, Robert C. "Bob". Alberta. *Eye Opener* (newspaper). Populist. 1904-22. *1940*
Eells, Edwin. Dawes Act (US, 1887). Indians (agencies). Land Tenure. Skokomish Indian Reservation. Washington. 1871-95. *970*
Egalitarianism. American Revolution. Historiography. Social change. 1775-83. 20c. *494*
—. Authority. Disciples of Christ. Republicanism. 1780-1820. *907*
Ehringhaus, J. C. B. Legislation. North Carolina. Social Security Act (US, 1935). Unemployment insurance. 1935-37. *2556*
Eight-hour day. Business. California (San Francisco). Construction. Law and Order Committee. Strikes. 1916-17. *2232*
—. Central Labor Union. Knights of Labor. Labor Unions and Organizations. Massachusetts (Boston). Strikes. 1886. *1321*
Eisenhower, Dwight D. (administration). Federal Policy. Legislation. Public Welfare. Reform. 1950-60. *2659*
Election Laws. Apportionment. Attorneys General. Courts. Intergovernmental Relations. Voting Rights Act (US, 1965; Section 5). 1965-77. *2801*
—. Dorr's Rebellion. *Luther* v. *Borden* (US, 1849). Rhode Island. State government. Supreme Court. 1842-49. *591*
—. Goebel, William. Government Regulation. Kentucky. Railroads. Taylor, William S. 1887-1900. *961*
Elections *See also* Election Laws; Political Campaigns; Presidents; Primaries; Referendum; Suffrage; Voting and Voting Behavior.
—. Antilabor sentiments. Canada, western. Immigration. Ku Klux Klan. 1921-30's. *1603*
—. Breckinridge, Robert J., Jr. Breckinridge, William C. P. Courts. Kentucky. Negroes. Testimony. 1866-69. *1096*
—. Bulkley, Robert J. Ohio. Prohibition. Senate. 1918-30. *2445*
—. California. Capital punishment. Courts. 1954-72. *2791*
—. California. Ralston, Jackson. Reform. Single tax. 1932-38. *2504*
—. Community control. Mexican Americans. Texas (Crystal City). 1910-75. *2739*
—. Congress. Constitutional Amendments (14th, 15th). Federal Election Campaign Act (US, 1971, 1974). Supreme Court. Voting Rights Act (US, 1965). 1965-75. *2767*
—. Connecticut. Peace Movements. 1919-39. *1617*
—. Democratic Party. Louisiana. Military Occupation. Reconstruction. Rousseau, Lovell H. 1868-69. *990*
—. McKinley, William. Ohio. Republican Party. Working class. 1891-93. *1355*
—. Morgan, Thomas John. Socialism. United Labor Party (platform). 1886-96. *1342*
—. Negroes. Politics. Reconstruction. Tennessee (Shelby County). 1865-76. *1160*
—. Ohio (Cincinnati). Physicians. Professionalism. Progressivism. Public health. 1890-1900. *2021*
—. Political Attitudes. South Dakota (Lake County). Woman suffrage. 1885-90. *1098*
Elections (congressional). American Tobacco Company. Kentucky. Populism. 1886-92. *1365*
—. Loyalty. Reconstruction. Virginia. 1865. *960*
Elections (gubernatorial). Progressivism. Tennessee. ca 1890-1906. *2081*
Elections (mayoral). Dever, William. Ethnic groups. Illinois (Chicago). Negroes. Prohibition. 1923-27. *2350*

SUBJECT INDEX

Elections, municipal. City Politics. Knights of Labor. Negroes. Political Reform. Virginia (Richmond). 1886-88. *1303*
Elections (presidential). Adams, John Quincy. Democratic Party. Jackson, Andrew. Slavery. Whig Party. 1828-44. *737*
—. Butler, Benjamin F. (papers). People's Party. Third Parties. 1884. *1027*
—. California. Progressive Party. 1924. *2413*
—. California. Racism. Republican Party. Slavery. 1860. *757*
—. Civil rights. Democratic Party. South Carolina. 1948-72. *1630*
—. Civil War. Negroes. Political Participation. Republican Party. 1864. *1224*
—. Compromise of 1877. Democratic Party. Reconstruction. Republican Party. Woodward, C. Vann. 1876-77. *1086*
—. Conservatism. Mississippi. Segregation. Sillers, Walter. State Legislatures. 1948-64. *2677*
—. Hoover, Herbert C. Progressivism. Republican Party. Senate. 1930-32. *2369*
—. Long, Huey P. Roosevelt, Franklin D. Share-Our-Wealth movement. 1932-36. *2595*
—. New York. Prohibition. Republican Party. 1884. *1473*
Elections (provincial). Communist Party. Cooperative Commonwealth Federation. Saskatchewan. 1930's. *1680*
Elementary and Secondary Education Act (Title I; US, 1965). Education. 1965-76. *2968*
Elementary Education *See also* Kindergarten.
—. Boycotts. Christianity. Jews. New York City. Religion in the Public Schools. 1905-06. *2298*
—. Carden, Georgiana. Compulsory Education. Mexican Americans. Migrant Labor. 1920's. *2383*
—. Florida. Peabody Fund. Reconstruction. Segregation. 1869-76. *1433*
—. Ohio (Cincinnati). Urbanization. 1870-1914. *205*
Eliot, Samuel A. Antislavery Sentiments. Fugitive Slave Act (US, 1850). Massachusetts (Boston). Patriotism. Unitarianism. 1850-60. *752*
Eliot, William Greenleaf. Curricula. Higher education. Missouri (St. Louis). Trans-Mississippi West. Washington University. 1853-87. *189*
Elites *See also* Decisionmaking; Social Classes; Social Status.
—. Agricultural Labor. Political Culture. 1946-72. *1773*
—. Air Pollution. Pennsylvania (Pittsburgh). Reform. Smoke. Tilbury, Corwin D. 1890's-1918. *1961*
—. American Institute for Education. Educational Reform. Massachusetts. Nationalism. Rural schools. 1830-37. *839*
—. Antislavery Sentiments. Cultural imperialism. Great Britain. 18c-19c. *765*
—. California State Agricultural Society. Farmers. Grange. 1870's-80's. *1385*
—. City Government. Human Development Corporation. Missouri (St. Louis). Negroes. Poor. War on Poverty. 1964-75. *2935*
—. Colonial government. North Carolina. Regulator movement. Social change. 1760-75. *502*
—. Conservatism. Ontario (Ottawa). Political Leadership. Public Welfare. 1880-1912. *1310*
—. DuBois, W. E. B. Education. Negroes. Social problems. 1897-1963. *1565*
—. DuBois, W. E. B. Intellectuals. Negroes. Talented Tenth strategy. 1895-1919. *2090*
—. DuBois, W. E. B. Liberal education. Negroes. Talented Tenth strategy. 1890's-1963. *1591*
—. Educational reform. Niles Bill (Ohio, 1898). Ohio (Toledo). Progressive Era. School boards. 1890's. *2328*
—. Hays, Samuel P. Ideology. Professionalism. Progressivism. Wiebe, Robert. 20c. *1971*
—. Kansas. Negroes. Politics. Republican Party. Waller, John Lewis. 1878-1900. *468*
—. Medical education. Social status. 1890-1973. *1784*
—. Politics. Race relations. Riots. 1960's-70's. *2857*
Elkins, Stanley M. Abolition Movement. Historiography. 1829-60. 1954-76. *760*
Elkins, Stanley M. (review article). Abolitionists. Slavery. Transcendentalism. 1830-63. 1959-73. *791*
Elkins, Stephen B. Reform. Republican Party. State Politics. West Virginia. White, Albert B. 1901-05. *1895*
Ellery, William, Jr. Colleges and Universities. Rhode Island (Newport). Stiles, Ezra. 1770. *486*

Employment

Ellis, George E. City Government. Michigan (Grand Rapids). Progressivism. 1894-1921. *2106*
Ely, Richard T. Bascom, John. Commons, John R. Social gospel. Wisconsin, University of. 1870-1910. *1017*
Emancipation *See also* Freedmen.
—. Abolition Movement. Proslavery Sentiments. Radicals and Radicalism. 1790-1865. *637*
—. African Baptist Church. Education. Meachum, John Berry. Missouri (St. Louis). Negroes. 1815-54. *395*
—. African Colonization Movement. Georgia. Liberia. Tubman, Emily. 1816-57. *655*
—. American Colonization Society. Liberia. North Carolina. Slaveholders. 1800-60. *708*
—. Breckinridge, Robert J. Kentucky. State Politics. 1830-49. *677*
—. Cedar Creek Monthly Meeting. Farms. Friends, Society of. Moorman, Clark Terrell. Ohio. Virginia (Caroline County). 1766-1814. *743*
—. Chase, Salmon Portland. Republicans, Radical. 1861-64. *1005*
—. Civil War. Ohio. Racism. State Politics. 1863-65. *1182*
—. Colonization. Lincoln, Abraham. Negroes. 1852-65. *747*
—. Colonization. Lincoln, Abraham. Negroes. 1861-65. *1138*
—. Colonization. Mississippi Colonization Society. 1831-60. *685*
—. Economics. South. 1860's. *1213*
—. Freedmen. South. Whites. 1865-66. *969*
—. Owen, Robert Dale. Tennessee (Nashoba). Utopias. Wright, Frances (letters). 1820-29. *718*
Emancipation Car (collection). Antislavery Sentiments. Music. Simpson, Joshua McCarter. 1854. *627*
Emancipation Party. Abolition Movement. Breckinridge, Robert J. Breckinridge, William Lewis. Constitutions, State. Kentucky. Presbyterians. 1849. *676*
Emancipation Proclamation. Civil Rights. Civil War. Lincoln, Abraham. 1854-63. *1230*
—. Civil War. Illinois Volunteers. Republican Party. 1862-63. *1087*
—. Freedmen. Liberty. Lincoln, Abraham. Republican Party. 1862. *1131*
—. Lincoln and Lincolniana. Republican Party. 1863-64. *1199*
—. New Jersey. Peace Movements. State legislatures. 1864. *1009*
Emerson, Arthur L. Brotherhood of Timber Workers. Industrial Workers of the World. Labor Disputes. Louisiana, western. Lumber and Lumbering. Texas, eastern. 1900-16. *2207*
Emerson, Ralph Waldo. Addams, Jane. Dewey, John. Dix, Dorothea. Pragmatism. Transcendentalism. 1830's-1960's. *231*
—. Antinomianism. Puritans. Sermons. 1820's-30's. *570*
Emery, Sarah E. Van De Vort. Populism. Rhetoric. 1887-95. *1393*
Emigration *See also* Demography; Immigration; Population; Race Relations; Refugees.
—. American Colonization Society. Liberia. Negroes. 19c. *688*
—. Antislavery Sentiments. Civil War. Douglas, H. Ford. Military Service. Negroes. 1854-65. *666*
—. Bibb, Henry. Canada. Negroes. Separatism. USA. 1830-60. *672*
—. Civil War. Haiti. Negroes. 1860-64. *1254*
—. Ethiopia (Addis Ababa). Ford, Arnold. Negroes. 1930-35. *2436*
—. Kansas-Nebraska Act (US, 1854). Slavery. Wisconsin. 1850's. *690*
Eminent domain. Cohen, Julius Henry. Housing. New York. 1920's-30's. *2370*
Emmons, Glenn L. Bureau of Indian Affairs. Indians. Social Policy. Tribes. 1953-61. *2660*
—. Bureau of Indian Affairs. Indians (reservations). Industrialization. 1953-60. *2661*
Employment *See also* Discrimination, Employment; Occupations; Unemployment.
—. Agriculture Department. Equal opportunity. Federal policy. 1964-76. *2744*
—. Anthony, Lucy. Equal opportunity. Feminism. Shaw, Anna Howard. 1865-1919. *330*
—. Asian Americans. Ethnicity. Legislation. Naturalization. Racism. 1850-20c. *65*

Employment

—. Attitudes. Blind. Education. Pennsylvania. Pittsburgh Workshop for the Blind. 19c-1939. *1670*
—. Beecher, Catharine. Education. Professionalization. Women. 1823-75. *182*
—. Bilbo, Theodore G. Fair Employment Practices Committee. Filibusters. Mississippi. Racism. Senate. 1941-46. *2617*
—. Civil Rights. Federal Government. Public Policy. State Government. 20c. *1572*
—. Civil Rights Movement. Sex roles. Women's Liberation Movement. 1950's-75. *2905*
—. Civilian Conservation Corps. Environment. South Dakota. 1933-42. *2519*
—. Coal Mines and Mining. Mitchell, John. United Mine Workers of America. 1897-1907. *2213*
—. Construction. Ickes, Harold. Negroes. Public Works Administration. Quotas. 1933-40. *2535*
—. Corporations. Hoover, Herbert C. Labor Unions and Organizations. 1919-29. *2465*
—. Depressions. Federal Emergency Relief Administration. 1933-40. *2606*
—. Economic Conditions. Equal opportunity. Law. Negroes. Occupations. 1954-72. *1785*
—. Education. Sex roles. Social Classes. Women. 1964-74. *2919*
—. Feminism. Organizations. Racism. Social classes. World War II. 1942-45. *2629*
—. Housing. Negroes. Racism. Voting and Voting Behavior. 1960's-70's. *2810*
—. Immigrants. Law Enforcement. Maximum hours laws. State Government. Women. 1920. *2398*
—. Minorities in Politics. Negroes. New Deal. Roosevelt, Franklin D. 1930-42. *2586*
—. Reform. Servants. 1892-1920. *2271*
—. Women's liberation movement. World War II. 1920's-70's. *1529*
End Poverty In California (program). California. Democratic Party. Political Campaigns (gubernatorial). Sinclair, Upton. ca 1933-34. *2592*
Energy. Air pollution. Cities. Industry. Legislation. 1880-1920. *38*
—. Air pollution. Clean Air Act (US, 1970). Demography. Fiscal Policy. State Government. 1970-79. *2719*
English Canadians. Attitudes. Canada. Race. Sex. Woman Suffrage. ca 1877-1918. *1*
—. Canada. Family. Woman suffrage. 1877-1918. *111*
—. Canada. Immigrants. Propaganda. Puttee, Arthur. Radicals and Radicalism. Water Conservation. ca 1888-1913. *1327*
English language. Anderson, James T. M. Anglicization. Ethnic groups. Immigrants. Public schools. Saskatchewan. 1918-23. *1856*
English, William H. Congress. Constitutions, State. Kansas. Proslavery Sentiments. 1857-58. *629*
Enlightenment. Abolition Movement. Christianity. Morality. Nationalism. Phillips, Wendell. 1830-84. *716*
Entertainers. Adoption. Baker, Josephine. Civil rights. Negroes. World War II. 1940-75. *358*
Environment *See also* Conservation of Natural Resources; Ecology.
—. Air pollution. Legislation. Public Policy. 1967-78. *2763*
—. Cities. Citizen Lobbies. Consumers. Noise pollution. Reform. 1893-1932. *1684*
—. Civilian Conservation Corps. Employment. South Dakota. 1933-42. *2519*
—. Frontier and Pioneer Life. Historiography. 1492-1978. *51*
—. Highway Engineering. Lancaster, Samuel Christopher. Oregon (Columbia River Highway). ca 1900-41. *1931*
Environmental law. Army Corps of Engineers. Refuse Act (US, 1899). Waterways. 1876-1971. *977*
Environmental policy. Great Britain. Interest groups. 1970's. *2742*
Environmental protection. California (San Francisco Bay area). Consumers. Government regulation. Housing. Local government. Suburbs. 1940-80. *2718*
Environmental Protection Agency. Equal Employment Opportunity Commission. Labor. Occupational Safety and Health Act (US, 1970). Safety. Women. 1970-76. *2698*
Environmentalism. City Life. Law. Pennsylvania (Philadelphia). 1750-84. *496*
Epidemics *See also* names of contagious diseases, e.g. Smallpox, etc.

—. Cholera. Missouri (St. Louis). Public Health. 1849-67. *862*
Episcopal Church, Protestant. Allin, John M. Civil rights. Clergy. Mississippi. Political Attitudes. 1964-73. *2795*
—. Antislavery Sentiments. Civil War. Jay, John, II. 1840-65. *773*
—. Black power. Church and Social Problems. Economic Aid. General Convention Special Program. Self-determination. 1963-75. *2850*
—. Civil rights movement. Race Relations. Theology. 1800-1965. *2849*
—. Clergy. Ingraham, Joseph Holt. Novels. Penal reform. Public Schools. Tennessee (Nashville). 1847-51. *584*
—. Conservatism. DuBose, William Porcher. Miles, James Warley. Murphy, Edgar Gardner. South. Theology. 1840-1920. *62*
—. Councils and Synods. Delegates. Kinsolving, George Herbert. Texas. Veto. Women. 1921-70. *2347*
—. Crapsey, Algernon Sidney. Heresy. New York (Rochester). Reform. St. Andrew's Church. Trials. 1879-1927. *454*
—. Education. Louisiana (New Orleans). Polk, Leonidas L. Slavery. 1805-65. *730*
—. Huntington, James Otis Sargent. Monasticism. Order of the Holy Cross. 1878-90. *1061*
—. Missouri (St. Louis). 1880-1920. *52*
—. Murphy, Edgar Gardner. Southern Education Board. 1900-13. *2118*
—. Nebraska (Omaha). Social Change. 1856-1919. *1494*
—. New York City. Newspapers. Racism. Riots. St. Philip's Church. Williams, Peter, Jr. 1830-50. *671*
Epstein, Abraham. Legislation. Pensions. Voluntary associations. 1920-35. *1777*
Equal Employment Opportunity Commission. Congress. Feminism. Sex Discrimination. 1964-74. *2920*
—. Environmental Protection Agency. Labor. Occupational Safety and Health Act (US, 1970). Safety. Women. 1970-76. *2698*
Equal Legal Rights Amendment. Federation of Business and Professional Women's Clubs. Texas. Women. 1957-72. *2909*
Equal opportunity. Agriculture Department. Employment. Federal policy. 1964-76. *2744*
—. American Psychological Association. Lancaster Press. Psychologists for Social Action. Racism. 1969-73. *2885*
—. Anthony, Lucy. Employment. Feminism. Shaw, Anna Howard. 1865-1919. *330*
—. Bethune, Mary McLeod. National Youth Administration. Negroes. Public Policy. Youth. 1935-44. *2594*
—. Business. Croly, Herbert. Federal Trade Commission Act (US, 1914). Progressivism. 1900's-10's. *2227*
—. Civil Rights Act (US, 1964; Title VII). Courts. Discrimination, employment. 1964-78. *2932*
—. Civilian Conservation Corps. Negroes. New Deal. 1933-42. *2514*
—. Colleges and Universities. Maryland. Negroes. 1908-75. *1860*
—. Democratic Party. Jacksonianism. Social theory. Wealth. 1836-46. *537*
—. Discrimination, Employment. Law. Public policy. 1964-72. *2949*
—. Economic Conditions. Employment. Law. Negroes. Occupations. 1954-72. *1785*
—. Educational policy. Law. 1954-74. *2852*
—. Louisiana Education Association. Negroes. School Integration. Teachers. 1901-70. *1857*
Equal rights. Colorado. Negroes. Reconstruction. 1865-67. *1134*
—. Discrimination. Homosexuals. 20c. *1677*
—. Integration. Prison reform. Women. 1820's-1900. *1451*
Equal Rights Amendment. Bible. Constitutional Amendments (19th). State Legislatures. Tennessee. Women. 1876-1974. *2904*
—. Florida. National Women's Party. Politics. West, Helen Hunt. Women. 1917-52. *1727*
—. National Women's Party. Social Feminists. Woman suffrage. 1920-23. *2376*
Equal Rights League. Pennsylvania. Public schools. School Integration. 1834-81. *208*
Equality. Attitudes. Lincoln, Abraham. 1830's-65. *642*
Boston Daily Evening Voice (newspaper). Labor Unions and Organizations. Massachusetts. Race Relations. Working Class. 1864-67. *998*
—. *Brown* v. *Board of Education* (US, 1954). Desegregation. Negroes. Public Schools. 1950's-74. *2817*

—. California. Woman suffrage. 1895-1911. *2160*
—. Carpetbaggers. Post, Louis F. Progressive era. Reconstruction. 1868-1925. *306*
—. Catholic Worker Movement. Human Rights. Public policy. 1933-78. *1678*
—. Christianity. Civil rights. Negroes. 19c-20c. *126*
—. Civil Rights. Discrimination. Negroes. Political Attitudes. Reconstruction. Texas. 1865-70. *1200*
—. Civil rights. Judicial Process. Liberty. 1960-79. *2772*
—. Class struggle. French language. Intellectuals. Nationalism. Quebec. 1960's-70's. *2693*
—. Clergy. Mormons. Negroes. Women. 1860-1979. *91*
—. DuBois, W. E. B. Wilson, Woodrow. 1911-18. *1952*
—. Federal government. Negroes. New York. States' rights. 1865-73. *1154*
—. Lobbying. New York City. State Legislatures. Strachan, Grace. Teachers. Wages. Women. 1907-11. *2202*
—. Social Status. Women. 1900-70's. *1568*
Eskimos *See also* Aleuts.
—. Alaska Native Claims Settlement Act (US, 1971). Aleuts. Indians. 1971-78. *2745*
—. Alaska Reorganization Act (US, 1936). Aleuts. Federal Policy. Indians. 1936-45. *2574*
—. Bureau of Indian Affairs. California (Alcatraz Island). Ideology. Indians. Political Protest. 1969-78. *2757*
Espionage Act of 1917. Conscientious Objectors. North Dakota. O'Hare, Kate Richards. Pacifism. World War I. 1900-25. *2131*
Ethics *See also* Medical Ethics; Morality; Values.
—. Advertising. Journalism. Progressivism. 1890's-1920's. *1910*
Ethiopia (Addis Ababa). Emigration. Ford, Arnold. Negroes. 1930-35. *2436*
Ethnic consciousness. Africa. Blyden, Edward Wilmot. Intellectuals. Negroes. ca 1832-65. *557*
—. Black Nationalism. Culture. 1960-75. *2883*
Ethnic Groups *See also* Minorities.
—. Anderson, James T. M. Anglicization. English language. Immigrants. Public schools. Saskatchewan. 1918-23. *1856*
—. Čačić, Tomo. Kjelt, Ole. Krat, Pavlo. Leftism. Mäkelä, A. B. Political Protest. Puttee, Arthur. Scarlett, Sam. 1907-34. *1561*
—. California. Educational Tests and Measurements. IQ tests. Progressivism. Students. 1917-21. *2300*
—. Democratic Party. Educational reform. Junior High Schools. Massachusetts (Somerville). Middle Classes. Progressivism. 1912-24. *2335*
—. Dever, William. Elections (mayoral). Illinois (Chicago). Negroes. Prohibition. 1923-27. *2350*
—. Imperialism. James, William. Race Relations. 1899-1910. *2033*
—. International Institute. Pluralism. Social services. 1910-79. *74*
—. Labor Unions and Organizations. Ohio (Cincinnati). Working class. 1893-1920. *2247*
—. Negroes. School Integration. 1964-78. *2879*
—. Pluralism. Political Power. 1950's-70's. *1592*
Ethnic studies. DuBois, W. E. B. Education. German Americans. Irish Americans. Woodson, Carter G. 1649-1972. *188*
Ethnicity. Asian Americans. Employment. Legislation. Naturalization. Racism. 1850-20c. *65*
—. California (San Francisco). Educational Reform. Religion. 1918-20. *2333*
—. Cities. Negroes. Race Relations. Social organization. Valentine, Charles. 1865-1975. *1697*
—. Democracy. Democratic Party. Nebraska. Prohibition. Republican Party. 1907-20. *1937*
—. Depressions. Progressive education. Race. 1929-45. *2513*
—. Douglass, Frederick. Justice. 19c. 1975. *657*
—. Indians. Political Protest. Religion. 1964-78. *2738*
—. Irish Americans. Land League. Radicals and Radicalism. Reform. Working class. 1880-83. *997*
—. Local option. Michigan. Prohibition. 1889-1917. *1928*
Ethnographers. Educators. Evangelism. Indians (reservations). Pueblo Indians (Hopi). Sullivan, John H. Taylor, Charles A. 1870-89. *1050*

Ethnography. Federal policy. Indians. Morgan, Lewis Henry. 1848-78. *1059*
Ethnology *See also* Acculturation; Anthropology; Negroes; Race Relations.
—. Douglass, Frederick. Speeches, Addresses, etc. 1854. *700*
Eugenics *See also* Birth Control.
—. Birth control. Feminism. Prostitution. 1890's. *1006*
—. Class struggle. Fisher, Irving. Progressivism. Racism. 1890's-1920. *1869*
—. Phrenology. 19c. *236*
Eugenics movement. Birth control. Feminism. Politics. 1915-74. *1588*
Europe *See also* Europe, Western.
—. Dewey, John. Educational Reform. Progressivism. 1800-1960. *1866*
—. Health. Women. Working Conditions. 1869-1979. *47*
—. Intellectuals. Social change. Utopias. 1930's-70's. *1675*
—. Pressure Groups. Women. 1888-1920's. *48*
—. Revivals. 1400-1900. *81*
Europe, Western. Canada. Social policy. USA. Welfare state. 1890-1970. *160*
Euthanasia. Great Britain. Medicine. Tollemache, Lionel A. Williams, Samuel D., Jr. 1870's-90's. *1452*
Evangelical Alliance. Beecher, Lyman. Great Britain. Temperance Movements. World Temperance Convention. 1846. *889*
Evangelicalism. Abolition Movement. Birney, James. Clergy. Smith, Gerrit. Stanton, H. B. Weld, Theodore Dwight. 1820-50. *744*
—. Abolition Movement. Blanchard, Jonathan. 1830's-80's. *455*
—. Antislavery sentiments. Religion. South. 1820-30. *758*
—. Colleges and Universities. Oberlin College. Ohio. Women. 1835-50. *796*
—. Jones, Charles Colcock. Race Relations. South. Utopias. 1804-63. *567*
—. Reform. Slavery. Stringfellow, Thornton. Virginia. 1800-70. *633*
—. Self-expression. Women. 1800-50. *799*
Evangelism. Abolition Movement. Congregationalism. Finney, Charles Grandison. South. 1833-69. *632*
—. Abolition Movement. Friendship. Tappan, Lewis. 1830-61. *645*
—. Christian Catholic Church. Dowie, John Alexander. Illinois (Zion). 1888-1907. *1512*
—. Converts. Louisiana (New Orleans). Protestant Churches. Slavery. 1800-61. *732*
—. Ecumenism. Protestantism. Social change. Social justice. Student Christian Movement. 19c-20c. *5*
—. Educators. Ethnographers. Indians (reservations). Pueblo Indians (Hopi). Sullivan, John H. Taylor, Charles A. 1870-89. *1050*
—. Keeble, Marshall. Race relations. 1878-1968. *412*
—. Michigan. Political parties. State Legislatures. 1837-61. *578*
—. Reform. Wright, Henry Clarke. 1820-60. *447*
Evans, Arthur. Canada, western. Communist Party. Labor. 1930's. *1658*
Evans, Warren Felt. Idealism. Mental healing. Mysticism. Romanticism. 1864-89. *1480*
Everett Mill. Massachusetts (Lawrence). Polish Americans. Radicals and Radicalism. Strikes. Textile Industry. Women. 1912. *2252*
Evolution. Education. LeConte, Joseph. 1875-1900. *1435*
—. LeConte, Joseph. Science. Sex roles. Women's rights. 1890's. *1115*
Executive Order 8802. Defense industries. Discrimination. March on Washington Movement. Military. Randolph, A. Philip. Webster, Milton. 1941-44. *2635*
Executive Power *See also* Presidents.
—. Civil rights. Kennedy, John F. Legislation. 1961-64. *2858*
—. Federal Regulation. Politics. President's Advisory Council on Executive Organization. Public Administration. Reform. 1937-79. *1705*
—. Intergovernmental Relations. Local Government. Ohio. Police. State Government. 1902-25. *2100*
Exercise. Attitudes. Health. New England. Recreation. Transcendentalism. 1830-60. *572*
Exiles. Allen, William G. Attitudes. Colonization. Great Britain. Negroes. New York Central College at McGrawville. 1820-78. *290*

Experimental Schools. *See* Free Schools.
Extradition. Canada. Courts. Fugitive slaves. Happy, Jesse. Kentucky. Testimony. 1793-1838. *748*
Eye Opener (newspaper). Alberta. Edwards, Robert C. "Bob". Populist. 1904-22. *1940*

F

Factionalism. Militancy. United Automobile Workers of America. 1937-41. *2482*
Factories. Architecture. Automobile Industry and Trade. Ford, Henry. Kahn, Albert. 1869-1942. 1900H. *1779*
—. Industrial Technology. Labor Disputes. National Cash Register Company. 1895-1913. *2249*
Fagan, Mark. City Politics. New Jersey (Jersey City). Progressivism. 1896-1907. *2279*
—. New Jersey (Jersey City). Progressives. Single tax. Taxation. 1901-17. *2278*
Fair Employment Practices Committee. American Federation of Labor. Discrimination, Employment. Federal Government. Labor Unions and Organizations. Shipbuilding. West Coast Master Agreement. World War II. 1939-46. *2627*
—. Bilbo, Theodore G. Employment. Filibusters. Mississippi. Racism. Senate. 1941-46. *2617*
—. Civil rights. Congress. Discrimination, employment. Roosevelt, Franklin D. (administration). World War II. 1941-46. *2640*
—. Discrimination. Negroes. Railroads. Southeastern Carriers Conference. World War II. 1941-45. *2630*
—. Discrimination, employment. Minorities. South. World War II. 1941-45. *2644*
Fair Labor Standards Act (US, 1938). Minimum wage. 1938-77. *1768*
Fairbairn, R. Edis. Canada. Pacifism. United Church of Canada. World War II. 1939. *2646*
Fairfield School for Boys. Agriculture. Boys. Juvenile Delinquency. Ohio. Reformatories. Values. 1840-84. *242*
Family *See also* Divorce; Marriage; Women.
—. Abortion. Sex roles. 19c-20c. *37*
—. Attitudes. Federal Government. Public welfare. 1962-80. *2929*
—. Canada. English Canadians. Woman suffrage. 1877-1918. *111*
—. Child Welfare. Foster homes. Immigration. Jews. New York City. Working class. 1900-05. *2061*
—. Child-rearing. Democracy. Infants. Spock, Benjamin *(Baby and Child Care)*. 1917-50. *1589*
—. Cities. Morality. Progressivism. Recreation. Reform. Socialization. 1890-1920. *1990*
—. Feminism. 1960-80. *2912*
—. Feminism. Journalism. Tarbell, Ida M. 1900-30. *1688*
—. Feminism. Ontario. 1875-1900. *1055*
—. Iakovos, Archbishop. Morality. Orthodox Eastern Church (Greek; congresses). Social Conditions. 1960-80. *2726*
—. Labor. Social Organization. Women. 1600-1970's. *54*
—. New York. Noyes, John Humphrey. Oneida Community. Religion. Sex. 1848-80. *271*
—. Reform. 1820-70. *583*
—. Sexuality. Social Theory. Sumner, William Graham. 1870's-1910. *985*
Far Western States *See also* individual states (including Alaska and Hawaii).
—. Indian Claims Commission. Kalispel Indians. 1950-65. *1549*
—. International Longshoremen's and Warehousemen's Union. Labor Unions and Organizations. 1934-37. *2481*
Farber, Myron. Courts. Freedom of the press. *New York Times* (newspaper). Reporters and Reporting. 1975-79. *2781*
Farley, Harriet. Dall, Caroline. Feminism. Letters. Working Class. 1850. *794*
Farm Security Administration. Delmo Housing Corporation. Missouri. Southern Tenant Farmers' Union. Tenancy. 1939-80. *1821*
Farm tenancy. Mississippi. Protestant Churches. Theology. 1936-40. *2525*
—. Political Protest. Socialism. Texas. 1901-17. *2216*
Farmer Labor party. Canada. Coldwell, Major J. Political Leadership. Progressivism. Social Democracy. 1907-32. *471*

Farmer, S. J. Dixon, Frederick John. Independent Labour Party. Manitoba. Single tax. 1920-49. *1791*
Farmer-Labor Party. Amlie, Thomas. Hard, Herbert. New Deal. Ohio Farmer-Labor Progressive Federation. Third Parties. 1930-40. *2543*
—. Amlie, Thomas. New Deal. Wisconsin. 1930-38. *2544*
—. Depressions. New Deal. Oregon Commonwealth Federation. Political Factions. 1933-38. *2545*
—. Michigan. New Deal. State Politics. 1933-37. *2541*
—. Minnesota. State politics. Swedish Americans. 1922-44. *1631*
—. Political Leadership. Radicals and Radicalism. Saskatchewan. Socialism. 1932-34. *1607*
Farmers. Agricultural Adjustment Administration. Depressions. Federal Policy. New Deal. New York, western. 1934. *2487*
—. Agricultural Labor. Industrial Workers of the World. Labor Disputes. Ranchers. Washington (Yakima Valley). 1910-36. *2569*
—. Agricultural reform. Editors and Editing. Poe, Clarence Hamilton. *Progressive Farmer* (periodical). South. 1899-1964. *1555*
—. Alabama. Negroes. Southern Improvement Company. Virginia. 1900-20. *2172*
—. Alberta. Alienation. Economic Conditions. Political Protest. 1921-79. *2948*
—. American Revolution (antecedents). New York. North Carolina. South Carolina. 1760's-70's. *484*
—. Arizona (Salt River Valley). Depressions. Japanese Americans. Race Relations. 1934-35. *2469*
—. Arkansas (northwestern). Brothers of Freedom. 1880's. *1372*
—. Bowen, Albert E., Jr. Nonpartisan League. North Dakota. Townley, Arthur C. 1914-15. *2054*
—. Business. Construction. Railroads. Utopias. Western States. 1880's-90's. *1511*
—. Business. Nonpartisan League. North Dakota. Politics. Townley, Arthur C. 1880-1959. *1667*
—. California State Agricultural Society. Elites. Grange. 1870's-80's. *1385*
—. Cherokee Indians. Grange. Indian Territory. 1870's. *1374*
—. Civil Disturbances. Regulators. South Carolina. 1730-80. *490*
—. Colored Farmers' Alliance. Negroes. South. ca 1886-95. *1172*
—. Communism. Political Protest. South Dakota. United Farmers League. 1923-34. *2409*
—. Depressions. Government. Great Plains. Letters. New Deal. 1930-40. *2476*
—. Education. Negroes. Tuskegee Institute. Washington, Booker T. 1881-1915. *1186*
—. Grange. Oklahoma. Saskatchewan. Socialism. Texas. 1900-45. *1714*
—. Idaho. Intellectuals. McKaig, Robert Raymond. Nonpartisan League. North Dakota. ca 1920-45. *2406*
—. Idaho. Irrigation. Progressive Party. State Politics. 1914-22. *2012*
—. Ideology. Old Northwest. Populism. Rhetoric. 1870's-80's. *1388*
—. Industrial Workers of the World. Orchards. Strikes. Washington (Yakima Valley). 1933. *2568*
—. McNary-Haugen bill. Montana. Pacific Northwest. Prices. Tariff. 1920-29. *2410*
—. Methodology. Southern Farmers' Alliance. 1884-90. *1391*
—. Oklahoma. Socialism. 1900's-10. *2063*
—. Political Parties. Radicals and radicalism. 1892-1930. *1682*
—. Shays' Rebellion. Social Classes. 1770's-87. *580*
Farmers' Alliance. Agricultural Organizations. Historiography. North Carolina. ca 1888-91. *1379*
—. Alexander, Sydenham B. Carr, Elias. Leadership. North Carolina. Polk, Leonidas L. Upper Classes. 1887-95. *1392*
—. *Alliance-Independent* (newspaper). Burrows, Jabez. Nebraska (Gage County). 1887-99. *1383*
—. Curricula. Iowa State Agricultural College. State Legislatures. Wallace, Henry. 1884-91. *1416*
—. Democratic Party. North Carolina. State Politics. Vance, Zebulon B. 1880-90. *1366*

Farmers' Educational and Cooperative Union of America. Agricultural Cooperatives. Consumers' United Stores. Nonpartisan League. North Dakota. 1916-19. *2259*
—. Agricultural Cooperatives. Labor Unions and Organizations. North Dakota (Burleigh County; Still). 1913-78. *2288*
—. Knappen, Howard P. North Dakota. 1913-20. *2260*
Farmer's Union of Alberta. Alberta (Edmonton). Kyforuk, Peter. Manitoba. Ukrainian Labour-Farmer Association. 1912-30's. *1828*
Farms. Catholic Church. New Deal. 1930's. *2591*
—. Cedar Creek Monthly Meeting. Emancipation. Friends, Society of. Moorman, Clark Terrell. Ohio. Virginia (Caroline County). 1766-1814. *743*
—. Forney, Jacob. Hurt, Garland. Indians (reservations). Utah Superintendency of Indian Affairs. 1850-62. *539*
Farwell, Arthur Burrage. Hyde Park Protective Association. Illinois (Chicago). Prohibition. Reform. 1885-1936. *1912*
Fascism. American Federation of Labor. Gompers, Samuel. Immigration. Jingoism. Racism. 1850-1924. *394*
Fashion. Commercials. Hygiene. Television. Women. Women's Liberation Movement. 1970's. *2921*
Federal aid to education. Catholic Church. Church Schools. Congress. Roosevelt, Eleanor. Spellman, Francis J. 1949-50. *2669*
—. Harrison, Byron Patton. Legislation. Mississippi. 1936-41. *2597*
Federal Bureau of Investigation. Civil Rights. Cold War. Detention. National security. Truman, Harry S. (administration). 1945-52. *2685*
—. Civil Rights. Roosevelt, Franklin D. 1936-80. *1716*
—. Hoover, J. Edgar. Radicals and Radicalism. Surveillance. 1919-21. *2461*
Federal Council of Churches of Christ in America. Methodist Federation for Social Service. North, Frank M. Social Creed of Methodism. Ward, Harry F. 1907-12. *1956*
Federal Election Campaign Act (US, 1971, 1974). Congress. Constitutional Amendments (14th, 15th). Elections. Supreme Court. Voting Rights Act (US, 1965). 1965-75. *2767*
Federal Emergency Relief Administration. Depressions. Employment. 1933-40. *2606*
Federal Employers' Liability Act (US, 1908). Accidents. Courts. Management. Railroads. Safety Appliances Act (US, 1893). Working Conditions. 1890-1913. *2117*
Federal Farm Loan Act (US, 1916). Banking. Bulkley, Robert J. Federal Reserve Act (US, 1913). Progressivism. 1906-30. *363*
Federal Government *See also* names of individual agencies, bureaus, and departments, e.g. Bureau of Indian Affairs, Office of Education, but State Department, Defense Department, etc.; Civil Service; Congress; Constitutions; Government; Legislation; Supreme Court.
—. Agricultural policy. Dawes Act (US, 1887). Indians (reservations). Kiowa Indians. Oklahoma. 1869-1901. *1062*
—. American Federation of Labor. Discrimination, Employment. Fair Employment Practices Committee. Labor Unions and Organizations. Shipbuilding. West Coast Master Agreement. World War II. 1939-46. *2627*
—. American Indian Movement. Deloria, Vine, Jr. Indians. Political Protest. South Dakota. Wounded Knee (occupation). 1877-1970's. *2712*
—. American Plan. Council of National Defense. Prostitution. Social policy. Venereal disease. Voluntary associations. World War I. 1917-21. *2048*
—. Ammons, Elias. Coal. Colorado. Strikes. Wilson, Woodrow. 1914. *2228*
—. Arkansas (Little Rock). Collins, LeRoy. Courts. Florida. Political Speeches. School integration. 1957. *2688*
—. Attitudes. Family. Public welfare. 1962-80. *2929*
—. Authority. Citizenship. Constitutional Amendments (13th, 14th, 15th). Freedmen. Reconstruction. 1865-70. *1132*
—. Boarding schools. Children. Indians. 1920-60's. *1864*
—. Bureaucracies. Business. Disability insurance. Social Security. 1900-40. *1829*

—. Business. Canada. Labor Unions and Organizations. Social control. Unemployment Insurance Act (Canada, 1941). Wages. 1910-41. *2623*
—. Canada. Education. Indians. Métis. 1940-70. *2959*
—. Canada. Physical Education and Training. 1850-1972. *33*
—. Canada. Social policy. Unemployment. 1918-21. *1816*
—. Canadian Labour Congress. Cooperative Commonwealth Federation. Industrial relations. Trades and Labour Congress of Canada. World War II. 1939-46. *2634*
—. Capitalism. Corporations. General Electric Company. Labor Unions and Organizations. Liberalism. 1920-33. *2412*
—. Cherokee Indians. Georgia. Land (cessions). Payne, John Howard (letter). Ross, John (chief). 1820's-30's. *575*
—. Cities. Civil rights movement. Local Government. Negroes. 1933-70. *1686*
—. Civil Rights. Employment. Public Policy. State Government. 20c. *1572*
—. Civil Rights Act (US, 1875). Constitutional Amendments (13th, 14th). Negroes. 1875-83. *1113*
—. Coal Mines and Mining. Pennsylvania. Roosevelt, Theodore. Strikes. 1902. *2218*
—. Collier, John. Indians. Liberalism. Roosevelt, Franklin D. (administration). Truman, Harry S. (administration). 1933-53. *1629*
—. Connecticut Asylum for the Deaf and Dumb. Kentucky Deaf and Dumb Asylum. Public Welfare. 1819-26. *901*
—. Debo, Angie (personal account). Indians. Public Opinion. Reform. 1969-76. *2703*
—. Debs, Eugene V. Illinois (Blue Island). Pullman Strike. Strikes. 1894. *1317*
—. Decisionmaking. Interest Groups. Legislation. Politics. Women. 1970's. *2911*
—. Desegregation. Law enforcement. Public Schools. South. 1954-73. *2824*
—. Equality. Negroes. New York. States' rights. 1865-73. *1154*
—. Frazier, Lynn J. Governors. Indians. North Dakota. Progressivism. 1916-40. *1538*
—. Hoover, Herbert C. Public welfare. Roosevelt, Franklin D. 1920-37. *2345*
—. House of Representatives. Intervention. Negroes. Population. South. Voting Rights Act (US, 1965). 1940-75. *2802*
—. Indians. Nebraska Historical Society. Omaha Indians. Returned Students of Omaha. Speeches, Addresses, etc. 1920's. *2442*
—. Legislation. Nevada. Newspapers. Racism. 1866-68. *976*
—. Legislation. Public Welfare. United Mine Workers of America (Welfare and Retirement Fund). 1945-70's. *2658*
—. Local Government. Massachusetts (Boston; South End). Middle Classes. Neighborhoods. Poor. Urban revitalization. 1960's-70's. *2694*
—. Medical care. Poor. Public Health. 1960-77. *2982*
—. Negroes. Segregation. 1916-29. *2392*
—. New Deal. Press. Progressivism. Reform. 1890's-1930's. *1534*
—. New York (Buffalo). Political protest. Social consciousness. 1965-76. *2747*
—. Rent control. 1940-47. *2633*
—. School integration. State Government. 1954-77. *2825*
—. Segregation. Trotter, William Monroe. Wilson, Woodrow. 1913-14. *2016*
Federal Policy *See also* Domestic Policy.
—. Acculturation. Canada. Indians. Sifton, Clifford. 1896-1905. *1012*
—. Agricultural Adjustment Administration. Depressions. Farmers. New Deal. New York, western. 1934. *2487*
—. Agriculture. Cheyenne and Arapaho Reservation. Indians. Oklahoma. 1869-80. *1063*
—. Agriculture Department. Employment. Equal opportunity. 1964-76. *2744*
—. Alaska Reorganization Act (US, 1936). Aleuts. Eskimos. Indians. 1936-45. *2574*
—. Arizona (Tucson). Camp Grant Affair. Indian Wars. 1871. *1037*
—. Assimilation. Collier, John. Indian Reorganization Act (US, 1934). 1933-45. *2530*
—. Bauer, Catherine. Public housing. Reform. Wagner-Steagall Act (US, 1937). Wood, Edith Elmer. 1890's-1940's. *2479*
—. Canada. Housing. 1970-79. *2950*

—. Cherokee Indians. Indians. New Deal. North Carolina, western. 1930's. *2607*
—. Civil rights. Interest Groups. Populism. Private sector. Racism. Wallace, George C. 1960's. *2899*
—. Competency commissions. Indians. Land allotment. 1913-20. *2031*
—. Conservation movement. Lumber and Lumbering. Pacific Northwest. Property rights. Public Lands. 1870's-90's. *1323*
—. Defense Policy. Industry. Labor Unions and Organizations. World War II. 1939-41. *2593*
—. Discrimination. Freedmen's Bureau. Mississippi. Reconstruction. State Government. 1865. *1227*
—. Eisenhower, Dwight D. (administration). Legislation. Public Welfare. Reform. 1950-60. *2659*
—. Ethnography. Indians. Morgan, Lewis Henry. 1848-78. *1059*
—. Gun Control. 1919-38. *1726*
—. Hayes, Rutherford B. Indians. 1877-81. *988*
—. Health. Nixon, Richard M. (administration). 1971-76. *2985*
—. Immigration. Negroes. 1917-29. *2382*
—. Indians. Meriam, Lewis (*Problem of Indian Administration*). Reform. Social conditions. 1920-28. *2362*
—. Nutrition. Public Health. 1906-79. *1525*
—. Presidents. Public welfare. 1933-78. *1793*
Federal Programs. Agricultural Adjustment Act (1933). Iowa. New Deal. Wallace, Henry Agard. 1933-34. *2537*
—. Assimilation. Cheyenne River Indian Reservation. Identity. Indians. Sioux Indians. 1889-1917. *45*
—. Education, Experimental Methods. Local Government. RAND Corporation. 1965-80. *2961*
—. Food stamps. Reform. 1930-77. *1872*
—. Freedmen. Georgia (Atlanta). North. Reconstruction. Religious organizations. 1865-69. *1273*
—. Legislation. Medicine and State. 1965-77. *2979*
—. Medical care. Poor. 1963-76. *2975*
Federal Regulation *See also* Economic Regulations; Government Regulation.
—. Antibiotics. Conflict of interest. Food and Drug Administration. Periodicals. Pharmacy. Welch, Henry. 1953-62. *2676*
—. Billboards. Congress. Highway Beautification Act (US, 1965). Land use. 1965-79. *2716*
—. Business. Freight and Freightage. Hepburn Act (US, 1906). Interstate Commerce Commission. 1905-06. *2282*
—. California. Chinese. Constitutions, State. Labor reform. Workingmen's Party of California. 1877-82. *1358*
—. Child Labor Act (US, 1916). Cotton. Textile Industry. 1907-16. *2002*
—. Consumer Product Safety Commission. Safety. 1972-77. *2721*
—. Consumer protection. Drugs. Legislation. Methodology. 1962-73. *2956*
—. Decisionmaking. Democracy. Social policy. 1970-75. *2734*
—. Drugs. Kefauver, Estes. Senate Subcommittee on Antitrust and Monopoly. South. 1950's-60's. *2939*
—. Executive power. Politics. President's Advisory Council on Executive Organization. Public Administration. Reform. 1937-79. *1705*
—. Medical care. Physicians. Professional Standards Review Organization Program. Social Security Act (US, 1935; Title XX, 1972). 1965-80. *2978*
Federal Reserve Act (US, 1913). Banking. Bulkley, Robert J. Federal Farm Loan Act (US, 1916). Progressivism. 1906-30. *363*
Federal Reserve System. Attitudes. Democracy. Income tax. Reform. Wilson, Woodrow. 1913-21. *1994*
Federal Subsistence Homesteads Corporation. Iowa (Granger). Ligutti, Luigi. New Deal. 1934-51. *2585*
Federal Trade Commission. Advertising. 1914-38. *1817*
Federal Trade Commission Act (US, 1914). Business. Croly, Herbert. Equal opportunity. Progressivism. 1900's-10's. *2227*
Federalism *See also* Federal Government.
—. Legislation. Progressivism. States' rights. 1880-1930. *1959*
Fédération Nationale Saint-Jean-Baptiste. Catholic Church. Feminism. Gérin-Lajoie, Marie. Quebec. 1907-33. *1039*

Federation of Business and Professional Women's Clubs. Breckinridge, Madeline McDowell. Kentucky Equal Rights Association. Woman suffrage. 1908-20. *2157*
—. Equal Legal Rights Amendment. Texas. Women. 1957-72. *2909*
Federation of Organized Trades and Labor Unions. American Federation of Labor. Knights of Labor. Labor Unions and Organizations. Ohio (Columbus). 1881-86. *1309*
Fell, Margaret. Feminism. Friends, Society of. Great Britain (Lancashire). Pennsylvania (Philadelphia). Women. 1670's. *498*
Fellowship of Reconciliation. Antiwar Sentiment. World War II. 1940-41. *2655*
Felt, Louie. Anderson, May. *Children's Friend* (periodical). Periodicals. Primary Association. Religious education. Utah. 1880-1940. *80*
Felton, Rebecca Latimer. Georgia. Politics. Senate. Woman suffrage. 1860's-1922. *423*
Female Charitable Society. Domestics. Girls. Industrialization. Massachusetts (Salem). 1800-40. *882*
Female Moral Reform Society. Morality. New York (Utica). Reform. Social Organization. 1830's-40's. *808*
Female seminary movement. Discrimination, Educational. Women. 1818-91. *202*
Feminism *See also* Women's Liberation Movement.
—. Abolition movement. Chapman, Maria Weston. Child, Lydia Maria. Stanton, Elizabeth Cady. ca 1830-40. *558*
—. Abolition Movement. Journalism. Lowry, Sylvanus B. Minnesota. Swisshelm, Jane Grey. 1815-84. *385*
—. Abolition Movement. Minnesota. St. Cloud *Visitor* (newspaper). Swisshelm, Jane Grey. 1857-62. *814*
—. Abolition Movement. Pennsylvania. Philadelphia Female Anti-Slavery Society. 1833-40. *616*
—. Abolition Movement. Sex roles. Social Change. 1820's-80. *798*
—. Advice columns. Dix, Dorothy. Louisiana. New Orleans *Picayune* (newspaper). 1895-1900. *980*
—. Alcott, Louisa May. Letters. Woman suffrage. 1853-85. *811*
—. American Revolution. Political theory. Republicans (Radical). Warren, Mercy Otis. 1760's-1805. *523*
—. Anarchism and Anarchists. deCleyre, Voltairine. Human Rights. 1800's-90's. *1046*
—. Anthony, Lucy. Employment. Equal opportunity. Shaw, Anna Howard. 1865-1919. *330*
—. Anthony, Susan B. Book Collecting. 1869-1903. *285*
—. Architecture. Communalism. Gilman, Charlotte Perkins. Housing. 1870-1920. *42*
—. Atherton, Gertrude. Authors. Novels. 1890's-1910's. *333*
—. Austin, Alice Constance. California (Llano del Rio). Housework. Howland, Marie Stevens. Mexico (Topolobampo). Utopias. 1874-1917. *929*
—. Barry, Robertine (pseud. Françoise). Gleason, Anne-Marie (pseud. Madeleine). Journalism. Quebec. Social Conditions. 1900-19. *1535*
—. Beecher, Henry Ward. New York City. Radicals and Radicalism. Sex. Vanderbilt, Cornelius. Woodhull, Victoria Claflin. 1868-90's. *336*
—. Bentham, Jeremy. Birth control. Carlile, Richard. Great Britain. Owen, Robert Dale. Place, Francis. Propaganda. Wright, Frances. 1790-1840. *817*
—. Birth control. Eugenics. Prostitution. 1890's. *1006*
—. Birth control. Eugenics movement. Politics. 1915-74. *1588*
—. Birth control. Sex roles. 1870's-80's. *1007*
—. Blackwell, Elizabeth. Medical Education. Pennsylvania (Philadelphia). 1821-1910. *809*
—. Blackwell, Henry B. Editors and Editing. Politics. Stone, Lucy. *Women's Journal* (periodical). 1870-1914. *1047*
—. Book reviews. Literary Criticism. Porter, Katherine Anne. 1922-29. *2373*
—. Bourassa, Henri. Canada. Divorce. Woman suffrage. 1913-25. *1698*
—. Bourne, Randolph. Political Commentary. Progressive education. Socialism. 1886-1918. *425*
—. Breckinridge, Sophonisba. 1880's-1948. *457*
—. Business. Illinois (Chicago). Philanthropy. Schmidt, Minna Moscherosch. 1886-1961. *315*

—. California. Gilman, Charlotte Perkins. New England. 1880's-1935. *287*
—. Canada. Civil Rights. Government. Great Britain. USA. 1850-20c. *79*
—. Canada. Literature. McClung, Nellie L. Politics. Reform. 1873-1930's. *1689*
—. Canada. National Council of Women of Canada. 1893-1929. *1690*
—. Catholic Church. Fédération Nationale Saint-Jean-Baptiste. Gérin-Lajoie, Marie. Quebec. 1907-33. *1039*
—. Catholic Church. Quebec. Religious Orders. Women. 1640-1975. *21*
—. Chafe, William. Historiography. O'Neill, William. Sexual revolution. ca 1920-70. *2374*
—. Charleston *News and Courier* (newspaper). Dawson, Francis Warrington. Dawson, Sarah Morgan. Reconstruction. South Carolina. 1870's. *973*
—. Civil Rights. Economic Research and Action Project. National Organization for Women. Student Nonviolent Coordinating Committee. 1960's. *2906*
—. Class consciousness. Great Britain. Labor Unions and Organizations. USA. Women's Trade Union League. 1890-1925. *2226*
—. Colorado (Boulder). Women's Christian Temperance Union. 1874-1967. *232*
—. Commission on the Status and Role of Women in the United Methodist Church. Methodism. Social Organizations. 1869-1974. *72*
—. Communism. Flynn, Elizabeth Gurley. ca 1890-1920. *282*
—. Congress. Equal Employment Opportunity Commission. Sex Discrimination. 1964-74. *2920*
—. Cooperative Commonwealth Federation. Leftism. Ontario (Toronto). Women's Joint Committee. 1930's. *1638*
—. Dall, Caroline. Farley, Harriet. Letters. Working Class. 1850. *794*
—. Darwinism. Women. 1850-1920. *88*
—. Dewey, John (letters). Klyce, Scudder. 1915-31. *1536*
—. Divorce. Marriage. Reform. Stanton, Elizabeth Cady. 1840-90. *1010*
—. Domesticity. Economic independence. Education. 1960's-70's. *2903*
—. Domesticity. Howe, Julia Ward. Motherhood. Reform. 1844-85. *349*
—. Economic conditions. Sex. Social Classes. 1600-1900. *36*
—. Education. Troy Female Seminary. Values. Willard, Emma Hart. 1822-72. *810*
—. Employment. Organizations. Racism. Social classes. World War II. 1942-45. *2629*
—. Family. 1960-80. *2912*
—. Family. Journalism. Tarbell, Ida M. 1900-30. *1688*
—. Family. Ontario. 1875-1900. *1055*
—. Fell, Margaret. Friends, Society of. Great Britain (Lancashire). Pennsylvania (Philadelphia). Women. 1670's. *498*
—. Firestone, Shulamith. Fuller, Margaret. Gilman, Charlotte Perkins. Godwin, Mary Wollstonecraft. Science. 1759-1972. *64*
—. Fuller, Margaret. Godwin, Mary Wollstonecraft. 1792-19c. *812*
—. Fuller, Margaret. Hawthorne, Nathaniel *(The Blithedale Romance)*. James, Henry *(Bostonians)*. Politics. Sex. 19c. *795*
—. Fuller, Margaret. Jefferson, Thomas. Journalism. Social criticism. 1840-50. *272*
—. Fuller, Margaret. New England. Radicals and Radicalism. Transcendentalism. 1810-50. *311*
—. Gage, Frances Dana. *Ohio Cultivator* (newspaper). Tracy-Cutler, Hannah Maria. 1845-55. *800*
—. Georgia. Peace Movements. Rankin, Jeannette. 1924-73. *352*
—. Great Britain. Hill, Claibourne M. USA. 1914. *1929*
—. Holiness Movement. Palmer, Phoebe. Wesley, Susanna. 1732-1973. *17*
—. Holley, Marrietta *(My Opinion)*. Literature. 1870-1926. *983*
—. Human Relations. Politics. Radicals and Radicalism. Values. 19c-1929. *29*
—. Identity. 1820's-60. *804*
—. Industry. Legislation. Progressivism. 1919-33. *2401*
—. Journalism. Swisshelm, Jane Grey. ca 1835-84. *328*
—. Kansas. Nichols, Clarina I. H. (papers). 1839-56. *338*
—. Kansas. Nichols, Clarina I. H. (papers). 1857-85. *337*

—. Kindergarten. Motherhood. Progressivism. 1860-1920. *1932*
—. Labor. Love. Speeches, Addresses, etc. Stanton, Elizabeth Cady. 1868-70. *992*
—. Labor Unions and Organizations. Lobbying. Middle Classes. Suffrage. Women's Trade Union League. ca 1903-20. *1980*
—. Lectures. Wright, Frances. 1820's-30's. *813*
—. Leftism. New York City. Prisons. Smedley, Agnes *(Cell Mates)*. 1918. *2019*
—. Literary characters. Novels. Rives, Amèlie. South. 1863-1945. *377*
—. Literature. Negroes. Stowe, Harriet Beecher. Truth, Soujourner. 1850's-90's. *802*
—. Literature. Utopias. 19c-20c. *267*
—. Lloyd, Lola Maverick. Peace Movements. 1914-44. *451*
—. Lockwood, Belva Bennett (letters). Political Campaigns (presidential). 1884. *1116*
—. Maryland, University of. Oral history. Sex Discrimination. 1968-78. *2913*
—. Massachusetts Association Opposed to the Further Extension of the Suffrage to Women. Political campaigns. Sex roles. Socialism. Woman suffrage. 1895-1915. *2166*
—. Mencken, H. L. Morality. 1900-56. *1641*
—. Mental health system. Social conditions. 20c. *2918*
—. Morality. Physical Education and Training. Sexuality. Women. 19c. *101*
—. Morality. Politics. Women. 19c-20c. *142*
—. Ontario (Toronto). 1870's-1910's. *421*
—. Pacific Area. Pan-Pacific and Southeast Asia Women's Association. 1928-70's. *1610*
—. Pennsylvania Council of Republican Women. Pinchot, Cornelia. 1920's-30's. *2509*
—. Poetry. 1850-91. *19*
—. Protestant Churches. Social Conditions. South. Women. 1920's. *2339*
—. Religion. 1967-76. *2916*
—. Rhetoric. Speeches, Addresses, etc. Stanton, Elizabeth Cady ("The Solitude of Self"). 1892. *964*
—. South. Thomas, Ella Gertrude Clanton (journal). 1848-89. *383*
Feminization. Historiography. Protestantism. Welter, Barbara. Women. 1820's-30's. 1970's. *910*
Ferm, Alexis Constantine. Education. Ferm, Elizabeth Byrne. Individualism. 1880's-1970's. *847*
Ferm, Elizabeth Byrne. Education. Ferm, Alexis Constantine. Individualism. 1880's-1970's. *847*
Fernandez, John F. O. Catholic Church. Laity. Parishes. Virginia (Norfolk). 1815-20. *905*
Fessenden, Samuel. Abolition movement. Free Soil movement. Liberty Party. Maine. State Politics. Willey, Austin. 1830's-48. *682*
Fiction *See also* Novels.
—. Cable, George Washington. Gardens. 1886-1925. *2*
—. Canada. Christianity. Labor. Social gospel. 1890's. *1354*
—. Homosexuality. Periodicals. Women. 1900-20. *1930*
Filene, Edward A. Industrial democracy. Massachusetts (Boston). Reform. 1890-1937. *1787*
Filibusters. Bilbo, Theodore G. Employment. Fair Employment Practices Committee. Mississippi. Racism. Senate. 1941-46. *2617*
Filipino Labor Union. Agricultural Labor. California (Salinas). Lettuce. Strikes. 1934. *2499*
Film industry. Blacklisting. Communists. Courts. Hollywood Ten. *Young v. MPAA* (US, 1965). 1947-73. *1736*
—. Griffith, David W. *(Birth of a Nation)*. Negroes. Racism. 1915-18. *1918*
Films. Attitudes. *Intolerance* (film). Progressivism. 1916. *1965*
—. *Birth of a Nation* (film). Griffith, David W. Negroes. Temperance Movements. 1900-20. *2087*
Films (documentary). Armies. Heisler, Stuart. *Negro Soldier* (film). Propaganda. Race Relations. World War II. 1944. *2621*
Finch, John (letter). New York (Finger Lakes area). Skaneateles Community. Utopias. 1843-45. *925*
Fincke, William. Brockwood Labor College. Education. Labor. 1919-37. *1614*
Finland *See also* Scandinavia.
—. Australia. Canada. Kurikka, Matti. Utopias. 1883-1915. *1707*

Finley, James B. Assimilation. Indians (agencies). Methodist Church. Missions and Missionaries. Ohio. Shaw, John. 1820-24. *581*
Finley, Robert. American Colonization Society. Racism. 1816-40. *648*
Finney, Charles Grandison. Abolition Movement. Congregationalism. Evangelism. South. 1833-69. *632*
—. Protestantism. 1815-65. *569*
Finnish Americans. Borg, Selma Josefina. Centennial Exposition of 1876. Lectures. Music. Pennsylvania (Philadelphia). Women's rights. 1858-90. *399*
—. British Columbia (Harmony Island). Kurikka, Matti. Utopias. 1901-05. *1628*
—. Imatra I (association). Labor Unions and Organizations. New York City (Brooklyn). 1890-1921. *2011*
—. Immigrants. Labor. Minnesota (Smithville). Socialism. Work People's College. 1900-20. *2315*
—. Iron Industry. Labor Unions and Organizations. Minnesota. Minnesota (Mesabi Range). Radicals and Radicalism. 1914-17. *2253*
Finnish Canadians. Canada. Editors and Editing. Kurikka, Matti. Mäkelä, A. B. Newspapers. Socialism. 1900-32. *464*
Finns. Canada. Immigrants. Labor Unions and Organizations. Radicals and Radicalism. 1918-26. *2407*
Fire insurance. Antitrust. Courts. Kansas City Board of Fire Underwriters. Law enforcement. Missouri. 1889-99. *1336*
Firearms Control Regulations Act (US, 1975). District of Columbia. Gun control. Methodology. US Conference of Mayors (report). 1975-80. *2778*
Firestone, Harvey S. Garvey, Marcus. Land. Leases. Liberia. Negroes. Universal Negro Improvement Association. 1926. *2402*
Firestone, Shulamith. Feminism. Fuller, Margaret. Gilman, Charlotte Perkins. Godwin, Mary Wollstonecraft. Science. 1759-1972. *64*
Fiscal Policy. Air pollution. Clean Air Act (US, 1970). Demography. Energy. State Government. 1970-79. *2719*
Fisher, Irving. Class struggle. Eugenics. Progressivism. Racism. 1890's-1920. *1869*
—. Congress. Progressive era. Public health. 1906-13. *2115*
—. Depressions. Economic Reform. Roosevelt, Franklin D. 1930's. *2468*
Fisher, Walter L. City Government. Illinois (Chicago). Reform. 1880-1910. *347*
Fisher, Walter Lowrie. Ballinger-Pinchot Controversy. Conservation. Interior Department. 1911-13. *1957*
Fisk University. Johnson, Charles S. Negroes. Race relations. UNESCO. 1900-56. *346*
—. Race Relations. Tennessee (Nashville). Youth Movements. 1909-26. *2397*
Five Civilized Tribes. Civil Rights. Indian-White Relations. 18c-20c. *1581*
—. Dawes Commission. Freedmen. Homesteading and Homesteaders. Indian Territory. 1893-1905. *1083*
Five-Day Plan. Economic Reform. Hicks, Mary. Hicks, Mildred. 1931-40. *2589*
Flathead Indian Reservation. Dawes Act (US, 1887). Indians. Land Tenure. Montana. Salish (Flathead) Indians. 1887-1904. *1075*
Fletcher, Alice Cunningham. Artifacts. Dawes Act (US, 1887). Indians (reservations). 1880's-90's. *968*
Fletcher, Benjamin Harrison. Crime and Criminals. Industrial Workers of the World. Labor. Longshoremen. Negroes. 1910-33. *437*
Fletcher, Horace. Hygiene. Mastication. Nutrition. 1890-1910. *2120*
Flexner Report. American Medical Association. Carnegie Foundation. Medical education. Reform. 1910-32. *2297*
—. Brookings, Robert. Medical education. Missouri (St. Louis). Reform. Washington University. 1910-16. *2318*
—. Legal education. Medical education. Reed Report (1921). 1910-74. *1862*
—. Medicine. Professionalism. Progressive era. Social control. 1910. *2317*
Flint, Austin. Medical Education. 1830's-70's. *256*
Florida *See also* South.
—. Acculturation. Collier, John. Indians. North Carolina. Schools. Seminole Indians. 1927-54. *1851*

—. Alabama (Selma). Civil Rights. Collins, LeRoy. Community Relations Service. Demonstrations. 1965-68. *2897*
—. American Missionary Association. Civil Rights. Education. Freedmen. 1864-74. *1245*
—. Arkansas (Little Rock). Collins, LeRoy. Courts. Federal Government. Political Speeches. School integration. 1957. *2688*
—. Attitudes. Roosevelt, Theodore. South. Washington, Booker T. 1901. *2080*
—. *Brown v. Board of Education* (US, 1954). Collins, LeRoy. State Legislatures. Supreme Court. 1954-61. *2664*
—. City Government. Civil rights movement. Negroes. Public services. 1960-76. *2814*
—. Civil Rights Act (US, 1964). School Integration. Supreme Court decisions. 1954-64. *2686*
—. Colored National Labor Union. Labor Unions and Organizations. National Union of Negro Labor. Negroes. Race Relations. Reconstruction. 1865-75. *1259*
—. Crime and criminals. Rebellions. Slavery. ca 1820-65. *659*
—. Elementary education. Peabody Fund. Reconstruction. Segregation. 1869-76. *1433*
—. Equal Rights Amendment. National Women's Party. Politics. West, Helen Hunt. Women. 1917-52. *1727*
—. Governors. Public Policy. Race relations. 1954-76. *1552*
—. Indian-White Relations. Pelota (game). Spain. 1675-84. *9*
—. Justice Department. Labor recruitment. New York City. Peonage. Quackenbos, Mary Grace. Turpentine industry. 1905-10. *2267*
—. Law. Race Relations. Segregation. Social customs. 1865-1977. *141*
—. Menard, John Willis. Negroes. Political Leadership. 1871-90. *283*
—. Negroes. Political attitudes. Reconstruction. Republican Party. Walls, Josiah T. 1867-85. *1192*
—. Women. 1890-1978. *1550*
Florida (Hernando County). Bootlegging. Depressions. Law enforcement. Liquor. Prohibition. 1929-33. *2359*
Florida (Jacksonville). Desegregation. Public schools. Students. 1960's-70's. *2834*
—. Negroes. Political Participation. 1887-1907. *1125*
Florida (Kissimmee). Civil Rights. Friends of the Florida Seminoles. Indians. Seminole Indians. Tiger, Tom. 1898-99. *1100*
Florida (Lee County). Koreshan Unity. Politics. Sects, Religious. Teed, Cyrus Reed. Utopias. 1880-1909. *1516*
Florida (Leon County). Carse, George B. Freedmen's Bureau. Reconstruction. Republican Party. 1867-70. *1074*
—. Convict lease system. Corporal punishment. Law Reform. Tabert, Martin. 1921-23. *2354*
Florida (Miami). Civil Rights Organizations. Discrimination. Louisiana (New Orleans). Murray, Hugh T., Jr. (reminiscences). 1959-60. *2871*
—. Law Enforcement. Prohibition. Smuggling. 1896-1920. *1948*
—. Nation, Carry. Temperance Movements. 1908-13. *1949*
Florida (Tampa). Civil rights. Demonstrations. Desegregation. Fort, Clarence. Lane, Julian. Negroes. 1960. *2902*
Florida, University of. Courts. Discrimination, educational. Hawkins, Virgil Darnell. Lawyers. Legal education. 1949-76. *1554*
Flynn, Dennis T. House of Representatives. McGuire, Bird S. Oklahoma. Progressivism. 1901-07. *1905*
Flynn, Elizabeth Gurley. Communism. Feminism. ca 1890-1920. *282*
Follen, Charles Theodore Christian. Abolition Movement. Harvard University. May, Samuel. 1824-42. *753*
Folsom, James E. Alabama. Civil Rights. Democratic Party. Negroes. State Government. Women. 1947-58. *2668*
Foltz, Clara Shortridge. California (San Diego). Lawyers. Women. 1872-1930. *413*
Food Adulteration and Inspection. Allen, Robert McDowell. Kentucky. Progressivism. Scovell, Melville Amasa. 1898-1916. *2125*
Food and Drug Administration. Antibiotics. Conflict of interest. Federal regulation. Periodicals. Pharmacy. Welch, Henry. 1953-62. *2676*

—. Great Plains. Labor. Radicals and Radicalism. Social change. Veblen, Thorstein. World War I. 1918. *1922*
Food Consumption *See also* Nutrition.
—. Abel, Mary Hinman. Aladdin Ovens. Atkinson, Edward. Massachusetts (Boston). New England Kitchen. Richards, Ellen H. Working Class. 1889-97. *1467*
Food, Drug, and Cosmetic Act (US, 1938). Consumers. Drugs. Regulation. 1938-78. *1818*
Food Stamp Act (US, 1964). Public Welfare. 1939-77. *2937*
Food stamps. Federal Programs. Reform. 1930-77. *1872*
Football. Higher education. Military training. Morality. 1890-1930. *2327*
—. Johnson, Owen *(Stover at Yale)*. Muckraking. Progressivism. 1911-20. *1998*
Foote, Edward Bliss. Birth control. Medicine. New York. 1858-1906. *543*
Foraker, Joseph B. Constitution League. Discrimination. Hepburn Bill, Warner-Foraker Amendment (1906). Jim Crow laws. Negroes. Railroads. Washington, Booker T. (and Committee of 12). 1906. *1919*
Ford, Arnold. Emigration. Ethiopia (Addis Ababa). Negroes. 1930-35. *2436*
Ford, Henry. Architecture. Automobile Industry and Trade. Factories. Kahn, Albert. 1869-1942. 1900H. *1779*
Ford Motor Company of Canada. Labor Law. Ontario (Windsor). United Automobile Workers (Canadian Region). 1946. *2682*
Foreign Mission School. American Board of Commissioners for Foreign Missions. Assimilation. Connecticut (Cornwall). Indian-White Relations. Students. 1816-27. *829*
Foreign Policy *See also* Defense Policy.
—. Dewey, John. Pacifism. War. 1918-32. *1615*
—. Economic policy. New Deal. Public works. Roosevelt, Franklin D. 1933. *2555*
—. Imports. International Steel Cartel. Labor. Steel Workers Organizing Committee. US Steel Corporation. 1937. *2538*
—. International Labor Organization. Isolationism. New Deal. Perkins, Frances. Roosevelt, Franklin D. 1921-34. *2570*
—. International Relations. Isolationism. League of Nations Association. Peace. 1934-38. *2466*
Foreign Relations *See also* Boundaries; Diplomacy; Tariff.
—. Abolition Movement. Anderson, John. Canada. Great Britain. Politics. USA. 1860-61. *734*
—. Abolition movement. Confederate States of America. Cuba. Spain. 1860-68. *1145*
—. *Advocate of Peace* (periodical). American Peace Society. Pacifism. Public Opinion. 1837-1932. *59*
—. Berry pickers. California (El Monte). Japan. Mexico. Strikes. 1933. *2522*
Forest and Farm Workers Union. Hall, Covington. Labor Unions and Organizations. Louisiana. Lumber and Lumbering. Socialism. 1907-16. *2192*
Forest Service. California (Eight Mile, Blue Creek). Indians. Religious liberty. Supreme Court. 1975. *2785*
—. Economic Development. Minnesota, northeastern. Public Policy. Superior National Forest. Wilderness. 1923-26. *2437*
Forests and Forestry *See also* Lumber and Lumbering.
—. Conservation of natural resources. Pacific Northwest. 1889-1913. *2052*
Forney, Jacob. Farms. Hurt, Garland. Indians (reservations). Utah Superintendency of Indian Affairs. 1850-62. *539*
Forrester, Alexander. Educators. Nova Scotia (Truro). ca 1848-69. *842*
Forssell, G. D. Iowa. Lectures. Minnesota. Progressivism. Social Conditions. 1890-95. *957*
Fort, Clarence. Civil rights. Demonstrations. Desegregation. Florida (Tampa). Lane, Julian. Negroes. 1960. *2902*
Fort Huachuca. Arizona. Bai-a-lil-le (medicine man). Civil Rights. Courts. Education. Indian Rights Association. Navajo Indians. Utah, southeastern. 1906-09. *2043*
Fort McIntosh. Negroes. Riots. Texas (Laredo). 25th Infantry, US (Company D). 1899. *1143*
Fort Sill. Apache Indians (Chiricahua, Ojo Caliente). Interior Department. Land allotment. Oklahoma. Prisoners of war. War Department. 1909-13. *2170*

Fort Valley High and Industrial School. Education. Georgia. Negroes. Torbert, James H. 1897-1911. *2296*
Fort Valley State College. Colleges and Universities (black). Georgia (Peach County). *Hunnicutt et al. v. Burge et al.* (Georgia, 1972). Racism. School Integration. 1972-78. *2800*
Forts. *See* names of specific forts, e.g. Fort Bragg.
Fortune, Timothy Thomas. Civil rights. Editors and Editing. Negroes. 1881-1928. *95*
Foster, Abigail Kelley. Abolition Movement. Foster, Stephen Symonds. Psychohistory. Radicals and Radicalism. 1820-77. *288*
Foster, Frank K. Comte, Auguste. Gompers, Samuel. Ideology. Labor Unions and Organizations. McGregor, Hugh. Spencer, Herbert. 1876-1900. *1295*
Foster homes. Child Welfare. Family. Immigration. Jews. New York City. Working class. 1900-05. *2061*
Foster, Richard B. (address). Missouri. Negroes. Reconstruction. Teachers. 1869. *1170*
Foster, Stephen Symonds. Abolition Movement. Foster, Abigail Kelley. Psychohistory. Radicals and Radicalism. 1820-77. *288*
Foster, William Z. Carlson, Oliver (reminiscences). Communist Party. Politburo. Radek, Karl. Trotskyism. USSR. 1924-35. *1548*
—. Communist Party. Socialist Party. 1881-1921. *304*
Foundations. Gates, Frederick T. Medical education. Physicians. Research, Clinical. Rockefeller, John D. 1910-39. *1833*
Founding Fathers. Kansas-Nebraska Act (US, 1854). Lincoln, Abraham. Reconstruction. Republicanism. 1854-65. *1058*
Fourth of July. Attitudes. Civil Rights. Declaration of Independence. Jefferson, Thomas. Negroes. 1776. 1800-50. *724*
Fox, George. Friends, Society of. Pennsylvania. Slave trade. 1656-1754. *522*
Fox, Ruth May. Diaries. Suffrage. Utah. Women. 1865-95. *1119*
Fram, Leon (reminiscences). Anti-Nazi Movements. Boycotts. Jews. League for Human Rights. Michigan (Detroit). 1930's-40's. *2507*
France *See also* French Revolution.
—. Cabet, Etienne. Icarians. Iowa (New Icaria, Corning). Utopias. 1852-98. *1502*
—. Collective Bargaining. Great Britain. Labor. 18c-20c. *167*
—. Colonialism. Madagascar. Waller, John L. 1891-95. *1282*
—. Communes. Considerant, Victor Prosper. Land. Texas, northern. Travel. 1852-69. *265*
—. Madagascar. Negroes. Press. Waller, John L. 1890's. *1281*
Franchise. *See* Citizenship; Suffrage.
Franciscan Sisters of Chicago. Addams, Jane. Dudzik, Mary Theresa. Illinois. Polish Americans. Social Work. 1860-1918. *369*
Frank, Jerome (review article). Harvard Law School. Law. 1870-1930. *2341*
Frankfurter, Felix. Depressions. Keynes, John Maynard. New Deal. Public works. 1932-35. *2473*
Franklin, Benjamin. Indians. Massacres. Pamphlets. Paxton Boys. Pennsylvania. 1764. *499*
—. Inoculation. Medical Research. 1730-50. *532*
Franklin, James. City Government. Editorials. Freedom of the Press. Inoculation. Massachusetts (Boston). *New England Courant* (newspaper). Smallpox. 1721. *535*
Fraud. Arapaho Indians. Cheyenne Indians. Dawes Act (US, 1887). Indians (agencies). Land allotment. Oklahoma. 1910's. *1888*
Frazier, Lynn J. Federal Government. Governors. Indians. North Dakota. Progressivism. 1916-40. *1538*
Free Schools. Educational Reform. Howland, John. Legislation. Rhode Island. 1757-1838. *431*
Free Soil movement. Abolition movement. Fessenden, Samuel. Liberty Party. Maine. State Politics. Willey, Austin. 1830's-48. *682*
Free Soil Party. Antislavery Sentiments. Illinois. Racism. Republican Party. 1848-60. *740*
Free Speech (newspaper). Lynching. Negroes. Tennessee (Memphis). Wells, Ida B. 1892. *1128*
Freedmen. Abolition Movement. Labor. Race relations. Slavery. 1830-63. *613*
—. African Society. Colonization. Hopkins, Samuel. Rhode Island (Providence). Sierra Leone. 1789-95. *614*
—. Agricultural Labor. Economic Structure. Racism. Reconstruction. Texas. 1865-74. *1263*
—. Alabama. Bureau of Refugees, Freedmen, and Abandoned Lands. Reconstruction. 1865-67. *1223*
—. Alabama. Labor. Plantations. Sharecropping. 1865-67. *1198*
—. American Freedmen's Inquiry Commission. Civil War. Johnson, Andrew. 1863. *1260*
—. American Missionary Association. Cardozo, Francis Louis. Education. Reconstruction. South Carolina (Charleston). State Politics. 1865-70. *1243*
—. American Missionary Association. Civil Rights. Education. Florida. 1864-74. *1245*
—. American Missionary Association. Congregationalism. Georgia (Liberty County). 1870-80's. *1247*
—. Authority. Citizenship. Constitutional Amendments (13th, 14th, 15th). Federal government. Reconstruction. 1865-70. *1132*
—. Authority. South. Teaching. Women. 1865-70. *1425*
—. Black capitalism. Civil War. Davis Bend colony. Eaton, John, Jr. Mississippi. 1862-66. *1249*
—. Cardozo, Francis Louis. Political rights. Reconstruction. South Carolina. Union League. 1870. *1268*
—. Cherokee Indians. Indian Territory. Racism. 1839-88. *1165*
—. Christianity. Education. Presbyterians. 1872-1900. *1272*
—. Civil Rights. Constitutional Amendments (13th, 14th, 15th). Politics. Reconstruction. 1865-77. *1188*
—. Civil rights. Louisiana Purchase. Treaty of Cession (1804). 1797-1804. *590*
—. Civil War. Louisiana (New Orleans). Negroes, free. Political Attitudes. Politics. Social Classes. 1860-65. *1275*
—. Dawes Commission. Five Civilized Tribes. Homesteading and Homesteaders. Indian Territory. 1893-1905. *1083*
—. Emancipation. South. Whites. 1865-66. *969*
—. Emancipation Proclamation. Liberty. Lincoln, Abraham. Republican Party. 1862. *1131*
—. Federal programs. Reconstruction. Religious organizations. Georgia (Atlanta). North. 1865-69. *1273*
—. *Freedom's Journal* (newspaper). Negroes. Negroes (free). Press. 1827-29. *713*
—. Hartzell, Joseph C. Methodist Church. Missions and Missionaries. Republican Party. South. 1870-73. *1208*
—. Homesteading and Homesteaders. Louisiana. Reconstruction. 1865-83. *1233*
—. House of Representatives. Murray, George Washington. Republican Party. South Carolina. Suffrage. 1893-97. *1163*
—. Intellectuals. Negroes, free. Politics. Social theory. South. 1870's-90's. *1274*
—. Louisiana (Madison Parish). Plantations. Race Relations. Reconstruction. 1863-74. *978*
—. North. Race Relations. Schools. Teachers. Virginia (Lexington). 1867. *1405*
Freedmen's Bureau. Alabama. Gardner, Samuel S. (letter). Negro Suffrage. Reconstruction. 1867. *1180*
—. Alabama. Racism. Reconstruction. Swayne, Wager. 1865-68. *1279*
—. American Missionary Association. Colleges and Universities. Mississippi. Negroes. Tougaloo College. 1865-69. *1141*
—. Archives, National. Public Records. Reconstruction. Texas. 1865-76. *1147*
—. Armies. Civil War. Maryland. Reconstruction. Reform. 1864-68. *1162*
—. Carse, George B. Florida (Leon County). Reconstruction. Republican Party. 1867-70. *1074*
—. Contracts. Planters. Sharecropping. South. 1865-68. *1258*
—. Courts. Howard, Oliver Otis. Reconstruction. South. 1865-68. *1229*
—. Courts. Justice. Negroes. Reconstruction. Texas. 1865-68. *1146*
—. Diaries. Hopkins, Sterling. Reconstruction. Virginia. 1868. *1056*
—. Discrimination. Federal Policy. Mississippi. Reconstruction. State Government. 1865. *1227*
—. Discrimination. Johnson, Andrew. Law. Reconstruction. 1865-66. *1226*
—. Education. Negroes. Texas. 1865-70. *1174*
—. Kentucky. Noble, Thomas. Race Relations. Reconstruction. Schools. 1865-70. *1190*
—. Kirkland, William S. Reconstruction. Texas. 1865-70. *1261*
—. Race relations. Schools. West Virginia (Berkeley, Jefferson counties). 1865-68. *1264*
—. West Virginia (Berkeley, Jefferson counties). 1865-68. *1077*
Freedmen's Bureau Act (US, 1865). Congress. Refugees. 1864-65. *1091*
Freedmen's Savings Bank. Alabama. Banking. Negroes. 1865-74. *1191*
Freedmen's Village. Land Tenure. Race Relations. Virginia (Arlington). 1872-1900. *1183*
Freedom. Fugitive Slaves. Latimer, George. Law. Massachusetts (Boston). Sewall, Samuel E. Shaw, Lemuel. ca 1790-1890. *784*
—. Individualism. Property. Social mobility. Socialism. 1750-1979. *85*
Freedom Colony. DeBernardi, G. B. Depressions. Kansas. Labor Exchange. Utopias. 1894-1905. *1510*
Freedom of Assembly *See also* Freedom of Speech; Riots.
—. American Civil Liberties Union. Associated Silk Workers Union. Freedom of Speech. New Jersey (Paterson). Strikes. 1924. *2378*
—. Anti-German sentiment. Bouck, William. Grange. Public Opinion. Vigilantes. Washington (Walla Walla). World War I. 1918. *2161*
Freedom of Speech *See also* Freedom of the Press.
—. American Civil Liberties Union. Associated Silk Workers Union. Freedom of Assembly. New Jersey (Paterson). Strikes. 1924. *2378*
—. Anti-Communist Movements. Letters. Ontario (Toronto). Police. Political Repression. 1931. *1724*
—. *Blackwell v. Issaquena County Board of Education* (US, 1966). *Burnside v. Byars* (US, 1966). Courts. Students. *Tinker v. Des Moines Community School District* (US, 1969). 1870-1969. *1728*
—. California (Fresno). Clyde, Edward M. Industrial Workers of the World. 1911. *2151*
—. California (Fresno). Industrial Workers of the World. 1910-11. *2138*
—. California (San Diego). Industrial Workers of the World. Mexico (Tijuana). 1911-12. *2162*
—. Chafee, Zechariah, Jr. Civil Rights. 1919-57. *1729*
—. City Politics. Industrial Workers of the World. Iowa (Sioux City). Short, Wallace. 1918-24. *2134*
—. Georgia. Obscenity. *Stanley v. Georgia* (US, 1969). Supreme Court. 1968-79. *2765*
—. Industrial Workers of the World. Labor Disputes. Washington (Aberdeen). 1911-12. *2150*
—. Industrial Workers of the World. Political Protest. Pratt, N. S. Washington (Spokane). 1909-10. *2132*
—. National Women's Party. Woman Suffrage. 1912-19. *2129*
—. Oklahoma. Political Repression. Vigilantes. World War I. 1914-17. *2137*
—. Pacifism. Virginia, University of. Whipple, Leon. World War I. 1917. *2130*
Freedom of the Press *See also* Censorship.
—. City Government. Editorials. Franklin, James. Inoculation. Massachusetts (Boston). *New England Courant* (newspaper). Smallpox. 1721. *535*
—. Courts. Farber, Myron. *New York Times* (newspaper). Reporters and Reporting. 1975-79. *2781*
—. Editorials. Newspapers. 1920. 1940. *1719*
Freedom Singers. Civil rights movement. Georgia (Albany; Harlem district). NAACP. Reagon, Bernice Johnson (interview). 1960-77. *2880*
Freedom Summers. Civil rights movement. Sex Discrimination. Women. 1960-65. *2882*
Freedom's Journal (newspaper). Abolition Movement. Cornish, Samuel E. Journalism. Negroes. Presbyterian Church. 1820's-59. *467*
—. Freedmen. Negroes. Negroes (free). Press. 1827-29. *713*
Freight and Freightage *See also* Railroads.
—. Agriculture. Populism. Prices. Railroads. 1870-97. *1360*
—. Business. Federal Regulation. Hepburn Act (US, 1906). Interstate Commerce Commission. 1905-06. *2282*
French Canadian Americans. Belgian Americans. Independent Textile Workers. Rhode Island (Woonsocket). Working Class. 1931-50's. *1767*

French Canadians. American Federation of Labor. Gompers, Samuel. Quebec. 1900-14. *1741*
—. Angers, François-Albert. Canada. Catholic Church. Pacifism. Values. 1940-79. *1595*
—. Antitrust. Hamel, Philippe. Nationalism. Public Utilities. Quebec (Quebec). 1929-34. *1757*
French language. Catholic Church. Church and State. Langevin, Adélard. Manitoba. Politics. Private schools. 1890-1916. *1410*
—. Catholic Church. Church schools. Langevin, Louis Philippe Adélard. Laurier, Wilfrid. Liberal Party. Prairie Provinces. Religion in the Public Schools. 1890-1915. *185*
—. Charter of the French Language (1977). Politics. Provincial government. Quebec. 1977-78. *2766*
—. Class struggle. Equality. Intellectuals. Nationalism. Quebec. 1960's-70's. *2693*
French Revolution. American Revolution. Canada. Ideology. 1775-1838. *139*
Freudianism. Literature. Women's liberation movement. 1946-70's. *1599*
—. New York City (Greenwich Village). Psychoanalysis. Radicals and Radicalism. Sex. 1913-20. *1936*
Friedlander, Alice G. Oregon (Portland). Speeches, Addresses, etc. Woman Suffrage. 1893. *1095*
Friends of the Florida Seminoles. Civil Rights. Florida (Kissimmee). Indians. Seminole Indians. Tiger, Tom. 1898-99. *1100*
Friends, Society of. Abolition Movement. American Revolution. Pennsylvania. Woolman, John. 1758-88. *530*
—. Abolition movement. Dugdale, Joseph A. Reform. 1810-96. *297*
—. Africans' School. Benezet, Anthony. Education. Negroes. Pennsylvania (Philadelphia). 1770's-80's. *487*
—. American Revolution. Diaries. Drinker family. Pennsylvania (Philadelphia). Prisoners. Virginia (Winchester). 1777-81. *526*
—. Antislavery Sentiments. Benezet, Anthony. 1759-84. *509*
—. Antislavery Sentiments. Boycotts. Cotton. Great Britain. 1840-60. *608*
—. Antislavery Sentiments. British North America. Social problems. Woolman, John. 1720-72. *478*
—. Antislavery Sentiments. Civil War. Jones, James Parnell. Maine. Military Service. 1850's-64. *320*
—. Antislavery Sentiments. North America. 1671-1771. *524*
—. Attitudes. New York (Auburn). Pennsylvania. Prisons. Reform. Religion. 1787-1845. *874*
—. Black nationalism. Colonization. Cuffe, Paul. Sierra Leone. 1810's. *694*
—. British North America. Great Britain. Slavery. 1757-61. *519*
—. Cedar Creek Monthly Meeting. Emancipation. Farms. Moorman, Clark Terrell. Ohio. Virginia (Caroline County). 1766-1814. *743*
—. Charities. Pennsylvania (Philadelphia). Society for Organizing Charitable Relief and Repressing Mendicancy. 1800-1900. *250*
—. Confederate States of America. Conscientious objectors. North Carolina. 1861-65. *1124*
—. Crime and Criminals. Peace bonds. Pennsylvania (Philadelphia). 1680-1829. *492*
—. Dunkards. Mennonites. Militarism. Pacifism. 1900-78. *1571*
—. Education. Girls. Ontario. 1790-1820. *852*
—. Fell, Margaret. Feminism. Great Britain (Lancashire). Pennsylvania (Philadelphia). Women. 1670's. *498*
—. Fox, George. Pennsylvania. Slave trade. 1656-1754. *522*
—. Humanism. Intellectuals. Penn, William. Radicals and Radicalism. 1650-1700. *474*
—. Indian Wars. Nonviolence. Paxton riots. Pennsylvania (Philadelphia). 1764-67. *497*
—. Pennsylvania Hospital for the Sick Poor. Pennsylvania (Philadelphia). Poor. 18c. *533*
Friendship. Abolition Movement. Evangelism. Tappan, Lewis. 1830-61. *645*
Frontier and Pioneer Life *See also* Cowboys; Homesteading and Homesteaders; Indians.
—. Compulsory education. Industrialization. Social change. 1870's. *1408*
—. Environment. Historiography. 1492-1978. *51*
—. Kentucky. Medical Education. Mitchell, Thomas Duche. Reform. 1809-65. *325*
Frontier Nursing Service. Breckinridge, Mary. Kentucky. Nurses and Nursing. 1925-65. *1559*

Fruitlands (community). Alcott, Amos Bronson. Lane, Charles. Massachusetts. Transcendentalism. Utopias. 1840-50. *922*
Fugitive Slave Act (US, 1850). Antislavery Sentiments. Eliot, Samuel A. Massachusetts (Boston). Patriotism. Unitarianism. 1850-60. *752*
—. Kentucky (Boone, Bourbon counties). Michigan (Cass County). Slaveholders. 1830-60. *786*
—. Methodist Church. Newspapers. Slavery. 1850. *684*
Fugitive Slaves. Abolition movement. Anderson, John. Canada. Great Britain. Trials. USA. 1860-61. *733*
—. Abolition Movement. Craft, Ellen. Craft, William. Great Britain. 1848-65. *611*
—. Abolitionists. Government. Great Britain. Law. Slave Trade. 1834-61. *774*
—. Abolitionists. Negroes. Pennsylvania (Pittsburgh). Philanthropic Society. 1830's-60. *610*
—. Canada. Courts. Extradition. Happy, Jesse. Kentucky. Testimony. 1793-1838. *748*
—. Civil War. Contraband programs. Louisiana, southern. Military Occupation. 1862-65. *1219*
—. Freedom. Latimer, George. Law. Massachusetts (Boston). Sewall, Samuel E. Shaw, Lemuel. ca 1790-1890. *784*
Fuller, Margaret. Feminism. Firestone, Shulamith. Gilman, Charlotte Perkins. Godwin, Mary Wollstonecraft. Science. 1759-1972. *64*
—. Feminism. Godwin, Mary Wollstonecraft. 1792-19c. *812*
—. Feminism. Hawthorne, Nathaniel *(The Blithedale Romance)*. James, Henry *(Bostonians)*. Politics. Sex. 19c. *795*
—. Feminism. Jefferson, Thomas. Journalism. Social criticism. 1840-50. *272*
—. Feminism. New England. Radicals and Radicalism. Transcendentalism. 1810-50. *311*
Fullilove v. Klutznick (US, 1980). Affirmative action. Discrimination. Minorities. *Regents of the University of California v. Allan Bakke* (US, 1978). Supreme Court. *United Steelworkers of America v. Weber* (US, 1979). 1970's. *2782*
—. Affirmative action. *United Steelworkers of America v. Weber* (US, 1979). 1979-81. *2786*
Fundamentalism. Civil War. Constitutional Amendments. Lincoln, Abraham. National Fast Day. National Reform Association. 1787-1945. *1484*
—. Democracy. Education. Local Politics. Social Change. Vigilantism. 1920's. *2375*
—. Long, Huey P. North Central States. Populism. Progressivism. Smith, Gerald L. K. 1934-48. *362*
—. Matthews, Mark Allison. Presbyterian Church. Washington (Seattle). 1900-40. *430*
Furman, Richard. Attitudes. Baptists. Church and Social Problems. Slavery. 1807-23. *695*

G

Gabriel's Insurrection. American Colonization Society. Monroe, James. Prosser, Gabriel. Slave revolts. Virginia. 1800. *698*
Gage, Frances Dana. Feminism. *Ohio Cultivator* (newspaper). Tracy-Cutler, Hannah Maria. 1845-55. *800*
Galveston Plan of 1907. Charities. Immigration. Industrial Removal Office. Jews. Migration, Internal. New York City. 1890-1914. *1476*
Gambling. Barkley, Alben. Kentucky. Louisville Churchmen's Federation. Progressivism. 1917-27. *2438*
Gandhi, Mahatma. Civil rights movement. King, Martin Luther, Jr. Nonviolence. Political Protest. 1950's-60's. *2878*
—. Civil rights movement. King, Martin Luther, Jr. Social change. 1959-68. *2822*
Garden cities. City Planning. New Jersey. Radburn (settlement). Suburbs. 1927-79. *1532*
—. Davis, Alexander Jackson. Haskell, Llewellyn S. Idealism. New Jersey (West Orange; Llewellyn Park). Suburbs. 1853-57. *943*
Garden City Movement. Business. Consumer cooperative movements. Nelson, Nelson O. Progressivism. 1890's-1918. *2240*
Gardens. Cable, George Washington. Fiction. 1886-1925. *2*
Gardner, Charles W. Abolition Movement. Constitutional conventions, state. Disfranchisement. Hinton, Frederick A. Negroes. Pennsylvania. 1838. *596*

Gardner, Samuel S. (letter). Alabama. Freedmen's Bureau. Negro Suffrage. Reconstruction. 1867. *1180*
Garland, Hamlin. Determinism. Indians. Reform. 1890-1923. *2111*
Garland, Rufus King. Arkansas. Greenback Party. State politics. Tobey, Charles E. 1876-82. *952*
Garment industry. Illinois (Chicago). Men. Strikes. 1910-11. *2286*
—. Illinois (Chicago). O'Reilly, Mary. Socialist Party. Strikes. Women. Zeh, Nellie M. 1910. *2183*
—. International Ladies' Garment Workers' Union. Texas. Women. 1933-50. *1770*
—. Jews. Labor movement. 1920's-30's. *1751*
—. Labor. Massachusetts (Boston). Women. 1869. *1287*
—. Labor. New York City. Women. 1831-69. *820*
Garnet, Henry Highland. Abolition Movement. Douglass, Frederick. Negroes. Political Factions. 1840-49. *742*
—. Abolition Movement. Reform. Speeches, Addresses, etc. 1843. *729*
Garrett, Thomas. Burris, Samuel D. Delaware. Hunn, John. Tubman, Harriet. Underground Railroad. 1820-60. *712*
Garrison, William Lloyd. Abolition Movement. American Anti-Slavery Society. Douglass, Frederick. 1833-51. *770*
—. Abolition movement. "Boston Clique". Individualism. Interpersonal Relations. 1830-40. *646*
—. Abolition Movement. Civil War (antecedents). Ohio. Western Antislavery Society. 1835-61. *650*
—. Abolition Movement. Connecticut (Canterbury). Crandall, Prudence. Racism. Sexism. 1830-40. *550*
—. Abolition Movement. New England. Racism. 1841. *717*
Garvey, Marcus. Africa. Negroes. Nkrumah, Kwame. 1920's-75. *2422*
—. Black Nationalism. 1914-30's. *2418*
—. Black nationalism. Communism. Depressions. New York City (Harlem). 1931-39. *2561*
—. Black Nationalism. New York City (Harlem). Universal Negro Improvement Association. 1919-26. *2358*
—. California (Los Angeles). Negroes. Universal Negro Improvement Association. 1920's. *2455*
—. Clergy. Community affairs. Negroes. New York (Buffalo). Universal Negro Improvement Association. 1830's-1920's. *2458*
—. Colonial policy. Italy. Pan-Africanism. Universal Negro Improvement Association. USA. 1920-23. *2371*
—. Colonization. Liberia. Negroes. Universal Negro Improvement Association. 1914-24. *2342*
—. Firestone, Harvey S. Land. Leases. Liberia. Negroes. Universal Negro Improvement Association. 1926. *2402*
—. Ideology. Jamaica. Negroes. Pan-Africanism. 1887-1927. *401*
—. Negroes. Religion. Universal Negro Improvement Association. 1920's. *2351*
Garvin, Lucius F. C. Political reform. Rhode Island. State Politics. 1876-1922. *343*
Gary, Elbert H. Mitchel, John Purroy. New York City (Committee on Unemployment and Relief). Progressives. Unemployment. 1914-17. *2058*
Gates, Frederick T. Foundations. Medical education. Physicians. Research, Clinical. Rockefeller, John D. 1910-39. *1833*
General Convention Special Program. Black power. Church and Social Problems. Economic Aid. Episcopal Church, Protestant. Self-determination. 1963-75. *2850*
General Education Board. Depressions. Public policy. Rockefeller, John D. Secondary education. Social change. 1930's. *2478*
General Electric Company. Capitalism. Corporations. Federal government. Labor Unions and Organizations. Liberalism. 1920-33. *2412*
—. Corporations. New Deal. 1933-40. *2550*
General Motors. Automobile Industry and Trade. Canada. Labor Disputes. 1927-30. *1798*
General Tire Company. Murray, Rex. Ohio (Akron). Strikes. Strikes. 1934-35. *2565*
Genetics. New York. Noyes, John Humphrey. Oneida Community. 1848-86. *1518*

Genovese, Eugene D. Land reform. Race relations. Reconstruction. Social Classes. South Carolina (Edgefield County). Woodward, C. Vann. 1865-90. *963*

George, Henry. Adams, Henry Brooks. Ideology. Industrialization. Philosophy of History. Social criticism. 1870's-1910's. *1073*

—. Canada. Economic Reform. Industry. Poverty. Progress (concept). Social gospel. ca 1879-99. *975*

—. Capitalism. Politics. Progressivism. Single tax. 1880-1920. *2188*

—. Crime and Criminals. Land. Monopolies. Property. Technology. 19c-20c. *1033*

—. Delaware. Political Parties. Reform. Single Tax movement. 1890's. *1085*

—. Economic Theory. Income. Landlords and Tenants. Population. Taxation. Technology. 1871-83. *1064*

—. Great Britain. Hyndman, Henry M. Ireland. Land Reform. Marxism. 1882-89. *1057*

—. Post, Louis F. Single tax movement. 1872-98. *965*

George Peabody College. Educational Administration. Nashville, University of. Payne, William Howard. Teacher training. Tennessee. 1875-1901. *1411*

Georgia *See also* South.

—. African Colonization Movement. Emancipation. Liberia. Tubman, Emily. 1816-87. *655*

—. Agricultural Reform. Hunt, Henry Alexander. Negroes. North Carolina. 1890-1938. *1744*

—. American Colonization Society. Colonization. Liberia. Negroes. 1816-60. *705*

—. Anti-Radicals. Ashburn, George W. (murder). Reconstruction. Trials. 1868. *987*

—. Baptists. *Brown* v. *Board of Education* (US, 1954). Desegregation. Supreme Court. 1954-61. *2662*

—. Blakely Institute. Dewey, John. Kilpatrick, William Heard. Progressive education. 19c-20c. *2301*

—. Burnside, Thomas E. Crawford, George W. Dueling. Law. 1809-28. *545*

—. Cherokee Indians. Federal government. Land (cessions). Payne, John Howard (letter). Ross, John (chief). 1820's-30's. *575*

—. Civil Rights. Columbus *Enquirer-Sun* (newspaper). Harris, Julian LaRose. Journalism. 1920's. *2439*

—. Civil rights. Methodist Church. Tilly, Dorothy. 1900's-70. *438*

—. Cocking, Walter D. Higher education. Negroes. Talmadge, Eugene. 1937-43. *2620*

—. Convict lease system. Economic Conditions. Prisons. Racism. 1868-1909. *1044*

—. Cooperative Workers of America. Hoover, Hiram F. Negroes. Secret Societies. South Carolina. 1886-87. *1197*

—. Education. Fort Valley High and Industrial School. Negroes. Torbert, James H. 1897-1911. *2296*

—. Felton, Rebecca Latimer. Politics. Senate. Woman suffrage. 1860's-1922. *423*

—. Feminism. Peace Movements. Rankin, Jeannette. 1924-73. *352*

—. Freedom of speech. Obscenity. *Stanley* v. *Georgia* (US, 1969). Supreme Court. 1968-79. *2765*

—. Liberia. Tubman, Emily. 1818-85. *317*

—. National Recovery Administration. State Government. Strikes. Talmadge, Eugene. Textile industry. 1934. *2467*

—. Negro Suffrage. Populism. Reform. Watson, Thomas E. 1880-1922. *27*

—. Negroes. Political Attitudes. Progressive Party. Roosevelt, Theodore. Wilson, Woodrow. 1912. *2038*

—. Negroes. Savannah Men's Sunday Club. Social Change. 1905-11. *1970*

—. Race relations. Rhetoric. Washington, Booker T. (Atlanta Exposition Address). 1895. *1167*

Georgia (Albany; Harlem district). Civil rights movement. Freedom Singers. NAACP. Reagon, Bernice Johnson (interview). 1960-77. *2880*

Georgia (Atlanta). Cities. Illinois (Chicago). New Jersey (Newark). Water supply. 1860-1923. *32*

—. City Politics. Jackson, Maynard. Negroes. Political Leadership. 1965-77. *2847*

—. Civil Rights. Ebenezer Baptist Church. King, Martin Luther, Jr. (tribute). 1968. 1977. *2842*

—. Columbians, Inc. Patriotism. Racism. 1946-47. *2665*

—. Communist Party. Herndon, Angelo. International Labor Defense. Negroes. 1932-37. *2548*

—. Economic Conditions. Political change. Race Relations. 1960's-73. *2812*

—. Educational reform. Illinois (Chicago). New York City. Progressivism. Teachers. 1890-1920. *2336*

—. Federal programs. Freedmen. North. Reconstruction. Religious organizations. 1865-69. *1273*

—. Revivals. Sunday, William Ashley ("Billy"). 1917. *1882*

Georgia (Darien). Antislavery Sentiments. Bain, John Mackintosh. Economic Conditions. Petitions. 1736-55. *518*

Georgia Equal Rights Association. Negroes. Reconstruction. Republican Party. Union League. 1865-80. *1214*

Georgia (Griffin). American Colonization Society. Liberia. Moss, William (letters). Slavery. 1853-57. *654*

Georgia (Jasper County). Sons of Temperance (Ocmulgee Division No. 40). Temperance Movements. 1848-49. *897*

Georgia (Liberty County). American Missionary Association. Congregationalism. Freedmen. 1870-80's. *1247*

Georgia (Peach County). Colleges and Universities (black). Fort Valley State College. *Hunnicutt et al.* v. *Burge et al.* (Georgia, 1972). Racism. School Integration. 1972-78. *2800*

Georgia Railroad. Discrimination, Employment. Negroes. Strikes. 1909. *2220*

Georgia, University of. Cocking, Walter D. Holley, Joseph Winthrop. Racism. Talmadge, Eugene. 1941. *2643*

—. Columbus *Enquirer-Sun* (newspaper). Harris, Julian LaRose. Student activism. 1920-29. *2416*

Gérin-Lajoie, Marie. Catholic Church. Fédération Nationale Saint-Jean-Baptiste. Feminism. Quebec. 1907-33. *1039*

German Americans. Abolition Movement. Gymnastics. Turnverein (club). 1850-70. *606*

—. Americanization. World War I. 1914-17. *1935*

—. Communia (settlement). Iowa (Volga Township). Swiss Americans. Utopias. 1847-64. *926*

—. DuBois, W. E. B. Education. Ethnic studies. Irish Americans. Woodson, Carter G. 1649-1972. *188*

—. Irish Americans. Local politics. New York City. Riots. Temperance Movements. 1857. *585*

—. Labor Unions and Organizations. Progressivism. Socialism. Wisconsin. 1900-12. *2103*

Germany *See also* component parts, e.g. Bavaria, Prussia, etc.

—. Canada. Hjelt, Ole. Labour Party. Nazism. Norway. Socialism. 1908-28. *321*

—. Gymnastics. New England. Physical Education and Training. 1820's. *838*

Germer, Adolph. Coal miners. Illinois (Virden). Socialism. Strikes. United Mine Workers of America. 1893-1900. *1291*

Ghettos. Black Muslims. Malcolm X. Political Leadership. Race Relations. 1940-65. *461*

Ghost Dance. Bureau of American Ethnology. Indians. Mooney, James. Peyote. Research. 1891-1921. *1110*

—. Indians. Revitalization movements. Social Organization. 1889. *967*

GI movement. Political Protest. Vietnam War. 1960's-70's. *2727*

Gibbons, James. Catholic Church. Knights of Labor. Social Theory. Taschereau, Elzéar Alexandre. 1880's. *1351*

Gibson, George Howard. *Alliance-Independent* (newspaper). Christian Socialism. Nebraska. Populism. *Wealth Makers* (newspaper). 1893-96. *1397*

Giddings, Joshua Reed. Abolition Movement. Ohio. Radicals and Radicalism. State Politics. 1840-60. *651*

Gillespie v. *Palmer* (US, 1866). Negro Suffrage. Wisconsin (Milwaukee). 1849-66. *1173*

Gillett, Emma M. District of Columbia. Legal education. Mussey, Ellen Spencer. Washington College of Law. Women. 1869-1949. *426*

Gilman, Catheryne Cooke. Reform. Social work. Women. 1904-54. *344*

Gilman, Charlotte Perkins. Architecture. Communalism. Feminism. Housing. 1870-1920. *42*

—. California. Feminism. New England. 1880's-1935. *287*

—. Feminism. Firestone, Shulamith. Fuller, Margaret. Godwin, Mary Wollstonecraft. Science. 1759-1972. *64*

Girl Scouts of America. Identity. Low, Juliette. Sex roles. 1900-20. *452*

Girls. Canada. Home economics. Hoodless, Adelaide. Public schools. 1890's-1900's. *215*

—. Domestics. Female Charitable Society. Industrialization. Massachusetts (Salem). 1800-40. *882*

—. Education. Friends, Society of. Ontario. 1790-1820. *852*

—. Juvenile Delinquency. Massachusetts (Lancaster). Socialization. State Industrial School for Girls. 1856-1905. *1443*

—. Lancaster Industrial School for Girls. Massachusetts. Reformatories. ca 1850-70. *1444*

—. Prizes. Schools. 1820-50. *553*

Gitlow v. *New York* (US, 1925). Civil rights. Constitutional Amendments (14th). Sanford, Edward Terry. Supreme Court. ca 1890-1930. *2399*

Gitteau, William B. Hamilton, J. Kent. Ohio (Toledo). Progressivism. Public Schools. Reform. 1898-1921. *2330*

Gladden, Washington. Bushnell, Horace. Christianity. Economic conditions. Politics. Social gospel. Youth. 1836-1918. *995*

—. Cities. Congregationalism. Ohio (Columbus). Reform. Social gospel. 1850's-1914. *396*

Glass, Carter. Collectivism. Liberals. National Recovery Administration. New Deal. 1933-35. *2533*

Glasscock, William E. Coal Mines and Mining. Martial law. National Guard. United Mine Workers of America. Violence. West Virginia (Cabin Creek, Paint Creek). 1912-13. *2176*

Gleason, Anne-Marie (pseud. Madelene). Barry, Robertine (pseud. Françoise). Feminism. Journalism. Quebec. Social Conditions. 1900-19. *1535*

Glennon, John J. Catholic Church. Church Schools. Missouri (St. Louis). Ritter, Joseph E. School Integration. 1935-47. *1850*

Globe. Labor. Liberalism. Newspapers. Ontario. 1885-90. *1332*

Godwin, Mary Wollstonecraft. Feminism. Firestone, Shulamith. Fuller, Margaret. Gilman, Charlotte Perkins. Science. 1759-1972. *64*

—. Feminism. Fuller, Margaret. 1792-19c. *812*

Godwin, Parke. Antislavery Sentiments. Brook Farm. Utopias. 1837-47. *587*

Goebel, William. Election Laws. Government Regulation. Kentucky. Railroads. Taylor, William S. 1887-1900. *961*

Goiter. Goler, George W. Iodine. New York (Rochester). Water supply. 1923-32. *2395*

Gold Coast. Colonization. Negroes. Sam, Alfred Charles. 1913-16. *1997*

Gold Mines and Mining. Alaska (Douglas Island). Labor Unions and Organizations. Strikes. Treadwell Mines. Western Federation of Miners. 1905-10. *2209*

Gold Rushes. British Columbia. California. Discrimination. Negroes. Race Relations. 1849-66. *592*

Goler, George W. Goiter. Iodine. New York (Rochester). Water supply. 1923-32. *2395*

Gompers, Samuel. American Federation of Labor. Brotherhood of Painters and Decorators. Labor Disputes. Voluntarism. 1894-1900. *1306*

—. American Federation of Labor. Fascism. Immigration. Jingoism. Racism. 1850-1924. *394*

—. American Federation of Labor. French Canadians. Quebec. 1900-14. *1741*

—. American Federation of Labor. Iglesias Pantín, Santiago. Labor Unions and Organizations. Puerto Rico. 1897-1920's. *2210*

—. American Federation of Labor. Labor. Socialism. 1893-95. *1304*

—. American Federation of Labor. Labor Unions and Organizations. Military. Preparedness. Wilson, Woodrow. 1914-17. *2000*

—. Communism. Pan American Federation of Labor. Political Attitudes. 1920's. *2457*

—. Comte, Auguste. Foster, Frank K. Ideology. Labor Unions and Organizations. McGregor, Hugh. Spencer, Herbert. 1876-1900. *1295*

—. Lenin, V. I. (views). Socialist Party. USSR. 1912-18. *1991*

Gonzales, Rodolfo "Corky". Crusade for Justice. Mexican Americans. Southwest. 1966-72. *2735*

Gordon, Jean. Child Labor Law (Louisiana, 1908). Louisiana (New Orleans). New York. Theatrical Syndicate. 1908-12. *1968*
Gospel Temperance Movement. Canada. Revivalism. Rine, D.I.K. 1877-82. *1439*
Gough, John B. Temperance Movements. 1828-86. *895*
Gould, Jay. Knights of Labor. Missouri (Sedalia). Modernization. Railroads. Strikes. 1885-86. *1292*
Government *See also* City Government; Civil Service; Constitutions; Federal Government; Local Government; Politics; Provincial Government; Public Administration; State Government.
—. Abolitionists. Fugitive slaves. Great Britain. Law. Slave Trade. 1834-61. *774*
—. Atlantic Provinces. Boardinghouses. Labor. Merchant Marine. ca 1850's-90's. *996*
—. Business. Economic planning. Labor Unions and Organizations. Liberalism. 1920-40. *1788*
—. Canada. Civil Rights. Feminism. Great Britain. USA. 1850-20c. *79*
—. Coal Mines and Mining. Health and safety regulations. Ohio. 1869-81. *1319*
—. Constitutional Law. Supreme Court. 1950-75. *1557*
—. Depressions. Farmers. Great Plains. Letters. New Deal. 1930-40. *2476*
—. Indians. Social change. 1960-76. *2743*
—. Labor movement. Labor Unions and Organizations. Voluntarism. 1890's-1930's. *1760*
—. Land. Saskatchewan. Settlement. 1929-35. *1796*
—. Liberalism. Progressivism. Richberg, Donald Randall. 1900-60. *274*
—. Private sector. Unemployment. 18c-1979. *260*
Government Regulation *See also* Federal Regulation.
—. Agriculture. Maryland (Baltimore). 1750-1820. *149*
—. Business. Pressure Groups. Public interest. 1975-79. *2953*
—. California (San Francisco Bay area). Consumers. Environmental protection. Housing. Local government. Suburbs. 1940-80. *2718*
—. Cummins, Albert B. Iowa (Davenport). Law Enforcement. Liquor. Riots. State Politics. 1907-08. *1880*
—. Election Laws. Goebel, William. Kentucky. Railroads. Taylor, William S. 1887-1900. *961*
—. North Carolina. Populism. Progressivism. Railroads. Russell, Daniel. 1894-98. *1369*
Government, Resistance to *See also* Revolution.
—. Church and State. Jehovah's Witnesses. Persecution. Theology. 1870's-1960's. *136*
Governors. Attitudes. Economic Growth. Segregation. South. 1950-69. *1533*
—. Capital punishment. Cruce, Lee. Negroes. Oklahoma. White supremacy. 1911-15. *1907*
—. Civil rights. Johnson, Andrew. Negroes. Tennessee. 1862-65. *972*
—. Crothers, Austin Lane. Maryland. Progressivism. 1904-12. *1896*
—. Federal Government. Frazier, Lynn J. Indians. North Dakota. Progressivism. 1916-40. *1538*
—. Florida. Public Policy. Race relations. 1954-76. *1552*
—. Kennon, Robert F. Louisiana. Reform. 1948-56. *2674*
Graduate schools. Desegregation. Discrimination. Educational. Lawsuits. Negroes. North Carolina. Professional training. 1930-51. *1835*
Grady, John (letters). Haywood, William Dudley. Industrial Workers of the World. Schuyler, Mont. USSR. 1921-22. *2425*
Grain elevators. Agricultural Cooperatives. Nebraska. 1900-15. *2263*
Grain Growers Guide (periodical). Chipman, George. Editors and Editing. Manitoba (Winnipeg). Reform. Social movements. 1905-30. *1637*
Grambling State University. Adams, Charles P. Colleges and Universities. Louisiana. Negroes. 1896-1928. *1836*
Grand Trunk Railway. Brotherhood of Locomotive Engineers. Canada. Strikes. 1876-77. *1333*
Grange. Anti-German sentiment. Bouck, William. Freedom of Assembly. Public Opinion. Vigilantes. Washington (Walla Walla). World War I. 1918. *2161*

—. California State Agricultural Society. Elites. Farmers. 1870's-80's. *1385*
—. Cherokee Indians. Farmers. Indian Territory. 1870's. *1374*
—. Farmers. Oklahoma. Saskatchewan. Socialism. Texas. 1900-45. *1714*
Granite Industry. Cerasoli, Mose (memoir). Labor. Labor Disputes. Vermont. 1913-38. *1807*
Grape industry. California. Labor Unions and Organizations. Strikes. United Farm Workers Union. 1966-70. *2934*
Great Awakening (2d). Pennsylvania. Reform. 1794-1860. *562*
Great Britain *See also* Ireland.
—. Abolition Movement. American Colonization Society. Colonization. Cresson, Elliot. Liberia. 1831-33. *609*
—. Abolition Movement. Anderson, John. Canada. Foreign Relations. Politics. USA. 1860-61. *734*
—. Abolition movement. Anderson, John. Canada. Fugitive Slaves. Trials. USA. 1860-61. *733*
—. Abolition Movement. Craft, Ellen. Craft, William. Fugitive slaves. 1848-65. *611*
—. Abolition movement. Douglass, Frederick. 1845-47. *649*
—. Abolition Movement. Historiography. Protestantism. 18c-19c. *792*
—. Abolition Movement. Novels. Victor, Metta V. 1861. *749*
—. Abolitionists. Fugitive slaves. Government. Law. Slave Trade. 1834-61. *774*
—. Allen, William G. Attitudes. Colonization. Exiles. Negroes. New York Central College at McGrawville. 1820-78. *290*
—. Antislavery Sentiments. Boycotts. Cotton. Friends, Society of. 1840-60. *608*
—. Antislavery Sentiments. Cultural imperialism. Elites. 18c-19c. *765*
—. Antislavery Sentiments. Greeley, Horace. Labor. Marx, Karl. New York *Tribune*. 1851-62. *764*
—. Antislavery Sentiments. Massachusetts (Salem). Negroes. Remond, Sarah Parker. Women. 1856-87. *294*
—. Antislavery Sentiments. Protestantism. 1846. *696*
—. Antislavery Sentiments. Sutherland, Duchess of (Harriet Howard). Tyler, Julia Gardiner. Women. 1842-89. *723*
—. Armies. Discrimination. White, Walter F. World War II. 1943-44. *2626*
—. Arthur, George. Colonial Government. Ontario (Upper Canada). Reform. 1837-41. *571*
—. Barnett, Samuel Augustus. Cities. Education. Poor. Progressivism. 1880's-1913. *2294*
—. Beecher, Lyman. Evangelical Alliance. Temperance Movements. World Temperance Convention. 1846. *889*
—. Bentham, Jeremy. Birth control. Carlile, Richard. Feminism. Owen, Robert Dale. Place, Francis. Propaganda. Wright, Frances. 1790-1840. *817*
—. Borden, Robert Laird. Canada. *Champion* (periodical). Woman suffrage. Women's Social and Political Union. 1910-18. *1737*
—. British North America. Friends, Society of. Slavery. 1757-61. *519*
—. Brownson, Orestes A. Catholic University of Ireland. Ireland. Newman, John Henry. 1853-54. *911*
—. Canada. Civil Rights. Feminism. Government. USA. 1850-20c. *79*
—. Canada. Counter Culture. Press, underground. USA. 1957-72. *2990*
—. Canada. Wartime Elections Act (Canada, 1917). Woman Suffrage. 1917. *1721*
—. Children. Education. Nutrition. 1890-1920. *2053*
—. Church and State. Education. India. Secularization. 19c. *198*
—. Cities. Community organizations. Social problems. 1960's-70's. *2746*
—. City planning. 1845-1974. *92*
—. Class consciousness. Feminism. Labor Unions and Organizations. USA. Women's Trade Union League. 1890-1925. *2226*
—. Coal Mines and Mining. Illinois. Labor Unions and Organizations. Legislation. Lobbying. 1861-72. *1312*
—. Cobden, Richard. Millenarianism. Nonconformists. Peace movements. 1840-60. *582*
—. Collective Bargaining. France. Labor. 18c-20c. *167*
—. Common law. Constitutional Amendments (4th). Searches. 15c-18c. *512*

—. Crime and Criminals. Plea bargaining. 17c-20c. *109*
—. DeLeon, Daniel. Socialism. 1880-1917. *177*
—. Economic History Association (annual meeting). Higher Education. Research. 19c-20c. 1977. *191*
—. Education. Jefferson, Thomas. Milton, John. 17c-19c. *833*
—. Environmental policy. Interest groups. 1970's. *2742*
—. Euthanasia. Medicine. Tollemache, Lionel A. Williams, Samuel D., Jr. 1870's-90's. *1452*
—. Feminism. Hill, Claibourne M. USA. 1914. *1929*
—. George, Henry. Hyndman, Henry M. Ireland. Land Reform. Marxism. 1882-89. *1057*
—. Humanitarianism. Ideology. USA. ca 1660-19c. *531*
—. Judicial Process. Law. Plea bargaining. 18c-20c. *128*
—. Labor Unions and Organizations. Massachusetts. 1130-1790. *473*
—. Labor Unions and Organizations. Steel industry. 1888-1912. *155*
—. Law reform. New England. Puritans. 1620-60. *501*
—. Public Schools. Sports. Upper Canada. Upper Classes. 1830-75. *210*
—. Social status. Women. 1925-65. *1551*
—. Utopias. 19c-20c. *270*
Great Britain (Lancashire). Fell, Margaret. Feminism. Friends, Society of. Pennsylvania (Philadelphia). Women. 1670's. *498*
Great Plains *See also* North Central States.
—. Canada. Pietism. Prairie Radicals. 1890-1975. *1530*
—. Depressions. Farmers. Government. Letters. New Deal. 1930-40. *2476*
—. Depressions. Radicals and Radicalism. State Politics. 1930-36. *2520*
—. Food and Drug Administration. Labor. Radicals and Radicalism. Social change. Veblen, Thorstein. World War I. 1918. *1922*
Great Society. Johnson, Lyndon B. Public Welfare. Rhetoric. 1963-65. *2764*
—. Johnson, Lyndon B. (administration). Public Welfare. Social Conditions. 1964-76. *2936*
Greeley, Horace. Antislavery Sentiments. Great Britain. Labor. Marx, Karl. New York *Tribune*. 1851-62. *764*
—. Civil War (antecedents). Reform. Secession. Slavery. 1860-61. *781*
Green, Ann Terry. Abolition Movement. Assassination. Lovejoy, Elijah P. Marriage. Phillips, Wendell. 1830-67. *779*
Green Corn Rebellion, 1917. Labor Unions and Organizations. Oklahoma. Radicals and Radicalism. Working Class Union. 1914-17. *2284*
Green Mountain Freeman (newspaper). Abolition Movement. Liberty Party. Poland, Joseph. State politics. Vermont. 1840-48. *683*
Greenback Party. Arkansas. Garland, Rufus King. State politics. Tobey, Charles E. 1876-82. *952*
Greenbelt new towns. Agriculture Department. Poor. Tugwell, Rexford Guy. 1935-36. *2560*
Grenell, Judson K. Knights of Labor. Labadie, Joseph. Michigan (Detroit). Socialist Labor Party. 1877-86. *1334*
Griffith, David W. *Birth of a Nation* (film). Films. Negroes. Temperance Movements. 1900-20. *2087*
Griffith, David W. (*Birth of a Nation*). Film industry. Negroes. Racism. 1915-18. *1918*
Grimes, John. Abolition movement. *New Jersey Freeman* (newspaper). Reform. 1844-50. *623*
Grimké, Angelina. Abolition Movement. Anthony, Susan B. Mott, Lucretia. Stanton, Elizabeth Cady. Woman Suffrage. ca 1820-60. *549*
Grimké, Sarah Moore. Christianity. Nature. Paul, Saint. Social organization. Women. 1c. 1830's. *807*
Grimké, Sarah Moore (letter). Sex discrimination. Women. 1853. *803*
Grinnell College. Colleges and Universities. Iowa. Sex roles. Women. 1884-1917. *221*
Grip (periodical). Bengough, John Wilson. City government. Ontario (Toronto). Political Reform. Protestantism. 1873-1910. *370*
Griscom, John H. (letters). Public Health. Reform. Sanitation. Shattuck, Lemuel. 1843-47. *863*
Gross, Tabbs. *Arkansas Freeman* (newspaper). Negroes. Political Commentary. Reconstruction. Republican Party. 1869-70. *1203*

Gun Control. Crime and Criminals. Massachusetts (Boston). 1974-76. *2784*
—. District of Columbia. Firearms Control Regulations Act (US, 1975). Methodology. US Conference of Mayors (report). 1975-80. *2778*
—. Federal Policy. 1919-38. *1726*
Gurowski, Adam. Abolition Movement. Poland. Radicals and Radicalism. 1849-66. *449*
Gymnastics. Abolition Movement. German Americans. Turnverein (club). 1850-70. *606*
—. California (San Francisco). Lewis, Dioclesius. Parot, Adele. 1860's-70's. *1404*
—. Germany. New England. Physical Education and Training. 1820's. *838*

H

Haiti. Civil War. Emigration. Negroes. 1860-64. *1254*
—. Negroes. Revolution. 1791-1861. *639*
Halifax Mechanics' Institute. Adult education. Middle Classes. Nova Scotia. Working class. 1830's-40's. *845*
Hall, Covington. Forest and Farm Workers Union. Labor Unions and Organizations. Louisiana. Lumber and Lumbering. Socialism. 1907-16. *2192*
Hall, G. Stanley. Adolescence. Boy Scouts of America. Boys' Clubs. Educational reform. ca 1890-1910. *2074*
—. Children. Playgrounds. Progressivism. 1880-1920. *1909*
—. Education. Minorities. Social Status. 1870's-1920. *2323*
Hall, Herbert. Devereux Mansion. Massachusetts (Marblehead). Mental Illness. Occupational therapy. Work Cure Program. 1912-23. *1969*
Hall, Lyman W. Antislavery Sentiments. Kansas-Nebraska Act (US, 1854). Ohio (Portage County). Political Parties. 1852-56. *619*
Hamel, Philippe. Antitrust. French Canadians. Nationalism. Public Utilities. Quebec (Quebec). 1929-34. *1757*
Hamilton, J. Kent. Gitteau, William B. Ohio (Toledo). Progressivism. Public Schools. Reform. 1898-1921. *2330*
Hamilton, Joseph G. de Roulhac. Constitutions, State (reform). North Carolina. Progressivism. Sikes, Enoch W. State Legislatures. 1898-1913. *2091*
Hamilton Manufacturing Company. Cotton. Labor Disputes. Massachusetts (Lowell). Social mobility. Textile Industry. Women. 1836-60. *818*
Hammond, John Hays. Militarism. Peace Movements. 1898-1914. *2017*
Hampton, Isabel. Addams, Jane. Illinois (Chicago). Johns Hopkins Hospital Training School for Nurses. Maryland (Baltimore). Nurses and Nursing. Professionalization. Social Work. 1889-1910. *1461*
Hampton, Wade. Chamberlain, Daniel H. Reconstruction. South Carolina. State Politics. 1877. *1054*
Hancock, George B. Civil rights. Jackson, Luther P. Negroes. Virginia. Young, Plummer B. 1930-45. *1583*
Hancock, Winfield Scott. Louisiana. Military. Mower, Joseph Anthony. Reconstruction. Texas. 1865-68. *989*
Handicapped Children *See also* Blind.
—. Institutionalization. 1900. *1944*
Handicrafts. *See* Home Economics.
Hapgood, William P. Columbia Conserve Company. Indiana (Indianapolis). Industrial Relations. 1917-43. *1789*
Happy, Jesse. Canada. Courts. Extradition. Fugitive slaves. Kentucky. Testimony. 1793-1838. *748*
Haralson, J. Alabama. Negro Suffrage. Reconstruction. Republican Party. 1867-82. *1252*
Hard, Herbert. Amlie, Thomas. Farmer-labor Party. New Deal. Ohio Farmer-Labor Progressive Federation. Third Parties. 1930-40. *2543*
Hardin, William J. Colorado (Denver). Negroes. 1863-73. *1135*
—. Colorado, northeastern. Kansas, northeastern. Langston, Charles H. Negro suffrage. 1865-67. *1133*
Harlan, John Marshall. Civil Rights. Supreme Court. 1877-1911. *1122*

—. Discrimination, Educational. *Joseph W. Cumming, James S. Harper and John Ladeveze v. School Board of Richmond County, Ga.* (US, 1899). Public Schools. Supreme Court. ca 1896-1907. *1194*
Harlem Renaissance. Art. Johnson, Charles S. Racism. 1920's. *2426*
Harmony Society. Christianity. Communes. Pennsylvania (Economy). Pittman, Clara. Socialist Laws (Germany, 1878). 1878-79. *1499*
—. City Planning. Communes. Indiana (New Harmony). Pennsylvania (Economy, Harmony). Social customs. 1820's-1905. *919*
—. Indiana (New Harmony). Rapp, George. Utopias. 1814-47. *937*
—. Koreshan Unity. Mexico (Topolobampo). Olombia. Utopias. 1879-93. *1500*
—. Pennsylvania. Rapp, George. State Legislatures. Utopias. 1805-07. *913*
—. Pennsylvania (Economy). vonWrede, Friedrich Wilhelm. 1842. *924*
Harpers Ferry raid. Abolition Movement. Brown, John. Civil War (antecedents). Sanborn, Franklin Benjamin. 1854-60. *707*
—. Abolition Movement. Brown, John. North Carolina. Sectional Conflict. State Politics. 1840-60. *675*
—. Antislavery movement. Brown, John. Vietnam War. Violence. Weathermen. 1800-61. 1960-75. *105*
—. Antislavery Sentiments. Brown, John. Massachusetts. 1859. *706*
—. Brown, John. Civil War (antecedents). North Carolina. Slavery. Social Psychology. 1859-60. *612*
—. Brown, John. Civil War (antecedents). West Virginia. White, Edward. 1859. *783*
—. Brown, John. Costello, Michael A. (letter). 1859-60. *630*
—. Brown, John. Race relations. 1858-59. *722*
Harrais, Margaret Keenan. Alaska (Valdez). 1902-62. *398*
Harris, Cicero. Harris, Robert. Harris, William. Negroes. Reconstruction. South. Teaching. 1864-70. *1278*
Harris, Julian LaRose. Civil Rights. Columbus *Enquirer-Sun* (newspaper). Georgia. Journalism. 1920's. *2439*
—. Columbus *Enquirer-Sun* (newspaper). Georgia. University of. Student activism. 1920-29. *2416*
Harris, Robert. Harris, Cicero. Harris, William. Negroes. Reconstruction. South. Teaching. 1864-70. *1278*
Harris, William. Harris, Cicero. Harris, Robert. Negroes. Reconstruction. South. Teaching. 1864-70. *1278*
Harrison, Byron Patton. Federal aid to education. Legislation. Mississippi. 1936-41. *2597*
Harrison, Hubert H. International Colored Unity League. Journalism. Liberty League of Negro Americans. Negroes. New York City (Harlem). Socialist Party. 1911-27. *1676*
Harrison, Pat. Senate. Social Security Act (US, 1935). 1934-35. *2598*
Harrison, Preston E. Big Spring State Hospital. Medical care. Mental Illness. Texas (western). 1946-77. *2981*
Hartz, Louis. Debs, Eugene V. Hillquit, Morris. Liberalism. Locke, John. Marxism. Political culture. 20c. *1986*
Hartzell, Joseph C. Freedmen. Methodist Church. Missions and Missionaries. Republican Party. South. 1870-73. *1208*
Harvard College. Legal education. Massachusetts. 1766-1840. *194*
Harvard Law School. Frank, Jerome (review article). Law. 1870-1930. *2341*
Harvard University. Abolition Movement. Follen, Charles Theodore Christian. May, Samuel. 1824-40. *753*
—. Corporal punishment. Eaton, Nathaniel. Massachusetts (Cambridge). Puritans. Trials. 1638. *495*
Harvard University, Houghton Library, Blagden Papers. Abolition movement. Letters. Phillips, Wendell. 1840-80. 1977-79. *605*
Harvey, Oliver. Civil rights. Duke University Medical Center. Labor Unions and Organizations. North Carolina (Durham). 1930's-70's. *2938*
Hasidism. Authority. Charisma. Counter Culture. Unification Church. 1960-80. *2986*
Haskell, Llewellyn S. Davis, Alexander Jackson. Garden cities. Idealism. New Jersey (West Orange; Llewellyn Park). Suburbs. 1853-57. *943*

Hastie, William H. Armies. Military recruitment. Negroes. Press. World War II. 1940-42. *2638*
—. Military. Negroes. Racism. Stimson, Henry L. World War II. 1940-43. *2636*
—. Military reform. Racism. World War II. 1940-43. *2637*
Hastings, Charles. Neighborhood Workers' Association. Ontario (Toronto). Poverty. Public health. 1910-21. *1527*
Haverford College Library (Quaker Collection). Abolition Movement. New Hampshire. Portsmouth Anti-Slavery Society. Rogers, Nathaniel Peabody. 1830-46. *316*
Hawaiians. State Politics. 1900-80. *2736*
Hawkins, Virgil Darnell. Courts. Discrimination, educational. Florida, University of. Lawyers. Legal education. 1949-76. *1554*
Hawthorne First Relay Assembly Test Room. Productivity. Research. Working Conditions. 1927-32. *2428*
Hawthorne, Nathaniel *(The Blithedale Romance)*. Feminism. Fuller, Margaret. James, Henry *(Bostonians)*. Politics. Sex. 19c. *795*
Hay, Henry (interview). Communist Party. Homosexuality. Mattachine Society. 1950-53. *2672*
Hayden, Lewis. Abolition Movement. Massachusetts (Boston). 1811-89. *420*
Hayes, Michael P. Brown, W. G. Herridge, W. D. Saskatchewan. United Reform Movement. 1938-40. *1664*
Hayes, Rutherford B. Congress. Mormons. Polygamy. Woman Suffrage. 1877-81. *1089*
—. Federal policy. Indians. 1877-81. *988*
Haymarket Riot (1886). Iowa. Socialism. Trumbull, Matthew Mark. 1826-94. *296*
Hays, Samuel P. Elites. Ideology. Professionalism. Progressivism. Wiebe, Robert. 20c. *1971*
Haywood, William Dudley. Grady, John (letters). Industrial Workers of the World. Schuyler, Mont. USSR. 1921-22. *2425*
—. Labor Unions and Organizations. Socialism. 1890-1928. *371*
Health. Attitudes. Exercise. New England. Recreation. Transcendentalism. 1830-60. *572*
—. Authority. Constitutional Amendments (1st). Religious liberty. Supreme Court. 1963-79. *2769*
—. City Government. New York City. Progressivism. Public baths. 1890-1915. *2121*
—. Europe. Women. Working Conditions. 1869-1979. *47*
—. Federal Policy. Nixon, Richard M. (administration). 1971-76. *2985*
—. Ladies' Physiological Institute of Boston and Vicinity. Massachusetts. Middle Classes. Physiology. Women. 1848-59. *902*
—. Medicine. 17c-20c. *2980*
—. Medicines, Patent. Nebraska (Omaha). Sanitation. 1870-1900. *1456*
Health and safety regulations. Coal Mines and Mining. Government. Ohio. 1869-81. *1319*
Health reform. Alcott, William A. "Christian Physiology". ca 1829-60. *903*
Hearst, William Randolph. New Deal. Progressivism. 1930-35. *2488*
Heisler, Stuart. Armies. Films (documentaries). *Negro Soldier* (film). Propaganda. Race Relations. World War II. 1944. *2621*
Henrietta Hebrew Benevolent Society. Ancker, Henrietta. California (San Bernardino). Charities. Jews. 1870-91. *1479*
Hepburn Act (US, 1906). Business. Federal Regulation. Freight and Freightage. Interstate Commerce Commission. 1905-06. *2282*
—. Cattlemen. Corn Belt Meat Producers' Association. Iowa. 1900-10. *2229*
Hepburn Bill, Warner-Foraker Amendment (1906). Constitution League. Discrimination. Foraker, Joseph B. Jim Crow laws. Negroes. Railroads. Washington, Booker T. (and Committee of 12). 1906. *1919*
Heresy. Crapsey, Algernon Sidney. Episcopal Church, Protestant. New York (Rochester). Reform. St. Andrew's Church. Trials. 1879-1927. *454*
Herndon, Angelo. Communist Party. Georgia (Atlanta). International Labor Defense. Negroes. 1932-37. *2548*
Herridge, W. D. Brown, W. G. Hayes, Michael P. Saskatchewan. United Reform Movement. 1938-40. *1664*
Hersey, John. Abolition Movement. Methodist Church. Millenarianism. Perfectionism. 1786-1862. *541*

Hibernian Anti-Slavery Society. Antislavery Sentiments. Ireland. Webb, Richard Davis. 1837-61. *736*
Hicks, Mary. Economic Reform. Five-Day Plan. Hicks, Mildred. 1931-40. *2589*
Hicks, Mildred. Economic Reform. Five-Day Plan. Hicks, Mary. 1931-40. *2589*
Higher Education *See also* Adult Education; Colleges and Universities; Junior Colleges.
—. Attitudes. Dewey, John. Reserve Officers' Training Corps. 1920-38. *1847*
—. Baldwin, Theron. Protestantism. Society for the Promotion of Collegiate and Theological Education at the West. 1843-73. *192*
—. Brewer, Fisk Parsons. Integration. South Carolina, University of. 1873-76. *1438*
—. Carnegie, Andrew. Pensions. Retirement. 1901-18. *2214*
—. Christianity. Corporations. Education, Finance. Social Darwinism. 1860-1930. *206*
—. Cocking, Walter D. Georgia. Negroes. Talmadge, Eugene. 1937-43. *2620*
—. Colorado (Aspen). Educational Reform. Paepcke, Walter. 1949-51. *2666*
—. Curricula. Eliot, William Greenleaf. Missouri (St. Louis). Trans-Mississippi West. Washington University. 1853-87. *189*
—. Economic History Association (annual meeting). Great Britain. Research. 19c-20c. 1977. *191*
—. Football. Military training. Morality. 1890-1930. *2327*
—. Liberal arts. Reform. South. 1850-60. *854*
—. Lowry, Morrow B. Lowry, Morrow B. (letter). Pennsylvania. Women's rights. 1868. *1413*
—. Negroes. Philanthropy. Whites. 1861-1920. *1234*
—. Religion. Social change. 1960's-70's. *2974*
—. Women. 1850-1970. *197*
Highway Beautification Act (US, 1965). Billboards. Congress. Federal Regulation. Land use. 1965-79. *2716*
Highway Engineering. Environment. Lancaster, Samuel Christopher. Oregon (Columbia River Highway). ca 1900-41. *1931*
Hill, Claibourne M. Feminism. Great Britain. USA. 1914. *1929*
Hillquit, Morris. American Socialist Party. Marxism. Political Reform. Socialism. 1901-14. *1942*
—. Debs, Eugene V. Hartz, Louis. Liberalism. Locke, John. Marxism. Political culture. 20c. *1986*
—. Jews. New York City. Socialism. 1890's-1933. *1713*
Hillsdale College. Adrian College. Michigan. Oberlin College. Ohio. Olivet College. 1833-70. *851*
Hinton, Frederick A. Abolition Movement. Constitutional conventions, state. Disfranchisement. Gardner, Charles W. Negroes. Pennsylvania. 1838. *596*
Hippies. Counter Culture. Cynics. 1960's-73. *2991*
Hiram House. Bellamy, George. Ohio (Cleveland). Settlement houses. 1896-1914. *1958*
Historians. Abolitionists. Psychohistory. 1800-60. 1930's-60's. *720*
—. Agricultural labor. California. McWilliams, Carey. 1939. *2587*
Historic Peace Churches (meeting). Kansas (Newton). Krehbiel, H. P. Pacifism. 1935-36. *2534*
Historiography *See also* Historians; Philosophy of History; Quantitative Methods.
—. Abolition Movement. Elkins, Stanley M. 1829-60. 1954-76. *760*
—. Abolition Movement. Great Britain. Protestantism. 18c-19c. *792*
—. Abolition Movement. Negroes. 1830-60. *754*
—. Agricultural Organizations. Farmers' Alliance. North Carolina. ca 1888-91. *1379*
—. Alabama. Reconstruction. Revisionism. 1884-1971. *1069*
—. American Revolution. Egalitarianism. Social change. 1775-83. 20c. *494*
—. American Revolution. Women. 1770's-1970's. *49*
—. Black Power. Civil Rights. South. 1954-72. *1542*
—. Carpetbaggers. Ideology. Mississippi. Reconstruction. Reformers. 1865-76. *1013*
—. Cash, W. J. Social change. South. 1830-1940. *1653*
—. Chafe, William. Feminism. O'Neill, William. Sexual revolution. ca 1920-70. *2374*

—. Civil War. Reconstruction. 1861-77. ca 1950-74. *984*
—. Congress. Negroes. Reconstruction. South. 1860's-1978. *1175*
—. Depressions. Hughes, Charles Evans. New Deal. Supreme Court. 1930's. 1950's-60's. *2572*
—. Economics. Education. Political systems. Social classes. 1840-20c. *219*
—. Environment. Frontier and Pioneer Life. 1492-1978. *51*
—. Feminization. Protestantism. Welter, Barbara. Women. 1820's-30's. 1970's. *910*
—. Imperialism. Leuchtenburg, William E. Progressivism. 1890's-1910's. 1952-74. *2089*
—. Imperialism. Leuchtenburg, William E. Progressivism. 1898-1916. 1952-75. *2023*
—. *Journal of Negro History* (periodical). Negroes. Woodson, Carter G. 1916-75. *1708*
—. Louisiana (New Orleans). Negroes. Political Leadership. Reconstruction. ca 1800-75. *1239*
—. Mugwumps. Political Reform. Republican Party. 1880's. 1910-79. *956*
—. Negroes. 17c-19c. 1960-76. *503*
—. Negroes. Roosevelt, Franklin D. (administration). USSR. World War II. 1939-45. *2648*
—. Political Leadership. Progressivism. Quantitative Methods. 1950's-77. *1914*
—. Progressivism. 1900-20's. *1988*
—. Quebec. Social Credit. 1936-65. *1765*
—. Race Relations. Washington, Booker T. 1898-1972. *1161*
—. Reconstruction. 1865-1979. *1000*
—. Reform. Values. 1780-1979. *57*
—. Republicans, Liberal. 1872. 1870's-1975. *1004*
—. Slave Revolts. South Carolina (Charleston). Vesey, Denmark. Wade, Richard (review article). 1821-22. 1964. *686*
—. Woman suffrage. 1868-1977. *117*
History *See also* particular branches of history, e.g. business history, oral history, psychohistory, science, history of; Philosophy of History.
—. Christianity. Religious liberty. Rhode Island. Williams, Roger. 17c. *514*
—. Institute for Advanced Study. Mathematics. New Jersey (Princeton). Research. Social Sciences. 1930-79. *2435*
Hjelt, Ole. Canada. Germany. Labour Party. Nazism. Norway. Socialism. 1908-28. *321*
Hoadly, George. Coal Mines and Mining. Ohio (Hocking Valley). Strikes. 1884-85. *1322*
Hocking Valley. Coal Mines and Mining. Lewis, John Llewellyn. Ohio, southeastern. Strikes. United Mine Workers of America. 1927. *2447*
Hoel, Chamberlain. Cooperatives. Oregon (Salem). Reform. 1852-65. *326*
Hoffman, Christian Balzac. Economic Reform. Kansas. Socialism. 1872-1915. *389*
Hofstadter, Richard. Colorado. Populism. Progressive movement. 1890-1910. 1950's. *1375*
Holiness Movement. Feminism. Palmer, Phoebe. Wesley, Susanna. 1732-1973. *17*
Holley, Joseph Winthrop. Cocking, Walter D. Georgia, University of. Racism. Talmadge, Eugene. 1941. *2643*
Holley, Marrietta *(My Opinion)*. Feminism. Literature. 1870-1926. *983*
Hollingsworth, Leta. Psychology. Women. 1886-1938. *1885*
Hollywood Ten. Blacklisting. Communists. Courts. Film industry. *Young v. MPAA* (US, 1965). 1947-73. *1736*
Home Economics *See also* Consumers; Food Consumption.
—. Bevier, Isabel. Illinois, University of. Women. 1900-21. *2295*
—. Canada. Girls. Hoodless, Adelaide. Public schools. 1890's-1900's. *215*
—. Curricula. Domesticity. Progressivism. Sex roles. 1900-20. *2314*
Home Employment Cooperative Company. Bennett, William H. Communitarianism. Missouri (Dallas County). Utopias. 1894-1905. *1507*
—. Colorado Cooperative Company. Communitarianism. Labor Exchange. Politics. Pragmatism. 1890-1905. *1508*
Homeopathy. Coeducation. Medical Education. Ohio (Cincinnati). Pulte Medical College. 1873-79. *1403*
Homesteading and Homesteaders. Clapp, Elsie Ripley. Education. New Deal. Roosevelt, Eleanor. West Virginia (Arthurdale). 1933-44. *2477*

—. Dawes Commission. Five Civilized Tribes. Freedmen. Indian Territory. 1893-1905. *1083*
—. Freedmen. Louisiana. Reconstruction. 1865-83. *1233*
—. Interior Department. Minnesota (Duluth). Public Housing. Resettlement Administration. 1936-47. *2510*
—. McCabe, Edward Preston. Migration, Internal. Negroes. Oklahoma. 1891-94. *1204*
Homicide. *See* Murder.
Homosexuality. Attitudes. 1870's-1900's. *8*
—. Communist Party. Hay, Henry (interview). Mattachine Society. 1950-53. *2672*
—. Fiction. Periodicals. Women. 1900-20. *1930*
Homosexuals. Discrimination. Equal rights. 20c. *1677*
Hoodless, Adelaide. Canada. Girls. Home economics. Public schools. 1890's-1900's. *215*
Hookworms. Poor. Rockefeller Sanitary Commission for the Eradication of Hookworm Disease. South. Stiles, Charles W. 1900-14. *2109*
Hoover Dam. Boulder Canyon Project. Colorado River. Industrial Workers of the World. Nevada. Strikes. 1931. *2433*
—. Boulder Canyon Project. Industrial Workers of the World. Nevada. Six Companies, Inc. Strikes. 1931. *2434*
Hoover, Herbert C. American Petroleum Institute. Ecology. Oil Industry and Trade. Politics. Pollution. 1921-26. *2365*
—. Child Welfare. Voluntary associations. War relief. 1914-31. *364*
—. Corporations. Employment. Labor Unions and Organizations. 1919-29. *2465*
—. Dix, I. F. Local politics. Self-help. Unemployed Citizens' League. Washington (Seattle). 1931-32. *2417*
—. Elections (presidential). Progressivism. Republican Party. Senate. 1930-32. *2369*
—. Federal Government. Public welfare. Roosevelt, Franklin D. 1920-37. *2345*
Hoover, Hiram F. Cooperative Workers of America. Georgia. Negroes. Secret Societies. South Carolina. 1886-87. *1197*
Hoover, J. Edgar. Federal Bureau of Investigation. Radicals and Radicalism. Surveillance. 1919-21. *2461*
Hopedale Community. Ballou, Adin Augustus. Draper, E. D. Massachusetts (Milford). Utopias. 1824-56. *917*
—. Ballou, Adin Augustus. Massachusetts (Milford). Religion. Utopias. 1830-42. *938*
Hopkins, Harry. New Deal. Politics. 1912-40. *414*
Hopkins, Samuel. African Society. Colonization. Freedmen. Rhode Island (Providence). Sierra Leone. 1789-95. *614*
—. American Revolution. Antislavery Sentiments. Congregationalism. Rhode Island (Newport). ca 1770-1803. *511*
—. Edwards, Jonathan. New Divinity (doctrines). New England. Theology. 1730-1803. *479*
Hopkins, Sterling. Diaries. Freedmen's Bureau. Reconstruction. Virginia. 1868. *1056*
Hospitals *See also* Clinics.
—. Baltimore City Hospital. Maryland. 1772-1964. *238*
—. Children. Massachusetts (Boston). New York City. Pediatrics. Pennsylvania (Philadelphia). 1776-1976. *249*
—. Cholera. City Government. Massachusetts (Springfield). Sanitation. 1865-70. *1471*
—. Codman, Ernest Amory. Medicine (practice of). 1910-23. *2056*
—. Discrimination. Mercy Hospital (proposed). Negroes. Ohio (Cleveland). 1927-30. *2380*
—. New York (Rochester). 19c. *240*
House Committee on Un-American Activities. Anti-Communist Movements. Negroes. Robeson, Paul. Robinson, Jackie. USSR. 1949. *2684*
House of Commons. Canada. Legislation. Liberal Party. Political Change. Progressive Party. 1920's. *1574*
House of Refuge for Colored Children. Juvenile Delinquency. Negroes. Pennsylvania (Philadelphia). 1828-60's. *872*
House of Representatives *See also* Legislation; Senate.
—. Ashley, James M. Civil War. Negro Suffrage. Ohio (Toledo). Reconstruction. 1861-62. *1019*
—. Ashley, James M. Constitutional Amendments (13th). Nationalism. Ohio. Political Parties. 1848-65. *1097*

—. Carpetbaggers. Negroes. Reconstruction. Republican Party. Scalawags. South. 1868-72. *1036*
—. Democratic Party. Human Rights. New Jersey. Norton, Mary T. Women. 1920-30. *2415*
—. Federal Government. Intervention. Negroes. Population. South. Voting Rights Act (US, 1965). 1940-75. *2802*
—. Flynn, Dennis T. McGuire, Bird S. Oklahoma. Progressivism. 1901-07. *1905*
—. Freedmen. Murray, George Washington. Republican Party. South Carolina. Suffrage. 1893-97. *1163*
—. Illinois. Logan, John A. Republicans, Radical. 1866-68. *1028*
—. Illinois (Chicago). Politics. Sabath, Adolph Joachim. 1907-32. *298*
—. Langston, John Mercer. Negroes. State Politics. Virginia. 1849-97. *300*
—. Montana. Pacifism. Rankin, Jeannette. 1880-1973. *465*
—. Montana. Political Campaigns (congressional). Rankin, Jeannette. Republican Party. Woman suffrage. 1900-16. *2142*
—. Republicans, Radical. Texas. 1870-73. *1088*
Housework. Austin, Alice Constance. California (Llano del Rio). Feminism. Howland, Marie Stevens. Mexico (Topolobampo). Utopias. 1874-1917. *929*
Housing *See also* City Planning; Discrimination; Housing; Landlords and Tenants; Public Housing.
—. Architecture. Communalism. Feminism. Gilman, Charlotte Perkins. 1870-1920. *42*
—. Attitudes. Negroes. Ohio (Toledo). Racism. United Automobile Workers of America. 1967-73. *2805*
—. California (San Francisco Bay area). Consumers. Environmental protection. Government regulation. Local government. Suburbs. 1940-80. *2718*
—. Canada. Federal Policy. 1970-79. *2950*
—. Cincinnati Better Housing League. Ohio. Race relations. 1916-39. *1573*
—. Cohen, Julius Henry. Eminent domain. New York. 1920's-30's. *2370*
—. Community services. Education. Indian-White relations. North Carolina Commission of Indian Affairs. ca 1700-1978. *108*
—. Employment. Negroes. Racism. Voting and Voting Behavior. 1960's-70's. *2810*
—. Kentucky (Louisville). NAACP. Segregation. Supreme Court. 1914-17. *2126*
—. Kentucky (Louisville). Poverty. Progressivism. 1900-10. *1927*
—. Negroes. New Deal. Pennsylvania (Philadelphia). 1930's. *2475*
Housing and Urban Development Act (US, 1965, Section 23). Illinois (Chicago). Law. Negroes. Public Housing Authority. Segregation. 1964-75. *2856*
Howard Association. Cholera. Louisiana (New Orleans). Philanthropy. Public health. Yellow fever. 1837-78. *235*
Howard, John. Architecture. Attitudes. Boston Prison Discipline Society. Crime and Criminals. Kingston Penitentiary. Ontario. ca 1830-50. *899*
Howard, Martin. Attitudes. Law. Murder. North Carolina. Slavery. 1765-91. *515*
Howard, Oliver Otis. Courts. Freedmen's Bureau. Reconstruction. South. 1865-68. *1229*
Howard, Robert. Labor Disputes. Massachusetts (Fall River). Textile industry. 1860-85. *1346*
Howard University. Civil rights. Nabrit, James Madison, Jr. Negroes. 1927-60. *439*
—. Congress. District of Columbia. Education, Finance. Politics. 1879-1928. *186*
Howe, Frederic C. Cities. Democracy. Liberalism. Progressivism. ca 1890-1940. *2013*
Howe, Joseph. Adult education. Educators. Nova Scotia. 1827-66. *844*
Howe, Julia Ward. Feminism. Motherhood. Reform. 1844-85. *349*
Howell, Clark. Cotton. Educational Reform. Phillips, Ulrich B. Progressivism. 1903-05. *2062*
Howells, William Dean. Attitudes. Capitalism. Cities. 1860-1900. *979*
Howland, John. Educational Reform. Free Schools. Legislation. Rhode Island. 1757-1838. *431*
Howland, Marie Stevens. Austin, Alice Constance. California (Llano del Rio). Feminism. Housework. Mexico (Topolobampo). Utopias. 1874-1917. *929*

Hoyt, David Starr. Antislavery Sentiments. *Arabia* (vessel). Arms Trade. Kansas. New England Emigrant Aid Company. 1855-59. *741*
Hudson, Hosea. Alabama (Birmingham). Communist Party. Negroes. South. 1920's-70's. *404*
Hughes, Charles Evans. Depressions. Historiography. New Deal. Supreme Court. 1930's. 1950's-60's. *2572*
—. New York Public Service Commission Law (1907). Public opinion. Public utilities. Railroads. 1907-09. *2200*
Hughes, Howard. Censorship. Legion of Decency. Motion Picture Producers and Distributors of America. *Outlaw* (film). Russell, Jane. 1940-49. *2649*
Hull House. Addams, Jane. Education. Ideology. Illinois (Chicago). Women. 1875-1930. *411*
—. Addams, Jane. Education. Illinois (Chicago). Working class. 1890's. *1426*
Human Development Corporation. City Government. Elites. Missouri (St. Louis). Negroes. Poor. War on Poverty. 1964-75. *2935*
Human Relations *See also* Discrimination; Family; Labor; Marriage; Race Relations.
—. Douglass, Frederick. Letters. 1846-94. *390*
—. Feminism. Politics. Radicals and Radicalism. Values. 19c-1929. *29*
—. Radicals and Radicalism. Sex. Wright, Henry Clarke. 1830-66. *805*
Human Rights. Anarchism and Anarchists. deCleyre, Voltairine. Feminism. 1800's-90's. *1046*
—. Catholic Worker Movement. Equality. Public policy. 1933-78. *1678*
—. Child Welfare. Law. Pressure Groups. 1978. *1639*
—. Child Welfare. Psychology. 1873-1914. 1970's. *143*
—. Civil rights. Negroes. Political Protest. 1954-78. *2774*
—. Democratic Party. House of Representatives. New Jersey. Norton, Mary T. Women. 1920-30. *2415*
—. DuBois, W. E. B. Negroes. Women. 1910-20. *1874*
—. Indian-White Relations. Jackson, Helen Hunt (*Century of Dishonor*). 1879-85. *1045*
—. Medical Reform. Mental Illness. Packard, Elizabeth. 1863-97. *356*
Humanism. Friends, Society of. Intellectuals. Penn, William. Radicals and Radicalism. 1650-1700. *474*
Humanitarian organizations. New York City. Reform. 1845-60. *877*
Humanitarianism. City Government. New York City. 1790-1860. *876*
—. Great Britain. Ideology. USA. ca 1660-19c. *531*
Humphrey, Hubert H. Communist Control Act (US,1954). Liberalism. McCarthy, Joseph R. 1954. *2675*
Humphrey, James K. Adventists. New York City (Harlem). Race Relations. Sabbath Day Adventist Church. Utopia Park. 1920's-30's. *1648*
Humphrey, R. M. Agricultural Reform. Arkansas. Colored Farmers' Alliance. Cotton. Strikes. 1891. *1171*
—. Colored Farmers' Alliance. Labor Unions and Organizations. Negroes. South. Strikes. 1876-91. *1150*
Hunn, John. Burris, Samuel D. Delaware. Garrett, Thomas. Tubman, Harriet. Underground Railroad. 1820-60. *712*
Hunnicutt et al. v. *Burge et al.* (Georgia, 1972). Colleges and Universities. Fort Valley State College. Georgia (Peach County). Racism. School Integration. 1972-78. *2800*
Hunt, Henry Alexander. Agricultural Reform. Georgia. Negroes. North Carolina. 1890-1938. *1744*
Hunting. Agriculture. Dewdney, Edgar. Indians (reservations). Northwest Territories. Saskatchewan. 1879-84. *1038*
Huntington, James Otis Sargent. Episcopal Church, Protestant. Monasticism. Order of the Holy Cross. 1878-90. *1061*
Huntley, Chet. Big Sky development. Conservation. Montana. Resorts. 1970-73. *2755*
Hurt, Garland. Farms. Forney, Jacob. Indians (reservations). Utah Superintendency of Indian Affairs. 1850-62. *539*
Hutchins, Robert M. Chicago, University of. Curricula. Education. 1930-77. *1839*

Hutchinson, Anne. Antinomian controversy. Massachusetts Bay Colony. Women. 1630-43. *520*
—. Bradstreet, Anne. Literature. Massachusetts Bay Colony. Religion. Social change. Women. 1630's-70's. *489*
Hyde, Ida H. Dohrn, Anton. Italy. Naples Zoological Station. Scientific Experiments and Research. Women. 1896-97. *1434*
Hyde Park Protective Association. Farwell, Arthur Burrage. Illinois (Chicago). Prohibition. Reform. 1885-1936. *1912*
Hydrotherapy. Adventists. Jackson, James Caleb. Medical reform. New York (Dansville). White, Ellen G. 1864-65. *1470*
Hygiene. American Medical Association. Cities. Public Health. 1820-80. *879*
—. Commercials. Fashion. Television. Women. Women's Liberation Movement. 1970's. *2921*
—. Fletcher, Horace. Mastication. Nutrition. 1890-1910. *2120*
Hyndman, Henry M. George, Henry. Great Britain. Ireland. Land Reform. Marxism. 1882-89. *1057*

I

Iakovos, Archbishop. Family. Morality. Orthodox Eastern Church (Greek; congresses). Social Conditions. 1960-80. *2726*
Icaria (colony). Cabet, Etienne. Illinois. Newspapers. Political Theory. Social Theory. Utopias. 1820's-56. *941*
—. Cabet, Etienne. Illinois (Nauvoo). Utopias. 1848-56. *915*
—. Cabet, Etienne. Utopias. 1840-95. *264*
Icarians. Cabet, Etienne. France. Iowa (New Icaria, Corning). Utopias. 1852-98. *1502*
Ickes, Harold. Construction. Employment. Negroes. Public Works Administration. Quotas. 1933-40. *2535*
Idaho *See also* Far Western States.
—. Alexander, Moses. Industrial Workers of the World. Labor reform. 1914-17. *2152*
—. Crime and Criminals. Industrial Workers of the World. Labor Law. State Government. 1917-33. *2088*
—. Davis, David W. Industrial Workers of the World. Nonpartisan League. Public opinion. Socialist Party. 1919-26. *2405*
—. Discrimination. Mormons. Politics. 1880-95. *1120*
—. Farmers. Intellectuals. McKaig, Robert Raymond. Nonpartisan League. North Dakota. ca 1920-45. *2406*
—. Farmers. Irrigation. Progressive Party. State Politics. 1914-22. *2012*
—. National American Woman Suffrage Association. Woman Suffrage. 1896-1920. *2149*
—. Prohibition. State Politics. 1932-35. *2575*
Idaho (Twin Falls). Kidnapping. O'Hare, Kate Richards. Socialism. Speeches, Addresses, etc. Utah. 1921. *2404*
Idaho, University of. Morrill Act (US, 1862). Washington State University. 1862-92. *1407*
Ideal States. See Utopias.
Idealism. Davis, Alexander Jackson. Garden cities. Haskell, Llewellyn S. New Jersey (West Orange; Llewellyn Park). Suburbs. 1853-57. *943*
—. Evans, Warren Felt. Mental healing. Mysticism. Romanticism. 1864-89. *1480*
Identity. Afro-American history. 1800-60. *576*
—. Alberta. Blackfoot Indians (Blood). Indians. Menominee Indians. Militancy. Wisconsin. 1950's-60's. *1685*
—. Assimilation. Cheyenne River Indian Reservation. Federal Programs. Indians. Sioux Indians. 1889-1917. *45*
—. Autobiography. Progressivism. Psychohistory. Reformers. ca 1860-1920. *366*
—. Feminism. 1820's-60. *804*
—. Girl Scouts of America. Low, Juliette. Sex roles. 1900-20. *452*
Ideology. Abolition Movement. Anti-Catholicism. Massachusetts (Boston). Riots. Social Classes. 1834-35. *555*
—. Abolition Movement. Proslavery Sentiments. South Carolina. 1776-1861. *660*
—. Abortion. 1965-80. *2722*
—. Abortion. Social Classes. 1970's. *2741*
—. Acculturation. Educational Reform. Industrialization. Pennsylvania. Social control. 1880-1910. *1420*
—. Adams, Henry Brooks. George, Henry. Industrialization. Philosophy of History. Social criticism. 1870's-1910's. *1073*

Ideology

—. Addams, Jane. Education. Hull House. Illinois (Chicago). Women. 1875-1930. *411*
—. American Revolution. Canada. French Revolution. 1775-1838. *139*
—. American Revolution. Civil Rights. Constitutional Law. 1776-1976. *134*
—. Assimilation. Black nationalism. Literature. Religion. Women. 1890-1925. *1654*
—. Black power. Political Leadership. 1960's-79. *2876*
—. Bond, Hugh Lennox. Maryland. Racism. Republicans (Radical). ca 1861-68. *1002*
—. Bureau of Indian Affairs. California (Alcatraz Island). Eskimos. Indians. Political Protest. 1969-78. *2757*
—. Canada. Civil service. Labor Unions and Organizations. Middle Classes. 1918-28. *1820*
—. Capitalism. Slavery. South. 19c. *766*
—. Carpetbaggers. Historiography. Mississippi. Reconstruction. Reformers. 1865-76. *1013*
—. Colleges and Universities. Education. Sex roles. Women. 19c-20c. *213*
—. Comte, Auguste. Foster, Frank K. Gompers, Samuel. Labor Unions and Organizations. McGregor, Hugh. Spencer, Herbert. 1876-1900. *1295*
—. Declaration of Independence. Radicals and Radicalism. Religion. Utopias. 1730's-1890's. *269*
—. DuBois, W. E. B. Integration. Negro Renaissance. 1903-74. *1543*
—. Elites. Hays, Samuel P. Professionalism. Progressivism. Wiebe, Robert. 20c. *1971*
—. Farmers. Old Northwest. Populism. Rhetoric. 1870's-80's. *1388*
—. Garvey, Marcus. Jamaica. Negroes. Pan-Africanism. 1887-1927. *401*
—. Great Britain. Humanitarianism. USA. ca 1660-19c. *531*
—. Industrial Conference, 1st. Labor Unions and Organizations. Management. Wilson, Woodrow. 1919. *2225*
—. North. Protestantism. Public Schools. Republican Party. Western states. 1870-1930. *204*
—. Politics. Populism. Walsh, Thomas J. ca 1890-1900. *1361*
Iglesias Pantín, Santiago. American Federation of Labor. Gompers, Samuel. Labor Unions and Organizations. Puerto Rico. 1897-1920's. *2210*
Illinois *See also* North Central States.
—. Addams, Jane. Dudzik, Mary Theresa. Franciscan Sisters of Chicago. Polish Americans. Social Work. 1860-1918. *369*
—. Adventists. Jones, Alonzo Trevier. Religious liberty. Sunday. World's Columbian Exposition (Chicago, 1893). 1893. *1492*
—. Antislavery Sentiments. Coles, Edward. Jefferson, Thomas. 1809-68. *689*
—. Antislavery Sentiments. Free Soil Party. Racism. Republican Party. 1848-60. *740*
—. Bishop Hill Colony. Communalism. Economic growth. Swedish Americans. Westward Movement. 1846-59. *935*
—. Bishop Hill Colony. Daily life. Jansson, Erik. Letters. Swedish Americans. Utopias. 1847-56. *939*
—. Bishop Hill Colony. Immigrants. Janssonists. Swedish Americans. Utopias. 1846-60. *920*
—. Bishop Hill Colony. Janssonists. Letters. Swedes. 1847. *936*
—. Bradwell, Myra. Lawyers. Sex Discrimination. Supreme Court (decision). 1873-1894. *1114*
—. Business. Capitalism. Legislation. Workmen's compensation. 1905-12. *2189*
—. Cabet, Etienne. Icaria (colony). Newspapers. Political Theory. Social Theory. Utopias. 1820's-56. *941*
—. Child labor. Law. Women. 1890-1920. *1955*
—. Coal Mines and Mining. Great Britain. Labor Unions and Organizations. Legislation. Lobbying. 1861-72. *1312*
—. Congress. Keller, Kent. Liberalism. New Deal. 1930-42. *2608*
—. Democratic Party. Republican Party. Slavery. Trumbull, Lyman. 1855-72. *323*
—. Education. Jefferson, Thomas. Lincoln, Abraham. 1820-62. *835*
—. House of Representatives. Logan, John A. Republicans, Radical. 1866-68. *1028*
—. Legislation. Reform. Wages. Women. Working Conditions. 1893-1917. *2187*
—. Local Government. Lochner, Louis Paul. Peace Movements. People's Council of America for Democracy and Peace. State Government. 1917. *2104*

—. People's Party. Political Attitudes. Populism. 1880-92. *1398*
—. Prisons. State Government. 1831-1903. *230*
—. Sanitation. 1865-1900. *1449*
Illinois Association Opposed to the Extension of Suffrage to Women. Suffrage. Women Remonstrants of the State of Illinois. 1886-1923. *132*
Illinois (Blue Island). Debs, Eugene V. Federal Government. Pullman Strike. Strikes. 1894. *1317*
Illinois (Bureau County). Abolition Movement. Bryant, John Howard. Bryant, Julian. Civil War. Lovejoy, Owen. Military Service. Negroes. 1831-65. *607*
Illinois (Canton). City Politics. Prohibition. Socialist Party. Whalen, Homer. 1911-20. *2093*
Illinois (Chicago). Addams, Jane. Education. Hull House. Ideology. Women. 1875-1930. *411*
—. Addams, Jane. Education. Hull House. Working class. 1890's. *1426*
—. Addams, Jane. Hampton, Isabel. Johns Hopkins Hospital Training School for Nurses. Maryland (Baltimore). Nurses and Nursing. Professionalization. Social Work. 1889-1910. *1461*
—. American Committee on Italian Migration. Immigration. Italian Americans. Reform. 1952-67. *2701*
—. Anderson, Mary. Labor Unions and Organizations. Nestor, Agnes. Robins, Margaret Dreier. Women. Women's Trade Union League. Working conditions. 1903-20. *2190*
—. Anglophobia. Censorship. City Politics. Libraries. Public Schools. Thompson, William Hale. 1927. *2454*
—. Baseball. Business. City life. Social change. Values. 1865-70. *1001*
—. Berry, George L. Newspapers. Strikes. 1912-14. *2274*
—. Bradwell, Myra. Law reform. Women's rights. 1855-92. *1034*
—. Brown v. Board of Education (US, 1954). Constitutional Amendments (14th). School integration. South. 1954-77. *2777*
—. Burnham, Daniel Hudson. City planning. Moody, Walter D. (Wacker's Manual of the Plan of Chicago). Progressivism. Publicity. Reform. 1909-11. *2071*
—. Business. Feminism. Philanthropy. Schmidt, Minna Moscherosch. 1886-1961. *315*
—. Catholic Church. Mundelein, George. 20c. *1621*
—. Charities. Negroes. Social problems. 1890-1917. *1979*
—. Charities Organization Society Movement. Public Welfare. 1880-1930. *1996*
—. Child Welfare. Off-the-Street Club. 1890's. *1477*
—. Cities. Georgia (Atlanta). New Jersey (Newark). Water supply. 1860-1923. *32*
—. Cities. Playgrounds. Progressivism. 1894-1917. *2027*
—. City Government. Fisher, Walter L. Reform. 1880-1910. *347*
—. Civil rights movement. Negroes. School integration. 1936. *2523*
—. Dever, William. Elections (mayoral). Ethnic groups. Negroes. Prohibition. 1923-27. *2350*
—. Dunne, Edward F. Educational Reform. Progressives. 1905-10. *2299*
—. Educational reform. Georgia (Atlanta). New York City. Progressivism. Teachers. 1890-1920. *2336*
—. Farwell, Arthur Burrage. Hyde Park Protective Association. Prohibition. Reform. 1885-1936. *1912*
—. Garment industry. Men. Strikes. 1910-11. *2286*
—. Garment Industry. O'Reilly, Mary. Socialist Party. Strikes. Women. Zeh, Nellie M. 1910. *2183*
—. House of Representatives. Politics. Sabath, Adolph Joachim. 1907-32. *298*
—. Housing and Urban Development Act (US, 1965, Section 23). Law. Negroes. Public Housing Authority. Segregation. 1964-75. *2856*
—. Immigrants' Protective League. 1908-21. *2007*
—. Labor reform. Morgan, Elizabeth Chambers. 1874-97. *1341*
—. Local Politics. Negroes. Public schools. 1910-41. *1845*

—. Militia. Police. Riots. Strikes. Wages. 1877. *1343*
—. Novels. Social Conditions. 1890-1910. *1963*
—. Post, Louis F. Progressivism. *Public* (newspaper). Single tax movement. 1898-1919. *1904*
Illinois (Chicago; Back of the Yards). Labor Unions and Organizations. Meat packing industry. Polish Americans. Strikes. 1921. *2424*
Illinois (Cook County). Aid to Families with Dependent Children. Mothers' pensions. Public Welfare. 1911-75. *2107*
Illinois Intercollegiate Prohibition Association. Colleges and Universities. Prohibition. Protestantism. 1893-1920. *2059*
Illinois (Nauvoo). Cabet, Etienne. Icaria (colony). Utopias. 1848-56. *915*
Illinois (Pullman). American Railway Union. California. Strikes. 1893-94. *1337*
—. Labor Unions and Organizations. Pullman strike. Railroads. 1880-94. *1325*
Illinois, University of. Bevier, Isabel. Home economics. Women. 1900-21. *2295*
Illinois (Virden). Coal miners. Germer, Adolph. Socialism. Strikes. United Mine Workers of America. 1893-1900. *1291*
Illinois Volunteers. Civil War. Emancipation Proclamation. Republican Party. 1862-63. *1087*
Illinois (Zion). Christian Catholic Church. Dowie, John Alexander. Evangelism. 1888-1907. *1512*
Illiteracy. Education. Kentucky Illiteracy Commission. Kentucky (Rowan County). Stewart, Cora Wilson. 1910-20. *2325*
Imatra I (association). Finnish Americans. Labor Unions and Organizations. New York City (Brooklyn). 1890-1921. *2011*
Imber, Naphtali Herz *(The Fall of Jerusalem)*. Bible. Myths and Symbols. Populism. 1856-1909. *1371*
Immigrants. Abolitionists. Irish Americans. Nationalism. ca 1830's-50's. *715*
—. Anderson, James T. M. Anglicization. English language. Ethnic groups. Public schools. Saskatchewan. 1918-23. *1856*
—. Bishop Hill Colony. Illinois. Janssonists. Swedish Americans. Utopias. 1846-60. *920*
—. Boycotts. Irish Americans. Labor. New York City. Working conditions. 1880-86. *1311*
—. Canada. English Canadians. Propaganda. Puttee, Arthur. Radicals and Radicalism. Water Conservation. ca 1888-1913. *1327*
—. Canada. Finns. Labor Unions and Organizations. Radicals and Radicalism. 1918-26. *2407*
—. Catholic Church. Irish Americans. McMahon, Patrick. Poor. Quebec (Quebec). St. Bridget's Home. 1847-1972. *244*
—. Compulsory education. Missouri (St. Louis). Public Schools. Truancy. 1905-07. *2313*
—. Deportation. Labor Unions and Organizations. Mexican Americans. New Deal. 1930's. *2500*
—. Educational Reform. New York (Buffalo). Public Schools. 1890-1916. *2332*
—. Employment. Law Enforcement. Maximum hours law. State Government. Women. 1920. *2398*
—. Finnish Americans. Labor. Minnesota (Smithville). Socialism. Work People's College. 1900-20. *2315*
—. Industrial Workers of the World. New Jersey (Paterson). Strikes. Textile Industry. Violence. 1913. *2254*
—. Industrial Workers of the World. New York (Little Falls). Strikes. Textile Industry. Women. 1912. *2269*
—. Italian Americans. Labor movement. ca 1880-1927. *175*
Immigrants' Protective League. Illinois (Chicago). 1908-21. *2007*
Immigration *See also* Assimilation; Demography; Deportation; Emigration; Naturalization; Population; Race Relations; Refugees; Social Problems.
—. American Committee on Italian Migration. Illinois (Chicago). Italian Americans. Reform. 1952-67. *2701*
—. American Federation of Labor. Fascism. Gompers, Samuel. Jingoism. Racism. 1850-1924. *394*
—. Antilabor sentiments. Canada, western. Elections. Ku Klux Klan. 1921-30's. *1603*
—. Argell, James B. Chinese Exclusion Act (US, 1882). Congress. Diplomacy. 1876-82. *947*
—. Asian Canadians. British Columbia. Politics. Racism. 1850-1914. *1524*

Immigration

—. Asians. Conservatism. Methodist Episcopal Church. Social Gospel. 1865-1908. *1029*
—. Asians. Negroes. Newlands, Francis. Progressives. West Coast. 1904-17. *2067*
—. British Columbia. Chinese. Japanese. Suffrage. 1935-49. *1725*
—. British Columbia (Trail). Consolidated Mining and Smelting Company. Mine, Mill and Smelter Workers, International Union of. Strikes. World War I. 1916-17. *1810*
—. California. Chinese Americans. Nativism. *Sacramento Union* (newspaper). 1850-82. *12*
—. California (San Francisco). Charities. Voluntary Associations. ca 1850-60. *885*
—. Charities. Galveston Plan of 1907. Industrial Removal Office. Jews. Migration, Internal. New York City. 1890-1914. *1476*
—. Child Welfare. Family. Foster homes. Jews. New York City. Working class. 1900-05. *2061*
—. Chinese. Labor Unions and Organizations. Powderly, Terence V. 1897-1902. *1052*
—. Federal Policy. Negroes. 1917-29. *2382*
—. Industrialization. Kamprath, William B. Labor (unskilled). New York (Buffalo). Vocational education. 1907-21. *2312*
—. Industrialization. Morality. Muckraking. Periodicals. 1900-09. *2047*
—. Japanese. Miller, Kelly. Negroes. Race Relations. 1906-24. *1601*
—. Poland. Polish Americans. Socialists. 1883-1914. *39*

Imperialism *See also* Colonialism; Militarism.
—. Ethnic groups. James, William. Race Relations. 1899-1910. *2033*
—. Historiography. Leuchtenburg, William E. Progressivism. 1890's-1910's. 1952-74. *2089*
—. Historiography. Leuchtenburg, William E. Progressivism. 1898-1916. 1952-75. *2023*

Imports. Foreign policy. International Steel Cartel. Labor. Steel Workers Organizing Committee. US Steel Corporation. 1937. *2538*

Impoundment. Russian Revolution (October). *Shilka* (vessel). Washington (Seattle). 1917. *2009*

Income. Canada. Child welfare. Legislation. Mothers. 1916-70's. *1814*
—. Canada. Legislation. Mothers. Public Welfare. ca 1900-39. *1815*
—. Civil rights. Economic conditions. Public Policy. 1948-75. *2861*
—. Civil Rights Act (US, 1964; Title VIII). Discrimination, Employment. Negroes. Women. 1964-70's. *2839*
—. Economic Theory. George, Henry. Landlords and Tenants. Population. Taxation. Technology. 1871-83. *1064*
—. Negroes. Social Status. 1954-74. *1823*

Income (redistribution). LaFollette, Philip F. National Progressives of America. Politics. Wisconsin. 1930-38. *2551*
—. Politics. Public policy. 1961-73. *2951*

Income tax. Attitudes. Democracy. Federal Reserve System. Reform. Wilson, Woodrow. 1913-21. *1994*

Independent Labour Party. Dixon, Frederick John. Farmer, S. J. Manitoba. Single tax. 1920-49. *1791*

Independent Textile Workers. Belgian Americans. French Canadian Americans. Rhode Island (Woonsocket). Working Class. 1931-50's. *1767*

India. Church and State. Education. Great Britain. Secularization. 19c. *198*

Indian Citizenship Act (US, 1924). Citizenship. Coolidge, Calvin. Political Reform. 1924. *2446*

Indian Civil Rights Act (US, 1968). Civil Rights. Natural law. Pueblo Indians. *Santa Clara Pueblo v. Martinez* (US, 1977). Tribal government. 1939-77. *2789*

Indian Claims Commission. Far Western States. Kalispel Indians. 1950-65. *1549*

Indian Reorganization Act (US, 1934). Assimilation. Collier, John. Federal Policy. 1933-45. *2530*
—. Bureau of Indian Affairs. Meriam Report (1928). 1928-34. *2444*
—. Dawes Act (US, 1887). Indian Rights Association. Indians. Land allotment. 1887-1934. *153*

Indian Rights Association. Arizona. Bai-a-lil-le (medicine man). Civil Rights. Education. Fort Huachuca. Navajo Indians. Utah, southeastern. 1906-09. *2043*
—. Assimilation. New York. Roosevelt, Theodore. 1890-1910. *1014*

SUBJECT INDEX

—. Civil Service Commissioner. Indian-White Relations. Roosevelt, Theodore. Welsh, Herbert. 1889-95. *1011*
—. Dawes Act (US, 1887). Indian Reorganization Act (US, 1934). Indians. Land allotment. 1887-1934. *153*

Indian Territory. Cherokee Indians. Farmers. Grange. 1870's. *1374*
—. Cherokee Indians. Freedmen. Racism. 1839-88. *1165*
—. Dawes Commission. Five Civilized Tribes. Freedmen. Homesteading and Homesteaders. 1893-1905. *1083*

Indian Wars *See also* Indians (tribal warfare); Massacres.
—. Arizona (Tucson). Camp Grant Affair. Federal Policy. 1871. *1037*
—. Colorado. Sand Creek Massacre. Soule, Silas S. 1859-65. *44*
—. Friends, Society of. Nonviolence. Paxton riots. Pennsylvania (Philadelphia). 1764-67. *497*

Indiana *See also* North Central States.
—. Automobile Industry and Trade. Labor. New Deal. Ohio. United Automobile Workers of America. 1935-40. *2542*
—. Civil Rights Act (US, 1964). Democratic Party. Primaries (presidential). Wallace, George C. Welsh, Matthew E. 1964. *2900*
—. Debs, Eugene V. Debs, Theodore. Labor Unions and Organizations. Sebree, Shubert (letters). 1890-1930's. *418*
—. Discrimination, Educational. NAACP. Negroes. ca 1869-1975. *211*
—. New Harmony (colony). Utopias. 1824-58. *916*

Indiana (Gary). Air pollution. City Government. Reform. US Steel Corporation. 1956-73. *2723*
—. Americanization. Labor Unions and Organizations. Polish Americans. United States Steel Corporation. 1906-20. *2178*
—. Brown, Willis. Juvenile delinquency. 1910-12. *2075*
—. Martial law. Steel industry. Strikes. 1919. *2244*

Indiana (Indianapolis). Columbia Conserve Company. Hapgood, William P. Industrial Relations. 1917-43. *1789*

Indiana (New Harmony). Anarchism and Anarchists. Libertarianism. Ohio (Cincinnati). Utopias. Warren, Joseph. 1818-74. *302*
—. City Planning. Communes. Harmony Society. Pennsylvania (Economy, Harmony). Social customs. 1820's-1905. *919*
—. Harmony Society. Rapp, George. Utopias. 1814-47. *937*

Indians *See also* terms beginning with the word Indian; names of Indian tribes, e.g. Delaware Indians; Acculturation; Aleuts; Asians; Eskimos; Metis; Tribes.
—. Abolitionists. Assimilation. 1820-80. *563*
—. Acculturation. American Indian Defense Association. Collier, John. Religious liberty. 1920-26. *2427*
—. Acculturation. Canada. Federal Policy. Sifton, Clifford. 1896-1905. *1012*
—. Acculturation. Collier, John. Florida. North Carolina. Schools. Seminole Indians. 1927-54. *1851*
—. Agriculture. Cheyenne and Arapaho Reservation. Federal Policy. Oklahoma. 1869-80. *1063*
—. Alaska Native Claims Settlement Act (US, 1971). Aleuts. Eskimos. 1971-78. *2745*
—. Alaska Reorganization Act (US, 1936). Aleuts. Eskimos. Federal Policy. 1936-45. *2574*
—. Alberta. Blackfoot Indians (Blood). Identity. Menominee Indians. Militancy. Wisconsin. 1950's-60's. *1685*
—. American Indian Federation. Bureau of Indian Affairs. Collier, John. Jamison, Alice Lee. New Deal. Political activism. 1930's-50's. *354*
—. American Indian Movement. Deloria, Vine, Jr. Federal Government. Political Protest. South Dakota. Wounded Knee (occupation). 1877-1970's. *2712*
—. American Indian Movement. Pine Ridge Indian Reservation. South Dakota. Wounded Knee (occupation). 1972-75. *2749*
—. American Indian Movement. Sioux Indians (Oglala). South Dakota (Wounded Knee). 1973. *2709*
—. Americas (North and South). Bureau of Indian Affairs. Collier, John. Inter-American Institute. 1930's-50's. *1662*
—. Anthropology. Pan-Indianism. Parker, Arthur C. Seneca Indians. 1881-1925. *355*

Indians

—. Antislavery Sentiments. 1830-94. *6*
—. Arapaho Indians. Cheyenne Indians. Mennonites. Missions and Missionaries. 1880-1900. *1030*
—. Arizona. Assimilation. Education. Industrial Arts Education. Phoenix Indian School. 1890-1901. *1437*
—. Arizona (Page). Discrimination, employment. Industrial Relations. Navajo Construction Workers Associations. Office of Navajo Labor Relations. 1971-77. *2944*
—. Assimilation. British Columbia. Schools. 1890-1920. *1861*
—. Assimilation. Cheyenne River Indian Reservation. Federal Programs. Identity. Sioux Indians. 1889-1917. *45*
—. Assimilation. Draper, Andrew Sloan. Education. 1880's-1913. *1424*
—. Assimilation. Education. Micmac Indians. Nova Scotia. Public policy. Religion. 1605-1872. *209*
—. Assimilation. Education. Self-determination. 1960's-70's. *2963*
—. Assimilation. Racism. Reform. 1880-1900. *944*
—. Attitudes. Missions and Missionaries. Presbyterian Church. 1837-93. *13*
—. Baptists. Crawford, Isabel. Kiowa Indians. Missions and Missionaries. Oklahoma (Wichita Mountains). Women's American Baptist Home Missionary Society. 1893-1961. *393*
—. Boarding schools. Children. Federal Government. 1920-60's. *1864*
—. Bureau of American Ethnology. Ghost Dance. Mooney, James. Peyote. Research. 1891-1921. *1110*
—. Bureau of Indian Affairs. California (Alcatraz Island). Eskimos. Ideology. Political Protest. 1969-78. *2757*
—. Bureau of Indian Affairs. Collier, John. New Deal. 1933-45. *2600*
—. Bureau of Indian Affairs. Educational policy. Medill, William. 1845-49. *836*
—. Bureau of Indian Affairs. Emmons, Glenn L. Social Policy. Tribes. 1953-61. *2660*
—. Bureau of Indian Affairs. Self-determination. 1945-75. *1545*
—. California. Compensation. Land claims. 1821-1963. *173*
—. California. Jackson, Helen Hunt *(Ramona)*. Mission Indians. Ponca Indians. Removals, forced. Schurz, Carl. 1873-84. *1051*
—. California (Eight Mile, Blue Creek). Forest Service. Religious liberty. Supreme Court. 1975. *2785*
—. California (San Diego). Jackson, Helen Hunt *(Ramona)*. 1882-84. *951*
—. Canada. Courts. Lavell, Jeannette. Political participation. Women's Liberation Movement. 1869-1979. *2914*
—. Canada. Education. Federal government. Métis. 1940-70. *2959*
—. Cherokee Indians. Citizenship. South. 1817-29. *598*
—. Cherokee Indians. Federal Policy. New Deal. North Carolina, western. 1930's. *2607*
—. Children. Poor. Saint Vincent de Paul Society. 1900-10. *2036*
—. Citizenship. Constitutional Amendments (14th). Law. ca 1776-1934. *131*
—. Civil Rights. Florida (Kissimmee). Friends of the Florida Seminoles. Seminole Indians. Tiger, Tom. 1898-99. *1100*
—. Collier, John. Federal Government. Liberalism. Roosevelt, Franklin D. (administration). Truman, Harry S. (administration). 1933-53. *1629*
—. Competency commissions. Federal Policy. Land allotment. 1913-20. *2031*
—. Dawes Act (US, 1887). Flathead Indian Reservation. Land Tenure. Montana. Salish (Flathead) Indians. 1887-1904. *1075*
—. Dawes Act (US, 1887). Indian Reorganization Act (US, 1934). Indian Rights Association. Land allotment. 1887-1934. *153*
—. Debo, Angie (personal account). Federal Government. Public Opinion. Reform. 1969-76. *2703*
—. Determinism. Garland, Hamlin. Reform. 1890-1923. *2111*
—. Education. Manuscripts. Wisconsin. 1820-50. *848*
—. Ethnicity. Political Protest. Religion. 1964-78. *2738*
—. Ethnography. Federal policy. Morgan, Lewis Henry. 1848-78. *1059*

Indians

—. Federal Government. Frazier, Lynn J. Governors. North Dakota. Progressivism. 1916-40. *1538*
—. Federal government. Nebraska Historical Society. Omaha Indians. Returned Students of Omaha. Speeches, Addresses, etc. 1920's. *2442*
—. Federal policy. Hayes, Rutherford B. 1877-81. *988*
—. Federal Policy. Meriam, Lewis *(Problem of Indian Administration)*. Reform. Social conditions. 1920-28. *2362*
—. Franklin, Benjamin. Massacres. Pamphlets. Paxton Boys. Pennsylvania. 1764. *499*
—. Ghost Dance. Revitalization movements. Social Organization. 1889. *967*
—. Government. Social change. 1960-76. *2743*
—. Labor Unions and Organizations. Navajo Indians. Southwest. 1958-78. *2945*
—. Lawsuits. Legislation. Public Welfare. 1957-77. *2706*
—. Religious liberty. 1609-1976. *145*

Indians (agencies) *See also* Indians (reservations).

—. Abolition Movement. Artifacts. California. Citrus industry. Rust, Horatio Nelson. 1850's-1906. *276*
—. Arapaho Indians. Cheyenne Indians. Dawes Act (US, 1887). Fraud. Land allotment. Oklahoma. 1910's. *1888*
—. Assimilation. Finley, James B. Methodist Church. Missions and Missionaries. Ohio. Shaw, John. 1820-24. *581*
—. California, southern. Jackson, Helen Hunt *(Century of Dishonor; Ramona)*. 1881-84. *1048*
—. Citizenship. Civil Rights. Crook, George. Political Corruption. Whites. 1870's-80's. *993*
—. Dawes Act (US, 1887). Eells, Edwin. Land Tenure. Skokomish Indian Reservation. Washington. 1871-95. *970*

Indians (reservations) *See also* Indians (agencies).

—. Agricultural policy. Dawes Act (US, 1887). Federal government. Kiowa Indians. Oklahoma. 1869-1901. *1062*
—. Agriculture. Blackfoot Indians. Cattle Raising. Montana. 1885-1935. *104*
—. Agriculture. Dewdney, Edgar. Hunting. Northwest Territories. Saskatchewan. 1879-84. *1038*
—. Artifacts. Dawes Act (US, 1887). Fletcher, Alice Cunningham. 1880's-90's. *968*
—. Bureau of Indian Affairs. Emmons, Glenn L. Industrialization. 1953-60. *2661*
—. Civilian Conservation Corps (Indian Division). Depressions. Sioux Indians. South Dakota. 1933-42. *2486*
—. Economic Policy. Prisons. Reform. 19c. *158*
—. Educators. Ethnographers. Evangelism. Pueblo Indians (Hopi). Sullivan, John H. Taylor, Charles A. 1870-89. *1050*
—. Farms. Forney, Jacob. Hurt, Garland. Utah Superintendency of Indian Affairs. 1850-62. *539*

Indians (tribal warfare) *See also* Indian Wars.

—. Acculturation. Creek Indians. 1865-1978. *68*

Indian-White Relations. Alaska. Assimilation. Brady, John Green. Economic Conditions. Tlingit Indians. 1878-1906. *1016*

—. American Board of Commissioners for Foreign Missions. Assimilation. Connecticut (Cornwall). Foreign Mission School. Students. 1816-27. *829*
—. Apes, William. Massachusetts (Mashpee). Reform. Wampanoag Indians. 1830-40. *600*
—. Bureau of Indian Affairs. Christianity. Iowa. Schools. Winnebago Indians. 1834-48. *850*
—. California. Civil War. Reform. Republican Party. 1860-70. *971*
—. California. Paiute Indians. Winnemucca, Sarah (Paiute). 1840's-91. *419*
—. Canada. Education. 1978. *2972*
—. Centennial Celebrations. Jackson, Helen Hunt. National Self-image. 1881. 1975. *1079*
—. Cherokee Indians. Christianity. Missions and Missionaries. Property. Social Change. Women. 19c. *107*
—. Civil Rights. Five Civilized Tribes. 18c-20c. *1581*
—. Civil Service Commissioner. Indian Rights Association. Roosevelt, Theodore. Welsh, Herbert. 1889-95. *1011*
—. Community services. Education. Housing. North Carolina Commission of Indian Affairs. ca 1700-1978. *108*

SUBJECT INDEX

—. Florida. Pelota (game). Spain. 1675-84. *9*
—. Human Rights. Jackson, Helen Hunt *(Century of Dishonor)*. 1879-85. *1045*
—. Legislation. New Mexico (Taos; Blue Lake). Pueblo Indians. Rites and Ceremonies. 20c. *1718*

Individualism. Abolition movement. "Boston Clique". Garrison, William Lloyd. Interpersonal Relations. 1830-40. *646*

—. *Actualité Économique* (periodical). Cooperative movement. Minville, Esdras. Nationalism. Quebec (Gaspé Peninsula). 1924-40. *1794*
—. *Actualité Économique* (periodical). Cooperative movement. Minville, Esdras. Quebec (Gaspé Peninsula). 1924-43. *1795*
—. Baptists, Southern. Politics. Social problems. 18c-1976. *31*
—. Chippewa Lumber and Boom Company. Deitz, John F. Weyerhaeuser, Frederick. Wisconsin (Cameron Dam). 1900-24. *1967*
—. Colleges and Universities. Curricula. Education. Negroes. 1890-1970's. *1853*
—. Colorado. Conservation of natural resources. Progressives. 1896-1910. *2028*
—. Conservatism. Olmsted, Frederick Law. 19c. *1041*
—. Education. Ferm, Alexis Constantine. Ferm, Elizabeth Byrne. 1880's-1970's. *847*
—. Freedom. Property. Social mobility. Socialism. 1750-1979. *85*
—. James, William. Political Reform. 1870's-1900. *341*

Industrial arts education. Africa. Pan-Africanism. Racism. South. 1879-1940. *214*

—. Agriculture. Negroes. North. Philanthropy. South. 1902-35. *1832*
—. Alabama. Negroes. Tuskegee Institute. Washington, Booker T. 1870's-90's. *1189*
—. Arizona. Assimilation. Education. Indians. Phoenix Indian School. 1890-1901. *1437*
—. Educational Policy. Negroes. Speeches, Addresses, etc. Washington, Booker T. 1884-1904. *1283*
—. Negroes. North. Progressive era. South. 1900-15. *2306*

Industrial Conference, 1st. Ideology. Labor Unions and Organizations. Management. Wilson, Woodrow. 1919. *2225*

Industrial Conference, 2d. Industrial democracy. Labor Reform. Labor Unions and Organizations. Wilson, Woodrow. 1919-20. *2180*

Industrial democracy. Filene, Edward A. Massachusetts (Boston). Reform. 1890-1937. *1787*

—. Industrial Conference, 2d. Labor Reform. Labor Unions and Organizations. Wilson, Woodrow. 1919-20. *2180*

Industrial Rayon Corporation. Strikes. Textile Workers Organizing Committee. Virginia (Covington). 1937-38. *2508*

Industrial Relations *See also* Collective Bargaining; Labor Unions and Organizations; Strikes.

—. Arizona (Page). Discrimination, employment. Indians. Navajo Construction Workers Associations. Office of Navajo Labor Relations. 1971-77. *2944*
—. Armaments Industry. Connecticut (Bridgeport). Technology. World War I. 1915-19. *2182*
—. British Columbia. Depressions. National Unemployed Workers' Association. Unemployment. Workers' Unity League. 1930-39. *1830*
—. Canadian Labour Congress. Cooperative Commonwealth Federation. Federal Government. Trades and Labour Congress of Canada. World War II. 1939-46. *2634*
—. Christianity. Massachusetts (Lawrence). Scudder, Vida Dutton. Women. 1912. *2196*
—. Collar Laundry Union. Irish Americans. New York (Troy). Women. 1864-69. *1352*
—. Columbia Conserve Company. Hapgood, William P. Indiana (Indianapolis). 1917-43. *1789*
—. Coopers' International Union. Mechanization. Standard Oil Company of Ohio. 1870's. *1313*
—. Knights of Labor. Politics. Rhode Island. 1880's. *1289*
—. Migration, Internal. Negroes. Pine industry. South. Working conditions. ca 1912-26. *1577*
—. Pennsylvania. Steel industry. 1800-1959. *174*

Industrial Removal Office. Charities. Galveston Plan of 1907. Immigration. Jews. Migration, Internal. New York City. 1890-1914. *1476*

Industrial Workers

Industrial revolution. Agrarianism. Bellamy, Edward *(Looking Backward 2000-1887)*. Utopias. ca 1865-1900. *1517*

Industrial safety. Accidents. California. Tanneries. Working Conditions. 1901-80. *2751*

—. Reform. "Safety First" (slogan). Young, Robert J. ca 1900-16. *1886*

Industrial Technology. Factories. Labor Disputes. National Cash Register Company. 1895-1913. *2249*

Industrial Workers of the World. Agricultural labor. California. Cannery and Agricultural Workers Industrial Union. Radicals and Radicalism. 1909-39. *1756*

—. Agricultural Labor. Farmers. Labor Disputes. Ranchers. Washington (Yakima Valley). 1910-36. *2569*
—. Alaska (Nome). American Federation of Labor. Labor Unions and Organizations. 1905-20. *2208*
—. Alexander, Moses. Idaho. Labor reform. 1914-17. *2152*
—. American Federation of Labor. Armies. Labor Disputes. Nevada (Goldfield). Western Federation of Miners. 1904-08. *2287*
—. American Federation of Labor. Louisiana. Marine Transport Workers. Sailors' Union. Strikes. United Fruit Company. 1913. *2193*
—. American Federation of Labor. One Big Union. Washington. 1919. *2179*
—. Arizona (Bisbee). Labor Unions and Organizations. Mining. Strikes. 1917. *2186*
—. Arizona (Bisbee). Shattuck Mine. Strikes. 1917. *2285*
—. Boulder Canyon Project. Colorado River. Hoover Dam. Nevada. Strikes. 1931. *2433*
—. Boulder Canyon Project. Hoover Dam. Nevada. Six Companies, Inc. Strikes. 1931. *2434*
—. Brotherhood of Timber Workers. Emerson, Arthur L. Labor Disputes. Louisiana, western. Lumber and Lumbering. Texas, eastern. 1900-16. *2207*
—. Brotherhood of Timber Workers. Louisiana. Lumber and Lumbering. Race Relations. Texas. 1910-13. *2215*
—. California (Fresno). Clyde, Edward M. Freedom of speech. 1911. *2151*
—. California (Fresno). Freedom of speech. 1910-11. *2138*
—. California (San Diego). Freedom of speech. Mexico (Tijuana). 1911-12. *2162*
—. California (Wheatland). Migrant Labor. State Government. Strikes. Trials. 1913-17. *2198*
—. Canada. Communist Party. Labor Unions and Organizations. Scarlett, Sam. 1900-41. *278*
—. Canada, western. Labor Unions and Organizations. Radicals and Radicalism. 1905-14. *1786*
—. Cigar industry. Pennsylvania (McKees Rocks, Pittsburgh). Pressed Steel Car Company. Steel Industry. Strikes. 1909-13. *2235*
—. City Politics. Freedom of speech. Iowa (Sioux City). Short, Wallace. 1918-24. *2134*
—. Coal Mines and Mining. Colorado. Strikes. 1927. *2411*
—. Courts. Labor. New Jersey (Paterson). Progressivism. Quinlan, Patrick. 1913-17. *2275*
—. Crime and Criminals. Fletcher, Benjamin Harrison. Labor. Longshoremen. Negroes. 1910-33. *437*
—. Crime and Criminals. Idaho. Labor Law. State Government. 1917-33. *2088*
—. Davis, David W. Idaho. Nonpartisan League. Public opinion. Socialist Party. 1919-26. *2405*
—. Domestics. Labor Unions and Organizations. Progressive era. Street, Jane (letter). 1917. *2224*
—. Farmers. Orchards. Strikes. Washington (Yakima Valley). 1933. *2568*
—. Freedom of Speech. Labor Disputes. Washington (Aberdeen). 1911-12. *2150*
—. Freedom of Speech. Political Protest. Pratt, N. S. Washington (Spokane). 1909-10. *2132*
—. Grady, John (letters). Haywood, William Dudley. Schuyler, Mont. USSR. 1921-22. *2425*
—. Immigrants. New Jersey (Paterson). Strikes. Textile Industry. Violence. 1913. *2254*
—. Immigrants. New York (Little Falls). Strikes. Textile Industry. Women. 1912. *2269*
—. Justice Department. Labor Unions and Organizations. Nebraska. Public opinion. World War I. 1915-20. *2113*
—. Kansas. Prisons. 1915-20. *1993*

Industrial Workers

—. Kansas. Radicals and Radicalism. Red Scare. Trials. 1917-19. *2148*
—. Kansas (Wichita). Labor Unions and Organizations. Oil Industry and Trade. Trials. *United States* v. *C. W. Anderson et al.* (US, 1919). World War I. 1917-19. *2171*
—. Labor. 1909-20. *2292*
—. Labor Disputes. Mines. Nevada (Goldfield, Tonopah). 1901-22. *2262*
—. Labor Disputes. Ohio (Toledo). Radicals and Radicalism. US Bureau of Investigation. 1918-20. *1906*
—. Labor Unions and Organizations. Nebraska. 1914-20. *2283*
—. Labor Unions and Organizations. Strikes. Washington (Yakima Valley). 1933. *2496*
—. Metal and Machinery Workers' Industrial Union (440). Ohio (Cleveland). 1918-50. *1826*
—. Ohio (Akron). Rubber. Strikes. 1913. *2290*
—. *Verona* (vessel). Violence. Washington. Washington (Everett). 1916. *2122*
Industrialists. Courts. Juvenile Delinquency. Middle Classes. Philanthropy. Reform. 1890-99. *1472*
—. Labor history (sources). New York (Buffalo). Police reports. Strikes. 1890-1913. *152*
Industrialization *See also* Economic Growth; Modernization.
—. Acculturation. Educational Reform. Ideology. Pennsylvania. Social control. 1880-1910. *1420*
—. Adams, Henry Brooks. George, Henry. Ideology. Philosophy of History. Social criticism. 1870's-1910's. *1073*
—. Attitudes. Canada, western. Labor Unions and Organizations. Radicals and Radicalism. Working class. 1897-1919. *1745*
—. Attitudes. Rhode Island (Pawtucket). Strikes. Textile industry. Working Class. 1824. *821*
—. Bureau of Indian Affairs. Emmons, Glenn L. Indians (reservations). 1953-60. *2661*
—. Carpetbaggers. Civil rights. Constitutional conventions, state. Reconstruction. South. 1867-69. *1021*
—. *Charities and the Commons* (periodical). Pennsylvania. *Pittsburgh Survey* (1909). Social Surveys. 1907-14. *2029*
—. Child labor. Iowa. Labor Unions and Organizations. Women. 1900's. *1984*
—. Colleges and Universities. Educational Reform. North Carolina, University of. Social Change. 1850-75. *1406*
—. Compulsory education. Frontier and Pioneer Life. Social change. 1870's. *1408*
—. Compulsory education. Labor. 1890-1930. *2326*
—. Cooke, Parsons. Massachusetts (Ware). Missions and Missionaries. Puritans. 19c. *906*
—. Domestics. Female Charitable Society. Girls. Massachusetts (Salem). 1800-40. *882*
—. Immigration. Kamprath, William B. Labor (unskilled). New York (Buffalo). Vocational education. 1907-21. *2312*
—. Immigration. Morality. Muckraking. Periodicals. 1900-09. *2047*
—. Knights of Labor. Knights of St. Crispin. Labor Unions and Organizations. Ontario (Toronto). 1856-90. *1318*
—. Knights of St. Crispin. Loyalism. Massachusetts (Lynn). Radicals and Radicalism. Working class. 1820-90. *1298*
—. Labor Unions and Organizations. Negroes. Race Relations. 19c-20c. *1819*
—. Political Attitudes. Populism. Slavery. South. 1860-96. *1382*
—. Railroads. Women. 1890's. *962*
Industry *See also* individual industries, e.g. Iron Industry, etc.; Industrialization; Management.
—. Air pollution. Cities. Energy. Legislation. 1880-1920. *38*
—. Attitudes. National War Labor Board. Public Policy. Sex roles. Wages. Women. World War I. 1918-19. *2191*
—. Beverly School. Education, Experimental Methods. Massachusetts. 1900-17. *2321*
—. Canada. Economic Reform. George, Henry. Poverty. Progress (concept). Social gospel. ca 1879-99. *975*
—. Commission on Industrial Accidents. Provincial Government. Quebec. Workmen's Compensation. 1890-1978. *1584*
—. Defense Policy. Federal Policy. Labor Unions and Organizations. World War II. 1939-41. *2593*
—. Feminism. Legislation. Progressivism. 1919-33. *2401*

Subject Index

—. Mortality. Muckraking. Occupations. Reform. 1890-1910. *2112*
—. Railroads. Strikes. 1877. *1353*
Inequality. Labor movement. Monopolies. 1830's-1982. *825*
Infants. Child-rearing. Democracy. Family. Spock, Benjamin *(Baby and Child Care)*. 1917-50. *1589*
Ingraham, Joseph Holt. Clergy. Episcopal Church, Protestant. Novels. Penal reform. Public Schools. Tennessee (Nashville). 1847-51. *584*
Inoculation. City Government. Editorials. Franklin, James. Freedom of the Press. Massachusetts (Boston). *New England Courant* (newspaper). Smallpox. 1721. *535*
—. Franklin, Benjamin. Medical Research. 1730-50. *532*
Insanity. *See* Mental Illness.
Institute for Advanced Study. History. Mathematics. New Jersey (Princeton). Research. Social Sciences. 1930-79. *2435*
Institutionalization. Handicapped children. 1900. *1944*
Institutions. Charities. Ontario (Toronto). Social work. ca 1875-1920. *246*
—. Civil rights. Negroes. Organizations. Sit-ins. South. 1960. *2868*
—. Commons, John R. Conservatism. Labor history. 1884-1935. *156*
—. Democracy. New Left. 1965-72. *2707*
—. Progressivism. Social Organization. Violence. 1880's-1910's. *2082*
Insurrections. *See* Rebellions.
Integration *See also* Assimilation.
—. Alabama (Tuscaloosa). Civil rights movement. Clergy. 1976-77. *2796*
—. Baseball. Brooklyn Dodgers (team). Montreal Royals (team). Negroes. Press. Rickey, Branch. Robinson, Jackie. 1945-47. *2690*
—. Brewer, Fisk Parsons. Higher education. South Carolina, University of. 1873-76. *1438*
—. Civil rights movement. Public policy. 1945-76. *1623*
—. Community control. Education. Negroes. New York City (Brooklyn). Politics. 1882-1902. *1181*
—. DuBois, W. E. B. Ideology. Negro Renaissance. 1903-74. *1543*
—. Equal rights. Prison reform. Women. 1820's-1900. *1451*
—. Litigation. NAACP. North. Public schools. 1954-75. *2841*
—. Missions and Missionaries. Presbyterian Church. 1562-1977. *15*
Intellectuals. Africa. Blyden, Edward Wilmot. Ethnic consciousness. Negroes. ca 1832-65. *557*
—. Anarchism and Anarchists. Kropotkin, Pëtr. Lectures. Russia. 1897-1901. *1501*
—. Attitudes. Letters. Slavery. Social Classes. 1830-60. *790*
—. Catholic Church. Democracy. Liberalism. Racism. 1924-59. *1560*
—. Class struggle. Equality. French language. Nationalism. Quebec. 1960's-70's. *2693*
—. Collectivism. National Association of Corporation Schools. Steinmetz, Charles Proteus. Utopias. 1910-17. *1950*
—. Colleges and Universities. Liberalism. Political Attitudes. Socialism. 1880-95. *1072*
—. Colleges and Universities. Political Protest. Radicals and Radicalism. Students. 1963-77. *2750*
—. Communist Party. Culture. Negroes. New York City (Harlem). Popular Front. 1935-39. *2562*
—. Crosby, Ernest Howard. Reformers. Tolstoy, Lev Nikolaevich, Count. 1878-1907. *334*
—. Cruse, Harold. Culture. Methodology. Negroes. 1910-75. *1519*
—. DuBois, W. E. B. Elites. Negroes. Talented Tenth strategy. 1895-1919. *2090*
—. Europe. Social change. Utopias. 1930's-70's. *1675*
—. Farmers. Idaho. McKaig, Robert Raymond. Nonpartisan League. North Dakota. ca 1920-45. *2406*
—. Freedmen. Negroes, free. Politics. Social theory. South. 1870's-90's. *1274*
—. Friends, Society of. Humanism. Penn, William. Radicals and Radicalism. 1650-1700. *474*
—. Law Enforcement. Radicals and Radicalism. World War I. 1914-20. *2158*
—. Liberalism. Lippmann, Walter. Politics. 1890-1974. *427*
—. Literature. Pacifism. Tolstoy, Leo. ca 1890's. *1080*

Interpersonal Relations

—. Socialism. Socialist Party. 1901-17. *1953*
Intelligence service. Canada, western. Conspiracy. Labor Disputes. One Big Union. Royal Canadian Mounted Police. 1919. *1612*
Inter-American Institute. Americas (North and South). Bureau of Indian Affairs. Collier, John. Indians. 1930's-50's. *1662*
Interest Groups *See also* Political Factions; Pressure Groups.
—. Civil rights. Federal Policy. Populism. Private sector. Racism. Wallace, George C. 1960's. *2899*
—. Compulsory Education. Educational reform. Pennsylvania. Social Problems. 1880-1911. *200*
—. Decisionmaking. Federal Government. Legislation. Politics. Women. 1970's. *2911*
—. Environmental policy. Great Britain. 1970's. *2742*
—. Local government. Political Reform. Social change. Taxation. 1960's. *2947*
—. Political Participation. Poor. 1960's. *2732*
Intergovernmental Relations. Apportionment. Attorneys General. Courts. Election Laws. Voting Rights Act (US, 1965; Section 5). 1965-77. *2801*
—. Executive Power. Local Government. Ohio. Police. State Government. 1902-25. *2100*
Interior Department. Apache Indians (Chiricahua, Ojo Caliente). Fort Sill. Land allotment. Oklahoma. Prisoners of war. War Department. 1909-13. *2170*
—. Ballinger-Pinchot Controversy. Conservation. Fisher, Walter Lowrie. 1911-13. *1957*
—. Homesteading and Homesteaders. Minnesota (Duluth). Public Housing. Resettlement Administration. 1936-47. *2510*
Internal Migration. *See* Migration, Internal.
International Brotherhood of Boilermakers, Iron Shipbuilders and Helpers of America. California (Sausalito). Discrimination. *James* v. *Marinship* (California, 1945). Labor. Negroes. Shipbuilding. 1940-48. *2653*
International Brotherhood of Pulp, Sulphite, and Paper Mill Workers. American Federation of Labor. Labor Unions and Organizations. Militancy. Paper industry. 1933-35. *2615*
International Colored Unity League. Harrison, Hubert H. Journalism. Liberty League of Negro Americans. Negroes. New York City (Harlem). Socialist Party. 1911-27. *1676*
International Institute. Ethnic Groups. Pluralism. Social services. 1910-79. *74*
International Labor Defense. Communist Party. Georgia (Atlanta). Herndon, Angelo. Negroes. 1932-37. *2548*
International Labor Organization. Foreign Policy. Isolationism. New Deal. Perkins, Frances. Roosevelt, Franklin D. 1921-34. *2570*
International Ladies' Garment Workers' Union. American Federation of Labor. Jews. Labor Unions and Organizations. 1930's. *1740*
—. Congress. London, Meyer. Socialism. 1914-22. *2212*
—. Garment industry. Texas. Women. 1933-50. *1770*
International Law *See also* Boundaries; Military Law; Refugees; Slave Trade.
—. American Peace Society. 1816-1978. *223*
International Longshoremen's and Warehousemen's Union. Far Western States. Labor Unions and Organizations. 1934-37. *2481*
—. Race relations. South Central and Gulf States. 1866-1920. *2236*
International Relations. Foreign Policy. Isolationism. League of Nations Association. Peace. 1934-38. *2466*
International Steel Cartel. Foreign policy. Imports. Labor. Steel Workers Organizing Committee. US Steel Corporation. 1937. *2538*
International Union of Catholic Women's Leagues (congress). Catholic Church. Italy (Rome). Quebec. Woman suffrage. 1922. *1734*
International Workingmen's Association. Boston Eight Hour League. Labor Unions and Organizations. Marxism. McNeill, George. New York. Steward, Ira. 1860-89. *1307*
International Workingmen's Association (Section 15). Louisiana (New Orleans). 1871. *1293*
International, 1st. Marxism. Sorge, Friedrich Adolph. 1852-1906. *1305*
International, 2d. Political Leadership. Socialist Party. 1889-1914. *1053*
Internment. Japanese Americans. Martial law. Tule Lake Camp. World War II. 1941-44. *2641*
Interpersonal Relations *See also* Human Relations.

Interpersonal Relations

—. Abolition movement. "Boston Clique". Garrison, William Lloyd. Individualism. 1830-40. *646*
Interstate Commerce Commission. Business. Federal Regulation. Freight and Freightage. Hepburn Act (US, 1906). 1905-06. *2282*
Intervention. Federal Government. House of Representatives. Negroes. Population. South. Voting Rights Act (US, 1965). 1940-75. *2802*
Interventionism. Anglo-Saxonism. Reform. Strong, Josiah. 1885-1915. *71*
Intolerance (film). Attitudes. Films. Progressivism. 1916. *1965*
Investments. Bartol, Cyrus. Massachusetts (Boston, Manchester). Real estate. Transcendentalism. 1850-96. *1015*
Iodine. Goiter. Goler, George W. New York (Rochester). Water supply. 1923-32. *2395*
Iowa *See also* North Central States.
—. Adams, Mary Newbury. Self-image. Social status. Women. 1850-1900. *1042*
—. Agricultural Adjustment Act (1933). Federal Programs. New Deal. Wallace, Henry Agard. 1933-34. *2537*
—. Bloomer, Amelia. Savery, Anne. State Politics. Woman suffrage. Woodhull, Victoria Claflin. 1868-72. *1111*
—. Bureau of Indian Affairs. Christianity. Indian-White Relations. Schools. Winnebago Indians. 1834-48. *850*
—. Cattlemen. Corn Belt Meat Producers' Association. Hepburn Act (US, 1906). 1900-10. *2229*
—. Child labor. Industrialization. Labor Unions and Organizations. Women. 1900's. *1984*
—. Colleges and Universities. Grinnell College. Sex roles. Women. 1884-1917. *221*
—. Educational Reform. Public schools. 1890-1900. *1421*
—. Educators. Modernization. Public schools. 1890-1900. *1422*
—. Forssell, G. D. Lectures. Minnesota. Progressivism. Social Conditions. 1890-95. *957*
—. Haymarket Riot (1886). Socialism. Trumbull, Matthew Mark. 1826-94. *296*
—. Kneeland, Abner. Salubria (community). Utopias. 1827-44. *914*
—. Men. Referendum. Voting and Voting Behavior. Woman suffrage. 1916. *2159*
—. Political parties. Prohibition. State Politics. 19c. *1445*
Iowa (Davenport). Cummins, Albert B. Government regulation. Law Enforcement. Liquor. Riots. State Politics. 1907-08. *1880*
Iowa (Des Moines). NAACP. 1915-30. *2015*
Iowa (Granger). Federal Subsistence Homesteads Corporation. Ligutti, Luigi. New Deal. 1934-51. *2585*
Iowa (New Icaria, Corning). Cabet, Etienne. France. Icarians. Utopias. 1852-98. *1502*
Iowa (Sioux City). City Politics. Freedom of speech. Industrial Workers of the World. Short, Wallace. 1918-24. *2134*
Iowa State Agricultural College. Curricula. Farmers' Alliance. State Legislatures. Wallace, Henry. 1884-91. *1416*
Iowa (Volga Township). Communia (settlement). German Americans. Swiss Americans. Utopias. 1847-64. *926*
IQ tests. California. Educational Tests and Measurements. Ethnic groups. Progressivism. Students. 1917-21. *2300*
Ireland *See also* Great Britain.
—. Anti-Catholicism. Urbanization. 1920-29. *2363*
—. Antislavery Sentiments. Hibernian Anti-Slavery Society. Webb, Richard Davis. 1837-61. *736*
—. Antislavery Sentiments. Irish Americans. O'Connell, Daniel. 1824-44. *735*
—. Brownson, Orestes A. Catholic University of Ireland. Great Britain. Newman, John Henry. 1853-54. *911*
—. Counter culture. ca 1970's. *2993*
—. George, Henry. Great Britain. Hyndman, Henry M. Land Reform. Marxism. 1882-89. *1057*
Ireland (Belfast). Abolition movement. Douglass, Frederick. Presbyterian Church. Smyth, Thomas. 1846. *697*
Ireland (Limerick). Irish Americans. Labor Unions and Organizations. Leadership. McCarthy, Patrick Henry. Youth. 1863-80. *402*
Irish Americans. Abolitionists. Immigrants. Nationalism. ca 1830's-50's. *715*
—. Antislavery Sentiments. Ireland. O'Connell, Daniel. 1824-44. *735*

SUBJECT INDEX

—. Boycotts. Immigrants. Labor. New York City. Working conditions. 1880-86. *1311*
—. California (San Francisco). Catholic Church. City Politics. Progressivism. Yorke, Peter C. 1900's. *2114*
—. Catholic Church. Immigrants. McMahon, Patrick. Poor. Quebec (Quebec). St. Bridget's Home. 1847-1972. *244*
—. Collar Laundry Union. Industrial Relations. New York (Troy). Women. 1864-69. *1352*
—. DuBois, W. E. B. Education. Ethnic studies. German Americans. Woodson, Carter G. 1649-1972. *188*
—. Ethnicity. Land League. Radicals and Radicalism. Reform. Working class. 1880-83. *997*
—. German Americans. Local politics. New York City. Riots. Temperance Movements. 1857. *585*
—. Ireland (Limerick). Labor Unions and Organizations. Leadership. McCarthy, Patrick Henry. Youth. 1863-80. *402*
—. Jones, Mary Harris. Labor Disputes. Speeches, Addresses, etc. 1870's-1920's. *170*
—. Knights of Father Mathew. Missouri (St. Louis). Temperance Movements. 1850-1930. 1900H. *259*
Iron Industry *See also* Steel Industry.
—. Finnish Americans. Labor Unions and Organizations. Minnesota. Minnesota (Mesabi Range). Radicals and Radicalism. 1914-17. *2253*
Irrigation. Farmers. Idaho. Progressive Party. State Politics. 1914-22. *2012*
Isolationism. American Peace Mobilization. Communist Party USA. World War II (antecedents). 1939-41. *2651*
—. Foreign Policy. International Labor Organization. New Deal. Perkins, Frances. Roosevelt, Franklin D. 1921-34. *2570*
—. Foreign Policy. International Relations. League of Nations Association. Peace. 1934-38. *2466*
Italian Americans. American Committee on Italian Migration. Illinois (Chicago). Immigration. Reform. 1952-67. *2701*
—. Immigrants. Labor movement. ca 1880-1927. *175*
—. Labor. Radicals and Radicalism. Rhode Island. 1905-30. *1753*
Italy *See also* Tuscany, Venetian Republic, etc.
—. Beccaria, Cesare. Capital punishment. Penal reform. 1764-97. *890*
—. Colonial policy. Garvey, Marcus. Pan-Africanism. Universal Negro Improvement Association. USA. 1920-23. *2371*
—. Dohrn, Anton. Hyde, Ida H. Naples Zoological Station. Scientific Experiments and Research. Women. 1896-97. *1434*
Italy (Rome). Catholic Church. International Union of Catholic Women's Leagues (congress). Quebec. Woman suffrage. 1922. *1734*

J

Jackson, Andrew. Adams, John Quincy. Democratic Party. Elections (presidential). Slavery. Whig Party. 1828-44. *737*
Jackson, Helen Hunt. Centennial Celebrations. Indian-White Relations. National Self-image. 1881. 1975. *1079*
Jackson, Helen Hunt *(Century of Dishonor)*. Human Rights. Indian-White Relations. 1879-85. *1045*
Jackson, Helen Hunt *(Century of Dishonor; Ramona)*. California, southern. Indians (agencies). 1881-84. *1048*
Jackson, Helen Hunt *(Ramona)*. California. Indians. Mission Indians. Ponca Indians. Removals, forced. Schurz, Carl. 1873-84. *1051*
—. Indians. 1882-84. *951*
Jackson, James Caleb. Adventists. Hydrotherapy. Medical reform. New York (Dansville). White, Ellen G. 1864-65. *1470*
Jackson, Luther P. Civil rights. Hancock, George B. Negroes. Virginia. Young, Plummer B. 1930-45. *1583*
Jackson, Maynard. City Politics. Georgia (Atlanta). Negroes. Political Leadership. 1965-77. *2847*
Jacksonianism. Democratic Party. Equal opportunity. Social theory. Wealth. 1836-46. *537*
Jacobs, Pattie Ruffner. Alabama. Woman suffrage. 1900's-20. *2145*
Jails. *See* Prisons.

Jewish Peace

Jamaica. Garvey, Marcus. Ideology. Negroes. Pan-Africanism. 1887-1927. *401*
James, Ada. Political Equality League. Referendum. Willis, Olympia Brown. Wisconsin. Woman Suffrage Association. 1912. *2141*
James, Henry *(Bostonians)*. Feminism. Fuller, Margaret. Hawthorne, Nathaniel *(The Blithedale Romance)*. Politics. Sex. 19c. *795*
James v. *Marinship* (California, 1945). California (Sausalito). Discrimination. International Brotherhood of Boilermakers, Iron Shipbuilders and Helpers of America. Labor. Negroes. Shipbuilding. 1940-48. *2653*
James, William. Ethnic groups. Imperialism. Race Relations. 1899-1910. *2033*
—. Individualism. Political Reform. 1870's-1900. *341*
Jamison, Alice Lee. American Indian Federation. Bureau of Indian Affairs. Collier, John. Indians. New Deal. Political activism. 1930's-50's. *354*
Janesville Associated Charities. Attitudes. Middle Classes. Poor. Wisconsin. 1870-1900. *1450*
Jansson, Erik. Bishop Hill Colony. Daily life. Illinois. Letters. Swedish Americans. Utopias. 1847-56. *939*
Janssonists. Bishop Hill Colony. Illinois. Immigrants. Swedish Americans. Utopias. 1846-60. *920*
—. Bishop Hill Colony. Illinois. Letters. Swedes. 1847. *936*
Japan. Berry pickers. California (El Monte). Foreign Relations. Mexico. Strikes. 1933. *2522*
Japanese. Attitudes. Canada. Citizenship. USA. World War II. 1941-58. *1730*
—. British Columbia. Chinese. Immigration. Suffrage. 1935-49. *1725*
—. Immigration. Miller, Kelly. Negroes. Race Relations. 1906-24. *1601*
Japanese Americans. Agricultural labor. California (San Joaquin Valley). Mexican Americans. Nisei Farmers League. United Farm Workers Union. 1971-77. *2926*
—. Arizona (Salt River Valley). Depressions. Farmers. Race Relations. 1934-35. *2469*
—. Baptists. Discrimination. Resettlement. World War II. 1890-1970. *1651*
—. Chinese Americans. Discrimination. Economic Conditions. Nativism. Social Status. 1840's-1978. *83*
—. Civic Unity Committee. Defense industries. Negroes. Race relations. Washington (Seattle). World War II. 1940-45. *2624*
—. Internment. Martial law. Tule Lake Camp. World War II. 1941-44. *2641*
Japanese Americans (Nikkei). Lumber and Lumbering. Oregon (Toledo). Pacific Spruce Corporation. Riots. 1925-26. *2453*
Japanese Americans (Sansei). Assimilation. Social Customs. 1968-76. *2758*
Japanese Canadians. Alberta. Chinese Canadians. Racism. 1920-50. *1657*
—. British Columbia. Canada. Chinese Canadians. Military Service. World War II. 1939-45. *2647*
—. British Columbia. Minorities. Public schools. 1900-72. *1562*
—. Canada. Race Relations. Removals, forced. World War II. 1890's-1940's. *1694*
Japanese (Issei). Agriculture. Arizona (Salt River Valley). Discrimination. Race Relations. 1934-35. *2582*
Jay, John, II. Antislavery Sentiments. Civil War. Episcopal Church, Protestant. 1840-65. *773*
Jefferson, Thomas. Antislavery Sentiments. Coles, Edward. Illinois. 1809-68. *689*
—. Attitudes. Civil Rights. Declaration of Independence. Fourth of July. Negroes. 1776. 1800-50. *724*
—. Calhoun, John C. Slavery. South. 1830's-40's. *787*
—. Education. Great Britain. Milton, John. 17c-19c. *833*
—. Education. Illinois. Lincoln, Abraham. 1820-62. *835*
—. Feminism. Fuller, Margaret. Journalism. Social criticism. 1840-50. *272*
Jehovah's Witnesses. Church and State. Government, Resistance to. Persecution. Theology. 1870's-1960's. *136*
Jesus People. Christianity. Youth Movements. 1960's. *2695*
Jewish Peace Fellowship. Peace Movements. World War II. 1943. *2654*

Jewish Welfare Federation of Detroit. Charities. Michigan. Social Organizations. 1926. *2367*
Jews *See also* Judaism.
—. Abolition movement. Reform. 1850-63. *750*
—. American Federation of Labor. International Ladies' Garment Workers' Union. Labor Unions and Organizations. 1930's. *1740*
—. American, Sadie. Congress of Jewish Women. Solomon, Hannah G. Women. World Parliament of Religions. World's Columbian Exposition (Chicago, 1893). 1893. *1488*
—. Americanization. Educational Alliance. New York City (Lower East Side). 1890-1914. *2310*
—. Ancker, Henrietta. California (San Bernardino). Charities. Henrietta Hebrew Benevolent Society. 1870-91. *1479*
—. Anti-Nazi Movements. Boycotts. Fram, Leon (reminiscences). League for Human Rights. Michigan (Detroit). 1930's-40's. *2507*
—. Assimilation. Education. Labor movement. Socialism. 1880's-1945. *100*
—. Boycotts. Christianity. Elementary Education. New York City. Religion in the Public Schools. 1905-06. *2298*
—. Brin, Fanny Fligelman. Minnesota (Minneapolis). Peace. Women. 1913-60's. *453*
—. Charities. Galveston Plan of 1907. Immigration. Industrial Removal Office. Migration, Internal. New York City. 1890-1914. *1476*
—. Child Welfare. Family. Foster homes. Immigration. New York City. Working class. 1900-05. *2061*
—. Cincinnati Union Bethel. Ohio. Settlement houses. 1838-1903. *225*
—. Civil rights movement. South. 1954-70. *2823*
—. Discrimination. Negroes. Racism. 1890-1915. *1938*
—. Educational Reform. New York City. Richman, Julia. Women. 1880-1912. *289*
—. Garment industry. Labor movement. 1920's-30's. *1751*
—. Hillquit, Morris. New York City. Socialism. 1890's-1933. *1713*
—. Labor movement. 1890's-1930's. *1790*
—. Labor movement. Public opinion. Stereotypes. 1880's-1915. *2211*
—. Labor Unions and Organizations. Malkiel, Theresa Serber. New York City. Socialist Party. Women. 1900's-14. *2035*
—. Lawyers. Social mobility. 20c. *1522*
—. Leftism. 1880's-1970's. *61*
—. New York City. Social Classes. Socialism. United Hebrew Trades. 1877-1926. *1340*
Jim Crow laws. Arkansas. Negroes. Political Leadership. Segregation. 1890's. *1193*
—. Constitution League. Discrimination. Foraker, Joseph B. Hepburn Bill, Warner-Foraker Amendment (1906). Negroes. Railroads. Washington, Booker T. (and Committee of 12). 1906. *1919*
—. Discrimination, Employment. NAACP. Negroes. Tennessee (Memphis). 1900-37. *1750*
—. Negroes. Railroads. Separate coach bills. South Carolina. 1880-98. *1215*
Jingoism. American Federation of Labor. Fascism. Gompers, Samuel. Immigration. Racism. 1850-1924. *394*
Johns Hopkins Hospital Training School for Nurses. Addams, Jane. Hampton, Isabel. Illinois (Chicago). Maryland (Baltimore). Nurses and Nursing. Professionalization. Social Work. 1889-1910. *1461*
Johnson, Andrew. American Freedmen's Inquiry Commission. Civil War. Freedmen. 1863. *1260*
—. Civil rights. Governors. Negroes. Tennessee. 1862-65. *972*
—. Discrimination. Freedmen's Bureau. Law. Reconstruction. 1865-66. *1226*
Johnson, Andrew N. Alabama (Mobile). Black Capitalism. Editors and Editing. Republican Party. Tennessee (Nashville). 1890-1920. *273*
Johnson, Charles S. Art. Harlem Renaissance. Racism. 1920's. *2426*
—. Fisk University. Negroes. Race relations. UNESCO. 1900-56. *346*
Johnson, James Weldon. NAACP. Negroes. White, Walter F. 1909-35. *1647*
Johnson, Lyndon B. Attitudes. Civil rights. Negroes. 1930's-68. *1531*
—. Civil rights. Negro Suffrage. Political Reform. 1960's. *2855*

—. Civil Rights movement. Long, Huey P. Radicals and Radicalism. South. 1920-70. *1706*
—. Great Society. Public Welfare. Rhetoric. 1963-65. *2764*
—. Rhetoric. Social movements. War on Poverty. 1965-66. *2954*
Johnson, Lyndon B. (administration). Civil rights. Negroes. 1963-69. *2866*
—. Great Society. Public Welfare. Social Conditions. 1964-76. *2936*
Johnson, Owen *(Stover at Yale)*. Football. Muckraking. Progressivism. 1911-20. *1998*
Joint Committee on the Care of Motherless Infants. Child Welfare. New York City. 1860-1907. *1475*
Jones, Alonzo Trevier. Adventists. Illinois. Religious liberty. Sunday. World's Columbian Exposition (Chicago, 1893). 1893. *1492*
Jones, Charles Colcock. Evangelicalism. Race Relations. South. Utopias. 1804-63. *567*
—. Missions and Missionaries. Presbyterian Church. Slavery. South. 1825-63. *776*
Jones Family (group). Oklahoma (Cleveland, Pottawatomie counties). Sedition. Trials. Working Class Union. World War I. 1917. *2155*
Jones, James Parnell. Antislavery Sentiments. Civil War. Friends, Society of. Maine. Military Service. 1850's-64. *320*
Jones, Mary Harris. Irish Americans. Labor Disputes. Speeches, Addresses, etc. 1870's-1920's. *170*
Jones, Samuel Milton. City Government. Ohio (Toledo). Reform. 1850's-1904. *280*
Jordan, David Starr. Antimilitarism. Democracy. World War I. 1898-1917. *1867*
Joseph W. Cumming, James S. Harper and John Ladeveze v. School Board of Richmond County, Ga. (US, 1899). Discrimination, Educational. Harlan, John Marshall. Public Schools. Supreme Court. ca 1896-1907. *1194*
Journal of Negro History (periodical). Historiography. Negroes. Woodson, Carter G. 1916-75. *1708*
Journalism *See also* Editors and Editing; Films; Freedom of the Press; Newspapers; Periodicals; Press; Reporters and Reporting.
—. Abolition Movement. Cornish, Samuel E. *Freedom's Journal* (newspaper). Negroes. Presbyterian Church. 1820's-59. *467*
—. Abolition Movement. Feminism. Lowry, Sylvanus B. Minnesota. Swisshelm, Jane Grey. 1815-84. *385*
—. Advertising. Ethics. Progressivism. 1890's-1920's. *1910*
—. Anthony, Susan B. *Revolution* (newspaper). Stanton, Elizabeth Cady. Woman Suffrage. 1868-70. *1108*
—. *Appeal to Reason* (newspaper). Kansas (Girard). Muckraking. Socialism. 1901-20. *2041*
—. Barry, Robertine (pseud. Françoise). Feminism. Gleason, Anne-Marie (pseud. Madeleine). Quebec. Social Conditions. 1900-19. *1535*
—. Boosterism. California (Los Angeles). City Government. Progressivism. Willard, Charles Dwight. 1888-1914. *319*
—. Canada. Catholic Church. Social Theory. Somerville, Henry. 1915-53. *284*
—. Civil Rights. Columbus *Enquirer-Sun* (newspaper). Georgia. Harris, Julian LaRose. 1920's. *2439*
—. Douglass, Frederick. New York City. Racism. 1841-47. *408*
—. Family. Feminism. Tarbell, Ida M. 1900-30. *1688*
—. Feminism. Fuller, Margaret. Jefferson, Thomas. Social criticism. 1840-50. *272*
—. Feminism. Swisshelm, Jane Grey. ca 1835-84. *328*
—. Harrison, Hubert H. International Colored Unity League. Liberty League of Negro Americans. Negroes. New York City (Harlem). Socialist Party. 1911-27. *1676*
—. Labor Unions and Organizations. Marxism. Negroes. Political protest. Randolph, A. Philip. ca 1911-75. *382*
—. Lectures. Minnesota. Political activism. Populism. Valesh, Eva McDonald. 1866-1956. *345*
—. McKelway, Alexander. Murphy, Edgar Gardner. Page, Walter Hines. South. 1890-1916. *1876*
Journals. *See* Diaries; Periodicals.
Judaism. *See also* Jews.
—. Agriculture. Krauskopf, Joseph. Reform. 1880's-1923. *2098*

—. Beth Ha Medrosh Hagodol synagogue. Colorado (Denver). Kauvar, Charles E. H. Progressivism. 1902-71. *428*
Judges *See also* Courts; Lawyers.
—. Attitudes. School Integration. South. 1954-70. *2833*
—. California (Los Angeles). Children's Court of Conciliation. Lindsey, Benjamin Barr. 1894-1943. *357*
Judicial Administration. Black, Hugo. Constitutional Amendments (1st). Due process. 1936-79. *1717*
—. Juvenile delinquency. Progressivism. Sex discrimination. 1890's-1910's. *2072*
—. Labor. Populism. Supreme courts, state. Western States. 1893-1902. *1024*
Judicial process. Civil rights. Constitutional Law. Douglas, William O. Liberalism. Supreme Court. 1928-77. *1715*
—. Civil rights. Equality. Liberty. 1960-79. *2772*
—. Great Britain. Law. Plea bargaining. 18c-20c. *128*
—. Juvenile Courts. 19c-1970's. *112*
Judicial reform. Congress. Progressivism. Supreme Court. Taft, William H. 1920-25. *2400*
Judicial review. Civil Rights. Constitutional Amendments (14th). Supreme Court. 19c-20c. *144*
Judiciary. Butler Bill. Local politics. Proslavery Sentiments. 1850's. *663*
Junior Colleges. California. Lange, Alexis. Progressivism. 1890-1920. *2308*
Junior High Schools. Democratic Party. Educational reform. Ethnic groups. Massachusetts (Somerville). Middle Classes. Progressivism. 1912-24. *2335*
Jury. Constitutional Amendments (1st). Decisionmaking. 1940's-75. *1732*
—. Constitutions, State. Lobbying. South Carolina. Women. 1921-67. *1731*
Justice. Courts. Freedmen's Bureau. Negroes. Reconstruction. Texas. 1865-68. *1146*
—. Douglass, Frederick. Ethnicity. 19c. 1975. *657*
Justice Department. Florida. Labor recruitment. New York City. Peonage. Quackenbos, Mary Grace. Turpentine industry. 1905-10. *2267*
—. Industrial Workers of the World. Labor Unions and Organizations. Nebraska. Public opinion. World War I. 1915-20. *2113*
—. Lawsuits. Negroes. School Integration. South. 1957-68. *2811*
Juvenile Courts. Colorado (Denver). Lindsey, Benjamin Barr. 1901-20's. *1902*
—. Education. Probation. 1899-1917. *2073*
—. Judicial Process. 19c-1970's. *112*
Juvenile Delinquency *See also* Child Welfare; Children; Juvenile Courts.
—. Agriculture. Boys. Fairfield School for Boys. Ohio. Reformatories. Values. 1840-84. *242*
—. Brown, Willis. Indiana (Gary). 1910-12. *2075*
—. Courts. Industrialists. Middle Classes. Philanthropy. Reform. 1890-99. *1472*
—. Girls. Massachusetts (Lancaster). Socialization. State Industrial School for Girls. 1856-1905. *1443*
—. House of Refuge for Colored Children. Negroes. Pennsylvania (Philadelphia). 1828-60's. *872*
—. Judicial Administration. Progressivism. Sex discrimination. 1890's-1910's. *2072*
—. Ontario (Penetanguishene). Reformatories. 1880-1905. *1618*

K

Kahn, Albert. Architecture. Automobile Industry and Trade. Factories. Ford, Henry. 1869-1942. 1900H. *1779*
Kalispel Indians. Far Western States. Indian Claims Commission. 1950-65. *1549*
Kamprath, William B. Immigration. Industrialization. Labor (unskilled). New York (Buffalo). Vocational education. 1907-21. *2312*
Kansas *See also* Western States.
—. Antislavery Sentiments. *Arabia* (vessel). Arms Trade. Hoyt, David Starr. New England Emigrant Aid Company. 1855-59. *741*
—. Antislavery Sentiments. Editors and Editing. Newspapers. Religion. Rhetoric. 1855-58. *680*
—. Attitudes. Boundaries. Civil War (antecedents). Missouri. Slavery. 1854-56. *634*

Kansas
— . Catholic Church. Protestantism. Religion in the Public Schools. 1861-1900. *1409*
— . Clemens, Gaspar Christopher. Socialism. 1885-90's. *959*
— . Congress. Constitutions, State. English, William H. Proslavery Sentiments. 1857-58. *629*
— . Conservatism. Constitutional law. New Deal. Newspapers. Supreme Court. 1934-35. *2502*
— . Court of Visitation. Populism. Railroads. Republican Party. State Legislatures. 1890-1900. *1386*
— . DeBernardi, G. B. Depressions. Freedom Colony. Labor Exchange. Utopias. 1894-1905. *1510*
— . Economic Reform. Hoffman, Christian Balzac. Socialism. 1872-1915. *389*
— . Economic reform. Politics. Rightmire, William F. Southern Farmers' Alliance. 1886-92. *1380*
— . Elites. Negroes. Politics. Republican Party. Waller, John Lewis. 1878-1900. *468*
— . Feminism. Nichols, Clarina I. H. (papers). 1839-56. *338*
— . Feminism. Nichols, Clarina I. H. (papers). 1857-85. *337*
— . Industrial Workers of the World. Prisons. 1915-20. *1993*
— . Industrial Workers of the World. Radicals and Radicalism. Red Scare. Trials. 1917-19. *2148*
— . Land Reform. Rogers, John R. Union Labor Party. 1838-1901. *1023*
— . Lease, Mary Elizabeth. Political Speeches. Populism. 1871-1933. *293*
— . Liberty bonds. Mennonites. Pacifism. Vigilantism. World War I. 1918. *2146*
— . Newspapers. Political Commentary. Populism. State Politics. Vincent, Henry. 1886-91. *1384*
— . Populism. Progressivism. Social Classes. 1885-1917. *10*
Kansas City Board of Fire Underwriters. Antitrust. Courts. Fire insurance. Law enforcement. Missouri. 1889-99. *1336*
Kansas (Elk County). Crandall, Prudence. Spiritualism. Temperance Movements. Women's rights. 1877-95. *1487*
Kansas (Girard). *Appeal to Reason* (newspaper). Journalism. Muckraking. Socialism. 1901-20. *2041*
Kansas (Newton). Historic Peace Churches (meeting). Krehbiel, H. P. Pacifism. 1935-36. *2534*
Kansas, northeastern. Colorado, northeastern. Hardin, William J. Langston, Charles H. Negro suffrage. 1865-67. *1133*
Kansas State Penitentiary. Barnard, Kate. Oklahoma. Prisons. Reform. 1908-09. *1974*
Kansas (Wichita). Industrial Workers of the World. Labor Unions and Organizations. Oil Industry and Trade. Trials. *United States v. C. W. Anderson et al.* (US, 1919). World War I. 1917-19. *2171*
Kansas-Nebraska Act (US, 1854). Antislavery Sentiments. Hall, Lyman W. Ohio (Portage County). Political Parties. 1852-56. *619*
— . Emigration. Slavery. Wisconsin. 1850's. *690*
— . Founding Fathers. Lincoln, Abraham. Reconstruction. Republicanism. 1854-65. *1058*
Kauvar, Charles E. H. Beth Ha Medrosh Hagodol synagogue. Colorado (Denver). Judaism. Progressivism. 1902-71. *428*
Keeble, Marshall. Evangelism. Race relations. 1878-1968. *412*
Keeney, Frank. Coal Mines and Mining. United Mine Workers of America. West Virginia. 1916-31. *1755*
Keep America Out of War Congress. Antiwar Sentiment. Socialist Party. Thomas, Norman. Villard, Oswald Garrison. World War II (antecedents). 1938-41. *2501*
Kefauver, Estes. Drugs. Federal regulation. Senate Subcommittee on Antitrust and Monopoly. South. 1950's-60's. *2939*
Keller, Helen. New Jersey (Montclair). Socialism. Speeches, Addresses, etc. 1890-1913. *1916*
Keller, Kent. Congress. Illinois. Liberalism. New Deal. 1930-42. *2608*
Kellogg, Merritt (diary). Adventists. Medicine (practice of). Trall, Russell Thacher. 1844-77. *894*
Keniston, Kenneth. Abolition Movement. Pacifism. Violence. 1830-65. *644*
Kennedy, Jane. Antiwar Sentiment. Civil rights. Oral history. Political Protest. Vietnam War. Women. 1964-77. *2724*

Kennedy, John F. Civil rights. Congress. Democratic Party. 1960-63. *2840*
— . Civil rights. Executive Power. Legislation. 1961-64. *2858*
— . Domestic Policy. Mental Retardation Facilities and Community Mental Health Centers Construction Act (US, 1963). Politics. Social Security Act (US, 1935; amended, 1963). 1961-63. *2976*
— . Mississippi. Negroes. Political Protest. Voting Rights Act (US, 1965). 1960-72. *2863*
— . New Left. Nixon, Richard M. Popular culture. Social change. 1960-69. *2754*
Kennon, Robert F. Governors. Louisiana. Reform. 1948-56. *2674*
Kentucky *See also* South; South Central and Gulf States.
— . Abolition Movement. Breckinridge, Robert J. Breckinridge, William Lewis. Constitutions, State. Emancipation Party. Presbyterians. 1849. *676*
— . Allen, Robert McDowell. Food Adulteration and Inspection. Progressivism. Scovell, Melville Amasa. 1898-1916. *2125*
— . American Tobacco Company. Elections (congressional). Populism. 1886-92. *1365*
— . Antislavery Sentiments. Clergy. Racism. 1791-1824. *603*
— . Antislavery sentiments. Pendleton, James Madison. Tennessee. 1849-60. *674*
— . Attitudes. Colonization. Slavery. South. 1816-50. *602*
— . Barkley, Alben. Gambling. Louisville Churchmen's Federation. Progressivism. 1917-27. *2438*
— . Beckham, John C. W. McCreary, James B. Progressivism. State Government. Willson, Augustus E. 1899-1915. *1894*
— . Berea College. Education. Negroes. 1858-1908. *1225*
— . Breckinridge, Mary. Frontier Nursing Service. Nurses and Nursing. 1925-65. *1559*
— . Breckinridge, Robert J. Emancipation. State Politics. 1830-49. *677*
— . Breckinridge, Robert J., Jr. Breckinridge, William C. P. Courts. Elections. Negroes. Testimony. 1866-69. *1096*
— . Canada. Courts. Extradition. Fugitive slaves. Happy, Jesse. Testimony. 1793-1838. *748*
— . Civil Rights. Negroes. Newspapers. Reconstruction. 1866-72. *1176*
— . Civil War. Croxton, John Thomas. Law. Military Service. Republican Party. 1855-74. *392*
— . Courts. Debts. Desha, Joseph. 1819-26. *823*
— . Debts. Law Reform. Legislation. 1790-1839. *824*
— . Education. Negroes. 1800-1954. *216*
— . Education, Finance. Negroes. Segregation. State Government. 1865-1954. *1178*
— . Election Laws. Goebel, William. Government Regulation. Railroads. Taylor, William S. 1887-1900. *961*
— . Freedmen's Bureau. Noble, Thomas. Race Relations. Reconstruction. Schools. 1865-70. *1190*
— . Frontier and Pioneer Life. Medical Education. Mitchell, Thomas Duche. Reform. 1809-65. *325*
— . McChesney, Henry V. Morrow, Edwin P. Political Campaigns (gubernatorial). Prohibition. Stanley, Augustus Owsley. 1915. *1873*
— . Negro Suffrage. Political Parties. 1865-82. *1177*
— . Political Reform. Progressivism. Stanley, A. O. State Politics. 1902-19. *1897*
— . Populism. State Politics. 1870-1900. *1367*
Kentucky (Bell County, London). American Civil Liberties Union. Civil rights. Miners. Trials. 1932-38. *2601*
Kentucky (Bell, Harlan counties). Coal Mines and Mining. Labor Disputes. Political Corruption. 1920-39. *2489*
Kentucky (Boone, Bourbon counties). Fugitive Slave Act (US, 1850). Michigan (Cass County). Slaveholders. 1830-60. *786*
Kentucky Deaf and Dumb Asylum. Connecticut Asylum for the Deaf and Dumb. Federal government. Public Welfare. 1819-26. *901*
Kentucky Equal Rights Association. Breckinridge, Madeline McDowell. Federation of Business and Professional Women's Clubs. Woman suffrage. 1908-20. *2157*
Kentucky Illiteracy Commission. Education. Illiteracy. Kentucky (Rowan County). Stewart, Cora Wilson. 1910-20. *2325*

Kjelt
Kentucky (Louisville). Bingham, Robert Worth. City government. Progressivism. Reform. 1905-10. *1926*
— . Housing. NAACP. Segregation. Supreme Court. 1914-17. *2126*
— . Housing. Poverty. Progressivism. 1900-10. *1927*
— . Negroes. School Integration. 1954-77. *2799*
— . Woman Suffrage. 1828-1920. *124*
Kentucky (Rowan County). Education. Illiteracy. Kentucky Illiteracy Commission. Stewart, Cora Wilson. 1910-20. *2325*
Kern, John W. Labor Law. Senate. Workman's Compensation Act (US, 1916). 1908-17. *2221*
Kesey, Ken. Counter Culture. LSD. Political Theory. Wolfe, Thomas Kennerly, Jr. 1964-68. *2992*
Keynes, John Maynard. Depressions. Frankfurter, Felix. New Deal. Public works. 1932-35. *2473*
Kibbey, Joseph H. Arizona. Schools. Segregation. 1908-12. *2309*
Kidnapping. Idaho (Twin Falls). O'Hare, Kate Richards. Socialism. Speeches, Addresses, etc. Utah. 1921. *2404*
Kilby, Thomas E. Alabama. Coal. Strikes. United Mine Workers of America. 1890-1929. *2448*
Killebrew, Joseph Buckner. Agrarianism. New South movement. South. ca 1870-1910. *1026*
Kilpatrick, William Heard. Blakely Institute. Dewey, John. Georgia. Progressive education. 19c-20c. *2301*
Kimball, Sarah Melissa Granger. Mormons. Utah. Woman Suffrage. 15th Ward Relief Society. 1818-98. *397*
Kindergarten. Curricula. Morality. Progressive education. 1860-1920. *184*
— . Feminism. Motherhood. Progressivism. 1860-1920. *1932*
King, Martin Luther, Jr. Abernathy, Ralph. Alabama (Birmingham). Civil rights. Demonstrations. Shuttlesworth, Fred L. 1956-79. *2809*
— . Alabama (Birmingham). Civil Rights. Negroes. Nonviolence. Political Protest. 1962. *2843*
— . Alabama (Montgomery). Boycotts. Leadership. Negroes. New York City (Harlem). Powell, Adam Clayton, Jr. 1941-56. *307*
— . Christianity. Civil Rights. Transcendentalism. 1840's-50. 1950's-60. *2815*
— . Civil Disobedience. Nonviolence. Race relations. 1954-68. *2891*
— . Civil rights. Negroes. Nonviolence. 1950's-68. *2826*
— . Civil rights. Political Protest. 1955-68. *2854*
— . Civil rights movement. Gandhi, Mahatma. Nonviolence. Political Protest. 1950's-60's. *2878*
— . Civil rights movement. Gandhi, Mahatma. Social change. 1959-68. *2822*
— . Civil Rights Movement. Negroes. Social Conditions. 1968-79. *2806*
— . Civil Rights Organizations. Leadership. Negroes. Southern Christian Leadership Conference. 1957-73. *2828*
— . Race relations. 1968. *2901*
King, Martin Luther, Jr. ("Letter from Birmingham Jail"). Civil rights. Literature. Rhetoric. 1963. *2807*
— . Negroes. Nonviolence. Rhetoric. 1963. *2869*
King, Martin Luther, Jr. (tribute). Civil Rights. Ebenezer Baptist Church. Georgia (Atlanta). 1968. 1977. *2842*
Kingston Penitentiary. Architecture. Attitudes. Boston Prison Discipline Society. Crime and Criminals. Howard, John. Ontario. ca 1830-50. *899*
— . Artisans. Convict labor. Machinists. Ontario. Petitions. 1833-36. *826*
Kinsey, Alfred C. Attitudes. Scientific Experiments and Research. Sex. ca 1940-77. *2678*
Kinsolving, George Herbert. Councils and Synods. Delegates. Episcopal Church, Protestant. Texas. Veto. Women. 1921-70. *2347*
Kiowa Indians. Agricultural policy. Dawes Act (US, 1887). Federal government. Indians (reservations). Oklahoma. 1869-1901. *1062*
— . Baptists. Crawford, Isabel. Indians. Missions and Missionaries. Oklahoma (Wichita Mountains). Women's American Baptist Home Missionary Society. 1893-1961. *393*
Kirkland, William S. Freedmen's Bureau. Reconstruction. Texas. 1865-70. *1261*
Kjelt, Ole. Čačić, Tomo. Ethnic Groups. Krat, Pavlo. Leftism. Mäkelä, A. B. Political Protest. Puttee, Arthur. Scarlett, Sam. 1907-34. *1561*

Klyce, Scudder. Dewey, John (letters). Feminism. 1915-31. *1536*
Knappen, Howard P. Farmers Educational and Cooperative Union of America. North Dakota. 1913-20. *2260*
Kneeland, Abner. Iowa. Salubria (community). Utopias. 1827-44. *914*
Knights of Father Mathew. Irish Americans. Missouri (St. Louis). Temperance Movements. 1850-1930. 1900H. *259*
Knights of Labor. American Federation of Labor. Federation of Organized Trades and Labor Unions. Labor Unions and Organizations. Ohio (Columbus). 1881-86. *1309*
—. Baughman Brothers (company). Boycotts. Richmond Typographical Union. Virginia. 1886-88. *1290*
—. Canada. Catholic Church. Labor Unions and Organizations. Taschereau, Elzéar-Alexandre. 1884-94. *1350*
—. Catholic Church. Gibbons, James. Social Theory. Taschereau, Elzéar Alexandre. 1880's. *1351*
—. Central Labor Union. Eight-hour day. Labor Unions and Organizations. Massachusetts (Boston). Strikes. 1886. *1321*
—. City Politics. Elections, municipal. Negroes. Political Reform. Virginia (Richmond). 1886-88. *1303*
—. Coal Mines and Mining. Race Relations. United Mine Workers of America. West Virginia, southern. 1880-94. *1140*
—. Gould, Jay. Missouri (Sedalia). Modernization. Railroads. Strikes. 1885-86. *1292*
—. Grenell, Judson. Labadie, Joseph. Michigan (Detroit). Socialist Labor Party. 1877-86. *1334*
—. Industrial Relations. Politics. Rhode Island. 1880's. *1289*
—. Industrialization. Knights of St. Crispin. Labor Unions and Organizations. Ontario (Toronto). 1856-90. *1318*
—. Labor Unions and Organizations. Negroes. South. 1880-87. *1187*
—. Labor Unions and Organizations. Pennsylvania (Scranton). Politics. Powderly, Terence V. 1876-1900. *361*
—. Powderly, Terence V. Temperance Movements. 1878-93. *1356*
—. Race relations. South. 1880-87. *1217*
—. South. ca 1885-88. *1328*
Knights of St. Crispin. Industrialization. Knights of Labor. Labor Unions and Organizations. Ontario (Toronto). 1856-90. *1318*
—. Industrialization. Loyalism. Massachusetts (Lynn). Radicals and Radicalism. Working class. 1820-90. *1298*
Know-Nothing Party. Anti-Catholicism. Maine. Morrill, Anson P. Nativism. Working class. 1854-55. *588*
—. Antislavery Sentiments. Massachusetts. Nativism. Republican Party. Voting and Voting Behavior. 1850's. *538*
—. Louisiana. Political leadership. Social Classes. 1845-60. *542*
—. Political Parties. 1853-56. *559*
Kollontai, Aleksandra. Communism. Norway. Propaganda. Russia. World War I. 1915-16. *2046*
Koreshan Unity. Florida (Lee County). Politics. Sects, Religious. Teed, Cyrus Reed. Utopias. 1880-1909. *1516*
—. Harmony Society. Mexico (Topolobampo). Olombia. Utopias. 1879-93. *1500*
Krat, Pavlo. Čačic, Tomo. Ethnic Groups. Kjelt, Ole. Leftism. Mäkelä, A. B. Political Protest. Puttee, Arthur. Scarlett, Sam. 1907-34. *1561*
—. Canada. Socialism. Ukrainian Canadians. ca 1902-52. *365*
Krauskopf, Joseph. Agriculture. Judaism. Reform. 1880's-1923. *2098*
Krehbiel, H. P. Historic Peace Churches (meeting). Kansas (Newton). Pacifism. 1935-36. *2534*
Kropotkin, Pëtr. Anarchism and Anarchists. Intellectuals. Lectures. Russia. 1897-1901. *1501*
Krutch, Joseph Wood. Ecology. Materialism. Values. 1920's-70. *1660*
Krzycki, Leo. Labor Unions and Organizations. Polish Americans. Radicals and Radicalism. Socialist Party. 1900's-66. *391*
Ku Klux Klan. Anti-Catholicism. Clergy. Protestantism. Republican Party. Rhode Island. 1915-32. *2441*
—. Anti-Catholicism. Protestantism. Saskatchewan. 1927-30. *1547*
—. Antilabor sentiments. Canada, western. Elections. Immigration. 1921-30's. *1603*
—. Arizona. 1921-25. *2338*
—. Local Politics. Nevada. Vigilantism. 1920-29. *2449*
—. Negroes. Reconstruction. South Carolina. 1868-71. *1076*
—. Oklahoma (Lawton). 1921-29. *2355*
—. Oregon (Tillamook). Social change. 1920's. *2456*
Kurikka, Matti. Australia. Canada. Finland. Utopias. 1883-1915. *1707*
—. British Columbia (Harmony Island). Finnish Americans. Utopias. 1901-05. *1628*
—. Canada. Editors and Editing. Finnish Canadians. Mäkelä, A. B. Newspapers. Socialism. 1900-32. *464*
Kyforuk, Peter. Alberta (Edmonton). Farmer's Union of Alberta. Manitoba. Ukrainian Labour-Farmer Association. 1912-30's. *1828*

L

La Raza Unida Party. Chavez, Cesar. Mexican Americans. 1968-73. *2711*
Labadie, Joseph. Grenell, Judson. Knights of Labor. Michigan (Detroit). Socialist Labor Party. 1877-86. *1334*
Labor *See also* Agricultural Labor; Capitalism; Child Labor; Collective Bargaining; Communism; Employment; Industrial Relations; Labor Law; Migrant Labor; Socialism; Strikes; Syndicalism; Unemployment; Unemployment Insurance; Wages; Working Class; Working Conditions.
—. Abolition Movement. Freedmen. Race relations. Slavery. 1830-63. *613*
—. Agricultural College Act (US, 1862). Agriculture. Mechanics' Mutual Protection (society). New York. People's College. 1843-60's. *1427*
—. Alabama. Freedmen. Plantations. Sharecropping. 1865-67. *1198*
—. American Federation of Labor. Carmody, John. Civil Works Administration. New Deal. 1933-34. *2584*
—. American Federation of Labor. Gompers, Samuel. Socialism. 1893-95. *1304*
—. Antislavery Sentiments. Great Britain. Greeley, Horace. Marx, Karl. New York Tribune. 1851-62. *764*
—. Atlantic Provinces. Boardinghouses. Government. Merchant Marine. ca 1850's-90's. *996*
—. Automobile Industry and Trade. Indiana. New Deal. Ohio. United Automobile Workers of America. 1935-40. *2542*
—. Behavior. Management, scientific. 1870-1920. *1330*
—. Boycotts. Immigrants. Irish Americans. New York City. Working conditions. 1880-86. *1311*
—. British Columbia. Legislation. Natural resources. New Democratic Party. Public Policy. Social Democracy. Taxation. 1972-75. *2942*
—. Brockwood Labor College. Education. Fincke, William. 1919-37. *1614*
—. Bulosan, Carlos. Literature. Marxism. 1931-56. *432*
—. Bureaucracies. Corporations. Poor. Social Classes. War on Poverty. 1960's. *2925*
—. California (Sausalito). Discrimination. International Brotherhood of Boilermakers, Iron Shipbuilders and Helpers of America. *James* v. *Marinship* (California, 1945). Negroes. Shipbuilding. 1940-48. *2653*
—. Canada. Christianity. Fiction. Social gospel. 1890's. *1354*
—. Canada, western. Communist Party. Evans, Arthur. 1930's. *1658*
—. Capitalism. Leisure. Social Organization. 1890-1920's. *151*
—. Cerasoli, Mose (memoir). Granite Industry. Labor Disputes. Vermont. 1913-38. *1807*
—. Civil War. Mississippi. Negroes. Vicksburg (battle). 1862. *1220*
—. Civil Works Administration. New Deal. 1933-39. *2484*
—. Civil-Military Relations. Publicity. War Manpower Commission. Women. World War II. 1942-45. *2650*
—. Collective Bargaining. France. Great Britain. 18c-20c. *167*
—. Compulsory education. Industrialization. 1890-1930. *2326*
—. Congress of Industrial Organizations. New Hampshire (Berlin). Nonpartisan League. Political Parties. 1932-36. *2497*
—. Courts. Industrial Workers of the World. New Jersey (Paterson). Progressivism. Quinlan, Patrick. 1913-17. *2275*
—. Crime and Criminals. Fletcher, Benjamin Harrison. Industrial Workers of the World. Longshoremen. Negroes. 1910-33. *437*
—. Economic Conditions. New Deal. Texas. 1929-39. *2573*
—. Economic Regulations. National Recovery Administration. Negroes. South. Wages. 1933-34. *2576*
—. Editorials. *Miners' Magazine*. Poetry. Songs. Western Federation of Miners. 1900-07. *2293*
—. Environmental Protection Agency. Equal Employment Opportunity Commission. Occupational Safety and Health Act (US, 1970). Safety. Women. 1970-76. *2698*
—. Family. Social Organization. Women. 1600-1970's. *54*
—. Feminism. Love. Speeches, Addresses, etc. Stanton, Elizabeth Cady. 1868-70. *992*
—. Finnish Americans. Immigrants. Minnesota (Smithville). Socialism. Work People's College. 1900-20. *2315*
—. Food and Drug Administration. Great Plains. Radicals and Radicalism. Social change. Veblen, Thorstein. World War I. 1918. *1922*
—. Foreign policy. Imports. International Steel Cartel. Steel Workers Organizing Committee. US Steel Corporation. 1937. *2538*
—. Garment Industry. Massachusetts (Boston). Women. 1869. *1287*
—. Garment Industry. New York City. Women. 1831-69. *820*
—. *Globe*. Liberalism. Newspapers. Ontario. 1885-90. *1332*
—. Industrial Workers of the World. 1909-20. *2292*
—. Italian Americans. Radicals and Radicalism. Rhode Island. 1905-30. *1753*
—. Judicial Administration. Populism. Supreme courts, state. Western States. 1893-1902. *1024*
—. Letters. Negroes. Riley, William R. Tennessee. United Mine Workers of America. 1892-95. *1201*
—. Local Politics. Missouri. Racism. Reconstruction. St. Louis *Daily Press* (newspaper). 1864-66. *1339*
—. Luther, Seth. Reform. Rhode Island. 1795-1863. *342*
—. Match industry. Quebec (Hull). Syndicat Catholique des Allumeftières. Women. 1919-24. *1775*
—. Mechanization. Production control. 19c-20c. *165*
—. Mexican Americans. Southwest. 1896-1915. *1908*
—. Mining. Western states. 1892-1904. *1335*
—. Negroes. Prisons. Tennessee. 1830-1915. *96*
—. New Deal. Radicals and Radicalism. Working class. 1930's. *2524*
—. New Jersey (Passaic). Strikes. Textile industry. Working conditions. 1875-1926. *2366*
—. New York (Rochester). Socialism. 1917-19. *1978*
—. Occupations. Sex discrimination. Social Change. 1950-70. *1813*
—. Red baiting. Socialism. Working conditions. 1871-1920. *154*
—. Reform. Social status. Women. 1830-60. *309*
—. Sex roles. Women's Liberation Movement. 19c-20c. *46*
—. Social change. South. 19c-20c. *150*
—. Violence. ca 1880-1920. *157*
Labor Church. Casson, Herbert N. Massachusetts (Lynn). Socialism. Working class. 1893-98. *1498*
Labor Department. Atlanta University. Negroes. Social Conditions. 1897-1907. *1964*
—. Lobbying. 1864-1913. *2219*
Labor Disputes *See also* Strikes.
—. Agricultural Labor. Farmers. Industrial Workers of the World. Ranchers. Washington (Yakima Valley). 1910-36. *2569*
—. Alberta (Drumheller Valley). One Big Union. United Mine Workers of America. 1919. *1827*
—. American Federation of Labor. Armies. Industrial Workers of the World. Nevada (Goldfield). Western Federation of Miners. 1904-08. *2287*
—. American Federation of Labor. Brotherhood of Painters and Decorators. Gompers, Samuel. Voluntarism. 1894-1900. *1306*

—. Automobile Industry and Trade. Canada. General Motors. 1927-30. *1798*
—. Brotherhood of Timber Workers. Emerson, Arthur L. Industrial Workers of the World. Louisiana, western. Lumber and Lumbering. Texas, eastern. 1900-16. *2207*
—. California (San Francisco). Chamber of Commerce Law and Order Committee. Chipman, Miner. 1915-19. *2233*
—. California (San Francisco). Law and Order Committee. Longshoremen. Strikes. 1916. *2234*
—. Canada, western. Conspiracy. Intelligence service. One Big Union. Royal Canadian Mounted Police. 1919. *1612*
—. Cerasoli, Mose (memoir). Granite Industry. Labor. Vermont. 1913-38. *1807*
—. Coal Mines and Mining. Kentucky (Bell, Harlan counties). Political Corruption. 1920-39. *2489*
—. Coal Mines and Mining. Mingo War. United Mine Workers of America. Violence. West Virginia (southern). 1919-22. *2389*
—. Congress of Industrial Organizations. New Deal. Newspapers. South. 1930-39. *2614*
—. Cotton. Hamilton Manufacturing Company. Massachusetts (Lowell). Social mobility. Textile Industry. Women. 1836-60. *818*
—. Factories. Industrial Technology. National Cash Register Company. 1895-1913. *2249*
—. Freedom of Speech. Industrial Workers of the World. Washington (Aberdeen). 1911-12. *2150*
—. Howard, Robert. Massachusetts (Fall River). Textile industry. 1860-85. *1346*
—. Industrial Workers of the World. Mines. Nevada (Goldfield, Tonopah). 1901-22. *2262*
—. Industrial Workers of the World. Ohio (Toledo). Radicals and Radicalism. US Bureau of Investigation. 1918-20. *1906*
—. Irish Americans. Jones, Mary Harris. Speeches, Addresses, etc. 1870's-1920's. *170*
—. Michigan (Battle Creek). Open shop movement. Post, Charles William. 1895-1920. *2239*
—. Norway. Norwegian Americans. Press. Thrane, Marcus. USA. 1886-94. *1285*
—. Pennsylvania (Tioga County). 1865-1905. *1326*
Labor Exchange. Colorado Cooperative Company. Communitarianism. Home Employment Cooperative Company. Politics. Pragmatism. 1890-1905. *1508*
—. DeBernardi, G. B. Depressions. Freedom Colony. Kansas. Utopias. 1894-1905. *1510*
Labor history. Commons, John R. Conservatism. Institutions. 1884-1935. *156*
Labor history (sources). Industrialists. New York (Buffalo). Police reports. Strikes. 1890-1913. *152*
Labor Law *See also* Child Labor; Collective Bargaining; Labor Unions and Organizations; Strikes.
—. American Federation of Labor. Buck's Stove and Range Company. Courts. 1907-11. *2222*
—. Courts. Discrimination, Employment. Women. 1876-1979. *43*
—. Crime and Criminals. Idaho. Industrial Workers of the World. State Government. 1917-33. *2088*
—. Ford Motor Company of Canada. Ontario (Windsor). United Automobile Workers (Canadian Region). 1946. *2682*
—. Kern, John W. Senate. Workman's Compensation Act (US, 1916). 1908-17. *2221*
Labor movement. Abolition Movement. Attitudes. North. 1820-65. *638*
—. American Federation of Labor. Bombing. California (Los Angeles). *Los Angeles Times.* McNamara case. Progressives. 1910-14. *2265*
—. Assimilation. Education. Jews. Socialism. 1880's-1945. *100*
—. Capitalism. 1860-1920. *164*
—. Garment industry. Jews. 1920's-30's. *1751*
—. Government. Labor Unions and Organizations. Voluntarism. 1890's-1930's. *1760*
—. Immigrants. Italian Americans. ca 1880-1927. *175*
—. Inequality. Monopolies. 1830's-1982. *825*
—. Jews. 1890's-1930's. *1790*
—. Jews. Public opinion. Stereotypes. 1880's-1915. *2211*
—. Marxism. Sorge, Friedrich Adolph. 1866-76. *1308*
—. Middle Classes. Schools, summer. South. Women. 1927-41. *1580*
—. Women. Working Conditions. 1840's. *828*

Labor Non-Partisan League. Legislation. Political representation. Working conditions. 1936-38. *2605*
Labor recruitment. Florida. Justice Department. New York City. Peonage. Quackenbos, Mary Grace. Turpentine industry. 1905-10. *2267*
Labor reform. Alexander, Moses. Idaho. Industrial Workers of the World. 1914-17. *2152*
—. California. Chinese. Constitutions, State. Federal Regulation. Workingmen's Party of California. 1877-82. *1358*
—. Canada. Royal Commission of Inquiry into the Relations between Capital and Labour. 1886-89. *1314*
—. Canada, western. Regionalism. Socialism. 1918-19. *1764*
—. Children. Progressivism. Rhetoric. 1904-16. *1917*
—. Coal Mines and Mining. Colorado. Roche, Josephine. Roosevelt, Franklin D. (administration). Social work. 1886-1976. *1772*
—. Illinois (Chicago). Morgan, Elizabeth Chambers. 1874-97. *1341*
—. Industrial Conference, 2d. Industrial democracy. Labor Unions and Organizations. Wilson, Woodrow. 1919-20. *2180*
—. Lowell Female Labor Reform Association. New England. Textile Industry. Women. 1845-47. *819*
—. New York (Little Falls). Strikes. Textile Industry. Women. 1912. *2268*
—. Progressivism. Social Classes. Women. 1882-1917. *2230*
—. Steel industry. Twelve-hour day. 1887-1923. *2384*
Labor Union of Alabama. Alabama. National Negro Labor Union. Negroes. Politics. Rapier, James T. Reconstruction. 1837-75. *1253*
Labor Unions and Organizations *See also* names of labor unions and organizations, e.g. American Federation of Labor, United Automobile Workers, etc.; Collective Bargaining; Labor Law; Strikes; Syndicalism.
—. Adventists. 1877-1903. *1344*
—. Agricultural Adjustment Administration. Depressions. Sharecroppers. Southern Tenant Farmers' Union. ca 1930's. *2602*
—. Agricultural Cooperatives. Farmers Educational and Cooperative Union of America. North Dakota (Burleigh County; Still). 1913-78. *2288*
—. Agricultural Cooperatives. Quebec. 1900-30. *1743*
—. Agricultural labor. 1900-79. *1781*
—. Agricultural labor. Boycotts. Race relations. South Carolina. 1886-95. *1196*
—. Agricultural Labor. California. National Industrial Recovery Act (US, 1933). 1933-34. *2495*
—. Alabama (Gadsden). 1930-43. *2549*
—. Alaska (Anchorage). Lewis, Lena Morrow. Railroads. Socialist Party. World War I. 1916-18. *2001*
—. Alaska (Douglas Island). Gold Mines and Mining. Strikes. Treadwell Mines. Western Federation of Miners. 1905-10. *2209*
—. Alaska (Nome). American Federation of Labor. Industrial Workers of the World. 1905-20. *2208*
—. Alberta (Cardiff, Edmonton). Chaban, Teklia. Coal Mines and Mining. Ukrainian Canadians. 1914-20's. *469*
—. American Federation of Labor. Communist Party. Radicals and Radicalism. Trade Union Unity League. 1933-35. *2494*
—. American Federation of Labor. Discrimination, Employment. Fair Employment Practices Committee. Federal Government. Shipbuilding. West Coast Master Agreement. World War II. 1939-46. *2627*
—. American Federation of Labor. Federation of Organized Trades and Labor Unions. Knights of Labor. Ohio (Columbus). 1881-86. *1309*
—. American Federation of Labor. Gompers, Samuel. Iglesias Pantín, Santiago. Puerto Rico. 1897-1920's. *2210*
—. American Federation of Labor. Gompers, Samuel. Military. Preparedness. Wilson, Woodrow. 1914-17. *2000*
—. American Federation of Labor. International Brotherhood of Pulp, Sulphite, and Paper Mill Workers. Militancy. Paper industry. 1933-35. *2615*
—. American Federation of Labor. International Ladies' Garment Workers' Union. Jews. 1930's. *1740*

—. Americanization. Indiana (Gary). Polish Americans. United States Steel Corporation. 1906-20. *2178*
—. Amherst Federation of Labor. Economic Conditions. Nova Scotia (Amherst). Strikes. 1901-31. *1801*
—. Anderson, Mary. Illinois (Chicago). Nestor, Agnes. Robins, Margaret Dreier. Women. Women's Trade Union League. Working conditions. 1903-20. *2190*
—. Antiwar sentiment. Socialism. World War I. 1914-17. *1982*
—. Arizona (Bisbee). Industrial Workers of the World. Mining. Strikes. 1917. *2186*
—. Attitudes. Canada, western. Industrialization. Radicals and Radicalism. Working class. 1897-1919. *1745*
—. Automobile Industry and Trade. Communist Party. 1920-33. *2394*
—. Automobile Industry and Trade. Communist Party USA. Michigan (Detroit). 1920's-1935. *1799*
—. Automobile Industry and Trade. League of Revolutionary Black Workers. Michigan (Detroit). Negroes. 1968-73. *2832*
—. Bell Telephone System. Labor Unions and Organizations. 1919-37. *1809*
—. Bell Telephone System. Labor Unions and Organizations. 1919-37. *1809*
—. *Boston Daily Evening Voice* (newspaper). Equality. Massachusetts. Race Relations. Working Class. 1864-67. *998*
—. Boston Eight Hour League. International Workingmen's Association. Marxism. McNeill, George. New York. Steward, Ira. 1860-89. *1307*
—. Brewing industry. Workmen's compensation. 1910-12. *2204*
—. British Columbia (Vancouver). Women. 1900-15. *1803*
—. British Columbia (Vancouver Island). Canadian Collieries (Dunsmuir) Limited. Coal Mines and Mining. Strikes. United Mine Workers of America. 1912-14. *2251*
—. Business. Canada. Federal Government. Social control. Unemployment Insurance Act (Canada, 1941). Wages. 1910-41. *2623*
—. Business. Economic planning. Government. Liberalism. 1920-40. *1788*
—. Business. New Deal. Taft-Hartley Act (US, 1947). Wagner Act (US, 1935). World War II. 1935-47. *1749*
—. California. Grape industry. Strikes. United Farm Workers Union. 1966-70. *2934*
—. California. Lobbying. Progressives. 1900-19. *1898*
—. California (Los Angeles). Congress of Industrial Organizations. Mexican Americans. 1938-50. *1521*
—. Canada. Catholic Church. Knights of Labor. Taschereau, Elzéar-Alexandre. 1884-94. *1350*
—. Canada. Civil service. Ideology. Middle Classes. 1918-28. *1820*
—. Canada. Communist Party. Industrial Workers of the World. Scarlett, Sam. 1900-41. *278*
—. Canada. Finns. Immigrants. Radicals and Radicalism. 1918-26. *2407*
—. Canada. Working class. 1845-75. *161*
—. Canada, western. Industrial Workers of the World. Radicals and Radicalism. 1905-14. *1786*
—. Canada (western). One Big Union. Radicals and Radicalism. Socialism. 1917-19. *1746*
—. Capitalism. Corporations. Federal government. General Electric Company. Liberalism. 1920-33. *2412*
—. Catholic Church. Polish Americans. Political Leadership. Progressivism. Socialism. Wisconsin (Milwaukee). 1900-30. *1663*
—. Central Labor Union. Eight-hour day. Knights of Labor. Massachusetts (Boston). Strikes. 1886. *1321*
—. Child labor. Industrialization. Iowa. Women. 1900's. *1984*
—. Chinese. Immigration. Powderly, Terence V. 1897-1902. *1052*
—. Christianity. Church and Social Problems. Socialism. 1880-1913. *2175*
—. Civil rights. Duke University Medical Center. Harvey, Oliver. North Carolina (Durham). 1930's-70's. *2938*
—. Civil Rights. Mexican Americans. North Central States. Social Organizations. 1900-76. *1659*
—. Class consciousness. Feminism. Great Britain. USA. Women's Trade Union League. 1890-1925. *2226*
—. Class struggle. South. 1810-1975. *162*

Labor Unions

—. Clerical workers. Women's Trade Union League. 1900-30. *1759*
—. Coal miners. Strikes. 1881-94. *1284*
—. Coal Mines and Mining. Davis, Richard L. Letters-to-the-editor. *National Labor Tribune.* Negroes. United Mine Workers of America. ca 1890-1900. *1139*
—. Coal Mines and Mining. Great Britain. Illinois. Legislation. Lobbying. 1861-72. *1312*
—. Coal Mines and Mining. One Big Union. Saskatchewan. 1907-45. *1782*
—. Coal Mines and Mining. Racism. Strikes. United Mine Workers of America. 1894-1920. *2272*
—. Coal Mines and Mining. Texas (Thurber). 1880's-1920's. *2238*
—. Colored Farmers' Alliance. Humphrey, R. M. Negroes. South. Strikes. 1876-91. *1150*
—. Colored National Labor Union. Florida. National Union of Negro Labor. Negroes. Race Relations. Reconstruction. 1865-75. *1259*
—. Communist Party. Mexico. 1935-39. *2540*
—. Communitarianism. 1880-1900. *1040*
—. Comte, Auguste. Foster, Frank K. Gompers, Samuel. Ideology. McGregor, Hugh. Spencer, Herbert. 1876-1900. *1295*
—. Congress of Industrial Organizations. Management. National Industrial Recovery Act (US, 1933). National Labor Relations Act (US, 1935). South. Textile Industry. 1933-41. *2613*
—. Constitutions. Editorials. New Deal. Periodicals. Supreme Court. 1935-37. *2503*
—. Corporations. Employment. Hoover, Herbert C. 1919-29. *2465*
—. Debs, Eugene V. Debs, Theodore. Indiana. Sebree, Shubert (letters). 1890-1930's. *418*
—. Defense Policy. Federal Policy. Industry. World War II. 1939-41. *2593*
—. DeLeon, Daniel. 1893-1908. *172*
—. Deportation. Immigrants. Mexican Americans. New Deal. 1930's. *2500*
—. Discrimination. Mexican Americans. North Central States. Steel Industry. 1919-45. *1802*
—. Discrimination. National Colored Labor Union. National Labor Union. Negroes. 1866-72. *1137*
—. Domestics. Industrial Workers of the World. Progressive era. Street, Jane (letter). 1917. *2224*
—. Ethnic groups. Ohio (Cincinnati). Working class. 1893-1920. *2247*
—. Far Western States. International Longshoremen's and Warehousemen's Union. 1934-37. *2481*
—. Feminism. Lobbying. Middle Classes. Suffrage. Women's Trade Union League. ca 1903-20. *1980*
—. Finnish Americans. Imatra I (association). New York City (Brooklyn). 1890-1921. *2011*
—. Finnish Americans. Iron Industry. Minnesota. Minnesota (Mesabi Range). Radicals and Radicalism. 1914-17. *2253*
—. Forest and Farm Workers Union. Hall, Covington. Louisiana. Lumber and Lumbering. Socialism. 1907-16. *2192*
—. German Americans. Progressivism. Socialism. Wisconsin. 1900-12. *2103*
—. Government. Labor movement. Voluntarism. 1890's-1930's. *1760*
—. Great Britain. Massachusetts. 1130-1790. *473*
—. Great Britain. Steel industry. 1888-1912. *155*
—. Green Corn Rebellion, 1917. Oklahoma. Radicals and Radicalism. Working Class Union. 1914-17. *2284*
—. Haywood, William Dudley. Socialism. 1890-1928. *371*
—. Ideology. Industrial Conference, 1st. Management. Wilson, Woodrow. 1919. *2225*
—. Illinois (Chicago; Back of the Yards). Meat packing industry. Polish Americans. Strikes. 1921. *2424*
—. Illinois (Pullman). Pullman strike. Railroads. 1880-94. *1325*
—. Indians. Navajo Indians. Southwest. 1958-78. *2945*
—. Industrial Conference, 2d. Industrial democracy. Labor Reform. Wilson, Woodrow. 1919-20. *2180*
—. Industrial Workers of the World. Justice Department. Nebraska. Public opinion. World War I. 1915-20. *2113*

—. Industrial Workers of the World. Kansas (Wichita). Oil Industry and Trade. Trials. *United States* v. *C. W. Anderson et al.* (US, 1919). World War I. 1917-19. *2171*
—. Industrial Workers of the World. Nebraska. 1914-20. *2283*
—. Industrial Workers of the World. Strikes. Washington (Yakima Valley). 1933. *2496*
—. Industrialization. Knights of Labor. Knights of St. Crispin. Ontario (Toronto). 1856-90. *1318*
—. Industrialization. Negroes. Race Relations. 19c-20c. *1819*
—. Ireland (Limerick). Irish Americans. Leadership. McCarthy, Patrick Henry. Youth. 1863-80. *402*
—. Jews. Malkiel, Theresa Serber. New York City. Socialist Party. Women. 1900's-14. *2035*
—. Journalism. Marxism. Negroes. Political protest. Randolph, A. Philip. ca 1911-75. *382*
—. Knights of Labor. Negroes. South. 1880-87. *1187*
—. Knights of Labor. Pennsylvania (Scranton). Politics. Powderly, Terence V. 1876-1900. *361*
—. Krzycki, Leo. Polish Americans. Radicals and Radicalism. Socialist Party. 1900's-66. *391*
—. Lewis, John Llewellyn. Reorganized United Mine Workers of America. 1920-33. *2357*
—. Libraries, public. Women. 1917-20. *2243*
—. *Life and Labor* (periodical). Women's Trade Union League. 1911-21. *2231*
—. Longshoremen. Louisiana (New Orleans). Race Relations. 1850's-1976. *176*
—. Lumber and Lumbering. Washington. Workmen's compensation. 1911. *2280*
—. Management. 1900-20. *2245*
—. Maryland. NAACP. Negroes. Teachers. 1930's. *2610*
—. Massachusetts (Lynn). Shoe Industry. Working class. 1895-1925. *2197*
—. Mexican Americans. Socialism. Texas. 1900-20. *2291*
—. Mormons. Utah. 1850-96. *1297*
—. National Trades and Labour Congress. Ontario (Kitchener). Quebec. Trades and Labour Congress of Canada. 1892-1902. *1805*
—. Negroes. Radicals and Radicalism. Socialism. 1865-1900. *1232*
—. New Deal. Radicals and Radicalism. 1930-39. *2546*
—. New York. Women. 1900-20. *2266*
—. New York. Women's Trade Union League. ca 1903-10. *2205*
—. New York City. Women's Trade Union League. 1903-14. *1924*
—. Ohio. Toledo Mechanics' Association. Willey, Austin. 1843. *827*
—. Pennsylvania (Allegheny-Kiskiminetas Valley). United Mine Workers of America. Violence. 1913-19. *2241*
—. Piedmont Plateau. Textile industry. 1901-32. *1792*
—. South. 1920's-74. *2930*
—. South. Textile industry. ca 1949-75. *1800*
—. United Electrical, Radio and Machine Workers of America. 1933-37. *2505*
—. Women. ca 1880-1925. *159*
—. Women's Trade Union League. 1870-1920. *53*
Labor (unskilled). Immigration. Industrialization. Kamprath, William B. New York (Buffalo). Vocational education. 1907-21. *2312*
Labour Party. Canada. Communist Party. Methodism. Smith, Albert Edward. Social Gospel. 1893-1924. *410*
—. Canada. Germany. Hjelt, Ole. Nazism. Norway. Socialism. 1908-28. *321*
Ladies' Physiological Institute of Boston and Vicinity. Health. Massachusetts. Middle Classes. Physiology. Women. 1848-59. *902*
LaFollette, Philip F. Depressions. New Deal. Progressivism. Roosevelt, Franklin D. Wisconsin Works Bill (1935). 1935. *2552*
—. Income (redistribution). National Progressives of America. Politics. Wisconsin. 1930-38. *2551*
LaFollette, Robert Marion. Nominations to Office. Presidency. Republican Party. Roosevelt, Theodore. 1910-12. *2022*
LaGuardia, Fiorello. City Politics. Civil rights. Liberalism. New York City. Powell, Adam Clayton, Jr. 1941-43. *2619*

Laity. Catholic Church. Fernandez, John F. O. Parishes. Virginia (Norfolk). 1815-20. *905*
Lancaster Industrial School for Girls. Girls. Massachusetts. Reformatories. ca 1850-70. *1444*
Lancaster, Joseph. English. Educational Policy. Public schools. *Richmond Enquirer* (newspaper). Ritchie, Thomas. Virginia. 1803-50. *840*
Lancaster Press. American Psychological Association. Equal opportunity. Psychologists for Social Action. Racism. 1969-73. *2885*
Lancaster, Samuel Christopher. Environment. Highway Engineering. Oregon (Columbia River Highway). ca 1900-41. *1931*
Land *See also* Agriculture; Eminent Domain; Land Tenure; Public Lands; Real Estate.
—. Communes. Considerant, Victor Prosper. France. Texas, northern. Travel. 1852-69. *265*
—. Crime and Criminals. George, Henry. Monopolies. Property. Technology. 19c-20c. *1033*
—. Firestone, Harvey S. Garvey, Marcus. Leases. Liberia. Negroes. Universal Negro Improvement Association. 1926. *2402*
—. Government. Saskatchewan. Settlement. 1929-35. *1796*
Land allotment. Apache Indians (Chiricahua, Ojo Caliente). Fort Sill. Interior Department. Oklahoma. Prisoners of war. War Department. 1909-13. *2170*
—. Arapaho Indians. Cheyenne Indians. Dawes Act (US, 1887). Fraud. Indians (agencies). Oklahoma. 1910's. *1888*
—. Competency commissions. Federal Policy. Indians. 1913-20. *2031*
—. Dawes Act (US, 1887). Indian Reorganization Act (US, 1934). Indian Rights Association. Indians. 1887-1934. *153*
Land (cessions). Cherokee Indians. Federal government. Georgia. Payne, John Howard (letter). Ross, John (chief). 1820's-30's. *575*
Land claims. California. Compensation. Indians. 1821-1963. *173*
Land League. Ethnicity. Irish Americans. Radicals and Radicalism. Reform. Working class. 1880-83. *997*
Land reform. Agrarianism. Southern Tenant Farmers' Union. 1933-40. *2511*
—. Alberta. Cooperative Commonwealth Federation. Leadership. Social credit. United Farmers of Alberta. 1930's. *1748*
—. Economic dependence. Negroes. Reconstruction. 1861-1900. *1155*
—. Genovese, Eugene D. Race relations. Reconstruction. Social Classes. South Carolina (Edgefield County). Woodward, C. Vann. 1865-90. *963*
—. George, Henry. Great Britain. Hyndman, Henry M. Ireland. Marxism. 1882-89. *1057*
—. Kansas. Rogers, John R. Union Labor Party. 1838-1901. *1023*
Land Tenure *See also* Real Estate.
—. Dawes Act (US, 1887). Eells, Edwin. Indians (agencies). Skokomish Indian Reservation. Washington. 1871-95. *970*
—. Dawes Act (US, 1887). Flathead Indian Reservation. Indians. Montana. Salish (Flathead) Indians. 1887-1904. *1075*
—. Freedmen's Village. Race Relations. Virginia (Arlington). 1872-1900. *1183*
—. Political Reform. Populism. Rogers, John R. State Politics. Washington. 1890-1900. *1363*
Land use. Billboards. Congress. Federal Regulation. Highway Beautification Act (US, 1965). 1965-79. *2716*
Landlords and Tenants *See also* Housing; Rent Control.
—. Economic Theory. George, Henry. Income. Population. Taxation. Technology. 1871-83. *1064*
Landscape architecture. Olmsted, Frederick Law. Reform. 19c. *955*
Lane, Charles. Alcott, Amos Bronson. Fruitlands (community). Massachusetts. Transcendentalism. Utopias. 1840-50. *922*
Lane, Julian. Civil rights. Demonstrations. Desegregation. Florida (Tampa). Fort, Clarence. Negroes. 1960. *2902*
Lane Seminary. Antislavery Sentiments. Debates. Ohio (Cincinnati; Walnut Hills). 1829-34. *692*
Lange, Alexis. California. Junior Colleges. Progressivism. 1890-1920. *2308*
Langevin, Adélard. Catholic Church. Church and State. French language. Manitoba. Politics. Private schools. 1890-1916. *1410*

Langevin, Louis Philippe Adélard. Catholic Church. Church schools. French language. Laurier, Wilfrid. Liberal Party. Prairie Provinces. Religion in the Public Schools. 1890-1915. *185*

Langston, Charles H. Colorado, northeastern. Hardin, William J. Kansas, northeastern. Negro suffrage. 1865-67. *1133*

Langston, John Mercer. House of Representatives. Negroes. State Politics. Virginia. 1849-97. *300*

Lanius, Henry E. Leader, George M. Legislation. Pennsylvania. Political leadership. Special education. 1820-1956. *1838*

Latimer, George. Freedom. Fugitive Slaves. Law. Massachusetts (Boston). Sewall, Samuel E. Shaw, Lemuel. ca 1790-1890. *784*

Lau v. Nichols (US, 1974). Bilingual education. California. Chacone-Moscone Bilingual Bicultural Education Act (1976). Civil Rights Act (US, 1964). Supreme Court. 1965-76. *2966*

Laurens, Henry. Philosophy. Republicanism. South Carolina. 1764-77. *483*

Laurier, Wilfrid. Catholic Church. Church schools. French language. Langevin, Louis Philippe Adélard. Liberal Party. Prairie Provinces. Religion in the Public Schools. 1890-1915. *185*

Lavell, Jeannette. Canada. Courts. Indians. Political participation. Women's Liberation Movement. 1869-1979. *2914*

Law *See also* terms beginning with the word legal; Constitutional Law; Courts; Criminal Law; Election Laws; International Law; Judges; Judicial Administration; Judicial Process; Jury; Lawyers; Legislation; Martial Law; Military Law; Police.

—. Abolitionists. Fugitive slaves. Government. Great Britain. Slave Trade. 1834-61. *774*
—. Abolitionists. Slavery. South. Supreme courts, state. 1810-60. *775*
—. Attitudes. Howard, Martin. Murder. North Carolina. Slavery. 1765-91. *515*
—. Birth control. Medicine and State. Public Policy. 19c. *40*
—. Burnside, Thomas E. Crawford, George W. Dueling. Georgia. 1809-28. *545*
—. California (San Francisco). Chinese Americans. Negroes. Political Leadership. Racism. 1865-75. *1184*
—. Canada. Civil rights. Mexico. USA. Violence. 18c-1974. *119*
—. Child labor. Illinois. Women. 1890-1920. *1955*
—. Child Welfare. Human Rights. Pressure Groups. 1978. *1639*
—. Citizenship. Constitutional Amendments (14th). Indians. ca 1776-1934. *131*
—. City Life. Environmentalism. Pennsylvania (Philadelphia). 1750-84. *496*
—. Civil War. Croxton, John Thomas. Kentucky. Military Service. Republican Party. 1855-74. *392*
—. Civil War. Mississippi. Negroes. Reconstruction. 1857-70. *114*
—. Civil War (antecedents). Constitutions. Slavery. 1830-60. *763*
—. Colleges and universities. School Integration. 19c-20c. *2886*
—. Discrimination. Freedmen's Bureau. Johnson, Andrew. Reconstruction. 1865-66. *1226*
—. Discrimination. Employment. Equal opportunity. Public policy. 1964-72. *2949*
—. Divorce. Massachusetts. Women. 1692-1786. *480*
—. Due process. Virginia. 1634-1700. *507*
—. Economic Conditions. Employment. Equal opportunity. Negroes. Occupations. 1954-72. *1785*
—. Educational policy. Equal opportunity. 1954-74. *2852*
—. Florida. Race Relations. Segregation. Social customs. 1865-1977. *141*
—. Frank, Jerome (review article). Harvard Law School. 1870-1930. *2341*
—. Freedom. Fugitive Slaves. Latimer, George. Massachusetts (Boston). Sewall, Samuel E. Shaw, Lemuel. ca 1790-1890. *784*
—. Great Britain. Judicial Process. Plea bargaining. 18c-20c. *128*
—. Housing and Urban Development Act (US, 1965, Section 23). Illinois (Chicago). Negroes. Public Housing Authority. Segregation. 1964-75. *2856*
—. Liberalism. Radicals and Radicalism. Social change. 1953-78. *1579*
—. Louisiana. Slavery. 1685-1766. *505*

—. Louisiana. Slavery. 1724-66. *508*
—. Mormons. Utah. ca 1830-80. *1104*
—. New Mexico. Social Customs. Women. 16c-1975. *1720*
—. Occupations. Segregation. Sex Discrimination. Women. 20c. *2910*
—. Racism. 1619-1896. *127*
—. Scandinavia. Self-awareness. Social Change. Women's Liberation Movement. 1840-1977. *35*

Law and Order Committee. Business. California (San Francisco). Construction. Eight-hour day. Strikes. 1916-17. *2232*
—. California (San Francisco). Labor Disputes. Longshoremen. Strikes. 1916. *2234*

Law Enforcement. Alien Anarchist Act (US, 1918). Anti-Communist Movements. Congress. Leftism. Post, Louis F. 1919-20. *2352*
—. Antitrust. Courts. Fire insurance. Kansas City Board of Fire Underwriters. Missouri. 1889-99. *1336*
—. Bootlegging. Depressions. Florida (Hernando County). Liquor. Prohibition. 1929-33. *2359*
—. Civil Disturbances. Conscription, Military. 1963-76. *2725*
—. Civil Rights Act (US, 1875). Supreme Court. 1875-83. *1159*
—. Cummins, Albert B. Government regulation. Iowa (Davenport). Liquor. Riots. State Politics. 1907-08. *1880*
—. Desegregation. Federal Government. Public Schools. South. 1954-76. *2824*
—. Drugs. Utah. 1967-71. *2770*
—. Employment. Immigrants. Maximum hours laws. State Government. Women. 1920. *2398*
—. Florida (Miami). Prohibition. Smuggling. 1896-1920. *1948*
—. Intellectuals. Radicals and Radicalism. World War I. 1914-20. *2158*
—. Mine, Mill and Smelter Workers, International Union of. Nicaragua. Silex, Humberto. Southwest. 1932-78. *1739*
—. Northwest Territories. Prohibition. Royal Canadian Mounted Police. 1874-91. *1460*

Law Reform. Anti-Imperialism. Attitudes. Mugwumps. NAACP. Storey, Moorfield. 1870's-1929. *462*
—. Anti-lynching law of 1894. Ohio. Smith, Harry C. Tourgée, Albion W. 1890-96. *1453*
—. Barnard, Kate. Child labor. Oklahoma. 1904-24. *1877*
—. Bradwell, Myra. Illinois (Chicago). Women's rights. 1855-92. *1034*
—. Capital punishment. Public Opinion. Rhode Island. 1838-52. *888*
—. Convict lease system. Corporal punishment. Florida (Leon County). Tabert, Martin. 1921-23. *2354*
—. Debts. Kentucky. Legislation. 1790-1839. *824*
—. Great Britain. New England. Puritans. 1620-60. *501*

Lawsuits. Desegregation. Discrimination, Educational. Graduate schools. Negroes. North Carolina. Professional training. 1930-51. *1835*
—. Indians. Legislation. Public Welfare. 1957-77. *2706*
—. Justice Department. Negroes. School Integration. South. 1957-68. *2811*

Lawyers *See also* Judges.
—. Bradwell, Myra. Illinois. Sex Discrimination. Supreme Court (decision). 1873-1894. *1114*
—. California (San Diego). Foltz, Clara Shortridge. Women. 1872-1930. *413*
—. Catholic Church. Pennsylvania. Progressivism. Smith, Walter George. 1900-22. *1891*
—. Courts. Discrimination, educational. Florida, University of. Hawkins, Virgil Darnell. Legal education. 1949-76. *1554*
—. Jews. Social mobility. 20c. *1522*
—. Lobbying. New Jersey. Philbrook, Mary. Women's Liberation Movement. 1895-1947. *409*
—. Marshall, Thurgood. Maryland, University of, School of Law. Murray, Donald G. NAACP. School Integration. 1930-54. *2531*
—. NAACP. Race relations. 1909-76. *1646*

Leader, George M. Lanius, Henry E. Legislation. Pennsylvania. Political leadership. Special education. 1820-1956. *1838*

Leadership *See also* Political Leadership.
—. Alabama (Montgomery). Boycotts. King, Martin Luther, Jr. Negroes. New York City (Harlem). Powell, Adam Clayton, Jr. 1941-56. *307*

—. Alberta. Cooperative Commonwealth Federation. Land reform. Social credit. United Farmers of Alberta. 1930's. *1748*
—. Alexander, Sydenham B. Carr, Elias. Farmers' Alliance. North Carolina. Polk, Leonidas L. Upper Classes. 1887-95. *1392*
—. Associated Charities. Charities. Massachusetts (Fall River, Lynn). Men. Social Policy. Women. 1880-1900. *1447*
—. Baptists, Southern. Race Relations. Texas. 1954-68. *2890*
—. Childhood. Religion. Secularism. Sex roles. Women. 1636-1930. *381*
—. Civil Rights Organizations. King, Martin Luther, Jr. Negroes. Southern Christian Leadership Conference. 1957-73. *2828*
—. Ireland (Limerick). Irish Americans. Labor Unions and Organizations. McCarthy, Patrick Henry. Youth. 1863-80. *402*
—. Miller, Kelly. Negroes. 1877-1918. *470*
—. Negro Young People's Congress. South. 1902. *2026*
—. Negroes. Reconstruction. South. 1867-75. *1211*
—. Negroes. Segregation. Urbanization. Virginia (Richmond). 1900-20. *1947*

League for Human Rights. Anti-Nazi Movements. Boycotts. Fram, Leon (reminiscences). Jews. Michigan (Detroit). 1930's-40's. *2507*

League for Social Reconstruction. Cooperative Commonwealth Federation. Regina Manifesto. Saskatchewan. Underhill, Frank. 1933. *1611*

League of Nations Association. Foreign Policy. International Relations. Isolationism. Peace. 1934-38. *2466*

League of Nations Covenant. American Peace Society. Pacifism. Paris Peace Conference. 1914-19. *2066*

League of Revolutionary Black Workers. Automobile Industry and Trade. Labor Unions and Organizations. Michigan (Detroit). Negroes. 1968-73. *2832*

League of Women for Community Service. Massachusetts (Boston). Negroes. Voluntary Associations. Women. 1918-77. *1575*

League of Women Voters. Alabama. National American Woman Suffrage Association. Woman Suffrage. 1919-21. *2450*

Lease, Mary Elizabeth. Kansas. Political Speeches. Populism. 1871-1933. *293*

Leases. Firestone, Harvey S. Garvey, Marcus. Land. Liberia. Negroes. Universal Negro Improvement Association. 1926. *2402*

LeConte, Joseph. Education. Evolution. 1875-1900. *1435*
—. Evolution. Science. Sex roles. Women's rights. 1890's. *1115*

Lectures *See also* Speeches, Addresses, etc.
—. Anarchism and Anarchists. Intellectuals. Kropotkin, Pëtr. Russia. 1897-1901. *1501*
—. Borg, Selma Josefina. Centennial Exposition of 1876. Finnish Americans. Music. Pennsylvania (Philadelphia). Women's rights. 1858-90. *399*
—. Coates, Sarah (letters). Ohio. Physiology. Women. 1850. *881*
—. Feminism. Wright, Frances. 1820's-30's. *813*
—. Forssell, G. D. Iowa. Minnesota. Progressivism. Social Conditions. 1890-95. *957*
—. Journalism. Minnesota. Political activism. Populism. Valesh, Eva McDonald. 1866-1956. *345*

Leftism *See also* Communism; New Left; Radicals and Radicalism; Socialism.
—. Alien Anarchist Act (US, 1918). Anti-Communist Movements. Congress. Law Enforcement. Post, Louis F. 1919-20. *2352*
—. American Federation of Labor. American Labor Union. Washington. Western Federation of Miners. 1880's-1920. *171*
—. Antiwar sentiment. Colleges and Universities. Political Protest. 1920-36. *2483*
—. Berrigan, Daniel. Berrigan, Philip. Catholic Church. Church and state. Murray, John Courtney. 1950's-70's. *1605*
—. Bliss, William D. P. Christianity. Social Gospel. 1876-1926. *20*
—. Čačić, Tomo. Ethnic Groups. Kjelt, Ole. Krat, Pavlo. Mäkelä, A. B. Political Protest. Puttee, Arthur. Scarlett, Sam. 1907-34. *1561*
—. Civil Rights. Negroes. Robeson, Paul. Singers. 1898-1976. *379*
—. Civil rights movement. Models. Political attitudes. Students. 1960's-70's. *2714*

Leftism

—. Cooperative Commonwealth Federation. Feminism. Ontario (Toronto). Women's Joint Committee. 1930's. *1638*
—. Feminism. New York City. Prisons. Smedley, Agnes *(Cell Mates)*. 1918. *2019*
—. Jews. 1880's-1970's. *61*
Legal education. Courts. Discrimination, educational. Florida, University of. Hawkins, Virgil Darnell. Lawyers. 1949-76. *1554*
—. District of Columbia. Gillett, Emma M. Mussey, Ellen Spencer. Washington College of Law. Women. 1869-1949. *426*
—. Flexner Report. Medical education. Reed Report (1921). 1910-74. *1862*
—. Harvard College. Massachusetts. 1766-1840. *194*
Legion of Decency. Censorship. Hughes, Howard. Motion Picture Producers and Distributors of America. *Outlaw* (film). Russell, Jane. 1940-49. *2649*
Legislation *See also* Congress; Law.
—. Air pollution. Cities. Energy. Industry. 1880-1920. *38*
—. Air pollution. Environment. Public Policy. 1967-78. *2763*
—. Alabama. Political Parties. Reconstruction. 1867. *1251*
—. Asian Americans. Employment. Ethnicity. Naturalization. Racism. 1850-20c. *65*
—. Border States. Congress. Loyalty oath. Republican Party. South. 1861-67. *950*
—. British Columbia. Labor. Natural resources. New Democratic Party. Public Policy. Social Democracy. Taxation. 1972-75. *2942*
—. Bureau of Surface Mine Reclamation. Mining. Pennsylvania. 1961-73. *2762*
—. Bureaucracies. Centralization. Missouri. Public schools. State government. 1853. *846*
—. Business. Capitalism. Illinois. Workmen's compensation. 1905-12. *2189*
—. Canada. Child welfare. Income. Mothers. 1916-70's. *1814*
—. Canada. House of Commons. Liberal Party. Political Change. Progressive Party. 1920's. *1574*
—. Canada. Income. Mothers. Public Welfare. ca 1900-39. *1815*
—. Civil rights. Congress. Democratic Party. Partisanship. Regionalism. Republican Party. 1963-72. *2803*
—. Civil rights. Congress. Demonstrations. Public opinion. 1957-77. *2813*
—. Civil rights. Executive Power. Kennedy, John F. 1961-64. *2858*
—. Civil rights. Population. Race Relations. Riots. Tennessee (Memphis). 1865-66. *1209*
—. Coal Mines and Mining. Great Britain. Illinois. Labor Unions and Organizations. Lobbying. 1861-72. *1312*
—. Consumer protection. Drugs. Federal regulation. Methodology. 1962-73. *2956*
—. Debts. Kentucky. Law Reform. 1790-1839. *824*
—. Decisionmaking. Federal Government. Interest Groups. Politics. Women. 1970's. *2911*
—. Delaware. DuPont, Pierre S. Educational Reform. 1890's-1921. *2452*
—. Depressions. Provincial government. Public Welfare. Quebec. Taschereau, Louis Alexandre. ca 1934-36. *1700*
—. Educational Reform. Free Schools. Howland, John. Rhode Island. 1757-1838. *431*
—. Ehringhaus, J. C. B. North Carolina. Social Security Act (US, 1935). Unemployment insurance. 1935-37. *2556*
—. Eisenhower, Dwight D. (administration). Federal Policy. Public Welfare. Reform. 1950-60. *2659*
—. Epstein, Abraham. Pensions. Voluntary associations. 1920-35. *1777*
—. Federal aid to education. Harrison, Byron Patton. Mississippi. 1936-41. *2597*
—. Federal Government. Nevada. Newspapers. Racism. 1866-68. *976*
—. Federal government. Public Welfare. United Mine Workers of America (Welfare and Retirement Fund). 1945-70's. *2658*
—. Federal programs. Medicine and State. 1965-77. *2979*
—. Federalism. Progressivism. States' rights. 1880-1930. *1959*
—. Feminism. Industry. Progressivism. 1919-33. *2401*
—. Illinois. Reform. Wages. Women. Working Conditions. 1893-1917. *2187*
—. Indians. Lawsuits. Public Welfare. 1957-77. *2706*

SUBJECT INDEX

—. Indian-White Relations. New Mexico (Taos; Blue Lake). Pueblo Indians. Rites and Ceremonies. 20c. *1718*
—. Labor Non-Partisan League. Political representation. Working conditions. 1936-38. *2605*
—. Lanius, Henry E. Leader, George M. Pennsylvania. Political leadership. Special education. 1820-1956. *1838*
—. Minimum wage. Occupations. Ohio. Sex Discrimination. Women. 1914-33. *1539*
—. Minimum wage. State government. Washington. 1913-25. *1822*
—. Mormons. Tobacco. Utah. 1896-1923. *2440*
—. Pennsylvania (Philadelphia). Segregation. Streetcars. 1850's-70. *1156*
—. Political Parties. Public Welfare. 1933-54. *1812*
Legislators. Blue law. Louisiana. Negroes. Reconstruction. State Legislatures. 1867-75. *1276*
Leisure *See also* Recreation.
—. Capitalism. Labor. Social Organization. 1890-1920's. *151*
Leland, Henry. Detroit Citizens League. Michigan. Progressivism. Social Classes. 1912-24. *1925*
Lenin, V. I. (views). Gompers, Samuel. Socialist Party. USSR. 1912-18. *1991*
Lenroot, Irvine L. Ansell, Samuel T. Chamberlain, George. Congress. Crowder, Enoch H. Military law. Progressivism. 1916-20. *2408*
Letters *See also* names of individuals with the subdivision letters, e.g. Jefferson, Thomas (letters).
—. Abolition Movement. Cass, William D. Methodist Episcopal Church (General Conference). 1844. *693*
—. Abolition movement. Harvard University, Houghton Library, Blagden Papers. Phillips, Wendell. 1840-80. 1977-79. *605*
—. Alcott, Louisa May. Feminism. Woman suffrage. 1853-85. *811*
—. American Revolution. Literature. Massachusetts. Warren, Mercy Otis. 1740-1814. *460*
—. Anti-Communist Movements. Freedom of Speech. Ontario (Toronto). Police. Political Repression. 1931. *1724*
—. Antislavery Sentiments. Brown, John. Douglass, Frederick. 1851-56. *725*
—. Attitudes. Intellectuals. Slavery. Social Classes. 1830-60. *790*
—. Bishop Hill Colony. Daily life. Illinois. Jansson, Erik. Swedish Americans. Utopias. 1847-56. *939*
—. Bishop Hill Colony. Illinois. Janssonists. Swedes. 1847. *936*
—. Bradford, George Partridge. Brook Farm. Daily life. Massachusetts. Utopias. 1841. *932*
—. Dall, Caroline. Farley, Harriet. Feminism. Working Class. 1850. *794*
—. DeLeon, Daniel. Socialist Labor Party. 1896-1904. *2094*
—. Depressions. Farmers. Government. Great Plains. New Deal. 1930-40. *2476*
—. Douglass, Frederick. Human Relations. 1846-94. *390*
—. Economic conditions. Mann, Mary Tyler Peabody. Ohio. Poorhouses. 1795-1858. *884*
—. Labor. Negroes. Riley, William R. Tennessee. United Mine Workers of America. 1892-95. *1201*
—. Lloyd, Henry Demarest. Morgan, Thomas John. Social Democratic Party. Socialist Labor Party. 1897-1901. *1349*
Letters-to-the-editor. Coal Mines and Mining. Davis, Richard L. Labor Unions and Organizations. *National Labor Tribune*. Negroes. United Mine Workers of America. ca 1890-1900. *1139*
Lettuce. Agricultural Labor. California (Salinas). Filipino Labor Union. Strikes. 1934. *2499*
Leuchtenburg, William E. Historiography. Imperialism. Progressivism. 1890's-1910's. 1952-74. *2089*
—. Historiography. Imperialism. Progressivism. 1898-1916. 1952-75. *2023*
Lewis, Dioclesius. California (San Francisco). Gymnastics. Parot, Adele. 1860's-70's. *1404*
—. Medical reform. Morality. Rhythmics. Sex. Women. 1860-1970's. *1481*
Lewis, John Llewellyn. Coal Mines and Mining. Hocking Valley, Ohio, southeastern. Strikes. United Mine Workers of America. 1927. *2447*

Liberia

—. Labor Unions and Organizations. Reorganized United Mine Workers of America. 1920-33. *2357*
Lewis, Lena Morrow. Alaska (Anchorage). Labor Unions and Organizations. Railroads. Socialist Party. World War I. 1916-18. *2001*
Libel. Buffalo Medical College. Loomis, Horatio N. Medical Education. Midwifery. New York. Obstetrics. White, James Platt. 1850. *869*
—. Moore, William. Pennsylvania. Political Theory. Provincial legislatures. Smith, William. 1750-60. *516*
Liberal Advocate (newspaper). Dogberry, Obediah. New York (Rochester). Religious liberty. 1832-34. *589*
Liberal arts. Higher education. Reform. South. 1850-60. *854*
Liberal education. DuBois, W. E. B. Elites. Negroes. Talented Tenth strategy. 1890's-1963. *1591*
Liberal Party. Canada. House of Commons. Legislation. Political Change. Progressive Party. 1920's. *1574*
—. Catholic Church. Church schools. French language. Langevin, Louis Philippe Adélard. Laurier, Wilfrid. Prairie Provinces. Religion in the Public Schools. 1890-1915. *185*
Liberal Republican Party. Reconstruction. ca 1870-72. *945*
Liberalism. Anarchism and Anarchists. Political Protest. Social criticism. 1960-68. *2705*
—. Baker, Ray Stannard. Civil rights. DuBois, W. E. B. Negroes. Wilmer, Cary Breckenridge (interview). 1900-10. *2110*
—. Business. Economic planning. Government. Labor Unions and Organizations. 1920-40. *1788*
—. Capitalism. Corporations. Federal government. General Electric Company. Labor Unions and Organizations. 1920-33. *2412*
—. Catholic Church. Democracy. Intellectuals. Racism. 1924-59. *1560*
—. Cities. Democracy. Howe, Frederic C. Progressivism. ca 1890-1940. *2013*
—. City Politics. Civil rights. LaGuardia, Fiorello. New York City. Powell, Adam Clayton, Jr. 1941-43. *2619*
—. Civil Rights. Constitutional Amendments (1st). Political Attitudes. 1954-74. *2768*
—. Civil rights. Constitutional Law. Douglas, William O. Judicial process. Supreme Court. 1928-77. *1715*
—. Colleges and Universities. Intellectuals. Political Attitudes. Socialism. 1880-95. *1072*
—. Collier, John. Federal Government. Indians. Roosevelt, Franklin D. (administration). Truman, Harry S. (administration). 1933-53. *1629*
—. Communist Control Act (US, 1954). Humphrey, Hubert H. McCarthy, Joseph R. 1954. *2675*
—. Communitarianism. Democracy. Progressive Era. 1890-1920's. *2049*
—. Congress. Illinois. Keller, Kent. New Deal. 1930-42. *2608*
—. Counts, George S. Educational reform. Race. 1929-54. *2379*
—. Debs, Eugene V. Hartz, Louis. Hillquit, Morris. Locke, John. Marxism. Political culture. 20c. *1986*
—. Depressions. New Deal. Political activism. Socialist Party. Unemployment. 1929-36. *1804*
—. Editors and Editing. Milton, George Fort. New Deal. Tennessee. 1930's. *2521*
—. *Globe*. Labor. Newspapers. Ontario. 1885-90. *1332*
—. Government. Progressivism. Richberg, Donald Randall. 1900-60. *274*
—. Intellectuals. Lippmann, Walter. Politics. 1890-1974. *427*
—. Law. Radicals and Radicalism. Social change. 1953-73. *1579*
—. New Deal. New Left. Political Theory. Welfare state. 1932-66. *1738*
—. *New Republic* (periodical). Progressivism. Science and Society. 1914-20. *2040*
—. Partisanship. Professionalism. Public welfare. State government. 1960's-70's. *2952*
—. Social Classes. Voting and Voting Behavior. 1960's-70's. *2731*
Liberals. Amlie, Thomas. Economic programs. New Deal. Politics. Wisconsin. 1931-39. *2609*
—. Civil rights. Minorities in Politics. New York City. 1963-70's. *2728*
—. Collectivism. Glass, Carter. National Recovery Administration. New Deal. 1933-35. *2533*
Liberia *See also* Africa, West.

—. Abolition Movement. American Colonization Society. Colonization. Cresson, Elliot. Great Britain. 1831-33. *609*
—. African Colonization Movement. Emancipation. Georgia. Tubman, Emily. 1816-57. *655*
—. American Colonization Society. Black nationalism. Delany, Martin Robinson. 1820-58. *620*
—. American Colonization Society. Colonization. Georgia. Negroes. 1816-20. *705*
—. American Colonization Society. Crummell, Alexander. Education. Negroes. 1853-73. *1126*
—. American Colonization Society. Emancipation. North Carolina. Slaveholders. 1800-60. *708*
—. American Colonization Society. Emigration. Negroes. 19c. *688*
—. American Colonization Society. Georgia (Griffin). Moss, William (letters). Slavery. 1853-57. *654*
—. Colonization. Garvey, Marcus. Negroes. Universal Negro Improvement Association. 1914-24. *2342*
—. Colonization. Methodist Episcopal Church. Missions and Missionaries. Negroes. Sierra Leone. 1833-48. *641*
—. Firestone, Harvey S. Garvey, Marcus. Land. Leases. Negroes. Universal Negro Improvement Association. 1926. *2402*
—. Georgia. Tubman, Emily. 1818-85. *317*
—. Negroes. Republican Party. Turner, James Milton. 1865-77. *1195*
Libertarianism. Anarchism and Anarchists. Indiana (New Harmony). Ohio (Cincinnati). Utopias. Warren, Joseph. 1818-74. *302*
Liberty. American Revolution (antecedents). Conservatism. North Carolina. Political Corruption. Regulators. 1766-71. *481*
—. Civil rights. Equality. Judicial Process. 1960-79. *2772*
—. Emancipation Proclamation. Freedmen. Lincoln, Abraham. Republican Party. 1862. *1131*
Liberty bonds. Kansas. Mennonites. Pacifism. Vigilantism. World War I. 1918. *2146*
Liberty League of Negro Americans. Harrison, Hubert H. International Colored Unity League. Journalism. Negroes. New York City (Harlem). Socialist Party. 1911-27. *1676*
Liberty Party. Abolition movement. Fessenden, Samuel. Free Soil movement. Maine. State Politics. Willey, Austin. 1830's-48. *682*
—. Abolition Movement. *Green Mountain Freeman* (newspaper). Poland, Joseph. State politics. Vermont. 1840-48. *683*
—. Abolition Movement. New York. 1840-48. *687*
—. Abolition Movement. Ohio. South. 1838-50. *670*
—. Antislavery Sentiments. Bailey, Gamaliel. Chase, Salmon Portland. Ohio. Republican Party. 1836-60. *668*
—. Antislavery sentiments. New Hampshire. State Politics. 1840-48. *677*
—. Democratic Party. Negro suffrage. New York. Referendum. Whig Party. 1840-47. *595*
Libraries *See also* names of individual libraries.
—. Anglophobia. Censorship. City Politics. Illinois (Chicago). Public Schools. Thompson, William Hale. 1927. *2454*
Libraries (public). Countryman, Gratia Alta. Minnesota (Minneapolis). Reform. Women. 1890's-1953. *424*
—. Labor Unions and Organizations. Women. 1917-20. *2243*
—. New Deal. 1933-39. *2480*
Life and Labor (periodical). Labor Unions and Organizations. Women's Trade Union League. 1911-21. *2231*
Ligutti, Luigi. Federal Subsistence Homesteads Corporation. Iowa (Granger). New Deal. 1934-51. *2585*
Lincoln, Abraham. Attitudes. Equality. 1830's-65. *642*
—. Censorship. Chicago *Times*. Civil War. Newspapers. 1863-64. *1118*
—. Civil Rights. Civil War. Emancipation Proclamation. 1854-63. *1230*
—. Civil War. Constitutional Amendments. Fundamentalism. National Fast Day. National Reform Association. 1787-1945. *1484*
—. Civil War. Louisiana (New Orleans). Negroes. Reconstruction. Suffrage. 1860-67. *1130*
—. Civil War. Political Theory. Revolution. Slavery. Social change. 1850-65. *1060*
—. Colonization. Emancipation. Negroes. 1852-65. *747*

—. Colonization. Emancipation. Negroes. 1861-65. *1138*
—. Douglas, Stephen A. Morality. Political Attitudes. Slavery. 1850's. *738*
—. Education. Illinois. Jefferson, Thomas. 1820-62. *835*
—. Emancipation Proclamation. Freedmen. Liberty. Republican Party. 1862. *1131*
—. Founding Fathers. Kansas-Nebraska Act (US, 1854). Reconstruction. Republicanism. 1854-65. *1058*
Lincoln and Lincolniana. Emancipation Proclamation. Republican Party. 1863-64. *1199*
Lincoln, Mary Todd. Attitudes. Domesticity. Stanton, Elizabeth Cady. Stowe, Harriet Beecher. 1830-80. *443*
Lincoln University. Education. Lindsay, Lizzie A. Missouri (Jefferson City). Negroes. Turner, James Milton. 1865-75. *1179*
Lindsay, Lizzie A. Education. Lincoln University. Missouri (Jefferson City). Negroes. Turner, James Milton. 1865-75. *1179*
Lindsey, Benjamin Barr. California (Los Angeles). Children's Court of Conciliation. Judges. 1894-1943. *357*
—. Colorado (Denver). Juvenile Courts. 1901-20's. *1902*
Lippmann, Walter. Intellectuals. Liberalism. Politics. 1890-1974. *427*
Liquor. Bootlegging. Depressions. Florida (Hernando County). Law enforcement. Prohibition. 1929-33. *2359*
—. Cummins, Albert B. Government regulation. Iowa (Davenport). Law Enforcement. Riots. State Politics. 1907-08. *1880*
Literary characters. Feminism. Novels. Rives, Amélie. South. 1863-1945. *377*
Literary Criticism. Book reviews. Feminism. Porter, Katherine Anne. 1922-29. *2373*
Literature *See also* Authors; Autobiography; Books; Fiction; Journalism; Novels; Poetry.
—. Agrarianism. Davidson, Donald. Mims, Edwin. South. 1923-58. *1656*
—. American Revolution. Letters. Massachusetts. Warren, Mercy Otis. 1740-1814. *460*
—. Assimilation. Black nationalism. Ideology. Religion. Women. 1890-1925. *1654*
—. Bradstreet, Anne. Hutchinson, Anne. Massachusetts Bay Colony. Religion. Social change. Women. 1630's-70's. *489*
—. Bulosan, Carlos. Labor. Marxism. 1931-56. *432*
—. Canada. Feminism. McClung, Nellie L. Politics. Reform. 1873-1930's. *1689*
—. Civil rights. King, Martin Luther, Jr. ("Letter from Birmingham Jail"). Rhetoric. 1963. *2807*
—. Donnelly, Ignatius. Populism. 1831-90's. *1359*
—. Feminism. Holley, Marrietta (*My Opinion*). 1870-1926. *983*
—. Feminism. Negroes. Stowe, Harriet Beecher. Truth, Soujourner. 1850's-90's. *802*
—. Feminism. Utopias. 19c-20c. *267*
—. Freudianism. Women's liberation movement. 1946-70's. *1599*
—. Intellectuals. Pacifism. Tolstoy, Leo. ca 1890's. *1080*
—. MacLane, Mary. Montana (Butte). Women. 1902-29. *384*
—. Mennonites. Pacifism. 20c. *1693*
—. Motherhood. Sex roles. Women. 1785-1815. *793*
—. Negroes. Radicals and Radicalism. Wright, Richard. 1920-60. *305*
—. Negroes. Wright, Richard. 1908-60. *348*
—. Sex roles. Social Change. Women. 19c. *78*
Litigation. Integration. NAACP. North. Public schools. 1954-73. *2841*
Little, Malcolm. *See* Malcolm X.
Livingston, Edward. Capital punishment. Public Opinion. ca 1800-30. *887*
Llano del Rio Co-operative Colony. Communes. Louisiana (Vernon Parish). Socialism. 1917-38. *1655*
Lloyd, Henry Demarest. Corruthers, James B. (letters). 1870-1903. *378*
—. Letters. Morgan, Thomas John. Social Democratic Party. Socialist Labor Party. 1897-1901. *1349*
Lloyd, Lola Maverick. Feminism. Peace Movements. 1914-44. *451*
Lobbying *See also* Citizen Lobbies; Interest Groups; Political Factions.
—. Agricultural Organizations. National Board of Farm Organizations. 1917-27. *1769*

—. California. Labor Unions and Organizations. Progressives. 1900-19. *1898*
—. Coal Mines and Mining. Great Britain. Illinois. Labor Unions and Organizations. Legislation. 1861-72. *1312*
—. Colleges and Universities. Douglass, Mabel Smith. Middle Classes. New Jersey College for Women. Women. 1911-18. *2324*
—. Constitutions, State. Jury. South Carolina. Women. 1921-67. *1731*
—. Equality. New York City. State Legislatures. Strachan, Grace. Teachers. Wages. Women. 1907-11. *2202*
—. Feminism. Labor Unions and Organizations. Middle Classes. Suffrage. Women's Trade Union League. ca 1903-20. *1980*
—. Labor Department. 1864-1913. *2219*
—. Lawyers. New Jersey. Philbrook, Mary. Women's Liberation Movement. 1895-1947. *409*
Local Government *See also* Local Politics; Public Administration.
—. Antitrust. New Jersey (Jersey City). Railroads. Taxation. 1901-07. *2276*
—. California (San Francisco Bay area). Consumers. Environmental protection. Government regulation. Housing. Suburbs. 1940-80. *2718*
—. Cities. Civil rights movement. Federal government. Negroes. 1933-70. *1686*
—. Education, Experimental Methods. Federal programs. RAND Corporation. 1965-80. *2961*
—. Executive Power. Intergovernmental Relations. Ohio. Police. State Government. 1902-25. *2100*
—. Federal Government. Massachusetts (Boston; South End). Middle Classes. Neighborhoods. Poor. Urban revitalization. 1960's-70's. *2694*
—. Illinois. Lochner, Louis Paul. Peace Movements. People's Council of America for Democracy and Peace. State Government. 1917. *2104*
—. Interest Groups. Political Reform. Social change. Taxation. 1960's. *2947*
—. Manitoba (Winnipeg). Queen, John. Socialism. Taxation. 1909-42. *1645*
—. Political Corruption. Socialist Party. Voting and Voting Behavior. 1910-14. *1879*
Local option. Ethnicity. Michigan. Prohibition. 1889-1917. *1928*
—. Louisiana (Shreveport). Prohibition. Voting and Voting Behavior. 1950-52. *2680*
Local Politics *See also* Local Government.
—. Alabama (Bullock, Greene, Wilcox counties). Decisionmaking. Negroes. 1971-72. *2819*
—. Butler Bill. Judiciary. Proslavery Sentiments. 1850's. *663*
—. Committee of Fifteen. New York City. Tammany Hall. 1900-01. *1934*
—. Democracy. Education. Fundamentalism. Social Change. Vigilantism. 1920's. *2375*
—. Dix, I. F. Hoover, Herbert C. Self-help. Unemployed Citizens' League. Washington (Seattle). 1931-32. *2417*
—. German Americans. Irish Americans. New York City. Riots. Temperance Movements. 1857. *585*
—. Illinois (Chicago). Negroes. Public schools. 1910-41. *1845*
—. Ku Klux Klan. Nevada. Vigilantism. 1920-29. *2449*
—. Labor. Missouri. Racism. Reconstruction. St. Louis *Daily Press* (newspaper). 1864-66. *1339*
—. Pennsylvania (Reading). Socialist Party. Women. ca 1927-38. *1666*
Lochner, Louis Paul. Illinois. Local Government. Peace Movements. People's Council of America for Democracy and Peace. State Government. 1917. *2104*
Locke, John. Debs, Eugene V. Hartz, Louis. Hillquit, Morris. Liberalism. Marxism. Political culture. 20c. *1986*
Lockwood, Belva Bennett (letters). Feminism. Political Campaigns (presidential). 1884. *1116*
Logan, John A. Congress. House of Representatives. Illinois. Republicans, Radical. 1866-68. *1028*
London, Jack. Australia. Strikes. 1908-09. *2246*
—. Bellamy, Edward. Socialism. Utopias. 1888-1920. *262*
—. Propaganda. Socialism. 1905-08. *2123*
London, Meyer. Congress. International Ladies' Garment Workers' Union. Socialism. 1914-22. *2212*
Long, Huey P. Civil Rights movement. Johnson, Lyndon B. Radicals and Radicalism. South. 1920-70. *1706*

Long

—. Depressions. Louisiana. Politics. Share-Our-Wealth movement. Smith, Gerald L. K. 1930's. *2527*
—. Economic Reform. Share-Our-Wealth movement. 1932-35. *2485*
—. Education. Louisiana. Working Class. 1928-35. *2515*
—. Elections (presidential). Roosevelt, Franklin D. Share-Our-Wealth movement. 1932-36. *2595*
—. Fundamentalism. North Central States. Populism. Progressivism. Smith, Gerald L. K. 1934-48. *362*
—. Louisiana. Populism. Progressivism. State Government. 1891-1935. *1566*
—. New Deal. Reform. 1933-35. *2490*
—. Political Leadership. Share-Our-Wealth movement. 1928-35. *2526*
Longfellow, Henry Wadsworth *(Poems on Slavery)*. Antislavery Sentiments. Massachusetts (Cambridge). 1842. *665*
Longshoremen. California (San Francisco). Labor Disputes. Law and Order Committee. Strikes. 1916. *2234*
—. California (San Francisco). Strikes. 1934-39. *2529*
—. Christianity. Oxford Group movement. Strikes. Washington (Seattle). 1921-34. *2604*
—. Crime and Criminals. Fletcher, Benjamin Harrison. Industrial Workers of the World. Labor. Negroes. 1910-33. *437*
—. Labor Unions and Organizations. Louisiana (New Orleans). Race Relations. 1850's-1976. *176*
Loomis, Horatio N. Buffalo Medical College. Libel. Medical Education. Midwifery. New York. Obstetrics. White, James Platt. 1850. *869*
Los Angeles Times. American Federation of Labor. Bombing. California (Los Angeles). Labor movement. McNamara case. Progressives. 1910-14. *2265*
—. Class Struggle. McNamara case. Progressivism. Radicals and Radicalism. Steffens, Lincoln. 1908-12. *2083*
Louisiana *See also* South; South Central and Gulf States.
—. Adams, Charles P. Colleges and Universities. Grambling State University. Negroes. 1896-1928. *1836*
—. Advice columns. Dix, Dorothy. Feminism. New Orleans *Picayune* (newspaper). 1895-1900. *980*
—. American Federation of Labor. Industrial Workers of the World. Marine Transport Workers. Sailors' Union. Strikes. United Fruit Company. 1913. *2193*
—. Andry plantation. Slave revolts. 1801-12. *625*
—. Armies. Banks, Nathaniel Prentiss. Civil War. Education. 1863-65. *1218*
—. Blue law. Legislators. Negroes. Reconstruction. State Legislatures. 1867-75. *1276*
—. Brotherhood of Timber Workers. Industrial Workers of the World. Lumber and Lumbering. Race Relations. Texas. 1910-13. *2215*
—. Carpetbaggers. Negroes. Republican Party. State Politics. 1868. *1136*
—. Constitutions, State. Slidell, John. Suffrage. 1812-52. *601*
—. Democratic Party. Elections. Military Occupation. Reconstruction. Rousseau, Lovell H. 1868-69. *990*
—. Depressions. Long, Huey P. Politics. Share-Our-Wealth movement. Smith, Gerald L. K. 1930's. *2527*
—. Education. Long, Huey P. Working Class. 1928-35. *2515*
—. Forest and Farm Workers Union. Hall, Covington. Labor Unions and Organizations. Lumber and Lumbering. Socialism. 1907-16. *2192*
—. Freedmen. Homesteading and Homesteaders. Reconstruction. 1865-83. *1233*
—. Governors. Kennon, Robert F. Reform. 1948-56. *2674*
—. Hancock, Winfield Scott. Military. Mower, Joseph Anthony. Reconstruction. Texas. 1865-68. *989*
—. Know-Nothing Party. Political leadership. Social Classes. 1845-60. *542*
—. Law. Slavery. 1685-1766. *505*
—. Law. Slavery. 1724-66. *508*
—. Long, Huey P. Populism. Progressivism. State Government. 1891-1935. *1566*
—. Military Occupation. Negro Suffrage. Reconstruction. Sheridan, Philip H. 1865-67. *991*

—. Negroes. Ray, John. Republican Party. Scalawags. ca 1836-88. *463*
—. Newspapers. Political Campaigns (presidential). Slavery. Two-party system. 1834-36. *661*
—. Oil Industry and Trade. Strikes. Texas. 1917-18. *2237*
—. Ostracism. Reconstruction. Scalawags. State Politics. Terrorism. 1866-78. *1081*
Louisiana Child Labor Laws (1908-1912). Child labor. Theater. 1908-12. *2050*
Louisiana Education Association. Equal opportunity. Negroes. School Integration. Teachers. 1901-70. *1857*
Louisiana (Madison Parish). Freedmen. Plantations. Race Relations. Reconstruction. 1863-74. *978*
Louisiana (New Orleans). Child Labor Law (Louisiana, 1908). Gordon, Jean. New York. Theatrical Syndicate. 1908-12. *1968*
—. Cholera. Howard Association. Philanthropy. Public health. Yellow fever. 1837-78. *235*
—. City Government. School Integration. 1952-61. *2679*
—. Civil Rights Organizations. Discrimination. Florida (Miami). Murray, Hugh T., Jr. (reminiscences). 1959-60. *2871*
—. Civil War. Freedmen. Negroes, free. Political Attitudes. Politics. Social Classes. 1860-65. *1275*
—. Civil War. Lincoln, Abraham. Negroes. Reconstruction. Suffrage. 1860-67. *1130*
—. Converts. Evangelism. Protestant Churches. Slavery. 1800-61. *732*
—. Crime and Criminals. Prohibition. 1918-33. *2386*
—. Education. Episcopal Church, Protestant. Polk, Leonidas L. Slavery. 1805-65. *730*
—. Historiography. Negroes. Political Leadership. Reconstruction. ca 1800-75. *1239*
—. International Workingmen's Association (Section 15). 1871. *1293*
—. Labor Unions and Organizations. Longshoremen. Race Relations. 1850's-1976. *176*
—. Metropolitan Police Force. Negroes. Politics. Riots. Whites. 1868. *1168*
—. Public opinion. Street, Electric Railway and Motor Coach Employees of America. Strikes. 1929-30. *2353*
Louisiana Purchase. Civil rights. Freedmen. Treaty of Cession (1804). 1797-1804. *590*
Louisiana (St. Landry). Race Relations. Reconstruction. Republican Party. Riots. 1868. *1151*
Louisiana (Shreveport). Local option. Prohibition. Voting and Voting Behavior. 1950-52. *2680*
Louisiana, southern. Civil War. Contraband programs. Fugitive slaves. Military Occupation. 1862-65. *1219*
Louisiana State Prison (Angola). Agriculture. Convict Labor. Prisons. Working Conditions. 1900-78. *1701*
Louisiana State University. Mims, Mary Williams. Teachers. 1910-67. *387*
Louisiana (Vernon Parish). Communes. Llano del Rio Co-operative Colony. Socialism. 1917-38. *1655*
Louisiana, western. Brotherhood of Timber Workers. Emerson, Arthur L. Industrial Workers of the World. Labor Disputes. Lumber and Lumbering. Texas, eastern. 1900-16. *2207*
—. Brotherhood of Timber Workers. Lumber and Lumbering. Race Relations. Southern Lumber Operators' Association. Texas, eastern. 1911-13. *2217*
Louisville Churchmen's Federation. Barkley, Alben. Gambling. Kentucky. Progressivism. 1917-27. *2438*
Love. Feminism. Labor. Speeches, Addresses, etc. Stanton, Elizabeth Cady. 1868-70. *992*
Lovejoy, Elijah P. Abolition Movement. Assassination. Green, Ann Terry. Marriage. Phillips, Wendell. 1830-67. *759*
Lovejoy, Owen. Abolition Movement. Bryant, John Howard. Bryant, Julian. Civil War. Illinois (Bureau County). Military Service. Negroes. 1831-65. *607*
Low, Juliette. Girl Scouts of America. Identity. Sex roles. 1900-20. *452*
Lowell Female Labor Reform Association. Labor reform. New England. Textile Industry. Women. 1845-47. *819*
Lowry, Morrow B. Higher education. Lowry, Morrow B. (letter). Pennsylvania. Women's rights. 1868. *1413*

Lowry, Morrow B. (letter). Higher education. Lowry, Morrow B. Pennsylvania. Women's rights. 1868. *1413*
Lowry, Sylvanus B. Abolition Movement. Feminism. Journalism. Minnesota. Swisshelm, Jane Grey. 1815-84. *385*
Loyalism. Industrialization. Knights of St. Crispin. Massachusetts (Lynn). Radicals and Radicalism. Working class. 1820-90. *1298*
Loyalty *See also* Patriotism.
—. Elections, congressional. Reconstruction. Virginia. 1865. *960*
Loyalty oath. Border States. Congress. Legislation. Republican Party. South. 1861-67. *950*
LSD. Counter Culture. Kesey, Ken. Political Theory. Wolfe, Thomas Kennerly, Jr. 1964-68. *2992*
Lucifer's Lantern (periodical). Atheism. Mormons. Schroeder, Theodore. Utah. 1889-1900. *1486*
Ludlow Massacre. Coal Mines and Mining. Colorado Fuel and Iron Company. National Guard. Strikes. 1913-14. *2206*
Lukens Iron Works. Authority. Paternalism. Pennsylvania (Coatesville). Profits. Strikes. 1886. *1347*
—. Paternalism. Pennsylvania (Coatesville). Strikes. 1886. *1348*
Lumber and Lumbering. Brotherhood of Timber Workers. Emerson, Arthur L. Industrial Workers of the World. Labor Disputes. Louisiana, western. Texas, eastern. 1900-16. *2207*
—. Brotherhood of Timber Workers. Industrial Workers of the World. Louisiana. Race Relations. Texas. 1910-13. *2215*
—. Brotherhood of Timber Workers. Louisiana, western. Race Relations. Southern Lumber Operators' Association. Texas, eastern. 1911-13. *2217*
—. Community Participation in Politics. Michigan (Bay City, Saginaw). Strikes. 1880's. *1320*
—. Conservation movement. Federal Policy. Pacific Northwest. Property rights. Public Lands. 1870's-90's. *1323*
—. Forest and Farm Workers Union. Hall, Covington. Labor Unions and Organizations. Louisiana. Socialism. 1907-16. *2192*
—. Japanese Americans (Nikkei). Oregon (Toledo). Pacific Spruce Corporation. Riots. 1925-26. *2453*
—. Labor Unions and Organizations. Washington. Workmen's compensation. 1911. *2280*
Lunn, George. New York (Schenectady). Socialist Party. Voting and Voting Behavior. Working Class. 1911-16. *1946*
Luther, Seth. Labor. Reform. Rhode Island. 1795-1863. *342*
Luther v. Borden (US, 1849). Dorr's Rebellion. Election Laws. Rhode Island. State government. Supreme Court. 1842-49. *591*
Lutheran Church (North Carolina Synod). Clergy. Negroes. 1865-89. *1228*
Lynch, James (letters). Methodist Episcopal Church. Mississippi. Negroes. Reconstruction. 1868-69. *1166*
Lynching. Ames, Jessie Daniel. Association of Southern Women for the Prevention of Lynching. Racism. South. Women. 1930's. *2516*
—. Ames, Jessie Daniel. Association of Southern Women for the Prevention of Lynching. South. Women. 1928-42. *2553*
—. Association of Southern Women for the Prevention of Lynching. Negroes. South. Women. 1930-42. *2472*
—. *Free Speech* (newspaper). Negroes. Tennessee (Memphis). Wells, Ida B. 1892. *1128*

M

Mabey, Charles R. Strikes. United Mine Workers of America. Utah (Carbon County). 1922. *2429*
Machinists. Artisans. Convict labor. Kingston Penitentiary. Ontario. Petitions. 1833-36. *826*
MacKinnon, Murdoch. Anti-Catholicism. Education, Finance. Saskatchewan. School Act (amended). Scott, Walter. 1913-26. *1849*
MacLane, Mary. Literature. Montana (Butte). Women. 1902-29. *384*
Madagascar. Colonialism. France. Waller, John L. 1891-95. *1282*
—. France. Negroes. Press. Waller, John L. 1890's. *1281*

Madison College. Adventists. Battle Creek College. Michigan. Sutherland, Edward A. Tennessee. 1897-1904. *2331*
Magazines. *See* Periodicals.
Maine *See also* New England; Northeastern or North Atlantic States.
—. 1830-50. *566*
—. Abolition movement. Fessenden, Samuel. Free Soil movement. Liberty Party. State Politics. Willey, Austin. 1830's-48. *682*
—. Anti-Catholicism. Know-Nothing Party. Morrill, Anson P. Nativism. Working class. 1854-55. *588*
—. Antislavery Sentiments. Civil War. Friends, Society of. Jones, James Parnell. Military Service. 1850's-64. *320*
Mäkelä, A. B. Čačić, Tomo. Ethnic Groups. Kjelt, Ole. Krat, Pavlo. Leftism. Political Protest. Puttee, Arthur. Scarlett, Sam. 1907-34. *1561*
—. Canada. Editors and Editing. Finnish Canadians. Kurikka, Matti. Newspapers. Socialism. 1900-32. *464*
Makonnen, T. Ras. Africa. DuBois, W. E. B. Pan-Africanism. USA. 1919-73. *2881*
Malcolm X. Black Muslims. Ghettos. Political Leadership. Race Relations. 1940-65. *461*
Malkiel, Theresa Serber. Jews. Labor Unions and Organizations. New York City. Socialist Party. Women. 1900's-14. *2035*
Man with the Muck-Rake (speech). Political Speeches. Rhetoric. Roosevelt, Theodore. 1906. *2014*
Management *See also* Collective Bargaining; Industrial Relations.
—. Accidents. Courts. Federal Employers' Liability Act (US, 1908). Railroads. Safety Appliances Act (US, 1893). Working Conditions. 1890-1913. *2117*
—. Congress of Industrial Organizations. Labor Unions and Organizations. National Industrial Recovery Act (US, 1933). National Labor Relations Act (US, 1935). South. Textile Industry. 1933-41. *2613*
—. Education. Negroes. Whites. 1652-1972. *183*
—. Ideology. Industrial Conference, 1st. Labor Unions and Organizations. Wilson, Woodrow. 1919. *2225*
—. Labor Unions and Organizations. 1900-20. *2245*
Management, scientific. Behavior. Labor. 1870-1920. *1330*
—. Buckeye Steel Castings Company. Bush, S. P. Ohio (Columbus). Social Work. Steel Industry. 1890-1920. *2181*
—. Progressivism. Taylor, Frederick W. 1880's-1900's. *2248*
Manitoba *See also* Prairie Provinces.
—. Alberta (Edmonton). Farmer's Union of Alberta. Kyforuk, Peter. Ukrainian Labour-Farmer Association. 1912-30's. *1828*
—. Catholic Church. Church and State. French language. Langevin, Adélard. Politics. Private schools. 1890-1916. *1410*
—. Catholic Church. Church Schools. McCarthy, D'Alton. Provincial legislatures. 1870-90. *1429*
—. Dixon, Frederick John. Farmer, S. J. Independent Labour Party. Single tax. 1920-49. *1791*
Manitoba (Winnipeg). Chipman, George. Editors and Editing. *Grain Growers Guide* (periodical). Reform. Social movements. 1905-30. *1637*
—. Local Government. Queen, John. Socialism. Taxation. 1909-42. *1645*
—. Penner, Jacob. Russia. Socialist Party. 1900-65. *406*
Mann Act (US, 1910). Progressivism. Prostitution. Women. 1910. *2003*
Mann, Mary Tyler Peabody. Economic conditions. Letters. Ohio. Poorhouses. 1795-1858. *884*
Manning, Joseph C. Alabama. Democratic Party. Populism. State Politics. 1892-96. *1387*
Manual training. Educational Reform. Missouri (St. Louis). Woodward, Calvin. 1897-1914. *2305*
Manual Training School. Education. Maryland (Baltimore). Newell, Alexander McFadden. Politics. Shepherd, Henry Elliot. 1876-94. *1428*
Manuscripts *See also* Documents.
—. Education. Indians. Wisconsin. 1820-50. *848*
Maoism. China. Strong, Anna Louise. USSR. 1919-70. *324*

March on Washington Movement. Brotherhood of Sleeping Car Porters. National Negro Congress. Negroes. Randolph, A. Philip. 1925-41. *353*
—. Defense industries. Discrimination. Executive Order 8802. Military. Randolph, A. Philip. Webster, Milton. 1941-44. *2635*
Mare Island Mutiny. California (San Francisco Bay). Courts Martial and Courts of Inquiry. Navies. Negroes. Port Chicago Naval Magazine. Race relations. 1944-48. *2652*
Marine Transport Workers. American Federation of Labor. Industrial Workers of the World. Louisiana. Sailors' Union. Strikes. United Fruit Company. 1913. *2193*
Maritime Provinces *See also* Atlantic Provinces.
—. Medicine, practice of. Professionalization. 1867-1914. *1020*
Maritime Rights Movement. Atlantic Provinces. Reform. Regionalism. 1900-25. *1578*
Marketing. Agriculture and Government. Canadian Chamber of Agriculture. 1935-45. *1780*
Marriage *See also* Divorce; Family; Sex; Women.
—. Abolition Movement. Assassination. Green, Ann Terry. Lovejoy, Elijah P. Phillips, Wendell. 1830-67. *759*
—. Divorce. Feminism. Reform. Stanton, Elizabeth Cady. 1840-90. *1010*
Marsh, Benjamin C. City Planning. National Conference on City Planning. Poor. Population. 1900-17. *1987*
Marsh, Leonard *(Report)*. Canada. Social Security. Socialism. Welfare state. 1930-44. *1771*
Marshall, John. *Dred Scott* v. *Sandford* (US, 1857). Slavery. Supreme Court. Taney, Roger Brooke. 1820-60. *785*
Marshall, Thurgood. Lawyers. Maryland, University of, School of Law. Murray, Donald G. NAACP. School Integration. 1930-54. *2531*
Martial law. Coal Mines and Mining. Glasscock, William E. National Guard. United Mine Workers of America. Violence. West Virginia (Cabin Creek, Paint Creek). 1912-13. *2176*
—. Indiana (Gary). Steel industry. Strikes. 1919. *2244*
—. Internment. Japanese Americans. Tule Lake Camp. World War II. 1941-44. *2641*
Marx, Karl. Antislavery Sentiments. Great Britain. Greeley, Horace. Labor. New York *Tribune.* 1851-62. *764*
Marxism *See also* Anarchism and Anarchists; Class Struggle; Communism; Social Democratic Party; Socialism; Syndicalism.
—. American Socialist Party. Hillquit, Morris. Political Reform. Socialism. 1901-14. *1942*
—. Boston Eight Hour League. International Workingmen's Association. Labor Unions and Organizations. McNeill, George. New York. Steward, Ira. 1860-89. *1307*
—. Bulosan, Carlos. Labor. Literature. 1931-56. *432*
—. Capitalism. Carver, George Washington. Myths and Symbols. Race Relations. South. 1896-1950's. *1604*
—. Debs, Eugene V. Hartz, Louis. Hillquit, Morris. Liberalism. Locke, John. Political culture. 20c. *1986*
—. George, Henry. Great Britain. Hyndman, Henry M. Ireland. Land Reform. 1882-89. *1057*
—. International, 1st. Sorge, Friedrich Adolph. 1852-1906. *1305*
—. Journalism. Labor Unions and Organizations. Negroes. Political protest. Randolph, A. Philip. ca 1911-75. *382*
—. Labor movement. Sorge, Friedrich Adolph. 1866-76. *1308*
Maryland. Armies. Civil War. Freedmen's Bureau. Reconstruction. Reform. 1864-68. *1162*
—. Baltimore City Hospital. Hospitals. 1772-1964. *238*
—. Bond, Hugh Lennox. Ideology. Racism. Republicans (Radical). ca 1861-68. *1002*
—. Colleges and Universities. Equal opportunity. Negroes. 1908-75. *1860*
—. Crothers, Austin Lane. Governors. Progressivism. 1904-12. *1896*
—. Labor Unions and Organizations. NAACP. Negroes. Teachers. 1930's. *2610*
Maryland (Baltimore). Addams, Jane. Hampton, Isabel. Illinois (Chicago). Johns Hopkins Hospital Training School for Nurses. Nurses and Nursing. Professionalization. Social Work. 1889-1910. *1461*
—. Agriculture. Government Regulation. 1750-1820. *149*

—. American Moral Reform Society. Civil Rights. Negroes (free). Watkins, William. 1801-58. *339*
—. City government. Construction. Schools. Urban reform. 1870-1900. *1402*
—. City Government. Negroes. Political protest. Public schools. 1865-1900. *1271*
—. City Government. Negroes. Republican Party. 1890-1931. *1593*
—. City Politics. Progressivism. 1895-1911. *1920*
—. Congress of Industrial Organizations. Negroes. 1930-41. *2580*
—. Education. Manual Training School. Newell, Alexander McFadden. Politics. Shepherd, Henry Elliot. 1876-94. *1428*
Maryland, University of. Feminism. Oral history. Sex Discrimination. 1968-78. *2913*
Maryland, University of, School of Law. Lawyers. Marshall, Thurgood. Murray, Donald G. NAACP. School Integration. 1930-54. *2531*
Mass Media *See also* Films; Newspapers; Radio; Television.
—. Democracy. Publicity. Reform. 1900-29. *1624*
Mass Transit. Boycotts. Negroes. Segregation. Virginia. 1904-07. *2154*
—. Missouri. Modernization. Monopolies. St. Louis Transit Company. Strikes. 1900. *2257*
Massachusetts *See also* New England; Northeastern or North Atlantic States.
—. Abolition Movement. Andover Seminary. Theology. 1825-35. *767*
—. Abolition Movement. Negroes (free). Remond, Charles Lenox. 1838-63. *459*
—. Alcott, Amos Bronson. Fruitlands (community). Lane, Charles. Transcendentalism. Utopias. 1840-50. *922*
—. American Institute for Education. Educational Reform. Elites. Nationalism. Rural schools. 1830-37. *839*
—. American Revolution. Letters. Literature. Warren, Mercy Otis. 1740-1814. *460*
—. Antislavery Sentiments. Brown, John. Harpers Ferry raid. 1859. *706*
—. Antislavery Sentiments. Know-Nothing Party. Nativism. Republican Party. Voting and Voting Behavior. 1850's. *538*
—. Baptists. Church and state. 1630-60. *510*
—. Beverly School. Education, Experimental Methods. Industry. 1900-17. *2321*
—. Blair, Nora Schelter. Brook Farm. Education, Experimental Methods. Personal narratives. Pratt, Frederick. Ripley, George. Utopias. 1841-47. *934*
—. *Boston Daily Evening Voice* (newspaper). Equality. Labor Unions and Organizations. Race Relations. Working Class. 1864-67. *998*
—. Boston Dispensary. Clinics. Davis, Michael M. 1910-20. *2051*
—. Boston Prison Discipline Society. Charlestown State Prison. Penal reform. 1804-78. *860*
—. Bradford, George Partridge. Brook Farm. Daily life. Letters. Utopias. 1841. *932*
—. Constitutional Amendments (19th; ratification). Woman suffrage. 1900-19. *2167*
—. Divorce. Law. Women. 1692-1786. *480*
—. Girls. Lancaster Industrial School for Girls. Reformatories. ca 1850-70. *1444*
—. Great Britain. Labor Unions and Organizations. 1130-1790. *473*
—. Harvard College. Legal education. 1766-1840. *194*
—. Health. Ladies' Physiological Institute of Boston and Vicinity. Middle Classes. Physiology. Women. 1848-59. *902*
—. Oral history. Sullivan, Anna (interview). Textile Workers Union of America. Women. 1918-76. *403*
—. Political Campaigns. Referendum. Woman suffrage. 1895-1920. *2140*
Massachusetts Association Opposed to the Further Extension of the Suffrage to Women. Feminism. Political campaigns. Sex roles. Socialism. Woman suffrage. 1895-1915. *2166*
Massachusetts Bay Colony. Antinomian controversy. Hutchinson, Anne. Women. 1630-43. *520*
—. Bradstreet, Anne. Hutchinson, Anne. Literature. Religion. Social change. Women. 1630's-70's. *489*
Massachusetts (Boston). Abel, Mary Hinman. Aladdin Ovens. Atkinson, Edward. Food Consumption. New England Kitchen. Richards, Ellen H. Working Class. 1889-97. *1467*

Massachusetts

—. Abolition Movement. American Union for the Relief and Improvement of the Colored Race. 1835-37. *761*
—. Abolition Movement. Anti-Catholicism. Ideology. Riots. Social Classes. 1834-35. *555*
—. Abolition Movement. Hayden, Lewis. 1811-89. *420*
—. Africa. Colonization. Cuffe, Paul. Negroes. 1810-15. *728*
—. American Revolution. Slavery. Wheatley, Phillis (letter). Whigs. 1767-80. *504*
—. Antiabolition sentiments. Clergy. Conservatism. Constitutions. Missouri (St. Louis). Unitarianism. 1828-57. *751*
—. Antibusing movement. Models. Political Protest. Social Organizations. 1970's. *2895*
—. Antislavery Sentiments. Eliot, Samuel A. Fugitive Slave Act (US, 1850). Patriotism. Unitarianism. 1850-60. *752*
—. Asylums. Mental Illness. Poor. 1847-1920. *261*
—. Baptists. Negroes. 1800-73. *565*
—. Busing. Community Participation. Political Protest. 1977-78. *2894*
—. Capital punishment. Public Opinion. 1836-54. *886*
—. Central Labor Union. Eight-hour day. Knights of Labor. Labor Unions and Organizations. Strikes. 1886. *1321*
—. Children. Hospitals. New York City. Pediatrics. Pennsylvania (Philadelphia). 1776-1976. *249*
—. Children. Pennsylvania (Philadelphia). Progressivism. Recreation. 1886-1911. *1985*
—. City Government. Editorials. Franklin, James. Freedom of the Press. Inoculation. *New England Courant* (newspaper). Smallpox. 1721. *535*
—. Civil Rights. Roberts, Sarah C. *Sarah C. Roberts* v. *City of Boston* (Massachusetts, 1850). School Integration. 1849-50. 1950's. *834*
—. Crime and Criminals. Gun Control. 1974-76. *2784*
—. Educational Reform. Negroes. Separatist Movements. Smith, Thomas Paul. 1848-49. *855*
—. Filene, Edward A. Industrial democracy. Reform. 1890-1937. *1787*
—. Freedom. Fugitive Slaves. Latimer, George. Law. Sewall, Samuel E. Shaw, Lemuel. ca 1790-1890. *784*
—. Garment Industry. Labor. Women. 1869. *1287*
—. League of Women for Community Service. Negroes. Voluntary Associations. Women. 1918-77. *1575*
—. Negroes. ca 1800-60. *560*
—. Social Customs. Temperance movements. Values. Working class. 1838-40. *868*
Massachusetts (Boston, Manchester). Bartol, Cyrus. Investments. Real estate. Transcendentalism. 1850-96. *1015*
Massachusetts (Boston, Quincy). Adams, Charles Francis. Conservation. Parks. 1880's-90's. *1070*
Massachusetts (Boston; South End). Federal Government. Local Government. Middle Classes. Neighborhoods. Poor. Urban revitalization. 1960's-70's. *2694*
Massachusetts (Cambridge). Antislavery Sentiments. Longfellow, Henry Wadsworth (*Poems on Slavery*). 1842. *665*
—. Corporal punishment. Eaton, Nathaniel. Harvard University. Puritans. Trials. 1638. *495*
Massachusetts (Fall River). Howard, Robert. Labor Disputes. Textile industry. 1860-85. *1346*
Massachusetts (Fall River, Lynn). Associated Charities. Charities. Leadership. Men. Social Policy. Women. 1880-1900. *1447*
Massachusetts (Haverhill). Shoe Industry. Strikes. Women. 1895. *1288*
Massachusetts (Lancaster). Girls. Juvenile Delinquency. Socialization. State Industrial School for Girls. 1856-1905. *1443*
Massachusetts (Lawrence). Christianity. Industrial Relations. Scudder, Vida Dutton. Women. 1912. *2196*
—. Everett Mill. Polish Americans. Radicals and Radicalism. Strikes. Textile Industry. Women. 1912. *2252*
Massachusetts (Lowell). Cotton. Hamilton Manufacturing Company. Labor Disputes. Social mobility. Textile Industry. Women. 1836-60. *818*

SUBJECT INDEX

—. Strikes. Values. Women. 1820-50. *548*
Massachusetts (Lynn). Casson, Herbert N. Labor Church. Socialism. Working class. 1893-98. *1498*
—. Industrialization. Knights of St. Crispin. Loyalism. Radicals and Radicalism. Working class. 1820-90. *1298*
—. Labor Unions and Organizations. Shoe Industry. Working class. 1895-1925. *2197*
Massachusetts (Marblehead). Devereux Mansion. Hall, Herbert. Mental Illness. Occupational therapy. Work Cure Program. 1912-23. *1969*
Massachusetts (Marlboro). Public Opinion. Shoe Industry. Strikes. 1898-99. *1300*
Massachusetts (Mashpee). Apes, William. Indian-white relations. Reform. Wampanoag Indians. 1830-40. *600*
Massachusetts (Milford). Ballou, Adin Augustus. Draper, E. D. Hopedale Community. Utopias. 1824-56. *917*
—. Ballou, Adin Augustus. Hopedale Community. Religion. Utopias. 1830-42. *938*
Massachusetts (Salem). Antislavery lecturer. Great Britain. Negroes. Remond, Sarah Parker. Women. 1856-87. *294*
—. Domestics. Female Charitable Society. Girls. Industrialization. 1800-40. *882*
Massachusetts (Somerville). Democratic Party. Educational reform. Ethnic groups. Junior High Schools. Middle Classes. Progressivism. 1912-24. *2335*
Massachusetts (Springfield). Abolition Movement. Riots. Thompson, George. 1851. *667*
—. Cholera. City Government. Hospitals. Sanitation. 1865-70. *1471*
Massachusetts (Ware). Cooke, Parsons. Industrialization. Missions and Missionaries. Puritans. 19c. *906*
Massachusetts, western. Alcohol. Prohibition. Romanelli, John. 1919-20. *2069*
—. *Chicopee News*. Massachusetts (Westfield). Newspapers. Prostitution. 1911. *2102*
Massachusetts (Westfield). *Chicopee News*. Massachusetts, western. Newspapers. Prostitution. 1911. *2102*
Massacres. Franklin, Benjamin. Indians. Pamphlets. Paxton Boys. Pennsylvania. 1764. *499*
Mastication. Fletcher, Horace. Hygiene. Nutrition. 1890-1910. *2120*
Match industry. Labor. Quebec (Hull). Syndicat Catholique des Allumettières. Women. 1919-24. *1775*
Materialism. Ecology. Krutch, Joseph Wood. Values. 1920's-70. *1660*
Mathematics. History. Institute for Advanced Study. New Jersey (Princeton). Research. Social Sciences. 1930-79. *2435*
Mather, Cotton. Attitudes. New England. Sermons. Women. 1650-1800. *493*
—. Clergy. Medicine. *Nishmath-chajim* (concept). 1700-22. *534*
Mathews, Henry M. Baltimore and Ohio Railroad. Railroads. Strikes. West Virginia (Martinsburg, Berkeley County). 1877. *1301*
Mathews, Shailer. Modernism. Science. Social gospel. Theology. 1864-1930. *446*
Mattachine Society. Communist Party. Hay, Henry (interview). Homosexuality. 1950-53. *2672*
Matthews, Mark Allison. Fundamentalism. Presbyterian Church. Washington (Seattle). 1900-40. *430*
Maurin, Peter ("Easy Essays"). Catholic Worker Movement. Political Theory. 1920's-33. *2419*
Maximum hours laws. Employment. Immigrants. Law Enforcement. State Government. Women. 1920. *2398*
May, Samuel. Abolition Movement. Follen, Charles Theodore Christian. Harvard University. 1824-42. *753*
McAlister, Alexander W. North Carolina. Public Welfare. 1910-45. *1569*
McCabe, Edward Preston. Homesteading and Homesteaders. Migration, Internal. Negroes. Oklahoma. 1891-94. *1204*
—. Migration, Internal. Negroes. Newspapers. Oklahoma (Langston). 1850-1920. *1246*
McCalla, Daniel. Presbyterian Church. 1770's-1809. *299*
McCarthy, D'Alton. Catholic Church. Church Schools. Manitoba. Provincial legislatures. 1870-90. *1429*
McCarthy, Joseph R. Communist Control Act (US,1954). Humphrey, Hubert H. Liberalism. 1954. *2675*

Medical Care

McCarthy, Patrick Henry. Ireland (Limerick). Irish Americans. Labor Unions and Organizations. Leadership. Youth. 1863-80. *402*
McChesney, Henry V. Kentucky. Morrow, Edwin P. Political Campaigns (gubernatorial). Prohibition. Stanley, Augustus Owsley. 1915. *1873*
McClung, Nellie L. Canada. Feminism. Literature. Politics. Reform. 1873-1930's. *1689*
—. Canada. Methodist Church. Ordination. United Church of Canada. Women. 1915-46. *1597*
McCreary, James B. Beckham, John C. W. Kentucky. Progressivism. State Government. Willson, Augustus E. 1899-1915. *1894*
McCumber, Porter James. Conservatism. McKenzie, Alexander John. North Dakota. Political reform. Republican Party. Suffrage. Women. 1898-1933. *435*
McDonough, David. Africa. American Colonization Society. Colonization. Medical Education. Presbyterian Church. Slavery. 1840-50. *710*
McGregor, Hugh. Comte, Auguste. Foster, Frank K. Gompers, Samuel. Ideology. Labor Unions and Organizations. Spencer, Herbert. 1876-1900. *1295*
McGuire, Bird S. Flynn, Dennis T. House of Representatives. Oklahoma. Progressivism. 1901-07. *1905*
McIntosh, Lachlan. American Revolution. Attitudes. Slavery. South. Wealth. 1775-87. *517*
McKaig, Robert Raymond. Farmers. Idaho. Intellectuals. Nonpartisan League. North Dakota. ca 1920-45. *2406*
McKelway, Alexander. Journalism. Murphy, Edgar Gardner. Page, Walter Hines. South. 1890-1916. *1876*
McKenzie, Alexander John. Conservatism. McCumber, Porter James. North Dakota. Political reform. Republican Party. Suffrage. Women. 1898-1933. *435*
McKinley, William. Elections. Ohio. Republican Party. Working class. 1891-93. *1355*
McLean, Mary Hancock. Medicine (practice of). Missouri (St. Louis). Women. 1883-1930. *359*
McMahon, Patrick. Catholic Church. Immigrants. Irish Americans. Poor. Quebec (Quebec). St. Bridget's Home. 1847-79. *244*
McNamara case. American Federation of Labor. Bombing. California (Los Angeles). Labor movement. *Los Angeles Times*. Progressives. 1910-14. *2265*
—. Christianity. Class Struggle. *Los Angeles Times*. Progressivism. Radicals and Radicalism. Steffens, Lincoln. 1908-12. *2083*
McNary-Haugen bill. Farmers. Montana. Pacific Northwest. Prices. Tariff. 1920-29. *2410*
McNeill, George. Boston Eight Hour League. International Workingmen's Association. Labor Unions and Organizations. Marxism. New York. Steward, Ira. 1860-89. *1307*
McWilliams, Carey. Agricultural labor. California. Historians. 1939. *2587*
Meachum, John Berry. African Baptist Church. Education. Emancipation. Missouri (St. Louis). Negroes. 1815-54. *395*
Mead, George Herbert. 1894-1927. *322*
Mead, Margaret. Scholars. Social sciences. Talbot, Marion. Thompson, Helen. Women. 1900-20's. *2065*
Meadows, Clarence W. Educational reform. Public Schools. Strayer, George D. Trent, W. W. West Virginia Education Association. 1932-58. *1837*
Meat packing industry. Illinois (Chicago; Back of the Yards). Labor Unions and Organizations. Polish Americans. Strikes. 1921. *2424*
Mechanics' Mutual Protection (society). Agricultural College Act (US, 1862). Agriculture. Labor. New York. People's College. 1843-60's. *1427*
Mechanization. Coopers' International Union. Industrial Relations. Standard Oil Company of Ohio. 1870's. *1313*
—. Labor. Production control. 19c-20c. *165*
Medical Care *See also* terms beginning with the word health.
—. Arizona (Tucson; Tent City). Baptists. Comstock, Oliver E. St. Luke's-in-the-Desert Hospital. 1907-37. *1596*
—. Arkansas. Mental illness. 1870's-1970's. *234*
—. Arkansas (Lee County). Clinics. Cooperatives. Negroes. 1960's-70's. *2977*

—. Big Spring State Hospital. Harrison, Preston E. Mental Illness. Texas (western). 1946-77. *2981*
—. Charities. Progressivism. Scientific management. 1900-20. *2064*
—. Child Welfare Commission. Socialism. Wisconsin (Milwaukee). 1911-12. *2032*
—. Coal Mines and Mining. United Mine Workers of America (Welfare and Retirement Fund). 1946-78. *1747*
—. Federal Government. Poor. Public Health. 1960-77. *2982*
—. Federal Programs. Poor. 1963-76. *2975*
—. Federal regulation. Physicians. Professional Standards Review Organization Program. Social Security Act (US, 1935; Title XX, 1972). 1965-80. *2978*
—. Mormon, Square. Poor People's Health Council. Race relations. Rossville Health Center. Tennessee (Fayette County). 1960's-70's. *2821*
—. Neighborhoods. Ohio (Cincinnati; Mohawk-Brighton). Phillips, Wilbur C. 1917-20. *2037*
Medical Education. Africa. American Colonization Society. Colonization. McDonough, David. Presbyterian Church. Slavery. 1840-50. *710*
—. American Medical Association. Carnegie Foundation. Flexner Report. Reform. 1910-32. *2297*
—. American Medical Association. Medical reform. 1895-1915. *2319*
—. Auburn Medical Institution. New York. 1825. *830*
—. Biochemistry. Medical Reform. 1890-1920. *1992*
—. Blackwell, Elizabeth. Feminism. Pennsylvania (Philadelphia). 1821-1910. *809*
—. Brookings, Robert. Flexner Report. Missouri (St. Louis). Reform. Washington University. 1910-16. *2318*
—. Buffalo Medical College. Libel. Loomis, Horatio N. Midwifery. New York. Obstetrics. White, James Platt. 1850. *869*
—. Cincinnati College of Medicine and Surgery. Ohio. Women. 1875-1910. *966*
—. Coeducation. Homeopathy. Ohio (Cincinnati). Pulte Medical College. 1873-79. *1403*
—. Columbia University (Medical School). New York City. Professionalization. 1760's. *488*
—. Elites. Social status. 1890-1973. *1784*
—. Flexner Report. Legal education. Reed Report (1921). 1910-74. *1862*
—. Flint, Austin. 1830's-70's. *256*
—. Foundations. Gates, Frederick T. Physicians. Research, Clinical. Rockefeller, John D. 1910-39. *1833*
—. Frontier and Pioneer Life. Kentucky. Mitchell, Thomas Duche. Reform. 1809-65. *325*
—. Meharry Medical College. Negroes. Tennessee (Nashville). 1860's-1970's. *226*
—. Polyclinics. Specialization. 1880-1900. *1431*
Medical ethics. Cabot, Richard C. 1906-16. *1900*
—. Cuba. Medical research. Reed, Walter. Yellow fever. 1900-01. *1883*
Medical reform. Adventists. Bible. 1800's-63. *867*
—. Adventists. Hydrotherapy. Jackson, James Caleb. New York (Dansville). White, Ellen G. 1864-65. *1470*
—. American Medical Association. Medical education. 1895-1915. *2319*
—. Arkansas. Pharmacy. Physicians. 1880-1910. *243*
—. Biochemistry. Medical Education. 1890-1920. *1992*
—. Blanchet, François. Quebec. 1776-1824. *861*
—. Canniff, William. Ontario (Toronto). Public health. 1869-90. *1468*
—. Childbirth. Twilight sleep. Women. 1914-15. *2004*
—. Human Rights. Mental Illness. Packard, Elizabeth. 1863-97. *356*
—. Lewis, Dioclesius. Morality. Rhythmics. Sex. Women. 1860-1970's. *1481*
—. Mental health. Professionalization. Territorial Government. Washington. 1853-75. *1459*
—. Middle Classes. Women. 1820-70. *893*
Medical research. Cuba. Medical ethics. Reed, Walter. Yellow fever. 1900-01. *1883*
—. Franklin, Benjamin. Inoculation. 1730-50. *532*
Medical societies. Women. 19c. *1032*
Medicine *See also* headings beginning with the word medical; Bacteriology; Clinics; Hospitals; Nurses and Nursing; Pharmacy; Physicians.

—. Abolitionists. Brown, William Wells. Negroes. Remond, Sarah Parker. Ruggles, David. Smith, James McCune. Tubman, Harriet. 1810-85. *329*
—. American Medical Association. Sex Discrimination. 1847-1910. *1031*
—. Americas (North and South). Columbia University College of Pharmacy. Pharmacy. Rusby, Henry Hurd. Scientific Expeditions. ca 1880-1930. *286*
—. Birth control. Foote, Edward Bliss. New York. 1858-1906. *543*
—. Black lung disease. Coal Mine Health and Safety Act (US, 1969; amended, 1972). Coal Mines and Mining. Strikes, wildcat. United Mine Workers of America. Workmen's Compensation. 1968-72. *2717*
—. City Government. Reform. Refuse disposal. Sanitation. Technology. Wisconsin (Milwaukee). 1867-1911. *1466*
—. Clergy. Mather, Cotton. *Nishmath-chajim* (concept). 1700-22. *534*
—. Euthanasia. Great Britain. Tollemache, Lionel A. Williams, Samuel D., Jr. 1870's-90's. *1452*
—. Flexner Report. Professionalism. Progressive era. Social control. 1910. *2317*
—. Health. 17c-20c. *2980*
—. Mental illness. State Government. 1700-1977. *247*
—. Mesmerism. Phrenology. Psychology. Sunderland, La Roy. 1820-68. *880*
—. Social change. Therapeutics. 19c. *252*
Medicine and State *See also* Public Health.
—. American Medical Association. Public health. 1860's-1917. *224*
—. Birth control. Law. Public Policy. 19c. *40*
—. Federal programs. Legislation. 1965-77. *2979*
Medicine (practice of) *See also* Diseases; Nurses and Nursing.
—. Adventists. Kellogg, Merritt (diary). Trall, Russell Thacher. 1844-77. *894*
—. American Medical Association. Arkansas Medical Society. Brinkley, John R. Quackery. 1920-42. *2583*
—. Andral, Gabriel. Bloodletting. Denman, Thomas. Dewees, William P. Obstetrics. 1800-1945. *254*
—. Anesthesia. Childbirth. Twilight sleep movement. Women. 1902-23. *2034*
—. Attitudes. Chiropractic. Cults. Science. 1850's-1970's. *229*
—. Bureaucracies. California (San Francisco). Municipal Clinic. Venereal disease. 1911. *2084*
—. Codman, Ernest Amory. Hospitals. 1910-23. *2056*
—. Maritime Provinces. Professionalization. 1867-1914. *1020*
—. McLean, Mary Hancock. Missouri (St. Louis). Women. 1883-1930. *359*
Medicine, preventive. 1880-1910. *241*
—. Milk scandal. Political Corruption. Progressivism. Public health. Rhode Island (Providence). 1913. *1915*
—. Occupations. Public health. Rosen, George. Social History. 1930's-77. *442*
Medicines, Patent. Health. Nebraska (Omaha). Sanitation. 1870-1900. *1456*
Medill, William. Bureau of Indian Affairs. Educational policy. Indians. 1845-49. *836*
Medrick, George. Coal Mines and Mining. Diaries. Pennsylvania, western. Strikes. United Mine Workers of America. 1927. *2372*
Meharry Medical College. Medical education. Negroes. Tennessee (Nashville). 1860's-1970's. *226*
Memoirs. *See* individual names with the subdivision (memoir); Autobiography.
Men. Associated Charities. Charities. Leadership. Massachusetts (Fall River, Lynn). Social Policy. Women. 1880-1900. *1447*
—. Economic opportunity. Educational achievements. Sex Discrimination. Women. 1962. 1973. *2908*
—. Garment industry. Illinois (Chicago). Strikes. 1910-11. *2286*
—. Iowa. Referendum. Voting and Voting Behavior. Woman suffrage. 1916. *2159*
Menard, John Willis. Florida. Negroes. Political Leadership. 1871-90. *283*
Mencken, H. L. Feminism. Morality. 1900-56. *1641*

Mendez v. *Westminster* (California, 1946). California (Orange County). Mexican Americans. Public schools. Segregation (*de jure, de facto*). 1850-1970's. *1865*
Mennonites. Alberta (Linden). Church Schools. Courts. Religious Liberty. 1977-78. *2780*
—. Arapaho Indians. Cheyenne Indians. Indians. Missions and Missionaries. 1880-1900. *1030*
—. Civil service. Conscription, military. World War II. 1930's-45. *2632*
—. Dunkards. Friends, Society of. Militarism. Pacifism. 1900-78. *1571*
—. Kansas. Liberty bonds. Pacifism. Vigilantism. World War I. 1918. *2146*
—. Literature. Pacifism. 20c. *1693*
—. Social consciousness. 1890-1905. *1945*
Menominee Indians. Alberta. Blackfoot Indians (Blood). Identity. Indians. Militancy. Wisconsin. 1950's-60's. *1685*
Mental healing. Evans, Warren Felt. Idealism. Mysticism. Romanticism. 1864-89. *1480*
Mental health. Medical Reform. Professionalization. Territorial Government. Washington. 1853-75. *1459*
—. Physicians. Psychiatry. 1917-41. *1541*
Mental health system. Feminism. Social conditions. 20c. *2918*
Mental Illness *See also* Psychiatry.
—. Aged. Crime and Criminals. Deinstitutionalization. 19c-20c. *227*
—. Arkansas. Medical care. 1870's-1970's. *234*
—. Asylums. Decarceration. 1950's-75. *2983*
—. Asylums. Massachusetts (Boston). Poor. 1847-1920. *261*
—. Asylums. New Brunswick. Nova Scotia. 1749-1900. *228*
—. Big Spring State Hospital. Harrison, Preston E. Medical care. Texas (western). 1946-77. *2981*
—. Crime and Criminals. Deinstitutionalization. 1960's-70's. *2984*
—. Devereux Mansion. Hall, Herbert. Massachusetts (Marblehead). Occupational therapy. Work Cure Program. 1912-23. *1969*
—. Human Rights. Medical Reform. Packard, Elizabeth. 1863-97. *356*
—. Medicine. State Government. 1700-1977. *247*
Mental Retardation Facilities and Community Mental Health Centers Construction Act (US, 1963). Domestic Policy. Kennedy, John F. Politics. Social Security Act (US, 1935; amended, 1963). 1961-63. *2976*
Merchant Marine. Atlantic Provinces. Boardinghouses. Government. Labor. ca 1850's-90's. *996*
Mercy Hospital (proposed). Discrimination. Hospitals. Negroes. Ohio (Cleveland). 1927-30. *2380*
Meriam, Lewis (*Problem of Indian Administration*). Federal Policy. Indians. Reform. Social conditions. 1920-28. *2362*
Meriam Report (1928). Bureau of Indian Affairs. Indian Reorganization Act (US, 1934). 1928-34. *2444*
Merton, Thomas. Cities. Nonviolence. Reform. Social criticism. 1960's. *2737*
Mesmerism. Medicine. Phrenology. Psychology. Sunderland, La Roy. 1820-68. *880*
Metal and Machinery Workers' Industrial Union (440). Industrial Workers of the World. Ohio (Cleveland). 1918-50. *1826*
Methodism. Canada. Children. 1850-1900. *1495*
—. Canada. Communist Party. Labour Party. Smith, Albert Edward. Social Gospel. 1893-1924. *410*
—. Canada. Social gospel. 1890-1914. *23*
—. Commission on the Status and Role of Women in the United Methodist Church. Feminism. Social Organizations. 1869-1974. *72*
—. Protestantism. Values. 1784-1924. *56*
Methodist Church. Abolition Movement. Hersey, John. Millenarianism. Perfectionism. 1786-1862. *541*
—. Antislavery sentiments. Baptists. Presbyterian Church. South. 1740-1860. *699*
—. Assimilation. Finley, James B. Indians (agencies). Missions and Missionaries. Ohio. Shaw, John. 1820-24. *581*
—. Bible. Religion in the Public Schools. Wisconsin. 1846-90. *1418*
—. Canada. McClung, Nellie L. Ordination. United Church of Canada. Women. 1915-46. *1597*
—. Civil rights. Georgia. Tilly, Dorothy. 1900's-70. *438*

Methodist Church

—. Freedmen. Hartzell, Joseph C. Missions and Missionaries. Republican Party. South. 1870-73. *1208*
—. Fugitive Slave Act (US, 1850). Newspapers. Slavery. 1850. *684*
—. Social Organizations. Temperance movements. 1919-72. *1613*

Methodist Episcopal Church. Asbury, Francis. Coke, Thomas. Slavery. 1780-1816. *624*
—. Asians. Conservatism. Immigration. Social Gospel. 1865-1908. *1029*
—. Bishops. Peck, Jesse T. Social gospel. 1850-83. *1025*
—. Colonization. Liberia. Missions and Missionaries. Negroes. Sierra Leone. 1833-48. *641*
—. Documents. Slave Revolts. Turner, Nat. Virginia. 1831-32. *908*
—. Lynch, James (letters). Mississippi. Negroes. Reconstruction. 1868-69. *1166*
—. Missions and Missionaries. Women's Foreign Missionary Society. 1869-1900. *1491*

Methodist Episcopal Church (General Conference). Abolition Movement. Cass, William D. Letters. 1844. *693*

Methodist Episcopal Church, South. Candler, Warren A. Political Campaigns (presidential). Prohibition. Religion. Smith, Alfred E. 1928. *2344*

Methodist Federation for Social Service. American League for Peace and Democracy. Social criticism. Ward, Harry F. 1900-40. *376*
—. Federal Council of Churches of Christ in America. North, Frank M. Social Creed of Methodism. Ward, Harry F. 1907-12. *1956*

Methodist Protestant Church. Shaw, Anna Howard. Social Gospel. Woman suffrage. 1880-1919. *448*
—. Women. 19c. *77*

Methodology See also Models; Quantitative Methods; Research.
—. Consumer protection. Drugs. Federal regulation. Legislation. 1962-73. *2956*
—. Cruse, Harold. Culture. Intellectuals. Negroes. 1910-75. *1519*
—. District of Columbia. Firearms Control Regulations Act (US, 1975). Gun control. US Conference of Mayors (report). 1975-80. *2778*
—. Farmers. Southern Farmers' Alliance. 1884-90. *1391*
—. Oral history. Paul, Alice (memoirs). Woman Suffrage. 1912-77. *335*
—. Political Protest. Psychoanalysis. Social conditions. Students. 1900-75. *1616*

Metis. Canada. Education. Federal government. Indians. 1940-70. *2959*

Metropolitan Areas See also terms beginning with the word urban; Cities.
—. Discrimination, housing. School integration. 1945-77. *1858*
—. Missions and Missionaries. Presbyterian Church. 1869-1977. *84*
—. Race Relations. Segregation, residential. 1960-70. *2896*

Metropolitan Police Force. Louisiana (New Orleans). Negroes. Politics. Riots. Whites. 1868. *1168*

Mexican Americans. Agricultural labor. California (San Joaquin Valley). Japanese Americans. Nisei Farmers League. United Farm Workers Union. 1971-77. *2926*
—. Boycotts. Presbyterian Church. Public schools. Segregation. Texas (San Angelo). 1910-15. *2303*
—. California (Los Angeles). Congress of Industrial Organizations. Labor Unions and Organizations. 1938-50. *1521*
—. California (Los Angeles). Curricula. Educational reform. Public schools. 1920's-30's. *1842*
—. California (Los Angeles). Pacific Electric Railroad. Strikes. 1900-03. *2289*
—. California (Orange County). *Mendez* v. *Westminster* (California, 1946). Public schools. Segregation *(de jure, de facto)*. 1850-1970's. *1865*
—. Carden, Georgiana. Compulsory Education. Elementary education. Migrant Labor. 1920's. *2383*
—. Chavez, Cesar. La Raza Unida Party. 1968-73. *2711*
—. Citizenship. Courts. Nationality. Race. 1846-97. *135*
—. Civil Rights. Labor Unions and Organizations. North Central States. Social Organizations. 1900-76. *1659*
—. Community control. Elections. Texas (Crystal City). 1910-75. *2739*
—. Crusade for Justice. Gonzales, Rodolfo "Corky". Southwest. 1966-72. *2735*
—. Deportation. Immigrants. Labor Unions and Organizations. New Deal. 1930's. *2500*
—. Discrimination. Labor Unions and Organizations. North Central States. Steel Industry. 1919-45. *1802*
—. Discrimination. Political Participation. 1930-75. *1679*
—. Labor. Southwest. 1896-1915. *1908*
—. Labor Unions and Organizations. Socialism. Texas. 1900-20. *2291*
—. Minorities in Politics. Public Schools. Self-perception. Texas (southern). 1930's-69. *1863*
—. Nationalism. Poetry. 1945-77. *1711*
—. Political activism. Primer Congreso Mexicanista (1911). Texas (Laredo). 1910-11. *2010*
—. Racism. Sterilization. Women. 20c. *2704*
—. Social consciousness. Theater, guerrilla. 1965-76. *2710*

Mexican War. Abolition Movement. Antiwar sentiment. Ohio. Propaganda. Protestant Churches. 1847. *561*
—. Corwin, Thomas. Political Speeches. Whig Party. 1847. *540*

Mexico. Armies. Drugs. New Mexico (Columbus). Pershing, John J. Prostitution. Venereal disease. 1916-17. *2068*
—. Berry pickers. California (El Monte). Foreign Relations. Japan. Strikes. 1933. *2522*
—. Canada. Civil rights. Law. USA. Violence. 18c-1974. *119*
—. Communist Party. Labor Unions and Organizations. 1935-39. *2540*

Mexico (Tijuana). California (San Diego). Freedom of speech. Industrial Workers of the World. 1911-12. *2162*

Mexico (Topolobampo). Austin, Alice Constance. California (Llano del Rio). Feminism. Housework. Howland, Marie Stevens. Utopias. 1874-1917. *929*
—. Harmony Society. Koreshan Unity. Olombia. Utopias. 1879-93. *1500*

Michigan See also North Central States.
—. Adrian College. Hillsdale College. Oberlin College. Ohio. Olivet College. 1833-70. *851*
—. Adventists. Battle Creek College. Madison College. Sutherland, Edward A. Tennessee. 1897-1904. *2331*
—. Catholic Church. Church and State. Compulsory education. Politics. 1920-25. *2348*
—. Charities. Jewish Welfare Federation of Detroit. Social Organizations. 1926. *2367*
—. Children. Coldwater State Public School. Crime and Criminals. Protestantism. 1874-96. *1430*
—. Children. Prisons. Reformatories. 1851-58. *900*
—. Detroit Citizens League. Leland, Henry. Progressivism. Social Classes. 1912-24. *1925*
—. Ethnicity. Local option. Prohibition. 1889-1917. *1928*
—. Evangelism. Political parties. State Legislatures. 1837-61. *578*
—. Farmer-Labor Party. New Deal. State Politics. 1933-37. *2541*

Michigan (Battle Creek). Labor Disputes. Open shop movement. Post, Charles William. 1895-1920. *2239*

Michigan (Bay City, Saginaw). Community Participation in Politics. Lumber and Lumbering. Strikes. 1880's. *1320*

Michigan (Beaver Island). Michigan, Lake. Strang, James Jesse. Utopias. Wisconsin (Voree). 1820-56. *942*

Michigan (Cass County). Fugitive Slave Act (US, 1850). Kentucky (Boone, Bourbon counties). Slaveholders. 1830-60. *786*

Michigan (Detroit). Anti-Nazi Movements. Boycotts. Fram, Leon (reminiscences). Jews. League for Human Rights. 1930's-40's. *2507*
—. Automobile Industry and Trade. Communist Party USA. Labor Unions and Organizations. 1920's-1935. *1799*
—. Automobile Industry and Trade. Labor Unions and Organizations. League of Revolutionary Black Workers. Negroes. 1968-73. *2832*
—. Dancey, John C. Discrimination. Urban League. Washington, Forrester B. 1916-39. *1696*
—. Grenell, Judson. Knights of Labor. Labadie, Joseph. Socialist Labor Party. 1877-86. *1334*

Michigan (Grand Rapids). City Government. Ellis, George E. Progressivism. 1894-1921. *2106*

Michigan, Lake. Michigan (Beaver Island). Strang, James Jesse. Utopias. Wisconsin (Voree). 1820-56. *942*

Michigan (Pontiac). Public schools. Race relations. School Integration. 1971-74. *2827*

Micmac Indians. Assimilation. Education. Indians. Nova Scotia. Public policy. Religion. 1605-1872. *209*
—. Bromley, Walter. Charities. Nova Scotia. Poverty. Self-help. 1813-25. *870*

Micronesia. Pacific Dependencies (US). Self-determination. Social Conditions. 1947-80. *2776*

Middle Classes. Adult education. Halifax Mechanics' Institute. Nova Scotia. Working class. 1830's-40's. *845*
—. Attitudes. Janesville Associated Charities. Poor. Wisconsin. 1870-1900. *1450*
—. California (Orange County). Oneida Community. Religion. Social Organization. Townerites. 1848-1900's. *1514*
—. Canada. Civil service. Ideology. Labor Unions and Organizations. 1918-28. *1820*
—. Colleges and Universities. Douglass, Mabel Smith. Lobbying. New Jersey College for Women. Women. 1911-18. *2324*
—. Courts. Industrialists. Juvenile Delinquency. Philanthropy. Reform. 1890-99. *1472*
—. Democratic Party. Educational reform. Ethnic groups. Junior High Schools. Massachusetts (Somerville). Progressivism. 1912-24. *2335*
—. Discrimination, Educational. Disfranchisement. Negro Suffrage. North Carolina. Progressivism. Public Finance. Whites. 1880-1910. *2316*
—. Federal Government. Local Government. Massachusetts (Boston; South End). Neighborhoods. Poor. Urban revitalization. 1960's-70's. *2694*
—. Feminism. Labor Unions and Organizations. Lobbying. Suffrage. Women's Trade Union League. ca 1903-20. *1980*
—. Health. Ladies' Physiological Institute of Boston and Vicinity. Massachusetts. Physiology. Women. 1848-59. *902*
—. Labor movement. Schools, summer. South. Women. 1927-41. *1580*
—. Medical reform. Women. 1820-70. *893*
—. Political Reform. Progressivism. ca 1880-1920. *1871*
—. Progressivism. Reform. Voting and Voting Behavior. Wisconsin. 1890's-1917. *2127*

Midwifery. Buffalo Medical College. Libel. Loomis, Horatio N. Medical Education. New York. Obstetrics. White, James Platt. 1850. *869*

Migrant Labor. California (Wheatland). Industrial Workers of the World. State Government. Strikes. Trials. 1913-17. *2198*
—. Carden, Georgiana. Compulsory Education. Elementary education. Mexican Americans. 1920's. *2383*

Migration, Internal See also Resettlement.
—. Charities. Galveston Plan of 1907. Immigration. Industrial Removal Office. Jews. New York City. 1890-1914. *1476*
—. Civil Rights. Constitutions. Supreme Court. 1780's-1977. *138*
—. Homesteading and Homesteaders. McCabe, Edward Preston. Negroes. Oklahoma. 1891-94. *1204*
—. Industrial Relations. Negroes. Pine industry. South. Working conditions. ca 1912-26. *1577*
—. McCabe, Edward Preston. Negroes. Newspapers. Oklahoma (Langston). 1850-1920. *1246*

Miles, James Warley. Conservatism. DuBose, William Porcher. Episcopal Church, Protestant. Murphy, Edgar Gardner. South. Theology. 1840-1920. *62*

Militancy. Alberta. Blackfoot Indians (Blood). Identity. Indians. Menominee Indians. Wisconsin. 1950's-60's. *1685*
—. American Federation of Labor. International Brotherhood of Pulp, Sulphite, and Paper Mill Workers. Labor Unions and Organizations. Paper industry. 1933-35. *2615*
—. Catto, Octavius V. Civil Rights. Pennsylvania (Philadelphia). 1861-71. *440*
—. Civil rights. Negroes. Religion. 1960's-70's. *2844*
—. Factionalism. United Automobile Workers of America. 1937-41. *2482*

Militarism See also Civil-Military Relations; Imperialism.

—. Dunkards. Friends, Society of. Mennonites. Pacifism. 1900-78. *1571*
—. Hammond, John Hays. Peace Movements. 1898-1914. *2017*
Military *See also* headings beginning with the words military and paramilitary; Armies; Civil-Military Relations; Conscription, Military; Defense Policy; Navies.
—. Alabama. Racism. Randolph, Ryland. Reconstruction. Trials. Tuscaloosa *Independent Monitor*. 1868. *986*
—. American Federation of Labor. Gompers, Samuel. Labor Unions and Organizations. Preparedness. Wilson, Woodrow. 1914-17. *2000*
—. Defense industries. Discrimination. Executive Order 8802. March on Washington Movement. Randolph, A. Philip. Webster, Milton. 1941-44. *2635*
—. Hancock, Winfield Scott. Louisiana. Mower, Joseph Anthony. Reconstruction. Texas. 1865-68. *989*
—. Hastie, William H. Negroes. Racism. Stimson, Henry L. World War II. 1940-43. *2636*
—. Sex roles. Women. World War II. 1941-44. *2628*
Military Law *See also* Courts Martial and Courts of Inquiry.
—. Ansell, Samuel T. Chamberlain, George. Congress. Crowder, Enoch H. Lenroot, Irvine L. Progressivism. 1916-20. *2408*
Military Occupation. Civil War. Contraband programs. Fugitive slaves. Louisiana, southern. 1862-65. *1219*
—. Cuba. Progressivism. Wood, Leonard. 1899-1902. *1951*
—. Democratic Party. Elections. Louisiana. Reconstruction. Rousseau, Lovell H. 1868-69. *990*
—. Louisiana. Negro Suffrage. Reconstruction. Sheridan, Philip H. 1865-67. *991*
Military Organization. Army. Civilian Conservation Corps. Negroes. 1933-42. *2528*
Military Recruitment *See also* Conscription, Military.
—. American Revolution. Negroes. 1770-1802. *527*
—. Armies. Hastie, William H. Negroes. Press. World War II. 1940-42. *2638*
—. Association for Promoting Colored Volunteers. Civil War. Negroes. New York. Race Relations. Union League. 1861-65. *1255*
Military reform. Hastie, William H. Racism. World War II. 1940-43. *2637*
Military Service. Abolition Movement. Bryant, John Howard. Bryant, Julian. Civil War. Illinois (Bureau County). Lovejoy, Owen. Negroes. 1831-65. *607*
—. Antislavery Sentiments. Civil War. Douglas, H. Ford. Emigration. Negroes. 1854-65. *666*
—. Antislavery Sentiments. Civil War. Friends, Society of. Jones, James Parnell. Maine. 1850's-64. *320*
—. British Columbia. Canada. Chinese Canadians. Japanese Canadians. World War II. 1939-45. *2647*
—. Civil War. Croxton, John Thomas. Kentucky. Law. Republican Party. 1855-74. *392*
Military Service (enlistees). Discrimination, Employment. Navies. Negroes. Race Relations. Segregation. 1798-1970's. 1970D 1900H. *41*
Military training. Football. Higher education. Morality. 1890-1930. *2327*
—. Muldoon, William. Physicians. Public health. Wood, Leonard. 1890-1915. *2044*
Military-industrial complex. Armaments Industry. 1900-60's. *1650*
Militia. Illinois (Chicago). Police. Riots. Strikes. Wages. 1877. *1343*
Milk scandal. Medicine, preventive. Political Corruption. Progressivism. Public health. Rhode Island (Providence). 1913. *1915*
Mill, John Stuart. Taylor, Harriet. Women's rights. ca 1850-73. *806*
Millenarianism *See also* Premillenarianism.
—. Abolition Movement. Hersey, John. Methodist Church. Perfectionism. 1786-1862. *541*
—. Black Muslims. Christianity. 1920-79. *1585*
—. Cobden, Richard. Great Britain. Nonconformists. Peace movements. 1840-60. *582*
Miller, Franklin, and Stevenson (firm). Bancroft, Joseph and Sons Company. Delaware (Wilmington). Scientific management. Textile Industry. 1911-27. *2281*

Miller, Kelly. Immigration. Japanese. Negroes. Race Relations. 1906-24. *1601*
—. Leadership. Negroes. 1877-1918. *470*
Milton, George Fort. Editors and Editing. Liberalism. New Deal. Tennessee. 1930's. *2521*
Milton, John. Education. Great Britain. Jefferson, Thomas. 17c-19c. *833*
Mims, Edwin. Agrarianism. Davidson, Donald. Literature. South. 1923-58. *1656*
Mims, Mary Williams. Louisiana State University. Teachers. 1910-67. *387*
Mine, Mill and Smelter Workers, International Union of. British Columbia (Trail). Consolidated Mining and Smelting Company. Immigration. Strikes. World War I. 1916-17. *1810*
—. Law Enforcement. Nicaragua. Silex, Humberto. Southwest. 1932-78. *1739*
Miner, Myrtilla. District of Columbia. Education. Negroes. Spiritualism. 1851-1955. *190*
Miners. American Civil Liberties Union. Civil rights. Kentucky (Bell County, London). Trials. 1932-38. *2601*
—. National Industrial Recovery Act (US, 1933). New Deal. Roosevelt, Eleanor. Subsistence Homesteads Program. West Virginia (Arthurdale). 1930-46. *2492*
Miners' Magazine. Editorials. Labor. Poetry. Songs. Western Federation of Miners. 1900-07. *2293*
Mines. Industrial Workers of the World. Labor Disputes. Nevada (Goldfield, Tonopah). 1901-22. *2262*
Mingo War. Coal Mines and Mining. Labor Disputes. United Mine Workers of America. Violence. West Virginia (southern). 1919-22. *2389*
Minimum wage. Fair Labor Standards Act (US, 1938). 1938-77. *1768*
—. Legislation. Occupations. Ohio. Sex Discrimination. Women. 1914-33. *1539*
—. Legislation. State government. Washington. 1913-25. *1822*
Mining *See also* specific kinds of mining, e.g. Silver Mining.
—. Arizona (Bisbee). Industrial Workers of the World. Labor Unions and Organizations. Strikes. 1917. *2186*
—. Bureau of Surface Mine Reclamation. Legislation. Pennsylvania. 1961-73. *2762*
—. Coal, anthracite. Pennsylvania. Strikes. United Mine Workers of America. 1922-23. *2391*
—. Labor. Western states. 1892-1904. *1335*
Ministers. *See* Clergy.
Minnesota *See also* North Central States.
—. Abolition Movement. Feminism. Journalism. Lowry, Sylvanus B. Swisshelm, Jane Grey. 1815-84. *385*
—. Abolition Movement. Feminism. St. Cloud *Visitor* (newspaper). Swisshelm, Jane Grey. 1857-62. *814*
—. Farmer-Labor Party. State politics. Swedish Americans. 1922-44. *1631*
—. Finnish Americans. Iron Industry. Labor Unions and Organizations. Minnesota (Mesabi Range). Radicals and Radicalism. 1914-17. *2253*
—. Forssell, G. D. Iowa. Lectures. Progressivism. Social Conditions. 1890-95. *957*
—. Journalism. Lectures. Political activism. Populism. Valesh, Eva McDonald. 1866-1956. *345*
—. Politics. Public Policy. Welfare Mothers Movement. 1960-72. *2933*
—. Workmen's compensation. 1909-13. *2173*
Minnesota (Duluth). Homesteading and Homesteaders. Interior Department. Public Housing. Resettlement Administration. 1936-47. *2510*
Minnesota (Mesabi Range). Finnish Americans. Iron Industry. Labor Unions and Organizations. Minnesota. Radicals and Radicalism. 1914-17. *2253*
Minnesota (Minneapolis). Brin, Fanny Fligelman. Jews. Peace. Women. 1913-60's. *453*
—. Countryman, Gratia Alta. Libraries (public). Reform. Women. 1890's-1953. *424*
—. Socialism. VanLear, Thomas. 1910-20. *2042*
Minnesota, northeastern. Economic Development. Forest Service. Public Policy. Superior National Forest. Wilderness. 1923-26. *2437*
Minnesota (St. Paul). Adams, John Quincy (1848-1922). Negroes. *Western Appeal* (newspaper). 1888-1922. *1269*
—. Baptists. Bishop, Harriet E. Women. 1847-83. *295*

Minnesota (Smithville). Finnish Americans. Immigrants. Labor. Socialism. Work People's College. 1900-20. *2315*
Minnesota, University of. Academic freedom. Schaper, William A. World War I. 1917. *2143*
Minorities *See also* Discrimination; Ethnic Groups; Nationalism; Population; Racism; Segregation.
—. Affirmative action. Discrimination. *Fullilove* v. *Klutznick* (US, 1980). *Regents of the University of California* v. *Allan Bakke* (US, 1978). Supreme Court. *United Steelworkers of America* v. *Weber* (US, 1979). 1970's. *2782*
—. British Columbia. Japanese Canadians. Public schools. 1900-72. *1562*
—. City Politics. Community Action Programs. Decisionmaking. Rhode Island (Providence). 1965-69. *2940*
—. Civil Rights. Supreme Court. 1886-1972. *73*
—. Colleges and Universities. Education, Experimental Methods. New York, City University of. 1847-1980. *196*
—. Decentralization Act (1969). New York City (Brooklyn, Lower East Side). Public Schools. School boards. 1969-73. *2965*
—. Discrimination, employment. Fair Employment Practices Committee. South. World War II. 1941-45. *2644*
—. Education. Hall, G. Stanley. Social Status. 1870's-1920. *2323*
—. Pluralism. Race relations. 1968-73. *2697*
Minorities in Politics. Civil rights. Liberals. New York City. 1963-70's. *2728*
—. Employment. Negroes. New Deal. Roosevelt, Franklin D. 1930-42. *2586*
—. Mexican Americans. Public Schools. Self-perception. Texas (southern). 1930's-69. *1863*
—. Mississippi. Negroes. Voting Rights Act (US, 1965). 1960-74. *2848*
—. Missouri (St. Louis). Negroes. Republican Party. Wheeler, John W. 1870-1915. *1142*
—. Negroes. Political Leadership. Reconstruction. Texas. 1865-90's. *1148*
Minville, Esdras. *Actualité Économique* (periodical). Cooperative movement. Individualism. Nationalism. Quebec (Gaspé Peninsula). 1924-40. *1794*
—. *Actualité Économique* (periodical). Cooperative movement. Individualism. Quebec (Gaspé Peninsula). 1924-43. *1795*
Mission Indians. California. Indians. Jackson, Helen Hunt *(Ramona)*. Ponca Indians. Removals, forced. Schurz, Carl. 1873-84. *1051*
Missions and Missionaries. Abolition Movement. American Free Baptist Mission Society. Baptists. Schisms. 1830-69. *702*
—. Abolitionists. Childhood. 1800-60. *789*
—. Arapaho Indians. Cheyenne Indians. Indians. Mennonites. 1880-1900. *1030*
—. Assimilation. Finley, James B. Indians (agencies). Methodist Church. Ohio. Shaw, John. 1820-24. *581*
—. Associates of Dr. Bray. Bray, Thomas. Church of England. Education. Negroes. 1717-77. *500*
—. Attitudes. Indians. Presbyterian Church. 1837-93. *13*
—. Baptists. Crawford, Isabel. Indians. Kiowa Indians. Oklahoma (Wichita Mountains). Women's American Baptist Home Missionary Society. 1893-1961. *393*
—. Baptists. Education. Negroes. South. 1862-81. *1240*
—. Canada. Christianity. Sex roles. Women. 1815-99. *1490*
—. Cherokee Indians. Christianity. Indian-White Relations. Property. Social Change. Women. 19c. *107*
—. Colonization. Liberia. Methodist Episcopal Church. Negroes. Sierra Leone. 1833-48. *641*
—. Cooke, Parsons. Industrialization. Massachusetts (Ware). Puritans. 19c. *906*
—. Freedmen. Hartzell, Joseph C. Methodist Church. Republican Party. South. 1870-73. *1208*
—. Integration. Presbyterian Church. 1562-1977. *15*
—. Jones, Charles Colcock. Presbyterian Church. Slavery. South. 1825-63. *776*
—. Methodist Episcopal Church. Women's Foreign Missionary Society. 1869-1900. *1491*
—. Metropolitan Areas. Presbyterian Church. 1869-1977. *84*

—. Nova Scotia. Raymond, Eliza Ruggles. Sierra Leone (Sherbro Island). Slaves. 1839-50. *621*
—. Organizations. Protestant Churches. Women. 1870's-90's. *1493*
Mississippi *See also* South; South Central and Gulf States.
—. Alcorn University. Negroes. Race Relations. Revels, Hiram Rhodes. Senate. ca 1870's. *1256*
—. Allin, John M. Civil rights. Clergy. Episcopal Church, Protestant. Political Attitudes. 1964-73. *2795*
—. American Missionary Association. Colleges and Universities. Freedmen's Bureau. Negroes. Tougaloo College. 1865-69. *1141*
—. Bilbo, Theodore G. Employment. Fair Employment Practices Committee. Filibusters. Racism. Senate. 1941-46. *2617*
—. Black capitalism. Civil War. Davis Bend colony. Eaton, John, Jr. Freedmen. 1862-66. *1249*
—. Boycotts. Negroes. Police brutality (alleged). Robinson, Alfred. United League. 1966-78. *2893*
—. Carpetbaggers. Historiography. Ideology. Reconstruction. Reformers. 1865-76. *1013*
—. Carter, William Hodding, Jr. Editors and Editing. Political Reform. Race Relations. ca 1930-60. *340*
—. Civil War. Labor. Negroes. Vicksburg (battle). 1862. *1220*
—. Civil War. Law. Negroes. Reconstruction. 1857-70. *114*
—. Conservatism. Elections, presidential. Segregation. Sillers, Walter. State Legislatures. 1948-64. *2677*
—. Discrimination. Federal Policy. Freedmen's Bureau. Reconstruction. State Government. 1865. *1227*
—. Farm tenancy. Protestant Churches. Theology. 1936-40. *2525*
—. Federal aid to education. Harrison, Byron Patton. Legislation. 1936-41. *2597*
—. Kennedy, John F. Negroes. Political Protest. Voting Rights Act (US, 1965). 1960-72. *2863*
—. Lynch, James (letters). Methodist Episcopal Church. Negroes. Reconstruction. 1868-69. *1166*
—. Minorities in Politics. Negroes. Voting Rights Act (US, 1965). 1960-74. *2848*
—. Negroes. Political Leadership. 1965-70. *2884*
—. Negroes. Public Opinion. Revels, Hiram Rhodes. Senate. 1870. *1202*
—. Ord, Edward Otho Cresap. Reconstruction. 1867-68. *982*
Mississippi Colonization Society. Colonization. Emancipation. 1831-60. *685*
Mississippi Valley, upper. Utopias. 1840's. *927*
Missouri *See also* North Central States.
—. American Missionary Association. Civil War. Education. Negroes. 1862-65. *1241*
—. Antitrust. Courts. Fire insurance. Kansas City Board of Fire Underwriters. Law enforcement. 1889-99. *1336*
—. Attitudes. Boundaries. Civil War (antecedents). Kansas. Slavery. 1854-56. *634*
—. Bureaucracies. Centralization. Legislation. Public schools. State government. 1853. *846*
—. Child Welfare. Children's Code Commission. 1915-19. *2060*
—. Children. St. Louis Children's Hospital. Women. 1879-1979. *237*
—. Delmo Housing Corporation. Farm Security Administration. Southern Tenant Farmers' Union. Tenancy. 1939-80. *1821*
—. Foster, Richard B. (address). Negroes. Reconstruction. Teachers. 1869. *1170*
—. Labor. Local Politics. Racism. Reconstruction. St. Louis *Daily Press* (newspaper). 1864-66. *1339*
—. Mass Transit. Modernization. Monopolies. St. Louis Transit Company. Strikes. 1900. *2257*
Missouri (Dallas County). Bennett, William H. Communitarianism. Home Employment Cooperative Company. Utopias. 1894-1905. *1507*
Missouri (Jefferson City). Education. Lincoln University. Lindsay, Lizzie A. Negroes. Turner, James Milton. 1865-75. *1179*
Missouri (St. Louis). African Baptist Church. Education. Emancipation. Meachum, John Berry. Negroes. 1815-54. *395*
—. Air Pollution. Smoke. 1891-1924. *1962*

—. Antiabolition sentiments. Clergy. Conservatism. Constitutions. Massachusetts (Boston). Unitarianism. 1828-57. *751*
—. Brookings, Robert. Flexner Report. Medical education. Reform. Washington University. 1910-16. *2318*
—. Catholic Church. Church Schools. Glennon, John J. Ritter, Joseph E. School Integration. 1935-47. *1850*
—. Cholera. Epidemics. Public Health. 1849-67. *862*
—. City Government. Elites. Human Development Corporation. Negroes. Poor. War on Poverty. 1964-75. *2935*
—. City Government. Political Reform. Progressivism. 1893-1904. *2199*
—. Compulsory education. Immigrants. Public Schools. Truancy. 1905-07. *2313*
—. Curricula. Eliot, William Greenleaf. Higher education. Trans-Mississippi West. Washington University. 1853-87. *189*
—. Educational Reform. Manual training. Woodward, Calvin. 1897-1914. *2305*
—. Educational Theory. Vocational Education. Washington University (Manual Training School). Woodward, Calvin. 1879-1910. *1412*
—. Episcopal Church, Protestant. 1880-1920. *52*
—. Irish Americans. Knights of Father Mathew. Temperance Movements. 1850-1930. 1900H. *259*
—. McLean, Mary Hancock. Medicine (practice of). Women. 1883-1930. *359*
—. Minorities in Politics. Negroes. Republican Party. Wheeler, John W. 1870-1915. *1142*
—. Negroes. School Integration. 1954-55. *2667*
—. Political Leadership. Racism. Social Classes. Strikes. Workingmen's Party. 1877. *1338*
Missouri (Sedalia). Gould, Jay. Knights of Labor. Modernization. Railroads. Strikes. 1885-86. *1292*
Mitchel, John Purroy. Educational reform. New York City. 1914-17. *2322*
—. Gary, Elbert H. New York City (Committee on Unemployment and Relief). Progressives. Unemployment. 1914-17. *2058*
Mitchell, John. Coal Mines and Mining. Employment. United Mine Workers of America. 1897-1907. *2213*
Mitchell, John P. Editors and Editing. Race Relations. *Richmond Planet* (newspaper). Virginia. ca 1883-1929. *407*
Mitchell, Maria. Association for the Advancement of Women. Education. Science. Women. 1870-89. *1035*
Mitchell, Thomas Duche. Frontier and Pioneer Life. Kentucky. Medical Education. Reform. 1809-65. *325*
Mobile Harbor Act (Alabama, 1842). Alabama. Negroes. Petitions. Prisons. Seamen. State Legislatures. 1849. *727*
Mobile *Register* (newspaper). Alabama. Brown, John. 1859. *626*
Mobility. See Social Mobility.
Models *See also* Methodology.
—. Antibusing movement. Massachusetts (Boston). Political Protest. Social Organizations. 1970's. *2895*
—. Civil rights movement. Leftism. Political attitudes. Students. 1960's-70's. *2714*
—. Education. Research and Development Centers program. 1960's-70's. *2964*
Modernism. Mathews, Shailer. Science. Social gospel. Theology. 1864-1930. *446*
Modernization *See also* Economic Theory; Industrialization; Social Change.
—. Educators. Iowa. Public schools. 1890-1900. *1422*
—. Gould, Jay. Knights of Labor. Missouri (Sedalia). Railroads. Strikes. 1885-86. *1292*
—. Mass Transit. Missouri. Monopolies. St. Louis Transit Company. Strikes. 1900. *2257*
Monasticism. Episcopal Church, Protestant. Huntington, James Otis Sargent. Order of the Holy Cross. 1878-90. *1061*
Monopolies *See also* Antitrust; Capitalism; Railroads.
—. Crime and Criminals. George, Henry. Land. Property. Technology. 19c-20c. *1033*
—. Inequality. Labor movement. 1830's-1982. *825*
—. Mass Transit. Missouri. Modernization. St. Louis Transit Company. Strikes. 1900. *2257*
Monroe, James. American Colonization Society. Gabriel's Insurrection. Prosser, Gabriel. Slave revolts. Virginia. 1800. *698*

Montana *See also* Western States.
—. Agriculture. Blackfoot Indians. Cattle Raising. Indians (reservations). 1885-1935. *104*
—. American Railway Union. Railroads. Strikes. 1894. *1357*
—. Big Sky development. Conservation. Huntley, Chet. Resorts. 1970-73. *2755*
—. Blackwell, Henry B. Constitutional conventions, state. Woman suffrage. 1889. *1121*
—. Congress. Rankin, Jeannette. Woman suffrage. 1913-18. *466*
—. Constitutions, State. Rankin, Jeannette. Woman suffrage. 1889-1914. *129*
—. Dawes Act (US, 1887). Flathead Indian Reservation. Indians. Land Tenure. Salish (Flathead) Indians. 1887-1904. *1075*
—. Farmers. McNary-Haugen bill. Pacific Northwest. Prices. Tariff. 1920-29. *2410*
—. House of Representatives. Pacifism. Rankin, Jeannette. 1880-1973. *465*
—. House of Representatives. Political Campaigns (congressional). Rankin, Jeannette. Republican Party. Woman suffrage. 1900-16. *2142*
—. National Park Service. Roosevelt, Theodore. Wildlife conservation. Yellowstone National Park. 1883-1918. *2079*
Montana (Butte). Literature. MacLane, Mary. Women. 1902-29. *384*
Montgomery *Herald* (newspaper). Alabama. Duke, Jesse C. Editors and Editing. Negroes. Political Commentary. Republican Party. 1886-1916. *1185*
Montreal Royals (team). Baseball. Brooklyn Dodgers (team). Integration. Negroes. Press. Rickey, Branch. Robinson, Jackie. 1945-47. *2690*
Moody, Walter D. (*Wacker's Manual of the Plan of Chicago*). Burnham, Daniel Hudson. City planning. Illinois (Chicago). Progressivism. Publicity. Reform. 1909-11. *2071*
Mooney, James. Bureau of American Ethnology. Ghost Dance. Indians. Peyote. Research. 1891-1921. *1110*
Mooney, Tom. Bombing. California (San Francisco). San Quentin Prison. Socialist Party. Trials. 1916-42. *2020*
Moore, William. Libel. Pennsylvania. Political Theory. Provincial legislatures. Smith, William. 1750-60. *516*
Moorman, Clark Terrell. Cedar Creek Monthly Meeting. Emancipation. Farms. Friends, Society of. Ohio. Virginia (Caroline County). 1766-1814. *743*
Morality *See also* Ethics; Values.
—. Abolition Movement. Christianity. Enlightenment. Nationalism. Phillips, Wendell. 1830-84. *716*
—. Benson, Ezra Taft. Mormons. Political Leadership. Presbyterian Church. Wallace, Henry A. 1933-60. *434*
—. Business. Cooperative Association of America. Democracy. Peck, Bradford (*World a Department Store*). Utopias. 1880-1925. *263*
—. Cities. Family. Progressivism. Recreation. Reform. Socialization. 1890-1920. *1990*
—. Cities. Public baths. Public health. 1880-1910. *1455*
—. Crime and Criminals. Education. Pennsylvania. Wickersham, James P. 1866-81. *1401*
—. Curricula. Kindergarten. Progressive education. 1860-1920. *184*
—. Dabney, Robert Lewis. Presbyterian Church. South. Texas, University of (Austin). Union Seminary. 1865-96. *1084*
—. Douglas, Stephen A. Lincoln, Abraham. Political Attitudes. Slavery. 1850's. *738*
—. Family. Iakovos, Archbishop. Orthodox Eastern Church (Greek; congresses). Social Conditions. 1960-80. *2726*
—. Female Moral Reform Society. New York (Utica). Reform. Social Organization. 1830's-40's. *808*
—. Feminism. Mencken, H. L. 1900-56. *1641*
—. Feminism. Physical Education and Training. Sexuality. Women. 19c. *101*
—. Feminism. Politics. Women. 19c-20c. *142*
—. Football. Higher education. Military training. 1890-1930. *2327*
—. Immigration. Industrialization. Muckraking. Periodicals. 1900-09. *2047*
—. Lewis, Dioclesius. Medical reform. Rhythmics. Sex. Women. 1860-1970's. *1481*
—. New York. Progressivism. Prohibition. Smith, Alfred E. Whitman, Charles. Woman Suffrage. 1911-18. *2116*

—. New York, upstate. Teaching. 1970-80. *2962*
—. Political parties. Slavery. 1828-36. *701*
—. Politics. Women. 19c-20c. *118*
—. Reform. Sex. 19c. *102*
Morgan, Elizabeth Chambers. Illinois (Chicago). Labor reform. 1874-97. *1341*
Morgan, Lewis Henry. Ethnography. Federal policy. Indians. 1848-78. *1059*
Morgan, Thomas John. Elections. Socialism. United Labor Party (platform). 1886-96. *1342*
—. Letters. Lloyd, Henry Demarest. Social Democratic Party. Socialist Labor Party. 1897-1901. *1349*
Morlan, Robert Loren. Nonpartisan League. North Dakota. Populism. 1910's-1920's. *1881*
Mormon, Square. Medical care. Poor People's Health Council. Race relations. Rossville Health Center. Tennessee (Fayette County). 1960's-70's. *2821*
Mormons. Atheism. *Lucifer's Lantern* (periodical). Schroeder, Theodore. Utah. 1889-1900. *1486*
—. Benson, Ezra Taft. Morality. Political Leadership. Presbyterian Church. Wallace, Henry A. 1933-60. *434*
—. Clergy. Equality. Negroes. Women. 1860-1979. *91*
—. Congress. Hayes, Rutherford B. Polygamy. Woman Suffrage. 1877-81. *1089*
—. Constitutional Amendments (21st). Prohibition. Utah. 1932-33. *2393*
—. Diaries. Musser, Elise Furer. Political Leadership. Utah. 1897-1967. *301*
—. Discrimination. Idaho. Politics. 1880-95. *1120*
—. Editors and Editing. Utah. *Woman's Exponent* (periodical). Women. 1872-1914. *3*
—. Kimball, Sarah Melissa Granger. Utah. Woman Suffrage. 15th Ward Relief Society. 1818-98. *397*
—. Labor Unions and Organizations. Utah. 1850-96. *1297*
—. Law. Utah. ca 1830-80. *1104*
—. Legislation. Tobacco. Utah. 1896-1923. *2440*
—. Prohibition. Utah. 1900's-1910's. *2039*
—. Snow, Eliza Roxey. Women. 1830-90. *75*
—. Statehood. Utah. Woman suffrage. 1867-96. *1090*
—. Utah. Woman Suffrage. 1895. *1123*
Morrill Act (US, 1862). Idaho, University of. Washington State University. 1862-92. *1407*
Morrill, Anson P. Anti-Catholicism. Know-Nothing Party. Maine. Nativism. Working class. 1854-55. *588*
Morris, Thomas. Antislavery movement. Ohio. State Legislatures. 1836-39. *711*
Morrow, Edwin P. Kentucky. McChesney, Henry V. Political Campaigns (gubernatorial). Prohibition. Stanley, Augustus Owsley. 1915. *1873*
Morrow, Prince Albert. Attitudes. Sex. 1890-1915. *1899*
Mortality. Industry. Muckraking. Occupations. Reform. 1890-1910. *2112*
—. Negroes. 19c-20c. *251*
Moss, William (letters). American Colonization Society. Georgia (Griffin). Liberia. Slavery. 1853-57. *654*
Motherhood. Domesticity. Feminism. Howe, Julia Ward. Reform. 1844-85. *349*
—. Feminism. Kindergarten. Progressivism. 1860-1920. *1932*
—. Literature. Sex roles. Women. 1785-1815. *793*
Mothers. Canada. Child welfare. Income. Legislation. 1916-70's. *1814*
—. Canada. Income. Legislation. Public Welfare. ca 1900-39. *1815*
Mothers' pensions. Aid to Families with Dependent Children. Illinois (Cook County). Public Welfare. 1911-75. *2107*
Motion Picture Producers and Distributors of America. Censorship. Hughes, Howard. Legion of Decency. *Outlaw* (film). Russell, Jane. 1940-49. *2649*
Moton, Robert Russa. Negroes. Politics. Scott, Emmett Jay. Tuskegee Institute. Washington, Booker T. 1915-25. *1643*
Mott, Lucretia. Abolition Movement. Anthony, Susan B. Grimké, Angelina. Stanton, Elizabeth Cady. Woman Suffrage. ca 1820-60. *549*
Movies. *See* Films.
Mower, Joseph Anthony. Hancock, Winfield Scott. Louisiana. Military. Reconstruction. Texas. 1865-68. *989*

Muckraking. *Appeal to Reason* (newspaper). Journalism. Kansas (Girard). Socialism. 1901-20. *2041*
—. Football. Johnson, Owen *(Stover at Yale)*. Progressivism. 1911-20. *1998*
—. Immigration. Industrialization. Morality. Periodicals. 1900-09. *2047*
—. Industry. Mortality. Occupations. Reform. 1890-1910. *2112*
Mugwumps. Anti-Imperialism. Attitudes. Law Reform. NAACP. Storey, Moorfield. 1870's-1929. *462*
—. Historiography. Political Reform. Republican Party. 1880's. 1910-79. *956*
Muir, John. California. Carr, Jeanne Caroline Smith. Wilderness. Wisconsin. 1850's-1903. *277*
Muldoon, William. Military training. Physicians. Public health. Wood, Leonard. 1890-1915. *2044*
Mundelein, George. Catholic Church. Illinois (Chicago). 20c. *1621*
Municipal Clinic. Bureaucracies. California (San Francisco). Medicine (practice of). Venereal disease. 1911. *2084*
Municipal League of Seattle. City Government. Progressivism. Reform. Washington (Seattle). 1910-20. *2045*
Munitions. *See* Armaments Industry.
Murder *See also* Assassination; Capital Punishment.
—. Attitudes. Howard, Martin. Law. North Carolina. Slavery. 1765-91. *515*
Murphy, Edgar Gardner. Conservatism. DuBose, William Porcher. Episcopal Church, Protestant. Miles, James Warley. South. Theology. 1840-1920. *62*
—. Episcopal Church, Protestant. Southern Education Board. 1900-13. *2118*
—. Journalism. McKelway, Alexander. Page, Walter Hines. South. 1890-1916. *1876*
Murray, Donald G. Lawyers. Marshall, Thurgood. Maryland, University of, School of Law. NAACP. School Integration. 1930-54. *2531*
Murray, George Washington. Freedmen. House of Representatives. Republican Party. South Carolina. Suffrage. 1893-97. *1163*
Murray, Hugh T., Jr. (reminiscences). Civil Rights Organizations. Discrimination. Florida (Miami). Louisiana (New Orleans). 1959-60. *2871*
Murray, John Courtney. Berrigan, Daniel. Berrigan, Philip. Catholic Church. Church and state. Leftism. 1950's-70's. *1605*
Murray, Rex. General Tire Company. Ohio (Akron). Strikes. Strikes. 1934-35. *2565*
Music *See also* Musicians; Radio.
—. Antislavery Sentiments. *Emancipation Car* (collection). Simpson, Joshua McCarter. 1854. *627*
—. Borg, Selma Josefina. Centennial Exposition of 1876. Finnish Americans. Lectures. Pennsylvania (Philadelphia). Women's rights. 1858-90. *399*
Musicians. Black Nationalism. Negroes. Robeson, Paul. 1914-45. *1692*
Musser, Elise Furer. Diaries. Mormons. Political Leadership. Utah. 1897-1967. *301*
Mussey, Ellen Spencer. District of Columbia. Gillett, Emma M. Legal education. Washington College of Law. Women. 1869-1949. *426*
Muste, Abraham J. Christianity. Niebuhr, Reinhold. Pacifism. Political Theory. Thomas, Norman. 1914-38. *1668*
—. Radicals and Radicalism. Unemployed Leagues. 1932-36. *2577*
Mysticism. Evans, Warren Felt. Idealism. Mental healing. Romanticism. 1864-89. *1480*
Myths and Symbols. Bible. Imber, Naphtali Herz *(The Fall of Jerusalem)*. Populism. 1856-1909. *1371*
—. Capitalism. Carver, George Washington. Marxism. Race Relations. South. 1896-1950's. *1604*

N

NAACP. Anti-Imperialism. Attitudes. Law Reform. Mugwumps. Storey, Moorfield. 1870's-1929. *462*
—. Army. Committee on Participation of Negroes in the National Defense Program. Negroes. Pittsburgh *Courier* (newspaper). Segregation. 1937-40. *2506*
—. Attica State Prison. Negroes. New York. Prisons. 1932. *2462*

—. Civil rights movement. Freedom Singers. Georgia (Albany; Harlem district). Reagon, Bernice Johnson (interview). 1960-77. *2880*
—. Civil rights movement. Negroes. South Dakota. 1804-1970. *4*
—. Class consciousness. Negroes. Pennsylvania (Philadelphia). Race. 1930's. *2566*
—. Craft, Juanita. Durham, William J. Smith, Antonio Maceo. Texas. White, Lulu B. 1933-50. *1586*
—. Democratic Party. Negro Suffrage. Primaries. *Smith* v. *Allwright* (US, 1944). South. Supreme Court. 1890's-1944. *1722*
—. Democratic Party. Negro Suffrage. Primaries. Supreme Court. Texas. 1927-45. *1723*
—. Discrimination, Educational. Indiana. Negroes. ca 1869-1975. *211*
—. Discrimination, Employment. Jim Crow laws. Negroes. Tennessee (Memphis). 1900-37. *1750*
—. Housing. Kentucky (Louisville). Segregation. Supreme Court. 1914-17. *2126*
—. Integration. Litigation. North. Public schools. 1954-73. *2841*
—. Iowa (Des Moines). 1915-30. *2015*
—. Johnson, James Weldon. Negroes. White, Walter F. 1909-35. *1647*
—. Labor Unions and Organizations. Maryland. Negroes. Teachers. 1930's. *2610*
—. Lawyers. Marshall, Thurgood. Maryland, University of, School of Law. Murray, Donald G. School Integration. 1930-54. *2531*
—. Lawyers. Race relations. 1909-76. *1646*
—. Nominations to Office. North Carolina. Parker, John J. Supreme Court. White, Walter F. 1930. *2385*
—. Progressivism. Whites. 1909-10. *2095*
Nabrit, James Madison, Jr. Civil rights. Howard University. Negroes. 1927-60. *439*
Naples Zoological Station. Dohrn, Anton. Hyde, Ida H. Italy. Scientific Experiments and Research. Women. 1896-97. *1434*
Nardella, Luigi (interview). Rhode Island. Strikes. Textile Industry. 1922. *2349*
Nashville, University of. Educational Administration. George Peabody College. Payne, William Howard. Teacher training. Tennessee. 1875-1901. *1411*
Nation, Carry. Florida (Miami). Temperance Movements. 1908-13. *1949*
—. Oklahoma. Temperance Movements. 1867-1911. *1440*
National American Woman Suffrage Association. Alabama. League of Women Voters. Woman Suffrage. 1919-21. *2450*
—. Idaho. Woman Suffrage. 1896-1920. *2149*
National Association of Colored Women. Negroes. Reform. Terrell, Mary Church. Woman Suffrage. 1892-1954. *312*
National Association of Corporation Schools. Collectivism. Intellectuals. Steinmetz, Charles Proteus. Utopias. 1910-17. *1950*
National Board of Farm Organizations. Agricultural Organizations. Lobbying. 1917-27. *1769*
National Brotherhood of Operative Potters. Pottery. Strikes. Tariff. 1894. *1345*
National Cash Register Company. Factories. Industrial Technology. Labor Disputes. 1895-1913. *2249*
—. Ohio (Dayton). Patterson, John H. Physical Education and Training. Working Conditions. 1890-1915. *169*
National Catholic Welfare Conference. Catholic Church. National Council of Catholic Women. Peace Movements. Women. 1919-46. *1636*
National Colored Labor Union. Discrimination. Labor Unions and Organizations. National Labor Union. Negroes. 1866-72. *1137*
National Conference on City Planning. City Planning. Marsh, Benjamin C. Poor. Population. 1900-17. *1987*
National Consumers' League. Consumers. Progressive era. Women. 1900-23. *2124*
National Council of Catholic Women. Catholic Church. National Catholic Welfare Conference. Peace Movements. Women. 1919-46. *1636*
National Council of Women of Canada. Canada. Feminism. 1893-1929. *1690*
National Fast Day. Civil War. Constitutional Amendments. Fundamentalism. Lincoln, Abraham. National Reform Association. 1787-1945. *1484*
National Guard *See also* Militia.
—. Coal Mines and Mining. Colorado Fuel and Iron Company. Ludlow Massacre. Strikes. 1913-14. *2206*

National Guard

—. Coal Mines and Mining. Glasscock, William E. Martial law. United Mine Workers of America. Violence. West Virginia (Cabin Creek, Paint Creek). 1912-13. *2176*
National Industrial Recovery Act (US, 1933). Agricultural Labor. California. Labor Unions and Organizations. 1933-34. *2495*
—. Congress of Industrial Organizations. Labor Unions and Organizations. Management. National Labor Relations Act (US, 1935). South. Textile Industry. 1933-41. *2613*
—. Miners. New Deal. Roosevelt, Eleanor. Subsistence Homesteads Program. West Virginia (Arthurdale). 1930-46. *2492*
National Labor Relations Act (US, 1935). Congress of Industrial Organizations. Labor Unions and Organizations. Management. National Industrial Recovery Act (US, 1933). South. Textile Industry. 1933-41. *2613*
National Labor Tribune. Coal Mines and Mining. Davis, Richard L. Labor Unions and Organizations. Letters-to-the-editor. Negroes. United Mine Workers of America. ca 1890-1900. *1139*
National Labor Union. Discrimination. Labor Unions and Organizations. National Colored Labor Union. Negroes. 1866-72. *1137*
National Maritime Union. Communist Party. Negroes. Racism. United Electrical, Radio and Machine Workers of America. World War II. 1941-45. *2622*
National Miners Union. Carbon County Coal Strike (1933). Strikes. United Mine Workers of America. Utah. 1900-39. *2571*
—. Negroes. Pennsylvania, western. United Mine Workers of America. 1925-31. *2420*
National Negro Congress. Brotherhood of Sleeping Car Porters. March on Washington Movement. Negroes. Randolph, A. Philip. 1925-41. *353*
—. Bunche, Ralph. Negroes. New Deal. Political Attitudes. 1930-39. *2532*
National Negro Labor Union. Alabama. Labor Union of Alabama. Negroes. Politics. Rapier, James T. Reconstruction. 1837-75. *1253*
National Organization for Women. Civil Rights. Economic Research and Action Project. Feminism. Student Nonviolent Coordinating Committee. 1960's. *2906*
National Park Service. Montana. Roosevelt, Theodore. Wildlife conservation. Yellowstone National Park. 1883-1918. *2079*
National Parks and Reserves *See also* Wildlife Conservation.
—. Conservation of Natural Resources. Economic Growth. 1870's - 1973. *90*
—. Recreation. Western States. Wilderness Act (US, 1964). 1864-1976. *7*
National Progressives of America. Income (redistribution). LaFollette, Philip F. Politics. Wisconsin. 1930-38. *2551*
National Recovery Administration. Collectivism. Glass, Carter. Liberals. New Deal. 1933-35. *2533*
—. Economic Conditions. New Deal. Supreme Court. Virginia. 1933-35. *2517*
—. Economic Regulations. Labor. Negroes. South. Wages. 1933-34. *2576*
—. Georgia. State Government. Strikes. Talmadge, Eugene. Textile industry. 1934. *2467*
National Reform Association. Civil War. Constitutional Amendments. Fundamentalism. Lincoln, Abraham. National Fast Day. 1787-1945. *1484*
National School Service (bulletin). Patriotism. Public Schools. Reform. 1918-19. *2337*
National Security *See also* Defense Policy.
—. Academic freedom. Ohio State University. Rugg, Harold Ordway. Speeches, Addresses, etc. 1951. *2771*
—. Civil Rights. Cold War. Detention. Federal Bureau of Investigation. Truman, Harry S. (administration). 1945-52. *2685*
—. Peace Movements. Preparedness. 1941-71. *1564*
National Self-image. Centennial Celebrations. Indian-White Relations. Jackson, Helen Hunt. 1881. 1975. *1079*
National Textile Workers Union. North Carolina (Gastonia). Strikes. Textile Industry. Weisbord, Vera Buch (reminiscence). 1929. *2459*
National Trades and Labour Congress. Labor Unions and Organizations. Ontario (Kitchener). Quebec. Trades and Labour Congress of Canada. 1892-1902. *1805*

SUBJECT INDEX

National Unemployed Workers' Association. British Columbia. Depressions. Industrial Relations. Unemployment. Workers' Unity League. 1930-39. *1830*
National Union of Negro Labor. Colored National Labor Union. Florida. Labor Unions and Organizations. Negroes. Race Relations. Reconstruction. 1865-75. *1259*
National War Labor Board. Attitudes. Industry. Public Policy. Sex roles. Wages. Women. World War I. 1918-19. *2191*
National Welfare Rights Organization. Political Protest. Public Welfare. 1967-74. *2941*
National Women's Party. Equal Rights Amendment. Florida. Politics. West, Helen Hunt. Women. 1917-52. *1727*
—. Equal Rights Amendment. Social Feminists. Woman suffrage. 1920-23. *2376*
—. Freedom of Speech. Woman Suffrage. 1912-19. *2129*
National Youth Administration. Bethune, Mary McLeod. Equal opportunity. Negroes. Public Policy. Youth. 1935-44. *2594*
—. Bethune, Mary McLeod. Negroes. New Deal. 1930-40. *2578*
Nationalism *See also* Anti-Imperialism; Minorities; Patriotism; Self-Determination; Separatist Movements.
—. Abolition Movement. Christianity. Enlightenment. Morality. Phillips, Wendell. 1830-84. *716*
—. Abolitionists. Immigrants. Irish Americans. ca 1830's-50's. *715*
—. *Actualité Économique* (periodical). Cooperative movement. Individualism. Minville, Esdras. Quebec (Gaspé Peninsula). 1924-40. *1794*
—. American Institute for Education. Educational Reform. Elites. Massachusetts. Rural schools. 1830-37. *839*
—. Antitrust. French Canadians. Hamel, Philippe. Public Utilities. Quebec (Quebec). 1929-34. *1757*
—. Ashley, James M. Constitutional Amendments (13th). House of Representatives. Ohio. Political Parties. 1848-65. *1097*
—. Class struggle. Equality. French language. Intellectuals. Quebec. 1960's-70's. *2693*
—. Mexican Americans. Poetry. 1945-77. *1711*
Nationality. Citizenship. Courts. Mexican Americans. Race. 1846-97. *135*
Nativism. Anti-Catholicism. Chinese Americans. Pacific Northwest. Racism. ca 1840-1945. *11*
—. Anti-Catholicism. Know-Nothing Party. Maine. Morrill, Anson P. Working class. 1854-55. *588*
—. Antislavery Sentiments. Know-Nothing Party. Massachusetts. Republican Party. Voting and Voting Behavior. 1850's. *538*
—. California. Chinese Americans. Immigration. *Sacramento Union* (newspaper). 1850-82. *12*
—. Carroll, Anna Ella. Probasco, Harriet. Women. 1840's-61. *797*
—. Chinese Americans. Discrimination. Economic Conditions. Japanese Americans. Social Status. 1840's-1978. *83*
Natural law. Civil Rights. Indian Civil Rights Act (US, 1968). Pueblo Indians. *Santa Clara Pueblo v. Martinez* (US, 1977). Tribal government. 1939-77. *2789*
Natural Resources *See also* Conservation of Natural Resources; Forests and Forestry; Wilderness.
—. British Columbia. Labor. Legislation. New Democratic Party. Public Policy. Social Democracy. Taxation. 1972-75. *2942*
Naturalization *See also* Citizenship.
—. Asian Americans. Employment. Ethnicity. Legislation. Racism. 1850-20c. *65*
Nature *See also* Ecology; Wilderness.
—. Christianity. Grimké, Sarah Moore. Paul, Saint. Social organization. Women. 1c. 1830's. *807*
Navajo Construction Workers Associations. Arizona (Page). Discrimination, employment. Indians. Industrial Relations. Office of Navajo Labor Relations. 1971-77. *2944*
Navajo Indians. Arizona. Bai-a-lil-le (medicine man). Civil Rights. Courts. Education. Fort Huachuca. Indian Rights Association. Utah, southeastern. 1906-09. *2043*
—. California. Courts. Peyote. Religious Liberty. 1964. *2792*
—. Indians. Labor Unions and Organizations. Southwest. 1958-78. *2945*
Navajo-Hopi Long Range Rehabilitation Act (US, 1950). War on Poverty. Youth. 1950-60's. *1783*

Negro Suffrage

Naval Construction. *See* Shipbuilding.
Naval Recruiting and Enlistment. *See* Military Recruitment.
Navies *See also* headings beginning with the word naval; Military; Shipbuilding.
—. California (San Francisco Bay). Courts Martial and Courts of Inquiry. Mare Island Mutiny. Negroes. Port Chicago Naval Magazine. Race relations. 1944-48. *2652*
—. Discrimination, Employment. Military Service (enlistees). Negroes. Race Relations. Segregation. 1798-1970's. 1970D 1900H. *41*
Navy League (Woman's Section). Preparedness. Sex roles. Suffrage. Woman's Peace Party. World War I. 1914-18. *2092*
Nazism. Canada. Germany. Hjelt, Ole. Labour Party. Norway. Socialism. 1908-28. *321*
Nebraska *See also* Western States.
—. Agricultural Cooperatives. Grain elevators. 1900-15. *2263*
—. Agriculture. Droughts. Politics. Populism. 1880's-90's. *1395*
—. *Alliance-Independent* (newspaper). Christian Socialism. Gibson, George Howard. Populism. *Wealth Makers* (newspaper). 1893-96. *1397*
—. Democracy. Democratic Party. Ethnicity. Prohibition. Republican Party. 1907-20. *1937*
—. Democratic Party. Political Parties. Populism. 1890's. *1394*
—. Industrial Workers of the World. Justice Department. Labor Unions and Organizations. Public opinion. World War I. 1915-20. *2113*
—. Industrial Workers of the World. Labor Unions and Organizations. 1914-20. *2283*
Nebraska (Gage County). *Alliance-Independent* (newspaper). Burrows, Jabez. Farmers' Alliance. 1887-99. *1383*
Nebraska Historical Society. Federal government. Indians. Omaha Indians. Returned Students of Omaha. Speeches, Addresses, etc. 1920's. *2442*
Nebraska (Omaha). Civil Rights. Negroes. Quality of life. Social services. Urban League. World War II. 1928-50. *2639*
—. Episcopal Church, Protestant. Social Change. 1856-1919. *1494*
—. Health. Medicines, Patent. Sanitation. 1870-1900. *1456*
Nebraska, University of. Colleges and Universities. Physical Education and Training. Women. 1879-1923. *220*
Negro Labor Committee. Crosswaith, Frank R. New York City (Harlem). 1925-39. *1824*
Negro Renaissance. DuBois, W. E. B. Ideology. Integration. 1903-74. *1543*
Negro Soldier (film). Armies. Films (documentaries). Heisler, Stuart. Propaganda. Race Relations. World War II. 1944. *2621*
Negro Suffrage. Alabama. Freedmen's Bureau. Gardner, Samuel S. (letter). Reconstruction. 1867. *1180*
—. Alabama. Haralson, J. Reconstruction. Republican Party. 1867-82. *1252*
—. Ashley, James M. Civil War. House of Representatives. Ohio (Toledo). Reconstruction. 1861-62. *1019*
—. Civil rights. Johnson, Lyndon B. Political Reform. 1960's. *2855*
—. Colorado, northeastern. Hardin, William J. Kansas, northeastern. Langston, Charles H. 1865-67. *1133*
—. Democratic Party. Liberty Party. New York. Referendum. Whig Party. 1840-47. *595*
—. Democratic Party. NAACP. Primaries. *Smith v. Allwright* (US, 1944). South. Supreme Court. 1890's-1944. *1722*
—. Democratic Party. NAACP. Primaries. Supreme Court. Texas. 1927-45. *1723*
—. Discrimination, Educational. Disfranchisement. Middle Classes. North Carolina. Progressivism. Public Finance. Whites. 1880-1910. *2316*
—. Economic Conditions. Race Relations. Washington, Booker T. 1895. *1149*
—. Georgia. Populism. Reform. Watson, Thomas E. 1880-1922. *27*
—. *Gillespie v. Palmer* (US, 1866). Wisconsin (Milwaukee). 1849-66. *1173*
—. Kentucky. Political Parties. 1865-82. *1177*
—. Louisiana. Military Occupation. Reconstruction. Sheridan, Philip H. 1865-67. *991*
—. New York. Referendum. Republican Party. 1846-69. *120*
—. North Carolina. Red Shirt Movement. Social Classes. Terrorism. Whites. 1898-1900. *1067*

SOCIAL REFORM AND REACTION IN AMERICA: AN ANNOTATED BIBLIOGRAPHY 311

Negro Suffrage

—. Racism. Reconstruction. Rhetoric. Ridicule. South. 1866-70. *1207*
—. Republican Party. Wisconsin. 1857. *599*
Negro (term). Discrimination. Editors and Editing. Publishers and Publishing. 1898-1975. *1590*
Negro Young People's Congress. Leadership. South. 1902. *2026*
Negroes *See also* Afro-American Studies; Black Capitalism; Black Muslims; Black Nationalism; Black Power; Civil War; Confederate States of America; Discrimination; Race Relations; Racism; Reconstruction; Slavery.
—. Abolition Movement. Bryant, John Howard. Bryant, Julian. Civil War. Illinois (Bureau County). Lovejoy, Owen. Military Service. 1831-65. *607*
—. Abolition Movement. Christology. New York. Ward, Samuel Ringgold. 1839-51. *618*
—. Abolition Movement. Clergy. 1830-60. *653*
—. Abolition movement. Constitutional Amendments (15th). Douglass, Frederick. Theology. 1825-86. *777*
—. Abolition Movement. Constitutional conventions, state. Disfranchisement. Gardner, Charles W. Hinton, Frederick A. Pennsylvania. 1838. *596*
—. Abolition Movement. Cornish, Samuel E. *Freedom's Journal* (newspaper). Journalism. Presbyterian Church. 1820's-59. *467*
—. Abolition Movement. Douglass, Frederick. Garnet, Henry Highland. Political Factions. 1840-49. *742*
—. Abolition Movement. Historiography. 1830-60. *754*
—. Abolition Movement. Truth, Sojourner. 1825-60. *445*
—. Abolitionists. Brown, William Wells. Medicine. Remond, Sarah Parker. Ruggles, David. Smith, James McCune. Tubman, Harriet. 1810-85. *329*
—. Abolitionists. Fugitive Slaves. Pennsylvania (Pittsburgh). Philanthropic Society. 1830's-60. *610*
—. Adams, Charles P. Colleges and Universities. Grambling State University. Louisiana. 1896-1928. *1836*
—. Adams, John Quincy (1848-1922). Minnesota (St. Paul). *Western Appeal* (newspaper). 1888-1922. *1269*
—. Adoption. Baker, Josephine. Civil rights. Entertainers. World War II. 1940-75. *358*
—. Affirmative action. City Government. Discrimination, employment. Ohio (Cincinnati). 1963-67. *2888*
—. Affirmative action. Education. School Integration. 17c-20c. *2845*
—. Africa. Blyden, Edward Wilmot. Ethnic consciousness. Intellectuals. ca 1832-65. *557*
—. Africa. Colonization. Cuffe, Paul. Massachusetts (Boston). 1810-15. *728*
—. Africa. Colonization. New Jersey Colonization Society. 1815-48. *745*
—. Africa. Garvey, Marcus. Nkrumah, Kwame. 1920's-75. *2422*
—. Africa, West. Blyden, Edward Wilmot. New York. 1850-1912. *291*
—. African Baptist Church. Education. Emancipation. Meachum, John Berry. Missouri (St. Louis). 1815-54. *395*
—. Africans' School. Benezet, Anthony. Education. Friends, Society of. Pennsylvania (Philadelphia). 1770's-80's. *487*
—. Afro-American Studies. Education. 1674-1917. *212*
—. Agricultural Reform. Georgia. Hunt, Henry Alexander. North Carolina. 1890-1938. *1744*
—. Agriculture. Industrial Arts Education. North. Philanthropy. South. 1902-35. *1832*
—. Alabama. American Missionary Association. Education. Talladega College. 1865-79. *1244*
—. Alabama. Banking. Freedmen's Savings Bank. 1865-74. *1191*
—. Alabama. Civil Rights. Democratic Party. Folsom, James E. State Government. Women. 1947-58. *2668*
—. Alabama. Duke, Jesse C. Editors and Editing. Montgomery *Herald* (newspaper). Political Commentary. Republican Party. 1886-1916. *1185*
—. Alabama. Farmers. Southern Improvement Company. Virginia. 1900-20. *2172*
—. Alabama. Industrial Arts Education. Tuskegee Institute. Washington, Booker T. 1870's-90's. *1189*
—. Alabama. Labor Union of Alabama. National Negro Labor Union. Politics. Rapier, James T. Reconstruction. 1837-75. *1253*

—. Alabama. Mobile Harbor Act (Alabama, 1842). Petitions. Prisons. Seamen. State Legislatures. 1849. *727*
—. Alabama (Birmingham). Civil Rights. King, Martin Luther, Jr. Nonviolence. Political Protest. 1962. *2843*
—. Alabama (Birmingham). Communist Party. Hudson, Hosea. South. 1920's-70's. *404*
—. Alabama (Bullock, Greene, Wilcox counties). Decisionmaking. Local Politics. 1971-72. *2819*
—. Alabama (Montgomery). Boycotts. King, Martin Luther, Jr. Leadership. New York City (Harlem). Powell, Adam Clayton, Jr. 1941-56. *307*
—. Alabama State College. Education. Paterson, William Burns. 1878-1915. *1257*
—. Alcorn University. Mississippi. Race Relations. Revels, Hiram Rhodes. Senate. ca 1870's. *1256*
—. Allen, William G. Attitudes. Colonization. Exiles. Great Britain. New York Central College at McGrawville. 1820-78. *290*
—. American Colonization Society. Colonization. Georgia. Liberia. 1816-60. *705*
—. American Colonization Society. Crummell, Alexander. Education. Liberia. 1853-73. *1126*
—. American Colonization Society. Emigration. Liberia. 19c. *688*
—. American Federation of Labor. Brotherhood of Sleeping Car Porters. Randolph, A. Philip. 1867-1935. *70*
—. American Federation of State, County, and Municipal Employees. Oral history. Roberts, Lillian. 1920's-70's. *417*
—. American Missionary Association. Civil War. Education. Missouri. 1862-65. *1241*
—. American Missionary Association. Colleges and Universities. Freedmen's Bureau. Mississippi. Tougaloo College. 1865-69. *1141*
—. American Missionary Association. Congregationalism. South. 1846-80. *1242*
—. American Moral Reform Society. Pennsylvania (Philadelphia). Reform. Whipper, William. 1830-76. *386*
—. American Revolution. Military Recruitment. 1770-1802. *527*
—. *Amos 'n' Andy* (program). Boycotts. Comic strips. Radio. Stereotypes. 1930's. *2588*
—. Anti-Communist Movements. House Committee on Un-American Activities. Robeson, Paul. Robinson, Jackie. USSR. 1949. *2684*
—. Antioch College. Colleges and Universities. Ohio (Yellow Springs). Segregation. 1966-69. *2864*
—. Antislavery Sentiments. Civil War. Douglas, H. Ford. Emigration. Military Service. 1854-65. *666*
—. Antislavery Sentiments. Great Britain. Massachusetts (Salem). Remond, Sarah Parker. Women. 1856-87. *294*
—. Antislavery Sentiments. Newspapers. Ontario. *Provincial Freeman* (newspaper). Shadd, Mary Ann. 1852-93. *351*
—. Appalachia. Reconstruction. Republican Party. State Politics. 1865-1900. *1216*
—. Arkansas. Constitutions, State (conventions). Reconstruction. 1868. *1250*
—. Arkansas. Disasters. Droughts. Plantations. Red Cross. Sharecroppers. 1930-31. *2463*
—. Arkansas. Jim Crow laws. Political Leadership. Segregation. 1890's. *1193*
—. Arkansas. Race Relations. Republican Party. 1867-1925. *115*
—. *Arkansas Freeman* (newspaper). Gross, Tabbs. Political Commentary. Reconstruction. Republican Party. 1869-70. *1203*
—. Arkansas (Lee County). Clinics. Cooperatives. Medical care. 1960's-70's. *2977*
—. Armies. Bates, Edward. Civil War. Politics. Wages. 1861-64. *1129*
—. Armies. Hastie, William H. Military recruitment. Press. World War II. 1940-42. *2638*
—. Army. Civilian Conservation Corps. Military Organization. 1933-42. *2528*
—. Army. Committee on Participation of Negroes in the National Defense Program. NAACP. Pittsburgh *Courier* (newspaper). Segregation. 1937-40. *2506*
—. Asians. Immigration. Newlands, Francis. Progressives. West Coast. 1904-17. *2067*
—. Associates of Dr. Bray, Thomas. Church of England. Education. Missions and Missionaries. 1717-77. *500*

—. Association for Promoting Colored Volunteers. Civil War. Military Recruitment. New York. Race Relations. Union League. 1861-65. *1255*
—. Association of Southern Women for the Prevention of Lynching. Lynching. South. Women. 1930-42. *2472*
—. Atlanta University. Labor Department. Social Conditions. 1897-1907. *1964*
—. Attica State Prison. NAACP. New York. Prisons. 1932. *2462*
—. Attitudes. Civil Rights. Declaration of Independence. Fourth of July. Jefferson, Thomas. 1776. 1800-50. *724*
—. Attitudes. Civil rights. Johnson, Lyndon B. 1930's-68. *1531*
—. Attitudes. Housing. Ohio (Toledo). Racism. United Automobile Workers of America. 1967-73. *2805*
—. Attitudes. Political Power. 1952-72. *1626*
—. Attitudes. Whites. 1963-77. *2818*
—. Automobile Industry and Trade. Labor Unions and Organizations. League of Revolutionary Black Workers. Michigan (Detroit). 1968-73. *2832*
—. Baker, Ray Stannard. Civil rights. DuBois, W. E. B. Liberalism. Wilmer, Cary Breckenridge (interview). 1900-10. *2110*
—. Baptists. Education. Missions and Missionaries. South. 1862-81. *1240*
—. Baptists. Massachusetts (Boston). 1800-73. *565*
—. Baptists, Southern. Education. Paternalism. 1880's-90's. *1266*
—. Barber, Jesse Max. *Voice of the Negro* (periodical). Washington, Booker T. 1904-07. *1966*
—. Baseball. Brooklyn Dodgers (team). Integration. Montreal Royals (team). Press. Rickey, Branch. Robinson, Jackie. 1945-47. *2690*
—. Berea College. Education. Kentucky. 1858-1908. *1225*
—. Bethune, Mary McLeod. Equal opportunity. National Youth Administration. Public Policy. Youth. 1935-44. *2594*
—. Bethune, Mary McLeod. National Youth Administration. New Deal. 1930-40. *2578*
—. Bibb, Henry. Canada. Emigration. Separatism. USA. 1830-60. *672*
—. *Birth of a Nation* (film). Films. Griffith, David W. Temperance Movements. 1900-20. *2087*
—. Black Nationalism. Musicians. Robeson, Paul. 1914-45. *1692*
—. Blue law. Legislators. Louisiana. Reconstruction. State Legislatures. 1867-75. *1276*
—. Boycotts. Mass Transit. Segregation. Virginia. 1904-07. *2154*
—. Boycotts. Mississippi. Police brutality (alleged). Robinson, Alfred. United League. 1966-78. *2893*
—. Breckinridge, Robert J., Jr. Breckinridge, William C. P. Courts. Elections. Kentucky. Testimony. 1866-69. *1096*
—. British Columbia. California. Discrimination. Gold Rushes. Race Relations. 1849-66. *592*
—. Brotherhood of Sleeping Car Porters. March on Washington Movement. National Negro Congress. Randolph, A. Philip. 1925-41. *353*
—. *Brown* v. *Board of Education* (US, 1954). Desegregation. Equality. Public Schools. 1950's-74. *2817*
—. *Brown* v. *Board of Education* (US, 1954). Educators. School Integration. 1954-75. *2838*
—. Buffalo Cooperative Economic Society, Inc. Nelson, Ezekiel E. New York (Buffalo). 1928-61. *1762*
—. Bunche, Ralph. National Negro Congress. New Deal. Political Attitudes. 1930-39. *2532*
—. Cain, Richard Harvey. Politics. Reconstruction. Social conditions. South Carolina. 1850's-87. *375*
—. California. Political activism. Religion. 1850-73. *76*
—. California (Los Angeles). Garvey, Marcus. Universal Negro Improvement Association. 1920's. *2455*
—. California (San Francisco). Chinese Americans. Law. Political Leadership. Racism. 1865-75. *1184*
—. California (San Francisco). Churches. Civil rights. Pressure groups. 1860's. *1221*

—. California (San Francisco Bay). Courts Martial and Courts of Inquiry. Mare Island Mutiny. Navies. Port Chicago Naval Magazine. Race relations. 1944-48. *2652*
—. California (Sausalito). Discrimination. International Brotherhood of Boilermakers, Iron Shipbuilders and Helpers of America. *James* v. *Marinship* (California, 1945). Labor. Shipbuilding. 1940-48. *2653*
—. Capital punishment. Cruce, Lee. Governors. Oklahoma. White supremacy. 1911-15. *1907*
—. Carpetbaggers. House of Representatives. Reconstruction. Republican Party. Scalawags. South. 1868-72. *1036*
—. Carpetbaggers. Louisiana. Republican Party. State Politics. 1868. *1136*
—. Carver, George Washington. Scientists. 1900-75. *380*
—. Catholic University of America. Colleges and Universities. Discrimination. District of Columbia. Wesley, Charles H. 1914-48. *2304*
—. Census Bureau. Cornell University. Economics. Progressivism. Racism. Willcox, Walter F. 1895-1910. *1870*
—. Centennial Celebrations. Douglass, Frederick. Pennsylvania (Philadelphia). 1876. *1157*
—. Charities. Illinois (Chicago). Social problems. 1890-1917. *1979*
—. Charleston City Railway Company. Desegregation. Reconstruction. South Carolina. Streetcars. 1867. *1169*
—. Christianity. Civil rights. Equality. 19c-20c. *126*
—. Church Schools. Colleges and universities, black. Tennessee. 1865-1920. *2307*
—. Cincinnati Colored School system. Discrimination, Educational. Economic Conditions. Ohio. Social Change. 19c. *832*
—. Cities. Civil disturbances. Political Participation. Social change. 1960's-70's. *2798*
—. Cities. Civil rights movement. Federal government. Local Government. 1933-70. *1686*
—. Cities. Educational Reform. Public Schools. South. Teachers. 1865-90. *1238*
—. Cities. Ethnicity. Race Relations. Social organization. Valentine, Charles. 1865-1975. *1697*
—. City Government. Civil rights movement. Florida. Public services. 1960-76. *2814*
—. City Government. Elites. Human Development Corporation. Missouri (St. Louis). Poor. War on Poverty. 1964-75. *2935*
—. City Government. Maryland (Baltimore). Political protest. Public schools. 1865-1900. *1271*
—. City Government. Maryland (Baltimore). Republican Party. 1890-1931. *1593*
—. City Politics. Elections, municipal. Knights of Labor. Political Reform. Virginia (Richmond). 1886-88. *1303*
—. City Politics. Georgia (Atlanta). Jackson, Maynard. Political Leadership. 1965-77. *2847*
—. Civic Unity Committee. Defense industries. Japanese Americans. Race relations. Washington (Seattle). World War II. 1940-45. *2624*
—. Civil Rights. Clark, Peter Humphries. Ohio (Cincinnati). Politics. 1880's-1925. *350*
—. Civil rights. Communist Party. Economic conditions. New York City (Harlem). Political Protest. 1930's. *2563*
—. Civil rights. Congress. Truman, Harry S. 1949-50. *2687*
—. Civil rights. Demonstrations. Desegregation. Florida (Tampa). Fort, Clarence. Lane, Julian. 1960. *2902*
—. Civil Rights. Demonstrations. Oklahoma (Oklahoma City). Restaurants. 1958-64. *2835*
—. Civil Rights. Discrimination. Equality. Political Attitudes. Reconstruction. Texas. 1865-70. *1200*
—. Civil rights. Economic Conditions. 1960's-70's. *2829*
—. Civil rights. Editors and Editing. Fortune, Timothy Thomas. 1881-1928. *95*
—. Civil rights. Governors. Johnson, Andrew. Tennessee. 1862-65. *972*
—. Civil rights. Hancock, George B. Jackson, Luther P. Virginia. Young, Plummer B. 1930-45. *1583*
—. Civil rights. Howard University. Nabrit, James Madison, Jr. 1927-60. *439*
—. Civil rights. Human rights. Political Protest. 1954-78. *2774*

—. Civil rights. Institutions. Organizations. Sit-ins. South. 1960. *2868*
—. Civil rights. Johnson, Lyndon B. (administration). 1963-69. *2866*
—. Civil Rights. Kentucky. Newspapers. Reconstruction. 1866-72. *1176*
—. Civil rights. King, Martin Luther, Jr. Nonviolence. 1950's-68. *2826*
—. Civil Rights. Leftism. Robeson, Paul. Singers. 1898-1976. *379*
—. Civil rights. Militancy. Religion. 1960's-70's. *2844*
—. Civil Rights. Nebraska (Omaha). Quality of life. Social services. Urban League. World War II. 1928-50. *2639*
—. Civil Rights. Newspapers. 1946-72. *2874*
—. Civil Rights. Pemberton, Caroline Hollingsworth. Pennsylvania (Philadelphia). Socialist Party. 1896-1903. *1158*
—. Civil Rights. Political Protest. Press. 1950-76. *2875*
—. Civil rights. Politics. Racism. 1940's. *1622*
—. Civil rights. Republican Party. Voting and Voting Behavior. 1846-69. *597*
—. Civil Rights. Sociology. South. Work, Monroe Nathan. 1900-45. *388*
—. Civil Rights. Turner, James Milton. 1865-1915. *313*
—. Civil Rights Act (US, 1866). Constitutional Amendments (14th, 15th). Reconstruction. Republican Party. States' rights. ca 1865-77. *953*
—. Civil Rights Act (US, 1875). Constitutional Amendments (13th, 14th). Federal Government. 1875-83. *1113*
—. Civil Rights Act (US, 1964; Title VIII). Discrimination, Employment. Income. Women. 1964-70's. *2839*
—. Civil rights movement. Illinois (Chicago). School integration. 1936. *2523*
—. Civil Rights Movement. King, Martin Luther, Jr. Social Conditions. 1968-79. *2806*
—. Civil rights movement. NAACP. South Dakota. 1804-1970. *4*
—. Civil rights movement. Nonviolence. Political Protest. 1955-65. *1709*
—. Civil rights movement. Politics. Riots. Tennessee (Columbia). Truman, Harry S. 1946. *2657*
—. Civil Rights Organizations. King, Martin Luther, Jr. Leadership. Southern Christian Leadership Conference. 1957-73. *2828*
—. Civil War. Elections (presidential). Political Participation. Republican Party. 1864. *1224*
—. Civil War. Emigration. Haiti. 1860-64. *1254*
—. Civil War. Labor. Mississippi. Vicksburg (battle). 1862. *1220*
—. Civil War. Law. Mississippi. Reconstruction. 1857-70. *114*
—. Civil War. Lincoln, Abraham. Louisiana (New Orleans). Reconstruction. Suffrage. 1860-67. *1130*
—. Civil War. Political Protest. State Politics. Suffrage. Tennessee. 1864-65. *1144*
—. Civil War. Reconstruction. Slavery. Women. 19c. *331*
—. Civilian Conservation Corps. Equal opportunity. New Deal. 1933-42. *2514*
—. Clark, Peter Humphries. Education. Ohio (Cincinnati). Socialism. 1849-81. *1197*
—. Class consciousness. NAACP. Pennsylvania (Philadelphia). Race. 1930's. *2566*
—. Clergy. Community affairs. Garvey, Marcus. New York (Buffalo). Universal Negro Improvement Association. 1830's-1920's. *2458*
—. Clergy. Equality. Mormons. Women. 1860-1979. *91*
—. Clergy. Lutheran Church (North Carolina Synod). 1865-89. *1228*
—. Coal Mines and Mining. Davis, Richard L. Labor Unions and Organizations. Letters-to-the-editor. *National Labor Tribune.* United Mine Workers of America. ca 1890-1900. *1139*
—. Coal Mines and Mining. Oregon Improvement Company. Strikebreakers. Washington (King County). 1891. *1265*
—. Cocking, Walter D. Georgia. Higher education. Talmadge, Eugene. 1937-43. *2620*
—. Colleges and Universities. Curricula. Education. Individualism. 1890-1970's. *1833*
—. Colleges and Universities. Equal opportunity. Maryland. 1908-75. *1860*
—. Colleges and Universities. Russwurm, John. 1823-1973. *181*

—. Colleges and universities, black. 1854-1978. *195*
—. Colleges and Universities (black). 1890-1974. *1843*
—. Colonization. Emancipation. Lincoln, Abraham. 1852-65. *747*
—. Colonization. Emancipation. Lincoln, Abraham. 1861-65. *1138*
—. Colonization. Garvey, Marcus. Liberia. Universal Negro Improvement Association. 1914-24. *2342*
—. Colonization. Gold Coast. Sam, Alfred Charles. 1913-16. *1997*
—. Colonization. Liberia. Methodist Episcopal Church. Missions and Missionaries. Sierra Leone. 1833-48. *641*
—. Colonization. Ohio (Cincinnati). Ontario (Wilberforce). 1829-56. *604*
—. Colorado. Equal rights. Reconstruction. 1865-67. *1134*
—. Colorado (Denver). Hardin, William J. 1863-73. *1135*
—. Colored Farmers' Alliance. Farmers. South. ca 1886-95. *1172*
—. Colored Farmers' Alliance. Humphrey, R. M. Labor Unions and Organizations. South. Strikes. 1876-91. *1150*
—. Colored National Labor Union. Florida. Labor Unions and Organizations. National Union of Negro Labor. Race Relations. Reconstruction. 1865-75. *1259*
—. Communist Party. Culture. Intellectuals. New York City (Harlem). Popular Front. 1935-39. *2562*
—. Communist Party. Georgia (Atlanta). Herndon, Angelo. International Labor Defense. 1932-37. *2548*
—. Communist Party. National Maritime Union. Racism. United Electrical, Radio and Machine Workers of America. World War II. 1941-45. *2622*
—. Community control. Education. Integration. New York City (Brooklyn). Politics. 1882-1902. *1181*
—. Congress. Historiography. Reconstruction. South. 1860's-1978. *1175*
—. Congress of Industrial Organizations. Maryland (Baltimore). 1930-41. *2580*
—. Conservatism. DuBois, W. E. B. Periodicals. Race relations. Radicals and Radicalism. Washington, Booker T. 1900-10. *1983*
—. Constitution League. Discrimination. Foraker, Joseph B. Hepburn Bill, Warner-Foraker Amendment (1906). Jim Crow laws. Railroads. Washington, Booker T. (and Committee of 12). 1906. *1919*
—. Constitutional Amendments (19th). *Crisis* (periodical). DuBois, W. E. B. Woman Suffrage. 1910-34. *1712*
—. Constitutional Amendments (24th). Political participation. Voter registration. Voting Rights Act (US, 1965). 1964-67. *2892*
—. Constitutional conventions. Ohio. Progressive era. Smith, Harry. Suffrage. 1863-1912. *2165*
—. Construction. Employment. Ickes, Harold. Public Works Administration. Quotas. 1933-40. *2535*
—. Cooperative Workers of America. Georgia. Hoover, Hiram F. Secret Societies. South Carolina. 1886-87. *1197*
—. Cooperatives. DuBois, W. E. B. Economic Theory. 1940. *2498*
—. Courts. Discrimination, Educational. District of Columbia. Public schools. 1804-1974. *1844*
—. Courts. Freedmen's Bureau. Justice. Reconstruction. Texas. 1865-68. *1146*
—. Crime and Criminals. Fletcher, Benjamin Harrison. Industrial Workers of the World. Labor. Longshoremen. 1910-33. *437*
—. Cruse, Harold. Culture. Intellectuals. Methodology. 1910-75. *1519*
—. Curaçao. Political Protest. Social change. 1960's-70's. *2797*
—. Decisionmaking. Desegregation. Political power. South. Teachers. Voting and Voting Behavior. 1950's-60's. *2831*
—. Delaware. DuPont, Pierre S. Philanthropy. Public Schools. 1918-30. *2451*
—. Democratic Party. Political participation. Poverty. South. 1960's. *2837*
—. Depressions. Progressive education. South. 1930-45. *2512*
—. Desegregation. Discrimination, Educational. Graduate schools. Lawsuits. North Carolina. Professional training. 1930-51. *1835*

Negroes

—. Dever, William. Elections (mayoral). Ethnic groups. Illinois (Chicago). Prohibition. 1923-27. *2350*
—. Discrimination. Fair Employment Practices Committee. Railroads. Southeastern Carriers Conference. World War II. 1941-45. *2630*
—. Discrimination. Hospitals. Mercy Hospital (proposed). Ohio (Cleveland). 1927-30. *2380*
—. Discrimination. Jews. Racism. 1890-1915. *1938*
—. Discrimination. Labor Unions and Organizations. National Colored Labor Union. National Labor Union. 1866-72. *1137*
—. Discrimination. Public Welfare. South. 1865-90. *1236*
—. Discrimination, Educational. Indiana. NAACP. ca 1869-1975. *211*
—. Discrimination, Employment. 1890-1970. *1763*
—. Discrimination, Employment. Georgia Railroad. Strikes. 1909. *2220*
—. Discrimination, Employment. Jim Crow laws. NAACP. Tennessee (Memphis). 1900-37. *1750*
—. Discrimination, Employment. Military Service (enlistees). Navies. Race Relations. Segregation. 1798-1970's. 1970D 1900H. *41*
—. District of Columbia. Education. Miner, Myrtilla. Spiritualism. 1851-1955. *190*
—. Documents. Slavery. Social Conditions. 1774-1841. *788*
—. Downing, George T. Public schools. Rhode Island (Newport). School Integration. 1855-66. *841*
—. DuBois, W. E. B. Education. Elites. Social problems. 1897-1963. *1565*
—. DuBois, W. E. B. Elites. Intellectuals. Talented Tenth strategy. 1895-1919. *2090*
—. DuBois, W. E. B. Elites. Liberal education. Talented Tenth strategy. 1890's-1963. *1591*
—. DuBois, W. E. B. Human rights. Women. 1910-20. *1874*
—. Economic Conditions. Employment. Equal opportunity. Law. Occupations. 1954-72. *1785*
—. Economic Conditions. Race Relations. Social change. Violence. 1960's. *2851*
—. Economic dependence. Land reform. Reconstruction. 1861-1900. *1155*
—. Economic Regulations. Labor. National Recovery Administration. South. Wages. 1933-34. *2576*
—. Education. Education Department. Reconstruction. 1867. *1277*
—. Education. Farmers. Tuskegee Institute. Washington, Booker T. 1881-1915. *1186*
—. Education. Fort Valley High and Industrial School. Georgia. Torbert, James H. 1897-1911. *2296*
—. Education. Freedmen's Bureau. Texas. 1865-70. *1174*
—. Education. Kentucky. 1800-1954. *216*
—. Education. Lincoln University. Lindsay, Lizzie A. Missouri (Jefferson City). Turner, James Milton. 1865-75. *1179*
—. Education. Management. Whites. 1652-1972. *183*
—. Education. North Carolina. Reconstruction. School Integration. 1865-67. *1127*
—. Education, Finance. Kentucky. Segregation. State Government. 1865-1954. *1178*
—. Educational Policy. Industrial Arts Education. Speeches, Addresses, etc. Washington, Booker T. 1884-1904. *1283*
—. Educational Reform. Massachusetts (Boston). Separatist Movements. Smith, Thomas Paul. 1848-49. *855*
—. Educational Reform. Pennsylvania (Philadelphia). White, Jacob C., Jr. 1857-1902. *441*
—. Educational theory. Washington, Booker T. 1881-1915. *193*
—. Elections. Politics. Reconstruction. Tennessee (Shelby County). 1865-76. *1160*
—. Elites. Kansas. Politics. Republican Party. Waller, John Lewis. 1878-1900. *468*
—. Emigration. Ethiopia (Addis Ababa). Ford, Arnold. 1930-35. *2436*
—. Employment. Housing. Racism. Voting and Voting Behavior. 1960's-70's. *2810*
—. Employment. Minorities in Politics. New Deal. Roosevelt, Franklin D. 1930-42. *2586*
—. Equal opportunity. Louisiana Education Association. School Integration. Teachers. 1901-70. *1857*
—. Equality. Federal government. New York. States' rights. 1865-73. *1154*

SUBJECT INDEX

—. Ethnic Groups. School Integration. 1964-78. *2879*
—. Federal Government. House of Representatives. Intervention. Population. South. Voting Rights Act (US, 1965). 1940-75. *2802*
—. Federal Government. Segregation. 1916-29. *2392*
—. Federal Policy. Immigration. 1917-29. *2382*
—. Feminism. Literature. Stowe, Harriet Beecher. Truth, Soujourner. 1850's-90's. *802*
—. Film industry. Griffith, David W. (*Birth of a Nation*). Racism. 1915-18. *1918*
—. Firestone, Harvey S. Garvey, Marcus. Land. Leases. Liberia. Universal Negro Improvement Association. 1926. *2402*
—. Fisk University. Johnson, Charles S. Race relations. UNESCO. 1900-56. *346*
—. Florida. Menard, John Willis. Political Leadership. 1871-90. *283*
—. Florida. Political attitudes. Reconstruction. Republican Party. Walls, Josiah T. 1867-85. *1192*
—. Florida (Jacksonville). Political Participation. 1887-1907. *1125*
—. Fort McIntosh. Riots. Texas (Laredo). 25th Infantry, US (Company D). 1899. *1143*
—. Foster, Richard B. (address). Missouri. Reconstruction. Teachers. 1869. *1170*
—. France. Madagascar. Press. Waller, John L. 1890's. *1281*
—. *Free Speech* (newspaper). Lynching. Tennessee (Memphis). Wells, Ida B. 1892. *1128*
—. Freedmen. *Freedom's Journal* (newspaper). Negroes (free). Press. 1827-29. *713*
—. Garvey, Marcus. Ideology. Jamaica. Pan-Africanism. 1887-1927. *401*
—. Garvey, Marcus. Religion. Universal Negro Improvement Association. 1920's. *2351*
—. Georgia. Political Attitudes. Progressive Party. Roosevelt, Theodore. Wilson, Woodrow. 1912. *2038*
—. Georgia. Savannah Men's Sunday Club. Social Change. 1905-11. *1970*
—. Georgia Equal Rights Association. Reconstruction. Republican Party. Union League. 1865-80. *1214*
—. Haiti. Revolution. 1791-1861. *639*
—. Harris, Cicero. Harris, Robert. Harris, William. Reconstruction. South. Teaching. 1864-70. *1278*
—. Harrison, Hubert H. International Colored Unity League. Journalism. Liberty League of Negro Americans. New York City (Harlem). Socialist Party. 1911-27. *1676*
—. Hastie, William H. Military. Racism. Stimson, Henry L. World War II. 1940-43. *2636*
—. Higher education. Philanthropy. Whites. 1861-1920. *1234*
—. Historiography. 17c-19c. 1960-76. *503*
—. Historiography. *Journal of Negro History* (periodical). Woodson, Carter G. 1916-75. *1708*
—. Historiography. Louisiana (New Orleans). Political Leadership. Reconstruction. ca 1800-75. *1239*
—. Historiography. Roosevelt, Franklin D. (administration). USSR. World War II. 1939-45. *2648*
—. Homesteading and Homesteaders. McCabe, Edward Preston. Migration, Internal. Oklahoma. 1891-94. *1204*
—. House of Refuge for Colored Children. Juvenile Delinquency. Pennsylvania (Philadelphia). 1828-60's. *872*
—. House of Representatives. Langston, John Mercer. State Politics. Virginia. 1849-97. *300*
—. Housing. New Deal. Pennsylvania (Philadelphia). 1930's. *2475*
—. Housing and Urban Development Act (US, 1965, Section 23). Illinois (Chicago). Law. Public Housing Authority. Segregation. 1964-75. *2856*
—. Illinois (Chicago). Local Politics. Public schools. 1910-41. *1845*
—. Immigration. Japanese. Miller, Kelly. Race Relations. 1906-24. *1601*
—. Income. Social Status. 1954-74. *1823*
—. Industrial Arts Education. North. Progressive era. South. 1900-15. *2306*
—. Industrial Relations. Migration, Internal. Pine industry. South. Working conditions. ca 1912-26. *1577*
—. Industrialization. Labor Unions and Organizations. Race Relations. 19c-20c. *1819*
—. Jim Crow laws. Railroads. Separate coach bills. South Carolina. 1880-98. *1215*

Negroes

—. Johnson, James Weldon. NAACP. White, Walter F. 1909-35. *1647*
—. Journalism. Labor Unions and Organizations. Marxism. Political protest. Randolph, A. Philip. ca 1911-75. *382*
—. Justice Department. Lawsuits. School Integration. South. 1957-68. *2811*
—. Kennedy, John F. Mississippi. Political Protest. Voting Rights Act (US, 1965). 1960-72. *2863*
—. Kentucky (Louisville). School Integration. 1954-77. *2799*
—. King, Martin Luther, Jr. ("Letter from Birmingham Jail"). Nonviolence. Rhetoric. 1963. *2869*
—. Knights of Labor. Labor Unions and Organizations. South. 1880-87. *1187*
—. Ku Klux Klan. Reconstruction. South Carolina. 1868-71. *1076*
—. Labor. Letters. Riley, William R. Tennessee. United Mine Workers of America. 1892-95. *1201*
—. Labor. Prisons. Tennessee. 1830-1915. *96*
—. Labor Unions and Organizations. Maryland. NAACP. Teachers. 1930's. *2610*
—. Labor Unions and Organizations. Radicals and Radicalism. Socialism. 1865-1900. *1232*
—. Leadership. Miller, Kelly. 1877-1918. *470*
—. Leadership. Reconstruction. South. 1867-75. *1211*
—. Leadership. Segregation. Urbanization. Virginia (Richmond). 1900-20. *1947*
—. League of Women for Community Service. Massachusetts (Boston). Voluntary Associations. Women. 1918-77. *1575*
—. Liberia. Republican Party. Turner, James Milton. 1865-77. *1195*
—. Literature. Radicals and Radicalism. Wright, Richard. 1920-60. *305*
—. Literature. Wright, Richard. 1908-60. *348*
—. Louisiana. Ray, John. Republican Party. Scalawags. ca 1836-88. *463*
—. Louisiana (New Orleans). Metropolitan Police Force. Politics. Riots. Whites. 1868. *1168*
—. Lynch, James (letters). Methodist Episcopal Church. Mississippi. Reconstruction. 1868-69. *1166*
—. Massachusetts (Boston). ca 1800-60. *560*
—. McCabe, Edward Preston. Migration, Internal. Newspapers. Oklahoma (Langston). 1850-1920. *1246*
—. Medical education. Meharry Medical College. Tennessee (Nashville). 1860's-1970's. *226*
—. Minorities in Politics. Mississippi. Voting Rights Act (US, 1965). 1960-74. *2848*
—. Minorities in Politics. Missouri (St. Louis). Republican Party. Wheeler, John W. 1870-1915. *1142*
—. Minorities in Politics. Political Leadership. Reconstruction. Texas. 1865-90's. *1148*
—. Mississippi. Political Leadership. 1965-70. *2884*
—. Mississippi. Public Opinion. Revels, Hiram Rhodes. Senate. 1870. *1202*
—. Missouri (St. Louis). School Integration. 1954-55. *2667*
—. Mortality. 19c-20c. *251*
—. Moton, Robert Russa. Politics. Scott, Emmett Jay. Tuskegee Institute. Washington, Booker T. 1915-25. *1643*
—. National Association of Colored Women. Reform. Terrell, Mary Church. Woman Suffrage. 1892-1954. *312*
—. National Miners Union. Pennsylvania, western. United Mine Workers of America. 1925-31. *2420*
—. Nelson, Alice Dunbar. South. Women. World War I. 1917-18. *1890*
—. New York City (Jamaica). Public schools. Segregation. 1895-1900. *1210*
—. Newspapers. Political Protest. Race Relations. World War II. 1941-45. *2625*
—. Pennsylvania. Suffrage. 1780-1900. *137*
—. Pennsylvania (Philadelphia). Race Relations. Riots. 1968. *2820*
—. *Plessy vs. Ferguson* (US, 1896). Segregation. Supreme Court (decisions). 1896. *1212*
—. Political Parties. Race relations. Virginia (Richmond). 1865. *1231*
—. Populism. Press. Republican Party. 1890-96. *1152*
—. Protestantism. Socialism. Woodbey, George Washington. 1902-15. *1939*
—. Radicals and Radicalism. Reconstruction. Republican Party. South Carolina (Beaufort County). 1865-88. *1003*
—. Readjuster Party. State debt. Virginia. 1879-83. *1222*

—. Reconstruction. South Carolina, University of. 1873-77. *1248*
—. Riots. Social Organization. 1960's. *2793*
—. Sex Discrimination. Women's Liberation Movement. 1960-75. *2733*
—. Voluntary associations. 20c. *1632*
—. Voluntary Associations. ca 1780-1830. *873*
—. Woman suffrage. 1850-1900. *1270*
Negroes (free). Abolition Movement. Massachusetts. Remond, Charles Lenox. 1838-63. *459*
—. Africa. Colonization. Schools. 1816-33. *837*
—. American Colonization Society. Rhetoric. Slavery. Social Status. Whites. 1831-34. *615*
—. American Moral Reform Society. Civil Rights. Maryland (Baltimore). Watkins, William. 1801-58. *339*
—. Civil War. Freedmen. Louisiana (New Orleans). Political Attitudes. Politics. Social Classes. 1860-65. *1275*
—. Freedmen. *Freedom's Journal* (newspaper). Negroes. Press. 1827-29. *713*
—. Freedmen. Intellectuals. Politics. Social theory. South. 1870's-90's. *1274*
Neighborhood Workers' Association. Hastings, Charles. Ontario (Toronto). Poverty. Public health. 1910-21. *1527*
Neighborhoods. Cities. Public Lands. Trust for Public Land. 1975-80. *2756*
—. Federal Government. Local Government. Massachusetts (Boston; South End). Middle Classes. Poor. Urban revitalization. 1960's-70's. *2694*
—. Medical care. Ohio (Cincinnati; Mohawk-Brighton). Phillips, Wilbur C. 1917-20. *2037*
—. New York City. Socialism. Working class. 1908-18. *2006*
Nelson, Alice Dunbar. Negroes. South. Women. World War I. 1917-18. *1890*
Nelson, Ezekiel E. Buffalo Cooperative Economic Society, Inc. Negroes. New York (Buffalo). 1928-61. *1762*
Nelson, Nelson O. Business. Consumer cooperative movements. Garden City Movement. Progressivism. 1890's-1918. *2240*
—. Businessmen. Cooperatives. Profit-sharing. 1886-1904. *1329*
Neo-Populism. Agrarianism. Political Change. Populism. Progressivism. 1676-1972. *30*
Nestor, Agnes. Anderson, Mary. Illinois (Chicago). Labor Unions and Organizations. Robins, Margaret Dreier. Women. Women's Trade Union League. Working conditions. 1903-20. *2190*
Neurology. Progressivism. Psychoanalysis. Putnam, James Sackson. Social change. 1895-1918. *2108*
—. Psychiatry. Social work. 1830's-1920's. *248*
Nevada *See also* Far Western States.
—. Boulder Canyon Project. Colorado River. Hoover Dam. Industrial Workers of the World. Strikes. 1931. *2433*
—. Boulder Canyon Project. Hoover Dam. Industrial Workers of the World. Six Companies, Inc. Strikes. 1931. *2434*
—. Federal Government. Legislation. Newspapers. Racism. 1866-68. *976*
—. Ku Klux Klan. Local Politics. Vigilantism. 1920-29. *2449*
—. Prohibition. State Politics. 1880-1933. *257*
Nevada (Goldfield). American Federation of Labor. Armies. Industrial Workers of the World. Labor Disputes. Western Federation of Miners. 1904-08. *2287*
Nevada (Goldfield, Tonopah). Industrial Workers of the World. Labor Disputes. Mines. 1901-22. *2262*
Nevada (Las Vegas). New Deal. Public works. 1933-40. *2554*
Nevada, University of. Clapp, Hannah Keziah. Educators. Woman Suffrage. 1824-1908. *456*
New Brunswick *See also* Atlantic Provinces.
—. Alberta. Populism. Radicals and Radicalism. Saskatchewan. Social organization. 1950's-70's. *2700*
—. Asylums. Mental Illness. Nova Scotia. 1749-1900. *228*
—. Education. Socialism. Stuart, Henry Harvey. 1873-1952. *310*
New Brunswick (Saint John). Charities. Newfoundland (Saint John's). Nova Scotia (Halifax). Poverty. Unemployment. 1815-60. *871*

New Deal. Agricultural Adjustment Act (1933). Federal Programs. Iowa. Wallace, Henry Agard. 1933-34. *2537*
—. Agricultural Adjustment Administration. Depressions. Farmers. Federal Policy. New York, western. 1934. *2487*
—. Agricultural Adjustment Administration. Soil Conservation Service. 1933-41. *2581*
—. Agricultural Policy. Association of Southern Commissioners of Agriculture. Cotton. South. Tennessee (Memphis). 1936-37. *2567*
—. Agricultural Reform. Catholic Church. Roosevelt, Franklin D. (administration). Social Theory. 1933-39. *2590*
—. American Federation of Labor. Carmody, John. Civil Works Administration. Labor. 1933-34. *2584*
—. American Indian Federation. Bureau of Indian Affairs. Collier, John. Indians. Jamison, Alice Lee. Political activism. 1930's-50's. *354*
—. Amlie, Thomas. Economic programs. Liberals. Politics. Wisconsin. 1931-39. *2609*
—. Amlie, Thomas. Farmer-labor Party. Hard, Herbert. Ohio Farmer-Labor Progressive Federation. Third Parties. 1930-40. *2543*
—. Amlie, Thomas. Farmer-Labor Party. Wisconsin. 1930-38. *2544*
—. Amlie, Thomas. Radicals and Radicalism. Roosevelt, Franklin D. Wisconsin. 1930-39. *1672*
—. Automobile Industry and Trade. Indiana. Labor. Ohio. United Automobile Workers of America. 1935-40. *2542*
—. Bethune, Mary McLeod. National Youth Administration. Negroes. 1930-40. *2578*
—. Bunche, Ralph. National Negro Congress. Negroes. Political Attitudes. 1930-39. *2532*
—. Bureau of Indian Affairs. Collier, John. Indians. 1933-45. *2600*
—. Bureau of Indian Affairs. Collier, John. Public Administration. Social sciences. 1933-45. *2599*
—. Business. Labor Unions and Organizations. Taft-Hartley Act (US, 1947). Wagner Act (US, 1935). World War II. 1935-47. *1749*
—. Catholic Church. Farms. 1930's. *2591*
—. Cherokee Indians. Federal Policy. Indians. North Carolina, western. 1930's. *2607*
—. Civil Works Administration. Labor. 1933-39. *2484*
—. Civilian Conservation Corps. Economic Conditions. Vermont. 1933-42. *2596*
—. Civilian Conservation Corps. Equal opportunity. Negroes. 1933-42. *2514*
—. Clapp, Elsie Ripley. Education. Homesteading and Homesteaders. Roosevelt, Eleanor. West Virginia (Arthurdale). 1933-44. *2477*
—. Collectivism. Glass, Carter. Liberals. National Recovery Administration. 1933-35. *2533*
—. Comintern (7th Congress). Communist Party. Socialist Party. 1935-39. *2547*
—. Congress. Illinois. Keller, Kent. Liberalism. 1930-42. *2608*
—. Congress. Roosevelt, Franklin D. Social Security Act (US, 1935). Unemployment insurance. 1934-35. *2471*
—. Congress of Industrial Organizations. Labor Disputes. Newspapers. South. 1930-39. *2614*
—. Congressmen. Politics. Roosevelt, Franklin D. Virginia. Woodrum, Clifton A. 1922-45. *433*
—. Conservation of Natural Resources. Cooke, Morris L. Rural Electrification Administration. 1933-51. *2491*
—. Conservatism. Constitutional law. Kansas. Newspapers. Supreme Court. 1934-35. *2502*
—. Conservatism. Creel, George. Progressivism. Works Progress Administration. 1900-53. *1520*
—. Constitutions. Editorials. Labor Unions and Organizations. Periodicals. Supreme Court. 1935-37. *2503*
—. Corporations. General Electric Company. 1933-40. *2550*
—. Deportation. Immigrants. Labor Unions and Organizations. Mexican Americans. 1930's. *2500*
—. Depressions. Farmer-Labor Party. Oregon Commonwealth Federation. Political Factions. 1933-38. *2545*
—. Depressions. Farmers. Government. Great Plains. Letters. 1930-40. *2476*
—. Depressions. Frankfurter, Felix. Keynes, John Maynard. Public works. 1932-35. *2473*
—. Depressions. Historiography. Hughes, Charles Evans. Supreme Court. 1930's. 1950's-60's. *2572*

—. Depressions. LaFollette, Philip F. Progressivism. Roosevelt, Franklin D. Wisconsin Works Bill (1935). 1935. *2552*
—. Depressions. Liberalism. Political activism. Socialist Party. Unemployment. 1929-36. *1804*
—. Economic Conditions. Labor. Texas. 1929-39. *2573*
—. Economic Conditions. National Recovery Administration. Supreme Court. Virginia. 1933-35. *2517*
—. Economic planning. Public policy. 1932-41. *2539*
—. Economic policy. Foreign Policy. Public works. Roosevelt, Franklin D. 1933. *2555*
—. Editors and Editing. Liberalism. Milton, George Fort. Tennessee. 1930's. *2521*
—. Employment. Minorities in Politics. Negroes. Roosevelt, Franklin D. 1930-42. *2586*
—. Farmer-Labor Party. Michigan. State Politics. 1933-37. *2541*
—. Federal government. Press. Progressivism. Reform. 1890's-1930's. *1534*
—. Federal Subsistence Homesteads Corporation. Iowa (Granger). Ligutti, Luigi. 1934-51. *2585*
—. Foreign Policy. International Labor Organization. Isolationism. Perkins, Frances. Roosevelt, Franklin D. 1921-34. *2570*
—. Hearst, William Randolph. Progressivism. 1930-35. *2488*
—. Hopkins, Harry. Politics. 1912-40. *414*
—. Housing. Negroes. Pennsylvania (Philadelphia). 1930's. *2475*
—. Labor. Radicals and Radicalism. Working class. 1930's. *2524*
—. Labor Unions and Organizations. Radicals and Radicalism. 1930-39. *2546*
—. Liberalism. New Left. Political Theory. Welfare state. 1932-66. *1738*
—. Libraries (public). 1933-39. *2480*
—. Long, Huey P. Reform. 1933-35. *2490*
—. Miners. National Industrial Recovery Act (US, 1933). Roosevelt, Eleanor. Subsistence Homesteads Program. West Virginia (Arthurdale). 1930-46. *2492*
—. Nevada (Las Vegas). Public works. 1933-40. *2554*
—. Political Attitudes. Public Welfare. South Dakota. 1930's-70's. *2470*
—. Political Participation. Roosevelt, Eleanor. Women. 1900-36. *372*
—. Progressives. Roosevelt, Franklin D. Senate. 1935-36. *2557*
—. Progressives. Senate. 1933-34. *2558*
New Democratic Party. British Columbia. Labor Legislation. Natural resources. Public Policy. Social Democracy. Taxation. 1972-75. *2942*
New Divinity (doctrines). Edwards, Jonathan. Hopkins, Samuel. New England. Theology. 1730-1803. *479*
New England *See also* individual states; Northeastern or North Atlantic States.
—. Abolition Movement. Civil War (antecedents). Parker, Theodore. Violence. 1850-60. *635*
—. Abolition Movement. Garrison, William Lloyd. Racism. 1841. *717*
—. Agriculture. Nutrition. Reformers. 1873-1907. *1465*
—. Antinomianism. Arminianism. Puritans. 1630-60. *482*
—. Attitudes. Exercise. Health. Recreation. Transcendentalism. 1830-60. *572*
—. Attitudes. Mather, Cotton. Sermons. Women. 1650-1800. *493*
—. Attitudes. Puritans. Slavery. 1641-1776. *521*
—. Backus, Isaac. Baptists. Religious liberty. 1754-89. *513*
—. California. Feminism. Gilman, Charlotte Perkins. 1880's-1935. *287*
—. Edwards, Jonathan. Hopkins, Samuel. New Divinity (doctrines). Theology. 1730-1803. *479*
—. Feminism. Fuller, Margaret. Radicals and Radicalism. Transcendentalism. 1810-50. *311*
—. Germany. Gymnastics. Physical Education and Training. 1820's. *838*
—. Great Britain. Law reform. Puritans. 1620-60. *501*
—. Labor reform. Lowell Female Labor Reform Association. Textile Industry. Women. 1845-47. *819*
—. Puritans. Slavery. 1652-1795. *528*

New England Courant (newspaper). City Government. Editorials. Franklin, James. Freedom of the Press. Inoculation. Massachusetts (Boston). Smallpox. 1721. *535*

New England Emigrant Aid Company. Antislavery Sentiments. *Arabia* (vessel). Arms Trade. Hoyt, David Starr. Kansas. 1855-59. *741*

New England Kitchen. Abel, Mary Hinman. Aladdin Ovens. Atkinson, Edward. Food Consumption. Massachusetts (Boston). Richards, Ellen H. Working Class. 1889-97. *1467*

New Era Union. Caryl, Charles W. Colorado. Progressive Era. Racial thought. Utopias. 1858-1926. *1509*

New federalism. Civil rights. Prisoners. Supreme courts, state. 1969-80. *2773*

New Hampshire *See also* New England; Northeastern or North Atlantic States.

—. Abolition Movement. Haverford College Library (Quaker Collection). Portsmouth Anti-Slavery Society. Rogers, Nathaniel Peabody. 1830-46. *316*

—. Antislavery sentiments. Liberty Party. State Politics. 1840-48. *681*

—. Authors. Churchill, Winston (1871-1947). Progressivism. ca 1900-47. *292*

—. Bass, Robert P. Boston and Maine Railroad. Churchill, Winston (1871-1947). Progressivism. Republican Party. 1890-1912. *1868*

New Hampshire (Berlin). Congress of Industrial Organizations. Labor. Nonpartisan League. Political Parties. 1932-36. *2497*

New Harmony (colony). Indiana. Utopias. 1824-58. *916*

New Jersey *See also* Northeastern or North Atlantic States.

—. Attitudes. Paterson, William. Slavery. 1785-1804. *739*

—. City Planning. Garden cities. Radburn (settlement). Suburbs. 1927-79. *1532*

—. Colleges and Universities. Educators. Pennsylvania. Professionalization. 1870-1915. *201*

—. Corporal punishment. Educational Reform. Schools. 1800-1972. *1432*

—. Democratic Party. House of Representatives. Human Rights. Norton, Mary T. Women. 1920-30. *2415*

—. Education. Raritan Bay Union. Utopias. 1853-61. *940*

—. Educational reform. Princeton University. Wilson, Woodrow. 1902-10. *2334*

—. Emancipation Proclamation. Peace Movements. State legislatures. 1864. *1009*

—. Lawyers. Lobbying. Philbrook, Mary. Women's Liberation Movement. 1895-1947. *409*

—. New York City. Patterson Strike Pageant. Strikes. Theater. 1913. *2250*

New Jersey (Bayonne). Polish Americans. Standard Oil Company of New Jersey. Strikes. 1915-16. *2203*

New Jersey College for Women. Colleges and Universities. Douglass, Mabel Smith. Lobbying. Middle Classes. Women. 1911-18. *2324*

New Jersey Colonization Society. Africa. Colonization. Negroes. 1815-48. *745*

New Jersey Freeman (newspaper). Abolition movement. Grimes, John. Reform. 1844-50. *623*

New Jersey (Jersey City). Antitrust. Local Government. Railroads. Taxation. 1901-07. *2276*

—. City Politics. Fagan, Mark. Progressivism. 1896-1907. *2279*

—. Fagan, Mark. Progressives. Single tax. Taxation. 1901-17. *2278*

—. Progressivism. Whittier House. 1890-1917. *2105*

New Jersey (Montclair). Keller, Helen. Socialism. Speeches, Addresses, etc. 1890-1913. *1916*

New Jersey (Newark). Cities. Georgia (Atlanta). Illinois (Chicago). Water supply. 1860-1923. *32*

—. Presbyterian Church. See, Isaac M. Sermons. Women. 1876. *1485*

New Jersey (Passaic). Labor. Strikes. Textile industry. Working conditions. 1875-1926. *2366*

New Jersey (Paterson). American Civil Liberties Union. Associated Silk Workers Union. Freedom of Assembly. Freedom of Speech. Strikes. 1924. *2378*

—. Courts. Industrial Workers of the World. Labor. Progressivism. Quinlan, Patrick. 1913-17. *2275*

—. Immigrants. Industrial Workers of the World. Strikes. Textile Industry. Violence. 1913. *2254*

—. Silk industry. Strikes. 1913-24. *1761*

New Jersey (Perth Amboy, Red Bank). Communes. North American Phalanx. Raritan Bay Union. Spring, Marcus. 1843-59. *930*

New Jersey (Princeton). History. Institute for Advanced Study. Mathematics. Research. Social Sciences. 1930-79. *2435*

New Jersey (West Orange; Llewellyn Park). Davis, Alexander Jackson. Garden cities. Haskell, Llewellyn S. Idealism. Suburbs. 1853-57. *943*

New Left *See also* Communism; Leftism; Radicals and Radicalism; Socialism.

—. Anarchism and Anarchists. Rightists. Youth Movements. 1968-73. *2708*

—. Antiwar Sentiment. Conscription, Military. Students. Vietnam War. 1965-71. *2696*

—. Democracy. Institutions. 1965-72. *2707*

—. Kennedy, John F. Nixon, Richard M. Popular culture. Social change. 1960-69. *2754*

—. Liberalism. New Deal. Political Theory. Welfare state. 1932-66. *1738*

—. Students. Youth Movements. 1905-70. *2760*

New Mexico *See also* Western States.

—. Anti-Saloon League. Prohibition. 1910-17. *1901*

—. Bilingual education. Spanish language. 1968-78. *2957*

—. Law. Social Customs. Women. 16c-1975. *1720*

New Mexico (Albuquerque). Congregationalism. Education. Prohibition. Social gospel. 1900-17. *2101*

New Mexico (Columbus). Armies. Drugs. Mexico. Pershing, John J. Prostitution. Venereal disease. 1916-17. *2068*

New Mexico (Taos; Blue Lake). Indian-White Relations. Legislation. Pueblo Indians. Rites and Ceremonies. 20c. *1718*

New Orleans *Picayune* (newspaper). Advice columns. Dix, Dorothy. Feminism. Louisiana. 1895-1900. *980*

New Republic (periodical). Liberalism. Progressivism. Science and Society. 1914-20. *2040*

New South movement. Agrarianism. Killebrew, Joseph Buckner. South. ca 1870-1910. *1026*

New York *See also* Northeastern or North Atlantic States.

—. Abolition Movement. Christology. Negroes. Ward, Samuel Ringgold. 1839-51. *618*

—. Abolition Movement. Liberty Party. 1840-48. *687*

—. Africa, West. Blyden, Edward Wilmot. Negroes. 1850-1912. *291*

—. Agricultural College Act (US, 1862). Agriculture. Labor. Mechanics' Mutual Protection (society). People's College. 1843-60's. *1427*

—. American Revolution (antecedents). Farmers. North Carolina. South Carolina. 1760's-70's. *484*

—. Assimilation. Indian Rights Association. Roosevelt, Theodore. 1890-1910. *1014*

—. Association for Promoting Colored Volunteers. Civil War. Military Recruitment. Negroes. Race Relations. Union League. 1861-65. *1255*

—. Attica State Prison. NAACP. Negroes. Prisons. 1932. *2462*

—. Auburn Medical Institution. Medical Education. 1825. *830*

—. Birth control. Foote, Edward Bliss. Medicine. 1858-1906. *543*

—. Boston Eight Hour League. International Workingmen's Association. Labor Unions and Organizations. Marxism. McNeill, George. Steward, Ira. 1860-89. *1307*

—. Buffalo Medical College. Libel. Loomis, Horatio N. Medical Education. Midwifery. Obstetrics. White, James Platt. 1850. *869*

—. Capital punishment. Constitutional Conventions, state. Progressivism. 1915. *1923*

—. Child Labor Law (Louisiana, 1908). Gordon, Jean. Louisiana (New Orleans). Theatrical Syndicate. 1908-12. *1968*

—. Cities. Philanthropy. Social problems. 1830-60. *878*

—. Cohen, Julius Henry. Eminent domain. Housing. 1920's-30's. *2370*

—. Democratic Party. Liberty Party. Negro suffrage. Referendum. Whig Party. 1840-47. *595*

—. Education. Troy Female Seminary. Willard, Emma Hart. Women. 1809-70. *436*

—. Elections (presidential). Prohibition. Republican Party. 1884. *1473*

—. Equality. Federal government. Negroes. States' rights. 1865-73. *1154*

—. Family. Noyes, John Humphrey. Oneida Community. Religion. Sex. 1848-80. *271*

—. Genetics. Noyes, John Humphrey. Oneida Community. 1848-86. *1518*

—. Labor Unions and Organizations. Women. 1900-20. *2266*

—. Labor Unions and Organizations. Women's Trade Union League. ca 1903-10. *2205*

—. Morality. Progressivism. Prohibition. Smith, Alfred E. Whitman, Charles. Woman Suffrage. 1911-18. *2116*

—. Negro suffrage. Referendum. Republican Party. 1846-69. *120*

—. Noyes, John Humphrey. Oneida Community. Sex. Social Status. Women. 1848-79. *266*

—. Platt, Thomas C. Progressivism. Public policy. Republican Party. State politics. 1890-1910. *2030*

—. Prison Association. Reform. Rehabilitation. 1844-62. *875*

—. Prison reform. Smith, Alfred E. 1903-28. *2360*

—. Prohibition. Voting and Voting Behavior. 1846. *896*

—. Referendum. Wald, Lillian D. Woman Suffrage. 1917. *2135*

New York (Auburn). Attitudes. Friends, Society of. Pennsylvania. Prisons. Reform. Religion. 1787-1845. *874*

New York (Buffalo). Buffalo Cooperative Economic Society, Inc. Negroes. Nelson, Ezekiel E. 1928-61. *1762*

—. Clergy. Community affairs. Garvey, Marcus. Negroes. Universal Negro Improvement Association. 1830's-1920's. *2458*

—. Educational Reform. Immigrants. Public Schools. 1890-1916. *2332*

—. Federal government. Political protest. Social consciousness. 1965-76. *2747*

—. Immigration. Industrialization. Kamprath, William B. Labor (unskilled). Vocational education. 1907-21. *2312*

—. Industrialists. Labor history (sources). Police reports. Strikes. 1890-1913. *152*

New York Central College at McGrawville. Allen, William G. Attitudes. Colonization. Exiles. Great Britain. Negroes. 1820-78. *290*

New York City. Antislavery Sentiments. Petitions. 1829-39. *679*

—. Beecher, Henry Ward. Feminism. Radicals and Radicalism. Sex. Vanderbilt, Cornelius. Woodhull, Victoria Claflin. 1868-90's. *336*

—. Boycotts. Christianity. Elementary Education. Jews. Religion in the Public Schools. 1905-06. *2298*

—. Boycotts. Immigrants. Irish Americans. Labor. Working conditions. 1880-86. *1311*

—. Charities. City government. Reform. Subsidies. 1870-98. *1463*

—. Charities. Galveston Plan of 1907. Immigration. Industrial Removal Office. Jews. Migration, Internal. 1890-1914. *1476*

—. Child Welfare. Family. Foster homes. Immigration. Jews. Working class. 1900-05. *2061*

—. Child Welfare. Joint Committee on the Care of Motherless Infants. 1860-1907. *1475*

—. Children. Hospitals. Massachusetts (Boston). Pediatrics. Pennsylvania (Philadelphia). 1776-1976. *249*

—. Cities. Pollution. Public Health. Reform. Refuse disposal. Waring, George E., Jr. 1880-1917. *69*

—. City Government. Health. Progressivism. Public baths. 1890-1915. *2121*

—. City Government. Humanitarianism. 1790-1860. *876*

—. City Politics. Civil rights. LaGuardia, Fiorello. Liberalism. Powell, Adam Clayton, Jr. 1941-43. *2619*

—. City politics. Public Health. Social policy. Tuberculosis. 1889-1900. *1941*

—. Civil rights. Liberals. Minorities in Politics. 1963-70's. *2728*

—. Columbia University (Medical School). Medical education. Professionalization. 1760's. *488*

—. Committee of Fifteen. Local Politics. Tammany Hall. 1900-01. *1934*

—. Communists. Radicals and Radicalism. "Rank and File" movement. Social work. 1931-51. *1600*

—. Douglass, Frederick. Journalism. Racism. 1841-47. *408*
—. Educational reform. Georgia (Atlanta). Illinois (Chicago). Progressivism. Teachers. 1890-1920. *2336*
—. Educational Reform. Jews. Richman, Julia. Women. 1880-1912. *289*
—. Educational reform. Mitchel, John Purroy. 1914-17. *2322*
—. Episcopal Church, Protestant. Newspapers. Racism. Riots. St. Philip's Church. Williams, Peter, Jr. 1830-50. *671*
—. Equality. Lobbying. State Legislatures. Strachan, Grace. Teachers. Wages. Women. 1907-11. *2202*
—. Feminism. Leftism. Prisons. Smedley, Agnes (*Cell Mates*). 1918. *2019*
—. Florida. Justice Department. Labor recruitment. Peonage. Quackenbos, Mary Grace. Turpentine industry. 1905-10. *2267*
—. Garment Industry. Labor. Women. 1831-69. *820*
—. German Americans. Irish Americans. Local politics. Riots. Temperance Movements. 1857. *585*
—. Hillquit, Morris. Jews. Socialism. 1890's-1933. *1713*
—. Humanitarian organizations. Reform. 1845-60. *877*
—. Jews. Labor Unions and Organizations. Malkiel, Theresa Serber. Socialist Party. Women. 1900's-14. *2035*
—. Jews. Social Classes. Socialism. United Hebrew Trades. 1877-1926. *1340*
—. Labor Unions and Organizations. Women's Trade Union League. 1903-14. *1924*
—. Neighborhoods. Socialism. Working class. 1908-18. *2006*
—. New Jersey. Patterson Strike Pageant. Strikes. Theater. 1913. *2250*
—. Race Relations. Social Problems. Urban League. 1919-59. *1652*
—. Riis, Jacob August. Urban reform. 1895-97. *1999*
New York City (Brooklyn). Community control. Education. Integration. Negroes. Politics. 1882-1902. *1181*
—. Finnish Americans. Imatra I (association). Labor Unions and Organizations. 1890-1921. *2011*
New York City (Brooklyn, Lower East Side). Decentralization Act (1969). Minorities. Public Schools. School boards. 1969-73. *2965*
New York City (Brownsville, Ocean Hill). Decentralization. Educational Policy. Public Opinion. 1962-71. *2971*
New York City (Committee on Unemployment and Relief). Gary, Elbert H. Mitchel, John Purroy. Progressives. Unemployment. 1914-17. *2058*
New York City (Greenwich Village). Freudianism. Psychoanalysis. Radicals and Radicalism. Sex. 1913-20. *1936*
—. Progressive era. 1900-20. *2018*
New York City (Harlem). Adventists. Humphrey, James K. Race Relations. Sabbath Day Adventist Church. Utopia Park. 1920's-30's. *1648*
—. Alabama (Montgomery). Boycotts. King, Martin Luther, Jr. Leadership. Negroes. Powell, Adam Clayton, Jr. 1941-56. *307*
—. Black nationalism. Communism. Depressions. Garvey, Marcus. 1931-39. *2561*
—. Black Nationalism. Garvey, Marcus. Universal Negro Improvement Association. 1919-26. *2358*
—. Civil rights. Communist Party. Economic conditions. Negroes. Political Protest. 1930's. *2563*
—. Communist Party. Culture. Intellectuals. Negroes. Popular Front. 1935-39. *2562*
—. Crosswaith, Frank R. Negro Labor Committee. 1925-39. *1824*
—. Harrison, Hubert H. International Colored Unity League. Journalism. Liberty League of Negro Americans. Negroes. Socialist Party. 1911-27. *1676*
New York City (Jamaica). Negroes. Public schools. Segregation. 1895-1900. *1210*
New York City (Lower East Side). Americanization. Educational Alliance. Jews. 1890-1914. *2310*
New York, City University of. Colleges and Universities. Education, Experimental Methods. Minorities. 1847-1980. *196*
New York (Dansville). Adventists. Hydrotherapy. Jackson, James Caleb. Medical reform. White, Ellen G. 1864-65. *1470*

New York (Finger Lakes area). Finch, John (letter). Skaneateles Community. Utopias. 1843-45. *925*
New York House of Refuge. Children. Education. Reformatories. 1800-30. *898*
New York (Little Falls). Immigrants. Industrial Workers of the World. Strikes. Textile Industry. Women. 1912. *2269*
—. Labor Reform. Strikes. Textile Industry. Women. 1912. *2268*
New York Public Service Commission Law (1907). Hughes, Charles Evans. Public opinion. Public utilities. Railroads. 1907-09. *2200*
New York (Rochester). Crapsey, Algernon Sidney. Episcopal Church, Protestant. Heresy. Reform. St. Andrew's Church. Trials. 1879-1927. *454*
—. Dogberry, Obediah. *Liberal Advocate* (newspaper). Religious liberty. 1832-34. *589*
—. Goiter. Goler, George W. Iodine. Water supply. 1923-32. *2395*
—. Hospitals. 19c. *240*
—. Labor. Socialism. 1917-19. *1978*
—. Radicals and Radicalism. Religion. Revivalism. 1830-56. *568*
New York (Schenectady). Lunn, George. Socialist Party. Voting and Voting Behavior. Working Class. 1911-16. *1946*
New York Times (newspaper). Courts. Farber, Myron. Freedom of the press. Reporters and Reporting. 1975-79. *2781*
New York *Tribune*. Antislavery Sentiments. Great Britain. Greeley, Horace. Labor. Marx, Karl. 1851-62. *764*
New York (Troy). Collar Laundry Union. Industrial Relations. Irish Americans. Women. 1864-69. *1352*
New York, upstate. Abolition movement. Petitions. Political participation. Women. 1838-39. *586*
—. Abolition Movement. Smith, Gerrit. 1840-50. *647*
—. Morality. Teaching. 1970-80. *2962*
New York (Utica). Abolition Movement. Democratic Party. Proslavery Sentiments. Riots. 1835. *709*
—. Female Moral Reform Society. Morality. Reform. Social Organization. 1830's-40's. *808*
New York, western. Agricultural Adjustment Administration. Depressions. Farmers. Federal Policy. New Deal. 1934. *2487*
Newell, Alexander McFadden. Education. Manual Training School. Maryland (Baltimore). Politics. Shepherd, Henry Elliot. 1876-94. *1428*
Newfoundland (Saint John's). Charities. New Brunswick (Saint John). Nova Scotia (Halifax). Poverty. Unemployment. 1815-60. *871*
Newlands, Francis. Asians. Immigration. Negroes. Progressives. West Coast. 1904-17. *2067*
Newman, John Henry. Brownson, Orestes A. Catholic University of Ireland. Great Britain. Ireland. 1853-54. *911*
News. Periodicals. Women's rights. 1922-76. *1544*
Newspapers *See also* Editors and Editing; Freedom of the Press; Journalism; Periodicals; Press; Reporters and Reporting.
—. Africa, West. Black Nationalism. Colonization. Oklahoma. Sam, Alfred Charles. 1913-14. *2008*
—. Anarchism and Anarchists. Oregon. Portland *Firebrand* (newspaper). Radicals and Radicalism. 1895-98. *1112*
—. Anti-Communist Movements. Washington State Committee on Un-American Activities. 1948-49. *2656*
—. Antislavery Sentiments. Editors and Editing. Kansas. Religion. Rhetoric. 1855-58. *680*
—. Antislavery Sentiments. Negroes. Ontario. *Provincial Freeman* (newspaper). Shadd, Mary Ann. 1852-93. *351*
—. Berry, George L. Illinois (Chicago). Strikes. 1912-14. *2274*
—. Cabet, Etienne. Icaria (colony). Illinois. Political Theory. Social Theory. Utopias. 1820's-56. *941*
—. Canada. Editors and Editing. Finnish Canadians. Kurikka, Matti. Mäkelä, A. B. Socialism. 1900-32. *464*
—. Censorship. Chicago *Times*. Civil War. Lincoln, Abraham. 1863-64. *1118*
—. *Chicopee News*. Massachusetts, western. Massachusetts (Westfield). Prostitution. 1911. *2102*
—. Civil Rights. Kentucky. Negroes. Reconstruction. 1866-72. *1176*

—. Civil Rights. Negroes. 1946-72. *2874*
—. Colorado. Public opinion. Woman suffrage. 1870's. *1099*
—. Congress of Industrial Organizations. Labor Disputes. New Deal. South. 1930-39. *2614*
—. Conservatism. Constitutional law. Kansas. New Deal. Supreme Court. 1934-35. *2502*
—. Duniway, Abigail Scott. Oregon (Portland). Utah. Wells, Emmeline B. Woman suffrage. 19c. *1092*
—. Editorials. Freedom of the Press. 1920. 1940. *1719*
—. Episcopal Church, Protestant. New York City. Racism. Riots. St. Philip's Church. Williams, Peter, Jr. 1830-50. *671*
—. Federal Government. Legislation. Nevada. Racism. 1866-68. *976*
—. Fugitive Slave Act (US, 1850). Methodist Church. Slavery. 1850. *684*
—. *Globe*. Labor. Liberalism. Ontario. 1885-90. *1332*
—. Kansas. Political Commentary. Populism. State Politics. Vincent, Henry. 1886-91. *1384*
—. Louisiana. Political Campaigns (presidential). Slavery. Two-party system. 1834-36. *661*
—. McCabe, Edward Preston. Migration, Internal. Negroes. Oklahoma (Langston). 1850-1920. *1246*
—. Negroes. Political Protest. Race Relations. World War II. 1941-45. *2625*
—. Race Relations. Sex. Smith, Lillian. South. 20c. *422*
Nicaragua. Law Enforcement. Mine, Mill and Smelter Workers, International Union of. Silex, Humberto. Southwest. 1932-78. *1739*
Nichols, Clarina I. H. (papers). Feminism. Kansas. 1839-56. *338*
—. Feminism. Kansas. 1857-85. *337*
Niebuhr, Reinhold. Christianity. Muste, Abraham J. Pacifism. Political Theory. Thomas, Norman. 1914-38. *1668*
Niles Bill (Ohio, 1898). Educational reform. Elites. Ohio (Toledo). Progressive Era. School boards. 1890's. *2328*
Nisei Farmers League. Agricultural labor. California (San Joaquin Valley). Japanese Americans. Mexican Americans. United Farm Workers Union. 1971-77. *2926*
Nishmath-chajim (concept). Clergy. Mather, Cotton. Medicine. 1700-22. *534*
Nixon, Richard M. Kennedy, John F. New Left. Popular culture. Social change. 1960-69. *2754*
Nixon, Richard M. (administration). Federal Policy. Health. 1971-76. *2985*
Nkrumah, Kwame. Africa. Garvey, Marcus. Negroes. 1920's-75. *2422*
Noble, Thomas. Freedmen's Bureau. Kentucky. Race Relations. Reconstruction. Schools. 1865-70. *1190*
Noise pollution. Cities. Citizen Lobbies. Consumers. Environment. Reform. 1893-1932. *1684*
—. Cities. Progressivism. Reform. 1900-30. *1683*
Nominations to Office. LaFollette, Robert Marion. Presidency. Republican Party. Roosevelt, Theodore. 1910-12. *2022*
—. NAACP. North Carolina. Parker, John J. Supreme Court. White, Walter F. 1930. *2385*
Nonconformists. Cobden, Richard. Great Britain. Millenarianism. Peace movements. 1840-60. *582*
Nonpartisan League. Agricultural Cooperatives. Consumers' United Stores. Farmers Educational and Cooperative Union of America. North Dakota. 1916-19. *2259*
—. Agricultural cooperatives. North Dakota. Socialist Party. 1915-20's. *2024*
—. Bowen, Albert E., Jr. Farmers. North Dakota. Townley, Arthur C. 1914-15. *2054*
—. Business. Farmers. North Dakota. Politics. Townley, Arthur C. 1880-1959. *1667*
—. Congress of Industrial Organizations. Labor. New Hampshire (Berlin). Political Parties. 1932-36. *2497*
—. Davis, David W. Idaho. Industrial Workers of the World. Public opinion. Socialist Party. 1919-26. *2405*
—. Farmers. Idaho. Intellectuals. McKaig, Robert Raymond. North Dakota. ca 1920-43. *2406*
—. Morlan, Robert Loren. North Dakota. Populism. 1910's-1920's. *1881*
—. North Dakota. Press. 1915-16. *2055*

Nonviolence. Alabama (Birmingham). Civil Rights. King, Martin Luther, Jr. Negroes. Political Protest. 1962. *2843*
—. Cities. Merton, Thomas. Reform. Social criticism. 1960's. *2737*
—. Civil Disobedience. King, Martin Luther, Jr. Race relations. 1954-68. *2891*
—. Civil rights. King, Martin Luther, Jr. Negroes. 1950's-68. *2826*
—. Civil rights movement. Gandhi, Mahatma. King, Martin Luther, Jr. Political Protest. 1950's-60's. *2878*
—. Civil rights movement. Negroes. Political Protest. 1955-65. *1709*
—. Friends, Society of. Indian Wars. Paxton riots. Pennsylvania (Philadelphia). 1764-67. *497*
—. King, Martin Luther, Jr. ("Letter from Birmingham Jail"). Negroes. Rhetoric. 1963. *2869*
Norfolk *Journal and Guide* (newspaper). Race Relations. Virginia. Washington, Booker T. Young, Plummer B. 1904-20's. *2096*
Normal School. *See* Teachers Colleges.
North. Abolition Movement. Attitudes. Labor movement. 1820-65. *638*
—. Agriculture. Industrial Arts Education. Negroes. Philanthropy. South. 1902-35. *1832*
—. Cities. School Integration. South. 1954-77. *2830*
—. Civil War. Pacifism. 1864. *946*
—. Courts. *Prigg* v. *Pennsylvania* (US, 1842). Slavery. Supreme Court. 1842-57. *636*
—. Federal programs. Freedmen. Georgia (Atlanta). Reconstruction. Religious organizations. 1865-69. *1273*
—. Freedmen. Race Relations. Schools. Teachers. Virginia (Lexington). 1867. *1405*
—. Ideology. Protestantism. Public Schools. Republican Party. Western states. 1870-1930. *204*
—. Industrial Arts Education. Negroes. Progressive era. South. 1900-15. *2306*
—. Integration. Litigation. NAACP. Public schools. 1954-73. *2841*
North America. Antislavery Sentiments. Friends, Society of. 1671-1771. *524*
North American Aviation. California (Inglewood). Communist Party. Strikes. United Automobile Workers of America. 1941. *2642*
North American Phalanx. Communes. New Jersey (Perth Amboy, Red Bank). Raritan Bay Union. Spring, Marcus. 1843-59. *930*
North Carolina *See also* South.
—. Abolition Movement. Brown, John. Harpers Ferry raid. Sectional Conflict. State Politics. 1840-60. *675*
—. Acculturation. Collier, John. Florida. Indians. Schools. Seminole Indians. 1927-54. *1851*
—. Agricultural Organizations. Farmers' Alliance. Historiography. ca 1888-91. *1379*
—. Agricultural Organizations. Southern Farmers' Alliance. Women. ca 1880-1900. *1373*
—. Agricultural Reform. Georgia. Hunt, Henry Alexander. Negroes. 1890-1938. *1744*
—. Alexander, Sydenham B. Carr, Elias. Farmers' Alliance. Leadership. Polk, Leonidas L. Upper Classes. 1887-95. *1392*
—. American Colonization Society. Emancipation. Liberia. Slaveholders. 1800-60. *708*
—. American Revolution. Race relations. Slave revolts. 1775-1802. *622*
—. American Revolution. Slave revolts. 1750-1775. *529*
—. American Revolution (antecedents). Conservatism. Liberty. Political Corruption. Regulators. 1766-71. *481*
—. American Revolution (antecedents). Farmers. New York. South Carolina. 1760's-70's. *484*
—. Attitudes. Howard, Martin. Law. Murder. Slavery. 1765-91. *515*
—. Brown, John. Civil War (antecedents). Harpers Ferry raid. Slavery. Social Psychology. 1859-60. *612*
—. California. Sermons. Sermons. Social Conditions. 1969-78. *2729*
—. Colonial government. Elites. Regulator movement. Social change. 1760-75. *502*
—. Confederate States of America. Conscientious objectors. Friends, Society of. 1861-65. *1124*
—. Conservatism. Democratic Party. Primaries, gubernatorial. Progressivism. 1890-1920. *2340*
—. Constitutions, State (reform). Hamilton, Joseph G. de Roulhac. Progressivism. Sikes, Enoch W. State Legislatures. 1898-1913. *2091*
—. Democratic Party. Farmers' Alliance. State Politics. Vance, Zebulon B. 1880-90. *1366*
—. Desegregation. Discrimination, Educational. Graduate schools. Lawsuits. Negroes. Professional training. 1930-51. *1835*
—. Discrimination, Educational. Disfranchisement. Middle Classes. Negro Suffrage. Progressivism. Public Finance. Whites. 1880-1910. *2316*
—. Education. Negroes. Reconstruction. School Integration. 1865-67. *1127*
—. Ehringhaus, J. C. B. Legislation. Social Security Act (US, 1935). Unemployment insurance. 1935-37. *2556*
—. Government Regulation. Populism. Progressivism. Railroads. Russell, Daniel. 1894-98. *1369*
—. McAlister, Alexander W. Public Welfare. 1910-45. *1569*
—. NAACP. Nominations to Office. Parker, John J. Supreme Court. White, Walter F. 1930. *2385*
—. Negro Suffrage. Red Shirt Movement. Social Classes. Terrorism. Whites. 1898-1900. *1067*
North Carolina Commission of Indian Affairs. Community services. Education. Housing. Indian-White relations. ca 1700-1978. *108*
North Carolina (Durham). Civil rights. Duke University Medical Center. Harvey, Oliver. Labor Unions and Organizations. 1930's-70's. *2938*
North Carolina (Gastonia). Communism. Novels. Poor. Strikes. Textile Industry. Whites. 1929-34. *2361*
—. National Textile Workers Union. Strikes. Textile Industry. Weisbord, Vera Buch (reminiscence). 1929. *2459*
—. Novels. Strikes. Textile Industry. 1929-30's. *2431*
North Carolina (Greensboro). Desegregation. Political Protest. Sit-ins. 1950's-60's. *2816*
North Carolina, University of. Colleges and Universities. Educational Reform. Industrialization. Social Change. 1850-75. *1406*
North Carolina, western. Cherokee Indians. Federal Policy. Indians. New Deal. 1930's. *2607*
North Carolina (Whittier). Prohibition. Robbins, Raymond. 1920's-32. *2343*
North Carolina (Wilmington). Alabama (Mobile). Cowan, Jacob. Slave Revolts. Walker, David (*Appeal*). 1829-31. *726*
North Central States *See also* individual states; Great Plains; North; Old Northwest.
—. Bellamy, Edward (*Looking Backward 2000-1887*). Economic Theory. Populism. 1880's-90's. *1377*
—. Civil Rights. Labor Unions and Organizations. Mexican Americans. Social Organizations. 1900-76. *1659*
—. Communist Party. Political Leadership. Ruthenberg, Charles Emil. USSR. 1919-27. *2414*
—. Discrimination. Labor Unions and Organizations. Mexican Americans. Steel Industry. 1919-45. *1802*
—. Fundamentalism. Long, Huey P. Populism. Progressivism. Smith, Gerald L. K. 1934-48. *362*
North Dakota *See also* Western States.
—. Agricultural Cooperatives. Consumers' United Stores. Farmers Educational and Cooperative Union of America. Nonpartisan League. 1916-19. *2259*
—. Agricultural cooperatives. Nonpartisan League. Socialist Party. 1915-20's. *2024*
—. Bowen, Albert E., Jr. Farmers. Nonpartisan League. Townley, Arthur C. 1914-15. *2054*
—. Business. Farmers. Nonpartisan League. Politics. Townley, Arthur C. 1880-1959. *1667*
—. Conscientious Objectors. Espionage Act of 1917. O'Hare, Kate Richards. Pacifism. World War I. 1900-25. *2131*
—. Conservatism. McCumber, Porter James. McKenzie, Alexander John. Political reform. Republican Party. Suffrage. Women. 1898-1933. *435*
—. Farmers. Idaho. Intellectuals. McKaig, Robert Raymond. Nonpartisan League. ca 1920-45. *2406*
—. Farmers Educational and Cooperative Union of America. Knappen, Howard P. 1913-20. *2260*
—. Federal Government. Frazier, Lynn J. Governors. Indians. Progressivism. 1916-40. *1538*
—. Morlan, Robert Loren. Nonpartisan League. Populism. 1910's-1920's. *1881*
—. Nonpartisan League. Press. 1915-16. *2055*
North Dakota (Burleigh County; Still). Agricultural Cooperatives. Farmers Educational and Cooperative Union of America. Labor Unions and Organizations. 1913-78. *2288*
North Dakota Workmen's Compensation Bureau. Rice, Hazel F. (account). Transportation. Working conditions. 1919-22. *2432*
North, Frank M. Federal Council of Churches of Christ in America. Methodist Federation for Social Service. Social Creed of Methodism. Ward, Harry F. 1907-12. *1956*
Northeastern or North Atlantic States *See also* individual states; New England; North.
—. Amalgamated Clothing Workers of America. Craton, Ann Washington. Women. 1915-44. *367*
Northwest Territories. Agriculture. Dewdney, Edgar. Hunting. Indians (reservations). Saskatchewan. 1879-84. *1038*
—. Law Enforcement. Prohibition. Royal Canadian Mounted Police. 1874-91. *1460*
Norton, Mary T. Democratic Party. House of Representatives. Human Rights. New Jersey. Women. 1920-30. *2415*
Norway *See also* Scandinavia.
—. Canada. Germany. Hjelt, Ole. Labour Party. Nazism. Socialism. 1908-28. *321*
—. Communism. Kollontai, Aleksandra. Propaganda. Russia. World War I. 1915-16. *2046*
—. Labor disputes. Norwegian Americans. Press. Thrane, Marcus. USA. 1886-94. *1285*
Norwegian Americans. Ager, Waldemar Theodore. Editors and Editing. Novels. *Reform* (newspaper). Temperance Movements. 1893-1941. *368*
—. Labor disputes. Norway. Press. Thrane, Marcus. USA. 1886-94. *1285*
Nova Scotia *See also* Atlantic Provinces.
—. Adult education. Colonial Government. ca 1820-35. *843*
—. Adult education. Educators. Howe, Joseph. 1827-66. *844*
—. Adult education. Halifax Mechanics' Institute. Middle Classes. Working class. 1830's-40's. *845*
—. Antigonish Movement. Catholic Church. Rural Development. Social change. ca 1928-73. *1854*
—. Assimilation. Education. Indians. Micmac Indians. Public policy. Religion. 1605-1872. *209*
—. Asylums. Mental Illness. New Brunswick. 1749-1900. *228*
—. Bromley, Walter. Charities. Micmac Indians. Poverty. Self-help. 1813-25. *870*
—. Missions and Missionaries. Raymond, Eliza Ruggles. Sierra Leone (Sherbro Island). Slaves. 1839-50. *621*
Nova Scotia (Amherst). Amherst Federation of Labor. Economic Conditions. Labor Unions and Organizations. Strikes. 1901-31. *1801*
Nova Scotia, eastern. Adult education. Antigonish Movement. Capitalism. Coady, Moses. Cooperatives. 1930-40. *1742*
Nova Scotia (Halifax). Charities. New Brunswick (Saint John). Newfoundland (Saint John's). Poverty. Unemployment. 1815-60. *871*
Nova Scotia (Truro). Educators. Forrester, Alexander. ca 1848-69. *842*
Novels. Abolition Movement. Great Britain. Victor, Metta V. 1861. *749*
—. Ager, Waldemar Theodore. Editors and Editing. Norwegian Americans. *Reform* (newspaper). Temperance Movements. 1893-1941. *368*
—. Atherton, Gertrude. Authors. Feminism. 1890's-1910's. *333*
—. Clergy. Episcopal Church, Protestant. Ingraham, Joseph Holt. Penal reform. Public Schools. Tennessee (Nashville). 1847-51. *584*
—. Communism. North Carolina (Gastonia). Poor. Strikes. Textile Industry. Whites. 1929-34. *2361*
—. Feminism. Literary characters. Rives, Amèlie. South. 1863-1945. *377*
—. Illinois (Chicago). Social Conditions. 1890-1910. *1963*
—. North Carolina (Gastonia). Strikes. Textile Industry. 1929-30's. *2431*
—. Olerich, Henry. Utopias. 1851-1927. *1506*
—. Politics. Radicals and Radicalism. Religion. Social change. 1915-71. *1691*
—. Populism. Utopias. 1893-97. *1008*

Novels
—. Utopias. 1880's-90's. *1513*
Noyes, John Humphrey. Authority. Charisma. Oneida Community. 1875-81. *1515*
—. Family. New York. Oneida Community. Religion. Sex. 1848-80. *271*
—. Genetics. New York. Oneida Community. 1848-86. *1518*
—. New York. Oneida Community. Sex. Social Status. Women. 1848-79. *266*
Nugent, John. Socialism. West Virginia State Federation of Labor. 1901-14. *2177*
Nurses and Nursing *See also* Children; Hospitals; Red Cross.
—. Addams, Jane. Hampton, Isabel. Illinois (Chicago). Johns Hopkins Hospital Training School for Nurses. Maryland (Baltimore). Professionalization. Social Work. 1889-1910. *1461*
—. Breckinridge, Mary. Frontier Nursing Service. Kentucky. 1925-65. *1559*
Nutrition *See also* Food Consumption.
—. Agriculture. New England. Reformers. 1873-1907. *1465*
—. Children. Education. Great Britain. 1890-1920. *2053*
—. Federal Policy. Public Health. 1906-79. *1525*
—. Fletcher, Horace. Hygiene. Mastication. 1890-1910. *2120*
Nye Committee. Detzer, Dorothy. Peace Movements. Politics. Women's International League for Peace and Freedom. 1920-34. *2430*

O

Oberlin College. Adrian College. Hillsdale College. Michigan. Ohio. Olivet College. 1833-70. *851*
—. Colleges and Universities. Evangelicalism. Ohio. Women. 1835-50. *796*
Obscenity. Freedom of speech. Georgia. *Stanley* v. *Georgia* (US, 1969). Supreme Court. 1968-79. *2765*
Obstetrics. Andral, Gabriel. Bloodletting. Denman, Thomas. Dewees, William P. Medicine (practice of). 1800-1945. *254*
—. Buffalo Medical College. Libel. Loomis, Horatio N. Medical Education. Midwifery. New York. White, James Platt. 1850. *869*
Occult Sciences. Behavior. Counter Culture. 1960's-70's. *2988*
Occupational Safety and Health Act (US, 1970). Environmental Protection Agency. Equal Employment Opportunity Commission. Labor. Safety. Women. 1970-76. *2698*
Occupational therapy. Devereux Mansion. Hall, Herbert. Massachusetts (Marblehead). Mental Illness. Work Cure Program. 1912-23. *1969*
Occupations. Economic Conditions. Employment. Equal opportunity. Law. Negroes. 1954-72. *1785*
—. Industry. Mortality. Muckraking. Reform. 1890-1910. *2112*
—. Labor. Sex discrimination. Social Change. 1950-70. *1813*
—. Law. Segregation. Sex Discrimination. Women. 20c. *2910*
—. Legislation. Minimum wage. Ohio. Sex Discrimination. Women. 1914-33. *1539*
—. Medicine, preventive. Public health. Rosen, George. Social History. 1930's-77. *442*
—. Political Attitudes. Student activism. 1960's-70's. *2715*
O'Connell, Daniel. Antislavery Sentiments. Ireland. Irish Americans. 1824-44. *735*
Octavia Hill Association. Pennsylvania (Philadelphia). Public Welfare. ca 1890-1909. *2097*
Office of Navajo Labor Relations. Arizona (Page). Discrimination, employment. Indians. Industrial Relations. Navajo Construction Workers Associations. 1971-77. *2944*
Off-the-Street Club. Child Welfare. Illinois (Chicago). 1890's. *1477*
O'Hare, Kate Richards. Conscientious Objectors. Espionage Act of 1917. North Dakota. Pacifism. World War I. 1900-25. *2131*
—. Idaho (Twin Falls). Kidnapping. Socialism. Speeches, Addresses, etc. Utah. 1921. *2404*
—. Socialist Party. Women. 1901-17. *1878*
Ohio *See also* North Central States.
—. Abolition Movement. Antiwar sentiment. Mexican War. Propaganda. Protestant Churches. 1847. *561*

—. Abolition Movement. Civil War (antecedents). Garrison, William Lloyd. Western Antislavery Society. 1835-61. *650*
—. Abolition Movement. Giddings, Joshua Reed. Radicals and Radicalism. State Politics. 1840-60. *651*
—. Abolition Movement. Liberty Party. South. 1838-50. *670*
—. Adrian College. Hillsdale College. Michigan. Oberlin College. Olivet College. 1833-70. *851*
—. Agriculture. Boys. Fairfield School for Boys. Juvenile Delinquency. Reformatories. Values. 1840-84. *242*
—. Alternative schools. Cincinnati School Board. 1972-79. *2973*
—. Anti-Catholicism. Political Systems. Republican Party. Slavery. Whig Party. 1850's. *564*
—. Anti-lynching law of 1894. Law Reform. Smith, Harry C. Tourgée, Albion W. 1890-96. *1453*
—. Anti-Saloon League of America. Prohibition. 1880-1912. *258*
—. Antislavery movement. Morris, Thomas. State Legislatures. 1836-39. *711*
—. Antislavery Sentiments. Bailey, Gamaliel. Chase, Salmon Portland. Liberty Party. Republican Party. 1836-60. *668*
—. Antislavery Sentiments. Political attitudes. Revivals. Voting and Voting Behavior. 1825-70. *664*
—. Ashley, James M. Constitutional Amendments (13th). House of Representatives. Nationalism. Political Parties. 1848-65. *1097*
—. Assimilation. Finley, James B. Indians (agencies). Methodist Church. Missions and Missionaries. Shaw, John. 1820-24. *581*
—. Autobiography. Tappan, Benjamin. 1773-1823. *416*
—. Automobile Industry and Trade. Indiana. Labor. New Deal. United Automobile Workers of America. 1935-40. *2542*
—. Black Laws (Ohio, 1804, 1807). State Politics. 1837-49. *593*
—. Bulkley, Robert J. Elections. Prohibition. Senate. 1918-30. *2445*
—. Cedar Creek Monthly Meeting. Emancipation. Farms. Friends, Society of. Moorman, Clark Terrell. Virginia (Caroline County). 1766-1814. *743*
—. Cincinnati Better Housing League. Housing. Race relations. 1916-39. *1573*
—. Cincinnati College of Medicine and Surgery. Medical Education. Women. 1875-1910. *966*
—. Cincinnati Colored School system. Discrimination, Educational. Economic Conditions. Negroes. Social Change. 19c. *832*
—. Cincinnati Union Bethel. Jews. Settlement houses. 1838-1903. *225*
—. Civil War. Emancipation. Racism. State Politics. 1863-65. *1182*
—. Coal Mines and Mining. Government. Health and safety regulations. 1869-81. *1319*
—. Coates, Sarah (letters). Lectures. Physiology. Women. 1850. *881*
—. Colleges and Universities. Evangelicalism. Oberlin College. Women. 1835-50. *796*
—. Company towns. Social Classes. Steel Industry. Strikes. 1937. *2474*
—. Constitutional conventions. Negroes. Progressive era. Smith, Harry. Suffrage. 1863-1912. *2165*
—. Economic conditions. Letters. Mann, Mary Tyler Peabody. Poorhouses. 1795-1858. *884*
—. Elections. McKinley, William. Republican Party. Working class. 1891-93. *1355*
—. Executive Power. Intergovernmental Relations. Local Government. Police. State Government. 1902-25. *2100*
—. Labor Unions and Organizations. Toledo Mechanics' Association. Willey, Austin. 1843. *827*
—. Legislation. Minimum wage. Occupations. Sex Discrimination. Women. 1914-33. *1539*
—. Prohibition. Woman's Christian Temperance Union. 1874-85. *1483*
Ohio (Akron). General Tire Company. Murray, Rex Strikes. Strikes. 1934-35. *2565*
—. Industrial Workers of the World. Rubber. Strikes. 1913. *2290*
Ohio (Cincinnati). Affirmative action. City Government. Discrimination, employment. Negroes. 1963-67. *2888*

—. Anarchism and Anarchists. Indiana (New Harmony). Libertarianism. Utopias. Warren, Joseph. 1818-74. *302*
—. Antislavery sentiments. Bailey, Gamaliel. 1840's. *669*
—. Cary, Samuel Fenton. Temperance movements. 1845-1900. *1448*
—. Central Labor Union. Strikes. 1886. *1331*
—. City government. Public health. ca 1800-50. *891*
—. Civil Rights. Clark, Peter Humphries. Negroes. Politics. 1880's-1925. *350*
—. Clark, Peter Humphries. Education. Negroes. Socialism. 1849-81. *332*
—. Coeducation. Homeopathy. Medical Education. Pulte Medical College. 1873-79. *1403*
—. Colonization. Negroes. Ontario (Wilberforce). 1829-56. *604*
—. Communes. Owen, Robert Dale. Utopias. 1820's-50's. *933*
—. Demonstrations. Protestant Churches. Temperance Movements. Women's Christian Temperance Union. 1874. *1446*
—. Elections. Physicians. Professionalism. Progressivism. Public health. 1890-1900. *2021*
—. Elementary Education. Urbanization. 1870-1914. *205*
—. Ethnic groups. Labor Unions and Organizations. Working class. 1893-1920. *2247*
Ohio (Cincinnati; Mohawk-Brighton). Medical care. Neighborhoods. Phillips, Wilbur C. 1917-20. *2037*
Ohio (Cincinnati; Walnut Hills). Antislavery Sentiments. Debates. Lane Seminary. 1829-34. *692*
Ohio (Cleveland). Bellamy, George. Hiram House. Settlement houses. 1896-1914. *1958*
—. City Politics. Draper, Andrew Sloan. Educational Reform. 1892-94. *1423*
—. Discrimination. Hospitals. Mercy Hospital (proposed). Negroes. 1927-30. *2380*
—. Industrial Workers of the World. Metal and Machinery Workers' Industrial Union (440). 1918-50. *1826*
Ohio (Columbus). American Federation of Labor. Federation of Organized Trades and Labor Unions. Knights of Labor. Labor Unions and Organizations. 1881-86. *1309*
—. Buckeye Steel Castings Company. Bush, S. P. Management, scientific. Social Work. Steel Industry. 1890-1920. *2181*
—. Cities. Congregationalism. Gladden, Washington. Reform. Social gospel. 1850's-1914. *396*
Ohio Cultivator (newspaper). Feminism. Gage, Frances Dana. Tracy-Cutler, Hannah Maria. 1845-55. *800*
Ohio (Dayton). National Cash Register Company. Patterson, John H. Physical Education and Training. Working Conditions. 1890-1915. *169*
Ohio Farmer-Labor Progressive Federation. Amlie, Thomas. Farmer-labor Party. Hard, Herbert. New Deal. Third Parties. 1930-40. *2543*
Ohio (Hocking Valley). Coal Mines and Mining. Hoadly, George. Strikes. 1884-85. *1322*
—. Coal Mines and Mining. Strikebreakers. Violence. 1884-85. *1296*
Ohio (Lisbon). Beilhardt, Jacob. Sex. Spirit Fruit Society. Utopias. 1865-1908. *1505*
Ohio (Lower Maumee Valley). Antislavery Sentiments. Underground Railroad. 1815-67. *782*
Ohio, northeastern. Abolition Movement. Wright, Elizur, Jr. 1829-32. *643*
Ohio (Portage County). Antislavery Sentiments. Hall, Lyman W. Kansas-Nebraska Act (US, 1854). Political Parties. 1852-56. *619*
Ohio, southeastern. Coal Mines and Mining. Hocking Valley. Lewis, John Llewellyn. Strikes. United Mine Workers of America. 1927. *2447*
Ohio State University. Academic freedom. National security. Rugg, Harold Ordway. Speeches, Addresses, etc. 1951. *2771*
Ohio (Toledo). Ashley, James M. Civil War. House of Representatives. Negro Suffrage. Reconstruction. 1861-62. *1019*
—. Attitudes. Housing. Negroes. Racism. United Automobile Workers of America. 1967-73. *2805*
—. City Government. Jones, Samuel Milton. Reform. 1850's-1904. *280*

Ohio

—. Educational reform. Elites. Niles Bill (Ohio, 1898). Progressive Era. School boards. 1890's. *2328*
—. Gitteau, William B. Hamilton, J. Kent. Progressivism. Public Schools. Reform. 1898-1921. *2330*
—. Industrial Workers of the World. Labor Disputes. Radicals and Radicalism. US Bureau of Investigation. 1918-20. *1906*
Ohio (Yellow Springs). Antioch College. Colleges and Universities. Negroes. Segregation. 1966-69. *2864*
Oil Industry and Trade. American Petroleum Institute. Ecology. Hoover, Herbert C. Politics. Pollution. 1921-26. *2365*
—. American Petroleum Institute. Pollution. Texas (Gulf Coast). 1900-70. *1797*
—. Congress of Industrial Organizations. Texas. World War II. 1942-43. *2631*
—. Industrial Workers of the World. Kansas (Wichita). Labor Unions and Organizations. Trials. *United States* v. *C. W. Anderson et al.* (US, 1919). World War I. 1917-19. *2171*
—. Louisiana. Strikes. Texas. 1917-18. *2237*
Oklahoma *See also* Indian Territory; South; South Central and Gulf States.
—. Africa, West. Black Nationalism. Colonization. Newspapers. Sam, Alfred Charles. 1913-14. *2008*
—. Agricultural policy. Dawes Act (US, 1887). Federal government. Indians (reservations). Kiowa Indians. 1869-1901. *1062*
—. Agriculture. Cheyenne and Arapaho Reservation. Federal Policy. Indians. 1869-80. *1063*
—. Apache Indians (Chiricahua, Ojo Caliente). Fort Sill. Interior Department. Land allotment. Prisoners of war. War Department. 1909-13. *2170*
—. Arapaho Indians. Cheyenne Indians. Dawes Act (US, 1887). Fraud. Indians (agencies). Land allotment. 1910's. *1888*
—. Barnard, Kate. Child labor. Law Reform. 1904-24. *1877*
—. Barnard, Kate. Kansas State Penitentiary. Prisons. Reform. 1908-09. *1974*
—. Capital punishment. Cruce, Lee. Governors. Negroes. White supremacy. 1911-15. *1907*
—. Constitutional Conventions, state. Democrats. Woman Suffrage. 1870-1907. *146*
—. Constitutional conventions, state. Politics. Woman suffrage. 1906. *2144*
—. Farmers. Grange. Saskatchewan. Socialism. Texas. 1900-45. *1714*
—. Farmers. Socialism. 1900's-10. *2063*
—. Flynn, Dennis T. House of Representatives. McGuire, Bird S. Progressivism. 1901-07. *1905*
—. Freedom of speech. Political Repression. Vigilantes. World War I. 1914-17. *2137*
—. Green Corn Rebellion, 1917. Labor Unions and Organizations. Radicals and Radicalism. Working Class Union. 1914-17. *2284*
—. Homesteading and Homesteaders. McCabe, Edward Preston. Migration, Internal. Negroes. 1891-94. *1204*
—. Nation, Carry. Temperance Movements. 1867-1911. *1440*
—. Prisons. Reform. 1910-67. *1553*
—. Socialist Party. 1916-18. *1893*
Oklahoma (Cleveland, Pottawatomie counties). Jones Family (group). Sedition. Trials. Working Class Union. World War I. 1917. *2155*
Oklahoma (Langston). McCabe, Edward Preston. Migration, Internal. Negroes. Newspapers. 1850-1920. *1246*
Oklahoma (Lawton). Ku Klux Klan. 1921-29. *2355*
Oklahoma (Oklahoma City). Bohanon, Luther. Courts. School Integration. 1955-79. *2808*
—. Civil Rights. Demonstrations. Negroes. Restaurants. 1958-64. *2835*
Oklahoma (Wichita Mountains). Baptists. Crawford, Isabel. Indians. Kiowa Indians. Missions and Missionaries. Women's American Baptist Home Missionary Society. 1893-1961. *393*
Old Northwest *See also* North Central States.
—. Abolition Movement. Christian Anti-Slavery Convention. 1830-60. *704*
—. Farmers. Ideology. Populism. Rhetoric. 1870's-80's. *1388*
Older, Fremont. California. Editors and Editing. Reporters and Reporting. San Francisco *Bulletin*. Women. 1895-1925. *1887*

Olerich, Henry. Behavior. Child development. Education, Experimental Methods. 1897-1902. *2311*
—. Novels. Utopias. 1851-1927. *1506*
Olivet College. Adrian College. Hillsdale College. Michigan. Oberlin College. Ohio. 1833-70. *851*
Olmsted, Frederick Law. Conservatism. Individualism. 19c. *1041*
—. Landscape architecture. Reform. 19c. *955*
Olombia. Harmony Society. Koreshan Unity. Mexico (Topolobampo). Utopias. 1879-93. *1500*
Omaha Indians. Federal government. Indians. Nebraska Historical Society. Returned Students of Omaha. Speeches, Addresses, etc. 1920's. *2442*
One Big Union. Alberta (Drumheller Valley). Labor disputes. United Mine Workers of America. 1919. *1827*
—. American Federation of Labor. Industrial Workers of the World. Washington. 1919. *2179*
—. Canada, western. Conspiracy. Intelligence service. Labor Disputes. Royal Canadian Mounted Police. 1919. *1612*
—. Canada (western). Labor Unions and Organizations. Radicals and Radicalism. Socialism. 1917-19. *1746*
—. Coal Mines and Mining. Labor Unions and Organizations. Saskatchewan. 1907-45. *1782*
Oneida Community. Authority. Charisma. Noyes, John Humphrey. 1875-81. *1515*
—. California (Orange County). Middle Classes. Religion. Social Organization. Townerites. 1848-1900's. *1514*
—. Family. New York. Noyes, John Humphrey. Religion. Sex. 1848-80. *271*
—. Genetics. New York. Noyes, John Humphrey. 1848-86. *1518*
—. New York. Noyes, John Humphrey. Sex. Social Status. Women. 1848-79. *266*
—. Religion. Utopias. 1837-86. *921*
O'Neill, William. Chafe, William. Feminism. Historiography. Sexual revolution. ca 1920-70. *2374*
Ontario. Antislavery Sentiments. Negroes. Newspapers. *Provincial Freeman* (newspaper). Shadd, Mary Ann. 1852-93. *351*
—. Architecture. Attitudes. Boston Prison Discipline Society. Crime and Criminals. Howard, John. Kingston Penitentiary. ca 1830-50. *899*
—. Artisans. Convict labor. Kingston Penitentiary. Machinists. Petitions. 1833-36. *826*
—. Communist Party. Quebec (Cowansville). Silk industry. Strikes. 1931. *1778*
—. Education. Friends, Society of. Girls. 1790-1820. *852*
—. Family. Feminism. 1875-1900. *1055*
—. *Globe*. Labor. Liberalism. Newspapers. 1885-90. *1332*
—. Prisons. Rehabilitation. 1884-1900. *1482*
—. Prohibition. Racism. Reform. 1890-1915. *18*
—. Temperance movements. USA. 1828-50. *859*
Ontario (Kitchener). Labor Unions and Organizations. National Trades and Labour Congress. Quebec. Trades and Labour Congress of Canada. 1892-1902. *1805*
Ontario (Ottawa). City Politics. Public Health. Reform. Typhoid fever. 1911-12. *1635*
—. Conservatism. Elites. Political Leadership. Public Welfare. 1880-1912. *1310*
Ontario (Penetanguishene). Juvenile Delinquency. Reformatories. 1880-1905. *1618*
Ontario School Act (1871). Conflict and Conflict Resolution. Ryerson, Egerton. Secondary education. 1850's-80's. *1415*
Ontario (Toronto). Anti-Communist Movements. Freedom of Speech. Letters. Police. Political Repression. 1931. *1724*
—. Bell Canada. Strikes. Telephone operators. Women. 1907. *1808*
—. Bengough, John Wilson. City government. *Grip* (periodical). Political Reform. Protestantism. 1873-1910. *370*
—. Canniff, William. Medical Reform. Public health. 1869-90. *1468*
—. Charities. Institutions. Social work. ca 1875-1920. *246*
—. Charities. Social Control. Tramps. 1870-90. *1065*
—. City government. Progressivism. Wickett, Samuel Morley. 1900-15. *1703*
—. Collective bargaining. Organizational Theory. Printing. 19c. *178*

—. Cooperative Commonwealth Federation. Feminism. Leftism. Women's Joint Committee. 1930's. *1638*
—. Feminism. 1870's-1910's. *421*
—. Hastings, Charles. Neighborhood Workers' Association. Poverty. Public health. 1910-21. *1527*
—. Industrialization. Knights of Labor. Knights of St. Crispin. Labor Unions and Organizations. 1856-90. *1318*
—. Recreation. Sabbatarianism. Tobogganing. 1912. *1609*
Ontario (Upper Canada). Arthur, George. Colonial Government. Great Britain. Reform. 1837-41. *571*
—. Crime and Criminals. Prisons. Reform. 1835-50. *857*
Ontario (Wilberforce). Colonization. Negroes. Ohio (Cincinnati). 1829-56. *604*
Ontario (Windsor). Ford Motor Company of Canada. Labor Law. United Automobile Workers (Canadian Region). 1946. *2682*
Open shop movement. Labor Disputes. Michigan (Battle Creek). Post, Charles William. 1895-1920. *2239*
Oral History *See also* Personal Narratives.
—. American Federation of State, County, and Municipal Employees. Negroes. Roberts, Lillian. 1920's-70's. *417*
—. Antiwar Sentiment. Civil rights. Kennedy, Jane. Political Protest. Vietnam War. Women. 1964-77. *2724*
—. Feminism. Maryland, University of. Sex Discrimination. 1968-78. *2913*
—. Massachusetts. Sullivan, Anna (interview). Textile Workers Union of America. Women. 1918-76. *403*
—. Methodology. Paul, Alice (memoirs). Woman Suffrage. 1912-77. *335*
Orchards. Farmers. Industrial Workers of the World. Strikes. Washington (Yakima Valley). 1933. *2568*
Ord, Edward Otho Cresap. Mississippi. Reconstruction. 1867-68. *982*
Order of the Holy Cross. Episcopal Church, Protestant. Huntington, James Otis Sargent. Monasticism. 1878-90. *1061*
Ordination. Canada. McClung, Nellie L. Methodist Church. United Church of Canada. Women. 1915-46. *1597*
—. Clergy. United Brethren in Christ. Women. 1889. *1489*
—. Presbyterian Church (Committee of Four). Women. 1926-30. *2346*
Oregon *See also* Far Western States.
—. Anarchism and Anarchists. Newspapers. Portland *Firebrand* (newspaper). Radicals and Radicalism. 1895-98. *1112*
—. Burt, Armistead. Calhoun, John C. Compromise of 1850. Congress. Slavery. Wilmot Proviso. ca 1846-60. *691*
—. Constitutions, State. Duniway, Abigail Scott. Voting rights. Woman Suffrage. 1860's-1912. *1093*
—. Portland *Oregonian*. Reporters and Reporting. Woman Suffrage. 1869-1905. *1101*
Oregon (Columbia River Highway). Environment. Highway Engineering. Lancaster, Samuel Christopher. ca 1900-41. *1931*
Oregon Commonwealth Federation. Depressions. Farmer-Labor Party. New Deal. Political Factions. 1933-38. *2545*
Oregon Improvement Company. Coal Mines and Mining. Negroes. Strikebreakers. Washington (King County). 1891. *1265*
Oregon (Portland). City Planning. World War II. 1940-45. *2616*
—. Duniway, Abigail Scott. Newspapers. Utah. Wells, Emmeline B. Woman suffrage. 19c. *1092*
—. Friedlander, Alice G. Speeches, Addresses, etc. Woman Suffrage. 1893. *1095*
—. Sabin, Ellen B. Teaching. Wisconsin. Women. 1850-95. *405*
Oregon (Salem). Cooperatives. Hoel, Chamberlain. Reform. 1852-65. *326*
Oregon (Tillamook). Ku Klux Klan. Social change. 1920's. *2456*
Oregon (Toledo). Japanese Americans (Nikkei). Lumber and Lumbering. Pacific Spruce Corporation. Riots. 1925-26. *2453*
O'Reilly, Mary. Garment Industry. Illinois (Chicago). Socialist Party. Strikes. Women. Zeh, Nellie M. 1910. *2183*
Organizational Theory *See also* Public Administration.
—. Collective bargaining. Ontario (Toronto). Printing. 19c. *178*

Organizations *See also* specific organizations by name; Social Organizations; Voluntary Associations.
—. Anti-Saloon League. Russell, Howard Hyde. Temperance movements. 1895-1900. *1464*
—. Civil rights. Institutions. Negroes. Sit-ins. South. 1960. *2868*
—. Employment. Feminism. Racism. Social classes. World War II. 1942-45. *2629*
—. Missions and Missionaries. Protestant Churches. Women. 1870's-90's. *1493*
Orthodox Eastern Church (Greek; congresses). Family. Iakovos, Archbishop. Morality. Social Conditions. 1960-80. *2726*
Ostracism. Alabama. Politics. Reconstruction. Republican Party. 1865-80. *1082*
—. Louisiana. Reconstruction. Scalawags. State Politics. Terrorism. 1866-78. *1081*
Outlaw (film). Censorship. Hughes, Howard. Legion of Decency. Motion Picture Producers and Distributors of America. Russell, Jane. 1940-49. *2649*
Owen, Robert Dale. Bentham, Jeremy. Birth control. Carlile, Richard. Feminism. Great Britain. Place, Francis. Propaganda. Wright, Frances. 1790-1840. *817*
—. Communes. Ohio (Cincinnati). Utopias. 1820's-50's. *933*
—. Communes. Sex roles. Women. 1824-28. *931*
—. Emancipation. Tennessee (Nashoba). Utopias. Wright, Frances (letters). 1820-29. *718*
Oxford Group movement. Christianity. Longshoremen. Strikes. Washington (Seattle). 1921-34. *2604*

P

Pacific Area. Feminism. Pan-Pacific and Southeast Asia Women's Association. 1928-70's. *1610*
Pacific Dependencies (US). Micronesia. Self-determination. Social Conditions. 1947-80. *2776*
Pacific Electric Railroad. California (Los Angeles). Mexican Americans. Strikes. 1900-03. *2289*
Pacific Northwest. Anti-Catholicism. Chinese Americans. Nativism. Racism. ca 1840-1945. *11*
—. Conservation movement. Federal Policy. Lumber and Lumbering. Property rights. Public Lands. 1870's-90's. *1323*
—. Conservation of natural resources. Forests and Forestry. 1889-1913. *2052*
—. DeVoe, Emma Smith. Duniway, Abigail Scott. Woman suffrage. 1854-1912. *130*
—. Farmers. McNary-Haugen bill. Montana. Prices. Tariff. 1920-29. *2410*
—. Prohibition. Reform. Weed, Ada M. Women's rights. 1858-1910. *327*
Pacific Spruce Corporation. Japanese Americans (Nikkei). Lumber and Lumbering. Oregon (Toledo). Riots. 1925-26. *2453*
Pacifism *See also* Conscientious Objectors; Peace Movements.
—. Abolition Movement. Keniston, Kenneth. Violence. 1830-65. *644*
—. *Advocate of Peace* (periodical). American Peace Society. Foreign Relations. Public Opinion. 1837-1932. *59*
—. American Peace Society. League of Nations Covenant. Paris Peace Conference. 1914-19. *2066*
—. Angers, François-Albert. Canada. Catholic Church. French Canadians. Values. 1940-79. *1595*
—. Buttrick, George Arthur. Presbyterian Church. 1915-74. *1563*
—. Canada. Fairbairn, R. Edis. United Church of Canada. World War II. 1939. *2646*
—. Christianity. Conscientious objectors. Thomas, Norman. World War I. 1915-18. *2136*
—. Christianity. Muste, Abraham J. Niebuhr, Reinhold. Political Theory. Thomas, Norman. 1914-38. *1668*
—. Civil War. North. 1864. *946*
—. Conscientious Objectors. Espionage Act of 1917. North Dakota. O'Hare, Kate Richards. World War I. 1900-25. *2131*
—. Dewey, John. Foreign policy. War. 1918-32. *1615*
—. Dunkards. Friends, Society of. Mennonites. Militarism. 1900-78. *1571*
—. Freedom of speech. Virginia, University of. Whipple, Leon. World War I. 1917. *2130*
—. Historic Peace Churches (meeting). Kansas (Newton). Krehbiel, H. P. 1935-36. *2534*

—. House of Representatives. Montana. Rankin, Jeannette. 1880-1973. *465*
—. Intellectuals. Literature. Tolstoy, Leo. ca 1890's. *1080*
—. Kansas. Liberty bonds. Mennonites. Vigilantism. World War I. 1918. *2146*
—. Literature. Mennonites. 20c. *1693*
Packard, Elizabeth. Human Rights. Medical Reform. Mental Illness. 1863-97. *356*
Padmore, George. Blyden, Edward Wilmot. DuBois, W. E. B. Pan-Africanism. 1776-1963. *25*
Paepcke, Walter. Colorado (Aspen). Educational Reform. Higher Education. 1949-51. *2666*
Page, Walter Hines. Journalism. McKelway, Alexander. Murphy, Edgar Gardner. South. 1890-1916. *1876*
Paint Creek-Cabin Creek Strike. *Socialist and Labor Star* (newspaper). Strikes. Thompson, Wyatt Hamilton. West Virginia. 1912-13. *2195*
Paiute Indians. California. Indian-White Relations. Winnemucca, Sarah (Paiute). 1840's-91. *419*
Palmer, Phoebe. Feminism. Holiness Movement. Wesley, Susanna. 1732-1973. *17*
Pamphlets. Communist Party. Rhetoric. 1929-39. *1540*
—. Franklin, Benjamin. Indians. Massacres. Paxton Boys. Pennsylvania. 1764. *499*
Pan American Federation of Labor. Communism. Gompers, Samuel. Political Attitudes. 1920's. *2457*
Pan-Africanism. Africa. DuBois, W. E. B. Makonnen, T. Ras. USA. 1919-73. *2881*
—. Africa. Industrial arts education. Racism. South. 1879-1940. *214*
—. Black Power. Carmichael, Stokely. Political Theory. 1965-73. *2860*
—. Blyden, Edward Wilmot. DuBois, W. E. B. Padmore, George. 1776-1963. *25*
—. Colonial policy. Garvey, Marcus. Italy. Universal Negro Improvement Association. USA. 1920-23. *2371*
—. Garvey, Marcus. Ideology. Jamaica. Negroes. 1887-1927. *401*
Pan-Indianism. Anthropology. Indians. Parker, Arthur C. Seneca Indians. 1881-1925. *355*
Pan-Pacific and Southeast Asia Women's Association. Feminism. Pacific Area. 1928-70's. *1610*
Paper industry. American Federation of Labor. International Brotherhood of Pulp, Sulphite, and Paper Mill Workers. Labor Unions and Organizations. Militancy. 1933-35. *2615*
Parents. Authority. Communications Behavior. Public Schools. Textbooks. West Virginia (Kanawha County). 1974. *2958*
—. California (Alum Rock). Education. Public Schools. Vouchers. 1960's-70's. *2960*
Paris Peace Conference. American Peace Society. League of Nations Covenant. Pacifism. 1914-19. *2066*
Parishes. Catholic Church. Fernandez, John F. O. Laity. Virginia (Norfolk). 1815-20. *905*
Park, Robert Ezra. Congo Reform Association. Race relations. Tuskegee Institute. 1905-13. *2025*
Parker, Arthur C. Anthropology. Indians. Pan-Indianism. Seneca Indians. 1881-1925. *355*
Parker, John J. NAACP. Nominations to Office. North Carolina. Supreme Court. White, Walter F. 1930. *2385*
Parker, Theodore. Abolition Movement. Civil War (antecedents). New England. Violence. 1850-60. *635*
Parks. Adams, Charles Francis. Conservation. Massachusetts (Boston, Quincy). 1880's-90's. *1070*
Parliaments *See also* House of Commons.
—. Bourassa, Henri. Canada. Progressives. 1926. *1633*
—. Canada. Criminal law. 1892-1902. *1107*
Parochial Schools. *See* Church Schools; Religious Education.
Parot, Adele. California (San Francisco). Gymnastics. Lewis, Dioclesius. 1860's-70's. *1404*
Parties, Political. *See* Political Parties.
Partisan Review (periodical). Editors and Editing. Socialism. Stalinism. 1930's. *2493*
Partisanship. Civil rights. Congress. Democratic Party. Legislation. Regionalism. Republican Party. 1963-72. *2803*
—. Liberalism. Professionalism. Public welfare. State government. 1960's-70's. *2952*
Pass Strike of 1932. Alberta. British Columbia. Coal Mines and Mining. Depressions. 1920's-30's. *1811*

Pastoralism. Communes. Suburbs. 1950's-1970's. *2987*
Paternalism. Authority. Lukens Iron Works. Pennsylvania (Coatesville). Profits. Strikes. 1886. *1347*
—. Baptists, Southern. Education. Negroes. 1880's-90's. *1266*
—. Lukens Iron Works. Pennsylvania (Coatesville). Strikes. 1886. *1348*
Paterson, William. Attitudes. New Jersey. Slavery. 1785-1804. *739*
Paterson, William Burns. Alabama State College. Education. Negroes. 1878-1915. *1257*
Patriotism *See also* Loyalty; Naturalization.
—. Antislavery Sentiments. Eliot, Samuel A. Fugitive Slave Act (US, 1850). Massachusetts (Boston). Unitarianism. 1850. *752*
—. Columbians, Inc. Georgia (Atlanta). Racism. 1946-47. *2665*
—. *National School Service* (bulletin). Public Schools. Reform. 1918-19. *2337*
Patronage. Douglass, Frederick. Politics. Republican Party. 1870-95. *1235*
Patterson, John H. National Cash Register Company. Ohio (Dayton). Physical Education and Training. Working Conditions. 1890-1915. *169*
Patterson Strike Pageant. New Jersey. New York City. Strikes. Theater. 1913. *2320*
Paul, Alice. South Carolina. Woman suffrage. ca 1891-1919. *2128*
Paul, Alice (memoirs). Methodology. Oral history. Woman Suffrage. 1912-77. *335*
Paul, Saint. Christianity. Grimké, Sarah Moore. Nature. Social organization. Women. 1c. 1830's. *807*
Paxton Boys. Franklin, Benjamin. Indians. Massacres. Pamphlets. Pennsylvania. 1764. *499*
Paxton riots. Friends, Society of. Indian Wars. Nonviolence. Pennsylvania (Philadelphia). 1764-67. *497*
Payne, John Howard (letter). Cherokee Indians. Federal government. Georgia. Land (cessions). Ross, John (chief). 1820's-30's. *575*
Payne, William Howard. Educational Administration. George Peabody College. Nashville, University of. Teacher training. Tennessee. 1875-1901. *1411*
Payne-Aldrich Tariff (1909). Businessmen. Reformers. Tariff. 1905-09. *2201*
Peabody Fund. Elementary education. Florida. Reconstruction. Segregation. 1869-76. *1433*
Peace *See also* Pacifism.
—. Brin, Fanny Fligelman. Jews. Minnesota (Minneapolis). Women. 1913-60's. *453*
—. Foreign Policy. International Relations. Isolationism. League of Nations Association. 1934-38. *2466*
Peace bonds. Crime and Criminals. Friends, Society of. Pennsylvania (Philadelphia). 1680-1829. *492*
Peace Movements *See also* Antiwar Sentiment.
—. Catholic Church. National Catholic Welfare Conference. National Council of Catholic Women. Women. 1919-46. *1636*
—. Cobden, Richard. Great Britain. Millenarianism. Nonconformists. 1840-60. *582*
—. Connecticut. Elections. 1919-39. *1617*
—. Demonstrations. Public opinion. Vietnam War. ca 1965-73. *2752*
—. Detzer, Dorothy. Nye Committee. Politics. Women's International League for Peace and Freedom. 1920-34. *2430*
—. Emancipation Proclamation. New Jersey. State legislatures. 1864. *1009*
—. Feminism. Georgia. Rankin, Jeannette. 1924-73. *352*
—. Feminism. Lloyd, Lola Maverick. 1914-44. *451*
—. Hammond, John Hays. Militarism. 1898-1914. *2017*
—. Illinois. Local Government. Lochner, Louis Paul. People's Council of America for Democracy and Peace. State Government. 1917. *2104*
—. Jewish Peace Fellowship. World War II. 1943. *2654*
—. National security. Preparedness. 1941-71. *1564*
Peace research. 19c-1975. *97*
Peck, Bradford *(World a Department Store)*. Business. Cooperative Association of America. Democracy. Morality. Utopias. 1880-1925. *263*
Peck, Jesse T. Bishops. Methodist Episcopal Church. Social gospel. 1850-83. *1025*

Pedagogy. *See* Teaching.
Pediatrics. Children. Hospitals. Massachusetts (Boston). New York City. Pennsylvania (Philadelphia). 1776-1976. *249*
Peffer, William A. Reconstruction. State Politics. Tennessee. 1865-69. *949*
Pelota (game). Florida. Indian-White Relations. Spain. 1675-84. *9*
Pemberton, Caroline Hollingsworth. Civil Rights. Negroes. Pennsylvania (Philadelphia). Socialist Party. 1896-1903. *1158*
Penal reform. Beccaria, Cesare. Capital punishment. Italy. 1764-97. *890*
—. Boston Prison Discipline Society. Charlestown State Prison. Massachusetts. 1804-78. *860*
—. Clergy. Episcopal Church, Protestant. Ingraham, Joseph Holt. Novels. Public Schools. Tennessee (Nashville). 1847-51. *584*
Pendleton, James Madison. Antislavery sentiments. Kentucky. Tennessee. 1849-60. *674*
Penn, William. Friends, Society of. Humanism. Intellectuals. Radicals and Radicalism. 1650-1700. *474*
Penner, Jacob. Manitoba (Winnipeg). Russia. Socialist Party. 1900-65. *406*
Pennsylvania *See also* Northeastern or North Atlantic States.
—. Abolition Movement. American Revolution. Friends, Society of. Woolman, John. 1758-88. *530*
—. Abolition Movement. Constitutional conventions, state. Disfranchisement. Gardner, Charles W. Hinton, Frederick A. Negroes. 1838. *596*
—. Abolition Movement. Feminism. Philadelphia Female Anti-Slavery Society. 1833-40. *616*
—. Abortion. Antiabortion movement. Anti-Saloon League. Politics. Pressure groups. Prohibition. 1890-1978. *1640*
—. Acculturation. Educational Reform. Ideology. Industrialization. Social control. 1880-1910. *1420*
—. Anti-Catholicism. Politics. Social Change. 1682-1774. *477*
—. Attitudes. Blind. Education. Employment. Pittsburgh Workshop for the Blind. 19c-1939. *1670*
—. Attitudes. Friends, Society of. New York (Auburn). Prisons. Reform. Religion. 1787-1845. *874*
—. Bureau of Surface Mine Reclamation. Legislation. Mining. 1961-73. *2762*
—. Catholic Church. Lawyers. Progressivism. Smith, Walter George. 1900-22. *1891*
—. Charities. Friends, Society of. Pennsylvania (Philadelphia). Society for Organizing Charitable Relief and Repressing Mendicancy. 1800-1900. *250*
—. *Charities and the Commons* (periodical). Industrialization. *Pittsburgh Survey* (1909). Social Surveys. 1907-14. *2029*
—. Coal, anthracite. Mining. Strikes. United Mine Workers of America. 1922-23. *2391*
—. Coal Mines and Mining. Federal government. Roosevelt, Theodore. Strikes. 1902. *2218*
—. Colleges and Universities. Educators. New Jersey. Professionalization. 1870-1915. *201*
—. Compulsory Education. Educational reform. Interest groups. Social Problems. 1880-1911. *200*
—. Crime and Criminals. Education. Morality. Wickersham, James P. 1866-81. *1401*
—. Equal Rights League. Public schools. School Integration. 1834-81. *208*
—. Fox, George. Friends, Society of. Slave trade. 1656-1754. *522*
—. Franklin, Benjamin. Indians. Massacres. Pamphlets. Paxton Boys. 1764. *499*
—. Great Awakening (2d). Reform. 1794-1860. *562*
—. Harmony Society. Rapp, George. State Legislatures. Utopias. 1805-07. *913*
—. Higher education. Lowry, Morrow B. Lowry, Morrow B. (letter). Women's rights. 1868. *1413*
—. Industrial Relations. Steel industry. 1800-1959. *174*
—. Lanius, Henry E. Leader, George M. Legislation. Political leadership. Special education. 1820-1956. *1838*
—. Libel. Moore, William. Political Theory. Provincial legislatures. Smith, William. 1750-60. *516*
—. Negroes. Suffrage. 1780-1900. *137*
—. Politics. Public welfare. 1967-73. *2943*

Pennsylvania (Allegheny-Kiskiminetas Valley). Labor Unions and Organizations. United Mine Workers of America. Violence. 1913-19. *2241*
—. Steel Industry. Strikes. 1919. *2242*
Pennsylvania (Bethlehem). Schwab, Charles M. Steel industry. Strikes. 1910. *2223*
Pennsylvania (Coatesville). Authority. Lukens Iron Works. Paternalism. Profits. Strikes. 1886. *1347*
—. Lukens Iron Works. Paternalism. Strikes. 1886. *1348*
Pennsylvania Council of Republican Women. Feminism. Pinchot, Cornelia. 1920's-30's. *2509*
Pennsylvania (Economy). Christianity. Communes. Harmony Society. Pittman, Clara. Socialist Laws (Germany, 1878). 1878-79. *1499*
—. Harmony Society. vonWrede, Friedrich Wilhelm. 1842. *924*
Pennsylvania (Economy, Harmony). City Planning. Communes. Harmony Society. Indiana (New Harmony). Social customs. 1820's-1905. *919*
Pennsylvania Hall. Abolition movement. Pennsylvania (Philadelphia). Riots. Women. 1833-37. *617*
Pennsylvania Hospital for the Sick Poor. Friends, Society of. Pennsylvania (Philadelphia). Poor. 18c. *533*
Pennsylvania (Lancaster). City Politics. Urban reform. 1921-30. *2377*
Pennsylvania (McKees Rocks, Pittsburgh). Cigar industry. Industrial Workers of the World. Pressed Steel Car Company. Steel Industry. Strikes. 1909-13. *2235*
Pennsylvania (Philadelphia). Abolition movement. Pennsylvania Hall. Riots. Women. 1833-37. *617*
—. Africans' School. Benezet, Anthony. Education. Friends, Society of. Negroes. 1770's-80's. *487*
—. American Moral Reform Society. Negroes. Reform. Whipper, William. 1830-76. *386*
—. American Revolution. Diaries. Drinker family. Friends, Society of. Prisoners. Virginia (Winchester). 1777-81. *526*
—. Antislavery Sentiments. Slavery. Trials. Williamson, Passmore. 1855. *628*
—. Blackwell, Elizabeth. Feminism. Medical Education. 1821-1910. *809*
—. Books. Child-rearing. Education. Protestantism. Republicanism. 1780-1835. *577*
—. Borg, Selma Josefina. Centennial Exposition of 1876. Finnish Americans. Lectures. Music. Women's rights. 1858-90. *399*
—. Bureaucrats. Public housing. 1929-41. *1528*
—. Catto, Octavius V. Civil Rights. Militancy. 1861-71. *440*
—. Centennial Celebrations. Douglass, Frederick. Negroes. 1876. *1157*
—. Charities. Friends, Society of. Pennsylvania. Society for Organizing Charitable Relief and Repressing Mendicancy. 1800-1900. *250*
—. Charities. Social work. Society for Organizing Charitable Relief and Repressing Mendicancy. Women. 1864-1909. *1474*
—. Children. Hospitals. Massachusetts (Boston). New York City. Pediatrics. 1776-1976. *249*
—. Children. Massachusetts (Boston). Progressivism. Recreation. 1886-1911. *1985*
—. City Life. Environmentalism. Law. 1750-84. *496*
—. Civil Rights. Negroes. Pemberton, Caroline Hollingsworth. Socialist Party. 1896-1903. *1158*
—. Class consciousness. NAACP. Negroes. Race. 1930's. *2566*
—. Crime and Criminals. Friends, Society of. Peace bonds. 1680-1829. *492*
—. Depressions. Public Welfare. 1820-28. *544*
—. Education. Women. Young Ladies Academy. 1780's-90's. *552*
—. Educational Reform. Negroes. White, Jacob C., Jr. 1857-1902. *441*
—. Fell, Margaret. Feminism. Friends, Society of. Great Britain (Lancashire). Women. 1670's. *498*
—. Friends, Society of. Indian Wars. Nonviolence. Paxton riots. 1764-67. *497*
—. Friends, Society of. Pennsylvania Hospital for the Sick Poor. Poor. 18c. *533*
—. House of Refuge for Colored Children. Juvenile Delinquency. Negroes. 1828-60's. *872*
—. Housing. Negroes. New Deal. 1930's. *2475*
—. Legislation. Segregation. Streetcars. 1850's-70. *1156*

—. Negroes. Race Relations. Riots. 1968. *2820*
—. Octavia Hill Association. Public Welfare. ca 1890-1909. *2097*
Pennsylvania (Pittsburgh). Abolitionists. Fugitive Slaves. Negroes. Philanthropic Society. 1830's-60. *610*
—. Air Pollution. Elites. Reform. Smoke. Tilbury, Corwin D. 1890's-1918. *1961*
—. Steel Industry. Strikes. 1919. *2174*
Pennsylvania (Reading). Local Politics. Socialist Party. Women. ca 1927-38. *1666*
Pennsylvania (Scranton). Knights of Labor. Labor Unions and Organizations. Politics. Powderly, Terence V. 1876-1900. *361*
Pennsylvania (Tioga County). Labor Disputes. 1865-1905. *1326*
Pennsylvania, western. Coal Mines and Mining. Diaries. Medrick, George. Strikes. United Mine Workers of America. 1927. *2372*
—. National Miners Union. Negroes. United Mine Workers of America. 1925-31. *2420*
Pensions *See also* Aged.
—. Carnegie, Andrew. Higher education. Retirement. 1901-18. *2214*
—. Epstein, Abraham. Legislation. Voluntary associations. 1920-35. *1777*
Peonage. Florida. Justice Department. Labor recruitment. New York City. Quackenbos, Mary Grace. Turpentine industry. 1905-10. *2267*
People's College. Agricultural College Act (US, 1862). Agriculture. Labor. Mechanics' Mutual Protection (society). New York. 1843-60's. *1427*
People's Council of America for Democracy and Peace. Illinois. Local Government. Lochner, Louis Paul. Peace Movements. State Government. 1917. *2104*
People's Legislative Service. Congress. Progressivism. Roll-call voting. 1922-29. *2423*
People's Party. Butler, Benjamin F. (papers). Elections (presidential). Third Parties. 1884. *1027*
—. Illinois. Political Attitudes. Populism. 1880-92. *1398*
Perfectionism. Abolition Movement. Hersey, John. Methodist Church. Millenarianism. 1786-1862. *541*
Periodicals *See also* Editors and Editing; Freedom of the Press; Newspapers; Press.
—. Anderson, May. *Children's Friend* (periodical). Felt, Louie. Primary Association. Religious education. Utah. 1880-1940. *80*
—. Antibiotics. Conflict of interest. Federal regulation. Food and Drug Administration. Pharmacy. Welch, Henry. 1953-62. *2676*
—. Assemblies of God. Church of God. Civil rights movement. Presbyterian Church, Southern. South. 1950's-60's. *2804*
—. Citizen Lobbies. Conscription, Military. Political Protest. Protestant Churches. 1940-59. *1570*
—. Conservatism. DuBois, W. E. B. Negroes. Race relations. Radicals and Radicalism. Washington, Booker T. 1900-10. *1983*
—. Constitutions. Editorials. Labor Unions and Organizations. New Deal. Supreme Court. 1935-37. *2503*
—. Fiction. Homosexuality. Women. 1900-20. *1930*
—. Immigration. Industrialization. Morality. Muckraking. 1900-09. *2047*
—. News. Women's rights. 1922-76. *1544*
Perkins, Frances. Foreign Policy. International Labor Organization. Isolationism. New Deal. Roosevelt, Franklin D. 1921-34. *2570*
Persecution *See also* Civil Rights; Religious Liberty.
—. Church and State. Government. Resistance to. Jehovah's Witnesses. Theology. 1870's-1960's. *136*
Pershing, John J. Armies. Drugs. Mexico. New Mexico (Columbus). Prostitution. Venereal disease. 1916-17. *2068*
Personal Narratives *See also* Autobiography; Diaries; Oral History.
—. Blair, Nora Schelter. Brook Farm. Education, Experimental Methods. Massachusetts. Pratt, Frederick. Ripley, George. Utopias. 1841-47. *934*
Peters, J. Sidney. Anti-Saloon League. Prohibition. Virginia. 1916-20. *1943*
Petitions. Abolition movement. New York, upstate. Political participation. Women. 1838-39. *586*
—. Alabama. Mobile Harbor Act (Alabama, 1842). Negroes. Prisons. Seamen. State Legislatures. 1849. *727*

Petitions

—. Antislavery Sentiments. Bain, John Mackintosh. Economic Conditions. Georgia (Darien). 1736-55. *518*
—. Antislavery Sentiments. New York City. 1829-39. *679*
—. Artisans. Convict labor. Kingston Penitentiary. Machinists. Ontario. 1833-36. *826*
Peyote. Bureau of American Ethnology. Ghost Dance. Indians. Mooney, James. Research. 1891-1921. *1110*
—. California. Courts. Navajo Indians. Religious Liberty. 1964. *2792*
Pharmacy. Americas (North and South). Columbia University College of Pharmacy. Medicine. Rusby, Henry Hurd. Scientific Expeditions. ca 1880-1930. *286*
—. Antibiotics. Conflict of interest. Federal regulation. Food and Drug Administration. Periodicals. Welch, Henry. 1953-62. *2676*
—. Arkansas. Medical Reform. Physicians. 1880-1910. *243*
Philadelphia Female Anti-Slavery Society. Abolition Movement. Feminism. Pennsylvania. 1833-40. *616*
Philanthropic Society. Abolitionists. Fugitive Slaves. Negroes. Pennsylvania (Pittsburgh). 1830's-60. *610*
Philanthropy *See also* Charities.
—. Agriculture. Industrial Arts Education. Negroes. North. South. 1902-35. *1832*
—. Business. Feminism. Illinois (Chicago). Schmidt, Minna Moscherosch. 1886-1961. *315*
—. Cholera. Howard Association. Louisiana (New Orleans). Public health. Yellow fever. 1837-78. *235*
—. Cities. New York. Social problems. 1830-60. *878*
—. Courts. Industrialists. Juvenile Delinquency. Middle Classes. Reform. 1890-99. *1472*
—. Delaware. DuPont, Pierre S. Negroes. Public Schools. 1918-30. *2451*
—. Higher education. Negroes. Whites. 1861-1920. *1234*
Philbrook, Mary. Lawyers. Lobbying. New Jersey. Women's Liberation Movement. 1895-1947. *409*
Philippines. Educational policy. USA. 1900-13. *2320*
Phillips, Ulrich B. Cotton. Educational Reform. Howell, Clark. Progressivism. 1903-05. *2062*
Phillips, Wendell. Abolition Movement. Assassination. Green, Ann Terry. Lovejoy, Elijah P. Marriage. 1830-67. *759*
—. Abolition Movement. Christianity. Enlightenment. Morality. Nationalism. 1830-84. *716*
—. Abolition movement. Harvard University, Houghton Library, Blagden Papers. Letters. 1840-80. 1977-79. *605*
—. Abolitionists. Alcott, Amos Bronson. Civil War (antecedents). Weld, Theodore Dwight. 1830-60. *721*
Phillips, Wilbur C. Medical care. Neighborhoods. Ohio (Cincinnati; Mohawk-Brighton). 1917-20. *2037*
Philosophy *See also* Ethics; Mysticism; Pragmatism; Transcendentalism.
—. Dewey, John. Education. 1909-30's. *373*
—. Education. 18c-20c. *1841*
—. Laurens, Henry. Republicanism. South Carolina. 1764-77. *483*
Philosophy of History *See also* Historiography.
—. Adams, Henry Brooks. George, Henry. Ideology. Industrialization. Social criticism. 1870's-1910's. *1073*
Phoenix Indian School. Arizona. Assimilation. Education. Indians. Industrial Arts Education. 1890-1901. *1437*
Phrenology. Eugenics. 19c. *236*
—. Medicine. Mesmerism. Psychology. Sunderland, La Roy. 1820-68. *880*
Physical Education and Training *See also* Sports.
—. Beecher, Catharine. Sex roles. Women. 1830's-40's. *815*
—. Canada. Federal government. 1850-1972. *33*
—. Colleges and Universities. Nebraska, University of. Women. 1879-1923. *220*
—. Feminism. Morality. Sexuality. Women. 19c. *101*
—. Germany. Gymnastics. New England. 1820's. *838*
—. National Cash Register Company. Ohio (Dayton). Patterson, John H. Working Conditions. 1890-1915. *169*
—. Recreation. Women. 1776-1865. *573*
—. Teacher training. 1850's-60's. *856*

SUBJECT INDEX

—. Wisconsin, University of. Women. 1863-1913. *1436*
Physicians. Arkansas. Medical Reform. Pharmacy. 1880-1910. *243*
—. Birth control. Dickenson, Robert Latou. Sanger, Margaret. Values. Women. 1830-1970. *87*
—. Chiropractic. 1885-1980. *1454*
—. Elections. Ohio (Cincinnati). Professionalism. Progressivism. Public health. 1890-1900. *2021*
—. Federal regulation. Medical care. Professional Standards Review Organization Program. Social Security Act (US, 1935; Title XX, 1972). 1965-80. *2978*
—. Foundations. Gates, Frederick T. Medical education. Research, Clinical. Rockefeller, John D. 1910-39. *1833*
—. Mental health. Psychiatry. 1917-41. *1541*
—. Military training. Muldoon, William. Public health. Wood, Leonard. 1890-1915. *2044*
—. Temperance movements. 1800-60. *864*
Physiology. Coates, Sarah (letters). Lectures. Ohio. Women. 1850. *881*
—. Health. Ladies' Physiological Institute of Boston and Vicinity. Massachusetts. Middle Classes. Women. 1848-59. *902*
Piedmont Plateau. Labor Unions and Organizations. Textile industry. 1901-32. *1792*
Pietism. Canada. Great Plains. Prairie Radicals. 1890-1975. *1530*
Pinchot, Cornelia. Feminism. Pennsylvania Council of Republican Women. 1920's-30's. *2509*
Pinchot, Gifford. Coal, anthracite. Strikes. United Mine Workers of America. 1925-26. *2390*
Pine industry. Industrial Relations. Migration, Internal. Negroes. South. Working conditions. ca 1912-26. *1577*
Pine Ridge Indian Reservation. American Indian Movement. Indians. South Dakota. Wounded Knee (occupation). 1972-75. *2749*
Pittman, Clara. Christianity. Communes. Harmony Society. Pennsylvania (Economy). Socialist Laws (Germany, 1878). 1878-79. *1499*
Pittsburgh *Courier* (newspaper). Army. Committee on Participation of Negroes in the National Defense Program. NAACP. Negroes. Segregation. 1937-40. *2506*
Pittsburgh Survey (1909). *Charities and the Commons* (periodical). Industrialization. Pennsylvania. Social Surveys. 1907-14. *2029*
Pittsburgh Workshop for the Blind. Attitudes. Blind. Education. Employment. Pennsylvania. 19c-1939. *1670*
Place, Francis. Bentham, Jeremy. Birth control. Carlile, Richard. Feminism. Great Britain. Owen, Robert Dale. Propaganda. Wright, Frances. 1790-1840. *817*
Plantations. Alabama. Freedmen. Labor. Sharecropping. 1865-67. *1198*
—. Arkansas. Disasters. Droughts. Negroes. Red Cross. Sharecroppers. 1930-31. *2463*
—. Freedmen. Louisiana (Madison Parish). Race Relations. Reconstruction. 1863-74. *978*
Planters. Contracts. Freedmen's Bureau. Sharecropping. South. 1865-68. *1258*
Platt, Thomas C. New York. Progressivism. Public policy. Republican Party. State politics. 1890-1910. *2030*
Playgrounds. Children. Hall, G. Stanley. Progressivism. 1880-1920. *1909*
—. Cities. Illinois (Chicago). Progressivism. 1894-1917. *2027*
Plea bargaining. California (Alameda County). Courts. Sentencing. 1880-1970's. *122*
—. Courts. Sentencing. 19c. *125*
—. Crime and Criminals. Great Britain. 17c-20c. *109*
—. Great Britain. Judicial Process. Law. 18c-20c. *128*
Plessy vs. Ferguson (US, 1896). Negroes. Segregation. Supreme Court (decisions). 1896. *1212*
Plug-uglies. Class conflict. Commission on Industrial Relations. Progressive era. Violence. 1890-1920. *1981*
Pluralism. Affirmative action. Civil rights. Supreme Court. 1970-80. *2779*
—. Ethnic Groups. International Institute. Social services. 1910-79. *74*
—. Ethnic groups. Political Power. 1950's-70's. *1592*
—. Minorities. Race relations. 1968-73. *2697*
Poe, Clarence Hamilton. Agricultural reform. Editors and Editing. Farmers. *Progressive Farmer* (periodical). South. 1899-1964. *1555*

Political Attitudes

Poetry. Antislavery Sentiments. Connecticut. Dwight, Theodore. 1788-1829. *640*
—. Editorials. Labor. *Miners' Magazine*. Songs. Western Federation of Miners. 1900-07. *2293*
—. Feminism. 1850-91. *19*
—. Mexican Americans. Nationalism. 1945-77. *1711*
Poland. Abolition Movement. Gurowski, Adam. Radicals and Radicalism. 1849-66. *449*
—. Immigration. Polish Americans. Socialists. 1883-1914. *39*
Poland, Joseph. Abolition Movement. *Green Mountain Freeman* (newspaper). Liberty Party. State politics. Vermont. 1840-48. *683*
Police *See also* Crime and Criminals; Criminal Law; Law Enforcement; Prisons.
—. American Federation of Labor. Armies. Streetcars. Strikes. Tennessee (Knoxville). 1919-20. *2185*
—. Anti-Communist Movements. Freedom of Speech. Letters. Ontario (Toronto). Political Repression. 1931. *1724*
—. Community relations. Race Relations. Riots. 1940-49. *2689*
—. Executive Power. Intergovernmental Relations. Local Government. Ohio. State Government. 1902-25. *2100*
—. Illinois (Chicago). Militia. Riots. Strikes. Wages. 1877. *1343*
—. Women. 1905-75. *1702*
Police brutality (alleged). Boycotts. Mississippi. Negroes. Robinson, Alfred. United League. 1966-78. *2893*
Police reports. Industrialists. Labor history (sources). New York (Buffalo). Strikes. 1890-1913. *152*
Polish Americans. Addams, Jane. Dudzik, Mary Theresa. Franciscan Sisters of Chicago. Illinois. Social Work. 1860-1918. *369*
—. Americanization. Indiana (Gary). Labor Unions and Organizations. United States Steel Corporation. 1906-20. *2178*
—. Catholic Church. Labor Unions and Organizations. Political Leadership. Progressivism. Socialism. Wisconsin (Milwaukee). 1900-30. *1663*
—. Everett Mill. Massachusetts (Lawrence). Radicals and Radicalism. Strikes. Textile Industry. Women. 1912. *2252*
—. Illinois (Chicago; Back of the Yards). Labor Unions and Organizations. Meat packing industry. Strikes. 1921. *2424*
—. Immigration. Poland. Socialists. 1883-1914. *39*
—. Krzycki, Leo. Labor Unions and Organizations. Radicals and Radicalism. Socialist Party. 1900's-66. *391*
—. New Jersey (Bayonne). Standard Oil Company of New Jersey. Strikes. 1915-16. *2203*
Politburo. Carlson, Oliver (reminiscences). Communist Party. Foster, William Z. Radek, Karl. Trotskyism. USSR. 1924-35. *1548*
Political activism. American Indian Federation. Bureau of Indian Affairs. Collier, John. Indians. Jamison, Alice Lee. New Deal. 1930's-50's. *354*
—. Bias. Public Policy. 1952-76. *2753*
—. California. Negroes. Religion. 1850-73. *76*
—. Depressions. Liberalism. New Deal. Socialist Party. Unemployment. 1929-36. *1804*
—. Journalism. Lectures. Minnesota. Populism. Valesh, Eva McDonald. 1866-1956. *345*
—. Mexican Americans. Primer Congreso Mexicanista (1911). Texas (Laredo). 1910-11. *2010*
Political Attitudes. Allin, John M. Civil rights. Clergy. Episcopal Church, Protestant. Mississippi. 1964-73. *279⁵*
—. Antislavery Sentiments. ꭎio. Revivals. Voting and Voting Behavior. 1825-70. *664*
—. Bunche, Ralph. National Negro Congress. Negroes. New Deal. 1930-39. *2532*
—. Capitalism. Depressions. Radicals and Radicalism. Texas. 1929-33. *2460*
—. City government. Reform. Texas (Beaumont). 1902-09. *1977*
—. Civil Rights. Constitutional Amendments (1st). Liberalism. 1954-74. *2768*
—. Civil Rights. Discrimination. Equality. Negroes. Reconstruction. Texas. 1865-70. *1200*
—. Civil rights movement. Leftism. Models. Students. 1960's-70's. *2714*
—. Civil War. Freedmen. Louisiana (New Orleans). Negroes, free. Politics. Social Classes. 1860-65. *1275*

Political Attitudes

—. Colleges and Universities. Intellectuals. Liberalism. Socialism. 1880-95. *1072*
—. Colleges and Universities. Radicals and Radicalism. Students. 1943-70. *1537*
—. Communism. Gompers, Samuel. Pan American Federation of Labor. 1920's. *2457*
—. Douglas, Stephen A. Lincoln, Abraham. Morality. Slavery. 1850's. *738*
—. Elections. South Dakota (Lake County). Woman suffrage. 1885-90. *1098*
—. Florida. Negroes. Reconstruction. Republican Party. Walls, Josiah T. 1867-85. *1192*
—. Georgia. Negroes. Progressive Party. Roosevelt, Theodore. Wilson, Woodrow. 1912. *2038*
—. Illinois. People's Party. Populism. 1880-92. *1398*
—. Industrialization. Populism. Slavery. South. 1860-96. *1382*
—. New Deal. Public Welfare. South Dakota. 1930's-70's. *2470*
—. Occupations. Student activism. 1960's-70's. *2715*
—. Populism. Social Change. Texas. ca 1880-1900. *1396*
—. Reformers. Religion. Settlement Movement. 1880's-90's. *1462*

Political Campaigns See also Elections; Political Speeches.

—. Allen, Ella. Baker, Charlotte. California (San Diego). Woman suffrage. 1911. *2147*
—. Arizona. Congressional Union for Woman Suffrage. Democratic Party. Women. 1914. 1916. *2164*
—. Feminism. Massachusetts Association Opposed to the Further Extension of the Suffrage to Women. Sex roles. Socialism. Woman suffrage. 1895-1915. *2166*
—. Massachusetts. Referendum. Woman suffrage. 1895-1920. *2140*

Political Campaigns (congressional). California. Sinclair, Upton. Socialist Party. ca 1920. *2464*
—. House of Representatives. Montana. Rankin, Jeannette. Republican Party. Woman suffrage. 1900-16. *2142*

Political Campaigns (gubernatorial). California. Democratic Party. End Poverty In California (program). Sinclair, Upton. ca 1933-34. *2592*
—. Kentucky. McChesney, Henry V. Morrow, Edwin P. Prohibition. Stanley, Augustus Owsley. 1915. *1873*

Political Campaigns (presidential). Candler, Warren A. Methodist Episcopal Church, South. Prohibition. Religion. Smith, Alfred E. 1928. *2344*
—. Feminism. Lockwood, Belva Bennett (letters). 1884. *1116*
—. Louisiana. Newspapers. Slavery. Two-party system. 1834-36. *661*

Political Change. Agrarianism. Neo-Populism. Populism. Progressivism. 1676-1972. *30*
—. Canada. House of Commons. Legislation. Liberal Party. Progressive Party. 1920's. *1574*
—. Economic Conditions. Georgia (Atlanta). Race Relations. 1960's-73. *2812*
—. Women's Liberation Movement. 19c-1970's. *58*

Political Commentary. Alabama. Duke, Jesse C. Editors and Editing. Montgomery *Herald* (newspaper). Negroes. Republican Party. 1886-1916. *1185*
—. *Arkansas Freeman* (newspaper). Gross, Tabbs. Negroes. Reconstruction. Republican Party. 1869-70. *1203*
—. Bourne, Randolph. Feminism. Progressive education. Socialism. 1886-1918. *425*
—. Kansas. Newspapers. Populism. State Politics. Vincent, Henry. 1886-91. *1384*
—. Steffens, Lincoln. 1900's-30's. *2119*

Political Corruption See also Elections; Lobbying; Political Reform.
—. American Revolution (antecedents). Conservatism. Liberty. North Carolina. Regulators. 1766-71. *481*
—. Citizenship. Civil Rights. Crook, George. Indians (agencies). Whites. 1870's-80's. *993*
—. Coal Mines and Mining. Kentucky (Bell, Harlan counties). Labor Disputes. 1920-39. *2489*
—. Local Government. Socialist Party. Voting and Voting Behavior. 1910-14. *1879*
—. Medicine, preventive. Milk scandal. Progressivism. Public health. Rhode Island (Providence). 1913. *1915*
—. Prohibition. Wyoming (Casper). 1919-33. *2388*

SUBJECT INDEX

Political Culture. Agricultural Labor. Elites. 1946-72. *1773*
—. Debs, Eugene V. Hartz, Louis. Hillquit, Morris. Liberalism. Locke, John. Marxism. 20c. *1986*

Political Economy. See Economics.
Political Equality League. James, Ada. Referendum. Willis, Olympia Brown. Wisconsin. Woman Suffrage Association. 1912. *2141*

Political Factions See also Interest Groups; Lobbying.
—. Abolition Movement. Douglass, Frederick. Garnet, Henry Highland. Negroes. 1840-49. *742*
—. Democratic Party. Douglas, Stephen A. Sanders, George. Young America movement. 1850's. *547*
—. Depressions. Farmer-Labor Party. New Deal. Oregon Commonwealth Federation. 1933-38. *2545*
—. Populism. Washington State People's Party. Washington (Whitman County, Ellensburg). ca 1891-98. *1389*

Political Leadership. Arkansas. Jim Crow laws. Negroes. Segregation. 1890's. *1193*
—. Benson, Ezra Taft. Morality. Mormons. Presbyterian Church. Wallace, Henry A. 1933-60. *434*
—. Black Muslims. Ghettos. Malcolm X. Race Relations. 1940-65. *461*
—. Black power. Ideology. 1960's-79. *2876*
—. California (San Francisco). Chinese Americans. Law. Negroes. Racism. 1865-75. *1184*
—. Canada. Coldwell, Major J. Farmer Labor party. Progressivism. Social Democracy. 1907-32. *471*
—. Catholic Church. Labor Unions and Organizations. Polish Americans. Progressivism. Socialism. Wisconsin (Milwaukee). 1900-30. *1663*
—. City Politics. Georgia (Atlanta). Jackson, Maynard. Negroes. 1965-77. *2847*
—. Communist Party. North Central States. Ruthenberg, Charles Emil. USSR. 1919-27. *2414*
—. Conservatism. Elites. Ontario (Ottawa). Public Welfare. 1880-1912. *1310*
—. Diaries. Mormons. Musser, Elise Furer. Utah. 1897-1967. *301*
—. Farmer-Labor Party. Radicals and Radicalism. Saskatchewan. Socialism. 1932-34. *1607*
—. Florida. Menard, John Willis. Negroes. 1871-90. *283*
—. Historiography. Louisiana (New Orleans). Negroes. Reconstruction. ca 1800-75. *1239*
—. Historiography. Progressivism. Quantitative Methods. 1950's-77. *1914*
—. International, 2d. Socialist Party. 1889-1914. *1053*
—. Know-Nothing Party. Louisiana. Social Classes. 1845-60. *542*
—. Lanius, Henry E. Leader, George M. Legislation. Pennsylvania. Special education. 1820-1956. *1838*
—. Long, Huey P. Share-Our-Wealth movement. 1928-35. *2526*
—. Minorities in Politics. Negroes. Reconstruction. Texas. 1865-90's. *1148*
—. Mississippi. Negroes. 1965-70. *2884*
—. Missouri (St. Louis). Racism. Social Classes. Strikes. Workingmen's Party. 1877. *1338*
—. Reform. Schurz, Carl. 1852-1906. *458*

Political participation. Abolition movement. New York, upstate. Petitions. Women. 1838-39. *586*
—. Abolition movement. Rantoul, Robert, Jr. 1820's-56. *303*
—. Canada. Courts. Indians. Lavell, Jeannette. Women's Liberation Movement. 1869-1979. *2914*
—. Cities. Civil disturbances. Negroes. Social change. 1960's-70's. *2798*
—. Civil War. Elections (presidential). Negroes. Republican Party. 1864. *1224*
—. Constitutional Amendments (24th). Negroes. Voter registration. Voting Rights Act (US, 1965). 1964-67. *2892*
—. Cooperative Commonwealth Federation. Saskatchewan. United Farmers of Canada. 1930-45. *1606*
—. Democratic Party. Negroes. Poverty. South. 1960's. *2837*
—. Discrimination. Mexican Americans. 1930-75. *1679*
—. Florida (Jacksonville). Negroes. 1887-1907. *1125*
—. Interest Groups. Poor. 1960's. *2732*

Political Protest

—. New Deal. Roosevelt, Eleanor. Women. 1900-36. *372*
—. Roosevelt, Theodore. Woman suffrage. 1899-1919. *2163*
—. Student activism. 1960's. *2692*

Political Parties See also names of political parties, e.g. Democratic Party, Republican Party, etc.; Elections; Political Campaigns; Third Parties.
—. Alabama. Legislation. Reconstruction. 1867. *1251*
—. Antislavery Sentiments. Hall, Lyman W. Kansas-Nebraska Act (US, 1854). Ohio (Portage County). 1852-56. *619*
—. Ashley, James M. Constitutional Amendments (13th). House of Representatives. Nationalism. Ohio. 1848-65. *1097*
—. Congress of Industrial Organizations. Labor. New Hampshire (Berlin). Nonpartisan League. 1932-36. *2497*
—. Cooperative Commonwealth Federation. Saskatchewan. Socialism. 1928-44. *1681*
—. Delaware. George, Henry. Reform. Single Tax movement. 1890's. *1085*
—. Democratic Party. Nebraska. Populism. 1890's. *1394*
—. Evangelism. Michigan. State Legislatures. 1837-61. *578*
—. Farmers. Radicals and radicalism. 1892-1930. *1682*
—. Iowa. Prohibition. State Politics. 19c. *1445*
—. Kentucky. Negro Suffrage. 1865-82. *1177*
—. Know-Nothing Party. 1853-56. *559*
—. Legislation. Public Welfare. 1933-54. *1812*
—. Morality. Slavery. 1828-36. *701*
—. Negroes. Race relations. Virginia (Richmond). 1865. *1231*

Political Power. Attitudes. Negroes. 1952-72. *1626*
—. Christian Science. Eddy, Mary Baker. Women. 1879-99. *999*
—. Decisionmaking. Desegregation. Negroes. South. Teachers. Voting and Voting Behavior. 1950's-60's. *2831*
—. Ethnic groups. Pluralism. 1950's-70's. *1592*

Political Protest See also Civil Disobedience; Civil Disturbances; Demonstrations; Revolution; Riots; Youth Movements.
—. 1900-81. *1665*
—. Alabama (Birmingham). Civil Rights. King, Martin Luther, Jr. Negroes. Nonviolence. 1962. *2843*
—. Alabama (Lowndes County). Black Power. Civil Rights. 1965-75. *2853*
—. Alberta. Alienation. Economic Conditions. Farmers. 1921-79. *2948*
—. American Indian Movement. Deloria, Vine, Jr. Federal Government. Indians. South Dakota. Wounded Knee (occupation). 1877-1970's. *2712*
—. Anarchism and Anarchists. Liberalism. Social criticism. 1960-68. *2705*
—. Antibusing movement. Massachusetts (Boston). Models. Social Organizations. 1970's. *2895*
—. Antiwar Sentiment. Civil rights. Kennedy, Jane. Oral history. Vietnam War. Women. 1964-77. *2724*
—. Antiwar sentiment. Colleges and Universities. Leftism. 1920-36. *2483*
—. Bibliographies. Communes. Counter culture. Social change. 1963-73. *2989*
—. Black power. Self-improvement. Sociology. 1960's-70's. *2859*
—. Bureau of Indian Affairs. California (Alcatraz Island). Eskimos. Ideology. Indians. 1969-78. *2757*
—. Busing. Community Participation. Massachusetts (Boston). 1977-78. *2894*
—. Čačić, Tomo. Ethnic Groups. Kjelt, Ole. Krat, Pavlo. Leftism. Mäkelä, A. B. Puttee, Arthur. Scarlett, Sam. 1907-34. *1561*
—. Canada. Economic opportunity. Social Classes. USA. 1960-74. *2702*
—. Citizen Lobbies. Conscription, Military. Periodicals. Protestant Churches. 1940-59. *1570*
—. City Government. Maryland (Baltimore). Negroes. Public schools. 1865-1900. *1271*
—. Civil rights. Communist Party. Economic conditions. Negroes. New York City (Harlem). 1930's. *2563*
—. Civil rights. Human rights. Negroes. 1954-78. *2774*
—. Civil rights. King, Martin Luther, Jr. 1955-68. *2854*
—. Civil Rights. Negroes. Press. 1950-76. *2875*
—. Civil rights movement. Gandhi, Mahatma. King, Martin Luther, Jr. Nonviolence. 1950's-60's. *2878*

—. Civil rights movement. Negroes. Nonviolence. 1955-65. *1709*
—. Civil War. Negroes. State Politics. Suffrage. Tennessee. 1864-65. *1144*
—. Colleges and Universities. Educational Reform. West. 1964-74. *2967*
—. Colleges and Universities. Intellectuals. Radicals and Radicalism. Students. 1963-77. *2750*
—. Communism. Farmers. South Dakota. United Farmers League. 1923-34. *2409*
—. Coxey, Jacob S. District of Columbia. Unemployment. 1894. *1302*
—. Curaçao. Negroes. Social change. 1960's-70's. *2797*
—. Desegregation. North Carolina (Greensboro). Sit-ins. 1950's-60's. *2816*
—. Ethnicity. Indians. Religion. 1964-78. *2738*
—. Farm tenancy. Socialism. Texas. 1901-17. *2216*
—. Federal government. New York (Buffalo). Social consciousness. 1965-76. *2747*
—. Freedom of Speech. Industrial Workers of the World. Pratt, N. S. Washington (Spokane). 1909-10. *2132*
—. GI movement. Vietnam War. 1960's-70's. *2727*
—. Journalism. Labor Unions and Organizations. Marxism. Negroes. Randolph, A. Philip. ca 1911-75. *382*
—. Kennedy, John F. Mississippi. Negroes. Voting Rights Act (US, 1965). 1960-72. *2863*
—. Methodology. Psychoanalysis. Social conditions. Students. 1900-75. *1616*
—. National Welfare Rights Organization. Public Welfare. 1967-74. *2941*
—. Negroes. Newspapers. Race Relations. World War II. 1941-45. *2625*
—. Social movements. Trials. 1920-79. *1526*
Political Reform *See also* names of reform movements, e.g. Progressivism, etc.; Lobbying; Political Corruption.
—. American Socialist Party. Hillquit, Morris. Marxism. Socialism. 1901-14. *1942*
—. Arkansas. Constitutions, State (proposed). Progressivism. 1917-18. *2005*
—. Arkansas Community Organizations for Reform Now. Community Participation in Politics. 1960's-70. *2730*
—. Bengough, John Wilson. City government. *Grip* (periodical). Ontario (Toronto). Protestantism. 1873-1910. *370*
—. Buckley, Christopher A. California (San Francisco). City Politics. Progressivism. 1890's. *1892*
—. Carter, William Hodding, Jr. Editors and Editing. Mississippi. Race Relations. ca 1930-60. *340*
—. Cities. Civil Engineering. Pollution. 1840-1920. *94*
—. Citizenship. Coolidge, Calvin. Indian Citizenship Act (US, 1924). 1924. *2446*
—. City Government. Missouri (St. Louis). Progressivism. 1893-1904. *2199*
—. City Politics. Elections, municipal. Knights of Labor. Negroes. Virginia (Richmond). 1886-88. *1303*
—. Civil rights. Johnson, Lyndon B. Negro Suffrage. 1960's. *2855*
—. Conservatism. McCumber, Porter James. McKenzie, Alexander John. North Dakota. Republican Party. Suffrage. Women. 1898-1933. *435*
—. Garvin, Lucius F. C. Rhode Island. State Politics. 1876-1922. *343*
—. Historiography. Mugwumps. Republican Party. 1880's. 1910-79. *956*
—. Individualism. James, William. 1870's-1900. *341*
—. Interest Groups. Local government. Social change. Taxation. 1960's. *2947*
—. Kentucky. Progressivism. Stanley, A. O. State Politics. 1902-19. *1897*
—. Land tenure. Populism. Rogers, John R. State Politics. Washington. 1890-1900. *1363*
—. Middle Classes. Progressivism. ca 1880-1920. *1871*
—. Progressivism. Prohibition. Richards, Richard Olsen. South Dakota. Taxation. 1902-30. *1913*
Political representation. Labor Non-Partisan League. Legislation. Working conditions. 1936-38. *2003*
Political Repression. Anti-Communist Movements. Freedom of Speech. Letters. Ontario (Toronto). Police. 1931. *1724*
—. Freedom of speech. Oklahoma. Vigilantes. World War I. 1914-17. *2137*

Political rights. Cardozo, Francis Louis. Freedmen. Reconstruction. South Carolina. Union League. 1870. *1268*
Political socialization. Civil rights movement. Radicals and Radicalism. Student activism. ca 1955-75. *2713*
Political Speeches *See also* Debates; Speeches, Addresses, etc.
—. Arkansas (Little Rock). Collins, LeRoy. Courts. Federal Government. Florida. School integration. 1957. *2688*
—. Corwin, Thomas. Mexican War. Whig Party. 1847. *540*
—. Democracy. Prohibition. Women. 1920-34. *2356*
—. Kansas. Lease, Mary Elizabeth. Populism. 1871-1933. *293*
—. Man with the Muck-Rake (speech). Rhetoric. Roosevelt, Theodore. 1906. *2014*
Political Systems. Anti-Catholicism. Ohio. Republican Party. Slavery. Whig Party. 1850's. *564*
—. Economics. Education. Historiography. Social classes. 1840-20c. *219*
Political Theory *See also* kinds of political theory, e.g. Democracy.
—. American Revolution. Feminism. Republicans (Radical). Warren, Mercy Otis. 1760's-1805. *523*
—. Black Power. Carmichael, Stokely. Pan-Africanism. 1965-73. *2860*
—. Cabet, Etienne. Icaria (colony). Illinois. Newspapers. Social Theory. Utopias. 1820's-56. *941*
—. Catholic Worker Movement. Maurin, Peter ("Easy Essays"). 1920's-33. *2419*
—. Chamberlain, John. Conservatism. Radicals and Radicalism. 1920's-65. *275*
—. Christianity. Muste, Abraham J. Niebuhr, Reinhold. Pacifism. Thomas, Norman. 1914-38. *1668*
—. Civil War. Lincoln, Abraham. Revolution. Slavery. Social change. 1850-65. *1060*
—. Counter Culture. Kesey, Ken. LSD. Wolfe, Thomas Kennerly, Jr. 1964-68. *2992*
—. Libel. Moore, William. Pennsylvania. Provincial legislatures. Smith, William. 1750-60. *516*
—. Liberalism. New Deal. New Left. Welfare state. 1932-66. *1738*
Political Violence. *See* Terrorism; Violence.
Politics *See also* headings beginning with the word political; City Politics; Elections; Government; Intergovernmental Relations; Lobbying; Local Politics; Minorities in Politics; Presidents; State Politics.
—. Abolition Movement. Anderson, John. Canada. Foreign Relations. Great Britain. USA. 1860-61. *734*
—. Abortion. Antiabortion movement. Anti-Saloon League. Pennsylvania. Pressure groups. Prohibition. 1890-1978. *1640*
—. Agrarianism. Attitudes. Social Organization. 1890's-1970's. *1546*
—. Agriculture. Droughts. Nebraska. Populism. 1880's-90's. *1395*
—. Alabama. Labor Union of Alabama. National Negro Labor Union. Negroes. Rapier, James T. Reconstruction. 1837-75. *1253*
—. Alabama. Ostracism. Reconstruction. Republican Party. 1865-80. *1082*
—. American Land Company. Andrew, John A. Reconstruction. South. 1865-67. *1066*
—. American Petroleum Institute. Ecology. Hoover, Herbert C. Oil Industry and Trade. Pollution. 1921-26. *2365*
—. Americans for Democratic Action. Civil rights. 1948. *2673*
—. Amlie, Thomas. Economic programs. Liberals. New Deal. Wisconsin. 1931-39. *2609*
—. Anti-Catholicism. Pennsylvania. Social Change. 1682-1774. *477*
—. Armies. Bates, Edward. Civil War. Negroes. Wages. 1861-64. *1129*
—. Asian Canadians. British Columbia. Immigration. Racism. 1850-1914. *1524*
—. Baptists, Southern. Individualism. Social problems. 18c-1976. *31*
—. Birth control. Eugenics movement. Feminism. 1915-74. *1588*
—. Blackwell, Henry B. Editors and Editing. Feminism. Stone, Lucy. *Women's Journal* (periodical). 1870-1914. *1047*
—. Bushnell, Horace. Christianity. Economic conditions. Gladden, Washington. Social gospel. Youth. 1836-1918. *995*

—. Business. Farmers. Nonpartisan League. North Dakota. Townley, Arthur C. 1880-1959. *1667*
—. Cain, Richard Harvey. Negroes. Reconstruction. Social conditions. South Carolina. 1850's-87. *375*
—. Canada. Feminism. Literature. McClung, Nellie L. Reform. 1873-1930's. *1689*
—. Capitalism. George, Henry. Progressivism. Single tax. 1880-1920. *2188*
—. Catholic Church. Church and State. Compulsory education. Michigan. 1920-25. *2348*
—. Catholic Church. Church and State. French language. Langevin, Adélard. Manitoba. Private schools. 1890-1916. *1410*
—. Charter of the French Language (1977). French language. Provincial government. Quebec. 1977-78. *2766*
—. Chesnutt, Charles W. Race relations. Washington, Booker T. 1880-1915. *1153*
—. Cities. Volunteerism. Women. 1820-1978. *34*
—. Civil Rights. Clark, Peter Humphries. Negroes. Ohio (Cincinnati). 1880's-1925. *350*
—. Civil Rights. Constitutional Amendments (13th, 14th, 15th). Freedmen. Reconstruction. 1865-77. *1188*
—. Civil rights. Negroes. Racism. 1940's. *1622*
—. Civil rights movement. Negroes. Riots. Tennessee (Columbia). Truman, Harry S. 1946. *2657*
—. Civil War. Freedmen. Louisiana (New Orleans). Negroes, free. Political Attitudes. Social Classes. 1860-65. *1275*
—. Colorado Cooperative Company. Communitarianism. Home Employment Cooperative Company. Labor Exchange. Pragmatism. 1890-1905. *1508*
—. Community control. Education. Integration. Negroes. New York City (Brooklyn). 1882-1902. *1181*
—. Congress. District of Columbia. Education. Finance. Howard University. 1879-1928. *186*
—. Congressmen. New Deal. Roosevelt, Franklin D. Virginia. Woodrum, Clifton A. 1922-45. *433*
—. Constitutional conventions, state. Oklahoma. Woman suffrage. 1906. *2144*
—. Decisionmaking. Federal Government. Interest Groups. Legislation. Women. 1970's. *2911*
—. Democracy. Social Change. Women. 1634-1935. *106*
—. Depressions. Long, Huey P. Louisiana. Share-Our-Wealth movement. Smith, Gerald L. K. 1930's. *2527*
—. Detzer, Dorothy. Nye Committee. Peace Movements. Women's International League for Peace and Freedom. 1920-34. *2430*
—. Discrimination. Idaho. Mormons. 1880-95. *1120*
—. Domestic Policy. Kennedy, John F. Mental Retardation Facilities and Community Mental Health Centers Construction Act (US, 1963). Social Security Act (US, 1935; amended, 1963). 1961-63. *2976*
—. Douglass, Frederick. Patronage. Republican Party. 1870-95. *1235*
—. Economic reform. Kansas. Rightmire, William F. Southern Farmers' Alliance. 1886-92. *1380*
—. Education. Manual Training School. Maryland (Baltimore). Newell, Alexander McFadden. Shepherd, Henry Elliot. 1876-94. *1428*
—. Elections. Negroes. Reconstruction. Tennessee (Shelby County). 1865-76. *1160*
—. Elites. Kansas. Negroes. Republican Party. Waller, John Lewis. 1878-1900. *468*
—. Elites. Race relations. Riots. 1960's-70's. *2857*
—. Equal Rights Amendment. Florida. National Women's Party. West, Helen Hunt. Women. 1917-52. *1727*
—. Executive power. Federal Regulation. President's Advisory Council on Executive Organization. Public Administration. Reform. 1937-79. *1705*
—. Felton, Rebecca Latimer. Georgia. Senate. Woman suffrage. 1860's-1922. *423*
—. Feminism. Fuller, Margaret. Hawthorne, Nathaniel (*The Blithedale Romance*). James, Henry (*Bostonians*). Sex. 19c. *795*
—. Feminism. Human Relations. Radicals and Radicalism. Values. 19c-1929. *29*
—. Feminism. Morality. Women. 19c-20c. *142*

—. Florida (Lee County). Koreshan Unity. Sects, Religious. Teed, Cyrus Reed. Utopias. 1880-1909. *1516*
—. Freedmen. Intellectuals. Negroes, free. Social theory. South. 1870's-90's. *1274*
—. Hopkins, Harry. New Deal. 1912-40. *414*
—. House of Representatives. Illinois (Chicago). Sabath, Adolph Joachim. 1907-32. *298*
—. Ideology. Populism. Walsh, Thomas J. ca 1890-1900. *1361*
—. Income (redistribution). LaFollette, Philip F. National Progressives of America. Wisconsin. 1930-38. *2551*
—. Income redistribution. Public policy. 1961-73. *2951*
—. Industrial Relations. Knights of Labor. Rhode Island. 1880's. *1289*
—. Intellectuals. Liberalism. Lippmann, Walter. 1890-1974. *427*
—. Knights of Labor. Labor Unions and Organizations. Pennsylvania (Scranton). Powderly, Terence V. 1876-1900. *361*
—. Louisiana (New Orleans). Metropolitan Police Force. Negroes. Riots. Whites. 1868. *1168*
—. Minnesota. Public Policy. Welfare Mothers Movement. 1960-72. *2933*
—. Morality. Women. 19c-20c. *118*
—. Moton, Robert Russa. Negroes. Scott, Emmett Jay. Tuskegee Institute. Washington, Booker T. 1915-25. *1643*
—. Novels. Radicals and Radicalism. Religion. Social change. 1915-71. *1691*
—. Pennsylvania. Public welfare. 1967-73. *2943*
—. Premillenarianism. Social Conditions. 1920's-50's. *1704*
—. Race Relations. Student Nonviolent Coordinating Committee. Values. 1961-66. *2889*
—. Reconstruction. Republican Party. Wisconsin. 1865-73. *981*
—. Revivals. 19c. *556*
Polk, Leonidas L. Alexander, Sydenham B. Carr, Elias. Farmers' Alliance. Leadership. North Carolina. Upper Classes. 1887-95. *1392*
—. Education. Episcopal Church, Protestant. Louisiana (New Orleans). Slavery. 1805-65. *730*
Polls. *See* Public Opinion.
Pollution *See also* Air Pollution; Noise Pollution.
—. American Petroleum Institute. Ecology. Hoover, Herbert C. Oil Industry and Trade. Politics. 1921-26. *2365*
—. American Petroleum Institute. Oil Industry and Trade. Texas (Gulf Coast). 1900-70. *1797*
—. Cities. Civil Engineering. Political reform. 1840-1920. *94*
—. Cities. New York City. Public Health. Reform. Refuse disposal. Waring, George E., Jr. 1880-1917. *69*
Polyclinics. Medical Education. Specialization. 1880-1900. *1431*
Polygamy. Congress. Hayes, Rutherford B. Mormons. Woman Suffrage. 1877-81. *1089*
Ponca Indians. California. Indians. Jackson, Helen Hunt *(Ramona)*. Mission Indians. Removals, forced. Schurz, Carl. 1873-84. *1051*
Poor *See also* Poverty.
—. Agriculture Department. Greenbelt new towns. Tugwell, Rexford Guy. 1935-36. *2560*
—. Asylums. Massachusetts (Boston). Mental Illness. 1847-1920. *261*
—. Attitudes. Janesville Associated Charities. Middle Classes. Wisconsin. 1870-1900. *1450*
—. Barnett, Samuel Augustus. Cities. Education. Great Britain. Progressivism. 1880's-1913. *2294*
—. Bureaucracies. Corporations. Labor. Social Classes. War on Poverty. 1960's. *2925*
—. Catholic Church. Immigrants. Irish Americans. McMahon, Patrick. Quebec (Quebec). St. Bridget's Home. 1847-1972. *244*
—. Charities. Church of England. City government. South Carolina (Charleston; St. Phillip's Parish). 1712-75. *536*
—. Children. Indians. Saint Vincent de Paul Society. 1900-10. *2036*
—. City Government. Elites. Human Development Corporation. Missouri (St. Louis). Negroes. War on Poverty. 1964-75. *2935*
—. City Planning. Marsh, Benjamin C. National Conference on City Planning. Population. 1900-17. *1987*
—. Communism. North Carolina (Gastonia). Novels. Strikes. Textile Industry. Whites. 1929-34. *2361*

—. Federal Government. Local Government. Massachusetts (Boston; South End). Middle Classes. Neighborhoods. Urban revitalization. 1960's-70's. *2694*
—. Federal Government. Medical care. Public Health. 1960-77. *2982*
—. Federal Programs. Medical care. 1963-76. *2975*
—. Friends, Society of. Pennsylvania Hospital for the Sick Poor. Pennsylvania (Philadelphia). 18c. *533*
—. Hookworms. Rockefeller Sanitary Commission for the Eradication of Hookworm Disease. South. Stiles, Charles W. 1900-14. *2109*
—. Interest Groups. Political Participation. 1960's. *2732*
Poor People's Health Council. Medical care. Mormon, Square. Race relations. Rossville Health Center. Tennessee (Fayette County). 1960's-70's. *2821*
Poorhouses. Economic conditions. Letters. Mann, Mary Tyler Peabody. Ohio. 1795-1858. *884*
Popular Culture *See also* Daily Life; Social Conditions.
—. Kennedy, John F. New Left. Nixon, Richard M. Social change. 1960-69. *2754*
Popular Front. Communist Party. Culture. Intellectuals. Negroes. New York City (Harlem). 1935-39. *2562*
Population *See also* names of ethnic or racial groups, e.g. Jews, Negroes, etc.; Aged; Birth Control; Census; Demography; Eugenics; Migration, Internal; Mortality.
—. City Planning. Marsh, Benjamin C. National Conference on City Planning. Poor. 1900-17. *1987*
—. Civil rights. Legislation. Race Relations. Riots. Tennessee (Memphis). 1865-66. *1209*
—. Economic Theory. George, Henry. Income. Landlords and Tenants. Taxation. Technology. 1871-83. *1064*
—. Federal Government. House of Representatives. Intervention. Negroes. South. Voting Rights Act (US, 1965). 1940-75. *2802*
—. Woman suffrage. Women's Liberation Movement. Wyoming. 1869-1920. *1102*
Populism. Agrarianism. Neo-Populism. Political Change. Progressivism. 1676-1972. *30*
—. Agrarianism. Radicals and Radicalism. Wisconsin. Working class. 19c. *1399*
—. Agrarianism. South. 1865-1900. *1378*
—. Agriculture. Droughts. Nebraska. Politics. 1880's-90's. *1395*
—. Agriculture. Freight and Freightage. Prices. Railroads. 1870-97. *1360*
—. Alabama. Democratic Party. Manning, Joseph C. State Politics. 1892-96. *1387*
—. Alberta. Cooperative Commonwealth Federation. Russia. Saskatchewan. Social Credit Party. USA. 1870's-1940's. *14*
—. Alberta. New Brunswick. Radicals and Radicalism. Saskatchewan. Social organization. 1950's-70's. *2700*
—. *Alliance-Independent* (newspaper). Christian Socialism. Gibson, George Howard. Nebraska. *Wealth Makers* (newspaper). 1893-96. *1397*
—. American Tobacco Company. Elections (congressional). Kentucky. 1886-92. *1365*
—. Bellamy, Edward *(Looking Backward 2000-1887)*. Economic Theory. North Central States. 1880's-90's. *1377*
—. Bible. Imber, Naphtali Herz *(The Fall of Jerusalem)*. Myths and Symbols. 1856-1909. *1371*
—. Business. Civil rights. Rhetoric. 1870-1900. *1370*
—. Civil rights. Federal Policy. Interest Groups. Private sector. Racism. Wallace, George C. 1960's. *2899*
—. Colorado. Hofstadter, Richard. Progressive movement. 1890-1910. 1950's. *1375*
—. Colorado. Progressivism. 1900. *1376*
—. Court of Visitation. Kansas. Railroads. Republican Party. State Legislatures. 1890-1900. *1386*
—. Democratic Party. Nebraska. Political Parties. 1890's. *1394*
—. Donnelly, Ignatius. Literature. 1831-90's. *1359*
—. Economic Policy. Prairie Provinces. Tariff. 1879. 1920-79. *1368*
—. Economics. 1880-1900. *1362*
—. Emery, Sarah E. Van De Vort. Rhetoric. 1887-95. *1393*
—. Farmers. Ideology. Old Northwest. Rhetoric. 1870's-80's. *1388*

—. Fundamentalism. Long, Huey P. North Central States. Progressivism. Smith, Gerald L. K. 1934-48. *362*
—. Georgia. Negro Suffrage. Reform. Watson, Thomas E. 1880-1922. *27*
—. Government Regulation. North Carolina. Progressivism. Railroads. Russell, Daniel. 1894-98. *1369*
—. Ideology. Politics. Walsh, Thomas J. ca 1890-1900. *1361*
—. Illinois. People's Party. Political Attitudes. 1880-92. *1398*
—. Industrialization. Political Attitudes. Slavery. South. 1860-96. *1382*
—. Journalism. Lectures. Minnesota. Political activism. Valesh, Eva McDonald. 1866-1956. *345*
—. Judicial Administration. Labor. Supreme courts, state. Western States. 1893-1902. *1024*
—. Kansas. Lease, Mary Elizabeth. Political Speeches. 1871-1933. *293*
—. Kansas. Newspapers. Political Commentary. State Politics. Vincent, Henry. 1886-91. *1384*
—. Kansas. Progressivism. Social Classes. 1885-1917. *10*
—. Kentucky. State Politics. 1870-1900. *1367*
—. Land tenure. Political Reform. Rogers, John R. State Politics. Washington. 1890-1900. *1363*
—. Long, Huey P. Louisiana. Progressivism. State Government. 1891-1935. *1566*
—. Morlan, Robert Loren. Nonpartisan League. North Dakota. 1910's-1920's. *1881*
—. Negroes. Press. Republican Party. 1890-96. *1152*
—. Novels. Utopias. 1893-97. *1008*
—. Political Attitudes. Social Change. Texas. ca 1880-1900. *1396*
—. Political Factions. Washington State People's Party. Washington (Whitman County, Ellensburg). ca 1891-98. *1389*
—. Reformers. State Legislatures. West. 1890's. *1364*
—. Social criticism. 1880's-1890's. *1390*
—. South. 1850's-90's. *1381*
Populist. Alberta. Edwards, Robert C. "Bob". *Eye Opener* (newspaper). 1904-22. *1940*
Port Chicago Naval Magazine. California (San Francisco Bay). Courts Martial and Courts of Inquiry. Mare Island Mutiny. Navies. Negroes. Race relations. 1944-48. *2652*
Porter, Katherine Anne. Book reviews. Feminism. Literary Criticism. 1922-29. *2373*
Portland *Firebrand* (newspaper). Anarchism and Anarchists. Newspapers. Oregon. Radicals and Radicalism. 1895-98. *1112*
Portland *Oregonian*. Oregon. Reporters and Reporting. Woman Suffrage. 1869-1905. *1101*
Ports. Businessmen. Progressives. Washington (Seattle). 1911-20. *2184*
Portsmouth Anti-Slavery Society. Abolition Movement. Haverford College Library (Quaker Collection). New Hampshire. Rogers, Nathaniel Peabody. 1830-46. *316*
Post, Charles William. Labor Disputes. Michigan (Battle Creek). Open shop movement. 1895-1920. *2239*
Post, Louis F. Alien Anarchist Act (US, 1918). Anti-Communist Movements. Congress. Law Enforcement. Leftism. 1919-20. *2352*
—. Carpetbaggers. Equality. Progressive era. Reconstruction. 1868-1925. *306*
—. George, Henry. Single tax movement. 1872-98. *965*
—. Illinois (Chicago). Progressivism. *Public* (newspaper). Single tax movement. 1898-1919. *1904*
—. Progressivism. Single Tax Movement. 1898-1913. *1903*
Pottery. National Brotherhood of Operative Potters. Strikes. Tariff. 1894. *1345*
Poverty *See also* Charities; Economic Conditions; Poor; Public Welfare.
—. Abolition Movement. Attitudes. Competition. Economic Structure. ca 1830-60. *656*
—. Blumer, Herbert. Public Policy. Social problems. 1960's-73. *2924*
—. Bromley, Walter. Charities. Micmac Indians. Nova Scotia. Self-help. 1813-25. *870*
—. Canada. Economic Reform. George, Henry. Industry. Progress (concept). Social gospel. ca 1879-99. *975*
—. Charities. New Brunswick (Saint John). Newfoundland (Saint John's). Nova Scotia (Halifax). Unemployment. 1815-60. *871*
—. Cities. Criminal Law. 1780-1840. *892*

—. Democratic Party. Negroes. Political participation. South. 1960's. *2837*
—. Hastings, Charles. Neighborhood Workers' Association. Ontario (Toronto). Public health. 1910-21. *1527*
—. Housing. Kentucky (Louisville). Progressivism. 1900-10. *1927*
Powderly, Terence V. Chinese. Immigration. Labor Unions and Organizations. 1897-1902. *1052*
—. Knights of Labor. Labor Unions and Organizations. Pennsylvania (Scranton). Politics. 1876-1900. *361*
—. Knights of Labor. Temperance Movements. 1878-93. *1356*
Powell, Adam Clayton, Jr. Alabama (Montgomery). Boycotts. King, Martin Luther, Jr. Leadership. Negroes. New York City (Harlem). 1941-56. *307*
—. City Politics. Civil rights. LaGuardia, Fiorello. Liberalism. New York City. 1941-43. *2619*
Pragmatism. Addams, Jane. Dewey, John. Dix, Dorothea. Emerson, Ralph Waldo. Transcendentalism. 1830's-1960's. *231*
—. Colorado Cooperative Company. Communitarianism. Home Employment Cooperative Company. Labor Exchange. Politics. 1890-1905. *1508*
—. Science. Social change. 1900-40. *1608*
Prairie Provinces *See also* Alberta; Manitoba; Saskatchewan.
—. Catholic Church. Church schools. French language. Langevin, Louis Philippe Adélard. Laurier, Wilfrid. Liberal Party. Religion in the Public Schools. 1890-1915. *185*
—. Economic Policy. Populism. Tariff. 1879. 1920-79. *1368*
—. Woman Suffrage. 1890's-1920's. *1735*
Prairie Radicals. Canada. Great Plains. Pietism. 1890-1975. *1530*
Prairie States. *See* individual states by name; Great Plains.
Pratt, Frederick. Blair, Nora Schelter. Brook Farm. Education, Experimental Methods. Massachusetts. Personal narratives. Ripley, George. Utopias. 1841-47. *934*
Pratt, N. S. Freedom of Speech. Industrial Workers of the World. Political Protest. Washington (Spokane). 1909-10. *2132*
Premillenarianism. Politics. Social Conditions. 1920's-50's. *1704*
Preparedness. American Federation of Labor. Gompers, Samuel. Labor Unions and Organizations. Military. Wilson, Woodrow. 1914-17. *2000*
—. National security. Peace Movements. 1941-71. *1564*
—. Navy League (Woman's Section). Sex roles. Suffrage. Woman's Peace Party. World War I. 1914-18. *2092*
Presbyterian Church. Abolition Movement. Anderson, Isaac. Southern and Western Theological Seminary. Tennessee (Maryville). 1819-50's. *574*
—. Abolition Movement. Beecher, Lyman. Colonization. 1820-50. *768*
—. Abolition Movement. Civil War (antecedents). South. Stanton, Robert. 1840-55. *731*
—. Abolition Movement. Cornish, Samuel E. *Freedom's Journal* (newspaper). Journalism. Negroes. 1820's-59. *467*
—. Abolition movement. Douglass, Frederick. Ireland (Belfast). Smyth, Thomas. 1846. *697*
—. Africa. American Colonization Society. Colonization. McDonough, David. Medical Education. Slavery. 1840-50. *710*
—. American Revolution. Antislavery sentiments. Racism. 1750-1818. *769*
—. Antislavery sentiments. Baptists. Methodist Church. South. 1740-1860. *699*
—. Attitudes. Indians. Missions and Missionaries. 1837-93. *13*
—. Benson, Ezra Taft. Morality. Mormons. Political Leadership. Wallace, Henry A. 1933-60. *434*
—. Bible. Constitutions, State. Religious Education. Supreme courts (state). Wisconsin. 1848-90. *1419*
—. Bible. Sexuality. 1975-80. *2740*
—. Boycotts. Mexican Americans. Public schools. Segregation. Texas (San Angelo). 1910-15. *2303*
—. Buttrick, George Arthur. Pacifism. 1915-74. *1563*
—. Christianity. Strong, William. Supreme Court. 1864-80. *1497*

—. Dabney, Robert Lewis. Morality. South. Texas, University of (Austin). Union Seminary. 1865-96. *1084*
—. Fundamentalism. Matthews, Mark Allison. Washington (Seattle). 1900-40. *430*
—. Integration. Missions and Missionaries. 1562-1977. *15*
—. Jones, Charles Colcock. Missions and Missionaries. Slavery. South. 1825-63. *776*
—. McCalla, Daniel. 1770's-1809. *299*
—. Metropolitan Areas. Missions and Missionaries. 1869-1977. *84*
—. New Jersey (Newark). See, Isaac M. Sermons. Women. 1876. *1485*
—. Slavery. Stowe, Harriet Beecher. 1830's-1870's. *909*
—. Social justice. 1770-1977. *50*
—. Women. 1800-1975. *82*
Presbyterian Church (Committee of Four). Ordination. Women. 1926-30. *2346*
Presbyterian Church, Southern. Assemblies of God. Church of God. Civil rights movement. Periodicals. South. 1950's-60's. *2804*
—. Bible. Race relations. South. 1861-1980. *98*
—. Bible. Sabbath. South. 1861-1959. *103*
Presbyterians. Abolition Movement. Breckinridge, Robert J. Breckinridge, William Lewis. Constitutions, State. Emancipation Party. Kentucky. 1849. *676*
—. Christianity. Education. Freedmen. 1872-1900. *1272*
Preservation. California. Community Participation in Politics. Conservation movement. 1970's. *2699*
Presidency *See also* Executive Power.
—. LaFollette, Robert Marion. Nominations to Office. Republican Party. Roosevelt, Theodore. 1910-12. *2022*
Presidents *See also* names of individual presidents.
—. Federal Policy. Public welfare. 1933-78. *1793*
President's Advisory Council on Executive Organization. Executive power. Federal Regulation. Politics. Public Administration. Reform. 1937-79. *1705*
President's Commission on Olympic Sports. Amateur Sports Act (US, 1978). Competition. Sports. 1960's-70's. *2783*
Press *See also* Books; Editors and Editing; Journalism; Newspapers; Periodicals; Reporters and Reporting.
—. Armies. Hastie, William H. Military recruitment. Negroes. World War II. 1940-42. *2638*
—. Baseball. Brooklyn Dodgers (team). Integration. Montreal Royals (team). Negroes. Rickey, Branch. Robinson, Jackie. 1945-47. *2690*
—. Civil Rights. Negroes. Political Protest. 1950-76. *2875*
—. Federal government. New Deal. Progressivism. Reform. 1890's-1930's. *1534*
—. France. Madagascar. Negroes. Waller, John L. 1890's. *1281*
—. Freedmen. *Freedom's Journal* (newspaper). Negroes. Negroes (free). 1827-29. *713*
—. Labor disputes. Norway. Norwegian Americans. Thrane, Marcus. USA. 1886-94. *1285*
—. Negroes. Populism. Republican Party. 1890-96. *1152*
—. Nonpartisan League. North Dakota. 1915-16. *2055*
Press, underground. Canada. Counter Culture. Great Britain. USA. 1957-72. *2990*
Pressed Steel Car Company. Cigar industry. Industrial Workers of the World. Pennsylvania (McKees Rocks, Pittsburgh). Steel Industry. Strikes. 1909-13. *2235*
Pressure Groups *See also* Interest Groups.
—. Abortion. Antiabortion movement. Anti-Saloon League. Pennsylvania. Politics. Prohibition. 1890-1978. *1640*
—. Business. Government regulation. Public interest. 1975-79. *2953*
—. California (San Francisco). Churches. Civil rights. Negroes. 1860's. *1221*
—. Child Welfare. Human Rights. Law. 1978. *1639*
—. Europe. Women. 1888-1920's. *48*
Preston School of Industry. California. Education. Prisons. Rehabilitation. Youth. 1894-1955. *1558*
Prices *See also* Wages.
—. Agriculture. Freight and Freightage. Populism. Railroads. 1870-97. *1360*

—. Farmers. McNary-Haugen bill. Montana. Pacific Northwest. Tariff. 1920-29. *2410*
Prigg v. *Pennsylvania* (US, 1842). Courts. North. Slavery. Supreme Court. 1842-57. *636*
Primaries *See also* Elections; Voting and Voting Behavior.
—. Courts. Democratic Party. Segregation. South Carolina. Waring, J. Waties. 1947-52. *2683*
—. Democratic Party. NAACP. Negro Suffrage. *Smith* v. *Allwright* (US, 1944). South. Supreme Court. 1890's-1944. *1722*
—. Democratic Party. NAACP. Negro Suffrage. Supreme Court. Texas. 1927-45. *1723*
Primaries, gubernatorial. Conservatism. Democratic Party. North Carolina. Progressivism. 1890-1920. *2340*
Primaries (presidential). Civil Rights Act (US, 1964). Democratic Party. Indiana. Wallace, George C. Welsh, Matthew E. 1964. *2900*
Primary Association. Anderson, May. *Children's Friend* (periodical). Felt, Louie. Periodicals. Religious education. Utah. 1880-1940. *80*
Primary Education. *See* Elementary Education.
Primer Congreso Mexicanista (1911). Mexican Americans. Political activism. Texas (Laredo). 1910-11. *2010*
Princeton University. Educational reform. New Jersey. Wilson, Woodrow. 1902-10. *2334*
Printing *See also* Books.
—. Collective bargaining. Ontario (Toronto). Organizational Theory. 19c. *178*
Prison Association. New York. Reform. Rehabilitation. 1844-62. *875*
Prison reform. Equal rights. Integration. Women. 1820's-1900. *1451*
—. New York. Smith, Alfred E. 1903-28. *2360*
Prisoners. American Revolution. Diaries. Drinker family. Friends, Society of. Pennsylvania (Philadelphia). Virginia (Winchester). 1777-81. *526*
—. Civil rights. New federalism. Supreme courts, state. 1969-80. *2773*
Prisoners of war. Apache Indians (Chiricahua, Ojo Caliente). Fort Sill. Interior Department. Land allotment. Oklahoma. War Department. 1909-13. *2170*
Prisons *See also* Crime and Criminals; Criminal Law; Police.
—. Agriculture. Convict Labor. Louisiana State Prison (Angola). Working Conditions. 1900-78. *1701*
—. Alabama. Mobile Harbor Act (Alabama, 1842). Negroes. Petitions. Seamen. State Legislatures. 1849. *727*
—. Attica State Prison. NAACP. Negroes. New York. 1932. *2462*
—. Attitudes. Friends, Society of. New York (Auburn). Pennsylvania. Reform. Religion. 1787-1845. *874*
—. Barnard, Kate. Kansas State Penitentiary. Oklahoma. Reform. 1908-09. *1974*
—. California. Education. Preston School of Industry. Rehabilitation. Youth. 1894-1955. *1558*
—. Children. Michigan. Reformatories. 1851-58. *900*
—. Convict lease system. Economic Conditions. Georgia. Racism. 1868-1909. *1044*
—. Crime and Criminals. Ontario (Upper Canada). Reform. 1835-50. *857*
—. Economic Policy. Indians (reservations). Reform. 19c. *158*
—. Feminism. Leftism. New York City. Smedley, Agnes (*Cell Mates*). 1918. *2019*
—. Illinois. State Government. 1831-1903. *230*
—. Industrial Workers of the World. Kansas. 1915-20. *1993*
—. Labor. Negroes. Tennessee. 1830-1915. *96*
—. Oklahoma. Reform. 1910-67. *1553*
—. Ontario. Rehabilitation. 1884-1900. *1482*
—. Public opinion. 1790-1978. *239*
Private Schools *See also* Church Schools.
—. Catholic Church. Church and State. French language. Langevin, Adélard. Manitoba. Politics. 1890-1916. *1410*
Private sector. Civil rights. Federal Policy. Interest Groups. Populism. Racism. Wallace, George C. 1960's. *2899*
—. Government. Unemployment. 18c-1979. *260*
Prizes. Girls. Schools. 1820-50. *553*
Probasco, Harriet. Carroll, Anna Ella. Nativism. Women. 1840's-61. *797*
Probation. Education. Juvenile Courts. 1899-1917. *2073*

Production control. Labor. Mechanization. 19c-20c. *165*
Productivity. Hawthorne First Relay Assembly Test Room. Research. Working Conditions. 1927-32. *2428*
Professional Standards Review Organization Program. Federal regulation. Medical care. Physicians. Social Security Act (US, 1935; Title XX, 1972). 1965-80. *2978*
Professional training. Desegregation. Discrimination, Educational. Graduate schools. Lawsuits. Negroes. North Carolina. 1930-51. *1835*
Professionalism. Elections. Ohio (Cincinnati). Physicians. Progressivism. Public health. 1890-1900. *2021*
—. Elites. Hays, Samuel P. Ideology. Progressivism. Wiebe, Robert. 20c. *1971*
—. Flexner Report. Medicine. Progressive era. Social control. 1910. *2317*
—. Liberalism. Partisanship. Public welfare. State government. 1960's-70's. *2952*
Professionalization. Addams, Jane. Hampton, Isabel. Illinois (Chicago). Johns Hopkins Hospital Training School for Nurses. Maryland (Baltimore). Nurses and Nursing. Social Work. 1889-1910. *1461*
—. Beecher, Catharine. Education. Employment. Women. 1823-75. *182*
—. Bureaucracies. Public welfare. 1900-29. *1825*
—. Colleges and Universities. Educators. New Jersey. Pennsylvania. 1870-1915. *201*
—. Columbia University (Medical School). Medical education. New York City. 1760's. *488*
—. Maritime Provinces. Medicine, practice of. 1867-1914. *1020*
—. Medical Reform. Mental health. Territorial Government. Washington. 1853-75. *1459*
Profits. Authority. Lukens Iron Works. Paternalism. Pennsylvania (Coatesville). Strikes. 1886. *1347*
Profit-sharing. Businessmen. Cooperatives. Nelson, Nelson O. 1886-1904. *1329*
Progress (concept). Canada. Economic Reform. George, Henry. Industry. Poverty. Social gospel. ca 1879-99. *975*
Progressive education. Blakely Institute. Dewey, John. Georgia. Kilpatrick, William Heard. 19c-20c. *2301*
—. Bourne, Randolph. Feminism. Political Commentary. Socialism. 1886-1918. *425*
—. California. ca 1930-40. *2518*
—. Curricula. Kindergarten. Morality. 1860-1920. *184*
—. Depressions. Ethnicity. Race. 1929-45. *2513*
—. Depressions. Negroes. South. 1930-45. *2512*
—. Sex roles. Women. 1880-1940. *179*
Progressive era. Carpetbaggers. Equality. Post, Louis F. Reconstruction. 1868-1925. *306*
—. Caryl, Charles W. Colorado. New Era Union. Racial thought. Utopias. 1858-1926. *1509*
—. Class conflict. Commission on Industrial Relations. Plug-uglies. Violence. 1890-1920. *1981*
—. Communitarianism. Democracy. Liberalism. 1890-1920's. *2049*
—. Congress. Fisher, Irving. Public health. 1906-13. *2115*
—. Constitutional conventions. Negroes. Ohio. Smith, Harry. Suffrage. 1863-1912. *2165*
—. Consumers. National Consumers' League. Women. 1900-23. *2124*
—. Domestics. Industrial Workers of the World. Labor Unions and Organizations. Street, Jane (letter). 1917. *2224*
—. Educational reform. Elites. Niles Bill (Ohio, 1898). Ohio (Toledo). School boards. 1890's. *2328*
—. Flexner Report. Medicine. Professionalism. Social control. 1910. *2317*
—. Industrial Arts Education. Negroes. North. South. 1900-15. *2306*
—. New York City (Greenwich Village). 1900-20. *2018*
—. Reformatories. Shank, Corwin. Washington (Monroe). 1904-18. *1972*
Progressive Farmer (periodical). Agricultural reform. Editors and Editing. Farmers. Poe, Clarence Hamilton. South. 1899-1964. *1555*
Progressive movement. Altruism. Public policy. Technology. 1900-17. 1973. *1933*
—. Colorado. Hofstadter, Richard. Populism. 1890-1910. 1950's. *1375*
Progressive Party. California. Elections (presidential). 1924. *2413*
—. Canada. House of Commons. Legislation. Liberal Party. Political Change. 1920's. *1574*

—. Farmers. Idaho. Irrigation. State Politics. 1914-22. *2012*
—. Georgia. Negroes. Political Attitudes. Roosevelt, Theodore. Wilson, Woodrow. 1912. *2038*
Progressives. American Federation of Labor. Bombing. California (Los Angeles). Labor movement. *Los Angeles Times*. McNamara case. 1910-14. *2265*
—. Asians. Immigration. Negroes. Newlands, Francis. West Coast. 1904-17. *2067*
—. Bourassa, Henri. Canada. Parliaments. 1926. *1633*
—. Businessmen. Ports. Washington (Seattle). 1911-20. *2184*
—. California. Labor Unions and Organizations. Lobbying. 1900-19. *1898*
—. Colorado. Conservation of natural resources. Individualism. 1896-1910. *2028*
—. Community centers. Country life movement. Religion. Rural Settlements. 1900's-20's. *2099*
—. Dunne, Edward F. Educational Reform. Illinois (Chicago). 1905-10. *2299*
—. Economic reform. Record, George L. 1859-1933. *2277*
—. Fagan, Mark. New Jersey (Jersey City). Single tax. Taxation. 1901-17. *2278*
—. Gary, Elbert H. Mitchel, John Purroy. New York City (Committee on Unemployment and Relief). Unemployment. 1914-17. *2058*
—. New Deal. Roosevelt, Franklin D. Senate. 1935-36. *2557*
—. New Deal. Senate. 1933-34. *2558*
—. Social change. 1890-1917. *1989*
—. Urban reform. 1890-1910. *2057*
Progressivism. Adams, Alva B. Colorado. State Politics. Sweet, William. 1922-24. *2403*
—. Advertising. Ethics. Journalism. 1890's-1920's. *1910*
—. Agrarianism. Neo-Populism. Political Change. Populism. 1676-1972. *30*
—. Alaska (Nome). Robins, Raymond. 1897-1925. *314*
—. Alexander, George. California (Los Angeles). City Government. Reform. ca 1909-13. *2070*
—. Allen, Robert McDowell. Food Adulteration and Inspection. Kentucky. Scovell, Melville Amasa. 1898-1916. *2125*
—. Allendale Farm. Boys. Bradley, Edward. 1894-1937. *1875*
—. Anarchist Scare (1908). Radicals and Radicalism. Social movements. 1900-10. *2139*
—. Ansell, Samuel T. Chamberlain, George. Congress. Crowder, Enoch H. Lenroot, Irvine L. Military law. 1916-20. *2408*
—. Arkansas. Constitutions, State (proposed). Political Reform. 1917-18. *2005*
—. Art criticism. Culture. 1900's. *1973*
—. Attitudes. Films. *Intolerance* (film). 1916. *1965*
—. Authors. Churchill, Winston (1871-1947). New Hampshire. ca 1900-47. *292*
—. Autobiography. Identity. Psychohistory. Reformers. ca 1860-1920. *366*
—. Banking. Bulkley, Robert J. Federal Farm Loan Act (US, 1916). Federal Reserve Act (US, 1913). 1906-30. *363*
—. Barkley, Alben. Gambling. Kentucky. Louisville Churchmen's Federation. 1917-27. *2438*
—. Barnett, Samuel Augustus. Cities. Education. Great Britain. Poor. 1880's-1913. *2294*
—. Bass, Robert P. Boston and Maine Railroad. Churchill, Winston (1871-1947). New Hampshire. Republican Party. 1890-1912. *1868*
—. Beckham, John C. W. Kentucky. McCreary, James B. State Government. Willson, Augustus E. 1899-1915. *1894*
—. Behavior. Reform. Sex. 1890-1920. *1995*
—. Beth Ha Medrosh Hagodol synagogue. Colorado (Denver). Judaism. Kauvar, Charles E. H. 1902-71. *428*
—. Bingham, Robert Worth. City government. Kentucky (Louisville). Reform. 1905-10. *1926*
—. Blaine, John J. Republican Party. Senate. Wisconsin. 1927-33. *2421*
—. Boosterism. California (Los Angeles). City Government. Journalism. Willard, Charles Dwight. 1888-1914. *319*
—. Buckley, Christopher A. California (San Francisco). City Politics. Political Reform. 1890's. *1892*

—. Burnham, Daniel Hudson. City planning. Illinois (Chicago). Moody, Walter D. *(Wacker's Manual of the Plan of Chicago).* Publicity. Reform. 1909-11. *2071*
—. Business. Campbell, Thomas M. Democratic Party. State Government. Texas. 1907-11. *2264*
—. Business. Consumer cooperative movements. Garden City Movement. Nelson, Nelson O. 1890's-1918. *2240*
—. Business. Croly, Herbert. Equal opportunity. Federal Trade Commission Act (US, 1914). 1900's-10's. *2227*
—. California. Educational Tests and Measurements. Ethnic groups. IQ tests. Students. 1917-21. *2300*
—. California. Junior Colleges. Lange, Alexis. 1890-1920. *2308*
—. California (San Francisco). Catholic Church. City Politics. Irish Americans. Yorke, Peter C. 1900's. *2114*
—. California (San Francisco). City Government. Crime and Criminals. Prostitution. 1910-14. *2085*
—. Canada. Coldwell, Major J. Farmer Labor party. Political Leadership. Social Democracy. 1907-32. *471*
—. Capital punishment. Constitutional Conventions, state. New York. 1915. *1923*
—. Capitalism. George, Henry. Politics. Single tax. 1880-1920. *2188*
—. Catholic Church. Labor Unions and Organizations. Polish Americans. Political Leadership. Socialism. Wisconsin (Milwaukee). 1900-30. *1663*
—. Catholic Church. Lawyers. Pennsylvania. Smith, Walter George. 1900-22. *1891*
—. Census Bureau. Cornell University. Economics. Negroes. Racism. Willcox, Walter F. 1895-1910. *1870*
—. Charities. Medical care. Scientific management. 1900-20. *2064*
—. Children. Hall, G. Stanley. Playgrounds. 1880-1920. *1909*
—. Children. Labor reform. Rhetoric. 1904-16. *1917*
—. Children. Massachusetts (Boston). Pennsylvania (Philadelphia). Recreation. 1886-1911. *1985*
—. Christianity. Class Struggle. *Los Angeles Times*. McNamara case. Radicals and Radicalism. Steffens, Lincoln. 1908-12. *2083*
—. Cities. Democracy. Howe, Frederic C. Liberalism. ca 1890-1940. *2013*
—. Cities. Family. Morality. Recreation. Reform. Socialization. 1890-1920. *1990*
—. Cities. Illinois (Chicago). Playgrounds. 1894-1917. *2027*
—. Cities. Noise pollution. Reform. 1900-30. *1683*
—. City Government. Ellis, George E. Michigan (Grand Rapids). 1894-1921. *2106*
—. City Government. Health. New York City. Public baths. 1890-1915. *2121*
—. City Government. Missouri (St. Louis). Political Reform. 1893-1904. *2199*
—. City Government. Municipal League of Seattle. Reform. Washington (Seattle). 1910-20. *2045*
—. City government. Ontario (Toronto). Wickett, Samuel Morley. 1900-15. *1703*
—. City Politics. Fagan, Mark. New Jersey (Jersey City). 1896-1907. *2279*
—. City Politics. Maryland (Baltimore). 1895-1911. *1920*
—. Class struggle. Eugenics. Fisher, Irving. Racism. 1890's-1920. *1869*
—. Colorado. Populism. 1900. *1376*
—. Congress. Judicial reform. Supreme Court. Taft, William H. 1920-25. *2400*
—. Congress. People's Legislative Service. Roll-call voting. 1922-29. *2423*
—. Conservatism. Creel, George. New Deal. Works Progress Administration. 1900-53. *1520*
—. Conservatism. Democratic Party. North Carolina. Primaries, gubernatorial. 1890-1920. *2340*
—. Conservatism. Saskatchewan. 1920's. *1556*
—. Constitutions, State (reform). Hamilton, Joseph G. de Roulhac. North Carolina. Sikes, Enoch W. State Legislatures. 1898-1913. *2091*
—. Cotton. Educational Reform. Howell, Clark. Phillips, Ulrich B. 1903-05. *2062*
—. Courts. Industrial Workers of the World. Labor. New Jersey (Paterson). Quinlan, Patrick. 1913-17. *2275*

Progressivism

—. Crawford, Coe Isaac. Republican Party. Roosevelt, Theodore. South Dakota. State Politics. 1912-14. *2076*
—. Crothers, Austin Lane. Governors. Maryland. 1904-12. *1896*
—. Cuba. Military occupation. Wood, Leonard. 1899-1902. *1951*
—. Curricula. Domesticity. Home economics. Sex roles. 1900-20. *2314*
—. Democratic Party. Educational reform. Ethnic groups. Junior High Schools. Massachusetts (Somerville). Middle Classes. 1912-24. *2335*
—. Depressions. LaFollette, Philip F. New Deal. Roosevelt, Franklin D. Wisconsin Works Bill (1935). 1935. *2552*
—. Detroit Citizens League. Leland, Henry. Michigan. Social Classes. 1912-24. *1925*
—. Dewey, John. Education. Social change. 1890-1979. *1834*
—. Dewey, John. Educational Reform. Europe. 1800-1960. *1866*
—. Discrimination, Educational. Disfranchisement. Middle Classes. Negro Suffrage. North Carolina. Public Finance. Whites. 1880-1910. *2316*
—. Educational reform. Georgia (Atlanta). Illinois (Chicago). New York City. Teachers. 1890-1920. *2336*
—. Elections. Ohio (Cincinnati). Physicians. Professionalism. Public health. 1890-1900. *2021*
—. Elections (gubernatorial). Tennessee. ca 1890-1906. *2081*
—. Elections (presidential). Hoover, Herbert C. Republican Party. Senate. 1930-32. *2369*
—. Elites. Hays, Samuel P. Ideology. Professionalism. Wiebe, Robert. 20c. *1971*
—. Federal Government. Frazier, Lynn J. Governors. Indians. North Dakota. 1916-40. *1538*
—. Federal government. New Deal. Press. Reform. 1890's-1930's. *1534*
—. Federalism. Legislation. States' rights. 1880-1930. *1959*
—. Feminism. Industry. Legislation. 1919-33. *2401*
—. Feminism. Kindergarten. Motherhood. 1860-1920. *1932*
—. Flynn, Dennis T. House of Representatives. McGuire, Bird S. Oklahoma. 1901-07. *1905*
—. Football. Johnson, Owen *(Stover at Yale).* Muckraking. 1911-20. *1998*
—. Forssell, G. D. Iowa. Lectures. Minnesota. Social Conditions. 1890-95. *957*
—. Fundamentalism. Long, Huey P. North Central States. Populism. Smith, Gerald L. K. 1934-48. *362*
—. German Americans. Labor Unions and Organizations. Socialism. Wisconsin. 1900-12. *2103*
—. Gitteau, William B. Hamilton, J. Kent. Ohio (Toledo). Public Schools. Reform. 1898-1921. *2330*
—. Government. Liberalism. Richberg, Donald Randall. 1900-60. *274*
—. Government Regulation. North Carolina. Populism. Railroads. Russell, Daniel. 1894-98. *1369*
—. Hearst, William Randolph. New Deal. 1930-35. *2488*
—. Historiography. 1900-20's. *1988*
—. Historiography. Imperialism. Leuchtenburg, William E. 1890's-1910's. 1952-74. *2089*
—. Historiography. Imperialism. Leuchtenburg, William E. 1898-1916. 1952-75. *2023*
—. Historiography. Political Leadership. Quantitative Methods. 1950's-77. *1914*
—. Housing. Kentucky (Louisville). Poverty. 1900-10. *1927*
—. Illinois (Chicago). Post, Louis F. *Public* (newspaper). Single tax movement. 1898-1919. *1904*
—. Institutions. Social Organization. Violence. 1880's-1910's. *2082*
—. Judicial Administration. Juvenile delinquency. Sex discrimination. 1890's-1910's. *2072*
—. Kansas. Populism. Social Classes. 1885-1917. *10*
—. Kentucky. Political Reform. Stanley, A. O. State Politics. 1902-19. *1897*
—. Labor Reform. Social Classes. Women. 1882-1917. *2230*
—. Liberalism. *New Republic* (periodical). Science and Society. 1914-20. *2040*
—. Long, Huey P. Louisiana. Populism. State Government. 1891-1935. *1566*
—. Management, scientific. Taylor, Frederick W. 1880's-1900's. *2248*

—. Mann Act (US, 1910). Prostitution. Women. 1910. *2003*
—. Medicine, preventive. Milk scandal. Political Corruption. Public health. Rhode Island (Providence). 1913. *1915*
—. Middle Classes. Political Reform. ca 1880-1920. *1871*
—. Middle Classes. Reform. Voting and Voting Behavior. Wisconsin. 1890's-1917. *2127*
—. Morality. New York. Prohibition. Smith, Alfred E. Whitman, Charles. Woman Suffrage. 1911-18. *2116*
—. NAACP. Whites. 1909-10. *2095*
—. Neurology. Psychoanalysis. Putnam, James Sackson. Social change. 1895-1918. *2108*
—. New Jersey (Jersey City). Whittier House. 1890-1917. *2105*
—. New York. Platt, Thomas C. Public policy. Republican Party. State politics. 1890-1910. *2030*
—. Political Reform. Prohibition. Richards, Richard Olsen. South Dakota. Taxation. 1902-30. *1913*
—. Post, Louis F. Single Tax Movement. 1898-1913. *1903*
—. South. 1890-1920. *1960*
Prohibition. Abortion. Antiabortion movement. Anti-Saloon League. Pennsylvania. Politics. Pressure groups. 1890-1978. *1640*
—. Adventists. Constitutional Amendments (21st). 1932-34. *2612*
—. Alaska. Women's Christian Temperance Union. 1842-1917. *255*
—. Alcohol. Massachusetts, western. Romanelli, John. 1919-20. *2069*
—. Anti-Saloon League. New Mexico. 1910-17. *1901*
—. Anti-Saloon League. Peters, J. Sidney. Virginia. 1916-20. *1943*
—. Anti-Saloon League of America. Ohio. 1880-1912. *258*
—. Arizona. 1914. *1911*
—. Bootlegging. Depressions. Florida (Hernando County). Law enforcement. Liquor. 1929-33. *2359*
—. Bulkley, Robert J. Elections. Ohio. Senate. 1918-30. *2445*
—. Candler, Warren A. Methodist Episcopal Church, South. Political Campaigns (presidential). Religion. Smith, Alfred E. 1928. *2344*
—. Catholic Church. Zurcher, George. 1884-1920's. *1442*
—. City Politics. Illinois (Canton). Socialist Party. Whalen, Homer. 1911-20. *2093*
—. Colleges and Universities. Illinois Intercollegiate Prohibition Association. Protestantism. 1893-1920. *2059*
—. Colorado (Denver). Wickersham Committee (1931). 1907-33. *2381*
—. Congregationalism. Education. New Mexico (Albuquerque). Social gospel. 1900-17. *2101*
—. Constitutional Amendments (18th). 1920-33. *2387*
—. Constitutional Amendments (18th). Dean Act (1919). State Legislatures. Texas. 1917-33. *2368*
—. Constitutional Amendments (18th and 21st). Democratic Party. Raskob, John J. Roosevelt, Franklin D. 1928-33. *2536*
—. Constitutional Amendments (21st). Mormons. Utah. 1932-33. *2393*
—. Crime and Criminals. Louisiana (New Orleans). 1918-33. *2386*
—. Democracy. Democratic Party. Ethnicity. Nebraska. Republican Party. 1907-20. *1937*
—. Democracy. Political Speeches. Women. 1920-34. *2356*
—. Dever, William. Elections (mayoral). Ethnic groups. Illinois (Chicago). Negroes. 1923-27. *2350*
—. Elections (presidential). New York. Republican Party. 1884. *1473*
—. Ethnicity. Local option. Michigan. 1889-1917. *1928*
—. Farwell, Arthur Burrage. Hyde Park Protective Association. Illinois (Chicago). Reform. 1885-1936. *1912*
—. Florida (Miami). Law Enforcement. Smuggling. 1896-1920. *1948*
—. Idaho. State Politics. 1932-35. *2575*
—. Iowa. Political parties. State Politics. 19c. *1445*
—. Kentucky. McChesney, Henry V. Morrow, Edwin P. Political Campaigns (gubernatorial). Stanley, Augustus Owsley. 1915. *1873*

—. Law Enforcement. Northwest Territories. Royal Canadian Mounted Police. 1874-91. *1460*
—. Local option. Louisiana (Shreveport). Voting and Voting Behavior. 1950-52. *2680*
—. Morality. New York. Progressivism. Smith, Alfred E. Whitman, Charles. Woman Suffrage. 1911-18. *2116*
—. Mormons. Utah. 1900's-1910's. *2039*
—. Nevada. State Politics. 1880-1933. *257*
—. New York. Voting and Voting Behavior. 1846. *896*
—. North Carolina (Whittier). Robbins, Raymond. 1920's-32. *2343*
—. Ohio. Woman's Christian Temperance Union. 1874-85. *1483*
—. Ontario. Racism. Reform. 1890-1915. *18*
—. Pacific Northwest. Reform. Weed, Ada M. Women's rights. 1858-1910. *327*
—. Political Corruption. Wyoming (Casper). 1919-33. *2388*
—. Political Reform. Progressivism. Richards, Richard Olsen. South Dakota. Taxation. 1902-30. *1913*
—. Women's Organization for National Prohibition Reform. 1929-33. *2396*
Proletariat. *See* Working class.
Propaganda *See also* Advertising; Public Opinion.
—. Abolition Movement. Antiwar sentiment. Mexican War. Ohio. Protestant Churches. 1847. *561*
—. Antislavery Sentiments. 1693-1859. *140*
—. Armies. Films (documentaries). Heisler, Stuart. *Negro Soldier* (film). Race Relations. World War II. 1944. *2621*
—. Bentham, Jeremy. Birth control. Carlile, Richard. Feminism. Great Britain. Owen, Robert Dale. Place, Francis. Wright, Frances. 1790-1840. *817*
—. Canada. English Canadians. Immigrants. Puttee, Arthur. Radicals and Radicalism. Water Conservation. ca 1888-1913. *1327*
—. Catholic Church. École Sociale Populaire. Quebec (Montreal). Syndicalism. Working Class. 1911-49. *1806*
—. Communalism. Cooperatives. 1830's-50's. *546*
—. Communism. Kollontai, Aleksandra. Norway. Russia. World War I. 1915-16. *2046*
—. London, Jack. Socialism. 1905-08. *2123*
Property *See also* Eminent Domain; Income; Real Estate.
—. Cherokee Indians. Christianity. Indian-White Relations. Missions and Missionaries. Social Change. Women. 19c. *107*
—. Crime and Criminals. George, Henry. Land. Monopolies. Technology. 19c-20c. *1033*
—. Freedom. Individualism. Social mobility. Socialism. 1750-1979. *85*
Property rights. Conservation movement. Federal Policy. Lumber and Lumbering. Pacific Northwest. Public Lands. 1870's-90's. *1323*
—. Reconstruction. South. State legislatures. Women. 1865-95. *1103*
Proslavery Sentiments *See also* Antislavery Sentiments.
—. Abolition Movement. Democratic Party. New York (Utica). Riots. 1835. *709*
—. Abolition Movement. Emancipation. Radicals and Radicalism. 1790-1865. *637*
—. Abolition Movement. Ideology. South Carolina. 1776-1861. *660*
—. Butler, Benjamin F. Civil War. 1861-64. *1018*
—. Butler Bill. Judiciary. Local politics. 1850's. *663*
—. Congress. Constitutions, State. English, William H. Kansas. 1857-58. *629*
Prosser, Gabriel. American Colonization Society. Gabriel's Insurrection. Monroe, James. Slave revolts. Virginia. 1800. *698*
Prostitution. 1870-1920. *28*
—. American Plan. Council of National Defense. Federal government. Social policy. Venereal disease. Voluntary associations. World War I. 1917-21. *2048*
—. Armies. Drugs. Mexico. New Mexico (Columbus). Pershing, John J. Venereal disease. 1916-17. *2068*
—. Birth control. Eugenics. Feminism. 1890's. *1006*
—. California (San Francisco). City Government. Crime and Criminals. Progressivism. 1910-14. *2085*
—. *Chicopee News.* Massachusetts, western. Massachusetts (Westfield). Newspapers. 1911. *2102*

—. Mann Act (US, 1910). Progressivism. Women. 1910. *2003*
Protest Marches. *See* Demonstrations; Political Protest.
Protestant Churches *See also* names of churches, e.g. Methodist Church, etc.; Protestantism.
—. Abolition Movement. Antiwar sentiment. Mexican War. Ohio. Propaganda. 1847. *561*
—. Church and Social Problems. Clergy. Reform. 1960's-70's. *2748*
—. Citizen Lobbies. Conscription, Military. Periodicals. Political Protest. 1940-59. *1570*
—. Converts. Evangelism. Louisiana (New Orleans). Slavery. 1800-61. *732*
—. Demonstrations. Ohio (Cincinnati). Temperance Movements. Women's Christian Temperance Union. 1874. *1446*
—. Farm tenancy. Mississippi. Theology. 1936-40. *2525*
—. Feminism. Social Conditions. South. Women. 1920's. *2339*
—. Missions and Missionaries. Organizations. Women. 1870's-90's. *1493*
Protestantism *See also* Evangelism; Fundamentalism; Noncomformists.
—. Abolition Movement. Great Britain. Historiography. 18c-19c. *792*
—. Adolescence. Boys. Canada. USA. Young Men's Christian Association. 1870-1920. *63*
—. Anti-Catholicism. Clergy. Ku Klux Klan. Republican Party. Rhode Island. 1915-32. *2441*
—. Anti-Catholicism. Ku Klux Klan. Saskatchewan. 1927-30. *1547*
—. Antislavery Sentiments. Great Britain. 1846. *696*
—. Baldwin, Theron. Higher education. Society for the Promotion of Collegiate and Theological Education at the West. 1843-73. *192*
—. Bengough, John Wilson. City government. *Grip* (periodical). Ontario (Toronto). Political Reform. 1873-1910. *370*
—. Bible. Catholic Church. Desmond, Humphrey. Religion in the Public Schools. Wisconsin. *Wisconsin ex rel. Frederick Weiss et al.* vs. *District School Board of School District 8* (1890). 1888-90. *1414*
—. Books. Child-rearing. Education. Pennsylvania (Philadelphia). Republicanism. 1780-1835. *577*
—. Catholic Church. Kansas. Religion in the Public Schools. 1861-1900. *1409*
—. Children. Coldwater State Public School. Crime and Criminals. Michigan. 1874-96. *1430*
—. Colleges and Universities. Illinois Intercollegiate Prohibition Association. Prohibition. 1893-1920. *2059*
—. Ecumenism. Evangelism. Social change. Social justice. Student Christian Movement. 19c-20c. *5*
—. Feminization. Historiography. Welter, Barbara. Women. 1820's-30's. 1970's. *910*
—. Finney, Charles Grandison. 1815-65. *569*
—. Ideology. North. Public Schools. Republican Party. Western states. 1870-1930. *204*
—. Methodism. Values. 1784-1924. *56*
—. Negroes. Socialism. Woodbey, George Washington. 1902-15. *1939*
—. Sex roles. Sunday School Movement. Women. 1790-1880. *180*
—. Social change. Women. World Council of Churches. 1945-75. *2917*
—. Talmage, Thomas DeWitt. 1869-1902. *1496*
Providence Association of Mechanics and Manufacturers. Educational reform. Rhode Island. Working Class. 1790's-1850. *853*
Provincial Freeman (newspaper). Antislavery Sentiments. Negroes. Newspapers. Ontario. Shadd, Mary Ann. 1852-93. *351*
Provincial Government. Catholic Church. Church and State. Public Charities Act (Canada, 1921). Quebec. Recessions. 1921-26. *1699*
—. Charter of the French Language (1977). French language. Politics. Quebec. 1977-78. *2766*
—. Commission on Industrial Accidents. Industry. Quebec. Workmen's Compensation. 1890-1978. *1584*
—. Depressions. Legislation. Public Welfare. Quebec. Taschereau, Louis Alexandre. ca 1934-36. *1700*
Provincial legislatures. Catholic Church. Church Schools. Manitoba. McCarthy, D'Alton. 1870-90. *1429*
—. Libel. Moore, William. Pennsylvania. Political Theory. Smith, William. 1750-60. *516*
Psychiatry *See also* Mental Illness; Psychology.

—. Mental health. Physicians. 1917-41. *1541*
—. Neurology. Social work. 1830's-1920's. *248*
Psychoanalysis *See also* Psychology.
—. Freudianism. New York City (Greenwich Village). Radicals and Radicalism. Sex. 1913-20. *1936*
—. Methodology. Political Protest. Social conditions. Students. 1900-75. *1616*
—. Neurology. Progressivism. Putnam, James Sackson. Social change. 1895-1918. *2108*
Psychohistory. Abolition Movement. Foster, Abigail Kelley. Foster, Stephen Symonds. Radicals and Radicalism. 1820-77. *288*
—. Abolitionists. Historians. 1800-60. 1930's-60's. *720*
—. Autobiography. Identity. Progressivism. Reformers. ca 1860-1920. *366*
Psychologists for Social Action. American Psychological Association. Equal opportunity. Lancaster Press. Racism. 1969-73. *2885*
Psychology *See also* Psychiatry; Psychoanalysis; Social Psychology.
—. Child Welfare. Human Rights. 1873-1914. 1970's. *143*
—. Hollingsworth, Leta. Women. 1886-1938. *1885*
—. Medicine. Mesmerism. Phrenology. Sunderland, La Roy. 1820-68. *880*
Public Administration *See also* Bureaucracies; Civil Service; Civil-Military Relations; Government.
—. Bureau of Indian Affairs. Collier, John. New Deal. Social sciences. 1933-45. *2599*
—. Executive power. Federal Regulation. Politics. President's Advisory Council on Executive Organization. Reform. 1937-79. *1705*
Public baths. Cities. Morality. Public health. 1880-1910. *1455*
—. City Government. Health. New York City. Progressivism. 1890-1915. *2121*
Public Charities Act (Canada, 1921). Catholic Church. Church and State. Provincial Government. Quebec. Recessions. 1921-26. *1699*
Public Finance. Discrimination, Educational. Disfranchisement. Middle Classes. Negro Suffrage. North Carolina. Progressivism. Whites. 1880-1910. *2316*
Public Health *See also* terms beginning with the word health; Diseases; Epidemics; Food Adulteration and Inspection; Hospitals; Medicine; Pollution; Sanitation; Water Supply.
—. Alabama. Diseases. 1839-1930. *2078*
—. American Medical Association. Cities. Hygiene. 1820-80. *879*
—. American Medical Association. Medicine and State. 1860's-1917. *224*
—. Bacteriology. Canada. Cities. 1900-30. *1644*
—. California (San Francisco). Chinatowns. Chinese Americans. Racism. 1870-1970. *1078*
—. Canniff, William. Medical Reform. Ontario (Toronto). 1869-90. *1468*
—. Cholera. Epidemics. Missouri (St. Louis). 1849-67. *862*
—. Cholera. Howard Association. Louisiana (New Orleans). Philanthropy. Yellow fever. 1837-78. *235*
—. Cities. Morality. Public baths. 1880-1910. *1455*
—. Cities. New York City. Pollution. Reform. Refuse disposal. Waring, George E., Jr. 1880-1917. *69*
—. Cities. Technology. Wastewater. Water Supply. 1850-1930. 1900H. *99*
—. City government. Ohio (Cincinnati). ca 1800-50. *891*
—. City politics. New York City. Social policy. Tuberculosis. 1889-1900. *1941*
—. City Politics. Ontario (Ottawa). Reform. Typhoid fever. 1911-12. *1635*
—. Congress. Fisher, Irving. Progressive era. 1906-13. *2115*
—. Diseases. 1870-1920. *253*
—. Elections. Ohio (Cincinnati). Physicians. Professionalism. Progressivism. 1890-1900. *2021*
—. Federal Government. Medical care. Poor. 1960-77. *2982*
—. Federal Policy. Nutrition. 1906-79. *1525*
—. Griscom, John H. (letters). Reform. Sanitation. Shattuck, Lemuel. 1843-47. *863*
—. Hastings, Charles. Neighborhood Workers' Association. Ontario (Toronto). Poverty. 1910-21. *1527*
—. Medicine, preventive. Milk scandal. Political Corruption. Progressivism. Rhode Island (Providence). 1913. *1915*

—. Medicine, preventive. Occupations. Rosen, George. Social History. 1930's-77. *442*
—. Military training. Muldoon, William. Physicians. Wood, Leonard. 1890-1915. *2044*
—. Sociology. Urbanization. 20c. *1671*
Public housing. Bauer, Catherine. Federal Policy. Reform. Wagner-Steagall Act (US, 1937). Wood, Edith Elmer. 1890's-1940's. *2479*
—. Bureaucrats. Pennsylvania (Philadelphia). 1929-41. *1528*
—. District of Columbia. Redevelopment. 1943-46. *2618*
—. Homesteading and Homesteaders. Interior Department. Minnesota (Duluth). Resettlement Administration. 1936-47. *2510*
Public Housing Authority. Housing and Urban Development Act (US, 1965, Section 23). Illinois (Chicago). Law. Negroes. Segregation. 1964-75. *2856*
Public interest. Business. Government regulation. Pressure Groups. 1975-79. *2953*
Public Lands. Cities. Neighborhoods. Trust for Public Land. 1975-80. *2756*
—. Conservation movement. Federal Policy. Lumber and Lumbering. Pacific Northwest. Property rights. 1870's-90's. *1323*
Public (newspaper). Illinois (Chicago). Post, Louis F. Progressivism. Single tax movement. 1898-1919. *1904*
Public Opinion *See also* Propaganda.
—. Abortion. 1800-1973. *93*
—. *Advocate of Peace* (periodical). American Peace Society. Foreign Relations. Pacifism. 1837-1932. *59*
—. American Revolution. Colleges and universities. State Legislatures. 1775-83. *485*
—. Anti-German sentiment. Bouck, William. Freedom of Assembly. Grange. Vigilantes. Washington (Walla Walla). World War I. 1918. *2161*
—. Antiwar Sentiment. Christianity. World War I. 1898-1918. *1889*
—. Capital punishment. Law Reform. Rhode Island. 1838-52. *888*
—. Capital punishment. Livingston, Edward. ca 1800-30. *887*
—. Capital punishment. Massachusetts (Boston). 1836-54. *886*
—. Civil rights. Congress. Demonstrations. Legislation. 1957-77. *2813*
—. Civil rights. Racism. 1820-1975. *147*
—. Colorado. Newspapers. Woman suffrage. 1870's. *1099*
—. Davis, David W. Idaho. Industrial Workers of the World. Nonpartisan League. Socialist Party. 1919-26. *2405*
—. Debo, Angie (personal account). Federal Government. Indians. Reform. 1969-76. *2703*
—. Decentralization. Educational Policy. New York City (Brownsville, Ocean Hill). 1962-71. *2971*
—. Demonstrations. Peace movements. Vietnam War. ca 1965-73. *2752*
—. Educational reform. 1960-80. *2970*
—. Hughes, Charles Evans. New York Public Service Commission Law (1907). Public utilities. Railroads. 1907-09. *2200*
—. Industrial Workers of the World. Justice Department. Labor Unions and Organizations. Nebraska. World War I. 1915-20. *2113*
—. Jews. Labor movement. Stereotypes. 1880's-1915. *2211*
—. Louisiana (New Orleans). Street, Electric Railway and Motor Coach Employees of America. Strikes. 1929-30. *2353*
—. Massachusetts (Marlboro). Shoe Industry. Strikes. 1898-99. *1300*
—. Mississippi. Negroes. Revels, Hiram Rhodes. Senate. 1870. *1202*
—. Prisons. 1790-1978. *239*
Public Policy. Air pollution. Environment. Legislation. 1967-78. *2763*
—. Altruism. Progressive movement. Technology. 1900-17. 1973. *1933*
—. Assimilation. Education. Indians. Micmac Indians. Nova Scotia. Religion. 1605-1872. *209*
—. Attitudes. Industry. National War Labor Board. Sex roles. Wages. Women. World War I. 1918-19. *2191*
—. Bethune, Mary McLeod. Equal opportunity. National Youth Administration. Negroes. Youth. 1935-44. *2594*
—. Bias. Political activism. 1952-76. *2753*
—. Birth control. Law. Medicine and State. 19c. *40*

Public Policy

—. Blumer, Herbert. Poverty. Social problems. 1960's-73. *2924*
—. British Columbia. Labor. Legislation. Natural resources. New Democratic Party. Social Democracy. Taxation. 1972-75. *2942*
—. Canada. Citizen Lobbies. Consumers' Association of Canada. 1947-77. *1587*
—. Canada. Colleges and Universities. Social Sciences. 1920-49. *1576*
—. Canada. Social security. USA. 1935-75. *1776*
—. Catholic Worker Movement. Equality. Human Rights. 1933-78. *1678*
—. Civil rights. Economic conditions. Income. 1948-75. *2861*
—. Civil Rights. Employment. Federal Government. State Government. 20c. *1572*
—. Civil rights movement. Integration. 1945-76. *1623*
—. Depressions. General Education Board. Rockefeller, John D. Secondary education. Social change. 1930's. *2478*
—. Discrimination, Employment. Equal opportunity. Law. 1964-72. *2949*
—. Economic Development. Forest Service. Minnesota, northeastern. Superior National Forest. Wilderness. 1923-26. *2437*
—. Economic planning. New Deal. 1932-41. *2539*
—. Florida. Governors. Race relations. 1954-76. *1552*
—. Income redistribution. Politics. 1961-73. *2951*
—. Minnesota. Politics. Welfare Mothers Movement. 1960-72. *2933*
—. New York. Platt, Thomas C. Progressivism. Republican Party. State politics. 1890-1910. *2030*

Public Records. Archives, National. Freedmen's Bureau. Reconstruction. Texas. 1865-76. *1147*

Public Schools *See also* Junior High Schools; Rural Schools; Schools.
—. Alabama (Mobile County). 1826. *831*
—. Anderson, James T. M. Anglicization. English language. Ethnic groups. Immigrants. Saskatchewan. 1918-23. *1856*
—. Anderson, James T. M. Anti-Catholicism. Saskatchewan. School Act (amended). Secularization. 1929-34. *1848*
—. Anglophobia. Censorship. City Politics. Illinois (Chicago). Libraries. Thompson, William Hale. 1927. *2454*
—. Authority. Communications Behavior. Parents. Textbooks. West Virginia (Kanawha County). 1974. *2958*
—. Boycotts. Mexican Americans. Presbyterian Church. Segregation. Texas (San Angelo). 1910-15. *2303*
—. British Columbia. Japanese Canadians. Minorities. 1900-72. *1562*
—. *Brown* v. *Board of Education* (US, 1954). Desegregation. Equality. Negroes. 1950's-74. *2817*
—. Bureaucracies. Centralization. Legislation. Missouri. State government. 1853. *846*
—. California (Alum Rock). Education. Parents. Vouchers. 1960's-70's. *2960*
—. California (Los Angeles). Curricula. Educational reform. Mexican Americans. 1920's-30's. *1842*
—. California (Orange County). *Mendez* v. *Westminster* (California, 1946). Mexican Americans. Segregation (de jure, de facto). 1850-1970's. *1865*
—. Canada. Girls. Home economics. Hoodless, Adelaide. 1890's-1900's. *215*
—. Cities. Educational Reform. Negroes. South. Teachers. 1865-90. *1238*
—. City Government. Maryland (Baltimore). Negroes. Political protest. 1865-1900. *1271*
—. Clergy. Episcopal Church, Protestant. Ingraham, Joseph Holt. Novels. Penal reform. Tennessee (Nashville). 1847-51. *584*
—. Compulsory education. Immigrants. Missouri (St. Louis). Truancy. 1905-07. *2313*
—. Courts. Discrimination, Educational. District of Columbia. Negroes. 1804-1974. *1844*
—. Decentralization Act (1969). Minorities. New York City (Brooklyn, Lower East Side). School boards. 1969-73. *2965*
—. Delaware. DuPont, Pierre S. Negroes. Philanthropy. 1918-30. *2451*
—. Desegregation. Federal Government. Law enforcement. South. 1954-73. *2824*
—. Desegregation. Florida (Jacksonville). Students. 1960's-70's. *2834*

SUBJECT INDEX

—. Discrimination, Educational. Harlan, John Marshall. *Joseph W. Cumming, James S. Harper and John Ladeveze* v. *School Board of Richmond County, Ga.* (US, 1899). Supreme Court. ca 1896-1907. *1194*
—. Downing, George T. Negroes. Rhode Island (Newport). School Integration. 1855-66. *841*
—. Dukhobors. Saskatchewan. 1905-50. *1855*
—. Educational Policy. 1840's-80's. *218*
—. Educational Policy. Lancaster, Joseph. *Richmond Enquirer* (newspaper). Ritchie, Thomas. Virginia. 1803-50. *840*
—. Educational Reform. Immigrants. New York (Buffalo). 1890-1916. *2332*
—. Educational Reform. Iowa. 1890-1900. *1421*
—. Educational reform. Meadows, Clarence W. Strayer, George D. Trent, W. W. West Virginia Education Association. 1932-58. *1837*
—. Educational reform. Social Classes. 1787-1973. *203*
—. Educators. Iowa. Modernization. 1890-1900. *1422*
—. Equal Rights League. Pennsylvania. School Integration. 1834-81. *208*
—. Giteau, William B. Hamilton, J. Kent. Ohio (Toledo). Progressivism. Reform. 1898-1921. *2330*
—. Great Britain. Sports. Upper Canada. Upper Classes. 1830-75. *210*
—. Ideology. North. Protestantism. Republican Party. Western states. 1870-1930. *204*
—. Illinois (Chicago). Local Politics. Negroes. 1910-41. *1845*
—. Integration. Litigation. NAACP. North. 1954-73. *2841*
—. Mexican Americans. Minorities in Politics. Self-perception. Texas (southern). 1930's-69. *1863*
—. Michigan (Pontiac). Race relations. School Integration. 1971-74. *2827*
—. *National School Service* (bulletin). Patriotism. Reform. 1918-19. *2337*
—. Negroes. New York City (Jamaica). Segregation. 1895-1900. *1210*
—. Reform. Socialism. Wisconsin (Milwaukee). Working class. 1890-1920. *2329*
—. School Integration. 1954-1976. *2846*

Public services. City Government. Civil rights movement. Florida. Negroes. 1960-76. *2814*

Public Utilities *See also* Corporations; Railroads; Water Supply.
—. Antitrust. French Canadians. Hamel, Philippe. Nationalism. Quebec (Quebec). 1929-34. *1757*
—. Hughes, Charles Evans. New York Public Service Commission Law (1907). Public opinion. Railroads. 1907-09. *2200*

Public Welfare *See also* Charities; Child Welfare; Children; Hospitals; Poorhouses; Social Security; Social Work.
—. 1932-64. *1582*
—. Aid to Families with Dependent Children. Illinois (Cook County). Mothers' pensions. 1911-75. *2107*
—. Alden, Augustus E. Brownlow, William G. Carpetbaggers. City Government. Education. Reconstruction. Republican Party. Tennessee (Nashville). 1865-69. *1049*
—. Angers, François-Albert. Catholic Church. Quebec. Social justice. 1950-80. *2931*
—. Attitudes. Family. Federal Government. 1962-80. *2929*
—. British Columbia (Vancouver). 1919-20. *1642*
—. Bureaucracies. Professionalization. 1900-29. *1825*
—. Canada. City Government. Depressions. ca 1930-40. *1695*
—. Canada. Income. Legislation. Mothers. ca 1900-39. *1815*
—. Charities Organization Society Movement. Illinois (Chicago). 1880-1930. *1996*
—. Connecticut Asylum for the Deaf and Dumb. Federal government. Kentucky Deaf and Dumb Asylum. 1819-26. *901*
—. Conservatism. Elites. Ontario (Ottawa). Political Leadership. 1880-1912. *1310*
—. Courts. 1925-75. *1774*
—. Depressions. Legislation. Provincial government. Quebec. Taschereau, Louis Alexandre. ca 1934-36. *1700*
—. Depressions. Pennsylvania (Philadelphia). 1820-28. *544*
—. Discrimination. Negroes. South. 1865-90. *1236*

Puritans

—. Eisenhower, Dwight D. (administration). Federal Policy. Legislation. Reform. 1950-60. *2659*
—. Federal Government. Hoover, Herbert C. Roosevelt, Franklin D. 1920-37. *2345*
—. Federal government. Legislation. United Mine Workers of America (Welfare and Retirement Fund). 1945-70's. *2658*
—. Federal Policy. Presidents. 1933-78. *1793*
—. Food Stamp Act (US, 1964). 1939-77. *2937*
—. Great Society. Johnson, Lyndon B. Rhetoric. 1963-65. *2764*
—. Great Society. Johnson, Lyndon B. (administration). Social Conditions. 1964-76. *2936*
—. Indians. Lawsuits. Legislation. 1957-77. *2706*
—. Legislation. Political Parties. 1933-54. *1812*
—. Liberalism. Partisanship. Professionalism. State government. 1960's-70's. *2952*
—. McAlister, Alexander W. North Carolina. 1910-45. *1569*
—. National Welfare Rights Organization. Political Protest. 1967-74. *2941*
—. New Deal. Political Attitudes. South Dakota. 1930's-70's. *2470*
—. Octavia Hill Association. Pennsylvania (Philadelphia). ca 1890-1909. *2097*
—. Pennsylvania. Politics. 1967-73. *2943*
—. Reform. Welfare State. 1935-80. *2946*
—. Scholarship. *Social Service Review* (periodical). Social work. 1927-77. *1567*

Public Welfare Amendments (1962). Social services. 1962-76. *2928*

Public works. Depressions. Frankfurter, Felix. Keynes, John Maynard. New Deal. 1932-35. *2473*
—. Economic policy. Foreign Policy. New Deal. Roosevelt, Franklin D. 1933. *2555*
—. Nevada (Las Vegas). New Deal. 1933-40. *2554*

Public Works Administration. Construction. Employment. Ickes, Harold. Negroes. Quotas. 1933-40. *2535*

Publicity *See also* Advertising; Propaganda.
—. Burnham, Daniel Hudson. City planning. Illinois (Chicago). Moody, Walter D. *(Wacker's Manual of the Plan of Chicago).* Progressivism. Reform. 1909-11. *2071*
—. Civil-Military Relations. Labor. War Manpower Commission. Women. World War II. 1942-45. *2650*
—. Democracy. Mass Media. Reform. 1900-29. *1624*

Publishers and Publishing *See also* Books; Editors and Editing; Press; Printing.
—. Abolitionists. Antislavery materials. Censorship. 1852-55. *772*
—. Discrimination. Editors and Editing. Negro (term). 1898-1975. *1590*

Pueblo Indians. Civil Rights. Indian Civil Rights Act (US, 1968). Natural law. *Santa Clara Pueblo* v. *Martinez* (US, 1977). Tribal government. 1939-77. *2789*
—. Indian-White Relations. Legislation. New Mexico (Taos; Blue Lake). Rites and Ceremonies. 20c. *1718*

Pueblo Indians (Hopi). Educators. Ethnographers. Evangelism. Indians (reservations). Sullivan, John H. Taylor, Charles A. 1870-89. *1050*

Puerto Rico. American Federation of Labor. Gompers, Samuel. Iglesias Pantín, Santiago. Labor Unions and Organizations. 1897-1920's. *2210*

Pullman Strike. Debs, Eugene V. Federal Government. Illinois (Blue Island). Strikes. 1894. *1317*
—. Illinois (Pullman). Labor Unions and Organizations. Railroads. 1880-94. *1325*

Pulte Medical College. Coeducation. Homeopathy. Medical Education. Ohio (Cincinnati). 1873-79. *1403*

Puritans *See also* Church of England; Congregationalism; Noncomformists.
—. Antinomianism. 1630's. *491*
—. Antinomianism. Arminianism. New England. 1630-60. *482*
—. Antinomianism. Emerson, Ralph Waldo. Sermons. 1820's-30's. *570*
—. Attitudes. New England. Slavery. 1641-1776. *521*
—. Cooke, Parsons. Industrialization. Massachusetts (Ware). Missions and Missionaries. 19c. *906*
—. Corporal punishment. Eaton, Nathaniel. Harvard University. Massachusetts (Cambridge). Trials. 1638. *495*

Puritans

—. Great Britain. Law reform. New England. 1620-60. *501*
—. New England. Slavery. 1652-1795. *528*
Putnam, James Sackson. Neurology. Progressivism. Psychoanalysis. Social change. 1895-1918. *2108*
Puttee, Arthur. Čačić, Tomo. Ethnic Groups. Kjelt, Ole. Krat, Pavlo. Leftism. Mäkelä, A. B. Political Protest. Scarlett, Sam. 1907-34. *1561*
—. Canada. English Canadians. Immigrants. Propaganda. Radicals and Radicalism. Water Conservation. ca 1888-1913. *1327*

Q

Quackenbos, Mary Grace. Florida. Justice Department. Labor recruitment. New York City. Peonage. Turpentine industry. 1905-10. *2267*
Quackery. American Medical Association. Arkansas Medical Society. Brinkley, John R. Medicine (practice of). 1920-42. *2583*
Quakers. *See* Friends, Society of.
Quality of life. Civil Rights. Nebraska (Omaha). Negroes. Social services. Urban League. World War II. 1928-50. *2639*
Quantitative Methods *See also* Methodology.
—. Historiography. Political Leadership. Progressivism. 1950's-77. *1914*
Quebec. Agrarianism. Angers, François-Albert. Cooperatives. Economic Theory. 1930-80. *1594*
—. Agricultural Cooperatives. Labor Unions and Organizations. 1900-30. *1743*
—. Agricultural Cooperatives. Syndicalism. 1922-79. *1758*
—. Agricultural Organizations. 1760-1930. 1900H. *148*
—. American Federation of Labor. French Canadians. Gompers, Samuel. 1900-14. *1741*
—. Angers, François-Albert. Catholic Church. Public welfare. Social justice. 1950-80. *2931*
—. Barry, Robertine (pseud. Françoise). Feminism. Gleason, Anne-Marie (pseud. Madeleine). Journalism. Social Conditions. 1900-19. *1535*
—. Blanchet, François. Medical reform. 1776-1824. *861*
—. Catholic Church. Church and State. Provincial Government. Public Charities Act (Canada, 1921). Recessions. 1921-26. *1699*
—. Catholic Church. Fédération Nationale Saint-Jean-Baptiste. Feminism. Gérin-Lajoie, Marie. 1907-33. *1039*
—. Catholic Church. Feminism. Religious Orders. Women. 1640-1975. *21*
—. Catholic Church. International Union of Catholic Women's Leagues (congress). Italy (Rome). Woman suffrage. 1922. *1734*
—. Charter of the French Language (1977). French language. Politics. Provincial government. 1977-78. *2766*
—. Class struggle. Equality. French language. Intellectuals. Nationalism. 1960's-70's. *2693*
—. Commission on Industrial Accidents. Industry. Provincial Government. Workmen's Compensation. 1890-1978. *1584*
—. Cooperatives. 1940-78. *2955*
—. Depressions. Legislation. Provincial government. Public Welfare. Taschereau, Louis Alexandre. ca 1934-36. *1700*
—. Historiography. Social Credit. 1936-65. *1765*
—. Labor Unions and Organizations. National Trades and Labour Congress. Ontario (Kitchener). Trades and Labour Congress of Canada. 1892-1902. *1805*
Quebec (Cowansville). Communist Party. Ontario. Silk industry. Strikes. 1931. *1778*
Quebec (Gaspé Peninsula). *Actualité Économique* (periodical). Cooperative movement. Individualism. Minville, Esdras. 1924-43. *1795*
—. *Actualité Économique* (periodical). Cooperative movement. Individualism. Minville, Esdras. Nationalism. 1924-40. *1794*
—. Catholic Church. Ross, François Xavier. Social Conditions. 1923-45. *374*
Quebec (Hull). Labor. Match industry. Syndicat Catholique des Allumettières. Women. 1919-24. *1775*
Quebec (Montreal). Catholic Church. École Sociale Populaire. Propaganda. Syndicalism. Working Class. 1911-49. *1806*
—. Strikes. Teamsters, International Brotherhood of. 1864. *1315*

Quebec (Quebec). Antitrust. French Canadians. Hamel, Philippe. Nationalism. Public Utilities. 1929-34. *1757*
—. Catholic Church. Immigrants. Irish Americans. McMahon, Patrick. Poor. St. Bridget's Home. 1847-1972. *244*
Queen, John. Local Government. Manitoba (Winnipeg). Socialism. Taxation. 1909-42. *1645*
Quinlan, Patrick. Courts. Industrial Workers of the World. Labor. New Jersey (Paterson). Progressivism. 1913-17. *2275*
Quotas. Construction. Employment. Ickes, Harold. Negroes. Public Works Administration. 1933-40. *2535*

R

Race. Attitudes. Canada. English Canadians. Sex. Woman Suffrage. ca 1877-1918. *1*
—. Citizenship. Courts. Mexican Americans. Nationality. 1846-97. *135*
—. Class consciousness. NAACP. Negroes. Pennsylvania (Philadelphia). 1930's. *2566*
—. Counts, George S. Educational reform. Liberalism. 1929-34. *2379*
—. Depressions. Ethnicity. Progressive education. 1929-45. *2513*
Race Relations *See also* Acculturation; Busing; Discrimination; Emigration; Ethnology; Human Relations; Immigration; Indian-White Relations; Negroes.
—. Abolition Movement. Freedmen. Labor. Slavery. 1830-63. *613*
—. Adventists. Humphrey, James K. New York City (Harlem). Sabbath Day Adventist Church. Utopia Park. 1920's-30's. *1648*
—. Agricultural labor. Boycotts. Labor Unions and Organizations. South Carolina. 1886-95. *1196*
—. Agriculture. Arizona (Salt River Valley). Discrimination. Japanese (Issei). 1934-35. *2582*
—. Alcorn University. Mississippi. Negroes. Revels, Hiram Rhodes. Senate. ca 1870's. *1256*
—. American Revolution. North Carolina. Slave revolts. 1775-1802. *622*
—. Arizona (Salt River Valley). Depressions. Farmers. Japanese Americans. 1934-35. *2469*
—. Arkansas. Negroes. Republican Party. 1867-1928. *115*
—. Arkansas. Republican Party. 1890's-1924. *2364*
—. Armies. Films (documentaries). Heisler, Stuart. *Negro Soldier* (film). Propaganda. World War II. 1944. *2621*
—. Association for Promoting Colored Volunteers. Civil War. Military Recruitment. Negroes. New York. Union League. 1861-65. *1255*
—. Authority. Reconstruction. Rhetoric. 1865-68. *1206*
—. Baptists, Southern. Leadership. Texas. 1954-68. *2890*
—. Bible. Presbyterian Church, Southern. South. 1861-1980. *98*
—. Black Muslims. Ghettos. Malcolm X. Political Leadership. 1940-65. *461*
—. *Boston Daily Evening Voice* (newspaper). Equality. Labor Unions and Organizations. Massachusetts. Working Class. 1864-67. *998*
—. British Columbia. California. Discrimination. Gold Rushes. Negroes. 1849-66. *592*
—. Brotherhood of Timber Workers. Industrial Workers of the World. Louisiana. Lumber and Lumbering. Texas. 1910-13. *2215*
—. Brotherhood of Timber Workers. Louisiana, western. Lumber and Lumbering. Southern Lumber Operators' Association. Texas, eastern. 1911-13. *2217*
—. Brown, John. Harpers Ferry raid. 1858-59. *722*
—. California (San Francisco Bay). Courts Martial and Courts of Inquiry. Mare Island Mutiny. Navies. Negroes. Port Chicago Naval Magazine. 1944-48. *2652*
—. Canada. Japanese Canadians. Removals, forced. World War II. 1890's-1940's. *1694*
—. Capitalism. Carver, George Washington. Marxism. Myths and Symbols. South. 1896-1950's. *1604*
—. Carter, William Hodding, Jr. Editors and Editing. Mississippi. Political Reform. ca 1930-60. *340*
—. Chesnutt, Charles W. Politics. Washington, Booker T. 1880-1915. *1153*

Race Relations

—. Cincinnati Better Housing League. Housing. Ohio. 1916-39. *1573*
—. Cities. Ethnicity. Negroes. Social organization. Valentine, Charles. 1865-1975. *1697*
—. Civic Unity Committee. Defense industries. Japanese Americans. Negroes. Washington (Seattle). World War II. 1940-45. *2624*
—. Civil Disobedience. King, Martin Luther, Jr. Nonviolence. 1954-68. *2891*
—. Civil rights. 1960-70's. *2836*
—. Civil rights. Legislation. Population. Riots. Tennessee (Memphis). 1865-66. *1209*
—. Civil rights movement. Episcopal Church, Protestant. Theology. 1800-1965. *2849*
—. Civil rights movement. South. Women. 1960's. *2907*
—. Class conflict. Segregation. South. 1865-90's. *1280*
—. Coal Mines and Mining. Knights of Labor. United Mine Workers of America. West Virginia, southern. 1880-94. *1140*
—. Colored Farmers' Alliance. Tennessee. 1888-91. *1164*
—. Colored National Labor Union. Florida. Labor Unions and Organizations. National Union of Negro Labor. Negroes. Reconstruction. 1865-75. *1259*
—. Community relations. Police. Riots. 1940-49. *2689*
—. Congo Reform Association. Park, Robert Ezra. Tuskegee Institute. 1905-13. *2025*
—. Conservatism. DuBois, W. E. B. Negroes. Periodicals. Radicals and Radicalism. Washington, Booker T. 1900-10. *1983*
—. Discrimination, Employment. Military Service (enlistees). Navies. Negroes. Segregation. 1798-1970's. 1970D 1900H. *41*
—. Economic Conditions. Georgia (Atlanta). Political change. 1960's-73. *2812*
—. Economic Conditions. Negro suffrage. Washington, Booker T. 1895. *1149*
—. Economic Conditions. Negroes. Social change. Violence. 1960's. *2851*
—. Editors and Editing. Mitchell, John P. *Richmond Planet* (newspaper). Virginia. ca 1883-1929. *407*
—. Elites. Politics. Riots. 1960's-70's. *2857*
—. Ethnic groups. Imperialism. James, William. 1899-1910. *2033*
—. Evangelicalism. Jones, Charles Colcock. South. Utopias. 1804-63. *567*
—. Evangelism. Keeble, Marshall. 1878-1968. *412*
—. Fisk University. Johnson, Charles S. Negroes. UNESCO. 1900-56. *346*
—. Fisk University. Tennessee (Nashville). Youth Movements. 1909-26. *2397*
—. Florida. Governors. Public Policy. 1954-76. *1552*
—. Florida. Law. Segregation. Social customs. 1865-1977. *141*
—. Freedmen. Louisiana (Madison Parish). Plantations. Reconstruction. 1863-74. *978*
—. Freedmen. North. Schools. Teachers. Virginia (Lexington). 1867. *1405*
—. Freedmen's Bureau. Kentucky. Noble, Thomas. Reconstruction. Schools. 1865-70. *1190*
—. Freedmen's Bureau. Schools. West Virginia (Berkeley, Jefferson counties). 1865-68. *1264*
—. Freedmen's Village. Land Tenure. Virginia (Arlington). 1872-1900. *1183*
—. Genovese, Eugene D. Land reform. Reconstruction. Social Classes. South Carolina (Edgefield County). Woodward, C. Vann. 1865-90. *963*
—. Georgia. Rhetoric. Washington, Booker T. (Atlanta Exposition Address). 1895. *1167*
—. Historiography. Washington, Booker T. 1898-1972. *1161*
—. Immigration. Japanese. Miller, Kelly. Negroes. 1906-24. *1601*
—. Industrialization. Labor Unions and Organizations. Negroes. 19c-20c. *1819*
—. International Longshoremen's and Warehousemen's Union. South Central and Gulf States. 1866-1920. *2236*
—. King, Martin Luther, Jr. 1968. *2901*
—. Knights of Labor. South. 1880-87. *1217*
—. Labor Unions and Organizations. Longshoremen. Louisiana (New Orleans). 1850's-1976. *1776*
—. Lawyers. NAACP. 1909-76. *1646*
—. Louisiana (St. Landry). Reconstruction. Republican Party. Riots. 1868. *1151*

Race Relations

—. Medical care. Mormon, Square. Poor People's Health Council. Rossville Health Center. Tennessee (Fayette County). 1960's-70's. *2821*
—. Metropolitan areas. Segregation, residential. 1960-70. *2896*
—. Michigan (Pontiac). Public schools. School Integration. 1971-74. *2827*
—. Minorities. Pluralism. 1968-73. *2697*
—. Negroes. Newspapers. Political Protest. World War II. 1941-45. *2625*
—. Negroes. Pennsylvania (Philadelphia). Riots. 1968. *2820*
—. Negroes. Political Parties. Virginia (Richmond). 1865. *1231*
—. New York City. Social Problems. Urban League. 1919-59. *1652*
—. Newspapers. Sex. Smith, Lillian. South. 20c. *422*
—. Norfolk *Journal and Guide* (newspaper). Virginia. Washington, Booker T. Young, Plummer B. 1904-20's. *2096*
—. Politics. Student Nonviolent Coordinating Committee. Values. 1961-66. *2889*
—. Race Relations. 1954-75. *2898*
—. Race Relations. 1954-75. *2898*
—. Reform. Social gospel. 1877-98. *1043*
—. School integration. Supreme Court decisions. 1954-74. *2865*
—. Segregation. South. 1865-90. *1237*
—. Social change. 1915-78. *1661*
—. West Virginia Human Rights Commission. 1961-66. *2887*

Racism. Abolition Movement. Africa. American Colonization Society. Colonization. Republicanism. ca 1815-35. *762*
—. Abolition Movement. Connecticut (Canterbury). Crandall, Prudence. Garrison, William Lloyd. Sexism. 1830-40. *550*
—. Abolition Movement. Garrison, William Lloyd. New England. 1841. *717*
—. Abolitionists. Antislavery sentiments. 1646-1974. *110*
—. Africa. Industrial arts education. Pan-Africanism. South. 1879-1940. *214*
—. Agricultural Labor. Economic Structure. Freedmen. Reconstruction. Texas. 1865-74. *1263*
—. Alabama. Freedmen's Bureau. Reconstruction. Swayne, Wager. 1865-68. *1279*
—. Alabama. Military. Randolph, Ryland. Reconstruction. Trials. Tuscaloosa *Independent Monitor*. 1868. *986*
—. Alberta. Chinese Canadians. Japanese Canadians. 1920-50. *1657*
—. American Colonization Society. Finley, Robert. 1816-40. *648*
—. American Federation of Labor. Fascism. Gompers, Samuel. Immigration. Jingoism. 1850-1924. *394*
—. American Psychological Association. Equal opportunity. Lancaster Press. Psychologists for Social Action. 1969-73. *2885*
—. American Revolution. Antislavery sentiments. Presbyterian Church. 1750-1818. *769*
—. Ames, Jessie Daniel. Association of Southern Women for the Prevention of Lynching. Lynching. South. Women. 1930's. *2516*
—. Anti-Catholicism. Chinese Americans. Nativism. Pacific Northwest. ca 1840-1945. *11*
—. Antislavery Sentiments. Clergy. Kentucky. 1791-1824. *603*
—. Antislavery Sentiments. Free Soil Party. Illinois. Republican Party. 1848-60. *740*
—. Art. Harlem Renaissance. Johnson, Charles S. 1920's. *2426*
—. Asian Americans. Employment. Ethnicity. Legislation. Naturalization. 1850-20c. *65*
—. Asian Canadians. British Columbia. 1900-50. *1674*
—. Asian Canadians. British Columbia. Immigration. Politics. 1850-1914. *1524*
—. Assimilation. Indians. Reform. 1880-1900. *944*
—. Attitudes. Housing. Negroes. Ohio (Toledo). United Automobile Workers of America. 1967-73. *2805*
—. Bacon's Rebellion. Class struggle. Slavery. Social control. Virginia. 1660-92. *472*
—. Bakke, Allan. *Regents of the University of California v. Allan Bakke* (US, 1978). Social change. 1960's-78. *2794*
—. Baptists, Southern. Churches. Education. Reconstruction. 1865-76. *1267*
—. Bilbo, Theodore G. Employment. Fair Employment Practices Committee. Filibusters. Mississippi. Senate. 1941-46. *2617*
—. Bond, Hugh Lennox. Ideology. Maryland. Republicans (Radical). ca 1861-68. *1002*
—. California. Elections (presidential). Republican Party. Slavery. 1860. *757*
—. California. Slavery. State Politics. 1849-60. *755*
—. California (San Francisco). Chinatowns. Chinese Americans. Public health. 1870-1970. *1078*
—. California (San Francisco). Chinese Americans. Law. Negroes. Political Leadership. 1865-75. *1184*
—. Caryl, Charles W. Colorado. New Era Union. Progressive Era. Utopias. 1858-1926. *1509*
—. Catholic Church. Democracy. Intellectuals. Liberalism. 1924-59. *1560*
—. Census Bureau. Cornell University. Economics. Negroes. Progressivism. Willcox, Walter F. 1895-1910. *1870*
—. Charleston *Daily Courier* (newspaper). Charleston *Mercury* (newspaper). Constitutional conventions, state. Reconstruction. South Carolina. 1867-68. *1205*
—. Cherokee Indians. Freedmen. Indian Territory. 1839-88. *1165*
—. Civil rights. Federal Policy. Interest Groups. Populism. Private sector. Wallace, George C. 1960's. *2899*
—. Civil rights. Negroes. Politics. 1940's. *1622*
—. Civil rights. Public Opinion. 1820-1975. *147*
—. Civil rights. Spooner, John Coit. 1897-1907. *2156*
—. Civil War. Emancipation. Ohio. State Politics. 1863-65. *1182*
—. Class struggle. Eugenics. Fisher, Irving. Progressivism. 1890's-1920. *1869*
—. Coal Mines and Mining. Labor Unions and Organizations. Strikes. United Mine Workers of America. 1894-1920. *2272*
—. Cocking, Walter D. Georgia, University of. Holley, Joseph Winthrop. Talmadge, Eugene. 1941. *2643*
—. Colleges and Universities (black). Fort Valley State College. Georgia (Peach County). *Hunnicutt et al. v. Burge et al.* (Georgia, 1972). School Integration. 1972-78. *2800*
—. Columbians, Inc. Georgia (Atlanta). Patriotism. 1946-47. *2665*
—. Communist Party. National Maritime Union. Negroes. United Electrical, Radio and Machine Workers of America. World War II. 1941-45. *2622*
—. Convict lease system. Economic Conditions. Georgia. Prisons. 1868-1909. *1044*
—. Discrimination. Jews. Negroes. 1890-1915. *1938*
—. Douglass, Frederick. Journalism. New York City. 1841-47. *408*
—. Economic Conditions. Reconstruction. Social Classes. South. 1865-76. *1071*
—. Employment. Feminism. Organizations. Social classes. World War II. 1942-45. *2629*
—. Employment. Housing. Negroes. Voting and Voting Behavior. 1960's-70's. *2810*
—. Episcopal Church, Protestant. New York City. Newspapers. Riots. St. Philip's Church. Williams, Peter, Jr. 1830-50. *671*
—. Federal Government. Legislation. Nevada. Newspapers. 1866-68. *976*
—. Film industry. Griffith, David W. *(Birth of a Nation)*. Negroes. 1915-18. *1918*
—. Hastie, William H. Military. Negroes. Stimson, Henry L. World War II. 1940-43. *2636*
—. Hastie, William H. Military reform. World War II. 1940-43. *2637*
—. Labor. Local Politics. Missouri. Reconstruction. St. Louis *Daily Press* (newspaper). 1864-66. *1339*
—. Law. 1619-1896. *127*
—. Mexican Americans. Sterilization. Women. 20c. *2704*
—. Missouri (St. Louis). Political Leadership. Social Classes. Strikes. Workingmen's Party. 1877. *1338*
—. Negro Suffrage. Reconstruction. Rhetoric. Ridicule. South. 1866-70. *1207*
—. Ontario. Prohibition. Reform. 1890-1915. *18*
—. South Carolina Association. South Carolina (Charleston). Vigilantes. 1823-50's. *618*

Radburn (settlement). City Planning. Garden cities. New Jersey. Suburbs. 1927-79. *1332*
Radek, Karl. Carlson, Oliver (reminiscences). Communist Party. Foster, William Z. Politburo. Trotskyism. USSR. 1924-35. *1548*

Radicals

Radicals and Radicalism *See also* Leftism; Political Reform; Revolution.
—. Abolition Movement. Emancipation. Proslavery Sentiments. 1790-1865. *637*
—. Abolition Movement. Foster, Abigail Kelley. Foster, Stephen Symonds. Psychohistory. 1820-77. *288*
—. Abolition Movement. Giddings, Joshua Reed. Ohio. State Politics. 1840-60. *651*
—. Abolition Movement. Gurowski, Adam. Poland. 1849-66. *449*
—. Agrarianism. Populism. Wisconsin. Working class. 19c. *1399*
—. Agricultural labor. California. Cannery and Agricultural Workers Industrial Union. Industrial Workers of the World. 1909-39. *1756*
—. Alberta. New Brunswick. Populism. Saskatchewan. Social organization. 1950's-70's. *2700*
—. American Federation of Labor. Communist Party. Labor Unions and Organizations. Trade Union Unity League. 1933-35. *2494*
—. Amlie, Thomas. New Deal. Roosevelt, Franklin D. Wisconsin. 1930-39. *1672*
—. Anarchism and Anarchists. Newspapers. Oregon. Portland *Firebrand* (newspaper). 1895-98. *1112*
—. Anarchist Scare (1908). Progressivism. Social movements. 1900-10. *2139*
—. Antiwar Sentiment. Vietnam War. Violence. 1960's-70's. *2761*
—. Attitudes. Canada, western. Industrialization. Labor Unions and Organizations. Working class. 1897-1919. *1745*
—. Beecher, Henry Ward. Feminism. New York City. Sex. Vanderbilt, Cornelius. Woodhull, Victoria Claflin. 1868-90's. *336*
—. Canada. English Canadians. Immigrants. Propaganda. Puttee, Arthur. Water Conservation. ca 1888-1913. *1327*
—. Canada. Finns. Immigrants. Labor Unions and Organizations. 1918-26. *2407*
—. Canada. Socialism. 1890-99. *1316*
—. Canada, western. Industrial Workers of the World. Labor Unions and Organizations. 1905-14. *1786*
—. Canada (western). Labor Unions and Organizations. One Big Union. Socialism. 1917-19. *1746*
—. Capitalism. Depressions. Political Attitudes. Texas. 1929-33. *2460*
—. Chamberlain, John. Conservatism. Political Theory. 1920's-65. *275*
—. Christianity. Class Struggle. *Los Angeles Times*. McNamara case. Progressivism. Steffens, Lincoln. 1908-12. *2083*
—. Civil Rights movement. Johnson, Lyndon B. Long, Huey P. South. 1920-70. *1706*
—. Civil rights movement. Political socialization. Student activism. ca 1955-75. *2713*
—. Colleges and Universities. Intellectuals. Political Protest. Students. 1963-77. *2750*
—. Colleges and Universities. Political Attitudes. Students. 1943-70. *1537*
—. Communists. New York City. "Rank and File" movement. Social work. 1931-51. *1600*
—. Conservatism. DuBois, W. E. B. Negroes. Periodicals. Race relations. Washington, Booker T. 1900-10. *1983*
—. Declaration of Independence. Ideology. Religion. Utopias. 1730's-1890's. *269*
—. Depressions. Great Plains. State Politics. 1930-36. *2520*
—. Ethnicity. Irish Americans. Land League. Reform. Working class. 1880-83. *997*
—. Everett Mill. Massachusetts (Lawrence). Polish Americans. Strikes. Textile Industry. Women. 1912. *2252*
—. Farmer-Labor Party. Political Leadership. Saskatchewan. Socialism. 1932-34. *1607*
—. Farmers. Political Parties. 1892-1930. *1682*
—. Federal Bureau of Investigation. Hoover, J. Edgar. Surveillance. 1919-21. *2461*
—. Feminism. Fuller, Margaret. New England. Transcendentalism. 1810-50. *311*
—. Feminism. Human Relations. Politics. Values. 19c-1929. *29*
—. Finnish Americans. Iron Industry. Labor Unions and Organizations. Minnesota. Minnesota (Mesabi Range). 1914-17. *2253*
—. Food and Drug Administration. Great Plains. Labor. Social change. Veblen, Thorstein. World War I. 1918. *1922*
—. Freudianism. New York City (Greenwich Village). Psychoanalysis. Sex. 1913-20. *1936*
—. Friends, Society of. Humanism. Intellectuals. Penn, William. 1650-1700. *474*

—. Green Corn Rebellion, 1917. Labor Unions and Organizations. Oklahoma. Working Class Union. 1914-17. *2284*
—. Human Relations. Sex. Wright, Henry Clarke. 1830-66. *805*
—. Industrial Workers of the World. Kansas. Red Scare. Trials. 1917-19. *2148*
—. Industrial Workers of the World. Labor Disputes. Ohio (Toledo). US Bureau of Investigation. 1918-20. *1906*
—. Industrialization. Knights of St. Crispin. Loyalism. Massachusetts (Lynn). Working class. 1820-90. *1298*
—. Intellectuals. Law Enforcement. World War I. 1914-20. *2158*
—. Italian Americans. Labor. Rhode Island. 1905-30. *1753*
—. Krzycki, Leo. Labor Unions and Organizations. Polish Americans. Socialist Party. 1900's-66. *391*
—. Labor. New Deal. Working class. 1930's. *2524*
—. Labor Unions and Organizations. Negroes. Socialism. 1865-1900. *1232*
—. Labor Unions and Organizations. New Deal. 1930-39. *2546*
—. Law. Liberalism. Social change. 1953-73. *1579*
—. Literature. Negroes. Wright, Richard. 1920-60. *305*
—. Muste, Abraham J. Unemployed Leagues. 1932-36. *2577*
—. Negroes. Reconstruction. Republican Party. South Carolina (Beaufort County). 1865-88. *1003*
—. New York (Rochester). Religion. Revivalism. 1830-56. *568*
—. Novels. Politics. Religion. Social change. 1915-71. *1691*
—. Social Organization. Woman suffrage. 19c. *116*
—. Students for a Democratic Society. Youth Movements. 1950's. 1960's. *2720*
Radio. *Amos 'n' Andy* (program). Boycotts. Comic strips. Negroes. Stereotypes. 1930's. *2588*
Railroad Carmen's Strike (1911-15). Scientific management. Strikes. Working class. 1903-22. *2256*
Railroads *See also* Eminent Domain; Freight and Freightage.
—. Accidents. Courts. Federal Employers' Liability Act (US, 1908). Management. Safety Appliances Act (US, 1893). Working Conditions. 1890-1913. *2117*
—. Agriculture. Freight and Freightage. Populism. Prices. 1870-97. *1360*
—. Alaska (Anchorage). Labor Unions and Organizations. Lewis, Lena Morrow. Socialist Party. World War I. 1916-18. *2001*
—. American Railway Union. Montana. Strikes. 1894. *1357*
—. Antitrust. Local Government. New Jersey (Jersey City). Taxation. 1901-07. *2276*
—. Armies. Strikes. Values. 1877. 1894. *1294*
—. Baltimore and Ohio Railroad. Mathews, Henry M. Strikes. West Virginia (Martinsburg, Berkeley County). 1877. *1301*
—. Business. Construction. Farmers. Utopias. Western States. 1880's-90's. *1511*
—. Constitution League. Discrimination. Foraker, Joseph B. Hepburn Bill, Warner-Foraker Amendment (1906). Jim Crow laws. Negroes. Washington, Booker T. (and Committee of 12). 1906. *1919*
—. Court of Visitation. Kansas. Populism. Republican Party. State Legislatures. 1890-1900. *1386*
—. Discrimination. Fair Employment Practices Committee. Negroes. Southeastern Carriers Conference. World War II. 1941-45. *2630*
—. Election Laws. Goebel, William. Government Regulation. Kentucky. Taylor, William S. 1887-1900. *961*
—. Gould, Jay. Knights of Labor. Missouri (Sedalia). Modernization. Strikes. 1885-86. *1292*
—. Government Regulation. North Carolina. Populism. Progressivism. Russell, Daniel. 1894-98. *1369*
—. Hughes, Charles Evans. New York Public Service Commission Law (1907). Public opinion. Public utilities. 1907-09. *2200*
—. Illinois (Pullman). Labor Unions and Organizations. Pullman strike. 1880-94. *1325*
—. Industrialization. Women. 1890's. *962*
—. Industry. Strikes. 1877. *1353*

—. Jim Crow laws. Negroes. Separate coach bills. South Carolina. 1880-98. *1215*
—. Strikes. Violence. Working class. 1877. *1299*
Ralston, Jackson. California. Elections. Reform. Single tax. 1932-38. *2504*
Ranchers. Agricultural Labor. Farmers. Industrial Workers of the World. Labor Disputes. Washington (Yakima Valley). 1910-36. *2569*
RAND Corporation. Education, Experimental Methods. Federal programs. Local Government. 1965-80. *2961*
Randolph, A. Philip. American Federation of Labor. Brotherhood of Sleeping Car Porters. Negroes. 1867-1935. *70*
—. Brotherhood of Sleeping Car Porters. March on Washington Movement. National Negro Congress. Negroes. 1925-41. *353*
—. Defense industries. Discrimination. Executive Order 8802. March on Washington Movement. Military. Webster, Milton. 1941-44. *2635*
—. Journalism. Labor Unions and Organizations. Marxism. Negroes. Political protest. ca 1911-75. *382*
Randolph, Ryland. Alabama. Military. Racism. Reconstruction. Trials. Tuscaloosa *Independent Monitor*. 1868. *986*
"Rank and File" movement. Communists. New York City. Radicals and Radicalism. Social work. 1931-51. *1600*
Rankin, Jeannette. Congress. Montana. Woman suffrage. 1913-18. *466*
—. Constitutions, State. Montana. Woman suffrage. 1889-1914. *129*
—. Feminism. Georgia. Peace Movements. 1924-73. *352*
—. House of Representatives. Montana. Pacifism. 1880-1973. *465*
—. House of Representatives. Montana. Political Campaigns (congressional). Republican Party. Woman suffrage. 1900-16. *2142*
Rantoul, Robert, Jr. Abolition movement. Political Participation. 1820's-56. *303*
Rapier, James T. Alabama. Labor Union of Alabama. National Negro Labor Union. Negroes. Politics. Reconstruction. 1837-75. *1253*
Rapp, George. Harmony Society. Indiana (New Harmony). Utopias. 1814-47. *937*
—. Harmony Society. Pennsylvania. State Legislatures. Utopias. 1805-07. *913*
Raritan Bay Union. Communes. New Jersey (Perth Amboy, Red Bank). North American Phalanx. Spring, Marcus. 1843-59. *930*
—. Education. New Jersey. Utopias. 1853-61. *940*
Raskob, John J. Constitutional Amendments (18th and 21st). Democratic Party. Prohibition. Roosevelt, Franklin D. 1928-33. *2536*
Rauschenbusch, Walter. Baptists. Dahlberg, Edwin (interview). 1914-18. *444*
Ray, John. Louisiana. Negroes. Republican Party. Scalawags. ca 1836-88. *463*
Raymond, Eliza Ruggles. Missions and Missionaries. Nova Scotia. Sierra Leone (Sherbro Island). Slaves. 1839-50. *621*
Readjuster Party. Negroes. State debt. Virginia. 1879-83. *1222*
Reagon, Bernice Johnson (interview). Civil rights movement. Freedom Singers. Georgia (Albany; Harlem district). NAACP. 1960-77. *2880*
Real Estate *See also* Eminent Domain; Land Tenure.
—. Bartol, Cyrus. Investments. Massachusetts (Boston, Manchester). Transcendentalism. 1850-96. *1015*
Reapportionment. *See* Apportionment.
Rebellions *See also* particular mutinies, insurrections, and rebellions by name, e.g. Kronstadt Mutiny, Warsaw ghetto uprising; Political Protest; Revolution.
—. Crime and criminals. Florida. Slavery. ca 1820-65. *659*
Recessions *See also* Depressions.
—. Catholic Church. Church and State. Provincial Government. Public Charities Act (Canada, 1921). Quebec. 1921-26. *1699*
Reclamation Movement. California. Ecology. 1874-1974. *163*
Reconstruction *See also* Carpetbaggers; Confederate States of America; Emancipation; Freedmen; Ku Klux Klan; Negroes.
—. Agricultural Labor. Economic Structure. Freedmen. Racism. Texas. 1865-74. *1263*
—. Alabama. Bureau of Refugees, Freedmen, and Abandoned Lands. Freedmen. 1865-67. *1223*

—. Alabama. Freedmen's Bureau. Gardner, Samuel S. (letter). Negro Suffrage. 1867. *1180*
—. Alabama. Freedmen's Bureau. Racism. Swayne, Wager. 1865-68. *1279*
—. Alabama. Haralson, J. Negro Suffrage. Republican Party. 1867-82. *1252*
—. Alabama. Historiography. Revisionism. 1884-1971. *1069*
—. Alabama. Labor Union of Alabama. National Negro Labor Union. Negroes. Politics. Rapier, James T. 1837-75. *1253*
—. Alabama. Legislation. Political Parties. 1867. *1251*
—. Alabama. Military. Racism. Randolph, Ryland. Trials. Tuscaloosa *Independent Monitor*. 1868. *986*
—. Alabama. Ostracism. Politics. Republican Party. 1865-80. *1082*
—. Alden, Augustus E. Brownlow, William G. Carpetbaggers. City Government. Education. Public welfare. Republican Party. Tennessee (Nashville). 1865-69. *1049*
—. American Land Company. Andrew, John A. Politics. South. 1865-67. *1066*
—. American Missionary Association. Cardozo, Francis Louis. Education. Freedmen. South Carolina (Charleston). State Politics. 1865-70. *1243*
—. Anti-Radicals. Ashburn, George W. (murder). Georgia. Trials. 1868. *987*
—. Appalachia. Negroes. Republican Party. State Politics. 1865-1900. *1216*
—. Archives, National. Freedmen's Bureau. Public Records. Texas. 1865-76. *1147*
—. Arkansas. Constitutions, State (conventions). Negroes. 1868. *1250*
—. *Arkansas Freeman* (newspaper). Gross, Tabbs. Negroes. Political Commentary. Republican Party. 1869-70. *1203*
—. Armies. Civil War. Freedmen's Bureau. Maryland. Reform. 1864-68. *1162*
—. Ashley, James M. Civil War. House of Representatives. Negro Suffrage. Ohio (Toledo). 1861-62. *1019*
—. Authority. Citizenship. Constitutional Amendments (13th, 14th, 15th). Federal government. Freedmen. 1865-70. *1132*
—. Authority. Race Relations. Rhetoric. 1865-68. *1206*
—. Baptists, Southern. Churches. Education. Racism. 1865-76. *1267*
—. Blue law. Legislators. Louisiana. Negroes. State Legislatures. 1867-75. *1276*
—. Cain, Richard Harvey. Negroes. Politics. Social conditions. South Carolina. 1850's-87. *375*
—. Cardozo, Francis Louis. Freedmen. Political rights. South Carolina. Union League. 1870. *1268*
—. Carpetbaggers. Civil rights. Constitutional conventions, state. Industrialization. South. 1867-69. *1021*
—. Carpetbaggers. Equality. Post, Louis F. Progressive era. 1868-1925. *306*
—. Carpetbaggers. Historiography. Ideology. Mississippi. Reformers. 1865-76. *1013*
—. Carpetbaggers. House of Representatives. Negroes. Republican Party. Scalawags. South. 1868-72. *1036*
—. Carse, George B. Florida (Leon County). Freedmen's Bureau. Republican Party. 1867-70. *1074*
—. Chamberlain, Daniel H. Hampton, Wade. South Carolina. State Politics. 1877. *1054*
—. Charleston City Railway Company. Desegregation. Negroes. South Carolina. Streetcars. 1867. *1169*
—. Charleston *Daily Courier* (newspaper). Charleston *Mercury* (newspaper). Constitutional conventions, state. Racism. South Carolina. 1867-68. *1205*
—. Charleston *News and Courier* (newspaper). Dawson, Francis Warrington. Dawson, Sarah Morgan. Feminism. South Carolina. 1870's. *973*
—. City Government. Republican Party. South. 1865-75. *1068*
—. Civil Rights. Constitutional Amendments (13th, 14th, 15th). Freedmen. Politics. 1865-77. *1188*
—. Civil Rights. Constitutional Amendments (14th). 1865-68. *1109*
—. Civil Rights. Discrimination. Equality. Negroes. Political Attitudes. Texas. 1865-70. *1200*
—. Civil Rights. Kentucky. Negroes. Newspapers. 1866-72. *1176*

Reconstruction

—. Civil Rights Act (US, 1866). Constitutional Amendments (14th, 15th). Negroes. Republican Party. States' rights. ca 1865-77. *953*
—. Civil War. Confiscations. Congress. Constitutional Law. Debates. 1861-65. *1105*
—. Civil War. Historiography. 1861-77. ca 1950-74. *984*
—. Civil War. Law. Mississippi. Negroes. 1857-70. *114*
—. Civil War. Lincoln, Abraham. Louisiana (New Orleans). Negroes. Suffrage. 1860-67. *1130*
—. Civil War. Negroes. Slavery. Women. 19c. *331*
—. Colorado. Equal rights. Negroes. 1865-67. *1134*
—. Colored National Labor Union. Florida. Labor Unions and Organizations. National Union of Negro Labor. Negroes. Race Relations. 1865-75. *1259*
—. Compromise of 1877. Democratic Party. Elections (presidential). Republican Party. Woodward, C. Vann. 1876-77. *1086*
—. Congress. Historiography. Negroes. South. 1860's-1978. *1175*
—. Constitutional conventions, state. Delegates. Virginia. 1867-68. *1022*
—. Courts. Freedmen's Bureau. Howard, Oliver Otis. South. 1865-68. *1229*
—. Courts. Freedmen's Bureau. Justice. Negroes. Texas. 1865-68. *1146*
—. Democratic Party. Elections. Louisiana. Military Occupation. Rousseau, Lovell H. 1868-69. *990*
—. Diaries. Freedmen's Bureau. Hopkins, Sterling. Virginia. 1868. *1056*
—. Discrimination. Federal Policy. Freedmen's Bureau. Mississippi. State Government. 1865. *1227*
—. Discrimination. Freedmen's Bureau. Johnson, Andrew. Law. 1865-66. *1226*
—. Economic Conditions. Racism. Social Classes. South. 1865-76. *1071*
—. Economic dependence. Land reform. Negroes. 1861-1900. *1155*
—. Education. Education Department. Negroes. 1867. *1277*
—. Education. Negroes. North Carolina. School Integration. 1865-67. *1127*
—. Elections. Negroes. Politics. Tennessee (Shelby County). 1865-76. *1160*
—. Elections, congressional. Loyalty. Virginia. 1865. *960*
—. Elementary education. Florida. Peabody Fund. Segregation. 1869-76. *1433*
—. Federal programs. Freedmen. Georgia (Atlanta). North. Religious organizations. 1865-69. *1273*
—. Florida. Negroes. Political attitudes. Republican Party. Walls, Josiah T. 1867-85. *1192*
—. Foster, Richard B. (address). Missouri. Negroes. Teachers. 1869. *1170*
—. Founding Fathers. Kansas-Nebraska Act (US, 1854). Lincoln, Abraham. Republicanism. 1854-65. *1058*
—. Freedmen. Homesteading and Homesteaders. Louisiana. 1865-83. *1233*
—. Freedmen. Louisiana (Madison Parish). Plantations. Race Relations. 1863-74. *978*
—. Freedmen's Bureau. Kentucky. Noble, Thomas. Race Relations. Schools. 1865-70. *1190*
—. Freedmen's Bureau. Kirkland, William S. Texas. 1865-70. *1261*
—. Genovese, Eugene D. Land reform. Race relations. Social Classes. South Carolina (Edgefield County). Woodward, C. Vann. 1865-90. *963*
—. Georgia Equal Rights Association. Negroes. Republican Party. Union League. 1865-80. *1214*
—. Hancock, Winfield Scott. Louisiana. Military. Mower, Joseph Anthony. Texas. 1865-68. *989*
—. Harris, Cicero. Harris, Robert. Harris, William. Negroes. South. Teaching. 1864-70. *1278*
—. Historiography. 1865-1979. *1000*
—. Historiography. Louisiana (New Orleans). Negroes. Political Leadership. ca 1800-75. *1239*
—. Ku Klux Klan. Negroes. South Carolina. 1868-71. *1076*
—. Labor. Local Politics. Missouri. Racism. St. Louis *Daily Press* (newspaper). 1864-66. *1339*
—. Leadership. Negroes. South. 1867-75. *1211*
—. Liberal Republican Party. ca 1870-72. *945*

—. Louisiana. Military Occupation. Negro Suffrage. Sheridan, Philip H. 1865-67. *991*
—. Louisiana. Ostracism. Scalawags. State Politics. Terrorism. 1866-78. *1081*
—. Louisiana (St. Landry). Race Relations. Republican Party. Riots. 1868. *1151*
—. Lynch, James (letters). Methodist Episcopal Church. Mississippi. Negroes. 1868-69. *1166*
—. Minorities in Politics. Negroes. Political Leadership. Texas. 1865-90's. *1148*
—. Mississippi. Ord, Edward Otho Cresap. 1867-68. *982*
—. Negro Suffrage. Racism. Rhetoric. Ridicule. South. 1866-70. *1207*
—. Negroes. Radicals and Radicalism. Republican Party. South Carolina (Beaufort County). 1865-88. *1003*
—. Negroes. South Carolina, University of. 1873-77. *1248*
—. Peffer, William A. State Politics. Tennessee. 1865-69. *949*
—. Politics. Republican Party. Wisconsin. 1865-73. *981*
—. Property rights. South. State legislatures. Women. 1865-95. *1103*
Record, George L. Economic reform. Progressives. 1859-1933. *2277*
Recreation *See also* Community Centers; Leisure; Resorts; Sports.
—. Attitudes. Exercise. Health. New England. Transcendentalism. 1830-60. *572*
—. Children. Massachusetts (Boston). Pennsylvania (Philadelphia). Progressivism. 1886-1911. *1985*
—. Cities. Family. Morality. Progressivism. Reform. Socialization. 1890-1920. *1990*
—. National Parks and Reserves. Western States. Wilderness Act (US, 1964). 1864-1976. *7*
—. Ontario (Toronto). Sabbatarianism. Tobogganing. 1912. *1609*
—. Physical Education and Training. Women. 1776-1865. *573*
Red baiting. Labor. Socialism. Working conditions. 1871-1920. *154*
Red Cross *See also* Disasters; Refugees.
—. Arkansas. Disasters. Droughts. Negroes. Plantations. Sharecroppers. 1930-31. *2463*
—. Barton, Clara. War. Women. 1860's-90's. *1457*
Red scare. Civil Rights. Smith, Alfred E. 1919-20. *2133*
—. Industrial Workers of the World. Kansas. Radicals and Radicalism. Trials. 1917-19. *2148*
Red Shirt Movement. Negro Suffrage. North Carolina. Social Classes. Terrorism. Whites. 1898-1900. *1067*
Redevelopment. District of Columbia. Public housing. 1943-46. *2618*
Reed Report (1921). Flexner Report. Legal education. Medical education. 1910-74. *1862*
Reed, Walter. Cuba. Medical ethics. Medical research. Yellow fever. 1900-01. *1883*
Referendum. Democratic Party. Liberty Party. Negro suffrage. New York. Whig Party. 1840-47. *595*
—. Iowa. Men. Voting and Voting Behavior. Woman suffrage. 1916. *2159*
—. James, Ada. Political Equality League. Willis, Olympia Brown. Wisconsin. Woman Suffrage Association. 1912. *2141*
—. Massachusetts. Political Campaigns. Woman suffrage. 1895-1920. *2140*
—. Negro suffrage. New York. Republican Party. 1846-69. *120*
—. New York. Wald, Lillian D. Woman Suffrage. 1917. *2135*
Reform *See also* specific kinds of reform, e.g. Economic Reform, Political Reform, etc.; reform movements, e.g. Abolition Movements, Temperance Movements, etc.; Social Conditions; Social Problems; Utopias.
—. 19c-1973. *24*
—. Abolition Movement. American Revolution. ca 1770-1899. *779*
—. Abolition movement. Dugdale, Joseph A. Friends, Society of. 1810-96. *297*
—. Abolition Movement. Garnet, Henry Highland. Speeches, Addresses, etc. 1843. *729*
—. Abolition movement. Grimes, John. *New Jersey Freeman* (newspaper). 1844-50. *623*
—. Abolition movement. Jews. 1850-63. *750*
—. Abolition Movement. Sexuality. 1830-65. *780*
—. Agriculture. Judaism. Krauskopf, Joseph. 1880's-1923. *2098*
—. Air pollution. City Government. Indiana (Gary). US Steel Corporation. 1956-73. *2723*

—. Air Pollution. Elites. Pennsylvania (Pittsburgh). Smoke. Tilbury, Corwin D. 1890's-1918. *1961*
—. Alabama. Baptists, Southern. Social Conditions. 1877-90. *974*
—. Alexander, George. California (Los Angeles). City Government. Progressivism. ca 1909-13. *2070*
—. American Committee on Italian Migration. Illinois (Chicago). Immigration. Italian Americans. 1952-67. *2701*
—. American Medical Association. Bureaucracies. Decisionmaking. 1960's. *2759*
—. American Medical Association. Carnegie Foundation. Flexner Report. Medical education. 1910-32. *2297*
—. American Moral Reform Society. Negroes. Pennsylvania (Philadelphia). Whipper, William. 1830-76. *386*
—. Anglo-Saxonism. Interventionism. Strong, Josiah. 1885-1915. *71*
—. Apes, William. Indian-white relations. Massachusetts (Mashpee). Wampanoag Indians. 1830-40. *600*
—. Armies. Civil War. Freedmen's Bureau. Maryland. Reconstruction. 1864-68. *1162*
—. Arthur, George. Colonial Government. Great Britain. Ontario (Upper Canada). 1837-41. *571*
—. Assimilation. Indians. Racism. 1880-1900. *944*
—. Atlantic Provinces. Maritime Rights Movement. Regionalism. 1900-25. *1578*
—. Attitudes. Democracy. Federal Reserve System. Income tax. Wilson, Woodrow. 1913-21. *1994*
—. Attitudes. Friends, Society of. New York (Auburn). Pennsylvania. Prisons. Religion. 1787-1845. *874*
—. Attitudes. Slavery. Tennessee, western. 1820-40. *771*
—. Barnard, Kate. Kansas State Penitentiary. Oklahoma. Prisons. 1908-09. *1974*
—. Bauer, Catherine. Federal Policy. Public housing. Wagner-Steagall Act (US, 1937). Wood, Edith Elmer. 1890's-1940's. *2479*
—. Behavior. Progressivism. Sex. 1890-1920. *1995*
—. Bingham, Robert Worth. City government. Kentucky (Louisville). Progressivism. 1905-10. *1926*
—. Brookings, Robert. Flexner Report. Medical education. Missouri (St. Louis). Washington University. 1910-16. *2318*
—. Burnham, Daniel Hudson. City planning. Illinois (Chicago). Moody, Walter D. *(Wacker's Manual of the Plan of Chicago).* Progressivism. Publicity. 1909-11. *2071*
—. California. Civil War. Indian-White Relations. Republican Party. 1860-70. *971*
—. California. Elections. Ralston, Jackson. Single tax. 1932-38. *2504*
—. Canada. Feminism. Literature. McClung, Nellie L. Politics. 1873-1930's. *1689*
—. Charities. City government. New York City. Subsidies. 1870-98. *1463*
—. Chipman, George. Editors and Editing. *Grain Growers Guide* (periodical). Manitoba (Winnipeg). Social movements. 1905-30. *1637*
—. Church and Social Problems. Clergy. Protestant Churches. 1960's-70's. *2748*
—. Cities. Citizen Lobbies. Consumers. Environment. Noise pollution. 1893-1932. *1684*
—. Cities. Congregationalism. Gladden, Washington. Ohio (Columbus). Social gospel. 1850's-1914. *396*
—. Cities. Family. Morality. Progressivism. Recreation. Socialization. 1890-1920. *1990*
—. Cities. Merton, Thomas. Nonviolence. Social criticism. 1960's. *2737*
—. Cities. New York City. Pollution. Public Health. Refuse disposal. Waring, George E., Jr. 1880-1917. *69*
—. Cities. Noise pollution. Progressivism. 1900-30. *1683*
—. Cities. Sanitation. Women. 1880-1917. *1975*
—. City Government. Fisher, Walter L. Illinois (Chicago). 1880-1910. *347*
—. City Government. Jones, Samuel Milton. Ohio (Toledo). 1850's-1904. *280*
—. City Government. Medicine. Refuse disposal. Sanitation. Technology. Wisconsin (Milwaukee). 1867-1911. *1466*
—. City Government. Municipal League of Seattle. Progressivism. Washington (Seattle). 1910-20. *2045*

—. City government. Political attitudes. Texas (Beaumont). 1902-09. *1977*
—. City Politics. Ontario (Ottawa). Public Health. Typhoid fever. 1911-12. *1635*
—. Civil War (antecedents). Greeley, Horace. Secession. Slavery. 1860-61. *781*
—. Class struggle. Standard of living. Working class. 1950's-73. *2923*
—. Cooperatives. Hoel, Chamberlain. Oregon (Salem). 1852-65. *326*
—. Countryman, Gratia Alta. Libraries (public). Minnesota (Minneapolis). Women. 1890's-1953. *424*
—. Courts. Industrialists. Juvenile Delinquency. Middle Classes. Philanthropy. 1890-99. *1472*
—. Crapsey, Algernon Sidney. Episcopal Church, Protestant. Heresy. New York (Rochester). St. Andrew's Church. Trials. 1879-1927. *454*
—. Crime and Criminals. Ontario (Upper Canada). Prisons. 1835-50. *857*
—. Debo, Angie (personal account). Federal Government. Indians. Public Opinion. 1969-76. *2703*
—. Delaware. George, Henry. Political Parties. Single Tax movement. 1890's. *1085*
—. Democracy. Mass Media. Publicity. 1900-29. *1624*
—. Determinism. Garland, Hamlin. Indians. 1890-1923. *2111*
—. Divorce. Feminism. Marriage. Stanton, Elizabeth Cady. 1840-90. *1010*
—. Domesticity. Feminism. Howe, Julia Ward. Motherhood. 1844-85. *349*
—. Economic Policy. Indians (reservations). Prisons. 19c. *158*
—. Education. 1870's-1970's. *222*
—. Eisenhower, Dwight D. (administration). Federal Policy. Legislation. Public Welfare. 1950-60. *2659*
—. Elkins, Stephen B. Republican Party. State Politics. West Virginia. White, Albert B. 1901-05. *1895*
—. Employment. Servants. 1892-1920. *2271*
—. Ethnicity. Irish Americans. Land League. Radicals and Radicalism. Working class. 1880-83. *997*
—. Evangelicalism. Slavery. Stringfellow, Thornton. Virginia. 1800-70. *633*
—. Evangelism. Wright, Henry Clarke. 1820-60. *447*
—. Executive power. Federal Regulation. Politics. President's Advisory Council on Executive Organization. Public Administration. 1937-79. *1705*
—. Family. 1820-70. *583*
—. Farwell, Arthur Burrage. Hyde Park Protective Association. Illinois (Chicago). Prohibition. 1885-1936. *1912*
—. Federal government. New Deal. Press. Progressivism. 1890's-1930's. *1534*
—. Federal Policy. Indians. Meriam, Lewis (*Problem of Indian Administration*). Social conditions. 1920-28. *2362*
—. Federal Programs. Food stamps. 1930-77. *1872*
—. Female Moral Reform Society. Morality. New York (Utica). Social Organization. 1830's-40's. *808*
—. Filene, Edward A. Industrial democracy. Massachusetts (Boston). 1890-1937. *1787*
—. Frontier and Pioneer Life. Kentucky. Medical Education. Mitchell, Thomas Duche. 1809-65. *325*
—. Georgia. Negro Suffrage. Populism. Watson, Thomas E. 1880-1922. *27*
—. Gilman, Catheryne Cooke. Social work. Women. 1904-54. *344*
—. Gitteau, William B. Hamilton, J. Kent. Ohio (Toledo). Progressivism. Public Schools. 1898-1921. *2330*
—. Governors. Kennon, Robert F. Louisiana. 1948-56. *2674*
—. Great Awakening (2d). Pennsylvania. 1794-1860. *562*
—. Griscom, John H. (letters). Public Health. Sanitation. Shattuck, Lemuel. 1843-47. *863*
—. Higher education. Liberal arts. South. 1850-60. *854*
—. Historiography. Values. 1780-1979. *57*
—. Humanitarian organizations. New York City. 1845-60. *877*
—. Illinois. Legislation. Wages. Women. Working Conditions. 1893-1917. *2187*
—. Industrial safety. "Safety First" (slogan). Young, Robert J. ca 1900-16. *1886*
—. Industry. Mortality. Muckraking. Occupations. 1890-1910. *2112*

—. Labor. Luther, Seth. Rhode Island. 1795-1863. *342*
—. Labor. Social status. Women. 1830-60. *309*
—. Landscape architecture. Olmsted, Frederick Law. 19c. *955*
—. Long, Huey P. New Deal. 1933-35. *2490*
—. Middle Classes. Progressivism. Voting and Voting Behavior. Wisconsin. 1890's-1917. *2127*
—. Morality. Sex. 19c. *102*
—. National Association of Colored Women. Negroes. Terrell, Mary Church. Woman Suffrage. 1892-1954. *312*
—. *National School Service* (bulletin). Patriotism. Public Schools. 1918-19. *2337*
—. New York. Prison Association. Rehabilitation. 1844-62. *875*
—. Oklahoma. Prisons. 1910-67. *1553*
—. Ontario. Prohibition. Racism. 1890-1915. *18*
—. Pacific Northwest. Prohibition. Weed, Ada M. Women's rights. 1858-1910. *327*
—. Political Leadership. Schurz, Carl. 1852-1906. *458*
—. Public Schools. Socialism. Wisconsin (Milwaukee). Working class. 1890-1920. *2329*
—. Public welfare. Welfare State. 1935-80. *2946*
—. Race Relations. Social gospel. 1877-98. *1043*
—. Social change. South. Williams, Claude. Williams, Joyce. 1930's-70's. *400*
Reform (newspaper). Ager, Waldemar Theodore. Editors and Editing. Norwegian Americans. Novels. Temperance Movements. 1893-1941. *368*
Reformatories. Agriculture. Boys. Fairfield School for Boys. Juvenile Delinquency. Ohio. Values. 1840-84. *242*
—. Children. Education. New York House of Refuge. 1800-30. *898*
—. Children. Michigan. Prisons. 1851-58. *900*
—. Girls. Lancaster Industrial School for Girls. Massachusetts. ca 1850-70. *1444*
—. Juvenile Delinquency. Ontario (Penetanguishene). 1880-1905. *1618*
—. Progressive Era. Shank, Corwin. Washington (Monroe). 1904-18. *1972*
Reformers. Agriculture. New England. Nutrition. 1873-1907. *1465*
—. Autobiography. Identity. Progressivism. Psychohistory. ca 1860-1920. *366*
—. Businessmen. Payne-Aldrich Tariff (1909). Tariff. 1905-09. *2201*
—. Carpetbaggers. Historiography. Ideology. Mississippi. Reconstruction. 1865-76. *1013*
—. Crosby, Ernest Howard. Intellectuals. Tolstoy, Lev Nikolaevich, Count. 1878-1907. *334*
—. Political attitudes. Religion. Settlement Movement. 1880's-90's. *1462*
—. Populism. State Legislatures. West. 1890's. *1364*
Refugees See also Exiles.
—. Congress. Freedmen's Bureau Act (US, 1865). 1864-65. *1091*
Refuse Act (US, 1899). Army Corps of Engineers. Environmental law. Waterways. 1876-1971. *977*
Refuse disposal. Cities. New York City. Pollution. Public Health. Reform. Waring, George E., Jr. 1880-1917. *69*
—. City Government. Medicine. Reform. Sanitation. Technology. Wisconsin (Milwaukee). 1867-1911. *1466*
Regents of the University of California v. *Allan Bakke* (US, 1978). Affirmative action. Discrimination. *Fullilove* v. *Klutznick* (US, 1980). Minorities. Supreme Court. *United Steelworkers of America* v. *Weber* (US, 1979). 1970's. *2782*
—. Bakke, Allan. Racism. Social change. 1960's-78. *2794*
Regina Manifesto. Cooperative Commonwealth Federation. League for Social Reconstruction. Saskatchewan. Underhill, Frank. 1933. *1611*
Regional development. Appalachia. City Planning. Tennessee, eastern. Virginia, southwestern. 1890-1929. *1710*
—. Appalachian Regional Development Act (US, 1965). Economic Development. Social Conditions. 1965-75. *2927*
Regionalism. Atlantic Provinces. Maritime Rights Movement. Reform. 1900-25. *1578*
—. Canada, western. Labor reform. Socialism. 1918-19. *1764*
—. Civil rights. Congress. Democratic Party. Legislation. Partisanship. Republican Party. 1963-72. *2803*

Regulation See also specific kinds of regulation, e.g. Federal Regulation.
—. Consumers. Drugs. Food, Drug, and Cosmetic Act (US, 1938). 1938-78. *1818*
Regulator movement. Colonial government. Elites. North Carolina. Social change. 1760-75. *502*
Regulators. American Revolution (antecedents). Conservatism. Liberty. North Carolina. Political Corruption. 1766-71. *481*
—. Civil Disturbances. Farmers. South Carolina. 1730-80. *490*
Rehabilitation. California. Education. Preston School of Industry. Prisons. Youth. 1894-1955. *1558*
—. New York. Prison Association. Reform. 1844-62. *875*
—. Ontario. Prisons. 1884-1900. *1482*
Religion See also Atheism; Christianity; Clergy; Councils and Synods; Ecumenism; Missions and Missionaries; Mysticism; Revivals; Sects, Religious; Sermons; Theology.
—. 1790-1815. *858*
—. Antislavery Sentiments. Editors and Editing. Kansas. Newspapers. Rhetoric. 1855-58. *680*
—. Antislavery sentiments. Evangelicalism. South. 1820-30. *758*
—. Assimilation. Black nationalism. Ideology. Literature. Women. 1890-1925. *1654*
—. Assimilation. Education. Indians. Micmac Indians. Nova Scotia. Public policy. 1605-1872. *209*
—. Attitudes. Friends, Society of. New York (Auburn). Pennsylvania. Prisons. Reform. 1787-1845. *874*
—. Ballou, Adin Augustus. Hopedale Community. Massachusetts (Milford). Utopias. 1830-42. *938*
—. Baseball. Social change. Values. 1892-1934. *1669*
—. Bradstreet, Anne. Hutchinson, Anne. Literature. Massachusetts Bay Colony. Social change. Women. 1630's-70's. *489*
—. California. Negroes. Political activism. 1850-73. *76*
—. California (Orange County). Middle Classes. Oneida Community. Social Organization. Townerites. 1848-1900's. *1514*
—. California (San Francisco). Educational Reform. Ethnicity. 1918-20. *2333*
—. Candler, Warren A. Methodist Episcopal Church, South. Political Campaigns (presidential). Prohibition. Smith, Alfred E. 1928. *2344*
—. Childhood. Leadership. Secularism. Sex roles. Women. 1636-1930. *381*
—. Civil rights. Militancy. Negroes. 1960's-70's. *2844*
—. Community centers. Country life movement. Progressives. Rural Settlements. 1900's-20's. *2099*
—. Declaration of Independence. Ideology. Radicals and Radicalism. Utopias. 1730's-1890's. *269*
—. Ethnicity. Indians. Political Protest. 1964-78. *2738*
—. Family. New York. Noyes, John Humphrey. Oneida Community. Sex. 1848-80. *271*
—. Feminism. 1967-76. *2916*
—. Garvey, Marcus. Negroes. Universal Negro Improvement Association. 1920's. *2351*
—. Higher education. Social change. 1960's-70's. *2974*
—. New York (Rochester). Radicals and Radicalism. Revivalism. 1830-56. *568*
—. Novels. Politics. Radicals and Radicalism. Social change. 1915-71. *1691*
—. Oneida Community. Utopias. 1837-86. *921*
—. Political attitudes. Reformers. Settlement Movement. 1880's-90's. *1462*
—. Rush, Benjamin. 1770's-1813. *318*
Religion in the Public Schools. Bible. Catholic Church. Desmond, Humphrey. Protestantism. Wisconsin. *Wisconsin ex rel. Frederick Weiss et al. vs. District School Board of School District 8* (1890). 1888-90. *1414*
—. Bible. Methodist Church. Wisconsin. 1846-90. *1418*
—. Boycotts. Christianity. Elementary Education. Jews. New York City. 1905-06. *2298*
—. Catholic Church. Church schools. French language. Langevin, Louis Philippe Adélard. Laurier, Wilfrid. Liberal Party. Prairie Provinces. 1890-1915. *185*
—. Catholic Church. Kansas. Protestantism. 1861-1900. *1409*

Religious Education *See also* Church Schools; Religion in the Public Schools; Theology.
— . Anderson, May. *Children's Friend* (periodical). Felt, Louie. Periodicals. Primary Association. Utah. 1880-1940. *80*
— . Bible. Constitutions, State. Presbyterian Church. Supreme courts (state). Wisconsin. 1848-90. *1419*
— . Catholic Church. Saskatchewan. Youth. 1870-1978. *207*
Religious Liberty *See also* Church and State; Persecution.
— . Acculturation. American Indian Defense Association. Collier, John. Indians. 1920-26. *2427*
— . Adventists. Illinois. Jones, Alonzo Trevier. Sunday. World's Columbian Exposition (Chicago, 1893). 1893. *1492*
— . Alberta (Linden). Church Schools. Courts. Mennonites. 1977-78. *2780*
— . American Revolution. Baptists. 1775-1800. *506*
— . Authority. Constitutional Amendments (1st). Health. Supreme Court. 1963-79. *2769*
— . Backus, Isaac. Baptists. New England. 1754-89. *513*
— . Baptists. Virginia. 1600-1800. *525*
— . California. Courts. Navajo Indians. Peyote. 1964. *2792*
— . California (Eight Mile, Blue Creek). Forest Service. Indians. Supreme Court. 1975. *2785*
— . Christianity. History. Rhode Island. Williams, Roger. 17c. *514*
— . Dogberry, Obediah. *Liberal Advocate* (newspaper). New York (Rochester). 1832-34. *589*
— . Indians. 1609-1976. *145*
Religious Orders *See also* religious orders by name.
— . Catholic Church. Feminism. Quebec. Women. 1640-1975. *21*
Religious organizations. Federal programs. Freedmen. Georgia (Atlanta). North. Reconstruction. 1865-69. *1273*
Religious Persecution. *See* Persecution.
Religious Revivals. *See* Revivals.
Remond, Charles Lenox. Abolition Movement. Massachusetts. Negroes (free). 1838-63. *459*
Remond, Sarah Parker. Abolitionists. Brown, William Wells. Medicine. Negroes. Ruggles, David. Smith, James McCune. Tubman, Harriet. 1810-85. *329*
— . Antislavery Sentiments. Great Britain. Massachusetts (Salem). Negroes. Women. 1856-87. *294*
Removals, forced. California. Indians. Jackson, Helen Hunt *(Ramona)*. Mission Indians. Ponca Indians. Schurz, Carl. 1873-84. *1051*
— . Canada. Japanese Canadians. Race Relations. World War II. 1890's-1940's. *1694*
Rent control. Federal government. 1940-47. *2633*
Reorganized United Mine Workers of America. Labor Unions and Organizations. Lewis, John Llewellyn. 1920-33. *2357*
Reporters and Reporting *See also* Editors and Editing; Journalism; News; Press.
— . Alabama. Civil rights movement. *Southern Courier* (newspaper). 1965-68. *2873*
— . California. Editors and Editing. Older, Fremont. San Francisco *Bulletin*. Women. 1895-1925. *1887*
— . Courts. Farber, Myron. Freedom of the press. *New York Times* (newspaper). 1975-79. *2781*
— . Oregon. Portland *Oregonian*. Woman Suffrage. 1869-1905. *1101*
Republican Party. Abolition Movement. American Abolition Society. 1855-58. *719*
— . Alabama. Duke, Jesse C. Editors and Editing. Montgomery *Herald* (newspaper). Negroes. Political Commentary. 1886-1916. *1185*
— . Alabama. Haralson, J. Negro Suffrage. Reconstruction. 1867-82. *1252*
— . Alabama. Ostracism. Politics. Reconstruction. 1865-80. *1082*
— . Alabama (Mobile). Black Capitalism. Editors and Editing. Johnson, Andrew N. Tennessee (Nashville). 1890-1920. *273*
— . Alden, Augustus E. Brownlow, William G. Carpetbaggers. City Government. Education. Public welfare. Reconstruction. Tennessee (Nashville). 1865-69. *1049*
— . Anti-Catholicism. Clergy. Ku Klux Klan. Protestantism. Rhode Island. 1915-32. *2441*
— . Anti-Catholicism. Ohio. Political Systems. Slavery. Whig Party. 1850's. *564*

— . Antislavery Sentiments. Bailey, Gamaliel. Chase, Salmon Portland. Liberty Party. Ohio. 1836-60. *668*
— . Antislavery Sentiments. Free Soil Party. Illinois. Racism. 1848-60. *740*
— . Antislavery Sentiments. Know-Nothing Party. Massachusetts. Nativism. Voting and Voting Behavior. 1850's. *538*
— . Appalachia. Negroes. Reconstruction. State Politics. 1865-1900. *1216*
— . Arkansas. Negroes. Race Relations. 1867-1928. *115*
— . Arkansas. Race Relations. 1890's-1924. *2364*
— . *Arkansas Freeman* (newspaper). Gross, Tabbs. Negroes. Political Commentary. Reconstruction. 1869-70. *1203*
— . Bass, Robert P. Boston and Maine Railroad. Churchill, Winston (1871-1947). New Hampshire. Progressivism. 1890-1912. *1868*
— . Blaine, John J. Progressivism. Senate. Wisconsin. 1927-33. *2421*
— . Border States. Congress. Legislation. Loyalty oath. South. 1861-67. *950*
— . California. Civil War. Indian-White Relations. Reform. 1860-70. *971*
— . California. Elections (presidential). Racism. Slavery. 1860. *757*
— . California. Slavery. 1852-56. *756*
— . Carpetbaggers. House of Representatives. Negroes. Reconstruction. Scalawags. South. 1868-72. *1036*
— . Carpetbaggers. Louisiana. Negroes. State Politics. 1868. *1136*
— . Carse, George B. Florida (Leon County). Freedmen's Bureau. Reconstruction. 1867-70. *1074*
— . City Government. Maryland (Baltimore). Negroes. 1890-1931. *1593*
— . City Government. Reconstruction. South. 1865-75. *1068*
— . Civil rights. Congress. Democratic Party. Legislation. Partisanship. Regionalism. 1963-72. *2803*
— . Civil rights. Negroes. Voting and Voting Behavior. 1846-59. *597*
— . Civil Rights Act (US, 1866). Constitutional Amendments (14th, 15th). Negroes. Reconstruction. States' rights. ca 1865-77. *953*
— . Civil War. Croxton, John Thomas. Kentucky. Law. Military Service. 1855-74. *392*
— . Civil War. Elections (presidential). Negroes. Political Participation. 1864. *1224*
— . Civil War. Emancipation Proclamation. Illinois Volunteers. 1862-63. *1087*
— . Compromise of 1877. Democratic Party. Elections (presidential). Reconstruction. Woodward, C. Vann. 1876-77. *1086*
— . Conservatism. McCumber, Porter James. McKenzie, Alexander John. North Dakota. Political reform. Suffrage. Women. 1898-1933. *435*
— . Court of Visitation. Kansas. Populism. Railroads. State Legislatures. 1890-1900. *1386*
— . Crawford, Coe Isaac. Progressivism. Roosevelt, Theodore. South Dakota. State Politics. 1912-14. *2076*
— . Democracy. Democratic Party. Ethnicity. Nebraska. Prohibition. 1907-20. *1937*
— . Democratic Party. Illinois. Slavery. Trumbull, Lyman. 1855-72. *323*
— . Douglass, Frederick. Patronage. Politics. 1870-95. *1235*
— . Elections. McKinley, William. Ohio. Working class. 1891-93. *1355*
— . Elections (presidential). Hoover, Herbert C. Progressivism. Senate. 1930-32. *2369*
— . Elections (presidential). New York. Prohibition. 1884. *1473*
— . Elites. Kansas. Negroes. Politics. Waller, John Lewis. 1878-1900. *468*
— . Elkins, Stephen B. Reform. State Politics. West Virginia. White, Albert B. 1901-05. *1895*
— . Emancipation Proclamation. Freedmen. Liberty. Lincoln, Abraham. 1862. *1131*
— . Emancipation Proclamation. Lincoln and Lincolniana. 1863-64. *1199*
— . Florida. Negroes. Political attitudes. Reconstruction. Walls, Josiah T. 1867-85. *1192*
— . Freedmen. Hartzell, Joseph C. Methodist Church. Missions and Missionaries. South. 1870-73. *1208*

— . Freedmen. House of Representatives. Murray, George Washington. South Carolina. Suffrage. 1893-97. *1163*
— . Georgia Equal Rights Association. Negroes. Reconstruction. Union League. 1865-80. *1214*
— . Historiography. Mugwumps. Political Reform. 1880's. 1910-79. *956*
— . House of Representatives. Montana. Political Campaigns (congressional). Rankin, Jeannette. Woman suffrage. 1900-16. *2142*
— . Ideology. North. Protestantism. Public Schools. Western states. 1870-1930. *204*
— . LaFollette, Robert Marion. Nominations to Office. Presidency. Roosevelt, Theodore. 1910-12. *2022*
— . Liberia. Negroes. Turner, James Milton. 1865-77. *1195*
— . Louisiana. Negroes. Ray, John. Scalawags. ca 1836-88. *463*
— . Louisiana (St. Landry). Race Relations. Reconstruction. Riots. 1868. *1151*
— . Minorities in Politics. Missouri (St. Louis). Negroes. Wheeler, John W. 1870-1915. *1142*
— . Negro suffrage. New York. Referendum. 1846-69. *120*
— . Negro suffrage. Wisconsin. 1857. *599*
— . Negroes. Populism. Press. 1890-96. *1152*
— . Negroes. Radicals and Radicalism. Reconstruction. South Carolina (Beaufort County). 1865-88. *1003*
— . New York. Platt, Thomas C. Progressivism. Public policy. State politics. 1890-1910. *2030*
— . Politics. Reconstruction. Wisconsin. 1865-73. *981*
— . Senter, DeWitt Clinton. Suffrage. Tennessee. 1869-70. *954*
Republicanism. Abolition Movement. Africa. American Colonization Society. Colonization. Racism. ca 1815-35. *762*
— . Authority. Disciples of Christ. Egalitarianism. 1780-1820. *907*
— . Books. Child-rearing. Education. Pennsylvania (Philadelphia). Protestantism. 1780-1835. *577*
— . Founding Fathers. Kansas-Nebraska Act (US, 1854). Lincoln, Abraham. Reconstruction. 1854-65. *1058*
— . Laurens, Henry. Philosophy. South Carolina. 1764-77. *483*
Republicans, Liberal. Historiography. 1872. 1870's-1975. *1004*
Republicans (Radical). American Revolution. Feminism. Political theory. Warren, Mercy Otis. 1760's-1805. *523*
— . Bond, Hugh Lennox. Ideology. Maryland. Racism. ca 1861-68. *1002*
— . Chase, Salmon Portland. Emancipation. 1861-64. *1005*
— . House of Representatives. Illinois. Logan, John A. 1866-68. *1028*
— . House of Representatives. Texas. 1870-73. *1088*
Research *See also* Methodology.
— . Bureau of American Ethnology. Ghost Dance. Indians. Mooney, James. Peyote. 1891-1921. *1110*
— . Economic History Association (annual meeting). Great Britain. Higher Education. 19c-20c. 1977. *191*
— . Hawthorne First Relay Assembly Test Room. Productivity. Working Conditions. 1927-32. *2428*
— . History. Institute for Advanced Study. Mathematics. New Jersey (Princeton). Social Sciences. 1930-79. *2435*
Research and Development Centers program. Education. Models. 1960's-70's. *2964*
Research, Clinical. Foundations. Gates, Frederick T. Medical education. Physicians. Rockefeller, John D. 1910-39. *1833*
Reserve Officers' Training Corps. Attitudes. Dewey, John. Higher education. 1920-38. *1847*
Resettlement *See also* Settlement.
— . Baptists. Discrimination. Japanese Americans. World War II. 1890-1970. *1651*
Resettlement Administration. Homesteading and Homesteaders. Interior Department. Minnesota (Duluth). Public Housing. 1936-47. *2510*
Resorts. Big Sky development. Conservation. Huntley, Chet. Montana. 1970-73. *2755*
Restaurants. Civil Rights. Demonstrations. Negroes. Oklahoma (Oklahoma City). 1958-64. *2835*
Retarded. *See* Handicapped.
Retirement. Carnegie, Andrew. Higher education. Pensions. 1901-18. *2214*

Returned Students of Omaha. Federal government. Indians. Nebraska Historical Society. Omaha Indians. Speeches, Addresses, etc. 1920's. *2442*

Reunion (community). Communes. Considerant, Victor Prosper. Texas. 1854-59. *918*

Revels, Hiram Rhodes. Alcorn University. Mississippi. Negroes. Race Relations. Senate. ca 1870's. *1256*

—. Mississippi. Negroes. Public Opinion. Senate. 1870. *1202*

Revisionism. Alabama. Historiography. Reconstruction. 1884-1971. *1069*

Revitalization movements. Ghost Dance. Indians. Social Organization. 1889. *967*

Revivalism. Canada. Gospel Temperance Movement. Rine, D.I.K. 1877-82. *1439*

—. New York (Rochester). Radicals and Radicalism. Religion. 1830-56. *568*

Revivals *See also* Great Awakening.

—. Antislavery Sentiments. Ohio. Political attitudes. Voting and Voting Behavior. 1825-70. *664*

—. Europe. 1400-1900. *81*

—. Georgia (Atlanta). Sunday, William Ashley ("Billy"). 1917. *1882*

—. Politics. 19c. *556*

Revolution *See also* specific revolutions by name, e.g. Glorious Revolution, French Revolution, etc.; American Revolution; Civil Disturbances; Government, Resistance to; Radicals and Radicalism; Rebellions; Riots.

—. American Revolution. 1760's-70's. 1960's-70's. *26*

—. Civil War. Lincoln, Abraham. Political Theory. Slavery. Social change. 1850-65. *1060*

—. Communist Party. Rhetoric. Russian Revolution. 1917-20. *1976*

—. Haiti. Negroes. 1791-1861. *639*

—. Women's liberation movement. 1960's-70's. *2915*

Revolution (newspaper). Anthony, Susan B. Journalism. Stanton, Elizabeth Cady. Woman Suffrage. 1868-70. *1108*

Rhetoric *See also* Lectures; Political Speeches.

—. American Colonization Society. Negroes, free. Slavery. Social Status. Whites. 1831-34. *615*

—. Antislavery Sentiments. Editors and Editing. Kansas. Newspapers. Religion. 1855-58. *680*

—. Authority. Race Relations. Reconstruction. 1865-68. *1206*

—. *Brown v. Board of Education* (US, 1954). School Integration. 1954-78. *2670*

—. Business. Civil rights. Populism. 1870-1900. *1370*

—. Children. Labor reform. Progressivism. 1904-16. *1917*

—. Civil rights. King, Martin Luther, Jr. ("Letter from Birmingham Jail"). Literature. 1963. *2807*

—. Communist Party. Pamphlets. 1929-39. *1540*

—. Communist Party. Revolution. Russian Revolution. 1917-20. *1976*

—. Emery, Sarah E. Van De Vort. Populism. 1887-95. *1393*

—. Farmers. Ideology. Old Northwest. Populism. 1870's-80's. *1388*

—. Feminism. Speeches, Addresses, etc. Stanton, Elizabeth Cady ("The Solitude of Self"). 1892. *964*

—. Georgia. Race relations. Washington, Booker T. (Atlanta Exposition Address). 1895. *1167*

—. Great Society. Johnson, Lyndon B. Public Welfare. 1963-65. *2764*

—. Johnson, Lyndon B. Social movements. War on Poverty. 1965-66. *2954*

—. King, Martin Luther, Jr. ("Letter from Birmingham Jail"). Negroes. Nonviolence. 1963. *2869*

—. Man with the Muck-Rake (speech). Political Speeches. Roosevelt, Theodore. 1906. *2014*

—. Negro Suffrage. Racism. Reconstruction. Ridicule. South. 1866-70. *1207*

Rhode Island *See also* New England; Northeastern or North Atlantic States.

—. Anti-Catholicism. Clergy. Ku Klux Klan. Protestantism. Republican Party. 1915-32. *2441*

—. Capital punishment. Law Reform. Public Opinion. 1838-52. *888*

—. Christianity. History. Religious liberty. Williams, Roger. 17c. *514*

—. Dorr's Rebellion. Election Laws. *Luther* v. *Borden* (US, 1849). State government. Supreme Court. 1842-49. *591*

—. Educational Reform. Free Schools. Howland, John. Legislation. 1757-1838. *431*

—. Educational reform. Providence Association of Mechanics and Manufacturers. Working Class. 1790's-1850. *853*

—. Garvin, Lucius F. C. Political reform. State Politics. 1876-1922. *343*

—. Industrial Relations. Knights of Labor. Politics. 1880's. *1289*

—. Italian Americans. Labor. Radicals and Radicalism. 1905-30. *1753*

—. Labor. Luther, Seth. Reform. 1795-1863. *342*

—. Nardella, Luigi (interview). Strikes. Textile Industry. 1922. *2349*

Rhode Island (Newport). American Revolution. Antislavery Sentiments. Congregationalism. Hopkins, Samuel. ca 1770-1803. *511*

—. Colleges and Universities. Ellery, William, Jr. Stiles, Ezra. 1770. *486*

—. Downing, George T. Negroes. Public schools. School Integration. 1855-66. *841*

Rhode Island (Pawtucket). Attitudes. Industrialization. Strikes. Textile industry. Working Class. 1824. *821*

—. Class conflict. Strikes. Textile Industry. 1790-1824. *822*

Rhode Island (Providence). African Society. Colonization. Freedmen. Hopkins, Samuel. Sierra Leone. 1789-95. *614*

—. City Politics. Community Action Programs. Decisionmaking. Minorities. 1965-69. *2940*

—. Medicine, preventive. Milk scandal. Political Corruption. Progressivism. Public health. 1913. *1915*

Rhode Island (Woonsocket). Belgian Americans. French Canadian Americans. Independent Textile Workers. Working Class. 1931-50's. *1767*

Rhythmics. Lewis, Dioclesius. Medical reform. Morality. Sex. Women. 1860-1970's. *1481*

Rice, Hazel F. (account). North Dakota Workmen's Compensation Bureau. Transportation. Working conditions. 1919-22. *2432*

Richards, Ellen H. Abel, Mary Hinman. Aladdin Ovens. Atkinson, Edward. Food Consumption. Massachusetts (Boston). New England Kitchen. Working Class. 1889-97. *1467*

Richards, Richard Olsen. Political Reform. Progressivism. Prohibition. South Dakota. Taxation. 1902-30. *1913*

Richberg, Donald Randall. Government. Liberalism. Progressivism. 1900-60. *274*

Richman, Julia. Educational Reform. Jews. New York City. Women. 1880-1912. *289*

Richmond Enquirer (newspaper). Educational Policy. Lancaster, Joseph. Public schools. Ritchie, Thomas. Virginia. 1803-50. *840*

Richmond Planet (newspaper). Editors and Editing. Mitchell, John P. Race Relations. Virginia. ca 1883-1929. *407*

Richmond Typographical Union. Baughman Brothers (company). Boycotts. Knights of Labor. Virginia. 1886-88. *1290*

Rickey, Branch. Baseball. Brooklyn Dodgers (team). Integration. Montreal Royals (team). Negroes. Press. Robinson, Jackie. 1945-47. *2690*

Ridicule. Negro Suffrage. Racism. Reconstruction. Rhetoric. South. 1866-70. *1207*

Rightists. Anarchism and Anarchists. New Left. Youth Movements. 1968-73. *2708*

Rightmire, William F. Economic reform. Kansas. Politics. Southern Farmers' Alliance. 1886-92. *1380*

Riis, Jacob August. New York City. Urban reform. 1895-97. *1999*

Riley, William R. Labor. Letters. Negroes. Tennessee. United Mine Workers of America. 1892-95. *1201*

Rincon School. California (San Francisco). Educational Reform. Swett, John. 1853-62. *849*

Rine, D.I.K. Canada. Gospel Temperance Movement. Revivalism. 1877-82. *1439*

Riots *See also* Civil Disturbances; Demonstrations; Strikes.

—. Abolition Movement. Anti-Catholicism. Ideology. Massachusetts (Boston). Social Classes. 1834-35. *555*

—. Abolition Movement. Democratic Party. New York (Utica). Proslavery Sentiments. 1835. *709*

—. Abolition Movement. Massachusetts (Springfield). Thompson, George. 1851. *667*

—. Abolition movement. Pennsylvania Hall. Pennsylvania (Philadelphia). Women. 1833-37. *617*

—. Civil rights. Legislation. Population. Race Relations. Tennessee (Memphis). 1865-66. *1209*

—. Civil rights movement. Negroes. Politics. Tennessee (Columbia). Truman, Harry S. 1946. *2657*

—. Community relations. Police. Race Relations. 1940-49. *2689*

—. Cummins, Albert B. Government regulation. Iowa (Davenport). Law Enforcement. Liquor. State Politics. 1907-08. *1880*

—. Elites. Politics. Race relations. 1960's-70's. *2857*

—. Episcopal Church, Protestant. New York City. Newspapers. Racism. St. Philip's Church. Williams, Peter, Jr. 1830-50. *671*

—. Fort McIntosh. Negroes. Texas (Laredo). 25th Infantry, US (Company D). 1899. *1143*

—. German Americans. Irish Americans. Local politics. New York City. Temperance Movements. 1857. *585*

—. Illinois (Chicago). Militia. Police. Strikes. Wages. 1877. *1343*

—. Japanese Americans (Nikkei). Lumber and Lumbering. Oregon (Toledo). Pacific Spruce Corporation. 1925-26. *2453*

—. Louisiana (New Orleans). Metropolitan Police Force. Negroes. Politics. Whites. 1868. *1168*

—. Louisiana (St. Landry). Race Relations. Reconstruction. Republican Party. 1868. *1151*

—. Negroes. Pennsylvania (Philadelphia). Race Relations. 1968. *2820*

—. Negroes. Social Organization. 1960's. *2793*

Ripley, George. Blair, Nora Schelter. Brook Farm. Education, Experimental Methods. Massachusetts. Personal narratives. Pratt, Frederick. Utopias. 1841-47. *934*

Ritchie, Thomas. Educational Policy. Lancaster, Joseph. Public schools. *Richmond Enquirer* (newspaper). Virginia. 1803-50. *840*

Rites and Ceremonies. Indian-White Relations. Legislation. New Mexico (Taos; Blue Lake). Pueblo Indians. 20c. *1718*

Ritter, Joseph E. Catholic Church. Church Schools. Glennon, John J. Missouri (St. Louis). School Integration. 1935-47. *1850*

Rives, Amélie. Feminism. Literary characters. Novels. South. 1863-1945. *377*

Robbins, Raymond. North Carolina (Whittier). Prohibition. 1920's-32. *2343*

Roberts, Lillian. American Federation of State, County, and Municipal Employees. Negroes. Oral history. 1920's-70's. *417*

Roberts, Sarah C. Civil Rights. Massachusetts (Boston). *Sarah C. Roberts* v. *City of Boston* (Massachusetts, 1850). School Integration. 1849-50. 1950's. *834*

Robeson, Paul. Anti-Communist Movements. House Committee on Un-American Activities. Negroes. Robinson, Jackie. USSR. 1949. *2684*

—. Black Nationalism. Musicians. Negroes. 1914-45. *1692*

—. Civil Rights. Leftism. Negroes. Singers. 1898-1976. *379*

Robins, Margaret Dreier. Anderson, Mary. Illinois (Chicago). Labor Unions and Organizations. Nestor, Agnes. Women. Women's Trade Union League. Working conditions. 1903-20. *2190*

Robins, Raymond. Alaska (Nome). Progressivism. 1897-1925. *314*

Robinson, Alfred. Boycotts. Mississippi. Negroes. Police brutality (alleged). United League. 1966-78. *2893*

Robinson, Jackie. Anti-Communist Movements. House Committee on Un-American Activities. Negroes. Robeson, Paul. USSR. 1949. *2684*

—. Baseball. Brooklyn Dodgers (team). Integration. Montreal Royals (team). Negroes. Press. Rickey, Branch. 1945-47. *2690*

Roche, Josephine. Coal Mines and Mining. Colorado. Labor reform. Roosevelt, Franklin D. (administration). Social work. 1886-1976. *1772*

Rockefeller, John D. Depressions. General Education Board. Public policy. Secondary education. Social change. 1930's. *2478*

—. Foundations. Gates, Frederick T. Medical education. Physicians. Research, Clinical. 1910-39. *1833*

Rockefeller Sanitary Commission for the Eradication of Hookworm Disease. Hookworms. Poor. South. Stiles, Charles W. 1900-14. *2109*

Rogers, John R. Kansas. Land Reform. Union Labor Party. 1838-1901. *1023*
—. Land tenure. Political Reform. Populism. State Politics. Washington. 1890-1900. *1363*
Rogers, Nathaniel Peabody. Abolition Movement. Haverford College Library (Quaker Collection). New Hampshire. Portsmouth Anti-Slavery Society. 1830-46. *316*
Roll-call voting. Congress. People's Legislative Service. Progressivism. 1922-29. *2423*
Roman Catholic Church. *See* Catholic Church.
Romanelli, John. Alcohol. Massachusetts, western. Prohibition. 1919-20. *2069*
Romanticism. Evans, Warren Felt. Idealism. Mental healing. Mysticism. 1864-89. *1480*
Roosevelt, Eleanor. Catholic Church. Church Schools. Congress. Federal aid to education. Spellman, Francis J. 1949-50. *2669*
—. Clapp, Elsie Ripley. Education. Homesteading and Homesteaders. New Deal. West Virginia (Arthurdale). 1933-44. *2477*
—. Miners. National Industrial Recovery Act (US, 1933). New Deal. Subsistence Homesteads Program. West Virginia (Arthurdale). 1930-46. *2492*
—. New Deal. Political Participation. Women. 1900-36. *372*
Roosevelt, Franklin D. Amlie, Thomas. New Deal. Radicals and Radicalism. Wisconsin. 1930-39. *1672*
—. Civil Rights. Federal Bureau of Investigation. 1936-80. *1716*
—. Congress. New Deal. Social Security Act (US, 1935). Unemployment insurance. 1934-35. *2471*
—. Congressmen. New Deal. Politics. Virginia. Woodrum, Clifton A. 1922-45. *433*
—. Constitutional Amendments (18th and 21st). Democratic Party. Prohibition. Raskob, John J. 1928-33. *2536*
—. Depressions. Economic Reform. Fisher, Irving. 1930's. *2468*
—. Depressions. LaFollette, Philip F. New Deal. Progressivism. Wisconsin Works Bill (1935). 1935. *2552*
—. Economic policy. Foreign Policy. New Deal. Public works. 1933. *2555*
—. Elections (presidential). Long, Huey P. Share-Our-Wealth movement. 1932-36. *2595*
—. Employment. Minorities in Politics. Negroes. New Deal. 1930-42. *2586*
—. Federal Government. Hoover, Herbert C. Public welfare. 1920-37. *2345*
—. Foreign Policy. International Labor Organization. Isolationism. New Deal. Perkins, Frances. 1921-34. *2570*
—. New Deal. Progressives. Senate. 1935-36. *2557*
Roosevelt, Franklin D. (administration). Agricultural Reform. Catholic Church. New Deal. Social Theory. 1933-39. *2590*
—. Civil rights. Congress. Discrimination, employment. Fair Employment Practices Committee. World War II. 1941-46. *2640*
—. Coal Mines and Mining. Colorado. Labor reform. Roche, Josephine. Social work. 1886-1976. *1772*
—. Collier, John. Federal Government. Indians. Liberalism. Truman, Harry S. (administration). 1933-53. *1629*
—. Historiography. Negroes. USSR. World War II. 1939-45. *2648*
Roosevelt, Theodore. Assimilation. Indian Rights Association. New York. 1890-1910. *1014*
—. Attitudes. Florida. South. Washington, Booker T. 1901. *2080*
—. Civil Service Commissioner. Indian Rights Association. Indian-White Relations. Welsh, Herbert. 1889-95. *1011*
—. Coal Mines and Mining. Federal government. Pennsylvania. Strikes. 1902. *2218*
—. Crawford, Coe Isaac. Progressivism. Republican Party. South Dakota. State Politics. 1912-14. *2076*
—. Georgia. Negroes. Political Attitudes. Progressive Party. Wilson, Woodrow. 1912. *2038*
—. LaFollette, Robert Marion. Nominations to Office. Presidency. Republican Party. 1910-12. *2022*
—. Man with the Muck-Rake (speech). Political Speeches. Rhetoric. 1906. *2014*
—. Montana. National Park Service. Wildlife conservation. Yellowstone National Park. 1883-1918. *2079*
—. Political Participation. Woman suffrage. 1899-1919. *2163*

Rosen, George. Medicine, preventive. Occupations. Public health. Social History. 1930's-77. *442*
Ross, François Xavier. Catholic Church. Quebec (Gaspé Peninsula). Social Conditions. 1923-45. *374*
Ross, John (chief). Cherokee Indians. Federal government. Georgia. Land (cessions). Payne, John Howard (letter). 1820's-30's. *575*
Rossville Health Center. Medical care. Mormon, Square. Poor People's Health Council. Race relations. Tennessee (Fayette County). 1960's-70's. *2821*
Rousseau, Lovell H. Democratic Party. Elections. Louisiana. Military Occupation. Reconstruction. 1868-69. *990*
Royal Canadian Mounted Police. Canada, western. Conspiracy. Intelligence service. Labor Disputes. One Big Union. 1919. *1612*
—. Law Enforcement. Northwest Territories. Prohibition. 1874-91. *1460*
Royal Commission of Inquiry into the Relations between Capital and Labour. Canada. Labor Reform. 1886-89. *1314*
Rubber. Industrial Workers of the World. Ohio (Akron). Strikes. 1913. *2290*
Rugg, Harold Ordway. Academic freedom. National security. Ohio State University. Speeches, Addresses, etc. 1951. *2771*
Ruggles, David. Abolitionists. Brown, William Wells. Medicine. Negroes. Remond, Sarah Parker. Smith, James McCune. Tubman, Harriet. 1810-85. *329*
Rural Cemetery Movement. Cemeteries. 1804-35. *579*
Rural Development. Antigonish Movement. Catholic Church. Nova Scotia. Social change. ca 1928-73. *1854*
Rural Electrification Administration. Conservation of Natural Resources. Cooke, Morris L. New Deal. 1933-51. *2491*
Rural Life. *See* Country Life.
Rural Schools. Agricultural Production. Cities. Country Life Movement. Educational Reform. 1900-20. *2302*
—. American Institute for Education. Educational Reform. Elites. Massachusetts. Nationalism. 1830-37. *839*
Rural Settlements *See also* Settlement; Villages.
—. Community centers. Country life movement. Progressives. Religion. 1900's-20's. *2099*
Rusby, Henry Hurd. Americas (North and South). Columbia University College of Pharmacy. Medicine. Pharmacy. Scientific Expeditions. ca 1880-1930. *286*
Rush, Benjamin. Religion. 1770's-1813. *318*
Ruskin (colony). Tennessee. Utopias. Wayland, Julius Augustus. 1894-1901. *1503*
Russell, Daniel. Government Regulation. North Carolina. Populism. Progressivism. Railroads. 1894-98. *1369*
Russell, Howard Hyde. Anti-Saloon League. Organizations. Temperance movements. 1895-1900. *1464*
Russell, Jane. Censorship. Hughes, Howard. Legion of Decency. Motion Picture Producers and Distributors of America. *Outlaw* (film). 1940-49. *2649*
Russia *See also* Finland; Poland; USSR.
—. Alberta. Cooperative Commonwealth Federation. Populism. Saskatchewan. Social Credit Party. USA. 1870's-1940's. *14*
—. Anarchism and Anarchists. Intellectuals. Kropotkin, Pëtr. Lectures. 1897-1901. *1501*
—. Communism. Kollontai, Aleksandra. Norway. Propaganda. World War I. 1915-16. *2046*
—. Manitoba (Winnipeg). Penner, Jacob. Socialist Party. 1900-65. *406*
Russian Revolution. Communist Party. Revolution. Rhetoric. 1917-20. *1976*
Russian Revolution (October). Impoundment. *Shilka* (vessel). Washington (Seattle). 1917. *2009*
Russwurm, John. Colleges and Universities. Negroes. 1823-1973. *181*
Rust, Horatio Nelson. Abolition Movement. Artifacts. California. Citrus industry. Indians (agencies). 1850's-1906. *276*
Ruthenberg, Charles Emil. Communist Party. North Central States. Political Leadership. USSR. 1919-27. *2414*
Ryerson, Egerton. Conflict and Conflict Resolution. Ontario School Act (1871). Secondary education. 1850's-80's. *1415*

S

Sabath, Adolph Joachim. House of Representatives. Illinois (Chicago). Politics. 1907-32. *298*
Sabbatarianism. Ontario (Toronto). Recreation. Tobogganing. 1912. *1609*
Sabbath. Bible. Presbyterian Church, Southern. South. 1861-1959. *103*
Sabbath Day Adventist Church. Adventists. Humphrey, James K. New York City (Harlem). Race Relations. Utopia Park. 1920's-30's. *1648*
Sabin, Ellen B. Oregon (Portland). Teaching. Wisconsin. Women. 1850-95. *405*
Sacramento Union (newspaper). California. Chinese Americans. Immigration. Nativism. 1850-82. *12*
Safety. Consumer Product Safety Commission. Federal Regulation. 1972-77. *2721*
—. Environmental Protection Agency. Equal Employment Opportunity Commission. Labor. Occupational Safety and Health Act (US, 1970). Women. 1970-76. *2698*
Safety Appliances Act (US, 1893). Accidents. Courts. Federal Employers' Liability Act (US, 1908). Management. Railroads. Working Conditions. 1890-1913. *2117*
"Safety First" (slogan). Industrial safety. Reform. Young, Robert J. ca 1900-16. *1886*
Sailors' Union. American Federation of Labor. Industrial Workers of the World. Louisiana. Marine Transport Workers. Strikes. United Fruit Company. 1913. *2193*
St. Andrew's Church. Crapsey, Algernon Sidney. Episcopal Church, Protestant. Heresy. New York (Rochester). Reform. Trials. 1879-1927. *454*
St. Bridget's Home. Catholic Church. Immigrants. Irish Americans. McMahon, Patrick. Poor. Quebec (Quebec). 1847-1972. *244*
St. Cloud *Visitor* (newspaper). Abolition Movement. Feminism. Minnesota. Swisshelm, Jane Grey. 1857-62. *814*
St. Louis Children's Hospital. Children. Missouri. Women. 1879-1979. *237*
St. Louis *Daily Press* (newspaper). Labor. Local Politics. Missouri. Racism. Reconstruction. 1864-66. *1339*
St. Louis Transit Company. Mass Transit. Missouri. Modernization. Monopolies. Strikes. 1900. *2257*
St. Luke's-in-the-Desert Hospital. Arizona (Tucson; Tent City). Baptists. Comstock, Oliver E. Medical care. 1907-37. *1596*
St. Philip's Church. Episcopal Church, Protestant. New York City. Newspapers. Racism. Riots. Williams, Peter, Jr. 1830-50. *671*
Saint Vincent de Paul Society. Children. Indians. Poor. 1900-10. *2036*
Salaries. *See* Wages.
Salish (Flathead) Indians. Dawes Act (US, 1887). Flathead Indian Reservation. Indians. Land Tenure. Montana. 1887-1904. *1075*
Salubria (community). Iowa. Kneeland, Abner. Utopias. 1827-44. *914*
Sam, Alfred Charles. Africa, West. Black Nationalism. Colonization. Newspapers. Oklahoma. 1913-14. *2008*
—. Colonization. Gold Coast. Negroes. 1913-16. *1997*
San Francisco *Bulletin*. California. Editors and Editing. Older, Fremont. Reporters and Reporting. Women. 1895-1925. *1887*
San Quentin Prison. Bombing. California (San Francisco). Mooney, Tom. Socialist Party. Trials. 1916-42. *2020*
Sanborn, Franklin Benjamin. Abolition Movement. Brown, John. Civil War (antecedents). Harpers Ferry raid. 1854-60. *707*
Sand Creek Massacre. Colorado. Indian Wars. Soule, Silas S. 1859-65. *44*
Sanders, George. Democratic Party. Douglas, Stephen A. Political Factions. Young America movement. 1850's. *547*
Sanford, Edward Terry. Civil rights. Constitutional Amendments (14th). *Gitlow* v. *New York* (US, 1925). Supreme Court. ca 1890-1930. *2399*
Sanger, Margaret. Birth control. Dickenson, Robert Latou. Physicians. Values. Women. 1830-1970. *87*
Sanitation *See also* Cemeteries; Pollution, Public Health; Water Supply.
—. Cholera. City Government. Hospitals. Massachusetts (Springfield). 1865-70. *1471*
—. Cities. Reform. Women. 1880-1917. *1975*

—. City Government. Medicine. Reform. Refuse disposal. Technology. Wisconsin (Milwaukee). 1867-1911. *1466*
—. City planning. Diseases. 1840-90. *245*
—. Griscom, John H. (letters). Public Health. Reform. Shattuck, Lemuel. 1843-47. *863*
—. Health. Medicines, Patent. Nebraska (Omaha). 1870-1900. *1456*
—. Illinois. 1865-1900. *1449*
Santa Clara Pueblo v. Martinez (US, 1977). Civil Rights. Indian Civil Rights Act (US, 1968). Natural law. Pueblo Indians. Tribal government. 1939-77. *2789*
Sarah C. Roberts v. City of Boston (Massachusetts, 1850). Civil Rights. Massachusetts (Boston). Roberts, Sarah C. School Integration. 1849-50. 1950's. *834*
Saskatchewan See also Prairie Provinces.
—. Agriculture. Dewdney, Edgar. Hunting. Indians (reservations). Northwest Territories. 1879-84. *1038*
—. Alberta. Cooperative Commonwealth Federation. Populism. Russia. Social Credit Party. USA. 1870's-1940's. *14*
—. Alberta. New Brunswick. Populism. Radicals and Radicalism. Social organization. 1950's-70's. *2700*
—. Anderson, James T. M. Anglicization. English language. Ethnic groups. Immigrants. Public schools. 1918-23. *1856*
—. Anderson, James T. M. Anti-Catholicism. Public schools. School Act (amended). Secularization. 1929-34. *1848*
—. Anti-Catholicism. Education, Finance. MacKinnon, Murdoch. School Act (amended). Scott, Walter. 1913-26. *1849*
—. Anti-Catholicism. Ku Klux Klan. Protestantism. 1927-30. *1547*
—. Brown, W. G. Hayes, Michael P. Herridge, W. D. United Reform Movement. 1938-40. *1664*
—. Catholic Church. Cooperative Commonwealth Federation. Socialism. 1930-50. *1620*
—. Catholic Church. Religious Education. Youth. 1870-1978. *207*
—. Coal Mines and Mining. Labor Unions and Organizations. One Big Union. 1907-45. *1782*
—. Communist Party. Cooperative Commonwealth Federation. Elections (provincial). 1930's. *1680*
—. Conservatism. Progressivism. 1920's. *1556*
—. Cooperative Commonwealth Federation. League for Social Reconstruction. Regina Manifesto. Underhill, Frank. 1933. *1611*
—. Cooperative Commonwealth Federation. Political Participation. United Farmers of Canada. 1930-45. *1606*
—. Cooperative Commonwealth Federation. Political Parties. Socialism. 1928-44. *1681*
—. Dukhobors. Public schools. 1905-50. *1855*
—. Farmer-Labor Party. Political Leadership. Radicals and Radicalism. Socialism. 1932-34. *1607*
—. Farmers. Grange. Oklahoma. Socialism. Texas. 1900-45. *1714*
—. Government. Land. Settlement. 1929-35. *1796*
—. Saskatoon Women Teachers' Association. Teachers. Women. 1918-70's. *1627*
—. Saskatoon Women Teachers' Association. Saskatchewan. Teachers. Women. 1918-70's. *1627*
Savannah Men's Sunday Club. Georgia. Negroes. Social Change. 1905-11. *1970*
Savery, Anne. Bloomer, Amelia. Iowa. State Politics. Woman suffrage. Woodhull, Victoria Claflin. 1868-72. *1111*
Scalawags. Carpetbaggers. House of Representatives. Negroes. Reconstruction. Republican Party. South. 1868-72. *1036*
—. Louisiana. Negroes. Ray, John. Republican Party. ca 1836-88. *463*
—. Louisiana. Ostracism. Reconstruction. State Politics. Terrorism. 1866-78. *1081*
Scandinavia. Law. Self-awareness. Social Change. Women's Liberation Movement. 1840-1977. *35*
Scarlett, Sam. Čačić, Tomo. Ethnic Groups. Kjelt, Ole. Krat, Pavlo. Leftism. Mäkelä, A. B. Political Protest. Puttee, Arthur. 1907-34. *1561*
—. Canada. Communist Party. Industrial Workers of the World. Labor Unions and Organizations. 1900-41. *278*
Schaper, William A. Academic freedom. Minnesota, University of. World War I. 1917. *2143*

Schisms. Abolition Movement. American Free Baptist Mission Society. Baptists. Missions and Missionaries. 1830-69. *702*
—. Abolition Movement. Sects, Religious. ca 1840-60. *703*
Schmidt, Minna Moscherosch. Business. Feminism. Illinois (Chicago). Philanthropy. 1886-1961. *315*
Scholars. Mead, Margaret. Social sciences. Talbot, Marion. Thompson, Helen. Women. 1900-20's. *2065*
Scholarship. Public Welfare. *Social Service Review* (periodical). Social work. 1927-77. *1567*
School Act (amended). Anderson, James T. M. Anti-Catholicism. Public schools. Saskatchewan. Secularization. 1929-34. *1848*
—. Anti-Catholicism. Education, Finance. MacKinnon, Murdoch. Saskatchewan. Scott, Walter. 1913-26. *1849*
School boards. Decentralization Act (1969). Minorities. New York City (Brooklyn, Lower East Side). Public Schools. 1969-73. *2965*
—. Educational reform. Elites. Niles Bill (Ohio, 1898). Ohio (Toledo). Progressive Era. 1890's. *2328*
School Busing. *See* Busing.
School Integration See also Busing.
—. Affirmative action. Education. Negroes. 17c-20c. *2845*
—. Arkansas (Little Rock). Collins, LeRoy. Courts. Federal Government. Florida. Political Speeches. 1957. *2688*
—. Attitudes. Judges. South. 1954-70. *2833*
—. Bohanon, Luther. Courts. Oklahoma (Oklahoma City). 1955-79. *2808*
—. *Brown v. Board of Education* (US, 1954). Constitutional Amendments (14th). Illinois (Chicago). South. 1954-77. *2777*
—. *Brown v. Board of Education* (US, 1954). Educators. Negroes. 1954-75. *2838*
—. *Brown v. Board of Education* (US, 1954). Rhetoric. 1954-78. *2670*
—. Byrd, Harry F. Chambers, Lenoir. Editors and Editing. Virginia. 1955-59. *2681*
—. Catholic Church. Church Schools. Glennon, John J. Missouri (St. Louis). Ritter, Joseph E. 1935-47. *1850*
—. Cities. North. South. 1954-77. *2830*
—. City Government. Louisiana (New Orleans). 1952-61. *2679*
—. Civil Rights. Massachusetts (Boston). Roberts, Sarah C. *Sarah C. Roberts v. City of Boston* (Massachusetts, 1850). 1849-50. 1950's. *834*
—. Civil Rights Act (US, 1964). Florida. Supreme Court decisions. 1954-64. *2686*
—. Civil rights movement. Illinois (Chicago). Negroes. 1936. *2523*
—. Colleges and universities. Law. 19c-20c. *2886*
—. Colleges and Universities (black). Fort Valley State College. Georgia (Peach County). *Hunnicutt et al. v. Burge et al.* (Georgia, 1972). Racism. 1972-78. *2800*
—. Congress. Courts. 1950's-70's. *2877*
—. Discrimination, housing. Metropolitan areas. 1945-77. *1858*
—. Downing, George T. Negroes. Public schools. Rhode Island (Newport). 1855-66. *841*
—. Education. Negroes. North Carolina. Reconstruction. 1865-67. *1127*
—. Equal opportunity. Louisiana Education Association. Negroes. Teachers. 1901-70. *1857*
—. Equal Rights League. Pennsylvania. Public schools. 1834-81. *208*
—. Ethnic Groups. Negroes. 1964-78. *2879*
—. Federal government. State Government. 1954-77. *2825*
—. Justice Department. Lawsuits. Negroes. South. 1957-68. *2811*
—. Kentucky (Louisville). Negroes. 1954-77. *2799*
—. Lawyers. Marshall, Thurgood. Maryland, University of, School of Law. Murray, Donald G. NAACP. 1930-54. *2531*
—. Michigan (Pontiac). Public schools. Race relations. 1971-74. *2827*
—. Missouri (St. Louis). Negroes. 1954-55. *2667*
—. Public Schools. 1954-1976. *2846*
—. Race Relations. Supreme Court decisions. 1954-74. *2865*
—. Supreme Court. 1877-1977. *1831*
—. Tennessee (Memphis). White flight. 1963-76. *2969*

Schools See also Church Schools; Colleges and Universities; Education; Free Schools; Junior Colleges; Junior High Schools; Private Schools; Public Schools; Rural Schools; Students; Teaching.
—. Acculturation. Collier, John. Florida. Indians. North Carolina. Seminole Indians. 1927-54. *1851*
—. Africa. Colonization. Negroes (free). 1816-33. *837*
—. Arizona. Kibbey, Joseph H. Segregation. 1908-12. *2309*
—. Assimilation. British Columbia. Indians. 1890-1920. *1861*
—. Bureau of Indian Affairs. Christianity. Indian-White Relations. Iowa. Winnebago Indians. 1834-48. *850*
—. City government. Construction. Maryland (Baltimore). Urban reform. 1870-1900. *1402*
—. Corporal punishment. Educational Reform. New Jersey. 1800-1972. *1432*
—. Freedmen. North. Race Relations. Teachers. Virginia (Lexington). 1867. *1405*
—. Freedmen's Bureau. Kentucky. Noble, Thomas. Race Relations. Reconstruction. 1865-70. *1190*
—. Freedmen's Bureau. Race relations. West Virginia (Berkeley, Jefferson counties). 1865-68. *1264*
—. Girls. Prizes. 1820-50. *553*
Schools, summer. Labor movement. Middle Classes. South. Women. 1927-41. *1580*
Schroeder, Theodore. Atheism. *Lucifer's Lantern* (periodical). Mormons. Utah. 1889-1900. *1486*
Schurz, Carl. California. Indians. Jackson, Helen Hunt *(Ramona).* Mission Indians. Ponca Indians. Removals, forced. 1873-84. *1051*
—. Political Leadership. Reform. 1852-1906. *458*
Schuyler, Mont. Grady, John (letters). Haywood, William Dudley. Industrial Workers of the World. USSR. 1921-22. *2425*
Schwab, Charles M. Pennsylvania (Bethlehem). Steel industry. Strikes. 1910. *2223*
Science See also headings beginning with the word scientific; Bacteriology; Ethnology; Mathematics.
—. Association for the Advancement of Women. Education. Mitchell, Maria. Women. 1870-89. *1035*
—. Attitudes. Chiropractic. Cults. Medicine (practice of). 1850's-1970's. *229*
—. Education. Women. ca 1800-60. *816*
—. Evolution. LeConte, Joseph. Sex roles. Women's rights. 1890's. *1115*
—. Feminism. Firestone, Shulamith. Fuller, Margaret. Gilman, Charlotte Perkins. Godwin, Mary Wollstonecraft. 1759-1972. *64*
—. Mathews, Shailer. Modernism. Social gospel. Theology. 1864-1930. *446*
—. Pragmatism. Social change. 1900-40. *1608*
—. Vegetarianism. 1850's. *904*
Science and Society. Liberalism. *New Republic* (periodical). Progressivism. 1914-20. *2040*
Scientific Expeditions See also names of specific expeditions.
—. Americas (North and South). Columbia University College of Pharmacy. Medicine. Pharmacy. Rusby, Henry Hurd. ca 1880-1930. *286*
Scientific Experiments and Research. Attitudes. Kinsey, Alfred C. Sex. ca 1940-77. *2678*
—. Dohrn, Anton. Hyde, Ida H. Italy. Naples Zoological Station. Women. 1896-97. *1434*
Scientific management. Bancroft, Joseph and Sons Company. Delaware (Wilmington). Miller, Franklin, and Stevenson (firm). Textile Industry. 1911-27. *2281*
—. Charities. Medical care. Progressivism. 1900-20. *2064*
—. Railroad Carmen's Strike (1911-15). Strikes. Working class. 1903-22. *2256*
Scientists See also names of individual scientists.
—. Boas, Franz. Discrimination. Wilder, Burt G. 1900-15. *1884*
—. Carver, George Washington. Negroes. 1900-75. *380*
Scott, Emmett Jay. Moton, Robert Russa. Negroes. Politics. Tuskegee Institute. Washington, Booker T. 1915-25. *1643*
Scott, Walter. Anti-Catholicism. Education, Finance. MacKinnon, Murdoch. Saskatchewan. School Act (amended). 1913-26. *1849*
Scovell, Melville Amasa. Allen, Robert McDowell. Food Adulteration and Inspection. Kentucky. Progressivism. 1898-1916. *2125*

Scudder, Vida Dutton. Christianity. Industrial Relations. Massachusetts (Lawrence). Women. 1912. *2196*
Seamen. Alabama. Mobile Harbor Act (Alabama, 1842). Negroes. Petitions. Prisons. State Legislatures. 1849. *727*
Searches. Common law. Constitutional Amendments (4th). Great Britain. 15c-18c. *512*
Sebree, Shubert (letters). Debs, Eugene V. Debs, Theodore. Indiana. Labor Unions and Organizations. 1890-1930's. *418*
Secession *See also* States' Rights.
—. Civil War (antecedents). Greeley, Horace. Reform. Slavery. 1860-61. *781*
Secondary Education *See also* Adult Education; Junior High Schools; Private Schools; Public Schools.
—. Conflict and Conflict Resolution. Ontario School Act (1871). Ryerson, Egerton. 1850's-80's. *1415*
—. Depressions. General Education Board. Public policy. Rockefeller, John D. Social change. 1930's. *2478*
Secret Societies. Cooperative Workers of America. Georgia. Hoover, Hiram F. Negroes. South Carolina. 1886-87. *1197*
Sectional Conflict. Abolition Movement. Brown, John. Harpers Ferry raid. North Carolina. State Politics. 1840-60. *675*
Sects, Religious. Abolition Movement. Schisms. ca 1840-60. *703*
—. Florida (Lee County). Koreshan Unity. Politics. Teed, Cyrus Reed. Utopias. 1880-1909. *1516*
Secularism. Childhood. Leadership. Religion. Sex roles. Women. 1636-1930. *381*
Secularization. Anderson, James T. M. Anti-Catholicism. Public schools. Saskatchewan. School Act (amended). 1929-34. *1848*
—. Church and State. Education. Great Britain. India. 19c. *198*
Sedition. Jones Family (group). Oklahoma (Cleveland, Pottawatomie counties). Trials. Working Class Union. World War I. 1917. *2155*
See, Isaac M. New Jersey (Newark). Presbyterian Church. Sermons. Women. 1876. *1485*
Segregation *See also* Desegregation; Discrimination; Minorities; Negroes.
—. Antioch College. Colleges and Universities. Negroes. Ohio (Yellow Springs). 1966-69. *2864*
—. Arizona. Kibbey, Joseph H. Schools. 1908-12. *2309*
—. Arkansas. Jim Crow laws. Negroes. Political Leadership. 1890's. *1193*
—. Army. Committee on Participation of Negroes in the National Defense Program. NAACP. Negroes. Pittsburgh *Courier* (newspaper). 1937-40. *2506*
—. Attitudes. Economic Growth. Governors. South. 1950-69. *1533*
—. Boycotts. Mass Transit. Negroes. Virginia. 1904-07. *2154*
—. Boycotts. Mexican Americans. Presbyterian Church. Public schools. Texas (San Angelo). 1910-15. *2303*
—. Civil rights. Supreme Court. Vinson, Frederick M. 1946-53. *2671*
—. Class conflict. Race relations. South. 1865-90's. *1280*
—. Colleges and Universities (black). State Government. Texas. 1876-1947. *1846*
—. Conservatism. Elections, presidential. Mississippi. Sillers, Walter. State Legislatures. 1948-64. *2677*
—. Courts. Democratic Party. Primaries. South Carolina. Waring, J. Waties. 1947-52. *2683*
—. Discrimination, Employment. Military Service (enlistees). Navies. Negroes. Race Relations. 1798-1970's. 1970D 1900H. *41*
—. Education, Finance. Kentucky. Negroes. State Government. 1865-1954. *1178*
—. Elementary education. Florida. Peabody Fund. Reconstruction. 1869-76. *1433*
—. Federal Government. Negroes. 1916-29. *2392*
—. Federal Government. Trotter, William Monroe. Wilson, Woodrow. 1913-14. *2016*
—. Florida. Law. Race Relations. Social customs. 1865-1977. *141*
—. Housing. Kentucky (Louisville). NAACP. Supreme Court. 1914-17. *2126*

—. Housing and Urban Development Act (US, 1965, Section 23). Illinois (Chicago). Law. Negroes. Public Housing Authority. 1964-75. *2856*
—. Law. Occupations. Sex Discrimination. Women. 20c. *2910*
—. Leadership. Negroes. Urbanization. Virginia (Richmond). 1900-20. *1947*
—. Legislation. Pennsylvania (Philadelphia). Streetcars. 1850's-70. *1156*
—. Negroes. New York City (Jamaica). Public schools. 1895-1900. *1210*
—. Negroes. *Plessy vs. Ferguson* (US, 1896). Supreme Court (decisions). 1896. *1212*
—. Race relations. South. 1865-90. *1237*
Segregation *(de jure, de facto)*. California (Orange County). *Mendez* v. *Westminster* (California, 1946). Mexican Americans. Public schools. 1850-1970's. *1865*
Segregation, residential. Metropolitan areas. Race Relations. 1960-70. *2896*
Self-awareness. Law. Scandinavia. Social Change. Women's Liberation Movement. 1840-1977. *35*
Self-determination. Assimilation. Education. Indians. 1960's-70's. *2963*
—. Black power. Church and Social Problems. Economic Aid. Episcopal Church, Protestant. General Convention Special Program. 1963-75. *2850*
—. Bureau of Indian Affairs. Indians. 1945-75. *1545*
—. Micronesia. Pacific Dependencies (US). Social Conditions. 1947-80. *2776*
Self-expression. Evangelicalism. Women. 1800-50. *799*
Self-help. Black nationalism. Bruce, John Edward. Economic independence. 1874-1924. *16*
—. Bromley, Walter. Charities. Micmac Indians. Nova Scotia. Poverty. 1813-25. *870*
—. Dix, I. F. Hoover, Herbert C. Local politics. Unemployed Citizens' League. Washington (Seattle). 1931-32. *2417*
Self-image. Adams, Mary Newbury. Iowa. Social status. Women. 1850-1900. *1042*
Self-improvement. Black power. Political Protest. Sociology. 1960's-70's. *2859*
Self-perception. Mexican Americans. Minorities in Politics. Public Schools. Texas (southern). 1930's-69. *1863*
Seminole Indians. Acculturation. Collier, John. Florida. Indians. North Carolina. Schools. 1927-54. *1851*
—. Civil Rights. Florida (Kissimmee). Friends of the Florida Seminoles. Indians. Tiger, Tom. 1898-99. *1100*
Senate *See also* House of Representatives; Legislation.
—. Alcorn University. Mississippi. Negroes. Race Relations. Revels, Hiram Rhodes. ca 1870's. *1256*
—. Bilbo, Theodore G. Employment. Fair Employment Practices Committee. Filibusters. Mississippi. Racism. 1941-46. *2617*
—. Blaine, John J. Progressivism. Republican Party. Wisconsin. 1927-33. *2421*
—. Bulkley, Robert J. Elections. Ohio. Prohibition. 1918-30. *2445*
—. Elections (presidential). Hoover, Herbert C. Progressivism. Republican Party. 1930-32. *2369*
—. Felton, Rebecca Latimer. Georgia. Politics. Woman suffrage. 1860's-1922. *423*
—. Harrison, Pat. Social Security Act (US, 1935). 1934-35. *2598*
—. Kern, John W. Labor Law. Workman's Compensation Act (US, 1916). 1908-17. *2221*
—. Mississippi. Negroes. Public Opinion. Revels, Hiram Rhodes. 1870. *1202*
—. New Deal. Progressives. 1933-34. *2558*
—. New Deal. Progressives. Roosevelt, Franklin D. 1935-36. *2557*
Senate Subcommittee on Antitrust and Monopoly. Drugs. Federal regulation. Kefauver, Estes. South. 1950's-60's. *2939*
Seneca Indians. Anthropology. Indians. Pan-Indianism. Parker, Arthur C. 1881-1925. *355*
Senior, Clarence. Continental Congress of Workers and Farmers. Socialist Party. 1933. *2611*
Sentencing. California (Alameda County). Courts. Plea bargaining. 1880-1970's. *122*
—. Courts. Plea bargaining. 19c. *125*
Senter, DeWitt Clinton. Republican Party. Suffrage. Tennessee. 1869-70. *954*
Sentinels of the Republic. Capitalism. Conservatism. Coolidge, Louis Arthur. 1900-25. *450*

Separate coach bills. Jim Crow laws. Negroes. Railroads. South Carolina. 1880-98. *1215*
Separatism. Bibb, Henry. Canada. Emigration. Negroes. USA. 1830-60. *672*
Separatist Movements. Educational Reform. Massachusetts (Boston). Negroes. Smith, Thomas Paul. 1848-49. *855*
Serials. *See* Periodicals.
Sermons. Antinomianism. Emerson, Ralph Waldo. Puritans. 1820's-30's. *570*
—. Attitudes. Mather, Cotton. New England. Women. 1650-1800. *493*
—. California. North Carolina. Sermons. Social Conditions. 1969-78. *2729*
—. California. North Carolina. Sermons. Social Conditions. 1969-78. *2729*
—. New Jersey (Newark). Presbyterian Church. See, Isaac M. Women. 1876. *1485*
Servants. Employment. Reform. 1892-1920. *2271*
Settlement *See also* Colonization; Frontier and Pioneer Life; Homesteading and Homesteaders; Resettlement; Rural Settlements.
—. Government. Land. Saskatchewan. 1929-35. *1796*
Settlement houses. Bellamy, George. Hiram House. Ohio (Cleveland). 1896-1914. *1958*
—. Cincinnati Union Bethel. Jews. Ohio. 1838-1903. *225*
Settlement Movement. Political attitudes. Reformers. Religion. 1880's-90's. *1462*
Seventh-Day Adventists. *See* Adventists.
Sewall, Samuel E. Freedom. Fugitive Slaves. Latimer, George. Law. Massachusetts (Boston). Shaw, Lemuel. ca 1790-1890. *784*
Sex *See also* Homosexuality; Men; Women.
—. Attitudes. Canada. English Canadians. Race. Woman Suffrage. ca 1877-1918. *1*
—. Attitudes. Kinsey, Alfred C. Scientific Experiments and Research. ca 1940-77. *2678*
—. Attitudes. Morrow, Prince Albert. 1890-1915. *1899*
—. Beecher, Henry Ward. Feminism. New York City. Radicals and Radicalism. Vanderbilt, Cornelius. Woodhull, Victoria Claflin. 1868-90's. *336*
—. Behavior. Progressivism. Reform. 1890-1920. *1995*
—. Beilhardt, Jacob. Ohio (Lisbon). Spirit Fruit Society. Utopias. 1865-1908. *1505*
—. Economic conditions. Feminism. Social Classes. 1600-1900. *36*
—. Family. New York. Noyes, John Humphrey. Oneida Community. Religion. 1848-80. *271*
—. Feminism. Fuller, Margaret. Hawthorne, Nathaniel *(The Blithedale Romance)*. James, Henry *(Bostonians)*. Politics. 19c. *795*
—. Freudianism. New York City (Greenwich Village). Psychoanalysis. Radicals and Radicalism. 1913-20. *1936*
—. Human Relations. Radicals and Radicalism. Wright, Henry Clarke. 1830-66. *805*
—. Lewis, Dioclesius. Medical reform. Morality. Rhythmics. Women. 1860-1970's. *1481*
—. Morality. Reform. 19c. *102*
—. New York. Noyes, John Humphrey. Oneida Community. Social Status. Women. 1848-79. *266*
—. Newspapers. Race Relations. Smith, Lillian. South. 20c. *422*
Sex Discrimination. American Medical Association. Medicine. 1847-1910. *1031*
—. Bradwell, Myra. Illinois. Lawyers. Supreme Court (decision). 1873-1894. *1114*
—. Civil rights movement. Freedom Summers. Women. 1960-65. *2882*
—. Congress. Equal Employment Opportunity Commission. Feminism. 1964-74. *2920*
—. Economic opportunity. Educational achievements. Men. Women. 1962. 1973. *2908*
—. Feminism. Maryland, University of. Oral history. 1968-78. *2913*
—. Grimké, Sarah Moore (letter). Women. 1853. *803*
—. Judicial Administration. Juvenile delinquency. Progressivism. 1890's-1910's. *2072*
—. Labor. Occupations. Social Change. 1950-70. *1813*
—. Law. Occupations. Segregation. Women. 20c. *2910*
—. Legislation. Minimum wage. Occupations. Ohio. Women. 1914-33. *1539*
—. Negroes. Women's Liberation Movement. 1960-75. *2133*
Sex roles. Abolition Movement. Feminism. Social Change. 1820's-80. *798*
—. Abortion. Family. 19c-20c. *37*

Sex roles

—. Addams, Jane. Values. 1880-1920. *281*
—. Addams, Jane. Women. Youth. 1860-89. *308*
—. Attitudes. Industry. National War Labor Board. Public Policy. Wages. Women. World War I. 1918-19. *2191*
—. Beecher, Catharine. Physical Education and Training. Women. 1830's-40's. *815*
—. Birth control. Feminism. 1870's-80's. *1007*
—. Canada. Christianity. Missions and Missionaries. Women. 1815-99. *1490*
—. Centennial Exposition of 1876. Values. Women. World's Columbian Exposition (Chicago, 1893). 1876-93. *948*
—. Childhood. Leadership. Religion. Secularism. Women. 1636-1930. *381*
—. Civil Rights Movement. Employment. Women's Liberation Movement. 1950's-75. *2905*
—. Colleges and Universities. Education. Ideology. Women. 19c-20c. *213*
—. Colleges and Universities. Grinnell College. Iowa. Women. 1884-1917. *221*
—. Communes. Owen, Robert Dale. Women. 1824-28. *931*
—. Curricula. Domesticity. Home economics. Progressivism. 1900-20. *2314*
—. Education. Employment. Social Classes. Women. 1964-74. *2919*
—. Evolution. LeConte, Joseph. Science. Women's rights. 1890's. *1115*
—. Feminism. Massachusetts Association Opposed to the Further Extension of the Suffrage to Women. Political campaigns. Socialism. Woman suffrage. 1895-1915. *2166*
—. Girl Scouts of America. Identity. Low, Juliette. 1900-20. *452*
—. Labor. Women's Liberation Movement. 19c-20c. *46*
—. Literature. Motherhood. Women. 1785-1815. *793*
—. Literature. Social Change. Women. 19c. *78*
—. Military. Women. World War II. 1941-44. *2628*
—. Navy League (Woman's Section). Preparedness. Suffrage. Woman's Peace Party. World War I. 1914-18. *2092*
—. Progressive education. Women. 1880-1940. *179*
—. Protestantism. Sunday School Movement. Women. 1790-1880. *180*
Sexism. Abolition Movement. Connecticut (Canterbury). Crandall, Prudence. Garrison, William Lloyd. Racism. 1830-40. *550*
Sexual revolution. Chafe, William. Feminism. Historiography. O'Neill, William. ca 1920-70. *2374*
Sexuality. Abolition Movement. Reform. 1830-65. *780*
—. Attitudes. 1650-1976. *123*
—. Bible. Presbyterian Church. 1975-80. *2740*
—. Family. Social Theory. Sumner, William Graham. 1870's-1910. *985*
—. Feminism. Morality. Physical Education and Training. Women. 19c. *101*
Shadd, Mary Ann. Antislavery Sentiments. Negroes. Newspapers. Ontario. *Provincial Freeman* (newspaper). 1852-93. *351*
Shakers. Children. Education. 1780-1900. *912*
Shank, Corwin. Progressive Era. Reformatories. Washington (Monroe). 1904-18. *1972*
Sharecroppers. Agricultural Adjustment Administration. Depressions. Labor Unions and Organizations. Southern Tenant Farmers' Union. ca 1930's. *2602*
—. Arkansas. Disasters. Droughts. Negroes. Plantations. Red Cross. 1930-31. *2463*
Sharecropping. Alabama. Freedmen. Labor. Plantations. 1865-67. *1198*
—. Contracts. Freedmen's Bureau. Planters. South. 1865-68. *1258*
Share-Our-Wealth movement. Depressions. Long, Huey P. Louisiana. Politics. Smith, Gerald L. K. 1930's. *2527*
—. Economic Reform. Long, Huey P. 1932-35. *2485*
—. Elections (presidential). Long, Huey P. Roosevelt, Franklin D. 1932-36. *2595*
—. Long, Huey P. Political Leadership. 1928-35. *2526*
Shattuck, Lemuel. Griscom, John H. (letters). Public Health. Reform. Sanitation. 1843-47. *863*
Shattuck Mine. Arizona (Bisbee). Industrial Workers of the World. Strikes. 1917. *2285*

Shaw, Anna Howard. Anthony, Lucy. Employment. Equal opportunity. Feminism. 1865-1919. *330*
—. Methodist Protestant Church. Social Gospel. Woman suffrage. 1880-1919. *448*
Shaw, John. Assimilation. Finley, James B. Indians (agencies). Methodist Church. Missions and Missionaries. Ohio. 1820-24. *581*
Shaw, Lemuel. Freedom. Fugitive Slaves. Latimer, George. Law. Massachusetts (Boston). Sewall, Samuel E. ca 1790-1890. *784*
Shays' Rebellion. Farmers. Social Classes. 1770's-87. *580*
Shepherd, Henry Elliot. Education. Manual Training School. Maryland (Baltimore). Newell, Alexander McFadden. Politics. 1876-94. *1428*
Sheridan, Philip H. Louisiana. Military Occupation. Negro Suffrage. Reconstruction. 1865-67. *991*
Shilka (vessel). Impoundment. Russian Revolution (October). Washington (Seattle). 1917. *2009*
Shipbuilding. American Federation of Labor. Discrimination, Employment. Fair Employment Practices Committee. Federal Government. Labor Unions and Organizations. West Coast Master Agreement. World War II. 1939-46. *2627*
—. California (Sausalito). Discrimination. International Brotherhood of Boilermakers, Iron Shipbuilders and Helpers of America. *James v. Marinship* (California, 1945). Labor. Negroes. 1940-48. *2653*
Shoe Industry. Labor Unions and Organizations. Massachusetts (Lynn). Working class. 1895-1925. *2197*
—. Massachusetts (Haverhill). Strikes. Women. 1895. *1288*
—. Massachusetts (Marlboro). Public Opinion. Strikes. 1898-99. *1300*
Short, Wallace. City Politics. Freedom of speech. Industrial Workers of the World. Iowa (Sioux City). 1918-24. *2134*
Shuttlesworth, Fred L. Abernathy, Ralph. Alabama (Birmingham). Civil rights. Demonstrations. King, Martin Luther, Jr. 1956-79. *2809*
Sierra Leone *See also* Africa, West.
—. African Society. Colonization. Freedmen. Hopkins, Samuel. Rhode Island (Providence). 1789-95. *614*
—. Black nationalism. Colonization. Cuffe, Paul. Friends, Society of. 1810's. *694*
—. Colonization. Liberia. Methodist Episcopal Church. Missions and Missionaries. Negroes. 1833-48. *641*
Sierra Leone (Sherbro Island). Missions and Missionaries. Nova Scotia. Raymond, Eliza Ruggles. Slaves. 1839-50. *621*
Sifton, Clifford. Acculturation. Canada. Federal Policy. Indians. 1896-1905. *1012*
Sikes, Enoch W. Constitutions, State (reform). Hamilton, Joseph G. de Roulhac. North Carolina. Progressivism. State Legislatures. 1898-1913. *2091*
Silex, Humberto. Law Enforcement. Mine, Mill and Smelter Workers, International Union of. Nicaragua. Southwest. 1932-78. *1739*
Silk industry. Communist Party. Ontario. Quebec (Cowansville). Strikes. 1931. *1778*
—. New Jersey (Paterson). Strikes. 1913-24. *1761*
Sillers, Walter. Conservatism. Elections, presidential. Mississippi. Segregation. State Legislatures. 1948-64. *2677*
Simpson, Joshua McCarter. Antislavery Sentiments. *Emancipation Car* (collection). Music. 1854. *627*
Sin. Attitudes. 1830's-60's. *554*
Sinclair, Upton. California. Democratic Party. End Poverty In California (program). Political Campaigns (gubernatorial). ca 1933-34. *2592*
—. California. Political Campaigns (congressional). Socialist Party. ca 1920. *2464*
—. *Collier's Weekly*. Socialism. Sumner, William Graham. 1900-04. *1921*
Singers. Civil Rights. Leftism. Negroes. Robeson, Paul. 1898-1976. *379*
Single tax. California. Elections. Ralston, Jackson. Reform. 1932-38. *2504*
—. Capitalism. George, Henry. Politics. Progressivism. 1880-1920. *2188*
—. Dixon, Frederick John. Farmer, S. J. Independent Labour Party. Manitoba. 1920-49. *1791*
—. Fagan, Mark. New Jersey (Jersey City). Progressives. Taxation. 1901-17. *2278*

Single Tax movement. Delaware. George, Henry. Political Parties. Reform. 1890's. *1085*
—. George, Henry. Post, Louis F. 1872-98. *965*
—. Illinois (Chicago). Post, Louis F. Progressivism. *Public* (newspaper). 1898-1919. *1904*
—. Post, Louis F. Progressivism. 1898-1913. *1903*
Sioux Indians. Assimilation. Cheyenne River Indian Reservation. Federal Programs. Identity. Indians. 1889-1917. *45*
—. Civilian Conservation Corps (Indian Divison). Depressions. Indians (reservations). South Dakota. 1933-42. *2486*
Sioux Indians (Oglala). American Indian Movement. Indians. South Dakota (Wounded Knee). 1973. *2709*
Sit-ins. Civil rights. Institutions. Negroes. Organizations. South. 1960. *2868*
—. Desegregation. North Carolina (Greensboro). Political Protest. 1950's-60's. *2816*
Six Companies, Inc. Boulder Canyon Project. Hoover Dam. Industrial Workers of the World. Nevada. Strikes. 1931. *2434*
Skaneateles Community. Finch, John (letter). New York (Finger Lakes area). Utopias. 1843-45. *925*
Skokomish Indian Reservation. Dawes Act (US, 1887). Eells, Edwin. Indians (agencies). Land Tenure. Washington. 1871-95. *970*
Slave Revolts. Alabama (Mobile). Cowan, Jacob. North Carolina (Wilmington). Walker, David (*Appeal*). 1829-31. *726*
—. American Colonization Society. Gabriel's Insurrection. Monroe, James. Prosser, Gabriel. Virginia. 1800. *698*
—. American Revolution. North Carolina. 1750-1775. *529*
—. American Revolution. North Carolina. Race relations. 1775-1802. *622*
—. Andry plantation. Louisiana. 1801-12. *625*
—. Documents. Methodist Episcopal Church. Turner, Nat. Virginia. 1831-32. *908*
—. Historiography. South Carolina (Charleston). Vesey, Denmark. Wade, Richard (review article). 1821-22. 1964. *686*
Slave Trade. Abolitionists. Fugitive slaves. Government. Great Britain. Law. 1834-61. *774*
—. Fox, George. Friends, Society of. Pennsylvania. 1656-1754. *522*
Slaveholders. Abolition Movement. Bacon, Leonard. 1830-61. *746*
—. American Colonization Society. Emancipation. Liberia. North Carolina. 1800-60. *708*
—. Fugitive Slave Act (US, 1850). Kentucky (Boone, Bourbon counties). Michigan (Cass County). 1830-60. *786*
Slavery *See also* Abolition Movement; Antislavery Sentiments; Emancipation; Freedmen; Fugitive Slaves; Negroes; Proslavery Sentiments; Slave Trade.
—. Abolition Movement. Freedmen. Labor. Race relations. 1830-63. *613*
—. Abolitionists. Elkins, Stanley M. (review article). Transcendentalism. 1830-63. 1959-73. *791*
—. Abolitionists. Law. South. Supreme courts, state. 1810-60. *775*
—. Adams, John Quincy. Democratic Party. Elections (presidential). Jackson, Andrew. Whig Party. 1828-44. *737*
—. Africa. American Colonization Society. Colonization. McDonough, David. Medical Education. Presbyterian Church. 1840-50. *710*
—. American Colonization Society. Georgia (Griffin). Liberia. Moss, William (letters). 1853-57. *654*
—. American Colonization Society. Negroes, free. Rhetoric. Social Status. Whites. 1831-34. *615*
—. American Revolution. Attitudes. McIntosh, Lachlan. South. Wealth. 1775-87. *517*
—. American Revolution. Massachusetts (Boston). Wheatley, Phillis (letter). Whigs. 1767-80. *504*
—. Anti-Catholicism. Ohio. Political Systems. Republican Party. Whig Party. 1850's. *564*
—. Antislavery Sentiments. Pennsylvania (Philadelphia). Trials. Williamson, Passmore. 1855. *628*
—. Asbury, Francis. Coke, Thomas. Methodist Episcopal Church. 1780-1816. *624*
—. Attitudes. Baptists. Church and Social Problems. Furman, Richard. 1807-23. *695*

Slavery

—. Attitudes. Boundaries. Civil War (antecedents). Kansas. Missouri. 1854-56. *634*
—. Attitudes. Colonization. Kentucky. South. 1816-50. *602*
—. Attitudes. Howard, Martin. Law. Murder. North Carolina. 1765-91. *515*
—. Attitudes. Intellectuals. Letters. Social Classes. 1830-60. *790*
—. Attitudes. New England. Puritans. 1641-1776. *521*
—. Attitudes. New Jersey. Paterson, William. 1785-1804. *739*
—. Attitudes. Reform. Tennessee, western. 1820-40. *771*
—. Bacon's Rebellion. Class struggle. Racism. Social control. Virginia. 1660-92. *472*
—. Baptists. Wayland, Francis. 1830-45. *662*
—. British North America. Friends, Society of. Great Britain. 1757-61. *519*
—. Brown, John. Civil War (antecedents). Harpers Ferry raid. North Carolina. Social Psychology. 1859-60. *612*
—. Burt, Armistead. Calhoun, John C. Compromise of 1850. Congress. Oregon. Wilmot Proviso. ca 1846-60. *691*
—. Calhoun, John C. Jefferson, Thomas. South. 1830's-40's. *787*
—. California. Elections (presidential). Racism. Republican Party. 1860. *757*
—. California. Racism. State Politics. 1849-60. *755*
—. California. Republican Party. 1852-56. *756*
—. Capitalism. Ideology. South. 19c. *766*
—. Christianity. Social Organization. 1740-76. *476*
—. Civil Rights. Civil War. Constitutional Amendments (14th, 15th). Supreme Court. Woman Suffrage. 1863-75. *1106*
—. Civil War. Lincoln, Abraham. Political Theory. Revolution. Social change. 1850-65. *1060*
—. Civil War. Negroes. Reconstruction. Women. 19c. *331*
—. Civil War (antecedents). Constitutions. Law. 1830-60. *763*
—. Civil War (antecedents). Greeley, Horace. Reform. Secession. 1860-61. *781*
—. Converts. Evangelism. Louisiana (New Orleans). Protestant Churches. 1800-61. *732*
—. Courts. North. *Prigg* v. *Pennsylvania* (US, 1842). Supreme Court. 1842-57. *636*
—. Crime and criminals. Florida. Rebellions. ca 1820-65. *659*
—. Democratic Party. Illinois. Republican Party. Trumbull, Lyman. 1855-72. *323*
—. Documents. Negroes. Social Conditions. 1774-1841. *788*
—. Douglas, Stephen A. Lincoln, Abraham. Morality. Political Attitudes. 1850's. *738*
—. *Dred Scott* v. *Sandford* (US, 1857). Marshall, John. Supreme Court. Taney, Roger Brooke. 1820-60. *785*
—. Education. Episcopal Church, Protestant. Louisiana (New Orleans). Polk, Leonidas L. 1805-65. *730*
—. Emigration. Kansas-Nebraska Act (US, 1854). Wisconsin. 1850's. *690*
—. Evangelicalism. Reform. Stringfellow, Thornton. Virginia. 1800-70. *633*
—. Fugitive Slave Act (US, 1850). Methodist Church. Newspapers. 1850. *684*
—. Industrialization. Political Attitudes. Populism. South. 1860-96. *1382*
—. Jones, Charles Colcock. Missions and Missionaries. Presbyterian Church. South. 1825-63. *776*
—. Law. Louisiana. 1685-1766. *505*
—. Law. Louisiana. 1724-66. *508*
—. Louisiana. Newspapers. Political Campaigns (presidential). Two-party system. 1834-36. *661*
—. Morality. Political parties. 1828-36. *701*
—. New England. Puritans. 1652-1795. *528*
—. Presbyterian Church. Stowe, Harriet Beecher. 1830's-1870's. *909*
—. South. 1789-1860. *652*
Slaves. Missions and Missionaries. Nova Scotia. Raymond, Eliza Ruggles. Sierra Leone (Sherbro Island). 1839-50. *621*
Slidell, John. Constitutions, State. Louisiana. Suffrage. 1812-52. *601*
Slums. *See* Cities; Ghettos.
Smallpox. City Government. Editorials. Franklin, James. Freedom of the Press. Inoculation. Massachusetts (Boston). *New England Courant* (newspaper). 1721. *535*

Smedley, Agnes. China. Chu Teh. Communism. Sorge, Richard. 1893-1950. *360*
Smedley, Agnes (*Cell Mates*). Feminism. Leftism. New York City. Prisons. 1918. *2019*
Smith, Albert Edward. Canada. Communist Party. Labour Party. Methodism. Social Gospel. 1893-1924. *410*
Smith, Alfred E. Candler, Warren A. Methodist Episcopal Church, South. Political Campaigns (presidential). Prohibition. Religion. 1928. *2344*
—. Civil Rights. Red scare. 1919-20. *2133*
—. Morality. New York. Progressivism. Prohibition. Whitman, Charles. Woman Suffrage. 1911-18. *2116*
—. New York. Prison reform. 1903-28. *2360*
Smith, Antonio Maceo. Craft, Juanita. Durham, William J. NAACP. Texas. White, Lulu B. 1933-50. *1586*
Smith, Gerald L. K. Depressions. Long, Huey P. Louisiana. Politics. Share-Our-Wealth movement. 1930's. *2527*
—. Fundamentalism. Long, Huey P. North Central States. Populism. Progressivism. 1934-48. *362*
Smith, Gerrit. Abolition Movement. Birney, James. Clergy. Evangelicalism. Stanton, H. B. Weld, Theodore Dwight. 1820-50. *744*
—. Abolition Movement. New York (upstate). 1840-50. *647*
Smith, Harry. Constitutional conventions. Negroes. Ohio. Progressive era. Suffrage. 1863-1912. *2165*
Smith, Harry C. Anti-lynching law of 1894. Law Reform. Ohio. Tourgée, Albion W. 1890-96. *1453*
Smith, James McCune. Abolitionists. Brown, William Wells. Medicine. Negroes. Remond, Sarah Parker. Ruggles, David. Tubman, Harriet. 1810-85. *329*
Smith, Lillian. Newspapers. Race Relations. Sex. South. 20c. *422*
Smith, Thomas Paul. Educational Reform. Massachusetts (Boston). Negroes. Separatist Movements. 1848-49. *855*
Smith v. *Allwright* (US, 1944). Democratic Party. NAACP. Negro Suffrage. Primaries. South. Supreme Court. 1890's-1944. *1722*
Smith, Walter George. Catholic Church. Lawyers. Pennsylvania. Progressivism. 1900-22. *1891*
Smith, William. Libel. Moore, William. Pennsylvania. Political Theory. Provincial legislatures. 1750-60. *516*
Smoke. Air Pollution. Elites. Pennsylvania (Pittsburgh). Reform. Tilbury, Corwin D. 1890's-1918. *1961*
—. Air Pollution. Missouri (St. Louis). 1891-1924. *1962*
Smuggling. Florida (Miami). Law Enforcement. Prohibition. 1896-1920. *1948*
Smyth, Thomas. Abolition movement. Douglass, Frederick. Ireland (Belfast). Presbyterian Church. 1846. *697*
Snow, Eliza Roxey. Mormons. Women. 1830-90. *75*
Social Change *See also* Economic Growth; Industrialization; Modernization.
—. Abolition Movement. Feminism. Sex roles. 1820's-80. *798*
—. American Revolution. Egalitarianism. Historiography. 1775-83. 20c. *494*
—. Anti-Catholicism. Pennsylvania. Politics. 1682-1774. *477*
—. Antigonish Movement. Catholic Church. Nova Scotia. Rural Development. ca 1928-73. *1854*
—. Bakke, Allan. Racism. *Regents of the University of California* v. *Allan Bakke* (US, 1978). 1960's-78. *2794*
—. Baseball. Business. City life. Illinois (Chicago). Values. 1865-70. *1001*
—. Baseball. Religion. Values. 1892-1934. *1669*
—. Bibliographies. Communes. Counter culture. Political Protest. 1963-73. *2989*
—. Black Power. 1963-68. *2867*
—. Bradstreet, Anne. Hutchinson, Anne. Literature. Massachusetts Bay Colony. Religion. Women. 1630's-70's. *489*
—. California (Oakland). Strikes. 1946-47. *2691*
—. Cash, W. J. Historiography. South. 1830-1940. *1653*
—. Cherokee Indians. Christianity. Indian-White Relations. Missions and Missionaries. Property. Women. 19c. *107*
—. Cincinnati Colored School system. Discrimination, Educational. Economic Conditions. Negroes. Ohio. 19c. *832*

Social Classes

—. Cities. Civil disturbances. Negroes. Political Participation. 1960's-70's. *2798*
—. Civil rights movement. Gandhi, Mahatma. King, Martin Luther, Jr. 1959-68. *2822*
—. Civil War. Lincoln, Abraham. Political Theory. Revolution. Slavery. 1850-65. *1060*
—. Colleges and Universities. Educational Reform. Industrialization. North Carolina, University of. 1850-75. *1406*
—. Colonial government. Elites. North Carolina. Regulator movement. 1760-75. *502*
—. Compulsory education. Frontier and Pioneer Life. Industrialization. 1870's. *1408*
—. Curaçao. Negroes. Political Protest. 1960's-70's. *2797*
—. Democracy. Education. Fundamentalism. Local Politics. Vigilantism. 1920's. *2375*
—. Democracy. Politics. Women. 1634-1935. *106*
—. Depressions. General Education Board. Public policy. Rockefeller, John D. Secondary education. 1930's. *2478*
—. Dewey, John. Education. Progressivism. 1890-1979. *1834*
—. Douglass, Frederick. Violence. ca 1840-95. *658*
—. Economic Conditions. Negroes. Race Relations. Violence. 1960's. *2851*
—. Ecumenism. Evangelism. Protestantism. Social justice. Student Christian Movement. 19c-20c. *5*
—. Episcopal Church, Protestant. Nebraska (Omaha). 1856-1919. *1494*
—. Europe. Intellectuals. Utopias. 1930's-70's. *1675*
—. Food and Drug Administration. Great Plains. Labor. Radicals and Radicalism. Veblen, Thorstein. World War I. 1918. *1922*
—. Georgia. Negroes. Savannah Men's Sunday Club. 1905-11. *1970*
—. Government. Indians. 1960-76. *2743*
—. Higher education. Religion. 1960's-70's. *2974*
—. Interest Groups. Local government. Political Reform. Taxation. 1960's. *2947*
—. Kennedy, John F. New Left. Nixon, Richard M. Popular culture. 1960-69. *2754*
—. Ku Klux Klan. Oregon (Tillamook). 1920's. *2456*
—. Labor. Occupations. Sex discrimination. 1950-70. *1813*
—. Labor. South. 19c-20c. *150*
—. Law. Liberalism. Radicals and Radicalism. 1953-73. *1579*
—. Law. Scandinavia. Self-awareness. Women's Liberation Movement. 1840-1977. *35*
—. Literature. Sex roles. Women. 19c. *78*
—. Medicine. Therapeutics. 19c. *252*
—. Neurology. Progressivism. Psychoanalysis. Putnam, James Jackson. 1895-1918. *2108*
—. Novels. Politics. Radicals and Radicalism. Religion. 1915-71. *1691*
—. Political Attitudes. Populism. Texas. ca 1880-1900. *1396*
—. Pragmatism. Science. 1900-40. *1608*
—. Progressives. 1890-1917. *1989*
—. Protestantism. Women. World Council of Churches. 1945-75. *2917*
—. Race relations. 1915-78. *1661*
—. Reform. South. Williams, Claude. Williams, Joyce. 1930's-70's. *400*
—. Women. 1700-1976. *86*
Social Classes *See also* Class Struggle; Elites; Middle Classes; Social Mobility; Social Status; Upper Classes; Working Class.
—. Abolition Movement. Anti-Catholicism. Ideology. Massachusetts (Boston). Riots. 1834-35. *555*
—. Abortion. Ideology. 1970's. *2741*
—. Attitudes. Intellectuals. Letters. Slavery. 1830-60. *790*
—. Bureaucracies. Corporations. Labor. Poor. War on Poverty. 1960's. *2925*
—. Canada. Economic opportunity. Political Protest. USA. 1960-74. *2702*
—. Civil War. Freedmen. Louisiana (New Orleans). Negroes, free. Political Attitudes. Politics. 1860-65. *1275*
—. Company towns. Ohio. Steel Industry. Strikes. 1937. *2474*
—. Detroit Citizens League. Leland, Henry. Michigan. Progressivism. 1912-24. *1925*
—. Economic conditions. Feminism. Sex. 1600-1900. *36*
—. Economic Conditions. Racism. Reconstruction. South. 1865-76. *1071*
—. Economics. Education. Historiography. Political systems. 1840-20c. *219*

Social Classes

—. Education. Employment. Sex roles. Women. 1964-74. *2919*
—. Educational reform. Public Schools. 1787-1973. *203*
—. Employment. Feminism. Organizations. Racism. World War II. 1942-45. *2629*
—. Farmers. Shays' Rebellion. 1770's-87. *580*
—. Genovese, Eugene D. Land reform. Race relations. Reconstruction. South Carolina (Edgefield County). Woodward, C. Vann. 1865-90. *963*
—. Jews. New York City. Socialism. United Hebrew Trades. 1877-1926. *1340*
—. Kansas. Populism. Progressivism. 1885-1917. *10*
—. Know-Nothing Party. Louisiana. Political leadership. 1845-60. *542*
—. Labor Reform. Progressivism. Women. 1882-1917. *2230*
—. Liberalism. Voting and Voting Behavior. 1960's-70's. *2731*
—. Missouri (St. Louis). Political Leadership. Racism. Strikes. Workingmen's Party. 1877. *1338*
—. Negro Suffrage. North Carolina. Red Shirt Movement. Terrorism. Whites. 1898-1900. *1067*
Social Conditions *See also* Cities; Counter Culture; Daily Life; Economic Conditions; Family; Labor; Marriage; Migration, Internal; Popular Culture; Social Classes; Social Mobility; Social Problems; Social Surveys; Standard of Living.
—. Alabama. Baptists, Southern. Reform. 1877-90. *974*
—. Appalachian Regional Development Act (US, 1965). Economic Development. Regional development. 1965-75. *2927*
—. Atlanta University. Labor Department. Negroes. 1897-1907. *1964*
—. Barry, Robertine (pseud. Françoise). Feminism. Gleason, Anne-Marie (pseud. Madeleine). Journalism. Quebec. 1900-19. *1535*
—. Cain, Richard Harvey. Negroes. Politics. Reconstruction. South Carolina. 1850's-87. *375*
—. California. North Carolina. Sermons. Sermons. 1969-78. *2729*
—. Catholic Church. Quebec (Gaspé Peninsula). Ross, François Xavier. 1923-45. *374*
—. Civil Rights Movement. King, Martin Luther, Jr. Negroes. 1968-79. *2806*
—. Documents. Negroes. Slavery. 1774-1841. *788*
—. Family. Iakovos, Archbishop. Morality. Orthodox Eastern Church (Greek; congresses). 1960-80. *2726*
—. Federal Policy. Indians. Meriam, Lewis (*Problem of Indian Administration*). Reform. 1920-28. *2362*
—. Feminism. Mental health system. 20c. *2918*
—. Feminism. Protestant Churches. South. Women. 1920's. *2339*
—. Forssell, G. D. Iowa. Lectures. Minnesota. Progressivism. 1890-95. *957*
—. Great Society. Johnson, Lyndon B. (administration). Public Welfare. 1964-76. *2936*
—. Illinois (Chicago). Novels. 1890-1910. *1963*
—. Methodology. Political Protest. Psychoanalysis. Students. 1900-75. *1616*
—. Micronesia. Pacific Dependencies (US). Self-determination. 1947-80. *2776*
—. Politics. Premillenarianism. 1920's-50's. *1704*
Social consciousness. Federal government. New York (Buffalo). Political protest. 1965-76. *2747*
—. Mennonites. 1890-1905. *1945*
—. Mexican Americans. Theater, guerrilla. 1965-76. *2710*
Social control. Acculturation. Educational Reform. Ideology. Industrialization. Pennsylvania. 1880-1910. *1420*
—. Bacon's Rebellion. Class struggle. Racism. Slavery. Virginia. 1660-92. *472*
—. Business. Canada. Federal Government. Labor Unions and Organizations. Unemployment Insurance Act (Canada, 1941). Wages. 1910-41. *2623*
—. Charities. Ontario (Toronto). Tramps. 1870-90. *1065*
—. Flexner Report. Medicine. Professionalism. Progressive era. 1910. *2317*
Social credit. Alberta. Cooperative Commonwealth Federation. Land reform. Leadership. United Farmers of Alberta. 1930's. *1748*
—. Historiography. Quebec. 1936-65. *1765*

SUBJECT INDEX

Social Credit Party. Alberta. Cooperative Commonwealth Federation. Populism. Russia. Saskatchewan. USA. 1870's-1940's. *14*
Social Creed of Methodism. Federal Council of Churches of Christ in America. Methodist Federation for Social Service. North, Frank M. Ward, Harry F. 1907-12. *1956*
Social criticism. Adams, Henry Brooks. George, Henry. Ideology. Philosophy of History. 1870's-1910's. *1073*
—. American League for Peace and Democracy. Methodist Federation for Social Service. Ward, Harry F. 1900-40. *376*
—. Anarchism and Anarchists. Liberalism. Political Protest. 1960-68. *2705*
—. Cities. Merton, Thomas. Nonviolence. Reform. 1960's. *2737*
—. Feminism. Fuller, Margaret. Jefferson, Thomas. Journalism. 1840-50. *272*
—. Populism. 1880's-1890's. *1390*
Social Customs. Assimilation. Japanese Americans (Sansei). 1968-76. *2758*
—. City Planning. Communes. Harmony Society. Indiana (New Harmony). Pennsylvania (Economy, Harmony). 1820's-1905. *919*
—. Florida. Law. Race Relations. Segregation. 1865-1917. *141*
—. Law. New Mexico. Women. 16c-1975. *1720*
—. Massachusetts (Boston). Temperance movements. Values. Working class. 1838-40. *868*
Social Darwinism. Christianity. Corporations. Education, Finance. Higher education. 1860-1930. *206*
Social Democracy. British Columbia. Labor. Legislation. Natural resources. New Democratic Party. Public Policy. Taxation. 1972-75. *2942*
—. Canada. Coldwell, Major J. Farmer Labor party. Political Leadership. Progressivism. 1907-32. *471*
Social Democratic Party *See also* Marxism; Socialism.
—. Letters. Lloyd, Henry Demarest. Morgan, Thomas John. Socialist Labor Party. 1897-1901. *1349*
Social Feminists. Equal Rights Amendment. National Women's Party. Woman suffrage. 1920-23. *2376*
Social Gospel. Asians. Conservatism. Immigration. Methodist Episcopal Church. 1865-1908. *1029*
—. Bascom, John. Commons, John R. Ely, Richard T. Wisconsin, University of. 1870-1910. *1017*
—. Bishops. Methodist Episcopal Church. Peck, Jesse T. 1850-83. *1025*
—. Bliss, William D. P. Christianity. Leftism. 1876-1926. *20*
—. Bushnell, Horace. Christianity. Economic conditions. Gladden, Washington. Politics. Youth. 1836-1918. *995*
—. Canada. Christianity. Fiction. Labor. 1890's. *1354*
—. Canada. Communist Party. Labour Party. Methodism. Smith, Albert Edward. 1893-1924. *410*
—. Canada. Economic Reform. George, Henry. Industry. Poverty. Progress (concept). ca 1879-99. *975*
—. Canada. Methodism. 1890-1914. *23*
—. Cities. Congregationalism. Gladden, Washington. Ohio (Columbus). Reform. 1850's-1914. *396*
—. Congregationalism. Education. New Mexico (Albuquerque). Prohibition. 1900-17. *2101*
—. Mathews, Shailer. Modernism. Science. Theology. 1864-1930. *446*
—. Methodist Protestant Church. Shaw, Anna Howard. Woman suffrage. 1880-1919. *448*
—. Race Relations. Reform. 1877-98. *1043*
Social History. Medicine, preventive. Occupations. Public health. Rosen, George. 1930's-77. *442*
Social justice. Angers, François-Albert. Catholic Church. Public welfare. Quebec. 1950-80. *2931*
—. Ecumenism. Evangelism. Protestantism. Social change. Student Christian Movement. 19c-20c. *5*
—. Presbyterian Church. 1770-1977. *50*
Social mobility. Cotton. Hamilton Manufacturing Company. Labor Disputes. Massachusetts (Lowell). Textile Industry. Women. 1836-60. *818*
—. Freedom. Individualism. Property. Socialism. 1750-1979. *85*
—. Jews. Lawyers. 20c. *1522*

Social Psychology

Social movements. Anarchist Scare (1908). Progressivism. Radicals and Radicalism. 1900-10. *2139*
—. Chipman, George. Editors and Editing. *Grain Growers Guide* (periodical). Manitoba (Winnipeg). Reform. 1905-30. *1637*
—. Johnson, Lyndon B. Rhetoric. War on Poverty. 1965-66. *2954*
—. Political Protest. Trials. 1920-79. *1526*
Social Organization. Agrarianism. Attitudes. Politics. 1890's-1970's. *1546*
—. Alberta. New Brunswick. Populism. Radicals and Radicalism. Saskatchewan. 1950's-70's. *2700*
—. California (Orange County). Middle Classes. Oneida Community. Religion. Townerites. 1848-1900's. *1514*
—. Capitalism. Labor. Leisure. 1890-1920's. *151*
—. Christianity. Grimké, Sarah Moore. Nature. Paul, Saint. Women. 1c. 1830's. *807*
—. Christianity. Slavery. 1740-76. *476*
—. Cities. Ethnicity. Negroes. Race Relations. Valentine, Charles. 1865-1975. *1697*
—. Communes. 19c-1976. *268*
—. Family. Labor. Women. 1600-1970's. *54*
—. Female Moral Reform Society. Morality. New York (Utica). Reform. 1830's-40's. *808*
—. Ghost Dance. Indians. Revitalization movements. 1889. *967*
—. Institutions. Progressivism. Violence. 1880's-1910's. *2082*
—. Negroes. Riots. 1960's. *2793*
—. Radicals and Radicalism. Woman suffrage. 19c. *116*
Social Organizations. Antibusing movement. Massachusetts (Boston). Models. Political Protest. 1970's. *2895*
—. Charities. Jewish Welfare Federation of Detroit. Michigan. 1926. *2367*
—. Civil Rights. Labor Unions and Organizations. Mexican Americans. North Central States. 1900-76. *1659*
—. Commission on the Status and Role of Women in the United Methodist Church. Feminism. Methodism. 1869-1974. *72*
—. Methodist Church. Temperance movements. 1919-72. *1613*
Social policy. American Plan. Council of National Defense. Federal government. Prostitution. Venereal disease. Voluntary associations. World War I. 1917-21. *2048*
—. Associated Charities. Charities. Leadership. Massachusetts (Fall River, Lynn). Men. Women. 1880-1900. *1447*
—. Bureau of Indian Affairs. Emmons, Glenn L. Indians. Tribes. 1953-61. *2660*
—. Canada. Europe, Western. USA. Welfare state. 1890-1970. *160*
—. Canada. Federal government. Unemployment. 1918-21. *1816*
—. City politics. New York City. Public Health. Tuberculosis. 1889-1900. *1941*
—. Decisionmaking. Democracy. Federal regulation. 1970-75. *2734*
Social Problems *See also* Charities; Child Labor; Crime and Criminals; Divorce; Emigration; Housing; Immigration; Juvenile Delinquency; Migrant Labor; Prostitution; Public Welfare; Race Relations; Unemployment.
—. Antislavery Sentiments. British North America. Friends, Society of. Woolman, John. 1720-72. *478*
—. Baptists, Southern. Individualism. Politics. 18c-1976. *31*
—. Blumer, Herbert. Poverty. Public Policy. 1960's-73. *2924*
—. Charities. Illinois (Chicago). Negroes. 1890-1917. *1979*
—. Cities. Community organizations. Great Britain. 1960's-70's. *2746*
—. Cities. New York. Philanthropy. 1830-60. *878*
—. Communes. Utopias. 1865-1914. *1504*
—. Compulsory Education. Educational reform. Interest groups. Pennsylvania. 1880-1911. *200*
—. DuBois, W. E. B. Education. Elites. Negroes. 1897-1963. *1565*
—. New York City. Race Relations. Urban League. 1919-59. *1652*
Social Psychology *See also* Human Relations.
—. Behavior. Censorship. Cities. 1960's-70's. *2788*
—. Brown, John. Civil War (antecedents). Harpers Ferry raid. North Carolina. Slavery. 1859-60. *612*

Social Reform. *See* specific kinds of reform, e.g. Agricultural Reform, Penal Reform.
Social Sciences *See also* Economics; Social Change; Sociology.
—. Bureau of Indian Affairs. Collier, John. New Deal. Public Administration. 1933-45. *2599*
—. Canada. Colleges and Universities. Public policy. 1920-49. *1576*
—. History. Institute for Advanced Study. Mathematics. New Jersey (Princeton). Research. 1930-79. *2435*
—. Mead, Margaret. Scholars. Talbot, Marion. Thompson, Helen. Women. 1900-20's. *2065*
Social Security *See also* Pensions; Unemployment Insurance.
—. Bureaucracies. Business. Disability insurance. Federal government. 1900-40. *1829*
—. Canada. Marsh, Leonard *(Report)*. Socialism. Welfare state. 1930-44. *1771*
—. Canada. Public Policy. USA. 1935-75. *1776*
Social Security Act (US, 1935). Congress. New Deal. Roosevelt, Franklin D. Unemployment insurance. 1934-35. *2471*
—. Ehringhaus, J. C. B. Legislation. North Carolina. Unemployment insurance. 1935-37. *2556*
—. Harrison, Pat. Senate. 1934-35. *2598*
Social Security Act (US, 1935; amended, 1963). Domestic Policy. Kennedy, John F. Mental Retardation Facilities and Community Mental Health Centers Construction Act (US, 1963). Politics. 1961-63. *2976*
Social Security Act (US, 1935; Title XX, 1972). Federal regulation. Medical care. Physicians. Professional Standards Review Organization Program. 1965-80. *2978*
Social Service Review (periodical). Public Welfare. Scholarship. Social work. 1927-77. *1567*
Social services. Civil Rights. Nebraska (Omaha). Negroes. Quality of life. Urban League. World War II. 1928-50. *2639*
—. Ethnic Groups. International Institute. Pluralism. 1910-79. *74*
—. Public Welfare Amendments (1962). 1962-76. *2928*
Social status. Adams, Mary Newbury. Iowa. Self-image. Women. 1850-1900. *1042*
—. American Colonization Society. Negroes, free. Rhetoric. Slavery. Whites. 1831-34. *615*
—. Chinese Americans. Discrimination. Economic Conditions. Japanese Americans. Nativism. 1840's-1978. *83*
—. Education. Hall, G. Stanley. Minorities. 1870's-1920. *2323*
—. Elites. Medical education. 1890-1973. *1784*
—. Equality. Women. 1900-70's. *1568*
—. Great Britain. Women. 1925-65. *1551*
—. Income. Negroes. 1954-74. *1823*
—. Labor. Reform. Women. 1830-60. *309*
—. New York. Noyes, John Humphrey. Oneida Community. Sex. Women. 1848-79. *266*
Social Structure. *See* Social Organization; Social Status.
Social Surveys *See also* Sociology.
—. *Charities and the Commons* (periodical). Industrialization. Pennsylvania. *Pittsburgh Survey* (1909). 1907-14. *2029*
Social Theory. Agricultural Reform. Catholic Church. New Deal. Roosevelt, Franklin D. (administration). 1933-39. *2590*
—. Cabet, Etienne. Icaria (colony). Illinois. Newspapers. Political Theory. Utopias. 1820's-56. *941*
—. Canada. Catholic Church. Journalism. Somerville, Henry. 1915-53. *284*
—. Catholic Church. Gibbons, James. Knights of Labor. Taschereau, Elzéar Alexandre. 1880's. *1351*
—. Democratic Party. Equal opportunity. Jacksonianism. Wealth. 1836-46. *537*
—. Family. Sexuality. Sumner, William Graham. 1870's-1910. *985*
—. Freedmen. Intellectuals. Negroes, free. Politics. South. 1870's-90's. *1274*
Social Welfare. *See* Public Welfare.
Social Work *See also* Charities; Public Welfare.
—. Addams, Jane. Dudzik, Mary Theresa. Franciscan Sisters of Chicago. Illinois. Polish Americans. 1860-1918. *369*
—. Addams, Jane. Hampton, Isabel. Illinois (Chicago). Johns Hopkins Hospital Training School for Nurses. Maryland (Baltimore). Nurses and Nursing. Professionalization. 1889-1910. *1461*
—. Buckeye Steel Castings Company. Bush, S. P. Management, scientific. Ohio (Columbus). Steel Industry. 1890-1920. *2181*

—. Charities. Institutions. Ontario (Toronto). ca 1875-1920. *246*
—. Charities. Pennsylvania (Philadelphia). Society for Organizing Charitable Relief and Repressing Mendicancy. Women. 1864-1909. *1474*
—. Coal Mines and Mining. Colorado. Labor reform. Roche, Josephine. Roosevelt, Franklin D. (administration). 1886-1976. *1772*
—. Communists. New York City. Radicals and Radicalism. "Rank and File" movement. 1931-51. *1600*
—. Community organizing. Education. 1920-39. *1523*
—. Gilman, Catheryne Cooke. Reform. Women. 1904-54. *344*
—. Neurology. Psychiatry. 1830's-1920's. *248*
—. Public Welfare. Scholarship. *Social Service Review* (periodical). 1927-77. *1567*
—. Wittenmyer, Annie Turner. Women's Christian Temperance Union. ca 1855-1900. *1441*
Socialism *See also* Capitalism; Communism; Labor; Labor Unions and Organizations; Leftism; Maoism; Marxism; Pensions; Social Democratic Party; Stalinism; Syndicalism; Utopias.
—. American Federation of Labor. Gompers, Samuel. Labor. 1893-95. *1304*
—. American Socialist Party. Hillquit, Morris. Marxism. Political Reform. 1901-14. *1942*
—. Anti-Catholicism. Capitalism. DeLeon, Daniel. 1891-1914. *55*
—. Antiwar sentiment. Labor Unions and Organizations. World War I. 1914-17. *1982*
—. *Appeal to Reason* (newspaper). Journalism. Kansas (Girard). Muckraking. 1901-20. *2041*
—. Assimilation. Education. Jews. Labor movement. 1880's-1945. *100*
—. Bellamy, Edward. London, Jack. Utopias. 1888-1920. *262*
—. Bourne, Randolph. Feminism. Political Commentary. Progressive education. 1886-1918. *425*
—. Canada. Editors and Editing. Finnish Canadians. Kurikka, Matti. Mäkelä, A. B. Newspapers. 1900-32. *464*
—. Canada. Germany. Hjelt, Ole. Labour Party. Nazism. Norway. 1908-28. *321*
—. Canada. Krat, Pavlo. Ukrainian Canadians. ca 1902-52. *365*
—. Canada. Marsh, Leonard *(Report)*. Social Security. Welfare state. 1930-44. *1771*
—. Canada. Radicals and Radicalism. 1890-99. *1316*
—. Canada, western. Labor reform. Regionalism. 1918-19. *1764*
—. Canada (western). Labor Unions and Organizations. One Big Union. Radicals and Radicalism. 1917-19. *1746*
—. *Canadian Forum*. Culture. 1920-34. *1649*
—. Casson, Herbert N. Labor Church. Massachusetts (Lynn). Working class. 1893-98. *1498*
—. Catholic Church. Cooperative Commonwealth Federation. Saskatchewan. 1930-50. *1620*
—. Catholic Church. Labor Unions and Organizations. Polish Americans. Political Leadership. Progressivism. Wisconsin (Milwaukee). 1900-30. *1663*
—. Child Welfare Commission. Medical care. Wisconsin (Milwaukee). 1911-12. *2032*
—. Christianity. Church and Social Problems. Labor Unions and Organizations. 1880-1913. *2175*
—. Clark, Peter Humphries. Education. Negroes. Ohio (Cincinnati). 1849-81. *332*
—. Clemens, Gaspar Christopher. Kansas. 1885-90's. *959*
—. Coal miners. Germer, Adolph. Illinois (Virden). Strikes. United Mine Workers of America. 1893-1900. *1291*
—. Colleges and Universities. Intellectuals. Liberalism. Political Attitudes. 1880-95. *1072*
—. *Collier's Weekly*. Sinclair, Upton. Sumner, William Graham. 1900-04. *1921*
—. Communes. Llano del Rio Co-operative Colony. Louisiana (Vernon Parish). 1917-38. *1655*
—. Congress. International Ladies' Garment Workers' Union. London, Meyer. 1914-22. *2212*
—. Cooperative Commonwealth Federation. Political Parties. Saskatchewan. 1928-44. *1681*
—. Corey, Lewis. 1940-53. *1625*
—. DeLeon, Daniel. Great Britain. 1880-1917. *177*
—. Economic Reform. Hoffman, Christian Balzac. Kansas. 1872-1915. *389*

—. Editors and Editing. *Partisan Review* (periodical). Stalinism. 1930's. *2493*
—. Education. New Brunswick. Stuart, Henry Harvey. 1873-1952. *310*
—. Elections. Morgan, Thomas John. United Labor Party (platform). 1886-96. *1342*
—. Farm tenancy. Political Protest. Texas. 1901-17. *2216*
—. Farmer-Labor Party. Political Leadership. Radicals and Radicalism. Saskatchewan. 1932-34. *1607*
—. Farmers. Grange. Oklahoma. Saskatchewan. Texas. 1900-45. *1714*
—. Farmers. Oklahoma. 1900's-10. *2063*
—. Feminism. Massachusetts Association Opposed to the Further Extension of the Suffrage to Women. Political campaigns. Sex roles. Woman suffrage. 1895-1915. *2166*
—. Finnish Americans. Immigrants. Labor. Minnesota (Smithville). Work People's College. 1900-20. *2315*
—. Forest and Farm Workers Union. Hall, Covington. Labor Unions and Organizations. Louisiana. Lumber and Lumbering. 1907-16. *2192*
—. Freedom. Individualism. Property. Social mobility. 1750-1979. *85*
—. German Americans. Labor Unions and Organizations. Progressivism. Wisconsin. 1900-12. *2103*
—. Haymarket Riot (1886). Iowa. Trumbull, Matthew Mark. 1826-94. *296*
—. Haywood, William Dudley. Labor Unions and Organizations. 1890-1928. *371*
—. Hillquit, Morris. Jews. New York City. 1890's-1933. *1713*
—. Idaho (Twin Falls). Kidnapping. O'Hare, Kate Richards. Speeches, Addresses, etc. Utah. 1921. *2404*
—. Intellectuals. Socialist Party. 1901-17. *1953*
—. Jews. New York City. Social Classes. United Hebrew Trades. 1877-1926. *1340*
—. Keller, Helen. New Jersey (Montclair). Speeches, Addresses, etc. 1890-1913. *1916*
—. Labor. New York (Rochester). 1917-19. *1978*
—. Labor. Red baiting. Working conditions. 1871-1920. *154*
—. Labor Unions and Organizations. Mexican Americans. Texas. 1900-20. *2291*
—. Labor Unions and Organizations. Negroes. Radicals and Radicalism. 1865-1900. *1232*
—. Local Government. Manitoba (Winnipeg). Queen, John. Taxation. 1909-42. *1645*
—. London, Jack. Propaganda. 1905-08. *2123*
—. Minnesota (Minneapolis). VanLear, Thomas. 1910-20. *2042*
—. Negroes. Protestantism. Woodbey, George Washington. 1902-15. *1939*
—. Neighborhoods. New York City. Working class. 1908-18. *2006*
—. Nugent, John. West Virginia State Federation of Labor. 1901-14. *2177*
—. Public Schools. Reform. Wisconsin (Milwaukee). Working class. 1890-1920. *2329*
—. Student League for Industrial Democracy. 1905-21. *2077*
Socialist and Labor Star (newspaper). Paint Creek-Cabin Creek Strike. Strikes. Thompson, Wyatt Hamilton. West Virginia. 1912-13. *2195*
Socialist Labor Party. DeLeon, Daniel. Letters. 1896-1904. *2094*
—. Grenell, Judson. Knights of Labor. Labadie, Joseph. Michigan (Detroit). 1877-86. *1334*
—. Letters. Lloyd, Henry Demarest. Morgan, Thomas John. Social Democratic Party. 1897-1901. *1349*
Socialist Laws (Germany, 1878). Christianity. Communes. Harmony Society. Pennsylvania (Economy). Pittman, Clara. 1878-79. *1499*
Socialist Party. Agricultural cooperatives. Nonpartisan League. North Dakota. 1915-20's. *2024*
—. Alaska (Anchorage). Labor Unions and Organizations. Lewis, Lena Morrow. Railroads. World War I. 1916-18. *2001*
—. Antiwar Sentiment. Keep America Out of War Congress. Thomas, Norman. Villard, Oswald Garrison. World War II (antecedents). 1938-41. *2501*
—. Bombing. California (San Francisco). Mooney, Tom. San Quentin Prison. Trials. 1916-42. *2020*
—. California. Political Campaigns (congressional). Sinclair, Upton. ca 1920. *2464*

Socialist Party

—. City Politics. Illinois (Canton). Prohibition. Whalen, Homer. 1911-20. *2093*
—. Civil Rights. Negroes. Pemberton, Caroline Hollingsworth. Pennsylvania (Philadelphia). 1896-1903. *1158*
—. Coal Mines and Mining. Debs, Eugene V. Strikes. West Virginia. 1912-14. *2194*
—. Comintern (7th Congress). Communist Party. New Deal. 1935-39. *2547*
—. Communist Party. Foster, William Z. 1881-1921. *304*
—. Continental Congress of Workers and Farmers. Senior, Clarence. 1933. *2611*
—. Davis, David W. Idaho. Industrial Workers of the World. Nonpartisan League. Public opinion. 1919-26. *2405*
—. Depressions. Liberalism. New Deal. Political activism. Unemployment. 1929-36. *1804*
—. Garment Industry. Illinois (Chicago). O'Reilly, Mary. Strikes. Women. Zeh, Nellie M. 1910. *2183*
—. Gompers, Samuel. Lenin, V. I. (views). USSR. 1912-18. *1991*
—. Harrison, Hubert H. International Colored Unity League. Journalism. Liberty League of Negro Americans. Negroes. New York City (Harlem). 1911-27. *1676*
—. Intellectuals. Socialism. 1901-17. *1953*
—. International, 2d. Political Leadership. 1889-1914. *1053*
—. Jews. Labor Unions and Organizations. Malkiel, Theresa Serber. New York City. Women. 1900's-14. *2035*
—. Krzycki, Leo. Labor Unions and Organizations. Polish Americans. Radicals and Radicalism. 1900's-66. *391*
—. Local Government. Political Corruption. Voting and Voting Behavior. 1910-14. *1879*
—. Local Politics. Pennsylvania (Reading). Women. ca 1927-38. *1666*
—. Lunn, George. New York (Schenectady). Voting and Voting Behavior. Working Class. 1911-16. *1946*
—. Manitoba (Winnipeg). Penner, Jacob. Russia. 1900-65. *406*
—. O'Hare, Kate Richards. Women. 1901-17. *1878*
—. Oklahoma. 1916-18. *1893*
—. Utah. Women. 1900-20. *2086*
—. Woman suffrage. Working Class. 1901-12. *1954*
Socialists. Immigration. Poland. Polish Americans. 1883-1914. *39*
Socialization *See also* Political Socialization.
—. Attitudes. Education. Women's studies. 1600-1974. *187*
—. Cities. Family. Morality. Progressivism. Recreation. Reform. 1890-1920. *1990*
—. Girls. Juvenile Delinquency. Massachusetts (Lancaster). State Industrial School for Girls. 1856-1905. *1443*
Society for Organizing Charitable Relief and Repressing Mendicancy. Charities. Friends, Society of. Pennsylvania (Philadelphia). 1800-1900. *250*
—. Charities. Pennsylvania (Philadelphia). Social work. Women. 1864-1909. *1474*
Society for the Promotion of Collegiate and Theological Education at the West. Baldwin, Theron. Higher education. Protestantism. 1843-73. *192*
Sociology *See also* Cities; Emigration; Family; Immigration; Labor; Marriage; Population; Race Relations; Slavery; Social Classes; Social Conditions; Social Organization; Social Problems; Social Surveys.
—. Black power. Political Protest. Self-improvement. 1960's-70's. *2859*
—. Civil Rights. Negroes. South. Work, Monroe Nathan. 1900-45. *388*
—. Public Health. Urbanization. 20c. *1671*
Soil Conservation Service. Agricultural Adjustment Administration. New Deal. 1933-41. *2581*
Solomon, Hannah G. American, Sadie. Congress of Jewish Women. Jews. Women. World Parliament of Religions. World's Columbian Exposition (Chicago, 1893). 1893. *1488*
Somerville, Henry. Canada. Catholic Church. Journalism. Social Theory. 1915-53. *284*
Songs. Editorials. Labor. *Miners' Magazine*. Poetry. Western Federation of Miners. 1900-07. *2293*
Sons of Temperance. Brownlow, William Gannaway. Temperance Movements. Tennessee. 1851-67. *865*
Sons of Temperance (Ocmulgee Division No. 40). Georgia (Jasper County). Temperance Movements. 1848-49. *897*

Sorge, Friedrich Adolph. International, 1st. Marxism. 1852-1906. *1305*
—. Labor movement. Marxism. 1866-76. *1308*
Sorge, Richard. China. Chu Teh. Communism. Smedley, Agnes. 1893-1950. *360*
Soule, Silas S. Colorado. Indian Wars. Sand Creek Massacre. 1859-65. *44*
South *See also* individual states by name; South Central and Gulf States; Southeastern States.
—. Abolition Movement. Civil War (antecedents). Presbyterian Church. Stanton, Robert. 1840-55. *731*
—. Abolition Movement. Congregationalism. Evangelism. Finney, Charles Grandison. 1833-69. *632*
—. Abolition Movement. Liberty Party. Ohio. 1838-50. *670*
—. Abolitionists. Law. Slavery. Supreme courts, state. 1810-60. *775*
—. Africa. Industrial arts education. Pan-Africanism. Racism. 1879-1940. *214*
—. Agrarianism. Davidson, Donald. Literature. Mims, Edwin. 1923-58. *1656*
—. Agrarianism. Killebrew, Joseph Buckner. New South movement. ca 1870-1910. *1026*
—. Agrarianism. Populism. 1865-1900. *1378*
—. Agricultural Policy. Association of Southern Commissioners of Agriculture. Cotton. New Deal. Tennessee (Memphis). 1936-37. *2567*
—. Agricultural reform. Editors and Editing. Farmers. Poe, Clarence Hamilton. *Progressive Farmer* (periodical). 1899-1964. *1555*
—. Agriculture. Industrial Arts Education. Negroes. North. Philanthropy. 1902-35. *1832*
—. Alabama (Birmingham). Communist Party. Hudson, Hosea. Negroes. 1920's-70's. *404*
—. American Land Company. Andrew, John A. Politics. Reconstruction. 1865-67. *1066*
—. American Missionary Association. Congregationalism. Negroes. 1846-80. *1242*
—. American Revolution. Attitudes. McIntosh, Lachlan. Slavery. Wealth. 1775-87. *517*
—. American Revolution (antecedents). Taxation. 1755-85. *475*
—. Ames, Jessie Daniel. Association of Southern Women for the Prevention of Lynching. Lynching. Racism. Women. 1930's. *2516*
—. Ames, Jessie Daniel. Association of Southern Women for the Prevention of Lynching. Lynching. Women. 1928-42. *2553*
—. Antislavery sentiments. Baptists. Methodist Church. Presbyterian Church. 1740-1860. *699*
—. Antislavery Sentiments. Clergy. Congregationalism. Connecticut. 1790-95. *631*
—. Antislavery sentiments. Evangelicalism. Religion. 1820-30. *758*
—. Assemblies of God. Church of God. Civil rights movement. Periodicals. Presbyterian Church, Southern. 1950's-60's. *2804*
—. Association of Southern Women for the Prevention of Lynching. Lynching. Negroes. Women. 1930-42. *2472*
—. Attitudes. Colonization. Kentucky. Slavery. 1816-50. *602*
—. Attitudes. Economic Growth. Governors. Segregation. 1950-69. *1533*
—. Attitudes. Florida. Roosevelt, Theodore. Washington, Booker T. 1901. *2080*
—. Attitudes. Judges. School Integration. 1954-70. *2833*
—. Authority. Freedmen. Teaching. Women. 1865-70. *1425*
—. Baptists. Education. Missions and Missionaries. Negroes. 1862-81. *1240*
—. Bible. Presbyterian Church, Southern. Race relations. 1861-1980. *98*
—. Bible. Presbyterian Church, Southern. Sabbath. 1861-1959. *103*
—. Black Nationalism. Colleges and universities. Student activism. 1890-1972. *1673*
—. Black Power. Civil Rights. Historiography. 1954-72. *1542*
—. Border States. Congress. Legislation. Loyalty oath. Republican Party. 1861-67. *950*
—. *Brown v. Board of Education* (US, 1954). Constitutional Amendments (14th). Illinois (Chicago). School integration. 1954-77. *2777*
—. Calhoun, John C. Jefferson, Thomas. Slavery. 1830's-40's. *787*
—. Capitalism. Carver, George Washington. Marxism. Myths and Symbols. Race Relations. 1896-1950's. *1604*
—. Capitalism. Ideology. Slavery. 19c. *766*

—. Carpetbaggers. Civil rights. Constitutional conventions, state. Industrialization. Reconstruction. 1867-69. *1021*
—. Carpetbaggers. House of Representatives. Negroes. Reconstruction. Republican Party. Scalawags. 1868-72. *1036*
—. Cash, W. J. Historiography. Social change. 1830-1940. *1653*
—. Cherokee Indians. Citizenship. Indians. 1817-29. *598*
—. Cities. Educational Reform. Negroes. Public Schools. Teachers. 1865-90. *1238*
—. Cities. North. School Integration. 1954-77. *2830*
—. City Government. Reconstruction. Republican Party. 1865-75. *1068*
—. Civil rights. Institutions. Negroes. Organizations. Sit-ins. 1960. *2868*
—. Civil Rights. Negroes. Sociology. Work, Monroe Nathan. 1900-45. *388*
—. Civil rights movement. Jews. 1954-70. *2823*
—. Civil Rights movement. Johnson, Lyndon B. Long, Huey P. Radicals and Radicalism. 1920-70. *1706*
—. Civil rights movement. Race Relations. Women. 1960's. *2907*
—. Class conflict. Race relations. Segregation. 1865-90's. *1280*
—. Class struggle. Labor unions and organizations. 1810-1975. *162*
—. Colored Farmers' Alliance. Farmers. Negroes. ca 1886-95. *1172*
—. Colored Farmers' Alliance. Humphrey, R. M. Labor Unions and Organizations. Negroes. Strikes. 1876-91. *1150*
—. Congress. Historiography. Negroes. Reconstruction. 1860's-1978. *1175*
—. Congress of Industrial Organizations. Labor Disputes. New Deal. Newspapers. 1930-39. *2614*
—. Congress of Industrial Organizations. Labor Unions and Organizations. Management. National Industrial Recovery Act (US, 1933). National Labor Relations Act (US, 1935). Textile Industry. 1933-41. *2613*
—. Conservatism. DuBose, William Porcher. Episcopal Church, Protestant. Miles, James Warley. Murphy, Edgar Gardner. Theology. 1840-1920. *62*
—. Contracts. Freedmen's Bureau. Planters. Sharecropping. 1865-68. *1258*
—. Courts. Freedmen's Bureau. Howard, Oliver Otis. Reconstruction. 1865-68. *1229*
—. Dabney, Robert Lewis. Morality. Presbyterian Church. Texas, University of (Austin). Union Seminary. 1865-96. *1084*
—. Decisionmaking. Desegregation. Negroes. Political power. Teachers. Voting and Voting Behavior. 1950's-60's. *2831*
—. Democratic Party. NAACP. Negro Suffrage. Primaries. *Smith v. Allwright* (US, 1944). Supreme Court. 1890's-1944. *1722*
—. Democratic Party. Negroes. Political participation. Poverty. 1960's. *2837*
—. Depressions. Negroes. Progressive education. 1930-45. *2512*
—. Desegregation. Federal Government. Law enforcement. Public Schools. 1954-73. *2824*
—. Discrimination. Negroes. Public Welfare. 1865-90. *1236*
—. Discrimination, employment. Fair Employment Practices Committee. Minorities. World War II. 1941-45. *2644*
—. Drugs. Federal regulation. Kefauver, Estes. Senate Subcommittee on Antitrust and Monopoly. 1950's-60's. *2939*
—. Economic Conditions. Racism. Reconstruction. Social Classes. 1865-76. *1071*
—. Economic Regulations. Labor. National Recovery Administration. Negroes. Wages. 1933-34. *2576*
—. Economics. Emancipation. 1860's. *1213*
—. Emancipation. Freedmen. Whites. 1865-66. *969*
—. Evangelicalism. Jones, Charles Colcock. Race Relations. Utopias. 1804-63. *567*
—. Federal Government. House of Representatives. Intervention. Negroes. Population. Voting Rights Act (US, 1965). 1940-75. *2802*
—. Feminism. Literary characters. Novels. Rives, Amèlie. 1863-1945. *377*
—. Feminism. Protestant Churches. Social Conditions. Women. 1920's. *2339*
—. Feminism. Thomas, Ella Gertrude Clanton (journal). 1848-89. *383*
—. Freedmen. Hartzell, Joseph C. Methodist Church. Missions and Missionaries. Republican Party. 1870-73. *1208*

—. Freedmen. Intellectuals. Negroes, free. Politics. Social theory. 1870's-90's. *1274*
—. Harris, Cicero. Harris, Robert. Harris, William. Negroes. Reconstruction. Teaching. 1864-70. *1278*
—. Higher education. Liberal arts. Reform. 1850-60. *854*
—. Hookworms. Poor. Rockefeller Sanitary Commission for the Eradication of Hookworm Disease. Stiles, Charles W. 1900-14. *2109*
—. Industrial Arts Education. Negroes. North. Progressive era. 1900-15. *2306*
—. Industrial Relations. Migration, Internal. Negroes. Pine industry. Working conditions. ca 1912-26. *1577*
—. Industrialization. Political Attitudes. Populism. Slavery. 1860-96. *1382*
—. Jones, Charles Colcock. Missions and Missionaries. Presbyterian Church. Slavery. 1825-63. *776*
—. Journalism. McKelway, Alexander. Murphy, Edgar Gardner. Page, Walter Hines. 1890-1916. *1876*
—. Justice Department. Lawsuits. Negroes. School Integration. 1957-68. *2811*
—. Knights of Labor. ca 1885-88. *1328*
—. Knights of Labor. Labor Unions and Organizations. Negroes. 1880-87. *1187*
—. Knights of Labor. Race relations. 1880-87. *1217*
—. Labor. Social change. 19c-20c. *150*
—. Labor movement. Middle Classes. Schools, summer. Women. 1927-41. *1580*
—. Labor Unions and Organizations. 1920's-74. *2930*
—. Labor Unions and Organizations. Textile industry. ca 1949-75. *1800*
—. Leadership. Negro Young People's Congress. 1902. *2026*
—. Leadership. Negroes. Reconstruction. 1867-75. *1211*
—. Negro Suffrage. Racism. Reconstruction. Rhetoric. Ridicule. 1866-70. *1207*
—. Negroes. Nelson, Alice Dunbar. Women. World War I. 1917-18. *1890*
—. Newspapers. Race Relations. Sex. Smith, Lillian. 20c. *422*
—. Populism. 1850's-90's. *1381*
—. Progressivism. 1890-1920. *1960*
—. Property rights. Reconstruction. State legislatures. Women. 1865-95. *1103*
—. Race relations. Segregation. 1865-90. *1237*
—. Reform. Social change. Williams, Claude. Williams, Joyce. 1930's-70's. *400*
—. Slavery. 1789-1860. *652*
—. Woman Suffrage. 1830-1945. *22*
South Carolina *See also* South.
—. Abolition Movement. Ideology. Proslavery Sentiments. 1776-1861. *660*
—. Agricultural labor. Boycotts. Labor Unions and Organizations. Race relations. 1886-95. *1196*
—. American Revolution (antecedents). Farmers. New York. North Carolina. 1760's-70's. *484*
—. Cain, Richard Harvey. Negroes. Politics. Reconstruction. Social conditions. 1850's-87. *375*
—. Cardozo, Francis Louis. Freedmen. Political rights. Reconstruction. Union League. 1870. *1268*
—. Chamberlain, Daniel H. Hampton, Wade. Reconstruction. State Politics. 1877. *1054*
—. Charleston City Railway Company. Desegregation. Negroes. Reconstruction. Streetcars. 1867. *1169*
—. Charleston *Daily Courier* (newspaper). Charleston *Mercury* (newspaper). Constitutional conventions, state. Racism. Reconstruction. 1867-68. *1205*
—. Charleston *News and Courier* (newspaper). Dawson, Francis Warrington. Dawson, Sarah Morgan. Feminism. Reconstruction. 1870's. *973*
—. Civil Disturbances. Farmers. Regulators. 1730-80. *490*
—. Civil rights. Democratic Party. Elections (presidential). 1948-72. *1630*
—. Constitutions, State. Jury. Lobbying. Women. 1921-67. *1731*
—. Cooperative Workers of America. Georgia. Hoover, Hiram F. Negroes. Secret Societies. 1886-87. *1197*
—. Courts. Democratic Party. Primaries. Segregation. Waring, J. Waties. 1947-52. *2683*
—. Freedmen. House of Representatives. Murray, George Washington. Republican Party. Suffrage. 1893-97. *1163*
—. Jim Crow laws. Negroes. Railroads. Separate coach bills. 1880-98. *1215*
—. Ku Klux Klan. Negroes. Reconstruction. 1868-71. *1076*
—. Laurens, Henry. Philosophy. Republicanism. 1764-77. *483*
—. Paul, Alice. Woman suffrage. ca 1891-1919. *2128*
—. Temperance Movements. 1880-1940. *233*
—. Woman suffrage. 1912-20. *2169*
—. Woman suffrage. Young, Virginia Durant. 1890-1903. *1117*
South Carolina Association. Racism. South Carolina (Charleston). Vigilantes. 1823-50's. *678*
South Carolina (Beaufort County). Negroes. Radicals and Radicalism. Reconstruction. Republican Party. 1865-88. *1003*
South Carolina (Charleston). American Missionary Association. Cardozo, Francis Louis. Education. Freedmen. Reconstruction. State Politics. 1865-70. *1243*
—. Historiography. Slave Revolts. Vesey, Denmark. Wade, Richard (review article). 1821-22. 1964. *686*
—. Racism. South Carolina Association. Vigilantes. 1823-50's. *678*
South Carolina (Charleston; St. Phillip's Parish). Charities. Church of England. City government. Poor. 1712-75. *536*
South Carolina (Edgefield County). Genovese, Eugene D. Land reform. Race relations. Reconstruction. Social Classes. Woodward, C. Vann. 1865-90. *963*
South Carolina, University of. Brewer, Fisk Parsons. Higher education. Integration. 1873-76. *1438*
—. Negroes. Reconstruction. 1873-77. *1248*
South Central and Gulf States *See also* individual states by name; South.
—. International Longshoremen's and Warehousemen's Union. Race relations. 1866-1920. *2236*
South Dakota *See also* Western States.
—. American Indian Movement. Deloria, Vine, Jr. Federal Government. Indians. Political Protest. Wounded Knee (occupation). 1877-1970's. *2712*
—. American Indian Movement. Indians. Pine Ridge Indian Reservation. Wounded Knee (occupation). 1972-75. *2749*
—. Civil rights movement. NAACP. Negroes. 1804-1970. *4*
—. Civilian Conservation Corps. Employment. Environment. 1933-42. *2519*
—. Civilian Conservation Corps (Indian Division). Depressions. Indians (reservations). Sioux Indians. 1933-42. *2486*
—. Communism. Farmers. Political Protest. United Farmers League. 1923-34. *2409*
—. Crawford, Coe Isaac. Progressivism. Republican Party. Roosevelt, Theodore. State Politics. 1912-14. *2076*
—. New Deal. Political Attitudes. Public Welfare. 1930's-70's. *2470*
—. Political Reform. Progressivism. Prohibition. Richards, Richard Olsen. Taxation. 1902-30. *1913*
South Dakota (Lake County). Elections. Political Attitudes. Woman suffrage. 1885-90. *1098*
South Dakota (Wounded Knee). American Indian Movement. Indians. Sioux Indians (Oglala). 1973. *2709*
Southeastern Carriers Conference. Discrimination. Fair Employment Practices Committee. Negroes. Railroads. World War II. 1941-45. *2630*
Southern and Western Theological Seminary. Abolition Movement. Anderson, Isaac. Presbyterian Church. Tennessee (Maryville). 1819-50's. *574*
Southern Baptist Convention. Women. 1860-1975. *60*
Southern Christian Leadership Conference. Civil Rights Organizations. King, Martin Luther, Jr. Leadership. Negroes. 1957-73. *2828*
Southern Courier (newspaper). Alabama. Civil rights movement. Reporters and Reporting. 1965-68. *2873*
Southern Education Board. Episcopal Church, Protestant. Murphy, Edgar Gardner. 1900-13. *2118*
Southern Farmers' Alliance. Agricultural Organizations. North Carolina. Women. ca 1880-1900. *1373*
—. Economic reform. Kansas. Politics. Rightmire, William F. 1886-92. *1380*
—. Farmers. Methodology. 1884-90. *1391*
Southern Improvement Company. Alabama. Farmers. Negroes. Virginia. 1900-20. *2172*
Southern Lumber Operators' Association. Brotherhood of Timber Workers. Louisiana, western. Lumber and Lumbering. Race Relations. Texas, eastern. 1911-13. *2217*
Southern Tenant Farmers' Union. Agrarianism. Land reform. 1933-40. *2511*
—. Agricultural Adjustment Administration. Depressions. Labor Unions and Organizations. Sharecroppers. ca 1930's. *2602*
—. Delmo Housing Corporation. Farm Security Administration. Missouri. Tenancy. 1939-80. *1821*
Southwest *See also* individual states; Far Western States.
—. Crusade for Justice. Gonzales, Rodolfo "Corky". Mexican Americans. 1966-72. *2735*
—. Indians. Labor Unions and Organizations. Navajo Indians. 1958-78. *2945*
—. Labor. Mexican Americans. 1896-1915. *1908*
—. Law Enforcement. Mine, Mill and Smelter Workers, International Union of. Nicaragua. Silex, Humberto. 1932-78. *1739*
Spain. Abolition movement. Confederate States of America. Cuba. Foreign Relations. 1860-68. *1145*
—. Florida. Indian-White Relations. Pelota (game). 1675-84. *9*
Spanish language. Bilingual education. New Mexico. 1968-78. *2957*
Special Education *See also* Blind; Handicapped Children; Vocational Education.
—. Lanius, Henry E. Leader, George M. Legislation. Pennsylvania. Political leadership. 1820-1956. *1838*
Special Interest Groups. *See* Interest Groups; Political Factions; Pressure Groups.
Specialization. Medical Education. Polyclinics. 1880-1900. *1431*
Speeches, Addresses, etc. *See also* Lectures; Political Speeches.
—. Abolition Movement. Garnet, Henry Highland. Reform. 1843. *729*
—. Academic freedom. National security. Ohio State University. Rugg, Harold Ordway. 1951. *2771*
—. Douglass, Frederick. Ethnology. 1854. *700*
—. Educational Policy. Industrial Arts Education. Negroes. Washington, Booker T. 1884-1904. *1283*
—. Federal government. Indians. Nebraska Historical Society. Omaha Indians. Returned Students of Omaha. 1920's. *2442*
—. Feminism. Labor. Love. Stanton, Elizabeth Cady. 1868-70. *992*
—. Feminism. Rhetoric. Stanton, Elizabeth Cady ("The Solitude of Self"). 1892. *964*
—. Friedlander, Alice G. Oregon (Portland). Woman Suffrage. 1893. *1095*
—. Idaho (Twin Falls). Kidnapping. O'Hare, Kate Richards. Socialism. Utah. 1921. *2404*
—. Irish Americans. Jones, Mary Harris. Labor Disputes. 1870's-1920's. *170*
—. Keller, Helen. New Jersey (Montclair). Socialism. 1890-1913. *1916*
—. Women's rights. Wright, Frances. 1828-30. *801*
Spellman, Francis J. Catholic Church. Church Schools. Congress. Federal aid to education. Roosevelt, Eleanor. 1949-50. *2669*
Spencer, Herbert. Comte, Auguste. Foster, Frank K. Gompers, Samuel. Ideology. Labor Unions and Organizations. McGregor, Hugh. 1876-1900. *1295*
Spirit Fruit Society. Beilhardt, Jacob. Ohio (Lisbon). Sex. Utopias. 1865-1908. *1505*
Spiritualism. Crandall, Prudence. Kansas (Elk County). Temperance Movements. Women's rights. 1877-95. *1487*
—. District of Columbia. Education. Miner, Myrtilla. Negroes. 1851-1955. *190*
Spock, Benjamin *(Baby and Child Care)*. Child-rearing. Democracy. Family. Infants. 1917-50. *1589*
Spooner, John Coit. Civil rights. Racism. 1897-1907. *2156*
Sports *See also* Physical Education and Training.
—. Amateur Athletic Union. Colleges and Universities. Women. 1890's-1936. *1766*
—. Amateur Sports Act (US, 1978). Competition. President's Commission on Olympic Sports. 1960's-70's. *2783*

—. Communist Party. Depressions. 1920's-40's. *2564*
—. Great Britain. Public Schools. Upper Canada. Upper Classes. 1830-75. *210*
Spring, Marcus. Communes. New Jersey (Perth Amboy, Red Bank). North American Phalanx. Raritan Bay Union. 1843-59. *930*
Stalinism. Editors and Editing. *Partisan Review* (periodical). Socialism. 1930's. *2493*
Standard of living. Class struggle. Reform. Working class. 1950's-73. *2923*
Standard Oil Company of New Jersey. New Jersey (Bayonne). Polish Americans. Strikes. 1915-16. *2203*
Standard Oil Company of Ohio. Coopers' International Union. Industrial Relations. Mechanization. 1870's. *1313*
Stanley, A. O. Kentucky. Political Reform. Progressivism. State Politics. 1902-19. *1897*
Stanley, Augustus Owsley. McChesney, Henry V. Morrow, Edwin P. Political Campaigns (gubernatorial). Prohibition. 1915. *1873*
Stanley v. Georgia (US, 1969). Freedom of speech. Georgia. Obscenity. Supreme Court. 1968-79. *2765*
Stanton, Elizabeth Cady. Abolition Movement. Anthony, Susan B. Grimké, Angelina. Mott, Lucretia. Woman Suffrage. ca 1820-60. *549*
—. Abolition movement. Chapman, Maria Weston. Child, Lydia Maria. Feminism. ca 1830-40. *558*
—. Anthony, Susan B. Journalism. *Revolution* (newspaper). Woman Suffrage. 1868-70. *1108*
—. Attitudes. Domesticity. Lincoln, Mary Todd. Stowe, Harriet Beecher. 1830-80. *443*
—. Divorce. Feminism. Marriage. Reform. 1840-90. *1010*
—. Feminism. Labor. Love. Speeches, Addresses, etc. 1868-70. *992*
Stanton, Elizabeth Cady ("The Solitude of Self"). Feminism. Rhetoric. Speeches, Addresses, etc. 1892. *964*
Stanton, H. B. Abolition Movement. Birney, James. Clergy. Evangelicalism. Smith, Gerrit. Weld, Theodore Dwight. 1820-50. *744*
Stanton, Robert. Abolition Movement. Civil War (antecedents). Presbyterian Church. South. 1840-55. *731*
State debt. Negroes. Readjuster Party. Virginia. 1879-83. *1222*
State Government *See also* Constitutions, State; Governors; State Legislatures; State Politics; States' Rights; Territorial Government.
—. Air pollution. Clean Air Act (US, 1970). Demography. Energy. Fiscal Policy. 1970-79. *2719*
—. Alabama. Civil Rights. Democratic Party. Folsom, James E. Negroes. Women. 1947-58. *2668*
—. Beckham, John C. W. Kentucky. McCreary, James B. Progressivism. Willson, Augustus E. 1899-1915. *1894*
—. Bureaucracies. Centralization. Legislation. Missouri. Public schools. 1853. *846*
—. Business. Campbell, Thomas M. Democratic Party. Progressivism. Texas. 1907-11. *2264*
—. California (Wheatland). Industrial Workers of the World. Migrant Labor. Strikes. Trials. 1913-17. *2198*
—. Civil Rights. Employment. Federal Government. Public Policy. 20c. *1572*
—. Coal Mines and Mining. Convict labor. Strikes. Tennessee. 1891-93. *1286*
—. Coal Mines and Mining. Strikes. United Mine Workers of America. West Virginia (Paint Creek). 1912-13. *2270*
—. Colleges and Universities (black). Segregation. Texas. 1876-1947. *1846*
—. Crime and Criminals. Idaho. Industrial Workers of the World. Labor Law. 1917-33. *2088*
—. Discrimination. Federal Policy. Freedmen's Bureau. Mississippi. Reconstruction. 1865. *1227*
—. Dorr's Rebellion. Election Laws. *Luther* v. *Borden* (US, 1849). Rhode Island. Supreme Court. 1842-49. *591*
—. Education, Finance. Kentucky. Negroes. Segregation. 1865-1954. *1178*
—. Employment. Immigrants. Law Enforcement. Maximum hours laws. Women. 1920. *2398*
—. Executive Power. Intergovernmental Relations. Local Government. Ohio. Police. 1902-25. *2100*
—. Federal government. School integration. 1954-77. *2825*

—. Georgia. National Recovery Administration. Strikes. Talmadge, Eugene. Textile industry. 1934. *2467*
—. Illinois. Local Government. Lochner, Louis Paul. Peace Movements. People's Council of America for Democracy and Peace. 1917. *2104*
—. Illinois. Prisons. 1831-1903. *230*
—. Legislation. Minimum wage. Washington. 1913-25. *1822*
—. Liberalism. Partisanship. Professionalism. Public welfare. 1960's-70's. *2952*
—. Long, Huey P. Louisiana. Populism. Progressivism. 1891-1935. *1566*
—. Medicine. Mental illness. 1700-1977. *247*
State Industrial School for Girls. Girls. Juvenile Delinquency. Massachusetts (Lancaster). Socialization. 1856-1905. *1443*
State Legislatures. Alabama. Mobile Harbor Act (Alabama, 1842). Negroes. Petitions. Prisons. Seamen. 1849. *727*
—. American Revolution. Colleges and universities. Public Opinion. 1775-83. *485*
—. Antislavery movement. Morris, Thomas. Ohio. 1836-39. *711*
—. Bible. Constitutional Amendments (19th). Equal Rights Amendment. Tennessee. Women. 1876-1974. *2904*
—. Blue law. Legislators. Louisiana. Negroes. Reconstruction. 1867-75. *1276*
—. *Brown* v. *Board of Education* (US, 1954). Collins, LeRoy. Florida. Supreme Court. 1954-61. *2664*
—. Conservatism. Elections, presidential. Mississippi. Segregation. Sillers, Walter. 1948-64. *2677*
—. Constitutional Amendments (18th). Dean Act (1919). Prohibition. Texas. 1917-33. *2368*
—. Constitutions, State (reform). Hamilton, Joseph G. de Roulhac. North Carolina. Progressivism. Sikes, Enoch W. 1898-1913. *2091*
—. Court of Visitation. Kansas. Populism. Railroads. Republican Party. 1890-1900. *1386*
—. Curricula. Farmers' Alliance. Iowa State Agricultural College. Wallace, Henry. 1884-91. *1416*
—. Emancipation Proclamation. New Jersey. Peace Movements. 1864. *1009*
—. Equality. Lobbying. New York City. Strachan, Grace. Teachers. Wages. Women. 1907-11. *2202*
—. Evangelism. Michigan. Political parties. 1837-61. *578*
—. Harmony Society. Pennsylvania. Rapp, George. Utopias. 1805-07. *913*
—. Populism. Reformers. West. 1890's. *1364*
—. Property rights. Reconstruction. South. Women. 1865-95. *1103*
State Politics *See also* Elections; Governors; Political Campaigns; Political Parties; State Government.
—. Abolition Movement. Brown, John. Harpers Ferry raid. North Carolina. Sectional Conflict. 1840-60. *675*
—. Abolition movement. Fessenden, Samuel. Free Soil movement. Liberty Party. Maine. Willey, Austin. 1830's-48. *682*
—. Abolition Movement. Giddings, Joshua Reed. Ohio. Radicals and Radicalism. 1840-60. *651*
—. Abolition Movement. *Green Mountain Freeman* (newspaper). Liberty Party. Poland, Joseph. Vermont. 1840-48. *683*
—. Adams, Alva B. Colorado. Progressivism. Sweet, William. 1922-24. *2403*
—. Alabama. Democratic Party. Manning, Joseph C. Populism. 1892-96. *1387*
—. American Missionary Association. Cardozo, Francis Louis. Education. Freedmen. Reconstruction. South Carolina (Charleston). 1865-70. *1243*
—. Antislavery sentiments. Liberty Party. New Hampshire. 1840-48. *681*
—. Appalachia. Negroes. Reconstruction. Republican Party. 1865-1900. *1216*
—. Arkansas. Garland, Rufus King. Greenback Party. Tobey, Charles E. 1876-82. *952*
—. Black Laws (Ohio, 1804, 1807). Ohio. 1837-49. *593*
—. Bloomer, Amelia. Iowa. Savery, Anne. Woman suffrage. Woodhull, Victoria Claflin. 1868-72. *1111*
—. Breckinridge, Robert J. Emancipation. Kentucky. 1830-49. *677*
—. California. Racism. Slavery. 1849-60. *755*
—. Carpetbaggers. Louisiana. Negroes. Republican Party. 1868. *1136*

—. Chamberlain, Daniel H. Hampton, Wade. Reconstruction. South Carolina. 1877. *1054*
—. Civil War. Emancipation. Ohio. Racism. 1863-65. *1182*
—. Civil War. Negroes. Political Protest. Suffrage. Tennessee. 1864-65. *1144*
—. Crawford, Coe Isaac. Progressivism. Republican Party. Roosevelt, Theodore. South Dakota. 1912-14. *2076*
—. Cummins, Albert B. Government regulation. Iowa (Davenport). Law Enforcement. Liquor. Riots. 1907-08. *1880*
—. Democratic Party. Farmers' Alliance. North Carolina. Vance, Zebulon B. 1880-90. *1366*
—. Depressions. Great Plains. Radicals and Radicalism. 1930-36. *2520*
—. Elkins, Stephen B. Reform. Republican Party. West Virginia. White, Albert B. 1901-05. *1895*
—. Farmer-Labor Party. Michigan. New Deal. 1933-37. *2541*
—. Farmer-Labor Party. Minnesota. Swedish Americans. 1922-44. *1631*
—. Farmers. Idaho. Irrigation. Progressive Party. 1914-22. *2012*
—. Garvin, Lucius F. C. Political reform. Rhode Island. 1876-1922. *343*
—. Hawaiians. 1900-80. *2736*
—. House of Representatives. Langston, John Mercer. Negroes. Virginia. 1849-97. *300*
—. Idaho. Prohibition. 1932-35. *2575*
—. Iowa. Political parties. Prohibition. 19c. *1445*
—. Kansas. Newspapers. Political Commentary. Populism. Vincent, Henry. 1886-91. *1384*
—. Kentucky. Political Reform. Progressivism. Stanley, A. O. 1902-19. *1897*
—. Kentucky. Populism. 1870-1900. *1367*
—. Land tenure. Political Reform. Populism. Rogers, John R. Washington. 1890-1900. *1363*
—. Louisiana. Ostracism. Reconstruction. Scalawags. Terrorism. 1866-78. *1081*
—. Nevada. Prohibition. 1880-1933. *257*
—. New York. Platt, Thomas C. Progressivism. Public policy. Republican Party. 1890-1910. *2030*
—. Peffer, William A. Reconstruction. Tennessee. 1865-69. *949*
Statehood. Mormons. Utah. Woman suffrage. 1867-96. *1090*
States' Rights *See also* Secession.
—. Civil Rights Act (US, 1866). Constitutional Amendments (14th, 15th). Negroes. Reconstruction. Republican Party. ca 1865-77. *953*
—. Equality. Federal government. Negroes. New York. 1865-73. *1154*
—. Federalism. Legislation. Progressivism. 1880-1930. *1959*
Statute. *See* Law; Legislation.
Steel Industry *See also* Iron Industry.
—. Buckeye Steel Castings Company. Bush, S. P. Management, scientific. Ohio (Columbus). Social Work. 1890-1920. *2181*
—. Cigar industry. Industrial Workers of the World. Pennsylvania (McKees Rocks, Pittsburgh). Pressed Steel Car Company. Strikes. 1909-13. *2235*
—. Company towns. Ohio. Social Classes. Strikes. 1937. *2474*
—. Discrimination. Labor Unions and Organizations. Mexican Americans. North Central States. 1919-45. *1802*
—. Great Britain. Labor Unions and Organizations. 1888-1912. *155*
—. Indiana (Gary). Martial law. Strikes. 1919. *2244*
—. Industrial Relations. Pennsylvania. 1800-1959. *174*
—. Labor Reform. Twelve-hour day. 1887-1923. *2384*
—. Pennsylvania (Allegheny-Kiskiminetas Valley). Strikes. 1919. *2242*
—. Pennsylvania (Bethlehem). Schwab, Charles M. Strikes. 1910. *2223*
—. Pennsylvania (Pittsburgh). Strikes. 1919. *2174*
Steel Workers Organizing Committee. Foreign policy. Imports. International Steel Cartel. Labor. US Steel Corporation. 1937. *2538*
Steffens, Lincoln. Christianity. Class Struggle. *Los Angeles Times*. McNamara case. Progressivism. Radicals and Radicalism. 1908-12. *2083*
—. Political Commentary. 1900's-30's. *2119*

Steinmetz

Steinmetz, Charles Proteus. Collectivism. Intellectuals. National Association of Corporation Schools. Utopias. 1910-17. *1950*
Stereotypes. *Amos 'n' Andy* (program). Boycotts. Comic strips. Negroes. Radio. 1930's. *2588*
—. Jews. Labor movement. Public opinion. 1880's-1915. *2211*
Sterilization. Mexican Americans. Racism. Women. 20c. *2704*
Steward, Ira. Boston Eight Hour League. International Workingmen's Association. Labor Unions and Organizations. Marxism. McNeill, George. New York. 1860-89. *1307*
Stewart, Cora Wilson. Education. Illiteracy. Kentucky Illiteracy Commission. Kentucky (Rowan County). 1910-20. *2325*
Stiles, Charles W. Hookworms. Poor. Rockefeller Sanitary Commission for the Eradication of Hookworm Disease. South. 1900-14. *2109*
Stiles, Ezra. Colleges and Universities. Ellery, William, Jr. Rhode Island (Newport). 1770. *486*
Stimson, Henry L. Hastie, William H. Military. Negroes. Racism. World War II. 1940-43. *2636*
Stone, Lucy. Blackwell, Henry B. Editors and Editing. Feminism. Politics. *Women's Journal* (periodical). 1870-1914. *1047*
Storey, Moorfield. Anti-Imperialism. Attitudes. Law Reform. Mugwumps. NAACP. 1870's-1929. *462*
Stowe, Harriet Beecher. Antislavery sentiments. Christianity. Civil War. ca 1850-80. *673*
—. Attitudes. Domesticity. Lincoln, Mary Todd. Stanton, Elizabeth Cady. 1830-80. *443*
—. Feminism. Literature. Negroes. Truth, Sojourner. 1850's-90's. *802*
—. Presbyterian Church. Slavery. 1830's-1870's. *909*
Strachan, Grace. Equality. Lobbying. New York City. State Legislatures. Teachers. Wages. Women. 1907-11. *2202*
Strang, James Jesse. Michigan (Beaver Island). Michigan, Lake. Utopias. Wisconsin (Voree). 1820-56. *942*
Strategy. *See* Military Strategy.
Strayer, George D. Educational reform. Meadows, Clarence W. Public Schools. Trent, W. W. West Virginia Education Association. 1932-58. *1837*
Street, Electric Railway and Motor Coach Employees of America. Louisiana (New Orleans). Public opinion. Strikes. 1929-30. *2353*
Street, Jane (letter). Domestics. Industrial Workers of the World. Labor Unions and Organizations. Progressive era. 1917. *2224*
Streetcars. American Federation of Labor. Armies. Police. Strikes. Tennessee (Knoxville). 1919-20. *2185*
—. Charleston City Railway Company. Desegregation. Negroes. Reconstruction. South Carolina. 1867. *1169*
—. Legislation. Pennsylvania (Philadelphia). Segregation. 1850's-70. *1156*
Strikebreakers. Coal Mines and Mining. Negroes. Oregon Improvement Company. Washington (King County). 1891. *1265*
—. Coal Mines and Mining. Ohio (Hocking Valley). Violence. 1884-85. *1296*
Strikes *See also* Civil Disturbances; Collective Bargaining; Labor Unions and Organizations; Syndicalism.
—. 1830-1910. *166*
—. Agricultural Labor. California (Salinas). Filipino Labor Union. Lettuce. 1934. *2499*
—. Agricultural Reform. Arkansas. Colored Farmers' Alliance. Cotton. Humphrey, R. M. 1891. *1171*
—. Alabama. Coal. Kilby, Thomas E. United Mine Workers of America. 1890-1929. *2448*
—. Alaska (Douglas Island). Gold Mines and Mining. Labor Unions and Organizations. Treadwell Mines. Western Federation of Miners. 1905-10. *2209*
—. American Civil Liberties Union. Associated Silk Workers Union. Freedom of Assembly. Freedom of Speech. New Jersey (Paterson). 1924. *2378*
—. American Federation of Labor. Armies. Police. Streetcars. Tennessee (Knoxville). 1919-20. *2185*
—. American Federation of Labor. Industrial Workers of the World. Louisiana. Marine Transport Workers. Sailors' Union. United Fruit Company. 1913. *2193*
—. American Railway Union. California. Illinois (Pullman). 1893-94. *1337*

SUBJECT INDEX

—. American Railway Union. Montana. Railroads. 1894. *1357*
—. Amherst Federation of Labor. Economic Conditions. Labor Unions and Organizations. Nova Scotia (Amherst). 1901-31. *1801*
—. Ammons, Elias. Coal. Colorado. Federal Government. Wilson, Woodrow. 1914. *2228*
—. Antiforeign sentiments. Utah (Carbon County). Utah Fuel Company. 1902-04. *2258*
—. Arizona (Bisbee). Industrial Workers of the World. Labor Unions and Organizations. Mining. 1917. *2186*
—. Arizona (Bisbee). Industrial Workers of the World. Shattuck Mine. 1917. *2285*
—. Arizona (Globe). Copper Mines and Mining. Western Federation of Miners. 1917. *2261*
—. Arizona (Globe). Copper Mines and Mining. Western Federation of Miners. World War I. 1917. *2255*
—. Armies. Railroads. Values. 1877. 1894. *1294*
—. Attitudes. Industrialization. Rhode Island (Pawtucket). Textile industry. Working Class. 1824. *821*
—. Australia. London, Jack. 1908-09. *2246*
—. Authority. Lukens Iron Works. Paternalism. Pennsylvania (Coatesville). Profits. 1886. *1347*
—. Baltimore and Ohio Railroad. Mathews, Henry M. Railroads. West Virginia (Martinsburg, Berkeley County). 1877. *1301*
—. Bell Canada. Ontario (Toronto). Telephone operators. Women. 1907. *1808*
—. Berry, George L. Illinois (Chicago). Newspapers. 1912-14. *2274*
—. Berry pickers. California (El Monte). Foreign Relations. Japan. Mexico. 1933. *2522*
—. Boulder Canyon Project. Colorado River. Hoover Dam. Industrial Workers of the World. Nevada. 1931. *2433*
—. Boulder Canyon Project. Hoover Dam. Industrial Workers of the World. Nevada. Six Companies, Inc. 1931. *2434*
—. British Columbia (Trail). Consolidated Mining and Smelting Company. Immigration. Mine, Mill and Smelter Workers, International Union of. World War I. 1916-17. *1810*
—. British Columbia (Vancouver Island). Canadian Collieries (Dunsmuir) Limited. Coal Mines and Mining. Labor Unions and Organizations. United Mine Workers of America. 1912-14. *2251*
—. Brotherhood of Locomotive Engineers. Canada. Grand Trunk Railway. 1876-77. *1333*
—. Business. California (San Francisco). Construction. Eight-hour day. Law and Order Committee. 1916-17. *2232*
—. California. Grape industry. Labor Unions and Organizations. United Farm Workers Union. 1966-70. *2934*
—. California (Inglewood). Communist Party. North American Aviation. United Automobile Workers of America. 1941. *2642*
—. California (Los Angeles). Mexican Americans. Pacific Electric Railroad. 1900-03. *2289*
—. California (Oakland). Social change. 1946-47. *2691*
—. California (San Francisco). Labor Disputes. Law and Order Committee. Longshoremen. 1916. *2234*
—. California (San Francisco). Longshoremen. 1934-39. *2529*
—. California (Wheatland). Industrial Workers of the World. Migrant Labor. State Government. Trials. 1913-17. *2198*
—. Canada. Winnipeg General Strike (1919). 1920-70. *1752*
—. Carbon County Coal Strike (1933). National Miners Union. United Mine Workers of America. Utah. 1900-39. *2571*
—. Central Labor Union. Eight-hour day. Knights of Labor. Labor Unions and Organizations. Massachusetts (Boston). 1886. *1321*
—. Central Labor Union. Ohio (Cincinnati). 1886. *1331*
—. Christianity. Longshoremen. Oxford Group movement. Washington (Seattle). 1921-34. *2604*
—. Cigar industry. Industrial Workers of the World. Pennsylvania (McKees Rocks, Pittsburgh). Pressed Steel Car Company. Steel Industry. 1909-13. *2235*
—. Class conflict. Rhode Island (Pawtucket). Textile Industry. 1790-1824. *822*
—. Coal, anthracite. Mining. Pennsylvania. United Mine Workers of America. 1922-23. *2391*

Strikes

—. Coal, anthracite. Pinchot, Gifford. United Mine Workers of America. 1925-26. *2390*
—. Coal miners. Germer, Adolph. Illinois (Virden). Socialism. United Mine Workers of America. 1893-1900. *1291*
—. Coal miners. Labor Unions and Organizations. 1881-94. *1284*
—. Coal Mines and Mining. Colorado. Industrial Workers of the World. 1927. *2411*
—. Coal Mines and Mining. Colorado Fuel and Iron Company. Ludlow Massacre. National Guard. 1913-14. *2206*
—. Coal Mines and Mining. Colorado (Las Animas, Huerfano counties). United Mine Workers of America. 1904-14. *2273*
—. Coal Mines and Mining. Convict labor. State Government. Tennessee. 1891-93. *1286*
—. Coal Mines and Mining. Debs, Eugene V. Socialist Party. West Virginia. 1912-14. *2194*
—. Coal Mines and Mining. Diaries. Medrick, George. Pennsylvania, western. United Mine Workers of America. 1927. *2372*
—. Coal Mines and Mining. Federal government. Pennsylvania. Roosevelt, Theodore. 1902. *2218*
—. Coal Mines and Mining. Hoadly, George. Ohio (Hocking Valley). 1884-85. *1322*
—. Coal Mines and Mining. Hocking Valley. Lewis, John Llewellyn. Ohio, southeastern. United Mine Workers of America. 1927. *2447*
—. Coal Mines and Mining. Labor Unions and Organizations. Racism. United Mine Workers of America. 1894-1920. *2272*
—. Coal Mines and Mining. State Government. United Mine Workers of America. West Virginia (Paint Creek). 1912-13. *2270*
—. Colored Farmers' Alliance. Humphrey, R. M. Labor Unions and Organizations. Negroes. South. 1876-91. *1150*
—. Communism. North Carolina (Gastonia). Novels. Poor. Textile Industry. Whites. 1929-34. *2361*
—. Communist Party. Ontario. Quebec (Cowansville). Silk industry. 1931. *1778*
—. Community Participation in Politics. Lumber and Lumbering. Michigan (Bay City, Saginaw). 1880's. *1320*
—. Company towns. Ohio. Social Classes. Steel Industry. 1937. *2474*
—. Cowboys. Western States. Working conditions. 1870-90. *1324*
—. Debs, Eugene V. Federal Government. Illinois (Blue Island). Pullman Strike. 1894. *1317*
—. Discrimination, Employment. Georgia Railroad. Negroes. 1909. *2220*
—. Everett Mill. Massachusetts (Lawrence). Polish Americans. Radicals and Radicalism. Textile Industry. Women. 1912. *2252*
—. Farmers. Industrial Workers of the World. Orchards. Washington (Yakima Valley). 1933. *2568*
—. Garment industry. Illinois (Chicago). Men. 1910-11. *2286*
—. Garment Industry. Illinois (Chicago). O'Reilly, Mary. Socialist Party. Women. Zeh, Nellie M. 1910. *2183*
—. General Tire Company. Murray, Rex. Ohio (Akron). Strikes. 1934-35. *2565*
—. General Tire Company. Murray, Rex. Ohio (Akron). Strikes. 1934-35. *2565*
—. Georgia. National Recovery Administration. State Government. Talmadge, Eugene. Textile industry. 1934. *2467*
—. Gould, Jay. Knights of Labor. Missouri (Sedalia). Modernization. Railroads. 1885-86. *1292*
—. Illinois (Chicago). Militia. Police. Riots. Wages. 1877. *1343*
—. Illinois (Chicago; Back of the Yards). Labor Unions and Organizations. Meat packing industry. Polish Americans. 1921. *2424*
—. Immigrants. Industrial Workers of the World. New Jersey (Paterson). Textile Industry. Violence. 1913. *2254*
—. Immigrants. Industrial Workers of the World. New York (Little Falls). Textile Industry. Women. 1912. *2269*
—. Indiana (Gary). Martial law. Steel industry. 1919. *2244*
—. Industrial Rayon Corporation. Textile Workers Organizing Committee. Virginia (Covington). 1937-38. *2508*
—. Industrial Workers of the World. Labor Unions and Organizations. Washington (Yakima Valley). 1933. *2496*
—. Industrial Workers of the World. Ohio (Akron). Rubber. 1913. *2290*

Strikes

—. Industrialists. Labor history (sources). New York (Buffalo). Police reports. 1890-1913. *152*
—. Industry. Railroads. 1877. *1353*
—. Labor. New Jersey (Passaic). Textile industry. Working conditions. 1875-1926. *2366*
—. Labor Reform. New York (Little Falls). Textile Industry. Women. 1912. *2268*
—. Louisiana. Oil Industry and Trade. Texas. 1917-18. *2237*
—. Louisiana (New Orleans). Public opinion. Street, Electric Railway and Motor Coach Employees of America. 1929-30. *2353*
—. Lukens Iron Works. Paternalism. Pennsylvania (Coatesville). 1886. *1348*
—. Mabey, Charles R. United Mine Workers of America. Utah (Carbon County). 1922. *2429*
—. Mass Transit. Missouri. Modernization. Monopolies. St. Louis Transit Company. 1900. *2257*
—. Massachusetts (Haverhill). Shoe Industry. Women. 1895. *1288*
—. Massachusetts (Lowell). Values. Women. 1820-50. *548*
—. Massachusetts (Marlboro). Public Opinion. Shoe Industry. 1898-99. *1300*
—. Missouri (St. Louis). Political Leadership. Racism. Social Classes. Workingmen's Party. 1877. *1338*
—. Nardella, Luigi (interview). Rhode Island. Textile Industry. 1922. *2349*
—. National Brotherhood of Operative Potters. Pottery. Tariff. 1894. *1345*
—. National Textile Workers Union. North Carolina (Gastonia). Textile Industry. Weisbord, Vera Buch (reminiscence). 1929. *2459*
—. New Jersey. New York City. Patterson Strike Pageant. Theater. 1913. *2250*
—. New Jersey (Bayonne). Polish Americans. Standard Oil Company of New Jersey. 1915-16. *2203*
—. New Jersey (Paterson). Silk industry. 1913-24. *1761*
—. North Carolina (Gastonia). Novels. Textile Industry. 1929-30's. *2431*
—. Paint Creek-Cabin Creek Strike. *Socialist and Labor Star* (newspaper). Thompson, Wyatt Hamilton. West Virginia. 1912-13. *2195*
—. Pennsylvania (Allegheny-Kiskiminetas Valley). Steel Industry. 1919. *2242*
—. Pennsylvania (Bethlehem). Schwab, Charles M. Steel industry. 1910. *2223*
—. Pennsylvania (Pittsburgh). Steel Industry. 1919. *2174*
—. Quebec (Montreal). Teamsters, International Brotherhood of. 1864. *1315*
—. Railroad Carmen's Strike (1911-15). Scientific management. Working class. 1903-22. *2256*
—. Railroads. Violence. Working class. 1877. *1299*
Strikes, wildcat. Black lung disease. Coal Mine Health and Safety Act (US, 1969; amended, 1972). Coal Mines and Mining. Medicine. United Mine Workers of America. Workmen's Compensation. 1968-72. *2717*
Stringfellow, Thornton. Evangelicalism. Reform. Slavery. Virginia. 1800-70. *633*
Strong, Anna Louise. China. Maoism. USSR. 1919-70. *324*
Strong, Josiah. Anglo-Saxonism. Interventionism. Reform. 1885-1915. *71*
Strong, William. Christianity. Presbyterian Church. Supreme Court. 1864-80. *1497*
Stuart, Henry Harvey. Education. New Brunswick. Socialism. 1873-1952. *310*
Student activism. Arkansas Agricultural, Mechanical, and Normal College. Arkansas, University of, Pine Bluff. Black Nationalism. Colleges and Universities. 1972-73. *2872*
—. Black Nationalism. Colleges and universities. South. 1890-1972. *1673*
—. Civil rights movement. Political socialization. Radicals and Radicalism. ca 1955-75. *2713*
—. Columbus *Enquirer-Sun* (newspaper). Georgia, University of. Harris, Julian LaRose. 1920-29. *2416*
—. Occupations. Political Attitudes. 1960's-70's. *2715*
—. Political Participation. 1960's. *2692*
Student Christian Movement. Ecumenism. Evangelism. Protestantism. Social change. Social justice. 19c-20c. *5*
Student League for Industrial Democracy. Socialism. 1905-21. *2077*

Student Nonviolent Coordinating Committee. Civil Rights. Economic Research and Action Project. Feminism. National Organization for Women. 1960's. *2906*
—. Politics. Race Relations. Values. 1961-66. *2889*
Students *See also* Colleges and Universities; Schools.
—. Alabama, University of. Attitudes. Desegregation. 1963-74. *2870*
—. American Board of Commissioners for Foreign Missions. Assimilation. Connecticut (Cornwall). Foreign Mission School. Indian-White Relations. 1816-27. *829*
—. Antiwar Sentiment. Conscription, Military. New Left. Vietnam War. 1965-71. *2696*
—. *Blackwell* v. *Issaquena County Board of Education* (US, 1966). *Burnside* v. *Byars* (US, 1966). Courts. Freedom of Speech. *Tinker* v. *Des Moines Community School District* (US, 1969). 1870-1969. *1728*
—. California. Educational Tests and Measurements. Ethnic groups. IQ tests. Progressivism. 1917-21. *2300*
—. Civil rights movement. Leftism. Models. Political attitudes. 1960's-70's. *2714*
—. Colleges and Universities. Intellectuals. Political Protest. Radicals and Radicalism. 1963-77. *2750*
—. Colleges and Universities. Political Attitudes. Radicals and Radicalism. 1943-70. *1537*
—. Desegregation. Florida (Jacksonville). Public schools. 1960's-70's. *2834*
—. Methodology. Political Protest. Psychoanalysis. Social conditions. 1900-75. *1616*
—. New Left. Youth Movements. 1905-70. *2760*
Students for a Democratic Society. Radicals and Radicalism. Youth Movements. 1950's. 1960's. *2720*
Subsidies. Charities. City government. New York City. Reform. 1870-98. *1463*
Subsistence Homesteads Program. Miners. National Industrial Recovery Act (US, 1933). New Deal. Roosevelt, Eleanor. West Virginia (Arthurdale). 1930-46. *2492*
Suburbs. California (San Francisco Bay area). Consumers. Environmental protection. Government regulation. Housing. Local government. 1940-80. *2718*
—. City Planning. Garden cities. New Jersey. Radburn (settlement). 1927-79. *1532*
—. Communes. Pastoralism. 1950's-1970's. *2987*
—. Davis, Alexander Jackson. Garden cities. Haskell, Llewellyn S. Idealism. New Jersey (West Orange; Llewellyn Park). 1853-57. *943*
Suffrage *See also* Naturalization; Negro Suffrage; Voter Registration; Voting and Voting Behavior; Woman Suffrage.
—. British Columbia. Chinese. Immigration. Japanese. 1935-49. *1725*
—. Civil War. Lincoln, Abraham. Louisiana (New Orleans). Negroes. Reconstruction. 1860-67. *1130*
—. Civil War. Negroes. Political Protest. State Politics. Tennessee. 1864-65. *1144*
—. Conservatism. McCumber, Porter James. McKenzie, Alexander John. North Dakota. Political reform. Republican Party. Women. 1898-1933. *435*
—. Constitutional conventions. Negroes. Ohio. Progressive era. Smith, Harry. 1863-1912. *2165*
—. Constitutions, State. Louisiana. Slidell, John. 1812-52. *601*
—. Diaries. Fox, Ruth May. Utah. Women. 1865-95. *1119*
—. Feminism. Labor Unions and Organizations. Lobbying. Middle Classes. Women's Trade Union League. ca 1903-20. *1980*
—. Freedmen. House of Representatives. Murray, George Washington. Republican Party. South Carolina. 1893-97. *1163*
—. Illinois Association Opposed to the Extension of Suffrage to Women. Women Remonstrants of the State of Illinois. 1886-1923. *132*
—. Navy League (Woman's Section). Preparedness. Sex roles. Woman's Peace Party. World War I. 1914-18. *2092*
—. Negroes. Pennsylvania. 1780-1900. *137*
—. Republican Party. Senter, DeWitt Clinton. Tennessee. 1869-70. *954*
Sullivan, Anna (interview). Massachusetts. Oral history. Textile Workers Union of America. Women. 1918-76. *403*

Supreme Court

Sullivan, John H. Educators. Ethnographers. Evangelism. Indians (reservations). Pueblo Indians (Hopi). Taylor, Charles A. 1870-89. *1050*
Sumner, William Graham. *Collier's Weekly.* Sinclair, Upton. Socialism. 1900-04. *1921*
—. Family. Sexuality. Social Theory. 1870's-1910. *985*
Sunday. Adventists. Illinois. Jones, Alonzo Trevier. Religious liberty. World's Columbian Exposition (Chicago, 1893). 1893. *1492*
Sunday School Movement. Protestantism. Sex roles. Women. 1790-1880. *180*
Sunday, William Ashley ("Billy"). Georgia (Atlanta). Revivals. 1917. *1882*
Sunderland, La Roy. Medicine. Mesmerism. Phrenology. Psychology. 1820-68. *880*
Superior National Forest. Economic Development. Forest Service. Minnesota, northeastern. Public Policy. Wilderness. 1923-26. *2437*
Supreme Court. Affirmative action. Civil rights. Pluralism. 1970-80. *2779*
—. Affirmative action. Discrimination. *Fullilove* v. *Klutznick* (US, 1980). Minorities. *Regents of the University of California* v. *Allan Bakke* (US, 1978). *United Steelworkers of America* v. *Weber* (US, 1979). 1970's. *2782*
—. Authority. Constitutional Amendments (1st). Health. Religious liberty. 1963-79. *2769*
—. Baptists. *Brown* v. *Board of Education* (US, 1954). Desegregation. Georgia. 1954-61. *2662*
—. Bilingual education. California. Chacone-Moscone Bilingual Bicultural Education Act (1976). Civil Rights Act (US, 1964). *Lau* v. *Nichols* (US, 1974). 1965-76. *2966*
—. *Brown* v. *Board of Education* (US, 1954). Collins, LeRoy. Florida. State Legislatures. 1954-61. *2664*
—. Burger, Warren E. Civil Rights. 1975-78. *2775*
—. Burger, Warren E. Civil Rights. ca 1970-75. *2790*
—. California (Eight Mile, Blue Creek). Forest Service. Indians. Religious liberty. 1975. *2785*
—. Christianity. Presbyterian Church. Strong, William. 1864-80. *1497*
—. Civil Rights. Civil War. Constitutional Amendments (14th, 15th). Slavery. Woman Suffrage. 1863-75. *1106*
—. Civil rights. Constitutional Amendments (14th). *Gitlow* v. *New York* (US, 1925). Sanford, Edward Terry. ca 1890-1930. *2399*
—. Civil Rights. Constitutional Amendments (14th). Judicial review. 19c-20c. *144*
—. Civil rights. Constitutional Law. Douglas, William O. Judicial process. Liberalism. 1928-77. *1715*
—. Civil Rights. Constitutions. Migration, internal. 1780's-1977. *138*
—. Civil Rights. Harlan, John Marshall. 1877-1911. *1122*
—. Civil Rights. Minorities. 1886-1972. *73*
—. Civil rights. Segregation. Vinson, Frederick M. 1946-53. *2671*
—. Civil Rights Act (US, 1875). Law Enforcement. 1875-83. *1159*
—. Congress. Constitutional Amendments (14th, 15th). Elections. Federal Election Campaign Act (US, 1971, 1974). Voting Rights Act (US, 1965). 1965-75. *2767*
—. Congress. Judicial reform. Progressivism. Taft, William H. 1920-25. *2400*
—. Conservatism. Constitutional law. Kansas. New Deal. Newspapers. 1934-35. *2502*
—. Constitutional Law. Government. 1950-75. *1557*
—. Constitutions. Editorials. Labor Unions and Organizations. New Deal. Periodicals. 1935-37. *2503*
—. Courts. North. *Prigg* v. *Pennsylvania* (US, 1842). Slavery. 1842-57. *636*
—. Democratic Party. NAACP. Negro Suffrage. Primaries. *Smith* v. *Allwright* (US, 1944). South. 1890's-1944. *1722*
—. Democratic Party. NAACP. Negro Suffrage. Primaries. Texas. 1927-45. *1723*
—. Depressions. Historiography. Hughes, Charles Evans. New Deal. 1930's. 1950's-60's. *2572*
—. Discrimination, Educational. Harlan, John Marshall. *Joseph W. Cumming, James S. Harper and John Ladeveze* v. *School Board of Richmond County, Ga.* (US, 1899). Public Schools. ca 1896-1907. *1194*
—. Dorr's Rebellion. Election Laws. *Luther* v. *Borden* (US, 1849). Rhode Island. State government. 1842-49. *591*

Supreme Court
—. *Dred Scott* v. *Sandford* (US, 1857). Marshall, John. Slavery. Taney, Roger Brooke. 1820-60. *785*
—. Economic Conditions. National Recovery Administration. New Deal. Virginia. 1933-35. *2517*
—. Freedom of speech. Georgia. Obscenity. *Stanley* v. *Georgia* (US, 1969). 1968-79. *2765*
—. Housing. Kentucky (Louisville). NAACP. Segregation. 1914-17. *2126*
—. NAACP. Nominations to Office. North Carolina. Parker, John J. White, Walter F. 1930. *2385*
—. School Integration. 1877-1977. *1831*
Supreme Court (decision). Bradwell, Myra. Illinois. Lawyers. Sex Discrimination. 1873-1894. *1114*
Supreme Court decisions. Civil Rights Act (US, 1964). Florida. School Integration. 1954-64. *2686*
—. Negroes. *Plessy vs. Ferguson* (US, 1896). Segregation. 1896. *1212*
—. Race Relations. School integration. 1954-74. *2865*
Supreme courts, state. Abolitionists. Law. Slavery. South. 1810-60. *775*
—. Bible. Constitutions, State. Presbyterian Church. Religious Education. Wisconsin. 1848-90. *1419*
—. Civil rights. New federalism. Prisoners. 1969-80. *2773*
—. Judicial Administration. Labor. Populism. Western States. 1893-1902. *1024*
Surveillance. Federal Bureau of Investigation. Hoover, J. Edgar. Radicals and Radicalism. 1919-21. *2461*
Sutherland, Duchess of (Harriet Howard). Antislavery Sentiments. Great Britain. Tyler, Julia Gardiner. Women. 1842-89. *723*
Sutherland, Edward A. Adventists. Battle Creek College. Madison College. Michigan. Tennessee. 1897-1904. *2331*
Swayne, Wager. Alabama. Freedmen's Bureau. Racism. Reconstruction. 1865-68. *1279*
Swedenborg, Emanuel. Arthur, Timothy Shay *(Ten Nights in a Bar-Room)*. Temperance Movements. 18c. 1854. *883*
Swedes. Bishop Hill Colony. Illinois. Janssonists. Letters. 1847. *936*
Swedish Americans. Bishop Hill Colony. Communalism. Economic growth. Illinois. Westward Movement. 1846-59. *935*
—. Bishop Hill Colony. Daily life. Illinois. Jansson, Erik. Letters. Utopias. 1847-56. *939*
—. Bishop Hill Colony. Illinois. Immigrants. Janssonists. Utopias. 1846-60. *920*
—. Farmer-Labor Party. Minnesota. State politics. 1922-44. *1631*
Sweet, William. Adams, Alva B. Colorado. Progressivism. State Politics. 1922-24. *2403*
Swett, John. California (San Francisco). Educational Reform. Rincon School. 1853-62. *849*
Swiss Americans. Communia (settlement). German Americans. Iowa (Volga Township). Utopias. 1847-64. *926*
Swisshelm, Jane Grey. Abolition Movement. Feminism. Journalism. Lowry, Sylvanus B. Minnesota. 1815-84. *385*
—. Abolition Movement. Feminism. Minnesota. St. Cloud *Visitor* (newspaper). 1857-62. *814*
—. Feminism. Journalism. ca 1835-84. *328*
Syndicalism *See also* Anarchism and Anarchists; Communism; Labor Unions and Organizations; Socialism.
—. Agricultural Cooperatives. Quebec. 1922-79. *1758*
—. Canadian Seamen's Union. Communists. 1936-49. *1754*
—. Catholic Church. École Sociale Populaire. Propaganda. Quebec (Montreal). Working Class. 1911-49. *1806*
Syndicat Catholique des Allumeftières. Labor. Match industry. Quebec (Hull). Women. 1919-24. *1775*
Synods. *See* Councils and Synods.

T

Tabert, Martin. Convict lease system. Corporal punishment. Florida (Leon County). Law Reform. 1921-23. *2354*
Taft, William H. Congress. Judicial reform. Progressivism. Supreme Court. 1920-25. *2400*

Taft-Hartley Act (US, 1947). Business. Labor Unions and Organizations. New Deal. Wagner Act (US, 1935). World War II. 1935-47. *1749*
Talbot, Marion. Mead, Margaret. Scholars. Social sciences. Thompson, Helen. Women. 1900-20's. *2065*
Talented Tenth strategy. DuBois, W. E. B. Elites. Intellectuals. Negroes. 1895-1919. *2090*
—. DuBois, W. E. B. Elites. Liberal education. Negroes. 1890's-1963. *1591*
Talladega College. Alabama. American Missionary Association. Education. Negroes. 1865-79. *1244*
Talmadge, Eugene. Cocking, Walter D. Georgia. Higher education. Negroes. 1937-43. *2620*
—. Cocking, Walter D. Georgia, University of. Holley, Joseph Winthrop. Racism. 1941. *2643*
—. Georgia. National Recovery Administration. State Government. Strikes. Textile industry. 1934. *2467*
Talmage, Thomas DeWitt. Protestantism. 1869-1902. *1496*
Tammany Hall. Committee of Fifteen. Local Politics. New York City. 1900-01. *1934*
Taney, Roger Brooke. *Dred Scott* v. *Sandford* (US, 1857). Marshall, John. Slavery. Supreme Court. 1820-60. *785*
Tanneries. Accidents. California. Industrial safety. Working Conditions. 1901-80. *2751*
Tappan, Benjamin. Autobiography. Ohio. 1773-1823. *416*
Tappan, Lewis. Abolition Movement. Evangelism. Friendship. 1830-61. *645*
Tarbell, Ida M. Family. Feminism. Journalism. 1900-30. *1688*
Tariff *See also* Smuggling.
—. Businessmen. Payne-Aldrich Tariff (1909). Reformers. 1905-09. *2201*
—. Economic Policy. Populism. Prairie Provinces. 1879. 1920-79. *1368*
—. Farmers. McNary-Haugen bill. Montana. Pacific Northwest. Prices. 1920-29. *2410*
—. National Brotherhood of Operative Potters. Pottery. Strikes. 1894. *1345*
Taschereau, Elzéar Alexandre. Catholic Church. Gibbons, James. Knights of Labor. Social Theory. 1880's. *1351*
Taschereau, Elzéar-Alexandre. Canada. Catholic Church. Knights of Labor. Labor Unions and Organizations. 1884-94. *1350*
Taschereau, Louis Alexandre. Depressions. Legislation. Provincial government. Public Welfare. Quebec. ca 1934-36. *1700*
Taxation *See also* Income Tax; Tariff.
—. American Revolution (antecedents). South. 1755-85. *475*
—. Antitrust. Local Government. New Jersey (Jersey City). Railroads. 1901-07. *2276*
—. British Columbia. Labor. Legislation. Natural resources. New Democratic Party. Public Policy. Social Democracy. 1972-75. *2942*
—. Economic Theory. George, Henry. Income. Landlords and Tenants. Population. Technology. 1871-83. *1064*
—. Fagan, Mark. New Jersey (Jersey City). Progressives. Single tax. 1901-17. *2278*
—. Interest Groups. Local government. Political Reform. Social change. 1960's. *2947*
—. Local Government. Manitoba (Winnipeg). Queen, John. Socialism. 1909-42. *1645*
—. Political Reform. Progressivism. Prohibition. Richards, Richard Olsen. South Dakota. 1902-30. *1913*
Taylor, Charles A. Educators. Ethnographers. Evangelism. Indians (reservations). Pueblo Indians (Hopi). Sullivan, John H. 1870-89. *1050*
Taylor, Frederick W. Management, scientific. Progressivism. 1880's-1900's. *2248*
Taylor, Harriet. Mill, John Stuart. Women's rights. ca 1850-73. *806*
Taylor, William S. Election Laws. Goebel, William. Government Regulation. Kentucky. Railroads. 1887-1900. *961*
Teacher training. Educational Administration. George Peabody College. Nashville, University of. Payne, William Howard. Tennessee. 1875-1901. *1411*
—. Physical Education and Training. 1850's-60's. *856*
Teachers *See also* Educators; Teaching.
—. American Federation of Teachers. Women's Liberation Movement. 1916-73. *1687*
—. Cities. Educational Reform. Negroes. Public Schools. South. 1865-90. *1238*

—. Decisionmaking. Desegregation. Negroes. Political power. South. Voting and Voting Behavior. 1950's-60's. *2831*
—. Educational reform. Georgia (Atlanta). Illinois (Chicago). New York City. Progressivism. 1890-1920. *2336*
—. Equal opportunity. Louisiana Education Association. Negroes. School Integration. 1901-70. *1857*
—. Equality. Lobbying. New York City. State Legislatures. Strachan, Grace. Wages. Women. 1907-11. *2202*
—. Foster, Richard B. (address). Missouri. Negroes. Reconstruction. 1869. *1170*
—. Freedmen. North. Race Relations. Schools. Virginia (Lexington). 1867. *1405*
—. Labor Unions and Organizations. Maryland. NAACP. Negroes. 1930's. *2610*
—. Louisiana State University. Mims, Mary Williams. 1910-67. *387*
—. Saskatchewan. Saskatoon Women Teachers' Association. Women. 1918-70's. *1627*
Teachers colleges. 19c. *199*
Teaching *See also* Education; Kindergarten; Schools; Teachers.
—. Authority. Freedmen. South. Women. 1865-70. *1425*
—. Harris, Cicero. Harris, Robert. Harris, William. Negroes. Reconstruction. South. 1864-70. *1278*
—. Morality. New York, upstate. 1970-80. *2962*
—. Oregon (Portland). Sabin, Ellen B. Wisconsin. Women. 1850-95. *405*
Teamsters, International Brotherhood of. Quebec (Montreal). Strikes. 1864. *1315*
Technology *See also* Agricultural Technology and Research; Industrial Technology; Science; Science and Society.
—. Altruism. Progressive movement. Public policy. 1900-17. 1973. *1933*
—. Armaments Industry. Connecticut (Bridgeport). Industrial Relations. World War I. 1915-19. *2182*
—. Cities. Public Health. Wastewater. Water Supply. 1850-1930. 1900H. *99*
—. City Government. Medicine. Reform. Refuse disposal. Sanitation. Wisconsin (Milwaukee). 1867-1911. *1466*
—. Crime and Criminals. George, Henry. Land Monopolies. Property. 19c-20c. *1033*
—. Economic Theory. George, Henry. Income. Landlords and Tenants. Population. Taxation. 1871-83. *1064*
Teed, Cyrus Reed. Florida (Lee County). Koreshan Unity. Politics. Sects, Religious. Utopias. 1880-1909. *1516*
Telephone operators. Bell Canada. Ontario (Toronto). Strikes. Women. 1907. *1808*
Television. Commercials. Fashion. Hygiene. Women. Women's Liberation Movement. 1970's. *2921*
Temperance Movements. Ager, Waldemar Theodore. Editors and Editing. Norwegian Americans. Novels. *Reform* (newspaper). 1893-1941. *368*
—. Anti-Saloon League. Organizations. Russell, Howard Hyde. 1895-1900. *1464*
—. Arthur, Timothy Shay *(Ten Nights in a Bar-Room)*. Swedenborg, Emanuel. 18c. 1854. *883*
—. Beecher, Lyman. Evangelical Alliance. Great Britain. World Temperance Convention. 1846. *889*
—. *Birth of a Nation* (film). Films. Griffith, David W. Negroes. 1900-20. *2087*
—. Brownlow, William Gannaway. Editors and Editing. Tennessee. *Whig* (newspaper). 1838-1913. *866*
—. Brownlow, William Gannaway. Sons of Temperance. Tennessee. 1851-67. *865*
—. Cary, Samuel Fenton. Ohio (Cincinnati). 1845-1900. *1448*
—. Crandall, Prudence. Kansas (Elk County). Spiritualism. Women's rights. 1877-95. *1487*
—. Demonstrations. Ohio (Cincinnati). Protestant Churches. Women's Christian Temperance Union. 1874. *1446*
—. Florida (Miami). Nation, Carry. 1908-13. *1949*
—. Georgia (Jasper County). Sons of Temperance (Ocmulgee Division No. 40). 1848-49. *897*
—. German Americans. Irish Americans. Local politics. New York City. Riots. 1857. *585*
—. Gough, John B. 1828-86. *895*
—. Irish Americans. Knights of Father Mathew. Missouri (St. Louis). 1850-1930. 1900H. *259*

Temperance Movements

—. Knights of Labor. Powderly, Terence V. 1878-93. *1356*
—. Massachusetts (Boston). Social Customs. Values. Working class. 1838-40. *868*
—. Methodist Church. Social Organizations. 1919-72. *1613*
—. Nation, Carry. Oklahoma. 1867-1911. *1440*
—. Ontario. USA. 1828-50. *859*
—. Physicians. 1800-60. *864*
—. South Carolina. 1880-1940. *233*
—. Willard, Frances. 1870's-90's. *1478*
—. Women. 1873-74. *958*
Tenancy. Delmo Housing Corporation. Farm Security Administration. Missouri. Southern Tenant Farmers' Union. 1939-80. *1821*
Tennessee *See also* South; South Central and Gulf States.
—. Adventists. Battle Creek College. Madison College. Michigan. Sutherland, Edward A. 1897-1904. *2331*
—. Antislavery sentiments. Kentucky. Pendleton, James Madison. 1849-60. *674*
—. Bible. Constitutional Amendments (19th). Equal Rights Amendment. State Legislatures. Women. 1876-1974. *2904*
—. Brownlow, William Gannaway. Editors and Editing. Temperance Movements. *Whig* (newspaper). 1838-51. *866*
—. Brownlow, William Gannaway. Sons of Temperance. Temperance Movements. 1851-67. *865*
—. Church Schools. Colleges and universities, black. Negroes. 1865-1920. *2307*
—. Civil rights. Governors. Johnson, Andrew. Negroes. 1862-65. *972*
—. Civil War. Negroes. Political Protest. State Politics. Suffrage. 1864-65. *1144*
—. Coal Mines and Mining. Convict labor. State Government. Strikes. 1891-93. *1286*
—. Colored Farmers' Alliance. Race Relations. 1888-91. *1164*
—. Editors and Editing. Liberalism. Milton, George Fort. New Deal. 1930's. *2521*
—. Educational Administration. George Peabody College. Nashville, University of. Payne, William Howard. Teacher training. 1875-1901. *1411*
—. Elections (gubernatorial). Progressivism. ca 1890-1906. *2081*
—. Labor. Letters. Negroes. Riley, William R. United Mine Workers of America. 1892-95. *1201*
—. Labor. Negroes. Prisons. 1830-1915. *96*
—. Peffer, William A. Reconstruction. State Politics. 1865-69. *949*
—. Republican Party. Senter, DeWitt Clinton. Suffrage. 1869-70. *954*
—. Ruskin (colony). Utopias. Wayland, Julius Augustus. 1894-1901. *1503*
Tennessee (Clinton). Baptists. Desegregation. Turner, Paul. Violence. 1956. *2663*
Tennessee (Columbia). Civil rights movement. Negroes. Politics. Riots. Truman, Harry S. 1946. *2657*
Tennessee, eastern. Appalachia. City Planning. Regional development. Virginia, southwestern. 1890-1929. *1710*
Tennessee (Fayette County). Medical care. Mormon, Square. Poor People's Health Council. Race relations. Rossville Health Center. 1960's-70's. *2821*
Tennessee (Knoxville). American Federation of Labor. Armies. Police. Streetcars. Strikes. 1919-20. *2185*
Tennessee (Maryville). Abolition Movement. Anderson, Isaac. Presbyterian Church. Southern and Western Theological Seminary. 1819-50's. *574*
Tennessee (Memphis). Agricultural Policy. Association of Southern Commissioners of Agriculture. Cotton. New Deal. South. 1936-37. *2567*
—. Bimetallism. Democrats, silver. 1895-96. *994*
—. Civil rights. Legislation. Population. Race Relations. Riots. 1865-66. *1209*
—. Discrimination, Employment. Jim Crow laws. NAACP. Negroes. 1900-37. *1750*
—. *Free Speech* (newspaper). Lynching. Negroes. Wells, Ida B. 1892. *1128*
—. School Integration. White flight. 1963-76. *2969*
Tennessee (Nashoba). Emancipation. Owen, Robert Dale. Utopias. Wright, Frances (letters). 1820-29. *718*

SUBJECT INDEX

Tennessee (Nashville). Alabama (Mobile). Black Capitalism. Editors and Editing. Johnson, Andrew N. Republican Party. 1890-1920. *273*
—. Alden, Augustus E. Brownlow, William G. Carpetbaggers. City Government. Education. Public welfare. Reconstruction. Republican Party. 1865-69. *1049*
—. Clergy. Episcopal Church, Protestant. Ingraham, Joseph Holt. Novels. Penal reform. Public Schools. 1847-51. *584*
—. Fisk University. Race Relations. Youth Movements. 1909-26. *2397*
—. Medical education. Meharry Medical College. Negroes. 1860's-1970's. *226*
Tennessee (Shelby County). Elections. Negroes. Politics. Reconstruction. 1865-76. *1160*
Tennessee, western. Attitudes. Reform. Slavery. 1820-40. *771*
Tenure. Academic freedom. American Association of University Professors. Civil Rights. 1915-70. *1733*
Terrell, Mary Church. National Association of Colored Women. Negroes. Reform. Woman Suffrage. 1892-1954. *312*
Territorial Government *See also* State Government.
—. Medical Reform. Mental health. Professionalization. Washington. 1853-75. *1459*
Terrorism *See also* Assassination; Crime and Criminals.
—. Louisiana. Ostracism. Reconstruction. Scalawags. State Politics. 1866-78. *1081*
—. Negro Suffrage. North Carolina. Red Shirt Movement. Social Classes. Whites. 1898-1900. *1067*
Testimony. Breckinridge, Robert J., Jr. Breckinridge, William C. P. Courts. Elections. Kentucky. Negroes. 1866-69. *1096*
—. Canada. Courts. Extradition. Fugitive slaves. Happy, Jesse. Kentucky. 1793-1838. *748*
Texas *See also* South; South Central and Gulf States.
—. Agricultural Labor. Economic Structure. Freedmen. Racism. Reconstruction. 1865-74. *1263*
—. Archives, National. Freedmen's Bureau. Public Records. Reconstruction. 1865-76. *1147*
—. Baptists, Southern. Leadership. Race Relations. 1954-68. *2890*
—. Brotherhood of Timber Workers. Industrial Workers of the World. Louisiana. Lumber and Lumbering. Race Relations. 1910-13. *2215*
—. Business. Campbell, Thomas M. Democratic Party. Progressivism. State Government. 1907-11. *2264*
—. Capitalism. Depressions. Political Attitudes. Radicals and Radicalism. 1929-33. *2460*
—. Civil Rights. Discrimination. Equality. Negroes. Political Attitudes. Reconstruction. 1865-70. *1200*
—. Colleges and Universities (black). Segregation. State Government. 1876-1947. *1846*
—. Communes. Considerant, Victor Prosper. Reunion (community). 1854-59. *918*
—. Congress of Industrial Organizations. Oil Industry and Trade. World War II. 1942-43. *2631*
—. Constitutional Amendments (18th). Dean Act (1919). Prohibition. State Legislatures. 1917-33. *2368*
—. Councils and Synods. Delegates. Episcopal Church, Protestant. Kinsolving, George Herbert. Veto. Women. 1921-70. *2347*
—. Courts. Freedmen's Bureau. Justice. Negroes. Reconstruction. 1865-68. *1146*
—. Craft, Juanita. Durham, William J. NAACP. Smith, Antonio Maceo. White, Lulu B. 1933-50. *1586*
—. Democratic Party. NAACP. Negro Suffrage. Primaries. Supreme Court. 1927-45. *1723*
—. Economic Conditions. Labor. New Deal. 1929-39. *2573*
—. Education. Freedmen's Bureau. Negroes. 1865-70. *1174*
—. Equal Legal Rights Amendment. Federation of Business and Professional Women's Clubs. Women. 1957-72. *2909*
—. Farm tenancy. Political Protest. Socialism. 1901-17. *2216*
—. Farmers. Grange. Oklahoma. Saskatchewan. Socialism. 1900-45. *1714*
—. Freedmen's Bureau. Kirkland, William S. Reconstruction. 1865-70. *1261*
—. Garment industry. International Ladies' Garment Workers' Union. Women. 1933-50. *1770*

Textile industry

—. Hancock, Winfield Scott. Louisiana. Military. Mower, Joseph Anthony. Reconstruction. 1865-68. *989*
—. House of Representatives. Republicans, Radical. 1870-73. *1088*
—. Labor Unions and Organizations. Mexican Americans. Socialism. 1900-20. *2291*
—. Louisiana. Oil Industry and Trade. Strikes. 1917-18. *2237*
—. Minorities in Politics. Negroes. Political Leadership. Reconstruction. 1865-90's. *1148*
—. Political Attitudes. Populism. Social Change. ca 1880-1900. *1396*
Texas (Beaumont). City government. Political attitudes. Reform. 1902-09. *1977*
Texas (Crystal City). Community control. Elections. Mexican Americans. 1910-75. *2739*
Texas, eastern. Brotherhood of Timber Workers. Emerson, Arthur L. Industrial Workers of the World. Labor Disputes. Louisiana, western. Lumber and Lumbering. 1900-16. *2207*
—. Brotherhood of Timber Workers. Louisiana, western. Lumber and Lumbering. Race Relations. Southern Lumber Operators' Association. 1911-13. *2217*
Texas (Gulf Coast). American Petroleum Institute. Oil Industry and Trade. Pollution. 1900-70. *1797*
Texas (Laredo). Fort McIntosh. Negroes. Riots. 25th Infantry, US (Company D). 1899. *1143*
—. Mexican Americans. Political activism. Primer Congreso Mexicanista (1911). 1910-11. *2010*
Texas, northern. Communes. Considerant, Victor Prosper. France. Land. Travel. 1852-69. *265*
Texas (San Angelo). Boycotts. Mexican Americans. Presbyterian Church. Public schools. Segregation. 1910-15. *2303*
Texas (southern). Mexican Americans. Minorities in Politics. Public Schools. Self-perception. 1930's-69. *1863*
Texas (Thurber). Coal Mines and Mining. Labor Unions and Organizations. 1880's-1920's. *2238*
Texas, University of (Austin). Dabney, Robert Lewis. Morality. Presbyterian Church. South. Union Seminary. 1865-96. *1084*
Texas (western). Big Spring State Hospital. Harrison, Preston E. Medical care. Mental Illness. 1946-77. *2981*
Textbooks. Authority. Communications Behavior. Parents. Public Schools. West Virginia (Kanawha County). 1974. *2958*
Textile industry. Attitudes. Industrialization. Rhode Island (Pawtucket). Strikes. Working Class. 1824. *821*
—. Bancroft, Joseph and Sons Company. Delaware (Wilmington). Miller, Franklin, and Stevenson (firm). Scientific management. 1911-27. *2281*
—. Child Labor Act (US, 1916). Cotton. Federal regulation. 1907-16. *2002*
—. Class conflict. Rhode Island (Pawtucket). Strikes. 1790-1824. *822*
—. Communism. North Carolina (Gastonia). Novels. Poor. Strikes. Whites. 1929-34. *2361*
—. Congress of Industrial Organizations. Labor Unions and Organizations. Management. National Industrial Recovery Act (US, 1933). National Labor Relations Act (US, 1935). South. 1933-41. *2613*
—. Cotton. Hamilton Manufacturing Company. Labor Disputes. Massachusetts (Lowell). Social mobility. Women. 1836-60. *818*
—. Everett Mill. Massachusetts (Lawrence). Polish Americans. Radicals and Radicalism. Strikes. Women. 1912. *2252*
—. Georgia. National Recovery Administration. State Government. Strikes. Talmadge, Eugene. 1934. *2467*
—. Howard, Robert. Labor Disputes. Massachusetts (Fall River). 1860-85. *1346*
—. Immigrants. Industrial Workers of the World. New Jersey (Paterson). Strikes. Violence. 1913. *2254*
—. Immigrants. Industrial Workers of the World. New York (Little Falls). Strikes. Women. 1912. *2269*
—. Labor. New Jersey (Passaic). Strikes. Working conditions. 1875-1926. *2366*
—. Labor reform. Lowell Female Labor Reform Association. New England. Women. 1845-47. *819*
—. Labor Reform. New York (Little Falls). Strikes. Women. 1912. *2268*
—. Labor Unions and Organizations. Piedmont Plateau. 1901-32. *1792*

Textile industry
—. Labor Unions and Organizations. South. ca 1949-75. *1800*
—. Nardella, Luigi (interview). Rhode Island. Strikes. 1922. *2349*
—. National Textile Workers Union. North Carolina (Gastonia). Strikes. Weisbord, Vera Buch (reminiscence). 1929. *2459*
—. North Carolina (Gastonia). Novels. Strikes. 1929-30's. *2431*
Textile Workers Organizing Committee. Industrial Rayon Corporation. Strikes. Virginia (Covington). 1937-38. *2508*
Textile Workers Union of America. Massachusetts. Oral history. Sullivan, Anna (interview). Women. 1918-76. *403*
Theater *See also* Films.
—. Child labor. Louisiana Child Labor Laws (1908-1912). 1908-12. *2050*
—. New Jersey. New York City. Patterson Strike Pageant. Strikes. 1913. *2250*
Theater, guerrilla. Mexican Americans. Social consciousness. 1965-76. *2710*
Theatrical Syndicate. Child Labor Law (Louisiana, 1908). Gordon, Jean. Louisiana (New Orleans). New York. 1908-12. *1968*
Theology *See also* Atheism; Christianity; Ethics; Mysticism; Religion.
—. Abolition Movement. Andover Seminary. Massachusetts. 1825-35. *767*
—. Abolition movement. Constitutional Amendments (15th). Douglass, Frederick. Negroes. 1825-86. *777*
—. Church and State. Government, Resistance to. Jehovah's Witnesses. Persecution. 1870's-1960's. *136*
—. Civil rights movement. Episcopal Church, Protestant. Race Relations. 1800-1965. *2849*
—. Conservatism. DuBose, William Porcher. Episcopal Church, Protestant. Miles, James Warley. Murphy, Edgar Gardner. South. 1840-1920. *62*
—. Edwards, Jonathan. Hopkins, Samuel. New Divinity (doctrines). New England. 1730-1803. *479*
—. Farm tenancy. Mississippi. Protestant Churches. 1936-40. *2525*
—. Mathews, Shailer. Modernism. Science. Social gospel. 1864-1930. *446*
Theosophy. California (Point Loma). Communes. Tingley, Katherine Augusta Westcott. Universal Brotherhood and Theosophical Society. 1897-1942. *1619*
Therapeutics. Medicine. Social change. 19c. *252*
Third Parties. Amlie, Thomas. Farmer-labor Party. Hard, Herbert. New Deal. Ohio Farmer-Labor Progressive Federation. 1930-40. *2543*
—. Butler, Benjamin F. (papers). Elections (presidential). People's Party. 1884. *1027*
Thomas, Ella Gertrude Clanton (journal). Feminism. South. 1848-89. *383*
Thomas, Norman. Antiwar Sentiment. Keep America Out of War Congress. Socialist Party. Villard, Oswald Garrison. World War II (antecedents). 1938-41. *2501*
—. Christianity. Conscientious objectors. Pacifism. World War I. 1915-18. *2136*
—. Christianity. Muste, Abraham J. Niebuhr, Reinhold. Pacifism. Political Theory. 1914-38. *1668*
Thompson, George. Abolition Movement. Massachusetts (Springfield). Riots. 1851. *667*
Thompson, Helen. Mead, Margaret. Scholars. Social sciences. Talbot, Marion. Women. 1900-20's. *2065*
Thompson, William Hale. Anglophobia. Censorship. City Politics. Illinois (Chicago). Libraries. Public Schools. 1927. *2454*
Thompson, Wyatt Hamilton. Paint Creek-Cabin Creek Strike. *Socialist and Labor Star* (newspaper). Strikes. West Virginia. 1912-13. *2195*
Thrane, Marcus. Labor disputes. Norway. Norwegian Americans. Press. USA. 1886-94. *1285*
Tiger, Tom. Civil Rights. Florida (Kissimmee). Friends of the Florida Seminoles. Indians. Seminole Indians. 1898-99. *1100*
Tilbury, Corwin D. Air Pollution. Elites. Pennsylvania (Pittsburgh). Reform. Smoke. 1890's-1918. *1961*
Tilly, Dorothy. Civil rights. Georgia. Methodist Church. 1900's-70. *438*
Tingley, Katherine Augusta Westcott. California (Point Loma). Communes. Theosophy. Universal Brotherhood and Theosophical Society. 1897-1942. *1619*

Tinker v. Des Moines Community School District (US, 1969). Blackwell v. Issaquena County Board of Education (US, 1966). Burnside v. Byars (US, 1966). Courts. Freedom of Speech. Students. 1870-1969. *1728*
Tlingit Indians. Alaska. Assimilation. Brady, John Green. Economic Conditions. Indian-White Relations. 1878-1906. *1016*
Tobacco. Legislation. Mormons. Utah. 1896-1923. *2440*
Tobey, Charles E. Arkansas. Garland, Rufus King. Greenback Party. State politics. 1876-82. *952*
Tobogganing. Ontario (Toronto). Recreation. Sabbatarianism. 1912. *1609*
Toledo Mechanics' Association. Labor Unions and Organizations. Ohio. Willey, Austin. 1843. *827*
Tollemache, Lionel A. Euthanasia. Great Britain. Medicine. Williams, Samuel D., Jr. 1870's-90's. *1452*
Tolstoy, Leo. Intellectuals. Literature. Pacifism. ca 1890's. *1080*
Tolstoy, Lev Nikolaevich, Count. Crosby, Ernest Howard. Intellectuals. Reformers. 1878-1907. *334*
Torbert, James H. Education. Fort Valley High and Industrial School. Georgia. Negroes. 1897-1911. *2296*
Tougaloo College. American Missionary Association. Colleges and Universities. Freedmen's Bureau. Mississippi. Negroes. 1865-69. *1141*
Tourgée, Albion W. Anti-lynching law of 1894. Law Reform. Ohio. Smith, Harry C. 1890-96. *1453*
Tourism *See also* Resorts.
—. Chinatowns. ca 1880-1940. *1634*
Townerites. California (Orange County). Middle Classes. Oneida Community. Religion. Social Organization. 1848-1900's. *1514*
Townley, Arthur C. Bowen, Albert E., Jr. Farmers. Nonpartisan League. North Dakota. 1914-15. *2054*
—. Business. Farmers. Nonpartisan League. North Dakota. Politics. 1880-1959. *1667*
Tracy-Cutler, Hannah Maria. Feminism. Gage, Frances Dana. *Ohio Cultivator* (newspaper). 1845-55. *800*
Trade Regulations *See also* Tariff.
—. Agriculture and Government. Antioption struggle. Commodity exchanges. 1890-94. *1400*
Trade Union Movements. *See* Labor Movement.
Trade Union Unity League. American Federation of Labor. Communist Party. Labor Unions and Organizations. Radicals and Radicalism. 1933-35. *2494*
Trade Unions. *See* Labor Unions and Organizations.
Trades and Labour Congress of Canada. Canadian Labour Congress. Cooperative Commonwealth Federation. Federal Government. Industrial relations. World War II. 1939-46. *2634*
—. Labor Unions and Organizations. National Trades and Labour Congress. Ontario (Kitchener). Quebec. 1892-1902. *1805*
Trall, Russell Thacher. Adventists. Kellogg, Merritt (diary). Medicine (practice of). 1844-77. *894*
Tramps. Charities. Ontario (Toronto). Social Control. 1870-90. *1065*
Transcendentalism. Abolitionists. Elkins, Stanley M. (review article). Slavery. 1830-63. 1959-73. *791*
—. Addams, Jane. Dewey, John. Dix, Dorothea. Emerson, Ralph Waldo. Pragmatism. 1830's-1960's. *231*
—. Alcott, Amos Bronson. Fruitlands (community). Lane, Charles. Massachusetts. Utopias. 1840-50. *922*
—. Attitudes. Exercise. Health. New England. Recreation. 1830-60. *572*
—. Bartol, Cyrus. Investments. Massachusetts (Boston, Manchester). Real estate. 1850-96. *1015*
—. Brisbane, Albert. Brook Farm. Channing, William Henry. 1840-46. *923*
—. Christianity. Civil Rights. King, Martin Luther, Jr. 1840's-50's. 1950's-60's. *2815*
—. Feminism. Fuller, Margaret. New England. Radicals and Radicalism. *311*
Trans-Mississippi West *See also* individual states.
—. Curricula. Eliot, William Greenleaf. Higher education. Missouri (St. Louis). Washington University. 1853-87. *189*

Transportation *See also* names of transportation vehicles, e.g. Automobiles, Ships, Buses, Trucks, Railroads, etc.; Commerce; Freight and Freightage; Mass Transit; Merchant Marine; Waterways.
—. North Dakota Workmen's Compensation Bureau. Rice, Hazel F. (account). Working conditions. 1919-22. *2432*
Travel. Communes. Considerant, Victor Prosper. France. Land. Texas, northern. 1852-69. *265*
Treadwell Mines. Alaska (Douglas Island). Gold Mines and Mining. Labor Unions and Organizations. Strikes. Western Federation of Miners. 1905-10. *2209*
Treaty of Cession (1804). Civil rights. Freedmen. Louisiana Purchase. 1797-1804. *590*
Trent, W. W. Educational reform. Meadows, Clarence W. Public Schools. Strayer, George D. West Virginia Education Association. 1932-58. *1837*
Trials *See also* Courts Martial and Courts of Inquiry; Crime and Criminals.
—. Abolition movement. Anderson, John. Canada. Fugitive Slaves. Great Britain. USA. 1860-61. *733*
—. Alabama. Military. Racism. Randolph, Ryland. Reconstruction. Tuscaloosa *Independent Monitor*. 1868. *986*
—. American Civil Liberties Union. Civil rights. Kentucky (Bell County, London). Miners. 1932-38. *2601*
—. Anti-Radicals. Ashburn, George W. (murder). Georgia. Reconstruction. 1868. *987*
—. Antislavery Sentiments. Pennsylvania (Philadelphia). Slavery. Williamson, Passmore. 1855. *628*
—. Bombing. California (San Francisco). Mooney, Tom. San Quentin Prison. Socialist Party. 1916-42. *2020*
—. California (Wheatland). Industrial Workers of the World. Migrant Labor. State Government. Strikes. 1913-17. *2198*
—. Corporal punishment. Eaton, Nathaniel. Harvard University. Massachusetts (Cambridge). Puritans. 1638. *495*
—. Crapsey, Algernon Sidney. Episcopal Church, Protestant. Heresy. New York (Rochester). Reform. St. Andrew's Church. 1879-1927. *454*
—. Industrial Workers of the World. Kansas. Radicals and Radicalism. Red Scare. 1917-19. *2148*
—. Industrial Workers of the World. Kansas (Wichita). Labor Unions and Organizations. Oil Industry and Trade. *United States v. C. W. Anderson et al.* (US, 1919). World War I. 1917-19. *2171*
—. Jones Family (group). Oklahoma (Cleveland, Pottawatomie counties). Sedition. Working Class Union. World War I. 1917. *2155*
—. Political Protest. Social movements. 1920-79. *1526*
Tribal government. Civil Rights. Indian Civil Rights Act (US, 1968). Natural law. Pueblo Indians. *Santa Clara Pueblo v. Martinez* (US, 1977). 1939-77. *2789*
Tribes *See also* names of specific tribes.
—. Bureau of Indian Affairs. Emmons, Glenn L. Indians. Social Policy. 1953-61. *2660*
Trotskyism. 1930's-40. *2559*
—. Carlson, Oliver (reminiscences). Communist Party. Foster, William Z. Politburo. Radek, Karl. USSR. 1924-35. *1548*
Trotter, William Monroe. Federal Government. Segregation. Wilson, Woodrow. 1913-14. *2016*
Troy Female Seminary. Education. Feminism. Values. Willard, Emma Hart. 1822-72. *810*
—. Education. New York. Willard, Emma Hart. Women. 1809-70. *436*
Truancy. Compulsory education. Immigrants. Missouri (St. Louis). Public Schools. 1905-07. *2313*
Truman, Harry S. Civil rights. Congress. Negroes. 1949-50. *2687*
—. Civil rights movement. Negroes. Politics. Riots. Tennessee (Columbia). 1946. *2657*
Truman, Harry S. (administration). Civil Rights. Cold War. Detention. Federal Bureau of Investigation. National security. 1945-52. *2685*
—. Collier, John. Federal Government. Indians. Liberalism. Roosevelt, Franklin D. (administration). 1933-53. *1629*
Trumbull, Lyman. Democratic Party. Illinois. Republican Party. Slavery. 1855-72. *323*

Trumbull, Matthew Mark. Haymarket Riot (1886). Iowa. Socialism. 1826-94. *296*
Trust for Public Land. Cities. Neighborhoods. Public Lands. 1975-80. *2756*
Truth, Sojourner. Abolition Movement. Negroes. 1825-60. *445*
Truth, Soujourner. Feminism. Literature. Negroes. Stowe, Harriet Beecher. 1850's-90's. *802*
Tuberculosis. City politics. New York City. Public Health. Social policy. 1889-1900. *1941*
Tubman, Emily. African Colonization Movement. Emancipation. Georgia. Liberia. 1816-57. *655*
—. Georgia. Liberia. 1818-85. *317*
Tubman, Harriet. Abolitionists. Brown, William Wells. Medicine. Negroes. Remond, Sarah Parker. Ruggles, David. Smith, James McCune. 1810-85. *329*
—. Burris, Samuel D. Delaware. Garrett, Thomas. Hunn, John. Underground Railroad. 1820-60. *712*
Tugwell, Rexford Guy. Agriculture Department. Greenbelt new towns. Poor. 1935-36. *2560*
Tule Lake Camp. Internment. Japanese Americans. Martial law. World War II. 1941-44. *2641*
Turner, James Milton. Civil Rights. Negroes. 1865-1915. *313*
—. Education. Lincoln University. Lindsay, Lizzie A. Missouri (Jefferson City). Negroes. 1865-75. *1179*
—. Liberia. Negroes. Republican Party. 1865-77. *1195*
Turner, Nat. Documents. Methodist Episcopal Church. Slave Revolts. Virginia. 1831-32. *908*
Turner, Paul. Baptists. Desegregation. Tennessee (Clinton). Violence. 1956. *2663*
Turnverein (club). Abolition Movement. German Americans. Gymnastics. 1850-70. *606*
Turpentine industry. Florida. Justice Department. Labor recruitment. New York City. Peonage. Quackenbos, Mary Grace. 1905-10. *2267*
Tuscaloosa *Independent Monitor*. Alabama. Military. Racism. Randolph, Ryland. Reconstruction. Trials. 1868. *986*
Tuskegee Institute. Alabama. Industrial Arts Education. Negroes. Washington, Booker T. 1870's-90's. *1189*
—. Congo Reform Association. Park, Robert Ezra. Race relations. 1905-13. *2025*
—. Education. Farmers. Negroes. Washington, Booker T. 1881-1915. *1186*
—. Moton, Robert Russa. Negroes. Politics. Scott, Emmett Jay. Washington, Booker T. 1915-25. *1643*
Twelve-hour day. Labor Reform. Steel industry. 1887-1923. *2384*
Twilight sleep. Childbirth. Medical Reform. Women. 1914-15. *2004*
Twilight sleep movement. Anesthesia. Childbirth. Medicine (practice of). Women. 1902-23. *2034*
Two-party system. Louisiana. Newspapers. Political Campaigns (presidential). Slavery. 1834-36. *661*
Tyler, Julia Gardiner. Antislavery Sentiments. Great Britain. Sutherland, Duchess of (Harriet Howard). Women. 1842-89. *723*
Typhoid fever. City Politics. Ontario (Ottawa). Public Health. Reform. 1911-12. *1635*
Typography. *See* Printing.

U

Ukrainian Canadians. Alberta (Cardiff, Edmonton). Chaban, Teklia. Coal Mines and Mining. Labor Unions and Organizations. 1914-20's. *469*
—. Canada. Krat, Pavlo. Socialism. ca 1902-52. *365*
Ukrainian Labour-Farmer Association. Alberta (Edmonton). Farmer's Union of Alberta. Kyforuk, Peter. Manitoba. 1912-30's. *1828*
Underground Railroad. Antislavery Sentiments. Ohio (Lower Maumee Valley). 1815-67. *782*
—. Burris, Samuel D. Delaware. Garrett, Thomas. Hunn, John. Tubman, Harriet. 1820-60. *712*
Underhill, Frank. Cooperative Commonwealth Federation. League for Social Reconstruction. Regina Manifesto. Saskatchewan. 1933. *1611*
Unemployed Citizens' League. Dix, I. F. Hoover, Herbert C. Local politics. Self-help. Washington (Seattle). 1931-32. *2417*
Unemployed Leagues. Muste, Abraham J. Radicals and Radicalism. 1932-36. *2577*

Unemployment *See also* Employment; Unemployment Insurance.
—. British Columbia. Depressions. Industrial Relations. National Unemployed Workers' Association. Workers' Unity League. 1930-39. *1830*
—. Canada. Federal government. Social policy. 1918-21. *1816*
—. Charities. New Brunswick (Saint John). Newfoundland (Saint John's). Nova Scotia (Halifax). Poverty. 1815-60. *871*
—. Coxey, Jacob S. District of Columbia. Political Protest. 1894. *1302*
—. Depressions. Liberalism. New Deal. Political activism. Socialist Party. 1929-36. *1804*
—. Gary, Elbert H. Mitchel, John Purroy. New York City (Committee on Unemployment and Relief). Progressives. 1914-17. *2058*
—. Government. Private sector. 18c-1979. *260*
Unemployment insurance. Congress. New Deal. Roosevelt, Franklin D. Social Security Act (US, 1935). 1934-35. *2471*
—. Ehringhaus, J. C. B. Legislation. North Carolina. Social Security Act (US, 1935). 1935-37. *2556*
Unemployment Insurance Act (Canada, 1941). Business. Canada. Federal Government. Labor Unions and Organizations. Social control. Wages. 1910-41. *2623*
UNESCO. Fisk University. Johnson, Charles S. Negroes. Race relations. 1900-56. *346*
Unification Church. Authority. Charisma. Counter Culture. Hasidism. 1960-80. *2986*
Union Labor Party. Kansas. Land Reform. Rogers, John R. 1838-1901. *1023*
Union League. Association for Promoting Colored Volunteers. Civil War. Military Recruitment. Negroes. New York. Race Relations. 1861-65. *1255*
—. Cardozo, Francis Louis. Freedmen. Political rights. Reconstruction. South Carolina. 1870. *1268*
—. Georgia Equal Rights Association. Negroes. Reconstruction. Republican Party. 1865-80. *1214*
Union Seminary. Dabney, Robert Lewis. Morality. Presbyterian Church. South. Texas, University of (Austin). 1865-96. *1084*
Unions. *See* Labor Unions and Organizations.
Unitarianism. Antiabolition sentiments. Clergy. Conservatism. Constitutions. Massachusetts (Boston). Missouri (St. Louis). 1828-57. *751*
—. Antislavery Sentiments. Eliot, Samuel A. Fugitive Slave Act (US, 1850). Massachusetts (Boston). Patriotism. 1850-60. *752*
United Automobile Workers (Canadian Region). Ford Motor Company of Canada. Labor Law. Ontario (Windsor). 1946. *2682*
United Automobile Workers of America. Attitudes. Housing. Negroes. Ohio (Toledo). Racism. 1967-73. *2805*
—. Automobile Industry and Trade. Indiana. Labor. New Deal. Ohio. 1935-40. *2542*
—. California (Inglewood). Communist Party. North American Aviation. Strikes. 1941. *2642*
—. Factionalism. Militancy. 1937-41. *2482*
United Brethren in Christ. Clergy. Ordination. Women. 1889. *1489*
United Church of Canada. Canada. Fairbairn, R. Edis. Pacifism. World War II. 1939. *2646*
—. Canada. McClung, Nellie L. Methodist Church. Ordination. Women. 1915-46. *1597*
United Electrical, Radio and Machine Workers of America. Communist Party. National Maritime Union. Negroes. Racism. World War II. 1941-45. *2622*
—. Labor Unions and Organizations. 1933-37. *2505*
United Farm Workers Union. Agricultural labor. California (San Joaquin Valley). Japanese Americans. Mexican Americans. Nisei Farmers League. 1971-77. *2926*
—. California. Grape industry. Labor Unions and Organizations. Strikes. 1966-70. *2934*
United Farmers League. Communism. Farmers. Political Protest. South Dakota. 1923-34. *2409*
United Farmers of Alberta. Alberta. Cooperative Commonwealth Federation. Land reform. Leadership. Social credit. 1930's. *1748*
United Farmers of Canada. Cooperative Commonwealth Federation. Political Participation. Saskatchewan. 1930-45. *1606*
United Fruit Company. American Federation of Labor. Industrial Workers of the World. Louisiana. Marine Transport Workers. Sailors' Union. Strikes. 1913. *2193*

United Hebrew Trades. Jews. New York City. Social Classes. Socialism. 1877-1926. *1340*
United Labor Party (platform). Elections. Morgan, Thomas John. Socialism. 1886-96. *1342*
United League. Boycotts. Mississippi. Negroes. Police brutality (alleged). Robinson, Alfred. 1966-78. *2893*
United Mine Workers of America. Alabama. Coal. Kilby, Thomas E. Strikes. 1890-1929. *2448*
—. Alberta (Drumheller Valley). Labor disputes. One Big Union. 1919. *1827*
—. Black lung disease. Coal Mine Health and Safety Act (US, 1969; amended, 1972). Coal Mines and Mining. Medicine. Strikes, wildcat. Workmen's Compensation. 1968-72. *2717*
—. British Columbia (Vancouver Island). Canadian Collieries (Dunsmuir) Limited. Coal Mines and Mining. Labor Unions and Organizations. Strikes. 1912-14. *2251*
—. Carbon County Coal Strike (1933). National Miners Union. Strikes. Utah. 1900-39. *2571*
—. Coal, anthracite. Mining. Pennsylvania. Strikes. 1922-23. *2391*
—. Coal, anthracite. Pinchot, Gifford. Strikes. 1925-26. *2390*
—. Coal miners. Germer, Adolph. Illinois (Virden). Socialism. Strikes. 1893-1900. *1291*
—. Coal Mines and Mining. Colorado (Las Animas, Huerfano counties). Strikes. 1904-14. *2273*
—. Coal Mines and Mining. Davis, Richard L. Labor Unions and Organizations. Letters-to-the-editor. *National Labor Tribune*. Negroes. ca 1890-1900. *1139*
—. Coal Mines and Mining. Diaries. Medrick, George. Pennsylvania, western. Strikes. 1927. *2372*
—. Coal Mines and Mining. Employment. Mitchell, John. 1897-1907. *2213*
—. Coal Mines and Mining. Glasscock, William E. Martial law. National Guard. Violence. West Virginia (Cabin Creek, Paint Creek). 1912-13. *2176*
—. Coal Mines and Mining. Hocking Valley. Lewis, John Llewellyn. Ohio, southeastern. Strikes. 1927. *2447*
—. Coal Mines and Mining. Keeney, Frank. West Virginia. 1916-31. *1755*
—. Coal Mines and Mining. Knights of Labor. Race Relations. West Virginia, southern. 1880-94. *1140*
—. Coal Mines and Mining. Labor Disputes. Mingo War. Violence. West Virginia (southern). 1919-22. *2389*
—. Coal Mines and Mining. Labor Unions and Organizations. Racism. Strikes. 1894-1920. *2272*
—. Coal Mines and Mining. State Government. Strikes. West Virginia (Paint Creek). 1912-13. *2270*
—. Labor. Letters. Negroes. Riley, William R. Tennessee. 1892-95. *1201*
—. Labor Unions and Organizations. Pennsylvania (Allegheny-Kiskiminetas Valley). Violence. 1913-19. *2241*
—. Mabey, Charles R. Strikes. Utah (Carbon County). 1922. *2429*
—. National Miners Union. Negroes. Pennsylvania, western. 1925-31. *2420*
United Mine Workers of America (Welfare and Retirement Fund). Coal Mines and Mining. Medical care. 1946-78. *1747*
—. Federal government. Legislation. Public Welfare. 1945-70's. *2658*
United Reform Movement. Brown, W. G. Hayes, Michael P. Herridge, W. D. Saskatchewan. 1938-40. *1664*
United States. *See* terms beginning with the word American, United States, and US; states; regions, e.g. New England, Western States, etc.; British North America; also names of government agencies and departments, e.g. Bureau of Indian Affairs, State Department, etc.
United States v. *C. W. Anderson et al.* (US, 1919). Industrial Workers of the World. Kansas (Wichita). Labor Unions and Organizations. Oil Industry and Trade. Trials. World War I. 1917-19. *2171*
United Steelworkers of America v. *Weber* (US, 1979). Affirmative action. Discrimination. *Fullilove* v. *Klutznick* (US, 1980). Minorities. *Regents of the University of California* v. *Allan Bakke* (US, 1978). Supreme Court. 1970's. *2782*
—. Affirmative action. *Fullilove* v. *Klutznick* (US, 1980). 1979-81. *2786*

Universal Brotherhood and Theosophical Society. California (Point Loma). Communes. Theosophy. Tingley, Katherine Augusta Westcott. 1897-1942. *1619*
Universal Negro Improvement Association. Black Nationalism. Garvey, Marcus. New York City (Harlem). 1919-26. *2358*
—. California (Los Angeles). Garvey, Marcus. Negroes. 1920's. *2455*
—. Clergy. Community affairs. Garvey, Marcus. Negroes. New York (Buffalo). 1830's-1920's. *2458*
—. Colonial policy. Garvey, Marcus. Italy. Pan-Africanism. USA. 1920-23. *2371*
—. Colonization. Garvey, Marcus. Liberia. Negroes. 1914-24. *2342*
—. Firestone, Harvey S. Garvey, Marcus. Land. Leases. Liberia. Negroes. 1926. *2402*
—. Garvey, Marcus. Negroes. Religion. 1920's. *2351*
Universities. *See* Colleges and Universities; Higher Education.
Upper Canada. Great Britain. Public Schools. Sports. Upper Classes. 1830-75. *210*
Upper Classes. Alexander, Sydenham B. Carr, Elias. Farmers' Alliance. Leadership. North Carolina. Polk, Leonidas L. 1887-95. *1392*
—. Great Britain. Public Schools. Sports. Upper Canada. 1830-75. *210*
Urban League. Civil Rights. Nebraska (Omaha). Negroes. Quality of life. Social services. World War II. 1928-50. *2639*
—. Dancey, John C. Discrimination. Michigan (Detroit). Washington, Forrester B. 1916-39. *1696*
—. New York City. Race Relations. Social Problems. 1919-59. *1652*
Urban reform. City government. Construction. Maryland (Baltimore). Schools. 1870-1900. *1402*
—. City Politics. Pennsylvania (Lancaster). 1921-30. *2377*
—. New York City. Riis, Jacob August. 1895-97. *1999*
—. Progressives. 1890-1910. *2057*
Urban revitalization. Federal Government. Local Government. Massachusetts (Boston; South End). Middle Classes. Neighborhoods. Poor. 1960's-70's. *2694*
Urbanization *See also* City Planning; Modernization.
—. Anti-Catholicism. Ireland. 1920-29. *2363*
—. Elementary Education. Ohio (Cincinnati). 1870-1900. *205*
—. Leadership. Negroes. Segregation. Virginia (Richmond). 1900-20. *1947*
—. Public Health. Sociology. 20c. *1671*
US Bureau of Investigation. Industrial Workers of the World. Labor Disputes. Ohio (Toledo). Radicals and Radicalism. 1918-20. *1906*
US Conference of Mayors (report). District of Columbia. Firearms Control Regulations Act (US, 1975). Gun control. Methodology. 1975-80. *2778*
US Steel Corporation. Air pollution. City Government. Indiana (Gary). Reform. 1956-73. *2723*
—. Americanization. Indiana (Gary). Labor Unions and Organizations. Polish Americans. 1906-20. *2178*
—. Foreign policy. Imports. International Steel Cartel. Labor. Steel Workers Organizing Committee. 1937. *2538*
USSR *See also* Russia.
—. Anti-Communist Movements. House Committee on Un-American Activities. Negroes. Robeson, Paul. Robinson, Jackie. 1949. *2684*
—. Carlson, Oliver (reminiscences). Communist Party. Foster, William Z. Politburo. Radek, Karl. Trotskyism. 1924-35. *1548*
—. China. Maoism. Strong, Anna Louise. 1919-70. *324*
—. Communist Party. North Central States. Political Leadership. Ruthenberg, Charles Emil. 1919-27. *2414*
—. Gompers, Samuel. Lenin, V. I. (views). Socialist Party. 1912-18. *1991*
—. Grady, John (letters). Haywood, William Dudley. Industrial Workers of the World. Schuyler, Mont. 1921-22. *2425*
—. Historiography. Negroes. Roosevelt, Franklin D. (administration). World War II. 1939-45. *2648*
Utah *See also* Far Western States.
—. Anderson, May. *Children's Friend* (periodical). Felt, Louie. Periodicals. Primary Association. Religious education. 1880-1940. *80*

—. Atheism. *Lucifer's Lantern* (periodical). Mormons. Schroeder, Theodore. 1889-1900. *1486*
—. Carbon County Coal Strike (1933). National Miners Union. Strikes. United Mine Workers of America. 1900-39. *2571*
—. Constitutional Amendments (21st). Mormons. Prohibition. 1932-33. *2393*
—. Diaries. Fox, Ruth May. Suffrage. Women. 1865-95. *1119*
—. Diaries. Mormons. Musser, Elise Furer. Political Leadership. 1897-1967. *301*
—. Drugs. Law Enforcement. 1967-71. *2770*
—. Duniway, Abigail Scott. Newspapers. Oregon (Portland). Wells, Emmeline B. Woman suffrage. 19c. *1092*
—. Editors and Editing. Mormons. *Woman's Exponent* (periodical). Women. 1872-1914. *3*
—. Idaho (Twin Falls). Kidnapping. O'Hare, Kate Richards. Socialism. Speeches, Addresses, etc. 1921. *2404*
—. Kimball, Sarah Melissa Granger. Mormons. Woman Suffrage. 15th Ward Relief Society. 1818-98. *397*
—. Labor Unions and Organizations. Mormons. 1850-96. *1297*
—. Law. Mormons. ca 1830-80. *1104*
—. Legislation. Mormons. Tobacco. 1896-1923. *2440*
—. Mormons. Prohibition. 1900's-1910's. *2039*
—. Mormons. Statehood. Woman suffrage. 1867-96. *1090*
—. Mormons. Woman Suffrage. 1895. *1123*
—. Socialist Party. Women. 1900-20. *2086*
Utah (Carbon County). Antiforeign sentiments. Strikes. Utah Fuel Company. 1902-04. *2258*
—. Mabey, Charles R. Strikes. United Mine Workers of America. 1922. *2429*
Utah Fuel Company. Antiforeign sentiments. Strikes. Utah (Carbon County). 1902-04. *2258*
Utah, southeastern. Arizona. Bai-a-lil-le (medicine man). Civil Rights. Courts. Education. Fort Huachuca. Indian Rights Association. Navajo Indians. 1906-09. *2043*
Utah Superintendency of Indian Affairs. Farms. Forney, Jacob. Hurt, Garland. Indians (reservations). 1850-62. *539*
Utilities. *See* Public Utilities.
Utopia Park. Adventists. Humphrey, James K. New York City (Harlem). Race Relations. Sabbath Day Adventist Church. 1920's-30's. *1648*
Utopias *See also* Communes.
—. Agrarianism. Bellamy, Edward (*Looking Backward 2000-1887*). Industrial revolution. ca 1865-1900. *1517*
—. Alcott, Amos Bronson. Fruitlands (community). Lane, Charles. Massachusetts. Transcendentalism. 1840-50. *922*
—. Anarchism and Anarchists. Indiana (New Harmony). Libertarianism. Ohio (Cincinnati). Warren, Joseph. 1818-74. *302*
—. Antislavery Sentiments. Brook Farm. Godwin, Parke. 1837-47. *587*
—. Austin, Alice Constance. California (Llano del Rio). Feminism. Housework. Howland, Marie Stevens. Mexico (Topolobampo). 1874-1917. *929*
—. Australia. Canada. Finland. Kurikka, Matti. 1883-1915. *1707*
—. Ballou, Adin Augustus. Draper, E. D. Hopedale Community. Massachusetts (Milford). 1824-56. *917*
—. Ballou, Adin Augustus. Hopedale Community. Massachusetts (Milford). Religion. 1830-42. *938*
—. Beilhardt, Jacob. Ohio (Lisbon). Sex. Spirit Fruit Society. 1865-1908. *1505*
—. Bellamy, Edward. London, Jack. Socialism. 1888-1920. *262*
—. Bennett, William H. Communitarianism. Home Employment Cooperative Company. Missouri (Dallas County). 1894-1905. *1507*
—. Bishop Hill Colony. Daily life. Illinois. Jansson, Erik. Letters. Swedish Americans. 1847-56. *939*
—. Bishop Hill Colony. Illinois. Immigrants. Janssonists. Swedish Americans. 1846-60. *920*
—. Blair, Nora Schelter. Brook Farm. Education, Experimental Methods. Massachusetts. Personal narratives. Pratt, Frederick. Ripley, George. 1841-47. *934*
—. Bradford, George Partridge. Brook Farm. Daily life. Letters. Massachusetts. 1841. *932*

—. British Columbia (Harmony Island). Finnish Americans. Kurikka, Matti. 1901-05. *1628*
—. Business. Construction. Farmers. Railroads. Western States. 1880's-90's. *1511*
—. Business. Cooperative Association of America. Democracy. Morality. Peck, Bradford (*World a Department Store*). 1880-1925. *263*
—. Cabet, Etienne. France. Icarians. Iowa (New Icaria, Corning). 1852-98. *1502*
—. Cabet, Etienne. Icaria (colony). 1840-95. *264*
—. Cabet, Etienne. Icaria (colony). Illinois. Newspapers. Political Theory. Social Theory. 1820's-56. *941*
—. Cabet, Etienne. Icaria (colony). Illinois (Nauvoo). 1848-56. *915*
—. Caryl, Charles W. Colorado. New Era Union. Progressive Era. Racial thought. 1858-1926. *1509*
—. Collectivism. Intellectuals. National Association of Corporation Schools. Steinmetz, Charles Proteus. 1910-17. *1950*
—. Communes. Ohio (Cincinnati). Owen, Robert Dale. 1820's-50's. *933*
—. Communes. Social problems. 1865-1914. *1504*
—. Communia (settlement). German Americans. Iowa (Volga Township). Swiss Americans. 1847-64. *926*
—. DeBernardi, G. B. Depressions. Freedom Colony. Kansas. Labor Exchange. 1894-1905. *1510*
—. Declaration of Independence. Ideology. Radicals and Radicalism. Religion. 1730's-1890's. *269*
—. Education. New Jersey. Raritan Bay Union. 1853-61. *940*
—. Emancipation. Owen, Robert Dale. Tennessee (Nashoba). Wright, Frances (letters). 1820-29. *718*
—. Europe. Intellectuals. Social change. 1930's-70's. *1675*
—. Evangelicalism. Jones, Charles Colcock. Race Relations. South. 1804-63. *567*
—. Feminism. Literature. 19c-20c. *267*
—. Finch, John (letter). New York (Finger Lakes area). Skaneateles Community. 1843-45. *925*
—. Florida (Lee County). Koreshan Unity. Politics. Sects, Religious. Teed, Cyrus Reed. 1880-1909. *1516*
—. Great Britain. 19c-20c. *270*
—. Harmony Society. Indiana (New Harmony). Rapp, George. 1814-47. *937*
—. Harmony Society. Koreshan Unity. Mexico (Topolobampo). Olombia. 1879-93. *1500*
—. Harmony Society. Pennsylvania. Rapp, George. State Legislatures. 1805-09. *913*
—. Indiana. New Harmony (colony). 1824-58. *916*
—. Iowa. Kneeland, Abner. Salubria (community). 1827-44. *914*
—. Michigan (Beaver Island). Michigan, Lake. Strang, James Jesse. Wisconsin (Voree). 1820-56. *942*
—. Mississippi Valley, upper. 1840's. *927*
—. Novels. 1880's-90's. *1513*
—. Novels. Olerich, Henry. 1851-1927. *1506*
—. Novels. Populism. 1893-97. *1008*
—. Oneida Community. Religion. 1837-86. *921*
—. Ruskin (colony). Tennessee. Wayland, Julius Augustus. 1894-1901. *1503*

V

Valentine, Charles. Cities. Ethnicity. Negroes. Race Relations. Social organization. 1865-1975. *1697*
Valesh, Eva McDonald. Journalism. Lectures. Minnesota. Political activism. Populism. 1866-1956. *345*
Values *See also* Attitudes; Public Opinion.
—. Addams, Jane. Sex roles. 1880-1920. *281*
—. Agriculture. Boys. Fairfield School for Boys. Juvenile Delinquency. Ohio. Reformatories. 1840-84. *242*
—. Angers, François-Albert. Canada. Catholic Church. French Canadians. Pacifism. 1940-79. *1595*
—. Armies. Railroads. Strikes. 1877. 1894. *1294*
—. Baseball. Business. City life. Illinois (Chicago). Social change. 1865-70. *1001*
—. Baseball. Religion. Social change. 1892-1934. *1669*

—. Birth control. Dickenson, Robert Latou. Physicians. Sanger, Margaret. Women. 1830-1970. *87*
—. Centennial Exposition of 1876. Sex roles. Women. World's Columbian Exposition (Chicago, 1893). 1876-93. *948*
—. Ecology. Krutch, Joseph Wood. Materialism. 1920's-70. *1660*
—. Education. Feminism. Troy Female Seminary. Willard, Emma Hart. 1822-72. *810*
—. Feminism. Human Relations. Politics. Radicals and Radicalism. 19c-1929. *29*
—. Historiography. Reform. 1780-1979. *57*
—. Massachusetts (Boston). Social Customs. Temperance movements. Working class. 1838-40. *868*
—. Massachusetts (Lowell). Strikes. Women. 1820-50. *548*
—. Methodism. Protestantism. 1784-1924. *56*
—. Politics. Race Relations. Student Nonviolent Coordinating Committee. 1961-66. *2889*
Vance, Zebulon B. Democratic Party. Farmers' Alliance. North Carolina. State Politics. 1880-90. *1366*
Vanderbilt, Cornelius. Beecher, Henry Ward. Feminism. New York City. Radicals and Radicalism. Sex. Woodhull, Victoria Claflin. 1868-90's. *336*
VanLear, Thomas. Minnesota (Minneapolis). Socialism. 1910-20. *2042*
Veblen, Thorstein. Food and Drug Administration. Great Plains. Labor. Radicals and Radicalism. Social change. World War I. 1918. *1922*
Vegetarianism. Science. 1850's. *904*
Venereal disease. American Plan. Council of National Defense. Federal government. Prostitution. Social policy. Voluntary associations. World War I. 1917-21. *2048*
—. Armies. Drugs. Mexico. New Mexico (Columbus). Pershing, John J. Prostitution. 1916-17. *2068*
—. Bureaucracies. California (San Francisco). Medicine (practice of). Municipal Clinic. 1911. *2084*
Vermont *See also* New England; Northeastern or North Atlantic States.
—. Abolition Movement. *Green Mountain Freeman* (newspaper). Liberty Party. Poland, Joseph. State politics. 1840-48. *683*
—. Cerasoli, Mose (memoir). Granite Industry. Labor. Labor Disputes. 1913-38. *1807*
—. Civilian Conservation Corps. Economic Conditions. New Deal. 1933-42. *2596*
—. Constitutions, State. Woman suffrage. 1870. *1094*
—. Woman Suffrage. 1883-1917. *113*
Vermont Pilgrims ("Mummyjums"). Bullard, Isaac. Christianity. 1817-24. *928*
Verona (vessel). Industrial Workers of the World. Violence. Washington. Washington (Everett). 1916. *2122*
Vesey, Denmark. Historiography. Slave Revolts. South Carolina (Charleston). Wade, Richard (review article). 1821-22. 1964. *686*
Veto. Councils and Synods. Delegates. Episcopal Church, Protestant. Kinsolving, George Herbert. Texas. Women. 1921-70. *2347*
Vicksburg (battle). Civil War. Labor. Mississippi. Negroes. 1862. *1220*
Victor, Metta V. Abolition Movement. Great Britain. Novels. 1861. *749*
Vietnam War. Antislavery movement. Brown, John. Harpers Ferry Raid. Violence. Weathermen. 1800-61. 1960-75. *105*
—. Antiwar Sentiment. Civil rights. Kennedy, Jane. Oral history. Political Protest. Women. 1964-77. *2724*
—. Antiwar Sentiment. Conscription, Military. New Left. Students. 1965-71. *2696*
—. Antiwar Sentiment. Radicals and Radicalism. Violence. 1960's-70's. *2761*
—. Demonstrations. Peace movements. Public opinion. ca 1965-73. *2752*
—. GI movement. Political Protest. 1960's-70's. *2727*
Vigilantes. Anti-German sentiment. Bouck, William. Freedom of Assembly. Grange. Public Opinion. Washington (Walla Walla). World War I. 1918. *2161*
—. Freedom of speech. Oklahoma. Political Repression. World War I. 1914-17. *2137*
—. Racism. South Carolina Association. South Carolina (Charleston). 1823-50's. *678*
Vigilantism. Democracy. Education. Fundamentalism. Local Politics. Social Change. 1920's. *2375*
—. Kansas. Liberty bonds. Mennonites. Pacifism. World War I. 1918. *2146*

—. Ku Klux Klan. Local Politics. Nevada. 1920-29. *2449*
Villard, Oswald Garrison. Antiwar Sentiment. Keep America Out of War Congress. Socialist Party. Thomas, Norman. World War II (antecedents). 1938-41. *2501*
Vincent, Henry. Kansas. Newspapers. Political Commentary. Populism. State Politics. 1886-91. *1384*
Vinson, Frederick M. Civil rights. Segregation. Supreme Court. 1946-53. *2671*
Violence. Abolition Movement. Civil War (antecedents). New England. Parker, Theodore. 1850-60. *635*
—. Abolition Movement. Keniston, Kenneth. Pacifism. 1830-65. *644*
—. Antislavery movement. Brown, John. Harpers Ferry Raid. Vietnam War. Weathermen. 1800-61. 1960-75. *105*
—. Antiwar Sentiment. Radicals and Radicalism. Vietnam War. 1960's-70's. *2761*
—. Baptists. Desegregation. Tennessee (Clinton). Turner, Paul. 1956. *2663*
—. Canada. Civil rights. Law. Mexico. USA. 18c-1974. *119*
—. Class conflict. Commission on Industrial Relations. Plug-uglies. Progressive era. 1890-1920. *1981*
—. Coal Mines and Mining. Glasscock, William E. Martial law. National Guard. United Mine Workers of America. West Virginia (Cabin Creek, Paint Creek). 1912-13. *2176*
—. Coal Mines and Mining. Labor Disputes. Mingo War. United Mine Workers of America. West Virginia (southern). 1919-22. *2389*
—. Coal Mines and Mining. Ohio (Hocking Valley). Strikebreakers. 1884-85. *1296*
—. Douglass, Frederick. Social change. ca 1840-95. *658*
—. Economic Conditions. Negroes. Race Relations. Social change. 1960's. *2851*
—. Immigrants. Industrial Workers of the World. New Jersey (Paterson). Strikes. Textile Industry. 1913. *2254*
—. Industrial Workers of the World. *Verona* (vessel). Washington. Washington (Everett). 1916. *2122*
—. Institutions. Progressivism. Social Organization. 1880's-1910's. *2082*
—. Labor. ca 1880-1920. *157*
—. Labor Unions and Organizations. Pennsylvania (Allegheny-Kiskiminetas Valley). United Mine Workers of America. 1913-19. *2241*
—. Railroads. Strikes. Working class. 1877. *1299*
Virginia *See also* South.
—. Alabama. Farmers. Negroes. Southern Improvement Company. 1900-20. *2172*
—. American Colonization Society. Gabriel's Insurrection. Monroe, James. Prosser, Gabriel. Slave revolts. 1800. *698*
—. Anti-Saloon League. Peters, J. Sidney. Prohibition. 1916-20. *1943*
—. Bacon's Rebellion. Class struggle. Racism. Slavery. Social control. 1660-92. *472*
—. Baptists. Church and state. 1775-1810. *594*
—. Baptists. Religious Liberty. 1600-1800. *525*
—. Baughman Brothers (company). Boycotts. Knights of Labor. Richmond Typographical Union. 1886-88. *1290*
—. Boycotts. Mass Transit. Negroes. Segregation. 1904-07. *2154*
—. Byrd, Harry F. Chambers, Lenoir. Editors and Editing. School Integration. 1955-59. *2681*
—. Civil rights. Hancock, George B. Jackson, Luther P. Negroes. Young, Plummer B. 1930-45. *1583*
—. Congressmen. New Deal. Politics. Roosevelt, Franklin D. Woodrum, Clifton A. 1922-45. *433*
—. Constitutional conventions, state. Delegates. Reconstruction. 1867-68. *1022*
—. Diaries. Freedmen's Bureau. Hopkins, Sterling. Reconstruction. 1868. *1056*
—. Documents. Methodist Episcopal Church. Slave Revolts. Turner, Nat. 1831-32. *908*
—. Due process. Law. 1634-1700. *507*
—. Economic Conditions. National Recovery Administration. New Deal. Supreme Court. 1933-35. *2517*
—. Editors and Editing. Mitchell, John P. Race Relations. *Richmond Planet* (newspaper). ca 1883-1929. *407*
—. Educational Policy. Lancaster, Joseph. Public schools. *Richmond Enquirer* (newspaper). Ritchie, Thomas. 1803-50. *840*
—. Elections, congressional. Loyalty. Reconstruction. 1865. *960*

—. Evangelicalism. Reform. Slavery. Stringfellow, Thornton. 1800-70. *633*
—. House of Representatives. Langston, John Mercer. Negroes. State Politics. 1849-97. *300*
—. Negroes. Readjuster Party. State debt. 1879-83. *1222*
—. Norfolk *Journal and Guide* (newspaper). Race Relations. Washington, Booker T. Young, Plummer B. 1904-20's. *2096*
Virginia (Arlington). Freedmen's Village. Land Tenure. Race Relations. 1872-1900. *1183*
Virginia (Caroline County). Cedar Creek Monthly Meeting. Emancipation. Farms. Friends, Society of. Moorman, Clark Terrell. Ohio. 1766-1814. *743*
Virginia (Covington). Industrial Rayon Corporation. Strikes. Textile Workers Organizing Committee. 1937-38. *2508*
Virginia (Lexington). Freedmen. North. Race Relations. Schools. Teachers. 1867. *1405*
Virginia (Norfolk). Catholic Church. Fernandez, John F. O. Laity. Parishes. 1815-20. *905*
Virginia (Richmond). City Politics. Elections, municipal. Knights of Labor. Negroes. Political Reform. 1886-88. *1303*
—. Leadership. Negroes. Segregation. Urbanization. 1900-20. *1947*
—. Negroes. Political Parties. Race relations. 1865. *1231*
Virginia, southwestern. Appalachia. City Planning. Regional development. Tennessee, eastern. 1890-1929. *1710*
Virginia, University of. Freedom of speech. Pacifism. Whipple, Leon. World War I. 1917. *2130*
Virginia (Winchester). American Revolution. Diaries. Drinker family. Friends, Society of. Pennsylvania (Philadelphia). Prisoners. 1777-81. *526*
Vocational Education *See also* Industrial Arts Education.
—. Educational Theory. Missouri (St. Louis). Washington University (Manual Training School). Woodward, Calvin. 1879-1910. *1412*
—. Immigration. Industrialization. Kamprath, William B. Labor (unskilled). New York (Buffalo). 1907-21. *2312*
Voice of the Negro (periodical). Barber, Jesse Max. Negroes. Washington, Booker T. 1904-07. *1966*
Voluntarism. American Federation of Labor. Brotherhood of Painters and Decorators. Gompers, Samuel. Labor Disputes. 1894-1900. *1306*
—. Government. Labor movement. Labor Unions and Organizations. 1890's-1930's. *1760*
Voluntary associations. American Plan. Council of National Defense. Federal government. Prostitution. Social policy. Venereal disease. World War I. 1917-21. *2048*
—. California (San Francisco). Charities. Immigration. ca 1850-60. *885*
—. Child Welfare. Hoover, Herbert C. War relief. 1914-31. *364*
—. Epstein, Abraham. Legislation. Pensions. 1920-35. *1777*
—. League of Women for Community Service. Massachusetts (Boston). Negroes. Women. 1918-77. *1575*
—. Negroes. 20c. *1632*
—. Negroes. ca 1780-1830. *873*
Volunteerism. Cities. Politics. Women. 1820-1978. *34*
vonWrede, Friedrich Wilhelm. Harmony Society. Pennsylvania (Economy). 1842. *924*
Voter registration. Constitutional Amendments (24th). Negroes. Political participation. Voting Rights Act (US, 1965). 1964-67. *2892*
Voting and Voting Behavior *See also* Elections; Roll-call Voting; Suffrage.
—. Antislavery Sentiments. Know-Nothing Party. Massachusetts. Nativism. Republican Party. 1850's. *538*
—. Antislavery Sentiments. Ohio. Political attitudes. Revivals. 1825-70. *664*
—. Civil rights. Negroes. Republican Party. 1846-69. *597*
—. Decisionmaking. Desegregation. Negroes. Political power. South. Teachers. 1950's-60's. *2831*
—. Discrimination. -1973. *133*
—. Employment. Housing. Negroes. Racism. 1960's-70's. *2810*
—. Iowa. Men. Referendum. Woman suffrage. 1916. *2159*
—. Liberalism. Social Classes. 1960's-70's. *2731*

Voting

—. Local Government. Political Corruption. Socialist Party. 1910-14. *1879*
—. Local option. Louisiana (Shreveport). Prohibition. 1950-52. *2680*
—. Lunn, George. New York (Schenectady). Socialist Party. Working Class. 1911-16. *1946*
—. Middle Classes. Progressivism. Reform. Wisconsin. 1890's-1917. *2127*
—. New York. Prohibition. 1846. *896*
Voting rights. Constitutions, State. Duniway, Abigail Scott. Oregon. Woman Suffrage. 1860's-1912. *1093*
Voting Rights Act (US, 1965). Congress. Constitutional Amendments (14th, 15th). Elections. Federal Election Campaign Act (US, 1971, 1974). Supreme Court. 1965-75. *2767*
—. Constitutional Amendments (24th). Negroes. Political participation. Voter registration. 1964-67. *2892*
—. Federal Government. House of Representatives. Intervention. Negroes. Population. South. 1940-75. *2802*
—. Kennedy, John F. Mississippi. Negroes. Political Protest. 1960-72. *2863*
—. Minorities in Politics. Mississippi. Negroes. 1960-74. *2848*
Voting Rights Act (US, 1965; Section 5). Apportionment. Attorneys General. Courts. Election Laws. Intergovernmental Relations. 1965-77. *2801*
Vouchers. California (Alum Rock). Education. Parents. Public Schools. 1960's-70's. *2960*

W

Wade, Richard (review article). Historiography. Slave Revolts. South Carolina (Charleston). Vesey, Denmark. 1821-22. 1964. *686*
Wage-price controls. Corporations. World War II. 1941-45. *2645*
—. War. 20c. *168*
Wages *See also* Minimum Wage; Prices.
—. Armies. Bates, Edward. Civil War. Negroes. Politics. 1861-64. *1129*
—. Attitudes. Industry. National War Labor Board. Public Policy. Sex roles. Women. World War I. 1918-19. *2191*
—. Business. Canada. Federal Government. Labor Unions and Organizations. Social control. Unemployment Insurance Act (Canada, 1941). 1910-41. *2623*
—. Economic Regulations. Labor. National Recovery Administration. Negroes. South. 1933-34. *2576*
—. Equality. Lobbying. New York City. State Legislatures. Strachan, Grace. Teachers. Women. 1907-11. *2202*
—. Illinois. Legislation. Reform. Women. Working Conditions. 1893-1917. *2187*
—. Illinois (Chicago). Militia. Police. Riots. Strikes. 1877. *1343*
Wagner Act (US, 1935). Business. Labor Unions and Organizations. New Deal. Taft-Hartley Act (US, 1947). World War II. 1935-47. *1749*
Wagner-Steagall Act (US, 1937). Bauer, Catherine. Federal Policy. Public housing. Reform. Wood, Edith Elmer. 1890's-1940's. *2479*
Wald, Lillian D. New York. Referendum. Woman Suffrage. 1917. *2135*
Walker, David *(Appeal)*. Alabama (Mobile). Cowan, Jacob. North Carolina (Wilmington). Slave Revolts. 1829-31. *726*
Wallace, George C. Civil rights. Federal Policy. Interest Groups. Populism. Private sector. Racism. 1960's. *2899*
—. Civil Rights Act (US, 1964). Democratic Party. Indiana. Primaries (presidential). Welsh, Matthew E. 1964. *2900*
Wallace, Henry. Curricula. Farmers' Alliance. Iowa State Agricultural College. State Legislatures. 1884-91. *1416*
Wallace, Henry A. Benson, Ezra Taft. Morality. Mormons. Political Leadership. Presbyterian Church. 1933-60. *434*
Wallace, Henry Agard. Agricultural Adjustment Act (1933). Federal Programs. Iowa. New Deal. 1933-34. *2537*
Waller, John L. Colonialism. France. Madagascar. 1891-95. *1282*
—. France. Madagascar. Negroes. Press. 1890's. *1282*
Waller, John Lewis. Elites. Kansas. Negroes. Politics. Republican Party. 1878-1900. *468*

Walls, Josiah T. Florida. Negroes. Political attitudes. Reconstruction. Republican Party. 1867-85. *1192*
Walsh, Thomas J. Ideology. Politics. Populism. ca 1890-1900. *1361*
Wampanoag Indians. Apes, William. Indian-white relations. Massachusetts (Mashpee). Reform. 1830-40. *600*
War *See also* names of wars, battles, etc., e.g. American Revolution, Gettysburg (battle), etc.; Antiwar Sentiment; Civil War; International Law; Military; Peace; Prisoners of War; Refugees.
—. Barton, Clara. Red Cross. Women. 1860's-90's. *1457*
—. Dewey, John. Foreign policy. Pacifism. 1918-32. *1615*
—. Wage-price controls. 20c. *168*
War Department. Apache Indians (Chiricahua, Ojo Caliente). Fort Sill. Interior Department. Land allotment. Oklahoma. Prisoners of war. 1909-13. *2170*
War Manpower Commission. Civil-Military Relations. Labor. Publicity. Women. World War II. 1942-45. *2650*
War on Poverty. Bureaucracies. Corporations. Labor. Poor. Social Classes. 1960's. *2925*
—. City Government. Elites. Human Development Corporation. Missouri (St. Louis). Negroes. Poor. 1964-75. *2935*
—. Johnson, Lyndon B. Rhetoric. Social movements. 1965-66. *2954*
—. Navajo-Hopi Long Range Rehabilitation Act (US, 1950). Youth. 1950-60's. *1783*
War Relief *See also* Red Cross.
—. Child Welfare. Hoover, Herbert C. Voluntary associations. 1914-31. *364*
Ward, Harry F. American League for Peace and Democracy. Methodist Federation for Social Service. Social criticism. 1900-40. *376*
—. Federal Council of Churches of Christ in America. Methodist Federation for Social Service. North, Frank M. Social Creed of Methodism. 1907-12. *1956*
Ward, Samuel Ringgold. Abolition Movement. Christology. Negroes. New York. 1839-51. *618*
Waring, George E., Jr. Cities. New York City. Pollution. Public Health. Reform. Refuse disposal. 1880-1917. *69*
Waring, J. Waties. Courts. Democratic Party. Primaries. Segregation. South Carolina. 1947-52. *2683*
Warren, Joseph. Anarchism and Anarchists. Indiana (New Harmony). Libertarianism. Ohio (Cincinnati). Utopias. 1818-74. *302*
Warren, Mercy Otis. American Revolution. Feminism. Political theory. Republicans (Radical). 1760's-1805. *523*
—. American Revolution. Letters. Literature. Massachusetts. 1740-1814. *460*
Wartime Elections Act (Canada, 1917). Canada. Great Britain. Woman Suffrage. 1917. *1721*
Washington *See also* Far Western States.
—. American Federation of Labor. American Labor Union. Leftism. Western Federation of Miners. 1880's-1920. *171*
—. American Federation of Labor. Industrial Workers of the World. One Big Union. 1919. *2179*
—. Dawes Act (US, 1887). Eells, Edwin. Indians (agencies). Land Tenure. Skokomish Indian Reservation. 1871-95. *970*
—. Industrial Workers of the World. *Verona* (vessel). Violence. Washington (Everett). 1916. *2122*
—. Labor Unions and Organizations. Lumber and Lumbering. Workmen's compensation. 1911. *2280*
—. Land tenure. Political Reform. Populism. Rogers, John R. State Politics. 1890-1900. *1363*
—. Legislation. Minimum wage. State government. 1913-25. *1822*
—. Medical Reform. Mental health. Professionalization. Territorial Government. 1853-75. *1459*
Washington (Aberdeen). Freedom of Speech. Industrial Workers of the World. Labor Disputes. 1911-12. *2150*
Washington, Booker T. Alabama. Industrial Arts Education. Negroes. Tuskegee Institute. 1870's-90's. *1189*
—. Attitudes. Florida. Roosevelt, Theodore. South. 1901. *2080*
—. Barber, Jesse Max. Negroes. *Voice of the Negro* (periodical). 1904-07. *1966*

—. Chesnutt, Charles W. Politics. Race relations. 1880-1915. *1153*
—. Conservatism. DuBois, W. E. B. Negroes. Periodicals. Race relations. Radicals and Radicalism. 1900-10. *1983*
—. Economic Conditions. Negro suffrage. Race Relations. 1895. *1149*
—. Education. Farmers. Negroes. Tuskegee Institute. 1881-1915. *1186*
—. Educational Policy. Industrial Arts Education. Negroes. Speeches, Addresses, etc. 1884-1904. *1283*
—. Educational theory. Negroes. 1881-1915. *193*
—. Historiography. Race Relations. 1898-1972. *1161*
—. Moton, Robert Russa. Negroes. Politics. Scott, Emmett Jay. Tuskegee Institute. 1915-25. *1643*
—. Norfolk *Journal and Guide* (newspaper). Race Relations. Virginia. Young, Plummer B. 1904-20's. *2096*
Washington, Booker T. (and Committee of 12). Constitution League. Discrimination. Foraker, Joseph B. Hepburn Bill, Warner-Foraker Amendment (1906). Jim Crow laws. Negroes. Railroads. 1906. *1919*
Washington, Booker T. (Atlanta Exposition Address). Georgia. Race relations. Rhetoric. 1895. *1167*
Washington College of Law. District of Columbia. Gillett, Emma M. Legal education. Mussey, Ellen Spencer. Women. 1869-1949. *426*
Washington (Everett). Industrial Workers of the World. *Verona* (vessel). Violence. Washington. 1916. *2122*
Washington, Forrester B. Dancey, John C. Discrimination. Michigan (Detroit). Urban League. 1916-39. *1696*
Washington (King County). Coal Mines and Mining. Negroes. Oregon Improvement Company. Strikebreakers. 1891. *1265*
Washington (Monroe). Progressive Era. Reformatories. Shank, Corwin. 1904-18. *1972*
Washington (Seattle). Businessmen. Ports. Progressives. 1911-20. *2184*
—. Christianity. Longshoremen. Oxford Group movement. Strikes. 1921-34. *2604*
—. City Government. Municipal League of Seattle. Progressivism. Reform. 1910-20. *2045*
—. Civic Unity Committee. Defense industries. Japanese Americans. Negroes. Race relations. World War II. 1940-45. *2624*
—. Dix, I. F. Hoover, Herbert C. Local politics. Self-help. Unemployed Citizens' League. 1931-32. *2417*
—. Fundamentalism. Matthews, Mark Allison. Presbyterian Church. 1900-40. *430*
—. Impoundment. Russian Revolution (October). *Shilka* (vessel). 1917. *2009*
Washington (Spokane). Freedom of Speech. Industrial Workers of the World. Political Protest. Pratt, N. S. 1909-10. *2132*
Washington State Committee on Un-American Activities. Anti-Communist Movements. Newspapers. 1948-49. *2656*
Washington State People's Party. Political Factions. Populism. Washington (Whitman County, Ellensburg). ca 1891-98. *1389*
Washington State University. Morrill Act (US, 1862). 1862-92. *1407*
Washington University. Brookings, Robert. Flexner Report. Medical education. Missouri (St. Louis). Reform. 1910-16. *2318*
—. Curricula. Eliot, William Greenleaf. Higher education. Missouri (St. Louis). Trans-Mississippi West. 1853-87. *189*
Washington University (Manual Training School). Educational Theory. Missouri (St. Louis). Vocational Education. Woodward, Calvin. 1879-1910. *1412*
Washington (Walla Walla). Anti-German sentiment. Bouck, William. Freedom of Assembly. Grange. Public Opinion. Vigilantes. World War I. 1918. *2161*
Washington (Whitman County, Ellensburg). Political Factions. Populism. Washington State People's Party. ca 1891-98. *1389*
Washington (Yakima Valley). Agricultural Labor. Farmers. Industrial Workers of the World. Labor Disputes. Ranchers. 1910-36. *2569*
—. Farmers. Industrial Workers of the World. Orchards. Strikes. 1933. *2568*
—. Industrial Workers of the World. Labor Unions and Organizations. Strikes. 1933. *2496*
Wastewater. Cities. Public Health. Technology. Water Supply. 1850-1930. 1900H. *99*

Water Conservation *See also* Water Supply.
—. Canada. English Canadians. Immigrants. Propaganda. Puttee, Arthur. Radicals and Radicalism. ca 1888-1913. *1327*
Water Supply *See also* Irrigation; Water Conservation.
—. Cities. Georgia (Atlanta). Illinois (Chicago). New Jersey (Newark). 1860-1923. *32*
—. Cities. Public Health. Technology. Wastewater. 1850-1930. 1900H. *99*
—. Goiter. Goler, George W. Iodine. New York (Rochester). 1923-32. *2395*
Waterways. Army Corps of Engineers. Environmental law. Refuse Act (US, 1899). 1876-1971. *977*
Watkins, William. American Moral Reform Society. Civil Rights. Maryland (Baltimore). Negroes (free). 1801-58. *339*
Watson, Thomas E. Georgia. Negro Suffrage. Populism. Reform. 1880-1922. *27*
Wayland, Francis. Baptists. Slavery. 1830-45. *662*
Wayland, Julius Augustus. Ruskin (colony). Tennessee. Utopias. 1894-1901. *1503*
Wealth. American Revolution. Attitudes. McIntosh, Lachlan. Slavery. South. 1775-87. *517*
—. Democratic Party. Equal opportunity. Jacksonianism. Social theory. 1836-46. *537*
Wealth Makers (newspaper). *Alliance-Independent* (newspaper). Christian Socialism. Gibson, George Howard. Nebraska. Populism. 1893-96. *1397*
Weathermen. Antislavery movement. Brown, John. Harpers Ferry Raid. Vietnam War. Violence. 1800-61. 1960-75. *105*
Webb, Richard Davis. Antislavery Sentiments. Hibernian Anti-Slavery Society. Ireland. 1837-61. *736*
Webster, Milton. Defense industries. Discrimination. Executive Order 8802. March on Washington Movement. Military. Randolph, A. Philip. 1941-44. *2635*
Weed, Ada M. Pacific Northwest. Prohibition. Reform. Women's rights. 1858-1910. *327*
Weisbord, Vera Buch (reminiscence). National Textile Workers Union. North Carolina (Gastonia). Strikes. Textile Industry. 1929. *2459*
Welch, Henry. Antibiotics. Conflict of interest. Federal regulation. Food and Drug Administration. Periodicals. Pharmacy. 1953-62. *2676*
Weld, Theodore Dwight. Abolition Movement. Birney, James. Clergy. Evangelicalism. Smith, Gerrit. Stanton, H. B. 1820-50. *744*
—. Abolitionists. Alcott, Amos Bronson. Civil War (antecedents). Phillips, Wendell. 1830-60. *721*
Welfare. *See* Public Welfare.
Welfare Mothers Movement. Minnesota. Politics. Public Policy. 1960-72. *2933*
Welfare state. Canada. Europe, Western. Social policy. USA. 1890-1970. *160*
—. Canada. Marsh, Leonard *(Report).* Social Security. Socialism. 1930-44. *1771*
—. Liberalism. New Deal. New Left. Political Theory. 1932-66. *1738*
—. Public welfare. Reform. 1935-80. *2946*
Wells, Emmeline B. Duniway, Abigail Scott. Newspapers. Oregon (Portland). Utah. Woman suffrage. 19c. *1092*
Wells, Ida B. *Free Speech* (newspaper). Lynching. Negroes. Tennessee (Memphis). 1892. *1128*
Welsh, Herbert. Civil Service Commissioner. Indian Rights Association. Indian-White Relations. Roosevelt, Theodore. 1889-95. *1011*
Welsh, Matthew E. Civil Rights Act (US, 1964). Democratic Party. Indiana. Primaries (presidential). Wallace, George C. 1964. *2900*
Welter, Barbara. Feminization. Historiography. Protestantism. Women. 1820's-30's. 1970's. *910*
Wesley, Charles H. Catholic University of America. Colleges and Universities. Discrimination. District of Columbia. Negroes. 1914-48. *2304*
Wesley, Susanna. Feminism. Holiness Movement. Palmer, Phoebe. 1732-1973. *17*
West. Colleges and Universities. Educational Reform. Political Protest. 1964-74. *2967*
—. Populism. Reformers. State Legislatures. 1890's. *1364*
West Coast. Asians. Immigration. Negroes. Newlands, Francis. Progressives. 1904-17. *2067*

West Coast Master Agreement. American Federation of Labor. Discrimination, Employment. Fair Employment Practices Committee. Federal Government. Labor Unions and Organizations. Shipbuilding. World War II. 1939-46. *2627*
West, Helen Hunt. Equal Rights Amendment. Florida. National Women's Party. Politics. Women. 1917-52. *1727*
West Virginia. Brown, John. Civil War (antecedents). Harpers Ferry raid. White, Edward. 1859. *783*
—. Coal Mines and Mining. Debs, Eugene V. Socialist Party. Strikes. 1912-14. *2194*
—. Coal Mines and Mining. Keeney, Frank. United Mine Workers of America. 1916-31. *1755*
—. Elkins, Stephen B. Reform. Republican Party. State Politics. White, Albert B. 1901-05. *1895*
—. Paint Creek-Cabin Creek Strike. *Socialist and Labor Star* (newspaper). Strikes. Thompson, Wyatt Hamilton. 1912-13. *2195*
West Virginia (Arthurdale). Clapp, Elsie Ripley. Education. Homesteading and Homesteaders. New Deal. Roosevelt, Eleanor. 1933-44. *2477*
—. Miners. National Industrial Recovery Act (US, 1933). New Deal. Roosevelt, Eleanor. Subsistence Homesteads Program. 1930-46. *2492*
West Virginia (Berkeley, Jefferson counties). Freedmen's Bureau. 1865-68. *1077*
—. Freedmen's Bureau. Race relations. Schools. 1865-68. *1264*
West Virginia (Cabin Creek, Paint Creek). Coal Mines and Mining. Glasscock, William E. Martial law. National Guard. United Mine Workers of America. Violence. 1912-13. *2176*
West Virginia Education Association. Educational reform. Meadows, Clarence W. Public Schools. Strayer, George D. Trent, W. W. 1932-58. *1837*
West Virginia Human Rights Commission. Race relations. 1961-66. *2887*
West Virginia (Kanawha County). Authority. Communications Behavior. Parents. Public Schools. Textbooks. 1974. *2958*
West Virginia (Martinsburg, Berkeley County). Baltimore and Ohio Railroad. Mathews, Henry M. Railroads. Strikes. 1877. *1301*
West Virginia (Paint Creek). Coal Mines and Mining. State Government. Strikes. United Mine Workers of America. 1912-13. *2270*
West Virginia, southern. Coal Mines and Mining. Knights of Labor. Race Relations. United Mine Workers of America. 1880-94. *1140*
—. Coal Mines and Mining. Labor Disputes. Mingo War. United Mine Workers of America. Violence. 1919-22. *2389*
West Virginia State Federation of Labor. Nugent, John. Socialism. 1901-14. *2177*
Western Antislavery Society. Abolition Movement. Civil War (antecedents). Garrison, William Lloyd. Ohio. 1835-61. *650*
Western Appeal (newspaper). Adams, John Quincy (1848-1922). Minnesota (St. Paul). Negroes. 1888-1922. *1269*
Western Federation of Miners. Alaska (Douglas Island). Gold Mines and Mining. Labor Unions and Organizations. Strikes. Treadwell Mines. 1905-10. *2209*
—. American Federation of Labor. American Labor Union. Leftism. Washington. 1880's-1920. *171*
—. American Federation of Labor. Armies. Industrial Workers of the World. Labor Disputes. Nevada (Goldfield). 1904-08. *2287*
—. Arizona (Globe). Copper Mines and Mining. Strikes. 1917. *2261*
—. Arizona (Globe). Copper Mines and Mining. Strikes. World War I. 1917. *2255*
—. Editorials. Labor. *Miners' Magazine.* Poetry. Songs. 1900-07. *2293*
Western States *See also* individual states; Far Western States; Southwest; Trans-Mississippi West.
—. Business. Construction. Farmers. Railroads. Utopias. 1880's-90's. *1511*
—. Cowboys. Strikes. Working conditions. 1870-90. *1324*
—. Ideology. North. Protestantism. Public Schools. Republican Party. 1870-1930. *204*
—. Judicial Administration. Labor. Populism. Supreme courts, state. 1893-1902. *1024*
—. Labor. Mining. 1892-1904. *1335*

—. National Parks and Reserves. Recreation. Wilderness Act (US, 1964). 1864-1976. *7*
Westward Movement *See also* Cowboys; Frontier and Pioneer Life.
—. Bishop Hill Colony. Communalism. Economic growth. Illinois. Swedish Americans. 1846-59. *935*
Weyerhaeuser, Frederick. Chippewa Lumber and Boom Company. Deitz, John F. Individualism. Wisconsin (Cameron Dam). 1900-24. *1967*
Whalen, Homer. City Politics. Illinois (Canton). Prohibition. Socialist Party. 1911-20. *2093*
Wheatley, Phillis (letter). American Revolution. Massachusetts (Boston). Slavery. Whigs. 1767-80. *504*
Wheeler, John W. Minorities in Politics. Missouri (St. Louis). Negroes. Republican Party. 1870-1915. *1142*
Whig (newspaper). Brownlow, William Gannaway. Editors and Editing. Temperance Movements. Tennessee. 1838-51. *866*
Whig Party. Adams, John Quincy. Democratic Party. Elections (presidential). Jackson, Andrew. Slavery. 1828-44. *737*
—. Anti-Catholicism. Ohio. Political Systems. Republican Party. Slavery. 1850's. *564*
—. Corwin, Thomas. Mexican War. Political Speeches. 1847. *540*
—. Democratic Party. Liberty Party. Negro suffrage. New York. Referendum. 1840-47. *595*
Whigs. American Revolution. Massachusetts (Boston). Slavery. Wheatley, Phillis (letter). 1767-80. *504*
Whipper, William. American Moral Reform Society. Negroes. Pennsylvania (Philadelphia). Reform. 1830-76. *386*
Whipple, Leon. Freedom of speech. Pacifism. Virginia, University of. World War I. 1917. *2130*
White, Albert B. Elkins, Stephen B. Reform. Republican Party. State Politics. West Virginia. 1901-05. *1895*
White, Edward. Brown, John. Civil War (antecedents). Harpers Ferry raid. West Virginia. 1859. *783*
White, Ellen G. Adventists. Hydrotherapy. Jackson, James Caleb. Medical reform. New York (Dansville). 1864-65. *1470*
White flight. School Integration. Tennessee (Memphis). 1963-76. *2969*
White, Jacob C., Jr. Educational Reform. Negroes. Pennsylvania (Philadelphia). 1857-1902. *441*
White, James Platt. Buffalo Medical College. Libel. Loomis, Horatio N. Medical Education. Midwifery. New York. Obstetrics. 1850. *869*
White, Lulu B. Craft, Juanita. Durham, William J. NAACP. Smith, Antonio Maceo. Texas. 1933-50. *1586*
White supremacy. Capital punishment. Cruce, Lee. Governors. Negroes. Oklahoma. 1911-15. *1907*
White, Walter F. Armies. Discrimination. Great Britain. World War II. 1943-44. *2626*
—. Johnson, James Weldon. NAACP. Negroes. 1909-35. *1647*
—. NAACP. Nominations to Office. North Carolina. Parker, John J. Supreme Court. 1930. *2385*
Whites. American Colonization Society. Negroes, free. Rhetoric. Slavery. Social Status. 1831-34. *615*
—. Attitudes. Negroes. 1963-77. *2818*
—. Citizenship. Civil Rights. Crook, George. Indians (agencies). Political Corruption. 1870's-80's. *993*
—. Communism. North Carolina (Gastonia). Novels. Poor. Strikes. Textile Industry. 1929-34. *2361*
—. Discrimination, Educational. Disfranchisement. Middle Classes. Negro Suffrage. North Carolina. Progressivism. Public Finance. 1880-1910. *2316*
—. Education. Management. Negroes. 1652-1972. *183*
—. Emancipation. Freedmen. South. 1865-66. *969*
—. Higher education. Negroes. Philanthropy. 1861-1920. *1234*
—. Louisiana (New Orleans). Metropolitan Police Force. Negroes. Politics. Riots. 1868. *1168*
—. NAACP. Progressivism. 1909-10. *2095*
—. Negro Suffrage. North Carolina. Red Shirt Movement. Social Classes. Terrorism. 1898-1900. *1067*

Whitman, Charles. Morality. New York. Progressivism. Prohibition. Smith, Alfred E. Woman Suffrage. 1911-18. *2116*
Whittier House. New Jersey (Jersey City). Progressivism. 1890-1917. *2105*
Wickersham Committee (1931). Colorado (Denver). Prohibition. 1907-33. *2381*
Wickersham, James P. Crime and Criminals. Education. Morality. Pennsylvania. 1866-81. *1401*
Wickett, Samuel Morley. City government. Ontario (Toronto). Progressivism. 1900-15. *1703*
Wiebe, Robert. Elites. Hays, Samuel P. Ideology. Professionalism. Progressivism. 20c. *1971*
Wilder, Burt G. Boas, Franz. Discrimination. Scientists. 1900-15. *1884*
Wilderness *See also* Conservation of Natural Resources; Forests and Forestry; National Parks and Reserves; Nature.
—. California. Carr, Jeanne Caroline Smith. Muir, John. Wisconsin. 1850's-1903. *277*
—. Economic Development. Forest Service. Minnesota, northeastern. Public Policy. Superior National Forest. 1923-26. *2437*
Wilderness Act (US, 1964). National Parks and Reserves. Recreation. Western States. 1864-1976. *7*
Wildlife Conservation *See also* Forests and Forestry; Great Plains; National Parks and Reserves; Natural Resources.
—. Montana. National Park Service. Roosevelt, Theodore. Yellowstone National Park. 1883-1918. *2079*
Willard, Charles Dwight. Boosterism. California (Los Angeles). City Government. Journalism. Progressivism. 1888-1914. *319*
Willard, Emma Hart. Education. Feminism. Troy Female Seminary. Values. 1822-72. *810*
—. Education. New York. Troy Female Seminary. Women. 1809-70. *436*
Willard, Frances. Temperance movements. 1870's-90's. *1478*
Willcox, Walter F. Census Bureau. Cornell University. Economics. Negroes. Progressivism. Racism. 1895-1910. *1870*
Willey, Austin. Abolition movement. Fessenden, Samuel. Free Soil movement. Liberty Party. Maine. State Politics. 1830's-48. *682*
—. Labor Unions and Organizations. Ohio. Toledo Mechanics' Association. 1843. *827*
Williams, Claude. Reform. Social change. South. Williams, Joyce. 1930's-70's. *400*
Williams, Joyce. Reform. Social change. South. Williams, Claude. 1930's-70's. *400*
Williams, Peter, Jr. Episcopal Church, Protestant. New York City. Newspapers. Racism. Riots. St. Philip's Church. 1830-50. *671*
Williams, Roger. Christianity. History. Religious liberty. Rhode Island. 17c. *514*
Williams, Samuel D., Jr. Euthanasia. Great Britain. Medicine. Tollemache, Lionel A. 1870's-90's. *1452*
Williamson, Passmore. Antislavery Sentiments. Pennsylvania (Philadelphia). Slavery. Trials. 1855. *628*
Willis, Olympia Brown. James, Ada. Political Equality League. Referendum. Wisconsin. Woman Suffrage Association. 1912. *2141*
Willson, Augustus E. Beckham, John C. W. Kentucky. McCreary, James B. Progressivism. State Government. 1899-1915. *1894*
Wilmer, Cary Breckenridge (interview). Baker, Ray Stannard. Civil rights. DuBois, W. E. B. Liberalism. Negroes. 1900-10. *2110*
Wilmot Proviso. Burt, Armistead. Calhoun, John C. Compromise of 1850. Congress. Oregon. Slavery. ca 1846-60. *691*
Wilson, Woodrow. American Federation of Labor. Gompers, Samuel. Labor Unions and Organizations. Military. Preparedness. 1914-17. *2000*
—. Ammons, Elias. Coal. Colorado. Federal Government. Strikes. 1914. *2228*
—. Attitudes. Democracy. Federal Reserve System. Income tax. Reform. 1913-21. *1994*
—. DuBois, W. E. B. Equality. 1911-18. *1952*
—. Educational reform. New Jersey. Princeton University. 1902-10. *2334*
—. Federal Government. Segregation. Trotter, William Monroe. 1913-14. *2016*
—. Georgia. Negroes. Political Attitudes. Progressive Party. Roosevelt, Theodore. 1912. *2038*
—. Ideology. Industrial Conference, 1st. Labor Unions and Organizations. Management. 1919. *2225*
—. Industrial Conference, 2d. Industrial democracy. Labor Reform. Labor Unions and Organizations. 1919-20. *2180*
—. Woman suffrage. 1913-20. *2153*
Winnebago Indians. Bureau of Indian Affairs. Christianity. Indian-White Relations. Iowa. Schools. 1834-48. *850*
Winnemucca, Sarah (Paiute). California. Indian-White Relations. Paiute Indians. 1840's-91. *419*
Winnipeg General Strike (1919). Canada. Strikes. 1920-70. *1752*
Wisconsin *See also* North Central States.
—. Agrarianism. Populism. Radicals and Radicalism. Working class. 19c. *1399*
—. Alberta. Blackfoot Indians (Blood). Identity. Indians. Menominee Indians. Militancy. 1950's-60's. *1685*
—. Amlie, Thomas. Economic programs. Liberals. New Deal. Politics. 1931-39. *2609*
—. Amlie, Thomas. Farmer-Labor Party. New Deal. 1930-38. *2544*
—. Amlie, Thomas. New Deal. Radicals and Radicalism. Roosevelt, Franklin D. 1930-39. *1672*
—. Attitudes. Janesville Associated Charities. Middle Classes. Poor. 1870-1900. *1450*
—. Bennett Law (Wisconsin, 1890). Church and state. Compulsory Education. 1890. *1417*
—. Bible. Catholic Church. Desmond, Humphrey. Protestantism. Religion in the Public Schools. *Wisconsin ex rel. Frederick Weiss et al.* vs. *District School Board of School District 8* (1890). 1888-90. *1414*
—. Bible. Constitutions, State. Presbyterian Church. Religious Education. Supreme courts (state). 1848-90. *1419*
—. Bible. Methodist Church. Religion in the Public Schools. 1846-90. *1418*
—. Blaine, John J. Progressivism. Republican Party. Senate. 1927-33. *2421*
—. California. Carr, Jeanne Caroline Smith. Muir, John. Wilderness. 1850's-1903. *277*
—. Education. Indians. Manuscripts. 1820-50. *848*
—. Emigration. Kansas-Nebraska Act (US, 1854). Slavery. 1850's. *690*
—. German Americans. Labor Unions and Organizations. Progressivism. Socialism. 1900-12. *2103*
—. Income (redistribution). LaFollette, Philip F. National Progressives of America. Politics. 1930-38. *2551*
—. James, Ada. Political Equality League. Referendum. Willis, Olympia Brown. Woman Suffrage Association. 1912. *2141*
—. Middle Classes. Progressivism. Reform. Voting and Voting Behavior. 1890's-1917. *2127*
—. Negro suffrage. Republican Party. 1857. *599*
—. Oregon (Portland). Sabin, Ellen B. Teaching. Women. 1850-95. *405*
—. Politics. Reconstruction. Republican Party. 1865-73. *981*
Wisconsin (Cameron Dam). Chippewa Lumber and Boom Company. Deitz, John F. Individualism. Weyerhaeuser, Frederick. 1900-24. *1967*
Wisconsin ex rel. Frederick Weiss et al. vs. *District School Board of School District 8* (1890). Bible. Catholic Church. Desmond, Humphrey. Protestantism. Religion in the Public Schools. Wisconsin. 1888-90. *1414*
Wisconsin (Milwaukee). Catholic Church. Labor Unions and Organizations. Polish Americans. Political Leadership. Progressivism. Socialism. 1900-30. *1663*
—. Child Welfare Commission. Medical care. Socialism. 1911-12. *2032*
—. City Government. Medicine. Reform. Refuse disposal. Sanitation. Technology. 1867-1911. *1466*
—. *Gillespie* v. *Palmer* (US, 1866). Negro Suffrage. 1849-66. *1173*
—. Public Schools. Reform. Socialism. Working class. 1890-1920. *2329*
Wisconsin, University of. Bascom, John. Commons, John R. Ely, Richard T. Social gospel. 1870-1910. *1017*
—. Physical Education and Training. Women. 1863-1913. *1436*
Wisconsin (Voree). Michigan (Beaver Island). Michigan, Lake. Strang, James Jesse. Utopias. 1820-56. *942*
Wisconsin Works Bill (1935). Depressions. LaFollette, Philip F. New Deal. Progressivism. Roosevelt, Franklin D. 1935. *2552*
Wittenmyer, Annie Turner. Social work. Women's Christian Temperance Union. ca 1855-1900. *1441*
Wolfe, Thomas Kennerly, Jr. Counter Culture. Kesey, Ken. LSD. Political Theory. 1964-68. *2992*
Woman Suffrage. Abolition Movement. Anthony, Susan B. Grimké, Angelina. Mott, Lucretia. Stanton, Elizabeth Cady. ca 1820-60. *549*
—. Alabama. Jacobs, Pattie Ruffner. 1900's-20. *2145*
—. Alabama. League of Women Voters. National American Woman Suffrage Association. 1919-21. *2450*
—. Alcott, Louisa May. Feminism. Letters. 1853-85. *811*
—. Allen, Ella. Baker, Charlotte. California (San Diego). Political Campaigns. 1911. *2147*
—. Anthony, Susan B. Journalism. *Revolution* (newspaper). Stanton, Elizabeth Cady. 1868-70. *1108*
—. Attitudes. Canada. English Canadians. Race. Sex. ca 1877-1918. *1*
—. Baptists, Southern. 1910-20. *2168*
—. Blackwell, Henry B. Constitutional conventions, state. Montana. 1889. *1121*
—. Bloomer, Amelia. Iowa. Savery, Anne. State Politics. Woodhull, Victoria Claflin. 1868-72. *1111*
—. Borden, Robert Laird. Canada. *Champion* (periodical). Great Britain. Women's Social and Political Union. 1910-18. *1737*
—. Bourassa, Henri. Canada. Divorce. Feminism. 1913-25. *1698*
—. Breckinridge, Madeline McDowell. Federation of Business and Professional Women's Clubs. Kentucky Equal Rights Association. 1908-20. *2157*
—. California. Equality. 1895-1911. *2160*
—. Canada. English Canadians. Family. 1877-1918. *111*
—. Canada. Great Britain. Wartime Elections Act (Canada, 1917). 1917. *1721*
—. Catholic Church. International Union of Catholic Women's Leagues (congress). Italy (Rome). Quebec. 1922. *1734*
—. Civil Rights. Civil War. Constitutional Amendments (14th, 15th). Slavery. Supreme Court. 1863-75. *1106*
—. Clapp, Hannah Keziah. Educators. Nevada, University of. 1824-1908. *456*
—. Colorado. Newspapers. Public opinion. 1870's. *1099*
—. Congress. Hayes, Rutherford B. Mormons. Polygamy. 1877-81. *1089*
—. Congress. Montana. Rankin, Jeannette. 1913-18. *466*
—. Constitutional Amendments (19th). *Crisis* (periodical). DuBois, W. E. B. Negroes. 1910-34. *1712*
—. Constitutional Amendments (19th; ratification). Massachusetts. 1900-19. *2167*
—. Constitutional Conventions, state. Democrats. Oklahoma. 1870-1907. *146*
—. Constitutional conventions, state. Oklahoma. Politics. 1906. *2144*
—. Constitutions, State. Duniway, Abigail Scott. Oregon. Voting rights. 1860's-1912. *1093*
—. Constitutions, State. Montana. Rankin, Jeannette. 1889-1914. *129*
—. Constitutions, State. Vermont. 1870. *1094*
—. DeVoe, Emma Smith. Duniway, Abigail Scott. Pacific Northwest. 1854-1912. *130*
—. Duniway, Abigail Scott. Newspapers. Oregon (Portland). Utah. Wells, Emmeline B. 19c. *1092*
—. Elections. Political Attitudes. South Dakota (Lake County). 1885-90. *1098*
—. Equal Rights Amendment. National Women's Party. Social Feminists. 1920-23. *2376*
—. Felton, Rebecca Latimer. Georgia. Politics. Senate. 1860's-1922. *423*
—. Feminism. Massachusetts Association Opposed to the Further Extension of the Suffrage to Women. Political campaigns. Sex roles. Socialism. 1895-1915. *2166*
—. Freedom of Speech. National Women's Party. 1912-19. *2129*
—. Friedlander, Alice G. Oregon (Portland). Speeches, Addresses, etc. 1893. *1095*
—. Historiography. 1868-1977. *117*
—. House of Representatives. Montana. Political Campaigns (congressional). Rankin, Jeannette. Republican Party. 1900-16. *2142*
—. Idaho. National American Woman Suffrage Association. 1896-1920. *2149*
—. Iowa. Men. Referendum. Voting and Voting Behavior. 1916. *2159*

Woman Suffrage — SUBJECT INDEX — Women

—. Kentucky (Louisville). 1828-1920. *124*
—. Kimball, Sarah Melissa Granger. Mormons. Utah. 15th Ward Relief Society. 1818-98. *397*
—. Massachusetts. Political Campaigns. Referendum. 1895-1920. *2140*
—. Methodist Protestant Church. Shaw, Anna Howard. Social Gospel. 1880-1919. *448*
—. Methodology. Oral history. Paul, Alice (memoirs). 1912-77. *335*
—. Morality. New York. Progressivism. Prohibition. Smith, Alfred E. Whitman, Charles. 1911-18. *2116*
—. Mormons. Statehood. Utah. 1867-96. *1090*
—. Mormons. Utah. 1895. *1123*
—. National Association of Colored Women. Negroes. Reform. Terrell, Mary Church. 1892-1954. *312*
—. Negroes. 1850-1900. *1270*
—. New York. Referendum. Wald, Lillian D. 1917. *2135*
—. Oregon. Portland *Oregonian*. Reporters and Reporting. 1869-1905. *1101*
—. Paul, Alice. South Carolina. ca 1891-1919. *2128*
—. Political Participation. Roosevelt, Theodore. 1899-1919. *2163*
—. Population. Women's Liberation Movement. Wyoming. 1869-1920. *1102*
—. Prairie Provinces. 1890's-1920's. *1735*
—. Radicals and Radicalism. Social Organization. 19c. *116*
—. Socialist Party. Working Class. 1901-12. *1954*
—. South. 1830-1945. *22*
—. South Carolina. 1912-20. *2169*
—. South Carolina. Young, Virginia Durant. 1890-1903. *1117*
—. Vermont. 1883-1917. *113*
—. Wilson, Woodrow. 1913-20. *2153*
Woman Suffrage Association. James, Ada. Political Equality League. Referendum. Willis, Olympia Brown. Wisconsin. 1912. *2141*
Woman's Christian Temperance Union. Ohio. Prohibition. 1874-85. *1483*
Woman's *Exponent* (periodical). Editors and Editing. Mormons. Utah. Women. 1872-1914. *3*
Woman's Peace Party. Navy League (Woman's Section). Preparedness. Sex roles. Suffrage. World War I. 1914-18. *2092*
Women *See also* Divorce; Family; Feminism; Marriage; Prostitution; Sex Discrimination; Woman Suffrage.
—. Abolition movement. New York, upstate. Petitions. Political participation. 1838-39. *586*
—. Abolition movement. Pennsylvania Hall. Pennsylvania (Philadelphia). Riots. 1833-37. *617*
—. Adams, Mary Newbury. Iowa. Self-image. Social status. 1850-1900. *1042*
—. Addams, Jane. Education. Hull House. Ideology. Illinois (Chicago). 1875-1930. *411*
—. Addams, Jane. Sex roles. Youth. 1860-89. *308*
—. Agricultural Organizations. North Carolina. Southern Farmers' Alliance. ca 1880-1900. *1373*
—. Alabama. Civil Rights. Democratic Party. Folsom, James E. Negroes. State Government. 1947-58. *2668*
—. Amalgamated Clothing Workers of America. Craton, Ann Washington. Northeastern or North Atlantic States. 1915-44. *367*
—. Amateur Athletic Union. Colleges and Universities. Sports. 1890's-1936. *1766*
—. American Historical Association (Coordinating Committee of Women in the History Profession). 1966-72. *2922*
—. American Revolution. Historiography. 1770's-1970's. *49*
—. American, Sadie. Congress of Jewish Women. Jews. Solomon, Hannah G. World Parliament of Religions. World's Columbian Exposition (Chicago, 1893). 1893. *1488*
—. Ames, Jessie Daniel. Association of Southern Women for the Prevention of Lynching. Lynching. Racism. South. 1930's. *2516*
—. Ames, Jessie Daniel. Association of Southern Women for the Prevention of Lynching. Lynching. South. 1928-42. *2553*
—. Anderson, Mary. Illinois (Chicago). Labor Unions and Organizations. Nestor, Agnes. Robins, Margaret Dreier. Women's Trade Union League. Working conditions. 1903-20. *2190*

—. Anesthesia. Childbirth. Medicine (practice of). Twilight sleep movement. 1902-23. *2034*
—. Antinomian controversy. Hutchinson, Anne. Massachusetts Bay Colony. 1630-43. *520*
—. Antislavery Sentiments. Great Britain. Massachusetts (Salem). Negroes. Remond, Sarah Parker. 1856-87. *294*
—. Antislavery Sentiments. Great Britain. Sutherland, Duchess of (Harriet Howard). Tyler, Julia Gardiner. 1842-89. *723*
—. Antiwar Sentiment. Civil rights. Kennedy, Jane. Oral history. Political Protest. Vietnam War. 1964-77. *2724*
—. Arizona. Congressional Union for Woman Suffrage. Democratic Party. Political Campaigns. 1914. 1916. *2164*
—. Assimilation. Black nationalism. Ideology. Literature. Religion. 1890-1925. *1654*
—. Associated Charities. Charities. Leadership. Massachusetts (Fall River, Lynn). Men. Social Policy. 1880-1900. *1447*
—. Association for the Advancement of Women. Education. Mitchell, Maria. Science. 1870-89. *1035*
—. Association of Southern Women for the Prevention of Lynching. Lynching. Negroes. South. 1930-42. *2472*
—. Attitudes. Industry. National War Labor Board. Public Policy. Sex roles. Wages. World War I. 1918-19. *2191*
—. Attitudes. Mather, Cotton. New England. Sermons. 1650-1800. *493*
—. Authority. Freedmen. South. Teaching. 1865-70. *1425*
—. Baptists. Bishop, Harriet E. Minnesota (St. Paul). 1847-83. *295*
—. Baptists, Southern. 1700-1974. *66*
—. Barton, Clara. Red Cross. War. 1860's-90's. *1457*
—. Beecher, Catharine. Education. Employment. Professionalization. 1823-75. *182*
—. Beecher, Catharine. Physical Education and Training. Sex roles. 1830's-40's. *815*
—. Bell Canada. Ontario (Toronto). Strikes. Telephone operators. 1907. *1808*
—. Bevier, Isabel. Home economics. Illinois, University of. 1900-21. *2295*
—. Bible. Constitutional Amendments (19th). Equal Rights Amendment. State Legislatures. Tennessee. 1876-1974. *2904*
—. Birth control. Dickenson, Robert Latou. Physicians. Sanger, Margaret. Values. 1830-1970. *87*
—. Bradstreet, Anne. Hutchinson, Anne. Literature. Massachusetts Bay Colony. Religion. Social change. 1630's-70's. *489*
—. Brin, Fanny Fligelman. Jews. Minnesota (Minneapolis). Peace. 1913-60's. *453*
—. British Columbia (Vancouver). Labor Unions and Organizations. 1900-15. *1803*
—. California. Editors and Editing. Older, Fremont. Reporters and Reporting. San Francisco *Bulletin*. 1895-1925. *1887*
—. California (San Diego). Foltz, Clara Shortridge. Lawyers. 1872-1930. *413*
—. Canada. Christianity. Missions and Missionaries. Sex roles. 1815-99. *1490*
—. Canada. McClung, Nellie L. Methodist Church. Ordination. United Church of Canada. 1915-46. *1597*
—. Canada. Young Women's Christian Association. 1870-1900. *1469*
—. Carroll, Anna Ella. Nativism. Probasco, Harriet. 1840's-61. *797*
—. Catholic Church. Feminism. Quebec. Religious Orders. 1640-1975. *21*
—. Catholic Church. National Catholic Welfare Conference. National Council of Catholic Women. Peace Movements. 1919-46. *1636*
—. Centennial Exposition of 1876. Sex roles. Values. World's Columbian Exposition (Chicago, 1893). 1876-93. *948*
—. Charities. Pennsylvania (Philadelphia). Social work. Society for Organizing Charitable Relief and Repressing Mendicancy. 1864-1909. *1474*
—. Cherokee Indians. Christianity. Indian-White Relations. Missions and Missionaries. Property. Social Change. 19c. *107*
—. Child labor. Illinois. Law. 1890-1920. *1955*
—. Child labor. Industrialization. Iowa. Labor Unions and Organizations. 1900's. *1984*
—. Childbirth. Medical Reform. Twilight sleep. 1914-15. *2004*
—. Childhood. Leadership. Religion. Secularism. Sex roles. 1636-1930. *381*
—. Children. Missouri. St. Louis Children's Hospital. 1879-1979. *237*

—. Christian Science. Eddy, Mary Baker. Political power. 1879-99. *999*
—. Christianity. Grimké, Sarah Moore. Nature. Paul, Saint. Social organization. 1c. 1830's. *807*
—. Christianity. Industrial Relations. Massachusetts (Lawrence). Scudder, Vida Dutton. 1912. *2196*
—. Cincinnati College of Medicine and Surgery. Medical Education. Ohio. 1875-1910. *966*
—. Cities. Politics. Volunteerism. 1820-1978. *34*
—. Cities. Reform. Sanitation. 1880-1917. *1975*
—. Civil Rights Act (US, 1964; Title VIII). Discrimination, Employment. Income. Negroes. 1964-70's. *2839*
—. Civil rights movement. Freedom Summers. Sex Discrimination. 1960-65. *2882*
—. Civil rights movement. Race Relations. South. 1960's. *2907*
—. Civil War. Negroes. Reconstruction. Slavery. 19c. *331*
—. Civil-Military Relations. Labor. Publicity. War Manpower Commission. World War II. 1942-45. *2650*
—. Clergy. Equality. Mormons. Negroes. 1860-1979. *91*
—. Clergy. Ordination. United Brethren in Christ. 1889. *1489*
—. Coates, Sarah (letters). Lectures. Ohio. Physiology. 1850. *881*
—. Collar Laundry Union. Industrial Relations. Irish Americans. New York (Troy). 1864-69. *1352*
—. Colleges and Universities. Douglass, Mabel Smith. Lobbying. Middle Classes. New Jersey College for Women. 1911-18. *2324*
—. Colleges and Universities. Education. Ideology. Sex roles. 19c-20c. *213*
—. Colleges and Universities. Evangelicalism. Oberlin College. Ohio. 1835-50. *796*
—. Colleges and Universities. Grinnell College. Iowa. Sex roles. 1884-1917. *221*
—. Colleges and Universities. Nebraska, University of. Physical Education and Training. 1879-1923. *220*
—. Commercials. Fashion. Hygiene. Television. Women's Liberation Movement. 1970's. *2921*
—. Communes. Owen, Robert Dale. Sex roles. 1824-28. *931*
—. Conservatism. McCumber, Porter James. McKenzie, Alexander John. North Dakota. Political reform. Republican Party. Suffrage. 1898-1933. *435*
—. Constitutions, State. Jury. Lobbying. South Carolina. 1921-67. *1731*
—. Consumers. National Consumers' League. Progressive era. 1900-23. *2124*
—. Cotton. Hamilton Manufacturing Company. Labor Disputes. Massachusetts (Lowell). Social mobility. Textile Industry. 1836-60. *818*
—. Councils and Synods. Delegates. Episcopal Church, Protestant. Kinsolving, George Herbert. Texas. Veto. 1921-70. *2347*
—. Countryman, Gratia Alta. Libraries (public). Minnesota (Minneapolis). Reform. 1890's-1953. *424*
—. Courts. Discrimination, Employment. Labor law. 1876-1979. *43*
—. Darwinism. Feminism. 1850-1920. *88*
—. Decisionmaking. Federal Government. Interest Groups. Legislation. Politics. 1970's. *2911*
—. Democracy. Political Speeches. Prohibition. 1920-34. *2356*
—. Democracy. Politics. Social Change. 1634-1935. *106*
—. Democratic Party. House of Representatives. Human Rights. New Jersey. Norton, Mary T. 1920-30. *2415*
—. Diaries. Fox, Ruth May. Suffrage. Utah. 1865-95. *1119*
—. Discrimination, Educational. Female seminary movement. 1818-91. *202*
—. District of Columbia. Gillett, Emma M. Legal education. Mussey, Ellen Spencer. Washington College of Law. 1869-1949. *426*
—. Divorce. Law. Massachusetts. 1692-1786. *480*
—. Dohrn, Anton. Hyde, Ida H. Italy. Naples Zoological Station. Scientific Experiments and Research. 1896-97. *1434*
—. DuBois, W. E. B. Human rights. Negroes. 1910-20. *1874*
—. Economic opportunity. Educational achievements. Men. Sex Discrimination. 1962. 1973. *2908*

Women

—. Editors and Editing. Mormons. Utah. *Woman's Exponent* (periodical). 1872-1914. *3*
—. Education. Employment. Sex roles. Social Classes. 1964-74. *2919*
—. Education. New York. Troy Female Seminary. Willard, Emma Hart. 1809-70. *436*
—. Education. Pennsylvania (Philadelphia). Young Ladies Academy. 1780's-90's. *552*
—. Education. Science. ca 1800-60. *816*
—. Educational Reform. Jews. New York City. Richman, Julia. 1880-1912. *289*
—. Employment. Immigrants. Law Enforcement. Maximum hours laws. State Government. 1920. *2398*
—. Environmental Protection Agency. Equal Employment Opportunity Commission. Labor. Occupational Safety and Health Act (US, 1970). Safety. 1970-76. *2698*
—. Equal Legal Rights Amendment. Federation of Business and Professional Women's Clubs. Texas. 1957-72. *2909*
—. Equal rights. Integration. Prison reform. 1820's-1900. *1451*
—. Equal Rights Amendment. Florida. National Women's Party. Politics. West, Helen Hunt. 1917-52. *1727*
—. Equality. Lobbying. New York City. State Legislatures. Strachan, Grace. Teachers. Wages. 1907-11. *2202*
—. Equality. Social Status. 1900-70's. *1568*
—. Europe. Health. Working Conditions. 1869-1979. *47*
—. Europe. Pressure Groups. 1888-1920's. *48*
—. Evangelicalism. Self-expression. 1800-50. *799*
—. Everett Mill. Massachusetts (Lawrence). Polish Americans. Radicals and Radicalism. Strikes. Textile Industry. 1912. *2252*
—. Family. Labor. Social Organization. 1600-1970's. *54*
—. Fell, Margaret. Feminism. Friends, Society of. Great Britain (Lancashire). Pennsylvania (Philadelphia). 1670's. *498*
—. Feminism. Morality. Physical Education and Training. Sexuality. 19c. *101*
—. Feminism. Morality. Politics. 19c-20c. *142*
—. Feminism. Protestant Churches. Social Conditions. South. 1920's. *2339*
—. Feminization. Historiography. Protestantism. Welter, Barbara. 1820's-30's. 1970's. *910*
—. Fiction. Homosexuality. Periodicals. 1900-20. *1930*
—. Florida. 1890-1978. *1550*
—. Garment Industry. Illinois (Chicago). O'Reilly, Mary. Socialist Party. Strikes. Zeh, Nellie M. 1910. *2183*
—. Garment industry. International Ladies' Garment Workers' Union. Texas. 1933-50. *1770*
—. Garment Industry. Labor. Massachusetts (Boston). 1869. *1287*
—. Garment Industry. Labor. New York City. 1831-69. *820*
—. Gilman, Catheryne Cooke. Reform. Social work. 1904-54. *344*
—. Great Britain. Social status. 1925-65. *1551*
—. Grimké, Sarah Moore (letter). Sex discrimination. 1853. *803*
—. Health. Ladies' Physiological Institute of Boston and Vicinity. Massachusetts. Middle Classes. Physiology. 1848-59. *902*
—. Higher education. 1850-1970. *197*
—. Hollingsworth, Leta. Psychology. 1886-1938. *1885*
—. Illinois. Legislation. Reform. Wages. Working Conditions. 1893-1917. *2187*
—. Immigrants. Industrial Workers of the World. New York (Little Falls). Strikes. Textile Industry. 1912. *2269*
—. Industrialization. Railroads. 1890's. *962*
—. Jews. Labor Unions and Organizations. Malkiel, Theresa Serber. New York City. Socialist Party. 1900's-14. *2035*
—. Labor. Match industry. Quebec (Hull). Syndicat Catholique des Allumeftières. 1919-24. *1775*
—. Labor. Reform. Social status. 1830-60. *309*
—. Labor movement. Middle Classes. Schools, summer. South. 1927-41. *1580*
—. Labor movement. Working Conditions. 1840's. *828*
—. Labor reform. Lowell Female Labor Reform Association. New England. Textile Industry. 1845-47. *819*
—. Labor Reform. New York (Little Falls). Strikes. Textile Industry. 1912. *2268*

—. Labor Reform. Progressivism. Social Classes. 1882-1917. *2230*
—. Labor Unions and Organizations. ca 1880-1925. *159*
—. Labor Unions and Organizations. Libraries, public. 1917-20. *2243*
—. Labor Unions and Organizations. New York. 1900-20. *2266*
—. Law. New Mexico. Social Customs. 16c-1975. *1720*
—. Law. Occupations. Segregation. Sex Discrimination. 20c. *2910*
—. League of Women for Community Service. Massachusetts (Boston). Negroes. Voluntary Associations. 1918-77. *1575*
—. Legislation. Minimum wage. Occupations. Ohio. Sex Discrimination. 1914-33. *1539*
—. Lewis, Dioclesius. Medical reform. Morality. Rhythmics. Sex. 1860-1970's. *1481*
—. Literature. MacLane, Mary. Montana (Butte). 1902-29. *384*
—. Literature. Motherhood. Sex roles. 1785-1815. *793*
—. Literature. Sex roles. Social Change. 19c. *78*
—. Local Politics. Pennsylvania (Reading). Socialist Party. ca 1927-38. *1666*
—. Mann Act (US, 1910). Progressivism. Prostitution. 1910. *2003*
—. Massachusetts. Oral history. Sullivan, Anna (interview). Textile Workers Union of America. 1918-76. *403*
—. Massachusetts (Haverhill). Shoe Industry. Strikes. 1895. *1288*
—. Massachusetts (Lowell). Strikes. Values. 1820-50. *548*
—. McLean, Mary Hancock. Medicine (practice of). Missouri (St. Louis). 1883-1930. *359*
—. Mead, Margaret. Scholars. Social sciences. Talbot, Marion. Thompson, Helen. 1900-20's. *2065*
—. Medical reform. Middle Classes. 1820-70. *893*
—. Medical societies. 19c. *1032*
—. Methodist Protestant Church. 19c. *77*
—. Mexican Americans. Racism. Sterilization. 20c. *2704*
—. Military. Sex roles. World War II. 1941-44. *2628*
—. Missions and Missionaries. Organizations. Protestant Churches. 1870's-90's. *1493*
—. Morality. Politics. 19c-20c. *118*
—. Mormons. Snow, Eliza Roxey. 1830-90. *75*
—. Negroes. Nelson, Alice Dunbar. South. World War I. 1917-18. *1890*
—. New Deal. Political Participation. Roosevelt, Eleanor. 1900-36. *372*
—. New Jersey (Newark). Presbyterian Church. See, Isaac M. Sermons. 1876. *1485*
—. New York. Noyes, John Humphrey. Oneida Community. Sex. Social Status. 1848-79. *266*
—. O'Hare, Kate Richards. Socialist Party. 1901-17. *1878*
—. Ordination. Presbyterian Church (Committee of Four). 1926-30. *2346*
—. Oregon (Portland). Sabin, Ellen B. Teaching. Wisconsin. 1850-95. *405*
—. Physical Education and Training. Recreation. 1776-1865. *573*
—. Physical Education and Training. Wisconsin, University of. 1863-1913. *1436*
—. Police. 1905-75. *1702*
—. Presbyterian Church. 1800-1975. *82*
—. Progressive education. Sex roles. 1880-1940. *179*
—. Property rights. Reconstruction. South. State legislatures. 1865-95. *1103*
—. Protestantism. Sex roles. Sunday School Movement. 1790-1880. *180*
—. Protestantism. Social change. World Council of Churches. 1945-75. *2079*
—. Saskatchewan. Saskatoon Women Teachers' Association. Teachers. 1918-70's. *1627*
—. Social Change. 1700-1976. *86*
—. Socialist Party. Utah. 1900-20. *2086*
—. Southern Baptist Convention. 1860-1975. *60*
—. Temperance Movements. 1873-74. *958*
Women Remonstrants of the State of Illinois. Illinois Association Opposed to the Extension of Suffrage to Women. Suffrage. 1886-1923. *132*

Women's American Baptist Home Missionary Society. Baptists. Crawford, Isabel. Indians. Kiowa Indians. Missions and Missionaries. Oklahoma (Wichita Mountains). 1893-1961. *393*
Women's Christian Temperance Union. Alaska. Prohibition. 1842-1917. *255*
—. Colorado (Boulder). Feminism. 1881-1967. *232*
—. Demonstrations. Ohio (Cincinnati). Protestant Churches. Temperance Movements. 1874. *1446*
—. Social work. Wittenmyer, Annie Turner. ca 1855-1900. *1441*
Women's Foreign Missionary Society. Methodist Episcopal Church. Missions and Missionaries. 1869-1900. *1491*
Women's International League for Peace and Freedom. Detzer, Dorothy. Nye Committee. Peace Movements. Politics. 1920-34. *2430*
Women's Joint Committee. Cooperative Commonwealth Federation. Feminism. Leftism. Ontario (Toronto). 1930's. *1638*
Women's Journal (periodical). Blackwell, Henry B. Editors and Editing. Feminism. Politics. Stone, Lucy. 1870-1914. *1047*
Women's Liberation Movement. American Federation of Teachers. Teachers. 1916-73. *1687*
—. Canada. Courts. Indians. Lavell, Jeannette. Political participation. 1869-1979. *2914*
—. Child care centers. 1854-1973. *89*
—. Civil Rights Movement. Employment. Sex roles. 1950's-75. *2905*
—. Commercials. Fashion. Hygiene. Television. Women. 1970's. *2921*
—. Employment. World War II. 1920's-70's. *1529*
—. Freudianism. Literature. 1946-70's. *1599*
—. Labor. Sex roles. 19c-20c. *46*
—. Law. Scandinavia. Self-awareness. Social Change. 1840-1977. *35*
—. Lawyers. Lobbying. New Jersey. Philbrook, Mary. 1895-1947. *409*
—. Negroes. Sex Discrimination. 1960-75. *2733*
—. Political change. 19c-1970's. *58*
—. Population. Woman suffrage. Wyoming. 1869-1920. *1102*
—. Revolution. 1960's-70's. *2915*
Women's Organization for National Prohibition Reform. Prohibition. 1929-33. *2396*
Women's rights. Borg, Selma Josefina. Centennial Exposition of 1876. Finnish Americans. Lectures. Music. Pennsylvania (Philadelphia). 1858-90. *399*
—. Bradwell, Myra. Illinois (Chicago). Law reform. 1855-92. *1034*
—. Crandall, Prudence. Kansas (Elk County). Spiritualism. Temperance Movements. 1877-95. *1487*
—. Evolution. LeConte, Joseph. Science. Sex roles. 1890's. *1115*
—. Higher education. Lowry, Morrow B. Lowry, Morrow B. (letter). Pennsylvania. 1868. *1413*
—. Mill, John Stuart. Taylor, Harriet. ca 1850-73. *806*
—. News. Periodicals. 1922-76. *1544*
—. Pacific Northwest. Prohibition. Reform. Weed, Ada M. 1858-1910. *327*
—. Speeches, Addresses, etc. Wright, Frances. 1828-30. *801*
Women's Social and Political Union. Borden, Robert Laird. Canada. *Champion* (periodical). Great Britain. Woman suffrage. 1910-18. *1737*
Women's studies. Attitudes. Education. Socialization. 1600-1974. *187*
Women's Trade Union League. Anderson, Mary. Illinois (Chicago). Labor Unions and Organizations. Nestor, Agnes. Robins, Margaret Dreier. Women. Working conditions. 1903-20. *2190*
—. Class consciousness. Feminism. Great Britain. Labor Unions and Organizations. USA. 1890-1925. *2226*
—. Clerical workers. Labor Unions and Organizations. 1900-30. *1759*
—. Feminism. Labor Unions and Organizations. Lobbying. Middle Classes. Suffrage. ca 1903-20. *1980*
—. Labor Unions and Organizations. 1870-1920. *53*
—. Labor Unions and Organizations. *Life and Labor* (periodical). 1911-21. *2231*
—. Labor Unions and Organizations. New York. ca 1903-10. *2205*
—. Labor Unions and Organizations. New York City. 1903-14. *1924*

Wood, Edith Elmer. Bauer, Catherine. Federal Policy. Public housing. Reform. Wagner-Steagall Act (US, 1937). 1890's-1940's. *2479*
Wood, Leonard. Cuba. Military occupation. Progressivism. 1899-1902. *1951*
—. Military training. Muldoon, William. Physicians. Public health. 1890-1915. *2044*
Woodbey, George Washington. Negroes. Protestantism. Socialism. 1902-15. *1939*
Woodhull, Victoria Claflin. Beecher, Henry Ward. Feminism. New York City. Radicals and Radicalism. Sex. Vanderbilt, Cornelius. 1868-90's. *336*
—. Bloomer, Amelia. Iowa. Savery, Anne. State Politics. Woman suffrage. 1868-72. *1111*
Woodrum, Clifton A. Congressmen. New Deal. Politics. Roosevelt, Franklin D. Virginia. 1922-45. *433*
Woodson, Carter G. DuBois, W. E. B. Education. Ethnic studies. German Americans. Irish Americans. 1649-1972. *188*
—. Historiography. *Journal of Negro History* (periodical). Negroes. 1916-75. *1708*
Woodward, C. Vann. Compromise of 1877. Democratic Party. Elections (presidential). Reconstruction. Republican Party. 1876-77. *1086*
—. Genovese, Eugene D. Land reform. Race relations. Reconstruction. Social Classes. South Carolina (Edgefield County). 1865-90. *963*
Woodward, Calvin. Educational Reform. Manual training. Missouri (St. Louis). 1897-1914. *2305*
—. Educational Theory. Missouri (St. Louis). Vocational Education. Washington University (Manual Training School). 1879-1910. *1412*
Woolman, John. Abolition Movement. American Revolution. Friends, Society of. Pennsylvania. 1758-88. *530*
—. Antislavery Sentiments. British North America. Friends, Society of. Social problems. 1720-72. *478*
Work Cure Program. Devereux Mansion. Hall, Herbert. Massachusetts (Marblehead). Mental Illness. Occupational therapy. 1912-23. *1969*
Work, Monroe Nathan. Civil Rights. Negroes. Sociology. South. 1900-45. *388*
Work People's College. Finnish Americans. Immigrants. Labor. Minnesota (Smithville). Socialism. 1900-20. *2315*
Workers. See Labor; Working Class.
Workers' Unity League. British Columbia. Depressions. Industrial Relations. National Unemployed Workers' Association. Unemployment. 1930-39. *1830*
Working Class *See also* Labor; Social Classes.
—. Abel, Mary Hinman. Aladdin Ovens. Atkinson, Edward. Food Consumption. Massachusetts (Boston). New England Kitchen. Richards, Ellen H. 1889-97. *1467*
—. Addams, Jane. Education. Hull House. Illinois (Chicago). 1890's. *1426*
—. Adult education. Halifax Mechanics' Institute. Middle Classes. Nova Scotia. 1830's-40's. *845*
—. Agrarianism. Populism. Radicals and Radicalism. Wisconsin. 19c. *1399*
—. Anti-Catholicism. Know-Nothing Party. Maine. Morrill, Anson P. Nativism. 1854-55. *588*
—. Attitudes. Canada, western. Industrialization. Labor Unions and Organizations. Radicals and Radicalism. 1897-1919. *1745*
—. Attitudes. Industrialization. Rhode Island (Pawtucket). Strikes. Textile industry. 1824. *821*
—. Belgian Americans. French Canadian Americans. Independent Textile Workers. Rhode Island (Woonsocket). 1931-50's. *1767*
—. *Boston Daily Evening Voice* (newspaper). Equality. Labor Unions and Organizations. Massachusetts. Race Relations. 1864-67. *998*
—. Canada. Labor Unions and Organizations. 1845-75. *161*
—. Casson, Herbert N. Labor Church. Massachusetts (Lynn). Socialism. 1893-98. *1498*
—. Catholic Church. École Sociale Populaire. Propaganda. Quebec (Montreal). Syndicalism. 1911-49. *1806*
—. Child Welfare. Family. Foster homes. Immigration. Jews. New York City. 1900-05. *2061*
—. Class struggle. Reform. Standard of living. 1950's-73. *2923*

—. Dall, Caroline. Farley, Harriet. Feminism. Letters. 1850. *794*
—. Education. Long, Huey P. Louisiana. 1928-35. *2515*
—. Educational reform. Providence Association of Mechanics and Manufacturers. Rhode Island. 1790's-1850. *853*
—. Elections. McKinley, William. Ohio. Republican Party. 1891-93. *1355*
—. Ethnic groups. Labor Unions and Organizations. Ohio (Cincinnati). 1893-1920. *2247*
—. Ethnicity. Irish Americans. Land League. Radicals and Radicalism. Reform. 1880-83. *997*
—. Industrialization. Knights of St. Crispin. Loyalism. Massachusetts (Lynn). Radicals and Radicalism. 1820-90. *1298*
—. Labor. New Deal. Radicals and Radicalism. 1930's. *2524*
—. Labor Unions and Organizations. Massachusetts (Lynn). Shoe Industry. 1895-1925. *2197*
—. Lunn, George. New York (Schenectady). Socialist Party. Voting and Voting Behavior. 1911-16. *1946*
—. Massachusetts (Boston). Social Customs. Temperance movements. Values. 1838-40. *868*
—. Neighborhoods. New York City. Socialism. 1908-18. *2006*
—. Public Schools. Reform. Socialism. Wisconsin (Milwaukee). 1890-1920. *2329*
—. Railroad Carmen's Strike (1911-15). Scientific management. Strikes. 1903-22. *2256*
—. Railroads. Strikes. Violence. 1877. *1299*
—. Socialist Party. Woman suffrage. 1901-12. *1954*
Working Class Union. Green Corn Rebellion, 1917. Labor Unions and Organizations. Oklahoma. Radicals and Radicalism. 1914-17. *2284*
—. Jones Family (group). Oklahoma (Cleveland, Pottawatomie counties). Sedition. Trials. World War I. 1917. *2155*
Working Conditions. Accidents. California. Industrial safety. Tanneries. 1901-80. *2751*
—. Accidents. Courts. Federal Employers' Liability Act (US, 1908). Management. Railroads. Safety Appliances Act (US, 1893). 1890-1913. *2117*
—. Agriculture. Convict Labor. Louisiana State Prison (Angola). Prisons. 1900-78. *1701*
—. Anderson, Mary. Illinois (Chicago). Labor Unions and Organizations. Nestor, Agnes. Robins, Margaret Dreier. Women. Women's Trade Union League. 1903-20. *2190*
—. Boycotts. Immigrants. Irish Americans. Labor. New York City. 1880-86. *1311*
—. Cowboys. Strikes. Western States. 1870-90. *1324*
—. Europe. Health. Women. 1869-1979. *47*
—. Hawthorne First Relay Assembly Test Room. Productivity. Research. 1927-32. *2428*
—. Illinois. Legislation. Reform. Wages. Women. 1893-1917. *2187*
—. Industrial Relations. Migration, Internal. Negroes. Pine industry. South. ca 1912-26. *1577*
—. Labor. New Jersey (Passaic). Strikes. Textile industry. 1875-1926. *2366*
—. Labor. Red baiting. Socialism. 1871-1920. *154*
—. Labor movement. Women. 1840's. *828*
—. Labor Non-Partisan League. Legislation. Political representation. 1936-38. *2605*
—. National Cash Register Company. Ohio (Dayton). Patterson, John H. Physical Education and Training. 1890-1915. *169*
—. North Dakota Workmen's Compensation Bureau. Rice, Hazel F. (account). Transportation. 1919-22. *2432*
Workingmen's Party. Missouri (St. Louis). Political Leadership. Racism. Social Classes. Strikes. 1877. *1338*
Workingmen's Party of California. California. Chinese. Constitutions, State. Federal Regulation. Labor reform. 1877-82. *1358*
Workman's Compensation Act (US, 1916). Kern, John W. Labor Law. Senate. 1908-17. *2221*
Workmen's Compensation. Coal Mine Health and Safety Act (US, 1969; amended, 1972). Coal Mines and Mining. Medicine. Strikes, wildcat. United Mine Workers of America. 1968-72. *2717*
—. Brewing industry. Labor Unions and Organizations. 1910-12. *2204*
—. Business. Capitalism. Illinois. Legislation. 1905-12. *2189*

—. Commission on Industrial Accidents. Industry. Provincial Government. Quebec. 1890-1978. *1584*
—. Labor Unions and Organizations. Lumber and Lumbering. Washington. 1911. *2280*
—. Minnesota. 1909-13. *2173*
Works Progress Administration. Conservatism. Creel, George. New Deal. Progressivism. 1900-53. *1520*
World Council of Churches. Protestantism. Social change. Women. 1945-75. *2917*
World Parliament of Religions. American, Sadie. Congress of Jewish Women. Jews. Solomon, Hannah G. Women. World's Columbian Exposition (Chicago, 1893). 1893. *1488*
World Temperance Convention. Beecher, Lyman. Evangelical Alliance. Great Britain. Temperance Movements. 1846. *889*
World War I *See also* battles and campaigns by name.
—. Academic freedom. Minnesota, University of. Schaper, William A. 1917. *2143*
—. Alaska (Anchorage). Labor Unions and Organizations. Lewis, Lena Morrow. Railroads. Socialist Party. 1916-18. *2001*
—. American Plan. Council of National Defense. Federal government. Prostitution. Social policy. Venereal disease. Voluntary associations. 1917-21. *2048*
—. Americanization. German Americans. 1914-17. *1935*
—. Anti-German sentiment. Bouck, William. Freedom of Assembly. Grange. Public Opinion. Vigilantes. Washington (Walla Walla). 1918. *2161*
—. Antimilitarism. Democracy. Jordan, David Starr. 1898-1917. *1867*
—. Antiwar Sentiment. Christianity. Public Opinion. 1898-1918. *1889*
—. Antiwar sentiment. Labor Unions and Organizations. Socialism. 1914-17. *1982*
—. Arizona (Globe). Copper Mines and Mining. Strikes. Western Federation of Miners. 1917. *2255*
—. Armaments Industry. Connecticut (Bridgeport). Industrial Relations. Technology. 1915-19. *2182*
—. Attitudes. Industry. National War Labor Board. Public Policy. Sex roles. Wages. Women. 1918-19. *2191*
—. British Columbia (Trail). Consolidated Mining and Smelting Company. Immigration. Mine, Mill and Smelter Workers, International Union of. Strikes. 1916-17. *1810*
—. Christianity. Conscientious objectors. Pacifism. Thomas, Norman. 1915-18. *2136*
—. Communism. Kollontai, Aleksandra. Norway. Propaganda. Russia. 1915-16. *2046*
—. Conscientious Objectors. Espionage Act of 1917. North Dakota. O'Hare, Kate Richards. Pacifism. 1900-25. *2131*
—. Food and Drug Administration. Great Plains. Labor. Radicals and Radicalism. Social change. Veblen, Thorstein. 1918. *1922*
—. Freedom of speech. Oklahoma. Political Repression. Vigilantes. 1914-17. *2137*
—. Freedom of speech. Pacifism. Virginia, University of. Whipple, Leon. 1917. *2130*
—. Industrial Workers of the World. Justice Department. Labor Unions and Organizations. Nebraska. Public opinion. 1915-20. *2113*
—. Industrial Workers of the World. Kansas (Wichita). Labor Unions and Organizations. Oil Industry and Trade. Trials. *United States v. C. W. Anderson et al.* (US, 1919). 1917-19. *2171*
—. Intellectuals. Law Enforcement. Radicals and Radicalism. 1914-20. *2158*
—. Jones Family (group). Oklahoma (Cleveland, Pottawatomie counties). Sedition. Trials. Working Class Union. 1917. *2155*
—. Kansas. Liberty bonds. Mennonites. Pacifism. Vigilantism. 1918. *2146*
—. Navy League (Woman's Section). Preparedness. Sex roles. Suffrage. Woman's Peace Party. 1914-18. *2092*
—. Negroes. Nelson, Alice Dunbar. South. Women. 1917-18. *1890*
World War II *See also* battles and campaigns by name.
—. Adoption. Baker, Josephine. Civil rights. Entertainers. Negroes. 1940-75. *358*
—. American Federation of Labor. Discrimination, Employment. Fair Employment Practices Committee. Federal Government. Labor Unions and Organizations. Shipbuilding. West Coast Master Agreement. 1939-46. *2627*

World War II

—. Antiwar Sentiment. Fellowship of Reconciliation. 1940-41. *2655*
—. Armies. Discrimination. Great Britain. White, Walter F. 1943-44. *2626*
—. Armies. Films (documentaries). Heisler, Stuart. *Negro Soldier* (film). Propaganda. Race Relations. 1944. *2621*
—. Armies. Hastie, William H. Military recruitment. Negroes. Press. 1940-42. *2638*
—. Attitudes. Canada. Citizenship. Japanese. USA. 1941-58. *1730*
—. Baptists. Discrimination. Japanese Americans. Resettlement. 1890-1970. *1651*
—. British Columbia. Canada. Chinese Canadians. Japanese Canadians. Military Service. 1939-45. *2647*
—. Business. Labor Unions and Organizations. New Deal. Taft-Hartley Act (US, 1947). Wagner Act (US, 1935). 1935-47. *1749*
—. Canada. Fairbairn, R. Edis. Pacifism. United Church of Canada. 1939. *2646*
—. Canada. Japanese Canadians. Race Relations. Removals, forced. 1890's-1940's. *1694*
—. Canadian Labour Congress. Cooperative Commonwealth Federation. Federal Government. Industrial relations. Trades and Labour Congress of Canada. 1939-46. *2634*
—. City Planning. Oregon (Portland). 1940-45. *2616*
—. Civic Unity Committee. Defense industries. Japanese Americans. Negroes. Race relations. Washington (Seattle). 1940-45. *2624*
—. Civil rights. Congress. Discrimination, employment. Fair Employment Practices Committee. Roosevelt, Franklin D. (administration). 1941-46. *2640*
—. Civil Rights. Nebraska (Omaha). Negroes. Quality of life. Social services. Urban League. 1928-50. *2639*
—. Civil service. Conscription, military. Mennonites. 1930's-45. *2632*
—. Civil-Military Relations. Labor. Publicity. War Manpower Commission. Women. 1942-45. *2650*
—. Communist Party. National Maritime Union. Negroes. Racism. United Electrical, Radio and Machine Workers of America. 1941-45. *2622*
—. Congress of Industrial Organizations. Oil Industry and Trade. Texas. 1942-43. *2631*
—. Corporations. Wage-price controls. 1941-45. *2645*
—. Defense Policy. Federal Policy. Industry. Labor Unions and Organizations. 1939-41. *2593*
—. Discrimination. Fair Employment Practices Committee. Negroes. Railroads. Southeastern Carriers Conference. 1941-45. *2630*
—. Discrimination, employment. Fair Employment Practices Committee. Minorities. South. 1941-45. *2644*
—. Employment. Feminism. Organizations. Racism. Social classes. 1942-45. *2629*
—. Employment. Women's liberation movement. 1920's-70's. *1529*
—. Hastie, William H. Military. Negroes. Racism. Stimson, Henry L. 1940-43. *2636*
—. Hastie, William H. Military reform. Racism. 1940-43. *2637*
—. Historiography. Negroes. Roosevelt, Franklin D. (administration). USSR. 1939-45. *2648*
—. Internment. Japanese Americans. Martial law. Tule Lake Camp. 1941-44. *2641*
—. Jewish Peace Fellowship. Peace Movements. 1943. *2654*
—. Military. Sex roles. Women. 1941-44. *2628*
—. Negroes. Newspapers. Political Protest. Race Relations. 1941-45. *2625*

World War II (antecedents). American Peace Mobilization. Communist Party USA. Isolationism. 1939-41. *2651*
—. Antiwar Sentiment. Keep America Out of War Congress. Socialist Party. Thomas, Norman. Villard, Oswald Garrison. 1938-41. *2501*

World's Columbian Exposition (Chicago, 1893). Adventists. Illinois. Jones, Alonzo Trevier. Religious liberty. Sunday. 1893. *1492*
—. American, Sadie. Congress of Jewish Women. Jews. Solomon, Hannah G. Women. World Parliament of Religions. 1893. *1488*
—. Centennial Exposition of 1876. Sex roles. Values. Women. 1876-93. *948*

Wounded Knee (occupation). American Indian Movement. Deloria, Vine, Jr. Federal Government. Indians. Political Protest. South Dakota. 1877-1970's. *2712*
—. American Indian Movement. Indians. Pine Ridge Indian Reservation. South Dakota. 1972-75. *2749*

Wright, Elizur, Jr. Abolition Movement. Ohio, northeastern. 1829-32. *643*

Wright, Frances. Bentham, Jeremy. Birth control. Carlile, Richard. Feminism. Great Britain. Owen, Robert Dale. Place, Francis. Propaganda. 1790-1840. *817*
—. Feminism. Lectures. 1820's-30's. *813*
—. Speeches, Addresses, etc. Women's rights. 1828-30. *801*

Wright, Frances (letters). Emancipation. Owen, Robert Dale. Tennessee (Nashoba). Utopias. 1820-29. *718*

Wright, Henry Clarke. Evangelism. Reform. 1820-60. *447*
—. Human Relations. Radicals and Radicalism. Sex. 1830-66. *805*

Wright, Richard. Literature. Negroes. 1908-60. *348*
—. Literature. Negroes. Radicals and Radicalism. 1920-60. *305*

Wyoming *See also* Western States.
—. Population. Woman suffrage. Women's Liberation Movement. 1869-1920. *1102*

Wyoming (Casper). Political Corruption. Prohibition. 1919-33. *2388*

Y

Yellow fever. Cholera. Howard Association. Louisiana (New Orleans). Philanthropy. Public health. 1837-78. *235*
—. Cuba. Medical ethics. Medical research. Reed, Walter. 1900-01. *1883*

Yellowstone National Park. Montana. National Park Service. Roosevelt, Theodore. Wildlife conservation. 1883-1918. *2079*

Yorke, Peter C. California (San Francisco). Catholic Church. City Politics. Irish Americans. Progressivism. 1900's. *2114*

Young America movement. Democratic Party. Douglas, Stephen A. Political Factions. Sanders, George. 1850's. *547*

Young Ladies Academy. Education. Pennsylvania (Philadelphia). Women. 1780's-90's. *552*

Young Men's Christian Association. Adolescence. Boys. Canada. Protestantism. USA. 1870-1920. *63*

Young, Plummer B. Civil rights. Hancock, George B. Jackson, Luther P. Negroes. Virginia. 1930-45. *1583*
—. Norfolk *Journal and Guide* (newspaper). Race Relations. Virginia. Washington, Booker T. 1904-20's. *2096*

Young, Robert J. Industrial safety. Reform. "Safety First" (slogan). ca 1900-16. *1886*

Young v. *MPAA* (US, 1965). Blacklisting. Communists. Courts. Film industry. Hollywood Ten. 1947-73. *1736*

Young, Virginia Durant. South Carolina. Woman suffrage. 1890-1903. *1117*

Young Women's Christian Association. Canada. Women. 1870-1900. *1469*

Youth *See also* Adolescence; Children; Youth Movements.
—. Addams, Jane. Sex roles. Women. 1860-89. *308*
—. Bethune, Mary McLeod. Equal opportunity. National Youth Administration. Negroes. Public Policy. 1935-44. *2594*
—. Bushnell, Horace. Christianity. Economic conditions. Gladden, Washington. Politics. Social gospel. 1836-1918. *995*
—. California. Education. Preston School of Industry. Prisons. Rehabilitation. 1894-1955. *1558*
—. Catholic Church. Religious Education. Saskatchewan. 1870-1978. *207*
—. Ireland (Limerick). Irish Americans. Labor Unions and Organizations. Leadership. McCarthy, Patrick Henry. 1863-80. *402*
—. Navajo-Hopi Long Range Rehabilitation Act (US, 1950). War on Poverty. 1950-60's. *1783*

Youth Movements *See also* Demonstrations.
—. Anarchism and Anarchists. New Left. Rightists. 1968-73. *2708*
—. Christianity. Jesus People. 1960's. *2695*
—. Fisk University. Race Relations. Tennessee (Nashville). 1909-26. *2397*
—. New Left. Students. 1905-70. *2760*
—. Radicals and Radicalism. Students for a Democratic Society. 1950's. 1960's. *2720*

Yugoslavia. Čačić, Tomo. Canada. Communist Party. Croatians. ca 1913-69. *415*

Z

Zeh, Nellie M. Garment Industry. Illinois (Chicago). O'Reilly, Mary. Socialist Party. Strikes. Women. 1910. *2183*

Zurcher, George. Catholic Church. Prohibition. 1884-1920's. *1442*

15th Ward Relief Society. Kimball, Sarah Melissa Granger. Mormons. Utah. Woman Suffrage. 1818-98. *397*

25th Infantry, US (Company D). Fort McIntosh. Negroes. Riots. Texas (Laredo). 1899. *1143*

AUTHOR INDEX

A

Abbey, Sue Wilson 2338
Abbott, Carl 2616
Abel, Emily K. 2294
Abeles, Ronald P. 2793
Abernathy, Mollie C. 2339
Abrahams, Edward H. 1359
Abrahamson, James L. 1867
Abrams, Douglas Carl 2340
Accinelli, Robert D. 2466
Ackerman, Bruce A. 2341
Adams, David Wallace 1087
Adams, Paul K. 1401
Adams, Pauline 1393
Aday, Lu Ann 2975
Agan, Thomas 1868
Agre, Gene P. 2903
Ahern, Wilbert H. 944 945
Akers, Charles W. 504
Akin, Edward N. 1125
Akpan, M. B. 1126 2342
Albin, Mel 308
Aldrich, Mark 1360 1869 1870
Aldridge, Delores P. 1831
Alexander, Roberta Sue 1127
Allain, Mathé 505
Allen, Bernadene V. 2794
Allen, Ernest 1519
Allen, Howard W. 1871 1914
Allen, Jeffrey Brooke 602 603
Allen, Jodie T. 1872
Allen, John E. 2467
Allen, Margaret V. 272
Allen, Theodore 472
Allen, William R. 2468
Almaraz, Felix D., Jr. 2957
Alschuler, Albert W. 109
Alsikafi, M. H. 2819
Alsobrook, David E. 273
Altschuler, Glenn C. 1923
Alvis, Joel L., Jr. 2795
Ammerman, Nancy T. 2796
Amsden, Jon 1284
Anders, Leslie 946
Andersen, Arlow W. 1285
Andersen, Ronald 2975
Anderson, David L. 947
Anderson, James D. 1832 2172
Anderson, William A. 2797 2798
Andrew, John 829
Andrews, Andrea R. 1402
Andrews, Edward Deming 912
Andrews, Faith 912
Andrews, William D. 948
Annunziata, Frank 274 275 1520 1738
Ansley, Fran 1286
Anstey, Roger 792
Apostol, Jane 276 277
Appleton, Thomas H., Jr. 1873
Aptheker, Bettina 1128 1874
Aptheker, Herbert 110
Arber, Sara 2919
Arendale, Marirose 2904
Argersinger, Peter H. 949
Armand, Laura 2806
Arndt, Karl J. R. 913 1499 1500
Arnez, Nancy L. 2799
Arnold, Frank 1739
Aron, William S. 2692
Arroyo, Luis Leobardo 1521
Ashby, LeRoy 1875 2343
Asher, Robert 1740 2173 2174
Ashworth, John 537
Askol'dova, S. M. 2175
Atwater, Edward C. 830
Aubéry, Pierre 2693
Auerbach, Jerold S. 1522
Auger, Deborah A. 2694
August, Jack 2469
Austin, Michael J. 1523
Avery, Donald H. 278 1524
Avery, Inda 2470
Avillo, Philip J., Jr. 950 1088
Avrich, Paul 1501

Axinn, June 222

B

Babcock, Robert 1741
Babu, B. Ramesh 2471
Bacchi, Carol 1 111
Baehre, Rainer 857
Bailey, Hugh C. 1876
Bailey, Kenneth R. 2176
Bailey, Robert J. 2617
Baily, Marilyn 604
Bainbridge, William Sims 2443
Baker, Mary Roys 473
Baker, Robert A. 506
Baldasty, Gerald J. 2656
Baldwin, Roger 279
Balswick, Jack 2695
Bammi, Vivek 1525
Banks, Carol M. 1137
Banner, Lois W. 858
Banning, Evelyn I. 951
Baral, J. K. 2696
Barber, Henry E. 2472
Barbour, Hugh 474
Barclay, Morgan J. 280
Barjenbruch, Judith 952
Barkan, Steven E. 1526
Barker, Fred A. 2177
Barker-Benfield, G. J. 281
Barkey, Charles H. 2801
Barlett, Irving H. 605
Barlow, William 1403
Barnard, Kate 1877
Barnes, Joseph W. 589
Barnes, William R. 2618
Barney, Robert Knight 606 1404
Barron, F. L. 859
Barron, Milton L. 2697
Bartow, Beverly 2295
Basen, Neil K. 1878
Basilick, Linda 2770
Baskerville, Stephen W. 2473
Bassett, Michael 1879
Bateman, Herman E. 1880
Bates, J. Leonard 1361
Bator, Paul Adolphus 1527
Bauer, Anne 860
Baughman, James L. 2474
Baum, Dale 538 1881
Baum, Gregory 1742
Bauman, John F. 1528 2475
Bauman, Mark K. 1882 2344
Baxandall, Rosalyn Fraad 1287
Baxandall, Rosalynn Fraad 282
Beales, Ross W., Jr. 1405
Bean, William B. 1883
Beardsley, Edward H. 1884
Beatty, Bess 283
Beauchamp, Claude 148 1743
Beauchamp, Gorman 262
Beck, Jeanne M. 284
Beck, Leonard N. 285
Becker, Robert A. 475
Beddow, James B. 2476
Beeler, Dorothy 2657
Beeten, Neil 2178
Beezer, Bruce G. 2477
Behr, Ted 2947
Bell, Brenda 1286
Bell, Carolyn 2698
Bellamy, Donnie D. 1744 2296 2800
Belz, Herman 1091 1129 1130 1131
Bender, George A. 286
Bendixen, Alfred 2
Benedict, Michael Les 953
Benjamin, Daniel K. 2606
Benjamin, Ludy T., Jr. 1885
Bennett, Dianne 1886
Bennett, Donald C. 2993
Bennion, Sherilyn Cox 3 1092 1887
Bercuson, David Jay 1745 1746 2179
Berens, John F. 1716
Berfield, Karen 607

Berger, Alan L. 2986
Berger, Bennett M. 2987
Bergesen, Albert 1132
Berkin, Carol Ruth 40 78 287 417 552 1352 1529 2065 2092 2516 2906
Berkowitz, Edward D. 1829 2345 2658 2659 2976
Berliner, Howard S. 2297
Bernard, Joel 288
Berney, Barbara 1747
Bernier, Jacques 861
Bernson, Sarah L. 4
Bernstein, Ilene N. 2725
Berrol, Selma 289
Berthrong, Donald J. 1888
Berwanger, Eugene H. 1133 1134 1135
Best, Gary Dean 2180
Beth, Loren P. 1717
Betke, Carl 1748
Betten, Neil 1523
Bicha, Karel D. 1362 1363 1364 1530
Biebel, Charles D. 2478
Bigham, Darrel E. 1889
Biklen, Sari Knopp 179
Billings, Warren M. 507
Billington, Louis 608
Billington, Monroe 1531
Binder, Arnold 112
Binion, Gayle 2801
Binning, F. Wayne 954 1136
Birch, Eugenie Ladner 1532 2479
Birrell, A. J. 1439
Black, Earl 1533
Black, Merle 2802 2803
Blackett, R. J. M. 290 609 610 611
Blackford, Mansel G. 2181
Blackwelder, Julia Kirk 2804
Blake, Cecil A. 291
Blanchard, Margaret A. 1534
Bland, Gaye K. 1365
Bland, Sidney R. 2128
Blaser, Kent 612
Blayney, Michael S. 2480
Blewett, Mary H. 1288
Blick, Boris 1502
Bloch, Herman D. 1137
Bloch, Ruth H. 793
Blochowiak, Mary Ann 1440
Blocker, Jack S., Jr. 1441
Blodgett, Geoffrey 292 955 956
Bloom, Leonard 2298
Blouet, Brian W. 1395
Blumberg, Dorothy Rose 293
Blume, Norman 2805
Blumenthal, Dan 2977
Bochin, Hal W. 540
Bodemann, Y. Michal 2988
Bodine, John J. 1718
Boender, Debra R. 2660
Boffard, Jean-Claude 2806
Bogardus, Ralph F. 957
Bogin, Ruth 294
Boivin, Aurélien 1535
Boles, John B. 541
Bolin, Winifred D. Wandersee 295
Bollinger, Heil D. 5
Bolt, Christine 6 638 699 765 774 789
Bonacich, Edna 613
Bonney, Margaret Atherton 914
Bonthius, Andrew 2481
Borden, Morton 1484
Bordin, Ruth 958
Borisiuk, V. I. 1749
Borit, G. S. 1138
Born, Kate 1750
Boryczka, Ray 2482
Bos, Johanna W. H. 2740
Bosmajian, Haig A. 2129 2765 2807
Boston, Ray 296
Boulton, Scot W. 2808
Bouthillier, Guy 2766
Bowen, Norman 2806
Bower, Robert K. 297
Bowers, William J. 2784

Bowles, Dorothy 1719
Boxerman, Burton A. 298
Boyd, Lois A. 1485
Boydston, Jo Ann 1536
Boylan, Anne M. 180
Brabham, Robin 1406
Brackenridge, R. Douglas 2346
Braden, Anne 2809
Bradley, Michael R. 476
Brady, James E. 1442
Brandes, Joseph 1751
Brasseaux, Carl A. 508
Braungart, Margaret M. 1537
Braungart, Richard G. 1537
Brax, Ralph S. 2483
Breen, William J. 1890
Breily, Ronald 1538
Bremer, William W. 2484
Brenzel, Barbara M. 1443 1444
Brewer, Paul W. 862
Briceland, Alan V. 299
Bridenthal, Renate 48
Brier, Stephen 1139 1140 1284
Brinkley, Alan 2485
Briscoe, Jerry B. 2699
Brito, Patricia 1539
Britts, Maurice W. 181
Brodhead, Michael J. 959
Bromberg, Alan B. 300 960 1366 2130
Bromert, Roger 2486
Brommel, Bernard J. 2131
Brooks, George E., Jr. 614
Brooks, Juanita 301
Brown, Delindus R. 615
Brown, E. Richard 1833
Brown, Ira V. 616 617
Brown, Lawrence L. 2347
Brown, Lorne 1752
Brown, Steve 2511
Brown, Thomas Elton 2348
Brown, Thomas J. 1367
Browne, Gary L. 149
Broyles, Glen J. 2132
Brudnoy, David 1486
Bruns, Roger A. 509
Bryan, C. Hobson 2819
Brym, Robert J. 2700
Bryson, Thomas A. 1891
Buchanan, Jess 1407
Buchholtz, C. W. 7
Buchstein, Frederick D. 302
Bucki, Cecelia F. 2182
Buckley, Thomas E. 510
Buhle, Mari Jo 36 2183
Buhle, Paul 1289 1753 2349
Bukowski, Douglas 2350
Bulkley, Peter B. 2487
Bullock, Robert D., Jr. 303
Bullock, Charles S., III 2810 2811
Bullough, Vern L. 8
Bullough, William A. 1892
Burbank, Garin 1714 1893
Burckel, Nicholas C. 961 1894 1895 1896 1897
Burgchardt, Carl R. 1540
Burger, John S. 322
Burger, Robert H. 2958
Burgess, Charles 1408
Burke, Padraic 2184
Burke, Ronald K. 618
Burkett, Randall K. 2351
Burki, Mary Ann Mason 1898
Burman, Stephen 2812
Burnett, Joe R. 1834
Burnham, John C. 1541 1899
Burns, Augustus M., III 1835
Burns, Chester R. 1900
Burran, James A. 1901 2185
Burson, George S., Jr. 1542
Burstein, Paul 2813
Burstyn, Joan N. 182 962
Burt, Larry W. 2661
Burton, Vernon 963
Bush, Robert D. 915
Bushnell, Amy 9
Butchart, Ronald Eugene 429
Butler, Janet G. 301
Butler, Johnnella 1543
Butler, Matilda 1544

Butler, Raymond V. 1545
Buttel, Frederick H. 1546
Button, James 2814
Bykov, Vil' 304
Byrkit, James W. 2186

C

Cain, Lee C. 831
Calderwood, William 1547
Calkins, David L. 832
Calvert, Robert A. 1714
Campanaro, Giorgio G. 390
Campbell, Ballard C. 1445
Campbell, Clarice T. 1141
Campbell, D'Ann 1902
Campbell, Finley C. 305
Campbell, Karlyn Kohrs 964
Candela, Joseph L., Jr. 2187
Candeloro, Dominic 306 965 1903 1904 2188 2299 2352
Cangi, Ellen Corwin 966
Cantor, Milton 821
Capeci, Dominic J., Jr. 307 2619
Cardinal, Eric J. 619
Carey, Patrick W. 905
Carlisle, Rodney 620
Carlisle, Rodney P. 2488
Carlson, Oliver 1548
Carmony, Donald F. 916
Carney, George O. 1905
Carpenter, Gerald 2353
Carper, James Carothers 1409
Carper, N. Gordon 2354
Carr, Joe Daniel 2489
Carriere, Marcus 542
Carriker, Robert C. 1549
Carroll, Berenice A. 54 213 2226
Carroll, Michael P. 967
Carruthers, Iva E. 183
Carson, Ruth 968
Cart, Theodore W. 536
Carter, Dan T. 969
Carter, David G. 1843
Carter, Doris Dorcas 1836
Carter, George E. 2815
Carter, L. Edward 2355
Carter, Paul A. 2356
Carvalho, Joseph, III 1290
Carver, Joan S. 1550
Cary, Francine C. 263
Cary, Lorin Lee 1291 1906 2357
Casdorph, Paul D. 1837
Casey, Orben J. 1907
Casillas, Mike 1908
Casino, Joseph J. 477
Cassedy, James H. 863 864
Cassity, Michael J. 150 1292 2490
Castile, George P. 970
Castrovinci, Joseph L. 2189
Cauthen, Irby B., Jr. 833
Cavaioli, Frank J. 2701
Cavallo, Dominick 184 308 1909
Celenza, James 2349
Chafe, William 2816
Chafetz, Janet Saltzman 1551
Chalmers, John W. 2959
Chambers-Schiller, Lee 309
Chandler, Robert 971
Chapman, James K. 310
Chapman, Paul Davis 2300
Cherry, Robert 2923
Chevigny, Bell Gale 311
Chicoineau, Jacques C. 264
Chipman, Donald D. 2301
Chittenden, Elizabeth F. 312 1093
Choquette, Robert 185
Christadler, Martin 1965
Christensen, Lawrence O. 313 1142
Christian, Garna L. 1143
Christian, Marcus 590
Christian, William A., Sr. 478
Christians, Clifford G. 1910
Christie, Jean 2491
Cimprich, John 972 1144

AUTHOR INDEX

Cirillo, Vincent J. 543
Clanton, O. Gene 10 959
Clark, E. Culpepper 973
Clark, Malcolm, Jr. 11
Clark, Nancy Tisdale 1911
Clark, Roger W. 1446
Clark, S. D. 2702
Clarke, John Henrik 2358
Clayton, John 1912
Clement, Priscilla Ferguson 544
Cleveland, Len G. 545 2662
Cleveland, Mary L. 2663
Clifford, Deborah P. 113 1094
Clow, Richmond L. 1913
Cloward, Richard 2941
Cloyd, Daniel Lee 974
Clubb, Jerome M. 1871 1914
Cluster, Dick 2880
Cofer, Richard 2359
Coffey, David M. 917
Cohen, Abby 1915
Cohen, David K. 2817 2960
Cohen, Ronald D. 2075
Colburn, David R. 1552 2133 2360
Cole, Babalola 186
Cole, Cheryl L. 12
Cole, Terrence 314
Coleburn, David R. 2664
Coleman, Michael C. 13
Collins, Thomas W. 2969
Comeau, Robert 1754
Comeault, Gilbert-L 1410
Condran, John G. 2818
Conforti, Joseph A. 479 511
Conklin, Forrest 865 866
Conley, John A. 1553
Conlin, Joseph R. 2113 2171 2207 2235 2254 2269 2290 2411 2434 2569
Conn, Sandra 2190
Conner, Valerie J. 2191
Conway, J. F. 14 1368
Conway, Jill 187
Coode, Thomas H. 2492
Cook, Bernard A. 1293 2192 2193
Cook, James F. 2620
Cook, Ramsay 975
Cook, Sylvia 2361
Coombs, David W. 2819
Cooney, Terry A. 2493
Cooper, Algia R. 1554
Cooper, Jerry M. 1294
Cooper, Richard J. 1838
Coray, Michael S. 976
Corbin, David A. 1755 2194 2195
Corcoran, Theresa 2196
Corner, George W. 2820
Cortada, James W. 1145
Corwin, Margaret 315
Coté, Joseph A. 1555
Cotkin, George B. 1295 1296
Cott, Nancy F. 480
Cotton, Carol 1916
Courville, L. D. 1556
Cousins, Leone B. 621
Couto, Richard 2821
Covell, Ruth M. 2978
Cowdrey, Albert E. 977
Cox, Archibald 1557
Cox, J. Robert 1917
Cox, Steven 316
Craven, Martha Jacquelyn 317
Creagh, Ronald 546
Creed, David A. 978
Crider, Gregory L. 979
Cripps, Thomas 1918 2621
Critchlow, Donald T. 2362 2622
Crofts, Daniel W. 1919
Crooks, James B. 1920
Crouch, Archie 15
Crouch, Barry A. 1146 1147 1148
Crouch, Ben M. 2848
Crouchett, Lawrence P. 188
Crow, Jeffrey J. 622 1369
Crow, Leslie 1558
Crowder, Ralph L. 16
Crowe Carrasco, Carol 1559
Crowley, Weldon S. 318
Cudd, John 623
Cuddihy, William 512
Cuddy, Edward 2363

Culbert, David 2621
Culley, Margaret 980
Culton, Donald R. 319
Cumberland, William H. 2134
Cumbler, John T. 1447 2197
Cummings, Melbourne 1149
Cuneo, Carl J. 2623
Current, Richard N. 981
Currie, James T. 114 982
Curry, Jane 983
Curry, Richard O. 984
Curtis, Bruce 985 1921
Curtis, Peter H. 320
Czajka, John L. 2919
Czuchlewski, Paul E. 1560

D

DaCosta, Emilia Viotti 792
Dahlie, Jorgen 321 1561 1562
Damiani, Alessandro 2494
Damsteegt, P. Gerard 867
Danbom, David B. 547 1922 2302
Daniel, Cletus E. 1756 2198 2495 2496
Daniel, Mike 986
Daniel, W. Harrison 624
Daniell, Elizabeth Otto 987
Daniels, Doris 2135
Dann, Martin 1150
Dannenbaum, Jed 1448
Darling, Arthur Burr 834
Datta, Lois-Ellin 2961
Davenport, F. Gorvin 1449
Davidson, Charles N., Jr. 1563
Davidson, Rondel V. 918
Davies, J. Kenneth 1297
Davin, Eric Leif 2497
Davis, Cullom 443
Davis, David Brion 792
Davis, Harold Eugene 223
Davis, Rodney O. 1487
Davis, Ronald L. F. 2199
Davison, Kenneth E. 988
Dawley, Alan 1298
Dawson, Joseph G., III 989 990 991
Dayton, Donald W. 17
Dayton, Lucille Sider 17
Dearstyne, Bruce W. 2200
DeBenedetti, Charles 1564
Debo, Angie 2703
Debouzy, Marianne 1299
DeCanio, Stephen J. 1829
Decarie, M. G. 18
Decker, Barry 2979
Deegan, Mary Jo 322
Delatte, Carolyn E. 1151
DelCastillo, Adelaida R. 2704
DeLeon, Arnoldo 2303
Deleon, David 2705
Dell, George W. 1839
Deloria, Vine, Jr. 2706
DeMarco, Joseph P. 2498
Dennis, Rutledge M. 1565
Dennison, George M. 591
Desjarlais, Lionel 1840 1841
Dethloff, Henry C. 1566
Detzer, David W. 2201
Deutrich, Mabel E. 107 372 586 2594 2628 2650
DeWitt, Howard A. 2499
Dickersin, Gail 19
DiClerico, Robert 2707
Dikshit, Om 2822
Dillard, Tom W. 115 2364
Dillingham, George A. 1411
Diner, Steven J. 1567
Dinnerstein, Leonard 2823
DiNunzio, Mario R. 323
Dinwoodie, D. H. 2500
Dirks, Patricia 1757
Dixon, Blase 2304
Dixon, Ruth B. 1568
Dobelstein, Andrew 1569
Dodd, Jill Siegel 868
Dodd, Martin H. 1300
Doenecke, Justus D. 2501
Doherty, Robert E. 2202
Doherty, William T., Jr. 1301
Dolgoff, Sam 2708
Dollar, Clyde D. 2709
Donahue, Francis 2710 2711
Dormon, James H. 625
Dorsey, George 2203

Douglas, Paul H. 919
Drachman, Virginia G. 869
Drago, Edmund L. 1152
Drake, Douglas C. 2365
Draughon, Ralph Brown, Jr. 626
Drescher, Nuala McGann 2204
Drescher, Seymour 6 638 699 765 774 789
Dressner, Richard B. 20 1923
Droker, Howard A. 2624
Dublin, Thomas 548 794 818
DuBois, Ellen 116 549 992
Dudley, J. Wayne 2665
Duffy, John 224
Duke, David C. 324
Dumont-Johnson, Micheline 21
Dunbar, Robert G. 2410
Dunlay, Thomas W. 993
Dunn, Joe P. 1570
Duram, James C. 2136 2502 2503
Durnbaugh, Donald 1571
Dybdahl, Tom 1648
Dye, Charles M. 189 1412 2305
Dye, Nancy Schrom 1924 2205
Dynes, Russell R. 2797

E

Eakin, Paul John 795
Eaklor, Vicki L. 627
Earle, Chester B. 2767
Earle, Valerie A. 2767
Early, Francis H. 819
Eaton, Clement 22
Eberson, Frederick 325
Ebner, Michael H. 2366
Echols, James P. 2504
Eckert, Ralph Lowell 628
Edelman, Marian Wright 2824
Edelstein, Frederick S. 2825
Edgar, Irving I. 2367
Edid, Maralyn 2947
Edmund, T. 2826
Edwards, G. Thomas 326 327
Edwards, Malcolm 592
Efthim, Helen 2827
Eger, Martin 2962
Egerton, John 1503
Eggers, Robert J. 4
Eggert, Gerald G. 1302
Ehrlich, Richard L. 1347 1348
Eichler, Margrit 117
Eisenberg, John M. 994
Ekirch, A. Roger 481
Eklund, Monica 2206
Elbert, E. Duane 629
Elder, Arlene A. 1153
Elenbaas, Jack D. 1925
Elliott, Josephine M. 916 937
Ellis, William E. 995 1926 1927
Ellsworth, Edward W. 835
Elmen, Paul 920
Elshtain, Jean Bethke 118
Elusche, Michael 190
Ely, James W., Jr. 630
Emery, George N. 23
Enck, Henry S. 2306
Endres, Kathleen 328
Engelmann, Larry 1928
Erickson, Leonard 593
Erlich, Howard S. 1370
Ernst, Joy S. 1929
Erskine, Hazel 2768
Erwin, Robert 24
Esedebe, P. Olisanwuche 25
Essig, James David 631 632
Evans, Sara M. 2905 2906 2907
Everett, Dianna 2368
Eversole, Theodore W. 225
Eyestone, Robert 1572

F

Fabbri, Dennis E. 2492
Faderman, Lillian 1930
Fahl, Ronald J. 1931

Fairbanks, Robert B. 1573
Fairclough, Adam 2828
Fairweather, Gordon L. 119
Falcone, David J. 1574
Faler, Paul 1298
Falk, Leslie A. 226 329
Farley, Ena L. 1154 1575
Farley, Reynolds 2829
Farrar, Eleanor 2960
Faucher, Albert 1758
Faust, Clarence 2666
Faust, Drew Gilpin 633
Faust, Richard H. 836
Featherman, David L. 2908
Feaver, George 2712
Feinman, Ronald L. 2369
Feinstein, Karen Wolk 1932
Feldberg, Roslyn L. 1759
Fellman, Michael 549 558 634 635 653 656 687 736 737 744 759 779 784 790
Felt, Jeremy P. 1933 1934
Felton, Barbara J. 227
Fendrich, James M. 2713 2714 2715
Ferguson, Barry 1576
Ferling, John 26
Fernandez, Ronald 1935
Ferrari, Art 2924
Fetner, Gerald 2370
Fickle, James E. 1577 2207
Field, Alexander J. 191
Field, Phyllis F. 120 595
Fierce, Milfred C. 1155
Fiering, Norman S. 531
Figgures, Cleopatra 1843
Filesi, Teobaldo 2371
Filippelli, Ronald L. 2372 2505
Findlay, James 192
Fineman, Joseph 1175
Fingard, Judith 870 871 996
Fingerhut, Eugene R. 27
Fink, Gary M. 1140 1328 1755 1760 1792 1800 2237 2353 2389 2467 2631
Fink, Leon 1303
Finkelman, Paul 636
Finkelstein, Barbara 2903
Finkle, Lee 2506 2625
Finn, Barbara R. 330
Finn, J. F. 1304
Fishbein, Leslie 28 1936
Fisher, Jeanne Y. 801
Fitzgerald, Michael R. 2830
Fladeland, Betty L. 637
Flanders, Jane 2373
Fleckner, John A. 1450
Fleming, Cynthia Griggs 2307
Fleming, John E. 331
Flinn, William L. 1546
Flora, Peter 160
Flowers, Ronald B. 2769
Floyd, Charles F. 2716
Fogarty, Robert S. 921 1504 1505
Fogelson, Nancy 1761
Foley, Douglas E. 1863
Folsom, Burton W., Jr. 1937
Foner, Eric 638 997
Foner, Philip S. 332 998 1156 1157 1158 1305 1413 1938 1939
Fones-Wolf, Elizabeth 1306
Fones-Wolf, Kenneth 1306 1307
Foran, Max 1940
Forbes, E. R. T. 1578
Fordham, Monroe 639 1762
Forrey, Carolyn 333
Foster, James C. 2208 2209
Foster, Stephen 482
Fowler, James H., II 2137
Fowler, Robert Booth 1579
Fox, Daniel M. 1941 2717
Fox, Margery 999
Fox, Richard W. 1942
Fram, Leon 2507
Francis, Daniel 228
Francis, Richard 922 923
Frank, Miriam 1308
Franklin, Benjamin, V. 640
Franklin, D. Bruce 641
Franklin, John Hope 1000 1159
Franklin, Vincent P. 837
Fraser, Hugh H. 1943

Fraser, Walter J., Jr. 536 1160
Frech, Laura P. 483
Frederick, Peter J. 334
Frederickson, George M. 642
Frederickson, Mary 1580
Freedman, Estelle B. 29 1451 2374
Freedman, Stephen 1001
Freeman, Richard B. 1763 2831
Freeman, Ruges R. 2667
Freidel, Frank 30
French, David 643
French, Larry 1581
Fretz, L. A. 1582
Frey, Cecile P. 872
Friedberger, Mark 1944
Frieden, Bernard J. 2718
Friedland, Roger 2925
Friedlander, Alice G. 1095
Friedman, Lawrence J. 550 644 645 646 647 648 1161
Friedman, Lawrence M. 121 122
Friesen, Gerald 1764
Friesen, Gerhard K. 924
Friesen, Steven 1945
Fry, Amelia E. 335
Fry, Joseph A. 2508
Fryer, Judith 336
Fugita, Stephen S. 2926
Fuke, Richard Paul 1002 1162
Fulkerson, Gerald 649
Furlow, John W., Jr. 2509
Furman, Necah Stewart 1720
Fursenko, A. A. 484
Fye, W. Bruce 1452

G

Gaboury, William J. 1163
Gaddy, C. Welton 31
Gadlin, Howard 123
Gaffield, Chad 1946
Gagnon, Gabriel 1765
Gaither, Gerald H. 1164
Galishoff, Stuart 32
Gallagher, Edward A. 2308
Galliher, John F. 2770
Galvin, Miles 2210
Gamble, Douglas A. 650 651
Gambone, Joseph A. 337 338
Game, Kingsley W. 2719
Gammage, Judie K. 2909
Gammon, Tim 1165
Gardner, Bettye J. 339
Gardner, Booker T. 193
Garrison, Bruce M. 340
Garrison, George R. 341
Garson, Robert A. 2375
Gartner, Lloyd P. 1371
Garvey, Timothy J. 2510
Gates, Margaret 2910
Gavins, Raymond 1583 1947
Gawalt, Gerard W. 194
Gear, James L. 33
Gehley, Dennis M. 2927
Geidel, Peter 2376
Geiger, John O. 1414
Gelb, Joyce 2911
Geldbach, Erich 838
Gelfand, Mark I. 2855
Geller, Gloria 1721
Gelston, Arthur Lewis 1003
Genest, Jean 1584
Genini, Ronald 2138
Genovese, Eugene D. 652
George, Carol V. R. 653
George, Paul S. 1948 1949
Gerber, David A. 1453
Gerber, Ellen 1766
Gerber, Richard Allan 1004
Gerstle, Gary 1767
Gersuny, Carl 342 343
Gerteis, Louis S. 1005
Gerz, Richard J., Jr. 2377
Geschwender, James A. 2832
Gianakos, Perry E. 1585
Gidney, R. D. 1415
Gietschier, Steven P. 2771
Gifford, James M. 551 654 655
Gilbert, James B. 1950
Gilbert, Jess 2511

Gilbert, Neil 2928
Gildemeister, Glen A. 1309
Giles, Michael W. 2833 2834
Gill, Mary E. 2309
Gillette, Howard, Jr. 1951
Gillette, Michael L. 1586
Gillis, Peter 1310
Gilman, Elizabeth 344
Gilman, Rhoda R. 345
Gilpin, Patrick J. 346
Ginzberg, Lori D. 796
Gittell, Marilyn 34
Glaberman, Martin 1308
Glanz, Rudolph 2211
Glaser, Martha 2378
Glassberg, David 1455
Glazier, Kenneth M. 1952
Gleberzon, William I. 1953
Glickstein, Jonathan A. 656
Gloster, Hugh M. 195
Goedeken, Edward A. 1416
Goff, John S. 2309
Gold, Carol 35
Goldberg, Gordon J. 2212
Goldman, Robert 151
Goldman, Sheldon 1715
Goldstein, Jonah 1587
Goldstein, Leslie Friedman 657 658
Goldstein, Robert J. 2139
Golomb, Deborah Grand 1488
Gonzales, Gilbert C. 1842
Goodenow, Ronald K. 2379 2512 2513
Goodman, Cary 2310
Goodwin, Leonard 2929
Gordon, Ann D. 36 552
Gordon, Audri 204
Gordon, Fred 2720
Gordon, Linda 37 1006 1007 1287 1588 1954
Gordon, Lynn 1955
Gordon, Mary MacDougall 839
Gordon, Michael A. 1311
Gorelick, Sherry 196
Gorrell, Donald K. 1489 1956
Gottlieb, Amy Zahl 1312
Gould, Alan B. 347 1957
Gounard, J.-F 348
Gowaskie, Joseph M. 2213
Gower, Calvin W. 2514
Grabowski, Harry G. 2721
Grabowski, John J. 1958
Graebner, William 1589 1886 1959 2214
Grafton, Carl 2668
Graham, Hugh Davis 2772
Graham, Patricia Albjerg 197
Granade, Ray 659
Granberg, Beth Wellman 2722
Granberg, Donald 2722
Grandfield, Robert S. 2140
Grant, Donald L. 1590
Grant, H. Roger 925 926 927 1008 1502 1505 1506 1507 1508 1509 1510 1511 2311
Grant, Jim 2930
Grant, Marilyn 2141
Grant, Mary H. 349
Grant, Mildred Bricker 1590
Grant, Philip A., Jr. 2669
Grantham, Dewey W. 1960
Gravely, William B. 1166
Graves, Carl R. 2835
Gray, Noel 2836
Grech, John D. 2312
Green, Dan S. 1591
Green, James R. 2215 2216 2292
Green, Jesse C., Jr. 594
Green, Jim 2217
Green, Joe L. 2515
Green, Nancy 553
Greenbaum, William 1592
Greenberg, Kenneth S. 660
Greene, Larry A. 1009
Greene, Suzanne Ellery 1593
Greene, William Robert 230
Greenstone, J. David 231
Greer, Edward 2723
Grenz, Stanley J. 513
Gribbin, William 554
Griffin, Barbara J. 840
Griffin, William 2380
Griffith, Elisabeth 1010

Grinder, Robert Dale 38 1961 1962
Groniowski, Krzysztof 39
Grosch, Anthony R. 1963
Gross, Harriet Engel 2724
Grossman, Joel B. 1579
Grossman, Jonathan 1768 1964 2218 2219
Grossman, Lawrence 350 841
Grube, John 1594 1595 2931
Guethlein, Carol 124
Guggisberg, Hans R. 514
Guither, Harold D. 1400
Gura, Philip F. 906
Guth, James L. 1769
Gutiérrez, Armando 1659
Gutman, Herbert G. 1313
Gwozdz, Kathe Palmero 532

H

Haas, Kenneth C. 2773
Habibuddin, S. M. 198
Hachey, Thomas 2626
Hackett, Derek 661
Hadwiger, Donald 1714
Hagan, John 2725
Hagan, William T. 1011
Halbrooks, G. Thomas 662
Hales, Jean Gould 797
Hall, D. J. 1012
Hall, Dick 1596
Hall, Jacquelyn Dowd 2516
Hall, Kermit L. 663
Haller, Mark H. 125
Hallett, Mary E. 1597
Ham, F. Gerald 928
Hamilton, Charles V. 2837
Hammett, Hugh B. 2220
Hammett, Theodore M. 555
Hammond, John L. 556 664
Hancock, Harold B. 351
Haney, James E. 2838
Hansen, James E., II 2381
Hansen, Miriam 1965
Hansot, Elisabeth 217
Harakas, Stanley S. 2726
Hardaway, Roger D. 2142
Harding, Susan 2912
Harding, Vincent 126
Hardy, B. Carmon 512
Hardy, Richard J. 2839 2861
Harkins, Michael J. 1456
Harlan, Louis R. 1966
Harper, John Paull 40
Harring, Sidney L. 152
Harris, J. John, III 1843 1853
Harris, Janet 665
Harris, Katherine 232
Harris, Robert L., Jr. 666 873
Harris, Ted C. 352
Harris, William C. 1013
Harris, William H. 353 2627
Harrison, Theresa A. 667
Harrod, Frederick S. 41
Harrold, Stanley C., Jr. 668 669 670
Hart, John 2840
Hartmann, Susan M. 2628 2629
Harvey, Fernand 1314
Harvey, Robert Paton 842
Hass, Paul H. 1967
Hasselmo, Nils 1631
Hastie, William H. 1598
Hatch, Nathan O. 907
Haughton, Virginia 2221
Hauptman, Laurence M. 354 1014
Hauser, Robert M. 2908
Havighurst, Robert J. 2963
Hawes, Joseph M. 121 874 892 1472 1702
Hayden, Dolores 42 929
Hayden, J. Carleton 2774
Hayes, James R. 2727
Haymes, Howard J. 1599
Haynes, John Earl 1600
Hayward, Mark D. 1813
Head, Faye E. 1968
Headon, Christopher 1490
Heale, M. J. 875 876 877 878
Heap, Margaret 1315
Heath, Alden R. 1512
Heath, Frederick M. 233
Heath, Robert L. 1167
Heath, William G., Jr. 1015

Heck, Edward V. 2775
Heidenheimer, Arnold J. 160
Heinemann, Ronald L. 2517
Helfand, Barry 2222
Hellwig, David J. 1601 2382
Henderson, Alexa B. 2630
Henderson, Steven T. 1602
Hendrick, Irving G. 2383 2518
Hendrickson, Kenneth E., Jr. 2519
Henker, Fred O., III 234
Henle, Ellen Langenheim 1457
Hennesey, Melinda Meek 1168
Henningson, Berton E., Jr. 1372
Henson, Tom M. 1603
Herbst, Jurgen 199 485 486
Herbst, Robert L. 2841
Hercher, Gail Pike 1969
Heriksen, Thomas H. 557
Herman, Alan 2520
Hersh, Blanche Glassman 558 798
Hertz, Edwin 2728
Hertz, Susan H. 2933
Hertzberg, Hazel Whitman 355
Hessen, Robert 2223
Hewitt, John H. 671
Hield, Melissa 1770
Higginbotham, A. Leon, Jr. 127
Higginbotham, Don 515
Hildebrand, Reginald F. 908
Hildreth, Peggy Bassett 235
Hill, Ann Corinne 43
Hill, Charles 2384
Hill, Claibourne M. 1929
Hilts, Victor L. 236
Himelhoch, Myra Samuels 356
Hinckley, Ted C. 1016 1458 2776
Hine, Darlene Clark 1722 1723 2385
Hine, William C. 1169
Hines, Linda O. 1604 1970
Hitchcock, James 1605
Hite, Roger W. 672
Hobby, Daniel T. 2224
Hobson, Julius, Jr. 1844
Hobson, Wayne K. 1971
Hodges, James A. 2521
Hoeveler, J. David, Jr. 1017
Hoffer, Peter C. 516
Hoffman, Abraham 2522
Hoffman, George 1606 1607
Hoig, Stan 44
Holford, David M. 153
Holl, Jack M. 1972
Holland, Antonio F. 1170
Hollander, Russell 1459
Hollinger, David A. 1608
Holmes, Harry D. 2199
Holmes, Joseph L. 154
Holmes, William F. 1171 1172
Holt, James 155
Holt, Michael F. 559
Holzhueter, John O. 1173
Holzner, Burkart 2964
Homel, Gene Howard 1316 1609
Homel, Michael W. 1845 2523
Hooper, Paul F. 1610
Hoopes, James 1973
Horn, Michiel 1611 1724 1771
Hornbein, Marjorie 357 1772
Hornbuckle, Jim 1581
Hornick, Nancy Slocum 487
Hornsby, Alton, Jr. 1174 1846 2842 2843
Horowitz, Murray M. 1018
Horowitz, Robert F. 1019
Horrall, Stan W. 1460 1612
Horton, James Oliver 560
Hosmer, John H. 1175
Hougen, Harvey R. 1974
Hougland, James G., Jr. 1613
Hovet, Theodore R. 673 909

Howard, Victor B. 561 674 675 676 677 1096 1176 1177 1178
Howell, Colin D. 1020
Howlett, Charles F. 1614 1615 1847
Hoxie, Frederick E. 45
Hoy, Suellen M. 1975
Hubbell, John T. 2143
Hudis, Paula M. 1813
Hudson, Gossie Harold 358 1179
Hudson, Hosea 404
Hudson, Winthrop S. 799
Huel, Raymond 1848 1849
Hulm, Richard L. 1180
Hume, Richard L. 1021 1022
Humphrey, David C. 488
Hunsaker, David M. 2670
Hunt, Janet G. 2844
Hunt, Larry L. 2844
Hunt, Marion 237 359
Hunt, Thomas C. 1417 1418 1419
Hunt, Vilma R. 47
Hurd, Richard W. 2524 2934
Hurst, Marsha 1181
Hurt, R. Douglas 1023 1024
Hurwitz, Edith F. 48
Hurwitz, Haggai 2225
Hutson, James H. 49
Hyman, Drew W. 2943
Hynson, Leon O. 1025

I

Ickstadt, Heinz 1513
Iglitzin, Lynne B. 58
Ilkka, Richard J. 1976
Illick, Joseph E. 1616
Ingram, Anne G. 2913
Irvin, Dale T. 50
Isaac, Amos 2777
Isaac, Paul E. 1977
Issel, William 200 1420
Isserman, Maurice 156 1978
Ives, Richard 2313

J

Jable, J. Thomas 562
Jacklin, Thomas M. 2525
Jackson, Harvey H. 517 518
Jackson, Joy J. 2386
Jackson, Philip 1979
Jackson, W. Sherman 1097 1182
Jacobs, Wilbur R. 51
Jacobsen, Timothy C. 1026
Jacoby, Robin Miller 1980 2226
Jaenicke, Douglas Walter 2227
Jaffe, Philip J. 360
James, Edward T. 361 1027
James, Felix 1183 1260
James, Janet Wilson 1461
James, Louise Boyd 2144
Jamieson, Duncan R. 879
Jamieson, Kathleen 2914
Janick, Herbert 1617
Janiewski, Dolores 820
January, Alan F. 678
Jeansonne, Glen 362 2526 2527
Jebsen, Harry, Jr. 1317
Jedlicka, Davor 251
Jeffrey, Julie Roy 1373
Jeffreys-Jones, Rhodri 157 1981
Jemison, Marie Stokes 2145
Jemnitz, János 1982
Jenkins, J. Craig 1773
Jenkins, William D. 363 2314
Jennings, Clara Murphy 2865
Jennings, Judith 519
Jennings, Mary Kay 1098
Jensen, Billie Barnes 1099 2228
Jentz, John B. 679
Jervey, Edward D. 880
Johnsen, Leigh Dana 1184
Johnson, Abby Arthur 1983
Johnson, Charles 2528
Johnson, Clyde 2631

Johnson, David W. 680
Johnson, James P. 364
Johnson, Keach 1421 1422 1984 2229
Johnson, Reinhard O. 681 682 683
Johnson, Roberta Ann 142
Johnson, Ronald M. 1423 1424 1983
Johnson, Ronald N. 1323
Johnson, Whittington B. 2671
Jonas, Donald E. 1792
Jones, Allen W. 1185 1186 1970
Jones, Andrew 1618
Jones, Bartlett C. 2387
Jones, Edward D., III 2778
Jones, Faustine C. 2845
Jones, Jacqueline 125
Jones, James P. 1028
Jones, Leon 2846
Jones, Mack H. 2847
Jones, Ronald W. 52
Jones, Russell M. 265
Jones, Walter R. 2388
Jordan, Daniel P. 630 2389
Jordan, Philip D. 1029
Joubert, Paul E. 2848
Judd, Dennis R. 2935
Juhnke, James C. 1030 2146
Justin, Meryl S. 1031

K

Kadzielski, Mark A. 1985
Kagan, Paul 1619
Kahn, Lawrence M. 2529
Kalberg, Stephen 1462
Kambeitz, Teresita 1620
Kanarek, Harold K. 2390 2391
Kane, Richard D. 2392
Kann, Kenneth 1187
Kann, Mark E. 1986
Kantor, Harvey 1987
Kantowicz, Edward R. 1621
Kaplan, Barry J. 1463
Kater, John L., Jr. 2849 2850
Katz, Harriet 1426
Katz, Jonathan 2672
Kaufman, Martin 1032
Kaushik, R. P. 1188
Kaye, Frances W. 800
Kazymyra, Nadia O. 365
Kealey, Gregory S. 1318
Keane, Patrick 843 844 845
Kearnes, John 2393
Kedro, Milan James 366
Keeran, Roger R. 2394
Keim, Albert N. 2632
Keller, Charles 158
Keller, Ralph A. 684
Keller, Rosemary Skinner 1491
Kelley, Don Quinn 1189
Kelley, Mary 221 349 452 1010 2314 2629
Kellog, Peter J. 1622 2673
Kelly, John M. 1033
Kelly, Lawrence C. 2530
Kelly, William R. 2851
Kemper, Donald J. 1850
Kendall, Kathleen Edgerton 801
Kenneally, James J. 53
Kennedy, David M. 1988
Kennedy, Susan Estabrook 2230 2231
Kent, Lori 2443
Kerber, Linda K. 563
Kern, Louis J. 266
Kerr, K. Austin 1319 1464
Kerr, Norwood Allen 685
Kersey, Harry A., Jr. 1100 1851
Kerson, Toba Schwaber 238
Kerstein, Robert J. 2935
Kessler, Lauren 1101
Kessler-Harris, Alice 54 159 367
Keubler, Edward J. 2531
Kilar, Jeremy W. 1320
Kilde, Clarence 368
Kilson, Martin 1623
Kimball, Philip Clyde 1190
Kimble, Cary 2980
Kinard, Harriet H. 233

King, Anne 489
King, John L., Jr. 1191
Kirby, John B. 2532
Kirchmann, George 930
Kirkland, Edward C. 1465
Kirp, David L. 2852
Kirschner, Don S. 1624 1989 1990
Kirst, Michael W. 217
Kirwan, Kent A. 55
Klehr, Harvey 1625 1991
Kleiman, Michael P. 1626
Klein, Rachel N. 490
Kleiner, Lydia 403
Kleinman, Max L. 686
Kline, Lawrence O. 56
Klingman, Peter D. 1192
Knawa, Anne Marie 369
Kneeland, Marilyn 2147
Koehler, Lyle 520
Koeniger, A. Cash 2533
Kogan, Herman 1034
Kohler, Robert E. 1992
Kohlstedt, Sally Gregory 881 1035
Kohn, Lawrence A. 2395
Kojder, Apolonja Maria 1627
Kolchin, Peter 1036
Kolehmainen, John I. 1628
Koller, Norman B. 2729
Kolmerton, Carol A. 931
Koontz, Claudia 48
Kopkind, Andrew 2730 2853
Koppes, Clayton R. 1629 1993 2148
Koroleva, A. P. 2854
Kostiainen, Auvo 2315
Kousser, J. Morgan 1193 1194 2316
Kozenko, B. D. 1994
Kraditor, Aileen S. 57
Krasner, Michael A. 2965
Kraut, Alan M. 595 687
Kravetz, Diane 2918
Kreider, Robert 2534
Kremer, Gary R. 1170 1195
Kremm, Thomas W. 564 1196 1197
Kress, Sylvia H. 1198
Kreuter, Gretchen 295 344 345 385 424 453
Kroll, Michael A. 239
Kronick, Jane C. 498
Krug, Mark M. 1199
Kruman, Marie W. 2535
Kudrle, Robert T. 160
Kuehl, Warren F. 59
Kulik, Gary B. 821 822
Kunitz, Stephen J. 2317
Kurland, Philip B. 1774
Kurtz, Michael L. 2674
Kushner, Howard I. 1995
Kusmer, Kenneth L. 1996
Kutcher, Stan 370
Kyvig, David E. 2396 2536

L

Ladd, Everett Carll, Jr. 2731
Lamb, Charles M. 2779
Lambert, Roger C. 2537
Lamis, Alec Peter 1630
Lammen, A. 688 1997
Lamon, Lester C. 2397
Lamoureaux, David 1998
Landes, Elisabeth M. 2398
Landry, Kenneth 1535
Lane, James B. 1999
Lang, Amy Schrager 491
Lang, Daniel W. 1427
Langbein, John H. 128
Langdon, Steven 161
Langellier, J. Phillip 1037
Langhorne, Elizabeth 689
Langley, Stephen 2749
Lansing, Marjorie 58
Lapitskii, M. I. 371
Lapointe, Michelle 1775
Larmour, Jean 1038
Larson, Bruce L. 1631
Larson, Simeon 2000
Larson, T. A. 129 130 1102 2149
Lash, Joseph P. 372
Laska, Lewis L. 2399
Lasser, Carol S. 882
Lau, Estelle Pau-on 2966
Lauderbaugh, Richard A. 2538
Lauderdale, William B. 1852
Lauricella, Francis, Jr. 883
Lavigne, Marie 1039
Lavine, T. Z. 2915
Lawler, Pat 2001
Lawr, D. A. 1415
Lawrence, Ken 162
Lawson, Alan 373
Lawson, David C. 59
Lawson, Steven F. 2400 2855
Layng, Anthony 1632
Lazerow, Jama 1321
Lazin, Frederick A. 2856
Lea, Arden J. 2002
Leab, Daniel J. 2003
Leavitt, Judith Walzer 1466 2004
Lebedum, Jean 802
Lebowitz, Neil H. 2633
Lebsock, Suzanne D. 1103
Ledbetter, Billy D. 1200
Ledbetter, Calvin R., Jr. 2005
Lee, Carol F. 1725
Lee, Everett S. 251
Lee, Juliet A. 690
Lee, Lawrence B. 163
Lee, R. Alton 131 691
Leff, Carol Skalnik 1726
Leff, Mark H. 1726
Leinenweber, Charles 2006
LeMoignan, Michel 374
Lemons, J. Stanley 2401
Leonard, Henry B. 2007
Leotta, Louis 1777
Lepawsky, Albert 2539
Lernack, Paul 492
Lerner, Gerda 803
Lesick, Lawrence T. 692
Leslie, W. Bruce 201
Letsinger, Norman H. 60
Levenstein, Harvey 1467 2540
Lévesque, Andrée 1778
Levesque, George A. 565
Levi, Margaret 2732
Levi, Steven C. 2232 2233 2234
Levin, Herman 222
Levitan, Sar A. 2936
Levitt, Joseph 1633
Levstik, Frank R. 884 1322
Levy, Joanne 2780
Lewallen, Kenneth A. 2008
LeWarne, Charles Pierce 1040 2009 2150 2151
Lewis, Anthony 2781
Lewis, David L. 1779
Lewis, Diane K. 2733
Lewis, Robert 1041
Lewis, Ronald L. 375 1201
Lewis, Vashti 2402
Lex, Louise Moede 1042
Libby, Billy W. 1202
Libecap, Gary D. 1323
Liebman, Arthur 61
Light, Ivan 1634
Lillard, Richard G. 2967
Lilley, William, III 2734
Limón, José E. 2010
Lindsay, Beverly 1853
Linford, Orma 1104
Link, Eugene P. 376
Lipsky, Michael 2857
Liski, Ilkka 2011
Littlefield, Daniel F., Jr. 1203 1204 1374
Livingston, John C. 2403
Lloyd, Sheila 1635
Locke, William R. 693
Lockett, Darby Richardson 2916
Logue, Cal M. 1205 1206 1207
Lojek, Helen 377
Loomis, Sally 694
Lopez, David E. 1324
Lord, Donald C. 2858
Lotz, Jim 1854
Lovejoy, David B., Jr. 240
Loveland, Anne C. 695 1208
Lovett, Bobby L. 1209
Lovett, Clara M. 2092
Lovin, Hugh T. 2012 2152 2404 2405 2406 2541 2542 2543 2544 2545
Lubove, Roy 2013
Lucas, Stephen E. 2014
Lucie, Patricia M. L. 1105 1106
Luckingham, Bradford 885
Ludmerer, Kenneth M. 2318
Luebbering, Ken 846
Luebke, Frederick C. 1395
Lufkin, Jack 2015
Lujan, Phillip 2789
Luker, Ralph E. 62 1043
Lunardini, Christine A. 2016
Luning Prak, N. 1325
Lurie, Jonathan 378 1430 1400
Lutzker, Michael A. 2017
Lynch, Acklyn R. 379
Lynch, John E. 2917
Lynch, Patrick 2235
Lynd, Staughton 2497 2546
Lynn, Kenneth S. 2018
Lyons, John 1855

M

Mabee, Carleton 1210
MacCarthy, Esther 1636
MacDonald, A. P., Jr. 2859
MacDonald, Maurice 2937
MacDougall, Heather A. 1468
MacDowell, Laurel Sefton 2634
Mackey, Philip English 886 887 888
Mackinley, Peter W. 521
MacKinnon, Jan 2019
MacKinnon, Steve 2019
Mackintosh, Barry 380
Maclear, J. F. 696 697 889
MacLeod, David 63
Macleod, R. C. 1107
MacPherson, Ian 1637 1780
Madden, Edward H. 341
Maestro, Marcello 890
Magdol, Edward 1211
Magner, Lois N. 64
Maidment, Richard A. 1212 2782
Majka, Linda C. 1781
Makahonuk, Glen 1782
Mal'kov, V. L. 2020 2547
Mallett, Richard P. 566
Malmsheimer, Lonna M. 493
Mambretti, Catherine Cole 132
Mancini, Matthew J. 1044
Maniha, Barbara B. 381
Maniha, John K. 381
Manley, John 1638
Marable, Manning 382 522 1543
Marcus, Alan I. 241 891 2021
Marcus, Irwin M. 1326
Marden, David 1783
Marecek, Jeanne 2918
Margolin, C. R. 1639
Margolis, Michael 1640
Margulies, Herbert F. 2022 2408
Marin, Christine 2735
Marina, William 494
Mark, Arthur 847
Markowitz, Gerald E. 1784 2023 2319
Markowitz, Judith B. 523
Marks, Bayly Ellen 1428
Marmor, Theodore R. 160
Maroney, James C. 2236 2237 2238
Marr, William L. 1213
Marsden, Michael T. 1045
Marsh, Margaret S. 1046
Marszalek, John F. 698
Martin, Charles H. 2548 2549
Martin, Edward A. 1641
Martin, Tony 2635
Martinson, Henry R. 2024
Masel-Walters, Lynne 1047 1108
Mason, Karen Oppenheim 2919
Massey, Mary Elizabeth 383
Mathes, Valerie Sherer 1048
Mathews, Allan 2409
Mathews, Donald G. 567 699
Mathews, James W. 932
Mathias, Frank F. 823
Matsudaira, Martin "Mich" 65
Mattern, Carolyn J. 384
Matters, Diane L. 1642
Matthews, Carl S. 1643
Matthews, Fred H. 2025
Matthews, Jean V. 804
Matthews, John Michael 1214 2026
Matthews, Linda M. 1215
Maxwell, John Francis 524
May, Glenn A. 2320
Mbatia, O. L. E. 1785
McArthur, Benjamin 1492 2027
McAuliffe, Mary S. 2675
McBeth, Harry Leon 66
McBride, David 596
McBride, Paul W. 2321
McBride, Robert M. 1049
McCarthy, Abigail 385
McCarthy, G. Michael 1375 1376 2028
McCluskey, Audrey 700
McCluskey, John 700
McCluskey, Stephen C. 1050
McClymer, John F. 2029
McConnell, Virginia 1051
McConville, Ed 2938
McCormack, A. Ross 1327 1786
McCormack, Donald J. 2860
McCormick, Richard L. 2030
McCormick, Richard P. 386
McCrone, Donald J. 2839
McCuaig, Katherine 1644
McCurley, James 99
McDonald, James 2749
McDonald, Rita 2410
McDonnell, Janet 2031
McElroy, James L. 568
McFadyen, Richard E. 2676 2939
McFarland, Charles K. 2153
McFaul, John M. 701
McGinnis, Ronald L. 2862
McGinty, Garnie W. 387
McGlen, Nancy E. 79
McGovern, James R. 1727
McGraw, Patricia Washington 1203
McGregor-Alegado, Davianna 2736
McGuire, Phillip 2636 2637 2638
McGuire, Thomas 2956
McHugh, Christine 1377
McInerny, Dennis Q. 2737
McKay, Robert B. 133
McKee, Delber L. 1052
McKenna, Angus 67
McKinney, Gordon B. 1216
McKivigan, John R. 702 703 704
McKillop, A. B. 1645
McLaren, Angus 67
McLaughlin, Doris B. 2239
McLaughlin, Milbrey Wallin 2968
McLaughlin, Tom L. 597
McLaurin, Melton A. 1217 1328
McLear, Patrick E. 1378
McLoughlin, William G. 598
McMahan, Ronald L. 2411
McManus, Michael J. 599
McMath, Robert C., Jr. 1379 1380
McMillen, Neil R. 2863
McMurry, Linda O. 388
McQuaid, Kim 600 1329 1787 1788 1789 1829 2240 2345 2412 2550 2659
McShane, Clay 94
Medicine, Bea 2738
Megehee, Mark K. 68
Meier, August 1646 1647 2154
Melcher, Daniel P. 2413
Melder, Keith 202
Melis, Caroline 1856
Melosi, Martin V. 32 38 69 94 99 1503 1684 1975
Melton, Thomas L. 2677
Melvin, Patricia Mooney 2032
Mendelson, Wallace 1109 1715
Mennel, Robert M. 242
Merelman, Richard M. 203
Mergen, Bernard 70 1790
Mesar, Joe 1648
Messner, William F. 1218 1219 1220
Meyer, John W. 204
Meyer, Paul R. 71
Meyerhuber, Carl I., Jr. 2241 2242
Meyers, Michael 2864
Michaels, Patricia 389
Middleton, Ernest J. 1857
Migliorino, Ellen Ginzburg 390
Mihelich, Dennis N. 2639
Milden, James W. 2243
Miller, Eugene 391
Miller, J. R. 1429
Miller, James C., III 2734
Miller, Janet A. 205
Miller, John E. 2551 2552
Miller, Kathleen Atkinson 2553
Miller, Larry C. 2033
Miller, Lawrence G. 2034
Miller, Michael V. 2739
Miller, Randall M. 705
Miller, Rex 392
Miller, Sally M. 1053 2035
Millett, Stephen M. 2414
Mills, Allen 1649 1791
Mims, Jasper, Jr. 2865
Miroff, Bruce 2866
Mitchell, Betty L. 706 707
Mitchell, Gary 2415
Mitchell, Memory F. 708
Mitchell, Norma Taylor 72
Mitchinson, Wendy 1469 1493
Mithun, Jacqueline S. 2867
Mittlebeeler, Emmet V. 824
Moehring, Eugene P. 2554
Moen, Phyllis 2929
Moens, Gabriel 73
Mohl, Raymond A. 74 892 2244 2322
Mohler, Dorothy A. 2036
Molander, Earl A. 1650
Mondello, Salvatore 393 1651
Monteleone, Renato 394
Montesano, Philip M. 1221
Montgomery, David 164 165 166 1330 2245 2292
Mooney-Melvin, Patricia 2037
Moore, Carol 2981
Moore, James R. 2555
Moore, James T. 1222
Moore, Jesse T., Jr. 1652
Moore, John H. 2246
Moore, John S. 525
Moore, Kathryn McDaniel 495
Moore, Kenny 2783
Moore, N. Webster 395
Moore, Robert J. 1054
Moorhead, James H. 569
Mora, Magdalena 2704
Moranian, Suzanne Elizabeth 848
Morantz, Regina Markell 893 2678
Morgan, David R. 2830
Morgan, Thomas S., Jr. 2556
Morris, Aldon 2868
Morris, James M. 933 1331
Morrison, Howard Alexander 709
Morrison, Joseph L. 1653
Morrison, W. R. 1055
Morton, Desmond 1332 1333
Morton, Michael 2155
Moses, L. G. 1110
Moses, Wilson Jeremiah 1654
Motley, Constance B. 134
Mott, Wesley T. 570 2869
Mount, Eric, Jr. 2740
Moyers, David M. 243
Muchinske, David 2323
Mueller, Samuel A. 1613
Mugleston, William F. 1056 2038 2416
Muir, Donal 2870
Mulder, John M. 396
Mulder, Ronald A. 2557 2558
Mullaney, Marie Marmo 2324
Muller, Mary Lee 2679
Mullins, William H. 2417
Mulvay, Jill C. 75 397
Munsey, Sylvia Falconer 398

AUTHOR INDEX

Murison, Barbara C. 571
Murphy, Larry George 76
Murrah, Bill 1655
Murray, Andrew E. 710
Murray, Hugh T., Jr. 2871
Musselman, Barbara L. 2247
Musselman, Thomas H. 2680
Myers, Beverlee A. 2982
Myers, Constance Ashton 2559
Myers, John B. 1223
Myerson, Joel 934
Myhra, David 2560
Myhrman, Anders 399

N

Nagel, Joane 204
Naison, Mark 400 2561 2562 2563 2564
Nam, Tae Y. 2872
Nash, Gary B. 533
Neal, Diane 1196 1197
Neal, Nevin E. 2153
Neary, Kevin 1640
Neary, Peter 1524
Neitz, Mary Jo 2741
Nelms, Willie E., Jr. 2325
Nelson, Carol Ann 117
Nelson, Daniel 2248 2249 2565
Nelson, H. Viscount 2566
Nelson, Larry E. 1224 2039
Nelson, Lawrence J. 2567
Nelson, Paul David 1225
Nelson, Richard 2956
Nelson, Ronald E. 935
Neuchterlein, James A. 2040
Neuenschwander, John A. 711
Neufeld, Maurice F. 825
Newbill, James G. 2568 2569
Newton, Bernard 1057
Newton, James E. 712
Nichols, John E. 1728
Nieman, Donald G. 1226 1227
Nitoburg, E. L. 2418
Noblit, George W. 2969
Nochlin, Linda 2250
Nolan, Dennis R. 1792
Noll, Mark A. 206
Noll, William T. 77
Noon, Thomas R. 1228
Noonan, Brian 207
Nord, David Paul 2041 2042
Nordin, Kenneth D. 713
Norrell, R. Jefferson 2873
Norris, John 2251
Norton, John E. 936
Norton, Mary Beth 40 78 287 417 552 1352 1529 2065 2516 2906
Noun, Louise 1111
Novitsky, Anthony 2419
Nowicka, Ewa 401
Nuechterlein, James A. 2640
Numbers, Ronald L. 894 1470
Nyden, Linda 2420

O

Oakes, James 1229
Oates, Stephen B. 1058 1230
Oberweiser, David 1059
O'Brien, John T. 1231
O'Brien, Michael 1656
O'Brien, Patrick G. 2421
O'Connell, Lucille 2252
O'Connor, Karen 79
O'Donnell, L. A. 402
Oestreicher, Richard 1334
Ofari, Earl 1232
O'Farrell, M. Brigid 403
Offiong, Daniel A. 2422
O'Gallagher, Marianna 244
Oh, John C. H. 1793
O'Kelly, Charlotte G. 2874 2875
Okihiro, Gary Y. 2641
Olin, Spencer C., Jr. 1514 1515
Ollila, Douglas J. 2253
Olsen, Otto H. 1060
Olson, David J. 2857
Olssen, Erik 2423
Olton, Charles S. 496

Oman, Susan Staker 80
O'Neal, David L. 714
Orfield, Gary 1858
O'Riordan, Timothy 2742
Ornstein, Allan C. 1859
Orr, J. Edwin 81
Osborne, James D. 2254
Osofsky, Gilbert 715 716
Osterman, Paul 2326
Ostrower, Gary B. 2570
Oubre, Claude F. 1233
Overstreet, Daphne 2255
Owram, Doug 1576

P

Pace, David 2681
Pacyga, Dominic A. 2424
Padilla, Fernando V. 135
Painter, Nell 404
Paisley, William 1544
Palley, Marian Lief 2911
Palmer, Bruce 1381 1382
Palmer, Bryan D. 826 2256 2425
Palmer, Howard 1657
Papanikolas, Helen Z. 2571
Paradis, Ruth 1794 1795
Park, Roberta J. 572 573
Parker, Harold M., Jr. 574
Parker, James R. 2156
Parker, Keith A. 1658
Parman, Donald L. 2043 2743
Parra, Ricardo 1659
Parrish, E. 2572
Patenaude, Lionel 2573
Patterson, John S. 717
Patterson, R. S. 1430
Pau On Lau, Estelle 405
Pavich, Paul N. 1660
Payne, John Howard 575
Payne, William C. 2744
Payne-Gaposchkin, Cecilia Helena 718
Paz, D. G. 1061 1494
Pearlman, Michael 2044 2327
Pearson, Carol 267
Pearson, Ralph L. 2426
Pederson, Roger A. 1972
Peeps, J. M. Stephen 1234
Peitzman, Steven J. 1431
Peltzman, Sam 2956
Pendergrass, Lee F. 2045
Penfield, Janet Harbison 82
Penner, Norman 406
Pennington, William D. 1062 1063
Penton, M. James 136
Perkal, M. Leon 719
Perkey, Elton A. 1383
Perret, Karen 2745
Perrotta, John A. 2940
Perrow, Charles 1773
Perry, Clay 407
Perry, Lewis 549 558 634 653 656 687 720 721 736 737 744 759 779 784 790 805
Perry, Patsy Brewington 408
Perry, Thelma D. 722
Peskin, Allan 1086
Petersen, William 83
Peterson, Jon A. 245
Peterson, Paul E. 2876
Peterson, Richard H. 1335
Petrella, Frank 1064
Petrick, Barbara 409
Petrov, D. O. 2046
Petryshyn, J. 410
Pettigrew, Thomas F. 1661
Phaneuf, Margaret M. 1471
Phillips, J. O. C. 411
Phillips, Loretta 895
Phillips, Paul D. 412
Phillips, Prentice 895
Philp, Kenneth R. 1662 2427 2574
Pickvance, C. G. 2746
Piehler, Harold 1384
Pienkos, Donald E. 1663
Pierce, Glenn A. 2784
Pilling, Arnold R. 2785
Piott, Steven L. 1336 2047 2257
Pitcher, Brian L. 2428
Pitre, Merline 1235
Pitsula, James M. 246 1065 1664

Pitzer, Donald E. 937
Pivar, David J. 2048
Piven, Frances Fox 1665 2941
Platt, Anthony 1472
Plaut, Eric A. 247
Plesur, Milton 1398 2116
Pocock, Emil 1473
Poethig, Richard P. 84
Polk, Barbara Bovee 1551
Polos, Nicholas C. 413 849
Polsby, Daniel D. 2877
Porter, Melba Dean 2157
Powell, Allan Kent 2258 2429
Powell, David O. 1403
Powell, Elwin H. 2747
Powell, Lawrence N. 1066
Powell, T. J. D. 1796
Powell, Thomas F. 85
Prather, H. Leon, Sr. 1067
Pratt, Joseph A. 1797
Pratt, William C. 1666
Prendergast, James A. 1798
Prescott, Gerald L. 1385
Press, Donald E. 1386
Price, David E. 2049
Price, Edward J., Jr. 137 208
Price, William S., Jr. 515
Prickett, James R. 1799 2642
Pride, Nancy 2050
Prieur, Vincent 268
Prude, Jonathan 1729
Pruden, George B., Jr. 536
Pruitt, Paul, Jr. 1387
Pumphrey, Ralph E. 2051
Purdy, Virginia C. 107 372 586 2594 2628 2650
Putney, Martha S. 1860

Q

Quarles, Benjamin 576 724 725
Quen, Jacques M. 248
Quinley, Harold E. 2748
Quinn, Larry 2575

R

Rabinowitz, Howard N. 1068 1236 1237 1238
Rachleff, Marshall 726 727
Radbill, Kenneth A. 526
Radbill, Samuel X. 249
Rader, Frank J. 414
Raeithel, Get 86
Raichle, Donald R. 1432
Rainard, R. Lyn 1516
Rainbolt, Rosemary 2430
Rakestraw, Lawrence 2052
Ralston, Helen 209
Ramsey, B. Carlyle 2643
Rand, Ivan C. 2682
Rankin, David C. 1239
Rao, K. L. Seshagiri 2878
Raper, Arthur F. 2576
Rasporich, Anthony 415
Ratcliffe, Donald J. 416
Rauch, Julia B. 250 1474
Ravitch, Diane 2879 2970
Ray, William W. 1337
Rayman, Ronald 850
Raynor, Bruce 1800
Reagon, Bernice Johnson 2880
Redford, James 1861
Reed, Harry A. 728 729
Reed, James 87
Reed, Merl E. 1140 1328 1755 1792 1800 2237 2353 2389 2467 2631 2644
Reese, William J. 2053 2328 2329 2330
Reid, Bill G. 1667
Reid, John D. 251
Reid, Robert 1069
Reilly, John M. 2431
Reilly, Nolan 1801
Reilly, Timothy F. 730 731 732
Reimen, Jacqueline 2158
Reinders, Robert C. 733 734
Reinhart, Cornel J. 1388
Reinier, Jacqueline S. 577

Remele, Larry 2054 2055 2259 2260
Remley, Mary L. 1436
Resnick, Philip 2942
Retzer, Joseph D. 2729
Reverby, Susan 417 869 902 1287 1833 2034 2056 2319
Reyburn, Phil 418
Reynolds, John F. 578
Riach, Douglas C. 735 736
Rice, Hazel F. 2432
Rich, David 827
Richards, Leonard L. 737
Richardson, Fredrick 1240
Richardson, Joe M. 1241 1242 1243 1244 1245
Richey, Elinor 419
Richey, Susan 1668
Rickabaugh, Carey G. 2786
Riddle, Thomas W. 1389
Ridge, Martin 1390
Riell, Robert B. 2261
Riess, Steven 1669
Rietveld, Ronald D. 738
Riley, Stephen T. 1070
Rimlinger, Gaston 167
Ringenbach, Paul T. 2057
Ringenberg, William C. 851
Rios, Victor 1659
Ritchie, Donald A. 2058
Rittenhouse, Floyd O. 2331
Ritti, R. Richard 2943
Rivers, Larry E. 1670
Robbins, Lynn Arnold 2944 2945
Robbins, Thomas 2787
Robboy, Anita W. 420
Robboy, Stanley J. 420
Roberson, Jere W. 1246
Roberts, Clarence N. 2059
Roberts, Terry 210
Roberts, Wayne 421
Roberts, Wesley A. 527
Robertson, Darrel M. 910
Robinson, Armstead L. 1071
Robinson, Donald Allen 2920
Robinson, Jo Ann 422
Rocha, Guy Louis 2262 2433 2434
Rockoff, Hugh 168 2645
Rodgers, Harrell R., Jr. 2788 2810
Rodgers, James 269
Rodine, Floyd 2263
Roediger, David R. 1338 1339
Rogers, Evelyna Keadle 423
Rogers, George A. 1247
Rogers, Raymond S. 2789
Rogers, T. W. 138
Rogers, William Warren 2080
Rohde, Nancy Freeman 424
Rollins, Richard M. 938
Romanofsky, Peter 1475 1476 2060 2061
Romero, Patricia W. 2881
Roof, Wade Clark 2896
Rooke, Patricia 1430
Roos, Philip D. 2749
Roosevelt, Jinx 425
Roper, John Herbert 1248 2062
Rorabaugh, W. J. 896 897
Rosales, Francisco A. 1802
Rosen, Ellen 2063
Rosen, F. Bruce 1433
Rosen, George 1671 2064
Rosenberg, Charles E. 87 252 1461 1992
Rosenberg, Leonard B. 739
Rosenberg, Rosalind 88 2065
Rosenberger, Homer T. 2066
Rosenkrantz, Barbara Gutmann 253
Rosenof, Theodore 1672
Rosenthal, Bernard 528
Rosenthal, Joel 1673
Rosenthal, Star 1803
Rosenzweig, Roy 1804 2577
Rosner, David 869 902 1784 1833 2034 2577
Ross, B. Joyce 2578
Ross, Dorothy 1072
Ross, Ruth 58
Ross, Steven Joseph 1249
Rothman, Sheila M. 89
Rothman, Stanley 2750
Rothschild, Mary Aickin 2882

Rothwell, David R. 2646
Rottier, Catherine M. 426
Rotundo, Barbara 579
Rouillard, Jacques 1805
Rovere, Richard H. 427
Rowland, Andrew 2751
Rowley, William D. 2067
Roy, Patricia E. 1674 2647
Royce, Marion V. 852
Rozett, John M. 740
Rubenstein, Susannah 247
Rubinoff, Michael W. 428
Rudé, George 139
Rudwick, Elliott 1646 1647 2154
Ruether, Rosemary Radford 807
Ruffin, Thomas F. 601
Rulon, Philip Reed 429
Runcie, John 2883
Runte, Alfred 90
Ruppert, Peter 1675
Rury, John 2266
Russell, C. Allyn 430
Russell, Joseph J. 211
Russell, William D. 91
Russo, Francis X. 431
Rutherford, Phillip R. 741
Ryan, James Gilbert 2579
Ryan, Mary P. 808
Ryan, Thomas G. 2159
Ryan, Thomas R. 911
Ryon, Roderick M. 2580

S

Sahli, Nancy 809
St. Amant, Jean-Claude 1806
St. Hilaire, Joseph M.ar 1250
Saito, Makoto 2435
Sakolsky, R. 2971
Salamon, Lester M. 2884
Salmon-Cox, Leslie 2964
Saloutos, Theodore 2581
Samuels, Wilfred D. 1676
San Juan, E., Jr. 432
Sanders, Bernard 1807
Sandos, James A. 2068
Sangster, Joan 1808
Sansoucy, Debra P. 2069
Sargent, James E. 433
Sargent, Lyman Tower 270
Sarkissian, Wendy 92
Sarotte, Georges-Michel 1677
Sato, Susie 2582
Sauer, R. 93
Saunders, R. Frank, Jr. 1247
Sawyer, Jack 2885
Schacht, John N. 1809
Schaffer, Ronald 2160
Schallhorn, Cathlyn 1477
Schappes, Morris U. 1340
Schapsmeier, Edward L. 434
Schapsmeier, Frederick H. 434
Scharnau, Ralph William 1341 1342
Scher, Richard K. 1552 2664 2814
Schiesl, Martin J. 2070
Schiller, Bradley R. 2946
Schleppi, John R. 169
Schlereth, Thomas J. 2071
Schlossman, Steven L. 898 2072 2073 2074 2075
Schlup, Leonard 435 2076
Schmelzer, Janet 2264
Schneider, Albert J. 2583
Schneirov, Richard 1343
Schnell, R. L. 2077
Scholten, Pat Creech 170
Schoonover, Shirley G. 2078
Schor, Joel 742
Schreiber, E. M. 2752
Schroeder, Fred E. H. 2921
Schudson, Michael 1862
Schullery, Paul 2079
Schultz, Stanley K. 94
Schultze, Quentin J. 1910
Schwab, John J. 2898
Schwantes, Carlos A. 171 1112 1344 2161
Schwartz, Bonnie Fox 2584
Schwartz, Michael H. 1391
Schwartz, Mildred A. 1730
Schwarz, Philip J. 743

AUTHOR INDEX

Schweninger, Loren 1251 1252 1253
Schwieder, Dorothy 2585
Sclar, Elliott 2947
Scott, Andrew M. 1073
Scott, Ann Firor 436 810
Scott, Donald M. 744
Scott, Osborne 212
Scott, Stanley 1810
Scott, William B. 2683
Scott, William R. 2436
Scull, Andrew T. 2983 2984
Seager, Allen 1811
Searle, R. Newell 2437
Sears, James M. 2586
Seaton, Douglas P. 745
Segers, Mary C. 1678
Séguy, Jean 2989
Sehr, Timothy J. 746
Seller, Maxine 2332
Selvin, David F. 2587
Semple, Neil 1495
Senn, David J. 2885
Seraile, William 95 437 1254 1255
Seretan, L. Glen 172
Servín, Manuel P. 1679
Setterdahl, Lilly 939
Severn, John K. 2080
Sewell, George A. 1256
Sexton, Robert F. 2438
Shade, William G. 853
Shaffer, Arthur H. 356
Shaffer, Stephen D. 2753
Shahan, J. M. 2081
Shanahan, Donald G., Jr. 173
Shankman, Arnold 438 1731 2439 2588 2589
Shanks, Rosalie 2162
Shapiro, Edward S. 2082 2590 2591
Shapiro, Herbert 2083 2265
Sharpless, John 2266
Sheeler, J. Reuben 439
Shelden, Randall G. 96
Sherer, Robert G. 1257
Shin, Yongsock 251
Shinn, Marybeth 227
Shlomowitz, Ralph 1258
Shockley, Ann Allen 140
Shofner, Jerrell H. 141 1074 1259 2267
Shotliff, Don A. 1345
Shpotov, B. M. 580
Shrader, Victor L. 2333
Shtob, Teresa 34
Shumsky, Neil Larry 2084 2085
Siddall, A. Clair 254
Siegel, Richard L. 2768
Silcox, Harry C. 440 441
Sillito, John R. 2086
Silver, George A. 442
Silverman, Eliane Leslau 2163
Silverman, Jason H. 747 748
Silverman, Joan 2087
Silvia, Philip T., Jr. 1346
Simmons, Adele 213
Simmons, Michael K. 749
Simon, Daniel T. 1802
Simon, John Y. 1260
Simon, Rita James 1732
Sims, Norman H. 1910
Sims, Robert C. 2088
Sinclair, Barbara Deckard 1812
Sinclair, Peter R. 1680 1681
Singer, David J. 97
Singer, Donald L. 2592
Siracusa, Joseph M. 2089
Sivachev, N. V. 2593 2648
Skaggs, Julian C. 1347 1348
Skakkebaek, Mette 1682
Skidmore, Max 2754
Skidmore, P. G. 1478
Skinner, James M. 2649
Sklar, Kathryn Kish 443
Skoglund, John E. 444
Skogstad, Grace 2948
Slaughter, Sheila 1733
Sloan, David 497
Sloan, Jan Butin 1434
Smallwood, James 1261 1263
Smilor, Raymond W. 1683 1684
Smith, Arthur B., Jr. 2949
Smith, Becky 255
Smith, Burton M. 1075

Smith, Charles U. 2886
Smith, Dale C. 256
Smith, Douglas C. 2887
Smith, Dowell H. 2749
Smith, Elaine M. 2594
Smith, Grace Ferguson 445
Smith, Harold T. 257
Smith, John S. H. 2440
Smith, Kenneth 446
Smith, Lawrence B. 2950
Smith, Norman W. 2441
Smith, Robert E. 581
Smith, Robert T. 2755
Smith, Ronald A. 2684
Smith, W. Elwood 1863
Smylie, James H. 98
Snapp, Meredith A. 2164
Snyder, David 1813 2851
Snyder, Robert E. 2268 2269 2595
Sokolow, Jayme A. 447 750 940
Sowell, Thomas 83
Spackman, S. G. F. 1113
Spates, James L. 2990
Spavins, Thomas 2956
Spector, Robert M. 1114
Speizman, Milton D. 498
Spencer, Ralph W. 448
Spiegel, S. Arthur 2888
Spiers, Fiona E. 2090
Spindler, George D. 1685
Spindler, Louise S. 1685
Spivey, Donald 214
Sponholtz, Lloyd L. 258 2165
Sprague, Stuart Seely 2270
Springer, W. F. 2442
Stafford, Walter W. 1686
Stagg, J. C. A. 1076
Stamp, Robert M. 215
Stange, Douglas C. 751 752 753
Stanke, Michael J. 754
Stanley, Gerald 755 756 757
Stark, Rodney 2443
Starr, Paul 2985
Stasik, Florian 449
Stealey, John Edmund, III 1077 1264
Steamer, Robert J. 2790
Steelman, Joseph F. 2091
Steelman, Lala Carr 1392
Steffens, Pete 499
Stefon, Frederick J. 2444
Stegh, Leslie J. 2445
Stein, Gary C. 2446
Stein, Peter R. 2756
Steinson, Barbara J. 2092
Stephens, Lester D. 1115 1435
Stern, Madeleine B. 811 1116
Stern, Marjorie 1687
Stern, Mark 1265
Stern, Norton B. 1479
Stern, Sheldon M. 450
Stetson, Frederick R. 2596
Stevens, Errol Wayne 2093
Stevenson, James A. 2094
Stevenson, Janet 451
Stevenson, Louise L. 2166
Stewart, James Brewer 758 759 760
Stewart, Joseph, Jr. 2811
Stinson, Robert 1688
Stirn, James R. 761
Stodder, Jim 176
Stone, Judith F. 2717
Stoper, Emily 142 2889
Storey, John W. 1266 1267 2890
Stow, Robert N. 1349
Strasser, Susan M. 2271
Straub, Eleanor F. 2650
Straw, Richard A. 2272 2447 2448
Streifford, David M. 762
Strickland, Charles E. 452
Strom, Sharon Hartman 2167
Strong-Boag, Veronica 1689 1690 1814 1815
Strout, Cushing 1691
Strozier, Charles B. 443
Struna, Nancy 1436
Struthers, James 1816
Stuckey, Sterling 1692
Stueck, William 2095
Stuhler, Barbara 295 344 345 385 424 453
Suderman, Elmer F. 1693

Suggs, George G., Jr. 2273
Suggs, Henry Lewis 2096
Sullivan, Margaret LoPiccolo 259
Sumners, Bill 2168
Sutherland, John F. 2097 2098
Sveino, Per 2891
Swain, Martha H. 2597 2598
Swallow, Craig A. 2449
Swanson, Edith 2898
Swanson, Merwin 2099
Swanton, Carolyn 454
Swart, Stanley L. 2100
Sweat, Edward F. 1268
Sweet, Leonard 446
Swenson, Mary E. 2450
Swetnam, George 174
Switzer, Walter E. 2791
Sylvain, Philippe 1350 1351
Szasz, Ferenc M. 763 957 1496
Szasz, Margaret Connell 1864 2101

T

Taft, Philip 2274
Taggart, Robert 2936
Taggart, Robert J. 2334 2451 2452
Takanishi, Ruby 143
Talbot, Steve 2757
Tanaka, June K. 1694
Tanaka, Ron 2758
Tanaka, Stefan 2453
Tarleau, Alison T. 2715
Tarr, Joel A. 99
Tatalovich, Raymond 2759
Taylor, Antoinette Elizabeth 1117 2169
Taylor, C. J. 899
Taylor, David V. 1269
Taylor, Graham D. 2599 2600
Taylor, John H. 1695
Taylor, Paul F. 2601
Taylor, Richard S. 455
Taylor, Sally 764
Teaford, Jon C. 1497
Teaham, John F. 1480
Tedlow, Richard S. 1817
Temin, Peter 1818
Temperley, Howard 765 766
Tenney, Craig D. 1118
Terbor-Penn, Rosalyn 1270
Terchek, Ronald J. 2892
Terrell, Karen A. 2102
Testi, Arnaldo 2103
Thatcher, Linda 1119
Thavenet, Dennis 900
Theoharis, Athan 2685
Theriot, Nancy M. 812
Thomas, Bettye C. 1271
Thomas, Richard W. 1696 1819
Thomas, Robert David 271
Thomison, Dennis 2454
Thompson, Ernest T. 1272
Thompson, J. Earl, Jr. 767 768 769
Thomson, Anthony 1820
Thornbery, Jerry 1273
Thornton, Emma 1393
Thrasher, Sue 2602
Thurner, Arthur W. 2104
Thurow, Lester C. 2951
Tillery, Tyrone 770
Tilly, Bette B. 771
Timberlake, C. L. 216
Tobin, Eugene M. 2105 2275 2276 2277 2278 2279
Tokarczyk, Roman 2760
Tolbert, Emory 2455
Toll, William 1274 1697 2456
Tomatsu, Hidenori 144
Tomberlin, Joseph A. 2686
Tomlins, Christopher L. 2603
Topping, Eva Catafygiotu 813
Torode, Brian 2993
Torto, Raymond 2947
Toth, Charles W. 2457
Totton, Kathryn Dunn 456
Towey, Martin G. 259
Towle, W. Wilder 1821
Toy, Eckard, V., Jr. 2604
Trask, David Stephens 1394 1395

Trattner, Walter I. 901
Trauner, Joan B. 1078
Travis, Anthony R. 457 2106 2107
Treckel, Paula A. 814
Trefousse, Hans L. 458
Tremblay, Marc-Adélard 2972
Trendel, Robert 772 773
Trennert, Robert A. 1437
Trifiro, Luigi 1734
Tripp, Joseph F. 1822 2280
Trofimenkoff, Susan Mann 1698
Trunk, Isaiah 100
Tucker, E. Bruce 2108
Tullos, Allen 2109
Tulsky, Fredric 2893
Tumminelli, Roberto 941
Tunnell, Ted 1275
Turbin, Carole 1352
Turcheneske, John Anthony, Jr. 2170
Turley, David M. 774
Turner, Frederick W., III 1079
Turner, James 1396
Tushnet, Mark 775
Tuttle, William M., Jr. 2110
Tyack, David B. 204 217 218 219
Tyner, Wayne C. 776
Tyor, Peter L. 261
Tyrrell, Alexander 582

U

Ueda, Reed 2335
Ullmo, Sylvia 1353
Ulmer, Barbara 536
Underhill, Lonnie E. 1204 1374 2111
Urban, Wayne R. 2336
Useem, Bert 2894 2895
Uselding, Paul 2112
Uslaner, Eric M. 2952
Usselman, Steven W. 2281

V

Valerina, A. F. 2605
VanDeburg, William L. 777 778
VanHorne, John C. 500
VanValey, Thomas L. 2896
Vasquez, John A. 2761
Vaughan, Philip H. 2687
Vaughn, Stephen 2337
Vaughn, William P. 1438
Veach, Rebecca Monroe 443
Vecoli, Rudolph J. 175
Verbrugge, Martha H. 902
Vernon, John M. 2721
Vertinsky, Patricia 101 815 1481
Vietor, Richard H. K. 2282 2762 2763
Vigod, B. L. 1699 1700
Villemez, Wayne J. 1823
Vincent, Charles 1276
Vipond, May 1354
Vodicka, John 1701
Vogel, David 2953
Vogel, Lise 828
Vogel, Morris J. 87 252 1461 1992
Voisey, Paul 1735

W

Wagaman, David G. 2113 2283
Wagy, Thomas R. 2688 2897
Waksmundski, John 1355
Waldrip, Donald R. 2973
Walker, Samuel 1356 1397 1702 2651 2689
Walker, Thomas G. 2833
Wallace, Les 459
Wallach, Stephanie 2072
Wallis, John Joseph 2606
Walsh, Brian 2993
Walsh, Harry 1080
Walsh, James P. 2114
Walter, John C. 1824

Walters, Ronald G. 102 583 779 780
Ward, F. Champion 2666
Ward, Geoffrey C. 443
Ward, Paul L. 2974
Warden, G. B. 501
Warheit, George J. 2898
Warner, Deborah Jean 816
Warner, Margaret Humphreys 534
Warren, Donald R. 1277
Warrick, Sherry 2284
Waserman, Manfred 2115
Wasserman, Ira M. 2899
Watkins, Ralph 2458
Watson, Alan D. 529
Watson, Fred 2285
Watson, James R. 2193
Wax, Darold D. 530
Weales, Gerald 460
Weathersby, Robert W., II 584
Weaver, Bill L. 2690
Weaver, John C. 1703
Webber, Irving L. 2819
Weber, Paul J. 55
Weber, Ronald E. 2952
Weed, Frank J. 1825
Weeks, Charles J. 2607
Weeks, Louis B. 103
Weeks, Robert P. 942
Weiler, N. Sue 2286
Weinbaum, Paul O. 585
Weiner, Nella Fermi 817
Weisberger, Bernard A. 781
Weisbord, Vera Buch 2459
Weiss, Samuel A. 461
Weiss, Stuart L. 2608 2609
Welch, Richard E., Jr. 462
Wellman, Judith 586
Wells, Dave 176
Wells, Merle W. 1120
Wendler, Marilyn V. 782
Wennersten, John R. 587 2610
Werly, John M. 1704
Wertheim, Larry M. 1736
Wessel, Thomas R. 104
Wesser, Robert F. 2116
West, Earle H. 1278
Wetherell, Donald G. 1482
Wetta, Frank J. 1081
Wetzel, Kurt 2117
Weyant, Jane G. 854
Wharton, Leslie 1498
Wheeler, Joanne E. 1398
Wheeler, Leslie 1121
Whisenhunt, Donald W. 2460 2611
Whitaker, F. M. 1483
White, Arthur O. 855
White, Earl Bruce 2171 2287
White, Edward 783
White, G. Edward 1122
White, Jean Bickmore 1123
White, Kenneth B. 1279
White, Larry 2612
White, Ronald C., Jr. 2118
White, W. Thomas 1357
Whitfield, Stephen J. 2119
Whitmore, Allan R. 588
Whittenburg, James P. 502
Whorton, James C. 903 904 2120
Wiecek, William M. 784 785
Wiggins, Sarah Woolfolk 1082
Wilcox, Jerome E. 2896
Wilke, Phyllis Kay 220
Willhelm, Sidney M. 2901
Williams, C. Arthur, Jr. 260
Williams, David 2461
Williams, E. Russ, Jr. 463
Williams, Lillian S. 2462
Williams, Marilyn Thornton 2121
Williams, Robert J. 1705
Williams, Ronnie 1083
Williams, T. Harry 1706
Williams, William J. 2122
Willson, Carolyn 2123
Wilson, Benjamin C. 786
Wilson, C. Edward 535
Wilson, Charles Reagan 1084
Wilson, J. Donald 464 1707
Wilson, Joan Hoff 465
Wilson, John 151
Wilson, R. Jackson 1517

AUTHOR INDEX

Wilson, Richard Guy 943
Wilson, William J. 1280
Wiltshire, Susan Ford 787
Winer, Jane L. 2981
Winestine, Belle Fligelman 466
Winfield, Betty Houchin 2656
Winston, Michael R. 788 1708
Wirmark, Bo 1709
Wise, Leah 2602
Wiswell, Candace Hinson 1823
Witheridge, David E. 145
Wold, Frances 2288
Wolfe, Allis Rosenberg 2124
Wolfe, Margaret Ripley 1710 2125
Wolfe, Nancy T. 1085
Wollenberg, Charles 1865 2289 2652 2653
Wolman, Philip J. 2691
Wolseley, Roland E. 467
Wood, James R. 1613
Wood, Peter H. 503
Wood, Randall B. 468
Woodruff, Nan E. 2463
Woods, Randall B. 1281 1282
Woodward, C. Vann 1086
Wortman, Roy T. 1826 2290
Woywitka, Anne B. 469 1827 1828
Wright, George C. 2126
Wright, James R., Jr. 146
Wright, W. D. 470
Wyatt, Philip R. 1518
Wyatt-Brown, Bertram 105 789 790 791
Wyche, Billy H. 2613 2614
Wyman, Roger E. 1399 2127

X

Xenakis, Jason 2991

Y

Yang, Kuo-shih 1866
Ybarra-Frausto, Tomás 1711
Yellin, Jean Fagan 1712
Yellowitz, Irwin 1713
Yosie, Terry F. 99
Young, Alfred 1283
Young, James D. 177
Young, Louise M. 106
Young, Mary E. 107
Young, Michael 2654
Young, Walter D. 471

Z

Zainaldin, James S. 261
Zamora, Emilio, Jr. 2291
Zanger, Martin 2464
Zangrando, Joanna Schneider 2922
Zangrando, Robert L. 147
Zarefsky, David 2764 2954
Zashin, Elliot M. 2992
Zeigler, Earle F. 856
Zeitzer, Glen 2655
Zerker, Sally 178
Ziebarth, Marilyn 1619
Zieger, Robert H. 2465 2615
Zimmerman, Joan G. 221
Zuber, Richard L. 1124

LIST OF PERIODICALS

A

Academe: Bulletin of the AAUP
Acadiensis: Journal of the History of the Atlantic Region [Canada]
Acta Poloniae Historica [Poland]
Action Nationale [Canada]
Adventist Heritage
Africa [Italy]
Afro-Americans in New York Life and History
Agricultural History
Alabama Historical Quarterly
Alabama Review
Alaska Journal (ceased pub 1980)
Alberta History [Canada]
Amerasia Journal
American Archivist
American Art Journal
American Behavioral Scientist
American Benedictine Review
American Book Collector (ceased pub 1976)
American Economic Review
American Heritage
American Historical Review
American History Illustrated
American Indian Quarterly: A Journal of Anthropology, History and Literature
American Jewish Historical Quarterly (see American Jewish History)
American Jewish History
American Journal of Economics and Sociology
American Journal of Legal History
American Journal of Political Science
American Journal of Sociology
American Literary Realism, 1870-1910
American Literature
American Political Science Review
American Politics Quarterly
American Quarterly
American Review of Canadian Studies
American Scholar
American Society of International Law. Proceedings (issues for 1970-73 appeared under the title American Journal of International Law)
American Sociological Review
American Studies in Scandinavia [Norway]
American Studies (Lawrence, KS)
American West
Americas: A Quarterly Review of Inter-American Cultural History (Academy of American Franciscan History)
Amerikastudien/American Studies [German Federal Republic]
Anglican Theological Review
Annals of Iowa
Annals of the American Academy of Political and Social Science
Annals of Wyoming
ANZHES Journal: Journal of the Australian and New Zealand History of Education Society [Australia]
Arizona and the West
Arkansas Historical Quarterly
Art in America
Asian & Pacific Quarterly of Cultural and Social Affairs [South Korea]
Atlantis: A Women's Studies Journal [Canada]
Australian Journal of Politics and History [Australia]
Aztlán

B

Baptist History and Heritage
BC Studies [Canada]
Beiträge zur Geschichte der Arbeiterbewegung [German Democratic Republic]
Biography
Black Scholar
Brigham Young University Studies
British Journal of Sociology [Great Britain]
Bulletin of National Taiwan Normal University (see Shih-ta Hsüeh-pao = Bulletin of National Taiwan Normal University) [Taiwan]
Bulletin of the Committee on Archives of the United Church of Canada [Canada]
Bulletin of the History of Medicine
Bulletin of the John Rylands University Library of Manchester [Great Britain]
Bulletin of the United Church of Canada (see Bulletin of the Committee on Archives of the United Church of Canada) [Canada]
Business History Review

C

Cahiers Internationaux d'Histoire Économique et Sociale [Italy]
California Historical Quarterly (see California History)
California History
Canada: An Historical Magazine (ceased pub 1976) [Canada]
Canadian Dimension [Canada]
Canadian Ethnic Studies = Études Ethniques au Canada [Canada]
Canadian Historical Association Historical Papers (see Historical Papers) [Canada]
Canadian Historical Review [Canada]
Canadian Journal of History = Annales Canadiennes d'Histoire [Canada]
Canadian Journal of History of Sport = Revue Canadienne de l'Histoire des Sports [Canada]
Canadian Journal of History of Sport and Physical Education (see Canadian Journal of History of Sport = Revue Canadienne de l'Histoire des Sports) [Canada]
Canadian Journal of Political Science = Revue Canadienne de Science Politique [Canada]
Canadian Review of American Studies [Canada]
Canadian Review of Sociology and Anthropology = Revue Canadienne de Sociologie et d'Anthropologie [Canada]
Canadian Review of Studies in Nationalism = Revue Canadienne des Études sur le Nationalisme [Canada]
Capitol Studies (see Congressional Studies)
Catalyst [Canada]
Catholic Historical Review
Centennial Review
Chicago History
Christian Scholar's Review
Chronicles of Oklahoma
Church History
Cincinnati Historical Society Bulletin
Civil Liberties Review (ceased pub 1979)
Civil War History
Clio
Clio Medica [Netherlands]
Colby Library Quarterly
Colorado Magazine (superseded by Colorado Heritage)
Colorado Quarterly
Communautés: Archives Internationales de Sociologie de la Coopération et du Developpement [France]
Communication Monographs
Concordia Historical Institute Quarterly
Congress and the Presidency: A Journal of Capital Studies
Congressional Studies (see Congress and the Presidency)
Continuity
Criminal Justice History
Crisis

D

Daedalus
Dalhousie Review [Canada]
Delaware History
Dialogue: A Journal of Mormon Thought
Diplomatic History

E

Early American Literature
Education and Urban Society
Éire-Ireland
Encounter [Great Britain]
Environmental Review
Essex Institute Historical Collections
Ethnic and Racial Studies [Great Britain]
Europa Ethnica [Austria]
Explorations in Ethnic Studies

F

Feminist Studies
Fides et Historia
Filson Club History Quarterly
Florida Historical Quarterly
Forest History (see Journal of Forest History)
Foundations: A Baptist Journal of History and Theology
Frankfurter Hefte [German Federal Republic]
French-American Review
Frontiers

G

Gandhi Marg [India]
Georgia Historical Quarterly
Georgia Life (ceased pub 1980)
Georgia Review
Geschichte in Wissenschaft und Unterricht [German Federal Republic]
Great Plains Journal
Greek Orthodox Theological Review

H

Harvard Educational Review
Harvard Library Bulletin
Hayes Historical Journal
Historian
Historic Preservation
Historical Journal [Great Britain]
Historical Journal of Massachusetts
Historical Journal of Western Massachusetts (see Historical Journal of Massachusetts)
Historical Magazine of the Protestant Episcopal Church
Historical New Hampshire
Historical News [New Zealand]
Historical Papers = Communications Historiques [Canada]
Historical Reflections = Réflexions Historiques [Canada]
History of Childhood Quarterly: The Journal of Psychohistory (see Journal of Psychohistory)
History of Education [Great Britain]
History of Education Quarterly
History of Political Economy
History Teacher
Huntington Library Quarterly

I

Idaho Yesterdays
Indian Historian (see Wassaje Indian Historian)
Indian Journal of American Studies [India]
Indian Journal of Politics [India]
Indian Political Science Review [India]
Indiana History Bulletin
Indiana Magazine of History
Indiana Social Studies Quarterly
Industrial and Labor Relations Review
Inquiry [Norway]
International Journal of African Historical Studies
International Journal of Contemporary Sociology
International Journal of Women's Studies [Canada]
International Migration = Migrations Internationales = Migraciones Internacionales [Netherlands]
International Review of History and Political Science [India]
International Review of Social History [Netherlands]
International Security
International Social Science Review
Irish Historical Studies [Republic of Ireland]
Isis
Italian Americana

J

Japan Interpreter [Japan]
Jewish Social Studies
Journal for the Scientific Study of Religion
Journal of African History [Great Britain]
Journal of African Studies
Journal of African-Afro-American Affairs
Journal of American History
Journal of American Studies [Great Britain]
Journal of Arizona History
Journal of Black Studies
Journal of Canadian Studies = Revue d'Études Canadiennes [Canada]
Journal of Cherokee Studies
Journal of Church and State
Journal of Communication
Journal of Contemporary History [Great Britain]
Journal of Economic History
Journal of Ecumenical Studies
Journal of Ethnic Studies

Journal of Family History: Studies in Family, Kinship, and Demography
Journal of Forest History
Journal of General Education
Journal of Imperial and Commonwealth History [Great Britain]
Journal of Interdisciplinary History
Journal of Intergroup Relations
Journal of Library History, Philosophy, and Comparative Librarianship
Journal of Mississippi History
Journal of Negro Education
Journal of Negro History
Journal of Peace Research [Norway]
Journal of Political and Military Sociology
Journal of Political Economy
Journal of Political Science
Journal of Politics
Journal of Popular Culture
Journal of Presbyterian History
Journal of Psychohistory
Journal of San Diego History
Journal of Social History
Journal of Social Issues
Journal of Southern History
Journal of Sport History
Journal of the American Academy of Religion
Journal of the American Institute of Planners (see Journal of the American Planning Association)
Journal of the American Planning Association
Journal of the Canadian Church Historical Society [Canada]
Journal of the History of Ideas
Journal of the History of Medicine and Allied Sciences
Journal of the History of the Behavioral Sciences
Journal of the Illinois State Historical Society
Journal of the Lancaster County Historical Society
Journal of the Rutgers University Library
Journal of the University of Bombay [India]
Journal of the West
Journal of Urban History
Journalism History
Journalism Quarterly

K

Kansas Historical Quarterly (superseded by Kansas History)
Kansas History
Kokkagakkai Zasshi [Japan]

L

Labor History
Labour = Travailleur [Canada]
Land Economics
Latin American Perspectives
Law & Society Review
Library Quarterly
Lincoln Herald
Literature of Liberty
Louisiana History
Louisiana Studies (see Southern Studies: An Interdisciplinary Journal of the South)

M

Maine Historical Society Quarterly
Marxist Perspectives (ceased pub 1980)
Maryland Historian
Maryland Historical Magazine
Massachusetts Historical Society Proceedings
Massachusetts Review
Mennonite Life
Methodist History
Michigan Jewish History
Mid-America
Midwest Quarterly
Midwest Review
Military Affairs
Military History of Texas and the Southwest
Milwaukee History
Minnesota History
Mississippi Quarterly
Missouri Historical Review
Missouri Historical Society. Bulletin (superseded by Gateway Heritage)
Montana: Magazine of Western History
Monthly Labor Review
Mouvement Social [France]
Movimento Operaio e Socialista [Italy]

N

Nebraska History
Negro History Bulletin
Nevada Historical Society Quarterly
New England Historical and Genealogical Register
New England Quarterly
New Jersey History
New Mexico Historical Review
New Scholar
New York Affairs
New York History
New-England Galaxy
New-York Historical Society Quarterly (suspended pub 1979)
Niagara Frontier
North Carolina Historical Review
North Dakota History
North Dakota Quarterly
North Louisiana Historical Association Journal
Northwest Ohio Quarterly: a Journal of History and Civilization
Norwegian Contributions to American Studies
Norwegian-American Studies
Nova Scotia Historical Quarterly (see Nova Scotia Historical Review) [Canada]
Nova Scotia Historical Review [Canada]
Novaia i Noveishaia Istoriia [Union of Soviet Socialist Republic]

O

Ohio History
Old Northwest
Old-Time New England
Ontario History [Canada]
Oregon Historical Quarterly

P

Pacific Historian
Pacific Historical Review
Pacific Northwest Quarterly
Pacific Northwesterner
Pacific Sociological Review
Paedagogica Historica [Belgium]
Palimpsest
Pan-African Journal [Kenya]
Panhandle-Plains Historical Review
Parameters
Párttörténeti Közlemények [Hungary]
Past and Present [Great Britain]
Peace and Change
Pennsylvania Folklife
Pennsylvania History
Pennsylvania Magazine of History and Biography
Perspectives in American History
Pharmacy in History
Philippine Studies [Philippines]
Phylon
Plains Anthropologist
Plural Societies [Netherlands]
Policy Studies Journal
Polish American Studies
Political Science Quarterly
Political Theory: an International Journal of Political Philosophy
Politico [Italy]
Politics [Australia]
Politics & Society
Polity
Population Studies [Great Britain]
Potomac Review
Prairie Forum [Canada]
Presidential Studies Quarterly
Proceedings of the Academy of Political Science
Proceedings of the American Antiquarian Society
Proceedings of the American Philosophical Society
Proceedings of the South Carolina Historical Association
Prologue: the Journal of the National Archives
Psychiatry: Journal for the Study of Interpersonal Processes
Psychohistory Review
Public Administration [Great Britain]
Public Historian
Public Interest
Public Opinion Quarterly
Public Policy
Public Welfare

Q

Quaker History
Quarterly Journal of Speech
Quarterly Journal of the Library of Congress

R

Radical America
Radical History Review
Recherches Sociographiques [Canada]
Records of the American Catholic Historical Society of Philadelphia
Red River Valley Historian
Red River Valley Historical Review
Register of the Kentucky Historical Society
Religion in Life (ceased pub 1980)
Renaissance and Modern Studies [Great Britain]
Research in Economic History
Research Studies
Review of Politics
Review of Radical Political Economics
Reviews in American History
Revista de Ciencias Sociales [Puerto Rico]
Revue de l'Université d'Ottawa (see University of Ottawa Quarterly = Revue de l'Université d'Ottawa) [Canada]
Revue d'Histoire de l'Amérique Française [Canada]
Revue Française d'Études Américaines [France]
Rhode Island History
Richmond County History
Rochester History
Rocky Mountain Social Science Journal (see Social Science Journal)
Rural Sociology

S

San José Studies
Saskatchewan History [Canada]
Scandinavian Journal of History [Sweden]
Scandinavian Review
Science and Society
Sessions d'Étude: Société Canadienne d'Histoire de l'Église Catholique (published simultaneously in one volume with Study Sessions: Canadian Catholic Historical Association) [Canada]
Shih-ta Hsüeh-pao = Bulletin of National Taiwan Normal University [Taiwan]
Signs: Journal of Women in Culture and Society
Social Forces
Social History = Histoire Sociale [Canada]
Social Problems
Social Review [Great Britain]
Social Science (see International Social Science Review)
Social Science History
Social Science Journal
Social Science Quarterly
Social Service Review
Social Studies
Societas
Society
Sociological Analysis
Sociological Inquiry
Sociological Quarterly
Sociology and Social Research
Sound Heritage [Canada]
Soundings (Nashville, TN)
South Atlantic Quarterly
South Carolina Historical Magazine
South Dakota History
Southern California Quarterly
Southern Exposure
Southern Humanities Review
Southern Literary Journal
Southern Quarterly
Southern Review
Southern Speech Communication Journal
Southern Studies: An Interdisciplinary Journal of the South
Southwest Economy and Society
Southwestern Historical Quarterly
Spiegel Historiael [Netherlands]
Stadion [German Federal Republic]
State Government
Storia Contemporanea [Italy]
Studia Nauk Politycznych [Poland]
Studies: An Irish Quarterly Review of Letters, Philosophy and
Studies in Comparative Communism
Studies in History and Society (suspended pub 1977)
Studies in the American Renaissance
Study Sessions: Canadian Catholic Historical Association (published simultaneously in one volume with Sessions d'Étude: Société Canadienne d'Histoire de l'Église Catholique) [Canada]
Supreme Court Historical Society Yearbook
Survey [Great Britain]

LIST OF PERIODICALS

Swedish

Swedish Pioneer Historical Quarterly (see Swedish American Historical Quarterly)
Synthesis

T

Tampa Bay History
Teachers College Record
Tennessee Historical Quarterly
Tequesta
Texana (ceased pub 1974)
Towson State Journal of International Affairs
Transactions of the Conference Group for Social and Administrative History
Transactions of the Historical and Scientific Society of Manitoba (superseded by Manitoba History) [Canada]
Transactions of the Royal Society of Canada = Mémoires de la Société Royale du Canada [Canada]
Turun Historiallinen Arkisto [Finland]

U

Umoja: A Scholarly Journal of Black Studies
United States Naval Institute Proceedings
University of Turku, Institute of General History. Publications (ceased pub 1977) [Finland]
Urban Affairs Quarterly

Urban History Review = Revue d'Histoire Urbaine [Canada]
Urban Review
Urban Studies [Great Britain]
Urbanism Past and Present
Utah Historical Quarterly

V

Vermont History
Vestnik Moskovskogo Universiteta, Seriia 9: Istoriia (superseded by Vestnik Moskovskogo Universiteta, Seriia 8: Istoriia) [Union of Soviet Socialist Republic]
Virginia Cavalcade
Virginia Magazine of History and Biography
Virginia Quarterly Review
Voprosy Istorii [Union of Soviet Socialist Republic]

W

Wasseje Indian Historian
West Tennessee Historical Society Papers
West Texas Historical Association Year Book
West Virginia History
Western American Literature
Western Historical Quarterly
Western Illinois Regional Studies

Western Pennsylvania Historical Magazine
Western Political Quarterly
Western Speech (see Western Journal of Speech Communication)
Western Speech Communication (see Western Journal of Speech Communication)
Western States Jewish Historical Quarterly
William and Mary Quarterly
Wilson Quarterly
Winterthur Portfolio
Wisconsin Magazine of History
Women's Studies
Working Papers for a New Society (see Working Papers Magazine)
Working Papers from the Regional Economic History Center
Working Papers Magazine
World Affairs

Y

Yale University Library Gazette
Yivo Annual of Jewish Social Science
Youth and Society

Z

Z Pola Walki [Poland]

LIST OF ABSTRACTERS

A
Aimone, A. C.
Aldrich, R.
Alvis, R.
Anderson, B. P.
Andrew, J. A., III
Athey, L. L.
Atkins, L. R.

B
Baatz, S.
Bailey, E. C.
Balmuth, D.
Barach, M. J.
Barnard, R. S.
Bassett, T. D. S.
Bassler, G.
Bauer, K. J.
Baylen, J. O.
Beaber, P. A.
Beck, P. J.
Bedford, W. B.
Beecher, L. N.
Belles, A. G.
Benthuysen, R. Van
Billigmeier, J. C.
Blaser, L. K.
Blethen, H. T.
Blum, G. P.
Bobango, G. J.
Bolton, G. A.
Bowers, D. E.
Bradford, J. C.
Brewster, D. E.
Broussard, J. H.
Burckel, N. C.
Burnett, B.
Burnett, R.
Buschen, J. J.
Bushnell, D.
Butchart, R. E.
Butcher, K.

C
Calkin, H. L.
Cameron, D. D.
Campbell, E. R.
Carp, E. W.
Castillo, R. Griswold del
Chan, L. B.
Chaput, D.
Chard, D. F.
Cleyet, G. P.
Coleman, J. S.
Coleman, P. J.
Collins, D. N.
Colwell, J. L.
Conner, S. P.
Coutinho, J. V.

D
D'Aniello, C.
Davison, S. R.
Dejevsky, N.
Dewees, A. C.
Dibert, M.
Dibert, M. D.
Dickinson, J. N.
Dietz, J. L.
Dodd, D.
Drysdale, A.
Dubay, R. W.
Duff, J. B.

E
Eid, L. V.
Eminhizer, E. E.
Engler, D. J.
English, J. C.
Erlebacher, A.
Evans, A. J.

F
Fahl, R. J.
Falk, J. D.
Farmerie, S. A.
Feingold, M.
Fenske, B. L.
Findling, J. E.
Fortner, R. S.
Fox, N. G. Sapper/G.
Frank, S. H.
Frenkley, N.
Frey, M. L.
Friedel, J. N.
Fulton, R. T.

G
Gagnon, G. O.
Gammage, J. K.
Garland, A. N.
Genung, M.
Geyer, M.
Gibson, E.
Gilmont, K. E.
Glasrud, B. A.
Grant, C. L.

H
Hardacre, P. H.
Harling, F. F.
Harrow, S.
Hartig, T. H.
Hartigan, F. X.
Hazelton, J. L.
Heitzman-Wojcicka, H.
Held, C. H.
Herrick, J. M.
Herstein, S. R.
Hewlett, G. A.
Hidas, P. I.
Hilliker, J. F.
Hillje, J. W.
Hinnebusch, P. D.
Hively, W. R.
Hobson, W. K.
Hoffman, A.
Holland, B.
Holzinger, J.
Homan, G. D.
Hopkins, C.
Horn, D. E.
Hough, C. M.
Houston, R. C.
Howell, A.
Howell, A. W.
Howell, R.
Huff, A. E.
Human, V. L.
Hunley, J. D.
Hyslop, E. C.

I
Iklé, F. W.
Ingram, J. L.

J
Jirran, R. J.
Johnson, B. D.
Johnson, D. W.
Johnson, E. D.
Johnson, E. S.
Johnson, L. F.

K
Kascus, M. A.
Kaufman, M.
Kearns, W. A.
Kennedy, P. W.
Kennedy, S. E.
Kerens, S.
Keyser, E. L.
Kicklighter, J. A.
Knafla, L. A.
Kobayashi, T.
Krenkel, J. H.
Krogstad, E. E.
Kubicek, R. V.
Kuntz, N. A.
Kurland, G.

L
Lake, G. L.
Lambert, D. K.
Larson, A. J.
LeBlanc, A. E.
Ledbetter, B. D.
Lederer, N.
Lee, J. M.
Leedom, J. W.
Leedom, J/J. W.
Legan, M. S.
Leonard, I. M.
Lester, E. R.
Levy, D.
Libbey, G. H.
Linkfield, T. P.
Lokken, R. N.
Lovin, H. T.
Lowitt, R.
Lucas, M. B.

M
Maloney, L. M.
Marks, H. S.
Marr, W. L.
Marshall, P. C.
Marti, D. B.
Maxted, L. R.
McArthur, J. N.
McCarthy, E.
McCarthy, J. M.
McCarthy, M. M.
McDonald, D. R.
McGinty, G. W.
McIntyre, W. D.
McKinney, G. B.
McKinstry, E. R.
McLaughlin, P. L.
McNeill, C. A.
Meyers, R. C.
Migliazzo, A. C.
Miller, R. M.
Moen, N. W.
Moore, J.
Morrison, S. C.
Mtewa, M.
Mulligan, W. H., Jr.
Munro, G. E.
Murdock, E. C.
Mycue, D. J.
Myers, R. C.

N
Neal, D. C.
Neville, J. D.
Newton, C. A.
Nielson, D. G.
Noble, R. E.
Novitsky, A. W.

O
Oaks, R. F.
Ohrvall, C. W.
Olbrich, W. L.
Olson, C. W.
Olson, G. L.
Osur, A. M.
Overbeck, J. A.
Oxley, A. P.

P
Packer, V. A.
Panting, G. E.
Papalas, A. J.
Parker, H. M.
Paul, B. J.
Paul, J. F.
Petersen, P. L.
Pickens, D. K.
Piersen, W. D.
Pliska, S. R.
Porter, B. S.
Powell, J.
Powell, L. N.
Powers, T. L.
Pragman, J. H.
Puffer, K. J.
Pusateri, C. J.

Q
Quéripel, S. R.
Quinlivan, M. E.

R
Reed, J. B.
Reith, L. J.
Richardson, T. P.
Rilee, V. P.
Ring, D. F.
Ritter, R. V.
Rollins, R. M.
Rosenfield, M. D.
Rosenthal, F.
Russell, L. A.

S
Sapper, N. G.
Sarna, J. D.
Sassoon, T.
Savitt, T. L.
Schoenberg, P. E.
Schoonover, T. D.
Schroeder, G. R.
Schulz, C. B.
Selleck, R. G.
Sevilla, S.
Sherer, R. G.
Shergold, P. R.
Sicher, E. R.
Simmerman, T.
Sirriyeh, E. M.
Sliwoski, R. S.
Smith, D. L.
Smith, G. L.
Smith, J. D.
Smith, L.
Smith, L. C.
Smith, L. D.
Smith, R. A.
Smith, S. R.
Smith, T. W.
Smoot, J. G.
Snow, K. C.
Soff, H. G.
Spira, T.
Sprague, S. S.
Stack, R. E.
Stickney, E. P.
Stockstill, M.
Stoesen, A. R.
Storey, B. A.
Strausbaugh, M. R.
Street, J. B.
Street, N. J.
Strom, S. C.
Summers, N.
Susskind, J. L.
Sussman, B.
Sweetland, J. H.
Swift, D. C.

T
Talley, K. A.
Tate, M. L.
Taylorson, P. J.
Tennyson, B. D.
Thacker, J. W.
Thomson, H. F.
Tomlinson, R. H.
Tomlinson-Brown, S.
Touchstone, D. B.
Trauth, M. P.
Travis, P.
Truschel, L. W.
Tull, J.

V
Valliant, R. B.
Vance, M. M.
VanWyk, L.
Velicer, L. F.
Verardo, D. R.
Vexler, R. I.
Vivian, J. F.

W
Walker, W. T.
Ward, G. W. R.
Ward, H. M.
Watson, C. A.
Wechman, R. J.
Wendel, T. H.
Wentworth, M. J.
West, K. B.
Whitham, W. B.
Wiederrecht, A. E.
Wiegand, W. A.
Williamson, N. A.
Wilson, M. T.
Woehrmann, P. J.
Wood, C. W.
Woodward, R. L.
Woolfe, L.
Wurster, H. W.

Y
Yanchisin, D. A.
Yerburgh, M. R.

Z
Zabel, O. H.
Ziewacz, L. E.
Zornow, W. F.

LIST OF ABBREVIATIONS

A.	Author-prepared Abstract
Acad.	Academy, Academie, Academia
Agric.	Agriculture, Agricultural
AIA	Abstracts in Anthropology
Akad.	Akademie
Am.	America, American
Ann.	Annals, Annales, Annual, Annali
Anthrop.	Anthropology, Anthropological
Arch.	Archives
Archaeol.	Archaeology, Archaeological
Art.	Article
Assoc.	Association, Associate
Biblio.	Bibliography, Bibliographical
Biog.	Biography, Biographical
Bol.	Boletim, Boletin
Bull.	Bulletin
c.	century (in index)
ca.	circa
Can.	Canada, Canadian, Canadien
Cent.	Century
Coll.	College
Com.	Committee
Comm.	Commission
Comp.	Compiler
DAI	Dissertation Abstracts International
Dept.	Department
Dir.	Director, Direktor
Econ.	Economy, Econom-.
Ed.	Editor, Edition
Educ.	Education, Educational
Geneal.	Genealogy, Genealogical, Genealogique
Grad.	Graduate
Hist.	History, Hist-.
IHE	Indice Historico Espanol
Illus.	Illustrated, Illustration
Inst.	Institute, Institut-.
Int.	International, Internacional, Internationaal, Internationaux, Internazionale
J.	Journal, Journal-prepared Abstract
Lib.	Library, Libraries
Mag.	Magazine
Mus.	Museum, Musee, Museo
Nac.	Nacional
Natl.	National, Nationale
Naz.	Nazionale
Phil.	Philosophy, Philosophical
Photo.	Photograph
Pol.	Politics, Political, Politique, Politico
Pr.	Press
Pres.	President
Pro.	Proceedings
Publ.	Publishing, Publication
Q.	Quarterly
Rev.	Review, Revue, Revista, Revised
Riv.	Rivista
Res.	Research
RSA	Romanian Scientific Abstracts
S.	Staff-prepared Abstract
Sci.	Science, Scientific
Secy.	Secretary
Soc.	Society, Societe, Sociedad, Societa
Sociol.	Sociology, Sociological
Tr.	Transactions
Transl.	Translator, Translation
U.	University, Universi-.
US	United States
Vol.	Volume
Y.	Yearbook

Abbreviations also apply to feminine and plural forms.
Abbreviations not noted above are based on *Webster's Third New International Dictionary* and the *United States Government Printing Office Style Manual.*

NO LONGER THE PROPERTY
OF THE
UNIVERSITY OF R.I. LIBRARY